BASEBALL PROSPECTUS 2024

The Essential Guide to the 2024 Season

Edited by Patrick Dubuque, Bryan Grosnick and Ginny Searle

Michael Ajeto, Maitreyi Anantharaman, Davy Andrews, Lucas Apostoleris, Lindsay Ballant, Michael Baumann, Demetrius Bell, Grant Brisbee, Zach Buchanan, Russell A. Carleton, Ben Carsley, Alex Chamberlain, Justin Choi, Michael Clair, Ben Clemens, Alex Convery, Zach Crizer, Mario Delgado Genzor, Alex Eisert, Daniel R. Epstein, James Fegan, Catherine Galanti, Mike Gianella, Steven Goldman, Nathan Graham, Nathan Grimm, Ben Hatch, Jon Hegglund, Scott Hines, Tim Jackson, Kyle Kishimoto, Justin Klugh, Jeremy Koo, Rob Mains, Kelsey McKinney, Andrew Mearns, Sam Miller, Jake Mintz, Dan Moore, Marc Normandin, Robert Orr, Jeffrey Paternostro, Mike Pielucci, Kate Preusser, Tommy Rancel, Esteban Rivera, David Roth, Shaker Samman, Janice Scurio, Jarrett Seidler, Jordan Shusterman, Steve Sladkowski, Ben Spanier, Matt Sussman, Jon Tayler, Lauren Theisen, Matt Trueblood, Eli Walsh, Alexandra Whitley, Roy Wood Jr.

Craig Goldstein and Andrew Mearns, Associate Editors
Robert Au, Harry Pavlidis and Amy Pircher, Statistics Editors

Library of Congress Cataloging-in-Publication Data:
paperback
ISBN-10: 1960115014
ISBN-13: 978-1960115010, 978-1960115027, 978-1960115034

Project Credits
Cover Design: Ginny Searle
Interior Design and Production: Amy Pircher, Robert Au
Layout: Amy Pircher, Robert Au

Cover Photos
Front Cover: Adley Rutschman. © Tommy Gilligan-USA TODAY Sports

Baseball icon courtesy of Uberux, from https://www.shareicon.net/author/uberux

Manufactured in the United States of America
10 9 8 7 6 5 4 3 2 1

Table of Contents

Statistical Introduction

by Bryan Grosnick

Over the past 30 years, Baseball Prospectus has been synonymous with taking a measurable and observable view of the sport of baseball. Since both our website and the Annual have started publication, sabermetrics and sports analytics in general have exploded in terms of both importance and popularity. And as this time has passed, we've learned more and more about the numbers and statistics that *matter* in baseball. As our view of baseball and the numbers that populate it change, so do the statistics we present to you in this book and on our website.

The drive to explore the analytics behind baseball performance doesn't mean that we can't enjoy the aesthetics of the sport, the thrill of competition and the joy of team athletics (though perhaps not the *Athletics team*, this past year). There's a false choice between the fun of baseball and the intricacies of statistical analysis. What we're hoping these metrics and numbers do is allow us to investigate and enjoy deeper the games we've watched, are watching or will watch. *"Was Mickey Mantle a better center fielder than Willie Mays?" "Why did the Blue Jays just remove Jose Berríos from this game in the fourth inning?" "How many home runs do you think Shohei Ohtani will hit in 2024?"* Our statistics may help you answer these questions, or ask and answer millions more.

If or when you have a question about any of the numbers in this book, how these metrics are developed, or how best to use them, our door is always open to you. Please stop by the Baseball Prospectus website, check out our Glossary or engage directly with our team. We love what we do here, and thrive on sharing our work with all of you.

(Programming note: The "proprietary" statistics here at Baseball Prospectus—you know, the ones you have to buy this book or visit our website to discover, many of them beginning with "Deserved"—are crafted from publicly-available data. While we built frameworks to extract meaning from the numbers and then share those advanced analytics with you, those underlying statistics themselves are freely available.)

Offense

To get a picture of a hitter's overall offensive production over a span of time—whether over a season or a career—start with Deserved Runs Created Plus (**DRC+**). Developed by Jonathan Judge and our stats team, this number encompasses everything that a hitter does while at the plate. Whether the player made an out, got a hit, walked, or moved a runner over with a sacrifice, a player's contribution in the batter's box is included in this number.

DRC+ is also a scaled metric: **A DRC+ of 100 roughly means that the hitter provided league-average offensive performance over that span**. One point of DRC is worth 1% better (or worse than average). If a DRC+ of 100 is about average for the league, then a DRC+ of 150 is outstanding—50% better than a league-average hitter—and puts you in the upper echelon of players. On the other hand, a DRC+ of 75 means that you'd better be an outstanding defender, because you're dragging the lineup down by being 25% worse than the league average.

However, DRC+ doesn't just take the hitting *events* and create a number, but it also includes *context* for all those events. The model uses inputs like the ballpark where the events happened, opposing pitcher success, the offensive environment of the league, the temperature on the day of the game, Statcast data and more ... and then uses those contextual factors to weigh the events that occurred as more or less impactful. So not only is DRC+ a great way to tell how successful a player performed, but it also is the single best way we have to identify how successful that hitter will be *in the future*.

After the hitter reaches base (or makes an out on the play), DRC+'s job is done. We use our ice-cold Baserunning Runs (**BRR**) metric to give runners credit for what they do on the basepaths. This number is more than just stolen base attempts—it also includes advancing on an outfield fly, scooting over on a soft grounder or taking an extra base after a teammate's hit.

Defense

In 2023, the Baseball Prospectus team overhauled the way we quantify defense. Today, our key holistic defensive metric is Deserved Runs Prevented Deserved Runs Prevented (**DRP**). DRP tallies up the total positive or negative value that a fielder provides in run prevention. Now, quantifying defense is a little more challenging than pitching or hitting—those actions take place in a much more one-on-one dynamic. Instead of using the "zone" data (which relies on private, subjective information entered by individuals) that many other advanced defensive metrics use, DRP pulls public Statcast play-by-play data as the primary input to our model.

The biggest component of DRP is **RDA** (Range Defense Added), which are the outs made on balls in play fielded by each individual player...but DRP also includes elements taking into account outfield assists and the prevention of baserunners taking extra bags on balls in play. This works for most positions on the field, but then there are the players who take up the most difficult, taxing and critical defensive position in a team's alignment: catchers. So we handle them differently.

There's so much extra work involved with catchers—not only do they field their position like everyone else, they prevent baserunners from swiping bases, block pitches that otherwise would sail right to the backstop and "frame" pitches to make them more or less likely to be called strikes.

This skill—"pitch framing" or "presentation"—used to be hard to quantify, so the public wasn't aware of just how much it affects run prevention. Today, our mixed-model approach does the trick, pulling in pitch tracking data, adjusting for context factors like pitcher, batter, umpire and home-field advantage, and producing a number of strikes that the catcher is adding to (or subtracting from) a pitcher's performance. We take these strikes and convert them to runs using linear weights, and that gives us another item to take into account for backstops.

Framing runs have a pretty significant effect on a catcher's overall defensive value, even though framing skill is on the rise throughout baseball as its importance has been measured. We stack those framing runs with the runs gained or lost from pitch blocking and preventing stolen bases, which results in Catching Defense Added (**CDA**), our metric evaluating how well catchers catch. Combine that with the occasional need to field balls in play, and *voila*, we get DRP for catchers.

Pitching

To best identify a pitcher's contribution to their team, we have to try and separate the effects of pitching from the effects of the other defenders on the field. Pitchers do have some (but not complete) influence on balls in play, and our signature pitching metric is designed to isolate a hurler's contribution while staying as independent as possible from the impact of a team's defenders.

That brings us to Deserved Run Average (**DRA**), our core pitching metric that evaluates a pitcher's performance in a way that *looks a lot like earned run average (ERA), but is actually very different*. First, DRA is scaled to runs allowed per nine innings instead of ERA, so you can expect DRA to be a little higher than what you'd normally expect from ERA.

To build out a pitcher's DRA, we start with the individual event data for everything a pitcher does on the mound. Then, we adjust the value of these events based on environmental factors like park, batter, catcher, home-field advantage,

pitcher role and temperature. Our multilevel-model approach pulls together these events and factors in much the same way we do in our DRC+ and baserunning models to get a final DRA number.

While DRA is a useful metric that helps us align our expectations of runs allowed in a way that looks like the old-school ERA statistic...you're not going to see it in this book. Why? Because we like to focus on **DRA-**, which is the cousin of our DRC+ number for hitters, but a little easier to read. Like DRC+, DRA- compares performance to league-average. A DRA- of 100 is middle-of-the-road, roughly league-average. The big difference between DRA- and DRC+, though, is that with DRA- *a lower number is better*. (This makes sense, because we're used to wanting low ERA and runs-allowed numbers when examining pitcher stats.) A DRA- of 75 is representative of pitcher performance about 25% better than the league's average, and a DRA- of 150 is representative of a pitcher who has been having an extremely rough go of it.

Projections

We know many readers value this book for our projections—a look into the potential future that could help you win your fantasy league, make a savvy bar bet or mystify your co-workers or family members. Enter **PECOTA**, Baseball Prospectus' signature, proprietary projection system. No longer the original product built by Nate Silver in the early '00s, the new PECOTA takes into account the player's past performance, information on the tendencies of professional ballplayers in the major, minor and overseas leagues, and other factors like the effects of age and the positions they play.

One of PECOTA's strengths is that it provides a probability distribution for outcomes in addition to your standard estimate. The point estimate you see in this book is the median forecast, but to see the detailed range of potential outcomes, you can subscribe to our website (baseballprospectus.com). Remember: All forecasts and projections have uncertainty, but by sharing the level of uncertainty of our forecasts and what the probability distribution looks like, we provide greater transparency along with accuracy.

Now let's get to the fun part—a detailed breakdown of all the numbers you'll find in the book for 2024.

Team Prospectus

Most of this book is composed of our 30 team chapters for each major-league franchise. (Yes, despite everything that happened in 2023, the Athletics still get a chapter. No, this is not going to be the final Athletics joke.) On the first page of each chapter, you get a large box full of information, as well as a snazzy stadium diagram. An example—the 2023 National League West champion Los Angeles Dodgers—is displayed on the following page.

We start with the team name, and underneath that is the team's un-adjusted win-loss record and division ranking. Below that, you'll find a dozen important statistics that tell you how the team performed, holistically, over the course of the previous season...as well as insight into what the construction of the team looks like. Each stat not only carries the metric's value, but also the ordinal ranking among all 30 MLB franchises. (Here, 1st always is the "best" rank, while 30th is the "worst.")

Pythag (short for "Pythagenpat") is an adjusted version of the team's 2023 winning percentage, and it's calculated based on runs scored per game (**RS/G**) and runs allowed per game (**RA/G**). Those numbers are run through a version of Bill James' Pythagorean formula that has been refined and improved by David Smyth and Brandon Heipp. We also include Deserved Winning Percentage (**dWin%**), which uses the frameworks that underpin DRC+ and DRA (along with depth charts) to estimate team runs scored and allowed in 2023 as the inputs for the same Pythagenpat formula used above. Then we have **Payroll**, which is the combined salary of all of the team's players, as well as Marginal Dollars per Marginal Win (**M$/MW**). The latter metric, developed by Doug Pappas, tells us how much money the team spent to earn production above the replacement level.

At the top of the right-hand column, we give Defensive Efficiency Rating (**DER**), which indicates the percentage of balls in play converted to outs for the team and serves as a quick shorthand for team fielding skill. **DRC+** indicates the overall offensive ability of the team as compared to league average, and **DRA-** indicates the overall pitching ability of the team. We also share Fielding Independent Pitching (**FIP**), which is another pitching metric that resembles ERA, but is based *only* on strikeouts, walks and home runs recorded by the team's pitchers. Finally, we have **B-Age** to tell us the average age of a team's batters (weighted by plate appearances), and **P-Age** to do the same for the team's pitchers (weighted by innings pitched). For these final two rankings, 1st corresponds to the youngest team, while 30th corresponds to the oldest.

The next major part of this stat box focuses on the team's home ballpark. We begin with a detailed diagram of the stadium's dimensions, including the distances from home plate to the outfield walls. Then, we include a few short bullet points about the playing surface and the history of the park, before moving onto another graphic that displays the height of the wall from the left field pole to the right field pole.

On to **Park Factors**, a table that helps explain how each stadium helps affect different events on the baseball diamond. These park factors are also indexes where 100 is average; a factor of 110 means that the park inflates the relative statistic by 10% while a factor of 90 means the park deflates the relative stat by 10%. Most of these park factors are broken down by handedness, as we share **Runs** (runs scored), **Runs/LH** (runs produced by left-handed hitters),

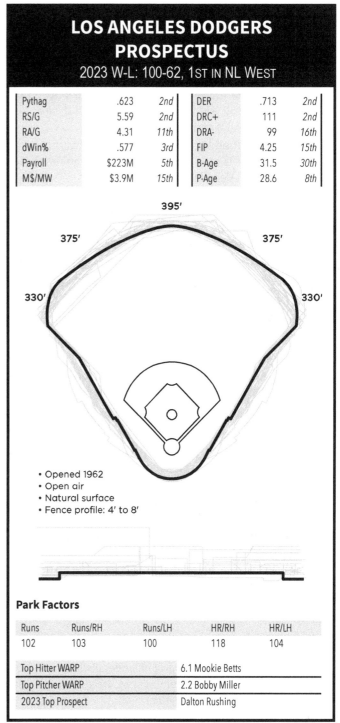

LOS ANGELES DODGERS PROSPECTUS
2023 W-L: 100-62, 1ST IN NL WEST

Pythag	.623	2nd	DER	.713	2nd
RS/G	5.59	2nd	DRC+	111	2nd
RA/G	4.31	11th	DRA-	99	16th
dWin%	.577	3rd	FIP	4.25	15th
Payroll	$223M	5th	B-Age	31.5	30th
M$/MW	$3.9M	15th	P-Age	28.6	8th

- Opened 1962
- Open air
- Natural surface
- Fence profile: 4' to 8'

Park Factors

Runs	Runs/RH	Runs/LH	HR/RH	HR/LH
102	103	100	118	104

Top Hitter WARP	6.1 Mookie Betts
Top Pitcher WARP	2.2 Bobby Miller
2023 Top Prospect	Dalton Rushing

Runs/RH (runs produced by right-handed hitters), **HR/LH** (home runs by left-handed hitters) and **HR/RH** (home runs by right-handed hitters).

Finally, we list the team's best hitter and pitcher by Wins Above Replacement Player (**WARP**)—which we'll get to in a little bit later in this section—as well as the team's top prospect as judged by our prospect evaluators.

On the second page of the team chapter, you'll find three line graphs. The first is **Payroll History**, which plots the team's payroll over the past decade as well as comparing it to the MLB average payroll and the team's division's average payroll. These figures are current as of January 1, 2024, and will ultimately change before Opening Day, so check out Baseball Prospectus' Cot's Baseball Contracts page for the most up-to-date contract data.

The second graph is **Future Commitments**, stretching five years out into the future. This notes the team's upcoming guaranteed payroll outlays—if any exist—and are also compared to the MLB and divisional averages.

Farm System Ranking, the third graph, displays how the franchise's minor-league talent fared in our rankings each year over the past decade.

The final team box is the **Personnel** section, which notes some of the most important decision-makers for each franchise, mostly high-level operations staff (roles like president of baseball operations and general manager), as well as the team's field manager. We're also proud to share any former Baseball Prospectus staff members who are currently part of the organization.

Position Players

All of that team-centric data is followed by a carefully crafted essay about the team, and that would be enough for most books. But not this one—it's time for the individual player comments! Here come 60-70 individual breakdowns of the most important major- and minor-league players for each franchise. (Please note that the text of these comments comes with the author's byline or two, but that's only a rough guide—players moved around in the offseason and the comments are not guaranteed to match each franchise's byline.)

Players are listed with the franchise that employed them in early January 2024. For players that changed teams after the first week of January, look to their previous team's chapter. We also have a free agent chapter for the most notable players without a team as of this book's publication. (Less notable FAs will appear in their previous team's chapter.)

Each player gets a "stat block" and a written comment. Our example this year is 2023 American League batting champion Yandy Díaz. First we list the player's name and primary position—we'll get to multi-position players a little later—before sharing key biographical details like birthdate, age (as of June 30, 2023), handedness, height and weight, and origin for entering the league.

Inside the stat block, we share the following identifying information for each season listed for the player: **YEAR**, **TM**, **LVL** (level of affiliated play) and **AGE**. Then it's on to what we call the "baseball card" stats or the primary stats you see

in most fantasy baseball leagues: **PA** (plate appearances), **R** (runs), **HR** (home runs), **RBI** (runs batted in) and **SB** (stolen bases).

Next it's the bridge between old school and new school. There's the "slash line" first: These stats are unadjusted, and include **AVG** (batting average), **OBP** (on-base percentage) and **SLG** (slugging percentage). Then we include **BABIP** (batting average on balls in play), which helps us understand the percentage of times that a ball hit into play ended up as a hit. We include this metric because it can help us identify if a batter has been lucky or not. An outrageously high BABIP *can* mean that a hitter had better luck than average, but the great hitters of our era also tend to post high BABIPs. (So do speedy hitters who put the ball on the ground a lot.)

New to this year's stat box (but not to advanced statistics) is **SLGCON** (slugging percentage on contact). This number shows a player's slugging percentage just for balls put into play, and reflects the production side of exit velocity, demonstrating how much power they converted into extra bases. Following this we include rates two of the "three true outcomes": **BB%** (walk rate) and **K%** (strikeout rate). This shares the percentage of all plate appearances where a hitter either walks or strikes out.

Another new addition to our stat boxes this year is a set of four plate discipline metrics. These next four rates help us understand a hitter's contact ability and approach in a more granular way than simple batting average. **ZSw%** (zone swing percentage) tells us how often a hitter swings at balls inside the strike zone, while **ZCon%** (zone contact percentage) tells us how often a hitter makes contact on those pitches swung at inside the strike zone. Their partners are **OSw%** (out-of-zone swing percentage), which is how often the hitter is swinging at pitches out of the strike zone and **OCon%** (out-of-zone contact percentage), which is how often the hitter makes contact on those pitches that they swung at. These are powerful statistics but might take some work to internalize: Be sure to check the "Average of Everything" essay to note what "good" and "bad" numbers look like for these and other stats.

The other major new addition to our stat boxes this year are metrics that have become increasingly critical for understanding how well a player hits: **LA** (launch angle) and **90th EV** (90th-percentile exit velocity). Launch angle gives us a picture of the average angle at which a player lofts the ball into the air on balls in play—too much launch angle and they're popping the ball up, too little and they're driving balls into the ground. 90th EV gives us a picture of how much

Yandy Díaz 1B Born: 08/08/91 Age: 32 Bats: R Throws: R Height: 6'2" Weight: 215 Origin: IFA, 2013

YEAR	TM	LVL	AGE	PA	R	HR	RBI	SB	AVG/OBP/SLG	BABIP	SLGCON	BB%	K%	ZSw%	ZCon%	OSw%	OCon%	LA	90th EV	DRC+	BRR	DRP	WARP
2021	TB	MLB	29	541	62	13	64	1	.256/.353/.387	.286	.474	12.8%	15.7%	69.7%	87.6%	22.3%	64.7%	6.7	108.0	112	-0.3	0.4	2.3
2022	TB	MLB	30	558	71	9	57	3	.296/.401/.423	.323	.484	14.0%	10.8%	66.1%	91.1%	22.9%	73.9%	7.8	108.1	141	0.2	0.9	4.2
2023	TB	MLB	31	600	95	22	78	0	.330/.410/.522	.367	.636	10.8%	15.7%	67.5%	89.0%	23.3%	65.2%	6.0	108.9	134	0.1	0.1	3.9
2024 DC	TB	MLB	32	621	70	14	68	2	.274/.364/.408	.303	.486	11.6%	14.0%							124	-0.1	0.4	3.1

2023 GP: 1B (118), DH (13), 3B (6)   Comps: Terry Pendleton (69), Jeff Cirillo (63), Ken McMullen (62)

Logan Webb RHP Born: 11/18/96   Age: 27   Height: 6'1"   Weight: 220   Origin: Round 4, 2014 Draft (#118 overall)

YEAR	TM	LVL	AGE	G (GS)	IP	W-L	SV	K	WHIP	ERA	CSP	BB%	K%	HR%	GB%	ZSw%	ZCon%	OSw%	OCon%	BABIP	SLGCON	DRA-	WARP
2021	SF	MLB	24	27 (26)	148¹	11-3	0	158	1.11	3.03	53.7%	6.0%	26.5%	1.5%	60.9%	61.0%	85.9%	37.1%	55.8%	.312	.466	63	4.3
2022	SF	MLB	25	32 (32)	192¹	15-9	0	163	1.16	2.90	52.9%	6.2%	20.7%	1.4%	56.6%	63.7%	87.2%	35.5%	61.9%	.294	.446	82	3.6
2023	SF	MLB	26	33 (33)	216	11-13	0	194	1.07	3.25	48.2%	3.6%	22.8%	2.4%	62.0%	62.7%	89.9%	36.8%	67.0%	.303	.491	74	5.5
2024 DC	SF	MLB	27	29 (29)	189¹	14-10	0	146	1.22	3.43	50.6%	5.8%	18.5%	1.7%	59.3%					.298	.449	81	3.6

2023 Arsenal: CH (87.5), SI (92.3), SL (84.3), FA (92.7)   *Comps: Dan Haren (79), Roy Halladay (78), Matt Garza (77)*

damage the hitter is doing to the ball and their best swings; it's not quite the hardest they can hit a ball, but it tells us what happens when the hitter really drives a pitch, ignoring outliers.

The last four statistics are designed to tell the whole picture of a player's performance. **DRC+** (Deserved Runs Created Plus) we've talked about before, and it gives us the hitter's total expected contribution at the plate, compared to the league average. **BRR** (Baserunning Runs) accounts for all baserunning events, not just thefts of second, third and home. **DRP** (Deserved Runs Prevented) gives us the whole picture of the player's defensive value, by number of runs above average allowed or prevented.

And last, but certainly not least, is **WARP** (Wins Above Replacement Player), a holistic metric for total player value. This takes into account deserved runs above average (a major input for DRC+), BRR, and DRP, then adjusts based on the positions the fielder played during the season. It's a cumulative statistic, and players are credited for all their plate appearances based on performance above "replacement level," or the play quality of players that are freely available after the start of the season.

Just below the player's most recent season, you'll find future data: That's the PECOTA projection and comparables. We'll talk about those a bit more in an upcoming section. And lastly, this year we've included **2023 GP** (2023 games played) below the stat box, which indicates what fielding positions were played, and for how many games (in parentheses).

Catchers

We've said it before: Catchers are special. Their defensive responsibilities are more massive than fielders at other positions, so to accurately gauge their value, we create a separate box just for their unique catching stats. Here's our Annual's cover model, Adley Rutschman, as an example.

Adley Rutschman

YEAR	TM	P. COUNT	FRM RUNS	BLK RUNS	THRW RUNS	TOT RUNS
2021	BOW	7738	12.8	0.6	0.2	13.6
2021	NOR	4199	3.2	0.1	0.1	3.4
2022	NOR	1095	0.0	0.1	-0.3	-0.2
2022	BAL	12228	10.7	0.2	0.3	11.2
2023	BAL	15491	12.7	0.0	0.2	12.9
2024	BAL	15632	12.7	0.1	0.0	12.8

YEAR and **TM** are the same columns you'd find in the stat boxes for position players and pitchers. **P. COUNT** (pitch count) tells us the number of pitches thrown to that catcher, including swinging strikes, fouls and balls in play. **FRM RUNS** (framing runs) is the total value in runs that the catcher provided or lost by receiving the pitch in a way that influenced the umpire to call a strike. **BLK RUNS** (blocking runs) is the total value in runs above or below average for the catcher's ability to prevent wild pitches and passed balls. **THRW RUNS** (throwing runs) is the total value in runs that the catcher provided or lost from throwing out base stealers *and* preventing them from attempting to steal as well. (Don't worry, this takes into account factors like pitcher delivery and speed of the baserunner.) **TOT RUNS** (total runs) is the sum of the previous three metrics, a total run value for the catcher's framing, blocking and throwing.

Pitchers

This year's example for our pitcher stat block is the 2023 MLB leader in innings pitched, San Francisco Giants hurler Logan Webb. Just like with our position players, the block leads off with biographical information at the top, followed by the same **YEAR**, **TM**, **LVL** and **AGE** columns present for the position players.

The first set of statistics are those more traditional "baseball card" or fantasy-relevant statistics: **G (GS)** (games pitched, with games started in parentheses), **W-L** (win-loss record), **SV** (saves), **K** (strikeouts) on the counting side, **WHIP** (walks plus hits per inning pitched) and **ERA** (earned run average) to help identify pitching skill and outcomes on a rate basis.

Our first proprietary metric for pitchers is **CSP** (called strike probability), and it shows the likelihood of any pitch thrown by this hurler to result in a called strike. This metric is adjusted and controls for factors like handedness, umpire, pitch type, count and location.

Next up are the useful rate stats that tell us quite a bit about a pitcher's effectiveness based on outcomes. **BB%** (walk rate) tells us what percentage of batters a pitcher walks, **K%** (strikeout rate) tells us what percentage of batters a pitcher strikes out and **HR%** (home run rate) tells us what percentage of batters a pitcher allows to smash a ball over the fence. These three give us our fielding-independent rates, but just as important is **GB%** (ground-ball percentage). That's the percentage of all batted balls in play hit on the ground, including both outs and hits...usually the higher this rate, the better. (Please note that this is based on the same subjectively entered observational data we talked about in the fielding section, but it's still very useful.)

This year, we've included the same new plate discipline metrics you'll see in the position player section: **ZSw%** (zone swing percentage), **ZCon%** (zone contact percentage), **OSw%** (out-of-zone swing percentage) and **OCon%** (out-of-zone contact percentage). These metrics can also help tell a pitcher's story, particularly if we compare how many swings a pitcher is getting outside of the zone (a great outcome for pitchers), or compare a thrower's ZSw% to their ZCon% to see how much trouble a hitter has getting a bead on their pitches over the plate.

We also include **BABIP** and **SLGCON** to tell the story of what kind of contact a pitcher allows. BABIP is slightly more useful for pitchers than hitters, as league-average BABIP for pitchers usually sits between .290-.300, and deviations from this can be markers of poor supporting defense or bad luck. SLGCON indicates how frequently extra-base hits result from a pitcher's balls in play, which can be telling for both current and future performance.

At the far side of the stat box, you'll see **DRA-**, which we've laid out as our best measure of current and future expected pitching performance. Anything lower than 100 indicates better-than-league-average performance, while numbers above 100 are not so good.

WARP is on the same scale as it is for hitters, so you can compare value across two very different types of players. However, WARP is calculated specifically for pitching outcomes with DRA as the primary output, and it's cumulative for the number of innings pitched. This is why you often see that relief pitchers have a lower WARP than you might initially expect. WARP also doesn't take leverage into account, so if you believe that clutch late-inning pitching performance provides extra value, you may choose to value those high-leverage relief pitchers differently.

New to this year's edition is a small line below the stat box that indicates **Arsenal**, listing out all of a pitcher's types of pitches thrown in order of usage, along with their median velocity. The abbreviations you'll see for different pitches are: **FA** (four-seam fastball), **FC** (cut fastball or cutter), **HC** (hard cutter), **FS** (splitter), **SI** (sinker), **SW** (sweeper), **SL** (slider), **CU** (curveball), **KC** (knuckle curve), **CS** (slow curve), **KN** (knuckleball), **SB** (screwball) and **CH** (changeup). (Fun fact: This list can also be found, almost in its entirety, below Yu Darvish's player comment in the San Diego Padres team chapter.)

PECOTA

As promised, now we can talk a little more about PECOTA, our signature projection system. Each of the player comments in this book includes a PECOTA projection for 2024, and all those projections for the player for 2024 are as of our *early January press date*.

PECOTA stats are projected for the park context as indicated by the team abbreviation, and all PECOTA projections represent a player's estimated *major-league*

performance. If you see a minor-leaguer's PECOTA projections, these are the numbers they'd project for with a rapid jump to the big leagues.

It's important to note that PECOTA doesn't just factor in the player's expected performance on a rate basis, it also adjusts for how much playing time they'll have available to record that performance. Our Depth Charts staff estimates playing time for each player based on their team's roster and depth chart, and those projections are noted as **2024 DC**. So what happens for players who aren't projected for major-league playing time because they're a prospect or a minor-league organizational player? These players get marked as **2024 non**, and their projection is for 251 plate appearances or 50 innings pitched.

Lastly, we have the comparables, listed in the book as **Comps** for short. You'll see three names, and these are the highest-scoring comparable players in the modeling process built by the BP Stats team. These three "targets" are examples of people who followed extremely similar career paths up to the player's age and in the context of their era. Next to each name you'll find a number that indicates the strength of the comparison; 100 indicates a perfect match, and 60 indicates an average match. These comps are meant to be backward-facing, and they match the age of the hitter to the age of the target. For example, if Adolis García is entering his age-31 season and he pulls a comparison to Nelson Cruz, his career is being compared up to Cruz's age-31 season...not the decade of work that came after that year or his career as a whole.

Managers

Near the end of this book, you'll find a section dedicated to those statistics for each major-league manager. We've pulled together a number of metrics from each manager's last five years on the bench. For more information on all the stats back there and what they mean, please visit the Glossary at www.baseballprospectus.com.

Those managers are ordered by **wRM+** (weighted reliever management plus), a metric that was developed by Rob Arthur and Rian Watt to measure how well a manager syncs up their best relievers to the biggest moments of leverage in a game. wRM+ takes into account both DRA and a scale called Leverage Index (which is provided by our friends at FanGraphs). Like many of our other metrics, wRM+ is scaled to league average; a wRM+ of 105 means that a manager used his relief pitching options about five percent better than average. On the other hand, a wRM+ of 95 tells us that the manager leveraged his relief pitchers about five percent worse than average.

A manager isn't solely responsible for a team's wRM+, and we know this because the metric's correlation with each manager isn't strong. It is, however, statistically significant, so we can tell that a team's manager has some effect on that number.

The Average of Everything

by Patrick Dubuque

Now that you've ostensibly purchased a book full of baseball statistics, here's a confession: Baseball statistics are tricky. It's more than just learning all of the various metrics and their various purposes, and memorizing their obscure acronyms. There's also the painstaking labor of internalizing them. Every baseball statistic balances somewhere on a spectrum with two ends: descriptive and predictive. Evaluating that result requires two steps, understanding what happened and also understanding whether it was good or bad.

This is why you still see batting averages splashed across every television broadcast. It's not that batting average is a wonderful way to describe a player's offensive output; it's also not the worst, but there are dozens better, and some of them even simpler. But people *get* average. They can react to it automatically, the way a musician can play a song without having to think about their hands. This is the ultimate state of enlightenment when it comes to stats. Unfortunately, it's not easy, and it's getting harder and harder.

Not only is the analytical landscape growing more intricate by the year, as already demonstrated by our ever-growing Statistical Introduction preceding this essay, but those years have come faster as well. Our ordinarily languid sport has seen seismic shifts in the past few years, between the tactical hyper-optimization of pitching and defense, new rules and even variations within the ball itself. Fortunately, we're not dealing with the same level of transformation common in basketball or football, where the numbers of a single generation prior feel like a completely different sport. Still, it's harder to know what a "good" number is than it used to be.

This is the reason BP uses index stats for its flagship, all-encompassing evaluative metrics, DRC+ and DRA-. These stats are simple to read: 100 is average. Above 100 is good for hitters; below 100 is good for pitchers. But the price of that accessibility is that the metric loses all ability to describe what actually happened. In these cases, that's actually fine: Because they roll up hundreds or thousands of tiny additions or subtractions in value across a season's worth of pitches, swings, and balls in play, description would be impossible anyway. But the numbers that go into those final scores, the inputs, still need to be countable. This is why the secondary summary stats like BRR, DRP and CDA are all still run-based; because the value of those components hasn't yet been internalized by baseball fans at large, it's still useful to

compare their relative value to each other. Being a 90th-percentile framer isn't the same as being a 90th-percentile arm in left, for example.

This, then, is a handy little guide to provide you with context for what you're about to absorb. Using every qualified hitter and pitcher and ranking them, it provides percentile rankings for the major statistics, as well as a name to attach as a signpost. For these tables, we're using starters with at least 120 innings pitched, since only 47 pitchers managed to qualify for the ERA title last year.

1. Value Stats: Starting Pitching

	ERA	Earned Run Average		WHIP	Walks + Hits Per Inning
99	2.25	Blake Snell	99	0.98	Gerrit Cole
90	3.14	Shohei Ohtani	90	1.07	Corbin Burnes
70	3.57	Seth Lugo	70	1.15	Aaron Nola
50	3.86	Freddy Peralta	50	1.23	Shane Bieber
30	4.48	Reid Detmers	30	1.34	Grayson Rodriguez
10	5.19	Hunter Brown	10	1.47	Kyle Freeland
1	6.28	Jordan Lyles	1	1.59	Trevor Williams

	IP/GS	Innings Per Games Started		FIP	Fielding Independent Pitching
99	6.60	Sandy Alcantara	99	2.82	Sonny Gray
90	6.06	Pablo López	90	3.20	Logan Webb
70	5.75	Sonny Gray	70	3.84	Logan Gilbert
50	5.62	Kyle Bradish	50	4.07	Clayton Kershaw
30	5.36	Dylan Cease	30	4.48	Michael Lorenzen
10	5.12	Ryne Nelson	10	5.21	Ryne Nelson
1	4.69	Michael Kopech	1	6.44	Michael Kopech

	DRA-	Deserved Run Average		WARP	Wins Above Replacement Player
99	72	Zach Eflin	99	5.5	Logan Webb
90	81	Shohei Ohtani	90	3.8	Justin Steele
70	90	Yu Darvish	70	2.7	Alex Cobb
50	100	Clarke Schmidt	50	1.8	Bailey Ober
30	109	Zack Greinke	30	1.1	Zack Greinke
10	124	Patrick Corbin	10	0.0	Trevor Williams
1	148	Tyler Anderson	1	-1.9	Tyler Anderson

League-wide starting pitcher ERA has fluctuated nearly three-quarters of a run in the last decade, from 3.82 in baseball's little ice age of 2014 to 4.54 during the peak of the juiced-ball chaos in 2019. Thanks to rule adjustments, we're closer to the upper end after 2023 (4.45). That our median falls so much lower than that is a demonstration of just how many subpar innings each year are devoted to replacement starters. Still, the median starter is good for just around 2.0 WARP despite the diminished innings totals.

2. Discipline Stats: Starting Pitching

	Z-Swing%	In-Zone Swing Rate		Z-Con%	In-Zone Contact Rate
99	60.1%	Charlie Morton	99	75.8%	Spencer Strider
90	64.6%	Shane Bieber	90	80.7%	Tyler Anderson
70	66.9%	Framber Valdez	70	83.2%	Andrew Heaney
50	68.8%	Clayton Kershaw	50	84.4%	Clayton Kershaw
30	70.6%	Andrew Heaney	30	87.0%	Seth Lugo
10	72.5%	Sandy Alcantara	10	88.7%	Taijuan Walker
1	75.6%	Lance Lynn	1	91.4%	Patrick Corbin

	O-Swing%	Out-of-Zone Swing Rate		O-Con%	Out-of-Zone Contact Rate
99	40.0%	Joe Ryan	99	40.2%	Tyler Glasnow
90	36.8%	Logan Webb	90	51.4%	Kodai Senga
70	34.0%	Logan Gilbert	70	56.8%	Justin Steele
50	32.9%	Patrick Sandoval	50	60.8%	Logan Allen
30	31.7%	Hunter Brown	30	63.6%	Dean Kremer
10	29.7%	Wade Miley	10	67.5%	Ryne Nelson
1	25.9%	Jake Irvin	1	74.6%	Miles Mikolas

	BABIP	Batting Average on Balls in Play		SLGCON	Slugging Percentage on Contact
99	.236	Wade Miley	99	.431	Sonny Gray
90	.265	Justin Verlander	90	.475	Tanner Bibee
70	.279	Merrill Kelly	70	.513	George Kirby
50	.293	Dean Kremer	50	.546	Seth Lugo
30	.309	Miles Mikolas	30	.570	Patrick Corbin
10	.320	Justin Steele	10	.611	Nick Pivetta
1	.353	Jack Flaherty	1	.702	Luke Weaver

The first step to moving beyond simple walk and strikeout rates is to think about how pitchers attack the plate and attempt to get the upper hand on batters. O-Swing%, also described as Chase Rate, is the most commonly discussed of these metrics, and refers to how often a pitcher can make a hitter swing at pitches that aren't strikes. Avoiding contact on those "bad" pitches is also desirable—a strike is always a good thing—but given how much harder it is to square up a pitch outside the zone, it's more gravy than meat. Getting free strikes by freezing batters on pitches in the zone is equally valuable, but harder to replicate. But the most underrated of the plate discipline stats might be Z-Con%, which is what happens when a pitcher throws a strike that the batter can't hit anyway. That's the optimal result of a pitch, but keep in mind that it doesn't take into account how often the pitcher is throwing strikes, just *how often* he gets away with it.

You're familiar with BABIP, an old friend of the sabermetric community. For a long time, BABIP was considered to be out of a pitcher's control, and while that turned out to be overstated, it's still a key source of variance for pitchers from year to year. The stat's less-famous brother, SLGCON, takes the same idea but applies slugging percentage instead, counting home runs rather than ignoring them.

3. Rate Stats: Starting Pitching

	K%	Strikeout Rate		BB%	Walk Rate
99	36.8%	Spencer Strider	99	2.5%	George Kirby
90	29.1%	Kodai Senga	90	4.8%	Bryce Miller
70	25.5%	Aaron Nola	70	6.6%	Kyle Bradish
50	22.7%	Logan Webb	50	7.3%	Yu Darvish
30	20.3%	Alex Cobb	30	8.3%	Lance Lynn
10	16.1%	Zack Greinke	10	10.2%	Tylor Megill
1	13.9%	Kyle Freeland	1	15.5%	Michael Kopech

	HR%	Home Run Rate		GB%	Ground-ball Rate
99	1.1%	Sonny Gray	99	62.0%	Logan Webb
90	2.2%	Kyle Hendricks	90	50.0%	Bryce Elder
70	2.7%	Justin Verlander	70	45.0%	Merrill Kelly
50	3.0%	Mitch Keller	50	42.2%	Zac Gallen
30	3.6%	Cristian Javier	30	39.4%	Yusei Kikuchi
10	4.3%	Kyle Freeland	10	34.7%	Spencer Strider
1	5.4%	Lance Lynn	1	25.7%	Cristian Javier

As strikeout rates continue to climb, it demands a perpetual re-evaluation of what average is. While walk rates have stayed surprisingly steady over the years, strikeouts have plateaued around the 22-23% range since the arrival of the "launch angle revolution" that arrived with the juiced ball in 2015-2016. The home run rate, similarly, hasn't quite reached the peak of 2019 and 2020, but is still far closer to it than the "normal" rates that came before.

4. Catcher Defense

	ThrR	Throwing Runs		BlkR	Blocking Runs
99	2.8	Gabriel Moreno	99	0.6	Gabriel Moreno
90	1.3	Sean Murphy	90	0.1	Gary Sánchez
70	0.3	J.T. Realmuto	70	0.0	Jose Trevino
50	0.0	Tyler Stephenson	50	0.0	Adley Rutschman
30	-0.1	Austin Hedges	30	-0.1	Jonah Heim
10	-0.4	Tom Murphy	10	-0.2	Ryan Jeffers
1	-1.3	Austin Barnes	1	-0.5	Shea Langeliers

	FrmR	Framing Runs		CDA	Catcher Defense Added
99	24.2	Austin Hedges	99	24.8	Patrick Bailey
90	8.6	Jake Rogers	90	9.0	Sean Murphy
70	2.8	Gary Sánchez	70	3.0	Yasmani Grandal
50	0.4	Will Smith	50	0.1	Austin Barnes
30	-2.9	Yainer Diaz	30	-3.2	Matt Thaiss
10	-8.9	Francisco Mejía	10	-9.0	Gabriel Moreno
1	-16.8	Martín Maldonado	1	-17.8	Martín Maldonado

The obvious takeaway here is that Gabriel Moreno is extremely good at a lot of the things one does as a catcher. He was also a pretty terrible catcher last year, because the value of framing remains, despite rumors of its demise, vastly more important than throwing or blocking. While it's counterintuitive, think of it this way: Turning a 1-1 count from 2-1 to 1-2 drastically reduces the average batter's chances of success in an at-bat. Now imagine having literally thousands and thousands of chances to twist the count in the pitcher's favor.

The other obvious takeaway here is that there are still aspects to catcher defense that we can't quantify, between handling pitching staffs and gamecalling. At least, Martín Maldonado had better hope there are.

5. Slash Stats: Hitting

	AVG	Batting Average		OBP	On-Base Percentage
99	.354	Luis Arraez	99	.416	Ronald Acuña Jr.
90	.289	Masataka Yoshida	90	.370	Christian Yelich
70	.271	Ke'Bryan Hayes	70	.346	Nico Hoerner
50	.260	Max Kepler	50	.328	Dansby Swanson
30	.248	J.D. Davis	30	.315	Luis Robert Jr.
10	.229	Jake Cronenworth	10	.296	Hunter Renfroe
1	.191	Giancarlo Stanton	1	.250	Brenton Doyle

	SLG	Slugging Percentage		ISO	Isolated Slugging Percentage
99	.654	Shohei Ohtani	99	.350	Shohei Ohtani
90	.512	Jorge Soler	90	.241	Nolan Gorman
70	.467	Willson Contreras	70	.201	Lourdes Gurriel Jr.
50	.437	Alec Bohm	50	.175	Elly De La Cruz
30	.407	Jonathan India	30	.154	Xander Bogaerts
10	.359	Geraldo Perdomo	10	.112	Dominic Smith
1	.296	Tim Anderson	1	.051	Tim Anderson

Again, a reminder that .260 may be the median batting average for starters, but the league average itself was .248, just three points higher than non-pitchers hit in 1968, the Year of the Pitcher. Modern baseball is on the low end of the spectrum in terms of OBP, thanks to that lowered batting average, but ISO, or slugging percentage minus batting average, remains as high as it's ever been, as everyone outside of Luis Arraez swings for the bleachers.

OPS, the favorite shorthand for offensive performance for decades, isn't included in the book because it's simple math to add OBP and SLG together, and we need all the space we can get. But a median .260/.325/.440 line means that you're hoping for something around a .765 mark. Still, better to just use an adjusted stat like OPS+, wRC+ or DRC+. Not only does it make it easier to compare players across eras, it solves the problem of various park effects.

6. BIP Stats: Batting

	Z-Swing%	In-Zone Swing Rate		Z-Con%	In-Zone Contact Rate
99	85.9%	Corey Seager	99	95.1%	Steven Kwan
90	75.8%	M. Yoshida	90	90.3%	Justin Turner
70	71.9%	Bobby Witt Jr.	70	87.5%	Ketel Marte
50	68.8%	Matt Chapman	50	84.7%	Julio Rodríguez
30	66.1%	Austin Hays	30	82.2%	Brandon Drury
10	61.2%	Jace Peterson	10	78.1%	Brenton Doyle
1	55.2%	Lars Nootbaar	1	73.4%	Nolan Jones

	O-Swing%	Out-of-Zone Swing Rate		O-Con%	Out-of-Zone Contact Rate
99	17.1%	Edouard Julien	99	89.4%	Luis Arraez
90	24.1%	Kyle Schwaber	90	72.8%	Lars Nootbaar
70	29.5%	Carlos Santana	70	66.5%	Bo Bichette
50	32.4%	E. Hernández	50	60.8%	Yasmani Grandal
30	35.6%	Cody Bellinger	30	56.2%	Marcell Ozuna
10	40.1%	Elias Díaz	10	48.8%	Tyler Stephenson
1	50.0%	Salvador Perez	1	33.5%	Ryan Noda

	BABIP	Batting Average on Balls in Play		SLGCON	Slugging Percentage on Contact
99	.401	Nolan Jones	99	.938	Aaron Judge
90	.345	Austin Hays	90	.703	Jorge Soler
70	.319	Matt Chapman	70	.623	Jeimer Candelario
50	.301	A. Benintendi	50	.567	Lourdes Gurriel Jr.
30	.289	Ozzie Albies	30	.526	Jonathan India
10	.265	Alejandro Kirk	10	.452	Jurickson Profar
1	.205	Pete Alonso	1	.331	Tony Kemp

Just as with pitchers, understanding plate discipline is a vital step in understanding hitters; perhaps more so, since on the public side we lack the tools to quantify the swing path the way we can with the spin, break and location of the pitch. The goal, unsurprisingly, is to swing at strikes as much as possible and balls as little as possible, and hit what you can. But as obvious as that is, it can still present red flags, particularly for young hitters, whose plate discipline skills might not be fully formed. Nolan Jones, for example, does a ton of damage on contact, but unless he can make more of it, he's going to have a hard time repeating his fantastic rookie season.

One of the problems with walk rate is that it makes it difficult to distinguish between discerning hitters and passive ones. A hitter with a low zone-swing rate like Lars Nootbaar is probably hurting himself by taking too many hittable pitches and putting himself into unfavorable pitchers' counts. Meanwhile, SLGCON again represents damage on contact from a productivity standpoint, to be paired with exit velocity below. The same way that not all hitters are going to gravitate toward the same BABIP, based on their swing tendencies, not all exit velocities result in the same outcomes. SLGCON tells you what happened, which is a useful thing sometimes.

7. Rate Stats: Hitting

	BB%	Walk Rate		K%	Strikeout Rate
99	19.2%	Aaron Judge	99	5.5%	Luis Arraez
90	13.6%	Robbie Grossman	90	14.3%	Andrew Benintendi
70	10.2%	Carlos Correa	70	18.3%	George Springer
50	8.7%	Anthony Volpe	50	21.6%	Bryan Reynolds
30	6.9%	Alec Bohm	30	23.9%	Randy Arozarena
10	5.2%	Amed Rosario	10	29.9%	Kyle Schwarber
1	3.3%	Salvador Perez	1	35.0%	Brenton Doyle

	LA	Average Launch Angle		90th EV	90th Percentile Exit Velocity
99	22.8	Jack Suwinski	99	112.4	Giancarlo Stanton
90	18.6	Willy Adames	90	108.3	Christopher Morel
70	15.3	Bobby Witt Jr.	70	106.4	Spencer Torkelson
50	13.1	Corey Seager	50	104.8	Mookie Betts
30	10.8	Carlos Correa	30	103.7	Jeremy Peña
10	6.8	Juan Soto	10	101.8	Robbie Grossman
1	1.5	Alek Thomas	1	97.3	Tony Kemp

Walks are the post-hype statistic of modern analytics, but they remain valuable. One of the reasons they've lost some of their luster is that we've moved beyond the stats they've been hidden by, particularly batting average. But the other reason is that the industry has moved toward the individual variables that go into walks, like the plate discipline stats above. Walks are messy things: they can be the result of being feared, being selective or being passive.

Exit velocity, meanwhile, remains in the statistical *zeitgeist*, thanks in part to the relative lack of public hitting metrics compared to the pitching side. The important thing to keep in mind, as Stanton ably reminds, is that exit velocity only matters if you can get the ball to exit, and even then mostly if you can get it in the air. A high-velocity, low-angle ball in play is a single at best. It's a reminder that EV is a great tool for player analysis, but it's only one tool.

8. Value Stats: Hitting

	DRC+	Deserved Runs Created		BRR	Baserunning Runs
99	176	Ronald Acuña Jr.	99	3.8	Ronald Acuña Jr.
90	132	Pete Alonso	90	1.1	Ozzie Albies
70	113	Marcus Semien	70	0.5	Jack Suwinski
50	105	J.P. Crawford	50	0.1	Bryce Harper
30	95	DJ LeMahieu	30	-0.3	Michael Conforto
10	84	Javier Báez	10	-0.6	Alex Bregman
1	59	Martín Maldonado	1	-1.3	Ty France

	DRP	Deserved Runs Prevented		WARP	Wins Above Replacement Player
99	25.3	Patrick Bailey	99	9.5	Ronald Acuña Jr.
90	4.0	Ke'Bryan Hayes	90	3.8	Gleyber Torres
70	1.0	Ty France	70	2.1	Alex Verdugo
50	0.1	Adolis García	50	1.4	Eddie Rosario
30	-1.1	Corey Seager	30	0.8	Nick Allen
10	-3.7	Jurickson Profar	10	0.1	Christian Bethancourt
1	-17.2	Martín Maldonado	1	-2.3	Martín Maldonado

And now we arrive at the evaluative stats. DRC+ is an index stat, which means above 100 is good and below 100 is bad. It's useful to note, however, just how tight the band is around the median: 40% of all starting hitters posted a DRC+ within 10 points of the median. Baserunning and defensive run values, by definition, are going to be centered around zero, and the vast majority of runners and fielders (outside the very best and worst catchers) will supply some portion of a win through their secondary skills.

Meanwhile, in terms of WARP, a couple of guys weren't very helpful to our middling aims here. Both Acuña and Maldonado surpassed the usual standards last year; traditionally the scale tends to top out at around eight in a standard Mike Trout season, and the worst player in baseball, when not a catcher, is in the -1.5 range. Still, the old rule of thumb remains generally true: Four wins is an All-Star, two wins is a starter, one win is a second-division starter and zero is still replacement level.

Now that you've taken a lay of the land, it might be good to throw a bookmark here so you can refer to it later while perusing the stat lines throughout the book. But as one last treat, since we've dug up the data already, you're probably wondering who the most average starters in baseball are. We can calculate this, without much rigor, by simply taking all the categories above (ignoring the catcher breakdowns) and calculating each player's standard deviations away from the mean for each one, then adding them together. In layman's terms: the player who's closest to the middle the most is the winner.

Rk	StDev	Hitters	Rk	StDev	Pitchers
5	6.28	Taylor Ward	5	6.23	Dean Kremer
4	6.12	Spencer Steer	4	6.13	Yu Darvish
3	5.96	Carlos Santana	3	5.60	Jon Gray
2	5.29	Luis Rengifo	2	5.05	Clayton Kershaw
1	4.37	Jeimer Candelario	1	4.76	Reid Detmers

So there you have it: Jeimer Candelario and Reid Detmers were the most average hitter and pitcher last year, not in terms of value, but in terms of distinctiveness. That's by no means an insult; just like vanilla is a miracle flavor embedded in so much of what we eat, baseball teams can't win championships without some average in them. They deserved to be celebrated. In moderation, naturally.

—Patrick Dubuque is the managing editor of Baseball Prospectus.

The 2023 Rules Changes: It's Not That Simple

by Rob Mains

The 2023 season ushered in the most consequential changes to MLB's rule book since—pick your favorite—the introduction of the designated hitter, regulating ballpark dimensions, various adjustments to the mound and strike zone, allowing pitchers to throw overhand or eliminating the ability of outfielders retire baserunners by hitting them with a thrown ball ("soaking" the runner) prior to reaching a base. Some fundamentally altered the way the game was played. Others were window dressing.

Though I am not a journalist—few applied math majors are—I will present this in inverted pyramid format, starting with the most consequential of the changes.

The Pitch Clock (or, as MLB calls it, the Pitch Timer)

Rule changes generally don't get the blood going, but there sure was a lot of *sturm und drang* over limiting the time between pitches to 15 seconds with the bases empty and 20 seconds with runners on base. To one camp, this was going to be the salvation of baseball, transforming it from a plodding game that would otherwise never appeal to Millennials and Gen Zs with truncated attention spans. To the other, it was a sacrilege, defiling the team sport that doesn't have a clock.

Of course, the pitch clock is hardly a new innovation. Limiting the time between pitches has been in the rulebook for over a century. What's new, after various failed attempts, is the will to enforce it.

So did it work? This graph displays the average time for 8.5-inning (i.e., home team doesn't bat in the last of the ninth) and 9-inning games over the past five years, 2020 excluded.

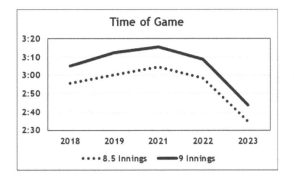

The average nine-inning game took 3:15 in 2021. That dropped by over half an hour, to 2:44, in 2023. (The introduction of PitchCom yielded a savings of about six minutes in 2022.) Games in which the home team didn't bat in the ninth fell about the same, from 3:04 to 2:35. If you went to four games a year, you spent an average of two fewer hours at the ballpark than you had in 2021.

But it's not quite that simple.

Teams learned from experience. The time between pitches expanded steadily over the season, from 18.3 seconds in April to 19.1 in August and September.

Multiply that by the average of 148 pitches per game and you've added a couple minutes to each game. Hurlers began milking every second, recharging as much as possible before every max-effort pitch. Managers, pitching coaches and catchers learned when to initiate their walks out to the mound, and pitchers and batters learned the limits on when they could call time. As a result, the length-of-game difference between 2023 and the prior season narrowed throughout the year.

Minutes Saved per Game, 2023 vs. 2022

Month	8.5 Innings	9 Innings
April	27.1	30.5
May	27.0	27.8
June	22.4	26.7
July	21.8	25.2
August	24.1	21.1
September	17.4	18.0

Compared to 2022, the time savings per game dropped from around half an hour in April to less than 20 minutes in September.

Did the pitch clock shorten the time of games? Absolutely. But don't be surprised if it creeps up a bit in 2024. It was on that trajectory through 2023. MLB's cognizant of this, and will reduce the time between pitches with runners on base from 20 to 18 seconds this year.

Banning the Shift

This was another controversial move. Some fans felt that fielding grounders in short right field to throw out a runner at first wasn't real baseball. Others felt that dictating where fielders could stand wasn't real baseball, akin to banning zone defenses in football. And there were doubts about the effect it would have.

The effect, it turns out, was positive, if not quite exactly as intended. Pulled groundballs—the type of batted balls most often gobbled up by that third infielder on one side of second—generated a .193 batting average in 2021 and a .192 average in 2022. That rose to .204 in 2023. The batting average on pulled line drives (granted, most of those wind up in the outfield) rose from .683 in 2021 and .678 in 2022 to .685 in 2023.

But it's not quite that simple.

First, the benefit applied solely to left-handed batters. Their pulled grounders generated a .180 average in 2023 compared to .147 in 2022 and .156 in 2021, when shifts predominated. Their batting average on liners went from .661 in 2022 to .689 last year. For right-handed batters, who were shifted less frequently, their .220 average on pulled grounders was exactly the same as in 2022 and only two points above 2021's .218. Their .552 batting average on pulled liners was higher than 2022's .548 but lower than 2021's .553.

Second, it wasn't just grounders. For lefties, pulled balls hit into the air—most of which wind up out of the reach of shifted infielders—generated a .562 average in 2023, 28 points higher than the year before. That's almost as good as the 33-point increase on pulled grounders. Right-handed batters' average on pulled air balls was four points higher than in 2022, outpacing their flat performance on pulled grounders.

Overall, batters in 2023 raised their batting average on pulled grounders by 12 points (.192 to .204) and on pulled liners by 6 points (.663 to .669), less than the 13 points by which they raised their batting average on pulled fly balls (.479 to .492). The difference in BABIP for pulled fly balls was negative, down 10 points, but that's because homers were up. (The vast majority of fly-ball base hits—around 80%--are home runs.) *Banning the shift helped batters on batted balls that the shift hardly affected more than those that it did.* Hitting over the shift remained a sound strategy even when there wasn't a shift. Which makes sense: as BP author Russell A. Carleton has stated, the shift grew in response to the rising tide of pull-heavy flyballers, not the other way around.

And it played out that way on other batted balls. For those hit up the middle or to the opposite field—where, in theory, defenses should have benefited from not having an infielder out of the usual position—batting averages on grounders increased by five points, from .286 to .291. Batting averages on balls hit in the air increased more, from .321 to .327.

Further, banning the shift was supposed to usher in a renaissance in contact hitting, with the Luis Arraezes of the world taking playing time from the Joey Gallos. It didn't work that way. In 2022, MLB batters struck out in 22.4% of plate appearances. In 2023, no longer forced into all-or-nothing swings to get the ball over shifted infielders, they struck out in…22.7% of plate appearances, the highest proportion ever for non-pitchers (excluding 2020). What went wrong?

Incentives, that's what. The shift was tough on left-handed pull hitters in particular. Take Gallo. He pulled nearly 55% of balls in play in 2022. Hitting into the shift, he batted .127 on pulled grounders in 2021 and .071 in 2022. Without the shift, that rose to .172 in 2023. The Twins signed Gallo and traded Arraez last offseason, in part for that arbitrage: Sacrifice Arraez's contact skills for the opportunity to get more from Gallo in a no-shift environment. Banning the shift created an incentive to utilize batters like Gallo more, not less.

In 2022, batters in the top quartile for pulled balls—those who pulled it 46.5% or more of the time—struck out in 23.6% of their plate appearances and accounted for, naturally, 25% of plate appearances. In 2023, with the shift now banned, batters who pulled 46.5% of batted balls struck out almost an identical amount, 23.5%, but now accounted for 38% of plate appearances. Notably pull-happy hitters went from representing two in eight plate appearances to better than three in eight. They brought their strikeouts along with them. Groundballs declined as a percentage of batted balls, from 42.7% to 42.3%.

Left-handed batters hit better on pulled grounders with the shift banned. But they hit even better on balls in the air. Righties saw no particular benefit. And by banning the shift, MLB encouraged managers to give more at bats to the high-strikeout pull hitters who were most penalized by shifts, resulting in less contact, not more.

Baserunning

Pitchers can reset the pitch clock by stepping off the rubber. In order to prevent that loophole from delaying games, pitchers are now limited to two "disengagements" per plate appearance. If they step off a third time, they have to pick off the runner or they're charged with a balk. Consequently, this provided baserunners with the license to take larger leads. This rule change, along with a three-inch increase in the base size and stepped-up enforcement of the balk rule, it was felt, would yield more stolen bases.

And did it ever. There were 3,503 stolen bases in 2022, a 41% increase from 2022 and 58% more than in 2021. The average of 0.72 per game was the most in 26 years. Stolen bases weren't back to the artificial turf-inflated (and lack of knowledge of run expectancy-inflated) days of the 1980s, but it was a far cry from the start of the decade, when stolen bases were at a nadir not seen since the Deadball II era of the 1960s.

But it's not that simple, though in this case, the underlying trends were *better* than what we saw in aggregate.

The stolen base numbers are impressive enough. But while they didn't set any records, the success of basestealers in 2023 did.

When evaluating basestealing, the concept of "break-even"—the success rate above which the attempt increases run expectancy—is calculable but nebulous. It depends on the run environment (the more scoring, the less attractive one-run strategies like stealing), the number of outs (the downside of getting caught is greater with no outs than with one), the team's scoring needs (stealing when needing just one run is a smarter strategy than when needing multiple runs), and the players involved (aggregate statistics don't capture the speed of the runner, the skill of the pitcher and catcher to hold the runner on, and the ability of the batter to advance the runner). So far this century, the theoretical breakeven for steals of second is a little under 75% with one or two outs, just under 70% with two down. Attempts to steal third have a breakeven of about 80% with no outs, 70% with one out, and nearly 90% with two outs (those make sense when you think about it).

In 2022, the league successfully stole at a 75.4% rate, an MLB record. Basestealers equaled or exceeded the theoretical break-even for all situations except attempted steals of third with no outs, which occurred only 48 times. (Most attempts to steal third come with one out.)

The stolen base success rate rocketed up to 80.2% in 2023, obliterating the old record. The success rates for steals of second and third were above break-even for all out states for the first time since caught stealings were recorded in 1950. But the pattern of when steals occurred over the season is informative.

Teams stole about 0.7 bases per game through the season's first five months, even as the success rate, already well above breakeven, climbed. Only in September was there a marked increase in stolen base attempts and a corresponding dip in the success rate (to a level still well above breakeven). That could be a pattern we'll see duplicated in 2024—more stolen bases in exchange for a lower (but still outstanding) success rate.

The disengagement rule didn't affect baserunners only when they were trying to steal a base. Bigger leads gave runners more of an opportunity to take an extra base on base hits. In the following graphs, the dotted line represents the 2017-22 average (excluding 2020). These figures reflect only runners with the next base unoccupied who advanced on hits, not on errors.

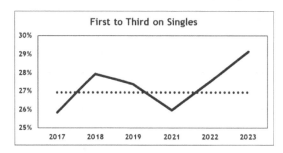

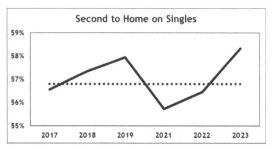

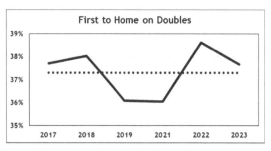

Baserunners took an extra base on base hits at an above-average rate in 2023. It took a while for them to get the hang of it: Runners went from first to third on singles at a 27.7% clip in April and May, 29.9% the rest of the year. With the exception of runners on first when a double is hit (the least-frequent of the three opportunities to take an extra base), the rate for the full season in 2023 exceeded each of the preceding five seasons.

The rules affecting baserunning were, relative to MLB's goals, wildly successful.

Position Players Pitching

This change didn't attract the headlines, nor the heat, of the other new rules. Both the players and the owners were concerned about the explosion of position players pitching in recent years. It had gone from an amusing novelty in blowouts to *de rigeur*.

MLB tried to tamp down on position player pitching in the 2019 collective bargaining agreement. It limited position players pitching to games in which a team was ahead by six or more runs or in extra innings. With COVID-19, though, and concerns over the workload of pitchers, the new rule was waived in both 2020 and 2021. Position players—who didn't appear as pitchers in a single game as recently as 2006—took the mound 89 times in 2021. The new restriction on position players pitching was finally implemented in May of 2022, but it didn't stem the tide of position players pitching, which reached a record 132 for the year.

Last year, MLB stiffened the rules. Position players are now allowed to pitch only if their team is trailing by eight or more runs or leading by ten or more runs. (They're still allowed, without restriction, in extra innings.)

But it's not quite that simple.

On the micro level, the change was a success. Position player pitching appearances in 2023 declined by 13%.

On a macro level, though?

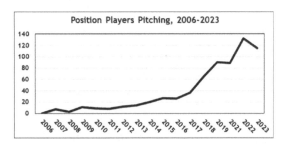

There were 115 position player pitching appearances in 2023. True, that's fewer than 2022's 132. But it's also 25 more than any other season in history. If watching Tampa Bay's Luke Raley give up seven runs in an inning and two thirds (as he did on May 20 against Toronto) or seeing the Angels' Eduardo Escobar retire all five batters he faced (September 15 against Detroit) is your idea of fun, fear not.

⚾ ⚾ ⚾

MLB's rule changes were, from a public relations standpoint, a success. Game times were significantly shortened, even if the time savings declined as the season progressed. Pull hitters had more success with shifts disallowed, even if the contact rate went down and the improved performance was across the board, not just balls hit into the departed shirt. Baserunners stole more bases and took more extra bases and could do so again this year. And position player pitching declined, if to still-high levels. The controversy the proposals engendered didn't hurt gameplay or the public image.

Whether MLB can keep the streak going when it inevitably implements automated balls and strikes, well, it's not quite that simple.

—Rob Mains is an author of Baseball Prospectus. Thanks to Robert Au and Tom Gieryn for research assistance.[1]

---

1. Data retrieved from Baseball Prospectus Leaderboards, Statcast Baseball Savant and Sports-Reference's Stathead Baseball; Information sources: Ben Lindbergh, "The Forgotten History of MLB's Pitch Clock," The Ringer, March 29 2023; Russell A. Carleton, "The Afterlife of the Shift," Baseball Prospectus, July 12 2023

ARIZONA DIAMONDBACKS

Essay by Zach Buchanan

Player comments by Justin Choi and BP staff

In October, as the Diamondbacks prepared to host their first playoff game in six years, an article made its way around the clubhouse. Arizona may have led the Dodgers 2-0 in their best-of-five National League Division Series, wrote *The Los Angeles Times*, but the Dodgers would be facing elimination in a comfortable setting: Arizona's Chase Field. "We're going to feel like we're going to play at home," said Dodgers outfielder and erstwhile Diamondback David Peralta. The comment rankled some of Peralta's former teammates, perhaps because it had the ring of truth.

Often over the years at Chase Field, the crowd contingent cheering for the home squad has been drowned out by those in other jerseys. NL West matchups are dominated by Dodger blue and Giants orange, and visits from other storied franchises—the Cubs, the Cardinals, the Yankees—similarly change the complexion of the stands. "When the Dodgers played at Chase Field this season," the *Times* article noted, "the average crowd was 27% larger than when they did not." It's such a frequent phenomenon that the Diamondbacks lean into it, often hoping to face the big-name teams on weekends or major holidays to boost attendance.

This October, however, the Diamondbacks had the last laugh. Not only did they crush a team that had historically crushed them, with a Game 3 win highlighted by four homers in one inning, the sellout Chase Field crowd was painted heavily in tones of teal, red and black. For the rest of Arizona's surprising run to the World Series, the franchise's typical home-field disadvantage ceased to exist. Even in a miserable Game 4 loss to the Rangers—a lopsided affair that might have given a regular-season crowd an early push toward the parking lot—the stands remained packed until the end.

Such a level of hometown support was new to the Diamondbacks, who have long struggled to build a rabid following in the desert. Enthusiasm abounded when the franchise debuted in 1998, with attendance topping three million in Arizona's first two seasons. The Diamondbacks received an additional bump in support when they won a championship in 2001. That team and its stars still retain a legendary aura in the Valley of the Sun, partly because little has been done since to dim its glow. Arizona has made the playoffs just four times in the past two decades, and never

ARIZONA DIAMONDBACKS PROSPECTUS
2023 W-L: 84-78, 2ND IN NL WEST

Pythag	.491	16th	DER	.698	13th
RS/G	4.60	15th	DRC+	100	15th
RA/G	4.70	20th	DRA-	100	17th
dWin%	.510	16th	FIP	4.36	19th
Payroll	$116M	21st	B-Age	27.9	11th
M$/MW	$2.7M	8th	P-Age	28.8	11th

407'

376'   376'

330'   335'

- Opened 1998
- Retractable roof
- Synthetic surface
- Fence profile: 7'6" to 25'

Park Factors

Runs	Runs/RH	Runs/LH	HR/RH	HR/LH
100	99	101	95	100

Top Hitter WARP	4.5 Corbin Carroll
Top Pitcher WARP	4.5 Zac Gallen
2023 Top Prospect	Jordan Lawlar

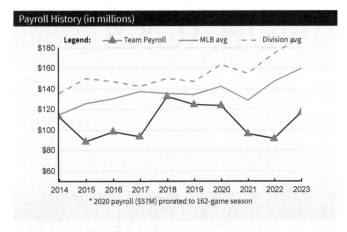

Payroll History (in millions)

Legend: ▲ Team Payroll — MLB avg - - Division avg

* 2020 payroll ($57M) prorated to 162-game season

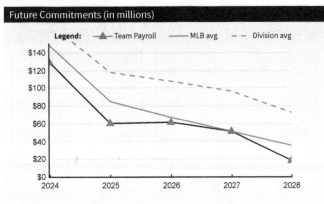

Future Commitments (in millions)

Legend: ▲ Team Payroll — MLB avg - - Division avg

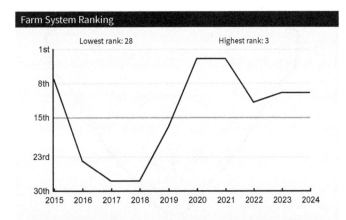

Farm System Ranking

Lowest rank: 28   Highest rank: 3

Personnel

President & Chief Executive Officer
Derrick Hall

Executive Vice President & General Manager
Mike Hazen

Sr. Vice President & Assistant General Manager
Amiel Sawdaye

Vice President, Research & Development
Mike Fitzgerald

Manager
Torey Lovullo

BP Alumni
Tucker Blair
Jason Parks

in consecutive years. The average gap between postseason appearances during that span was more than five years, meaning a good Diamondbacks team came around less often than February 29th.

But now, more than perhaps at any point in their history, the Diamondbacks appear built for sustained success. They are good—arguably better than their 84-78 record, as they showed throughout the postseason—and they are young. Their stars are either locked up long-term, like Corbin Carroll and Ketel Marte, or still in their pre-arbitration seasons. High-end prospects like Jordan Lawlar and Druw Jones could claim roles in the future. General manager Mike Hazen, who enters his eighth season and has held the position longer than anyone else in franchise history, factors the long-term into every decision he makes. For the first time in 20 years, they are poised to consistently win and to train their fans to expect good things. "We see there's an opportunity here," Hazen told *The Arizona Republic* after the season. There is also a challenge.

Phoenix is an odd market, populous but filled with transplants who bring their own baseball loyalties. In 2021, census data showed it was the fastest-growing city in the country, according to *The New York Times*, and an *Axios* analysis earlier this year determined that the population of the metropolitan Phoenix area has grown by five million people since 2000. The newcomers may seek the sun in the desert, but they first sprouted from the ground elsewhere. They bring their own sports histories, and sometimes the Diamondbacks have a hard time competing.

As one of the two youngest teams in the league, only now are the Diamondbacks benefiting from a generation of Arizonans who grew up watching them. The seven- and eight-year-olds who achieved sports consciousness watching Arizona win a title in 2001 are just now starting families and passing down their heirloom baseball rooting interests. The first generation of Diamondbacks fans also grew up watching star players leave and solid teams underachieve. If their attention was rewarded with a playoff appearance, further investment was met only with disappointment.

But entering 2024, coming off an energizing World Series run and with money to add to its intriguing cast of characters, a far-fetched idea now appears more plausible.

Can the Diamondbacks finally turn Phoenix into a baseball town?

⚾ ⚾ ⚾

The early years of Diamondbacks baseball both spoiled fans and doomed them. Eager to build a winner from scratch, team founder Jerry Colangelo opened the franchise coffers to make an early splash. The Diamondbacks lost 97 games in their inaugural season, but quickly spent to add big names like Luis Gonzalez, Randy Johnson and Steve Finley that offseason. A 100-win season followed in year two and the 2000 squad boasted the seventh-highest Opening Day payroll in the game, according to Cot's Contracts. The 2002 team, buoyed by the previous year's World Series win, ranked fourth. Johnson won four Cy Youngs in Arizona, Gonzalez had a 57-homer season and All-Stars appeared all over the diamond. Those teams were star-studded and expensive. And, eventually, they were old.

Beginning in 2003, Arizona's veteran core started to break down. Yet, they were still under contract and many were owed deferred payments for years after their deals expired. In 2004, as the Diamondbacks lost 111 games, they found themselves aging, injured and deep in debt with no young players ready to fill the team's many holes. Midway through that season, Colangelo was ousted by current owner Ken Kendrick, who was cast as the villain as the ownership group tried to get the club's finances in order.

Years of penny-pinching followed, during which Kendrick faced a steep learning curve as the organization's control person. The 2002 team ran an Opening Day payroll of more than $102 million, per Cot's, and not until 2014 did Kendrick again authorize spending into nine digits. The Phoenix metropolitan area is one of the largest media markets in the country, but Arizona's payroll climbed into the top half of the league only once, in that 2014 campaign. Arizona lost 98 games that year.

In the interim, Kendrick and the Diamondbacks struggled with impatience. They shuffled through managers and general managers, with the owner habitually nudging his decision-makers into making moves he preferred. After an 81-81 season in 2012, he expressed discontent with homegrown star Justin Upton and pushed general manager Kevin Towers to trade him in a deal that returned little other than light-hitting shortstop Nick Ahmed. Entering 2016, a year after firing Towers and hiring Dave Stewart and Tony La Russa, Kendrick signed star pitcher Zack Greinke largely without their input. At $34 million per year, Greinke was paid appropriately, but the Diamondbacks weren't one big, expensive piece away from contention. Arizona lost 93 games in Greinke's first year, and Kendrick once again changed regimes.

The Hazen era has followed, and it's been a healthier one, even if the road has been no less bumpy. Hazen tweaked the club into a playoff team his first year, then struggled to keep it competitive while rebuilding the farm system and infrastructure under the hood. A contention-minded team face-planted in in 2021 and lost 110 games, but Kendrick did not clean house. More than at any point during his stewardship, Kendrick has given his GM rope to shape the team as he sees fit. There have been whiffs—the Madison Bumgarner signing, several of Hazen's trade additions in the early years—but none that have meaningfully muddied the club's long-term picture.

Few prospects Hazen has traded have turned into stars elsewhere. Several he's acquired—Carroll in the draft and Marte, Gabriel Moreno and Zac Gallen in trades—have achieved stardom. And the Diamondbacks aren't bracing for painful impending departures. They enter 2024 with only two notable players (Christian Walker and Paul Sewald) poised to

hit free agency. Marte and Carroll are controllable through 2028 and 2031, respectively. Others like Moreno, Geraldo Perdomo, Alek Thomas and Brandon Pfaadt have yet to reach arbitration.

GMs love nothing more than a good, controllable core, and the Diamondbacks should be in a position to add. They still owe Bumgarner $14 million for 2024, but Kendrick said entering the offseason that the team's surprise postseason run boosted revenue to the point that he'll make "not insubstantial investments" in the team's roster. After running a $116 million payroll in 2023, the organization's fourth-highest ever, it's possible the team could eclipse its record $131 million Opening Day tally from 2018.

Arizona had the 11th-lowest attendance in 2023, although most of the excitement they generated came in the postseason. Despite playing in a metropolitan area of nearly five million people, the Diamondbacks haven't ranked higher than 15th since 2004. They built a winner fast, but didn't build it right, and support withered as they struggled for two decades to figure out the correct formula.

Now they're poised to finally build something sustainably, and they think fans will come.

⚾   ⚾   ⚾

The Diamondbacks don't have to look far to prove that Phoenix will support a winning team. Not long ago, and just two blocks down from Chase Field, they watched it firsthand. In 2021, after missing the playoffs for 10 straight years and being godawful for many seasons in the interim, the Phoenix Suns engineered a galvanizing run to the NBA Finals. The Valley of the Sun, mostly known for hosting Super Bowls, Final Fours and other events that depend on welcoming tourists from elsewhere, burned with a new civic pride.

Murals popped up on the side of buildings featuring the likenesses of Suns stars Devin Booker and Chris Paul. In the postseason, fans flocked to Sky Harbor Airport to welcome the team back from the road. The Suns don't make for a perfect analogue—they have been in Arizona longer than any other pro team, and have enjoyed more and longer windows of contention—but they've kept winning since and the city has kept supporting them. Now the Diamondbacks just made their own unexpected run at a title, and they too seem to be at the start of something, rather than the end.

The key is to keep it up. The Suns, it's worth noting, kept striking while the iron was hot, swinging pricey trades for established stars in Kevin Durant and Bradley Beal. One basketball star inevitably has a far greater effect on a team's fortunes than one baseball star, but the Suns responded to the pressure of their return to prominence with gutsy moves to get even better. Though the Diamondbacks surely will spend more entering 2024—a willingness they demonstrated by taking on the final $11 million owed to third baseman Eugenio Suárez from the Mariners—it remains to be seen if they'll ever again open the vault like they did for Greinke eight years ago.

Building off the surprise success of 2023 is essential if the Diamondbacks ever want a fanbase too large to manually count between innings. Their playoff drought before 2023 was hardly long, but whatever postseason excitement they generated was incredibly short-lived. "It can't be so spread out and sporadic like it's been," said team president and CEO Derrick Hall. "Not getting back to the playoffs for four, five, six, seven years, you're going to erode your fanbase." Before 2023, Arizona's had been slowly wilting. In recent seasons, retention of season ticket holders hovered around 80%-85%, Hall said—not a precipitous drop, but "still a decline." Interest dipped so much that *The Arizona Republic* began listing prep sports before the Diamondbacks on their website menu.

These days, the picture is understandably rosier. Arizona has added season ticket holders rather than lost them, and the team has seen a boost in merchandise sales. Though the changing TV landscape presents a tough knot to untangle—Arizona was one of two teams dropped by bankrupt Bally Sports at midseason, with MLB taking over broadcasts for the rest of the year—Hall said the team's internal viewership data showed a meaningful boost in fans watching from home, with a 20% increase in average household rating and a 35% jump in average households per game.

Continued winning means more money, which the Diamondbacks promise means more roster investments. If those are made wisely, they should redound to more wins. That's on top of whatever long-overdue improvements Arizona makes to Chase Field, which Hall said for next season include new LED lights and upgrades to the sound system and video boards, as well as a "quick fix" to the stadium's troublesome retractable roof. More now than at any point in the past, the Diamondbacks have all the ingredients for success.

They have talent and youth, the ability to spend and the right front office to entrust with the wallet. Already battle-tested in the playoffs, they're poised to be buoyed by outside additions and from within their own minor-league system. They have piqued the interest of a population that has long regarded them with indifference. It may be too early to expect murals of Carroll and Gallen to dot the Phoenix landscape, but after failing to draw two million fans since the pandemic, perhaps Chase Field will look fuller in 2024 with occupants more homogeneously dressed in the home team's colors. The Diamondbacks got their fans' attention. Now they've got to keep it.

"You don't want to lose them and hope they come back," Hall said. "You've got to maintain that fanbase. Right now, we've got momentum."

—*Zach Buchanan is a baseball writer based in Phoenix.*

HITTERS

Nick Ahmed SS   Born: 03/15/90   Age: 34   Bats: R   Throws: R   Height: 6'2"   Weight: 201   Origin: Round 2, 2011 Draft (#85 overall)

YEAR	TM	LVL	AGE	PA	R	HR	RBI	SB	AVG/OBP/SLG	BABIP	SLGCON	BB%	K%	ZSw%	ZCon%	OSw%	OCon%	LA	90th EV	DRC+	BRR	DRP	WARP
2021	AZ	MLB	31	473	46	5	38	7	.221/.280/.339	.279	.445	7.2%	22.0%	69.8%	82.9%	35.8%	59.9%	9.9	102.1	69	0.1	3.8	0.2
2022	AZ	MLB	32	54	7	3	7	0	.231/.259/.442	.265	.622	3.7%	27.8%	71.1%	89.9%	31.6%	47.2%	6.8	101.1	69	0.0	-0.4	-0.1
2023	AZ	MLB	33	210	14	2	17	5	.212/.257/.303	.278	.411	5.7%	24.8%	67.8%	81.2%	34.7%	59.1%	12.6	102.1	73	0.1	-0.8	-0.1
2024 non	AZ	MLB	34	251	22	4	23	5	.225/.282/.336	.279	.441	6.8%	22.4%							74	0.0	1.4	0.2

2023 GP: SS (65), DH (3)   *Comps: Leo Durocher (72), Larry Bowa (70), Alfredo Griffin (69)*

If these were the Diamondbacks of old, they might have allotted Ahmed more playing time, allowing him to find his footing after a shoulder injury kept him off the field for most of 2022. But that team now exists solely in the past, and so does Ahmed. The meteoric rise of Geraldo Perdomo convinced the D-Backs of today to crown a new starting shortstop. And by the time Jordan Lawlar was called up, the writing was on the wall: They designated Ahmed for assignment in September and released him shortly thereafter. Defensively, he's still a sight to behold, but his glove no longer makes up for a limp bat that will only get droopier with age. Letting him go was the correct decision. As is usually the case, though, it's a bummer. Ahmed was the D-Backs' longest-tenured player, the last connection to an era of Arizona baseball that featured Paul Goldschmidt, Robbie Ray, AJ Pollock and many others. Those squads were atrocious for years, became World Series contenders in 2017, then slid back down again—and through it all, Ahmed was there, making slick play after slick play, the one metronomic constant.

Jorge Barrosa CF   Born: 02/17/01   Age: 23   Bats: S   Throws: L   Height: 5'5"   Weight: 165   Origin: IFA, 2017

YEAR	TM	LVL	AGE	PA	R	HR	RBI	SB	AVG/OBP/SLG	BABIP	SLGCON	BB%	K%	ZSw%	ZCon%	OSw%	OCon%	LA	90th EV	DRC+	BRR	DRP	WARP
2021	VIS	A	20	163	30	3	16	9	.333/.389/.449	.404	.569	4.3%	19.0%							111	1.4	3.7	1.3
2021	HIL	A+	20	272	41	4	21	20	.256/.332/.405	.304	.505	8.1%	17.6%							110	-0.2	6.5	1.9
2022	HIL	A+	21	43	5	1	6	4	.300/.349/.450	.324	.514	4.7%	11.6%							117	0.6	-0.6	0.2
2022	AMA	AA	21	510	85	12	51	22	.276/.374/.438	.314	.537	12.7%	15.7%							113	1.5	1.3	2.8
2023	RNO	AAA	22	502	91	13	65	15	.274/.394/.456	.313	.570	15.9%	16.3%	61.9%	86.7%	28.9%	65.3%			111	0.5	-2.5	1.7
2024 DC	AZ	MLB	23	63	6	1	6	2	.230/.315/.350	.280	.455	10.0%	19.4%							88	0.0	0	0.1

2023 GP: CF (94), LF (22), RF (4)   *Comps: Jake Cave (62), Albert Almora Jr. (59), Dustin Fowler (56)*

The diminutive Barrosa is squarely in the running for the title of "Most Underrated D-Backs Prospect." His ability to work both sides of the plate, steal bases, and track down balls in center field are all attributes that elevate him above the generic fourth-outfielder type. He's still not what you'd call an everyday player—at least not the kind you plan around—but Barrosa filling in for a sidelined regular, going on a BABIP-fueled rampage and showing up on defensive highlight reels, providing two to three wins above replacement is totally how Arizona would make the playoffs again.

Corbin Carroll OF Born: 08/21/00 Age: 23 Bats: L Throws: L Height: 5'10" Weight: 165 Origin: Round 1, 2019 Draft (#16 overall)

YEAR	TM	LVL	AGE	PA	R	HR	RBI	SB	AVG/OBP/SLG	BABIP	SLGCON	BB%	K%	ZSw%	ZCon%	OSw%	OCon%	LA	90th EV	DRC+	BRR	DRP	WARP
2021	HIL	A+	20	29	9	2	5	3	.435/.552/.913	.571	1.312	20.7%	24.1%							113	-0.4	0.7	0.2
2022	AMA	AA	21	277	62	16	39	20	.313/.430/.643	.379	.918	14.8%	24.5%							125	2.4	1.2	2.1
2022	RNO	AAA	21	157	25	7	22	11	.287/.408/.535	.345	.742	15.3%	22.9%	59.6%	87.0%	21.5%	53.1%			114	1.8	5.2	1.4
2022	AZ	MLB	21	115	13	4	14	2	.260/.330/.500	.333	.712	7.0%	27.0%	61.5%	80.9%	33.3%	59.1%	9.1	102.6	90	0.3	1.9	0.5
2023	AZ	MLB	22	645	116	25	76	54	.285/.362/.506	.325	.650	8.8%	19.4%	67.2%	87.3%	32.0%	66.7%	10.6	106.0	116	2.9	10.8	4.5
2024 DC	AZ	MLB	23	592	70	20	77	31	.267/.354/.478	.318	.618	9.5%	20.4%							127	1.3	11.6	5.0

2023 GP: LF (74), RF (64), CF (44), DH (3)   *Comps: Andrew Benintendi (68), Christian Yelich (65), Cody Bellinger (63)*

Let's put aside the statistics and accolades for a moment here, and stop to imagine the pressure Carroll must have faced heading into 2023. He was the D-Backs' number one prospect, the future face of a rebuilding franchise. He signed a massive contract extension *before* he exhausted his rookie eligibility. Yet somehow, Carroll lived up to the hype—and more. What kind of rookie hits 25 home runs and swipes more than 50 bags with a 5-foot-11, 165-pound frame? Carroll is a marvel to watch: He makes up for a relative lack of raw power with quick hands and an uppercut swing, allowing him to drive balls in the air with consistency and authority. He seems to have a preternatural sense for when to attempt a stolen base, which, coupled with his plus-plus speed, means he's seldom caught. And in the postseason, the razzle-dazzle continued, putting Carroll on the radar of baseball fans nationwide. Many things went Arizona's way last season. But Carroll's immediate ascendance to superstardom must be the most satisfying of them all.

Dominic Fletcher OF Born: 09/02/97 Age: 26 Bats: L Throws: L Height: 5'6" Weight: 185 Origin: Round 2, 2019 Draft (#75 overall)

YEAR	TM	LVL	AGE	PA	R	HR	RBI	SB	AVG/OBP/SLG	BABIP	SLGCON	BB%	K%	ZSw%	ZCon%	OSw%	OCon%	LA	90th EV	DRC+	BRR	DRP	WARP
2021	AMA	AA	23	440	60	15	56	3	.264/.314/.445	.320	.611	5.7%	24.8%							95	0.4	4.7	1.6
2022	AMA	AA	24	142	28	7	34	4	.346/.408/.591	.385	.735	9.2%	17.6%							106	0.5	0.8	0.7
2022	RNO	AAA	24	449	70	5	38	5	.301/.368/.452	.369	.581	9.4%	19.6%	67.6%	90.3%	36.6%	70.2%			99	-5.4	11.9	1.9
2023	RNO	AAA	25	334	71	10	45	5	.291/.399/.500	.340	.644	12.6%	18.6%	71.7%	86.6%	30.2%	65.7%			110	-1.2	0.4	1.4
2023	AZ	MLB	25	102	10	2	14	0	.301/.350/.441	.377	.577	6.9%	21.6%	66.3%	85.5%	36.4%	69.2%	7.0	100.9	86	-0.1	-1.0	0.0
2024 DC	AZ	MLB	26	259	24	4	26	4	.245/.312/.381	.300	.487	7.7%	20.2%							91	-0.2	-1.1	0.2

2023 GP: CF (14), RF (12), LF (4)   *Comps: Lorenzo Cain (65), Kevin Kiermaier (65), Tyler Naquin (64)*

It took a Corbin Carroll injury for the D-Backs to finally have a use for Fletcher, whom they called up in late April. He hit the ground running, but a subsequent slump and Carroll's return made for a May demotion. Fletcher found his way back to the big-league roster in late June… and only lasted about a week. All this was seemingly not enough misery, so the Baseball Gods punished Fletcher with a fractured finger that prematurely ended his 2023 season. 'Tis the life of a platoon fourth outfielder on a team whose weakness isn't your position. Concerns about his ability to hit aside, he looked extremely comfortable in the outfield during his cup of coffee. Together with Alek Thomas, Fletcher makes center field a no-fly zone.

Lourdes Gurriel Jr. LF/DH Born: 10/10/93 Age: 30 Bats: R Throws: R Height: 6'4" Weight: 215 Origin: IFA, 2016

YEAR	TM	LVL	AGE	PA	R	HR	RBI	SB	AVG/OBP/SLG	BABIP	SLGCON	BB%	K%	ZSw%	ZCon%	OSw%	OCon%	LA	90th EV	DRC+	BRR	DRP	WARP
2021	TOR	MLB	27	541	62	21	84	1	.276/.319/.466	.305	.585	5.9%	18.9%	69.6%	85.6%	37.9%	63.2%	10.4	104.4	114	-0.3	-3.2	2.5
2022	TOR	MLB	28	493	52	5	52	3	.291/.343/.400	.346	.489	6.3%	16.8%	69.9%	87.6%	33.0%	65.1%	11.0	104.1	110	-0.5	-1.4	1.9
2023	AZ	MLB	29	592	65	24	82	5	.261/.309/.463	.282	.569	5.6%	17.4%	70.7%	89.9%	33.2%	68.0%	10.8	103.6	114	-0.1	-1.8	2.3
2024 DC	AZ	MLB	30	506	54	16	61	3	.265/.315/.426	.289	.512	6.1%	15.7%							108	-0.2	-2.6	1.5

2023 GP: LF (95), DH (50), 1B (1)   *Comps: Cleon Jones (84), Lou Piniella (83), Eddie Rosario (82)*

Few players are as inconsistently consistent as Gurriel Jr., who goes through hot streaks and slumps, power outages and BABIP slumps, and yet always winds up in the same place. Fortunately, it's a pretty good place. The secondary piece in the Moreno-Varsho trade quickly asserted that the Diamondbacks won the trade, hitting .311/.359/.547 through the end of May, before the gravitational forces of his career line pulled him back like a tractor beam. Meanwhile, in an effort to stave off defensive decline, Gurriel Jr. improved his reaction time at the expense of the quality of his routes. In other words, once he saw an incoming ball, he immediately took off, optimization be damned. And it worked, for the most part. That summarizes his career in general, really: There's a perfect version of him in there, one that marries athleticism and technique, gets the liners to drop while staying healthy enough to put the flies over the fence, lets the bad pitches by, makes the most of his speed. That hypothetical Gurriel Jr. is a star. The one we have is still pretty good.

─────── ★ ★ ★ *2024 Top 101 Prospect* **#81** ★ ★ ★ ───────

Druw Jones CF Born: 11/28/03 Age: 20 Bats: R Throws: R Height: 6'4" Weight: 180 Origin: Round 1, 2022 Draft (#2 overall)

YEAR	TM	LVL	AGE	PA	R	HR	RBI	SB	AVG/OBP/SLG	BABIP	SLGCON	BB%	K%	ZSw%	ZCon%	OSw%	OCon%	LA	90th EV	DRC+	BRR	DRP	WARP
2023	DIAR	ROK	19	32	8	0	2	3	.222/.344/.222	.300	.300	15.6%	21.9%										
2023	VIS	A	19	131	19	2	9	6	.252/.366/.351	.347	.506	15.3%	26.0%							100	1.3	1.1	0.5
2024 non	AZ	MLB	20	251	19	2	20	0	.211/.273/.294	.322	.466	7.0%	33.8%							62	0.0	0	-0.4

2023 GP: CF (34), DH (7)   *Comps: Daniel Mateo (79), Austin Jackson (74), Joe Benson (71)*

There's not much to report here, despite Jones being arguably the top prospect in Arizona's farm system following Corbin Carroll's graduation (also see: Lawlar, Jordan). That's because a freak shoulder injury just three weeks after signing and then a quad strain in early 2023 have limited Jones to a mere 172 plate appearances in pro ball. The lack of a meaningful sample size, unreliable to begin with due to those injuries, means there's no reason to change our outlook on Jones. In this case, starting from a clean slate seems like the right decision. Recall that his massive raw power and terrific instincts in the outfield, both near-unprecedented for someone of his age, were what propelled him to the top of draft boards in 2022. The double-whammy of injuries in his first professional season might have slowed him down, but it's way too early to say they have altered his ultimate destination: star center fielder for the Diamondbacks.

★ ★ ★ *2024 Top 101 Prospect* **#14** ★ ★ ★

Jordan Lawlar **SS**   Born: 07/17/02   Age: 21   Bats: R   Throws: R   Height: 6'1"   Weight: 190   Origin: Round 1, 2021 Draft (#6 overall)

YEAR	TM	LVL	AGE	PA	R	HR	RBI	SB	AVG/OBP/SLG	BABIP	SLGCON	BB%	K%	ZSw%	ZCon%	OSw%	OCon%	LA	90th EV	DRC+	BRR	DRP	WARP
2022	VIS	A	19	208	44	9	32	24	.351/.447/.603	.437	.833	13.0%	23.1%							120	1.0	-1.1	1.1
2022	HIL	A+	19	130	31	3	17	13	.288/.385/.477	.382	.679	12.3%	25.4%							109	3.6	-1.8	0.8
2022	AMA	AA	19	97	18	4	11	2	.212/.299/.353	.259	.526	10.3%	28.9%							85	0.2	-0.2	0.1
2023	AMA	AA	20	410	77	15	48	33	.263/.366/.474	.310	.636	11.5%	21.7%							101	5.3	-3.3	1.6
2023	RNO	AAA	20	80	18	5	19	3	.358/.438/.612	.365	.745	11.3%	15.0%	72.3%	83.8%	21.5%	52.9%			114	-0.4	-0.6	0.3
2023	AZ	MLB	20	34	2	0	0	1	.129/.206/.129	.200	.200	5.9%	32.4%	70.4%	84.2%	28.7%	39.1%	11.2	86.3	73	0.0	0.2	0.0
2024 DC	AZ	MLB	21	199	19	5	20	6	.223/.296/.359	.284	.500	8.0%	25.3%							86	-0.1	0.4	0.4

2023 GP: SS (13)   *Comps: Xander Bogaerts (56), Carlos Correa (53), Adalberto Mondesi (52)*

Prospects in the mirror are closer than they appear, especially these days. When Lawlar was first drafted in 2021, many saw him as someone who'd progress quickly through the minors. But his arrival in the show, just two years later, probably surprised even the most optimistic proponents. It's a well-deserved promotion. Hitting-wise, Lawlar has never encountered a genuine wall in the pros, and he removed any lingering doubts about his hit tool by posting a strikeout rate of 15% in Triple-A. The Diamondbacks needed an extra jolt to propel themselves towards October baseball, saw that one of their top prospects was raking, and made the decision. Unfortunately, Lawlar wasn't much help. And although it's just 30 plate appearances, *maaaybe* we need to heed caution to how he whiffed and whiffed and whiffed, especially against breaking balls. Then again, Lawlar's cup of coffee did showcase his stellar plate discipline, so it wasn't all a wash. Let's hope he can record an exit velocity over 100 mph in 2024, allowing us to let out a sigh of relief, and say, "See, nothing to worry about!"

Kyle Lewis **DH**   Born: 07/13/95   Age: 28   Bats: R   Throws: R   Height: 6'4"   Weight: 222   Origin: Round 1, 2016 Draft (#11 overall)

YEAR	TM	LVL	AGE	PA	R	HR	RBI	SB	AVG/OBP/SLG	BABIP	SLGCON	BB%	K%	ZSw%	ZCon%	OSw%	OCon%	LA	90th EV	DRC+	BRR	DRP	WARP
2021	SEA	MLB	25	147	15	5	11	2	.246/.333/.392	.307	.548	10.9%	25.2%	75.6%	71.9%	26.3%	53.3%	17.4	106.2	100	0.1	-2.2	0.4
2022	TAC	AAA	26	174	29	12	34	0	.245/.362/.517	.267	.745	14.9%	25.9%	75.4%	75.6%	28.1%	50.4%			111	-1.2	-1.4	0.5
2022	SEA	MLB	26	62	6	3	5	0	.143/.226/.304	.147	.459	8.1%	30.6%	76.7%	76.8%	32.4%	41.1%	16.2	105.5	92	0.0	-0.6	0.0
2023	RNO	AAA	27	293	55	17	80	0	.371/.457/.641	.426	.837	13.3%	19.8%	66.5%	80.9%	29.3%	66.3%			123	-1.4	-1.1	1.5
2023	AZ	MLB	27	54	2	1	2	0	.157/.204/.255	.241	.433	5.6%	38.9%	72.5%	69.7%	31.0%	54.5%	23.8	100.8	61	0.0	-0.1	-0.1
2024 non	AZ	MLB	28	251	28	9	30	0	.231/.314/.398	.282	.553	10.1%	25.2%							101	0.0	-3.6	0.4

2023 GP: DH (11), LF (3)   *Comps: Matt Murton (53), Wily Mo Pena (50), Johan Camargo (48)*

The sheer discrepancy between his Triple-A and big-league slashline in 2023 suggests that the former AL Rookie of the Year winner is forever destined to reside in Quad-A purgatory. On top of that, Lewis still can't stay healthy for long enough to prove that he belongs on a major-league roster, meaning his time as a relevant baseball name is ticking down fast. The last window of opportunity is this upcoming season, assuming another team gives him one last opportunity. But if he fails once more, Lewis will likely go down as one of the biggest "What ifs?" in recent memory.

Evan Longoria **3B/DH**   Born: 10/07/85   Age: 38   Bats: R   Throws: R   Height: 6'1"   Weight: 213   Origin: Round 1, 2006 Draft (#3 overall)

YEAR	TM	LVL	AGE	PA	R	HR	RBI	SB	AVG/OBP/SLG	BABIP	SLGCON	BB%	K%	ZSw%	ZCon%	OSw%	OCon%	LA	90th EV	DRC+	BRR	DRP	WARP
2021	SF	MLB	35	291	45	13	46	1	.261/.351/.482	.305	.659	12.0%	23.4%	66.6%	81.8%	23.6%	59.7%	15.4	105.5	111	-0.2	-0.4	1.3
2022	SAC	AAA	36	25	3	0	0	0	.333/.360/.417	.500	.625	4.0%	32.0%	60.5%	73.1%	31.5%	58.8%			78	-1.5	-0.6	-0.2
2022	SF	MLB	36	298	31	14	42	0	.244/.315/.451	.297	.656	9.1%	27.9%	65.6%	79.1%	29.1%	57.2%	18.5	105.8	103	-0.2	-0.9	0.7
2023	AZ	MLB	37	237	25	11	28	0	.223/.295/.422	.277	.645	9.7%	30.8%	61.1%	82.0%	31.5%	57.8%	15.9	107.0	77	-0.2	0.3	0.0
2024 non	AZ	MLB	38	251	28	9	30	0	.228/.308/.400	.283	.566	9.6%	26.5%							98	0.0	-0.2	0.6

2023 GP: 3B (41), DH (25)   *Comps: Scott Rolen (81), Matt Williams (77), Brooks Robinson (75)*

If 2023 was Longoria's last season, it wasn't the flashiest, nor the most memorable. But not every baseball icon needs a storybook ending to be remembered for decades to come. In a way, Longoria's brief stay in Arizona, considering the arc of his career, was an appropriate sendoff: A star on a small-market team, Longoria seldom received the intense limelight reserved for big city sports celebrities. Instead, he quietly put up stellar numbers year after year, excelling at all parts of the game. And even as his body began to rust, Longoria never became a burden—not to a team, and certainly not to a fandom. As a Diamondback, he fulfilled his duties as both a platoon bat and a veteran leader for a team brimming with up-and-coming players. Sure, it would have been awesome to see Longoria ride off into a glorious sunset, just as Albert Pujols did in 2022. But nothing will change what he's accomplished, whether we've reached the coda or not.

Jansel Luis **MI**   Born: 03/06/05   Age: 19   Bats: S   Throws: R   Height: 6'0"   Weight: 170   Origin: IFA, 2022

YEAR	TM	LVL	AGE	PA	R	HR	RBI	SB	AVG/OBP/SLG	BABIP	SLGCON	BB%	K%	ZSw%	ZCon%	OSw%	OCon%	LA	90th EV	DRC+	BRR	DRP	WARP
2022	DSL DBR	ROK	17	178	33	1	14	8	.335/.393/.404	.379	.464	6.7%	11.8%										
2023	DIAB	ROK	18	105	18	3	12	9	.297/.381/.495	.324	.592	8.6%	14.3%										
2023	VIS	A	18	155	19	4	15	7	.257/.310/.417	.314	.550	5.2%	22.6%							94	0.0	-1.3	0.3
2024 non	AZ	MLB	19	251	18	3	20	0	.210/.254/.306	.316	.480	4.7%	33.7%							55	0.0	0	-0.6

2023 GP: 2B (29), SS (26), DH (7)   *Comps: Rougned Odor (81), Omar Estévez (79), Paul Kelly (78)*

As is often the case for teenage infield prospects, the bounds on Luis' potential are basically nonexistent; it's tough to give an estimate of someone who hasn't even finished growing. But by the eye test—the only reliable test at this point—Luis seems promising. Most evaluators agree that he's athletic enough to stick at shortstop, which is rare: Scouting reports tend to be pessimistic about anyone's capacity to handle one of baseball's most arduous positions. Then there's the fact that he's a legitimate switch hitter. His left-handed swing is tailor-made for hard, airborne contact; his right-handed swing lacks polish, but is nonetheless advanced for someone of his age. Right now, Luis' biggest weakness is his lack of discipline at the plate. Let's be honest, though: Who among us were disciplined when we were 18? It's understandable that Luis wants to show off his burgeoning power, and it's safe to assume that he'll become more patient as he matures.

Ketel Marte 2B   Born: 10/12/93   Age: 30   Bats: S   Throws: R   Height: 6'1"   Weight: 210   Origin: IFA, 2010

YEAR	TM	LVL	AGE	PA	R	HR	RBI	SB	AVG/OBP/SLG	BABIP	SLGCON	BB%	K%	ZSw%	ZCon%	OSw%	OCon%	LA	90th EV	DRC+	BRR	DRP	WARP
2021	AZ	MLB	27	374	52	14	50	2	.318/.377/.532	.352	.646	8.3%	16.0%	67.7%	89.8%	30.2%	71.3%	9.9	107.3	122	-0.1	-7.2	1.9
2022	AZ	MLB	28	558	68	12	52	5	.240/.321/.407	.276	.512	9.9%	18.1%	66.9%	85.0%	32.0%	71.7%	13.4	106.4	109	0.0	0.3	2.3
2023	AZ	MLB	29	650	94	25	82	8	.276/.358/.485	.300	.600	10.9%	16.8%	69.1%	87.5%	27.2%	64.0%	10.7	106.7	121	0.1	-0.3	3.6
2024 DC	AZ	MLB	30	616	70	18	74	5	.263/.345/.439	.298	.542	10.2%	17.1%							120	0.0	-1.5	3.1

2023 GP: 2B (145), DH (5), CF (2), SS (1)   *Comps: Lou Whitaker (71), Roberto Alomar (70), Billy Herman (69)*

We'll look back on 2019 as the year that allowed line-drive hitters with unassuming physiques to set career-highs in home runs, subsequently inflating our expectations for their future outputs. Marte was one of the poster children for the launch angle revolution back then, but after his power numbers dwindled in the seasons to follow, he was written off as a fluke, a product of an abnormally lively ball. And yet by any WAR metric he was an All-Star in 2023. You can change the official baseball, but you can't change what's inherent to a player: Marte regularly records some of the highest maximum exit velocities in the league. He's carried an above-average barrel rate in every season since his breakout year, if you exclude an uncharacteristically poor (and truncated) 2020 showing. That's alongside a consistent sub-20% strikeout rate, which is just… *chef's kiss*. Marte is a fantastic second baseman regardless of the environment he's in, or the environment of his critics.

Jake McCarthy RF   Born: 07/30/97   Age: 26   Bats: L   Throws: L   Height: 6'2"   Weight: 215   Origin: Round 1, 2018 Draft (#39 overall)

YEAR	TM	LVL	AGE	PA	R	HR	RBI	SB	AVG/OBP/SLG	BABIP	SLGCON	BB%	K%	ZSw%	ZCon%	OSw%	OCon%	LA	90th EV	DRC+	BRR	DRP	WARP
2021	AMA	AA	23	156	25	6	23	17	.241/.333/.489	.318	.736	10.9%	29.5%							100	2.1	-7.0	0.0
2021	RNO	AAA	23	212	38	9	31	12	.262/.330/.508	.306	.683	9.4%	23.1%							104	1.2	-5.5	0.4
2021	AZ	MLB	23	70	11	2	4	3	.220/.333/.373	.324	.611	11.4%	32.9%	72.1%	76.0%	28.7%	33.3%	1.1	100.6	73	0.0	0.0	0.0
2022	RNO	AAA	24	165	33	5	27	11	.369/.457/.596	.412	.706	11.5%	13.3%	69.7%	88.7%	26.7%	56.3%			118	-1.2	-4.1	0.4
2022	AZ	MLB	24	354	53	8	43	23	.283/.342/.427	.349	.559	6.5%	21.5%	74.9%	83.1%	33.9%	52.5%	6.3	102.5	96	1.5	1.9	1.3
2023	RNO	AAA	25	221	42	9	36	15	.360/.416/.594	.383	.696	7.7%	13.1%	79.9%	90.2%	26.6%	63.0%			115	-0.6	-0.5	1.0
2023	AZ	MLB	25	312	37	2	16	26	.243/.318/.326	.305	.421	8.3%	19.9%	71.9%	89.3%	34.0%	60.5%	5.9	99.3	87	1.1	4.1	0.9
2024 DC	AZ	MLB	26	361	35	7	38	23	.250/.318/.393	.294	.491	7.4%	17.9%							96	0.7	1.5	1.0

2023 GP: RF (84), CF (12), DH (1)   *Comps: Jackie Bradley Jr. (55), Corey Hart (54), Josh Reddick (53)*

Last year's *BP Annual* comment pondered whether McCarthy is a speed-power guy or merely a speed guy. Six months of baseball later, we're leaning more towards the latter. McCarthy enjoyed a bite-sized breakout in 2022, but many signs pointed to it being unsustainable. Sure enough, his swing reverted to its original form the following season, leading to more grounders and fewer hard-hit balls. McCarthy's fall to Earth isn't a massive loss for the D-Backs, who have plenty of outfield options. But it's a loss for baseball fans, for whom speed-power guys are eye candy.

Gabriel Moreno C   Born: 02/14/00   Age: 24   Bats: R   Throws: R   Height: 5'11"   Weight: 195   Origin: IFA, 2016

YEAR	TM	LVL	AGE	PA	R	HR	RBI	SB	AVG/OBP/SLG	BABIP	SLGCON	BB%	K%	ZSw%	ZCon%	OSw%	OCon%	LA	90th EV	DRC+	BRR	DRP	WARP
2021	LAR	WIN	21	73	11	1	8	2	.279/.397/.361	.327	.440	15.1%	15.1%										
2021	MSS	WIN	21	100	16	1	18	0	.329/.410/.494	.370	.583	13.0%	13.0%	55.0%	81.8%	36.8%	57.1%						
2021	NH	AA	21	145	29	8	45	1	.373/.441/.651	.398	.788	9.7%	15.2%							147	0.6	-2.3	1.2
2022	BUF	AAA	22	267	35	3	39	7	.315/.386/.420	.377	.518	9.0%	16.9%							115	-2.8	1.1	1.1
2022	TOR	MLB	22	73	10	1	7	0	.319/.356/.377	.350	.426	5.5%	11.0%	61.9%	89.0%	36.7%	68.5%	5.8	103.7	113	0.0	1.2	0.5
2023	AZ	MLB	23	380	33	7	50	6	.284/.339/.408	.338	.523	7.6%	19.7%	59.5%	91.5%	30.3%	65.6%	4.3	103.1	98	0.1	-9.2	0.5
2024 DC	AZ	MLB	24	438	43	9	44	6	.260/.322/.381	.300	.469	7.5%	16.8%							102	-0.1	3	2.0

2023 GP: C (104)   *Comps: Salvador Perez (66), John Ryan Murphy (64), Francisco Mejía (63)*

YEAR	TM	P. COUNT	FRM RUNS	BLK RUNS	THRW RUNS	TOT RUNS
2021	MSS	1282			0.4	0.4
2021	NH	4215	-2.5	0.1	0.6	-1.8
2022	BUF	7046	-3.2	0.1	4.1	1.0
2022	TOR	2527	1.1	0.0	0.5	1.6
2023	AZ	13798	-11.4	0.6	2.8	-8.0
2024	AZ	15632	-0.6	0.4	3.1	3.0

Just how good is Moreno? It's a question more difficult to answer than you might think. The catcher started generating buzz within scouting circles after he slugged .650 in 2021 across Double- and Triple-A, but his batted ball data at the major-league level suggests those numbers were somewhat inflated. He employs a flat swing, which allows Moreno to flick letter-high fastballs the other way, but also makes him vulnerable to down-and-in sinkers. Behind the plate, Moreno is competent at blocking pitches and gunning down would-be base stealers, but his framing currently rates as well below average. And while he's known for his athleticism, that has yet to translate into runs, either via stolen or extra bases. The repeating pattern of "Moreno has or does X, but lacks Y" raises the question, "Does Moreno need more time to refine certain aspects of his game, or are those flaws here to stay?" There may not be an evaluator, professional or amateur, who can confidently answer that question as of this writing.

Kevin Newman IF   Born: 08/04/93   Age: 30   Bats: R   Throws: R   Height: 6'1"   Weight: 195   Origin: Round 1, 2015 Draft (#19 overall)

YEAR	TM	LVL	AGE	PA	R	HR	RBI	SB	AVG/OBP/SLG	BABIP	SLGCON	BB%	K%	ZSw%	ZCon%	OSw%	OCon%	LA	90th EV	DRC+	BRR	DRP	WARP
2021	PIT	MLB	27	554	50	5	39	6	.226/.265/.309	.236	.336	4.9%	7.4%	63.5%	95.2%	30.1%	76.8%	9.6	100.6	86	0.2	0.9	1.2
2022	IND	AAA	28	53	6	0	6	0	.396/.434/.458	.442	.524	5.7%	11.3%							113	0.8	-0.5	0.3
2022	PIT	MLB	28	309	31	2	24	8	.274/.316/.372	.322	.446	5.2%	15.5%	66.1%	92.8%	35.2%	74.0%	12.4	101.1	97	0.2	-1.9	0.7
2023	LOU	AAA	29	44	6	0	3	0	.211/.318/.211	.267	.267	11.4%	18.2%	65.3%	83.0%	23.3%	42.9%			87	0.1	-0.5	0.0
2023	CIN	MLB	29	253	28	3	28	8	.253/.311/.364	.280	.429	6.7%	13.4%	63.0%	89.5%	32.4%	77.8%	12.1	101.1	112	0.1	-1.8	1.0
2024 non	AZ	MLB	30	251	22	3	22	4	.249/.303/.344	.274	.394	6.6%	11.9%							85	0.1	-1.2	0.2

2023 GP: 3B (24), SS (19), 2B (16), 1B (9), DH (7)   *Comps: Darwin Barney (55), Eduardo Núñez (54), Erik González (54)*

The utility infielder was dealt to the Reds ahead of 2023 and, even on a roster that seemingly added a talented and exciting infielder every other week, Newman played all over the place and stood at the plate well enough to hang around most of the season in between an oblique strain and a bout of gastritis. That performance wasn't enough to make him indispensable among all those infielders, as he was released at the end of September, but another team searching for infield depth might offer the first-ever genuine and welcoming utterance of "hello, Newman."

Geraldo Perdomo SS   Born: 10/22/99   Age: 24   Bats: S   Throws: R   Height: 6'2"   Weight: 203   Origin: IFA, 2016

YEAR	TM	LVL	AGE	PA	R	HR	RBI	SB	AVG/OBP/SLG	BABIP	SLGCON	BB%	K%	ZSw%	ZCon%	OSw%	OCon%	LA	90th EV	DRC+	BRR	DRP	WARP
2021	AMA	AA	21	344	51	6	32	8	.231/.351/.357	.299	.498	13.7%	23.5%							104	0.3	1.6	1.4
2021	AZ	MLB	21	37	5	0	1	0	.258/.378/.419	.320	.520	16.2%	16.2%	63.2%	77.8%	19.4%	57.1%	16.5	98.3	99	0.0	0.0	0.1
2022	AZ	MLB	22	500	58	5	40	9	.195/.285/.262	.243	.345	10.0%	20.6%	60.1%	87.7%	23.5%	67.2%	8.8	99.1	78	0.5	6.4	1.0
2023	AZ	MLB	23	495	71	6	47	16	.246/.353/.359	.295	.455	12.9%	17.4%	59.1%	90.8%	21.2%	70.8%	14.1	98.2	96	0.9	-3.4	1.1
2024 DC	AZ	MLB	24	445	43	7	41	11	.230/.333/.348	.269	.427	12.1%	16.1%							95	0.1	2.2	1.5

2023 GP: SS (116), 2B (28), 3B (16)   *Comps: Luis Ordaz (66), Abraham O. Nunez (66), Ketel Marte (62)*

Geraldo Perdomo: major-league shortstop. Believe it or not, that title was once in jeopardy; after a glum rookie season, Perdomo seemed destined for a utility role. But he broke out in his sophomore year, and for a brief moment in April, he was also the hottest hitter on the planet. Yes, it took some divine intervention, and his cooling off as the weather warmed up came to the surprise of no one with even a basic understanding of Baseball Savant. Not all of it was a fluke, however. Perdomo has a genuine knack for pulling the ball and producing shallow line drives, often dropping mere inches from the foul line, meaning he'll always be somewhat disliked by advanced metrics. But you know what no model could possibly dislike? His 98th percentile chase rate, meaning he swung at fewer balls than almost anyone in the majors. The DRC+ he ultimately ended up with seems like a reasonable guideline for how Perdomo will fare in the future.

Jace Peterson 3B   Born: 05/09/90   Age: 34   Bats: L   Throws: R   Height: 6'0"   Weight: 215   Origin: Round 1, 2011 Draft (#58 overall)

YEAR	TM	LVL	AGE	PA	R	HR	RBI	SB	AVG/OBP/SLG	BABIP	SLGCON	BB%	K%	ZSw%	ZCon%	OSw%	OCon%	LA	90th EV	DRC+	BRR	DRP	WARP
2021	NAS	AAA	31	64	12	5	19	1	.236/.344/.582	.258	.889	14.1%	29.7%							122	-0.2	-0.6	0.3
2021	MIL	MLB	31	302	36	6	31	10	.247/.348/.367	.310	.497	12.6%	22.5%	59.1%	82.7%	25.5%	55.3%	12.2	102.8	94	0.3	0.1	0.8
2022	MIL	MLB	32	328	44	8	34	12	.236/.316/.382	.303	.542	10.1%	25.9%	57.1%	84.8%	26.8%	52.4%	9.2	102.3	86	0.6	0.3	0.4
2023	OAK	MLB	33	324	30	6	28	11	.221/.313/.324	.279	.446	11.1%	23.8%	61.1%	85.5%	25.9%	55.7%	15.1	101.5	93	0.4	0.0	0.8
2023	AZ	MLB	33	106	5	0	9	4	.183/.276/.258	.246	.348	10.4%	22.6%	61.6%	88.7%	27.0%	51.4%	10.5	98.1	86	0.1	0.1	0.2
2024 DC	AZ	MLB	34	93	9	2	9	3	.219/.310/.347	.273	.468	10.6%	22.6%							85	0.1	-0.5	0.0

2023 GP: 3B (112), 2B (21), DH (3), P (2), 1B (1), LF (1)   *Comps: Nick Punto (66), Mark McLemore (62), Alex Cora (53)*

Peterson initially agreed to a two-year contract with Oakland, where he didn't do much with the bat and was traded for a smattering of prospect capital. In Arizona, he eventually formed the strong half of a third base platoon with fellow veteran Evan Longoria, but still couldn't muster up the strength to hit, even in a more specialized role. Peterson is a utility man's utility man, a human Swiss Army knife, but the rust on his various tools has become noticeable, and half the blades won't come out. The Diamondbacks will probably run him back next year; it won't cost them much, and a player like Peterson, even in a diminished state, is plenty valuable for his versatility. It wouldn't be surprising, though, if this marks the beginning of the end.

Emmanuel Rivera 3B   Born: 06/29/96   Age: 28   Bats: R   Throws: R   Height: 6'2"   Weight: 225   Origin: Round 19, 2015 Draft (#579 overall)

YEAR	TM	LVL	AGE	PA	R	HR	RBI	SB	AVG/OBP/SLG	BABIP	SLGCON	BB%	K%	ZSw%	ZCon%	OSw%	OCon%	LA	90th EV	DRC+	BRR	DRP	WARP
2021	OMA	AAA	25	282	48	19	57	3	.286/.348/.592	.300	.766	7.8%	20.6%							126	-1.7	4.0	1.9
2021	KC	MLB	25	98	13	1	5	2	.256/.316/.333	.324	.435	8.2%	21.4%	70.6%	89.1%	32.2%	54.8%	7.7	105.2	83	0.0	-0.1	0.1
2022	MAY	WIN	26	150	12	0	14	2	.303/.340/.338	.344	.384	4.7%	11.3%							107	-0.1	-2.5	0.1
2022	OMA	AAA	26	85	12	3	5	1	.307/.388/.520	.357	.661	11.8%	18.8%							107	-0.1	-2.5	0.1
2022	KC	MLB	26	211	24	6	22	0	.237/.284/.399	.281	.520	5.2%	21.8%	75.1%	86.0%	32.4%	59.7%	9.4	105.2	97	-0.2	0.4	0.5
2022	AZ	MLB	26	148	22	6	18	1	.227/.304/.424	.267	.589	8.1%	25.0%	73.9%	84.3%	33.1%	51.4%	10.8	103.0	97	-0.3	0.1	0.3
2023	RNO	AAA	27	129	23	5	25	1	.330/.395/.598	.348	.713	9.3%	14.0%	74.8%	87.7%	23.7%	53.2%			117	0.1	2.1	0.8
2023	AZ	MLB	27	283	32	4	29	1	.261/.314/.358	.313	.458	7.8%	19.8%	71.1%	86.6%	29.9%	51.5%	11.4	103.4	95	-0.2	0.1	0.7
2024 DC	AZ	MLB	28	197	20	5	21	1	.244/.304/.389	.291	.504	7.2%	21.3%							95	-0.1	0.1	0.3

2023 GP: 3B (65), 1B (12), DH (9)   *Comps: Luis Jimenez (60), Danny Valencia (56), Chone Figgins (56)*

From 2022 to '23, Rivera increased his hard-hit rate by eight percentage points (good!), but saw his barrel rate decrease by 3.4 percentage points (bad!). Here, the bad outweighs the good. Even if you start hitting 'em harder, it's meaningless if you're doing so at suboptimal launch angles. This, combined with the fact that he suddenly turned into a pumpkin against four-seam fastballs, tells us that the issue probably lies in *how* Rivera's bat is colliding with the ball. So no, he's not a lost cause. Maybe he's a little late against the hard stuff, or maybe his swing path is a little out of whack. An offseason of work should be enough to provide Rivera an offensive pick-me-up and return him to role-player status.

Kevin Sim　IF　Born: 02/07/02　Age: 22　Bats: R　Throws: R　Height: 6'2"　Weight: 210　Origin: Round 5, 2023 Draft (#148 overall)

YEAR	TM	LVL	AGE	PA	R	HR	RBI	SB	AVG/OBP/SLG	BABIP	SLGCON	BB%	K%	ZSw%	ZCon%	OSw%	OCon%	LA	90th EV	DRC+	BRR	DRP	WARP
2023	VIS	A	21	123	14	3	14	1	.255/.333/.400	.329	.557	8.1%	25.2%							97	0.2	-0.9	0.0
2024 non	AZ	MLB	22	251	19	3	20	0	.212/.266/.302	.331	.493	5.7%	35.8%							60	0.0	0	-0.7

2023 GP: 3B (18), 1B (7), 2B (6), DH (2)　　　　　　　　　　　Comps: JC Encarnacion (85), Spencer Steer (85), Deibinson Romero (84)

Sim is the son of former KBO player Shim Jeong-soo, who hit 300 home runs in his career and was bestowed the nickname 'Hercules.' Staying true to his lineage, Sim led all prospects at last year's MLB Draft Combine in hard-hit balls and left an undeniable impression on scouts, including those working for the Diamondbacks. It's true that he doesn't have a standout tool other than his raw power. But if you believe what years of baseball data can tell us, one positive is that he doesn't strike out too often for someone with an uppercut swing—and that could signal a future improvement to his hit tool.

Eugenio Suárez　3B　Born: 07/18/91　Age: 32　Bats: R　Throws: R　Height: 5'11"　Weight: 213　Origin: IFA, 2008

YEAR	TM	LVL	AGE	PA	R	HR	RBI	SB	AVG/OBP/SLG	BABIP	SLGCON	BB%	K%	ZSw%	ZCon%	OSw%	OCon%	LA	90th EV	DRC+	BRR	DRP	WARP
2021	CIN	MLB	29	574	71	31	79	0	.198/.286/.428	.224	.647	9.8%	29.8%	66.9%	85.5%	28.8%	50.1%	18.6	106.2	91	-0.7	-0.7	1.2
2022	SEA	MLB	30	629	76	31	87	0	.236/.332/.459	.302	.718	11.6%	31.2%	65.8%	81.0%	27.4%	46.5%	20.0	105.2	112	-0.7	0.5	2.4
2023	SEA	MLB	31	694	68	22	96	2	.232/.323/.391	.314	.609	10.1%	30.8%	68.5%	80.9%	30.0%	48.4%	19.2	105.1	82	-0.9	2.7	0.8
2024 DC	AZ	MLB	32	584	63	21	69	0	.209/.300/.380	.271	.576	10.0%	30.1%							91	0.0	0.3	0.9

2023 GP: 3B (159), DH (3)　　　　　　　　　　　　　　　　Comps: Billy Nash (69), Ken McMullen (69), Evan Longoria (68)

Suárez joined Kyle Schwarber in defending their respective leagues' strikeout crowns, with each racking up career-high totals that ranked inside the top six on the all-time single-season leaderboard. But unlike Schwarber, whose barrage of titanic dingers continued to compensate for the boatload of Ks, Suárez's power production went in the wrong direction. While a career year with the glove paired with exceptional durability helped him maintain respectable value amidst his sharp downtick in pop, his future as a reliable middle-of-the-order bat is suddenly in question. With the Mariners' stated intentions to cut down on the lineup's collective propensity to whiff and their less transparent but painfully obvious goal of cutting payroll, a trade of Suárez and his $11 million salary for 2024 emerged as likely. That said, salary dumping a fan favorite who consistently professed "Good Vibes Only" was an appropriately bleak start to Seattle's winter. The D-Backs, meanwhile, still riding the wave from their unlikely pennant, were an ideal beneficiary on the other end of the deal. Adding a flawed but functional veteran in Suárez both addressed a severe need at third base while adding a beloved personality that any clubhouse would happily welcome.

Alek Thomas　CF　Born: 04/28/00　Age: 24　Bats: L　Throws: L　Height: 5'11"　Weight: 175　Origin: Round 2, 2018 Draft (#63 overall)

YEAR	TM	LVL	AGE	PA	R	HR	RBI	SB	AVG/OBP/SLG	BABIP	SLGCON	BB%	K%	ZSw%	ZCon%	OSw%	OCon%	LA	90th EV	DRC+	BRR	DRP	WARP
2021	AMA	AA	21	329	54	10	41	8	.283/.374/.507	.335	.656	11.2%	19.8%							119	-0.6	-1.0	1.6
2021	RNO	AAA	21	166	32	8	18	5	.369/.434/.658	.439	.852	9.0%	20.5%							119	0.4	4.0	1.4
2022	RNO	AAA	22	131	25	4	19	5	.322/.397/.539	.351	.639	10.7%	13.7%	74.2%	85.9%	32.2%	69.4%			110	-1.8	-0.4	0.4
2022	AZ	MLB	22	411	45	8	39	4	.231/.275/.344	.263	.427	5.4%	18.0%	62.9%	85.1%	39.8%	64.6%	2.6	104.2	80	1.7	5.2	1.2
2023	RNO	AAA	23	128	24	3	31	2	.348/.409/.518	.396	.630	9.4%	15.6%	61.2%	93.7%	31.9%	65.2%			105	1.9	-1.9	0.5
2023	AZ	MLB	23	402	51	9	39	9	.230/.273/.374	.273	.486	4.7%	21.4%	64.1%	88.3%	39.2%	60.5%	1.5	104.1	83	0.6	4.1	1.1
2024 DC	AZ	MLB	24	457	44	10	48	7	.252/.312/.400	.302	.504	6.8%	19.4%							96	0.6	4.2	1.9

2023 GP: CF (117), DH (2)　　　　　　　　　　　　　　　Comps: Dustin Fowler (63), Byron Buxton (62), Melky Cabrera (61)

When evaluating a prospect, we tend to write off one lackluster season as an adjustment period. But after two lackluster seasons in a row, we sometimes want to prod him with a long stick and exclaim, "C'mon, do something!" If Thomas' continued struggles in the majors are making you impatient, it's understandable. For all his talents, the young outfielder can't stop chasing after bad pitches, or stop driving the ball into the ground. Well, he *does* show patience at the plate… when he's supposed to be aggressive, that is. While the league as a whole in 2023 swung at 73% of pitches in the middle of the zone, Thomas swung at 68% of them. That might not seem like a major difference, but there's almost no value in taking a middle-middle pitch. It's catastrophic, then, to be below-average in a statistic like that. This is an area Thomas should be able to address quickly, with good results to follow. Elevating and celebrating, as much as it's important, can come later.

Cristofer Torin　MI　Born: 05/26/05　Age: 19　Bats: R　Throws: R　Height: 5'10"　Weight: 155　Origin: IFA, 2022

YEAR	TM	LVL	AGE	PA	R	HR	RBI	SB	AVG/OBP/SLG	BABIP	SLGCON	BB%	K%	ZSw%	ZCon%	OSw%	OCon%	LA	90th EV	DRC+	BRR	DRP	WARP
2022	DSL DBB	ROK	17	202	45	0	26	21	.333/.465/.434	.376	.496	18.3%	9.9%										
2023	DIAR	ROK	18	126	31	2	13	15	.320/.437/.427	.333	.468	16.7%	7.1%										
2023	VIS	A	18	156	16	2	11	6	.236/.314/.300	.287	.382	9.0%	19.2%							94	-0.5	-1.0	0.3
2024 non	AZ	MLB	19	251	18	2	19	0	.208/.257/.287	.271	.389	5.3%	24.3%							53	0.0	0	-0.7

2023 GP: SS (36), 2B (27), DH (2)　　　　　　　　　　　　Comps: Leury García (73), Luis Urías (73), Wenceel Pérez (68)

An 18-year-old signed out of Venezuela, Torin has perhaps the most coveted prospect profile in existence: a switch-hitting shortstop. Its value lies in the margin for error it provides. As long as Torin is at least average with both the bat and the glove, he'll be courted by infield-starved major league teams for years to come. But, as baseball fans know, becoming merely decent at a sport whose participants are some of the best athletes in the world is a Herculean feat. Case in point: Torin looked overwhelmed in his first matchups against true professional pitchers. His resolve has been tested—it's now time to see whether the youngin' can return the favor.

★ ★ ★ *2024 Top 101 Prospect* **#35** ★ ★ ★

Tommy Troy **SS**   Born: 01/17/02   Age: 22   Bats: R   Throws: R   Height: 5'10"   Weight: 197   Origin: Round 1, 2023 Draft (#12 overall)

YEAR	TM	LVL	AGE	PA	R	HR	RBI	SB	AVG/OBP/SLG	BABIP	SLGCON	BB%	K%	ZSw%	ZCon%	OSw%	OCon%	LA	90th EV	DRC+	BRR	DRP	WARP
2023	HIL	A+	21	99	13	4	16	8	.247/.343/.447	.304	.644	12.1%	26.3%						94	-1.0	-1.8	0.0
2024 non	AZ	MLB	22	251	21	4	22	0	.215/.277/.317	.289	.448	7.0%	27.2%						68	0.0	0	-0.1

2023 GP: SS (22), DH (5)   *Comps: Trevor Story (79), Marcus Semien (77), Anderson Tejeda (77)*

While at Stanford, Troy showcased devastating, easy bat speed and the ability to lift the ball, earning him a top-15 overall selection in the draft. It's not clear where he'll end up on the dirt—the Snakes stuck him at the six post-draft and while it wasn't always pretty, that could be chalked up to some loose bone fragments in his foot, which were removed following the season. His bat will carry the offensive profile wherever he ends up, and he should have the athleticism and arm for either second or third. His swing decisions have looked solid of late, but the history there is more "mixed" than "pristine" and will be something to track in the coming season. This Troy might not launch a thousand ships, but 25+ homers seems well within reach.

A.J. Vukovich **CF**   Born: 07/20/01   Age: 22   Bats: R   Throws: R   Height: 6'2"   Weight: 210   Origin: Round 4, 2020 Draft (#119 overall)

YEAR	TM	LVL	AGE	PA	R	HR	RBI	SB	AVG/OBP/SLG	BABIP	SLGCON	BB%	K%	ZSw%	ZCon%	OSw%	OCon%	LA	90th EV	DRC+	BRR	DRP	WARP
2021	VIS	A	19	276	42	10	42	10	.259/.322/.449	.329	.653	6.9%	27.9%						94	-0.7	-9.2	-0.3
2021	HIL	A+	19	124	13	3	20	6	.298/.315/.438	.367	.570	2.4%	22.6%						108	0.0	-0.8	0.4
2022	HIL	A+	20	448	55	15	69	35	.274/.308/.450	.330	.599	4.0%	23.4%						113	1.1	-2.2	1.8
2022	AMA	AA	20	45	6	2	9	1	.295/.311/.432	.379	.613	2.2%	28.9%						92	-0.2	-0.5	0.0
2023	AMA	AA	21	507	84	24	96	20	.263/.333/.485	.331	.708	9.1%	28.4%						90	0.7	6.7	1.8
2024 non	AZ	MLB	22	251	23	6	26	6	.227/.276/.361	.312	.538	5.4%	30.9%						77	0.0	0	0.0

2023 GP: CF (69), LF (33), 3B (15), RF (9), 1B (7), DH (4)   *Comps: Randal Grichuk (58), Miguel Vargas (58), Josh Vitters (57)*

Vukovich was drafted as a third baseman, but he never really had the chops. The solution? Transitioning to center field, which seems to be a patented D-Backs remedy. According to scouting reports, he's been solid there. You might have assumed otherwise, but the reason that Vukovich had trouble at third was his lack of dexterity, which isn't much of an issue in the outfield. What he does possess is agility, especially for someone of his size. He'll have to keep practicing, because without a defensive home, Vukovich is nigh unplayable. For worse, he embodies the all-power, all-strikeout, no-walk slugger archetype, which is so one-dimensional that it lies below abstract thought. The odds that Vukovich becomes a legitimate center fielder are still fairly slim. But by baseball standards, they're enough to warrant (some) expectations.

Christian Walker **1B**   Born: 03/28/91   Age: 33   Bats: R   Throws: R   Height: 6'0"   Weight: 208   Origin: Round 4, 2012 Draft (#132 overall)

YEAR	TM	LVL	AGE	PA	R	HR	RBI	SB	AVG/OBP/SLG	BABIP	SLGCON	BB%	K%	ZSw%	ZCon%	OSw%	OCon%	LA	90th EV	DRC+	BRR	DRP	WARP
2021	AZ	MLB	30	445	55	10	46	0	.244/.315/.382	.307	.519	8.5%	23.8%	83.2%	79.5%	32.8%	60.1%	15.9	105.0	85	0.1	-0.8	0.0
2022	AZ	MLB	31	667	84	36	94	2	.242/.327/.477	.248	.615	10.3%	19.6%	70.1%	86.8%	27.5%	55.5%	17.2	106.4	130	-0.5	1.3	3.9
2023	AZ	MLB	32	661	86	33	103	11	.258/.333/.497	.272	.635	9.4%	19.2%	73.1%	83.4%	31.0%	57.2%	16.2	106.2	116	-0.1	1.7	2.9
2024 DC	AZ	MLB	33	630	75	26	83	3	.252/.328/.447	.284	.582	9.2%	20.8%							117	-0.2	0.7	2.7

2023 GP: 1B (152), DH (4)   *Comps: David Segui (74), Babe Dahlgren (72), Paul Konerko (70)*

If you had a nickel for every unheralded first baseman who had a second breakout season at age 31, then followed it up with a near-identical campaign, you'd have a single nickel, which has zero value in this hyper-inflated economy. Walker has solidified himself as one of the top first basemen in the league. A poster child for why average exit velocity isn't everything, he's exceptionally skilled at creating hard-hit, pulled balls that stay in the air just long enough, the primary source of his production at the plate. The downside is that failing to meet even one of those three criteria could turn a surefire hit into an out, but at this point, we should be confident in Walker's ability to churn out a sufficient number of batted balls within a specific range. If he starts losing bat speed—well, we can worry about that later. Besides, Walker has solid plate discipline and an admirable strikeout rate for a slugger, which shields D-Backs fans from the experience Twins and Yankees fans had when watching the mercurial Joey Gallo.

PITCHERS

Madison Bumgarner **LHP**   Born: 08/01/89   Age: 34   Height: 6'4"   Weight: 240   Origin: Round 1, 2007 Draft (#10 overall)

YEAR	TM	LVL	AGE	G (GS)	IP	W-L	SV	K	WHIP	ERA	CSP	BB%	K%	HR%	GB%	ZSw%	ZCon%	OSw%	OCon%	BABIP	SLGCON	DRA-	WARP
2021	AZ	MLB	31	26(26)	146¹	7-10	0	124	1.18	4.67	56.3%	6.4%	20.2%	3.9%	33.0%	67.8%	85.7%	32.7%	65.8%	.267	.566	119	-0.1
2022	AZ	MLB	32	30(30)	158²	7-15	0	112	1.44	4.88	53.5%	7.0%	16.0%	3.6%	36.6%	71.5%	86.8%	30.4%	72.8%	.307	.590	151	-2.6
2023	AZ	MLB	33	4(4)	16²	0-3	0	10	2.40	10.26	46.2%	16.7%	11.1%	4.4%	35.9%	77.7%	88.9%	20.9%	68.2%	.350	.726	175	-0.5
2024 non	AZ	MLB	34	58(0)	50	2-2	0	36	1.49	5.74	52.8%	8.6%	16.2%	4.1%	35.5%					.297	.585	126	-0.5

2023 Arsenal: FA (89.6), FC (86.3), CU (77.2), CH (84.3)   *Comps: CC Sabathia (70), Vida Blue (67), Frank Tanana (65)*

In Major League Baseball, a drama/sitcom/thriller which has been running for over a century, Bumgarner once played the role of a curmudgeonly ace. Much to the audience's delight, he was regularly provoked by younger, flamboyant stars like Yasiel Puig, providing the show with a sense of comedic tension. But it was his brilliance on the mound that made the character work. In particular, Bumgarner's postseason dominance acted as a counterpoint to his sullen demeanor. Even if you didn't like the man, you couldn't help but admire him. Over the years, however, the writers began emphasizing Bumgarner's flaws, ostensibly for comedic effect. This decision is apparent in the D-Backs arc, as Bumgarner was reduced to a soft-tossing crybaby, bereft of any redeemable qualities. Such "Flanderization"—the regrettable process of whittling down a character to their most superficial traits—hastened the demise of a fan-favorite anti-hero. Thankfully, Bumgarner was written out of the show early on in 2023.

Miguel Castro RHP   Born: 12/24/94   Age: 29   Height: 6'7"   Weight: 201   Origin: IFA, 2012

YEAR	TM	LVL	AGE	G(GS)	IP	W-L	SV	K	WHIP	ERA	CSP	BB%	K%	HR%	GB%	ZSw%	ZCon%	OSw%	OCon%	BABIP	SLGCON	DRA-	WARP
2021	NYM	MLB	26	69(2)	70¹	3-4	0	77	1.29	3.45	50.2%	14.2%	25.4%	2.3%	51.4%	59.5%	76.2%	31.2%	57.9%	.241	.429	100	0.7
2022	NYY	MLB	27	34(0)	29	5-0	0	31	1.45	4.03	49.7%	11.5%	23.7%	1.5%	47.5%	61.0%	75.4%	30.0%	57.9%	.321	.537	99	0.3
2023	AZ	MLB	28	75(0)	64²	6-6	7	60	1.18	4.31	49.9%	9.3%	22.4%	3.0%	43.3%	63.4%	83.3%	32.2%	58.5%	.251	.480	95	0.9
2024 DC	AZ	MLB	29	50(0)	53²	3-2	2	54	1.38	4.45	49.3%	10.8%	22.9%	2.8%	46.4%					.291	.526	99	0.3

2023 Arsenal: SI (96.8), SL (83.9), CH (91.5)   *Comps: Michael Jackson (58), Eric O'Flaherty (56), Huston Street (56)*

You often hear that someone or something is "greater than the sum of its parts." But for Castro, the converse is true: He is, for unclear reasons, less than his separate components. In theory, if you add up his flamin' hot sinker, sweepy slide piece, and monster extension from a 6-foot-7 frame, you should end up with a devastating set-up man. In reality, Castro is a middling middle reliever who has D-Backs fans stewing when he takes the mound. He's going to need a better attack plan against lefty batters if he wants to stick around; his changeup isn't much, and you can only do so much with a righty-exclusive, sinker-slider arsenal.

Zach Davies RHP   Born: 02/07/93   Age: 31   Height: 6'0"   Weight: 180   Origin: Round 26, 2011 Draft (#785 overall)

YEAR	TM	LVL	AGE	G(GS)	IP	W-L	SV	K	WHIP	ERA	CSP	BB%	K%	HR%	GB%	ZSw%	ZCon%	OSw%	OCon%	BABIP	SLGCON	DRA-	WARP
2021	CHC	MLB	28	32(32)	148	6-12	0	114	1.60	5.78	49.9%	11.2%	17.1%	3.7%	41.4%	69.1%	88.4%	29.8%	64.8%	.311	.605	134	-1.2
2022	AZ	MLB	29	27(27)	134¹	2-5	0	102	1.30	4.09	51.5%	9.1%	17.9%	3.7%	42.0%	67.6%	84.7%	27.7%	70.1%	.258	.516	114	0.3
2023	RNO	AAA	30	3(3)	13¹	1-0	0	6	2.18	8.77		10.8%	9.2%	1.5%	40.4%	73.1%	93.4%	25.5%	57.1%	.412	.627	119	
2023	AZ	MLB	30	18(18)	82¹	2-5	0	72	1.66	7.00	45.1%	10.3%	19.1%	2.7%	43.6%	63.1%	89.8%	27.1%	62.6%	.348	.588	118	0.2
2024 non	AZ	MLB	31	58(0)	50	2-2	0	39	1.46	4.93	48.2%	9.9%	18.0%	3.0%	41.9%					.296	.529	109	0.0

2023 Arsenal: SI (89.7), FA (89.6), CH (80.8), FC (87.6), CU (77.1), SL (81.7), SW (78.5)   *Comps: Sidney Ponson (81), Mike Pelfrey (80), Bill Gullickson (79)*

GRIM REAPER: It is time to go.

DAVIES: Did I... did I have a good career?

REAPER: No. Well... I can't say for sure; it's a tough question. I mean, you were never really a big ground-ball guy, even during your prime, and it's not like you were *that* great at limiting free passes. You sort of stayed around a league-average ERA, which was enough to get you some of those one-year contracts. Sucks that you had to deal with injuries in your latest season, though. Seems like your team could have used a fourth starter in the playoffs.

DAVIES: Wait, I thought you were going to say I was the best. Or something like that!

REAPER: Hey, I'm the guy with the scythe, not the glowing wings.

Zac Gallen RHP   Born: 08/03/95   Age: 28   Height: 6'2"   Weight: 189   Origin: Round 3, 2016 Draft (#106 overall)

YEAR	TM	LVL	AGE	G(GS)	IP	W-L	SV	K	WHIP	ERA	CSP	BB%	K%	HR%	GB%	ZSw%	ZCon%	OSw%	OCon%	BABIP	SLGCON	DRA-	WARP
2021	AZ	MLB	25	23(23)	121¹	4-10	0	139	1.29	4.30	53.5%	9.4%	26.6%	3.6%	43.6%	64.4%	86.8%	30.4%	62.4%	.289	.590	83	2.2
2022	AZ	MLB	26	31(31)	184	12-4	0	192	0.91	2.54	51.6%	6.6%	26.9%	2.1%	45.6%	64.1%	86.6%	36.2%	66.0%	.237	.436	84	3.4
2023	AZ	MLB	27	34(34)	210	17-9	0	220	1.12	3.47	47.3%	5.6%	26.0%	2.6%	42.2%	66.7%	86.5%	33.9%	56.6%	.301	.530	82	4.5
2024 DC	AZ	MLB	28	29(29)	180²	13-8	0	182	1.19	3.69	49.3%	7.0%	24.3%	3.1%	43.1%					.288	.540	87	2.9

2023 Arsenal: FA (93.6), KC (82.4), CH (86.9), FC (90.3), SL (87.7)   *Comps: Don Drysdale (87), Matt Cain (86), Don Wilson (86)*

Gallen is nicknamed 'The Milkman' because his last name sounds like a unit of measurement for milk. That's pretty much it; monikers are the one aspect of the game that they really were better at a century ago. But there are more ways than this homophonic pun that Gallen resembles milk. See, on its own, milk is a bland, creamy mixture—essentially flavorless. Gallen's fastball, the foundation of his arsenal, is by itself a painfully plain offering. He lobs it down the middle a lot, too, and you wonder why hitters don't crush it more often. But the value of milk lies in its versatility. With the help of just a few extra ingredients, it can transform into butter, cheese, or even ice cream. Similarly, when Gallen pairs his B-tier fastball with his curveball, changeup, or cutter, he elevates it into an A-tier product. The secret lies in how Gallen constructs pitch sequences and tunnels, though of course, we may never get to find out what it is. After a two-year run of excellence, however, there's no denying that his approach works. That's the beauty of Gallen: He seems ordinary at first, yet is anything but.

Kevin Ginkel RHP   Born: 03/24/94   Age: 30   Height: 6'4"   Weight: 235   Origin: Round 22, 2016 Draft (#659 overall)

YEAR	TM	LVL	AGE	G(GS)	IP	W-L	SV	K	WHIP	ERA	CSP	BB%	K%	HR%	GB%	ZSw%	ZCon%	OSw%	OCon%	BABIP	SLGCON	DRA-	WARP
2021	AZ	MLB	27	32(0)	28¹	0-1	0	31	1.55	6.35	53.0%	10.9%	24.0%	5.4%	41.5%	68.2%	86.3%	30.2%	58.3%	.311	.753	101	0.3
2022	RNO	AAA	28	30(0)	30²	2-1	9	45	1.14	1.17		9.8%	36.6%	0.8%	43.1%	62.7%	77.0%	32.5%	51.0%	.344	.500	73	0.7
2022	AZ	MLB	28	30(0)	29¹	1-1	1	30	1.30	3.38	55.4%	8.9%	24.2%	0.8%	50.0%	61.8%	87.8%	33.9%	53.7%	.321	.457	84	0.5
2023	RNO	AAA	29	4(0)	5	1-0	1	11	0.80	0.00		0.0%	57.9%	0.0%	75.0%	66.7%	44.4%	47.7%	38.1%	.500	.625	64	0.2
2023	AZ	MLB	29	60(0)	65¹	9-1	4	70	0.98	2.48	46.9%	9.1%	27.6%	1.2%	49.7%	69.3%	85.1%	32.7%	46.9%	.244	.417	81	1.4
2024 DC	AZ	MLB	30	50(0)	53²	3-3	6	62	1.24	3.59	49.2%	9.5%	27.3%	2.7%	45.0%					.289	.529	83	0.7

2023 Arsenal: FA (95.9), SL (86.7), SI (95)   *Comps: Nick Vincent (69), Michael Kohn (67), Kevin Quackenbush (67)*

It's fun whenever pitchers practice alchemy, splitting one pitch into two or fusing two pitches into one. Ginkel, it turns out, is something of a scientist himself. In 2023, he developed two distinct fastballs—a four-seamer and a sinker from his old fastball, which used to be in a so-called 'dead zone' of subpar vertical and horizontal movement. Such a fastball has no purpose, being mediocre at both generating whiffs and soft contact. By assigning a specific role to each type of fastball (four-seamers for whiffs, sinkers for soft contact), Ginkel broke out and became one of the few bullpen arms the D-Backs could rely on. He's not going to avoid the long ball forever, but it seems clear that he's a better pitcher now than he ever was.

Tommy Henry LHP Born: 07/29/97   Age: 26   Height: 6'3"   Weight: 205   Origin: Round 2, 2019 Draft (#74 overall)

YEAR	TM	LVL	AGE	G (GS)	IP	W-L	SV	K	WHIP	ERA	CSP	BB%	K%	HR%	GB%	ZSw%	ZCon%	OSw%	OCon%	BABIP	SLGCON	DRA-	WARP
2021	AMA	AA	23	23(23)	115²	4-6	0	135	1.46	5.21		10.8%	27.4%	4.9%	38.7%					.335	.718	84	1.8
2022	RNO	AAA	24	21(21)	113	4-4	0	103	1.31	3.74		9.5%	21.7%	2.3%	44.1%	72.1%	80.0%	30.6%	61.5%	.295	.481	90	1.3
2022	AZ	MLB	24	9(9)	47	3-4	0	36	1.45	5.36	56.8%	10.2%	17.6%	4.9%	38.6%	74.5%	84.3%	28.2%	60.7%	.276	.594	141	-0.5
2023	AZ	MLB	25	17(16)	89	5-4	0	64	1.36	4.15	48.0%	9.2%	16.8%	3.1%	36.0%	70.2%	85.0%	33.3%	66.9%	.278	.514	130	-0.3
2024 DC	AZ	MLB	26	16(16)	89	5-6	0	71	1.53	5.72	50.7%	9.6%	17.9%	3.8%	36.9%					.307	.587	125	-0.4

2023 Arsenal: FA (90.8), CU (79.4), CH (84.2), SL (83.7), SW (82.9)   *Comps: Brett Oberholtzer (81), Scott Diamond (80), Andrew Suárez (80)*

Can Henry make a name for himself without an uptick in velocity? Sure, but he's going to have to start pitching like somebody who throws 91, not 97. It's unfortunate that left elbow inflammation discontinued his first season as a full-time starter, as we might have missed out on planned adjustments to his repertoire. While his fastball is the weakest of all D-Backs rookies, his trio of off-speed stuff is formidable—and that's what Henry, upon returning, should lean on. The all too common prescription for a young, flailing starter is to move (i.e. banish) him to the bullpen, but to force Henry into a bullpen role would be a mistake. He has a starter's repertoire, and he deserves the opportunity to be on the mound every fifth day, or at least prove otherwise.

Drey Jameson RHP Born: 08/17/97   Age: 26   Height: 6'0"   Weight: 165   Origin: Round 1, 2019 Draft (#34 overall)

YEAR	TM	LVL	AGE	G (GS)	IP	W-L	SV	K	WHIP	ERA	CSP	BB%	K%	HR%	GB%	ZSw%	ZCon%	OSw%	OCon%	BABIP	SLGCON	DRA-	WARP
2021	HIL	A+	23	13(12)	64¹	2-4	0	77	1.21	3.92		6.7%	28.5%	3.3%	52.6%					.319	.569	95	0.7
2021	AMA	AA	23	8(8)	46¹	3-2	0	68	1.21	4.08		9.3%	35.1%	3.1%	38.5%					.327	.614	79	0.8
2022	AMA	AA	24	4(4)	18²	2-1	0	23	0.91	2.41		5.6%	32.4%	0.0%	55.8%					.302	.395	63	0.5
2022	RNO	AAA	24	22(21)	114	5-12	0	109	1.59	6.95		8.2%	21.2%	4.1%	48.2%	68.4%	82.8%	27.2%	60.2%	.351	.697	101	0.6
2022	AZ	MLB	24	4(4)	24¹	3-0	0	24	1.11	1.48	59.4%	7.1%	24.5%	2.0%	56.1%	70.8%	82.4%	29.9%	56.7%	.281	.455	86	0.4
2023	RNO	AAA	25	5(5)	28	4-0	0	24	1.43	5.79		8.9%	19.5%	1.6%	44.2%	64.8%	83.5%	24.8%	64.4%	.325	.542	104	0.2
2023	AZ	MLB	25	15(3)	40²	3-1	1	37	1.43	3.32	48.8%	10.3%	21.3%	3.4%	46.6%	65.0%	84.4%	32.7%	50.0%	.304	.547	96	0.6
2024 non	AZ	MLB	26	58(0)	50	2-2	0	48	1.40	4.76	52.1%	8.7%	21.9%	3.0%	47.3%					.312	.557	106	0.1

2023 Arsenal: SI (95), SW (85.4), FA (97.2), CH (89.2), CU (80.7), FC (90.1)   *Comps: Dillon Peters (63), A.J. Griffin (63), Zach Plesac (62)*

The award for trendiest pitch arsenal on the D-Backs goes to Jameson, whose east-to-west slider and dual fastballs are so hot right now. Not wanting to be typecast as a future reliever, Jameson also showed off a much-improved changeup in 2023. He altered its shape by adding three ticks of velocity *and* three inches of downward movement. That's a remarkable achievement, given the (generally) inverse relationship between those variables. The effort paid off: Lefty batters averaged .190 and whiffed a third of the time against Jameson's changeup, despite it often being nowhere near the edges of the zone. Of course, because we can't have anything nice, Jameson underwent Tommy John surgery in September. Although he'll be out for the entirety of next season, don't you dare forget about him—if all four of his pitches are ever in sync for an extended period, the Snakes might have a no. 3 starter.

Bryce Jarvis RHP Born: 12/26/97   Age: 26   Height: 6'2"   Weight: 195   Origin: Round 1, 2020 Draft (#18 overall)

YEAR	TM	LVL	AGE	G (GS)	IP	W-L	SV	K	WHIP	ERA	CSP	BB%	K%	HR%	GB%	ZSw%	ZCon%	OSw%	OCon%	BABIP	SLGCON	DRA-	WARP
2021	AMA	AA	23	8(8)	35	1-2	0	40	1.40	5.66		11.2%	26.3%	5.3%	43.6%					.286	.685	106	0.1
2022	AMA	AA	24	25(25)	106²	3-6	0	110	1.88	8.27		11.9%	21.8%	5.3%	39.3%					.381	.781	119	-0.7
2023	AMA	AA	25	3(3)	14	2-1	0	17	1.07	3.86		12.7%	30.9%	0.0%	48.4%					.258	.333	90	0.2
2023	RNO	AAA	25	24(16)	92¹	7-5	0	96	1.49	5.26		11.2%	23.4%	2.4%	39.6%	66.3%	81.5%	29.1%	54.2%	.322	.567	92	1.3
2023	AZ	MLB	25	11(1)	23²	2-1	0	12	0.97	3.04	47.8%	9.8%	13.0%	3.3%	43.7%	73.2%	89.0%	22.6%	66.0%	.162	.357	111	0.1
2024 DC	AZ	MLB	26	13(5)	30	1-2	0	24	1.53	5.57	47.8%	10.8%	18.1%	3.6%	39.4%					.298	.562	121	-0.2

2023 Arsenal: FA (95.5), SL (84.5), CH (84.5), CU (81.5)   *Comps: Adrian Houser (66), Kyle McPherson (64), Paul Clemens (63)*

As more organizations incorporate granular pitch data into their draft models, Jarvis might be the last pick of his kind. Recall that his velocity spike led to an unexpected, but defensible, first-round selection in 2020. Jarvis has held that gain all throughout his pro career. In this regard, the scouts were dead-on. But Jarvis' fastball shape is poor, enough that his heater is a legitimate weakness. This issue could have been mitigated somewhat if his secondaries had developed nicely over the years, but he still has trouble commanding them, as evidenced by how shaky he was during his first 11 big league outings. Granted, nobody could have anticipated that Jarvis would end up with below-average command. But his fastball provides a valuable lesson: In today's game, it's exceedingly difficult to compensate for a lack of movement with raw velocity.

Merrill Kelly RHP Born: 10/14/88   Age: 35   Height: 6'2"   Weight: 202   Origin: Round 8, 2010 Draft (#251 overall)

YEAR	TM	LVL	AGE	G (GS)	IP	W-L	SV	K	WHIP	ERA	CSP	BB%	K%	HR%	GB%	ZSw%	ZCon%	OSw%	OCon%	BABIP	SLGCON	DRA-	WARP
2021	AZ	MLB	32	27(27)	158	7-11	0	130	1.29	4.44	56.0%	6.1%	19.5%	3.1%	43.3%	70.5%	88.2%	30.7%	63.5%	.305	.550	96	1.8
2022	AZ	MLB	33	33(33)	200¹	13-8	0	177	1.14	3.37	54.1%	7.6%	22.0%	2.6%	42.9%	68.9%	83.4%	33.1%	65.5%	.269	.488	94	2.6
2023	AZ	MLB	34	30(30)	177²	12-8	0	187	1.19	3.29	45.8%	9.6%	25.9%	2.8%	45.0%	68.8%	82.9%	36.5%	61.4%	.279	.522	91	2.8
2024 DC	AZ	MLB	35	29(29)	174²	12-9	0	159	1.26	3.99	51.0%	8.4%	21.6%	3.3%	43.3%					.279	.531	92	2.3

2023 Arsenal: FA (92.5), CH (88.8), HC (91.2), SI (92.5), KC (82.3), SL (85.6)   *Comps: Tim Hudson (79), Justin Verlander (78), Jeff Samardzija (78)*

Along with kimchi and BTS, Kelly is one of the most successful South Korean exports to the United States. In case you don't know or forgot, his story goes as follows: Once stuck in the upper levels of the Rays' minor-league organization, Kelly got an opportunity with the SK Wyverns (now SSG Landers) of the KBO, where he gradually honed his command and started striking out more and more hitters. Impressed, the D-Backs offered him a modest but, at the time, unprecedented contract in the winter of 2018. (Remember, he had no prior experience in the big leagues.) Since then, Kelly has been arguably their most effective—and durable—starting pitcher. He tried out a few new tricks in 2023, including a slider that complements an already deep arsenal. Even still, the changeup remains the crown jewel of Kelly's pitch mix. Baseball Savant tells us that it ranks in the 100th percentile for off-speed pitch run value; the fact that it was in the 20th percentile in 2019 demonstrates just how far Kelly has come as a finesse pitcher, one of the few remaining today.

★ ★ ★ *2024 Top 101 Prospect* **#74** ★ ★ ★

Yu-Min Lin   LHP   Born: 07/12/03   Age: 20   Height: 5'11"   Weight: 160   Origin: IFA, 2021

YEAR	TM	LVL	AGE	G(GS)	IP	W-L	SV	K	WHIP	ERA	CSP	BB%	K%	HR%	GB%	ZSw%	ZCon%	OSw%	OCon%	BABIP	SLGCON	DRA-	WARP
2022	DIAR	ROK	18	7(7)	23	0-2	0	41	0.65	2.35		7.0%	47.7%	0.0%	51.4%					.250	.343		
2022	VIS	A	18	7(7)	33¹	2-0	0	50	1.41	2.97		11.4%	35.7%	1.4%	31.5%					.408	.625	84	0.4
2023	HIL	A+	19	13(13)	60¹	1-3	0	76	1.14	3.43		9.3%	32.1%	1.3%	46.3%					.333	.504	73	1.3
2023	AMA	AA	19	11(11)	61	5-2	0	64	1.23	4.28		10.0%	24.7%	2.7%	46.0%					.276	.494	86	1.1
2024 DC	*AZ*	*MLB*	*20*	*11(3)*	*23²*	*1-1*	*0*	*23*	*1.48*	*5.32*		*11.1%*	*21.4%*	*3.6%*	*36.8%*					*.296*	*.586*	*116*	*0.0*

Comps: Tyler Skaggs (75), Julio Teheran (69), Dylan Bundy (68)

According to all known archaic prejudices in player evaluation, there is no way Lin should be a legitimate prospect. He sometimes sits below 90 mph on his fastball and possesses an unassuming physique. Lin, of course, strikes out batter after batter anyways, because he doesn't care what scouts think is impossible. He compensates for a lack of velocity with a low arm slot and tons of vertical break, placing changeups down-and-away with ease and precision. He currently has a below-average breaking ball, but with all the recent advancements in pitch design, constructing one that suits him shouldn't be a big hassle. True, he did run into a bit of a wall in Double-A. It's possible that a 1st-percentile fastball velocity, no matter how good your command or secondary pitches are, is a death knell. Even so, out of all the soft-tossers out there, it's Lin who has the best chance of breaking into the big leagues.

Joe Mantiply   LHP   Born: 03/01/91   Age: 33   Height: 6'4"   Weight: 219   Origin: Round 27, 2013 Draft (#816 overall)

YEAR	TM	LVL	AGE	G(GS)	IP	W-L	SV	K	WHIP	ERA	CSP	BB%	K%	HR%	GB%	ZSw%	ZCon%	OSw%	OCon%	BABIP	SLGCON	DRA-	WARP
2021	AZ	MLB	30	57(0)	39²	0-3	0	38	1.56	3.40	55.6%	9.6%	21.5%	0.6%	44.6%	60.1%	81.7%	37.1%	58.7%	.370	.595	89	0.6
2022	AZ	MLB	31	69(0)	60	2-5	2	61	1.08	2.85	54.3%	2.5%	25.1%	2.5%	54.3%	64.3%	84.6%	43.5%	55.6%	.319	.488	71	1.5
2023	RNO	AAA	32	11(1)	12¹	1-0	0	11	1.78	7.30		6.9%	19.0%	3.4%	41.9%	61.5%	78.0%	32.5%	67.5%	.390	.667	85	0.3
2023	AZ	MLB	32	35(3)	39	2-2	0	28	1.13	4.62	49.5%	5.7%	17.8%	2.5%	53.3%	64.9%	84.5%	38.9%	67.4%	.267	.500	94	0.6
2024 DC	*AZ*	*MLB*	*33*	*45(0)*	*48¹*	*3-2*	*0*	*39*	*1.33*	*4.25*	*52.8%*	*6.8%*	*18.6%*	*2.3%*	*49.9%*					*.307*	*.497*	*96*	*0.3*

2023 Arsenal: SI (89.6), SL (80.3), CH (82), FA (90.5)   *Comps: Adam Kolarek (40), Javy Guerra (39), T.J. McFarland (38)*

Oh, no. Mantiply is supposed to be the ultimate gem in the rough, the antithesis to modern baseball's obsession with raw velocity and movement, a 27th-round pick whose unlikely ascent to the upper echelon of relieverdom is representative of what's so great about baseball. But he dealt with intermittent injuries all throughout 2023, which might have contributed to a notable erosion in breaking ball command. Because of this, Mantiply's fastball, which barely sits above 90 mph, became an easier target for opposing hitters: They swung more often against it but swung less often against his off-speed offerings, taking them for balls. The results were a barrage of hard contact and early, solemn departures from the mound. Mantiply has a realistic opportunity to redeem himself next season, but his post-breakout campaign was a cruel reminder that the margin of error for someone like himself is, unfortunately, thin.

Justin Martinez   RHP   Born: 07/30/01   Age: 22   Height: 6'3"   Weight: 180   Origin: IFA, 2018

YEAR	TM	LVL	AGE	G(GS)	IP	W-L	SV	K	WHIP	ERA	CSP	BB%	K%	HR%	GB%	ZSw%	ZCon%	OSw%	OCon%	BABIP	SLGCON	DRA-	WARP
2021	VIS	A	19	7(7)	23	1-3	0	24	1.74	6.65		14.0%	22.4%	0.9%	56.9%					.381	.547	96	0.2
2022	HIL	A+	20	13(0)	27	1-2	1	44	1.30	2.67		12.3%	38.6%	0.9%	49.1%					.385	.509	79	0.5
2023	RNO	AAA	21	47(0)	49¹	2-1	9	67	1.64	4.20		21.2%	29.6%	1.3%	56.5%	65.2%	77.8%	30.4%	40.6%	.286	.467	79	0.6
2023	AZ	MLB	21	10(0)	10	0-0	1	14	2.40	12.60	41.4%	19.3%	24.6%	3.5%	46.7%	62.2%	76.5%	27.9%	55.8%	.393	.767	96	0.1
2024 DC	*AZ*	*MLB*	*22*	*19(0)*	*21¹*	*1-1*	*0*	*27*	*1.55*	*5.09*	*41.4%*	*16.0%*	*27.9%*	*2.9%*	*43.3%*					*.295*	*.574*	*108*	*0.0*

2023 Arsenal: FA (100.6), FS (88.8), SL (89.2)   *Comps: Miguel Castro (59), Andrés Muñoz (54), Carlos Martinez (54)*

At the suggestion of Jeffrey Paternostro and the *BP* Prospect Staff, this author went to Martinez's Baseball Savant page and saw how many times he had to click the "Load Random Video" button before seeing a strike.

The answer: 11. It took 11 videos for Martinez to throw a pitch in the zone. If we (generously) assume that he throws a strike 50% of the time, the odds that you'll see only one strike in 11 videos is 0.00537, or a little more than 0.5%. And if we (more realistically) assume that he throws a strike 25% of the time, the odds soar to a whopping… 15.5%. But what are the odds that Martinez improves his atrocious command, you ask? Come back later when we have a way to model that.

Scott McGough   RHP   Born: 10/31/89   Age: 34   Height: 5'11"   Weight: 190   Origin: Round 5, 2011 Draft (#164 overall)

YEAR	TM	LVL	AGE	G(GS)	IP	W-L	SV	K	WHIP	ERA	CSP	BB%	K%	HR%	GB%	ZSw%	ZCon%	OSw%	OCon%	BABIP	SLGCON	DRA-	WARP
2023	AZ	MLB	33	63(1)	70¹	2-7	9	86	1.28	4.73	47.3%	10.0%	28.6%	4.7%	48.1%	66.5%	85.0%	34.9%	46.7%	.272	.650	79	1.6
2024 DC	*AZ*	*MLB*	*34*	*40(0)*	*43*	*2-2*	*0*	*48*	*1.27*	*4.18*	*47.3%*	*8.7%*	*26.4%*	*3.7%*	*32.1%*					*.293*	*.595*	*96*	*0.3*

2023 Arsenal: FA (93.5), FS (85.8), SL (86.6)   *Comps: Blake Parker (40), Nick Vincent (40), Brad Boxberger (38)*

It must have been somewhat surreal for McGough, standing on a major-league mound once again, eight years after he made his debut in 2015. How does one measure a year in a life, let alone eight? There are the usual quantitative methods: three minor-league organizations, followed by four years in Japan with the Yakult Swallows; the three NPB All-Star selections that came along with them; the two-year, $6.25 million contract the Diamondbacks offered, allowing McGough to return to the U.S. in triumph. But life isn't accurately measured in accolades or monetary figures. It's measured in countless bullpen sessions, language barriers, cultural differences, worries, thoughts of whether it's a fruitless endeavor, this pursuit of a major-league mound. To us, McGough's disappearance was a blip on the radar, if that. To him, it was everything—and more.

Mark Melancon RHP Born: 03/28/85 Age: 39 Height: 6'1" Weight: 215 Origin: Round 9, 2006 Draft (#284 overall)

YEAR	TM	LVL	AGE	G (GS)	IP	W-L	SV	K	WHIP	ERA	CSP	BB%	K%	HR%	GB%	ZSw%	ZCon%	OSw%	OCon%	BABIP	SLGCON	DRA-	WARP
2021	SD	MLB	36	64(0)	64²	4-3	39	59	1.22	2.23	54.4%	9.4%	22.3%	1.5%	56.7%	67.2%	88.5%	29.6%	63.7%	.284	.421	85	1.1
2022	AZ	MLB	37	62(0)	56	3-10	18	35	1.50	4.66	53.7%	8.5%	14.2%	2.0%	43.2%	71.3%	88.5%	31.0%	64.0%	.315	.466	115	0.1
2024 non	AZ	MLB	39	58(0)	50	2-2	0	35	1.46	4.92	52.4%	8.8%	16.1%	2.6%	47.5%					.305	.506	109	0.0

2023 Arsenal: HC (88.8), KC (79.8), FS (82.3)   *Comps: Mike Timlin (80), Chad Qualls (80), Joakim Soria (80)*

No, Melancon hasn't retired yet. If you're wondering why you didn't hear a peep from him, blame a shoulder injury that kept the closer sidelined all season long. But this may as well be the end for Melancon. At age 38, it would take a conspiracy to make his sluggish repertoire effective in today's fast-paced game. That it *did* work for so many years, though, is an accomplishment worth highlighting. Melancon never accumulated many whiffs, even during his prime, but something about his cutter and curveball kept the ball on the ground and, vitally, in the park. Since the start of integration, 1,641 pitchers have tossed at least 500 innings. Among them, Melancon is tied for the 49th-lowest home-per-nine rate (0.54)—for comparison, Mariano Rivera is tied for 34th-lowest (0.50). Who knows, maybe he'll come back for one last ride, and once again baffle baseball writers with his fielding-dependent pitching.

Kyle Nelson LHP Born: 07/08/96 Age: 27 Height: 6'1" Weight: 175 Origin: Round 15, 2017 Draft (#462 overall)

YEAR	TM	LVL	AGE	G (GS)	IP	W-L	SV	K	WHIP	ERA	CSP	BB%	K%	HR%	GB%	ZSw%	ZCon%	OSw%	OCon%	BABIP	SLGCON	DRA-	WARP
2021	COL	AAA	24	25(0)	25²	0-1	1	30	1.68	6.66		16.8%	25.2%	0.8%	39.1%					.324	.478	89	0.5
2021	CLE	MLB	24	10(0)	9²	0-0	0	8	1.86	9.31	55.0%	16.3%	16.3%	0.0%	38.7%	57.5%	80.4%	29.2%	53.6%	.323	.387	129	-0.1
2022	AZ	MLB	25	43(1)	37	2-1	0	30	1.08	2.19	50.6%	9.3%	19.9%	0.7%	39.4%	69.1%	84.9%	34.7%	60.3%	.243	.385	106	0.2
2023	AZ	MLB	26	68(2)	56	7-4	0	67	1.30	4.18	48.6%	5.9%	28.0%	5.0%	35.7%	70.8%	86.5%	38.2%	46.7%	.331	.695	82	1.2
2024 DC	AZ	MLB	27	45(0)	48¹	3-2	0	52	1.38	4.60	49.8%	10.1%	24.6%	3.1%	37.3%					.305	.563	102	0.2

2023 Arsenal: SL (85.4), FA (92), FC (88.1), CH (83.7)   *Comps: Chasen Shreve (55), Tanner Scott (52), Aaron Bummer (52)*

To the naked eye, it might seem like Nelson faltered in his second season with the D-Backs. After all, his ERA nearly doubled. But it'd be remiss to not mention how much Nelson's command improved—especially that of his slider, which he consistently placed down-and-away to lefties, who chased after it to no avail. Unfortunately, when Nelson did make a mistake, he turned into a punching bag at the local gym, in the sense that hitters big and small delivered bloop-hit jabs or home-run hooks. Of course, part of being a fastball-slider reliever is that you'll always be susceptible to some hard contact. History does tell us that better days are ahead for Nelson and his ilk; at the very least, they're not going away any time soon.

Ryne Nelson RHP Born: 02/01/98 Age: 26 Height: 6'3" Weight: 184 Origin: Round 2, 2019 Draft (#56 overall)

YEAR	TM	LVL	AGE	G (GS)	IP	W-L	SV	K	WHIP	ERA	CSP	BB%	K%	HR%	GB%	ZSw%	ZCon%	OSw%	OCon%	BABIP	SLGCON	DRA-	WARP
2021	HIL	A+	23	8(8)	39¹	4-1	0	59	0.89	2.52		9.1%	38.3%	1.9%	29.5%					.240	.487	85	0.6
2021	AMA	AA	23	14(14)	77	3-3	0	104	1.19	3.51		8.2%	32.9%	4.1%	38.0%					.312	.635	89	0.8
2022	RNO	AAA	24	26(26)	136	10-5	0	128	1.39	5.43		7.9%	21.6%	4.2%	36.0%	71.8%	82.6%	32.0%	65.4%	.301	.627	108	0.1
2022	AZ	MLB	24	3(3)	18¹	1-1	0	16	0.82	1.47	60.9%	8.7%	23.2%	2.9%	25.5%	63.9%	84.2%	25.4%	58.8%	.156	.413	107	0.1
2023	RNO	AAA	25	4(4)	21²	0-1	0	9	1.20	3.74		8.0%	10.2%	3.4%	39.1%	66.3%	86.1%	30.8%	72.5%	.242	.426	115	
2023	AZ	MLB	25	29(27)	144	8-8	0	96	1.42	5.31	52.7%	7.4%	15.5%	3.9%	36.8%	72.4%	85.8%	29.2%	65.9%	.301	.622	124	-0.1
2024 DC	AZ	MLB	26	16(16)	82¹	4-6	0	59	1.48	5.57	53.4%	8.1%	16.3%	3.9%	36.0%					.303	.586	123	-0.3

2023 Arsenal: FA (94.4), SW (81.7), CH (83.4), SL (85.6), CU (76)   *Comps: Daniel Gossett (79), Adam Morgan (79), Eli Morgan (78)*

As a rookie Nelson pitched like Spencer Strider, but not in a good way. The movement on Nelson's fastball is great but not otherworldly, and the velocity on it is merely so-so. If you chuck that kind of heater down the pipe time and time again, you're going to get hit hard. Strider can get away, or rather find success, with so-called mistakes; Nelson can't. Perhaps aware of his shortcomings, he cut down on his fastball usage as the season progressed, but that failed to provide even a respite for the beleaguered 25-year-old. There's no quick remedy here. In order to succeed at the major-league level, Nelson needs to make better use of his four secondary pitches, either by throwing more of them for strikes or finding a golden ratio between their usage rates, though "both" is probably the correct answer. The good news: He's at minimum a back-of-the-rotation starter, despite all the various hiccups.

Brandon Pfaadt RHP Born: 10/15/98 Age: 25 Height: 6'4" Weight: 220 Origin: Round 5, 2020 Draft (#149 overall)

YEAR	TM	LVL	AGE	G (GS)	IP	W-L	SV	K	WHIP	ERA	CSP	BB%	K%	HR%	GB%	ZSw%	ZCon%	OSw%	OCon%	BABIP	SLGCON	DRA-	WARP
2021	VIS	A	22	7(7)	40¹	2-2	0	57	0.89	3.12		4.4%	35.6%	3.1%	40.0%					.267	.537	94	0.4
2021	HIL	A+	22	9(9)	58	5-4	0	67	0.91	2.48		6.2%	29.5%	2.2%	39.9%					.246	.483	100	0.4
2021	AMA	AA	22	6(6)	33¹	1-1	0	36	1.32	4.59		4.9%	25.4%	8.5%	30.6%					.291	.796	99	0.2
2022	AMA	AA	23	19(19)	105¹	6-6	0	144	1.25	4.53		4.3%	32.2%	4.3%	34.9%					.372	.725	68	2.5
2022	RNO	AAA	23	10(10)	61²	5-1	0	74	0.99	2.63		5.8%	30.6%	3.7%	29.8%	69.3%	75.2%	35.6%	50.9%	.270	.533	102	0.3
2023	RNO	AAA	24	12(12)	60²	6-2	0	69	1.24	3.71		6.3%	27.1%	4.3%	35.7%	69.3%	85.2%	31.5%	50.9%	.308	.645	88	1.0
2023	AZ	MLB	24	19(18)	96	3-9	0	94	1.41	5.72	51.6%	6.2%	22.3%	5.2%	32.2%	67.3%	83.4%	34.5%	61.5%	.316	.705	101	1.1
2024 DC	AZ	MLB	25	23(23)	117²	7-7	0	105	1.26	4.50	51.6%	6.2%	21.2%	4.0%	33.0%					.292	.589	103	0.8

2023 Arsenal: FA (93.6), SW (84), CH (86.6), SI (93.2), CU (78.8)   *Comps: Daniel Gossett (77), Tyler Duffey (76), Joe Ross (71)*

We've been tricked, we've been backstabbed, and we've been, quite possibly, bamboozled by Pfaadt's reputation as a prospect. We were told that Pfaadt was capable of generating swings and misses with all the components of his arsenal, and that, in context, his numbers in the hitter-friendly Pacific Coast League were impressive. But Pfaadt's turbulent rookie season uncovered key details. On the bright side, there's no doubting that his sweeper is a plus-plus pitch: Nobody's hitting it, not even the best lefty sluggers. The shape of his fastball, however, left much to be desired, and it became clear that his curveball and changeup command were still works in progress. Yes, he's not going to allow two home runs per nine next season. There isn't much reason for concern, despite that ERA. Pfaadt just isn't as big-league ready as we might have hoped, which is perfectly okay. This is a pitching prospect with tons of room for growth, who just happened to have to be the number three starter on a playoff team.

Eduardo Rodriguez LHP Born: 04/07/93   Age: 31   Height: 6'2"   Weight: 231   Origin: IFA, 2010

YEAR	TM	LVL	AGE	G (GS)	IP	W-L	SV	K	WHIP	ERA	CSP	BB%	K%	HR%	GB%	ZSw%	ZCon%	OSw%	OCon%	BABIP	SLGCON	DRA-	WARP
2021	BOS	MLB	28	32(31)	157²	13-8	0	185	1.39	4.74	51.8%	7.0%	27.4%	2.8%	44.0%	69.3%	81.6%	34.6%	62.8%	.364	.622	82	3.0
2022	DET	MLB	29	17(17)	91	5-5	0	72	1.33	4.05	52.2%	8.7%	18.4%	3.1%	42.8%	66.7%	86.1%	33.4%	76.5%	.279	.507	114	0.2
2023	DET	MLB	30	26(26)	152²	13-9	0	143	1.15	3.30	49.8%	7.7%	23.0%	2.4%	40.3%	68.9%	83.3%	32.0%	64.2%	.275	.481	104	1.5
2024 DC	AZ	MLB	31	26(26)	150¹	10-8	0	134	1.34	4.48	50.0%	7.8%	20.7%	3.2%	41.0%					.301	.547	102	1.2

2023 Arsenal: FA (92.3), FC (88.9), CH (86.2), SI (92.5), SL (84.8)   Comps: Jon Lester (81), Cole Hamels (78), Tom Glavine (78)

Platonically, there isn't much to recommend Arizona—a dry puckered kiss from a least-favorite aunt—over California, a veritable Barbieland of beaches and sunshine. However, there are understandable financial reasons one would prefer to make a large pile of money in the Grand Canyon State vs. the Golden State (Very Big Holes are an indisputably great place to hide money, preferably in canvas "$" sacks). This is an argument lost on Tigers fans, many of whom hate E-Rod with a passion reserved for Canadian coins and Ohio State after he nixed a trade deadline move to LA as too far from home...yet signed a four-year deal with the D-Backs this offseason. It's funny to imagine the avuncular Rodriguez as such a lightning rod for fury; his stuff is as serviceable as ever, although he profiles better as a comfortable mid-rotation arm for the Snakes rather than anchoring the top of a young and inconsistent lineup, as was the case in Detroit.

Andrew Saalfrank LHP Born: 08/18/97   Age: 26   Height: 6'3"   Weight: 205   Origin: Round 6, 2019 Draft (#182 overall)

YEAR	TM	LVL	AGE	G (GS)	IP	W-L	SV	K	WHIP	ERA	CSP	BB%	K%	HR%	GB%	ZSw%	ZCon%	OSw%	OCon%	BABIP	SLGCON	DRA-	WARP
2022	HIL	A+	24	25(0)	39²	3-2	0	53	1.26	2.95		10.4%	30.6%	1.2%	71.7%					.309	.434	91	0.6
2022	AMA	AA	24	13(0)	14	1-0	0	17	1.50	5.14		13.4%	25.4%	3.0%	45.0%					.263	.475	82	0.2
2023	AMA	AA	25	21(0)	33¹	4-0	1	45	1.29	2.70		14.2%	31.9%	0.0%	65.3%					.307	.384	69	0.9
2023	RNO	AAA	25	23(0)	30²	4-2	1	48	1.21	2.35		11.7%	37.5%	1.6%	60.0%	60.5%	81.4%	34.8%	37.3%	.323	.531	55	0.6
2023	AZ	MLB	25	10(0)	10¹	0-0	0	6	1.06	0.00	42.5%	9.8%	14.6%	0.0%	74.2%	73.2%	85.4%	42.0%	54.8%	.226	.226	96	0.1
2024 DC	AZ	MLB	26	45(0)	48¹	3-2	0	57	1.37	3.90	42.5%	11.7%	26.9%	1.8%	56.8%					.308	.488	87	0.6

2023 Arsenal: SI (92.2), KC (83.8)   Comps: Andrew Vasquez (50), Travis Bergen (49), Danny Coulombe (48)

It's curious that the Internet, which returns results on the most esoteric topics imaginable given the right parameters, houses very little information on Saalfrank. What are his hopes? His dreams? His favorite type of sandwich? The world appears indifferent. He seems to have fallen under the radar despite having put up a 37.5% strikeout rate in Triple-A. It's not that Saalfrank is some gargantuan diamond in the rough, but that his seam-shifted-wake-friendly sinker and screwy curveball are enough to make him be at least a competent middle reliever. Once this paragraph makes its way online and into the intestines of the Cthulhu that is SEO, we may see Saalfrank rise a few spots on the search engine hierarchy, just above bovine psychology.

Paul Sewald RHP Born: 05/26/90   Age: 34   Height: 6'3"   Weight: 219   Origin: Round 10, 2012 Draft (#320 overall)

YEAR	TM	LVL	AGE	G (GS)	IP	W-L	SV	K	WHIP	ERA	CSP	BB%	K%	HR%	GB%	ZSw%	ZCon%	OSw%	OCon%	BABIP	SLGCON	DRA-	WARP
2021	SEA	MLB	31	62(0)	64²	10-3	11	104	1.02	3.06	53.9%	9.1%	39.4%	3.8%	25.9%	68.1%	71.5%	34.6%	50.2%	.256	.600	68	1.7
2022	SEA	MLB	32	65(0)	64	5-4	20	72	0.77	2.67	53.9%	7.0%	29.8%	4.1%	30.9%	72.7%	72.9%	31.1%	53.2%	.159	.449	85	1.1
2023	SEA	MLB	33	45(0)	43	3-1	21	60	1.02	2.93	50.8%	8.3%	35.5%	3.0%	28.4%	69.2%	71.0%	30.4%	61.5%	.281	.538	81	0.9
2023	AZ	MLB	33	20(0)	17²	0-1	13	20	1.47	3.57	44.7%	12.5%	25.0%	3.8%	36.7%	73.5%	84.3%	33.8%	62.7%	.289	.583	102	0.2
2024 DC	AZ	MLB	34	50(0)	53²	3-6	35	66	1.19	3.62	51.8%	9.3%	29.7%	3.5%	30.0%					.280	.582	85	0.7

2023 Arsenal: FA (92.4), SL (84.1)   Comps: Kirby Yates (78), Brad Brach (75), Darren O'Day (70)

The Sewald of today was literally created in a lab—well, a pitching lab, but a lab nonetheless, where the Mariners instructed him to embrace his low arm slot and feel for supination, which help generate glove-side movement. Many pitchers have undergone data-driven transformations since, but few have been quite as effective—or consistent—as the one-time Met. Here's someone who throws two and only two pitches, who doesn't have the lopsided platoon splits that plague other two-pitch relievers, and who rarely, if ever, gets hurt. What more would you want from a closer? Acquiring Sewald at the deadline made Torey Lovullo's life a little easier. Tie game? Time for Sewald to pitch! Save situation? Time for Sewald to pitch! Just need a clean inning? TFSTP!

Landon Sims RHP Born: 01/03/01   Age: 23   Height: 6'2"   Weight: 227   Origin: Round 1, 2022 Draft (#34 overall)

YEAR	TM	LVL	AGE	G (GS)	IP	W-L	SV	K	WHIP	ERA	CSP	BB%	K%	HR%	GB%	ZSw%	ZCon%	OSw%	OCon%	BABIP	SLGCON	DRA-	WARP
2023	DIAB	ROK	22	5(4)	6	0-1	0	5	1.33	4.50		12.5%	20.8%	0.0%	37.5%					.313	.312		
2023	VIS	A	22	7(7)	15²	0-3	0	19	1.53	6.89		11.0%	26.0%	4.1%	34.1%					.317	.690	88	0.0
2024 non	AZ	MLB	23	58(0)	50	2-2	0	43	1.59	6.13		11.2%	18.9%	4.2%	35.2%					.302	.615	132	-0.6

Comps: Trey McLoughlin (89), Juan Minaya (79), A.J. Bogucki (78)

Research for this comment included typing the name 'Landon Sims' in Twitter's search bar multiple times. Each time, the latest results were from 2022 or 2021—a clear sign that a once-touted prospect had been erased from the public's collective memory. It's a shame, because Sims is undoubtedly talented, and the fact that he was selected 24th overall in 2022 is no accident. But Sims went under the knife almost immediately after holding up his jersey and smiling, and upon returning, his former velocity wasn't there, nor was the signature sharp break on his slider. It's unclear whether he's found some of his old pizzazz after 20-or-so innings in 2023; we'll have to wait until the upcoming season to give a proper verdict. It is worth noting that we're already past the point where, if Sims' velocity didn't take a major hit, we should be seeing signs of its return. No news, in this case, is bad news.

Peter Strzelecki RHP Born: 10/24/94 Age: 29 Height: 6'2" Weight: 216 Origin: Undrafted Free Agent, 2018

YEAR	TM	LVL	AGE	G (GS)	IP	W-L	SV	K	WHIP	ERA	CSP	BB%	K%	HR%	GB%	ZSw%	ZCon%	OSw%	OCon%	BABIP	SLGCON	DRA-	WARP
2021	BLX	AA	26	36(0)	47	0-2	1	65	1.26	3.45		8.5%	32.7%	2.5%	38.9%					.343	.625	89	0.7
2021	NAS	AAA	26	4(0)	5	0-0	0	6	1.00	3.60		5.0%	30.0%	5.0%	38.5%					.300	.636	77	0.1
2022	NAS	AAA	27	27(0)	31²	4-0	3	50	0.88	2.84		8.3%	41.7%	3.3%	32.8%					.259	.649	70	0.9
2022	MIL	MLB	27	30(0)	35	2-1	1	40	1.23	2.83	51.6%	10.1%	27.0%	1.4%	31.5%	64.0%	78.8%	34.0%	56.2%	.295	.483	93	0.5
2023	NAS	AAA	28	7(0)	7²	0-0	1	11	1.43	7.04		11.1%	30.6%	0.0%	25.0%	71.4%	72.5%	38.9%	51.4%	.350	.550	95	0.1
2023	RNO	AAA	28	13(0)	12¹	0-1	0	16	2.27	8.76		24.6%	24.6%	0.0%	19.4%	59.6%	73.5%	20.6%	51.4%	.387	.548	111	0.0
2023	MIL	MLB	28	36(0)	35²	3-5	0	37	1.18	4.54	47.9%	6.4%	23.7%	1.9%	38.6%	67.3%	78.1%	30.7%	64.6%	.299	.495	100	0.4
2023	AZ	MLB	28	1(0)	1¹	0-0	0	0	2.25	0.00	40.7%	28.6%	0.0%	0.0%	20.0%	75.0%	88.9%	18.2%	75.0%	.200	.200	99	0.0
2024 DC	AZ	MLB	29	13(0)	16	1-1	0	18	1.31	4.43	49.3%	10.2%	26.2%	3.4%	34.1%					.289	.581	99	0.1

2023 Arsenal: FA (92.2), SW (81), SI (91.4), CH (84)   Comps: Ryan O'Rourke (78), Jordan Weems (74), Tyler Kinley (72)

Oops, darn it, there goes another breakout reliever whose sophomore season ended up a disappointment. Strzelecki put up some dandy numbers for Milwaukee in 2022, and he looked to be an integral part of the team's bullpen coming into '23. But alarm bells started going off when his fastball velocity was down by a tick and a half. Not long after, batters caught up to this decline in stuff, and the Brewers eventually demoted Strzelecki. Arizona acquired him at the deadline, but Brent Strom's famous voodoo magic was no use: Strzelecki made exactly one appearance for his new team, in which he walked two batters, struck out none, and still sat 91 instead of 93. The offseason should give Strom and the coaching staff time to come up with a more drastic measure: an incantation, or a Ouija board, perhaps.

Ryan Thompson RHP Born: 06/26/92 Age: 32 Height: 6'5" Weight: 210 Origin: Round 23, 2014 Draft (#676 overall)

YEAR	TM	LVL	AGE	G (GS)	IP	W-L	SV	K	WHIP	ERA	CSP	BB%	K%	HR%	GB%	ZSw%	ZCon%	OSw%	OCon%	BABIP	SLGCON	DRA-	WARP
2021	TB	MLB	29	36(0)	34	3-2	0	37	1.03	2.38	56.6%	6.7%	27.6%	2.2%	47.7%	64.2%	79.3%	37.7%	63.9%	.277	.523	80	0.7
2022	TB	MLB	30	47(0)	42²	3-3	3	39	1.17	3.80	52.5%	6.1%	21.5%	2.2%	49.6%	63.4%	84.4%	35.2%	65.7%	.282	.469	87	0.7
2023	DUR	AAA	31	13(0)	19¹	4-0	1	24	1.19	3.26		13.9%	30.4%	0.0%	61.4%	61.4%	82.0%	29.5%	56.9%	.273	.326	85	0.4
2023	TB	MLB	31	18(0)	17²	1-2	0	12	1.19	6.11	50.8%	9.2%	15.8%	2.6%	46.3%	60.6%	88.8%	25.6%	65.9%	.235	.472	91	0.3
2023	AZ	MLB	31	13(0)	13	0-0	1	9	0.54	0.69	58.8%	2.2%	20.0%	2.2%	79.4%	66.2%	88.7%	30.6%	72.7%	.152	.294	89	0.2
2024 DC	AZ	MLB	32	40(0)	43	2-2	0	34	1.26	3.74	53.8%	8.2%	18.6%	2.2%	52.0%					.279	.458	86	0.5

2023 Arsenal: SI (90.8), SW (78.5), FA (91.8), FS (83.4)   Comps: Blake Parker (63), Josh Fields (56), Dan Otero (55)

For all the fuss *Moneyball* made about medieval baseball organizations ignoring players due to perceived defects, there's a disappointing lack of pitchers with truly funky deliveries in today's game. Thompson, in that sense, is a blessing. No other right-hander uses a sidearm motion as drastic and as angular as he. How the entire package works is a mystery, but it just does, so we're content to sit and watch in silence, sporadically nodding in appreciation. In 2023, Thompson had an off year with the Rays, who designated him for assignment in August. The D-Backs made the smart move of picking up him and encouraging him to throw his sinker *a lot* more often. It worked brilliantly. Don't question the logistics of how he ties up the league's deadliest sluggers with 89-mph fastballs. All you have to do is watch, then nod.

Blake Walston LHP Born: 06/28/01 Age: 23 Height: 6'5" Weight: 175 Origin: Round 1, 2019 Draft (#26 overall)

YEAR	TM	LVL	AGE	G (GS)	IP	W-L	SV	K	WHIP	ERA	CSP	BB%	K%	HR%	GB%	ZSw%	ZCon%	OSw%	OCon%	BABIP	SLGCON	DRA-	WARP
2021	VIS	A	20	8(8)	43¹	2-2	0	60	1.18	3.32		9.4%	33.3%	2.2%	43.7%					.303	.602	86	0.6
2021	HIL	A+	20	11(11)	52¹	2-3	0	57	1.30	4.13		7.1%	25.2%	5.3%	36.8%					.288	.658	120	-0.2
2022	HIL	A+	21	4(4)	17²	1-0	0	27	1.13	2.55		9.6%	37.0%	0.0%	48.7%					.333	.395	81	0.3
2022	AMA	AA	21	21(21)	106¹	7-3	0	110	1.45	5.16		8.5%	24.0%	3.5%	34.0%					.345	.681	83	1.6
2023	RNO	AAA	22	30(30)	149¹	12-6	0	104	1.57	4.52		14.0%	15.6%	1.4%	37.0%	71.5%	85.4%	27.5%	62.7%	.296	.450	118	-0.6
2024 DC	AZ	MLB	23	5(5)	21²	1-2	0	17	1.62	5.96		11.3%	17.3%	3.2%	35.0%					.311	.563	128	-0.1

2023 Arsenal: FA (91), SL (85.8), SW (82.3), CH (84.5), CU (75.9)   Comps: Foster Griffin (77), Kyle Lobstein (73), Gabriel Ynoa (72)

Walston made a whopping 30 starts in Triple-A last year, demonstrating that he's got quite the appetite for innings. But, for the most part, they were tough to swallow: Walston was constantly battling himself, having lost a grip on his otherwise solid repertoire. And though a portion of his struggles can be explained by the bouncy castle that is the Pacific Coast League, it's alarming that his acclaimed changeup, which let Walston get away with a middling fastball velocity, deteriorated the most. The D-Backs added him to the 40-man roster during the offseason, so he'll presumably get a chance to work things out against big league hitters. It'll be a challenge, but a challenge might be just what he needs.

LINEOUTS

Hitters

HITTER	POS	TM	LVL	AGE	PA	R	HR	RBI	SB	AVG/OBP/SLG	BABIP	SLGCON	BB%	K%	ZSw%	ZCon%	OSw%	OCon%	LA	90th EV	DRC+	BRR	DRP	WARP
Blaze Alexander	SS	RNO	AAA	24	305	45	8	52	2	.291/.408/.457	.398	.689	13.8%	27.2%	71.4%	78.0%	29.3%	44.8%			89	3.5	-2.5	0.4
Andrés Chaparro	CI	SWB	AAA	24	601	82	25	89	4	.247/.331/.444	.277	.592	10.8%	21.8%	71.8%	86.0%	32.0%	50.2%			96	-1.6	0.8	1.3
Gino Groover	3B	HIL	A+	21	100	13	1	14	1	.264/.340/.379	.278	.423	8.0%	9.0%							112	-0.4	0.3	0.3
Jose Herrera	C	RNO	AAA	26	119	19	2	14	0	.257/.364/.376	.304	.469	12.6%	16.8%	61.4%	92.9%	29.6%	54.3%			100	-1.8	0.2	0.2
	C	AZ	MLB	26	120	15	0	7	1	.208/.296/.257	.292	.366	10.8%	25.0%	58.4%	90.6%	23.0%	61.2%	10.3	97.8	77	-0.1	-10.3	-0.9
Jack Hurley	CF	VIS	A	21	42	3	1	5	3	.265/.405/.471	.400	.762	16.7%	31.0%							99	-0.8	0.1	0.0
	CF	HIL	A+	21	88	12	1	6	6	.293/.341/.415	.411	.596	5.7%	28.4%							79	-0.1	0.0	0.0
Ivan Melendez	CI	SRR	WIN	23	93	12	2	13	1	.241/.355/.405	.321	.582	10.8%	25.8%	78.8%	68.3%	23.2%	47.8%						
	CI	HIL	A+	23	256	36	18	43	4	.270/.352/.593	.350	.957	8.2%	33.6%							125	-0.3	6.3	2.1
	CI	AMA		23	170	29	12	33	0	.275/.335/.556	.361	.914	5.9%	35.3%							77	-0.6	-0.1	-0.1
Kristian Robinson	OF	DIAR	ROK	22	27	3	1	4	1	.296/.296/.519	.389	.737	0.0%	29.6%	100.0%	100.0%	0.0%							
	OF	VIS	A	22	189	29	9	26	20	.288/.407/.538	.400	.857	12.7%	30.7%							113	0.9	-4.4	0.6
	OF	HIL	A+	22	39	6	2	6	2	.265/.359/.441	.368	.714	10.3%	33.3%							88	-0.6	0.0	0.0
Ruben Santana	3B	DIAB	ROK	18	211	33	4	35	7	.316/.389/.487	.410	.664	8.1%	23.7%	90.0%	100.0%	20.0%	66.7%						
Pavin Smith	RF	RNO	AAA	27	290	45	9	49	2	.318/.428/.506	.360	.630	15.9%	16.2%	62.0%	87.7%	25.6%	68.7%			111	-4.1	1.6	0.7
	RF	AZ	MLB	27	228	26	7	30	1	.188/.317/.325	.209	.425	15.4%	19.7%	61.4%	91.4%	24.7%	58.5%	13.8	103.9	113	-0.1	-1.4	0.7
Gian Zapata	OF	DSL AZR	ROK	17	141	23	9	30	3	.274/.362/.573	.324	.893	9.2%	29.8%										

Given that Jordan of the Red Sox is stuck in Double-A, **Blaze Alexander** will likely become the first player in major-league history named Blaze. He's a nimble shortstop with a cannon for an arm, making this a win for both the D-Backs' infield depth and nominative determinism. ⓧ In another era, #Free**AndrésChaparro** would have been a trending topic on Yankees Twitter. Since Twitter technically doesn't exist anymore and we have a better idea of what makes a Triple-A hitter successful, that didn't exactly happen—though he still had his share of #stans. ⓧ Owing to his transcendental bat control, **Gino Groover** became a second-round pick out of NC State. He needs a defensive home and a little more loft to his swing, but anything contact-related is gravy. ⓧ In an alternative universe, where the 39-man roster is convention, **Jose Herrera** would not be on it. But in our universe, where the number is 40, he's the backup backup catcher for the D-Backs. ⓧ **Jack Hurley** projects to be a power-oriented, around-average corner outfielder. (*Warning: High strikeout and chase rates may apply. Check your carrier for more information.*) ⓧ Whether **Ivan Melendez** becomes a late-blooming power bat like Brent Rooker will largely depend on his adjustments to higher-level pitching. His swinging-strike rate may be ghastly, but it'd be premature to write off the former Golden Spikes Award winner. ⓧ For someone who missed three seasons' worth of baseball due to legal issues, **Kristian Robinson** fared surprisingly well in his return. He also cleared waivers in August, a demonstration of the height of the mountain he has yet to climb. ⓧ The combination of **Ruben Santana**'s pull-side strength, throwing arm, and consistent hustle makes him a name worth paying attention to. ⓧ This was originally a snarky comment about how one-dimensional **Pavin Smith** is. But you don't disrespect someone with a .364 postseason on-base percentage—as a pinch-hitter, no less. ⓧ The D-Backs' selection of **Gian Zapata** came from their simple, yet effective international draft model: IF position_projection == 'CF' // THEN 'draft' // ELSE 'no_draft'

Pitchers

PITCHER	TM	LVL	AGE	G (GS)	IP	W-L	SV	K	WHIP	ERA	CSP	BB%	K%	HR%	GB%	ZSw%	ZCon%	OSw%	OCon%	BABIP	SLGCON	DRA-	WARP
Slade Cecconi	RNO	AAA	24	23 (23)	116¹	5-9	0	118	1.38	6.11		7.1%	23.3%	4.7%	33.5%	66.1%	84.4%	32.1%	59.3%	.310	.666	103	0.8
	AZ	MLB	24	7 (4)	27	0-1	0	20	1.15	4.33	53.4%	3.6%	18.0%	3.6%	37.6%	73.7%	89.0%	25.6%	62.5%	.284	.583	112	0.1
Tyler Chatwood	BRD	A	33	7 (1)	7¹	0-1	0	4	1.23	4.91		19.4%	12.9%	3.2%	76.2%	82.7%	90.7%	26.4%	62.5%	.100	.286	106	0.0
	RNO	AAA	33	5 (0)	5¹	0-0	0	2	0.75	1.69		5.0%	10.0%	0.0%	52.9%	73.3%	86.4%	35.3%	66.7%	.176	.250	86	
Yilber Diaz	HIL	A+	22	22 (22)	87²	2-10	0	124	1.33	5.03		13.0%	33.0%	3.5%	38.4%					.297	.642	82	1.7
	AMA	AA	22	3 (3)	15	1-0	0	16	1.40	3.60		14.1%	25.0%	1.6%	38.5%					.289	.421	106	0.0
Luis Frías	RNO	AAA	25	27 (0)	31²	3-0	4	36	0.95	3.13		7.3%	29.3%	2.4%	32.9%	70.0%	80.7%	32.8%	47.9%	.247	.487	84	0.4
	AZ	MLB	25	29 (0)	31	1-0	0	26	1.52	4.06	47.2%	12.2%	18.7%	2.2%	41.5%	72.1%	80.6%	31.9%	62.4%	.297	.532	111	0.2
Tyler Gilbert	RNO	AAA	29	30 (7)	74²	7-3	0	88	1.54	5.30		7.7%	26.1%	3.0%	37.3%	67.2%	80.4%	31.4%	58.9%	.378	.641	76	1.2
	AZ	MLB	29	11 (0)	17¹	0-2	0	19	1.50	5.19	48.8%	6.9%	26.4%	2.8%	41.7%	70.4%	78.9%	31.0%	62.5%	.413	.750	92	0.3
Dylan Ray	HIL	A+	22	22 (22)	99¹	7-6	0	123	1.17	3.81		7.9%	30.4%	2.0%	48.6%					.321	.516	77	2.0
	AMA	AA	22	3 (3)	14	1-2	0	15	1.79	8.36		11.9%	22.4%	4.5%	28.6%					.359	.775	111	0.0
Ricardo Yan	VIS	A	20	18 (18)	81	1-9	0	105	1.14	4.33		9.9%	30.6%	1.5%	48.9%					.288	.489	64	1.4
	HIL	A+	20	5 (3)	22²	1-0	0	33	0.93	1.19		12.4%	37.1%	1.1%	52.4%					.220	.333	52	0.3

Slade Cecconi throws gas but is hindered by his poor fastball shape, as are numerous D-Backs pitching prospects. He's gonna need a ticket to ride. Ⓧ Yes, **Tyler Chatwood** is alive and well. He still hasn't had the chance to properly show off his new sinker-cutter tandem, but hopefully his minor-league pact with the D-Backs will give him a long-awaited and long-deserved opportunity. Ⓧ **Yilber Diaz** has the fastball shape but not the command. If he and Slade Cecconi swapped bodies a lá *Freaky Friday*, the D-Backs would have two late-inning options. Ⓧ The masculine urge to add a cutter, believing it will fix all your pitching woes, was just too strong for **Luis Frías** to resist. What good is a quasi-breaking ball if your four-seamer gets obliterated? Ⓧ This is your annual reminder that **Tyler Gilbert** tossed a no-hitter in his *major-league debut*. Although he's been not-as-great ever since, his three-mph uptick in velocity might inspire a team to try to rediscover his glory day. Ⓧ It's a *teeny* bit disappointing that **Caden Grice** will focus exclusively on pitching as a pro. But it makes sense: Grice the pitcher already has two polished secondaries, whereas Grice the hitter is an aggressive lefty with big power but an inflexible swing. Maybe they'll kill the NL DH? Ⓧ Four years ago, **Corbin Martin** seemed a sure bet to become the most famous Corbin on the D-Backs. After multiple injuries and subsequent surgeries, that prospect (pun intended) is now all but off the table. Ⓧ Armed with a riding fastball and a plummeting curveball that complements it, **Dylan Ray** is slowly but gradually building himself up to be a legitimate starting pitcher. He struggled in a brief stop at Double-A, but remember, development is never just a straight line. Ⓧ **Chris Rodriguez**'s one-inning, two-run outing in Single-A on September 10th wasn't just a bullpen appearance in an already lopsided match, it was the culmination of over two years away from the game. He lost the entirety of the 2022 season and most of the two seasons before and after it undergoing, recovering from and rehabbing two shoulder surgeries. While still technically on a rehab assignment, he made the jump up to Triple-A almost immediately after that game, and finished his season with two more short relief appearances in Salt Lake City. Ⓧ There's video of **Ricardo Yan** striking out the side in Single-A Visalia, and it's a pleasure to watch as he bamboozles each hitter with his deceptive, coil-like delivery. He can ride his sinker and sweeper all the way to the majors, so long as he picks up a little bit of velocity.

ATLANTA BRAVES

Essay by Justin Klugh

Player comments by Demetrius Bell and BP staff

The nightmare isn't always the same.

Sometimes it's Kim Batiste lining a game-winning double straight through Terry Pendleton. Sometimes it's Rhys Hoskins spiking his bat so hard your house falls down. Sometimes it's the Phanatic's acidic saliva dissolving Blooper's head down to the skull.

The nightmare isn't always the same, but it comes from the same pain: The Braves broke off triple-digit wins only to have some low-seed, starry-eyed Phillies team end their season.

Pain typically teaches a lesson. But the Braves just don't want to learn it.

Fortunately, you'll never return to the moment a loss actually happened—the actual instant it was all over, when you didn't feel grace or dignity or hard-earned wisdom. You were just *mad*, reaching for any excuse, justification, or piece of trash to throw—anything to keep that pain from reaching your heart.

The Braves are supposed to *be* that pain; not feel it. They're supposed to roll into the World Series with underdog guts in their cleats and slap around whatever AL squad has the nerve to show up. Every Wild Card wonder, every team of destiny, every cute little story about some guys that just *believed*—they're all supposed to end in Atlanta.

All those teams—Phillies or not—with their 87 wins and their third-place finishes, know one thing the Braves don't: You can know how to win without learning how to lose.

When the Braves won it all in 1995, it was seen as the beginning of a dynasty. That's why every time they lost in the postseason—and they lost *so many* times—they had in most cases been viewed as the inevitable winners. The Braves are only two years removed from their last championship in 2021, yet have somehow earned a reputation as chokers. Two years after they'd won in 1995, things sounded pretty much the same as they took on the Marlins in the 1997 NLCS.

If Florida was a team of destiny, then their destiny seemed to be to die: Coming into the playoffs, Alex Fernandez tore his rotator cuff. Kevin Brown got a stomach virus. Moises Alou injured his hand. Bobby Bonilla had the flu. Jim Leyland contracted walking pneumonia. Jeff Conine had just seen *The Ice Storm* and was still pretty bummed about it. And still

ATLANTA BRAVES PROSPECTUS
2023 W-L: 104-58, 1ST IN NL EAST

Pythag	.633	1st	DER	.688	24th
RS/G	5.85	1st	DRC+	121	1st
RA/G	4.42	13th	DRA-	96	12th
dWin%	.635	1st	FIP	4.11	8th
Payroll	$203M	8th	B-Age	28.3	16th
M$/MW	$3.3M	10th	P-Age	30.1	23rd

400'

385'   375'

335'   325'

- Opened 2017
- Open air
- Natural surface
- Fence profile: 6' to 16'

Park Factors

Runs	Runs/RH	Runs/LH	HR/RH	HR/LH
100	98	102	94	109

Top Hitter WARP	9.4 Ronald Acuña Jr.
Top Pitcher WARP	4.9 Spencer Strider
2023 Top Prospect	Hurston Waldrep

Payroll History (in millions)

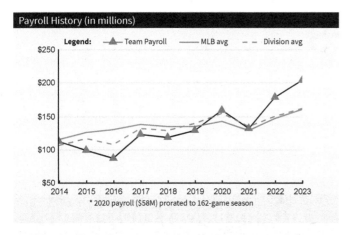

Legend: ▲ Team Payroll — MLB avg --- Division avg

* 2020 payroll ($58M) prorated to 162-game season

Future Commitments (in millions)

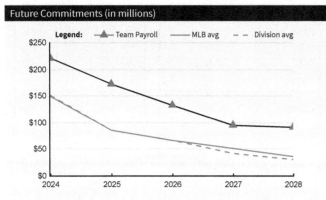

Legend: ▲ Team Payroll — MLB avg --- Division avg

Farm System Ranking

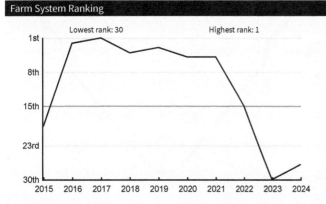

Lowest rank: 30   Highest rank: 1

Personnel

**President, Baseball Operations
& General Manager**
Alex Anthopoulos

**Senior Vice President, Baseball
Development**
Mike Fast

**Assistant General Manager,
Research and Development**
Jason Paré

**Assistant General Manager,
Player Development**
Ben Sestanovich

Manager
Brian Snitker

BP Alumni
Mike Fast
Jason Paré
Ronit Shah
Will Siskel
Colin Wyers

the Marlins managed to, according to one Atlanta columnist, "...snatch the spot reserved for the Braves in the World Series."

Baseball doesn't take reservations, no matter how loudly you demand to see the playoffs' manager. But there can't be many more signs that you're not deserving of victory than getting outclassed by a bunch of sick Fish. It didn't happen because the seeding was bad or the format was dumb or the reporters reported. It happened because when the game ended, the 101-win Braves just didn't have the numbers. It's just baseball, played within the confines of two potential outcomes, and the Braves couldn't, in a seven-game series, reach out and grab the one they preferred before the Marlins had won Game 6.

Every team is a team of destiny. Just usually not the one they want.

The sting fades, the scar remains. Losing is just something that happens—something you live with. It turns into trauma, it turns into motivation and occasionally you can turn it into somebody else's pain. But that all comes from facing the other way. If you just stand there, staring at it, all you're going to feel is that same sting over, and over and over again. Every call to change the format met by a shrug. Every claim of media malpractice met by a laugh. Every fear that your *guys* didn't let you down, the *system* did, drowned out by the cheer of the winning team's crowd.

But losing isn't *meant* to feel good. That's why everybody looks so undignified trying to fight it with anything other than offense.

The Braves had plenty of that in the '90s. But every year after 1995, an underdog found its way past them. Their era of dominance ended after the 2005 postseason—their last go at being more than just the villains in someone's Cinderella story. In fact, by then, they were telling one of their own: The 2005 Braves weren't a dominating force; they were 18 rookies, a bunch of injured veterans and a bullpen trying sweatily to contain implosion after implosion.

In Game 4 of that year's NLDS against the Astros, they led 6-1 with only six outs to go. Then Lance Berkman grand slammed a 2-1 pitch straight through the heart of Atlanta, and the Astros soon tied it up.

The Braves clung to the scoreboard for the next six hours. It took the longest postseason game of all time, but Houston eventually walked it off in the 18th.

"Adversity helps you," said Joey Devine, a 21-year-old Braves pitcher who'd started the year at North Carolina State. "If you learn how to overcome it." Chipper Jones, in his mid-30s, saw it differently: "This will sting for a long time."

A sting subsides. But nothing fades faster than glory.

"Atlanta's run of divisional dominance is one of the greatest records in baseball history," wrote one columnist, "but the Braves' inability to win more than one championship ring during the run stands as one of the game's greatest failures."

The league changed. The playoffs changed. Atlanta was in them and out of them. They broke through again in 2021, winning it all, but it wasn't enough. A year later, they weren't the defending champs anymore, and that meant something was wrong. So they stocked up on arms. Filled the lineup with bats. Gave everybody deals that will keep them Braves forever. They made hard choices and then made people forget them by winning 104 games. And at the end of it, their reward was the chance to win three more against—

No, no, no, no, *no*. The Phillies?! *Again?!?*

How does this seeding make sense? How do the *playoffs* make sense? How is the reward for having the best record in baseball a flight to *Philadelphia?!* To play against the team that beer belly'd them out of the postseason in '93 and spiked a bat off their heads in '22*?!*

It all happened in slow motion. Sure, Game 2 was fun. But since the end result of *that* was Orlando Arcia's hot mic moment, Bryce Harper's iconic stare and a disingenuous debate on media ethics, well. The fun faded even faster than the glory.

The Braves lost, again; in the NLDS, again. To the Phillies. Again.

Losing to that team and its fans feels like watching a serial killer charm a jury. Harper knew all he had to do was stare because the fans were going to do most of the legwork. They yelled at Arcia until he appeared to have a meltdown in the dugout and hoisted Blooper's severed head on a stick at an Eagles tailgate after threatening to eat him on social media. Oh, did you hear about them being granted sainthood because they clapped for one of their players?

Can you imagine if they did something that actually *impacted* the game, like throwing trash on the field?

You want to go back to when things made *sense*. Maybe sometime around June, when the Braves were doing what they did best: scoring 4-5 runs before the opposing pitcher had his shoes tied. It feels great to be the team that can ruin a nice summer weekend in Philadelphia, then hop on a plane out of town. Unfortunately for the Braves, every summer has a fall.

And so, the nightmares come again: Runs pouring in on an endless series of bases-loaded catcher interference calls. Harper staring at Arcia until he crumbles into dust and blows away in a sausage-scented South Philly breeze. The Phanatic laying an egg that hatches a baby Ronald Acuna Jr. and gently placing a tiny Phillies hat on his head.

This is where you could really use an answer: A breathing exercise, or perhaps a certain blend of tea. Something into which you can channel the emotions you built up for the Braves over the course of a wish-fulfillment regular season, followed by a postseason you couldn't believe was happening.

After 2005, some fans embraced the cleansing nature of fire, burning hats and jerseys. Some turned to other sports, other teams or other interests, like they wouldn't just let them down, too. Some died, Braves fandom etched into their obituaries, a footnote between the names of their beloved grandchildren and where to send some flowers.

There is no answer. There is only more baseball. And it gets played whether you're watching from the stands or buried in the ground.

How do you "fix" a team that leads the league in batting average, hits, runs and hits that knocked in runs; the only team that hit over 300 dingers and the only team to slug over .500 in 2023? Spencer Strider and even a half-asleep pitching staff should be able to make that work. And they did, for 162 games, dancing and whooping on the Phillies' own field as they clinched their playoff spot and sealed their doom.

The Braves are probably tired of clenching their fists every time somebody shrugs, smirks and says, "That's baseball!" So they're not trying to learn how to lose. They're trying to never do it again. They're trading for players and then cutting them, revving their engines before the light turns green.

Making the playoffs? Hell, you only need 84 wins to get in now. The Braves can manage 84 wins by late August. And they'll never *have* to learn how to lose if they just stop doing it. They're not up against any particular team, they're up against the teeth-grinding riddle of baseball's postseason: *Anything can happen if you get in.* But the Braves don't want "anything." They want to win. By January, they were one of the only non-Dodgers teams to take steps toward addressing that specific issue.

Trading their only position playing prospect who could have been a factor in 2024 for Chris Sale was very "Braves": It happened with no warning to the public, it was lauded by the giddy writers on the Braves beat and the front office immediately followed it up with a contract extension. The 34-year-old Sale joined a roster in January that is entirely locked up through 2026, and most through 2028. He may make 30 starts next year, or zero, but Atlanta is just praying for four or five very specific ones.

Attempts to elicit control over a force like baseball is like trying to catch the wind in a net. But what else can they do but fight an unwinnable war against chaos; a war you never win, just one you learn to survive.

Because even a team that's learned how to lose—a team whose fans can do it with grace, dignity and with their heads held high, or at least the ability to get over it—has lost. And loss is something nobody wants to experience, no matter how many excuses they've prepared.

People want to win. But when they don't, they'll settle for being right. And when they're wrong, they'll pick their favorite version of the truth. And they'll sleep with it under their pillows at night and think everything played a part in this conspiracy except the final score. All because the Braves played 104 games that went their way and a couple in October that didn't.

But everybody's got to learn how to lose, because some day, everybody's going to do it.

—*Justin Klugh is an author of Baseball Prospectus.*

HITTERS

Ronald Acuña Jr. RF Born: 12/18/97 Age: 26 Bats: R Throws: R Height: 6'0" Weight: 205 Origin: IFA, 2014

YEAR	TM	LVL	AGE	PA	R	HR	RBI	SB	AVG/OBP/SLG	BABIP	SLGCON	BB%	K%	ZSw%	ZCon%	OSw%	OCon%	LA	90th EV	DRC+	BRR	DRP	WARP
2021	ATL	MLB	23	360	72	24	52	17	.283/.394/.596	.311	.835	13.6%	23.6%	69.5%	78.0%	24.4%	61.0%	18.3	111.1	164	0.5	3.6	4.4
2022	ATL	MLB	24	533	71	15	50	29	.266/.351/.413	.331	.566	9.9%	23.6%	75.5%	81.1%	29.7%	64.9%	10.9	108.5	124	1.4	3.3	3.5
2023	ATL	MLB	25	735	149	41	106	73	.337/.416/.596	.338	.685	10.9%	11.4%	73.1%	87.1%	26.8%	70.1%	7.4	111.0	176	3.8	2.5	9.4
2024 DC	ATL	MLB	26	677	91	29	96	49	.294/.382/.500	.316	.607	11.1%	15.3%							151	1.4	4.7	6.8

2023 GP: RF (156), DH (2)   *Comps: Hank Aaron (78), Ellis Valentine (77), Mookie Betts (76)*

During the first inning on Opening Day last season, Acuña reached base and handily avoided two pickoff attempts. Well aware of the new rules, on the very next pitch following pickoff no. 2 he took off for second and swiped it. That was the start of a historic season for Acuña; he hit his first homer in the second game and began his journey to joining the 40/40 Club. Not only did he reach it, he actually did plenty of renovation work while he was there and built his own wing. When Acuña was finished, he was the only player in baseball history with 40 homers and 70 stolen bases in the same season. The part that's bone-chilling for his rivals is that 50/50 seems like a real possibility if Acuña can continue to stay healthy. The possibilities are endless for any other new clubs that he could create by himself in the future.

Ozzie Albies 2B Born: 01/07/97 Age: 27 Bats: S Throws: R Height: 5'8" Weight: 165 Origin: IFA, 2013

YEAR	TM	LVL	AGE	PA	R	HR	RBI	SB	AVG/OBP/SLG	BABIP	SLGCON	BB%	K%	ZSw%	ZCon%	OSw%	OCon%	LA	90th EV	DRC+	BRR	DRP	WARP
2021	ATL	MLB	24	686	103	30	106	20	.259/.310/.488	.278	.613	6.9%	18.7%	83.9%	84.0%	41.6%	64.9%	21.1	103.1	105	0.8	1.6	3.2
2022	ATL	MLB	25	269	36	8	35	3	.247/.294/.409	.270	.505	5.9%	17.5%	83.5%	86.9%	45.6%	68.2%	17.2	100.7	90	-0.1	-0.4	0.5
2023	ATL	MLB	26	660	96	33	109	13	.280/.336/.513	.289	.626	7.0%	16.2%	80.1%	88.5%	39.7%	68.5%	16.6	102.8	113	1.1	-0.3	3.1
2024 DC	ATL	MLB	27	594	69	23	78	13	.261/.322/.452	.281	.549	7.3%	16.3%							114	0.5	0.5	2.8

2023 GP: 2B (148)   *Comps: Roberto Alomar (82), Bobby Doerr (81), Rod Carew (79)*

Nobody was feeling the optimistic vibes last spring more than Albies. Atlanta's longtime second baseman deserves credit for being one of the first and most prominent names to predict that his good buddy Ronald Acuña Jr. would put up a 40/40 season. He also predicted that both he and Michael Harris II would join Acuña in the 40/40 club, so maybe we should just credit him for buying multiple lottery tickets instead of just one. While Albies himself didn't come close to going 40/40, he should still be quite happy with his performance; he returned to the upper echelons of second basemen after a tough, injury-plagued 2022. His DRC+ was not far off from his career high, his BRR suggested that he was still plenty effective as a baserunner and he also posted a career-high isolated power. This was the type of bounce-back campaign that Albies needed.

―――――――――――――――――― ★ ★ ★ *2024 Top 101 Prospect* **#98** ★ ★ ★ ――――――――――――――――――

Ignacio Alvarez SS Born: 04/11/03 Age: 21 Bats: R Throws: R Height: 5'11" Weight: 190 Origin: Round 5, 2022 Draft (#155 overall)

YEAR	TM	LVL	AGE	PA	R	HR	RBI	SB	AVG/OBP/SLG	BABIP	SLGCON	BB%	K%	ZSw%	ZCon%	OSw%	OCon%	LA	90th EV	DRC+	BRR	DRP	WARP
2022	BRA	ROK	19	51	11	1	5	4	.279/.392/.419	.306	.486	13.7%	11.8%										
2022	AUG	A	19	71	14	0	6	4	.294/.493/.373	.357	.452	26.8%	12.7%							134	0.5	-1.4	0.4
2023	ROM	A+	20	501	62	7	66	16	.284/.395/.391	.341	.494	13.2%	17.4%							121	1.7	10.7	3.8
2024 non	ATL	MLB	21	251	21	2	20	0	.222/.301/.308	.268	.383	9.0%	17.9%							76	0.0	0	0.1

2023 GP: SS (107), DH (8), 3B (1)   *Comps: Ehire Adrianza (73), Junior Lake (73), Matt Tuiasosopo (72)*

There wasn't much fanfare surrounding Alvarez's entry into Atlanta's system as a fifth-round pick from Riverside City College in 2022. While he still doesn't have light-tower power, fancy footwork or blazing speed going for him, he's become one of the Braves' top prospects by doing the simple things well. He doesn't chase balls, he's good at hitting pitches in the strike zone and he has become a very reliable defender at shortstop. He's proven to be sure-handed with a very strong arm, with a knack for constantly getting the first step right when it comes to getting to ground balls. Alvarez may not have been on everybody's radar when he was drafted, but if he continues his generalized progress, that'll change.

Orlando Arcia SS Born: 08/04/94 Age: 29 Bats: R Throws: R Height: 6'0" Weight: 187 Origin: IFA, 2010

YEAR	TM	LVL	AGE	PA	R	HR	RBI	SB	AVG/OBP/SLG	BABIP	SLGCON	BB%	K%	ZSw%	ZCon%	OSw%	OCon%	LA	90th EV	DRC+	BRR	DRP	WARP
2021	GWN	AAA	26	322	54	17	37	5	.282/.351/.516	.272	.594	9.6%	11.8%							133	1.2	4.4	2.7
2021	MIL	MLB	26	11	0	0	1	0	.091/.091/.091	.125	.125	0.0%	27.3%	65.0%	76.9%	43.5%	70.0%	-0.3	103.0	102	0.0	0.0	0.0
2021	ATL	MLB	26	78	9	2	13	1	.214/.282/.343	.245	.444	9.0%	20.5%	72.1%	82.2%	35.4%	58.6%	9.8	101.1	89	0.0	-0.5	0.1
2022	ATL	MLB	27	234	25	9	30	0	.244/.316/.416	.278	.551	9.0%	21.8%	63.9%	86.5%	31.1%	53.0%	12.0	104.8	108	0.1	-0.9	0.8
2023	ATL	MLB	28	533	66	17	65	1	.264/.321/.420	.301	.531	7.3%	19.1%	67.9%	83.1%	29.7%	62.8%	5.6	103.4	111	0.0	-2.5	2.3
2024 DC	ATL	MLB	29	505	51	13	55	1	.243/.304/.382	.281	.482	7.3%	19.2%							95	-0.3	2.5	1.7

2023 GP: SS (139)   *Comps: Elvis Andrus (66), Jose Offerman (63), Rick Auerbach (63)*

Despite returning to relative relevancy in 2022, Arcia still wasn't expected to start 2023 as the first-choice shortstop for Atlanta. That was supposed to be either Vaughn Grissom or Braden Shewmake's job heading into the new season, with Arcia slotting in as a veteran insurance policy. Instead, Arcia parlayed a solid-if-unspectacular spring training into a starting role and proceeded to finally have the type of season that was expected of him back when he was a hot prospect. He combined steady defense with a productive campaign at the plate while also being a reliable baserunner. He's also got an 80-grade staredown, as he demonstrated to Bryce Harper in the NLDS. Fittingly, Arcia's breakout rendered the three-year extension he signed in March another absolute bargain for Atlanta—it truly warms the heart.

Sabin Ceballos 3B/DH Born: 08/17/02 Age: 21 Bats: R Throws: R Height: 6'3" Weight: 225 Origin: Round 3, 2023 Draft (#94 overall)

YEAR	TM	LVL	AGE	PA	R	HR	RBI	SB	AVG/OBP/SLG	BABIP	SLGCON	BB%	K%	ZSw%	ZCon%	OSw%	OCon%	LA	90th EV	DRC+	BRR	DRP	WARP
2023	AUG	A	20	35	3	1	6	0	.281/.343/.375	.400	.571	8.6%	31.4%							96	0.2	-0.1	0.1
2024 non	ATL	MLB	21	251	19	2	19	0	.207/.265/.289	.286	.411	6.4%	27.8%							57	0.0	0	-0.7

2023 GP: 3B (10), DH (4)

Ceballos charted a unique path to affiliated ball, going from his native San Juan, Puerto Rico to San Jacinto JC in Texas to the Oregon Ducks before finally being drafted by the Braves in the third round of the 2023 draft. He took that journey while speaking softly and carrying a big stick—which is to say that he got here mostly due to his bat. He has a solid hit tool, demonstrating an ability to spray the ball all over the field. He's also got an intriguing amount of power, only adding to his allure with the bat. While he does possess a bit of a rocket arm, he may not have the speed to stick around at third base and might be moving to the opposite corner of the diamond. Either way, Ceballos has a bat that should play as he embarks on his first full season of professional baseball.

Travis d'Arnaud C Born: 02/10/89 Age: 35 Bats: R Throws: R Height: 6'2" Weight: 210 Origin: Round 1, 2007 Draft (#37 overall)

YEAR	TM	LVL	AGE	PA	R	HR	RBI	SB	AVG/OBP/SLG	BABIP	SLGCON	BB%	K%	ZSw%	ZCon%	OSw%	OCon%	LA	90th EV	DRC+	BRR	DRP	WARP
2021	ATL	MLB	32	229	21	7	26	0	.220/.284/.388	.260	.519	7.4%	23.1%	76.4%	85.0%	32.6%	57.7%	6.3	106.4	78	-0.3	5.2	0.8
2022	ATL	MLB	33	426	61	18	60	0	.268/.319/.472	.306	.611	4.5%	21.1%	70.1%	82.0%	40.6%	62.2%	12.0	104.0	102	-0.4	8.2	2.4
2023	ATL	MLB	34	292	31	11	39	0	.225/.288/.397	.258	.530	7.2%	22.9%	77.6%	77.5%	31.9%	59.8%	10.4	105.3	93	-0.2	2.6	1.1
2024 DC	ATL	MLB	35	336	34	10	38	0	.238/.298/.389	.288	.524	6.5%	23.8%							94	0.0	2.1	1.1

2023 GP: C (63), DH (8)

Comps: Mike Lieberthal (76), Don Slaught (73), Terry Steinbach (73)

YEAR	TM	P. COUNT	FRM RUNS	BLK RUNS	THRW RUNS	TOT RUNS
2021	ATL	7703	6.3	0.0	0.1	6.3
2022	ATL	14462	10.7	0.2	-0.1	10.7
2023	ATL	8891	4.4	0.0	-0.7	3.7
2024	ATL	8418	2.5	-0.1	-0.3	2.1

There was plenty of intrigue as to how the Braves would go about finding space for both Sean Murphy and d'Arnaud after the team decided to upgrade their battery of backstops over the 2022-23 offseason. Would they utilize d'Arnaud as a DH? Would Murphy fit in the lineup whenever d'Arnaud got behind the plate? Would they split playing time, with Murphy being the primary catcher and d'Arnaud functioning as a more typical backup? The final option ended up being the answer, and d'Arnaud went from being one of the top hitting catchers in baseball in 2022 to being a fine backup option in 2023. Atlanta was able to get good production from their primary DH, in a marked departure from the first year of the role's implementation on the Senior Circuit, which freed up d'Arnaud to focus on providing value when Murphy needed a breather. The vet was perfectly capable of giving what was needed. His output at the plate was once again solid, and while his days as a defensive dynamo might be behind him, his pitch framing is still a sight to behold on his best days.

David Fletcher MI Born: 05/31/94 Age: 30 Bats: R Throws: R Height: 5'9" Weight: 185 Origin: Round 6, 2015 Draft (#195 overall)

YEAR	TM	LVL	AGE	PA	R	HR	RBI	SB	AVG/OBP/SLG	BABIP	SLGCON	BB%	K%	ZSw%	ZCon%	OSw%	OCon%	LA	90th EV	DRC+	BRR	DRP	WARP
2021	LAA	MLB	27	665	74	2	47	15	.262/.297/.324	.287	.359	4.7%	9.0%	61.5%	95.7%	35.2%	83.8%	7.7	96.9	94	0.3	-0.4	1.9
2022	SL	AAA	28	51	3	0	1	1	.204/.235/.224	.238	.262	3.9%	13.7%	52.8%	92.1%	33.3%	75.8%			98	0.5	-0.7	0.1
2022	LAA	MLB	28	228	20	2	17	1	.255/.288/.333	.268	.360	3.1%	7.0%	60.1%	92.9%	38.6%	81.4%	14.4	94.4	106	-0.1	0.8	1.0
2023	SL	AAA	29	380	57	4	38	6	.330/.382/.428	.345	.460	7.1%	6.3%	67.6%	95.4%	38.9%	84.2%			108	-0.3	0.3	1.4
2023	LAA	MLB	29	97	7	2	12	0	.247/.302/.326	.256	.362	7.2%	9.3%	67.2%	89.1%	37.9%	76.4%	7.8	98.3	105	0.1	0.1	0.4
2024 DC	ATL	MLB	30	198	18	2	17	2	.277/.321/.358	.298	.399	5.7%	9.0%							96	0.0	0.2	0.5

2023 GP: SS (18), 2B (14), 3B (3)

Comps: Wally Backman (73), Lenny Harris (72), Sandy Alomar Sr. (71)

Fletcher was one of the teacher's pets in Joe Maddon's classroom, but wasn't looked on quite as kindly by substitute teacher Phil Nevin. He was outrighted to Salt Lake twice, which is almost exactly like being sent to the principal's office but with much higher stakes. During his time in the majors, though, his characteristic low-strikeout, contact-heavy batting style was still in effect, providing him a .628 OPS that might have been much more palatable without the ugly BABIP. Over 89 at-bats, Fletcher still shored up 22 hits and only struck out nine times. In that span, he was walked seven times—including once, intentionally, by JP Sears, in an October game that was meaningless for both the Angels and A's. None of that was enough to prevent him from being moved in a bad money-for-bad money deal over the winter.

Douglas Glod CF Born: 01/20/05 Age: 19 Bats: R Throws: R Height: 5'9" Weight: 185 Origin: IFA, 2022

YEAR	TM	LVL	AGE	PA	R	HR	RBI	SB	AVG/OBP/SLG	BABIP	SLGCON	BB%	K%	ZSw%	ZCon%	OSw%	OCon%	LA	90th EV	DRC+	BRR	DRP	WARP
2022	DSL BRA	ROK	17	128	23	2	13	3	.202/.352/.356	.288	.544	17.2%	28.1%										
2023	BRA	ROK	18	207	29	5	25	6	.224/.386/.398	.330	.660	18.4%	30.9%										
2024									No projection														

2023 GP: RF (18), CF (17), LF (8), DH (4)

The Braves made a couple of splashy signings in the International Free Agent market ahead of the 2022 season, and one of those players was Glod. Regarded as one of the consensus top-30 international prospects when he was signed, Glod had a tough debut season in the Dominican Summer League, but started to come into his own last season for Atlanta's FCL Championship-winning team. While his strikeout rate remained too high for comfort, he showcased more power at the plate. Though he spent 2023 in center field, it's likely that his speed won't be enough to stay there and he'll eventually move to a corner outfield spot.

Michael Harris II CF Born: 03/07/01 Age: 23 Bats: L Throws: L Height: 6'0" Weight: 195 Origin: Round 3, 2019 Draft (#98 overall)

YEAR	TM	LVL	AGE	PA	R	HR	RBI	SB	AVG/OBP/SLG	BABIP	SLGCON	BB%	K%	ZSw%	ZCon%	OSw%	OCon%	LA	90th EV	DRC+	BRR	DRP	WARP
2021	ROM	A+	20	420	55	7	64	27	.294/.362/.436	.349	.547	8.3%	18.1%							116	1.9	11.4	3.5
2022	MIS	AA	21	196	33	5	33	11	.305/.372/.506	.364	.652	8.7%	19.9%							118	0.5	1.5	1.2
2022	ATL	MLB	21	441	75	19	64	20	.297/.339/.514	.361	.694	4.8%	24.3%	69.5%	85.9%	41.2%	56.6%	4.4	108.4	108	1.4	0.3	2.2
2023	ATL	MLB	22	539	76	18	57	20	.293/.331/.477	.334	.597	4.6%	18.7%	67.7%	83.6%	42.2%	66.1%	7.6	108.2	116	1.4	0.8	3.3
2024 DC	ATL	MLB	23	538	56	15	63	19	.268/.321/.428	.323	.554	6.1%	21.1%							108	0.5	-0.2	2.5

2023 GP: CF (138)   Comps: Vada Pinson (66), Mookie Betts (66), Heinie Mueller (62)

In 1994, legendary Atlanta rap duo OutKast stormed onto the hip-hop scene with their debut album *Southernplayalisticadillacmuzik*. As is typical when it comes to hit albums from newcomers on the scene, the attention slowly but surely turned to whatever was in store next. It's very difficult to live up to expectations when your first album is a smash success, but OutKast managed to exceed them with their follow-up album *ATLiens*. If Harris' rookie season in 2022 was his version of *Southernplayalisticadillacmuzik*, then 2023 was his rendition of *ATLiens*. Despite a shaky start at the plate, he continued to bring the noise with the stick while flourishing on the basepaths and especially in the field with his glove. It was the follow-up offering that has established Harris as a true star on the baseball scene rather than a flash in the pan; now it's time to see if he'll be ready to deliver his version of *Aquemini* as he enters his third big-league season.

Jarred Kelenic OF Born: 07/16/99 Age: 24 Bats: L Throws: L Height: 6'1" Weight: 206 Origin: Round 1, 2018 Draft (#6 overall)

YEAR	TM	LVL	AGE	PA	R	HR	RBI	SB	AVG/OBP/SLG	BABIP	SLGCON	BB%	K%	ZSw%	ZCon%	OSw%	OCon%	LA	90th EV	DRC+	BRR	DRP	WARP
2021	TAC	AAA	21	143	29	9	28	6	.320/.392/.624	.323	.757	10.5%	15.4%							125	-1.5	-0.9	0.7
2021	SEA	MLB	21	377	41	14	43	6	.181/.265/.350	.216	.511	9.5%	28.1%	68.1%	87.4%	33.7%	53.7%	14.6	104.0	84	0.2	-4.5	0.4
2022	TAC	AAA	22	394	58	18	65	9	.295/.365/.557	.339	.726	8.9%	20.8%	69.3%	87.1%	30.5%	52.7%			108	1.5	4.2	2.1
2022	SEA	MLB	22	181	20	7	17	5	.141/.221/.313	.167	.500	8.8%	33.7%	69.4%	72.5%	32.2%	56.7%	18.7	104.6	78	0.0	-0.5	0.0
2023	TAC	AAA	23	43	8	1	5	1	.306/.395/.472	.400	.680	14.0%	25.6%	72.3%	80.9%	27.5%	46.7%			89	-1.0	-1.2	-0.1
2023	SEA	MLB	23	416	44	11	49	13	.253/.327/.419	.359	.650	9.9%	31.7%	67.2%	80.8%	32.5%	44.8%	10.4	106.6	67	0.5	0.9	-0.4
2024 DC	ATL	MLB	24	393	39	11	42	8	.209/.289/.368	.286	.562	9.2%	31.1%							82	0.1	-0.1	0.1

2023 GP: LF (79), RF (21), CF (8), DH (3)   Comps: Melvin Nieves (54), Fernando Martinez (51), Byron Buxton (47)

As if hitting .180 over his first two big-league seasons wasn't sobering enough, Kelenic learned a new life lesson in Year Three in the form of anger management. After a nine-pitch battle in July with Minnesota's fearsome final boss Jhoan Duran ended with a ?, Kelenic returned to the dugout and let out his frustration with a swift kick of the Gatorade cooler. The result: a broken foot, a teary-eyed apology and four weeks on the shelf. By the time he returned, memories of a promising April in which he appeared on track for the long-awaited breakout suddenly felt faint. Still, his early-season exploits were a reminder that even amidst struggles, Kelenic has a knack for hitting the ball over the fence—and sometimes *way* over the fence. His 482-foot blast on April 12 off a 98-mph fastball from Julian Merryweather crashed down in a section of the center field bleachers at Wrigley Field rarely visited by batted balls. The advanced hit tool Kelenic was lauded for as an amateur may never come to be, but his thunderous in-game power and high-energy playstyle should ensure a long career for Kelenic in some form. Abruptly jettisoned to Atlanta in stunning fashion as an unexpected vehicle for Seattle's salary dump spree, Kelenic now has the opportunity to operate in an environment without the pressure of becoming the next big thing.

David McCabe 3B Born: 03/25/00 Age: 24 Bats: S Throws: R Height: 6'3" Weight: 230 Origin: Round 4, 2022 Draft (#125 overall)

YEAR	TM	LVL	AGE	PA	R	HR	RBI	SB	AVG/OBP/SLG	BABIP	SLGCON	BB%	K%	ZSw%	ZCon%	OSw%	OCon%	LA	90th EV	DRC+	BRR	DRP	WARP
2022	AUG	A	22	118	14	1	23	0	.260/.347/.350	.333	.479	12.7%	22.9%							100	-2.3	-1.0	0.1
2023	SRR	WIN	23	92	13	0	8	1	.271/.435/.357	.452	.610	22.8%	31.5%	55.6%	74.3%	20.0%	51.7%						
2023	AUG	A	23	176	26	8	25	1	.267/.381/.493	.333	.727	15.3%	26.7%							133	-1.8	-0.2	0.9
2023	ROM	A+	23	348	37	9	50	9	.281/.388/.428	.332	.553	15.2%	19.0%							122	-1.7	-8.1	0.9
2024 non	ATL	MLB	24	251	23	4	23	0	.226/.302/.338	.291	.467	9.3%	24.2%							82	0.0	0	0.1

2023 GP: 3B (118), DH (19), 1B (7)   Comps: Leonard Davis (83), Mark Sobolewski (79), Mitch Delfino (73)

When the Braves drafted McCabe with the 125th overall pick of the 2022 draft, it was clear that they were banking on his power eventually breaking out at some point. It didn't happen during his initial go-around as a pro, but McCabe finally started hitting them long and far on a regular basis in 2023. He also managed to cut down on his strikeout rate, another facet of his professional debut that had observers questioning whether or not he could make it as a big-league hitter. He's starting to affirmatively answer those questions now. Additionally, his improvements on defense and his arm strength are making it plausible that you could place him at any corner and be fine. McCabe didn't make a loud arrival in Atlanta's system, but he's making noise now.

Sean Murphy C Born: 10/04/94 Age: 29 Bats: R Throws: R Height: 6'3" Weight: 228 Origin: Round 3, 2016 Draft (#83 overall)

YEAR	TM	LVL	AGE	PA	R	HR	RBI	SB	AVG/OBP/SLG	BABIP	SLGCON	BB%	K%	ZSw%	ZCon%	OSw%	OCon%	LA	90th EV	DRC+	BRR	DRP	WARP
2021	OAK	MLB	26	448	47	17	59	0	.216/.306/.405	.257	.570	8.9%	25.4%	69.4%	84.0%	31.8%	53.5%	15.4	106.4	96	-0.4	10.0	2.6
2022	OAK	MLB	27	612	67	18	66	1	.250/.332/.426	.290	.554	9.2%	20.3%	72.8%	84.5%	33.5%	63.6%	11.9	106.3	125	-0.5	5.7	4.5
2023	ATL	MLB	28	438	65	21	68	0	.251/.365/.478	.286	.651	11.2%	22.4%	71.3%	83.2%	26.7%	56.1%	13.2	108.3	125	-0.5	9.2	3.9
2024 DC	ATL	MLB	29	449	52	16	55	0	.235/.330/.414	.276	.555	10.0%	22.4%							112	-0.4	6	3.0

2023 GP: C (102), DH (5)   *Comps: J.P. Arencibia (70), Chris Iannetta (68), Carlos Santana (67)*

YEAR	TM	P. COUNT	FRM RUNS	BLK RUNS	THRW RUNS	TOT RUNS
2021	OAK	14783	11.4	0.0	0.4	11.7
2022	OAK	16561	7.0	0.4	1.0	8.4
2023	ATL	14440	8.4	0.4	1.3	10.0
2024	ATL	14430	4.8	0.3	0.9	5.9

We just got done seeing the Oakland-to-Atlanta instant offense pipeline work in Atlanta's favor with Matt Olson, so it wasn't particularly surprising to see Murphy receive a boost in leaving the spacious Oakland Coliseum for a hitter-friendly environment. What was surprising was seeing Murphy go from being simply a good hitter for a catcher to being a good hitter, period (though DRC+ saw the breakthrough plainly in 2022). His slugging and isolated power spiked, firmly entrenching him among the best power-hitting catchers in baseball. He did this while increasing his walk rate for the third straight season, so he was getting on base more often even when he wasn't putting his bat's extra oomph to good use. The boost in offense didn't come at the expense of defense, either—Murphy was just as effective behind the plate as he had been in Oakland and adjusted pretty well to this new world of increased stolen base attempts. Murphy wasn't in dire need of a change of scenery, but it didn't take long to transform his new house into a loving home.

Matt Olson 1B Born: 03/29/94 Age: 30 Bats: L Throws: R Height: 6'5" Weight: 225 Origin: Round 1, 2012 Draft (#47 overall)

YEAR	TM	LVL	AGE	PA	R	HR	RBI	SB	AVG/OBP/SLG	BABIP	SLGCON	BB%	K%	ZSw%	ZCon%	OSw%	OCon%	LA	90th EV	DRC+	BRR	DRP	WARP
2021	OAK	MLB	27	673	101	39	111	4	.271/.371/.540	.269	.675	13.1%	16.8%	72.7%	83.1%	28.6%	66.1%	16.3	108.0	139	-0.2	-0.7	4.7
2022	ATL	MLB	28	699	86	34	103	0	.240/.325/.477	.274	.659	10.7%	24.3%	75.4%	77.1%	31.9%	61.6%	16.1	108.0	122	-0.4	0.9	3.3
2023	ATL	MLB	29	720	127	54	139	1	.283/.389/.604	.302	.832	14.4%	23.2%	73.8%	76.0%	29.1%	65.0%	16.4	109.4	141	-0.3	0.5	5.2
2024 DC	ATL	MLB	30	638	95	39	106	0	.259/.366/.530	.288	.726	13.4%	23.3%							145	0.0	0.4	4.9

2023 GP: 1B (162)   *Comps: Boog Powell (79), Prince Fielder (76), Kent Hrbek (75)*

Olson not only acclimated to his new, hitter-friendly environment in Cobb County, but also got well-acquainted with slugging in every other ballpark in the National League and beyond. Olson smacked two dingers against the Nationals in the second game of the season and went ahead and added 52 more to that tally by the time he was done. After spending most of 2022 making fixes to his swing, it was clear he'd come across a winning formula in explosive fashion. He admitted to swinging too hard in the past and dialed things back a bit; Olson certainly wasn't swinging too softly last year, finding a beautiful and happy medium. We know what Olson can really do at the plate. Now it's time to see if he can keep doing it.

Marcell Ozuna DH Born: 11/12/90 Age: 33 Bats: R Throws: R Height: 6'1" Weight: 225 Origin: IFA, 2008

YEAR	TM	LVL	AGE	PA	R	HR	RBI	SB	AVG/OBP/SLG	BABIP	SLGCON	BB%	K%	ZSw%	ZCon%	OSw%	OCon%	LA	90th EV	DRC+	BRR	DRP	WARP
2021	GIG	WIN	30	90	10	4	13	0	.316/.389/.519	.333	.621	11.1%	14.4%										
2021	ATL	MLB	30	208	21	7	26	0	.213/.288/.356	.244	.472	9.1%	22.1%	73.5%	78.7%	32.7%	63.5%	15.2	107.4	95	0.0	-1.1	0.5
2022	GIG	WIN	31	61	8	1	6	0	.212/.328/.327	.244	.405	14.8%	16.4%										
2022	ATL	MLB	31	507	56	23	56	2	.226/.274/.413	.252	.557	6.1%	24.1%	68.6%	82.0%	36.6%	57.9%	17.1	106.9	109	-0.2	-2.7	1.6
2023	ATL	MLB	32	592	84	40	100	0	.274/.346/.558	.293	.747	9.6%	22.6%	71.9%	83.8%	31.6%	56.2%	15.8	108.0	133	-0.4	-0.1	3.6
2024 DC	ATL	MLB	33	566	70	26	79	2	.249/.320/.454	.280	.601	8.9%	22.2%							117	-0.2	-0.8	2.3

2023 GP: DH (141), LF (2)   *Comps: Rondell White (73), Frank Thomas (69), Bob Watson (68)*

The first two seasons of Ozuna's contract extension with the Braves were calamitous. He was a designated hitter who seemingly couldn't hit anymore and had also run afoul of the law twice in those two seasons. Ozuna started 2023 just as poorly at the plate, and it seemed like his future was either going to be on the bench or in another organization entirely. However, something weird happened in mid-May: He started hitting the ball and getting on base again. It wasn't just a hot streak, either, as Ozuna got back on track following a mid-season slump and ultimately recorded one of the best power-hitting seasons of his career. The turnaround was somehow simultaneously shocking and unsurprising, as the peripherals always suggested that there was still something there. Still, this all felt extremely unlikely considering how poorly things had been going for Ozuna.

Austin Riley 3B Born: 04/02/97 Age: 27 Bats: R Throws: R Height: 6'3" Weight: 240 Origin: Round 1, 2015 Draft (#41 overall)

YEAR	TM	LVL	AGE	PA	R	HR	RBI	SB	AVG/OBP/SLG	BABIP	SLGCON	BB%	K%	ZSw%	ZCon%	OSw%	OCon%	LA	90th EV	DRC+	BRR	DRP	WARP
2021	ATL	MLB	24	662	91	33	107	0	.303/.367/.531	.368	.742	7.9%	25.4%	73.7%	83.8%	35.4%	56.5%	14.7	108.2	118	-0.1	2.2	4.0
2022	ATL	MLB	25	693	90	38	93	2	.273/.349/.528	.315	.727	8.2%	24.2%	77.2%	83.5%	34.7%	56.1%	13.3	109.0	135	0.0	5.4	5.2
2023	ATL	MLB	26	715	117	37	97	3	.281/.345/.516	.324	.707	8.3%	24.1%	71.8%	81.3%	31.6%	57.3%	13.8	109.3	114	0.0	3.7	3.9
2024 DC	ATL	MLB	27	640	79	28	89	2	.263/.335/.466	.309	.629	8.1%	23.2%							126	-0.1	6.7	4.5

2023 GP: 3B (159)   *Comps: Ron Santo (73), Ryan Zimmerman (73), José Ramírez (71)*

By this point in Riley's career, what he can do at the plate isn't particularly shocking anymore. He was once again well-above average with the bat, slamming over 30 homers for the third season in a row. None of that is new. What *is* new: Riley took some pretty big strides with his glove in 2023. He started to look a lot more consistent at the hot corner, making routine plays while still providing highlight-reel efforts on occasion. This culminated with a ridiculous finish to Game 2 of the NLDS, when Riley ranged toward the middle of the infield to cut off a throw from Michael Harris II, relaying the ball to first and catching Bryce Harper for a game-ending 8-5-3 double play. While he's still not an elite defender, Riley is confident enough to make plays like that, serving to make him an even more well-rounded star.

Ambioris Tavarez SS   Born: 11/12/03   Age: 20   Bats: R   Throws: R   Height: 5'11"   Weight: 168   Origin: IFA, 2021

YEAR	TM	LVL	AGE	PA	R	HR	RBI	SB	AVG/OBP/SLG	BABIP	SLGCON	BB%	K%	ZSw%	ZCon%	OSw%	OCon%	LA	90th EV	DRC+	BRR	DRP	WARP
2022	BRA	ROK	18	69	12	1	8	3	.277/.304/.385	.459	.676	4.3%	40.6%										
2023	AUG	A	19	480	61	7	34	21	.216/.319/.337	.388	.636	9.2%	40.8%							69	-1.3	0.5	0.2
2024 non	ATL	MLB	20	251	18	2	19	0	.204/.257/.288	.404	.591	5.6%	47.5%							54	0.0	0	-0.6

2023 GP: SS (91), DH (17)   *Comps: Jeison Guzmán (81), Wilber Sanchez (81), Maikol Escotto (79)*

It's important to remember that while Tavarez didn't exactly have a banner campaign on the farm last season, he was 19 years old for the entirety of it. This was also the first season when he got a real and substantial number of at-bats, as the Braves didn't participate in the Dominican Summer League in 2021 and the next summer he was coming off of an offseason surgery. He still has potential to hit for power, but his main issue at the moment is hitting the ball in the first place. What got him into trouble a lot was the fact that he's been swinging wild and free when it comes to his plate discipline. Being young, wild and free might work for Wiz Khalifa, but Tavarez will have to get his plate approach under control if he's going to make any real noise going forward. The raw talent and the tools are there, but he's definitely a wild card at the moment.

PITCHERS

Aaron Bummer LHP   Born: 09/21/93   Age: 30   Height: 6'3"   Weight: 215   Origin: Round 19, 2014 Draft (#558 overall)

YEAR	TM	LVL	AGE	G (GS)	IP	W-L	SV	K	WHIP	ERA	CSP	BB%	K%	HR%	GB%	ZSw%	ZCon%	OSw%	OCon%	BABIP	SLGCON	DRA-	WARP
2021	CHW	MLB	27	62(0)	56¹	5-5	2	75	1.26	3.51	54.1%	12.0%	31.0%	1.2%	76.9%	59.8%	85.8%	30.8%	44.9%	.298	.391	63	1.6
2022	CHW	MLB	28	32(0)	26²	2-1	2	30	1.50	2.36	50.1%	8.5%	25.6%	1.7%	62.7%	53.7%	86.3%	27.0%	52.8%	.384	.527	74	0.6
2023	CHW	MLB	29	61(0)	58¹	5-5	0	78	1.53	6.79	46.3%	13.5%	29.2%	1.5%	58.8%	51.4%	84.2%	32.4%	51.2%	.340	.531	81	1.3
2024 DC	ATL	MLB	30	48(0)	51²	4-2	0	62	1.27	3.27	49.1%	11.3%	28.2%	1.5%	62.0%					.295	.443	75	0.9

2023 Arsenal: SI (94.7), SW (82.6), FC (87.4), FA (94.9), CH (88.1)   *Comps: Luis Avilán (66), Rex Brothers (64), Jeurys Familia (63)*

From 2019 to 2022, Aaron Bummer was one of the most devastating left-handed relievers in baseball, with an extreme funk to his delivery and a unique pitch mix. His ascension was somewhat of a mystery until the public side of the baseball world learned about seam-shifted wake, the reason why hitters always seemed to be swinging at a place where his upper 90s sinker never quite seemed to go. Hitters caught up, but after two seasons of underperforming his peripherals, the reliever started to lean on his excellent sweeper more and more. More sweepers meant more strikeouts but also more walks: now when Bummer was unlucky with base hits it was happening with runners on. The metrics see 2023 as a fluke disaster, in keeping with the team he pitched for. The Braves will test that premise after trading for Bummer in November.

Jesse Chavez RHP   Born: 08/21/83   Age: 40   Height: 6'1"   Weight: 175   Origin: Round 42, 2002 Draft (#1252 overall)

YEAR	TM	LVL	AGE	G (GS)	IP	W-L	SV	K	WHIP	ERA	CSP	BB%	K%	HR%	GB%	ZSw%	ZCon%	OSw%	OCon%	BABIP	SLGCON	DRA-	WARP
2021	GWN	AAA	37	13(0)	20	1-0	2	27	1.00	2.25		10.4%	35.1%	1.3%	57.1%					.275	.425	84	0.4
2021	ATL	MLB	37	30(4)	33²	3-2	0	36	1.01	2.14	55.3%	8.3%	27.1%	0.0%	43.0%	62.1%	87.3%	27.3%	72.0%	.267	.381	89	0.5
2022	LAA	MLB	38	11(0)	10²	1-0	0	10	1.78	7.59	55.7%	8.0%	20.0%	4.0%	36.1%	62.1%	84.4%	25.6%	71.9%	.382	.750	93	0.1
2022	CHC	MLB	38	3(0)	5²	0-0	0	3	1.59	6.35	54.9%	8.3%	12.5%	4.2%	26.3%	66.7%	82.1%	14.0%	83.3%	.333	.632	91	0.1
2022	ATL	MLB	38	46(1)	53	3-3	0	61	1.19	2.72	53.1%	6.4%	28.0%	2.3%	41.5%	63.3%	78.4%	35.2%	67.4%	.324	.550	81	1.0
2023	ATL	MLB	39	36(1)	34²	1-0	1	39	1.10	1.56	45.7%	8.3%	27.1%	1.4%	51.1%	59.4%	74.6%	29.6%	68.2%	.273	.427	85	0.7
2024 non	ATL	MLB	40	58(0)	50	2-2	0	49	1.30	4.41	51.2%	8.3%	22.9%	3.7%	40.6%					.291	.569	101	0.2

2023 Arsenal: HC (88.7), SI (91.1), CH (85), CU (76)   *Comps: Elmer Dessens (64), Mike Timlin (60), Chad Qualls (60)*

There's a strong chance that had Chavez not suffered a microfracture taking a comebacker to the shin, 2023 would've gone down as one of the best seasons of his career. The stylish hat collector also took to collecting souls on the mound, as he was on his way to posting a career-high strikeout while avoiding giving up any serious amounts of hard contact. His cut fastball reached a whiff percentage that he hadn't sniffed since the early stages of his career, and even when opposing hitters caught up with it they weren't able to do any real damage. After spending most of his career as a journeyman, Chavez has seemingly found his home in Atlanta—it's just a shame that it took a decade and a half to get here.

Yonny Chirinos RHP   Born: 12/26/93   Age: 30   Height: 6'2"   Weight: 225   Origin: IFA, 2012

YEAR	TM	LVL	AGE	G (GS)	IP	W-L	SV	K	WHIP	ERA	CSP	BB%	K%	HR%	GB%	ZSw%	ZCon%	OSw%	OCon%	BABIP	SLGCON	DRA-	WARP
2022	CSC	A	28	3(2)	6¹	0-1	0	6	1.74	11.37		6.3%	18.8%	3.1%	45.5%					.381	.864	101	0.1
2022	DUR	AAA	28	5(5)	16	0-0	0	13	1.06	2.81		9.5%	20.6%	3.2%	54.5%	76.9%	80.0%	34.6%	33.3%	.220	.395	92	0.3
2022	TB	MLB	28	2(1)	7	1-0	0	6	1.14	0.00	58.5%	3.3%	20.0%	0.0%	77.3%	72.1%	87.1%	31.6%	66.7%	.318	.409	87	0.1
2023	DUR	AAA	29	5(4)	19¹	0-1	0	17	1.40	4.66		9.3%	19.8%	1.2%	56.7%	73.5%	85.6%	28.8%	55.3%	.305	.433	96	0.3
2023	ATL	MLB	29	5(5)	22¹	1-1	0	22	1.79	9.27	50.1%	6.7%	21.0%	4.8%	52.0%	72.6%	86.9%	34.4%	65.4%	.400	.716	109	0.2
2023	TB	MLB	29	15(4)	62²	4-4	0	31	1.24	4.02	50.3%	7.6%	11.8%	3.8%	44.2%	71.6%	90.7%	30.1%	71.8%	.245	.525	117	0.2
2024 non	ATL	MLB	30	58(0)	50	2-2	0	34	1.43	4.99	50.0%	8.1%	15.5%	2.9%	46.1%					.300	.521	111	-0.1

2023 Arsenal: SI (92.7), FS (85.2), SL (89), FA (93.2)   *Comps: Trevor Williams (65), Nick Tropeano (62), José Ureña (61)*

If anybody can illustrate how much of a mirage April performance can be, it's Chirinos. The cruelest month went about as well as Chirinos could've asked, as he pitched 14 innings and only gave up one run. April showers brought anything but May flowers, though. Chirinos struggled through May and continued the descent as spring faded, with his nadir coming during a late-June start in which the Royals tagged him for eight runs over 5 ⅓ innings. Eventually, Tampa Bay shipped him to Atlanta, where things didn't get much better: Chirinos eventually ended the season on the 60-day IL with an elbow injury. The only thing that seemed to go right was that his splitter continued to be a very effective pitch—well, that and April. He'll always have April.

Luis De Avila   LHP   Born: 05/29/01   Age: 23   Height: 5'9"   Weight: 215   Origin: IFA, 2017

YEAR	TM	LVL	AGE	G (GS)	IP	W-L	SV	K	WHIP	ERA	CSP	BB%	K%	HR%	GB%	ZSw%	ZCon%	OSw%	OCon%	BABIP	SLGCON	DRA-	WARP
2021	ROYG	ROK	20	3 (0)	5¹	0-0	0	5	1.69	3.38		18.5%	18.5%	0.0%	58.8%					.235	.412		
2021	COL	A	20	24 (0)	52¹	5-4	0	59	1.68	5.16		7.8%	24.2%	1.6%	59.6%					.406	.606	87	0.8
2022	ROM	A+	21	24 (24)	126¹	6-8	0	129	1.27	3.49		8.4%	24.2%	2.1%	60.6%					.306	.486	98	1.1
2023	MIS	AA	22	25 (25)	123¹	6-10	0	125	1.30	3.28		11.7%	24.0%	1.5%	51.2%					.289	.458	86	1.6
2024 non	ATL	MLB	23	58 (0)	50	2-2	0	42	1.57	5.41		11.2%	18.4%	2.7%	46.5%					.311	.529	117	-0.2

2023 Arsenal: SI (90.5), SL (82.1), CH (87.5), FC (88.9), FA (90.6)   Comps: Anthony Banda (54), Ryan Rolison (53), Brock Burke (52)

The road to the bigs has been a long and winding one for De Avila. He joined the Rockies on an international deal back in 2017 and struggled at the Rookie level in 2018 before being suspended 72 games for a positive PED test ahead of 2019. Colorado let him go afterwards and while he eventually signed with the Royals, he lost 2020 due to the pandemic. He wouldn't pitch in another game until 2021, when Kansas City used him as a reliever. That designation changed when the Braves took him in the Minor League Rule 5 Draft before the 2022 season; he's been starting ever since. De Avila doesn't have an overpowering fastball, but he's made huge strides with his curveball while his sinker and changeup have helped him get a ton of soft outs on the ground. He was getting it done mostly in Double-A in 2023, but he saw some action in Triple-A as well, meaning that it's only a matter of time before his winding path to the Show leads to a spot start here and there.

Bryce Elder   RHP   Born: 05/19/99   Age: 25   Height: 6'2"   Weight: 220   Origin: Round 5, 2020 Draft (#156 overall)

YEAR	TM	LVL	AGE	G (GS)	IP	W-L	SV	K	WHIP	ERA	CSP	BB%	K%	HR%	GB%	ZSw%	ZCon%	OSw%	OCon%	BABIP	SLGCON	DRA-	WARP
2021	ROM	A+	22	9 (9)	45	2-1	0	55	1.29	2.60		10.3%	28.4%	1.0%	58.6%					.316	.470	79	1.0
2021	MIS	AA	22	9 (9)	56	7-1	0	60	1.00	3.21		7.8%	27.5%	3.2%	58.7%					.244	.489	86	1.0
2021	GWN	AAA	22	7 (7)	36²	2-3	0	40	1.04	2.21		13.6%	27.2%	0.7%	53.5%					.200	.314	81	0.9
2022	GWN	AAA	23	18 (17)	105	6-5	0	97	1.19	4.46		7.3%	22.2%	3.2%	55.6%					.275	.527	81	2.4
2022	ATL	MLB	23	10 (9)	54	2-4	0	47	1.24	3.17	50.6%	10.1%	20.7%	1.8%	48.7%	65.9%	89.8%	34.3%	62.4%	.268	.437	108	0.3
2023	GWN	AAA	24	1 (1)	6	0-0	0	4	1.00	6.00		4.3%	17.4%	4.3%	61.1%	61.3%	89.5%	27.3%	50.0%	.235	.444	100	0.1
2023	ATL	MLB	24	31 (31)	174²	12-4	0	128	1.28	3.81	45.4%	8.6%	17.5%	2.6%	50.0%	68.6%	87.1%	32.2%	62.3%	.275	.485	111	1.0
2024 DC	ATL	MLB	25	16 (16)	90²	7-5	0	69	1.42	4.72	46.4%	9.2%	17.4%	2.7%	49.7%					.295	.505	105	0.6

2023 Arsenal: SI (89.7), SL (83), CH (85.2), FA (90.9)   Comps: Jarred Cosart (70), Michael Fulmer (70), Alex Cobb (70)

You're not meant to understand enigmas. Was 2023 a successful season for Elder? Yes, unquestionably. He managed to become a fixture in Atlanta's rotation following his call-up, and even earned himself a trip to the All-Star game. His slider went from average to the best tool in his arsenal and his breaking stuff befuddled hitters into soft contact for most of the season. What made the season so enigmatic was that Elder managed to succeed while pitching to contact with a four-seamer that hits 91 mph on a good day. That should be a recipe for disaster, and it usually was disastrous whenever the fastball wasn't located properly. And yet, on the whole, it worked. It's not a process that should work in baseball's current era, but that's the thing about enigmas: They don't need to be understood to be appreciated.

Max Fried   LHP   Born: 01/18/94   Age: 30   Height: 6'4"   Weight: 190   Origin: Round 1, 2012 Draft (#7 overall)

YEAR	TM	LVL	AGE	G (GS)	IP	W-L	SV	K	WHIP	ERA	CSP	BB%	K%	HR%	GB%	ZSw%	ZCon%	OSw%	OCon%	BABIP	SLGCON	DRA-	WARP
2021	ATL	MLB	27	28 (28)	165²	14-7	0	158	1.09	3.04	56.9%	6.1%	23.7%	2.2%	51.0%	69.5%	86.5%	32.1%	56.7%	.281	.476	78	3.5
2022	ATL	MLB	28	30 (30)	185¹	14-7	0	170	1.01	2.48	51.3%	4.4%	23.2%	1.6%	50.3%	69.0%	85.7%	37.2%	60.6%	.280	.423	77	4.0
2023	GWN	AAA	29	3 (3)	9	0-2	0	10	1.78	5.00		10.3%	25.6%	5.1%	52.0%	72.6%	95.6%	32.1%	70.6%	.435	.833	86	0.2
2023	ATL	MLB	29	14 (14)	77²	8-1	0	80	1.13	2.55	44.4%	5.8%	25.7%	2.3%	57.8%	67.9%	84.7%	32.5%	56.9%	.310	.474	80	1.7
2024 DC	ATL	MLB	30	26 (26)	147²	12-6	0	139	1.20	3.41	50.7%	6.2%	22.6%	2.1%	52.8%					.302	.483	81	2.8

2023 Arsenal: FA (94.2), CU (74.3), CH (86.4), SI (93.5), SL (86.8), SW (82.1)   Comps: Atlee Hammaker (76), Tom Glavine (71), Dock Ellis (71)

In 2022, Fried's regular season was ended by a stomach ailment. The illness impacted his playoff performance and complicated Atlanta's pitching plans. In 2023, Fried's regular season was ended by a blister. The blister impacted his playoff performance and complicated Atlanta's pitching plans. Sadly, the blister was one of a series of roadblocks over a season when he was unable to ever escape first gear. He strained his left hamstring on Opening Day, and upon returning only made four more starts before going back on the IL with a strained left forearm. While you're always happy to avoid the worst when it comes to elbows, that malady still cost Fried three months. When he was actually on the mound, he was typically sharp and his curveball was as disgusting as ever. He doesn't need a return to form so much as a return to health. Here's hoping that next year's entry doesn't include the phrase "In 2024, Fried's regular season came to an end…"

Drue Hackenberg   RHP   Born: 04/01/02   Age: 22   Height: 6'2"   Weight: 220   Origin: Round 2, 2023 Draft (#59 overall)

YEAR	TM	LVL	AGE	G (GS)	IP	W-L	SV	K	WHIP	ERA	CSP	BB%	K%	HR%	GB%	ZSw%	ZCon%	OSw%	OCon%	BABIP	SLGCON	DRA-	WARP
2024 non	ATL	MLB	22	58 (0)	50	2-2	0	46	1.60	5.95		12.7%	20.3%	4.0%	38.3%					.297	.600	128	-0.5

Comps: Andrew Bellatti (25), Tommy Romero (24), Jorgan Cavanerio (23)

Despite not being so highly rated a prospect as many of the players who were selected around him in the second round of the 2023 Draft, Hackenberg brings valuable college experience and success to the table. That's something that the Braves value when it comes to selecting pitchers, so it wasn't a major shock to see him chosen with the 59th overall pick. Atlanta likely figures that he's got the stuff to be really good in the future—his sinker can induce ground balls for outs and his slider can miss bats. The main issue is that he doesn't have a real out pitch; the sooner that changes, the better. He was a starter at Virginia Tech and he'll likely be a back-end starter if he can put his arsenal together.

Brad Hand LHP Born: 03/20/90 Age: 34 Height: 6'3" Weight: 224 Origin: Round 2, 2008 Draft (#52 overall)

YEAR	TM	LVL	AGE	G (GS)	IP	W-L	SV	K	WHIP	ERA	CSP	BB%	K%	HR%	GB%	ZSw%	ZCon%	OSw%	OCon%	BABIP	SLGCON	DRA-	WARP
2021	TOR	MLB	31	11 (0)	8²	0-2	0	5	1.85	7.27	57.9%	7.3%	12.2%	7.3%	30.3%	73.1%	85.7%	27.7%	60.9%	.333	.719	109	0.0
2021	WAS	MLB	31	41 (0)	42²	5-5	21	42	1.15	3.59	56.7%	9.9%	23.1%	2.7%	40.2%	62.3%	85.8%	23.9%	68.1%	.239	.486	106	0.3
2021	NYM	MLB	31	16 (0)	13¹	1-0	0	14	1.28	2.70	54.1%	9.1%	25.5%	1.8%	48.6%	60.2%	85.7%	26.5%	63.9%	.324	.588	90	0.2
2022	PHI	MLB	32	55 (0)	45	3-2	5	38	1.33	2.80	55.9%	11.6%	19.2%	1.0%	40.5%	60.9%	88.5%	25.2%	68.9%	.273	.414	124	-0.1
2023	ATL	MLB	33	20 (0)	18	2-2	1	18	1.39	7.50	46.9%	7.6%	22.8%	2.5%	30.2%	58.0%	90.8%	29.9%	63.6%	.354	.620	99	0.2
2023	COL	MLB	33	40 (0)	35²	3-1	0	41	1.43	4.54	47.9%	10.2%	26.1%	2.5%	37.1%	64.8%	88.2%	30.4%	56.8%	.341	.670	95	0.5
2024 non	ATL	MLB	34	58 (0)	50	2-2	0	47	1.37	4.79	52.3%	9.6%	21.7%	3.4%	36.4%					.289	.555	107	0.0

2023 Arsenal: SW (81.1), FA (92.7), SI (92.8), FC (86.6)   Comps: Dave Righetti (66), Arthur Rhodes (62), Tug McGraw (59)

Though Hand's run prevention remained solid in 2022, DRA- looked at his worst walk rate in a decade (and worst K-rate in nearly as long) and assigned the worst figure of his 13-year career. It really seemed like the baseball grim reaper was coming, and joining up with Colorado to start off last season appeared another grim portend. That's not where you want to be if you're a journeyman lefty who is finding it more and more difficult to get batters to chase and whiff. Looking solely at ERA, one might assume those bad omens came to fruition. However, Hand was able to get his strikeout percentage up to 26% while he was with the Rockies, a number better than anything he'd put up since his time in Cleveland. That was enough to get him sent off to a locale that was still hitter-friendly, but much less so than Colorado: Atlanta. Though another stretch of poor batted-ball luck only resulted in more earned runs, Hand's walks and strikeouts normalized and he wound up with a DRA- identical to his career line. He's an old Hand, and he proved there's still enough in the tank to be a nifty relief option. He also completed his NL East jersey collection, for good measure.

Raisel Iglesias RHP Born: 01/04/90 Age: 34 Height: 6'2" Weight: 190 Origin: IFA, 2014

YEAR	TM	LVL	AGE	G (GS)	IP	W-L	SV	K	WHIP	ERA	CSP	BB%	K%	HR%	GB%	ZSw%	ZCon%	OSw%	OCon%	BABIP	SLGCON	DRA-	WARP
2021	LAA	MLB	31	65 (0)	70	7-5	34	103	0.93	2.57	54.4%	4.4%	37.7%	4.0%	39.5%	69.5%	69.0%	40.8%	45.6%	.290	.614	62	2.1
2022	LAA	MLB	32	39 (0)	35²	2-6	16	48	1.07	4.04	55.3%	6.2%	32.9%	3.4%	29.9%	68.1%	82.1%	37.8%	49.2%	.296	.593	77	0.8
2022	ATL	MLB	32	28 (0)	26¹	0-0	1	30	0.84	0.34	48.0%	5.0%	30.0%	0.0%	40.6%	71.6%	74.3%	44.4%	55.8%	.270	.323	78	0.6
2023	ATL	MLB	33	58 (0)	55²	5-4	33	68	1.19	2.75	45.4%	6.5%	29.4%	3.0%	42.6%	73.6%	80.1%	39.8%	51.4%	.312	.555	80	1.2
2024 DC	ATL	MLB	34	54 (0)	57¹	4-5	41	68	1.12	3.31	49.9%	6.4%	29.0%	3.4%	38.1%					.293	.570	80	0.8

2023 Arsenal: CH (89.5), FA (95.3), SI (95), SL (84.7)   Comps: Jim Gott (80), Kevin Gregg (79), Alejandro Pena (78)

When you look at Iglesias' body of work between 2022 and 2023, the two years feature somewhat similar results. However, there was one big difference in 2023: hitters apparently figured out his sinker and fastball. Opposing batters had an xBA of .387 and an actual batting average of .519 against his sinker, while the fastball earned its .327 batting average against. So how did Iglesias still log a solid season? His changeup and slider were equally nasty, as the changeup was hit to a meager .166 line and the slider elicited a barely there .056 BA. The changeup was his most-used pitch and the slider his least-used, with the fastball and sinker wedged in the middle, like two dry McDouble patties between two of the tastiest, richest pretzel buns one could find.

Joe Jiménez RHP Born: 01/17/95 Age: 29 Height: 6'3" Weight: 277 Origin: Undrafted Free Agent, 2013

YEAR	TM	LVL	AGE	G (GS)	IP	W-L	SV	K	WHIP	ERA	CSP	BB%	K%	HR%	GB%	ZSw%	ZCon%	OSw%	OCon%	BABIP	SLGCON	DRA-	WARP
2021	DET	MLB	26	52 (0)	45¹	6-1	1	57	1.52	5.96	53.7%	16.7%	27.1%	2.9%	34.5%	73.6%	80.1%	28.4%	47.6%	.269	.593	123	-0.1
2022	DET	MLB	27	62 (0)	56²	3-2	2	77	1.09	3.49	58.2%	5.6%	33.3%	1.7%	32.6%	71.7%	77.6%	37.9%	57.4%	.328	.529	70	1.4
2023	ATL	MLB	28	59 (0)	56¹	0-3	0	73	1.15	3.04	51.4%	5.9%	30.7%	3.8%	28.2%	70.2%	78.8%	35.0%	49.2%	.304	.630	84	1.2
2024 DC	ATL	MLB	29	54 (0)	57¹	4-2	3	69	1.22	4.03	53.7%	8.6%	28.4%	3.8%	32.0%					.289	.604	93	0.5

2023 Arsenal: FA (95.4), SL (84.4), CH (89.8)   Comps: Kelvin Herrera (67), Trevor Gott (65), Dan Miceli (62)

There are countless examples of relievers who found lightning in a bottle for one season before, just as quickly, it dissipated. Jiménez had spent a few years trying to find the electricity he unleashed in 2022, and he sure pitched like he was determined not to lose it. His high strikeout percentage and low walk rate both stayed in the same neighborhood as during his breakout campaign, and his adjustment from Comerica Park to Truist Park went off without a serious hitch. The biggest concern was that if and when hitters made contact with Jiménez's offerings, it was usually hard and loud. With that being said, it was still a huge challenge for opposing batters to even connect; a fastball-slider combo proved a formidable 1-2 punch. It sure seems like Jiménez is planning on harnessing the lightning for as long as he possibly can.

Pierce Johnson RHP Born: 05/10/91 Age: 33 Height: 6'2" Weight: 202 Origin: Round 1, 2012 Draft (#43 overall)

YEAR	TM	LVL	AGE	G (GS)	IP	W-L	SV	K	WHIP	ERA	CSP	BB%	K%	HR%	GB%	ZSw%	ZCon%	OSw%	OCon%	BABIP	SLGCON	DRA-	WARP
2021	SD	MLB	30	63 (2)	58²	3-4	0	77	1.26	3.22	54.0%	11.1%	31.6%	2.5%	33.1%	61.8%	82.8%	32.9%	52.9%	.308	.577	91	0.8
2022	ELP	AAA	31	5 (0)	5	0-0	1	6	0.40	1.80		0.0%	35.3%	0.0%	54.5%	69.4%	72.0%	45.5%	40.0%	.182	.364	90	0.1
2022	SD	MLB	31	15 (0)	14¹	1-2	0	21	1.53	5.02	59.4%	12.5%	32.8%	1.6%	57.1%	65.1%	70.2%	22.5%	76.5%	.382	.543	73	0.3
2023	ATL	MLB	32	24 (0)	23²	1-1	0	32	0.89	0.76	46.0%	5.6%	36.0%	3.4%	55.8%	63.0%	82.4%	45.9%	45.3%	.265	.538	84	0.5
2023	COL	MLB	32	43 (0)	39	1-5	13	58	1.85	6.00	45.9%	13.3%	30.9%	3.7%	27.6%	64.3%	83.4%	30.2%	48.5%	.412	.767	83	0.8
2024 DC	ATL	MLB	33	48 (0)	51²	4-2	0	66	1.24	3.72	49.9%	10.4%	30.1%	3.5%	35.5%					.285	.583	87	0.6

2023 Arsenal: CU (85.4), FA (96), SL (88.9), SW (86.9)   Comps: Jared Hughes (64), Ryan Tepera (64), Hector Neris (63)

Johnson has been a solid reliever for most of his career, but in 2023 he undertook his biggest challenge yet: Pitching in Colorado. This posed a stern challenge, as he posted what would've been career-high walk and home run rates during his Mile High stint. He also managed to record a career-high strikeout percentage, and an 83 DRA- suggested he was doing just fine. It was enough to catch the attention of the Braves, who brought him from 5,200 feet above sea level to the more-manageable Truist Park, situated 4,150 feet closer to sea level. Pitchers often see a bounce in their numbers leaving Coors Field, but Johnson pitched as if he'd been given a new lease on baseball life, maintaining his DRA- while also posting a microscopic ERA and issuing just five bases on balls. Some people love the Rocky Mountains, but it appears that Johnson was more at home in the Appalachian foothills.

Cade Kuehler RHP Born: 05/24/02 Age: 22 Height: 6'0" Weight: 215 Origin: Round 2, 2023 Draft (#70 overall)

YEAR	TM	LVL	AGE	G (GS)	IP	W-L	SV	K	WHIP	ERA	CSP	BB%	K%	HR%	GB%	ZSw%	ZCon%	OSw%	OCon%	BABIP	SLGCON	DRA-	WARP
2023	AUG	A	21	2(2)	7	0-0	0	8	0.71	0.00		15.4%	30.8%	0.0%	64.3%					.071	.071	98	0.1
2024 non	ATL	MLB	22	58(0)	50	2-2	0	47	1.71	6.57		12.8%	20.2%	4.0%	36.8%					.320	.630	139	-0.8

Comps: Carlos Hernández (26), Jeff Ferrell (26), Greg Weissert (26)

After logging a ton of innings for the Campbell Camels over three years and becoming the university's first player to make it onto the U.S. Collegiate National Team, Kuehler landed with the Braves. It's not a shock that he's ended up here, as Atlanta has made a habit out of selecting experienced college arms with their top picks. What remains to be seen is whether or not Kuehler will eventually make a push for the big leagues as a starter or a reliever. He's hit 98 on the radar gun with his four-seamer, and that's not the only nasty stuff in the arsenal. However, he's had issues with command, which could dictate his career path. The stuff makes him an intriguing prospect, but utilizing it will require Kuehler to pare his repertoire down and get his location under control.

Reynaldo López RHP Born: 01/04/94 Age: 30 Height: 6'1" Weight: 225 Origin: IFA, 2012

YEAR	TM	LVL	AGE	G (GS)	IP	W-L	SV	K	WHIP	ERA	CSP	BB%	K%	HR%	GB%	ZSw%	ZCon%	OSw%	OCon%	BABIP	SLGCON	DRA-	WARP
2021	CLT	AAA	27	10(10)	39	1-6	0	50	1.90	7.62		11.1%	26.5%	3.2%	38.8%					.431	.759	110	0.3
2021	CHW	MLB	27	20(9)	57²	4-4	0	55	0.95	3.43	54.7%	5.9%	24.8%	4.5%	39.0%	70.9%	81.3%	32.4%	65.7%	.222	.573	98	0.6
2022	CHW	MLB	28	61(1)	65¹	6-4	0	63	0.95	2.76	53.3%	4.3%	24.8%	0.4%	38.8%	69.4%	80.2%	37.2%	59.9%	.287	.427	80	1.3
2023	CHW	MLB	29	43(0)	42	2-5	4	52	1.31	4.29	45.6%	12.4%	29.2%	3.9%	37.5%	75.3%	77.6%	32.2%	57.4%	.268	.573	88	0.8
2023	CLE	MLB	29	12(0)	11	1-0	0	12	0.82	0.00	48.1%	10.0%	30.0%	0.0%	56.5%	80.0%	86.7%	34.0%	42.4%	.217	.217	95	0.2
2023	LAA	MLB	29	13(0)	13	0-2	2	19	1.54	2.77	45.0%	13.3%	31.7%	1.7%	34.4%	67.9%	71.9%	42.6%	60.6%	.355	.531	85	0.3
2024 DC	ATL	MLB	30	48(0)	51²	4-2	0	57	1.27	4.06	50.4%	9.5%	25.9%	3.6%	37.7%					.282	.568	94	0.4

2023 Arsenal: FA (98.1), SL (88.1), CH (88.6), CU (76.4)

Comps: Tom Murphy (70), Wade Davis (70), LaTroy Hawkins (69)

López added considerable velo for the third consecutive year, consistently outputting triple digits and striking out more than a batter per inning for the first time in his career. But he also walked hitters at the highest rate of any full season yet, thanks to a few too many spiked sliders plus fastballs that sailed far too high. After nearly seven years on the White Sox, López took a tour of the AL in 2023's second half, landing in Anaheim at the trade deadline before being claimed on waivers by Cleveland for the final month, in which he didn't allow a run and demonstrated better control than any other point during the season. He'll find a new home in Atlanta this year, possibly joined by his good buddy Lucas Giolito. After three transactions together in the past decade, they may simply be a package deal.

Adam Maier RHP Born: 11/26/01 Age: 22 Height: 6'0" Weight: 203 Origin: Round 7, 2022 Draft (#215 overall)

When he arrived at the University of British Columbia in Canada back in 2020, Maier had precisely zero attention from MLB clubs—despite being a two-way player. He abandoned his two-way aspirations early on due to the pandemic-shortened '20 and '21 seasons, with velocity that ran up to 97 mph surely helping to influence the permanent focus on mound work. Maier's appearances in the Cape Cod Baseball League in the summer of 2021, even over a short sample, caught the eyes of the Oregon Ducks (as well as some big-league scouts). He didn't get a ton of time to show off what he could do at Oregon, either, due to an elbow injury; what he did do was impressive enough to convince the Braves to draft him with their seventh-round pick in 2022. Maier still has yet to make his pro debut, but at this point he's used to taking the scenic route.

A.J. Minter LHP Born: 09/02/93 Age: 30 Height: 6'0" Weight: 215 Origin: Round 2, 2015 Draft (#75 overall)

YEAR	TM	LVL	AGE	G (GS)	IP	W-L	SV	K	WHIP	ERA	CSP	BB%	K%	HR%	GB%	ZSw%	ZCon%	OSw%	OCon%	BABIP	SLGCON	DRA-	WARP
2021	GWN	AAA	27	7(0)	7¹	0-0	6	10	0.41	0.00		12.0%	40.0%	0.0%	41.7%					.000	.000	90	0.1
2021	ATL	MLB	27	61(0)	52¹	3-6	0	57	1.22	3.78	53.7%	9.0%	25.8%	0.9%	46.5%	68.3%	78.1%	33.2%	52.5%	.300	.493	78	1.1
2022	ATL	MLB	28	75(0)	70	5-4	5	94	0.91	2.06	51.9%	5.5%	34.7%	1.8%	38.4%	71.8%	76.0%	36.7%	54.0%	.289	.494	69	1.8
2023	ATL	MLB	29	70(0)	64²	3-6	10	82	1.19	3.76	47.9%	8.1%	31.5%	2.3%	34.4%	72.6%	80.2%	33.3%	49.0%	.331	.542	82	1.4
2024 DC	ATL	MLB	30	54(0)	57¹	4-2	8	68	1.18	3.51	50.2%	8.3%	28.6%	3.3%	38.2%					.288	.557	84	0.7

2023 Arsenal: FA (96), FC (89.6), CH (86.8)

Comps: Rex Brothers (65), Ken Giles (63), B.J. Ryan (62)

Had the Braves made a deep playoff run in 2023, Minter's quip after a dramatic win in Game 2 of the NLDS—where he suggested that the comeback Atlanta made was down to nothing but "heart and nuts"—would've been seen on t-shirts across the South. Instead, it'll just be remembered in these pages as a mantra for how Minter was able to eventually turn his 2023 around. From late-April through May, Minter had a nightmarish run of 15 appearances in which he had a 3.90 FIP but a ghastly 10.93 ERA. Still, Brian Snitker kept the faith that Minter would eventually figure things out and kept on rolling him out there for appearances. By the end of the season, Minter's cFIP and DRA were essentially salvaged; he ended up having another good campaign as a high-leverage reliever for the Braves. It sure helped that Snitker had the heart to stay faithful in his ability and Minter had the nuts and determination to turn his year around.

Charlie Morton RHP   Born: 11/12/83   Age: 40   Height: 6'5"   Weight: 215   Origin: Round 3, 2002 Draft (#95 overall)

YEAR	TM	LVL	AGE	G(GS)	IP	W-L	SV	K	WHIP	ERA	CSP	BB%	K%	HR%	GB%	ZSw%	ZCon%	OSw%	OCon%	BABIP	SLGCON	DRA-	WARP
2021	ATL	MLB	37	33(33)	185²	14-6	0	216	1.04	3.34	54.2%	7.7%	28.6%	2.1%	47.5%	64.9%	83.2%	31.9%	52.9%	.271	.457	71	4.6
2022	ATL	MLB	38	31(31)	172	9-6	0	205	1.23	4.34	52.7%	8.7%	28.2%	3.8%	39.4%	63.5%	85.0%	33.0%	51.9%	.293	.605	90	2.6
2023	ATL	MLB	39	30(30)	163¹	14-12	0	183	1.43	3.64	43.7%	11.6%	25.6%	2.0%	43.2%	60.1%	82.0%	32.1%	51.7%	.323	.528	104	1.6
2024 DC	ATL	MLB	40	28(28)	148²	11-7	0	182	1.31	4.33	49.5%	9.8%	28.4%	3.4%	41.6%					.303	.590	98	1.5

2023 Arsenal: CU (82.4), FA (95), CH (86), SL (89.1), SI (94.3)   *Comps: Kevin Brown (74), Max Scherzer (73), Dennis Martinez (71)*

Shortly after the Braves clinched the NL East title for the sixth straight season, Morton was interviewed on Bally Sports South, providing emotional, eloquent answers: He expressed sadness at the thought of potentially being separated from this particular squad. The tone of the interview made it seem as if Morton was preparing to make his exit from the league after 16 seasons. Had that been it for Morton, then it was a solid swan song. His curveball was as good as it had ever been, he induced a ton of whiffs with his knee-buckler and he combined it with a strong changeup to sit down plenty of batters. He did have trouble with walks, posting his highest walk rate since his rookie season, and his DRA was as high as it's ever been. Still, his performance was perfectly capable, even before the age adjustment. Atlanta exercised his $20 option at the start of the offseason, so the crafty vet will have at least one more go-around.

Penn Murfee RHP   Born: 05/02/94   Age: 30   Height: 6'2"   Weight: 195   Origin: Round 33, 2018 Draft (#988 overall)

YEAR	TM	LVL	AGE	G(GS)	IP	W-L	SV	K	WHIP	ERA	CSP	BB%	K%	HR%	GB%	ZSw%	ZCon%	OSw%	OCon%	BABIP	SLGCON	DRA-	WARP
2021	ARK	AA	27	10(10)	52¹	5-2	0	62	1.34	4.13		8.7%	27.1%	3.9%	40.1%					.308	.623	101	0.3
2021	TAC	AAA	27	16(4)	26¹	2-1	0	35	1.41	4.44		13.0%	30.4%	1.7%	41.3%					.328	.548	91	0.2
2022	TAC	AAA	28	5(0)	8	2-0	2	10	0.38	0.00		7.4%	37.0%	0.0%	42.9%	55.8%	83.3%	37.7%	55.0%	.077	.077	90	0.1
2022	SEA	MLB	28	64(1)	69¹	4-0	0	76	0.95	2.99	52.5%	6.6%	27.9%	2.6%	33.0%	70.4%	85.6%	35.3%	59.5%	.243	.460	83	1.3
2023	SEA	MLB	29	16(0)	14	1-2	0	16	1.07	1.29	43.5%	17.2%	27.6%	1.7%	45.2%	61.4%	76.5%	39.3%	58.2%	.138	.300	96	0.2
2024 non	ATL	MLB	30	58(0)	50	2-2	0	52	1.30	4.32	50.6%	9.8%	24.6%	3.6%	35.9%					.282	.565	98	0.3

2023 Arsenal: SW (79.4), FA (88.3), SI (88.2)   *Comps: Tyler Kinley (55), Kyle McGowin (55), Seth Lugo (53)*

The latest chapter in Murfee's unlikely odyssey from college infielder to side-winding big-league reliever featured the ultimate, if unfortunate, coronation so many arms before him have experienced: UCL surgery. Things appeared a bit off in the early going when Murfee's funky four-seamer was more 87-88 mph than the 89-91 range he occupied as a rookie, but he was still getting outs thanks to his deceptive delivery and splendid sweeper. A lost second half pushed Murfee down and eventually off Seattle's ultra-deep reliever depth chart, prompting a few journeys through waivers that eventually landed him with Atlanta, where he'll rehab in hopes of resuming his effective middle-relief duties in short order.

Owen Murphy RHP   Born: 09/27/03   Age: 20   Height: 6'1"   Weight: 190   Origin: Round 1, 2022 Draft (#20 overall)

YEAR	TM	LVL	AGE	G(GS)	IP	W-L	SV	K	WHIP	ERA	CSP	BB%	K%	HR%	GB%	ZSw%	ZCon%	OSw%	OCon%	BABIP	SLGCON	DRA-	WARP
2022	AUG	A	18	3(3)	7	0-1	0	10	1.57	7.71		18.8%	31.3%	0.0%	62.5%					.313	.438	119	0.0
2023	AUG	A	19	18(18)	72²	6-3	0	97	1.24	4.71		9.1%	31.4%	2.6%	32.4%					.316	.602	93	1.0
2023	ROM	A+	19	3(3)	17	0-1	0	16	1.47	4.76		5.5%	21.9%	1.4%	32.1%					.385	.588	95	0.1
2024 non	ATL	MLB	20	58(0)	50	2-2	0	40	1.50	5.53		10.5%	17.9%	4.0%	31.9%					.288	.580	121	-0.3

Comps: Spencer Adams (75), Sem Robberse (74), Arodys Vizcaíno (73)

The word that gets bandied about a ton when it comes to Murphy is "upside." The 20th-overall pick from 2022 possesses a ton of it; he used a lively fastball and a plus slider, with a curveball and changeup to complement them, in order to rack up a hefty strikeout rate of just over 10 per nine innings. He also showed plenty of encouraging signs with his command, as he was able to get his walk rate down to something respectable after he came out of the gates looking a bit wild at times. With all of that being said, it appears that Murphy's Law was in effect whenever he actually gave up contact: If he got hit, it was usually for extra bases or over the fence. That'll be what Murphy has to work on next. Considering all that he has going for him, he's going to be given as much time as he needs to work on it.

Angel Perdomo LHP   Born: 05/07/94   Age: 30   Height: 6'8"   Weight: 265   Origin: IFA, 2011

YEAR	TM	LVL	AGE	G(GS)	IP	W-L	SV	K	WHIP	ERA	CSP	BB%	K%	HR%	GB%	ZSw%	ZCon%	OSw%	OCon%	BABIP	SLGCON	DRA-	WARP
2021	NAS	AAA	27	14(1)	14	1-0	0	25	0.86	1.29		7.7%	48.1%	1.9%	34.8%					.333	.545	73	0.4
2021	MIL	MLB	27	19(0)	17	1-0	0	28	1.65	6.35	52.8%	20.3%	35.4%	5.1%	39.4%	65.5%	69.9%	24.1%	60.8%	.276	.812	94	0.2
2022	DUR	AAA	28	21(2)	29²	4-2	0	48	0.94	2.12		10.2%	40.7%	1.7%	30.9%	57.1%	83.3%	38.7%	16.7%	.264	.481	69	0.9
2023	IND	AAA	29	20(0)	22²	1-1	1	35	1.28	3.18		16.5%	36.1%	2.1%	39.5%	66.9%	60.7%	29.6%	46.1%	.268	.558	80	0.6
2023	PIT	MLB	29	30(0)	29	3-2	0	44	1.10	3.72	51.9%	9.4%	37.6%	2.6%	32.2%	67.9%	76.0%	26.5%	50.7%	.333	.649	77	0.7
2024 non	ATL	MLB	30	58(0)	50	2-2	0	68	1.24	3.75	51.6%	12.3%	31.8%	3.2%	36.3%					.269	.570	86	0.6

2023 Arsenal: FA (94), SL (83.4), CH (90.4)   *Comps: Jake Diekman (69), Mike Dunn (68), Matt Grace (68)*

The former Brewer Perdomo struggled with command in his last major-league stint, but a change of scenery has done wonders for him. He's no longer afraid of throwing the fastball over the plate, letting it go where it may, which sets up his slider to generate some of the weakest contact in the league. The fastball hasn't suffered from this paradigm shift, either: it generates as many swings and misses as before and gets even more called strikes from its increased presence in the zone. When the hitter does make contact, the above-average vertical break often leads to a routine fly ball. While he's only performed as a lefty specialist so far, he has the makeup to be a trusted pair of hands out of Pittsburgh's 'pen for years to come.

JR Ritchie RHP   Born: 06/26/03   Age: 21   Height: 6'2"   Weight: 185   Origin: Round 1, 2022 Draft (#35 overall)

YEAR	TM	LVL	AGE	G (GS)	IP	W-L	SV	K	WHIP	ERA	CSP	BB%	K%	HR%	GB%	ZSw%	ZCon%	OSw%	OCon%	BABIP	SLGCON	DRA-	WARP
2022	AUG	A	19	3 (3)	10	0-0	0	10	1.10	2.70		10.5%	26.3%	2.6%	47.8%					.273	.522	103	0.1
2023	AUG	A	20	4 (4)	13¹	0-1	0	25	1.05	5.40		5.7%	47.2%	0.0%	32.0%					.440	.560	64	0.4
2024 non	ATL	MLB	21	58 (0)	50	2-2	0	46	1.43	5.20		10.1%	20.8%	4.1%	34.4%					.288	.591	115	-0.2

Comps: Drew Hutchison (50), Justin Nicolino (47), Mason Thompson (46)

Baseball-wise, things were initially going well in 2023 for Ritchie, as his first four starts back in Low-A Augusta saw him strike out nearly half of opponents. Sadly, his 2023 season came to an end at that point due to Tommy John surgery, which will likely cost him the entire 2024 season. The small sample size is still enough to get you excited for what Ritchie can bring to the table in 2025, with a sharp slider topping off an impressive repertoire of pitches. Off the field, Ritchie used his time away from the game to help raise money for those affected by the wildfire disaster in Maui. His efforts to help give back to a place he called his second home were a whole lot more meaningful than any efforts he made on the field.

Chris Sale LHP   Born: 03/30/89   Age: 35   Height: 6'6"   Weight: 180   Origin: Round 1, 2010 Draft (#13 overall)

YEAR	TM	LVL	AGE	G (GS)	IP	W-L	SV	K	WHIP	ERA	CSP	BB%	K%	HR%	GB%	ZSw%	ZCon%	OSw%	OCon%	BABIP	SLGCON	DRA-	WARP
2021	POR	AA	32	2 (2)	7¹	0-0	0	15	0.95	2.45		3.3%	50.0%	3.3%	38.5%					.417	.923	74	0.2
2021	WOR	AAA	32	2 (2)	9²	1-0	0	15	1.14	0.93		10.0%	37.5%	0.0%	28.6%					.333	.571	96	0.2
2021	BOS	MLB	32	9 (9)	42²	5-1	0	52	1.34	3.16	51.6%	6.6%	28.4%	3.3%	47.0%	68.2%	79.7%	35.3%	62.6%	.358	.609	91	0.6
2022	BOS	MLB	33	2 (2)	5²	0-1	0	5	1.06	3.18	57.7%	4.0%	20.0%	0.0%	50.0%	60.9%	92.9%	21.4%	75.0%	.278	.389	119	0.0
2023	WOR	AAA	34	2 (2)	6¹	0-0	0	10	0.95	0.00		8.0%	40.0%	0.0%	46.2%	60.0%	85.7%	47.2%	48.0%	.308	.385	86	0.1
2023	BOS	MLB	34	20 (20)	102²	6-5	0	125	1.13	4.30	47.1%	6.8%	29.4%	3.5%	37.3%	63.4%	80.7%	37.3%	57.8%	.291	.618	89	1.8
2024 DC	ATL	MLB	35	23 (23)	113¹	8-5	0	130	1.18	3.81	48.4%	7.8%	27.4%	3.5%	39.4%					.286	.570	89	1.6

2023 Arsenal: FA (94.3), SL (78.2), CH (86.1), SI (93.5)   *Comps: Clayton Kershaw (78), Pedro Martinez (76), CC Sabathia (75)*

Sale's 11.1 K/9 over his career is the highest in MLB history with a minimum of 1,000 innings pitched. It's important to put that in print because it's one of those records that's so fragile it's destined to shatter, but he kept it in bubble wrap by barely pitching from 2020-2022. He put his record back on the line last year, but his strikeout rate was just a hair below his career 30.5% mark. After recovering from every arm injury known to humankind, his velocity is hardly diminished at all from his peak. It wasn't a perfect season—he missed two months with shoulder inflammation, and when he was on the mound his command occasionally abandoned him. When he located properly though, he looked like the Sale of old, pitching well enough to keep his name in the record books a little longer.

Spencer Schwellenbach RHP   Born: 05/31/00   Age: 24   Height: 6'1"   Weight: 200   Origin: Round 2, 2021 Draft (#59 overall)

YEAR	TM	LVL	AGE	G (GS)	IP	W-L	SV	K	WHIP	ERA	CSP	BB%	K%	HR%	GB%	ZSw%	ZCon%	OSw%	OCon%	BABIP	SLGCON	DRA-	WARP
2023	AUG	A	23	13 (13)	51¹	4-2	0	41	1.15	2.63		7.2%	19.6%	1.4%	50.0%					.281	.408	105	0.4
2023	ROM	A+	23	3 (3)	13²	1-0	0	14	0.37	1.98		2.2%	30.4%	0.0%	40.0%					.133	.167	86	0.0
2024 non	ATL	MLB	24	58 (0)	50	2-2	0	37	1.57	6.03		9.0%	16.5%	3.8%	38.0%					.315	.587	131	-0.6

Comps: Walker Lockett (49), Dakota Bacus (49), Cody Morris (48)

It took a while, but we finally got to see what Schwellenbach could do as a pitcher once his recovery from Tommy John surgery was complete, and he proved why he was taken so early in the 2021 Draft. His start to the season wasn't as smooth, which might have been expected given that he'd gone under the knife almost immediately after being drafted. However, once he got into a groove and was able to work on his three-pitch combo of a fastball, slider and changeup, Schwellenbach lined up favorably against nearly any pitching prospect in Atlanta's system. There may have been a remote possibility that he'd return to the field as a position player if he was unable to get going, but it now appears that his future on the mound is set in stone. The upside is there; it's just a matter of tapping into that potential.

AJ Smith-Shawver RHP   Born: 11/20/02   Age: 21   Height: 6'3"   Weight: 205   Origin: Round 7, 2021 Draft (#217 overall)

YEAR	TM	LVL	AGE	G (GS)	IP	W-L	SV	K	WHIP	ERA	CSP	BB%	K%	HR%	GB%	ZSw%	ZCon%	OSw%	OCon%	BABIP	SLGCON	DRA-	WARP
2021	BRA	ROK	18	4 (4)	8¹	0-1	0	16	1.68	8.64		26.3%	42.1%	5.3%	33.3%					.200	.833		
2022	AUG	A	19	17 (17)	68²	3-4	0	103	1.35	5.11		13.0%	34.4%	1.3%	32.9%					.338	.574	86	1.3
2023	ROM	A+	20	3 (3)	14	1-0	0	23	0.71	0.00		7.7%	44.2%	0.0%	32.0%					.240	.320	97	0.1
2023	MIS	AA	20	2 (2)	7	1-0	0	9	1.14	0.00		10.3%	31.0%	0.0%	23.5%					.294	.529	105	0.1
2023	GWN	AAA	20	10 (10)	41	2-2	0	47	1.27	4.17		15.2%	27.5%	2.3%	36.7%	66.9%	79.8%	31.2%	55.6%	.234	.459	99	0.6
2023	ATL	MLB	20	6 (5)	25¹	1-0	0	20	1.11	4.26	45.7%	10.5%	19.0%	6.7%	37.0%	73.5%	82.0%	26.7%	71.2%	.152	.534	118	0.1
2024 DC	ATL	MLB	21	20 (11)	68	4-3	0	63	1.45	4.94	45.7%	12.1%	21.0%	3.5%	34.6%					.278	.556	109	0.2

2023 Arsenal: FA (94.6), SL (84.9), CU (76.9), FS (86.2)   *Comps: Randall Delgado (68), Jacob Turner (64), Taijuan Walker (63)*

If Smith-Shawver's season was a '90s movie, you'd expect it to start during his appearance in Game 3 of the 2023 NLDS, deploying a magical record scratch to freeze everything in the vicinity so the (at the time) 20-year-old could ask the fans watching at home, "You're probably wondering how I ended up in this situation?" It's a pertinent question, since we're talking about a guy who started the season in High-A. The Braves have regularly given prospects on whom they're high a rocket-ship ride towards the top of the system, and Smith-Shawver earned his with a formidable fastball-slider duo that bewildered minor-league batters. His performance in big-league spot starts and a solid showing in pre-postseason workouts led to the shocking appearance on the playoff roster. If there's a sequel this October, seeing the Texan back in a big moment will require little explanation.

Spencer Strider   RHP   Born: 10/28/98   Age: 25   Height: 6'0"   Weight: 195   Origin: Round 4, 2020 Draft (#126 overall)

YEAR	TM	LVL	AGE	G(GS)	IP	W-L	SV	K	WHIP	ERA	CSP	BB%	K%	HR%	GB%	ZSw%	ZCon%	OSw%	OCon%	BABIP	SLGCON	DRA-	WARP
2021	AUG	A	22	4(4)	15¹	0-0	0	32	0.72	0.59		8.8%	56.1%	0.0%	25.0%					.300	.474	53	0.5
2021	ROM	A+	22	3(3)	14²	0-0	0	24	1.02	2.45		9.7%	38.7%	1.6%	43.3%					.276	.448	82	0.3
2021	MIS	AA	22	14(14)	63	3-7	0	94	1.22	4.71		10.9%	35.3%	2.3%	30.7%					.321	.619	80	1.3
2021	ATL	MLB	22	2(0)	2¹	1-0	0	0	1.29	3.86	56.0%	11.1%	0.0%	11.1%	25.0%	93.3%	92.9%	43.5%	60.0%	.143	.625	119	0.0
2022	ATL	MLB	23	31(20)	131²	11-5	0	202	0.99	2.67	54.6%	8.5%	38.3%	1.3%	40.3%	69.2%	76.3%	35.0%	48.2%	.292	.457	58	4.1
2023	ATL	MLB	24	32(32)	186²	20-5	0	281	1.09	3.86	47.4%	7.6%	36.8%	2.9%	34.7%	72.0%	75.8%	38.4%	40.7%	.316	.595	73	4.9
2024 DC	ATL	MLB	25	29(29)	169	14-6	0	245	1.10	3.10	50.1%	8.8%	35.5%	3.6%	36.6%					.287	.608	76	3.4

2023 Arsenal: FA (97.5), SL (85.8), CH (87.1)   Comps: Walker Buehler (73), Matt Harvey (73), Sonny Gray (69)

If this whole "baseball" thing doesn't work out for Strider, then he could find a future down multiple branching paths. He could very well start his own music review website, which could rival anything *Pitchfork* has going on—all you have to do is Google "Art Vandelay Rating System" and you'll come across an interview that Strider did with *Foolish Baseball*. He could also go into stand-up comedy with a focus on deadpan comedy, though it's hard to imagine that his "no fans" routine would go over well in Philadelphia or New York. Fortunately for Strider, baseball is working for him and it's working fabulously, at that. He's still pumping in 102-mph heaters with alarming regularity and he's been actively developing his slider as a consistent put-out pitch, while also peppering in a tricky changeup every now and then. Strider had a fantastic season on the mound, and there's still plenty of room for him to get better. That's good news for the Braves and bad news for rival teams—plus those who would prefer that he focus on reviewing indie rock going forward.

Darius Vines   RHP   Born: 04/30/98   Age: 26   Height: 6'1"   Weight: 190   Origin: Round 7, 2019 Draft (#217 overall)

YEAR	TM	LVL	AGE	G(GS)	IP	W-L	SV	K	WHIP	ERA	CSP	BB%	K%	HR%	GB%	ZSw%	ZCon%	OSw%	OCon%	BABIP	SLGCON	DRA-	WARP
2021	AUG	A	23	8(8)	36	2-0	0	48	0.94	2.25		7.0%	33.6%	2.1%	51.8%					.256	.482	66	1.0
2021	ROM	A+	23	14(14)	75	4-4	0	81	1.05	3.24		6.3%	27.0%	4.0%	43.5%					.255	.545	93	0.9
2022	MIS	AA	24	20(20)	107	7-4	0	127	1.21	3.95		6.7%	28.5%	3.6%	43.5%					.312	.576	86	1.9
2022	GWN	AAA	24	7(5)	33²	1-0	0	29	1.28	3.21		9.8%	20.3%	0.7%	42.0%					.283	.449	98	0.5
2023	BRA	ROK	25	2(2)	6	0-0	0	7	0.50	0.00		0.0%	35.0%	0.0%	76.9%					.231	.231		
2023	ROM	A+	25	2(2)	9	0-0	0	14	1.00	4.00		8.6%	40.0%	5.7%	27.8%					.250	.722	78	0.2
2023	GWN	AAA	25	6(5)	34¹	3-2	0	28	1.22	2.36		9.4%	20.1%	3.6%	41.2%	76.4%	78.9%	38.6%	47.6%	.261	.500	96	0.6
2023	ATL	MLB	25	5(2)	20¹	1-0	0	14	1.08	3.98	46.4%	8.3%	16.7%	3.6%	40.3%	70.6%	86.9%	33.3%	58.7%	.203	.517	117	0.1
2024 DC	ATL	MLB	26	31(5)	51	3-2	0	44	1.40	4.91	46.4%	8.6%	19.7%	3.6%	38.7%					.298	.567	110	0.1

2023 Arsenal: FA (90), FC (85.4), CH (81.4), SL (80.9)   Comps: Jefry Rodriguez (70), James Marvel (66), Tyler Wilson (65)

Thanks to the fifth starting job in Atlanta's rotation being less of a permanent position and more of a suggestion, the revolving door eventually offered Vines an opportunity to show his stuff at the major-league level. He was given the unenviable task of making his big-league debut in the pitcher-unfriendly confines of Coors Field; he responded by pitching six innings and only giving up two runs. He was able to do this by sticking to what got him to The Show: strong control and command of his pitches. His changeup has a tendency to confound opposing batters, and he's capable of painting the corners with his breaking pitches (particularly his curveball) at an impressive level of accuracy. Vines isn't going to overwhelm anybody with his stuff, as his heater tops out in the low-to-mid 90s if he's giving it all he's got. Still, if he can retain the ability to miss bats on a regular basis and keep hard contact to a minimum, Vines can avoid withering in the harsh big-league sun.

─────────────── ★ ★ ★ *2024 Top 101 Prospect* **#30** ★ ★ ★ ───────────────
Hurston Waldrep   RHP   Born: 03/01/02   Age: 22   Height: 6'2"   Weight: 210   Origin: Round 1, 2023 Draft (#24 overall)

YEAR	TM	LVL	AGE	G(GS)	IP	W-L	SV	K	WHIP	ERA	CSP	BB%	K%	HR%	GB%	ZSw%	ZCon%	OSw%	OCon%	BABIP	SLGCON	DRA-	WARP
2023	ROM	A+	21	3(3)	12	0-0	0	17	0.75	0.75		11.1%	37.8%	0.0%	69.6%					.174	.217	77	0.3
2023	MIS	AA	21	3(3)	10	0-1	0	11	1.50	2.70		15.6%	24.4%	2.2%	73.1%					.280	.462	98	
2024 DC	ATL	MLB	22	5(5)	21²	1-1	0	24	1.52	5.32		12.3%	24.1%	3.4%	40.5%					.309	.590	115	0.0

2023 Arsenal: FA (95.7), SL (86.9), FS (87.7)   Comps: Luis Severino (25), Bruce Rondón (25), Nick Struck (24)

After a college career that took him from Southern Miss in Hattiesburg to the College World Series with Florida, Waldrep ended up making it back to his home state after the Braves selected him with the 24th overall pick of the 2023 Draft. After an extremely eventful NCAA Tournament run for his final collegiate act, it would've been understandable if Waldrep took his time getting adjusted to the professional game. Instead, an impressive arsenal—a 97-mph heater, a split change that can miss plenty of bats and a solid slider—rocketed Waldrep all the way to Triple-A in his first professional season. His ascent was so rapid (he never recorded more than 12 innings at any level between Low-A and Triple-A) that it seemed possible that Waldrep could've snuck his way onto Atlanta's postseason roster. He might have done so, if he could improve the command. Once that occurs, Waldrep won't be too far away from living a lot of Georgia kids' dreams and pitching for the local big-league club.

Allan Winans RHP   Born: 08/10/95   Age: 28   Height: 6'2"   Weight: 165   Origin: Round 17, 2018 Draft (#500 overall)

YEAR	TM	LVL	AGE	G (GS)	IP	W-L	SV	K	WHIP	ERA	CSP	BB%	K%	HR%	GB%	ZSw%	ZCon%	OSw%	OCon%	BABIP	SLGCON	DRA-	WARP
2021	BRK	A+	25	12 (0)	19²	1-2	0	16	0.92	1.83		9.2%	21.1%	0.0%	61.5%					.220	.280	93	0.2
2021	BNG	AA	25	14 (0)	27¹	1-1	3	29	0.73	1.65		7.8%	28.2%	2.9%	53.1%					.148	.391	94	0.3
2022	MIS	AA	26	8 (8)	44¹	1-4	0	44	1.17	2.44		4.7%	23.2%	1.1%	56.5%					.318	.438	86	0.8
2022	GWN	AAA	26	4 (3)	15	0-1	0	16	1.33	6.00		9.1%	24.2%	3.0%	46.3%					.308	.561	104	0.2
2023	GWN	AAA	27	23 (17)	126¹	9-4	1	113	1.08	2.85		7.1%	22.3%	2.2%	49.9%	64.9%	83.6%	34.9%	55.1%	.263	.453	85	3.1
2023	ATL	MLB	27	6 (6)	32¹	1-2	0	34	1.39	5.29	51.7%	5.7%	24.1%	3.5%	45.4%	60.4%	88.5%	37.5%	57.9%	.348	.653	96	0.5
2024 DC	*ATL*	*MLB*	*28*	*23 (3)*	*37¹*	*2-2*	*0*	*29*	*1.34*	*4.52*	*51.7%*	*7.2%*	*18.1%*	*2.8%*	*44.6%*					*.300*	*.521*	*102*	*0.3*

2023 Arsenal: CH (83.1), SI (89.6), SW (78.9), FA (90)   Comps: *Glenn Sparkman (61), Sam Gaviglio (60), Andrew Albers (58)*

Winans started last season in Triple-A; it was safe to assume, with Atlanta's struggles to find consistent back-end starters, that he'd eventually be thrown into spot-start duty. That eventuality came in July, but it was his second career start that brought him into the limelight. Winans showed up as the 27th man for a doubleheader against the Mets and contributed seven shutout innings toward a stunning 21-3 win; a four-pitch combo of a four-seamer, changeup, sinker and slider worked to near-perfection for the former Mets 17th-round selection. New York got their revenge in his next start, but Winans has at least earned the shot at more spot starts.

LINEOUTS

Hitters

HITTER	POS	TM	LVL	AGE	PA	R	HR	RBI	SB	AVG/OBP/SLG	BABIP	SLGCON	BB%	K%	ZSw%	ZCon%	OSw%	OCon%	LA	90th EV	DRC+	BRR	DRP	WARP
Ehire Adrianza	SS	GWN	AAA	33	30	1	0	0	0	.143/.200/.214	.160	.240	6.7%	10.0%	71.4%	88.6%	24.6%	64.3%			95	-1.5		
	SS	ATL	MLB	33	11	0	0	0	0	.000/.091/.000		.000	9.1%	36.4%	60.9%	92.9%	33.3%	70.0%	10.5	101.2	91		-0.1	0.0
Charlie Culberson	1B	GWN	AAA	34	107	7	1	10	3	.204/.234/.255	.288	.397	4.7%	32.7%	71.2%	75.4%	44.9%	52.8%			74	1.0	0.1	0.1
	1B	ATL	MLB	34	1	0	0	0	0	1.000/1.000/1.000	1.000	1.000	0.0%	0.0%	100.0%	0.0%	66.7%	50.0%	-20.0	80.8	88	0.0	0.0	0.0
Luis Guanipa	OF	DSL BRA	ROK	17	208	34	4	17	20	.238/.361/.384	.289	.508	11.1%	20.2%										
Kevin Pillar	LF	ATL	MLB	34	206	29	9	32	4	.228/.248/.416	.255	.558	2.9%	24.3%	72.4%	84.0%	44.2%	61.1%	17.9	103.2	84	0.1	-0.9	0.1
Chadwick Tromp	C	GWN	AAA	28	268	32	10	33	0	.210/.336/.384	.230	.506	16.0%	20.1%	60.8%	82.5%	31.9%	66.0%			108	-0.6	1.5	1.2
	C	ATL	MLB	28	16	1	0	1	0	.125/.125/.188	.222	.333	0.0%	43.8%	64.0%	87.5%	51.4%	57.9%	22.7	99.5	78	-0.1	-0.1	0.0
Andrew Velazquez	SS	GWN	AAA	28	64	4	0	4	1	.217/.266/.250	.371	.429	6.3%	39.1%	70.2%	75.0%	39.0%	40.4%			61	0.1	0.1	0.1
	SS	SL	AAA	28	92	15	3	7	7	.203/.337/.392	.250	.569	16.3%	25.0%	74.8%	67.4%	33.2%	56.3%			101	0.8	2.1	0.5
	SS	LAA	MLB	28	94	12	2	3	13	.173/.264/.284	.245	.451	10.6%	31.9%	77.6%	70.3%	33.7%	52.9%	2.8	99.9	72	0.4	-1.2	-0.1
Luke Waddell	MI	MIS	AA	24	446	57	8	64	26	.290/.395/.403	.319	.476	14.6%	12.8%							120	0.4	12.7	3.6
	MI	GWN	AAA	24	131	16	0	10	3	.221/.346/.279	.247	.326	15.3%	11.5%	63.7%	87.6%	24.2%	78.1%			105	0.1	-0.8	0.4
Forrest Wall	OF	GWN	AAA	27	411	62	8	43	52	.280/.372/.427	.351	.572	12.7%	21.9%	57.7%	87.4%	22.5%	62.4%			104	3.6	-3.7	1.6
	OF	ATL	MLB	27	15	6	1	2	5	.462/.533/.846	.625	1.222	13.3%	26.7%	53.1%	94.1%	33.8%	84.6%	15.5	99.0	83	0.1	-0.1	0.0
Luke Williams	UT	OKC	AAA	26	198	31	6	29	11	.268/.364/.452	.331	.628	12.1%	23.7%	73.0%	81.0%	29.5%	52.2%			103	3.0	-4.1	0.6
	UT	GWN	AAA	26	216	31	6	24	17	.251/.343/.396	.291	.510	12.0%	19.4%	70.2%	88.0%	27.3%	50.8%			95	2.1	0.2	0.7
	UT	ATL	MLB	26	9	1	0	0	3	.000/.000/.000		.000	0.0%	44.4%	84.6%	90.9%	41.2%	42.9%	32.8	98.2	78	0.1	0.0	0.0
	UT	LAD	MLB	26	10	0	0	0	1	.100/.100/.100	.143	.143	0.0%	30.0%	76.9%	70.0%	41.7%	50.0%	1.0	95.9	78	0.0	0.0	0.0

Ehire Adrianza is basically your definitional replacement player. Injuries kept him at exactly zero WARP, but at the same time, this is his lane; he really seems destined to stay on this path going forward. ⊗ In mid-July, **Charlie Culberson** got his only plate appearance and base hit of the 2023 season. That might be the last hit he gets for a while—not because he's washed out of baseball, but because he's decided to go down the path of relief pitching. Maybe you'll see him in a bullpen near you? ⊗ It's fairly damning that on the eve of the second season in **Leury García's** three-year, $16.5 million contract, the White Sox released him. It's even more damning that afterward, no other team picked him up to pad their Triple-A depth. ⊗ The Braves made a huge splash in the International Free Agent market when they brought in **Luis Guanipa** on a $2.5 million deal. At a glance, he figures to be a captivating prospect: He may be on the wiry side but he swings a very quick bat, and he's got power to go with his hit tool, plus a ton of speed to go along with it. Guanipa has "leadoff hitter" written all over him. ⊗ Following an injury-plagued 2022 campaign spent far more in Triple-A than in the majors, it seemed safe to assume another season down the depth chart was in the cards for **Kevin Pillar**. Instead, he stuck around with the Braves and ended up filling a standard fourth outfielder role. His performance was nowhere near the level that he'd reached in Toronto, but simply being back in the majors beats riding the buses in the minors. ⊗ On August 11, 2020, **Chadwick Tromp** watched four pitches and walked to first base. Since that fateful day at the height of the pandemic, he hasn't had a single major-league walk. He's now up to 102 consecutive plate appearances without a free pass. Stay tuned to see if that changes in time for the 2025 edition! ⊗ **Andrew Velazquez**'s season peaked in June, when he managed to draw the fury of Lance Lynn simply by bunting his way onto first for a single. The baseball gods may have sided with Lynn on this one, as Velazquez eventually ended his season with arguably the most bunt-averse organization in all of MLB. Go figure. ⊗ Atlanta spent the offseason clearing out their upper-minors middle infield depth, leaving a great opportunity for **Luke Waddell**. While he lacks for any power, he makes excellent swing decisions and is short to the ball. A plus hit tool and some light positional flexibility should carry him to the majors. ⊗ It may have taken 10 seasons, but 2023 was the year it finally happened for **Forrest Wall**. The 35th-overall pick of the 2014 draft finally made it over the minor-league wall and into big-league paradise. Maybe he can stick around as a fourth outfielder! ⊗ On September 20, **Luke Williams** stole two bases in the ninth inning of a deadlocked game. Those were half of his four stolen bases all season; unfortunately, he did all that just to get thrown out at home by Nick Castellanos, who caught a pop fly in foul territory that nobody wanted him to catch and justified himself with a strike to the plate.

Pitchers

PITCHER	TM	LVL	AGE	G (GS)	IP	W-L	SV	K	WHIP	ERA	CSP	BB%	K%	HR%	GB%	ZSw%	ZCon%	OSw%	OCon%	BABIP	SLGCON	DRA-	WARP
Kolby Allard	GWN	AAA	25	2 (2)	6²	0-0	0	8	1.20	2.70		7.1%	28.6%	0.0%	27.8%	59.3%	84.4%	28.3%	60.0%	.333	.389	101	0.1
	ATL	MLB	25	4 (3)	12¹	0-1	0	13	1.62	6.57	49.8%	7.1%	23.2%	3.6%	30.8%	68.2%	89.7%	34.2%	51.3%	.378	.641	115	0.1
Dylan Dodd	GWN	AAA	25	16 (14)	74²	4-6	0	67	1.55	5.91		9.1%	20.4%	4.3%	44.2%	73.2%	83.9%	35.9%	62.7%	.333	.642	97	1.2
	ATL	MLB	25	7 (7)	34¹	2-2	0	15	1.89	7.60	57.3%	7.3%	9.1%	5.5%	35.3%	74.1%	86.6%	33.2%	70.5%	.346	.684	154	-0.6
Tommy Doyle	ABQ	AAA	27	33 (0)	37	4-4	8	41	1.27	3.41		11.7%	26.6%	3.2%	49.5%	72.2%	80.2%	39.3%	44.7%	.267	.526	75	0.6
	COL	MLB	27	15 (0)	23²	0-1	0	18	1.52	6.85	45.0%	12.6%	17.5%	4.9%	43.1%	76.1%	84.3%	33.5%	50.7%	.269	.625	112	0.1
Daysbel Hernández	ROM	A+	26	6 (0)	5¹	2-0	0	6	1.88	8.44		19.2%	23.1%	3.8%	26.7%					.286	.600	139	-0.1
	MIS	AA	26	12 (0)	14	1-0	2	19	0.64	0.00		10.0%	38.0%	0.0%	30.8%					.154	.154	84	0.2
	GWN	AAA	26	5 (0)	5¹	0-0	0	11	0.94	1.69		14.3%	52.4%	0.0%	33.3%	82.1%	68.8%	28.2%	35.0%	.333	.800	84	0.1
	ATL	MLB	26	4 (0)	3²	1-0	0	6	2.45	7.36	42.1%	15.0%	30.0%	5.0%	27.3%	77.8%	81.0%	39.3%	50.0%	.500	.818	98	0.0
Ray Kerr	ELP	AAA	28	36 (0)	36	6-0	10	42	1.14	2.25		11.7%	29.0%	1.4%	43.0%	68.3%	80.4%	33.0%	49.1%	.262	.424	76	0.8
	SD	MLB	28	22 (0)	27	1-1	0	35	1.26	4.33	47.8%	7.9%	30.7%	4.4%	39.1%	66.7%	82.0%	32.4%	46.8%	.317	.765	91	0.4
Dylan Lee	GWN	AAA	28	7 (0)	7¹	1-1	0	4	1.50	6.14		10.0%	13.3%	10.0%	43.5%	68.9%	90.3%	34.0%	61.1%	.250	.783	108	0.1
	ATL	MLB	28	24 (1)	23²	1-0	0	24	1.35	4.18	49.2%	7.9%	23.8%	4.0%	37.7%	71.3%	78.2%	40.2%	58.9%	.317	.582	94	0.4
Lucas Luetge	GWN	AAA	36	21 (0)	24	2-1	0	26	1.46	3.75		8.4%	24.3%	3.7%	44.4%	62.0%	83.6%	32.0%	59.3%	.324	.556	86	0.5
	ATL	MLB	36	12 (0)	13²	1-0	0	14	1.76	7.24	40.0%	10.8%	21.5%	3.1%	41.9%	68.4%	88.1%	36.7%	71.0%	.366	.571	101	0.2
Jackson Stephens	GWN	AAA	29	12 (4)	24²	1-1	0	26	1.09	3.28		4.0%	26.0%	1.0%	38.5%	66.5%	78.9%	35.2%	57.8%	.344	.516	89	0.5
	ATL	MLB	29	5 (0)	12	0-0	0	11	1.50	3.00	47.1%	9.6%	21.2%	1.9%	38.9%	69.2%	84.1%	34.8%	61.7%	.353	.486	96	0.2

It was a rough year for **Kolby Allard**, who started the season on the IL with a strained oblique and ended it on the IL with shoulder nerve inflammation. His reunion tour in Atlanta was forestalled in brutal fashion, and now it's an open question if he'll be able to get any sort of comeback tour going. ⓧ As promising as were **Ian Anderson**'s 2020 and 2021 seasons, that's how mortifying 2022 and 2023 ended up being. He started the year in Triple-A and made one calamitous start before being shut down for the season and requiring Tommy John surgery. At least now he can work on his command, hopefully without his elbow bothering him. ⓧ You'd be hard-pressed to find a more winding path to the 2023 Salt River Rafters' roster than **Dylan Dodd**'s: He began the season in Atlanta's big-league rotation following a strong spring, then proceeded to crash back to Earth. He showed promise in his MLB debut, but it went downhill from there; he spent the vast majority of the season in Triple-A, where injuries forced a smaller workload than in 2022. Hence the AFL invite. ⓧ **Tommy Doyle**'s selection in 2017 came at the beginning of a Rockies' trend of drafting college pitchers early, a pattern that, despite all odds, continued after him. He returned to the majors after a torn labrum, and it was like he hadn't missed a day. (Don't look up what the day before looked like.) ⓧ In July, **Daysbel Hernández** struck out the side in his MLB debut, putting his domineering fastball-slider combo to effective use. He also got a chance to show off that combo in the NLDS, where he was one of the only Atlanta pitchers to escape unscathed during the Game 3 onslaught. ⓧ Fun fact: **Ray Kerr** had the second-highest strikeout rate among Padres relievers last season, minimum 20 innings pitched. That probably says more about San Diego's bullpen than it does him, but his curveball is a legit swing-and-miss offering. ⓧ For the vast majority of April and May, it sure seemed **Dylan Lee** was gearing up to pick up where he left off in 2022: He only surrendered two earned runs over the season's first month. It would've been nice to see what was next, but his left shoulder got inflamed and cost him most of the rest of the season, eventually requiring surgery. ⓧ You won't see many situations where a pitcher's primary offering resulted in a .565 batting average against while his other pitches, thrown half the time, were hit to a .111 tune—but that's exactly the kind of weird fact a **Lucas Luetge** season never fails to provide. ⓧ Usually when a pitcher is struggling, news of a serious injury will give those struggles crucial context. When **Tyler Matzek**'s velocity and overall performance suffered a sudden and precipitous dip, a torn UCL suddenly made it all make sense. The jury's still out on how that rehabilitation compares to his having overcome the yips. ⓧ **Darren O'Day** retired a full year ago, but don't act like you'd be surprised if he just showed up in the sixth inning of some random June game against the Pirates and got three lazy fly outs. ⓧ It's a shame about the limitations of sending a book off to print in January, because we don't yet know if the Braves will successfully trade **Jackson Stephens** to the Atlanta Braves, with the Pirates somehow eating $2 million in dead money. The future is so exciting. ⓧ **Huascar Ynoa** spent all that time in 2022 not punching benches only for his pitching elbow to betray him at the end of the season, when he came down with a torn UCL. Ynoa figures to be ready for spring training, when he and that lively heater of his will have a lot to prove to get back in the big-league rotation.

BALTIMORE ORIOLES

Essay by Lindsay Ballant

Player comments by Jake Mintz and BP staff

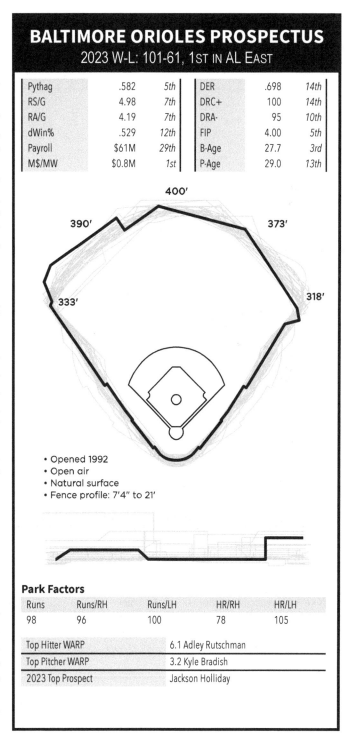

BALTIMORE ORIOLES PROSPECTUS
2023 W-L: 101-61, 1ST IN AL EAST

Pythag	.582	5th	DER	.698	14th
RS/G	4.98	7th	DRC+	100	14th
RA/G	4.19	7th	DRA-	95	10th
dWin%	.529	12th	FIP	4.00	5th
Payroll	$61M	29th	B-Age	27.7	3rd
M$/MW	$0.8M	1st	P-Age	29.0	13th

400'
390'
373'
333'
318'

- Opened 1992
- Open air
- Natural surface
- Fence profile: 7'4" to 21'

Park Factors

Runs	Runs/RH	Runs/LH	HR/RH	HR/LH
98	96	100	78	105

Top Hitter WARP	6.1 Adley Rutschman
Top Pitcher WARP	3.2 Kyle Bradish
2023 Top Prospect	Jackson Holliday

Forty years ago, I witnessed the one—and only, so far in my lifetime—World Series championship won by my team. I was 11 months old. My only memory of this comes in the form of an inherited relic—a polaroid photograph of my father on the sofa with an O's trucker hat on, and me, on his lap, holding a plastic Orioles cup larger than my head. Like many fandom origin stories, we inherit such unrequited fidelity to a team generationally, through family, whether blood or found. Others, if not duty-bound, have the free will to choose a team based on, usually, who's dominating the sport at the time, and exercise the right to be a fair-weather fan (shoutout to the '90s diaspora of Chicago Bulls fans). Fair-weather fandom is a perfectly legitimate origin story. Winning a lot of games is fun and exciting, and being fun and exciting to watch attracts more fans, regardless of geography. For those of us who form lifelong bonds, a team can be that family member to whom you're loyal no matter what they do, no matter how many times they break your heart.

For my parents' generation, it must've been a no-brainer to be Orioles fans. Their formative years overlapped with the most successful in franchise history. Imagine if over 18 years *your* team held the best winning percentage in baseball (.588), won six AL pennants and three titles. Sign me up. For many, however, fandom comes with no such dynasties, and no such guarantees. Casting aside location-based deference, there were many more desirable teams to hitch a wagon to in my youth before pledging allegiance to Birdland. Much like affording a house or having a retirement plan, it's much harder for my generation to be Orioles fans.

Luckily, the present-day Orioles are making it easy to be a fan again.

⚾   ⚾   ⚾

Baltimore fans have been waiting for this ever since they were promised a contending team and a new era when executive vice president and general manager Mike Elias was hired in December of 2018. He then brought on first-time manager Brandon Hyde. For four years thereafter, fans were given an IOU instead of a major-league caliber roster, with the assurance that the Process must be Trusted: The

43

Payroll History (in millions)

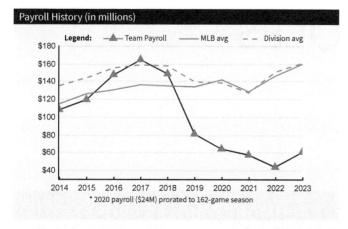

Legend: ▲ Team Payroll — MLB avg --- Division avg

$180
$160
$140
$120
$100
$80
$60
$40

2014 2015 2016 2017 2018 2019 2020 2021 2022 2023

* 2020 payroll ($24M) prorated to 162-game season

Future Commitments (in millions)

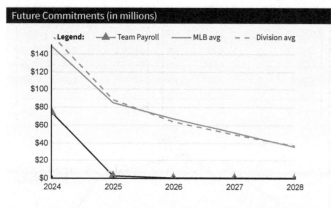

Legend: ▲ Team Payroll — MLB avg --- Division avg

$140
$120
$100
$80
$60
$40
$20
$0

2024 2025 2026 2027 2028

Farm System Ranking

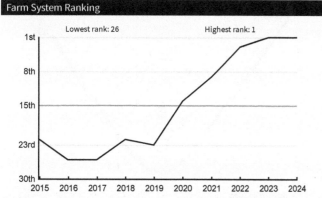

Lowest rank: 26   Highest rank: 1

1st

8th

15th

23rd

30th

2015 2016 2017 2018 2019 2020 2021 2022 2023 2024

Personnel

Executive Vice President and General Manager
Mike Elias

Vice President & Assistant General Manager, Analytics
Sig Mejdal

Assistant General Manager, Baseball Operations
Eve Rosenbaum

Director, Baseball Systems
Di Zou

Vice President, Player Development and Domestic Scouting
Matt Blood

Manager
Brandon Hyde

BP Alumni
Kevin Carter

---

tank—er, I mean, "rebuild"—was a painful but necessary reality, the dynasty was forthcoming, the contention window would be wide open for the next decade.

The echoes of 1983 were inescapable. That spring, a fella by the name of Cal Ripken Jr. had just won Rookie of the Year; by mid-July of last season infielder and former top prospect Gunnar Henderson was a frontrunner for AL Rookie of the Year. Then: one of the building blocks of the Oriole Way, catcher Rick Dempsey, slashed his way to World Series MVP by hitting .385 with a .923 slugging percentage over the series. Summer 2023: Former number-one draft pick and face of the franchise Adley Rutschman, a switch-hitting unicorn of a catcher, was living up to expectations in his first full season in the majors. After a bombastic manager's retirement left big shoes to fill going into the '83 season, a journeyman minor-league coach got the call-up to lead a major-league team for the first time.

Last year's squad started the season with 18 wins in the month of April—a franchise record—and headed into May with the third-best record in the majors (with the unfortunate luck of sharing a division with the 23-6 Rays). The 1983 World Series champion team suffered two separate seven-game losing streaks during the regular season; the worst streak last year was two separate four-game skids. While those blips were enough to flip Orioles Twitter into freakout mode, it wasn't enough to tarnish their perfect run of 52 series without being swept (except for That One Series, which we'll return to later), stretching to 91 when combined with the prior season—pure, uncut nostalgia for a city that takes pride in its consecutive streaks. And if April's success seemed like a fluke thanks to an easy schedule, the Orioles never dipped below a 54% winning percentage for a single month of the regular season. The '83 team finished one win out of the best record in the AL; this team reached the century mark in Ws for the first time in the Camden Yards era. Every Orioles team in history up until last year that hit the 100-win threshold went on to compete in the World Series. Was Bradish, Gibson, Kremer, Means & Rodriguez the next McGregor, Boddicker, Davis, Flanagan & Palmer? The 40-year parallels wrote themselves.

⚾   ⚾   ⚾

"I think our goal this year is to make the playoffs [in 2023] and put ourselves in a better position to make the playoffs," Mike Elias declared in December of 2022, after overseeing his first winning season since taking over. Early in 2023 he quipped: "I believe that our rebuild is behind us." In a year when the Birds were largely projected to come in fourth or fifth in the AL East, they emerged as the number one seed in the American League.

The young core touted as the future of the franchise came to fruition. They were led by Henderson, whose slow start will barely register as a footnote in the history books, Rutschman, Félix Bautista (one of the best closers in baseball) and starter Grayson Rodriguez, who had long been advertised as baseball's most promising pitching prospect. We saw flashes of what the rest of a potential future squad will look like in Heston Kjerstad and Colton Cowser. These welcome additions filled out the roster for perennial performers like Cedric Mullins and Anthony Santander, who both contributed some of their best career numbers that were—*finally*—capitalized upon by a playoff-contending team.

Of course, getting to 100 wins requires contributions from everyone. Resourcefulness in the overlooked and the undervalued is, after all, what landed former scout-turned general manager Elias and analytics lead and assistant GM Sig Mejdal at the helm of a franchise with notoriously frugal ownership. The acquisitions of Adam Frazier, Kyle Gibson, Aaron Hicks and Ryan O'Hearn didn't make for splashy headlines, nor did it satisfy the expectations of those who took Elias' "It's liftoff from here" affirmation to foreshadow a pursuit of a marquee name or two. They did, however, fulfill Elias' promise of upgrades by nibbling at the margins, squeezing everything they could from those modest signings. O'Hearn in particular boasted a 1.1 WARP after five years in Kansas City accumulating 0.3 total.

If the benchmark for thrilling baseball is a hero's journey narrative compacted within nine innings, this team provided that drama nearly every night. Nearly half their wins were comebacks, and no team won more one-run games. Whenever there was a dip, the top-ranked farm system was there to provide a continuous stream of fresh talent. Even when they lost Bautista to a devastating injury in August, the O's kept steamrolling with a dominant 18-11 record to finish off the regular season. The starters had maxed out their career innings and the bullpen was running on fumes, but the wins kept coming. Like magic.

Then came October.

⚾   ⚾   ⚾

In many respects, last year's postseason felt completely detached from the regular season across the league, as Wild Card teams made quick work of the league's two 100-win teams in the divisional round. Still, it was a bitter pill to see an improbable rise to secure that one seed, only to be defeated by the Rangers—who limped into a postseason slot on an 18-24 stretch run. Veteran skipper Bruce Bochy was always a step ahead of Hyde's clever platooning, which had, in part, earned him the AL Manager of the Year award. Down one run in the ninth, Henderson misread a sign and made an ill-advised, and easily rebuffed, stolen base attempt. It was a metaphorical kill shot.

And just like that, what started out as a bang ended in a whimper. Eight straight playoff losses, a streak dating back to 2014, is suddenly the longest active in the majors. Swept for the first time in 91 straight series, on a national stage. It was hard to reconcile the crescendo of such a historic season ending with such a sudden drop off a cliff.

For a team that carried a redemption arc narrative throughout the season, it was cold comfort to be the the the lone club occupying the middle sliver of the Venn diagram of extremes—one of three teams with over 100 wins in the regular season and one of three teams with a 100-loss season just two years prior. That the two 100-losses-two-years-prior teams eventually became the World Series contenders felt like some hyper-specific storyline created in a lab to make O's fans apoplectic, as we sat through the slick, worst-to-first pre-game programming from our living rooms for someone else's teams.

Still, the disappointment of the conclusion doesn't erase the breakthrough success of 2023, though it does lead to some heavy questions: What's next, how do they get there and what impediments are blocking the franchise from ascending to that next step.

⚾   ⚾   ⚾

One of the many perks of an improbable season on the field is that it served as a welcome distraction from the antics of acting owner, John P. Angelos, son of longtime owner Peter, who remains incapacitated from assuming managerial responsibilities of the franchise. It's not often that you hear chants of "sell the team" from the fanbase of a club occupying first place, but last year, Angelos the younger earned that dubious distinction.

Whether it was publicly berating a columnist who inquired about the team finances during a rare press conference (while promising to share said financials with the media before the start of the season, which...surprise! never happened), or privately berating one of his own employees, as news broke amidst the late season playoff run that beloved play-by-play commentator, Kevin Brown, was suspended from the MASN broadcast booth for contextualizing the Orioles dramatic improvement against the Tampa Bay Rays compared to recent seasons, John's fixation on burying inconvenient truths had the team going viral for all the wrong reasons. The eldest boy's pathetic attempts to control the narrative backfired once again, when he set up an in-game a photo-op standing alongside Maryland Governor Wes Moore, surrounded by a sellout crowd there to see their team clinch the AL East, to announce an official "lease agreement" keeping the team in Baltimore for the next 30 years—except it wasn't *actually* a lease agreement but a non-binding legal framework, that both sides walked back after the publicity stunt. A long-term lease was eventually finalized, though not before Angelos dragged negotiations down to the wire with hopes of securing more than the already guaranteed $600 million of taxpayer subsidized funding in order to redevelop surrounding parts of the stadium in his vision (and to pad his wallet), paid for by the state.

Birdland can breathe a sigh of relief that the team will stay in Baltimore for the next generation, but our young core may not. John poured cold water on the thought of any lengthy contracts—despite being the third-lowest payroll in the league in a market equivalent to the Padres, who had the third-highest payroll in all of baseball. And while Elias and the rest of the front office certainly deserve high praise for the turnaround, it's nearly impossible to separate the austerity ethos of Angelos from his first lieutenant, who appears to be just as invested as his boss in perfecting the *Moneyball* 2.0 model.

Ⓧ   Ⓧ   Ⓧ

There's been much debate on what "the right way" is to build a winning baseball club, with the implication that spending money for high-dollar players is some sort of cheat code to winning, while others argue that intentionally tanking for high draft picks is another form of rigging the system. While spending is a risky proposition, using the excuse of bloated rosters as a shield in order to *never* spend is not just No Fun, from a fan's perspective. It runs the greater risk of wasting the prime years of a meticulously built young core by depriving them of a few key assets—priced at market value—that could bring the team over the top. What was the point of saving all that money over half a decade if there's none left to invest in talent when the team really needs it?

There's a poetic irony to the Orioles being bested by the Rangers last year. Both teams underwent recent rebuilds and had their share of throwaway seasons—but Texas put their chips on the table, significantly increased payroll and went for it—and they have the trophy to show for it. Thus, the "right way" of building a winning team, at least the past few years, appears to combine both approaches—building out a competitive farm system *and* meaningful spending to fill in the gaps. If, during the offseason, the Orioles had doubled their payroll, they'd still be under the league average. And therein lies the frustration with the Minimum Viable Product approach to constructing a contender—when you come up short, there's plenty of instances to point to where saving came at the expense of winning.

If that '83 championship season is regarded as the North Star, then it also ought to serve as a warning for just how quickly fortunes can unravel. There's a reason that we don't talk about the seasons *after* 1983. Despite retaining many of the same stars and despite celebrated individual performances and near-comebacks, the numbers didn't add up. The dormancy of the next decade was, after all, how John's father ended up as majority owner of the club in the first place.

Even the most discerning of BP readers knows you can't put projection charts on streetlight banners; you can't wrap a bus in prospect rankings. For nearly half a decade, Baltimore has waited patiently as promises of a successful future baseball club awaited. Now that the future has arrived, there's no going back from a 101-win season, Rookie of the Year, Manager of the Year, Executive of the Year, number-one overall prospect, number-one ranked farm system, AL East Division Champions and number-one AL seed. There's nothing left to prove on paper. The criteria for the front office's performance evaluation is no longer abstract growth charts, it's maintaining the dominance demonstrated last season and bringing the pennant back to Baltimore. The players and coaches are all in, the city is all in—the big question is whether the executive suite will go all in, too.

Ⓧ   Ⓧ   Ⓧ

Ten years ago, when the Orioles were embarking upon their previous renaissance, I found myself, once again, rekindling my inherited fandom with my father, who was in the hospital that summer. The year previous was the first time Baltimore had reached the postseason since 1997, thanks to a new GM and a new manager, and some promising young homegrown talent (including a guy by the name of Manny Machado) combined with some more solid, developed players who had played through the preceding lean years (like a center fielder by the name of Adam Jones), and some promising young pitching prospects (a few guys by the name of Zach Britton and Kevin Gausman). "Those doubles are going to turn into homers," my dad remarked from his hospital bed, in reference to the 21-year-old Machado's league-leading tally that season. He wanted to make sure I brought my laptop on a specific day so we could use it to watch Gausman's major-league debut; he had high hopes for the young man.

Unfortunately, my father didn't live to see the apex of that era—he passed in June of that year, before the dominant 2014 run to the ALCS. My last hours spent with him were, in fact, watching a pretty unremarkable loss to the Blue Jays on my laptop from his bed in the rehabilitation facility.

While some of my father's ashes are scattered at the sculpture garden at the Hall of Fame in Cooperstown, I kept some for a future World Series celebration here in Baltimore. Hopefully, all of us won't have to wait too much longer. ▪

—Lindsay Ballant is the art director of The Baffler.

HITTERS

★ ★ ★ *2024 Top 101 Prospect* **#13** ★ ★ ★

Samuel Basallo **C/1B** Born: 08/13/04 Age: 19 Bats: L Throws: R Height: 6'3" Weight: 180 Origin: IFA, 2021

YEAR	TM	LVL	AGE	PA	R	HR	RBI	SB	AVG/OBP/SLG	BABIP	SLGCON	BB%	K%	ZSw%	ZCon%	OSw%	OCon%	LA	90th EV	DRC+	BRR	DRP	WARP
2021	DSL OR1	ROK	16	154	18	5	19	1	.239/.338/.410	.278	.539	12.3%	20.8%									0.4	
2022	ORI	ROK	17	180	22	6	32	1	.278/.350/.424	.322	.554	8.3%	20.6%										
2023	DEL	A	18	352	52	12	60	7	.299/.384/.503	.357	.660	11.6%	20.7%							125	-0.9	-0.4	1.7
2023	ABD	A+	18	115	21	8	24	5	.333/.443/.688	.353	.868	16.5%	17.4%							140	0.4	0.4	0.9
2024 non	*BAL*	*MLB*	*19*	*251*	*24*	*6*	*26*	*0*	*.237/.299/.380*	*.318*	*.547*	*7.5%*	*28.0%*							*90*	*0.0*	*0*	*0.5*

2023 GP: C (68), 1B (28), DH (15)

Comps: Keibert Ruiz (61), Jason Heyward (55), Wander Franco (52)

YEAR	TM	P. COUNT	FRM RUNS	BLK RUNS	THRW RUNS	TOT RUNS
2021	DSL OR1	1866			0.0	0.0
2022	ORI	2212			0.7	0.7
2023	DEL	7449	-1.8	0.6	2.2	1.0
2023	ABD	2214	-0.6	0.1	0.4	-0.1
2024	*BAL*	*6956*	*-1.9*	*0.2*	*0.6*	*-1.1*

Shed-sized, teenage catchers with elite raw power to all fields are hardly a dime a dozen, especially ones who strike out less than the league average. Basallo, the new Baltimore regime's first major international signing after decades of ignoring Latin American amateurs, had a phenomenal 2023. He put himself on the prospect map with 20 taters across three levels, and while the defensive chops are still a work in progress, the dude is a 19-year-old catcher set to spend most of 2024 in Double-A. Basallo is Baltimore's best shot at extending their outrageous run of no. 1 overall prospects—Rutschman, Henderson and Holliday—to four.

★ ★ ★ *2024 Top 101 Prospect* **#82** ★ ★ ★

Enrique Bradfield Jr. **CF** Born: 12/02/01 Age: 22 Bats: L Throws: L Height: 6'1" Weight: 170 Origin: Round 1, 2023 Draft (#17 overall)

YEAR	TM	LVL	AGE	PA	R	HR	RBI	SB	AVG/OBP/SLG	BABIP	SLGCON	BB%	K%	ZSw%	ZCon%	OSw%	OCon%	LA	90th EV	DRC+	BRR	DRP	WARP
2023	DEL	A	21	77	15	0	6	20	.302/.494/.340	.348	.409	24.7%	11.7%							142	2.7	3.6	1.2
2024 non	*BAL*	*MLB*	*22*	*251*	*21*	*2*	*19*	*0*	*.213/.301/.298*	*.255*	*.365*	*10.0%*	*16.9%*							*73*	*0.0*	*0*	*0.0*

2023 GP: CF (19), LF (5), RF (1)

Comps: Keenyn Walker (84), Eduardo Sosa (74), Ender Inciarte (69)

Baltimore's newest first-round pick is one of the fastest people you will ever watch play baseball. In 22 non-Complex minor-league games, Bradfield stole 24 bags. Across three years at Vanderbilt he swiped 141, setting the school record halfway through his junior year. He's a spectacularly entertaining center field defender with a shot to be a perennial Gold Glover. But...can he hit? Bradfield didn't homer in his first taste of pro ball, but still posted an above-average DRC+ because (1) he makes fantastic swing decisions and (2) his speed turns outs into singles and singles into doubles. If he can somehow get the isolated power over .100, Bradfield could be one of the most captivating and distinct players in baseball.

★ ★ ★ *2024 Top 101 Prospect* **#51** ★ ★ ★

Colton Cowser **OF** Born: 03/20/00 Age: 24 Bats: L Throws: R Height: 6'2" Weight: 220 Origin: Round 1, 2021 Draft (#5 overall)

YEAR	TM	LVL	AGE	PA	R	HR	RBI	SB	AVG/OBP/SLG	BABIP	SLGCON	BB%	K%	ZSw%	ZCon%	OSw%	OCon%	LA	90th EV	DRC+	BRR	DRP	WARP
2021	ORIO	ROK	21	25	8	1	8	3	.500/.560/.773	.588	.944	12.0%	16.0%									-1.5	
2021	DEL	A	21	124	22	1	26	4	.347/.476/.429	.418	.532	17.7%	15.3%							124	-1.1	0.2	0.7
2022	ABD	A+	22	278	42	4	22	16	.258/.385/.410	.374	.627	16.2%	28.4%							112	4.2	-5.1	1.2
2022	BOW	AA	22	224	49	10	33	2	.341/.469/.568	.446	.840	16.1%	25.4%							127	-1.4	0.7	1.3
2022	NOR	AAA	22	124	23	5	11	0	.219/.339/.429	.290	.672	10.5%	30.6%							90	1.8	2.1	0.6
2023	NOR	AAA	23	399	72	17	62	9	.300/.417/.520	.390	.778	16.0%	26.8%	62.0%	81.8%	23.2%	45.9%			116	-0.7	-2.4	1.7
2023	BAL	MLB	23	77	15	0	4	1	.115/.286/.148	.175	.231	16.9%	28.6%	62.9%	78.9%	24.4%	63.5%	5.9	103.6	81	0.1	0.4	0.1
2024 DC	*BAL*	*MLB*	*24*	*93*	*10*	*2*	*9*	*1*	*.223/.330/.363*	*.310*	*.547*	*12.2%*	*29.4%*							*99*	*0.0*	*0.6*	*0.3*

2023 GP: RF (12), CF (10), LF (7)

Comps: Andrew Stevenson (64), Josh Reddick (57), Jake Marisnick (50)

The former no. 5 overall pick underwhelmed in his first big league cup of coffee, as his trademark plate discipline spiraled into an overly passive approach. Overreacting to such a small sample is often unwise, but Cowser looked lost enough during his debut stretch to warrant legitimate concern. Back among the youths, Cowser kept raking in Triple-A while continuing to walk at his usual strong clip. But a glance at Cowser's Triple-A heat map raises serious questions about his ability to impact anything on the outer half of the dish from both righties and lefties. If he were a no-doubt defensive center fielder, Cowser could find a role as a walk-happy pull machine, but his glove is below-average at best. Cowser remains an exciting, unique, flawed player who should get another run of big league time in '24, if he doesn't get traded for a starting pitcher first.

Jud Fabian OF Born: 09/27/00 Age: 23 Bats: R Throws: L Height: 6'1" Weight: 195 Origin: Round 2, 2022 Draft (#67 overall)

YEAR	TM	LVL	AGE	PA	R	HR	RBI	SB	AVG/OBP/SLG	BABIP	SLGCON	BB%	K%	ZSw%	ZCon%	OSw%	OCon%	LA	90th EV	DRC+	BRR	DRP	WARP
2022	DEL	A	21	52	16	3	9	0	.386/.481/.841	.438	1.057	15.4%	17.3%							134	0.9	2.0	0.6
2022	ABD	A+	21	30	1	0	4	0	.167/.300/.208	.235	.312	16.7%	26.7%							88	-0.3	0.0	0.0
2023	ABD	A+	22	237	35	9	43	19	.281/.392/.490	.352	.718	15.6%	25.7%							120	0.0	-0.3	1.5
2023	BOW	AA	22	288	36	15	31	12	.176/.314/.399	.233	.731	15.3%	37.5%							87	-0.8	6.3	1.1
2024 non	BAL	MLB	23	251	25	6	26	5	.222/.307/.362	.343	.604	10.0%	36.0%							90	0.0	0	0.5

2023 GP: CF (65), LF (22), RF (19), DH (12)　　　　Comps: Tito Polo (62), Kala Ka'aihue (61), Bubba Starling (61)

Meet your new three-true-outcomes overlord. Fabian is an above-average center fielder with plus speed who walked, homered or struckout in 58% of his 288 plate appearances in Double-A. The defensive outlook and raw juice gives him some latitude, but there are very few productive big leaguers with strikeout rates around Fabian's 37.5% in Double-A. Considering the surplus of position-player talent in Baltimore's system, it seems unlikely that Fabian will get the necessary chance to fail and learn in the big leagues with the Birds, whenever the time comes, but it turns out there are 29 other teams.

Adam Frazier 2B Born: 12/14/91 Age: 32 Bats: L Throws: R Height: 5'10" Weight: 180 Origin: Round 6, 2013 Draft (#179 overall)

YEAR	TM	LVL	AGE	PA	R	HR	RBI	SB	AVG/OBP/SLG	BABIP	SLGCON	BB%	K%	ZSw%	ZCon%	OSw%	OCon%	LA	90th EV	DRC+	BRR	DRP	WARP
2021	PIT	MLB	29	428	58	4	32	5	.324/.388/.448	.359	.509	8.2%	10.7%	68.5%	93.3%	31.9%	79.7%	14.8	98.3	119	0.2	0.9	2.7
2021	SD	MLB	29	211	25	1	11	5	.267/.327/.335	.299	.381	6.2%	10.9%	67.3%	93.0%	35.5%	78.8%	7.0	97.7	110	0.2	0.2	1.1
2022	SEA	MLB	30	602	61	3	42	11	.238/.301/.311	.268	.359	7.6%	12.1%	69.5%	92.1%	35.0%	77.0%	13.2	99.2	99	-0.5	0.8	1.8
2023	BAL	MLB	31	455	59	13	60	11	.240/.300/.396	.258	.474	7.0%	14.9%	67.6%	90.1%	34.9%	68.6%	15.2	99.8	94	0.3	-4.9	0.6
2024 DC	BAL	MLB	32	477	44	7	45	12	.252/.315/.361	.286	.431	7.4%	14.6%							92	0.1	0.3	0.9

2023 GP: 2B (130), RF (7), LF (3), DH (2)　　　　Comps: Cookie Rojas (71), Johnny Ray (71), Nellie Fox (68)

The man nicknamed "Captain Slapdick" by Mariners fans in 2022 for his wet-noodle bat and propensity for rolling over grounders to second was Baltimore's big offensive free agent acquisition. Not exactly the "blast off" that GM Mike Elias had promised O's fans after the 2022 trade deadline. And while Frazier wasn't Trea Turner or Aaron Judge, he was perfectly respectable as a tough-to-strikeout veteran platoon starter with more power than expected. Yes, Frazier's game is about as sexy as a trip to the DMV, but every good ballclub needs an Adam Frazier or at least the concept of an Adam Frazier. In fact, we all do. Not every day can be Christmas or New Year's or Brian Roberts; some days have to be Adam Frazier, and that's okay.

Austin Hays LF Born: 07/05/95 Age: 29 Bats: R Throws: R Height: 5'11" Weight: 200 Origin: Round 3, 2016 Draft (#91 overall)

YEAR	TM	LVL	AGE	PA	R	HR	RBI	SB	AVG/OBP/SLG	BABIP	SLGCON	BB%	K%	ZSw%	ZCon%	OSw%	OCon%	LA	90th EV	DRC+	BRR	DRP	WARP
2021	BAL	MLB	25	529	73	22	71	4	.256/.308/.461	.286	.591	5.3%	20.2%	63.7%	90.0%	34.1%	56.5%	12.3	104.6	110	0.3	0.7	2.6
2022	BAL	MLB	26	582	66	16	60	2	.250/.306/.413	.289	.525	5.8%	19.6%	69.7%	90.2%	38.2%	59.7%	11.6	103.3	101	-0.1	2.1	2.1
2023	BAL	MLB	27	566	76	16	67	5	.275/.325/.444	.345	.609	6.7%	24.9%	66.1%	87.0%	34.1%	53.3%	10.9	105.2	97	0.2	0.7	1.5
2024 DC	BAL	MLB	28	540	54	14	59	4	.246/.305/.390	.301	.523	6.6%	23.2%							100	-0.1	-0.1	1.4

2023 GP: LF (137), CF (7), RF (5), DH (3)　　　　Comps: Joe Rudi (57), Jerry Morales (56), Vernon Wells (56)

Hays has seen a lot. He made his MLB debut with the Birds at age 21, way back in September of 2017. Seth Smith played in that game, so it's been a minute. Now a seasoned 28-year-old, Hays has survived the entirety of Baltimore's rebuild and rebirth. The regular outfield for the 110-loss 2021 Orioles was Hays in left, Cedric Mullins in center and Anthony Santander in right. Sound familiar? Given the space to develop on subpar ball clubs, Hays has steadily developed into a perfectly sufficient everyday outfielder. A hot first half earned him an All-Star nod—he actually started the game in Seattle after injuries bounced Mike Trout and Aaron Judge—but tailed off as the season wore on. The epitome of a Role-5 player, Hays is neither a problem nor a solution. With two more seasons until he reaches free agency, he gets to remain the Orioles starting left fielder unless his production suddenly falls off a cliff.

Gunnar Henderson SS/3B Born: 06/29/01 Age: 23 Bats: L Throws: R Height: 6'3" Weight: 220 Origin: Round 2, 2019 Draft (#42 overall)

YEAR	TM	LVL	AGE	PA	R	HR	RBI	SB	AVG/OBP/SLG	BABIP	SLGCON	BB%	K%	ZSw%	ZCon%	OSw%	OCon%	LA	90th EV	DRC+	BRR	DRP	WARP
2021	DEL	A	20	157	30	8	39	5	.312/.369/.574	.404	.853	8.9%	29.3%							108	0.8	3.4	1.0
2021	ABD	A+	20	289	34	9	35	11	.230/.343/.432	.313	.673	13.8%	30.1%							98	-1.9	3.5	0.9
2022	BOW	AA	21	208	41	8	35	12	.312/.452/.573	.350	.756	19.7%	18.3%							138	1.1	0.8	1.7
2022	NOR	AAA	21	295	60	11	41	10	.288/.390/.504	.374	.733	12.9%	26.4%							110	1.3	-0.2	1.3
2022	BAL	MLB	21	132	12	4	18	1	.259/.348/.440	.333	.622	12.1%	25.8%	67.3%	81.3%	22.8%	56.9%	1.9	107.1	111	0.1	0.0	0.5
2023	BAL	MLB	22	622	100	28	82	10	.255/.325/.489	.306	.683	9.0%	25.6%	68.0%	82.5%	30.6%	58.6%	11.6	106.9	114	0.5	2.1	3.3
2024 DC	BAL	MLB	23	579	66	20	72	11	.247/.327/.436	.310	.611	9.9%	25.7%							114	0.4	2.8	3.0

2023 GP: 3B (84), SS (83), DH (11)　　　　Comps: Rafael Devers (64), Ryan Zimmerman (57), Jay Bruce (56)

During his time as a prospect, Henderson was hyped as the type of player who might one day earn a statue of himself outside a stadium. But for the first two months of 2023, the eventual AL Rookie of the Year took that sentiment far too literally, blasting past the word "selective" and even "passive" toward downright "statuesque." From Opening Day until June 1, Henderson swung at just 68.8% of in-zone pitches with two strikes, far and away the lowest rate in MLB. But from that point until the end of the season Henderson's 20-game rolling zone-swing rate jumped more than 20 percentage points. The surface level results, predictably, followed. A monster June, during which the 22-year-old posted a .994 OPS, rocketed him into awards conversation. He would go on to dominate that conversation for the remainder of the season, winning the award by a unanimous vote. A capable defender at both left-side infield spots who's just starting to hone his approach and tap into his light-tower raw power, Henderson is a franchise cornerstone set to make All-Star teams until his body grows old or the planet disintegrates.

★ ★ ★ *2024 Top 101 Prospect* **#1** ★ ★ ★

Jackson Holliday SS Born: 12/04/03 Age: 20 Bats: L Throws: R Height: 6'0" Weight: 185 Origin: Round 1, 2022 Draft (#1 overall)

YEAR	TM	LVL	AGE	PA	R	HR	RBI	SB	AVG/OBP/SLG	BABIP	SLGCON	BB%	K%	ZSw%	ZCon%	OSw%	OCon%	LA	90th EV	DRC+	BRR	DRP	WARP
2022	ORI	ROK	18	33	6	1	3	3	.409/.576/.591	.400	.650	30.3%	6.1%										
2022	DEL	A	18	57	8	0	6	1	.238/.439/.333	.313	.438	26.3%	17.5%							124	-0.1	-0.1	0.3
2023	DEL	A	19	67	15	2	16	3	.396/.522/.660	.500	.875	20.9%	19.4%							123	1.3	0.4	0.6
2023	ABD	A+	19	259	52	5	35	17	.314/.452/.488	.405	.660	19.3%	20.8%							139	-3.1	1.4	1.8
2023	BOW	AA	19	164	28	3	15	3	.338/.421/.507	.425	.667	12.8%	20.7%							108	1.9	-1.2	0.7
2023	NOR	AAA	19	91	18	2	9	1	.267/.396/.400	.321	.517	17.6%	18.7%	71.1%	84.0%	21.2%	53.8%			103	-0.4	-0.8	0.1
2024 DC	BAL	MLB	20	462	45	7	43	3	.241/.333/.362	.309	.488	11.5%	22.6%							100	0.0	0	1.7

2023 GP: SS (98), 2B (20), DH (4), 3B (2)   *Comps: Ozzie Albies (60), Jason Heyward (46), Xander Bogaerts (43)*

The best prospect in baseball checks every box: the hair, the pedigree, the surface-level stats, the up-the-middle defense, the exit velocity numbers, the swing decisions, the hair. There's very, very little not to like. There's always a chance the hit tool plays down a grade once he reaches the big leagues and has to adjust to the best pitchers in the world, but up until now, Holliday has done nothing but wow. As a 19 year old, he set three levels of the minors ablaze before earning a late season call-up to Triple-A. Given his background—you might be familiar with his pops, Matt—Jackson has essentially been a professional baseball player since his 12th birthday. That experience and comfort oozes out through every aspect of his game. He's not the most naturally gifted shortstop, but has a magnificent internal clock and looks at least competent defensively. His at-bats are mature beyond his years and lead to fantastic swing decisions. The bright lights of the majors won't faze him whenever he debuts early in 2024. That Druw Jones—who many outlets ranked first in Holliday's 2022 draft—barely treaded water in Low-A while Holliday was inspiring calls for a late-season MLB debut, only adds to the mystique. Holliday is set to hit 30 bombs a year and make All-Star Games for the next decade.

★ ★ ★ *2024 Top 101 Prospect* **#41** ★ ★ ★

Heston Kjerstad RF Born: 02/12/99 Age: 25 Bats: L Throws: R Height: 6'3" Weight: 205 Origin: Round 1, 2020 Draft (#2 overall)

YEAR	TM	LVL	AGE	PA	R	HR	RBI	SB	AVG/OBP/SLG	BABIP	SLGCON	BB%	K%	ZSw%	ZCon%	OSw%	OCon%	LA	90th EV	DRC+	BRR	DRP	WARP
2022	DEL	A	23	98	17	2	17	0	.463/.551/.650	.565	.825	13.3%	17.3%							127	-0.4	-0.1	0.6
2022	ABD	A+	23	186	28	3	20	1	.233/.312/.362	.302	.509	8.6%	25.3%							77	0.5	2.3	0.3
2023	BOW	AA	24	206	30	11	23	3	.310/.383/.576	.324	.693	7.3%	15.0%							135	-2.6	-2.3	1.0
2023	NOR	AAA	24	337	57	10	32	2	.298/.371/.498	.356	.650	8.0%	20.5%	71.5%	87.8%	36.9%	53.3%			100	-0.2	0.1	1.0
2023	BAL	MLB	24	33	3	2	3	0	.233/.281/.467	.278	.700	6.1%	30.3%	63.0%	86.2%	37.2%	41.4%	19.5	105.9	99	0.0	0.0	0.1
2024 DC	BAL	MLB	25	251	23	6	26	1	.228/.289/.366	.287	.497	6.5%	24.6%							83	0.0	-0.2	0.2

2023 GP: DH (6), LF (3), RF (1)   *Comps: Raul Ibanez (58), Alex Presley (55), Gaby Sanchez (54)*

After missing the entire 2021 season with a heart issue, Kjerstad used 2022 to get back up to speed before reasserting himself as a legit top prospect in 2023. The former no. 2 overall pick performed well in Triple-A before a late-season big-league call-up left him as the last O's hitter off the postseason roster. Juice this legit, matched up with Kjerstad's league-average zone contact rate, is an alluring combination that could see the corner outfielder smash plenty of dingers in the big leagues. Despite the Orioles' glut of outfielders—albeit most of whom with less prospect seniority—he's unlikely to be left off the major-league roster for long.

Jorge Mateo SS Born: 06/23/95 Age: 29 Bats: R Throws: R Height: 6'1" Weight: 200 Origin: IFA, 2012

YEAR	TM	LVL	AGE	PA	R	HR	RBI	SB	AVG/OBP/SLG	BABIP	SLGCON	BB%	K%	ZSw%	ZCon%	OSw%	OCon%	LA	90th EV	DRC+	BRR	DRP	WARP
2021	SD	MLB	26	93	10	2	6	5	.207/.250/.322	.276	.467	2.2%	29.0%	69.8%	76.1%	31.6%	54.5%	9.9	103.6	76	0.1	1.1	0.2
2021	BAL	MLB	26	116	9	2	8	5	.280/.328/.421	.359	.570	6.0%	24.1%	68.5%	84.1%	39.7%	51.9%	17.0	104.0	73	0.0	-0.1	0.0
2022	BAL	MLB	27	533	63	13	50	35	.221/.267/.379	.286	.539	5.1%	27.6%	72.7%	81.9%	38.6%	50.5%	14.6	104.3	71	2.0	2.0	0.3
2023	BAL	MLB	28	350	58	7	34	32	.217/.267/.340	.267	.458	6.3%	23.4%	67.2%	85.6%	37.2%	54.3%	10.0	105.7	81	1.4	5.3	1.0
2024 DC	BAL	MLB	29	120	11	2	12	9	.223/.277/.346	.283	.469	6.2%	25.2%							78	0.1	0.6	0.2

2023 GP: SS (110), CF (4), DH (2)   *Comps: Pat Valaika (63), Erik González (62), Niko Goodrum (51)*

Decades from now, when the rising temperatures of our planet bring a cavalcade of catastrophe and doom, we will pull the next generation aside for a chat. Great grandchildren will inquire about the past—a simpler, more peaceful world—as the ice caps melt and the rising sea forces all 40 MLB teams to take turns playing at Coors Field. And those of us fortunate enough to have paid witness, to have seen the magic with our own eyes, will carry on the wonder that was Jorge Mateo's April 2023. Like our current society, Mateo's hot start was built on a bed of unsustainable lies, but boy, was it fun while it lasted. Time, as it always does, revealed the truth: that .347/.395/.667 March/April slash would not hold. Mateo is still an incredibly entertaining and somewhat valuable player—he can run, he can play shortstop and center, he can handle lefties—but he's not the savior of this world, or the next.

★ ★ ★ *2024 Top 101 Prospect* **#15** ★ ★ ★

Coby Mayo 3B   Born: 12/10/01   Age: 22   Bats: R   Throws: R   Height: 6'5"   Weight: 230   Origin: Round 4, 2020 Draft (#103 overall)

YEAR	TM	LVL	AGE	PA	R	HR	RBI	SB	AVG/OBP/SLG	BABIP	SLGCON	BB%	K%	ZSw%	ZCon%	OSw%	OCon%	LA	90th EV	DRC+	BRR	DRP	WARP
2021	ORIB	ROK	19	84	17	3	13	6	.324/.429/.535	.364	.655	13.1%	15.5%									2.1	
2021	DEL	A	19	125	27	5	26	5	.311/.416/.547	.373	.725	12.8%	20.8%							118	1.3	-3.3	0.4
2022	ABD	A+	20	288	50	14	49	5	.251/.326/.494	.275	.653	9.4%	21.5%							142	-1.6	3.2	2.3
2022	BOW	AA	20	145	21	5	20	0	.250/.331/.398	.365	.654	8.3%	34.5%							92	0.5	0.7	0.4
2023	BOW	AA	21	347	48	17	44	4	.307/.424/.603	.384	.861	14.7%	24.8%							134	-2.5	1.2	2.1
2023	NOR	AAA	21	267	36	12	55	1	.267/.393/.512	.315	.716	15.7%	23.2%	60.2%	83.0%	25.6%	55.8%			114	0.6	-0.9	0.8
2024 DC	BAL	MLB	22	95	10	2	10	0	.237/.321/.385	.310	.542	9.9%	26.6%							105	0.0	0	0.3

2023 GP: 3B (102), 1B (28), DH (12)   *Comps: Austin Riley (73), Evan Longoria (71), Joey Gallo (66)*

A big man with a magnificently violent hack, Mayo is probably Baltimore's best offensive prospect not named Holliday. His future defensive home is almost certainly first base or an outfield corner, but it probably won't bother folks; this guy can really rake. Despite that busy, chaotic swing, Mayo tends to remain impressively connected and short throughout his motion, which helps play up his imposing pull power. He's an incredibly physical kid, and with his swing decision making trending in a positive direction, this is a potential middle-of-the-order force just a call-up away from Camden Yards.

James McCann C   Born: 06/13/90   Age: 34   Bats: R   Throws: R   Height: 6'3"   Weight: 235   Origin: Round 2, 2011 Draft (#76 overall)

YEAR	TM	LVL	AGE	PA	R	HR	RBI	SB	AVG/OBP/SLG	BABIP	SLGCON	BB%	K%	ZSw%	ZCon%	OSw%	OCon%	LA	90th EV	DRC+	BRR	DRP	WARP
2021	NYM	MLB	31	412	29	10	46	1	.232/.294/.349	.304	.504	7.8%	27.9%	71.0%	84.9%	36.7%	58.2%	9.4	103.4	72	-0.3	0.1	0.2
2022	NYM	MLB	32	191	19	3	18	3	.195/.257/.282	.244	.383	5.8%	24.1%	70.0%	84.8%	39.7%	56.5%	16.3	104.1	89	-0.1	2.8	0.7
2023	BAL	MLB	33	226	25	6	26	3	.222/.269/.377	.274	.520	4.0%	25.2%	70.6%	85.2%	42.2%	48.6%	16.2	104.2	89	-0.2	-0.1	0.5
2024 DC	BAL	MLB	34	212	19	4	20	2	.222/.280/.336	.293	.482	6.2%	27.6%							77	-0.1	-0.7	0.1

2023 GP: C (59), DH (7), 1B (2), P (1)   *Comps: Yorvit Torrealba (62), Joe Oliver (61), Bob Boone (59)*

YEAR	TM	P. COUNT	FRM RUNS	BLK RUNS	THRW RUNS	TOT RUNS
2021	NYM	13581	1.8	-0.1	0.3	2.0
2022	NYM	7385	4.1	-0.2	0.2	4.1
2023	BAL	7836	-0.2	-0.1	0.7	0.4
2024	BAL	8418	-1.0	-0.2	0.6	-0.6

Baltimore took the veteran backstop off the Mets' hands in December '22 for nothing more than a PTBNL. Even though the Orioles assumed just five of the remaining $24 million on McCann's contract, he was still the third-highest paid player on Baltimore's roster all season. Backing up Adley Rutschman is good work if you can get it, and McCann delivered an admirable performance as the prototypical experienced second-string catcher. Pitchers loved throwing to him, hitters loved talking to him and McCann went from Queens scapegoat to Baltimore clubhouse cog. Winning cures everything, especially if your help isn't really required.

Ryan McKenna OF   Born: 02/14/97   Age: 27   Bats: R   Throws: R   Height: 5'11"   Weight: 195   Origin: Round 4, 2015 Draft (#133 overall)

YEAR	TM	LVL	AGE	PA	R	HR	RBI	SB	AVG/OBP/SLG	BABIP	SLGCON	BB%	K%	ZSw%	ZCon%	OSw%	OCon%	LA	90th EV	DRC+	BRR	DRP	WARP
2021	NOR	AAA	24	123	25	11	23	7	.307/.423/.683	.345	1.015	17.1%	26.8%							145	-0.7	1.0	1.1
2021	BAL	MLB	24	197	20	2	14	1	.183/.292/.266	.312	.474	12.2%	37.6%	69.8%	74.2%	28.2%	52.7%	10.9	102.2	56	0.2	2.1	-0.2
2022	BAL	MLB	25	172	23	2	11	2	.237/.294/.340	.350	.525	6.4%	32.0%	75.2%	78.4%	34.6%	41.9%	15.4	103.0	60	0.2	2.4	0.0
2023	NOR	AAA	26	61	14	3	7	2	.182/.262/.418	.226	.676	9.8%	34.4%	67.0%	79.4%	27.3%	41.7%			80	0.2	-1.4	0.0
2023	BAL	MLB	26	139	23	2	18	5	.254/.316/.361	.354	.537	6.5%	28.8%	71.4%	83.1%	39.2%	45.2%	9.9	105.9	68	0.3	1.6	0.1
2024 DC	BAL	MLB	27	91	8	2	9	2	.207/.280/.329	.292	.509	8.1%	31.9%							76	0.0	0.9	0.1

2023 GP: RF (55), CF (25), LF (15), P (1), DH (1)   *Comps: Lewis Brinson (56), Delino DeShields (55), Lee Tinsley (53)*

On the second day of the season, McKenna dropped a routine pop fly that would have been the final out of an outrageous 8-7 Orioles victory over the Red Sox. Instead, the ball doinked off the heel of his mitt, and the next batter, Adam Duvall, roped a two-run walk-off bomb that made McKenna an early-season scapegoat. While he started the season as Baltimore's fourth outfielder, inconsistent play and the arrival of Aaron Hicks, Colton Cowser and eventually Heston Kjerstad pushed McKenna down the depth chart. By season's end, the speedy Maine native was shuttling back between Camden Yards and Triple-A Norfolk every few weeks. In a tragic bit of misfortune, McKenna was in Triple-A during the O's playoff clinch celebration on September 18th and the O's division clinch celebration on September 28th, with a trip back to Baltimore sandwiched in between. He's on the outside of Baltimore's 2024 outfield rotation, hoping to warrant a shot with a second-division team looking for a buy-low center field option.

Ryan Mountcastle 1B   Born: 02/18/97   Age: 27   Bats: R   Throws: R   Height: 6'4"   Weight: 220   Origin: Round 1, 2015 Draft (#36 overall)

YEAR	TM	LVL	AGE	PA	R	HR	RBI	SB	AVG/OBP/SLG	BABIP	SLGCON	BB%	K%	ZSw%	ZCon%	OSw%	OCon%	LA	90th EV	DRC+	BRR	DRP	WARP
2021	BAL	MLB	24	586	77	33	89	4	.255/.309/.487	.297	.697	7.0%	27.5%	76.1%	77.7%	42.2%	58.1%	16.8	105.8	107	0.1	0.0	1.9
2022	BAL	MLB	25	609	62	22	85	4	.250/.305/.423	.303	.586	7.1%	25.3%	80.0%	80.2%	41.2%	58.1%	16.0	106.6	114	0.0	0.6	2.3
2023	BAL	MLB	26	470	64	18	68	3	.270/.328/.452	.315	.604	7.9%	22.8%	75.9%	85.9%	40.8%	54.4%	12.1	107.0	111	-0.2	0.4	1.6
2024 DC	BAL	MLB	27	517	56	17	61	3	.248/.309/.406	.299	.549	7.5%	23.8%							105	-0.1	0.7	1.4

2023 GP: 1B (90), DH (23)   *Comps: Paul Konerko (61), Richie Sexson (60), Ricky Jordan (59)*

In May, the Orioles social media team mic'd up Mountcastle during pre-game for one of those behind the scenes-style videos. At one point, he delivers a scathingly accurate assessment of himself: "My natural face just has a stupid smile on it." That's also a great way to describe Mountcastle the player. Like his face, his offensive approach is equally approachable and inflexible. The man loves to swing, he loves to chase, he loves to hit. When he makes contact with a baseball, it's the equivalent of a warm smile, but there are many times in life where other facial expressions are the most prudent course of action. If Mountcastle keeps grinning his way through that hack-happy approach, he's a reliable, average first baseman who scorches the ball and doesn't offer much else. Still, that's a pretty nice life.

Cedric Mullins CF   Born: 10/01/94   Age: 29   Bats: L   Throws: L   Height: 5'9"   Weight: 175   Origin: Round 13, 2015 Draft (#403 overall)

YEAR	TM	LVL	AGE	PA	R	HR	RBI	SB	AVG/OBP/SLG	BABIP	SLGCON	BB%	K%	ZSw%	ZCon%	OSw%	OCon%	LA	90th EV	DRC+	BRR	DRP	WARP
2021	BAL	MLB	26	675	91	30	59	30	.291/.360/.518	.322	.654	8.7%	18.5%	64.2%	86.4%	32.9%	69.9%	14.1	103.4	120	1.4	6.7	5.4
2022	BAL	MLB	27	672	89	16	64	34	.258/.318/.403	.299	.508	7.0%	18.8%	73.8%	84.6%	34.8%	67.2%	16.2	103.0	92	2.1	5.9	2.6
2023	BAL	MLB	28	455	51	15	74	19	.233/.305/.416	.271	.554	9.5%	22.2%	73.9%	82.1%	31.4%	63.3%	20.8	103.3	88	0.6	2.7	1.3
2024 DC	BAL	MLB	29	570	61	17	66	26	.249/.320/.413	.294	.538	8.5%	20.9%							105	0.5	3.9	2.8

2023 GP: CF (110), DH (3)   Comps: Jackie Bradley Jr. (70), Mickey Rivers (64), Marvell Wynne (64)

When Mullins hit the IL with a right groin injury on May 29, the O's leadoff man was reemerging as one of the more dynamic center fielders in the sport. Through 54 games Mullins had a .263/.356/.479 slash line with eight homers and 13 steals to go along with outstanding outfield defense. But that unfortunate groin injury, suffered while running out a ground ball, completely torpedoed Mullins' season. From his return on June 24 until the end of the season, Mullins slashed .205/.257/.357 with a .263 xWOBA and then went 0-for-12 in the Orioles' brief October soirée. Lower body injuries for a player like Mullins, who relies so much on his speed to create value, are particularly concerning, but a full offseason of R&R should give him a clean slate heading into 2024. He remains entrenched as the Orioles starting center fielder, but might find himself hitting further down the lineup as the Hendersons, Rutschmans, Kjerstads and Hollidays of the world continue matriculating toward greatness.

Connor Norby 2B   Born: 06/08/00   Age: 24   Bats: R   Throws: R   Height: 5'9"   Weight: 180   Origin: Round 2, 2021 Draft (#41 overall)

YEAR	TM	LVL	AGE	PA	R	HR	RBI	SB	AVG/OBP/SLG	BABIP	SLGCON	BB%	K%	ZSw%	ZCon%	OSw%	OCon%	LA	90th EV	DRC+	BRR	DRP	WARP
2021	DEL	A	21	126	17	3	17	5	.283/.413/.434	.352	.606	16.7%	22.2%							113	0.3	-0.1	0.6
2022	ABD	A+	22	209	27	8	20	6	.237/.311/.425	.277	.581	8.6%	23.9%							105	0.8	-0.6	0.7
2022	BOW	AA	22	296	58	17	46	10	.298/.389/.571	.322	.746	11.5%	19.9%							122	-1.3	-0.7	1.3
2022	NOR	AAA	22	42	7	4	7	0	.359/.405/.718	.333	.824	7.1%	11.9%							120	-0.2	1.2	0.3
2023	NOR	AAA	23	633	104	21	92	10	.290/.359/.483	.347	.638	9.0%	21.6%	73.6%	84.6%	35.3%	64.1%			100	0.9	1.0	1.5
2024 DC	BAL	MLB	24	62	6	1	6	1	.231/.292/.360	.283	.465	7.0%	22.9%							87	0.0	0	0.1

2023 GP: 2B (105), LF (27), RF (5), DH (3), SS (1)   Comps: Scott Kingery (70), Nick Senzel (58), Alberto Callaspo (56)

Oh wow, what a surprise: an upper-minors Orioles hitting prospect with awesome swing decisions, solid pop and defensive nebulousness. We're fast approaching the too-many-cooks portion of Baltimore's developmental explosion and Norby is a perfect example of the organization's growing list of redundancies. The power numbers regressed a tad in 2023, with a hard-hit percentage below the MLB average, but Norby remains a likely big leaguer. The chances of him entrenching himself with Baltimore are slim, but an org with a softer MLB roster could give Norby a shot.

Ryan O'Hearn 1B   Born: 07/26/93   Age: 30   Bats: L   Throws: L   Height: 6'3"   Weight: 220   Origin: Round 8, 2014 Draft (#243 overall)

YEAR	TM	LVL	AGE	PA	R	HR	RBI	SB	AVG/OBP/SLG	BABIP	SLGCON	BB%	K%	ZSw%	ZCon%	OSw%	OCon%	LA	90th EV	DRC+	BRR	DRP	WARP
2021	OMA	AAA	27	82	22	12	25	3	.375/.451/.931	.333	1.175	11.0%	18.3%							177	1.0	-0.3	1.0
2021	KC	MLB	27	254	23	9	29	0	.225/.268/.369	.277	.527	5.1%	28.0%	74.3%	81.2%	35.2%	55.8%	14.5	105.9	77	-0.1	-0.6	-0.2
2022	KC	MLB	28	145	14	1	16	0	.239/.290/.321	.313	.434	5.5%	24.1%	68.7%	86.2%	35.2%	61.1%	12.8	106.1	81	0.1	-0.5	0.0
2023	NOR	AAA	29	52	11	4	13	0	.354/.404/.729	.433	1.029	7.7%	26.9%	66.7%	75.9%	25.0%	51.6%			113	0.8	-1.1	0.2
2023	BAL	MLB	29	368	48	14	60	5	.289/.322/.480	.340	.629	4.1%	22.3%	72.4%	86.7%	34.7%	61.5%	11.9	105.1	105	-0.2	-0.3	1.0
2024 DC	BAL	MLB	30	332	36	12	41	2	.255/.303/.424	.299	.555	5.8%	22.3%							101	-0.2	-0.8	0.6

2023 GP: 1B (70), RF (23), DH (14), LF (6)   Comps: Justin Smoak (58), Carlos Pena (52), J.T. Snow (52)

Not even the Orioles believed in O'Hearn, who obliterated the baseball in spring training, but was assigned to Norfolk out of camp. They had plenty of reason not to: In his five years as a Royal, O'Hearn was the epitome of a baseball afterthought, a first baseman on a small-market team who didn't hit. But then Ryan Mountcastle got hurt, so O'Hearn joined the O's the second week in April and never left, solidifying himself as one of the most shocking, out-of-nowhere stories of the season. Much of his shocking success was a result of never having to face a lefty, but the under-the-hood numbers support his massive jump. O'Hearn, with the help of a private hitting instructor, learned how to hit fastballs, which is kind of a big deal if you want to be a big leaguer. Unless he gets bitten by a venomous snake, he'll be a key platoon contributor in '24.

Joey Ortiz MI   Born: 07/14/98   Age: 25   Bats: R   Throws: R   Height: 5'9"   Weight: 190   Origin: Round 4, 2019 Draft (#108 overall)

YEAR	TM	LVL	AGE	PA	R	HR	RBI	SB	AVG/OBP/SLG	BABIP	SLGCON	BB%	K%	ZSw%	ZCon%	OSw%	OCon%	LA	90th EV	DRC+	BRR	DRP	WARP
2021	ABD	A+	22	89	14	0	8	3	.289/.382/.434	.373	.569	11.2%	20.2%							104	0.2	0.6	0.4
2021	BOW	AA	22	67	11	4	9	1	.233/.313/.467	.238	.609	9.0%	20.9%							113	0.8	0.5	0.4
2022	BOW	AA	23	485	69	15	71	2	.269/.337/.455	.298	.559	8.5%	16.7%							130	-0.1	6.7	3.7
2022	NOR	AAA	23	115	22	4	14	6	.346/.400/.567	.381	.678	7.8%	14.8%							113	-0.4	0.0	0.5
2023	NOR	AAA	24	389	66	9	58	11	.321/.378/.507	.373	.632	8.2%	17.7%	65.3%	89.6%	36.8%	71.6%			108	3.5	2.2	2.0
2023	BAL	MLB	24	34	4	0	4	0	.212/.206/.242	.280	.333	0.0%	26.5%	61.4%	85.7%	40.0%	63.6%	0.3	108.5	94	0.0	0.0	0.1
2024 DC	BAL	MLB	25	59	5	1	6	1	.236/.295/.353	.276	.442	7.0%	18.0%							86	0.0	-0	0.1

2023 GP: 2B (7), 3B (4), SS (3)   Comps: Kevin Frandsen (62), José Osuna (61), Chris Taylor (60)

Like most other ballclubs, the Orioles can only field nine dudes at a time. Unlike most other ballclubs, the Orioles are packed with young offensive talent like a nine-year-old's suitcase. Ortiz was one of the unfortunate souls lost in that math problem. The undersized, wiry infielder might have played 100 games last season had he been on the 2021 Orioles or the 2023 Tigers. Instead, he tallied just 34 forgettable plate appearances in 15 games across three separate big-league stints. Impressively, Ortiz kept raking in Triple-A despite the yo-yo-esque nature of his season. Drafted as a defensive specialist with inflated offensive numbers courtesy of college baseball's version of Coors Field, Ortiz's game has gone the other way since joining the Orioles. He's still a potential impact big leaguer, and a sufficiently capable defensive shortstop with a solid offensive track record in the upper minors, but it's increasingly unlikely Ortiz makes his name as an Oriole. There can only be so many big fish in the infield; this one is starting to smell a bit like trade bait.

BASEBALL PROSPECTUS 2024

Adley Rutschman C
Born: 02/06/98　Age: 26　Bats: S　Throws: R　Height: 6'2"　Weight: 230　Origin: Round 1, 2019 Draft (#1 overall)

YEAR	TM	LVL	AGE	PA	R	HR	RBI	SB	AVG/OBP/SLG	BABIP	SLGCON	BB%	K%	ZSw%	ZCon%	OSw%	OCon%	LA	90th EV	DRC+	BRR	DRP	WARP
2021	BOW	AA	23	358	61	18	55	1	.271/.392/.508	.279	.630	15.4%	15.9%							141	0.3	13.2	4.3
2021	NOR	AAA	23	185	25	5	20	2	.312/.405/.490	.364	.621	13.0%	17.8%							123	-0.6	3.6	1.4
2022	NOR	AAA	24	53	5	3	7	0	.233/.377/.442	.206	.514	13.2%	11.3%	72.7%	87.5%	16.1%	100.0%			132	-0.3	-0.3	0.3
2022	BAL	MLB	24	470	70	13	42	4	.254/.362/.445	.291	.567	13.8%	18.3%	63.5%	90.4%	25.7%	68.8%	15.7	103.5	123	0.1	9.2	3.9
2023	BAL	MLB	25	687	84	20	80	1	.277/.374/.435	.303	.526	13.4%	14.7%	61.3%	90.6%	26.8%	74.9%	12.7	104.2	132	-0.3	10.8	6.1
2024 DC	BAL	MLB	26	597	69	16	69	0	.260/.359/.418	.280	.497	12.7%	13.5%							123	0.0	12.9	5.2

2023 GP: C (110), DH (46)

Comps: Tyler Flowers (66), Will Smith (63), Martín Maldonado (63)

CHARM CITY GOLDEN RETRIEVER RESCUE: ADOPTIONS AVAILABLE

YEAR	TM	P. COUNT	FRM RUNS	BLK RUNS	THRW RUNS	TOT RUNS
2021	BOW	7738	12.8	0.6	0.2	13.6
2021	NOR	4199	3.2	0.1	0.1	3.4
2022	NOR	1095	0.0	0.1	-0.3	-0.2
2022	BAL	12228	10.7	0.2	0.3	11.2
2023	BAL	15491	12.7	0.0	0.2	12.9
2024	BAL	15632	12.7	0.1	0.0	12.8

Adley is a 26-year-old catcher with so much love to give a good team. Affable and high-energy, he's good with pitchers of all ages, from rookies to seniors. He thrives best in a high-offense environment and loves to go for walks. He possesses 85th percentile "fetch" skills in preventing passed balls and wild pitches, and is eager to jump up in meeting strangers attempting to nab second base, though could work on his skills as a guardian against steals. Alas, the hidden-ball trick won't work on him as his chase rate is well below league-average. Overall projection: a very good boy.

Anthony Santander RF/DH
Born: 10/19/94　Age: 29　Bats: S　Throws: R　Height: 6'2"　Weight: 230　Origin: IFA, 2011

YEAR	TM	LVL	AGE	PA	R	HR	RBI	SB	AVG/OBP/SLG	BABIP	SLGCON	BB%	K%	ZSw%	ZCon%	OSw%	OCon%	LA	90th EV	DRC+	BRR	DRP	WARP
2021	BAL	MLB	26	438	54	18	50	1	.241/.286/.433	.275	.577	5.3%	23.1%	72.4%	82.3%	37.3%	64.7%	18.0	106.5	98	-0.1	-7.8	0.3
2022	BAL	MLB	27	647	78	33	89	0	.240/.318/.455	.248	.577	8.5%	18.9%	67.6%	86.6%	34.3%	67.7%	21.5	106.1	124	-0.4	-9.8	2.6
2023	BAL	MLB	28	656	81	28	95	5	.257/.325/.472	.299	.636	8.4%	23.2%	67.7%	83.1%	37.7%	69.4%	20.5	106.2	107	-0.5	-4.7	1.6
2024 DC	BAL	MLB	29	559	66	24	75	2	.244/.314/.444	.267	.569	8.1%	19.9%							111	-0.3	-7.8	1.3

2023 GP: RF (97), DH (47), 1B (12), LF (1)

Comps: Ruben Sierra (76), Wally Post (73), Josh Reddick (72)

Pull the baseball in the air, kids. That is, if you want to make a living. Santander had the second highest fly-ball rate in baseball—that's called elevating and celebrating—and many, many of those flies were to the pull side. But Santander has become more than just that, with his 41 doubles ranking third in all of baseball. Combine all that with a league-average walk rate and you have a player capable of hitting in the middle of a good team's order. The former Rule 5 pick has one year left on his current contract, which has made Santander the center of trade speculation, given the cornucopia of Orioles outfield prospects. Even for a ruthlessly long-sighted team like Baltimore, trading away a dependable middle-of-the-order presence like Santander would be surprising. But if the O's underperform in the first half, don't be shocked if the highest paid player on Baltimore's 2024 roster—suck it, Craig Kimbrel—gets dealt before he hits the open market. That Santander, acquired by the old front office regime, endured the years to make it to the postseason as a key contributor is incredible.

Ramón Urías 3B
Born: 06/03/94　Age: 30　Bats: R　Throws: R　Height: 5'10"　Weight: 185　Origin: IFA, 2010

YEAR	TM	LVL	AGE	PA	R	HR	RBI	SB	AVG/OBP/SLG	BABIP	SLGCON	BB%	K%	ZSw%	ZCon%	OSw%	OCon%	LA	90th EV	DRC+	BRR	DRP	WARP
2021	NOR	AAA	27	101	14	4	12	1	.258/.340/.483	.317	.672	8.9%	24.8%							105	0.2	0.0	0.4
2021	BAL	MLB	27	296	33	7	38	1	.279/.361/.412	.369	.581	9.5%	25.7%	67.7%	80.2%	25.6%	61.9%	5.2	104.4	104	0.0	-0.1	1.2
2022	BAL	MLB	28	445	50	16	51	1	.248/.305/.414	.287	.548	6.7%	22.0%	74.1%	79.4%	31.0%	59.9%	10.7	104.4	96	0.0	3.6	1.3
2023	BAL	MLB	29	396	45	4	42	3	.264/.328/.375	.355	.521	6.8%	25.5%	71.4%	80.7%	33.9%	57.8%	7.8	103.6	75	0.0	-0.9	-0.1
2024 DC	BAL	MLB	30	222	21	5	22	1	.236/.303/.358	.303	.493	7.3%	25.1%							91	0.0	0.2	0.4

2023 GP: 3B (92), 2B (22), 1B (13), DH (3)

Comps: Alberto Callaspo (48), Chris Stynes (47), Kevin Kouzmanoff (47)

Urías, a 2022 Gold Glove winner, is starting to look like the odd man out among Baltimore's abundance of infielders. It didn't help that both sides of his game took a dramatic step back in 2023, due at least in part to a nagging heel issue, and not the Ric Flair kind. The batted-ball data went from sufficient to pool noodle-ish, while the defensive metrics hinted toward a bag of hurled tomatoes instead of another Gold Glove. He currently leads his younger brother, Luis, in career WAR by a score of 7.4 to 7.0. Definitely keep an eye on that barnstorming showdown.

Jordan Westburg IF Born: 02/18/99 Age: 25 Bats: R Throws: R Height: 6'2" Weight: 210 Origin: Round 1, 2020 Draft (#30 overall)

YEAR	TM	LVL	AGE	PA	R	HR	RBI	SB	AVG/OBP/SLG	BABIP	SLGCON	BB%	K%	ZSw%	ZCon%	OSw%	OCon%	LA	90th EV	DRC+	BRR	DRP	WARP
2021	DEL	A	22	91	18	3	24	5	.366/.484/.592	.500	.894	13.2%	26.4%							114	0.8	-2.2	0.3
2021	ABD	A+	22	285	41	8	41	9	.286/.389/.469	.372	.665	12.3%	24.9%							114	0.5	2.3	1.6
2021	BOW	AA	22	130	15	4	14	3	.232/.323/.429	.282	.600	10.8%	24.6%							96	0.3	1.7	0.5
2022	BOW	AA	23	209	32	9	32	3	.247/.344/.473	.310	.688	12.4%	27.3%							113	1.6	-0.5	1.0
2022	NOR	AAA	23	413	64	18	74	9	.273/.361/.508	.318	.676	10.7%	21.8%							113	-1.2	-2.6	1.5
2023	NOR	AAA	24	301	57	18	54	6	.295/.372/.567	.328	.745	9.6%	21.3%	72.0%	80.7%	27.9%	46.2%			126	0.0	-5.0	1.4
2023	BAL	MLB	24	228	26	3	23	4	.260/.311/.404	.336	.553	7.0%	24.6%	71.7%	83.6%	30.8%	57.2%	13.9	105.9	80	0.2	-0.3	0.1
2024 DC	BAL	MLB	25	436	43	11	46	6	.241/.306/.385	.310	.539	7.7%	26.1%							99	0.0	-0.9	1.1

2023 GP: 2B (50), 3B (29), DH (1)   Comps: Erik González (59), Sean Rodríguez (59), Chris Nelson (58)

In a 228-plate appearance sample, Westburg's rookie season was the epitome of average. No shame in that; some of us live our whole lives dreaming of being average. The Mississippi State product debuted in late June and held his own for the rest of the season, mixing in starts at both second and third base, depending on the hand of the pitcher, the health of the first baseman and the barometer. He showed less power in that limited big-league run than he had in the upper minors, but his batted-ball data looked kosher enough to believe there's more juice in the tank. With Gunnar Henderson now entrenched at shortstop and Jackson Holliday the impending long-term option at second base, Westburg should have a chance to prove himself as Baltimore's third baseman of the future.

Creed Willems C Born: 06/04/03 Age: 21 Bats: L Throws: R Height: 6'0" Weight: 225 Origin: Round 8, 2021 Draft (#227 overall)

YEAR	TM	LVL	AGE	PA	R	HR	RBI	SB	AVG/OBP/SLG	BABIP	SLGCON	BB%	K%	ZSw%	ZCon%	OSw%	OCon%	LA	90th EV	DRC+	BRR	DRP	WARP
2021	ORIO	ROK	18	25	3	0	1	0	.182/.280/.227	.267	.333	8.0%	28.0%									-0.1	
2022	DEL	A	19	246	21	4	23	0	.190/.264/.321	.252	.464	5.7%	27.6%							83	-0.3	-4.4	-0.1
2023	DEL	A	20	120	20	8	28	2	.302/.442/.615	.356	.881	16.7%	24.2%							131	-0.6	-1.1	0.6
2023	ABD	A+	20	311	22	9	47	0	.192/.267/.319	.237	.463	8.4%	27.7%							80	0.9	-6.2	0.0
2024 non	BAL	MLB	21	251	20	5	22	0	.199/.258/.312	.300	.500	6.3%	35.3%							59	0.0	0	-0.5

2023 GP: C (58), DH (25), 1B (23)   Comps: Roberto Peña (65), Alex Monsalve (61), Ben Rortvedt (58)

Willems looks and plays like a bit character from *Eastbound and Down*. He got a massive bonus as an amateur in the eighth round back in 2021, but looked overmatched by pro pitching immediately. Things went better in a Low-A rerun for the first few months of 2023, but then Willems got promoted to High-A and got exposed to the tune of a .586 OPS over 311 plate appearances. He's a fun, one-dimensional player who might become a Mexican Pacific Winter League icon, but is unlikely to ever impact the baseball above Double-A. One anonymous scout simply said: "He stinks, I'm not sure why you're asking about him," which is both disrespectful and insightful.

YEAR	TM	P. COUNT	FRM RUNS	BLK RUNS	THRW RUNS	TOT RUNS
2022	DEL	7037	-7.7	0.2	1.2	-6.3
2023	DEL	2333	-1.2	0.2	0.4	-0.6
2023	ABD	5849	-6.7	-0.2	0.6	-6.3
2024	BAL	6956	-4.3	0.3	0.3	-3.7

PITCHERS

Bryan Baker RHP Born: 12/02/94 Age: 29 Height: 6'6" Weight: 235 Origin: Round 11, 2016 Draft (#320 overall)

YEAR	TM	LVL	AGE	G (GS)	IP	W-L	SV	K	WHIP	ERA	CSP	BB%	K%	HR%	GB%	ZSw%	ZCon%	OSw%	OCon%	BABIP	SLGCON	DRA-	WARP
2021	BUF	AAA	26	39 (0)	41¹	6-1	11	48	0.85	1.31		10.2%	28.9%	0.6%	41.8%					.175	.250	86	0.9
2021	TOR	MLB	26	1 (0)	1	0-0	0	1	1.00	0.00	51.1%	0.0%	25.0%	0.0%	0.0%	100.0%	62.5%	18.2%	50.0%	.333	.333	82	0.0
2022	BAL	MLB	27	66 (2)	69²	4-3	1	76	1.23	3.49	55.4%	8.9%	26.1%	1.0%	41.4%	69.1%	76.7%	28.3%	65.8%	.311	.438	84	1.3
2023	NOR	AAA	28	13 (0)	13¹	1-1	0	18	1.88	6.75		12.1%	27.3%	3.0%	35.0%	63.7%	81.9%	34.2%	56.6%	.395	.700	90	0.2
2023	BAL	MLB	28	46 (0)	45	4-3	0	51	1.27	3.60	47.6%	12.9%	27.4%	2.2%	34.5%	73.5%	82.4%	30.0%	65.9%	.276	.500	94	0.7
2024 DC	BAL	MLB	29	15 (0)	17¹	1-1	0	17	1.34	4.36	51.9%	10.4%	23.2%	3.5%	37.5%					.277	.551	100	0.1

2023 Arsenal: FA (95.9), SL (86.4), CH (80.8), CU (83.9)   Comps: Brad Brach (77), Dillon Maples (77), Jake Diekman (77)

Baker entered Game 2 of the ALDS—a must-win for the Orioles after a brutal Game 1 loss—in a crucial spot. Grayson Rodriguez had just gotten his socks rocked, sent packing after just an inning and two thirds. But the O's were only down 5-2 in the top of the third, a surmountable mountain, a hill really. In came Baker with a clean frame. He dirtied things up pretty swiftly. After inducing a leadoff flyout, Baker walked three consecutive Rangers, got yanked and watched helplessly from the dugout as Mitch Garver hit a series-defining ding-dong off Jacob Webb. It was a cruel but appropriate coda to Baker's season; the red-bearded reliever allowed 54% of inherited baserunners to score in 2023 (league average is around 32%). Regression may come, but it often doesn't come in time.

Mike Baumann RHP   Born: 09/10/95   Age: 28   Height: 6'4"   Weight: 240   Origin: Round 3, 2017 Draft (#98 overall)

YEAR	TM	LVL	AGE	G(GS)	IP	W-L	SV	K	WHIP	ERA	CSP	BB%	K%	HR%	GB%	ZSw%	ZCon%	OSw%	OCon%	BABIP	SLGCON	DRA-	WARP
2021	BOW	AA	25	10(10)	38²	3-2	0	39	1.22	4.89		11.1%	24.1%	3.7%	44.2%					.237	.515	96	0.4
2021	NOR	AAA	25	6(6)	27	1-1	0	26	1.15	2.00		12.0%	24.1%	0.0%	37.7%					.261	.313	97	0.4
2021	BAL	MLB	25	4(0)	10	1-1	0	5	1.90	9.90	58.4%	12.0%	10.0%	4.0%	36.8%	81.6%	88.7%	22.2%	58.3%	.306	.632	132	-0.1
2022	NOR	AAA	26	20(9)	60	2-6	1	81	1.32	4.20		9.6%	31.2%	2.3%	58.2%	66.7%	83.3%	38.9%	71.4%	.327	.523	66	1.9
2022	BAL	MLB	26	13(4)	34¹	1-3	0	23	1.51	4.72	58.1%	6.0%	15.4%	2.0%	49.6%	75.2%	90.3%	30.2%	71.7%	.357	.535	99	0.3
2023	NOR	AAA	27	6(0)	6	0-0	1	9	1.00	0.00		21.7%	39.1%	0.0%	55.6%	71.8%	67.9%	30.9%	47.6%	.111	.111	88	0.1
2023	BAL	MLB	27	60(0)	64²	10-1	0	61	1.31	3.76	46.8%	12.1%	22.3%	2.6%	42.4%	70.2%	85.7%	32.5%	58.4%	.266	.500	105	0.6
2024 DC	BAL	MLB	28	43(0)	46¹	3-2	0	41	1.39	4.48	50.8%	10.6%	20.4%	2.9%	43.4%					.283	.518	102	0.2

2023 Arsenal: FA (96.5), KC (87.4), SL (91.1), FC (93.4), CH (89.7), SW (84.3)   *Comps: André Rienzo (52), Joel Payamps (52), Pedro Villarreal (50)*

You've watched this scene a million times: a player enduring an in-game interview with the TV broadcast while teammates bombard him with a series of juvenile pranks and distractions. On August 6, 2023, Baumann found himself in this exact spot. There he sat, in the O's home bullpen, a headset draped over his cap, his shoelaces tied together, a waterfall of sunflower seeds pouring down his front courtesy of Danny Coulombe. But amidst this adversity, Baumann offered a shockingly insightful and self-aware quip. "Relievers are like offensive linemen," he told the home broadcast. "People don't really know who you are unless you really mess up." There's no better way to describe Baumann's 2023. The dude threw over 60 innings of above-average ball and few noticed. He'll be a reliable, if unspectacular, part of Baltimore's 2024 'pen, unless he isn't. Relievers are like offensive linemen, if you haven't heard.

Félix Bautista RHP   Born: 06/20/95   Age: 29   Height: 6'8"   Weight: 285   Origin: IFA, 2012

YEAR	TM	LVL	AGE	G(GS)	IP	W-L	SV	K	WHIP	ERA	CSP	BB%	K%	HR%	GB%	ZSw%	ZCon%	OSw%	OCon%	BABIP	SLGCON	DRA-	WARP
2021	ABD	A+	26	11(0)	15	0-2	2	28	1.13	1.20		16.1%	45.2%	1.6%	30.4%					.273	.478	85	0.2
2021	BOW	AA	26	12(0)	13¹	0-1	4	24	0.98	0.67		19.3%	42.1%	0.0%	47.6%					.095	.190	85	0.2
2021	NOR	AAA	26	17(0)	18¹	1-3	5	25	1.09	2.45		12.0%	33.3%	1.3%	30.0%					.263	.474	85	0.4
2022	BAL	MLB	27	65(0)	65²	4-4	15	88	0.93	2.19	55.9%	9.1%	34.8%	2.8%	42.6%	72.2%	76.3%	34.1%	51.0%	.231	.475	66	1.8
2023	BAL	MLB	28	56(0)	61	8-2	33	110	0.92	1.48	43.6%	11.0%	46.4%	1.7%	36.4%	74.1%	66.8%	36.7%	41.6%	.274	.455	65	1.8
2024 non	BAL	MLB	29	58(0)	50	2-2	0	80	1.08	2.71	49.1%	11.1%	39.0%	3.2%	38.5%					.268	.592	68	1.1

2023 Arsenal: SI (99.6), FS (88.6), CU (86.4), FA (99.8)   *Comps: John Axford (71), Ryan O'Rourke (70), Dillon Maples (70)*

Only three relief seasons in MLB history have been definitively more dominant than Bautista's 2023: Edwin Díaz's 2022, Craig Kimbrel's 2012, and Craig Kimbrel's 2017. For five months, "The Mountain" was unfathomably excellent, delivering scoreless outings in 49 out of 56 chances, while allowing multiple runs in a single outing just once all season. Why? It's pretty simple. The 6-foot-8 Bautista's triple-digit heater looks like it's being dropped down an elevator shaft, while his dastardly splitter was literally the most untouchable pitch in baseball. He single-handedly transformed Baltimore's ninth innings into an inevitability, which enabled Manager of the Year Brandon Hyde to be much more aggressive with his other relief options. To the chagrin of Baltimoreans and ball-lovers everywhere, Bautista's UCL went kablooey in late August. While the club left the window open for a potential October return, it was not to be. He underwent surgery in late September and will miss the whole 2024 season.

Kyle Bradish RHP   Born: 09/12/96   Age: 27   Height: 6'3"   Weight: 215   Origin: Round 4, 2018 Draft (#121 overall)

YEAR	TM	LVL	AGE	G(GS)	IP	W-L	SV	K	WHIP	ERA	CSP	BB%	K%	HR%	GB%	ZSw%	ZCon%	OSw%	OCon%	BABIP	SLGCON	DRA-	WARP
2021	BOW	AA	24	3(3)	13²	1-0	0	26	0.88	0.00		9.6%	50.0%	0.0%	47.6%					.333	.429	84	0.2
2021	NOR	AAA	24	21(19)	86²	5-5	0	105	1.43	4.26		10.3%	27.8%	2.6%	43.2%					.336	.600	93	1.5
2022	BOW	AA	25	2(2)	8	1-0	0	9	0.13	0.00		0.0%	36.0%	0.0%	43.8%					.063	.062	93	0.1
2022	NOR	AAA	25	4(4)	19²	2-1	0	23	0.81	1.83		5.3%	30.7%	1.3%	50.0%					.234	.396	83	0.4
2022	BAL	MLB	25	23(23)	117²	4-7	0	111	1.40	4.90	56.6%	9.0%	21.8%	3.3%	45.3%	68.9%	88.2%	28.9%	56.6%	.314	.556	94	1.5
2023	BAL	MLB	26	30(30)	168²	12-7	0	168	1.04	2.83	47.9%	6.6%	25.0%	2.1%	48.9%	65.8%	88.7%	30.8%	51.2%	.271	.454	87	3.2
2024 DC	BAL	MLB	27	29(29)	163	11-8	0	151	1.25	3.74	51.2%	7.9%	21.9%	2.4%	47.6%					.290	.493	88	2.5

2023 Arsenal: SW (88.1), HC (94.5), SI (94.8), KC (84.8), CH (90.6)   *Comps: Anthony DeSclafani (71), Kyle Hendricks (67), Domingo Germán (65)*

Nothing to see here, just the best season by an Orioles starting pitcher in over two decades, one that culminated in a well-deserved fourth-place Cy Young finish. Bradish became the first Orioles starter to earn a vote since Erik Bedard in 2007 and delivered the highest Cy Young finish by an Orioles starter since Mike Mussina in 1999. Those accomplishments are all the more impressive when you consider that the 28th pitch of Bradish season was a laser-beam comebacker off his foot that sent him to the IL for much of April. And things didn't totally click for the 27-year-old righty until early June, mostly because Bradish's pedestrian four-seamer was getting predictably pulverized. Because Bradish falls off to the first base side of the rubber when he throws, his release point is extremely over-the-top, which makes the four-seamer very hittable. So Bradish tinkered with his usage rates, deprioritizing the four-seamer in favor of a sinker that he picked up in 2022, and voilà, the rocket took off. From July onward, Bradish had a 2.14 ERA across 16 starts with more than a strikeout per inning and an opposing .245 xWOBA. His stellar nine-strikeout playoff start only solidified himself as one of the more exciting hurlers in the American League. For an Orioles organization so thirsty for frontline, controllable starting pitching, Bradish's breakout was one of the most exciting developments in a season full of exciting developments.

Yennier Cano RHP   Born: 03/09/94   Age: 30   Height: 6'4"   Weight: 245   Origin: IFA, 2019

YEAR	TM	LVL	AGE	G (GS)	IP	W-L	SV	K	WHIP	ERA	CSP	BB%	K%	HR%	GB%	ZSw%	ZCon%	OSw%	OCon%	BABIP	SLGCON	DRA-	WARP
2021	WCH	AA	27	12 (0)	18¹	3-1	1	28	1.20	1.47		6.2%	34.6%	1.2%	72.3%					.348	.468	80	0.3
2021	STP	AAA	27	30 (1)	51¹	2-2	4	58	1.44	3.86		12.8%	25.7%	1.8%	60.6%					.315	.496	86	1.0
2022	NOR	AAA	28	11 (0)	16²	0-1	1	20	1.50	4.32		10.7%	26.7%	4.0%	51.1%					.318	.596	81	0.4
2022	STP	AAA	28	20 (0)	23²	1-1	3	25	0.93	1.90		6.7%	28.1%	2.2%	64.9%					.259	.444	81	0.6
2022	BAL	MLB	28	3 (0)	4¹	0-1	0	7	3.23	18.69	51.2%	18.5%	25.9%	0.0%	53.3%	69.0%	96.6%	32.9%	56.5%	.600	.600	89	0.1
2022	MIN	MLB	28	10 (0)	13²	1-0	0	14	2.05	9.22	50.7%	15.7%	20.0%	4.3%	50.0%	54.5%	85.5%	35.4%	68.8%	.341	.738	104	0.1
2023	BAL	MLB	29	72 (0)	72²	1-4	8	65	1.00	2.11	49.3%	4.6%	23.0%	1.4%	57.9%	68.3%	84.2%	35.5%	59.0%	.284	.438	76	1.8
2024 DC	BAL	MLB	30	55 (0)	58	4-3	7	51	1.31	3.92	49.7%	8.4%	20.3%	2.1%	54.0%					.295	.474	90	0.6

2023 Arsenal: SI (96.4), CH (90.9), SL (87.4), FA (96.7)   Comps: Chris Hatcher (74), Andrew Kittredge (74), Eric Yardley (74)

There was a moment during the ninth inning of one of Baltimore's improbable 101 wins when the camera flashed from an unflappable Cano atop the Camden Yards mound to Orioles GM Mike Elias, somewhere in the stands with a grin of joyful disbelief on his face. So many things go into building a contender, so much planning, crafting, and for the Orioles in particular, long-term vision boarding. That Cano, a promising, but relatively unknown trade throw-in blossomed into one of the American League's best relievers within the span of a year seemed equally shocking to the man running the Orioles as it did everyone else around baseball. In 2022, Cano allowed 23 runs in 18 MLB innings, which even certain shellfish understand is not good. In 2023, Cano did not allow an earned run until the 18th appearance of his season on May 19th. He didn't walk a batter until May 25th. And while there were signs throughout the summer that the magic might be wearing off, Cano and the 96-mph chunk of lead he calls a sinker just kept the good times rolling. With the addition of Craig Kimbrel, Cano will start the year as Baltimore's 8th inning guy/fireman/Swiss Army knife, but given the mercurial nature of Kimbrel's highwire act nowadays, Cano could quickly return to the closing role he stepped into in September of 23 after Félix Bautista's arm went pop.

Danny Coulombe   LHP   Born: 10/26/89   Age: 34   Height: 5'10"   Weight: 190   Origin: Round 25, 2012 Draft (#776 overall)

YEAR	TM	LVL	AGE	G (GS)	IP	W-L	SV	K	WHIP	ERA	CSP	BB%	K%	HR%	GB%	ZSw%	ZCon%	OSw%	OCon%	BABIP	SLGCON	DRA-	WARP
2021	MIN	MLB	31	29 (1)	34¹	3-2	0	33	1.22	3.67	56.2%	5.0%	23.7%	3.6%	42.4%	74.5%	88.2%	36.7%	59.1%	.323	.592	89	0.5
2022	MIN	MLB	32	10 (0)	12¹	0-0	0	9	1.30	1.46	50.4%	17.0%	17.0%	0.0%	37.1%	73.1%	75.4%	30.6%	62.2%	.200	.265	122	0.0
2023	BAL	MLB	33	61 (0)	51¹	5-3	2	58	1.11	2.81	43.4%	5.7%	27.6%	1.9%	44.2%	63.5%	81.9%	36.1%	58.9%	.308	.460	78	1.2
2024 DC	BAL	MLB	34	55 (0)	58	4-3	2	61	1.28	4.04	47.5%	7.8%	24.6%	2.9%	41.7%					.305	.546	95	0.4

2023 Arsenal: SL (86.1), SW (82.3), SI (91.1), FA (91.3), KC (80.3), CH (77.6)   Comps: Jake Diekman (66), Aaron Loup (65), Tony Sipp (60)

Who doesn't love an age-33 breakout season? Coulombe spent the better part of a decade bouncing around bullpens as an anonymous back-of-the-roster junky lefty. Then *bang*, he started throwing a cutter nearly 50% of the time and now he's world famous—well, at least he's more famous than before. Better to be recognized when you're old than when you're gone. Coulombe's cutter really is the secret sauce here: He hides it phenomenally from a bizarre, anti-extension release that hitters can't seem to pick up. Relievers are more volatile than Jose Canseco's Twitter feed circa 2013, but Coulombe's 2023 was more than smoke and mirrors.

Shintaro Fujinami   RHP   Born: 04/12/94   Age: 30   Height: 6'6"   Weight: 180   Origin: IFA, 2023

YEAR	TM	LVL	AGE	G (GS)	IP	W-L	SV	K	WHIP	ERA	CSP	BB%	K%	HR%	GB%	ZSw%	ZCon%	OSw%	OCon%	BABIP	SLGCON	DRA-	WARP
2023	OAK	MLB	29	34 (7)	49¹	5-8	0	51	1.66	8.57	47.4%	13.0%	22.1%	2.6%	37.9%	68.9%	76.8%	26.9%	53.6%	.331	.585	106	0.4
2023	BAL	MLB	29	30 (0)	29²	2-0	2	32	1.21	4.85	45.6%	11.9%	25.4%	2.4%	41.6%	73.1%	76.1%	28.7%	65.9%	.243	.506	102	0.3
2024 non	BAL	MLB	30	58 (0)	50	2-2	0	53	1.45	5.14	46.7%	11.5%	23.8%	3.6%	31.8%					.295	.593	113	-0.1

2023 Arsenal: FA (98.5), FS (92.9), FC (88.5), SW (84.4), SL (84.7), SI (95.6), CU (75.4)   Comps: Derek Law (97), Matt Karchner (90), Kyle Barraclough (88)

Mt. Fuji is the quintessential bullpen roller coaster: a flamethrowing, control-seeking specimen equally capable of complete dominance or total catastrophe. Signed by Oakland as a starter last offseason, Fujinami's time in the rotation was hilariously short-lived, as he allowed 24 runs in 15 innings through his first four starts. The O's acquired Fuji at the deadline, buying as low as low has ever been bought, and got a slightly more honed version; the strikeout rate went up and the walk rate went down. There's a closer in here somewhere—fellow Oriole Félix Bautista is really the only other pitcher who throws this hard with this much extension—but for now, Fujinami is the patron saint of bullpen volatility.

DL Hall   LHP   Born: 09/19/98   Age: 25   Height: 6'2"   Weight: 210   Origin: Round 1, 2017 Draft (#21 overall)

YEAR	TM	LVL	AGE	G (GS)	IP	W-L	SV	K	WHIP	ERA	CSP	BB%	K%	HR%	GB%	ZSw%	ZCon%	OSw%	OCon%	BABIP	SLGCON	DRA-	WARP
2021	BOW	AA	22	7 (7)	31²	2-0	0	56	1.01	3.13		12.5%	43.8%	3.1%	59.3%					.240	.556	80	0.6
2022	NOR	AAA	23	22 (18)	76²	3-7	0	125	1.45	4.70		14.2%	36.1%	2.9%	35.5%	75.0%	81.0%	31.7%	46.2%	.327	.625	60	2.6
2022	BAL	MLB	23	11 (1)	13²	1-1	1	19	1.68	5.93	54.2%	9.4%	29.7%	0.0%	46.2%	70.2%	71.2%	34.2%	69.8%	.436	.526	93	0.2
2023	NOR	AAA	24	17 (11)	49	1-2	1	70	1.39	4.22		13.8%	32.3%	3.2%	42.9%	62.7%	76.9%	25.9%	45.1%	.295	.562	81	1.2
2023	BAL	MLB	24	18 (0)	19¹	3-0	0	23	1.19	3.26	45.9%	6.2%	28.4%	2.5%	47.2%	73.2%	76.8%	34.1%	59.5%	.314	.547	83	0.4
2024 DC	BAL	MLB	25	43 (0)	46¹	3-2	0	56	1.32	3.88	48.9%	11.5%	28.0%	2.6%	43.4%					.290	.525	90	0.5

2023 Arsenal: FA (95.8), SL (88.1), CH (85), SW (85.9), CU (81.3)   Comps: Scott Elbert (65), Darwinzon Hernández (64), Josh Hader (63)

Since the dawn of time, baseball prognosticators have been debating whether or not Hall is a starting pitcher. Unfortunately, his 2023 season did little to answer that question. The southpaw was effective, but struggled to throw strikes and experienced a velocity dip in mid-May. The O's sent him back to the complex to regain his strength and health. When Hall returned to the Norfolk Tides in early August, he did so as a reliever—and a particularly effective one. That earned Hall a late-August big-league call, where he tantalized in short stints while the O's hurtled toward October. The good news for Hall: He's almost certainly a valuable arm on this competitive Orioles team. The bad news: Now that the Birds are good, Hall may have run out of time to be a starter. A million things could happen, but the O's are likely to add pitchers in free agency to their already crowded mix, potentially pushing Hall and his electric heater to the bullpen for good. As a reliever, though, he's a real multi-inning weapon, which may answer the starter/reliever question once and for all.

Cole Irvin LHP Born: 01/31/94 Age: 30 Height: 6'4" Weight: 225 Origin: Round 5, 2016 Draft (#137 overall)

YEAR	TM	LVL	AGE	G(GS)	IP	W-L	SV	K	WHIP	ERA	CSP	BB%	K%	HR%	GB%	ZSw%	ZCon%	OSw%	OCon%	BABIP	SLGCON	DRA-	WARP
2021	OAK	MLB	27	32(32)	178¹	10-15	0	125	1.33	4.24	56.0%	5.5%	16.3%	3.0%	37.6%	72.3%	84.4%	35.1%	74.4%	.305	.515	125	-0.7
2022	OAK	MLB	28	30(30)	181	9-13	0	128	1.16	3.98	56.7%	4.9%	17.3%	3.4%	37.0%	71.5%	86.3%	35.8%	68.3%	.274	.510	117	0.2
2023	NOR	AAA	29	9(9)	49¹	6-3	0	30	1.28	4.38		4.2%	14.2%	3.8%	45.0%	65.6%	89.0%	33.6%	79.7%	.286	.515	106	0.6
2023	BAL	MLB	29	24(12)	77¹	1-4	0	68	1.28	4.42	51.6%	6.3%	20.2%	3.3%	41.2%	70.4%	86.5%	35.1%	67.8%	.293	.540	116	0.3
2024 DC	BAL	MLB	30	35(15)	96	5-6	0	66	1.33	4.75	55.0%	5.7%	15.8%	3.3%	37.3%					.296	.533	110	0.3

2023 Arsenal: FA (92.4), SI (91.9), CH (84.2), FC (85.5), SW (77.3), CU (76.1)   *Comps: Dave Roberts (74), Paul Maholm (73), Wade Miley (73)*

No matter how his Baltimore tenure turns out, Irvin will always be the first player acquired for a prospect in the Mike Elias era. The former A's "ace" was straight cheeks for the first few weeks of the season and got sent down to Triple-A pretty swiftly. However, the lefty made a lasting mark on the 2023 Orioles when he ideated (alongside Keegan Akin) the infamous water "homer hose" that the O's used as a home run celebration throughout the year. When Irvin returned from his minor-league rejuvenation in June, he posted a 3.22 ERA and 4.25 FIP, exactly why Baltimore emptied out the farm system for him. Irvin is a valuable bulk boy when healthy, but is unlikely to provide a more lasting contribution than the dong bong. Retire his number.

Seth Johnson RHP Born: 09/19/98 Age: 25 Height: 6'1" Weight: 205 Origin: Round 1, 2019 Draft (#40 overall)

YEAR	TM	LVL	AGE	G(GS)	IP	W-L	SV	K	WHIP	ERA	CSP	BB%	K%	HR%	GB%	ZSw%	ZCon%	OSw%	OCon%	BABIP	SLGCON	DRA-	WARP
2021	CSC	A	22	23(16)	93²	6-6	0	115	1.27	2.88		8.3%	29.0%	1.8%	48.0%					.336	.531	89	1.4
2022	BG	A+	23	7(7)	27	1-1	0	41	1.26	3.00		10.0%	37.3%	3.6%	31.0%					.352	.741	89	0.4
2024 DC	BAL	MLB	25	3(3)	12²	1-1	0	12	1.47	5.25		10.6%	20.5%	3.7%	36.9%					.294	.564	117	0.0

Comps: Austin Ross (39), Enderson Franco (39), Dakota Bacus (39)

The Orioles snagged Johnson from Tampa in the 2022 Trey Mancini deal, even though Johnson was slated for Tommy John surgery. He returned toward the end of 2023 and ran through a quick refresher, making five outings across four different levels. Already 24, Johnson's bizarre pitching timeline—he also converted from the infield in college—means his most likely scenario is an eventual trip to the bullpen. He has a mature fastball and an enticing slider, but as for the other stuff? The developmental clock was already ticking.

Craig Kimbrel RHP Born: 05/28/88 Age: 36 Height: 6'0" Weight: 215 Origin: Round 3, 2008 Draft (#96 overall)

YEAR	TM	LVL	AGE	G(GS)	IP	W-L	SV	K	WHIP	ERA	CSP	BB%	K%	HR%	GB%	ZSw%	ZCon%	OSw%	OCon%	BABIP	SLGCON	DRA-	WARP
2021	CHC	MLB	33	39(0)	36²	2-3	23	64	0.71	0.49	47.9%	9.5%	46.7%	0.7%	33.3%	60.8%	72.5%	36.2%	37.8%	.203	.305	72	0.9
2021	CHW	MLB	33	24(0)	23	2-2	1	36	1.22	5.09	49.3%	10.2%	36.7%	5.1%	26.5%	67.3%	75.8%	32.2%	37.7%	.295	.809	80	0.5
2022	LAD	MLB	34	63(0)	60	6-7	22	72	1.32	3.75	52.8%	10.8%	27.7%	1.5%	38.7%	67.3%	81.1%	29.9%	54.7%	.313	.516	97	0.7
2023	PHI	MLB	35	71(0)	69	8-6	23	94	1.04	3.26	47.1%	10.1%	33.8%	3.6%	34.2%	67.6%	75.9%	29.9%	49.7%	.239	.550	81	1.5
2024 DC	BAL	MLB	36	49(0)	52	3-6	35	66	1.23	3.87	48.8%	10.6%	30.0%	3.7%	33.8%					.273	.591	91	0.5

2023 Arsenal: FA (95.9), KC (86.3), SW (85.2), CH (89.3)   *Comps: Kenley Jansen (91), Aroldis Chapman (85), Armando Benitez (83)*

Old dog, new tricks: A reborn Kimbrel achieved more extension and spin on his (once) legendary two-pitch arsenal, helping flatten out his fastball a smidge and add depth to his legendary curve. The results weren't astounding, at least not compared to the olden days. Nevertheless, pitching coach Caleb Cotham and the Phillies turned back Kimbrel's clock farther than the Dodgers (often lauded for the ability to "fix" players) could do, at least until October's dying days. This is a career in its twilight, but it's an illustrious career with an historic trajectory that, despite very recently appearing kaput, retains a flicker of hope. Father Time takes no prisoners, but Kimbrel may have bought his Hall of Fame aspirations a new lease on life. Then again, he may have made a deal with the devil, given his horribly—in the eyes of some Phillies fans, unforgivably—ill-timed postseason implosion. The Orioles still believe, though, signing him to help cover the loss of Félix Bautista to injury.

Dean Kremer RHP Born: 01/07/96 Age: 28 Height: 6'2" Weight: 210 Origin: Round 14, 2016 Draft (#431 overall)

YEAR	TM	LVL	AGE	G(GS)	IP	W-L	SV	K	WHIP	ERA	CSP	BB%	K%	HR%	GB%	ZSw%	ZCon%	OSw%	OCon%	BABIP	SLGCON	DRA-	WARP
2021	NOR	AAA	25	17(13)	62¹	1-5	0	69	1.30	4.91		7.4%	25.6%	3.3%	46.6%					.313	.590	87	1.2
2021	BAL	MLB	25	13(13)	53²	0-7	0	47	1.64	7.55	57.9%	10.2%	19.2%	6.9%	30.2%	69.4%	87.7%	27.2%	64.1%	.297	.751	141	-0.6
2022	NOR	AAA	26	2(2)	7	0-0	0	13	0.43	0.00		8.0%	52.0%	0.0%	44.4%					.111	.222	75	0.2
2022	BAL	MLB	26	22(21)	125¹	8-7	0	87	1.25	3.23	55.2%	6.6%	17.0%	2.1%	39.2%	69.7%	86.6%	36.4%	65.3%	.300	.479	107	0.8
2023	BAL	MLB	27	32(32)	172²	13-5	0	157	1.31	4.12	47.9%	7.5%	21.4%	3.7%	39.8%	70.5%	83.6%	31.2%	63.6%	.293	.543	102	1.8
2024 DC	BAL	MLB	28	29(29)	157¹	9-10	0	139	1.36	4.62	51.3%	7.9%	20.4%	3.2%	38.6%					.302	.551	106	0.9

2023 Arsenal: FA (94.6), FC (88.7), SI (91.9), CH (85.3), CU (78.1), SW (83.1)   *Comps: Chase De Jong (62), Kyle Gibson (60), Hector Noesí (59)*

Kremer added a sinker in 2023 that was decently effective at inducing soft contact and also allowed his four-seam fastball to play up a tick. That new offering was instrumental in allowing him to post a career high in starts and innings; only sentient pitching machine Kyle Gibson threw more often for the O's. Kremer remains a respectable back-of-the-rotation option, but his lack of a wipeout secondary limits his ceiling and proved to be his downfall in the decisive third game of the ALDS. Because he doesn't have an intimidating breaker, Kremer has to be pinpoint-accurate with his fastball command to get outs against the game's best lineups. With Gibson gone in free agency, Kremer could step into that innings-eater role, but the Orioles should avoid a situation where he's relied upon to start in October, unless they can help him develop a more get-out-of-jail-free off-speed pitch.

Chayce McDermott RHP   Born: 08/22/98   Age: 25   Height: 6'3"   Weight: 197   Origin: Round 4C, 2021 Draft (#132 overall)

YEAR	TM	LVL	AGE	G (GS)	IP	W-L	SV	K	WHIP	ERA	CSP	BB%	K%	HR%	GB%	ZSw%	ZCon%	OSw%	OCon%	BABIP	SLGCON	DRA-	WARP
2021	FAY	A	22	6(4)	18¹	0-0	0	33	1.15	3.44		13.5%	44.6%	4.1%	45.2%					.286	.710	80	0.3
2022	ASH	A+	23	19(10)	72	6-1	0	114	1.39	5.50		13.4%	35.4%	2.8%	46.2%					.318	.608	79	1.4
2022	BOW	AA	23	6(6)	26²	1-1	0	36	1.39	6.07		17.4%	31.3%	6.1%	35.6%					.192	.797	92	0.5
2023	BOW	AA	24	16(14)	68¹	5-6	1	88	1.26	3.56		15.3%	30.7%	2.1%	33.8%					.243	.461	88	1.4
2023	NOR	AAA	24	10(8)	50²	3-2	0	64	1.01	2.49		11.7%	31.2%	1.5%	32.7%	67.0%	79.3%	29.6%	47.0%	.218	.422	81	1.3
2024 DC	BAL	MLB	25	6(6)	27	1-2	0	31	1.48	4.99		13.8%	25.9%	3.6%	34.7%					.282	.583	111	0.1

2023 Arsenal: FA (94), SL (83.9), SW (81.4), CU (76), CH (84.5)   Comps: Kyle McPherson (73), A.J. Griffin (72), Mike Baumann (71)

Another high-carry heater in a system full of high-carry heaters. McDermott's fastball command still leaves much to be desired, but his two distinct secondary breakers enabled a spectacular 2023 season despite a pretty gaudy walk rate. If you like him, he's a potential mid-rotation starter with three plus pitches who'll grow into his body and learn how to locate the heater. If you don't, you're betting the lack of fastball command eventually pushes him to the bullpen, where he'll rack up swings and misses in short, tightrope stints.

John Means LHP   Born: 04/24/93   Age: 31   Height: 6'4"   Weight: 230   Origin: Round 11, 2014 Draft (#331 overall)

YEAR	TM	LVL	AGE	G (GS)	IP	W-L	SV	K	WHIP	ERA	CSP	BB%	K%	HR%	GB%	ZSw%	ZCon%	OSw%	OCon%	BABIP	SLGCON	DRA-	WARP
2021	BAL	MLB	28	26(26)	146²	6-9	0	134	1.03	3.62	54.4%	4.4%	22.7%	5.1%	32.6%	73.4%	76.4%	32.8%	71.4%	.241	.563	112	0.5
2022	BAL	MLB	29	2(2)	8	0-0	0	7	1.25	3.38	53.2%	5.9%	20.6%	0.0%	36.0%	79.7%	85.1%	34.2%	69.2%	.320	.375	114	0.0
2023	BOW	AA	30	3(3)	7¹	0-1	0	10	1.09	6.14		6.5%	32.3%	3.2%	55.6%					.294	.611	78	0.2
2023	NOR	AAA	30	3(3)	14¹	1-0	0	12	1.19	2.51		10.3%	20.7%	1.7%	38.5%	75.8%	75.0%	28.5%	62.2%	.263	.410	97	0.2
2023	BAL	MLB	30	4(4)	23²	1-2	0	10	0.72	2.66	50.1%	4.5%	11.4%	4.5%	28.8%	72.4%	87.6%	36.6%	78.9%	.130	.403	138	-0.2
2024 DC	BAL	MLB	31	28(28)	151¹	9-9	0	118	1.29	4.43	51.6%	6.2%	18.3%	3.2%	33.6%					.293	.537	104	1.1

2023 Arsenal: FA (91.8), CH (81), SL (85.7), KC (77.9)   Comps: Matthew Boyd (49), Dallas Keuchel (49), Anthony DeSclafani (47)

Means' extended journey back from Tommy John was a grave reminder that the reconstructive elbow surgery is far from a magic bullet. The affable lefty went under the knife in April 2022, but a variety of setbacks kept Means off a big league mound until early September 2023. Much changed about the Orioles over those 17 months, with the team transforming from a laughing stock to a plucky Cinderella to an AL East frontrunner. But when Means finally returned, he looked like the same reliable, unspectacular no. 3 starter he'd been before the layoff, minus the strikeouts. A bout of elbow soreness bumped Means from a playoff start (and off the playoff roster altogether), but there are no indications that's a lingering issue to worry about. He's a ball-in-play machine, which given the new Camden Yards dimensions, is a more feasible plan than the last time he pitched a full season.

Cionel Pérez LHP   Born: 04/21/96   Age: 28   Height: 6'0"   Weight: 175   Origin: IFA, 2016

YEAR	TM	LVL	AGE	G (GS)	IP	W-L	SV	K	WHIP	ERA	CSP	BB%	K%	HR%	GB%	ZSw%	ZCon%	OSw%	OCon%	BABIP	SLGCON	DRA-	WARP
2021	LOU	AAA	25	31(0)	30¹	1-2	2	41	1.29	3.26		10.1%	31.8%	0.8%	49.3%					.342	.473	79	0.7
2021	CIN	MLB	25	25(0)	24	1-2	0	25	1.71	6.37	54.2%	18.0%	22.5%	4.5%	51.5%	65.4%	80.3%	22.2%	49.2%	.262	.615	101	0.2
2022	BAL	MLB	26	66(0)	57²	7-1	1	55	1.16	1.40	55.2%	9.0%	23.5%	0.9%	51.0%	67.2%	84.0%	32.1%	53.4%	.284	.377	89	0.9
2023	BAL	MLB	27	65(0)	53¹	4-2	3	44	1.56	3.54	48.7%	10.9%	17.8%	0.8%	60.5%	67.0%	87.9%	29.3%	65.5%	.323	.429	95	0.8
2024 DC	BAL	MLB	28	49(0)	52	3-2	0	45	1.43	4.32	51.6%	10.7%	19.4%	1.9%	54.4%					.298	.465	97	0.3

2023 Arsenal: SI (96.4), SW (83.9), FA (97), CU (83.8)   Comps: Kyle Ryan (52), Chasen Shreve (51), Scott Elbert (48)

It was a tale of two seasons for the skinny Cuban lefty. Pérez tinkered with a curveball in the first half and it went very poorly. He fell down Brandon Hyde's "how much do I trust this guy" ranking and looked like a candidate to be jettisoned off the roster. Then he came back from some forearm soreness in late July and posted a 1.64 ERA with nearly a K an inning in his last 31 appearances. Why? He stopped throwing the curveball and leaned more on his high-90s sinker. He's the best lefty in Baltimore's bullpen.

Alex Pham RHP   Born: 10/09/99   Age: 24   Height: 5'11"   Weight: 165   Origin: Round 19, 2021 Draft (#557 overall)

YEAR	TM	LVL	AGE	G (GS)	IP	W-L	SV	K	WHIP	ERA	CSP	BB%	K%	HR%	GB%	ZSw%	ZCon%	OSw%	OCon%	BABIP	SLGCON	DRA-	WARP
2021	DEL	A	21	3(0)	5	2-0	0	5	0.60	0.00		0.0%	27.8%	0.0%	38.5%					.231	.308	107	0.0
2022	DEL	A	22	6(0)	11¹	0-0	2	15	1.32	1.59		14.3%	30.6%	0.0%	51.9%					.296	.370	104	0.1
2022	ABD	A+	22	11(0)	20²	5-2	0	30	1.40	5.66		12.6%	34.5%	2.3%	50.0%					.364	.651	90	0.3
2023	ABD	A+	23	12(10)	51¹	3-3	0	76	1.05	2.45		12.1%	36.7%	2.4%	37.1%					.240	.490	90	0.6
2023	BOW	AA	23	14(9)	60²	0-2	1	54	0.99	2.67		7.2%	23.0%	2.1%	44.5%					.239	.390	92	1.1
2024 non	BAL	MLB	24	58(0)	50	2-2	0	48	1.51	5.38		11.1%	21.7%	3.8%	37.2%					.303	.595	118	-0.2

Comps: Drew Anderson (65), Walker Lockett (63), Luis Castillo (62)

Pham is a short, twitchy, senior sign whose breakout caught the eye of many scouts in 2023 thanks to a 2.57 ERA and 10.4 K/9 in 112 innings. He's also the exact sum of his parts; nothing wows you, nothing worries you. A short arm action creates tons of deception and allows Pham's four pitches to play up. Even though the fastball can reach 95 at times, that's not what draws the eye; he simply doesn't beat himself by making bad pitches. He's an athletic pitcher who knows how to mix his arsenal and should carve out a nice big-league career as a back-end bulk guy/swingman. Easy to watch, easy to like.

Cade Povich LHP Born: 04/12/00 Age: 24 Height: 6'3" Weight: 185 Origin: Round 3, 2021 Draft (#98 overall)

YEAR	TM	LVL	AGE	G(GS)	IP	W-L	SV	K	WHIP	ERA	CSP	BB%	K%	HR%	GB%	ZSw%	ZCon%	OSw%	OCon%	BABIP	SLGCON	DRA-	WARP
2021	FTM	A	21	3(2)	8	0-0	0	16	1.00	1.13		5.7%	45.7%	0.0%	33.3%	59.5%	63.6%	24.5%	76.9%	.400	.667	91	0.1
2022	CR	A+	22	16(16)	78²	6-8	0	107	1.23	4.46		7.7%	31.8%	2.7%	44.5%					.326	.602	83	1.5
2022	ABD	A+	22	2(2)	12	2-0	0	15	0.50	0.00		4.8%	35.7%	0.0%	45.8%					.167	.167	86	0.2
2022	BOW	AA	22	6(5)	23¹	2-2	0	26	1.37	6.94		10.7%	25.2%	4.9%	39.4%					.267	.615	88	0.4
2023	BOW	AA	23	18(18)	81¹	6-7	0	118	1.36	4.87		10.5%	33.4%	3.4%	43.8%					.343	.668	72	2.3
2023	NOR	AAA	23	10(10)	45¹	2-3	0	53	1.35	5.36		14.7%	26.9%	3.0%	42.1%	61.0%	78.7%	27.5%	56.8%	.241	.482	89	0.8
2024 DC	BAL	MLB	24	6(6)	27	1-2	0	29	1.41	4.77		11.0%	24.2%	3.5%	37.2%					.292	.566	108	0.1

2023 Arsenal: FA (93.8), FC (89.9), CH (84.4), SW (81), CU (77)　　　　Comps: Eric Lauer (76), Sean Nolin (74), Nick Pivetta (69)

During the 2022 deadline, the O's traded away All-Star closer Jorge López to Minnesota for a smorgasbord of pitching prospects, including Povich. At the time, it seemed like GM Mike Elias was being too conservative, too pessimistic about his present and too rosy about his future. But then every single thing about that trade went perfectly, including Povich's ascension up Baltimore prospect lists as perhaps the best pitcher in a farm full of bats. Povich might have three legit plus secondaries—slider, curve, change—which obscure a relatively meh fastball. Thankfully, Povich throws with his left hand. If the heater shape, speed or command take a step forward, this is a pitchability southpaw who could work in the middle of a rotation. If the fastball is dried in cement, he's more of a back-end type.

Grayson Rodriguez RHP Born: 11/16/99 Age: 24 Height: 6'5" Weight: 230 Origin: Round 1, 2018 Draft (#11 overall)

YEAR	TM	LVL	AGE	G(GS)	IP	W-L	SV	K	WHIP	ERA	CSP	BB%	K%	HR%	GB%	ZSw%	ZCon%	OSw%	OCon%	BABIP	SLGCON	DRA-	WARP
2021	ABD	A+	21	5(5)	23¹	3-0	0	40	0.69	1.54		5.7%	45.5%	2.3%	42.5%					.237	.450	69	0.6
2021	BOW	AA	21	18(18)	79²	6-1	0	121	0.87	2.60		7.1%	39.0%	2.6%	37.8%					.252	.534	83	1.4
2022	NOR	AAA	22	14(14)	69²	6-1	0	97	0.93	2.20		7.7%	35.8%	0.7%	42.1%	60.6%	74.4%	42.2%	46.5%	.280	.433	58	2.5
2023	NOR	AAA	23	8(8)	41¹	4-0	0	56	1.09	1.96		11.2%	33.1%	2.4%	47.3%	69.1%	73.4%	35.8%	49.6%	.250	.478	76	1.2
2023	BAL	MLB	23	23(23)	122	7-4	0	129	1.34	4.35	48.9%	8.2%	25.0%	3.1%	46.9%	70.0%	83.1%	35.0%	58.8%	.323	.577	86	2.4
2024 DC	BAL	MLB	24	29(29)	157¹	10-8	0	167	1.21	3.34	48.9%	8.9%	25.4%	2.4%	45.5%					.283	.491	80	3.1

2023 Arsenal: FA (97.5), CH (84), SW (82.3), CU (80), FC (90.1)　　　　Comps: Luis Severino (63), Drew Hutchison (63), Archie Bradley (63)

You can divide Rodriguez's debut season into four distinct chapters. He debuted on April 5 and for two months performed like a batting-cage pitching machine, posting a catastrophic 7.35 ERA in his first 10 starts with the highest hard-hit rate in MLB. Then he went back to Triple-A, made a few mechanical adjustments and returned to the Orioles in late July with a rejuvenated upper 90s heater. From that point until the end of the regular season "G-Rod" was sensational, posting a 2.58 ERA and a 2.76 FIP in 13 starts. Then, against the Rangers in ALDS Game 2, a pumped-up Rodriguez was allergic to the strike zone, walking four and allowing five runs while recording just five outs in Baltimore's season-defining 11-8 loss. But the current outlook is undeniably positive. One overexcited afternoon in October did not undo the immense strides made by Rodriguez during the latter half of the season. He started Game 2 of a playoff series as a 24-year-old rookie for a reason—well, two reasons. The Orioles didn't have enough starting pitching. The current shape of Rodriguez's fastball might limit him from ever becoming a true, *take your lunch money, shove your head down the toilet* type of ace, but there's enough else here to feel optimistic about him becoming a rotation stalwart in Baltimore.

Jacob Webb RHP Born: 08/15/93 Age: 30 Height: 6'2" Weight: 210 Origin: Round 18, 2014 Draft (#553 overall)

YEAR	TM	LVL	AGE	G(GS)	IP	W-L	SV	K	WHIP	ERA	CSP	BB%	K%	HR%	GB%	ZSw%	ZCon%	OSw%	OCon%	BABIP	SLGCON	DRA-	WARP
2021	GWN	AAA	27	24(0)	24	1-2	6	34	1.00	3.00		7.1%	34.3%	2.0%	42.1%					.278	.519	76	0.6
2021	ATL	MLB	27	34(0)	34¹	5-4	1	33	1.51	4.19	53.0%	9.2%	21.6%	2.6%	34.3%	75.8%	75.7%	39.4%	60.3%	.340	.583	109	0.2
2022	RNO	AAA	28	6(0)	5¹	0-0	0	7	2.06	10.13		11.5%	26.9%	3.8%	37.5%	62.2%	78.6%	33.9%	70.0%	.467	.812	89	0.1
2022	GWN	AAA	28	28(0)	30¹	2-3	3	35	0.99	5.34		5.0%	28.9%	3.3%	41.0%	73.3%	72.7%	35.7%	40.0%	.270	.564	81	0.7
2023	SL	AAA	29	16(1)	17¹	1-3	1	21	1.85	6.75		14.0%	24.4%	0.0%	40.4%	73.2%	77.9%	33.3%	54.7%	.392	.529	94	0.2
2023	LAA	MLB	29	29(0)	31²	1-1	1	34	1.36	3.98	44.8%	14.3%	24.3%	4.3%	36.9%	66.1%	78.5%	31.8%	57.1%	.221	.566	102	0.3
2023	BAL	MLB	29	25(0)	22	0-0	0	23	1.18	3.27	46.4%	10.9%	25.0%	0.0%	36.8%	78.1%	71.2%	45.5%	59.0%	.281	.393	100	0.3
2024 DC	BAL	MLB	30	49(0)	52	3-2	0	58	1.30	4.24	47.5%	9.9%	25.7%	3.3%	37.3%					.287	.564	98	0.3

2023 Arsenal: FA (94.8), CH (85.8), SW (83.9)　　　　Comps: Derek Law (71), Kevin Quackenbush (70), Austin Brice (69)

The juggernaut, pitching-loaded Los Angeles Angels (can you smell the sarcasm?) designated Webb for assignment on August 5 despite a totally respectable 113 ERA+. There was a bit of FIP magic involved there, but still, it's not like the Angels were swimming in lockdown relievers. So the O's, at the time somewhat bereft of healthy arms, scooped Webb up and he was sensational down the stretch. Yes, he gave up the backbreaking Mitch Garver grand slam on the first pitch he threw in ALDS Game 2, but Webb's fastball has above-average velocity and shape, which allow his two more pedestrian off-speed pitches to work. He's a non-embarrassing low-leverage bullpen option.

Tyler Wells RHP   Born: 08/26/94   Age: 29   Height: 6'8"   Weight: 260   Origin: Round 15, 2016 Draft (#453 overall)

YEAR	TM	LVL	AGE	G (GS)	IP	W-L	SV	K	WHIP	ERA	CSP	BB%	K%	HR%	GB%	ZSw%	ZCon%	OSw%	OCon%	BABIP	SLGCON	DRA-	WARP
2021	BAL	MLB	26	44 (0)	57	2-3	4	65	0.91	4.11	57.0%	5.4%	29.0%	4.0%	21.2%	73.1%	77.6%	40.8%	63.4%	.228	.531	99	0.6
2022	BAL	MLB	27	23 (23)	103²	7-7	0	76	1.14	4.25	55.2%	6.6%	18.0%	3.8%	36.6%	70.9%	82.3%	35.7%	64.2%	.247	.505	107	0.6
2023	BOW	AA	28	3 (3)	8²	0-0	0	7	1.04	3.12		8.6%	20.0%	5.7%	20.0%					.174	.542	111	0.1
2023	NOR	AAA	28	7 (0)	6	0-0	1	7	1.83	9.00		13.8%	24.1%	3.4%	38.9%	58.7%	77.8%	33.3%	47.8%	.353	.722	93	0.1
2023	BAL	MLB	28	25 (20)	118²	7-6	1	117	0.99	3.64	46.9%	7.2%	24.9%	5.3%	32.4%	68.4%	81.6%	32.6%	62.3%	.200	.567	109	0.9
2024 DC	*BAL*	*MLB*	*29*	*42 (16)*	*114²*	*7-6*	*0*	*107*	*1.26*	*4.21*	*51.2%*	*7.7%*	*22.2%*	*3.7%*	*32.5%*					*.282*	*.561*	*99*	*0.9*

2023 Arsenal: FA (92.8), FC (88.7), CH (85.5), SL (84.2), CU (74.5), SW (86.3)   *Comps: Felipe Paulino (56), Garrett Richards (54), Matt Garza (54)*

Wells had perhaps the single weirdest season of any big-league hurler. During the first half, the lanky Oklahoman was bizarrely (and unsustainably) effective, slapping together a league-leading 0.93 WHIP with a bottom-five 1.81 HR/9 to post a 3.18 ERA across 104 ⅔ innings. Sure, opponents had a hilarious .202 batting average on balls in play, but Wells was solidifying himself as a flawed but useful pitcher. Then, during a three-start stretch directly following the All-Star Break, the bottom fell out. The fastball command evaporated and Wells, who'd already reached a career high in innings, was sent to Triple-A for some R&R. There, he de-loaded into a relief role and returned to Baltimore in September as a member of the bullpen. Across seven scoreless outings—four down the stretch and in all three games of the ALDS—Wells the Reliever was masterful. The heater velocity ticked up and he allowed just two of the 27 batters he faced to reach base. With Félix Bautista out for 2024 there's a chance the O's commit to Wells—the only person in the clubhouse who physically looks the closer eye-to-eye—as a late-inning replacement.

LINEOUTS

Hitters

HITTER	POS	TM	LVL	AGE	PA	R	HR	RBI	SB	AVG/OBP/SLG	BABIP	SLGCON	BB%	K%	ZSw%	ZCon%	OSw%	OCon%	LA	90th EV	DRC+	BRR	DRP	WARP
Dylan Beavers	OF	ABD	A+	21	369	46	9	48	22	.273/.369/.463	.338	.634	13.6%	22.8%							117	-0.6	-4.6	1.4
	OF	BOW	AA	21	157	29	2	12	5	.321/.417/.478	.410	.627	12.7%	20.4%							105	0.2	0.1	0.6
Frederick Bencosme	MI	ABD	A+	20	476	60	2	49	28	.246/.338/.319	.288	.380	11.6%	14.1%							109	1.8	-3.6	1.6
Billy Cook	UT	MSS	WIN	24	81	8	4	13	2	.215/.358/.462	.278	.769	16.0%	32.1%	53.8%	85.7%	27.6%	37.5%						
	UT	BOW	AA	24	501	64	24	81	30	.251/.320/.456	.290	.634	8.4%	25.0%							106	0.5	11.0	2.8
Hudson Haskin	CF	NOR	AAA	24	95	14	3	13	5	.268/.368/.463	.422	.792	6.3%	35.8%	66.7%	79.4%	37.0%	48.7%			87	0.2	-0.3	0.1
Sam Hilliard	OF	ATL	MLB	29	78	15	3	6	4	.236/.295/.431	.389	.795	7.7%	42.3%	64.5%	68.1%	26.3%	37.8%	19.8	110.1	64	0.2	0.1	0.0
Mac Horvath	IF	DEL	A	21	64	11	2	5	9	.308/.422/.500	.412	.743	15.6%	26.6%							104	0.4	0.5	0.3
Josh Lester	3B	NOR	AAA	28	470	62	23	87	2	.257/.307/.475	.302	.661	6.6%	26.0%	73.4%	83.7%	38.1%	47.8%			90	0.5	4.8	1.4
	3B	BAL	MLB	28	23	0	0	4	0	.182/.217/.182	.267	.267	4.3%	30.4%	60.5%	82.6%	42.6%	56.5%	-1.8	102.7	78	0.0	0.0	0.0
Michael Perez	C	SYR	AAA	30	270	27	9	27	0	.204/.309/.352	.488	.488	12.6%	23.7%	67.2%	85.4%	32.3%	58.6%			88	-1.0	-1.6	0.3
	C	NYM	MLB	30	8	1	0	0	0	.500/.500/.625	.571	.714	0.0%	12.5%	66.7%	100.0%	35.3%	66.7%	16.3	109.1	97	0.1	0.0	0.0
Kyle Stowers	OF	NOR	AAA	25	283	42	17	49	3	.245/.364/.511	.278	.758	14.1%	26.9%	77.0%	77.8%	30.7%	39.8%			106	-2.1	3.8	1.0
	OF	BAL	MLB	25	33	1	0	0	0	.067/.152/.067	.111	.111	9.1%	36.4%	75.5%	75.7%	37.7%	46.2%	16.7	104.6	70	-0.1	-0.2	-0.1
Braylin Tavera	OF	ORI	ROK	18	133	15	4	20	13	.262/.391/.421	.293	.536	16.5%	17.3%	50.0%	50.0%	21.4%	33.3%						
Terrin Vavra	RF	NOR	AAA	26	68	12	2	9	2	.333/.382/.524	.396	.660	4.4%	19.1%	81.3%	74.0%	29.9%	63.2%			101	-0.7	0.2	0.2
	RF	BAL	MLB	26	56	9	0	5	1	.245/.315/.245	.324	.324	8.9%	21.4%	78.1%	80.0%	31.9%	56.8%	6.2	102.0	91	0.0	-0.7	0.0
Max Wagner	3B/2B	ABD	A+	21	360	60	10	36	26	.234/.356/.401	.297	.574	14.2%	25.0%							109	2.2	-2.9	1.6
	3B/2B	BOW	AA	21	119	16	3	18	1	.252/.303/.414	.338	.597	5.9%	28.6%							85	0.9	1.0	0.2

Dylan Beavers is a solid weeknight meal missing an ingredient. He's not suited for center, and not powerful enough for a corner. He's in an environment that will make the most out of his skillset, but at the same time, he might just be a chicken nugget in an organization full of steak.   ⚾ **Frederick Bencosme** was a pick to click before the 2023 season, but failed to showcase any significant power. For now, he's an up-down utility type who can pick it pretty well at a few different spots.   ⚾ A 24-year-old pull-heavy power bat in a system overflowing with them, **Billy Cook** generates a lot of power from a wide stance that relies a bit too much on his upper half and somewhat limits the rest of his offensive game. Before long, the O's will trade him for the 19-year-old version of himself, in case that one breaks out.   ⚾ A great runner who suffered from a bunch of lower body injuries that washed out most of his 2023 season, **Hudson Haskin** went unselected in the Rule 5 draft. His bat needs to take a small step forward if he's to fulfill his fate as a stereotypical fifth outfielder.   ⚾ A DRC+ in the 60s, earned with a strikeout rate in the 40s against a walk rate in the single digits, will make it very difficult to stick around the majors for long. This is the predicament into which **Sam Hilliard** played himself, and which it'll take a big change to escape.   ⚾ There wasn't too much new to glean from **Mac Horvath's** brief 99 plate appearance sample. He's another prototypical Orioles draftee: a college slugger with good swing decisions who can drive the baseball in the air to the pull side, but lacks an obvious defensive home. Take a drink.   ⚾ Utility journeyman **Josh Lester** went 4-for-22 in the bigs last year. He has some fun exit velocity numbers, but besides a Triple-A Home Run Derby there's not much to see here unless he commits to chasing down Mike Hessman for the all-time lead in International League homers.   ⚾ **Michael Perez** saw his major-league playing time dwindle last year. Catch-and-throw backstops without much bat now seem to be more likely to be a third or fourth catcher in an organization, rather than playing second fiddle.   ⚾ **Kyle Stowers** was one of the few O's prospects whose stock declined in 2023. The bleach-blonde surfer-haired outfielder made the Opening Day roster, then spent April collecting strikeouts like it was a hobby before making his permanent residence in Norfolk.   ⚾ **Braylin Tavera** was a big-money bonus guy out of the Dominican Republic in 2021 who emerged from the fray at Baltimore's Florida Complex last season. A wiry, athletic outfielder with an advanced approach and power projection, he's done nothing to dispel his early buzz.   ⚾ A strained right shoulder limited **Terrin Vavra** to just 43 games across three levels in what was a key year for the light-hitting utility man. Barring a devastating outbreak of mumps among the O's infield, Vavra's lasting contribution to the MLB world may be the inspiration for a mythical, since-deleted Foolish Baseball tweet.   ⚾ **Max Wagner** exploded up draft boards in 2022 with a 27-dinger season at Clemson that got him picked in the second round as a draft-eligible sophomore. It's a delightfully smooth swing that's fun to watch and easy to like, but Wagner failed to seperate himself from the pack offensively in 2023. Some guys just need to repeat a level.

Pitchers

PITCHER	TM	LVL	AGE	G (GS)	IP	W-L	SV	K	WHIP	ERA	CSP	BB%	K%	HR%	GB%	ZSw%	ZCon%	OSw%	OCon%	BABIP	SLGCON	DRA-	WARP
Keegan Akin	NOR	AAA	28	5 (1)	8	0-0	0	14	0.25	1.13		3.8%	53.8%	3.8%	36.4%	62.2%	57.1%	41.9%	42.3%	.000	.364	82	0.2
	BAL	MLB	28	24 (1)	23²	2-2	0	27	1.77	6.85	52.1%	6.3%	24.1%	1.8%	34.6%	67.1%	82.3%	39.0%	64.9%	.434	.662	92	0.4
Justin Armbruester	BOW	AA	24	12 (12)	62	3-2	0	43	1.15	2.47		7.5%	17.1%	2.0%	31.0%					.260	.438	124	0.2
	NOR	AAA	24	14 (13)	59¹	3-4	0	66	1.47	4.70		12.1%	24.9%	3.4%	31.1%	67.7%	78.4%	35.8%	62.8%	.291	.594	101	0.7
Trace Bright	ABD	A+	22	22 (18)	82²	2-6	0	127	1.33	4.35		13.2%	35.0%	2.2%	37.6%					.314	.579	80	1.4
	BOW	AA	22	4 (3)	17	1-0	0	20	1.24	2.12		11.3%	28.2%	1.4%	50.0%					.293	.415	85	0.4
Tucker Davidson	KC	MLB	27	20 (1)	19²	0-1	0	15	1.42	5.03	45.7%	9.1%	17.0%	4.5%	38.7%	70.6%	88.3%	32.8%	62.3%	.281	.590	103	0.2
	LAA	MLB	27	18 (0)	31²	1-1	2	31	1.74	6.54	47.2%	7.4%	20.9%	1.4%	47.1%	61.3%	87.5%	35.5%	61.5%	.416	.627	99	0.4
Luis De León	ORI	ROK	20	6 (6)	27¹	2-0	0	36	1.35	1.65		12.0%	30.8%	0.0%	64.1%					.359	.453		0.4
	DEL	A	20	9 (5)	26¹	3-1	0	31	1.25	2.39		14.2%	27.4%	0.0%	73.8%					.262	.277	86	0.4
Mychal Givens	NOR	AAA	33	8 (0)	8²	0-0	0	7	1.27	7.27		10.5%	18.4%	5.3%	40.0%	57.7%	75.6%	20.3%	61.5%	.217	.520	107	0.1
	BAL	MLB	33	6 (0)	4	0-1	0	2	2.50	11.25	43.0%	27.3%	9.1%	0.0%	46.2%	77.1%	88.9%	27.8%	80.0%	.308	.417	113	0.0
Jonathan Heasley	OMA	AAA	26	32 (15)	94²	2-5	1	88	1.62	6.85		10.5%	20.5%	4.7%	38.1%	68.2%	82.1%	31.3%	59.9%	.321	.720	110	0.7
	KC	MLB	26	12 (0)	15	0-0	0	9	1.27	7.20	50.3%	3.2%	14.3%	7.9%	25.5%	75.6%	80.9%	35.1%	69.6%	.261	.720	119	0.0
Joey Krehbiel	NOR	AAA	30	35 (0)	39¹	1-1	3	32	1.58	3.89		14.2%	18.2%	4.0%	46.6%	68.3%	83.9%	31.0%	59.3%	.270	.534	108	0.4
	BAL	MLB	30	6 (0)	5	1-0	0	5	0.80	1.80	46.9%	10.5%	26.3%	5.3%	25.0%	57.1%	95.0%	20.0%	33.3%	.091	.500	99	0.1
Dillon Tate	NOR	AAA	29	8 (0)	6²	0-1	0	6	3.00	13.50		20.0%	15.0%	0.0%	37.5%	67.3%	86.5%	20.6%	50.0%	.500	.625	129	0.0
Peter Van Loon	BOW	AA	24	18 (11)	53²	2-7	1	70	1.49	6.04		9.5%	29.0%	5.0%	32.4%					.344	.750	92	1.0
Nick Vespi	NOR	AAA	27	36 (0)	38²	4-0	7	41	1.14	2.33		8.4%	26.5%	1.9%	45.5%	72.7%	78.9%	33.2%	44.4%	.286	.515	86	0.8
	BAL	MLB	27	9 (0)	14¹	1-0	0	9	1.23	4.30	48.6%	3.4%	15.3%	3.4%	46.8%	70.8%	92.1%	34.5%	61.5%	.311	.596	103	0.2
Austin Voth	NOR	AAA	31	9 (3)	15¹	0-0	0	20	1.89	5.28		12.3%	27.4%	1.4%	40.9%	62.5%	77.3%	35.5%	61.4%	.442	.636	80	0.4
	BAL	MLB	31	25 (0)	34²	1-2	0	34	1.56	5.19	46.0%	9.4%	21.3%	3.8%	33.3%	67.0%	82.3%	33.6%	66.7%	.327	.604	106	0.3
Bruce Zimmermann	NOR	AAA	28	21 (21)	99²	4-7	0	110	1.55	4.42		8.7%	24.6%	1.1%	45.5%	71.0%	81.9%	35.0%	49.1%	.378	.551	85	2.4
	BAL	MLB	28	7 (0)	13¹	2-0	0	14	1.28	4.72	47.2%	0.0%	23.0%	4.9%	48.9%	73.3%	84.1%	38.8%	48.0%	.333	.659	91	0.2

It was a waste of a year for the fire-hydrant lefty **Keegan Akin**, who pitched poorly before a back issue sidelined him for the entire second half. If healthy, he's bullpen depth; if unhealthy, he's a West Michigan University alum who loves hunting in his free time. ⓧ **Justin Armbruester** has a potentially special high-ride fastball with tons of vertical movement. If he can just charge up that heater up from his 92.4 mph average in 2023, it could be a real weapon in the Tyler Wells mold. ⓧ **Jackson Baumeister** never made it all click during his two years at Florida State, but the Orioles liked his potential and athleticism enough to pop him 63rd overall in the 2023 draft. The six-foot-four righty has phenomenal lower-half flexibility which allows for a unique low-release fastball that has tons of carry. ⓧ Fifth-rounder **Trace Bright's** high-ride heater and overhand curve could have rocketed him up the system as a reliever. Instead, the O's opted to develop the lanky righty as a starter, yielding decent results in '23. ⓧ Following stints with the Angels and Royals after being cast off by the Braves, **Tucker Davidson** finally landed with a club that shares his interest in analytics when the Orioles claimed the lefty on waivers. That would have been a real mind-pretzel of a sentence to read even a few years ago, so if you're a time traveler reading this book, sorry, and also please put the book down, there's literally so much else that needs doing. ⓧ Lanky Dominican right-hander **Luis de Leon** was fantastic across two levels (Complex and Low-A) despite an organizational directive that had him throwing nearly 45% changeups at times. That strategy makes long-term sense given De Leon already has two plus pitches (mid-90s fastball and a slider) and could be a future MLB starter if the changeup comes along. ⓧ The fun-to-watch sidewinder **Mychal Givens** signed a one-year homecoming deal with the Birds last winter, but threw just four horrific innings for the big-league club and was released in August. Not much else to see here. ⓧ The Royals gave up on **Jonathan Heasley** as a starter and moved him to the bullpen, where his fastball ticked way up in some shorter outings but batters continued to make hard contact against it, as they did against all of his pitches except the slider. As Jorge Luis Borges said, rain falling on a three-headed monster is still rain, and hittable pitches coming out of the bullpen are still hittable pitches. ⓧ Most relievers are random chance, a game of blindfolded darts in the back of a moving semi. **Joey Krehbiel** was a key cog of Baltimore's 2022 pen that helped the club surpass expectations, but then saw his stuff tick down in spring and didn't make the team out of camp. A former teammate of his once nicknamed him "Big Husky," so it's a shame Krehbiel is unlikely to ever get famous enough for that moniker to catch on. ⓧ **Dillon Tate** was penciled in as Baltimore's set-up man after solidifying himself as one of the game's more reliable relievers in 2021 and 2022. Instead, his right forearm started barking in spring training and never stopped. He didn't throw a competitive pitch after June 21, and his decision to bypass elbow surgery also makes his 2024 status murky. ⓧ **Peter Van Loon** is a 16th-rounder who carved across 88 ⅔ innings in 2022, but was limited by injuries during the regular season last year. There's not much of note in his pitch mix either. Do you think Van Loons hate car fanatics? ⓧ Long-locked lefty **Nick Vespi** was a tornado of bullpen dominance in Triple-A, but didn't experience the same success in the bigs. It's below-average raw stuff from a deceptive southpaw release that would be dominant in, say, the Dominican Winter League. That's meant as a compliment, honest. ⓧ **Austin Voth** skirted certain death throughout a magical 2022 that saw him rack up 83 quality MLB innings. Then the other shoe dropped. Injuries played a part, but he also struggled to rack up outs whenever he was healthy. Voth or die, baby. ⓧ **Bruce Zimmermann** was one of just two pitchers in 2023 to throw at least ten innings and not walk a single batter. Somehow, that did not earn him a single Cy Young vote.

BOSTON RED SOX

Essay by Alex Convery

Player comments by Daniel R. Epstein and BP staff

Near the ending of Andrew Dominik's 2012 film, *Killing Them Softly* (not a baseball movie!), Brad Pitt's character, a hitman looking to collect, stands at a bar facing the man who hired him. Times are tough, the man explains, when confronted about the reduced pay. It's a recession. With Obama's inauguration speech ringing out from the television, the promise of hope mixed with the cold reality of life as it is, Pitt looks at his employer and says "America's not a country, it's just a business."

Baseball is a business too. It's been a business since 1870, five years after Appomattox, which is to say: for a long time. Fans know this. When buying a ticket to a game, there's little illusion where that money goes.

The cynic, or, say, the hitman at the bar, might say that fandom has become a business too. Or maybe it's a promise—an often one-sided and unspoken one, but, a promise that if you, the fan, provide capital by supporting a team, the team will in turn use the capital to offer competitive baseball. There's a spectrum to which each team upholds or breaks this promise; some do both simultaneously. Winning is a business, just like losing can be a business (see: Dick Monfort and the Rockies).

The Red Sox are a business. Hell, this is the franchise that sold Babe Ruth for the rights to stage a play. Fenway Park was built over marshland in the Back Bay because the land was cheap. The ticket prices at Fenway are perpetually near the top of the league, beers feel like they're served in Dixie cups and it's still one of the only parks where you can pay top dollar to sit behind a pole. Despite all this, since John Henry and company assumed ownership of the team, they've, for the most part, upheld their end of the promise. The Red Sox win. And, as the saying goes, winning fixes everything.

It should, at least. And yet the organization finds itself at an existential crossroads heading into the 2024 season. "Existential" may sound dramatic, but a franchise doesn't go through three executive leaders in the span of eight years without some form of deep seated angst. There are plenty of reasons for this, but at its core, this conflict is driven by a fanbase fatigued with being asked to view the team strictly as a business the way the GM and owners do. Or to put it more simply: fatigued with the idea of fandom as business.

BOSTON RED SOX PROSPECTUS
2023 W-L: 78-84, 5TH IN AL EAST

Pythag	.498	14th	DER	.682	28th
RS/G	4.77	11th	DRC+	101	10th
RA/G	4.79	21st	DRA-	93	7th
dWin%	.547	8th	FIP	4.38	20th
Payroll	$181M	12th	B-Age	29.2	25th
M$/MW	$5.5M	20th	P-Age	29.7	20th

- Opened 1912
- Open air
- Natural surface
- Fence profile: 3' to 37'

Park Factors

Runs	Runs/RH	Runs/LH	HR/RH	HR/LH
106	106	106	96	87

Top Hitter WARP	4.5 Rafael Devers
Top Pitcher WARP	3.0 Nick Pivetta
2023 Top Prospect	Roman Anthony

61

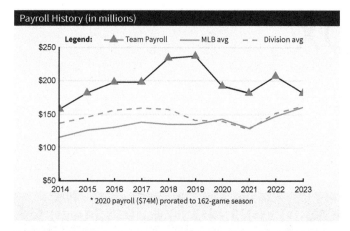

Payroll History (in millions)

Legend: ▲ Team Payroll — MLB avg --- Division avg

$250
$200
$150
$100
$50

2014 2015 2016 2017 2018 2019 2020 2021 2022 2023

* 2020 payroll ($74M) prorated to 162-game season

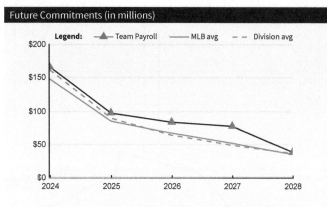

Future Commitments (in millions)

Legend: ▲ Team Payroll — MLB avg --- Division avg

$200
$150
$100
$50
$0

2024 2025 2026 2027 2028

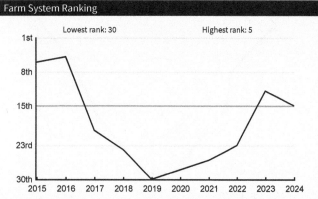

Farm System Ranking

Lowest rank: 30   Highest rank: 5

1st
8th
15th
23rd
30th

2015 2016 2017 2018 2019 2020 2021 2022 2023 2024

Personnel

Chief Baseball Officer
Criag Breslow

Executive Vice President, Assistant General Manager
Raquel Ferreira

Executive Vice President, Assistant General Manager
Eddie Romero

Senior Vice President, Baseball Operations
Ben Crockett

Senior Vice President, Assistant General Manager
Michael Groopman

Manager
Alex Cora

BP Alumni
Spencer Bingol
Todd Gold
Mike Groopman
Jason Karegeannes

Trading Mookie Betts was business. It was justified to fans under such pretenses, Chaim Bloom explaining: "It's part of a larger goal, to put ourselves in position to compete and win sustainably for as many years as we can. Using our resources is a means to that end. What we wanted was to get under the CBT in service of that larger goal."

Nothing he's saying is wrong—but he's talking about trading the franchise's best homegrown player since Ted Williams like a CEO talking about an investment on a quarterly earnings call with shareholders. It may be a larger goal, in his eyes, but it's in no way a grander one.

The Betts trade was an obvious inflection point, but the rubicon was crossed on September 1, 2020. That afternoon, the Red Sox' official Twitter account posted (and quickly deleted) a RESET button meme when it became official that the team had successfully slipped under the luxury tax threshold, thus resetting their ability to spend without penalty in the years to come. The tweet was a blatant admittal of motive, asking fans to celebrate a strategic manipulation of the balance sheet the same way they would post a graphic celebrating a victory over the Orioles on a random Tuesday in July. It shattered the fourth wall of fandom, the equivalent of Brad Pitt stopping in the middle of his monologue to smirk at the camera.

It's not the same. Even if resetting the luxury tax was an effort to continue beating the Orioles on random summer Tuesdays to come, it's not the same. And treating it as such was saying the quiet part out loud.

Ultimately, Bloom was fired for doing what he was hired to do, just as his predecessor was.

Hiring Dave Dombrowski in 2015 was business. The Red Sox tasked Dombrowski with building a contender immediately, even if it cost capital—prospect and financial. And he did just that, in his usual way. He traded Yoán Moncada and Michael Kopech. He spent nearly half a billion dollars over the course of three offseasons. And the Red Sox did win. They ripped off three straight division titles for the first time in franchise history, all capped off with the 2018 championship. But it didn't take a scouting expert to look down the pipeline and realize there wasn't much internal help on the way post-2018. Dombrowski exhausted budget, prospects and everything else to win. It worked. And it got him fired.

Ownership's directive to Dave Dombrowski when hired: *Do whatever it takes to win a world series even if it costs prospect capital to do so.*

Four years later: *Well done, but did you need to trade all the prospects?*

So, they changed course again. They brought in Bloom, part of the Tampa hive-mind perpetually winning more with less. This aggravated a segment of the fanbase who viewed his hiring not as a quest for sustainability, but simply as a cost-cutting measure.

Complaining that the Red Sox were being run too much like the Rays always rang hollow. The Rays have been the most stable team in the AL East over their 15-year run that started in 2008. That stability is exactly what Boston had in mind when hiring Bloom. Look no further than the Dodgers hiring of Andrew Friedman in 2014 (and the sustained success that followed in Los Angeles) to see Boston's line of thinking. It was always possible to marry efficiency with a larger scale.

But the Bloom era was ultimately defined by too many round pegs in square holes. Enrique Hernández at shortstop. Jackie Bradley Jr.'s bat in the everyday order. Relying on a broken 36-year-old Corey Kluber to be an innings eater. Arguably his best acquisition, Kyle Schwarber, was greatly neutralized by playing him at first base. Inactivity and half-measures at the past two trade deadlines ultimately doomed him. Sitting a few games out of the Wild Card both years, Bloom failed to bring in meaningful reinforcements, forcing the question whether he wanted to improve the team at each deadline to begin with. What began as patience started to look like passivity.

Somehow, it ended with Kyle Barraclough. Plucked from the Atlantic League in June, the one-time long ago closer Barraclough was pitching well in the minors, but on August 28, with the Sox' playoff hopes on life support, he entered a do-or-die game against the Astros. It quickly became just a die game. He proceeded to give up ten runs over the next 4 1/3 innings, as the theoretically contending Red Sox had run out of pitchers. As Alex Cora stated after the game: "This is who we have." A damning statement on Bloom, one that only grew louder with the vitriol of fans and local media in the days to come. It's hard not to look at that game and think that's the night that the Red Sox decided to fire Bloom. Who could have guessed it would be Kyle Barraclough?

Ultimately, fans spoke with the loudest tool they have available: their wallets. Attendance across baseball was up in 2023, but not in Boston. Average attendance at Fenway slipped to 12th overall, their lowest rank since 2001. The franchise is a long way from the infamous decade-long sellout streak that started in 2003, and Bloom ultimately paid the price for that—fair or not. The life of a hired gun is always a risky one.

Ownership's directive to Chaim Bloom when hired: *Do whatever it takes to rebuild the farm system.*

Four years later: *Well done, but did the major-league team have to be so bad?*

What future potential would you sacrifice to win today? Dombrowski's answer was just about everything. Bloom's was just about nothing. Neither was satisfactory to the team that hired them; the fans, notably, were not consulted. This, of course, begs the question: what does the organization want? How is success defined in Boston?

With that question lingering, and the smell of blood still hanging in the abattoir, it's no surprise that the upper-tier baseball operation candidates tabbed as potential successors, David Stearns, Sam Fuld, Brandon Gomes, Jon Daniels (and upwards of ten total candidates according to certain reports) declined to interview for the role. It seems prudent not to accept a job where listening to your boss will get you fired.

So, that leaves Craig Breslow, by all accounts an exciting hire given the available options. His pitching development wizardry with the Cubs is an obvious selling point given the lack of quality pitching depth in the system over the last three years. In many ways, the organization seems well-positioned for the sustainable success Bloom was chasing. Triston Casas looks destined to protect Rafael Devers in the lineup for years to come, forming one of the more formidable power tandems in the sport. Brayan Bello showed flashes of ace-potential, landing a few too many four-seam fastballs in the lower half of the strike zone shy of an elite season. And while there's not a sure thing behind him, Garret Whitlock, Tanner Houck and Kutter Crawford are an intriguing stable of arms. One can imagine Alex Cora deploying the trio creatively in October. But they have to get there first.

The farm is in the best shape it's been since the mid-2010s, when Betts, Devers and Benintendi represented hope for the next young core. Marcelo Mayer, Roman Anthony, Miguel Bleis and Ceddanne Rafaela now represent the same. The future should be bright. Of course, there's a chance they may not play a game for the Red Sox at all, depending on the urgency Breslow feels to leverage prospect capital for a competitive team next year. Such is the crossroads the organization finds itself at.

But that's the future. The present is still the present, and that's the tense the Red Sox have had the hardest time living in. Since the moment Mookie Betts was traded, Red Sox fans have experienced an emotion common in the post-Moneyball era (just ask an A's fan), a reconciliation of one's love of the game juxtaposed with the inherent greed that underpins the sport and business' existence. They've struggled to think about the game, and not think about thinking about the game. It's a fair question, right? If the team is just a business, then why care at all? I can't say it better than Roger Angell, so I won't try:

> *"It is foolish and childish, on the face of it, to affiliate ourselves with anything so insignificant and patently contrived and commercially exploitative as a professional sports team. It's almost unanswerable. Almost. What is left out of this calculation, it seems to be, is the business of caring—caring deeply and passionately, really caring—which is a capacity or an emotion that has almost gone out of our lives. Naïveté—the infantile and ignoble joy that sends a grown man or woman to dancing in the middle of the night over the haphazardous flight of a distant ball—seems a small price to pay for such a gift."*

The business of caring. The only business that ultimately matters to a fan. It's helpless and futile and irrational. It's often unwise and certainly one-sided. But it's what brings fans to the park to begin with. A team, even just a player, to care about.

During my one trip to Fenway last year, a painful three-game sweep by the visiting Blue Jays, my Dad and I met up with one of his old roommates, a lifelong New Englander. He looked at my hat and shook his head: "I'm boycotting the team, I just don't like the way they're running things." There's no question that there's a contingent of the fanbase in the same boat, the attendance numbers reflect as much. The funny part is when we got into discussing the loss the night before, it quickly became apparent that he had watched every pitch, and had plenty to say about Cora's bullpen management. There's nothing more Boston than boycotting a team but still having complaints about the sixth-inning reliever.

The point is: fans want to care. It's up to the Red Sox to give them reason to do so again.

—Alex Convery is a baseball blogger turned screenwriter, and authored AIR (2023).

HITTERS

Wilyer Abreu OF
Born: 06/24/99   Age: 25   Bats: L   Throws: L   Height: 5'10"   Weight: 215   Origin: IFA, 2017

YEAR	TM	LVL	AGE	PA	R	HR	RBI	SB	AVG/OBP/SLG	BABIP	SLGCON	BB%	K%	ZSw%	ZCon%	OSw%	OCon%	LA	90th EV	DRC+	BRR	DRP	WARP
2021	ASH	A+	22	331	52	16	50	10	.268/.363/.495	.353	.755	11.5%	29.9%							104	-2.3	2.2	1.2
2022	CC	AA	23	411	81	15	54	23	.249/.399/.459	.325	.683	19.0%	26.3%							115	2.4	-3.4	2.0
2022	POR	AA	23	168	25	4	19	8	.242/.399/.375	.325	.578	21.4%	26.8%							109	-3.0	-1.4	0.3
2023	WOR	AAA	24	363	67	22	65	8	.274/.391/.538	.290	.716	16.3%	20.4%	67.8%	85.4%	27.7%	55.0%			124	0.1	4.9	2.6
2023	BOS	MLB	24	85	10	2	14	3	.316/.388/.474	.431	.679	10.6%	27.1%	67.8%	77.3%	29.4%	54.7%	12.4	105.9	99	0.0	-1.2	0.1
2024 DC	BOS	MLB	25	296	33	8	33	8	.241/.344/.398	.313	.559	12.6%	24.9%							108	-0.3	-3	0.8

2023 GP: LF (12), CF (12), RF (3)   Comps: Lucas Duda (61), Yonder Alonso (60), Eric Thames (60)

Abreu isn't a lot of things. He isn't the breakout prospect of the Red Sox system … but only because of the subject of the next comment in this book. He isn't a pitcher…but his outfield throws average 94.7 mph. He isn't a true center fielder because he probably isn't 215 pounds anymore…but he isn't a liability in a corner spot either. He isn't the strikeout machine scouts feared a year ago whose propensity to chase capped his hit tool at 40…in fact, he demonstrated superb awareness of the strike zone in his five weeks in Boston. He isn't a dead-pull hitter…he sprayed 26 of his 53 batted balls to the left of second base. He isn't a nameless throw-in prospect from the Christian Vázquez trade anymore because he isn't just a potential fourth outfielder—he's much more.

───────── ★   ★   ★ *2024 Top 101 Prospect* **#8** ★   ★   ★ ─────────

Roman Anthony OF
Born: 05/13/04   Age: 20   Bats: L   Throws: R   Height: 6'2"   Weight: 200   Origin: Round 2, 2022 Draft (#79 overall)

YEAR	TM	LVL	AGE	PA	R	HR	RBI	SB	AVG/OBP/SLG	BABIP	SLGCON	BB%	K%	ZSw%	ZCon%	OSw%	OCon%	LA	90th EV	DRC+	BRR	DRP	WARP
2022	RSX	ROK	18	40	5	0	7	1	.429/.475/.486	.469	.548	10.0%	10.0%										
2022	SAL	A	18	43	2	0	5	0	.189/.279/.243	.206	.273	11.6%	9.3%							110	0.3	0.3	0.2
2023	SAL	A	19	202	27	1	18	11	.228/.376/.316	.285	.417	18.8%	18.8%							120	-1.2	-0.3	0.9
2023	GVL	A+	19	245	41	12	38	2	.294/.412/.569	.410	.899	16.3%	30.6%							117	-2.7	2.7	1.0
2023	POR	AA	19	44	10	1	8	3	.343/.477/.543	.393	.655	18.2%	13.6%							116	0.6	1.0	0.3
2024 non	BOS	MLB	20	251	23	4	22	5	.221/.307/.333	.301	.474	10.3%	26.9%							83	0.0	0	0.3

2023 GP: CF (68), RF (19), DH (19), LF (1)   Comps: Jarred Kelenic (61), Cristian Pache (56), Jo Adell (55)

That swing. It's one of *those* left-handed swings—as pristine and powerful as the first rays of sun over the ocean on a clear morning. The numbers support the aesthetics: few prospects reach Double-A in their first full year out of high school, and even fewer pair a robust 17.5% walk rate with a modest 24.2% strikeout rate in their age-19 season. Also, Anthony's hard-hit rate and exit velocities were some of the best in the minors regardless of age. He hasn't fully activated his over-the-fence potential yet and needs to lift the ball more consistently, but if you watch him swing the bat, you won't need any metrics to tell you what kind of prospect he has become. It doesn't take all morning to recognize a sunrise.

Christian Arroyo 2B
Born: 05/30/95   Age: 29   Bats: R   Throws: R   Height: 6'1"   Weight: 220   Origin: Round 1, 2013 Draft (#25 overall)

YEAR	TM	LVL	AGE	PA	R	HR	RBI	SB	AVG/OBP/SLG	BABIP	SLGCON	BB%	K%	ZSw%	ZCon%	OSw%	OCon%	LA	90th EV	DRC+	BRR	DRP	WARP
2021	WOR	AAA	26	38	4	0	2	1	.091/.184/.121	.136	.190	5.3%	31.6%							83	0.3	-0.6	0.0
2021	BOS	MLB	26	181	22	6	25	1	.262/.324/.445	.325	.608	4.4%	24.3%	77.3%	81.6%	42.4%	64.3%	9.2	103.9	90	0.1	0.4	0.5
2022	BOS	MLB	27	300	32	6	36	5	.286/.322/.414	.326	.502	4.3%	16.3%	78.9%	90.1%	42.8%	66.0%	8.8	105.0	113	0.0	0.1	1.4
2023	WOR	AAA	28	71	5	0	2	1	.138/.211/.169	.170	.208	8.5%	16.9%	86.2%	89.4%	39.4%	47.5%			85	0.2	-1.6	-0.1
2023	BOS	MLB	28	206	23	3	24	1	.241/.268/.369	.295	.480	3.4%	21.8%	81.0%	84.3%	43.7%	60.5%	11.0	102.2	90	0.0	0.3	0.4
2024 non	BOS	MLB	29	251	23	5	25	3	.241/.292/.358	.292	.464	5.5%	21.0%							84	0.0	0.4	0.2

2023 GP: 2B (62), 3B (4), SS (4)   Comps: Hernán Pérez (52), Brandon Phillips (51), Jose Vidro (51)

Statistics tell a story. These are the plot elements of Arroyo's 2023 season:

1. **Exposition**: His 20 hits in spring training led the Red Sox and he compiled an .844 OPS in the Grapefruit League.
2. **Conflict**: After a slow start, he went 8-16 with two walks, two doubles and a home run from April 29 to May 6, but a hamstring strain waylaid him for the next month.
3. **Rising Action**: He returned in June determined to resume his hot streak, but only managed a .252 on-base percentage from June 5 through August 2.
4. **Climax**: Boston designated him for assignment.
5. **Resolution**: His offense bottomed out in Triple-A and his future in baseball remains unclear.

Not all stories have a happy ending, but he set up a redemption arc in the sequel—assuming he can find a publisher.

Miguel Bleis   RF   Born: 03/01/04   Age: 20   Bats: R   Throws: R   Height: 6'0"   Weight: 170   Origin: IFA, 2021

YEAR	TM	LVL	AGE	PA	R	HR	RBI	SB	AVG/OBP/SLG	BABIP	SLGCON	BB%	K%	ZSw%	ZCon%	OSw%	OCon%	LA	90th EV	DRC+	BRR	DRP	WARP
2021	DSL RSR	ROK	17	136	17	4	17	7	.252/.331/.420	.283	.532	8.8%	18.4%									-1.8	
2022	RSX	ROK	18	167	28	5	27	18	.301/.353/.542	.394	.769	6.0%	26.9%										
2023	SAL	A	19	142	18	1	16	11	.230/.282/.325	.304	.466	7.0%	26.8%						92	0.1	5.2	0.8	
2024 non	BOS	MLB	20	251	18	2	19	0	.206/.253/.289	.299	.430	5.1%	31.2%						53	0.0	0	-0.7	

2023 GP: RF (13), CF (11), DH (7)   Comps: Agustin Ruiz (74), Rymer Liriano (68), Jose Carlos Urena (66)

Bleis suffered a left shoulder subluxation in May, which is a fancy medical term meaning the bone popped out of its socket. Action movies teach us there are two ways to fix this. A) Slam it into a door to bang it back in place, then continue fighting bad guys like it never happened, or B) Overcome a grim prognosis with a workout montage. Our protagonist did the second thing. He spent most of 2023 building strength after surgery rather than resuming baseball activities. For this type of injury, it's recommended to avoid the type of motion that caused it in the first place, which was … swinging a bat. The film's turning point will be his return to Salem, either stronger than ever or as a tragic martyr for some other hero to avenge.

Triston Casas   1B   Born: 01/15/00   Age: 24   Bats: L   Throws: R   Height: 6'5"   Weight: 244   Origin: Round 1, 2018 Draft (#26 overall)

YEAR	TM	LVL	AGE	PA	R	HR	RBI	SB	AVG/OBP/SLG	BABIP	SLGCON	BB%	K%	ZSw%	ZCon%	OSw%	OCon%	LA	90th EV	DRC+	BRR	DRP	WARP
2021	SCO	WIN	21	97	19	1	11	0	.372/.495/.487	.475	.633	17.5%	18.6%	84.6%	63.6%	21.7%	60.0%						
2021	POR	AA	21	329	57	13	52	6	.284/.395/.484	.323	.627	14.9%	19.1%							128	-0.8	-6.2	1.4
2021	WOR	AAA	21	42	6	1	7	1	.242/.381/.485	.280	.640	19.0%	19.0%							107	-0.4	0.0	0.1
2022	WOR	AAA	22	317	45	11	38	0	.273/.382/.481	.323	.648	14.5%	21.5%							101	0.7	-1.1	0.9
2022	BOS	MLB	22	95	11	5	12	1	.197/.358/.408	.208	.585	20.0%	24.2%	60.4%	80.2%	23.3%	62.7%	3.0	103.3	102	0.0	-0.1	0.2
2023	BOS	MLB	23	502	66	24	65	0	.263/.367/.490	.317	.693	13.9%	25.1%	69.0%	77.9%	25.9%	60.5%	16.1	107.8	122	-0.5	-1.8	2.2
2024 DC	BOS	MLB	24	584	68	20	71	1	.236/.339/.417	.295	.580	12.5%	24.7%							111	-0.6	-1.7	1.7

2023 GP: 1B (125), DH (3)   Comps: Anthony Rizzo (66), Logan Morrison (63), Prince Fielder (61)

Every Sox player bleeds red for Boston, but that's a happenstance of hemoglobin. Casas took his devotion a step further, painting his fingernails red and toenails white all year. While he led the league wire-to-wire in nail polish consumption, his bat wasn't as consistent in the first half and he took a .398 slugging percentage into the All-Star break. Then he homered in each of the first three games of the second half and remained one of MLB's hottest hitters the rest of the way. By season's end, the only qualified players whose walk rate (13.9%), strikeout rate (25.1%) and ISO (.226) were all better than his were Shohei Ohtani, Matt Olson and Juan Soto. Keeping statistical company with some of baseball's best while rebuking traditional norms of masculinity makes him an easy player to support.

Yu Chang   IF   Born: 08/18/95   Age: 28   Bats: R   Throws: R   Height: 6'1"   Weight: 180   Origin: IFA, 2013

YEAR	TM	LVL	AGE	PA	R	HR	RBI	SB	AVG/OBP/SLG	BABIP	SLGCON	BB%	K%	ZSw%	ZCon%	OSw%	OCon%	LA	90th EV	DRC+	BRR	DRP	WARP
2021	COL	AAA	25	66	9	4	13	1	.322/.394/.610	.417	.900	7.6%	28.8%							92	0.1	-1.1	0.1
2021	CLE	MLB	25	251	32	9	39	1	.228/.267/.426	.281	.601	4.4%	27.5%	72.6%	88.7%	34.3%	50.8%	19.4	104.2	76	0.1	0.0	-0.1
2022	CLE	MLB	26	10	0	0	0	0	.000/.000/.000		.000	0.0%	70.0%	52.9%	55.6%	46.7%	57.1%	35.3	103.8	61		0.0	0.0
2022	PIT	MLB	26	49	5	1	2	0	.167/.286/.262	.261	.458	8.2%	36.7%	72.0%	78.0%	33.9%	42.5%	20.5	100.2	77	0.0	0.1	0.0
2022	TB	MLB	26	105	11	3	12	0	.260/.305/.385	.324	.536	6.7%	25.7%	69.9%	87.9%	30.0%	58.8%	13.3	105.9	76	0.1	-0.1	0.0
2022	BOS	MLB	26	26	3	0	1	0	.150/.346/.250	.231	.385	19.2%	26.9%	66.0%	77.4%	33.3%	56.0%	4.3	104.6	58	0.0	-0.1	-0.1
2023	WOR	AAA	27	66	10	3	10	2	.323/.364/.500	.370	.633	6.1%	19.7%	71.9%	87.8%	35.0%	52.4%			102	0.4	0.5	0.2
2023	BOS	MLB	27	112	12	6	18	4	.162/.200/.352	.169	.521	2.7%	30.4%	68.4%	86.3%	39.7%	35.8%	9.3	104.0	76	0.0	-0.9	0.0
2024 non	BOS	MLB	28	251	25	7	28	2	.225/.286/.374	.287	.528	6.5%	27.3%							84	0.0	-1.1	0.1

2023 GP: SS (33), 2B (4), 1B (2), 3B (1), DH (1)   Comps: Sean Rodríguez (49), Chris Owings (48), Anderson Hernandez (48)

In the seventh inning of a Red Sox-Athletics game on July 9, A's batter Brent Rooker hit a grounder up the middle with a runner on first and no one out. Just before it reached second baseman Christian Arroyo, Chang, playing shortstop, intercepted it on the run. He took five steps towards second base but failed to beat the runner to the bag, then pivoted and threw too late to get the out at first. He achieved -1.7 DRP at shortstop last year in only 378 ⅔ innings at the position, in part due to those poor instincts on display that day against Oakland. At the plate, his 30.4% strikeout rate was nearly twice as high as his batting average; it's no wonder the club designated him for assignment in August. He'll be on the move again this winter, still looking to make a play.

Bobby Dalbec 3B
Born: 06/29/95   Age: 29   Bats: R   Throws: R   Height: 6'4"   Weight: 225   Origin: Round 4, 2016 Draft (#118 overall)

YEAR	TM	LVL	AGE	PA	R	HR	RBI	SB	AVG/OBP/SLG	BABIP	SLGCON	BB%	K%	ZSw%	ZCon%	OSw%	OCon%	LA	90th EV	DRC+	BRR	DRP	WARP
2021	BOS	MLB	26	453	50	25	78	2	.240/.298/.494	.316	.789	6.2%	34.4%	72.0%	71.4%	34.2%	46.8%	17.4	108.5	102	0.0	-0.4	1.0
2022	BOS	MLB	27	353	40	12	39	3	.215/.283/.369	.293	.588	8.2%	33.4%	68.2%	76.7%	32.2%	48.8%	16.0	105.6	77	-0.2	-0.1	-0.3
2023	WOR	AAA	28	493	82	33	79	18	.269/.381/.557	.364	.943	13.0%	34.3%	60.7%	66.7%	28.6%	42.9%			119	0.1	1.1	2.6
2023	BOS	MLB	28	53	6	1	1	1	.204/.264/.306	.450	.714	7.5%	52.8%	67.0%	60.7%	35.5%	42.9%	13.7	108.8	53	0.0	0.1	-0.2
2024 DC	BOS	MLB	29	249	28	10	31	4	.209/.292/.398	.324	.714	8.7%	40.0%							91	0.1	-0.1	0.2

2023 GP: 1B (15), 3B (2), DH (2), 2B (1), SS (1)   Comps: Chris Shelton (52), Tyler White (51), Tyler Moore (50)

Dalbec led all Triple-A players in home runs—a feat to be proud of, even if he would've preferred to be playing in Fenway. His power hasn't gone away, but the Red Sox left him in Worcester for most of the season, likely influenced by his 34.3% strikeout rate in the minors. He didn't get consistent run with the big club until Triston Casas got hurt in mid-September, and he failed to make much of the opportunity. So, now what? He spent more time manning third base and right field than first base in Triple-A, probably in the hopes of carving a path to a major-league role as a four-corners bench bat who can do damage against lefties. It's a good idea, because there sure isn't a big-league spot for another backup first baseman who strikes out too much.

Rafael Devers 3B
Born: 10/24/96   Age: 27   Bats: L   Throws: R   Height: 6'0"   Weight: 235   Origin: IFA, 2013

YEAR	TM	LVL	AGE	PA	R	HR	RBI	SB	AVG/OBP/SLG	BABIP	SLGCON	BB%	K%	ZSw%	ZCon%	OSw%	OCon%	LA	90th EV	DRC+	BRR	DRP	WARP
2021	BOS	MLB	24	664	101	38	113	5	.279/.352/.538	.307	.710	9.3%	21.5%	80.0%	76.9%	36.4%	65.6%	13.0	108.4	140	0.3	-3.9	5.3
2022	BOS	MLB	25	614	84	27	88	3	.295/.358/.521	.329	.655	8.1%	18.6%	78.0%	78.8%	40.0%	63.4%	11.4	108.0	131	-0.2	-2.6	3.5
2023	BOS	MLB	26	656	90	33	100	5	.271/.351/.500	.292	.639	9.5%	19.2%	78.6%	76.2%	36.7%	70.9%	12.6	108.6	132	-0.4	-1.9	4.5
2024 DC	BOS	MLB	27	634	80	27	89	4	.271/.351/.481	.312	.617	9.3%	20.1%							130	-0.2	-5	3.6

2023 GP: 3B (151), DH (2), SS (1)   Comps: Richie Hebner (80), George Brett (80), Eddie Mathews (79)

Raphael is no one's favorite turtle. Leonardo is the leader, Michelangelo is the party animal and Donatello is the brain. That doesn't leave much room for the dude in red to stand out. Devers received a big contract extension while the other homegrown stars did not, which thrust him into the miscast Leonardo role by default. He's become a durable, consistent producer—the unrivaled star of the team with a fearsome bat and defense you can put up with (for now). A four-win player is a great supporting character who brings depth and intrigue to a championship-caliber roster but, just like his ninja namesake, might not have sufficient juice to build the entire show around. Even though he's the best Rafael the Sox could want, he won't overcome a three-turtle deficit by himself.

Jarren Duran CF
Born: 09/05/96   Age: 27   Bats: L   Throws: R   Height: 6'2"   Weight: 205   Origin: Round 7, 2018 Draft (#220 overall)

YEAR	TM	LVL	AGE	PA	R	HR	RBI	SB	AVG/OBP/SLG	BABIP	SLGCON	BB%	K%	ZSw%	ZCon%	OSw%	OCon%	LA	90th EV	DRC+	BRR	DRP	WARP
2021	WOR	AAA	24	283	46	16	36	16	.258/.357/.516	.288	.708	10.6%	23.3%							117	1.8	-3.9	1.3
2021	BOS	MLB	24	112	17	2	10	2	.215/.241/.336	.318	.537	3.6%	35.7%	71.9%	78.9%	38.4%	48.5%	8.8	103.5	46	0.1	1.0	-0.2
2022	WOR	AAA	25	307	49	10	38	18	.283/.349/.491	.352	.665	8.5%	23.8%							101	3.2	5.7	1.8
2022	BOS	MLB	25	223	23	3	17	7	.221/.283/.363	.302	.525	6.3%	28.3%	71.3%	84.3%	33.7%	51.8%	6.9	102.7	87	0.6	3.8	0.9
2023	BOS	MLB	26	362	46	8	40	24	.295/.346/.482	.381	.661	6.6%	24.9%	74.8%	87.7%	33.9%	55.8%	10.5	107.2	85	0.9	3.5	1.0
2024 DC	BOS	MLB	27	554	54	13	60	23	.241/.308/.403	.305	.536	7.2%	23.1%							93	0.9	4.7	1.7

2023 GP: CF (75), LF (27), RF (1), DH (1)   Comps: Abraham Almonte (60), Steven Duggar (60), Jackie Bradley Jr. (58)

After sending up caution flags in his first two laps around MLB, Duran finally appeared to turn another corner. His topline batting stats improved substantially and he cut down on the boneheaded defense and baserunning mistakes that characterized his 2022 campaign. His hitting numbers don't hold up if you pop the hood, though. His DRC+ was even lower than the previous year's and his BABIP is unsustainable. He did improve his hard-hit rate from 38.0% to 46.3%, bashed more line drives with fewer grounders and decreased his strikeout rate from 28.3% to 24.9%. A center fielder with improving plate discipline and batted-ball characteristics along with positive defense and baserunning metrics is still a sports car, but more like a Miata than a Corvette. He ended the race with a flat tire, as turf toe put him in the garage in August.

Vaughn Grissom SS
Born: 01/05/01   Age: 23   Bats: R   Throws: R   Height: 6'2"   Weight: 210   Origin: Round 11, 2019 Draft (#337 overall)

YEAR	TM	LVL	AGE	PA	R	HR	RBI	SB	AVG/OBP/SLG	BABIP	SLGCON	BB%	K%	ZSw%	ZCon%	OSw%	OCon%	LA	90th EV	DRC+	BRR	DRP	WARP
2021	AUG	A	20	328	52	5	33	13	.311/.402/.446	.360	.541	10.4%	14.9%							127	1.6	1.7	2.3
2021	ROM	A+	20	52	12	2	10	3	.378/.519/.595	.375	.688	21.2%	9.6%							139	0.9	-0.7	0.4
2022	ROM	A+	21	344	62	11	55	20	.312/.404/.487	.332	.562	9.3%	11.6%							142	0.7	0.9	3.0
2022	MIS	AA	21	98	10	3	12	7	.363/.408/.516	.405	.610	4.1%	14.3%							122	0.8	1.0	0.7
2022	ATL	MLB	21	156	24	5	18	5	.291/.353/.440	.350	.579	7.1%	21.8%	72.2%	88.0%	38.5%	58.0%	9.2	101.4	99	0.1	-0.7	0.4
2023	GWN	AAA	22	468	74	8	61	13	.330/.419/.501	.376	.601	12.0%	14.1%	70.3%	87.6%	29.9%	61.3%			117	3.0	0.2	2.4
2023	ATL	MLB	22	80	5	0	9	0	.280/.313/.347	.344	.433	2.5%	18.8%	74.8%	89.8%	38.4%	63.8%	5.0	101.6	89	0.0	-0.9	0.1
2024 DC	BOS	MLB	23	380	37	6	37	7	.258/.331/.378	.308	.466	7.6%	17.4%							101	-0.1	-1.3	1.0

2023 GP: SS (19), 2B (4)   Comps: Ketel Marte (60), Dickie Thon (54), José Peraza (53)

As soon as Dansby Swanson left town, it was all but assumed that Grissom would take up the starting shortstop role. Despite having a solid spring on paper, the Braves decided to go with Orlando Arcia; after getting an extended taste of the bigs in 2022, Grissom commenced last season in Gwinnett. Grissom's bat has never been a concern—the biggest question is whether or not he can play good enough defense at a position that requires a reliable glove. While he showed signs of real improvement on that front, the jury's still out as to whether or not Grissom will stick in the middle infield once he eventually returns to the majors for good. Though the next step may have been deferred for nearly the entire regular season, he was "rewarded" by being called upon as the team's last hope in the NLDS.

Blaze Jordan CI Born: 12/19/02 Age: 21 Bats: R Throws: R Height: 6'2" Weight: 220 Origin: Round 3, 2020 Draft (#89 overall)

YEAR	TM	LVL	AGE	PA	R	HR	RBI	SB	AVG/OBP/SLG	BABIP	SLGCON	BB%	K%	ZSw%	ZCon%	OSw%	OCon%	LA	90th EV	DRC+	BRR	DRP	WARP
2021	RSX	ROK	18	76	12	4	19	1	.362/.408/.667	.396	.821	7.9%	17.1%									0.7	
2021	SAL	A	18	38	7	2	7	0	.250/.289/.444	.269	.571	5.3%	21.1%							113	0.3	-1.1	0.1
2022	SAL	A	19	415	48	8	57	4	.286/.357/.446	.329	.545	8.9%	16.1%							116	1.0	1.7	2.4
2022	GVL	A+	19	106	12	4	11	1	.301/.387/.441	.387	.621	10.4%	25.5%							87	-2.2	-2.6	-0.4
2023	GVL	A+	20	322	48	12	55	2	.324/.385/.533	.349	.637	8.7%	14.6%							119	0.1	-4.1	1.5
2023	POR	AA	20	203	19	6	31	0	.254/.296/.402	.268	.472	5.9%	13.8%							103	-2.9	2.8	0.6
2024 non	BOS	MLB	21	251	22	5	24	0	.234/.285/.352	.280	.448	5.9%	20.2%							79	0.0	0	-0.1

2023 GP: 1B (65), 3B (51), DH (6)   Comps: Chris Marrero (59), Josh Vitters (56), Josh Naylor (56)

Jordan is several years removed from his amateur days of hitting the ball a mile on YouTube. He conquered the low minors in his age-20 season and could reach MLB by late 2024. At this inflection point, his future looks like it will take one of four possible paths: 1) prototypical mashing first baseman who cracks windows on Lansdowne Street regularly; 2) bat-first third baseman who rotates at DH with Rafael Devers because it's hard to discern which of them is a bigger defensive liability. 3) weak side of a first-base platoon (if Triston Casas falls apart); 4) Just-missed prospect who finds out the hard way how difficult it is to succeed as a right-right first baseman—in other words, Bobby Dalbec. But first, a return to Double-A awaits, where the pitchers throw just a bit harder than they do on YouTube.

★ ★ ★ *2024 Top 101 Prospect* **#32** ★ ★ ★

Marcelo Mayer SS Born: 12/12/02 Age: 21 Bats: L Throws: R Height: 6'2" Weight: 188 Origin: Round 1, 2021 Draft (#4 overall)

YEAR	TM	LVL	AGE	PA	R	HR	RBI	SB	AVG/OBP/SLG	BABIP	SLGCON	BB%	K%	ZSw%	ZCon%	OSw%	OCon%	LA	90th EV	DRC+	BRR	DRP	WARP
2021	RSX	ROK	18	107	25	3	17	7	.275/.377/.440	.361	.625	14.0%	25.2%									-0.5	
2022	SAL	A	19	308	46	9	40	16	.286/.406/.504	.375	.730	16.6%	25.3%							121	2.3	-0.5	1.8
2022	GVL	A+	19	116	15	4	13	1	.265/.379/.449	.338	.638	14.7%	25.0%							91	0.1	2.3	0.5
2023	GVL	A+	20	164	23	7	34	5	.290/.366/.524	.343	.704	10.4%	22.6%							117	0.1	-1.4	0.8
2023	POR	AA	20	190	20	6	20	4	.189/.254/.355	.220	.500	7.9%	25.8%							88	0.2	0.5	0.4
2024 non	BOS	MLB	21	251	22	5	24	4	.223/.290/.346	.306	.506	7.9%	29.1%							79	0.0	0	0.2

2023 GP: SS (71), DH (7), 3B (1)   Comps: Richard Urena (63), Lucius Fox (61), Cole Tucker (60)

On May 7 in Asheville, Mayer started the game 3-for-3 with a single, a double and a home run. In his fourth at-bat, he laced a line drive into the gap. He sped around second pursuing the cycle, but slipped and landed awkwardly on his shoulder. The ailment shelved him for a week, but when he returned, his swing wasn't quite right. From May 14 through August 2, he slashed .190/.256/.366 across High-A and Double-A until the organization shut him down for the rest of the season to let his shoulder heal properly. Assuming he returns to full health this spring, he will resume his place as one of the game's top prospects and continue his rampage through the minor leagues, perhaps with the newfound wisdom that there's a difference between hustle and rushing back from an injury.

Reese McGuire C Born: 03/02/95 Age: 29 Bats: L Throws: R Height: 6'0" Weight: 233 Origin: Round 1, 2013 Draft (#14 overall)

YEAR	TM	LVL	AGE	PA	R	HR	RBI	SB	AVG/OBP/SLG	BABIP	SLGCON	BB%	K%	ZSw%	ZCon%	OSw%	OCon%	LA	90th EV	DRC+	BRR	DRP	WARP
2021	TOR	MLB	26	217	22	1	10	0	.253/.310/.343	.318	.442	6.9%	20.3%	72.0%	87.4%	33.3%	63.6%	12.2	101.4	86	-0.1	7.1	1.2
2022	CHW	MLB	27	166	12	0	10	0	.225/.261/.285	.283	.364	3.6%	19.9%	69.8%	91.4%	36.0%	58.5%	12.1	100.3	79	-0.1	0.5	0.2
2022	BOS	MLB	27	108	13	3	12	1	.337/.377/.500	.411	.653	5.6%	21.3%	61.0%	94.2%	44.3%	66.3%	11.5	100.0	91	-0.1	0.7	0.3
2023	BOS	MLB	28	206	15	1	16	2	.267/.310/.358	.366	.500	5.3%	25.7%	63.4%	83.3%	44.3%	70.3%	2.9	100.2	72	-0.2	2.9	0.4
2024 DC	BOS	MLB	29	243	20	3	21	2	.234/.294/.338	.295	.433	6.5%	20.9%							73	-0.2	4.2	0.5

2023 GP: C (62), DH (1)   Comps: Miguel Montero (57), Jorge Alfaro (56), A.J. Pierzynski (54)

YEAR	TM	P. COUNT	FRM RUNS	BLK RUNS	THRW RUNS	TOT RUNS
2021	TOR	8862	7.5	0.0	0.7	8.3
2022	CHW	6759	1.6	-0.2	0.1	1.5
2022	BOS	4029	1.5	-0.1	0.0	1.3
2023	BOS	7476	3.2	0.0	0.3	3.6
2024	BOS	9620	3.9	0.1	0.1	4.2

Having a lefty-hitting catcher can be like going apple-picking late in the season. It seems like a fun idea, but when you get to the orchard, the trees are all picked over and you're left with a bag of pitted, gnarly apples that you're never going to eat. McGuire is ostensibly a lefty-hitting catcher, but that descriptor falsely implies that he *hits*. His pitch recognition metrics cratered as he swung at fewer strikes and more pitches out of the zone than at any point in his career. See those launch angle and 90th percentile exit velocity stats? They're among the lowest in the game, so when he succeeded in making contact, it mostly produced weak ground balls. Alas, the orchard's last remnants don't taste as good as what's available in the produce section.

Adalberto Mondesi SS Born: 07/27/95 Age: 28 Bats: S Throws: R Height: 6'1" Weight: 200 Origin: IFA, 2011

YEAR	TM	LVL	AGE	PA	R	HR	RBI	SB	AVG/OBP/SLG	BABIP	SLGCON	BB%	K%	ZSw%	ZCon%	OSw%	OCon%	LA	90th EV	DRC+	BRR	DRP	WARP
2021	KC	MLB	25	136	19	6	17	15	.230/.271/.452	.299	.687	4.4%	31.6%	84.6%	77.6%	39.9%	43.7%	15.8	104.8	80	0.5	-0.2	0.1
2022	KC	MLB	26	54	3	0	3	5	.140/.204/.140	.233	.233	7.4%	37.0%	73.9%	69.2%	33.1%	35.7%	5.1	101.8	68	0.1	0.3	0.0
2024 non	BOS	MLB	28	251	23	6	25	13	.219/.278/.351	.315	.547	6.9%	33.4%							75	0.3	-0.1	0.0

Comps: Wilmer Flores (45), Javier Báez (45), Jhonny Peralta (44)

Let's take a glass-half-full approach first. Mondesi was technically one of Boston's best defensive shortstops in 2023. Their collective -8.3 DRP was last in the AL at the position, but his was 0.0 because he never played a single game. (Oops, that's too negative. Let's start over.) ... Believe it or not, the Red Sox won the Mondesi trade. Josh Taylor was atrocious for the Royals, giving up 17 runs in 17 ⅔ innings. An awful player is worse than one who doesn't play at all, right? The infielder experienced setback after setback from his April 2022 ACL tear. (Ugh. Nope, too negative again. This is hard.) ... Mondesi earned $3,045,000 in 2023, which is fortunate for him because he may never play in the majors again. (Nailed it!)

Tyler O'Neill   LF   Born: 06/22/95   Age: 29   Bats: R   Throws: R   Height: 5'11"   Weight: 200   Origin: Round 3, 2013 Draft (#85 overall)

YEAR	TM	LVL	AGE	PA	R	HR	RBI	SB	AVG/OBP/SLG	BABIP	SLGCON	BB%	K%	ZSw%	ZCon%	OSw%	OCon%	LA	90th EV	DRC+	BRR	DRP	WARP
2021	STL	MLB	26	537	89	34	80	15	.286/.352/.560	.366	.860	7.1%	31.3%	74.8%	77.9%	34.2%	48.2%	18.1	108.4	118	1.3	6.2	4.0
2022	STL	MLB	27	383	56	14	58	14	.228/.308/.392	.277	.567	9.9%	26.9%	68.8%	80.0%	31.7%	54.1%	13.7	106.0	92	0.3	1.5	1.1
2023	MEM	AAA	28	31	4	0	3	0	.231/.355/.269	.316	.368	16.1%	22.6%	67.3%	85.7%	24.1%	57.1%			91	-1.2	-0.6	-0.1
2023	STL	MLB	28	266	27	9	21	5	.231/.312/.403	.284	.561	10.5%	25.2%	69.7%	85.6%	30.2%	53.8%	15.2	106.0	99	0.1	0.3	0.8
2024 DC	BOS	MLB	29	506	57	18	61	16	.237/.321/.408	.293	.562	9.4%	24.9%							104	0.6	2.1	1.9

2023 GP: LF (58), CF (13), DH (1)   Comps: Greg Vaughn (54), Randal Grichuk (52), Carlos González (52)

O'Neill entered the 2023 season having made five trips to the IL between the last two seasons. Unfortunately, no greater fate awaited him in the months ahead. The 28-year-old owns two Gold Gloves, but when he has managed to get on the field lately, his maddeningly inconsistent plate production caused patience to run thin among fans despite his potential to mash in addition to his more obvious talents with speed and defense. The organization, it seems, was not quite as fed up as were the fans; the pile-up in the St. Louis outfield wasn't cleared at the trade deadline as widely predicted. The Cardinals' nightmare year wasn't the end of their reshuffling the deck, though; come December, O'Neill was moved to Boston and another of the league's scarlet-clad clubs. Two seasons of weak contact and IL time have faded the memory of 2021, when he finished above Freddie Freeman in NL MVP voting, but the Red Sox are hoping that guy's still in there.

★   ★   ★   *2024 Top 101 Prospect*   **#59**   ★   ★   ★

Ceddanne Rafaela   OF/SS   Born: 09/18/00   Age: 23   Bats: R   Throws: R   Height: 5'9"   Weight: 165   Origin: IFA, 2017

YEAR	TM	LVL	AGE	PA	R	HR	RBI	SB	AVG/OBP/SLG	BABIP	SLGCON	BB%	K%	ZSw%	ZCon%	OSw%	OCon%	LA	90th EV	DRC+	BRR	DRP	WARP
2021	SAL	A	20	432	73	10	53	23	.251/.305/.424	.288	.530	5.8%	18.3%							110	1.6	11.0	3.1
2022	CAG	WIN	21	76	10	1	8	5	.262/.368/.369	.333	.490	11.8%	21.1%										
2022	GVL	A+	21	209	37	9	36	14	.330/.368/.594	.409	.801	4.8%	24.4%							110	0.1	-3.6	0.6
2022	POR	AA	21	313	45	12	50	14	.278/.324/.500	.310	.640	5.1%	19.8%							107	-0.5	6.0	1.8
2023	POR	AA	22	266	40	6	37	30	.294/.332/.441	.351	.568	5.3%	20.7%							90	1.5	5.3	1.2
2023	WOR	AAA	22	219	40	14	42	6	.312/.370/.618	.348	.815	5.5%	21.9%	73.2%	84.3%	45.0%	53.8%			108	-1.0	4.9	1.3
2023	BOS	MLB	22	89	11	2	5	3	.241/.281/.386	.333	.582	4.5%	31.5%	75.5%	80.6%	42.2%	58.4%	7.7	102.8	65	0.1	0.2	0.0
2024 DC	BOS	MLB	23	467	43	12	50	21	.226/.273/.376	.297	.530	4.4%	27.8%							78	-0.1	2	0.5

2023 GP: CF (20), SS (5), 2B (4), DH (1)   Comps: Franklin Gutierrez (54), Dalton Pompey (53), Ryan Kalish (51)

Twice upon a (recent) time, the Red Sox had a speedy, undersized infielder with a unique first name who developed into an excellent defensive outfielder with a smooth swing and surprising pop. Rafaela makes it thrice, but there's a wide spectrum of outcomes between Enrique Hernández and Mookie Betts, and his ability to figure out major-league breaking pitches will determine whether he falls closer to the former or the latter. Getting on base enough to bat in the top half of the lineup will be a challenge due to his hyper-aggressive approach and low walk rate, but he's already Boston's best defensive outfielder. All that's left to do is to give him everyday playing time—and keep the Dodgers away from him.

Rob Refsnyder   OF   Born: 03/26/91   Age: 33   Bats: R   Throws: R   Height: 6'0"   Weight: 203   Origin: Round 5, 2012 Draft (#187 overall)

YEAR	TM	LVL	AGE	PA	R	HR	RBI	SB	AVG/OBP/SLG	BABIP	SLGCON	BB%	K%	ZSw%	ZCon%	OSw%	OCon%	LA	90th EV	DRC+	BRR	DRP	WARP
2021	STP	AAA	30	80	13	5	14	0	.318/.425/.621	.327	.774	15.0%	16.3%							133	0.9	1.7	0.8
2021	MIN	MLB	30	157	21	2	12	1	.245/.325/.324	.327	.475	10.8%	25.5%	65.8%	80.3%	21.5%	57.1%	10.2	106.1	80	-0.1	-1.1	0.1
2022	WOR	AAA	31	182	31	6	28	4	.306/.429/.524	.386	.733	15.4%	23.1%							123	0.4	-1.5	1.0
2022	BOS	MLB	31	177	25	6	21	1	.307/.384/.497	.394	.710	8.5%	26.0%	63.0%	79.6%	27.3%	67.8%	13.3	103.9	124	0.0	-1.6	0.9
2023	BOS	MLB	32	243	31	1	28	7	.248/.365/.317	.316	.413	13.6%	19.3%	64.5%	82.4%	22.5%	65.6%	12.0	102.2	100	0.4	-1.5	0.6
2024 DC	BOS	MLB	33	170	17	3	16	3	.238/.337/.358	.297	.466	11.0%	20.8%							98	0.0	-1.6	0.3

2023 GP: LF (54), CF (15), DH (7), RF (6)   Comps: John Moses (48), Emil Brown (40), Donovan Solano (40)

In the event of a blackout, it's important to be prepared with candles, flashlights, blankets and maybe a deck of cards. Refsnyder's swing-change-fueled power surge from 2022 proved to be short-lived as his groundball rate climbed from 37.3% to 43.3% and his fly-ball rate fell below 20% for the first time since 2017. Fortunately, the vet's emergency power-outage kit included a reduced swing rate, especially on pitches outside of the zone, and a stellar walk rate to keep his on-base percentage alight. Despite his lack of thump, he can keep the lights on as a fourth outfielder as long as his ability to collect free passes doesn't run out of batteries.

Pablo Reyes   IF   Born: 09/05/93   Age: 30   Bats: R   Throws: R   Height: 5'8"   Weight: 175   Origin: IFA, 2012

YEAR	TM	LVL	AGE	PA	R	HR	RBI	SB	AVG/OBP/SLG	BABIP	SLGCON	BB%	K%	ZSw%	ZCon%	OSw%	OCon%	LA	90th EV	DRC+	BRR	DRP	WARP
2021	NAS	AAA	27	153	26	4	20	1	.226/.301/.368	.239	.450	9.8%	15.7%							104	0.4	0.4	0.6
2021	MIL	MLB	27	87	12	1	3	4	.256/.333/.359	.306	.444	10.3%	17.2%	59.3%	87.5%	29.4%	75.4%	15.4	100.2	91	0.1	0.0	0.2
2022	NAS	AAA	28	432	63	11	59	15	.273/.348/.439	.305	.531	9.0%	15.5%	50.0%	80.0%	39.5%	70.6%			112	-1.9	3.3	2.0
2022	MIL	MLB	28	16	1	0	0	0	.267/.313/.267	.308	.308	6.3%	12.5%	61.5%	100.0%	39.4%	76.9%	-4.2	93.0	97	0.0	-0.1	0.0
2023	POR	AA	29	33	4	1	3	3	.222/.364/.370	.250	.476	18.2%	18.2%							109	0.5	-1.6	0.0
2023	WOR	AAA	29	26	6	2	4	1	.280/.308/.520	.238	.565	3.8%	7.7%	57.8%	84.6%	26.2%	72.7%			109	0.5	-0.6	0.1
2023	LV	AAA	29	91	13	1	10	3	.257/.385/.351	.353	.510	17.6%	25.3%	59.9%	86.6%	25.7%	59.4%			99	0.2	-0.5	0.3
2023	BOS	MLB	29	185	27	2	20	7	.287/.339/.377	.315	.432	7.6%	11.4%	63.1%	90.9%	26.3%	75.2%	13.5	102.5	113	0.2	-1.3	0.8
2024 DC	BOS	MLB	30	90	9	1	8	3	.247/.317/.356	.292	.441	8.3%	16.9%							90	0.0	-0.9	0.1

2023 GP: SS (31), 2B (30), 3B (4), P (2), 1B (2), DH (2)   Comps: Jason Bartlett (50), Darwin Barney (50), Miguel Rojas (48)

If the percentage of walks is a walk rate and the percentage of strikeouts is a strikeout rate, shouldn't the percentage of hits be a hit rate? The term "batting average" hearkens to an earlier era when the stat was considered so synonymous with hitting prowess that it was practically all anyone needed to know. In those days, Reyes' 2023 campaign would have been hailed as a breakout. Boston turned to him to stabilize their middle infield sinkhole after Oakland—Oakland!—released him in May, and he blooped and dunked his way into Sox fans' hearts. His 86.1% contact rate was superb, but with little power and few walks, his production was way too dependent on his inflated BABIP to be repeatable. He's a scrappy underdog who's easy to love, but keep in mind the Red Sox lost 22 games last year in which they outhit their opponent—second-most in MLB behind Kansas City's 23. Singles only get you so far.

Trevor Story SS   Born: 11/15/92   Age: 31   Bats: R   Throws: R   Height: 6'2"   Weight: 209   Origin: Round 1, 2011 Draft (#45 overall)

YEAR	TM	LVL	AGE	PA	R	HR	RBI	SB	AVG/OBP/SLG	BABIP	SLGCON	BB%	K%	ZSw%	ZCon%	OSw%	OCon%	LA	90th EV	DRC+	BRR	DRP	WARP
2021	COL	MLB	28	595	88	24	75	20	.251/.329/.471	.293	.641	8.9%	23.4%	74.9%	83.5%	34.5%	56.5%	17.6	105.7	106	0.8	-1.8	2.6
2022	BOS	MLB	29	396	53	16	66	13	.238/.303/.434	.309	.660	8.1%	30.8%	70.2%	78.5%	36.7%	57.4%	18.4	105.6	97	0.8	0.0	1.1
2023	WOR	AAA	30	38	6	3	6	1	.313/.421/.719	.333	.958	13.2%	21.1%	74.6%	87.2%	31.5%	41.4%			106	0.3	-0.7	0.1
2023	BOS	MLB	30	168	12	3	14	10	.203/.250/.316	.290	.485	5.4%	32.7%	69.9%	78.7%	35.1%	51.2%	15.7	103.9	63	0.3	1.1	-0.1
2024 DC	BOS	MLB	31	570	59	18	66	19	.226/.299/.391	.298	.569	8.0%	28.7%							90	0.5	-2.4	1.1

2023 GP: SS (36), DH (6), 2B (1)   *Comps: Cal Ripken Jr. (67), Nomar Garciaparra (67), Joe Cronin (66)*

82.3, 79.1, 76.1. Those were the average velocities of Story's throws each year from 2020-2022. At that rate of decline, he'd have been throwing beer-league softball speed by the end of his contract. Elbow surgery reversed the trend and his arm averaged 81.2 mph in 2023. That was still only in the 25th percentile, but it was enough to shift him back to the six. Now the Red Sox finally have a shortstop who rakes ... what's that? He doesn't rake anymore? There's no surgical fix for that. After so-so offensive seasons in 2021 and 2022, he swung at air more often than a windmill. The 168 plate appearances he managed aren't enough for a referendum on an eight-year veteran, but with four years remaining on his deal, this contract has the potential to bounce just like too many of his throws to first.

──────────────── ★ ★ ★ *2024 Top 101 Prospect* **#47** ★ ★ ★ ────────────────

Kyle Teel C   Born: 02/15/02   Age: 22   Bats: L   Throws: R   Height: 6'1"   Weight: 190   Origin: Round 1, 2023 Draft (#14 overall)

YEAR	TM	LVL	AGE	PA	R	HR	RBI	SB	AVG/OBP/SLG	BABIP	SLGCON	BB%	K%	ZSw%	ZCon%	OSw%	OCon%	LA	90th EV	DRC+	BRR	DRP	WARP
2023	GVL	A+	21	66	10	0	9	1	.377/.485/.453	.465	.571	16.7%	16.7%							105	1.7	1.9	0.6
2023	POR	AA	21	39	3	1	11	2	.323/.462/.484	.474	.750	20.5%	28.2%							99	-0.6	-0.1	0.0
2024 non	BOS	MLB	22	251	22	3	21	6	.223/.305/.320	.298	.447	9.8%	25.0%							79	0.0	0	0.3

2023 GP: C (20), DH (6)

The Teel name draws a lot of water in the North Jersey sports scene, but are elite athletes born or bred? Teel's father, Garett, was a catcher in the Dodgers system and established a baseball academy in Passaic County. His younger brother, Aidan, is a promising pitcher who followed him to the University of Virginia. His second cousin, Mike, was the greatest

Comps: Shane Peterson (77), Dominic Smith (73), Sam Travis (70)

YEAR	TM	P. COUNT	FRM RUNS	BLK RUNS	THRW RUNS	TOT RUNS
2023	GVL	1984	1.9	0.1	0.3	2.4
2024	BOS	6956	0.2	0.2	0.0	0.3

quarterback in Rutgers University's modern history and an NFL draft pick. Kyle may surpass them all: He earned a first-round selection by slashing .407/.475/.655 as a junior at Virginia, then continued raking in the pros. He's an exceptional runner for a catcher and a good receiver with a world-class arm. He's capable of anything except settling the nature vs. nurture debate, and has the potential to make the rest of the Teels known foremost as "Kyle's relatives."

Enmanuel Valdez 2B   Born: 12/28/98   Age: 25   Bats: L   Throws: R   Height: 5'8"   Weight: 191   Origin: IFA, 2015

YEAR	TM	LVL	AGE	PA	R	HR	RBI	SB	AVG/OBP/SLG	BABIP	SLGCON	BB%	K%	ZSw%	ZCon%	OSw%	OCon%	LA	90th EV	DRC+	BRR	DRP	WARP
2021	ASH	A+	22	318	52	21	72	5	.254/.313/.541	.254	.708	7.9%	21.1%							113	-0.4	3.4	1.7
2021	CC	AA	22	98	11	5	18	0	.256/.367/.512	.286	.700	13.3%	22.4%							113	0.4	0.7	0.5
2022	TOR	WIN	23	75	8	1	6	0	.179/.243/.299	.224	.408	6.7%	24.0%										
2022	CC	AA	23	205	40	11	45	4	.357/.463/.649	.438	.901	16.6%	22.9%							132	-2.5	-4.1	0.8
2022	WOR	AAA	23	195	26	7	30	3	.237/.309/.422	.283	.584	9.7%	24.6%							102	0.0	0.2	0.6
2022	SUG	AAA	23	173	26	10	32	1	.296/.347/.560	.306	.685	6.4%	16.8%	75.1%	80.5%	36.7%	68.9%			119	-1.9	0.2	0.8
2023	WOR	AAA	24	232	38	10	41	4	.254/.388/.476	.288	.638	17.7%	20.7%	62.5%	87.1%	23.4%	55.8%			115	-1.8	-1.5	0.6
2023	BOS	MLB	24	149	17	6	19	5	.266/.311/.453	.323	.618	5.4%	24.8%	60.0%	84.8%	33.1%	64.5%	10.3	102.3	98	0.1	0.1	0.4
2024 DC	BOS	MLB	25	122	13	4	14	2	.242/.322/.415	.290	.541	9.4%	21.4%							103	-0.1	-0	0.4

2023 GP: 2B (47), SS (1), DH (1)   *Comps: Brandon Lowe (59), Scooter Gennett (54), Derek Dietrich (53)*

We've evolved beyond sizeism at second base. Jose Altuve is 5'6" and has 209 career home runs. The 6'4" DJ LeMahieu has four Gold Gloves. The stereotype for a 5'8" second baseman is a slap-and-dash singles hitter with no power, bullet speed and a great glove, but Valdez's .187 ISO was seventh at the position in 2023 with a minimum of 100 plate appearances. In fairness, he also lacks the positive tropes regarding his stature. His 26.4 ft/s sprint speed was only 28th percentile and his defense was tough to swallow. While he makes a fair amount of contact, his walk rate didn't carry over to MLB and he won't come anywhere near the five batting titles Altuve and LeMahieu share. But hey, if a small second baseman wants to be an iron-gloved power hitter, now's the time. Go for it, short king.

Connor Wong C   Born: 05/19/96   Age: 28   Bats: R   Throws: R   Height: 6'1"   Weight: 190   Origin: Round 3, 2017 Draft (#100 overall)

YEAR	TM	LVL	AGE	PA	R	HR	RBI	SB	AVG/OBP/SLG	BABIP	SLGCON	BB%	K%	ZSw%	ZCon%	OSw%	OCon%	LA	90th EV	DRC+	BRR	DRP	WARP
2021	WOR	AAA	25	208	22	8	26	7	.256/.288/.442	.323	.624	4.3%	27.9%							87	0.7	-0.2	0.5
2021	BOS	MLB	25	14	3	0	1	0	.308/.357/.538	.667	1.167	7.1%	50.0%	59.3%	50.0%	28.6%	60.0%	9.4	103.5	64	0.0	0.0	0.0
2022	WOR	AAA	26	355	47	15	44	7	.288/.349/.489	.341	.650	7.6%	22.5%							109	-1.5	4.4	1.6
2022	BOS	MLB	26	56	8	1	7	0	.188/.273/.313	.250	.469	8.9%	28.6%	62.5%	83.6%	38.3%	52.9%	2.9	107.0	84	0.1	-0.5	0.0
2023	BOS	MLB	27	403	55	9	36	8	.235/.288/.385	.341	.603	5.5%	33.3%	71.0%	79.1%	38.2%	50.9%	14.7	105.5	63	-0.2	-8.1	-1.1
2024 DC	BOS	MLB	28	361	33	9	37	5	.215/.273/.351	.291	.513	5.8%	29.6%							71	-0.1	-1.8	-0.1

2023 GP: C (121), 2B (4), DH (1)   Comps: Jett Bandy (63), Kevin Plawecki (60), Grayson Greiner (59)

Wong was the starting catcher for the Red Sox last season, but ... why? It wasn't his bat; he was the second-worst hitter in MLB according to DRC+ with a minimum of 400 plate appearances. It wasn't his defense either, as he finished 95th out of 102 catchers in DRP due to substandard pitch framing. At his age, he wasn't a prospect in the conventional sense. Most of the time, he didn't even have the platoon advantage over left-handed backup Reese McGuire. What did Boston see in him that—ah! Found it! His eight stolen bases as a catcher trailed only J.T. Realmuto's 16. Those sweet, sweet steals kept him in the lineup despite, uh, everything else. Yeah, that must be it, because it seems like there's nothing else to see here.

YEAR	TM	P. COUNT	FRM RUNS	BLK RUNS	THRW RUNS	TOT RUNS
2021	WOR	6625	0.3	0.0	0.2	0.4
2021	BOS	499	0.0	0.0	0.0	0.0
2022	WOR	7985	2.9	-0.1	2.1	4.9
2022	BOS	2342	-0.1	0.0	-0.1	-0.2
2023	BOS	15687	-8.4	-0.1	0.5	-8.1
2024	BOS	14430	-2.1	-0.1	0.4	-1.8

Nick Yorke 2B   Born: 04/02/02   Age: 22   Bats: R   Throws: R   Height: 5'11"   Weight: 200   Origin: Round 1, 2020 Draft (#17 overall)

YEAR	TM	LVL	AGE	PA	R	HR	RBI	SB	AVG/OBP/SLG	BABIP	SLGCON	BB%	K%	ZSw%	ZCon%	OSw%	OCon%	LA	90th EV	DRC+	BRR	DRP	WARP
2021	SAL	A	19	346	59	10	47	11	.323/.413/.500	.353	.595	11.8%	13.6%							144	-4.9	7.0	3.0
2021	GVL	A+	19	96	17	4	15	2	.333/.406/.571	.407	.774	11.5%	22.9%							116	0.3	-1.0	0.4
2022	GVL	A+	20	373	48	11	45	8	.231/.303/.365	.288	.506	8.8%	25.2%							92	-2.1	5.3	1.0
2023	POR	AA	21	506	74	13	61	18	.268/.350/.435	.339	.599	10.1%	24.1%							102	2.6	-0.2	1.4
2024 DC	BOS	MLB	22	64	6	1	6	1	.233/.298/.349	.312	.500	7.2%	26.2%							81	0.0	0	0.0

2023 GP: 2B (96), DH (14)   Comps: Manuel Margot (51), Omar Estévez (50), Randal Grichuk (49)

The Battle of Saratoga in 1777. Tina Turner in 1984. The Patriots against the Falcons in 2017. Yorke in 2023. Three of these are among the greatest comebacks of all time (not telling which three). The other is a darn good comeback nevertheless. Yorke made a radical swing change to a setup holding the bat like a sledgehammer at a "test-your-strength" carnival game. This resulted in more searing line drives and fewer pull-side grounders, even though it cost some bat control for a hit-tool-forward batter. That's something to keep an eye on, but the once-and-future prospect also made substantial defensive improvements, going from a 40-grade second baseman to the best defender at the position in the Eastern League, as voted by opposing managers. I guess what we're saying here is that while *Private Dancer* was a great album, it's got nothing on Yorke looking like he'll seize Boston's starting keystone job in 2024.

Masataka Yoshida LF/DH   Born: 07/15/93   Age: 30   Bats: L   Throws: R   Height: 5'8"   Weight: 192   Origin: IFA, 2022

YEAR	TM	LVL	AGE	PA	R	HR	RBI	SB	AVG/OBP/SLG	BABIP	SLGCON	BB%	K%	ZSw%	ZCon%	OSw%	OCon%	LA	90th EV	DRC+	BRR	DRP	WARP
2023	BOS	MLB	29	580	71	15	72	8	.289/.338/.445	.316	.524	5.9%	14.0%	60.5%	87.1%	31.4%	74.5%	4.0	104.8	123	-0.5	0.9	3.2
2024 DC	BOS	MLB	30	622	69	15	70	5	.283/.355/.431	.310	.495	8.5%	11.8%							119	-0.3	0.1	2.9

2023 GP: LF (87), DH (49)   Comps: Mike Greenwell (89), Mickey Hatcher (89), Melky Cabrera (88)

When Yoshida arrived from Japan a year ago, there were two schools of thought on his transition to MLB. Either he would win a batting title or fail to catch up to fastballs—there was no middle ground. As is often the case, the reality was somewhere in the huge space between Carl Yastrzemski and Rusney Castillo. Overall, he had a productive offensive season without big counting stats, but if you're looking for a Sox legend to comp him to, you might have to look at his negative attributes. For example, one could say he combined the skills of Ted Williams (outfield glove), Wade Boggs (enormous home-road splits), Dustin Pedroia (size and power) and Rafael Devers (speed). The total package looks something like Mike Greenwell, but not in his MVP-caliber 1988 season *or* his '90s decline phase. With four more years on his contract, we'll have plenty of time to either find a better comparison point, or for Yoshida to write his own name in Red Sox lore.

PITCHERS

Brayan Bello RHP   Born: 05/17/99   Age: 25   Height: 6'1"   Weight: 195   Origin: IFA, 2017

YEAR	TM	LVL	AGE	G (GS)	IP	W-L	SV	K	WHIP	ERA	CSP	BB%	K%	HR%	GB%	ZSw%	ZCon%	OSw%	OCon%	BABIP	SLGCON	DRA-	WARP
2021	GVL	A+	22	6 (6)	31²	5-0	0	45	1.01	2.27		5.7%	36.9%	2.5%	52.9%					.328	.529	69	0.8
2021	POR	AA	22	15 (15)	63²	2-3	0	87	1.41	4.66		8.6%	31.1%	1.8%	44.8%					.381	.621	83	1.1
2022	POR	AA	23	7 (7)	37¹	4-2	0	48	0.80	1.69		8.5%	33.8%	2.1%	61.0%					.192	.395	70	1.1
2022	WOR	AAA	23	11 (10)	58²	6-2	0	81	1.19	2.76		10.0%	33.8%	1.3%	61.5%					.326	.522	58	2.1
2022	BOS	MLB	23	13 (11)	57¹	2-8	0	55	1.78	4.71	50.6%	10.1%	20.5%	0.4%	54.9%	67.1%	83.9%	33.2%	61.8%	.404	.541	98	0.6
2023	BOS	MLB	24	28 (28)	157	12-11	0	132	1.34	4.24	46.6%	6.7%	19.8%	3.6%	56.1%	70.8%	84.5%	33.1%	62.5%	.307	.578	88	2.9
2024 DC	BOS	MLB	25	29 (29)	163	10-10	0	136	1.37	4.23	47.5%	8.3%	19.5%	2.1%	55.1%					.313	.491	95	1.9

2023 Arsenal: SI (95.2), CH (86.3), FA (95.7), SL (85.2), SW (86.2), FC (89.1)   Comps: Mitch Keller (68), Tyler Mahle (68), Erik Johnson (67)

When Bello gave up eight runs over 7 ⅓ innings in his first two appearances and got sent straight back to Worcester, Alex Cora said, "This is about now. This is not about his future." Back in the bigs by the end of April, it became clear that Bello's future was *now*. Meanwhile, Boston's *now* became more about *their* future. (It's all very Marty McFly/Doctor Who, with the present and future colliding.) The important thing is that his changeup and sinker both averaged about 10 inches of run and neutralized righties and lefties alike. Now, the minors are decidedly in his past ... and his future as a mid-rotation starter has started happening now. Somehow. (There's probably a flux capacitor or TARDIS involved.)

Brennan Bernardino LHP   Born: 01/15/92   Age: 32   Height: 6'4"   Weight: 180   Origin: Round 26, 2014 Draft (#785 overall)

YEAR	TM	LVL	AGE	G (GS)	IP	W-L	SV	K	WHIP	ERA	CSP	BB%	K%	HR%	GB%	ZSw%	ZCon%	OSw%	OCon%	BABIP	SLGCON	DRA-	WARP
2021	JAL	WIN	29	23(4)	35²	2-3	0	41	1.09	3.53		5.5%	28.1%	0.7%	54.5%					.341	.461		
2022	JAL	WIN	30	9(9)	42¹	3-3	0	31	1.09	2.34		7.1%	18.2%	0.6%	61.0%					.270	.352		
2022	TAC	AAA	30	23(0)	32²	2-0	2	35	0.86	2.20		8.0%	28.0%	0.8%	55.8%	59.8%	79.7%	23.9%	56.9%	.224	.377	82	0.5
2022	SEA	MLB	30	2(0)	2¹	0-1	0	0	2.14	3.86	61.4%	15.4%	0.0%	0.0%	45.5%	85.7%	100.0%	15.0%	100.0%	.273	.300	109	0.0
2023	BOS	MLB	31	55(6)	50²	2-1	0	58	1.30	3.20	50.2%	8.3%	26.9%	1.9%	48.5%	62.6%	84.5%	23.6%	56.1%	.338	.537	87	1.0
2024 DC	BOS	MLB	32	39(0)	42	2-2	0	37	1.28	4.04	50.6%	8.7%	21.0%	2.7%	45.3%					.289	.500	92	0.4

2023 Arsenal: SI (91.1), SW (77.7), CH (82.8)   Comps: Grant Dayton (60), Louis Head (57), Zac Rosscup (54)

A half-step can redefine a season. On September 14, Bernardino nearly wriggled out of a bases-loaded, two-out jam against the Yankees when DJ LeMahieu grounded out to second base to end the inning ... except the out call at first base was overturned on a challenge, letting a run score. Three pitches later, Aaron Judge hit a grand slam. Those were five of the 19 runs he allowed all year, and they would've never happened if the original call had been upheld. That doesn't absolve him of all culpability, and it highlights a gaping platoon split—he allowed an .872 OPS to right-handed hitters as opposed to .459 to lefties. He's a classic low-slot sinker/slider slinger, but he might need to workshop his little-used changeup to keep right-handed hitters in check. Otherwise, he can hope the batter in front of Judge runs a little more slowly next time.

Isaiah Campbell RHP   Born: 08/15/97   Age: 26   Height: 6'4"   Weight: 230   Origin: Round 2, 2019 Draft (#76 overall)

YEAR	TM	LVL	AGE	G (GS)	IP	W-L	SV	K	WHIP	ERA	CSP	BB%	K%	HR%	GB%	ZSw%	ZCon%	OSw%	OCon%	BABIP	SLGCON	DRA-	WARP
2021	EVE	A+	23	5(0)	19¹	3-1	0	20	0.98	2.33		7.7%	25.6%	2.6%	48.0%					.234	.468	87	0.3
2022	EVE	A+	24	19(4)	33	1-0	10	35	0.85	0.82		8.1%	28.5%	1.6%	53.8%					.211	.372	92	0.4
2022	ARK	AA	24	14(0)	13	0-4	1	24	1.15	3.46		3.6%	42.9%	3.6%	30.0%					.423	.821	60	0.4
2023	ARK	AA	25	23(0)	24	6-0	5	27	1.04	2.63		7.4%	28.4%	2.1%	60.7%					.271	.443	80	0.5
2023	SEA	MLB	25	27(0)	28²	4-1	1	33	1.22	2.83	45.6%	10.8%	27.5%	1.7%	39.7%	69.2%	85.7%	32.4%	53.1%	.282	.458	95	0.4
2024 DC	BOS	MLB	26	33(0)	36	2-2	0	36	1.38	4.65	45.6%	9.3%	23.3%	3.3%	40.2%					.310	.571	104	0.1

2023 Arsenal: FA (95.1), FC (86.5), SL (82.1)   Comps: Steve Cishek (82), Tyler Zuber (81), Fautino De Los Santos (80)

Campbell's swift evolution from accomplished college starter to reliable big-league bullpen arm continued on without a hitch, as he proved effective in a low-leverage role as a rookie. Ironically, his highest-leverage appearance of the season came in a situation where a sizable portion of his own fans were rooting against him. One day after Seattle was mathematically eliminated from postseason contention, Campbell closed out a 1-0 victory against the top of the Rangers lineup in Game 162 for his first career save—which helped clinch the AL West for the rival Astros in the waning hours of the regular season. Though a strong note to end the season on, and one that aged awfully well as Texas proceeded to win its next 11 road games en route to a championship, a significant promotion up the bullpen hierarchy seems unlikely based on how his fastball-slider combo stacks up with the high-powered arsenals of his fellow reliever friends.

Max Castillo RHP   Born: 05/04/99   Age: 25   Height: 6'2"   Weight: 280   Origin: IFA, 2015

YEAR	TM	LVL	AGE	G (GS)	IP	W-L	SV	K	WHIP	ERA	CSP	BB%	K%	HR%	GB%	ZSw%	ZCon%	OSw%	OCon%	BABIP	SLGCON	DRA-	WARP
2021	NH	AA	22	21(20)	102	11-4	0	89	1.38	4.85		7.9%	20.2%	2.7%	43.8%					.312	.540	105	0.6
2022	LAR	WIN	23	8(7)	30²	3-2	0	21	1.21	4.11		5.5%	16.5%	1.6%	47.5%					.292	.408		
2022	NH	AA	23	6(6)	29	3-1	0	35	1.21	3.10		11.5%	28.7%	2.5%	49.3%					.261	.563	86	0.6
2022	OMA	AAA	23	7(6)	21¹	1-1	0	22	2.06	8.44		8.0%	19.5%	2.7%	32.5%					.416	.727	117	0.1
2022	BUF	AAA	23	5(3)	27¹	2-0	0	29	0.73	0.66		10.0%	29.0%	2.0%	45.0%					.138	.317	87	0.6
2022	TOR	MLB	23	9(2)	20²	0-0	0	20	0.97	3.05	48.9%	6.2%	24.7%	4.9%	51.8%	66.7%	85.1%	34.1%	64.5%	.212	.518	94	0.3
2022	KC	MLB	23	5(4)	18²	0-2	0	17	1.77	9.16	52.1%	11.2%	19.1%	4.5%	40.0%	74.1%	83.0%	30.5%	67.2%	.345	.672	111	0.1
2023	OMA	AAA	24	22(21)	116	6-7	0	94	1.25	4.58		5.7%	19.2%	6.3%	38.6%	68.1%	86.9%	32.2%	65.9%	.258	.648	101	1.7
2023	KC	MLB	24	7(0)	20¹	0-1	0	10	1.43	4.43	49.6%	10.1%	11.2%	2.2%	40.3%	70.3%	88.2%	32.1%	77.8%	.281	.492	121	0.0
2024 DC	BOS	MLB	25	15(6)	39	2-3	0	28	1.49	5.50	50.2%	7.9%	16.1%	3.5%	41.6%					.316	.565	121	-0.2

2023 Arsenal: FA (93.4), SL (83.8), CH (87.2)   Comps: José Ureña (61), Kyle Wright (59), Kohl Stewart (59)

The Royals acquired the solidly built, workmanlike Castillo in the Whit Merrifield trade as an MLB-adjacent, durable arm. The hope was he'd be able to spackle over innings on the strength of his changeup and whiff-inducing slider, with an ability to flex between the rotation and a relief role. Instead, Castillo spent most of the season toiling in the mines of the PCL, failing to miss bats and giving up an explosive 2.4 home runs per nine innings. No one yearns for that.

Kutter Crawford RHP   Born: 04/01/96   Age: 28   Height: 6'1"   Weight: 195   Origin: Round 16, 2017 Draft (#491 overall)

YEAR	TM	LVL	AGE	G(GS)	IP	W-L	SV	K	WHIP	ERA	CSP	BB%	K%	HR%	GB%	ZSw%	ZCon%	OSw%	OCon%	BABIP	SLGCON	DRA-	WARP
2021	POR	AA	25	10(10)	46¹	3-2	0	64	0.82	3.30		2.9%	37.2%	4.1%	39.8%					.271	.634	84	0.8
2021	WOR	AAA	25	10(9)	48¹	3-4	0	67	1.32	5.21		7.2%	32.1%	2.4%	33.1%					.370	.672	88	0.9
2021	BOS	MLB	25	1(1)	2	0-1	0	2	3.50	22.50	49.3%	15.4%	15.4%	7.7%	11.1%	70.0%	57.1%	48.6%	83.3%	.500	1.286	125	0.0
2022	WOR	AAA	26	6(4)	24¹	1-0	0	23	1.44	5.18		5.4%	20.7%	4.5%	38.3%					.316	.613	98	0.3
2022	BOS	MLB	26	21(12)	77¹	3-6	0	77	1.42	5.47	56.8%	8.7%	23.1%	3.6%	31.0%	70.1%	81.9%	30.9%	61.7%	.322	.616	112	0.3
2023	BOS	MLB	27	31(23)	129¹	6-8	0	135	1.11	4.04	47.0%	6.8%	25.6%	3.2%	35.0%	74.1%	80.4%	36.8%	63.0%	.269	.539	96	1.8
2024 DC	BOS	MLB	28	24(24)	116¹	6-7	0	115	1.26	4.16	50.3%	7.4%	23.8%	3.5%	33.8%					.301	.573	96	1.2

2023 Arsenal: FA (93.7), FC (88.7), KC (79.5), SW (82.2), FS (82.6), SL (83.1)   *Comps: Chris Stratton (56), Tyler Wilson (53), Stephen Fife (52)*

Any builder, handyperson or tinkerer knows it isn't enough to have lots of tools—you have to anticipate the right one to use in each situation. Sometimes the thingamabob will do the job, but not as well as the whatchamacallit. Crawford has plenty of gadgets and doodads in his toolbox—four-seamer, curveball, sweeper, slider and *of course* cutter—but it was his changeup that made the biggest difference last year. He transformed it from a traditional *cambio* to more of a split-change, which paired better with his four-seamer against left-handed hitters especially: Their OPS against him plummeted from .967 in 2022 to .675 last season. When facing batters for a third time, they slashed .356/.385/.688 against him, but as a five-and-dive starter, he's the whiz of Boston's workshop.

Cooper Criswell RHP   Born: 07/24/96   Age: 27   Height: 6'6"   Weight: 200   Origin: Round 13, 2018 Draft (#391 overall)

YEAR	TM	LVL	AGE	G(GS)	IP	W-L	SV	K	WHIP	ERA	CSP	BB%	K%	HR%	GB%	ZSw%	ZCon%	OSw%	OCon%	BABIP	SLGCON	DRA-	WARP
2021	RCT	AA	24	12(12)	70¹	6-4	0	85	1.08	3.71		2.7%	29.2%	3.1%	48.5%					.319	.583	89	1.1
2021	SL	AAA	24	9(9)	47	3-5	0	43	1.47	6.51		5.7%	20.4%	3.8%	40.8%					.353	.658	115	-0.2
2021	LAA	MLB	24	1(1)	1¹	0-1	0	0	4.50	20.25	51.9%	0.0%	0.0%	0.0%	60.0%	76.5%	100.0%	29.2%	100.0%	.600	.900	112	0.0
2022	ANG	ROK	25	5(5)	13	0-0	0	19	1.00	2.08		3.8%	36.5%	0.0%	33.3%					.367	.467		
2022	DUR	AAA	25	11(3)	36²	2-1	0	33	1.01	4.17		4.1%	22.8%	2.1%	51.4%	59.1%	92.3%	40.0%	57.1%	.277	.452	79	0.9
2022	TB	MLB	25	1(1)	3¹	0-0	0	4	0.90	2.70	65.8%	7.7%	30.8%	0.0%	62.5%	56.0%	71.4%	30.0%	66.7%	.250	.250	87	0.1
2023	DUR	AAA	26	23(17)	84²	4-4	2	80	1.30	3.93		6.2%	21.6%	2.2%	50.8%	61.4%	86.4%	34.7%	62.7%	.319	.484	87	1.8
2023	TB	MLB	26	10(0)	33	1-1	0	27	1.55	5.73	50.0%	7.3%	17.9%	4.0%	42.2%	64.3%	88.2%	31.6%	73.0%	.330	.620	103	0.3
2024 non	BOS	MLB	27	58(0)	50	2-2	0	34	1.31	4.49	51.0%	6.1%	15.7%	2.9%	43.7%					.293	.509	102	0.2

2023 Arsenal: SI (89), SW (76.6), FC (83.8), CH (84.2)   *Comps: Tyler Wilson (61), Craig Stammen (58), Tyler Cloyd (58)*

Criswell joined a long list of fungible arms that Tampa Bay used to make up the many, many innings they lost to injury. All 10 of his appearances out of the bullpen spanned multiple innings, with nearly half of his outings going at least 12 outs deep. Despite long limbs to go with those long outings, Criswell is more of a finesse pitcher, tossing four offerings that averaged under 90 mph. In a typical showing, he would mix in an upper-80s "heater" with a sweeping disco slider in ... you know, *the late-70s*. Under the tutelage of Kyle Snyder, he added a cutter that spun in a few ticks higher than the slider and a changeup to keep things interesting. The results were underwhelming for the most part, but the extension he gets and the drop on all four of his offerings earned him a big-league contract to fill out Boston's pitching staff.

Lucas Giolito RHP   Born: 07/14/94   Age: 29   Height: 6'6"   Weight: 245   Origin: Round 1, 2012 Draft (#16 overall)

YEAR	TM	LVL	AGE	G(GS)	IP	W-L	SV	K	WHIP	ERA	CSP	BB%	K%	HR%	GB%	ZSw%	ZCon%	OSw%	OCon%	BABIP	SLGCON	DRA-	WARP
2021	CHW	MLB	26	31(31)	178²	11-9	0	201	1.10	3.53	58.9%	7.2%	27.9%	3.8%	33.3%	73.3%	77.3%	34.3%	53.4%	.270	.566	89	2.7
2022	CHW	MLB	27	30(30)	161²	11-9	0	177	1.44	4.90	56.1%	8.7%	25.4%	3.4%	38.6%	68.9%	83.9%	33.0%	54.1%	.340	.634	104	1.3
2023	CHW	MLB	28	21(21)	121	6-6	0	131	1.22	3.79	48.0%	8.3%	25.8%	3.9%	34.5%	68.7%	83.4%	32.1%	54.1%	.279	.603	100	1.4
2023	CLE	MLB	28	6(6)	30²	1-4	0	39	1.50	7.04	45.4%	11.6%	28.3%	8.0%	32.5%	69.1%	88.0%	33.3%	52.5%	.264	.878	104	0.3
2023	LAA	MLB	28	6(6)	32²	1-5	0	34	1.47	6.89	46.2%	10.1%	22.8%	6.7%	43.8%	66.1%	83.1%	30.8%	47.2%	.267	.766	114	0.1
2024 DC	BOS	MLB	29	31(31)	175¹	11-10	0	186	1.28	4.15	52.4%	8.7%	25.3%	3.4%	36.8%					.298	.575	95	2.0

2023 Arsenal: FA (93.3), CH (81), SL (84.2), CU (78.3), SI (91.9)   *Comps: Jon Garland (72), Jim Maloney (71), Joe Coleman (71)*

Giolito has been one of the most omnipresent pitchers in baseball since his callup, qualifying (or being one out away from qualifying) for the ERA title in six consecutive seasons. Combined with consistently above-average results, he might have appeared an attractive candidate for prospective free agent buyers this offseason, especially in a league where innings are at a premium. But after a midseason trade to the Angels (that sent top catching prospect Edgar Quero the other way) and subsequent waiver claim by Cleveland, things really fell off the rails. His walk rate ballooned, and when he did find the zone his pitches were thrown right down Broadway and got absolutely hammered. There's plenty to work with here, though: His slider and changeup can still elicit above-average whiff rates when not left over the heart of the plate. But that return to form is hardly a guarantee. Giolito may have played himself out of a nine-figure contract, and will likely end up taking a short-term prove-it deal.

Tanner Houck RHP   Born: 06/29/96   Age: 28   Height: 6'5"   Weight: 226   Origin: Round 1, 2017 Draft (#24 overall)

YEAR	TM	LVL	AGE	G(GS)	IP	W-L	SV	K	WHIP	ERA	CSP	BB%	K%	HR%	GB%	ZSw%	ZCon%	OSw%	OCon%	BABIP	SLGCON	DRA-	WARP
2021	WOR	AAA	25	6(6)	21	0-2	0	26	1.24	5.14		7.8%	28.9%	1.1%	53.7%					.340	.547	90	0.4
2021	BOS	MLB	25	18(13)	69	1-5	1	87	1.13	3.52	50.2%	7.4%	30.5%	1.4%	48.5%	68.0%	82.6%	33.6%	52.1%	.319	.473	77	1.5
2022	BOS	MLB	26	32(4)	60	5-4	8	56	1.18	3.15	49.7%	8.9%	22.7%	1.2%	50.9%	68.9%	84.8%	33.8%	53.6%	.289	.398	87	1.0
2023	WOR	AAA	27	3(3)	8²	0-0	0	10	0.92	2.08		8.6%	28.6%	0.0%	77.3%	67.3%	78.8%	38.9%	45.7%	.227	.227	76	0.2
2023	BOS	MLB	27	21(21)	106	6-10	0	99	1.37	5.01	48.4%	8.9%	21.4%	3.0%	52.7%	67.0%	84.6%	33.8%	53.3%	.299	.547	91	1.8
2024 DC	BOS	MLB	28	24(24)	123²	7-7	0	118	1.33	4.12	48.9%	9.0%	22.4%	2.3%	51.3%					.309	.504	93	1.5

2023 Arsenal: SL (84.1), SI (93.6), FS (87.9), FC (91.9), FA (94.1), SW (83.8)   *Comps: Danny Salazar (60), Dinelson Lamet (60), Dan Straily (60)*

Houck finally got the chance to start, and in doing so turned his name into a contraction. For example, *Houck'ome his strikeout rate was down nine points from two years earlier?* Well, he experimented off and on with pitch-to-contact offerings such as a sinker and a cutter rather than his swing-and-miss slider and four-seamer. *Then Houck'ome he couldn't decide on a pitch mix?* Because nothing worked against lefties, as is often the case for righty sidearmers. They didn't hit the slider much, but destroyed all his other pitches and accounted for 11 of the 14 home runs he served up. *Okay, so Houck'ome the Red Sox kept him in the rotation?* (Sigh.) They didn't have anyone better to take his place.

Joe Jacques LHP   Born: 03/11/95   Age: 29   Height: 6'4"   Weight: 210   Origin: Round 33, 2018 Draft (#984 overall)

YEAR	TM	LVL	AGE	G (GS)	IP	W-L	SV	K	WHIP	ERA	CSP	BB%	K%	HR%	GB%	ZSw%	ZCon%	OSw%	OCon%	BABIP	SLGCON	DRA-	WARP
2021	IND	AAA	26	37(0)	48	3-1	1	53	1.42	4.31		9.3%	24.8%	2.3%	49.6%					.339	.550	114	0.3
2022	IND	AAA	27	37¹	29(0)	4-1	2	27	1.26	3.62		7.8%	17.6%	2.6%	50.9%					.292	.472	112	0.3
2023	WOR	AAA	28	33(1)	39	1-3	1	35	1.15	2.54		8.0%	21.6%	2.5%	60.0%	59.2%	85.1%	30.7%	65.6%	.269	.444	91	0.8
2023	BOS	MLB	28	23(1)	26²	2-1	1	20	1.58	5.06	50.1%	8.2%	16.4%	1.6%	62.8%	56.9%	91.6%	25.8%	65.6%	.361	.560	98	0.3
2024 DC	BOS	MLB	29	21(0)	24	1-1	0	18	1.46	4.88	50.1%	8.8%	16.8%	2.1%	54.3%					.315	.487	107	0.0

2023 Arsenal: SI (91.3), SL (77.4), CH (85.3)   *Comps: Sam Clay (64), Colt Hynes (61), Sammy Solís (59)*

Cows no longer exist in the wild and 33rd-round picks no longer exist in the draft. Both species now serve only to feed more dominant creatures. When Jacques offered up his 91-mph sinker, opposing batters saw a juicy hamburger. When he featured his lackluster slider, they saw a filet mignon. The Sox only brought him into games they were already losing for his final 10 appearances of the season, often letting opponents pound him like ground beef. Still, it's a great accomplishment for a 28-year-old rookie to overcome his draft status and reach the majors at all. It's better to be on the menu than extinct.

Kenley Jansen RHP   Born: 09/30/87   Age: 36   Height: 6'5"   Weight: 265   Origin: IFA, 2004

YEAR	TM	LVL	AGE	G (GS)	IP	W-L	SV	K	WHIP	ERA	CSP	BB%	K%	HR%	GB%	ZSw%	ZCon%	OSw%	OCon%	BABIP	SLGCON	DRA-	WARP
2021	LAD	MLB	33	69(0)	69	4-4	38	86	1.04	2.22	57.3%	12.9%	30.9%	1.4%	37.3%	69.9%	73.6%	33.9%	55.2%	.216	.367	89	1.0
2022	ATL	MLB	34	65(0)	64	5-2	41	85	1.05	3.38	57.7%	8.5%	32.7%	3.1%	29.1%	67.7%	79.4%	35.4%	60.9%	.259	.544	78	1.4
2023	BOS	MLB	35	51(0)	44²	3-6	29	52	1.28	3.63	51.0%	9.0%	27.7%	2.7%	20.5%	69.6%	76.3%	38.0%	62.3%	.313	.547	99	0.6
2024 DC	BOS	MLB	36	51(0)	54	3-6	36	62	1.28	4.10	54.2%	9.9%	27.5%	3.5%	28.6%					.294	.585	94	0.4

2023 Arsenal: HC (94.4), SL (84.2), SI (95.4)   *Comps: Craig Kimbrel (91), Joakim Soria (86), Michael Jackson (85)*

James Brown best describes what happened to Jansen's primary offering in 2023. "Like a dull knife/just ain't cuttin'/just talkin' loud/then saying nothin'." He brought his cutter usage back up to 78.8% after it had dropped to the 60-65% range the three previous years. He also jumped its velo back up to 94.5 mph from the low 90s. What his cutter failed to do was, uh, cut. It lost 81% of its horizontal movement, decreasing from 4.9 inches to 0.9. The upshot was career worsts in DRA-, WHIP and strikeout rate. If he wants to Get On Up in save situations next year, he might need to find a Brand New Bag to make opponents Get Up Offa That Thing.

Corey Kluber RHP   Born: 04/10/86   Age: 38   Height: 6'4"   Weight: 210   Origin: Round 4, 2007 Draft (#134 overall)

YEAR	TM	LVL	AGE	G (GS)	IP	W-L	SV	K	WHIP	ERA	CSP	BB%	K%	HR%	GB%	ZSw%	ZCon%	OSw%	OCon%	BABIP	SLGCON	DRA-	WARP
2021	NYY	MLB	35	16(16)	80	5-3	0	82	1.34	3.83	52.0%	9.7%	24.0%	2.3%	43.0%	66.7%	87.1%	33.7%	51.7%	.311	.516	104	0.6
2022	TB	MLB	36	31(31)	164	10-10	0	139	1.21	4.34	55.3%	3.0%	20.2%	2.9%	35.1%	68.5%	85.3%	37.4%	63.3%	.318	.540	97	1.9
2023	BOS	MLB	37	15(9)	55	3-6	1	42	1.64	7.04	48.0%	8.2%	16.3%	6.6%	30.0%	69.9%	85.8%	33.6%	69.1%	.301	.737	140	-0.5
2024 non	BOS	MLB	38	58(0)	50	2-2	0	38	1.39	5.18	52.4%	6.9%	17.6%	3.9%	34.3%					.301	.574	116	-0.2

2023 Arsenal: SW (80.8), FC (86.3), SI (88.4), CH (82.5), FA (88.5)   *Comps: Zack Greinke (72), Max Scherzer (71), Mike Mussina (69)*

Kluber is not an old man. However, the average American's life expectancy is 79.1 years, and the two-time Cy Young Award recipient is nearing that mid-point. Should he start living like he's on the back nine of life, taking up activities like aqua yoga, birding, arts and crafts, or lawn bowling to stay active? Maybe. Because after allowing 17 home runs in 55 innings, pitching in the majors probably won't be one his regular endeavors for much longer. His last appearance was a three-inning save on June 20—the first and only save of his career. After that, he landed on the IL with shoulder inflammation, then was shut down for good during a rehab attempt five weeks later. A second act of board games and croquet awaits, if this really is the end of his run.

Chris Martin RHP   Born: 06/02/86   Age: 38   Height: 6'8"   Weight: 224   Origin: Round 21, 2005 Draft (#627 overall)

YEAR	TM	LVL	AGE	G (GS)	IP	W-L	SV	K	WHIP	ERA	CSP	BB%	K%	HR%	GB%	ZSw%	ZCon%	OSw%	OCon%	BABIP	SLGCON	DRA-	WARP
2021	ATL	MLB	35	46(0)	43¹	2-4	1	33	1.27	3.95	60.0%	3.3%	18.2%	2.2%	48.9%	76.0%	86.5%	34.1%	62.9%	.338	.500	86	0.7
2022	LAD	MLB	36	26(0)	24²	3-1	2	34	0.53	1.46	58.2%	1.1%	37.0%	1.1%	42.9%	71.3%	79.8%	44.6%	67.9%	.200	.309	59	0.8
2022	CHC	MLB	36	34(0)	31¹	1-0	0	40	1.34	4.31	55.5%	3.0%	30.1%	3.8%	51.7%	75.4%	79.7%	31.7%	61.5%	.393	.727	60	1.0
2023	BOS	MLB	37	55(0)	51¹	4-1	3	46	1.03	1.05	54.9%	4.0%	23.1%	1.0%	49.7%	73.2%	80.6%	42.7%	69.7%	.301	.396	82	1.1
2024 DC	BOS	MLB	38	63(0)	66	4-3	4	55	1.21	3.70	56.0%	5.0%	20.2%	2.6%	46.7%					.306	.510	87	0.7

2023 Arsenal: FC (92.5), FA (95.8), SI (95.1), FS (88.3), SL (86.7), SW (84.4)   *Comps: Blake Parker (53), Luis García (51), Joe Smith (50)*

Great pitching is timeless even if its descriptors aren't. Forty years ago, Martin's season would've been celebrated for his minuscule ERA. Twenty years ago, his nearly complete elimination of two of the three true outcomes—walks and home runs—would have been the main story. Today, we know his declining strikeout rate can be attributed to a career-high 35.7% cutter usage. The pitch generates fewer whiffs but more weak contact, which resulted in an 84.5-mph average exit velocity—the fifth-lowest in MLB (minimum 30 innings). Even without as many strikeouts as usual, he allowed only one run over his final 33 ⅔ innings from June 9 through the end of the season. Entering his age-38 campaign, he's proving to be just as enduring as a 1-2-3 eighth inning.

Chris Murphy LHP Born: 06/05/98 Age: 26 Height: 6'1" Weight: 186 Origin: Round 6, 2019 Draft (#197 overall)

YEAR	TM	LVL	AGE	G (GS)	IP	W-L	SV	K	WHIP	ERA	CSP	BB%	K%	HR%	GB%	ZSw%	ZCon%	OSw%	OCon%	BABIP	SLGCON	DRA-	WARP
2021	GVL	A+	23	14(14)	68¹	5-3	0	81	1.24	4.21		8.0%	28.3%	5.9%	38.8%					.281	.718	103	0.4
2021	POR	AA	23	7(6)	33	3-2	0	47	1.30	5.45		9.4%	34.1%	2.9%	33.8%					.356	.675	96	0.3
2022	POR	AA	24	15(13)	76²	4-5	0	91	1.00	2.58		10.2%	29.8%	2.0%	35.9%					.229	.436	94	1.3
2022	WOR	AAA	24	15(15)	75¹	3-6	0	58	1.57	5.50		12.0%	17.0%	2.3%	45.8%					.305	.558	127	0.0
2023	WOR	AAA	25	15(9)	52²	2-3	0	61	1.78	6.32		12.3%	24.2%	2.8%	41.3%	70.4%	80.9%	31.8%	56.3%	.378	.623	93	1.0
2023	BOS	MLB	25	20(0)	47²	1-2	1	49	1.41	4.91	45.0%	8.0%	23.1%	2.4%	42.8%	73.2%	84.8%	30.3%	65.6%	.326	.560	88	0.9
2024 DC	BOS	MLB	26	15(6)	37²	2-2	0	33	1.47	4.97	45.0%	10.3%	20.1%	3.0%	40.3%					.308	.543	109	0.1

2023 Arsenal: FA (94), FC (87.9), CU (75.9), CH (84.8), SW (79.1)   Comps: Scott Barlow (66), Conner Menez (65), Rob Zastryzny (64)

Even though the Red Sox dropkicked Murphy back to Worcester the first three times they tried him out, he found himself shipping up to Boston to finish out the season at the end of September. His changeup is his best weapon, as he threw 55 of them without giving up a base hit. Both his slider and curveball played well too, but his bland four-seamer got smoked by opposing hitters as evidenced by his zone-contact rate. He's in the mix for a bullpen role this year, but hopefully with fewer trips on the Triple-A shuttle. The greatest accomplishment of his debut season was becoming the top search result for "Chris Murphy Boston," beating out approximately 10,000 guys who grew up in Southie.

Luis Perales RHP Born: 04/14/03 Age: 21 Height: 6'1" Weight: 160 Origin: IFA, 2019

YEAR	TM	LVL	AGE	G (GS)	IP	W-L	SV	K	WHIP	ERA	CSP	BB%	K%	HR%	GB%	ZSw%	ZCon%	OSw%	OCon%	BABIP	SLGCON	DRA-	WARP
2022	RSX	ROK	19	9(7)	25	0-1	0	34	0.76	1.08		9.6%	36.2%	0.0%	44.0%					.200	.306		
2022	SAL	A	19	4(4)	10²	0-1	0	16	1.97	3.38		21.2%	30.8%	1.9%	33.3%					.391	.583	103	0.1
2023	SAL	A	20	13(13)	53¹	4-4	0	71	1.24	3.21		12.4%	31.4%	0.9%	37.1%					.295	.451	77	1.1
2023	GVL	A+	20	8(8)	36¹	0-3	0	44	1.68	4.95		13.2%	26.3%	4.8%	32.0%					.337	.714	106	0.3
2024 non	BOS	MLB	21	58(0)	50	2-2	0	49	1.66	6.15		14.0%	21.2%	4.0%	32.4%					.299	.619	131	-0.6

Comps: Robert Stephenson (70), A.J. Cole (68), Akeem Bostick (67)

When you read a menu at a restaurant, they don't put the side dishes first; when you're talking about a pitching prospect, you don't start the conversation with the breaking and off-speed stuff. Perales has a chef's choice heater, touching 98 with ride to induce whiffs at the top of the zone. There's a slider, changeup, and cutter on the plate as well, which he throws with varying degrees of consistency. Given his troubling walk rates and diminutive stature, there's relief risk in his profile, but he plays for the right organization to ignore size concerns. Even if he can't throw enough strikes or season his secondaries enough for a starting role, he can let it rip with the four-seamer as a strikeout machine out of the bullpen. When it comes to pitching, high cheese is always the best main course.

Nick Pivetta RHP Born: 02/14/93 Age: 31 Height: 6'5" Weight: 210 Origin: Round 4, 2013 Draft (#136 overall)

YEAR	TM	LVL	AGE	G (GS)	IP	W-L	SV	K	WHIP	ERA	CSP	BB%	K%	HR%	GB%	ZSw%	ZCon%	OSw%	OCon%	BABIP	SLGCON	DRA-	WARP
2021	BOS	MLB	28	31(30)	155	9-8	1	175	1.30	4.53	56.7%	9.8%	26.5%	3.6%	38.2%	69.8%	85.0%	31.7%	59.9%	.290	.595	100	1.5
2022	BOS	MLB	29	33(33)	179²	10-12	0	175	1.38	4.56	56.6%	9.4%	22.6%	3.5%	38.5%	68.6%	84.4%	32.0%	63.8%	.300	.570	106	1.2
2023	BOS	MLB	30	38(16)	142²	10-9	1	183	1.12	4.04	46.8%	8.5%	31.2%	3.9%	36.3%	66.3%	82.4%	37.3%	56.3%	.269	.614	83	3.0
2024 DC	BOS	MLB	31	28(28)	148²	9-9	0	161	1.27	4.07	52.8%	9.2%	25.9%	3.6%	37.8%					.289	.576	94	1.7

2023 Arsenal: FA (94.8), KC (79.6), SL (87.7), SW (84.5), FS (84.4)   Comps: Ray Washburn (76), Stan Bahnsen (68), Esteban Loaiza (68)

This can't be right. We're getting reports that Pivetta was … good?! Don't worry, his trademark frustrating inconsistency didn't go away—if anything it amplified. He had a 6.30 ERA through seven starts and was bumped out of the rotation in May. From then on, he filled every role from starter to closer and anything in between. On July 17, he threw six no-hit innings with 12 strikeouts. Five days later, he faced only three batters, retiring them all. On the 31st, he had a spot start that lasted into the eighth inning. He picked up a sweeper along the way which became a true swing-and-miss offering, leading to a career-best 31.2% strikeout rate. It's faint praise to say that he was the best pitcher on the Red Sox by WARP and DRA-, but using him as a Swiss Army Knife somehow synergizes with his tendency toward chaos.

Joely Rodríguez LHP Born: 11/14/91 Age: 32 Height: 6'1" Weight: 223 Origin: IFA, 2009

YEAR	TM	LVL	AGE	G (GS)	IP	W-L	SV	K	WHIP	ERA	CSP	BB%	K%	HR%	GB%	ZSw%	ZCon%	OSw%	OCon%	BABIP	SLGCON	DRA-	WARP
2021	NYY	MLB	29	21(0)	19	1-0	0	17	1.42	2.84	50.2%	7.6%	21.5%	1.3%	50.0%	64.8%	88.1%	34.5%	47.4%	.370	.500	80	0.4
2021	TEX	MLB	29	31(0)	27¹	1-3	1	30	1.61	5.93	50.0%	9.4%	23.4%	2.3%	63.1%	66.3%	78.2%	37.7%	59.2%	.363	.543	79	0.6
2022	NYM	MLB	30	55(0)	50¹	2-4	0	57	1.35	4.47	50.3%	12.0%	26.4%	1.4%	53.0%	51.2%	80.8%	37.0%	61.3%	.307	.450	87	0.8
2023	POR	AA	31	5(0)	5¹	0-0	0	6	0.94	1.69		10.0%	30.0%	5.0%	75.0%					.182	.500	88	0.1
2023	WOR	AAA	31	7(0)	6	1-0	0	9	2.00	4.50		3.4%	31.0%	0.0%	63.2%	62.2%	71.4%	49.2%	61.3%	.611	.722	77	0.2
2023	BOS	MLB	31	11(0)	11	0-0	0	14	1.73	6.55	44.9%	11.8%	27.5%	3.9%	45.2%	53.5%	91.3%	33.3%	53.5%	.379	.710	90	0.2
2024 non	BOS	MLB	32	58(0)	50	2-2	0	53	1.36	4.13	49.3%	10.0%	24.6%	2.4%	49.1%					.308	.518	93	0.4

2023 Arsenal: SI (91.2), CH (86.4), SL (83.3), FA (91.1)   Comps: Jake Diekman (58), Sam Freeman (56), Fernando Abad (55)

Ballplayers seem to have body parts that the rest of us don't; Rodríguez injured several of them. He missed time for his right oblique, left shoulder, and right hip in 2023. Following a setback from his third separate IL stint, Alex Cora told reporters, "It's tough because he was throwing the ball well. The upper hip, the outside of it." First of all, *was he?* Velocity on all of his pitches was down three or four miles per hour from a few years ago and his fastball had the spin rate of a rotisserie chicken. Besides, 19 baserunners in 11 innings speaks for itself. Secondly, *what is an upper hip? What is "the outside of it?"* Athletes are just built different.

John Schreiber   RHP   Born: 03/05/94   Age: 30   Height: 6'2"   Weight: 224   Origin: Round 15, 2016 Draft (#445 overall)

YEAR	TM	LVL	AGE	G (GS)	IP	W-L	SV	K	WHIP	ERA	CSP	BB%	K%	HR%	GB%	ZSw%	ZCon%	OSw%	OCon%	BABIP	SLGCON	DRA-	WARP
2021	WOR	AAA	27	33(8)	66¹	3-3	1	65	1.31	2.71		9.3%	23.2%	1.1%	48.9%					.314	.460	98	0.9
2021	BOS	MLB	27	1(0)	3	0-0	0	5	1.67	3.00	49.5%	7.7%	38.5%	0.0%	42.9%	60.9%	85.7%	33.3%	63.6%	.571	.857	86	0.1
2022	WOR	AAA	28	7(0)	12¹	2-1	0	15	0.97	1.46		6.1%	30.6%	4.1%	50.0%					.250	.567	87	0.3
2022	BOS	MLB	28	64(0)	65	4-4	8	74	0.98	2.22	51.7%	7.4%	28.8%	1.2%	56.9%	67.0%	76.8%	32.1%	53.8%	.269	.459	66	1.8
2023	BOS	MLB	29	46(2)	46²	2-1	1	53	1.41	3.86	47.6%	12.3%	26.0%	2.9%	41.8%	66.5%	81.4%	28.2%	65.9%	.302	.575	93	0.7
2024 DC	BOS	MLB	30	51(0)	54	3-2	2	56	1.24	3.68	49.3%	9.1%	24.6%	2.6%	45.9%					.290	.510	85	0.7

2023 Arsenal: SW (81.1), FA (93.4), SI (93), CH (88.2)   *Comps: Evan Scribner (65), Noé Ramirez (65), Evan Marshall (64)*

Schreiber's throwing motion is like a fallen trebuchet. He extends the ball behind his body to the second baseman, then bends low and flings it sidearm. His low slot gives his sweeper artificial horizontal movement and his four-seamer appears to rise. This made him one of MLB's top relievers in 2022. In 2023, he was still among the best in the game—against right-handed hitters only. Lefties stopped chasing his pitches out of the strike zone, mostly laying off those back-foot sweepers and sitting on fastballs, leading to more walks, bad counts and loud sounds off the bat. Even when they did chase, they connected more often, as the outside-the-zone contact rate against him skyrocketed. A reliever who mows down righty batters is still a weapon, but if he can't improve against lefties, well, there's a reason no one uses catapults in battle anymore.

Garrett Whitlock   RHP   Born: 06/11/96   Age: 28   Height: 6'5"   Weight: 222   Origin: Round 18, 2017 Draft (#542 overall)

YEAR	TM	LVL	AGE	G (GS)	IP	W-L	SV	K	WHIP	ERA	CSP	BB%	K%	HR%	GB%	ZSw%	ZCon%	OSw%	OCon%	BABIP	SLGCON	DRA-	WARP
2021	BOS	MLB	25	46(0)	73¹	8-4	2	81	1.10	1.96	55.8%	5.7%	27.2%	2.0%	49.7%	70.5%	79.6%	34.5%	60.6%	.304	.495	69	1.9
2022	BOS	MLB	26	31(9)	78¹	4-2	6	82	1.02	3.45	57.7%	4.8%	26.4%	3.2%	40.8%	70.3%	78.2%	34.0%	56.2%	.271	.526	78	1.6
2023	WOR	AAA	27	4(4)	15	0-0	0	17	1.27	1.20		3.2%	27.4%	1.6%	35.7%	64.4%	81.6%	35.1%	56.5%	.400	.634	88	0.3
2023	BOS	MLB	27	22(10)	71²	5-5	1	72	1.33	5.15	50.5%	4.3%	23.7%	4.3%	43.5%	69.2%	84.1%	36.3%	53.5%	.342	.671	87	1.4
2024 DC	BOS	MLB	28	57(0)	60	4-2	0	58	1.20	3.70	54.2%	5.8%	23.4%	2.8%	43.0%					.308	.531	87	0.8

2023 Arsenal: SI (94.2), CH (82.6), SW (79.8)   *Comps: Garrett Mock (63), Dave Borkowski (56), Adrian Houser (54)*

Whitlock threw two innings in his final appearance of last season and gave up just a seeing-eye single through the infield while striking out three. He held his hands a little higher in the set position, which was all the difference he needed to generate six swinging strikes on 33 pitches. Maybe it was a timing mechanism; maybe he had been tipping his pitches—there was more than a three-inch difference in average horizontal release point between his breaking and off-speed pitches for most of the year. With his MLB-best 7.6 feet of extension and fantastic walk rate, he should've been more effective, but his sinker and changeup were annihilated in most of his previous outings when he wasn't dogged by hip and elbow ailments. Could it have been such a simple fix as bringing his hands higher when coming set? Who knows, but he probably wishes he'd have tried it months earlier.

Josh Winckowski   RHP   Born: 06/28/98   Age: 26   Height: 6'4"   Weight: 215   Origin: Round 15, 2016 Draft (#462 overall)

YEAR	TM	LVL	AGE	G (GS)	IP	W-L	SV	K	WHIP	ERA	CSP	BB%	K%	HR%	GB%	ZSw%	ZCon%	OSw%	OCon%	BABIP	SLGCON	DRA-	WARP
2021	POR	AA	23	21(20)	100	8-3	0	88	1.30	4.14		7.0%	20.5%	2.3%	50.3%					.300	.489	100	0.8
2021	WOR	AAA	23	2(2)	12	1-1	0	13	0.67	2.25		6.7%	28.9%	2.2%	50.0%					.148	.357	94	0.2
2022	WOR	AAA	24	13(12)	61¹	2-4	0	62	1.22	3.82		7.1%	24.3%	1.6%	52.9%					.312	.483	85	1.3
2022	BOS	MLB	24	15(14)	70¹	5-7	0	44	1.59	5.89	56.0%	8.5%	13.9%	3.2%	52.3%	66.5%	89.3%	27.4%	69.6%	.322	.582	109	0.4
2023	BOS	MLB	25	60(1)	84¹	4-4	3	82	1.42	2.88	48.9%	8.4%	22.3%	2.5%	51.4%	70.5%	83.5%	33.2%	58.2%	.331	.522	87	1.6
2024 DC	BOS	MLB	26	51(0)	54	3-2	0	43	1.36	4.23	51.8%	8.4%	18.8%	2.3%	50.7%					.304	.491	95	0.5

2023 Arsenal: SI (96.4), FC (88.7), SL (85.4), CH (92.7), FA (96.1), CU (80.5)   *Comps: Anthony Bass (64), Paul Blackburn (64), Gabriel Ynoa (63)*

A pitching staff is like a salad. There are a few tomatoes and croutons here and there to stand out and give it zest, but most of it is plain old lettuce. Leafy greens fill the plate and provide structure even though they're nobody's favorite veggies, and Winckowski is romaine. Note that this is an upgrade from his rookie year, during which he looked so wilted that he didn't belong in the bowl at all. He increased his cutter usage from 10.1% to 35.3% and settled in as an effective sinker/slider/cutter multi-inning bullpen arm. However, his excellent ERA was the product of an elevated 80.6% strand rate, which isn't supported by his thoroughly average batted-ball data. Bullpens and salads both need filler, but no matter how much you dress him, he'll never pop like a carrot or slice of radish (Radatz?).

LINEOUTS

Hitters

HITTER	POS	TM	LVL	AGE	PA	R	HR	RBI	SB	AVG/OBP/SLG	BABIP	SLGCON	BB%	K%	ZSw%	ZCon%	OSw%	OCon%	LA	90th EV	DRC+	BRR	DRP	WARP
Antonio Anderson	3B	SAL	A	18	28	2	0	1	0	.185/.214/.222	.278	.333	3.6%	32.1%							89	-0.8	0.0	0.0
Yoeilin Cespedes	SS	DSL RSXB	ROK	17	209	37	6	38	1	.346/.392/.560	.368	.641	6.7%	11.5%										
David Hamilton	SS	WOR	AAA	25	469	74	17	54	57	.247/.363/.438	.297	.606	15.1%	23.2%	62.0%	87.1%	27.9%	65.0%			105	2.8	4.4	2.2
	SS	BOS	MLB	25	39	2	0	0	2	.121/.256/.182	.174	.261	15.4%	25.6%	55.7%	92.3%	32.2%	62.1%	16.8	98.0	88	0.0	-0.1	0.1
Nathan Hickey	C	GVL	A+	23	82	13	4	9	0	.294/.402/.588	.356	.833	14.6%	24.4%							124	-1.0	-0.9	0.3
	C	POR	AA	23	335	49	15	56	3	.258/.352/.474	.323	.690	11.9%	27.2%							116	1.7	-7.5	1.1
Chase Meidroth	IF	GVL	A+	21	97	19	2	14	4	.338/.495/.459	.442	.630	21.6%	20.6%							134	-2.5	0.0	0.3
	IF	POR	AA	21	396	59	7	43	9	.255/.386/.375	.315	.494	14.9%	19.7%							130	3.0	-1.2	2.2
Mikey Romero	IF	SAL	A	19	105	11	0	9	2	.217/.288/.304	.260	.373	8.6%	16.2%							101	-0.6	0.6	0.4
Nazzan Zanetello	SS	RSX	ROK	18	45	6	0	1	5	.139/.311/.222	.238	.381	20.0%	33.3%										

Boston gave third-round pick **Antonio Anderson** an overslot bonus to forgo his commitment to Georgia Tech. The rules say he couldn't play for both at once, which is just as well, because combining a yellow jacket with red socks would be a fashion disaster. ⦿ **Yoeilin Cespedes** was Boston's splashiest international amateur signing of the 2023 class with a $1.4 million bonus. No, he's not related to any other Y. Cespedes in professional baseball, but he's making a name for himself with outstanding hand-eye coordination and surprising pop for his small frame. ⦿ **David Hamilton** led all Triple-A players in steals, posted a phenomenal 15.1% walk rate, played all three up-the-middle positions and even showed a little power. He's as versatile as Forrest Gump, and nearly as likely to quietly show up in a team photo this year. ⦿ **Nathan Hickey** led Portland in OPS, but his throws from behind the plate look like 50 Cent's ceremonial first pitch. He allowed 129 stolen bases and threw out only 10 runners. He needs to switch positions and/or improve his arm if he wants to get rich (or die tryin'). ⦿ In a stiff rebuke of nominative determinism, **Chase Meidroth** was one of the most patient hitters in the minor leagues. If he maintains his 16.2% walk rate as he climbs the ladder, they'll have to write "Won't-Chase Meidroth" on his big-league *per diem* checks. ⦿ It's too early to use the "B" word for 2022 first-round pick **Mikey Romero**, but if he does become the thing that rhymes with dust, his 2023 season will have been the first red flag. Let's hope his poor hitting was caused by a sore back that limited him to 34 games. ⦿ **Nazzan Zanetello** has as many professional hits as he does *N*s and *Z*s in his name. The 2023 second-round pick made it to the Carolina League but only played one game there before an injury ended his season.

Pitchers

PITCHER	TM	LVL	AGE	G (GS)	IP	W-L	SV	K	WHIP	ERA	CSP	BB%	K%	HR%	GB%	ZSw%	ZCon%	OSw%	OCon%	BABIP	SLGCON	DRA-	WARP
Kyle Barraclough	WOR	AAA	33	14 (13)	74	8-1	0	62	1.31	3.65		14.8%	20.4%	3.0%	35.8%	69.6%	81.0%	29.9%	58.7%	.234	.472	103	0.9
	BOS	MLB	33	3 (0)	7²	1-1	0	4	2.61	12.91	45.6%	8.7%	6.5%	37.5%	72.1%	90.9%	25.3%	62.5%	.379	.839	131	0.0
Richard Fitts	SOM	AA	23	27 (27)	152²	11-5	0	163	1.14	3.48		6.8%	25.9%	3.5%	40.8%					.276	.534	90	2.9
Justin Garza	WOR	AAA	29	24 (0)	28	2-1	2	28	1.50	4.82		11.6%	23.1%	2.5%	39.0%	70.0%	84.0%	29.9%	57.6%	.338	.526	98	0.4
	BOS	MLB	29	17 (1)	18¹	0-2	0	17	1.85	7.36	47.7%	13.2%	18.7%	3.3%	34.4%	69.1%	83.5%	26.7%	68.5%	.328	.650	118	0.0
Wikelman Gonzalez	GVL	A+	21	15 (15)	63	6-3	0	105	1.44	5.14		15.1%	37.6%	1.8%	43.8%					.352	.594	72	1.4
	POR	AA	21	10 (10)	48¹	3-1	0	63	1.14	2.42		14.1%	31.8%	1.0%	37.1%					.243	.365	92	1.0
Dinelson Lamet	COL	MLB	30	16 (4)	25²	1-4	0	31	2.34	11.57	45.4%	16.4%	23.1%	4.5%	43.8%	72.3%	85.5%	23.9%	56.1%	.432	.897	107	0.2
	BOS	MLB	30	1 (0)	2	0-0	0	1	2.50	13.50	47.7%	9.1%	9.1%	9.1%	33.3%	87.5%	92.9%	25.0%	66.7%	.375	.778	110	0.0
Mauricio Llovera	SAC	AAA	27	17 (2)	20²	1-0	1	24	1.06	3.92		7.1%	28.6%	4.8%	42.3%	56.1%	81.9%	27.6%	48.2%	.250	.615	80	0.4
	BOS	MLB	27	25 (0)	29²	1-3	0	24	1.52	5.46	55.6%	9.4%	17.3%	1.4%	50.0%	60.4%	87.5%	25.0%	69.0%	.313	.454	98	0.4
	SF	MLB	27	5 (0)	5¹	1-0	0	5	1.13	1.69	47.9%	9.5%	23.8%	4.8%	35.7%	66.7%	95.5%	25.6%	70.0%	.231	.615	96	0.1
Bryan Mata	WOR	AAA	24	9 (7)	27	0-3	0	28	2.19	6.33		21.3%	19.9%	0.7%	44.3%	64.2%	81.5%	21.4%	58.4%	.359	.487	122	0.0
Noah Song	GVL	A+	26	7 (6)	21²	1-2	0	15	1.38	4.15		11.5%	15.6%	3.1%	34.3%					.250	.522	126	0.0
Brandon Walter	WOR	AAA	26	21 (18)	94	3-5	0	88	1.43	4.60		8.5%	21.3%	2.4%	49.5%	65.3%	85.7%	36.2%	64.6%	.325	.534	88	2.0
	BOS	MLB	26	9 (0)	23	0-0	1	16	1.70	6.26	51.0%	6.6%	15.1%	2.8%	42.7%	73.2%	90.8%	30.3%	70.5%	.367	.585	116	0.1
Greg Weissert	SWB	AAA	28	38 (0)	40¹	5-3	10	58	1.09	2.90		10.1%	34.3%	3.0%	43.5%	51.9%	78.6%	32.2%	54.4%	.256	.562	77	1.1
	NYY	MLB	28	17 (0)	20	0-0	0	22	1.45	4.05	48.8%	9.2%	25.3%	3.4%	48.2%	68.4%	76.0%	23.2%	62.2%	.346	.582	88	0.4

"Ough" makes many different sounds. **Kyle Barraclough** had a rough go, coughing up 24 baserunners out of 46 batters faced. He thought he ought to get another chance, though the bough was broken, so he had to plough through on minor-league dough. ⦿ It's not often we can describe a guy who was once stuck in the bullpen at Auburn a pleasant surprise and a minor-league workhorse. But after leading all of Double-A in innings last year, **Richard Fitts** that description. ⦿ It isn't easy for normal human-sized pitchers to reach MLB, so we're not going to make any quips about **Justin Garza**'s 5-foot-10, 170-pound frame. His scattershot command is fair game, though, and his inability to locate his pitches brought his season up shor—never mind. ⦿ **Wikelman Gonzalez** has the build of a batboy, but it's not his size that counts—it's the mid-90s fastball and wipeout secondaries. He led all full-season minor-league pitchers with a 35.2% strikeout rate, so some other 165-pound kid will have to collect the foul balls. ⦿ Remember when **Dinelson Lamet** received down-ballot Cy Young votes in 2020, three years before he got mercilessly blasted out of two different organizations? [deep sigh] So does he; so does he. ⦿ Back home in Korea, **Chansol Lee**'s fastball blew batters away at 153 kph. That's good enough for him to jump directly to MLB with a $300,000 bonus while spurning a first-round selection in the KBO draft—but remember conversion rates: In America, that fastball is only 95 mph. ⦿ The Spanish word *llavero* translates to "key ring" in English. Unfortunately for the Red Sox, (**Mauricio**) **Llovera**'s minor-league production didn't translate much at all. ⦿ **Bryan Mata** answered the "starter or reliever" question, albeit not the way he would've liked. He missed four months with a lat strain, but walking 30 out of 141 batters is the more concerning issue. Now out of options, he has to answer the much-worse "major leaguer or not" question. ⦿ **Noah Song** is a veteran who has yet to become a rookie. He returned from more than three years of active duty in the US Navy with a creaky back and a fastball several ticks lower than when he last pitched in 2019. A baseball-centric offseason could reinvigorate his post-service career. ⦿ This is not 'Nam; this is baseball. There are rules. **Brandon Walter's** velocity never returned after a 2022 injury and hitters stayed calmer than you are in the box against him, refusing to let him mark it zero on the scoreboard. ⦿ **Greg Weissert's** sweeper might go BRRR and cause delightfully bad swings here and there, but his command still leaves a lot to be desired. The Yankees evidently agreed; after optioning him on Opening Day Eve, they did it four more different times in 2023.

CHICAGO CUBS

Essay by Roy Wood Jr.

Player comments by Nathan Grimm and BP staff

Every child should have a pet or a favorite sports team—both teach you how to deal with loss.

It's important for kids to experience the *feeling* of loss, but not so much so that they become completely hopeless and in disarray. But sports don't just help us deal with pain, they also help give us a chance to practice cautious optimism. Sports help keep us honest about the moments in our own life where we feel optimistic. After a few failed runs at a championship, you start to learn how to keep your level of optimism from getting dangerously low, or rising unrealistically high.

In that sense, the Chicago Cubs are the perfect team to keep a child even-keeled.

To a certain extent, and for a particular generation, the Cubs *are* baseball. Not winning—not in the slightest—but baseball as an idea, standing in an outfield, having a beer in the bleachers. The Cubs had history without specificity, a general feel. Big plans abandoned and forgotten, summers enjoyed and wasted. Anything can be Cubs baseball if you squint. It's time spent, without any more detail necessary or allowed.

More often than not, sports fandom is generational. A father passes his misery down to his son or daughter, who then retells it to a grandchild. But for those of us who are first-generation sports fans, our path to choosing our team can be a little different, especially if it's a sport that no one in the neighborhood cares about. I enjoyed baseball as a child, and to this day I cannot tell you where that love came from.

I did not grow up in a baseball town. (At least until Michael Jordan came to Birmingham.) In Alabama, we loved Bo Jackson but couldn't name the other eight people in the Royals' starting lineup. And we loved Frank Thomas...but in those days you would be hard pressed to find anyone that knew the Big Hurt's baseball stats better than they knew his numbers as the star tight end for Auburn.

I also did not grow up in a baseball home. As far as I know, my parents never played organized sports. My father sure didn't—a car crash as a 13-year-old damaged his hip In such a way that he never regained full mobility. And my mom, well...let's go back to one of my old Little League seasons. Every year, they did the annual parents-versus-kids softball

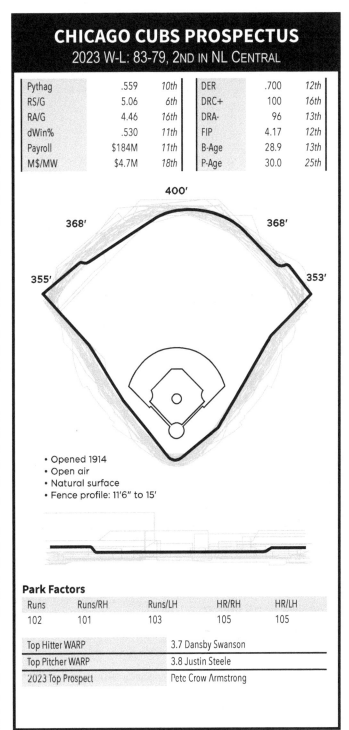

CHICAGO CUBS PROSPECTUS
2023 W-L: 83-79, 2ND IN NL CENTRAL

Pythag	.559	10th	DER	.700	12th
RS/G	5.06	6th	DRC+	100	16th
RA/G	4.46	16th	DRA-	96	13th
dWin%	.530	11th	FIP	4.17	12th
Payroll	$184M	11th	B-Age	28.9	13th
M$/MW	$4.7M	18th	P-Age	30.0	25th

400'
368'   368'
355'   353'

- Opened 1914
- Open air
- Natural surface
- Fence profile: 11'6" to 15'

Park Factors

Runs	Runs/RH	Runs/LH	HR/RH	HR/LH
102	101	103	105	105

Top Hitter WARP	3.7 Dansby Swanson
Top Pitcher WARP	3.8 Justin Steele
2023 Top Prospect	Pete Crow Armstrong

Payroll History (in millions)

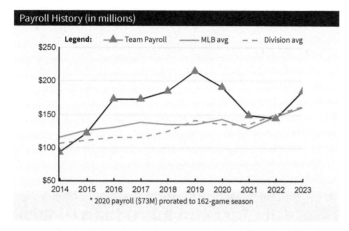

Legend: ▲ Team Payroll — MLB avg - - Division avg

* 2020 payroll ($73M) prorated to 162-game season

Future Commitments (in millions)

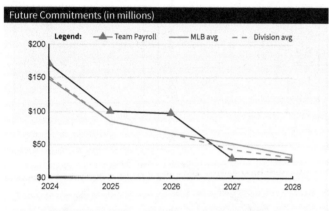

Legend: ▲ Team Payroll — MLB avg - - Division avg

Farm System Ranking

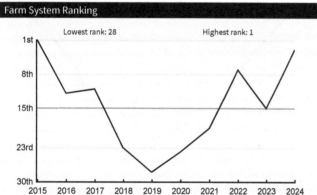

Lowest rank: 28   Highest rank: 1

Personnel

President, Baseball Operations
Jed Hoyer

General Manager
Carter Hawkins

Assistant General Manager
Ehsan Bokhari

Vice President, Player Development
Jared Banner

Vice President, Baseball Operations
Greg Davey

Vice President, Research & Development
Chris Moore

Manager
Craig Counsell

BP Alumni
Bryan Cole

game. My mom was a lifetime college professor, and she got a hit through a series of *Bad News Bears*-ass errors. She made the turn past second base and was barrelling towards third, and in seconds her face goes from the sheer joy of being excited that she got a hit to the sheer terror of knowing she was going too fast and was about to overrun third base.

(I played Little League on the west side of Birmingham, Alabama in the Central Park neighborhood. We played on Keenon Field, and Keenon Field had some unique features, because it was crammed into an elementary school parking lot. There was little to no foul territory down the baselines, so there was third base, and immediately behind it was the third base coaches' box, and immediately behind *that* was a huge, rusty fence. The kind of fence that would for sure give you hepatitis or tetanus or whatever other diseases you catch from a fence.)

It's less than six feet from third base to the fence, so Little Leaguers turning past third to home would sometimes swing too wide and scrape their arm as they went for home plate. And if you were headed to third base at Keenon Field, you *have* to know how to slide.

I looked at my mother's face and I could see her doing the velocity calculations versus the amount of space she had left to slow down. She was going to have to slide but, clearly, she didn't know how. So my mother stumbled, tumbled, rolled and somersaulted through third base smack into the hepatitis fence. Tagged out, the inning was over. And that was the last day my mother did anything remotely athletic.

I should have known at that moment that athleticism would never be in my genes.

⚾   ⚾   ⚾

I spent the early 1990s copying the batting stances of Jerome Walton, Mark Grace and Andre Dawson—to varying degrees of failure. But I was hooked and happy to be a fan, even if no one else in my house or my town was.

My fandom was solidified in 1989 when the Cubs went to the NLCS and lost to the San Francisco Giants. What I thought would be an amazing run for the next decade turned sour really fast. Sid Bream slid into history, Greg Maddux left the friendly confines and suddenly Birmingham was a city full of Atlanta Braves fans. It would be almost a decade (1998) before the club saw the playoffs again. (Of course, they were promptly swept by Atlanta.)

Then there was 2003, 2007 and 2008, then on to the current run where, since 2015, the Cubs have made it to the postseason more times than not. The team has never had a 10-year stretch this fruitful. Not even when they were back-to-back champs pre-Prohibition did they make so many trips to the postseason.

This is the right balance. You can't expect your team to win all the time...unless you are a fan of the Yankees or the Dallas Cowboys. I think every sports team has to sell a little optimism to their fanbase, but good sports organizations know that every now and then they have to deliver on that promise.

⚾ ⚾ ⚾

I played Little League in Memphis but I don't think I saw baseball on television until we got to Birmingham. I was born in New York City, so my basic assumption is that—without parental supervision—I would become a Mets fan. I loved Dwight Gooden and Darryl Strawberry, but I learned very fast that the only way I could ever see them on TV in Alabama during the 1980s was when they played the Chicago Cubs.

The Cubs, like the Braves, benefited from a superstation that carried them on multiple cable packages across the country. But the biggest difference between the Cubs and the Braves is that the Cubs came on television during the day, when I did not have to compete with my father for control over the single television in the house that had a cable box. If the Braves had 1:00 PM baseball games that I could watch all day during the summer and after school, this essay might be about Ronald Acuña's 40-70 journey instead.

It started as only watching baseball when the Mets were playing, but I eventually switched sides. Inevitably I fell in love with the Cubs, Harry Caray and Steve Stone.

One day, while watching baseball in the afternoon, my father came into the room. He never paid much attention to what I was watching on TV, but when he saw it was the Cubs he paused for a moment and sat down. "I used to do a radio show with Ernie Banks," he mumbled.

(Now, just because my father did not play any sports did not mean he did not have a healthy love and respect for athletes. My father was a radio news reporter: He covered conflicts and crises on every continent but Antarctica. In between those travels he ended up in Chicago for a while at WVON radio. He struck up a relationship with Ernie Banks and eventually the two of them hosted a weekly radio show together.)

When it was clear to him that I had no idea who Ernie Banks was, he proceeded to explain to me his history and what he meant to so many black people in Chicago while playing on Chicago's predominantly white North Side. I thought it was really cool that my father knew Ernie Banks and he thought it was pretty cool that I enjoyed baseball.

It would be the last time he and I ever really discussed sports.

⚾ ⚾ ⚾

Chicago blew a few leads in September that probably could have kept them in the hunt, but in hindsight when you look at what the Arizona Diamondbacks accomplished, they were just white-hot. Sometimes it's just someone else's movie. Still, after blowing that lead in the Wild Card race in September, I wondered if they were heading back to their losing ways...then the Cubs went and hired the most expensive manager in the game over the offseason: Craig Counsell. The team made a huge addition, but it came with the cost of well-loved David Ross.

Some Cubs fans describe seeing David Ross leave Wrigley as one the most painful sights since seeing Anthony Rizzo in Yankee pinstripes. This offseason's sudden change in the clubhouse keeps you balanced. David Ross out, Craig Counsell in. On the one hand, it can give a Cubs fan hope that maybe there will be more major moves made...another Dansby Swanson-type signing or a big trade. Perhaps the return of Cody Bellinger, a humble arrival who made so many friends so quickly. On the other hand, this is the same organization that has chosen over the years to say goodbye, one by one, to the players who were the architects of the 2016 journey.

Each of these decisions to move on from the magic of 2016 disappointed many of us in Cub Nation, but ultimately life itself is about tough choices and making them swiftly and fearlessly before figuring out a way to continue on. (There's another lesson sports can teach kids.) Considering how close the Cubs were in the Wild Card in 2023, I would say that they figured that out.

To be a Cubs fan over the age of 30 is to constantly look at the clock waiting for it to strike midnight so you can see that the beautiful Cinderella "always in the playoffs" slipper fall from your feet, returning to the team that didn't make the playoffs for 39 years in a row. But I think if the last nine years have shown us anything, it's that this is an organization that wants to compete every year and expects to do so. Gone are the days when it was enough for the club to fill up Wrigley and distract them with some other, better team three hours a day. That's one of those changes where it's time for us Cub fans to accept that.

⚾ ⚾ ⚾

When my son was born in 2016, the only things I wanted to pass down to him were a decent work ethic and the love of sports. And as far as that thing I mentioned earlier about learning loss and optimism...well, I travel far too much for work to ever consider being a pet owner. So, sports it is.

I'm not sure if the sport he eventually comes to love will be baseball. (It's not polling too high with him right now.) It's the kind of sport where it helps to play around the neighborhood, and he's growing up in the concrete confines of New York City. Stickball is all but dead, and the city doesn't lend itself to the space needed for seven to 10 kids in the neighborhood to go out and play with a tennis ball, as I did every year in the expanse of neighborhoods and parks in Alabama.

He and I play a little pepper ball, and soft toss when we can. I even let him take a few swings in that VR headset virtual batting cage software, but it still seems like basketball and tennis are his things for now. Nonetheless, he loves watching the sport and a few trips to Wrigley Field with me have helped.

At first, I really wanted to raise a Cubs fan and maybe a baseball player, but as I've gotten older I realize I just wanted to raise a baseball fan. I said it before, more often than not sports fandom is generational. My son was born to a Cubs fan and a Brewers fan. To save my son from bonding with the blue and gold, I agreed that his mother could raise him as a Packers fan. It's looking like the Chicago Cubs are going to be competitive for a very long time, so he'll have to get his thrill of disappointment from the Packers rather than Anthony Young and his 27 consecutive losses.

Cub fans are so used to hedging their bets. For years we did not know how to accept winning; then we got to a place where we expected it. These Cubs are different from Ernie Banks' Cubs, and it looks like they're different from the ones I grew up with too. They won't only teach him about loss, or how to keep expectations low. Things change over the generations, and now we find our balance.

—Roy Wood Jr. is an Emmy-nominated producer, comedian and writer based in New York City.

HITTERS

★ ★ ★ *2024 Top 101 Prospect* **#80** ★ ★ ★

Kevin Alcántara CF Born: 07/12/02 Age: 21 Bats: R Throws: R Height: 6'6" Weight: 188 Origin: IFA, 2018

YEAR	TM	LVL	AGE	PA	R	HR	RBI	SB	AVG/OBP/SLG	BABIP	SLGCON	BB%	K%	ZSw%	ZCon%	OSw%	OCon%	LA	90th EV	DRC+	BRR	DRP	WARP
2021	YNK	ROK	18	31	5	1	3	2	.370/.452/.519	.500	.737	12.9%	25.8%									-0.6	
2021	CUB	ROK	18	107	27	4	21	3	.337/.415/.609	.443	.875	12.1%	26.2%									-4.3	
2022	MB	A	19	495	76	15	85	14	.273/.360/.451	.345	.633	11.1%	24.8%								108	2.9	3.9	2.5
2023	MSS	WIN	20	89	10	5	23	2	.253/.326/.532	.319	.824	7.9%	31.5%	70.6%	75.0%	39.3%	63.6%						
2023	SB	A+	20	408	65	12	66	15	.286/.341/.466	.353	.631	7.6%	23.8%								106	3.0	6.5	2.2
2024 non	CHC	MLB	21	251	22	5	24	0	.227/.281/.351	.310	.516	6.2%	29.3%								77	0.0	0	0.1

2023 GP: CF (100), RF (11), DH (9)   *Comps: Manuel Margot (85), Cameron Maybin (82), Victor Robles (79)*

That Alcántara is routinely described as the Cubs prospect with the highest upside, and yet was ranked the sixth-best prospect on our list last winter, speaks to the distance between now and some nebulous then. He continued to take steps toward that end in 2023, reaching Double-A by September while demonstrating all the tools that have made him a darling of ceiling fetishists. He also showed the ability to make in-season adjustments, parlaying some small mechanical and approach adjustments into a .338/.416/.579 line in the second half. Assuming he begins the 2024 season at Double-A, perhaps the distance between now and the majors will prove to be shorter than that between his current and idealized forms.

Jorge Alfaro C/DH Born: 06/11/93 Age: 31 Bats: R Throws: R Height: 6'2" Weight: 249 Origin: IFA, 2010

YEAR	TM	LVL	AGE	PA	R	HR	RBI	SB	AVG/OBP/SLG	BABIP	SLGCON	BB%	K%	ZSw%	ZCon%	OSw%	OCon%	LA	90th EV	DRC+	BRR	DRP	WARP
2021	MIA	MLB	28	311	22	4	30	8	.244/.283/.342	.354	.515	3.5%	31.8%	79.6%	79.4%	45.8%	53.1%	2.1	109.0	59	0.1	3.9	0.1
2022	SD	MLB	29	274	25	7	40	1	.246/.285/.383	.364	.620	4.0%	35.8%	81.8%	72.8%	50.2%	50.7%	8.3	109.1	59	0.0	-2.9	-0.7
2023	WOR	AAA	30	191	22	6	30	4	.320/.366/.520	.391	.689	4.7%	22.5%	81.6%	82.1%	53.7%	51.2%			99	0.0	-0.7	0.5
2023	JAX	AAA	30	73	3	0	6	0	.200/.274/.262	.265	.354	6.8%	23.3%	82.9%	75.9%	41.5%	42.4%			77	0.7	0.2	0.1
2023	COL	MLB	30	32	2	1	4	0	.161/.188/.387	.222	.632	0.0%	37.5%	80.5%	90.9%	54.5%	41.7%	2.3	103.1	91	0.0	0.0	0.0
2023	BOS	MLB	30	20	0	0	0	0	.118/.250/.118	.143	.143	10.0%	15.0%	82.1%	95.7%	40.0%	43.8%	-15.6	105.1	80	0.0	-0.2	0.0
2024 non	CHC	MLB	31	251	21	5	24	1	.207/.258/.328	.292	.500	4.5%	32.3%							63	-0.1	-1.6	-0.4

2023 GP: C (8), DH (7)   *Comps: Welington Castillo (55), Sandy León (54), Wilson Ramos (53)*

After splitting the first six years of his career evenly between the Phillies and Marlins, Alfaro played for three teams over the last two calendar years. He rejoined Miami on a minor-league deal late last summer, where he registered an OPS south of .600 with the Triple-A Jumbo Shrimp. That wasn't much better than what he did in the major leagues, where his trademark ability to stretch the zone like a pair of pants worn exclusively on Thanksgiving placed him among the league's bottom-25 batters by OPS (minimum 50 PA). This 1960s-inspired free love for swinging continued to undercut Alfaro's ability to even come close to working a walk, making for an ugly combo that has sapped any ability to impact the ball. That prevented him cracking Miami's woof-worthy catcher tandem and has reduced him to familiar organizational depth.

YEAR	TM	P. COUNT	FRM RUNS	BLK RUNS	THRW RUNS	TOT RUNS
2021	MIA	7948	4.6	-0.2	0.5	5.0
2022	SD	8855	-1.7	-0.4	0.2	-1.9
2023	JAX	1563	0.0	0.0	0.3	0.3
2023	WOR	4133	-0.4	-0.1	-0.7	-1.2
2023	COL	203	-0.1	0.0	0.0	-0.1
2023	BOS	579	-0.2	0.0	0.0	-0.2
2024	CHC	6956	-1.5	-0.1	0.0	-1.7

Miguel Amaya C Born: 03/09/99 Age: 25 Bats: R Throws: R Height: 6'0" Weight: 230 Origin: IFA, 2015

YEAR	TM	LVL	AGE	PA	R	HR	RBI	SB	AVG/OBP/SLG	BABIP	SLGCON	BB%	K%	ZSw%	ZCon%	OSw%	OCon%	LA	90th EV	DRC+	BRR	DRP	WARP
2021	TNS	AA	22	106	11	1	13	2	.215/.406/.304	.281	.421	19.8%	20.8%							127	1.0	0.3	0.8
2022	CUB	ROK	23	44	4	2	4	0	.216/.341/.378	.273	.583	15.9%	29.5%										
2022	TNS	AA	23	116	15	4	19	0	.278/.379/.485	.343	.681	12.1%	24.1%							115	-1.9	0.0	0.3
2023	TNS	AA	24	56	9	4	8	1	.273/.411/.659	.333	1.074	14.3%	30.4%							112	0.4	-0.3	0.3
2023	IOW	AAA	24	60	5	1	10	0	.313/.450/.479	.424	.676	18.3%	23.3%	57.3%	87.3%	29.3%	48.8%			107	-0.2	0.1	0.2
2023	CHC	MLB	24	156	17	5	18	0	.214/.329/.359	.264	.516	7.7%	25.6%	66.7%	84.8%	29.9%	51.0%	18.1	103.7	101	-0.1	1.7	0.7
2024 DC	CHC	MLB	25	245	25	6	25	0	.216/.317/.356	.281	.507	9.0%	26.1%							93	0.0	3.6	1.1

2023 GP: C (41), DH (9)   *Comps: Austin Romine (55), Tomás Nido (52), Pedro Severino (52)*

The Cubs will likely enter the 2024 season with a May-December backstop tandem, with Amaya representing the youthful counterpart to Yan Gomes' veteran presence. Amaya debuted last season after Tommy John surgery and a Lisfranc fracture in his left foot ensured his path to the majors was anything but linear. In his introduction to the bigs, he lifted the ball as often as Pete Alonso and Brent Rooker, two hulking sluggers. That tendency allowed nine extra-base hits, but dragged down his batting average, too. His defense, meanwhile, was good enough to ensure he's a part of the team's plans, even if the bat is more Yan Gomes than Johnny Gomes.

YEAR	TM	P. COUNT	FRM RUNS	BLK RUNS	THRW RUNS	TOT RUNS
2021	TNS	1942	0.3	-0.1	0.4	0.7
2023	TNS	1632	0.5	-0.1	-0.2	0.1
2023	IOW	1997	-0.1	0.0	0.3	0.2
2023	CHC	4815	2.8	0.0	-0.2	2.6
2024	CHC	8418	3.9	0.0	-0.3	3.6

★ ★ ★ *2024 Top 101 Prospect* **#84** ★ ★ ★

Moises Ballesteros C/1B   Born: 11/08/03   Age: 20   Bats: L   Throws: R   Height: 5'7"   Weight: 195   Origin: IFA, 2021

YEAR	TM	LVL	AGE	PA	R	HR	RBI	SB	AVG/OBP/SLG	BABIP	SLGCON	BB%	K%	ZSw%	ZCon%	OSw%	OCon%	LA	90th EV	DRC+	BRR	DRP	WARP
2021	DSL CUBR	ROK	17	187	22	3	25	6	.266/.396/.390	.299	.462	16.6%	12.8%									3.0	
2022	CUB	ROK	18	110	12	7	18	0	.268/.355/.536	.268	.667	11.8%	17.3%										
2022	MB	A	18	129	17	3	15	0	.248/.349/.394	.300	.531	14.0%	21.7%							104	-1.5	-1.2	0.2
2023	MB	A	19	241	28	8	32	5	.274/.394/.457	.284	.539	16.6%	12.4%							140	-4.3	0.1	1.3
2023	SB	A+	19	231	33	6	31	2	.300/.364/.463	.350	.595	9.5%	19.5%							113	-1.0	-1.6	0.5
2024 non	CHC	MLB	20	251	22	4	23	0	.226/.292/.339	.277	.446	8.0%	21.5%							78	0.0	0	0.2

2023 GP: C (76), 1B (26), DH (14)   *Comps: Freddie Freeman (68), Jake Bauers (67), Daric Barton (65)*

The exact phrase "built like a fire hydrant" was used twice by BP writers in 2023, both times to describe Ballesteros. (Past players who have garnered the comparison include Willians Astudillo, Jedd Gyorko and Yoenis Céspedes, among others.) Any publicity is good publicity, as they say, so Ballesteros drawing that comparison at least means he's giving writers reason to talk about him. That'll happen when you hit .285/.375/.449 across three levels while showing good bat-to-ball skills and an advanced approach for a 19-year-old. Fire hydrants are notorious for being unathletic—sedentary, even—so Ballesteros will likely have to stick behind the plate to realize his full potential, and his ability to remain there is the biggest question moving forward. Only recently celebrating his 20th birthday, it's a question that doesn't require a definitive answer in 2024.

★ ★ ★ *2024 Top 101 Prospect* **#65** ★ ★ ★

Owen Caissie OF   Born: 07/08/02   Age: 21   Bats: L   Throws: R   Height: 6'3"   Weight: 190   Origin: Round 2, 2020 Draft (#45 overall)

YEAR	TM	LVL	AGE	PA	R	HR	RBI	SB	AVG/OBP/SLG	BABIP	SLGCON	BB%	K%	ZSw%	ZCon%	OSw%	OCon%	LA	90th EV	DRC+	BRR	DRP	WARP
2021	CUB	ROK	18	136	20	6	20	1	.349/.478/.596	.500	.929	19.1%	28.7%									-5.0	
2021	MB	A	18	90	15	1	9	0	.233/.367/.329	.356	.533	17.8%	31.1%							92	-0.4	0.7	0.2
2022	SB	A+	19	433	57	11	58	11	.254/.349/.402	.350	.598	11.5%	28.6%							94	3.8	1.1	1.6
2023	TNS	AA	20	528	77	22	84	7	.289/.398/.519	.407	.829	14.4%	31.1%							107	0.2	3.7	2.4
2024 DC	CHC	MLB	21	30	3	1	3	0	.241/.324/.375	.368	.588	10.0%	34.0%							96	0.0	0	0.1

2023 GP: RF (101), DH (12), LF (6)   *Comps: Dylan Carlson (64), Giancarlo Stanton (60), Justin Williams (60)*

Hey look, it's another promising Cubs outfield prospect. With Pete Crow-Armstrong and Alexander Canario reaching the highest level in 2023, Caissie is a step behind his peers, but that's no knock on his ultimate upside. The big-bodied 21-year-old combines tremendous power with a good knowledge of the strike zone...and a swing-and-miss problem that could be his downfall. Three-true-outcome players are more acceptable in today's game than ever before, but they're not the kind of guys who supplant more well-rounded hitters that the Cubs appear to have in the pipeline. The good news for Caissie is that with Crow-Armstrong and Canario arriving in Chicago, he's got time to work on those holes in his swing without the bleacher bums clamoring for a premature promotion, or subsequent demotion.

Alexander Canario OF   Born: 05/07/00   Age: 24   Bats: R   Throws: R   Height: 5'11"   Weight: 165   Origin: IFA, 2016

YEAR	TM	LVL	AGE	PA	R	HR	RBI	SB	AVG/OBP/SLG	BABIP	SLGCON	BB%	K%	ZSw%	ZCon%	OSw%	OCon%	LA	90th EV	DRC+	BRR	DRP	WARP
2021	SJ	A	21	274	43	9	29	15	.235/.325/.433	.307	.648	12.0%	28.8%							98	1.0	0.9	1.0
2021	SB	A+	21	182	19	9	28	6	.224/.264/.429	.248	.589	5.5%	25.3%							106	-1.7	2.8	0.8
2022	SB	A+	22	100	17	7	22	3	.281/.360/.584	.383	.963	10.0%	35.0%							110	-0.6	0.4	0.4
2022	TNS	AA	22	350	51	24	61	17	.248/.329/.552	.269	.781	10.3%	26.0%							117	0.0	1.1	2.0
2022	IOW	AAA	22	84	16	6	14	3	.231/.386/.538	.231	.795	15.5%	25.0%							115	0.2	-0.1	0.4
2023	CUB	ROK	23	26	6	1	5	0	.286/.423/.619	.333	.812	15.4%	19.2%										
2023	SB	A+	23	46	4	0	7	0	.256/.370/.282	.400	.440	13.0%	30.4%							82	-0.2	-0.1	0.0
2023	IOW	AAA	23	161	23	8	35	2	.276/.342/.524	.344	.760	9.3%	28.0%	75.2%	78.6%	30.6%	50.8%			90	-0.6	4.0	0.6
2023	CHC	MLB	23	17	1	1	6	0	.294/.294/.647	.500	1.222	0.0%	47.1%	87.0%	65.0%	52.6%	50.0%	17.6	104.4	68	0.0	-0.2	-0.1
2024 DC	CHC	MLB	24	218	22	7	26	5	.219/.282/.389	.296	.595	7.2%	32.0%							85	-0.2	-1	0.1

2023 GP: DH (4), LF (1), CF (1), RF (1)   *Comps: Michael Chavis (46), Wilkin Ramirez (46), Justin Huber (45)*

That Canario is already being compared to human windmills like Adam Duvall and Teoscar Hernández is either promising or discouraging, depending on your perspective. The pro would be, hey, those guys are solid, productive big-league hitters. The con would be that if that's his ceiling, it's a bit disappointing given the incredibly loud raw power he possesses. That doesn't even address the question of where he plays on a Cubs team that's already running short on at-bats to dole out. The good news is that we should know a lot more in short order, as after a September cup of coffee with the big club, he seems headed for a chance to sink or swim at the highest level early in 2024.

★ ★ ★ *2024 Top 101 Prospect* **#20** ★ ★ ★

Pete Crow-Armstrong   OF   Born: 03/25/02   Age: 22   Bats: L   Throws: L   Height: 5'11"   Weight: 184   Origin: Round 1, 2020 Draft (#19 overall)

YEAR	TM	LVL	AGE	PA	R	HR	RBI	SB	AVG/OBP/SLG	BABIP	SLGCON	BB%	K%	ZSw%	ZCon%	OSw%	OCon%	LA	90th EV	DRC+	BRR	DRP	WARP
2021	SLU	A	19	32	6	0	4	2	.417/.563/.500	.556	.667	21.9%	18.8%	75.0%	85.7%	32.4%	59.1%			119	0.1	1.6	0.3
2022	MB	A	20	183	39	7	27	13	.354/.443/.557	.415	.704	12.0%	18.0%							121	0.7	2.8	1.3
2022	SB	A+	20	288	50	9	34	19	.287/.333/.498	.353	.673	4.9%	24.0%							87	0.5	0.3	0.6
2023	TNS	AA	21	342	68	14	60	27	.289/.371/.527	.351	.727	9.1%	24.0%							110	3.4	-0.2	1.9
2023	IOW	AAA	21	158	30	6	22	10	.271/.350/.479	.368	.720	9.5%	29.7%	77.2%	74.7%	40.1%	58.4%			78	0.2	4.5	0.6
2023	CHC	MLB	21	19	3	0	1	2	.000/.176/.000		.000	15.8%	36.8%	84.4%	55.6%	29.3%	58.3%	5.1	105.0	90	0.1	-0.2	0.0
2024 DC	CHC	MLB	22	396	38	9	42	19	.235/.296/.393	.326	.579	6.5%	29.7%							86	0.4	-3.6	0.3

2023 GP: CF (13)   *Comps: Dalton Pompey (65), Mookie Betts (60), Matt Kemp (59)*

It's not uncommon for a first-round draft pick to show up on prospect lists early, before falling off as it becomes clear he doesn't have the juice. It's another thing for a premium draft pick to be left off top-100 (or, ahem, Top 101) lists for years, only to rocket up the list as Crow-Armstrong did ahead of the 2023 season. This wasn't simply a case of being overlooked, of course—the hype came with a 2022 swing change that gave him more (read: some) in-game power, elevating him from a speedy, glove-first outfield prospect to a triple threat. He delivered on that promise with another good season in 2023, one that ended with him batting atop the lineup for the Cubs on the final day of the regular season. It remains to be seen whether the leadoff job sticks, but the part where he's in a Cubs uniform seems like a safe bet.

Brennen Davis   OF   Born: 11/02/99   Age: 24   Bats: R   Throws: R   Height: 6'0"   Weight: 210   Origin: Round 2, 2018 Draft (#62 overall)

YEAR	TM	LVL	AGE	PA	R	HR	RBI	SB	AVG/OBP/SLG	BABIP	SLGCON	BB%	K%	ZSw%	ZCon%	OSw%	OCon%	LA	90th EV	DRC+	BRR	DRP	WARP
2021	SB	A+	21	32	6	2	5	2	.321/.406/.607	.350	.773	9.4%	18.8%							113	0.0	-0.3	0.1
2021	TNS	AA	21	316	50	13	36	6	.252/.367/.474	.344	.746	11.4%	30.7%							105	-1.0	0.8	1.1
2021	IOW	AAA	21	68	10	4	12	0	.268/.397/.536	.297	.732	16.2%	22.1%							113	-0.9	-1.9	0.1
2022	IOW	AAA	22	174	16	4	13	0	.191/.322/.319	.258	.506	13.2%	29.9%							87	-1.4	1.4	0.3
2023	IOW	AAA	23	257	27	4	26	9	.187/.296/.279	.231	.379	8.6%	22.6%	76.6%	76.4%	35.0%	59.0%			78	-0.8	4.9	0.6
2024 non	CHC	MLB	24	251	22	5	23	4	.212/.281/.326	.296	.490	7.1%	30.4%							72	0.0	0	-0.2

2023 GP: RF (37), LF (23), DH (11)   *Comps: Dalton Pompey (47), Daz Cameron (45), Domingo Santana (43)*

If you're hunting for optimism with regards to Davis' future, consider starting somewhere other than his stat line. It won't be found in his injury history, either, as a core muscle surgery in June stole another half-season's worth of development. All that's left, then, is to squint and visualize the promise he once held, which still exists somewhere within Davis even after consecutive underwhelming years in the high minors. It wouldn't be the first time a post-hype prospect put together a healthy season and reminded everyone of why they liked him in the first place, so we're not yet out on the outfielder as a potential impact player in the majors. That said, you can only squint so much before your eyes are just closed.

Yan Gomes   C   Born: 07/19/87   Age: 36   Bats: R   Throws: R   Height: 6'2"   Weight: 212   Origin: Round 10, 2009 Draft (#310 overall)

YEAR	TM	LVL	AGE	PA	R	HR	RBI	SB	AVG/OBP/SLG	BABIP	SLGCON	BB%	K%	ZSw%	ZCon%	OSw%	OCon%	LA	90th EV	DRC+	BRR	DRP	WARP
2021	OAK	MLB	33	140	19	5	17	0	.221/.264/.366	.250	.480	4.3%	22.1%	70.2%	90.2%	42.6%	60.9%	20.6	102.5	97	0.0	-1.6	0.4
2021	WAS	MLB	33	235	30	9	35	0	.271/.323/.454	.309	.579	5.5%	20.0%	66.7%	89.5%	34.6%	68.0%	10.4	103.4	103	-0.1	4.5	1.5
2022	CHC	MLB	34	293	23	8	31	2	.235/.260/.365	.252	.439	2.7%	16.0%	71.9%	89.6%	41.8%	69.8%	9.6	101.2	111	-0.2	0.8	1.5
2023	CHC	MLB	35	419	44	10	63	1	.267/.315/.408	.309	.518	5.0%	19.3%	70.7%	85.8%	39.6%	64.2%	15.6	103.1	100	-0.4	-7.8	0.8
2024 DC	CHC	MLB	36	380	37	10	41	1	.244/.294/.379	.285	.480	5.2%	20.0%							88	-0.3	-4.9	0.3

2023 GP: C (103), DH (12)   *Comps: Nick Hundley (69), Mike Lieberthal (67), Don Slaught (66)*

A Google search for Barry University yields a section of notable alumni, with thumbnails in rows of six. It's understandable that Gomes doesn't appear in the first row, with names like Shaquille O'Neal and Flo Rida occupying prominent spots, but it's nevertheless jarring that one has to scroll down to the sixth to find the Cubs backstop, one rung below a gold-medal rower from the 1920s. Toiling in relative obscurity as a decent hitter at position without decent hitters, last season he caught the most innings he's logged since 2018. Did that

YEAR	TM	P. COUNT	FRM RUNS	BLK RUNS	THRW RUNS	TOT RUNS
2021	OAK	4367	-1.0	0.0	0.1	-1.0
2021	WAS	8701	4.7	0.3	0.6	5.6
2022	CHC	9685	0.9	0.2	1.1	2.2
2023	CHC	13560	-7.4	0.0	1.3	-6.2
2024	CHC	14430	-6.4	0.0	1.3	-5.1

workload lead to his defense being considerably worse than it's ever been in a full season? Correlation doesn't equal causation, but it's worth wondering. The permanent arrival of Miguel Amaya in 2024 will offer some more respite for the pride of Barry University.

Ian Happ   LF   Born: 08/12/94   Age: 29   Bats: S   Throws: R   Height: 6'0"   Weight: 205   Origin: Round 1, 2015 Draft (#9 overall)

YEAR	TM	LVL	AGE	PA	R	HR	RBI	SB	AVG/OBP/SLG	BABIP	SLGCON	BB%	K%	ZSw%	ZCon%	OSw%	OCon%	LA	90th EV	DRC+	BRR	DRP	WARP
2021	CHC	MLB	26	535	63	25	66	9	.226/.323/.434	.281	.654	11.6%	29.2%	68.1%	78.0%	27.3%	50.0%	9.9	104.9	89	0.1	-0.6	1.2
2022	CHC	MLB	27	641	72	17	72	9	.271/.342/.440	.336	.594	9.0%	23.2%	73.5%	81.5%	31.7%	58.8%	10.8	105.1	99	-0.2	4.0	2.4
2023	CHC	MLB	28	691	86	21	84	14	.248/.360/.431	.299	.585	14.3%	22.1%	68.1%	82.9%	27.2%	60.0%	13.2	104.1	111	0.1	2.5	3.1
2024 DC	CHC	MLB	29	624	72	19	73	8	.241/.346/.413	.289	.549	12.7%	21.4%							113	0.1	1.4	2.9

2023 GP: LF (154), DH (4)   *Comps: Joc Pederson (71), Adolfo Phillips (70), John Briggs (69)*

Happ turned in a career-high 25 homers in 2021 and batted a career-best .271 in 2022, but it's not hard to argue that this past season was his best all-around performance to date. He did it by taking bits and pieces of both of those previous seasons and blending them into something better, swinging less than he did in 2022 (44.4%) and coming up empty less than ever (10.1%). Swinging less and making more contact when you do swing is often a good combination. So, too, is the combo of Happ and the Cubs, as an April extension will keep him on the city's North Side through the 2026 season.

Nico Hoerner 2B Born: 05/13/97 Age: 27 Bats: R Throws: R Height: 6'1" Weight: 200 Origin: Round 1, 2018 Draft (#24 overall)

YEAR	TM	LVL	AGE	PA	R	HR	RBI	SB	AVG/OBP/SLG	BABIP	SLGCON	BB%	K%	ZSw%	ZCon%	OSw%	OCon%	LA	90th EV	DRC+	BRR	DRP	WARP
2021	CHC	MLB	24	170	13	0	16	5	.302/.382/.369	.360	.444	10.0%	14.7%	70.1%	91.5%	33.3%	68.4%	7.7	102.3	99	0.1	0.0	0.6
2022	CHC	MLB	25	517	60	10	55	20	.281/.327/.410	.300	.465	5.4%	11.0%	66.4%	93.7%	36.0%	75.0%	10.6	101.9	109	1.4	6.0	3.0
2023	CHC	MLB	26	688	98	9	68	43	.283/.346/.383	.312	.442	7.1%	12.1%	61.8%	93.9%	32.8%	78.3%	10.4	101.1	105	2.3	-2.7	2.5
2024 DC	CHC	MLB	27	586	57	9	57	27	.269/.333/.378	.289	.427	7.2%	10.4%							105	1.0	-1.9	2.0

2023 GP: 2B (135), SS (20), DH (1)
Comps: Luis Castillo (61), Erick Aybar (59), Chick Galloway (59)

Hoerner is not, by any objective measurement, a burner. And yet no baserunner benefited more from the rule changes MLB enacted to encourage stolen bases. Hoerner's 43 steals last season were fifth-most in the majors despite the fact that his sprint speed—consider this acknowledgement that sprint speed doesn't fully capture base-stealing ability—actually decreased from 2022 to 2023. He's always been a good hitter regardless of what he does on the basepaths, capable of laying the bat on the ball in any section of the zone, but the added speed component took his offensive game to another level. Now the rest of the baseball world just needs to catch up, pun fully intended.

Nick Madrigal 3B Born: 03/05/97 Age: 27 Bats: R Throws: R Height: 5'8" Weight: 175 Origin: Round 1, 2018 Draft (#4 overall)

YEAR	TM	LVL	AGE	PA	R	HR	RBI	SB	AVG/OBP/SLG	BABIP	SLGCON	BB%	K%	ZSw%	ZCon%	OSw%	OCon%	LA	90th EV	DRC+	BRR	DRP	WARP
2021	CHW	MLB	24	215	30	2	21	1	.305/.349/.425	.324	.464	5.1%	7.9%	62.0%	98.0%	33.7%	83.2%	1.3	98.5	110	0.1	-0.1	1.1
2022	CHC	MLB	25	228	19	0	7	3	.249/.305/.282	.286	.324	6.1%	11.8%	62.6%	94.5%	31.9%	82.5%	-0.9	98.8	103	0.0	0.4	0.9
2023	IOW	AAA	26	70	18	1	7	0	.424/.514/.678	.471	.769	11.4%	10.0%	50.5%	100.0%	29.9%	81.8%			119	-0.4	0.5	0.3
2023	CHC	MLB	26	294	34	2	28	10	.263/.311/.352	.283	.386	3.4%	8.2%	59.8%	96.6%	33.9%	82.9%	3.4	99.3	103	0.5	2.7	1.4
2024 DC	CHC	MLB	27	396	37	5	37	6	.284/.337/.383	.300	.418	5.7%	7.7%							109	0.2	3.1	1.9

2023 GP: 3B (72), 2B (14), DH (4)
Comps: Steve Lombardozzi (56), César Hernández (54), Johnny Giavotella (54)

Since reaching the majors, Madrigal has only ever called the city of Chicago home. That's about the only stability he's had in his four-year MLB career, though, as injuries—last season it was a pair of IL stints related to his right hamstring—have limited him to 846 plate appearances since 2020. He also hasn't been able to settle in anywhere defensively, sliding over to third base to accommodate the signing of Dansby Swanson that pushed Nico Hoerner to the keystone. He's not a prototypical third baseman, so that arrangement—defensively, on the active roster, perhaps with the Cubs altogether—may not be permanent, either. Thankfully for Madrigal, home is where the heart is, so maybe he's actually been at home the entire time.

Matt Mervis 1B Born: 04/16/98 Age: 26 Bats: L Throws: R Height: 6'2" Weight: 225 Origin: Round 39, 2016 Draft (#1174 overall)

YEAR	TM	LVL	AGE	PA	R	HR	RBI	SB	AVG/OBP/SLG	BABIP	SLGCON	BB%	K%	ZSw%	ZCon%	OSw%	OCon%	LA	90th EV	DRC+	BRR	DRP	WARP
2021	MB	A	23	289	38	9	42	6	.204/.309/.367	.236	.503	12.5%	22.8%							106	-0.5	5.5	1.3
2022	SB	A+	24	108	17	7	29	0	.350/.389/.650	.412	.878	4.6%	24.1%							138	1.0	2.3	1.1
2022	TNS	AA	24	230	34	14	51	2	.300/.370/.596	.322	.771	8.7%	20.0%							133	-0.6	3.1	1.8
2022	IOW	AAA	24	240	41	15	39	0	.297/.383/.593	.294	.713	10.4%	14.6%							134	0.5	-0.7	1.6
2023	IOW	AAA	25	441	77	22	78	2	.282/.399/.533	.327	.737	15.2%	22.7%	72.8%	80.5%	30.0%	48.4%			110	1.3	1.3	1.6
2023	CHC	MLB	25	99	8	3	11	0	.167/.242/.289	.218	.448	8.1%	32.3%	73.4%	83.1%	33.9%	41.2%	8.5	109.8	92	-0.1	-0.1	0.1
2024 DC	CHC	MLB	26	356	38	12	42	1	.216/.297/.394	.272	.564	8.9%	27.4%							89	-0.2	-0.1	0.2

2023 GP: 1B (27)
Comps: Jared Walsh (68), Chris Shaw (67), Ji Man Choi (54)

After getting blocked by the likes of Frank Schwindel, Alfonso Rivas and Eric Hosmer, Mervis finally got his long-awaited shot at the bigs—and promptly fell on his face. As denoted by DRC+, though, it wasn't the disaster his slash line pretends; he hit the ball hard but right at people, and put an uncharacteristic number of them on the ground. David Ross lost patience with him by mid-June, and he was banished back to Iowa to beat up on Triple-A pitching. With fewer than 100 plate appearances, it feels a little too soon to slap the Quad-A label on Mervis, especially given the peripherals, but it didn't stop Chicago from anointing Christopher Morel as the team's 2024 first baseman heading into camp. Mervis deserves to be playing in the majors somewhere; if the Cubs feel they're too good to wait on him to develop, there are plenty of teams out there that aren't.

Christopher Morel DH Born: 06/24/99 Age: 25 Bats: R Throws: R Height: 5'11" Weight: 145 Origin: IFA, 2015

YEAR	TM	LVL	AGE	PA	R	HR	RBI	SB	AVG/OBP/SLG	BABIP	SLGCON	BB%	K%	ZSw%	ZCon%	OSw%	OCon%	LA	90th EV	DRC+	BRR	DRP	WARP
2021	TNS	AA	22	417	59	17	64	16	.220/.300/.432	.276	.652	9.8%	29.7%							98	-0.8	6.0	1.7
2021	IOW	AAA	22	39	6	1	2	2	.257/.333/.371	.333	.520	10.3%	25.6%							88	1.3	-0.3	0.2
2022	TNS	AA	23	122	22	7	20	3	.306/.380/.565	.366	.782	8.2%	24.6%							110	0.6	0.8	0.7
2022	CHC	MLB	23	425	55	16	47	10	.235/.308/.433	.320	.678	8.9%	32.2%	73.1%	71.1%	35.2%	48.6%	9.0	106.1	92	0.5	-2.4	0.8
2023	IOW	AAA	24	134	31	11	31	4	.330/.425/.730	.429	1.135	12.7%	30.6%	68.8%	73.8%	37.1%	52.9%			121	0.2	-3.0	0.4
2023	CHC	MLB	24	429	62	26	70	6	.247/.313/.508	.303	.773	8.4%	31.0%	73.2%	79.6%	35.7%	42.7%	12.4	108.3	93	0.2	-0.7	0.6
2024 DC	CHC	MLB	25	565	66	25	76	11	.228/.299/.438	.304	.683	8.2%	32.6%							102	0.1	-0.5	1.4

2023 GP: DH (61), 2B (19), CF (12), LF (8), RF (8), 3B (5), SS (2)
Comps: Ian Happ (58), Teoscar Hernández (55), Dexter Fowler (54)

Morel came to chew bubblegum and swing really hard at pitches, and he's all out of bubblegum. It's tempting call the 24-year-old a poor man's Adolis García at the dish—the 2022 version, not the god-like 2023 iteration—but that might actually be a disservice to Morel, who mirrors García in a lot of ways while also showing a better batting eye than the Texas slugger early in his career. The big difference, then, is that while García's defense ensured his bat would stay in the lineup no matter how many times he swung and missed, Morel's shortcomings in the field forced the Cubs to relegate him to Triple-A to start the year and then use him primarily at designated hitter upon his promotion. While that's a viable path forward in today's MLB, the Cubs would surely prefer he once again follow in the footsteps of El Bombi and have that defensive light bulb go on as well. It's baby steps for now, as reports are that the Cubs will hand Morel a first baseman's glove when camp opens.

Jefferson Rojas SS   Born: 04/25/05   Age: 19   Bats: R   Throws: R   Height: 5'10"   Weight: 150   Origin: IFA, 2022

YEAR	TM	LVL	AGE	PA	R	HR	RBI	SB	AVG/OBP/SLG	BABIP	SLGCON	BB%	K%	ZSw%	ZCon%	OSw%	OCon%	LA	90th EV	DRC+	BRR	DRP	WARP
2022	DSL CUBB	ROK	17	169	27	1	19	15	.303/.391/.407	.336	.465	9.5%	10.7%										
2023	MB	A	18	307	48	7	31	13	.268/.345/.404	.320	.521	7.5%	19.9%							109	0.2	-0.5	1.5
2024 non	CHC	MLB	19	251	19	3	20	0	.208/.257/.300	.270	.410	4.9%	24.7%							57	0.0	0	-0.5

2023 GP: SS (61), DH (5), 2B (4)   *Comps: Kevin Made (92), Eduardo Garcia (84), Cole Tucker (84)*

There are some obscure millionaires in the world—a guy in Iowa who got all five white balls correct on a Mega Millions ticket but not the gold ball, perhaps, or an Arizona woman who came into a large settlement with a cereal conglomerate after finding a cockroach in her breakfast—and Rojas is among them, after the Cubs signed him for seven figures out of the Dominican Republic in 2022. In his first full season in the organization, the 18-year-old showed all the tools that would convince a club to shell out a cool mil, handling shortstop without issue while holding his own offensively in Low-A. It was enough to convince BP prospect writer Ben Spanier to tab him as a breakout prospect to watch for 2024, a breakout that would put him firmly on the prospect map if he's not there already. Obscure millionaire? Not for long.

───────────── ★ ★ ★ *2024 Top 101 Prospect* **#21** ★ ★ ★ ─────────────

Matt Shaw IF   Born: 11/06/01   Age: 22   Bats: R   Throws: R   Height: 5'11"   Weight: 185   Origin: Round 1, 2023 Draft (#13 overall)

YEAR	TM	LVL	AGE	PA	R	HR	RBI	SB	AVG/OBP/SLG	BABIP	SLGCON	BB%	K%	ZSw%	ZCon%	OSw%	OCon%	LA	90th EV	DRC+	BRR	DRP	WARP
2023	SB	A+	21	89	14	4	18	7	.393/.427/.655	.426	.764	4.5%	13.5%							129	-0.3	-1.7	0.4
2023	TNS	AA	21	70	10	3	9	6	.292/.329/.523	.314	.642	4.3%	17.1%							110	1.3	-0.4	0.2
2024 DC	CHC	MLB	22	30	3	1	3	1	.232/.278/.356	.265	.435	5.1%	17.2%							76	0.0	0	0.0

2023 GP: SS (20), 2B (10), DH (5), 3B (3)   *Comps: Howie Kendrick (78), Jose Altuve (77), Henry Alejandro Rodriguez (73)*

The book on college bats is that they're more pro-ready than their high school counterparts. Fun fact—that book is actually Shaw's biography. The 22-year-old went straight from tormenting Big Ten pitchers to hctoring minor-league arms, eventually graduating to Double-A before the year was over. If there are no concerns about his bat, then, there is some question about his ultimate defensive home, as he was drafted as a shortstop but may be better suited for second base in time. Those positions are occupied by Dansby Swanson and Nico Hoerner, respectively, for the near future in Chicago, but it's a good problem to have for the Cubs. It's also one that should present itself as soon as this year, if Shaw's bat keeps producing with each new chapter.

Seiya Suzuki RF   Born: 08/18/94   Age: 29   Bats: R   Throws: R   Height: 5'11"   Weight: 182   Origin: IFA, 2022

YEAR	TM	LVL	AGE	PA	R	HR	RBI	SB	AVG/OBP/SLG	BABIP	SLGCON	BB%	K%	ZSw%	ZCon%	OSw%	OCon%	LA	90th EV	DRC+	BRR	DRP	WARP
2022	CHC	MLB	27	446	54	14	46	9	.262/.336/.433	.326	.599	9.4%	24.7%	57.1%	87.6%	27.0%	62.3%	11.7	104.9	96	0.4	2.0	1.4
2023	CHC	MLB	28	583	75	20	74	6	.285/.357/.485	.341	.649	10.1%	22.3%	62.1%	86.1%	26.5%	66.7%	11.1	106.3	111	-0.1	3.5	2.6
2024 DC	CHC	MLB	29	582	69	21	74	8	.256/.343/.443	.289	.563	10.7%	18.9%							120	0.0	1.9	3.1

2023 GP: RF (132), DH (5)   *Comps: Gary Matthews (81), Nelson Cruz (79), Brian Jordan (79)*

After Suzuki missed the first two weeks of the season with a strained oblique, it was perhaps a foregone conclusion that his season would end better than it started. Few could have predicted just how well Suzuki would close, though, as he posted a 149 wRC+ in the season's second half and was, by the same metric, the fifth-best hitter in baseball in September. Our own DRC+ agreed—his 111 DRC+ was well above average, and much more promising than the 96 he registered in his rookie season. He made more contact, and harder contact, while getting around on pitches and pulling more line drives. It's just hard to find many flaws in his skill set, and he should arguably only continue to get better as he further acclimates to the North American game.

Dansby Swanson SS   Born: 02/11/94   Age: 30   Bats: R   Throws: R   Height: 6'1"   Weight: 190   Origin: Round 1, 2015 Draft (#1 overall)

YEAR	TM	LVL	AGE	PA	R	HR	RBI	SB	AVG/OBP/SLG	BABIP	SLGCON	BB%	K%	ZSw%	ZCon%	OSw%	OCon%	LA	90th EV	DRC+	BRR	DRP	WARP
2021	ATL	MLB	27	653	78	27	88	9	.248/.311/.449	.297	.627	8.0%	25.6%	74.7%	77.5%	29.0%	55.1%	14.4	104.4	101	0.1	2.8	2.7
2022	ATL	MLB	28	696	99	25	96	18	.277/.329/.447	.348	.624	7.0%	26.1%	73.8%	77.8%	30.5%	53.7%	15.8	104.8	110	2.0	10.8	4.5
2023	CHC	MLB	29	638	81	22	80	9	.244/.328/.416	.297	.572	10.3%	24.1%	72.7%	79.0%	28.9%	57.3%	13.1	104.4	107	0.2	9.1	3.7
2024 DC	CHC	MLB	30	621	69	21	74	13	.245/.321/.411	.299	.562	9.2%	24.1%							105	0.5	8.9	3.6

2023 GP: SS (147)   *Comps: Dave Concepcion (83), Jay Bell (80), Roy Smalley (72)*

At a glance, the 22 homers Swanson hit in his first year with the Cubs look like a decent approximation of the 25 he hit the year prior. Just a fly here and there knocked down in the Windy City, right? Wrong. Whereas Swanson had 26.4 expected homers in 2022, per Statcast—and 29.6 the year before that—the shortstop produced just 18 last year, thanks in large part to a drop in hard-hit balls and a rise in grounders. All that said, his Gold Glove-level defense and improved eye helped him to be a nearly four-win player even with the offensive step back. And while the shortstop did hit the IL for the first time since 2019 with a heel contusion that caused him to miss out on the All-Star game, his 147 games played go a long way toward helping him accrue that value. All told it'll go down as a successful start to the massive seven-year, $177 million contract he signed last offseason.

Mike Tauchman OF   Born: 12/03/90   Age: 33   Bats: L   Throws: L   Height: 6'1"   Weight: 220   Origin: Round 10, 2013 Draft (#289 overall)

YEAR	TM	LVL	AGE	PA	R	HR	RBI	SB	AVG/OBP/SLG	BABIP	SLGCON	BB%	K%	ZSw%	ZCon%	OSw%	OCon%	LA	90th EV	DRC+	BRR	DRP	WARP
2021	SAC	AAA	30	154	25	3	19	2	.266/.370/.438	.337	.609	13.0%	23.4%							95	1.8	-1.8	0.4
2021	SF	MLB	30	175	21	4	15	1	.178/.286/.283	.240	.430	12.6%	29.7%	72.4%	73.4%	21.5%	48.5%	9.5	102.0	73	0.1	0.8	0.1
2021	NYY	MLB	30	16	1	0	0	2	.214/.267/.286	.375	.500	6.3%	37.5%	86.8%	63.6%	18.8%	16.7%	18.8	99.9	73	0.0	0.1	0.0
2023	IOW	AAA	32	103	17	3	15	1	.278/.427/.443	.333	.603	20.4%	20.4%	67.3%	79.3%	19.0%	60.4%			115	0.1	0.5	0.6
2023	CHC	MLB	32	401	64	8	48	7	.252/.363/.377	.313	.506	14.0%	21.4%	66.0%	81.7%	22.7%	61.3%	8.0	103.6	95	0.2	-1.9	0.9
2024 DC	CHC	MLB	33	281	28	5	26	4	.227/.327/.344	.289	.462	11.9%	22.3%							91	0.1	-1.7	0.4

2023 GP: CF (81), DH (12), RF (10), LF (4)   *Comps: Tommy Pham (49), Eric Young Jr. (48), Craig Gentry (45)*

Tauchman went from minor-league free-agent signing to Cubs leadoff hitter in the span of six months, taking over the top spot in the lineup in mid-June and holding it through the end of the season. What does that guarantee him moving forward? Absolutely nothing, including but not limited to a major-league contract. Or, at least, he might have to get a new address if he's to stay in the bigs, as the Cubs have holdovers Ian Happ and Seiya Suzuki and a handful of young, promising outfielders—notably Pete Crow-Armstrong and Alexander Canario, among others—in tow. This is a guy who spent the 2022 season in Japan, though, so he's no stranger to having to do things the hard way. That's life when you're Mike Tauchman—it's tough, man.

★ ★ ★ *2024 Top 101 Prospect* **#91** ★ ★ ★

James Triantos 2B/DH   Born: 01/29/03   Age: 21   Bats: R   Throws: R   Height: 6'1"   Weight: 195   Origin: Round 2, 2021 Draft (#56 overall)

YEAR	TM	LVL	AGE	PA	R	HR	RBI	SB	AVG/OBP/SLG	BABIP	SLGCON	BB%	K%	ZSw%	ZCon%	OSw%	OCon%	LA	90th EV	DRC+	BRR	DRP	WARP
2021	CUB	ROK	18	109	27	6	19	3	.327/.376/.594	.351	.723	6.4%	16.5%									-1.0	
2022	MB	A	19	504	74	7	50	20	.272/.335/.386	.315	.469	7.7%	16.1%							112	3.2	-6.5	2.0
2023	MSS	WIN	20	95	18	3	15	9	.425/.505/.700	.484	.848	12.6%	14.7%	50.0%	100.0%	13.0%	66.7%						
2023	SB	A+	20	350	43	4	46	16	.285/.363/.390	.309	.444	9.7%	10.6%							120	2.3	0.2	1.9
2024 non	CHC	MLB	21	251	20	3	21	0	.220/.275/.311	.256	.378	6.0%	16.0%							66	0.0	0	-0.4

2023 GP: 2B (62), DH (20), 3B (10), CF (10), SS (1), LF (1)   Comps: José Peraza (68), Jahmai Jones (65), Dilson Herrera (63)

This is unscientific, but forced to choose between elite contact ability or elite power as a core attribute—assuming that the other, then, is a deficiency, or at least a work in progress—we assume most players would choose to be blessed with an innate ability to put bat to ball and hope the power comes with age or mechanics tweaks. In a world where contact is king, Triantos would be royalty. The 20-year-old continues to connect with exceptional consistency, striking out just over 10% of the time in a 2023 season spent mostly at High-A. Will the power come? If his performance in the Arizona Fall League is any indication, the answer is: maybe. It's a step in the right direction, if nothing else, and offers hope that he can still be an impact player at the highest level despite his defensive shortcomings.

Patrick Wisdom 3B   Born: 08/27/91   Age: 32   Bats: R   Throws: R   Height: 6'2"   Weight: 220   Origin: Round 1, 2012 Draft (#52 overall)

YEAR	TM	LVL	AGE	PA	R	HR	RBI	SB	AVG/OBP/SLG	BABIP	SLGCON	BB%	K%	ZSw%	ZCon%	OSw%	OCon%	LA	90th EV	DRC+	BRR	DRP	WARP
2021	CHC	MLB	29	375	54	28	61	4	.231/.305/.518	.318	.946	8.5%	40.8%	76.9%	69.9%	33.2%	42.3%	19.7	108.0	87	0.0	0.2	0.7
2022	CHC	MLB	30	534	67	25	66	8	.207/.298/.426	.274	.699	9.9%	34.3%	72.3%	74.4%	30.8%	45.6%	21.0	106.8	91	0.1	-2.0	0.5
2023	CHC	MLB	31	302	43	23	46	4	.205/.289/.500	.237	.854	9.9%	36.8%	72.7%	74.3%	28.4%	51.6%	21.9	107.9	92	0.0	-1.2	0.5
2024 DC	CHC	MLB	32	521	66	29	77	9	.213/.299/.451	.268	.719	9.7%	33.3%							104	0.0	-1.3	1.3

2023 GP: 3B (61), 1B (14), DH (11), LF (5), RF (4), 2B (1)   Comps: Todd Frazier (58), Josh Donaldson (55), Mike Napoli (54)

Wisdom surfaces in the national consciousness from time to time when he goes on a homer binge like the one he orchestrated in April, socking eight homers in his first 14 games. The holes in his swing are so known and so pronounced, though, that few expected what we were seeing was some new trick from this old dog. The skeptics were proven right when Wisdom went ice cold—he finished the first half hitting .190/.279/.451 with a 39.1% strikeout percentage, even with the hot start baked in—and in the season's second half he was relegated to a bench role behind Nick Madrigal. The contrast between the two, and the decision to side with Madrigal, says a lot about how the organization views the hot corner moving forward.

PITCHERS

Adbert Alzolay RHP   Born: 03/01/95   Age: 29   Height: 6'1"   Weight: 208   Origin: IFA, 2012

YEAR	TM	LVL	AGE	G (GS)	IP	W-L	SV	K	WHIP	ERA	CSP	BB%	K%	HR%	GB%	ZSw%	ZCon%	OSw%	OCon%	BABIP	SLGCON	DRA-	WARP
2021	CHC	MLB	26	29(21)	125²	5-13	1	128	1.16	4.58	56.6%	6.6%	24.7%	4.8%	43.8%	67.4%	81.1%	34.4%	60.5%	.270	.601	86	2.1
2022	CHC	MLB	27	6(0)	13¹	2-1	0	19	0.83	3.38	55.9%	3.8%	36.5%	1.9%	40.0%	67.0%	78.0%	39.1%	48.8%	.276	.567	84	0.2
2023	CHC	MLB	28	58(0)	64	2-5	22	67	1.02	2.67	50.0%	5.1%	26.5%	2.0%	42.3%	71.6%	82.4%	34.5%	53.6%	.290	.470	79	1.4
2024 DC	CHC	MLB	29	55(0)	58²	4-6	28	62	1.23	3.93	53.2%	7.5%	24.9%	3.1%	42.5%					.298	.549	90	0.6

2023 Arsenal: SL (87.4), SI (95.5), FA (95.6), FC (91), CH (88.5)   Comps: Alex Colomé (64), Dinelson Lamet (59), Joe Kelly (58)

If Alzolay wasn't going to be the frontline starter some hoped he could be, the next best outcome was emerging as a dominant reliever. That brilliance killed two birds with one stone for the Cubs; they both avoided their once-top prospect becoming a disappointing major leaguer while also finding a solution to the closer question that faced them when the season began. Alzolay has always enjoyed excellent movement on his breaking stuff, but the move to the bullpen added just enough flame to his sinker to pair off the slider effectively, giving hitters two planes of movement to worry about. The right forearm strain suffered in mid-September is worth monitoring, especially given his history of healthy concerns, but he returned to pitch in the season's final weekend, easing concerns that it might linger.

Javier Assad RHP   Born: 07/30/97   Age: 26   Height: 6'1"   Weight: 200   Origin: IFA, 2015

YEAR	TM	LVL	AGE	G (GS)	IP	W-L	SV	K	WHIP	ERA	CSP	BB%	K%	HR%	GB%	ZSw%	ZCon%	OSw%	OCon%	BABIP	SLGCON	DRA-	WARP
2021	TNS	AA	23	21(20)	93	4-8	0	74	1.54	5.32		7.6%	17.7%	2.9%	41.8%					.341	.580	119	0.0
2022	TNS	AA	24	15(14)	71²	4-1	0	74	1.34	2.51		9.4%	24.7%	2.0%	43.3%					.330	.526	96	0.9
2022	IOW	AAA	24	8(7)	36²	1-2	0	37	1.04	2.95		4.7%	24.8%	2.7%	46.1%					.276	.461	88	0.7
2022	CHC	MLB	24	9(8)	37²	2-2	0	30	1.46	3.11	50.9%	12.0%	18.1%	2.4%	41.4%	69.8%	88.2%	32.4%	62.4%	.277	.466	122	-0.1
2023	CHC	MLB	25	32(10)	109¹	5-3	0	94	1.23	3.05	47.5%	9.1%	20.9%	2.9%	46.0%	67.1%	88.3%	26.3%	63.4%	.269	.506	100	1.2
2024 DC	CHC	MLB	26	30(15)	94²	5-6	0	73	1.42	4.83	48.4%	9.4%	17.6%	2.9%	44.1%					.295	.522	106	0.4

2023 Arsenal: SI (92.8), FC (89.1), FA (93.3), SW (80.8), CU (76.7), CH (85.1)   Comps: Stephen Fife (64), Gabriel Ynoa (63), A.J. Griffin (62)

It would be lazy and frankly inaccurate to compare Assad to teammate Kyle Hendricks, but there is something to the "Analysts Hate Him! This Cubs Pitcher's One Weird Trick To Get Hitters Out" aspect of Assad's game. Like Hendricks, the 26-year-old has consistently gotten outs at the major-league level despite advanced metrics that suggest he shouldn't. Unlike Hendricks, Assad does it with a six-pitch mix that, while not generating whiffs, keeps hitters off balance enough that they hit the ball softer and on the ground more often than they do against his colleagues. The Cubs look set to carry most of their 2023 starting rotation into 2024, and that's not including guys like Hayden Wesneski and Ben Brown, so Assad's near future could be bulk relief or as a really good sixth starter option. Much like any one of those six pitches, though, it's nice to have a guy like Assad in your back pocket in case he's needed, or if some analyst is giving you trouble on the street.

Brad Boxberger   RHP   Born: 05/27/88   Age: 36   Height: 5'10"   Weight: 211   Origin: Round 1, 2009 Draft (#43 overall)

YEAR	TM	LVL	AGE	G (GS)	IP	W-L	SV	K	WHIP	ERA	CSP	BB%	K%	HR%	GB%	ZSw%	ZCon%	OSw%	OCon%	BABIP	SLGCON	DRA-	WARP
2021	MIL	MLB	33	71(0)	64²	5-4	4	83	1.07	3.34	55.4%	9.4%	31.2%	3.0%	37.1%	69.5%	72.4%	27.4%	59.3%	.257	.521	87	1.1
2022	MIL	MLB	34	70(0)	64	4-3	1	68	1.23	2.95	56.8%	10.1%	25.4%	2.2%	33.9%	61.3%	79.9%	29.0%	68.7%	.284	.485	97	0.7
2023	CHC	MLB	35	22(0)	20	0-1	2	17	1.30	4.95	49.0%	13.1%	20.2%	3.6%	43.6%	61.6%	84.7%	25.5%	62.7%	.231	.527	107	0.2
2024 non	CHC	MLB	36	58(0)	50	2-2	0	47	1.41	4.88	54.2%	10.5%	21.3%	3.7%	38.4%					.285	.568	108	0.0

2023 Arsenal: FA (91.7), SL (87.2), CH (81.6)   *Comps: Tyler Clippard (85), Steve Cishek (84), Greg Holland (84)*

It's easy to look at that 2023 innings pitched total and surmise that the same right forearm strain that cost Boxberger 4 ½ months also contributed to him having his worst season since 2019. But even when he was ostensibly healthy, closing out two games for the Cubs in the season's first month, his fastball velocity was already down more than a tick where it sat in 2022. Does that matter for a guy who topped out at 94 mph during his heyday? It's hard to say, but there's clear evidence that the pitch, which he threw half the time, was ineffective, generating few whiffs and registering poor results. In our 2023 comment, the last line urged readers to "trust the track record" with regards to Boxberger's outlook. Between the diminished velocity, the forearm strain that lingered into the offseason and the fact that he'll turn 36 years old next year, we may be better off trusting what we know about player archetypes when projecting Boxberger's future.

Ben Brown   RHP   Born: 09/09/99   Age: 24   Height: 6'6"   Weight: 210   Origin: Round 33, 2017 Draft (#983 overall)

YEAR	TM	LVL	AGE	G (GS)	IP	W-L	SV	K	WHIP	ERA	CSP	BB%	K%	HR%	GB%	ZSw%	ZCon%	OSw%	OCon%	BABIP	SLGCON	DRA-	WARP
2021	JS	A+	21	4(2)	12	0-0	0	14	1.58	7.50		13.0%	25.9%	3.7%	46.9%					.333	.594	90	0.2
2022	JS	A+	22	16(15)	73	3-5	0	105	1.04	3.08		7.7%	35.4%	2.4%	43.0%					.291	.524	88	1.0
2022	TNS	AA	22	7(7)	31	3-0	0	44	1.48	4.06		9.5%	32.1%	2.2%	40.5%					.395	.649	91	0.5
2023	TNS	AA	23	4(4)	20	2-0	0	30	0.95	0.45		7.8%	39.0%	1.3%	48.8%					.308	.425	68	0.7
2023	IOW	AAA	23	22(15)	72²	6-8	0	100	1.53	5.33		15.8%	31.1%	2.8%	35.7%	62.2%	77.4%	29.7%	48.7%	.321	.645	89	1.5
2024 DC	CHC	MLB	24	12(3)	25²	1-1	0	30	1.39	4.68		11.6%	27.2%	3.7%	36.1%					.297	.603	103	0.1

2023 Arsenal: FA (95.8), SL (85.8), SW (86.8), CH (89.9)   *Comps: Maikel Cleto (67), José Ramirez (62), Brad Peacock (61)*

In a piece from May 2023, BP fantasy writer Jesse Roche identified four pitching standouts at the Triple-A level: Gavin Williams, who graduated and was terrific in the majors; Bobby Miller, who graduated and was terrific in the majors; Andrew Abbott, who graduated and was terrific in the majors; and Brown, who … stayed at Triple-A. Brown ran into trouble in June, suffered an oblique injury in early August, and upon his return was moved to the bullpen in hopes he might be able to aid the postseason-minded, Alzolay-missing Cubs. Unfortunately, he never got straightened out, leaving us waiting until at least 2024 for his debut. Despite that, little has changed with regards to his bright future at the highest level, and his inclusion on the aforementioned list is certainly promising for the prospects of early success in the majors.

Jose Cuas   RHP   Born: 06/28/94   Age: 30   Height: 6'3"   Weight: 195   Origin: Round 11, 2015 Draft (#331 overall)

YEAR	TM	LVL	AGE	G (GS)	IP	W-L	SV	K	WHIP	ERA	CSP	BB%	K%	HR%	GB%	ZSw%	ZCon%	OSw%	OCon%	BABIP	SLGCON	DRA-	WARP
2021	NWA	AA	27	22(0)	32¹	3-1	3	32	1.18	1.95		5.3%	24.1%	0.8%	53.3%					.333	.429	81	0.6
2021	OMA	AAA	27	3(0)	5	1-0	0	4	0.60	0.00		5.6%	22.2%	0.0%	50.0%					.167	.167	83	0.1
2022	OMA	AAA	28	22(0)	22¹	0-3	3	21	1.07	1.61		7.4%	22.1%	1.1%	62.5%					.262	.355	91	0.4
2022	KC	MLB	28	47(0)	37²	4-2	1	34	1.67	3.58	52.4%	13.3%	18.9%	1.1%	49.1%	60.1%	79.5%	29.9%	66.1%	.327	.482	107	0.2
2023	KC	MLB	29	45(1)	41²	3-0	0	52	1.61	4.54	46.1%	10.9%	27.1%	3.1%	40.0%	66.6%	80.4%	30.6%	51.1%	.367	.658	96	0.6
2023	CHC	MLB	29	27(1)	23²	0-2	1	19	1.31	3.04	40.1%	14.0%	19.0%	2.0%	53.1%	67.8%	82.5%	30.5%	60.7%	.242	.406	106	0.2
2024 DC	CHC	MLB	30	50(0)	52²	3-2	0	54	1.38	4.65	46.6%	10.4%	23.2%	3.0%	44.7%					.296	.544	102	0.2

2023 Arsenal: SI (92.9), SL (82.5), FA (92.4), CH (87.8)

Few players have a backstory as neat as Cuas, one that took him through independent baseball and self-employment. Unfortunately, his rags-to-pre-arbitration-riches origins may be the most interesting thing about him as a pitcher. The Cubs found him compelling enough to trade for him at the deadline, sending Nelson Velázquez to the Royals in return, but his insistence on pounding right-handed hitters with sinkers capped his upside despite good whiff rates on his slider and four-seam fastball. Adding the four-seamer was a good start; the next step is phasing out the sinker, which did more harm than good, and leaning on his strikeout offerings instead. And if he does? Well, it may not be the most tantalizing chapter of his story, but it could end up being the most fruitful.

Jackson Ferris   LHP   Born: 01/15/04   Age: 20   Height: 6'4"   Weight: 195   Origin: Round 2, 2022 Draft (#47 overall)

YEAR	TM	LVL	AGE	G (GS)	IP	W-L	SV	K	WHIP	ERA	CSP	BB%	K%	HR%	GB%	ZSw%	ZCon%	OSw%	OCon%	BABIP	SLGCON	DRA-	WARP
2023	MB	A	19	18(18)	56	2-3	0	77	1.21	3.38		13.9%	32.5%	0.4%	53.7%					.283	.420	76	1.2
2024 non	CHC	MLB	20	58(0)	50	2-2	0	49	1.59	5.82		13.6%	21.6%	3.8%	36.9%					.293	.593	125	-0.4

Comps: Kodi Medeiros (87), Mick Abel (86), A.J. Alexy (85)

A year ago, Ferris was a projection. A lanky, hard-throwing, left-handed projection that the Cubs paid nearly twice the slot amount to sign after taking him in the second round of the 2022 MLB Draft, but a projection nonetheless. With a sampling of Low-A pitching under his belt, the 19-year-old allows for description with more certainty, if only a bit more. But even more than other prospects, Ferris is a rough draft, with pitches that still need polishing and pairing, mechanics to smooth, conditioning. The Cubs went out and got Ferris because they saw a nice blank canvas to work with, given his feel for spin and his body; the work is just beginning.

Michael Fulmer RHP   Born: 03/15/93   Age: 31   Height: 6'3"   Weight: 224   Origin: Round 1, 2011 Draft (#44 overall)

YEAR	TM	LVL	AGE	G (GS)	IP	W-L	SV	K	WHIP	ERA	CSP	BB%	K%	HR%	GB%	ZSw%	ZCon%	OSw%	OCon%	BABIP	SLGCON	DRA-	WARP
2021	DET	MLB	28	52 (4)	69²	5-6	14	73	1.28	2.97	49.6%	6.7%	24.6%	2.4%	45.7%	70.1%	81.2%	35.4%	56.5%	.323	.518	82	1.3
2022	DET	MLB	29	41 (0)	39¹	3-4	2	39	1.25	3.20	53.3%	11.8%	23.1%	0.6%	32.7%	66.4%	82.5%	28.7%	52.3%	.264	.375	107	0.3
2022	MIN	MLB	29	26 (0)	24¹	2-2	1	22	1.56	3.70	45.7%	7.5%	20.6%	2.8%	37.3%	74.1%	85.3%	35.1%	56.0%	.375	.649	114	0.1
2023	CHC	MLB	30	58 (1)	57	3-5	2	65	1.33	4.42	45.5%	11.8%	27.4%	3.0%	39.4%	67.0%	85.0%	32.2%	40.8%	.304	.590	88	1.0
2024 non	CHC	MLB	31	58 (0)	50	2-2	0	54	1.36	4.55	47.9%	10.1%	25.0%	3.4%	39.9%					.298	.572	102	0.2

2023 Arsenal: SW (83.3), FA (94.3), SL (90), SI (95), CH (90)   Comps: Wade Davis (69), Tom Murphy (68), Daniel Hudson (68)

The comment in the 2023 edition of the Annual surmised that there "aren't many new places for Fulmer to go from here." Fulmer, presumably an avid Annual reader, dropped an Usher "watch this" GIF and did what the commenter said he couldn't, adding a sweeper that he threw 30.6% of the time en route to a successful season pitching in the back end of the Cubs' bullpen. On the surface, the season wasn't as impressive as his 2022 turn, but under the hood he was improved — his 90 DRA- was the second-best mark of his career, and he struck out a career-best 27.4% of batters faced. The Cubs would surely like to have him back in the mix in 2024, but his progress surely turned some heads outside of Chicago as well. We'll have to wait until 2025 to see whether Fulmer has a new trick up his sleeve after he underwent UCL revision surgery in October.

Kyle Hendricks RHP   Born: 12/07/89   Age: 34   Height: 6'3"   Weight: 190   Origin: Round 8, 2011 Draft (#264 overall)

YEAR	TM	LVL	AGE	G (GS)	IP	W-L	SV	K	WHIP	ERA	CSP	BB%	K%	HR%	GB%	ZSw%	ZCon%	OSw%	OCon%	BABIP	SLGCON	DRA-	WARP
2021	CHC	MLB	31	32 (32)	181	14-7	0	131	1.35	4.77	54.4%	5.6%	16.7%	3.9%	43.4%	65.6%	87.9%	36.9%	70.2%	.302	.588	113	0.5
2022	CHC	MLB	32	16 (16)	84¹	4-6	0	66	1.29	4.80	51.5%	6.7%	18.5%	4.2%	36.3%	64.0%	85.2%	34.2%	65.6%	.285	.590	125	-0.2
2023	IOW	AAA	33	5 (5)	20¹	2-1	0	20	1.33	5.75		7.1%	23.5%	2.4%	39.7%	66.0%	85.1%	31.9%	61.0%	.345	.596	95	0.3
2023	CHC	MLB	33	24 (24)	137	6-8	0	93	1.20	3.74	46.1%	4.7%	16.1%	2.2%	46.3%	62.7%	87.8%	36.4%	69.1%	.284	.474	105	1.3
2024 DC	CHC	MLB	34	28 (28)	156²	9-10	0	108	1.32	4.60	50.6%	5.9%	16.2%	3.1%	42.8%					.300	.531	103	1.1

2023 Arsenal: CH (80.7), SI (87.6), FA (87.8), KC (73.4)   Comps: Charles Nagy (82), Freddy Garcia (80), Alex Cobb (80)

If there's a silver lining to the capsule tear in his right shoulder that cost Hendricks the second half of the 2022 season, it's that no arm injury could conceivably make Hendricks throw any softer than he already did. In fact, it was probably more likely he emerged from the ordeal with more juice; it wouldn't be the first time a soft-tossing righty in a Cubs hat miraculously found new life on his heater after a major injury. Alas, Hendricks had no such luck, but his consolation prize was a bounce-back season that saw him return to his pre-injury ways—namely, generating weak contact on the strength of a devastating changeup that was once again one of the best in the league. All told, it was the 33-year-old's best season since the abbreviated 2020 campaign, and it came at a good time with the Cubs holding an option for his 2024 season. You can't teach an old dog new tricks, they say, but fortunately for Hendricks, the old tricks still work just fine.

—————————————— ★ ★ ★ *2024 Top 101 Prospect* **#27** ★ ★ ★ ——————————————

Cade Horton RHP   Born: 08/20/01   Age: 22   Height: 6'1"   Weight: 211   Origin: Round 1, 2022 Draft (#7 overall)

YEAR	TM	LVL	AGE	G (GS)	IP	W-L	SV	K	WHIP	ERA	CSP	BB%	K%	HR%	GB%	ZSw%	ZCon%	OSw%	OCon%	BABIP	SLGCON	DRA-	WARP
2023	MB	A	21	4 (4)	14¹	0-0	0	21	0.84	1.26		7.3%	38.2%	1.8%	33.3%					.241	.400	86	0.2
2023	SB	A+	21	11 (11)	47	3-3	0	65	1.00	3.83		6.5%	35.1%	3.2%	45.8%					.287	.542	58	1.5
2023	TNS	AA	21	6 (6)	27	1-1	0	31	1.07	1.33		10.1%	28.4%	0.0%	37.3%					.273	.338	86	
2024 DC	CHC	MLB	22	12 (3)	25²	1-1	0	26	1.39	4.86		9.6%	23.6%	3.8%	35.6%					.302	.595	107	0.1

Comps: Matt Manning (84), Chris Archer (81), Mitch Keller (81)

In our preseason writeup of Cubs prospects, the BP Prospect Team noted that underslot signing Horton didn't have a long track record as a pitcher while at the University of Oklahoma and thus "might see larger gains in a pro development program than you would from a more advanced college arm." That checked out. A year further removed from Tommy John surgery, the 22-year-old dominated the low minors, posting a ruthless 33.5% strikeout percentage across three levels. By year's end, Horton was dispatching Double-A hitters with a new curve and split-change to go with his plus slider and fastball, so there's no reason he shouldn't begin the 2024 season in Knoxville at the very least. Where he finishes the season? Given the aggressive nature of pitcher promotions in 2023, nobody should be surprised if it's on a mound in Wrigley Field.

Brandon Hughes LHP   Born: 12/01/95   Age: 28   Height: 6'2"   Weight: 215   Origin: Round 16, 2017 Draft (#495 overall)

YEAR	TM	LVL	AGE	G (GS)	IP	W-L	SV	K	WHIP	ERA	CSP	BB%	K%	HR%	GB%	ZSw%	ZCon%	OSw%	OCon%	BABIP	SLGCON	DRA-	WARP
2021	SB	A+	25	8 (0)	11¹	2-1	0	17	0.97	1.59		8.7%	37.0%	2.2%	33.3%					.261	.458	86	0.2
2021	TNS	AA	25	18 (0)	30²	0-0	1	43	1.21	1.76		10.1%	33.3%	2.3%	32.9%					.318	.522	78	0.7
2022	IOW	AAA	26	5 (0)	10¹	1-0	0	12	0.58	0.00		5.6%	33.3%	0.0%	31.8%					.182	.227	88	0.2
2022	CHC	MLB	26	57 (0)	57²	2-3	8	68	1.09	3.12	52.7%	8.8%	28.5%	4.6%	34.0%	69.8%	80.5%	34.7%	48.0%	.233	.585	101	0.5
2023	IOW	AAA	27	11 (0)	11	2-0	0	9	2.45	9.00		15.3%	15.3%	5.1%	22.5%	71.6%	80.9%	31.1%	50.0%	.405	.872	133	-0.1
2023	CHC	MLB	27	17 (0)	13²	0-3	0	17	1.61	7.24	41.8%	12.7%	27.0%	3.2%	29.7%	67.9%	80.7%	30.3%	42.6%	.353	.611	98	0.2
2024 non	CHC	MLB	28	58 (0)	50	2-2	0	60	1.36	4.62	50.1%	10.2%	27.4%	3.4%	33.1%					.307	.606	103	0.1

2023 Arsenal: SL (83.2), FA (93.6), SI (93.8)   Comps: Ryan O'Rourke (63), Brad Wieck (62), Jeff Beliveau (61)

It's a nifty coincidence that Hughes had an identical DRA- (101) and Contextual FIP (98) in his 2022 and 2023 seasons, considering that a good deal of context is required to understand how the two seasons could go so differently while looking so similar under the hood. Unlike in that brilliant 2022 rookie campaign, very little went right for Hughes this past season, between knee issues, and a knee debridement procedure in late June ended his season. When on the field, his surface numbers were tarnished by a .343 BABIP and 59.4% strand rate. It's unwise to assume much in this game, but if both his luck and his health normalize, an output somewhere between his 2022 and 2023 numbers should be the expectation for 2024.

Shota Imanaga LHP   Born: 09/01/93   Age: 30   Height: 5'10"   Weight: 175   Origin: IFA, 2024

YEAR	TM	LVL	AGE	G(GS)	IP	W-L	SV	K	WHIP	ERA	CSP	BB%	K%	HR%	GB%	ZSw%	ZCon%	OSw%	OCon%	BABIP	SLGCON	DRA-	WARP
2024 DC	CHC	MLB	30	26(26)	145	8-10	0	142	1.29	5.07		6.2%	23.3%	5.4%	18.7%					.295	.680	115	0.2

Imanaga isn't the guy you wanted. He won't win the Cy Young and no club offered him $325 million. Sorry. But if we compare him with the other starter who jumped from Japan statistically, rather than just through scouting, he holds his own in several respects. He led qualified NPB hurlers with a 29.2% strikeout rate and 174 punchouts—five more than that other fellow. His fastball sits in the low 90s, but averages 20 inches of induced vertical break, which will help it play above its velocity. His splitter is a swing-and-miss weapon and he manipulates a plethora of breaking and off-speed offerings to keep hitters off balance. Homers are a problem, yes, but he consistently stays ahead in the count and rarely issues walks. Maybe he's more Nestor Cortes than Gerrit Cole, but consider him a silver medal rather than a consolation prize.

Mark Leiter Jr. RHP   Born: 03/13/91   Age: 33   Height: 6'0"   Weight: 210   Origin: Round 22, 2013 Draft (#661 overall)

YEAR	TM	LVL	AGE	G(GS)	IP	W-L	SV	K	WHIP	ERA	CSP	BB%	K%	HR%	GB%	ZSw%	ZCon%	OSw%	OCon%	BABIP	SLGCON	DRA-	WARP
2021	ERI	AA	30	8(4)	25²	2-4	0	35	1.29	5.26		7.2%	31.5%	3.6%	34.8%					.350	.734	89	0.4
2021	TOL	AAA	30	17(15)	89	8-4	0	110	1.01	3.34		6.4%	30.5%	2.8%	46.4%					.275	.528	83	2.0
2022	IOW	AAA	31	6(6)	22	0-3	0	32	1.23	5.32		6.4%	34.0%	4.3%	30.9%					.333	.655	79	0.5
2022	CHC	MLB	31	35(4)	67²	2-7	3	73	1.14	3.99	52.8%	8.9%	25.9%	3.5%	48.0%	60.7%	85.2%	32.8%	53.7%	.251	.531	92	0.9
2023	CHC	MLB	32	69(0)	64¹	1-3	4	77	1.12	3.50	44.0%	8.9%	28.6%	2.6%	45.6%	64.9%	81.0%	30.4%	49.5%	.270	.545	83	1.3
2024 DC	CHC	MLB	33	55(0)	58²	4-3	4	65	1.18	3.65	48.0%	8.4%	26.6%	3.1%	44.7%					.281	.532	84	0.8

2023 Arsenal: FS (84.9), SI (91.5), FC (88.9), CU (73.6), FA (91.5)   Comps: Carlos Torres (55), Blake Treinen (52), Ryan Tepera (51)

The 2016 film *Split* is about a man with dissociative identity disorder, so if we're making a movie about Leiter's second act we'll have to settle for *Splitter*. That's been the star of the show anyway, as Leiter uncovered its value in 2022 and dramatically upped his usage of the split-finger pitch in 2023, throwing it one third of the time. That's a smart decision when it yields a .134 batting average against and .223 slugging percentage and generates whiffs nearly half the time. (Mostly against lefties—the sequel will be called *Splits* and will explore whether the 32-year-old will ever figure out how to retire righties.) Leiter will likely never be an all-weather closer, and the Cubs have better options for saves on most days, but he's quietly been pretty good for two years now and should at least have a guaranteed bullpen role moving forward. This story has a happy ending.

Julian Merryweather RHP   Born: 10/14/91   Age: 32   Height: 6'4"   Weight: 215   Origin: Round 5, 2014 Draft (#158 overall)

YEAR	TM	LVL	AGE	G(GS)	IP	W-L	SV	K	WHIP	ERA	CSP	BB%	K%	HR%	GB%	ZSw%	ZCon%	OSw%	OCon%	BABIP	SLGCON	DRA-	WARP
2021	TOR	MLB	29	13(1)	13	0-1	2	12	1.31	4.85	62.5%	7.3%	21.8%	7.3%	39.5%	67.6%	84.1%	31.3%	66.7%	.265	.676	103	0.1
2022	TOR	MLB	30	26(1)	26²	0-3	0	23	1.43	6.75	57.6%	5.9%	19.3%	3.4%	47.1%	74.3%	91.4%	35.7%	53.7%	.333	.627	92	0.4
2023	CHC	MLB	31	69(0)	72	5-1	2	98	1.31	3.38	46.0%	11.9%	32.3%	2.6%	41.1%	67.6%	81.5%	33.6%	42.6%	.313	.527	78	1.7
2024 DC	CHC	MLB	32	55(0)	58²	4-3	8	70	1.28	4.08	49.5%	10.0%	28.0%	3.6%	41.7%					.291	.586	92	0.5

2023 Arsenal: SL (87.2), FA (98.3), CH (81.6), SW (84.4)   Comps: Marcus Walden (55), Jacob Barnes (52), George Kontos (52)

Merryweather has been a tantalizing talent for as long as we can remember, which is to say, since 2014. You're saying people remember times before 2014? Impossible. Since time immemorial, Merryweather had an intriguing right arm attached to a body that rarely let him show off that talent. He managed to stay relatively healthy in 2023, though, and parlayed that health into his best season as a major-league pitcher. Despite being 32 years old, the long path to get here means he'll remain a Cub for the foreseeable future, a boon for the team after they got him for nothing on the waiver wire this past winter. Barring the unforeseeable—and, boy, if you think our memory is bad, wait until you hear about our ability to see the future—Merryweather will remain an important piece of the Cubs' high-leverage bullpen plans moving forward.

Daniel Palencia RHP   Born: 02/05/00   Age: 24   Height: 5'11"   Weight: 160   Origin: IFA, 2020

YEAR	TM	LVL	AGE	G(GS)	IP	W-L	SV	K	WHIP	ERA	CSP	BB%	K%	HR%	GB%	ZSw%	ZCon%	OSw%	OCon%	BABIP	SLGCON	DRA-	WARP
2021	MB	A	21	7(7)	27	1-0	0	38	1.30	3.67		15.7%	33.0%	1.7%	20.7%					.268	.474	114	0.0
2021	STK	A	21	6(6)	14¹	0-2	0	14	1.60	6.91		9.2%	21.5%	4.6%	40.5%					.359	.707	105	0.0
2022	SB	A+	22	21(20)	75¹	1-3	0	98	1.21	3.94		11.1%	31.1%	2.2%	46.0%					.290	.494	64	2.2
2023	TNS	AA	23	5(5)	15¹	0-0	0	18	1.30	5.87		13.6%	27.3%	4.5%	41.0%					.222	.579	108	0.2
2023	IOW	AAA	23	13(0)	13²	0-0	2	18	1.46	7.90		10.6%	27.3%	1.5%	36.8%	67.4%	71.9%	39.1%	54.5%	.324	.579	101	0.2
2023	CHC	MLB	23	27(0)	28¹	5-3	0	33	1.27	4.45	43.6%	11.8%	27.7%	2.5%	35.7%	70.2%	77.7%	32.8%	56.7%	.288	.522	96	0.4
2024 DC	CHC	MLB	24	44(0)	47	3-2	0	53	1.50	5.59	43.6%	11.9%	24.9%	4.1%	35.9%					.307	.638	120	-0.3

2023 Arsenal: FA (98.5), SL (89.7), SI (98.7), CU (83.4), CH (87.9)   Comps: Junior Fernández (70), Mauricio Cabrera (67), Jandel Gustave (67)

In January 2023, the BP prospect staff was asked to identify prospects who missed the Top 101 but had a chance to crack the list in 2024. Palencia made that list, but he won't be on this year's: Not because he took a step back, but because he shot from High-A to half a season in the bigs. A triple-digit fastball and devastating slider will do that, as the playoff-minded Cubs saw a need for his power arm in their bullpen rather than toiling away in the minors. What does that mean for his development, and his progress as a starter in particular? That's the question, one the Cubs will answer when they're not chasing ships. His inability to develop a clear third offering may relegate him to the bullpen full-time from here on. It's pretty clear that wherever he ends up, though, he'll be doing it at the highest level.

Michael Rucker RHP Born: 04/27/94 Age: 30 Height: 6'1" Weight: 195 Origin: Round 11, 2016 Draft (#344 overall)

YEAR	TM	LVL	AGE	G (GS)	IP	W-L	SV	K	WHIP	ERA	CSP	BB%	K%	HR%	GB%	ZSw%	ZCon%	OSw%	OCon%	BABIP	SLGCON	DRA-	WARP
2021	IOW	AAA	27	19(0)	39¹	3-0	0	49	1.35	4.81		5.4%	29.3%	4.8%	46.7%					.364	.748	81	0.9
2021	CHC	MLB	27	20(0)	28¹	0-0	1	30	1.52	6.99	50.8%	8.7%	23.8%	4.0%	45.8%	72.4%	83.8%	34.7%	50.0%	.346	.659	92	0.4
2022	IOW	AAA	28	10(0)	15¹	1-0	0	13	1.50	1.17		11.8%	19.1%	0.0%	48.9%					.319	.383	104	0.2
2022	CHC	MLB	28	41(0)	54²	3-1	0	50	1.28	3.95	52.3%	8.7%	21.8%	3.5%	44.7%	74.2%	83.6%	32.6%	59.1%	.278	.522	95	0.7
2023	IOW	AAA	29	13(2)	21¹	0-1	2	19	0.80	1.69		6.5%	24.7%	2.6%	41.5%	69.8%	82.7%	31.8%	49.2%	.196	.346	90	0.4
2023	CHC	MLB	29	35(0)	40¹	2-1	0	40	1.44	4.91	42.4%	10.8%	22.7%	3.4%	51.8%	69.8%	86.7%	28.2%	52.3%	.306	.589	92	0.6
2024 DC	*CHC*	*MLB*	*30*	*26(0)*	*29¹*	*2-1*	*0*	*29*	*1.36*	*4.50*	*48.0%*	*8.8%*	*22.7%*	*3.1%*	*45.8%*					*.305*	*.547*	*100*	*0.1*

2023 Arsenal: FA (94.9), FC (89.6), SL (86.1), CU (81), CH (90.4), SI (93.8)　　　　　　　*Comps: Rob Scahill (64), Tyler Duffey (60), Gonzalez Germen (59)*

Among pitchers with at least 40 innings pitched in 2023, Rucker's 0.34 was the lowest Average Leverage Index. That's not a stat you put on your résumé, but hey, as New Found Glory said, at least he's known for something. What he should perhaps strive to be known for is a trimmed-down arsenal, as you rarely see relievers throwing five pitches as Rucker did last season. He uses his hard slider as almost a splitter, dropping it out of the zone, which works well enough. The 95-mph four-seamer that he threw roughly 40% of the time really didn't, grading out as his worst pitch. The 29-year-old will try to diagnose the cause in the offseason. And if he can't? Well, they probably have an Average Leverage Index for the minors, too.

Drew Smyly LHP Born: 06/13/89 Age: 35 Height: 6'2" Weight: 188 Origin: Round 2, 2010 Draft (#68 overall)

YEAR	TM	LVL	AGE	G (GS)	IP	W-L	SV	K	WHIP	ERA	CSP	BB%	K%	HR%	GB%	ZSw%	ZCon%	OSw%	OCon%	BABIP	SLGCON	DRA-	WARP
2021	ATL	MLB	32	29(23)	126²	11-4	0	117	1.37	4.48	58.3%	7.5%	21.4%	4.9%	38.4%	71.6%	87.0%	33.7%	56.9%	.300	.629	108	0.7
2022	CHC	MLB	33	22(22)	106¹	7-8	0	91	1.19	3.47	58.1%	5.8%	20.4%	3.6%	40.6%	72.8%	83.5%	36.6%	61.7%	.275	.540	117	0.1
2023	CHC	MLB	34	41(23)	142¹	11-11	0	141	1.43	5.00	45.8%	8.9%	22.5%	4.2%	34.5%	67.1%	83.6%	34.2%	60.3%	.307	.642	113	0.7
2024 DC	*CHC*	*MLB*	*35*	*44(0)*	*47*	*3-2*	*0*	*43*	*1.31*	*4.48*	*52.0%*	*7.9%*	*21.6%*	*3.7%*	*35.8%*					*.294*	*.564*	*101*	*0.3*

2023 Arsenal: KC (78.7), SI (92.2), FC (88.8)　　　　　　　*Comps: Floyd Bannister (74), Ricky Nolasco (70), Rick Reuschel (69)*

Only 13 pitchers in baseball had both double-digit wins and double-digit losses last season, and you better believe we're telling you that weirdly specific stat because Smyly was one of them. Of those 13 pitchers, none threw fewer innings than Smyly's 142 ⅓. The guy was just a magnet for decisions, good and bad. What conclusions can we draw from these statistics? Few, really, but it's hard to find something new or interesting to say about the 34-year-old, who's been around and been doing his thing—moderate strikeouts, moderate baserunners, literally a nearly perfectly average career DRA- of 99—for more than a decade now. The Cubs did shift him to relief midyear, and he thrived in the role, even as the rest of the bullpen fell apart down the stretch. He's got one more year left on his current deal, so we're at least guaranteed to see Smyly doing the aforementioned thing a little longer on the North Side.

Justin Steele LHP Born: 07/11/95 Age: 28 Height: 6'2" Weight: 205 Origin: Round 5, 2014 Draft (#139 overall)

YEAR	TM	LVL	AGE	G (GS)	IP	W-L	SV	K	WHIP	ERA	CSP	BB%	K%	HR%	GB%	ZSw%	ZCon%	OSw%	OCon%	BABIP	SLGCON	DRA-	WARP
2021	CHC	MLB	25	20(9)	57	4-4	0	59	1.35	4.26	54.7%	10.9%	23.8%	4.8%	49.7%	64.9%	82.4%	30.3%	57.8%	.264	.603	97	0.6
2022	CHC	MLB	26	24(24)	119	4-7	0	126	1.35	3.18	56.6%	9.8%	24.6%	1.6%	51.1%	68.9%	84.6%	30.4%	60.6%	.318	.470	93	1.6
2023	CHC	MLB	27	30(30)	173¹	16-5	0	176	1.17	3.06	51.5%	5.0%	24.6%	2.0%	48.9%	72.2%	87.7%	36.1%	56.8%	.320	.504	80	3.8
2024 DC	*CHC*	*MLB*	*28*	*29(29)*	*169*	*10-9*	*0*	*157*	*1.31*	*4.07*	*53.6%*	*7.8%*	*21.7%*	*2.4%*	*48.8%*					*.305*	*.507*	*92*	*2.2*

2023 Arsenal: HC (92), SW (83.5), SI (92), CU (81.4), CH (87.5)　　　　　　　*Comps: Framber Valdez (61), Drew Pomeranz (58), Marco Gonzales (57)*

In his first 27 starts of the 2023 season, Steele had lifted himself from near-obscurity to a shining beacon of hope for those looking for a Cy Young alternative to Blake Snell and his 13.3% walk rate. It didn't happen, as he and his team stumbled in the final month, but any questions surrounding Steele's legitimacy have since been silenced. A shift to being a primarily two-pitch pitcher in the second half of 2022 elevated his game to another level, and even though we've been taught that starting pitchers need more than two viable pitches to be effective, it no longer applies if they're both good enough. Steele doubled down and threw his four-seam fastball and sweeping slider a combined 96.5% of the time last year. Lefties did slug .473 against him last year; you can choose to consider that a red flag, or do the math on how that factors into the total line and see it as a path toward getting even better.

Jameson Taillon RHP Born: 11/18/91 Age: 32 Height: 6'5" Weight: 230 Origin: Round 1, 2010 Draft (#2 overall)

YEAR	TM	LVL	AGE	G (GS)	IP	W-L	SV	K	WHIP	ERA	CSP	BB%	K%	HR%	GB%	ZSw%	ZCon%	OSw%	OCon%	BABIP	SLGCON	DRA-	WARP
2021	NYY	MLB	29	29(29)	144¹	8-6	0	140	1.21	4.30	56.3%	7.3%	23.2%	4.0%	33.9%	71.5%	82.1%	35.9%	61.5%	.273	.568	107	0.8
2022	NYY	MLB	30	32(32)	177¹	14-5	0	151	1.13	3.91	53.4%	4.4%	20.7%	3.6%	40.4%	71.4%	87.1%	34.3%	63.2%	.278	.552	100	1.7
2023	CHC	MLB	31	30(29)	154¹	8-10	1	140	1.28	4.84	49.6%	6.3%	21.4%	4.1%	38.0%	69.2%	84.6%	33.7%	67.8%	.292	.575	105	1.5
2024 DC	*CHC*	*MLB*	*32*	*24(24)*	*126¹*	*7-8*	*0*	*104*	*1.27*	*4.34*	*52.5%*	*6.5%*	*19.6%*	*3.6%*	*38.4%*					*.291*	*.553*	*99*	*1.2*

2023 Arsenal: FA (93.8), FC (88.6), KC (80.7), SW (81), SI (94.1), CH (86.6)　　　　　　　*Comps: Rick Wise (79), Brad Penny (79), Charles Nagy (79)*

Ignoring those pesky results for a moment, Taillon actually made two pretty interesting and promising changes this past season. The first was the addition of a sweeper—pitch number seven—that ended up being his best pitch against righties. The second was an increased reliance on his curveball against lefties, which was similarly effective. His next step will be figuring out how to get those lefties out more often, as the .266/.340/.514 line that they put up last year won't get it done. But perhaps most of all, Taillon might need to be more creative. Usually when a guy is throwing six or seven pitches, the conventional wisdom is that he should trim that down, lean more into his strengths. In Taillon's case, he might actually need to blend more: Seeking to get ahead in the count, the righty threw first-pitch fastballs 77% of the time. It netted him a career-high 70% first-strike rate, but because fastballs are his worst offerings, it also resulted in a .714 slugging against. PitchCom randomization might be a better strategy. That said, a strong finish to the year, including a 2.76 ERA in September, should at least give Taillon confidence—if not solutions—heading into 2024.

Keegan Thompson RHP Born: 03/13/95 Age: 29 Height: 6'1" Weight: 210 Origin: Round 3, 2017 Draft (#105 overall)

YEAR	TM	LVL	AGE	G(GS)	IP	W-L	SV	K	WHIP	ERA	CSP	BB%	K%	HR%	GB%	ZSw%	ZCon%	OSw%	OCon%	BABIP	SLGCON	DRA-	WARP
2021	CHC	MLB	26	32(6)	53¹	3-3	1	55	1.48	3.38	56.8%	12.8%	22.6%	3.7%	42.2%	71.0%	84.5%	28.4%	60.8%	.273	.556	114	0.1
2022	CHC	MLB	27	29(17)	115	10-5	1	108	1.27	3.76	54.6%	8.9%	22.3%	3.3%	40.3%	67.2%	84.7%	30.9%	61.1%	.282	.548	104	0.9
2023	IOW	AAA	28	20(0)	30	3-0	0	40	1.90	8.10		15.8%	27.4%	5.5%	32.1%	65.6%	76.8%	30.6%	51.4%	.356	.835	101	0.4
2023	CHC	MLB	28	19(0)	28²	2-2	1	26	1.36	4.71	47.0%	15.2%	20.8%	1.6%	39.2%	66.5%	83.2%	26.3%	57.9%	.234	.390	111	0.2
2024 DC	CHC	MLB	29	38(0)	41	2-2	0	42	1.45	5.02	53.7%	11.7%	22.9%	3.5%	39.7%					.293	.573	109	0.0

2023 Arsenal: FA (94.2), FC (89.6), CU (82.2), SW (84.5), CH (89.9)   *Comps: Joe Kelly (62), Rafael Montero (58), Mike Wright Jr. (58)*

Sometimes you have to feel for second-division players who suddenly find themselves in first-division organizations. When the Cubs made their push toward playoff contention, Thompson suddenly found his services unneeded, and instead of helping out as a jack-of-all-trades swingman, he spent 2023 serving as a reliever-of-all-midwest states. Despite the wall suddenly erected between himself and a major-league per diem, he did little to knock it down, walking too many batters as he lost some of his ability to get hitters to chase. If Chicago remains too successful to make use of him, at least Thompson will reach free agency in 2028.

Hayden Wesneski RHP Born: 12/05/97 Age: 26 Height: 6'3" Weight: 210 Origin: Round 6, 2019 Draft (#195 overall)

YEAR	TM	LVL	AGE	G(GS)	IP	W-L	SV	K	WHIP	ERA	CSP	BB%	K%	HR%	GB%	ZSw%	ZCon%	OSw%	OCon%	BABIP	SLGCON	DRA-	WARP
2021	HV	A+	23	7(7)	36¹	1-1	0	47	0.91	1.49		6.7%	35.1%	1.5%	51.9%					.293	.455	77	0.8
2021	SOM	AA	23	15(15)	83	8-4	0	92	1.18	4.01		6.4%	26.7%	3.2%	43.6%					.305	.570	94	0.9
2021	SWB	AAA	23	3(2)	11	2-1	0	12	1.36	3.27		10.9%	26.1%	0.0%	41.4%					.345	.448	99	0.2
2022	SWB	AAA	24	19(19)	89²	6-7	0	83	1.15	3.51		7.5%	22.4%	2.4%	40.9%					.270	.502	95	1.5
2022	IOW	AAA	24	5(4)	20²	0-2	0	23	1.21	5.66		9.3%	26.7%	1.2%	47.2%					.308	.462	96	0.3
2022	CHC	MLB	24	6(4)	33	3-2	0	33	0.94	2.18	56.2%	5.3%	25.0%	2.3%	46.1%	71.6%	78.3%	33.1%	66.7%	.244	.443	95	0.4
2023	IOW	AAA	25	5(5)	20	1-0	0	28	1.00	1.35		10.1%	35.4%	2.5%	37.2%	69.7%	77.2%	32.7%	46.9%	.244	.476	89	0.4
2023	CHC	MLB	25	34(11)	89¹	3-5	0	83	1.28	4.63	49.7%	8.4%	21.9%	5.3%	40.0%	64.0%	85.9%	29.9%	63.2%	.261	.609	98	1.1
2024 DC	CHC	MLB	26	29(8)	60	3-3	0	53	1.30	4.30	51.0%	8.2%	20.9%	3.2%	40.9%					.290	.536	97	0.5

2023 Arsenal: SW (82.1), FA (94.6), SI (93), FC (88.8), CH (84.2)   *Comps: Luis Cessa (66), Shaun Anderson (65), Brandon Workman (65)*

There's something very aesthetically pleasing about Wesneski's pitch percentage chart—just five, different colored lines hovering across the page, each nearly perfectly horizontal and none intersecting with the others. Of course, practically, that's not a great thing, as the 25-year-old entered last season needing to find another offering to pair with his near-elite sweeper, and he didn't seem to look for it. That sweeper still did its thing, and he threw it a ton accordingly, but that lack of another swing-and-miss pitch plagued him all season. Because of that, by year's end he was pitching exclusively out of the bullpen—not what anyone had in mind after his dazzling debut in September 2022. That may be his permanent home if he doesn't find a way to get lefties out consistently, and fast.

★ ★ ★ *2024 Top 101 Prospect* **#94** ★ ★ ★

Jordan Wicks LHP Born: 09/01/99 Age: 24 Height: 6'3" Weight: 220 Origin: Round 1, 2021 Draft (#21 overall)

YEAR	TM	LVL	AGE	G(GS)	IP	W-L	SV	K	WHIP	ERA	CSP	BB%	K%	HR%	GB%	ZSw%	ZCon%	OSw%	OCon%	BABIP	SLGCON	DRA-	WARP
2021	SB	A+	21	4(4)	7	0-0	0	5	1.43	5.14		9.4%	15.6%	0.0%	37.5%					.304	.435	117	0.0
2022	SB	A+	22	16(16)	66²	4-3	0	86	1.25	3.65		6.0%	30.6%	1.8%	45.1%					.363	.552	69	1.8
2022	TNS	AA	22	8(8)	28	0-3	0	35	1.25	4.18		9.1%	28.9%	4.1%	50.0%					.284	.556	83	0.5
2023	TNS	AA	23	13(13)	58¹	4-0	0	69	1.17	3.39		8.0%	29.0%	3.8%	40.3%					.286	.599	83	1.3
2023	IOW	AAA	23	7(7)	33	3-0	0	30	1.18	3.82		9.6%	22.2%	2.2%	44.0%	64.4%	87.9%	31.7%	56.0%	.264	.489	89	0.7
2023	CHC	MLB	23	7(7)	34²	4-1	0	24	1.27	4.41	42.1%	7.5%	16.3%	3.4%	47.3%	73.7%	86.3%	32.2%	65.3%	.269	.533	125	0.0
2024 DC	CHC	MLB	24	19(19)	81¹	4-6	0	67	1.41	4.85	42.1%	8.6%	18.8%	3.2%	44.0%					.301	.541	107	0.4

2023 Arsenal: CH (81.4), FA (92.3), SI (91.6), FC (89.2), CU (78.2), SW (81.7)   *Comps: Robert Dugger (70), Eric Lauer (67), Patrick Corbin (66)*

A few years ago, we might have labeled the rookie Wicks a potential sleeper, stumping for him to up the usage of his changeup—the pitch that's very clearly his meal ticket—and tick down usage of his four-seam fastball in turn. We now live in a baseball climate where pitchers are encouraged to lead with their best pitch, though, and so there will be no pounding of the table after Wicks came out and threw his changeup nearly 30% of the time in his first seven MLB starts. It was the fastball that got knocked around, but the pitch graded out as above-average in the minors and should at least be serviceable moving forward. And if the curveball, which showed well in an admittedly very limited sample size, is a weapon against righties as well? This candle could burn bright for a long time.

LINEOUTS

Hitters

HITTER	POS	TM	LVL	AGE	PA	R	HR	RBI	SB	AVG/OBP/SLG	BABIP	SLGCON	BB%	K%	ZSw%	ZCon%	OSw%	OCon%	LA	90th EV	DRC+	BRR	DRP	WARP
Pablo Aliendo	C	TNS	AA	22	375	49	16	61	5	.231/.332/.458	.301	.710	10.9%	30.4%						99	0.6	-1.9	0.9
David Bote	IF	IOW	AAA	30	425	61	14	61	7	.258/.361/.456	.311	.621	12.5%	22.6%	71.3%	83.9%	30.2%	48.1%		99	-1.4	-1.5	1.0
Alexis Hernandez	SS	CUB	ROK	18	150	25	3	25	9	.315/.407/.515	.494	.838	12.0%	33.3%						99			
Eric Hosmer	1B/DH	CHC	MLB	33	100	7	2	14	0	.234/.280/.330	.299	.449	6.0%	25.0%	68.5%	81.7%	40.6%	70.1%	3.3	104.6	88	0.0	0.1	0.1
Miles Mastrobuoni	3B	IOW	AAA	27	165	35	2	14	9	.295/.448/.473	.409	.678	21.8%	23.6%	52.9%	81.4%	22.3%	67.6%		112	-1.1	-0.5	0.5
	3B	CHC	MLB	27	149	24	1	5	13	.241/.308/.301	.310	.396	8.7%	21.5%	51.2%	84.6%	28.2%	68.0%	11.8	101.2	84	0.4	-0.1	0.2
Haydn McGeary	1B	SB	A+	23	90	9	3	13	3	.368/.467/.592	.439	.750	14.4%	17.8%						123	-1.9	0.1	0.3
	1B	TNS	AA	23	442	56	16	75	4	.255/.382/.435	.311	.613	15.2%	23.8%						114	-2.6	2.5	1.9
BJ Murray Jr.	3B	TNS	AA	23	542	71	16	74	14	.263/.382/.462	.333	.647	15.1%	23.8%						115	-2.0	-4.8	1.4
Edwin Ríos	DH	IOW	AAA	29	176	26	6	20	0	.263/.364/.454	.370	.704	11.4%	30.7%	66.7%	81.4%	36.2%	50.6%		90	1.3	-2.9	0.1
	DH	CHC	MLB	29	34	3	1	2	0	.071/.235/.214	.091	.500	14.7%	47.1%	70.3%	75.6%	30.3%	37.0%	20.6	103.1	71	0.0	0.0	0.0
Josh Rivera	IF	SB	A+	22	103	18	2	12	1	.250/.320/.402	.323	.561	8.7%	25.2%						95	-1.8	0.6	0.1
Brian Serven	C	ABQ	AAA	28	162	14	5	20	0	.199/.241/.331	.258	.500	4.9%	31.5%	73.7%	82.7%	45.2%	46.0%		70	0.0	0.9	0.0
	C	COL	MLB	28	23	0	0	1	0	.130/.130/.174	.231	.308	0.0%	43.5%	59.5%	68.2%	45.0%	38.9%	19.7	98.0	67	0.0	1.1	0.1
Luis Vazquez	SS	TNS	AA	23	258	38	11	40	4	.284/.340/.483	.346	.671	6.2%	25.2%						98	2.0	1.6	1.0
	SS	IOW	AAA	23	270	34	9	40	6	.257/.381/.428	.302	.572	14.1%	20.7%	70.3%	80.3%	34.5%	57.7%		101	-1.4	1.5	0.9

A jump in his 90th-percentile exit velocity drove an impressive offensive campaign for **Pablo Aliendo** in 2023, one that put him on prospect maps—if still on the periphery. Catchers who can actually catch can live on that periphery for a long time. ⓧ When you give a guy a five-year, $16 million contract, 14 homers and seven steals in just 99 games should be a welcome contribution. The problem is, 30-year-old **David Bote** spent the entire 2023 season at Triple-A. ⓧ The carrying tool for **Alexis Hernandez** coming stateside was his speed. The 19-year-old is also excelling at the primary task of many international signings, growing correctly, as he's already starting to get his newfound young adult strength into batted balls. ⓧ When the Cubs signed **Eric Hosmer** and later Edwin Ríos last offseason, people asked, what are they going to do with all these first basemen? The answer, at least in Hosmer's case, was release them—the 34-year-old was cut loose in May after two disappointing months. ⓧ **Miles Mastrobuoni** is one of those guys whose value to an MLB team is derived from the fact that he brings about seven different gloves to the ballpark every day. You might say he's a jack of all trades, Mastr ... you know what, never mind. ⓧ There's a lot to like about **Haydn McGeary** as a concept—a big, strong first baseman that doesn't strike out much and walks a lot is a recipe for success. In practice, the 24-year-old needs to turn more hard-hit grounders into line drives and home runs to carry his pedestrian glove to The Show. ⓧ Sadly, the "B" in **BJ Murray Jr.** doesn't stand for "Bill," no matter how much we all wish it did. Still, the *Groundhog Day* star and Cubs fanatic might soon view the younger Murray as a son if the 23-year-old continues to make Futures Game appearances, as he did in 2023. And if he does repeat in 2024? Well, it wouldn't be the first time a Murray had déjà vu. ⓧ Tantalizing power has always been **Edwin Ríos**' meal ticket; the problem is, he makes so little contact that he usually goes hungry. After being granted free agency in October, the 29-year-old will be on the hunt for his next meal this winter. ⓧ A college bat who turned 23 years old a few days after the season ended, **Josh Rivera** went from the University of Florida to High-A in the course of a few weeks this past summer. The aggressive promotion didn't seem to faze him, suggesting the infielder could be a quick riser through the Cubs' system. ⓧ **Brian Serven** pummeled Triple-A pitching as a 27-year-old in 2022, earning a timeshare at catcher in the majors down the stretch. Those gains didn't stick, although his glovework probably still merits the Austin Hedges "hold your nose and bat him ninth half the time anyway" treatment. ⓧ **Luis Vázquez** showed enough with the stick (and the eye) on his second pass through the high minors to grab a spot on the Cubs' 40-man after the 2023 season. That's about as exciting as we can make a future utility man sound, so let's hope it worked.

Pitchers

PITCHER	TM	LVL	AGE	G (GS)	IP	W-L	SV	K	WHIP	ERA	CSP	BB%	K%	HR%	GB%	ZSw%	ZCon%	OSw%	OCon%	BABIP	SLGCON	DRA-	WARP
Michael Arias	MB	A	21	11 (11)	42¹	1-4	0	64	1.16	2.55		14.5%	37.2%	0.6%	40.2%					.284	.415	79	0.8
	SB	A+	21	11 (11)	39	0-6	0	46	1.74	5.77		14.4%	25.6%	1.1%	44.8%					.388	.562	102	0.5
Richard Bleier	IOW	AAA	36	5 (0)	5²	0-0	0	2	1.94	6.35		17.2%	6.9%	0.0%	27.3%	69.0%	93.1%	43.9%	69.0%	.286	.500	120	0.0
	BOS	MLB	36	27 (0)	30²	1-0	0	16	1.37	5.28	51.7%	3.8%	12.1%	3.8%	52.8%	71.4%	88.7%	41.6%	73.8%	.317	.552	100	0.4
Colten Brewer	SWB	AAA	30	15 (2)	20	0-0	0	23	0.70	1.35		7.8%	29.9%	2.6%	45.7%	68.9%	69.2%	30.4%	45.5%	.136	.304	87	0.4
	NYY	MLB	30	3 (0)	8¹	0-0	0	4	1.08	4.32	51.0%	8.8%	11.8%	8.8%	61.5%	65.3%	87.5%	27.3%	60.0%	.130	.692	99	0.1
Nick Burdi	IOW	AAA	30	21 (0)	19²	0-0	4	33	1.53	3.20		15.4%	36.3%	1.1%	36.8%	62.6%	70.7%	27.6%	49.3%	.405	.632	80	0.5
	CHC	MLB	30	3 (0)	3	0-0	0	4	2.00	9.00	42.3%	20.0%	26.7%	0.0%	25.0%	78.9%	73.3%	46.2%	55.6%	.375	.857	110	0.0
Luis Devers	SB	A+	23	15 (14)	56¹	4-5	0	62	1.44	5.11		12.8%	24.8%	1.6%	34.9%					.310	.469	105	0.0
Tyler Duffey	IOW	AAA	32	36 (2)	45¹	4-1	2	53	1.10	3.77		12.6%	29.1%	3.8%	33.7%	64.0%	78.1%	31.4%	51.1%	.206	.545	97	0.7
	CHC	MLB	32	1 (0)	2	0-0	0	3	0.50	4.50	39.1%	0.0%	42.9%	14.3%	0.0%	72.7%	100.0%	30.0%	50.0%	.000	1.000	100	0.0
Kohl Franklin	SB	A+	23	5 (5)	19¹	0-2	0	30	1.29	2.79		14.0%	34.9%	2.3%	28.6%					.275	.500	82	0.4
	TNS	AA	23	21 (21)	85²	4-10	0	86	1.49	5.99		10.0%	22.7%	5.0%	45.3%					.311	.671	106	-0.8
Drew Gray	CUB	ROK	20	3 (3)	6¹	0-0	0	11	1.42	5.68		20.7%	37.9%	0.0%	50.0%					.300	.500		
	MB	A	20	11 (11)	27²	0-3	0	45	1.52	4.23		18.4%	36.0%	0.0%	53.8%					.365	.423	92	0.4
Shane Greene	IOW	AAA	34	9 (7)	25²	2-1	0	27	1.32	1.75		10.9%	24.5%	1.8%	24.6%	60.9%	77.2%	27.1%	61.7%	.299	.449	114	0.2
	CHC	MLB	34	2 (0)	3	0-0	0	3	1.33	0.00	47.2%	16.7%	25.0%	0.0%	57.1%	50.0%	87.5%	15.4%	25.0%	.286	.429	99	0.0
Codi Heuer	IOW	AAA	26	15 (0)	12²	0-1	0	15	2.05	7.82		17.5%	23.8%	3.2%	27.0%	76.0%	73.7%	32.9%	61.1%	.371	.649	123	0.0
Caleb Kilian	IOW	AAA	26	25 (24)	120¹	8-3	0	95	1.32	4.56		7.0%	18.6%	3.3%	44.7%	67.8%	86.0%	28.5%	63.9%	.299	.560	95	2.1
	CHC	MLB	26	3 (1)	5¹	0-1	0	5	2.81	16.88	52.0%	6.1%	15.2%	0.0%	50.0%	77.6%	91.1%	25.0%	66.7%	.591	.727	102	0.1
Luke Little	SB	A+	22	5 (4)	17¹	0-0	0	21	1.10	0.52		9.5%	28.4%	0.0%	53.7%					.293	.341	83	0.3
	TNS	AA	22	23 (0)	34²	3-2	0	63	1.38	3.12		18.2%	40.9%	0.6%	50.0%					.345	.455	69	0.4
	IOW	AAA	22	8 (0)	11²	2-0	1	21	1.29	1.54		13.7%	41.2%	0.0%	36.4%	58.2%	80.7%	23.8%	41.4%	.364	.455	74	0.3
	CHC	MLB	22	7 (0)	6²	0-0	0	12	1.35	0.00	42.5%	13.3%	40.0%	0.0%	61.5%	57.9%	66.7%	26.9%	33.3%	.385	.583	82	0.1

If you can whip a ball across the diamond from shortstop, you can probably throw it pretty hard from a mound, too, right? The Cubs had that thought when they snapped up **Michael Arias** off waivers in 2021. The move has already paid dividends, with Arias showing both an electric fastball and decent secondaries in the low minors. ⓫ It's actually sort of incredible that **Richard Bleier** has existed as a reliever—and a successful one, at that—all these years despite a career 13.6% strikeout percentage. At 36 years old, it's safe to assume that they're not coming; job offers remain to be seen. ⓫ **Colten Brewer** is an excellent pick for not only the "Name All The 2023 Yankees" Sporcle Quiz, but also any future Yankees/Red Sox (or Yankees/Hanshin Tigers!) Immaculate Grid intersections. ⓫ Like his return to the majors, **Nick Burdi**'s return to these pages for the first time since 2021 will be brief. After working his way back from a second Tommy John surgery, Burdi then enjoyed bouts of appendicitis and ulnar nerve irritation before the clock ran out on him. ⓫ The organization's minor-league pitcher of the year in 2022, **Luis Devers** won't be retaining his title, though he did cap the season with 41 strikeouts in his final 28 ⅓ innings of work. ⓫ The Cubs had 21 different players make multiple relief appearances in 2023 and **Tyler Duffey** wasn't one of them. They did promote him and put him on the mound in Game 162, so Duffey can at least say he got to pitch in October—which is more than most Cubs pitchers can say. ⓫ It's not going to take much for **Kohl Franklin** to become the greatest Kohl in MLB history—0.1 WARP would suffice. Based on that homer rate in Double-A, it might also take far too much. ⓫ Former 2021 third-round pick **Drew Gray** came back from Tommy John and pitched like a guy coming back from Tommy John. Command is a long-term concern, but for now all that really matters is that he knows how to grip a changeup and that he's having a good time. ⓫ By pitching a single major-league inning, **Shane Greene** finds himself on the exact line between having his usefulness wrung out by the MLB reliever shuttle process, and having it be neat that he's still around to have his usefulness wrung out by the MLB reliever shuttle process. ⓫ Since being traded for Craig Kimbrel in 2021, **Codi Heuer** has torn his UCL and broken his elbow. He's probably had a ton of minor bad things happen to him, too, hangnails and stolen packages and failed water heaters, but fans only care about the big stuff. ⓫ **Caleb Kilian** got three MLB appearances for the second straight year. Around them he was a pretty good Triple-A pitcher in 2022, and a pretty forgettable one at Triple-A last year in 2023. That's a problem, because at 26 years old, forgettable isn't far from forgotten. ⓫ There is quite literally nothing small about **Luke Little**, from his 6-foot-8-inch frame to his triple-digit velocity. The Cubs, size queens that they are, couldn't help but notice that he was packing heat(ers) and gave the 23-year-old a month-long audition in September, one he almost certainly passed. ⓫ **Ethan Roberts** is yet another promising Cubs pitching prospect whose progression got halted by the dreaded elbow tear. He and his employer will spend 2024 sorting through what's left of his arm, sort of like an unboxing video but for a person's livelihood. ⓫ Tommy John surgery ahead of the 2023 MLB Draft surely didn't help **Jaxon Wiggins'** stock, but the Cubs still saw fit to take him at no. 68 overall. That speaks to how they view the right-hander's upside, one he'll work to make good on when he returns to the mound this summer.

CHICAGO WHITE SOX

Essay by James Fegan

Player comments by Esteban Rivera and BP staff

If you missed Charlie Kaufman's 2008 film *Synecdoche, New York*, you missed 124 minutes of runtime that contained at least as many, if not more genuinely upbeat moments than the 101-loss 2023 White Sox, and with a comparable body count to boot.

As much as the film's larger themes—loss, regret and a project of enormous personal hubris contorting into a living mausoleum for a series of naïve ambitions—align to the narrative arc of this embattled ballclub, a particular metaphor stabs directly at its heart. In the early portions of the film, a woman named Hazel purchases a home that is actively ablaze. While touring the home through the rising smoke, she airs concerns that the roaring fire will someday kill her. The realtor does not dismiss this for a second. It's worth noting that the mounting burn damage does make for a more affordable acquisition price.

Near the end of the film, Hazel indeed dies of smoke inhalation by way of—*get this*—living in the burning house. Sometimes the exchange for upfront cost savings is an existentially larger bill coming due in the end.

In *Synecdoche*, somehow this inevitable and clearly telegraphed fate still provides a sense of shock and tragedy when it finally arrives. Maybe it's because Hollywood largely pretends smoke inhalation doesn't exist, and has people running the equivalent of first-to-third through walls of flame all the time. But we see this person living and operating beside the inferno as a daily act. They have their standard supply of triumphs, disappointments, rising and falling actions, and the flames that will someday consume them become mere background scenery. She gets married, for Pete's sake, and has kids! Kids who live in the burning house!

Just a ridiculous movie that I paid money to see multiple times. Separately, I was once a White Sox partial season-ticket holder.

Despite it all, Hazel has some late-in-the-game moments that make it feel possible she can achieve some measure of happiness, and that being constantly surrounded by the fire that will surely kill her might just be the idiosyncratic trappings to her underdog love story. Which is to say that within the past seven years, the White Sox have both possessed the consensus top farm system in the sport, had a

CHICAGO WHITE SOX PROSPECTUS
2023 W-L: 61-101, 4TH IN AL CENTRAL

Pythag	.375	28th	DER	.692	18th
RS/G	3.96	29th	DRC+	92	26th
RA/G	5.19	26th	DRA-	106	26th
dWin%	.421	28th	FIP	4.73	26th
Payroll	$181M	13th	B-Age	28.4	22nd
M$/MW	$12.9M	28th	P-Age	29.6	15th

400'
377'
372'
330'
335'

- Opened 1991
- Open air
- Natural surface
- Fence profile: 8'

Park Factors

Runs	Runs/RH	Runs/LH	HR/RH	HR/LH
100	100	101	105	104

Top Hitter WARP	2.9 Luis Robert Jr.
Top Pitcher WARP	1.5 Gregory Santos
2023 Top Prospect	Colson Montgomery

Payroll History (in millions)

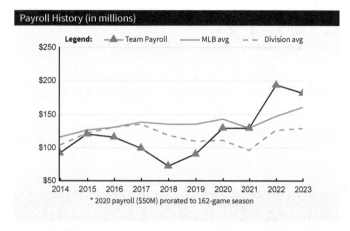

* 2020 payroll ($50M) prorated to 162-game season

Future Commitments (in millions)

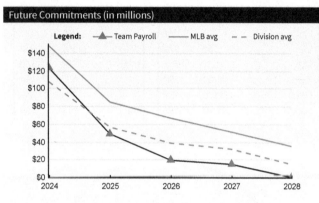

Farm System Ranking

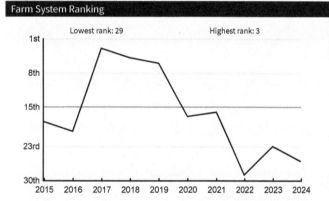

Personnel

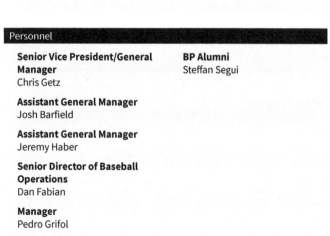

Senior Vice President/General Manager
Chris Getz

Assistant General Manager
Josh Barfield

Assistant General Manager
Jeremy Haber

Senior Director of Baseball Operations
Dan Fabian

Manager
Pedro Grifol

BP Alumni
Steffan Segui

player earn the MVP trophy, employed a nationally renowned broadcaster, held a lead in a decisive playoff game and won 93 games in a season, despite being very much the Chicago White Sox the entire time.

"It's a big decision, how one prefers to die," the realtor offers during the showing. Every top baseball executive surely anticipates that their tenure is likely to end with them being blamed for every shortcoming, taking bullets for others and never openly acknowledging the constraints placed upon them by ownership, and yet they decide to forge ahead anyway. But perhaps former GM Rick Hahn still took a moment to be surprised that his long-awaited tenure, one he hoped to define by a decisive swing for an all-encompassing rebuild, would instead be most remembered for his boss shockingly hiring Tony La Russa at the moment of his plan's realization. And it ended by his being fired alongside Ken Williams, as if they were a package deal without distinct ideas.

But for the last several years, the White Sox have been that burning house, where succumbing to its flames was a possibility—nay, inevitability—at all times. Their failings in foundational elements of organizational structure have mostly been fodder for caustic, privately told jokes by industry veterans. But when they bubbled up into publicly acknowledged issues and the odor of smoke became impossible to ignore, they have been responded to in a manner of someone who sees their ceiling cave in and begins Googling DIY construction tips as embers fill their living room, rather than evacuating...or you know, extinguishing the fire in some dedicated manner.

The post-2016 rebuild that once prompted the Sox to envision multiple championships was notable because no team had ever touted such a bounty of controllable major-league assets while simultaneously being utterly hopeless going forward. They wound up losing 284 games in three years, but cashing out all their trade chips for highly ranked prospects was just the path of least resistance compared to examining how they arrived at such a predicament. Even their multi-year efforts have had the hallmarks and rapidly diminishing returns of a quick fix.

In kind, it's ironic that Chris Getz has been promoted to general manager and tasked with a quick turnaround amid the wreckage of the 2023 season. Because ahead of 2017, Getz was brought in to initiate a gradual modernization of a troubled Sox player development system that already had arguably the most important crop of prospects in franchise history moving through it, breathing in all that smoke.

Ahead of the press conference introducing Getz as GM last September, longtime Sox chairman Jerry Reinsdorf stated his confidence that a team that has been blackening into ash for the last two and a half seasons could quickly return to contention. Concrete details were not given. He rooted some of that faith in what he feels is a greatly improved quality of players coming into the organization since Mike Shirley took over the scouting director job from Nick Hostetler after the 2019 draft.

Set aside briefly whether it was necessary to take a potshot at a still-present Sox employee, or whether Jake Burger's post-trade deadline flourish with the Miami Marlins represents the Sox not getting as much return as other teams would have from Hostetler's drafts. Following the logic of the comment, the Sox made a vitally needed change at scouting director, right *after* they had picked fourth overall in 2018, and third in 2019—the highest picks they would receive as part of their intentional tanking and rebuilding cycle.

All our eulogies could wind up a retelling of how we fishtailed down the road of life, over-correcting in response to all our mistakes well after the opportunity to meaningfully address them had passed. In Chicago's case that oversteer was Lance Lynn, the big trade for a playoff-caliber starting pitcher that an up-and-coming Sox team needed. That is, needed earlier: He arrived right after a dormant 2020 trade deadline, a playoff series loss defined by his absence and manager Rick Renteria getting axed as he struggled to navigate through the pitching shortfall. That trade return Dane Dunning matured into an effective back-end starter for a World Series winning Rangers team, while Lynn's late-career prime, contract extension and the White Sox relevance all ended simultaneously, is somehow just a footnote.

The protagonist's estranged younger daughter, Olive, is sort of the MacGuffin of *Synecdoche*; something for the hero to spend a lifetime hopelessly longing for against all reason. For the White Sox that's been a healthy and productive season from Eloy Jiménez. But just as a late in life reunion between father and daughter is a weird and unsatisfying weak scene in the film, almost anti-comedy in its broadness, the Sox nearly coaxed a career-high in games played from Jiménez this past year by finally resigning him to DH (mostly). A convoluted upper leadership structure made it such that it was hard to find consensus on decisive action until after flames had charred a vital wing of the house beyond recognition. So Jiménez's shift was just in time for the toll of countless injuries and resulting arrested development to sap power and lift from his bat, while the roster still teemed with poor defenders who are DH candidates themselves.

And sure, it's typical for how the timing of the trade deadline and end of season management changes line up. But the White Sox fired Williams and Hahn three weeks after the duo teamed up to deal seven players at the end of July, in a desperate effort to restock an organization that had grown catastrophically bereft of both pitching and catching talent at their upper levels.

These are probably not the most telling examples of the White Sox kind of just operating peacefully alongside their own mounting destruction over the last several years. Driving Jason Benetti out of town and downgrading the television broadcast in the middle of a period where the on-field product isn't worthwhile on its own doesn't really fit with this trend, but is rather just an independently embarrassing thing. But as the brain is deprived of crucial oxygen and your lungs filled with pollutants, the memories and moments that flood the consciousness are more random than expository.

The "people ruining themselves through the obvious results of their own actions" genre has been popular for a few dozen centuries. But even while admiring its construction in so many ways, I cannot in good conscience recommend *Synecdoche* to anyone. Not after I tried to get my wife to watch it and she, a literal mental health therapist, demanded it shut off barely a third of the way in because it was "too depressing."

But should you indulge your curiosity, at least try to get to the part where Phillip Seymour Hoffman's character wins a prestigious and lucrative MacArthur "genius" grant right in time for his family life and physical health to start completely breaking down in response. The last two White Sox teams, predictably waylaid by injuries with little fallback plan and more encumbered by infighting at multiple levels as their dreams diminished, were by far the most expensive rosters in franchise history. When Hoffman's character is richer than he's ever been in his life but can't get his leg to stop spasming, it very well could have been a scene from a Sox training room.

Ask any White Sox employee and they would probably say the worst thing about the 2023 season was losing all those games, everyone being miserable about it and a bunch of their friends getting fired. Maybe a fan would note the psychic whiplash of seeing two of their 2022 All-Stars having their team options declined to save money at the end of 2023. You can certainly see where they're coming from with that. But for my money, there was a striking level of insult in the White Sox being largely unable to crack any of those "most disappointing teams" lists. It's not that the pundits thought the team would be incredible; it's that the failure was so deep as to feel predestined.

Sure, the Mets built the most expensive team ever and wound up selling at the deadline. And no one ever expects a Cardinals team to look like less than the sum of their parts. But the Yankees and Red Sox are both at threat level midnight for having what would constitute typical White Sox seasons. The Padres, long the White Sox' Sisyphean twins on the left coast, posted a winning record and have had to call into question everything about themselves.

The White Sox have not been favorites for a time now, but this time last year were largely viewed as having the talent to win a barren AL Central—in the unlikely event that they got out of their own way. That it not only turned into 101 losses and the sixth-worst season in a not particularly strong franchise history, but also set off a wave of public recriminations and triggered a front office bloodletting and roster overhaul, and only the juiciest bits inspired even morbid curiosity from the baseball world is...just not the most flattering development.

Recall your most life-altering and personally crushing failure, and now imagine if all your peers reacted like they kind of saw it coming from a good ways off, shrugging helplessly, because the smoke was visible for miles. ▦

—James Fegan is a Chicago-based writer and reporter.

HITTERS

Andrew Benintendi LF   Born: 07/06/94   Age: 30   Bats: L   Throws: L   Height: 5'9"   Weight: 180   Origin: Round 1, 2015 Draft (#7 overall)

YEAR	TM	LVL	AGE	PA	R	HR	RBI	SB	AVG/OBP/SLG	BABIP	SLGCON	BB%	K%	ZSw%	ZCon%	OSw%	OCon%	LA	90th EV	DRC+	BRR	DRP	WARP
2021	KC	MLB	26	538	63	17	73	8	.276/.324/.442	.309	.551	6.7%	18.0%	75.9%	82.6%	36.0%	69.8%	15.6	102.0	110	0.0	1.1	2.8
2022	KC	MLB	27	390	40	3	39	4	.320/.387/.398	.366	.468	10.0%	13.3%	77.1%	85.2%	30.5%	72.5%	11.0	101.3	119	0.4	1.6	2.4
2022	NYY	MLB	27	131	14	2	12	4	.254/.331/.404	.303	.517	9.9%	19.1%	73.6%	88.3%	31.5%	60.0%	16.9	102.4	116	0.4	0.5	0.8
2023	CHW	MLB	28	621	72	5	45	13	.262/.326/.356	.301	.423	8.4%	14.3%	71.8%	85.9%	33.9%	73.5%	14.6	99.5	97	0.1	-1.8	1.4
2024 DC	CHW	MLB	29	631	62	10	61	10	.265/.337/.374	.306	.451	9.1%	15.3%							103	0.1	-0.7	1.9

2023 GP: LF (147), DH (1)   Comps: Tim Raines (70), Carl Crawford (67), Goose Goslin (66)

Turns out that if you have hamate procedures twice in 10 years, your power will pay the price. From a pure ISO perspective, Benintendi's line held from 2022 to 2023. But BABIP isn't just a thing that happens to you each year; if you look deeper into the rate at which he put the barrel on the ball and made hard contact, fears about Benintendi's ability to drive the ball are already at DEFCON 2. (Lower is worse; yes, it's weird.) In the first season of a five-year, $75 million contract, the left fielder's short and medium term prospects look awfully bleak. Maybe if Benintendi was still playing average defense, one could squint to find some optimism, but his range (specifically moving towards the wall) reached a career low. Although Benintendi has shown a knack for playing to his park's dimensions as time goes by, it's questionable whether he has the physical skills to do that anymore. At least he's out of hamates?

Oscar Colás RF   Born: 09/17/98   Age: 25   Bats: L   Throws: L   Height: 5'11"   Weight: 209   Origin: IFA, 2022

YEAR	TM	LVL	AGE	PA	R	HR	RBI	SB	AVG/OBP/SLG	BABIP	SLGCON	BB%	K%	ZSw%	ZCon%	OSw%	OCon%	LA	90th EV	DRC+	BRR	DRP	WARP
2022	WS	A+	23	268	37	7	42	1	.311/.369/.475	.375	.611	8.2%	20.1%							108	-1.5	-4.2	0.6
2022	BIR	AA	23	225	39	14	33	1	.306/.364/.563	.355	.763	6.2%	24.0%							122	0.7	1.0	1.5
2022	CLT	AAA	23	33	5	2	4	1	.387/.424/.645	.588	1.053	6.1%	36.4%	66.7%	75.0%	61.1%	45.5%			79	0.2	-0.3	0.0
2023	CLT	AAA	24	238	36	9	29	2	.272/.345/.465	.322	.619	9.2%	22.3%	70.9%	84.4%	40.6%	62.3%			96	0.5	-0.8	0.7
2023	CHW	MLB	24	263	32	5	19	4	.216/.257/.314	.281	.443	4.6%	27.0%	70.0%	83.5%	44.9%	55.0%	6.4	107.0	67	0.1	-1.0	-0.5
2024 DC	CHW	MLB	25	501	47	12	52	5	.234/.287/.366	.305	.512	5.9%	27.0%							81	-0.1	-2.4	-0.1

2023 GP: RF (69), CF (8), DH (2)   Comps: Joey Terdoslavich (67), Kyle Parker (65), Omar Quintanilla (63)

It's almost always dubious to take a prospect from Double-A and ink him into the Opening Day lineup, but if you're insistent, Colás had the numbers to back it up. He put the ball in play with authority and had a visually whippy, quick swing. The only question was the hit tool, and as 2023 went on it stopped being a question; pitchers quickly manipulated his weakness against breaking stuff to their advantage. Worse still, his athleticism couldn't translate into any defensive value sufficient to give him time to learn on the job; this in turn called his coaching into question. Colás still has the physical skills to develop into a solid hitter, but this type of decision, with no backup plan, was a key reason for the White Sox bottoming out so hard.

Jacob Gonzalez SS   Born: 05/30/02   Age: 22   Bats: L   Throws: R   Height: 6'2"   Weight: 200   Origin: Round 1, 2023 Draft (#15 overall)

YEAR	TM	LVL	AGE	PA	R	HR	RBI	SB	AVG/OBP/SLG	BABIP	SLGCON	BB%	K%	ZSw%	ZCon%	OSw%	OCon%	LA	90th EV	DRC+	BRR	DRP	WARP
2023	KAN	A	21	137	16	1	13	1	.207/.328/.261	.242	.330	14.6%	16.8%							113	-0.8	4.2	1.1
2024 non	CHW	MLB	22	251	19	2	19	0	.206/.278/.287	.269	.391	8.2%	23.6%							61	0.0	0	-0.3

2023 GP: SS (33), DH (1)   Comps: Niuman Romero (85), Ricardo Cubillan (84), Josh Prince (84)

Where a hitter's hands start when swinging—high, medium, or low—doesn't necessarily matter, as long as they result in a clean bat path through the strike zone. Gonzalez holds his hands up high, and his natural rotational motion pulls them downward to get low pitches. But that same looping swing leaves him vulnerable against professional power-pitching, especially up in the zone. The result is that Gonzalez is always a little behind, and it leads to catching up to hard pitches, and punching at them rather than driving them. His movement at shortstop carries that same sense of latency, the jump just a little laggy, and if it's a portent for a move to third, Gonzalez is going to have to figure out his swing in a hurry.

Yasmani Grandal C   Born: 11/08/88   Age: 35   Bats: S   Throws: R   Height: 6'2"   Weight: 225   Origin: Round 1, 2010 Draft (#12 overall)

YEAR	TM	LVL	AGE	PA	R	HR	RBI	SB	AVG/OBP/SLG	BABIP	SLGCON	BB%	K%	ZSw%	ZCon%	OSw%	OCon%	LA	90th EV	DRC+	BRR	DRP	WARP
2021	CLT	AAA	32	25	3	1	1	0	.273/.360/.455	.385	.714	8.0%	32.0%							95	0.0	0.3	0.1
2021	CHW	MLB	32	375	60	23	62	0	.240/.420/.520	.246	.736	23.2%	21.9%	51.3%	84.7%	19.1%	58.3%	13.6	107.8	135	-0.6	1.3	3.2
2022	CLT	AAA	33	38	6	2	5	0	.379/.526/.621	.360	.667	23.7%	5.3%	53.5%	87.0%	10.8%	42.9%			142	-0.2	-0.1	0.3
2022	CHW	MLB	33	376	15	5	27	1	.202/.301/.269	.249	.355	12.0%	21.0%	60.4%	86.0%	24.1%	63.8%	12.1	104.1	93	-1.6	4.0	1.2
2023	CHW	MLB	34	405	33	8	33	0	.234/.309/.339	.284	.444	8.9%	21.2%	62.4%	84.4%	31.3%	60.8%	11.0	102.7	95	-0.8	1.9	1.3
2024 DC	CHW	MLB	35	273	29	7	29	0	.229/.320/.362	.274	.478	11.2%	21.3%							95	-0.6	2.7	1.1

2023 GP: C (92), DH (16), 1B (6)   Comps: Brian McCann (73), Del Crandall (67), Ivey Wingo (64)

Father Time remains undefeated. After years of struggling through the molecular attrition that is everyday catching, Grandal managed to stay healthy in 2023, only to discover that the pain-free body he remembered was no longer the one he has. The two skills that made him an unheralded star and then a well-compensated one, his plate discipline and defense, have eroded; he's now merely average at both, and power on contact has departed him as well. Those surface numbers are actually a touch higher than where the batted ball data has him, as he's sloughed off five ticks of exit velocity in two years. Perhaps backup work will slow the passage of time, at least in terms of cartilage.

YEAR	TM	P. COUNT	FRM RUNS	BLK RUNS	THRW RUNS	TOT RUNS
2021	CHW	10543	2.8	-0.2	0.1	2.7
2022	CHW	9319	6.8	-0.4	-0.7	5.6
2023	CHW	12014	4.1	0.0	-0.2	3.9
2024	*CHW*	*6956*	*3.0*	*-0.2*	*-0.1*	*2.7*

Calvin Harris C   Born: 11/15/01   Age: 22   Bats: L   Throws: R   Height: 6'0"   Weight: 215   Origin: Round 4, 2023 Draft (#116 overall)

YEAR	TM	LVL	AGE	PA	R	HR	RBI	SB	AVG/OBP/SLG	BABIP	SLGCON	BB%	K%	ZSw%	ZCon%	OSw%	OCon%	LA	90th EV	DRC+	BRR	DRP	WARP
2023	KAN	A	21	130	14	1	19	0	.241/.362/.315	.294	.400	15.4%	17.7%						104	-0.9	3.0	0.7
2024 non	*CHW*	*MLB*	*22*	*251*	*20*	*2*	*19*	*0*	*.209/.280/.293*	*.262*	*.381*	*8.1%*	*20.7%*						*64*	*0.0*	*0*	*-0.2*

2023 GP: C (26), DH (7)   *Comps: Federico Hernandez (84), Edgar Cabral (81), Sandy León (80)*

YEAR	TM	P. COUNT	FRM RUNS	BLK RUNS	THRW RUNS	TOT RUNS
2023	KAN	3195	1.9	0.3	0.0	2.2
2024	*CHW*	*6956*	*0.2*	*0.5*	*0.1*	*0.7*

If this system has anything, it's future backup catchers. Harris, a 2023 fourth-rounder, has a short, quick swing that lets him create ideal launch to the opposite field against righties and big pull-side pop against lefties. He also controls the zone well, making good decisions about when to open up the zone or lock it down. The ball doesn't really do anything when he does have to hit it, but he has a year or two to figure that part out. Reports on Harris' glovework were less rosy coming out of college, but he put together solid framing numbers in Low-A, meaning that in this case "backup catcher" might just be an aesthetic label and not a descriptive one.

Eloy Jiménez   DH   Born: 11/27/96   Age: 27   Bats: R   Throws: R   Height: 6'4"   Weight: 240   Origin: IFA, 2013

YEAR	TM	LVL	AGE	PA	R	HR	RBI	SB	AVG/OBP/SLG	BABIP	SLGCON	BB%	K%	ZSw%	ZCon%	OSw%	OCon%	LA	90th EV	DRC+	BRR	DRP	WARP
2021	CLT	AAA	24	41	3	1	2	0	.263/.293/.395	.375	.625	4.9%	34.1%							78	-0.1	0.6	0.1
2021	CHW	MLB	24	231	23	10	37	0	.249/.303/.437	.293	.596	6.9%	24.7%	75.7%	80.2%	39.4%	50.8%	8.2	106.5	100	-0.1	-0.4	0.7
2022	CLT	AAA	25	63	8	2	6	0	.246/.317/.351	.279	.444	9.5%	19.0%	69.6%	82.1%	34.4%	66.7%			105	-1.5	-0.6	0.0
2022	CHW	MLB	25	327	40	16	54	0	.295/.358/.500	.337	.664	8.6%	22.0%	71.8%	78.4%	35.4%	57.8%	7.5	107.6	133	-0.2	-1.1	2.0
2023	CHW	MLB	26	489	50	18	64	0	.272/.317/.441	.305	.554	6.1%	19.0%	72.7%	83.9%	39.2%	55.1%	5.9	108.4	117	-0.3	-0.4	1.9
2024 DC	*CHW*	*MLB*	*27*	*578*	*69*	*23*	*76*	*0*	*.271/.328/.450*	*.321*	*.596*	*7.2%*	*22.6%*							*118*	*0.0*	*-1.5*	*2.5*

2023 GP: DH (105), RF (14)   *Comps: Delmon Young (59), Raul Mondesi (58), Billy Butler (58)*

Jiménez has cracked the 20-home run barrier exactly once, in his rookie season. To be fair, he would have blown past it in 2020 if not for the pandemic, but otherwise the majority of his career has become defined by injury, inconsistency, or both. Chicago's cleanup hitter only went on the IL once all season—for an appendectomy—but his bat took a few other breaks. He struggled to barrel up pitches, especially in the second half, where he cut both his strikeout and home run rate nearly in half as he searched for an answer. Compared to 2022, Jiménez kept his extreme internal rotation on his front foot in his stance, but the lead leg is significantly wider. The result? He has more torso bend and less hip hinge. It's as if he's creating inorganic torso bend as a compensation for no longer creating the necessary rotation and depth in his hips. If 90% of the game is half mental, so is hitting for power; if anything, it's easier to fix a mechanical issue than a torn pectoral muscle. That said, it's also easier to fix a mechanical issue than *prevent* a torn pectoral muscle in a player prone to injury, and believing that Jiménez will be more durable in his late 20s is more a question of faith than science as he approaches the first of two contract option years.

Korey Lee   C   Born: 07/25/98   Age: 25   Bats: R   Throws: R   Height: 6'2"   Weight: 210   Origin: Round 1, 2019 Draft (#32 overall)

YEAR	TM	LVL	AGE	PA	R	HR	RBI	SB	AVG/OBP/SLG	BABIP	SLGCON	BB%	K%	ZSw%	ZCon%	OSw%	OCon%	LA	90th EV	DRC+	BRR	DRP	WARP
2021	ASH	A+	22	121	24	3	14	1	.330/.397/.459	.402	.588	9.9%	19.8%							112	-0.6	0.1	0.5
2021	CC	AA	22	203	25	8	27	3	.254/.320/.443	.275	.547	8.4%	17.2%							116	1.3	-1.4	1.1
2021	SUG	AAA	22	38	2	0	4	0	.229/.263/.343	.296	.462	5.3%	23.7%							83	0.1	-1.1	-0.1
2022	SUG	AAA	23	446	74	25	76	12	.238/.307/.483	.281	.704	8.1%	28.5%	77.4%	78.9%	34.2%	46.7%			93	2.1	5.9	1.6
2022	HOU	MLB	23	26	1	0	4	0	.160/.192/.240	.250	.375	3.8%	34.6%	74.0%	81.1%	46.0%	52.2%	10.8	100.8	72	0.0	-1.4	-0.1
2023	CLT	AAA	24	55	2	0	4	1	.255/.309/.275	.448	.483	5.5%	40.0%	68.8%	72.7%	37.0%	45.5%			65	-0.3	0.4	-0.1
2023	SUG	AAA	24	302	37	5	32	12	.283/.328/.406	.369	.553	5.6%	24.8%	74.9%	78.7%	39.3%	50.0%			84	2.8	-2.9	0.3
2023	CHW	MLB	24	70	4	1	3	0	.077/.143/.138	.091	.200	7.1%	28.6%	80.3%	79.8%	35.8%	50.0%	8.8	99.9	79	0.0	-1.9	-0.1
2024 DC	*CHW*	*MLB*	*25*	*151*	*13*	*3*	*14*	*3*	*.211/.261/.330*	*.290*	*.495*	*5.5%*	*30.6%*							*66*	*0.1*	*-5.2*	*-0.6*

2023 GP: C (23)   *Comps: Alex Jackson (58), Sandy León (58), John Ryan Murphy (55)*

YEAR	TM	P. COUNT	FRM RUNS	BLK RUNS	THRW RUNS	TOT RUNS
2021	ASH	2963	-0.5	-0.1	0.0	-0.6
2021	CC	5227	-1.3	-0.9	0.3	-1.9
2022	SUG	10554	4.9	-1.0	1.4	5.3
2022	HOU	1041	-1.3	0.0	0.0	-1.3
2023	CLT	1442	-0.1	0.0	0.3	0.2
2023	SUG	8656	-2.8	-0.5	0.2	-3.1
2023	CHW	3413	-1.3	-0.1	0.2	-1.2
2024	*CHW*	*6012*	*-4.9*	*-0.2*	*-0.1*	*-5.2*

While Grandal wraps up a long and successful career, Lee is checking every room for traps. Once considered the catcher of the future in Houston, the Astros looked at him, looked at the decaying form of Martín Maldonado, and decided that having nine hitters in a lineup was overrated. In 2023 he was shipped to Chicago for Kendall Graveman at the deadline, and the White Sox, lacking any depth at the position, were happy to take him in. Still, the holes in Lee's profile are undeniable. Visually, his swing is compelling. He has quiet movements that result in respectable rotational power, but the sub-.225 xwOBA against center-cut fastballs might be a signal: His steep vertical entry before he starts his downswing may be related to his lack of barrel awareness since there are only a handful of hitters who are successful with such a jagged motion. Whether Chicago is the right organization to guide Lee is unclear.

Nicky Lopez IF   Born: 03/13/95   Age: 29   Bats: L   Throws: R   Height: 5'11"   Weight: 180   Origin: Round 5, 2016 Draft (#163 overall)

YEAR	TM	LVL	AGE	PA	R	HR	RBI	SB	AVG/OBP/SLG	BABIP	SLGCON	BB%	K%	ZSw%	ZCon%	OSw%	OCon%	LA	90th EV	DRC+	BRR	DRP	WARP
2021	KC	MLB	26	565	78	2	43	22	.300/.365/.378	.347	.444	8.7%	13.1%	64.6%	91.2%	30.4%	74.4%	1.3	99.2	106	1.3	3.3	2.9
2022	KC	MLB	27	480	51	0	20	13	.227/.281/.273	.265	.319	6.0%	13.1%	68.7%	86.9%	34.3%	76.3%	4.3	98.6	90	1.3	1.4	1.2
2023	ATL	MLB	28	72	13	1	12	2	.277/.333/.369	.309	.436	6.9%	13.9%	76.7%	84.8%	33.9%	64.3%	-1.2	100.2	104	0.1	-0.1	0.3
2023	KC	MLB	28	190	19	0	13	4	.213/.323/.281	.262	.346	11.1%	15.8%	67.2%	86.9%	32.2%	66.2%	0.5	96.8	100	0.4	0.8	0.7
2024 DC	CHW	MLB	29	300	26	2	24	6	.244/.321/.324	.294	.398	9.1%	16.7%							87	0.4	-1.2	0.3

2023 GP: 2B (49), 3B (29), SS (11), 1B (4), P (2), LF (2), DH (1)   *Comps: Alexi Casilla (62), Chris Getz (62), Eric Sogard (58)*

This was yet another season of Lopez sticking to his script. The script: playing fine defense, hitting for average and offering intangibles so solid that he's welcome in any clubhouse. It was enough for two clubhouses in 2023, as the Royals took a flier on recently waived reliever Taylor Hearn at the cost of sending Lopez to Atlanta. He adapted to his new, high-powered environment by putting up some of the best offensive numbers of his career—you know he was feeling good when he even hit a ball over the outfield fence as a treat! It's clear that Lopez is purely a role player at this point in his career, but he plays his role very well.

Martín Maldonado C   Born: 08/16/86   Age: 37   Bats: R   Throws: R   Height: 6'0"   Weight: 230   Origin: Round 27, 2004 Draft (#803 overall)

YEAR	TM	LVL	AGE	PA	R	HR	RBI	SB	AVG/OBP/SLG	BABIP	SLGCON	BB%	K%	ZSw%	ZCon%	OSw%	OCon%	LA	90th EV	DRC+	BRR	DRP	WARP
2021	HOU	MLB	34	426	40	12	36	0	.172/.272/.300	.221	.455	11.0%	29.8%	63.0%	82.0%	26.8%	51.3%	17.8	101.1	66	-0.8	-2.0	-0.3
2022	HOU	MLB	35	379	40	15	45	0	.186/.248/.352	.228	.531	5.8%	30.6%	71.5%	82.5%	34.0%	45.1%	14.6	102.9	71	-1.2	5.8	0.5
2023	HOU	MLB	36	407	33	15	36	0	.191/.258/.348	.260	.565	7.4%	34.2%	67.3%	76.8%	34.1%	47.5%	16.6	102.8	59	-0.4	-17.2	-2.3
2024 DC	CHW	MLB	37	176	16	5	18	0	.189/.262/.325	.259	.510	7.8%	33.0%							64	0.0	-5.3	-0.7

2023 GP: C (116), P (1)   *Comps: Jeff Mathis (71), Steve Yeager (66), Russell Martin (66)*

YEAR	TM	P. COUNT	FRM RUNS	BLK RUNS	THRW RUNS	TOT RUNS
2021	HOU	16739	-0.6	0.1	0.8	0.4
2022	HOU	15040	6.6	-0.1	1.6	8.0
2023	HOU	16674	-15.6	-0.1	-0.8	-16.6
2024	CHW	7215	-5.1	0.0	-0.2	-5.3

The last position player to post a WARP lower than Maldonado's 2023 performance was 15 years ago, and it was by Ryan Doumit, at -2.7. Don't pull your 2009 *BP Annual* off the shelf to double-check, though: We actually assigned the former Pirate a 3.2 in the text, saying "he'll never be a great defender, but he worked his way up to adequate." Not long afterward, catcher framing became a thing. Maldonado's legacy depends on the opposite revelation happening: Never a great hitter, he worked his way down to automatic out, his bat speed decaying to the point where he could yank the occasional hanging breaking ball down the line and nothing else. Worse still, the former defensive specialist lost all ability to frame, leaving the indictment of numbers you see above. Someday, maybe we'll unlock a method for evaluating all the aspects of catching that Maldonado does bring through his veteran presence, and that -2.3 WARP will be errata as well?

Yoán Moncada 3B   Born: 05/27/95   Age: 29   Bats: S   Throws: R   Height: 6'2"   Weight: 225   Origin: IFA, 2015

YEAR	TM	LVL	AGE	PA	R	HR	RBI	SB	AVG/OBP/SLG	BABIP	SLGCON	BB%	K%	ZSw%	ZCon%	OSw%	OCon%	LA	90th EV	DRC+	BRR	DRP	WARP
2021	CHW	MLB	26	616	74	14	61	3	.263/.375/.412	.350	.590	13.6%	25.5%	66.1%	82.2%	28.0%	57.4%	11.4	105.7	104	-0.1	0.5	2.5
2022	CLT	AAA	27	25	5	2	5	0	.318/.360/.636	.357	.933	8.0%	28.0%	76.9%	70.0%	35.0%	42.9%			109	-0.3	1.0	0.2
2022	CHW	MLB	27	433	41	12	51	2	.212/.273/.353	.265	.495	7.4%	26.3%	68.4%	83.5%	31.9%	55.0%	15.6	104.3	80	-0.1	5.7	0.6
2023	CLT	AAA	28	50	7	2	5	0	.409/.480/.636	.552	.903	12.0%	26.0%	59.8%	85.7%	29.3%	53.7%			100	-0.8	-1.1	0.0
2023	CHW	MLB	28	357	39	11	40	1	.260/.305/.425	.350	.626	5.6%	30.0%	67.9%	80.8%	32.7%	53.1%	12.5	104.9	73	-0.2	1.2	0.1
2024 DC	CHW	MLB	29	579	58	16	63	2	.235/.303/.384	.306	.546	7.9%	27.1%							92	-0.2	5.6	1.5

2023 GP: 3B (90)   *Comps: Rick Schu (67), Larry Parrish (65), Adrián Beltré (64)*

Moncada almost compels one to optimism. His swings from both sides of the plate still look beautiful. He may not hit the ball as hard as he did in 2018 and 2019, but his quiet rotation and consistent above-average swing variance allowed him to put the ball on the sweet spot on the bat, even in a down year like 2023. The resulting line drives are the key reason he can run an above-average BABIP even as he bleeds speed and pure power. Yet the optimism is strained: It seems like every other week he has a lower body injury that kills any possible rhythm he tries to build, and his plate discipline has disintegrated as a result. The pressure is on Moncada as he heads for an almost certain buyout of his $25 million 2025 contract option, followed by his first trip into free agency. Further removed from the IL, the third baseman finished strong, hitting .287/.332/.486 over his last 50 games. Prior, he had hit .216/.271/.353 in 143 games going back to the start of the 2022 season. One is worthy of another contract and a starting role, the other may have to wait a while for his next opportunity.

─────── ★ ★ ★ *2024 Top 101 Prospect* **#11** ★ ★ ★ ───────

Colson Montgomery SS   Born: 02/27/02   Age: 22   Bats: L   Throws: R   Height: 6'3"   Weight: 205   Origin: Round 1, 2021 Draft (#22 overall)

YEAR	TM	LVL	AGE	PA	R	HR	RBI	SB	AVG/OBP/SLG	BABIP	SLGCON	BB%	K%	ZSw%	ZCon%	OSw%	OCon%	LA	90th EV	DRC+	BRR	DRP	WARP
2021	WSX	ROK	19	111	16	0	7	0	.287/.396/.362	.375	.472	11.7%	19.8%									-2.7	
2022	KAN	A	20	205	31	4	26	0	.324/.424/.476	.402	.633	12.7%	20.5%							125	1.3	0.1	1.3
2022	WS	A+	20	164	22	5	14	1	.258/.387/.417	.282	.519	15.9%	15.9%							126	-0.7	0.6	1.0
2022	BIR	AA	20	52	5	2	7	0	.146/.192/.292	.156	.424	3.8%	28.8%							99	-0.3	-1.5	0.0
2023	GDD	WIN	21	86	9	3	20	0	.244/.302/.423	.314	.623	7.0%	29.1%	75.0%	80.0%	35.0%	14.3%						
2023	WSX	ROK	21	45	9	1	6	2	.353/.511/.588	.393	.690	24.4%	11.1%										
2023	WS	A+	21	82	15	3	10	0	.345/.537/.552	.425	.744	24.4%	18.3%							132	0.0	2.3	0.8
2023	BIR	AA	21	167	27	4	21	0	.244/.400/.427	.308	.589	15.0%	21.6%							114	0.6	-1.3	0.6
2024 DC	CHW	MLB	22	97	9	1	9	0	.224/.316/.336	.289	.460	10.3%	23.6%							87	0.0	0	0.2

2023 GP: SS (71), DH (12)   *Comps: Trevor Story (52), Shed Long Jr. (47), Didi Gregorius (47)*

The latter third of the first round of the 2021 draft was filled with talented infielders twho have blossomed in the minor leagues, Montgomery being one of them. He makes a ton of flush contact and displays high quality swing decisions for any player, regardless of age. From an eye test perspective, he has a smooth, balanced lefty stroke reminiscent of Joey Votto pre-leg kick. He was limited to 64 games in 2023 because of back and oblique injuries, but his results were still impressive. The next task for his offensive game is to develop a bit more lift with his lanky limbs, but those adjustments are more likely to come with better health, considering the difficulties of making upper body adjustments when ramping up mobility. Defensively there's work to do too—Montgomery is a big man even by the standards of modern shortstops and second base beckons. Fortunately for him, the Sox have as big a void there as they do at any other position. It's been a long, long wait since the days of Ray Durham.

Carlos Pérez C   Born: 09/10/96   Age: 27   Bats: R   Throws: R   Height: 5'11"   Weight: 205   Origin: IFA, 2014

YEAR	TM	LVL	AGE	PA	R	HR	RBI	SB	AVG/OBP/SLG	BABIP	SLGCON	BB%	K%	ZSw%	ZCon%	OSw%	OCon%	LA	90th EV	DRC+	BRR	DRP	WARP
2021	BIR	AA	24	441	46	13	59	1	.264/.313/.418	.269	.470	5.7%	10.2%							123	-0.4	-0.3	2.6
2022	CLT	AAA	25	465	53	21	76	2	.254/.316/.450	.234	.497	7.3%	8.6%	69.7%	90.1%	34.9%	77.6%			123	-3.1	6.3	2.8
2022	CHW	MLB	25	18	0	0	2	0	.222/.222/.333	.250	.375	0.0%	11.1%	70.0%	90.5%	41.3%	68.4%	16.2	98.4	98	0.0	-0.5	0.0
2023	CLT	AAA	26	312	31	12	34	0	.240/.295/.408	.242	.476	6.1%	13.1%	71.0%	93.1%	37.0%	76.4%			100	-0.7	0.3	0.9
2023	CHW	MLB	26	53	5	1	3	0	.204/.264/.347	.243	.447	7.5%	20.8%	63.9%	89.1%	40.8%	66.7%	12.5	101.8	90	0.0	-2.9	-0.2
2024 non	CHW	MLB	27	251	23	6	26	1	.216/.266/.347	.226	.404	5.3%	12.7%							71	0.0	-6.8	-0.7

2023 GP: C (20), DH (2)

Comps: Grayson Greiner (68), J.R. Towles (64), Izzy Molina (64)

Respect needs to be given to catchers who toil through the minor leagues for over eight years and finally get their shot. Pérez, who signed with the White Sox in 2014, came into power for the first time in his career in 2022, like an unexpected inheritance from a long-lost aunt. He continued to ride that wave last year and got not just a week-long cup of coffee, but the whole pot, playing in 27 games and staying on the active roster for nearly four months. He isn't the typical glove-first backup catcher, though: His best tool is his bat-to-ball ability, and if he can combine the power he added in '22 with a little more lift, he may carve out a role for himself as a hit-first backup.

YEAR	TM	P. COUNT	FRM RUNS	BLK RUNS	THRW RUNS	TOT RUNS
2021	BIR	11775	-1.7	0.3	1.5	0.1
2022	CLT	12674	2.1	-1.5	5.8	6.5
2022	CHW	806	-0.5	0.0	0.0	-0.5
2023	CLT	8220	-0.3	0.0	1.7	1.4
2023	CHW	1810	-3.1	-0.1	0.0	-3.2
2024	CHW	6956	-6.6	0.1	-0.3	-6.8

★ ★ ★ *2024 Top 101 Prospect* **#78** ★ ★ ★

Edgar Quero C   Born: 04/06/03   Age: 21   Bats: S   Throws: R   Height: 5'11"   Weight: 170   Origin: IFA, 2021

YEAR	TM	LVL	AGE	PA	R	HR	RBI	SB	AVG/OBP/SLG	BABIP	SLGCON	BB%	K%	ZSw%	ZCon%	OSw%	OCon%	LA	90th EV	DRC+	BRR	DRP	WARP
2021	ANG	ROK	18	116	21	4	24	1	.253/.440/.506	.327	.746	19.8%	24.1%									0.2	
2021	IE	A	18	42	2	1	6	1	.206/.310/.353	.316	.667	11.9%	38.1%							84	-0.8	-0.5	-0.1
2022	IE	A	19	515	86	17	75	12	.312/.435/.530	.360	.680	14.2%	17.7%							139	-2.5	-8.8	3.2
2023	RCT	AA	20	321	40	3	35	1	.246/.386/.332	.294	.419	17.1%	16.5%							115	-3.0	-1.6	1.1
2023	BIR	AA	20	134	12	3	22	0	.277/.366/.393	.311	.494	12.7%	17.2%							116	-1.2	-2.9	0.2
2024 DC	CHW	MLB	21	29	3	0	3	0	.226/.313/.334	.275	.450	10.2%	19.4%							86	0.0	0	0.1

2023 GP: C (95), DH (6)

Comps: Keibert Ruiz (65), Austin Hedges (62), Jahmai Jones (53)

Of all the players Chicago acquired at the 2023 trade deadline, none has a more promising future than Quero. At age 20, he was one of the top offensive catchers in Double-A. His profile is fueled by a combination of above-average bat-to-ball skills and good raw power. From a swing perspective, the power is more natural on the left-hand side. His slugging numbers aren't eye-popping, but he consistently makes flush contact. He can adjust his barrel and body to go down and get low breaking balls, but can also maintain strong posture and flick his hands at high heaters, especially from the left side. He has the look of an adjustable hitter with the numbers to show for it. His hands behind the plate, however,

YEAR	TM	P. COUNT	FRM RUNS	BLK RUNS	THRW RUNS	TOT RUNS
2021	ANG	1757			0.6	0.6
2021	IE	1468	-0.5	0.0	0.1	-0.4
2022	IE	11910	-11.4	0.9	0.8	-9.8
2023	BIR	4129	-2.4	0.3	0.2	-1.9
2023	RCT	9998	-2.0	-0.6	3.7	1.2
2024	CHW	1202	-0.5	0.0	0.1	-0.4

are a work in progress. He tends to stab when reaching across his body, which can be a problem with hard breaking balls. His athleticism does keep him in a good position to block pitches and work underneath the ball as a receiver. He still has to overcome the offensive stagnation that afflicts so many young catchers as they rise to Double-A and above, but the potential is there for Quero to give the White Sox their first enduringly above-average backstop since A.J. Pierzynski, if not Carlton Fisk.

Bryan Ramos 3B   Born: 03/12/02   Age: 22   Bats: R   Throws: R   Height: 6'2"   Weight: 190   Origin: IFA, 2018

YEAR	TM	LVL	AGE	PA	R	HR	RBI	SB	AVG/OBP/SLG	BABIP	SLGCON	BB%	K%	ZSw%	ZCon%	OSw%	OCon%	LA	90th EV	DRC+	BRR	DRP	WARP
2021	KAN	A	19	504	64	13	57	13	.244/.345/.415	.295	.558	10.1%	21.8%							103	1.4	0.9	1.8
2022	WS	A+	20	433	64	19	74	1	.275/.350/.471	.291	.579	9.2%	16.4%							125	2.6	-0.3	2.6
2022	BIR	AA	20	86	8	3	12	0	.225/.279/.375	.242	.462	5.8%	17.4%							107	-0.3	-0.2	0.3
2023	BIR	AA	21	342	46	14	48	4	.271/.369/.457	.319	.616	11.1%	21.9%							114	0.2	3.5	1.5
2024 non	CHW	MLB	22	251	23	6	25	2	.217/.283/.344	.277	.479	7.1%	25.8%							77	0.0	0	-0.1

2023 GP: 3B (87), DH (13)

Comps: Josh Vitters (73), Ryan Mountcastle (65), Nolan Arenado (63)

Ramos is in line to carry on the tradition of Cuban stars in the White Sox organization. His well-rounded performance for his league and age throughout his minor league career has been compelling, even with a flawed approach. As the 2023 season progressed, so did Ramos. His best months of the season came in August and September, when his raw pop played in tandem with his bat-to-ball skills, hitting nearly .290 and slugging above .500. His numbers demonstrate the kind of power he has, but his twitchy hands make it even more obvious. His combination of above-average bat speed and quiet lower half during his loading phase put him in a great position to manipulate his barrel and get to breaking balls down in the zone, especially on the inner third. On the defensive side, his below-average arm strength may end up moving him off third base down the line, but it was the only spot he played in during 2023.

Luis Robert Jr. CF   Born: 08/03/97   Age: 26   Bats: R   Throws: R   Height: 6'2"   Weight: 220   Origin: IFA, 2017

YEAR	TM	LVL	AGE	PA	R	HR	RBI	SB	AVG/OBP/SLG	BABIP	SLGCON	BB%	K%	ZSw%	ZCon%	OSw%	OCon%	LA	90th EV	DRC+	BRR	DRP	WARP
2021	CHW	MLB	23	296	42	13	43	6	.338/.378/.567	.394	.729	4.7%	20.6%	85.9%	83.8%	44.6%	55.7%	14.0	108.2	129	0.0	-1.5	2.2
2022	CHW	MLB	24	401	54	12	56	11	.284/.319/.426	.329	.535	4.2%	19.2%	84.2%	85.4%	47.2%	58.8%	10.2	107.3	114	0.5	-3.4	1.8
2023	CHW	MLB	25	595	90	38	80	20	.264/.315/.542	.314	.791	5.0%	28.9%	79.6%	81.5%	43.5%	47.5%	16.5	107.6	114	0.7	-4.0	2.9
2024 DC	CHW	MLB	26	583	72	29	85	17	.257/.310/.472	.306	.656	5.5%	26.1%							115	0.3	-6.2	2.6

2023 GP: CF (143)   *Comps: Matt Kemp (77), Mookie Betts (69), Vernon Wells (66)*

2023 was the year of La Pantera. After three straight years of being deprived of seeing what Luis Robert Jr. could do in a full season, his explosive power was fully realized, and he paired his great offense with incredible center field defense and quality baserunning. As the lone bright spot on the 2023 White Sox, Robert gave Chicago fans something to appreciate night in, night out—at least until September, when he finally went cold and missed the chance to be the first new member of the team 40-homer club since Todd Frazier in 2016. Robert's breakout was primarily fueled by his mastery of torque: After going from a wide to a neutral stance, and as a result adopting a closed stride, Robert was able to turn the outer third from a cold zone to a sizzling, boiling, devastating hot one. By cleaning up his rotational direction, he doubled his pull rate on outside fastballs year over year, a category that includes some of the best hitters in baseball. It wouldn't be surprising if Robert further improved in 2024. His swing has been optimized.

José Rodríguez IF   Born: 05/13/01   Age: 23   Bats: R   Throws: R   Height: 5'11"   Weight: 175   Origin: IFA, 2018

YEAR	TM	LVL	AGE	PA	R	HR	RBI	SB	AVG/OBP/SLG	BABIP	SLGCON	BB%	K%	ZSw%	ZCon%	OSw%	OCon%	LA	90th EV	DRC+	BRR	DRP	WARP
2021	KAN	A	20	361	58	9	32	20	.283/.328/.452	.317	.545	5.8%	15.8%							111	1.8	-8.9	0.9
2021	WS	A+	20	126	19	5	19	10	.361/.381/.538	.369	.604	4.0%	10.3%							138	-1.7	-4.0	0.4
2022	BIR	AA	21	484	75	11	68	40	.280/.340/.430	.308	.505	7.9%	13.6%							106	3.7	-1.4	2.0
2023	BIR	AA	22	404	63	18	54	28	.264/.297/.450	.305	.599	4.5%	23.5%							99	1.4	-1.1	1.0
2023	CLT	AAA	22	89	11	3	8	3	.253/.270/.379	.268	.446	2.2%	14.6%	70.6%	76.4%	50.3%	72.1%			95	-0.5	-1.7	-0.2
2023	CHW	MLB	22	0	1	0	0	0	.000/.000/.000														
2024 DC	CHW	MLB	23	97	8	2	9	4	.223/.262/.344	.270	.457	4.4%	22.4%							69	0.0	-0.1	-0.1

2023 GP: 2B (1)   *Comps: Henry Alejandro Rodriguez (72), Daniel Castro (62), Steve Lombardozzi (58)*

There's no shortage of stories in 2023 about players who flew through the minors with dominant, multi-level performances. Rodríguez probably isn't one of them. The combination of plus hit tool and bat speed are exciting, so much so that the speedy infielder couldn't wait to show them off, swinging at every pitch within (and sometimes out of) arm's reach. This isn't so much a criticism of the infielder himself, whose skills are undeniable. But given where the team stands, it's hard to understand the rush. Take some time, watch a few hundred plate appearances, develop an actual plan for him at the plate. After all, as long as we're talking about stories, the cautionary tale of Oscar Colás is *right there.*

Gavin Sheets RF   Born: 04/23/96   Age: 28   Bats: L   Throws: L   Height: 6'5"   Weight: 230   Origin: Round 2, 2017 Draft (#49 overall)

YEAR	TM	LVL	AGE	PA	R	HR	RBI	SB	AVG/OBP/SLG	BABIP	SLGCON	BB%	K%	ZSw%	ZCon%	OSw%	OCon%	LA	90th EV	DRC+	BRR	DRP	WARP
2021	CLT	AAA	25	254	36	11	46	1	.295/.362/.507	.344	.669	9.8%	21.7%							114	0.1	0.5	1.1
2021	CHW	MLB	25	179	23	11	34	0	.250/.324/.506	.264	.675	8.9%	22.3%	67.2%	88.2%	31.9%	66.7%	11.3	104.7	111	-0.1	-0.2	0.7
2022	CHW	MLB	26	410	34	15	53	0	.241/.295/.411	.272	.533	6.6%	21.0%	64.3%	84.5%	36.2%	69.7%	14.7	103.9	93	-0.4	-1.5	0.6
2023	CHW	MLB	27	344	24	10	43	1	.203/.267/.331	.222	.420	8.1%	19.2%	70.2%	86.0%	32.5%	67.4%	17.1	103.4	90	-0.1	-1.3	0.3
2024 DC	CHW	MLB	28	385	43	14	47	1	.248/.315/.417	.276	.519	8.1%	18.3%							104	-0.3	-0.8	0.9

2023 GP: RF (68), 1B (22), DH (11), LF (7)   *Comps: Lucas Duda (65), Domonic Brown (59), Dan Johnson (55)*

To put it bluntly, Sheets is not an outfielder, despite the fact that he is regularly carted out on the grass and asked to do an impression. The fact that he is forced to play two-thirds of his games in a corner outfield spot because the White Sox and their offseason plan—write Oscar Colás in with ink, close eyes, pray—is actively hurting his ability to do what he does best: hit the ball. It's not ideal being put in a position to fail by your own organization, but that alone isn't necessarily enough to explain Sheets' declining offensive performance. His vertical bat angle has decreased to a surprisingly flat level relative to his successful 2021, and it coincides directly with a drastic decrease in barrel and hard-hit rates. This is a hitter who desperately needs a swing adjustment, and without it, he won't resemble the righty masher that he was in the minors and during his rookie season. Note he's a career .208/.263/.318 hitter in road games—perhaps heckling from the bleachers is getting to him too. The fans know even if the White Sox don't.

Braden Shewmake MI   Born: 11/19/97   Age: 26   Bats: L   Throws: R   Height: 6'3"   Weight: 190   Origin: Round 1, 2019 Draft (#21 overall)

YEAR	TM	LVL	AGE	PA	R	HR	RBI	SB	AVG/OBP/SLG	BABIP	SLGCON	BB%	K%	ZSw%	ZCon%	OSw%	OCon%	LA	90th EV	DRC+	BRR	DRP	WARP
2021	MIS	AA	23	344	40	12	40	4	.228/.271/.401	.262	.522	4.9%	21.8%							100	-0.4	5.3	1.5
2022	GWN	AAA	24	307	37	7	25	9	.259/.316/.399	.298	.502	7.5%	18.6%	81.8%	88.9%	29.4%	60.0%			95	1.5	1.8	1.0
2023	GWN	AAA	25	526	79	16	69	27	.234/.298/.407	.264	.522	7.4%	19.8%	78.0%	78.8%	40.7%	59.7%			86	4.7	6.6	1.6
2023	ATL	MLB	25	4	0	0	0	0	.000/.000/.000		.000	0.0%	25.0%	80.0%	75.0%	75.0%	33.3%	-34.5	97.4	95		0.0	0.0
2024 DC	CHW	MLB	26	182	15	4	17	5	.208/.260/.331	.263	.448	5.6%	25.1%							63	0.0	-0.6	-0.3

2023 GP: SS (2)   *Comps: Luis Alfonso Cruz (60), Luis Hernandez (59), Tzu-Wei Lin (52)*

The spring training competition was presumed to be a formality when it came to the shortstop position in Atlanta. Vaughn Grissom seemed to be the heir apparent throughout the entire offseason, but Shewmake's strong spring suddenly brought him into the conversation. As it turned out, both of the young middle infielders ended up starting the season in Triple-A while Orlando Arcia became the starting shortstop. This worked out very well for Arcia as he became an All-Star, and it also worked out for Grissom as he thrived in Gwinnett. It didn't go so well for Shewmake, who struggled mightily at the plate and has gone from having potential to be an all-around threat to being projected as a defensive specialist—at best. He'll have to improve significantly at the plate in order to make a big-league impact.

Lenyn Sosa IF   Born: 01/25/00   Age: 24   Bats: R   Throws: R   Height: 6'0"   Weight: 180   Origin: IFA, 2016

YEAR	TM	LVL	AGE	PA	R	HR	RBI	SB	AVG/OBP/SLG	BABIP	SLGCON	BB%	K%	ZSw%	ZCon%	OSw%	OCon%	LA	90th EV	DRC+	BRR	DRP	WARP
2021	WS	A+	21	353	45	10	49	3	.290/.321/.443	.349	.576	4.0%	21.8%							98	0.4	6.3	1.6
2021	BIR	AA	21	121	10	1	7	0	.214/.240/.282	.273	.371	1.7%	23.1%							77	-0.2	2.4	0.3
2022	CAR	WIN	22	170	18	2	15	0	.272/.343/.384	.342	.504	8.2%	21.2%										
2022	BIR	AA	22	289	47	14	48	0	.331/.384/.549	.340	.650	7.3%	13.8%							136	1.5	3.1	2.5
2022	CLT	AAA	22	247	30	9	31	3	.296/.352/.469	.331	.579	7.3%	17.4%	71.3%	85.5%	37.4%	70.8%			108	0.3	0.0	1.0
2022	CHW	MLB	22	36	3	1	1	0	.114/.139/.229	.136	.348	2.8%	33.3%	70.0%	85.7%	55.7%	61.5%	5.8	102.8	85	0.0	-0.1	0.0
2023	CLT	AAA	23	308	41	17	44	0	.271/.313/.507	.310	.685	5.8%	24.4%	63.0%	79.7%	39.0%	62.3%			99	-1.6	1.8	0.9
2023	CHW	MLB	23	173	12	6	14	0	.201/.224/.348	.227	.460	2.9%	23.1%	65.5%	84.2%	42.4%	66.0%	13.9	102.8	86	0.0	0.4	0.3
2024 DC	CHW	MLB	24	120	12	4	13	1	.241/.280/.384	.292	.518	4.5%	23.8%							84	-0.2	-0.1	0.1

2023 GP: 2B (44), 3B (10)   Comps: Hanser Alberto (63), Hernán Pérez (60), Luis Rengifo (58)

Opposite-field power seems like a portent of skillfull hitting. When a player can let the ball travel and still get some lift in their bat path, they have a promising trait that gives them a few precious extra milliseconds to recognize pitches. Sosa has that trait. Of his six home runs in 2023, four were hit to the opposite field, including one off a 101-mph heater from Jhoan Duran. Counterintuitively, this ability has thus far been completely beside the point. When a hitter struggles to this extent and doesn't have a robust minor-league statistical profile, it's fair to question if they'll ever make it work, but there's something here. Sosa's ultra-aggressive approach has been his kryptonite, but if he can find just a *soupçon* of sangfroid, the swing skills are there for Sosa to be a power-first second baseman. For now, though, he's a power-only one.

Max Stassi C   Born: 03/15/91   Age: 33   Bats: R   Throws: R   Height: 5'10"   Weight: 200   Origin: Round 4, 2009 Draft (#123 overall)

YEAR	TM	LVL	AGE	PA	R	HR	RBI	SB	AVG/OBP/SLG	BABIP	SLGCON	BB%	K%	ZSw%	ZCon%	OSw%	OCon%	LA	90th EV	DRC+	BRR	DRP	WARP
2021	LAA	MLB	30	319	45	13	35	0	.241/.326/.426	.325	.663	8.8%	31.7%	66.5%	78.5%	29.7%	54.1%	11.7	104.1	85	-0.3	13.2	2.0
2022	LAA	MLB	31	375	32	9	30	0	.180/.267/.303	.239	.457	10.1%	29.9%	67.2%	79.2%	28.6%	45.7%	9.1	103.1	76	-0.4	-1.2	0.1
2024 DC	CHW	MLB	33	258	26	7	28	0	.214/.294/.359	.284	.532	8.9%	29.6%							85	0.0	6.8	1.2

Comps: Martín Maldonado (55), Sandy León (55), Chris Snyder (55)

YEAR	TM	P. COUNT	FRM RUNS	BLK RUNS	THRW RUNS	TOT RUNS
2021	LAA	11913	13.9	0.0	0.6	14.4
2022	LAA	13467	1.2	-0.4	-0.2	0.6
2024	CHW	9620	7.0	-0.1	-0.1	6.8

Hoping to recover from a disastrous 2022, Stassi's season was waylaid first by a hip injury that eventually landed him on the 60-day IL. As he was cleared to resume activities, he missed the balance of the season tending to a serious family medical issue, and the Angels continued to pay him while on the IL as he did so...up until they needed that money to slip under the CBT threshold late in the year. He'll get a fresh start, and possibly a starting job, on Chicago's south side in 2024. When he's right, Stassi provides a stable framing presence behind the plate and some thunder at it. Here's hoping he gets there; both the player and his new fans deserve a rebound.

Andrew Vaughn 1B   Born: 04/03/98   Age: 26   Bats: R   Throws: R   Height: 6'0"   Weight: 215   Origin: Round 1, 2019 Draft (#3 overall)

YEAR	TM	LVL	AGE	PA	R	HR	RBI	SB	AVG/OBP/SLG	BABIP	SLGCON	BB%	K%	ZSw%	ZCon%	OSw%	OCon%	LA	90th EV	DRC+	BRR	DRP	WARP
2021	CHW	MLB	23	469	56	15	48	1	.235/.309/.396	.271	.522	8.7%	21.5%	64.3%	86.4%	32.8%	61.5%	10.1	105.9	105	-0.3	-4.4	1.4
2022	CHW	MLB	24	555	60	17	76	0	.271/.321/.429	.301	.529	5.6%	17.3%	62.5%	88.6%	35.2%	65.9%	7.6	104.4	114	-1.0	-6.0	1.7
2023	CHW	MLB	25	615	67	21	80	0	.258/.314/.429	.299	.556	5.9%	21.0%	66.3%	88.3%	34.9%	60.2%	11.3	105.9	113	-1.0	0.1	2.2
2024 DC	CHW	MLB	26	619	68	21	76	0	.255/.316/.421	.292	.537	6.5%	19.8%							108	0.0	0.1	1.8

2023 GP: 1B (143), DH (8)   Comps: Nick Evans (68), Josh Bell (64), Nick Swisher (63)

The year is 2021. It's a beautiful sunny day in the Bronx. Vaughn steps to the plate against Aroldis Chapman with the White Sox down one in the top of the ninth and no runners on. Only a month into Vaughn's major-league career he's been given a great opportunity to show the kind of hitter he could be for his team against quality pitching. He takes a 100-mph heater just off the black to start the at-bat and get ahead in the count. After that, he gets a challenge 99-mph four-seamer in the heart of the plate. He responds with a 432-foot opposite-field shot over the Yankees' bullpen to tie the game. It seemed as though the slugger had arrived. And yet: After 1,600 plate appearances in the show, Vaughn sits at a 111 career DRC+ and just north of replacement-level production. His bottom-of-the-league struggles against sweepers and curveballs in 2023 (.167 xwOBA) have set him back immensely. Until he learns how to make body adjustments against these pitches, he'll continue to just be another second-division guy, and not the star hitter that was expected.

George Wolkow OF   Born: 01/11/06   Age: 18   Bats: L   Throws: R   Height: 6'7"   Weight: 239   Origin: Round 7, 2023 Draft (#209 overall)

YEAR	TM	LVL	AGE	PA	R	HR	RBI	SB	AVG/OBP/SLG	BABIP	SLGCON	BB%	K%	ZSw%	ZCon%	OSw%	OCon%	LA	90th EV	DRC+	BRR	DRP	WARP
2023	WSX	ROK	17	51	6	1	3	2	.225/.392/.325	.364	.565	17.6%	33.3%										
2024									No projection														

2023 GP: CF (7), RF (6)

Standing 6-foot-7 and weighing 240 lbs is enough to get a head start toward the best power projection in any draft class. Add that Wolkow was barely 17 on draft night and you have yourself an above-slot $1 million bonus player in the seventh round. The gargantuan size and left-handed swing are something to dream on, even if it's a long dream. Mechanics, unsurprisingly, are the primary concern for the local Chicago school kid, but the problem isn't about length, as it is for many tall players: Wolkow has a twitch in his hands that can disconnect his bat from his plane of rotation, which may explain his whiff troubles in high school ball. Wolkow offers as much promise as anyone, but remember, some blank slates go on to become Thomas Kinkades.

PITCHERS

Sean Burke RHP Born: 12/18/99 Age: 24 Height: 6'6" Weight: 230 Origin: Round 3, 2021 Draft (#94 overall)

YEAR	TM	LVL	AGE	G (GS)	IP	W-L	SV	K	WHIP	ERA	CSP	BB%	K%	HR%	GB%	ZSw%	ZCon%	OSw%	OCon%	BABIP	SLGCON	DRA-	WARP
2021	KAN	A	21	5 (5)	14	0-1	0	20	1.36	3.21		16.1%	32.3%	0.0%	43.3%					.321	.370	92	0.2
2022	WS	A+	22	6 (5)	28	2-1	0	31	1.29	2.89		10.6%	27.4%	2.7%	30.9%					.318	.588	114	0.0
2022	BIR	AA	22	19 (19)	73	2-7	0	99	1.44	4.81		10.4%	31.2%	3.5%	44.8%					.361	.665	83	1.4
2022	CLT	AAA	22	2 (2)	7	0-2	0	7	2.14	11.57		8.3%	19.4%	2.8%	34.6%	74.1%	95.0%	26.3%	40.0%	.440	.720	120	0.0
2023	CLT	AAA	23	9 (9)	36²	1-4	0	34	1.72	7.61		16.3%	20.5%	5.4%	37.5%	65.4%	84.8%	31.1%	61.7%	.287	.676	120	0.1
2024 DC	CHW	MLB	24	3 (3)	12²	0-1	0	12	1.59	5.91		12.5%	20.8%	4.1%	36.0%					.298	.615	127	-0.1

2023 Arsenal: FA (93), SL (84.2), CU (77.4), CH (84.7)   Comps: Carson LaRue (71), Jeremy Beasley (71), Cal Quantrill (69)

Burke is among a handful of altitudinous starters in the upper half of the White Sox system, but he isn't your typical lanky pitcher. Up until the moment he releases the ball, he's everything you want in a pitcher, moving athletically on the rubber without violent mechanics. He throws from his ear like an NFL quarterback, leading to success in the upper third with the heater and more whiffs on his curveball than any other secondary pitch. But that same snapping, tight delivery creates problems after the ball leaves the hand: His short arm action often fails to sync with his long stride down the mound, leading to control issues and laborious, 80-pitch starts. If he can start to channel the completion rate of fellow six-foot-six athlete Justin Herbert, and treat the plate like a receiver on a curl route, there's a future where he remains a starter.

Ky Bush LHP Born: 11/12/99 Age: 24 Height: 6'6" Weight: 240 Origin: Round 2, 2021 Draft (#45 overall)

YEAR	TM	LVL	AGE	G (GS)	IP	W-L	SV	K	WHIP	ERA	CSP	BB%	K%	HR%	GB%	ZSw%	ZCon%	OSw%	OCon%	BABIP	SLGCON	DRA-	WARP
2021	TRI	A+	21	5 (5)	12	0-2	0	20	1.58	4.50		9.3%	37.0%	0.0%	46.4%					.500	.643	103	0.1
2022	RCT	AA	22	21 (21)	103	7-4	0	101	1.18	3.67		6.8%	23.7%	3.3%	44.7%					.282	.538	93	1.4
2023	RCT	AA	23	6 (6)	26	1-3	0	33	1.42	5.88		12.6%	29.7%	5.4%	45.2%					.304	.738	87	0.0
2023	BIR	AA	23	9 (9)	41²	3-4	0	36	1.68	6.70		11.6%	19.0%	5.3%	42.3%					.319	.703	133	
2024 non	CHW	MLB	24	58 (0)	50	2-2	0	44	1.62	6.25		10.4%	19.3%	4.1%	37.9%					.319	.623	135	-0.7

Comps: Bailey Falter (70), Kyle Ryan (70), Jesse Biddle (70)

How cruel a year can be. Last winter, Bush was the fifth-ranked prospect in his organization and on the cusp of the majors. Granted, that organization was the Angels, and the reason they didn't call him up alongside everyone else with a pulse is that he strained an oblique and clearly failed to heal from it. After serving as the throw-in on the Lucas Giolito trade, Bush is going to have to pitch his way back into relevance, armed only with some left-side deception—he hides the ball behind his back hip in a manner similar to Jordan Montgomery. One thing not in his toolbelt at this point: an out pitch. There's no real reliever path here, so Bush will need to find both velocity and consistency to move up the ladder, the prospect equivalent of rolling boxcars.

Jonathan Cannon RHP Born: 07/19/00 Age: 23 Height: 6'6" Weight: 213 Origin: Round 3, 2022 Draft (#101 overall)

YEAR	TM	LVL	AGE	G (GS)	IP	W-L	SV	K	WHIP	ERA	CSP	BB%	K%	HR%	GB%	ZSw%	ZCon%	OSw%	OCon%	BABIP	SLGCON	DRA-	WARP
2022	KAN	A	21	3 (3)	6¹	0-0	0	3	0.95	1.42		9.1%	13.6%	0.0%	52.9%					.235	.235	111	0.0
2023	WS	A+	22	14 (14)	72²	5-2	0	67	1.22	3.59		8.2%	22.9%	2.4%	50.2%					.299	.558	97	0.7
2023	BIR	AA	22	11 (11)	48¹	1-4	0	39	1.57	5.77		6.7%	17.3%	3.6%	55.6%					.329	.584	97	
2024 non	CHW	MLB	23	58 (0)	50	2-2	0	33	1.57	5.88		9.0%	14.5%	3.5%	42.0%					.309	.565	128	-0.5

Comps: Duke Von Schamann (78), Collin Wiles (78), Jeff Ferrell (77)

You couldn't ask for a better baseball name, but don't check to see if it's accurate. Cannon isn't the triple-digit fireballing type, but he throws in the mid-90s and demonstrates a mechanical rhythm on the mound. With a hands-above-the-head motion to his windup, the young starter syncs up his upper and lower body very well, helping him to command his cutter and slider well despite the long arm action. There's no drawstring violence here, either. His rapid progress through the system and ability to handle a heavy workload are good signs for the future, but unlocking a breaking ball is necessary to complete his starter's arsenal.

Dylan Cease RHP Born: 12/28/95 Age: 28 Height: 6'2" Weight: 195 Origin: Round 6, 2014 Draft (#169 overall)

YEAR	TM	LVL	AGE	G (GS)	IP	W-L	SV	K	WHIP	ERA	CSP	BB%	K%	HR%	GB%	ZSw%	ZCon%	OSw%	OCon%	BABIP	SLGCON	DRA-	WARP
2021	CHW	MLB	25	32 (32)	165²	13-7	0	226	1.25	3.91	53.2%	9.6%	31.9%	2.8%	33.6%	67.5%	75.8%	33.8%	52.4%	.310	.572	85	2.9
2022	CHW	MLB	26	32 (32)	184	14-8	0	227	1.11	2.20	52.5%	10.4%	30.4%	2.1%	38.7%	67.4%	78.0%	35.8%	54.6%	.261	.466	80	3.7
2023	CHW	MLB	27	33 (33)	177	7-9	0	214	1.42	4.58	43.4%	10.1%	27.3%	2.4%	36.2%	70.3%	83.9%	32.0%	49.6%	.331	.587	108	1.4
2024 DC	CHW	MLB	28	29 (29)	160¹	8-11	0	190	1.31	4.18	48.2%	10.3%	27.8%	3.5%	37.3%					.293	.583	95	1.8

2023 Arsenal: FA (95.8), SL (86.5), KC (80.5), FS (74.5)   Comps: Trevor Bauer (84), Wade Miller (83), Ubaldo Jiménez (83)

Of all the regression that slammed into the 2023 White Sox, perhaps none was more shocking than that of Cease. Yes, his profile as a pitcher is a bit more volatile than most of the league's aces, but even with that as a prior, doubling your run total from 45 earned runs to 90 in similar volume is nothing short of absurd. However, when you've always walked on the edge with the free passes, and your slider goes from "double check the results" to "great," you can start to see how we got here. Chicago's volatility in the field didn't help, either, as the team's defense fell apart, both behind him and in terms of framing. It's fair to expect Cease's 2024 numbers to fall somewhere in between his fantastic 2022 and unfortunate 2023. Despite the slight velocity drop off, he still has one of the nastiest arsenals in all of baseball. It's hard to bet against that.

Garrett Crochet LHP   Born: 06/21/99   Age: 25   Height: 6'6"   Weight: 230   Origin: Round 1, 2020 Draft (#11 overall)

YEAR	TM	LVL	AGE	G (GS)	IP	W-L	SV	K	WHIP	ERA	CSP	BB%	K%	HR%	GB%	ZSw%	ZCon%	OSw%	OCon%	BABIP	SLGCON	DRA-	WARP
2021	CHW	MLB	22	54(0)	54¹	3-5	0	65	1.27	2.82	55.8%	11.7%	28.3%	0.9%	37.5%	63.8%	80.0%	29.3%	56.6%	.303	.432	91	0.8
2023	BIR	AA	24	6(0)	6	0-0	0	11	1.67	6.00		14.3%	39.3%	0.0%	53.8%					.462	.750	89	0.0
2023	CLT	AAA	24	6(0)	6¹	0-0	0	13	0.95	2.84		7.7%	50.0%	0.0%	70.0%	41.7%	65.0%	26.3%	55.0%	.400	.400	74	0.2
2023	CHW	MLB	24	13(0)	12²	0-2	0	12	1.97	3.55	46.2%	20.3%	18.8%	1.6%	31.6%	67.5%	79.0%	26.7%	63.0%	.306	.543	122	0.0
2024 DC	CHW	MLB	25	54(0)	57	3-3	7	68	1.42	4.65	52.4%	12.6%	27.0%	3.4%	38.3%					.292	.581	103	0.2

2023 Arsenal: FA (96.7), SL (84.8), CH (90.7)   Comps: Tim Collins (58), Caleb Ferguson (54), Eric O'Flaherty (54)

Crochet has had a whirlwind of a short career so far. After missing all of 2022 due to Tommy John surgery, the former Tennessee pitcher made his return in May and his mechanics were reminiscent of the early days of being a triple-digit touching outlier. The more careful, dreadfully normal, 97-mph 2023 Crochet was fine, but the extra velocity was what made him special. But it was clear after only a month of work that his body simply could not tolerate it, as he went on the injured list for three months battling shoulder inflammation. In his few September outings, Crochet's mechanics and velocity deteriorated relative to May. It may just be that his days of flying too close to the sun are over, and now he's just a good lefty reliever and not another potential Chris Sale.

Jake Eder LHP   Born: 10/09/98   Age: 25   Height: 6'4"   Weight: 215   Origin: Round 4, 2020 Draft (#104 overall)

YEAR	TM	LVL	AGE	G (GS)	IP	W-L	SV	K	WHIP	ERA	CSP	BB%	K%	HR%	GB%	ZSw%	ZCon%	OSw%	OCon%	BABIP	SLGCON	DRA-	WARP
2021	PNS	AA	22	15(15)	71¹	3-5	0	99	0.98	1.77		9.4%	34.5%	1.0%	50.3%					.261	.387	82	1.4
2023	JUP	A	24	3(3)	9²	0-2	0	10	1.55	4.66		10.6%	21.3%	0.0%	66.7%	69.2%	77.8%	33.3%	42.1%	.333	.467	80	0.1
2023	PNS	AA	24	6(6)	29²	2-1	0	38	1.28	3.94		12.9%	30.6%	3.2%	38.2%					.286	.567	102	-0.1
2023	BIR	AA	24	5(5)	17¹	0-3	0	22	2.42	11.42		15.6%	22.9%	3.1%	28.3%					.480	.811	153	
2024 DC	CHW	MLB	25	3(3)	13²	0-1	0	14	1.54	5.49		11.9%	22.4%	3.4%	39.1%					.307	.575	119	0.0

2023 Arsenal: FA (92.5), SL (79.9), CH (84.2)   Comps: Evan Kruczynski (66), Kyle McPherson (66), Dellin Betances (66)

There's often a two-step process when it comes to surprising deadline deals. Step one was the question: How did the White Sox get Eder, one of Miami's best prospects, for half a season of Jake Burger? Eventually, we reached step two: How did Eder suddenly become worth only the entrée portion of a value meal? The funky lefty dominated Double-A in 2021 before going under the knife for Tommy John surgery, and it looks like he picked up a few scars. He suffered the predictable loss of command on his return, which hadn't been strong to begin with. However, Eder still possesses one of the best sliders in the minors and the pedigree of a potential mid-rotation starter. In Miami, Eder's abbreviated timeline would've been challenged because of their organizational pitching depth, but Chicago presents him with a new opportunity, one that may allow him room for error.

Erick Fedde RHP   Born: 02/25/93   Age: 31   Height: 6'4"   Weight: 203   Origin: Round 1, 2014 Draft (#18 overall)

YEAR	TM	LVL	AGE	G (GS)	IP	W-L	SV	K	WHIP	ERA	CSP	BB%	K%	HR%	GB%	ZSw%	ZCon%	OSw%	OCon%	BABIP	SLGCON	DRA-	WARP
2021	WAS	MLB	28	29(27)	133¹	7-9	0	128	1.44	5.47	51.4%	8.1%	21.7%	3.9%	48.4%	67.8%	86.9%	29.3%	64.4%	.320	.616	94	1.7
2022	WAS	MLB	29	27(27)	127	6-13	0	94	1.63	5.81	53.5%	10.1%	16.4%	3.7%	42.0%	68.0%	87.6%	25.8%	70.9%	.321	.577	128	-0.6
2024 DC	CHW	MLB	31	26(26)	152²	8-10	0	145	1.27	3.98	51.7%	8.2%	22.6%	3.3%	43.1%					.286	.533	92	2.0

We regret to disappoint longtime *BP Annual* readers that the running joke about Fedde is dead. We can no longer quip over all of his pitches bleeding into each other and looking identical: It's not applicable anymore. After flunking out of MLB, he took a brand-new sweeper and reworked changeup to Korea, where he put up deGrom-esque numbers in a hitter-friendly environment and won the KBO's MVP award. Now a year after he couldn't find an MLB contract offer whatsoever, he's joining the White Sox on a two-year, $15 million deal. We know none of this is amusing or witty, but the matter at hand calls for serious consideration. He's no longer a punchline, so you'll have to find your laughs elsewhere in this book.

Chris Flexen RHP   Born: 07/01/94   Age: 30   Height: 6'3"   Weight: 219   Origin: Round 14, 2012 Draft (#440 overall)

YEAR	TM	LVL	AGE	G (GS)	IP	W-L	SV	K	WHIP	ERA	CSP	BB%	K%	HR%	GB%	ZSw%	ZCon%	OSw%	OCon%	BABIP	SLGCON	DRA-	WARP
2021	SEA	MLB	26	31(31)	179²	14-6	0	125	1.25	3.61	56.8%	5.4%	16.9%	2.6%	42.3%	72.2%	88.0%	33.2%	69.2%	.300	.506	103	1.4
2022	SEA	MLB	27	33(22)	137²	8-9	2	95	1.33	3.73	52.4%	8.6%	16.1%	2.9%	33.9%	75.5%	87.4%	32.6%	65.4%	.273	.498	127	-0.6
2023	ABQ	AAA	28	2(2)	9¹	1-0	0	11	1.07	0.96		13.5%	29.7%	2.7%	23.8%	74.6%	78.7%	30.8%	42.9%	.200	.429	112	0.1
2023	SEA	MLB	28	17(4)	42	0-4	0	29	1.86	7.71	46.2%	9.7%	14.8%	5.6%	41.9%	71.8%	86.9%	35.1%	61.9%	.350	.649	120	0.0
2023	COL	MLB	28	12(12)	60¹	2-4	0	45	1.54	6.27	46.9%	7.0%	16.7%	5.2%	35.6%	72.5%	88.6%	28.9%	62.9%	.321	.672	127	-0.1
2024 DC	CHW	MLB	29	32(3)	44¹	2-3	0	35	1.47	5.33	51.8%	8.1%	17.9%	3.7%	37.8%					.310	.576	118	-0.1

2023 Arsenal: FA (92.1), FC (88.2), CH (81.1), SL (81.4), SW (79.8), CU (71.4), SI (90.6)   Comps: Dick Bosman (68), Mike Pelfrey (65), Bill Lee (64)

After a KBO stint in 2020, Flexen returned to the majors to post a pair of solid campaigns as a starter and swingman in Seattle before regression took hold and the Mariners cut him loose. As all low-upside, DFA starters eventually do, Flexen found his way to the Rockies to finish out the campaign. He improved upon his ERA with Colorado, but then again, it was hard not to. Thanks to Flexen's over-the-top release point, his vertically oriented heater simply couldn't cut it at Coors. His changeup, however, remained effective throughout the entire season. The *cambio* has been his best offering since he returned stateside, benefitting from an extremely low spin rate that mitigates the backspin on it, enabling it to drop more. If Flexen scraps his ineffective four-seamer, he'll have to improve his cutter so that the change still has something hard to play off of. There's time still for reinvention, but there may not be a place for it.

Deivi García RHP   Born: 05/19/99   Age: 25   Height: 5'9"   Weight: 163   Origin: IFA, 2015

YEAR	TM	LVL	AGE	G (GS)	IP	W-L	SV	K	WHIP	ERA	CSP	BB%	K%	HR%	GB%	ZSw%	ZCon%	OSw%	OCon%	BABIP	SLGCON	DRA-	WARP
2021	SWB	AAA	22	24(22)	90²	3-7	0	97	1.88	6.85		15.6%	22.2%	4.8%	29.9%					.333	.716	119	0.3
2021	NYY	MLB	22	2(2)	8¹	0-2	0	7	1.44	6.48	53.6%	10.5%	18.4%	2.6%	23.1%	61.0%	83.3%	33.0%	58.1%	.280	.680	147	-0.1
2022	SOM	AA	23	6(6)	26²	2-1	0	37	1.05	5.40		7.0%	32.2%	5.2%	45.5%					.233	.615	81	0.6
2022	SWB	AAA	23	14(7)	37¹	2-4	0	39	1.71	7.96		13.4%	21.8%	3.9%	27.5%					.324	.689	130	-0.1
2023	SWB	AAA	24	28(1)	46	3-2	0	45	1.76	5.67		14.6%	20.5%	4.1%	38.6%	72.4%	75.6%	29.1%	55.0%	.308	.667	114	0.3
2023	CLT	AAA	24	7(0)	9	0-1	0	17	1.22	2.00		15.4%	43.6%	5.1%	25.0%	60.0%	71.4%	31.9%	43.2%	.214	.750	78	0.2
2023	CHW	MLB	24	6(0)	9¹	0-1	0	7	1.39	2.89	39.7%	19.0%	16.7%	2.4%	50.0%	54.7%	88.6%	26.9%	62.1%	.160	.400	116	0.0
2023	NYY	MLB	24	2(0)	5²	0-0	1	3	1.41	1.59	42.4%	16.0%	12.0%	4.0%	27.8%	89.8%	79.5%	20.6%	64.3%	.176	.588	119	0.0
2024 DC	CHW	MLB	25	47(0)	50²	3-3	0	49	1.59	5.92	46.1%	12.7%	21.3%	4.0%	35.7%					.301	.607	127	-0.4

2023 Arsenal: FA (95.4), CH (84.9), FC (89.3), CU (77.3), SW (80.4), SL (82.4)   Comps: Jacob Turner (46), Alex Reyes (43), Tyler Chatwood (42)

After years of trying to restore his pre-2020 form as a top prospect with an invisiball four-seamer, the Yankees finally gave up on the Deivi García Experience. With a ton of natural extension for a five-foot-nine pitcher, a low vertical approach angle and low release point, Deivi was able to fool hitters at the bottom of the strike zone with a pitch that seemed as if it never left the ground. Those same properties allowed the pitch to play up nicely at the top of the strike zone, but an offseason overhaul going into 2021 almost completely took away his strengths, and forever changed his career arc. Despite rediscovering his old velocity, his fastball never acquired its old movement, and a lack of command caused him to alternate between waste pitches and meatballs. This is one of those occasions that would seem to reward a change of scenery, but sometimes you can't go back home.

Tim Hill LHP   Born: 02/10/90   Age: 34   Height: 6'4"   Weight: 200   Origin: Round 32, 2014 Draft (#963 overall)

YEAR	TM	LVL	AGE	G (GS)	IP	W-L	SV	K	WHIP	ERA	CSP	BB%	K%	HR%	GB%	ZSw%	ZCon%	OSw%	OCon%	BABIP	SLGCON	DRA-	WARP
2021	SD	MLB	31	78(0)	59²	6-6	1	56	1.24	3.62	52.7%	9.0%	22.0%	3.5%	58.8%	65.8%	81.5%	30.0%	67.6%	.264	.518	79	1.2
2022	SD	MLB	32	55(0)	48	3-0	0	25	1.23	3.56	53.3%	7.0%	12.6%	0.5%	59.0%	66.9%	89.6%	28.9%	74.1%	.284	.364	97	0.5
2023	SD	MLB	33	48(0)	44¹	1-4	0	26	1.65	5.48	49.2%	6.9%	12.9%	3.5%	60.9%	69.7%	90.6%	34.3%	75.7%	.354	.599	98	0.6
2024 DC	CHW	MLB	34	47(0)	50²	3-3	7	32	1.46	4.93	51.1%	7.8%	14.3%	2.1%	56.7%					.310	.477	108	0.0

2023 Arsenal: FA (90.9), SI (88.9), FC (88), SL (83.1), CH (82.5)   Comps: Richard Bleier (63), George Sherrill (58), Will Harris (58)

By all rights, the three batter minimum should've relegated Hill to the dustbin, or at least to your local natural history museum alongside the dodo and the passenger pigeon. As a lefty sidearmer, he's death on his southpaw compatriots but vulnerable to right-handers, who have mashed him more or less every season—they slugged a Ruthian .602 against him in 2023. That he's carved out a career beyond his kind's extinction event is admirable, though it rested on the shaky ground, hucking 89-mph sinkers without anything approaching swing-and-miss stuff. That worked out surprisingly well in 2022, but DRA wasn't buying it, and lo, 2023 was the correction; despite a ground-ball rate that would make Derek Lowe blush, Hill gave up loads of hard contact before a sprained finger suffered in August ended his season early. A giant flying projectile brought an end to the dinosaurs; dozens of smaller ones cost Hill his roster spot in San Diego, which non-tendered him over the winter. The White Sox, evolution's last-chance saloon, signed him to a one-year deal for reasons best known to themselves.

Brent Honeywell RHP   Born: 03/31/95   Age: 29   Height: 6'2"   Weight: 195   Origin: Round 2, 2014 Draft (#72 overall)

YEAR	TM	LVL	AGE	G (GS)	IP	W-L	SV	K	WHIP	ERA	CSP	BB%	K%	HR%	GB%	ZSw%	ZCon%	OSw%	OCon%	BABIP	SLGCON	DRA-	WARP
2021	DUR	AAA	26	31(13)	81²	5-4	2	67	1.20	3.97		7.2%	20.0%	3.9%	41.5%					.268	.533	104	0.9
2021	TB	MLB	26	3(2)	4¹	0-0	0	4	1.85	8.31	57.1%	14.3%	19.0%	9.5%	42.9%	81.8%	85.2%	20.0%	66.7%	.250	.786	113	0.0
2022	ESC	WIN	27	7(6)	28	2-0	0	17	0.64	0.96		6.1%	17.2%	1.0%	42.1%					.147	.263		
2022	LV	AAA	27	11(0)	17¹	0-3	0	21	2.02	7.79		8.2%	24.7%	8.2%	35.7%	72.8%	82.4%	34.4%	55.4%	.447	.981	88	0.2
2023	CLT	AAA	28	4(4)	15¹	0-1	0	9	1.50	7.04		10.1%	13.0%	5.8%	38.0%	65.5%	82.4%	30.1%	74.5%	.261	.660	108	0.1
2023	CHW	MLB	28	4(0)	5²	0-0	0	3	2.12	11.12	49.6%	10.0%	10.0%	6.7%	47.8%	81.8%	86.1%	31.2%	50.0%	.333	.739	107	0.0
2023	SD	MLB	28	36(0)	46²	2-4	0	42	1.37	4.05	46.6%	9.8%	20.6%	3.9%	49.3%	72.2%	83.8%	28.1%	65.2%	.279	.544	97	0.6
2024 non	CHW	MLB	29	58(0)	50	2-2	0	39	1.47	5.22	47.4%	9.1%	17.7%	3.0%	45.1%					.304	.537	115	-0.2

2023 Arsenal: FA (95), CH (87.6), SW (81.7), SB (80.3), SI (95.4), FC (90.6), CU (80.1)   Comps: Robert Stephenson (48), Randall Delgado (46), Matt Magill (45)

In terms of advanced pitch-evaluation metrics, Honeywell's sweeper is the standout of his arsenal. In terms of more rudimentary pitch-counting metrics, it comes in a distant third behind a fastball and changeup that rate considerably below-average. And for all that, he's better known for the pitch he throws fourth-most, his vaunted screwball. It's not clear that the White Sox are going to be the team best equipped to maximize Honeywell's potential, iron out his pitch mix, or (perhaps) help him ditch the four-seamer for a sinker that better pairs with his best pitch. But the Padres ran into roster space problems and couldn't make room for him: Reverse order is how the waiver wire works, so this is his fate. Still, if he can manage 50 innings in a major-league bullpen, no matter how often he throws what, it'll have to be considered a success.

Seth Keener RHP   Born: 10/04/01   Age: 22   Height: 6'2"   Weight: 195   Origin: Round 3, 2023 Draft (#84 overall)

YEAR	TM	LVL	AGE	G (GS)	IP	W-L	SV	K	WHIP	ERA	CSP	BB%	K%	HR%	GB%	ZSw%	ZCon%	OSw%	OCon%	BABIP	SLGCON	DRA-	WARP
2023	WSX	ROK	21	4(2)	6	1-0	0	7	0.67	1.50		9.1%	31.8%	0.0%	38.5%					.154	.231		
2023	KAN	A	21	3(3)	6¹	0-1	0	7	1.74	7.11		6.7%	23.3%	3.3%	42.9%					.400	.571	85	0.0
2024 non	CHW	MLB	22	58(0)	50	2-2	0	41	1.65	6.42		11.3%	17.9%	4.1%	35.9%					.311	.609	138	-0.8

Comps: Luis Pena (26), Dean Kremer (26), Reiss Knehr (26)

Perhaps if he hadn't served on a Wake Forest team with one of the two best rotations in college baseball, Keener would have garnered a little more attention. Instead, he was a fourth starter, doomed to flip between starts and long relief as the schedule demanded. He started eight of his 23 total games as a junior, posting a 2.69 and allowing well below a baserunner per inning. On the strength of that showing, the White Sox scooped him up in the third round of the 2023 draft. He will be developed as a starter with a 60-grade sweeper and a heater that can get into the mid-90s. His changeup and fastball will become more important as he works into a full-time starter role, but if all else fails, he has a proven relief track record that he can fall back on.

Michael Kopech RHP   Born: 04/30/96   Age: 28   Height: 6'3"   Weight: 210   Origin: Round 1, 2014 Draft (#33 overall)

YEAR	TM	LVL	AGE	G (GS)	IP	W-L	SV	K	WHIP	ERA	CSP	BB%	K%	HR%	GB%	ZSw%	ZCon%	OSw%	OCon%	BABIP	SLGCON	DRA-	WARP
2021	CHW	MLB	25	44 (4)	69¹	4-3	0	103	1.13	3.50	56.0%	8.4%	36.1%	3.2%	37.6%	63.7%	75.1%	33.6%	56.0%	.304	.623	67	1.9
2022	CHW	MLB	26	25 (25)	119¹	5-9	0	105	1.19	3.54	53.6%	11.5%	21.3%	3.0%	35.6%	64.9%	85.1%	31.4%	63.0%	.223	.460	115	0.2
2023	CHW	MLB	27	30 (27)	129¹	5-12	0	134	1.59	5.43	43.6%	15.4%	22.7%	4.9%	35.0%	65.2%	82.0%	28.1%	60.7%	.265	.650	129	-0.4
2024 DC	CHW	MLB	28	29 (19)	107²	5-8	0	115	1.44	5.02	48.8%	12.5%	24.2%	3.9%	35.0%					.281	.588	110	0.3

2023 Arsenal: FA (95.4), SL (85.4), CH (88.9), SW (82.8), CU (80.4)   *Comps: Tyler Glasnow (65), Archie Bradley (61), Lucas Sims (59)*

Outside a five-start stretch between May and June, Kopech ranked among the worst pitchers in all of baseball in 2023. His vaunted four-seamer went from a weapon to a liability. From a pitch shape and value perspective, it was among one of the league's best, but all too often it was crushed. His command issues—perhaps due to a significant release point change—led to even more walks, more home runs and more barrels than ever before. The home runs and barrels, in turn, led to more walks, as Kopech found himself in fastball counts without a fastball to trust. The knee and shoulder troubles he dealt with throughout the year could have contributed, but as the case with many White Sox players, who's to say this will improve in 2024? Kopech failed to finish the fifth inning in four August starts, Chicago decided they'd rather watch José Ureña pitch, as damning a sentence as could be written. Kopech's final two starts were as an opener; the team will have to decide if a permanent move to the bullpen will salvage what's left of the young pitcher.

Jordan Leasure RHP   Born: 08/15/98   Age: 25   Height: 6'3"   Weight: 215   Origin: Round 14, 2021 Draft (#432 overall)

YEAR	TM	LVL	AGE	G (GS)	IP	W-L	SV	K	WHIP	ERA	CSP	BB%	K%	HR%	GB%	ZSw%	ZCon%	OSw%	OCon%	BABIP	SLGCON	DRA-	WARP
2021	RC	A	22	4 (0)	5²	1-0	0	6	1.41	4.76		12.0%	24.0%	8.0%	43.8%					.214	.750	109	0.0
2022	GL	A+	23	5 (0)	9¹	0-0	2	21	0.96	1.93		13.5%	56.8%	0.0%	27.3%					.364	.545	63	0.3
2022	TUL	AA	23	44 (0)	49¹	2-2	5	63	1.16	3.65		9.3%	30.9%	3.9%	24.6%					.265	.617	78	0.9
2023	TUL	AA	24	29 (0)	35	2-2	9	56	1.06	3.09		11.3%	39.7%	4.3%	45.6%					.242	.632	68	1.0
2023	CLT	AAA	24	15 (0)	13¹	0-2	2	23	1.80	6.07		12.3%	35.4%	4.6%	42.4%	58.8%	79.1%	30.7%	44.7%	.433	.939	72	0.4
2024 DC	CHW	MLB	25	10 (0)	12²	1-1	0	15	1.37	4.66		11.3%	26.6%	4.1%	35.6%					.283	.606	104	0.0

2023 Arsenal: FA (97.5), SL (88.5), CU (78.7)   *Comps: Shea Spitzbarth (69), Bobby Wahl (67), Steve Ames (66)*

How can you not be romantic about a Division II stud pushing his way to the big leagues? That development path isn't an easy one. After posting less than inspiring results through his first three years at the University of Tampa, Leasure turned it all around in 2021 and dominated across 38 ⅓ innings, with a 1.17 ERA and 60 strikeouts. Since then, he's been a solid high-leverage reliever in the Dodgers' system. But like other pitchers who came to Chicago via trade at the 2023 deadline, he largely struggled upon his arrival despite his strikeout numbers staying high. With a 70-grade heater and big time ride, Leasure has a future as at least a medium-leverage reliever, but he can't forget about the most important ingredient. No, not love, but command.

Cristian Mena RHP   Born: 12/21/02   Age: 21   Height: 6'2"   Weight: 170   Origin: IFA, 2019

YEAR	TM	LVL	AGE	G (GS)	IP	W-L	SV	K	WHIP	ERA	CSP	BB%	K%	HR%	GB%	ZSw%	ZCon%	OSw%	OCon%	BABIP	SLGCON	DRA-	WARP
2021	WSX	ROK	18	13 (12)	48¹	1-4	0	62	1.86	7.82		9.1%	27.0%	3.5%	48.6%					.442	.734		
2022	KAN	A	19	11 (11)	53²	1-2	0	66	1.12	2.68		7.0%	30.7%	0.9%	45.1%					.328	.455	86	1.0
2022	WS	A+	19	10 (10)	40²	1-3	0	47	1.50	4.65		12.3%	26.3%	2.2%	44.5%					.330	.556	89	0.5
2022	BIR	AA	19	3 (3)	10	0-1	0	13	1.70	6.30		2.2%	28.9%	2.2%	35.5%					.500	.839	98	0.1
2023	BIR	AA	20	23 (23)	114	7-6	0	136	1.35	4.66		11.3%	27.9%	3.5%	38.4%					.300	.613	93	1.1
2023	CLT	AAA	20	4 (4)	19²	1-1	0	20	1.78	5.95		9.8%	21.7%	1.1%	32.3%	66.3%	85.7%	33.5%	44.6%	.410	.565	99	0.2
2024 DC	CHW	MLB	21	3 (3)	13²	0-1	0	13	1.52	5.51		10.7%	21.6%	3.8%	35.3%					.310	.595	120	0.0

2023 Arsenal: FA (92.9), CU (83.3), CH (88.5), SW (83.6)   *Comps: Jacob Turner (52), Francis Martes (49), Tyler Skaggs (49)*

Someone in the White Sox org either really likes Mena, or really hates him. Despite being the age where undergrads are often trying to pin down majors, the 20-year-old is already built up to 130 innings and sitting on the doorstep of the major leagues. He's also getting trampled at every single level by lineups years older than him. Fastball location is somewhat to blame here, though you could argue that by putting their young, talented pitcher in a position where he can't afford to make mistakes the White Sox have rished hampering his development, like creating an artificial Coors environment. The best news for Mena is that Chicago is running out of levels to toss him into.

Nick Nastrini RHP   Born: 02/18/00   Age: 24   Height: 6'3"   Weight: 215   Origin: Round 4, 2021 Draft (#131 overall)

YEAR	TM	LVL	AGE	G (GS)	IP	W-L	SV	K	WHIP	ERA	CSP	BB%	K%	HR%	GB%	ZSw%	ZCon%	OSw%	OCon%	BABIP	SLGCON	DRA-	WARP
2021	RC	A	21	6(6)	13	0-0	0	30	1.00	2.08		12.7%	54.5%	3.6%	56.2%					.286	.938	74	0.3
2022	GL	A+	22	21(21)	86¹	5-3	0	127	1.16	3.86		10.7%	34.9%	3.3%	37.8%					.271	.595	81	1.7
2022	TUL	AA	22	6(6)	30¹	1-1	0	42	0.99	4.15		13.6%	35.6%	4.2%	35.6%					.167	.552	74	0.6
2023	BIR	AA	23	4(4)	21¹	3-0	0	31	1.27	4.22		7.4%	33.0%	1.1%	30.9%					.358	.519	80	
2023	TUL	AA	23	17(17)	73²	5-3	0	85	1.40	4.03		11.3%	26.1%	2.5%	33.5%					.302	.565	103	0.4
2023	CLT	AAA	23	4(4)	19²	1-2	0	23	1.02	4.12		12.7%	29.1%	2.5%	31.8%	70.7%	84.8%	29.6%	48.2%	.190	.500	84	0.3
2024 DC	CHW	MLB	24	6(6)	25²	1-2	0	28	1.46	5.12		11.7%	24.4%	3.7%	33.9%					.298	.597	112	0.1

2023 Arsenal: FA (93.9), CH (85), SL (85.8), KC (79.2)   Comps: Rogelio Armenteros (77), Ryan Helsley (77), Cody Martin (77)

Coming from the Dodgers for Joe Kelly at the trade deadline, Nastrini immediately positioned himself near the top of Chicago's prospect list. With a four-pitch mix and varying pitch shapes, the former UCLA Bruin is capable of getting out both lefties and righties, and odds are he'll get a shot to start. The phrase "four-pitch mix" often leads one to assume that all four are on the same level, but that's not true here; Nastrini's change is his strongest offering, but the fastball lost some bite last year and the 12-6 curve is well behind those and the slider. It's also a phrase that, when applied to back-end starters, connotes a level of command that Nastrini has never mastered. This is a man who needs to add feel, and he'll have to start by applying his strengths differently to hitters from both sides of the plate.

Peyton Pallette RHP   Born: 05/09/01   Age: 23   Height: 6'1"   Weight: 180   Origin: Round 2, 2022 Draft (#62 overall)

YEAR	TM	LVL	AGE	G (GS)	IP	W-L	SV	K	WHIP	ERA	CSP	BB%	K%	HR%	GB%	ZSw%	ZCon%	OSw%	OCon%	BABIP	SLGCON	DRA-	WARP
2023	KAN	A	22	22(22)	72	0-4	0	78	1.36	4.13		12.8%	24.4%	2.5%	37.0%					.266	.492	111	0.3
2024 non	CHW	MLB	23	58(0)	50	2-2	0	43	1.72	6.71		12.9%	18.5%	4.0%	34.1%					.312	.620	142	-0.9

Comps: Matt Marsh (86), Cory Rasmus (83), Cesar Rosado (82)

The White Sox have taken to using their second-round picks to select first-round talents recovering from Tommy John, with Pallette preceding 2023 choice Grant Taylor. The jury is out on that strategy, because it has to be. The former Razorback spent his first year of pro ball ramping up, peaking at four innings a start, while picking up the pieces of his arsenal. His curveball is the best in the system, spinning at over 3,000 rpm and capable of wiping out of the zone, while his fastball sits at an acceptable 93-95 mph. Mechanically, Pallette doesn't create much hip-shoulder separation and has struggled to find consistency with his delivery, leading to wildness. The change is about as consistent as you'd expect from a guy recovering from Tommy John. The parts are here for a successful starter, but the phrase "reliever fallback" exists for cases like these.

Gregory Santos RHP   Born: 08/28/99   Age: 24   Height: 6'2"   Weight: 190   Origin: IFA, 2015

YEAR	TM	LVL	AGE	G (GS)	IP	W-L	SV	K	WHIP	ERA	CSP	BB%	K%	HR%	GB%	ZSw%	ZCon%	OSw%	OCon%	BABIP	SLGCON	DRA-	WARP
2021	SAC	AAA	21	14(0)	15²	1-1	0	15	1.60	5.17		12.3%	20.5%	1.4%	63.0%					.333	.478	88	0.2
2021	SF	MLB	21	3(0)	2	0-2	0	3	3.50	22.50	53.3%	15.4%	23.1%	23.1%	37.5%	56.5%	92.3%	23.3%	42.9%	.400	1.750	108	0.0
2022	SAC	AAA	22	33(0)	33	1-2	1	34	1.48	4.91		13.5%	23.0%	2.7%	52.7%	70.8%	79.1%	33.5%	46.2%	.287	.573	89	0.4
2022	SF	MLB	22	2(0)	3²	0-0	0	2	1.64	4.91	57.5%	17.6%	11.8%	0.0%	75.0%	62.1%	94.4%	28.9%	54.5%	.250	.333	104	0.0
2023	CHW	MLB	23	60(0)	66¹	2-2	5	66	1.30	3.39	49.8%	5.9%	22.8%	0.7%	51.7%	65.7%	83.7%	37.2%	52.0%	.337	.423	78	1.5
2024 DC	CHW	MLB	24	54(0)	57	3-5	20	53	1.39	4.45	50.3%	9.6%	21.4%	2.5%	50.0%					.304	.509	99	0.3

2023 Arsenal: SL (91.7), SI (99.1), FA (99.1), SW (79.9)   Comps: Kelvin Herrera (55), Johnny Ruffin (48), Ryan Wagner (45)

The best way to describe Gregory Santos is absolutely wicked. Equipped with a triple-digit sinker and low-90s slider, Santos may be one of the nastiest pitchers the majors. Upon his arrival in Chicago after five years in San Francisco's system, he essentially nixed his four-seamer and dropped his release by almost half a foot. Of course, this resulted in a significant pitch mix change, but it also changed the outlook of Santos' career. It's incredible that pitchers can just do this; it's as if moving to a new city to start over actually made someone into a new person.

From a pitch design perspective, his higher arm slot was not conducive to his strengths. He throws a gyro-dominant slider, but pairing a hard fastball with undesirable pitch qualities took away from his ability to keep hitters honest against his sizzling breaking ball. By dropping his arm slot and leaning into his natural run his slider added horizontal movement, making it one of the best in the league. Even in his breakout, it's clear he is still learning how to use his sinker, but it's clear he will be quite alright even without an elite one. Hitters struggle to make contact against the slider, and he's shown a good ability to challenge it in the strike zone: He only gave up one extra-base hit on it all season.

★ ★ ★ *2024 Top 101 Prospect* **#57** ★ ★ ★

Noah Schultz **LHP**   Born: 08/05/03   Age: 20   Height: 6'9"   Weight: 220   Origin: Round 1, 2022 Draft (#26 overall)

YEAR	TM	LVL	AGE	G (GS)	IP	W-L	SV	K	WHIP	ERA	CSP	BB%	K%	HR%	GB%	ZSw%	ZCon%	OSw%	OCon%	BABIP	SLGCON	DRA-	WARP
2023	KAN	A	19	10(10)	27	1-2	0	38	0.85	1.33		5.8%	36.5%	2.9%	50.8%					.250	.508	73	0.7
2024 non	*CHW*	*MLB*	*20*	*58(0)*	*50*	*2-2*	*0*	*46*	*1.46*	*5.35*		*9.9%*	*20.7%*	*3.9%*	*35.9%*					*.299*	*.589*	*118*	*-0.2*

Comps: José Soriano (67), Luis Vega (65), Robbie Erlin (63)

Despite his limited pro track record, Schultz made a bid to be considered the organization's top pitching prospect after a dominant 27 innings with the Kannapolis Cannon Ballers. The left-hander is perhaps one of the most physically imposing pitchers in all of professional baseball, towering over the batter at six-foot-nine. Yet with a shockingly low arm slot, Schultz's game isn't all about pure power, even though he has that too. Schultz's surprisingly normal release point gives him one of the best horizontally oriented sliders across the minor leagues. That said, height has its disadvantages even outside airplanes: the youngster started 2023 with a flexor strain and ended it with a shoulder impingement. As his body and mechanics develop through his minor-league career, he'll have to adjust his tendency to drift his throwing shoulder forward too early in his delivery and better engage his scapula area to increase his rotational efficiency. The 26th-overall pick of the 2022 draft still has a lot of innings to pitch and the injury nexus to survive before all the positives here solidify into more than just a promising beginning, but so far so good.

Jared Shuster **LHP**   Born: 08/03/98   Age: 25   Height: 6'3"   Weight: 210   Origin: Round 1, 2020 Draft (#25 overall)

YEAR	TM	LVL	AGE	G (GS)	IP	W-L	SV	K	WHIP	ERA	CSP	BB%	K%	HR%	GB%	ZSw%	ZCon%	OSw%	OCon%	BABIP	SLGCON	DRA-	WARP
2021	ROM	A+	22	15(14)	58¹	2-0	0	73	1.06	3.70		6.4%	31.1%	4.3%	34.7%					.272	.637	95	0.6
2021	MIS	AA	22	3(3)	14²	0-0	0	17	1.64	7.36		7.4%	25.0%	7.4%	36.2%					.341	.844	90	0.2
2022	MIS	AA	23	17(16)	90²	6-7	0	106	0.96	2.78		6.2%	30.0%	2.3%	46.2%					.263	.457	81	1.9
2022	GWN	AAA	23	10(9)	48²	1-3	0	39	1.21	4.25		8.0%	19.4%	5.0%	45.1%	78.9%	93.3%	36.1%	46.2%	.246	.589	100	0.7
2023	GWN	AAA	24	16(16)	79	5-6	0	64	1.68	5.01		12.6%	17.9%	2.8%	43.1%	67.7%	82.4%	30.3%	60.6%	.329	.583	104	0.9
2023	ATL	MLB	24	11(11)	52²	4-3	0	30	1.50	5.81	48.0%	11.3%	13.0%	3.0%	34.1%	71.1%	88.7%	27.4%	59.4%	.277	.515	145	-0.6
2024 DC	*CHW*	*MLB*	*25*	*13(13)*	*62*	*2-6*	*0*	*46*	*1.56*	*5.82*	*48.0%*	*9.6%*	*16.4%*	*3.9%*	*35.0%*					*.305*	*.580*	*127*	*-0.3*

2023 Arsenal: FA (91.7), SL (85), CH (82.6)   *Comps: Adam Morgan (76), Dallas Keuchel (75), Zack Britton (74)*

The final two spots in Atlanta's rotation were up for grabs heading into spring training, and Shuster took advantage of the opportunity and pitched his way onto the Opening Day Roster. Both he and fellow surprise starter Dylan Dodd quickly realized that anything that happened at CoolToday Park in North Port, Florida was a million miles away from, say, Nationals Park in Washington D.C. That was where Shuster struggled in his MLB debut, and things didn't get much better in his home debut. He was sent down after his second start, but he got a second chance in May after Kyle Wright's shoulder started acting up. The slider and changeup worked well enough to miss bats, but opposing batters were rarely ever fooled by the fastball—Shuster's most-used offering. He could eventually find consistent work as a back-end starter, but there's still some progress to be made before he can fill that role.

Michael Soroka **RHP**   Born: 08/04/97   Age: 26   Height: 6'5"   Weight: 225   Origin: Round 1, 2015 Draft (#28 overall)

YEAR	TM	LVL	AGE	G (GS)	IP	W-L	SV	K	WHIP	ERA	CSP	BB%	K%	HR%	GB%	ZSw%	ZCon%	OSw%	OCon%	BABIP	SLGCON	DRA-	WARP
2022	GWN	AAA	24	5(5)	21	0-2	0	17	1.29	6.43		7.9%	19.1%	3.4%	58.7%					.283	.548	95	0.3
2023	GWN	AAA	25	17(17)	87	4-4	0	92	1.07	3.41		7.9%	25.9%	1.7%	41.9%	68.5%	79.7%	31.8%	59.1%	.267	.427	84	2.0
2023	ATL	MLB	25	7(6)	32¹	2-2	0	29	1.48	6.40	49.0%	8.3%	20.0%	6.2%	44.0%	68.9%	84.5%	28.2%	62.5%	.300	.717	105	0.3
2024 DC	*CHW*	*MLB*	*26*	*19(19)*	*87¹*	*3-7*	*0*	*75*	*1.34*	*4.42*	*48.3%*	*8.4%*	*19.9%*	*2.8%*	*44.0%*					*.296*	*.517*	*100*	*0.8*

2023 Arsenal: FA (93.1), SL (83.1), SI (92.6), CH (82.1)   *Comps: Jerome Williams (60), Tyler Skaggs (60), Chris Volstad (59)*

The fact that Soroka was finally able to make it back to the big leagues is an impressive feat on its own. After tearing his right Achilles tendon twice, along with sustaining an extremely unfortunate array of nagging injuries, it's a miracle and a testament to his determination that Soroka was able to get back on the mound in the Oakland Coliseum late last May. That determination will serve him well in the future as he attempts to re-establish himself in the bigs. His return to the majors was plagued by an alarming uptick in home run percentage; other than that, his numbers were actually pretty similar to those of his only full season to date. That's not to say that it's guaranteed that he's going to pick up where he left off in 2019, but Soroka already beat long odds to return to the majors—who's to say that he won't continue beating them?

Grant Taylor **RHP**   Born: 05/20/02   Age: 22   Height: 6'3"   Weight: 230   Origin: Round 2, 2023 Draft (#51 overall)

If not for an untimely bout of Tommy John surgery, Taylor would have likely been the third LSU starting pitcher to go in the 2023 first round. Instead, he dropped to 51st overall and was scooped up by the White Sox. His arm drag and extreme over-the-top arm slot make him a prototypical four-seam and curveball pitcher, but his future role will likely depend on his strength post-rehab. He demonstrated a violent delivery while at LSU, so the hope is to clean up some mechanical deficiencies with his arm and torso, while maintaining the plus shape of his four-seamer. If he does end up in the bullpen, a Nick Anderson-style of pitching is a likely outcome, as is, well, a second UCL repair. The tough thing about prospects is that they're like paperback mysteries: After you read a bunch of them, you get a feel for how each story's going to end.

Touki Toussaint RHP Born: 06/20/96   Age: 28   Height: 6'3"   Weight: 215   Origin: Round 1, 2014 Draft (#16 overall)

YEAR	TM	LVL	AGE	G (GS)	IP	W-L	SV	K	WHIP	ERA	CSP	BB%	K%	HR%	GB%	ZSw%	ZCon%	OSw%	OCon%	BABIP	SLGCON	DRA-	WARP
2021	GWN	AAA	25	7 (4)	20²	2-1	0	28	1.16	3.48		14.3%	33.3%	1.2%	61.0%					.275	.463	83	0.5
2021	ATL	MLB	25	11 (10)	50	3-3	0	48	1.30	4.50	55.6%	10.2%	22.2%	5.1%	46.4%	65.2%	86.6%	25.3%	52.8%	.252	.603	105	0.3
2022	HER	WIN	26	6 (6)	33	1-0	0	41	1.15	3.55		10.4%	30.6%	0.0%	56.4%					.324	.432		
2022	GWN	AAA	26	13 (8)	41²	2-2	0	53	1.61	6.26		13.0%	27.5%	3.6%	49.1%					.340	.688	84	0.9
2022	SL	AAA	26	9 (3)	13²	0-1	0	9	1.76	3.95		17.7%	14.5%	4.8%	48.8%	59.8%	92.7%	24.3%	73.0%	.263	.575	123	-0.1
2022	LAA	MLB	26	8 (2)	25¹	1-1	0	26	1.34	4.62	47.7%	17.6%	24.1%	1.9%	50.8%	66.7%	88.6%	29.1%	51.7%	.228	.373	101	0.2
2023	COL	AAA	27	20 (1)	37²	2-1	3	48	1.33	4.06		14.5%	30.2%	1.9%	48.2%	61.9%	82.6%	29.0%	40.9%	.293	.542	87	0.8
2023	CHW	MLB	27	19 (15)	83¹	4-6	0	83	1.42	4.97	43.2%	14.2%	22.7%	2.7%	48.4%	61.0%	87.0%	27.9%	58.4%	.265	.493	114	0.4
2023	CLE	MLB	27	1 (1)	3²	0-1	0	2	2.18	4.91	34.9%	26.3%	10.5%	0.0%	50.0%	60.0%	93.3%	28.1%	68.8%	.273	.400	131	0.0
2024 DC	CHW	MLB	28	23 (23)	104	4-9	0	111	1.49	4.95	45.6%	13.5%	23.6%	2.7%	46.9%					.292	.528	107	0.5

2023 Arsenal: CU (76.4), SI (93.1), FA (93.8), FS (87.7), SL (87)   *Comps: Chris Archer (54), Robert Stephenson (50), Vance Worley (50)*

For his birthday Toussaint got claimed on waivers, and it was the nicest thing anyone got him. The pitching-starved White Sox gave the fragile righty his longest run in a six-year career, and he used it to answer basically none of the questions that have plagued him since day one. The man still cannot aim. Among pitchers with at least 1,500 pitches, no one drew fewer swings than Toussaint. The obvious reason why: He threw the fourth-highest rate of balls on 0-0, second-highest on 1-0, and third-highest on 2-0. He and teammate Michael Kopech seemed to be trying to speedrun walks. It's a shame, because the man has a great breaking ball, but he'll never get a chance to use it, much less put hitters on their back foot before throwing it.

LINEOUTS

Hitters

HITTER	POS	TM	LVL	AGE	PA	R	HR	RBI	SB	AVG/OBP/SLG	BABIP	SLGCON	BB%	K%	ZSw%	ZCon%	OSw%	OCon%	LA	90th EV	DRC+	BRR	DRP	WARP
Hanser Alberto	3B/2B	CHW	MLB	30	90	11	3	16	0	.220/.261/.390	.224	.464	4.4%	14.4%	79.6%	87.8%	54.4%	71.3%	13.3	98.1	88	-0.1	-0.3	0.1
Yoelqui Céspedes	OF	BIR	AA	25	456	52	9	31	15	.214/.315/.326	.299	.496	9.9%	29.6%							82	-3.8	11.1	1.1
	OF	CLT	AAA	25	47	10	1	6	1	.362/.362/.553	.410	.650	0.0%	14.9%	96.1%	98.0%	56.4%	61.4%			95	-0.4	0.0	0.0
Paul DeJong	SS	MEM	AAA	29	40	9	2	14	0	.353/.450/.618	.500	.955	12.5%	30.0%	63.5%	76.5%	34.0%	60.0%			100	0.5	1.8	0.3
	SS	SF	MLB	29	50	2	1	5	0	.184/.180/.286	.242	.424	0.0%	32.0%	74.4%	75.4%	50.0%	41.5%	14.0	102.4	68	0.0	0.1	0.0
	SS	STL	MLB	29	306	38	13	32	4	.233/.297/.412	.289	.599	6.9%	28.4%	73.1%	78.9%	34.4%	49.1%	18.8	104.1	78	-0.2	0.6	0.2
	SS	TOR	MLB	29	44	1	0	1	0	.068/.068/.068	.115	.115	0.0%	40.9%	80.8%	81.0%	61.3%	34.7%	9.1	97.6	58	0.0	0.1	-0.1
Clint Frazier	OF	RR	AAA	28	60	6	1	4	0	.250/.350/.442	.364	.676	11.7%	30.0%	65.6%	81.0%	31.8%	50.0%			94	-0.1	-0.6	0.1
	OF	CLT	AAA	28	256	32	11	30	5	.231/.363/.442	.280	.657	15.6%	26.6%	66.5%	82.9%	25.0%	48.8%			100	0.0	8.4	1.5
	OF	CHW	MLB	28	76	10	0	3	4	.197/.303/.242	.302	.372	13.2%	30.3%	72.5%	87.3%	29.5%	51.6%	12.8	103.5	75	0.1	-0.5	-0.1
Romy Gonzalez	2B	CHW	MLB	26	97	11	3	14	7	.194/.208/.376	.273	.614	2.1%	37.1%	67.8%	79.2%	36.9%	40.5%	5.6	108.5	73	0.3	0.4	0.0
Adam Haseley	OF	CLT	AAA	27	313	39	6	24	10	.264/.338/.386	.306	.474	8.9%	16.6%	74.8%	85.3%	36.3%	61.9%			89	-0.7	1.8	0.8
	OF	CHW	MLB	27	39	6	0	2	1	.222/.282/.278	.286	.357	7.7%	20.5%	76.6%	83.7%	29.2%	42.1%	8.4	103.2	88	0.0	-0.2	0.0
Zach Remillard	IF	CLT	AAA	29	276	46	5	28	16	.235/.342/.355	.276	.451	12.3%	18.1%	64.5%	89.8%	28.6%	59.7%			99	1.7	4.8	1.2
	IF	CHW	MLB	29	160	16	1	18	4	.252/.295/.320	.367	.475	5.0%	30.0%	63.3%	81.1%	30.9%	39.8%	8.2	99.1	57	0.1	-0.1	-0.4
Chuckie Robinson	C	LOU	AAA	28	413	57	13	74	7	.290/.356/.450	.332	.568	7.7%	18.6%	75.8%	74.8%	41.4%	63.7%			100	-1.6	0.4	1.1
Terrell Tatum	CF	WS	A+	23	276	54	4	29	32	.268/.434/.421	.380	.629	21.0%	25.0%							119	0.4	-4.1	1.1
	CF	BIR	AA	23	276	35	2	22	15	.230/.361/.315	.340	.493	15.2%	29.0%							87	1.1	-0.7	0.5
Wilfred Veras	RF	WS	A+	20	402	52	11	63	18	.277/.316/.438	.346	.601	5.0%	25.1%							81	-1.1	1.6	1.1
	RF	BIR	AA	20	162	23	6	30	6	.309/.346/.533	.398	.750	4.9%	27.2%							94	1.0	-2.7	0.3

Hanser Alberto has never been an average hitter, doesn't play any position particularly well, and is one of the slowest runners in the league. He's also had an eight-year career and has made over $5 million. This is a beautiful success story. ⓧ If you watch **Yoelqui Céspedes** hit batting practice, you'd probably think this is one of the most physically gifted baseball players on earth. This is why a lot of scouts no longer watch batting practice. ⓧ After an infamous 3-for-44 stretch following his acquisition by Toronto at the trade deadline, **Paul DeJong** opened his Giants career with a 3-for-5 game, including a home run and driving in the winning run in extras. The subsequent 1-for-29 slide did not buy him a much longer stint in San Francisco. ⓧ **Clint Frazier** still possesses quick hands and feet, but his best skill might be his choice of employers; despite his whiff problems, Chicago's outfield situation might be his best bet to keep striking out at the major-league level in 2024. ⓧ After seeing his strikeout rate go up year after year, **Romy Gonzalez** finally found a way to stop waving at pitches in August. Unfortunately, it was by undergoing season-ending shoulder surgery. ⓧ The last time **Adam Haseley** hit a home run in a major-league park, Brian McCann was starting for the Braves, and he's one year away from being on the Hall of Fame ballot. It's just nice to be able to use something other than the pandemic to mark time, which also happened since Haseley hit a home run in a major-league park. ⓧ **Zach Remillard** can play any position except pitcher, catcher, and hitter. He's technically playable against lefties, generally not the sort of limitation you want in a utility infielder, but Chicago lost Leury García's number, so here we are. ⓧ Though **Chuckie Robinson** posted a great-for-a-catcher .806 OPS in 101 Triple-A games, it's been child's play for pitchers to send him back to the dugout in his brief major-league career. ⓧ Walks, speed, and defense: Those are **Terrell Tatum's** three carrying tools, and they might just be enough to earn him some playing time on the 2008 Oakland Athletics. In 2024, he might have to try hitting a ball or two into the air. ⓧ **Wilfred Veras** starts his hands like a jedi clutching their lightsaber before a duel, and he never really creates any depth with his barrel. This is a young player who needs to learn how to use his oblique and rear hip to rotate.

Pitchers

PITCHER	TM	LVL	AGE	G (GS)	IP	W-L	SV	K	WHIP	ERA	CSP	BB%	K%	HR%	GB%	ZSw%	ZCon%	OSw%	OCon%	BABIP	SLGCON	DRA-	WARP
Tanner Banks	CLT	AAA	31	13 (0)	23	2-0	0	30	1.30	3.13		3.2%	31.9%	3.2%	35.0%	67.2%	78.7%	33.9%	58.1%	.421	.729	80	0.6
	CHW	MLB	31	32 (3)	61	1-4	1	51	1.23	4.43	49.8%	6.3%	20.0%	3.9%	37.0%	70.3%	81.6%	27.6%	62.8%	.282	.608	106	0.5
Alex Colomé	CLT	AAA	34	33 (0)	33¹	4-1	2	26	1.59	3.24		9.6%	16.7%	1.3%	53.1%	79.5%	88.5%	37.0%	50.4%	.327	.464	95	0.5
	CHW	MLB	34	4 (0)	3	0-1	0	2	1.67	6.00	43.5%	20.0%	13.3%	6.7%	70.0%	86.4%	94.7%	35.0%	42.9%	.111	.600	95	0.0
Shane Drohan	POR	AA	24	6 (6)	34	5-0	0	36	0.82	1.32		7.0%	28.1%	0.8%	43.9%					.222	.268	85	0.7
	WOR	AAA	24	21 (19)	89	5-7	0	93	1.87	6.47		14.9%	21.9%	4.5%	36.6%	70.5%	84.4%	31.0%	57.4%	.346	.745	106	1.0
Jared Kelley	WS	A+	21	12 (5)	42	2-4	0	47	1.45	5.14		13.8%	26.0%	1.1%	44.0%					.318	.528	106	0.1
	BIR	AA	21	16 (0)	23	0-3	0	28	2.74	11.74		22.1%	21.4%	2.3%	38.6%					.463	.754	170	
Chad Kuhl	WAS	MLB	30	16 (5)	38¹	0-4	1	31	1.96	8.45	45.4%	15.0%	16.6%	4.3%	30.4%	65.9%	86.3%	24.8%	52.1%	.336	.714	144	-0.4
Jimmy Lambert	CLT	AAA	28	15 (0)	16¹	0-1	0	12	1.71	7.71		14.3%	15.6%	3.9%	32.1%	68.2%	74.4%	29.7%	66.7%	.286	.635	126	0.0
	CHW	MLB	28	35 (1)	37²	2-3	1	41	1.62	5.26	49.7%	11.6%	23.8%	5.8%	33.6%	66.7%	83.5%	29.0%	54.1%	.313	.771	103	0.4
Davis Martin	CLT	AAA	26	3 (3)	16	0-0	0	20	1.06	2.81		10.9%	31.3%	3.1%	30.6%	61.9%	78.1%	30.8%	45.8%	.235	.500	101	0.2
Tanner McDougal	KAN	A	20	21 (21)	69¹	0-3	0	80	1.40	4.15		14.3%	26.7%	1.7%	45.3%					.299	.470	88	1.1
Edgar Navarro	BIR	AA	25	7 (0)	9	1-0	0	6	0.89	0.00		15.6%	18.8%	0.0%	52.4%					.143	.190	106	0.1
	CLT	AAA	25	39 (0)	43²	2-2	3	38	1.53	4.33		16.2%	19.2%	0.5%	60.7%	64.1%	87.0%	28.4%	59.7%	.281	.397	103	0.6
	CHW	MLB	25	8 (0)	8²	0-0	0	9	1.50	7.27	49.4%	5.1%	23.1%	5.1%	53.8%	73.0%	89.1%	25.3%	63.6%	.375	.769	91	0.1
Nicholas Padilla	CLT	AAA	26	44 (0)	45²	2-3	5	54	1.93	5.52		17.6%	24.4%	2.3%	58.2%	60.7%	80.8%	28.6%	48.1%	.379	.636	97	0.8
	CHW	MLB	26	3 (0)	4²	0-1	0	6	2.14	5.79	41.0%	4.3%	26.1%	4.3%	12.5%	70.0%	85.7%	32.9%	47.8%	.533	.938	105	0.0
Sammy Peralta	CLT	AAA	25	29 (6)	69	5-6	0	68	1.30	5.09		6.4%	23.1%	3.1%	43.2%	65.2%	85.5%	33.1%	62.4%	.315	.564	93	1.2
	CHW	MLB	25	16 (0)	20	2-0	0	18	1.50	4.05	49.8%	12.2%	20.0%	2.2%	37.7%	67.3%	85.0%	30.9%	69.1%	.288	.508	107	0.2
Lane Ramsey	CLT	AAA	26	32 (0)	36	4-4	6	48	1.81	5.50		16.1%	28.6%	2.4%	32.6%	65.7%	77.5%	27.6%	57.4%	.391	.722	105	0.5
	CHW	MLB	26	21 (0)	20	1-0	0	18	1.70	5.85	46.8%	9.8%	19.6%	1.1%	35.4%	71.5%	88.2%	30.5%	57.8%	.381	.516	102	0.2
Jesse Scholtens	CLT	AAA	29	9 (9)	46²	2-2	0	45	1.24	4.44		6.8%	23.4%	4.7%	39.4%	72.5%	81.9%	32.0%	58.1%	.293	.614	97	0.7
	CHW	MLB	29	26 (11)	85	1-9	1	58	1.53	5.29	46.0%	8.0%	15.4%	4.0%	40.8%	69.2%	86.9%	29.6%	67.6%	.313	.551	123	0.0
Bryan Shaw	CLT	AAA	35	23 (0)	23²	2-1	4	26	1.39	4.94		16.5%	25.2%	1.9%	55.2%	70.5%	82.1%	25.9%	43.8%	.250	.404	95	0.4
	CHW	MLB	35	38 (0)	45²	0-0	4	40	1.23	4.14	47.6%	8.9%	21.1%	1.6%	40.2%	70.0%	83.2%	27.7%	64.8%	.290	.444	105	0.4
Alex Speas	FRI	AA	25	23 (0)	28¹	3-0	2	47	0.92	0.64		11.3%	40.9%	0.0%	50.0%					.250	.353	61	0.9
	RR	AAA	25	26 (1)	28¹	2-2	2	38	1.62	5.08		19.2%	29.2%	1.5%	54.7%	55.9%	78.0%	28.9%	47.1%	.306	.438	81	0.3
	TEX	MLB	25	3 (0)	2	0-0	0	4	3.50	13.50	35.1%	41.7%	33.3%	0.0%	0.0%	47.4%	88.9%	23.9%	54.5%	.667	.667	100	0.0

After nearly a decade in the minor leagues, **Tanner Banks** finally made his debut in 2022, carving out a role for himself as a multi-inning reliever due to his four-pitch mix. The good news for him is that the White Sox appear to be heading for another year of needing guys like Tanner Banks. ⑬ **Alex Colomé** is near the end of a successful decade-long career, having made the graceful descent from Minnesota to Colorado to Triple-A. It's always sad to see a fastball-exclusive pitcher go, especially one with a cutter as mean as his was back with Tampa. ⑬ Traffic advisory: Be on the lookout for **Shane Drohan**'s fastball command and secondaries consistency, last seen dislodged from a moving vehicle traveling southbound on I-495 between Portland and Worcester. If found, please report missing items to Guaranteed Rate Field—he changed Sox in the Rule 5 Draft. ⑬ **Matt Foster** lost the feel for his changeup, first through mechanical tinkering and then through the surgical kind. Hopefully, the extended rehab will allow him to discover his old arm slot and the magic therein. ⑬ **Jared Kelley** is the only pitcher for whom the extra-inning runner-on-second rule applies every inning, because he walks the first two batters every time out. ⑬ Released by the Nationals in June, **Chad Kuhl** turned down multiple offers to continue pitching in 2023 so he could focus on his wife Amanda's battle with cancer, as well as becoming an advocate for breast cancer research and treatment. ⑬ **Jimmy Lambert** averages 18 inches of induced vertical break on his fastball, and his curveball has vicious depth spinning in the opposite direction. Maybe he shouldn't have thrown the latter half as often as he did a slider that looked like a juicy T-bone steak to a cartoon shipwrecked castaway. ⑬ We're likely to see a lot of competition for the back of Chicago's starting rotation this spring. Luckily for **Davis Martin**, who had Tommy John surgery in May, we're likely to see a lot of competition throughout the summer as well. ⑬ In a way, it's a little unfair that we group statistics by seasons; **Tanner McDougal** struggled to throw strikes early in his return from Tommy John, but found the zone with his fastball later on in the summer. It's not *that* unfair, though. ⑬ **Edgar Navarro** has big-time vertical depth on his sinker, which could play nicely at the bottom of the zone against right-handed hitters. He can't throw strikes, thanks to a tendency to commit his lead hip too early, but that won't be a problem as long as he never allows a single hit. ⑬ On YouTube you can find a video entitled "**Nicholas Padilla** 2023 Highlights!" complete with exclamation mark. It is six pitches long. Perhaps the most remarkable aspect of it is that three of them landed in the strike zone. ⑬ Coming from the Division II powerhouse that is the University of Tampa as an 18th-rounder, **Sammy Peralta's** push to the majors in 2023 was an impressive feat. His deceptive arm slot results in significant arm-side run on his four-seamer, and provides hope he can serve as a lefty specialist at the back of a bullpen. ⑬ Other pitchers in the same neighborhood of arm-side four-seam run as **Lane Ramsey** throw a changeup or splitter, but he throws neither. Instead, he relies on a slider that has never worked very well despite the vertical plane. In a perfect pitch design world, he gets in the lab and dabbles with how to make the most of his ability to run the ball by adding a change or splitty. ⑬ Having dealt half their rotation at the deadline, the White Sox turned to contact maven **Jesse Scholtens** to start every fifth day down the stretch. Don't worry, though; it's over now. ⑬ Relievers never die. They just permanently underperform their peripherals. Somehow only and simultaneously already 35 years old, **Bryan Shaw** avoided the FIP Reaper at least one more time, thanks to only allowing five barrels in 127 batted balls. ⑬ From 2019-2022, **Alex Speas** threw only 17 ⅓ innings. Completing a full season including an MLB debut in 2023 was a success, but it must sting to get waived by the World Series champs the same day the postseason began. ⑬ **Garrett Wright** allowed basically the same number of hits and walks in three years as a college reliever at TCU. When he's on, he pairs a 97-mph heater with a hard slider; when he's off, he also pairs them, but he starts off facing in the wrong direction. It sounds like a simple fix, but nothing is simple for the White Sox.

CINCINNATI REDS

Essay by Steven Goldman

Player comments by Eli Walsh and BP staff

The 2023 season was the 100th anniversary of perhaps the greatest campaign by a starting pitcher in Reds history. In 1923, right-hander Dolf Luque, one of the game's first greats to hail from Cuba (the field being shamefully curtailed by the color line), went 27-8 with a 1.93 ERA in 322 innings. He led the National League in wins, ERA and shutouts (six) while allowing only two home runs—even in the Deadball Era, that rate was one-seventh the league average.

Luque, who was with the Reds from 1918 through 1929, also had one of the best pitching careers in Reds history, his 38.2 WAR (per Baseball-Reference) trailing only turn-of-the-20th century lefty Noodles Hahn and Luque teammate Eppa Rixey. There haven't been many more starting pitchers like them; whatever the overall success of the team, whoever the general manager, regardless of the sincerity of the owner, the Reds have largely gone from hand-to-mouth with starters, making their bed not with Mr. Ace, but Mr. Ace Enough for Our Budget. Sometimes it has worked. Mostly it hasn't.

Reds ownership has not only traditionally been parsimonious (to put it politely), but in the draft era the club has had as bad a record in the first round as any team. This is particularly true when it comes to discerning among the best amateur pitchers. The best of the Reds first-rounders were right-hander Gary Nolan (1966, 13th overall) and left-hander Don Gullett (1969, 14th overall) who were (a) both excellent pitchers whose careers were subsumed by injuries and (b) picked over 50 years ago. Never mind drafting a Justin Verlander or Clayton Kershaw in the years since; the Reds haven't even picked a Lance Lynn, certainly not in this century, although the futures of Nick Lodolo and Hunter Greene and 2023 first rounders Rhett Lowder and Ty Floyd remain to be written. Tellingly, in the 67-year history of the Cy Young Award, Reds pitchers have taken home exactly one trophy, earned during the pandemic-truncated 2020 season by a man unworthy of mention who would make a total of 21 appearances with the team.

Even the Big Red Machine's pitching was just good enough to keep up with one of the deepest lineups of all time, while the 1990 World Series winner (the team's last to date; in the 29-year run of this book we've gotten to write about only four

CINCINNATI REDS PROSPECTUS
2023 W-L: 82-80, 3RD IN NL CENTRAL

Pythag	.477	18th	DER	.692	20th
RS/G	4.83	9th	DRC+	89	29th
RA/G	5.07	23rd	DRA-	104	21st
dWin%	.441	26th	FIP	4.81	27th
Payroll	$83M	26th	B-Age	27.3	6th
M$/MW	$1.9M	3rd	P-Age	28.0	4th

- Opened 2003
- Open air
- Natural surface
- Fence profile: 8' to 12'

Park Factors

Runs	Runs/RH	Runs/LH	HR/RH	HR/LH
106	107	106	125	127

Top Hitter WARP	2.1 Jonathan India
Top Pitcher WARP	2.0 Hunter Greene
2023 Top Prospect	Noelvi Marte

Payroll History (in millions)

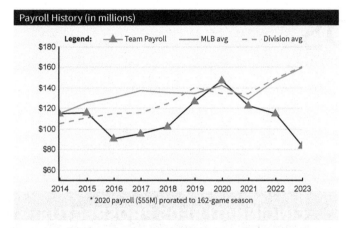

* 2020 payroll ($55M) prorated to 162-game season

Future Commitments (in millions)

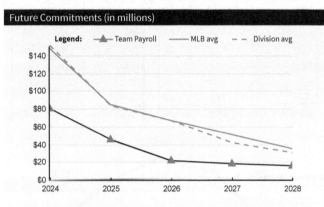

Farm System Ranking

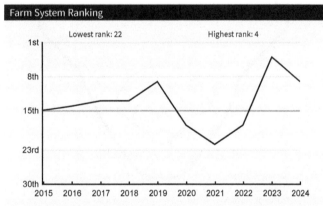

Personnel

President of Baseball Operations
Nick Krall

Senior Vice President & General Manager
Brad Meador

Vice President, Assistant General Manager
Sam Grossman

Vice President, Player Personnel
Chris Buckley

Vice President, Player Development
Shawn Pender

Manager
David Bell

Reds postseason teams) was famously reliant on its "Nasty Boys" bullpen trio of Norm Charlton, Rob Dibble and Randy Myers. While the Reds have gotten a handful of strong starting pitching performances since then—including, in this century, from the likes of Bronson Arroyo, Luis Castillo, Johnny Cueto, Sonny Gray and Aaron Harang—the team is still trying to assemble the next great rotation in Reds history. Arguably they've been fitfully efforting in this direction since 1967. As much as relief pitching has come to dominate the game, this remains something the Reds need to do—starting pitchers still throw nearly 60% of the innings.

The team's current shortfall is the result of errors, oversights and negligence in team-building demonstrated as recently as 2019-2020. In the former season, Reds starting pitchers had an ERA of 4.12 against a league average of 4.33; in the latter it was 3.50 against 4.41. By midseason 2022, none of the pitchers who compiled those records were still with the team. In some cases, the trades that took them away yielded promising returns: Castillo brought Noelvi Marte and organizational top prospect Edwin Arroyo, among others, from the Mariners; Sonny Gray returned another top prospect, Chase Petty, from the Twins; Tyler Mahle, also dealt to the Twins, netted Spencer Steer and Christian Encarnacion-Strand. (Not all of the moves were positive—Wade Miley has continued to pitch well, if infrequently, since being waived for cost-cutting reasons in November 2021.)

Yet, even if the Reds did well in recouping talent with the dissolution of this rotation, the aftermath distracts us from what the Reds did as a team when they had it. The answer: One fourth-place finish, and one quick exit from the postseason during the Wild Card round. The simple reason was that the hitters were as bad as the pitchers were good. In baseball, rebuilding requires the whole buffet of options, from internal player development to trades to free-agent signings. Acting as if the team is on its uppers means racing a series of unforgiving clocks—injury, arbitration, free agency—to put together a complete roster before expense and entropy pulls it apart again.

The evolving 2024 Reds would seem to be reasonably close to doing that, but at least as of this writing the front office has shown little urgency about getting there. Their biggest move to date has been adding free-agent infielder Jeimer Candelario on a three-year, $45 million contract. Candelario is a switch-hitting two-corner man who has hit .249/.324/.429 over the last three seasons. He would no doubt be a valuable player in the right context, but the Reds were already drowning in infielders and Candelario's addition (and absorption of scarce dollars) further muddles rather than clarifies the Reds' plans.

This odd zig-zag undermines confidence in the direction of a club that had shown great year-over-year improvement. If you consider the 2023 Reds in light of a 100-loss 2022 season, they had a very good year. Coming within a couple of losses of a Wild Card spot was a major accomplishment given the lack of hitting, pitching and defensive ability that characterized the preceding edition. It seems almost ungrateful to point out that the 2023 edition was only somewhat better at these things.

The starting rotation, while young and brimming with potential, is still mostly hypothetical. The many 25-and-under position players introduced or established last year—Steer, Encarnacion-Strand, Marte, Will Benson, Matt McClain and Elly De La Cruz among them—showed promise but also experienced growing pains. Five of the six are infielders. Steer will likely go to an outfield corner. That still leaves too many bodies for the available chairs, especially with the addition of Candelario and the continued presence of Jonathan India. In November, president of baseball operations Nick Krall denied that the club was looking to move India (while suggesting he too would be tried in the pastures), but the second baseman's stagnation and first-year arbitration eligibility and the upside of the younger players would seem likely to force his hand however much he might want to resist the inevitable.

Surely someone must go, if only to rationalize the roster—there is a thin line between depth and chaos—if only for pitching. The Curse of Luque still obtains. With the starting rotation subjected to the weird complacency of a bewitched organization, results didn't matter. Luke Weaver, who is somehow still dining out on post-first-round breakout potential after eight years and 144 games, recorded just two quality starts in 21 tries as a Red, the lowest percentage in the National League. Even Hugh "Losing Pitcher" Mulcahy was more reliable than that, and yet the Reds kept running him out to the mound into mid-August despite knowing what they were going to get. No Reds pitcher threw 150 innings, and it's possible no Reds pitcher is going to, even if Greene, Lodolo, Graham Ashcraft and Andrew Abbott retain varying degrees of potential for growth but, as with all pitchers, more than equal potential for further injuries—and then we begin again. Acquisition Frankie Montas reached the threshold once, in 2021, and failed to accumulate that many in the proceeding two seasons combined. Retooled ex-Padres swingman Nick Martinez is here too. He's never thrown 150 major-league innings either.

Every rebuilding team faces a moment when inchoate talent must be shaped into a roster that has a chance to win. As always, not choosing is a choice. See: the now-concluded quest to prove that Nick Senzel could play. Nearly 42 years ago, the 1982 Twins, rebuilding from the bottom up in the aftermath of free agency, gave 100 or more plate appearances to 11 rookies, arguably the largest youth movement by volume in history. This did not make the Twins an immediate success—the club went 60-102. The kids had to be sorted into keepers and discards. When the Twins finally won the World Series in 1987, five members of the class of '82 (Tom Brunansky, Randy Bush, Gary Gaetti, Kent Hrbek and Tim Laudner) were part of it. Six (Jim Eisenreich, Lenny Faedo, Randy Johnson the Lesser, Bobby Mitchell, Jesus Vega and Ron Washington) were not. You try solutions, they fail, and—contra Senzel—you move on.

Consider Elly De La Cruz. For about a month of 2023, De La Cruz was one of the most dynamic players in baseball—as of his 30th major-league game he was hitting .325/.363/.524 and had stolen 16 bases in 18 attempts. Then he lost the plot: From that point on he hit .191/.272/.355 in 68 games. As he went, so went the team. The Reds, 27-33 on the day of De La Cruz's debut, rode his torrid debut to a 22-8 record. They went 32-39 thereafter.

De La Cruz is only 22 and, with buckets of talent, was a consensus top-10 prospect coming into the 2023 season. It would be spectacularly premature to give up on him—heck, Mickey Mantle and Willie Mays both flailed at times during their rookie campaigns. Yet, in the hypothetical, unlikely case he continues on a Senzelian path, to persevere past the point of reason with him or with any of the current kids would be to restrict the team's evolution at a time when there is no time. If the hype of De La Cruz is too dazzling, consider Brandon Williamson, or the 5:1 strikeout-to-walk ratio of Encarnacion-Stroud, or the slumping Tyler Stephenson. Choosing entails risk, but ultimately the Reds will have to pick their nine guys and go forward. And then they'll have to find some pitchers.

As of this date, with far too little changed on a team that ended up in the almost/not quite pile, there's no reason to trust that current management and ownership will be as aggressive as they need to be. The talent is very nearly there, but the team portrait is half-finished. The Reds play in a division ripe for the taking, too. And yet they do not recognize their moment of great potential and great jeopardy: The Curse of Luque held illimitable dominion over all.

—Steven Goldman is a former EIC of Baseball Prospectus.

HITTERS

Edwin Arroyo SS Born: 08/25/03 Age: 20 Bats: S Throws: S Height: 6'0" Weight: 175 Origin: Round 2, 2021 Draft (#48 overall)

YEAR	TM	LVL	AGE	PA	R	HR	RBI	SB	AVG/OBP/SLG	BABIP	SLGCON	BB%	K%	ZSw%	ZCon%	OSw%	OCon%	LA	90th EV	DRC+	BRR	DRP	WARP
2021	RA12	WIN	17	65	6	0	2	1	.250/.333/.304	.333	.405	9.2%	21.5%										
2021	MRN	ROK	17	86	16	2	10	4	.211/.337/.324	.295	.511	11.6%	30.2%									-2.6	
2022	DBT	A	18	109	16	1	16	4	.227/.303/.381	.318	.561	8.3%	28.4%	82.8%	80.6%	33.1%	45.0%		80	-0.1	1.1	0.2
2022	MOD	A	18	410	76	13	67	21	.316/.385/.514	.386	.682	8.5%	22.0%						106	3.1	4.3	2.2
2023	DAY	A+	19	534	72	13	55	28	.248/.321/.427	.297	.559	9.0%	21.0%						106	4.2	-4.2	1.7
2024 non	CIN	MLB	20	251	21	4	23	0	.224/.279/.345	.295	.476	6.2%	25.8%						74	0.0	0	0.1

2023 GP: SS (116), DH (7)   *Comps: Royce Lewis (73), Matt Dominguez (70), Andrés Giménez (70)*

Arroyo's first full season in the Reds' system wasn't quite as flashy as his 2022 breakout, but the 20-year-old earned a late-season promotion to Double-A and still appears poised to be a well-rounded big leaguer. At the very least, Arroyo's defensive prowess will eventually earn him some time as a backup infielder or utility infielder. Of course, given the organization he plays for, there's a very real chance that doesn't happen in Cincinnati. If it does, he needs only seven major-league homers to surpass former pitcher Bronson for the most big flies in Reds history among players with the surname Arroyo. Don't worry, you don't have to look it up because we already did.

Will Benson   OF   Born: 06/16/98   Age: 26   Bats: L   Throws: L   Height: 6'5"   Weight: 230   Origin: Round 1, 2016 Draft (#14 overall)

YEAR	TM	LVL	AGE	PA	R	HR	RBI	SB	AVG/OBP/SLG	BABIP	SLGCON	BB%	K%	ZSw%	ZCon%	OSw%	OCon%	LA	90th EV	DRC+	BRR	DRP	WARP
2021	AKR	AA	23	332	63	14	42	14	.221/.374/.469	.301	.778	18.1%	31.3%							117	1.0	-4.2	1.4
2021	COL	AAA	23	107	7	3	9	0	.161/.271/.333	.250	.608	13.1%	39.3%							68	-0.5	-0.8	-0.1
2022	COL	AAA	24	401	75	17	45	16	.278/.426/.522	.340	.733	18.7%	22.7%							124	-2.5	4.2	2.5
2022	CLE	MLB	24	61	8	0	3	0	.182/.250/.200	.278	.306	4.9%	31.1%	60.0%	84.8%	26.1%	35.5%	8.6	104.6	66	0.0	0.1	0.0
2023	LOU	AAA	25	133	25	3	9	11	.206/.406/.402	.279	.629	24.1%	26.3%	65.3%	80.0%	18.1%	40.0%			100	-0.1	3.3	0.7
2023	CIN	MLB	25	329	51	11	31	19	.275/.365/.498	.391	.777	12.2%	31.3%	69.1%	77.8%	22.8%	48.0%	14.8	103.9	82	0.8	1.0	0.3
2024 DC	CIN	MLB	26	402	46	12	48	17	.230/.346/.421	.317	.634	13.6%	29.0%							109	0.6	0.8	1.7

2023 GP: RF (54), LF (46), DH (5), CF (4)   *Comps: Josh Reddick (57), Dexter Fowler (56), Anthony Santander (52)*

Between Benson and Nolan Jones, the Cleveland Guardians giving away immediately productive outfielders has graduated from fun bit to actual trend. The red flags are certainly present: a strikeout rate in excess of 30%, significant batted-ball luck, middling defensive skills that won't keep him in the lineup should he stop hitting. None of that mattered, though, last June 7, when he launched a mammoth walk-off home run against the Dodgers—his first as a big leaguer. Regardless of whether Benson irons out his approach at the plate, sometimes you just have to ride the wave for as long as it crests.

Jeimer Candelario   3B   Born: 11/24/93   Age: 30   Bats: S   Throws: R   Height: 6'2"   Weight: 222   Origin: IFA, 2010

YEAR	TM	LVL	AGE	PA	R	HR	RBI	SB	AVG/OBP/SLG	BABIP	SLGCON	BB%	K%	ZSw%	ZCon%	OSw%	OCon%	LA	90th EV	DRC+	BRR	DRP	WARP
2021	DET	MLB	27	626	75	16	67	0	.271/.351/.443	.333	.585	10.4%	21.6%	69.0%	85.7%	33.6%	64.2%	12.8	105.3	110	-0.1	-1.4	2.8
2022	DET	MLB	28	467	49	13	50	0	.217/.272/.361	.257	.484	6.0%	23.3%	74.7%	82.6%	36.2%	62.8%	13.6	102.8	91	-0.1	-0.2	0.6
2023	CHC	MLB	29	157	20	6	17	2	.234/.318/.445	.277	.622	10.8%	24.8%	62.7%	83.8%	31.3%	60.0%	11.5	104.9	101	0.1	0.2	0.5
2023	WAS	MLB	29	419	57	16	53	6	.258/.342/.481	.297	.632	8.6%	21.0%	70.0%	85.0%	32.6%	63.1%	15.4	104.5	106	0.0	0.4	1.7
2024 DC	CIN	MLB	30	534	60	18	66	3	.246/.324/.429	.292	.561	8.8%	21.6%							105	-0.1	-0.2	1.4

2023 GP: 3B (115), 1B (21), DH (8)   *Comps: Mike Moustakas (67), Mike Mowrey (66), Bob Bailey (66)*

In baseball, we tend to assume that players are who they've shown us to be. That's why it was so surprising that after two very good seasons in 2020 and 2021, the veteran Candelario took such a step backward in 2022. Signing a low-dollar, low-stakes contract with the Nationals last winter, the 30-year-old set about recapturing that prior form. What followed was a near-perfect reproduction of those good Tigers years, as everything under the hood looked almost identical from a plate discipline perspective. A career high in homers came at the expense of batting average, a tradeoff the utility of which is worth wondering about, but all in all it was a win for common baseball understanding. As Dennis Green might say, he is who we thought he was, and now he'll get to remind us via the most homer-friendly park in baseball.

Curt Casali   C   Born: 11/09/88   Age: 35   Bats: R   Throws: R   Height: 6'2"   Weight: 220   Origin: Round 10, 2011 Draft (#317 overall)

YEAR	TM	LVL	AGE	PA	R	HR	RBI	SB	AVG/OBP/SLG	BABIP	SLGCON	BB%	K%	ZSw%	ZCon%	OSw%	OCon%	LA	90th EV	DRC+	BRR	DRP	WARP
2021	SF	MLB	32	231	20	5	26	0	.210/.313/.350	.287	.522	11.3%	28.6%	76.1%	81.0%	24.5%	46.5%	23.7	99.7	82	-0.2	0.0	0.4
2022	SEA	MLB	33	50	7	1	3	0	.125/.300/.225	.160	.346	18.0%	28.0%	71.1%	78.3%	26.7%	59.4%	37.2	101.0	89	-0.1	0.0	0.1
2022	SF	MLB	33	126	13	4	14	0	.231/.325/.370	.300	.556	11.9%	28.6%	74.9%	81.2%	27.2%	54.0%	21.7	102.3	87	-0.2	-3.3	-0.1
2023	CIN	MLB	34	96	8	0	6	0	.175/.290/.200	.246	.281	11.5%	24.0%	70.6%	87.5%	24.9%	46.0%	18.2	99.1	80	-0.1	-1.2	0.0
2024 non	CIN	MLB	35	251	23	5	23	0	.204/.297/.319	.258	.438	10.1%	24.1%							77	0.0	-0.8	0.1

2023 GP: C (38), 1B (2), 3B (1)   *Comps: Chris Iannetta (56), Jason LaRue (53), Chad Kreuter (51)*

The Reds signed Casali with the intention that he'd provide depth behind Tyler Stephenson and Luke Maile, and hit a little bit to make up for his so-so defense behind the dish. The opposite happened, as Casali posted his worst OPS since his rookie season and a foot contusion cost him the entirety of the second half. As a result, the Reds declined his 2024 option, putting him in search of a new team for whom he could in theory provide depth behind the plate. Such is the life of the journeyman catcher.

YEAR	TM	P. COUNT	FRM RUNS	BLK RUNS	THRW RUNS	TOT RUNS
2021	SF	7929	0.9	0.0	0.1	1.0
2022	SEA	1883	0.3	0.0	-0.1	0.3
2022	SF	4825	-2.9	0.0	0.0	-2.9
2023	CIN	4053	-1.1	0.0	0.2	-0.9
2024	CIN	6956	-0.9	-0.1	0.2	-0.8

Cam Collier   3B/DH   Born: 11/20/04   Age: 19   Bats: L   Throws: R   Height: 6'2"   Weight: 210   Origin: Round 1, 2022 Draft (#18 overall)

YEAR	TM	LVL	AGE	PA	R	HR	RBI	SB	AVG/OBP/SLG	BABIP	SLGCON	BB%	K%	ZSw%	ZCon%	OSw%	OCon%	LA	90th EV	DRC+	BRR	DRP	WARP
2022	RED	ROK	17	35	7	2	4	0	.370/.514/.630	.421	.810	20.0%	17.1%										
2023	DBT	A	18	461	40	6	68	5	.246/.349/.356	.317	.489	12.4%	23.0%	59.4%	86.3%	36.6%	63.8%			99	-2.1	3.1	1.2
2024 non	CIN	MLB	19	251	19	2	19	0	.207/.271/.288	.292	.421	7.2%	28.6%							59	0.0	0	-0.6

2023 GP: 3B (72), DH (39)   *Comps: Marcos Vechionacci (82), Francisco Lindor (62), Dorssys Paulino (60)*

What do you do when one of your highest-ceiling hitting prospects can't slug over .400 in Low-A? The 2022 first-round pick played the entire season at 18 and—to his credit—wasn't an automatic out with Daytona, but six home runs in 111 games is what one would expect from an elite fielding middle infielder rather than a third baseman with some of the best raw power in the Reds' organization. Again, Collier is younger than a lot of players who will be drafted in July, so there's no need to hit the panic button or even edge a hand toward it. It would certainly be nice for Collier to start punishing pro pitching in games so no one starts side-eyeing that button, though.

Elly De La Cruz SS   Born: 01/11/02   Age: 22   Bats: S   Throws: R   Height: 6'5"   Weight: 200   Origin: IFA, 2018

YEAR	TM	LVL	AGE	PA	R	HR	RBI	SB	AVG/OBP/SLG	BABIP	SLGCON	BB%	K%	ZSw%	ZCon%	OSw%	OCon%	LA	90th EV	DRC+	BRR	DRP	WARP
2021	RED	ROK	19	55	13	3	13	2	.400/.455/.780	.531	1.114	7.3%	27.3%									0.3	
2021	DBT	A	19	210	22	5	29	8	.269/.305/.477	.372	.712	4.8%	31.0%	75.0%	80.6%	40.8%	52.7%			89	-0.7	9.7	1.2
2022	DAY	A+	20	306	53	20	52	28	.302/.359/.609	.389	.914	7.8%	30.7%							116	1.7	0.3	1.7
2022	CHA	AA	20	207	34	8	34	19	.305/.357/.553	.420	.833	7.7%	30.9%							96	2.2	1.5	0.9
2023	LOU	AAA	21	186	38	12	36	11	.297/.398/.633	.361	.926	14.0%	26.9%	61.5%	79.5%	29.9%	52.5%			117	-0.1	0.9	1.0
2023	CIN	MLB	21	427	67	13	44	35	.235/.300/.410	.336	.652	8.2%	33.7%	61.4%	81.3%	34.9%	57.6%	3.2	109.2	74	1.9	-3.0	0.0
2024 DC	CIN	MLB	22	553	59	19	68	42	.228/.297/.426	.309	.637	7.8%	30.8%							93	0.6	0.3	1.4

2023 GP: SS (69), 3B (32), DH (1)   *Comps: Chris Owings (66), Amed Rosario (61), Javier Báez (60)*

Well that sure was fun, wasn't it? De La Cruz's rookie year stats weren't so gilded as those of Corbin Carroll or even some of his teammates, but there's a case to be made that no other first-year player was as electric or just plain ol' fun to watch as De La Cruz at his best. It's certainly fair to be concerned about his second-half struggles: between August 1 and October 1, he logged a .647 OPS and 76 punchouts in 51 games. Even so, there are few players on the planet with the ability to hit and throw the ball as hard as he does. Every game De La Cruz steps between the lines, there's a chance he'll do at least one spectacular thing. Sometimes it's hitting for the cycle, sometimes it's just legging out an infield single. What's most evident from De La Cruz's at-times bombastic debut is that his potential in the coming years is pretty much unlimited—it's just a question of whether he can unlock it consistently.

Christian Encarnacion-Strand 3B   Born: 12/01/99   Age: 24   Bats: R   Throws: R   Height: 6'0"   Weight: 224   Origin: Round 4, 2021 Draft (#128 overall)

YEAR	TM	LVL	AGE	PA	R	HR	RBI	SB	AVG/OBP/SLG	BABIP	SLGCON	BB%	K%	ZSw%	ZCon%	OSw%	OCon%	LA	90th EV	DRC+	BRR	DRP	WARP
2021	FTM	A	21	92	17	4	18	2	.391/.424/.598	.526	.852	5.4%	28.3%	67.3%	80.0%	40.7%	61.4%			101	0.2	0.6	0.3
2022	CR	A+	22	330	52	20	68	7	.296/.370/.599	.353	.842	9.1%	25.8%							136	1.3	-0.8	2.3
2022	CHA	AA	22	148	13	7	29	0	.309/.351/.522	.376	.724	4.1%	25.7%							105	-1.0	-0.5	0.3
2022	WCH	AA	22	60	11	5	17	1	.333/.400/.685	.371	.925	6.7%	23.3%							112	0.2	-0.2	0.2
2023	LOU	AAA	23	316	65	20	62	2	.331/.405/.637	.377	.847	10.4%	21.8%	68.7%	82.4%	40.6%	60.7%			125	0.8	2.5	2.1
2023	CIN	MLB	23	241	29	13	37	2	.270/.328/.477	.336	.693	5.8%	28.6%	72.3%	83.6%	39.1%	54.6%	18.9	105.8	88	-0.1	0.0	0.2
2024 DC	CIN	MLB	24	423	50	18	57	1	.253/.314/.449	.313	.621	6.2%	26.1%							106	-0.3	-0	1.1

2023 GP: 1B (35), DH (24), 3B (9), RF (1)   *Comps: Ryan Braun (63), Nathaniel Lowe (61), Paul DeJong (60)*

Encarnacion-Strand had the chance, when he debuted in July, to set a record for the longest last name on the back of a jersey, as his surname's 18 characters surpass Simeon Woods Richardson's 16. Alas, "CES" went with just "Encarnacion" on his back. Regardless of what anyone called him, Encarnacion-Strand played pretty much exactly to his scouting report, combining a promising bat with mostly unconvincing work at both infield and outfield corners. He's most likely a first baseman or a DH long-term, but if he can bring the peripherals up to the 2023 stat line, the Reds will be happy to plug him in the lineup and let him cook. That's a big *if*, but he's raked at every previous level and that held up fine in the big leagues despite the protestations of DRC+.

Jake Fraley RF   Born: 05/25/95   Age: 29   Bats: L   Throws: L   Height: 6'0"   Weight: 206   Origin: Round 2, 2016 Draft (#77 overall)

YEAR	TM	LVL	AGE	PA	R	HR	RBI	SB	AVG/OBP/SLG	BABIP	SLGCON	BB%	K%	ZSw%	ZCon%	OSw%	OCon%	LA	90th EV	DRC+	BRR	DRP	WARP
2021	SEA	MLB	26	265	27	9	36	10	.210/.352/.369	.265	.552	17.4%	26.8%	64.2%	79.0%	22.4%	55.9%	12.4	102.7	92	0.3	1.4	0.9
2022	CIN	MLB	27	247	33	12	28	4	.259/.344/.468	.289	.623	10.5%	21.9%	71.4%	86.4%	28.8%	58.4%	14.0	102.6	109	0.3	1.5	1.2
2023	CIN	MLB	28	380	41	15	65	21	.256/.339/.443	.283	.562	9.7%	18.7%	77.7%	84.8%	33.2%	60.7%	16.5	102.7	101	0.8	2.9	1.4
2024 DC	CIN	MLB	29	339	41	13	44	11	.253/.343/.437	.296	.574	10.8%	21.2%							114	0.2	1.3	1.5

2023 GP: RF (55), LF (29), DH (23)   *Comps: David Murphy (56), Seth Smith (55), Brandon Nimmo (55)*

Most of Fraley's best play came in the first half: he walked nearly as often as he struck out and ran an OPS in the .800s into early August, when he suffered a stress fracture in his toe that kept him out for around a month. It's safe to say that after two productive seasons, when he's available Fraley has made himself into one of the few outfielders in whom Reds can have full confidence. Up-and-coming teams usually need late bloomers like these to fill out a roster. Barring any major trades, Fraley looks like he'll be wearing red for years to come—though he'd inspire more conviction if he could avoid the injured list for the first time in a half-decade.

TJ Friedl CF   Born: 08/14/95   Age: 28   Bats: L   Throws: L   Height: 5'10"   Weight: 180   Origin: Undrafted Free Agent, 2016

YEAR	TM	LVL	AGE	PA	R	HR	RBI	SB	AVG/OBP/SLG	BABIP	SLGCON	BB%	K%	ZSw%	ZCon%	OSw%	OCon%	LA	90th EV	DRC+	BRR	DRP	WARP
2021	LOU	AAA	25	448	59	12	36	13	.264/.357/.422	.288	.508	9.8%	14.5%							113	2.6	-10.6	1.5
2021	CIN	MLB	25	36	9	1	2	0	.290/.361/.419	.276	.448	11.1%	5.6%	66.0%	97.0%	24.4%	66.7%	24.0	100.6	103	0.0	-0.1	0.1
2022	LOU	AAA	26	241	33	8	38	10	.278/.371/.468	.327	.611	11.6%	19.9%							113	-0.2	-2.0	0.9
2022	CIN	MLB	26	258	33	8	25	7	.240/.314/.436	.251	.530	7.8%	15.5%	61.6%	90.9%	30.1%	65.0%	18.5	102.2	94	0.0	1.8	0.8
2023	CIN	MLB	27	556	73	18	66	27	.279/.352/.467	.308	.573	8.5%	16.2%	58.9%	90.7%	28.9%	68.5%	12.7	100.9	93	1.0	0.9	1.7
2024 DC	CIN	MLB	28	566	61	16	65	18	.250/.330/.415	.281	.504	8.6%	16.1%							103	0.6	-1.2	2.1

2023 GP: CF (126), LF (23), RF (2), DH (1)   *Comps: Steven Duggar (58), Dexter Fowler (56), Ángel Pagán (54)*

It's at this point we have to posit the question: Was Friedl's flowing mane holding him back? The undrafted 2016 free agent broke out in a big way in 2023 and tended to keep his lettuce pinned up for much of the season before cutting it short late in the summer. Through 94 games before debuting the cleaned-up look on August 11, he logged a .790 OPS. The rest of the way he OPSed .882. Hair or no hair, Friedl turned himself into one of the Reds' steadiest bats, serving as the lineup's spark plug for most of the season while providing an athletic and above-average glove at all three outfield spots. An unexpected breakout like Friedl's is the kind contending teams need beyond their superstars—it's just unfortunate it may have come at the cost of arguably the best hair on the team.

Jonathan India 2B Born: 12/15/96 Age: 27 Bats: R Throws: R Height: 6'0" Weight: 200 Origin: Round 1, 2018 Draft (#5 overall)

YEAR	TM	LVL	AGE	PA	R	HR	RBI	SB	AVG/OBP/SLG	BABIP	SLGCON	BB%	K%	ZSw%	ZCon%	OSw%	OCon%	LA	90th EV	DRC+	BRR	DRP	WARP
2021	CIN	MLB	24	631	98	21	69	12	.269/.376/.459	.326	.624	11.3%	22.3%	57.2%	84.1%	26.0%	60.4%	13.0	104.3	109	0.5	-0.9	3.0
2022	CIN	MLB	25	431	48	10	41	3	.249/.327/.378	.305	.500	7.2%	21.8%	58.0%	86.5%	28.9%	61.8%	14.7	103.5	101	-0.3	-3.0	1.0
2023	CIN	MLB	26	529	78	17	61	14	.244/.338/.407	.281	.536	9.8%	20.6%	58.5%	85.5%	22.0%	61.5%	15.3	103.9	108	1.0	-1.2	2.1
2024 DC	CIN	MLB	27	398	45	12	46	6	.247/.341/.403	.287	.514	9.3%	18.8%							109	0.0	-2	1.3

2023 GP: 2B (104), DH (15)   *Comps: Jim Gilliam (63), Frank Bolling (61), Tim Teufel (60)*

The former Rookie of the Year found himself on the outside looking in at the Reds' infield alignment halfway through 2023, following multiple prospect promotions throughout the summer. That spawned rumors that India was on the trade block as Cincinnati sought controllable starting pitching, but he stayed put at the trade deadline before missing most of the second half with plantar fasciitis. India's feet are ostensibly healthy going into 2024, but it remains to be seen whether they'll be planted in Great American Ball Park dirt on Opening Day.

Luke Maile C Born: 02/06/91 Age: 33 Bats: R Throws: R Height: 6'3" Weight: 225 Origin: Round 8, 2012 Draft (#272 overall)

YEAR	TM	LVL	AGE	PA	R	HR	RBI	SB	AVG/OBP/SLG	BABIP	SLGCON	BB%	K%	ZSw%	ZCon%	OSw%	OCon%	LA	90th EV	DRC+	BRR	DRP	WARP
2021	NAS	AAA	30	155	17	1	15	2	.225/.351/.318	.359	.519	14.2%	32.3%							77	-0.1	8.1	0.9
2021	MIL	MLB	30	34	6	0	3	0	.300/.382/.433	.391	.565	8.8%	20.6%	66.7%	84.6%	36.5%	54.8%	1.8	102.4	86	0.0	0.1	0.1
2022	CLE	MLB	31	206	19	3	17	0	.221/.301/.326	.291	.465	9.2%	26.2%	65.7%	81.7%	28.2%	54.7%	17.6	101.4	76	-0.2	0.5	0.2
2023	CIN	MLB	32	199	17	6	25	2	.235/.308/.391	.290	.538	7.0%	24.6%	66.7%	80.7%	26.4%	60.7%	13.5	102.9	84	-0.1	-3.8	0.0
2024 DC	CIN	MLB	33	181	17	4	17	1	.220/.298/.342	.283	.463	8.1%	24.5%							79	-0.2	0.3	0.2

2023 GP: C (71), P (4), DH (1)   *Comps: Jeff Mathis (59), Martín Maldonado (57), Sandy León (55)*

YEAR	TM	P. COUNT	FRM RUNS	BLK RUNS	THRW RUNS	TOT RUNS
2021	NAS	5546	8.5	0.0	0.0	8.5
2021	MIL	1125	0.3	0.0	0.0	0.3
2022	CLE	8237	0.6	0.1	0.9	1.6
2023	CIN	8624	-3.9	0.0	1.0	-2.9
2024	CIN	7215	0.2	0.0	0.2	0.3

Being a back-up catcher can be a pretty sweet gig. Call it the Jeff Mathis Corollary: you don't have to hit at all as long as you're excellent defensively. Last year, though, Maile didn't tear the cover off the ball *or* field particularly well, posting negative defensive and framing metrics for the first time in his career. Early in the offseason the Reds re-signed him anyway, both to be Tyler Stephenson's caddy and to maintain his status as a leader—in a very green clubhouse and among a young and talented rotation. Not bad for a back-up catcher who didn't quite catch as expected.

Trey Mancini 1B/DH Born: 03/18/92 Age: 32 Bats: R Throws: R Height: 6'3" Weight: 230 Origin: Round 8, 2013 Draft (#249 overall)

YEAR	TM	LVL	AGE	PA	R	HR	RBI	SB	AVG/OBP/SLG	BABIP	SLGCON	BB%	K%	ZSw%	ZCon%	OSw%	OCon%	LA	90th EV	DRC+	BRR	DRP	WARP
2021	BAL	MLB	29	616	77	21	71	0	.255/.326/.432	.308	.581	8.3%	23.2%	67.7%	80.1%	33.8%	58.1%	9.9	107.8	107	-0.4	0.3	1.9
2022	HOU	MLB	30	186	17	8	22	0	.176/.258/.364	.191	.517	9.7%	26.3%	67.9%	83.5%	36.2%	58.2%	14.3	103.4	76	-0.1	-0.7	-0.1
2022	BAL	MLB	30	401	39	10	41	0	.268/.347/.404	.326	.534	8.7%	21.4%	69.3%	82.9%	32.2%	56.9%	12.4	105.5	107	-0.1	-1.2	1.1
2023	CHC	MLB	31	263	31	4	28	0	.234/.299/.336	.327	.503	8.0%	29.7%	70.2%	79.4%	34.3%	49.5%	12.1	104.0	64	-0.3	-0.1	-0.6
2024 non	CIN	MLB	32	251	25	7	27	0	.226/.300/.367	.289	.516	8.3%	26.2%							89	0.0	-0.6	0.1

2023 GP: 1B (51), DH (22), RF (5)   *Comps: Jerry Morales (68), Ruben Sierra (67), Tony Clark (67)*

Mancini was seen as a good value signing by the Cubs prior to 2023, a veteran presence intended to support Chicago's young core and form half of a first base Voltron with Eric Hosmer. The robot they actually resembled was a Star Wars battle droid: wholly ineffective and easily dispatched by even the most novice of foes, be they Jedi or your garden variety pitcher. Mancini still started more games at first base for the Cubs than anyone not named Cody Bellinger, but Chicago designated him for assignment by late August. Aside from a short minor-league stint with the Reds, Mancini is presumably looking to turn the page on a generally unproductive 2023—just as Disney did with the Star Wars Expanded Universe immediately upon the franchise's acquisition.

★ ★ ★ *2024 Top 101 Prospect* **#25** ★ ★ ★

Noelvi Marte SS/3B Born: 10/16/01 Age: 22 Bats: R Throws: R Height: 6'0" Weight: 216 Origin: IFA, 2018

YEAR	TM	LVL	AGE	PA	R	HR	RBI	SB	AVG/OBP/SLG	BABIP	SLGCON	BB%	K%	ZSw%	ZCon%	OSw%	OCon%	LA	90th EV	DRC+	BRR	DRP	WARP
2021	MOD	A	19	478	87	17	69	23	.271/.368/.462	.326	.622	12.1%	22.2%							123	4.1	-1.1	3.1
2021	EVE	A+	19	33	4	0	2	1	.290/.333/.419	.450	.650	6.1%	33.3%							95	0.4	0.9	0.2
2022	DAY	A+	20	126	12	4	13	10	.292/.397/.443	.338	.566	13.5%	18.3%							112	-0.1	0.0	0.6
2022	EVE	A+	20	394	62	15	55	13	.275/.363/.462	.321	.612	10.7%	21.3%							115	-1.0	0.0	1.9
2023	CHA	AA	21	222	37	8	25	10	.281/.356/.464	.309	.576	9.9%	17.1%							116	-1.7	0.4	1.0
2023	LOU	AAA	21	167	31	3	20	8	.280/.365/.455	.330	.580	12.0%	18.6%	64.4%	87.4%	30.9%	50.9%			101	1.1	-0.8	0.5
2023	CIN	MLB	21	123	15	3	15	6	.316/.366/.456	.384	.584	6.5%	20.3%	66.7%	84.6%	30.4%	54.8%	2.1	107.9	90	0.2	-0.4	0.2
2024 DC	CIN	MLB	22	500	50	12	52	16	.245/.314/.377	.312	.510	7.9%	23.9%							94	0.3	-1	0.9

2023 GP: 3B (29), SS (4), 2B (1), DH (1)   *Comps: David Wright (61), Bo Bichette (58), Brett Lawrie (58)*

Marte has a somewhat similar profile to fellow infielder Christian Encarnacion-Strand, in that he hammers the ball and it remains to be seen where he'll stand in the field, long-term. Marte was already moved off shortstop as he entered his 20s, and may also have to move away from the hot corner to an outfield corner as his body matures. This has been his profile since he signed as a teenager out of the Dominican Republic, but it hasn't mattered too much because he rakes everywhere he goes. Even in a month's worth of games in the majors, he didn't show many signs of slowing up any time soon.

Matt McLain MI   Born: 08/06/99   Age: 24   Bats: R   Throws: R   Height: 5'8"   Weight: 180   Origin: Round 1, 2021 Draft (#17 overall)

YEAR	TM	LVL	AGE	PA	R	HR	RBI	SB	AVG/OBP/SLG	BABIP	SLGCON	BB%	K%	ZSw%	ZCon%	OSw%	OCon%	LA	90th EV	DRC+	BRR	DRP	WARP
2021	DAY	A+	21	119	15	3	19	10	.273/.387/.424	.329	.560	14.3%	20.2%							111	0.4	1.3	0.7
2022	CHA	AA	22	452	67	17	58	27	.232/.363/.453	.300	.689	15.5%	28.1%							129	2.5	-9.1	2.3
2023	LOU	AAA	23	180	30	12	40	10	.340/.467/.688	.385	.925	16.7%	20.6%	61.0%	80.0%	25.2%	61.1%			145	-1.3	1.6	1.5
2023	CIN	MLB	23	403	65	16	50	14	.290/.357/.507	.385	.740	7.7%	28.5%	59.0%	82.9%	29.6%	56.7%	13.9	104.1	86	0.5	2.8	0.9
2024 DC	CIN	MLB	24	529	60	18	64	17	.237/.325/.414	.305	.592	9.7%	26.8%							104	0.3	1.8	2.1

2023 GP: SS (53), 2B (37), DH (4)   *Comps: Ian Desmond (76), Paul DeJong (73), Tim Anderson (70)*

After the team futzed around with Jose Barrero at shortstop for the season's first couple months, McLain and Elly De La Cruz debuted in mid-May and early June to form a sort of symbiote at shortstop, if those correlated organisms out a third of the time and posted a BABIP well above the league average. The UCLA product still played as well as any member of Cincinnati's sterling rookie class, enough to limit some of the team's other young infielders to part-time work (though DRC+ was less than impressed). McLain may not line up at the six long-term—that's understandable when you play on the same team as De La Cruz—but his 2023 performance and well-rounded offensive profile make him a player around whom the Reds can plan for the next half-decade.

Wil Myers RF/1B   Born: 12/10/90   Age: 33   Bats: R   Throws: R   Height: 6'3"   Weight: 207   Origin: Round 3, 2009 Draft (#91 overall)

YEAR	TM	LVL	AGE	PA	R	HR	RBI	SB	AVG/OBP/SLG	BABIP	SLGCON	BB%	K%	ZSw%	ZCon%	OSw%	OCon%	LA	90th EV	DRC+	BRR	DRP	WARP
2021	SD	MLB	30	500	56	17	63	8	.256/.334/.434	.333	.638	10.8%	28.2%	66.4%	76.8%	31.2%	54.9%	10.6	104.0	84	0.2	-0.2	0.5
2022	ELP	AAA	31	38	3	2	3	0	.229/.289/.429	.250	.577	7.9%	23.7%	73.4%	78.7%	27.2%	50.0%			99	-0.5	-0.2	0.0
2022	SD	MLB	31	286	29	7	41	2	.261/.315/.398	.357	.594	7.3%	30.1%	64.8%	80.7%	31.7%	51.8%	13.0	103.5	83	0.2	0.7	0.2
2023	LOU	AAA	32	29	4	1	3	0	.185/.241/.296	.211	.400	6.9%	24.1%	65.5%	73.7%	27.0%	52.9%			98	0.0	-0.9	0.0
2023	CIN	MLB	32	141	11	3	12	2	.189/.257/.283	.273	.456	8.5%	34.0%	57.2%	77.0%	32.5%	44.1%	9.9	102.8	59	0.2	-0.7	-0.4
2024 non	CIN	MLB	33	251	25	7	27	3	.222/.291/.368	.303	.560	8.4%	31.0%							85	0.0	-0.9	0.0

2023 GP: RF (27), 1B (13), DH (4)   *Comps: Justin Upton (65), Candy Maldonado (63), Dwight Evans (62)*

On April 15, Myers went 4-5 with a double, two home runs and five RBI. He played 23 more games for the Reds after that date, recording more than one hit in only one and knocking just a singular additional double and home run. Myers was later jettisoned from the organization in late June after a month on the IL and remained a free agent all season. It's possible this is the end of the line for the former top prospect, but he has plenty of incentive to hang around for another year: He's less than a year of service time from passing the 10-year threshold, with all the benefits of pension and respect that milestone accords.

Spencer Steer 1B   Born: 12/07/97   Age: 26   Bats: R   Throws: R   Height: 5'11"   Weight: 185   Origin: Round 3, 2019 Draft (#90 overall)

YEAR	TM	LVL	AGE	PA	R	HR	RBI	SB	AVG/OBP/SLG	BABIP	SLGCON	BB%	K%	ZSw%	ZCon%	OSw%	OCon%	LA	90th EV	DRC+	BRR	DRP	WARP
2021	CR	A+	23	208	37	10	24	4	.274/.409/.506	.283	.625	16.8%	15.4%							143	2.5	-0.1	1.9
2021	WCH	AA	23	280	45	14	42	4	.241/.304/.470	.274	.665	7.1%	26.1%							99	0.6	2.7	1.1
2022	WCH	AA	24	156	27	8	30	1	.307/.385/.591	.318	.711	9.0%	14.7%							130	-0.5	1.3	1.1
2022	STP	AAA	24	232	39	12	32	2	.242/.345/.485	.248	.619	12.1%	18.5%							119	0.3	-1.3	1.1
2022	LOU	AAA	24	104	14	3	13	1	.293/.375/.467	.364	.623	8.7%	22.1%							100	0.5	-0.6	0.3
2022	CIN	MLB	24	108	12	2	8	0	.211/.306/.326	.269	.449	10.2%	24.1%	60.2%	88.3%	29.6%	65.8%	13.8	102.0	83	0.0	0.1	0.1
2023	CIN	MLB	25	665	74	23	86	15	.271/.356/.464	.318	.609	10.2%	20.9%	65.7%	85.6%	29.5%	61.6%	15.7	103.9	105	0.3	-2.6	1.9
2024 DC	CIN	MLB	26	565	62	18	66	7	.237/.322/.402	.278	.523	9.3%	20.9%							100	0.0	-2.9	1.2

2023 GP: 1B (73), 3B (47), LF (45), 2B (16), DH (6), RF (3)   *Comps: Brian Anderson (57), Nick Evans (57), Lucas Duda (57)*

The Tyler Mahle trade keeps looking worse and worse for Minnesota. First, Mahle's season was halted after five starts because he needed Tommy John surgery. Then, the Twins had to watch from a distance as the two players they dealt for Mahle—Steer and Christian Encarnacion-Strand—played like cornerstones for a lineup that's bursting with young talent. Steer played all over the diamond to accommodate the Reds' other infielders and keep his bat in the lineup, appearing mostly at first base, third base and in left field. As a result, Steer played in all but six of Cincinnati's games; he also led the team in home runs. Fair to say he was the most valuable Steer in the Midwest.

Tyler Stephenson C/DH   Born: 08/16/96   Age: 27   Bats: R   Throws: R   Height: 6'4"   Weight: 225   Origin: Round 1, 2015 Draft (#11 overall)

YEAR	TM	LVL	AGE	PA	R	HR	RBI	SB	AVG/OBP/SLG	BABIP	SLGCON	BB%	K%	ZSw%	ZCon%	OSw%	OCon%	LA	90th EV	DRC+	BRR	DRP	WARP
2021	CIN	MLB	24	402	56	10	45	0	.286/.366/.431	.333	.549	10.2%	18.7%	66.6%	91.3%	22.4%	60.0%	7.6	102.4	102	0.1	1.1	1.8
2022	CIN	MLB	25	183	24	6	35	1	.319/.372/.482	.409	.672	6.6%	25.7%	66.9%	82.5%	25.8%	54.2%	11.3	100.9	93	-0.2	-1.2	0.3
2023	CIN	MLB	26	517	59	13	56	0	.243/.317/.378	.314	.533	9.1%	26.1%	65.1%	82.6%	24.7%	48.8%	9.2	103.6	67	-0.8	-10.7	-1.6
2024 DC	CIN	MLB	27	465	48	12	50	0	.241/.320/.378	.313	.526	8.8%	25.6%							95	0.0	-2.5	1.2

2023 GP: C (92), DH (43), 1B (8)   *Comps: Derek Norris (67), Jimmie Wilson (66), Welington Castillo (63)*

YEAR	TM	P. COUNT	FRM RUNS	BLK RUNS	THRW RUNS	TOT RUNS
2021	CIN	10089	3.0	-0.4	-0.1	2.6
2022	CIN	6198	-0.6	-0.1	0.3	-0.4
2023	CIN	12140	-9.1	-0.2	0.0	-9.2
2024	CIN	15632	-1.9	-0.4	-0.1	-2.4

Stephenson looked like a franchise two-way catcher when he wasn't hurt in 2021 and 2022, so those Reds probably would have been over the moon to know he would appear in 142 games in 2023, including about 92 behind the dish. However, Stephenson's bat virtually disappeared even as his hard-hit rate increased and most of his numbers under the hood remained the same. But that's all right because he was a capable defensive backstop, right? Reader, he was not, posting a Defensive Runs Prevented mark of -10.0 that was among the worst in the league. Caveats about catching defensive metrics aside, it's tough sledding when your ostensible two-way catcher stops being good on either side of the ball.

PITCHERS

Andrew Abbott LHP   Born: 06/01/99   Age: 25   Height: 6'0"   Weight: 192   Origin: Round 2, 2021 Draft (#53 overall)

YEAR	TM	LVL	AGE	G (GS)	IP	W-L	SV	K	WHIP	ERA	CSP	BB%	K%	HR%	GB%	ZSw%	ZCon%	OSw%	OCon%	BABIP	SLGCON	DRA-	WARP
2021	DBT	A	22	4(3)	11	0-0	0	19	1.36	4.91		8.2%	38.8%	4.1%	48.0%	69.8%	67.6%	31.3%	42.3%	.391	.840	84	0.2
2022	DAY	A+	23	5(4)	27	3-0	0	40	0.85	0.67		6.8%	38.8%	1.0%	47.3%					.278	.382	76	0.6
2022	CHA	AA	23	20(20)	91	7-7	0	119	1.37	4.75		10.6%	30.8%	1.8%	43.4%					.360	.582	80	1.9
2023	CHA	AA	24	3(3)	15²	1-0	0	36	0.57	1.15		5.4%	64.3%	0.0%	41.2%					.353	.471	50	0.7
2023	LOU	AAA	24	7(7)	38¹	3-0	0	54	1.07	3.05		9.0%	34.8%	5.2%	37.2%	65.0%	78.4%	32.4%	50.0%	.244	.640	76	1.1
2023	CIN	MLB	24	21(21)	109¹	8-6	0	120	1.32	3.87	47.7%	9.6%	26.1%	3.5%	28.6%	68.1%	84.2%	31.8%	60.1%	.302	.602	112	0.6
2024 DC	CIN	MLB	25	19(19)	101	5-7	0	109	1.33	4.54	47.7%	9.8%	25.5%	4.2%	30.7%					.294	.612	100	0.9

2023 Arsenal: FA (92.7), SW (82.8), CU (80.8), CH (86.6)   Comps: Wade Miley (70), Matthew Boyd (67), Andrew Suárez (65)

It's a shame Abbott never got to appear in the same rotation as Luis Castillo, but the young southpaw did give the 2023 Reds a desperately needed dependable starter, with strikeout stuff to boot. Even considering that Abbott outpitched his DRA and didn't entirely alleviate command and control concerns, he's the kind of pitcher the Reds can build around alongside Hunter Greene and Nick Lodolo. The biggest red flag might be Abbott's final two months, over which he had an ERA north of six and opponents slashed .307/.382/.508. In other words, the answer to "who's on first?" was likely to be "opposing hitters."

Graham Ashcraft RHP   Born: 02/11/98   Age: 26   Height: 6'2"   Weight: 248   Origin: Round 6, 2019 Draft (#174 overall)

YEAR	TM	LVL	AGE	G (GS)	IP	W-L	SV	K	WHIP	ERA	CSP	BB%	K%	HR%	GB%	ZSw%	ZCon%	OSw%	OCon%	BABIP	SLGCON	DRA-	WARP
2021	DAY	A+	23	8(8)	38²	4-1	0	55	1.06	2.33		8.1%	34.2%	0.0%	54.5%					.322	.353	63	1.2
2021	CHA	AA	23	14(14)	72¹	7-3	0	74	1.13	3.36		8.2%	25.3%	1.4%	59.6%					.287	.417	87	1.2
2022	LOU	AAA	24	8(8)	35¹	3-2	0	35	1.67	2.29		9.9%	20.5%	0.0%	66.7%					.359	.400	96	0.5
2022	CIN	MLB	24	19(19)	105	5-6	0	71	1.42	4.89	54.9%	6.5%	15.3%	2.4%	54.4%	72.7%	89.5%	31.9%	67.7%	.314	.486	103	0.8
2023	CIN	MLB	25	26(26)	145²	7-9	0	111	1.37	4.76	49.1%	8.3%	17.8%	3.7%	47.5%	68.3%	87.6%	32.5%	61.6%	.293	.555	108	1.1
2024 DC	CIN	MLB	26	26(26)	142¹	8-10	0	106	1.43	4.85	51.3%	8.6%	17.0%	2.7%	49.6%					.306	.510	105	0.9

2023 Arsenal: HC (96), SW (88.3), SI (96.5)   Comps: David Buchanan (73), Ben Lively (72), Anthony DeSclafani (69)

Looking at the rate stats, one wouldn't expect Ashcraft to throw fastballs in the mid and upper 90s alongside sliders in the upper 80s, with a strikeout rate that's closer to Zack Greinke than Zack Wheeler. That's mostly a function of Ashcraft's poor fastball shape and characteristics that make the pitch far too hittable. Case in point: Ashcraft threw his cutter more than any other pitch in 2023, but against it opposing players hit .290 and slugged .434. He's a perfectly serviceable arm, but barring changes to his repertoire or better luck on all those ground balls, the Reds might be better off not giving Ashcraft 100+ innings again.

Fernando Cruz RHP   Born: 03/28/90   Age: 34   Height: 6'2"   Weight: 237   Origin: Round 6, 2007 Draft (#186 overall)

YEAR	TM	LVL	AGE	G (GS)	IP	W-L	SV	K	WHIP	ERA	CSP	BB%	K%	HR%	GB%	ZSw%	ZCon%	OSw%	OCon%	BABIP	SLGCON	DRA-	WARP
2022	LOU	AAA	32	51(0)	56	4-4	23	66	1.04	2.89		8.4%	29.3%	1.8%	41.2%					.267	.450	79	1.4
2022	CIN	MLB	32	14(2)	14²	0-1	0	21	1.23	1.23	48.1%	14.1%	32.8%	1.6%	39.4%	71.8%	73.2%	33.9%	52.6%	.250	.424	94	0.2
2023	CIN	MLB	33	58(2)	66	1-2	0	98	1.21	4.91	44.9%	10.0%	35.1%	2.2%	30.5%	71.0%	79.3%	34.8%	47.9%	.319	.608	78	1.5
2024 DC	CIN	MLB	34	36(0)	39	2-1	0	51	1.27	4.21	45.4%	10.0%	30.8%	4.2%	33.0%					.298	.639	93	0.3

2023 Arsenal: FS (81.5), FA (94.4), SL (88), CU (83.5), SI (92.8)   Comps: Caleb Thielbar (61), Pat Venditte (60), Steve Cishek (58)

More frequently than any other position, relievers post incredible statistics in complete anonymity. Enter Cruz, who was originally drafted as a third baseman, converted to pitching and floated around the minor, Mexican and independent leagues for more than a decade before making his MLB debut in 2022 and posting a 35% strikeout rate in 2023. That was mainly driven by a flat-out dominant splitter: He threw 409 of them, which returned just 11 hits and a .154 slugging percentage. The ERA wasn't sexy, but the DRA decidedly was; Cruz cemented himself as one of the Reds' best late-inning options ahead of Alexis Díaz.

Alexis Díaz RHP   Born: 09/28/96   Age: 27   Height: 6'2"   Weight: 224   Origin: Round 12, 2015 Draft (#355 overall)

YEAR	TM	LVL	AGE	G (GS)	IP	W-L	SV	K	WHIP	ERA	CSP	BB%	K%	HR%	GB%	ZSw%	ZCon%	OSw%	OCon%	BABIP	SLGCON	DRA-	WARP
2021	CHA	AA	24	35(0)	42¹	3-1	2	70	1.18	3.83		11.1%	38.9%	1.1%	43.0%					.333	.494	68	1.1
2022	CIN	MLB	25	59(0)	63²	7-3	10	83	0.96	1.84	50.4%	12.9%	32.5%	2.0%	29.9%	69.4%	78.0%	35.2%	46.2%	.180	.354	92	0.9
2023	CIN	MLB	26	71(0)	67¹	9-6	37	86	1.19	3.07	42.0%	12.6%	30.1%	1.4%	37.7%	70.1%	77.2%	32.6%	49.6%	.270	.440	87	1.2
2024 DC	CIN	MLB	27	62(0)	65¹	5-6	32	86	1.33	4.52	45.6%	12.0%	30.4%	4.1%	34.9%					.289	.633	98	0.4

2023 Arsenal: SL (87.6), FA (94.8)   Comps: Kyle Barraclough (93), Reyes Moronta (92), Ryan Cook (86)

While it wasn't quite as good as his older brother Edwin's 2022 performance, Díaz turned in one of the best relief seasons in baseball and earned his first All-Star nod after looking nearly unhittable for most of the spring and early summer. Even as he looked gassed for much of August and September, walking nearly as many as he struck out across 20 innings and blowing a pair of saves that potentially kept the Reds out of the playoffs, Díaz is the most important relief arm Cincinnati has going forward. There's a non-zero chance he becomes the better reliever in the family soon, too.

Buck Farmer   RHP   Born: 02/20/91   Age: 33   Height: 6'4"   Weight: 243   Origin: Round 5, 2013 Draft (#156 overall)

YEAR	TM	LVL	AGE	G (GS)	IP	W-L	SV	K	WHIP	ERA	CSP	BB%	K%	HR%	GB%	ZSw%	ZCon%	OSw%	OCon%	BABIP	SLGCON	DRA-	WARP
2021	TOL	AAA	30	9(0)	11¹	0-2	0	7	1.32	3.97		8.3%	14.6%	0.0%	36.1%					.306	.361	107	0.0
2021	RR	AAA	30	15(0)	15	2-1	8	15	1.13	3.60		9.8%	24.6%	1.6%	42.5%					.263	.395	87	0.1
2021	DET	MLB	30	36(0)	35¹	0-0	0	37	1.73	6.37	49.8%	12.3%	21.6%	5.3%	37.0%	68.8%	79.6%	31.3%	66.9%	.313	.673	130	-0.2
2022	LOU	AAA	31	20(0)	22¹	0-3	1	34	1.21	3.63		9.8%	37.0%	4.3%	28.6%					.311	.633	78	0.6
2022	CIN	MLB	31	44(0)	47	2-2	2	54	1.30	3.83	48.0%	12.6%	27.1%	1.0%	42.0%	67.4%	79.1%	34.7%	58.4%	.293	.436	94	0.6
2023	CIN	MLB	32	71(0)	75	4-5	3	70	1.16	4.20	45.7%	9.4%	22.7%	3.6%	32.5%	67.8%	77.4%	33.0%	59.7%	.244	.542	103	0.7
2024 DC	CIN	MLB	33	49(0)	52	3-2	0	53	1.38	4.85	46.8%	9.9%	23.6%	4.1%	36.8%					.296	.604	105	0.1

2023 Arsenal: FA (94.1), SW (83.2), CH (88.2), SL (84.6)   *Comps: Tommy Hunter (50), Matt Guerrier (49), Liam Hendriks (49)*

A decade into his major-league career, Farmer had one of his best efforts by WARP in 2023 and blew past his previous career-high innings total, finishing exactly two outs behind the Reds' most-used reliever, Ian Gibaut. Of course, Farmer also seeded plenty of opponent comebacks when it mattered most, posting an ERA north of five in 35 ⅓ innings from the start of July though the end of the season. It was a likely enough result to make a few Reds fans utter half of the spoonerism of Farmer's name down the stretch.

Ty Floyd   RHP   Born: 08/28/01   Age: 22   Height: 6'2"   Weight: 200   Origin: Round 1, 2023 Draft (#38 overall)

After tying a College World Series record by punching out 17 Florida hitters to help LSU win the national title, the Reds took Floyd with the 38th-overall pick. Much like their first-round pick Rhett Lowder, Floyd profiles as a quick-moving starter and pairs a rising mid-90s fastball with a slider and changeup that both project to be at least average pitches down the road. If it all breaks right, Floyd's the kind of pitcher who could reach the majors in the next couple years. The Reds will certainly be tickled pink if he does.

Ian Gibaut   RHP   Born: 11/19/93   Age: 30   Height: 6'3"   Weight: 250   Origin: Round 11, 2015 Draft (#328 overall)

YEAR	TM	LVL	AGE	G (GS)	IP	W-L	SV	K	WHIP	ERA	CSP	BB%	K%	HR%	GB%	ZSw%	ZCon%	OSw%	OCon%	BABIP	SLGCON	DRA-	WARP
2021	STP	AAA	27	32(1)	45	1-4	0	54	1.67	6.80		10.1%	26.0%	2.4%	48.9%					.389	.638	80	1.1
2021	MIN	MLB	27	3(0)	6²	0-0	0	4	1.35	2.70	58.6%	7.1%	14.3%	7.1%	52.4%	94.3%	84.8%	37.7%	57.7%	.263	.667	108	0.0
2022	COL	AAA	28	17(0)	19²	2-0	3	19	1.22	3.20		10.1%	24.1%	0.0%	51.9%					.308	.412	97	0.3
2022	CIN	MLB	28	33(0)	34²	1-2	1	48	1.62	4.67	52.8%	11.7%	31.2%	1.9%	39.8%	64.9%	82.1%	30.6%	62.3%	.412	.693	86	0.6
2022	CLE	MLB	28	1(0)	1¹	0-0	0	0	0.75	0.00	60.1%	0.0%	0.0%	0.0%	20.0%	61.5%	62.5%	40.0%	100.0%	.200	.200	91	0.0
2023	CIN	MLB	29	74(0)	75²	8-4	3	69	1.28	3.33	50.5%	8.8%	21.7%	2.5%	39.8%	72.4%	82.2%	34.2%	60.8%	.295	.484	90	1.3
2024 DC	CIN	MLB	30	49(0)	52	3-2	0	48	1.39	4.73	51.3%	9.8%	21.1%	3.5%	40.6%					.296	.555	103	0.2

2023 Arsenal: FA (95.3), FC (91.7), SW (84.1), CH (86.3)   *Comps: Tommy Kahnle (71), J.J. Hoover (66), Fernando Salas (66)*

Gibaut bounced across multiple organizations before 2023, when he suddenly found himself the Reds' set-up man, leading the bullpen in innings despite punching out hitters at a lower rate than in any other professional stint of at least seven innings. Go figure. Though he made his name as a changeup artist, Gibaut's fastball has been arguably his best pitch since joining Cincinnati, drawing a .291 slugging percentage from opposing hitters despite a fairly average shape. Repeat efforts from pop-up relievers like Gibaut aren't always a given, but going forward the Reds expect him to help anchor a sometimes-shaky bullpen unit.

Hunter Greene   RHP   Born: 08/06/99   Age: 24   Height: 6'5"   Weight: 242   Origin: Round 1, 2017 Draft (#2 overall)

YEAR	TM	LVL	AGE	G (GS)	IP	W-L	SV	K	WHIP	ERA	CSP	BB%	K%	HR%	GB%	ZSw%	ZCon%	OSw%	OCon%	BABIP	SLGCON	DRA-	WARP
2021	CHA	AA	21	7(7)	41	5-0	0	60	1.00	1.98		8.6%	37.0%	1.2%	41.2%					.301	.447	92	0.6
2021	LOU	AAA	21	14(14)	65¹	5-8	0	79	1.29	4.13		9.1%	28.6%	4.0%	45.2%					.306	.611	84	1.4
2022	LOU	AAA	22	3(3)	7	0-0	0	15	1.14	2.57		6.7%	50.0%	0.0%	33.3%					.500	.750	70	0.2
2022	CIN	MLB	22	24(24)	125²	5-13	0	164	1.21	4.44	52.8%	9.0%	30.9%	4.5%	30.1%	71.3%	76.4%	33.5%	55.9%	.281	.646	101	1.2
2023	LOU	AAA	23	3(3)	12	0-0	0	12	1.08	3.00		14.3%	24.5%	4.1%	36.7%	70.8%	78.4%	28.8%	35.3%	.143	.433	101	0.2
2023	CIN	MLB	23	22(22)	112	4-7	0	152	1.42	4.82	46.2%	9.6%	30.5%	3.8%	34.5%	70.4%	80.0%	33.9%	54.0%	.342	.731	88	2.0
2024 DC	CIN	MLB	24	26(26)	132	7-9	0	162	1.28	4.37	49.2%	9.8%	29.0%	4.3%	32.8%					.293	.633	96	1.4

2023 Arsenal: FA (98.7), SL (87.7), CH (91.5)   *Comps: Taijuan Walker (67), Luis Severino (67), Jack Flaherty (65)*

Greene has been almost exactly league-average since debuting in 2022, mixing tantalizing starts like his six-inning, no-hit, 11-strikeout performance against the Cubs in late May with others like his August 20 matchup against the Blue Jays, when he allowed five homers and eight earned runs over three innings. The unfortunate thing for Greene is that he was actually quite good for the season's first two months and change before hip soreness kept him off the mound for two months. His first start back from the IL was that clunker against Toronto, and he ultimately allowed 10 dingers in 38 ⅔ innings across his final eight starts. Greene has as much or more talent as any other pitcher who toed the rubber for the Reds in 2023. You'd sure like to see it for more than 120 innings at a time, though.

Kevin Herget RHP   Born: 04/03/91   Age: 33   Height: 5'10"   Weight: 185   Origin: Round 39, 2013 Draft (#1175 overall)

YEAR	TM	LVL	AGE	G (GS)	IP	W-L	SV	K	WHIP	ERA	CSP	BB%	K%	HR%	GB%	ZSw%	ZCon%	OSw%	OCon%	BABIP	SLGCON	DRA-	WARP
2021	COL	AAA	30	28(7)	80¹	7-5	2	85	1.31	4.48		6.7%	24.6%	5.2%	41.6%					.299	.665	101	1.0
2022	DUR	AAA	31	21(17)	97²	8-1	0	99	1.24	2.95		3.9%	24.4%	3.2%	36.0%	78.9%	85.9%	40.0%	69.6%	.333	.600	93	1.6
2022	TB	MLB	31	3(0)	7	0-1	0	4	1.29	7.71	57.5%	0.0%	13.3%	0.0%	34.6%	70.2%	87.9%	34.4%	68.2%	.346	.583	109	0.0
2023	LOU	AAA	32	34(5)	47¹	2-3	0	48	1.54	5.13		10.0%	22.7%	3.8%	41.0%	67.5%	73.7%	26.8%	64.3%	.336	.654	96	0.7
2023	CIN	MLB	32	14(0)	24¹	1-2	1	13	1.32	5.18	50.7%	5.7%	12.4%	3.8%	33.3%	67.6%	85.0%	31.7%	72.6%	.275	.571	116	0.1
2024 non	CIN	MLB	33	58(0)	50	2-2	0	36	1.37	5.12	51.9%	6.5%	16.7%	4.0%	35.2%					.296	.573	115	-0.2

2023 Arsenal: FA (92.6), CH (83.6), FC (85.5), CU (76.3), SL (82.4), SW (81), SI (92.9)   *Comps: Justin Miller (46), Javy Guerra (43), Dan Otero (42)*

If Herget had thrown enough innings to qualify (read: way more than 24 ⅓) he would have had one of the 15 worst hard-hit rates in the league at 44%—the same as Patrick Corbin. That doesn't tell the full story, though: Cy Young finalists Zac Gallen and Logan Webb had the third- and fourth-worst hard hit rates in the league, respectively. Other contact pitchers like Brady Singer and Framber Valdez also allowed hard contact at some of the highest rates in the league. Those guys can get away with it, of course, because they also throw devastating secondary pitches. Herget really only throws one, a changeup that actually isn't that devastating, on which opposing hitters slugged .619. Put simply, it's hard to succeed when you don't strike anyone out and your ostensible best pitch gets tattooed consistently.

Derek Law RHP   Born: 09/14/90   Age: 33   Height: 6'3"   Weight: 225   Origin: Round 9, 2011 Draft (#297 overall)

YEAR	TM	LVL	AGE	G (GS)	IP	W-L	SV	K	WHIP	ERA	CSP	BB%	K%	HR%	GB%	ZSw%	ZCon%	OSw%	OCon%	BABIP	SLGCON	DRA-	WARP
2021	STP	AAA	30	18(3)	28¹	1-1	4	28	1.31	2.54		10.3%	23.9%	0.9%	59.7%					.316	.377	96	0.5
2021	MIN	MLB	30	9(0)	15	0-0	0	14	1.60	4.20	56.9%	11.9%	20.9%	3.0%	44.4%	68.9%	78.0%	33.5%	48.3%	.326	.614	108	0.1
2022	LOU	AAA	31	6(0)	8	0-0	0	3	0.88	1.13		10.7%	10.7%	0.0%	72.7%					.182	.227	102	0.1
2022	TOL	AAA	31	33(0)	39	1-3	15	44	1.21	3.23		6.2%	27.2%	1.2%	44.9%					.333	.510	87	0.8
2022	CIN	MLB	31	15(0)	17²	2-2	0	15	1.47	4.08	50.8%	8.9%	19.0%	2.5%	50.0%	61.8%	92.6%	35.3%	63.6%	.321	.545	96	0.2
2022	DET	MLB	31	2(0)	2	0-1	0	2	2.50	4.50	53.2%	7.7%	15.4%	7.7%	33.3%	75.0%	66.7%	25.8%	50.0%	.375	1.000	97	0.0
2023	CIN	MLB	32	54(3)	55	4-6	2	45	1.38	3.60	45.2%	10.8%	18.8%	2.5%	39.8%	71.2%	82.4%	31.9%	58.7%	.278	.463	107	0.4
2024 non	CIN	MLB	33	58(0)	50	2-2	0	45	1.42	4.79	47.2%	9.4%	20.6%	3.0%	43.1%					.304	.543	106	0.1

2023 Arsenal: FC (92.3), FA (95.8), SL (86.7), SI (95), CU (79.1), CH (88.8)   *Comps: Javy Guerra (66), Bryan Shaw (58), Nick Vincent (57)*

For the first time since his rookie year, Law was more or less a dependable and above-average middle reliever for more than a handful of games at a time. Some of his success can be chalked up to batted-ball luck, given a DRA that edged over five, but the Reds were not exactly in any position to be picky about the useful relief innings they got beyond Alexis Díaz. The 33-year-old journeyman has come a long way since making a name for himself by posting preposterous strikeout-to-walk ratios in the minor leagues, and largely pitches to contact now. Nevertheless, a couple hundred hitters stepped into the box and fought the Law in 2023, and for the first time in a while, the Law won.

Nick Lodolo LHP   Born: 02/05/98   Age: 26   Height: 6'6"   Weight: 216   Origin: Round 1, 2019 Draft (#7 overall)

YEAR	TM	LVL	AGE	G (GS)	IP	W-L	SV	K	WHIP	ERA	CSP	BB%	K%	HR%	GB%	ZSw%	ZCon%	OSw%	OCon%	BABIP	SLGCON	DRA-	WARP
2021	CHA	AA	23	10(10)	44	2-1	0	68	0.91	1.84		5.2%	39.3%	0.6%	53.3%					.337	.433	77	1.0
2022	CIN	MLB	24	19(19)	103¹	4-7	0	131	1.25	3.66	52.9%	8.8%	29.7%	2.9%	45.6%	63.0%	82.0%	32.2%	51.0%	.322	.595	101	1.0
2023	CIN	MLB	25	7(7)	34¹	2-1	0	47	1.75	6.29	46.6%	6.0%	28.3%	6.0%	45.1%	61.1%	86.7%	36.2%	50.0%	.440	.890	83	0.7
2024 DC	CIN	MLB	26	19(19)	83¹	4-6	0	99	1.25	4.26	50.9%	8.5%	27.9%	3.3%	45.3%					.305	.575	93	1.0

2023 Arsenal: FA (93.9), SW (80.2), CH (87.9), SI (93.9)   *Comps: Patrick Corbin (52), Zack Britton (51), Justus Sheffield (50)*

Things looked great for Lodolo through three starts in April, after which he owned a K-BB% of 28%. He then proceeded to get shelled in his next four starts before he was ruled out for the rest of May with what was initially diagnosed as left calf tendinitis. That quickly transpired to actually be a tibia stress fracture, which put him out for June and July as he hit the 60-day IL. Lodolo got rehabbing in August, making a start each at three levels before suffering another stress fracture in the same left tibia, ending his season for good. Given how many starts the Reds gave to the Luke Weavers and Luis Cessas of the world—61 combined starts went to pitchers with a DRA- of 115 or worse—a healthy and effective Lodolo would fortify their rotation more than almost any other pitcher in the organization. Even with the latter half of his meager season, in which he allowed a minimum of two homers in all four starts, the advanced metrics judged him the best of any Cincinnati starter to take the hill at least four times. Of that group of 12, only Lodolo and Hunter Greene earned a DRA- starting with an eight... or a nine. A healthy campaign would be a game-changer, both for the 26-year-old and his organization. Of course, we're talking about a player whose 116 innings in 2022 between Triple-A and the majors were easily the most he'd ever thrown in a season, including college, so "healthy" is a relative term.

───────────── ★ ★ ★ *2024 Top 101 Prospect* **#49** ★ ★ ★ ─────────────

Rhett Lowder RHP   Born: 03/08/02   Age: 22   Height: 6'2"   Weight: 200   Origin: Round 1, 2023 Draft (#7 overall)

YEAR	TM	LVL	AGE	G (GS)	IP	W-L	SV	K	WHIP	ERA	CSP	BB%	K%	HR%	GB%	ZSw%	ZCon%	OSw%	OCon%	BABIP	SLGCON	DRA-	WARP
2024 DC	CIN	MLB	22	13(3)	19¹	1-2	0	16	1.67	6.63		12.2%	18.4%	4.6%	35.0%					.312	.635	138	-0.3

Fresh off his epic, win-or-go-home duel with eventual first-overall pick Paul Skenes in the College World Series semi-finals, the Reds plucked Lowder out of Wake Forest with the seventh-overall pick and promptly shut the right-hander down for the rest of the year. No matter, as Lowder has the tools to move quickly toward Cincinnati's rotation on the back of an excellent slider and changeup and above-average command. He also had some of the best hair of any 2023 draftee, which gives him a minor resemblance to Jeff Spicoli. Lowder probably won't be catching any tasty waves on the Ohio River, but his potential should start generating a cool buzz for Reds fans later this year.

Nick Martinez   RHP   Born: 08/05/90   Age: 33   Height: 6'1"   Weight: 200   Origin: Round 18, 2011 Draft (#564 overall)

YEAR	TM	LVL	AGE	G (GS)	IP	W-L	SV	K	WHIP	ERA	CSP	BB%	K%	HR%	GB%	ZSw%	ZCon%	OSw%	OCon%	BABIP	SLGCON	DRA-	WARP
2022	SD	MLB	31	47(10)	106¹	4-4	8	95	1.29	3.47	54.0%	9.2%	21.2%	3.3%	47.4%	67.2%	84.3%	34.2%	61.7%	.276	.521	97	1.2
2023	SD	MLB	32	63(9)	110¹	6-4	1	106	1.26	3.43	46.3%	8.7%	23.0%	2.6%	52.1%	65.1%	85.0%	34.9%	54.7%	.294	.476	86	2.1
2024 DC	CIN	MLB	33	52(16)	115¹	6-6	0	107	1.33	4.23	49.6%	9.0%	21.8%	3.0%	43.0%					.296	.530	94	1.2

2023 Arsenal: CH (81), SI (93.2), KC (82.1), FC (89.8), FA (93.5), SL (86.5)   *Comps: LaTroy Hawkins (64), Vern Ruhle (64), Jamey Wright (63)*

Across two seasons in San Diego, Martinez gave the Padres basically identical results, but unlike in *The Matrix*, this déjà vu isn't a sign of impending doom but of a pitcher in his natural place. As a starter, he was sublime, with a 2.32 ERA and .557 OPS against in 42 ⅔ innings. As a reliever, he was less productive working as a setup option in the late innings, though he handcuffed righties, holding them to a .603 OPS overall. Now primarily a sinker-changeup pitcher—the former his go-to option against righties, the latter reserved for southpaws—he gets by on weak contact and grounders and misses bats with the slow ball, which carried a whiff rate of 46.5%. None of this is particularly sexy, but for the right club—say, one that has minimal starting pitching depth and could use a versatile swingman but doesn't want to spend a lot in the process—Martinez is a perfect fit. And right on cue, the Reds signed the veteran to a two-year deal in the hopes that he can produce his Padres numbers *ad infinitum*.

Sam Moll   LHP   Born: 01/03/92   Age: 32   Height: 5'9"   Weight: 190   Origin: Round 3, 2013 Draft (#77 overall)

YEAR	TM	LVL	AGE	G (GS)	IP	W-L	SV	K	WHIP	ERA	CSP	BB%	K%	HR%	GB%	ZSw%	ZCon%	OSw%	OCon%	BABIP	SLGCON	DRA-	WARP
2021	RNO	AAA	29	21(0)	21²	0-0	0	30	1.57	5.82		14.9%	29.7%	3.0%	44.4%					.314	.611	77	0.4
2021	LV	AAA	29	12(0)	13²	1-1	2	17	1.24	2.63		9.1%	30.9%	3.6%	57.6%					.323	.606	80	0.2
2021	OAK	MLB	29	8(0)	10¹	0-0	0	8	1.26	3.48	54.8%	11.4%	18.2%	2.3%	44.8%	53.1%	91.2%	25.2%	73.1%	.250	.379	106	0.1
2022	OAK	MLB	30	53(0)	43¹	2-1	0	46	1.27	2.91	53.8%	11.8%	24.6%	2.7%	50.0%	64.1%	83.7%	26.1%	60.0%	.252	.470	94	0.5
2023	OAK	MLB	31	45(1)	37²	0-3	1	46	1.41	4.54	48.7%	11.2%	27.1%	0.6%	53.1%	61.1%	82.3%	31.0%	67.6%	.340	.490	88	0.7
2023	CIN	MLB	31	25(0)	24²	2-0	0	22	0.97	0.73	47.7%	11.2%	22.4%	1.0%	49.2%	60.2%	87.0%	30.7%	65.1%	.190	.297	92	0.4
2024 DC	CIN	MLB	32	42(0)	45²	3-2	0	43	1.40	4.54	50.6%	11.2%	21.7%	2.8%	48.5%					.290	.515	98	0.3

2023 Arsenal: SW (82.1), SI (93.7), FA (94.2), CH (86)   *Comps: Sam Freeman (47), Scott Alexander (44), Adam Kolarek (44)*

Sammy Spinrate was the Reds' lone addition at the August 1 trade deadline, and he ended up being arguably the team's best bullpen weapon not named Alexis Díaz in the second half, striking out nearly a quarter of batters while getting over half of batted balls on the ground. Moll is never going to blow anyone away, but his hellion of a slider generates ugly swings and weak contact and has helped him evolve into a somewhat-underrated southpaw. Getting away from the anonymity of the Oakland A's bullpen will help with that, while providing the Reds have another useful arm they can pencil in for a 2024 roster with playoff aspirations and a desperate need for dependable pitching.

Frankie Montas   RHP   Born: 03/21/93   Age: 31   Height: 6'2"   Weight: 255   Origin: IFA, 2009

YEAR	TM	LVL	AGE	G (GS)	IP	W-L	SV	K	WHIP	ERA	CSP	BB%	K%	HR%	GB%	ZSw%	ZCon%	OSw%	OCon%	BABIP	SLGCON	DRA-	WARP
2021	OAK	MLB	28	32(32)	187	13-9	0	207	1.18	3.37	53.1%	7.3%	26.6%	2.6%	42.3%	71.4%	80.8%	37.1%	57.6%	.298	.526	90	2.7
2022	NYY	MLB	29	8(8)	39²	1-3	0	33	1.54	6.35	53.6%	8.1%	17.8%	3.2%	43.8%	71.9%	84.1%	35.6%	59.7%	.325	.598	109	0.2
2022	OAK	MLB	29	19(19)	104²	4-9	0	109	1.14	3.18	52.8%	6.6%	25.8%	2.8%	44.9%	75.8%	84.0%	37.0%	56.7%	.290	.516	87	1.7
2023	NYY	MLB	30	1(0)	1¹	1-0	0	1	2.25	0.00	39.3%	14.3%	14.3%	0.0%	80.0%	66.7%	66.7%	35.3%	66.7%	.400	.600	94	0.0
2024 DC	CIN	MLB	31	24(24)	116¹	6-7	0	114	1.29	4.24	52.5%	7.9%	23.3%	3.5%	43.5%					.301	.561	94	1.3

2023 Arsenal: SI (94.6), FS (85.7), SL (88.8), FA (95.5)   *Comps: Justin Masterson (64), Dave Goltz (62), Tyson Ross (61)*

Most Yankees fans were wary of trusting too much in Montas after he pitched so poorly in wake of the 2022 trade deadline. But they at least hoped that he would, y'know, *pitch*. Surgery in February to repair that aching right shoulder rendered his 2023 a wash in a hurry and locked in the deal that brought him to the Bronx as one of the worst in Brian Cashman's tenure as GM. Montas' lone appearance was a stint in relief on September 30, when New York had already been eliminated.

Emilio Pagán   RHP   Born: 05/07/91   Age: 33   Height: 6'2"   Weight: 208   Origin: Round 10, 2013 Draft (#297 overall)

YEAR	TM	LVL	AGE	G (GS)	IP	W-L	SV	K	WHIP	ERA	CSP	BB%	K%	HR%	GB%	ZSw%	ZCon%	OSw%	OCon%	BABIP	SLGCON	DRA-	WARP
2021	SD	MLB	30	67(0)	63¹	4-3	0	69	1.17	4.83	55.2%	6.8%	26.2%	6.1%	23.0%	77.7%	77.7%	33.7%	57.9%	.253	.717	117	0.0
2022	MIN	MLB	31	59(0)	63	4-6	9	84	1.37	4.43	52.4%	9.5%	30.7%	4.4%	39.9%	73.0%	74.2%	38.0%	63.5%	.320	.696	78	1.3
2023	MIN	MLB	32	66(1)	69¹	5-2	1	65	0.95	2.99	51.6%	7.7%	23.8%	1.8%	31.2%	77.0%	81.6%	35.4%	64.5%	.222	.415	100	0.8
2024 DC	CIN	MLB	33	49(0)	52	3-2	4	52	1.29	4.44	52.3%	8.5%	23.7%	4.2%	31.9%					.290	.597	98	0.3

2023 Arsenal: FA (95.9), FC (87.7), FS (86), CU (81.9)   *Comps: Brad Brach (73), Pedro Báez (69), Steve Cishek (69)*

Of the 276 pitchers who threw at least 1,000 pitches in 2023, only one hurler—Twins teammate Joe Ryan—got foul balls on a higher percentage of his offerings than Pagán. Take the 244 pitchers who got at least 500 swings and go by rate, instead of overall pitches, and the picture hardly changes at all. This is a sticky skill; it lives somewhere in each pitcher's interactions of approach, velocity and movement. Pagán stood out in a similar way in 2022. In most other respects, though, his 2023 was much different than the previous campaign, and the changes were for the better (if you trust your eyes and the results) or much for the worse (if you like advanced numbers when you're projecting pitcher performance). Pagán missed far fewer bats in the zone last year, and his strikeout rate predictably crashed. He better than halved opponents' home-run rate, too, though, and he walked fewer hitters. Guys who allow a lot of foul balls, above all, expose themselves to a lot of variance. Hitters struggle to square them up—but they also get more chances to see the one mistake they need. Pagán avoided those mistakes last year, but that skill is much less sticky.

★ ★ ★ *2024 Top 101 Prospect* **#72** ★ ★ ★

Connor Phillips RHP   Born: 05/04/01   Age: 23   Height: 6'2"   Weight: 209   Origin: Round 2, 2020 Draft (#64 overall)

YEAR	TM	LVL	AGE	G (GS)	IP	W-L	SV	K	WHIP	ERA	CSP	BB%	K%	HR%	GB%	ZSw%	ZCon%	OSw%	OCon%	BABIP	SLGCON	DRA-	WARP
2021	MOD	A	20	16(16)	72	7-3	0	104	1.47	4.75		13.7%	32.3%	0.3%	41.2%					.361	.467	95	0.6
2022	DAY	A+	21	12(12)	64	4-3	0	90	1.11	2.95		12.5%	35.2%	2.0%	46.5%					.279	.516	96	0.8
2022	CHA	AA	21	12(12)	45²	1-5	0	60	1.80	4.93		15.7%	27.6%	1.4%	28.7%					.378	.571	125	-0.2
2023	CHA	AA	22	14(14)	64²	2-2	0	111	1.31	3.34		9.5%	39.1%	3.2%	39.3%					.374	.698	61	2.2
2023	LOU	AAA	22	11(10)	40¹	2-3	1	43	1.56	4.69		16.9%	24.2%	0.6%	47.1%	62.7%	84.9%	27.1%	61.4%	.311	.452	95	0.8
2023	CIN	MLB	22	5(5)	20²	1-1	0	26	1.50	6.97	48.9%	13.5%	27.1%	5.2%	33.9%	61.6%	86.7%	27.5%	60.7%	.255	.607	111	0.1
2024 DC	*CIN*	*MLB*	*23*	*13(3)*	*26*	*1-2*	*0*	*27*	*1.53*	*5.36*	*48.9%*	*13.5%*	*23.6%*	*3.8%*	*35.9%*					*.295*	*.589*	*113*	*0.0*

2023 Arsenal: FA (96.6), SW (84.5), CU (82.2), CH (91.1)   *Comps: Sean Reid-Foley (78), Chris Archer (74), Edward Cabrera (71)*

Through a combination of graduations, injuries and underperformance, at times last summer Phillips looked like arguably the best upper-minors starting pitching prospect in the Reds' system. That performance didn't entirely translate to Phillips' 10 starts in Triple-A or his five in the majors, where he didn't benefit from the pre-tacked baseball used in the first half of the Double-A Southern League season. He was also pushed up to the majors more quickly than the Reds may have wanted, after six other pitchers were made unavailable due to illness, injury or poor performance. Nevertheless, Phillips looks like a future mid-rotation starter, with a lack of consistent command holding back a high-90s fastball and two breaking balls that both have the potential to be above-average.

Lucas Sims RHP   Born: 05/10/94   Age: 30   Height: 6'2"   Weight: 213   Origin: Round 1, 2012 Draft (#21 overall)

YEAR	TM	LVL	AGE	G (GS)	IP	W-L	SV	K	WHIP	ERA	CSP	BB%	K%	HR%	GB%	ZSw%	ZCon%	OSw%	OCon%	BABIP	SLGCON	DRA-	WARP
2021	CIN	MLB	27	47(0)	47	5-3	7	76	1.11	4.40	53.5%	9.2%	39.0%	3.1%	26.8%	58.9%	79.5%	32.6%	45.9%	.308	.670	75	1.1
2022	CIN	MLB	28	6(0)	6²	1-0	1	5	1.65	9.45	46.1%	19.4%	16.1%	0.0%	52.6%	57.1%	82.1%	25.0%	75.0%	.263	.389	109	0.0
2023	CIN	MLB	29	67(0)	61	7-3	3	72	1.18	3.10	45.0%	15.1%	27.9%	1.9%	22.6%	67.7%	76.9%	31.2%	52.0%	.215	.469	109	0.4
2024 DC	*CIN*	*MLB*	*30*	*49(0)*	*52*	*3-2*	*4*	*70*	*1.30*	*4.37*	*46.6%*	*12.2%*	*31.4%*	*3.9%*	*29.0%*					*.287*	*.629*	*95*	*0.4*

2023 Arsenal: SW (83.9), FA (94.4), CU (78.4)   *Comps: Tyler Clippard (65), Michael Lorenzen (58), Carlos Marmol (57)*

What would you do as an omniscient god playing with your own customizable dollhouse? That's the inherent question of the video game series *The Sims,* in which players can choose between earnestly creating diverse and dynamic communities, wantonly killing various gibberish-spewing avatars or running sadistic experiments in eugenics. Beauty or barbarity are in the eyes of the beholder. A less conventional method of playing the game is designing one's player character to be a hard-throwing, high-strikeout reliever with command issues and deploying him to southern Ohio. And yet here we are, talking about the Reds' main set-up man—though he'll have trouble keeping up the roleplay without cutting the walk rate another 4% or so.

Brandon Williamson LHP   Born: 04/02/98   Age: 26   Height: 6'6"   Weight: 210   Origin: Round 2, 2019 Draft (#59 overall)

YEAR	TM	LVL	AGE	G (GS)	IP	W-L	SV	K	WHIP	ERA	CSP	BB%	K%	HR%	GB%	ZSw%	ZCon%	OSw%	OCon%	BABIP	SLGCON	DRA-	WARP
2021	EVE	A+	23	6(6)	31	2-1	0	59	1.00	3.19		8.1%	47.6%	3.2%	44.2%					.354	.731	77	0.6
2021	ARK	AA	23	13(13)	67¹	2-5	0	94	1.26	3.48		8.1%	33.0%	2.5%	36.6%					.353	.619	77	1.3
2022	CHA	AA	24	14(14)	67¹	5-2	0	74	1.50	4.14		13.4%	24.8%	1.7%	39.1%					.322	.534	105	0.5
2022	LOU	AAA	24	13(13)	55¹	1-5	0	49	1.63	4.07		14.5%	19.1%	1.6%	31.9%					.302	.488	127	0.0
2023	LOU	AAA	25	8(8)	34	2-4	0	27	1.88	6.62		12.1%	16.4%	4.2%	32.8%	71.2%	83.5%	25.6%	69.5%	.339	.661	140	-0.2
2023	CIN	MLB	25	23(23)	117	5-5	0	98	1.28	4.46	49.1%	7.9%	20.0%	3.7%	36.9%	68.8%	84.8%	29.8%	66.1%	.280	.553	119	0.2
2024 DC	*CIN*	*MLB*	*26*	*11(11)*	*57²*	*3-5*	*0*	*48*	*1.54*	*5.68*	*49.1%*	*10.6%*	*18.6%*	*4.0%*	*36.6%*					*.304*	*.588*	*121*	*-0.1*

2023 Arsenal: FA (92.9), FC (89.4), CH (84.1), SW (81.8), CU (73.1), SI (91.9)   *Comps: Wade Miley (73), Andrew Suárez (73), David Buchanan (70)*

Quick, who threw the second-most innings on the 2023 Reds behind Graham Ashcraft? If you guessed Hunter Greene, you're not very good at deciphering context clues. If you already knew it was Williamson, you probably follow the Reds more closely than most. Williamson, included in the Eugenio Suárez-Jesse Winker deal ahead of the 2022 season, debuted last May and remained in the majors for the rest of 2023, generally holding his own despite some uninspiring surface-level stats. There's still some bullpen risk here and you'd like to see Williamson strike out hitters at a better clip, but he's probably just as likely to settle in as a Platonic ideal fourth or fifth starter.

Alex Young LHP   Born: 09/09/93   Age: 30   Height: 6'3"   Weight: 220   Origin: Round 2, 2015 Draft (#43 overall)

YEAR	TM	LVL	AGE	G (GS)	IP	W-L	SV	K	WHIP	ERA	CSP	BB%	K%	HR%	GB%	ZSw%	ZCon%	OSw%	OCon%	BABIP	SLGCON	DRA-	WARP
2021	AZ	MLB	27	30(2)	41²	2-6	0	38	1.68	6.26	53.6%	10.4%	19.7%	5.7%	44.8%	68.4%	83.9%	36.6%	54.5%	.322	.700	114	0.1
2022	COL	AAA	28	30(0)	32	3-0	1	47	1.16	3.66		5.3%	35.6%	3.8%	51.9%					.347	.649	65	1.0
2022	SF	MLB	28	24(1)	26¹	1-1	0	20	1.48	2.39	48.6%	9.6%	17.5%	0.0%	53.7%	63.2%	88.5%	42.5%	54.1%	.341	.457	102	0.2
2022	CLE	MLB	28	1(0)	0¹	0-0	0	1	3.00	0.00	60.9%	0.0%	50.0%	0.0%	100.0%	100.0%	50.0%	50.0%	0.0%	1.000	2.000	82	0.0
2023	CIN	MLB	29	63(0)	53²	4-2	1	50	1.36	3.86	45.3%	8.5%	21.2%	4.2%	47.9%	68.8%	85.6%	38.6%	52.2%	.279	.567	89	0.9
2024 DC	*CIN*	*MLB*	*30*	*42(0)*	*45²*	*3-2*	*0*	*45*	*1.36*	*4.42*	*47.9%*	*8.6%*	*23.1%*	*2.9%*	*46.4%*					*.314*	*.545*	*97*	*0.3*

2023 Arsenal: SI (90.7), CH (85.9), SW (81.8), FA (91.6)   *Comps: Tyler Duffey (57), Vidal Nuño (55), Adam Conley (51)*

It's a tale as old as time: a lefty with too many pitches who can't hack it as a starter pares down his arsenal, moves to the bullpen and becomes a shutdown reliever. Toss Young on the pile. Outside of trade deadline acquisition Sam Moll, Young was far and away the Reds' best left-handed relief option all season, running 39% whiff rates with both his changeup and slider. He was also, like most of Cincinnati's other relievers, leaking oil down the stretch, allowing 13 earned runs in 12 ⅓ innings from Aug. 1 onwards—though that didn't prevent him from logging a career-best DRA- by a significant margin. In other words, you could say he was both a beauty and a beast in 2023. Check back next year to see whether Young might actually be cursed.

LINEOUTS

Hitters

HITTER	POS	TM	LVL	AGE	PA	R	HR	RBI	SB	AVG/OBP/SLG	BABIP	SLGCON	BB%	K%	ZSw%	ZCon%	OSw%	OCon%	LA	90th EV	DRC+	BRR	DRP	WARP
Jay Allen II	CF	DAY	A+	20	105	15	1	3	10	.154/.260/.220	.260	.392	7.6%	38.1%							65	1.0	-1.9	-0.1
Jose Barrero	SS/CF	LOU	AAA	25	335	47	19	57	20	.258/.333/.540	.324	.844	6.6%	31.3%	70.0%	85.0%	37.1%	42.7%			92	-0.7	-3.1	0.1
	SS/CF	CIN	MLB	25	149	15	2	17	3	.218/.295/.323	.307	.483	10.1%	29.5%	72.2%	78.8%	33.3%	43.8%	17.2	104.4	80	0.0	-2.2	-0.1
Ricardo Cabrera	SS	RED	ROK	18	175	41	5	21	21	.350/.469/.559	.437	.741	12.0%	20.0%										
	SS	DBT	A	18	27	7	0	2	3	.316/.519/.316	.429	.429	18.5%	18.5%	70.8%	82.4%	34.7%	52.0%			108	0.6	-0.6	0.1
Conner Capel	OF	LV	AAA	26	391	55	9	47	17	.252/.346/.402	.310	.533	11.8%	21.5%	65.0%	86.1%	24.9%	55.9%			92	-0.4	-1.2	0.9
	OF	OAK	MLB	26	86	6	0	3	5	.260/.372/.329	.396	.500	14.0%	29.1%	61.9%	80.8%	24.4%	48.9%	12.1	100.7	81	0.1	0.1	0.1
Stuart Fairchild	OF	LOU	AAA	27	114	19	4	13	3	.277/.384/.447	.344	.627	9.6%	23.7%	70.6%	82.6%	23.6%	44.8%			95	0.2	-2.3	0.1
	OF	CIN	MLB	27	255	34	5	28	10	.228/.321/.388	.306	.567	9.8%	27.1%	79.1%	76.6%	29.2%	44.3%	14.1	102.5	76	0.4	1.6	0.2
Austin Hendrick	RF	DAY	A+	22	516	55	14	47	19	.204/.271/.335	.298	.557	7.4%	35.9%							65	0.0	2.7	-0.5
Rece Hinds	RF	CHA	AA	22	461	63	23	98	20	.269/.330/.536	.358	.847	7.4%	32.8%							99	-1.6	3.7	1.6
Carlos Jorge	2B	DBT	A	19	356	70	9	36	31	.295/.400/.483	.356	.632	13.2%	19.7%	76.0%	80.1%	35.7%	60.9%			123	2.7	1.4	2.5
	2B	DAY	A+	19	94	8	3	14	1	.239/.277/.398	.321	.603	5.3%	31.9%							77	-1.0	-3.9	-0.4
Nick Martini	LF	LOU	AAA	33	417	64	15	65	0	.275/.393/.481	.325	.643	14.4%	20.9%	61.1%	86.1%	25.2%	60.5%			118	-0.3	-4.7	1.6
	LF	CIN	MLB	33	79	10	6	16	0	.264/.329/.583	.255	.737	6.3%	19.0%	68.8%	88.4%	30.7%	70.4%	23.5	103.3	114	0.0	-0.6	0.3
Sammy Stafura	SS	RED	ROK	18	53	7	1	6	0	.071/.212/.190	.100	.421	15.1%	43.4%										
Sal Stewart	3B/DH	DBT	A	19	387	55	10	60	10	.269/.395/.424	.300	.521	17.1%	15.2%	68.7%	84.0%	30.1%	75.7%			129	-2.0	0.9	2.3
	3B/DH	DAY	A+	19	131	16	2	11	5	.291/.397/.391	.330	.467	13.7%	13.7%							123	0.9	0.1	0.8
Logan Tanner	C	DBT	A	22	258	31	2	27	0	.202/.304/.307	.269	.438	13.2%	25.2%	66.8%	84.0%	26.6%	54.7%			89	0.3	4.6	0.8
Jason Vosler	IF	LOU	AAA	29	363	55	20	68	3	.240/.333/.482	.271	.689	12.4%	25.9%	67.8%	82.5%	28.5%	55.5%			100	-3.1	1.9	1.0
	IF	CIN	MLB	29	65	6	3	10	0	.161/.200/.371	.206	.622	4.6%	38.5%	72.6%	72.2%	31.6%	44.0%	26.4	102.3	74	0.0	0.1	-0.1
Austin Wynns	C	COL	MLB	32	131	11	1	8	1	.214/.273/.282	.282	.388	6.1%	24.4%	67.1%	78.9%	33.0%	63.9%	13.9	99.1	69	-0.3	3.4	0.3
	C	LAD	MLB	32	12	0	0	2	0	.182/.250/.273	.333	.500	8.3%	41.7%	53.8%	78.6%	33.3%	66.7%	18.7	96.8	82	-0.1	0.1	0.0

Jay Allen II is looking like a rough draft selection at the moment, having failed to hit at either level of A-ball as he enters his 20s. He still has time, and the Reds also took Matt McLain and Andrew Abbott in the same draft, but missing this badly on a first-round pick hurts. ⓧ **Jose Barrero** has yet to make good on his former prospect status and has been passed on the depth chart by several other infielders, even as he made improvements to his walk rate and more than tripled an obscene 22 DRC+ from 2022. At this point, the Cuban utility player's best shot at playing time might be with another organization. ⓧ Could I interest you in another promising middle infielder? **Ricardo Cabrera** torched the Arizona Complex League in 2023 and the 19-year-old looks poised for a productive full-season debut at Low-A Daytona. ⓧ You're tied for first place in your bar trivia league, and the final question projects onto the screen: "Who was the Opening Day designated hitter for the Oakland Athletics in 2023?" You better pray that **Conner Capel** happens to be on your trivia team, or that you can access your smartphone without anyone noticing. ⓧ There's no metric to specifically denote a player as an OF4/OF5, but the perfectly competent **Stuart Fairchild** could lead the league if such a stat existed. ⓧ **Austin Hendrick** has never delivered on his first-round draft pedigree, stalling in A-ball for three consecutive years. His power also disappeared in 2023, as he slugged just .336, leaving him without a carrying tool or really any standout tools to speak of. If there's a positive for Hendrick, it's that things can't really get any worse. ⓧ **Rece Hinds** still has massive power. He also still strikes out far too much and doesn't make enough contact to profile as anything other than a one-dimensional slugger. This has been your annual Rece Report. Check back next year for, in all likelihood, the same report, give or take another promotion now that he's made it to the high minors. ⓧ **Carlos Jorge** was excellent in his full-season debut in Low-A, but tailed off a bit after a late-season promotion to High-A Dayton. Defensively, he bounced between second base and center field and could be a big-league regular at either spot. ⓧ After a year playing in the KBO, **Nick Martini** ginned up his most productive stint yet in the majors, posting a .916 OPS in just 29 games. It may have earned him a shake as a bench outfielder in 2024. ⓧ **Sammy Stafura** has years of development ahead after the Reds drafted the New York prep shortstop in the second round of the 2023 draft, but he profiles as a future high-contact, speedy infielder who can stick at the six. ⓧ **Sal Stewart** is a young infielder with an advanced bat but an uncertain future defensive home; yes, another one. The Reds selected Stewart with the compensation pick the team received when former high school draftee and onetime-infielder Nick Castellanos signed with Philadelphia, making the Miami prep a fitting selection. ⓧ **Logan Tanner** caught exactly 30% of attempted base stealers in 63 Low-A games and posted decent blocking stats, but the 2022 second-rounder's modest production with the bat at Mississippi State simply hasn't translated to pro ball. ⓧ **Jason Vosler** can hit a little bit and play all over the place. Unfortunately for him, he doesn't really play any of those positions well. Unfortunately for the Reds, he didn't really hit much in 2023 either. ⓧ **Austin Wynns** hasn't lived up to his name during his short career, which officially entered journeyman status last season as he traversed three different teams. His primary accomplishment in 2023 was giving fans a break from seeing the other Rockies catchers.

Pitchers

PITCHER	TM	LVL	AGE	G (GS)	IP	W-L	SV	K	WHIP	ERA	CSP	BB%	K%	HR%	GB%	ZSw%	ZCon%	OSw%	OCon%	BABIP	SLGCON	DRA-	WARP
Julian Aguiar	DAY	A+	22	14 (14)	70¹	4-1	0	77	0.97	1.92		8.5%	27.2%	0.7%	52.5%					.240	.335	71	1.5
	CHA	AA	22	11 (11)	54²	4-4	0	61	1.28	4.28		5.6%	26.3%	2.6%	47.4%					.340	.608	72	
Tejay Antone	LOU	AAA	29	12 (0)	12	0-0	0	11	1.42	3.00		9.6%	21.2%	1.9%	48.6%	50.6%	86.7%	33.6%	56.4%	.324	.486	97	0.2
	CIN	MLB	29	5 (1)	5²	0-0	0	7	0.88	1.59	42.3%	9.5%	33.3%	0.0%	66.7%	40.6%	84.6%	41.4%	70.8%	.250	.333	89	0.1
Daniel Duarte	LOU	AAA	26	32 (0)	35	4-0	7	39	1.17	3.34		11.3%	25.8%	0.0%	52.3%	65.1%	81.0%	30.5%	56.1%	.273	.360	91	0.7
	CIN	MLB	26	31 (0)	31²	3-0	1	23	1.39	3.69	49.1%	14.7%	16.9%	3.7%	50.0%	71.3%	81.0%	29.3%	64.9%	.218	.451	107	0.3
Brett Kennedy	LOU	AAA	28	17 (16)	78²	4-4	0	72	1.50	4.81		9.0%	20.8%	2.6%	38.8%	74.3%	80.1%	32.9%	63.8%	.338	.576	94	1.3
	CIN	MLB	28	5 (2)	18	1-0	0	9	1.44	6.50	48.7%	8.4%	10.8%	1.2%	39.1%	67.7%	88.4%	26.2%	68.8%	.290	.550	122	0.0
Casey Legumina	LOU	AAA	26	26 (1)	31²	2-1	0	39	1.67	4.83		8.8%	26.5%	2.0%	45.2%	67.4%	76.9%	30.6%	61.0%	.411	.637	85	0.6
	CIN	MLB	26	11 (0)	12²	1-0	0	11	1.97	5.68	45.8%	14.8%	18.0%	4.9%	51.2%	64.4%	82.1%	26.8%	67.6%	.342	.756	102	0.1
Andrew Moore	DAY	A+	23	10 (0)	14¹	1-0	0	20	1.57	5.52		15.6%	31.3%	1.6%	51.5%					.375	.576	99	0.2
Connor Overton	CIN	MLB	29	3 (3)	11	0-1	0	9	2.36	11.45	47.4%	12.7%	16.4%	5.5%	43.6%	67.5%	92.6%	32.5%	48.7%	.444	.947	118	0.0
Chase Petty	DAY	A+	20	16 (16)	60	0-2	0	61	1.20	1.95		5.8%	25.1%	0.0%	59.6%					.349	.424	73	1.3
	CHA	AA	20	2 (2)	8	0-0	0	5	0.75	0.00		3.2%	16.1%	0.0%	44.0%					.200	.280	109	
Lyon Richardson	DBT	A	23	3 (3)	9	0-0	0	18	0.67	1.00		3.0%	54.5%	0.0%	46.2%	48.3%	78.6%	50.0%	34.5%	.385	.500	58	0.2
	CHA	AA	23	15 (15)	46	0-2	0	58	1.24	2.15		11.7%	30.9%	1.1%	48.1%					.317	.481	74	0.9
	LOU	AAA	23	6 (6)	14¹	0-1	0	24	1.81	9.42		21.7%	34.8%	0.0%	37.9%	59.5%	76.0%	29.1%	37.9%	.379	.571	83	0.2
	CIN	MLB	23	4 (4)	16²	0-2	0	12	1.92	8.64	46.1%	14.8%	14.8%	7.4%	48.0%	70.5%	86.0%	26.1%	76.9%	.229	.704	130	-0.1
Reiver Sanmartin	CIN	MLB	27	14 (0)	14	1-0	0	13	1.93	7.07	38.4%	14.3%	18.6%	2.9%	55.3%	62.0%	78.9%	37.0%	73.8%	.333	.543	105	0.1
Chasen Shreve	DET	MLB	32	47 (0)	41¹	1-2	0	42	1.38	4.79	43.5%	6.7%	23.3%	3.3%	44.8%	64.2%	84.4%	39.7%	63.2%	.331	.608	95	0.6
	CIN	MLB	32	3 (0)	3¹	0-0	0	3	0.90	2.70	42.4%	15.4%	23.1%	7.7%	25.0%	65.0%	84.6%	34.3%	41.7%	.000	.500	87	0.1
Carson Spiers	CHA	AA	25	28 (9)	83	8-3	0	106	1.35	3.69		11.3%	29.2%	1.7%	40.2%					.320	.548	83	0.1
	CIN	MLB	25	4 (2)	13	0-1	1	12	1.92	6.92	47.1%	10.9%	18.8%	1.6%	26.7%	69.2%	84.0%	33.9%	72.9%	.386	.545	114	0.1
Levi Stoudt	LOU	AAA	25	25 (19)	82¹	5-6	0	58	1.66	6.23		13.0%	15.1%	5.2%	33.5%	70.0%	87.3%	29.9%	67.5%	.270	.648	141	-0.6
	CIN	MLB	25	4 (2)	10¹	0-1	0	9	2.32	9.58	46.1%	14.5%	16.4%	1.8%	44.7%	67.9%	87.7%	25.0%	65.7%	.405	.676	108	0.1

Julian Aguiar's primary weapon is a nasty two-plane slider, but his mid-90s heater has mediocre shape and he doesn't have much of a change yet. He's likely to hang around the majors for a long time, starting as soon as this year, but lacks significant upside. ⊗ **Tejay Antone** is a good reliever who can't seem to catch a break, logging just five appearances in his return from a second Tommy John surgery before elbow tendonitis prematurely ended his season. ⊗ **Daniel Duarte** posted a 3.69 ERA across 30 ⅔ innings, but his DRA north of five feels more accurate given that he tallied roughly equal numbers of hits allowed, walks and strikeouts. ⊗ **Justin Dunn** lost all of 2023 to shoulder issues, then had surgery to repair his shoulder's anterior capsule in September, putting the former prospect involved in the Edwin Díaz and Eugenio Suárez trades out of action indefinitely. ⊗ **Vladimir Gutierrez** spent all of 2023 recovering from elbow reconstruction surgery, including a mid-August setback that caused the Reds to pause his minor-league rehab assignment. The Cuban right-hander should have a better chance to impact the team's pitching staff this year after a regular offseason. ⊗ The Reds took **Hunter Hollan**, a polished southpaw with unspectacular stuff out of Arkansas, in the third round of the 2023 draft. Despite a lanky frame and a fastball that sits in the low 90s, even without adding strength Hollan might just move quickly as a high-floor, low-ceiling fifth or sixth starter type. ⊗ Five years after debuting for a terrible Padres team, **Brett Kennedy** returned to the majors only to give up 13 runs in 18 innings and be unceremoniously released at season's end. ⊗ **Casey Legumina** avoided beaning anyone in his debut season, but still walked nearly as many hitters as he struck out and allowed eight earned runs in 12 ⅔ innings. ⊗ A raffle ticket reliever included in the Luis Castillo deal, even in a year derailed by injury and control issues **Andrew Moore** still flashed the kind of premium stuff that plays in the late innings. ⊗ **Connor Overton** failed to shift the league's perception of him as an organizational arm after three dreadful April starts that featured 14 runs allowed in just 11 innings. ⊗ **Chase Petty** is an athletic righty with a mid-90s fastball and an MLB-caliber slider. He's also steadily developing a changeup and continues to look like a future starter. The ingredients here are good. But you know what they say about hard-throwing prep pitchers: they're heartbreakers. ⊗ **Lyon Richardson** showed plenty of courage returning from Tommy John surgery and rocketing from A-ball to the majors, but after allowing 16 runs in 16 ⅔ innings, he may want to ask the wizard for better results. ⊗ After 14 mostly ineffective innings constituting his third big-league campaign, **Reiver Sanmartin** had Tommy John surgery in July, shelving the funky lefty for most of 2024. ⊗ **Cole Schoenwetter** was the Reds' fourth-round draft pick in 2023, out of a Southern California high school, and has three potentially above-average pitches between his fastball, spike curve and changeup. Schoenwetter is athletic but has plenty of development to come, with a thin frame that could stand to bulk up a bit in the coming years. ⊗ **Chasen Shreve** is living proof that being a capable southpaw reliever will keep teams…chasing…an arm down for a decade or more. ⊗ **Carson Spiers** was an undrafted free agent signing in 2020 and had steadily molded himself into the shape of a future back-end starter before debuting in the majors in 2023. The results weren't sexy, but he did strike out around a batter per inning in his brief cup of coffee and could get a more extended look in 2024. ⊗ **Levi Stoudt**'s days as a starter could be coming to an end, but there's a good chance he still has a few years ahead of him as a 95-and-a-slider reliever.

CLEVELAND GUARDIANS

Essay by Scott Hines

Player comments by Kyle Kishimoto and BP staff

Progressive Field can't be 30 years old...can it?

I remember the opening of that ballpark at the corner of Carnegie and Ontario like it was yesterday: a glittering jewel at the forefront of Major League Baseball's pivot away from cavernous multi-sport stadiums to retro-inspired stadia purpose-built for their teams.

I was 11 years old, and—

Hm. Wait a second. [checks driver's license]

Well, that's personally troubling news. It's hard for me to process this now, but the downtown Cleveland ballpark once known as Jacobs Field will celebrate its 30th birthday this spring. Once a cutting-edge newcomer, it's now the 11th-oldest ballpark in Major League Baseball, and it's likely to move up a few spots in that order in the coming years as older ballparks in Oakland, St. Petersburg and Kansas City are set to fall out of use. The new kid on the block is all grown up, but you know what?

Thirty's not such a bad place to be.

A 30th birthday can be a harrowing milestone for some, but it can be liberating, too. It's the point in one's life when you really start thinking about your direction in life. It's when you start thinking about who you really *are*.

I think often about the auxiliary bleachers.

You can spy them, albeit briefly, in a highlight from August 1996—one of my all-time favorite plays and a YouTube clip to which I often return—when Kenny Lofton climbed nearly over the center-field wall to rob Baltimore's B.J. Surhoff of a sure home run. It's only for a second, but if you know what you're looking for, they're there.

It's a bit hard to imagine now, given that the Guardians rarely play to a full house at Progressive Field, but there was a time when people would give anything just to get inside the gates. The club had spent decades playing to sparse crowds at Municipal Stadium. One of my earliest sports memories is banging the empty wooden seats around us to the beat of Queen's "We Will Rock You," even though we weren't about to rock anyone. Suddenly, though, Cleveland moved into a great new ballpark and became the most exciting team in all of baseball. They had power (Albert Belle, Jim Thome and

CLEVELAND GUARDIANS PROSPECTUS
2023 W-L: 76-86, 3RD IN AL CENTRAL

Pythag	.476	19th	DER	.701	10th
RS/G	4.09	27th	DRC+	97	19th
RA/G	4.30	8th	DRA-	105	23rd
dWin%	.465	23rd	FIP	4.23	14th
Payroll	$89M	25th	B-Age	27.3	10th
M$/MW	$2.5M	7th	P-Age	26.6	1st

405'

370'   375'

325'   325'

- Opened 1994
- Open air
- Natural surface
- Fence profile: 9' to 19'

Park Factors

Runs	Runs/RH	Runs/LH	HR/RH	HR/LH
98	98	99	88	105

Top Hitter WARP	4.8 José Ramírez
Top Pitcher WARP	1.7 Tanner Bibee
2023 Top Prospect	Chase DeLauter

Payroll History (in millions)

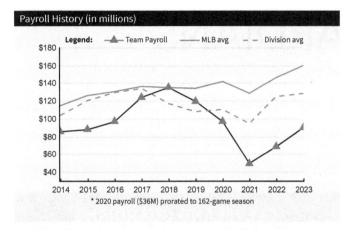

Legend: ▲ Team Payroll — MLB avg - - Division avg

* 2020 payroll ($36M) prorated to 162-game season

Future Commitments (in millions)

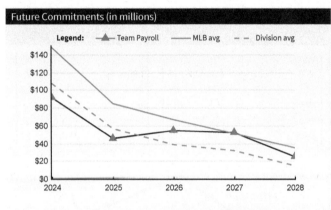

Legend: ▲ Team Payroll — MLB avg - - Division avg

Farm System Ranking

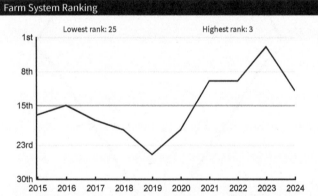

Lowest rank: 25   Highest rank: 3

Personnel

President, Baseball Operations Chris Antonetti	**Assistant General Manager** James Harris
General Manager Mike Chernoff	**Manager** Stephen Vogt
Executive Vice President & **Assistant General Manager** Matt Forman	**BP Alumni** Max Marchi Chris Mosch
Assistant General Manager Sky Andrecheck	Ethan Purser Keith Woolner
Assistant General Manager Eric Binder	

Manny Ramirez). They had speed (Lofton). They had gloves (Lofton and Omar Vizquel). They had *the* shutdown closer (Jose Mesa).

They had everything except space for everyone who wanted to get inside the ballpark.

The stadium's original capacity of 42,865 seats surely seemed sufficient when it was planned, but after the team won 100 games and their first pennant in a generation in 1995, it looked woefully inadequate. Hasty renovations were made. The left-field bleachers, originally a clean rectangle, received angled wings to boost their capacity. That wasn't enough, though, and so an additional set of "auxiliary" bleachers, seats that looked like they belonged at a high school football stadium or along a parade route, were added behind the permanent center-field stands. They only added 480 seats to the ballpark, but over the course of 81 sold-out home games, that was another 38,880 tickets, nearly a whole ballpark's worth of people who would get to see their favorite team play. Fans sat in those bleachers happily when they got the chance.

The sellout streak, 455 games over seven seasons, is well-known in franchise lore, and commemorated on signs within the stadium. But it underlines how unfathomable the idea of *reducing* the stadium's capacity would've sounded back then, back when I'd spend hours in line at a West Side Rini-Rego Stop-n-Shop Ticketmaster counter in December, hoping to *maybe* snag a few tickets to a Tuesday night game against the Royals in August. I'd try the call-in line hundreds of times until I got a ring instead of a busy signal, trying anything because I just *had* to see this team, had to see my superheroes in person.

There are some market-specific reasons why the Guardians don't sell out every game anymore, and some market-specific reasons why they *did* back in the 1990s. First of all, the Browns were gone. That was a big hole in the city's heart and its discretionary spending budget that Cleveland's baseball club was more than happy to fill. The city was also nearly a third larger then than it is now. There was a pent-up demand for winning baseball that was suddenly fulfilled, and it felt like a fairy tale. All of that is true.

Baseball's changed as a whole, though, too.

On Opening Day 1994, the average capacity of all 28 major-league stadiums was a shade under 52,000. On Opening Day 2024—pending various offseason tweaks—that number will be a lot closer to 42,000. That's roughly a 20% drop in average capacity, one that mirrors Jacobs/Progressive Field's reduction from 42,865 to 34,830 over the past 30 years. Sure, teams would still love to sell out every game just like Cleveland once did—but it's not entirely necessary, and the fewer empty seats that are available, the more demand can be stirred up for the ones a team *does* have. Television, linear or streaming, is the primary revenue source for MLB clubs, and the importance of actually selling tickets to a team's bottom line has dropped steadily for decades.

Even the butts that *do* get in the stadium aren't expected to spend as much time in their seats. There are gourmet concessions to patronize, beer gardens to hang out in, playgrounds and plazas to mill around. A fan who spends nine innings sitting in a seat and actually watching baseball is probably an outlier. A big-league stadium in the present day isn't just a place to watch a game. It's a place to go *and* watch a game in between all the other things to see and do there.

The way that we consume sports is just different in 2023 than it was in 1993. Sports are more present in people's day-to-day lives than ever, with near-instant access to any game, any score, any statistic and any opinion anyone could have about a game. Fans don't *have* to be inside the ballpark to ride along with their teams, and so those who are in the ballpark need a little bit more on offer than in summers past. One could take that as an indictment of short modern attention spans, a reflection of franchises' commitment to diversifying revenue streams or just be happy that there's beer other than Budweiser to drink nowadays.

Things have also changed for the Guardians on the field: The days of top-10 payrolls are well behind, and lately Cleveland's front office has had little choice but to to play the shell game of arbitration-year trades and dependence on continuously successful player development that seems to be the only path low-budget clubs see to contention. José Ramírez remains the indomitable, metronomic core of the offense, though Steven Kwan and his miniscule walk rate have been almost precisely as valuable through the outfielder's first two seasons and Andrés Giménez and the brothers Naylor make a capable enough supporting cast; while Aaron Civale was shipped out last summer and Shane Bieber appears destined to follow him out the door within the year, either via trade or free agency, Tanner Bibee, Triston McKenzie and Gavin Williams appear ready to lead the team's next crop of capable arms. Whether that will be enough for a return to the postseason, in which the Guardians have appeared in just two out of the last five Octobers (and won only series) is an open question, but no one can claim Cleveland isn't tinkering with the on-field product at least as frequently as it does the stadium those teams play in.

Progressive Field began undergoing a fresh round of renovations over the offseason, a series of changes that will stretch into the 2025 season. This isn't the first time the ballpark has gone under the knife. Major renovations in 2014 and 2015 reconfigured large areas of the facility, moving bullpens, adding a big bar and—most visibly—removing large chunks of the upper deck seating in favor of shipping-container-like structures that served as standing-room terraces available for rent to corporate groups and parties.

I *hated* the shipping containers.

I'm an architect, so I feel justified in objecting on purely aesthetic grounds; they were ugly. They ruined the pristine visuals of a ballpark that had balanced retro and modern in a way none of the other parks of its time managed to do. More than that, though, I objected as a fan. Those ugly

monstrosities in the right-field upper deck looked like a white flag, an admission that the glory days were over. They covered up the failure, not quite so literally as in St. Petersburg or the East Bay, but just as unseemly. That shouldn't fly here, not at the corner of Carnegie and Ontario. The boxes were awkward and ill-considered, a sign of a ballpark struggling to age gracefully.

The new renovations promise to bring back some grace and dignity.

First of all, the shipping containers are gone. (Thank heavens.) They're getting yanked out of the stadium, and if I had my way they'd be thrown into Lake Erie where they could serve out the rest of their days as party decks for the zebra mussels. The seats they covered up nearly a decade ago aren't coming back, though: Instead, the whole structure of the upper deck is being cut back, creating a much more permanent-seeming setting for open viewing terraces which will offer wide-open vistas of Cleveland from inside the ballpark. A similar cut-away will be made down the third-base line, and if I'm considering the angles correctly, that terrace should allow a hypothetical fan to view both the Cleveland Guardians baseball club *and* their namesake, the "Guardians of Traffic" flanking the Hope Memorial Bridge.

There's a whole portfolio of other changes in this renovation, including a "Dugout Club" bar behind home plate and the demise of the glassed-in Terrace Club restaurant behind the left-field foul pole (a spot that captured a particular, 1990s image of luxury encapsulated in Kevin McAllister's stay in the Plaza Hotel in *Home Alone 2*, and where I first tried duck breast). There will be expanded administration offices, a new building behind right field and renovations to the clubhouse. It's an ambitious project, but makes a heck of a lot more sense than deeming a park obsolete before it hits 30, like Leonardo DiCaprio dating.

I don't want to sound like I'm in the tank for the club's management here—they'll have to sign a second player to a second contract before I'll go to bat for them—but I'm optimistic about the future of this ballpark I love so dearly. The upcoming renovations, at least in the videos the team has offered up, promise a realization of maturity for a ballpark that's finally past its awkward teenage years. These changes are a bit like finally setting up a 401(k) or starting a daily skincare routine: They're things you do when you're old enough to quit fooling around and start acting like an adult.

At 30, you start to understand your limitations. You can't do the things you used to do, but that's alright—in fact, it'd be a lot more worrying if you *wanted* to keep doing them. You're not a kid anymore, and you're probably never going to be a kid again. You begin to have a true understanding of what you're capable of and who you really are.

My favorite part of The Jake—I'm sorry, I'm one of those people who still can't help but call it The Jake—has always been the left-field home-run porch. It's been the landing spot for countless Cleveland home runs, not least of them Rajai Davis' *maybe-we'll-finally-win-it-ah-well-nevertheless* game-tying laser in Game 7 of the 2016 World Series, but it's also the most elegant part of the park's design. It's the spot where Cleveland spills into the ballpark, and the ballpark spills into Cleveland. It's not some kitschy integration of an old warehouse building, and it's not an ersatz skyline made of team-controlled hotels. It's just an open door between the game and the city, a place you can walk up to on any of the 280-some days of the year without a game and peer in, dreaming about baseball.

These new renovations embrace that same pattern language. The ballpark isn't covering up its thinning hair with a shipping-container ballcap anymore. It's realizing that what's always served it best is the city it belongs to, and it's finally embracing it.

—Scott Hines is the publisher of Action Cookbook Newsletter.

HITTERS

Gabriel Arias IF   Born: 02/27/00   Age: 24   Bats: R   Throws: R   Height: 6'1"   Weight: 217   Origin: IFA, 2016

YEAR	TM	LVL	AGE	PA	R	HR	RBI	SB	AVG/OBP/SLG	BABIP	SLGCON	BB%	K%	ZSw%	ZCon%	OSw%	OCon%	LA	90th EV	DRC+	BRR	DRP	WARP
2021	COL	AAA	21	483	64	13	55	5	.284/.348/.454	.351	.607	8.1%	22.8%							101	-1.1	-1.8	1.3
2022	SAN	WIN	22	110	9	1	5	1	.202/.245/.269	.267	.368	4.5%	25.5%										
2022	COL	AAA	22	323	46	13	36	5	.240/.310/.406	.279	.557	7.7%	24.1%							95	0.6	-1.7	0.7
2022	CLE	MLB	22	57	9	1	5	1	.191/.321/.319	.267	.484	14.0%	28.1%	61.8%	76.4%	28.6%	47.5%	-2.7	106.0	83	0.0	0.0	0.0
2023	CLE	MLB	23	345	36	10	26	3	.210/.275/.352	.290	.550	8.1%	32.8%	79.6%	74.7%	37.3%	43.0%	4.0	106.9	65	-0.1	0.6	-0.4
2024 DC	CLE	MLB	24	257	23	6	25	3	.207/.272/.338	.288	.516	7.2%	31.8%							73	-0.1	0.8	0.0

2023 GP: SS (53), 1B (35), RF (19), 3B (14), DH (2), 2B (1)   Comps: J.P. Crawford (58), Ketel Marte (55), Jonathan Villar (53)

In his first season of regular big-league playing time, Arias validated many of the hit tool concerns associated with his profile in the minors. Only three hitters with at least 300 plate appearances swung and missed more than he on a per-pitch basis; he simply hasn't shown the plate coverage necessary to make up for his poor chase rate. Arias has prodigious raw power but hasn't been able to actualize it in games thanks to a high groundball rate and tendency to hit his fly balls away from the pull side. Where he *has* shined is on defense, serving in a utility role but playing a competent shortstop when stationed there. If his bat doesn't turn out well enough to be a starting shortstop, the fact that he's played well at five different positions will secure him a roster spot as an omnipositional bench player.

Will Brennan RF   Born: 02/02/98   Age: 26   Bats: L   Throws: L   Height: 6'0"   Weight: 200   Origin: Round 8, 2019 Draft (#250 overall)

YEAR	TM	LVL	AGE	PA	R	HR	RBI	SB	AVG/OBP/SLG	BABIP	SLGCON	BB%	K%	ZSw%	ZCon%	OSw%	OCon%	LA	90th EV	DRC+	BRR	DRP	WARP
2021	LC	A+	23	269	42	4	30	13	.290/.368/.441	.339	.538	9.3%	16.0%							116	-0.7	2.0	1.5
2021	AKR	AA	23	177	28	2	20	2	.280/.369/.360	.328	.446	10.2%	16.4%							107	0.0	-4.5	0.3
2022	AKR	AA	24	157	16	4	39	5	.311/.382/.504	.319	.571	10.8%	10.2%							130	-0.4	-2.4	0.8
2022	COL	AAA	24	433	53	9	68	15	.316/.367/.471	.342	.544	7.6%	12.2%							114	-0.2	-1.6	1.8
2022	CLE	MLB	24	45	6	1	8	2	.357/.400/.500	.378	.553	4.4%	8.9%	75.0%	87.0%	52.6%	75.6%	5.5	103.1	113	0.0	0.0	0.2
2023	CLE	MLB	25	455	41	5	41	13	.266/.299/.356	.296	.411	3.5%	12.5%	72.4%	86.6%	43.5%	75.2%	9.5	100.8	96	0.6	1.9	1.2
2024 DC	CLE	MLB	26	285	27	4	28	6	.278/.324/.391	.312	.458	5.7%	14.1%							104	0.2	0.5	0.9

2023 GP: RF (110), CF (11), LF (7), DH (4)   Comps: Charlie Blackmon (61), Chris Denorfia (55), Greg Allen (54)

In his first full major-league season, Brennan validated concerns about his approach at the plate and ability to consistently impact the ball despite a preternatural feel for contact. He finished the year in the 10th percentile or worse by average exit velocity, barrel rate, and chase rate, failing to eclipse the .300 OBP threshold. He did fare far better with the platoon advantage, but still didn't hit enough against righties to secure a job as the long-side platoon starter going forward. His skills on the bases and with the glove will play up in a more limited bench role going forward.

★ ★ ★ *2024 Top 101 Prospect* **#100** ★ ★ ★

Juan Brito IF   Born: 09/24/01   Age: 22   Bats: S   Throws: R   Height: 5'11"   Weight: 202   Origin: IFA, 2018

YEAR	TM	LVL	AGE	PA	R	HR	RBI	SB	AVG/OBP/SLG	BABIP	SLGCON	BB%	K%	ZSw%	ZCon%	OSw%	OCon%	LA	90th EV	DRC+	BRR	DRP	WARP
2021	RCK	ROK	19	109	20	3	11	5	.295/.406/.432	.354	.567	13.8%	19.3%									0.9	
2022	FRE	A	20	497	91	11	72	17	.286/.407/.470	.319	.571	15.7%	14.3%							128	-0.9	1.2	3.3
2023	LC	A+	21	161	29	4	14	3	.265/.379/.424	.282	.505	14.9%	13.0%							131	2.0	-0.6	1.1
2023	AKR	AA	21	374	46	10	60	3	.276/.373/.444	.310	.556	12.8%	16.8%							121	-2.0	-0.5	1.4
2024 DC	CLE	MLB	22	29	3	0	3	0	.225/.308/.346	.264	.429	10.0%	17.9%							87	0.0	0	0.1

2023 GP: 2B (76), 3B (32), SS (22), DH (6)   Comps: Vidal Bruján (66), Steve Lombardozzi (66), Alexi Amarista (65)

Brito joined the Guardians system in a one-for-one trade for Nolan Jones, whom the Guardians certainly didn't anticipate getting to all of his 70-grade raw power in games and slugging over .540. Brito is now one of about 100 contact-oriented middle infielders on Cleveland's 40-man roster, and reached as high as Triple-A last season. He possesses plus contact skills and a keen eye at the plate, posting the second-highest OBP, third-highest walk rate, and lowest strikeout rate of any Eastern League farmhands (with at least 350 plate appearances) 21 years old or under. He lacks premier over-the-fence power, but hits line drives at an above-average rate and still knocked 14 homers simply because he puts so many quality pitches in play. There are big questions about his defensive abilities at second base, and he's definitely not a shortstop, but Brito's bat will have him competing for regular infield reps alongside the likes of Brayan Rocchio and José Tena.

Kole Calhoun　RF　Born: 10/14/87　Age: 36　Bats: L　Throws: L　Height: 5'10"　Weight: 205　Origin: Round 8, 2010 Draft (#264 overall)

YEAR	TM	LVL	AGE	PA	R	HR	RBI	SB	AVG/OBP/SLG	BABIP	SLGCON	BB%	K%	ZSw%	ZCon%	OSw%	OCon%	LA	90th EV	DRC+	BRR	DRP	WARP
2021	AZ	MLB	33	182	17	5	17	0	.235/.297/.373	.281	.496	8.2%	22.5%	82.0%	81.7%	34.4%	49.7%	17.5	101.9	85	-0.2	-3.3	-0.2
2022	TEX	MLB	34	424	36	12	49	3	.196/.257/.330	.263	.508	6.4%	32.1%	79.5%	75.8%	37.9%	49.4%	15.6	104.4	64	-0.1	-4.0	-1.1
2023	SWB	AAA	35	105	24	4	18	0	.281/.390/.528	.333	.701	12.4%	21.0%	78.2%	77.5%	31.0%	55.1%			101	1.2	1.6	0.6
2023	OKC	AAA	35	161	22	5	28	0	.308/.366/.531	.339	.650	8.7%	16.1%	82.3%	86.8%	31.1%	50.0%			102	-1.2	0.0	0.5
2023	CLE	MLB	35	174	18	6	25	0	.217/.282/.376	.241	.492	7.5%	21.3%	77.7%	90.6%	30.0%	55.6%	20.5	102.2	96	-0.1	0.1	0.3
2024 non	*CLE*	*MLB*	*36*	*251*	*24*	*7*	*26*	*1*	*.220/.289/.361*	*.270*	*.488*	*7.6%*	*24.3%*							*81*	*-0.2*	*-3.1*	*-0.3*

2023 GP: 1B (25), DH (14), RF (3)　　　　　　　　　　　　　　　　　　　*Comps: Nick Markakis (66), Michael Tucker (65), Tommy Griffith (65)*

It looked like the end of the road for the veteran, but Cleveland came calling in August in need of reinforcements. Calhoun, along with much of the wave of Guardians waiver claims tasked with helping them run down the first-place Twins, simply didn't have enough in the tank. After selling at the trade deadline, the Guardians went 23-32. Now entering his age-36 season, it appears Calhoun may truly be done. Still, a career featuring four above-average full seasons by DRC+ and a Gold Glove award are nothing to scoff at, and a silver lining to his underwhelming Guardians tenure was reaching 10 years of service time—a milestone that places him in the top decile of players in big-league experience and grants him full access to MLB's pension plan.

Deyvison De Los Santos　CI　Born: 06/21/03　Age: 21　Bats: R　Throws: R　Height: 5'11"　Weight: 185　Origin: IFA, 2019

YEAR	TM	LVL	AGE	PA	R	HR	RBI	SB	AVG/OBP/SLG	BABIP	SLGCON	BB%	K%	ZSw%	ZCon%	OSw%	OCon%	LA	90th EV	DRC+	BRR	DRP	WARP
2021	DIA	ROK	18	95	19	5	17	1	.329/.421/.610	.415	.862	13.7%	25.3%									1.9	
2021	VIS	A	18	160	26	3	20	2	.276/.340/.421	.374	.598	8.1%	26.9%							95	1.0	5.8	1.0
2022	VIS	A	19	349	43	12	67	4	.329/.370/.513	.404	.698	6.3%	24.1%							98	-1.4	-4.6	0.5
2022	HIL	A+	19	166	24	9	33	1	.278/.307/.506	.365	.769	4.2%	32.5%							103	-2.8	-0.9	0.1
2022	AMA	AA	19	45	5	1	6	0	.231/.333/.359	.276	.467	11.1%	20.0%							100	0.0	-0.6	0.1
2023	AMA	AA	20	481	73	20	61	4	.254/.297/.431	.308	.596	5.2%	26.0%							80	-0.8	1.6	0.2
2024 DC	*CLE*	*MLB*	*21*	*98*	*8*	*2*	*9*	*1*	*.224/.263/.339*	*.305*	*.484*	*4.5%*	*29.9%*							*69*	*0.0*	*0*	*-0.2*

2023 GP: 3B (74), 1B (35), DH (7)　　　　　　　　　　　　　　　　　　*Comps: Hudson Potts (72), Isaac Paredes (61), Matt Dominguez (60)*

Depending on whom you ask, De Los Santos is either one of the Diamondbacks' top prospects, or one of their most flawed. You could choose to look at his plus-plus raw power and say, "Yes, I know he chases after everything and can't field, but you can't ignore such talent at a young age." Maybe you pair that age with the fact that his performance *did* improve after he turned 20. Or you could argue that his shortcomings, many of them correlative, leave a permanent stain on his profile. There's no right answer, of course, at least not yet, but players like De Los Santos do tend to end up at one extreme or the other, instead of at a middle ground. That's something to consider.

───────────────── ★　★　★　*2024 Top 101 Prospect*　**#31**　★　★　★ ─────────────────

Chase DeLauter　OF　Born: 10/08/01　Age: 22　Bats: L　Throws: L　Height: 6'4"　Weight: 235　Origin: Round 1, 2022 Draft (#16 overall)

YEAR	TM	LVL	AGE	PA	R	HR	RBI	SB	AVG/OBP/SLG	BABIP	SLGCON	BB%	K%	ZSw%	ZCon%	OSw%	OCon%	LA	90th EV	DRC+	BRR	DRP	WARP
2023	PEJ	WIN	21	95	16	4	23	5	.257/.358/.473	.224	.538	13.7%	9.5%	76.2%	93.8%	12.0%	100.0%						
2023	GUA	ROK	21	38	8	1	4	3	.286/.447/.500	.304	.609	21.1%	13.2%										
2023	LC	A+	21	176	24	4	31	3	.366/.403/.549	.403	.634	5.7%	12.5%							121	-0.9	-0.5	0.7
2023	AKR	AA	21	28	3	0	4	0	.364/.464/.409	.400	.474	17.9%	10.7%							116	0.0		
2024 non	*CLE*	*MLB*	*22*	*251*	*21*	*3*	*22*	*0*	*.233/.288/.337*	*.271*	*.411*	*6.3%*	*16.4%*							*75*	*0.0*	*0*	*0.0*

2023 GP: RF (36), CF (26), LF (8), DH (7)　　　　　　　　　　　　　　　*Comps: Josh Bell (82), Alex Kirilloff (78), Domonic Brown (72)*

DeLauter was one of the more interesting first-round draft selections in recent memory due to the varying evaluations on him from different sources. Eyeball scouts disliked the short finish to his swing and lack of premier college competition in a mid-major conference, yet models were all over his plus exit velocities and the fact that he mashed both on campus and on the Cape. The first half of his pro debut season was wiped out by a foot fracture, but his performance in High-A after he recovered seems to be a win for the data analysts. A scissor-kick swing limited his pull-side power, as he hit just four homers in 176 plate appearances, but he still slugged nearly .550 thanks to a high contact rate and ability to line doubles into the gaps. He made up for missed time in the Arizona Fall League, and may soon be knocking on the door of the majors if he can record an uninterrupted season.

Estevan Florial　OF　Born: 11/25/97　Age: 26　Bats: L　Throws: R　Height: 6'1"　Weight: 195　Origin: IFA, 2015

YEAR	TM	LVL	AGE	PA	R	HR	RBI	SB	AVG/OBP/SLG	BABIP	SLGCON	BB%	K%	ZSw%	ZCon%	OSw%	OCon%	LA	90th EV	DRC+	BRR	DRP	WARP
2021	SWB	AAA	23	362	65	13	41	13	.218/.315/.404	.291	.630	11.6%	30.9%							86	1.8	-1.4	0.7
2021	NYY	MLB	23	25	3	1	2	1	.300/.440/.550	.385	.786	20.0%	24.0%	72.1%	74.2%	26.9%	44.4%	6.1	101.9	88	0.0	-0.2	0.1
2022	SWB	AAA	24	461	66	15	46	39	.283/.368/.481	.398	.738	11.7%	30.4%							94	0.9	-0.6	1.2
2022	NYY	MLB	24	35	4	0	1	2	.097/.200/.097	.167	.167	8.6%	37.1%	75.0%	68.9%	30.0%	25.0%	10.4	102.5	79	0.0	-0.9	-0.1
2023	SWB	AAA	25	482	83	28	79	25	.284/.380/.565	.362	.872	13.7%	29.9%	73.3%	76.8%	25.9%	39.1%			100	0.2	1.8	1.6
2023	NYY	MLB	25	71	5	0	8	3	.230/.324/.311	.333	.463	9.9%	28.2%	74.6%	71.1%	24.4%	45.0%	17.6	103.6	79	0.0	-0.6	0.0
2024 DC	*CLE*	*MLB*	*26*	*126*	*13*	*3*	*14*	*5*	*.225/.306/.379*	*.324*	*.606*	*9.4%*	*32.8%*							*93*	*0.0*	*-1.4*	*0.1*

2023 GP: CF (19)　　　　　　　　　　　　　　　　　　　　*Comps: Todd Dunwoody (59), Jordan Schafer (59), Gerald Young (54)*

Although the longtime Baby Bomber was designated for assignment after briefly making the Opening Day roster, no one claimed this former top prospect. Thus began a long year of getting *far* too familiar with the former Steamtown Mall in Scranton, likely because the Yankees did not want to call him back up only to risk losing him via waivers. Though Florial had a power boost in 2023, the strikeout concerns that have shrouded him throughout his professional career lingered. Few were terribly shocked when he didn't do much upon his return to The Show in September.

Tyler Freeman IF Born: 05/21/99   Age: 25   Bats: R   Throws: R   Height: 6'0"   Weight: 190   Origin: Round 2, 2017 Draft (#71 overall)

YEAR	TM	LVL	AGE	PA	R	HR	RBI	SB	AVG/OBP/SLG	BABIP	SLGCON	BB%	K%	ZSw%	ZCon%	OSw%	OCon%	LA	90th EV	DRC+	BRR	DRP	WARP
2021	AKR	AA	22	180	26	2	19	4	.323/.372/.470	.357	.538	4.4%	11.7%							122	-0.8	1.3	1.1
2022	COL	AAA	23	343	51	6	44	6	.279/.371/.364	.296	.408	7.3%	9.3%							126	0.9	-3.4	1.7
2022	CLE	MLB	23	86	9	0	3	1	.247/.314/.286	.284	.333	4.7%	12.8%	69.3%	93.8%	37.0%	64.9%	10.3	103.3	107	0.1	-0.2	0.3
2023	COL	AAA	24	116	24	2	17	10	.319/.457/.462	.365	.560	12.9%	13.8%	63.5%	87.0%	25.8%	80.3%			119	1.3	0.4	0.7
2023	CLE	MLB	24	168	20	4	18	5	.242/.295/.366	.275	.455	6.0%	17.9%	66.2%	89.8%	33.5%	71.0%	5.6	103.6	97	0.2	-0.4	0.5
2024 DC	CLE	MLB	25	193	18	3	18	6	.248/.313/.351	.277	.413	6.6%	13.4%							92	0.1	-0.2	0.4

2023 GP: 3B (25), 2B (17), SS (11), DH (9), 1B (1), LF (1)   *Comps: Dawel Lugo (65), Andy LaRoche (60), Yairo Muñoz (57)*

Once a contact machine running sub-10% strikeout rates as he climbed through the minors, Freeman's hype as a bat-control demon has largely fizzled out, as he hit .242 with a sub-.300 OBP in limited majors action last season. He's squared up the ball more frequently to trade off with those whiffs, but he hits the ball on the ground too often and doesn't pull the ball enough to sneak his way into some decent game power—his below-average BABIP shows that simply putting the ball in play and hoping for the best isn't always an effective strategy. Defensively, his best strength is his versatility; he's capable at all four infield positions, though he looks best at second base. For now, Freeman looks fine as a fifth or sixth infielder on a poor offensive team, but will have to get on base a lot more to ascend to regular starter status.

Andrés Giménez 2B Born: 09/04/98   Age: 25   Bats: L   Throws: R   Height: 5'11"   Weight: 161   Origin: IFA, 2015

YEAR	TM	LVL	AGE	PA	R	HR	RBI	SB	AVG/OBP/SLG	BABIP	SLGCON	BB%	K%	ZSw%	ZCon%	OSw%	OCon%	LA	90th EV	DRC+	BRR	DRP	WARP
2021	COL	AAA	22	233	30	10	31	8	.287/.342/.502	.345	.682	5.2%	23.6%							107	-2.8	-1.8	0.5
2021	CLE	MLB	22	210	23	5	16	11	.218/.282/.351	.273	.493	5.2%	25.7%	74.3%	82.7%	46.2%	56.4%	8.3	104.3	71	0.4	0.9	0.1
2022	CLE	MLB	23	557	66	17	69	20	.297/.371/.466	.353	.604	6.1%	20.1%	70.7%	83.1%	42.2%	63.7%	10.8	102.9	122	1.8	1.4	3.6
2023	CLE	MLB	24	616	76	15	62	30	.251/.314/.399	.289	.499	5.2%	18.2%	70.5%	83.7%	44.0%	66.3%	12.0	102.3	93	0.8	2.5	1.7
2024 DC	CLE	MLB	25	562	60	15	64	24	.260/.329/.412	.306	.533	6.0%	20.3%							111	0.9	2.3	2.7

2023 GP: 2B (150)   *Comps: Francisco Lindor (58), Lou Bierbauer (54), Tony Kubek (53)*

Giménez' breakout 2022 season was a case study in everything that can go right for a highly aggressive hitter—he ambushed any pitch near his damage zone low and inside while showing off tremendous plate coverage. His inability to repeat that stellar campaign was indicative of everything that can go *wrong* for that kind of profile. His quality of contact precipitously declined as he connected on more bad pitches, taking a significant chunk out of his line-drive rate and exit velocities. Large year-to-year fluctuations on contact outcomes may be inevitable for Giménez, whose lack of selectivity means he has to roll the dice on what kind of pitches he puts in play. There are still two consistent aspects to his profile, though: He doesn't walk much but gets hit by pitches at Mark Canha levels, providing him a decent OBP floor. And of course there's his defense. Giménez has emerged as one of the league's finest fielders at the keystone, last year earning his first Gold Glove award. What we see from him offensively going forward should be somewhere between his past two efforts, and that's more than enough to make him a crucial position player on this roster.

Austin Hedges C Born: 08/18/92   Age: 31   Bats: R   Throws: R   Height: 6'1"   Weight: 220   Origin: Round 2, 2011 Draft (#82 overall)

YEAR	TM	LVL	AGE	PA	R	HR	RBI	SB	AVG/OBP/SLG	BABIP	SLGCON	BB%	K%	ZSw%	ZCon%	OSw%	OCon%	LA	90th EV	DRC+	BRR	DRP	WARP
2021	CLE	MLB	28	312	32	10	31	1	.178/.220/.308	.214	.442	4.8%	27.9%	73.5%	79.7%	38.0%	56.4%	17.8	103.2	54	-0.4	5.7	0.0
2022	CLE	MLB	29	338	26	7	30	2	.163/.241/.248	.193	.338	7.4%	23.1%	67.1%	82.2%	31.9%	57.6%	15.0	99.9	70	-0.5	8.3	0.8
2023	TEX	MLB	30	25	1	0	2	0	.208/.208/.208	.313	.312	0.0%	32.0%	70.7%	75.9%	35.6%	31.2%	20.8	100.5	101	0.0	2.0	0.3
2023	PIT	MLB	30	187	13	1	14	1	.180/.237/.230	.226	.303	5.9%	20.9%	73.3%	82.3%	35.7%	60.0%	11.4	100.2	70	-0.1	24.0	2.4
2024 DC	CLE	MLB	31	183	16	4	17	1	.204/.267/.311	.254	.419	6.8%	24.0%							64	-0.2	8.4	0.7

2023 GP: C (80), P (4)   *Comps: Jeff Mathis (71), Bill Bergen (67), Morgan Murphy (64)*

YEAR	TM	P. COUNT	FRM RUNS	BLK RUNS	THRW RUNS	TOT RUNS
2021	CLE	12266	6.9	0.2	0.3	7.4
2022	CLE	12981	10.7	0.3	-0.4	10.6
2023	PIT	8470	22.8	0.1	-0.1	22.8
2023	TEX	1007	2.1	0.0	0.0	2.1
2024	CLE	7215	8.3	0.1	-0.1	8.4

Austin Hedges' defensive prowess is so renowned that when we prompted ChatGPT to come up with a fun fact for him, it reeled off the following series of knee-slappers:

"Meet Austin Hedges, the catcher whose glove is so magical, it once caught a foul ball while ordering pizza for the pitcher. Rumor has it, his shin guards are made from the tears of baseballs that never made it past him. When he's not thwarting base stealers, he's practicing his secret skill of predicting pitches using a crystal ball. They say he doesn't block baseballs; he negotiates with them. Austin Hedges, where catching excellence meets comedy on the diamond!"

Two things are clear: First, AI is in no danger of taking over the jobs of Baseball Prospectus' writers. Second, Hedges' reputation is well-established.

Steven Kwan LF   Born: 09/05/97   Age: 26   Bats: L   Throws: L   Height: 5'9"   Weight: 170   Origin: Round 5, 2018 Draft (#163 overall)

YEAR	TM	LVL	AGE	PA	R	HR	RBI	SB	AVG/OBP/SLG	BABIP	SLGCON	BB%	K%	ZSw%	ZCon%	OSw%	OCon%	LA	90th EV	DRC+	BRR	DRP	WARP
2021	AKR	AA	23	221	42	7	31	4	.337/.411/.539	.354	.612	10.0%	10.4%							135	1.8	0.4	1.9
2021	COL	AAA	23	120	23	5	13	2	.311/.398/.505	.300	.547	11.7%	6.7%							137	1.6	1.4	1.2
2022	CLE	MLB	24	638	89	6	52	19	.298/.373/.400	.323	.447	9.7%	9.4%	55.2%	95.5%	26.2%	83.9%	11.6	98.5	120	1.1	8.6	4.6
2023	CLE	MLB	25	718	93	5	54	21	.268/.340/.370	.294	.419	9.7%	10.4%	59.1%	95.1%	27.6%	78.9%	10.3	97.5	108	1.3	7.6	3.6
2024 DC	CLE	MLB	26	662	67	9	65	17	.279/.352/.397	.296	.441	9.6%	9.0%							116	0.6	7.2	4.0

2023 GP: LF (153), DH (3)   Comps: Brandon Jones (62), Dave Sappelt (61), Mallex Smith (60)

Kwan's profile is near-perfectly optimized for someone who barrels the ball about once a month. He draws a good number of walks, hits a ton of soft line drives that find their way to the outfield grass, steals bases efficiently and has a feel for contact so proficient it makes you wonder if he's even playing the same sport as everyone else. In his sophomore season, pitchers found they could beat him with firm four-seamers and breaking balls in the dirt, resulting in a slightly reduced quality of contact. But even this diminished version of Kwan was still an above-average hitter and tremendous overall player, winning his second consecutive Gold Glove in left field. It's fun to see the titans of the game dominate at everything with ease, but it's oftentimes even more compelling to see players like Kwan who can maximize their output in spite of certain limitations.

Ramón Laureano RF   Born: 07/15/94   Age: 29   Bats: R   Throws: R   Height: 5'11"   Weight: 203   Origin: Round 16, 2014 Draft (#466 overall)

YEAR	TM	LVL	AGE	PA	R	HR	RBI	SB	AVG/OBP/SLG	BABIP	SLGCON	BB%	K%	ZSw%	ZCon%	OSw%	OCon%	LA	90th EV	DRC+	BRR	DRP	WARP
2021	OAK	MLB	26	378	43	14	39	12	.246/.317/.443	.304	.621	7.1%	25.9%	66.8%	84.6%	37.6%	60.6%	12.1	105.3	103	0.4	-1.7	1.5
2022	LV	AAA	27	44	10	0	2	2	.135/.273/.189	.192	.269	11.4%	25.0%	65.6%	78.6%	31.4%	65.9%			90	2.1	1.0	0.4
2022	OAK	MLB	27	383	49	13	34	11	.211/.287/.376	.262	.537	6.5%	27.2%	66.0%	84.4%	33.7%	51.1%	14.9	105.0	94	0.1	-3.7	0.5
2023	CLE	MLB	28	158	22	3	14	4	.243/.342/.382	.323	.547	10.1%	25.9%	63.7%	89.5%	30.8%	49.2%	12.1	103.2	83	-0.1	-0.3	0.1
2023	OAK	MLB	28	246	24	6	21	8	.213/.280/.364	.288	.539	6.9%	29.7%	71.8%	87.1%	34.0%	48.1%	13.6	103.6	82	0.1	0.0	0.1
2024 DC	CLE	MLB	29	486	48	12	51	17	.216/.301/.361	.276	.513	8.1%	26.3%							90	0.2	-1.6	0.5

2023 GP: RF (83), CF (20), DH (4)   Comps: B.J. Upton (65), Austin Jackson (65), Austin Kearns (64)

Oakland gave Laureano away for free on waivers a couple days after the trade deadline, possibly foreshadowing what was to come for Cleveland's late-season roster moves. After posting an .853 OPS through his first two seasons, Laureano's struggles against non-fastballs became well-documented, and opposing pitchers adjusted accordingly. He's been a below-average hitter since, but has continued to mash left-handed pitching—to the tune of a .270/.333/.460 slash line in 2023. He still provides defensive value in right field with a cannon of an arm, racking up nine outfield assists and putting the fear of God in any runner attempting to take an extra base. Going forward, it looks like he'll be platooned more, insulating him from a marked weakness against right-handed pitching.

─────────── ★ ★ ★ *2024 Top 101 Prospect* **#37** ★ ★ ★ ───────────

Kyle Manzardo 1B   Born: 07/18/00   Age: 23   Bats: L   Throws: R   Height: 6'0"   Weight: 205   Origin: Round 2, 2021 Draft (#63 overall)

YEAR	TM	LVL	AGE	PA	R	HR	RBI	SB	AVG/OBP/SLG	BABIP	SLGCON	BB%	K%	ZSw%	ZCon%	OSw%	OCon%	LA	90th EV	DRC+	BRR	DRP	WARP
2021	RAY	ROK	20	50	10	2	8	0	.349/.440/.605	.371	.703	8.0%	12.0%									0.1	
2022	BG	A+	21	275	53	17	55	0	.329/.436/.636	.343	.799	16.4%	16.7%							155	2.8	-0.6	2.7
2022	MTG	AA	21	122	18	5	26	1	.323/.402/.576	.333	.713	11.5%	15.6%							131	0.2	1.3	0.9
2023	PEJ	WIN	22	89	16	5	15	0	.241/.326/.532	.255	.700	10.1%	21.3%	58.8%	85.0%	26.2%	54.5%						
2023	DUR	AAA	22	313	33	11	38	1	.238/.342/.442	.269	.585	13.4%	20.8%	62.2%	88.0%	26.4%	64.0%			102	-3.5	0.0	0.6
2023	COL	AAA	22	92	16	6	16	0	.256/.348/.590	.233	.719	13.0%	15.2%	57.4%	84.9%	23.1%	72.5%			117	1.3	1.8	0.4
2024 DC	CLE	MLB	23	434	44	11	46	0	.232/.312/.380	.270	.487	9.7%	19.7%							96	0.0	0	0.6

2023 GP: 1B (94), DH (20)   Comps: Wes Bankston (69), Ronald Guzmán (67), Dominic Smith (65)

Manzardo was the only first baseman taken in the first 100 picks of his draft class, and the thunderous performance of his bat has validated the early selection. He's a disciplined hitter who's not easy to beat in the zone, and he's gained a bit of a power stroke, a new development since entering the pro ranks in line with an extreme batted-ball profile. Manzardo pulls more fly balls than almost anyone in affiliated baseball; big-league hitters with launch and spray distributions like his include Mookie Betts and Isaac Paredes, spelling hope for his power output even without chart-topping exit velocity. Manzardo was moved to Cleveland at the trade deadline for Aaron Civale, providing some much-needed thump to a farm system lacking in power bats.

Bo Naylor C   Born: 02/21/00   Age: 24   Bats: L   Throws: R   Height: 6'0"   Weight: 205   Origin: Round 1, 2018 Draft (#29 overall)

YEAR	TM	LVL	AGE	PA	R	HR	RBI	SB	AVG/OBP/SLG	BABIP	SLGCON	BB%	K%	ZSw%	ZCon%	OSw%	OCon%	LA	90th EV	DRC+	BRR	DRP	WARP
2021	AKR	AA	21	356	41	10	44	10	.188/.280/.332	.255	.517	10.4%	31.5%							82	-0.5	7.1	1.1
2022	AKR	AA	22	220	29	6	21	11	.271/.427/.471	.333	.645	20.5%	20.9%							122	1.3	-0.9	1.3
2022	COL	AAA	22	290	44	15	47	9	.257/.366/.514	.306	.741	12.8%	25.9%							113	-1.5	7.2	1.8
2022	CLE	MLB	22	8	0	0	0	0	.000/.000/.000		.000	0.0%	62.5%	75.0%	50.0%	28.6%	33.3%	37.8	104.2	66		0.0	0.0
2023	COL	AAA	23	270	45	13	48	2	.253/.393/.498	.273	.655	18.1%	19.3%	60.7%	82.1%	23.5%	66.7%			127	-1.0	0.5	1.7
2023	CLE	MLB	23	230	33	11	32	5	.237/.339/.470	.267	.641	13.0%	23.0%	67.6%	85.4%	27.7%	65.4%	21.0	101.9	103	0.0	4.4	1.4
2024 DC	CLE	MLB	24	389	43	12	44	6	.225/.324/.389	.270	.530	12.1%	23.0%							102	0.0	3.7	2.0

2023 GP: C (67)   Comps: Miguel Montero (56), John Ryan Murphy (50), Hank Conger (49)

In his first extended opportunity at the major-league level, Naylor absolutely showed out with both the bat and glove. He demonstrated incredible discipline for a 23-year old rookie while lifting the ball enough to hit 11 homers in just 230 plate appearances. Naylor joined Nolan Jones as the only two rookies with both an isolated power above .230 and walk rate above 12%. The one nit to pick in his offensive game is an overperformance of his expected stats, but he hits the ball in the air at Kyle Schwarber levels and pulls it enough to repeatedly knock homers without monster raw power; most of his homers to right field would have cleared the fence at nearly every ballpark. Naylor also silenced speculation about his long-term defensive home, keeping an extra five runs off the board with his framing abilities. After years of starting the likes of Yan Gomes, Austin Hedges and Roberto Pérez behind the dish, it looks like the Guardians have a middle-of-the-order hitter and defensive captain rolled into one.

YEAR	TM	P. COUNT	FRM RUNS	BLK RUNS	THRW RUNS	TOT RUNS
2021	AKR	10542	5.6	-0.5	1.5	6.6
2022	AKR	5951	-0.8	0.0	0.3	-0.5
2022	COL	8260	5.2	-0.5	0.8	5.5
2022	CLE	227	0.0	0.0	0.0	0.0
2023	COL	7053	1.6	-0.3	0.2	1.5
2023	CLE	8551	5.5	-0.1	-0.3	5.1
2024	CLE	13228	4.7	-0.5	-0.5	3.8

Josh Naylor 1B   Born: 06/22/97   Age: 27   Bats: L   Throws: L   Height: 5'11"   Weight: 250   Origin: Round 1, 2015 Draft (#12 overall)

YEAR	TM	LVL	AGE	PA	R	HR	RBI	SB	AVG/OBP/SLG	BABIP	SLGCON	BB%	K%	ZSw%	ZCon%	OSw%	OCon%	LA	90th EV	DRC+	BRR	DRP	WARP
2021	CLE	MLB	24	250	28	7	21	1	.253/.301/.399	.287	.495	5.6%	18.0%	69.9%	85.1%	41.8%	72.0%	8.8	106.3	102	0.0	-3.0	0.4
2022	COL	AAA	25	25	4	0	5	0	.200/.360/.300	.200	.300	20.0%	0.0%							118	-0.8	0.0	0.1
2022	CLE	MLB	25	498	47	20	79	6	.256/.319/.452	.268	.550	7.6%	16.1%	72.1%	90.2%	39.9%	71.3%	10.6	105.9	120	-0.3	0.1	2.3
2023	CLE	MLB	26	495	52	17	97	10	.308/.354/.489	.326	.576	6.7%	13.7%	76.6%	89.5%	44.4%	70.7%	12.7	105.7	129	0.0	0.2	2.9
2024 DC	CLE	MLB	27	583	65	18	71	8	.274/.331/.437	.299	.527	7.2%	15.6%							116	-0.3	0.1	2.4

2023 GP: 1B (91), DH (27), RF (1)   Comps: Ketel Marte (57), Dmitri Young (57), Anthony Rizzo (56)

After a breakout in his first full season, Naylor built on his excellent 2022 performance, even improving in some areas. The days of double-digit walk rates as a minor leaguer are long since past, but he's gotten more aggressive to take advantage of his plate coverage and put more balls in play. He's made far more solid contact, raising his BABIP by nearly 60 points, with nearly all of the improvement coming on ground balls. And after two years of absolute futility versus left-handed pitching, his results were platoon-neutral—he even struck out less against southpaws than righties. It's safe to say he's actualized the potential that once made him a highly touted prospect, although the shape of his production has been different than what was once expected.

Jhonkensy Noel LF   Born: 07/15/01   Age: 22   Bats: R   Throws: R   Height: 6'3"   Weight: 250   Origin: IFA, 2017

YEAR	TM	LVL	AGE	PA	R	HR	RBI	SB	AVG/OBP/SLG	BABIP	SLGCON	BB%	K%	ZSw%	ZCon%	OSw%	OCon%	LA	90th EV	DRC+	BRR	DRP	WARP
2021	LYN	A	19	162	36	11	40	2	.393/.426/.693	.421	.846	4.3%	16.7%							148	0.3	2.4	1.6
2021	LC	A+	19	111	13	8	25	3	.280/.351/.550	.328	.797	8.1%	27.9%							124	-1.0	0.5	0.6
2022	LC	A+	20	252	35	19	42	1	.219/.286/.509	.237	.784	7.1%	31.7%							114	-1.7	-3.4	0.6
2022	AKR	AA	20	278	43	13	42	2	.242/.338/.488	.271	.661	10.8%	22.7%							119	-1.5	1.3	1.5
2023	COL	AAA	21	585	81	27	85	1	.220/.303/.420	.249	.583	8.4%	24.8%	64.8%	80.0%	42.7%	59.1%			94	-2.7	10.8	2.2
2024 non	CLE	MLB	22	251	25	8	29	1	.223/.281/.382	.287	.556	6.0%	28.6%							85	0.0	0	0.1

2023 GP: LF (45), RF (40), 1B (28), 3B (20), DH (10)   Comps: Byron Buxton (42), Jo Adell (42), Victor Robles (40)

Noel is on a short list of guys who have a case for the greatest raw power in affiliated baseball—after bursting onto the scene with a 32-homer 2022 highlighted by a thunderous Futures Game appearance, last year he continued to show off his 80-grade exit velocities at the Triple-A level. But nearly every other aspect of his skillset is marginal. Noel chases at Ronny Mauricio levels, and his tendency to go after breaking balls led to plenty of mishit ground balls, a death sentence for someone who has to go yard regularly to succeed. He's a poor runner and won't sniff average range in an outfield corner. Don't be fooled by his DRP, which ranked second in the International League: His range was below-average, but he racked up a monstrous 15 outfield assists against baserunners who assumed the hulking slugger was merely a statue on the grass.

José Ramírez 3B   Born: 09/17/92   Age: 31   Bats: S   Throws: R   Height: 5'9"   Weight: 190   Origin: IFA, 2009

YEAR	TM	LVL	AGE	PA	R	HR	RBI	SB	AVG/OBP/SLG	BABIP	SLGCON	BB%	K%	ZSw%	ZCon%	OSw%	OCon%	LA	90th EV	DRC+	BRR	DRP	WARP
2021	CLE	MLB	28	636	111	36	103	27	.266/.355/.538	.256	.639	11.3%	13.7%	64.9%	92.8%	30.6%	75.9%	18.5	105.9	134	1.3	0.2	5.0
2022	CLE	MLB	29	685	90	29	126	20	.280/.355/.514	.279	.595	10.1%	12.0%	68.2%	92.5%	34.1%	76.4%	21.0	104.0	128	0.6	0.5	4.0
2023	CLE	MLB	30	691	87	24	80	28	.282/.356/.475	.285	.539	10.6%	10.6%	68.8%	92.0%	33.6%	75.2%	18.0	104.6	133	1.1	-1.9	4.8
2024 DC	CLE	MLB	31	639	79	25	87	27	.278/.357/.483	.285	.561	10.4%	12.2%							136	0.9	-0.8	4.7

2023 GP: 3B (125), DH (31)   Comps: Brooks Robinson (77), George Kell (75), Ron Santo (73)

What's left to say about Ramírez? He's essentially had the same line eight years running, averaging a 25/25 season with a 130-140 DRC+ alongside above-average defense at the hot corner. He's one of the most well-rounded superstars in the game. Among hitters with at least 4,000 plate appearances since the start of 2016, Ramírez, Bryce Harper and Mookie Betts are the only two who rank top-five in both isolated power and walk-to-strikeout ratio. No one has matched both his 208 homers and 182 stolen bases during that same timeframe. The only nit to pick in his most recent campaign was a slight decrease in power, though an improved DRC+ compared to 2022 could have been the result of his improved exit velocity and barrel rate. Two seasons into his long-term extension, the most lucrative in Cleveland's history, Ramírez has continued to show why he's worth every penny and much more.

Brayan Rocchio SS Born: 01/13/01   Age: 23   Bats: S   Throws: R   Height: 5'10"   Weight: 170   Origin: IFA, 2017

YEAR	TM	LVL	AGE	PA	R	HR	RBI	SB	AVG/OBP/SLG	BABIP	SLGCON	BB%	K%	ZSw%	ZCon%	OSw%	OCon%	LA	90th EV	DRC+	BRR	DRP	WARP
2021	LC	A+	20	288	45	9	33	14	.265/.337/.428	.319	.573	6.9%	22.6%							108	1.0	1.1	1.3
2021	AKR	AA	20	203	34	6	30	7	.293/.360/.505	.350	.650	6.4%	20.2%							112	-1.1	1.7	1.0
2022	AKR	AA	21	432	62	13	48	12	.265/.349/.432	.302	.551	9.7%	18.8%							114	2.9	1.9	2.4
2022	COL	AAA	21	152	21	5	16	2	.234/.298/.387	.241	.457	7.9%	13.8%							112	-0.1	-2.3	0.4
2023	COL	AAA	22	537	81	7	65	25	.280/.367/.421	.312	.490	11.2%	12.3%	70.5%	87.5%	31.5%	66.1%			101	1.5	0.7	1.8
2023	CLE	MLB	22	86	9	0	8	0	.247/.279/.321	.364	.481	4.7%	31.4%	67.7%	81.8%	46.7%	54.5%	2.0	97.4	63	0.0	0.0	-0.1
2024 DC	CLE	MLB	23	426	37	7	39	8	.218/.283/.336	.263	.434	7.3%	20.4%							76	-0.2	-1.1	-0.1

2023 GP: SS (18), 3B (6)   Comps: Tyler Pastornicky (69), Luis Sardinas (64), Ketel Marte (63)

After spending the past couple years alternately showcasing supreme contact skills and pull-side power, Rocchio went for the former option last year over a full Triple-A campaign, setting career-bests in strikeout and walk rate, but his worst showing in isolated power. He complemented his high-OBP profile with some speed, taking advantage of the new rules with 25 bags swiped. This solid performance earned him an August cup of coffee, where his plus approach crumbled as he indiscriminately swung at everything. He held his own at shortstop in Columbus, but played a bit of third during his call-up. Rocchio is still just 23 and it's far too early to say he won't be an everyday regular at the six, but he'll likely have to stay there given the added offensive responsibilities that come with playing the hot corner.

Jean Segura 3B Born: 03/17/90   Age: 34   Bats: R   Throws: R   Height: 5'10"   Weight: 220   Origin: IFA, 2007

YEAR	TM	LVL	AGE	PA	R	HR	RBI	SB	AVG/OBP/SLG	BABIP	SLGCON	BB%	K%	ZSw%	ZCon%	OSw%	OCon%	LA	90th EV	DRC+	BRR	DRP	WARP
2021	PHI	MLB	31	567	76	14	58	9	.290/.348/.436	.317	.514	6.9%	13.8%	65.6%	89.7%	36.3%	74.0%	5.9	105.1	115	0.5	1.9	3.5
2022	PHI	MLB	32	387	45	10	33	13	.277/.336/.387	.307	.463	6.5%	15.0%	66.2%	89.5%	38.0%	72.7%	4.4	104.7	115	0.4	0.4	2.0
2023	MIA	MLB	33	326	25	3	21	6	.219/.277/.279	.251	.331	6.7%	14.4%	65.8%	89.4%	41.0%	72.2%	2.7	103.6	98	0.0	0.4	1.0
2024 non	CLE	MLB	34	251	24	5	24	9	.255/.317/.360	.290	.432	7.1%	15.3%							95	0.2	0.5	0.6

2023 GP: 3B (84)

After inking a one-year deal with an option with the Marlins last winter, Segura lasted all of four months with the club before getting shipped out as a fiscal balance for Josh Bell. The Guardians promptly cut him and he didn't land with anyone else, even on a minor-league deal, the rest of the year. It's a little hard to say what went wrong aside from everything and nothing: A power decline that began in 2022 continued into last season, leaving the stout infielder with an emaciated .060 ISO. That's one thing when you're hitting for average, and another when every part of your slash line starts with a two. Far be it from us to reminisce for the days when a early-mid 30s player on a bad year automatically got a bounce-back contract (or at least an NRI), but Segura actually recorded better max and comparable 90th percentile and average exit velos as prior years. His launch angle was his lowest of the last three, but that seems like something an enterprising org could seek to fix for a popular clubhouse type.

Myles Straw CF Born: 10/17/94   Age: 29   Bats: R   Throws: R   Height: 5'10"   Weight: 178   Origin: Round 12, 2015 Draft (#349 overall)

YEAR	TM	LVL	AGE	PA	R	HR	RBI	SB	AVG/OBP/SLG	BABIP	SLGCON	BB%	K%	ZSw%	ZCon%	OSw%	OCon%	LA	90th EV	DRC+	BRR	DRP	WARP
2021	CLE	MLB	26	268	42	2	14	13	.285/.362/.377	.353	.476	10.8%	18.7%	58.8%	91.7%	26.4%	78.6%	13.8	100.3	99	0.6	4.7	1.6
2021	HOU	MLB	26	370	44	2	34	17	.262/.339/.326	.324	.417	10.3%	19.2%	63.3%	90.1%	24.6%	79.6%	10.8	99.0	92	0.6	5.1	1.8
2022	CLE	MLB	27	596	72	0	32	21	.221/.291/.273	.261	.326	9.1%	14.6%	58.6%	93.1%	27.3%	78.7%	9.6	98.9	88	2.3	8.2	2.4
2023	CLE	MLB	28	518	52	1	29	20	.238/.301/.297	.295	.375	8.1%	18.7%	61.0%	90.0%	30.5%	79.6%	9.1	98.6	80	0.9	5.3	1.3
2024 DC	CLE	MLB	29	479	40	3	38	18	.239/.310/.318	.277	.378	8.9%	14.4%							82	0.7	5.7	1.3

2023 GP: CF (145)   Comps: Billy Hamilton (60), Darren Lewis (57), Alex Diaz (54)

Perhaps nothing says more about the lack of thump in Straw's bat than the fact that no hitter saw a higher percentage of fastballs last season. He doesn't crush offspeed or breaking stuff, and simply doesn't impact the ball enough to damage pitchers' main offerings. He sat in the first percentile in barrel rate and expected slugging percentage, and his single home run across 518 plate appearances was infinity percent better than his 2022 mark. Though he'll never be a fearsome power hitter, he was an above-average regular in his first two seasons by WARP thanks to his elite glove in center field and efficient basestealing. But last season, he lost a step—he was one of the few players to be less effective at swiping bags under the new rules—while his defensive range fell to merely good rather than Gold Glove caliber. Quality defense at a premium position still made him a second-division regular, but Cleveland will have to hope it represents his floor rather than the start of an unfortunate trend. The final straw for this sort of player comes quickly.

José Tena SS Born: 03/20/01   Age: 23   Bats: L   Throws: R   Height: 5'11"   Weight: 195   Origin: IFA, 2017

YEAR	TM	LVL	AGE	PA	R	HR	RBI	SB	AVG/OBP/SLG	BABIP	SLGCON	BB%	K%	ZSw%	ZCon%	OSw%	OCon%	LA	90th EV	DRC+	BRR	DRP	WARP
2021	LC	A+	20	447	58	16	58	10	.281/.331/.467	.355	.652	6.0%	26.2%							102	1.6	-6.0	1.0
2022	AKR	AA	21	550	74	13	66	8	.264/.299/.411	.332	.561	4.5%	25.1%							86	0.5	-1.2	0.7
2023	AKR	AA	22	362	44	4	37	16	.260/.353/.370	.371	.559	11.3%	28.7%							88	-0.6	-4.1	0.2
2023	COL	AAA	22	66	9	4	11	0	.350/.394/.667	.425	.930	6.1%	25.8%	69.6%	78.2%	28.8%	55.6%			95	-1.1	1.6	0.2
2023	CLE	MLB	22	34	2	0	3	0	.226/.294/.290	.389	.500	8.8%	38.2%	62.9%	89.7%	29.2%	42.9%	13.4	99.2	63	0.0	-0.1	-0.1
2024 non	CLE	MLB	23	251	21	4	23	4	.205/.263/.321	.285	.478	6.3%	30.3%							62	-0.2	-1.7	-0.6

2023 GP: SS (10), 2B (3), 3B (3), DH (1)   Comps: Didi Gregorius (56), Jorge Polanco (55), Cristhian Adames (53)

Tena climbed all the way from Double-A to a big-league cup of coffee last year, but his performance didn't inspire the most confidence about a future everyday role. His swing-and-miss issues were as apparent as ever, and his previously free-swinging approach seemed to be more passive than anything else. Tena's slash lines hovered above water at each level thanks to inflated BABIPs, but he lacked the batted-ball profile to back them up; he never hit many line drives and lacked the raw power to hit balls out of the yard. At this point he's tracking more like a 40-man depth piece than a major-league mainstay, especially with the fierce competition for playing time in a crowded Cleveland infield.

George Valera OF Born: 11/13/00 Age: 23 Bats: L Throws: L Height: 6'0" Weight: 195 Origin: IFA, 2017

YEAR	TM	LVL	AGE	PA	R	HR	RBI	SB	AVG/OBP/SLG	BABIP	SLGCON	BB%	K%	ZSw%	ZCon%	OSw%	OCon%	LA	90th EV	DRC+	BRR	DRP	WARP
2021	LC	A+	20	263	45	16	43	10	.256/.430/.548	.276	.773	20.9%	22.1%							157	0.4	1.7	2.8
2021	AKR	AA	20	100	6	3	22	1	.267/.340/.407	.357	.625	11.0%	30.0%							93	-0.4	3.7	0.6
2022	AKR	AA	21	387	64	15	59	2	.264/.367/.470	.332	.674	13.4%	25.8%							109	-2.1	5.5	2.1
2022	COL	AAA	21	179	25	9	23	0	.221/.324/.448	.248	.633	12.3%	25.1%							106	-1.0	0.3	0.6
2023	GUA	ROK	22	26	5	1	3	2	.333/.423/.667	.375	.875	15.4%	19.2%										
2023	COL	AAA	22	312	40	10	35	1	.211/.343/.375	.268	.561	16.0%	27.2%	60.8%	74.8%	21.5%	48.0%			95	0.8	3.5	1.1
2024 DC	CLE	MLB	23	30	3	1	3	0	.224/.315/.367	.313	.588	10.8%	30.8%							95	0.0	0	0.1

2023 GP: CF (43), LF (22), RF (13), DH (7)   *Comps: Carlos González (47), Jesús Sánchez (45), Daz Cameron (44)*

Valera battled a wrist injury early in the season that put him on a lengthy cold streak, then missed a chunk of the minor-league season rehabbing, but took off in the second half and performed in line with his career norms. He demonstrates incredible pitch selection, and pulls the ball enough to amass extra-base hits even without immense raw juice. While Valera won't get himself out by chasing, he's concerningly vulnerable to offerings in the strike zone. Had he been in the majors, his in-zone whiff rate would rank third-worst among qualified hitters, and the Triple-A level featured significantly fewer firm fastballs up in the zone. He's still tracking like a low-average, high-OBP regular, especially if he continues playing a passable center field.

Mike Zunino C Born: 03/25/91 Age: 33 Bats: R Throws: R Height: 6'2" Weight: 235 Origin: Round 1, 2012 Draft (#3 overall)

YEAR	TM	LVL	AGE	PA	R	HR	RBI	SB	AVG/OBP/SLG	BABIP	SLGCON	BB%	K%	ZSw%	ZCon%	OSw%	OCon%	LA	90th EV	DRC+	BRR	DRP	WARP
2021	TB	MLB	30	375	64	33	62	0	.216/.301/.559	.231	.925	9.1%	35.2%	68.4%	72.3%	31.7%	44.3%	23.5	109.6	109	-0.4	6.8	2.7
2022	TB	MLB	31	123	7	5	16	0	.148/.195/.304	.185	.507	4.9%	37.4%	68.3%	79.1%	39.9%	38.5%	21.2	106.4	59	-0.1	2.0	0.0
2023	CLE	MLB	32	140	11	3	11	0	.177/.271/.306	.317	.603	10.7%	43.6%	64.9%	72.3%	34.3%	37.9%	15.1	106.3	48	-0.1	-1.1	-0.5
2024 non	CLE	MLB	33	251	26	10	30	0	.186/.265/.367	.271	.648	8.0%	39.4%							75	0.0	1.2	0.3

2023 GP: C (42)   *Comps: Jeff Mathis (68), Duffy Dyer (66), Marc Hill (61)*

YEAR	TM	P. COUNT	FRM RUNS	BLK RUNS	THRW RUNS	TOT RUNS
2021	TB	13711	8.6	-0.2	0.2	8.5
2022	TB	4610	3.0	-0.1	-0.1	2.8
2023	CLE	5615	-0.8	-0.2	0.2	-0.8
2024	CLE	6956	1.4	-0.2	0.1	1.3

The Guardians gave playing time to seven different catchers in 2023, and those not named Bo Naylor combined for below-replacement production, so it says something that Zunino was handed a midseason release even on a team without other options. He's one of the most extreme power hitters in baseball history; Zunino and Joey Gallo are the only batters with .400 career slugging percentages despite falling below the Mendoza line. But he didn't club 33 homers like he did with the Rays a couple seasons ago. He didn't even manage 20 as he did with Seattle on three occasions. He scraped a measly three long balls in 140 plate appearances with exit velocities and fly-ball rates significantly below his career norms. His 43.6% strikeout rate was dreadful even by his standards, and his once-tremendous framing abilities graded out as below-average. It was a year when everything went wrong for Zunino, whose days as a productive backstop seem to be behind him.

PITCHERS

Logan Allen LHP Born: 09/05/98 Age: 25 Height: 6'0" Weight: 190 Origin: Round 2, 2020 Draft (#56 overall)

YEAR	TM	LVL	AGE	G (GS)	IP	W-L	SV	K	WHIP	ERA	CSP	BB%	K%	HR%	GB%	ZSw%	ZCon%	OSw%	OCon%	BABIP	SLGCON	DRA-	WARP
2021	LC	A+	22	9(9)	51¹	5-0	0	67	0.97	1.58		6.5%	33.5%	1.5%	44.1%					.296	.492	80	1.1
2021	AKR	AA	22	12(10)	60	4-0	0	76	0.88	2.85		5.6%	32.9%	3.9%	28.8%					.238	.525	96	0.5
2022	AKR	AA	23	13(13)	73	5-3	0	104	1.10	3.33		7.5%	35.6%	3.1%	39.0%					.316	.628	79	1.8
2022	COL	AAA	23	14(14)	59²	4-4	0	73	1.56	6.49		10.7%	27.0%	3.0%	37.3%					.354	.636	101	0.8
2023	COL	AAA	24	5(5)	20¹	0-0	0	26	1.23	3.10		10.5%	30.2%	1.2%	43.1%	58.6%	78.0%	34.6%	54.9%	.300	.469	87	0.5
2023	CLE	MLB	24	24(24)	125¹	7-8	0	119	1.40	3.81	45.7%	8.9%	22.2%	3.0%	41.6%	69.5%	86.6%	32.9%	60.8%	.317	.558	113	0.6
2024 DC	CLE	MLB	25	23(23)	117²	7-7	0	110	1.37	4.47	45.7%	9.0%	21.6%	2.9%	41.2%					.300	.539	102	0.9

2023 Arsenal: FA (91.6), SL (78.9), CH (82.8), FC (86)   *Comps: Sean Nolin (74), Adam Morgan (74), Jakob Junis (73)*

The stereotype among left-handed college pitching prospects is that what they may lack in stuff, they make up in maturity and polish. Allen demonstrates why this rule exists, sitting in the low 90s but landing atop the strikeout leaderboard at each minor-league level. He was called up early in the season to replace an injured Shane Bieber and never looked back, finishing as the Guardians' third-most effective starter (but only the second-best rookie). Scouts were enamored with the shape of his fastball and sweeper, but his most effective pitch turned out to be his changeup—unique for its above-average drop and complete lack of horizontal movement. (Allen has denied it's a splitter or forkball, contrary to what pitch classification algorithms assert.) Batters slugged just .221 against it, and not one change was taken deep. Allen's ceiling is capped by average command and a middling rest of his arsenal, but his handedness and best pitch should give him a spot in the back of a rotation until the sun burns out (or the change does).

Scott Barlow RHP Born: 12/18/92 Age: 31 Height: 6'3" Weight: 210 Origin: Round 6, 2011 Draft (#194 overall)

YEAR	TM	LVL	AGE	G (GS)	IP	W-L	SV	K	WHIP	ERA	CSP	BB%	K%	HR%	GB%	ZSw%	ZCon%	OSw%	OCon%	BABIP	SLGCON	DRA-	WARP
2021	KC	MLB	28	71(0)	74¹	5-3	16	91	1.20	2.42	51.1%	9.2%	29.7%	1.3%	38.9%	63.2%	84.0%	35.8%	45.0%	.315	.492	85	1.3
2022	KC	MLB	29	69(0)	74¹	7-4	24	77	1.00	2.18	50.8%	7.6%	26.6%	3.1%	46.8%	59.2%	86.0%	38.9%	52.3%	.240	.459	76	1.7
2023	SD	MLB	30	25(0)	29¹	0-2	0	32	1.19	3.07	48.1%	9.8%	26.0%	0.8%	40.0%	59.3%	77.7%	30.7%	52.8%	.297	.423	91	0.5
2023	KC	MLB	30	38(0)	38²	2-4	13	47	1.55	5.35	43.2%	12.5%	26.7%	1.7%	44.3%	59.0%	88.1%	36.5%	54.0%	.347	.539	91	0.6
2024 DC	CLE	MLB	31	49(0)	52	3-2	0	61	1.28	3.95	47.9%	9.6%	27.2%	2.9%	42.3%					.297	.555	91	0.5

2023 Arsenal: CU (78.7), SL (83.2), FA (93.2), SW (82.8), SI (93.4)   *Comps: Matt Barnes (63), Andrew Chafin (62), Bobby Parnell (62)*

In 2023, Barlow went from the kind of out-of-nowhere exciting closer that last-place teams occasionally stumble into to the kind of walk-prone terrifying closer that last-place teams have by default. Flipped from Kansas City to San Diego for a pair of low-level pitchers, he was much better in southern California, slashing the free passes and benefiting from a BABIP dip. In that light, it's surprising that the Padres dealt him in the offseason despite a bullpen that could use the help; his upcoming raise via arbitration from last season's $5.3 million salary probably played a big part in that decision. Barlow's fastball is a problem, steadily clocking in at 93 mph after sitting 95 in years prior, but his curveball and slider remain the main attractions. Both were tough to square up in 2023; so long as that remains the case, he'll have a place in the late innings.

Jaime Barria RHP Born: 07/18/96 Age: 27 Height: 6'1" Weight: 210 Origin: IFA, 2013

YEAR	TM	LVL	AGE	G (GS)	IP	W-L	SV	K	WHIP	ERA	CSP	BB%	K%	HR%	GB%	ZSw%	ZCon%	OSw%	OCon%	BABIP	SLGCON	DRA-	WARP
2021	SL	AAA	24	10(10)	49	3-2	0	34	1.27	4.41		3.8%	16.2%	4.8%	36.5%					.280	.596	133	-0.8
2021	LAA	MLB	24	13(11)	56²	2-4	0	35	1.57	4.61	53.7%	7.6%	14.0%	3.2%	43.8%	71.5%	88.7%	29.0%	67.7%	.333	.560	123	-0.1
2022	LAA	MLB	25	35(1)	79¹	3-3	0	54	1.03	2.61	57.8%	6.0%	17.1%	3.5%	40.0%	71.6%	85.0%	34.8%	63.9%	.230	.483	102	0.7
2023	LAA	MLB	26	34(6)	82¹	2-6	0	62	1.47	5.68	48.1%	8.3%	17.1%	5.5%	36.2%	72.6%	84.6%	31.1%	64.5%	.286	.632	121	0.1
2024 DC	CLE	MLB	27	96(0)	100¹	5-5	0	75	1.42	5.17	51.7%	7.5%	17.0%	3.6%	38.5%					.302	.563	115	-0.2

2023 Arsenal: SL (85.7), FA (93), CH (84.6), SI (92.1)   Comps: Sean O'Sullivan (63), Jordan Lyles (62), Drew Hutchison (59)

Barria's star blazed bright for a moment, but may now be in danger of burning out. He started last year as a long reliever, then made a few spot starts and was shortly thereafter banished back to the bullpen. Despite a rocky start to his career, Barria was still one of the most underrated players on the Angels—if not in baseball as a whole—for a bit. However, his season was a story of two very disparate halves. Before the All-Star break he was cruising, posting a 3.33 ERA and 1.17 WHIP with 45 strikeouts, allowing eight home runs and 16 walks in 54 ⅓ innings. After the break, his numbers nosedived: a staggering 10.29 ERA, 2.07 WHIP, 36 runs allowed including 12 home runs and 14 walks against just 17 strikeouts—all in 28 innings, half his workload from the first half.

Tanner Bibee RHP Born: 03/05/99 Age: 25 Height: 6'2" Weight: 205 Origin: Round 5, 2021 Draft (#156 overall)

YEAR	TM	LVL	AGE	G (GS)	IP	W-L	SV	K	WHIP	ERA	CSP	BB%	K%	HR%	GB%	ZSw%	ZCon%	OSw%	OCon%	BABIP	SLGCON	DRA-	WARP
2022	LC	A+	23	12(12)	59	2-1	0	86	1.07	2.59		5.6%	37.2%	3.5%	37.4%					.344	.667	89	1.0
2022	AKR	AA	23	13(13)	73²	6-1	0	81	0.88	1.83		4.9%	28.4%	1.4%	34.2%					.260	.434	86	1.5
2023	COL	AAA	24	3(3)	15¹	2-0	0	19	1.04	1.76		13.1%	31.1%	0.0%	38.2%	59.8%	82.8%	28.2%	42.5%	.235	.265	97	0.2
2023	CLE	MLB	24	25(25)	142	10-4	0	141	1.18	2.98	47.8%	7.7%	24.1%	2.2%	36.5%	68.1%	81.4%	32.0%	61.8%	.287	.481	100	1.7
2024 DC	CLE	MLB	25	28(28)	156²	10-9	0	152	1.27	4.19	47.8%	8.1%	22.9%	3.4%	36.5%					.286	.554	97	1.6

2023 Arsenal: FA (95), SW (84.8), CH (83.9), CU (78.4)   Comps: Zach Plesac (80), Kyle Hendricks (78), Joe Ryan (77)

Bibee is your quintessential Cleveland pitching prospect. During the winter after he was drafted, a fairy sprinkled some Guardians dust on him, and the guy who had below-average stuff in college showed up in the minors sitting in the mid-90s while reaching back for eights and nines. It took just three starts in Triple-A to convince team brass to call him up to the big club just a year after his professional debut, and it's clear he was ready. Bibee demonstrated tremendous feel for his four-pitch mix—led by his slider, which drew chases and whiffs at an excellent rate. He immediately locked himself into the rotation and stayed there until a hip injury ended his season a few weeks early. But by then, he'd already proven his point. On a staff that had Shane Bieber, Triston McKenzie and Aaron Civale projected for the Opening Day rotation, the ultimate leader in ERA and innings was the guy who most had never heard of before he appeared at no. 52 on our preseason prospect list. With Bieber entering his final year before free agency, Bibee may well take his place atop the Guardians rotation.

Shane Bieber RHP Born: 05/31/95 Age: 29 Height: 6'3" Weight: 200 Origin: Round 4, 2016 Draft (#122 overall)

YEAR	TM	LVL	AGE	G (GS)	IP	W-L	SV	K	WHIP	ERA	CSP	BB%	K%	HR%	GB%	ZSw%	ZCon%	OSw%	OCon%	BABIP	SLGCON	DRA-	WARP
2021	CLE	MLB	26	16(16)	96²	7-4	0	134	1.21	3.17	56.1%	8.1%	33.1%	2.7%	44.9%	66.1%	81.1%	35.8%	42.3%	.327	.588	74	2.2
2022	CLE	MLB	27	31(31)	200	13-8	0	198	1.04	2.88	57.3%	4.6%	25.0%	2.3%	48.1%	69.0%	87.2%	34.9%	45.1%	.288	.472	76	4.5
2023	CLE	MLB	28	21(21)	128	6-6	0	107	1.23	3.80	48.6%	6.4%	20.1%	2.6%	47.3%	64.6%	90.0%	32.5%	55.4%	.295	.520	98	1.7
2024 DC	CLE	MLB	29	28(28)	167²	11-9	0	171	1.25	3.90	52.0%	6.9%	24.1%	2.8%	47.0%					.307	.538	91	2.3

2023 Arsenal: FA (91.6), SL (85), FC (86.8), KC (82.8), CH (87.4)   Comps: Félix Hernández (81), Aaron Nola (80), Ben Sheets (80)

Bieber's season was put on pause for two months with elbow inflammation, but his time on the mound constituted his most pedestrian performance in his career. The two ticks of velocity he lost in 2022 haven't come back, but more concerning was his decline in command. His slider and cutter, which he was previously able to locate with robotic accuracy just off the edge of the plate, ended up further away from the zone and easier for hitters to ignore. In the strike zone, he was easier to hit than ever, finishing the year with a below-average strikeout rate for the first time in his career. Entering a contract year, Bieber has more to prove than just how effective he is going forward; he'll also be looking to demonstrate his durability. Despite two 200-inning campaigns, he's never finished over 130 frames in consecutive seasons, thanks to unfortunately timed injuries and pandemics, but a return to form across a full season's workload still has the potential to transform his outlook in free agency.

Joey Cantillo LHP Born: 12/18/99 Age: 24 Height: 6'4" Weight: 225 Origin: Round 16, 2017 Draft (#468 overall)

YEAR	TM	LVL	AGE	G (GS)	IP	W-L	SV	K	WHIP	ERA	CSP	BB%	K%	HR%	GB%	ZSw%	ZCon%	OSw%	OCon%	BABIP	SLGCON	DRA-	WARP
2021	AKR	AA	21	5(1)	8	0-2	0	12	2.25	4.50		24.4%	29.3%	0.0%	42.1%					.421	.526	90	0.1
2022	AKR	AA	22	14(13)	60²	4-3	0	87	1.09	1.93		11.4%	35.5%	0.8%	41.7%					.288	.468	77	1.5
2023	AKR	AA	23	6(6)	24¹	1-0	0	35	1.15	1.85		14.4%	36.1%	2.1%	39.1%					.273	.533	83	0.6
2023	COL	AAA	23	20(18)	95	6-4	0	111	1.52	4.64		12.9%	26.1%	3.8%	38.8%	63.7%	74.5%	26.4%	55.8%	.307	.607	89	2.0
2024 DC	CLE	MLB	24	13(13)	54¹	2-4	0	61	1.48	4.99		12.6%	25.2%	3.3%	36.3%					.297	.581	110	0.2

2023 Arsenal: FA (93.6), CH (80.2), SL (84.5), CU (76.8)   Comps: Sean Reid-Foley (57), Josh Hader (53), Stephen Gonsalves (53)

After missing significant time in each of 2021 and '22, last season was Cantillo's most complete as a professional: He tossed 119 ⅓ innings, most of which came in the hitter-friendly International League. The lefty supplements his fastball with two plus secondaries, a changeup and a slider, each of which ran a swinging-strike rate over 20%. The change is one of the best in the minor leagues, getting a swing and miss about once every four uses—a higher rate than Devin Williams or Yennier Canó. Cantillo's stuff plays up thanks to changes in his arsenal based on batter handedness; he's basically fastball/slider only against lefties and fastball/changeup only versus righties, with the occasional curveball mixed in against each. His command is still a work in progress—he'll have to cut down his 13% walk rate—but the stuff is more than good enough to warrant a 2024 debut in the starting rotation.

Emmanuel Clase RHP Born: 03/18/98 Age: 26 Height: 6'2" Weight: 206 Origin: IFA, 2015

YEAR	TM	LVL	AGE	G (GS)	IP	W-L	SV	K	WHIP	ERA	CSP	BB%	K%	HR%	GB%	ZSw%	ZCon%	OSw%	OCon%	BABIP	SLGCON	DRA-	WARP
2021	CLE	MLB	23	71(0)	69²	4-5	24	74	0.96	1.29	53.6%	5.7%	26.5%	0.7%	67.7%	73.4%	82.7%	41.6%	47.3%	.263	.335	60	2.1
2022	CLE	MLB	24	77(0)	72²	3-4	42	77	0.73	1.36	55.6%	3.7%	28.4%	1.1%	62.8%	74.3%	81.4%	49.9%	55.2%	.223	.320	59	2.3
2023	CLE	MLB	25	75(0)	72²	3-9	44	64	1.16	3.22	51.7%	5.3%	21.2%	1.3%	55.2%	72.4%	83.7%	36.9%	53.6%	.296	.424	80	1.6
2024 DC	CLE	MLB	26	55(0)	58	4-6	36	54	1.22	3.37	53.2%	6.6%	22.2%	1.8%	58.5%					.303	.465	80	0.9

2023 Arsenal: HC (99.2), SL (91.3), SI (98.3), CU (82.8)   Comps: Huston Street (77), Mark Wohlers (72), Gregg Olson (71)

If it were 1993 instead of 2023, Clase and his league-leading 43 saves would likely have run away with the Rolaids Relief Man of the Year award. Unfortunately, that honor has been renamed, and its voters (a group of retired relievers) knew juuuust enough to consider his dozen blown saves, which also paced the league. The most statistically enlightened might also dock him for his -1.96 win probability added, second-worst among American League relief pitchers. Clase's worsened command and occasional struggles to hold velocity may have been the results of an immense workload, as he appeared in more games than any other pitcher over the past three seasons. His slight declines in swing-and-miss rates proved especially costly when his opponents were gifted runners in scoring position; on four occasions he surrendered walk-offs in extra innings. In total, he allowed more earned runs last year than in his 2021 and '22 seasons combined. Still, it's a testament to Clase's excellence that a season with a 3.14 ERA was disastrous by his standards. He'll likely return to form as one of the league's top closers, though you might not see him pitch in 75 games again.

Xzavion Curry RHP Born: 07/27/98 Age: 25 Height: 6'0" Weight: 195 Origin: Round 7, 2019 Draft (#220 overall)

YEAR	TM	LVL	AGE	G (GS)	IP	W-L	SV	K	WHIP	ERA	CSP	BB%	K%	HR%	GB%	ZSw%	ZCon%	OSw%	OCon%	BABIP	SLGCON	DRA-	WARP
2021	LYN	A	22	5(5)	25¹	3-0	0	38	0.63	1.07		4.3%	40.4%	1.1%	27.5%					.220	.333	72	0.6
2021	LC	A+	22	13(13)	67²	5-1	0	80	0.96	2.66		4.4%	29.6%	3.7%	30.9%					.261	.575	91	1.0
2022	AKR	AA	23	13(11)	69	5-3	0	80	1.09	3.65		6.7%	28.4%	3.2%	31.7%					.275	.502	102	0.9
2022	COL	AAA	23	12(10)	53	4-1	0	54	1.38	4.58		10.0%	23.5%	3.9%	36.2%					.287	.583	103	0.6
2022	CLE	MLB	23	2(2)	9¹	0-1	0	3	2.04	5.79	51.6%	12.8%	6.4%	2.1%	32.4%	67.8%	82.5%	25.5%	63.0%	.333	.486	135	-0.1
2023	CLE	MLB	24	41(9)	95	3-4	0	67	1.35	4.07	51.8%	7.4%	16.6%	3.0%	31.1%	72.1%	84.7%	30.4%	68.8%	.295	.533	120	0.1
2024 DC	CLE	MLB	25	49(6)	76²	4-4	0	56	1.41	5.12	51.8%	8.0%	16.6%	3.7%	31.6%					.291	.562	115	-0.1

2023 Arsenal: FA (92.8), SL (85.3), CU (75.2), CH (88.1)   Comps: Justin Grimm (58), Robert Dugger (53), Trevor Bell (48)

Curry's first full season in the majors went as well as you could expect for a pitcher who lacks the stuff to cut it in most rotations. Aside from a few spot starts, he primarily contributed two or three low-leverage innings at a time, pitching to a 4.07 ERA (though you may not be able to stomach the peripherals). Curry fills the zone with his fastball and slider, primarily because they aren't able to draw out-of-zone chases, inviting balls in play and keeping a low walk rate. He may not have enviable pitch model grades or ever be a high-leverage 'pen arm, but he covers so many innings from one bullpen slot that he's worth keeping around.

Daniel Espino RHP Born: 01/05/01 Age: 23 Height: 6'2" Weight: 225 Origin: Round 1, 2019 Draft (#24 overall)

YEAR	TM	LVL	AGE	G (GS)	IP	W-L	SV	K	WHIP	ERA	CSP	BB%	K%	HR%	GB%	ZSw%	ZCon%	OSw%	OCon%	BABIP	SLGCON	DRA-	WARP
2021	LYN	A	20	10(10)	42²	1-2	0	64	1.34	3.38		12.8%	35.6%	1.1%	48.4%					.352	.505	68	1.2
2021	LC	A+	20	10(10)	49	2-6	0	88	0.94	4.04		8.2%	45.1%	3.6%	31.1%					.280	.659	58	1.6
2022	AKR	AA	21	4(4)	18¹	1-0	0	35	0.71	2.45		5.9%	51.5%	5.9%	20.7%					.200	.828	71	0.5
2024 non	CLE	MLB	23	58(0)	50	2-2	0	62	1.29	4.27		10.5%	29.1%	4.0%	34.6%					.286	.619	97	0.3

Comps: Matt Manning (82), Drew Hutchison (80), Mitch Keller (80)

On April 29, 2022, Espino made his fourth start of the year, allowing one run over 4 ⅔ innings and continuing to absolutely lay waste to the Double-A level. He hasn't thrown a single pitch since, as the shoulder soreness that shut down his '22 season led to an anterior capsule surgery that will keep him out until midway through 2024. By that point, Espino will have missed over two full calendar years, and the 2021 campaign when he struck out 40% of batters while showing off triple-digit velocity and three plus pitches seems like a lifetime ago. Entering his age-23 season, it remains to be seen how much of his frontline stuff returns after a lengthy recovery and just a single uninterrupted minor-league campaign.

Amir Garrett LHP Born: 05/03/92 Age: 32 Height: 6'5" Weight: 239 Origin: Round 22, 2011 Draft (#685 overall)

YEAR	TM	LVL	AGE	G (GS)	IP	W-L	SV	K	WHIP	ERA	CSP	BB%	K%	HR%	GB%	ZSw%	ZCon%	OSw%	OCon%	BABIP	SLGCON	DRA-	WARP
2021	CIN	MLB	29	63(0)	47²	0-4	7	61	1.57	6.04	54.6%	13.5%	28.4%	4.2%	50.4%	61.9%	80.0%	31.5%	49.1%	.322	.669	86	0.8
2022	KC	MLB	30	60(0)	45¹	3-1	0	49	1.32	4.96	51.5%	16.3%	25.0%	0.0%	38.2%	64.5%	83.4%	28.8%	60.4%	.255	.349	116	0.1
2023	KC	MLB	31	27(0)	24¹	0-1	0	28	1.73	3.33	44.9%	17.9%	25.0%	3.6%	43.8%	68.5%	76.2%	25.5%	68.4%	.305	.613	100	0.3
2024 non	CLE	MLB	32	58(0)	50	2-2	0	57	1.50	4.87	49.0%	14.1%	25.4%	3.0%	43.1%					.294	.549	106	0.1

2023 Arsenal: SL (86.2), SI (94.9), FA (95.2)   Comps: Zack Britton (67), Andrew Chafin (64), J.C. Romero (63)

A lethal gyro slider and 97-mph heat from a lefty is usually a relief package that gets teams salivating, except when paired with command only marginally better than Rick Ankiel's. Garrett's walk rates look like the strikeout rates of a crafty back-end starter and he often misses spots towards the middle of the zone, which can get hammered by batters sitting meatball. His stuff is untouchable when properly executed, but given that he's over 300 innings into his big-league career with an ERA hovering near five, it's safe to say it usually isn't. DRA is more optimistic, at least. Entering free agency for the first time in his career, Garrett will get an opportunity with a team looking to hit the right tail of his wide variance in possible outcomes.

Steve Hajjar LHP   Born: 08/07/00   Age: 23   Height: 6'5"   Weight: 240   Origin: Round 2, 2021 Draft (#61 overall)

YEAR	TM	LVL	AGE	G (GS)	IP	W-L	SV	K	WHIP	ERA	CSP	BB%	K%	HR%	GB%	ZSw%	ZCon%	OSw%	OCon%	BABIP	SLGCON	DRA-	WARP
2022	FTM	A	21	12 (12)	43²	2-2	0	71	1.08	2.47		12.6%	40.8%	1.7%	34.2%	71.0%	68.6%	29.1%	49.6%	.289	.487	75	1.2
2022	DAY	A+	21	2 (2)	7	0-1	0	10	1.43	6.43		20.0%	33.3%	0.0%	21.4%					.286	.357	108	0.0
2023	GUA	ROK	22	2 (1)	7	1-1	0	7	1.71	3.86		18.8%	21.9%	0.0%	42.1%					.316	.474		
2023	LC	A+	22	14 (14)	57¹	3-4	0	58	1.55	3.61		20.2%	22.6%	1.6%	30.1%					.234	.400	155	-0.3
2024 non	CLE	MLB	23	58 (0)	50	2-2	0	55	1.77	6.36		17.0%	23.4%	3.4%	32.0%					.308	.612	133	-0.6

Comps: Kevin Siegrist (55), Blake Snell (54), Hector Perez (53)

Hajjar came to Cleveland as part of the trade that sent Will Benson to the Reds, his second move in two professional seasons. His pro debut put his big-time strikeout stuff on display—two potentially plus secondaries from the left side were simply too much for Low-A hitters to handle. But he also walked more than his fair share of batters and missed time with a shoulder injury. After a promotion to High-A, Hajjar's struggles to throw strikes became debilitating. He walked 22.5% of batters faced while uncorking 8 wild pitches in 14 games, also spending even more time on the injured list. The quality of stuff is still there, but he may have required the winter to fully overhaul his mechanics and rhythm on the mound.

Sam Hentges LHP   Born: 07/18/96   Age: 27   Height: 6'6"   Weight: 245   Origin: Round 4, 2014 Draft (#128 overall)

YEAR	TM	LVL	AGE	G (GS)	IP	W-L	SV	K	WHIP	ERA	CSP	BB%	K%	HR%	GB%	ZSw%	ZCon%	OSw%	OCon%	BABIP	SLGCON	DRA-	WARP
2021	CLE	MLB	24	30 (12)	68²	1-4	0	68	1.78	6.68	54.7%	10.1%	21.4%	3.1%	45.4%	68.7%	89.7%	30.6%	56.7%	.386	.647	110	0.3
2022	CLE	MLB	25	57 (0)	62	3-2	1	72	0.97	2.32	53.6%	7.8%	29.4%	1.2%	60.9%	67.1%	82.8%	36.3%	53.5%	.259	.383	73	1.5
2023	CLE	MLB	26	56 (0)	52¹	3-2	0	56	1.36	3.61	48.9%	8.1%	25.1%	0.9%	57.0%	64.7%	87.1%	31.0%	50.6%	.347	.466	82	1.1
2024 DC	CLE	MLB	27	49 (0)	52	3-2	0	51	1.31	3.76	52.2%	9.2%	22.9%	2.0%	52.8%					.299	.473	86	0.6

2023 Arsenal: KC (79.9), FA (95.7), SL (87.6), SI (95.5)   *Comps: Enny Romero (59), Anthony Misiewicz (56), Taylor Rogers (56)*

Just three pitchers allowed hard hits at a higher rate than Hentges, but each of them had an ERA at least a run worse, if not several. He limited damage by keeping the ball on the ground more than nearly anyone else, thanks to his high slot and the downhill plane of his pitches—even his four-seam fastball has less carry and more perceived drop than most offerings. He switched up his pitch usage, committing to a sinker/slider mix against fellow lefties while exclusively using his fastball and curveball to neutralize right-handed hitters. He actually ran reverse splits for the season, as the latter two offerings generated plenty of whiffs and grounders alike.

James Karinchak RHP   Born: 09/22/95   Age: 28   Height: 6'3"   Weight: 215   Origin: Round 9, 2017 Draft (#282 overall)

YEAR	TM	LVL	AGE	G (GS)	IP	W-L	SV	K	WHIP	ERA	CSP	BB%	K%	HR%	GB%	ZSw%	ZCon%	OSw%	OCon%	BABIP	SLGCON	DRA-	WARP
2021	COL	AAA	25	7 (0)	6	1-1	0	9	1.00	3.00		12.5%	37.5%	4.2%	33.3%					.182	.583	84	0.1
2021	CLE	MLB	25	60 (0)	55¹	7-4	11	78	1.21	4.07	55.6%	13.6%	33.2%	3.8%	39.8%	65.6%	73.5%	29.4%	61.5%	.228	.579	87	0.9
2022	COL	AAA	26	12 (0)	11	1-0	0	17	1.91	5.73		20.8%	32.1%	0.0%	24.0%					.400	.500	96	0.2
2022	CLE	MLB	26	38 (0)	39	2-0	3	62	1.10	2.08	54.1%	13.1%	38.8%	1.3%	23.7%	57.1%	78.7%	28.4%	50.0%	.270	.440	85	0.7
2023	COL	AAA	27	24 (0)	23¹	0-0	5	42	1.16	4.24		13.5%	43.8%	1.0%	24.4%	51.5%	79.3%	31.3%	50.0%	.325	.684	75	0.7
2023	CLE	MLB	27	44 (0)	39	2-5	0	52	1.33	3.23	42.0%	16.4%	30.4%	3.5%	28.4%	59.7%	80.1%	30.8%	60.1%	.220	.578	108	0.3
2024 DC	CLE	MLB	28	49 (0)	52	3-2	4	73	1.26	3.67	49.3%	13.6%	32.8%	3.4%	30.9%					.259	.586	85	0.6

2023 Arsenal: FA (95.1), CU (83.1)   *Comps: Carl Edwards Jr. (59), Henry Alberto Rodriguez (56), Nick Goody (56)*

We talk a lot about how the sweeping rule changes last season helped or hindered certain types of players, from the speedsters taking advantage of larger bases to hulking sluggers pulling grounders with no over shift to check them. But for Karinchak, that was the second time rule modifications messed up his groove in the past three years. First, it was the sticky stuff enforcement, a major blow to a guy whose ultra-vertical fastball and curveball rely entirely on spin-based movement. It took him a year to adjust, but he looked great in 2022. Then the pitch clock was implemented, and while most hurlers realized they didn't need to change all that much to avoid timer violations, Karinchak was one of the few who did. The most noticeable effect was a sudden inability to throw strikes, especially with the fastball. He also allowed homers at thrice the rate of his previous season, perhaps unsurprising given his refusal to impart horizontal movement on his pitches. Even if he returns to dominance this season, it's anyone's guess what new changes the league will throw at him in 2025.

Ben Lively RHP   Born: 03/05/92   Age: 32   Height: 6'4"   Weight: 235   Origin: Round 4, 2013 Draft (#135 overall)

YEAR	TM	LVL	AGE	G (GS)	IP	W-L	SV	K	WHIP	ERA	CSP	BB%	K%	HR%	GB%	ZSw%	ZCon%	OSw%	OCon%	BABIP	SLGCON	DRA-	WARP
2022	LOU	AAA	30	18(18)	77	2-5	0	79	1.35	4.09		8.4%	23.7%	1.8%	40.4%					.330	.532	110	0.6
2023	LOU	AAA	31	7(6)	32²	4-0	0	22	1.26	4.68		9.0%	16.4%	3.7%	45.5%	66.7%	85.3%	28.5%	77.4%	.258	.526	106	0.4
2023	CIN	MLB	31	19(12)	88²	4-7	0	79	1.36	5.38	50.6%	6.5%	20.6%	5.2%	38.8%	66.0%	86.9%	27.7%	63.8%	.297	.630	105	0.8
2024 DC	CLE	MLB	32	42(10)	74¹	3-4	0	58	1.42	5.19	50.6%	8.2%	17.6%	3.5%	39.3%					.296	.559	116	-0.1

2023 Arsenal: FA (90.9), SW (80.4), SI (91.5), CH (84.5), FC (88.7), CU (76.4)   Comps: Josh Tomlin (55), Kyle Lohse (54), Tim Redding (53)

The Reds originally drafted Lively all the way back in 2013, eventually trading him for Marlon Byrd the following year—which is a very 2014 transaction to make. Several organizations, waiver claims and a stint in the Korean league later, Lively returned to where it all began. He was tasked with starting meaningful games for the Reds, if only because the team was so desperate for pitchers; you, reading this right now, actually started three games for the 2023 Reds. In fairness, Lively did his job, which was to absorb some innings to avoid running the rookie pitchers into the ground, and filled the role perfectly admirably. Returning to the *Annual* for the first time since 2019, if his career's not lively it's at least live-ish, although now with the other team in Ohio.

Triston McKenzie RHP   Born: 08/02/97   Age: 26   Height: 6'5"   Weight: 165   Origin: Round 1, 2015 Draft (#42 overall)

YEAR	TM	LVL	AGE	G (GS)	IP	W-L	SV	K	WHIP	ERA	CSP	BB%	K%	HR%	GB%	ZSw%	ZCon%	OSw%	OCon%	BABIP	SLGCON	DRA-	WARP
2021	COL	AAA	23	5(5)	21¹	1-1	0	23	1.41	2.95		13.2%	25.3%	5.5%	26.8%					.255	.643	117	0.1
2021	CLE	MLB	23	25(24)	120	5-9	0	136	1.18	4.95	53.4%	11.7%	27.5%	4.2%	29.5%	70.0%	84.3%	35.8%	58.4%	.227	.559	118	0.0
2022	CLE	MLB	24	31(30)	191¹	11-11	0	190	0.95	2.96	58.6%	5.9%	25.6%	3.4%	33.1%	72.6%	82.2%	36.8%	59.6%	.238	.494	90	2.8
2023	COL	AAA	25	4(4)	14	0-1	0	15	1.21	5.14		8.9%	26.8%	8.9%	38.9%	58.5%	83.6%	29.0%	52.6%	.226	.750	96	0.2
2023	CLE	MLB	25	4(4)	16	0-3	0	16	1.56	5.06	45.3%	17.8%	21.9%	1.4%	34.1%	69.6%	83.3%	30.3%	59.6%	.256	.477	119	0.0
2024 DC	CLE	MLB	26	26(26)	142¹	9-8	0	150	1.33	4.53	55.3%	9.5%	24.6%	3.9%	33.5%					.287	.594	104	1.0

2023 Arsenal: FA (92.6), SL (85.1), CU (79)   Comps: Chris Archer (66), Jack Flaherty (65), Luis Severino (64)

Whenever a wire-framed hurler enters the pro ranks, it's *de rigueur* to question his durability and speculate whether he can remain a starter at all. The lack of confidence in McKenzie's ability to pitch a full season is what made his 2022 campaign such a triumph—relentlessly attacking the zone with his fastball and breaking balls for over 190 innings, he was practically an iron man by today's standards. He threw 48 more innings than he had in any other season since being drafted, and it appears that last year he paid the price for it. McKenzie missed the first two months of the year with a shoulder strain and made just two starts in June before being shut down again with a UCL strain. He and the Guardians opted against surgery, instead spending three more months rehabbing the injury. He would come back for two short starts in the last week of the season, walking nine batters while striking out just one. I wouldn't read into the control issues too heavily; that McKenzie returned at all at least indicates a healthy offseason to fully prepare for a rebound 2024.

Eli Morgan RHP   Born: 05/13/96   Age: 28   Height: 5'10"   Weight: 190   Origin: Round 8, 2017 Draft (#252 overall)

YEAR	TM	LVL	AGE	G (GS)	IP	W-L	SV	K	WHIP	ERA	CSP	BB%	K%	HR%	GB%	ZSw%	ZCon%	OSw%	OCon%	BABIP	SLGCON	DRA-	WARP
2021	COL	AAA	25	5(5)	22¹	0-1	0	21	1.39	4.03		12.0%	22.8%	1.1%	25.4%					.333	.448	120	0.1
2021	CLE	MLB	25	18(18)	89¹	5-7	0	81	1.25	5.34	54.2%	5.8%	21.4%	5.3%	30.0%	70.9%	85.1%	35.0%	65.0%	.282	.652	126	-0.4
2022	CLE	MLB	26	50(1)	66²	5-3	0	72	0.88	3.38	56.6%	5.1%	28.1%	3.9%	30.8%	71.8%	82.3%	36.0%	59.6%	.226	.545	89	1.0
2023	CLE	MLB	27	61(0)	67¹	5-2	1	75	1.44	4.01	46.4%	8.0%	25.1%	3.0%	40.7%	72.3%	83.0%	37.6%	56.6%	.337	.571	89	1.2
2024 DC	CLE	MLB	28	55(0)	58	4-2	0	57	1.27	4.26	51.6%	7.8%	23.0%	3.7%	35.5%					.286	.572	99	0.4

2023 Arsenal: FA (92.8), CH (78.8), SL (85.8), SW (85.1)   Comps: Tyler Duffey (70), André Rienzo (65), Trent Thornton (64)

Morgan's role on the Guardians' staff has transformed each year: As a rookie he was a starter who couldn't handle the order multiple times; as a sophomore he was a long reliever making frequent multi-inning appearances; in 2023 he completed his metamorphosis, settling into a one-inning cog on the bridge to Emmanuel Clase. Concurrent with the evolution in role has been a change in his pitching style. He reduced his fastball usage in exchange for more sliders, and changeups kept more balls in the yard but allowed more contact to be hit on a line. His wicked changeup is a weapon to keep lefties at bay, but a particularly ineffective slider shifted things too far in the reverse split direction, allowing fellow righties to tee off to the tune of a .490 slugging percentage. His overall output in terms of innings and DRA- were nearly unchanged from 2022, but the shape of that production drastically changed alongside his usage.

Doug Nikhazy LHP   Born: 08/11/99   Age: 24   Height: 6'0"   Weight: 210   Origin: Round 2, 2021 Draft (#58 overall)

YEAR	TM	LVL	AGE	G (GS)	IP	W-L	SV	K	WHIP	ERA	CSP	BB%	K%	HR%	GB%	ZSw%	ZCon%	OSw%	OCon%	BABIP	SLGCON	DRA-	WARP
2022	LC	A+	22	21(21)	93	4-4	0	118	1.37	3.19		16.9%	29.4%	2.0%	40.5%					.252	.456	94	1.2
2022	AKR	AA	22	3(3)	9¹	0-2	0	10	2.68	11.57		21.6%	19.6%	2.0%	53.3%					.448	.621	116	0.1
2023	AKR	AA	23	26(22)	102	4-8	0	128	1.62	4.94		15.4%	27.0%	2.7%	32.3%					.310	.608	100	1.5
2024 non	CLE	MLB	24	58(0)	50	2-2	0	53	1.76	6.32		16.3%	22.3%	3.4%	33.5%					.308	.606	132	-0.6

Comps: Joey Murray (79), Thomas Pannone (78), Trevor Stephan (78)

Given Cleveland's reputation for drafting pitchers with command and developing their stuff in the minor leagues, it's easy to see why they spent a 2021 second-round pick on Nikhazy, known at Ole Miss as a fearless zone-filler even without overpowering velocity. But since entering the pro ranks, he's struggled tremendously with command, walking nearly seven batters per nine. He also hasn't experienced the trademark Cleveland velocity bump, still sitting in the low-90s with his fastball, though it punches above its radar gun reading thanks to his extension and low release point from an undersized frame. Nikhazy's curveball and slider have the potential to end up as above-average offerings, but that won't mean much if he can't find the zone.

Nick Sandlin RHP   Born: 01/10/97   Age: 27   Height: 5'11"   Weight: 175   Origin: Round 2, 2018 Draft (#67 overall)

YEAR	TM	LVL	AGE	G (GS)	IP	W-L	SV	K	WHIP	ERA	CSP	BB%	K%	HR%	GB%	ZSw%	ZCon%	OSw%	OCon%	BABIP	SLGCON	DRA-	WARP
2021	CLE	MLB	24	34(0)	33²	1-1	0	48	1.13	2.94	52.7%	12.1%	34.0%	1.4%	41.7%	55.4%	77.7%	28.2%	50.0%	.271	.479	82	0.6
2022	COL	AAA	25	5(0)	4¹	0-0	0	3	1.62	8.31		21.1%	15.8%	5.3%	33.3%					.200	.636	102	0.1
2022	CLE	MLB	25	46(0)	44	5-2	0	41	1.16	2.25	50.4%	13.3%	22.8%	1.1%	55.4%	69.5%	82.4%	30.3%	57.0%	.227	.339	96	0.5
2023	CLE	MLB	26	61(0)	60	5-5	0	66	1.03	3.75	47.0%	10.0%	27.6%	5.0%	40.1%	65.0%	77.1%	32.6%	54.5%	.195	.566	88	1.1
2024 DC	*CLE*	*MLB*	*27*	*55(0)*	*58*	*4-2*	*0*	*68*	*1.34*	*4.24*	*49.1%*	*11.3%*	*27.0%*	*3.0%*	*43.7%*					*.290*	*.550*	*96*	*0.4*

2023 Arsenal: SL (79.2), FA (92.4), SI (92.6), CH (86)   Comps: *Arodys Vizcaíno (67), Corey Knebel (61), Diego Castillo (61)*

Sandlin has the profile of your classic sidearm reliever—fastballs sitting in the low 90s alongside a sweepy, low-slot breaking ball. The advantage of an ultra-flat frisbee slider is that it closely resembles a heater before bending off the plate; the downside is that when the pitch hangs up in the zone, it stays on plane with line-drive swings and can get crushed. Sandlin's slider resulted in six homers last year; over his first two seasons he allowed just four on all pitches combined. Despite that major uptick in homers, he put together a solid season and even cleaned up a considerable platoon split, making him useful as an all-purpose middle reliever rather than merely a specialist.

Trevor Stephan RHP   Born: 11/25/95   Age: 28   Height: 6'5"   Weight: 225   Origin: Round 3, 2017 Draft (#92 overall)

YEAR	TM	LVL	AGE	G (GS)	IP	W-L	SV	K	WHIP	ERA	CSP	BB%	K%	HR%	GB%	ZSw%	ZCon%	OSw%	OCon%	BABIP	SLGCON	DRA-	WARP
2021	CLE	MLB	25	43(0)	63¹	3-1	1	75	1.41	4.41	53.6%	11.0%	26.6%	5.3%	32.9%	71.9%	77.2%	29.1%	56.4%	.272	.674	104	0.5
2022	CLE	MLB	26	66(0)	63²	6-5	3	82	1.18	2.69	52.9%	6.7%	30.7%	1.1%	47.2%	67.5%	75.5%	38.4%	51.7%	.344	.500	71	1.6
2023	CLE	MLB	27	71(0)	68²	7-7	2	75	1.30	4.06	45.5%	8.8%	25.5%	2.0%	41.0%	73.9%	81.8%	35.3%	53.6%	.318	.549	92	1.1
2024 DC	*CLE*	*MLB*	*28*	*49(0)*	*52*	*3-2*	*2*	*61*	*1.28*	*4.12*	*50.0%*	*9.2%*	*27.3%*	*3.1%*	*40.4%*					*.298*	*.565*	*94*	*0.4*

2023 Arsenal: FA (95.1), FS (86.7), SL (85.6)   Comps: *Matt Barnes (77), Michael Feliz (75), Josh Staumont (73)*

Following a season when nearly everything seemed to click out of nowhere, Stephan experienced some regression. His splitter was still wonderful, earning whiffs on over one-fourth of pitches thrown despite almost never being aimed at the strike zone. But his fastball lost a tick of velocity and his slider faltered, often ending up flat and ready to crush. The result was that he became far more hittable in the zone and allowed plenty of loud contact, pushing his ERA closer to league-average. If he can't regain his velocity, Stephan's path to regaining elite form will likely involve scaling up the usage of his splitter, which he's used just a quarter of the time.

Noah Syndergaard RHP   Born: 08/29/92   Age: 31   Height: 6'6"   Weight: 242   Origin: Round 1, 2010 Draft (#38 overall)

YEAR	TM	LVL	AGE	G (GS)	IP	W-L	SV	K	WHIP	ERA	CSP	BB%	K%	HR%	GB%	ZSw%	ZCon%	OSw%	OCon%	BABIP	SLGCON	DRA-	WARP
2021	NYM	MLB	28	2(2)	2	0-1	0	2	1.50	9.00	57.1%	0.0%	25.0%	12.5%	16.7%	81.8%	100.0%	33.3%	40.0%	.400	1.167	122	0.0
2022	LAA	MLB	29	15(15)	80	5-8	0	64	1.21	3.83	56.9%	6.5%	18.9%	2.7%	44.4%	70.4%	83.6%	33.1%	66.2%	.277	.484	106	0.5
2022	PHI	MLB	29	10(9)	54²	5-2	0	31	1.32	4.12	55.5%	4.0%	13.7%	2.2%	39.0%	68.3%	91.2%	35.0%	73.0%	.320	.516	116	0.1
2023	OKC	AAA	30	2(2)	10	0-1	0	8	1.00	5.40		0.0%	20.5%	2.6%	32.3%	70.1%	85.1%	43.5%	63.0%	.300	.533	102	0.1
2023	CLE	MLB	30	6(6)	33¹	1-2	0	18	1.29	5.40	55.8%	6.9%	12.4%	6.9%	32.7%	75.6%	84.9%	26.3%	81.7%	.223	.602	127	-0.1
2023	LAD	MLB	30	12(12)	55¹	1-4	0	38	1.45	7.16	51.9%	3.7%	15.4%	4.9%	40.4%	69.7%	86.9%	30.3%	69.0%	.326	.661	125	-0.1
2024 non	*CLE*	*MLB*	*31*	*58(0)*	*50*	*2-2*	*0*	*32*	*1.39*	*5.10*	*54.0%*	*5.9%*	*14.8%*	*3.3%*	*40.2%*					*.305*	*.541*	*114*	*-0.2*

2023 Arsenal: SI (92.6), CH (87.5), FA (92.5), CU (78), FC (89.7), SL (84.8)   Comps: *Bill Gullickson (84), Matt Harvey (83), Alex Cobb (80)*

It's difficult to admit you're not what you once were, especially for professional athletes at the top of the world in their given craft. But after two seasons of his insistence otherwise, it's safe to conclude Syndergaard's breathtaking velocity from his early career won't be coming back. He's appeared for five teams since undergoing Tommy John surgery in 2021, and at this point is more than six ticks below where he sat as a former Mets co-ace. The attempts he's made to adapt to his physical limitations, like centering his arsenal around his sinker and changeup to get more ground balls, simply haven't been enough—his strikeout rate has fallen through the floor and his fastballs, which never had great shape to begin with, got hit harder and harder with diminished velocity. It's shocking to see such a fall from a former whiff machine entering his age-31 season. Syndergaard's glory days are long behind him, but there might be just one more team willing to give him a shot based on his pre-injury track record.

Gavin Williams RHP   Born: 07/26/99   Age: 24   Height: 6'6"   Weight: 250   Origin: Round 1, 2021 Draft (#23 overall)

YEAR	TM	LVL	AGE	G (GS)	IP	W-L	SV	K	WHIP	ERA	CSP	BB%	K%	HR%	GB%	ZSw%	ZCon%	OSw%	OCon%	BABIP	SLGCON	DRA-	WARP
2022	LC	A+	22	9(9)	45	2-1	0	67	0.87	1.40		8.3%	39.9%	0.0%	40.5%					.298	.361	73	1.1
2022	AKR	AA	22	16(16)	70	3-3	0	82	1.00	2.31		9.2%	29.1%	3.2%	35.5%					.219	.464	79	1.7
2023	AKR	AA	23	3(3)	14¹	1-0	0	20	0.63	0.63		5.7%	37.7%	0.0%	26.7%					.200	.267	89	0.3
2023	COL	AAA	23	9(9)	46	3-2	0	61	1.09	2.93		11.5%	33.3%	3.3%	40.4%	64.6%	76.3%	34.0%	49.3%	.250	.537	84	1.1
2023	CLE	MLB	23	16(16)	82	3-5	0	81	1.26	3.29	47.3%	10.7%	23.5%	2.3%	38.6%	70.8%	80.0%	31.2%	59.8%	.270	.502	111	0.5
2024 DC	*CLE*	*MLB*	*24*	*23(23)*	*115²*	*6-7*	*0*	*125*	*1.34*	*4.40*	*47.3%*	*10.6%*	*24.9%*	*3.4%*	*38.0%*					*.285*	*.567*	*100*	*1.0*

2023 Arsenal: FA (95.8), SL (85.1), KC (76.4), CH (88.7)   Comps: *Jake Faria (81), Matt Harvey (80), Dan Straily (77)*

The fastball and bullet slider that rocketed Williams up draft boards and through the minors have performed as advertised in the majors, racking up whiffs thanks to plus velocity and elite extension. The rest of his arsenal is still a work in progress, as the increased caliber of competition forced Williams to diversify his mix. He's especially struggled with locating the curveball and changeup, which he's thrown 23% of the time at the major-league level compared to just 14% at East Carolina. Lefty hitters, seeing more of his weaker offerings, enjoyed a 100-point boost in wOBA and triple the walk rate of their right-handed counterparts. Williams' 3.29 ERA ranked fourth in baseball among rookies with at least 15 starts (and second on his own team), but overperformed his DRA by over two runs. Refining his approach against lefties is the developmental priority, though he's also a candidate to simplify his arsenal and do what he does best—especially with hurlers like Spencer Strider and Justin Steele thriving with just two pitches, unburdened by subpar tertiary offerings.

LINEOUTS

Hitters

HITTER	POS	TM	LVL	AGE	PA	R	HR	RBI	SB	AVG/OBP/SLG	BABIP	SLGCON	BB%	K%	ZSw%	ZCon%	OSw%	OCon%	LA	90th EV	DRC+	BRR	DRP	WARP
Jaison Chourio	OF	GUA	ROK	18	189	40	1	25	19	.349/.476/.463	.451	.616	20.1%	19.6%										
	OF	LYN	A	18	42	7	0	3	1	.200/.310/.229	.333	.400	14.3%	35.7%							84	0.4	0.3	0.1
Jake Fox	OF	LC	A+	20	453	61	8	53	9	.256/.330/.398	.322	.535	9.9%	22.7%							96	-0.2	5.6	1.9
Welbyn Francisca	SS	DSL GUAB	ROK	17	179	34	3	24	11	.316/.419/.500	.395	.650	13.4%	19.6%										
David Fry	C	COL	AAA	27	117	18	4	19	2	.317/.402/.545	.364	.688	9.4%	17.9%	65.7%	83.8%	32.0%	67.1%			116	0.4	-0.2	0.6
	C	CLE	MLB	27	113	12	4	15	2	.238/.319/.416	.299	.592	7.1%	26.5%	75.3%	79.3%	42.4%	62.5%	16.7	101.8	83	-0.1	-4.0	-0.3
Cam Gallagher	C	CLE	MLB	30	149	6	0	7	0	.126/.154/.168	.184	.247	2.7%	30.9%	69.2%	84.5%	34.8%	65.1%	17.0	99.4	56	-0.2	2.8	0.0
Petey Halpin	CF	AKR	AA	21	510	55	9	38	12	.243/.312/.372	.311	.515	9.2%	24.7%							89	0.6	13.3	2.4
Cooper Ingle	C	LC	A+	21	69	8	0	10	2	.288/.464/.385	.341	.455	24.6%	11.6%							128	-0.7	-0.1	0.3
C.J. Kayfus	1B/LF	LYN	A	21	77	13	4	19	5	.271/.429/.542	.273	.681	19.5%	15.6%							133	-1.0	0.1	0.4
Bryan Lavastida	C	AKR	AA	24	247	31	4	33	9	.246/.367/.350	.282	.430	13.8%	15.4%							112	-2.0	-3.0	0.5
	C	COL	AAA	24	218	32	8	37	7	.233/.310/.407	.261	.542	10.1%	21.6%	67.4%	76.6%	27.5%	55.0%			91	0.9	0.7	0.6
Sandy León	C	COL	AAA	34	61	6	2	4	0	.220/.361/.400	.243	.513	16.4%	18.0%	51.6%	91.8%	30.8%	65.3%			110	-0.8	0.3	0.1
	C	TEX	MLB	34	44	4	0	4	0	.146/.186/.195	.286	.381	2.3%	45.5%	61.4%	79.6%	32.2%	68.4%	16.5	100.5	49	0.0	0.0	-0.1
Angel Martínez	IF	AKR	AA	21	437	55	11	60	10	.245/.321/.392	.282	.500	8.5%	19.0%							111	0.4	0.0	1.6
	IF	COL	AAA	21	154	17	3	19	1	.268/.320/.401	.340	.538	6.5%	23.4%	63.3%	80.6%	39.8%	69.2%			86	2.2	-0.9	0.2
Johnathan Rodriguez	OF	AKR	AA	23	363	42	18	55	3	.289/.364/.512	.359	.733	9.4%	26.7%							121	-0.6	6.9	2.5
	OF	COL	AAA	23	202	32	11	33	0	.280/.376/.560	.388	.899	12.4%	32.7%	65.0%	73.6%	34.2%	48.8%			92	0.5	1.8	0.5
Ralphy Velazquez	C	GUA	ROK	18	28	7	2	8	1	.348/.393/.739	.333	.944	10.7%	17.9%										
Kahlil Watson	SS	BEL	A+	20	243	26	7	22	14	.206/.337/.362	.268	.550	14.4%	28.0%							100	-1.0	-8.3	-0.2
	SS	LC	A+	20	98	15	5	16	11	.233/.306/.442	.254	.613	8.2%	24.5%							106	0.7	-1.1	0.3

Jaison Chourio had a solid stateside debut in Goodyear, putting up big numbers in the Arizona Complex League. But much of his success was predicated on conditions that won't be repeated as he climbs the ladder. He hit a ton of ground balls—ending up at first base thanks to questionable infield defense—had far more swing-and-miss than his strikeout rate would indicate, and hit just one homer in 39 games. ⊗ Originally drafted as a middle infielder, **Jake Fox** was converted to a full-time outfielder last season after the front office realized they couldn't roster eight bench infielders at a time. The stellar plate discipline he showed off in his first full pro season was mostly a mirage of facing pitchers with 20-grade command every night, but he still has average or better contact skills. ⊗ To the surprise of approximately no one, Cleveland's most notable signing from the 2023 international class was a switch-hitting middle infielder with a potentially plus hit tool. You can't read too much into the statline from **Welbyn Francisca**'s DSL season due to the vast differences in players' physicality, but his 148-pound frame launched 16 extra-base hits in 40 games; he was one of just a dozen hitters aged 17 or under to bat at least .315. ⊗ Perhaps nothing says more about the offensive struggles of the 2023 Guardians than **David Fry**'s run of September starts as the third or fourth hitter in the lineup. The multipositional rookie catcher provides value as a bench bat thanks to his versatility, but he's certainly not someone you'd like hitting anywhere near that high. ⊗ **Cam Gallagher** was joined by a trio of Austins (Hedges, Nola, Barnes) at the bottom of the OPS leaderboard among catchers; his .042 ISO and .154 OBP were almost impressively poor offensive numbers. His talents as a framer still give him big-league utility, but he'll have to hit more like Austin Wynns (career .597 OPS) than Austin Barnes to stick around. ⊗ **Petey Halpin** advanced a level for the third season in a row. His offensive numbers took a tumble as he was tested by Double-A pitching, but he was an absolute wizard with the glove in center field. He doesn't have the bat to be a future first-division regular, but should find utility as a fourth outfielder or even a glove-first starter in the Myles Straw mold. ⊗ **Cooper Ingle** has a good eye at the dish and excellent bat-to-ball skills, but little thump in his bat; any extra-base output in his future will come from liners into the gaps. In addition to catching, he played all over the field, including in the corner outfield and even at second base, but at least for now he'll be given the chance to prove himself as a full-time backstop. ⊗ Cleveland's proclivity for hit-over-power batsmen in the draft even extends to traditional power positions like first base: **C.J. Kayfus** possesses strong contact skills and a disciplined approach at the plate, but clubbed just one home run in over 200 plate appearances in wood-bat college summer leagues. The shape of his offensive performance will appear much more palatable if he sticks in the outfield. ⊗ **Bryan Lavastida** put himself on the prospect radar with big-time minor-league numbers after being drafted out of junior college in 2018, but failed to perform in a brief big-league stint in '22. He struggled with both the bat and glove after being outrighted to the minors, and will stay in the org as a depth catching option. ⊗ For the second year in a row, **Sandy León** made brief big-league appearances sandwiched by long stints in the minors or on the waiver wire. Such is the life of a veteran third catcher, the sure-handed glove who shouldn't be standing anywhere near a batter's box. He'll continue bouncing around the league, reappearing in the majors for a week at a time, for as long as he's willing to provide his replacement-level services. ⊗ I could copy-paste this description for about a dozen prospects in this system, but **Angel Martínez** is a switch hitter who makes a lot of contact and has built up experience at three infield spots. He's not a future All-Star, but there's a future multi-positional roster spot for him in the near future as long as he can bully his way past all the other guys just like him. ⊗ **Johnathan Rodriguez** was a third-round pick seven years ago and is finally making the *Annual* after being added to the 40-man roster to prevent him from reaching minor-league free agency. After filling out his frame, he's experienced a power breakout in the past two seasons, clubbing 55 homers and putting up plus exit velocities. He moves well enough to stick in a corner outfield spot, and the biggest remaining question for him now is whether he can actualize his raw power at the highest level despite concerning whiff issues. ⊗ For the fifth year in a row, Cleveland cut an under-slot deal with their top draft selection. **Ralphy Velazquez** was one of the top prep hitters in the draft, and while his defense behind the plate is iffy, he has the big-time power potential to still be a prospect even if he moves to first base or corner outfield. ⊗ **Kahlil Watson**, who came to Cleveland in the trade that sent Josh Bell to Miami, doesn't fit the Guardians' mold of hit-first middle infield prospects. Rather, he has loud physical tools that have been held back by a ton of swing-and-miss and mighty struggles against non-fastballs. He's still just 20 years old and has time to improve his pitch recognition skills, but the pace of his development has certainly fallen behind what was anticipated in his draft year.

Pitchers

PITCHER	TM	LVL	AGE	G (GS)	IP	W-L	SV	K	WHIP	ERA	CSP	BB%	K%	HR%	GB%	ZSw%	ZCon%	OSw%	OCon%	BABIP	SLGCON	DRA-	WARP
Tanner Burns	AKR	AA	24	29 (14)	86²	5-3	1	86	1.26	3.01		11.4%	23.9%	3.1%	38.0%					.263	.482	100	1.3
Will Dion	LC	A+	23	9 (4)	33²	3-0	0	41	1.01	1.87		7.5%	30.8%	0.8%	34.6%					.288	.425	81	0.6
	AKR	AA	23	17 (15)	83	3-4	0	88	1.11	2.60		7.6%	26.7%	1.8%	45.5%					.296	.462	80	2.0
Hunter Gaddis	COL	AAA	25	20 (15)	74¹	2-10	0	65	1.55	6.05		9.8%	19.2%	5.3%	35.6%	71.9%	82.0%	31.6%	60.1%	.298	.681	114	0.6
	CLE	MLB	25	11 (7)	42	2-1	0	24	1.31	4.50	51.2%	7.7%	13.2%	3.3%	26.4%	69.2%	88.1%	29.7%	72.7%	.261	.526	141	-0.4
Tim Herrin	COL	AAA	26	33 (0)	37¹	7-2	3	43	1.10	3.38		13.4%	28.9%	2.0%	61.6%	65.7%	74.5%	32.4%	55.5%	.217	.412	79	1.0
	CLE	MLB	26	23 (0)	27²	1-1	0	32	1.48	5.53	47.5%	9.9%	26.4%	2.5%	42.7%	67.0%	86.5%	31.9%	51.1%	.371	.583	84	0.6
Parker Messick	LYN	A	22	13 (13)	56²	3-2	0	61	1.09	3.02		6.0%	26.0%	0.4%	41.0%					.303	.442	80	1.2
	LC	A+	22	13 (11)	65	2-4	0	75	1.34	4.43		8.8%	26.3%	3.5%	38.5%					.317	.615	95	0.9
Daniel Norris	COL	AAA	30	22 (16)	67²	4-5	0	62	1.58	5.45		9.5%	20.3%	4.2%	44.5%	64.3%	82.4%	31.1%	63.3%	.330	.660	102	0.9
	CLE	MLB	30	7 (0)	12²	0-0	0	11	1.74	5.68	40.8%	19.0%	17.5%	4.8%	38.5%	72.4%	87.3%	26.9%	58.7%	.194	.526	120	0.0
Adam Oller	TAC	AAA	28	12 (12)	63²	6-4	0	62	1.57	5.51		9.7%	21.4%	4.5%	30.3%	64.8%	83.6%	31.3%	62.1%	.328	.684	110	0.3
	LV	AAA	28	12 (9)	50²	4-3	0	59	1.66	7.11		10.3%	25.2%	5.1%	29.7%	71.7%	84.8%	31.7%	55.5%	.353	.776	102	0.7
	OAK	MLB	28	9 (1)	19²	1-1	0	13	2.08	10.07	41.6%	11.9%	12.9%	5.0%	30.7%	79.9%	82.6%	25.4%	73.5%	.343	.681	129	-0.1

At some point during the season, the Guardians decided a pitcher with a 12% walk rate and an ineffective changeup was unlikely to crack it in the rotation, converting **Tanner Burns** to single-inning relief. He possesses an above-average breaking ball and looks like a future middle reliever now, especially if his low-90s fastball gains some zip in short bursts.   ⊗   In keeping with their model-driven draft trends, the Guardians took yet another high school prospect who was still 17 years old on draft day, using their savings to select a comp round-caliber player with the 58th-overall pick. **Alex Clemmey** has huge fastball velocity from the left side; his developmental priorities lie in secondary pitches that still have a ways to go.   ⊗   A former Day 2 pick from the 2021 Draft class, **Will Dion** has done nothing but perform since entering pro ball; he has a combined ERA of just 2.14 and spent most of 2023 in Double-A. His heater sits at just 90 mph, but has utility at the top of the zone thanks to premium carry; he supplements the pitch with a suite of well-commanded secondaries.   ⊗   After **Hunter Gaddis** posted ludicrous strikeout numbers at each level of the minors, his stuff appeared to hit a wall last year. In 11 appearances as a swingman, he fanned just 13% of hitters, less than half of his minor-league average. He has a path to contributing as an emergency bulk arm, but his ceiling is severely limited by his lack of swing-and-miss.   ⊗   I've always wanted to see an ultra-fast pitcher serve as a dedicated pinch runner, but while the converted outfield speedster **Anthony Gose** certainly fits the mold, he'll have to throw enough strikes to make the major-league roster in the first place after missing much of the past two seasons with Tommy John surgery.   ⊗   **Tim Herrin** has rare velocity for a lefty, sitting 95-97 with his fastball while throwing an upper-80s slider with equal proportion. He was hit hard at times, but also showed flashes of the brilliant stuff that shot him up minor-league strikeout leaderboards in 2022. His big-league outings included a few three-inning appearances as a middle-inning swingman, priming him for a bigger and more versatile role.   ⊗   Drafted out of Florida State as a polished lefty with plus command and a suite of secondary pitches, **Parker Messick** was exactly as advertised in his first pro season, throwing 120 innings across Low- and High-A with a better-than-average walk rate at each level. His stuff hasn't taken a huge leap forward, as some expected for a pitcher in Cleveland's system, but even if he goes the way of Marco Gonzales rather than Shane Bieber, there's still a lot to like about his big-league future.   ⊗   For a journeyman who's compiled the majority of his big-league career across three separate residencies in Detroit, it seems fitting that the latest stop for **Daniel Norris** was in Cleveland, just 90 miles away from the Motor City as the crow flies. Unfortunately, that distance was too far for his comfort, as he failed to reproduce the consistent mediocrity he put together over a decade with the Tigers; he was shipped back to nearby Columbus after just seven games in which he walked more batters than he struck out.   ⊗   Even by the impossibly bleak standards of the 2023 Oakland Athletics, **Adam Oller** struggled on the mound to an extreme degree, dooming him to a substantial stint attempting to get outs in the Pacific Coast League—no one's idea of a good time.

COLORADO ROCKIES

Essay by Mario Delgado Genzor

Player comments by Alex Eisert and BP staff

There's a town in Spain called Zaragoza, known for its extreme weather: intense, dry heat during the summer that turns into bone-chilling cold during the winter. And yet, this bipolar climate isn't even the most infamous aspect of my birthplace's environment. That title goes to a wind so intense, it even has its own name: *cierzo*, a cold, ever-present gust that can often reach streaks of over 50 mph, and sometimes peaks at or just past 60 mph. Just as rivers cut into the earth and shape it, the *cierzo* shapes Zaragoza's people.

Harsh conditions have shaped the mentality and behavior of humans across the globe for thousands of years, and the place where I'm from is no different. We're consistently stereotyped as stubborn, blunt and proud people, and that holds up in reality. Even our accent, the way we speak and our mannerisms, are directly influenced by the weather in which we build our lives. This is a simple fact of life none of us even needs to acknowledge—we merely accept it, one jacket at a time. Dumpsters have to be quite literally nailed down to the concrete so they won't tip over in the months where the wind is at its strongest. It's an adaptation unique to us, an outside factor we've found a way to tame and live with.

In baseball, that dynamic has proven no different. Players, fans and franchises have to deal with outside factors all the time. From a wind-blown home run that changes the outcome of a game, to poor attendance and greedy ownership that causes a team to relocate, baseball can't isolate itself from the outside world. But there is one external factor that stands head and shoulders above all else across the game today, a variable so game-altering that even after three decades many still don't know what to make of it: mile-high altitude. It's not certain the league fully understood what they were getting into when they placed a new expansion franchise in Colorado.

In many ways, the results have been mixed. The Rockies are one of professional sports' most unique franchises, simultaneously managing to toe the line between being infamous and faceless, between having a strong identity and drifting along aimlessly. They've collected more than a few superstar players, but after 30 years as a big league club, they've yet to claim a single division title. They've won 90 or more games three times in three decades, and have finished

COLORADO ROCKIES PROSPECTUS
2023 W-L: 59-103, 5TH IN NL WEST

Pythag	.365	29th	DER	.675	29th
RS/G	4.45	18th	DRC+	89	30th
RA/G	5.91	30th	DRA-	114	30th
dWin%	.384	30th	FIP	5.24	30th
Payroll	$172M	16th	B-Age	28.8	18th
M$/MW	$14.5M	29th	P-Age	30.0	17th

390' 415' 375' 347' 350'

- Opened 1995
- Open air
- Natural surface
- Fence profile: 8' to 16'6"

Park Factors

Runs	Runs/RH	Runs/LH	HR/RH	HR/LH
104	104	104	103	101

Top Hitter WARP	2.3 Nolan Jones
Top Pitcher WARP	1.7 Jake Bird
2023 Top Prospect	Adael Amador

Payroll History (in millions)

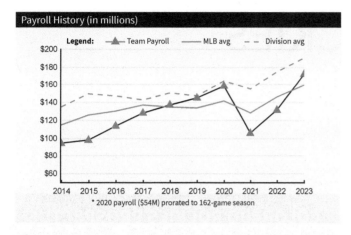

Legend: ▲ Team Payroll — MLB avg - - Division avg

* 2020 payroll ($54M) prorated to 162-game season

Future Commitments (in millions)

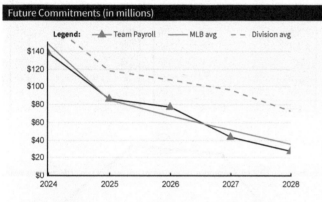

Legend: ▲ Team Payroll — MLB avg - - Division avg

Farm System Ranking

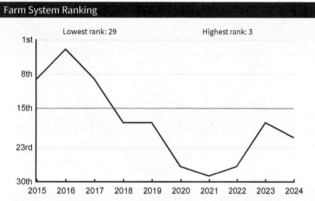

Lowest rank: 29   Highest rank: 3

Personnel

Senior VP & General Manager
Bill Schmidt

VP - International Scouting & Development
Rolando Fernandez

VP and AGM of Scouting
Danny Montgomery

VP and AGM of Baseball Operations
Zach Rosenthal

Manager
Bud Black

second or higher in their division four times in that span. In 22 of those 30 campaigns, they've finished 10 or more games back of the division winner. And in 2023 they reached a new low, losing a franchise record 103 games and finishing 41 games out of first place, a total 'bested' only by the prior year's 43 games back.

If winning and losing is all you're interested in, the Rockies won't even register in your radar. And yet, for those whose interest in the game of baseball goes far past pennants and World Series rings, the Rockies are a major source of fascination. They play half their games in the most unique environment in baseball history, one that affects their road games as well. There have been many attempts to tame altitude, but none have worked so far. And while there are some who might simply land on the conclusion that Denver baseball is doomed to being a curiosity at best, surrender feels unnecessary.

Rather, it's this entirely particular set of circumstances that makes the Rockies such an interesting challenge. As with human history, there is no eliminating your environment, there is only living with it and adapting in order to survive and thrive. It's easy to fall prey to a defeatist attitude in this situation, but what if we look at it from an entirely different angle? What if, instead of accepting that we're not going to enjoy easy, fertile success in rough lands, we attempt to carve out a living there? What if we could turn the proverbial pitcher's bogeyman that is Coors Field into a real advantage? In order to do that, we need to get the lay of the land.

First off, the thin air makes fly balls carry more than they do at sea level. This is a problem for obvious reasons—not only does it mean more extra-base hits, it also creates slightly different reads for outfielders. Perhaps most crucially, it means that fly-ball-oriented pitchers tend to walk a razor's edge in Colorado, which is relevant because most dominant strikeout pitchers tend to have fly-ball tendencies. And of course, there is no better outcome for a pitcher than getting strike three.

Second, and related to the first point: The outfield at Coors Field is huge, because the people who designed the place had a pretty good idea of the ludicrous amount of home runs that would be hit if the ballpark had normal dimensions. The expanse gives outfielders more grass to cover, which puts a premium on outfield defense and range in particular. It also means you're more likely to see things such as bloop hits, triples and extra bases taken in general. Many people would think of home runs when Coors Field comes up, but that's not the real differentiating factor that sets the park aside—BABIP is. If you manage to put the bat on the ball at Coors, especially if you lift it, you'll be rewarded more than anywhere else. To underline: for a pitcher, no place rewards a strikeout more than Coors Field.

And last, but certainly not least: The thin air actively changes the way pitches move. There have been many studies about this in the past, and even when the majors were getting started with baseball in Colorado, there was already a notion that a pitcher's curveball wouldn't curve the same when pitching there. We now know this extends well past just curveballs and affects all pitch types, especially fastballs, and this variance in pitch movement is a vital aspect of pitching in and out of elevation. The difficulty in getting acclimated to Colorado isn't just physical—losing multiple inches of movement on your pitches requires an adjustment in where you start a pitch, the target your catcher sets up for you, and so on.

This is the real dilemma of pitching at altitude. There's no ballpark in which punching tickets is more important than Coors Field, but Coors is also the one and only park that actively hampers the ability to strike people out in the first place. Fly balls carry, pitches move less; what is a hurler to do?

The Rockies themselves have tried a few different strategies throughout their history. They spent big on starters in free agency around the turn of the millennium, and watched both Mike Hampton and Denny Neagle go up in flames. They went all-in on sinkerballers, multiple times, only to eventually run into the low-ceiling nature of such a pitching staff. They patiently crafted a rotation of homegrown starters in the mid-to-late 2010s, but their outdated strategies and development methods ensured virtually none of those pitchers reached their ceiling, at least on a consistent basis. And then there's one infamous tactic worth examination, one the team used in 2012. Many of you will immediately know what I'm talking about.

The Rockies' piggyback rotation of 2012 is pretty infamous—widely mocked at the time and since, often thought of as an embarrassment that a major-league team couldn't find five worthy starters to give the ball to. And yet, the move made perfect sense then; Rockies starters had a brutal 6.28 ERA at the time the strategy was implemented, and quite frankly, the team really didn't have five good arms. As a result, they decided that trying anything was better than trying nothing, and set up a system involving a four-man rotation with strict pitch counts and specific piggyback relievers behind each starter. Looking back on it more than a decade later, it looks shockingly ahead of its time; if a team with a shortage of reliable starters tried this in 2024, many of us wouldn't bat an eyelash.

The point here isn't that piggybacking starters in a four-man rotation is the key to success at altitude; far from it. But it's a display of the important qualities required to survive and thrive in stressful environments: a willingness to think outside the box, act proactively and accept the inevitable risks. That, in its essence, is what you need if you want to not just get by, but have success in the harsh conditions that Coors Field creates. Conservative, risk-averse behavior will only lead to stagnation and eventual extinction.

The key to finding the right formula to pitch at Coors is to realize there is no one bullet-proof formula, no One Trick Doctors Hate that will enable a pitcher to overcome this obstacle all by itself. Are there some pitchers better suited for altitude than others? Sure: Upshot four-seamers that thrive on velocity and approach angle, hard breaking balls, splitters, pitchers with fastball utility and the ability to create multiple breaking ball shapes. But that's the specifics, and it's not what this is about. The point is that it's by embracing individuality, rather than a series of set-in-stone, cookie-cutter beliefs, that the Rockies will finally put themselves in a position to tame the place they call home. It's time for the franchise to start nailing their dumpsters down to the concrete so they don't tip over when the wind starts to arrive in full force.

This seems straightforward, but there is no guarantee the franchise will show itself willing to take a leap into the unknown. That in itself is a massive source of frustration for a fanbase that receives little to no feedback from management on just what the organization's baseball plans are for the near or even long-term future, and it's an even more heinous crime once you realize the inherent creativity that should come with being a sports franchise in such a radically different environment. No team should be more open to being different and unique and yet, one could argue no team has been buried deeper into a pit of mediocrity and stagnant thought process over the past decade than the Colorado Rockies. Heck, the team logo is still designed with Times New Roman!

And that's the true tragedy of this franchise. Baseball has been blessed with something entirely unique: a team that plays half its games in a completely alien environment, a set of conditions ripe for creative, aggressive minds. Coors contains enough imbalances and inefficiencies to occupy an enterprising analyst for eternity. And unlike many teams not located in major markets, the Rockies face no issues when it comes to stability, willingness to spend or fan attendance; Coors Field is beautiful and will be around for a long time, ownership has shown itself capable of spending significant amounts of money on players, the park is routinely filled with people no matter how bad the on-field product gets and Denver is a great sports city. What else could you possibly want?

The Colorado Rockies can be a model franchise that embraces the circumstances it lives with, instead of letting fear of them mold their outlook on how baseball should be played. But in order to do that, they must pop that warm, comfortable bubble they have created for themselves. Will they feel a cold breeze or two at first, as they start taming their environment? It's likely, yes. But over time, they will learn, and the myth that you can't pitch at Coors Field will disappear. That still won't solve all the challenges altitude presents, of course. Dealing with the ever-present issue of hitting on the road, for example, is another hurdle they must clear in due time, and that one has its own quirks. But you have to nail something down first. Dismantling the fear of Coors Field would go a long way in clearing the path for the Colorado Rockies to enter the modern era once and for all. And when they do, those dumpsters won't end up sideways on the street anymore.

—Mario Delgado Genzor is an author of Baseball Prospectus.

HITTERS

───────────────── ★ ★ ★ *2024 Top 101 Prospect* **#28** ★ ★ ★ ─────────────────

Adael Amador MI Born: 04/11/03 Age: 21 Bats: S Throws: R Height: 6'0" Weight: 200 Origin: IFA, 2019

YEAR	TM	LVL	AGE	PA	R	HR	RBI	SB	AVG/OBP/SLG	BABIP	SLGCON	BB%	K%	ZSw%	ZCon%	OSw%	OCon%	LA	90th EV	DRC+	BRR	DRP	WARP
2021	RCK	ROK	18	200	41	4	24	10	.299/.394/.445	.331	.541	13.5%	14.5%									-3.8	
2022	FRE	A	19	555	100	15	57	26	.292/.415/.445	.312	.524	15.7%	12.1%							122	4.3	-6.3	3.1
2023	SPO	A+	20	259	46	9	35	12	.302/.391/.514	.307	.582	12.0%	10.0%							139	0.1	-2.1	1.9
2023	HFD	AA	20	41	3	1	2	3	.143/.244/.229	.148	.296	9.8%	19.5%							107	0.4	-1.2	0.0
2024 non	*COL*	*MLB*	*21*	*251*	*23*	*5*	*24*	*8*	*.226/.300/.343*	*.246*	*.402*	*8.7%*	*13.1%*							*83*	*0.0*	*0*	*0.3*

2023 GP: SS (48), 2B (23)   *Comps: Carter Kieboom (75), Richard Urena (73), Ryan Mountcastle (71)*

The short-armed Amador is extremely quick to the baseball, allowing him to post the second-best contact rate among minor leaguers age 20 and under (min. 300 PAs). Alas, much of that contact was pulled on the ground: he was one of just five minor leaguers with a pull rate of at least 45% and a grounder rate of at least 55%. While this profile played in High-A, in his first taste of the shift-heavier Double-A, he struggled mightily. But it was a small sample, and he was also coming off of a fractured hamate; once fully healed, it would behoove him to sacrifice some of that elite contact for more loft in his swing. Even if he never does, the goal is something like a switch-hitting Thairo Estrada, a solid second baseman on the bulkier side.

Warming Bernabel 3B Born: 06/06/02 Age: 22 Bats: R Throws: R Height: 6'1" Weight: 180 Origin: IFA, 2018

YEAR	TM	LVL	AGE	PA	R	HR	RBI	SB	AVG/OBP/SLG	BABIP	SLGCON	BB%	K%	ZSw%	ZCon%	OSw%	OCon%	LA	90th EV	DRC+	BRR	DRP	WARP
2021	RCK	ROK	19	86	18	6	31	5	.432/.453/.743	.426	.887	5.8%	14.0%									2.5	
2021	FRE	A	19	94	9	1	7	4	.205/.287/.313	.232	.377	7.4%	14.9%							111	-0.9	0.6	0.4
2022	FRE	A	20	300	52	10	54	21	.317/.390/.504	.336	.592	9.7%	13.0%							127	-1.1	1.8	2.1
2022	SPO	A+	20	109	18	4	17	2	.305/.315/.486	.329	.580	1.8%	15.6%							114	0.1	-0.7	0.4
2023	RCK	ROK	21	36	9	2	8	0	.333/.389/.636	.360	.778	2.8%	16.7%										
2023	HFD	AA	21	322	30	6	28	2	.225/.270/.338	.271	.436	4.7%	21.1%							85	0.1	-1.1	0.2
2024 non	*COL*	*MLB*	*22*	*251*	*20*	*4*	*22*	*2*	*.217/.262/.322*	*.267*	*.420*	*4.8%*	*22.2%*							*63*	*0.0*	*0*	*-0.5*

2023 GP: 3B (85), DH (5)   *Comps: Isiah Kiner-Falefa (59), Brandon Drury (55), Miguel Andujar (55)*

Bernabel's age-20 heater in the minors came with some warning signs, as he posted the second-lowest walk rate in all of High-A during his time in Spokane. Unfortunately, not only was his 2023 walk rate hardly better, ranking sixth-worst in Double-A, but his DRC+ (64) and infield fly-ball rate (37.1%) were also in the bottom 10 at the level. In a sense, he's as uber-aggressive as the Rockies in their pursuit of high-variance corner bats that tend to flame out. To avoid joining that group, Bernabel will have to adjust his own approach.

Charlie Blackmon DH/RF Born: 07/01/86 Age: 38 Bats: L Throws: L Height: 6'3" Weight: 221 Origin: Round 2, 2008 Draft (#72 overall)

YEAR	TM	LVL	AGE	PA	R	HR	RBI	SB	AVG/OBP/SLG	BABIP	SLGCON	BB%	K%	ZSw%	ZCon%	OSw%	OCon%	LA	90th EV	DRC+	BRR	DRP	WARP
2021	COL	MLB	34	582	76	13	78	3	.270/.351/.411	.305	.499	9.3%	15.6%	68.1%	87.2%	31.5%	67.4%	10.5	104.8	111	0.1	2.4	2.8
2022	COL	MLB	35	577	60	16	78	4	.264/.314/.419	.304	.527	5.5%	18.9%	71.0%	87.1%	36.6%	65.8%	11.9	102.1	97	-0.1	0.3	1.2
2023	COL	MLB	36	413	57	8	40	4	.279/.363/.440	.307	.520	9.4%	13.3%	66.2%	87.3%	33.4%	70.3%	18.0	102.6	121	0.1	0.3	2.0
2024 DC	*COL*	*MLB*	*37*	*533*	*55*	*12*	*57*	*4*	*.253/.328/.391*	*.290*	*.477*	*8.2%*	*16.3%*							*101*	*0.1*	*0.3*	*1.3*

2023 GP: DH (61), RF (30)   *Comps: Paul Waner (73), Edd Roush (71), Al Oliver (71)*

Blackmon had an uneven and a tinge unlucky 13th season in Colorado. On the one hand, he had his best offensive showing since 2019. On the other hand … well, there was a cast from when an errant pitch fractured his right paw. The Rockies rewarded him all the same, signing him to a one-year extension worth $13 million to up the odds he ends his big-league career where it began. If this upcoming year proves to be Chuck Nazty's last, then allow us to be the first to write that he had a good run—particularly that four-year stretch, from 2016-19, when he was undeniably one of the best pure hitters in the game.

Kris Bryant RF/DH Born: 01/04/92 Age: 32 Bats: R Throws: R Height: 6'5" Weight: 230 Origin: Round 1, 2013 Draft (#2 overall)

YEAR	TM	LVL	AGE	PA	R	HR	RBI	SB	AVG/OBP/SLG	BABIP	SLGCON	BB%	K%	ZSw%	ZCon%	OSw%	OCon%	LA	90th EV	DRC+	BRR	DRP	WARP
2021	CHC	MLB	29	374	58	18	51	4	.267/.358/.503	.314	.692	10.4%	23.8%	75.9%	85.1%	30.0%	53.2%	13.4	103.5	101	0.0	0.2	1.3
2021	SF	MLB	29	212	28	7	22	6	.262/.344/.444	.311	.589	10.8%	21.7%	77.0%	84.3%	32.7%	49.0%	18.8	103.8	101	0.0	-0.1	0.8
2022	COL	MLB	30	181	28	5	14	0	.306/.376/.475	.338	.571	9.4%	14.9%	74.9%	90.5%	27.2%	54.1%	14.3	102.0	116	0.1	0.0	0.9
2023	COL	MLB	31	335	36	10	31	0	.233/.313/.367	.270	.474	8.7%	20.3%	73.1%	85.4%	27.5%	56.2%	14.9	102.2	98	-0.2	-2.2	0.4
2024 DC	*COL*	*MLB*	*32*	*490*	*52*	*14*	*54*	*0*	*.241/.322/.389*	*.289*	*.507*	*8.9%*	*21.0%*							*100*	*0.0*	*-1*	*0.9*

2023 GP: RF (46), DH (25), 1B (7), LF (1)   *Comps: Evan Longoria (78), David Wright (78), Scott Rolen (78)*

When Bryant signed with the Rockies prior to the 2022 season, the assumption was that he was trading his chance to enjoy team-level success for the opportunity to post some silly statistics in Coors Field. (Plus, you know, a great public education for his children—oh, and a lot of money.) That hasn't been the case; not because the Rockies have been better than expected, but because Bryant has been worse and more absent than projected. Indeed, it'll take him more than a month into his third season with the Rockies to appear in his 162nd game with the franchise. It'll take him longer than that if he's ever to get his Rockies career OPS over the .800 mark (it's at .740). To think that, given his age and injury history, these were supposed to be the best years of the deal. Bryant seems to be a likable fellow, and Colorado's fan base surely deserves something good. Here's hoping that his 2024 season reminds everyone why he once appeared to be on a Hall of Fame trajectory.

Cole Carrigg   UT   Born: 05/08/02   Age: 22   Bats: S   Throws: R   Height: 6'3"   Weight: 200   Origin: Round 2, 2023 Draft (#65 overall)

YEAR	TM	LVL	AGE	PA	R	HR	RBI	SB	AVG/OBP/SLG	BABIP	SLGCON	BB%	K%	ZSw%	ZCon%	OSw%	OCon%	LA	90th EV	DRC+	BRR	DRP	WARP
2023	RCK	ROK	21	57	13	2	13	7	.396/.464/.688	.500	.943	10.5%	22.8%										
2023	FRE	A	21	101	19	3	16	6	.326/.376/.554	.386	.708	6.9%	19.8%						108	0.3	-0.2	0.4
2024 non	COL	MLB	22	251	19	2	20	0	.219/.274/.317	.301	.451	6.2%	27.5%						66	0.0	0	-0.2

2023 GP: CF (15), SS (10), C (7), DH (5)   Comps: Andrew Toles (88), Corey Rosier (88), John Shelby (87)

The Rockies' second-round pick in the 2023 draft, Carrigg received reps at shortstop, catcher and in center field in his debut. He was also uncredited for his work in composing his own walk-up music, reconciling Fresno's general ledger accounts, and translating their PR statements into Latin. That versatility presents Colorado with a problem: go the safe route and use his athleticism to make him a reasonable middle infielder, roll the dice on getting themselves a great-hitting catcher, or stick him in the outfield and let him focus on maximizing his switch-hitting offense? Or see if he can learn them all at the same time, and risk spreading him too thin? Given the state of the farm, the Rockies might wish they could do the one thing he can't offer: playing multiple positions at once.

Harold Castro   2B   Born: 11/30/93   Age: 30   Bats: L   Throws: R   Height: 5'10"   Weight: 195   Origin: IFA, 2011

YEAR	TM	LVL	AGE	PA	R	HR	RBI	SB	AVG/OBP/SLG	BABIP	SLGCON	BB%	K%	ZSw%	ZCon%	OSw%	OCon%	LA	90th EV	DRC+	BRR	DRP	WARP
2021	DET	MLB	27	339	35	3	37	1	.283/.310/.359	.351	.465	4.1%	21.2%	73.0%	83.9%	48.0%	65.1%	10.0	100.6	84	-0.3	-0.8	0.4
2022	CAR	WIN	28	103	17	0	4	2	.374/.398/.384	.425	.437	1.9%	11.7%										
2022	DET	MLB	28	443	37	7	47	0	.271/.300/.381	.318	.469	3.8%	17.8%	70.4%	88.0%	43.9%	72.7%	11.5	101.3	97	-0.1	-1.2	0.7
2023	COL	MLB	29	270	24	1	31	1	.252/.275/.314	.332	.422	3.3%	24.4%	70.5%	85.9%	47.0%	57.5%	10.2	99.8	75	-0.1	0.3	0.0
2024 non	COL	MLB	30	251	21	3	22	1	.251/.292/.345	.316	.453	5.1%	22.2%							79	-0.1	-0.9	-0.1

2023 GP: 2B (68), CF (11), LF (5), SS (4), RF (3), DH (3), P (2), 3B (2)   Comps: Jonathan Herrera (49), Wally Backman (48), Jerry Remy (48)

Despite establishing himself as a below-average hitter and defender with little upside, Castro managed to secure plenty of reps in 2023, mostly as the strong side of a platoon at second base. Perhaps more befuddling, he managed to keep his roster spot even after Brendan Rodgers returned at the end of July, even wresting 46 plate appearances down the stretch from younger players on a rebuilding team. Maybe Castro possesses some intangibles that made his presence worth it, or maybe the Rockies were threatened to play him by some other Castros. Either way, from his pull-heavy groundball ways to his career-worst chase rate, there's little in his batted-ball profile or plate discipline that points to him being more than a replacement-level type.

Elias Díaz   C   Born: 11/17/90   Age: 33   Bats: R   Throws: R   Height: 6'1"   Weight: 223   Origin: IFA, 2008

YEAR	TM	LVL	AGE	PA	R	HR	RBI	SB	AVG/OBP/SLG	BABIP	SLGCON	BB%	K%	ZSw%	ZCon%	OSw%	OCon%	LA	90th EV	DRC+	BRR	DRP	WARP
2021	COL	MLB	30	371	52	18	44	0	.246/.310/.464	.249	.565	8.1%	16.2%	74.1%	88.0%	34.8%	57.2%	14.8	104.8	112	-0.2	3.2	2.5
2022	COL	MLB	31	381	29	9	51	0	.228/.281/.368	.270	.480	6.6%	21.5%	72.2%	86.2%	38.4%	66.3%	11.2	104.9	85	-0.5	-11.2	-0.6
2023	COL	MLB	32	526	48	14	72	1	.267/.316/.409	.324	.541	6.5%	22.4%	76.7%	82.4%	40.1%	57.4%	12.6	105.6	93	-0.4	-13.7	0.1
2024 DC	COL	MLB	33	453	45	13	50	0	.240/.297/.384	.293	.509	6.7%	22.7%							89	-0.3	-8.7	0.0

2023 GP: C (126), DH (8)

Comps: Luke Sewell (71), Travis d'Arnaud (71), Farmer Vaughn (70)

YEAR	TM	P. COUNT	FRM RUNS	BLK RUNS	THRW RUNS	TOT RUNS
2021	COL	12793	2.3	-0.1	2.6	4.7
2022	COL	14059	-10.3	-0.3	0.6	-10.0
2023	COL	16873	-14.2	0.0	1.7	-12.5
2024	COL	13228	-9.4	-0.2	1.0	-8.6

Colorado's lone All-Star representative in 2023, Díaz made good on his Midsummer Classic opportunity by hitting a decisive two-run homer off of Félix Bautista, earning MVP honors in the process. Whether he deserved to be on that stage or not in the first place is another story. He posted a second-straight season of extremely poor framing—costing the Rockies an estimated 10 runs again—and he put together another mediocre sum with his work at the plate. We could provide a bunch of complicated stats, but to summarize: It's bad when you swing at more pitches than ever in your career, with more of those swings being chases than ever, and make contact at your worst rate ever, all while pitchers are throwing the fewest strikes to you ever. With Drew Romo knocking on the door, Díaz's days as a starter are limited.

Brenton Doyle   CF   Born: 05/14/98   Age: 26   Bats: R   Throws: R   Height: 6'2"   Weight: 200   Origin: Round 4, 2019 Draft (#129 overall)

YEAR	TM	LVL	AGE	PA	R	HR	RBI	SB	AVG/OBP/SLG	BABIP	SLGCON	BB%	K%	ZSw%	ZCon%	OSw%	OCon%	LA	90th EV	DRC+	BRR	DRP	WARP
2021	SPO	A+	23	424	70	16	47	21	.279/.336/.454	.388	.691	7.1%	31.6%							96	-0.5	2.8	1.4
2022	HFD	AA	24	507	74	23	68	23	.246/.287/.450	.314	.677	4.5%	31.2%							88	2.8	10.7	2.2
2022	ABQ	AAA	24	41	8	3	9	0	.389/.463/.778	.550	1.217	12.2%	31.7%	66.1%	68.3%	31.6%	50.0%			94	0.1	1.5	0.2
2023	ABQ	AAA	25	57	12	5	8	1	.306/.404/.633	.400	1.033	14.0%	33.3%	76.1%	71.6%	32.1%	44.4%			104	0.6	0.0	0.3
2023	COL	MLB	25	431	48	10	48	22	.203/.250/.343	.295	.552	5.1%	35.0%	74.2%	78.1%	36.1%	43.0%	9.9	103.2	63	0.9	4.4	0.1
2024 DC	COL	MLB	26	508	47	14	54	20	.211/.265/.357	.304	.561	5.6%	34.3%							69	0.6	2.7	0.1

2023 GP: CF (125)   Comps: Adam Engel (70), Reggie Abercrombie (70), Matthew den Dekker (67)

Doyle is an athletic outlier. Ninety-eighth-percentile footspeed and 99th-percentile arm strength have made him an elite defender by any measure; he nearly hit 106 mph on a throw and tops out at around 30 feet per second when he's sprinting. To put those cartoonish features into cartoonish context, he's what you'd get if you gave the Popeye's strength to the Road Runner without weighing him down at all. The lean Doyle can hit the ball hard too, topping out at a solid 111 mph off the bat, but he'll have to trade some of his spinach for carrots if he really wants to improve on offense; his swing decisions made him the worst batter by DRC+ among any with his number of plate appearances. Coupled with a penchant for whiffs, those decisions resulted in a nearly 30-percentage-point difference between his strikeout and walk rates (also the largest among hitters by that cutoff). If he can get his bat into "well-below-average" territory instead of whatever last season represents, then his secondary skills will make him into a star.

★ ★ ★ *2024 Top 101 Prospect* **#87** ★ ★ ★

Yanquiel Fernandez   RF   Born: 01/01/03   Age: 21   Bats: L   Throws: L   Height: 6'2"   Weight: 198   Origin: IFA, 2019

YEAR	TM	LVL	AGE	PA	R	HR	RBI	SB	AVG/OBP/SLG	BABIP	SLGCON	BB%	K%	ZSw%	ZCon%	OSw%	OCon%	LA	90th EV	DRC+	BRR	DRP	WARP
2021	DSL ROC	ROK	18	202	29	6	34	0	.333/.406/.531	.361	.623	10.9%	12.9%									-3.7	
2022	FRE	A	19	523	76	21	109	5	.284/.340/.507	.330	.668	7.5%	21.8%							108	-3.3	3.4	2.1
2023	SPO	A+	20	268	47	17	64	1	.319/.354/.605	.332	.750	5.2%	17.9%							131	-1.3	3.6	2.0
2023	HFD	AA	20	237	20	8	25	0	.206/.262/.362	.276	.564	6.3%	32.9%							65	-1.2	0.5	-0.2
2024 non	COL	MLB	21	251	22	6	26	0	.222/.267/.362	.298	.528	5.1%	30.0%							73	0.0	0	-0.2

2023 GP: RF (103), DH (16)   *Comps: Jorge Bonifacio (62), Carlos González (57), Justin Williams (55)*

After a solid full-season debut in 2022, you couldn't say "Yanquiel Fernandez" without someone mentioning Yordan Alvarez. There's no denying that the hulking, lefty-swinging, positionless prospect bears passing resemblance to the Astros' star, and his minor-league statistics hadn't done much to detract from that comparison even halfway into 2023. Then Fernandez met his match in Double-A ,where a nearly 20% swinging-strike rate led to a 5-to-1 strikeout-to-walk ratio. Alvarez never posted a strikeout rate that high or a walk rate that low at any level, but he also didn't reach Double-A until he was 21. Fernandez will get his turn in his second chance at the level to start 2024, and we should avoid ruling the Alvarez comparisons premature until at least then. And maybe avoid making new ones, to play it safe.

Hunter Goodman   1B   Born: 10/08/99   Age: 24   Bats: R   Throws: R   Height: 5'11"   Weight: 210   Origin: Round 4, 2021 Draft (#109 overall)

YEAR	TM	LVL	AGE	PA	R	HR	RBI	SB	AVG/OBP/SLG	BABIP	SLGCON	BB%	K%	ZSw%	ZCon%	OSw%	OCon%	LA	90th EV	DRC+	BRR	DRP	WARP
2021	RCK	ROK	21	74	16	2	12	1	.300/.419/.517	.356	.674	12.2%	18.9%									0.1	
2022	FRE	A	22	321	53	22	68	4	.291/.368/.592	.324	.819	8.1%	24.3%							133	1.5	0.6	2.7
2022	SPO	A+	22	211	39	12	34	1	.315/.351/.589	.397	.853	5.2%	28.9%							104	2.0	1.1	1.0
2022	HFD	AA	22	47	5	2	4	1	.227/.277/.364	.267	.500	6.4%	25.5%							93	0.5	-0.2	0.1
2023	HFD	AA	23	400	53	25	78	0	.239/.325/.523	.252	.728	10.3%	24.5%							126	-0.8	1.3	2.4
2023	ABQ	AAA	23	67	15	9	33	0	.371/.418/.903	.389	1.244	6.0%	25.4%	64.8%	86.0%	39.9%	47.5%			118	-1.1	-0.4	0.1
2023	COL	MLB	23	77	6	1	17	1	.200/.247/.386	.277	.587	6.5%	31.2%	63.3%	83.9%	41.0%	45.0%	11.7	107.9	79	0.0	-0.3	-0.1
2024 DC	COL	MLB	24	318	34	12	40	1	.225/.282/.412	.286	.594	6.0%	28.7%							88	0.0	-1.4	0.1

2023 GP: RF (10), 1B (8), DH (3)   *Comps: Jordan Luplow (54), Aaron Cunningham (53), Kendrys Morales (50)*

Goodman demolished minor-league pitching to the tune of a combined 70 homers in his first two full years of pro ball. The last nine of those long balls came in just 67 Triple-A plate appearances, warranting a call-up at the end of August. As all those strikeout rates above may have suggested, Goodman struggled with the swing-and-miss in his cup of coffee, whiffing on 38% of his attempts. Beneath it all, though, above-average barrel and hard-hit rates hinted at the raw power that made him so good in the minors. His bat will play to some capacity; the biggest question is where. Drafted as a catcher, his ultimate home will probably be at first base, an outfield corner or DH. The Rockies have a logjam at each of those positions, though, so Goodman might want to call on any unscrupulous lawyers in the family to see if they can get him a change of scenery.

Nolan Jones   LF   Born: 05/07/98   Age: 26   Bats: L   Throws: R   Height: 6'4"   Weight: 195   Origin: Round 2, 2016 Draft (#55 overall)

YEAR	TM	LVL	AGE	PA	R	HR	RBI	SB	AVG/OBP/SLG	BABIP	SLGCON	BB%	K%	ZSw%	ZCon%	OSw%	OCon%	LA	90th EV	DRC+	BRR	DRP	WARP
2021	COL	AAA	23	407	60	13	48	10	.238/.356/.431	.327	.671	14.5%	30.0%							99	3.8	3.3	1.8
2022	COL	AAA	24	248	44	9	43	4	.276/.368/.463	.352	.660	12.5%	25.8%							111	-0.4	0.8	1.2
2022	CLE	MLB	24	94	10	2	13	0	.244/.309/.372	.358	.582	8.5%	33.0%	62.6%	71.6%	28.4%	67.2%	15.5	107.9	81	-0.1	0.6	0.1
2023	ABQ	AAA	25	187	38	12	42	5	.356/.481/.711	.432	1.000	17.6%	23.0%	48.5%	87.0%	24.0%	59.8%			125	-1.6	3.6	1.3
2023	COL	MLB	25	424	60	20	62	20	.297/.389/.542	.401	.826	12.5%	29.7%	59.4%	73.4%	28.9%	59.9%	9.8	107.6	121	0.8	-0.7	2.3
2024 DC	COL	MLB	26	544	61	17	64	13	.233/.329/.412	.311	.607	11.2%	28.3%							105	0.1	-2.3	1.7

2023 GP: LF (60), RF (34), 1B (10), CF (5), 3B (1)   *Comps: Domonic Brown (60), Eddie Rosario (54), David Dahl (53)*

Prior to the 2023 season, Jones came over to the Rockies in a prospect-for-prospect swap with the Guardians. (So much for another long-term Nolan at the hot corner in Colorado.) Worse, instead of trying Jones in the outfield corners to start the season, the Rockies stashed him in the minors in favor of scuffling veterans like Jurickson Profar, despite Colorado's obvious non-competitiveness. But Jones' raw power finally broke into games in Triple-A, as he topped his previous high in ISO by nearly 150 points; the Rockies couldn't ignore him, and he brought that breakout to the majors as one of their few bright spots. What's more, he kept his strikeout rate reasonable despite boom-or-bust tendencies in the minors and he demonstrated plus defense in the outfield thanks to his third baseman's arm. He could slot in nicely next to Brenton Doyle for years to come.

Dyan Jorge   SS   Born: 03/18/03   Age: 21   Bats: R   Throws: R   Height: 6'3"   Weight: 170   Origin: IFA, 2022

YEAR	TM	LVL	AGE	PA	R	HR	RBI	SB	AVG/OBP/SLG	BABIP	SLGCON	BB%	K%	ZSw%	ZCon%	OSw%	OCon%	LA	90th EV	DRC+	BRR	DRP	WARP
2022	DSL COL	ROK	19	218	35	4	20	13	.319/.404/.450	.365	.537	10.6%	14.2%										
2023	RCK	ROK	20	94	31	3	18	9	.370/.495/.644	.407	.770	20.2%	12.8%										
2023	FRE	A	20	215	29	0	22	10	.283/.322/.338	.337	.411	6.0%	16.3%							93	1.6	3.2	1.1
2024 non	COL	MLB	21	251	17	2	18	0	.207/.251/.280	.265	.365	4.8%	22.4%							49	0.0	0	-0.8

2023 GP: SS (59), 2B (11), DH (2)   *Comps: Eric Stamets (87), James Beresford (85), Calten Daal (85)*

Jorge, the Rockies' most expensive international signing in franchise history at $2.8 million, emerged from complex ball for the first time in 2023. Only held back for so long due to his status as a Cuban national, the 20-year-old was expected to mash in his first taste of the American minor-league system. However, like the "L" in his first name, Dyan's power was nowhere to be found, as he failed to homer and pounded 51.6% of his balls in play into the ground en route to a paltry .056 ISO. When he did manage to elevate, he popped up over a fifth of the time. Still, the high contact he's become known for was evident, as he ranked just outside the California League's top 10 in swinging-strike and strikeout rate. If the power becomes a sticking point further down the line, he could easily trade some contact for more pop, but don't count out more thump arriving naturally once his lanky frame begins to fill out.

Ryan McMahon 3B   Born: 12/14/94   Age: 29   Bats: L   Throws: R   Height: 6'2"   Weight: 219   Origin: Round 2, 2013 Draft (#42 overall)

YEAR	TM	LVL	AGE	PA	R	HR	RBI	SB	AVG/OBP/SLG	BABIP	SLGCON	BB%	K%	ZSw%	ZCon%	OSw%	OCon%	LA	90th EV	DRC+	BRR	DRP	WARP
2021	COL	MLB	26	596	80	23	86	6	.254/.331/.449	.306	.622	9.9%	24.7%	74.6%	79.0%	30.0%	56.0%	14.3	104.8	93	0.0	1.5	1.7
2022	COL	MLB	27	597	67	20	67	7	.246/.327/.414	.311	.590	10.1%	26.5%	66.1%	81.1%	29.2%	55.6%	11.0	106.6	95	-0.1	-1.9	0.9
2023	COL	MLB	28	627	80	23	70	5	.240/.322/.431	.326	.669	10.8%	31.6%	69.1%	75.4%	31.1%	54.9%	10.1	106.8	82	-0.4	0.3	0.6
2024 DC	COL	MLB	29	572	64	20	68	9	.228/.319/.405	.303	.602	10.8%	29.3%							100	-0.1	0.3	1.6

2023 GP: 3B (130), 2B (22), DH (3)   Comps: Howard Johnson (57), Michael Cuddyer (55), Graig Nettles (53)

In a day and age where unlimited growth is the default marketplace expectation, it's comforting to run across a player who rejects the idea out of hand. McMahon brings the same skill set to the table now that he did three years ago. He's a skilled defensive third baseman with a bat capable of launching 20+ home runs and finishing a few ticks away from the league-average mark. That's a perfectly good player, and one who should continue to make the Rockies' call to extend him look like a rare good decision.

Elehuris Montero 1B/DH   Born: 08/17/98   Age: 25   Bats: R   Throws: R   Height: 6'3"   Weight: 235   Origin: IFA, 2014

YEAR	TM	LVL	AGE	PA	R	HR	RBI	SB	AVG/OBP/SLG	BABIP	SLGCON	BB%	K%	ZSw%	ZCon%	OSw%	OCon%	LA	90th EV	DRC+	BRR	DRP	WARP
2021	HFD	AA	22	379	46	22	69	0	.279/.361/.523	.309	.725	11.3%	23.7%							124	0.2	-3.4	1.9
2021	ABQ	AAA	22	121	23	6	17	0	.278/.355/.546	.293	.670	8.3%	16.5%							114	-1.2	-0.8	0.4
2022	ABQ	AAA	23	297	44	15	54	4	.310/.392/.541	.354	.719	9.1%	21.2%	69.8%	86.3%	32.7%	47.1%			114	1.6	-5.5	1.0
2022	COL	MLB	23	185	21	6	20	0	.233/.270/.432	.318	.655	4.3%	32.4%	68.4%	82.2%	40.2%	41.9%	13.5	104.8	67	0.0	-0.1	-0.4
2023	ABQ	AAA	24	163	32	15	48	0	.359/.411/.718	.346	.895	8.6%	17.2%	57.0%	92.5%	37.0%	54.2%			131	1.0	0.0	1.2
2023	COL	MLB	24	307	40	11	39	0	.243/.290/.426	.352	.699	4.9%	36.2%	65.2%	83.5%	45.6%	40.2%	10.2	106.3	53	-0.3	-0.5	-1.2
2024 DC	COL	MLB	25	381	40	14	46	2	.222/.284/.399	.294	.599	6.2%	30.9%							86	-0.2	-0.5	0.0

2023 GP: 1B (55), DH (16), 3B (12)   Comps: Michael Chavis (55), Maikel Franco (55), Johan Camargo (53)

There are three E's in Montero's first and last names. There might be four A's on his scouting report. Montero's 2023 was a mirror-image of his debut '22 season: Once again, he lit up Triple-A, but couldn't stick in the majors due to a failure to hit non-fastballs. He's not a good enough fielder to overcome a below-average bat, and he's now on the shady side of 25. We suspect that he's one more poor run at the big-league level from being dismissed as a Quad-A player, making this a most pivotal season for his career prospects. (We don't want to alarm anyone, but we're beginning to think that the Arenado trade was a stinker for the Rockies.)

Benny Montgomery CF   Born: 09/09/02   Age: 21   Bats: R   Throws: R   Height: 6'4"   Weight: 200   Origin: Round 1, 2021 Draft (#8 overall)

YEAR	TM	LVL	AGE	PA	R	HR	RBI	SB	AVG/OBP/SLG	BABIP	SLGCON	BB%	K%	ZSw%	ZCon%	OSw%	OCon%	LA	90th EV	DRC+	BRR	DRP	WARP
2021	RCK	ROK	18	52	7	0	6	5	.340/.404/.383	.421	.474	9.6%	17.3%									0.4	
2022	FRE	A	19	264	48	6	42	9	.313/.394/.502	.429	.722	8.0%	26.9%							93	0.5	0.2	0.5
2023	SPO	A+	20	497	62	10	51	18	.251/.336/.370	.339	.535	10.5%	27.2%							91	-2.0	-7.6	-0.2
2024 non	COL	MLB	21	251	20	3	21	0	.222/.283/.317	.322	.477	6.7%	31.1%							71	0.0	0	-0.1

2023 GP: CF (102), DH (15), LF (9)   Comps: Charlie Fermaint (71), Angel Morales (71), Johan Mieses (63)

There are a lot of Montgomerys in baseball right now, but Benny's funky swing has always made him unique—he brings his hands down to his chest and winds them up before he even decides to swing. In the outfield, he doesn't seem to know what to do with his hands, either; per DRP, he was the 10th-worst fielder in all of High-A in 2023. A swing overhaul could be in store for the 21-year-old, who still has time to put it all together riding his elite speed to the majors in order to become the throwback player his first name suggests he can be.

Brendan Rodgers 2B   Born: 08/09/96   Age: 27   Bats: R   Throws: R   Height: 6'0"   Weight: 204   Origin: Round 1, 2015 Draft (#3 overall)

YEAR	TM	LVL	AGE	PA	R	HR	RBI	SB	AVG/OBP/SLG	BABIP	SLGCON	BB%	K%	ZSw%	ZCon%	OSw%	OCon%	LA	90th EV	DRC+	BRR	DRP	WARP
2021	COL	MLB	24	415	49	15	51	0	.284/.328/.470	.328	.601	4.6%	20.2%	75.8%	87.1%	35.2%	61.1%	6.6	105.2	101	-0.2	0.0	1.5
2022	COL	MLB	25	581	72	13	63	0	.266/.325/.408	.304	.505	7.9%	17.4%	74.3%	85.9%	30.7%	61.2%	4.9	105.4	112	0.2	4.2	3.1
2023	COL	MLB	26	192	21	4	20	0	.258/.313/.388	.316	.504	5.7%	21.4%	68.1%	87.7%	33.2%	54.5%	5.4	103.8	94	-0.1	0.5	0.5
2024 DC	COL	MLB	27	568	56	13	61	0	.252/.312/.390	.306	.501	6.6%	20.8%							96	0.0	3.1	1.6

2023 GP: 2B (43), DH (2)   Comps: Yolmer Sánchez (56), Erick Aybar (55), Brandon Phillips (55)

Heading into 2023, Rodgers was looking to build upon a career year, perhaps aiming to finally achieve the heights many projected him for when he was chosen third overall in '15. But after a Gold Glove and career-best DRC+ in 2022, he was felled by a dislocated left shoulder in spring training and forced to undergo surgery. It's a good thing he didn't take after his long-lost cousin Aaron and choose football, because this wasn't his first rodeo; he also underwent surgery on his right shoulder in 2019. Even though his throwing arm was spared this time, his defense—not to mention his offense—suffered upon his return. At the plate, he hit a ton of ground balls while seeing his discipline erode. Perhaps his frustration had boiled over or he simply wasn't fully up to speed when he came back, but the Rockies are counting on a bounceback from one of their infield quarterbacks regardless.

Drew Romo C   Born: 08/29/01   Age: 22   Bats: S   Throws: R   Height: 5'11"   Weight: 205   Origin: Round 1, 2020 Draft (#35 overall)

YEAR	TM	LVL	AGE	PA	R	HR	RBI	SB	AVG/OBP/SLG	BABIP	SLGCON	BB%	K%	ZSw%	ZCon%	OSw%	OCon%	LA	90th EV	DRC+	BRR	DRP	WARP
2021	FRE	A	19	339	48	6	47	23	.314/.345/.439	.348	.523	5.6%	14.7%							121	1.2	13.1	3.2
2022	SPO	A+	20	420	52	5	58	18	.254/.321/.372	.306	.474	8.3%	19.3%							100	0.0	8.3	2.1
2023	HFD	AA	21	368	45	13	48	6	.254/.313/.440	.277	.554	7.9%	18.2%							100	-1.9	3.3	1.3
2024 DC	COL	MLB	22	63	5	1	6	1	.227/.278/.346	.285	.457	5.7%	22.2%							70	0.0	0	0.0

2023 GP: C (85), DH (20) · *Comps: Chance Sisco (72), Salvador Perez (71), Sebastian Valle (69)*

YEAR	TM	P. COUNT	FRM RUNS	BLK RUNS	THRW RUNS	TOT RUNS
2021	FRE	9774	11.8	1.8	0.7	14.3
2022	SPO	7764	9.4	0.2	-0.1	9.5
2023	HFD	11988	1.2	-0.1	1.3	2.4
2024	COL	2405	0.9	0.2	0.1	1.1

Hunter Goodman's inability to develop as a catcher will probably become a moot point as soon as Romo reaches the majors. Though he had a bit of a down year defensively, Romo was still a net positive behind the dish in his first taste of the high minors in 2023, and he's only a year removed from a pair of elite framing seasons. He's no slouch with the bat either, with the above-average strikeout rates that DRC+ loves, with an encouraging glimpse of pop to boot. But his value remains largely tied to his defense; if he can regain his framing skills, Romo could be a bigger part of the Rockies' pitching turnaround than any shift on the pitching side itself.

Jacob Stallings C   Born: 12/22/89   Age: 34   Bats: R   Throws: R   Height: 6'5"   Weight: 225   Origin: Round 7, 2012 Draft (#226 overall)

YEAR	TM	LVL	AGE	PA	R	HR	RBI	SB	AVG/OBP/SLG	BABIP	SLGCON	BB%	K%	ZSw%	ZCon%	OSw%	OCon%	LA	90th EV	DRC+	BRR	DRP	WARP
2021	PIT	MLB	31	427	38	8	53	0	.246/.335/.369	.297	.478	11.5%	19.9%	67.2%	87.4%	25.7%	57.3%	10.8	101.6	91	-0.8	3.2	1.6
2022	MIA	MLB	32	384	25	4	34	0	.223/.292/.292	.280	.384	7.6%	21.6%	64.4%	88.6%	28.2%	58.0%	13.1	100.8	85	-0.4	-4.0	0.2
2023	MIA	MLB	33	276	22	3	20	0	.191/.278/.286	.249	.397	9.8%	24.3%	61.2%	88.6%	23.3%	53.2%	8.6	101.9	81	-0.6	1.4	0.5
2024 DC	COL	MLB	34	211	19	3	19	0	.220/.300/.324	.271	.419	9.2%	20.6%							77	0.0	1.4	0.3

2023 GP: C (82), P (7), DH (3) · *Comps: Ryan Hanigan (68), Gary Bennett (64), Cy Perkins (59)*

YEAR	TM	P. COUNT	FRM RUNS	BLK RUNS	THRW RUNS	TOT RUNS
2021	PIT	15291	3.6	0.3	0.6	4.6
2022	MIA	14818	-2.3	0.5	-0.4	-2.2
2023	MIA	10733	3.6	0.2	0.2	4.0
2024	COL	8418	1.1	0.2	0.0	1.3

Ah, Stallings. What a guy. He can wear the hell out of some catcher's gear. He makes a hat look good but also pulls off that Bald Guy With Facial Hair look without looking like a fuzzy thumb. And boy, is he tall! 6-foot-5 and every inch of it! That's nearly 80 inches of human! Unbelievable stuff!

When your backup catcher's OPS matches the area code for Port Angeles WA (564), his batting average is that of Newcastle, England (0191) and his defensive work is anything short of elite, it's necessary to prime oneself by listing other dangerously unimpressive things before dwelling on the backstop too much. Call it Stalling(s).

Sterlin Thompson 3B   Born: 06/26/01   Age: 23   Bats: L   Throws: R   Height: 6'4"   Weight: 200   Origin: Round 1, 2022 Draft (#31 overall)

YEAR	TM	LVL	AGE	PA	R	HR	RBI	SB	AVG/OBP/SLG	BABIP	SLGCON	BB%	K%	ZSw%	ZCon%	OSw%	OCon%	LA	90th EV	DRC+	BRR	DRP	WARP
2022	RCK	ROK	21	61	9	1	6	1	.273/.328/.382	.359	.538	3.3%	26.2%	65.0%	92.3%	33.3%	66.7%						
2022	FRE	A	21	50	9	1	4	2	.348/.380/.500	.441	.676	6.0%	24.0%							95	0.2	-1.5	0.0
2023	SRR	WIN	22	95	14	0	13	6	.342/.463/.487	.491	.712	17.9%	25.3%	59.7%	86.0%	24.8%	46.2%						
2023	SPO	A+	22	263	42	7	39	14	.323/.399/.520	.366	.636	8.7%	16.0%							133	-0.7	-1.8	1.5
2023	HFD	AA	22	144	14	7	17	3	.238/.333/.429	.264	.574	10.4%	22.2%							117	-0.6	-0.9	0.4
2024 non	COL	MLB	23	251	22	4	23	4	.226/.288/.341	.280	.449	6.9%	21.9%							77	0.0	0	-0.1

2023 GP: 3B (59), 2B (22), DH (14), RF (11), LF (10) · *Comps: Garin Cecchini (69), Tony Kemp (68), Yung-Chi Chen (66)*

One of Colorado's many lefty-swinging corner bats, Thompson did turn a bit of a corner in 2023, growing into some of the raw power that made him a first-rounder in 2022 and providing merely below-average defense at third after an atrocious showing the previous season. On a rate basis, DRP looked more fondly on his glovework, and he made just five errors in nearly 500 innings at the hot corner after committing three in under 100 frames in his debut. Still, he'll have to continue improving to really separate himself from the pack, and offense is the easiest path forward. Sterlin Silver Slugger is a better nickname than Sterlin Gold Glove, anyway.

Michael Toglia 1B/RF   Born: 08/16/98   Age: 25   Bats: S   Throws: L   Height: 6'5"   Weight: 226   Origin: Round 1, 2019 Draft (#23 overall)

YEAR	TM	LVL	AGE	PA	R	HR	RBI	SB	AVG/OBP/SLG	BABIP	SLGCON	BB%	K%	ZSw%	ZCon%	OSw%	OCon%	LA	90th EV	DRC+	BRR	DRP	WARP
2021	SPO	A+	22	330	50	17	66	7	.234/.333/.465	.275	.686	12.7%	27.6%							108	2.0	11.8	2.5
2021	HFD	AA	22	169	16	5	18	3	.217/.331/.406	.295	.630	13.6%	30.2%							93	-2.3	4.3	0.5
2022	HFD	AA	23	420	63	23	66	7	.234/.329/.466	.286	.716	12.1%	30.2%							113	1.9	0.0	2.0
2022	ABQ	AAA	23	75	11	7	17	0	.333/.413/.758	.405	1.136	12.0%	29.3%	66.9%	84.3%	25.4%	52.3%			114	-2.3	-0.1	0.1
2022	COL	MLB	23	120	10	2	12	1	.216/.275/.378	.338	.627	7.5%	36.7%	66.0%	78.9%	32.7%	45.3%	17.1	105.3	69	0.0	-0.2	-0.2
2023	ABQ	AAA	24	367	57	16	64	3	.256/.368/.474	.296	.646	14.4%	22.3%	68.7%	82.5%	25.0%	47.6%			110	0.5	-1.5	1.3
2023	COL	MLB	24	152	18	4	9	1	.163/.224/.284	.218	.440	6.6%	32.9%	72.9%	84.9%	34.1%	26.7%	16.9	106.0	65	0.0	0.1	-0.3
2024 DC	COL	MLB	25	186	18	5	20	2	.207/.288/.361	.282	.545	9.2%	30.5%							79	0.0	0.1	-0.1

2023 GP: 1B (26), RF (17), LF (1) · *Comps: Brandon Allen (52), Arismendy Alcántara (49), Moisés Sierra (48)*

Toglia progressed through the minors steadily, if unspectacularly, before a homer barrage in Triple-A earned him a late-season call-up in 2022. But he looked overmatched in the majors then, and he looked overmatched in 2023. Worse yet, in his time in the minors this past year, he didn't light up Triple-A as he had before. Toglia is a better fielder than the average first baseman, but a DRC+ in the 60s isn't going to cut it anywhere on the diamond, much less at the premier position for offense. It could be time to accept that he might never grow into his raw power, but on the bright side, sacrificing some loft for a more level swing could be what enables him to reach major-league breaking balls. Okay, probably not, but you know what they say about necessity.

Ezequiel Tovar SS   Born: 08/01/01   Age: 22   Bats: R   Throws: R   Height: 6'0"   Weight: 162   Origin: IFA, 2017

YEAR	TM	LVL	AGE	PA	R	HR	RBI	SB	AVG/OBP/SLG	BABIP	SLGCON	BB%	K%	ZSw%	ZCon%	OSw%	OCon%	LA	90th EV	DRC+	BRR	DRP	WARP
2021	SRR	WIN	19	96	10	3	10	2	.161/.219/.287	.167	.373	5.2%	20.8%	86.0%	85.7%	49.1%	57.7%						
2021	FRE	A	19	326	60	11	54	21	.309/.346/.510	.320	.585	4.3%	11.7%							132	2.5	8.1	3.3
2021	SPO	A+	19	143	19	4	18	3	.239/.266/.396	.252	.461	2.1%	13.3%							115	-1.0	-1.8	0.4
2022	HFD	AA	20	295	39	13	47	17	.318/.386/.545	.378	.720	8.5%	21.7%							113	1.4	0.9	1.6
2022	COL	MLB	20	35	2	1	2	0	.212/.257/.333	.261	.458	5.7%	25.7%	80.4%	81.1%	46.2%	54.1%	9.0	103.7	89	0.0	0.0	0.1
2023	COL	MLB	21	615	79	15	73	11	.253/.287/.408	.328	.571	4.1%	27.0%	79.2%	81.9%	46.5%	53.6%	12.5	104.1	76	0.4	-3.4	-0.1
2024 DC	COL	MLB	22	542	50	14	58	11	.233/.279/.378	.298	.519	4.8%	25.9%							79	-0.2	2.7	0.8

2023 GP: SS (153)   Comps: Carlos Correa (63), Ketel Marte (62), Starlin Castro (60)

Tovar joined forces with Brenton Doyle for arguably the best up-the-middle defense in the majors in 2023, but what they really need is to join forces on a quest to eat more carrots. Tovar probably has more upside with the bat, as a solid hit tool led to an above-average DRC+ at almost every minor-league stop, but he also swings at everything, and that simply won't fly in the majors. At least his defense will ensure that he'll continue to get an opportunity to work things through in the majors—though Tovar isn't the most fleet of foot, as evidenced by his subpar range and baserunning, his glove is brilliant, and he looks like the shortstop defender Brendan Rodgers couldn't be. Yet if Rodgers rebounds defensively in 2024, the Rockies would have an even better shot at the best up-the-middle defense in the league. That's one way to counteract an extreme hitting environment, but with Doyle and Tovar as fixtures in the lineup, the Rockies won't really be taking advantage of their home park themselves.

Alan Trejo IF   Born: 05/30/96   Age: 28   Bats: R   Throws: R   Height: 6'2"   Weight: 205   Origin: Round 16, 2017 Draft (#476 overall)

YEAR	TM	LVL	AGE	PA	R	HR	RBI	SB	AVG/OBP/SLG	BABIP	SLGCON	BB%	K%	ZSw%	ZCon%	OSw%	OCon%	LA	90th EV	DRC+	BRR	DRP	WARP
2021	ABQ	AAA	25	363	56	17	72	2	.278/.324/.569	.314	.742	6.3%	21.5%							100	-2.7	7.6	1.6
2021	COL	MLB	25	50	7	1	3	0	.217/.260/.326	.290	.484	6.0%	30.0%	68.4%	75.0%	41.1%	70.5%	10.7	101.2	70	0.0	-0.1	0.0
2022	ABQ	AAA	26	293	46	16	52	2	.296/.331/.551	.330	.719	3.4%	21.8%	76.3%	80.5%	43.3%	66.4%			98	0.5	2.2	1.0
2022	COL	MLB	26	125	15	4	17	1	.271/.312/.424	.337	.575	4.0%	24.8%	67.0%	85.9%	40.9%	60.9%	13.9	99.4	84	-0.1	-0.8	0.1
2023	JAL	WIN	27	76	2	0	6	0	.221/.276/.265	.294	.367	6.6%	25.0%										
2023	ABQ	AAA	27	54	9	1	4	2	.370/.463/.565	.485	.765	13.0%	22.2%	62.8%	79.7%	26.5%	66.7%			101	0.5	2.3	0.4
2023	COL	MLB	27	227	24	4	26	5	.232/.288/.343	.286	.455	7.0%	22.5%	70.5%	86.8%	34.1%	65.3%	14.1	99.3	78	0.0	-0.8	0.0
2024 DC	COL	MLB	28	27	3	1	3	0	.233/.288/.380	.280	.526	6.0%	21.2%							83	0.0	-0.2	0.0

2023 GP: 2B (49), 3B (23), SS (9), P (2), DH (1)   Comps: Grant Green (64), Erik González (63), Jason Bartlett (62)

Trejo earned a bigger role with the Rockies after taking steps forward offensively and defensively in 2022. While he solidified his gains with the glove and increased his versatility with more reps at third in 2023, his bat slid backward. That's mostly because his hard-hit rate fell to a miserable 22.6%, the fifth-worst among hitters with at least 200 PAs. Perhaps he should return to swinging like he's blindfolded; that is, after all, the Rockies' philosophy when it comes to inking new players. For Trejo though, it just might work—he managed a palatable output on pitches in the shadow and chase zones, just a little lower than his mark on pitches down the pipe, and he benefited from putting a few more of those pitches in play in 2022. Basically, he's put together a profile that can catch up when he's behind in the count, without the all-or-nothing early swings to make use of that recovery. Regardless, his defense will likely grant him a spot as a utilityman.

PITCHERS

Mason Albright LHP   Born: 11/26/02   Age: 21   Height: 6'0"   Weight: 190   Origin: Round 12, 2021 Draft (#351 overall)

YEAR	TM	LVL	AGE	G (GS)	IP	W-L	SV	K	WHIP	ERA	CSP	BB%	K%	HR%	GB%	ZSw%	ZCon%	OSw%	OCon%	BABIP	SLGCON	DRA-	WARP
2021	ANG	ROK	18	3 (2)	8	1-0	0	8	0.63	0.00		6.7%	26.7%	0.0%	40.0%					.150	.250		
2022	IE	A	19	12 (12)	48	0-4	0	53	1.98	9.00		9.7%	22.3%	5.0%	40.5%					.414	.890	130	-0.8
2023	IE	A	20	15 (14)	79²	9-4	0	86	1.23	3.62		6.0%	25.7%	3.0%	38.2%					.312	.570	87	0.9
2023	SPO	A+	20	5 (5)	25	2-0	0	24	1.44	2.88		11.2%	22.4%	3.7%	34.3%					.308	.652	105	0.1
2024 non	COL	MLB	21	58 (0)	50	2-2	0	42	1.60	6.25		10.1%	18.6%	4.2%	33.2%					.317	.621	135	-0.7

Comps: Dedgar Jimenez (54), Robert Gsellman (53), Foster Griffin (52)

All was indeed bright for Albright, as he amassed a 3.28 ERA across three stops in 2023. Acquired at the deadline in the Randal Grichuk/C.J. Cron deal, the lefty utilizes a delivery reminiscent to that of Clayton Kershaw, and he has a curveball to match. He rode the deuce to above-average strikeout and walk rates across 109.2 total innings, and his 14.8% swinging-strike rate ranked 21st among all minor-league hurlers with at least 100 frames. Now entering his age-21 season, the bigger concern is Albright's lack of a true third offering. Still, he's young enough that he has time to develop one, and even if he doesn't the curveball alone probably gives him a major-league future as a lefty specialist.

Chase Anderson RHP Born: 11/30/87 Age: 36 Height: 6'1" Weight: 210 Origin: Round 9, 2009 Draft (#276 overall)

YEAR	TM	LVL	AGE	G (GS)	IP	W-L	SV	K	WHIP	ERA	CSP	BB%	K%	HR%	GB%	ZSw%	ZCon%	OSw%	OCon%	BABIP	SLGCON	DRA-	WARP
2021	RR	AAA	33	5 (3)	15	0-1	0	14	1.47	4.20		11.9%	20.9%	7.5%	25.5%					.225	.682	115	0.1
2021	LHV	AAA	33	5 (5)	17¹	1-2	0	14	1.50	5.71		6.6%	18.4%	2.6%	37.5%					.352	.554	114	0.1
2021	PHI	MLB	33	14 (9)	48	2-4	0	35	1.48	6.75	52.9%	9.3%	16.3%	4.7%	35.7%	69.4%	80.1%	30.5%	70.5%	.281	.639	130	-0.3
2022	DUR	AAA	34	10 (1)	10	3-0	1	10	0.90	3.60		5.0%	25.0%	5.0%	35.7%					.192	.571	97	0.1
2022	TOL	AAA	34	17 (15)	70	4-3	0	62	1.39	4.63		8.9%	20.3%	4.6%	33.6%					.280	.620	122	0.1
2022	CIN	MLB	34	9 (7)	24	2-4	0	23	1.33	6.37	45.6%	14.6%	22.3%	2.9%	54.8%	69.4%	80.7%	32.7%	73.6%	.237	.500	96	0.3
2023	LOU	AAA	35	5 (5)	23	2-1	0	19	1.57	4.30		13.0%	19.0%	4.0%	32.8%	71.9%	75.3%	35.2%	61.5%	.302	.606	127	0.0
2023	COL	MLB	35	17 (17)	81¹	1-6	0	62	1.48	5.75	46.5%	9.0%	17.5%	4.8%	34.4%	72.7%	83.3%	28.6%	70.5%	.302	.616	125	-0.1
2023	TB	MLB	35	2 (0)	5	0-0	1	2	0.60	0.00	52.6%	5.6%	11.1%	0.0%	53.3%	65.7%	78.3%	27.0%	70.0%	.133	.133	112	0.0
2024 non	COL	MLB	36	58 (0)	50	2-2	0	39	1.51	5.71	48.0%	9.5%	17.3%	3.9%	35.9%					.300	.588	125	-0.4

2023 Arsenal: FC (89.3), FA (93.5), CH (84.1), SI (93.2), SW (80.6), CU (77.9)　　　Comps: Rodrigo Lopez (80), Jeff Suppan (76), Jason Marquis (74)

The ironic thing about baseball's most replaceable pitcher is that he's always out there replacing someone. The ubiquitous Anderson collected his most work since before the pandemic, sidling his way into Colorado's rotation and alternating either giving up one run or nine, depending on the alignment of the planets. For a 35-year-old who could have believably retired three years ago, Anderson's in a weird spot: He has enough life on his pitches, especially a refashioned cutter with better horizontal movement, to be a successful shuttle-level reliever. But his pedigree, and his platoon-resistant curve, make him too attractive to some desperate club as a mediocre starter. His numbers might be better in the former case, but it's hard to blame him for enjoying the MLB per diem, even if it means occasionally giving up home runs on three consecutive pitches.

Daniel Bard RHP Born: 06/25/85 Age: 39 Height: 6'4" Weight: 215 Origin: Round 1, 2006 Draft (#28 overall)

YEAR	TM	LVL	AGE	G (GS)	IP	W-L	SV	K	WHIP	ERA	CSP	BB%	K%	HR%	GB%	ZSw%	ZCon%	OSw%	OCon%	BABIP	SLGCON	DRA-	WARP
2021	COL	MLB	36	67 (0)	65²	7-8	20	80	1.60	5.21	52.6%	11.8%	26.3%	2.6%	42.0%	70.6%	79.3%	27.9%	53.1%	.355	.622	99	0.7
2022	COL	MLB	37	57 (0)	60¹	6-4	34	69	0.99	1.79	56.1%	10.2%	28.2%	1.2%	51.4%	65.9%	82.5%	28.4%	53.9%	.221	.361	79	1.2
2023	COL	MLB	38	50 (0)	49¹	4-2	1	47	1.70	4.56	47.8%	21.1%	20.3%	2.2%	36.7%	64.5%	84.9%	22.1%	64.2%	.244	.512	131	-0.2
2024 DC	COL	MLB	39	47 (0)	50²	2-3	3	54	1.47	5.07	51.9%	13.3%	23.9%	3.4%	41.4%					.285	.561	109	0.0

2023 Arsenal: SL (87.3), SI (95.2), FA (94.8), FC (89.3), SW (83.2), CH (88.1)　　　Comps: Pat Neshek (58), Rudy Seanez (57), Todd Jones (56)

Bard dominated as a young reliever before twin losses of command and velocity led to a seven-year exile from the majors, the last two years spent semi-retired and mentoring young Diamondbacks. But his pupils urged him to try one last comeback attempt, and from 2020-'22, Bard was miraculously capable and at times excellent in relief for the Rockies, earning Comeback Player of the Year honors, some MVP votes, and amassing a fine 26.9% strikeout rate. Then the control issues and inconsistency returned in a World Baseball Classic run that cost Jose Altuve his thumb and Bard his confidence. That's when the veteran decided to go public with his mental health battle. And though he couldn't restore his velocity or control down the stretch in 2023, he managed a palatable ERA, worked nearly 50 frames and inspired other players to open up about their own struggles with anxiety. Ultimately, forearm troubles ended his season, injecting more uncertainty into his final year under contract in 2024. But whatever happens, Bard's comeback will go down as one of baseball's most impactful.

Jake Bird RHP Born: 12/04/95 Age: 28 Height: 6'3" Weight: 200 Origin: Round 5, 2018 Draft (#156 overall)

YEAR	TM	LVL	AGE	G (GS)	IP	W-L	SV	K	WHIP	ERA	CSP	BB%	K%	HR%	GB%	ZSw%	ZCon%	OSw%	OCon%	BABIP	SLGCON	DRA-	WARP
2021	HFD	AA	25	10 (1)	20¹	1-0	0	23	1.33	2.21		7.7%	25.3%	1.1%	71.9%					.339	.456	90	0.3
2021	ABQ	AAA	25	29 (1)	38¹	5-1	0	36	1.38	3.99		11.7%	22.2%	1.9%	64.8%					.304	.476	84	0.5
2022	ABQ	AAA	26	22 (0)	26	2-2	2	34	0.96	2.77		8.5%	32.1%	2.8%	63.3%	59.1%	83.0%	32.6%	46.4%	.228	.467	69	0.6
2022	COL	MLB	26	38 (0)	47²	2-4	0	42	1.43	4.91	55.6%	10.9%	19.9%	3.3%	54.2%	65.6%	90.0%	21.4%	52.3%	.284	.547	99	0.5
2023	COL	MLB	27	70 (3)	89¹	3-3	0	77	1.35	4.33	52.4%	7.1%	20.2%	1.6%	52.6%	66.2%	88.3%	27.5%	58.8%	.333	.511	87	1.7
2024 DC	COL	MLB	28	60 (0)	63¹	3-3	3	48	1.39	4.58	53.4%	9.0%	17.4%	2.4%	51.7%					.297	.495	101	0.3

2023 Arsenal: SI (94.6), KC (81.7), FC (89.7), SL (86.3), CH (87.1)　　　Comps: Alan Busenitz (74), Dan Jennings (72), Kevin McCarthy (72)

The Rockies made Bird free range in his first full major-league season: Not counting the three times he served as an opener, the bearded right-hander's 84 ⅓ innings out of the 'pen last season tied for most in the majors. In a familiar tale, he notched a 2.82 ERA in 44 ⅔ innings on the road, yet he limped to a 5.84 mark over the exact same workload at home. His overall line still looked solid, but he'll be more likely to attain longevity if he can limit the damage in Colorado. As with fellow reliever Justin Lawrence, the velo on Bird's mid-90s sinker should play up in Coors, and the deception wrought by his funky, low three-quarters release should play anywhere. And unlike Lawrence, Bird has five pitches to play with and thus more room to customize his repertoire based on venue, which should enable him to take the next step at home. His gyro-heavy, low-spin sinker should work everywhere due to its reliance on gravity over air pressure, but it might serve him to step away from his Magnus-dependent curveball whenever he returns to Denver, instead turning to his slider-cutter combo when he's in need of a secondary pitch.

Ty Blach LHP Born: 10/20/90 Age: 33 Height: 6'1" Weight: 215 Origin: Round 5, 2012 Draft (#178 overall)

YEAR	TM	LVL	AGE	G (GS)	IP	W-L	SV	K	WHIP	ERA	CSP	BB%	K%	HR%	GB%	ZSw%	ZCon%	OSw%	OCon%	BABIP	SLGCON	DRA-	WARP
2021	DEL	A	30	10(10)	15	0-0	0	14	0.73	1.80		1.8%	24.6%	0.0%	51.2%					.244	.341	94	0.2
2022	ABQ	AAA	31	15(1)	36	1-5	0	20	1.44	4.50		5.1%	12.7%	1.9%	46.9%	65.7%	83.9%	33.1%	80.0%	.331	.492	113	-0.1
2022	COL	MLB	31	24(1)	44¹	1-0	1	29	1.40	5.89	58.4%	5.7%	15.0%	2.1%	41.7%	66.8%	85.5%	35.3%	71.1%	.322	.555	114	0.1
2023	ABQ	AAA	32	11(5)	30²	3-1	0	27	1.43	4.40		6.0%	20.3%	1.5%	54.1%	68.4%	89.9%	34.4%	63.6%	.354	.485	85	0.6
2023	COL	MLB	32	20(13)	78	3-3	0	50	1.64	5.54	50.7%	6.8%	14.2%	4.3%	38.2%	67.8%	93.5%	34.7%	72.0%	.346	.638	138	-0.6
2024 non	COL	MLB	33	58(0)	50	2-2	0	28	1.52	5.71	52.8%	6.7%	12.4%	3.4%	41.0%					.313	.545	125	-0.4

2023 Arsenal: FA (89.5), CH (80.2), SL (83.9), CU (79.2)   Comps: Tommy Milone (59), Chris Rusin (59), Ross Detwiler (58)

Per pitch modeling, Blach's cutter was the Rockies' best pitch in 2023, with its shape grading out at 70% better than league average. There was just one problem: None of the lefty's other offerings came in better than 30% *below* average. With nothing to work off of, the cutter was a net negative per run value; even Mariano Rivera had a decent two-seamer, and his cut-fastball was probably the best ever. Blach's ERA *was* about a run better in Coors than on the road, but that seemingly had more to do with HR/FB luck than any intrinsic advantage; the 99% active-spin sinker that he rolled with more than half the time had its two-plane movement greatly diminished by the thin air, the same air that couldn't boost the pitch beyond a career-low velocity despite offering less resistance than at sea level. He did hold same-handed hitters to significantly lower output, suggesting that the sinker and cutter could give him a future as a specialist, just probably not at a mile-high altitude. Sure enough, he elected free agency this offseason.

Matt Carasiti RHP Born: 07/23/91 Age: 32 Height: 6'2" Weight: 205 Origin: Round 6, 2012 Draft (#198 overall)

YEAR	TM	LVL	AGE	G (GS)	IP	W-L	SV	K	WHIP	ERA	CSP	BB%	K%	HR%	GB%	ZSw%	ZCon%	OSw%	OCon%	BABIP	SLGCON	DRA-	WARP
2022	SAC	AAA	30	23(0)	21²	3-2	1	28	2.03	8.31		12.7%	25.5%	3.6%	46.2%	65.2%	81.9%	29.6%	50.7%	.426	.815	90	0.3
2023	ABQ	AAA	31	25(0)	27	2-1	2	26	1.48	3.33		10.1%	21.8%	0.8%	51.2%	67.7%	89.8%	28.6%	59.2%	.346	.538	86	0.2
2023	COL	MLB	31	16(0)	24¹	1-0	1	16	1.60	6.29	52.0%	10.0%	14.5%	2.7%	56.1%	65.6%	82.5%	23.7%	63.0%	.316	.512	100	0.3
2024 non	COL	MLB	32	58(0)	50	2-2	0	43	1.49	5.32	51.7%	9.8%	19.1%	3.2%	40.6%					.307	.561	116	-0.2

2023 Arsenal: SI (95.4), FS (81.5), FC (91.8), FA (95)   Comps: Danny Coulombe (54), Pedro Strop (53), Casey Fien (53)

After making his major-league debut for the team in 2016, Carasiti spent a second season with the Rockies, sandwiching stints in four other MLB organizations, the Atlantic League, and Japan. This go-round didn't work out, but the right-hander has an interesting arsenal that could play in Colorado. Or, more specifically, one interesting pitch: a forkball that he threw more than Kodai Senga threw his own. Carasiti's fork averaged a cool 840 rpm in 2023, the third-lowest mark among pitches thrown at least 50 times last season. That made it almost entirely reliant on gravity, which still works at Coors as this book went to press. Except in this case it didn't, possibly because Carasiti was mainly reliant on a Magnus-heavy sinker. The Rockies outrighted him after the season, but it's worth keeping him around on the off chance that he can find the knife to his fork.

──────────────── ★ ★ ★ *2024 Top 101 Prospect* **#92** ★ ★ ★ ────────────────

Chase Dollander RHP Born: 10/26/01 Age: 22 Height: 6'2" Weight: 200 Origin: Round 1, 2023 Draft (#9 overall)

The Rockies' top pick in the 2023 draft and the ninth selection overall, Dollander's calling card is his fastball. It sits mid-90s and tops out at 99 mph, velocity that could play up with the thinner air at Coors creating less drag. Thanks to its effect on the pitch's carry, though, he'll have to use the heater less than the 65% of the time he did in 2023. He has a trio of secondary offerings, but turned to the curve and change a combined 14% in his last season at Tennessee; those two pitches seem more designed to keep left-handers honest. Meanwhile, Chase failed to get hitters to do just that for his primary breaking ball, a slider, cited by many as the reason for his inconsistent 2023 season after a dominant '22. Overall, Dollander has some good raw tools, but if the Rockies' history (complete with widely circulated pictures of Colorado's empty draft room) is any indication, we wouldn't bet on their analysts (analyst?) having a solid plan for him.

Ryan Feltner RHP Born: 09/02/96 Age: 27 Height: 6'4" Weight: 190 Origin: Round 4, 2018 Draft (#126 overall)

YEAR	TM	LVL	AGE	G (GS)	IP	W-L	SV	K	WHIP	ERA	CSP	BB%	K%	HR%	GB%	ZSw%	ZCon%	OSw%	OCon%	BABIP	SLGCON	DRA-	WARP
2021	SPO	A+	24	7(7)	37¹	3-1	0	45	1.18	2.17		11.5%	28.8%	0.6%	42.4%					.275	.374	90	0.5
2021	HFD	AA	24	13(13)	72²	5-2	0	80	1.24	2.85		7.4%	26.8%	2.3%	37.9%					.324	.552	100	0.6
2021	COL	MLB	24	2(2)	6¹	0-1	0	6	2.21	11.37	54.7%	15.2%	18.2%	9.1%	9.5%	65.6%	75.0%	19.8%	50.0%	.333	.950	128	0.0
2022	ABQ	AAA	25	11(11)	51²	5-1	0	60	1.30	3.83		8.1%	27.1%	2.3%	41.1%	65.2%	80.4%	27.2%	57.5%	.326	.583	90	0.6
2022	COL	MLB	25	20(19)	97¹	4-9	0	84	1.41	5.83	54.6%	8.2%	19.6%	3.7%	41.4%	69.8%	86.6%	27.7%	64.9%	.300	.589	114	0.3
2023	ABQ	AAA	26	2(2)	7¹	0-1	0	6	1.36	2.45		13.3%	20.0%	0.0%	45.0%	72.9%	82.9%	23.5%	43.8%	.300	.350	93	
2023	COL	MLB	26	10(10)	43¹	2-4	0	38	1.68	5.82	50.7%	13.9%	18.9%	1.0%	43.6%	62.6%	88.8%	29.5%	60.6%	.328	.462	115	0.2
2024 DC	COL	MLB	27	15(15)	64	2-6	0	53	1.50	5.28	53.2%	10.4%	18.9%	3.3%	40.9%					.306	.560	114	0.1

2023 Arsenal: SL (88.8), FA (95.2), SI (95), CH (84.4), CU (78.9), SW (81.7)   Comps: Tyler Cloyd (63), Spencer Turnbull (63), Trevor Richards (62)

Numbers aside, Feltner had a remarkable year. In a feat of incredible perseverance and courage, the right-hander returned to a major-league mound just four months after his last appearance left him with a skull fracture. That he tossed five shutout frames in his return was icing on the cake, but it speaks to the 27-year-old's latent potential; after all, he struck out upwards of 25% of hitters he faced away from Coors on the season. Granted, that also came with a 15.1% walk rate. Yet you can't help but feel there's a chance for him to figure it all out—his velocity continued its upward trajectory, he had among the best stuff of any Rockies starter last year and his spin profile should be well-suited for Coors. With Feltner's resolve, he just might put it all together in the coming years.

Kyle Freeland LHP Born: 05/14/93 Age: 31 Height: 6'4" Weight: 204 Origin: Round 1, 2014 Draft (#8 overall)

YEAR	TM	LVL	AGE	G (GS)	IP	W-L	SV	K	WHIP	ERA	CSP	BB%	K%	HR%	GB%	ZSw%	ZCon%	OSw%	OCon%	BABIP	SLGCON	DRA-	WARP
2021	ABQ	AAA	28	2 (2)	10	1-1	0	4	0.60	1.80		5.4%	10.8%	0.0%	76.7%					.133	.133	102	0.0
2021	COL	MLB	28	23 (23)	120²	7-8	0	105	1.42	4.33	52.4%	7.4%	20.4%	3.9%	44.0%	67.3%	88.6%	30.6%	63.6%	.328	.607	99	1.2
2022	COL	MLB	29	31 (31)	174²	9-11	0	131	1.41	4.53	53.0%	6.9%	17.1%	2.5%	42.2%	71.2%	88.3%	31.4%	65.1%	.319	.563	129	-0.9
2023	COL	MLB	30	29 (29)	155²	6-14	0	94	1.47	5.03	51.4%	6.2%	13.9%	4.3%	39.8%	73.0%	91.3%	33.1%	68.1%	.312	.596	129	-0.5
2024 DC	COL	MLB	31	28 (28)	148²	6-13	0	92	1.49	5.58	51.4%	7.1%	14.2%	3.4%	40.6%					.315	.561	122	-0.4

2023 Arsenal: SI (88.8), SL (84.5), FA (89), CU (80.8), CH (84.4)　　　　*Comps: Jeff Francis (83), Claude Osteen (82), Joe Saunders (82)*

Of the three lifetime Rockie starters who made their full-season debuts in 2017, Freeland has the lowest career ERA. Some of that is due to his outlier 2018 that earned him Cy Young consideration, but focusing only on that would ignore his other five seasons of above-average park-adjusted ERA. His 2023 falls in that group, but just barely, and it might be his last considering that it was Freeland's third season in a row with diminished velocity. He's already tried moving off his slower four-seamer; 2023 marked the lowest four-seam usage rate of his career and the highest sinker usage. His sinker didn't lose as much velo, and Freeland pours it into the zone at a steep angle. Yet sinkers don't generate as many whiffs, and Freeland's was demolished when it was put into play. Sinkers do, however, help sliders play up, as Freeland's turned in its best season since 2018. It often takes multiple attempts to rework an arsenal in the face of a velocity decline; Freeland's next try might include a more prominently featured slider.

Austin Gomber LHP Born: 11/23/93 Age: 30 Height: 6'5" Weight: 220 Origin: Round 4, 2014 Draft (#135 overall)

YEAR	TM	LVL	AGE	G (GS)	IP	W-L	SV	K	WHIP	ERA	CSP	BB%	K%	HR%	GB%	ZSw%	ZCon%	OSw%	OCon%	BABIP	SLGCON	DRA-	WARP
2021	COL	MLB	27	23 (23)	115¹	9-9	0	113	1.24	4.53	56.7%	8.4%	23.2%	4.1%	43.2%	65.8%	84.4%	31.5%	57.9%	.265	.566	100	1.1
2022	COL	MLB	28	33 (17)	124²	5-7	0	95	1.37	5.56	54.6%	6.4%	18.0%	3.8%	42.0%	71.5%	87.1%	32.7%	63.7%	.310	.595	117	0.1
2023	COL	MLB	29	27 (27)	139	9-9	0	87	1.49	5.50	52.2%	7.1%	14.4%	4.3%	40.9%	70.6%	87.7%	28.3%	66.8%	.314	.609	125	-0.2
2024 DC	COL	MLB	30	28 (28)	140¹	5-12	0	93	1.49	5.38	53.8%	7.7%	15.1%	3.2%	41.5%					.315	.549	117	-0.1

2023 Arsenal: FA (90.9), SL (85.1), CH (81.7), KC (77.8), SI (88.5)　　　　*Comps: Rick Waits (73), John Lannan (69), Ken Brett (69)*

The "prize" of the Nolan Arenado deal, Gomber's third season in Denver was his worst by many measures. Sure, he posted a career-high in innings (a season-ending back injury kept him from an even higher total), but his strikeout rate cratered, finishing third to last in the majors (just behind teammate Kyle Freeland) and dropping his K-BB% down to fourth to last (min. 100 IP). His most-used offering, a four-seamer, has cost him 40 runs over the past two seasons, the worst run value of any pitch in that time. For some reason, he used it even more in 2023 despite a career-worst velocity, and at the expense of his slider, the only pitch that has actually fooled batters. Clearly, the 99% active-spin, rise-reliant heater doesn't play in Coors, but what could the declining Gomber replace it with? Given the success of his slider, a cutter might be worth tinkering with. Ultimately, however, entering his age-30 season, there's little hope that the southpaw will be what salvages the fateful Arenado trade.

Gavin Hollowell RHP Born: 11/04/97 Age: 26 Height: 6'7" Weight: 215 Origin: Round 6, 2019 Draft (#189 overall)

YEAR	TM	LVL	AGE	G (GS)	IP	W-L	SV	K	WHIP	ERA	CSP	BB%	K%	HR%	GB%	ZSw%	ZCon%	OSw%	OCon%	BABIP	SLGCON	DRA-	WARP
2021	FRE	A	23	22 (0)	22	2-0	4	31	0.91	2.45		5.7%	35.6%	1.1%	44.0%					.286	.460	83	0.3
2022	HFD	AA	24	42 (0)	48²	4-2	16	64	0.90	3.14		7.4%	34.0%	1.6%	31.4%					.265	.452	89	0.9
2022	COL	MLB	24	6 (0)	7	0-2	0	8	1.57	7.71	52.0%	12.5%	25.0%	3.1%	25.0%	70.0%	78.6%	25.3%	57.1%	.316	.579	104	0.1
2023	ABQ	AAA	25	19 (0)	23¹	0-0	2	27	1.41	3.47		9.7%	26.2%	1.9%	43.1%	62.3%	78.2%	30.4%	60.3%	.333	.538	77	0.3
2023	COL	MLB	25	26 (0)	33²	2-0	1	32	1.46	5.88	48.9%	11.7%	20.8%	5.2%	32.7%	67.7%	77.8%	30.1%	68.6%	.256	.633	111	0.2
2024 DC	COL	MLB	26	54 (0)	57	3-2	0	57	1.36	4.77	49.3%	9.8%	23.3%	3.6%	33.4%					.295	.583	105	0.1

2023 Arsenal: FA (93.6), SW (82.4), SI (94), FC (86.9), CH (82.3)　　　　*Comps: Ryan Meisinger (80), Travis Bergen (79), Ryan Dull (79)*

Hollowell finally brought his funky slot to the majors for an extended stay after a brief debut in 2022. His low arm angle enables him to have the kind of side-spinning sinker that not only kills ride, but also looks like the mirror image of his slider from the hitter's standpoint. Unfortunately, Coors mutes the horizontal movement that comes with his sidespin, too. Hollowell has high spin rates on all of his pitches, and it's likely his sinker would run and his slider would sweep with the best of them if he didn't pitch half of his games in Colorado. With some luck and improved control, Hollowell could follow Justin Lawrence's path to improved performance on the road down the line (Hollowell actually pitched better in Denver in 2023), to pair with decent enough numbers at home thanks to a deceptive delivery and velocity. You might say that Hollo's well that ends well.

Dakota Hudson RHP Born: 09/15/94 Age: 29 Height: 6'5" Weight: 215 Origin: Round 1, 2016 Draft (#34 overall)

YEAR	TM	LVL	AGE	G (GS)	IP	W-L	SV	K	WHIP	ERA	CSP	BB%	K%	HR%	GB%	ZSw%	ZCon%	OSw%	OCon%	BABIP	SLGCON	DRA-	WARP
2021	SPR	AA	26	3 (3)	11²	1-0	0	7	1.11	0.77		11.4%	15.9%	0.0%	56.2%					.250	.406	103	0.1
2021	STL	MLB	26	2 (1)	8²	1-0	0	6	0.92	2.08	58.6%	2.9%	17.6%	0.0%	65.4%	70.4%	92.1%	31.2%	70.8%	.269	.346	84	0.1
2022	MEM	AAA	27	3 (3)	21	1-1	0	19	1.33	1.71		9.2%	21.8%	0.0%	49.2%					.339	.362	99	0.3
2022	STL	MLB	27	27 (26)	139²	8-7	0	78	1.45	4.45	54.2%	10.2%	13.1%	1.5%	53.6%	68.0%	91.8%	27.9%	67.0%	.303	.442	119	0.0
2023	MEM	AAA	28	11 (11)	48	5-4	0	39	1.85	6.00		7.6%	17.3%	2.2%	54.2%	70.5%	88.8%	33.4%	58.0%	.416	.671	98	0.8
2023	STL	MLB	28	18 (12)	81¹	6-3	0	45	1.50	4.98	48.9%	9.6%	12.7%	2.5%	51.3%	72.6%	89.5%	28.6%	62.1%	.305	.515	117	0.2
2024 DC	COL	MLB	29	37 (21)	126¹	5-10	0	81	1.54	5.31	51.0%	9.2%	14.3%	2.4%	52.6%					.314	.503	114	0.1

2023 Arsenal: SI (91.8), FC (85.3), FA (91.3), SL (81.3), CH (84.9)　　　　*Comps: Brandon Morrow (76), Dustin Hermanson (75), Darren Oliver (73)*

Hudson has been trying to rediscover his ability to mix up his pitches and throw them correctly since 2020, when he got Tommy John, that tragic milestone in any pitcher's story that's followed, or not followed, by a dramatic comeback. In the years since, Hudson has suffered from debilitating neck spasms and at one point couldn't raise his throwing arm. It took him a while to get back to the point that he could throw a pitch—but he did, and in July, the Cardinals brought him back to the majors. In August, they started letting him make regular starts. They weren't all good ones, but there were enough to indicate that the 29-year-old is not quite finished. He does appear, however, to be done in St. Louis after being non-tendered early in the offseason.

Karl Kauffmann RHP   Born: 08/15/97   Age: 26   Height: 6'2"   Weight: 200   Origin: Round 2, 2019 Draft (#77 overall)

YEAR	TM	LVL	AGE	G (GS)	IP	W-L	SV	K	WHIP	ERA	CSP	BB%	K%	HR%	GB%	ZSw%	ZCon%	OSw%	OCon%	BABIP	SLGCON	DRA-	WARP
2021	HFD	AA	23	19(18)	82	2-11	0	65	2.00	7.35		10.1%	16.0%	4.4%	52.5%					.379	.707	121	-0.3
2022	HFD	AA	24	15(15)	77²	5-4	0	84	1.35	4.06		10.4%	25.6%	2.7%	47.1%					.313	.573	100	1.0
2022	ABQ	AAA	24	13(13)	64	4-5	0	60	1.80	6.05		14.8%	19.7%	3.6%	52.3%	65.2%	81.6%	26.7%	64.8%	.317	.609	97	0.5
2023	ABQ	AAA	25	19(19)	92¹	3-5	0	61	1.81	6.43		9.8%	14.3%	2.6%	45.3%	72.1%	88.6%	31.9%	63.2%	.370	.577	124	-0.4
2023	COL	MLB	25	11(3)	35	2-5	0	16	1.66	8.23	42.4%	10.1%	10.1%	3.2%	41.0%	75.1%	89.4%	28.9%	73.6%	.316	.571	136	-0.2
2024 DC	COL	MLB	26	10(0)	12²	0-1	0	8	1.74	6.85	42.4%	10.7%	13.5%	3.6%	41.2%					.325	.578	144	-0.2

2023 Arsenal: SI (90.2), CH (85.1), SL (83.4), FA (90.4), FC (88.2), SW (81.4)   Comps: Thomas Eshelman (72), Brooks Raley (69), T.J. Zeuch (66)

The Rockies promoted Kauffman despite... well, the numbers are right there, folks. Predictably, he performed even worse in the majors, walking as many as he struck out—together with Daniel Bard, Kauffman represented half of the first pair of teammates to do that since 2018 (min. 30 IP). Unlike Bard, Kauffman could easily be outrighted without the sunk cost of a hefty contract, and the Rockies kicked him off the 40-man at the end of the year. He has some interesting pitches, including a splitter with plus drop and a one-seam sinker, but as anyone who's seen Andy Warhol's directorial output can attest, interesting and good aren't necessarily correlated.

Tyler Kinley RHP   Born: 01/31/91   Age: 33   Height: 6'4"   Weight: 220   Origin: Round 16, 2013 Draft (#472 overall)

YEAR	TM	LVL	AGE	G (GS)	IP	W-L	SV	K	WHIP	ERA	CSP	BB%	K%	HR%	GB%	ZSw%	ZCon%	OSw%	OCon%	BABIP	SLGCON	DRA-	WARP
2021	COL	MLB	30	70(0)	70¹	3-2	0	68	1.21	4.73	56.4%	8.8%	23.1%	4.1%	38.7%	76.2%	82.0%	33.1%	52.7%	.253	.571	98	0.7
2022	COL	MLB	31	25(0)	24	1-1	0	27	1.13	0.75	58.2%	6.0%	27.0%	0.0%	39.4%	76.0%	77.2%	35.4%	51.4%	.318	.394	84	0.4
2023	COL	MLB	32	18(0)	16¹	0-4	5	17	1.65	6.06	49.0%	7.9%	22.4%	3.9%	19.2%	73.8%	84.4%	30.4%	62.7%	.375	.694	107	0.1
2024 DC	COL	MLB	33	60(0)	63¹	3-4	9	60	1.32	4.44	52.9%	8.7%	22.2%	3.5%	35.5%					.293	.568	100	0.3

2023 Arsenal: SL (91.4), FA (96.7), CH (86.7)   Comps: Justin Miller (65), Brad Brach (63), Dan Otero (62)

In the fall of 2022, the Rockies chose to add Kinley—fresh off of the always-ominous flexor tendon repair—to their small group of players under guaranteed multi-year contracts. Perhaps Colorado was thinking, given their fealty when it comes to locking up healthy players, why not try some unhealthy ones? Of course, this strategy backfired too, as the injury seemingly blunted Kinley's sharp slider. The slide-piece saw a 10-percentage-point dip in swinging-strike rate on the season, accompanied by a loss of drop and cut. In fact, the pitch *backed* up on average; hitters didn't square it up when they did make contact. While increased velo may have diminished the slider, Kinley also averaged a career-high fastball velocity. Hitters kept teeing off the pitch despite that, but his ability to continue to max out post-surgery indicates he has something left in the tank.

Peter Lambert RHP   Born: 04/18/97   Age: 27   Height: 6'2"   Weight: 208   Origin: Round 2, 2015 Draft (#44 overall)

YEAR	TM	LVL	AGE	G (GS)	IP	W-L	SV	K	WHIP	ERA	CSP	BB%	K%	HR%	GB%	ZSw%	ZCon%	OSw%	OCon%	BABIP	SLGCON	DRA-	WARP
2021	SPO	A+	24	4(4)	7²	0-0	0	7	1.83	5.87		15.8%	18.4%	5.3%	47.8%					.286	.739	127	-0.1
2021	COL	MLB	24	2(2)	5²	0-0	0	3	2.47	11.12	56.4%	6.7%	10.0%	6.7%	52.0%	74.5%	80.0%	26.3%	70.0%	.435	.800	105	0.0
2022	ABQ	AAA	25	4(4)	8²	0-2	0	11	1.96	6.23		14.3%	26.2%	0.0%	37.5%	68.6%	75.0%	26.2%	52.4%	.458	.500	89	0.1
2023	ABQ	AAA	26	7(7)	21²	0-2	0	21	1.57	4.15		14.3%	21.4%	0.0%	30.6%	70.7%	84.0%	33.1%	55.0%	.328	.393	131	-0.2
2023	COL	MLB	26	25(11)	87¹	3-7	0	71	1.39	5.36	48.1%	7.5%	18.9%	4.8%	41.0%	71.2%	85.1%	30.0%	66.7%	.296	.674	111	0.5
2024 DC	COL	MLB	27	38(16)	108	4-8	0	87	1.49	5.39	48.6%	9.6%	18.1%	3.3%	41.1%					.309	.561	117	-0.1

2023 Arsenal: FA (93.5), SL (88.5), CH (86.4), SW (82.8), CU (78.2)   Comps: Sean O'Sullivan (52), Greg Reynolds (47), Dave Eiland (46)

Lambert had Tommy John surgery in 2020, and lingering elbow pain limited him to just 30 ⅓ professional innings in the following two seasons. With a clean bill of health coming into 2023, Lambert built up strength in the minors before taking on a swingman role in the majors. Ultimately, a biceps issue surfaced to end his season, but in between Lambert made good on his promise as a command-first prospect with an above-average walk rate. His strikeout numbers left something to be desired, especially for someone who tosses half of his innings at Coors; accordingly, he pitched to an ERA nearly two runs higher at home on the season. Beyond the lack of punchouts, Lambert's stuff isn't suited for high elevation; with above-average active and overall spin rates, the right-hander's arsenal plays better when he can utilize the Magnus effect to its fullest extent. In a vacuum, his spin profile made him a good candidate for the sweeper he added this past season, but not at Coors.

Justin Lawrence RHP   Born: 11/25/94   Age: 29   Height: 6'3"   Weight: 213   Origin: Round 12, 2015 Draft (#347 overall)

YEAR	TM	LVL	AGE	G (GS)	IP	W-L	SV	K	WHIP	ERA	CSP	BB%	K%	HR%	GB%	ZSw%	ZCon%	OSw%	OCon%	BABIP	SLGCON	DRA-	WARP
2021	ABQ	AAA	26	31(0)	32¹	6-5	13	30	1.36	4.73		8.5%	21.1%	2.1%	61.5%					.312	.484	95	0.2
2021	COL	MLB	26	19(0)	16²	1-0	0	17	2.40	8.64	48.8%	22.1%	19.8%	0.0%	48.0%	58.9%	87.9%	21.5%	54.3%	.429	.565	126	-0.1
2022	ABQ	AAA	27	28(0)	29¹	1-0	1	49	1.02	3.07		11.0%	41.5%	1.7%	40.7%	52.6%	81.1%	28.8%	37.8%	.288	.500	72	0.7
2022	COL	MLB	27	38(0)	42²	3-1	1	48	1.55	5.70	53.4%	11.5%	25.1%	1.6%	50.0%	62.0%	85.4%	28.3%	58.2%	.350	.542	87	0.7
2023	COL	MLB	28	69(0)	75	4-7	11	78	1.35	3.72	51.6%	11.0%	23.9%	1.5%	46.8%	59.2%	84.4%	26.6%	59.6%	.305	.492	91	1.2
2024 DC	COL	MLB	29	60(0)	63¹	3-5	15	61	1.37	4.32	51.9%	11.2%	22.1%	2.6%	46.4%					.287	.508	95	0.4

2023 Arsenal: SI (95.5), SW (84.1), CH (80.2)   Comps: Tayron Guerrero (70), Derek Law (69), Brad Brach (68)

At first glance, Lawrence might not have leapt out as the Rockies' best chance at a homegrown breakout in 2023. The sidearmer relies on high spin rates—his sweeper was the majors' third-spinniest—to generate side-to-side movement, a profile that depends on manipulating air pressure that just isn't there at 5,000 feet. Then again, the right-hander has two things going for him that always play at elevation: velocity, which in fact increases slightly due to less air resistance, and a deceptive low slot, which plays just about anywhere. After routinely hitting the high 90s in his debut season, Lawrence has settled in as more of a mid-90s guy, but his slot has gotten lower every year. That funk has enabled him to impart more backspin on the sweeper that, unlike a traditional slider, benefits from more lift as a popup-inducing pitch. And while his fastball velocity has plateaued, the sweeper has gotten harder each year. He threw it more than ever in 2023, and we just may see even more of it going forward.

Jake Madden   RHP   Born: 12/26/01   Age: 22   Height: 6'6"   Weight: 185   Origin: Round 4, 2022 Draft (#118 overall)

YEAR	TM	LVL	AGE	G (GS)	IP	W-L	SV	K	WHIP	ERA	CSP	BB%	K%	HR%	GB%	ZSw%	ZCon%	OSw%	OCon%	BABIP	SLGCON	DRA-	WARP
2023	FRE	A	21	6(6)	15	0-2	0	14	1.80	7.80		12.7%	19.7%	5.6%	50.0%					.318	.667	108	
2023	IE	A	21	14(14)	64¹	2-6	0	66	1.59	5.46		12.9%	21.9%	2.3%	52.4%					.309	.543	113	-0.2
2024 non	COL	MLB	22	58(0)	50	2-2	0	40	1.75	6.86		13.2%	16.8%	4.0%	38.8%					.308	.605	145	-1.0

Comps: Jorge López (96), Luke Albright (93), Sugar Ray Marimon (92)

The other half of the Rockies' return for Randal Grichuk and C.J. Cron, Madden was a higher draft pick than Mason Albright, but his first professional season left a lot to be desired. He ranked in the bottom 20 in both ERA and walk rate in A-ball (min. 70 IP) as a 21-year-old, suggesting that he may be better suited to play football video games than baseball. Meanwhile, his lanky 6-foot-6 frame could actually serve him more as a basketball player. Still, there's an opportunity for the right-hander to add more muscle, which could level up his fastball and already-plus changeup. That way, he could improve upon a middling swinging-strike rate and rack up strikeouts with whiffs, rather than batters taking everything because they're prepared to jump out of the box.

Germán Márquez   RHP   Born: 02/22/95   Age: 29   Height: 6'1"   Weight: 230   Origin: IFA, 2011

YEAR	TM	LVL	AGE	G (GS)	IP	W-L	SV	K	WHIP	ERA	CSP	BB%	K%	HR%	GB%	ZSw%	ZCon%	OSw%	OCon%	BABIP	SLGCON	DRA-	WARP
2021	COL	MLB	26	32(32)	180	12-11	0	176	1.27	4.40	58.4%	8.5%	23.3%	2.8%	51.3%	68.7%	85.6%	30.8%	50.7%	.297	.524	81	3.6
2022	COL	MLB	27	31(31)	181²	9-13	0	150	1.37	4.95	58.2%	8.1%	19.3%	3.9%	48.2%	70.8%	88.2%	32.9%	58.1%	.292	.594	103	1.5
2023	COL	MLB	28	4(4)	20	2-2	0	17	1.10	4.95	49.8%	3.8%	21.3%	5.0%	51.7%	71.3%	87.0%	33.7%	62.1%	.278	.684	91	0.3
2024 DC	COL	MLB	29	11(11)	64¹	4-4	0	55	1.34	4.32	56.4%	8.1%	20.1%	2.8%	48.8%					.305	.525	97	0.7

2023 Arsenal: FA (95.9), SL (88.6), SI (95.1), KC (87.1), CH (86.6)   *Comps: Sidney Ponson (75), Edwin Jackson (74), Jonathon Niese (73)*

While he's only posted one season with a sub-4.00 ERA in Coors, Márquez's ability to manage the hangover effect on the road has made him one of just four pitchers to post three 50-inning, sub-4.00 ERA seasons in away games as a Rockie. So, even after he underwent Tommy John surgery in May, it was widely expected that the Rockies would retain him in some form. Given that they were likely to buy out his $16 million option for next season, the two parties negotiated an incentive-laden two-year, $20 million extension in its place. This mirrors two-year deals handed out to Tommy John returnees Garrett Richards and James Paxton by the Padres and Red Sox, respectively, with the expectation that Márquez is unlikely to see much play, if any, during the first year of the contract. Those other pitchers saw some success in limited innings on those deals, but they weren't nearly as durable as Márquez prior to their operations, so with any luck, the longtime Rockie will have a full and healthy 2025.

Nick Mears   RHP   Born: 10/07/96   Age: 27   Height: 6'2"   Weight: 200   Origin: Undrafted Free Agent, 2018

YEAR	TM	LVL	AGE	G (GS)	IP	W-L	SV	K	WHIP	ERA	CSP	BB%	K%	HR%	GB%	ZSw%	ZCon%	OSw%	OCon%	BABIP	SLGCON	DRA-	WARP
2021	IND	AAA	24	17(0)	18²	2-2	1	25	1.34	5.30		11.0%	30.5%	2.4%	32.6%					.326	.533	79	0.5
2021	PIT	MLB	24	30(0)	23¹	1-0	0	23	1.63	5.01	51.7%	12.1%	21.5%	4.7%	39.4%	68.8%	81.5%	34.5%	66.7%	.303	.614	113	0.1
2022	IND	AAA	25	23(0)	24²	1-1	0	27	1.46	4.74		16.0%	25.5%	1.9%	40.3%					.283	.516	86	0.5
2022	PIT	MLB	25	2(0)	2	0-0	0	2	1.00	0.00	54.5%	12.5%	25.0%	0.0%	40.0%	100.0%	83.3%	42.1%	50.0%	.200	.200	95	0.0
2023	ABQ	AAA	26	24(0)	23²	4-1	1	39	1.61	6.08		20.6%	36.4%	0.9%	51.1%	59.1%	74.5%	32.2%	48.9%	.341	.523	75	0.2
2023	COL	MLB	26	16(0)	19¹	0-1	0	21	1.45	3.72	45.8%	16.1%	24.1%	1.1%	35.3%	60.1%	84.3%	30.2%	68.7%	.260	.451	108	0.1
2024 DC	COL	MLB	27	54(0)	57	3-3	0	64	1.47	4.80	47.9%	14.2%	25.2%	3.3%	38.6%					.283	.570	104	0.1

2023 Arsenal: FA (96), CU (80.4), SL (85.3), CH (88.3)   *Comps: Michael Tonkin (59), Jeremy Jeffress (57), Dan Altavilla (56)*

The Rockies sure are fond of relievers who walk nearly a hitter per inning in Triple-A. Mears is no exception. He's persisted through myriad injuries and personal tragedies (the least of which was being claimed off waivers by Colorado), and his ability to induce soft contact mitigated the impact of his still-bloated walk rate in the majors. He mainly relies on a mid-to-upper 90s four-seamer that plays up due to his over-the-top release, top-flight extension and ability to hide the ball well. The heater's carry was certainly impacted by the altitude, but deception and velo play everywhere. Meanwhile, the slider he added to pair with his hammer curve in 2022 *is* well-suited for Coors. Of the gyro variety, the pitch mainly relies on gravity to induce whiffs. With continued health and a bit more polish, Mears could be a good candidate for using different pitch mixes based on whether he's home or away.

Michael Prosecky   LHP   Born: 02/28/01   Age: 23   Height: 6'3"   Weight: 200   Origin: Round 6, 2022 Draft (#176 overall)

YEAR	TM	LVL	AGE	G (GS)	IP	W-L	SV	K	WHIP	ERA	CSP	BB%	K%	HR%	GB%	ZSw%	ZCon%	OSw%	OCon%	BABIP	SLGCON	DRA-	WARP
2023	FRE	A	22	21(21)	109	11-7	0	125	1.17	2.72		9.1%	27.6%	0.9%	45.2%					.303	.409	75	1.3
2024 non	COL	MLB	23	58(0)	50	2-2	0	44	1.50	5.44		10.3%	19.9%	3.6%	36.6%					.302	.575	119	-0.3

Comps: Austin Sodders (91), Steven Brault (89), David Peterson (88)

Prosecky pitched out of the bullpen for Louisville, but a successful 2023 in the Single-A rotation had him sipping champagne. Due to his late introduction to starting, the southpaw is still refining his third offering, a changeup, but he already owns a solid fastball/curve combo that lends him a high floor. A short, quick release helps him hide the ball, and his low-90s four-seamer jumps on hitters sooner than they'd expect. The deception also helps his two primary offerings—already a natural pairing—blend especially well. If he's moved back to the 'pen, his advanced age could have him uncorking heaters in the majors before long.

Cal Quantrill RHP Born: 02/10/95 Age: 29 Height: 6'3" Weight: 195 Origin: Round 1, 2016 Draft (#8 overall)

YEAR	TM	LVL	AGE	G (GS)	IP	W-L	SV	K	WHIP	ERA	CSP	BB%	K%	HR%	GB%	ZSw%	ZCon%	OSw%	OCon%	BABIP	SLGCON	DRA-	WARP
2021	CLE	MLB	26	40(22)	149²	8-3	0	121	1.18	2.89	52.7%	7.6%	19.6%	2.6%	42.8%	69.8%	83.6%	32.3%	70.1%	.270	.478	106	0.9
2022	CLE	MLB	27	32(32)	186¹	15-5	0	128	1.21	3.38	52.3%	6.1%	16.6%	2.7%	41.2%	69.7%	88.3%	34.9%	72.8%	.280	.476	113	0.6
2023	AKR	AA	28	2(2)	8²	1-0	0	7	1.04	1.04		5.9%	20.6%	2.9%	41.7%					.261	.417	98	0.1
2023	COL	AAA	28	3(3)	14	1-2	0	10	1.71	9.00		10.6%	15.2%	4.5%	29.2%	64.4%	87.5%	40.0%	78.6%	.311	.617	117	0.1
2023	CLE	MLB	28	19(19)	99²	4-7	0	58	1.46	5.24	45.7%	7.9%	13.1%	2.5%	40.4%	72.6%	85.1%	30.2%	74.8%	.300	.512	139	-0.9
2024 DC	COL	MLB	29	28(28)	143	5-12	0	95	1.47	5.43	49.8%	7.8%	15.1%	3.3%	40.4%					.310	.549	118	-0.1

2023 Arsenal: SI (93.8), FC (88.5), FA (94.1), FS (87.2), CU (82.6), CH (86)   Comps: Danny Cox (82), Mike Pelfrey (81), Kyle Gibson (81)

For years, one of the biggest questions about Quantrill was simply "when?" When was the guy with strikeout and walk numbers straight out of the 1980s going to put up results reflecting that? He had multiple successful seasons overperforming his peripherals thanks to a kitchen-sink arsenal that kept hitters guessing and a strong team defense that minimized the damage done by hard hits and barrels. That strategy relied on him flooding the zone with five different offerings, something he wasn't able to replicate in 2023. His CSP fell by almost seven points, and the uninspiring movement profiles of his pitches didn't draw chases off the plate. His struggles to earn strikes were reflected in his AL-worst K-BB% and CSW%. Quantrill may be regressing into the back-end starter type that many expected from the quality of his stuff, but to guarantee himself even that role he'll need to find the zone again.

Joe Rock LHP Born: 07/29/00 Age: 23 Height: 6'6" Weight: 200 Origin: Round 2, 2021 Draft (#68 overall)

YEAR	TM	LVL	AGE	G (GS)	IP	W-L	SV	K	WHIP	ERA	CSP	BB%	K%	HR%	GB%	ZSw%	ZCon%	OSw%	OCon%	BABIP	SLGCON	DRA-	WARP
2021	RCK	ROK	20	4(2)	8	1-0	0	11	0.75	1.13		3.4%	37.9%	0.0%	70.6%					.294	.294		
2022	SPO	A+	21	20(20)	107²	7-8	0	109	1.23	4.43		9.9%	24.0%	2.2%	44.7%					.270	.514	103	0.8
2022	HFD	AA	21	2(2)	8	0-0	0	11	1.75	10.12		13.2%	28.9%	5.3%	45.5%					.350	.727	84	0.2
2023	HFD	AA	22	19(19)	90	1-10	0	108	1.40	4.50		8.1%	27.3%	3.3%	43.8%					.345	.633	80	2.3
2024 non	COL	MLB	23	58(0)	50	2-2	0	45	1.52	5.66		10.2%	20.1%	3.9%	37.8%					.306	.597	123	-0.4

2023 Arsenal: SI (93.1), SL (84.9), CH (86.1)   Comps: JoJo Romero (57), Jayson Aquino (55), Brett Oberholtzer (55)

Despite Colorado's best efforts at systematically dismantling their pitching prospects, nominative determinism has put Rock on a collision course with Denver. The jury's still out on whether the 6-foot-6 boulder of a man will end up in the bullpen or rotation; if you're willing to look past his strand-rate-driven ERAs, he's seen his fair share of success as a starter in the minors, racking up strikeouts at an above-average clip with a whiff rate to match. Still, his low arm slot creates plenty of horizontal movement that could push him toward specialist status (especially if his changeup doesn't improve as a backup). Either way, Rock still has one more mountain to climb before reaching the majors in Triple-A, but he could arrive sooner than expected if the Rockies' pitching injuries pile up again.

Connor Seabold RHP Born: 01/24/96 Age: 28 Height: 6'2" Weight: 190 Origin: Round 3, 2017 Draft (#83 overall)

YEAR	TM	LVL	AGE	G (GS)	IP	W-L	SV	K	WHIP	ERA	CSP	BB%	K%	HR%	GB%	ZSw%	ZCon%	OSw%	OCon%	BABIP	SLGCON	DRA-	WARP
2021	WOR	AAA	25	11(11)	54	4-3	0	52	1.15	3.50		8.4%	22.9%	2.6%	30.9%					.261	.493	109	0.4
2021	BOS	MLB	25	1(1)	3	0-0	0	0	1.67	6.00	52.2%	16.7%	0.0%	8.3%	40.0%	63.2%	83.3%	29.2%	100.0%	.222	.700	122	0.0
2022	WOR	AAA	26	19(19)	86²	8-2	0	89	1.13	3.32		5.3%	24.7%	1.9%	38.6%					.303	.500	92	1.5
2022	BOS	MLB	26	5(5)	18¹	0-4	0	19	2.35	11.29	55.2%	8.2%	19.4%	5.1%	29.4%	72.0%	84.5%	32.4%	58.2%	.476	.926	124	-0.1
2023	ABQ	AAA	27	8(8)	31¹	1-2	0	36	1.72	7.47		5.4%	24.2%	2.0%	28.4%	70.8%	83.0%	39.9%	61.4%	.434	.680	88	-0.1
2023	COL	MLB	27	27(13)	87¹	1-7	0	67	1.65	7.52	52.7%	6.9%	16.4%	4.7%	32.7%	75.1%	84.8%	28.3%	63.7%	.340	.689	127	-0.2
2024 non	COL	MLB	28	58(0)	50	2-2	0	37	1.37	5.02	53.1%	6.9%	17.0%	3.5%	33.0%					.303	.562	111	-0.1

2023 Arsenal: FA (92.8), SL (85.4), CH (80.5), CU (78.5)   Comps: Tyler Wilson (62), Mike Wright Jr. (60), Ben Lively (58)

Judging by his name, moving from the Boston Harbor to landlocked and dry Colorado wouldn't do Seabold any favors. Judging from his arsenal, you wouldn't come to a much different conclusion. The right-hander relies primarily on a side-spinning four-seamer with a microscopic gyro degree. As a result, Seabold's heater combined with those of teammates Austin Gomber and Chris Flexen to make up half of the six worst pitches per run value in the majors. Seabold's changeup holds some promise at elevation, as the pitch's low overall and active spin rates enable gravity to do its thing even a mile high. But he'd need at least one more decent offering to even cut it as a reliever, as evidenced by the 7.31 ERA he posted out of the bullpen in 2023.

Antonio Senzatela RHP Born: 01/21/95 Age: 29 Height: 6'1" Weight: 236 Origin: IFA, 2011

YEAR	TM	LVL	AGE	G (GS)	IP	W-L	SV	K	WHIP	ERA	CSP	BB%	K%	HR%	GB%	ZSw%	ZCon%	OSw%	OCon%	BABIP	SLGCON	DRA-	WARP
2021	COL	MLB	26	28(28)	156²	4-10	0	105	1.34	4.42	56.9%	4.8%	15.7%	1.8%	50.4%	71.2%	87.8%	29.4%	66.2%	.326	.507	95	1.9
2022	COL	MLB	27	19(19)	92¹	3-7	0	54	1.69	5.07	54.3%	5.6%	13.1%	2.2%	48.9%	72.9%	91.8%	27.9%	67.6%	.386	.587	112	0.3
2023	COL	MLB	28	2(2)	7²	0-1	0	4	1.17	4.70	49.2%	6.7%	13.3%	10.0%	54.2%	75.5%	86.5%	28.2%	65.0%	.190	.708	107	0.1
2024 non	COL	MLB	29	58(0)	50	2-2	0	30	1.44	5.05	53.7%	6.6%	13.9%	2.7%	48.5%					.315	.514	111	-0.1

2023 Arsenal: FA (94.4), SL (85.6), CH (86.9), CU (77.8)   Comps: Jeff Suppan (68), Kyle Lohse (66), Mike Leake (66)

After Márquez went under the knife, Senzatela was the next longtime Rockie to undergo Tommy John surgery. Unlike Márquez, Senzatela also comes with a longer injury history, as he'd only just returned from a torn ACL suffered in 2022. He has the edge in one crucial area: his ERA has been half a run better than Márquez's in Coors, likely because Senzatela's four-seamer is below-average in terms of active spin percentage and average spin rate. Senzatela's heater is his primary offering, and it's successful because these below-average traits lead to less rise than hitters expect, a phenomenon only magnified in Coors with the thinner air further nullifying the Magnus effect. As a result, Senzatela's four-seamer approaches the plate at a steeper-than-average angle even after controlling for pitch height, and hitters tend to roll it over; his career groundball rate north of 50% is a testament to that. Even if his fastball velocity drops post-injury, its ideal-for-Coors spin profile portends some degree of future success in Denver.

Brent Suter LHP Born: 08/29/89   Age: 34   Height: 6'4"   Weight: 213   Origin: Round 31, 2012 Draft (#965 overall)

YEAR	TM	LVL	AGE	G (GS)	IP	W-L	SV	K	WHIP	ERA	CSP	BB%	K%	HR%	GB%	ZSw%	ZCon%	OSw%	OCon%	BABIP	SLGCON	DRA-	WARP
2021	MIL	MLB	31	61(1)	73¹	12-5	1	69	1.31	3.07	51.9%	7.7%	22.0%	2.9%	52.1%	72.2%	90.5%	32.1%	60.9%	.303	.530	89	1.1
2022	MIL	MLB	32	54(0)	66²	5-3	0	53	1.20	3.78	56.7%	8.1%	19.5%	3.3%	43.8%	71.5%	81.2%	31.6%	61.5%	.266	.518	105	0.5
2023	COL	MLB	33	57(2)	69¹	4-3	0	55	1.30	3.38	46.1%	8.6%	18.8%	1.0%	44.5%	66.5%	86.7%	27.6%	62.4%	.302	.432	99	0.8
2024 DC	COL	MLB	34	53(0)	56¹	3-2	0	46	1.33	4.23	50.7%	8.1%	19.2%	2.6%	44.4%					.294	.503	96	0.4

2023 Arsenal: HC (86.3), SI (88.3), CH (76.6), SL (76.8)   Comps: Brian Duensing (47), Dennis Cook (47), Craig Stammen (46)

Suter has always gotten by more on guile than pure stuff, as a twitchy delivery and unusual movement have propped up his mid-to-high 80s heater. As it happens, Suter and the Rockies were a match made in heaven: his four-seamer approaches the plate at an oddly steep angle due to a high gyro degree—it's maybe more similar to a cutter—and Coors doesn't mess with gravity. Regardless of altitude, the southpaw's velocity decline continued, and it's likely his four-seamer would have continued its overall tailspin if the Rockies hadn't had him add a sinker. Though the other fastball wasn't particularly effective itself, the four-seamer played off of it beautifully. By the time you read this, Suter should be part of a contender's bullpen.

Victor Vodnik RHP Born: 10/09/99   Age: 24   Height: 6'0"   Weight: 200   Origin: Round 14, 2018 Draft (#412 overall)

YEAR	TM	LVL	AGE	G (GS)	IP	W-L	SV	K	WHIP	ERA	CSP	BB%	K%	HR%	GB%	ZSw%	ZCon%	OSw%	OCon%	BABIP	SLGCON	DRA-	WARP
2021	MIS	AA	21	11(11)	33²	1-4	0	41	1.60	5.35		14.7%	27.3%	3.3%	52.9%					.333	.616	93	0.5
2022	MIS	AA	22	7(0)	7	0-0	1	14	1.00	0.00		10.7%	50.0%	0.0%	63.6%					.364	.455	83	0.1
2022	GWN	AAA	22	24(0)	27²	2-0	2	33	1.52	2.93		13.2%	27.3%	1.7%	52.9%					.353	.543	86	0.6
2023	HFD	AA	23	4(0)	6	0-0	2	9	0.83	0.00		4.3%	39.1%	0.0%	61.5%					.308	.385	85	0.1
2023	MIS	AA	23	30(0)	40²	3-1	4	56	1.25	3.10		14.5%	32.6%	1.2%	40.9%					.282	.465	80	1.0
2023	ABQ	AAA	23	8(0)	7	1-1	0	4	2.29	7.71		13.9%	11.1%	8.3%	44.4%	63.6%	88.6%	28.9%	75.0%	.333	.778	97	
2023	COL	MLB	23	6(0)	8²	1-0	0	12	2.08	8.31	47.0%	6.8%	27.3%	0.0%	62.1%	73.1%	84.2%	31.5%	64.7%	.517	.621	76	0.2
2024 DC	COL	MLB	24	35(0)	38	2-2	0	37	1.46	4.69	47.0%	12.4%	22.1%	2.8%	47.6%					.295	.523	102	0.1

2023 Arsenal: FA (97.4), CH (89.2), SL (85.2)   Comps: Phillippe Aumont (47), José Leclerc (47), Junior Fernández (43)

Half of the return for Pierce Johnson, Vodnik's stuff was tantalizing in a small-sample major-league debut, BABIP gods be damned. Armed with the name of an evil Bond-movie scientist and a high-90s heater, the right-hander leaned on it at a 71% clip. It's truly a weapon; not only does it benefit from plus velocity, but also plus extension, and it isn't overly reliant on active spin, so it should play in Coors. His changeup has typically graded out as his better secondary offering, and it mirrors his fastball quite well, but he's also been refining a slider. If his control and those secondaries improve, he could become an elite multi-inning fireman; if he remains wild, batters had better don their safety goggles.

LINEOUTS

Hitters

HITTER	POS	TM	LVL	AGE	PA	R	HR	RBI	SB	AVG/OBP/SLG	BABIP	SLGCON	BB%	K%	ZSw%	ZCon%	OSw%	OCon%	LA	90th EV	DRC+	BRR	DRP	WARP
Jamari Baylor	2B	FRE	A	22	139	32	7	27	6	.333/.475/.611	.446	.930	17.3%	26.6%							126	2.1	1.1	1.1
	2B	JS	A+	22	36	3	0	1	0	.172/.333/.172	.357	.357	16.7%	41.7%							96	-0.2	0.7	0.1
	2B	SPO	A+	22	64	10	1	8	6	.185/.313/.333	.290	.562	14.1%	34.4%							78	0.6	-1.1	0.0
Jordan Beck	OF	SPO	A+	22	341	62	20	72	11	.292/.378/.566	.319	.746	12.6%	20.8%							133	3.5	-0.3	2.7
	OF	HFD	AA	22	223	22	5	19	9	.240/.342/.406	.353	.645	13.5%	31.8%							84	0.9	3.3	0.6
Sean Bouchard	OF	ABQ	AAA	27	71	11	1	6	5	.222/.408/.315	.282	.425	23.9%	19.7%	45.9%	85.2%	13.9%	62.5%			99	0.3	0.7	0.3
	OF	COL	MLB	27	43	11	4	7	0	.316/.372/.684	.381	1.083	9.3%	32.6%	60.0%	92.9%	32.6%	36.7%	9.3	105.8	101	0.0	-0.6	0.1
Robert Calaz	OF	DSL COL	ROK	17	189	38	7	29	6	.325/.423/.561	.400	.772	11.6%	22.8%										
Julio Carreras	SS	GIG	WIN	23	60	14	3	11	6	.333/.424/.608	.389	.795	13.3%	20.0%	53.1%	76.5%	33.0%	62.1%						
	SS	HFD	AA	23	356	48	5	31	13	.235/.316/.334	.300	.452	9.3%	22.8%							93	5.4	3.2	1.7
	SS	ABQ	AAA	23	62	8	1	7	1	.255/.371/.373	.324	.514	16.1%	22.6%	68.0%	77.3%	30.0%	75.6%			90	-2.5	-0.6	-0.1
Yonathan Daza	OF	ABQ	AAA	29	181	22	2	19	4	.305/.350/.415	.340	.486	5.0%	13.3%	71.6%	90.7%	39.1%	73.7%			97	-2.8	-0.8	0.2
	OF	COL	MLB	29	80	8	0	7	1	.270/.304/.351	.323	.426	3.8%	16.3%	73.5%	92.8%	45.1%	65.8%	14.1	97.9	93	0.0	-0.7	0.1
Ryan Ritter	SS	FRE	A	22	295	53	18	58	6	.305/.405/.606	.356	.856	12.5%	24.4%							146	-0.6	-2.7	2.5
	SS	SPO	A+	22	201	33	6	26	12	.265/.367/.441	.406	.743	10.9%	34.3%							82	2.2	3.5	0.7
	SS	HFD	AA	22	29	4	0	1	2	.160/.276/.200	.286	.357	10.3%	37.9%							66	0.1	-0.1	0.0
Zac Veen	OF	HFD	AA	21	201	15	2	24	22	.209/.303/.308	.260	.411	11.4%	21.4%							83	-2.0	-0.9	0.0

The Rockies placed 23-year-old former Phillies third-rounder **Jamari Baylor** in A-ball to ease his transition to the team. There, he looked like one of the best hitters in the organization, but with a 16% swinging-strike rate despite his advanced age for the level, that says more about the state of the Rockies than it does about Baylor. ⓧ Given his uppercut swing, evaluators have long worried about **Jordan Beck**'s ability to make contact against upper-level pitching. Evaluators are often smart folks. If he can't get the hit tool in gear, he'll be more Lost Cause than Where It's At. ⓧ For the second season in a row, **Sean Bouchard** tantalized with small-sample major-league brilliance, and for the second time injuries threw up obstacles like the second act of a lazily written children's movie. Next we're going to see falling anvils. ⓧ **Robert Calaz** sounds more like the name of a wizard than a baseball player, but the 17-year-old international signee certainly had a magical debut with the bat in the DSL. However, he'll need some sorcery to develop into a serviceable defender. ⓧ **Julio Carreras** didn't improve meaningfully with the bat in his second crack at Double-A. But as a glove-first middle-infielder with a dash of speed, he should be able to hide in this farm system like a fugitive in a parade. ⓧ **Yonathan Daza** can hit a fastball, batting .333 against them in his career. Imagine what it'd be like if he ever worked a fastball count. ⓧ Rockies 2022 fourth-round pick **Ryan Ritter** traversed three levels in his first full professional season, mashing 24 homers along the way. The shortstop whiffs about as often as the Rockies do on middle-infield prospects, but his profile resembles their greatest success of recent years in Trevor Story. ⓧ 2020 first-rounder **Zac Veen**'s long swing had him behind many Double-A fastballs, a problem exacerbated by a wrist injury sustained shortly after his promotion in 2022. He tried playing through pain in 2023 before opting for surgery in July. The injury is unlikely to impact Veen's all-important speed.

Pitchers

PITCHER	TM	LVL	AGE	G (GS)	IP	W-L	SV	K	WHIP	ERA	CSP	BB%	K%	HR%	GB%	ZSw%	ZCon%	OSw%	OCon%	BABIP	SLGCON	DRA-	WARP
Jalen Beeks	DUR	AAA	29	20 (1)	25²	2-1	0	27	1.36	3.86		8.2%	24.5%	2.7%	56.8%	73.9%	83.8%	32.4%	51.9%	.324	.527	75	0.7
	TB	MLB	29	30 (8)	42¹	2-3	1	47	1.49	5.95	46.7%	10.9%	24.5%	2.1%	44.7%	67.1%	78.7%	30.1%	52.0%	.322	.533	97	0.6
Noah Davis	ABQ	AAA	26	14 (14)	60	1-4	0	45	1.45	4.50		13.2%	17.0%	2.6%	39.9%	66.6%	87.3%	26.3%	59.5%	.271	.512	121	-0.3
	COL	MLB	26	8 (6)	30	0-4	0	26	1.93	8.70	51.4%	10.3%	17.8%	4.1%	46.5%	69.1%	84.9%	28.2%	70.3%	.389	.670	110	0.2
Jaden Hill	SPO	A+	23	16 (16)	43²	0-9	0	57	1.81	9.48		11.5%	26.3%	5.1%	52.0%					.371	.810	92	0.6
Gabriel Hughes	SPO	A+	21	8 (8)	37²	4-3	0	54	1.19	5.50		9.3%	33.5%	3.1%	49.5%					.291	.656	78	0.7
	HFD	AA	21	6 (6)	29	2-2	0	29	1.55	7.14		8.3%	22.0%	5.3%	45.1%					.321	.744	100	0.4
Evan Justice	SPO	A+	24	10 (0)	9²	1-0	1	19	0.93	0.00		12.5%	47.5%	0.0%	50.0%					.308	.385	80	0.2
	HFD	AA	24	15 (0)	16	5-0	0	25	0.88	3.38		14.1%	39.1%	0.0%	21.4%					.179	.333	84	0.4
	ABQ	AAA	24	13 (0)	13	0-1	0	19	1.54	6.23		19.4%	30.6%	1.6%	32.1%	63.0%	70.7%	24.5%	54.1%	.259	.519	94	0.2
	COL	MLB	24	9 (0)	7¹	0-0	0	7	3.00	8.59	40.8%	19.0%	16.7%	0.0%	53.8%	55.9%	93.9%	20.9%	69.6%	.560	.640	104	0.1
Matt Koch	ABQ	AAA	32	29 (1)	34²	1-2	2	34	1.62	7.27		7.0%	21.5%	4.4%	25.9%	75.5%	85.2%	33.1%	53.2%	.365	.704	118	0.0
	COL	MLB	32	39 (1)	38²	3-2	0	27	1.29	5.12	50.5%	5.5%	16.6%	4.3%	50.4%	73.9%	87.6%	33.5%	58.7%	.288	.548	95	0.5
Carson Palmquist	SPO	A+	22	15 (15)	70	7-2	0	106	1.27	3.73		9.4%	35.7%	3.0%	31.8%					.361	.680	84	1.0
	HFD	AA	22	4 (4)	22¹	0-2	0	28	1.25	4.43		9.6%	29.8%	4.3%	37.5%					.288	.589	80	0.6
Riley Pint	ABQ	AAA	25	47 (0)	57¹	3-4	0	85	1.74	6.12		20.9%	31.1%	1.1%	55.3%	53.5%	79.7%	21.9%	43.0%	.336	.533	83	0.9
	COL	MLB	25	1 (0)	0¹	0-0	0	0	12.00	27.00	35.3%	60.0%	0.0%	0.0%	50.0%	57.1%	100.0%	0.0%		.500	1.000	111	0.0
Ryan Rolison	FRE	A	25	2 (2)	6	0-0	0	7	1.50	6.00		10.7%	25.0%	3.6%	38.9%					.294	.611	106	0.0
Jordy Vargas	FRE	A	19	13 (13)	64	6-3	0	69	1.23	4.22		9.1%	26.1%	1.5%	34.1%					.313	.497	90	0.8

Jalen Beeks was a bit better than his sub-6 ERA, but not good enough to justify paying him over a million dollars in arbitration. Best of luck in Coors Field! ⓧ **Noah Davis** has as many first names as he has bad fastballs. Though he shunned his four-seamer in 2023, his true-spin sinker cost him 10 runs thanks to the Coors effect; in limited action, his changeup cost him an additional six. ⓧ Tommy John surgery wiped out **Lucas Gilbreath**'s 2023 season, adding uncertainty to whether the southpaw reliever's velo uptick will stick. Luckily, he's used his time off to become a TikTok influencer and read up on analytics, both of which should at least help him improve the sliding-thumb action on his breaking ball. ⓧ **Jaden Hill**, who fell to the Rockies in the second round in 2021 due to Tommy John, finally made his full-season debut in 2023. Unfortunately for Hill, he looked like he was running up one the entire time. ⓧ **Gabriel Hughes**, the 10th-overall pick in the 2022 draft, didn't make it to 70 pro innings before undergoing Tommy John. When healthy, the big right-hander paired plus strikeout rates with decent enough walk and grounder rates, but struggled in tense situations, with a far-below-average strand rate. It's hard to blame him for having shaky confidence as a Rockies' farmhand. ⓧ In what can only be described as Rockies Law, **Evan Justice** received a promotion despite walking nearly a batter per inning in Triple-A. The lefty pairs a funky hitch in his delivery with an ability to hide the ball well, both of which work to keep hitters and himself off balance. ⓧ Prior to the 2023 season, **Matt Koch**'s preferred beverage was a cup of coffee; the last time he tossed more than 20 innings in the majors was back in 2018. Since that last long stint, he's played in Japan, traversed a handful of organizations and transitioned to full-time relief work, none of which meaningfully improved his skills. ⓧ Hello my baby, hello Mahoney. The Rockies welcomed third-round pick **Jack Mahoney** and his sweet-like-honey mid-90s heater with life and a solid feel for the strike zone. The right-hander didn't pitch a ton in college due to Tommy John, but he was South Carolina's best pitcher in 2023. ⓧ A third-rounder from 2022, towering southpaw **Carson Palmquist** strutted his strikeout stuff with a funky verging-on-sidearm delivery. He could be the first successful "-quist" since Willie bloomed as a utilityman for the Mariners in the 2000s. ⓧ Pour one out for **Riley Pint**, the former fourth-overall pick doomed to obscurity because he was drafted by the Rockies. The 25-year-old actually got to wear the green City Connect jersey, but spent most of the season in Triple-A where he notched a 53% strike rate, the second-lowest in the minors at any level (min. 50 IP). ⓧ The Rockies like to shroud their advanced analytics formulas in secrecy, extending the practice to player injuries as well. Shoulder surgery returnee **Ryan Rolison** made just four minor-league appearances before heading back on the IL with an "undisclosed" issue. A cursory glance at his Instagram, however, reveals he underwent another shoulder procedure in August. ⓧ Another high-pick college arm, **Sean Sullivan** parlayed a 75% usage rate on his fastball into a second-round selection in 2023. Despite low-90s velo, the heater is plus and the real concern for the Rockies is that lagging secondaries may sully the low-slot lefty's development as a starter. ⓧ **Jordy Vargas** succumbed to Tommy John surgery in his first try at full-season ball. His arms, as long as the Rockies' chances of making the playoffs in the next 10 years, portend an ability to maintain his mid-90s velocity and perhaps build on it, something he'll need to succeed in Coors given that his best secondary is a Magnus-heavy curveball.

DETROIT TIGERS

Essay by David Roth

Player comments by Nathan Graham, Kate Preusser and BP staff

For years, the Detroit Tigers were a lot easier to understand than they were to watch. The teams they put on the field were ragged and unintelligible and given to prolonged bouts of distressingly avant-garde baseball, but also they weren't really supposed to be much more than that. They were the teams that came before the teams to come, the contender that was forming somewhere over the horizon, or in the minors. The idea was that when all that nascent talent was just about ready, the team would make its move—add some big-league talent at big-league prices, bring it all together, and then rule the American League Central for a half-decade or so. Plenty of teams talk about this sort of thing, although many of them have found the teardown so gratifying (or just so cost effective) that they've proven reluctant to spring for the rebuild that was supposed to justify it. The Tigers were unique among this cohort in a number of ways, foremost among them being how poorly things went once they actually committed to trying.

Poorly enough, in fact, that it felt like something of a triumph that they were a fairly normal mediocre team in 2023. They finished second in an appalling division, and were both not very good and inarguably better than they'd looked the year before. In the end, they managed a win more than in 2021, which was the season that inspired them to treat 2022 as the season in which they would flip the switch and become contenders. Instead, that year became an abject 66-96 disaster that led to the firing of GM Al Avila. That rebuild is not complete, lord knows, but it isn't really abandoned, either. It is sort of starting again, and sort of just beginning in earnest; if there's any real accomplishment in that it's that it all feels a bit more legible, now.

There is a sense that the Tigers are moving up, although how quick and how steep that ascent will be is hard to know because it will depend largely on young players with brief or qualified or nonexistent track records of big-league success becoming successful big-leaguers. It would be foolish to presume to make any kind of diagnosis for this team's future when they are still so thoroughly in the waiting room. But after the lurid flameout of the team's underbaked and overly optimistic attempt to flip into contention, even 2023's transitional mediocrity counts as a sort of victory, and the

DETROIT TIGERS PROSPECTUS
2023 W-L: 78-84, 2ND IN AL CENTRAL

Pythag	.448	22nd	DER	.702	9th
RS/G	4.08	28th	DRC+	94	22nd
RA/G	4.57	19th	DRA-	101	18th
dWin%	.465	22nd	FIP	4.14	9th
Payroll	$122M	19th	B-Age	27.9	2nd
M$/MW	$3.4M	11th	P-Age	28.1	7th

412'
370'   365'
342'   330'

- Opened 2000
- Open air
- Natural surface
- Fence profile: 7' to 10'

Park Factors

Runs	Runs/RH	Runs/LH	HR/RH	HR/LH
97	97	97	88	86

Top Hitter WARP	2.4 Jake Rogers
Top Pitcher WARP	2.2 Tarik Skubal
2023 Top Prospect	Jackson Jobe

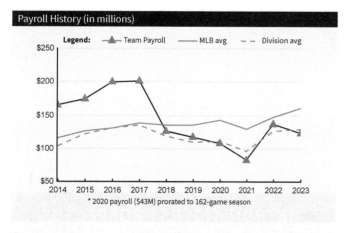

Payroll History (in millions)

Legend: Team Payroll — MLB avg — — Division avg

* 2020 payroll ($43M) prorated to 162-game season

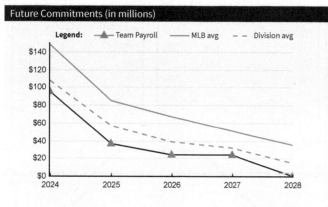

Future Commitments (in millions)

Legend: Team Payroll — MLB avg — — Division avg

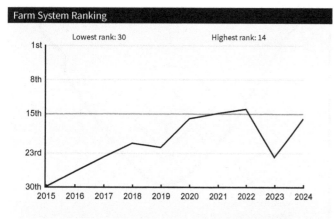

Farm System Ranking

Lowest rank: 30   Highest rank: 14

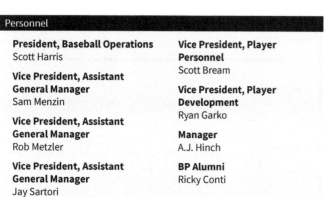

Personnel

President, Baseball Operations
Scott Harris

Vice President, Assistant General Manager
Sam Menzin

Vice President, Assistant General Manager
Rob Metzler

Vice President, Assistant General Manager
Jay Sartori

Vice President, Player Personnel
Scott Bream

Vice President, Player Development
Ryan Garko

Manager
A.J. Hinch

BP Alumni
Ricky Conti

way forward in 2024 seems...well, difficult and contingent, still, but plausible. With some luck, the 2024 edition should be easier to understand *and* easier to watch than the ones that came before.

If there is still a lot of ambiguity here, it's worth remembering that the American League Central will make a person ask difficult questions. Some of these questions are relative—for instance, "was the 2012 AL Central, which the Tigers topped with 88 wins and in which three of five teams lost 90 games or more, more dispiriting than the 2023 version, which featured two 100-loss teams and whose only team above .500 was the 87-win Twins?" It's a good question, or maybe just the interesting kind of bad question; I encourage you to have this debate, if you must, as quietly as possible and far from anyone whose opinions you value. But many of the questions raised by the AL Central are bigger, broader and heavier: Would a loving deity have permitted the seasons that the White Sox and Royals had in 2023 to happen at all, let alone simultaneously? How would one reconcile the existence of such a god with the realities of Jordan Lyles' 31 starts for those Royals, or Tim Anderson's entire campaign with the White Sox?

In a division that has delivered a classic staring-into-the-void experience for the last decade and change, the 2023 season was notable mostly for how defiantly the void stared back. Teams will have seasons, and in the case of some AL Central teams decades, that will make even the most sunny-sided fan wonder what any of this is actually for, and whether it can possibly be worth it. In the long run, this kind of existential malaise tends to work out, less because some satisfying answer gets revealed and more because the long run and the working-it-out are the point; that process is what baseball *is*, and is about, and what fans miss most when it isn't happening. It's a nice way to order and observe the passage of time, but it is admittedly nicer to observe in some divisions than others, and this is a division that does not so much cast doubt on all that as it taunts everyone who believes it. "Yes, yes, baseball is about time and work and patience, as much a devotional activity as it is leisure," the American League Central leers in response to any high-minded attempt to appreciate the game. "Great stuff, there. *Now watch MJ Melendez play the outfield.*"

In both the literal and figurative sense, the Detroit Tigers are a part of the American League Central. After those turns as a ghost-ridden ruin and a cautionary tale, they won 78 games, two more than the third-place Guardians, nine fewer than the division champion Twins—all factual statements, but also notably American League Central truths. The Tigers got where they got in some outwardly uninspiring ways—they had two winning months and four losing ones, outperformed their Pythagorean projection by five wins just to reach 78 wins, and still got there in large part by going 35-17 (.673) against the teams in their accursed division, which meant they were 43-67 (.390) against everyone else.

But credit where it is due: In a division so bleak that it is frequently difficult to parse, the Tigers looked and played like a fairly normal in-between team in 2023.

Every team in this division has a plan, but some of them are more overtly tragicomic or blithely doomed than others. It was fairly easy to understand what the Tigers were about in 2023, and it is easy to see what they might be in 2024—a team working to fit some low-commitment veterans around a core of promising but as-yet unproven homegrown talent. There are a lot of ways that it could go wrong, and only so many ways in which it might go right, and the presence of a bottomed-out Javy Báez anchors the broader concept in more or less the same ways that a garish and troublingly wet area rug might be said to tie a living room together. But you can sort of see how it might work, and get a sense of what the organization is trying to do. In this division, and for this organization, that is saying quite a bit.

⚾   ⚾   ⚾

Detroit's might-be cornerstones were high draft picks not long ago, and while all of them carry significant caveats into this season—these range from Spencer Torkelson's 1,088 below-average MLB plate appearances to some variously improbable and variously resolved health issues relating to virtually every other important young player—there is some reason for hope basically everywhere. Torkelson, whom the Tigers picked first overall in 2020, has underlying metrics that suggest he has been more unlucky than overmatched during his first two seasons in the bigs, and put up an .800 OPS after the All-Star break. Riley Greene, the fifth overall pick in 2019, looked actively good before going down with an elbow injury that ultimately required Tommy John surgery; he should be ready for Opening Day. The team seems content to let Colt Keith and Jace Jung claim the starting jobs at third and second, respectively, when they're ready; both have hit well enough in the minors to suggest that this could happen in 2024. Of the team's many unfinished pitching prospects, it can at least be said that Casey Mize (the first overall pick in 2018) is healthier than he has been in nearly two years, and that Jackson Jobe (third overall, 2021) looked good in the 64 minor-league innings he was healthy enough to pitch last season, and I guess also that it seems highly unlikely that Matt Manning (ninth overall, 2016) will once again have his left foot broken by comebackers twice in the same season. Reese Olson had a promising debut in 2023; Tarik Skubal returned from early-summer flexor tendon surgery to look like a viable staff ace down the stretch.

There are times in writing these kinds of essays when you become aware that you are, and pardon the newsroom jargon here, "just kind of saying a lot of names." If you are the sort of person who reads the essays in a book like this, you probably know some or all of those listed names; if you are someone who cares about the Detroit Tigers, you might have been thinking about these players for some time, and wondering why I left out Kerry Carpenter. But while many of

these players have been or still are vaunted prospects none of them has really spent much time as a productive big-leaguer just yet. (Carpenter, a 19th-round pick in 2019, put up a 120 OPS+ in 2023; I hope you're happy.) The main idea, in 2024, is to see if that changes. "We're going to be young," manager A.J. Hinch told *The Athletic* in December. "But that doesn't mean worse."

What the Tigers have built, mostly, is a vast store of accumulated vauntedness attached to a notably smaller amount of productive big-league baseball. This class of recent and pending player-development graduates could be anything, still, up to and including the foundation of a really good baseball team. They could also keep being what they have been—hurt, mostly, or affirmatively baffled, or stymied, or just miscast. It is easy to see how a GM might have looked at all this young talent, all of it seemingly ready or nearly so, and decided that the time was right to go for it. It is equally easy to see, with hindsight and from just about any vantage point in the wreckage left by that failure to launch, why that GM is no longer around.

Detroit's new regime has the same core of young players, and the same challenge, but thus far has taken a different approach. Avila shopped near the top of the free agent market in 2021 to sign Báez, who has been a disaster and whose struggles to catch up to fastballs in 2023 are ominous in the extreme, and Eduardo Rodriguez, who pitched well enough when available to opt out of his contract and sign a richer deal with Arizona over the winter. President of baseball operations Scott Harris and GM Jeff Greenberg have mostly focused on filling out the roster with identifiably cromulent veteran depth—the sort of affordable, useful, fungible players that function as the connective tissue on good big-league rosters. None of these players remotely qualify as splashy acquisitions—if I could interest you in some more names, Detroit's primary offseason acquisitions as this book goes to press are outfielder Mark Canha, starters Jack Flaherty and Kenta Maeda plus budget-priced relievers Shelby Miller (reanimated by the Dodgers) and Andrew Chafin (jarringly hirsute).

None of those players will be the deciding factor in whether the Tigers make the sort of leap in 2024 that they intended to make in 2022. They are not really those kinds of players. Leaving aside the open question of whether Chris Ilitch, one of the cadre of glum MLB heirs to have inherited baseball teams they seem mostly annoyed by, would be willing to pay for such a player should the situation arise, these moves can be explained by Harris and Greenberg not really thinking that these Tigers are quite that kind of team yet. Those veterans' presence, much like Kansas City's *Supermarket Sweep*-y romp through the lower-middle end of the free agent market this offseason, is both an attempt to make the team better by upgrading from below-average players to average ones and a nod to the fact that a sufficient critical mass of average players might be enough to hang around in a typical AL Central race. These are short and mostly unremarkable commitments, but they are better than nothing, and the players on whom these reasonable bets were placed seem reasonably likely to repay them.

None of that is very inspiring, really, but it is something—both a modified, limited answer in the affirmative on the vexingly fraught question of whether the team should "try to win baseball games" and a belated acknowledgment of how that kind of thing actually gets done. In the last few years, the Tigers have cycled through a number of organizational strategies without ever really getting any less in-between. Whatever they will or won't become will depend entirely upon players who have either only just begun to become whatever they will be; if Torkelson and Greene and Mize and the rest aren't good or just aren't available, the return-on-investment on Jack Flaherty won't mean much beyond how many and what kind of teenage prospects he brings back at the deadline. It's happening later than planned, and everyone involved carries bruises from the initial premature attempt, but the Tigers are about to figure out what all those high draft picks have amounted to.

Building out a player development and operations apparatus that helps the organization's young players figure things out in a more linear or just legible process and arrive a little less nascent and flaw-forward is the broader challenge facing this front office; it will be some time before anyone knows how well that goes. At the major-league level, the challenge is just as difficult but notably more direct. The pieces, or anyway *pieces*, are there, and it's now just a matter of seeing how and if they fit together. That's not an easy task, but relative to the opaque wishcasting and general drift of the previous regime it is at least recognizably *a task*. After years of American League Central-scented abstraction, in which the team cycled through various possible futures without ever generating anything like the necessary momentum to escape a persistently dreary present, the Tigers seem about ready to become some kind of baseball team. Whether that team is good or bad, that's still something like progress. ∎

—David Roth is a co-owner of Defector.

HITTERS

Akil Baddoo LF
Born: 08/16/98   Age: 25   Bats: L   Throws: L   Height: 6'1"   Weight: 214   Origin: Round 2, 2016 Draft (#74 overall)

YEAR	TM	LVL	AGE	PA	R	HR	RBI	SB	AVG/OBP/SLG	BABIP	SLGCON	BB%	K%	ZSw%	ZCon%	OSw%	OCon%	LA	90th EV	DRC+	BRR	DRP	WARP
2021	DET	MLB	22	461	60	13	55	18	.259/.330/.436	.335	.619	9.8%	26.5%	70.3%	76.1%	29.0%	58.5%	14.1	102.3	93	0.8	7.0	2.2
2022	TOL	AAA	23	131	14	3	15	7	.300/.405/.500	.366	.655	14.5%	19.8%							109	-1.2	1.7	0.6
2022	DET	MLB	23	225	30	2	9	9	.204/.289/.269	.289	.394	10.7%	28.4%	69.3%	81.3%	29.7%	54.8%	14.5	102.4	73	0.1	4.1	0.5
2023	TOL	AAA	24	49	6	1	7	2	.275/.388/.475	.333	.633	16.3%	20.4%	61.8%	92.7%	22.8%	57.7%			108	-1.6	-1.0	0.0
2023	DET	MLB	24	357	40	11	34	14	.218/.310/.372	.268	.520	11.8%	24.9%	68.8%	86.1%	28.8%	53.9%	10.5	104.3	103	0.8	5.8	1.8
2024 DC	DET	MLB	25	253	25	6	26	12	.228/.319/.376	.281	.506	11.4%	22.4%							97	0.4	3.9	1.1

2023 GP: LF (96), CF (5), RF (5), DH (5)   Comps: Robbie Grossman (54), Travis Snider (53), Oswaldo Arcia (52)

Like a new driver who once turned the wrong way down a one-way street (NOT based on a real incident), the 25-year-old Baddoo started to slowly reverse out of trouble after a downturn in 2022. He improved his approach against changeups and sliders, helping to cut down his strikeouts overall. He also found more barrels than he did in 2022, hitting double-digit home runs. Despite a quad injury that took him out of action for a month, he was on pace to set a new career high in four-baggers, despite not consistently barrelling up the ball. Although the quality of contact remains suspect, it's another area he's improved on over the prior season's campaign. Sometimes it just takes a little bit of time to figure out where all the gears are (again NOT BASED ON A REAL STORY).

Javier Báez SS
Born: 12/01/92   Age: 31   Bats: R   Throws: R   Height: 6'0"   Weight: 190   Origin: Round 1, 2011 Draft (#9 overall)

YEAR	TM	LVL	AGE	PA	R	HR	RBI	SB	AVG/OBP/SLG	BABIP	SLGCON	BB%	K%	ZSw%	ZCon%	OSw%	OCon%	LA	90th EV	DRC+	BRR	DRP	WARP
2021	NYM	MLB	28	186	32	9	22	5	.299/.371/.515	.390	.754	7.0%	28.5%	75.7%	77.4%	46.3%	48.5%	9.4	105.1	78	0.2	0.1	0.2
2021	CHC	MLB	28	361	48	22	65	13	.248/.292/.484	.330	.794	4.2%	36.3%	76.7%	69.1%	47.1%	49.8%	11.6	107.7	91	0.6	2.0	1.2
2022	DET	MLB	29	590	64	17	67	9	.238/.278/.393	.292	.534	4.4%	24.9%	69.0%	79.4%	48.8%	52.8%	9.5	105.2	86	1.0	-1.1	0.8
2023	DET	MLB	30	547	58	9	59	12	.222/.267/.325	.274	.431	4.4%	22.9%	68.5%	82.2%	46.7%	54.7%	9.2	105.5	84	0.4	-0.7	0.7
2024 DC	DET	MLB	31	546	51	14	57	9	.234/.283/.366	.294	.501	5.0%	25.4%							85	0.4	3.4	1.3

2023 GP: SS (130), DH (5)   Comps: Joe Cronin (64), Derek Jeter (61), Jeff Blauser (61)

Like a vaudeville melodrama where "paying the rent" is replaced with "strike out less," people—scouts, coaches, commenters, fans, some in these very pages—have long told Báez he has to get his plate discipline under control, only for him to put his glove on his head and respond "I won't strike out less!" And why would he do what anyone else says, when his approach got him to the majors at barely old enough to crush a celebratory beer, to All-Star nods and MVP votes at the pinnacle of his career? After descending from his 2018-2019 peak, Javy said "you win" and cut his ballooning strikeout rate down, mostly by laying off the sliders that had bedeviled him. But more contact only works if it's good contact, and he continued to expand the zone up, where he's often made hay out of what other players consider waste pitches, only with many fewer barrels. Rather than returning to Puerto Rico this offseason, El Mago is staying stateside and dedicating himself to strength training to try to address the aging cliff he's seemingly jumped off of; he'll need to avoid train tracks and villains with handlebar mustaches, so he better stay out of Detroit.

Justice Bigbie OF   Born: 01/24/99   Age: 25   Bats: R   Throws: R   Height: 6'2"   Weight: 200   Origin: Round 19, 2021 Draft (#555 overall)

YEAR	TM	LVL	AGE	PA	R	HR	RBI	SB	AVG/OBP/SLG	BABIP	SLGCON	BB%	K%	ZSw%	ZCon%	OSw%	OCon%	LA	90th EV	DRC+	BRR	DRP	WARP
2021	TIGW	ROK	22	84	9	1	14	0	.282/.381/.408	.345	.527	13.1%	19.0%									-1.5	
2021	TIGE	ROK	22	34	5	1	4	0	.179/.324/.286	.222	.421	17.6%	26.5%									-0.6	
2022	LAK	A	23	372	37	2	41	4	.258/.339/.358	.346	.490	7.5%	23.9%	72.7%	76.0%	34.0%	60.5%			90	-1.6	-4.0	0.3
2022	WM	A+	23	34	6	1	7	0	.387/.441/.613	.458	.760	5.9%	17.6%							102	-0.6	-0.2	0.0
2023	SRR	WIN	24	79	8	0	10	2	.265/.354/.309	.305	.362	12.7%	12.7%	73.8%	95.6%	24.5%	47.8%						
2023	WM	A+	24	155	25	6	27	1	.333/.400/.543	.381	.682	9.7%	18.1%							131	0.5	-2.2	0.8
2023	ERI	AA	24	272	51	12	43	5	.362/.421/.564	.382	.656	8.1%	12.5%							130	1.4	-1.9	1.8
2023	TOL	AAA	24	58	5	1	8	0	.275/.345/.392	.361	.556	8.6%	25.9%	72.2%	81.4%	40.7%	54.5%			88	-0.3	0.1	0.0
2024 non	DET	MLB	25	251	22	4	24	2	.240/.294/.351	.301	.466	5.8%	22.7%							82	0.0	0	0.0

2023 GP: LF (76), RF (39), DH (19)   *Comps: Tyson Auer (54), Steve Pearce (49), Brian Fletcher (48)*

The Tigers are still figuring out what they have in Bigbie after his breakout performance at the plate in 2023. Following mediocre production in his first two years, the old-for-his-level prospect suddenly started putting up Quad-A slugger numbers but without the Quad-A slugger whiff rates that usually kill that profile. He's not athletic (although capable of covering a corner outfield spot), and the bat speed is fringy, but for all the lack of fluidity he can still muscle pitches anywhere in the zone. It shouldn't work, and probably won't, and yet... He's the kind of prospect a team like the Tigers would rather not have room for, but might.

Miguel Cabrera DH   Born: 04/18/83   Age: 41   Bats: R   Throws: R   Height: 6'4"   Weight: 267   Origin: IFA, 1999

YEAR	TM	LVL	AGE	PA	R	HR	RBI	SB	AVG/OBP/SLG	BABIP	SLGCON	BB%	K%	ZSw%	ZCon%	OSw%	OCon%	LA	90th EV	DRC+	BRR	DRP	WARP
2021	DET	MLB	38	526	48	15	75	0	.256/.316/.386	.305	.514	7.6%	22.4%	69.4%	83.9%	34.3%	59.5%	10.2	105.4	105	-1.4	-0.2	1.3
2022	DET	MLB	39	433	25	5	43	1	.254/.305/.317	.324	.426	6.5%	23.3%	71.1%	81.2%	35.4%	61.2%	5.3	104.0	88	-1.1	0.0	0.2
2023	DET	MLB	40	370	21	4	34	0	.257/.322/.353	.317	.454	8.4%	20.0%	69.9%	83.1%	30.5%	57.6%	7.4	103.4	96	-0.7	0.0	0.5
2024 non	DET	MLB	41	251	24	5	24	0	.242/.306/.348	.296	.455	7.7%	21.4%							87	-0.6	-0.4	-0.1

2023 GP: DH (96), 1B (1)   *Comps: Eddie Murray (66), Albert Pujols (66), Steve Garvey (59)*

Steven Kwan tried to shoot a grounder past Cabrera, installed at first base in the final home game for the Tigers in 2023, but the ball rolled just close enough for the 40-year-old to show off some YMCA-grandpa-grade athleticism in the scoop. Cabrera ran it in himself, beating out the hustling Kwan, the ball cradled safely to his chest with one arm, the other one up to wave off the pitcher trailing to first base. Let that be how we all go out: one arm raised in triumph, running it out on our own terms. He also went 0-3, and let that also be how we all go out: with everyone politely choosing to forget that part.

Mark Canha LF   Born: 02/15/89   Age: 35   Bats: R   Throws: R   Height: 6'2"   Weight: 209   Origin: Round 7, 2010 Draft (#227 overall)

YEAR	TM	LVL	AGE	PA	R	HR	RBI	SB	AVG/OBP/SLG	BABIP	SLGCON	BB%	K%	ZSw%	ZCon%	OSw%	OCon%	LA	90th EV	DRC+	BRR	DRP	WARP
2021	OAK	MLB	32	625	93	17	61	12	.231/.358/.387	.274	.514	12.3%	20.5%	63.3%	84.9%	24.0%	66.1%	13.6	102.3	114	0.7	-1.3	3.3
2022	NYM	MLB	33	542	71	13	61	3	.266/.367/.403	.309	.510	8.9%	17.9%	62.4%	83.0%	28.0%	69.2%	11.0	103.1	119	-0.5	-0.7	2.9
2023	MIL	MLB	34	204	23	5	33	4	.287/.373/.427	.313	.503	8.3%	13.2%	63.7%	91.0%	28.2%	71.6%	15.0	103.2	108	0.1	-0.3	0.7
2023	NYM	MLB	34	303	28	6	29	7	.245/.343/.381	.279	.478	10.6%	17.2%	61.2%	86.6%	24.3%	67.4%	11.9	104.3	118	-0.1	-1.1	1.4
2024 DC	DET	MLB	35	451	48	9	45	5	.248/.346/.373	.285	.461	9.7%	16.4%							111	-0.1	-2.5	1.5

2023 GP: LF (68), DH (33), RF (26), 1B (18), 3B (4)   *Comps: Andrew McCutchen (62), Dusty Baker Jr. (60), Lu Blue (60)*

As ambrosial as an al pastor street taco, as delightful as a Hokkaido scallop over celery root with caviar ... Canha was a flavorful trade deadline addition to the Brewers lineup. His tenure in Milwaukee found him cooking an .800 OPS including five home runs and 33 RBI through 50 games played. The menu he's been carrying for the past four seasons through Oakland and New York includes his patience; his walk rate has dropped slightly but is still well above average. Significantly, his strikeout rate also decreased. Canha's Milwaukee numbers, including a wOBA north of .360 on fastballs, instilled enough confidence for Craig Counsell to place him fourth in the Brewers lineup and even give him a few stints at DH. The tough at-bats he serves and his steady contact numbers make it possible to stomach that lousy defense he offers in left field. Developing their own appetite for contention, the Detroit Tigers moved quickly in the offseason to order up the left fielder and solidify their lineup.

Kerry Carpenter RF/DH   Born: 09/02/97   Age: 26   Bats: L   Throws: R   Height: 6'2"   Weight: 220   Origin: Round 19, 2019 Draft (#562 overall)

YEAR	TM	LVL	AGE	PA	R	HR	RBI	SB	AVG/OBP/SLG	BABIP	SLGCON	BB%	K%	ZSw%	ZCon%	OSw%	OCon%	LA	90th EV	DRC+	BRR	DRP	WARP
2021	ERI	AA	23	461	57	15	74	5	.262/.319/.433	.299	.559	6.3%	20.4%							104	-0.4	-5.6	1.0
2022	ERI	AA	24	262	43	22	48	1	.304/.359/.646	.347	.923	6.1%	27.5%							136	0.2	-3.3	1.7
2022	TOL	AAA	24	138	17	8	27	2	.331/.420/.644	.330	.752	12.3%	12.3%							133	-0.6	-0.8	0.8
2022	DET	MLB	24	113	16	6	10	0	.252/.310/.485	.303	.704	5.3%	28.3%	70.7%	82.9%	37.2%	55.2%	14.8	102.6	91	0.0	0.0	0.2
2023	TOL	AAA	25	40	4	1	3	0	.171/.275/.286	.227	.435	12.5%	30.0%	59.5%	88.6%	31.1%	53.6%			90	0.2	-0.1	0.1
2023	DET	MLB	25	459	57	20	64	6	.278/.340/.471	.338	.650	7.0%	25.1%	72.9%	81.9%	38.1%	60.9%	13.2	103.9	100	0.2	0.7	1.2
2024 DC	DET	MLB	26	491	52	17	59	5	.239/.301/.415	.289	.569	6.7%	24.6%							101	-0.1	-0.1	1.1

2023 GP: RF (80), DH (27), LF (11)   *Comps: Lucas Duda (64), Andre Ethier (63), Corey Dickerson (62)*

A 19th-rounder who earned an August call-up in 2022 after revamping his swing and stance to elicit more power, Carpenter became an important feel-good story for an organization desperately short on them. A longer stay in the bigs in 2023 showed he's not just a Cinderella story—Carpenter continued to make hard, loud contact, barreling the ball with regularity. Magic always comes at a price, though, and the price of Carpenter's new cantilevered, full-extension swing is that he's going to be outfoxed by pitchers at times. A good team should be able to happily absorb Carpenter's elevated strikeout rate as a tradeoff for 20-plus homers, and the Tigers will, as well.

★ ★ ★ *2024 Top 101 Prospect* **#24** ★ ★ ★

Max Clark CF Born: 12/21/04 Age: 19 Bats: L Throws: L Height: 6'1" Weight: 205 Origin: Round 1, 2023 Draft (#3 overall)

YEAR	TM	LVL	AGE	PA	R	HR	RBI	SB	AVG/OBP/SLG	BABIP	SLGCON	BB%	K%	ZSw%	ZCon%	OSw%	OCon%	LA	90th EV	DRC+	BRR	DRP	WARP
2023	TIG	ROK	18	56	13	2	12	4	.283/.411/.543	.324	.694	16.1%	17.9%	82.4%	85.7%	15.0%	66.7%						
2023	LAK	A	18	51	5	0	7	1	.154/.353/.179	.250	.292	23.5%	29.4%	47.2%	84.0%	11.8%	44.4%			95	0.3	0.3	0.1
2024 non	DET	MLB	19	251	20	2	19	0	.206/.284/.288	.294	.425	9.1%	28.9%							64	0.0	0	-0.3

2023 GP: CF (23) *Comps: Leonardo Molina (68), José Sánchez (62), Michael Harris II (62)*

Clark's savvy social media presence and huge following made him arguably the most hyped prep draftee since Bryce Harper in 2009. However, he's not just a baseball Kardashian: There's substance and potential in the young lefty's game. He stood out on the summer circuit with his excellent bat-to-ball skills and advanced approach at the plate, recognizing spin well and rarely chasing out of the zone. His swing is geared for hard line drives, but there's plenty of bat speed and as his frame fills out, Clark is likely to produce above-average power numbers. He's a premium athlete with all the attributes necessary to become a five-tool standout—six if you include his ability to promote the other five.

Dillon Dingler C Born: 09/17/98 Age: 25 Bats: R Throws: R Height: 6'3" Weight: 210 Origin: Round 2, 2020 Draft (#38 overall)

YEAR	TM	LVL	AGE	PA	R	HR	RBI	SB	AVG/OBP/SLG	BABIP	SLGCON	BB%	K%	ZSw%	ZCon%	OSw%	OCon%	LA	90th EV	DRC+	BRR	DRP	WARP
2021	WM	A+	22	141	25	8	24	0	.287/.376/.549	.342	.779	9.2%	25.5%							127	2.1	5.0	1.5
2021	ERI	AA	22	208	24	4	20	1	.202/.264/.314	.272	.468	4.3%	29.8%							82	-0.3	5.5	0.8
2022	ERI	AA	23	448	56	14	58	1	.238/.333/.419	.335	.664	10.0%	31.9%							97	0.7	11.9	2.4
2023	ERI	AA	24	219	35	9	41	3	.253/.372/.462	.333	.706	12.3%	28.8%							108	1.7	1.3	1.1
2024 non	DET	MLB	25	251	23	5	25	1	.219/.287/.346	.315	.534	7.1%	32.4%							79	0.0	0	0.3

2023 GP: C (68), DH (21) *Comps: Carlos Corporán (55), John Hicks (53), Luke Montz (52)*

The offensive bar for major-league catchers is low, but right now it looks like Dingler might not even reach that threshold. Once one of the top prospects in the organization, Dingler's shine has faded due to his inability to adjust to upper-level pitching and a strikeout rate tracking upwards like the nation's student loan debt. Catchers are weird and development is not linear, so maybe Dingler rebounds in 2024 and begins to make just enough contact to take advantage of his plus raw pop. But at 25 years old and lacking prior offensive success in the upper minors, the odds don't seem much better than those student loans getting forgiven.

YEAR	TM	P. COUNT	FRM RUNS	BLK RUNS	THRW RUNS	TOT RUNS
2021	WM	3574	3.5	-0.3	1.6	4.8
2021	ERI	5952	4.4	0.5	0.8	5.7
2022	ERI	11712	6.3	-0.1	5.7	11.9
2023	ERI	5662	0.9	-0.1	0.7	1.5
2023	TOL	3279	1.2	0.1	1.0	2.3
2024	DET	6956	1.1	-0.2	0.8	1.7

Riley Greene CF Born: 09/28/00 Age: 23 Bats: L Throws: L Height: 6'3" Weight: 200 Origin: Round 1, 2019 Draft (#5 overall)

YEAR	TM	LVL	AGE	PA	R	HR	RBI	SB	AVG/OBP/SLG	BABIP	SLGCON	BB%	K%	ZSw%	ZCon%	OSw%	OCon%	LA	90th EV	DRC+	BRR	DRP	WARP
2021	ERI	AA	20	373	59	16	54	12	.298/.381/.525	.386	.763	11.0%	27.3%							112	1.8	4.0	2.4
2021	TOL	AAA	20	185	36	8	30	4	.308/.400/.553	.406	.815	11.9%	27.6%							105	1.5	-2.5	0.6
2022	TOL	AAA	21	68	10	1	6	3	.274/.338/.387	.340	.500	8.8%	20.6%							101	1.2	-1.4	0.2
2022	DET	MLB	21	418	46	5	42	1	.253/.321/.362	.354	.531	8.6%	28.7%	65.9%	83.5%	30.6%	60.5%	3.5	107.8	88	0.0	2.7	1.2
2023	DET	MLB	22	416	51	11	37	7	.288/.349/.447	.384	.640	8.4%	27.4%	69.4%	79.3%	30.8%	60.3%	6.9	107.5	97	0.0	-0.6	1.2
2024 DC	DET	MLB	23	570	56	13	60	7	.241/.311/.385	.318	.545	8.5%	26.7%							96	0.2	3.3	1.5

2023 GP: CF (79), DH (9), LF (6), RF (6) *Comps: Vernon Wells (56), Mel Hall (55), Corey Patterson (52)*

Everyone deserves hope. For Tigers fans, that came in the form of Greene taking a significant step forward in 2023, making more and better contact while playing a passable center field. Continued improvement in cutting down on his strikeouts and finding a happy launch angle middle ground between "threatening passing satellites" and "making a bid for King of the Moles" should go a long way in sustaining those improvements and delivering on his tremendous potential. Greene's season was cut short with an injury culminating in TJ surgery on his non-throwing arm, because Tigers fans aren't allowed to have *too* much hope lest the harmony of the celestial spheres be thrown off (yes, the same music that plays at the Comerica Park carousel), but he's slated to be on track to return by Opening Day 2024.

Andy Ibáñez 2B Born: 04/03/93 Age: 31 Bats: R Throws: R Height: 5'10" Weight: 205 Origin: IFA, 2015

YEAR	TM	LVL	AGE	PA	R	HR	RBI	SB	AVG/OBP/SLG	BABIP	SLGCON	BB%	K%	ZSw%	ZCon%	OSw%	OCon%	LA	90th EV	DRC+	BRR	DRP	WARP
2021	RR	AAA	28	129	21	7	27	1	.342/.411/.640	.356	.760	9.3%	14.0%							127	0.9	1.5	1.1
2021	TEX	MLB	28	272	31	7	25	0	.277/.321/.435	.297	.505	5.5%	12.9%	72.5%	88.5%	37.5%	67.9%	15.4	102.6	106	0.0	0.1	1.1
2022	RR	AAA	29	315	38	6	31	5	.255/.330/.390	.288	.470	8.9%	15.2%	73.9%	88.7%	31.7%	70.9%			95	-3.5	-1.5	0.3
2022	TEX	MLB	29	128	13	1	9	3	.218/.273/.277	.258	.337	7.0%	16.4%	73.9%	92.6%	28.8%	60.5%	15.2	101.4	95	0.1	0.1	0.2
2023	TOL	AAA	30	79	14	5	16	2	.297/.418/.609	.304	.780	16.5%	17.7%	72.9%	88.5%	29.1%	64.4%			122	-0.6	1.1	0.5
2023	DET	MLB	30	383	42	11	41	1	.264/.312/.433	.300	.537	6.3%	18.0%	71.4%	89.5%	39.8%	64.5%	12.9	103.3	112	-0.3	0.5	1.7
2024 DC	DET	MLB	31	220	21	5	22	2	.247/.304/.374	.284	.463	7.1%	17.5%							94	0.0	0.3	0.4

2023 GP: 2B (77), 3B (16), LF (13), RF (8), 1B (4), DH (4) *Comps: Tommy La Stella (56), Whit Merrifield (54), Mike Aviles (48)*

Ibáñez can play a lot of positions, but in Texas, he somehow found himself blocked at all of them. But a full-time audition with the Tigers showed the weaknesses in his game pretty clearly. Despite possessing solid bat-to-ball skills, Ibáñez lacks the kind of standout skill, like exceptional power or base-stealing or defense, needed to make him an everyday player. To borrow from the best short story in the English language, "Yours" by Mary Robison, "to own only a little talent…was an awful, plaguing thing." Ibáñez has much more than a little talent—as a major leaguer, he's one of the best baseball players in the world—but it still might not be enough. At least Detroit should offer him plenty of work as a fallback.

★ ★ ★ *2024 Top 101 Prospect* **#66** ★ ★ ★

Jace Jung **2B**   Born: 10/04/00   Age: 23   Bats: L   Throws: R   Height: 6'0"   Weight: 205   Origin: Round 1, 2022 Draft (#12 overall)

YEAR	TM	LVL	AGE	PA	R	HR	RBI	SB	AVG/OBP/SLG	BABIP	SLGCON	BB%	K%	ZSw%	ZCon%	OSw%	OCon%	LA	90th EV	DRC+	BRR	DRP	WARP
2022	WM	A+	21	134	16	1	13	1	.231/.373/.333	.300	.450	18.7%	20.9%							104	-1.6	3.4	0.6
2023	WM	A+	22	366	46	14	43	5	.254/.377/.465	.303	.641	15.3%	22.7%							125	-1.2	0.1	1.9
2023	ERI	AA	22	209	28	14	39	0	.284/.373/.563	.336	.811	11.0%	26.8%							128	0.1	2.5	1.4
2024 non	DET	MLB	23	251	25	6	26	0	.226/.309/.361	.297	.519	9.8%	26.9%							90	0.0	0	0.4

2023 GP: 2B (109), DH (24), 3B (8)   *Comps: Cory Spangenberg (68), Travis Blankenhorn (64), Enmanuel Valdez (64)*

Like many younger siblings, Jung has spent his life following in the footsteps of his older brother. Whether it was attending high school, enrolling at Texas Tech, or becoming a top draft selection, he's always been right on Josh's heels in terms of success on the diamond. We're not ready to say that the trend will continue in 2024 with Jace becoming a key cog to a World Series champion, but he is likely to hit his way to a major-league debut in Motown. The bat has a chance to be special, producing hard contact to all fields and above-average power numbers. His defensive limitations make it unlikely that a Gold Glove will ever grace Jung's trophy case, but that doesn't matter when you can hit like he can.

★ ★ ★ *2024 Top 101 Prospect* **#22** ★ ★ ★

Colt Keith **3B**   Born: 08/14/01   Age: 22   Bats: L   Throws: R   Height: 6'2"   Weight: 211   Origin: Round 5, 2020 Draft (#132 overall)

YEAR	TM	LVL	AGE	PA	R	HR	RBI	SB	AVG/OBP/SLG	BABIP	SLGCON	BB%	K%	ZSw%	ZCon%	OSw%	OCon%	LA	90th EV	DRC+	BRR	DRP	WARP
2021	LAK	A	19	181	32	1	21	4	.320/.436/.422	.422	.574	16.6%	21.5%	63.8%	87.2%	23.6%	63.3%			117	1.4	2.0	1.2
2021	WM	A+	19	76	7	1	6	0	.162/.250/.250	.250	.415	10.5%	35.5%							80	0.9	0.7	0.2
2022	WM	A+	20	216	38	9	31	4	.301/.370/.544	.343	.695	10.2%	19.4%							138	1.6	-1.8	1.5
2023	ERI	AA	21	276	43	14	50	2	.325/.391/.585	.386	.787	9.1%	22.8%							132	-2.0	-2.1	1.3
2023	TOL	AAA	21	301	45	13	51	1	.287/.369/.521	.320	.670	11.6%	19.3%	71.9%	84.7%	28.9%	56.5%			108	0.3	-2.1	0.7
2024 DC	DET	MLB	22	294	28	6	30	1	.241/.306/.384	.307	.523	7.8%	24.4%							93	0.0	0	0.6

2023 GP: 3B (62), 2B (41), DH (24)   *Comps: Corey Seager (63), Mike Moustakas (58), Nolan Gorman (57)*

Injuries limited Keith's time on the diamond in 2022, but he showed just enough at West Michigan and in the AFL to earn a spot at the back end of that year's Top 101 prospect list. Fully healthy in 2023, we saw a true breakout at the plate, as his power came alive without sacrificing contact ability. He's definitely a hit-first prospect, but there were enough gains made in the field to conclude that Keith will likely settle in as an adequate defender at the keystone. With no true red flags in his offensive profile and a track record of success in the high minors, Keith should be ready to take the field in Detroit sometime in 2024.

Hao-Yu Lee **2B**   Born: 02/03/03   Age: 21   Bats: R   Throws: R   Height: 5'9"   Weight: 190   Origin: IFA, 2021

YEAR	TM	LVL	AGE	PA	R	HR	RBI	SB	AVG/OBP/SLG	BABIP	SLGCON	BB%	K%	ZSw%	ZCon%	OSw%	OCon%	LA	90th EV	DRC+	BRR	DRP	WARP
2021	PHI	ROK	18	25	9	1	5	0	.364/.440/.773	.438	1.000	12.0%	20.0%	66.7%	90.0%	37.5%	46.7%					-0.1	
2022	CLR	A	19	302	37	7	50	10	.283/.384/.415	.338	.532	11.9%	18.9%	63.9%	85.5%	29.9%	60.8%			133	1.3	2.8	2.4
2022	JS	A+	19	40	5	1	2	3	.257/.350/.486	.320	.654	12.5%	22.5%							104	-0.2	-0.9	0.0
2023	JS	A+	20	285	35	5	26	14	.283/.372/.401	.340	.510	10.2%	18.6%							120	-0.2	3.4	1.6
2023	WM	A+	20	32	4	1	3	2	.214/.313/.429	.278	.632	9.4%	28.1%							97	-0.1	-0.1	0.1
2024 non	DET	MLB	21	251	21	3	22	0	.221/.284/.320	.280	.425	6.9%	22.8%							72	0.0	0	-0.2

2023 GP: 2B (67), 3B (8), SS (7), DH (4)   *Comps: Royce Lewis (67), Travis Denker (66), Cole Tucker (65)*

Detroit was fairly quiet at last year's trade deadline, but dealing Michael Lorenzen did net them a top-101 quality prospect in Lee. He features a quiet and compact swing geared to spraying hard line drives to all fields. While the bat-to-ball skills are plus, there's still development needed in the swing decisions, and Lee is sure to be tested in 2024 as he faces advanced pitching for the first time. The plentiful contact will never be loud, meaning Lee is unlikely to ever produce more than fringe-average power numbers. That lack of potent offensive impact, and his limitations with the glove, put a ton of pressure on Lee to hit his fair share of gappers if he's going to become an everyday infielder.

Eddys Leonard **SS**   Born: 11/10/00   Age: 23   Bats: R   Throws: R   Height: 5'11"   Weight: 195   Origin: IFA, 2017

YEAR	TM	LVL	AGE	PA	R	HR	RBI	SB	AVG/OBP/SLG	BABIP	SLGCON	BB%	K%	ZSw%	ZCon%	OSw%	OCon%	LA	90th EV	DRC+	BRR	DRP	WARP
2021	RC	A	20	308	59	14	57	6	.295/.399/.544	.362	.759	11.0%	24.0%							122	-0.1	1.3	1.9
2021	GL	A+	20	184	30	8	24	3	.299/.375/.530	.360	.713	9.2%	22.8%							117	-0.4	-5.3	0.4
2022	GL	A+	21	566	80	15	61	4	.264/.348/.435	.317	.573	8.0%	21.0%							109	1.3	-5.2	2.0
2023	TUL	AA	22	388	37	11	44	3	.254/.327/.411	.307	.543	7.5%	21.9%							88	-0.9	-2.3	0.4
2023	TOL	AAA	22	171	30	8	31	2	.302/.374/.530	.346	.705	9.9%	21.6%	74.8%	87.8%	38.5%	50.7%			99	-0.4	-1.0	0.4
2024 non	DET	MLB	23	251	23	5	25	2	.227/.286/.354	.287	.480	6.2%	24.3%							81	0.0	0	0.2

2023 GP: SS (107), CF (10), DH (6), 2B (4), LF (3), 3B (2)   *Comps: Yamaico Navarro (66), Eugenio Suárez (62), Mauricio Dubón (61)*

Adding Joe Kelly and Lance Lynn at the deadline created a 40-man roster crunch for the Dodgers, and Leonard was the casualty. For the low, low price of cash, the Tigers secured a high-contact, but free-swinging, versatile infielder who showed some surprising pop with the bat in 2023. An extremely streaky hitter, Leonard has been all-or-nothing at the plate during his professional career. However, he was trending upward, putting together good at-bats as a 22-year-old in Triple-A. Defensively, he can be plugged in at multiple infield and outfield positions to provide adequate but unremarkable glovework. There's not much in terms of talent blocking his path to Detroit, and a solid start to the year might just pave the way for Leonard to make a 2024 debut.

Justyn-Henry Malloy 3B   Born: 02/19/00   Age: 24   Bats: R   Throws: R   Height: 6'1"   Weight: 212   Origin: Round 6, 2021 Draft (#187 overall)

YEAR	TM	LVL	AGE	PA	R	HR	RBI	SB	AVG/OBP/SLG	BABIP	SLGCON	BB%	K%	ZSw%	ZCon%	OSw%	OCon%	LA	90th EV	DRC+	BRR	DRP	WARP
2021	AUG	A	21	147	23	5	21	4	.270/.388/.434	.318	.576	16.3%	20.4%							123	-0.4	-1.4	0.6
2022	ROM	A+	22	320	51	10	44	3	.304/.409/.479	.376	.663	14.7%	22.8%							126	1.0	-2.6	1.6
2022	MIS	AA	22	238	35	6	31	0	.268/.403/.421	.354	.615	18.1%	25.2%							113	0.9	-4.1	0.8
2022	GWN	AAA	22	33	5	1	6	2	.280/.424/.440	.300	.550	21.2%	15.2%							116	-1.4	0.3	0.1
2023	TOL	AAA	23	611	89	23	83	5	.277/.417/.474	.354	.690	18.0%	24.9%	59.9%	80.7%	19.5%	49.7%			117	0.5	-3.8	2.9
2024 non	DET	MLB	24	251	27	5	26	0	.245/.342/.373	.332	.540	12.0%	27.3%							106	0.0	0	0.9

2023 GP: 3B (60), DH (31), LF (29), RF (15)   Comps: Garin Cecchini (48), Jedd Gyorko (46), Michael Hermosillo (45)

As a three-true-outcomes, four-corners prospect, Malloy's walking a thin line if he hopes to become a lineup mainstay in Detroit. Despite getting temporarily blocked by the acquisition of Mark Canha, he'll likely get his shot at major-league playing time before long. But with an approach that borders on passive and fringe-average bat-to-ball skills, he might get carved up by big-league pitching. On the other hand, Malloy has shown the ability to make adjustments and find success at every minor-league stop, and might just do the same when the call comes this summer. It comes down to patience versus passivity at the plate: The majority of hitting is waiting for mistake pitches, but there are two kinds of mistakes. Taking balls is well and good, but eventually you have to do something with the strikes.

Nick Maton 3B   Born: 02/18/97   Age: 27   Bats: L   Throws: R   Height: 6'2"   Weight: 178   Origin: Round 7, 2017 Draft (#203 overall)

YEAR	TM	LVL	AGE	PA	R	HR	RBI	SB	AVG/OBP/SLG	BABIP	SLGCON	BB%	K%	ZSw%	ZCon%	OSw%	OCon%	LA	90th EV	DRC+	BRR	DRP	WARP
2021	LHV	AAA	24	252	29	5	27	3	.199/.332/.345	.252	.486	15.1%	23.8%							97	-1.4	-3.3	0.3
2021	PHI	MLB	24	131	16	2	14	2	.256/.323/.385	.364	.577	7.6%	29.8%	71.5%	79.2%	32.9%	49.5%	16.8	101.7	67	0.0	-0.4	-0.1
2022	LHV	AAA	25	250	33	5	35	3	.261/.368/.436	.327	.590	13.6%	22.0%	74.3%	80.8%	34.8%	37.5%			100	1.6	-4.7	0.4
2022	PHI	MLB	25	85	13	5	17	0	.250/.341/.514	.325	.860	11.8%	34.1%	71.3%	83.3%	34.2%	39.5%	17.8	99.5	84	0.0	0.0	0.1
2023	TOL	AAA	26	175	32	3	27	3	.293/.414/.457	.369	.621	15.4%	21.1%	73.6%	81.0%	28.3%	60.7%			95	-0.4	-0.1	0.4
2023	DET	MLB	26	293	29	8	32	1	.173/.288/.305	.206	.432	13.0%	24.9%	70.0%	79.7%	28.5%	50.7%	18.4	101.4	89	0.1	-0.8	0.4
2024 DC	DET	MLB	27	156	15	3	15	1	.208/.307/.337	.271	.474	11.2%	25.3%							84	0.0	-1	0.0

2023 GP: 3B (53), 2B (30), DH (13), SS (4)   Comps: Tzu-Wei Lin (52), Cody Asche (52), Carlos Asuaje (50)

Occasionally, Maton provides big, thrilling moments, ambushing fastballs for highlight-reel homers. Unfortunately, he often struggles to contain his enthusiasm to swing, chasing off-speed pitches and putting himself in poor counts. We've talked a lot about the aesthetics of "pitch face," the frozen grimace, often caught on baseball cards, of the pitcher mid-delivery. Maton, more than most batters, has a distinct "swing face," an open look of disbelief, which somewhat contrasts with his love of bat flips. Regardless of expression, he wasn't able to hang with the big cats all summer and found himself back in Triple-A. The Tigers' coaching staff will need him to complete the baseball equivalent of writing "I will not chase sliders in the opposite batters' box" a hundred times on a chalkboard.

★ ★ ★ *2024 Top 101 Prospect* #79 ★ ★ ★

Kevin McGonigle MI   Born: 08/18/04   Age: 19   Bats: L   Throws: R   Height: 5'10"   Weight: 187   Origin: Round 1, 2023 Draft (#37 overall)

YEAR	TM	LVL	AGE	PA	R	HR	RBI	SB	AVG/OBP/SLG	BABIP	SLGCON	BB%	K%	ZSw%	ZCon%	OSw%	OCon%	LA	90th EV	DRC+	BRR	DRP	WARP
2023	TIG	ROK	18	45	11	0	1	6	.273/.467/.333	.321	.393	24.4%	11.1%	80.0%	100.0%	43.8%	85.7%						
2023	LAK	A	18	48	7	1	5	2	.350/.438/.475	.371	.543	14.6%	10.4%	69.4%	88.2%	20.8%	72.7%			121	-1.0	0.8	0.3
2024 non	DET	MLB	19	251	20	2	20	0	.211/.278/.298	.278	.402	7.7%	24.3%							64	0.0	0	-0.3

2023 GP: SS (14), 2B (6), DH (1)

One of the top prep hitters available in the 2023 draft, McGonigle fits the mold of recent Tigers prospects with his advanced bat and questionable defensive home. Twelve games is a small sample size and High-A Lakeland is a long way from the major leagues, but McGonigle's post-draft performance there as a teenager was still impressive. With his glove, he'll likely end up as a second baseman ultimately but should hold his own there thanks to his solid instincts and sneaky quickness. That move down the defensive spectrum is going to put some pressure on his bat to not just make contact, but quality contact. Eventually, McGonigle and the Tigers are going to play everyone's favorite prospecting game: Hit Tool Roulette.

Zach McKinstry UT   Born: 04/29/95   Age: 29   Bats: L   Throws: R   Height: 6'0"   Weight: 180   Origin: Round 33, 2016 Draft (#1001 overall)

YEAR	TM	LVL	AGE	PA	R	HR	RBI	SB	AVG/OBP/SLG	BABIP	SLGCON	BB%	K%	ZSw%	ZCon%	OSw%	OCon%	LA	90th EV	DRC+	BRR	DRP	WARP
2021	OKC	AAA	26	171	35	7	21	4	.272/.368/.510	.287	.620	11.7%	15.2%							114	1.0	3.9	1.3
2021	LAD	MLB	26	172	19	7	29	1	.215/.263/.405	.262	.593	5.8%	29.1%	60.7%	86.1%	34.7%	57.6%	13.5	101.7	68	0.1	0.4	-0.1
2022	OKC	AAA	27	223	36	4	25	0	.335/.417/.487	.382	.589	12.1%	14.8%	67.6%	82.7%	28.9%	71.8%			112	-2.2	-1.6	0.7
2022	CHC	MLB	27	171	17	4	12	7	.206/.272/.361	.272	.523	7.6%	28.1%	65.5%	87.3%	33.4%	66.4%	12.0	101.7	72	0.5	-0.1	-0.1
2022	LAD	MLB	27	14	4	1	2	0	.091/.286/.364		.571	21.4%	28.6%	74.2%	82.6%	5.4%	0.0%	6.8	102.1	82	0.0	0.0	0.0
2023	DET	MLB	28	518	60	9	35	16	.231/.302/.351	.284	.464	8.5%	21.8%	68.6%	87.9%	30.2%	65.5%	17.6	102.4	91	0.9	0.2	1.1
2024 DC	DET	MLB	29	341	31	6	33	7	.225/.298/.355	.269	.456	8.6%	19.9%							84	0.1	-1.6	0.1

2023 GP: 3B (52), 2B (47), RF (38), SS (23), LF (22), CF (2), DH (2), P (1)   Comps: Ryan Flaherty (48), Roger Bernadina (46), Brock Holt (45)

McKinstry literally did the teen-movie cliche of taking off his glasses and changing his hair in hopes of revealing a full-time player underneath; alas, the platoon bat remained flat despite a scorching-hot start. However, the Tigers aren't in the position to turn down McKinstry's defensive utility and unique (to the Tigers) ability to Not Strike Out All The Time, so the pair grudgingly agreed to go steady for the rest of freshman year, at least until some better prospects come around.

Parker Meadows CF   Born: 11/02/99   Age: 24   Bats: L   Throws: R   Height: 6'5"   Weight: 205   Origin: Round 2, 2018 Draft (#44 overall)

YEAR	TM	LVL	AGE	PA	R	HR	RBI	SB	AVG/OBP/SLG	BABIP	SLGCON	BB%	K%	ZSw%	ZCon%	OSw%	OCon%	LA	90th EV	DRC+	BRR	DRP	WARP
2021	WM	A+	21	408	50	8	44	9	.208/.290/.330	.261	.457	9.1%	24.3%							94	1.7	-2.7	1.0
2022	WM	A+	22	67	16	4	7	0	.230/.288/.525	.256	.744	6.0%	26.9%							126	1.0	-1.6	0.4
2022	ERI	AA	22	489	64	16	51	17	.275/.354/.466	.309	.591	10.6%	18.4%							117	0.2	1.6	2.7
2023	TOL	AAA	23	517	78	19	65	19	.256/.337/.474	.305	.653	11.0%	23.8%	67.6%	86.0%	30.6%	59.6%			99	1.2	0.1	1.8
2023	DET	MLB	23	145	19	3	13	8	.232/.331/.368	.302	.523	11.7%	25.5%	62.1%	86.6%	29.4%	60.6%	17.4	104.2	90	0.3	1.4	0.5
2024 DC	DET	MLB	24	547	48	11	52	13	.207/.280/.343	.259	.462	8.2%	23.6%							74	0.5	5	0.7

2023 GP: CF (36), DH (1)   Comps: Jackie Bradley Jr. (66), Aaron Hicks (64), Mallex Smith (61)

Being able to cover center field is a lot like having strong study skills in college: You can be deficient in a lot of other ways and get away with it. Meadows maintained the game power that had long eluded him in the low minors, but saw a dip in his contact rate, showing a particular fondness for soft-breaking stuff away. But the upgrade he offers with the glove over Riley Greene, who's better suited to right fight, will buy him a season or two to figure it out (while his team is also figuring it out). In that sense, he and the Tigers are perfect for each other: He'll need to improve to hold his own as a first-division regular, and the Tigers probably need an improved version of him to get there.

Jake Rogers C   Born: 04/18/95   Age: 29   Bats: R   Throws: R   Height: 6'1"   Weight: 201   Origin: Round 3, 2016 Draft (#97 overall)

YEAR	TM	LVL	AGE	PA	R	HR	RBI	SB	AVG/OBP/SLG	BABIP	SLGCON	BB%	K%	ZSw%	ZCon%	OSw%	OCon%	LA	90th EV	DRC+	BRR	DRP	WARP
2021	DET	MLB	26	127	17	6	17	1	.239/.306/.496	.344	.836	8.7%	36.2%	63.6%	71.4%	30.6%	48.5%	25.3	104.3	69	0.1	-3.1	-0.3
2023	DET	MLB	28	365	47	21	49	1	.221/.286/.444	.268	.690	7.7%	32.3%	67.7%	77.0%	26.3%	50.0%	15.2	103.7	98	-0.2	10.7	2.4
2024 DC	DET	MLB	29	304	33	12	37	2	.215/.282/.395	.274	.596	7.7%	30.5%							90	-0.1	-3	0.5

2023 GP: C (99), DH (7), LF (1)   Comps: Cameron Rupp (65), Sandy León (58), Jonathan Lucroy (56)

YEAR	TM	P. COUNT	FRM RUNS	BLK RUNS	THRW RUNS	TOT RUNS
2021	DET	5067	-2.6	-0.1	0.2	-2.5
2023	DET	13597	9.6	0.1	0.2	10.0
2024	DET	12025	-2.7	-0.1	-0.2	-3.0

Perhaps, in growing his trademark mustache long enough to connect with his chest hair, Rogers was attempting to enact an ancient lycanthropic spell to derive more contact in his swing. It did not work. But if the goal was to unseat Eric Haase for the starting catching job in Detroit, job well done; especially if you consider the job of a modern-day MLB catcher to be providing plus defense and hitting the occasional tank while also putting up eye-wateringly bad strikeout rates. The mustache might be saying "the South will rise again," but the batting average sure isn't.

Spencer Torkelson 1B   Born: 08/26/99   Age: 24   Bats: R   Throws: R   Height: 6'1"   Weight: 220   Origin: Round 1, 2020 Draft (#1 overall)

YEAR	TM	LVL	AGE	PA	R	HR	RBI	SB	AVG/OBP/SLG	BABIP	SLGCON	BB%	K%	ZSw%	ZCon%	OSw%	OCon%	LA	90th EV	DRC+	BRR	DRP	WARP
2021	WM	A+	21	141	21	5	28	3	.312/.440/.569	.363	.765	17.0%	19.9%							128	0.4	-0.1	0.9
2021	ERI	AA	21	212	33	14	36	1	.263/.373/.560	.278	.784	14.2%	23.6%							139	-0.5	-1.5	1.4
2021	TOL	AAA	21	177	35	11	27	1	.238/.350/.531	.233	.703	13.0%	20.3%							120	-0.1	-1.0	0.7
2022	TOL	AAA	22	155	18	5	18	1	.229/.348/.389	.294	.567	14.8%	26.5%							98	-0.6	0.0	0.3
2022	DET	MLB	22	404	38	8	28	0	.203/.285/.319	.255	.441	9.2%	24.5%	68.9%	85.7%	28.8%	54.3%	15.0	105.5	86	-0.5	0.5	0.1
2023	DET	MLB	23	684	88	31	94	3	.233/.313/.446	.269	.621	9.8%	25.0%	69.6%	84.8%	28.3%	57.5%	17.2	106.4	110	-0.8	-2.2	1.9
2024 DC	DET	MLB	24	599	65	20	70	2	.227/.312/.394	.267	.531	10.0%	22.9%							102	-0.4	-0.8	1.2

2023 GP: 1B (154), DH (5)   Comps: Dominic Smith (57), Derrek Lee (52), Nick Johnson (49)

There's a plethora of permutations on the *Moneyball* "Billy, this is/his defect is" meme, but first-overall pick Torkelson, despite a dismal rookie campaign in 2022, has dodged those so far. Toiling away in relative obscurity in Detroit coupled with a 30+ homer season will do that. The thing that was supposed to make Tork an unstoppable force at the plate was his plus power, combined with a distaste for striking out; the latter has yet to translate at the next level, but when he makes contact it's so long and loud as to deliver him safely from the memelords. Torkelson was pitched to his weak point, low and away, a quarter of the time in 2023, and pitchers will continue to attack him there as long as he continues to swing and miss. The adjustments he makes going forward will determine if he's Jonah-Hill-whiteboard-dot-jpeg fodder or has Tigers fans resuscitating the classic "show [Tork] the money."

Matt Vierling RF   Born: 09/16/96   Age: 27   Bats: R   Throws: R   Height: 6'3"   Weight: 205   Origin: Round 5, 2018 Draft (#137 overall)

YEAR	TM	LVL	AGE	PA	R	HR	RBI	SB	AVG/OBP/SLG	BABIP	SLGCON	BB%	K%	ZSw%	ZCon%	OSw%	OCon%	LA	90th EV	DRC+	BRR	DRP	WARP
2021	REA	AA	24	102	16	6	16	5	.345/.422/.644	.369	.812	11.8%	17.6%							136	-0.1	3.5	1.1
2021	LHV	AAA	24	236	25	5	31	5	.248/.331/.359	.291	.463	10.2%	19.5%							99	-0.8	3.5	1.0
2021	PHI	MLB	24	77	11	2	6	2	.324/.364/.479	.420	.667	5.2%	26.0%	61.7%	85.1%	28.7%	57.8%	6.1	107.7	89	0.0	-0.2	0.1
2022	LHV	AAA	25	95	15	2	9	8	.271/.347/.459	.309	.557	10.5%	15.8%							117	0.7	-1.5	0.4
2022	PHI	MLB	25	357	41	6	32	7	.246/.297/.351	.290	.447	6.4%	19.6%	58.5%	88.4%	32.0%	67.6%	11.9	105.7	103	-0.2	1.4	1.4
2023	DET	MLB	26	530	63	10	44	6	.261/.329/.388	.321	.507	8.3%	21.1%	60.6%	87.2%	30.6%	69.8%	8.8	105.2	100	0.2	-0.8	1.5
2024 DC	DET	MLB	27	450	42	8	43	11	.238/.305/.353	.277	.438	7.8%	17.7%							89	0.2	-1.5	0.5

2023 GP: RF (58), LF (41), 3B (35), CF (31), 2B (1)   Comps: Abraham Almonte (50), Manuel Margot (49), Chris Denorfia (47)

The Yearling is the worst Pulitzer-winning novel-turned-movie, a lugubrious slog through the rural South featuring a heavy-handed parallel narrative between a poor, lonely child and an orphaned fawn that ends exactly as you think it does. Similarly, The Vierling found the world to be a harsh and unfeeling place when the World Series-contending Phillies dealt him to the perpetually disappointing Tigers. This did give Vierling a chance to grow into an everyday role, but an ongoing series of setup and swing changes failed to produce a hoped-for breakthrough season. And even worse, he didn't do the one thing the lefty-heavy Tigers needed him to do, which was mash lefty pitching. Maybe the breakthrough is yet to come, but to paraphrase another, much better writer, we think we've seen this film before: We didn't like the ending then, either.

PITCHERS

Beau Brieske RHP   Born: 04/04/98   Age: 26   Height: 6'3"   Weight: 200   Origin: Round 27, 2019 Draft (#802 overall)

YEAR	TM	LVL	AGE	G(GS)	IP	W-L	SV	K	WHIP	ERA	CSP	BB%	K%	HR%	GB%	ZSw%	ZCon%	OSw%	OCon%	BABIP	SLGCON	DRA-	WARP
2021	WM	A+	23	13(13)	62²	6-3	0	76	1.02	3.45		6.0%	30.2%	2.0%	35.4%					.289	.532	77	1.4
2021	ERI	AA	23	8(8)	44	3-1	0	40	1.00	2.66		4.7%	23.3%	1.2%	41.3%					.286	.433	108	0.2
2022	TOL	AAA	24	4(4)	17¹	0-2	0	19	1.27	4.15		7.0%	26.8%	4.2%	39.1%					.326	.667	99	0.2
2022	DET	MLB	24	15(15)	81²	3-6	0	54	1.20	4.19	56.3%	7.4%	15.9%	4.1%	37.1%	77.1%	84.2%	31.7%	79.1%	.242	.498	119	0.0
2023	TOL	AAA	25	9(1)	11¹	0-0	0	10	1.24	3.18		13.0%	21.7%	2.2%	26.7%	81.1%	78.3%	33.6%	52.8%	.241	.467	107	0.1
2023	DET	MLB	25	25(1)	35	2-3	2	31	1.37	3.60	43.7%	7.9%	20.4%	2.6%	42.2%	74.1%	85.5%	34.9%	68.6%	.305	.528	97	0.5
2024 DC	*DET*	*MLB*	*26*	*53(0)*	*56*	*3-3*	*0*	*40*	*1.38*	*4.74*	*51.5%*	*8.3%*	*16.6%*	*3.1%*	*38.3%*					*.286*	*.522*	*108*	*0.1*

2023 Arsenal: FA (96.7), CH (88.7), SI (95.9), SL (87.3), CU (81.6)   *Comps: Dillon Peters (67), Nick Martinez (66), Trevor Williams (65)*

What was originally thought to be a minor fatigue issue that might cost him a start or two ended up as an ulnar nerve entrapment that kept Brieske out of action for over a calendar year. The Tigers eased him back into the fold mid-June, and Brieske responded well, working in short bursts as a relief arm. His sinking fastball velocity was easily sitting in the mid-90s, complemented by his firm change and slider. He likes to live out of the zone with his secondaries, so the jump in chase rate he saw in 2023 is vital for him to maintain. The 2024 Tigers will have a lot of arms in competition for starters' innings, and it's likely Brieske will get pushed permanently to the bullpen, where A.J. Hinch can use him in late-inning, high-leverage situations.

Andrew Chafin LHP   Born: 06/17/90   Age: 34   Height: 6'2"   Weight: 235   Origin: Round 1, 2011 Draft (#43 overall)

YEAR	TM	LVL	AGE	G(GS)	IP	W-L	SV	K	WHIP	ERA	CSP	BB%	K%	HR%	GB%	ZSw%	ZCon%	OSw%	OCon%	BABIP	SLGCON	DRA-	WARP
2021	CHC	MLB	31	43(0)	39¹	0-2	0	37	0.84	2.06	57.2%	8.0%	24.7%	0.7%	49.5%	69.9%	85.0%	36.3%	57.6%	.204	.313	81	0.8
2021	OAK	MLB	31	28(0)	29¹	2-2	5	27	1.06	1.53	53.5%	6.0%	23.3%	2.6%	36.6%	71.0%	87.4%	38.1%	62.6%	.266	.443	87	0.5
2022	DET	MLB	32	64(0)	57¹	2-3	3	67	1.17	2.83	51.5%	7.8%	27.6%	2.1%	50.0%	69.7%	85.8%	33.9%	48.2%	.293	.477	77	1.2
2023	MIL	MLB	33	20(0)	17	1-1	0	14	1.41	5.82	42.2%	13.5%	18.9%	4.1%	46.9%	61.4%	88.7%	28.2%	59.6%	.239	.571	110	0.1
2023	AZ	MLB	33	43(0)	34¹	2-3	8	49	1.43	4.19	40.3%	12.0%	32.7%	2.0%	34.9%	61.8%	81.4%	37.0%	53.2%	.350	.627	89	0.6
2024 DC	*DET*	*MLB*	*34*	*53(0)*	*56*	*3-3*	*4*	*65*	*1.28*	*3.88*	*47.9%*	*9.6%*	*27.1%*	*2.8%*	*42.2%*					*.295*	*.544*	*91*	*0.5*

2023 Arsenal: SI (92.1), SL (83.4), FA (92), CH (86.1)   *Comps: Justin Wilson (66), Jake Diekman (63), Alan Embree (60)*

The Arizona Diamondbacks went to the World Series without Chafin, a very believable statement. He landed in Milwaukee at the trade deadline, where the Brewers were hoping for a reliable lefty arm out of the pen to support the beleaguered Hoby Milner and to compensate for losing Justin Wilson to injury. His post-trade line is a mixed bag, sometimes riding scoreless streaks, sometimes raising blood pressures all over Wisconsin. His walk rate inflated significantly from 2022, and he was used, albeit questionably, in plenty of high-leverage situations by Craig Counsell. Opponents hit him hard, placing him near the bottom of the league, and it didn't help that his slider lost a significant amount of horizontal movement. It'll be believable when another team goes to the World Series next year without Chafin, who signed a one-year deal with the Tigers.

José Cisnero RHP   Born: 04/11/89   Age: 35   Height: 6'3"   Weight: 258   Origin: IFA, 2007

YEAR	TM	LVL	AGE	G(GS)	IP	W-L	SV	K	WHIP	ERA	CSP	BB%	K%	HR%	GB%	ZSw%	ZCon%	OSw%	OCon%	BABIP	SLGCON	DRA-	WARP
2021	DET	MLB	32	67(0)	61²	4-4	4	62	1.33	3.65	53.1%	11.7%	23.4%	2.3%	44.6%	67.9%	79.6%	27.4%	70.2%	.281	.476	94	0.8
2022	TOL	AAA	33	6(0)	5²	1-0	0	6	0.71	3.18		4.5%	27.3%	0.0%	50.0%					.214	.357	91	0.1
2022	DET	MLB	33	28(0)	25	1-0	0	23	1.36	1.08	53.3%	18.1%	21.9%	0.0%	37.1%	68.2%	78.0%	26.8%	59.4%	.242	.290	116	0.0
2023	DET	MLB	34	63(0)	59¹	3-4	2	70	1.48	5.31	49.5%	9.4%	26.2%	3.7%	43.4%	70.9%	80.5%	30.4%	63.7%	.342	.638	92	1.0
2024 non	*DET*	*MLB*	*35*	*58(0)*	*50*	*2-2*	*0*	*51*	*1.38*	*4.65*	*50.6%*	*10.6%*	*23.2%*	*3.2%*	*40.8%*					*.291*	*.553*	*103*	*0.1*

2023 Arsenal: FA (95.9), SI (95.7), CU (84.8), CH (88.9), SL (87.6), FC (90), SW (82.4)   *Comps: Brad Boxberger (59), Justin Speier (57), Anthony Bass (57)*

After four solid seasons in Detroit where he largely outran his peripherals, Cisnero suffered death by BABIP and an acute case of dingeritis in his fifth year with the Tigers. The culprit: His sinker went out like an old water heater, losing more than half its whiff rate from 2022 and more than doubling its SLGCON, up to .563. The club put him on waivers prior to the postseason deadline, only to be ignored thanks to the Angels' estate sale. Cisnero was already on his second act in MLB, and age 34 might as well be Methuselah in MLB terms, but hey, Cher keeps threatening to retire, too.

Mason Englert RHP   Born: 11/01/99   Age: 24   Height: 6'4"   Weight: 206   Origin: Round 4, 2018 Draft (#119 overall)

YEAR	TM	LVL	AGE	G(GS)	IP	W-L	SV	K	WHIP	ERA	CSP	BB%	K%	HR%	GB%	ZSw%	ZCon%	OSw%	OCon%	BABIP	SLGCON	DRA-	WARP
2021	DE	A	21	19(19)	80²	6-3	0	90	1.23	4.35		7.6%	26.3%	1.2%	36.7%					.325	.514	113	0.2
2022	HIC	A+	22	21(21)	103¹	7-5	0	116	0.96	3.57		6.3%	28.3%	3.7%	41.4%					.234	.513	87	1.5
2022	FRI	AA	22	3(3)	15¹	1-1	0	20	1.24	4.11		7.7%	30.8%	1.5%	30.8%					.342	.538	83	0.2
2023	TOL	AAA	23	9(0)	11¹	1-0	0	19	1.76	7.15		7.4%	35.2%	7.4%	45.2%	71.1%	78.0%	33.6%	26.8%	.444	1.000	76	0.3
2023	DET	MLB	23	31(1)	56	4-3	0	41	1.50	5.46	49.3%	6.7%	16.2%	4.7%	38.3%	74.0%	84.2%	34.6%	64.3%	.307	.640	110	0.4
2024 DC	*DET*	*MLB*	*24*	*22(0)*	*24²*	*1-1*	*0*	*21*	*1.42*	*5.25*	*49.3%*	*8.1%*	*18.8%*	*3.6%*	*37.5%*					*.301*	*.577*	*118*	*-0.1*

2023 Arsenal: SL (84.5), FA (91.5), CH (83.9), CU (78.6), SW (80.9)   *Comps: Kendry Flores (69), J.B. Wendelken (65), Garrett Richards (64)*

A former over-slot fourth-round selection, Englert's professional debut was delayed nearly 35 months due to COVID and Tommy John surgery, but he showed enough during his brief run to convince the Tigers to pop him in last winter's Rule 5 draft. He was inconsistent working out of the bullpen, with strikeouts in particularly short supply, but with the required year under his belt, Detroit is now able to send him down to continue to refine his four-pitch arsenal. Nothing in his repertoire projects to be above-average but with additional time to develop, Englert could become a back-of-the-rotation innings-eater.

Alex Faedo RHP Born: 11/12/95 Age: 28 Height: 6'5" Weight: 225 Origin: Round 1, 2017 Draft (#18 overall)

YEAR	TM	LVL	AGE	G (GS)	IP	W-L	SV	K	WHIP	ERA	CSP	BB%	K%	HR%	GB%	ZSw%	ZCon%	OSw%	OCon%	BABIP	SLGCON	DRA-	WARP
2022	LAK	A	26	3(1)	10²	1-1	0	12	0.84	2.53		7.1%	28.6%	0.0%	38.5%	81.0%	78.4%	40.4%	31.6%	.231	.320	93	0.2
2022	DET	MLB	26	12(12)	53²	1-5	0	44	1.64	5.53	56.0%	10.2%	18.0%	2.9%	31.0%	70.6%	84.7%	29.9%	61.3%	.335	.585	142	-0.6
2023	TOL	AAA	27	7(7)	26¹	0-2	0	30	0.99	3.42		5.9%	29.4%	3.9%	30.3%	69.5%	80.2%	38.2%	47.3%	.258	.561	100	0.4
2023	DET	MLB	27	15(12)	64²	2-5	0	58	1.05	4.45	50.4%	7.6%	22.1%	4.6%	35.5%	67.3%	86.8%	32.3%	59.6%	.211	.533	106	0.6
2024 DC	DET	MLB	28	34(0)	37¹	2-2	0	31	1.37	4.86	52.8%	8.5%	19.4%	3.8%	33.7%					.286	.565	111	0.1

2023 Arsenal: FA (93), SL (82.6), CH (85.9)   Comps: Hector Noesí (66), Matt Andriese (63), Jerad Eickhoff (62)

Stop us if you've heard this one before: a young Tigers pitcher taken in the first round throws an underwhelming fastball and focuses more on soft contact than strikeouts. Unlike other players under this model, Faedo, as a three-pitch pitcher, throws his fastball almost half the time—a dangerous proposition given how often batters like to sidle up to it. But his slider and changeup, as he gains comfort with throwing them in the big-league environment, should clamor for more of a time-share in 2024. As a result, Faedo should fit in nicely with his fastball-pooh-poohing rotation-mates soon.

Jack Flaherty RHP Born: 10/15/95 Age: 28 Height: 6'4" Weight: 225 Origin: Round 1, 2014 Draft (#34 overall)

YEAR	TM	LVL	AGE	G (GS)	IP	W-L	SV	K	WHIP	ERA	CSP	BB%	K%	HR%	GB%	ZSw%	ZCon%	OSw%	OCon%	BABIP	SLGCON	DRA-	WARP
2021	STL	MLB	25	17(15)	78¹	9-2	0	85	1.06	3.22	55.7%	8.1%	26.4%	3.7%	39.0%	68.8%	82.9%	28.4%	54.3%	.236	.517	97	0.8
2022	SPR	AA	26	4(4)	16²	0-0	0	23	1.02	2.16		6.2%	35.4%	0.0%	26.3%					.342	.421	73	0.3
2022	STL	MLB	26	9(8)	36	2-1	0	33	1.61	4.25	52.4%	13.2%	19.8%	2.4%	41.1%	72.2%	82.1%	24.3%	58.8%	.314	.557	127	-0.1
2023	STL	MLB	27	20(20)	109²	7-6	0	106	1.55	4.43	44.9%	11.1%	21.9%	2.1%	45.1%	65.9%	84.5%	29.9%	60.6%	.346	.572	110	0.7
2023	BAL	MLB	27	9(7)	34²	1-3	0	42	1.67	6.75	44.6%	7.3%	25.5%	4.2%	35.5%	66.0%	79.0%	31.9%	60.0%	.390	.717	100	0.4
2024 DC	DET	MLB	28	24(24)	128²	7-9	0	134	1.34	4.32	47.7%	9.7%	24.0%	2.7%	41.7%					.297	.535	98	1.2

2023 Arsenal: FA (93.3), SL (84.4), KC (76.6), FC (88.9), CH (85.5), SI (90.2)   Comps: John Smoltz (75), Julio Teheran (74), Don Cardwell (73)

Flaherty went from marquee deadline addition to barely making the O's playoff roster in a jiffy. In 15 years, you'll look at his Baseball-Reference page and go, "He was on the Orioles?" Once considered one of the sport's best young arms, Flaherty now offers a disastrous combo of (1) lots of hits and (2) lots of walks. Trevor Williams was the only starter with at least 130 innings to post a worse WHIP in 2023. Some unknown future pitching coach may one day sprinkle developmental pixie dust and rediscover the version of Flaherty that finished fourth in the 2019 NL Cy Young, or at least take credit for it when the righty doesn't cough up that high-.300s BABIP again. Or, you know, maybe not. Some pitchers are just one-act plays.

Wilmer Flores RHP Born: 02/20/01 Age: 23 Height: 6'4" Weight: 225 Origin: IFA, 2020

YEAR	TM	LVL	AGE	G (GS)	IP	W-L	SV	K	WHIP	ERA	CSP	BB%	K%	HR%	GB%	ZSw%	ZCon%	OSw%	OCon%	BABIP	SLGCON	DRA-	WARP
2021	TIGW	ROK	20	3(2)	13	2-1	0	18	1.31	4.85		3.5%	31.6%	0.0%	58.8%					.441	.588		
2021	LAK	A	20	11(11)	53	4-3	0	72	1.30	3.40		9.8%	32.1%	0.4%	52.4%	63.5%	79.2%	31.4%	52.1%	.368	.448	99	0.6
2022	WM	A+	21	6(5)	19²	1-0	0	35	0.81	1.83		2.6%	45.5%	2.6%	57.9%					.333	.526	67	0.5
2022	ERI	AA	21	19(19)	83²	6-4	0	95	1.05	3.01		6.1%	27.5%	2.3%	45.7%					.280	.489	89	1.6
2023	WM	A+	22	3(3)	8¹	0-1	0	8	1.56	11.88		2.6%	21.1%	0.0%	55.6%					.444	.519	97	0.0
2023	ERI	AA	22	18(18)	80²	5-3	0	82	1.29	3.90		9.5%	24.3%	1.5%	48.6%					.313	.493	92	1.4
2024 DC	DET	MLB	23	13(3)	26	1-2	0	23	1.41	4.86		8.8%	20.2%	2.9%	40.8%					.305	.544	109	0.1

Comps: Mitch Keller (69), Jarred Cosart (66), Robert Gsellman (65)

Flores was the breakout of the Tigers' system in 2022, a former undrafted free agent signee who bullied Double-A hitters and looked poised to claim a spot in Detroit's beleaguered major-league rotation. In 2023, however, the pop-up prospect just got popped. The fastball velocity dipped early, forcing him to lean heavily on a mediocre-at-best changeup, which allowed Eastern League hitters to get their revenge and produce loud contact. Flores did provide a glimmer of hope in the fall, with the heater showing a bit more life and his two breakers surfacing as serviceable backup pitches.

Jason Foley RHP Born: 11/01/95 Age: 28 Height: 6'4" Weight: 215 Origin: Undrafted Free Agent, 2016

YEAR	TM	LVL	AGE	G (GS)	IP	W-L	SV	K	WHIP	ERA	CSP	BB%	K%	HR%	GB%	ZSw%	ZCon%	OSw%	OCon%	BABIP	SLGCON	DRA-	WARP
2021	TOL	AAA	25	32(0)	34²	1-1	2	36	1.53	4.41		12.4%	23.5%	3.3%	55.3%					.330	.602	95	0.6
2021	DET	MLB	25	11(0)	10¹	0-0	0	6	1.26	2.61	51.0%	11.1%	13.3%	2.2%	58.1%	65.2%	82.2%	25.6%	81.8%	.233	.484	112	0.0
2022	TOL	AAA	26	4(0)	5	1-0	0	6	1.20	3.60		4.8%	28.6%	4.8%	57.1%					.308	.571	96	0.1
2022	DET	MLB	26	60(0)	60¹	1-0	0	43	1.38	3.88	59.4%	4.3%	16.8%	0.8%	56.5%	71.7%	90.3%	30.9%	68.4%	.355	.442	74	1.4
2023	DET	MLB	27	70(0)	69	3-3	7	55	1.16	2.61	49.0%	5.4%	19.9%	0.7%	56.6%	66.1%	89.7%	35.4%	71.6%	.310	.431	83	1.4
2024 DC	DET	MLB	28	53(0)	56	3-2	0	36	1.35	4.34	53.2%	7.2%	14.7%	2.1%	54.5%					.293	.470	99	0.3

2023 Arsenal: SI (97.3), SL (88.6), CH (91.4), FA (96.7)   Comps: Kevin McCarthy (49), Jake Petricka (47), Ryan Pressly (47)

Foley artists recreate everyday sounds in movies, which makes nominative sense here, as Foley's modest strikeout numbers don't attract a ton of attention despite his ability to limit free passes and induce weak contact. But Foley isn't the typical low-stuff, high-command contact manager tinkering along in the background. He has leading-man stuff, with a bowling-ball sinker that averages 97 and kisses triple digits, capable of sounding like punching a slab of meat when it hits the catcher's mitt. The few times he does venture toward the top of the zone with the sinker, he can induce whiffs but seems to be under orders to pound the bottom of the zone to try to induce ground balls, which he does at an elite rate. A newer, hard (91 mph) changeup is a better whiff-getter and offsets an inconsistent slider that too often winds up in the fat part of the zone, but further refinement of his arsenal is needed to keep Foley from being mere background noise in the Tigers' bullpen.

Sawyer Gipson-Long RHP Born: 12/12/97 Age: 26 Height: 6'4" Weight: 225 Origin: Round 6, 2019 Draft (#179 overall)

YEAR	TM	LVL	AGE	G (GS)	IP	W-L	SV	K	WHIP	ERA	CSP	BB%	K%	HR%	GB%	ZSw%	ZCon%	OSw%	OCon%	BABIP	SLGCON	DRA-	WARP
2021	FTM	A	23	14(13)	67¹	5-5	0	95	1.32	4.54		6.1%	32.0%	2.0%	42.9%	67.7%	76.9%	39.2%	51.3%	.369	.635	98	0.8
2021	CR	A+	23	6(6)	29²	3-3	0	39	1.25	4.55		7.4%	32.2%	3.3%	37.0%					.348	.644	83	0.6
2022	CR	A+	24	10(10)	49²	5-2	0	52	0.93	1.99		6.8%	27.1%	2.1%	50.0%					.238	.421	89	0.8
2022	ERI	AA	24	7(7)	35²	2-2	0	35	1.29	4.54		6.0%	23.3%	4.7%	46.6%					.313	.686	101	0.5
2022	WCH	AA	24	8(7)	37²	3-4	0	35	1.38	7.17		3.6%	20.8%	3.0%	46.8%					.345	.598	89	0.4
2023	ERI	AA	25	14(13)	65	6-5	0	76	1.02	3.74		5.9%	29.8%	4.7%	43.8%					.260	.642	78	1.7
2023	TOL	AAA	25	8(6)	34²	2-3	0	50	1.36	5.45		9.2%	32.7%	5.2%	37.6%	62.5%	82.7%	36.6%	44.9%	.325	.729	79	0.9
2023	DET	MLB	25	4(4)	20	1-0	0	26	1.10	2.70	44.0%	9.8%	31.7%	2.4%	35.4%	63.7%	74.7%	36.8%	55.1%	.261	.542	99	0.2
2024 DC	DET	MLB	26	10(10)	41²	1-3	0	46	1.29	4.52	44.0%	7.5%	25.5%	3.8%	37.1%					.302	.612	105	0.3

2023 Arsenal: SL (82.3), CH (86.1), FA (93.8), SI (92.6), FC (87.5)   *Comps: Taylor Jungmann (68), Spencer Turnbull (67), Shane Greene (67)*

Late-season starts against the Angels, White Sox, A's and Royals made for a gentle beginning to the big-league career of Gipson-Long. He was more than up to the task against this daisy chain of opponents, finding success by leaning more heavily on his slider and change and using the fastball to steal a strike early. DRA-, which adjusts for quality of opponent, sees an average arm, though it'd be more impressive if Gipson-Long could find the corner more often with his slider, given how rarely MLB batters chased it. It's unreasonable to expect sub-three ERA's to continue, but SGL showed enough during his brief stint in Detroit to be considered a future swingman for the Tigers.

Tyler Holton LHP Born: 06/13/96 Age: 28 Height: 6'2" Weight: 200 Origin: Round 9, 2018 Draft (#279 overall)

YEAR	TM	LVL	AGE	G (GS)	IP	W-L	SV	K	WHIP	ERA	CSP	BB%	K%	HR%	GB%	ZSw%	ZCon%	OSw%	OCon%	BABIP	SLGCON	DRA-	WARP
2021	AMA	AA	25	18(7)	48¹	4-3	1	56	1.41	6.33		6.1%	26.2%	2.8%	52.5%					.366	.626	94	0.5
2021	RNO	AAA	25	8(4)	16	0-1	0	22	2.06	7.87		7.5%	27.5%	1.3%	44.2%					.510	.769	77	0.3
2022	AZ	MLB	26	10(0)	9	0-0	0	6	1.11	3.00	53.7%	5.1%	15.4%	2.6%	30.0%	74.1%	79.1%	37.6%	60.5%	.241	.400	121	0.0
2023	DET	MLB	27	59(1)	85¹	3-2	1	74	0.87	2.11	50.1%	5.6%	22.8%	2.8%	44.6%	67.9%	81.4%	33.0%	60.3%	.213	.402	93	1.3
2024 DC	DET	MLB	28	46(0)	49²	3-2	0	44	1.34	4.46	50.4%	7.4%	20.5%	2.9%	42.2%					.303	.533	102	0.2

2023 Arsenal: FA (91.7), CH (83), FC (88.1), SW (81.6), SI (91.2), CU (78.2)   *Comps: Robby Scott (69), Tyler Olson (68), Darin Downs (65)*

The teacher's pet of the Tigers' pitching development department, whose motto is ABSC (Always Be Soft-Contacting), lefty Holton relies on wrong-footing batters with an arsenal that's looking up at the Mariana Trench. It's not exciting, but that's by design, as the Tigers continue to assemble the Soviet architecture of pitching staffs: no-frills brute efficiency that nourishes the body but not the soul. To be fair to Holton, if that's true, last season he served up some of the most vitamin-fortified gruel science can imagine; hitters slugged (!) .219 on his four-seamer.

Brant Hurter LHP Born: 09/06/98 Age: 25 Height: 6'6" Weight: 250 Origin: Round 7, 2021 Draft (#195 overall)

YEAR	TM	LVL	AGE	G (GS)	IP	W-L	SV	K	WHIP	ERA	CSP	BB%	K%	HR%	GB%	ZSw%	ZCon%	OSw%	OCon%	BABIP	SLGCON	DRA-	WARP
2022	LAK	A	23	10(6)	42¹	3-3	0	57	0.94	2.98		3.6%	33.7%	2.4%	45.2%	67.0%	81.4%	38.7%	46.4%	.300	.534	80	1.1
2022	WM	A+	23	11(10)	50²	4-1	0	62	1.09	3.20		5.4%	30.4%	1.0%	57.8%					.333	.516	80	1.0
2022	ERI	AA	23	4(2)	13²	0-2	0	17	1.83	7.90		6.3%	26.6%	1.6%	51.2%					.476	.628	81	0.3
2023	ERI	AA	24	26(26)	118	6-7	0	133	1.19	3.28		6.6%	26.7%	1.4%	52.8%					.325	.495	84	2.7
2024 DC	DET	MLB	25	3(3)	12²	0-1	0	11	1.32	4.39		7.3%	20.4%	2.8%	42.1%					.301	.525	101	0.1

Comps: Framber Valdez (78), Matthew Boyd (72), Sean Hjelle (72)

You know how a pitcher will kind of saunter and strut, loose-limbed, after striking a batter out? Hurter somehow imbues that feeling into his actual pitching motion, a lackadaisical flap that makes his strikeouts feel more earned, or at least premeditated. While most Tigers pitching prospects scuffled this past season, Hurter was one of the few who took a clear step forward in his development. He's a low-slot lefty who pounds the zone with his plus sinker, slider and improving change. The heater lacks premium velocity and Hurter is not an arm that will fare well multiple times through an order, but his ability to avoid barrels and pitch from deceptive angles will allow him to get hitters out at the highest level.

★ ★ ★ *2024 Top 101 Prospect* **#17** ★ ★ ★

Jackson Jobe RHP Born: 07/30/02 Age: 21 Height: 6'2" Weight: 190 Origin: Round 1, 2021 Draft (#3 overall)

YEAR	TM	LVL	AGE	G (GS)	IP	W-L	SV	K	WHIP	ERA	CSP	BB%	K%	HR%	GB%	ZSw%	ZCon%	OSw%	OCon%	BABIP	SLGCON	DRA-	WARP
2022	LAK	A	19	18(18)	61²	2-5	0	71	1.36	4.52		9.3%	26.3%	4.4%	40.2%	69.3%	80.9%	32.6%	58.4%	.299	.652	103	0.9
2022	WM	A+	19	3(3)	15²	2-0	0	10	0.96	1.15		7.9%	15.9%	3.2%	40.4%					.178	.362	115	0.0
2023	LAK	A	20	6(6)	16	0-1	0	20	1.06	2.25		4.4%	29.4%	2.9%	27.9%	70.6%	72.7%	34.2%	64.7%	.293	.512	78	0.3
2023	WM	A+	20	8(8)	40	2-3	0	54	1.05	3.60		1.9%	33.8%	4.4%	43.7%					.337	.634	54	1.0
2023	ERI	AA	20	1(1)	6	0-0	0	6	0.67	0.00		0.0%	25.0%	0.0%	33.3%					.222	.222		
2024 non	DET	MLB	21	58(0)	50	2-2	0	42	1.45	5.65		7.9%	19.3%	4.5%	34.4%					.306	.616	125	-0.4

2023 Arsenal: FA (97), SL (83), FC (91.4), CH (86.4)   *Comps: Spencer Adams (58), Sean Reid-Foley (55), Jacob Turner (50)*

A contentious selection with the third-overall pick in 2021, Jobe looked like he might be headed towards the fate of so many other Tigers first-round pitching selections. Suffering an inconsistent first professional season and missing the first half of 2023 with lumbar spine inflammation, he supplied no shortage of concern about his long-term projection. However, once healthy in the second half of the season, Jobe looked again like a potential top-of-the-rotation arm, capable of dominating a lineup. He was carrying his mid-90s velocity deep into games and added a cutter to go along with his plus slider and change. A full, healthy season in 2024 and we might be talking about Jobe being the top minor-league arm in baseball—someone who falls off the prospect lists due to graduation rather than failure.

Alex Lange RHP   Born: 10/02/95   Age: 28   Height: 6'3"   Weight: 202   Origin: Round 1, 2017 Draft (#30 overall)

YEAR	TM	LVL	AGE	G(GS)	IP	W-L	SV	K	WHIP	ERA	CSP	BB%	K%	HR%	GB%	ZSw%	ZCon%	OSw%	OCon%	BABIP	SLGCON	DRA-	WARP
2021	TOL	AAA	25	19(0)	21²	2-1	1	27	1.80	4.57		17.0%	27.0%	0.0%	33.9%					.393	.536	95	0.4
2021	DET	MLB	25	36(0)	35²	1-3	1	39	1.49	4.04	52.2%	9.9%	24.1%	3.1%	44.2%	66.7%	85.8%	38.2%	51.2%	.323	.577	99	0.3
2022	DET	MLB	26	71(0)	63¹	7-4	0	82	1.23	3.41	49.0%	11.4%	30.3%	1.8%	54.2%	58.4%	82.2%	38.1%	38.8%	.288	.483	76	1.4
2023	DET	MLB	27	67(0)	66	7-5	26	79	1.33	3.68	36.2%	15.6%	27.4%	2.1%	50.3%	58.9%	84.4%	34.0%	44.4%	.245	.477	100	0.8
2024 DC	DET	MLB	28	53(0)	56	3-6	30	78	1.35	4.04	43.3%	12.8%	31.8%	2.4%	49.1%					.305	.550	91	0.5

2023 Arsenal: KC (87.1), SI (95.9), CH (89.4), FA (96.2)   *Comps: Ryne Stanek (76), Josh Staumont (75), Michael Mariot (74)*

In the Chinese zodiac, tigers are believed to be so powerful they ward off the three most common household disasters: fire, thieves and ghosts. As a Double Tiger (LSU *and* Detroit), Lange certainly embodies the first part: He doesn't let batters get hot against him, instead pounding balls straight into the earth, scattering broken kindling about. He doesn't let hitters steal from him, either, employing his deadly heavy curveball to keep would-be thieves of extra bases tethered to home plate. But the third leg of this stool is lacking. Rather than busting ghosts, he gives them safe, free passage to first base thanks to below-average command. Walks aren't an issue if you strike all the other hitters out, but if batters do manage to sneak a hit through the infield, all of a sudden that's a roaring heap of trouble. Time to find a proton pack and declare he ain't afraid of no MLB hitters.

Ty Madden RHP   Born: 02/21/00   Age: 24   Height: 6'3"   Weight: 215   Origin: Round 1, 2021 Draft (#32 overall)

YEAR	TM	LVL	AGE	G(GS)	IP	W-L	SV	K	WHIP	ERA	CSP	BB%	K%	HR%	GB%	ZSw%	ZCon%	OSw%	OCon%	BABIP	SLGCON	DRA-	WARP
2022	WM	A+	22	19(19)	87	6-4	0	84	1.09	3.10		7.2%	23.4%	2.8%	32.1%					.254	.469	123	-0.2
2022	ERI	AA	22	7(7)	35²	2-2	0	49	1.12	2.78		8.5%	34.5%	4.2%	46.9%					.293	.637	72	1.0
2023	ERI	AA	23	26(25)	118	3-4	0	146	1.28	3.43		10.2%	29.7%	3.3%	37.3%					.309	.613	86	2.6
2024 non	DET	MLB	24	58(0)	50	2-2	0	48	1.44	5.18		9.9%	21.7%	3.7%	33.2%					.299	.588	116	-0.2

Comps: Robert Dugger (84), Cory Abbott (83), Adam Warren (82)

Prospect writers are so boring. They're always going on and on about "consistency" and "repeatability" and "mechanics." Where's their awe at the unpredictable? Madden has put together just enough good days to accrue some buzz as a potential starter. In any given start—hell, in any given plate appearance—any pitch could be plus, or slap the backstop. Variety is the spice of life, someone once said, though they probably weren't holding a radar gun at the time. The upper-90s fastball and slider make for a good reliever fallback, but maybe not yet in any situation where you can't afford a hit batter or a homer.

Kenta Maeda RHP   Born: 04/11/88   Age: 36   Height: 6'1"   Weight: 185   Origin: IFA, 2016

YEAR	TM	LVL	AGE	G(GS)	IP	W-L	SV	K	WHIP	ERA	CSP	BB%	K%	HR%	GB%	ZSw%	ZCon%	OSw%	OCon%	BABIP	SLGCON	DRA-	WARP
2021	MIN	MLB	33	21(21)	106¹	6-5	0	113	1.30	4.66	52.9%	7.1%	24.9%	3.5%	39.0%	71.7%	83.7%	35.9%	54.7%	.318	.597	103	0.8
2023	STP	AAA	35	4(4)	13¹	0-0	0	17	1.13	2.03		9.1%	30.9%	1.8%	36.4%	64.3%	87.3%	24.8%	58.6%	.281	.394	93	0.2
2023	MIN	MLB	35	21(20)	104¹	6-8	0	117	1.17	4.23	47.2%	6.5%	27.3%	4.0%	32.1%	70.0%	85.4%	34.9%	54.4%	.293	.610	97	1.4
2024 DC	DET	MLB	36	23(23)	117²	6-7	0	114	1.20	3.86	48.5%	7.0%	23.2%	3.5%	35.3%					.280	.554	93	1.5

2023 Arsenal: FS (84.2), FA (91), SL (82.2), SW (80.4), SI (90.4), CU (76.6), FC (87.5)   *Comps: Jack Morris (78), Zack Greinke (78), Corey Kluber (78)*

Baseball gives us plenty of false beauties. Every year, there are a half-dozen hurlers who show up to throw 100 with a wicked slider and a changeup science just discovered last week. Those are puff. They're movie stars, playing a show designed to help you and then forget that time will soon gobble up that moment and eliminate it. Baseball is suffering from a real and increasing dearth of real people—people like Maeda. Despite the language barrier he faces, he's funny and personable, focused and fiery. He's also deeply damaged, both by the Tommy John surgery he had to undergo at an advanced age and by the ravages of time. Keep your superstars. The real joy in baseball lies in watching a 35-year-old with waning stuff and a newfangled countdown clock on him, reaching into the future over and over to pluck out the pitch that will flummox a far more talented opponent. Maeda has a couple years of that left.

Matt Manning RHP   Born: 01/28/98   Age: 26   Height: 6'6"   Weight: 195   Origin: Round 1, 2016 Draft (#9 overall)

YEAR	TM	LVL	AGE	G(GS)	IP	W-L	SV	K	WHIP	ERA	CSP	BB%	K%	HR%	GB%	ZSw%	ZCon%	OSw%	OCon%	BABIP	SLGCON	DRA-	WARP
2021	TOL	AAA	23	7(7)	32¹	1-3	0	36	1.55	8.07		6.9%	25.0%	7.6%	34.7%					.337	.823	110	0.3
2021	DET	MLB	23	18(18)	85¹	4-7	0	57	1.51	5.80	57.8%	8.6%	14.8%	2.6%	44.7%	66.2%	88.9%	30.6%	72.8%	.306	.533	134	-0.7
2022	TOL	AAA	24	6(6)	20¹	1-1	0	23	1.43	2.66		11.5%	26.4%	0.0%	47.2%					.358	.431	93	0.3
2022	DET	MLB	24	12(12)	63	2-3	0	48	1.17	3.43	56.5%	7.2%	18.3%	2.3%	41.0%	69.1%	85.9%	33.0%	62.7%	.259	.421	106	0.4
2023	TOL	AAA	25	3(3)	8²	0-0	0	9	1.85	0.00		20.5%	23.1%	0.0%	45.5%	82.2%	85.0%	22.1%	60.9%	.364	.409	104	0.1
2023	DET	MLB	25	15(15)	78	5-4	0	50	1.04	3.58	54.9%	6.6%	15.8%	3.5%	38.1%	68.7%	84.6%	25.8%	72.9%	.216	.455	119	0.1
2024 DC	DET	MLB	26	19(19)	101	5-8	0	74	1.46	5.21	56.2%	8.7%	16.5%	3.3%	40.8%					.296	.543	117	0.0

2023 Arsenal: FA (93.3), SW (82), CU (79.6), CH (87)   *Comps: Jarred Cosart (70), Drew Hutchison (69), Zach Eflin (69)*

At this point, Manning's lack of strikeouts is starting to look like a feature rather than a bug. Manning relies on his heater more than his postmodern-pitching colleagues, but he rarely got whiffs on it. And far from being a contact manager, batters hit him hard. The stingy parks of the AL Central protected him from accruing too much damage, but when you pop the hood on his 2023, this Motor City denizen is leaking oil. Maybe Manning could take a page out of the book of fellow first-rounder and Extension King Logan Gilbert and work on refining his secondaries, as Gilbert did in refining his slider and adding a splitter. The first step will be logging a healthy season, as Manning's 2023 was once again cut short—this time with a fractured foot.

Shelby Miller RHP Born: 10/10/90 Age: 33 Height: 6'3" Weight: 225 Origin: Round 1, 2009 Draft (#19 overall)

YEAR	TM	LVL	AGE	G (GS)	IP	W-L	SV	K	WHIP	ERA	CSP	BB%	K%	HR%	GB%	ZSw%	ZCon%	OSw%	OCon%	BABIP	SLGCON	DRA-	WARP
2021	IND	AAA	30	10(1)	14	2-1	0	22	0.93	3.86		5.4%	39.3%	1.8%	41.9%					.300	.484	78	0.3
2021	IOW	AAA	30	3(3)	10¹	0-0	0	15	0.97	1.74		14.3%	35.7%	2.4%	47.6%					.150	.333	99	0.2
2021	CHC	MLB	30	3(0)	2	0-0	0	1	6.00	31.50	52.2%	27.8%	5.6%	0.0%	41.7%	78.8%	88.5%	21.2%	90.9%	.583	.818	122	0.0
2021	PIT	MLB	30	10(0)	10²	0-1	0	7	1.41	5.06	58.1%	13.6%	15.9%	6.8%	36.7%	71.4%	71.7%	20.2%	66.7%	.222	.633	132	-0.1
2022	SWB	AAA	31	16(0)	21	2-2	4	25	0.90	1.71		7.1%	29.4%	1.2%	30.8%					.240	.373	95	0.3
2022	SAC	AAA	31	27(1)	32¹	0-2	8	44	1.24	3.62		11.0%	32.4%	2.2%	32.9%	62.7%	78.0%	28.2%	51.2%	.306	.581	90	0.4
2022	SF	MLB	31	4(0)	7	0-1	0	14	1.29	6.43	59.3%	10.0%	46.7%	0.0%	23.1%	51.6%	81.2%	27.7%	72.2%	.462	.692	78	0.1
2023	LAD	MLB	32	36(1)	42	3-0	1	42	0.90	1.71	50.4%	11.7%	25.8%	1.8%	38.0%	64.2%	81.1%	25.9%	60.0%	.167	.343	99	0.5
2024 DC	DET	MLB	33	46(0)	49²	3-2	0	48	1.33	4.37	52.2%	10.3%	22.4%	3.3%	37.7%					.275	.539	100	0.2

2023 Arsenal: FA (93.7), FS (85.9), SW (82.2), SI (93.5)   Comps: Wily Peralta (59), Oliver Pérez (59), Dennis Eckersley (58)

When he signed with the Dodgers for $1.5 million, Miller seemed sure to be one of the biggest bargains of the offseason. Armed with one of the flatter fastballs in MLB and a slider with upwards of 14 inches of sweep, Miller folded in a splitter to steel himself against the platoon splits that come with having a huge sweeping breaking ball. It worked, sort of. Miller posted a career-low .254 wOBA against left-handed batters, but also walked 17.1% of them, because he threw his splitter for a ball over 50% of the time. In this case, we actually *do* gotta hand it to him, as it's his first time throwing 40 innings since *Old Town Road* topped the charts.

Casey Mize RHP Born: 05/01/97 Age: 27 Height: 6'3" Weight: 212 Origin: Round 1, 2018 Draft (#1 overall)

YEAR	TM	LVL	AGE	G (GS)	IP	W-L	SV	K	WHIP	ERA	CSP	BB%	K%	HR%	GB%	ZSw%	ZCon%	OSw%	OCon%	BABIP	SLGCON	DRA-	WARP
2021	DET	MLB	24	30(30)	150¹	7-9	0	118	1.14	3.71	54.5%	6.7%	19.3%	3.9%	48.0%	66.6%	85.4%	29.8%	63.7%	.254	.531	110	0.6
2022	DET	MLB	25	2(2)	10	0-1	0	4	1.50	5.40	57.1%	4.4%	8.9%	2.2%	35.9%	69.6%	97.9%	27.0%	70.4%	.316	.590	127	0.0
2024 DC	DET	MLB	27	16(16)	74¹	3-6	0	55	1.39	4.82	53.5%	8.1%	16.9%	2.8%	44.4%					.295	.517	109	0.3

Comps: Daniel Mengden (65), Kyle Drabek (64), Erik Johnson (63)

After missing time in 2020 with a shoulder injury, and then missing most of 2022 and all of 2023 with an elbow injury that will-they-won't-they'd around until TJ surgery finally became a necessity, word on the street is Mize will enter 2024 ready to finally assume his rightful place in the Tigers rotation. That seat might not be quite as grand as in years past, with Tarik Skubal looking poised to become the staff ace. But a healthy Mize would be a huge boost to a pitching-poor club that's had to lean more on offensive contributions during this phase of the Tigers rebuild, which has been the equivalent of running out of milk while making omelets and substituting Elmer's glue.

Reese Olson RHP Born: 07/31/99 Age: 24 Height: 6'1" Weight: 160 Origin: Round 13, 2018 Draft (#395 overall)

YEAR	TM	LVL	AGE	G (GS)	IP	W-L	SV	K	WHIP	ERA	CSP	BB%	K%	HR%	GB%	ZSw%	ZCon%	OSw%	OCon%	BABIP	SLGCON	DRA-	WARP
2021	WIS	A+	21	14(14)	69	5-4	0	79	1.35	4.30		11.9%	26.9%	1.7%	43.4%					.312	.497	88	1.2
2021	WM	A+	21	2(2)	11	1-0	0	14	0.73	0.00		4.9%	34.1%	0.0%	44.0%					.240	.280	87	0.2
2021	ERI	AA	21	5(5)	24²	2-1	0	21	1.30	4.74		13.5%	20.2%	1.0%	49.3%					.250	.397	110	0.1
2022	ERI	AA	22	26(25)	119²	8-6	0	168	1.23	4.14		7.5%	33.1%	3.0%	42.1%					.337	.647	70	3.4
2023	TOL	AAA	23	10(10)	36²	2-3	0	47	1.75	6.38		12.6%	26.9%	2.9%	51.9%	61.3%	76.1%	33.2%	55.8%	.374	.696	85	0.9
2023	DET	MLB	23	21(18)	103²	5-7	0	103	1.12	3.99	46.9%	7.8%	24.4%	3.3%	42.1%	66.2%	86.7%	32.1%	52.8%	.255	.509	97	1.4
2024 DC	DET	MLB	24	24(24)	123²	6-9	0	124	1.39	4.65	46.9%	9.7%	23.0%	3.1%	41.8%					.300	.560	105	0.7

2023 Arsenal: SW (84.8), FA (94.9), SI (94.9), CH (87.8), CU (78.9)   Comps: Jake Faria (76), Joe Ross (74), Yordano Ventura (72)

Olson is the final boss of the Tigers' anti-fastball rotation, leading with a slider that drops like an airshow finale designed to make the crowd say "oooh" and leave batters shaking their heads as they trudge back to the dugout. He pairs it with a hard, tunneling changeup that also gets whiffs—when he can land it. But while the high-flying slider elicits whiffs aplenty, the rest of the arsenal remains grounded. His fastball and sinker regularly get hit hard, and while his surface numbers are shiny, there's trouble brewing in how hard and how often batters are able to achieve liftoff. Olson gets into bad counts too often, spurring the dingeritis that's dogged him since the minors. He'll have to find a way to get ahead more often if he doesn't want his wings clipped back to Toledo.

Tarik Skubal LHP Born: 11/20/96 Age: 27 Height: 6'3" Weight: 240 Origin: Round 9, 2018 Draft (#255 overall)

YEAR	TM	LVL	AGE	G (GS)	IP	W-L	SV	K	WHIP	ERA	CSP	BB%	K%	HR%	GB%	ZSw%	ZCon%	OSw%	OCon%	BABIP	SLGCON	DRA-	WARP
2021	DET	MLB	24	31(29)	149¹	8-12	0	164	1.26	4.34	58.0%	7.4%	25.9%	5.5%	38.4%	70.2%	80.9%	30.8%	58.7%	.278	.665	119	-0.1
2022	DET	MLB	25	21(21)	117²	7-8	0	117	1.16	3.52	56.7%	6.7%	24.5%	1.9%	46.2%	69.8%	84.2%	36.4%	58.5%	.301	.508	90	1.8
2023	TOL	AAA	26	3(3)	9²	0-0	0	13	0.93	1.86		8.1%	35.1%	2.7%	52.4%	62.2%	82.6%	29.9%	43.5%	.250	.476	80	0.3
2023	DET	MLB	26	15(15)	80¹	7-3	0	102	0.90	2.80	51.0%	4.5%	32.9%	1.3%	50.8%	70.3%	79.1%	37.6%	51.6%	.289	.458	71	2.2
2024 DC	DET	MLB	27	29(29)	157¹	10-9	0	177	1.11	3.03	55.1%	7.0%	27.5%	2.6%	45.3%					.282	.510	75	3.4

2023 Arsenal: FA (95.8), CH (84.2), SL (87.6), SI (95.7), CU (76.3)   Comps: Drew Smyly (64), Blake Snell (62), Alex Wood (61)

Like the kid who walks in on the first day of school with a cool new look, Skubal returned from the IL in July looking like he spent his summer lifting weights and reading fashion magazines. His fastball and sinker both had a little more oomph, but the real stunner was his changeup; the improved shape of this pitch paired with better command allowed him to throw it more often than ever, decreasing his reliance on a less-impressive slider. Despite increased usage of the *cambio*, batters were as helpless as ever flailing after the pitch. With another offseason to continue tinkering with the slider, it feels like soon everyone will be saying He's All That.

Spencer Turnbull RHP Born: 09/18/92 Age: 31 Height: 6'3" Weight: 210 Origin: Round 2, 2014 Draft (#63 overall)

YEAR	TM	LVL	AGE	G (GS)	IP	W-L	SV	K	WHIP	ERA	CSP	BB%	K%	HR%	GB%	ZSw%	ZCon%	OSw%	OCon%	BABIP	SLGCON	DRA-	WARP
2021	DET	MLB	28	9(9)	50	4-2	0	44	0.98	2.88	53.6%	6.0%	21.9%	1.0%	57.1%	70.6%	85.7%	32.6%	61.5%	.255	.377	85	0.9
2023	TOL	AAA	30	6(6)	21	0-1	0	25	1.95	6.86		10.8%	24.5%	2.0%	37.5%	60.6%	79.4%	27.7%	63.1%	.452	.766	93	0.3
2023	DET	MLB	30	7(7)	31	1-4	0	24	1.68	7.26	48.6%	10.3%	16.6%	3.4%	46.6%	64.3%	85.1%	31.7%	68.0%	.327	.602	114	0.1
2024 non	DET	MLB	31	58(0)	50	2-2	0	42	1.42	4.84	48.5%	9.1%	18.9%	2.7%	47.4%					.301	.526	107	0.0

2023 Arsenal: HC (93.6), SL (84.9), SI (93.8), CH (88.3), CU (78.8)　　　　Comps: Chris Bassitt (61), Jordan Zimmermann (61), Brian Lawrence (60)

My, how the Turnbull turntables have turned: throw a no-hitter in 2021, get non-tendered in 2023. TJ surgery shortened the distance between those two points, and a neck injury plus a cracked toenail accentuated by a case of the Detroit Malaise (for which Eduardo Rodriguez is seemingly Patient Zero) turned the telescope around entirely. Saying the quiet part out loud, Scott Harris said of Turnbull's non-tender that "both sides needed a fresh start," once Turnbull petitioned for and won an extra year of service time after being optioned to the minors during his recovery in August. Now a new team will get a chance to play with Turnbull's deep pitch arsenal (fun!) and try to help him lock in his command (less fun!). Still, go ahead and lock in "Spencer Turnbulls On Parade" as your fantasy baseball team name for 2024; we have a good feeling.

Andrew Vasquez LHP Born: 09/14/93 Age: 30 Height: 6'6" Weight: 235 Origin: Round 32, 2015 Draft (#950 overall)

YEAR	TM	LVL	AGE	G (GS)	IP	W-L	SV	K	WHIP	ERA	CSP	BB%	K%	HR%	GB%	ZSw%	ZCon%	OSw%	OCon%	BABIP	SLGCON	DRA-	WARP
2021	OKC	AAA	27	6(0)	6	0-0	0	11	1.33	3.00		7.7%	42.3%	0.0%	38.5%					.462	.538	72	0.1
2021	STP	AAA	27	33(0)	42¹	4-0	0	68	1.02	3.61		12.1%	37.4%	2.7%	60.8%					.216	.532	104	0.4
2021	LAD	MLB	27	2(0)	1²	0-0	0	3	0.60	0.00	64.0%	0.0%	50.0%	0.0%	100.0%	71.4%	70.0%	38.5%	80.0%	.333	.333	86	0.0
2022	BUF	AAA	28	10(0)	11	2-0	1	15	0.45	2.45		5.0%	37.5%	0.0%	66.7%					.143	.190	80	0.3
2022	SAC	AAA	28	14(0)	16¹	5-0	1	23	1.10	2.20		7.6%	34.8%	1.5%	27.8%	52.8%	86.2%	33.8%	50.0%	.343	.500	90	0.2
2022	TOR	MLB	28	9(0)	6²	0-0	0	6	1.35	8.10	51.1%	9.4%	18.8%	3.1%	50.0%	43.5%	90.0%	30.6%	50.0%	.263	.450	102	0.1
2022	SF	MLB	28	1(0)	2	0-0	0	4	0.50	0.00	55.2%	14.3%	57.1%	0.0%	50.0%	46.7%	100.0%	10.0%	0.0%	.000	.000	97	0.0
2023	DET	MLB	29	12(0)	8²	0-0	0	9	2.31	8.31	46.7%	18.4%	18.4%	0.0%	55.2%	57.7%	95.6%	32.0%	74.4%	.393	.536	98	0.1
2023	PHI	MLB	29	30(0)	39²	2-1	0	34	1.24	2.27	52.2%	8.2%	20.0%	2.4%	42.7%	58.7%	91.0%	26.9%	60.7%	.277	.443	98	0.5
2024 non	DET	MLB	30	58(0)	50	2-2	0	43	1.29	4.19	51.2%	9.2%	20.0%	2.5%	45.7%					.277	.483	94	0.4

2023 Arsenal: SW (80.5), SI (88.8), FA (89.2), CH (83.4)　　　　Comps: Danny Coulombe (51), Jake Diekman (49), Sam Freeman (49)

In an iconic episode of The Simpsons, Marge finds a pink Chanel suit at a discount store that magically propels her into a different social stratosphere. Similarly, Vasquez has made an MLB career out of a slider he throws a whopping 80% of the time, papering over his substandard fastball. But like Marge eventually runs out of ways to refashion her suit to impress the ladies at the country club, Vasquez also has only so much fabric to work with. Despite some shiny surface numbers and the most appealing thing to baseball execs, years of cost control, the Tigers let him walk this offseason. But that's okay, he wouldn't want to be a member of any club that would have this version of him as a member anyway.

Will Vest RHP Born: 06/06/95 Age: 29 Height: 6'0" Weight: 180 Origin: Round 12, 2017 Draft (#365 overall)

YEAR	TM	LVL	AGE	G (GS)	IP	W-L	SV	K	WHIP	ERA	CSP	BB%	K%	HR%	GB%	ZSw%	ZCon%	OSw%	OCon%	BABIP	SLGCON	DRA-	WARP
2021	TOL	AAA	26	23(0)	25²	1-3	2	25	1.36	4.91		7.3%	22.9%	2.8%	52.6%					.333	.560	85	0.5
2021	SEA	MLB	26	32(0)	35	1-0	0	27	1.60	6.17	54.6%	11.5%	17.3%	1.3%	39.8%	72.9%	81.4%	30.4%	70.8%	.343	.543	120	0.0
2022	DET	MLB	27	59(2)	63	3-3	1	63	1.33	4.00	56.3%	8.1%	23.2%	2.2%	49.2%	67.0%	83.8%	34.3%	65.9%	.320	.500	80	1.3
2023	DET	MLB	28	48(4)	48¹	2-1	2	56	1.10	2.98	49.4%	6.5%	28.1%	1.5%	44.2%	59.3%	85.4%	38.1%	64.5%	.294	.465	83	1.0
2024 DC	DET	MLB	29	53(0)	56	3-3	4	52	1.31	4.13	53.3%	9.0%	21.5%	2.8%	44.8%					.286	.515	95	0.4

2023 Arsenal: FA (95.3), SL (86.2), CH (87.3), SI (95)　　　　Comps: Hector Neris (65), Brad Brach (65), Tyler Kinley (64)

Vest didn't suffer a loss out of the bullpen until the final week of September, which is pretty impressive considering just how often the Tigers lost games last season. (To be fair, he did have a month-and-a-half-long stint on the IL with a knee issue padding those stats.) Alex Lange has a hold on the closer role in Detroit for now, but while Vest lags behind Lange in loudness of stuff, he more than makes up for in command of the zone. Keep an eye on him to usurp that closer role if Lange continues to struggle with his command. Nonetheless, a hand as steady as Vest's should still see plenty of action, whatever the inning.

Joey Wentz LHP Born: 10/06/97 Age: 26 Height: 6'5" Weight: 220 Origin: Round 1, 2016 Draft (#40 overall)

YEAR	TM	LVL	AGE	G (GS)	IP	W-L	SV	K	WHIP	ERA	CSP	BB%	K%	HR%	GB%	ZSw%	ZCon%	OSw%	OCon%	BABIP	SLGCON	DRA-	WARP
2021	LAK	A	23	5(5)	18²	0-3	0	24	1.66	6.75		9.5%	28.6%	6.0%	34.6%	62.4%	78.5%	22.6%	68.2%	.383	.880	110	0.1
2021	ERI	AA	23	13(13)	53¹	0-4	0	58	1.39	3.71		14.2%	24.9%	3.0%	33.3%					.256	.522	109	0.2
2022	TOL	AAA	24	12(11)	48¹	2-2	0	53	1.18	3.17		10.2%	27.0%	3.1%	39.3%					.267	.492	86	1.0
2022	DET	MLB	24	7(7)	32²	2-2	0	27	1.10	3.03	53.9%	9.6%	20.0%	1.5%	40.4%	69.1%	88.3%	28.7%	62.8%	.228	.440	121	0.0
2023	TOL	AAA	25	6(6)	28²	2-1	0	37	1.53	4.40		9.4%	28.9%	2.3%	29.5%	63.7%	81.0%	33.0%	55.6%	.387	.641	93	0.5
2023	DET	MLB	25	25(19)	105²	3-13	0	98	1.68	6.90	48.4%	9.6%	19.9%	5.1%	36.6%	71.3%	85.0%	30.3%	56.9%	.329	.682	138	-0.8
2024 DC	DET	MLB	26	46(6)	70²	3-4	0	64	1.49	5.33	49.4%	10.1%	20.2%	3.6%	36.9%					.302	.579	119	-0.2

2023 Arsenal: FA (93.6), FC (86), CH (85.2), CU (77.7)　　　　Comps: Kyle Lobstein (65), Adalberto Mejía (64), Mitch Keller (63)

Wentz's debut in 2022 wasn't a Scene but an Arms Race, as a moribund Oakland lineup proceeded to Light Him Up for six runs and chased him from the game in the third inning, causing A.J. Hinch to tell him Sugar, You're Going Down (to Toledo). Initially, there were whispers the Tigers had robbed Atlanta by acquiring shiny prospect Wentz for Shane Greene, but Atlanta might have known what they were doing. Wentz too often mars that with meltdowns, and doesn't have the kind of raw stuff that can bail him out of scrapes. His fastball is especially hittable (.682 SLGCON), another young Tigers pitcher with subpar stuff (The Kids Aren't Alright). He needs to show some more consistency next season, or it'll be the Tigers saying Thnks fr th Mmrs.

LINEOUTS

Hitters

HITTER	POS	TM	LVL	AGE	PA	R	HR	RBI	SB	AVG/OBP/SLG	BABIP	SLGCON	BB%	K%	ZSw%	ZCon%	OSw%	OCon%	LA	90th EV	DRC+	BRR	DRP	WARP
Max Anderson	2B	LAK	A	21	145	18	2	21	2	.289/.345/.445	.337	.559	8.3%	17.9%	80.0%	78.7%	43.7%	57.4%			102	-1.0	2.5	0.6
Roberto Campos	OF	WM	A+	20	371	34	5	53	4	.257/.313/.395	.320	.519	7.5%	21.8%							98	-2.5	-4.6	0.1
Isan Díaz	2B	TOL	AAA	27	27	6	2	6	0	.217/.333/.478	.188	.611	14.8%	18.5%	81.8%	77.8%	32.9%	62.5%			107	0.5	-0.1	0.1
	2B	SAC	AAA	27	108	22	7	19	3	.240/.324/.490	.314	.810	11.1%	35.2%	73.2%	77.4%	32.6%	41.6%			90	0.1	0.8	0.2
	2B	DET	MLB	27	5	0	0	0	0	.000/.000/.000		.000	0.0%	40.0%	71.4%	60.0%	40.0%	50.0%	39.4	92.7	92		0.0	0.0
	2B	SF	MLB	27	21	0	0	1	0	.053/.143/.053	.083	.083	9.5%	33.3%	60.6%	80.0%	20.0%	28.6%	12.2	102.6	85	0.0	0.0	0.0
Peyton Graham	IF	LAK	A	22	239	38	4	29	15	.232/.339/.355	.291	.480	11.7%	22.2%	67.1%	83.5%	29.0%	54.6%			103	0.0	-3.4	0.7
Carson Kelly	C	RNO	AAA	28	34	5	0	4	0	.345/.412/.448	.455	.619	8.8%	23.5%	60.3%	94.3%	35.7%	76.0%			97	0.9	-0.2	0.1
	C	AZ	MLB	28	92	6	1	6	1	.226/.283/.298	.295	.410	7.6%	25.0%	62.5%	83.0%	30.7%	54.5%	9.7	102.0	75	-0.1	-0.6	0.0
	C	DET	MLB	28	59	7	1	7	0	.173/.271/.269	.235	.400	11.9%	28.8%	65.3%	75.0%	28.7%	45.7%	26.5	100.3	84	0.0	-0.8	0.0
Ryan Kreidler	SS	LAK	A	25	25	7	1	6	1	.211/.400/.421	.333	.800	24.0%	36.0%	62.2%	65.2%	27.4%	47.1%			89	0.4	-0.8	0.0
	SS	TOL	AAA	25	209	31	11	42	11	.239/.349/.460	.272	.659	13.4%	25.4%	68.9%	80.9%	26.9%	43.7%			101	1.0	5.0	1.0
	SS	DET	MLB	25	18	2	0	0	0	.111/.111/.111	.182	.182	0.0%	38.9%	59.4%	78.9%	42.5%	35.3%	13.2	97.1	78	0.0	0.0	0.0
Andre Lipcius	1B	WM	A+	25	25	3	1	3	0	.286/.400/.476	.333	.625	16.0%	20.0%							111	-1.0	-0.3	0.0
	1B	TOL	AAA	25	419	53	11	58	0	.272/.363/.419	.311	.528	12.4%	17.7%	68.6%	81.1%	29.8%	69.4%			98	-0.4	-2.2	0.7
	1B	DET	MLB	25	38	3	1	4	0	.286/.342/.400	.346	.519	7.9%	21.1%	77.8%	83.7%	29.0%	62.1%	16.9	98.9	88	0.0	-0.4	0.0
Austin Meadows	LF	DET	MLB	28	21	0	0	2	0	.238/.238/.286	.278	.333	0.0%	14.3%	69.4%	92.0%	44.2%	73.7%	15.8	107.8	92	0.2	-0.1	0.1
Tyler Nevin	1B	TOL	AAA	26	385	63	15	58	4	.326/.400/.543	.364	.673	9.9%	16.9%	64.6%	84.5%	29.8%	68.5%			117	2.4	-6.2	1.5
	1B	DET	MLB	26	111	11	2	10	0	.200/.306/.316	.246	.429	10.8%	22.5%	71.3%	82.5%	25.0%	62.9%	14.0	101.2	89	-0.1	-0.6	0.1
Izaac Pacheco	3B	WM	A+	20	508	54	12	50	6	.211/.283/.352	.292	.542	9.3%	31.5%							78	1.9	4.6	0.4
Wenceel Pérez	UT	ERI	AA	23	343	56	6	28	19	.271/.353/.375	.306	.453	10.2%	15.2%							111	1.2	-2.0	1.2
	UT	TOL	AAA	23	160	29	3	19	6	.264/.394/.496	.313	.640	16.9%	18.1%	64.4%	86.2%	29.0%	64.1%			110	-2.5	-1.4	0.3
Donny Sands	C	TOL	AAA	27	371	32	5	36	1	.225/.318/.353	.272	.459	12.1%	19.9%	52.9%	88.8%	32.4%	63.9%			94	-4.5	1.4	0.6
Jonathan Schoop	2B/3B	DET	MLB	31	151	15	0	7	0	.213/.278/.272	.287	.374	8.6%	24.5%	77.0%	81.3%	36.0%	55.5%	11.5	105.8	80	-0.1	-0.3	0.1
Nick Solak	OF	TOL	AAA	28	221	26	2	20	2	.221/.340/.315	.201	.425	14.9%	21.3%	61.9%	79.9%	24.4%	60.0%			90	-0.4	-3.0	0.0
	OF	GWN	AAA	28	173	23	6	28	2	.272/.364/.444	.297	.540	9.8%	15.6%	60.7%	87.7%	31.0%	74.0%			115	-2.4	-2.8	0.3
	OF	ATL	MLB	28	0	1	0	0	0	.000/.000/.000													0.0	
	OF	DET	MLB	28	0	0	0	0	0	.000/.000/.000														

Max Anderson is no revolting blob when it comes to hitting. A prep star in Omaha, Anderson stayed close to home and flourished at Nebraska, becoming both the first Husker to hit over .400 in 22 years and a second-round selection by the Tigers. ⊗ A former big-money international signee, **Roberto Campos** looks the part of a slugging, corner outfielder. But until he can produce a slugging percentage that starts with a number higher than three, he shouldn't be considered one. ⊗ In the postscript to *Ball Four*, Jim Bouton tells of a New York radio DJ who once quizzed his listeners, "Who or what was, or is, a Dooley Womack?" We now know the answer: A Dooley Womack is a ballplayer most known for being traded for a more famous ballplayer, and it looks like **Isan Díaz** is going to finish his career as one. ⊗ One of the top college hitters available in the 2022 draft, **Peyton Graham** had all the characteristics of a quick climber. However, injuries and inconsistent performance at the plate have kept him from advancing past Low-A. ⊗ **Carson Kelly** went from the heir apparent to one of the greatest catchers of this generation, to high-profile trade return, to getting released, to landing with the Tigers. The rising arc of a prep catching prospect is longer than recorded human history; the fall, brutally short. ⊗ **Ryan Kreidler** earned a spot on the 2023 Opening Day roster but struggled to hit and then struggled to stay on the field, instead watching as other utility guys passed him on the depth chart. It seems unfair that ballplayers should have to deal with the horrors of old age at 25. ⊗ In a parallel universe, **Andre Lipcius** never signs with the Tigers. Instead he uses his nuclear engineering degree to monitor plants around the country from his desk at Oak Ridge, shipping out T437 control panels when needed. Is he happy? Is he successful? Does he become whatever the utility infielder equipment of nuclear engineers is? ⊗ The highlight of **Austin Meadow's** season—mostly lost to an ongoing battle with anxiety—was getting to spend spring training with his younger brother Parker, who at one point was photographed "caddying" the pair's gear into Lakeland. The vicissitudes of baseball are never-ending, but forcing a younger sibling to do one's gruntwork is eternal. ⊗ There might be plenty of time for father-son bonding this summer, with Phil now out as the manager in Los Angeles and **Tyler Nevin** posting an OPS+ of 72 last year in Detroit. ⊗ The Midwest League proved to be too much for **Izaac Pacheco** in 2023, with the more advanced High-A pitching sending his strikeout rate north of 30%. He'll have to make more consistent contact if he's to continue to climb the ladder. ⊗ Seven years after being signed, **Wenceel Pérez** is finally showing us who he is as a prospect. Not a star, not a bust, but a valuable utility player who should make his debut sometime in 2024. ⊗ Blocked by J.T. Realmuto in Philly, **Donny Sands** now has a clear path to playing time in Detroit. His ability to grind out at-bats and steal strikes behind the plate should earn him the opportunity to help handle the young Tigers pitching staff. ⊗ **Jonathan Schoop** has played Salieri to Manny Machado's Mozart of early '10s Orioles prospects, a division that only sharpened last year when Machado, as a Padre, composed a season on par with *Concertone for Two Violins*—mid, but not his worst work—while Schoop was sent home by the Tigers in July. ⊗ Every year there's one player who pings around the transaction wire like a five-year-old on Halloween hopped up on Skittles; last year that honor went to **Nick Solak**, who was with four different clubs before the season even started, and ended with a fifth. That he couldn't even find playing time with Detroit, team no. 5, tells you what you need to know about his current stock.

Pitchers

PITCHER	TM	LVL	AGE	G (GS)	IP	W-L	SV	K	WHIP	ERA	CSP	BB%	K%	HR%	GB%	ZSw%	ZCon%	OSw%	OCon%	BABIP	SLGCON	DRA-	WARP
Matthew Boyd	DET	MLB	32	15 (15)	71	5-5	0	73	1.32	5.45	45.6%	8.3%	24.1%	3.6%	38.4%	70.5%	82.7%	36.6%	52.8%	.302	.576	105	0.7
Miguel Díaz	TOL	AAA	28	49 (0)	57	2-4	14	73	1.40	5.05		10.2%	28.6%	1.2%	51.0%	68.8%	76.3%	30.2%	54.2%	.340	.549	77	1.5
	DET	MLB	28	12 (3)	14	1-0	0	16	0.93	0.64	45.6%	9.3%	29.6%	0.0%	39.4%	62.7%	82.7%	36.8%	60.9%	.242	.303	91	0.2
Heath Hembree	TOL	AAA	34	6 (0)	6	1-0	0	6	1.33	3.00		8.0%	24.0%	0.0%	23.5%	68.0%	79.4%	30.4%	42.9%	.353	.353	114	0.0
	DUR	AAA	34	8 (0)	7	3-1	2	8	1.57	1.29		15.6%	25.0%	0.0%	31.6%	70.2%	81.8%	32.3%	53.3%	.316	.389	122	0.0
	TB	MLB	34	1 (0)	1¹	0-0	0	2	0.75	0.00	39.1%	25.0%	50.0%	0.0%	100.0%	60.0%	100.0%	46.2%	33.3%	.000	.000	88	0.0
Garrett Hill	TOL	AAA	27	26 (4)	46¹	3-2	0	64	1.88	6.02		14.3%	28.7%	2.7%	44.2%	64.1%	75.5%	26.6%	55.3%	.430	.737	90	0.9
	DET	MLB	27	9 (0)	15²	0-0	1	14	2.11	9.19	47.6%	17.5%	17.5%	5.0%	43.1%	66.4%	83.1%	17.7%	71.0%	.326	.755	110	0.1
Troy Melton	LAK	A	22	7 (7)	26²	0-0	0	33	1.20	3.38		5.5%	30.0%	2.7%	45.7%	72.9%	69.0%	36.3%	60.7%	.343	.586	68	0.6
	WM	A+	22	16 (15)	65¹	3-1	0	61	1.12	2.48		6.7%	22.8%	0.7%	38.2%					.288	.475	88	0.8
Keider Montero	WM	A+	22	4 (4)	16	0-0	0	22	0.88	2.81		6.6%	36.1%	1.6%	51.4%					.265	.457	69	0.4
	ERI	AA	22	15 (15)	69¹	10-2	0	91	1.50	4.93		10.1%	29.6%	2.3%	40.8%					.375	.615	90	1.3
	TOL	AAA	22	8 (7)	42	5-2	0	47	1.33	4.93		7.7%	25.8%	4.4%	38.5%	70.2%	78.7%	33.3%	54.3%	.312	.690	84	0.8
Brendan White	TOL	AAA	24	29 (0)	37	3-2	0	50	1.51	4.14		6.8%	30.9%	2.5%	51.5%	66.2%	78.3%	28.4%	50.0%	.432	.711	72	1.1
	DET	MLB	24	33 (2)	40²	2-3	0	44	1.35	5.09	46.6%	8.5%	24.9%	2.3%	50.4%	63.7%	81.6%	37.1%	57.4%	.333	.541	89	0.7
Trey Wingenter	TOL	AAA	29	22 (0)	21	0-0	1	27	1.43	5.57		12.1%	29.7%	2.2%	40.4%	66.9%	80.4%	32.1%	43.5%	.340	.627	82	0.5
	DET	MLB	29	17 (0)	17	1-0	0	22	1.35	5.82	41.9%	9.2%	28.9%	2.6%	45.5%	75.5%	85.0%	35.0%	49.3%	.333	.605	87	0.3

Matthew Boyd deserves better than the injury cards he's been dealt; after missing most of the previous two seasons with flexor tendon surgery, he needed TJ surgery in 2023, putting an abrupt end on a promising start to the season. At least he got to celebrate his hometown Mariners ending the playoff drought as a member of the 2022 team; hopefully other, similarly happy, memories are ahead. ⦿ Signed to a minor-league deal in 2022, **Miguel Díaz** has been good enough to hang around but not good enough to carve out a permanent bullpen role. That might change after his solid September, where he was utilized as an opener and in some high-leverage situations. ⦿ **Heath Hembree** / It's me, Cathy / I've come home, because you walked the bases full / And the last batter broke a window…Oh it gets dark, it gets lonely / out here on the waiver wire / you tried a lot, but what you've got / is too wild, batters get so greedy / isn't it maybe time / to buy a car dealership / and come back home to Wuthering, Wuthering, Wuthering Heights? ⦿ Runs against **Garrett Hill** / Giving up nine per nine / Runs against Garrett Hill / Giving up nine per nine ⦿ An advanced college pitcher, **Troy Melton** did exactly what you'd expect against younger competition in A-ball: taunt them with references to Plato and Aristotle they couldn't possibly understand. Also, the upper-90s heat. ⦿ **Keider Montero** is a current starter and potential future reliever. He's got two above-average secondaries in his curve and slider, and a cursory changeup, but the hangup is a mid-90s fastball that lacks wiggle and takes a bruising a bit too often. There could be more velo in the tank as a reliever, which might offset that problem. ⦿ Claimed on waivers by the Tigers in March, **Freddy Pacheco** was put on the IL just two weeks later in need of a UCL procedure. He's likely to miss the entirety of the 2024 season. ⦿ **Trevor Rosenthal** is more active on Twitter than he's been on a big-league mound since his fever-dream comeback 2020 season. He'll hope to bring whatever he's got left in the tank and tax tips for the very wealthy to a new club this spring. ⦿ A lot of minor leaguers were left without support during the pandemic, but **Brendan White** simply coached himself into owning a solid fastball-slider combo. The four-seam looks a little flat to the eye, but he got a respectable 35.7% whiff rate on it in the majors. ⦿ An over-slot third-round selection, **Paul Wilson** is the son of former Giant lefty Trevor Wilson. He shares many of his father's qualities, including a strong fastball, power curve and, to a lesser extent, power eyebrows. ⦿ **Trey Wingenter** didn't do much in his limited time in Detroit to endear himself to the Motown faithful, but beneath the surface stats, he put on a pretty decent audition for his next employer, averaging 96 on the fastball and getting a fair number of chases on the slider.

HOUSTON ASTROS

Essay by Mike Pielucci

Player comments by Jon Tayler and BP staff

The dais at Globe Life Field is packed as Corey Seager fires the final salvo of the Texas Rangers' first championship season. His teammates are lined up behind him: home white jerseys, cream-colored World Series hats. Before them is a lagoon of people, hundreds of thousands deep.

Seager, typically laconic, is hardly the Ranger best suited to close out the post-parade ceremony in Arlington, but this is light work. His audience is happy and carefree and drunk, which means he could rile this lot up with just about anything.

He chose the boldest thing.

"I've just got one thing to say," he begins, with his head tilted down and his cap backward. "Everybody was wondering what would happen if the Rangers didn't win the World Series"—and here his teammates start to bob and laugh and shout in approval, all too content to follow where their best player is leading them—"I guess we'll never know!"

With that, he turns and nods his head in delight, off to dish out hand slaps and absorb back claps.

Those hundreds of thousands pop like a wrestling crowd on *Monday Night Raw*. Somewhere 250 miles south, I imagine Alex Bregman grimacing. If not him, then at least some of his Houston Astros teammates are, as their in-state rivals ape Bregman's infamous champagne toast weeks earlier after Houston edged Texas via tiebreak to capture the American League West.

How could they not? The Astros are unaccustomed to being the butt of the joke. They are baseball's provocateurs, its instigators. No franchise is more adept at extracting hate and disgust, vitriol and bile from its opponents—and those opponents' fans, and those fans' loved ones and just about everyone who hails from somewhere outside of South Texas. Trash cans have a great deal to do with that, of course, but so does naked fear. The Astros intimidate through results. That division title Bregman gloated about was their third in a row and sixth in seven years, the streak interrupted only by the pandemic-shortened 2020 season. Their seven-game playoff classic against Texas marked Houston's seventh consecutive ALCS berth. They have two World Series championships to show for their efforts, along with two more runner-up appearances.

HOUSTON ASTROS PROSPECTUS
2023 W-L: 90-72, 1ST IN AL WEST

Pythag	.580	6th	DER	.702	8th
RS/G	5.10	5th	DRC+	109	3rd
RA/G	4.31	9th	DRA-	98	14th
dWin%	.569	5th	FIP	4.33	17th
Payroll	$180M	14th	B-Age	29.2	28th
M$/MW	$3.8M	14th	P-Age	29.3	19th

409'

362'   373'

315'   326'

- Opened 2000
- Retractable roof
- Natural surface
- Fence profile: 7' to 25'

Park Factors

Runs	Runs/RH	Runs/LH	HR/RH	HR/LH
101	102	100	111	94

Top Hitter WARP	5.4 Kyle Tucker
Top Pitcher WARP	3.9 Framber Valdez
2023 Top Prospect	Zach Dezenzo

Payroll History (in millions)

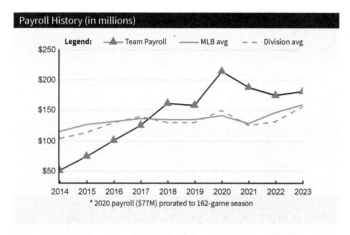

Legend: Team Payroll | MLB avg | Division avg

* 2020 payroll ($77M) prorated to 162-game season

Future Commitments (in millions)

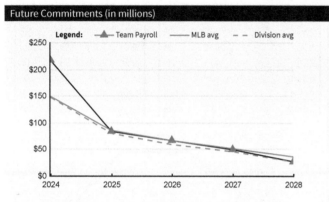

Legend: Team Payroll | MLB avg | Division avg

Farm System Ranking

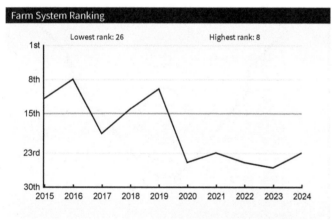

Lowest rank: 26   Highest rank: 8

Personnel

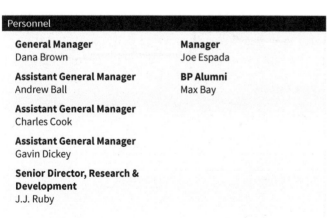

General Manager
Dana Brown

Assistant General Manager
Andrew Ball

Assistant General Manager
Charles Cook

Assistant General Manager
Gavin Dickey

Senior Director, Research & Development
J.J. Ruby

Manager
Joe Espada

BP Alumni
Max Bay

This is baseball's most successful operation since the Yankees of the late '90s and early aughts, largely because a cast of characters that is so spectacular has remained so static. An ace like Zack Greinke has aged out and the steady Michael Brantley just retired, while homegrown superstars Carlos Correa and George Springer left in free agency, but 2024 marks Jose Altuve's 14th season in Houston and Bregman's ninth. Justin Verlander is going on eight-ish years, depending on what fractions one assigns half seasons in 2017 (upon being acquired from Detroit at the trade deadline) and 2023 (upon being reacquired from the Mets at the same time of year), along with the 2020 and 2021 campaigns that got swallowed up by Tommy John surgery. Kyle Tucker and Framber Valdez showed up seven years ago. Yordan Alvarez has been around for five.

The team's power has never lied in inevitability; Houston has lost three of those ALCSes, and split the World Series appearances. But even in defeat, the Astros always maintained an air of irrepressibility. Beat them, perhaps, but know that they will be back—as division champs, then playoff contenders, then as a team playing for the pennant and sometimes even more. Your victories are temporary. Theirs are perpetual.

Last year felt different. No one had ever punked Houston the way Texas did, with the Rangers scoring 20 runs to the Astros' four in Games 6 and 7 at Minute Maid Park, then sending one final receipt weeks later via that Seager clapback. Texas was supposed to be finished after Game 5, shattered after that benches-clearing fracas between Adolis García and Martín Maldonado blunted their momentum before Altuve took Rangers closer José Leclerc deep for a stunning ninth-inning comeback. Houston was within a game of a third consecutive World Series appearance with two to play in their own building, against a team they swept by an aggregate score of 39-10 in their final three-game set in the regular season.

That one-two punch—a mental haymaker, an emotional uppercut—has walloped so many Astros opponents over these seven years, and history told us Texas would be no different. Then the Rangers got off the canvas and battered the defending champs into submission, hitting harder and faster than Houston could handle.

Perhaps we should have seen this coming. Aside from that 2020 runner-up finish to Oakland, in the A's last wheeze of excellence for the foreseeable future, nobody had clawed within five games of Houston in the division since 2017. Last year, the barbarians stormed the gate and refused to stand down. The Astros stared up at Texas, who wrapped up 2023 with the second-best run differential in baseball despite a buffoonish 16 losses in 20 late-season games, for the bulk of the regular season. They spent the late summer sweating out the resurgent Mariners, who went 38-15 in July and August, including taking six of seven games across two series in Houston. The Astros eked it out anyway, through what felt like canny and good old-fashioned stubbornness, and that plus a TikTok-sized media cycle comparing the merits of

Houston's playoff-clinching celebration to Texas'—it remains every bit as dumb as you remember—provided cloud cover for the Astros playing sub-.500 ball at home and limping into the playoffs with a 13-14 record in September and October.

But there is no hiding it now: the Astros are in middle age. That they could plausibly be arriving there only now, after the seven ALCS appearances and six division titles and four AL pennants and two World Series crowns, is astounding. Those Yankees were borderline decrepit in their seventh season after beginning the three-peat, running out 28-year-old Alex Rodriguez as their only everyday player under 30 and 27-year-old Javier Vazquez as their only similarly aged starter. Houston's closest analogue out west, the Los Angeles Dodgers, have given up the ghost of sustaining their own run from within, ripping up one bedrock after another—Corey Seager, Justin Turner, Kenley Jansen, Cody Bellinger and perhaps even Clayton Kershaw—and refreshing around high-priced imports like Shohei Ohtani, Yoshinobu Yamamoto and Freddie Freeman.

Not so in Houston, where Bregman and Valdez are only hitting their age-30 seasons, Tucker is 27 and Alvarez just 26. Flanking them are a passel of twentysomethings who all pass the ripe test, to some degree or another: Cristian Javier, Yainer Diaz, Jeremy Peña, Luis Garcia, Hunter Brown, Chas McCormick, Bryan Abreu. Why couldn't this go on for another run or five?

Except Altuve turns 34 in May, the same age at which Craig Biggio plummeted from his Hall of Fame peak. Presuming health—Altuve missed 72 games last year with multiple injuries—there is little reason to anticipate a similar drop-off: he turned in a 123 DRC+ in 410 plate appearances with contact metrics similar to his even-better 2022 campaign. Of course, he need only turn to his left and glance at José Abreu, three years his senior, for a reminder of how swiftly stardom can spoil. There is no escape hatch from the two years and $39 million remaining on Abreu's contract, nor is there much safety net to be found in a perpetually barren farm system, and so Houston has little choice but to trot him out and hope for better. After a season in which he sunk to a .237/.296/.383 slash line with -2.8 Deserved Runs Prevented, that could be eminently doable without saying too much.

Then there is Verlander, who will pitch this season at 41 years old. Important as his reacquisition was in the practical sense—he was the best starter moved at the trade deadline—it was that much more so on a symbolic level. The organization that was once so cutting edge that *Sports Illustrated* prophesied their first World Series win years ahead of time needed to turn backward for a solution. It almost worked, too. This version of Verlander was more deception than diesel, leaning on his curve over a diminished fastball and striking out just 7.98 batters per nine innings, his lowest full-season number since the 2014 campaign that seemed to signal the end of his run as one of baseball's premier aces. That didn't prevent him from re-asserting himself as Houston's most dependable starter—until his Game 4 outing against Texas, when six hits, four runs and just three strikeouts in 5 ⅔ innings laid bare how much closer he is to the end than the beginning.

Whether the Astros avoid the same fate depends on Verlander maintaining this wizened approach for another 25 starts this year, along with Altuve's bat staying quick and his body staying sturdy. It likely depends even more on that glut of players between them and the established younger core. Maybe that's Javier recapturing his velocity, and with it the form that made him one of the game's great breakouts in 2022. Or perhaps it's Diaz marrying his pop with patience after walking in just 2.9% of his plate appearances as a rookie. If not him, how about Peña, who could use a bit of each trait after dropping from 22 home runs to 10 without anywhere close to enough plate discipline to compensate? The rotation levels up if Brown channels the interminable Verlander comps into something more solid. Ditto if Garcia returns from Tommy John surgery in time to chew up innings in the back half of the season. It feels fanciful to expect even that from Lance McCullers Jr. after general manager Dana Brown braced the public not to see him until July, nearly two calendar years after McCullers' last major-league start. But if he regains any measure of health, his career 3.48 ERA, 3.76 DRA and 10.02 K/9 say plenty about what could be in the offing.

The Astros likely do not require all of those breakthroughs to make this transition a graceful one. They will need at least some, though, because those barbarians intend to lay siege. With Max Scherzer out until midseason and Jacob deGrom's recovery from a second Tommy John an unknown, Texas' rotation could be traditionally shambolic, but a World Series-winning lineup should be even better via full seasons from phenoms Evan Carter and Josh Jung (plus a likely cameo from Wyatt Langford, who is a better prospect than both). And miserly as the Mariners' offseason was, Seattle will augment Julio Rodríguez with arguably the best pitching in the American League. Both teams have younger stars than Houston, and deeper farm systems and, presumably, longer tails. They've already challenged the Astros—and, in Texas' case, overtaken them once. Each could plausibly do so again, for much longer.

Or they could not. It remains anyone's guess what happens next because there is no modern corollary to what the Astros are positioned to attempt. Teams this good, this long, should not be this primed for so much more.

Were we discussing another franchise, that would veer toward more naked appreciation. It's never so straightforward with Houston, which makes it all the more fitting that middle age on them figures to look less like desperation and grand gestures than intentioned, understated steps forward. It won't be enough to make them admired. But they'd settle for remaining feared a good while longer instead.

—Mike Pielucci is the sports editor at D Magazine.

HITTERS

José Abreu 1B Born: 01/29/87 Age: 37 Bats: R Throws: R Height: 6'3" Weight: 235 Origin: IFA, 2013

YEAR	TM	LVL	AGE	PA	R	HR	RBI	SB	AVG/OBP/SLG	BABIP	SLGCON	BB%	K%	ZSw%	ZCon%	OSw%	OCon%	LA	90th EV	DRC+	BRR	DRP	WARP
2021	CHW	MLB	34	659	86	30	117	1	.261/.351/.481	.293	.643	9.3%	21.7%	67.0%	84.5%	36.2%	58.0%	10.5	107.2	114	-0.3	0.0	2.5
2022	CHW	MLB	35	679	85	15	75	0	.304/.378/.446	.350	.546	9.1%	16.2%	67.3%	87.1%	33.2%	62.1%	8.2	107.6	148	-0.2	0.0	5.3
2023	HOU	MLB	36	594	62	18	90	0	.237/.296/.383	.276	.505	7.1%	21.9%	65.4%	84.3%	39.6%	61.3%	11.0	105.8	101	-0.4	-0.4	1.3
2024 DC	HOU	MLB	37	590	66	19	70	0	.256/.328/.415	.302	.539	7.8%	20.8%							109	-0.4	0.2	1.8

2023 GP: 1B (134), DH (7)   Comps: Eddie Murray (79), Adrián González (78), Steve Garvey (78)

Perpetually a slow starter in his MLB career, Abreu was no different in Astros orange, getting his tenure in Houston started with a ghastly .236 wOBA in March and April. While he rebounded in June, the year was marked with more ups and downs than Tesla stock, resulting in his worst full-season figures since coming stateside. What happened? The bulky slugger stopped hitting the ball like it owed him money, with multi-point plunges in hard-hit rate and xwOBAcon, a three-mph dip in average exit velocity, and a second straight season with an ISO starting with a one. Worse, what looked like a reversal in strikeout, whiff and chase rate in 2022 now looks more like a fluke, as Abreu went back to swinging with relative abandon. That strategy worked when he was producing elite thump, but it's less appealing when you're posting David Peralta numbers at Kyle Schwarber prices.

Jose Altuve 2B Born: 05/06/90 Age: 34 Bats: R Throws: R Height: 5'6" Weight: 166 Origin: IFA, 2007

YEAR	TM	LVL	AGE	PA	R	HR	RBI	SB	AVG/OBP/SLG	BABIP	SLGCON	BB%	K%	ZSw%	ZCon%	OSw%	OCon%	LA	90th EV	DRC+	BRR	DRP	WARP
2021	HOU	MLB	31	678	117	31	83	5	.278/.350/.489	.280	.576	9.7%	13.4%	65.8%	91.2%	35.6%	75.8%	15.2	102.9	111	0.3	2.0	3.6
2022	HOU	MLB	32	604	103	28	57	18	.300/.387/.533	.315	.639	10.9%	14.4%	64.8%	90.1%	31.8%	76.0%	16.0	102.2	137	1.9	-0.9	4.7
2023	HOU	MLB	33	410	76	17	51	14	.311/.393/.522	.348	.651	10.7%	17.3%	63.2%	89.3%	34.7%	73.2%	11.3	102.9	123	0.3	-0.4	2.4
2024 DC	HOU	MLB	34	603	73	23	78	14	.267/.348/.448	.286	.540	9.9%	15.3%							123	0.3	1.6	3.7

2023 GP: 2B (87), DH (1)   Comps: Roberto Alomar (79), Billy Herman (75), Frankie Frisch (74)

Will Altuve ever slow down? At the plate, the answer remains a firm "not yet." Since briefly appearing cooked (or at least lightly charred) during the shortened 2020 season, the diminutive All-Star has returned to his peak production. His early-30s power surge has continued apace, as has his newfound patience, and despite missing a big chunk of the first half with a broken hand, he looked like his usual self upon returning. And while his contact peripherals continue to predict his downfall thanks to his pedestrian exit velocities and barrel rates, he keeps right on chugging, thanks to his freakish ability to put bat on ball seemingly no matter the location. The tough question, if you're Astros brass, is how much longer you're willing to bet on one of baseball's biggest outliers continuing this run. The 2024 season will be the last year of the mega-extension Altuve signed in 2018, and while it's hard to imagine him in another uniform, Houston's leadership can't love the idea of throwing hands against the unstoppable progression of time, particularly as his defensive and baserunning value continues to sink. Helping Altuve's cause: the first half of 2023 proved decisively that the team doesn't have a handy replacement in house for him. He's still the straw that stirs the drink in south Texas.

Yordan Alvarez DH/LF Born: 06/27/97 Age: 27 Bats: L Throws: R Height: 6'5" Weight: 225 Origin: IFA, 2016

YEAR	TM	LVL	AGE	PA	R	HR	RBI	SB	AVG/OBP/SLG	BABIP	SLGCON	BB%	K%	ZSw%	ZCon%	OSw%	OCon%	LA	90th EV	DRC+	BRR	DRP	WARP
2021	HOU	MLB	24	598	92	33	104	1	.277/.346/.531	.320	.727	8.4%	24.2%	61.2%	89.3%	31.2%	61.9%	14.2	109.2	129	0.0	-0.8	3.8
2022	HOU	MLB	25	561	95	37	97	1	.306/.406/.613	.320	.791	13.9%	18.9%	66.4%	88.1%	27.3%	58.4%	12.6	109.9	163	-0.1	-1.1	5.7
2023	HOU	MLB	26	496	77	31	97	0	.293/.407/.583	.306	.752	13.9%	18.5%	65.2%	87.6%	29.8%	63.7%	17.5	109.9	161	-0.9	-1.2	4.7
2024 DC	HOU	MLB	27	570	82	30	90	0	.276/.380/.526	.300	.679	12.8%	19.3%							153	0.0	-1	5.0

2023 GP: DH (73), LF (40)   Comps: Frank Thomas (85), Hal Trosky Sr. (85), Eddie Murray (83)

Baseball isn't exempt from this endless era of remakes, reboots and sequels; the top prospect in baseball is Matt Holliday's kid. Consider, then, the idea of Alvarez as the second coming of David Ortiz, but in high-definition and with advanced CGI and VFX—and not the kind that turns every Marvel movie into blue-and-gray sludge. At his peak from 2003 through '08, Ortiz hit .297/.398/.598; over the last three years, Alvarez has hit .292/.385/.573, and in a more difficult run-scoring environment to boot. But this is a vibes-based link as well—Alvarez brings that same feeling of either giddy anticipation or holy terror when he steps to the plate, depending on your rooting interest. And like Ortiz, he somehow finds another level when the calendar flips to October: Alvarez almost single-handedly derailed the Rangers' World Series run by hitting a ridiculous .481/.531/.778 in the ALCS and finished the postseason with six homers in 11 games. You can't beat him with lefties, with break or spin or fade, or anywhere in the strike zone. Maybe the more apt comparison isn't Ortiz but Darkseid; at the end of the day, Yordan Alvarez is.

Luis Baez OF Born: 01/11/04 Age: 20 Bats: R Throws: R Height: 6'1" Weight: 205 Origin: IFA, 2022

YEAR	TM	LVL	AGE	PA	R	HR	RBI	SB	AVG/OBP/SLG	BABIP	SLGCON	BB%	K%	ZSw%	ZCon%	OSw%	OCon%	LA	90th EV	DRC+	BRR	DRP	WARP
2022	DSL HOUO	ROK	18	222	40	9	43	10	.305/.351/.552	.376	.762	6.3%	25.2%										
2023	AST	ROK	19	76	10	7	15	1	.271/.434/.661	.237	.867	21.1%	18.4%										
2023	FAY	A	19	179	20	4	23	0	.239/.324/.413	.311	.598	9.5%	26.8%							88	-0.6	0.9	0.3
2024 non	HOU	MLB	20	251	19	3	20	0	.204/.257/.295	.294	.442	5.7%	31.2%							55	0.0	0	-0.7

2023 GP: RF (31), LF (10), CF (10), DH (7)   Comps: Yorman Rodriguez (77), Elier Hernandez (75), Willy García (75)

The recipient of Houston's biggest international signing bonus in 2022, Baez obliterated the complex league in his first season stateside, showing excellent plate discipline and power. Quickly bumped up to A-ball, he slowed down there, but that should be expected for a 19-year-old facing older, tougher competition—besides, he still put up a .348 wOBA. Baez boasts elite bat speed and thump, with plus grades on his power and a big, physical frame that promises even more in the future. That's about all there is to him, as he's an average defender trending toward a corner outfield spot or first base and doesn't have much speed—not that you need fleet feet for a home run trot. To paraphrase a certain NBA Hall of Famer, the ceiling is the roof with Baez.

Michael Brantley   LF/DH   Born: 05/15/87   Age: 37   Bats: L   Throws: L   Height: 6'2"   Weight: 209   Origin: Round 7, 2005 Draft (#205 overall)

YEAR	TM	LVL	AGE	PA	R	HR	RBI	SB	AVG/OBP/SLG	BABIP	SLGCON	BB%	K%	ZSw%	ZCon%	OSw%	OCon%	LA	90th EV	DRC+	BRR	DRP	WARP
2021	HOU	MLB	34	508	68	8	47	1	.311/.362/.437	.337	.493	6.5%	10.4%	66.8%	92.6%	28.5%	82.0%	9.9	103.3	125	-0.7	-4.2	2.8
2022	HOU	MLB	35	277	28	5	26	1	.288/.370/.416	.311	.474	11.2%	10.8%	62.3%	93.7%	27.4%	77.3%	10.6	102.9	122	-0.5	-1.7	1.3
2023	SUG	AAA	36	64	7	1	12	0	.298/.453/.447	.277	.457	23.4%	1.6%	53.6%	92.5%	11.8%	82.4%			126	0.1	0.8	0.5
2023	HOU	MLB	36	57	7	2	7	0	.278/.298/.426	.255	.442	3.5%	3.5%	55.5%	96.7%	24.5%	81.5%	13.9	102.2	108	0.0	-0.6	0.1
2024 non	HOU	MLB	37	251	27	5	26	1	.289/.361/.409	.307	.455	9.6%	9.5%							120	-0.4	-4.6	0.8

2023 GP: LF (10), DH (4)   *Comps: Lou Brock (75), Garret Anderson (71), Heinie Manush (69)*

Brantley's 15th season in the majors lasted barely longer than two weeks (not counting the postseason) thanks to right shoulder surgery. Worse, recurring shoulder pain affected him even after he returned from the long layoff, probably contributing to his paltry numbers across that tiny sample. The good news is that none of that affected his eye at the plate, which remains well above average, and he still hit the ball hard. This was the second time Brantley's balky right shoulder has been operated on, and given his age it's not clear if his body is up to the rigors of a full season anymore. Even if he were permanently placed at DH, which he should be, given his lack of speed and range, he should be fit with a safety vest at all times. It's a bummer how aging players go out in bits and pieces, fading away like a flag in the sun.

Alex Bregman   3B   Born: 03/30/94   Age: 30   Bats: R   Throws: R   Height: 6'0"   Weight: 192   Origin: Round 1, 2015 Draft (#2 overall)

YEAR	TM	LVL	AGE	PA	R	HR	RBI	SB	AVG/OBP/SLG	BABIP	SLGCON	BB%	K%	ZSw%	ZCon%	OSw%	OCon%	LA	90th EV	DRC+	BRR	DRP	WARP
2021	HOU	MLB	27	400	54	12	55	1	.270/.355/.422	.286	.498	11.0%	13.3%	66.9%	92.8%	21.5%	71.2%	15.9	102.3	118	-0.5	-0.1	2.2
2022	HOU	MLB	28	656	93	23	93	1	.259/.366/.454	.260	.529	13.3%	11.7%	69.4%	90.8%	21.0%	72.7%	19.6	102.0	125	-1.0	3.2	3.8
2023	HOU	MLB	29	724	103	25	98	3	.262/.363/.441	.270	.512	12.7%	12.0%	62.6%	91.9%	21.5%	73.3%	17.7	101.6	122	-0.6	4.0	4.6
2024 DC	HOU	MLB	30	642	77	20	77	2	.262/.364/.428	.272	.494	12.5%	11.4%							125	-0.6	3	4.1

2023 GP: 3B (160), DH (1)   *Comps: Adrián Beltré (80), Ron Santo (79), David Wright (78)*

On the seventh day of June, Alex Bregman rested. To that point, he had started at third base in all 61 games of the Astros' season, but his streak was snapped on that Wednesday in Toronto, with Grae Kessinger taking his place at the hot corner in a 3-2 loss to the Blue Jays. The next day, Bregman was back at third; he wouldn't take another day off for the rest of the year. It's that kind of durability and consistency that's made him such a valuable part of the Astros; as GM Dana Brown told reporters during Winter Meetings, "He's a pillar for this club." It's a good analogy, as Bregman is basically a load-bearing column for Houston's nine-year dynasty. Only José Ramírez topped him in WARP among regular third basemen last season, and he finished fourth in DRC+. Defensively, he was a hair behind Austin Riley in DRP and ranked third overall. Yet, unless Brown and Houston's ownership take a big financial plunge, 2024 will be the last year that the Astros will benefit from Bregman's steady presence on the field and in the clubhouse, as free agency—and a $200 million-plus contract—await in the winter.

Victor Caratini   C   Born: 08/17/93   Age: 30   Bats: S   Throws: R   Height: 5'11"   Weight: 225   Origin: Round 2, 2013 Draft (#65 overall)

YEAR	TM	LVL	AGE	PA	R	HR	RBI	SB	AVG/OBP/SLG	BABIP	SLGCON	BB%	K%	ZSw%	ZCon%	OSw%	OCon%	LA	90th EV	DRC+	BRR	DRP	WARP
2021	SD	MLB	27	356	33	7	39	2	.227/.309/.323	.281	.437	9.8%	23.0%	67.2%	87.4%	29.5%	54.3%	8.4	106.8	86	-0.5	-5.0	0.3
2022	MIL	MLB	28	314	26	9	34	0	.199/.300/.342	.228	.454	9.9%	21.3%	62.3%	89.9%	27.0%	59.7%	6.9	104.8	91	-0.7	6.7	1.4
2023	MIL	MLB	29	226	23	7	25	1	.259/.327/.383	.296	.494	8.4%	19.9%	66.7%	84.1%	31.8%	72.0%	10.3	105.8	103	-0.3	3.6	1.3
2024 DC	HOU	MLB	30	284	29	7	29	0	.232/.315/.359	.270	.455	9.3%	18.8%							93	0.0	2.2	1.0

2023 GP: C (58), DH (2), 1B (1)   *Comps: Tucker Barnhart (62), Josh Thole (61), Marc Hill (60)*

YEAR	TM	P. COUNT	FRM RUNS	BLK RUNS	THRW RUNS	TOT RUNS
2021	SD	13376	-3.2	0.1	0.0	-3.2
2022	MIL	11736	8.5	0.2	0.4	9.1
2023	MIL	8114	4.2	0.0	-0.3	3.8
2024	HOU	9620	2.6	0.1	-0.4	2.3

The 2023 Brewers had the luxury of having not just one good framing catcher, but two. Caratini was a solid backup for William Contreras, offering occasional power when Contreras' bat was relocated to the DH spot. A glance at his line invokes thoughts of "not terrible," but also reflects the on-base ability, contact skills, and here-and-there homers you'd be grateful for from your backup veteran backstop. The Astros agreed, signing him to a lucrative (again, by backup catcher standards) two-year, $12 million contract to provide the same service in Houston, time-sharing with Yainer Diaz and letting the offense-forward starter leave the mask off every so often.

Kenedy Corona   OF   Born: 03/21/00   Age: 24   Bats: R   Throws: R   Height: 5'10"   Weight: 184   Origin: IFA, 2019

YEAR	TM	LVL	AGE	PA	R	HR	RBI	SB	AVG/OBP/SLG	BABIP	SLGCON	BB%	K%	ZSw%	ZCon%	OSw%	OCon%	LA	90th EV	DRC+	BRR	DRP	WARP
2021	FAY	A	21	224	30	2	22	19	.244/.306/.343	.318	.466	6.3%	23.7%							91	0.3	7.8	1.3
2022	FAY	A	22	188	32	9	30	8	.261/.346/.491	.298	.664	11.2%	22.9%							121	-0.1	4.1	1.4
2022	ASH	A+	22	279	56	10	37	20	.290/.373/.498	.353	.670	10.0%	22.6%							107	1.4	3.0	1.6
2023	ASH	A+	23	29	7	2	4	1	.360/.448/.600	.500	.938	13.8%	31.0%							105	1.3	0.3	0.3
2023	CC	AA	23	491	63	20	61	31	.244/.324/.449	.297	.635	9.8%	25.9%							101	1.3	8.9	2.7
2024 DC	HOU	MLB	24	64	6	1	6	3	.217/.281/.351	.294	.525	7.1%	29.5%							78	0.0	0	0.0

2023 GP: CF (64), RF (39), LF (13), DH (8)   *Comps: Chris Heisey (56), Jiandido Tromp (56), Mike Gerber (55)*

Corona has a name straight out of a Thomas Pynchon novel and a likely future as a fourth outfielder, which 2023 did not dispel. Though he has above-average power, too much of his contact goes straight into the dirt, and while his plus speed helps him there, it limits his offensive upside, making him more likely to be a glove-first regular for a second-division squad. Not that there's anything wrong with that; Corona grades out as an excellent fielder thanks to ample speed and a strong arm, and he should be able to handle center field and excel in the corners. The trick to pushing past that reserve ceiling will be elevation, which would pair nicely with his pull-happy tendencies; fewer strikeouts wouldn't hurt either. Given that the Astros acquired him *and* Blake Taylor from the Mets in exchange for 16 games of Jake Marisnick, it's pretty much all upside no matter how brightly Corona shines.

★ ★ ★ *2024 Top 101 Prospect* **#40** ★ ★ ★

Zach Dezenzo **3B**   Born: 05/11/00   Age: 24   Bats: R   Throws: R   Height: 6'4"   Weight: 220   Origin: Round 12, 2022 Draft (#373 overall)

YEAR	TM	LVL	AGE	PA	R	HR	RBI	SB	AVG/OBP/SLG	BABIP	SLGCON	BB%	K%	ZSw%	ZCon%	OSw%	OCon%	LA	90th EV	DRC+	BRR	DRP	WARP
2022	FAY	A	22	117	13	4	15	4	.255/.342/.402	.355	.631	10.3%	31.6%							95	0.8	1.3	0.5
2023	MSS	WIN	23	75	12	3	7	2	.231/.333/.446	.300	.674	10.7%	29.3%	73.7%	85.7%	19.2%	40.0%						
2023	ASH	A+	23	133	38	4	20	6	.407/.474/.628	.494	.826	12.0%	20.3%							123	1.7	-0.2	0.9
2023	CC	AA	23	277	42	14	41	16	.257/.339/.486	.320	.717	9.4%	28.5%							100	1.9	-4.3	0.4
2024 non	HOU	MLB	24	251	24	5	25	7	.231/.294/.358	.323	.539	7.1%	30.8%							84	0.0	0	0.2

2023 GP: 3B (81), 2B (12), 1B (10), DH (8)   *Comps: Danny Valencia (76), Bobby Dalbec (73), Kyle Reynolds (69)*

How much you believe in Dezenzo as a future major leaguer depends on two factors. The first is his bat, which he swings with frightening speed and produces MLB-caliber exit velocities (and has since his days at Ohio State). It's unfortunately attached to a below-average hit tool; while Dezenzo did his best Ted Williams imitation at High-A after a post-draft swing change, his contact issues resurfaced once he reached Corpus Christi, with a strikeout rate nearing 30%. The other concern is his glove: Though he played up the middle in college, his imposing frame translates better to a corner. The Astros used him at second occasionally, but he's seen more time at third; he seems unlikely to become the first Astro at the position to win a Gold Glove since 1974, but it's early and he's still learning. There's likely enough offense here that Dezenzo can make some kind of mark, and the Astros couldn't ask for much more from an under-slot 12th-round pick.

Yainer Diaz **C/DH**   Born: 09/21/98   Age: 25   Bats: R   Throws: R   Height: 6'0"   Weight: 195   Origin: IFA, 2016

YEAR	TM	LVL	AGE	PA	R	HR	RBI	SB	AVG/OBP/SLG	BABIP	SLGCON	BB%	K%	ZSw%	ZCon%	OSw%	OCon%	LA	90th EV	DRC+	BRR	DRP	WARP
2021	FAY	A	22	49	3	1	7	1	.229/.224/.333	.227	.364	0.0%	8.2%							115	0.0	1.6	0.4
2021	LYN	A	22	258	30	5	50	1	.314/.357/.464	.361	.563	5.8%	16.3%							115	-1.3	2.0	1.3
2021	ASH	A+	22	105	28	11	33	2	.396/.438/.781	.391	.949	7.6%	16.2%							156	-0.4	-1.3	0.9
2022	CC	AA	23	267	37	9	48	1	.316/.367/.504	.345	.603	7.9%	15.0%							115	0.6	4.0	1.7
2022	SUG	AAA	23	219	38	16	48	1	.294/.342/.587	.291	.728	5.9%	17.8%	76.7%	86.0%	42.3%	61.3%			119	0.4	-6.9	0.6
2022	HOU	MLB	23	9	0	0	1	0	.125/.222/.250	.167	.333	11.1%	22.2%	88.9%	100.0%	54.5%	41.7%	21.1	105.9	89		0.0	0.0
2023	HOU	MLB	24	377	51	23	60	1	.282/.308/.538	.292	.680	2.9%	19.6%	76.7%	84.9%	47.1%	59.7%	11.8	106.4	124	-0.2	-2.9	1.9
2024 DC	HOU	MLB	25	389	45	16	52	0	.268/.310/.456	.306	.585	4.7%	20.9%							112	0.0	-3.3	1.7

2023 GP: C (60), DH (38), 1B (8)   *Comps: Buster Posey (62), Mike Piazza (62), Kendrys Morales (61)*

YEAR	TM	P. COUNT	FRM RUNS	BLK RUNS	THRW RUNS	TOT RUNS
2021	ESC	1246			0.0	0.0
2021	LYN	5174	0.7	0.3	2.1	3.1
2021	ASH	1663	-1.1	0.0	-0.2	-1.2
2022	CC	3895	-1.2	0.0	2.8	1.5
2022	SUG	4537	-6.9	-0.1	-0.4	-7.4
2022	HOU	23	0.0	0.0	0.0	0.0
2023	HOU	6748	-2.4	0.1	0.1	-2.2
2024	HOU	13228	-4.1	0.1	0.7	-3.4

For the first time in five seasons, Houston's Opening Day lineup card won't list "Maldonado" at catcher. Instead, it'll be Diaz, thanks to a breakout year with the bat and the departure of Dusty Baker and his veteran binky. But before Diaz passes Go and collects $200, it's worth asking: is he the right man for the job? Working in his favor: the highest wOBA (.354) from a Houston backstop since Jason Castro in 2013. DRC+ thinks he earned every penny of his numbers. Working against him: Javier Báez-esque chase and walk rates, and struggles with spin. To be determined: his defense. Diaz's arm and blocking grade out favorably, but not his framing; per CDA, he's below-average overall. Then again, by CDA, the worst defensive catcher in baseball last year was … Martín Maldonado. With Baker no longer calling the shots and Diaz's bat too potent to stick in a reserve role, here's betting the starter job is his for at least next year, and likely longer.

Mauricio Dubón **UT**   Born: 07/19/94   Age: 29   Bats: R   Throws: R   Height: 6'0"   Weight: 173   Origin: Round 26, 2013 Draft (#773 overall)

YEAR	TM	LVL	AGE	PA	R	HR	RBI	SB	AVG/OBP/SLG	BABIP	SLGCON	BB%	K%	ZSw%	ZCon%	OSw%	OCon%	LA	90th EV	DRC+	BRR	DRP	WARP
2021	SAC	AAA	26	283	41	8	31	9	.332/.410/.498	.365	.589	10.2%	13.4%							117	2.0	-2.8	1.5
2021	SF	MLB	26	187	20	5	22	2	.240/.278/.377	.282	.493	4.8%	21.9%	68.8%	83.0%	37.9%	69.1%	13.7	101.1	87	-0.1	0.1	0.4
2022	HOU	MLB	27	216	21	3	16	2	.208/.254/.294	.222	.339	5.6%	12.0%	73.6%	87.7%	40.4%	80.4%	15.3	100.8	96	0.0	0.8	0.7
2022	SF	MLB	27	49	10	2	8	0	.239/.245/.391	.214	.429	2.0%	8.2%	73.0%	90.7%	43.6%	76.5%	22.9	102.3	127	0.1	0.1	0.4
2023	HOU	MLB	28	492	76	10	46	7	.278/.309/.411	.308	.484	3.9%	14.2%	75.3%	86.4%	44.6%	77.1%	9.7	102.3	107	0.7	0.3	2.1
2024 DC	HOU	MLB	29	268	25	5	27	5	.259/.305/.371	.288	.437	5.6%	14.3%							91	0.0	0.4	0.5

2023 GP: 2B (79), CF (29), SS (9), LF (9), 1B (2), RF (2), 3B (1)   *Comps: Cameron Maybin (49), DJ LeMahieu (48), Marlon Byrd (46)*

Inherent in the term "super-utility" is extreme usefulness. Dubón ably played every infield position but catcher and two of three outfield spots last season; odds are that if Dusty Baker had asked him to throw an inning or two, he would've gamely taken the mound to chuck some eephus curves. And there is value in that utility; by WARP, Dubon finished sixth among Astros position players despite not getting full-time work. But when you need drywall more than spackle, he's the wrong man for the job. Case in point: When Baker benched Chas McCormick during the ALCS and turned to Dubón not just in center but, in Games 4 and 5, near the top of the lineup. The result: a .300 average and nothing else, because he's an all-slap/no-slug contact pest in the mold of David Fletcher or Myles Straw. Dubón is a representative of cognitive dissonance: He does good work, and the less you see of him the better off things are going.

Corey Julks LF Born: 02/27/96 Age: 28 Bats: R Throws: R Height: 6'1" Weight: 185 Origin: Round 8, 2017 Draft (#241 overall)

YEAR	TM	LVL	AGE	PA	R	HR	RBI	SB	AVG/OBP/SLG	BABIP	SLGCON	BB%	K%	ZSw%	ZCon%	OSw%	OCon%	LA	90th EV	DRC+	BRR	DRP	WARP
2021	CC	AA	25	372	67	14	36	15	.287/.349/.491	.344	.654	8.6%	22.6%							114	-1.1	10.3	2.7
2022	SUG	AAA	26	590	100	31	89	22	.270/.351/.503	.301	.666	9.5%	21.7%	57.9%	86.9%	29.3%	58.5%			133	-0.3	-6.2	3.7
2023	SUG	AAA	27	129	26	3	11	6	.240/.388/.462	.282	.593	18.6%	17.8%	56.5%	86.0%	22.0%	61.8%			104	0.9	-0.2	0.2
2023	HOU	MLB	27	323	35	6	33	15	.245/.297/.352	.306	.471	6.8%	23.2%	62.3%	85.0%	34.1%	61.3%	16.9	104.4	84	0.3	-0.5	0.2
2024 DC	HOU	MLB	28	126	13	3	13	4	.237/.307/.378	.290	.500	8.3%	22.8%							93	0.0	-0.3	0.2

2023 GP: LF (69), DH (19), RF (1) Comps: Trevor Crowe (64), Noel Cuevas (60), Juan Carlos Perez (58)

After a season spent stomping on Triple-A pitching, the Astros were hoping for Corey to go "Julks Smash!" against major leaguers, but throughout the summer his OPS remained stubbornly in the .700 club. Anything that wasn't a fastball turned him into a windmill; his whiff rate against breaking balls and off-speed pitches broke 30%, with spin and sweep proving hard for him to square up. Nor did he show much patience at the plate, or do much with the strikes he did get. Most concerning of all, things got worse as the season went on; from mid-July through the end of August, Julks hit a miserable .088/.159/.123 in 63 plate appearances. His semi-regular playing time split between left field and DH vanished the moment Michael Brantley was ready for service. A spot on the 2024 roster, and perhaps the 40-man, will require him to figure out how to change reliably from Bruce Banner into his green alter-ego.

Joey Loperfido CF Born: 05/11/99 Age: 25 Bats: L Throws: R Height: 6'3" Weight: 220 Origin: Round 7, 2021 Draft (#208 overall)

YEAR	TM	LVL	AGE	PA	R	HR	RBI	SB	AVG/OBP/SLG	BABIP	SLGCON	BB%	K%	ZSw%	ZCon%	OSw%	OCon%	LA	90th EV	DRC+	BRR	DRP	WARP
2021	FAY	A	22	87	10	2	6	1	.116/.276/.261	.158	.474	9.2%	35.6%							85	1.2	-0.6	0.2
2022	FAY	A	23	348	51	9	45	30	.304/.399/.473	.379	.636	11.5%	21.8%							125	-2.2	4.6	2.3
2022	ASH	A+	23	113	19	3	24	2	.354/.434/.552	.443	.746	11.5%	22.1%							105	-0.1	-0.9	0.3
2023	ASH	A+	24	37	4	1	5	3	.265/.297/.529	.308	.692	5.4%	21.6%							112	-0.3	-0.7	0.1
2023	CC	AA	24	365	60	19	57	20	.296/.392/.548	.344	.738	12.9%	22.2%							126	-0.8	-3.5	1.8
2023	SUG	AAA	24	138	15	5	16	4	.235/.333/.403	.329	.649	11.6%	32.6%	66.0%	79.6%	31.9%	46.9%			80	-0.9	0.5	0.1
2024 DC	HOU	MLB	25	99	9	2	10	3	.226/.298/.355	.296	.500	8.1%	26.2%							84	0.0	0	0.1

2023 GP: CF (43), 2B (21), RF (20), 1B (19), LF (14), DH (8) Comps: Corey Brown (63), Ryan Flaherty (59), Mike Gerber (56)

Loperfido continues to fly through the Astros' system, going from draft pick to Triple-A in a mere two years. All he did at Double-A was mash, running a double-digit walk rate and a .252 ISO, and though his time in Sugar Land wasn't as sweet, it's clear that he's a bat to believe in thanks to some gaudy hard-hit rates. He's managed to add power to his game, too, albeit with too many groundballs in the mix. Less certain is his long-term defensive home. Houston has shuttled him between first, second and center field; while he's been fine up the middle, it's more likely that he settles in at the cold corner. Still, with his versatility and left-handed stroke, Loperfido is a realistic candidate to reach the big leagues sometime in 2024.

Brice Matthews SS Born: 03/16/02 Age: 22 Bats: R Throws: R Height: 6'0" Weight: 190 Origin: Round 1, 2023 Draft (#28 overall)

YEAR	TM	LVL	AGE	PA	R	HR	RBI	SB	AVG/OBP/SLG	BABIP	SLGCON	BB%	K%	ZSw%	ZCon%	OSw%	OCon%	LA	90th EV	DRC+	BRR	DRP	WARP
2023	FAY	A	21	150	22	4	11	16	.217/.373/.367	.289	.550	16.0%	26.7%							99	1.0	0.1	0.6
2024 non	HOU	MLB	22	251	21	3	21	0	.210/.282/.305	.314	.479	8.0%	32.7%							68	0.0	0	-0.1

2023 GP: SS (29), DH (6) Comps: Albert Cartwright (71), Jorge Flores (69), Tyler Kolodny (69)

While college draft picks are usually thought of as polished players closer to the majors than their high school counterparts, plenty are also raw and in need of refinement. Case in point: Astros 2023 first-rounder Matthews, a University of Nebraska product who remains a project. To be fair, he's not a formless lump of clay, putting up good numbers in his three years as a Cornhusker to go with plus speed and workable defense up the middle. What concerned evaluators going into the draft was his hit tool, though in his final season in the Big Ten, he did a better job making contact in the zone, allowing him to tap more into his sizable raw power. The task for the Astros, who are perilously short on middle infielders in their system, will be both improving Matthews' overall approach and seeing if he can stick at short, another topic where scouts are divided.

Chas McCormick OF Born: 04/19/95 Age: 29 Bats: R Throws: L Height: 6'0" Weight: 208 Origin: Round 21, 2017 Draft (#631 overall)

YEAR	TM	LVL	AGE	PA	R	HR	RBI	SB	AVG/OBP/SLG	BABIP	SLGCON	BB%	K%	ZSw%	ZCon%	OSw%	OCon%	LA	90th EV	DRC+	BRR	DRP	WARP
2021	HOU	MLB	26	320	47	14	50	4	.257/.319/.447	.341	.706	7.8%	32.5%	66.9%	71.5%	29.9%	51.7%	19.0	103.6	71	0.3	0.9	0.1
2022	HOU	MLB	27	407	47	14	44	4	.245/.332/.407	.308	.577	11.3%	26.0%	69.9%	76.1%	32.6%	54.5%	12.6	103.1	101	-0.1	2.5	1.7
2023	HOU	MLB	28	457	59	22	70	19	.273/.353/.489	.331	.689	8.8%	25.6%	70.8%	79.2%	33.2%	57.9%	14.7	103.0	96	0.7	1.0	1.4
2024 DC	HOU	MLB	29	523	60	19	64	15	.238/.321/.408	.295	.572	9.4%	25.7%							104	0.1	0.7	1.9

2023 GP: LF (59), CF (55), RF (24), DH (4) Comps: Ryan Raburn (61), Khris Davis (61), Tommy Pham (58)

While the rest of the baseball world laid roses at Dusty Baker's feet when he announced his retirement, McCormick probably didn't shed a tear. It's clear that the veteran manager and his erstwhile center fielder never got on the same page despite the latter's production. Reasons for the pair's disconnect abound—the scuttlebutt is that Baker was unhappy with McCormick's weight—but either way, a good year overall and a scorching stretch from early May through the end of August (.282/.360/.514) still wasn't enough to make him an everyday starter. Even in the postseason, Baker opted to give playing time in center to the punchless Mauricio Dubón. Amusingly enough, DRC+ thinks Baker was right to give McCormick the side-eye, thanks to a decline in walk rate and a BABIP spike unaccompanied by better quality of contact stats. Still, his overall numbers, improved defense and steady forward progression (and the team's lack of better options in center or left) suggest that McCormick should and will get more run from Joe Espada.

Jacob Melton CF Born: 09/07/00 Age: 23 Bats: L Throws: L Height: 6'3" Weight: 208 Origin: Round 2, 2022 Draft (#64 overall)

YEAR	TM	LVL	AGE	PA	R	HR	RBI	SB	AVG/OBP/SLG	BABIP	SLGCON	BB%	K%	ZSw%	ZCon%	OSw%	OCon%	LA	90th EV	DRC+	BRR	DRP	WARP
2022	FAY	A	21	86	11	4	13	4	.324/.424/.577	.396	.804	12.8%	23.3%							114	-1.0	0.3	0.3
2023	ASH	A+	22	394	73	18	42	41	.244/.338/.453	.272	.598	12.2%	21.1%							105	3.2	4.3	2.7
2023	CC	AA	22	56	10	5	13	5	.250/.304/.558	.258	.806	7.1%	28.6%							108	0.7	0.6	0.2
2024 non	HOU	MLB	23	251	23	5	24	15	.217/.285/.343	.284	.491	8.0%	27.0%							77	0.0	0	0.1

2023 GP: CF (48), DH (26), RF (17), LF (9)   *Comps: Luis Barrera (71), Brandon Jones (68), Adam Haseley (63)*

Coming off a strong final month in A-ball in 2022, Melton wasn't overwhelmed by High-A or Double-A, but he also didn't set either on fire. Worse, some of his numbers—looking at you, strikeout and walk rates—raise concern as to whether Melton has what it takes to solve upper-level pitching. It starts with a stiff swing that looks more like a product of the KBO or NPB, and while there's plenty of power in it, it's also vulnerable to breaking balls and middle-in fastballs. Equally strange is a propensity to hit the ball to all fields, but only in the air or on the ground; there aren't many line drives off his bat. Defensively, his plus speed makes him a center fielder for now, but "for now" is the key phrase; it's unlikely he sticks there long-term. Neither fish nor fowl, Melton has a cloudy future.

Jake Meyers CF Born: 06/18/96 Age: 28 Bats: R Throws: L Height: 6'0" Weight: 200 Origin: Round 13, 2017 Draft (#391 overall)

YEAR	TM	LVL	AGE	PA	R	HR	RBI	SB	AVG/OBP/SLG	BABIP	SLGCON	BB%	K%	ZSw%	ZCon%	OSw%	OCon%	LA	90th EV	DRC+	BRR	DRP	WARP
2021	SUG	AAA	25	304	52	16	51	10	.343/.408/.598	.389	.764	8.2%	19.4%							126	-1.0	13.6	3.2
2021	HOU	MLB	25	163	22	6	28	3	.260/.323/.438	.352	.667	6.1%	30.7%	67.6%	81.4%	31.6%	55.6%	9.3	103.7	75	0.1	-0.3	0.1
2022	SUG	AAA	26	170	26	7	18	2	.306/.406/.507	.343	.640	14.7%	17.6%	63.7%	86.5%	25.2%	54.8%			122	0.8	1.6	1.2
2022	HOU	MLB	26	160	13	1	15	2	.227/.269/.313	.344	.490	4.4%	33.8%	67.9%	79.2%	33.0%	53.7%	7.2	103.0	68	0.0	0.7	0.0
2023	HOU	MLB	27	341	42	10	33	5	.227/.296/.382	.283	.534	7.6%	25.8%	72.0%	85.6%	29.1%	48.4%	13.7	102.2	83	0.3	-0.3	0.5
2024 DC	HOU	MLB	28	346	34	9	37	4	.229/.299/.368	.284	.502	7.5%	24.2%							87	0.0	-0.9	0.6

2023 GP: CF (105), LF (2)   *Comps: Drew Stubbs (63), Roman Quinn (59), Marlon Byrd (57)*

At this point, there's not much to suggest that Meyers is more than a glove and a flat Nebraska accent. More walks, fewer strikeouts, and more power from the year prior only translated into a DRC+ in the Jackie Bradley Jr./Trent Grisham range, in large part because Meyers has no thump in his lumber. His average exit velocity and barrel rate were both in the fifth percentile, 13 of his 16 doubles were down the line, and while he does a decent job avoiding empty swings, not even Tony Gwynn in his prime could get by if only one out of every 20 balls is hit with any mustard. Good defense will keep Meyers employed as long as he wants, but it's a thin line between being the next generation's Kevin Kiermaier and being Joey Wiemer's clean-cut cousin.

Jeremy Peña SS Born: 09/22/97 Age: 26 Bats: R Throws: R Height: 6'0" Weight: 202 Origin: Round 3, 2018 Draft (#102 overall)

YEAR	TM	LVL	AGE	PA	R	HR	RBI	SB	AVG/OBP/SLG	BABIP	SLGCON	BB%	K%	ZSw%	ZCon%	OSw%	OCon%	LA	90th EV	DRC+	BRR	DRP	WARP
2021	EST	WIN	23	134	18	2	15	7	.291/.364/.410	.381	.565	8.2%	23.9%										
2021	AST	ROK	23	27	3	0	2	1	.348/.444/.478	.471	.647	7.4%	22.2%									0.2	
2021	SUG	AAA	23	133	22	10	19	5	.287/.346/.598	.325	.839	4.5%	26.3%							106	1.1	2.2	0.8
2022	HOU	MLB	24	558	72	22	63	11	.253/.289/.426	.298	.575	3.9%	24.2%	75.4%	86.4%	40.7%	49.1%	8.2	105.3	79	0.7	-0.7	0.3
2023	HOU	MLB	25	634	81	10	52	13	.263/.324/.381	.323	.491	6.8%	20.3%	74.9%	88.1%	38.4%	50.1%	5.5	103.7	94	0.5	0.4	1.8
2024 DC	HOU	MLB	26	579	58	15	63	14	.244/.300/.383	.298	.511	6.1%	23.1%							92	0.0	-0.5	1.4

2023 GP: SS (150)   *Comps: Tim Anderson (76), Eduardo Núñez (73), Eduardo Escobar (72)*

In 2023, Houston got as much if not more out of Peña than the man he once replaced in Carlos Correa. While the latter alternated between stiff and lost in Minnesota, the former married league-average hitting with acceptable defense to put together a fine if unexceptional season. Said season was missing a lot of the power that Peña showed off in his rookie campaign, as pitchers continued to work him down and away, forcing him to extend his arms. That led to empty swings and harmless grounders to the left side. But DRC+ thought highly of his walk rate going from atrocious to merely bad, and while that still comes with too much aggression, the combination may be an inescapable part of Peña's game. Houston will live with it so long as he remains in the red with the glove and especially for as long as he's cheap. That extends his leash through at least the next couple years, before escalating arbitration awards will force the Astros to make a decision on whether Peña joins Correa as a Texas ex.

Kyle Tucker RF Born: 01/17/97 Age: 27 Bats: L Throws: R Height: 6'4" Weight: 199 Origin: Round 1, 2015 Draft (#5 overall)

YEAR	TM	LVL	AGE	PA	R	HR	RBI	SB	AVG/OBP/SLG	BABIP	SLGCON	BB%	K%	ZSw%	ZCon%	OSw%	OCon%	LA	90th EV	DRC+	BRR	DRP	WARP
2021	HOU	MLB	24	567	83	30	92	14	.294/.359/.557	.304	.678	9.3%	15.9%	82.7%	86.7%	31.9%	67.1%	17.7	104.8	135	0.4	1.9	4.5
2022	HOU	MLB	25	609	71	30	107	25	.257/.330/.478	.261	.579	9.7%	15.6%	84.1%	87.9%	30.1%	64.1%	19.1	104.1	129	1.9	-0.4	4.0
2023	HOU	MLB	26	674	97	29	112	30	.284/.369/.517	.289	.616	11.9%	13.6%	73.4%	88.2%	26.3%	66.6%	15.2	104.7	147	1.2	-3.3	5.4
2024 DC	HOU	MLB	27	623	77	24	84	30	.271/.355/.473	.287	.566	11.1%	14.5%							132	0.9	-2.1	4.0

2023 GP: RF (153), DH (4)   *Comps: Johnny Callison (71), Rusty Staub (70), Shawn Green (69)*

While the bean counters in Houston strain to figure out how to pay Alex Bregman and Jose Altuve, what will it take to lock Tucker down long-term? The Tampa product spent his age-26 season proving that he's a key cog in the Astros' lineup, finishing a homer shy of a 30-30 season and setting new career highs in WARP and DRC+. There's no mystery as to how Tucker does it: He hits the ball hard and square, he rarely misses when he swings and he's exceptionally patient and he demolishes fastballs. Tucker ranked in the 80th percentile in SEAGER, a metric designed to measure selective aggression on hittable pitches. The only nit to pick is his mediocre defense in the cozy confines of Minute Maid, but that matters less when he's perpetually turning baseballs into leather-covered mush. A deserved payday draws ever closer.

PITCHERS

Bryan Abreu   RHP   Born: 04/22/97   Age: 27   Height: 6'1"   Weight: 225   Origin: IFA, 2013

YEAR	TM	LVL	AGE	G(GS)	IP	W-L	SV	K	WHIP	ERA	CSP	BB%	K%	HR%	GB%	ZSw%	ZCon%	OSw%	OCon%	BABIP	SLGCON	DRA-	WARP
2021	TOR	WIN	24	7(7)	26	1-4	0	28	1.31	2.42		9.8%	25.0%	0.0%	55.2%					.315	.342		
2021	SUG	AAA	24	15(0)	15¹	0-0	0	24	1.57	1.76		19.1%	35.3%	0.0%	51.6%					.355	.419	64	0.4
2021	HOU	MLB	24	31(0)	36	3-3	1	36	1.47	5.75	51.3%	11.2%	22.4%	2.5%	48.1%	72.8%	83.0%	29.6%	49.2%	.310	.549	101	0.3
2022	HOU	MLB	25	55(0)	60¹	4-0	2	88	1.18	1.94	50.0%	10.5%	35.5%	0.8%	47.7%	72.3%	78.1%	35.8%	40.9%	.336	.450	69	1.5
2023	HOU	MLB	26	72(0)	72	3-2	5	100	1.04	1.75	46.3%	10.8%	34.8%	2.1%	37.3%	64.8%	74.1%	31.3%	40.7%	.262	.480	77	1.7
2024 DC	HOU	MLB	27	50(0)	53¹	4-2	5	79	1.23	3.57	48.2%	11.6%	35.0%	3.0%	42.4%					.299	.593	82	0.7

2023 Arsenal: SL (87.5), FA (97.7), SI (96.7), KC (83.5)   *Comps: Carl Edwards Jr. (65), Ernesto Frieri (64), Dan Altavilla (63)*

Abreu is the dream of every fastball-slider righty, and for every pitching coach and front office cycling through three dozen of those arms every season. Still adding velocity—his four-seamer sits at a gaudy 97.6 mph—and featuring a slider that has above-average break and sweep, Abreu is borderline impossible to hit, with sub-.200 batting averages against and whiff rates above 37% on both his offerings. The slider became his primary pitch last season, with a usage rate just south of 60%; he threw it the majority of the time in nearly every count, even when he fell behind. (He also ditched a curveball that was at one point in his career his best pitch, because why not add more challenges if you're already this dominant?) That change, in turn, made the fastball that much harder to hit, save for the occasional pipe shot; its whiff rate shot up 10 points from 2022 to '23. It's a simple formula executed to perfection, and it's made Abreu one of the best non-closer relievers in the game.

Spencer Arrighetti   RHP   Born: 01/02/00   Age: 24   Height: 6'2"   Weight: 186   Origin: Round 6, 2021 Draft (#178 overall)

YEAR	TM	LVL	AGE	G(GS)	IP	W-L	SV	K	WHIP	ERA	CSP	BB%	K%	HR%	GB%	ZSw%	ZCon%	OSw%	OCon%	BABIP	SLGCON	DRA-	WARP
2021	FAY	A	21	4(2)	9²	2-1	0	16	0.52	2.79		5.6%	44.4%	2.8%	35.3%					.125	.353	95	0.1
2022	ASH	A+	22	22(13)	85²	6-5	2	124	1.56	5.04		11.7%	31.6%	1.5%	42.1%					.390	.606	91	1.0
2022	CC	AA	22	5(4)	21	1-1	0	28	1.05	3.43		11.1%	34.6%	3.7%	38.6%					.244	.568	67	0.5
2023	CC	AA	23	13(8)	60²	7-2	0	79	1.17	4.15		9.1%	31.2%	1.6%	32.4%					.312	.518	87	1.2
2023	SUG	AAA	23	15(13)	64	2-5	0	62	1.33	4.64		13.4%	23.1%	2.6%	33.3%	66.0%	84.9%	27.4%	54.5%	.266	.530	98	0.6
2024 DC	HOU	MLB	24	3(3)	13¹	1-1	0	14	1.41	4.87		11.4%	22.7%	3.6%	34.0%					.284	.579	107	0.1

2023 Arsenal: FA (92.4), SW (79.6), CH (86.8)   *Comps: Aaron Blair (73), Domingo Acevedo (73), José Cisnero (73)*

A slow start and a rough finish marred an otherwise solid season for Arrighetti, during which he earned a bump to Triple-A and briefly looked like a potential second-half call-up. The latter didn't come to pass, but it's not hard to see him making his way to Houston next year as a rotation fill-in *a la* J.P. France. Like France, Arrighetti makes do without an overpowering arsenal; his fastball averages 92 mph, and the best of his handful of breaking balls is a big sweeping slider that acts as his main whiff pitch. His three-quarters arm slot and flat approach angle help the heater play up, but he struggles to land the slider for strikes and savvier PCL hitters learned to lay off of it. Still, the stuff is there—Arrighetti just needs a little more time in the pot.

Hunter Brown   RHP   Born: 08/29/98   Age: 25   Height: 6'2"   Weight: 212   Origin: Round 5, 2019 Draft (#166 overall)

YEAR	TM	LVL	AGE	G(GS)	IP	W-L	SV	K	WHIP	ERA	CSP	BB%	K%	HR%	GB%	ZSw%	ZCon%	OSw%	OCon%	BABIP	SLGCON	DRA-	WARP
2021	CC	AA	22	13(11)	49¹	1-4	1	76	1.50	4.20		13.4%	35.0%	2.8%	45.5%					.379	.676	96	0.4
2021	SUG	AAA	22	11(8)	51	5-1	0	55	1.33	3.88		9.7%	25.5%	2.8%	52.5%					.311	.566	84	0.7
2022	SUG	AAA	23	23(14)	106	9-4	1	134	1.08	2.55		10.6%	31.5%	1.2%	54.3%	63.9%	81.0%	29.2%	54.2%	.271	.412	67	2.7
2022	HOU	MLB	23	7(2)	20¹	2-0	0	22	1.08	0.89	58.3%	8.8%	27.5%	0.0%	64.7%	64.1%	91.5%	32.0%	56.9%	.294	.412	84	0.4
2023	HOU	MLB	24	31(29)	155²	11-13	0	178	1.36	5.09	48.0%	8.3%	26.8%	3.9%	52.2%	66.8%	86.9%	31.6%	57.3%	.330	.648	79	3.5
2024 DC	HOU	MLB	25	26(26)	139²	10-6	0	141	1.27	3.68	48.9%	9.5%	23.8%	2.4%	52.0%					.286	.492	85	2.3

2023 Arsenal: FA (95.8), SL (91.9), KC (83.1), CH (88.3), SW (84.3), SI (95.2)   *Comps: Robinson Tejeda (71), Anthony Reyes (70), Nick Tropeano (69)*

Brown's brief 2022 illustrated the trouble with small samples, with good numbers on the surface undercut by peripheral stats—no homers allowed, a sky-high strand- and ground-ball rate—suggesting an unrepeatable performance lurking underneath. Lo and behold, in 2023 a lofty home run rate, a more reasonable strand rate and fewer ground balls all added up to worse numbers overall. Yet that's not the whole story either: DRA- thought that the Brown of 2022 and the Brown of 2023 were functionally the same pitcher. You don't need AI to see it: he ran identical strikeout, walk, swing and whiff rates. Now add a pinch of Statcast, which says, "hold on, not only was Brown's quality of contact generally worse in 2023—hence all the homers—but his stuff slipped, too." His fastball, a mile per hour slower last season, leaked into the heart of the strike zone too often, and his breakers couldn't find the edges. So was Brown bad, unlucky, secretly good, or something else in 2023? Consider this a vote for "a second-year pitcher figuring it out," and one who still shows plenty of promise.

Dylan Coleman   RHP   Born: 09/16/96   Age: 27   Height: 6'5"   Weight: 230   Origin: Round 4, 2018 Draft (#111 overall)

YEAR	TM	LVL	AGE	G(GS)	IP	W-L	SV	K	WHIP	ERA	CSP	BB%	K%	HR%	GB%	ZSw%	ZCon%	OSw%	OCon%	BABIP	SLGCON	DRA-	WARP
2021	NWA	AA	24	18(0)	24²	1-1	4	37	0.97	2.92		5.3%	38.9%	2.1%	50.9%					.333	.528	69	0.6
2021	OMA	AAA	24	27(0)	33	4-0	3	56	1.09	3.55		12.6%	41.5%	1.5%	36.2%					.304	.483	66	1.0
2021	KC	MLB	24	5(0)	6¹	0-0	0	7	0.95	1.42	56.7%	4.0%	28.0%	0.0%	23.5%	76.1%	71.4%	33.3%	76.2%	.294	.412	102	0.1
2022	KC	MLB	25	68(0)	68	5-2	0	71	1.24	2.78	51.3%	12.8%	24.6%	1.7%	41.7%	64.5%	76.1%	31.6%	59.2%	.247	.433	96	0.8
2023	OMA	AAA	26	32(0)	30²	1-5	2	48	1.70	4.70		21.8%	32.7%	2.0%	39.3%	60.4%	75.4%	27.1%	52.3%	.293	.557	94	0.5
2023	KC	MLB	26	23(1)	18¹	0-2	0	21	2.02	8.84	41.7%	19.8%	21.9%	3.1%	35.3%	58.0%	80.3%	25.4%	54.7%	.313	.625	122	0.0
2024 non	HOU	MLB	27	58(0)	50	2-2	0	61	1.46	4.88	49.0%	14.4%	27.4%	3.4%	38.4%					.281	.579	106	0.1

2023 Arsenal: FA (95.3), SW (81), FC (90.2)   *Comps: Brian Ellington (76), Kevin Quackenbush (75), Vic Black (72)*

In 1965, Kurt Vonnegut's master's thesis—on the patterns of familiar narratives like fairy tales—was rejected by the University of Chicago, infuriating Vonnegut, who fumed "it was rejected because it was so simple and looked like too much fun." Coleman would have done well to replicate Vonnegut's approach and kept things fun and simple; instead, he tweaked his arsenal to add a cutter, faded the fastball, and started throwing his slider more. He proceeded to endure a dreadful funhouse mirror version of his sterling rookie year, suffering not one but two demotions to Triple-A to try to get things going in the right direction. Maybe the tweaks were necessary due to declining fastball velocity, or maybe it was an intentional adjustment, but whatever the reason, Coleman's fastball got pummeled, and the new cutter didn't fare particularly well, either. All the while his command, never a strong suit, deserted him entirely. It could be that he's just deep in the woods with grandma's house still safely ahead, but he could also take Vonnegut's position towards the "apathetic" University of Chicago and invite those tweaks to "take a flying [redacted] at the mooooooooon."

Trey Dombroski LHP Born: 03/13/01 Age: 23 Height: 6'5" Weight: 235 Origin: Round 4, 2022 Draft (#133 overall)

YEAR	TM	LVL	AGE	G (GS)	IP	W-L	SV	K	WHIP	ERA	CSP	BB%	K%	HR%	GB%	ZSw%	ZCon%	OSw%	OCon%	BABIP	SLGCON	DRA-	WARP
2023	FAY	A	22	26(15)	119	7-9	1	148	1.12	3.71		7.3%	30.1%	3.1%	43.3%					.285	.578	82	2.3
2024 non	HOU	MLB	23	58(0)	50	2-2	0	45	1.48	5.50		9.4%	20.1%	4.1%	36.0%					.303	.604	121	-0.3

Comps: José Taveras (84), Jaime Arias (83), Anthony Shew (82)

Dombroski's name could double as a vanity plate for Bode Miller, a man who once wrote that his goal was to go "as fast as the natural universe would allow." Unfortunately for Dombroski, said universe has throttled his fastball; it sits in the high 80s, only occasionally touching the low 90s. Houston's ability to coax some more miles per hour out of him will likely be the difference between Dombroski settling in as a back-of-the-rotation arm and something more. The rest of the Dombrowski package works just fine: good breaking balls, a changeup that gets whiffs and a smooth delivery that allows him to throw strikes with regularity. A 30% strikeout rate in A-ball suggests that he can make his stuff work. If he can find those extra ticks on the fastball, it will be time to get excited.

J.P. France RHP Born: 04/04/95 Age: 29 Height: 6'0" Weight: 216 Origin: Round 14, 2018 Draft (#432 overall)

YEAR	TM	LVL	AGE	G (GS)	IP	W-L	SV	K	WHIP	ERA	CSP	BB%	K%	HR%	GB%	ZSw%	ZCon%	OSw%	OCon%	BABIP	SLGCON	DRA-	WARP
2021	CC	AA	26	8(5)	33²	3-2	0	50	1.25	4.28		9.9%	35.2%	1.4%	43.6%					.342	.618	75	0.7
2021	SUG	AAA	26	17(13)	80¹	6-1	0	107	1.31	3.59		11.0%	30.9%	3.5%	31.2%					.294	.594	90	0.8
2022	SUG	AAA	27	34(15)	110²	3-4	3	136	1.36	3.90		10.6%	28.3%	3.1%	33.7%	69.9%	80.3%	27.8%	51.2%	.304	.590	81	1.9
2023	SUG	AAA	28	5(3)	19¹	2-1	0	26	1.03	2.33		14.3%	33.8%	0.0%	54.3%	62.1%	76.8%	27.9%	46.0%	.225	.325	89	0.3
2023	HOU	MLB	28	24(23)	136¹	11-6	0	101	1.36	3.83	50.0%	8.1%	17.4%	3.3%	42.0%	66.1%	86.2%	27.9%	62.8%	.290	.513	113	0.7
2024 DC	HOU	MLB	29	23(23)	127	9-7	0	101	1.42	4.76	50.0%	9.5%	18.2%	3.2%	41.2%					.292	.530	106	0.7

2023 Arsenal: FA (93), FC (86.9), CH (81.5), KC (75.9), SW (80) *Comps: Spenser Watkins (61), Jason Alexander (60), Jerad Eickhoff (59)*

France has the name of a dime novel detective or a hard-bitten World War II sergeant, but the one in our reality is a bespectacled, mustachioed New Orleans native with a pitching arsenal straight out of 1974. France gets by on a parade of soft stuff and deception, throwing sliders, cutters, changeups, curveballs, smoke bombs, Wiffle Balls—whatever keeps hitters off his fastball long enough to turn a lineup over at least twice. When unexpectedly pressed into service by numerous rotation injuries he did that with regularity, completing five or more innings in 19 of his 23 starts. That doesn't mean he's well cast as a frontline starter on a contender: His Statcast contact and expected stats are a sea of blue (or *bleu*, rather), and DRA places him squarely alongside the likes of Miles Mikolas and Luke Weaver. It's the kind of profile that screams "NL Central fourth starter," and maybe his ultimate destiny awaits that fateful phone call from the Pirates. Until then, he'll remain at the back of Houston's rotation or atop Sugar Land's, trying to dodge the raindrops.

Luis Garcia RHP Born: 12/13/96 Age: 27 Height: 5'11" Weight: 244 Origin: IFA, 2017

YEAR	TM	LVL	AGE	G (GS)	IP	W-L	SV	K	WHIP	ERA	CSP	BB%	K%	HR%	GB%	ZSw%	ZCon%	OSw%	OCon%	BABIP	SLGCON	DRA-	WARP
2021	HOU	MLB	24	30(28)	155¹	11-8	0	167	1.18	3.48	55.4%	7.9%	26.4%	3.0%	38.3%	67.3%	79.7%	33.1%	55.3%	.291	.554	97	1.7
2022	HOU	MLB	25	28(28)	157¹	15-8	0	157	1.13	3.72	56.9%	7.3%	24.4%	3.6%	37.0%	72.3%	81.0%	32.6%	55.1%	.261	.544	91	2.3
2023	HOU	MLB	26	6(6)	27	2-2	0	31	1.30	4.00	45.0%	8.7%	27.0%	2.6%	26.0%	69.3%	82.3%	37.5%	52.4%	.319	.611	103	0.3
2024 DC	HOU	MLB	27	6(6)	33²	2-2	0	35	1.28	4.21	54.8%	8.4%	24.4%	3.7%	35.8%					.290	.585	96	0.4

2023 Arsenal: FC (85.8), FA (93.3), SW (78.9), CU (76.9), CH (85) *Comps: Brett Myers (61), Pedro Ramos (57), Ian Kennedy (57)*

It is a truth universally acknowledged, that a pitcher in possession of a plus pitch, must be in want of throwing it more. Such was the case for Garcia, who increased his cutter usage to a career high in 2022 and kept right on going in '23, tossing it 43% of the time. And why not? It boasted a whiff rate over 40% the year prior—a rate it matched last season—and helped him avoid hard contact far better than his fastball, which hitters tattooed. But it's also a pitch Garcia struggles to command. He aims it down and away to righties, where it occasionally nicks the corner of the strike zone but usually ends up two inches off the plate or in the dirt. More cutters, then, meant more strikeouts…and more walks. For now, that's the least of his issues: on May 1, Garcia left his start against the Giants with elbow tightness. A day later, he was on the injured list; two weeks after that, he was on the operating table undergoing Tommy John surgery. We likely won't see him again until 2025.

Colton Gordon LHP Born: 12/20/98 Age: 25 Height: 6'4" Weight: 225 Origin: Round 8, 2021 Draft (#238 overall)

YEAR	TM	LVL	AGE	G (GS)	IP	W-L	SV	K	WHIP	ERA	CSP	BB%	K%	HR%	GB%	ZSw%	ZCon%	OSw%	OCon%	BABIP	SLGCON	DRA-	WARP
2022	ASB	ROK	23	4(4)	7	0-1	0	11	0.57	0.00		3.8%	42.3%	0.0%	42.9%					.214	.357		
2022	ASO	ROK	23	2(1)	6	0-0	0	11	1.17	4.50		4.2%	45.8%	4.2%	30.0%					.455	1.250		
2022	FAY	A	23	5(3)	20¹	0-0	0	27	0.79	2.21		4.0%	36.0%	1.3%	53.3%					.273	.409	74	0.5
2022	ASH	A+	23	4(3)	20¹	2-0	1	29	0.79	2.66		3.9%	37.7%	2.6%	34.1%					.262	.545	68	0.5
2023	CC	AA	24	20(18)	93¹	4-5	1	121	1.19	3.95		9.1%	30.7%	2.3%	34.3%					.300	.535	87	2.2
2023	SUG	AAA	24	9(6)	35	3-2	0	30	1.74	4.63		13.5%	18.4%	4.9%	29.7%	63.4%	85.9%	34.0%	70.6%	.301	.640	120	
2024 DC	HOU	MLB	25	3(3)	12²	1-1	0	12	1.39	4.86		9.8%	21.1%	3.7%	33.3%					.288	.579	108	0.1

2023 Arsenal: FA (90.6), CU (73.6), CH (84.7), SW (78.1), FC (86), SI (91.1) *Comps: Sam Howard (79), Tyler Pill (75), Darin Gorski (75)*

"Colton" first appeared in the Social Security Administration's database of popular baby names in 1982, when it ranked 799th nationwide. By 1998, when Gordon was born, it had surged all the way to 106th; as any teacher can tell you, it's stayed relatively popular ever since. MLB registered its first Colton in 2015 and has since added two more to the ledger. Will Gordon be the fourth? Working in his favor: good command; a low release point combined with a flat fastball approach angle; and a sweeping slider that ties lefty hitters into knots. Working against him: pedestrian velocity and lots of time on the shelf owing to the pandemic and 2021 Tommy John surgery. Now healthy, he's making up for lost time, though he uncharacteristically struggled to throw strikes in his first taste of Triple-A. He'll go as far as his deception can take him, making him a likely back-end starter or lefty reliever.

Kendall Graveman RHP   Born: 12/21/90   Age: 33   Height: 6'2"   Weight: 200   Origin: Round 8, 2013 Draft (#235 overall)

YEAR	TM	LVL	AGE	G(GS)	IP	W-L	SV	K	WHIP	ERA	CSP	BB%	K%	HR%	GB%	ZSw%	ZCon%	OSw%	OCon%	BABIP	SLGCON	DRA-	WARP
2021	HOU	MLB	30	23(0)	23	1-1	0	27	1.39	3.13	47.9%	11.9%	26.7%	1.0%	56.1%	69.8%	81.4%	28.7%	59.2%	.339	.456	82	0.4
2021	SEA	MLB	30	30(0)	33	4-0	10	34	0.70	0.82	49.4%	6.6%	28.1%	1.7%	53.9%	63.3%	91.1%	35.4%	60.6%	.176	.303	80	0.7
2022	CHW	MLB	31	65(0)	65	3-4	6	66	1.40	3.18	51.6%	9.1%	23.2%	1.8%	54.2%	64.9%	80.2%	34.0%	64.4%	.324	.492	87	1.1
2023	CHW	MLB	32	45(0)	44	3-4	8	42	1.20	3.48	42.9%	10.8%	22.6%	3.2%	39.0%	63.5%	80.6%	32.3%	61.6%	.241	.496	108	0.3
2023	HOU	MLB	32	23(0)	22¹	2-2	0	24	1.52	2.42	41.7%	16.7%	25.0%	3.1%	35.7%	70.1%	80.9%	28.1%	52.1%	.288	.545	100	0.3
2024 DC	HOU	MLB	33	45(0)	48	3-2	0	49	1.35	4.42	46.9%	10.5%	23.5%	3.0%	46.1%					.290	.533	98	0.3

2023 Arsenal: SI (96.2), SL (87.2), FA (96.1), CH (88.6), CU (81.9)   *Comps: Jason Grilli (68), LaTroy Hawkins (63), David Weathers (63)*

It's a credit to Graveman's complete overhaul as a late-inning reliever the past three years that it's difficult to remember his first act as a strikeout-averse fifth starter in Oakland. Unless he can reverse some trends, however, his second act might also be coming to a close. The veteran struggled with his command, triggering a snowball effect: Not only did he have a particularly difficult time locating on three-ball counts, exaggerating his walk rate compared to his out-of-zone rate, but those extra hitter's counts led to prepared hitters elevating pitches that couldn't afford to miss the black. Houston tried to tinker by reducing Graveman's slider usage in favor of his four-seamer, which was always his best pitch in terms of results, if in no small part because of the surprise factor. He has one more year on his current contract to figure out how to revive his mojo.

Cristian Javier RHP   Born: 03/26/97   Age: 27   Height: 6'1"   Weight: 213   Origin: IFA, 2015

YEAR	TM	LVL	AGE	G(GS)	IP	W-L	SV	K	WHIP	ERA	CSP	BB%	K%	HR%	GB%	ZSw%	ZCon%	OSw%	OCon%	BABIP	SLGCON	DRA-	WARP
2021	HOU	MLB	24	36(9)	101¹	4-1	2	130	1.18	3.55	50.8%	12.5%	30.7%	3.8%	27.4%	73.4%	77.8%	28.5%	54.0%	.235	.554	115	0.2
2022	HOU	MLB	25	30(25)	148²	11-9	0	194	0.95	2.54	53.9%	8.9%	33.2%	2.9%	25.2%	71.7%	78.1%	33.4%	57.1%	.229	.485	81	2.9
2023	HOU	MLB	26	31(31)	162	10-5	0	159	1.27	4.56	45.1%	9.0%	23.1%	3.6%	25.7%	70.3%	82.2%	32.6%	59.2%	.273	.573	124	-0.1
2024 DC	HOU	MLB	27	29(29)	151¹	10-8	0	157	1.30	4.33	49.0%	9.7%	24.4%	3.7%	26.9%					.281	.581	99	1.4

2023 Arsenal: FA (92.8), SW (79.6), KC (76.7), CH (83.6)   *Comps: Blake Snell (64), Zack Wheeler (63), Nick Tropeano (63)*

What happened to Javier in 2023? Well, how much time do you have? In short: too many homers, not enough walks, a velocity dip on his four-seamer, and a slider that went from "banned by the Geneva Convention" to "safe for all ages." The pitch lost 10 points of whiff rate and about an inch of sweep, and that was enough to crater both it and, in turn, Javier's season. That's the kind of monoculture fragility he risks by throwing his four-seamer and slider 90% of the time; once the blight came for the latter he was left with a changeup and curveball that are more change-of-pace offerings than viable third or fourth pitches. While his fastball is still flat as Kansas atop the strike zone with hellacious backspin, it's easier to get under it when you can spit on the slider; hitters knocked it out of the park 21 times. Javier's velo decline and a change in release point suggest he wasn't performing at 100%, and the Astros will have to hope that a fix is as simple as better health.

Seth Martinez RHP   Born: 08/29/94   Age: 29   Height: 6'2"   Weight: 200   Origin: Round 17, 2016 Draft (#502 overall)

YEAR	TM	LVL	AGE	G(GS)	IP	W-L	SV	K	WHIP	ERA	CSP	BB%	K%	HR%	GB%	ZSw%	ZCon%	OSw%	OCon%	BABIP	SLGCON	DRA-	WARP
2021	SUG	AAA	26	36(0)	57²	5-3	0	78	0.95	2.81		8.7%	33.9%	2.2%	41.1%					.242	.496	74	1.1
2021	HOU	MLB	26	3(0)	3	0-0	0	3	2.67	15.00	55.7%	18.8%	18.8%	0.0%	30.0%	60.0%	77.8%	21.2%	71.4%	.500	.700	119	0.0
2022	SUG	AAA	27	14(0)	15	2-1	0	15	1.07	3.60		9.8%	24.6%	3.3%	51.3%	68.7%	72.2%	26.0%	61.8%	.216	.436	96	0.1
2022	HOU	MLB	27	29(0)	38²	1-1	0	38	1.03	2.09	53.1%	9.0%	24.5%	1.9%	40.2%	70.3%	78.6%	30.1%	67.3%	.235	.366	91	0.6
2023	SUG	AAA	28	19(0)	20	0-0	1	30	1.45	2.25		11.4%	34.1%	1.1%	44.7%	65.4%	78.3%	27.1%	42.1%	.391	.489	54	0.1
2023	HOU	MLB	28	35(0)	43	2-3	1	45	1.49	5.23	47.2%	9.7%	23.1%	2.6%	38.4%	70.0%	84.2%	28.6%	57.8%	.333	.592	98	0.5
2024 DC	HOU	MLB	29	19(0)	21¹	1-1	0	22	1.30	4.32	49.6%	9.7%	23.5%	3.5%	38.9%					.278	.559	97	0.1

2023 Arsenal: FA (91.2), SW (79.3), SI (90.4), CH (86.3)   *Comps: Paul Sewald (78), Andrew Kittredge (75), Wander Suero (75)*

The peril of throwing 91 mph on the regular is that you have zero margin for error. Case in point: Martinez, whose fastball will never be mistaken for an F-22, surviving a surprising rookie year with it sitting 92. When that slid closer to 90–91 in 2023, though, hitters had a far easier time with it. (While the difference between 92 and 90 mph over 60 feet and six inches is a matter of a single millisecond, that's not insignificant.) Martinez simply doesn't have the control and command to get away with that kind of fastball, even with a deceptive delivery. The increasingly inaccurately named fastball turned his sweeper from reliable whiff-getter to a hit-or-miss offering, which made Martinez look more like an up-and-down relief arm than someone who can count on steady employment as a middle-innings option. He'll need a new trick or that extra tick to differentiate himself from the crowd of undistinguished right-handers on Houston's bullpen depth chart.

Phil Maton RHP   Born: 03/25/93   Age: 31   Height: 6'2"   Weight: 206   Origin: Round 20, 2015 Draft (#597 overall)

YEAR	TM	LVL	AGE	G (GS)	IP	W-L	SV	K	WHIP	ERA	CSP	BB%	K%	HR%	GB%	ZSw%	ZCon%	OSw%	OCon%	BABIP	SLGCON	DRA-	WARP
2021	CLE	MLB	28	38(1)	41¹	2-0	0	61	1.35	4.57	52.4%	11.2%	34.3%	2.2%	40.4%	65.9%	74.4%	35.1%	45.0%	.356	.725	86	0.7
2021	HOU	MLB	28	27(0)	25¹	4-0	0	24	1.62	4.97	51.5%	10.1%	20.2%	1.7%	38.8%	71.5%	81.3%	37.2%	56.2%	.346	.538	103	0.2
2022	HOU	MLB	29	67(0)	65²	0-2	0	73	1.25	3.84	52.0%	8.5%	26.0%	3.6%	36.9%	69.6%	80.5%	33.8%	55.0%	.291	.581	100	0.7
2023	HOU	MLB	30	68(0)	66	4-3	1	74	1.12	3.00	46.8%	9.1%	27.0%	2.2%	42.2%	71.7%	77.4%	35.5%	53.2%	.270	.485	89	1.2
2024 DC	HOU	MLB	31	53(0)	56¹	3-2	0	64	1.27	4.13	49.9%	9.4%	26.7%	3.1%	39.8%					.292	.557	94	0.4

2023 Arsenal: CU (73.8), HC (89.2), SW (79.7), SI (88.4)   Comps: Jeremy Jeffress (66), Noé Ramirez (63), Shawn Kelley (63)

At the end of the 2022 season, Phil Maton broke a finger on his pitching hand by punching a locker. The reason for his anger? He had given up two runs and two hits in Houston's season finale against Philadelphia, including a single to Phillies infielder Nick Maton—his little brother. While big brothers everywhere will understand the particular fury that losing to younger siblings brings out, Maton's outburst cost him a playoff roster spot. Luckily, the Astros looked past it, and they were wise to; Phil halved his home run rate en route to the best year of his career. Part and parcel of that: a decision to make his curveball his primary pitch in place of his 89-mph fastball. The breaker has huge spin and great horizontal movement, making it difficult to barrel; batters had a hard-hit rate of just 18.1% on it. To make matters even better, while Phil shone, Nick struggled to a DRC+ of 88 with Detroit. Family bragging rights: re-established.

Rafael Montero RHP   Born: 10/17/90   Age: 33   Height: 6'0"   Weight: 190   Origin: IFA, 2011

YEAR	TM	LVL	AGE	G (GS)	IP	W-L	SV	K	WHIP	ERA	CSP	BB%	K%	HR%	GB%	ZSw%	ZCon%	OSw%	OCon%	BABIP	SLGCON	DRA-	WARP
2021	HOU	MLB	30	4(0)	6	0-1	0	5	0.83	0.00	52.1%	9.5%	23.8%	0.0%	50.0%	79.4%	74.1%	26.9%	64.3%	.214	.286	79	0.1
2021	SEA	MLB	30	40(0)	43¹	5-3	7	37	1.64	7.27	50.2%	7.4%	18.1%	2.0%	55.1%	71.4%	82.5%	37.9%	71.9%	.366	.559	87	0.7
2022	HOU	MLB	31	71(0)	68¹	5-2	14	73	1.02	2.37	48.0%	8.5%	27.0%	1.1%	51.7%	67.1%	74.9%	32.9%	67.7%	.262	.382	74	1.6
2023	HOU	MLB	32	68(0)	67¹	3-3	1	79	1.53	5.08	42.5%	9.7%	26.5%	3.7%	40.6%	74.0%	74.5%	33.4%	64.1%	.358	.683	92	1.1
2024 DC	HOU	MLB	33	50(0)	53¹	4-2	5	56	1.30	4.14	46.0%	9.2%	24.5%	2.9%	44.5%					.297	.544	94	0.4

2023 Arsenal: FA (96.2), CH (91.4), SI (95.5), SL (88.3)   Comps: Liam Hendriks (51), Tommy Hunter (50), LaTroy Hawkins (50)

The late-career surge that took Montero from Mets castoff to key piece of a championship bullpen broke on the rocks in 2023, as an elevated home run rate turned him into the Dominican Lance Lynn. Normally one of the more prolific worm-killers in the league, he saw his fly-ball rate shoot up 10 points, with corresponding increases in barrel rate, launch angle, average exit velocity and hard-hit rate. The culprit was the same pitch that made Montero a stud reliever: his fastball. With batters ready to see it on the regular—he threw it just shy of 50% of the time, a four-point jump from the season prior—they gripped and ripped, elevating it with regularity; its launch angle went from 14 degrees in 2022 to 26 last year. His lack of a good secondary, meanwhile, let hitters sit on the heater. Montero may need a new approach, or at least a less predictable old one.

Oliver Ortega RHP   Born: 10/02/96   Age: 27   Height: 6'0"   Weight: 165   Origin: IFA, 2015

YEAR	TM	LVL	AGE	G (GS)	IP	W-L	SV	K	WHIP	ERA	CSP	BB%	K%	HR%	GB%	ZSw%	ZCon%	OSw%	OCon%	BABIP	SLGCON	DRA-	WARP
2021	RCT	AA	24	25(0)	30²	2-3	5	46	1.50	6.16		9.4%	33.1%	2.2%	46.8%					.400	.628	82	0.6
2021	SL	AAA	24	9(0)	12	0-0	0	15	1.33	3.75		9.3%	27.8%	3.7%	44.1%					.281	.576	88	0.1
2021	LAA	MLB	24	8(0)	9¹	1-0	0	4	1.50	4.82	60.4%	5.1%	10.3%	2.6%	75.0%	61.4%	100.0%	26.8%	81.8%	.355	.500	93	0.1
2022	SL	AAA	25	23(0)	25²	2-1	2	27	1.64	5.96		6.6%	22.3%	2.5%	46.3%	59.7%	88.9%	33.7%	54.9%	.392	.696	93	0.3
2022	LAA	MLB	25	27(0)	34	1-3	1	33	1.47	3.71	54.9%	12.2%	22.3%	3.4%	50.0%	74.2%	90.7%	35.7%	57.6%	.300	.537	92	0.5
2023	STP	AAA	26	24(0)	34²	3-1	5	44	0.98	1.82		7.4%	32.6%	2.2%	47.5%	66.1%	77.3%	30.7%	48.4%	.276	.494	77	0.9
2023	MIN	MLB	26	10(0)	14²	0-1	0	14	1.23	4.30	50.7%	11.1%	22.2%	3.2%	31.7%	62.2%	77.0%	34.8%	60.4%	.231	.450	105	0.1
2024 DC	HOU	MLB	27	19(0)	21¹	1-1	0	19	1.31	4.07	54.2%	9.0%	20.4%	2.7%	46.1%					.284	.508	93	0.2

2023 Arsenal: KC (82.5), SW (84.3), SI (95.5), FA (95.3)   Comps: Cory Rasmus (65), Victor Alcántara (65), Travis Lakins Sr. (64)

For every two or three pitchers you saw rushing to add a sweeper in 2023, there was one doing as Ortega did: switching back in the other direction, in search of a breaking ball they can better command. In his case, it's the right move. Ortega's new, old-fashioned slider is more firm and vertical, and it misses plenty of bats without sailing into waste pitch territory. In a brief look in 2023, he showed that he can lead his arsenal with it against right-handed batters, and that he can throw it to lefties with some confidence—forcing them to adjust to two distinct breaking balls. He also traded in a four-seamer that big-league hitters obliterated in 2022 for a sinker that looks much more promising. There's something here.

Ryan Pressly RHP   Born: 12/15/88   Age: 35   Height: 6'2"   Weight: 206   Origin: Round 11, 2007 Draft (#354 overall)

YEAR	TM	LVL	AGE	G (GS)	IP	W-L	SV	K	WHIP	ERA	CSP	BB%	K%	HR%	GB%	ZSw%	ZCon%	OSw%	OCon%	BABIP	SLGCON	DRA-	WARP
2021	HOU	MLB	32	64(0)	64	5-3	26	81	0.97	2.25	58.3%	5.2%	32.4%	1.6%	55.1%	66.3%	85.7%	37.7%	45.5%	.298	.452	61	1.9
2022	HOU	MLB	33	50(0)	48¹	3-3	33	65	0.89	2.98	51.2%	7.1%	35.7%	2.2%	44.2%	67.6%	77.7%	37.4%	43.5%	.265	.455	68	1.3
2023	HOU	MLB	34	65(0)	65¹	4-5	31	74	1.07	3.58	46.3%	6.0%	27.6%	3.0%	54.8%	67.9%	87.4%	38.1%	45.2%	.272	.512	74	1.6
2024 DC	HOU	MLB	35	50(0)	53¹	4-5	38	60	1.14	3.10	50.3%	6.9%	27.3%	2.5%	50.4%					.296	.510	75	0.9

2023 Arsenal: SL (89.8), CU (82.1), FA (94.7), CH (89.8), SI (93.7)   Comps: Darren O'Day (83), Jonathan Papelbon (82), Francisco Cordero (81)

While Pressly was his usual strong self in 2023, there are signs that he's exiting the elite tier of closers and settling into regular decency. His strikeout rate dipped below 30% for the first time since he came to Houston, and while he's managed to arrest his velocity decline, he's also trying to feature his fastball less and less. In 2022, he made his slider his primary offering; in '23, the curveball supplanted the heater as option no. 2. That makes sense, as both breakers are whiff machines, but the curve in particular got whacked when thrown for a strike, with an eye-watering 55.3% hard-hit rate. Stealing outs with spin has been Pressly's modus operandi since the Astros swiped him from the Twins, but that's a tough strategy to execute in high-leverage spots if you don't have a fastball to keep hitters honest.

Ryne Stanek   RHP   Born: 07/26/91   Age: 32   Height: 6'4"   Weight: 226   Origin: Round 1, 2013 Draft (#29 overall)

YEAR	TM	LVL	AGE	G (GS)	IP	W-L	SV	K	WHIP	ERA	CSP	BB%	K%	HR%	GB%	ZSw%	ZCon%	OSw%	OCon%	BABIP	SLGCON	DRA-	WARP
2021	HOU	MLB	29	72 (0)	68¹	3-5	2	83	1.21	3.42	51.5%	12.8%	28.6%	2.8%	33.3%	72.9%	74.9%	30.9%	55.9%	.242	.470	106	0.4
2022	HOU	MLB	30	59 (0)	54²	2-1	1	62	1.23	1.15	50.5%	13.8%	27.7%	0.9%	38.9%	72.7%	75.0%	33.0%	52.6%	.264	.380	103	0.5
2023	HOU	MLB	31	55 (0)	50²	3-1	0	51	1.24	4.09	47.1%	9.9%	23.9%	3.8%	30.7%	78.0%	76.8%	33.8%	56.8%	.258	.532	108	0.4
2024 non	HOU	MLB	32	58 (0)	50	2-2	0	55	1.43	4.93	48.5%	11.4%	24.9%	3.9%	33.1%					.294	.606	109	0.0

2023 Arsenal: FA (98.1), FS (89.1), SL (88.6)   *Comps: Matt Barnes (68), Brad Boxberger (68), Pedro Strop (67)*

Once an opener and occasional setup man, Stanek settled into the creamy middle in his final year under contract with the Astros. If they were tied or trailing in the sixth, it was safe to assume he and his resplendent flowing hair would soon saunter into the game, "Still D.R.E." blasting in the background. But though Stanek has grown a lot with the Astros, he couldn't keep it home a lot, as more fly balls and more hard contact added up to more homers. Even with a fastball humming in at 98 mph, Stanek had a hard time avoiding barrels, and while he brought his walk rate down to a more reasonable figure, that came with a dip in strikeouts that neutered his overall value. As he worked in the strike zone more often and threw fewer splitters and sliders than the year prior, hitters picked up on it, swinging more and whiffing less. With that approach, it's hard to imagine Stanek ascending beyond middle reliever status.

Alonzo Tredwell   RHP   Born: 05/08/02   Age: 22   Height: 6'8"   Weight: 230   Origin: Round 2, 2023 Draft (#61 overall)

Tabbed by the Astros in the second round of the 2023 draft, Tredwell is built like Aaron Judge but throws about as hard as Aaron Nola. The good news is that his immense frame, long limbs and high arm slot produce elite extension and a flat approach angle at the top of the strike zone, with a fastball that boasts tons of vertical break. That's a good base for a potential back-end starter, with the possibility for more if his secondaries continue to develop; as of now, he flashes plus with a curveball, less so with a slider, and his changeup grades out as an incomplete. Converted from relief to the rotation in his final season at UCLA, he'll have to build his stamina and innings and continue to work on his non-fastballs after relying on heaters the majority of the time in college.

José Urquidy   RHP   Born: 05/01/95   Age: 29   Height: 6'0"   Weight: 217   Origin: IFA, 2015

YEAR	TM	LVL	AGE	G (GS)	IP	W-L	SV	K	WHIP	ERA	CSP	BB%	K%	HR%	GB%	ZSw%	ZCon%	OSw%	OCon%	BABIP	SLGCON	DRA-	WARP
2021	HOU	MLB	26	20 (20)	107	8-3	0	90	0.99	3.62	59.4%	4.5%	21.3%	4.0%	31.7%	72.1%	80.7%	34.6%	63.6%	.239	.524	112	0.3
2022	HOU	MLB	27	29 (28)	164¹	13-8	0	134	1.17	3.94	56.3%	5.6%	19.7%	4.3%	36.3%	72.1%	85.4%	35.6%	65.3%	.264	.556	113	0.5
2023	CC	AA	28	2 (2)	9	0-1	0	7	1.22	5.00		2.5%	17.5%	0.0%	29.0%					.323	.355	126	0.0
2023	HOU	MLB	28	16 (10)	63	3-3	1	45	1.43	5.29	44.7%	9.1%	16.4%	4.0%	36.5%	71.8%	82.7%	38.8%	66.0%	.281	.554	121	0.1
2024 DC	HOU	MLB	29	46 (6)	73¹	4-3	0	56	1.36	4.85	53.9%	7.0%	17.7%	3.7%	35.3%					.295	.562	109	0.2

2023 Arsenal: FA (93.2), CH (86.2), SW (80.8), KC (79.8), SI (93.8)   *Comps: Jerad Eickhoff (57), Dillon Gee (55), Jakob Junis (54)*

How did you spend your summer vacation? Urquidy had to stay inside, rehabbing a shoulder strain. To be fair, Houston's weather in high summer is roughly equivalent to walking through a car wash that dispenses bisque, so he probably didn't mind lounging in the air conditioning, but that injury sank his year. It's both tempting and hopeful to assume that his bum shoulder was behind his struggles, as his already mediocre strikeout rate fell into the cellar; it's never a good sign when your statistical neighbors are Chris Flexen and Trevor Williams. Walks, too, were a problem, though he was able to mitigate some of that extra traffic by tossing more changeups and sweepers and inducing lots of weak contact. But hitters destroyed his fastball, with a .632 slugging percentage against it, even as he avoided the strike zone more than ever. Urquidy will perpetually live or die based on how much trouble he can avoid with that four-seamer; here's hoping his next summer is spent figuring that out instead of gazing longingly out the window.

Framber Valdez   LHP   Born: 11/19/93   Age: 30   Height: 5'11"   Weight: 239   Origin: IFA, 2015

YEAR	TM	LVL	AGE	G (GS)	IP	W-L	SV	K	WHIP	ERA	CSP	BB%	K%	HR%	GB%	ZSw%	ZCon%	OSw%	OCon%	BABIP	SLGCON	DRA-	WARP
2021	HOU	MLB	27	22 (22)	134²	11-6	0	125	1.25	3.14	57.1%	10.1%	21.9%	2.1%	70.1%	61.7%	88.5%	28.6%	51.8%	.268	.436	80	2.7
2022	HOU	MLB	28	31 (31)	201¹	17-6	0	194	1.16	2.82	59.4%	8.1%	23.5%	1.3%	66.5%	65.5%	87.4%	31.3%	52.0%	.286	.412	78	4.3
2023	HOU	MLB	29	31 (31)	198	12-11	0	200	1.13	3.45	48.3%	7.1%	24.8%	2.4%	54.3%	66.9%	87.6%	32.4%	52.4%	.284	.504	85	3.9
2024 DC	HOU	MLB	30	31 (31)	196²	15-8	0	186	1.23	3.58	53.7%	7.8%	22.4%	2.2%	57.8%					.292	.474	83	3.5

2023 Arsenal: SI (95.3), CU (80.2), CH (90.1), SL (84.5), FC (89.5), FA (95.7), SW (85.1)   *Comps: CC Sabathia (77), Bob Gibson (75), Denny Neagle (74)*

On the surface, being called "The Grease" doesn't seem like a sign of respect, but for Valdez, *La Grasa* is a moniker that reflects his swaggy style as a natty dresser who routinely smells like the fragrance counter at a high-end department store. It's also a reflection of his supreme confidence, buoyed by a 2022 season in which he helped carry Houston to a championship. Last year brought more acclaim and accolades, with the lefty tossing a no-hitter in August against Cleveland, one in which he manufactured his usual double-digit outs on the ground. But the Valdez of 2023 was uncharacteristically airborne, running a career-worst ground-ball rate and a positive launch angle after years of living in the dirt. Despite (or due to?) upping the velocity on his sinker to 95 mph on average, he lost almost four inches of drop on it from the year prior. As you'd expect, that flatter sinker made him easier to beat in the strike zone. It's worth wondering if Valdez's heavy 2022 workload — 225 innings between the regular season and playoffs—had an effect. Or maybe all that cologne made it hard to get a good grip. Either way, Houston needs a greater *Grasa* in 2024.

Justin Verlander RHP   Born: 02/20/83   Age: 41   Height: 6'5"   Weight: 235   Origin: Round 1, 2004 Draft (#2 overall)

YEAR	TM	LVL	AGE	G (GS)	IP	W-L	SV	K	WHIP	ERA	CSP	BB%	K%	HR%	GB%	ZSw%	ZCon%	OSw%	OCon%	BABIP	SLGCON	DRA-	WARP
2022	HOU	MLB	39	28(28)	175	18-4	0	185	0.83	1.75	55.1%	4.4%	27.8%	1.8%	37.9%	75.4%	83.1%	36.8%	64.1%	.240	.384	71	4.3
2023	NYM	MLB	40	16(16)	94¹	6-5	0	81	1.14	3.15	47.2%	8.0%	21.0%	2.3%	38.1%	68.6%	87.1%	34.9%	63.6%	.258	.446	103	1.0
2023	HOU	MLB	40	11(11)	68	7-3	0	63	1.12	3.31	52.6%	4.9%	22.3%	3.2%	32.7%	70.6%	85.5%	35.6%	67.5%	.275	.530	106	0.6
2024 DC	HOU	MLB	41	26(26)	152²	11-7	0	137	1.21	4.07	51.5%	6.3%	21.6%	3.9%	35.2%					.281	.566	95	1.8

2023 Arsenal: FA (94.4), SL (87), CU (78.3), CH (85.2)   *Comps: Roger Clemens (79), Don Sutton (78), Tom Seaver (77)*

"You could not live with your own failure," Verlander told Jim Crane upon returning to Houston at the trade deadline. "Where did that bring you? Back to me." Okay, he probably didn't quote Thanos when donning the orange once again, but his return was about as inevitable. Swooped up by Steve Cohen as part of his winter spending spree, the 40-year-old strained his shoulder on the eve of Opening Day, missing a month. A 4.11 ERA through June suggested that maybe Cohen had overpaid for a name brand, but the rest of the Mets weren't any better; by the time the future Hall-of-Famer found his groove in July, it was too late for New York. The Astros, meanwhile, had a Verlander-shaped hole in their starting five that Crane was eager to fill with the real deal, and while the cost was high, in the words of America's favorite Malthusian warlord, that was a small price to pay for rotation salvation. It almost worked, too: Verlander pitched to a 3.31 ERA as an Astro to help Houston rally for another AL West title, but Jordan Montgomery out-dueled him in ALCS Game 1, and his Game 5 outing was a dud. A year and $43 million remain on his deal, most of which Cohen is footing, followed by a $35 million vesting option if he cracks 140 innings in 2024. Will the Astros want him in '25 at age 42? They can dread it and run from it, but Verlander arrives all the same.

LINEOUTS

Hitters

HITTER	POS	TM	LVL	AGE	PA	R	HR	RBI	SB	AVG/OBP/SLG	BABIP	SLGCON	BB%	K%	ZSw%	ZCon%	OSw%	OCon%	LA	90th EV	DRC+	BRR	DRP	WARP
Colin Barber	LF/DH	CC	AA	22	321	42	11	40	5	.244/.358/.433	.293	.594	14.0%	22.7%							101	-3.8	-4.2	0.4
Zach Cole	CF	FAY	A	22	312	48	11	46	25	.265/.397/.494	.381	.801	14.4%	31.1%							126	0.8	2.9	2.2
	CF	ASH	A+	22	175	31	8	19	12	.247/.349/.480	.341	.783	12.0%	33.1%							86	0.6	-1.5	0.4
Camilo Diaz	SS	DSL ASTB	ROK	17	195	29	4	15	7	.209/.374/.353	.326	.607	21.0%	32.8%										
Cam Fisher	OF	FAY	A	22	134	16	5	15	5	.273/.396/.500	.403	.833	16.4%	32.8%							108	-1.4	-3.4	0.0
Kenni Gomez	OF	AST	ROK	18	61	8	2	12	8	.208/.311/.321	.231	.415	9.8%	19.7%										
David Hensley	IF	SUG	AAA	27	293	42	6	36	9	.220/.365/.356	.307	.545	18.4%	20.8%	51.4%	82.2%	20.6%	52.7%			91	-0.1	2.7	0.7
	IF	HOU	MLB	27	94	12	1	3	1	.119/.213/.167	.188	.286	10.6%	37.2%	56.3%	77.6%	21.6%	54.3%	2.7	104.3	60	0.1	0.0	-0.2
Alberto Hernandez	SS	AST	ROK	19	169	23	2	20	9	.257/.375/.414	.315	.532	14.2%	18.3%										
Chase Jaworsky	SS	AST	ROK	18	38	4	0	2	0	.281/.395/.281	.346	.346	15.8%	15.8%										
Grae Kessinger	IF	SUG	AAA	25	230	37	6	32	2	.283/.397/.435	.331	.576	15.2%	19.6%	65.8%	84.0%	24.2%	67.5%			111	1.1	-2.2	0.8
	IF	HOU	MLB	25	45	3	1	1	0	.200/.289/.325	.259	.464	11.1%	26.7%	64.3%	73.3%	30.5%	62.1%	14.2	102.8	94	0.0	0.1	0.1
Pedro León	CF/2B	SUG	AAA	25	564	74	21	72	21	.244/.343/.435	.318	.650	11.2%	28.4%	71.6%	83.9%	33.9%	45.9%			93	0.5	-8.3	0.4
César Salazar	C	SUG	AAA	27	222	21	2	16	3	.191/.362/.272	.223	.336	14.0%	14.9%	67.2%	87.4%	26.6%	58.8%			102	-1.4	1.1	0.7
	C	HOU	MLB	27	19	1	0	0	0	.111/.158/.111	.167	.167	5.3%	31.6%	83.9%	80.8%	41.2%	61.9%	18.5	92.5	81	0.0	-0.5	0.0
Jon Singleton	1B	NAS	AAA	31	216	23	10	29	0	.258/.384/.483	.281	.628	17.1%	19.0%	67.2%	87.7%	20.1%	57.0%			118	-0.4	-1.5	0.8
	1B	SUG	AAA	31	148	27	12	28	1	.333/.446/.692	.368	.965	17.6%	23.0%	61.2%	86.1%	20.5%	41.8%			117	-0.9	0.5	0.6
	1B	HOU	MLB	31	73	8	2	10	0	.194/.301/.323	.204	.400	13.7%	16.4%	69.7%	91.8%	21.7%	47.1%	19.6	103.8	92	0.0	0.1	0.1
	1B	MIL	MLB	31	32	3	0	2	0	.103/.188/.138	.167	.222	9.4%	34.4%	58.7%	88.9%	34.0%	63.6%	11.8	100.4	97	0.0	0.0	0.1
Esmil Valencia	OF	DSL ASTO	ROK	17	211	35	2	24	11	.262/.346/.388	.301	.467	9.0%	14.7%										
Will Wagner	2B/3B	AST	ROK	24	25	5	0	2	1	.313/.542/.375	.333	.400	28.0%	4.0%										
	2B/3B	CC	AA	24	234	36	7	32	3	.309/.385/.507	.370	.656	11.1%	20.1%							111	-2.3	-1.0	0.6
	2B/3B	SUG	AAA	24	28	3	0	4	2	.577/.607/.692	.625	.750	7.1%	7.1%	55.8%	95.8%	19.2%	100.0%			103	0.8		

You can call **Colin Barber** ERCOT: just like Texas' energy grid, the power isn't there. Until it shows up, he projects as a second-tier corner outfielder or strong-side platoon bat. ⓧ **Zach Cole** is the kind of player you'd build in a baseball RPG: enormous power, plus speed, a cannon for an arm, an ideal physique. Only after you've started the game, though, do you realize you didn't leave enough points for a hit tool. ⓧ **Camilo Diaz** has a surfeit of tools, led by plus power and top-flight bat speed, that earned him an enormous signing bonus. We didn't see much of that offense in action, as he didn't put a ball in play in over half his Dominican League plate appearances. ⓧ Lefty-swinging **Cam Fisher** led the NCAA in home runs last season with One Weird Trick: relentlessly launching balls to the pull side. He may be a one-trick pony, but it's an impressive one. ⓧ Hyped as a potential breakout candidate, **Kenni Gomez** stumbled out of the blocks in the Gulf Coast League, where he produced groundouts and weak fly balls. Like a retiree from the Northeast, a return to West Palm Beach is in his future. ⓧ The six-foot-six **David Hensley** was asked to do his best Jose Altuve impression at season's start, replacing the injured All-Star at second base. An Altuve-sized .403 OPS over his first 86 plate appearances put an end to that act. ⓧ File **Alberto Hernandez**'s name away for later. He built on a solid pro debut in the Dominican Summer League with a better year on Florida's back fields, displaying plus plate discipline in the process. ⓧ **Chase Jaworski** is doomed to be nicknamed Jaws, though he's more mako than great white, with more speed than power to his game so far. He's also unlikely to stick at shortstop long-term. ⓧ Old heads will know **Grae Kessinger**'s grandfather, Don, a six-time All-Star and winner of two Gold Gloves back in the 1960s and 70s with the Cubs. Don's Zoomer reboot has the same profile: light stick, good glove, scrappiness for days. ⓧ **Pedro León** is at risk of going out like a lamb, contact skills compromising his elite pull-side power. Not helping is so-so defense wherever he goes, despite plus speed and a huge arm. ⓧ Third catcher **César Salazar** nearly became second catcher César Salazar for a brief moment before the Astros slammed down Victor Caratini ahead of him like the last brick in "The Cask of Amontillado." ⓧ Almost a decade after signing his infamous contract, there stood **Jon Singleton** in Game 6 of the ALCS, pinch-hitting with two outs and the bases loaded, his team down two. He worked the count full against a bone-weary Jose LeClerc, fouling off pitches, waiting for his moment. Then he struck out. ⓧ Lauded as the best pure hitter of Houston's 2023 international class, **Esmil Valencia** has a compact swing and a good feel for contact, giving him a potentially short runway to the majors if he clicks against more advanced pitching. ⓧ A better fit for positionless baseball before the shift ban, **Will Wagner** is miscast as a regular at second or third base. As a hitter, he's more of a gap-to-gap contact pest than a power threat. Essentially he has the Luis Arraez starter kit, though Wagner's ceiling isn't as high.

Pitchers

PITCHER	TM	LVL	AGE	G (GS)	IP	W-L	SV	K	WHIP	ERA	CSP	BB%	K%	HR%	GB%	ZSw%	ZCon%	OSw%	OCon%	BABIP	SLGCON	DRA-	WARP
Brandon Bielak	SUG	AAA	27	13 (11)	55	1-4	0	63	1.42	5.24		7.8%	25.8%	2.5%	49.1%	68.6%	85.4%	32.4%	59.4%	.346	.624	73	0.6
	HOU	MLB	27	15 (13)	80	5-6	0	62	1.53	3.83	45.9%	10.2%	17.6%	3.4%	50.0%	68.2%	85.2%	30.4%	63.6%	.312	.574	105	0.7
Ronel Blanco	SUG	AAA	29	15 (13)	73¹	7-4	0	81	1.17	3.68		12.3%	26.8%	3.3%	43.7%	69.7%	76.6%	32.7%	52.5%	.227	.489	78	0.3
	HOU	MLB	29	17 (7)	52	2-1	0	52	1.48	4.50	44.1%	12.4%	23.0%	5.3%	34.7%	78.3%	77.0%	33.2%	51.4%	.280	.629	116	0.2
Jake Bloss	FAY	A	22	5 (4)	16¹	1-1	0	20	1.53	2.76		15.9%	29.0%	0.0%	59.5%					.378	.444	110	0.0
Declan Cronin	CLT	AAA	25	47 (0)	51²	3-0	2	42	1.43	3.83		8.9%	18.7%	1.3%	54.8%	66.3%	83.6%	29.9%	59.6%	.331	.459	100	0.7
	CHW	MLB	25	9 (0)	11	0-1	0	8	1.64	9.00	50.4%	13.7%	15.7%	5.9%	52.9%	64.3%	92.6%	25.7%	64.3%	.258	.618	104	0.1
Shawn Dubin	SUG	AAA	27	20 (12)	55²	1-5	1	60	1.60	6.63		14.3%	23.3%	2.7%	41.9%	68.8%	80.8%	30.8%	57.3%	.310	.642	95	0.3
	HOU	MLB	27	3 (1)	9	0-0	0	11	1.67	7.00	43.6%	7.1%	26.2%	2.4%	44.4%	75.4%	87.8%	35.5%	52.6%	.423	.731	94	0.1
Matt Gage	SUG	AAA	30	34 (0)	37¹	1-1	0	39	1.63	4.58		12.0%	23.3%	3.0%	38.2%	61.8%	83.8%	32.6%	52.5%	.356	.654	87	0.2
	HOU	MLB	30	5 (0)	6²	0-0	0	8	1.35	2.70	46.2%	11.1%	29.6%	3.7%	43.8%	55.6%	68.0%	24.3%	55.6%	.357	.667	85	0.1
Michael Knorr	FAY	A	23	4 (2)	17¹	2-0	0	24	1.15	2.60		9.9%	33.8%	0.0%	55.0%					.325	.385	87	0.3
	ASH	A+	23	11 (8)	41	1-5	0	54	1.37	4.61		9.4%	30.0%	4.4%	38.0%					.310	.692	87	0.6
Rhett Kouba	CC	AA	23	23 (21)	110	7-5	0	118	1.07	3.27		5.1%	26.2%	2.7%	41.1%					.291	.512	84	2.5
	SUG	AAA	23	5 (3)	18	1-2	0	18	1.94	4.50		16.1%	20.7%	2.3%	50.0%	64.9%	85.0%	27.6%	61.1%	.365	.611	86	
Joel Kuhnel	LOU	AAA	28	21 (0)	24	1-2	0	15	1.75	7.12		9.7%	13.3%	1.8%	45.2%	66.9%	89.3%	34.6%	70.7%	.358	.554	118	0.1
	SUG	AAA	28	17 (0)	19²	1-1	1	16	1.58	5.03		5.7%	18.4%	2.3%	53.0%	75.3%	85.8%	34.1%	63.2%	.375	.600	73	0.3
	CIN	MLB	28	2 (0)	3¹	0-0	0	2	2.40	8.10	51.9%	11.8%	0.0%	0.0%	60.0%	63.0%	82.4%	33.3%	90.0%	.400	.533	101	0.0
	HOU	MLB	28	7 (0)	9²	0-0	0	3	1.34	4.66	52.3%	7.3%	7.3%	4.9%	55.9%	83.1%	85.2%	26.0%	63.2%	.250	.500	105	0.1
Parker Mushinski	SUG	AAA	27	32 (0)	31²	3-1	0	39	1.04	2.84		8.8%	31.2%	1.6%	55.6%	56.6%	80.0%	32.7%	54.0%	.286	.417	64	0.6
	HOU	MLB	27	14 (0)	14²	0-0	0	15	1.57	5.52	49.0%	5.8%	21.7%	7.2%	52.2%	62.6%	92.5%	37.8%	60.7%	.341	.826	90	0.2
Tayler Scott	OKC	AAA	31	19 (0)	19²	3-0	2	25	1.17	1.37		12.5%	31.3%	0.0%	39.5%	55.0%	84.1%	33.3%	52.9%	.302	.381	86	0.3
	LV	AAA	31	14 (0)	15²	2-0	3	17	0.70	1.72		5.4%	30.4%	0.0%	50.0%	60.0%	86.0%	32.1%	44.2%	.222	.257	69	
	OAK	MLB	31	8 (1)	8	0-0	0	7	1.63	3.38	47.7%	5.3%	18.4%	5.3%	42.9%	71.4%	85.0%	32.3%	63.3%	.346	.750	105	0.1
	LAD	MLB	31	6 (0)	6	0-0	0	6	1.67	9.00	46.0%	13.3%	26.7%	0.0%	29.4%	70.7%	86.2%	33.8%	58.3%	.353	.625	98	0.1
	BOS	MLB	31	4 (1)	3²	0-0	0	2	2.73	4.91	47.7%	20.0%	10.0%	5.0%	38.5%	62.9%	90.9%	19.0%	37.5%	.417	.846	119	0.0
Bennett Sousa	NAS	AAA	28	16 (0)	17	2-2	1	23	1.29	4.76		9.6%	31.5%	2.7%	57.1%	68.0%	75.0%	43.0%	45.5%	.325	.571	79	0.4
	MIL	MLB	28	2 (0)	2²	0-0	0	2	2.63	13.50	47.5%	14.3%	14.3%	7.1%	50.0%	85.0%	100.0%	28.6%	30.0%	.444	.800	100	0.0
	HOU	MLB	28	5 (0)	6¹	0-0	0	8	0.16	0.00	42.1%	0.0%	40.0%	0.0%	41.7%	71.9%	73.9%	39.6%	57.1%	.083	.083	89	0.1
Forrest Whitley	SUG	AAA	25	8 (6)	30	1-2	0	32	1.33	5.70		12.6%	23.7%	4.4%	44.4%	62.2%	85.8%	27.7%	64.3%	.230	.613	100	0.3

Brandon Bielak's best pitch is his changeup, so it only makes sense that the Astros had him double its usage rate, making it his second-most thrown pitch on the season. Unfortunately, every once in a while he had to throw his second-best pitch. ⓧ **Ronel Blanco** gave up too many homers as a starter, too many hits as a reliever and too many walks as a pitcher. And while his cutter grades out as plus, it's less a building block and more a gorgeous painting hung precariously on a dirty brick wall. ⓧ Stop us if you've heard this before: the Astros drafted a physically imposing right-hander with a hard, riding fastball and a big breaking ball. That's **Jake Bloss**, third-rounder out of Georgetown, who'll hope to become a rock in Houston's rotation or bullpen. ⓧ **Declan Cronin** got told about his big-league callup while in the middle of a timed online chess match, and had to forfeit when he took the call. In a sense, having to lose a game to join the White Sox is a fitting indoctrination. ⓧ **Shawn Dubin**, a graduate of NAIA Georgetown College who used to work as a roofer, made his MLB debut in June in relief against the Mets and struck out Francisco Lindor. He also gave up five runs in an inning. You win some, you lose some. ⓧ Former indy leaguer **Matt Gage** has a nice sweeper from the left side and the bad luck to have landed with a team and manager that had no interest in rostering lefty relievers. Maybe Joe Espada will see the good in him. ⓧ **Michael Knorr** was a two-true outcomes pitcher in High-A; a third of the batters he faced there homered or struck out. Such is life as a strike-thrower with good velocity but inconsistent breaking pitches. ⓧ **Rhett Kouba** walked almost as many batters in five games at Triple-A as he did over nearly an entire season in Double-A. That's not his style, as a pitcher with plus control, which he needs given his deep but unexciting arsenal. ⓧ **Joel Kuhnel** lost significant velocity on his fastball last season, going from 96.4 mph in 2022 on average to 94.2 in '23, with a corresponding decline in strikeout rate. Without heat or whiffs, he's a Quad-A arm and a lock to throw 15–20 bad major-league innings a year. ⓧ The year came and went without an appearance from **Lance McCullers Jr.** at any level, a strained forearm muscle in spring training leading to season-ending flexor tendon surgery in June. If all goes well, he should be back on the mound in 2024, but "if all goes well" might as well be his nickname at this point. ⓧ Houston's rotation couldn't stay healthy, but the bullpen had no such issues. That was to the detriment of **Parker Mushinski**, who spent another season putting up fine numbers in Triple-A. Like a lovesick teen, he's waiting for a call that won't come. ⓧ The well-traveled **Tayler Scott** was claimed off waivers twice last year by teams who were curious enough to fix either his sinker that wouldn't induce groundballs or the egregious spelling of his first name. ⓧ It was a long year for **Bennett Sousa**, who spent spring training with the Reds and the season itself going from Milwaukee to Detroit to Houston with multiple Triple-A stops in between. Hopefully he takes time in the offseason to let off some steam. ⓧ **Forrest Whitley** can't throw strikes or stay healthy, completing his collapse from one of baseball's most exciting pitching prospects into one who may never reach the majors. If he does, it'll likely be as a long reliever or swingman.

KANSAS CITY ROYALS

Essay by Maitreyi Anantharaman

Player comments by Kate Preusser and BP staff

Collin Snider's first pitch of the afternoon was a ball low and outside, and he never recovered. The second might have clipped the zone, just at the top, but you had to want to see a strike, and the home-plate umpire didn't. A third sailed high and away. So did another one—that was four—and one more after that. The sixth straight ball summoned Salvador Perez to the mound. He couldn't tame the wildness; Snider threw ball seven, and the catcher was back on the mound again after the eighth. Maybe Randy Arozarena, up next, would solve the problem. He had swung at every pitch thrown to him that day. But there were lines even he wouldn't cross. The ninth was low and away, the 10th inside. It wasn't something these Rays' announcers had ever seen before, they said. Seldom did disasters unfold this way, so painfully, sans any intervention. "Blindfolded, you could probably find the zone once out of 10 pitches," one of them reasoned. Snider's eyes stayed very much open and unobstructed as he defied the odds and threw his 11th straight ball and then a 12th and then lucky 13. Some hundred million years into this outing, Edwin Moscoso at last lifted his forearm to say strike one. And the fans in Kansas City, a good baseball town with a bad baseball team, gave their pitcher a cheer.

In a season carefully devised to wrangle time, Royals baseball had this funny way of taking longer. The losses, 106 of them, each told their own story about the franchise's near-decade of inaction. A famous image shows a wide-eyed cartoon dog wearing a nice bowler hat. He is huddled beside his coffee mug at a table, smoke overhead, while fire rages around him. "This is fine," the dog thinks. The comic is 10 years old. It's by an illustrator named, conveniently for this metaphor's sake, KC Green, and it extends beyond the two oft meme-d panels. In the full strip, the dog sits and sits in the flames, smoke overtaking the room, until finally his eyeballs melt from his skull. Green, once asked why only the first part ever caught on, wondered if there was something more hopeful in the lack of resolution. Without knowing his fate, we could still imagine the dog seized by urgency, leaping up from the table, saving himself with retinas intact.

I thought of this cartoon dog often while watching the Royals last year, when the club's dominant energy was "This is fine" even as the atmospheric state remained "on fire." The

KANSAS CITY ROYALS PROSPECTUS
2023 W-L: 56-106, 5TH IN AL CENTRAL

Pythag	.388	27th	DER	.689	22nd
RS/G	4.17	23rd	DRC+	96	20th
RA/G	5.30	28th	DRA-	109	27th
dWin%	.438	27th	FIP	4.72	25th
Payroll	$92M	24th	B-Age	26.6	1st
M$/MW	$9.7M	26th	P-Age	29.5	18th

- Opened 1973
- Open air
- Natural surface
- Fence profile: 9' to 11'

Park Factors

Runs	Runs/RH	Runs/LH	HR/RH	HR/LH
98	100	96	82	80

Top Hitter WARP	5.0 Bobby Witt Jr.
Top Pitcher WARP	1.8 Brady Singer
2023 Top Prospect	Blake Mitchell

Payroll History (in millions)

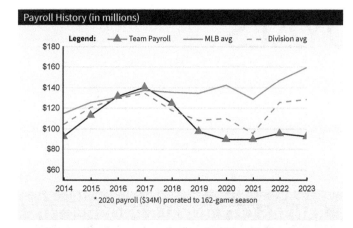

Legend: —▲— Team Payroll —— MLB avg - - - Division avg

* 2020 payroll ($34M) prorated to 162-game season

Future Commitments (in millions)

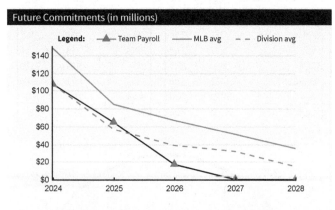

Legend: —▲— Team Payroll —— MLB avg - - - Division avg

Farm System Ranking

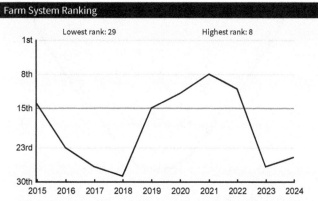

Lowest rank: 29   Highest rank: 8

Personnel

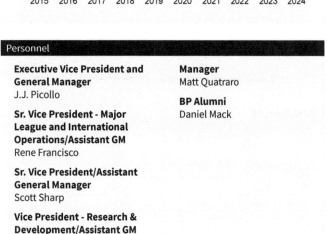

Executive Vice President and General Manager
J.J. Picollo

Sr. Vice President - Major League and International Operations/Assistant GM
Rene Francisco

Sr. Vice President/Assistant General Manager
Scott Sharp

Vice President - Research & Development/Assistant GM
Daniel Mack

Manager
Matt Quatraro

BP Alumni
Daniel Mack

team performed an impressive feat of gymnastics, finishing in last place and also with a single Top-101 prospect. Losing was always in the cards; owner John Sherman declared 2023 an "evaluation year" before the season began. It was an amusing image to return to throughout the summer, in those moments when, say, a reliever threw 13 straight balls or when another gave up the cycle before recording a single out in his debut. I imagined a stoic group of scientists jotting little notes in their lab report as the beaker bubbled over.

Stasis is contagious. It came to define Kansas City's pitching staff, the free agent and the homegrown prospect alike. Jordan Lyles, the veteran starter brought in on a two-year deal, reasoned that endurance could compensate for everything else. Asked whether he'd rather throw a scoreless five-inning start or a five-run complete game, he chose the complete game with no hesitation. To him, there was something virtuous in persistence, even in being persistently bad. An old college clip of Brady Singer enraged by pouring rain at his Super Regional start, once an account of his drive to compete, now seemed like an omen for his stubbornness. In hindsight, the nature of his anger was clear: He wasn't upset that the rain kept from pitching in a big game, but that the rain prevented him from doing something in exactly the way he'd always done it. There would never be a third pitch for him. Just the two. And he would throw them over and over, forever and ever, to whatever result.

Even the "shakeups" hardly registered. Dayton Moore was fired as president of the Royals late in the 2022 season, after a World Series win and 16 years with the team. But Sherman turned to an internal replacement, Moore's longtime deputy, J.J. Picollo. Picollo is a cipher. He once blamed the Royals' disastrous pitching outcomes on outside training facilities, where pitchers were "losing their identities." But he also testifies, if accidentally, to the value of doing things. At the deadline, he traded 35-year-old Aroldis Chapman to the Rangers in exchange for Cole Ragans, a 25-year-old left-handed starter coming off his second Tommy John surgery. Ragans, with the help of an outside facility, *had* assumed a new identity in the offseason. Suddenly he threw an upper-90s fastball and a slider that missed bats. It was an organizational victory so shocking one tended to chalk it up to accident. Was that fair? No. But what had the Royals ever done to earn the benefit of the doubt?

The team's rare fits of haste could be revealing. In July, Sherman began a long letter to fans recounting a recent meeting in the parking lot of Kauffman Stadium. On his way to a game against the Tigers, he'd been introduced to the widow of Dick Howser, who managed the 1985 World Series-winning Royals.

There are lessons in the life of Dick Howser. He reached the majors undeterred by his size; the high school growth spurt stopped for him at 5-foot-7 and 150 pounds. As a manager for the Yankees and then the Royals, he was no different: unimposing but effective. The late sportswriter Dave Andrews fashioned Howser into a martyr of sorts in a classic column about his "execution" at George Steinbrenner's hands. He'd made a stoic foil to Steinbrenner's bully, the kind of manager firm enough to resist ownership's overreach. But the words after Sherman's story were non-sequitur, the parking lot meeting simply reminding him of "the history, the legacy and the passion" of Royals fans, which in turn reminded him of the new stadium he wanted built and the various public funds it would require. That night at the K, Nancy Howser, whose husband's teams never finished worse than second place, watched the Royals fall to 27-68.

Sherman made his billions in the extraction business, and his zeal for the new stadium project has locals wondering whether he's been eyeing a sale of the team ever since he assumed controlling ownership in 2019. He appears likely to get his wish. Kansas City's mayor, Quinton Lucas, once campaigned on the new ballpark's superfluity. "We need a new downtown baseball stadium like I need a Maserati," his famous line went. But his position has softened since he took office, and when Oklahoma City agreed to an arena deal with a 95-5 public-private funding split last fall, considered a heist even by the standards of publicly funded stadiums, Lucas called such investment "wise" in a congratulatory tweet.

Only in slick stadium renderings have the Royals advanced a real vision for their future. One announces, on a vast video screen, that Salvador Perez, Bobby Witt Jr. and Brady Singer have led the Royals to a World Series. (Crown Vision, the video board shaped like the Royals' logo, hasn't survived the move.) Another shows fans filtering in and out of a ballpark district restaurant called, not to put too fine a point on it, Dante's Inferno.

In a new book, *Kingdom Quarterback*, the sportswriters Rustin Dodd and Mark Dent graft a biography of Patrick Mahomes onto a more sprawling urban history of Kansas City. Mahomes, leader of so many comeback drives, echoes a city seeking its own revival, they say. It's telling that the Royals are almost entirely absent from these pages. (The one baseball-focused chapter has to do with Mahomes, as a teenager, watching the ALCS and tweeting, "I really want the Royals to win.") The Royals may have little place in this book about football, but for a long time they have had just as little place in this book about action, about the love and daring that compels all kinds of Kansas Citians to confront what is broken or failing or wrong in their city and to do something about it.

In just three years, Dodd and Dent write, an organizing group called KC Tenants has formed a new power base in the city. Already it boasts real results: 71% of Kansas City voters approved a bond measure to fund affordable housing in the 2022 election thanks to the tenant union's campaigning. "The first thing you have to believe is that you will win," the group's co-founder Tara Raghuveer tells the authors. "If we don't start with that belief, we're not going to get anywhere."

No one could ever find that spirit reflected in the proud resignation of Jordan Lyles or in ownership's "open" letter to fans, always circling around the message and never arriving. The city turns elsewhere: to the tight end with the courage to ask out his crush or to the quarterback who bends the world to his will.

The genius of Mahomes—what makes him more fun to contemplate than the Kansas City Royals—is that he does think like KC Green's dapper dog. But he comes by that belief honestly, not on the waves of delusion or sloth. To him, this—13 seconds on the game clock, crummy receivers, a leg out of commission—is fine. Everything is fine because he will make it fine. Never do things seem finer than when Patrick Mahomes takes the field.

Forget how the cartoon ends. You can always get up from the table and put out the fire. And maybe the Royals have. When the offseason began, the team was "surprisingly aggressive" in trying to acquire starters, *The Athletic*'s Ken Rosenthal reported. Free-agent additions to the pitching staff—Seth Lugo, Michael Wacha, Will Smith and Chris Stratton—cast the "evaluation year" in a new light: Maybe there was more truth than bluster to that phrase—the team did lose 100 games, but their Pythagorean record was a full eight games better. The front office located the team's pressing issues in 2023 and addressed them. Three months into the offseason, only a handful of teams had spent more. However transformative these signings prove to be—they involve mostly low-risk veterans—the Royals are at least beginning the year with the belief that they can win. Maybe everything will be fine.

The player who often gave me such hope for the Royals was Bobby Witt Jr. I watched the 23-year-old shortstop late one night in what was shaping up to be a Royals-y loss to the Twins. The team had blown a lead in the top of the ninth, and was down in extra innings, though the bases were loaded with one out when Witt came up to bat. The general unseriousness in Kansas City belied Witt's talent. He struggled early in the year, but for a long and astonishing stretch of summer, he seemed impossible to get out. He played a loud and thrilling game, baseball at all its extremes. And he was facing another extreme in the flamethrowing closer Jhoan Duran that night. Witt fell down in the count, 1-2, but battled it back full. The next pitch was 102 mph and in on his hands. "A lot of us were joking that if we took that same swing it would have been a popout to the pull-side infielder," said Royals second baseman Michael Massey the day after Witt's walk-off grand slam. But it was Bobby Witt Jr. taking that swing. The pitcher's son from Texas stepped onto the field and laughed at the heat.

—Maitreyi Anantharaman is a co-owner of Defector.

HITTERS

Gavin Cross OF   Born: 02/13/01   Age: 23   Bats: L   Throws: L   Height: 6'1"   Weight: 210   Origin: Round 1, 2022 Draft (#9 overall)

YEAR	TM	LVL	AGE	PA	R	HR	RBI	SB	AVG/OBP/SLG	BABIP	SLGCON	BB%	K%	ZSw%	ZCon%	OSw%	OCon%	LA	90th EV	DRC+	BRR	DRP	WARP
2022	COL	A	21	123	20	7	22	4	.293/.423/.596	.355	.868	17.9%	25.2%							113	-2.0	-1.0	0.2
2023	QC	A+	22	407	49	12	58	23	.206/.300/.383	.262	.562	10.3%	27.8%							95	1.2	0.2	1.1
2024 non	KC	MLB	23	251	22	5	23	0	.208/.276/.327	.296	.500	7.7%	31.5%							69	0.0	0	-0.1

2023 GP: CF (89), RF (7), DH (6)

Comps: Brandon Jones (58), Greyson Jenista (53), Steven Sensley (53)

The strikeout issues that Cross worked to quell in college have reared up again in pro ball, but when he does make contact, it's generally of the long-and-loud variety. He torched baseballs even in the frosty Midwest League, and has shown at times he can utilize a patient approach in waiting for pitches to damage, but it's far from the plug-and-play advanced college bat for which many Royals fans had hoped with a top-10 selection in the 2022 Draft. A likely corner outfielder at the next level, Cross needs to find a way to unlock the big thump in his bat on a consistent basis before he finds himself at a tougher *Crossroads* than a Britney Spears vehicle.

Freddy Fermin C   Born: 05/16/95   Age: 29   Bats: R   Throws: R   Height: 5'9"   Weight: 200   Origin: IFA, 2015

YEAR	TM	LVL	AGE	PA	R	HR	RBI	SB	AVG/OBP/SLG	BABIP	SLGCON	BB%	K%	ZSw%	ZCon%	OSw%	OCon%	LA	90th EV	DRC+	BRR	DRP	WARP
2021	NWA	AA	26	303	45	10	45	1	.279/.356/.446	.310	.548	9.6%	16.5%							115	2.0	2.5	2.0
2022	OMA	AAA	27	348	44	15	56	1	.270/.365/.480	.290	.607	13.2%	17.8%							112	-1.6	3.4	1.6
2022	KC	MLB	27	7	1	0	0	0	.000/.000/.000		.000	0.0%	42.9%	69.2%	77.8%	27.3%	66.7%	14.5	99.1	77	0.0	-0.1	0.0
2023	OMA	AAA	28	58	12	5	14	0	.304/.448/.674	.281	.838	19.0%	15.5%	66.2%	81.1%	27.3%	66.7%			137	-0.6	1.1	0.5
2023	KC	MLB	28	235	26	9	32	0	.281/.321/.461	.323	.599	5.5%	21.3%	81.6%	87.5%	37.3%	59.4%	10.8	103.3	97	-0.1	0.5	0.9
2024 DC	KC	MLB	29	181	18	5	19	0	.247/.314/.383	.295	.492	8.0%	20.5%							99	-0.1	-1.3	0.5

2023 GP: C (65), DH (2)

Comps: Stephen Vogt (60), Curt Casali (60), Michael McKenry (55)

YEAR	TM	P. COUNT	FRM RUNS	BLK RUNS	THRW RUNS	TOT RUNS
2021	NWA	4481	1.1	0.1	0.4	1.6
2022	OMA	10286	-0.6	0.9	2.0	2.3
2022	KC	307	-0.1	0.0	0.0	-0.1
2023	OMA	1904	0.0	-0.1	0.2	0.1
2023	KC	8410	0.2	0.1	0.6	0.8
2024	KC	7215	-1.7	0.0	0.4	-1.3

As an undersized backstop, Fermin failed to command interest from teams as an amateur; the Royals finally signed him for under $10K as a 19-year-old, ancient in terms of international free agents. Fermin rewarded the Royals' faith by applying himself with vigor to learn both the strike zone and, in order to communicate with his pitchers, the English language. He also venerates fellow Venezuelan catcher Salvador Perez, his mentor and the player he now gets to back up in the big leagues. It's extremely current-era Royals to have the most feel-good story be a backup catcher, but it's also a pretty solid feel-good story.

Maikel Garcia 3B   Born: 03/03/00   Age: 24   Bats: R   Throws: R   Height: 6'0"   Weight: 180   Origin: IFA, 2016

YEAR	TM	LVL	AGE	PA	R	HR	RBI	SB	AVG/OBP/SLG	BABIP	SLGCON	BB%	K%	ZSw%	ZCon%	OSw%	OCon%	LA	90th EV	DRC+	BRR	DRP	WARP
2021	COL	A	21	237	40	1	26	24	.303/.409/.415	.352	.500	16.0%	13.9%							125	1.8	4.3	2.0
2021	QC	A+	21	243	38	3	24	11	.281/.351/.396	.331	.486	9.9%	16.5%							113	0.7	0.0	1.2
2022	NWA	AA	22	369	63	4	33	27	.291/.369/.409	.345	.502	11.1%	16.3%							111	1.7	0.3	1.9
2022	OMA	AAA	22	186	41	7	28	12	.274/.341/.463	.322	.623	9.1%	22.6%							106	-0.3	-1.2	0.5
2022	KC	MLB	22	23	1	0	2	0	.318/.348/.364	.412	.471	4.3%	21.7%	62.2%	87.0%	28.6%	81.2%	3.1	99.0	88	0.0	-0.1	0.0
2023	OMA	AAA	23	112	11	1	17	4	.242/.348/.347	.301	.452	14.3%	19.6%	54.7%	80.5%	21.0%	78.6%			108	-2.1	0.3	0.3
2023	KC	MLB	23	515	59	4	50	23	.272/.323/.358	.344	.476	7.4%	22.3%	64.7%	86.4%	24.7%	67.3%	6.0	104.6	86	0.7	0.7	0.9
2024 DC	KC	MLB	24	550	47	6	46	23	.238/.306/.332	.292	.419	8.3%	18.9%							83	-0.1	0.4	0.4

2023 GP: 3B (104), SS (14), DH (5), 2B (4)

Comps: Martín Prado (63), Yamaico Navarro (59), Jose Vizcaino (59)

The presence of Bobby Witt Jr. shunted the slick-gloved Garcia over to third base in the bigs, where he was equally stellar, but no one apprised his bat, which is still set to "pound ground," of the move. Short of dropping Garcia into the fountains at Kauffman and hoping he emerges Scott Rolen-sized, the adjustments will have to come in the box, namely by increasing his comically low average launch angle to something designed to find grass rather than dirt. A disciplined hitter in the box who doesn't often chase and makes consistent hard contact, it seems like Garcia should be finding more barrels than he is. Perhaps a quick jaunt east to see Rolen's Hoosiers, with a stopoff in IU's weight room, could help him out.

Tyler Gentry RF   Born: 02/01/99   Age: 25   Bats: R   Throws: R   Height: 6'0"   Weight: 210   Origin: Round 3, 2020 Draft (#76 overall)

YEAR	TM	LVL	AGE	PA	R	HR	RBI	SB	AVG/OBP/SLG	BABIP	SLGCON	BB%	K%	ZSw%	ZCon%	OSw%	OCon%	LA	90th EV	DRC+	BRR	DRP	WARP
2021	QC	A+	22	186	29	6	28	4	.259/.395/.449	.360	.717	15.6%	29.6%							101	-1.3	1.2	0.6
2022	QC	A+	23	152	22	5	23	2	.336/.434/.516	.447	.742	13.2%	25.7%							126	-0.9	-0.9	0.8
2022	NWA	AA	23	331	57	16	63	8	.321/.417/.555	.362	.731	12.1%	19.9%							129	-0.9	9.8	3.2
2023	OMA	AAA	24	572	69	16	71	14	.253/.370/.421	.309	.575	14.2%	22.2%	59.0%	82.3%	22.0%	55.9%			107	1.1	5.4	2.5
2024 DC	KC	MLB	25	128	12	2	12	2	.236/.322/.353	.314	.494	9.7%	25.7%							95	0.0	0	0.2

2023 GP: RF (112), DH (13), LF (4)

Comps: Francisco Peguero (67), Leandro Castro (66), Anthony Santander (61)

Gentry slowed down some while facing crafty Triple-A hurlers, with numbers that were damp not only compared to the lofty heights of his breakout year but also considering the offensive environment of the PCL. However, he put together a second-half campaign more akin to the heights of his 2022 season, bringing his blend of power plus solid plate discipline, and this spring will compete for a spot in a Royals outfield that's short on both those traits.

Asbel Gonzalez OF Born: 01/02/06 Age: 18 Bats: R Throws: R Height: 6'2" Weight: 170 Origin: IFA, 2023

YEAR	TM	LVL	AGE	PA	R	HR	RBI	SB	AVG/OBP/SLG	BABIP	SLGCON	BB%	K%	ZSw%	ZCon%	OSw%	OCon%	LA	90th EV	DRC+	BRR	DRP	WARP
2023	DSL ROYB	ROK	17	63	7	1	2	8	.196/.339/.275	.243	.368	11.1%	20.6%										
2023	DSL ROYG	ROK	17	110	18	0	16	9	.272/.364/.413	.305	.481	10.9%	11.8%										
2024									No projection														

2023 GP: CF (38), LF (4)

The Royals have gone heavy into Venezuela recently, signing eight players out of the country in 2023 as part of their largest-ever IFA class. Gonzalez is an intriguing find; after a strong debut, he represented the Royals at the DSL All-Star Game last July. He patrols the outfield with long, skinny legs that recall Bambi on the ice but nevertheless show plenty of coordination. Currently the "power" part of his power-speed combo is doubles and triples but again, his career is currently first-act *Bambi*, hopefully with a happier narrative arc.

Garrett Hampson UT Born: 10/10/94 Age: 29 Bats: R Throws: R Height: 5'11" Weight: 196 Origin: Round 3, 2016 Draft (#81 overall)

YEAR	TM	LVL	AGE	PA	R	HR	RBI	SB	AVG/OBP/SLG	BABIP	SLGCON	BB%	K%	ZSw%	ZCon%	OSw%	OCon%	LA	90th EV	DRC+	BRR	DRP	WARP
2021	COL	MLB	26	494	69	11	33	17	.234/.289/.380	.291	.513	6.7%	23.9%	64.5%	85.6%	29.1%	59.3%	12.9	101.1	72	0.2	3.5	0.6
2022	COL	MLB	27	226	29	2	15	12	.211/.287/.307	.294	.449	9.3%	27.9%	61.0%	88.5%	31.7%	56.1%	7.5	100.9	73	0.8	0.3	0.1
2023	JAX	AAA	28	103	17	0	5	6	.348/.412/.435	.416	.519	8.7%	14.6%	59.5%	84.0%	28.1%	73.0%			102	0.3	0.2	0.4
2023	MIA	MLB	28	252	30	3	23	5	.276/.349/.380	.379	.545	9.1%	26.6%	58.4%	83.3%	30.7%	59.6%	10.7	101.4	69	0.3	0.9	0.0
2024 DC	KC	MLB	29	180	16	3	16	5	.222/.291/.328	.285	.443	8.0%	23.7%							76	0.2	0.2	0.0

2023 GP: SS (30), CF (26), RF (21), 2B (13), LF (10), 3B (5), DH (2)   Comps: Darwin Barney (55), Johnny Giavotella (53), Ronny Cedeno (53)

While it appeared as though Hampson had simply forgotten his bat at the end of his stint in Colorado, he also repeatedly misplaced it in Miami. It could be anywhere. Manager Skip Schumacher apparently tried to put one of those Apple AirTags on it, but the battery died and left both men in a pickle. They should try painting it like the team's home run sculpture, or make it play Scott Stapp's "Marlins Will Soar," or attach it to Hampson's ankle like a Skip-It toy—just don't turn off the lights when it's around Arráez or he'll step into another ankle injury. Someone has got to try *something*, though Hampson and his disappearing bat are now the Royals' responsibility.

Kyle Isbel CF Born: 03/03/97 Age: 27 Bats: L Throws: R Height: 5'11" Weight: 190 Origin: Round 3, 2018 Draft (#94 overall)

YEAR	TM	LVL	AGE	PA	R	HR	RBI	SB	AVG/OBP/SLG	BABIP	SLGCON	BB%	K%	ZSw%	ZCon%	OSw%	OCon%	LA	90th EV	DRC+	BRR	DRP	WARP
2021	OMA	AAA	24	451	62	15	55	22	.269/.357/.444	.314	.578	10.0%	20.2%							108	-1.1	-2.3	1.6
2021	KC	MLB	24	83	16	1	7	2	.276/.337/.434	.385	.623	8.4%	27.7%	60.5%	92.3%	41.1%	59.5%	18.4	103.7	82	0.3	1.3	0.2
2022	KC	MLB	25	278	32	5	28	9	.211/.264/.340	.275	.481	5.8%	27.0%	62.8%	87.5%	35.5%	67.6%	10.1	103.5	66	0.1	2.2	0.0
2023	OMA	AAA	26	37	7	2	6	0	.290/.405/.548	.304	.680	16.2%	16.2%	65.3%	93.8%	30.6%	67.6%			110	0.2	0.1	0.2
2023	KC	MLB	26	313	45	5	34	7	.240/.282/.380	.283	.476	5.4%	18.8%	64.1%	91.6%	33.8%	63.1%	13.5	103.3	97	0.5	0.6	1.1
2024 DC	KC	MLB	27	375	34	7	37	10	.237/.296/.368	.281	.467	7.0%	19.5%							87	0.3	0	0.7

2023 GP: CF (89), DH (1)   Comps: Pablo Reyes (59), Matt Szczur (57), Jackie Bradley Jr. (57)

Jason Isbell is a Grammy-winning musician who unintentionally inspired the first-ballot HoF Tweet about "30–50 feral hogs." This Isbel is a Royals outfielder who entered the 2023 season looking to rebound from a disappointing sophomore campaign. Instead, he got off to a lumbering start before losing a month to a hamstring issue. After returning from injury in July, he made a change to his swing path to keep the bat in the zone longer and saw both his contact frequency and quality fatten up. The contact-focused Isbel still needs to be more selective at the plate, though, as demonstrated via his paltry walk rate. Plus contact with superior outfield defense should be a shoo-in for an Opening Day roster spot, but Isbel has to contend with the similarly defensively talented Drew Waters, and an outfield mix in Kansas City that's become more crowded since last season. There's always another 30–50 hogs to fend off, it seems.

Carter Jensen C/DH Born: 07/03/03 Age: 21 Bats: L Throws: R Height: 6'1" Weight: 210 Origin: Round 3, 2021 Draft (#78 overall)

YEAR	TM	LVL	AGE	PA	R	HR	RBI	SB	AVG/OBP/SLG	BABIP	SLGCON	BB%	K%	ZSw%	ZCon%	OSw%	OCon%	LA	90th EV	DRC+	BRR	DRP	WARP
2021	ROYG	ROK	17	65	8	1	7	4	.273/.385/.382	.400	.583	15.4%	29.2%									0.5	
2022	COL	A	18	485	66	11	50	8	.226/.363/.382	.275	.517	17.1%	21.2%							117	-2.8	1.5	2.3
2023	QC	A+	19	497	61	11	45	11	.211/.356/.363	.267	.520	18.5%	24.1%							113	-3.0	-3.7	1.8
2024 non	KC	MLB	20	251	22	3	21	0	.207/.305/.312	.281	.448	11.7%	26.5%							78	0.0	0	0.3

2023 GP: C (68), DH (48)   Comps: Francisco Peña (52), Aramis Ademan (49), Tirso Ornelas (48)

Is it possible that the Kansas City-born, lefty-hitting Jensen modeled his loft-heavy swing on longtime Royal Alex Gordon's? The Royals probably hope so, as they'd take Gordo's early-10s heater in a heartbeat from their catching prospect, but they'll probably have to settle for more of a three true outcomes type with passable defense behind the dish, which might deliver less overall value but an equal shot at a World Series game-tying dinger or two.

YEAR	TM	P. COUNT	FRM RUNS	BLK RUNS	THRW RUNS	TOT RUNS
2022	COL	6704	1.7	-1.6	2.2	2.3
2023	QC	9988	-2.0	-2.6	-0.1	-4.7
2024	KC	6956	0.1	-1.3	0.0	-1.2

Nick Loftin IF Born: 09/25/98   Age: 25   Bats: R   Throws: R   Height: 5'11"   Weight: 180   Origin: Round 1, 2020 Draft (#32 overall)

YEAR	TM	LVL	AGE	PA	R	HR	RBI	SB	AVG/OBP/SLG	BABIP	SLGCON	BB%	K%	ZSw%	ZCon%	OSw%	OCon%	LA	90th EV	DRC+	BRR	DRP	WARP
2021	QC	A+	22	410	67	10	57	11	.289/.373/.463	.323	.557	10.2%	14.6%							122	1.6	-3.1	2.1
2022	NWA	AA	23	425	78	12	47	24	.270/.354/.421	.288	.500	10.6%	13.4%							108	0.8	-3.6	1.4
2022	OMA	AAA	23	168	26	5	19	5	.216/.280/.359	.259	.491	6.0%	24.4%							89	0.3	-3.5	0.0
2023	ROY	ROK	24	26	10	1	5	1	.471/.615/.706	.538	.923	23.1%	15.4%										
2023	OMA	AAA	24	358	41	14	56	6	.270/.344/.444	.274	.522	9.5%	13.1%	67.2%	88.6%	33.4%	71.3%			109	-0.5	-1.4	1.1
2023	KC	MLB	24	68	10	0	10	2	.323/.368/.435	.392	.540	5.9%	17.6%	69.6%	83.1%	31.1%	71.7%	10.6	100.2	94	0.0	0.0	0.1
2024 DC	KC	MLB	25	156	14	3	15	4	.239/.302/.352	.277	.436	7.1%	17.1%							87	0.0	0	0.2

2023 GP: 1B (8), 2B (7), 3B (4), DH (2)   *Comps: Tommy Edman (55), Kendrys Morales (55), Tyler Austin (54)*

The Royals guarded their former first-rounder jealously last year, keeping him shut up in a tower in Omaha before he finally debuted in September, playing him sparingly down the stretch and then yanking him back from the AFL two weeks into that season. Maybe the Royals were slow-playing Loftin after a clean-up procedure on a bothersome meniscus cost him a month, or maybe they didn't want other teams to gaze too wantonly upon the plus-disciplined, potential speed-and-power threat, who despite providing some defensive flexibility is ultimately without an everyday position given this ballclub's current composition. Loftin will be fine, as long as he listens to Royal Bluebeard and stays out of that locked room labeled FORMER UTILITYMEN.

Michael Massey 2B Born: 03/22/98   Age: 26   Bats: L   Throws: R   Height: 6'0"   Weight: 195   Origin: Round 4, 2019 Draft (#109 overall)

YEAR	TM	LVL	AGE	PA	R	HR	RBI	SB	AVG/OBP/SLG	BABIP	SLGCON	BB%	K%	ZSw%	ZCon%	OSw%	OCon%	LA	90th EV	DRC+	BRR	DRP	WARP
2021	QC	A+	23	439	76	21	87	12	.289/.351/.531	.297	.644	7.5%	15.5%							132	1.0	-4.0	2.6
2022	NWA	AA	24	248	36	9	48	9	.305/.359/.495	.356	.657	8.5%	21.8%							101	0.9	0.8	0.9
2022	OMA	AAA	24	143	21	7	29	4	.325/.392/.595	.395	.824	9.1%	24.5%							101	0.1	3.2	0.7
2022	KC	MLB	24	194	16	4	17	3	.243/.307/.376	.304	.512	4.6%	23.7%	71.7%	82.1%	40.0%	57.2%	15.3	102.2	88	0.1	-1.3	0.2
2023	KC	MLB	25	461	42	15	55	6	.229/.274/.381	.261	.495	5.2%	21.5%	72.5%	86.9%	36.2%	63.4%	19.2	104.5	89	0.3	-1.3	0.6
2024 DC	KC	MLB	26	484	47	12	52	9	.241/.297/.386	.280	.494	6.1%	20.0%							93	0.1	-1.9	0.7

2023 GP: 2B (118), DH (9)   *Comps: Jemile Weeks (64), Kevin Frandsen (56), Logan Forsythe (54)*

Massey won the KC BBWAA chapter's 2023 "Mike Swanson Good Guy" award, given to the player who "best exemplifies a cooperative spirit with the beat writers who cover the team"—which feels like a grown-up version of the "classroom helper" award. On the field, he is somewhat of a teacher's pet: His defense at the keystone is superb, and in the box, he swings at the right pitches, makes a ton of contact and doesn't strike out much, while clubbing double-digit homers in his first full season. However, Massey pulled the ball more than all but a handful of players in MLB—naughty, naughty!—and the guys ahead of him on the list (think names like Albies, Schwarber, Muncy, Paredes) all hit about twice as many home runs, which is what Massey needs to do to sustain his low-average, contact-heavy approach. Hopefully his manager is stocked up on gold stars.

MJ Melendez OF Born: 11/29/98   Age: 25   Bats: L   Throws: R   Height: 6'1"   Weight: 190   Origin: Round 2, 2017 Draft (#52 overall)

YEAR	TM	LVL	AGE	PA	R	HR	RBI	SB	AVG/OBP/SLG	BABIP	SLGCON	BB%	K%	ZSw%	ZCon%	OSw%	OCon%	LA	90th EV	DRC+	BRR	DRP	WARP
2021	NWA	AA	22	347	58	28	65	2	.285/.372/.628	.286	.842	12.4%	21.9%							143	-0.7	-2.9	2.7
2021	OMA	AAA	22	184	37	13	38	1	.293/.413/.620	.310	.838	17.4%	21.2%							128	-1.4	-1.5	1.0
2022	OMA	AAA	23	91	7	2	6	3	.167/.286/.295	.204	.411	14.3%	24.2%							97	0.7	0.6	0.4
2022	KC	MLB	23	534	57	18	62	2	.217/.313/.393	.258	.550	12.4%	24.5%	68.4%	79.7%	27.4%	58.8%	15.3	104.8	115	0.2	-16.4	1.0
2023	KC	MLB	24	602	65	16	56	6	.235/.316/.398	.311	.584	10.3%	28.2%	71.8%	73.4%	29.8%	51.6%	17.2	105.2	89	0.5	4.0	1.2
2024 DC	KC	MLB	25	548	57	16	61	4	.220/.309/.385	.287	.569	10.9%	28.4%							98	0.1	2.6	1.6

2023 GP: RF (72), LF (58), DH (12), C (10), 1B (1)   *Comps: Max Kepler (54), Jarrod Saltalamacchia (51), Justin Smoak (51)*

YEAR	TM	P. COUNT	FRM RUNS	BLK RUNS	THRW RUNS	TOT RUNS
2021	NWA	7560	-3.1	-0.5	0.3	-3.3
2021	OMA	4305	-2.6	-0.3	0.4	-2.4
2022	OMA	2202	0.3	-0.2	0.0	0.1
2022	KC	9969	-17.5	-1.1	0.7	-17.9
2023	KC	1186	0.0	0.0	0.0	0.0
2024	KC	6956	-6.1	-0.4	0.1	-6.4

After slumping through most of the season, the Royals posted their only winning month in September, morphing into a Scrappy-Doo of a team that swept Cleveland and Houston back-to-back. One of the drivers of that month of success was Melendez, who made a slight adjustment around the All-Star Break, raising his hands, which helped him make consistently hard and loud contact; of his 16 homers, 10 came in July and later. He's still bedeviled by whiffs, including on an alarming number on fastballs right in the middle of the plate, but with high on-base players ahead of him and natural thump in his bat, Melendez just needs to make a little more contact to keep himself and his team punching above their weight. Take a flier on him in fantasy leagues while he's still catcher-eligible, as the conversion to corner outfielder seems to be complete.

★ ★ ★ *2024 Top 101 Prospect* **#96** ★ ★ ★

Blake Mitchell C Born: 08/03/04   Age: 19   Bats: L   Throws: R   Height: 6'1"   Weight: 202   Origin: Round 1, 2023 Draft (#8 overall)

YEAR	TM	LVL	AGE	PA	R	HR	RBI	SB	AVG/OBP/SLG	BABIP	SLGCON	BB%	K%	ZSw%	ZCon%	OSw%	OCon%	LA	90th EV	DRC+	BRR	DRP	WARP
2023	ROY	ROK	18	52	8	0	3	1	.147/.423/.176	.238	.300	32.7%	26.9%										
2024									No projection														

2023 GP: C (8), DH (5)

The Royals have a type and they stick to it, opting for the disciplined high-schooler Mitchell with their first-round selection in 2023 over the more free-swinging (and arguably better-regarded) UVA catcher Kyle Teel. However, this pick frustrated many Royals fans, comparing Teel's present production against Mitchell's future projections—*potential* plus power, *potential* plus hit—and considering the very real attrition rate of prep catching prospects. Mitchell has a rocket launcher for an arm and blocks well, thus appearing a solid bet to stay behind the plate, at least, but it's understandable that it's hard to sell current Royals fans on *potential* anything.

Vinnie Pasquantino 1B   Born: 10/10/97   Age: 26   Bats: L   Throws: L   Height: 6'4"   Weight: 245   Origin: Round 11, 2019 Draft (#319 overall)

YEAR	TM	LVL	AGE	PA	R	HR	RBI	SB	AVG/OBP/SLG	BABIP	SLGCON	BB%	K%	ZSw%	ZCon%	OSw%	OCon%	LA	90th EV	DRC+	BRR	DRP	WARP
2021	QC	A+	23	276	44	13	42	4	.291/.384/.565	.298	.673	12.0%	13.8%							144	-1.5	5.0	2.5
2021	NWA	AA	23	237	35	11	42	2	.310/.405/.560	.307	.644	13.1%	11.0%							140	0.1	-2.8	1.5
2022	OMA	AAA	24	313	52	18	70	3	.277/.371/.561	.258	.658	12.8%	12.5%							135	-0.9	0.9	2.1
2022	KC	MLB	24	298	25	10	26	1	.295/.383/.450	.306	.518	11.7%	11.4%	71.3%	92.3%	29.4%	73.8%	12.0	105.7	134	-0.6	0.1	1.8
2023	KC	MLB	25	260	24	9	26	0	.247/.324/.437	.250	.505	9.6%	11.9%	63.2%	91.1%	36.0%	73.2%	17.1	104.2	117	-0.3	-0.1	1.0
2024 DC	KC	MLB	26	517	57	15	61	3	.261/.337/.428	.276	.503	9.5%	13.1%							118	-0.7	-0.1	2.1

2023 GP: 1B (44), DH (17)   Comps: David Cooper (75), Mitch Moreland (75), Yonder Alonso (70)

Even the most diehard Royals fans can be forgiven if they forewent watching the remainder of the season after June 9, as no game better encapsulated the 2023 Royals season. Entering the day at 18-44, Kansas City lost a 3-2 affair to Baltimore. The game opened with Austin Hays homering on the first pitch Daniel Lynch IV threw, while the Royals offense only scared up three hits into the seventh inning; the real kicker, though, was the midgame loss of their breakout-candidate first baseman, with a torn labrum which would end his season. The good news is Pasquantino was an above-average hitter even while managing the shoulder injury in the 2022 season, so should return even better with his new robo-shoulder. The better news is that this year's June 9th game is scheduled against the Mariners, the one team in baseball that likes to trip over its own feet more than the Royals.

Salvador Perez C   Born: 05/10/90   Age: 34   Bats: R   Throws: R   Height: 6'3"   Weight: 255   Origin: IFA, 2006

YEAR	TM	LVL	AGE	PA	R	HR	RBI	SB	AVG/OBP/SLG	BABIP	SLGCON	BB%	K%	ZSw%	ZCon%	OSw%	OCon%	LA	90th EV	DRC+	BRR	DRP	WARP
2021	KC	MLB	31	665	88	48	121	1	.273/.316/.544	.298	.749	4.2%	25.6%	78.9%	80.8%	48.1%	53.7%	16.3	107.9	121	-0.6	-17.0	2.5
2022	KC	MLB	32	473	48	23	76	0	.254/.292/.465	.285	.616	3.8%	23.0%	78.2%	78.7%	45.7%	58.7%	18.2	106.3	109	-0.7	-13.9	0.5
2023	KC	MLB	33	580	59	23	80	0	.255/.292/.422	.294	.563	3.3%	23.3%	77.2%	81.9%	50.0%	58.5%	16.1	106.6	95	-1.2	-7.9	0.6
2024 DC	KC	MLB	34	550	63	24	74	0	.256/.299/.443	.299	.596	4.2%	24.1%							109	0.0	-13.3	1.1

2023 GP: C (91), DH (29), 1B (23)   Comps: Ted Simmons (76), Ivan Rodríguez (76), Joe Torre (73)

YEAR	TM	P. COUNT	FRM RUNS	BLK RUNS	THRW RUNS	TOT RUNS
2021	KC	17285	-15.3	-0.6	1.5	-14.4
2022	KC	10818	-14.2	0.0	0.8	-13.5
2023	KC	12450	-7.1	-0.2	-0.1	-7.4
2024	KC	14430	-12.3	-0.2	-0.6	-13.2

Unlike football teams that scatter "captain" patches like ticker-tape, MLB franchises dole out the "C" on jerseys with extreme prejudice; the Royals elected to offer it to their longest-tenured player only in the twilight of his career, at the beginning of the 2023 season. Sadly, the totem of the patch didn't inspire Perez's bat to greater heights, because time is a notorious thief. Still, Salvy remains one of the game's luminaries behind the dish, even if time eventually dictates that he take a majority of his plate appearances as "DH" rather than the other "C."

Nick Pratto 1B   Born: 10/06/98   Age: 25   Bats: L   Throws: L   Height: 6'1"   Weight: 225   Origin: Round 1, 2017 Draft (#14 overall)

YEAR	TM	LVL	AGE	PA	R	HR	RBI	SB	AVG/OBP/SLG	BABIP	SLGCON	BB%	K%	ZSw%	ZCon%	OSw%	OCon%	LA	90th EV	DRC+	BRR	DRP	WARP
2021	NWA	AA	22	275	44	15	43	7	.271/.404/.570	.349	.894	16.7%	29.1%							121	-1.8	-0.8	1.2
2021	OMA	AAA	22	270	54	21	55	5	.259/.367/.634	.282	.966	13.7%	28.5%							119	1.0	-1.1	1.2
2022	OMA	AAA	23	374	57	17	47	8	.228/.369/.449	.299	.720	15.8%	30.5%							106	-0.2	-2.2	1.1
2022	KC	MLB	23	182	18	7	20	0	.184/.271/.386	.250	.663	10.4%	36.3%	65.5%	76.6%	31.0%	48.9%	19.5	102.9	65	-0.1	0.2	-0.4
2023	OMA	AAA	24	131	14	4	17	0	.180/.290/.342	.222	.514	12.2%	28.2%	63.1%	89.1%	28.7%	53.2%			89	0.3	0.7	0.2
2023	KC	MLB	24	345	33	7	35	1	.232/.307/.353	.388	.643	8.4%	40.0%	59.5%	80.3%	30.3%	42.2%	13.8	104.6	57	0.1	-0.8	-1.1
2024 DC	KC	MLB	25	228	21	5	22	1	.187/.276/.330	.261	.523	9.6%	32.3%							72	-0.1	-0	-0.4

2023 GP: 1B (78), LF (16), RF (5)   Comps: Justin Smoak (61), Brandon Allen (56), Ronald Guzmán (49)

Ludwig Mies van der Rohe, who designed both the Seagram Building and the Barcelona Chair, said that designing skyscrapers was easy; it was the chairs that were difficult. First base in the big leagues is one of these deceptively difficult paradoxes, as Pratto found out: The once-vaunted prospect whiffed his way through a disappointing power-suck of a year, including a month-long IL stint with a groin injury which might have been a lowlight had the peripherals not been quite so alarming when he was on the field. He also failed to look comfortable at the cold corner, something that had been a strength of his. The defense will likely rebound, but he has to find a way to tap into his power at the plate, or Pratto will continue to find himself sitting on some mighty uncomfortable chairs.

Hunter Renfroe RF   Born: 01/28/92   Age: 32   Bats: R   Throws: R   Height: 6'1"   Weight: 230   Origin: Round 1, 2013 Draft (#13 overall)

YEAR	TM	LVL	AGE	PA	R	HR	RBI	SB	AVG/OBP/SLG	BABIP	SLGCON	BB%	K%	ZSw%	ZCon%	OSw%	OCon%	LA	90th EV	DRC+	BRR	DRP	WARP
2021	BOS	MLB	29	572	89	31	96	1	.259/.315/.501	.284	.668	7.7%	22.7%	67.8%	82.8%	35.6%	63.3%	16.0	108.4	116	-0.2	-2.1	2.6
2022	MIL	MLB	30	522	62	29	72	1	.255/.315/.492	.281	.660	7.5%	23.2%	67.6%	82.9%	34.6%	60.2%	17.7	106.8	113	-0.3	-3.8	1.9
2023	CIN	MLB	31	44	4	1	4	0	.128/.227/.205	.154	.296	11.4%	27.3%	72.5%	84.0%	29.8%	61.1%	10.9	104.0	93	0.0	-0.1	0.1
2023	LAA	MLB	31	504	56	19	56	0	.242/.304/.434	.279	.575	7.7%	22.4%	72.0%	82.0%	37.5%	62.0%	15.3	106.2	95	-0.2	-4.7	0.5
2024 DC	KC	MLB	32	498	55	19	62	0	.236/.300/.415	.272	.553	7.8%	22.5%							102	0.0	-4.9	0.8

2023 GP: RF (128), DH (7), 1B (5)   Comps: Glenallen Hill (74), Dan Ford (73), Jay Buhner (73)

Renfroe was part of a sextet of Angels who were shuttled through waivers in late August after the team, its postseason hopes and Shohei Ohtani's UCL were all torn asunder. Even amid arguably his worst full offensive season as a major leaguer, Renfroe offered the potential to sock a few dingers in Cincinnati's famously hitter-friendly confines and fortify a fairly doughy outfield group. He would subsequently post an OPS of .432 in 14 games, leading to a DFA in fewer than three weeks. Whoops! Renfroe was an above-average hitter as recently as 2022 and will be 32 for all of 2024, so there's still probably more in the tank here. The Royals concurred, signing him to a one-year deal with a player option Things getting *worse* after leaving Anaheim is a rare thing for a major leaguer these days, though he already managed it once.

Carson Roccaforte CF Born: 03/29/02   Age: 22   Bats: L   Throws: L   Height: 6'1"   Weight: 195   Origin: Round 2, 2023 Draft (#66 overall)

YEAR	TM	LVL	AGE	PA	R	HR	RBI	SB	AVG/OBP/SLG	BABIP	SLGCON	BB%	K%	ZSw%	ZCon%	OSw%	OCon%	LA	90th EV	DRC+	BRR	DRP	WARP
2023	COL	A	21	122	19	0	12	11	.257/.377/.356	.366	.514	15.6%	25.4%							101	-0.3	-2.3	0.1
2024 non	KC	MLB	22	251	19	2	19	0	.210/.280/.291	.306	.435	8.0%	30.1%							63	0.0	0	-0.3

2023 GP: CF (27), DH (3)   *Comps: Jiwan James (79), Ricardo Ferreira (77), Clete Thomas (72)*

Find something you love like the Royals love acquiring players with surnames that sound like small-town establishments that offer either the best or worst lasagna of one's life. The latest addition to this club, Roccaforte reminds some of a similarly Adriatic-surnamed erstwhile Royal in Andrew Benintendi, though he's taller, more athletic and speedier than his predecessor—if also somewhat lacking in the power department. But he's an on-base machine with great bat-to-ball skills who's poised to move quickly; sometimes, fast-casual fare tastes just as good.

Cayden Wallace 3B Born: 08/07/01   Age: 22   Bats: R   Throws: R   Height: 5'10"   Weight: 205   Origin: Round 2, 2022 Draft (#49 overall)

YEAR	TM	LVL	AGE	PA	R	HR	RBI	SB	AVG/OBP/SLG	BABIP	SLGCON	BB%	K%	ZSw%	ZCon%	OSw%	OCon%	LA	90th EV	DRC+	BRR	DRP	WARP
2022	COL	A	20	122	15	2	16	8	.294/.369/.468	.353	.586	9.8%	18.0%							112	-1.8	-0.2	0.4
2023	QC	A+	21	428	56	10	64	15	.261/.341/.431	.319	.574	9.8%	22.0%							109	-0.6	2.5	1.5
2023	NWA	AA	21	140	19	3	20	3	.236/.300/.362	.265	.442	8.6%	16.4%							103	1.6	-1.8	0.2
2024 non	KC	MLB	22	251	21	4	23	3	.224/.282/.337	.287	.453	6.7%	24.0%							75	0.0	0	-0.1

2023 GP: 3B (122), DH (8)   *Comps: Miguel Andujar (70), Brandon Drury (64), Dawel Lugo (62)*

Like a person who shows up at the potluck with a spread of store-bought chips and salsa after the Peking duck's been brought in, Wallace is a victim of timing. The Royals encouraged the former Razorback into a third base slot, just in time for the much flashier Maikel Garcia to assume the position at the big-league level. Wallace will need to outbid Garcia with his bat, which does possess a good amount of natural thump, or figure out how to make a good Bananas Foster on the fly.

Drew Waters OF Born: 12/30/98   Age: 25   Bats: S   Throws: R   Height: 6'0"   Weight: 185   Origin: Round 2, 2017 Draft (#41 overall)

YEAR	TM	LVL	AGE	PA	R	HR	RBI	SB	AVG/OBP/SLG	BABIP	SLGCON	BB%	K%	ZSw%	ZCon%	OSw%	OCon%	LA	90th EV	DRC+	BRR	DRP	WARP
2021	GWN	AAA	22	459	70	11	37	28	.240/.329/.381	.341	.588	10.2%	30.9%							85	2.1	13.2	2.2
2022	OMA	AAA	23	143	29	7	17	13	.295/.399/.541	.392	.815	14.0%	28.7%							99	1.1	1.5	0.6
2022	GWN	AAA	23	210	26	5	16	5	.246/.305/.393	.321	.560	7.6%	27.1%							83	1.4	2.2	0.6
2022	KC	MLB	23	109	14	5	18	0	.240/.324/.479	.353	.821	11.0%	36.7%	71.1%	78.0%	30.8%	51.2%	10.9	104.7	79	-0.1	-1.6	-0.1
2023	OMA	AAA	24	58	12	2	6	2	.327/.397/.635	.405	.846	10.3%	22.4%	72.3%	88.2%	32.8%	65.9%			107	0.3	1.0	0.4
2023	KC	MLB	24	337	40	8	32	16	.228/.300/.377	.321	.585	8.0%	31.8%	73.3%	80.6%	36.7%	50.3%	17.4	104.0	76	0.7	-0.3	0.1
2024 DC	KC	MLB	25	243	22	6	24	9	.213/.286/.356	.293	.531	8.2%	30.1%							81	0.2	-2.4	0.0

2023 GP: CF (50), RF (47), DH (6), LF (4)   *Comps: Tyler O'Neill (56), Oswaldo Arcia (51), Travis Snider (50)*

Waters' path to a starting job in the big leagues couldn't be any more clearly illuminated if there were aircraft marshallers holding comically oversized flashlights pointing to the Kauffman outfield—but he still has to land the plane. An oblique injury and lengthy rehab assignment that delayed his start to the season make it hard to judge if the switch hitter dialed back enough of his aggressiveness at the plate in his Fudd-like quest for huntin' bawwels, but to his credit, he found them at an above-average rate when he wasn't chasing sliders. The wiry defensive wizard isn't exactly a likely candidate as a TTO titan, but his quick, powerful swing can create the kind of effortless hard contact you see from ocean-sized men… though it also comes with those king-sized whiffs.

Bobby Witt Jr. SS Born: 06/14/00   Age: 24   Bats: R   Throws: R   Height: 6'1"   Weight: 200   Origin: Round 1, 2019 Draft (#2 overall)

YEAR	TM	LVL	AGE	PA	R	HR	RBI	SB	AVG/OBP/SLG	BABIP	SLGCON	BB%	K%	ZSw%	ZCon%	OSw%	OCon%	LA	90th EV	DRC+	BRR	DRP	WARP
2021	NWA	AA	21	279	44	16	51	14	.295/.369/.570	.339	.785	9.0%	24.0%							120	1.1	-2.8	1.4
2021	OMA	AAA	21	285	55	17	46	15	.285/.352/.581	.314	.778	9.1%	22.5%							114	-0.1	-6.2	0.8
2022	KC	MLB	22	632	82	20	80	30	.254/.294/.428	.295	.555	4.7%	21.4%	70.7%	82.9%	38.8%	64.7%	17.1	106.8	109	3.0	-14.5	1.4
2023	KC	MLB	23	694	97	30	96	49	.276/.319/.495	.295	.610	5.8%	17.4%	71.9%	85.6%	35.1%	64.9%	15.3	106.6	138	1.8	-6.8	5.0
2024 DC	KC	MLB	24	638	72	23	82	41	.268/.320/.454	.302	.568	6.1%	18.6%							117	0.7	-6.8	3.0

2023 GP: SS (149), DH (10)   *Comps: Bo Bichette (78), Corey Seager (77), Gleyber Torres (77)*

In a flex not seen since Bruce Springsteen released his first two albums months apart in 1973, baseball's newest "Junior" managed to one-up the success of his rookie year with an even better follow-up; no sophomore slump here. He followed up a 20/30 season with a 30/30 season, becoming the 45th player in MLB history to join that club, and was just one stolen base shy of 30/50. After a rough first year in the field by defensive metrics, he settled in well enough at shortstop that the Royals felt emboldened to install him there permanently. But the most impressive gains came in the box, where he largely stopped chasing fastballs up and away, cut down his strikeouts and raised his walk rate to above-average, becoming a constant on-base threat from the leadoff spot. That improved approach also helped him more consistently tap into his power, thrilling fans in Kauffman Stadium who have already retconned their Texas-born prodigy into a son of Missouri. Witt has a ways to go before he earns "The Boss" as a moniker, but he's already an Assistant Regional Manager in Kansas City.

PITCHERS

Nick Anderson RHP Born: 07/05/90 Age: 34 Height: 6'4" Weight: 205 Origin: Round 32, 2012 Draft (#995 overall)

YEAR	TM	LVL	AGE	G (GS)	IP	W-L	SV	K	WHIP	ERA	CSP	BB%	K%	HR%	GB%	ZSw%	ZCon%	OSw%	OCon%	BABIP	SLGCON	DRA-	WARP
2021	DUR	AAA	30	11 (0)	10²	0-0	0	12	1.22	5.06		2.3%	27.3%	4.5%	29.0%					.357	.767	91	0.2
2021	TB	MLB	30	6 (0)	6	0-1	1	1	1.00	4.50	55.8%	8.3%	4.2%	8.3%	14.3%	76.3%	82.8%	39.1%	80.0%	.105	.500	133	0.0
2022	DUR	AAA	31	17 (0)	16	1-0	1	12	1.44	5.62		4.3%	17.4%	7.2%	43.4%	84.2%	93.8%	35.0%	57.1%	.313	.679	99	0.2
2023	ATL	MLB	32	35 (0)	35¹	4-0	1	36	1.10	3.06	52.2%	6.4%	25.5%	2.1%	40.6%	65.2%	81.2%	33.2%	57.1%	.290	.505	88	0.6
2024 DC	KC	MLB	33	46 (0)	49	2-3	7	50	1.31	4.52	51.5%	7.2%	24.0%	3.6%	33.7%					.307	.592	106	0.1

2023 Arsenal: FA (94.4), SL (81)   Comps: James Hoyt (56), Blake Parker (55), Will Harris (54)

For the 35 innings that Anderson threw in 2023, he again looked like a gem of a reliever. His fastball velocity may not have been where it was during his early period of success in Florida, but it did go up a tick from his days of struggle in 2021. He leaned on a curveball that missed plenty of bats and became a bonafide out pitch. It propelled him back into high-leverage situations and it seemed as if he'd be a vital cog in Atlanta's bullpen down the stretch. Unfortunately, a July shoulder strain ended up costing him the rest of the big-league season and he was only able to return to action in a rehab stint in September. Anderson's new curveball-focused approach worked well and it wouldn't be shocking at all if he picks up this year right where he left off.

Jonathan Bowlan RHP Born: 12/01/96 Age: 27 Height: 6'6" Weight: 240 Origin: Round 2, 2018 Draft (#58 overall)

YEAR	TM	LVL	AGE	G (GS)	IP	W-L	SV	K	WHIP	ERA	CSP	BB%	K%	HR%	GB%	ZSw%	ZCon%	OSw%	OCon%	BABIP	SLGCON	DRA-	WARP
2021	NWA	AA	24	4 (4)	17	2-0	0	25	0.94	1.59		4.5%	37.9%	0.0%	50.0%					.342	.421	83	0.3
2022	ROY	ROK	25	7 (7)	19¹	0-1	0	26	1.71	5.12		4.5%	29.2%	1.1%	36.2%					.491	.786		
2022	NWA	AA	25	9 (9)	39	1-3	0	30	1.74	6.92		9.3%	16.4%	3.8%	42.4%					.352	.634	135	-0.6
2023	NWA	AA	26	10 (9)	35	1-5	0	47	1.63	7.20		7.9%	28.7%	4.3%	39.6%					.394	.758	85	0.6
2023	OMA	AAA	26	14 (12)	67	6-6	1	58	1.55	5.24		10.8%	19.6%	4.1%	40.8%	73.2%	83.5%	29.5%	58.9%	.309	.598	96	1.1
2023	KC	MLB	26	2 (1)	3	0-1	0	3	1.67	3.00	50.8%	0.0%	21.4%	7.1%	27.3%	88.5%	73.9%	33.3%	60.0%	.400	.727	109	0.0
2024 DC	KC	MLB	27	22 (3)	34²	1-2	0	31	1.51	5.61	50.8%	9.1%	19.8%	3.6%	36.0%					.317	.602	125	-0.2

2023 Arsenal: SL (85.9), FA (95.3), SI (94.9), CH (87.4), CU (76.8)   Comps: Zach Neal (50), Tyler Pill (47), Sam Gaviglio (45)

The second-round pick of the Royals' vaunted 2018 draft finally made it to the Show last year after being slowed by TJ, mostly because Kansas City was in worse need of arms than a zombie handball team. His plus command is still on the mend, but his mid-90s sinking fastball and plus slider seem to have emerged unscathed; in Double-A and Triple-A he put up punchout numbers that make the mouth water. It still largely feels like a relief profile thanks to an inconsistent changeup, but this Royals pitching staff needs arms, arrrrrrrms.

Jake Brentz LHP Born: 09/14/94 Age: 29 Height: 6'1" Weight: 205 Origin: Round 11, 2013 Draft (#325 overall)

YEAR	TM	LVL	AGE	G (GS)	IP	W-L	SV	K	WHIP	ERA	CSP	BB%	K%	HR%	GB%	ZSw%	ZCon%	OSw%	OCon%	BABIP	SLGCON	DRA-	WARP
2021	KC	MLB	26	72 (0)	64	5-2	2	76	1.28	3.66	51.1%	13.3%	27.3%	2.5%	48.1%	67.1%	80.5%	27.2%	51.7%	.255	.516	99	0.7
2022	KC	MLB	27	8 (0)	5¹	0-3	0	9	3.94	23.63	46.7%	26.3%	23.7%	2.6%	33.3%	53.7%	75.9%	20.0%	57.1%	.625	.941	115	0.0
2024 DC	KC	MLB	29	46 (0)	49	2-2	0	55	1.48	4.69	50.4%	13.7%	25.1%	2.5%	43.4%					.294	.531	104	0.1

Comps: Darin Downs (61), Jeff Beliveau (56), Rowan Wick (56)

The argument for shelling out for a personal espresso machine is that eventually, it saves money by replacing a daily coffee run—which, along with avocado toast, is apparently the only thing holding millennials back from home ownership. Perhaps that was the Royals' thinking in signing the hard-throwing lefty Brentz to a two-year deal, keeping him in the organization after he underwent Tommy John surgery in mid-2022: Why pick up a fastball-slider reliever on the open market when we have one at home? But as any at-home barista is quick to learn, more moving parts means more parts to break, and Brentz pitched all of 2 ⅔ minor-league innings in 2023 before suffering a season-ending lat strain. He'll enter his age-29 season with fewer than 70 big-league innings under his belt, along with lingering questions about how well he can command his stuff. The Royals will have to hope there's a new section on iFixit for relievers.

Chandler Champlain RHP Born: 07/23/99 Age: 24 Height: 6'5" Weight: 220 Origin: Round 9, 2021 Draft (#273 overall)

YEAR	TM	LVL	AGE	G (GS)	IP	W-L	SV	K	WHIP	ERA	CSP	BB%	K%	HR%	GB%	ZSw%	ZCon%	OSw%	OCon%	BABIP	SLGCON	DRA-	WARP
2022	TAM	A	22	16 (15)	73¹	2-5	0	94	1.24	4.30		6.2%	30.5%	3.6%	51.3%	70.7%	84.1%	36.9%	55.9%	.333	.632	88	1.6
2022	QC	A+	22	8 (7)	32	1-3	0	22	2.16	9.84		7.1%	14.1%	1.9%	39.7%					.466	.703	139	-0.3
2023	QC	A+	23	11 (11)	62¹	6-3	0	61	1.06	2.74		7.3%	24.7%	2.0%	51.8%					.270	.448	79	1.1
2023	NWA	AA	23	14 (14)	73	5-5	0	64	1.22	3.82		8.3%	21.2%	3.6%	42.6%					.268	.526	98	0.6
2024 non	KC	MLB	24	58 (0)	50	2-2	0	36	1.49	5.57		8.4%	16.4%	3.8%	38.6%					.303	.576	123	-0.4

Comps: Sterling Sharp (84), Nolan Kingham (82), David Buchanan (82)

Chandler's primetime soap opera name is more exciting than his damage-limiting stuff, which is more *PBS Newshour*, but he was able to crank his fastball up to the mid-90s and elevate it for whiffs against Double-A hitters. The heater, along with a pair of swing-and-miss secondaries, indicates he should be racking up more Ks than he has, but inconsistency in landing those secondaries has thus far capped his strikeout potential. When the big-bodied hurler is on, though, he looks every bit like his higher-profile potential rotation mates, none of whom even has an alliterative name.

Austin Cox LHP Born: 03/28/97 Age: 27 Height: 6'4" Weight: 235 Origin: Round 5, 2018 Draft (#152 overall)

YEAR	TM	LVL	AGE	G (GS)	IP	W-L	SV	K	WHIP	ERA	CSP	BB%	K%	HR%	GB%	ZSw%	ZCon%	OSw%	OCon%	BABIP	SLGCON	DRA-	WARP
2021	NWA	AA	24	15(15)	63	4-1	0	56	1.25	3.00		9.6%	21.5%	3.1%	34.1%					.271	.508	111	0.0
2022	OMA	AAA	25	29(24)	147¹	7-7	1	105	1.43	4.21		7.7%	16.2%	3.1%	37.2%					.303	.560	129	-0.2
2023	OMA	AAA	26	12(9)	47¹	2-1	0	39	1.39	3.61		10.8%	20.0%	6.2%	45.9%	69.0%	85.9%	29.0%	72.8%	.273	.697	104	0.6
2023	KC	MLB	26	24(3)	35²	0-1	1	33	1.26	4.54	47.2%	11.4%	22.1%	1.3%	36.1%	65.8%	79.9%	28.8%	59.6%	.274	.457	110	0.2
2024 non	KC	MLB	27	58(0)	50	2-2	0	44	1.50	5.59	47.2%	9.4%	19.6%	3.8%	36.0%					.309	.596	122	-0.4

2023 Arsenal: FA (91.4), SL (86.8), CH (83.4), CU (77.9) *Comps: Sugar Ray Marimon (65), Charlie Leesman (65), A.J. Schugel (65)*

The musical *Little Shop of Horrors* isn't just a collection of bops about a carnivorous plant, but a critique of capitalism and a warning about sacrificing one's own health and well-being for an employer. It's a lesson that would have served Cox well when, after taking a comebacker off his knee, he heroically tried to cover first base anyway, resulting in a full ACL tear that required surgery and ended his debut season. A true crafty lefty, he somehow turns worse-than-average stuff into more-than-average whiffs with his full starter's arsenal and ability to pound the corners gloveside, making righties reach and jamming lefties; he was non-tendered last fall but re-upped with KC on a minors deal, so we might suddenly see more of Cox in the Royals' rotation this year.

Steven Cruz RHP Born: 06/15/99 Age: 25 Height: 6'7" Weight: 225 Origin: IFA, 2017

YEAR	TM	LVL	AGE	G (GS)	IP	W-L	SV	K	WHIP	ERA	CSP	BB%	K%	HR%	GB%	ZSw%	ZCon%	OSw%	OCon%	BABIP	SLGCON	DRA-	WARP
2021	FTM	A	22	26(2)	46²	4-2	1	76	1.35	4.05		14.2%	36.0%	1.4%	46.5%	64.8%	68.4%	29.3%	47.9%	.316	.561	96	0.6
2022	WCH	AA	23	46(0)	56	1-4	4	72	1.59	5.14		13.6%	28.0%	1.6%	36.1%					.352	.563	75	1.1
2023	NWA	AA	24	29(0)	32²	0-0	9	42	1.22	2.20		14.6%	30.7%	0.7%	53.4%					.264	.315	80	0.5
2023	OMA	AAA	24	14(0)	17	0-1	0	22	1.29	6.88		13.9%	30.6%	4.2%	35.9%	66.9%	75.9%	31.7%	51.9%	.250	.579	94	0.3
2023	KC	MLB	24	10(4)	12²	0-0	0	15	1.74	4.97	43.7%	17.7%	24.2%	1.6%	37.1%	69.6%	84.4%	23.0%	57.1%	.294	.571	110	0.1
2024 DC	KC	MLB	25	46(0)	49	2-3	0	53	1.58	5.43	43.7%	14.3%	23.8%	3.1%	37.8%					.299	.570	119	-0.2

2023 Arsenal: FA (97.8), SI (97.3), SL (89.4), FC (92.6), CH (92) *Comps: Chad Sobotka (76), Keith Butler (75), Ryan Meisinger (73)*

Down the stretch, the Royals decided to load-test the chestnut "it doesn't matter how many batters you walk as long as you strike enough of 'em out" with their Oops! All Flamethrowers! bullpen. That approach was perhaps embodied the best by all 79 inches of Cruz, who came thrillingly close to both striking out and walking one batter per inning last season. With elite fastball velocity coming from a truly terrifying angle, he's at least the most interesting version of the archetype, but as any battle-tested preschool parent can tell you, *Don't Break the Ice!* is a fun game until it absolutely is not.

Carlos Hernández RHP Born: 03/11/97 Age: 27 Height: 6'4" Weight: 255 Origin: IFA, 2016

YEAR	TM	LVL	AGE	G (GS)	IP	W-L	SV	K	WHIP	ERA	CSP	BB%	K%	HR%	GB%	ZSw%	ZCon%	OSw%	OCon%	BABIP	SLGCON	DRA-	WARP
2021	OMA	AAA	24	6(6)	26¹	2-1	0	26	1.29	4.44		5.3%	23.0%	5.3%	43.6%					.306	.688	112	0.2
2021	KC	MLB	24	24(11)	85²	6-2	0	74	1.28	3.68	51.4%	11.5%	20.7%	2.0%	40.2%	73.1%	81.8%	30.0%	61.8%	.267	.436	123	-0.2
2022	OMA	AAA	25	12(11)	50	2-4	0	44	1.16	3.78		9.1%	21.2%	3.4%	36.6%					.232	.479	97	0.7
2022	KC	MLB	25	27(7)	56	0-5	0	35	1.84	7.39	54.3%	11.7%	13.2%	2.6%	36.7%	72.2%	83.2%	32.3%	67.0%	.339	.572	142	-0.7
2023	KC	MLB	26	67(4)	70	1-10	4	77	1.33	5.27	46.4%	10.3%	25.7%	3.3%	32.5%	74.2%	80.9%	35.3%	53.3%	.287	.598	102	0.7
2024 DC	KC	MLB	27	40(0)	43¹	2-3	7	44	1.45	5.04	50.0%	10.2%	23.1%	3.4%	36.0%					.308	.587	114	-0.1

2023 Arsenal: FA (99.4), SL (88.7), FS (88.8), CU (84.1) *Comps: Denny Bautista (66), Jeanmar Gómez (64), Anthony Swarzak (63)*

Hernández is built like a semitruck and his fastball comes at hitters like the brakes have been cut, so you can understand why the Royals chose to hold on to the controllable reliever at the trade deadline—especially after some pitch mix adjustments (namely, not throwing the bad ones anymore) and a newfound ability to find the zone produced a steep increase in strikeouts. Post-deadline Hernández did what relievers often do because they live, by nature, in small sample sizes: he struggled down the stretch, which infuriated the fanbase for breaking the cardinal rule of ABTR: Always Be Trading Relievers. But Hernández's runaway-truck velo isn't going anywhere; neither is the next trade deadline.

Brad Keller RHP Born: 07/27/95 Age: 28 Height: 6'5" Weight: 255 Origin: Round 8, 2013 Draft (#240 overall)

YEAR	TM	LVL	AGE	G (GS)	IP	W-L	SV	K	WHIP	ERA	CSP	BB%	K%	HR%	GB%	ZSw%	ZCon%	OSw%	OCon%	BABIP	SLGCON	DRA-	WARP
2021	KC	MLB	25	26(26)	133²	8-12	0	120	1.66	5.39	55.7%	10.4%	19.6%	2.9%	48.3%	68.8%	87.1%	28.7%	62.7%	.347	.590	120	-0.1
2022	KC	MLB	26	35(22)	139²	6-14	1	102	1.50	5.09	56.8%	9.2%	16.5%	2.8%	52.2%	71.7%	89.8%	32.3%	60.6%	.311	.523	101	1.3
2023	NWA	AA	27	6(0)	8²	2-0	0	8	1.27	4.15		10.8%	21.6%	2.7%	60.0%					.250	.480	97	0.1
2023	OMA	AAA	27	9(2)	9	0-3	0	5	3.56	15.00		35.6%	8.5%	1.7%	41.9%	55.3%	88.5%	16.0%	72.0%	.345	.586	160	-0.1
2023	KC	MLB	27	11(9)	45¹	3-4	0	31	1.92	4.57	43.6%	21.3%	14.7%	1.4%	57.6%	59.9%	90.2%	24.1%	58.2%	.302	.450	136	-0.3
2024 non	KC	MLB	28	58(0)	50	2-2	0	43	1.69	5.70	52.5%	14.1%	18.4%	2.4%	52.6%					.309	.513	120	-0.3

2023 Arsenal: HC (93.7), SW (84.5), CU (85.4), FS (91.2), SI (93.1), SL (87.3) *Comps: Mike Pelfrey (80), Scott Erickson (79), Storm Davis (79)*

Keller was 45 ⅓ innings into testing the boundaries of how much interest a back-end starter who doesn't strike anyone out could pique, having overhauled his arsenal at Driveline over the prior offseason, but shoulder impingement—and then the much scarier-sounding "symptoms associated with thoracic outlet syndrome"—shut him down for the season. A free agent whenever he's able to return to play, it's unclear which team will host the next stages of the Keller experiment; maybe the Royals again, as they've seemed to be setting up a Victorian-style Home for Boys With Soggy Shoulders.

Will Klein RHP   Born: 11/28/99   Age: 24   Height: 6'5"   Weight: 230   Origin: Round 5, 2020 Draft (#135 overall)

YEAR	TM	LVL	AGE	G (GS)	IP	W-L	SV	K	WHIP	ERA	CSP	BB%	K%	HR%	GB%	ZSw%	ZCon%	OSw%	OCon%	BABIP	SLGCON	DRA-	WARP
2021	QC	A+	21	36(0)	70¹	7-1	4	121	1.24	3.20		14.9%	40.9%	1.4%	50.8%					.312	.567	80	1.5
2022	NWA	AA	22	30(3)	43²	1-1	0	55	2.43	10.51		22.0%	23.7%	2.6%	44.8%					.419	.661	166	-1.5
2023	NWA	AA	23	21(0)	29¹	0-2	1	44	1.43	3.38		10.7%	33.6%	0.8%	45.1%					.391	.559	71	0.8
2023	OMA	AAA	23	28(1)	35	1-3	3	49	1.86	5.66		14.4%	28.2%	1.7%	44.8%	64.6%	80.3%	27.2%	42.7%	.398	.594	86	0.8
2024 DC	KC	MLB	24	8(0)	10²	0-1	0	12	1.56	5.20		14.8%	25.0%	2.9%	39.9%					.297	.552	114	0.0

2023 Arsenal: FA (97.5), SL (88.7), CU (81.6)   *Comps: Evan Phillips (76), Johnny Barbato (75), Jake Barrett (75)*

A welcome relief from the Royals' minor-league stable of pitch-to-contact hurlers, Klein has big, bad stuff: a triple-digit fastball, a true power curve and a wicked cutter, with the attendant wildness typical of those who rush their fastballs in where angels fear to tread. The Royals protected him from the Rule 5 Draft over the offseason, so expect to see a heavy dose of Klein as he competes for a bullpen spot this spring; keep some pearls handy for clutching.

Ben Kudrna RHP   Born: 01/30/03   Age: 21   Height: 6'3"   Weight: 175   Origin: Round 2, 2021 Draft (#43 overall)

YEAR	TM	LVL	AGE	G (GS)	IP	W-L	SV	K	WHIP	ERA	CSP	BB%	K%	HR%	GB%	ZSw%	ZCon%	OSw%	OCon%	BABIP	SLGCON	DRA-	WARP
2022	COL	A	19	17(17)	72¹	2-5	0	61	1.35	3.48		10.3%	19.6%	1.3%	39.4%					.292	.419	112	0.3
2023	COL	A	20	14(13)	68¹	4-3	0	70	1.42	3.56		10.3%	24.1%	2.4%	49.2%					.326	.529	91	1.0
2023	QC	A+	20	8(8)	40¹	1-4	0	34	1.66	5.36		8.5%	19.2%	4.0%	44.1%					.375	.659	97	0.5
2024 non	KC	MLB	21	58(0)	50	2-2	0	37	1.71	6.76		10.7%	15.8%	4.2%	36.8%					.321	.615	144	-0.9

Comps: Zack Littell (77), Jackson Stephens (76), Blayne Enlow (76)

As a prep prospect, Kudrna was known for his advanced secondaries—a bat-missing slider and promising changeup—moreso than his fastball. After a couple seasons of careful coddling by the Royals' player development staff, he's now added velocity to his heater, able to dial it up into the upper-90s while running it up and in on lefties; between the extra fuzz on the pitch and his ability to miss bats with his secondaries when he's got his command working, he should probably have the "contact-manager" label lifted any day now. Although he lost most of his strikeout gains in the move to High-A, another shot at befuddling batters in Quad Cities appears likely given his youth. Danza, Kudrna.

Sam Long LHP   Born: 07/08/95   Age: 29   Height: 6'1"   Weight: 185   Origin: Round 18, 2016 Draft (#540 overall)

YEAR	TM	LVL	AGE	G (GS)	IP	W-L	SV	K	WHIP	ERA	CSP	BB%	K%	HR%	GB%	ZSw%	ZCon%	OSw%	OCon%	BABIP	SLGCON	DRA-	WARP
2021	RIC	AA	25	4(4)	15	0-1	0	22	1.07	3.00		6.7%	36.7%	0.0%	41.2%					.353	.618	89	0.2
2021	SAC	AAA	25	11(3)	26¹	1-0	0	31	0.95	2.05		8.8%	30.4%	2.0%	45.2%					.233	.419	84	0.4
2021	SF	MLB	25	12(5)	40²	2-1	0	38	1.28	5.53	58.3%	8.5%	21.6%	2.8%	39.2%	68.0%	85.7%	33.1%	67.9%	.278	.542	107	0.2
2022	SAC	AAA	26	8(3)	16²	1-0	0	16	1.62	4.32		20.5%	20.5%	2.6%	30.4%	64.4%	80.3%	28.0%	72.4%	.205	.444	109	0.1
2022	SF	MLB	26	28(6)	42¹	1-3	1	33	1.25	3.61	58.2%	7.7%	18.2%	4.4%	38.3%	68.0%	79.8%	29.0%	64.7%	.250	.588	115	0.1
2023	SAC	AAA	27	4(0)	10	1-0	0	7	1.90	9.90		10.2%	14.3%	4.1%	43.2%	60.3%	93.6%	36.2%	60.5%	.343	.639	118	
2023	LV	AAA	27	11(0)	13²	1-0	4	13	1.46	3.95		10.0%	21.7%	0.0%	40.0%	63.2%	84.7%	27.0%	67.6%	.350	.474	82	
2023	OAK	MLB	27	40(1)	45	0-1	2	32	1.56	5.60	47.0%	10.6%	16.1%	2.5%	42.1%	67.6%	85.6%	34.5%	72.2%	.317	.535	111	0.3
2024 non	KC	MLB	28	58(0)	50	2-2	0	37	1.48	5.07	53.4%	9.9%	16.6%	2.9%	40.2%					.295	.525	112	-0.1

2023 Arsenal: FA (94.3), CU (77.5), SL (85.1), CH (86)   *Comps: Alex Young (56), Tyler Duffey (55), Anthony Banda (54)*

We all yearn for equality. In the case of Long, he treats all batters with the same vigor, which is what you want out of a human being, but not necessarily out of a late-inning lefty. With no discernible platoon splits, he relies on a disappearing curveball and an overhauled changeup (so overhauled it was categorized last year as a split-finger fastball). By giving batters a different look, he can burst into the game in any inning, and sometimes throw a second inning if he's feeling vivacious. Start calling him Sam Long Reliever.

Seth Lugo RHP   Born: 11/17/89   Age: 34   Height: 6'4"   Weight: 225   Origin: Round 34, 2011 Draft (#1032 overall)

YEAR	TM	LVL	AGE	G (GS)	IP	W-L	SV	K	WHIP	ERA	CSP	BB%	K%	HR%	GB%	ZSw%	ZCon%	OSw%	OCon%	BABIP	SLGCON	DRA-	WARP
2021	NYM	MLB	31	46(0)	46¹	4-3	1	55	1.29	3.50	55.6%	9.7%	28.2%	3.1%	41.7%	64.7%	79.2%	33.5%	54.3%	.307	.585	90	0.7
2022	NYM	MLB	32	62(0)	65	3-2	3	69	1.17	3.60	56.5%	6.6%	25.4%	3.3%	45.1%	62.6%	87.2%	27.8%	57.8%	.283	.522	81	1.3
2023	SD	MLB	33	26(26)	146¹	8-7	0	140	1.20	3.57	51.9%	6.0%	23.2%	3.1%	45.4%	66.1%	87.0%	29.2%	61.0%	.298	.548	91	2.4
2024 DC	KC	MLB	34	29(29)	163	9-10	0	152	1.28	4.00	53.0%	7.3%	22.1%	2.7%	44.3%					.301	.522	94	1.6

2023 Arsenal: FA (93.8), CU (80), SI (93.5), FC (87.9), CH (86.5), SW (81.4), SL (81.6)   *Comps: Joe Hesketh (67), Jose Mesa (64), Joe Kelly (63)*

Finally given the regular rotation spot he'd been seeking, Lugo rewarded the Padres' faith with a perfectly cromulent no. 3 or 4 starter season. His 91 DRA- ranked him along other such mid-rotation stalwarts as José Berríos, Merrill Kelly and Alex Cobb, and that feels like the proper place for the veteran righty. He's someone who gives you five or six good innings a start and makes you sweat bullets if he's on the mound for a postseason game. What separates Lugo from a more lucrative place in a contender's starting five is an overall lack of diversity. His approach didn't change in shifting out of relief, with three-fifths of his pitches either a four-seamer thrown reliably for strikes or the big-spin curveball he's leaned on for years, rounded out by a sinker to keep hitters honest. None of them add up to much swing-and-miss, though, and he paid a hefty third-time-through-the-order penalty (an .833 OPS against). But he's proven that he can hack it as a starter and will be compensated as such by a team desperate for them, signing a three-year, $45 million pact with the Royals.

BASEBALL PROSPECTUS 2024

Daniel Lynch IV LHP   Born: 11/17/96   Age: 27   Height: 6'6"   Weight: 200   Origin: Round 1, 2018 Draft (#34 overall)

YEAR	TM	LVL	AGE	G (GS)	IP	W-L	SV	K	WHIP	ERA	CSP	BB%	K%	HR%	GB%	ZSw%	ZCon%	OSw%	OCon%	BABIP	SLGCON	DRA-	WARP
2021	OMA	AAA	24	12(11)	57	4-3	0	62	1.61	5.84		7.0%	24.1%	3.9%	44.8%					.390	.731	98	0.8
2021	KC	MLB	24	15(15)	68	4-6	0	55	1.63	5.69	51.8%	10.0%	17.7%	2.9%	38.9%	72.8%	87.4%	31.7%	55.5%	.336	.583	155	-1.3
2022	KC	MLB	25	27(27)	131²	4-13	0	122	1.57	5.13	53.8%	8.7%	20.3%	3.5%	42.0%	72.8%	84.0%	33.8%	60.4%	.337	.591	117	0.2
2023	KC	MLB	26	9(9)	52¹	3-4	0	34	1.26	4.64	47.7%	7.2%	15.2%	4.0%	38.4%	70.6%	86.8%	34.0%	59.4%	.252	.512	137	-0.4
2024 DC	KC	MLB	27	6(6)	37¹	2-3	0	32	1.51	5.62	52.0%	8.2%	19.2%	3.5%	39.4%					.325	.587	126	-0.2

2023 Arsenal: FA (93), CH (84.4), FC (87.9), SW (80.7), SI (92.7)   *Comps: Matthew Boyd (68), Tommy Milone (68), David Huff (66)*

"Lynchian" as a visual style often involves a nightmarish juxtaposition of the menacing with the mundane, which is also a way to describe DLIV's career so far: a loud fastball that somehow doesn't strike anyone out, and a stable of serviceable off-speed pitches that occasionally like to slip their earthly bonds and become ungovernable. A shoulder strain that bothered him all year added to the ominosity, but there are tender shoots of hope: Lynch faded a slider in favor of a changeup, which became his most effective pitch. He also managed to get into the zone more often, limiting hard contact—though without improved strikeout rates. But with that thin curtain barely containing baseball's giants, it's a dangerous line to fire-walk.

Alec Marsh RHP   Born: 05/14/98   Age: 26   Height: 6'2"   Weight: 220   Origin: Round 2, 2019 Draft (#70 overall)

YEAR	TM	LVL	AGE	G (GS)	IP	W-L	SV	K	WHIP	ERA	CSP	BB%	K%	HR%	GB%	ZSw%	ZCon%	OSw%	OCon%	BABIP	SLGCON	DRA-	WARP
2021	NWA	AA	23	6(6)	25¹	1-3	0	42	1.30	4.97		12.3%	39.6%	3.8%	44.0%					.348	.760	69	0.6
2022	NWA	AA	24	25(25)	114¹	1-15	0	147	1.67	7.32		10.1%	27.4%	5.0%	39.8%					.364	.782	77	2.1
2022	OMA	AAA	24	2(2)	10	1-1	0	9	1.00	1.80		11.6%	20.9%	2.3%	32.1%					.148	.321	108	0.1
2023	NWA	AA	25	11(11)	47¹	3-3	0	56	1.58	5.32		11.3%	26.4%	1.9%	43.1%					.373	.605	85	0.7
2023	OMA	AAA	25	3(3)	15	2-0	0	19	1.33	2.40		10.6%	28.8%	1.5%	46.2%	71.8%	81.0%	34.5%	37.3%	.316	.459	86	0.3
2023	KC	MLB	25	17(8)	74¹	3-9	0	85	1.56	5.69	44.9%	11.4%	24.9%	4.7%	34.6%	66.3%	83.2%	32.3%	54.1%	.321	.741	111	0.5
2024 DC	KC	MLB	26	6(6)	28¹	1-2	0	32	1.48	5.41	44.9%	11.1%	24.8%	3.7%	35.4%					.310	.620	121	-0.1

2023 Arsenal: FA (94.4), CH (87.1), CU (81.2), SW (85.1), SL (87.4), SI (94.4)   *Comps: Jimmy Nelson (73), Anthony DeSclafani (71), Tyler Cloyd (70)*

Drafted highly in 2019 to be the latest head of the Royals' college pitching hydra, Marsh instead finds himself bogged down in the bullpen thanks to fringy command, which has kept him on the swampy edge of the big-league rotation. When he can spot his pitches, Marsh can rack up the whiffs with a four-seamer that rides up and a deep arsenal of secondaries (sweeper, slider, curve, change); he also adjusted his slider grip midseason to elicit more sweep, and the Royals now have him slinging it about as often as the heater. That's a pretty impressive in-season adjustment for a player in his first go-round in the bigs, but Marsh has to improve the command issues that have threatened to sink him throughout the minors, as too often those pitches wind up in the soggy part of the zone like errant shots from a balky NES zapper; no one wants to see that darn dog get the last laugh, though.

James McArthur RHP   Born: 12/11/96   Age: 27   Height: 6'7"   Weight: 230   Origin: Round 12, 2018 Draft (#347 overall)

YEAR	TM	LVL	AGE	G (GS)	IP	W-L	SV	K	WHIP	ERA	CSP	BB%	K%	HR%	GB%	ZSw%	ZCon%	OSw%	OCon%	BABIP	SLGCON	DRA-	WARP
2021	REA	AA	24	19(15)	74¹	2-6	0	78	1.30	4.48		7.2%	24.4%	2.8%	46.9%					.322	.574	99	0.6
2022	REA	AA	25	13(13)	57	2-6	0	65	1.61	5.05		10.0%	25.0%	3.8%	43.6%					.361	.706	100	0.8
2023	OMA	AAA	26	23(2)	40²	2-1	1	57	1.28	3.98		11.6%	31.5%	1.7%	50.5%	57.3%	83.4%	31.6%	39.2%	.292	.464	79	1.0
2023	LHV	AAA	26	5(4)	16	0-2	0	15	1.69	7.31		9.3%	20.0%	4.0%	43.1%	61.7%	86.4%	28.1%	52.9%	.362	.640	106	0.2
2023	KC	MLB	26	18(2)	23¹	1-0	4	23	0.94	4.63	51.3%	2.2%	25.6%	2.2%	57.8%	60.8%	87.5%	35.5%	56.9%	.290	.565	80	0.5
2024 DC	KC	MLB	27	51(0)	54¹	3-5	14	49	1.31	4.12	51.3%	8.7%	20.7%	2.4%	48.5%					.291	.497	95	0.4

2023 Arsenal: CU (82.4), SI (94.3), SL (86.6), FA (94.9), FC (91.8), CH (89)   *Comps: Scott Effross (64), Angel Sánchez (62), Warwick Saupold (62)*

Here's a rags-to-riches story worthy of Horatio Alger: McArthur arrived on the rails in Kansas City after being cast off in Philadelphia, and ended the season as the *de facto* Royals closer, complete with a sobriquet lovingly bestowed by Royals fans, "The General" (he'll save you some games). The myth of American exceptionalism applies to baseball, as well; Big Mac is blessed with six feet and seven inches of height that makes his lower-velo sinking fastball play up along a heavy curve and sweepy slider. His dreadful first outing as a Royal involved seven earned runs in one June inning followed by a quick demotion, and when he came back up in August the struggles continued, but he rebounded with a lights-out September in which he struck out 35% of batters without handing out a single walk. He has to maintain the gains he's made in command to prove that beautiful month wasn't a blip, but don't be surprised to see him descending from the fountains in center field at Kauffman to the tune of "I Think I'm Gonna Like It Here."

Frank Mozzicato LHP   Born: 06/19/03   Age: 21   Height: 6'3"   Weight: 175   Origin: Round 1, 2021 Draft (#7 overall)

YEAR	TM	LVL	AGE	G (GS)	IP	W-L	SV	K	WHIP	ERA	CSP	BB%	K%	HR%	GB%	ZSw%	ZCon%	OSw%	OCon%	BABIP	SLGCON	DRA-	WARP
2022	COL	A	19	19(19)	69	2-6	0	89	1.54	4.30		16.7%	29.1%	2.0%	53.4%					.314	.500	73	1.7
2023	COL	A	20	12(12)	56¹	2-5	0	85	1.24	3.04		14.5%	36.2%	2.1%	40.5%					.279	.539	85	1.1
2023	QC	A+	20	9(9)	36²	0-4	0	45	1.83	7.12		18.5%	25.3%	3.9%	41.4%					.293	.629	130	0.1
2024 non	KC	MLB	21	58(0)	50	2-2	0	53	1.77	6.71		16.1%	22.5%	4.4%	36.3%					.302	.650	141	-0.9

Comps: Tyler Matzek (77), Stephen Gonsalves (75), Robert Stephenson (72)

Like a finicky houseplant, the Royals have been as careful as possible with their cold-weather 2021 first-rounder, transplanting him gently from the icy temps of the Northeast, to the Arizona desert, and then to the sweltering swamps of the Carolinas before finally moving him to the Midwest League, where he's likely to remain as he works to string together consistent quality outings. Prep pitching prospects might be the orchids of the draft, desperately tricky to cultivate, but Mozzicato has tougher skin than most, led by a pair of surprisingly advanced secondaries in his devastating sharp curveball and changeup; unlike many of his contemporaries, he'll have the arguably easier task of building up his riding fastball (90-92 mph) to league-average rather than trying to coax a secondary pitch to blossom.

Cole Ragans LHP   Born: 12/12/97   Age: 26   Height: 6'4"   Weight: 190   Origin: Round 1, 2016 Draft (#30 overall)

YEAR	TM	LVL	AGE	G (GS)	IP	W-L	SV	K	WHIP	ERA	CSP	BB%	K%	HR%	GB%	ZSw%	ZCon%	OSw%	OCon%	BABIP	SLGCON	DRA-	WARP
2021	HIC	A+	23	10(10)	44¹	1-2	0	54	1.08	3.25		8.1%	31.2%	2.3%	40.4%					.300	.485	84	0.7
2021	FRI	AA	23	9(7)	36¹	3-1	0	33	1.62	5.70		12.0%	19.9%	4.8%	31.5%					.301	.734	123	-0.2
2022	FRI	AA	24	10(10)	51¹	5-3	0	65	1.17	2.81		9.1%	31.3%	2.9%	42.3%					.299	.533	67	1.2
2022	RR	AAA	24	8(8)	43¹	3-2	0	48	1.06	3.32		6.7%	27.0%	2.2%	47.4%	73.1%	74.8%	30.7%	69.0%	.273	.478	81	0.7
2022	TEX	MLB	24	9(9)	40	0-3	0	27	1.48	4.95	51.0%	9.2%	15.5%	3.4%	36.6%	80.2%	89.1%	33.7%	62.1%	.296	.550	147	-0.6
2023	OMA	AAA	25	4(4)	18²	2-1	0	22	1.50	4.82		12.3%	27.2%	1.2%	42.9%	73.6%	68.9%	33.2%	58.5%	.354	.469	85	0.4
2023	RR	AAA	25	3(3)	9²	0-0	0	15	1.14	2.79		15.4%	38.5%	2.6%	50.0%	65.2%	72.4%	31.0%	69.2%	.235	.500	87	0.2
2023	TEX	MLB	25	17(0)	24¹	2-3	0	24	1.40	5.92	46.9%	13.2%	22.6%	3.8%	40.3%	71.2%	78.5%	29.8%	64.4%	.254	.538	97	0.3
2023	KC	MLB	25	12(12)	71²	5-2	0	89	1.07	2.64	45.8%	9.4%	31.1%	1.0%	45.0%	72.8%	76.3%	34.8%	55.6%	.283	.417	87	1.3
2024 DC	*KC*	*MLB*	*26*	*29(29)*	*174²*	*10-10*	*0*	*194*	*1.30*	*3.94*	*47.4%*	*10.2%*	*26.1%*	*2.8%*	*41.3%*					*.292*	*.536*	*92*	*2.2*

2023 Arsenal: FA (96.6), CH (86.6), FC (91.7), CU (81.9), SL (86.9), SI (94.5)   *Comps: Framber Valdez (74), A.J. Griffin (66), Matthew Boyd (66)*

The Royals spent all that time and effort trying to draft a frontline pitcher and the Rangers just…gave them one. To be fair, Ragans' tenure as a Ranger didn't seem to denote "future star"; he lost time with back-to-back TJ surgeries and, upon his return, struggled with commanding the zone. But freed from Texas and the interminable Cole Hamels comparisons, this changeup-slinging lefty blossomed in a lighter shade of blue. His velocity spiked significantly across the board with the Royals, pushing the heater into the mid-90s and leaving the Hamels comps in the dust. But the real improvement was in Ragans' pitch selection, fueled by a pair of new offerings. The changeup remains a swing-and-miss weapon, but Ragans also paired the fastball with a newly developed gyro slider that's been especially deadly against lefties. To righties, he'll throw a cutter in on the hands and pour in the rest of a deep arsenal. Broken clocks and small-ish sample sizes apply, but so far Ragans looks like not only the steal of the trade deadline, but maybe of the decade. Rom-coms are right: sometimes you only find love when you stop looking for it.

Brady Singer RHP   Born: 08/04/96   Age: 27   Height: 6'5"   Weight: 215   Origin: Round 1, 2018 Draft (#18 overall)

YEAR	TM	LVL	AGE	G (GS)	IP	W-L	SV	K	WHIP	ERA	CSP	BB%	K%	HR%	GB%	ZSw%	ZCon%	OSw%	OCon%	BABIP	SLGCON	DRA-	WARP
2021	OMA	AAA	24	2(2)	4²	0-2	0	2	1.93	13.50		4.3%	8.7%	4.3%	52.6%					.412	.722	109	0.0
2021	KC	MLB	24	27(27)	128¹	5-10	0	131	1.55	4.91	54.1%	9.0%	22.4%	2.4%	50.6%	61.9%	85.1%	29.6%	58.4%	.350	.554	103	1.0
2022	OMA	AAA	25	3(3)	13²	1-0	0	11	0.88	3.29		7.5%	20.8%	5.7%	57.9%					.143	.474	100	0.2
2022	KC	MLB	25	27(24)	153¹	10-5	0	150	1.14	3.23	57.2%	5.6%	24.2%	2.9%	47.8%	61.6%	88.1%	29.8%	58.1%	.303	.513	79	3.2
2023	KC	MLB	26	29(29)	159²	8-11	0	133	1.45	5.52	49.5%	7.0%	18.9%	2.8%	49.6%	65.5%	89.4%	30.2%	57.1%	.330	.591	101	1.8
2024 DC	*KC*	*MLB*	*27*	*28(28)*	*151¹*	*8-10*	*0*	*127*	*1.37*	*4.56*	*52.7%*	*7.7%*	*19.3%*	*2.5%*	*48.5%*					*.309*	*.516*	*104*	*1.0*

2023 Arsenal: SI (92.4), SL (84.3), CH (88), FA (92.5)   *Comps: Stan Bahnsen (81), Ismael Valdez (81), Scott Erickson (80)*

Hamilton vs. Burr. Hemingway vs. Faulkner. Singer vs. Changeup. The question of what Singer's third pitch will be has loomed over his career, briefly spelled by a 2022 second-half breakout but returning last year, as the low-slot righty again struggled to begin the season. Singer's changeup, thrown reluctantly and exclusively to lefties, was actually effective when he did throw it, thanks largely to a grip change to make it tunnel better with his slider—which also featured a new grip intended to elicit more horizontal movement. Unfortunately, the gains on the slider were negligible, and might have cost Singer some command on his sinker, which got significantly worse: He struck out fewer hitters and walked more with the pitch than ever in his career, and when batters made contact, they torched it with regularity. The Dodgers were reportedly sniffing around Singer at the trade deadline, which tells you there's still a valuable pitcher in there, but that pitcher didn't appear consistently in 2023: Singer would follow up a sterling outing with a stinker, with little signs of any kind of upward trajectory. So maybe the real rivalry is Singer vs. Singer. Just kidding, it's actually Singer vs. The Royals, who rewarded him for his breakout campaign by taking him to arbitration over $375,000 prior to the 2023 season.

Chris Stratton RHP   Born: 08/22/90   Age: 33   Height: 6'2"   Weight: 205   Origin: Round 1, 2012 Draft (#20 overall)

YEAR	TM	LVL	AGE	G (GS)	IP	W-L	SV	K	WHIP	ERA	CSP	BB%	K%	HR%	GB%	ZSw%	ZCon%	OSw%	OCon%	BABIP	SLGCON	DRA-	WARP
2021	PIT	MLB	30	68(0)	79¹	7-1	8	86	1.30	3.63	56.4%	9.8%	25.5%	2.7%	41.0%	69.7%	86.0%	33.3%	53.7%	.293	.514	94	1.0
2022	STL	MLB	31	20(0)	22²	5-0	0	23	1.50	2.78	49.9%	12.2%	23.5%	0.0%	51.6%	67.6%	80.4%	32.2%	62.3%	.355	.410	94	0.3
2022	PIT	MLB	31	40(1)	40²	5-4	2	37	1.55	5.09	53.7%	7.2%	20.4%	2.2%	39.2%	68.5%	82.2%	38.0%	65.9%	.368	.595	100	0.4
2023	TEX	MLB	32	22(0)	29	1-0	0	22	1.10	3.41	46.5%	6.8%	18.8%	3.4%	33.7%	66.1%	87.0%	33.7%	75.8%	.244	.458	99	0.4
2023	STL	MLB	32	42(0)	53²	1-1	1	59	1.16	4.19	49.9%	7.7%	26.7%	1.8%	41.0%	68.9%	80.8%	31.0%	67.1%	.295	.529	84	1.1
2024 DC	*KC*	*MLB*	*33*	*46(0)*	*49*	*2-3*	*4*	*44*	*1.36*	*4.49*	*51.0%*	*8.6%*	*20.6%*	*3.0%*	*39.9%*					*.298*	*.537*	*104*	*0.1*

2023 Arsenal: FA (93.1), SL (86.9), CU (80.9), CH (86.6), SI (92)   *Comps: Doug Brocail (68), Paul Quantrill (62), Joe Kelly (61)*

Stratton has found himself on the move in consecutive deadline day deals, going to St. Louis from Pittsburgh in 2022 and to Arlington by way of St. Louis in 2023. Along the way, he's racked up the third most innings of any full-time reliever, trailing only Emmanual Clase of the Guardians and the always-funky Tyler Rogers of the Giants. Stratton doesn't have the benefit of the most unusual delivery in the majors or a 100 mph cutter to dice up hitters with, though. He's just got a rubber arm and a 93 mph four-seam fastball that misses far more bats than it has any right to; hitters only connected on 76.2% of their swings in the zone against the pitch. For reference, hitters squared up Hunter Greene's 100+ mph four-seamer 77.4% of the time. That uncanny ability to pound the zone without getting in trouble convinced the Royals to sign him to a one-year deal in the offseason, making it likely that Stratton makes a midseason switch for the third straight season once things go south in KC.

Michael Wacha RHP   Born: 07/01/91   Age: 33   Height: 6'6"   Weight: 215   Origin: Round 1, 2012 Draft (#19 overall)

YEAR	TM	LVL	AGE	G (GS)	IP	W-L	SV	K	WHIP	ERA	CSP	BB%	K%	HR%	GB%	ZSw%	ZCon%	OSw%	OCon%	BABIP	SLGCON	DRA-	WARP
2021	TB	MLB	29	29(23)	124²	3-5	0	121	1.31	5.05	57.7%	5.9%	22.9%	4.4%	41.9%	74.8%	85.4%	38.2%	64.9%	.313	.621	104	0.9
2022	BOS	MLB	30	23(23)	127¹	11-2	0	104	1.12	3.32	55.3%	6.0%	20.2%	3.5%	41.2%	73.5%	86.6%	33.6%	67.5%	.260	.524	103	1.1
2023	SD	MLB	31	24(24)	134¹	14-4	0	124	1.16	3.22	50.2%	7.8%	22.4%	2.7%	35.2%	67.9%	84.4%	33.1%	62.0%	.266	.504	105	1.2
2024 DC	KC	MLB	32	26(26)	145	8-9	0	124	1.29	4.28	52.9%	7.4%	20.2%	3.3%	38.2%					.288	.540	101	1.2

2023 Arsenal: CH (82), FA (92.4), FC (87.5), SI (92.2), CU (74.3), SL (80.2)   Comps: Milt Pappas (73), Bill Gullickson (73), Ismael Valdez (73)

Determined to show all the haters who doubted that he could once again dance on the razor's edge, Wacha went out and just about matched his 2022 ERA. There were some slight tweaks to his formula—a few more changeups, not as many cutters—and, per usual, an injured list stint for arm trouble. By and large, the veteran put up almost exactly the same numbers with San Diego that he did in Boston. Once again, it was his changeup and fastball doing the heavy lifting, even as the latter continued to leak velocity—it clocks in at just 92 mph now—with more dip on the former leading to more whiffs and, in turn, better results from the four-seamer. That changeup has been Wacha's meal ticket for a while now, and it's what keeps him firmly in the "useful back-end starter" bucket as opposed to the "scrounging for minor-league invites" crowd, where Dakota Hudson and Zach Davies chant "One of us! One of us!" His next magic trick: replicating those numbers in Kansas City, which signed him to a two-year, $32 million deal.

Beck Way RHP   Born: 08/06/99   Age: 24   Height: 6'4"   Weight: 200   Origin: Round 4, 2020 Draft (#129 overall)

YEAR	TM	LVL	AGE	G (GS)	IP	W-L	SV	K	WHIP	ERA	CSP	BB%	K%	HR%	GB%	ZSw%	ZCon%	OSw%	OCon%	BABIP	SLGCON	DRA-	WARP
2021	TAM	A	21	15(14)	47	3-1	0	54	1.11	2.68		14.9%	27.7%	1.0%	62.0%	67.4%	82.4%	28.1%	48.5%	.202	.311	88	0.7
2021	HV	A+	21	4(4)	16¹	1-2	0	29	1.65	7.71		12.0%	38.7%	4.0%	51.4%					.469	.971	84	0.3
2022	QC	A+	22	7(7)	35²	3-3	0	47	1.15	3.79		11.1%	30.7%	0.7%	41.0%					.288	.512	90	0.5
2022	HV	A+	22	15(15)	72¹	5-5	0	80	1.12	3.73		9.0%	27.6%	3.1%	46.1%					.271	.564	95	0.7
2023	NWA	AA	23	28(17)	79²	2-9	0	80	1.77	6.67		16.3%	20.7%	2.6%	43.2%					.315	.549	123	-0.8
2024 non	KC	MLB	24	58(0)	50	2-2	0	46	1.65	6.14		13.9%	19.8%	3.5%	39.8%					.298	.580	130	-0.6

Comps: Ryan Searle (67), Albert Abreu (62), Hunter Wood (62)

"Where It's At": in his fastball-slider combo, Way has two workable pitches and… well, that might be it, nudging him toward the bullpen. That doesn't necessarily make the Royals the "Loser" of the Andrew Benintendi trade, even if he's a "Lost Cause" for the rotation; but, as "Everybody's Gotta Learn Sometime," changeups are notoriously difficult to develop. Often, it's just better to "Pay No Mind" to expectations and say "Hell Yes" to the voices that are calling your name.

Kyle Wright RHP   Born: 10/02/95   Age: 28   Height: 6'4"   Weight: 215   Origin: Round 1, 2017 Draft (#5 overall)

YEAR	TM	LVL	AGE	G (GS)	IP	W-L	SV	K	WHIP	ERA	CSP	BB%	K%	HR%	GB%	ZSw%	ZCon%	OSw%	OCon%	BABIP	SLGCON	DRA-	WARP
2021	GWN	AAA	25	24(24)	137	10-5	0	137	1.18	3.02		8.0%	24.2%	1.6%	51.6%					.293	.475	88	2.7
2021	ATL	MLB	25	2(2)	6¹	0-1	0	6	1.89	9.95	55.2%	14.3%	17.1%	5.7%	40.0%	63.3%	81.6%	17.8%	38.5%	.294	.833	121	0.0
2022	ATL	MLB	26	30(30)	180¹	21-5	0	174	1.16	3.19	56.2%	7.2%	23.6%	2.6%	55.1%	65.8%	84.7%	34.6%	56.3%	.284	.474	78	3.8
2023	GWN	AAA	27	3(3)	11¹	0-2	0	14	1.41	6.35		10.4%	29.2%	2.1%	40.7%	58.7%	79.5%	18.9%	47.1%	.385	.667	96	0.2
2023	ATL	MLB	27	9(7)	31	1-3	0	34	1.84	6.97	47.3%	11.0%	21.9%	3.2%	59.0%	66.0%	90.1%	32.9%	57.8%	.372	.653	88	0.6
2024 non	KC	MLB	28	58(0)	50	2-2	0	48	1.30	3.95	53.2%	8.9%	22.2%	2.1%	52.7%					.298	.486	91	0.5

2023 Arsenal: KC (84.5), SI (93.2), FA (93.6), CH (88.5), SL (88.4)   Comps: José Ureña (65), Andrew Heaney (60), Jeff Locke (60)

It's mighty hard to climb uphill under the best of circumstances, and it's even more difficult to do so when you've got a bum limb holding you back. That was the case for Wright for most of 2023, following offseason shoulder issues that necessitated a cortisone injection. The recovery from this injection caused him to start the season on the IL. Upon his return in May, Wright made a few starts where he was ineffective at best and then went right back on the IL until September. By the time the end of the regular season rolled around, Wright had been sent to the bullpen after struggling in his first two starts back. He'll presumably be back in the rotation for 2024, when Atlanta will be hoping he again proves to be Mr. (W)right.

Angel Zerpa LHP   Born: 09/27/99   Age: 24   Height: 6'0"   Weight: 220   Origin: IFA, 2016

YEAR	TM	LVL	AGE	G (GS)	IP	W-L	SV	K	WHIP	ERA	CSP	BB%	K%	HR%	GB%	ZSw%	ZCon%	OSw%	OCon%	BABIP	SLGCON	DRA-	WARP
2021	QC	A+	21	8(8)	41²	4-0	0	53	0.96	2.59		4.8%	31.7%	1.2%	44.2%					.297	.495	83	0.8
2021	NWA	AA	21	13(13)	45¹	0-3	0	54	1.54	5.96		9.5%	27.0%	3.5%	47.6%					.370	.637	88	0.5
2021	KC	MLB	21	1(1)	5	0-1	0	4	0.80	0.00		5.0%	20.0%	0.0%	40.0%	60.0%	88.9%	31.6%	83.3%	.214	.308	119	0.0
2022	NWA	AA	22	13(13)	64	2-5	0	69	1.42	4.36		7.6%	24.8%	2.5%	46.5%					.354	.627	81	1.0
2022	OMA	AAA	22	6(6)	7²	0-0	0	0	0.78	1.17		14.3%	0.0%	0.0%	58.3%					.083	.125	111	0.1
2022	KC	MLB	22	3(2)	11	2-1	0	3	1.09	1.64	58.7%	6.8%	6.8%	4.5%	50.0%	66.2%	95.7%	24.4%	76.2%	.194	.395	128	-0.1
2023	NWA	AA	23	3(3)	8	0-0	0	7	1.00	1.13		9.7%	22.6%	3.2%	38.1%					.200	.429	103	0.1
2023	OMA	AAA	23	6(6)	26²	0-2	0	23	1.50	4.72		11.1%	19.7%	3.4%	38.0%	57.8%	86.9%	28.6%	53.1%	.307	.603	109	0.3
2023	KC	MLB	23	15(3)	42²	3-3	0	36	1.27	4.85	51.0%	4.4%	19.8%	3.8%	50.0%	73.9%	87.8%	30.0%	65.5%	.307	.586	96	0.6
2024 DC	KC	MLB	24	22(3)	34²	1-2	0	24	1.40	4.70	49.7%	8.2%	15.8%	2.5%	45.8%					.296	.496	107	0.1

2023 Arsenal: FA (94.7), SI (94.8), SL (86.3), CH (87)   Comps: Yohander Méndez (55), Daniel Norris (39), Jesús Luzardo (39)

The Royals sent Zerpa to the AFL last offseason, a rare assignment for an MLB-experienced pitcher: maybe it was to make up time after a shoulder issue delayed his start to the regular season, or maybe the Royals are still trying to puzzle out whether he's a back-end starter or a reliever. No matter how Kansas City opts to utilize Zerpa, the stuff remains the same: a mid-90s sinker that induces groundballs, a slurvy sweeper and excellent command of the strike zone. He doesn't miss bats, so this particular abecedary will have a dog-eared page at "C" for "contact management."

LINEOUTS

Hitters

HITTER	POS	TM	LVL	AGE	PA	R	HR	RBI	SB	AVG/OBP/SLG	BABIP	SLGCON	BB%	K%	ZSw%	ZCon%	OSw%	OCon%	LA	90th EV	DRC+	BRR	DRP	WARP
Matt Beaty	1B	OMA	AAA	30	57	7	2	9	0	.294/.368/.471	.302	.533	8.8%	10.5%	59.8%	92.3%	28.3%	71.9%			108	-0.1	0.6	0.1
	1B	SAC	AAA	30	129	14	4	23	0	.272/.406/.447	.316	.582	10.9%	18.6%	68.6%	89.6%	26.2%	62.3%			111	-0.2	-1.1	0.5
	1B	SF	MLB	30	5	1	0	1	0	.200/.200/.200	.333	.333	0.0%	40.0%	85.7%	100.0%	75.0%	66.7%	-17.5	73.7	94	0.0	0.0	0.0
	1B	KC	MLB	30	67	7	0	3	0	.232/.358/.304	.295	.386	9.0%	17.9%	66.3%	92.5%	34.2%	60.4%	9.2	96.8	91	-0.1	-0.1	0.1
Dairon Blanco	OF	OMA	AAA	30	208	37	3	19	47	.347/.444/.451	.416	.565	10.6%	16.8%	69.6%	83.7%	32.0%	60.4%			107	3.6	0.4	1.2
	OF	KC	MLB	30	138	19	3	18	24	.258/.324/.452	.330	.615	7.2%	23.9%	70.8%	83.2%	35.5%	53.2%	7.0	103.9	91	0.9	1.9	0.5
Jackie Bradley Jr.	OF	KC	MLB	33	113	10	1	6	0	.133/.188/.210	.173	.289	4.4%	25.7%	69.4%	80.0%	40.4%	51.6%	4.9	103.3	85	0.0	-0.8	0.1
Hunter Dozier	3B	KC	MLB	31	91	8	2	9	2	.183/.253/.305	.250	.472	8.8%	31.9%	74.4%	80.8%	30.3%	45.3%	12.9	103.2	77	0.0	-0.1	0.0
Matt Duffy	IF	KC	MLB	32	209	17	2	16	1	.251/.306/.325	.303	.408	5.7%	18.7%	65.8%	86.2%	33.8%	64.1%	8.8	99.9	93	0.0	0.2	0.4
Nate Eaton	CF	OMA	AAA	26	367	52	15	39	22	.252/.312/.441	.294	.593	7.9%	23.2%	70.4%	80.1%	39.3%	62.1%			89	2.1	6.1	1.3
	CF	KC	MLB	26	56	2	0	1	3	.075/.125/.075	.125	.125	3.6%	37.5%	69.1%	78.6%	35.4%	44.4%	10.2	99.3	63	0.1	0.3	-0.1
Diego Hernandez	CF	ROY	ROK	22	29	7	2	6	0	.440/.517/.760	.529	1.000	10.3%	20.7%										
	CF	NWA	AA	22	269	30	0	20	17	.245/.302/.290	.341	.407	5.9%	25.7%							75	3.0	-1.2	0.2
Logan Porter	C	OMA	AAA	27	448	52	13	48	1	.232/.339/.377	.291	.538	13.4%	25.2%	61.2%	81.6%	26.4%	51.2%			94	-1.6	0.2	0.9
	C	KC	MLB	27	38	4	1	3	0	.194/.324/.323	.263	.500	13.2%	28.9%	70.5%	81.4%	28.2%	41.7%	18.4	101.0	81	-0.1	0.5	0.1
Samad Taylor	UT	OMA	AAA	24	414	65	8	55	43	.301/.418/.466	.373	.624	15.9%	20.5%	57.7%	84.2%	27.8%	61.6%			117	1.9	-0.5	1.9
	UT	KC	MLB	24	69	11	0	4	8	.200/.279/.267	.308	.421	10.1%	31.9%	69.5%	74.4%	35.4%	61.8%	6.3	103.8	70	0.2	0.4	0.0
Tyler Tolbert	UT	NWA	AA	25	574	95	10	50	50	.276/.336/.419	.346	.555	7.0%	22.1%							86	2.6	1.8	1.3
Javier Vaz	UT	QC	A+	22	388	49	6	39	26	.270/.367/.390	.283	.432	12.6%	8.2%							128	-1.1	0.0	2.7
	UT	NWA	AA	22	130	17	2	12	4	.304/.391/.429	.348	.511	11.5%	13.8%							116	1.0	-3.9	0.3
Nelson Velázquez	OF	IOW	AAA	24	330	48	16	44	7	.253/.333/.469	.320	.703	9.7%	29.4%	75.5%	78.9%	33.4%	47.8%			89	-1.4	-5.7	0.1
	OF	KC	MLB	24	147	27	14	28	0	.233/.299/.579	.221	.856	7.5%	29.3%	72.6%	77.1%	31.2%	47.1%	18.5	106.1	120	0.0	-0.7	0.7
	OF	CHC	MLB	24	32	8	3	6	0	.241/.313/.621	.222	.857	9.4%	25.0%	79.6%	83.7%	38.2%	44.8%	1.8	105.5	95	0.0	-0.2	0.1
Trevor Werner	3B/DH	COL	A	22	135	32	8	36	8	.354/.459/.699	.432	.963	15.6%	23.0%							142	-1.7	-3.5	0.5

Shoutout to **Matt Beaty**'s near-career-high OBP: he walks in Beaty, like the night, which is falling quickly on his MLB career if the cold-cornerman now on the wrong side of 30 can't scare up some more slugging. ⊗ **Dairon Blanco** isn't like other 31-year-old rookies; he's a cool 31-year old rookie, with game-changing footspeed the envy of men a decade younger than him. Still, if you're Daironing a Blanc as to why the wretched Royals are rostering the light-hitting outfielder, it's all in the steals—71 across Triple-A and the majors despite just 346 PA. ⊗ **Jackie Bradley Jr.**'s recent *Annual* comments have focused on his defense, which is akin to when judges on singing competitions praise a performer's appearance first; the jig was finally up for JBJ in Kansas City, an ignominious swan song for a 10-year career, so let's choose to remember his MVP-winning performance in the 2018 ALCS rather than the sour notes at the end. ⊗ The second-worst thing about **Hunter Dozier**'s contract was that it's an easy enough cudgel for any clodpate can wield as a point about why Spending Money Is Bad, Actually. The first-worst thing about it was, sadly, Hunter Dozier last year. ⊗ **Matt Duffy** joined the Royals on a minor-league deal, both to balance a lefty-heavy lineup and to serve as high-OBP insurance/veteran presence in a lineup of excitable young'uns, then he kind of…never left. Surely somewhere there's a baseball player equivalent of Frank Grimes aghast that the ultra-light hitting Duffman wiggled his way onto at least one more big-league roster, but he doesn't need batting gloves, he's Matt Du— ⊗ **Nate Eaton**, who runs like a deer and can play every position on the field (including catcher and pitcher), would be a great bench option on a good team where he's surrounded by credible hitters. Alas, he plays for this iteration of the Royals.

⊗ True Royals Sickos were likely glued to LIDOM play last fall, where **Diego Hernandez**—who missed most of the season after dislocating his shoulder diving after a ball in spring training—showed off his flashy toolkit as a member of the Gigantes Del Cibao. "El Coffee," who's been working on shortening up his stroke to get more line-drive power and let his plus speed to the rest of the work, re-upped with KC on a minors deal after being non-tendered and will try to jolt his way back onto the 40-man roster. ⊗ Baseball is cruel to many but rewarded über-grinder **Logan Porter**, a former Royals minor-league clubbie signed post-draft as org filler and ticketed as a bullpen catcher, with a big-league debut in 2023: a reminder that sometimes there is still a round bit of sweetness in a world obsessed with pouring increasingly nuclear IBUs. ⊗ Speedster **Samad Taylor** had a dream debut in mid-June, when his first MLB hit capped a six-run comeback to deliver the Royals a walkoff win against the Angels, but the alarm went off the next morning and he spent the rest of the season tossing and turning between Omaha and Kansas City. ⊗ **Tyler Tolbert** is Dolly Parton-levels of likable, plays an excitingly athletic brand of defense wherever the team puts him, swipes base without being caught and was named the Royals MiLB Hitter of the Year despite not, uh, hitting all that much. We have no choice but to stan. ⊗ Raise your hand if you have been personally victimized by the Royals taking undersized premium defensive players with no power to speak of, then put your hand down, because **Javier Vaz** wasn't taken until the 15th round and has already punched well above his draft weight; his slash line actually improved after a promotion to the upper minors. ⊗ Just as a perfect sprinkle of bitters can enliven a flat cocktail, **Nelson Velázquez** brings some much-needed thump to the contact-focused Royals lineup. Some merely adopted the TTO life; he was born into it, prompting the strikeout-allergic Cubs to trade him into a niche in Kansas City, where he's so far brought the noise along with the pain of his high-strikeout approach. ⊗ **Trevor Werner** Herzog rejects the idea of controlling the zone as a bourgeois concept rooted in the desire for mediocrity and beigeness. We would like to see the baby, wherein the baby is a giant tater who shows up regularly enough to offset Werner's high-strikeout approach and general Teutonic indifference at the hot corner.

Pitchers

PITCHER	TM	LVL	AGE	G (GS)	IP	W-L	SV	K	WHIP	ERA	CSP	BB%	K%	HR%	GB%	ZSw%	ZCon%	OSw%	OCon%	BABIP	SLGCON	DRA-	WARP
Kris Bubic	KC	MLB	25	3 (3)	16	0-2	0	16	1.31	3.94	51.1%	2.9%	23.5%	1.5%	51.0%	76.9%	78.5%	34.3%	57.1%	.375	.510	96	0.2
Luis Cessa	ABQ	AAA	31	6 (6)	21¹	0-2	0	19	1.88	8.44		9.9%	18.8%	5.0%	43.1%	71.7%	88.6%	32.1%	57.4%	.379	.789	120	0.0
	ROC	AAA	31	16 (1)	20²	1-3	3	23	1.65	8.71		10.1%	23.2%	4.0%	39.1%	65.4%	84.6%	32.4%	52.2%	.333	.721	99	0.3
	CIN	MLB	31	7 (6)	26	1-4	0	11	2.23	9.00	49.1%	9.1%	8.3%	2.3%	37.0%	68.4%	90.2%	31.9%	79.1%	.413	.667	149	-0.4
Jonah Dipoto	NWA	AA	26	7 (0)	10¹	0-0	0	13	1.26	0.87		8.9%	28.9%	0.0%	61.5%					.346	.346	85	0.2
	OMA	AAA	26	36 (0)	40¹	3-2	0	47	1.54	4.24		14.9%	26.0%	4.4%	45.5%	59.7%	83.2%	25.1%	49.2%	.290	.614	95	0.7
Taylor Hearn	OMA	AAA	28	12 (0)	14²	0-0	2	22	1.70	2.45		13.4%	32.8%	1.5%	45.7%	73.3%	77.6%	30.8%	46.2%	.441	.600	75	0.3
	RR	AAA	28	24 (2)	39¹	2-2	0	54	1.50	3.66		13.4%	30.2%	1.1%	47.4%	63.6%	83.6%	26.9%	55.2%	.347	.526	73	1.0
	TEX	MLB	28	4 (0)	7	0-0	0	7	1.86	10.29	49.6%	11.8%	20.6%	2.9%	21.7%	76.6%	85.7%	25.7%	68.4%	.364	.522	108	0.1
	ATL	MLB	28	1 (0)	0¹	0-0	0	0	12.00	108.00	38.8%	40.0%	0.0%	20.0%	0.0%	87.5%	85.7%	12.5%	50.0%	.500	1.667	132	0.0
	KC	MLB	28	8 (0)	7²	0-0	0	8	1.83	8.22	48.2%	5.4%	21.6%	5.4%	40.7%	75.0%	83.3%	43.7%	63.2%	.400	.815	109	0.1
Marwys Jorge	DSL ROYG	ROK	17	11 (9)	30¹	0-2	1	28	1.35	4.15		14.4%	21.2%	0.0%	43.6%					.282	.377		
Jordan Lyles	KC	MLB	32	31 (31)	177²	6-17	0	120	1.24	6.28	47.7%	6.0%	16.0%	5.2%	33.0%	71.2%	89.2%	31.6%	65.0%	.256	.606	136	-1.2
John McMillon	COL	A	25	9 (0)	10²	1-0	4	21	0.94	3.38		14.0%	48.8%	0.0%	43.8%					.250	.312	78	0.2
	QC	A+	25	13 (0)	20	3-1	1	40	0.80	2.70		10.4%	51.9%	1.3%	39.3%					.259	.519	55	0.7
	NWA	AA	25	15 (0)	20²	3-2	5	30	1.11	0.87		13.6%	37.0%	0.0%	48.6%					.300	.450	75	0.4
	KC	MLB	25	4 (0)	4	0-0	0	8	0.25	2.25	40.4%	0.0%	61.5%	7.7%	20.0%	52.4%	81.8%	41.2%	14.3%	.000	.800	90	0.1
Matt Sauer	SOM	AA	24	14 (13)	68¹	6-4	0	83	1.14	3.42		10.3%	29.5%	3.9%	39.5%					.244	.563	89	1.2
Will Smith	TEX	MLB	33	60 (0)	57¹	2-7	22	55	1.06	4.40	45.6%	7.5%	24.3%	2.2%	29.2%	68.8%	84.3%	38.6%	55.8%	.262	.468	103	0.6
Josh Taylor	OMA	AAA	30	5 (0)	5¹	0-0	0	5	1.88	6.75		4.0%	20.0%	4.0%	42.1%	61.4%	88.9%	22.6%	42.9%	.444	.789	107	0.1
	KC	MLB	30	17 (1)	17²	1-3	0	26	1.75	8.15	45.8%	10.8%	31.3%	4.8%	45.8%	67.4%	85.3%	32.5%	47.7%	.409	.848	89	0.3
Anthony Veneziano	NWA	AA	25	8 (8)	42¹	5-1	0	48	0.99	2.13		3.0%	28.4%	3.0%	45.9%					.305	.505	75	1.2
	OMA	AAA	25	18 (17)	89²	5-4	0	79	1.41	4.22		11.2%	20.6%	2.3%	43.0%	68.7%	81.9%	32.2%	59.0%	.297	.528	96	1.4
	KC	MLB	25	2 (0)	2¹	0-0	0	1	1.71	0.00	49.2%	16.7%	8.3%	0.0%	33.3%	82.6%	94.7%	21.9%	42.9%	.222	.556	116	0.0

Kris Bubic was off to an exciting start to the season, having overhauled his repertoire with a new slider, a lower release point and a harder, flatter fastball. That was unfortunately enough to attract the attention of the baseball gods, who saw the potential of a Royals pitcher getting to have nice things and promptly zapped his UCL. Ⓧ **Luis Cessa** has seen his velocity decrease, his ERA spike and his role diminish from back-end swingman to Triple-A innings-eater. The Royals signed him to a minor-league deal to provide insurance for their higher-profile signings. Ⓧ It's starting to feel unlikely that **Jonah Dipoto** will follow dad Jerry into the big leagues; after finally conquering the Texas League, the command issues that have hunted the younger Dipoto reappeared in Triple-A. He continues to miss bats, spurred along by a new cutter, but misses the zone just as often. Then again, there's not *that* much difference between the late-90s Rockies and the current Royals. Ⓧ **Taylor Hearn** is a Texas-born, third-generation cowboy whose grandfather Cleo was a legend on the circuit known as "Mr. Black Rodeo." The Royals hoped to rein in the lanky lefty's command struggles, and he did post the best K:BB ratio of his career—but he also surrendered a truckload of hard contact and was sent to git along to the waiver wire. He elected to lasso the NPB's Hiroshima Toyo Carp as a free agent. Ⓧ **Marwys Jorge** was the best-regarded prospect out of Kansas City's blockbuster 2023 IFA signing class. Trained by former Royal Edinson Volquez, he features a power curve and is already able to get into the low 90s with his fastball at an age where other kids are seeing how far they can fit a pair of ski poles up their nose or whatever the latest viral challenge is. Ⓧ **Asa Lacy** has a name that sounds like it belongs on the list of The Four Hundred, but instead of swanky Gilded Age dinner tables he's been on the training table for most of his pro career. He'll try to bank some real time on the mound in 2024, but back injuries are even more demanding and capricious than Mrs. Astor. Ⓧ What's the line between "serviceable but unpleasant" and "untenable and repugnant?" Call it the **Jordan Lyles** Line, maybe, as Baltimore's innings-eater became Kansas City's lotus-eater. Hey, at least it's all-you-can-eat lotuses, as Lyles chewed up more innings than anyone else on staff, because Kauffman Stadium apparently houses America's lone remaining HomeTown Buffet. Ⓧ It is an *Annual* truth universally acknowledged that if there's a fastball-slider reliever who throws triple digits and has reached the upper minors, they at least get a lineout. The new-look Royals pitching development crew has been working with **John McMillon** to simplify his approach and harness his stuff; whether he's Wickham or Darcy will have to sort itself out on the moors next year (the Great Plains are basically the moors of America). Ⓧ The second of approximately 44 Yankees pitching prospects popped in December's Rule 5 Draft, **Matt Sauer** is a 95-and-a-slider masquerading as a starting pitcher prospect. He has a good shot to stick with the Royals, a team which, unlike the Yankees, does not generate six 95-and-a-slider guys out of their pitch lab every year. Ⓧ Quality relievers of a certain ilk earn the word *erstwhile* near the end of their career, usually after losing a tick off their fastball. It goes like this: **Will Smith**, erstwhile closer for the Rangers, didn't play a huge role in their postseason run, but somehow collected his third consecutive World Series ring. Ⓧ You know that weird camp song about the guy named Joe who works in a button factory and progressively gets more and more stress laid upon him until he snaps? Swap in Joe for **Josh Taylor**, who had a bad back with Boston, and then a bad back and a bad shoulder with KC, and has had bad command everywhere he's gone. Maybe if he turned the button with his right hand? Ⓧ Command issues and some plain old bad sequencing luck have occluded **Anthony Veneziano's** career so far, but he wields a heavy sinker and two solid off-speed offerings in the slider and changeup. The Magic 8 Ball will be given a good shake in Kansas City this season, where signs point to "yes, the Royals need arms." Ⓧ After a conservative 2022 draft, last July the Royals went back to their riverboat gambling ways by taking a high school battery with their first two picks. The pitching side of the duo, **Blake Wolters** impresses with a loud fastball and a slider that's mowed down hitters so far, but for Royals fans anxious to see him coming down the Missouri, he's still up in Montana somewhere. Ⓧ The Royals are not afraid of a cold-weather high school hurler, and **Hiro Wyatt** can create plenty of his own heat with a mid-90s fastball and a high-spin slider that moves like a wayward excavator—although some of that warmth might come from the redness of the flags around his shorter stature and high-effort delivery.

LOS ANGELES ANGELS

Essay by Dan Moore

Player comments by Catherine Galanti and BP staff

The beginning of the end was as enlightening as it was brutal. Even casual fans can recall the scene. Shohei Ohtani, pitching in relief for Team Japan, stares down teammate Mike Trout, representing Team USA, with two out in the ninth inning of the 2023 World Baseball Classic final. The crowd is on its feet, the tension coiled tight and intolerable in that way only truly great baseball can get. Though there's a sense of gravity to the moment—a weight of importance and improbability—which transcends baseball. The announcers call the moment "storybook." No one needs an explanation as to why.

Instead, we give ourselves over to it. We watch as Trout digs into the box, a pitbull pawing dirt. Ohtani, from the stretch and with grace, breathes and winds and lets rip a 100-mph fastball right down the middle of the plate. Trout swings through it with viciousness. The crowd exhales. The two fighters return to their corners.

Next, Ohtani uncorks a fastball that hits *102* on the gun; Trout takes it, for a ball. The dance continues, anticipation ratcheting with every pitch, until the count goes full, and now time slows down, as in a chess match. Trout is sitting fastball, has no choice really but to be sitting fastball, and understanding this, aware of the leverage he's afforded himself, perhaps, Ohtani glides and snaps an ambitious rococo sweeper that starts on the inside of the plate and veers like a magic trick off the other side. Trout swings and misses, and Ohtani rips off his cap and roars at the crowd, and in the split-second before he's engulfed by his teammates, you see it: the monster inside this man, uncaged, and the hype that's so long surrounded him incontrovertibly justified.

This is the enlightening part, and it elevates the moment. It's Jordan at Boston Garden in '86, Woods at Augusta in '97, Federer in the 2005 U.S. Open final, one of those rare sports moments that's as clarifying to witness as it is cathartic to live through, is clarifying *for* the catharsis, though exactly what it clarifies differs depending on your vantage. Specifically, whether you're watching from Orange County or some other far less miserable redoubt. Ohtani finishes the tournament with a 1.86 ERA. He batted .435.

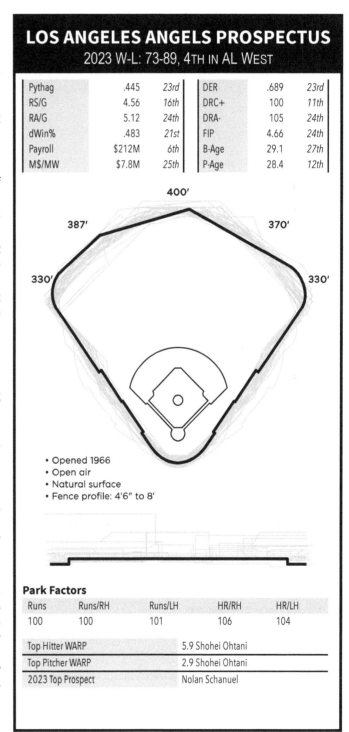

LOS ANGELES ANGELS PROSPECTUS
2023 W-L: 73-89, 4TH IN AL WEST

Pythag	.445	23rd	DER	.689	23rd
RS/G	4.56	16th	DRC+	100	11th
RA/G	5.12	24th	DRA-	105	24th
dWin%	.483	21st	FIP	4.66	24th
Payroll	$212M	6th	B-Age	29.1	27th
M$/MW	$7.8M	25th	P-Age	28.4	12th

400'
387'   370'
330'   330'

- Opened 1966
- Open air
- Natural surface
- Fence profile: 4'6" to 8'

Park Factors

Runs	Runs/RH	Runs/LH	HR/RH	HR/LH
100	100	101	106	104

Top Hitter WARP	5.9 Shohei Ohtani
Top Pitcher WARP	2.9 Shohei Ohtani
2023 Top Prospect	Nolan Schanuel

Payroll History (in millions)

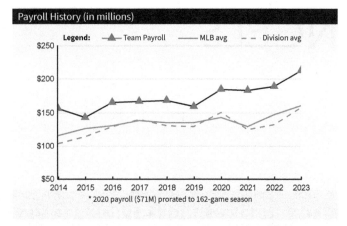

Legend: Team Payroll — MLB avg — Division avg

* 2020 payroll ($71M) prorated to 162-game season

Future Commitments (in millions)

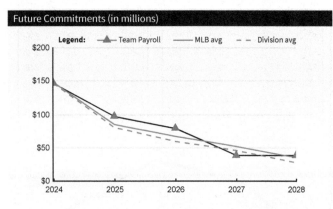

Legend: Team Payroll — MLB avg — Division avg

Farm System Ranking

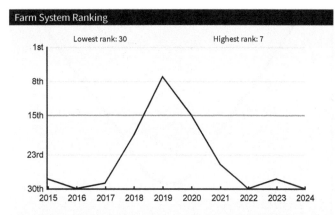

Lowest rank: 30   Highest rank: 7

Personnel

General Manager
Perry Minasian

Director, Player Procurement
David Haynes

Director, Player Development
Joey Prebysnki

Senior Director, Research & Development
Michael Lord

Manager
Ron Washingtron

BP Alumni
Matt Bishoff

Some stories are too sad for their own good. The sad parts consume the nice or redemptive things that came before, the way black holes swallow light. Movies in which dogs die generally fall into this category. So, too, now that it's over, does the story of the Los Angeles Angels in the era of Shohei Ohtani and Mike Trout—a story of persistent, near-mythopoeic mediocrity that reached its unceremonious end when Ohtani signed with the Dodgers as a free agent, in December of 2023, his contract a coda.

Call this, then, a reckoning. Few organizations in the history of sports have ever made such impotent use of bottled lightning. Those who forget history are condemned to repeat it, of course. We owe posterity a post-mortem.

⚾   ⚾   ⚾

The basics. For half a decade, the Angels rostered two of the best players in the history of baseball. Between them they hold five MVPs and two Rookie of the Year awards. Trout is the active leader in WARP, at 70.4, and until last year led all active players in career slugging (.582). Ohtani was the 2023 American League leader in both categories. He was also, before he got hurt, one of baseball's best pitchers. There are arguably no two people presently playing baseball who can do more to help a team win. And yet, the Angels during the Trout and Ohtani era could manage mostly only to lose. This would merely be a curiosity if it weren't for the corollary: the Angels front office could not manage, either for their sake or ours, to get baseball's best and most entertaining players into even one game that truly matters. We saw last spring what it's like, seeing Ohtani and Trout play for a trophy. The deprivation feels criminal. One imagines that, for Angels fans, it must also be mighty difficult to swallow.

What happened? Part of the problem was bad luck. The Angels signed Ohtani in 2018. He spent most of the next three seasons, including Trout's 2019 MVP run, either hurt or rehabbing something previously hurt, which meant he was not his normal self at the plate, and not allowed to be himself at all on the mound. He only truly became Ohtani, *world-uniting-two-way god* in 2021. That year, Trout appeared in just 36 games. The Angels finished the season 77-85.

There's more. Anthony Rendon—an MVP candidate in DC—has averaged just 50 games per season since signing with the Angels four years ago. That's bad luck! It's also bad luck that, in the games he *has* played in, he's generally forgotten how to hit. The Angels have rostered a number of players like this over the years: stars who tumbled off cliffs after signing contract extensions, players of promise—Patrick Sandoval, Taylor Ward, former top prospect and still-looked-to catcher of the future Logan O'Hoppe—who succumbed to injury or slumped into unreliability promptly after they were embedded in full-time support roles. O'Hoppe, for example, went down with a torn labrum in April of last year. He'd compiled four homers and 13 RBIs while providing excellent defense over the preceding three weeks. His replacement, Matt Thaiss, ended the season batting .214, and at least twice his defense actively lost games. All this just one season after catcher Max Stassi, fresh off a contract extension all his own, turned in one of the worst seasons from a catcher—offensive or defensive—in a quarter of a century.

This sort of thing would frustrate even well-run clubs. The difference between well-run clubs and the Angels, however, is that the latter is owned by Arte Moreno. In last year's *Annual*, David Roth posited that effective MLB owners must prove adept at two pursuits: spending money on big-league talent and the "unglamorous mold-abatement work" of scouting and development. Moreno, one of baseball's most meddlesome owners, is adept at neither. Instead he seems to build baseball teams the way Marvel casts sequels, or as children go shopping: drawn haphazardly to the shiniest names on the lowest shelves. He also appears earnestly ignorant of the fact that prospects don't grow on trees. As *The Athletic*'s Sam Blum has reported, the Angels harbor one of baseball's smallest scouting departments. In 2016, baseball analyst Keith Law wrote that the Angels' farm system was "the worst [he'd] ever seen." In the aftermath of 2023, they're back to where they began, owners of the weakest pipeline in baseball.

But even if reasons for the Angels' competitive insignificance are clear cut, what makes the team's languishing irredeemable, dramaturgically speaking, is a bit more nuanced. Why does the story linger with such rancor? One answer: the benign intentions of its antagonists—and the cruel hope they sustained within us as an audience.

Team owners come in degrees of despicability. The worst are those, born into their wealth, who don't seem to appreciate the dream that owning a pro baseball team in our eyes represents, and who in turn don't try hard enough to win. (Or, in the case of owners like John Fisher, who actively try *not* to try.) Moreno is not that kind of owner. He's the first-born son of immigrants. He fought in Vietnam. And he tries. He truly wanted to win with Ohtani and Trout. When pressed by *Sports Illustrated* about why he had turned down trade offers for Ohtani, in 2022, he responded, "We expect to be a playoff contender...I'm not going to sit here and wonder what happens in an outcome we're not planning for. That would be like a fighter going into the ring and thinking, 'What if I lose?' If he does that, he will lose."

This was only several months after Moreno had declined to sell the Angels, mind you, something he similarly explained with the justification, "I just couldn't do it."

Wherein lies the issue. Sadness is easier to swallow with a side of anger, regret less stunning when cut with dreams of vengeance. Moreno made mistakes; keeps making the same mistakes, in fact. But these mistakes have never been malicious; they're just dumb. Moreno understood what he'd stumbled upon, in Trout and Ohtani, years ago; that's why he signed Rendon (7 years; $245M). It's why he signed Zack Cozart (3 years; $38M). It's why he signed Justin Upton (5

years; $106M). It's why he gave David Fletcher $26M guaranteed. Was any of this sound baseball strategy? No. The result of these dispersals, made to the near exclusion of any infrastructural investment, was an organization so top-heavy it could be felled by a faint breeze. But was it willfully evil? Also no! Worse: it was earnest, the desperate, earnest striving of an aspirant hero attempting—and failing, over and over—to fly. And not really reading any research on the subject of heat and wax wings.

Still, the languishing of the Angels that occurred under Moreno's watch would not be what it is—would just be pitiful, as opposed to haunting—had it not occurred in the face of crushed hope. Much of which can be traced back to the Angels GM Perry Minasian.

Moreno hired Minasian as the Angels GM in November 2020. It was an unenviable gig. But Minasian bought in like a good company man, attempting as he was able to repurpose his boss' conception of sound baseball strategy into actually workable baseball strategy, slapping his name—one imagines reluctantly—on contracts he didn't want to sign. And most years, he provided Angels fans some hope that the team might compete.

There was a real sense that the 2023 Angels were going to be different. That Minasian, in spite of the multi-form infrastructural challenges he had to deal with, had done it: assembled a 26-man roster not far off from contention, a roster that, with a little luck, perhaps, would compete. Certainly that was the view on Opening Day, when even the most sober baseball minds were delightfully stoned off the WBC, and Ohtani suddenly seemed capable of winning games by himself, and a healthy Trout appeared poised to reshoulder his burden as the Angels' cornerstone. Some analysts even suggested the Angels were World Series contenders. Then the Angels started the year winning back-to-back series on the road against division rivals. They played above-.500 baseball through the All-Star break. Ohtani, for his part, played baseball better than he ever had, which is to say better than *anyone* ever had, hitting the ball harder and out of the park more often than any player in the majors while simultaneously throwing the ball harder and with more wicked snap than any pitcher in the majors. Other things were going right, too. Mickey Moniak, former top prospect, had a that'll-do-pig .982 OPS. And Trout managed to spend more time on the field than off it. He fractured the hamate bone in his left wrist on July 3. But he was expected back in August, and the Angels managed to close out July with a 54-49 record.

Recognizing the stakes, perhaps—the last chance to restore dignity to this era of Angels baseball—Minasian got on the phone. He sent highly ranked catching prospect Edgar Quero to the White Sox in return for Lucas Giolito and Reynaldo López, and picked up C.J. Cron and Randal Grichuk from the Rockies. The next day, in the first game of a doubleheader against Detroit, Ohtani pitched a complete-game shutout; the Angels won 6-0. The second game, Ohtani hit two home runs; the Angels won 11-4.

Now the hope was contagious. Suddenly, it *really* seemed like the Angels were not far off from contention. For a brief, delirious moment, it appeared Minasian had done it: delivered the main characters of this morbid canticle from the purgatory Moreno had imprisoned them all in, provided fans the competition they'd long been denied, delivered *all* of us from the clammy uncomfortable survivors' guilt we'd been barrelling towards. There was even talk of the Angels re-signing Ohtani after the season. As if a truly happy ending might be imminent after all. It was the reverse second-act break, the world suddenly opening up.

The Angels lost 16 of their next 21 games. They fell 10 games back of the AL Wild Card. The hitters Minasian traded for didn't hit. Giolito looked broken. Then, in the first game of a doubleheader against the Reds, the playoff push really unraveling now, came the *coup de grâce*. Ohtani, that game's starting pitcher, threw a pitch, grimaced, and stepped off the mound in pain. The Angels scratched him from his next start; manager Phil Nevin assured reporters the issue was "arm fatigue." But Ohtani was not fatigued. He'd torn his UCL—the same injury that had taken him off the mound for multiple years at the start of his six-year MLB career. He'd thrown his last pitch in an Angels uniform.

All this was bad enough. But then, 48 hours before MLB's waiver deadline, Ohtani practically still prostrate on the trainer's table, Minasian placed each of the players he had just traded for unceremoniously on waivers. The primary undignified goal was saving a few million dollars in off-season tax expenses. What it felt like was an admission of defeat, as anticlimactic as an off-screen death.

But that doesn't quite cut it, does it? More like it was a needlessly bleak *on*-screen death, some sick sort of euthanization carried out right there in front of the kids, drawn out to let the audience stew in it, slack-jawed. In an instant, the story was drained of its redemptive potential. From here on out it'd be Dickens without the change of heart, *Field of Dreams* if Shoeless Joe never showed up: a waste and a slog, arduous and for nothing. The opposite of storybook.

Certainly no one would learn anything from it. Moreno was back on his Marvel-casting grind as soon as the offseason started, making gestures to elite free agents, Ohtani included—blind, evidently, to the rudderless and broken state of his organization. Which was evident everywhere but most notably in the hearts and minds of his fans. Three months after the sell-off, Ohtani was a Dodger; the day he signed, dozens of Angels fans assembled spontaneously outside Angels stadium, to mourn together, like elephants. "It feels like a piece of me died," one fan told reporters. From his tone—dejected yet also disillusioned; stricken but slightly sardonic—he seemed to understand it had died in vain.

—Dan Moore is a writer from the Bay Area.

HITTERS

Jo Adell OF   Born: 04/08/99   Age: 25   Bats: R   Throws: R   Height: 6'3"   Weight: 215   Origin: Round 1, 2017 Draft (#10 overall)

YEAR	TM	LVL	AGE	PA	R	HR	RBI	SB	AVG/OBP/SLG	BABIP	SLGCON	BB%	K%	ZSw%	ZCon%	OSw%	OCon%	LA	90th EV	DRC+	BRR	DRP	WARP
2021	SL	AAA	22	339	57	23	69	8	.289/.342/.592	.351	.868	6.5%	29.2%							107	1.7	0.7	1.7
2021	LAA	MLB	22	140	17	4	26	2	.246/.295/.408	.298	.541	5.7%	22.9%	76.1%	77.3%	38.9%	61.4%	9.2	107.4	88	0.1	1.6	0.4
2022	SL	AAA	23	180	35	13	33	3	.239/.333/.587	.273	.919	11.1%	31.1%	69.5%	82.4%	31.6%	51.3%			100	1.9	-1.6	0.6
2022	LAA	MLB	23	285	22	8	27	4	.224/.264/.373	.338	.621	3.9%	37.5%	71.8%	71.7%	37.1%	51.8%	16.6	106.5	43	-0.1	0.9	-1.0
2023	SL	AAA	24	330	62	24	57	9	.273/.375/.586	.306	.853	12.1%	26.4%	72.1%	80.8%	29.5%	50.2%			117	2.2	-1.6	1.6
2023	LAA	MLB	24	62	7	3	6	1	.207/.258/.448	.300	.788	6.5%	40.3%	74.8%	77.1%	34.7%	36.5%	11.7	107.9	60	0.0	0.0	-0.1
2024 DC	LAA	MLB	25	389	42	16	49	4	.215/.281/.403	.277	.611	7.1%	31.4%							89	0.1	0.9	0.7

2023 GP: RF (9), CF (7), LF (2)   Comps: Melvin Nieves (51), Byron Buxton (51), Clint Frazier (43)

We've been waiting for Adell to transform into the advertised product pretty much since he got drafted, to get all the shiny bells and whistles the potential promised. While that day might not yet be here, it's at least getting closer—if you ignore DRC+. We're now facing the imminent impact of Adell's potential, and hopefully that doesn't mean a crash. His fielding was about as good as it's ever been, and like many Angels hitters last year, he was on track for a great season before being sidelined with injury. In Triple-A he raked 24 home runs, but he only got into 17 games at the MLB level. Accordingly, his hard-hit ball percentage and exit velocity were up, but so was his strikeout percentage, almost three points to 40.3%.

Trey Cabbage 1B   Born: 05/03/97   Age: 27   Bats: L   Throws: R   Height: 6'2"   Weight: 204   Origin: Round 4, 2015 Draft (#110 overall)

YEAR	TM	LVL	AGE	PA	R	HR	RBI	SB	AVG/OBP/SLG	BABIP	SLGCON	BB%	K%	ZSw%	ZCon%	OSw%	OCon%	LA	90th EV	DRC+	BRR	DRP	WARP
2021	WCH	AA	24	278	40	18	49	2	.262/.349/.533	.393	.970	11.2%	39.6%							88	1.4	-2.0	0.3
2022	RCT	AA	25	136	21	10	32	10	.327/.434/.664	.474	1.136	14.7%	34.6%							120	0.9	0.2	0.9
2023	SL	AAA	26	474	83	30	89	32	.306/.379/.596	.394	.902	9.5%	30.0%	74.8%	81.5%	38.3%	42.5%			107	1.0	-1.3	1.4
2023	LAA	MLB	26	56	5	1	7	1	.208/.232/.321	.370	.630	3.6%	46.4%	85.5%	67.6%	50.8%	26.9%	4.7	108.4	53	0.1	0.1	-0.2
2024 DC	LAA	MLB	27	184	21	7	24	6	.233/.299/.427	.332	.692	7.6%	35.1%							99	0.1	-0	0.4

2023 GP: 1B (9), RF (6), LF (3), CF (2)   Comps: Mark Hamilton (61), Rhyne Hughes (59), Jake Goebbert (54)

If ever there was someone who epitomized the minor-league grinder lifestyle, it's Cabbage. He was drafted out of high school in 2015 and spent the next eight seasons working through the Twins and Angels farm systems, finally getting his first callup in July of last year. The Angels' minor-league structure was, charitably, garbage, which—depending on one's perspective—makes it either difficult to be taken seriously or easy to stand out. Cabbage was doing something right, putting together one of only two 30-30 seasons across MiLB and being named the Angels Hitting Prospect of the Year. While his minor-league stats look far better than the numbers from his MLB debut, he still led the club's entire minor-league cohort in home runs, slugging and OPS (.975).

Willie Calhoun DH/RF   Born: 11/04/94   Age: 29   Bats: L   Throws: R   Height: 5'8"   Weight: 205   Origin: Round 4, 2015 Draft (#132 overall)

YEAR	TM	LVL	AGE	PA	R	HR	RBI	SB	AVG/OBP/SLG	BABIP	SLGCON	BB%	K%	ZSw%	ZCon%	OSw%	OCon%	LA	90th EV	DRC+	BRR	DRP	WARP
2021	TEX	MLB	26	284	26	6	25	0	.250/.310/.381	.267	.438	7.4%	12.0%	65.5%	88.5%	31.6%	78.1%	15.0	105.2	106	-0.1	-1.6	0.9
2022	SAC	AAA	27	170	24	5	23	0	.291/.376/.453	.311	.532	11.2%	12.9%	62.7%	90.9%	25.5%	73.3%			115	-0.4	-1.9	0.6
2022	RR	AAA	27	91	18	5	20	0	.217/.264/.410	.194	.486	6.6%	14.3%	55.2%	89.1%	35.5%	81.5%			117	0.6	-1.0	0.4
2022	SF	MLB	27	9	0	0	1	0	.125/.222/.125	.167	.167	11.1%	22.2%	50.0%	85.7%	33.3%	71.4%	25.4	99.7	121	0.2	0.0	0.1
2022	TEX	MLB	27	53	7	1	2	0	.136/.283/.273	.135	.316	15.1%	11.3%	57.5%	88.1%	23.2%	86.2%	13.8	106.5	111	0.0	0.0	0.2
2023	NYY	MLB	28	149	16	5	16	0	.239/.309/.403	.245	.474	9.4%	13.4%	56.8%	89.6%	28.7%	77.6%	12.2	104.4	99	-0.2	-0.7	0.2
2024 non	LAA	MLB	29	251	25	6	26	0	.249/.314/.377	.265	.432	8.1%	11.9%							95	0.0	-3.3	0.2

2023 GP: DH (26), RF (9), LF (3)   Comps: Casey Kotchman (52), Miguel Dilone (48), Terry Francona (46)

In one of many examples of Aaron Boone backing one of his players, he confidently declared the following on April 25: "No doubt in my mind Willie Calhoun can bang and is going to hit." With Giancarlo Stanton and Josh Donaldson on the IL already, Calhoun was going to get some looks in the lineup anyway, and after his skipper's show of support despite a 3-for-22 start, he at least looked respectable with a .774 OPS the rest of the way. Said "rest of the way" only entailed 37 games before Calhoun himself got hurt, and by the time he was healthy enough to return at the end of July, the Yankees decided that there weren't enough at-bats to go around. He was DFA'd and might end up replacing Shohei Ohtani as the Angels' DH, so Boone better be right.

C.J. Cron 1B   Born: 01/05/90   Age: 34   Bats: R   Throws: R   Height: 6'4"   Weight: 235   Origin: Round 1, 2011 Draft (#17 overall)

YEAR	TM	LVL	AGE	PA	R	HR	RBI	SB	AVG/OBP/SLG	BABIP	SLGCON	BB%	K%	ZSw%	ZCon%	OSw%	OCon%	LA	90th EV	DRC+	BRR	DRP	WARP
2021	COL	MLB	31	547	70	28	92	1	.281/.375/.530	.316	.705	11.0%	21.4%	68.4%	82.0%	33.2%	59.9%	16.2	108.0	133	-0.1	-0.4	3.4
2022	COL	MLB	32	632	79	29	102	0	.257/.315/.468	.307	.655	6.8%	25.9%	62.9%	86.8%	37.5%	63.1%	14.5	106.9	104	-0.7	0.0	1.5
2023	COL	MLB	33	224	31	11	32	0	.260/.304/.476	.289	.627	5.8%	22.3%	64.8%	81.0%	32.7%	58.7%	13.2	108.3	119	-0.5	-0.1	0.9
2023	LAA	MLB	33	54	7	1	5	0	.200/.259/.260	.265	.371	7.4%	27.8%	61.0%	85.1%	50.4%	61.3%	12.1	101.9	81	-0.1	0.0	0.0
2024 DC	LAA	MLB	34	443	52	19	59	0	.249/.314/.442	.295	.603	7.4%	24.4%							110	0.0	-0.4	1.4

2023 GP: 1B (61), DH (9)   Comps: Paul Konerko (83), Greg Colbrunn (82), Eric Karros (79)

After more than five seasons away, Cron's return to the Angels was less than triumphant. Including his stats from the greater portion of his campaign with the Rockies cushions the downfall of his lackluster 2023, but doesn't hide the reality that this was one of his worst seasons since debuting. The truth is, he wasn't doing enough to be worth the Angels' while. First base might be the only position where they weren't suffering for choice—in 2023, nine players made at least one appearance at first (including Jake Lamb, which says something). Cron's Mendoza-line hitting and .978 fielding percentage in just over 100 innings with the Angels might not have kept him in the mix long-term, even had he not departed in free agency.

Brandon Drury 2B/1B   Born: 08/21/92   Age: 31   Bats: R   Throws: R   Height: 6'2"   Weight: 230   Origin: Round 13, 2010 Draft (#404 overall)

YEAR	TM	LVL	AGE	PA	R	HR	RBI	SB	AVG/OBP/SLG	BABIP	SLGCON	BB%	K%	ZSw%	ZCon%	OSw%	OCon%	LA	90th EV	DRC+	BRR	DRP	WARP
2021	SYR	AAA	28	236	28	9	32	0	.257/.318/.449	.291	.582	8.1%	20.8%							107	-1.9	-1.9	0.5
2021	NYM	MLB	28	88	7	4	14	0	.274/.307/.476	.328	.645	3.4%	25.0%	66.4%	88.8%	41.9%	61.5%	11.4	105.4	77	0.0	-0.3	0.0
2022	SD	MLB	29	183	25	8	28	0	.238/.290/.435	.267	.579	4.9%	23.0%	67.0%	84.1%	34.5%	67.1%	16.5	105.3	89	-0.1	0.0	0.2
2022	CIN	MLB	29	385	62	20	59	2	.274/.335/.520	.306	.684	7.5%	21.8%	62.5%	87.4%	32.1%	67.6%	12.8	105.4	106	-0.2	0.1	1.2
2023	LAA	MLB	30	523	61	26	83	0	.262/.306/.497	.308	.691	4.8%	26.0%	69.9%	82.2%	38.1%	53.0%	12.0	105.6	97	-0.5	-0.7	1.1
2024 DC	LAA	MLB	31	506	56	20	65	0	.237/.291/.422	.287	.586	5.7%	26.1%							97	0.0	-0.7	0.9

2023 GP: 2B (92), 1B (47), DH (9)   Comps: Aramis Ramirez (71), Don Money (67), Brooks Robinson (66)

When considering the most iconic, influential, or beloved Angels of the 2023 season, one's mind instantly goes to Brandon Drury, right? Maybe it should. He was one of the healthiest and most consistent members of the lineup; yes, the bar is pretty low, but his reputation doesn't deserve to be besmirched like that. He kept his head down and his nose on the grindstone, playing the fourth-most games on the team (125), and was second in hits, home runs, RBI and runs scored (just behind Ohtani) with 127, 26, 83 and 61 respectively. His 1.3 WARP placed him fifth among the club's batters. It wasn't always showstopping, but there's nothing wrong with clocking in and clocking out if you're still getting the job done. Someone's still gotta put food on the table.

Eduardo Escobar 3B/2B   Born: 01/05/89   Age: 35   Bats: S   Throws: R   Height: 5'10"   Weight: 193   Origin: IFA, 2006

YEAR	TM	LVL	AGE	PA	R	HR	RBI	SB	AVG/OBP/SLG	BABIP	SLGCON	BB%	K%	ZSw%	ZCon%	OSw%	OCon%	LA	90th EV	DRC+	BRR	DRP	WARP
2021	MIL	MLB	32	199	27	6	25	0	.268/.342/.458	.313	.586	9.5%	19.6%	75.9%	85.1%	35.4%	67.9%	21.2	101.9	98	0.0	-0.3	0.5
2021	AZ	MLB	32	400	50	22	65	1	.246/.300/.478	.261	.621	7.3%	21.3%	72.2%	84.1%	34.8%	64.8%	20.9	103.4	106	0.1	-0.6	1.7
2022	NYM	MLB	33	542	58	20	69	0	.240/.295/.430	.281	.582	7.4%	23.8%	73.6%	82.8%	40.2%	61.3%	20.8	104.3	106	0.6	-6.8	1.0
2023	NYM	MLB	34	120	15	4	16	2	.236/.286/.409	.265	.523	6.7%	20.0%	66.7%	83.3%	39.4%	72.7%	12.4	102.3	79	0.0	-0.9	0.0
2023	LAA	MLB	34	189	17	2	15	0	.219/.259/.303	.301	.435	5.3%	28.6%	67.5%	77.0%	42.5%	60.1%	15.4	98.8	77	-0.1	-1.1	-0.1
2024 non	LAA	MLB	35	251	25	7	28	1	.234/.292/.383	.289	.524	7.1%	24.8%							88	0.0	-3	0.0

2023 GP: 3B (65), 2B (20), 1B (5), P (3), DH (3), SS (1)   Comps: Toby Harrah (68), Tim Wallach (64), Sal Bando (63)

Escobar played a little bit of everything as a utility infielder last season, appearing primarily at third, but getting some time at second as well as a few games at first and DH. Most interestingly, Escobar made three appearances out of the bullpen for the Angels, going 3⅓ innings and allowing just one run. Clearly, he didn't qualify for any league-wide recognition (no Angels pitcher did) but he does get to boast the fourth-best ERA amongst the Angels pitching staff. After being traded to the Angels in June, Escobar had better stats than he did in the first half of the season with the Mets—more hits, more runs scored, more total bases, more walks—though he took the tradeoff of more at bats at the cost of a lower slash line across the board. One of Escobar's greatest accomplishments of the season came off the field: He achieved a lifetime goal of becoming an American citizen in June, just days after being traded.

Randal Grichuk OF Born: 08/13/91 Age: 32 Bats: R Throws: R Height: 6'2" Weight: 216 Origin: Round 1, 2009 Draft (#24 overall)

YEAR	TM	LVL	AGE	PA	R	HR	RBI	SB	AVG/OBP/SLG	BABIP	SLGCON	BB%	K%	ZSw%	ZCon%	OSw%	OCon%	LA	90th EV	DRC+	BRR	DRP	WARP
2021	TOR	MLB	29	545	59	22	81	0	.241/.281/.423	.266	.544	5.0%	20.9%	73.9%	88.6%	37.4%	60.6%	16.3	107.2	97	-0.2	-3.2	1.5
2022	COL	MLB	30	538	60	19	73	4	.259/.299/.425	.309	.567	4.5%	23.6%	70.8%	87.3%	36.4%	58.9%	8.9	106.7	100	0.2	-4.7	1.2
2023	ABQ	AAA	31	36	6	0	3	0	.091/.167/.121	.111	.148	8.3%	16.7%	73.7%	85.7%	22.5%	62.5%			109	0.2	-0.3	0.1
2023	COL	MLB	31	263	40	8	27	2	.308/.365/.496	.363	.630	6.8%	19.4%	69.2%	87.6%	36.4%	55.2%	16.4	105.8	107	0.1	-4.4	0.5
2023	LAA	MLB	31	208	25	8	17	0	.216/.264/.412	.239	.537	5.3%	21.6%	67.4%	87.3%	39.8%	58.0%	11.2	107.0	82	0.1	-2.6	-0.1
2024 non	LAA	MLB	32	251	25	8	29	2	.243/.292/.395	.290	.522	5.6%	22.7%							92	0.0	-3.3	0.1

2023 GP: LF (65), RF (27), CF (22), DH (11)　　　Comps: Red Murray (70), Gary Matthews (70), Dusty Baker Jr. (69)

Grichuk matched his career-high in extra-base hits, and drew the second-most walks of his career, but his offensive output fell off the table alongside the altitude drop from Coors to Angel Stadium. However, after being placed on waivers twice in consecutive weeks down the stretch, the Angels' first pick from the 2011 Draft finished out the season strong, with an .817 OPS in his final 20 games before his first shot at free agency. He won't see any offers as lucrative as the five-year extension he signed with the Blue Jays back in 2019, but Grichuk proved he still had something to fight for.

Mickey Moniak OF Born: 05/13/98 Age: 26 Bats: L Throws: R Height: 6'2" Weight: 195 Origin: Round 1, 2016 Draft (#1 overall)

YEAR	TM	LVL	AGE	PA	R	HR	RBI	SB	AVG/OBP/SLG	BABIP	SLGCON	BB%	K%	ZSw%	ZCon%	OSw%	OCon%	LA	90th EV	DRC+	BRR	DRP	WARP
2021	LHV	AAA	23	409	42	15	65	5	.238/.299/.447	.280	.617	7.6%	24.7%							97	-1.7	-6.0	0.6
2021	PHI	MLB	23	37	3	1	3	0	.091/.167/.182	.125	.353	8.1%	43.2%	69.5%	73.2%	41.3%	38.7%	5.9	103.9	60	0.0	-0.1	-0.1
2022	REA	AA	24	25	5	1	6	0	.391/.400/.652	.471	.882	4.0%	24.0%							105	0.4	-1.4	0.0
2022	LHV	AAA	24	91	14	5	8	5	.277/.341/.518	.321	.705	8.8%	24.2%							106	0.3	-0.2	0.4
2022	PHI	MLB	24	50	4	0	2	0	.130/.184/.152	.222	.259	6.0%	38.0%	66.7%	82.6%	49.6%	51.8%	6.0	103.4	47	0.1	0.0	-0.1
2022	LAA	MLB	24	62	9	3	6	1	.200/.226/.417	.281	.714	1.6%	40.3%	81.1%	79.5%	46.0%	36.5%	26.0	107.6	61	0.0	0.1	-0.1
2023	SL	AAA	25	141	27	8	23	2	.308/.355/.585	.364	.800	5.0%	24.8%	84.1%	83.3%	42.2%	54.3%			109	1.6	-2.8	0.5
2023	LAA	MLB	25	323	35	14	45	6	.280/.307/.495	.397	.778	2.8%	35.0%	79.8%	74.1%	48.8%	46.3%	19.1	105.0	75	0.1	0.6	0.1
2024 DC	LAA	MLB	26	458	45	16	55	6	.219/.266/.399	.300	.616	4.9%	33.2%							78	0.1	2.2	0.2

2023 GP: CF (54), RF (16), LF (12)　　　Comps: David Dahl (56), Jake Cave (56), Joc Pederson (56)

Oh Mickey, you're so fine indeed. The former number one pick didn't fare quite how anyone expected in Philadelphia, but showed the glimmers he was scouted for over the course of the 2023 season in Anaheim, particularly when it came to power hitting. Moniak really came into his own last year, bumping up his barrel percentage to 12.6% from 7.9% the previous campaign, and dipping his weak and topped contact rates to all-time lows. Even for the less statistically minded out there, the numbers speak for themselves: he set a career high in home runs by over 10 (his 14 were good enough to tie him for sixth on the team) and he had 20 multi-hit games—in 2022, he only had three, and zero the year prior.

Mike Moustakas CI Born: 09/11/88 Age: 35 Bats: L Throws: R Height: 6'0" Weight: 225 Origin: Round 1, 2007 Draft (#2 overall)

YEAR	TM	LVL	AGE	PA	R	HR	RBI	SB	AVG/OBP/SLG	BABIP	SLGCON	BB%	K%	ZSw%	ZCon%	OSw%	OCon%	LA	90th EV	DRC+	BRR	DRP	WARP
2021	CIN	MLB	32	206	21	6	22	0	.208/.282/.372	.239	.496	8.7%	22.3%	70.0%	84.7%	38.6%	58.3%	18.6	106.2	89	-0.1	-0.6	0.3
2022	CIN	MLB	33	285	30	7	25	2	.214/.295/.345	.272	.492	8.4%	26.3%	74.3%	83.1%	41.6%	57.4%	19.7	104.1	78	-0.2	-0.2	-0.2
2023	COL	MLB	34	136	21	4	17	0	.270/.360/.435	.338	.617	12.5%	25.0%	66.5%	79.4%	29.0%	61.5%	20.8	104.6	101	-0.4	-0.1	0.3
2023	LAA	MLB	34	250	22	8	31	0	.236/.256/.371	.277	.500	2.4%	24.4%	75.3%	83.2%	43.9%	59.1%	17.0	103.9	79	-0.2	-0.5	0.0
2024 non	LAA	MLB	35	251	25	7	27	0	.224/.293/.364	.278	.497	7.6%	24.6%							83	0.0	-1.1	-0.1

2023 GP: 3B (52), 1B (50), DH (10)　　　Comps: Robin Ventura (67), Buddy Bell (60), Stan Hack (59)

In one of the more surprising moves of their funhouse mirror season, the Angels traded for Moustakas almost immediately after routing his Rockies, 25-1, in late June. Despite playing between 17 and 70 fewer games in an Angels uniform than his top-10 colleagues, he still slugged his way to a tie for ninth on the club in RBI before going down in mid-September with a forearm strain. Moose returned to the wild of free agency after having been "noncommittal" about a reunion. Go figure.

Zach Neto SS Born: 01/31/01 Age: 23 Bats: R Throws: R Height: 6'0" Weight: 185 Origin: Round 1, 2022 Draft (#13 overall)

YEAR	TM	LVL	AGE	PA	R	HR	RBI	SB	AVG/OBP/SLG	BABIP	SLGCON	BB%	K%	ZSw%	ZCon%	OSw%	OCon%	LA	90th EV	DRC+	BRR	DRP	WARP
2022	TRI	A+	21	31	2	1	4	1	.200/.355/.400	.200	.476	12.9%	12.9%							113	-0.3	-0.1	0.1
2022	RCT	AA	21	136	22	4	23	4	.320/.382/.492	.389	.645	5.9%	21.3%							99	-0.6	-0.3	0.3
2023	RCT	AA	22	34	10	3	10	3	.444/.559/.815	.563	1.158	17.6%	23.5%							118	0.4	0.0	0.2
2023	LAA	MLB	22	329	38	9	34	5	.225/.308/.377	.272	.514	6.1%	23.4%	70.4%	83.4%	30.9%	50.7%	14.7	104.4	97	0.0	1.2	1.1
2024 DC	LAA	MLB	23	519	52	13	54	10	.228/.306/.366	.286	.506	6.7%	24.9%							92	0.1	3.7	1.7

2023 GP: SS (84)　　　Comps: Gavin Cecchini (66), Jonathan Araúz (64), Luis Rengifo (60)

Neto was the first member of the 2022 draft class to debut, beating the likes of Jackson Holliday, Druw Jones and Kumar Rocker. That kind of precedent creates pressure, but Neto has taken it in stride, looking more like a veteran than a green prospect. He played more than half of the season with the Angels, hanging around after the call-up in mid-April until he was put on the IL in early August with back inflammation. His hitting was respectable, but it was defensively that Neto dazzled. In 84 games, he logged 114 putouts, 205 assists and 43 double plays. His range at shortstop was among the best: he ranked second in the American League for both range factor per nine innings and range factor per game.

Logan O'Hoppe C Born: 02/09/00   Age: 24   Bats: R   Throws: R   Height: 6'2"   Weight: 185   Origin: Round 23, 2018 Draft (#677 overall)

YEAR	TM	LVL	AGE	PA	R	HR	RBI	SB	AVG/OBP/SLG	BABIP	SLGCON	BB%	K%	ZSw%	ZCon%	OSw%	OCon%	LA	90th EV	DRC+	BRR	DRP	WARP
2021	PEJ	WIN	21	100	19	3	17	3	.299/.440/.519	.328	.645	21.0%	15.0%	63.2%	66.7%	24.0%	50.0%						
2021	JS	A+	21	358	43	13	48	6	.270/.335/.459	.294	.573	8.4%	17.6%							124	0.2	3.9	2.5
2021	REA	AA	21	57	6	3	7	0	.296/.333/.481	.310	.578	1.8%	15.8%							109	-0.3	-1.0	0.1
2021	LHV	AAA	21	23	2	1	3	0	.190/.261/.381	.188	.471	8.7%	17.4%							102	-0.3	-0.3	0.1
2022	REA	AA	22	316	48	15	45	6	.275/.392/.496	.289	.619	13.0%	16.5%							142	-0.1	-0.6	2.4
2022	RCT	AA	22	131	24	11	33	1	.306/.473/.673	.288	.868	22.1%	16.8%							167	0.1	2.2	1.7
2022	LAA	MLB	22	16	1	0	2	0	.286/.375/.286	.364	.364	12.5%	18.8%	72.4%	76.2%	29.0%	33.3%	23.9	91.9	94	0.0	-0.3	0.0
2023	LAA	MLB	23	199	23	14	29	0	.236/.296/.500	.240	.679	7.0%	24.1%	73.1%	83.6%	36.9%	46.7%	19.4	105.3	104	-0.1	-7.8	0.1
2024 DC	LAA	MLB	24	415	47	16	52	4	.233/.307/.409	.279	.562	8.4%	24.9%							101	-0.1	-8.8	0.7

2023 GP: C (49), DH (1)

Comps: Wilin Rosario (64), Salvador Perez (55), Ben Petrick (52)

YEAR	TM	P. COUNT	FRM RUNS	BLK RUNS	THRW RUNS	TOT RUNS
2021	PEJ	1520			0.0	0.0
2021	JS	8803	4.1	-0.1	0.6	4.6
2021	REA	1517	-0.6	-0.1	-0.3	-0.9
2021	LHV	819	-0.2	0.0	0.0	-0.2
2022	RCT	3867	2.0	-0.1	0.2	2.1
2022	REA	8259	-1.1	0.4	-0.5	-1.1
2022	LAA	638	-0.2	0.0	0.0	-0.2
2023	LAA	7516	-7.4	-0.1	-0.2	-7.8
2024	LAA	14430	-7.8	-0.1	-0.9	-8.8

If he isn't yet, O'Hoppe should be a cult favorite. While fans were deprived of seeing him healthy all year as he missed four months with a torn labrum, he bookended the season with two healthy stretches that proved what he's made of. His stats are strong, but as much as anything it's his clubhouse leadership—even as a rookie—that is setting him up as the franchise catcher going forward. Former manager Phil Nevin made comps to J.T. Realmuto and Yadier Molina both in physical ability and in work ethic; big shoes to fill for someone with only about 200 MLB at-bats. O'Hoppe's made those at-bats count, though. He shook off the rust from not playing for two thirds of the season and hit a clean .261/.292/.587 with nine homers, three doubles and 15 RBI in 25 games in the last month of the year—if that doesn't seem like an impressive number of runners plated, take a gander at who was breaking into the Angels lineup by September.

Kyren Paris SS Born: 11/11/01   Age: 22   Bats: R   Throws: R   Height: 6'0"   Weight: 180   Origin: Round 2, 2019 Draft (#55 overall)

YEAR	TM	LVL	AGE	PA	R	HR	RBI	SB	AVG/OBP/SLG	BABIP	SLGCON	BB%	K%	ZSw%	ZCon%	OSw%	OCon%	LA	90th EV	DRC+	BRR	DRP	WARP
2021	IE	A	19	136	29	2	18	16	.274/.434/.491	.429	.800	19.9%	30.1%							98	0.7	4.1	0.8
2021	TRI	A+	19	55	6	1	6	4	.231/.273/.365	.355	.594	3.6%	36.4%							88	-0.1	0.6	0.1
2022	TRI	A+	20	392	58	8	32	28	.229/.345/.387	.330	.602	12.5%	29.8%							104	3.7	-6.5	1.2
2022	RCT	AA	20	51	11	3	8	5	.359/.510/.641	.500	1.000	19.6%	27.5%							109	-0.2	-0.5	0.1
2023	RCT	AA	21	514	79	14	45	44	.255/.393/.417	.365	.655	17.1%	29.4%							105	5.6	6.2	3.0
2023	LAA	MLB	21	46	4	0	1	3	.100/.200/.100	.174	.174	8.7%	37.0%	74.7%	80.4%	32.5%	37.8%	2.6	104.7	68	0.0	0.0	0.0
2024 DC	LAA	MLB	22	123	12	2	11	5	.215/.307/.334	.335	.554	10.7%	35.3%							86	0.1	-0.2	0.2

2023 GP: SS (9), 2B (2), CF (2), DH (1)

Comps: Richard Urena (54), Ketel Marte (50), Amed Rosario (50)

Paris continued his strong start from 2022 and kept the momentum in Double-A this past season, putting a bit more pop in his swing and drawing even more walks than in his professional debut. He was rewarded with 15 games at the MLB level, getting the call-up when Luis Rengifo was out due to injury. Paris suffered a torn thumb ligament near the end of the season, the latest in a string of injuries disproportionately long for a career as sparse as his, but he should return in early 2024—hopefully with an extra-base hit and a SLG over .100 in the bigs.

Brett Phillips OF Born: 05/30/94   Age: 30   Bats: L   Throws: R   Height: 6'0"   Weight: 195   Origin: Round 6, 2012 Draft (#189 overall)

YEAR	TM	LVL	AGE	PA	R	HR	RBI	SB	AVG/OBP/SLG	BABIP	SLGCON	BB%	K%	ZSw%	ZCon%	OSw%	OCon%	LA	90th EV	DRC+	BRR	DRP	WARP
2021	TB	MLB	27	292	50	13	44	14	.206/.300/.427	.302	.771	11.3%	38.7%	64.5%	70.9%	23.1%	47.1%	18.1	103.1	69	1.0	5.7	0.6
2022	NOR	AAA	28	88	16	6	17	1	.277/.432/.631	.324	1.025	19.3%	28.4%							111	-0.1	-0.9	0.3
2022	TB	MLB	28	208	21	5	14	7	.147/.225/.250	.232	.465	7.7%	40.9%	63.9%	66.9%	26.4%	47.2%	19.0	102.2	33	1.1	2.8	-0.6
2022	BAL	MLB	28	17	1	0	1	0	.118/.118/.235	.250	.500	0.0%	52.9%	66.7%	64.3%	14.0%	66.7%	32.9	100.2	44	0.0	0.3	0.0
2023	SL	AAA	29	264	37	6	25	7	.230/.352/.366	.344	.619	15.9%	33.0%	66.8%	75.3%	22.3%	60.0%			78	-2.5	2.0	0.1
2023	LAA	MLB	29	71	9	3	6	3	.175/.268/.333	.333	.778	11.3%	50.7%	66.2%	63.8%	29.5%	30.4%	15.8	102.1	53	0.2	0.3	-0.1
2024 non	LAA	MLB	30	251	23	6	24	4	.176/.275/.317	.257	.530	11.0%	35.3%							67	0.5	1.7	0.0

2023 GP: CF (24), RF (4), LF (3), P (1), DH (1)

Comps: Ruben Rivera (53), Nate McLouth (52), Corey Patterson (51)

In the nicest way possible, Phillips is the whack-a-mole of the baseball world. It's not that he's a pest to get rid of—although his transaction history might suggest otherwise—it's just that right when you get used to seeing him in one place, he's suddenly in another. Warming up to him as a Brewer? He's a Royal now. Rays World Series hero? See you in Baltimore, buddy. Settling in as an Angel? Who knows where he'll be next year. He's the jack of all teams and master of none, though he can always be expected to turn up one place (on the diamond) sooner or later: He's not America's favorite position player pitcher for nothing. He's now extended his pitching appearance resume three years running, and who knows. Maybe one of these days he'll actually pick up a strikeout.

Nelson Rada CF Born: 08/24/05   Age: 18   Bats: L   Throws: L   Height: 5'10"   Weight: 160   Origin: IFA, 2022

YEAR	TM	LVL	AGE	PA	R	HR	RBI	SB	AVG/OBP/SLG	BABIP	SLGCON	BB%	K%	ZSw%	ZCon%	OSw%	OCon%	LA	90th EV	DRC+	BRR	DRP	WARP
2022	DSL ANG	ROK	16	206	50	1	26	27	.311/.446/.439	.365	.522	12.6%	12.6%										
2023	IE	A	17	540	94	2	48	55	.276/.395/.346	.348	.446	13.5%	18.1%							107	8.7	-4.0	2.4
2024 non	LAA	MLB	18	251	19	1	18	0	.215/.281/.289	.282	.386	7.5%	23.4%							63	0.0	0	-0.3

2023 GP: CF (115)

Comps: Wilmer Flores (58), Fernando Martinez (49), Carlos Tocci (46)

Rada impressed in his first taste of full-season ball, the majority of which he played as a minor. He appeared in all but five games of Inland Empire's season and recorded at least one hit in three-quarters of his appearances, putting the ball in play often but also showcasing an ability to take a walk. Those 55 stolen bases look even more impressive against just 11 caught stealings; the speedster also received an MiLB Gold Glove in the outfield, becoming the only Angels prospect to receive the award.

Anthony Rendon 3B Born: 06/06/90 Age: 34 Bats: R Throws: R Height: 6'1" Weight: 200 Origin: Round 1, 2011 Draft (#6 overall)

YEAR	TM	LVL	AGE	PA	R	HR	RBI	SB	AVG/OBP/SLG	BABIP	SLGCON	BB%	K%	ZSw%	ZCon%	OSw%	OCon%	LA	90th EV	DRC+	BRR	DRP	WARP
2021	LAA	MLB	31	249	24	6	34	0	.240/.329/.382	.267	.472	11.6%	16.5%	72.1%	89.0%	26.4%	69.3%	22.2	101.3	96	-0.2	-0.2	0.7
2022	LAA	MLB	32	193	15	5	24	2	.229/.326/.380	.258	.481	11.9%	18.1%	68.4%	85.4%	24.3%	70.6%	19.0	102.6	108	-0.1	0.9	0.8
2023	LAA	MLB	33	183	23	2	22	2	.236/.361/.318	.268	.388	13.7%	14.8%	66.1%	88.7%	20.7%	66.7%	16.3	101.7	110	-0.1	-0.5	0.8
2024 DC	LAA	MLB	34	335	35	7	33	1	.236/.334/.358	.265	.435	11.5%	15.4%							101	-0.3	-0.1	0.9

2023 GP: 3B (43) Comps: Buddy Bell (75), Heinie Groh (75), Brooks Robinson (72)

How do you describe Rendon's role on the Angels? He's like the chill uncle you see once a year, or the guy who comes in at a frat party to sink a celebrity shot in beer pong, only to leave you with the hardest cup configuration and a vague, sticky disappointment in the aftermath. If we do some quick math, his seven-year, $245 million contract breaks down to $35 million a year. Four years in, he's played fewer than 60 games a year—and fewer than 45 in 2023. Putting that all together, he made over $800,000 for every game he appeared in last year, and doesn't exactly show signs of getting healthier or less inclined to butt heads with media and fans alike. As of right now, he's projected to return from his tibia fracture in early 2024, but only time will tell how soon he'll be back—or for how long.

Luis Rengifo IF Born: 02/26/97 Age: 27 Bats: S Throws: R Height: 5'10" Weight: 195 Origin: IFA, 2013

YEAR	TM	LVL	AGE	PA	R	HR	RBI	SB	AVG/OBP/SLG	BABIP	SLGCON	BB%	K%	ZSw%	ZCon%	OSw%	OCon%	LA	90th EV	DRC+	BRR	DRP	WARP
2021	SL	AAA	24	228	46	8	32	13	.329/.386/.560	.357	.663	7.5%	14.0%							120	-0.8	-2.2	1.0
2021	LAA	MLB	24	190	22	6	18	1	.201/.246/.310	.220	.397	4.7%	20.0%	70.3%	81.5%	38.1%	63.7%	11.1	100.8	86	0.2	0.3	0.4
2022	SL	AAA	25	112	19	4	15	2	.313/.384/.525	.375	.693	10.7%	21.4%	67.5%	78.9%	31.2%	63.7%			107	2.1	0.9	0.7
2022	LAA	MLB	25	511	45	17	52	6	.264/.294/.429	.285	.512	3.3%	15.5%	77.6%	86.2%	42.5%	70.0%	10.0	102.4	116	0.5	-0.4	2.5
2023	LAA	MLB	26	445	55	16	51	6	.264/.339/.444	.293	.561	9.2%	18.4%	75.8%	86.3%	34.0%	60.2%	11.2	103.3	112	0.5	-0.7	2.0
2024 DC	LAA	MLB	27	536	57	16	62	7	.252/.315/.405	.289	.509	7.5%	18.8%							102	0.3	-0.7	1.6

2023 GP: 2B (65), SS (37), 3B (23), RF (11), LF (6), CF (4) Comps: Brandon Phillips (70), Martín Prado (60), Howie Kendrick (58)

Rengifo had a breakout year and was setting or tying career highs in every slash line stat before getting injured in the most Angels way possible, tearing his bicep taking swings in the on-deck circle in early September. While he was healthy, Rengifo was clutch in an injury-plagued lineup. He flew under the radar, but posted his second consecutive two-WARP season and logged innings at six different positions, establishing himself as one of the more elite super-utility guys in the game. He's on track to be healthy come the start of this season, and if he continues to be as versatile as he's proven thus far, could become known as a rare trade whiff for the Rays—and an even rarer win for Arte Moreno, who blocked the Angels front office from dealing him a couple years later.

Alberto Rios LF Born: 03/19/02 Age: 22 Bats: R Throws: R Height: 6'0" Weight: 203 Origin: Round 3, 2023 Draft (#79 overall)

YEAR	TM	LVL	AGE	PA	R	HR	RBI	SB	AVG/OBP/SLG	BABIP	SLGCON	BB%	K%	ZSw%	ZCon%	OSw%	OCon%	LA	90th EV	DRC+	BRR	DRP	WARP
2023	IE	A	21	145	19	3	18	7	.181/.269/.315	.225	.444	9.7%	25.5%							85	-0.4	-0.5	0.1
2024 non	LAA	MLB	22	251	19	3	20	0	.199/.255/.291	.277	.422	6.0%	29.0%							54	0.0	0	-0.8

2023 GP: LF (32), DH (4) Comps: Kel Jones (81), Estee Harris (81), Lane Adams (79)

Rios was drafted out of Stanford in the third round as the reigning Pac-12 Player of the Year. Primarily a catcher in his single year as a collegiate starter, he got reps exclusively as a left fielder in his first taste of professional ball; it's not yet clear whether the move is permanent or if it was simply an effort to preserve his legs. He struggled with his first taste of pro pitching, though he did slog through a .238 BABIP over 39 games between rookie ball and Low-A, a line that seems unlikely to repeat given the defensive caliber of low minors.

Alfonso Rivas 1B Born: 09/13/96 Age: 27 Bats: L Throws: L Height: 5'10" Weight: 190 Origin: Round 4, 2018 Draft (#113 overall)

YEAR	TM	LVL	AGE	PA	R	HR	RBI	SB	AVG/OBP/SLG	BABIP	SLGCON	BB%	K%	ZSw%	ZCon%	OSw%	OCon%	LA	90th EV	DRC+	BRR	DRP	WARP
2021	IOW	AAA	24	237	22	4	32	0	.284/.405/.411	.361	.547	14.8%	20.7%							115	-2.6	4.9	1.2
2021	CHC	MLB	24	49	7	1	3	0	.318/.388/.409	.481	.643	8.2%	32.7%	68.9%	86.3%	26.5%	55.6%	10.2	104.5	70	0.0	-0.2	-0.1
2022	IOW	AAA	25	106	15	1	10	0	.298/.368/.415	.409	.591	9.4%	26.4%							91	0.7	0.0	0.3
2022	CHC	MLB	25	287	27	3	25	6	.235/.322/.307	.344	.470	10.1%	30.3%	63.7%	87.2%	27.9%	53.9%	4.3	103.5	74	0.5	0.0	-0.3
2023	HER	WIN	26	70	14	3	12	4	.439/.543/.684	.537	.886	15.7%	18.6%										
2023	ELP	AAA	26	260	54	9	40	8	.332/.462/.582	.400	.766	18.8%	19.2%	60.2%	88.3%	24.9%	55.7%			118	-1.4	-0.9	1.1
2023	PIT	MLB	26	106	6	3	14	1	.234/.305/.436	.302	.631	6.6%	27.4%	62.8%	87.6%	31.7%	57.8%	10.7	104.6	76	-0.1	0.1	-0.1
2023	SD	MLB	26	17	2	0	1	0	.200/.294/.333	.375	.625	11.8%	41.2%	53.1%	76.5%	18.6%	12.5%	18.7	102.1	69	0.0	0.0	0.0
2024 DC	LAA	MLB	27	60	6	1	6	1	.229/.327/.357	.301	.514	11.2%	25.1%							96	0.0	0.1	0.1

2023 GP: 1B (47), LF (1) Comps: Justin Smoak (62), Brett Wallace (57), J.R. Phillips (56)

Rivas is a soft-hitting first baseman, which helps explain why he's in his fourth organization in five years, and ready to go five-for-six. His biggest strength is his swing path, which allows for great batted ball quality in most at-bats, giving him consistently excellent BABIPs. However, he generally ranks in the bottom of the league for power, a crucial skill for slow, lumbering first basemen. While he crushed the ball in the first half of the year in the offense-friendly PCL, he was simply present at the MLB level as a strong-side platoon hitter. He's good enough to come off the bench for most teams, but that's about as far as it goes.

Jorge Ruiz   LF   Born: 06/30/04   Age: 20   Bats: L   Throws: L   Height: 5'10"   Weight: 164   Origin: IFA, 2021

YEAR	TM	LVL	AGE	PA	R	HR	RBI	SB	AVG/OBP/SLG	BABIP	SLGCON	BB%	K%	ZSw%	ZCon%	OSw%	OCon%	LA	90th EV	DRC+	BRR	DRP	WARP
2021	DSL ANG	ROK	17	212	32	1	15	19	.270/.381/.362	.305	.423	10.4%	11.8%									-7.1	
2022	ANG	ROK	18	222	36	0	23	8	.335/.382/.414	.370	.459	5.4%	9.0%		85.7%	100.0%							
2023	IE	A	19	342	49	3	52	13	.304/.379/.419	.358	.512	8.2%	15.8%							112	4.2	0.2	2.0
2024 non	LAA	MLB	20	251	18	2	19	0	.214/.267/.297	.270	.383	5.7%	21.6%							58	0.0	0	-0.6

2023 GP: LF (56), RF (11), CF (9)   *Comps: Luis Domoromo (82), Telmito Agustin (76), Jesús Sánchez (76)*

Ruiz was a top-five hitter in the 66ers lineup, and though he didn't have a ton of pop, he was still seeing (and hitting) the ball well, cruising to the third-best slugging percentage on his team among everyone who had at least 300 PA for Inland Empire. His season ended in late July due to injury, but he's starting this season at 19 years old and is a lefty outfielder, which, for whatever it's worth, is a gap in the Angels' current lineup.

★ ★ ★ *2024 Top 101 Prospect* **#89** ★ ★ ★

Nolan Schanuel   1B   Born: 02/14/02   Age: 22   Bats: L   Throws: R   Height: 6'4"   Weight: 220   Origin: Round 1, 2023 Draft (#11 overall)

YEAR	TM	LVL	AGE	PA	R	HR	RBI	SB	AVG/OBP/SLG	BABIP	SLGCON	BB%	K%	ZSw%	ZCon%	OSw%	OCon%	LA	90th EV	DRC+	BRR	DRP	WARP
2023	RCT	AA	21	76	15	1	12	1	.333/.474/.467	.380	.549	21.1%	11.8%							122	-1.6	-0.1	0.2
2023	LAA	MLB	21	132	19	1	6	0	.275/.402/.330	.326	.400	15.2%	14.4%	66.5%	86.4%	23.9%	74.3%	6.2	97.7	111	0.0	-0.1	0.5
2024 DC	LAA	MLB	22	577	56	8	53	0	.240/.330/.350	.279	.426	10.5%	15.7%							95	0.0	-0.4	0.7

2023 GP: 1B (28), DH (1)   *Comps: Casey Kotchman (61), Andrés Blanco (57), Anthony Rizzo (56)*

Of the fastest-debuting players in MLB history since the institution of the Amateur Draft, three Angels crack the top 25 according to Baseball America, with one in each of the last two seasons. Neither of the other pair were faster than Schanuel, who made his debut in August just a month and change after being drafted 11th overall. Those 40 days weren't a wandering-in-the-desert scenario; he played 22 games in rookie ball, Low-A and Double-A collectively, where he racked up 27 hits, 15 RBI and 20 runs scored. Getting fast-tracked to the Show didn't bog him down, either—he reached base in all 29 big-league games in which he appeared, tied for the third-longest on-base streak to start an MLB career, and counting.

Michael Stefanic   2B/3B   Born: 02/24/96   Age: 28   Bats: R   Throws: R   Height: 5'8"   Weight: 180   Origin: Undrafted Free Agent, 2018

YEAR	TM	LVL	AGE	PA	R	HR	RBI	SB	AVG/OBP/SLG	BABIP	SLGCON	BB%	K%	ZSw%	ZCon%	OSw%	OCon%	LA	90th EV	DRC+	BRR	DRP	WARP
2021	RCT	AA	25	96	11	1	9	0	.345/.406/.437	.408	.528	7.3%	15.6%							116	-0.3	1.4	0.6
2021	SL	AAA	25	458	67	16	54	6	.334/.408/.505	.363	.596	9.8%	13.5%							126	0.6	-2.7	2.8
2022	SL	AAA	26	346	50	4	37	4	.314/.422/.425	.326	.460	13.9%	6.4%	61.3%	95.1%	20.9%	89.4%			130	-1.4	0.4	2.2
2022	LAA	MLB	26	69	5	0	0	0	.197/.279/.230	.245	.286	7.2%	17.4%	60.4%	89.1%	26.9%	66.7%	4.8	97.5	93	0.0	0.0	0.2
2023	SL	AAA	27	455	67	5	62	8	.365/.463/.467	.388	.511	13.2%	7.3%	61.9%	96.6%	23.4%	87.7%			120	-2.1	-4.1	1.7
2023	LAA	MLB	27	71	5	0	6	0	.290/.380/.355	.333	.407	11.3%	11.3%	63.3%	93.5%	23.9%	91.9%	8.8	97.8	104	0.0	-0.1	0.2
2024 DC	LAA	MLB	28	250	25	3	23	2	.265/.343/.359	.277	.392	8.9%	7.4%							105	-0.2	-0.5	0.8

2023 GP: 2B (12), 3B (8), DH (1)   *Comps: Breyvic Valera (62), Joey Wendle (62), Kelby Tomlinson (56)*

Similarly to Trey Cabbage, Stefanic was a tremendous minor-league hitter who struggled with consistency at the MLB level. He took home the MiLB batting title with a .365/.463/.467 slash line in Triple-A, walking 60 times and scoring and driving in more than that number. His first couple trips to the big leagues were nothing impressive, but credit where credit is due—he sorted out the shakiness from repeated Salt Lake-to-Anaheim-back-to-Salt Lake journeys and hit .400 in his last few weeks with the Angels. He's proven that he's one of the best hitters in the minors, and when he's allowed to stay in the bigs for longer than three games at a time, he managed to hit just as well there. He's no power hitter, with an on-base percentage healthily surpassing his slugging, but hey: Don't look a gift offensive infielder in the mouth.

Matt Thaiss   C   Born: 05/06/95   Age: 29   Bats: L   Throws: R   Height: 6'0"   Weight: 215   Origin: Round 1, 2016 Draft (#16 overall)

YEAR	TM	LVL	AGE	PA	R	HR	RBI	SB	AVG/OBP/SLG	BABIP	SLGCON	BB%	K%	ZSw%	ZCon%	OSw%	OCon%	LA	90th EV	DRC+	BRR	DRP	WARP
2021	SL	AAA	26	449	71	17	69	2	.280/.383/.496	.325	.655	13.4%	20.5%							110	-2.2	1.4	2.0
2021	LAA	MLB	26	8	1	0	0	0	.143/.250/.143	.167	.167	12.5%	12.5%	83.3%	100.0%	20.0%	33.3%	18.9	110.0	93	0.0	0.0	0.0
2022	SL	AAA	27	332	46	10	48	7	.268/.364/.451	.306	.574	13.0%	18.4%	71.1%	82.3%	21.7%	50.3%			103	-1.0	-5.2	0.5
2022	LAA	MLB	27	81	9	2	8	1	.217/.321/.319	.295	.489	13.6%	29.6%	75.0%	76.5%	26.6%	44.0%	7.5	102.6	83	0.0	-1.1	0.0
2023	LAA	MLB	28	307	32	9	31	2	.214/.319/.340	.272	.497	11.7%	27.0%	74.5%	71.7%	23.3%	52.8%	9.6	104.9	91	-0.5	-3.8	0.3
2024 DC	LAA	MLB	29	222	22	5	22	2	.209/.304/.345	.281	.511	10.7%	28.5%							84	-0.1	-3.8	0.0

2023 GP: C (82), DH (5), 1B (3)   *Comps: Justin Smoak (53), Martín Maldonado (49), Ryan McGuire (48)*

If Logan O'Hoppe was the bread of the Angels' catching sandwich last year, Thaiss was undoubtedly the meat. He stepped in after O'Hoppe (and then Max Stassi) were taken out of commission for much of the year, and did the work admirably. His playing time got beefed up significantly—he had never appeared in more than 50 games since his rookie 2019, but got the nod 95 times in 2023, including 82 starts behind the plate, five at DH and three at first. Seven years after his draft, Thaiss is starting to look like a first-round pick: His hitting stats got consistently better—impressive for a member of a platoon catcher squad

YEAR	TM	P. COUNT	FRM RUNS	BLK RUNS	THRW RUNS	TOT RUNS
2021	SL	8256	2.2	0.2	0.3	2.8
2022	SL	6755	-3.5	0.0	-0.7	-4.2
2022	LAA	1764	-0.9	0.0	0.0	-0.9
2023	LAA	10072	-1.8	-0.2	-0.5	-2.5
2024	LAA	8418	-3.7	0.0	-0.1	-3.8

and even more oversaturated first base miasma—and he was (mostly) dependable defensively. It's worth noting though, at catcher, Thaiss' original position, he committed eight errors, which ties him for sixth-most in MLB, a rating DRP heartily underscored.

Mike Trout CF   Born: 08/07/91   Age: 32   Bats: R   Throws: R   Height: 6'2"   Weight: 235   Origin: Round 1, 2009 Draft (#25 overall)

YEAR	TM	LVL	AGE	PA	R	HR	RBI	SB	AVG/OBP/SLG	BABIP	SLGCON	BB%	K%	ZSw%	ZCon%	OSw%	OCon%	LA	90th EV	DRC+	BRR	DRP	WARP
2021	LAA	MLB	29	146	23	8	18	2	.333/.466/.624	.456	.961	18.5%	28.1%	64.4%	78.3%	21.9%	60.8%	13.0	110.0	149	0.1	-0.1	1.6
2022	LAA	MLB	30	499	85	40	80	1	.283/.369/.630	.323	.923	10.8%	27.9%	68.3%	76.0%	26.0%	57.9%	24.8	109.1	146	-0.2	2.8	4.9
2023	LAA	MLB	31	362	54	18	44	2	.263/.367/.490	.335	.740	12.4%	28.7%	72.4%	78.3%	23.6%	53.3%	19.3	108.5	118	0.1	-1.2	2.0
2024 DC	LAA	MLB	32	522	73	30	82	1	.248/.348/.502	.293	.730	11.8%	27.3%							135	-0.1	-0.8	3.9

2023 GP: CF (79), DH (2) 　　　　　　　　　　　　　　　　　*Comps: Mickey Mantle (81), Ken Griffey Jr. (75), Cesar Cedeno (71)*

Years from now, our kids or grandkids will ask what it was like to watch Mike Trout. "It was incredible," we'll say. "Because of the catches he made? The home runs he hit?" the kids will clamor. We'll lean back on our hypothetical porch rocking chairs and take a drag from our hypothetical pipes. "Because he was the greatest player that never was."

Maybe that's a bit harsh. Trout has still accomplished plenty, and still has seven whole seasons remaining under contract to get back on track. But going back to 2020, he's missed more games than he's played. In 2023, he appeared in just 82 games due to a hamate bone fracture, and resurfaced for one single game before returning to the IL. Over his now decade-plus career, he's logged just four seasons with more than 150 games, and seven over 120.

Chad Wallach C   Born: 11/04/91   Age: 32   Bats: R   Throws: R   Height: 6'2"   Weight: 246   Origin: Round 5, 2013 Draft (#142 overall)

YEAR	TM	LVL	AGE	PA	R	HR	RBI	SB	AVG/OBP/SLG	BABIP	SLGCON	BB%	K%	ZSw%	ZCon%	OSw%	OCon%	LA	90th EV	DRC+	BRR	DRP	WARP
2021	SL	AAA	29	171	30	8	22	0	.223/.322/.432	.260	.621	11.7%	26.3%							97	1.0	1.2	0.7
2021	JAX	AAA	29	130	11	7	17	0	.204/.369/.427	.230	.647	17.7%	26.9%							121	-1.9	-0.1	0.6
2021	MIA	MLB	29	66	2	0	6	0	.200/.242/.267	.400	.571	4.5%	48.5%	63.2%	71.6%	38.9%	38.2%	8.3	101.6	37	-0.1	-0.3	-0.3
2022	SL	AAA	30	365	40	9	43	3	.219/.304/.361	.277	.513	9.9%	26.0%	74.4%	78.1%	27.4%	47.2%			75	-4.1	4.0	-0.1
2022	LAA	MLB	30	40	3	1	4	0	.143/.231/.257	.160	.346	10.0%	22.5%	73.9%	72.5%	29.3%	65.5%	17.8	103.3	90	-0.1	-0.1	0.1
2023	SL	AAA	31	43	6	2	8	1	.361/.442/.556	.393	.690	14.0%	16.3%	72.9%	76.5%	22.9%	47.4%			106	0.2	0.8	0.3
2023	LAA	MLB	31	172	18	7	15	0	.197/.259/.376	.258	.590	7.6%	33.1%	79.1%	73.4%	30.9%	39.8%	16.0	103.5	64	-0.2	-1.7	-0.3
2024 DC	LAA	MLB	32	29	3	1	3	0	.194/.266/.315	.261	.471	8.1%	30.0%							64	0.0	0	0.0

2023 GP: C (59), DH (2), 1B (1) 　　　　　　　　　　　　*Comps: Brett Hayes (61), Roberto Pérez (58), Martín Maldonado (58)*

There's no way to say this delicately. Wallach did what he was asked to do, which was to be a third- or fourth-string catcher on a terrifyingly fragile roster. Far from the first choice, he soldiered through anyway, and had a career year (of sorts)—mostly because after never appearing in more than 23 games, and suddenly finding oneself in 65, it's pretty easy to make those counting stats stack up. Next up in his Halos career, ideally, is surpassing the Mendoza line.

YEAR	TM	P. COUNT	FRM RUNS	BLK RUNS	THRW RUNS	TOT RUNS
2021	SL	2206	1.2	0.0	-0.1	1.1
2021	JAX	3580	-0.7	0.0	0.9	0.2
2021	MIA	2584	0.1	0.0	0.0	0.1
2022	SL	8644	4.1	-0.1	-1.0	3.0
2022	LAA	1455	0.1	0.0	0.0	0.1
2023	SL	1500	0.4	0.0	0.4	0.7
2023	LAA	7040	-0.6	-0.2	0.1	-0.7
2024	LAA	1202	0.1	0.0	0.0	0.0

Jared Walsh 1B   Born: 07/30/93   Age: 30   Bats: L   Throws: L   Height: 6'0"   Weight: 210   Origin: Round 39, 2015 Draft (#1185 overall)

YEAR	TM	LVL	AGE	PA	R	HR	RBI	SB	AVG/OBP/SLG	BABIP	SLGCON	BB%	K%	ZSw%	ZCon%	OSw%	OCon%	LA	90th EV	DRC+	BRR	DRP	WARP
2021	LAA	MLB	27	585	70	29	98	2	.277/.340/.509	.335	.714	8.2%	26.0%	70.1%	82.4%	34.8%	62.4%	8.0	107.7	106	0.0	0.6	1.8
2022	LAA	MLB	28	454	41	15	44	2	.215/.269/.374	.281	.554	5.9%	30.4%	67.7%	81.9%	34.0%	57.0%	10.4	105.9	72	-0.3	0.0	-0.7
2023	SL	AAA	29	225	28	9	28	0	.217/.360/.375	.320	.651	16.9%	34.7%	59.4%	69.8%	23.6%	57.8%			80	-0.1	-0.9	-0.1
2023	LAA	MLB	29	116	10	4	11	0	.125/.216/.279	.164	.492	9.5%	38.8%	66.8%	66.4%	30.4%	35.0%	18.5	104.6	61	0.0	-0.4	-0.3
2024 non	LAA	MLB	30	251	27	9	29	1	.223/.300/.390	.327	.647	9.0%	35.7%							93	-0.1	-0.1	0.2

2023 GP: 1B (29), RF (9), DH (1) 　　　　　　　　　　　*Comps: Doug Mientkiewicz (50), Scott Van Slyke (50), Tyler White (50)*

Look, most people can't have an All-Star year annually. But after garnering one All-Star nom, the expectation is that you'll continue to be a very good player afterwards. Walsh had his moment in 2021, and has never been the same since, seeing a steep dropoff in production in 2022 and an absolute implosion in 2023. He posted a dismal .125 average and .495 OPS in 39 games with the Angels and was sent to Salt Lake five times, including stints on the injured and temporarily inactive lists plus two banishments outright. Walsh's bat was sorely missed in the Angels lineup, but so was his presence at first base, where he played 118 and 128 games during the previous two seasons respectively. While there were many aspects of last season that the Angels wished turned out differently, relying on a fleet of temporary replacement first basemen instead of a proven anchor was a special kind of hurt.

Taylor Ward LF   Born: 12/14/93   Age: 30   Bats: R   Throws: R   Height: 6'1"   Weight: 200   Origin: Round 1, 2015 Draft (#26 overall)

YEAR	TM	LVL	AGE	PA	R	HR	RBI	SB	AVG/OBP/SLG	BABIP	SLGCON	BB%	K%	ZSw%	ZCon%	OSw%	OCon%	LA	90th EV	DRC+	BRR	DRP	WARP
2021	SL	AAA	27	59	15	4	10	2	.429/.525/.857	.515	1.135	15.3%	20.3%							113	0.6	-0.8	0.3
2021	LAA	MLB	27	237	33	8	33	1	.250/.332/.438	.301	.595	8.4%	23.2%	68.8%	85.0%	29.6%	56.2%	16.2	105.1	97	0.1	0.2	0.7
2022	LAA	MLB	28	564	73	23	65	5	.281/.360/.473	.325	.624	10.6%	21.3%	65.2%	85.3%	23.2%	62.0%	16.1	104.1	120	0.3	-0.7	3.0
2023	LAA	MLB	29	409	60	14	47	4	.253/.335/.421	.284	.543	9.5%	19.6%	68.4%	88.6%	26.7%	60.2%	14.5	103.9	112	-0.1	-1.2	1.6
2024 DC	LAA	MLB	30	563	64	19	68	5	.251/.332/.416	.286	.532	9.5%	19.2%							112	0.0	-1.1	2.2

2023 GP: LF (93), 1B (1) 　　　　　　　　　　　*Comps: Craig Monroe (56), Nelson Cruz (55), Danny Bautista (52)*

The 2023 season was unequivocally rough for the Angels, not just for the dissipation of the first legitimate playoff hopes in recent memory, but for the string of unusual and disheartening injuries that followed the team through the season. One of the most impactful injuries came in late July, on a high and inside sinker from Alek Manoah that simply didn't sink—hitting Ward in the face and fracturing his skull in three places. Ward didn't suffer a concussion and his eyesight wasn't damaged, but he required three plates to be inserted, and of course, his season was over. The timing couldn't have been worse for Ward (not that there's ever a convenient time to need extensive facial surgery), who had continued to establish himself as a dependable everyday player on both sides of the ball. In 2022, his best season so far, he finished the year with an OPS of .833. In the month leading up to that at-bat against Manoah in 2023, Ward had logged an OPS of 1.047.

Evan White 1B Born: 04/26/96 Age: 28 Bats: R Throws: L Height: 6'1" Weight: 219 Origin: Round 1, 2017 Draft (#17 overall)

YEAR	TM	LVL	AGE	PA	R	HR	RBI	SB	AVG/OBP/SLG	BABIP	SLGCON	BB%	K%	ZSw%	ZCon%	OSw%	OCon%	LA	90th EV	DRC+	BRR	DRP	WARP
2021	SEA	MLB	25	104	8	2	9	0	.144/.202/.237	.188	.348	5.8%	29.8%	71.8%	78.4%	30.6%	55.6%	19.0	104.2	70	0.0	0.0	-0.2
2022	TAC	AAA	26	107	14	7	16	0	.204/.308/.484	.190	.643	12.1%	21.5%	70.1%	84.5%	32.2%	55.3%			110	-0.5	-0.5	0.3
2024 non	LAA	MLB	28	251	23	7	26	0	.192/.262/.334	.247	.494	7.6%	28.9%							67	0.0	0	-0.6

2023 GP: 1B (2)   *Comps: Alfredo Marte (64), Joey Terdoslavich (61), Chris Shaw (59)*

It's possible that White's immense early struggles were damning enough to rule out any sort of meaningful future as a big leaguer. But three surgeries in three years—the most recent being a second season-ending hip surgery after just two games in 2023—have robbed White of the opportunity to prove much of anything, regardless of how bleak his on-field outlook looked. Suddenly, the pre-debut extension he signed was no longer just a massive whiff for Seattle from a pure baseball standpoint, its increasing commitments became entirely untenable from a payroll perspective, necessitating White's inclusion in the salary dump swap to the Braves. Atlanta promptly played hot potato with the $15 million owed to White over the next two years and flipped him to Anaheim, where he'll look to get healthy first and foremost, let alone live up to any last ounce of hype still remaining.

PITCHERS

Tyler Anderson LHP Born: 12/30/89 Age: 34 Height: 6'2" Weight: 220 Origin: Round 1, 2011 Draft (#20 overall)

YEAR	TM	LVL	AGE	G (GS)	IP	W-L	SV	K	WHIP	ERA	CSP	BB%	K%	HR%	GB%	ZSw%	ZCon%	OSw%	OCon%	BABIP	SLGCON	DRA-	WARP
2021	SEA	MLB	31	13(13)	63²	2-3	0	48	1.32	4.81	55.9%	4.8%	17.6%	4.0%	32.1%	74.6%	84.6%	41.6%	69.6%	.303	.612	126	-0.3
2021	PIT	MLB	31	18(18)	103¹	5-8	0	86	1.20	4.35	58.3%	5.8%	20.0%	3.7%	36.5%	74.2%	80.0%	34.0%	67.7%	.280	.542	104	0.7
2022	LAD	MLB	32	30(28)	178²	15-5	0	138	1.00	2.57	55.9%	4.8%	19.5%	2.0%	39.9%	70.8%	85.1%	38.7%	62.8%	.257	.443	103	1.5
2023	LAA	MLB	33	27(25)	141	6-6	0	119	1.49	5.43	46.7%	10.2%	18.9%	3.2%	30.1%	75.1%	80.5%	32.2%	58.8%	.302	.581	149	-1.9
2024 DC	LAA	MLB	34	26(26)	137¹	7-9	0	119	1.31	4.39	52.2%	7.9%	20.4%	3.4%	33.1%					.289	.546	100	1.2

2023 Arsenal: FA (90.1), CH (80), FC (85.4), SI (88.2), SL (81.4), SW (75.9), CU (72.5)   *Comps: Jason Vargas (78), Mark Buehrle (78), Wade Miley (77)*

Anderson was Mr. Average in some ways for the Angels—6-6 record, middle-of-the-pack ERA, and 20th out of the Angels' 39 (!) pitchers in WHIP—but his name was at the top of some lists, for better or for worse: He gave up the most earned runs of any member of the staff, but was top-five in strikeouts, and only two pitchers threw more innings. That's how averages work: some great and some terrible balance out to create a pitcher who's…fine. All those gains with the Dodgers immediately flew out the sunroof on the drive down the 5, of course, but that was basically to be expected given the involved organizations.

Sam Bachman RHP Born: 09/30/99 Age: 24 Height: 6'1" Weight: 235 Origin: Round 1, 2021 Draft (#9 overall)

YEAR	TM	LVL	AGE	G (GS)	IP	W-L	SV	K	WHIP	ERA	CSP	BB%	K%	HR%	GB%	ZSw%	ZCon%	OSw%	OCon%	BABIP	SLGCON	DRA-	WARP
2021	TRI	A+	21	5(5)	14¹	0-2	0	15	1.19	3.77		6.9%	25.9%	1.7%	65.8%					.324	.526	109	0.0
2022	RCT	AA	22	12(12)	43²	1-1	0	30	1.51	3.92		13.0%	15.5%	2.1%	54.1%					.282	.437	115	0.1
2023	RCT	AA	23	6(6)	26¹	3-2	0	29	1.33	5.81		16.9%	24.6%	2.5%	43.1%					.194	.444	114	0.2
2023	LAA	MLB	23	11(0)	17	1-2	1	14	1.65	3.18	45.6%	14.3%	18.2%	0.0%	58.8%	67.4%	88.5%	27.3%	43.1%	.333	.373	99	0.2
2024 DC	LAA	MLB	24	28(0)	30²	1-1	0	29	1.69	5.93	45.6%	13.6%	20.1%	2.6%	49.2%					.319	.543	125	-0.3

2023 Arsenal: SL (87.9), SI (96.8), CH (90.2)   *Comps: Miguel Castro (72), Anthony Bass (71), Dakota Hudson (71)*

Where to start with Bachman? The fact that he was the latest in a long tradition of Angels first-round pitcher draft picks, covering much of this century? His unconventional delivery that's generously described as a three-quarters arm slot? What about his billing as the starter of the future, only to be beset by injury in each of his three professional seasons this far? There are still a lot of question marks with Bachman, but he held it down out of the bullpen in his debut despite bypassing Triple-A entirely. If he can get healthy, he'll be in the mix for a starting role. Not even by default, though that's always a reasonable concern with the Angels' half-empty stable of arms.

Griffin Canning RHP Born: 05/11/96 Age: 28 Height: 6'2" Weight: 180 Origin: Round 2, 2017 Draft (#47 overall)

YEAR	TM	LVL	AGE	G (GS)	IP	W-L	SV	K	WHIP	ERA	CSP	BB%	K%	HR%	GB%	ZSw%	ZCon%	OSw%	OCon%	BABIP	SLGCON	DRA-	WARP
2021	LAA	MLB	25	14(13)	62²	5-4	0	62	1.48	5.60	55.2%	10.1%	22.4%	5.1%	36.0%	74.5%	79.6%	32.6%	54.9%	.298	.668	122	-0.1
2023	LAA	MLB	27	24(22)	127	7-8	0	139	1.24	4.32	49.4%	6.7%	25.9%	4.1%	42.4%	67.4%	84.5%	33.2%	49.9%	.297	.599	88	2.3
2024 DC	LAA	MLB	28	24(24)	133¹	7-9	0	141	1.29	4.27	49.5%	8.6%	24.7%	3.5%	40.3%					.294	.573	97	1.4

2023 Arsenal: FA (94.6), SL (88.4), CH (90.1), CU (81.7)   *Comps: Joe Musgrove (65), Nick Tropeano (65), Vance Worley (64)*

Canning is good: He's better than he's given credit for, and was especially effective after the All-Star Break. In the latter half, he had a 3.91 ERA, 11.55 strikeouts and 2.38 walks per nine, bolstering an already strong 9.9 K/9 and 2.6 BB/9 line on the entire year. Over 24 appearances, he set a career-high with 127 innings; in his final seven games, he posted a 3.49 ERA with 43 strikeouts in 38 ⅔ innings. Not only was he pitching more, he was pitching better than ever before, a pleasant surprise after missing the entirety of 2022 with a stress fracture in his back. Canning missed a couple games here and there throughout the season, but was primarily healthy, and improved the velo on his four-seam fastball by over a mile per hour. His whiff rate, strikeout rate and walk rate are all well above average, boding well for a potential move up in the rotation.

Adam Cimber RHP Born: 08/15/90 Age: 33 Height: 6'3" Weight: 195 Origin: Round 9, 2013 Draft (#268 overall)

YEAR	TM	LVL	AGE	G (GS)	IP	W-L	SV	K	WHIP	ERA	CSP	BB%	K%	HR%	GB%	ZSw%	ZCon%	OSw%	OCon%	BABIP	SLGCON	DRA-	WARP
2021	TOR	MLB	30	39 (0)	37¹	2-2	1	30	0.96	1.69	54.4%	3.4%	20.5%	1.4%	56.9%	69.7%	86.3%	38.2%	67.3%	.271	.393	86	0.6
2021	MIA	MLB	30	33 (0)	34¹	1-2	0	21	1.19	2.88	54.8%	7.9%	15.0%	0.0%	49.5%	71.3%	81.7%	27.6%	79.2%	.291	.379	95	0.4
2022	TOR	MLB	31	77 (0)	70²	10-6	4	58	1.12	2.80	55.8%	4.4%	19.8%	2.0%	41.1%	69.2%	84.0%	34.6%	71.0%	.294	.471	91	1.0
2023	TOR	MLB	32	22 (0)	20²	0-2	1	12	1.55	7.40	46.6%	7.4%	12.6%	6.3%	47.2%	66.3%	86.4%	31.1%	82.8%	.288	.634	106	0.2
2024 DC	LAA	MLB	33	34 (0)	37	2-2	0	24	1.35	4.79	53.3%	6.3%	14.6%	2.9%	44.8%					.295	.508	107	0.0

2023 Arsenal: FA (85.4), SW (74.8), SI (85.3)   *Comps: Dan Otero (66), Brandon Kintzler (64), Justin Miller (63)*

After two straight seasons of sub-3.00 ERA relief work, the funky right-hander with the pigeon-toed stance and submariner delivery looked set for another fine season with four straight shutout performances to begin the year. Unfortunately, it all unraveled after that; Cimber first hit the IL with a rhomboid strain before seeing his season end with a right shoulder impingement. In a baseball development world that always seems hellbent on delivering factory-like efficiency from its prospects, it's always a welcome sight to see a handmade one-of-a-kind like Cimber on the mound, so let's hope for health and a return to his bespoke form next season.

Caden Dana RHP Born: 12/17/03 Age: 20 Height: 6'4" Weight: 215 Origin: Round 11, 2022 Draft (#328 overall)

YEAR	TM	LVL	AGE	G (GS)	IP	W-L	SV	K	WHIP	ERA	CSP	BB%	K%	HR%	GB%	ZSw%	ZCon%	OSw%	OCon%	BABIP	SLGCON	DRA-	WARP
2022	ANG	ROK	18	3 (3)	6²	0-0	0	6	0.90	1.35		0.0%	24.0%	0.0%	42.1%					.316	.368		
2023	IE	A	19	3 (3)	15	1-1	0	18	0.80	1.20		10.5%	31.6%	1.8%	28.1%					.161	.312	96	0.2
2023	TRI	A+	19	11 (11)	53¹	2-4	0	71	1.29	4.22		10.7%	31.7%	1.3%	39.4%					.339	.556	85	0.8
2024 non	LAA	MLB	20	58 (0)	50	2-2	0	50	1.55	5.71		11.8%	22.0%	3.8%	34.4%					.308	.612	124	-0.4

Comps: Francis Martes (84), Julio Teheran (79), Sixto Sánchez (78)

If there's one thing the Angels love, it's paying way over slot value. It isn't quite clear whether the $1.5 million gamble for an 11th-round pick has paid off yet, but Dana has made significant strides since his selection in 2022, becoming one of the best-regarded prospects in a terrible system. Best not hold it against the cold-weather prep arm, though, who performed well in 14 starts before being shut down mid-summer for load management purposes; he certainly has the stuff to reach the big leagues—and with the Angels' aggressive promotions of late, that debut will likely come sooner than most expect. That's a different concern than whether he has the control and stamina to stick in the rotation, however.

Reid Detmers LHP Born: 07/08/99 Age: 24 Height: 6'2" Weight: 210 Origin: Round 1, 2020 Draft (#10 overall)

YEAR	TM	LVL	AGE	G (GS)	IP	W-L	SV	K	WHIP	ERA	CSP	BB%	K%	HR%	GB%	ZSw%	ZCon%	OSw%	OCon%	BABIP	SLGCON	DRA-	WARP
2021	RCT	AA	21	12 (12)	54	2-4	0	97	1.17	3.50		8.0%	43.1%	4.4%	33.9%					.361	.771	69	1.4
2021	SL	AAA	21	2 (2)	8	1-0	0	11	1.00	1.13		3.1%	34.4%	0.0%	31.6%					.368	.579	97	0.0
2021	LAA	MLB	21	5 (5)	20²	1-3	0	19	1.79	7.40	56.9%	10.9%	18.8%	5.0%	33.3%	68.0%	79.8%	30.4%	59.7%	.328	.681	147	-0.3
2022	LAA	MLB	22	25 (25)	129	7-6	0	122	1.21	3.77	55.0%	8.5%	22.6%	2.4%	36.1%	68.9%	80.8%	33.1%	65.1%	.278	.507	120	-0.1
2023	LAA	MLB	23	28 (28)	148²	4-10	0	168	1.35	4.48	47.8%	9.3%	26.1%	3.0%	36.7%	71.3%	83.0%	32.5%	56.7%	.318	.569	101	1.6
2024 DC	LAA	MLB	24	29 (29)	154¹	8-10	0	167	1.30	4.41	51.0%	9.5%	25.1%	3.8%	36.2%					.285	.578	100	1.4

2023 Arsenal: FA (94.4), SL (89.2), CU (74.7), CH (85), SI (93.6), SW (82.8)   *Comps: José Suarez (71), Tyler Skaggs (63), Arthur Rhodes (60)*

No one embodied Atlas laboring under his burden quite like Detmers last year. His sky-sized task was to carry a languishing Angels pitching staff, and by god did he drag them along as far as he could. His 148 ⅔ innings set the mark for the rest of the team. He surpassed his previous career-high pitches thrown by over 400, and his strikeout total by 45. For all that, he should have been set up with servants to answer his every whim, peeling grapes and fanning him with oversized palm branches. Instead, he got…nothing. Four wins, if you're counting, against double-digit losses. That doesn't seem like Atlas, it seems like Sisyphus, continually rolling his boulder up the hill, just hoping that he won't get crushed.

Carlos Estévez RHP Born: 12/28/92 Age: 31 Height: 6'6" Weight: 277 Origin: IFA, 2011

YEAR	TM	LVL	AGE	G (GS)	IP	W-L	SV	K	WHIP	ERA	CSP	BB%	K%	HR%	GB%	ZSw%	ZCon%	OSw%	OCon%	BABIP	SLGCON	DRA-	WARP
2021	COL	MLB	28	64 (0)	61²	3-5	11	60	1.49	4.38	57.1%	7.8%	22.2%	3.0%	44.9%	75.3%	82.7%	29.5%	60.8%	.354	.604	91	0.9
2022	COL	MLB	29	62 (0)	57	4-4	2	54	1.18	3.47	52.9%	9.8%	23.0%	3.0%	35.7%	78.3%	81.3%	29.1%	72.4%	.247	.503	109	0.3
2023	LAA	MLB	30	63 (0)	62¹	5-5	31	78	1.49	3.90	51.4%	11.0%	27.8%	2.5%	31.1%	73.7%	77.9%	33.0%	62.0%	.346	.560	94	0.9
2024 DC	LAA	MLB	31	64 (0)	67²	4-8	34	69	1.36	4.81	53.1%	9.7%	23.4%	4.1%	36.0%					.287	.596	107	0.0

2023 Arsenal: FA (97.1), SL (88.5), CH (89.5)   *Comps: Jeremy Jeffress (68), Manny Corpas (65), Mark Lowe (64)*

If Colorado is MLB's version of the moon, 2023 was Estévez's first terrestrial season. It went pretty well, as he paced the team with 31 saves, 20 more than his previous high-water mark—no other Angel compiled more than four. It was no surprise that Estévez's heater lost some rise outside of Coors' thin air, but his willingness to deploy it at the top of the zone increased—gravity might hurt fastball rise, but it helps keep fly balls in the park—and his four-seam whiff rate benefited. It was Estévez himself who felt the gravitational pull in the season's second half, as the first-time All-Star burned up on re-entry, with a 6.59 ERA compared to his otherworldly 1.80 mark in the first half of the season. He'll enter the 2024 as the bullpen's anchor.

Carson Fulmer RHP Born: 12/13/93 Age: 30 Height: 6'0" Weight: 210 Origin: Round 1, 2015 Draft (#8 overall)

YEAR	TM	LVL	AGE	G (GS)	IP	W-L	SV	K	WHIP	ERA	CSP	BB%	K%	HR%	GB%	ZSw%	ZCon%	OSw%	OCon%	BABIP	SLGCON	DRA-	WARP
2021	LOU	AAA	27	37 (2)	41	1-5	1	51	1.59	4.61		13.4%	27.3%	2.1%	49.5%					.343	.607	86	0.8
2021	CIN	MLB	27	20 (0)	25²	0-0	0	24	1.52	6.66	51.4%	11.2%	20.7%	2.6%	47.4%	64.3%	82.8%	29.9%	54.5%	.319	.568	110	0.1
2022	OKC	AAA	28	49 (1)	56²	6-6	12	62	1.25	2.86		14.5%	25.6%	1.7%	48.3%	71.3%	80.3%	34.4%	48.1%	.232	.454	74	1.2
2023	SL	AAA	29	12 (11)	41	0-2	0	33	1.78	5.27		14.8%	17.5%	2.6%	46.4%	66.0%	82.4%	26.0%	57.8%	.333	.610	111	0.2
2023	LAA	MLB	29	3 (1)	10	1-1	0	6	1.00	2.70	50.1%	10.3%	15.4%	2.6%	57.1%	62.0%	86.4%	25.6%	63.6%	.185	.429	106	0.1
2024 non	LAA	MLB	30	58 (0)	50	2-2	0	42	1.54	5.31	49.2%	12.2%	18.6%	2.7%	46.0%					.296	.523	115	-0.2

2023 Arsenal: CH (86.3), SI (92.6), CU (81.3), SL (87), FA (92.7)   Comps: Drew VerHagen (45), Dominic Leone (45), Anthony Bass (44)

What must class reunions be like for Carson Fulmer? His 2015 Vanderbilt draft class produced the more successful and better-known Dansby Swanson and Walker Buehler, and Tony Kemp and Mike Yastrzemski departed the program two years prior. At least in 2023 he was back on a big-league roster for the first time since 2020, when he started his brutal spin cycle of being signed and DFA'd by six teams (and the Pirates twice) before momentarily settling in Anaheim. Even with all that, his 2023 has got to be better cocktail party conversation than that of fellow Commodore compatriot Curt Casali, who recorded a sub-.500 OPS for the Reds over 80 major-league at-bats.

Luis García RHP Born: 01/30/87 Age: 37 Height: 6'2" Weight: 240 Origin: IFA, 2017

YEAR	TM	LVL	AGE	G (GS)	IP	W-L	SV	K	WHIP	ERA	CSP	BB%	K%	HR%	GB%	ZSw%	ZCon%	OSw%	OCon%	BABIP	SLGCON	DRA-	WARP
2021	SWB	AAA	34	18 (0)	17¹	1-2	11	19	1.10	3.63		4.3%	27.5%	2.9%	59.6%					.311	.543	84	0.4
2021	STL	MLB	34	34 (0)	33¹	1-1	2	34	0.99	3.24	60.0%	5.9%	25.2%	1.5%	46.7%	71.2%	79.5%	30.9%	45.9%	.256	.411	85	0.6
2022	SD	MLB	35	64 (0)	61	4-6	3	68	1.21	3.39	54.9%	6.6%	26.3%	1.2%	53.3%	66.4%	83.9%	33.0%	49.2%	.327	.437	68	1.6
2023	SD	MLB	36	61 (0)	59²	2-3	0	53	1.39	4.07	45.9%	9.0%	19.9%	2.2%	59.8%	69.8%	87.7%	32.3%	55.4%	.301	.481	84	1.2
2024 DC	LAA	MLB	37	52 (0)	55¹	3-2	0	51	1.31	4.14	50.3%	8.2%	21.3%	2.5%	52.2%					.300	.497	94	0.4

2023 Arsenal: SI (97.6), SW (81.5), FA (97.5), FS (88.5), HC (95.6)   Comps: Clay Carroll (77), Hector Carrasco (77), Matt Albers (77)

The ronin of journeyman middle relievers, García arrived in San Diego in 2022 on a two-year deal, joining his fifth different team in five seasons. In year one, he was excellent; in year two, he was mostly fine but lost a lot of whiffs, mostly on his slider, which he both struggled to locate and threw with less velocity (as he did his sinker, though both it and his four-seamer still broke 97 mph on the radar gun). That all added up to average performance, which will put bread on the table, but closer to Wonder Bread than home-made brioche. Unsurprisingly, then, García will next ply his trade for the Angels, who employed him all the way back in 2019 and who eagerly plucked him off the supermarket shelf to add to a bullpen that desperately needs average-or-better innings in bulk at affordable prices.

Jimmy Herget RHP Born: 09/09/93 Age: 30 Height: 6'3" Weight: 170 Origin: Round 6, 2015 Draft (#175 overall)

YEAR	TM	LVL	AGE	G (GS)	IP	W-L	SV	K	WHIP	ERA	CSP	BB%	K%	HR%	GB%	ZSw%	ZCon%	OSw%	OCon%	BABIP	SLGCON	DRA-	WARP
2021	RR	AAA	27	27 (0)	37²	2-2	3	48	1.06	2.63		7.6%	30.6%	3.2%	33.0%					.250	.495	98	0.2
2021	LAA	MLB	27	14 (0)	14²	2-2	0	18	1.30	4.30	52.7%	6.7%	30.0%	0.0%	44.4%	64.5%	81.2%	24.6%	38.2%	.417	.600	89	0.2
2021	TEX	MLB	27	4 (0)	4	0-1	0	2	1.25	9.00	61.5%	0.0%	11.1%	5.6%	40.0%	68.2%	93.3%	37.5%	50.0%	.286	.667	92	0.1
2022	LAA	MLB	28	49 (1)	69	2-1	9	63	0.91	2.48	55.5%	5.6%	23.7%	1.5%	41.1%	64.7%	86.0%	32.5%	56.7%	.246	.423	83	1.3
2023	SL	AAA	29	25 (0)	32²	1-2	1	36	1.29	4.68		9.6%	26.5%	3.7%	38.8%	65.6%	80.9%	26.9%	44.2%	.300	.595	79	0.5
2023	LAA	MLB	29	29 (1)	29	2-4	0	26	1.41	4.66	53.0%	6.3%	20.5%	5.5%	28.6%	67.3%	87.9%	28.0%	60.8%	.310	.703	107	0.2
2024 DC	LAA	MLB	30	52 (0)	55¹	3-2	2	47	1.29	4.41	54.0%	8.2%	19.9%	3.6%	36.4%					.277	.545	100	0.2

2023 Arsenal: CU (77.2), SL (85.3), SI (91.5), FS (85.8), FA (93)   Comps: Kevin Quackenbush (54), Danny Farquhar (54), Shawn Armstrong (54)

The cool thing about Herget isn't that he uses a variety of arm angles and has mastered lateral break to a degree most can only dream of. Nor is it that three of his pitches get more than 15 inches of total movement (and his slider is somehow the one that moves the least). It's that at 6-foot-3 and 170 pounds, he looks more beanpole than behemoth. He looks like he'd be more at ease in the tech support section of a Best Buy than on the mound making hitters duck for cover, but has sliced his way to a top-10 ranking in horizontal movement with both his curveball and sinker. Oh, also pretty cool is the fact that those two pitches end up nearly three feet apart by the time they get to the plate.

Camden Minacci RHP Born: 01/14/02 Age: 22 Height: 6'3" Weight: 215 Origin: Round 6, 2023 Draft (#174 overall)

YEAR	TM	LVL	AGE	G (GS)	IP	W-L	SV	K	WHIP	ERA	CSP	BB%	K%	HR%	GB%	ZSw%	ZCon%	OSw%	OCon%	BABIP	SLGCON	DRA-	WARP
2023	IE	A	21	7 (0)	8¹	0-0	0	10	2.28	5.40		2.3%	23.3%	0.0%	51.6%					.581	.700	71	0.0
2024 non	LAA	MLB	22	58 (0)	50	2-2	0	40	1.59	6.13		10.1%	17.5%	3.9%	36.7%					.312	.599	133	-0.6

Comps: Jordan Milbrath (26), Mitch Keller (26), Pedro Avila (26)

A sixth-round pick in the 2023 draft, Minacci might be a diamond in the rough for the Angels (and it is very rough). He's a highly rated closer and finished with the NCAA's sixth-most saves in his junior year at Wake Forest ahead of being drafted. He skipped rookie ball and went straight to Low-A Inland Empire, which might suggest that the Angels are looking to fast-track his development. The sooner the better; the Angels bullpen was among the league's worst by ERA, WHIP, walks issued, hits and runs allowed—you know, just every pitching statistic.

Zach Plesac   RHP   Born: 01/21/95   Age: 29   Height: 6'3"   Weight: 220   Origin: Round 12, 2016 Draft (#362 overall)

YEAR	TM	LVL	AGE	G (GS)	IP	W-L	SV	K	WHIP	ERA	CSP	BB%	K%	HR%	GB%	ZSw%	ZCon%	OSw%	OCon%	BABIP	SLGCON	DRA-	WARP
2021	CLE	MLB	26	25(25)	142²	10-6	0	100	1.20	4.67	55.5%	5.7%	16.7%	3.8%	44.5%	74.4%	84.2%	33.5%	64.6%	.264	.533	116	0.2
2022	CLE	MLB	27	25(24)	131²	3-12	0	100	1.32	4.31	56.0%	6.7%	17.6%	3.3%	40.0%	73.2%	85.4%	34.7%	65.8%	.288	.526	121	-0.1
2023	COL	AAA	28	19(18)	94²	5-6	0	71	1.48	6.08		10.3%	17.4%	7.3%	40.0%	75.2%	82.4%	30.5%	53.8%	.257	.724	101	1.2
2023	CLE	MLB	28	5(5)	21¹	1-1	0	14	1.97	7.59	52.8%	4.8%	13.3%	2.9%	50.0%	76.9%	90.2%	36.7%	64.9%	.415	.671	106	0.2
2024 DC	LAA	MLB	29	25(15)	77²	3-6	0	56	1.43	5.24	54.7%	7.2%	16.4%	3.7%	42.9%					.304	.562	117	0.0

2023 Arsenal: SL (85.2), FA (91.6), CH (84.2), CU (79.5)   Comps: Jakob Junis (63), Jerad Eickhoff (62), Trevor Williams (61)

Sometimes, work can be frustrating. You might have a meeting that doesn't go well, make an important decision that backfires or simply battle a headache all day. And when that happens, you may have the urge to yell "Rats!" (or some other words we can't print in this book) while angrily pacing the room. Well, when Plesac had a bad day at the office, his catharsis was to rip off his shirt, somehow breaking his pitching thumb in the process. A year later, his business dealings went awry again. As a majestic home run ball flew through the sky, Plesac turned his anger (and fist) towards the ground, enraged that Earth's gravity couldn't bring the ball down. This time, his pinky took the brunt of the force. No one likes working with a crankypants, so after five miserable starts where he couldn't strike a batter out to save his life, Plesac was designated for assignment and sent to Triple-A (where he had a 7.55 FIP). Place your bets on whether he'll be out of baseball before breaking his middle three fingers in anger.

Patrick Sandoval   LHP   Born: 10/18/96   Age: 27   Height: 6'3"   Weight: 190   Origin: Round 11, 2015 Draft (#319 overall)

YEAR	TM	LVL	AGE	G (GS)	IP	W-L	SV	K	WHIP	ERA	CSP	BB%	K%	HR%	GB%	ZSw%	ZCon%	OSw%	OCon%	BABIP	SLGCON	DRA-	WARP
2021	LAA	MLB	24	17(14)	87	3-6	1	94	1.21	3.62	51.5%	9.9%	25.9%	3.0%	50.7%	66.2%	78.5%	34.1%	51.3%	.266	.493	88	1.4
2022	LAA	MLB	25	27(27)	148²	6-9	0	151	1.34	2.91	54.1%	9.4%	23.7%	1.3%	46.6%	67.1%	83.1%	35.5%	54.4%	.320	.454	96	1.8
2023	LAA	MLB	26	28(28)	144²	7-13	0	128	1.51	4.11	46.3%	11.3%	19.6%	1.8%	46.3%	66.5%	82.9%	32.9%	57.7%	.309	.483	115	0.5
2024 DC	LAA	MLB	27	29(29)	151¹	8-11	0	148	1.46	4.69	49.7%	10.6%	22.1%	2.6%	46.6%					.310	.526	103	1.1

2023 Arsenal: SL (86.9), CH (83.1), FA (93), SI (93.3), CU (76.4), SW (81.6)   Comps: Robbie Ray (66), Matt Moore (64), Jake Odorizzi (64)

The only Angels starter who shouldered anything close to Reid Detmers' workload was Sandoval, who persevered through 144 ⅔ innings, and was similarly rewarded with a poor return on investment for his efforts. His zone percentage was slightly down from years past, which contributed to the not-so-proud distinction of handing out the eighth-most walks in all of baseball, and his strikeout percentage was down by over four points. One piece of good news does stand out, though: Sandoval added a sweeper to his arsenal this past year, bringing his pitch mix up to six. While he used the sweeper only 2.7% of the time, rays of hope are shining through already: namely, in the 21 plate appearances that ended on the pitch, he gave up just four hits and struck out seven.

Chase Silseth   RHP   Born: 05/18/00   Age: 24   Height: 6'0"   Weight: 217   Origin: Round 11, 2021 Draft (#321 overall)

YEAR	TM	LVL	AGE	G (GS)	IP	W-L	SV	K	WHIP	ERA	CSP	BB%	K%	HR%	GB%	ZSw%	ZCon%	OSw%	OCon%	BABIP	SLGCON	DRA-	WARP
2022	RCT	AA	22	15(15)	83	7-0	0	110	0.95	2.28		8.4%	34.4%	3.4%	48.9%					.247	.531	74	2.0
2022	LAA	MLB	22	7(7)	28²	1-3	0	24	1.57	6.59	55.0%	9.3%	18.6%	5.4%	44.6%	61.3%	87.7%	33.1%	57.0%	.310	.681	109	0.1
2023	SL	AAA	23	11(11)	45²	4-1	0	49	1.18	2.96		10.8%	26.3%	0.5%	55.7%	61.5%	84.8%	32.0%	54.3%	.292	.425	78	1.0
2023	LAA	MLB	23	16(8)	52¹	4-1	0	56	1.28	3.96	45.4%	11.8%	25.3%	4.1%	48.9%	62.8%	80.5%	30.8%	61.2%	.250	.562	92	0.8
2024 DC	LAA	MLB	24	23(23)	106¹	5-7	0	107	1.34	4.25	48.4%	10.3%	23.2%	3.0%	46.4%					.287	.530	96	1.1

2023 Arsenal: FA (94.9), SW (81.2), FS (87.3), SI (94.1), FC (90.8), SL (85.8), CU (79.2)   Comps: Edward Cabrera (70), Sean Reid-Foley (69), Jake Odorizzi (69)

The fact that any MLB team, even the Angels, would at any point be rocking with an eight-man rotation is astonishing, so don't worry if you aren't too familiar with the stylings of someone like Silseth. Regardless, maybe he should be given more credit. He threw twice as many innings in 2023 as the previous season and nobly handled the lack of trust created by a disastrous 2022 debut. Silseth struck out way more batters but still walks too many, and also serves up too many home runs. It's the Angels, though, so… grading on a curve. He also finished three games and picked up a hold, which could signify (Silseth-fy? Sorry) bullpen depth for a roster that desperately needs it.

José Soriano   RHP   Born: 10/20/98   Age: 25   Height: 6'3"   Weight: 220   Origin: IFA, 2016

YEAR	TM	LVL	AGE	G (GS)	IP	W-L	SV	K	WHIP	ERA	CSP	BB%	K%	HR%	GB%	ZSw%	ZCon%	OSw%	OCon%	BABIP	SLGCON	DRA-	WARP
2022	ANG	ROK	23	4(4)	8	0-0	0	11	0.75	0.00		6.9%	37.9%	0.0%	43.8%	91.7%	90.9%	34.8%	25.0%	.250	.375		
2023	RCT	AA	24	17(2)	23¹	0-2	1	31	1.46	4.24		15.4%	29.8%	1.0%	55.6%					.321	.444	81	0.5
2023	LAA	MLB	24	38(0)	42	1-3	0	56	1.33	3.64	42.3%	12.4%	30.3%	2.2%	51.5%	57.6%	86.4%	33.7%	39.6%	.309	.510	85	0.8
2024 DC	LAA	MLB	25	52(0)	55¹	3-2	0	70	1.37	4.26	42.3%	12.6%	28.6%	2.7%	47.6%					.295	.543	94	0.4

2023 Arsenal: KC (86.6), FA (98.6), SI (96.2), SL (89.9)   Comps: Chad Sobotka (77), Devin Williams (77), Dylan Coleman (77)

Congratulations, José! YOU are the winner of the "10th-best out-of-zone swing-and-miss-percentage in MLB" sweepstakes, which just goes to show anything is possible if one digs deep enough in the Statcast stockpiles. Soriano walks too many, but the spike curve is a legitimate weapon and he also gets a healthy amount of batted balls on the ground. Whether he can last in a high-leverage role is likely dependent more on the command than the 100-mph heater.

José Suarez LHP Born: 01/03/98 Age: 26 Height: 5'10" Weight: 225 Origin: IFA, 2014

YEAR	TM	LVL	AGE	G(GS)	IP	W-L	SV	K	WHIP	ERA	CSP	BB%	K%	HR%	GB%	ZSw%	ZCon%	OSw%	OCon%	BABIP	SLGCON	DRA-	WARP
2021	LAA	MLB	23	23(14)	98¹	8-8	0	85	1.23	3.75	52.1%	8.7%	20.6%	2.7%	47.6%	69.7%	83.7%	33.6%	62.8%	.269	.496	100	0.9
2022	LAA	MLB	24	22(20)	109	8-8	0	103	1.25	3.96	55.6%	7.1%	22.3%	3.0%	40.7%	69.2%	84.8%	37.7%	63.0%	.290	.534	101	1.0
2023	LAA	MLB	25	11(7)	33²	1-3	0	28	1.96	8.29	47.9%	12.1%	17.0%	6.1%	31.9%	70.2%	81.8%	32.5%	55.6%	.343	.737	147	-0.4
2024 DC	LAA	MLB	26	52(0)	55¹	3-3	0	51	1.48	5.30	52.2%	9.8%	20.5%	3.5%	38.1%					.307	.574	116	-0.1

2023 Arsenal: FA (92.4), CH (82.1), SW (77.7), SL (85.1), SI (91), FC (88), CU (76.2)   *Comps: Tyler Skaggs (67), Martín Pérez (59), Drew Hutchison (59)*

As they say: those who can do, and those who can't get sent to the Arizona Complex League. Before going on the 60-day IL in May, Suarez had already given up nine homers and 26 earned runs in six starts. The time away did him good, though—from when he came back in September through the end of the season, he gave up just five runs on nine hits in 9 ⅓ innings. That (complete) handful of runs looks pretty sweet compared to the double-digit ERA with which he hit the IL, though, and via the same trick in perspective the bump of nearly half by DRA- didn't look so bad compared to the doubled-up ERA, walk and home run rates. He got more whiffs, at least.

César Valdez RHP Born: 03/17/85 Age: 39 Height: 6'2" Weight: 225 Origin: IFA, 2005

YEAR	TM	LVL	AGE	G(GS)	IP	W-L	SV	K	WHIP	ERA	CSP	BB%	K%	HR%	GB%	ZSw%	ZCon%	OSw%	OCon%	BABIP	SLGCON	DRA-	WARP
2021	BAL	MLB	36	39(0)	46	2-2	8	45	1.65	5.87	54.0%	6.7%	21.4%	3.8%	47.3%	65.5%	84.0%	43.0%	59.1%	.380	.685	86	0.8
2022	SL	AAA	37	23(23)	146¹	10-5	0	123	1.09	3.94		3.8%	21.0%	2.4%	51.5%	69.2%	85.3%	45.5%	58.2%	.293	.525	84	2.3
2022	LAA	MLB	37	1(0)	1	0-0	0	0	2.00	9.00	62.5%	0.0%	0.0%	0.0%	80.0%	100.0%	87.5%	37.5%	100.0%	.400	.400	102	0.0
2023	SL	AAA	38	33(16)	114	4-7	0	94	1.71	6.95		6.1%	17.9%	4.0%	51.6%	68.1%	88.5%	39.4%	61.7%	.383	.683	93	1.3
2024 non	LAA	MLB	39	58(0)	50	2-2	0	35	1.39	4.93	53.4%	5.7%	16.2%	3.2%	45.0%					.312	.545	111	-0.1

2023 Arsenal: CH (79.3), SI (85.8)   *Comps: Elmer Dessens (48), Josh Tomlin (47), Collin McHugh (45)*

The Dos Equis commercials were wrong. That guy wasn't the most interesting man in the world—César Valdez is. Ranging from five to 15 years older than his contemporaries on the Salt Lake Bees roster, Valdez has had a lot more life to live—and he certainly has lived it. He's made 69 appearances at the MLB level, but has spent most of the last decade in the Mexican and International leagues, and debuted in Triple-A in 2009—around the time many of his teammates were starting to get serious about Little League. A veteran arm might not be a bad thing for the Angels, not only because Valdez was bound to learn a thing or two over 20 years of pro ball, but because durability like his is hard to find these days.

LINEOUTS

Hitters

HITTER	POS	TM	LVL	AGE	PA	R	HR	RBI	SB	AVG/OBP/SLG	BABIP	SLGCON	BB%	K%	ZSw%	ZCon%	OSw%	OCon%	LA	90th EV	DRC+	BRR	DRP	WARP
Jordyn Adams	OF	SL	AAA	23	480	74	15	67	44	.267/.351/.465	.352	.684	11.0%	27.7%	66.5%	78.0%	29.5%	47.3%			85	6.8	1.8	1.2
	OF	LAA	MLB	23	40	1	0	1	1	.128/.125/.128	.208	.217	0.0%	40.0%	78.9%	71.4%	43.3%	51.7%	6.3	102.6	62	0.0	-0.9	-0.2
Denzer Guzman	SS	IE	A	19	472	62	7	52	8	.239/.309/.371	.328	.536	8.9%	27.8%							85	1.6	-3.7	0.8
Dario Laverde	C	ANG	ROK	18	167	23	1	32	7	.306/.419/.455	.377	.592	16.8%	18.6%										
Charles Leblanc	IF	JAX	AAA	27	370	49	12	34	4	.252/.384/.423	.330	.617	16.5%	25.9%	61.9%	82.8%	21.3%	59.6%			107	1.1	0.5	1.3
Francisco Mejía	C	DUR	AAA	27	92	13	6	19	0	.326/.359/.593	.367	.785	4.3%	22.8%	69.0%	88.8%	41.0%	71.4%			101	0.7	-0.2	0.1
	C	TB	MLB	27	160	22	5	19	0	.227/.258/.400	.266	.536	3.8%	23.8%	71.3%	82.6%	52.7%	74.2%	18.8	100.7	79	0.0	-8.6	-0.7
Felix Morrobel	SS	DSL ANG	ROK	17	171	21	0	20	11	.286/.322/.335	.309	.365	4.7%	7.6%										
Adrian Placencia	2B	TRI	A+	20	480	59	9	46	24	.218/.354/.336	.303	.510	17.1%	27.7%							87	-0.4	1.0	0.7
	2B	RCT	AA	20	60	5	1	4	0	.170/.237/.226	.276	.414	6.7%	40.0%							68	0.1	0.0	0.0
Joe Redfield	CF	TRI	A+	21	53	8	1	8	2	.255/.340/.426	.306	.541	9.4%	18.9%							102	0.8	-0.9	0.2
Livan Soto	IF	RCT	AA	23	127	18	1	5	1	.206/.331/.271	.292	.397	15.0%	26.8%							94	-0.7	1.1	0.3
	IF	SL	AAA	23	350	48	8	42	0	.248/.347/.389	.313	.540	12.6%	23.7%	65.1%	83.4%	27.5%	61.8%			87	-1.0	0.6	0.1
	IF	LAA	MLB	23	12	2	0	0	0	.222/.417/.222	.286	.286	25.0%	16.7%	66.7%	94.4%	19.4%	57.1%	25.3	99.7	111	0.0	0.0	0.1

It's too bad that Salt Lake and Anaheim aren't too far apart, or else **Jordyn Adams** would have racked up lots of frequent flier miles for all the times he passed through John Wayne Airport. The speedy outfielder got called up four times within the last month and a half of the season, and is projected to officially arrive this year—though the power potential got left behind a while ago. ⊕ **Denzer Guzman** came into his own over the course of his final season as a teenager, logging plenty of extra-base hits in a full-season assignment to Low-A Inland Empire and continuing to take all his reps at shortstop. If he can cut down on strikeouts, he'll be among the next crop of Angels prospects fast-tracked to the majors. ⊕ In **Dario Laverde's** second season in Rookie ball, he averaged almost a hit per game, with 14 extra-base hits, and even seven stolen bases. He didn't quite walk more than he struck out again, but it was a close thing. ⊕ **Charles LeBlanc** took plate appearances at five different positions in Triple-A last year, and he arguably hit better than he ever has. He's a jack of all trades but master of none. ⊕ **Francisco Mejía** never was a good defensive catcher and is no longer a good hitter. Still, he will likely continue to get opportunities because the same can be said about a lot of people who play his position. ⊕ Seeing a 2005 birth year listed on a roster remains shocking, but **Felix Morrobel** held his own in his first taste of affiliated ball after signing for $900,000 out of the Dominican Republic last January. Morrobel was a DSL All-Star for his prodigious contact ability, nearly logging as many stolen bases as he did strikeouts, but will eventually need to showcase more power to cut it moving forward—even at the six. ⊕ After ranking seventh on the Angels' 2023 prospect list, **Adrian Placencia** tumbled 13 places after posting an OBP ahead of his SLG in both High-A and a brief taste of Double-A. The 17.1% walk rate in the former stint was plenty strong, but a .336 SLG had less to do with poor luck than with striking out in more than a quarter of chances. ⊕ A 2023 fourth-round pick, **Joe Redfield** hasn't had much chance to prove himself in the minors but crushed at Sam Houston State University. He led the Bearkats in slugging percentage, runs scored, home runs and total bases, and was second in batting average, walks, hits, stolen bases, and doubles. So try not to be too bearish despite the under-slot bonus. ⊕ A member of the nine-man revolving door at second base, **Livan Soto** appeared four times for the Angels in late May and early June. He hit ninth in each appearance, and was pinch-hit for twice. He did edge out Shohei Ohtani for the team's best OBP (no plate appearance minimum, natch), which might mark the only time his name and Ohtani's ever appear next to one another on a leaderboard.

BASEBALL PROSPECTUS 2024

Pitchers

PITCHER	TM	LVL	AGE	G (GS)	IP	W-L	SV	K	WHIP	ERA	CSP	BB%	K%	HR%	GB%	ZSw%	ZCon%	OSw%	OCon%	BABIP	SLGCON	DRA-	WARP
Kelvin Caceres	TRI	A+	23	11 (0)	11	0-0	5	21	1.18	2.45		11.1%	46.7%	0.0%	36.8%					.421	.556	81	0.2
	RCT	AA	23	34 (0)	33²	5-1	2	53	1.54	5.61		13.8%	33.3%	1.9%	50.6%					.355	.628	80	0.3
	SL	AAA	23	7 (0)	10	1-0	1	11	1.00	0.90		12.5%	27.5%	0.0%	69.6%	56.9%	85.4%	23.7%	38.9%	.217	.273	67	
	LAA	MLB	23	2 (0)	1¹	0-0	0	1	3.00	6.75	38.4%	25.0%	12.5%	0.0%	60.0%	70.0%	100.0%	30.8%	50.0%	.500	.500	117	0.0
Chris Clark	IE	A	21	6 (6)	19¹	0-2	0	22	1.40	4.66		5.8%	25.6%	1.2%	40.4%					.375	.684	79	
Davis Daniel	IE	A	26	4 (4)	20¹	1-1	0	28	0.98	1.77		6.3%	35.0%	0.0%	34.0%					.319	.489	70	
	LAA	MLB	26	3 (0)	12¹	1-1	0	9	1.30	2.19	46.1%	17.3%	17.3%	1.9%	47.1%	69.9%	89.2%	31.2%	64.1%	.182	.424	110	0.1
Ben Joyce	RCT	AA	22	14 (0)	15²	0-1	4	24	1.28	4.60		18.6%	34.3%	1.4%	21.4%					.222	.464	104	0.2
	LAA	MLB	22	12 (0)	10	1-1	0	10	1.80	5.40	44.7%	18.8%	20.8%	2.1%	46.4%	65.4%	81.1%	27.1%	65.6%	.296	.481	102	0.1
Jack Kochanowicz	TRI	A+	22	5 (5)	23²	1-0	0	14	1.06	1.52		3.1%	14.6%	0.0%	61.0%					.289	.307	99	0.2
	RCT	AA	22	16 (16)	70¹	4-5	0	55	1.46	6.53		7.1%	17.7%	4.8%	48.9%					.314	.656	114	0.4
Adam Kolarek	OKC	AAA	34	33 (0)	30	0-3	1	26	1.43	2.40		13.4%	20.5%	0.0%	53.1%	67.6%	79.1%	25.8%	77.5%	.329	.390	89	0.5
	NYM	MLB	34	4 (0)	4²	0-0	0	5	0.43	0.00	45.3%	5.9%	29.4%	0.0%	60.0%	60.9%	92.9%	26.8%	72.7%	.111	.111	84	0.1
	LAD	MLB	34	1 (0)	1¹	0-0	0	2	0.75	0.00	45.2%	0.0%	40.0%	0.0%	66.7%	62.5%	60.0%	36.4%	50.0%	.333	.333	78	0.0
Aaron Loup	LAA	MLB	35	55 (0)	48²	2-3	1	45	1.75	6.10	51.3%	8.7%	19.5%	2.6%	47.0%	67.5%	85.2%	35.0%	68.6%	.373	.589	97	0.7
Jorge Marcheco	IE	A	20	17 (17)	93	7-5	0	91	1.08	4.06		6.1%	24.1%	2.9%	34.6%					.269	.529	83	1.2
	TRI	A+	20	5 (5)	28²	3-1	0	33	0.87	1.88		2.8%	30.6%	3.7%	22.2%					.265	.569	113	0.0
José Marte	LAA	MLB	27	10 (0)	9¹	0-0	0	7	2.25	8.68	45.4%	14.6%	14.6%	6.3%	38.2%	68.2%	86.7%	28.0%	63.3%	.355	.812	115	0.0
Victor Mederos	RCT	AA	22	20 (20)	92	4-9	0	99	1.48	5.67		10.4%	23.9%	5.1%	46.4%					.298	.660	106	0.9
	LAA	MLB	22	3 (0)	3	0-0	0	3	2.67	9.00	45.9%	17.6%	17.6%	0.0%	60.0%	60.9%	92.9%	20.9%	66.7%	.500	.556	96	0.0
Reyes Moronta	SL	AAA	30	34 (0)	40²	4-2	6	52	1.55	3.32		19.7%	28.4%	1.6%	27.7%	66.9%	73.9%	27.4%	52.3%	.264	.484	93	0.6
	LAA	MLB	30	2 (0)	1¹	0-0	0	2	5.25	6.75	34.3%	27.3%	18.2%	9.1%	16.7%	66.7%	87.5%	30.6%	45.5%	.600	1.167	116	0.0
José Quijada	LAA	MLB	27	10 (0)	9	0-1	4	8	1.22	6.00	50.7%	7.3%	19.5%	0.0%	39.3%	67.1%	85.7%	38.6%	64.7%	.286	.321	102	0.1
Kenny Rosenberg	SL	AAA	27	20 (20)	100	7-7	0	120	1.51	4.95		10.3%	27.0%	3.1%	39.8%	71.1%	78.7%	30.1%	48.9%	.350	.632	87	1.9
	LAA	MLB	27	7 (3)	33	2-2	0	29	1.48	3.82	47.6%	9.6%	19.9%	2.1%	44.1%	70.8%	87.1%	31.5%	60.8%	.323	.500	107	0.2
Andrew Wantz	SL	AAA	27	22 (0)	25¹	0-0	5	29	1.58	4.62		12.6%	26.1%	4.5%	27.9%	72.6%	82.2%	35.0%	54.6%	.333	.676	93	0.5
	LAA	MLB	27	27 (3)	39¹	2-0	0	33	1.09	3.89	47.0%	9.4%	20.6%	2.5%	30.6%	74.0%	80.7%	30.1%	62.1%	.224	.459	112	0.2

Kelvin Caceres got his feet wet in the bigs last year after speeding through the final three minor-league levels, posting a better ground-ball rate at each stop ahead of debuting in game no. 159. If only he could post a walk rate in the single digits, it might be easier to believe the Angels have a legitimate find in the Dominican power righty. ⓲ A Harvard product, **Chris Clark** was the first pitcher the Angels selected in the 2023 draft. The fifth-rounder led the Ivy League in strikeouts (93) and collected double-figure strikeouts in three starts. He picked up right where he left off in Low-A, striking out more than a quarter of batters while walking just five of 86 opponents. ⓲ **Davis Daniel** put up the second-lowest batting average against amongst Angels pitchers (.167), not counting Eduardo Escobar, and recorded the staff's lowest ERA outside of Jake Lamb and Brett Phillips. It's a good thing not to count that trio, not only because it makes Daniel look better, but also because they're all position players no longer on the 40-man roster, whereas Daniel is, you know, an actual pitcher. ⓲ **Ben Joyce** only has three pitches (if we can count throwing a sweeper one singular time as "having a sweeper"), but for a rookie pitcher averaging 100.9 mph on the fastball, maybe not too much else is required. There's a cutter-y slider, for good measure, which might end up being a better pitch than the flat heater. ⓲ Well, this Kent is no Superman. **Barrett Kent** was hot and cold in his senior season ahead of being—get this—selected by the Angels in the later rounds and signed on an over-slot deal. He flashes high velo with inconsistent control; the slider and curveball are decent, and the changeup is a work in progress. For a 19-year-old it's a relatively complete arsenal, arguably justifying the aggressive promotion to Low-A even putting aside the Angels-ness of it all. ⓲ **Jack Kochanowicz** has undergone a makeover the likes of which is typically reserved for 2000s movies and catastrophic breakups. He got healthy, changed his arm slot and updated his pitch mix, switching from a four-seam to a two-seam fastball and boosting his changeup and sweeper. The new and improved Kochanowicz was thusly rewarded, being the only Angels prospect protected from December's Rule 5 draft. ⓲ Sidewinder **Adam Kolarek** made one scoreless appearance for the Dodgers in June and cleared waivers. He then got sold to the Mets and made four more scoreless appearances before eating another DFA and finishing out the season in Atlanta's system. The Angels being the Angels, Kolarek and his shiny 0.00 ERA landed a major-league deal in November to replace Aaron Loup as their designated aging LOOGY. ⓲ **Aaron Loup** in the Loup: another ground-ball rate of nearly half. Thrown for a Loup: a .373 BABIP. Thus the 6.10 ERA, though DRA- saw through it and actually assigned the aged lefty a better mark than in his first year with the Angels. A fat lot of good it did the guy who couldn't buy a groundout to save his life. It had to be enough to drive him—and the fans—Loupy. ⓲ **Jorge Marcheco** is a pitchability righty with a low-90s heater and fringy secondaries. That worked well enough in A-ball, but advanced batters should pose a significant challenge in the upper minors. ⓲ **José Marte** has appeared for the Angels in each of the preceding three seasons, never surpassing 11 appearances while his ERA stubbornly stuck around nine. He walked exactly as many as he struck out in limited action last season before a stress reaction in his elbow robbed him of a chance to log more innings or get his career WHIP into the ones. ⓲ While Marte at least got two outs in each of his appearances, **Victor Mederos** mastered even more of a disappearing act in his brief debut stint, including one appearance in which he gave up three hits and two runs, all while securing zero outs. ⓲ Given that 66 players dressed for the Angels last season (one short of a franchise record), it's nearly impossible to remember everyone. Don't sweat it if you don't remember Reyes Moronta; he didn't exactly make his appearances memorable, contributing 1 ⅓ innings over two games and allowing seven of 11 opponents to reach base. ⓲ **José Quijada**, the self-proclaimed "spicy guy" of the staff, seemed to be pretty mild and controlled on the mound, a distinct change from 2022, when he threw his four-seamer with reckless abandon, both in frequency and location. Too bad it only lasted for 10 games before his elbow popped. ⓲ After bouncing around in the Twins system for the better part of a decade (and spending a few seasons in the NPB), **Fernando Romero** is back in affiliated ball. He cobbled together an eight-inning season between three levels, moving up from rookie ball to Triple-A before electing free agency. ⓲ Do you hear that? It's a choir of angels (no pun intended) heralding the arrival of a potential legitimate long reliever. **Kenny Rosenberg** made a couple spot starts, but in three of four relief appearances, he contributed five innings. ⓲ For once, an Angels pitcher who doesn't leave something to be desired: in comparison to **Andrew Wantz** the rest of the staff had something Wantz-ing. Of pitchers who appeared in at least 25 games, he had the club's best ERA besides José Soriano and Matt Moore (who left the team in the August fire sale), picking up a tidy 2-0 record as a reliever, with three no-decisions as a starter.

LOS ANGELES DODGERS

Essay by Sam Miller

Player comments by Michael Ajeto and BP staff

There's a problem that philosophers struggle with known as moral luck. As rational beings, we generally don't blame (or credit) people for things that are outside of their control. (Armando Galarraga losing his perfect game on an umpire's bad call, John Fisher being born into owning-a-team levels of personal wealth, etc.) The problem, as the influential philosopher Thomas Nagel has written, is that far, far, far, *far* more is out of our control than we generally acknowledge.

For example, the Dodgers will quite possibly win a World Series (or several) in the next 10 years, and that will likely be facilitated by the triumphant signing of Shohei Ohtani, baseball's best player. We will appropriately celebrate the Dodgers' president of baseball operations, Andrew Friedman, for landing Ohtani when no other team could.

But consider, through Nagel's "four ways in which the natural objects of moral assessment are disturbingly subject to luck," how much of the Ohtani signing was contingent on external factors over which, even as team president, Friedman had little control:

1. Luck of One's Constitution

It was a constellation of the team's pre-existing characteristics—some partly under their control, some not—coupled with Ohtani's bespoke wishes that made the Dodgers the clear favorites to sign him, while at least two dozen other teams (who were perhaps equally desirous of and willing to pay him) were never even considered. The Dodgers might not have signed Ohtani, no matter how hard they tried, had Walter O'Malley moved his club to San Francisco instead of Los Angeles, had Frank McCourt been 10% better at owning the team, had Clayton Kershaw blown out his shoulder in 2009, had the Red Sox signed Mookie Betts to an extension in 2018, had Friedman chosen law instead of banking 25 years ago, had Ohtani preferred cold weather, etc.

2. Luck In One's Circumstances

Had the Angels simply been good over the past six seasons, Ohtani might never have gone to free agency, might have re-signed with the Angels if he had hit the open market, or might not have so heavily prioritized winning in his ultimate choice. The Angels being constantly bad was

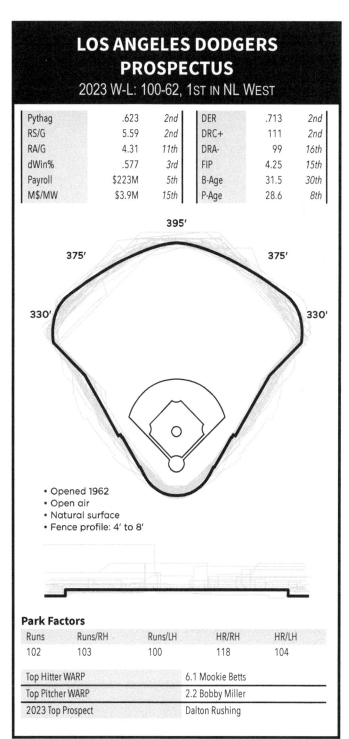

LOS ANGELES DODGERS PROSPECTUS
2023 W-L: 100-62, 1ST IN NL WEST

Pythag	.623	2nd	DER	.713	2nd
RS/G	5.59	2nd	DRC+	111	2nd
RA/G	4.31	11th	DRA-	99	16th
dWin%	.577	3rd	FIP	4.25	15th
Payroll	$223M	5th	B-Age	31.5	30th
M$/MW	$3.9M	15th	P-Age	28.6	8th

395'

375'   **375'**

330'   **330'**

- Opened 1962
- Open air
- Natural surface
- Fence profile: 4' to 8'

Park Factors

Runs	Runs/RH	Runs/LH	HR/RH	HR/LH
102	103	100	118	104

Top Hitter WARP	6.1 Mookie Betts
Top Pitcher WARP	2.2 Bobby Miller
2023 Top Prospect	Dalton Rushing

227

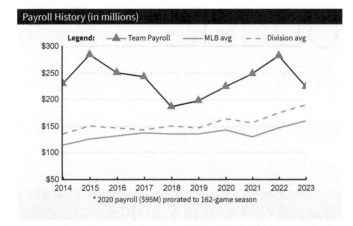

Payroll History (in millions)

Legend: ▲ Team Payroll — MLB avg - - - Division avg

*2020 payroll ($95M) prorated to 162-game season

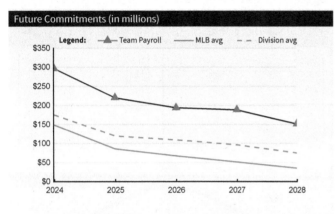

Future Commitments (in millions)

Legend: ▲ Team Payroll — MLB avg - - - Division avg

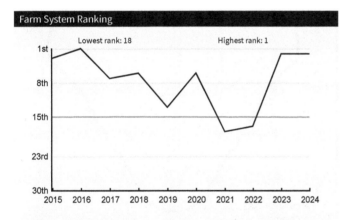

Farm System Ranking

Lowest rank: 18   Highest rank: 1

Personnel

President, Baseball Operations
Andrew Friedman

Executive Vice President & General Manager
Brandon Gomes

Senior Vice President, Baseball Operations
Josh Byrnes

Vice President & Assistant General Manager
Jeffrey Kingston

Vice President & Assistant General Manager
Alex Slater

Manager
Dave Roberts

outside the Dodgers' control, and not the obvious outcome of putting the world's two best players on the same team for six years, yet it was a prerequisite to Friedman having the opportunity to sign Ohtani this winter.

3. Luck In How One Is Determined By Antecedent Circumstances

It was to Friedman's great fortune that signing Ohtani was *so obviously right*. We are lucky when our best options are the ones that are easiest to choose—decisions that we don't resist, that aren't socially frowned upon, that don't challenge our identities and that aren't impossibly hard.

4. Luck In The Way One's Actions Turn Out

There's at least some possibility that Ohtani will bomb. If he doesn't—if he's the superstar we all expect him to be for at least several of the next 10 years, carrying the Dodgers to titles—then we'll forget that the alternative scenario of failure ever even existed.

The problem of moral luck is that it ends up affecting everything, from the circumstances of our birth to the flapping of unknown faraway butterflies to the uncertainty over whether humans even have free will at all. Nagel calls it a paradox. He says "the problem has no solution. Eventually nothing remains which can be ascribed to the responsible self, and we are left with nothing but a portion of the larger sequence of events, which can be deplored or celebrated, but not blamed or praised."

⚾   ⚾   ⚾

In the past three seasons, the Dodgers have won 317 games. That's more than any team has won in a three-year stretch since 1969-1971. For all that success, here's an example of the sort of beat-writer questions they faced at their post-postseason press conference last October:

"It does not sound like you feel significant changes need to be made to avoid a third consecutive organizational failure. Call me cynical—is this arrogance? How come you're not talking in terms of making significant changes?"

"Organizational failure" was actually Friedman's phrase, used first in 2022 and repeated in 2023 and perhaps just not thought of in time for the 2021 post-postseason conference. The Dodgers' last three playoff series have produced three of the six biggest upsets (by win differential) in MLB postseason history. Most recently, they failed to win a single game against the Diamondbacks, whose regular-season run differential last year was 222 runs worse than the Dodgers'. They failed to hold even a single *lead* against those Diamondbacks. They scored a total of six runs; the Diamondbacks scored seven runs before Dodgers pitching could get four outs.

The Dodgers, as a story-generating protagonist, are in a weird place: The first six months of their season generally have no suspense, while the last month (or less) of their season generally follows no reason. Because of this no-suspense/no-reason dynamic, these post-postseason press conferences are incredibly revealing. One of the most important things we can know about the Dodgers is how they view themselves. (As one reporter phrased it after the Diamondbacks series: "What story do you tell yourselves that makes this make sense?") How they view themselves tells us how they'll prepare for the future.

While Friedman does make statements in his post-postseason press conferences that suggest the accepting of responsibility—not just the "organizational failure" talk but also, of his own role, "I didn't do a good enough job"—one comes away suspecting he mostly thinks the Dodgers just got bad-lucked. Not necessarily bad-lucked in the obvious ways of, say, errant umpiring calls or horribly placed Bartmans, but in the several-levels-down types of luck suggested by Nagel.

Put them, let's say, in four baseball-specific categories:

1. The Luck Of Unrepresentative Outcomes

For example: In the 2023 NLDS, Clayton Kershaw allowed six runs without getting out of the first inning against the Diamondbacks, yes. But "*if we got to replay that inning* 100 times, I don't think that happens more than two or three times."

Likewise, Bobby Miller—the rookie who started that series' Game 2—failed to get out of the second inning, but again that was something like a mistake of probabilities. "I feel very strongly that Bobby Miller was ready for October. Obviously, he didn't pitch great in Game 2, but *had he pitched again* I would have bet on him." And Mookie Betts and Freddie Freeman went 1-for-21, and by Win Probability Added were the hitters most responsible for the club's loss, but that is just a glitch in logic: "Going into any postseason, Mookie and Freddie *would be* among the highest drafted."

So the Dodgers lost, but hypothetical versions of the Dodgers—versions arguably truer to their essential beings—would have won. It's basically: The only smart options were the ones we chose. Therefore, you can't blame us for choosing them, even if they went wrong.

2. The Luck of Bad Timing

On the 2022 loss: "In the regular season, we led baseball in every statistical category with runners in scoring position. And this series we were not. During the course of the season, we had peaks and valleys with runners in scoring position. This was a valley."

On 2023: "We scored over 900 runs for the first time in Los Angeles Dodgers history. It's the best offensive team we've had in this run. Obviously, there are three-game snippets throughout a year where our offense doesn't perform."

This accepts that performance has variance, and the variance is out of the players' control. Players can't make themselves better on a certain week. But, through bad luck, the playoffs can happen to fall on a week when they're all bad. "My point is how you define best team," Friedman says at one point. "I think it's about the hottest team. How much of that are things you can foresee in advance, as opposed to after the fact? I think that's a really important distinction."

3. The Luck Of 50/50 Outcomes

If you're presented with an almost impossible choice—a 55/45 choice—and you choose the 55, it's bad luck if the 45 comes up. If you're presented with a truly impossible choice—a 50/50 choice—that's already bad luck for you, because you can't really make any informed decision. Friedman, on manager Dave Roberts: "There are decisions that are 50/50 or 55/45, and if those moves would have worked out Dave would have gotten praise for them. Definitionally, if that's the case, which I genuinely believe, it's hard on the other side to be too critical. So many decisions like this don't have a clear right or wrong answer until after it plays out." (Needless to say from the premise of the question and answer, several of them have played out poorly for the Dodgers in recent postseasons.)

Similarly, when asked whether he needs to get more "postseason guys" who'll presumably elevate in October, he says the "noise and variance, year to year" is beyond human control. "We've had guys who've been incredible one year, not good the next. It's not just, 'Oh, he's a postseason player,' 'he's not.' We've seen it first hand. Look at Corey Seager's 2019 [awful], 2020 [transcendent], 2021 [awful]. It's just not that easy. If it was, I promise you, we would do that."

Friedman gave that answer before Seager carried the Rangers to the title and won the World Series MVP award, though those latter events arguably made his point stronger.

4. The Luck of It Being Luck-Based All The Way Down

This one means: Participating in a competitive field in which randomness is such a flattening variable is already a form of bad luck, at least for the "best" team. "If the vast majority of the time the best team always won the World Series and this time they did not, then it'd be easier to point fingers and isolate why," Friedman said. "I just don't see the view of the world of pointing fingers and firing someone for those reasons." If you're living in a shruggy world, you can't do much but shrug.

There's more I could add. He talks about specific batted-ball outcomes, his team hitting into hard outs and the other team getting low-probability homers. He muses, repeatedly, about whether there's "something there" or if it's "just baseball." The bulk of his answers suggest he feels a *lot* of it is "just baseball," out of his hands.

That's a lot of quotes, but they're important quotes, because the key thing to know about the Dodgers—a great team with a great farm system and the money and the will to keep it that way pretty much indefinitely—is whether they feel like they failed or were failed. They have reached a point where they can't really win more regular-season games than they already do. And they'll likely always be at a point where they can't control much of what happens in the postseason.

The question everybody wants answered is whether they feel the need to change—to fire Dave Roberts, or to sign different types of player, or to de-emphasize the regular season, or pursue austerity, or change their approach to starting pitching or young players or clubhouse guys, or something else. And the answer has seemed to be: No.

Friedman will acknowledge that what they've been doing has been unsuccessful. But he insists that it's been working, *to the extent he has any control.*

"Is the regular season just too different from the postseason," he's asked at one of these press conferences.

"No. It's longer."

⚾   ⚾   ⚾

So, a few months and roughly $1.2 billion spent since that post-postseason press conference, was signing Ohtani and Yoshinobu Yamamoto and trading for Tyler Glasnow significant change?

Narratives are rarely so tidy, so one could say yes or one could say no. I say no. The Dodgers, having previously committed to a fairly simple strategy predicated on winning the most possible regular-season games, continue to do that. They have neither blown past their previous efforts nor scaled them back nor pivoted unexpectedly.

To the degree there were specific criticisms after their latest postseason bow-out, they were:

The Dodgers choked in October, because maybe their players are not the right kind of postseason performers. Ohtani has (famously) no postseason experience, Yamamoto has no MLB experience at all and Glasnow's postseason ERA is 5.72. They're just all-the-time great players, that's all.

The Dodgers' playoff rotation was so compromised (by bad health, by inexperience and by being Lance Lynn) that they couldn't swagger into the postseason. Getting three potential aces could help. But the Dodgers clearly bet on upside over reliability with these moves, particularly looking at the length of each pitcher's contract.

The Dodgers don't have an "October" type of manager. Dave Roberts remains. And let me point this out: Since he took over as manager, the Dodgers have played 84 postseason games. Based on the regular-season winning percentages of the Dodgers and their opponents in those games, they "should" have won 45.6 postseason game. They have, in fact, won 45.

Let me also point this out: In the 2021 NLCS, they had a higher OBP and a higher SLG than Atlanta, so you could argue they outplayed the Braves. In the 2022 NLDS, they had a higher OBP and a higher SLG than San Diego, so you could argue they outplayed San Diego. They've played as well as they should have, by some standards—though, quoting Nagel once again, "everything we do belongs to a world that we have not created." You don't get to choose the standards by which you're judged, and those standards might also not be "fair."

Last year's series against Arizona was obviously a disaster on a whole new level, but you could also take that to just be proof that the range of baseball variance knows no limits. Anything can happen to anyone at any time. If it could happen to the Dodgers against the Diamondbacks, then it even could happen to...the Dodgers against the Diamondbacks.

But, okay, it's absolutely true that the Dodgers have failed three years in a row. They'll say it themselves. The irony is that all that failure—and the willingness to declare it failure—was a key part of their successful pitch to Ohtani.

"They said when they look back at the last 10 years, even though they made the playoffs every single year, one World Series ring, they consider that a failure," Ohtani said at his introductory press conference. "And when I heard that, I knew that they were all about winning, and that's exactly how I feel."

Which—if you believe Ohtani—would mean that the Dodgers would have been *less* likely to sign the world's best ballplayer if they'd won *more* World Series titles. How's that for a tradeoff? Check back in a few years, I guess, or ask your nearest philosopher.

—Sam Miller publishes the Pebble Hunting newsletter.

HITTERS

Mookie Betts **RF/2B** Born: 10/07/92 Age: 31 Bats: R Throws: R Height: 5'9" Weight: 180 Origin: Round 5, 2011 Draft (#172 overall)

YEAR	TM	LVL	AGE	PA	R	HR	RBI	SB	AVG/OBP/SLG	BABIP	SLGCON	BB%	K%	ZSw%	ZCon%	OSw%	OCon%	LA	90th EV	DRC+	BRR	DRP	WARP
2021	LAD	MLB	28	550	93	23	58	10	.264/.367/.487	.276	.597	12.4%	15.6%	65.4%	92.1%	24.8%	68.6%	19.0	103.3	125	0.3	-1.3	3.4
2022	LAD	MLB	29	639	117	35	82	12	.269/.340/.533	.272	.652	8.6%	16.3%	71.3%	93.0%	26.5%	66.8%	18.8	103.9	123	0.9	5.2	4.3
2023	LAD	MLB	30	693	126	39	107	14	.307/.408/.579	.316	.709	13.9%	15.4%	63.1%	92.5%	21.7%	66.9%	20.6	104.8	148	0.3	0.2	6.1
2024 DC	LAD	MLB	31	646	88	31	94	13	.270/.368/.493	.279	.591	11.9%	14.4%							138	0.3	0.9	5.1

2023 GP: RF (107), 2B (70), SS (16)   *Comps: Al Kaline (80), Hank Aaron (78), Frank Robinson (77)*

If ever there was a criticism of Betts' hitting prowess, it's that, when controlling for launch angle, he doesn't hit the ball all that hard. He's historically been much more akin to Kris Bryant than, say, Teoscar Hernández. That's perfectly reasonable, given his overall output, and especially so when contextualized with his 5-foot-9, 180-pound frame. And yet! Betts went ahead and had himself his best year at the plate since 2018, hitting, by far, the lowest percentage of ground balls of his career while posting his highest dynamic hard-hit percentage since 2020—and likely of his career, outside of 2018. Given the respective launch angle of his batted balls, Betts was *actually* hitting the ball hard in 2023, not just hitting balls at launch angles that are easier to hit hard. He did so by catching the ball out in front of the plate in order to maximize his ability to hit the ball to his pull-side, where it's easier to hit the ball hard, as well as drive it in the air—a sensible combination. Betts took a few years off (or, "off"), but in focusing on his power output, he's reasserted himself as one of the most talented hitters in MLB.

★ ★ ★ *2024 Top 101 Prospect* **#71** ★ ★ ★

Michael Busch **IF** Born: 11/09/97 Age: 26 Bats: L Throws: R Height: 6'1" Weight: 210 Origin: Round 1, 2019 Draft (#31 overall)

YEAR	TM	LVL	AGE	PA	R	HR	RBI	SB	AVG/OBP/SLG	BABIP	SLGCON	BB%	K%	ZSw%	ZCon%	OSw%	OCon%	LA	90th EV	DRC+	BRR	DRP	WARP
2021	TUL	AA	23	495	84	20	67	2	.267/.386/.484	.337	.707	14.1%	26.1%							112	0.4	7.2	3.0
2022	TUL	AA	24	137	31	11	29	1	.306/.445/.667	.355	1.000	17.5%	26.3%							127	0.1	-0.5	0.8
2022	OKC	AAA	24	504	87	21	79	3	.266/.343/.480	.327	.681	9.9%	26.0%	71.2%	79.3%	26.8%	60.8%			98	-2.4	-4.4	0.7
2023	OKC	AAA	25	469	85	27	90	4	.323/.431/.618	.356	.798	13.9%	18.8%	69.0%	87.6%	24.1%	62.3%			130	-3.7	7.1	2.9
2023	LAD	MLB	25	81	9	2	7	1	.167/.247/.292	.227	.467	9.9%	33.3%	69.7%	80.2%	32.4%	53.7%	5.5	105.3	76	0.0	-0.4	-0.1
2024 DC	*LAD*	*MLB*	*26*	*126*	*14*	*4*	*15*	*1*	*.228/.313/.410*	*.273*	*.561*	*9.8%*	*23.8%*							*101*	*0.0*	*-0.3*	*0.3*

2023 GP: 3B (13), DH (8), 1B (4), 2B (1), LF (1) *Comps: Chris Shaw (63), J.D. Davis (62), Josh Bell (60)*

There's not much (nothing) for Busch to prove at the minor-league level, which is good, given that he's 26. There's also not much to draw from in his 27 MLB games. He struggled defensively at third base, which wasn't exactly a surprise, and he also struggled to make contact as he got his feet wet against major-league pitchers. Busch ought to be afforded an acclimation period as he sees a higher level of pitching, but if we look past the elevated swinging-strike percentage and ground-ball rate, his batted ball numbers indicate that he's already exhibiting the ability to impact the ball. It just won't show up as game power, per se, until he converts that contact from ground balls and high flies to more standard fly balls and line drives.

Diego Cartaya **C** Born: 09/07/01 Age: 22 Bats: R Throws: R Height: 6'3" Weight: 219 Origin: IFA, 2018

YEAR	TM	LVL	AGE	PA	R	HR	RBI	SB	AVG/OBP/SLG	BABIP	SLGCON	BB%	K%	ZSw%	ZCon%	OSw%	OCon%	LA	90th EV	DRC+	BRR	DRP	WARP
2021	RC	A	19	137	31	10	31	0	.298/.409/.614	.353	.909	13.1%	27.0%							119	0.5	-4.0	0.4
2022	RC	A	20	163	31	9	31	0	.260/.405/.550	.321	.828	14.1%	27.0%							118	0.1	-1.2	0.8
2022	GL	A+	20	282	43	13	41	1	.251/.379/.476	.310	.705	14.2%	26.6%							109	0.6	-3.2	0.9
2023	TUL	AA	21	403	51	19	57	0	.189/.278/.379	.216	.565	9.2%	29.0%							94	0.6	-10.8	-0.2
2024 non	*LAD*	*MLB*	*22*	*251*	*25*	*7*	*26*	*0*	*.217/.291/.357*	*.306*	*.559*	*7.8%*	*32.6%*							*83*	*0.0*	*0*	*0.4*

2023 GP: C (68), DH (28) *Comps: Jacob Nottingham (56), Jorge Alfaro (51), Francisco Mejía (51)*

Just one year removed from ranking number one in our Dodgers prospect ranking, Cartaya has been supplanted by not one but *two* catchers. He's dropped all the way to number nine, which is partially because he was very bad, and partially because the Dodgers have a very strong system. In fairness to Cartaya, he was about three years young for the level, so it's hard to completely fault him for the aggressive assignment, and at the level where his particular profile often gets a wakeup call. He'll get plenty of chances to settle into Double-A, but regardless, we wouldn't sweat his 2023 struggles yet. The power is there, and defensively he can probably catch every day. The swing-and-miss in his game is just a bigger issue than previously thought.

YEAR	TM	P. COUNT	FRM RUNS	BLK RUNS	THRW RUNS	TOT RUNS
2021	RC	4422	-3.7	-1.0	1.0	-3.8
2022	RC	3762	-1.4	-0.9	1.0	-1.2
2022	GL	6178	-2.6	-1.2	0.8	-3.0
2023	TUL	9954	-9.6	-0.8	-1.2	-11.6
2024	*LAD*	*6956*	*-3.9*	*-0.9*	*-0.1*	*-4.9*

★ ★ ★ *2024 Top 101 Prospect* **#48** ★ ★ ★

Josue De Paula **RF** Born: 05/24/05 Age: 19 Bats: L Throws: L Height: 6'3" Weight: 185 Origin: Undrafted Free Agent, 2022

YEAR	TM	LVL	AGE	PA	R	HR	RBI	SB	AVG/OBP/SLG	BABIP	SLGCON	BB%	K%	ZSw%	ZCon%	OSw%	OCon%	LA	90th EV	DRC+	BRR	DRP	WARP
2022	DSL LADB	ROK	17	223	42	5	30	16	.349/.448/.522	.395	.626	14.3%	13.9%										
2023	RC	A	18	340	55	2	40	14	.284/.396/.372	.353	.475	13.5%	17.9%							109	0.2	-3.2	1.2
2024 non	*LAD*	*MLB*	*19*	*251*	*19*	*1*	*18*	*0*	*.206/.276/.282*	*.276*	*.389*	*7.8%*	*24.6%*							*59*	*0.0*	*0*	*-0.7*

2023 GP: RF (65), CF (6), DH (3) *Comps: Danry Vasquez (73), Jack Suwinski (71), Ramón Flores (68)*

It's never really a compliment to say that a ballplayer's on-base percentage outpaced their slugging percentage, and this isn't the exception, although it comes as close as it gets. De Paula, who accomplished the dubious feat at Low-A, frequently receives comparisons and projections that will make you blush. Aside from the robust power projection, we love the traits he's flashing, making great swing decisions as a result of strong pitch recognition at just 18 years of age. His anemic .089 isolated slugging percentage will surely grow, as he already boasts exit velocities you'd expect from older players, and he's only going to continue to fill out. He's vaulted himself from unlisted to the second spot on our Dodgers' top prospects list, currently projecting as an everyday corner outfielder with a sky-high ceiling.

Freddie Freeman **1B** Born: 09/12/89 Age: 34 Bats: L Throws: R Height: 6'5" Weight: 220 Origin: Round 2, 2007 Draft (#78 overall)

YEAR	TM	LVL	AGE	PA	R	HR	RBI	SB	AVG/OBP/SLG	BABIP	SLGCON	BB%	K%	ZSw%	ZCon%	OSw%	OCon%	LA	90th EV	DRC+	BRR	DRP	WARP
2021	ATL	MLB	31	695	120	31	83	8	.300/.393/.503	.321	.613	12.2%	15.4%	79.3%	84.1%	30.9%	69.8%	12.2	105.5	146	0.4	0.8	5.7
2022	LAD	MLB	32	708	117	21	100	13	.325/.407/.511	.359	.614	11.9%	14.4%	75.7%	85.5%	30.6%	71.8%	13.8	104.5	152	-0.2	0.9	6.0
2023	LAD	MLB	33	730	131	29	102	23	.331/.410/.567	.370	.700	9.9%	16.6%	78.4%	85.8%	30.6%	67.7%	15.4	105.2	139	0.6	-0.4	5.1
2024 DC	*LAD*	*MLB*	*34*	*661*	*80*	*20*	*82*	*11*	*.287/.371/.460*	*.320*	*.559*	*10.6%*	*15.8%*							*134*	*0.2*	*1*	*4.3*

2023 GP: 1B (161) *Comps: Keith Hernandez (79), Eddie Murray (78), Boog Powell (76)*

What is there to say other than that, in his age-33 season, Freeman continues to rake near career-best levels, aging so gracefully because he's equipped with one of the best swings in the world. By vertical bat angle (VBA), there are only three steeper swings in MLB. VBA is by no means without flaws, but it *is* correlated with what Freeman does well: When he puts the ball in play, it disproportionately lands for a hit. That's because his swing allows him to make consistent, flush contact at optimal launch angles, evidenced by his possession of one of the lowest mishit percentages In MLB, and one of the tightest standard deviations of launch angles. These traits allow him to consistently run BABIPs well above .300 over his career, which should allow him to avoid falling off a cliff as he ages. And if his year wasn't already good enough at the plate, he took advantage of the new rules, swiping 23 bags to nearly double his career-high.

Enrique Hernández SS   Born: 08/24/91   Age: 32   Bats: R   Throws: R   Height: 5'11"   Weight: 195   Origin: Round 6, 2009 Draft (#191 overall)

YEAR	TM	LVL	AGE	PA	R	HR	RBI	SB	AVG/OBP/SLG	BABIP	SLGCON	BB%	K%	ZSw%	ZCon%	OSw%	OCon%	LA	90th EV	DRC+	BRR	DRP	WARP
2021	BOS	MLB	29	585	84	20	60	1	.250/.337/.449	.278	.573	10.4%	18.8%	68.1%	88.1%	30.4%	60.6%	18.4	104.2	113	0.1	-4.4	2.9
2022	BOS	MLB	30	402	48	6	45	0	.222/.291/.338	.257	.421	8.5%	17.7%	71.6%	89.1%	33.5%	58.1%	17.1	103.7	94	0.0	-3.9	0.7
2023	LAD	MLB	31	185	19	5	30	1	.262/.308/.423	.283	.511	6.5%	15.7%	69.9%	88.2%	35.2%	69.8%	17.3	102.8	127	-0.1	-1.7	1.0
2023	BOS	MLB	31	323	38	6	31	3	.222/.279/.320	.267	.415	6.8%	21.1%	66.9%	84.5%	30.9%	58.4%	17.1	101.7	100	-0.2	-4.4	0.6
2024 DC	LAD	MLB	32	443	42	10	45	2	.232/.299/.360	.272	.458	7.7%	19.4%							86	0.0	-5.6	0.1

2023 GP: SS (74), 2B (36), CF (23), 3B (12), LF (11), 1B (10), RF (4)   Comps: Mickey Stanley (59), Paul Blair (57), Vernon Wells (56)

It was the second straight injury-plagued year for Hernández, who underwent a double hernia surgery less than two weeks after his last game of the season. By some standards, he was one of the worst hitters in MLB, whereas if you consult DRC+, he was an above-average hitter. The answer is probably somewhere in the middle. Hernández clearly hasn't been quite right the past few years, as he's watched his exit velocity numbers fall along with his hard-hit metrics, though it's worth noting that his max and 90th-percentile exit velos ticked up upon donning Dodgers blue (at the expense of his strikeout and walk rates). At this point, the odds are stacked against him—he's not getting any younger, and he's long been a liability against right-handed pitching—but there's a version of Hernández that can adequately play seven defensive positions while contributing positively with his bat. And that's nothing to say of his beneficial presence in the clubhouse.

Teoscar Hernández RF   Born: 10/15/92   Age: 31   Bats: R   Throws: R   Height: 6'2"   Weight: 215   Origin: IFA, 2011

YEAR	TM	LVL	AGE	PA	R	HR	RBI	SB	AVG/OBP/SLG	BABIP	SLGCON	BB%	K%	ZSw%	ZCon%	OSw%	OCon%	LA	90th EV	DRC+	BRR	DRP	WARP
2021	TOR	MLB	28	595	92	32	116	12	.296/.346/.524	.352	.716	6.1%	24.9%	77.7%	80.5%	34.5%	49.5%	13.4	107.8	124	0.5	2.4	4.0
2022	TOR	MLB	29	535	71	25	77	6	.267/.316/.491	.335	.706	6.4%	28.4%	72.0%	77.3%	33.0%	46.3%	11.8	107.9	99	0.1	3.0	1.8
2023	SEA	MLB	30	678	70	26	93	7	.258/.305/.435	.342	.657	5.6%	31.1%	74.7%	76.3%	39.1%	47.9%	12.6	107.3	98	-0.1	1.8	1.6
2024 DC	LAD	MLB	31	513	60	23	69	5	.246/.302/.440	.319	.649	6.2%	30.1%							101	-0.1	0.3	1.5

2023 GP: RF (135), DH (28)   Comps: Dan Ford (71), Sammy Sosa (70), Gary Matthews (70)

Landing in Seattle via trade entering his platform year was an especially tough bounce for Hernández on multiple fronts. Not only did he carry the burden as the Mariners' lone—albeit lackluster—major off-season offensive addition, he was also tasked with delivering such expected power production in the unfriendly confines of T-Mobile Park, with free agency looming all the while. Though he still hit the ball hard consistently, the mental and physical challenge of trying to slug in Seattle seemed to exacerbate Hernández aggressive approach for the worse. The splits were stark, in both process and results: .276 wOBA, .315 xwOBA at home, .353 wOBA, .354 xwOBA on the road. Factoring elite durability and a step forward with the glove in right field, it was still a largely respectable season for Hernández on the whole, just not the one for which he—or Seattle—had hoped.

Jason Heyward OF   Born: 08/09/89   Age: 34   Bats: L   Throws: L   Height: 6'5"   Weight: 240   Origin: Round 1, 2007 Draft (#14 overall)

YEAR	TM	LVL	AGE	PA	R	HR	RBI	SB	AVG/OBP/SLG	BABIP	SLGCON	BB%	K%	ZSw%	ZCon%	OSw%	OCon%	LA	90th EV	DRC+	BRR	DRP	WARP
2021	CHC	MLB	31	353	35	8	30	5	.214/.280/.347	.247	.439	7.6%	19.3%	62.1%	89.8%	32.8%	57.6%	7.6	105.4	89	0.1	-0.4	0.5
2022	CHC	MLB	32	151	15	1	10	1	.204/.278/.277	.260	.362	7.3%	21.2%	65.9%	78.9%	35.6%	63.6%	13.0	106.2	85	0.1	-0.6	0.2
2023	LAD	MLB	33	377	56	15	40	2	.269/.340/.473	.291	.585	9.0%	17.0%	66.1%	88.0%	33.0%	66.5%	15.5	104.0	110	-0.1	-0.4	1.5
2024 DC	LAD	MLB	34	391	40	10	42	3	.244/.320/.386	.278	.481	9.2%	17.6%							99	-0.1	-1.6	0.8

2023 GP: RF (90), CF (23), LF (7), 1B (6), DH (6)   Comps: Ruben Sierra (62), Harry Hooper (61), Rusty Staub (60)

In perhaps the least surprising development of the year, the Dodgers signed Heyward to a minor-league contract and he had his best year by DRC+ in a decade. It's hardly the first time the veteran has retooled his swing, but certainly one of few times it's yielded such significant results. By lowering his hands and reducing his hand movement, he was able to make more consistent contact and stave off the nagging ground-ball habit that's plagued him throughout his career. In particular, pitchers were unable to get fastballs past Heyward, as he cut down his whiff rate and posted the highest slugging percentage against fastballs of his career by 79 points. LA rewarded him handsomely for his comeback, ensuring he'll be back to serve as the strong side of their right-field platoon at least one more year.

───────────── ★ ★ ★ *2024 Top 101 Prospect* **#70** ★ ★ ★ ─────────────

Thayron Liranzo C/DH   Born: 07/05/03   Age: 21   Bats: S   Throws: R   Height: 6'3"   Weight: 195   Origin: IFA, 2021

YEAR	TM	LVL	AGE	PA	R	HR	RBI	SB	AVG/OBP/SLG	BABIP	SLGCON	BB%	K%	ZSw%	ZCon%	OSw%	OCon%	LA	90th EV	DRC+	BRR	DRP	WARP
2021	DSL SHO	ROK	17	85	11	1	9	3	.250/.393/.353	.340	.500	16.5%	23.5%									0.0	
2022	DOD	ROK	18	171	23	8	30	0	.236/.339/.486	.276	.679	12.3%	24.6%										
2023	RC	A	19	418	81	24	70	2	.272/.400/.562	.335	.833	16.7%	26.8%							145	1.1	-0.5	3.5
2024 non	LAD	MLB	20	251	24	5	25	0	.224/.300/.356	.348	.596	9.2%	36.0%							86	0.0	0	0.4

2023 GP: C (53), DH (29), 1B (14)   Comps: Diego Cartaya (86), Wil Myers (81), Gary Sánchez (80)

YEAR	TM	P. COUNT	FRM RUNS	BLK RUNS	THRW RUNS	TOT RUNS
2022	DOD	1386			0.0	0.0
2023	RC	7813	-1.8	-0.9	0.7	-2.1
2024	LAD	6956	-1.9	-0.5	0.2	-2.3

In perhaps our most aggressive ranking in the Dodgers' system, we have Liranzo as their fourth-ranked prospect. (And yes, that makes three catchers in the Dodgers' top 10 prospects.) Liranzo's numbers are eerily similar to Diego Cartaya's in Low-A, although Liranzo has the added challenge of being a switch-hitter on top of being 20 years old and still learning how to catch. His gaudy numbers are supported by elite exit velocities, which is to say that his output was well deserved. His contact skills could get exposed as he faces more quality pitching at higher levels, but Liranzo has extraordinary offensive potential for a catcher. We should learn a lot about the Dodgers' confidence in his defensive chops this year based on how often he plays at other positions.

Gavin Lux   SS   Born: 11/23/97   Age: 26   Bats: L   Throws: R   Height: 6'2"   Weight: 190   Origin: Round 1, 2016 Draft (#20 overall)

YEAR	TM	LVL	AGE	PA	R	HR	RBI	SB	AVG/OBP/SLG	BABIP	SLGCON	BB%	K%	ZSw%	ZCon%	OSw%	OCon%	LA	90th EV	DRC+	BRR	DRP	WARP
2021	OKC	AAA	23	74	18	1	10	0	.279/.338/.382	.346	.491	8.1%	20.3%							92	1.0	3.1	0.5
2021	LAD	MLB	23	381	49	7	46	4	.242/.328/.364	.300	.484	10.8%	21.8%	71.2%	87.4%	27.9%	56.6%	11.3	105.0	85	0.5	1.6	0.9
2022	LAD	MLB	24	471	66	6	42	7	.276/.346/.399	.341	.515	10.0%	20.2%	64.9%	85.0%	25.8%	61.0%	7.2	102.7	107	0.5	-0.3	1.9
2024 DC	LAD	MLB	26	476	46	8	46	10	.240/.318/.362	.293	.470	9.7%	20.3%							93	0.5	3.9	1.7

Comps: Asdrúbal Cabrera (53), Ketel Marte (53), Luis Sardinas (53)

Here's the thing about those sleepy spring training games: You never know when you're going to see someone ruin their life. Lux was running from second to third on a routine ground ball to the third baseman, and when he ducked mid-stride to avoid the throw, he blew out his knee, ending his season. Reports on his recovery were encouraging, which is fortunate, because the second baseman will be a shortstop when he gets back to work, thanks to the permanent relocation of Mookie Betts. Switching positions always puts more strain on the bat, and given that his expected numbers are still lagging behind his actual numbers—especially in the power department—Lux appears set up for a challenging 2024 campaign.

Manuel Margot   OF   Born: 09/28/94   Age: 29   Bats: R   Throws: R   Height: 5'11"   Weight: 180   Origin: IFA, 2011

YEAR	TM	LVL	AGE	PA	R	HR	RBI	SB	AVG/OBP/SLG	BABIP	SLGCON	BB%	K%	ZSw%	ZCon%	OSw%	OCon%	LA	90th EV	DRC+	BRR	DRP	WARP
2021	TB	MLB	26	464	55	10	57	13	.254/.313/.382	.281	.459	8.0%	15.1%	72.9%	87.3%	35.7%	69.2%	10.3	104.6	110	0.4	4.9	2.7
2022	TB	MLB	27	363	36	4	47	7	.274/.325/.375	.332	.470	6.6%	18.7%	75.4%	85.5%	37.4%	61.6%	9.1	105.2	103	0.3	1.4	1.4
2023	TB	MLB	28	336	39	4	38	9	.264/.310/.376	.306	.457	5.4%	16.4%	71.0%	85.0%	34.8%	61.7%	10.1	104.8	110	0.6	0.6	1.6
2024 DC	LAD	MLB	29	336	32	5	32	7	.258/.316/.368	.307	.456	7.1%	18.0%							94	0.1	0.8	0.8

2023 GP: CF (55), RF (43)   *Comps: Mike Hershberger (68), Gary Sutherland (60), Jose Cardenal (60)*

Remember last year when we wondered why the Rays would guarantee around $20 million dollars for a platoon outfielder? The best we could come up with was they must have had plans for him to do more in 2023. Well, Margot did pretty much the same thing he did a season ago … just not as well. He's a decent hitter that does not strike out a ton, but also does not walk much. He has below-average pop and is not a weapon on the bases. He missed a lot of time in 2022 with a knee injury, and seemingly lost a step in the outfield where his defensive metrics took a turn for the worse … then also missed time late in 2023 after a minor elbow procedure. He is still guaranteed $12 million, which is why he found himself as ballast for the Tyler Glasnow trade and likely out of a starting role.

Max Muncy   3B   Born: 08/25/90   Age: 33   Bats: L   Throws: R   Height: 6'0"   Weight: 215   Origin: Round 5, 2012 Draft (#169 overall)

YEAR	TM	LVL	AGE	PA	R	HR	RBI	SB	AVG/OBP/SLG	BABIP	SLGCON	BB%	K%	ZSw%	ZCon%	OSw%	OCon%	LA	90th EV	DRC+	BRR	DRP	WARP
2021	LAD	MLB	30	592	95	36	94	2	.249/.368/.527	.257	.695	14.0%	20.3%	61.1%	85.4%	20.6%	57.9%	15.4	106.8	143	-0.3	0.4	4.8
2022	LAD	MLB	31	565	69	21	69	2	.196/.329/.384	.227	.551	15.9%	25.0%	60.7%	80.8%	20.5%	57.2%	21.1	104.6	101	-0.1	-1.9	1.3
2023	LAD	MLB	32	579	95	36	105	1	.212/.333/.475	.221	.696	14.7%	26.4%	60.2%	80.4%	24.2%	52.6%	21.8	105.5	112	-0.1	-1.4	2.5
2024 DC	LAD	MLB	33	554	70	25	74	1	.219/.341/.427	.261	.619	14.4%	26.2%							116	-0.2	-2.8	2.3

2023 GP: 3B (124), DH (10)   *Comps: Mike Hegan (57), Chris Davis (57), Carlos Pena (56)*

If you thought 2022 was the beginning of his offensive descent…well…we'll see! Muncy returned to something closer to his previous production, ranking in the 59th percentile in wOBA, but 87th percentile in xwOBA. He may have lost his ability to be one of the top fastball demolishers—and his eye seems to have become significantly less discerning, or more desperate—but Muncy has maintained his ability to hit the slower stuff better than the majority of the league. Perhaps it's age-related, or maybe an intentional shift in approach—the Dodgers love these type of guys—but Muncy has quietly begun to become even more of an extreme fly ball and pull hitter than he's ever been. Over the past two years, he ranks in the 99th and 97th percentiles in those areas, respectively. The Dodgers are apparently still confident that he'll age relatively gracefully, as they awarded him a two-year, $24 million contract, which they probably ought to be, given that his dynamic hard-hit percentage indicates that he still possesses the ability to hit the ball hard as consistently as almost anyone.

Shohei Ohtani   RHP/DH   Born: 07/05/94   Age: 30   Bats: L   Throws: R   Height: 6'4"   Weight: 210   Origin: IFA, 2017

YEAR	TM	LVL	AGE	PA	R	HR	RBI	SB	AVG/OBP/SLG	BABIP	SLGCON	BB%	K%	ZSw%	ZCon%	OSw%	OCon%	LA	90th EV	DRC+	BRR	DRP	WARP
2021	LAA	MLB	26	639	103	46	100	26	.257/.372/.592	.303	.914	15.0%	29.6%	71.4%	75.8%	31.2%	50.5%	16.6	110.7	155	0.6	0.0	7.2
2022	LAA	MLB	27	666	90	34	95	11	.273/.356/.519	.320	.715	10.8%	24.2%	74.3%	79.4%	32.7%	60.5%	12.1	108.1	148	-0.2	0.0	5.3
2023	LAA	MLB	28	599	102	44	95	20	.304/.412/.654	.342	.918	15.2%	23.9%	71.6%	78.4%	34.1%	54.3%	13.3	111.0	165	0.8	0.0	5.9
2024 DC	LAD	MLB	29	624	93	38	105	17	.267/.374/.549	.319	.792	13.8%	26.4%							153	0.5	0	5.6

2023 GP: DH (134), P (23)   *Comps: Reggie Jefferson (77), Boog Powell (76), Kent Hrbek (76)*

YEAR	TM	LVL	AGE	G (GS)	IP	W-L	SV	K	WHIP	ERA	CSP	BB%	K%	HR%	GB%	ZSw%	ZCon%	OSw%	OCon%	BABIP	SLGCON	DRA-	WARP
2021	LAA	MLB	26	23 (23)	130¹	9-2	0	156	1.09	3.18	56.3%	8.3%	29.3%	2.8%	44.9%	69.8%	81.1%	30.3%	52.5%	.271	.524	78	2.8
2022	LAA	MLB	27	28 (28)	166	15-9	0	219	1.01	2.33	55.8%	6.7%	33.2%	2.1%	41.9%	69.6%	79.8%	32.0%	44.2%	.289	.494	64	4.7
2023	LAA	MLB	28	23 (23)	132	10-5	0	167	1.06	3.14	49.7%	10.4%	31.5%	3.4%	45.8%	67.2%	80.8%	29.8%	48.3%	.240	.520	81	2.9

2023 Arsenal: SW (83.9), FA (97), FC (89.9), SI (94.2), FS (88.1), SL (84.5), CU (75.4)

We're standing at the edge of a precipice now, anticipating a new era without fully understanding what that era entails. What does a world in which Ohtani is no longer an Angel look like? What will be done to finally, finally get him into the playoffs? In a sense, the buildup to this season is more exciting than when Ohtani originally signed in 2018—in the words of Boobie Miles in *Friday Night Lights*, "hype is something that's not for real. I'm all real."

Ohtani is indeed all real. Yes, there's been considerable pain associated with injury and the general malaise of putting up with the Angels, but in his tenure we saw some of the most soaring, euphoric highs the sport has had to offer in the last century; to be honest, Angels fans were pretty spoiled. Some of the nuance was undoubtedly lost on us—you can only see so many "firsts" before they start to blur. Those firsts are a well of possibility that seems never to run dry, but what has run out is the Angels' time, along with their wistful promises that each year would be different, just trust them. Ohtani's patience ran out too, the desire to live up to his true potential outweighing the inaction and indecision on the Angels' part. The final kick in the pants: Arte Moreno reportedly had the option to match the Dodgers' best and final offer, and declined.

Every team was waiting impatiently for Ohtani's contract to be up from the moment he signed it. His move into LA (actually, not just in name) is a turning point that could determine the landscape of baseball for years to come. Ohtani is likely to continue being Ohtani, but everything else will change.

James Outman CF Born: 05/14/97 Age: 27 Bats: L Throws: R Height: 6'3" Weight: 215 Origin: Round 7, 2018 Draft (#224 overall)

YEAR	TM	LVL	AGE	PA	R	HR	RBI	SB	AVG/OBP/SLG	BABIP	SLGCON	BB%	K%	ZSw%	ZCon%	OSw%	OCon%	LA	90th EV	DRC+	BRR	DRP	WARP
2021	GDD	WIN	24	83	17	3	11	2	.284/.422/.552	.390	.841	18.1%	27.7%	80.0%	75.0%	36.4%	12.5%						
2021	GL	A+	24	304	50	9	30	21	.250/.385/.472	.349	.731	14.8%	28.9%							120	1.4	-4.9	1.4
2021	TUL	AA	24	187	40	9	24	2	.289/.369/.518	.368	.748	9.6%	27.3%							98	0.7	1.5	0.8
2022	TUL	AA	25	307	59	16	45	7	.295/.394/.552	.386	.837	12.4%	29.0%							107	0.6	0.8	1.4
2022	OKC	AAA	25	252	42	15	61	6	.292/.390/.627	.343	.893	12.7%	25.0%	73.3%	80.6%	23.8%	46.8%			112	-2.4	2.7	1.2
2022	LAD	MLB	25	16	6	1	3	0	.462/.563/.846	1.000	1.833	12.5%	43.8%	70.4%	84.2%	33.3%	25.0%	16.5	109.5	55	0.0	0.0	0.0
2023	LAD	MLB	26	567	86	23	70	16	.248/.353/.437	.343	.699	12.0%	31.9%	71.4%	75.5%	27.7%	41.3%	16.0	105.0	84	1.1	3.2	1.4
2024 DC	*LAD*	*MLB*	*27*	*480*	*53*	*16*	*57*	*9*	*.219/.319/.401*	*.313*	*.646*	*10.6%*	*33.3%*							*101*	*0.3*	*1.5*	*1.9*

2023 GP: CF (135), LF (17), RF (6), DH (3)   *Comps: Aaron Altherr (56), Chris Duncan (55), Keon Broxton (54)*

Outman picked up right where he left off with his shot of espresso in 2022, hitting a home run in his first game of the season and tacking on two multi-home run games before April was over, and while an early summer slump sent his swing back to the drawing board, the resulting adjustments led to improved contact, as well as improved baserunning and defense in center field. If there are any existing question marks in his profile, it's the swing-and-miss in Outman's game—his strikeout and whiff rates are among the highest of qualified hitters—without the gaudy exit velocity numbers that usually accompany them. And while it's true that Outman doesn't post Ohtanian exit velocities, he shares two tricks with teammate Mookie Betts to make the most of the power he does have: He pulls fly balls and line drives more than almost anyone, and he avoids mishits. In other words, he's optimized his batted balls both horizontally and vertically. This thing could veer either way—and the late-season skid has our recency bias heightened—but there's a lot to build on here.

Andy Pages OF Born: 12/08/00 Age: 23 Bats: R Throws: R Height: 6'1" Weight: 212 Origin: IFA, 2018

YEAR	TM	LVL	AGE	PA	R	HR	RBI	SB	AVG/OBP/SLG	BABIP	SLGCON	BB%	K%	ZSw%	ZCon%	OSw%	OCon%	LA	90th EV	DRC+	BRR	DRP	WARP
2021	GL	A+	20	538	96	31	88	6	.265/.394/.539	.305	.771	14.3%	24.5%							139	1.4	-0.7	4.3
2022	TUL	AA	21	571	69	26	80	6	.236/.336/.468	.271	.657	10.9%	24.5%							97	1.6	7.3	2.7
2023	TUL	AA	22	142	23	3	25	7	.284/.430/.495	.364	.701	17.6%	22.5%							103	1.8	3.0	1.0
2024 DC	*LAD*	*MLB*	*23*	*64*	*7*	*2*	*7*	*1*	*.227/.318/.377*	*.288*	*.512*	*10.0%*	*24.9%*							*96*	*0.0*	*0*	*0.2*

2023 GP: CF (15), RF (12), LF (5), DH (2)   *Comps: Willy García (63), Aaron Cunningham (63), Ryan Kalish (61)*

Yet another extreme fly-ball hitter in the Dodgers' system, Pages has a steep swing that's geared to lift balls to his pull side, which he does enthusiastically. He's had success at every level of the minor leagues, and notably has limited strikeouts despite a healthy amount of swing-and-miss in his game. He had surgery for a torn labrum in his shoulder in June, after just one Triple-A game, but should be set to return at full-go come spring training. He's currently blocked, a reason why most folks heard about him first as part of some hypothetical trade, but there are several avenues to major-league playing time for him in 2024.

David Peralta LF Born: 08/14/87 Age: 36 Bats: L Throws: L Height: 6'1" Weight: 210 Origin: IFA, 2005

YEAR	TM	LVL	AGE	PA	R	HR	RBI	SB	AVG/OBP/SLG	BABIP	SLGCON	BB%	K%	ZSw%	ZCon%	OSw%	OCon%	LA	90th EV	DRC+	BRR	DRP	WARP
2021	AZ	MLB	33	538	57	8	63	2	.259/.325/.402	.303	.496	8.6%	17.1%	68.1%	88.3%	31.3%	64.4%	5.1	106.8	98	0.0	2.5	2.1
2022	TB	MLB	34	180	10	0	18	0	.255/.317/.335	.331	.446	7.8%	22.2%	71.6%	87.7%	35.8%	63.0%	13.1	104.0	78	0.0	-0.3	0.0
2022	AZ	MLB	34	310	29	12	41	1	.248/.316/.460	.292	.627	8.7%	23.9%	70.2%	84.9%	37.2%	55.1%	16.5	106.8	101	0.0	-0.8	0.9
2023	LAD	MLB	35	422	47	7	55	4	.259/.294/.381	.296	.466	4.7%	17.1%	75.6%	86.4%	38.1%	63.7%	8.1	105.1	101	0.0	-1.1	1.1
2024 DC	*LAD*	*MLB*	*36*	*341*	*32*	*6*	*34*	*2*	*.254/.309/.381*	*.303*	*.478*	*6.8%*	*19.1%*							*94*	*-0.1*	*-1.2*	*0.5*

2023 GP: LF (118), RF (12), DH (6)   *Comps: Charlie Jamieson (79), Jerry Lynch (75), Ken Griffey (75)*

Between average numbers at the plate and middling defense in the outfield, Peralta might be the most forgettable longtime veteran in the sport. As the Dodgers did their patented roster-juggling, waiting for Jason Heyward to go back to hitting like Jason Heyward, Peralta found himself in the strong side of a platoon in left. That went fine until the All-Star Break, at which point he hurt his elbow. Stars can pull that sort of thing off; guys like Peralta really can't, and he slumped to a .578 OPS in the second half before acquiescing to flexor tendon surgery. He's on a timetable to return to baseball shape next summer, if anyone remembers him by then.

Miguel Rojas SS Born: 02/24/89 Age: 35 Bats: R Throws: R Height: 6'0" Weight: 188 Origin: IFA, 2005

YEAR	TM	LVL	AGE	PA	R	HR	RBI	SB	AVG/OBP/SLG	BABIP	SLGCON	BB%	K%	ZSw%	ZCon%	OSw%	OCon%	LA	90th EV	DRC+	BRR	DRP	WARP
2021	MIA	MLB	32	539	66	9	48	13	.265/.322/.392	.295	.461	6.9%	13.7%	66.8%	91.4%	30.3%	63.6%	11.3	101.6	100	0.1	-1.2	1.8
2022	MIA	MLB	33	507	34	6	36	9	.236/.283/.323	.258	.371	5.1%	12.0%	66.8%	94.9%	33.7%	69.2%	10.0	101.3	101	0.1	0.0	1.7
2023	LAD	MLB	34	423	49	5	31	8	.236/.290/.322	.255	.368	6.1%	11.3%	69.0%	92.4%	35.3%	70.7%	10.6	101.4	105	0.1	7.3	2.5
2024 DC	LAD	MLB	35	95	9	2	9	2	.251/.308/.357	.276	.408	6.6%	12.4%							89	-0.1	0.8	0.3

2023 GP: SS (121), P (3), 2B (1), 3B (1), DH (1)   Comps: Rey Sanchez (68), Alfredo Griffin (67), Ozzie Smith (67)

It's got to be quite the jumpscare to have Trea Turner start 160 games at shortstop and then watch him walk away from your favorite team just to watch Rojas play the bulk of those games in his place. In fairness, that wasn't quite the plan—Gavin Lux, who was going to get lots of reps at shortstop, injured himself running the basepaths during spring training. And in even more fairness, Rojas filled his role admirably, having some tough luck with the bat, but playing consistent, dependable defense. Lux is set to return to an everyday role at shortstop, which will allow Rojas to serve in more of a natural bench role.

─────────── ★ ★ ★ *2024 Top 101 Prospect* **#36** ★ ★ ★ ───────────

Dalton Rushing C Born: 02/21/01 Age: 23 Bats: L Throws: R Height: 6'1" Weight: 220 Origin: Round 2, 2022 Draft (#40 overall)

YEAR	TM	LVL	AGE	PA	R	HR	RBI	SB	AVG/OBP/SLG	BABIP	SLGCON	BB%	K%	ZSw%	ZCon%	OSw%	OCon%	LA	90th EV	DRC+	BRR	DRP	WARP
2022	RC	A	21	128	27	8	30	1	.424/.539/.778	.472	.987	16.4%	16.4%							134	0.5	0.3	1.0
2023	GL	A+	22	381	55	15	53	1	.228/.404/.452	.276	.665	18.9%	24.4%							132	0.8	0.6	2.2
2024 non	LAD	MLB	23	251	25	5	24	0	.225/.326/.354	.299	.503	11.6%	26.0%							96	0.0	0	0.7

2023 GP: C (46), 1B (23), DH (19)   Comps: Julian Leon (71), Tony Sanchez (66), John Hicks (64)

YEAR	TM	P. COUNT	FRM RUNS	BLK RUNS	THRW RUNS	TOT RUNS
2022	RC	2546	1.1	-0.5	0.2	0.8
2023	GL	6156	1.8	-0.2	0.0	1.6
2024	LAD	6956	-0.1	-0.6	0.1	-0.6

We have Rushing as the top-ranked prospect in the Dodgers' system, which has him looking like a steal at the top of the second round. The catcher continued to rake after being promoted from Low- to High-A, with the only hiccups being a bump in strikeout percentage and a significant reduction in batting average. He was hit by a backswing on June 14th, and to that point had been slashing .265/.436/.503, so between an injury to point to and a profile incongruent from his results, a concussion and another fielding injury are as good an explanation as any. Rushing is trending upwards defensively and will likely be good enough to stick behind the dish. At this point, the big question might be whether or not he can stay healthy there.

Will Smith C Born: 03/28/95 Age: 29 Bats: R Throws: R Height: 5'10" Weight: 195 Origin: Round 1, 2016 Draft (#32 overall)

YEAR	TM	LVL	AGE	PA	R	HR	RBI	SB	AVG/OBP/SLG	BABIP	SLGCON	BB%	K%	ZSw%	ZCon%	OSw%	OCon%	LA	90th EV	DRC+	BRR	DRP	WARP
2021	LAD	MLB	26	501	71	25	76	3	.258/.365/.495	.274	.655	11.6%	20.2%	63.1%	85.9%	27.4%	67.6%	19.7	103.7	115	-0.4	4.2	3.5
2022	LAD	MLB	27	578	68	24	87	1	.260/.343/.465	.276	.573	9.7%	16.6%	65.4%	84.7%	27.3%	73.7%	18.7	104.0	132	-1.0	3.0	4.5
2023	LAD	MLB	28	554	80	19	76	3	.261/.359/.438	.277	.541	11.4%	16.1%	68.4%	84.5%	32.1%	75.7%	15.9	103.5	122	-0.6	0.2	3.5
2024 DC	LAD	MLB	29	499	62	18	64	1	.256/.355/.437	.278	.537	10.8%	16.1%							122	-0.5	0.3	3.2

2023 GP: C (111), DH (14)   Comps: Willson Contreras (65), Victor Martinez (64), Welington Castillo (64)

YEAR	TM	P. COUNT	FRM RUNS	BLK RUNS	THRW RUNS	TOT RUNS
2021	LAD	16176	6.2	0.0	0.1	6.3
2022	LAD	15036	5.9	0.0	-0.6	5.3
2023	LAD	15394	1.5	0.0	0.2	1.8
2024	LAD	15632	0.2	0.3	-0.2	0.3

After starting the season with three home runs in the first five games, Smith suffered a concussion that landed him on the injured list for over two weeks. Upon his return, he was promptly greeted with a pitch in the ribs. He struggled mightily down the stretch, no doubt due to the cumulative effects of multiple significant injuries throughout the season, as well as his particular trade. His exit velocities dropped, and he put the ball on the ground at a career-high rate, but by season's end still mustered a more-than-respectable 121 DRC+. Make no mistake, though, Smith remains a top-five catcher. He might not hit the ball at particularly high exit velocities—even when healthy—but he does consistently hit the ball hard, and at optimal launch angles. That catching, though, will wear a man down. Given how many prospects the Dodgers have at the position, before long the team might start thinking about how Smith could hit unburdened.

Chris Taylor UT Born: 08/29/90 Age: 33 Bats: R Throws: R Height: 6'1" Weight: 196 Origin: Round 5, 2012 Draft (#161 overall)

YEAR	TM	LVL	AGE	PA	R	HR	RBI	SB	AVG/OBP/SLG	BABIP	SLGCON	BB%	K%	ZSw%	ZCon%	OSw%	OCon%	LA	90th EV	DRC+	BRR	DRP	WARP
2021	LAD	MLB	30	582	92	20	73	13	.254/.344/.438	.337	.653	10.8%	28.7%	72.4%	77.0%	25.8%	47.3%	16.9	104.5	96	0.2	-0.2	1.9
2022	LAD	MLB	31	454	45	10	43	10	.221/.304/.373	.336	.620	9.7%	35.2%	77.8%	70.9%	28.0%	36.7%	20.4	103.5	68	0.2	-0.3	-0.3
2023	LAD	MLB	32	384	51	15	56	16	.237/.326/.420	.327	.667	10.7%	32.6%	74.0%	73.3%	27.5%	45.7%	21.6	104.6	84	0.6	0.7	0.5
2024 DC	LAD	MLB	33	328	34	10	36	10	.216/.304/.369	.307	.581	10.0%	32.6%							87	0.3	-0.7	0.4

2023 GP: LF (57), SS (31), 3B (28), DH (7), CF (5), 2B (3)   Comps: Billy Rogell (59), Jeffrey Leonard (58), Justin Upton (56)

For the better part of his career, Taylor has been one of the best in the league at putting the ball into play at optimal launch angles. From 2017 to 2021, he ranked in the 87th and 89th percentile in mishit and sweet-spot percentage, respectively. Although Taylor has maintained a high sweet spot percentage, his mishit percentage has begun to climb over the past two years, from 58.8% to 62.6%, indicating that the batted balls that he's lifting haven't been hit hard enough, too often turning into high fly outs and pop outs. It's also two straight years where Taylor has posted a strikeout rate over 30%, which doesn't bode well for a hitting profile already in decline.

Joendry Vargas SS Born: 11/08/05 Age: 18 Bats: R Throws: R Height: 6'4" Weight: 175 Origin: IFA, 2023

YEAR	TM	LVL	AGE	PA	R	HR	RBI	SB	AVG/OBP/SLG	BABIP	SLGCON	BB%	K%	ZSw%	ZCon%	OSw%	OCon%	LA	90th EV	DRC+	BRR	DRP	WARP
2023	DSL LADB	ROK	17	208	47	7	31	19	.328/.423/.529	.360	.643	14.4%	14.9%										
2024									No projection														

2023 GP: SS (28), DH (10), 3B (8), 2B (1)

One of the top prospects in the 2023 international class, Vargas has one of the highest ceilings in the organization. Dominican Summer League stats can be all-but-ignored, but since they're what we have, it's nice to see them align with our reports. (We have him ranked just outside of our Dodgers top 10.) Vargas has already exhibited a sound approach, power to all fields, and slick hands in the field. There's plenty of risk that he'll have to move off of shortstop as he adds to his frame, but he would project well as a third baseman and, in general, has the potential to be a five-tool player.

Miguel Vargas 3B/OF Born: 11/17/99 Age: 24 Bats: R Throws: R Height: 6'3" Weight: 205 Origin: IFA, 2017

YEAR	TM	LVL	AGE	PA	R	HR	RBI	SB	AVG/OBP/SLG	BABIP	SLGCON	BB%	K%	ZSw%	ZCon%	OSw%	OCon%	LA	90th EV	DRC+	BRR	DRP	WARP
2021	GL	A+	21	172	31	7	16	4	.314/.366/.532	.353	.669	5.2%	18.6%							121	-1.1	-2.5	0.6
2021	TUL	AA	21	370	67	16	60	7	.321/.386/.523	.344	.633	9.7%	15.4%							125	1.0	-1.3	2.2
2022	OKC	AAA	22	520	100	17	82	16	.304/.404/.511	.331	.619	13.7%	14.6%	73.2%	83.3%	24.6%	70.1%			120	1.4	-3.8	2.7
2022	LAD	MLB	22	50	4	1	8	1	.170/.200/.255	.206	.353	4.0%	26.0%	67.7%	76.1%	35.0%	75.0%	25.5	102.2	82	0.0	0.0	0.0
2023	OKC	AAA	23	285	45	10	43	8	.288/.407/.479	.341	.631	16.1%	20.0%	67.2%	82.1%	19.3%	72.8%			107	1.6	-2.7	0.6
2023	LAD	MLB	23	304	36	7	32	3	.195/.305/.367	.224	.482	12.5%	20.1%	71.0%	83.1%	22.7%	63.3%	16.7	102.4	95	-0.1	-0.9	0.6
2024 DC	LAD	MLB	24	130	14	3	14	2	.234/.324/.379	.271	.484	10.4%	18.4%							99	0.1	-0.1	0.3

2023 GP: 2B (78), 1B (5), DH (1)　　　　　　　　　　　　　　　　　*Comps: Jon Singleton (54), Aaron Cunningham (53), Christian Arroyo (53)*

Vargas has a lot of great traits. He has an exceptionally discerning eye—he played through a broken hand in spring training by sitting the bat on his shoulder, and carried that patience into the regular season—and he's historically made a lot of contact. Perhaps because of his feel for the strike zone, pitchers threw him fastballs 64.1% of the time, which means he saw more of them than 98% of hitters. There's also that he doesn't impact the ball particularly well, so pitchers might feel more comfortable piping a heater to him than, say, Jarred Kelenic. Vargas' primary issue right now as a hitter is that he's getting under the ball too often for a hitter that doesn't have plus raw power, which effectively results in automatic outs. The broken hand didn't magically improve his glove at second, sadly, which is perhaps why the Dodgers have stated they plan to use him in the outfield more.

PITCHERS

Yency Almonte RHP Born: 06/04/94 Age: 30 Height: 6'5" Weight: 223 Origin: Round 17, 2012 Draft (#537 overall)

YEAR	TM	LVL	AGE	G (GS)	IP	W-L	SV	K	WHIP	ERA	CSP	BB%	K%	HR%	GB%	ZSw%	ZCon%	OSw%	OCon%	BABIP	SLGCON	DRA-	WARP
2021	COL	MLB	27	48 (0)	47²	1-3	0	47	1.59	7.55	50.9%	13.4%	21.7%	4.1%	42.3%	68.0%	87.6%	29.5%	56.0%	.297	.642	122	-0.1
2022	OKC	AAA	28	14 (0)	18	0-1	3	28	0.83	4.00		1.4%	40.6%	4.3%	66.7%	55.1%	77.6%	39.9%	38.5%	.306	.641	61	0.5
2022	LAD	MLB	28	33 (0)	35¹	0-0	1	33	0.79	1.02	50.8%	7.4%	24.4%	1.5%	50.0%	63.8%	81.4%	34.3%	48.5%	.186	.322	86	0.6
2023	LAD	MLB	29	49 (0)	48	3-2	0	49	1.40	5.06	44.7%	11.5%	23.6%	2.9%	42.7%	62.7%	82.6%	30.6%	53.0%	.296	.511	95	0.7
2024 DC	LAD	MLB	30	49 (0)	52¹	4-2	3	54	1.28	4.14	47.5%	9.2%	24.2%	3.1%	44.5%					.287	.534	93	0.4

2023 Arsenal: SW (83), SI (95.9), FA (96.2), CH (89.6), FC (92.8)　　　　　*Comps: Evan Marshall (64), Matt Bowman (64), Luke Jackson (62)*

Unsustainable peripherals be damned, Almonte posted a 1.02 ERA over 35 ⅓ innings in 2022. You have to be doing something right to even luck into that, perhaps a devastating sweeper that ranked in the 78th percentile in strike percentage. Something happened in 2023 in which his ERA ballooned to nearly five times his 2022 total. Whatever the root cause, it's clear that it affected his sweeper, which dropped all the way to the 26th percentile. Our hunch is that his issues are release-based: He released the ball higher and closer to first base, with a slightly higher expected movement direction, indicating that he'd tinkered with his arm slot. The result is a sweeper with more spin efficiency than he'd had over the past several years, and pitches that, overall, had more generic shapes. Sometimes it's better to be lucky than average. Most of the time, really.

Walker Buehler RHP Born: 07/28/94 Age: 29 Height: 6'2" Weight: 185 Origin: Round 1, 2015 Draft (#24 overall)

YEAR	TM	LVL	AGE	G (GS)	IP	W-L	SV	K	WHIP	ERA	CSP	BB%	K%	HR%	GB%	ZSw%	ZCon%	OSw%	OCon%	BABIP	SLGCON	DRA-	WARP
2021	LAD	MLB	26	33 (33)	207²	16-4	0	212	0.97	2.47	55.3%	6.4%	26.0%	2.3%	44.0%	68.5%	84.4%	34.1%	57.1%	.250	.460	76	4.6
2022	LAD	MLB	27	12 (12)	65	6-3	0	58	1.29	4.02	52.8%	6.2%	21.2%	2.9%	47.7%	72.0%	86.6%	34.5%	58.9%	.312	.533	94	0.8
2024 DC	LAD	MLB	29	24 (24)	136	10-6	0	136	1.28	4.16	53.5%	7.4%	23.6%	3.2%	44.0%					.303	.556	94	1.6

2023 Arsenal: FA (94.1), FC (87.7), SI (92.8), CU (76.4), SL (83.4)　　　*Comps: Jim Palmer (91), Roger Clemens (90), Félix Hernández (89)*

The last we saw of Buehler was a highly diminished version of the pitcher he'd been for half a decade, with his K% dipping below league-average, and an ERA above it for the first time in his career. We theorized that his downfall could be attributed to the regression of his idiosyncratic mechanics, which allow him to leverage his slender frame to rotate his trunk efficiently and get to his over-the-top arm slot. This regression has resulted in a significant drop in his fastball's spin rate-to-velocity ratio, and its actual and expected movement direction veering more towards a generic fastball shape. For a pitcher whose fastball has disproportionately been his primary offering, this has rendered him half of the pitcher he was: bad fastball and solid secondaries, rather than elite fastball and solid secondaries. If his momentary reappearance in September is any indication—and given it's two innings' worth, it might not be—Buehler might have taken a positive step in terms of fastball shape, but he'll need his old fastball velocity to truly return to form.

Nabil Crismatt RHP Born: 12/25/94   Age: 29   Height: 6'1"   Weight: 220   Origin: IFA, 2011

YEAR	TM	LVL	AGE	G (GS)	IP	W-L	SV	K	WHIP	ERA	CSP	BB%	K%	HR%	GB%	ZSw%	ZCon%	OSw%	OCon%	BABIP	SLGCON	DRA-	WARP
2021	SD	MLB	26	45(0)	81¹	3-1	0	71	1.36	3.76	52.8%	6.8%	20.2%	2.8%	50.8%	66.6%	85.8%	34.9%	60.8%	.326	.541	87	1.3
2022	SD	MLB	27	50(1)	67¹	5-2	0	65	1.17	2.94	53.6%	7.9%	23.2%	1.8%	49.7%	64.9%	83.5%	36.2%	61.9%	.280	.487	86	1.1
2023	RNO	AAA	28	14(9)	47¹	4-3	0	44	1.63	6.85		8.3%	20.4%	4.6%	36.6%	67.9%	82.7%	34.6%	58.5%	.343	.682	98	0.1
2023	SD	MLB	28	7(0)	11	0-1	0	9	2.18	9.82	43.2%	12.3%	15.8%	5.3%	52.5%	59.2%	88.9%	35.5%	53.7%	.378	.700	97	0.1
2023	AZ	MLB	28	1(0)	2	0-1	0	3	1.00	0.00	40.7%	0.0%	37.5%	0.0%	40.0%	69.2%	55.6%	23.8%	40.0%	.400	.600	95	0.0
2024 non	LAD	MLB	29	58(0)	50	2-2	0	43	1.37	4.57	51.7%	8.1%	19.8%	2.8%	47.9%					.304	.526	102	0.2

2023 Arsenal: CH (81.8), CU (73.4), FA (88.8), SI (88.7), SL (84.5)   Comps: Tyler Duffey (47), Esmil Rogers (47), Tyler Thornburg (47)

All of us have bad days. Some of us have bad weeks, or months. Then there are the unfortunate few who experience an entire down year, which then takes additional years to recover from. In 2023, Crismatt had one of the most miserable years by a pitcher in recent memory. His command completely evaporated, as if he forgot how to pitch. After building up a 9.82 ERA, the Padres designated him for assignment. The D-Backs then signed Crismatt to a minor-league contract, but the easier level of competition made no difference. For some reason, Crismatt was no longer the pitcher he used to be. He made a single big league appearance in August, then slithered back down into the depths of Triple-A. His prior run of success in Triple-A lends confidence in his ability to rebound, as does his landing with the Dodgers on a minor league deal.

Caleb Ferguson LHP Born: 07/02/96   Age: 28   Height: 6'3"   Weight: 226   Origin: Round 38, 2014 Draft (#1149 overall)

YEAR	TM	LVL	AGE	G (GS)	IP	W-L	SV	K	WHIP	ERA	CSP	BB%	K%	HR%	GB%	ZSw%	ZCon%	OSw%	OCon%	BABIP	SLGCON	DRA-	WARP
2022	OKC	AAA	25	10(2)	7¹	0-1	0	13	1.91	7.36		10.8%	35.1%	2.7%	42.1%	66.7%	82.0%	27.7%	30.4%	.500	.842	76	0.1
2022	LAD	MLB	25	37(1)	34²	1-0	0	37	1.15	1.82	55.9%	12.0%	26.1%	0.7%	41.9%	70.1%	78.1%	27.9%	62.9%	.259	.395	100	0.3
2023	LAD	MLB	26	68(7)	60¹	7-4	3	70	1.44	3.43	50.5%	8.5%	25.9%	1.5%	47.9%	68.4%	84.1%	32.4%	55.1%	.364	.518	85	1.2
2024 DC	LAD	MLB	27	49(0)	52¹	4-2	5	58	1.28	4.00	51.9%	9.6%	26.0%	2.8%	45.1%					.296	.532	89	0.5

2023 Arsenal: FA (95.9), SL (86.7), SW (80.2)   Comps: Arodys Vizcaíno (56), Eric O'Flaherty (55), Kelvin Herrera (54)

Consider Ferguson cured of his home run problem, posting a home run-to-fly ball rate below 10% for the second consecutive year after averaging 20% his first three years in the league. After having success with his slow, steep slider in 2022, Ferguson moved towards a firmer, more gyro-heavy shape. The change, in general, was a positive one, but Ferguson saw some fastball regression, perhaps due to a higher arm angle, and thus steeper fastball shape. Like all relievers, and particularly Dodgers relievers, the overall line obscures hills and valleys, and he allowed his fair share of inherited runners to score. Ferguson and L.A. both wanted him to earn saves and free up Evan Phillips for a fireman role, but he couldn't justify the switch—his ERA in the eighth was 0.82, and in the ninth, it was 8.59. Fortunately, you only really have to be perfect when you're the closer; the set-up guy can just settle for being good.

★ ★ ★ *2024 Top 101 Prospect* **#67** ★ ★ ★

Nick Frasso RHP Born: 10/18/98   Age: 25   Height: 6'5"   Weight: 200   Origin: Round 4, 2020 Draft (#106 overall)

YEAR	TM	LVL	AGE	G (GS)	IP	W-L	SV	K	WHIP	ERA	CSP	BB%	K%	HR%	GB%	ZSw%	ZCon%	OSw%	OCon%	BABIP	SLGCON	DRA-	WARP
2021	DUN	A	22	3(2)	5	0-0	0	8	1.00	0.00		9.5%	38.1%	0.0%	45.5%	55.0%	63.6%	24.1%	57.1%	.273	.364	96	0.1
2022	DUN	A	23	7(7)	25²	0-0	0	42	0.82	0.70		8.2%	42.9%	0.0%	40.4%	67.6%	77.2%	40.3%	25.3%	.277	.362	75	0.7
2022	VAN	A+	23	3(3)	11	0-0	0	15	0.45	0.82		5.1%	38.5%	2.6%	40.9%					.095	.273	91	0.2
2022	TUL	AA	23	4(4)	11²	0-0	0	10	1.63	5.40		13.0%	18.5%	1.9%	35.1%					.306	.528	116	-0.1
2023	TUL	AA	24	21(21)	73²	3-4	0	94	1.25	3.91		7.6%	29.8%	1.3%	42.1%					.344	.529	80	1.7
2023	OKC	AAA	24	4(4)	19¹	1-2	0	13	1.34	3.26		8.3%	15.5%	0.0%	39.3%	65.5%	88.4%	27.7%	59.6%	.311	.393	100	
2024 DC	LAD	MLB	25	12(3)	26	2-1	0	25	1.35	4.54		8.9%	22.3%	3.1%	37.1%					.300	.545	101	0.2

2023 Arsenal: FA (93.7), SL (86.1), CH (83.4)   Comps: Yoanys Quiala (65), Joel Payamps (64), Sugar Ray Marimon (63)

Frasso is a headache for hitters. He uses his large frame to get down the mound toward the middle of the third base line and fire across his body, creating a unique angle to the plate. That adds deception to a running fastball that touches 100 and can create up to 20 inches of induced vertical break. His fastball alone would make him an effective reliever, but he's also crafting a changeup and slider that will help him avoid being limited to the bullpen. He tossed five or more innings in three of his last four starts, which is encouraging for someone only a couple years removed from Tommy John. His role won't come down to talent, but whether he can go two to three times through the lineup without getting tagged.

Tyler Glasnow RHP Born: 08/23/93   Age: 30   Height: 6'8"   Weight: 225   Origin: Round 5, 2011 Draft (#152 overall)

YEAR	TM	LVL	AGE	G (GS)	IP	W-L	SV	K	WHIP	ERA	CSP	BB%	K%	HR%	GB%	ZSw%	ZCon%	OSw%	OCon%	BABIP	SLGCON	DRA-	WARP
2021	TB	MLB	27	14(14)	88	5-2	0	123	0.93	2.66	61.2%	7.9%	36.2%	2.9%	45.3%	68.5%	78.4%	33.0%	37.1%	.250	.526	68	2.3
2022	TB	MLB	28	2(2)	6²	0-0	0	10	0.90	1.35	55.4%	7.7%	38.5%	3.8%	35.7%	63.4%	88.5%	37.0%	48.1%	.231	.500	88	0.1
2023	TB	MLB	29	21(21)	120	10-7	0	162	1.08	3.53	48.5%	7.6%	33.4%	2.7%	50.9%	67.6%	80.5%	33.6%	40.2%	.294	.546	72	3.2
2024 DC	LAD	MLB	30	24(24)	138¹	11-4	0	189	1.10	2.81	51.5%	8.4%	33.8%	2.9%	48.5%					.292	.551	69	3.5

2023 Arsenal: FA (96.5), SL (90.3), CU (84), CH (92.2)   Comps: Justin Verlander (75), Bob Gibson (75), Jim Bunning (75)

After missing most of the 2022 season recovering from Tommy John surgery and then the start of 2023 with an unrelated oblique injury, the Rays were happy to get 21 really good starts out of their ace. At full strength, Glasnow is one of the best pitchers in baseball. Since 2021, he has registered 295 strikeouts in 214 ⅔ innings, and he has allowed just around one baserunner per frame over the same period. Of course, 200-something innings in three years is not ideal, but the 120 he tossed last season were a career high. The stuff remains filthy, led by an upper-90s fastball, but last year he opted for more 90-mph sliders and showed a renewed interest in his changeup. His pitches are fast coming in and relatively fast coming back, but he has kept the ball in the yard and more than half the batted balls against him stayed on the ground. His $25 million price tag made him too rich for the Rays to keep, but his new team has no qualms about adding him to their collection of extremely expensive pitchers who carry significant injury risk.

Tony Gonsolin RHP Born: 05/14/94 Age: 30 Height: 6'3" Weight: 205 Origin: Round 9, 2016 Draft (#281 overall)

YEAR	TM	LVL	AGE	G (GS)	IP	W-L	SV	K	WHIP	ERA	CSP	BB%	K%	HR%	GB%	ZSw%	ZCon%	OSw%	OCon%	BABIP	SLGCON	DRA-	WARP
2021	OKC	AAA	27	3(3)	10¹	0-0	0	9	0.87	3.48		7.5%	22.5%	5.0%	35.7%					.154	.536	106	0.0
2021	LAD	MLB	27	15(13)	55²	4-1	0	65	1.35	3.23	53.6%	14.2%	27.2%	3.3%	36.4%	69.3%	82.8%	28.8%	51.7%	.254	.543	105	0.3
2022	LAD	MLB	28	24(24)	130¹	16-1	0	119	0.87	2.14	57.2%	7.0%	23.9%	2.2%	42.9%	69.1%	84.6%	34.8%	55.6%	.207	.404	89	2.0
2023	LAD	MLB	29	20(20)	103	8-5	0	82	1.22	4.98	46.0%	9.2%	18.9%	4.4%	35.6%	71.9%	89.2%	34.8%	64.2%	.235	.528	128	-0.3
2024 non	LAD	MLB	30	58(0)	50	2-2	0	45	1.34	4.53	51.3%	9.0%	21.1%	3.6%	38.0%					.287	.554	101	0.2

2023 Arsenal: FA (92.6), FS (83.1), SL (86.8), KC (81) *Comps: Chris Bassitt (58), Mike Clevinger (58), Zack Godley (55)*

Say what you will about Gonsolin, but if there's one thing he's always done, it's coax hitters into putting balls into play that consistently find their way into gloves. That wasn't the case this past year. His career xwOBA of .336 ballooned to .414 in 2023, indicating that he'd regressed from an above-average contact suppressor to a below-average one. The cause is likely a drop in arm slot—okay, the real cause is the UCL tear that Gonsolin pitched through, based on the heartening news that "he couldn't make it any worse"—that pushed him toward a far more generic fastball shape than in previous years, and at lower velocities. He's always been a pitcher that succeeds in spite of his fastball, not because of it, so his slider regression in particular is what inevitably made him a replacement-level pitcher.

Brusdar Graterol RHP Born: 08/26/98 Age: 25 Height: 6'1" Weight: 265 Origin: IFA, 2014

YEAR	TM	LVL	AGE	G (GS)	IP	W-L	SV	K	WHIP	ERA	CSP	BB%	K%	HR%	GB%	ZSw%	ZCon%	OSw%	OCon%	BABIP	SLGCON	DRA-	WARP
2021	OKC	AAA	22	17(0)	16²	2-2	1	20	1.02	6.48		7.2%	29.0%	1.4%	73.8%					.268	.381	83	0.3
2021	LAD	MLB	22	34(1)	33¹	3-0	0	27	1.41	4.59	60.3%	8.7%	18.0%	1.3%	57.7%	69.2%	88.5%	33.1%	65.1%	.314	.490	96	0.4
2022	LAD	MLB	23	46(1)	49²	2-4	4	43	0.99	3.26	57.9%	5.1%	21.8%	1.5%	63.8%	75.4%	82.7%	39.7%	72.1%	.261	.420	74	1.2
2023	LAD	MLB	24	68(1)	67¹	4-2	7	48	0.97	1.20	50.5%	4.7%	18.7%	1.2%	64.4%	68.1%	90.8%	35.2%	71.4%	.262	.370	78	1.6
2024 DC	LAD	MLB	25	49(0)	52¹	4-3	13	36	1.28	3.81	54.5%	6.9%	16.1%	1.8%	60.9%					.289	.438	87	0.6

2023 Arsenal: SI (98.7), SL (88.6), FC (95.7), FA (98.6), SW (88.1) *Comps: Roberto Osuna (63), Caleb Ferguson (62), Arodys Vizcaíno (60)*

Layperson or expert, most anyone who watches Graterol will comment about how he barely extends towards the plate when he pitches—and it's true! He looks like he's tossing batting practice. At 5.7 feet, he ranks in second percentile among all qualified pitchers in release extension, which is a supposed death knell for the modern pitcher. You want the ball as close to the plate as you can when you let it go, so the batter has the least time to see it. Graterol represents an example of pitching not being cookie cutter. His lack of extension allows him to throw from a higher point in space, providing him a steeper release to complement his arm slot and fastball shapes. He might not generate the strikeouts that were expected of him as a projected frontline starter, but consider 2023 yet another feather in Graterol's cap as he weaponizes his sinker to get hitters to pound baseballs into the ground.

Michael Grove RHP Born: 12/18/96 Age: 27 Height: 6'3" Weight: 200 Origin: Round 2, 2018 Draft (#68 overall)

YEAR	TM	LVL	AGE	G (GS)	IP	W-L	SV	K	WHIP	ERA	CSP	BB%	K%	HR%	GB%	ZSw%	ZCon%	OSw%	OCon%	BABIP	SLGCON	DRA-	WARP
2021	TUL	AA	24	21(19)	71	1-4	0	88	1.79	7.86		12.4%	26.0%	5.6%	34.8%					.351	.766	93	0.7
2022	TUL	AA	25	5(5)	16¹	0-1	0	22	0.98	2.76		7.5%	32.8%	1.5%	45.0%					.256	.513	69	0.4
2022	OKC	AAA	25	14(12)	59²	1-4	0	68	1.29	4.07		8.2%	26.7%	3.9%	40.0%	70.0%	86.1%	36.4%	57.1%	.297	.654	87	0.8
2022	LAD	MLB	25	7(6)	29¹	1-0	0	24	1.43	4.60	58.4%	7.5%	18.0%	4.5%	40.4%	71.4%	88.3%	34.2%	60.9%	.280	.576	106	0.2
2023	OKC	AAA	26	5(2)	13¹	0-0	0	22	0.90	2.70		1.9%	41.5%	3.8%	30.0%	63.5%	83.3%	41.2%	23.4%	.321	.633	74	0.1
2023	LAD	MLB	26	18(12)	69	2-3	0	73	1.48	6.13	49.2%	6.3%	24.2%	4.0%	39.6%	67.3%	86.2%	36.3%	54.8%	.364	.676	94	0.9
2024 DC	LAD	MLB	27	39(13)	86	5-4	0	83	1.35	4.71	51.4%	8.3%	22.4%	3.9%	38.8%					.300	.591	105	0.5

2023 Arsenal: SL (85.7), FA (94.9), CS (78.3), FC (89.2), CH (87.3), SI (93.6) *Comps: Randy Dobnak (71), Nick Martinez (69), Chase De Jong (68)*

Grove throws from an over-the-top arm slot and uses his steep release to try and complement the vertical approach angle of his fastball by throwing it lower in the zone than most pitchers. This might help his slider play up—hitters chase his slider over 40% of the time—but his fastball ranks in the second percentile in in-zone swing-and-miss percentage and gets barreled up frequently. Grove would benefit from elevating his four-seamer and folding in a one- or two-seam variety, which would further steepen his fastball's approach angle to better complement his slider's shape. Speaking of his slider, the only one that misses more bats than Grove's is Spencer Strider's, so regardless of what he does with his fastball, he ought to make his slider even more of a primary weapon than he did in 2023. He introduced a new cutter to even out his splits against lefties, but he actually had worse results because both his cutter and fastball were so dreadful against them. He'll need to perform some significant tweaking if he wants to start.

Kyle Hurt RHP Born: 05/30/98 Age: 26 Height: 6'3" Weight: 240 Origin: Round 5, 2020 Draft (#134 overall)

YEAR	TM	LVL	AGE	G (GS)	IP	W-L	SV	K	WHIP	ERA	CSP	BB%	K%	HR%	GB%	ZSw%	ZCon%	OSw%	OCon%	BABIP	SLGCON	DRA-	WARP
2021	RC	A	23	8(1)	16¹	1-2	1	28	1.35	5.51		13.9%	38.9%	1.4%	43.8%					.355	.531	83	0.3
2022	GL	A+	24	13(11)	40²	4-2	0	64	1.06	2.21		13.4%	39.0%	0.6%	50.0%					.267	.360	85	0.7
2022	TUL	AA	24	12(8)	31	1-5	0	45	2.32	9.29		21.9%	26.6%	1.8%	43.4%					.405	.613	114	-0.1
2023	TUL	AA	25	19(15)	65	2-3	0	110	1.28	4.15		11.8%	39.4%	2.5%	43.9%					.344	.679	62	2.0
2023	OKC	AAA	25	7(1)	27	2-1	0	42	1.11	3.33		10.1%	38.5%	2.8%	52.7%	64.4%	68.8%	34.8%	41.5%	.308	.593	58	
2023	LAD	MLB	25	1(0)	2	0-0	0	3	0.00	0.00	47.7%	0.0%	50.0%	0.0%	66.7%	70.0%	57.1%	50.0%	57.1%	.000	.000	87	0.0
2024 DC	LAD	MLB	26	12(3)	26	2-1	0	35	1.37	4.32	47.7%	13.5%	30.8%	3.3%	40.8%					.291	.587	95	0.3

2023 Arsenal: FA (95.5), CH (87.3), SL (84.2) *Comps: Josh James (41), Sean Poppen (41), Collin McHugh (41)*

Hurt is fascinating. At 1,878 rpm, he creates less raw spin with his fastball than almost anyone in baseball, which translates to a relatively generic shape. Much like Kevin Gausman, though, his ability to create splitter-like depth on his changeup allows his fastball to play up big time—it has a 15.8% swinging-strike rate at the minor-league level and it appears this will translate to the major leagues as well. A bad fastball isn't a bad fastball if hitters don't find out until it's too late—just ask Rich Hill. His changeup missed a staggering 31.9% of bats, clearing the path for Hurt to generate the second-highest K-BB% in MiLB in 2023, at 27.8%. He's got a curveball and slider too, but we won't talk about them until he tries throwing them regularly.

Hyun-Seok Jang   RHP   Born: 03/14/04   Age: 20   Height: 6'4"   Weight: 200   Origin: IFA, 2023

Projected to go first overall in the KBO draft, Jang elected to forego the exercise and sign with the Dodgers for $900,000. At just 19 years old, Jang's fastball sits around 94 mph with carry and has reportedly topped out at 97-98. His mid-80s slider appears to be his most developed secondary offering, and he has a curveball in the upper-70s that, while likely to be used as more of a get-me-over pitch to steal strikes rather than to get hitters to chase, gets huge depth. His low-80s changeup is reportedly the laggard of his repertoire, but again, he's a teenager. Between feel for supination and fastball velocity and shape that is already passable at the major-league level, Jang has a great foundation to work with, although we shouldn't expect to see him for several years.

Joe Kelly   RHP   Born: 06/09/88   Age: 36   Height: 6'1"   Weight: 174   Origin: Round 3, 2009 Draft (#98 overall)

YEAR	TM	LVL	AGE	G (GS)	IP	W-L	SV	K	WHIP	ERA	CSP	BB%	K%	HR%	GB%	ZSw%	ZCon%	OSw%	OCon%	BABIP	SLGCON	DRA-	WARP
2021	LAD	MLB	33	48(0)	44	2-0	2	50	0.98	2.86	55.8%	8.2%	27.5%	1.6%	58.4%	57.5%	86.4%	30.0%	50.8%	.227	.414	77	1.0
2022	CHW	MLB	34	43(1)	37	1-3	1	53	1.59	6.08	49.8%	13.5%	31.2%	1.2%	65.9%	55.7%	83.0%	32.7%	49.7%	.382	.567	78	0.8
2023	CHW	MLB	35	31(0)	29	1-5	1	41	1.31	4.97	46.7%	9.4%	32.0%	2.3%	56.2%	57.8%	86.8%	35.3%	50.4%	.329	.630	72	0.8
2023	LAD	MLB	35	11(0)	10¹	1-0	0	19	0.87	1.74	47.4%	15.0%	47.5%	0.0%	66.7%	53.3%	72.5%	31.9%	53.3%	.200	.200	69	0.3
2024 DC	LAD	MLB	36	49(0)	52¹	4-2	0	61	1.22	3.30	49.8%	10.7%	27.6%	2.2%	56.0%					.277	.474	76	0.9

2023 Arsenal: SI (98.9), SL (91.6), KC (89.8), FA (99.4), CH (89.1)   *Comps: Jason Grilli (78), Jose Mesa (74), LaTroy Hawkins (71)*

Since joining the Dodgers in 2019, nearly every full season of Kelly's has been typified by very strong peripherals, and mediocre results. Consider 2023 another tally to the "good process, meh outcome" tracker, with an ERA- 24% higher than his 71 DRA-. For the first time with the team, Kelly elected to de-emphasize his nearly 90-mph curveball in favor of a revamped slider that now has much more gyro spin and sits just shy of 92. His decision was a sound one, providing him with a more reliable wipeout pitch when he got to two strikes, which translated to a career-high K-BB% and utter dominance against righties. The Dodgers made it a priority to get him back, though not enough of one to let him keep his old number, which got assigned to some other guy. Still, he really does have great stuff.

Payton Martin   RHP   Born: 05/19/04   Age: 20   Height: 6'0"   Weight: 170   Origin: Round 17, 2022 Draft (#525 overall)

YEAR	TM	LVL	AGE	G (GS)	IP	W-L	SV	K	WHIP	ERA	CSP	BB%	K%	HR%	GB%	ZSw%	ZCon%	OSw%	OCon%	BABIP	SLGCON	DRA-	WARP
2023	RC	A	19	14(12)	39²	2-1	0	48	1.13	2.04		9.4%	30.2%	0.6%	55.8%					.315	.409	67	0.9
2024 non	LAD	MLB	20	58(0)	50	2-2	0	47	1.58	5.94		11.4%	20.7%	3.9%	37.8%					.312	.612	128	-0.5

Comps: Ben Brown (79), Matt Manning (78), Noah Syndergaard (73)

Thanks to the quirk of being a shortstop and not a pitcher, Martin's 17th-round selection looks like a potential trivia question for years, like Tom Brady being the quarterback drafted after Spergon Wynn. As with many shortstop converts, he possesses the hyperathleticism that translates to clean, efficient mechanics. Despite being shy of 20 years old, he's already starting to get his fastball into the mid-90s, with a mixture of carry and arm-side movement coveted by teams. He complements his fastball with a mid-80s slider that he used to dispatch Druw Jones in three pitches. He's one of the most underrated prospects in MLB, but probably not for long.

Dustin May   RHP   Born: 09/06/97   Age: 26   Height: 6'6"   Weight: 180   Origin: Round 3, 2016 Draft (#101 overall)

YEAR	TM	LVL	AGE	G (GS)	IP	W-L	SV	K	WHIP	ERA	CSP	BB%	K%	HR%	GB%	ZSw%	ZCon%	OSw%	OCon%	BABIP	SLGCON	DRA-	WARP
2021	LAD	MLB	23	5(5)	23	1-1	0	35	0.96	2.74	56.7%	6.5%	37.6%	4.3%	54.9%	65.5%	77.8%	30.1%	49.2%	.255	.588	67	0.6
2022	OKC	AAA	24	5(5)	19	1-0	0	33	1.05	1.89		7.6%	41.8%	2.5%	45.0%	65.6%	80.5%	36.5%	46.8%	.316	.650	63	0.5
2022	LAD	MLB	24	6(6)	30	2-3	0	29	1.17	4.50	52.3%	11.0%	22.8%	2.4%	50.6%	71.3%	80.6%	28.7%	51.3%	.237	.405	96	0.4
2023	LAD	MLB	25	9(9)	48	4-1	0	34	0.94	2.63	51.8%	8.6%	18.2%	0.5%	44.4%	69.4%	85.7%	28.4%	80.4%	.209	.313	105	0.4
2024 DC	LAD	MLB	26	10(10)	46¹	3-2	0	39	1.32	4.29	52.8%	9.1%	19.6%	2.9%	47.0%					.282	.507	96	0.5

2023 Arsenal: SI (96.9), FA (97.6), SW (86.7), FC (93.2), CH (91.2)   *Comps: Shelby Miller (61), Jack Flaherty (58), Carlos Martinez (58)*

May returned in 2023 possessing half of the swinging-strike generating ability that he did in prior years. Perhaps the most prominent tweak is that he shifted his release towards the first base side, narrowing the synthetic sweep that he creates on his breaking ball, as well as his cutter. Whiffs be damned, May was still able to create exceptionally pitcher-friendly contact, given that he still maintains a repertoire with lots of spin—of both the Magnus and non-Magnus variety—and side-to-side movement that help his pitches dart away from the barrel. He has as much potential as almost any other pitcher, but we won't see him until the latter half of 2024, if at all, as he underwent his second elbow surgery in three years in mid-July.

Bobby Miller RHP   Born: 04/05/99   Age: 25   Height: 6'5"   Weight: 220   Origin: Round 1, 2020 Draft (#29 overall)

YEAR	TM	LVL	AGE	G (GS)	IP	W-L	SV	K	WHIP	ERA	CSP	BB%	K%	HR%	GB%	ZSw%	ZCon%	OSw%	OCon%	BABIP	SLGCON	DRA-	WARP
2021	GL	A+	22	14(11)	47	2-2	0	56	0.87	1.91		5.9%	29.8%	0.5%	45.6%					.257	.336	84	0.9
2021	TUL	AA	22	3(3)	9¹	0-0	0	14	1.29	4.82		4.8%	33.3%	2.4%	52.0%					.375	.600	70	0.1
2022	TUL	AA	23	20(19)	91	6-6	0	117	1.20	4.45		8.1%	30.5%	2.1%	49.4%					.311	.481	61	2.5
2022	OKC	AAA	23	4(4)	21¹	1-1	0	28	1.08	3.38		7.1%	32.9%	4.7%	56.0%	67.8%	85.6%	35.1%	57.6%	.283	.600	75	0.4
2023	OKC	AAA	24	4(4)	14¹	1-1	0	12	1.19	5.65		9.8%	19.7%	3.3%	40.5%	67.0%	84.9%	29.2%	71.4%	.225	.500	120	0.0
2023	LAD	MLB	24	22(22)	124¹	11-4	0	119	1.10	3.76	48.0%	6.3%	23.6%	2.4%	46.8%	69.3%	81.8%	32.1%	59.4%	.277	.490	88	2.2
2024 DC	LAD	MLB	25	21(21)	120	9-5	0	117	1.29	4.14	48.0%	7.8%	22.9%	2.9%	46.1%					.301	.534	94	1.5

2023 Arsenal: FA (99.2), SI (98.8), CU (80.6), SL (89.7), CH (88.1), SW (85.4)   *Comps: Kyle Hendricks (77), Alex Cobb (77), Daniel Mengden (74)*

Not quite the distinguishing feat it might initially appear, Miller posted the highest WARP on the Dodgers last year, aided in part by none of their pitchers throwing even 135 innings. Still, Miller was the most effective Dodgers starter on a per-inning basis, with his success primarily coming in the form of contact suppression, using his big velo and strange pitch shapes to generate a .339 xwOBAcon, 30 points below the league average. Despite the successful rookie campaign, there are still hurdles to overcome. His ability to sit 99 masks the fact that he's within an inch of a dead-zone fastball and undistinguished by vertical approach angle as well. Perhaps, then, it's actually *more* impressive that he had the year that he did, given that he struggled to throw strikes with each of his secondaries. Miller's 90-mph gyro slider is sure to turn into one of the better pitches in MLB as he dials it in, and his curveball's huge shape is begging him to zone it, earning called strikes at his whim, a la Ross Stripling. Both ought to cover for any shortcomings related to his fastball's shape, velocity be damned. And once one of his secondaries emerges? Look out.

Evan Phillips RHP   Born: 09/11/94   Age: 29   Height: 6'2"   Weight: 215   Origin: Round 17, 2015 Draft (#510 overall)

YEAR	TM	LVL	AGE	G (GS)	IP	W-L	SV	K	WHIP	ERA	CSP	BB%	K%	HR%	GB%	ZSw%	ZCon%	OSw%	OCon%	BABIP	SLGCON	DRA-	WARP
2021	NOR	AAA	26	18(0)	25	1-1	0	35	1.40	5.04		13.2%	33.0%	4.7%	36.8%					.308	.764	86	0.5
2021	TB	MLB	26	1(0)	3	0-0	1	2	1.00	3.00	60.3%	0.0%	16.7%	8.3%	40.0%	64.0%	75.0%	38.9%	85.7%	.222	.600	104	0.0
2021	LAD	MLB	26	7(0)	10¹	1-1	0	9	1.26	3.48	57.8%	10.9%	19.6%	0.0%	54.8%	72.0%	86.1%	32.7%	57.6%	.258	.323	100	0.1
2022	LAD	MLB	27	64(0)	63	7-3	2	77	0.76	1.14	54.8%	6.4%	33.0%	0.9%	45.7%	64.0%	79.7%	29.8%	51.6%	.228	.331	69	1.6
2023	LAD	MLB	28	62(0)	61¹	2-4	24	66	0.83	2.05	50.1%	5.6%	28.2%	2.6%	42.8%	65.6%	82.1%	33.1%	51.8%	.222	.436	82	1.3
2024 DC	LAD	MLB	29	49(0)	52¹	4-4	31	58	1.21	3.77	52.4%	8.0%	26.6%	3.1%	42.8%					.294	.546	86	0.6

2023 Arsenal: SW (85.4), FC (93.2), FA (96.4), SI (95.6)   *Comps: Trevor Gott (68), Dominic Leone (68), David Aardsma (66)*

Phillips dominated once more as the Dodgers' primary closer, although he wasn't quite as overpowering as the previous year. A drop in his arm slot altered the shape of his four-seam fastball and cutter in particular, adding significant run to the former due to the adjusted arm slot and increase in active spin, as well as a shift in his latter's expected movement direction, creating more arm-side movement. The result was an improved fastball, due to its more unique shape, but significant regression in his ability to miss bats and create weak contact with his cutter, leaving him more vulnerable to left-handed hitters and widening his platoon splits. It's possible that the new cutter shape made it more difficult to get it in on the hands of lefties, as he more frequently let it leak out over the plate because, at 93 mph, even his lesser cutter should still overwhelm hitters. He'll have plenty of opportunities to get himself right, as he's still the most talented reliever on the roster.

River Ryan RHP   Born: 08/17/98   Age: 25   Height: 6'2"   Weight: 195   Origin: Round 11, 2021 Draft (#340 overall)

YEAR	TM	LVL	AGE	G (GS)	IP	W-L	SV	K	WHIP	ERA	CSP	BB%	K%	HR%	GB%	ZSw%	ZCon%	OSw%	OCon%	BABIP	SLGCON	DRA-	WARP
2022	RC	A	23	10(10)	33²	1-3	0	48	1.25	2.67		9.2%	33.8%	1.4%	51.2%					.351	.544	71	0.7
2022	GL	A+	23	5(3)	14	1-1	0	22	1.21	1.93		13.6%	37.3%	3.4%	55.2%					.259	.517	70	0.4
2023	TUL	AA	24	24(22)	97¹	1-6	0	98	1.25	3.33		10.7%	23.7%	1.9%	46.7%					.281	.439	91	1.4
2023	OKC	AAA	24	2(2)	7	0-1	0	12	2.00	10.29		5.7%	34.3%	5.7%	33.3%	74.6%	73.6%	31.3%	42.9%	.526	1.095	78	
2024 non	LAD	MLB	25	58(0)	50	2-2	0	48	1.47	5.18		10.8%	21.6%	3.5%	39.2%					.298	.578	114	-0.1

2023 Arsenal: FA (96.6), FC (87.9), CH (87.7), CU (82.5)

Another shortstop convert, Ryan sits in the mid-to-upper 90s with his fastball, which is supported by three interesting secondaries in his changeup, curveball, and cutter. Though perhaps a matter of sample size, Ryan has managed to throw a lot of strikes with his fastball, but hasn't yet been able to convert foul balls into whiffs. He's currently the most comfortable with his cutter, but he's demonstrated the ability to expertly kill spin with his 88-mph yo-yo changeup—it's essentially vertically neutral without the forces of gravity—while his low-80s curveball has huge depth and should allow him to steal strikes with ease. He generates whiffs with all four pitches, and the only thing left for him to do is refine his secondaries to throw more strikes so he can limit his walks.

Emmet Sheehan RHP   Born: 11/15/99   Age: 24   Height: 6'5"   Weight: 220   Origin: Round 6, 2021 Draft (#192 overall)

YEAR	TM	LVL	AGE	G (GS)	IP	W-L	SV	K	WHIP	ERA	CSP	BB%	K%	HR%	GB%	ZSw%	ZCon%	OSw%	OCon%	BABIP	SLGCON	DRA-	WARP
2021	RC	A	21	5(0)	13	3-0	0	27	1.15	4.15		8.9%	48.2%	3.6%	50.0%					.400	.773	77	0.3
2022	GL	A+	22	18(12)	63²	7-2	0	101	1.08	2.83		10.7%	38.7%	0.8%	41.1%					.310	.480	71	1.6
2023	TUL	AA	23	12(10)	53¹	4-1	0	88	0.88	1.86		10.9%	41.7%	2.4%	32.6%					.211	.453	67	1.5
2023	OKC	AAA	23	3(1)	9²	0-1	0	14	1.03	5.59		15.8%	36.8%	5.3%	41.2%	72.9%	74.4%	33.9%	43.9%	.133	.647	82	
2023	LAD	MLB	23	13(11)	60¹	4-1	1	64	1.19	4.92	45.1%	10.5%	25.8%	4.4%	33.1%	75.2%	81.5%	33.8%	53.2%	.240	.587	110	0.4
2024 DC	LAD	MLB	24	44(18)	114²	8-5	0	146	1.33	4.36	45.1%	11.7%	29.6%	3.8%	34.0%					.288	.616	97	1.1

2023 Arsenal: FA (95.3), SL (87.1), CH (82.9), SW (79.1)   *Comps: Cristian Javier (65), Dylan Cease (59), Rob Whalen (58)*

Sheehan has a strange, squatty delivery that he sits into and whips his arm across to create deception. His low-three-quarters arm slot adds even more deception, as the expected movement direction of his fastball is that of a pitcher who throws out of a higher slot. That he sits 95 mph with a -4.0° vertical approach angle makes it exceptionally hard to get on top of, which helps him convert it into lots of whiffs and pop-ups. Fastball aside, he's hardly lacking for stuff. He creates exceptional depth with his slider and changeup and somehow even more depth with his sweeper, which also cuts across 17 inches. The issue has long been that Sheehan struggles to throw strikes, which he did about as often as Lance Lynn and Jordan Lyles (derogatory). Sheehan ranked in the 76th percentile of secondary pitches in the "waste" zone, which means that he throws far too many non-competitive pitches when he goes away from his fastball. Part of success, after all, is allowing your enemies to fail themselves.

Gavin Stone RHP Born: 10/15/98 Age: 25 Height: 6'1" Weight: 175 Origin: Round 5, 2020 Draft (#159 overall)

YEAR	TM	LVL	AGE	G(GS)	IP	W-L	SV	K	WHIP	ERA	CSP	BB%	K%	HR%	GB%	ZSw%	ZCon%	OSw%	OCon%	BABIP	SLGCON	DRA-	WARP
2021	RC	A	22	18(17)	70	1-2	0	101	1.27	3.73		6.8%	34.2%	1.7%	46.9%					.381	.645	90	0.8
2021	GL	A+	22	5(5)	21	1-0	0	37	1.10	3.86		6.0%	44.6%	2.4%	56.1%					.410	.675	60	0.7
2022	GL	A+	23	6(6)	25	1-1	0	28	1.00	1.44		6.0%	28.0%	1.0%	53.8%					.281	.354	79	0.5
2022	TUL	AA	23	14(13)	73¹	6-4	0	107	1.21	1.60		9.9%	35.3%	0.3%	44.0%					.356	.423	57	2.2
2022	OKC	AAA	23	6(6)	23¹	2-1	0	33	0.94	1.16		8.6%	35.5%	1.1%	46.0%	70.7%	77.8%	37.4%	40.3%	.265	.460	71	0.5
2023	OKC	AAA	24	21(19)	100²	7-4	0	120	1.31	4.74		10.7%	27.8%	2.8%	44.3%	72.4%	77.9%	33.9%	50.1%	.294	.548	76	1.7
2023	LAD	MLB	24	8(4)	31	1-1	1	22	1.90	9.00	46.7%	8.6%	14.5%	5.3%	44.3%	70.4%	81.6%	38.1%	54.0%	.355	.719	112	0.2
2024 DC	LAD	MLB	25	36(10)	74²	5-3	0	80	1.33	4.22	46.7%	9.2%	25.0%	2.9%	42.3%					.307	.550	94	0.7

2023 Arsenal: CH (86), FA (94.3), SL (90.5), SI (94.8), SW (86.2), CU (78.8)   *Comps: Daniel Gossett (79), Trevor Oaks (73), Walker Lockett (73)*

In a world where the sluggers all sit fastball, Stone and his decoy changeup were dead on arrival. It's a beautiful pitch, designed to swoop out of the zone like a playful wood sprite, but advanced hitters could read the spin and wait for the four-seamer, which was excruciatingly average. After licking his wounds following three brutal spot starts and the subsequent demotion, Stone added a two-seam fastball upon his return in August. It rides a lot for a two-seamer, but its movement is between that of a four- and two-seamer, looking to the hitter like late break. The two-seamer is likely still in development, but would pair better with his changeup than his four-seamer and would tunnel better with his slider. This is his rookie season we're talking about, and one that came after waltzing through the minors, but with a 5.9 K-BB% on the year, Stone ought to experiment with *something*. What's he got to lose?

Julio Urías LHP Born: 08/12/96 Age: 27 Height: 6'0" Weight: 225 Origin: IFA, 2012

YEAR	TM	LVL	AGE	G(GS)	IP	W-L	SV	K	WHIP	ERA	CSP	BB%	K%	HR%	GB%	ZSw%	ZCon%	OSw%	OCon%	BABIP	SLGCON	DRA-	WARP
2021	LAD	MLB	24	32(32)	185²	20-3	0	195	1.02	2.96	58.2%	5.1%	26.2%	2.6%	40.0%	67.1%	83.4%	37.3%	64.0%	.276	.486	82	3.5
2022	LAD	MLB	25	31(31)	175	17-7	0	166	0.96	2.16	57.1%	6.0%	24.1%	3.3%	38.8%	69.6%	84.3%	36.4%	63.2%	.229	.469	92	2.4
2023	LAD	MLB	26	21(21)	117¹	11-8	0	117	1.16	4.60	51.6%	5.0%	24.3%	5.0%	36.6%	66.9%	84.2%	35.3%	62.6%	.285	.654	100	1.4
2024 non	LAD	MLB	27	58(0)	50	2-2	0	46	1.18	3.75	55.0%	6.3%	22.2%	3.3%	37.7%					.283	.534	89	0.5

2023 Arsenal: FA (92.8), CU (79.3), CH (86.2), FC (87)   *Comps: Frank Tanana (66), Milt Pappas (64), Madison Bumgarner (64)*

www.menstoppingviolence.org | Men Stopping Violence is a community-based activist organization in Atlanta that works to involve men in combating male violence against women.

The National Domestic Violence Hotline is 1-800-799-7233 and thehotline.org is a helpful starting point to find resources and information as to how to get help.

Alex Vesia LHP Born: 04/11/96 Age: 28 Height: 6'1" Weight: 209 Origin: Round 17, 2018 Draft (#507 overall)

YEAR	TM	LVL	AGE	G(GS)	IP	W-L	SV	K	WHIP	ERA	CSP	BB%	K%	HR%	GB%	ZSw%	ZCon%	OSw%	OCon%	BABIP	SLGCON	DRA-	WARP
2021	OKC	AAA	25	9(0)	9	0-0	2	19	0.67	1.00		9.4%	59.4%	0.0%	44.4%					.333	.333	67	0.2
2021	LAD	MLB	25	41(0)	40	3-1	1	54	0.98	2.25	52.3%	13.7%	33.5%	3.7%	25.3%	72.5%	66.5%	28.9%	51.9%	.143	.494	96	0.5
2022	LAD	MLB	26	63(0)	54¹	5-0	1	79	1.12	2.15	54.5%	10.6%	34.8%	0.9%	34.4%	69.3%	71.1%	32.9%	59.0%	.297	.412	83	1.0
2023	OKC	AAA	27	13(0)	13¹	1-1	0	22	1.20	3.38		10.9%	40.0%	3.6%	25.9%	61.0%	75.4%	34.1%	53.3%	.320	.630	81	0.3
2023	LAD	MLB	27	56(1)	49²	2-5	1	64	1.39	4.35	47.8%	7.8%	29.5%	3.2%	27.6%	74.7%	78.0%	32.0%	55.2%	.354	.612	85	1.0
2024 DC	LAD	MLB	28	49(0)	52¹	4-2	0	66	1.26	3.95	51.1%	10.3%	29.8%	3.6%	30.1%					.289	.595	89	0.5

2023 Arsenal: FA (94.5), SL (86), CH (85.7), SI (94)   *Comps: Jake Diekman (72), Jace Fry (69), Tommy Kahnle (69)*

With a motion reminiscent of Tyler Anderson's without the hesitation kick, Vesia uses a funky delivery to pair with his fastball, which he throws from an over-the-top arm slot (but low release) to create one of the flattest fastball shapes in MLB. Usually, over-the-top guys struggle to create enough induced vertical break to keep their fastball shape flat, but Vesia's combination of a low release, active spin, and velocity all get him over the hump and help his fastball beeline to the catcher's glove. Vesia weaponizes his fastball to stay above the barrel of hitters, getting hitters to pop out and get under the ball 12.7% and 38.8% of the time, respectively. You'd think that his accompanying gyro-heavy slider would make him an impossible at-bat, but he struggles to get hitters to expand the zone with it, in part because his slider ranks in the 14th percentile of all pitches in waste percentage, meaning he spikes it too often for hitters to be allured by it. He still keeps the walks plenty manageable, though.

Yoshinobu Yamamoto RHP   Born: 08/17/98   Age: 25   Height: 5'10"   Weight: 176   Origin: IFA, 2023

YEAR	TM	LVL	AGE	G (GS)	IP	W-L	SV	K	WHIP	ERA	CSP	BB%	K%	HR%	GB%	ZSw%	ZCon%	OSw%	OCon%	BABIP	SLGCON	DRA-	WARP
2024 DC	LAD	MLB	25	28(28)	154	12-5	0	157	1.11	3.12		6.4%	25.2%	2.7%	30.0%					.284	.514	75	3.4

The goal is to win the World Series every year. This should be obvious, but for many teams, it doesn't appear to be the case. The Dodgers reaffirmed that goal by acquiring Yamamoto after winning 100 games in the regular season and zero in the playoffs. They didn't lose solely because of slumps by Mookie Betts or Freddie Freeman, and the current DH-only version of Shohei Ohtani wouldn't have helped. The losing pitcher in the NLDS elimination game was Lance Lynn, who gave up three more home runs since you began reading this comment.

The pitching staff didn't just need an arm—it needed a savior. It required an heir to Clayton Kershaw's throne. In hindsight, it seems clear that all the Ohtani money and deferrals were a precursor to signing Yamamoto, who was arguably the best pitcher in the world last year. He's intended to be the ace, the promised one, the missing piece of the playoff puzzle who comes with more hype than perhaps any Japanese pitcher ever (excluding Ohtani). Contending for a Cy Young was a possibility before he signed, but with $325 million it becomes the expectation. Can he live up to that? At last, we're about to find out.

Ryan Yarbrough LHP   Born: 12/31/91   Age: 32   Height: 6'5"   Weight: 215   Origin: Round 4, 2014 Draft (#111 overall)

YEAR	TM	LVL	AGE	G (GS)	IP	W-L	SV	K	WHIP	ERA	CSP	BB%	K%	HR%	GB%	ZSw%	ZCon%	OSw%	OCon%	BABIP	SLGCON	DRA-	WARP
2021	TB	MLB	29	30(21)	155	9-7	0	117	1.23	5.11	52.5%	4.1%	17.9%	3.8%	35.2%	65.8%	85.8%	36.8%	70.3%	.293	.566	123	-0.4
2022	DUR	AAA	30	7(7)	27²	2-2	0	26	1.59	4.55		9.4%	20.3%	2.3%	37.9%					.345	.581	120	0.1
2022	TB	MLB	30	20(9)	80	3-8	0	61	1.38	4.50	53.6%	6.2%	17.2%	3.4%	37.2%	67.8%	81.6%	36.6%	72.5%	.306	.554	137	-0.7
2023	OMA	AAA	31	3(3)	14²	0-0	0	18	0.75	1.23		3.8%	34.0%	1.9%	42.4%	65.0%	78.5%	36.1%	52.3%	.250	.424	84	0.3
2023	KC	MLB	31	14(7)	51	4-5	0	29	1.20	4.24	52.0%	4.2%	13.7%	2.4%	37.5%	70.7%	85.5%	35.6%	68.5%	.288	.443	117	0.1
2023	LAD	MLB	31	11(2)	38²	4-2	2	38	1.27	4.89	50.9%	3.0%	23.0%	4.8%	40.8%	67.4%	79.8%	38.7%	67.9%	.321	.625	101	0.4
2024 DC	LAD	MLB	32	48(5)	71¹	5-3	0	54	1.29	4.63	51.9%	5.5%	17.8%	3.3%	37.4%					.301	.541	104	0.4

2023 Arsenal: FA (87.2), SW (72), FC (84.4), CH (78.7)   *Comps: Jarrod Washburn (82), Joe Saunders (82), Brian Anderson (80)*

As is often the case with pitchers with low arm slots, Yarbrough runs relatively extreme platoon splits, because lefties see the ball late, and righties see it out of his hand early. At his best, Yarbrough used his low, low-three-quarters delivery to neutralize lefties, his cutter to jam righties in on their hands and dotted changeups down and away, and through 2020, Yarbrough was able to mitigate his platoon splits. But between losing velo and his widening horizontal release point, he's now a liability against righties, and he's starting to regress against lefties too. He reshaped his cutter to give it more ride, but that didn't stop him from having the worst changeup run value per 100 pitches outside of Garrett Whitlock and Julio Urías. It'll still work, though, as long as he never walks another batter ever again.

LINEOUTS

Hitters

HITTER	POS	TM	LVL	AGE	PA	R	HR	RBI	SB	AVG/OBP/SLG	BABIP	SLGCON	BB%	K%	ZSw%	ZCon%	OSw%	OCon%	LA	90th EV	DRC+	BRR	DRP	WARP
Austin Barnes	C	LAD	MLB	33	200	15	2	11	2	.180/.256/.242	.222	.319	8.5%	21.5%	67.9%	83.9%	25.4%	65.2%	5.6	101.9	81	-0.3	0.0	0.3
Hunter Feduccia	C	OKC	AAA	26	380	61	11	57	0	.279/.387/.451	.336	.600	15.3%	20.8%	65.2%	85.3%	20.4%	59.3%			104	0.5	-1.5	1.1
Yeiner Fernandez	C	GL	A+	20	433	47	6	50	4	.273/.360/.375	.303	.442	10.9%	12.9%							118	0.9	-3.5	1.8
Jake Gelof	3B	RC	A	21	137	23	5	23	2	.225/.314/.433	.293	.658	11.7%	29.9%							94	-0.7	-1.2	-0.1
Kendall George	CF	DOD	ROK	18	71	11	0	7	11	.362/.451/.414	.429	.511	15.5%	15.5%										
	CF	RC	A	18	50	13	0	3	6	.381/.469/.429	.485	.545	12.0%	18.0%							100	0.9	-1.2	0.1
Trey Sweeney	SS	SOM	AA	23	472	67	13	49	20	.252/.367/.411	.294	.531	13.8%	19.1%							121	-1.0	1.9	2.6
Kolten Wong	2B	SEA	MLB	32	216	21	2	19	1	.165/.241/.227	.203	.297	7.4%	21.3%	69.8%	90.8%	30.0%	58.4%	13.0	99.7	73	0.2	0.3	0.0
	2B	LAD	MLB	32	34	4	2	8	2	.300/.353/.500	.318	.652	5.9%	20.6%	76.7%	93.5%	34.9%	51.7%	16.7	101.8	102	0.0	0.1	0.1

Austin Barnes posted the lowest DRC+ of his career outside of 2018, but on the other hand, he also regressed in the one area in which he's historically excelled: framing. Barnes' called strikes above average plummeted to a career-low, effectively eliminating any quantifiable value he has as a player. ⓧ At age 26, **Hunter Feduccia** isn't a prospect, instead part-timing his way up the ladder by splitting jobs with bigger names. He's also hit at every level, and given the kind of contracts Luke Maile and Carson Kelly got this offseason, he's got to be feeling pretty good about his résumé. ⓧ **Yeiner Fernandez** is about to experience the difficulty spike that is the jump to Double-A, hasn't translated his power into games, and his framing has a long way to go. Still, it's always fun to root for a 2B/C prospect, at least until it's proven that he really is just the former masquerading as the latter. ⓧ Having leveled the ACC before the draft with Glaus-like power, **Jake Gelof** employed the same swing in the minors and found that the ball didn't magically steer right toward it. When he gets a bad pitch, though, he can make stadium employees paint little memorials on upper-deck seats. ⓧ It's pretty rare that a team's most recent first-round pick only rates as a lineout, but that's a testament to the Dodgers system, as well as the ceiling of **Kendall George** and his slash-heavy, footspeed-oriented game. There will be time to rave about his elite contact skills in paragraph form as he heads toward the end of his teens. ⓧ Once a first-round pick, **Trey Sweeney** will only be a short-term big leaguer unless he can unlock something at the plate. He's less blocked in Chavez Ravine than he was in the Bronx, but he needs to develop his stick no matter the metropolitan area. ⓧ One of Seattle's key acquisitions last offseason, **Kolten Wong** managed just five multi-hit games and eight extra-base hits before hitting the waiver wire at the trade deadline. He hit a whammy in his first Dodgers plate appearance, after which the team chose not to press its luck.

Pitchers

PITCHER	TM	LVL	AGE	G (GS)	IP	W-L	SV	K	WHIP	ERA	CSP	BB%	K%	HR%	GB%	ZSw%	ZCon%	OSw%	OCon%	BABIP	SLGCON	DRA-	WARP
Maddux Bruns	RC	A	21	6 (6)	21	0-0	0	33	1.14	1.29		14.8%	37.5%	0.0%	41.5%					.268	.341	75	0.4
	GL	A+	21	20 (20)	76	0-7	0	93	1.45	4.74		15.8%	27.2%	2.0%	40.0%					.278	.533	111	0.4
Daniel Hudson	LAD	MLB	36	3 (0)	3	0-0	1	5	1.67	0.00	42.9%	21.4%	35.7%	0.0%	50.0%	82.6%	84.2%	29.3%	33.3%	.333	.500	100	0.0
Jared Karros	RC	A	22	19 (16)	70²	3-4	0	75	1.20	3.95		7.5%	25.7%	3.1%	40.2%					.292	.573	73	1.0
	GL	A+	22	3 (2)	13	1-0	1	11	0.69	0.69		2.1%	22.9%	2.1%	31.4%					.206	.343	102	0.1
Landon Knack	TUL	AA	25	12 (12)	57¹	2-0	0	61	0.94	2.20		5.4%	27.4%	1.3%	36.9%					.269	.442	87	1.1
	OKC	AAA	25	10 (10)	43	3-1	0	38	1.44	2.93		9.6%	20.2%	3.2%	34.4%	71.0%	82.6%	29.9%	62.6%	.304	.562	108	0.4
Ronan Kopp	GL	A+	20	30 (21)	72¹	0-4	1	107	1.31	2.99		16.7%	35.8%	2.0%	39.1%					.295	.518	86	1.6
Jimmy Nelson	OKC	AAA	34	29 (0)	27	1-1	0	34	1.93	5.00		23.5%	25.8%	1.5%	37.1%	54.0%	82.4%	26.4%	47.9%	.322	.517	103	0.1
Gus Varland	OKC	AAA	26	30 (1)	33¹	2-1	2	39	1.11	2.16		6.0%	29.3%	1.5%	43.0%	63.3%	84.6%	37.0%	61.0%	.321	.512	66	1.1
	MIL	MLB	26	8 (0)	8²	0-0	0	6	2.65	11.42	52.3%	15.7%	11.8%	5.9%	50.0%	64.1%	88.1%	17.9%	57.9%	.364	.722	113	0.0
	LAD	MLB	26	8 (0)	11²	1-1	0	14	1.71	3.09	41.1%	15.4%	26.9%	0.0%	46.7%	78.9%	83.9%	36.6%	51.0%	.414	.621	97	0.2
Kendall Williams	GL	A+	22	7 (7)	31²	1-2	0	27	0.95	1.99		7.9%	21.4%	1.6%	51.7%					.212	.360	94	0.5
	TUL	AA	22	8 (8)	39	3-3	0	33	1.36	3.92		13.3%	19.1%	0.6%	48.2%					.259	.393	106	0.1
	OKC	AAA	22	1 (1)	6	0-1	0	2	1.83	7.50		18.5%	7.4%	7.4%	25.0%	66.7%	88.5%	34.6%	61.1%	.222	.895	128	
Justin Wrobleski	GL	A+	22	25 (23)	102¹	4-4	0	109	1.25	2.90		8.3%	26.0%	1.4%	43.1%					.325	.493	81	1.8

He'll never escape discussion of his first name, but **Maddux Bruns** is veering into 1930s nickname territory, when they'd call the big clumsy first baseman "Tiny." The former first-rounder has all the stuff in the world, but what few barns remain in Southern California are all safe from him. ⓦ If you're going to lose a year and a half to shoulder issues, make your last baseball memory as good as **J.P. Feyereisen** did. Before leaving us he perfected a steep, dropping fastball at the top of the zone that worked as an out-pitch. If nothing else, he's found the blueprint for his success. ⓦ After toiling for years with arm injuries, **Daniel Hudson** finally overcame them, only to be felled instead by an MCL sprain. He mulled retirement for a few months but ultimately decided to give it one more go in 2024, signing an incentive-laden contract with the Dodgers. ⓦ It's always fun when a second-generation ballplayer follows his father's vocation, and even team, but not position. In just one pro season, 16th-rounder **Jarred Karros** (son of Eric) doubled his injury-plagued college inning count, and the steady work clearly did him good. ⓦ It's hard to know what **Landon Knack** is, since he's never quite healthy, but regardless he's dragging himself closer to a role in the big leagues. He has the deep arsenal of a starter, and the metrics of one of those old action figures that show "real battle damage." ⓦ Obvious future relievers with command issues rarely make the book at all, let alone in a system like this one. **Ronan Kopp** ranked 18th on BP's Dodgers prospect list in 2023, with the warning that he'd have to learn to throw strikes to stick around; he didn't, and he's still 18th, because the stuff got even nastier in the meantime. ⓦ The Dodgers keep sending **Jimmy Nelson** paychecks, the way that Renaissance-era benefactors would patronize the arts. Hokusai didn't make it until his early 50s, so maybe Nelson can squeeze another season's worth of life out of his arm at 35. ⓦ The sexual tension between **Alex Reyes** and not throwing strikes is too great, so the Dodgers declined his $3 million option for 2024. ⓦ Long arms are the ultimate scouting tradeoff: They're great for throwing filthy pitches and also walking every fifth batter. **Eriq Swan** pushes to the front of the line of command-challenged live arms, thanks to fairly clean mechanics to go with his cartoonishly long levers. ⓦ The last we saw of **Blake Treinen**, he'd transformed his profile by throwing more cutters at the expense of his demon sinker, while also taking his relatively generic slider and turning it into more of a sweeper to complement his other pitches. We'll see more after the Dodgers exercised their club option on him. ⓦ **Gus Varland**, as the first Gus in the majors in nearly a decade, has a legacy to protect. Let his brother Louie take care of the Varlands. The former Rule 5 pick appeared grateful to be returned by the Brewers; his time at both OKC and LA last year were massive improvements over his usual labors. ⓦ It's hard to imagine, but someday there's going to be a new generation of Justin Bruihls and Phil Bickfords in LA. It'll include groundballer **Kendall Williams**, who's starting now but seems destined to mop up the latter stages of 11-3 blowouts in a few years. ⓦ Some pitchers are suited for long hair, and that includes **Justin Wrobleski**, with his oops-all-limbs delivery and jab-step foot plant. The southpaw could develop into a solid starter in a couple years, given his four-pitch mix and plus change, or he could race to the majors quickly if the Dodgers need him in relief.

MIAMI MARLINS

Essay by Russell A. Carleton

Player comments by Tim Jackson and BP staff

There is a diner in every city that on Friday night/Saturday morning at 1:00 am becomes the nexus of the universe for a few hours. In no other place will you find second-shift workers, drunk college students, beleaguered new parents giddily grabbing food after their first date night in three months, the cast of a local community theater production celebrating Opening Night and, for good measure, some tourists who have decided to drive all night to get *there* by morning. And then there's Larry. Larry is somehow always there and has been since the place was opened in 1993. Every thread of humanity has wound its way through the diner tonight all joined in the pursuit of cheap breakfast food. It doesn't make any sense and yet it exists. Like any good diner founded in the 1990s, it still has some of its original teal décor, which it proudly wears and is at once gaudy and comforting. It's hard to say what exactly makes the diner stand out. It's mostly just a place that's open, and yet it made the playoffs.

The Miami Marlins of Florida are a weird nexus of the baseball universe and most of it has nothing to do with what's happening on the field. In baseball, there are the games themselves, and those are fun to watch. Each tells its own little story. But then there's the meta-game. That's the collection of forces that impact how the game unfolds. Over the last decade, baseball has seen extensive changes to how it is played, from the ascendance of the reliever, to the primary place in pitching strategy, to the near-extinction of "small ball" to the dominance of analytic thinking as the primary mover in the game. There will be more changes to the very culture of the game over the next decade, and if you want to understand those swirling winds, you'd do well to study Miami and the odd cast of characters that have stopped by to dine.

The Marlins' season opened with an all-too-rare "challenge trade" that by the end of the season kind of worked out for both sides. The Marlins sent pitcher Pablo López (and a couple of other minor leaguers) to the Twins in exchange for second baseman Luis Arraez. In a baseball universe where almost all the trades are either "your present for my future" or debt restructuring deals entirely disconnected from the players involved, it was the most

MIAMI MARLINS PROSPECTUS
2023 W-L: 84-78, 3RD IN NL EAST

Pythag	.462	21st	DER	.692	19th
RS/G	4.11	26th	DRC+	99	17th
RA/G	4.46	17th	DRA-	93	6th
dWin%	.539	9th	FIP	4.15	10th
Payroll	$93M	23rd	B-Age	29.8	29th
M$/MW	$2.0M	5th	P-Age	27.8	2nd

- Opened 2012
- Retractable roof
- Synthetic surface
- Fence profile: 7' to 11'6"

Park Factors

Runs	Runs/RH	Runs/LH	HR/RH	HR/LH
99	98	101	92	95

Top Hitter WARP	5.2 Luis Arraez
Top Pitcher WARP	3.2 Sandy Alcantara
2023 Top Prospect	Noble Meyer

Payroll History (in millions)

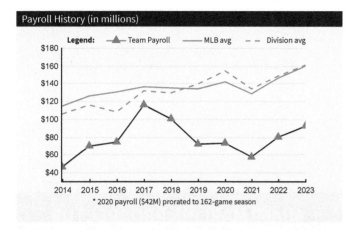

Legend: ▲ Team Payroll — MLB avg - - Division avg

* 2020 payroll ($42M) prorated to 162-game season

Future Commitments (in millions)

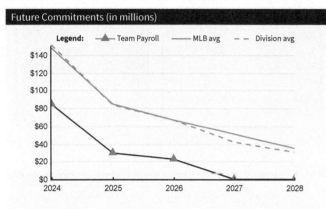

Legend: ▲ Team Payroll — MLB avg - - Division avg

Farm System Ranking

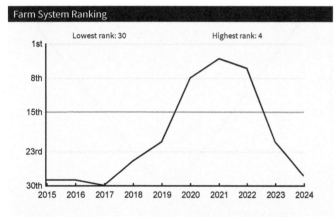

Lowest rank: 30   Highest rank: 4

Personnel

President of Baseball Operations
Peter Bendix

Assistant General Manager
Brian Chattin

Assistant General Manager
Daniel Greenlee

Assistant General Manager
Gabe Kapler

Assistant General Manager
Oz Ocampo

Manager
Skip Schumaker

BP Alumni
John Eshleman

fascinating trade of the off-season. How often does it happen that two All-Stars, and at that two All-Stars on the good side of 30, a pitcher and a hitter, are traded for each other?

The Marlins got what they hoped for. Arraez won the batting title—and say whatever you want about batting average, but if you hit .354, you're doing OK—and brought a kick to an offense that needed it. In fact, a lot fell apart for the Marlins in 2023. Jean Segura was no longer a sure thing. Mr. Joey Wendle's development was arrested. Jazz Chisholm Jr. went from the potential new "face" of MLB (along with a cover spot on the video game *MLB: The Show*) to the latest example of the "Madden curse." And yet...somehow, the Marlins made the playoffs. It was the expanded playoffs, but the *other* 84-win National League team that squeaked in made it to the World Series. A few things land differently, and maybe it could have been the Marlins, improbably fighting for their third World Series title in franchise history, despite the fact that after 31 years of existence, they have still never won a division title. If there is a poster child for what the modern expansion of the playoffs has wrought, it might just be wearing teal—at least on Fridays.

The Marlins won 84 games, even though they had not only a negative run differential, but one that pegged them as a 75-win team underneath it all. The secret to their success was an unreal 33-14 record in games decided by one run. When that happens for a team, the usual reasons come out. Maybe the Marlins had an outstanding bullpen. Except, they didn't really. Their bullpen had the 21st-best ERA in 2023. Maybe the Marlins just knew when to turn it on when it counted. The problem there is that extensive research has shown that there's no repeatable skill in coming through in the clutch, either at the individual or team level. Yes, the Marlins won those one-run games, but those are games that probably could have gone in either direction. Sometimes, you flip a coin 10 times and get seven heads. Sometimes the fish bite and sometimes they don't. The cold reality is that the Marlins weren't all that great a team in 2023. Just understand, fellow diners, that's the baseline we're starting from for 2024. This was a team that was just good enough to catch a lucky gust of wind.

In the time-honored tradition of the Manager of the Year Award going to the manager whose team had the most people who said "Wait, they're good?" about them, Skip Schumaker took home the trophy. If you only sorta paid attention to MLB through the season—or even if you paid detailed attention—you'd have been excused when at the end of the year, you noted that Miami was somehow in the playoff picture, and that was the first time you'd had that thought. For all we know, Schumaker could very well have been the glue that held it all together. Somewhere in the depths of the Marlin tank, maybe Schumaker had really made a deep connection with Avisaíl García or Jesús Luzardo and really was the person who pulled the best out of them. Maybe Schumaker was better at it than anyone else in the National Conference—sorry, League. Maybe not. I still think it's funny that we give out a Manager of the Year Award when most of what a manager does is completely invisible to all but the people behind that clubhouse door.

In September, the Marlins suffered an awful loss when ace pitcher Sandy Alcantara went on the injured list and then needed the dreaded Tommy John surgery. Alcantara will miss all of 2024. If there was a pitcher who could still claim the nearly faded title of "ace" in modern baseball, it was Alcantara. He was the only pitcher to notch 200 innings in both 2021 and 2022 and was on the way to hitting the mark in 2023, logging 184 ⅔ innings before an early September shutdown. In the age of "load management" for starters, Alcantara was one of the few outliers, routinely pitching into the (gasp!) seventh and eighth innings, being both good enough to not warrant being lifted for a reliever and seemingly strong enough to handle the load without breaking. Until something broke.

There is a great deal of discussion about the role of the starting pitcher in the modern game of baseball. MLB Commissioner Rob Manfred has identified the issue as one of concern. In a game which has for so long subtitled its events with the names of the two starting pitchers, it's bad for business when they're both out after the fifth inning, only to be replaced by a steady stream of one-inning wonders. Manfred has floated the idea of further restricting the number of pitchers that teams could keep on the active roster in the hopes that teams would be less tempted to go to the bullpen earlier in the game. But on the flip side, there is a growing realization that sharing the pitching load is a better strategy for getting 27 outs than having one player do it all.

Alcantara's injury is a data point in another ongoing argument. Do pitch counts and workload restrictions actually reduce the number of injuries that pitchers suffer? For those who long for the days of pitchers who could even regularly eclipse 200 innings, to say little of 250, Alcantara was proof of concept that this was still possible in the modern game. Until he wasn't.

After the season, the Marlins saw the resignation of their general manager, Kim Ng, who held the distinction of being the first woman to hold the post of GM for an MLB team and for that matter, any of the "major" sports teams in the United States. According to reports, Ng resigned in protest to the idea that the Marlins were looking to hire someone to be given the title President of Baseball Operations—who effectively would have become Ng's boss. Ng's departure, along with that of Derek Jeter, from the Marlins C-suite naturally led to the question of who was really the head chef in Miami. Were the Marlins being run on the charisma and charm of Jeter? The hard-won experience of Ng? Was someone else pulling the strings all along?

The answer now is that the Marlins are being run by new President of Baseball Operations Peter Bendix (disclosure: someone with whom I have shared a table a few times). Bendix comes from the Tampa Bay organization, where he rose from intern to general manager of the "other Florida team." By taking his talents to South Beach, he joins Andrew Friedman, Chaim Bloom and James Click—who have all emigrated from St. Petersburg to helm other teams, based on Tampa Bay's strong history of putting together competitive teams on a shoestring budget. And yes, analytics.

And so as we leave the diner and pay our check, we see a team struggling all at once with many of the threads that have run through baseball for the past decade, and indeed struggling with a lot of questions that we haven't fully solved. Was trading a good pitcher in López for a good hitter in Arraez a good idea? Is Arraez, a throwback to the high batting average days of 40 years ago, strangely undervalued in a world where the *acronymati* spit on the stat? What is the measure of a good manager and how big is that measure anyway? How much of it is luck masquerading as skill? How much of it is skill that no one ever sees? What are we to make of the role of luck more generally in the game? Did the Marlins really make the playoffs or just happened to slip into them? What is the status of the old-timey model of the starting pitcher? Is it officially gone forever? What is the role of leadership in a franchise and how well can a team that has never been known as an analytical powerhouse adapt to having someone who trained in those arts at the helm?

Welcome to the diner. Try the fish.

—Russell A. Carleton is an author of Baseball Prospectus.

HITTERS

Jacob Amaya SS   Born: 09/03/98   Age: 25   Bats: R   Throws: R   Height: 6'0"   Weight: 180   Origin: Round 11, 2017 Draft (#340 overall)

YEAR	TM	LVL	AGE	PA	R	HR	RBI	SB	AVG/OBP/SLG	BABIP	SLGCON	BB%	K%	ZSw%	ZCon%	OSw%	OCon%	LA	90th EV	DRC+	BRR	DRP	WARP
2021	TUL	AA	22	476	60	12	47	5	.216/.303/.343	.254	.455	10.9%	21.6%							94	-0.9	-3.8	0.7
2022	TUL	AA	23	216	39	9	26	3	.264/.370/.500	.267	.595	14.8%	13.4%							120	1.4	-2.2	1.2
2022	OKC	AAA	23	351	46	8	45	3	.259/.368/.381	.329	.531	14.0%	23.6%	63.2%	79.9%	23.0%	61.5%			102	-0.3	0.5	1.1
2023	JAX	AAA	24	566	85	15	65	6	.252/.345/.407	.288	.521	12.4%	18.7%	62.8%	85.8%	21.9%	70.7%			104	2.0	-2.7	1.6
2023	MIA	MLB	24	9	1	0	2	1	.222/.222/.222	.250	.250	0.0%	11.1%	57.1%	100.0%	50.0%	71.4%	-0.1	99.9	94	0.0	0.0	0.0
2024 DC	MIA	MLB	25	211	19	4	19	1	.223/.299/.333	.265	.423	9.1%	19.3%							82	-0.1	-1.3	0.1

2023 GP: SS (3), 2B (1)   *Comps: Abiatal Avelino (62), Pete Kozma (57), Dixon Machado (56)*

Amaya's first season in the Miami organization went, ahem, swimmingly. He drove the ball better than he has at every previous minor-league stop, save for a brief stretch at Double-A while still with the Dodgers, despite not selling out for power the way he did a couple of years ago. You won't mistake him for a masher, but he isn't swinging a Twizzler up there. He continued to pare down his strikeout rate, too. If there's a catch, it's that he endured another prolonged slump at the dish the way he has in the past, hitting only .208 in August before catching fire to finish the campaign. Acquired for Miguel Rojas as an option who could have more long-term impact, he won't be a star but he looks like a real major leaguer at the six for a Marlins club that needs one.

Luis Arraez 2B   Born: 04/09/97   Age: 27   Bats: L   Throws: R   Height: 5'10"   Weight: 175   Origin: IFA, 2013

YEAR	TM	LVL	AGE	PA	R	HR	RBI	SB	AVG/OBP/SLG	BABIP	SLGCON	BB%	K%	ZSw%	ZCon%	OSw%	OCon%	LA	90th EV	DRC+	BRR	DRP	WARP
2021	MIN	MLB	24	479	58	2	42	2	.294/.357/.376	.323	.424	9.0%	10.0%	63.0%	93.4%	30.0%	83.7%	10.2	99.0	114	0.0	0.5	2.6
2022	MIN	MLB	25	603	88	8	49	4	.316/.375/.420	.331	.456	8.3%	7.1%	64.1%	95.0%	29.3%	90.1%	12.9	99.4	125	-0.7	0.7	3.3
2023	MIA	MLB	26	617	71	10	69	3	.354/.393/.469	.362	.498	5.7%	5.5%	69.6%	94.4%	37.3%	89.4%	11.3	98.7	141	-0.4	2.2	5.2
2024 DC	MIA	MLB	27	611	65	8	63	4	.321/.377/.432	.336	.461	7.4%	5.9%							130	-0.4	2.5	4.2

2023 GP: 2B (134), 1B (12), DH (1)   *Comps: Gregg Jefferies (71), Nellie Fox (71), Dave Cash (69)*

When asked about her favorite novel after a trade with Minnesota in the winter, it's no coincidence that Marlins general manager Kim Ng told reporters, "*Arraez Were Watching God*" (which is a thing that definitely actually happened). The infielder's game is anathema to prevailing modern strategy, and Miami's bet on it was widely seen as awkward—especially considering how it forced Jazz Chisholm Jr. to move to center field. Then Arraez went and posted the highest batting average MLB has seen in more than a decade, in large part because he swung more and was able to erase the platoon split he'd previously displayed against lefties. He added a little more thump, too—a relative term, to be sure—by posting a career-best .115 isolated slugging mark. He's a star. With how he sprays singles to delight the masses, he might be a time traveler, too.

Josh Bell DH/1B   Born: 08/14/92   Age: 31   Bats: S   Throws: R   Height: 6'4"   Weight: 261   Origin: Round 2, 2011 Draft (#61 overall)

YEAR	TM	LVL	AGE	PA	R	HR	RBI	SB	AVG/OBP/SLG	BABIP	SLGCON	BB%	K%	ZSw%	ZCon%	OSw%	OCon%	LA	90th EV	DRC+	BRR	DRP	WARP
2021	WAS	MLB	28	568	75	27	88	0	.261/.347/.476	.276	.597	11.4%	17.8%	76.5%	83.9%	27.8%	61.8%	5.0	107.8	124	-0.4	-0.4	3.0
2022	SD	MLB	29	210	26	3	14	0	.192/.316/.271	.233	.353	15.2%	19.5%	66.0%	81.4%	25.6%	64.5%	6.2	105.9	114	-0.4	0.0	0.8
2022	WAS	MLB	29	437	52	14	57	0	.301/.384/.493	.324	.589	11.2%	14.0%	72.2%	86.0%	30.9%	70.4%	9.3	105.2	138	-0.9	0.0	2.8
2023	MIA	MLB	30	224	26	11	26	0	.270/.338/.480	.314	.653	8.9%	23.7%	69.9%	84.0%	31.1%	55.3%	10.0	105.9	124	-0.3	-0.1	1.1
2023	CLE	MLB	30	393	26	11	48	0	.233/.318/.383	.272	.500	10.9%	20.6%	72.2%	83.2%	32.8%	63.4%	9.2	107.3	100	-0.3	-0.2	0.7
2024 DC	MIA	MLB	31	590	67	19	70	0	.246/.332/.411	.284	.528	10.7%	19.9%							110	0.0	-0.4	1.9

2023 GP: DH (89), 1B (60)   *Comps: Justin Morneau (79), Joe Judge (78), Charlie Grimm (77)*

When the Guardians acquired a younger, cheaper version of Bell at the trade deadline in Kyle Manzardo, the Marlins were happy to snap up the displaced veteran in an effort to plug their first-base hole. It worked. Bell slashed a ringing .270/.338/.480 with Miami, miles better than the .233/.318/.383 he put up with Cleveland in spite of pitchers throwing him more junk to get him off all the four-seamers he was hammering. After suiting up with four teams in 366 days, Bell appears comfortable enough to keep performing in various locales even if he does so in unexpected ways. With the 31-year-old exercising a player option to stay in Miami this season, at least he'll have a chance to reprise his second-half role. He isn't good at first base, but being able to put up numbers in a difficult home park will keep him in the lineup. Being a switch hitter with thump for a team that likes to keep it weird and has lacked power helps, too.

Jon Berti IF   Born: 01/22/90   Age: 34   Bats: R   Throws: R   Height: 5'10"   Weight: 190   Origin: Round 18, 2011 Draft (#559 overall)

YEAR	TM	LVL	AGE	PA	R	HR	RBI	SB	AVG/OBP/SLG	BABIP	SLGCON	BB%	K%	ZSw%	ZCon%	OSw%	OCon%	LA	90th EV	DRC+	BRR	DRP	WARP
2021	MIA	MLB	31	271	35	4	19	8	.210/.311/.313	.265	.424	11.8%	22.5%	64.4%	86.3%	27.4%	66.0%	1.6	103.3	88	0.5	0.0	0.6
2022	MIA	MLB	32	404	47	4	28	41	.240/.324/.338	.308	.450	10.4%	22.0%	68.1%	86.1%	28.0%	57.5%	4.9	103.3	93	3.9	0.0	1.2
2023	MIA	MLB	33	424	53	7	33	16	.294/.344/.405	.349	.505	6.8%	18.2%	67.3%	88.3%	28.9%	66.2%	2.5	103.6	109	0.8	0.2	1.9
2024 DC	MIA	MLB	34	468	43	7	43	32	.242/.315/.344	.291	.434	8.8%	18.9%							91	1.3	-1.2	1.0

2023 GP: SS (64), 3B (41), LF (18), 2B (15), RF (1), DH (1)   *Comps: Craig Gentry (45), Larry Bowa (42), Jamey Carroll (42)*

In putting together his best campaign at 33 years of age, the late-blooming Berti offered a flavor for every kind of fan. He popped more extra-base hits than he ever has. While that number still isn't especially high, it also came with the most in-zone contact he's produced, putting him in the league's 85th percentile. The breakout complemented his ability to play all over the diamond. He played more games at more positions than ever before, making up for defense rated as a net negative. Overall, Berti's speed is still nearly elite, even if he only pushed for extra bases at an average rate. As the years go by, he pads his unique ledger the way a child does a pillow fort, slowly adding one more thing at a time.

Christian Bethancourt C   Born: 09/02/91   Age: 32   Bats: R   Throws: R   Height: 6'3"   Weight: 205   Origin: IFA, 2008

YEAR	TM	LVL	AGE	PA	R	HR	RBI	SB	AVG/OBP/SLG	BABIP	SLGCON	BB%	K%	ZSw%	ZCon%	OSw%	OCon%	LA	90th EV	DRC+	BRR	DRP	WARP
2021	IND	AAA	29	363	46	14	60	4	.281/.339/.468	.321	.601	7.7%	20.1%							109	1.3	-3.0	1.3
2022	TB	MLB	30	151	16	7	15	1	.255/.265/.436	.301	.591	1.3%	25.8%	79.2%	73.2%	50.7%	50.7%	9.8	106.3	90	0.0	1.6	0.5
2022	OAK	MLB	30	182	23	4	19	4	.249/.298/.385	.306	.508	5.5%	22.5%	84.1%	76.7%	43.1%	51.7%	9.2	108.0	95	0.1	0.1	0.4
2023	TB	MLB	31	332	49	11	33	1	.225/.254/.381	.278	.536	3.9%	27.4%	78.2%	77.5%	47.3%	48.5%	10.7	104.1	69	-0.1	1.1	0.1
2024 DC	MIA	MLB	32	189	17	5	20	2	.229/.270/.364	.300	.520	4.8%	28.8%							77	0.0	1.4	0.3

2023 GP: C (102), P (1)   *Comps: Dioner Navarro (58), Tom Prince (49), Muddy Ruel (47)*

Bethancourt was the Rays' primary backstop in 2023, making 89 starts behind the dish. Defensively, he was up to the task and earned positive marks for his framing and blocking ability. Runners were more successful than they were a year ago, but not all of that is on the catcher; the game itself was much different on the bases than in 2022. At the plate, Bethancourt remains a suborn puppy and still refuses to walk, with less than four percent of his appearances ending with a free pass. While that was not as big of an issue when his average on balls in play was above .300, that number has fallen about 30 points and his quality of contact has drooped in kind. Like most catchers with a solid glove and some pop, he'll continue to hang around the majors and ~~Cleveland~~ Miami will give him another shot in 2024.

YEAR	TM	P. COUNT	FRM RUNS	BLK RUNS	THRW RUNS	TOT RUNS
2021	IND	4070	-2.3	0.0	0.1	-2.2
2022	EST	1765			0.4	0.4
2022	OAK	1890	0.2	-0.1	0.3	0.4
2022	TB	4768	1.4	0.1	0.7	2.2
2023	TB	12547	1.9	-0.3	1.0	2.5
2024	MIA	7215	1.3	-0.1	0.3	1.5

Peyton Burdick OF   Born: 02/26/97   Age: 27   Bats: R   Throws: R   Height: 6'0"   Weight: 205   Origin: Round 3, 2019 Draft (#82 overall)

YEAR	TM	LVL	AGE	PA	R	HR	RBI	SB	AVG/OBP/SLG	BABIP	SLGCON	BB%	K%	ZSw%	ZCon%	OSw%	OCon%	LA	90th EV	DRC+	BRR	DRP	WARP
2021	PNS	AA	24	460	71	23	52	9	.231/.376/.472	.293	.739	16.5%	29.3%							133	0.3	-5.3	2.7
2021	JAX	AAA	24	31	5	0	1	0	.143/.226/.250	.235	.412	9.7%	35.5%							77	0.1	-1.4	-0.1
2022	JAX	AAA	25	430	74	15	58	13	.214/.326/.409	.272	.611	12.3%	27.9%	81.1%	66.7%	30.7%	48.8%			89	2.0	4.1	1.3
2022	MIA	MLB	25	102	8	4	11	1	.207/.284/.380	.283	.614	7.8%	34.3%	77.8%	76.6%	32.9%	47.3%	19.2	105.0	83	0.0	-0.5	0.1
2023	JAX	AAA	26	492	63	24	74	12	.219/.327/.448	.311	.783	11.6%	36.6%	72.6%	70.8%	31.1%	46.5%			87	1.5	8.9	1.5
2023	MIA	MLB	26	37	4	1	2	1	.182/.270/.333	.357	.733	8.1%	48.6%	76.6%	53.1%	36.0%	54.8%	17.5	108.1	55	0.0	-0.2	-0.1
2024 DC	MIA	MLB	27	157	15	5	17	3	.187/.270/.340	.280	.585	8.2%	37.6%							72	0.0	-0.8	-0.2

2023 GP: RF (11), CF (3), LF (1)   *Comps: Brandon Boggs (64), Mac Williamson (57), John Mayberry Jr. (56)*

When Homer Simpson played golf, he unwittingly tried to cheat by raising his score. After professional golfer Tom Kite told Homer that *lowering* one's mark was the traditional way to cheat at the game, Homer acknowledged, "that's one way." With Burdick's strikeout rate climbing all the way to 36.6% last year, it's unclear *what* the Marlins instructed him to do to get better. He hit for his typical power but also carried forward the holes in his game, and struck out in nearly half of his chances in a cup of coffee with the big-league outfit—thanks to an inability to make contact in the zone. Everyone loves a good dinger, but some whiffs displace too much air to ignore.

Jake Burger 3B   Born: 04/10/96   Age: 28   Bats: R   Throws: R   Height: 6'2"   Weight: 230   Origin: Round 1, 2017 Draft (#11 overall)

YEAR	TM	LVL	AGE	PA	R	HR	RBI	SB	AVG/OBP/SLG	BABIP	SLGCON	BB%	K%	ZSw%	ZCon%	OSw%	OCon%	LA	90th EV	DRC+	BRR	DRP	WARP
2021	CLT	AAA	25	340	46	18	54	0	.274/.332/.513	.330	.726	7.1%	26.8%							102	-2.4	-0.3	0.9
2021	CHW	MLB	25	42	5	1	3	0	.263/.333/.474	.409	.783	9.5%	35.7%	68.8%	75.0%	38.1%	48.9%	9.6	110.5	75	0.0	0.0	0.0
2022	CLT	AAA	26	168	22	5	16	0	.253/.351/.384	.299	.500	10.7%	20.2%	69.5%	88.8%	33.9%	43.8%			112	-0.5	-0.1	0.7
2022	CHW	MLB	26	183	20	8	26	0	.250/.302/.458	.324	.688	5.5%	30.6%	77.1%	79.4%	38.2%	45.2%	12.8	107.8	95	-0.1	-1.4	0.2
2023	CHW	MLB	27	323	44	25	52	1	.214/.279/.527	.225	.807	6.8%	31.6%	72.9%	80.7%	41.0%	45.5%	12.0	109.6	115	0.0	-0.2	1.5
2023	MIA	MLB	27	217	27	9	28	0	.303/.355/.505	.354	.662	4.6%	21.7%	75.6%	83.1%	40.8%	49.8%	13.1	111.3	96	0.1	-0.3	0.6
2024 DC	MIA	MLB	28	554	62	23	72	2	.236/.298/.427	.297	.622	6.3%	28.8%							103	-0.1	-2.9	1.3

2023 GP: 3B (102), DH (29), 1B (5), 2B (5)   *Comps: Chris Johnson (69), Gio Urshela (65), Eugenio Suárez (65)*

After years of injuries and bad vibes, Burger has a recipe that would make even a Kardashian salivate. His power appeared like the McRib, manifesting in triumph after years of brief glimpses and whispers of its existence. The biggest adjustment came post-trade, after which he chased less. Miami's lineup swung at more pitches out of the zone than all but nine teams (the White Sox were worst), so whether it's a sticky change will take time to suss out. Burger also registered plus defense for the first time in his career, though, so maybe it really was just about getting the hell out of Chicago.

Jazz Chisholm Jr. CF   Born: 02/01/98   Age: 26   Bats: L   Throws: R   Height: 5'11"   Weight: 184   Origin: IFA, 2015

YEAR	TM	LVL	AGE	PA	R	HR	RBI	SB	AVG/OBP/SLG	BABIP	SLGCON	BB%	K%	ZSw%	ZCon%	OSw%	OCon%	LA	90th EV	DRC+	BRR	DRP	WARP
2021	MIA	MLB	23	507	70	18	53	23	.248/.303/.425	.319	.618	6.7%	28.6%	64.9%	80.1%	35.9%	59.0%	8.9	106.0	74	1.2	-2.2	0.1
2022	MIA	MLB	24	241	39	14	45	12	.254/.325/.535	.294	.776	8.7%	27.4%	66.1%	80.2%	34.4%	52.2%	14.8	104.0	103	0.3	0.2	0.9
2023	MIA	MLB	25	383	50	19	51	22	.250/.304/.457	.318	.688	6.8%	30.8%	64.6%	73.2%	31.3%	50.8%	8.7	106.4	93	0.9	3.0	1.5
2024 DC	MIA	MLB	26	596	71	26	82	33	.243/.313/.454	.322	.687	8.0%	31.1%							110	0.9	3.9	3.4

2023 GP: CF (95), DH (1)   *Comps: Yoán Moncada (59), Jonathan Schoop (57), Javier Báez (57)*

Compared to Chisholm's incredible but injury-shortened 2022, his line last year might indicate he felt some hard regression, but his overall performance impressed, considering the circumstances. Even though he missed time with turf toe and an oblique strain, he was still healthier overall and embraced a transition to center field to accommodate the acquisition of Luis Arráez. He covered significant ground there, becoming the team's second-most valuable defender despite having had fewer opportunities than other regulars. In the face of all the interruptions he also managed to nearly be a league-average bat who chased less and became a more efficient base stealer. Having shown both flashes of star power and the traits of a glue guy, he remains the face of the franchise with a sky-high ceiling—even if he isn't currently the team's best player.

Bryan De La Cruz LF Born: 12/16/96   Age: 27   Bats: R   Throws: R   Height: 6'2"   Weight: 175   Origin: IFA, 2013

YEAR	TM	LVL	AGE	PA	R	HR	RBI	SB	AVG/OBP/SLG	BABIP	SLGCON	BB%	K%	ZSw%	ZCon%	OSw%	OCon%	LA	90th EV	DRC+	BRR	DRP	WARP
2021	TOR	WIN	24	69	6	1	12	0	.226/.290/.339	.260	.420	7.2%	17.4%										
2021	SUG	AAA	24	293	48	12	50	2	.324/.362/.518	.373	.662	5.8%	20.1%							111	1.9	-3.1	1.3
2021	MIA	MLB	24	219	17	5	19	1	.296/.356/.427	.380	.582	8.2%	24.2%	73.7%	88.6%	35.4%	56.8%	11.2	103.2	84	-0.1	-2.8	0.1
2022	TOR	WIN	25	136	14	1	9	1	.234/.301/.331	.308	.446	8.1%	23.5%										
2022	JAX	AAA	25	54	10	4	10	1	.320/.370/.620	.364	.838	7.4%	24.1%							112	0.6	3.4	0.6
2022	MIA	MLB	25	355	38	13	43	4	.252/.294/.432	.304	.594	5.4%	25.4%	72.2%	80.0%	34.1%	59.1%	9.9	105.5	102	-0.4	-3.2	0.8
2023	MIA	MLB	26	626	60	19	78	4	.257/.304/.411	.307	.545	6.4%	22.7%	70.2%	78.4%	36.4%	62.3%	11.9	104.5	95	-0.3	-4.2	0.9
2024 DC	MIA	MLB	27	491	50	15	57	2	.253/.303/.406	.310	.546	6.2%	24.0%							99	-0.4	-3.7	0.9

2023 GP: LF (142), RF (15), CF (7), DH (1)   *Comps: Marcell Ozuna (60), Harold Ramírez (57), Dexter Fowler (57)*

De La Cruz had a slightly down year that took him from average to palatable. After his first extended audition in the majors in 2021 he was primed for a breakout, one for which the Astros had never had any intention of waiting. But following some encouraging signs in 2022, year three in Miami wasn't a step in the right direction—or any discernible new one. His ability to barrel the ball declined from strong to middling, which can happen to a swing-happy guy whose in-zone contact rate sits the league's bottom 10%. With more than 1000 big-league plate appearances, Cruz isn't a reliable regular but could settle in nicely as a fourth outfielder who gets exposed less because he plays less.

Xavier Edwards UT Born: 08/09/99   Age: 24   Bats: S   Throws: R   Height: 5'10"   Weight: 175   Origin: Round 1, 2018 Draft (#38 overall)

YEAR	TM	LVL	AGE	PA	R	HR	RBI	SB	AVG/OBP/SLG	BABIP	SLGCON	BB%	K%	ZSw%	ZCon%	OSw%	OCon%	LA	90th EV	DRC+	BRR	DRP	WARP
2021	MTG	AA	21	337	40	0	27	19	.302/.377/.368	.348	.430	10.7%	12.5%							110	-1.2	0.6	1.3
2022	DUR	AAA	22	400	48	5	33	7	.246/.328/.350	.300	.445	10.8%	18.8%	70.0%	92.9%	30.2%	73.3%			91	-0.7	-1.9	0.5
2023	JAX	AAA	23	433	80	7	47	32	.351/.429/.457	.364	.497	12.0%	6.9%	70.4%	92.1%	29.6%	83.7%			117	3.3	-0.5	2.4
2023	MIA	MLB	23	84	12	0	3	5	.295/.329/.333	.359	.406	3.6%	16.7%	73.0%	86.9%	37.3%	69.6%	7.3	96.0	95	0.1	0.1	0.2
2024 DC	MIA	MLB	24	246	22	3	22	8	.256/.321/.349	.289	.405	8.0%	12.6%							91	0.0	-0	0.5

2023 GP: 2B (24), CF (4), DH (1)   *Comps: Martín Prado (69), Tyler Pastornicky (60), Dawel Lugo (57)*

In a brief 20-game stint precipitated by injuries elsewhere on the roster and September roster expansion, Edwards displayed how spicy the Marlins' slash-and-dash approach can get. Still, despite a saucy batting average and perfectly acceptable on-base percentage, his dearth of pop could be damning. He also illustrates how this approach can fall short if you're just about anyone other than teammate Luis Arraez. It's odd that he played second base exclusively in the majors despite Miami having no clear-cut options in his way at other positions and having tried him out at third, short, and center field in the minors before his call-ups.

Nick Fortes C Born: 11/11/96   Age: 27   Bats: R   Throws: R   Height: 5'11"   Weight: 198   Origin: Round 4, 2018 Draft (#117 overall)

YEAR	TM	LVL	AGE	PA	R	HR	RBI	SB	AVG/OBP/SLG	BABIP	SLGCON	BB%	K%	ZSw%	ZCon%	OSw%	OCon%	LA	90th EV	DRC+	BRR	DRP	WARP
2021	PNS	AA	24	226	21	3	23	5	.251/.338/.359	.289	.440	9.7%	15.9%							114	0.3	5.8	1.8
2021	JAX	AAA	24	152	16	4	21	0	.237/.322/.378	.248	.436	6.6%	11.8%							118	-1.9	-1.2	0.5
2021	MIA	MLB	24	34	6	4	7	1	.290/.353/.677	.263	.913	8.8%	23.5%	59.6%	94.1%	30.3%	60.9%	23.9	106.2	99	0.0	-1.0	0.0
2022	JAX	AAA	25	120	13	3	13	1	.257/.342/.381	.279	.455	9.2%	14.2%	73.1%	84.2%	28.0%	71.4%			113	0.5	3.6	0.9
2022	MIA	MLB	25	240	41	9	24	5	.230/.304/.392	.252	.494	7.5%	18.8%	64.0%	86.0%	32.4%	65.5%	15.7	104.6	103	0.3	1.7	1.1
2023	MIA	MLB	26	323	33	6	26	4	.204/.263/.299	.234	.374	5.3%	18.3%	64.6%	88.6%	31.4%	75.6%	12.7	102.6	89	0.1	4.6	1.3
2024 DC	MIA	MLB	27	316	29	7	31	6	.228/.293/.347	.253	.417	6.7%	15.6%							83	0.0	-1.6	0.4

2023 GP: C (104), DH (2)

Let's start with the bad news: Fortes was an absolutely dreadful hitter last year. Of guys who played at least as much as he did, he was the ninth-worst by DRC+ and dead last by OPS. Imagine the NBA players from the original *Space Jam* after they've had their skills slurped off by the aliens, or Uncle Rico from *Napoleon Dynamite* throwing a pass. Fortes was the baseball equivalent of that at the dish. Now the good news: When he was behind it was a different story. He ranked 18th in DRP, clearing the bar for a starting position by handling a talented and diverse pitching staff that was one of the best overall units in the league. You take the good with the bad when it comes to catchers, and given that Fortes is only entering his age-27 season there's still room for growth.

Comps: Martín Maldonado (66), Travis d'Arnaud (60), Austin Hedges (59)

YEAR	TM	P. COUNT	FRM RUNS	BLK RUNS	THRW RUNS	TOT RUNS
2021	PNS	6615	5.9	0.1	0.0	6.0
2021	JAX	3742	0.0	0.1	-0.4	-0.3
2021	MIA	744	-0.8	-0.1	0.0	-0.9
2022	JAX	3480	2.5	0.2	0.9	3.6
2022	MIA	7565	2.5	0.1	0.2	2.8
2023	MIA	13027	5.6	0.5	-0.4	5.6
2024	MIA	12025	-1.2	0.1	-0.4	-1.6

Avisaíl García OF   Born: 06/12/91   Age: 33   Bats: R   Throws: R   Height: 6'4"   Weight: 250   Origin: IFA, 2007

YEAR	TM	LVL	AGE	PA	R	HR	RBI	SB	AVG/OBP/SLG	BABIP	SLGCON	BB%	K%	ZSw%	ZCon%	OSw%	OCon%	LA	90th EV	DRC+	BRR	DRP	WARP
2021	MIL	MLB	30	515	68	29	86	8	.262/.330/.490	.291	.665	7.4%	23.5%	83.9%	77.2%	41.0%	51.9%	9.6	108.5	118	-0.1	-0.9	2.6
2022	JAX	AAA	31	34	3	0	2	2	.250/.353/.321	.389	.529	14.7%	32.4%							85	-0.4	0.7	0.1
2022	MIA	MLB	31	380	31	8	35	4	.224/.266/.317	.298	.456	4.5%	28.7%	83.3%	81.5%	42.9%	40.6%	3.1	106.8	67	0.0	-3.1	-0.8
2023	JAX	AAA	32	32	4	3	6	0	.259/.375/.667	.308	1.125	15.6%	34.4%	69.0%	80.0%	21.2%	52.9%			99	-0.9	2.2	0.2
2023	MIA	MLB	32	118	8	3	12	2	.185/.241/.315	.258	.493	5.1%	33.1%	76.3%	83.7%	38.4%	34.7%	10.4	106.9	72	0.0	-0.9	-0.2
2024 DC	MIA	MLB	33	365	35	10	38	4	.217/.287/.351	.286	.513	7.1%	28.6%							81	-0.1	-1	-0.2

2023 GP: RF (23), LF (10), DH (2), CF (1)   Comps: Jose Guillen (60), Roberto Clemente (57), Jermaine Dye (56)

The Get Up Kids are an emo band from Kansas who have written songs about typical things, like pivotal moments in relationships and frustration with oneself over imperfect timing and personal development. They've also written songs about less typical things, like going places with urgency just to remember you're alive, and the Massachusetts turnpike. These are things you might want to remember, hence the title of their seminal 1999 album, *Something to Write Home About*. The only way García's 2023 registers as such is if you consider it to have stunk so badly that you need to tell someone or risk passing out and hitting your head on your way to the floor. He registered just 118 plate appearances thanks to injury and performed almost as poorly as his career-worst 2022, offering little reason beyond hope for a bounce-back campaign next year.

Jordan Groshans CI   Born: 11/10/99   Age: 24   Bats: R   Throws: R   Height: 6'3"   Weight: 200   Origin: Round 1, 2018 Draft (#12 overall)

YEAR	TM	LVL	AGE	PA	R	HR	RBI	SB	AVG/OBP/SLG	BABIP	SLGCON	BB%	K%	ZSw%	ZCon%	OSw%	OCon%	LA	90th EV	DRC+	BRR	DRP	WARP
2021	NH	AA	21	316	46	7	40	0	.291/.367/.450	.347	.576	10.8%	19.3%							118	-1.2	-2.6	1.3
2022	BUF	AAA	22	279	30	1	24	2	.250/.348/.296	.303	.366	12.5%	16.5%							98	-0.4	-0.9	0.6
2022	JAX	AAA	22	133	14	2	10	1	.301/.398/.416	.344	.500	14.3%	14.3%							116	-0.4	-0.4	0.6
2022	MIA	MLB	22	65	9	1	2	0	.262/.308/.311	.319	.396	6.2%	20.0%	66.1%	89.5%	27.7%	68.3%	5.8	103.1	89	-0.1	-0.1	0.0
2023	JAX	AAA	23	528	60	6	60	0	.243/.339/.330	.292	.413	12.5%	17.4%	67.0%	87.8%	26.0%	63.4%			89	1.1	0.4	0.5
2024 DC	MIA	MLB	24	91	8	1	8	0	.240/.309/.327	.291	.409	8.6%	18.8%							84	-0.1	-0	0.0

2023 GP: 3B (77), 1B (41), DH (7)   Comps: Richard Urena (61), Ketel Marte (59), Christian Arroyo (58)

Just five qualified corner infielders registered an OPS below .700 this past season, and of that ignominious group only one was on a playoff club (thank you, Houston, for carrying the withering remains of José Abreu). Groshans has registered a mark above that in the upper minors just once: at Double-A in 2021, upon being acquired by Miami. It would be fair to argue that injuries have sapped not just his power but his ability to be effective in the box at all, but he registered 528 plate appearances in 2023 and still came up empty. A corner bat without thump is like Burger King without a catchy, incessant jingle: You can't remember the last time you thought of one.

Yuli Gurriel 1B   Born: 06/09/84   Age: 40   Bats: R   Throws: R   Height: 6'0"   Weight: 215   Origin: IFA, 2016

YEAR	TM	LVL	AGE	PA	R	HR	RBI	SB	AVG/OBP/SLG	BABIP	SLGCON	BB%	K%	ZSw%	ZCon%	OSw%	OCon%	LA	90th EV	DRC+	BRR	DRP	WARP
2021	HOU	MLB	37	605	83	15	81	1	.319/.383/.462	.336	.530	9.8%	11.2%	64.2%	91.0%	29.1%	79.3%	13.4	104.2	125	-0.4	-0.4	3.1
2022	HOU	MLB	38	584	53	8	53	8	.242/.288/.360	.266	.415	5.1%	12.5%	66.0%	92.5%	36.4%	77.0%	14.6	103.1	96	-0.5	0.5	0.8
2023	MIA	MLB	39	329	32	4	27	4	.245/.304/.359	.272	.421	7.9%	13.4%	65.4%	90.2%	32.5%	74.7%	16.3	102.7	110	0.1	0.2	1.1
2024 non	MIA	MLB	40	251	24	4	24	2	.256/.316/.370	.280	.425	7.3%	12.3%							95	-0.1	0.2	0.3

2023 GP: 1B (93), DH (3)   Comps: Mark Grace (76), Rod Carew (75), Bill Buckner (73)

A striking amount of what we said about Gurriel after 2022 rings true after 2023. His 13.4% strikeout rate represented a career worst, despite being a figure many major leaguers would do terrible things to obtain. Unfortunately, we're not building a Power Rangers-style Megazord of the best parts of various players to create a phenomenon of justice. The power didn't come back and he became even more vulnerable to all types of fastballs; on top of all that, he endured a further swoon at the end of the season. On a rate basis, his 108 games represent the fewest appearances he's made in a major-league season. He had one plate appearance in Miami's brief playoff series and struck out. He might still get the bat on the ball, but most everything else in the game could be signaling for Gurriel to call it quits the way it does for so many players.

Dane Myers CF   Born: 03/08/96   Age: 28   Bats: R   Throws: R   Height: 6'0"   Weight: 205   Origin: Round 6, 2017 Draft (#185 overall)

YEAR	TM	LVL	AGE	PA	R	HR	RBI	SB	AVG/OBP/SLG	BABIP	SLGCON	BB%	K%	ZSw%	ZCon%	OSw%	OCon%	LA	90th EV	DRC+	BRR	DRP	WARP
2021	LAK	A	25	60	15	0	9	5	.311/.450/.378	.519	.680	15.0%	33.3%	50.5%	80.4%	28.7%	55.6%			96	0.6	0.9	0.3
2021	ERI	AA	25	104	8	3	14	0	.278/.311/.443	.353	.614	3.8%	26.0%							90	-0.2	0.2	0.2
2022	ERI	AA	26	442	59	25	72	20	.268/.316/.506	.315	.713	5.2%	26.7%							127	-3.7	1.6	2.4
2022	TOL	AAA	26	46	5	0	5	1	.256/.304/.326	.393	.500	2.2%	32.6%							73	0.0	-1.2	-0.1
2023	PNS	AA	27	215	34	7	25	14	.291/.395/.462	.331	.579	12.6%	17.2%							122	0.5	1.7	1.4
2023	JAX	AAA	27	223	43	8	37	6	.339/.417/.516	.396	.664	10.3%	19.3%	62.3%	84.6%	32.1%	70.3%			110	1.2	-2.5	0.8
2023	MIA	MLB	27	70	9	1	9	1	.269/.286/.358	.354	.500	2.9%	27.1%	64.0%	80.0%	33.6%	65.2%	-1.0	107.2	71	0.0	0.2	0.0
2024 DC	MIA	MLB	28	121	12	3	13	4	.243/.302/.371	.297	.488	6.5%	22.2%							92	0.1	0.3	0.3

2023 GP: CF (19), LF (2), DH (1)   Comps: Ryan McBroom (61), Brandon Barnes (57), Matt McBride (52)

In the context of Miami prospect bats, Myers registers as a Goldilocks option. His ability to avoid strikeouts and his power registering as respectively moderate mean there isn't an obvious hole in his game like others. He can get swing happy, as evidenced in his brief call-up, but he makes enough useful contact that he remains competitive in the box. You might be tempted to wonder if he'd turn into a bigger threat if he focused more on contact to spray the ball around, or leaned into his power to find the barrel a bit more, but as a center fielder who has registered a DRC+ above 120 in upper minors stints in each of the last two years, all he truly needs is an extended opportunity to show he's just right for a big-league job.

Jesús Sánchez RF Born: 10/07/97 Age: 26 Bats: L Throws: R Height: 6'3" Weight: 222 Origin: IFA, 2014

YEAR	TM	LVL	AGE	PA	R	HR	RBI	SB	AVG/OBP/SLG	BABIP	SLGCON	BB%	K%	ZSw%	ZCon%	OSw%	OCon%	LA	90th EV	DRC+	BRR	DRP	WARP
2021	JAX	AAA	23	155	23	10	31	1	.348/.406/.652	.382	.821	7.7%	18.7%							140	0.6	6.0	1.8
2021	MIA	MLB	23	251	27	14	36	0	.251/.319/.489	.316	.745	8.0%	31.1%	70.7%	83.2%	36.7%	55.2%	8.9	107.8	91	0.0	1.5	0.7
2022	JAX	AAA	24	183	30	6	27	4	.308/.399/.465	.377	.617	11.5%	21.3%							119	1.1	-1.3	1.0
2022	MIA	MLB	24	343	38	13	36	1	.214/.280/.403	.258	.570	7.6%	26.8%	66.3%	82.5%	36.2%	56.5%	11.0	107.6	93	-0.3	-4.9	0.4
2023	MIA	MLB	25	402	43	14	52	3	.253/.327/.450	.321	.640	9.5%	26.6%	70.5%	81.1%	35.4%	55.7%	5.8	108.9	105	-0.2	-2.3	1.0
2024 DC	MIA	MLB	26	558	63	20	70	6	.240/.318/.429	.302	.605	9.2%	26.4%							107	-0.4	-1.2	1.7

2023 GP: RF (106), CF (9), LF (8), DH (1)   *Comps: Randal Grichuk (55), Jay Bruce (54), Jeremy Hermida (52)*

After a dreadful 2022, Sánchez bounced back with his healthiest year in the majors to date. His performance was fueled by a return to mashing fastballs, against which he registered a .511 slugging percentage that clocked in 65 points higher than the league average. It was critical in his return to form, given that he slugged almost 100 points worse against the offerings in 2022. Maybe it was timing, or something mechanical, or maybe it was Maybelline, but it was an even bigger deal since pitchers threw him more gas than they have since his rookie season. That reality, combined with a declining ability to do damage on the changeup, could make Sánchez's success more subject to the opposition's approach than his own skills.

PITCHERS

Sandy Alcantara RHP Born: 09/07/95 Age: 28 Height: 6'5" Weight: 200 Origin: IFA, 2013

YEAR	TM	LVL	AGE	G (GS)	IP	W-L	SV	K	WHIP	ERA	CSP	BB%	K%	HR%	GB%	ZSw%	ZCon%	OSw%	OCon%	BABIP	SLGCON	DRA-	WARP
2021	MIA	MLB	25	33 (33)	205²	9-15	0	201	1.07	3.19	54.6%	6.0%	24.0%	2.5%	52.8%	72.1%	83.0%	38.6%	57.9%	.273	.494	75	4.6
2022	MIA	MLB	26	32 (32)	228²	14-9	0	207	0.98	2.28	55.8%	5.6%	23.4%	1.8%	53.2%	71.7%	83.7%	38.9%	61.8%	.262	.434	69	5.6
2023	MIA	MLB	27	28 (28)	184²	7-12	0	151	1.21	4.14	49.8%	6.3%	19.8%	2.9%	51.1%	72.5%	83.4%	39.1%	61.7%	.289	.499	90	3.2
2024 non	MIA	MLB	28	58 (0)	50	2-2	0	42	1.23	3.70	52.7%	6.5%	20.3%	2.5%	50.9%					.293	.490	87	0.6

2023 Arsenal: SI (97.7), CH (91.2), FA (98.1), SL (90.1), CU (86.2)   *Comps: Félix Hernández (68), Dave Stieb (68), Matt Cain (67)*

It's rare to look at a pitcher's profile from year to year and see nearly identical rates in nearly all aspects of their approach: mix, movement, velocity, contact allowed, you name it. It's David Lynch levels of weird to see those mirrored efforts yield such disparate results, as was the case with 2023 Alcantara compared to the 2022 Cy Young-winning version.

He gave up more homers, but not more than he has typically through his career. He had less fortune on batted balls, but was still notably better than average. He even threw slightly fewer pitchers per batter faced and remained on pace for more than 200 innings, which would have marked three straight campaigns achieving the feat. Sometimes the game really is one of inches, or even fractions of inches. Shut down at the end of last season with a dreaded UCL sprain that led to Tommy John surgery, Alcantara will be out for the entire year.

Matt Barnes RHP Born: 06/17/90 Age: 34 Height: 6'4" Weight: 208 Origin: Round 1, 2011 Draft (#19 overall)

YEAR	TM	LVL	AGE	G (GS)	IP	W-L	SV	K	WHIP	ERA	CSP	BB%	K%	HR%	GB%	ZSw%	ZCon%	OSw%	OCon%	BABIP	SLGCON	DRA-	WARP
2021	BOS	MLB	31	60 (0)	54²	6-5	24	84	1.12	3.79	57.3%	9.0%	37.8%	3.6%	42.2%	62.9%	82.8%	36.7%	48.3%	.306	.617	66	1.5
2022	BOS	MLB	32	44 (0)	39²	0-4	8	34	1.44	4.31	53.2%	11.9%	19.3%	1.1%	44.1%	62.4%	84.3%	31.1%	55.6%	.296	.431	111	0.2
2023	MIA	MLB	33	24 (1)	21¹	1-0	0	20	1.64	5.48	43.4%	10.1%	20.2%	2.0%	48.5%	59.2%	94.0%	29.1%	62.7%	.348	.500	100	0.3
2024 non	MIA	MLB	34	58 (0)	50	2-2	0	50	1.38	4.52	49.7%	10.3%	23.2%	3.1%	44.2%					.296	.542	101	0.2

2023 Arsenal: KC (83.5), FA (93.7), FS (88.3), CH (88.1)   *Comps: Brad Boxberger (58), Greg Holland (57), Justin Wilson (55)*

Through June 1, Barnes was Miami's fifth-most used reliever. While not a go-to lockdown option, he was in the club's regular mix thanks to his ability to generate ground balls and limit home runs. That helped balance out his propensity to walk too many batters while not striking out enough, but his career-low fastball velocity (93.6 mph, down roughly a tick and a half from previous years) and inability to get swinging strikes were tipping the scales against him. Then he went on the shelf with a hip injury and eventually underwent season-ending surgery. At this point Barnes is a competent but low-ceiling middle reliever; the thrifty Marlins declined his option, putting him on the free-agent market with little leverage.

Archie Bradley RHP Born: 08/10/92 Age: 31 Height: 6'4" Weight: 215 Origin: Round 1, 2011 Draft (#7 overall)

YEAR	TM	LVL	AGE	G (GS)	IP	W-L	SV	K	WHIP	ERA	CSP	BB%	K%	HR%	GB%	ZSw%	ZCon%	OSw%	OCon%	BABIP	SLGCON	DRA-	WARP
2021	PHI	MLB	28	53 (0)	51	7-3	2	40	1.43	3.71	52.9%	9.8%	17.9%	2.2%	56.0%	69.9%	88.0%	31.7%	74.3%	.299	.506	96	0.6
2022	LAA	MLB	29	21 (0)	18²	0-1	2	15	1.29	4.82	57.0%	9.0%	19.2%	1.3%	58.9%	66.7%	86.0%	29.5%	69.2%	.291	.411	87	0.3
2023	JAX	AAA	30	14 (1)	26¹	0-2	1	21	1.25	5.47		9.9%	18.9%	4.5%	38.2%	62.4%	85.8%	29.9%	73.2%	.239	.587	113	0.2
2023	MIA	MLB	30	4 (0)	7¹	0-0	0	7	2.18	11.05	47.7%	7.7%	17.9%	5.1%	35.7%	60.0%	88.9%	31.5%	64.3%	.423	.821	107	0.1
2024 non	MIA	MLB	31	58 (0)	50	2-2	0	36	1.41	4.84	51.6%	8.4%	16.4%	2.8%	47.7%					.296	.512	108	0.0

2023 Arsenal: FA (93.2), SI (92.8), KC (79.9), SW (80.6), CH (84.6)   *Comps: Tyler Clippard (64), Kyle Farnsworth (62), Larry Sherry (62)*

It's been a couple of years since Bradley was both healthy and effective. After a slapstick entry to a benches-clearing brawl caused injuries that led to him pitching only 18 ⅔ innings in 2022, he barely managed to reach even a third of that total last year. Having signed a minor-league deal, he pitched well enough for Miami's Triple-A affiliate—including one five-inning start, because why not?— to get his contract selected and rejoin the majors. He got touched up in his first outing, threw four scoreless frames in his next two and then was devoured by the Braves for six runs and outrighted off the roster. His velocity continued to decline and he continued to try to throw five pitches to counter it. It was another weird year for a player who has collected weird moments like your mom does those odd, cute, awkward Snow Babies statues.

Huascar Brazoban   RHP   Born: 10/15/89   Age: 34   Height: 6'3"   Weight: 155   Origin: IFA, 2012

YEAR	TM	LVL	AGE	G (GS)	IP	W-L	SV	K	WHIP	ERA	CSP	BB%	K%	HR%	GB%	ZSw%	ZCon%	OSw%	OCon%	BABIP	SLGCON	DRA-	WARP
2022	JAX	AAA	32	27 (0)	45¹	2-0	0	59	1.06	3.18		8.8%	32.6%	3.3%	43.8%	80.4%	62.2%	39.5%	50.0%	.263	.553	65	1.4
2022	MIA	MLB	32	27 (0)	32	1-1	0	40	1.47	3.09	50.2%	14.9%	28.4%	2.1%	48.7%	71.6%	73.2%	32.4%	45.3%	.311	.532	93	0.4
2023	MIA	MLB	33	50 (0)	58²	5-2	0	65	1.43	4.14	44.0%	12.1%	25.3%	1.9%	51.0%	66.3%	80.6%	36.8%	55.9%	.318	.497	86	1.1
2024 DC	MIA	MLB	34	35 (0)	38	2-2	0	47	1.35	4.19	46.1%	10.8%	28.3%	2.7%	46.8%					.311	.551	94	0.3

2023 Arsenal: SL (87.7), CH (89.3), SI (96.2), FA (96.7)   Comps: Jumbo Díaz (66), Pat Venditte (65), Will Harris (63)

After becoming relevant in the major leagues again with Miami in 2022, following a five-year absence from affiliated ball, Brazoban proved he could continue to hang with the best of the best. He induced more grounders with three of his four pitches. Even against the exception to that rule, the sinker, almost 50% of batted balls went on the ground. This pivot gave his strikeout rate a haircut, but also helped curb his walks. As one of only a handful of relievers with a legitimate four-pitch mix, Brazoban carries traits that should keep him in bullpens, even with half a decade on many of his peers. That can be cool, anyway. Just look at the Fonz.

Edward Cabrera   RHP   Born: 04/13/98   Age: 26   Height: 6'5"   Weight: 217   Origin: IFA, 2015

YEAR	TM	LVL	AGE	G (GS)	IP	W-L	SV	K	WHIP	ERA	CSP	BB%	K%	HR%	GB%	ZSw%	ZCon%	OSw%	OCon%	BABIP	SLGCON	DRA-	WARP
2021	JUP	A	23	2 (2)	6	0-0	0	11	0.67	0.00		0.0%	47.8%	0.0%	36.4%	69.4%	72.0%	21.2%	36.4%	.364	.364	89	0.1
2021	PNS	AA	23	5 (5)	26	2-1	0	33	0.96	2.77		6.2%	34.0%	3.1%	48.3%					.296	.544	85	0.5
2021	JAX	AAA	23	6 (6)	29¹	1-3	0	48	1.40	3.68		14.7%	37.2%	3.1%	37.7%					.316	.746	77	0.7
2021	MIA	MLB	23	7 (7)	26¹	0-3	0	28	1.63	5.81	52.6%	15.8%	23.3%	5.0%	40.6%	71.3%	80.3%	27.4%	59.0%	.286	.710	118	0.0
2022	PNS	AA	24	2 (2)	6	0-0	0	8	0.17	0.00		5.0%	40.0%	0.0%	54.5%					.000	.000	98	0.1
2022	JAX	AAA	24	6 (6)	28²	2-2	0	39	1.15	3.77		10.3%	33.6%	1.7%	44.6%					.302	.523	76	0.7
2022	MIA	MLB	24	14 (14)	71²	6-4	0	75	1.07	3.01	49.3%	11.3%	25.8%	3.4%	44.8%	63.6%	80.8%	33.6%	56.7%	.207	.466	103	0.6
2023	JAX	AAA	25	5 (5)	28¹	3-1	0	30	1.13	2.22		10.6%	26.5%	1.8%	48.6%	64.5%	82.2%	36.3%	59.4%	.265	.420	80	0.7
2023	MIA	MLB	25	22 (20)	99²	7-7	0	118	1.44	4.24	40.0%	15.2%	27.2%	2.5%	55.3%	59.7%	85.4%	34.3%	54.2%	.285	.527	90	1.7
2024 DC	MIA	MLB	26	24 (24)	111²	6-7	0	130	1.33	3.89	44.1%	12.3%	27.0%	2.4%	49.9%					.283	.505	88	1.7

2023 Arsenal: CH (93), FA (96.4), CU (84.7), SI (96.5), SL (88.4)   Comps: Chris Archer (62), Robert Stephenson (60), Jarred Cosart (60)

Cabrera continued to be plagued by issues locating his four-seamer and sinker, with each hardly going for more strikes than balls. What's awkward is that he threw each pitch more than he did in 2022, when batted-ball fortune helped cover up flaws his peripherals couldn't hide. He got better action from his curveball and changeup, though, and pared down his slider usage to a borderline show-me pitch. Miami's track record with developing arms is well-established, but the biggest reason Cabrera threw so many innings was the rotation enduring a spate of injuries. If Cabrera can't figure out his heaters and sort out the ugly WHIP, the Marlins won't have to wait around to find other options.

JT Chargois   RHP   Born: 12/03/90   Age: 33   Height: 6'3"   Weight: 200   Origin: Round 2, 2012 Draft (#72 overall)

YEAR	TM	LVL	AGE	G (GS)	IP	W-L	SV	K	WHIP	ERA	CSP	BB%	K%	HR%	GB%	ZSw%	ZCon%	OSw%	OCon%	BABIP	SLGCON	DRA-	WARP
2021	TB	MLB	30	25 (0)	23²	5-1	0	24	1.23	1.90	48.3%	14.3%	24.5%	3.1%	44.1%	74.6%	91.3%	32.9%	57.6%	.214	.517	100	0.2
2021	SEA	MLB	30	31 (0)	30	1-0	0	29	0.97	3.00	55.3%	5.1%	24.6%	1.7%	44.9%	67.2%	85.0%	29.0%	46.2%	.276	.455	97	0.3
2022	DUR	AAA	31	10 (0)	5²	1-2	0	4	3.00	20.65		20.0%	11.4%	2.9%	27.3%					.429	.818	137	0.0
2022	TB	MLB	31	21 (3)	22¹	2-0	0	17	0.94	2.42	55.4%	5.8%	19.8%	3.5%	59.7%	64.7%	91.8%	36.4%	55.2%	.220	.516	85	0.4
2023	MIA	MLB	32	46 (5)	42¹	1-0	1	35	1.25	3.61	48.9%	10.3%	20.1%	1.7%	54.6%	59.7%	86.7%	26.2%	68.5%	.276	.491	92	0.7
2024 DC	MIA	MLB	33	47 (0)	50²	3-2	0	42	1.35	4.36	51.1%	9.4%	19.4%	2.7%	47.1%					.285	.500	99	0.3

2023 Arsenal: SI (96.3), SL (86.2), FA (95.8)   Comps: Darren O'Day (70), Nick Vincent (67), Grant Balfour (66)

Chargois took a step back in 2023, losing the gains he enjoyed from improved control. The consequences were steep. He lost whiffs on his sinker and slider. And, like a bad infomercial, there's more. He was still able to get a grounder from the sinker 57.1% of the time batters put it in play, which is awesome, but also a far cry from his elite 68.4% ground-ball rate on it the year before. In fact, 2023's mark was the worst he's posted with the sinker in a full season in his major-league career. His velocity is still there, though the breaking ball lost a tick, perhaps deliberately in an effort to better locate it. His season played out the way a knit sweater worn one too many times between washes does: slightly loose and unshapely, devoid of its cozy crispness. At the time of publishing, it's not yet confirmed that spending a few minutes in the dryer will similarly tighten up Chargois' game.

Johnny Cueto   RHP   Born: 02/15/86   Age: 38   Height: 5'11"   Weight: 229   Origin: IFA, 2004

YEAR	TM	LVL	AGE	G (GS)	IP	W-L	SV	K	WHIP	ERA	CSP	BB%	K%	HR%	GB%	ZSw%	ZCon%	OSw%	OCon%	BABIP	SLGCON	DRA-	WARP
2021	SF	MLB	35	22 (21)	114²	7-7	0	98	1.37	4.08	54.3%	6.1%	20.0%	3.1%	37.2%	73.6%	81.7%	33.8%	70.4%	.336	.597	100	1.0
2022	CLT	AAA	36	4 (4)	15²	0-1	0	17	1.21	5.17		6.3%	27.0%	4.8%	57.1%	72.0%	91.7%	36.4%	46.4%	.308	.643	85	0.3
2022	CHW	MLB	36	25 (24)	158¹	8-10	0	102	1.23	3.35	51.5%	5.1%	15.7%	2.3%	42.0%	71.4%	88.2%	34.9%	74.2%	.296	.492	112	0.6
2023	MIA	MLB	37	13 (10)	52¹	1-4	0	39	1.26	6.02	47.5%	6.9%	17.9%	7.8%	33.5%	72.2%	87.3%	38.7%	71.9%	.236	.675	125	-0.1
2024 non	MIA	MLB	38	58 (0)	50	2-2	0	31	1.45	5.58	50.6%	6.6%	14.0%	4.0%	36.5%					.300	.576	124	-0.4

2023 Arsenal: FA (92.1), SL (85.9), SI (92.1), CH (84.1), FC (87.8), CU (71.3)   Comps: Kevin Millwood (80), Tim Hudson (77), Jim Palmer (76)

After a season of smoke, mirrors and delight with the White Sox, Cueto had none of it going with Miami. He upped his strikeout rate by a couple percentage points, but still came in well below average as his walk rate jumped. Given his diminished skill set, it was the equivalent of putting a tablespoon of salt into a recipe that calls for a teaspoon. Cueto stranded runners at the same rate he has the last few years, which is to say he was thoroughly average at it, often a fine way to go through life. But when you give up the highest rate of home runs per nine innings since 2019, among any individual pitcher season lasting at least 50 innings, you're going to have a bad time. His 6.02 HR/9 made declining a 2024 option easy for Miami, and put him in line for another long winter of waiting to see if someone else was interested.

Enmanuel De Jesus LHP   Born: 12/10/96   Age: 27   Height: 6'3"   Weight: 190   Origin: IFA, 2013

YEAR	TM	LVL	AGE	G (GS)	IP	W-L	SV	K	WHIP	ERA	CSP	BB%	K%	HR%	GB%	ZSw%	ZCon%	OSw%	OCon%	BABIP	SLGCON	DRA-	WARP
2021	POR	AA	24	21(8)	59	5-2	1	71	1.56	3.97		9.6%	26.3%	0.7%	43.8%					.386	.567	104	0.3
2022	SAC	AAA	25	35(19)	101²	4-5	0	118	1.56	4.51		10.9%	25.2%	2.3%	42.1%	68.3%	82.0%	32.1%	57.2%	.351	.593	81	1.8
2023	JUP	A	26	2(2)	7¹	1-0	0	9	1.23	3.68		3.2%	29.0%	0.0%	52.4%	63.8%	93.3%	46.4%	56.2%	.381	.429	71	0.1
2023	JAX	AAA	26	17(16)	84²	4-5	1	61	1.69	4.78		13.3%	15.9%	2.3%	38.0%	72.0%	86.6%	33.7%	65.1%	.324	.556	119	0.1
2023	MIA	MLB	26	2(0)	6¹	0-0	0	5	2.05	11.37	48.1%	11.8%	14.7%	0.0%	40.9%	66.1%	81.1%	31.2%	60.0%	.409	.545	113	0.0
2024 non	MIA	MLB	27	58(0)	50	2-2	0	43	1.59	5.78	48.1%	10.6%	18.8%	2.9%	36.9%					.321	.563	124	-0.4

2023 Arsenal: FA (93.4), SL (79.7), CH (86.6), SI (93.9), CU (68)   Comps: Tanner Tully (36), Rob Zastryzny (35), Ryan Carpenter (35)

Word has it that De Jesus is into impressions. He does a killer Ray Romano, going around the clubhouse shouting "Deborah! [existential sigh]." One day in spring training he decided his next muse would be Edward Cabrera. He focused on every mannerism of his teammate, to the point that he couldn't put the mask away when he got to the mound in Triple-A, also imitating Cabrera's proclivity for free passes. The biggest tell was that he didn't even emulate the strikeouts—so he's just a four-pitch kitchen sink guy with a middling fastball and unimpressive slider. His changeup can be great, but is mitigated because it lacks anything to play off, lodging De Jesus firmly in the category of "organizational depth."

Calvin Faucher RHP   Born: 09/22/95   Age: 28   Height: 6'1"   Weight: 190   Origin: Round 10, 2017 Draft (#286 overall)

YEAR	TM	LVL	AGE	G (GS)	IP	W-L	SV	K	WHIP	ERA	CSP	BB%	K%	HR%	GB%	ZSw%	ZCon%	OSw%	OCon%	BABIP	SLGCON	DRA-	WARP
2021	WCH	AA	25	19(0)	30²	1-1	1	42	2.05	7.04		15.8%	27.6%	3.9%	47.1%					.423	.762	118	0.0
2021	DUR	AAA	25	11(3)	20¹	0-0	0	26	1.03	1.77		8.9%	32.9%	1.3%	37.0%					.289	.413	83	0.4
2022	DUR	AAA	26	34(4)	43	3-3	1	52	1.51	3.56		10.9%	27.1%	3.6%	45.4%					.333	.650	84	0.9
2022	TB	MLB	26	22(0)	21¹	2-3	1	21	1.69	5.48	55.0%	9.9%	20.8%	4.0%	40.6%	64.0%	86.7%	28.6%	61.0%	.338	.580	96	0.3
2023	DUR	AAA	27	8(1)	8²	0-1	0	13	1.50	1.04		17.9%	33.3%	0.0%	52.6%	71.9%	68.3%	33.1%	47.5%	.316	.316	89	0.2
2023	TB	MLB	27	17(4)	25²	1-1	0	25	1.68	7.01	48.7%	10.0%	20.8%	3.3%	48.8%	67.6%	87.7%	32.2%	60.4%	.346	.598	93	0.4
2024 DC	MIA	MLB	28	25(3)	39	2-2	0	37	1.46	4.84	51.3%	11.0%	21.2%	3.0%	43.4%					.301	.543	107	0.1

2023 Arsenal: FC (91.2), SW (87.3), FA (95.5), KC (85)   Comps: Preston Claiborne (73), Jacob Webb (72), Montana DuRapau (72)

Faucher started the season in a *de facto* opener role as he logged four opens in his first eight appearances, stretching 14 innings. Unfortunately for him, his right arm was not compliant with the usage. He landed on the injured list twice for arm-related issues before he was shut down for good in August. Even when healthy, things were not going his way; he allowed far too many hits and runs. The most intriguing part of his season was his move from being a two-pitch pitcher for the most part, to using a four-pitch medley, most likely in hopes he could get outs across multiple innings. His arm is lively enough to continue the experiment ... provided his arm is lively enough to pitch.

Braxton Garrett LHP   Born: 08/05/97   Age: 26   Height: 6'2"   Weight: 202   Origin: Round 1, 2016 Draft (#7 overall)

YEAR	TM	LVL	AGE	G (GS)	IP	W-L	SV	K	WHIP	ERA	CSP	BB%	K%	HR%	GB%	ZSw%	ZCon%	OSw%	OCon%	BABIP	SLGCON	DRA-	WARP
2021	JAX	AAA	23	18(18)	85²	5-4	0	86	1.23	3.89		9.0%	24.1%	2.8%	45.3%					.281	.522	112	0.6
2021	MIA	MLB	23	8(7)	34	1-2	0	32	1.82	5.03	53.0%	12.6%	20.1%	1.9%	36.2%	65.2%	87.2%	31.3%	66.9%	.398	.590	118	0.0
2022	JAX	AAA	24	7(7)	34¹	2-3	0	29	1.08	3.15		6.4%	20.6%	2.1%	52.0%	51.9%	85.7%	50.7%	61.8%	.253	.424	96	0.5
2022	MIA	MLB	24	17(17)	88	3-7	0	90	1.25	3.58	55.7%	6.4%	24.1%	2.4%	47.4%	62.3%	91.3%	38.7%	54.1%	.322	.548	103	0.7
2023	MIA	MLB	25	31(30)	159²	9-7	0	156	1.15	3.66	49.2%	4.4%	23.7%	3.0%	48.8%	62.8%	89.6%	35.3%	55.0%	.302	.562	90	2.7
2024 DC	MIA	MLB	26	28(28)	143	8-9	0	133	1.28	4.17	51.2%	6.8%	21.8%	2.7%	47.4%					.304	.526	96	1.6

2023 Arsenal: SI (90.6), SW (82.9), FC (87.5), FA (91), CH (84.2), CU (77.8)   Comps: Robbie Erlin (68), Homer Bailey (67), Zach Eflin (66)

Like a Pokémon, Garrett continued his evolution last year by subbing in a cutter for his four-seamer and leaning more into his sinker. A fascinating case given how a move to a more standard arm slot led to funkier angles on his stuff, he coaxed fewer whiffs out of the zone but due to the change generated weaker contact and gave up less offense overall. Getting guys to get themselves out is an impressive skill even if not a primary focus of pitcher development today. Despite fastball velocity that more closely resembles a sterno than a flamethrower, Garrett has rounded into a reliable rotation option who provides a unique look in a rotation with guys who dial it up to the high 90s.

Bryan Hoeing RHP   Born: 10/19/96   Age: 27   Height: 6'6"   Weight: 210   Origin: Round 7, 2019 Draft (#201 overall)

YEAR	TM	LVL	AGE	G (GS)	IP	W-L	SV	K	WHIP	ERA	CSP	BB%	K%	HR%	GB%	ZSw%	ZCon%	OSw%	OCon%	BABIP	SLGCON	DRA-	WARP
2021	BEL	A+	24	22(22)	121	7-6	0	96	1.27	4.83		4.6%	18.4%	2.5%	56.1%					.307	.527	103	1.1
2022	PNS	AA	25	4(4)	25²	2-1	0	26	0.94	0.35		3.9%	25.5%	0.0%	72.5%					.290	.377	87	0.4
2022	JAX	AAA	25	18(17)	94	7-5	0	49	1.44	5.07		8.6%	12.1%	3.4%	53.2%	65.9%	96.3%	21.3%	70.0%	.287	.542	131	-0.2
2022	MIA	MLB	25	8(1)	12²	1-1	0	6	1.89	12.08	51.4%	8.2%	9.8%	8.2%	52.0%	65.7%	96.9%	30.4%	74.5%	.318	.812	117	0.0
2023	JAX	AAA	26	7(4)	30²	1-0	0	37	0.95	2.35		3.3%	30.8%	2.5%	57.0%	61.7%	85.6%	41.9%	50.9%	.297	.571	73	0.9
2023	MIA	MLB	26	33(7)	70²	2-3	0	53	1.36	5.48	47.0%	8.2%	17.4%	4.3%	45.1%	64.9%	87.1%	30.5%	66.5%	.275	.624	105	0.6
2024 DC	MIA	MLB	27	44(3)	57²	3-3	0	38	1.35	4.61	47.7%	7.0%	15.4%	2.9%	46.2%					.293	.511	105	0.2

2023 Arsenal: SI (94.3), SL (83.3), FA (94.2), CH (85.8)   Comps: Paul Clemens (67), Greg Reynolds (61), Jeff Manship (59)

Hoeing plants seeds in hitters' minds with four different pitches, though he usually digs in with a sinker-slider combination that accounts for more than 80% of his offerings. The sinker turns into a worm burner that makes him bay leaf in himself, while the slider gets whiffs at a rate that is only radish. When it all comes together it feels like it was mint to be, but his ERA betrays how that hardly happened. He'll need a new wrinkle in order to prune his runs allowed. Perhaps the sage advice of the Marlins pitching development staff will help him reach a new level and achieve peas.

Jesús Luzardo LHP   Born: 09/30/97   Age: 26   Height: 6'0"   Weight: 218   Origin: Round 3, 2016 Draft (#94 overall)

YEAR	TM	LVL	AGE	G (GS)	IP	W-L	SV	K	WHIP	ERA	CSP	BB%	K%	HR%	GB%	ZSw%	ZCon%	OSw%	OCon%	BABIP	SLGCON	DRA-	WARP
2021	LV	AAA	23	8(8)	29	2-2	0	26	1.66	6.52		11.1%	19.3%	2.2%	47.2%					.349	.557	99	0.1
2021	OAK	MLB	23	13(6)	38	2-4	0	40	1.63	6.87	55.0%	9.2%	23.1%	6.4%	38.5%	69.3%	81.6%	28.4%	54.5%	.333	.748	123	-0.1
2021	MIA	MLB	23	12(12)	57¹	4-5	0	58	1.60	6.44	50.5%	12.1%	22.0%	3.4%	36.5%	74.5%	83.1%	33.5%	53.9%	.319	.679	125	-0.2
2022	JAX	AAA	24	2(2)	8²	0-0	0	9	0.81	2.08		11.4%	25.7%	0.0%	47.6%					.143	.143	91	0.2
2022	MIA	MLB	24	18(18)	100¹	4-7	0	120	1.04	3.32	54.7%	8.8%	30.0%	2.5%	40.7%	66.2%	79.9%	32.6%	52.7%	.254	.502	96	1.2
2023	MIA	MLB	25	32(32)	178²	10-10	0	208	1.21	3.58	45.3%	7.4%	28.1%	3.0%	40.7%	70.1%	82.6%	34.7%	50.9%	.312	.591	93	2.6
2024 DC	MIA	MLB	26	28(28)	154	9-9	0	176	1.26	4.05	48.8%	8.8%	27.0%	3.3%	40.3%					.297	.571	94	1.9

2023 Arsenal: FA (96.9), SL (85.2), CH (88.4), SI (96.7), FC (90.9)   Comps: Martín Pérez (51), Luis Severino (51), Jonathon Niese (50)

Luzardo took another step forward last season, finally figuring out his four-seamer and absolutely pounding the zone with it. He threw it a lot—more frequently than all but 15 qualified starters—and that's because the pitch got top-five results by chases and whiffs. For the first time in his career he was able to hammer the top of the zone (and above it when ahead), giving him a high-powered, no-frills weapon to pair with his dagger slider and worm-burning changeup. Luzardo's strikeout rate didn't explode, nor did his walk rate plummet, but that's because he was already compiling rates among the league's elite. What he has done is round into a stronger, more reliable pitcher who can pile up innings, providing another lights-out arm for the Marlins as they wait/hope/pray for a lineup that can even come close to complementing the pitching staff.

─────── ★ ★ ★ *2024 Top 101 Prospect* **#86** ★ ★ ★ ───────

Max Meyer RHP   Born: 03/12/99   Age: 25   Height: 6'0"   Weight: 196   Origin: Round 1, 2020 Draft (#3 overall)

YEAR	TM	LVL	AGE	G (GS)	IP	W-L	SV	K	WHIP	ERA	CSP	BB%	K%	HR%	GB%	ZSw%	ZCon%	OSw%	OCon%	BABIP	SLGCON	DRA-	WARP
2021	PNS	AA	22	20(20)	101	6-3	0	113	1.23	2.41		9.6%	27.2%	1.7%	52.7%					.304	.494	91	1.5
2021	JAX	AAA	22	2(2)	10	0-1	0	17	0.80	0.90		5.3%	44.7%	2.6%	47.4%					.278	.737	72	0.3
2022	JAX	AAA	23	12(12)	58	3-4	0	65	1.00	3.72		8.3%	28.4%	2.2%	51.0%	71.8%	92.9%	39.6%	52.4%	.246	.441	67	1.8
2022	MIA	MLB	23	2(2)	6	0-1	0	6	1.50	7.50	63.6%	7.7%	23.1%	7.7%	44.4%	69.8%	83.3%	30.4%	57.1%	.313	.889	103	0.1
2024 DC	MIA	MLB	25	13(13)	62	3-4	0	58	1.35	4.45	63.6%	9.4%	21.7%	3.1%	42.6%					.292	.538	101	0.5

Comps: Shane Bieber (46), Erik Johnson (46), Edward Cabrera (45)

We pick up with Meyer almost exactly where we left off in the 2023 *Annual*: He hasn't thrown a competitive pitch since leaving his second major-league game after two-thirds of a frame with an elbow injury that required Tommy John surgery. The righty was last rumored for a return to game action in the Arizona Fall League, though that never transpired. Should he come back at the same level, with a high-velocity fastball that has suboptimal shape and a biting high-80s slider, he'll become yet another weapon in the Marlins' stable of electric arms.

─────── ★ ★ ★ *2024 Top 101 Prospect* **#73** ★ ★ ★ ───────

Noble Meyer RHP   Born: 01/10/05   Age: 19   Height: 6'5"   Weight: 185   Origin: Round 1, 2023 Draft (#10 overall)

YEAR	TM	LVL	AGE	G (GS)	IP	W-L	SV	K	WHIP	ERA	CSP	BB%	K%	HR%	GB%	ZSw%	ZCon%	OSw%	OCon%	BABIP	SLGCON	DRA-	WARP
2023	JUP	A	18	3(3)	7	0-0	0	9	1.86	3.86		11.8%	26.5%	0.0%	42.9%	53.3%	87.5%	37.5%	44.4%	.450	.500	88	0.1
2024 non	MIA	MLB	19	58(0)	50	2-2	0	37	1.78	7.06		13.3%	15.6%	4.1%	34.4%					.305	.612	149	-1.1

2023 Arsenal: FA (93.8), SL (80.8), CU (74), CH (83.7)   Comps: Hunter Greene (26), Luis De La Rosa (26), Matt Heidenreich (26)

Noblesse oblige refers to the expectation that those blessed with elite societal positions or wealth have a duty to act generously to those with less privilege. Low-minors hitters might have hoped that Noble Meyer would take it easy on them, as befitting someone inked for $4.5 million out of Beaverton, Oregon. In brief, thoroughly controlled professional appearances, however, he set down nearly three in 10 opponents, though he did have the courtesy to walk nearly half as many batters. His fastball doesn't have ideal traits for today's game, coming in flatter than is ideal and into worse locations. He does flash three distinct breaking balls, which creates a lot to work with for an organization with some of the stronger pitching development in the league.

Patrick Monteverde LHP   Born: 09/24/97   Age: 26   Height: 6'2"   Weight: 200   Origin: Round 8, 2021 Draft (#239 overall)

YEAR	TM	LVL	AGE	G (GS)	IP	W-L	SV	K	WHIP	ERA	CSP	BB%	K%	HR%	GB%	ZSw%	ZCon%	OSw%	OCon%	BABIP	SLGCON	DRA-	WARP
2021	MRL	ROK	23	7(1)	14²	0-0	2	16	1.23	3.07		6.5%	25.8%	1.6%	46.3%					.325	.561		
2022	BEL	A+	24	15(15)	79	3-4	0	90	1.11	2.51		8.0%	27.9%	2.5%	34.2%					.280	.503	97	0.9
2022	PNS	AA	24	6(6)	30²	1-0	0	32	1.40	4.99		4.6%	24.4%	3.8%	41.3%					.368	.714	97	0.3
2023	PNS	AA	25	21(21)	114	10-5	0	114	1.20	3.32		9.9%	24.5%	2.8%	40.2%					.271	.530	92	2.1
2023	JAX	AAA	25	2(2)	8²	1-1	0	7	2.42	15.58		12.5%	14.6%	8.3%	17.1%	70.5%	81.8%	21.4%	66.7%	.355	.939	140	-0.1
2024 DC	MIA	MLB	26	13(3)	27	1-2	0	23	1.51	5.52		9.7%	19.3%	3.6%	33.3%					.309	.581	122	-0.1

2023 Arsenal: FA (89.5), CH (81.7), FC (85.2), CU (76.9)   Comps: Austin Warner (57), Evan Grills (56), Charlie Furbush (55)

Monteverde is a smaller, soft-tossing lefty whose four-pitch mix is deceptive thanks to his short, over-the-top arm motion. Despite fastball gas that tops out around 90 mph, he knows how to let his pitches mingle, including a cutter-ish thing that pushes the high 80s. At Double-A last year he ripped off five innings in at least 18 of 22 starts, an impressive detail considering pitchers average well under 100 pitches throughout the minors. His age and experience relative to his peers at the level might have something to do with that, and he'll need to establish himself higher up the ladder before it's easy to buy into him as another Marlins pitching development success story.

Roddery Muñoz RHP Born: 04/14/00 Age: 24 Height: 6'2" Weight: 210 Origin: IFA, 2018

YEAR	TM	LVL	AGE	G (GS)	IP	W-L	SV	K	WHIP	ERA	CSP	BB%	K%	HR%	GB%	ZSw%	ZCon%	OSw%	OCon%	BABIP	SLGCON	DRA-	WARP
2021	AUG	A	21	8(6)	29²	1-2	0	33	1.48	6.67		8.5%	25.6%	2.3%	37.6%					.366	.595	87	0.5
2022	ROM	A+	22	19(19)	89¹	8-4	0	105	1.37	4.03		9.5%	26.9%	2.3%	47.0%					.319	.556	85	1.4
2022	MIS	AA	22	3(3)	11	0-0	0	14	1.55	9.82		9.6%	26.9%	5.8%	45.5%					.310	.688	98	0.1
2023	BRA	ROK	23	5(3)	8	1-0	0	10	0.88	1.13		10.3%	34.5%	0.0%	53.3%					.267	.400		
2023	ROC	AAA	23	12(10)	38²	1-3	0	41	1.73	6.98		14.9%	22.7%	4.4%	42.0%	71.8%	80.1%	30.4%	47.2%	.308	.645	92	0.7
2023	GWN	AAA	23	16(0)	27¹	2-2	0	27	1.54	4.28		15.4%	22.0%	2.4%	45.9%	72.8%	81.0%	26.7%	58.6%	.282	.541	101	0.4
2024 DC	MIA	MLB	24	13(3)	25¹	1-2	0	24	1.65	6.14		12.4%	20.3%	3.8%	37.2%					.314	.615	132	-0.3

2023 Arsenal: FA (95.6), SL (89.2)　　　　　　　　　　Comps: Hunter Wood (64), Ofreidy Gómez (59), Dean Deetz (59)

Like all too many flamethrowing prospects, Muñoz has the kind of raw ability fans can dream on that all too often turns into the stuff of nightmares. A longtime Atlanta farmhand, he was promoted to Triple-A and moved to the bullpen in the hopes that his fastball/slider combination would be enough to make him a viable setup weapon. Instead, his command regressed and Atlanta lost him on waivers to the Nationals. The Nats moved him back to the rotation and it was a complete disaster. Muñoz's future is almost certainly in the late innings, but he's going to need to figure out the zone in short order.

Andrew Nardi LHP Born: 08/18/98 Age: 25 Height: 6'3" Weight: 215 Origin: Round 16, 2019 Draft (#471 overall)

YEAR	TM	LVL	AGE	G (GS)	IP	W-L	SV	K	WHIP	ERA	CSP	BB%	K%	HR%	GB%	ZSw%	ZCon%	OSw%	OCon%	BABIP	SLGCON	DRA-	WARP
2021	JUP	A	22	8(0)	15²	1-1	2	23	1.09	3.45		4.8%	37.1%	0.0%	54.3%	63.0%	72.1%	35.7%	53.7%	.400	.543	85	0.3
2021	BEL	A+	22	10(0)	19¹	2-1	0	27	1.29	4.66		4.9%	32.9%	4.9%	44.0%					.370	.720	93	0.3
2021	PNS	AA	22	11(0)	17¹	1-1	0	19	1.10	2.60		12.5%	26.4%	2.8%	45.2%					.200	.381	92	0.3
2022	PNS	AA	23	13(0)	19¹	2-2	2	31	0.98	1.40		5.3%	41.3%	1.3%	46.2%					.368	.538	69	0.5
2022	JAX	AAA	23	24(0)	31²	3-0	7	45	0.88	2.84		11.3%	36.3%	2.4%	31.7%	76.2%	87.5%	36.4%	50.0%	.183	.435	73	0.9
2022	MIA	MLB	23	13(0)	14²	1-1	0	24	2.66	9.82	56.2%	16.9%	28.9%	6.0%	22.2%	74.3%	78.0%	28.6%	53.4%	.500	1.044	117	0.0
2023	MIA	MLB	24	63(0)	57¹	8-1	3	73	1.15	2.67	45.1%	8.9%	30.8%	3.0%	43.9%	71.7%	82.0%	34.7%	55.3%	.290	.558	81	1.2
2024 DC	MIA	MLB	25	60(0)	63¹	4-3	4	74	1.28	4.05	47.7%	10.4%	27.5%	3.2%	39.0%					.287	.558	93	0.5

2023 Arsenal: FA (94.6), SW (82.8), CH (89.8)　　　　　　　Comps: José Quijada (72), Rex Brothers (68), Silvino Bracho (65)

Nardi's second taste of the big leagues went much better than his first. He kept his pitch mix almost identical, throwing his fastball more than 60% of the time and more often than all but 15 qualified relievers. The key for him was having better location. He perched a fastball at the top of the zone and pinpointed a slider down and away, executing a north-south game plan that leads to success in modern baseball; he mitigated any issues produced by the shape of his heater by coaxing more chases. In all, the gnarly results reflect how a small change can be a big deal—but also how sometimes things just break a pitcher's way.

Steven Okert LHP Born: 07/09/91 Age: 33 Height: 6'2" Weight: 202 Origin: Round 4, 2012 Draft (#148 overall)

YEAR	TM	LVL	AGE	G (GS)	IP	W-L	SV	K	WHIP	ERA	CSP	BB%	K%	HR%	GB%	ZSw%	ZCon%	OSw%	OCon%	BABIP	SLGCON	DRA-	WARP
2021	JAX	AAA	29	15(0)	20	2-0	4	29	0.85	1.80		5.3%	38.2%	1.3%	24.4%					.308	.450	81	0.5
2021	MIA	MLB	29	34(0)	36	3-1	0	40	1.03	2.75	51.9%	10.6%	28.2%	3.5%	32.5%	69.8%	76.3%	31.2%	59.1%	.221	.537	92	0.5
2022	MIA	MLB	30	60(0)	51¹	5-5	0	63	1.17	2.98	52.9%	11.8%	28.5%	3.2%	34.4%	65.6%	78.0%	31.1%	58.4%	.237	.517	99	0.5
2023	JAX	AAA	31	4(0)	5²	0-0	0	11	0.88	0.00		4.5%	50.0%	0.0%	50.0%	73.2%	63.3%	39.6%	57.1%	.400	.500	87	0.1
2023	MIA	MLB	31	64(2)	58²	3-2	0	73	1.26	4.45	46.9%	9.7%	29.6%	3.6%	23.6%	69.2%	77.4%	30.6%	55.4%	.299	.641	97	0.8
2024 DC	MIA	MLB	32	60(0)	63¹	4-2	0	77	1.24	3.95	49.9%	9.8%	28.7%	3.3%	30.2%					.288	.571	91	0.6

2023 Arsenal: SL (81.9), FA (93.8)　　　　　　　　　　Comps: Sam Freeman (60), Jerry Blevins (58), Brad Boxberger (57)

Okert may have been the least of Miami's three lefties last season, but that's no insult. Though he was barely better than average by DRA-, consistency produced the biggest contribution of his six-year career. He loaded up on his four-seamer more than ever, shooting it over the heart of the plate more than in any campaign since 2018. That helps explain how he gave up four of his nine homers on the heater, despite throwing it less than 40% of the time. He remained a slider monster, turning to the pitch the remainder of the time. It accrued a modest number of swings and misses, and lots of weak contact produced by getting chases out of the zone. Okert spells his given name with a "v" in the middle, but the results were pretty P-H phat.

Kaleb Ort RHP Born: 02/05/92 Age: 32 Height: 6'4" Weight: 248 Origin: Undrafted Free Agent, 2016

YEAR	TM	LVL	AGE	G (GS)	IP	W-L	SV	K	WHIP	ERA	CSP	BB%	K%	HR%	GB%	ZSw%	ZCon%	OSw%	OCon%	BABIP	SLGCON	DRA-	WARP
2021	WOR	AAA	29	42(0)	45¹	1-3	19	62	1.32	2.98		10.0%	31.0%	2.0%	34.5%					.333	.536	83	1.0
2021	BOS	MLB	29	1(0)	0¹	0-0	0	0	6.00	0.00	72.2%	33.3%	0.0%	0.0%	0.0%	80.0%	75.0%	14.3%	100.0%	.500	.500	102	0.0
2022	WOR	AAA	30	39(0)	40²	2-2	16	53	1.13	2.88		10.7%	31.5%	0.6%	37.9%					.293	.446	78	1.0
2022	BOS	MLB	30	25(0)	28¹	1-2	1	27	1.76	6.35	52.5%	11.2%	20.1%	3.0%	31.1%	73.6%	78.4%	29.1%	58.0%	.360	.596	126	-0.1
2023	WOR	AAA	31	13(0)	11²	1-2	1	16	1.37	1.54		15.1%	30.2%	1.9%	21.4%	63.5%	81.8%	18.2%	64.0%	.259	.464	112	0.1
2023	BOS	MLB	31	21(2)	23	1-2	0	24	1.57	6.26	46.4%	8.4%	22.4%	5.6%	28.8%	72.3%	85.2%	30.8%	71.4%	.328	.739	105	0.2
2024 non	MIA	MLB	32	58(0)	50	2-2	0	45	1.37	4.57	49.8%	10.2%	21.0%	3.2%	30.5%					.283	.537	103	0.1

2023 Arsenal: FA (96.2), SW (84.3), FC (91.4), CH (90.9)　　　　　Comps: Steve Delabar (61), James Hoyt (58), Blake Parker (58)

Visualize a slider in your mind's eye. Where does it hit the catcher's mitt? The only answer is at the bottom of the zone or below it. If it's higher than that, it probably gets smashed and doesn't reach the catcher at all. This is why Ort's slider had a 32.5% whiff rate, but still allowed an .808 slugging percentage. When he buried it down, he generated swings and misses. When he left it up, a fan got a souvenir. His fastball looked lively when he threw it for strikes, but a two-pitch pitcher can't survive if one of those two is a hanger. By the end of the season, he was a no-pitch pitcher because elbow inflammation landed him on the 60-day IL. He should visualize a more consistent, leather-slapping slider as he recuperates.

Eury Pérez RHP   Born: 04/15/03   Age: 21   Height: 6'8"   Weight: 220   Origin: IFA, 2019

YEAR	TM	LVL	AGE	G (GS)	IP	W-L	SV	K	WHIP	ERA	CSP	BB%	K%	HR%	GB%	ZSw%	ZCon%	OSw%	OCon%	BABIP	SLGCON	DRA-	WARP
2021	JUP	A	18	15(15)	56	2-3	0	82	0.95	1.61		9.5%	36.9%	0.9%	36.0%	73.2%	74.2%	33.2%	53.4%	.268	.386	78	1.4
2021	BEL	A+	18	5(5)	22	1-2	0	26	0.73	2.86		6.0%	31.3%	6.0%	37.7%					.133	.580	92	0.3
2022	PNS	AA	19	17(17)	75	3-3	0	106	1.16	4.08		8.0%	34.1%	2.9%	41.7%					.319	.622	79	1.6
2023	PNS	AA	20	8(8)	36²	3-1	0	54	0.93	3.19		7.0%	38.0%	3.5%	47.4%					.260	.603	64	1.0
2023	MIA	MLB	20	19(19)	91¹	5-6	0	108	1.13	3.15	45.4%	8.3%	28.9%	4.0%	25.3%	74.0%	78.6%	34.3%	49.5%	.264	.624	106	0.8
2024 DC	MIA	MLB	21	26(26)	134²	8-8	0	162	1.21	3.85	45.4%	8.8%	28.8%	3.6%	27.8%					.288	.597	90	1.9

2023 Arsenal: FA (97.5), SL (86.6), CU (81.3), CH (89.9)   Comps: Tyler Skaggs (67), Deivi García (65), Taijuan Walker (65)

Pérez was electric in his debut. Compared to rookies who threw at least 90 innings, his 20.8% strikeout-minus-walk rate is a top-10 mark in the last decade and the best by a Marlins arm since José Fernández in 2013. He got more chases out of the zone than the average pitcher and limited contact within it better than just about anyone. He accomplished this while being extremely four-seam and slider heavy, despite having two other legitimate options in his changeup and curveball. He also did it having started the year as a damn teenager. It's hard to say what his ceiling is, with it being so early in his career that he hasn't even fully built the frame. Maybe he'll just build out Miami's version of Ojai's Bart's Books, an outdoor dreamland of delights.

A.J. Puk LHP   Born: 04/25/95   Age: 29   Height: 6'7"   Weight: 248   Origin: Round 1, 2016 Draft (#6 overall)

YEAR	TM	LVL	AGE	G (GS)	IP	W-L	SV	K	WHIP	ERA	CSP	BB%	K%	HR%	GB%	ZSw%	ZCon%	OSw%	OCon%	BABIP	SLGCON	DRA-	WARP
2021	LV	AAA	26	29(4)	48²	2-5	1	58	1.64	6.10		8.4%	25.7%	5.3%	39.5%					.363	.762	91	0.4
2021	OAK	MLB	26	12(0)	13¹	0-3	0	16	1.80	6.07	56.6%	9.2%	24.6%	1.5%	52.4%	67.3%	81.9%	25.0%	61.8%	.415	.524	96	0.2
2022	OAK	MLB	27	62(0)	66¹	4-3	4	76	1.15	3.12	54.1%	8.2%	27.0%	2.5%	42.7%	67.1%	81.7%	30.9%	51.1%	.286	.518	90	1.0
2023	MIA	MLB	28	58(0)	56²	7-5	15	78	1.18	3.97	50.6%	5.4%	32.2%	4.1%	44.3%	64.6%	75.3%	33.1%	52.7%	.319	.644	73	1.5
2024 DC	MIA	MLB	29	60(0)	63¹	4-3	6	74	1.24	4.01	52.5%	7.9%	27.5%	3.3%	43.7%					.302	.574	93	0.5

2023 Arsenal: FA (95.9), SW (83.9), SI (95.3), FS (87.6)   Comps: Andrew Chafin (49), Michael Feliz (46), Tony Cingrani (46)

Puk more than doubled his career WARP with a stellar season that was more productive than 2022 over fewer innings, the first year in which he demonstrated he could stay healthy. His second-consecutive healthy campaign yielded the best strikeout and walk rates of his career. He leaned into being a two-pitch power reliever with a hellish four-seamer that was harder than ever for hitters to square up. It wasn't just that he got more chases, but that he was able to locate the heat in the zone more and also generate a career-best contact rate there. His slider remained a down-and-gloveside dagger that generated weak contact. We don't have advanced data on it, but it's fair to assume Puk's beard was also producing the best results so far: Perhaps he unlocked it all with a new shampoo and texture spray. Regardless, he's grown himself (and his facial hair) into a lockdown end-game option.

David Robertson RHP   Born: 04/09/85   Age: 39   Height: 5'11"   Weight: 195   Origin: Round 17, 2006 Draft (#524 overall)

YEAR	TM	LVL	AGE	G (GS)	IP	W-L	SV	K	WHIP	ERA	CSP	BB%	K%	HR%	GB%	ZSw%	ZCon%	OSw%	OCon%	BABIP	SLGCON	DRA-	WARP
2021	DUR	AAA	36	6(0)	6	0-0	0	12	0.83	0.00		4.5%	54.5%	0.0%	37.5%					.500	.500	76	0.2
2021	TB	MLB	36	12(1)	12	0-0	0	16	1.25	4.50	61.3%	8.0%	32.0%	4.0%	40.0%	68.1%	81.2%	21.9%	56.0%	.321	.633	98	0.1
2022	PHI	MLB	37	22(0)	23¹	1-3	6	30	1.37	2.70	51.0%	16.2%	30.3%	2.0%	43.4%	62.0%	81.2%	34.1%	51.8%	.275	.509	87	0.4
2022	CHC	MLB	37	36(0)	40¹	3-0	14	51	1.04	2.23	55.1%	11.5%	30.9%	2.4%	47.8%	63.6%	76.8%	29.9%	53.4%	.216	.440	87	0.7
2023	MIA	MLB	38	22(0)	21¹	2-4	4	30	1.59	5.06	46.7%	12.4%	30.9%	2.1%	40.7%	64.6%	77.9%	28.6%	54.7%	.385	.611	80	0.5
2023	NYM	MLB	38	40(0)	44	4-2	14	48	1.00	2.05	46.3%	7.6%	27.9%	2.9%	43.1%	61.9%	81.7%	35.2%	53.7%	.252	.481	84	0.9
2024 DC	MIA	MLB	39	47(0)	50	3-2	0	61	1.25	3.83	50.3%	10.1%	29.1%	3.4%	41.7%					.288	.567	89	0.5

2023 Arsenal: HC (93.4), KC (84.7), SL (86.1), SW (82.9), CH (87.8), SI (93.5)   Comps: Michael Jackson (74), Lee Smith (73), Rich Gossage (72)

Being a reliever is an act of committing oneself to play the hottest game show of 1882, *Lady or Tiger*. By all the advanced metrics, Robertson as a Marlin was a carbon copy of his excellent first half with the Mets. By the more nebulous metrics of "did fans wish he fell into an open manhole," it was a rough August for Miami's big bullpen acquisition, who blew three of his first seven save chances and then never saw another. Given that his curve and cutter are intact (he threw the latter harder than he had for years), some other team is going to get pretty good odds that the 39-year-old picks the right door next time.

Sixto Sánchez RHP   Born: 07/29/98   Age: 25   Height: 6'0"   Weight: 234   Origin: IFA, 2015

YEAR	TM	LVL	AGE	G (GS)	IP	W-L	SV	K	WHIP	ERA	CSP	BB%	K%	HR%	GB%	ZSw%	ZCon%	OSw%	OCon%	BABIP	SLGCON	DRA-	WARP
2024 DC	MIA	MLB	25	6(6)	27²	1-2	0	26	1.43	4.62	50.5%	9.6%	21.1%	2.4%	50.4%					.313	.518	103	0.2

Comps: Jacob Turner (60), Henderson Alvarez III (55), Alex Sanabia (52)

Last season, the former top prospect registered his first inning as a professional in three years. Unfortunately, it also happened to be the only inning he threw in a game all year. Sánchez's two-strikeout, one-walk performance was encouraging simply for having happened: His return from shoulder surgeries—yes, plural—was delayed for months because of soreness and myriad setbacks. The average rookie in the majors last year was 26. Sánchez is now just 25, but given the massive talent he displayed as a teenager, any discussion of him at this point is merely an ember glimmering in the ashes of former hopes.

Tanner Scott LHP   Born: 07/22/94   Age: 29   Height: 6'0"   Weight: 235   Origin: Round 6, 2014 Draft (#181 overall)

YEAR	TM	LVL	AGE	G (GS)	IP	W-L	SV	K	WHIP	ERA	CSP	BB%	K%	HR%	GB%	ZSw%	ZCon%	OSw%	OCon%	BABIP	SLGCON	DRA-	WARP
2021	BAL	MLB	26	62 (0)	54	5-4	0	70	1.57	5.17	51.4%	14.7%	27.9%	2.4%	52.9%	66.8%	82.0%	30.2%	38.7%	.318	.533	93	0.7
2022	MIA	MLB	27	67 (0)	62²	4-5	20	90	1.61	4.31	49.0%	15.9%	31.1%	1.7%	45.6%	66.0%	77.6%	33.0%	47.5%	.347	.566	97	0.7
2023	MIA	MLB	28	74 (0)	78	9-5	12	104	0.99	2.31	47.2%	7.8%	33.9%	1.0%	49.7%	66.7%	76.6%	38.4%	45.9%	.291	.422	71	2.1
2024 DC	MIA	MLB	29	60 (0)	63¹	4-6	31	84	1.25	3.43	48.6%	11.1%	31.3%	2.2%	48.7%					.299	.517	79	1.0

2023 Arsenal: SL (89.3), FA (96.7)   Comps: Ken Giles (67), B.J. Ryan (66), David Robertson (65)

After five years as a steady and effective lefty, in 2023 Scott became baseball's best relief-exclusive pitcher by WARP. He cut his walk rate in half and landed at 7.8%, the only single-digit mark of his career. He spotted his four-seamer consistently in the low-and-away corner for the first time in his career after typically trying to use it higher in the zone, where it played like an average pitch. His wipeout slider worked off the heat by falling out of the zone, leaving batters to flail at it before missing altogether—in much the same way one might attempt to reach the top shelf, only to extend too far and windmill to the ground. Batters whiffed at the breaker more than 20% of the time they offered; it took a few years in the sun, but he's finally become Tannest Scott.

Devin Smeltzer LHP   Born: 09/07/95   Age: 28   Height: 6'3"   Weight: 195   Origin: Round 5, 2016 Draft (#161 overall)

YEAR	TM	LVL	AGE	G (GS)	IP	W-L	SV	K	WHIP	ERA	CSP	BB%	K%	HR%	GB%	ZSw%	ZCon%	OSw%	OCon%	BABIP	SLGCON	DRA-	WARP
2021	MIN	MLB	25	1 (0)	4²	0-0	0	3	0.43	0.00	65.6%	5.9%	17.6%	0.0%	45.5%	76.0%	84.2%	29.6%	50.0%	.091	.100	97	0.1
2022	STP	AAA	26	15 (9)	50	3-4	0	47	1.60	7.56		6.9%	20.3%	4.3%	38.8%					.353	.738	121	0.1
2022	MIN	MLB	26	15 (12)	70¹	5-2	0	40	1.22	3.71	54.2%	6.6%	13.9%	4.5%	37.4%	66.3%	87.0%	33.6%	74.0%	.254	.529	133	-0.5
2023	JAX	AAA	27	20 (20)	86	5-10	0	70	1.71	6.38		12.2%	17.8%	5.1%	32.1%	68.5%	85.9%	32.7%	66.8%	.311	.695	133	-0.2
2023	MIA	MLB	27	9 (1)	22¹	0-1	0	16	1.48	6.45	49.4%	4.0%	16.0%	7.0%	35.5%	63.6%	88.3%	34.2%	69.1%	.319	.737	112	0.1
2024 non	MIA	MLB	28	58 (0)	50	2-2	0	36	1.52	5.83	52.7%	8.5%	16.1%	4.0%	35.6%					.304	.584	128	-0.5

2023 Arsenal: FA (89.4), CH (82.7), CU (74.8), SW (78.4), FC (83.7)   Comps: Paul Blackburn (65), Greg Reynolds (62), Brett Oberholtzer (62)

As a funk-based lefty whose fastball fails to crack 90 mph, Smeltzer's margin for error is wafer-thin. His career-best walk rate wasn't enough to make up for the slider and curveball, which combined to represent a quarter of his pitches thrown but lost their ability to generate swinging strikes. A changeup was his only real weapon, but was neutralized in part because he didn't have much to pair it with. He only made it into nine big-league games, five of which were in April. He was designated for assignment on four separate occasions. After the postseason concluded he elected free agency, though he eventually caught back on with Miami in early December. With a career DRA of 5.34, finding success would also mean redefining the lingering juvenilia phrase about whoever Smeltzer dealt-zer.

George Soriano RHP   Born: 03/24/99   Age: 25   Height: 6'2"   Weight: 210   Origin: IFA, 2015

YEAR	TM	LVL	AGE	G (GS)	IP	W-L	SV	K	WHIP	ERA	CSP	BB%	K%	HR%	GB%	ZSw%	ZCon%	OSw%	OCon%	BABIP	SLGCON	DRA-	WARP
2021	JUP	A	22	7 (7)	34	3-0	0	47	1.29	2.91		12.0%	31.3%	2.0%	51.2%	65.4%	76.4%	30.3%	50.6%	.299	.512	112	0.1
2021	BEL	A+	22	11 (11)	55¹	4-1	0	67	1.39	3.74		7.9%	27.8%	2.1%	37.3%					.366	.567	96	0.6
2022	PNS	AA	23	8 (6)	29	0-2	0	36	1.45	3.10		12.7%	26.9%	1.5%	34.2%					.311	.568	125	-0.1
2022	JAX	AAA	23	32 (0)	47	4-2	8	49	1.15	2.49		12.0%	25.7%	1.0%	35.1%	68.8%	63.6%	44.4%	41.7%	.259	.387	89	0.9
2023	JAX	AAA	24	17 (5)	25¹	1-2	0	27	1.70	5.33		11.6%	22.3%	2.5%	37.2%	63.3%	77.8%	31.5%	58.6%	.351	.653	107	0.3
2023	MIA	MLB	24	26 (1)	52	0-0	1	52	1.33	3.81	48.3%	10.1%	22.8%	2.6%	42.6%	64.2%	82.2%	29.3%	52.7%	.284	.503	95	0.8
2024 DC	MIA	MLB	25	60 (0)	63¹	4-3	0	65	1.48	5.19	48.3%	11.0%	22.9%	3.1%	40.0%					.310	.568	113	-0.2

2023 Arsenal: FA (94.7), SL (83.4), CH (88.8)   Comps: Nick Nelson (65), J.J. Hoover (60), Jonathan Holder (57)

Soriano broke into the majors in 2023 and produced his lowest walk rate since A-ball. He used a power changeup, which came in around 88 mph, to pummel the bottom arm-side section of the zone while slinging a softer, low-80s slider to his glove side. His 94ish-mph four-seamer is nothing to write home about and he could probably stand to throw it less. He didn't overwhelm major-league hitters but he mostly kept them in check, a fine accomplishment for a 24-year-old in his first taste of the major leagues.

Ryan Weathers LHP   Born: 12/17/99   Age: 24   Height: 6'1"   Weight: 230   Origin: Round 1, 2018 Draft (#7 overall)

YEAR	TM	LVL	AGE	G (GS)	IP	W-L	SV	K	WHIP	ERA	CSP	BB%	K%	HR%	GB%	ZSw%	ZCon%	OSw%	OCon%	BABIP	SLGCON	DRA-	WARP
2021	ELP	AAA	21	2 (2)	10	1-0	0	11	1.50	3.60		4.7%	25.6%	4.7%	46.7%					.393	.733	106	0.0
2021	SD	MLB	21	30 (18)	94²	4-7	1	72	1.38	5.32	54.9%	7.5%	18.0%	5.0%	43.6%	70.2%	85.5%	24.9%	71.8%	.299	.621	106	0.6
2022	ELP	AAA	22	31 (22)	123	7-7	0	88	1.79	6.73		10.1%	15.6%	5.5%	35.7%	74.6%	84.3%	29.3%	64.5%	.346	.714	140	-2.3
2022	SD	MLB	22	1 (1)	3²	0-0	0	3	2.73	9.82	51.7%	19.0%	14.3%	0.0%	50.0%	82.9%	82.8%	25.9%	57.1%	.429	.500	148	-0.1
2023	ELP	AAA	23	8 (8)	40²	1-2	0	52	1.57	4.20		13.5%	29.2%	2.8%	44.6%	68.2%	77.0%	30.4%	50.8%	.365	.653	85	0.9
2023	JAX	AAA	23	7 (7)	39	4-0	0	38	1.08	2.54		9.4%	25.5%	2.7%	46.4%	66.8%	78.3%	27.8%	59.3%	.258	.479	81	0.9
2023	MIA	MLB	23	3 (2)	13	0-2	0	14	1.92	7.62	45.5%	19.7%	23.0%	4.9%	25.7%	60.0%	84.8%	21.6%	52.8%	.323	.848	125	0.0
2023	SD	MLB	23	12 (10)	44²	1-6	0	29	1.61	6.25	49.1%	8.7%	14.8%	4.6%	38.9%	72.0%	82.0%	26.1%	66.7%	.329	.633	136	-0.3
2024 DC	MIA	MLB	24	41 (6)	67	3-4	0	58	1.50	5.31	51.4%	10.1%	19.4%	3.3%	40.3%					.306	.562	117	-0.1

2023 Arsenal: FA (95.4), CH (87.2), SW (81.1)   Comps: Bryse Wilson (69), Sean O'Sullivan (67), Ryan Feierabend (67)

Weathers started the year looking like a completely different pitcher than ever before. His average fastball velocity was all the way up to 96.2 mph in his first start, a mark it had never reached in the big leagues, with a more lively angle. He slowly declined over the next few weeks until the heater sat under 90 at the end of April. Shortly after that he was demoted, and then revealed to be injured, an order of operations best described as Weird Padre Stuff. He returned to the field with anonymity but, after being traded, was solid for Miami in three relief appearances where he carried higher velocity and threw more sliders. As far as future development, he's in the right organization to make the most of his skill set, whatever it looks like.

LINEOUTS

Hitters

HITTER	POS	TM	LVL	AGE	PA	R	HR	RBI	SB	AVG/OBP/SLG	BABIP	SLGCON	BB%	K%	ZSw%	ZCon%	OSw%	OCon%	LA	90th EV	DRC+	BRR	DRP	WARP
Kemp Alderman	OF	JUP	A	20	133	13	1	15	4	.205/.286/.316	.291	.474	5.3%	29.3%	83.6%	69.6%	42.5%	35.3%			79	-0.9	-4.5	-0.5
Jacob Berry	CI	PEJ	WIN	22	72	13	2	7	0	.262/.319/.446	.349	.659	6.9%	29.2%	77.8%	85.7%	36.2%	76.5%						
	CI	BEL	A+	22	345	28	4	37	5	.227/.278/.369	.275	.474	4.6%	20.3%							93	-0.5	6.0	1.3
	CI	PNS	AA	22	123	22	5	22	5	.248/.301/.442	.277	.575	7.3%	21.1%							106	0.3	-1.3	0.4
Vidal Bruján	IF	EST	WIN	25	69	8	0	8	10	.345/.441/.473	.432	.619	14.5%	18.8%	66.2%	96.2%	34.3%	73.5%						
	IF	DUR	AAA	25	276	41	10	32	19	.272/.362/.477	.302	.600	11.2%	17.8%	69.3%	87.4%	33.4%	70.1%			107	-3.0	6.2	1.2
	IF	TB	MLB	25	84	14	0	6	3	.171/.241/.197	.236	.273	6.0%	25.0%	73.3%	83.0%	37.4%	68.7%	10.0	99.1	79	0.1	-0.1	0.0
Yiddi Cappe	2B	BEL	A+	20	536	53	5	53	18	.220/.250/.308	.263	.386	3.4%	19.0%							83	-0.3	-4.0	0.2
Jonathan Davis	OF	TOL	AAA	31	141	21	5	20	5	.258/.336/.516	.307	.696	9.9%	22.7%	60.8%	83.3%	24.5%	55.0%			108	0.6	7.1	1.2
	OF	MIA	MLB	31	104	22	2	10	1	.244/.307/.378	.328	.557	6.7%	27.9%	63.8%	82.3%	26.9%	55.4%	6.4	100.8	72	0.1	-0.4	0.0
Jerar Encarnación	RF	JAX	AAA	25	516	63	26	76	6	.228/.347/.452	.348	.838	15.1%	38.8%	62.3%	67.2%	31.4%	44.8%			94	0.6	2.7	1.2
Troy Johnston	1B	PNS	AA	26	374	71	18	83	16	.296/.396/.567	.319	.712	11.2%	17.1%							132	0.2	7.1	3.3
	1B	JAX	AAA	26	226	31	8	33	8	.323/.403/.520	.381	.669	8.8%	19.5%	76.2%	84.4%	42.2%	61.9%			104	1.3	2.4	0.8
Joe Mack	C	BEL	A+	20	503	46	6	36	0	.218/.295/.287	.280	.390	8.3%	23.5%							81	-0.5	2.7	0.5
Victor Mesa Jr.	CF	PNS	AA	21	533	73	18	76	16	.242/.308/.412	.287	.551	7.7%	22.9%							96	5.2	8.5	2.8
Janero Miller	CF	DSL MIA	ROK	17	131	14	0	10	4	.239/.331/.310	.466	.614	10.7%	42.7%										
Antony Peguero	OF	MRL	ROK	18	180	24	0	21	6	.224/.311/.282	.299	.386	9.4%	23.3%										
Brock Vradenburg	1B	JUP	A	21	133	15	1	10	3	.236/.368/.291	.347	.438	16.5%	27.8%	61.9%	76.9%	16.5%	33.3%			89	0.5	-1.0	0.1

Contrary to reports, **Kemp Alderman** is not a local news anchor but a corner outfield bat who mashed his way through the SEC. His 1.149 OPS was the highest on the Ole Miss roster by 150 points. He struggled to replicate that talent in Low-A, where Miami placed him after selecting him in the second round, but represents all the things the big-league club has been unable to develop. ⓧ A total of nine home runs as a positionless bat who continues to get promoted despite his flaws makes **Jacob Berry** into a confounding David Lynch tale, minus the charm or payoff. He needs to have a big season to avoid being another miss for Miami's efforts at hitter development. Things looked better in Double-A, but the 2022 sixth-overall pick has more ground to make up than is desirable. ⓧ **Vidal Bruján** cannot hit baseballs, which makes his job very difficult. He'll get a chance to do this very difficult job slightly further south in Miami now! ⓧ Though there were reasons to overlook **Yiddi Cappe**'s mediocre Low-A performance in 2022 and focus on the tools, it's a tougher sell a year later and a level higher. An .088 isolated slugging was the eighth-worst qualified mark in the Midwest League; a .558 OPS was second-worst. Given that he pulls the ball more than half of the time, it's hard to feel encouraged about his ability to impact the ball on contact. ⓧ You might say **Jonathan Davis** "Got The Life," getting more plate appearances in the majors last year than ever before. Given his pallid results, you might also say he was "Coming Undone" in them. The way he hits, "Y'all Want A Single" might as well be his catch phrase. It's a pretty Marlins-y trait, though, something they keep "All In The Family." ⓧ The free-swinging nature of **Jerar Encarnación** finally started to manifest in more whiffs at Triple-A, where his willingness to attack along with the holes in his bat path produced a strikeout rate approaching 40%. He either has to start making more contact (hard) or lay off pitches he can't damage (less hard). ⓧ In return trips to both Double- and Triple-A, **Troy Johnston** showed out, OPSing over .900 in each stop. Unfortunately, it's not great to be repeating those levels at age 26. He lacks the thump to cut it in the majors, where his max and average exit velocities fall well short of the requirement. ⓧ **Joe Mack** was looking like a Three True Outcomes catcher in his early professional career, but his power continues to slip and now his walk and strikeout rates are squarely average. That leaves him as Just A Guy. Still only 20 years old, he could manifest new carrying traits as he acclimates to the full-season grind as a backstop. ⓧ **Victor Mesa Jr.** has started to blend the various traits he's shown as a professional, combining a solid eye with new-found power while playing a strong center field. Carrying those abilities through the high minors and into the majors would instantly make him a regular most any team would welcome. ⓧ Despite playing as both a center fielder and a pitcher before signing, **Janero Miller** resided exclusively on the mound in his DSL debut. He walked as many as he struck out, but threw a solid amount of strikes for a kid making his first professional appearance. He dabbles with four pitches—a four-seamer, slider, curveball, and changeup—and has a loose motion. ⓧ It's possible that **Antony Peguero** was trying to leverage his ability to put barrel to ball early in the season, at the cost of taking a walk. That could help explain how he drove the ball at a lesser rate in his second go-round of the Complex league, sacrificing strong contact for any contact at all. The ceiling isn't as high for him as it is for other prospects, but making the most of his hit tool could float him longer. ⓧ **Brock Vradenburg** was one of just four players to play in each of Michigan State's 55 games in the 2023 season. He was the team's most dangerous hitter, registering more walks than strikeouts on his way to knocking 39 extra-base hits. He's the kind of spicy meatball you hope to one day sandwich between the club's contact-oriented bats to create a tasty offense.

Pitchers

PITCHER	TM	LVL	AGE	G (GS)	IP	W-L	SV	K	WHIP	ERA	CSP	BB%	K%	HR%	GB%	ZSw%	ZCon%	OSw%	OCon%	BABIP	SLGCON	DRA-	WARP
Daniel Castano	JAX	AAA	28	17 (9)	61²	5-2	0	58	1.31	4.67		9.7%	21.6%	3.7%	45.1%	70.9%	81.2%	34.8%	57.4%	.262	.557	87	1.3
	MIA	MLB	28	2 (0)	3	0-0	0	4	3.33	21.00	50.2%	15.0%	20.0%	10.0%	61.5%	65.5%	89.5%	17.5%	57.1%	.455	1.154	102	0.0
Dax Fulton	PNS	AA	21	7 (6)	33	2-4	0	39	1.55	5.18		12.8%	26.4%	2.7%	54.5%					.333	.598	95	0.7
Jeff Lindgren	JAX	AAA	26	22 (17)	86²	6-6	0	59	1.38	4.88		12.6%	15.8%	4.0%	37.0%	68.3%	82.5%	29.0%	70.6%	.235	.545	125	0.0
	MIA	MLB	26	3 (0)	7	0-0	0	1	1.14	5.14	46.2%	14.3%	3.6%	0.0%	26.1%	75.7%	85.7%	24.6%	75.0%	.174	.304	123	0.0
Karson Milbrandt	JUP	A	19	12 (12)	52¹	3-3	0	52	1.45	5.33		11.4%	22.7%	1.7%	35.3%	76.6%	80.9%	30.3%	68.3%	.315	.531	104	0.2
	BEL	A+	19	11 (11)	43	0-3	0	41	1.63	4.60		12.3%	21.0%	0.5%	40.3%					.352	.504	113	0.2
Jacob Miller	JUP	A	19	14 (14)	59¹	2-4	0	50	1.20	4.70		10.1%	20.2%	1.2%	50.6%	70.8%	87.6%	31.8%	60.7%	.259	.416	87	0.7
Trevor Rogers	MIA	MLB	25	4 (4)	18	1-2	0	19	1.22	4.00	43.0%	7.6%	24.1%	2.5%	51.0%	61.4%	82.9%	40.7%	64.8%	.286	.451	98	0.2
Josh Simpson	JAX	AAA	25	25 (0)	34¹	1-1	0	59	1.54	4.19		14.6%	37.6%	2.5%	41.9%	54.1%	78.8%	29.3%	45.7%	.377	.694	73	1.0

The Marlins had a bullpen from hell that rode flaming steeds to the mound before feasting on opposing lineups, so there was no need to rush **Anthony Bender** back from Tommy John surgery for their playoff push. He was getting to the point of facing live hitters by the end of the season and should be back with his worm-burning sinker and swing-and-miss slider soon enough. ⊗ **Daniel Castano** continued his winding career path by making it into two major-league games and giving up seven earned runs. Should his baseball aspirations not work out, his nature as a soft-tossing lefty could land him a spot on the cable news circuit. ⊗ **Dax Fulton** ultimately took a step back because he couldn't stop walking batters, as if someone had cursed him and he couldn't keep himself from vomiting slugs in a story about a wizard boy. Worse yet, he went down with a UCL injury last May and shortly underwent elbow surgery; he'll miss the entire 2024 campaign. ⊗ **Jeff Lindgren** can only amp it up to about 90 mph, but his short motion and consistent location atop the zone make the velo play better than one might expect. He relies on four pitches, more as a matter of necessity than luxury: He's not fooling anyone into whiffs or grounders with funky shape or arm angle, instead working to unbalance hitters, much like a magician wearing a slightly off-putting cologne. ⊗ **Karson Milbrandt** has an arsenal of strong traits, but he hasn't yet been able to harness them. His fastball pushes the mid-90s and his changeup, as with many Marlin prospects, is strong. However, he continues to walk too many while striking out too few, and starting giving up fly balls like they were going out of style following a promotion to High-A. ⊗ Like a meal that tastes better as leftovers after all the flavors get to hang out, **Jacob Miller** repeated A-ball and got stronger as the season wore on. He approached a strikeout per inning at the end of the season. His modern repertoire—mid-90s gas, two legit breaking balls—is deep enough to turn the lineup over as a starter but could play in relief, too. ⊗ On the heels of an ugly 2022, **Trevor Rogers** didn't have much opportunity to bounce back, first suffering a bicep strain in his throwing arm and then a right lat tear in a rehab assignment. By the end of the regular season he was still just playing catch. With injuries compounding, questions remain as to whether Rogers can harness his changeup and develop a his fastball that can get outs against major-leaguers. ⊗ **Josh Simpson** has worked his way up the ladder by throwing gas and being wild, in much the same way a middle school boy would be after discovering stink bombs in the mid 1990s. He struggled at the start of the season but pared his walk rate and made a big jump in strikeouts as the summer came on, suggesting his game should play at the next level. ⊗ Standing 6-foot-5 and listed at 210 pounds, **Thomas White** resembles a sycamore tree at Glastonbury Grove in *Twin Peaks*: mysteriously wispy and yet representative of something potentially massive. Drafted as a late first-rounder, he flashed big strikeout stuff and lacked control in his professional debut. Like many draftees, it's possible he was too worn out to show his best self.

MILWAUKEE BREWERS

Essay by Patrick Dubuque

Player comments by Janice Scurio and BP staff

I.

My only direct experience with brewing came in undergrad. I split a house off-campus with four friends, as one does, and it worked out fine, in the sense that none of us were particularly tidy and none of us noticed. But one day, our alliance was briefly shattered. One of them decided that they were going to try to make beer. On the stove, in a big pot.

(I am not reporting this to cast judgment. I readily confess that once, in this same house, on that same stove, I once made boxed macaroni and cheese—my last meal in the house—only to find out, halfway through, that someone had used up all the milk. I decided to substitute double the butter. The meal worked like a charm: one bite, and I wasn't hungry anymore.)

The beer was this guy's double butter. He poured in the hops, dutifully stirred it around for a while until he got bored and a movie he liked came on TNT. By the time he got back to it...well. The house stank for days. I don't remember how it tasted; the odds that he threw it out and that I had some and blocked out the memory are about 50-50. But what I remember most is how hard he worked to salvage this mortally wounded ale and the sunk cost of his ingredients. It was dead, and not dead, at the same time. As long as he kept stirring.

As far as monomyths go, the struggle of the broke college student is as universal as the quest for the grail. There's a touch of pathos to it, of innocence lost, of a misguided battle against the inevitable. The dramatic irony is built in: It's simple to look back, with the wisdom of hindsight and adulthood, and see what the actors couldn't: how things fell apart before they fell apart.

It's true in baseball as well. Let the inscription be: Here li(v)e the Milwaukee Brewers.

II.

Brandon Woodruff spun on his heel and craned his head skyward. His four-seamer had bled back over the middle of the plate, top of the zone, and Jake Burger was waiting for it. It had already been a shaky fifth inning of a shaky final outing for the Brewers' co-ace, in what was to be his final warmup for the postseason. He'd struck out two on gifts from

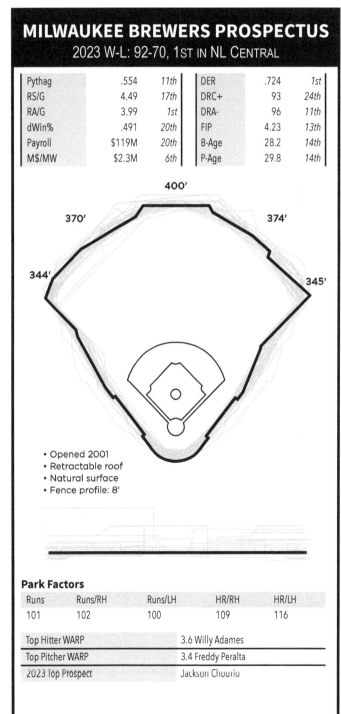

MILWAUKEE BREWERS PROSPECTUS
2023 W-L: 92-70, 1ST IN NL CENTRAL

Pythag	.554	11th	DER	.724	1st
RS/G	4.49	17th	DRC+	93	24th
RA/G	3.99	1st	DRA-	96	11th
dWin%	.491	20th	FIP	4.23	13th
Payroll	$119M	20th	B-Age	28.2	14th
M$/MW	$2.3M	6th	P-Age	29.8	14th

400'

370'   374'

344'   345'

- Opened 2001
- Retractable roof
- Natural surface
- Fence profile: 8'

Park Factors

Runs	Runs/RH	Runs/LH	HR/RH	HR/LH
101	102	100	109	116

Top Hitter WARP	3.6 Willy Adames
Top Pitcher WARP	3.4 Freddy Peralta
2023 Top Prospect	Jackson Chourio

Payroll History (in millions)

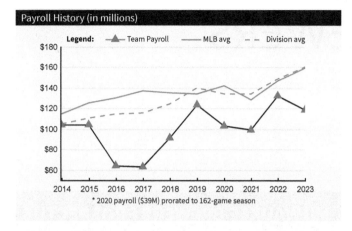

Legend: Team Payroll — MLB avg - - Division avg

* 2020 payroll ($39M) prorated to 162-game season

Future Commitments (in millions)

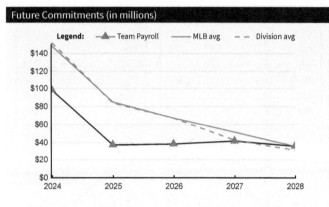

Legend: Team Payroll — MLB avg - - Division avg

Farm System Ranking

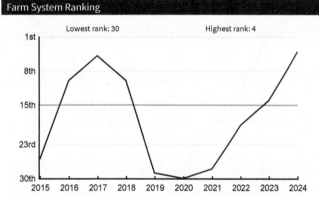

Lowest rank: 30   Highest rank: 4

Personnel

General Manager
Matt Arnold

Assistant General Manager
Karl Mueller

Assistant General Manager
Matt Kleine

Assistant General Manager
Will Hudgins

Manager
Pat Murphy

BP Alumni
James Fisher
Adam Hayes
Matt Kleine
Dan Turkenkopf

the umpire, each six inches off the plate, and given up a first-pitch single to Josh Bell. But Burger's exuberance wasn't matched by his timing, and Christian Yelich barely had to shuffle his feet before the ball fell into his glove.

It was the sort of evening that's easy to excuse. The final line was five innings, four runs, three of them from a single mistake pitch to Burger, back in the first. Woodruff was dead and not dead at the same time, and the only visible symptom was the radar gun. His final four-seamer, pitch no. 87 on the night, reached the plate at 94.9 mph, one digit shy of his usual velocity. After the game, the recaps scarcely mentioned his performance, focusing on a rare bullpen failure that ultimately gave up the winning run. Beneath the surface of his arm, at the cellular level, his story and Milwaukee's were already being written out.

On October 2, the day before the Brewers faced the Arizona Diamondbacks in the Wild Card round, manager Craig Counsell broke the news: Woodruff would not be joining them. They were seeking a second opinion on his reconstructed shoulder, and hoped to have him back for the next round. There would be no next round, and there would be no Woodruff. That same day, the David Stearns era officially came to an end, as the advisor signed on with the New York Mets. On October 4 the Brewers went home, swept. On October 13, Woodruff had anterior capsule surgery on his throwing shoulder, and will miss most if not all of the 2024 season. On November 7, Counsell left Milwaukee to helm the Chicago Cubs. On November 17, the Brewers non-tendered Woodruff. In the span of a month and a half, the Brewers collapsed like a cholera outbreak. There was scarcely time to mourn.

III.

Of the many things modern baseball has taken from us—mythology; simple, unlayered experiential appreciation; stadium beers that don't require a credit check—one of the most insidious thefts is our loss of immortality. People and dogs die, but though the names change, baseball teams are supposed to last forever. Rogers Hornsby can stare out the window and wait for spring, but that's because there always will be one; he never has to worry about the alternative. But while baseball teams once reset themselves like Charlie Brown with the first thaw, with everyone inside and out convinced that this would be *the* year, we no longer have the privilege of that innocence. Baseball teams die, too, now, and exist as a bloodline.

The Brewers almost felt like they could live forever. As Michael Baumann wrote in these pages last year, considering the end of the Stearns era, baseball's continual restructuring, its renewal, are a refutation of the Great Man Theory of History. Not only do teams, like nations, outlive their rulers, they exist as intricate webs of coordination. Trading David Stearns, talented as he was and is, for Matt Arnold wasn't supposed to be the deathblow it might have appeared. And it wasn't: The Brewers finished with the fifth-best record in baseball, and strolled to a postseason berth.

Not everything was entirely smooth. Woodruff missed four months of the season, and a little part of Corbin Burnes missed the whole thing, sending him to the worst season (94 DRA-) of his career. Nor could the team perform its usual trick of spinning 1.5-WARP players out of straw, struggling to fill holes at second and third all year, and ending with Brice Turang and Josh Donaldson weighing down the bottom of the order. Jesse Winker did little. Julio Teheran, given 11 starts, did a bit too much.

But it was all mostly fine, until the moment it wasn't. That's how death works, after all. It wasn't the loss of Stearns, or Counsell, or Woodruff, or the security of the Bally television revenue. It was all of them, all at once. This is the actuarial dilemma, and the root of all anxiety: nothing is ever *likely* to kill you. Something is guaranteed to.

IV.

In his 1658 work *Urne-Burial*, British scholar Thomas Browne catalogs a collection of ancient Saxon cremation pots unearthed in Norfolk. After laying out his field notes, he turns to the idea of ceremonial burial, and the seriousness of life that compels people to put so much care into the result of death. Following a series of melancholy thoughts about the finitude of life and legacy—"grave-stones tell the truth scarce fourty years: Generations passe while some trees stand, and old Families last not three oaks"—Browne admits that our best defense against the crushing weight of death is just not to think about it too much. That our deeds are forgotten isn't all bad, at least for our descendants. "To be ignorant of evils to come, and forgetful of evils past, is a mercifull provision of nature, whereby we digest the mixture of our few and evil dayes, and our delivered senses not relapsing into cutting remembrances, our sorrows are not kept raw by the edge of remembrances." Lives and seasons have to end, or there wouldn't be new ones.

Despite its embrace of life cycles, baseball is still bad at funerals; teams and players usually just disappear, coming back from injury or DFA or last night's loss until they don't, anymore. The funeral is supposed to be a middle ground between being forgotten and being remembered, a single shot of reflection and closure. Something within us propels us forward, keeps us from getting ensnared. Schopenhauer saw this as the will to live: a force more animalistic than holy, the way that the stepped-on ant keeps crawling in circles, or a pitcher volunteers for his third Tommy John surgery. Browne casts it more elegantly: "Life is a pure flame, and we live by an invisible Sun within us."

V.

The Milwaukee Brewers aren't dead yet, as of this writing. Their velocity is just down.

The team moved Mark Canha, Tyrone Taylor and Adrian Houser in cost-cutting moves, replacing them with Jake Bauers, Joe Ross and cheap in-house options. Because of arbitration raises, those moves have the roster's payroll almost exactly where they were before, hovering just above the league's bottom third. For their market, it's a healthy payroll, and they've allocated it wisely. But the days of February bargain hunting in cold markets is over, and it's unclear if owner Mark Attanasio will give his front office the flexibility to pounce should the opportunity arrive anyway.

Only three Brewers are guaranteed contracts after 2024: Christian Yelich, Jackson Chourio and Aaron Ashby. Freddy Peralta, Wade Miley and Colin Rea have options, either team or mutual. Two of the team's linchpins, Burnes and shortstop Willy Adames, will be eligible for free agency.

It's all too easy to imagine Milwaukee, sans Woodruff and with longtime Counsell lieutenant Pat Murphy now running the show, refusing to go gentle. It's easy because that's the preferable outcome: They're no longer the 92-win team they were in their halcyon days of 2023, but the NL Central is hardly a bloody battleground. The Reds, Cubs and Cardinals have yet to make any serious claims for the division, or to even decisively remedy their flawed rosters of yesteryear. We remain in what qualifies for Milwaukee baseball as a dynasty, and the fans are rubbing the defibrillators. They know Corbin Burnes is as good as gone; it's hard to believe he isn't gone already. One more season, they cry. Don't you die on me. One more.

VI.

I have children now. After a couple of decades off, boxed macaroni and cheese is part of my life again. I make it properly, because I'm an adult.

One of the defining traits of living with children is that they have a limited imagination. The popular conception is that children are incredible at imagining things, and that they lose this as they grow up. This is true. But it is limited. Children have little capacity for conceptualizing failure. They'll put their milk on the edge of the table, and you'll tell them "please don't put your milk on the edge of the table" and they'll ask why not and you'll tell them why not. They will hear your answer, process every single word of your explanation, then leave the milk on the edge of the table. Three minutes later they'll knock it over with their elbow and spill it all over the floor. They will stare at it.

This, and the other wondrous aspect of childlike wonder mentioned earlier, aren't entirely unrelated. It's why my friend kept stirring that pot of decaying hop-water, and why professional athletes achieve success: They can't imagine an end.

This, to be clear, is a virtue. You spend a lot of time as a parent managing the borders of your childrens' world. Santa is the one everyone talks about, and sadness bleeds into the frame whether we want it to or not. We are, as Schopenauer reminds us, creatures of want. But death is a tricky one: You don't technically have to teach your kids about it right away, unless a cat or a grandparent steps in for you. And there isn't really much reason to. You spend the vast majority of your life thinking about, or trying not to think about, the finite nature of existence. Anxiety can form on its own; there's little need to train it.

So for now, it's just macaroni and cheese. It isn't a problem that they want to eat it for every meal, that it probably supplies the nutritional equivalent of eight candy canes and the orange cheeze-with-a-Z will give them super-cancer. This is what the Brewers still barely are, the very edge of the logistical impossibility of Santa and the nagging feeling that mom and dad won't be around forever. The trick is to just hold on to it, to keep stirring, dumb as it feels, dumb as it is. The act of stirring the dead beer is living. Hopefully, Brewers fans get one more year of it before they can no longer stand the smell.

—Patrick Dubuque is the managing editor of Baseball Prospectus.

HITTERS

Willy Adames SS Born: 09/02/95 Age: 28 Bats: R Throws: R Height: 6'1" Weight: 214 Origin: IFA, 2015

YEAR	TM	LVL	AGE	PA	R	HR	RBI	SB	AVG/OBP/SLG	BABIP	SLGCON	BB%	K%	ZSw%	ZCon%	OSw%	OCon%	LA	90th EV	DRC+	BRR	DRP	WARP
2021	MIL	MLB	25	413	61	20	58	4	.285/.366/.521	.349	.731	11.4%	25.4%	73.6%	79.8%	30.5%	54.5%	15.3	105.1	95	0.4	-0.2	1.2
2021	TB	MLB	25	142	16	5	15	1	.197/.254/.371	.276	.605	7.0%	35.9%	74.7%	70.2%	35.6%	46.2%	23.5	104.4	105	0.0	-0.1	0.6
2022	MIL	MLB	26	617	83	31	98	8	.238/.298/.458	.278	.650	7.9%	26.9%	72.2%	81.8%	32.8%	56.0%	19.3	104.4	103	0.0	12.4	3.5
2023	MIL	MLB	27	638	73	24	80	5	.217/.310/.407	.259	.580	11.1%	25.9%	72.7%	81.4%	35.3%	52.8%	18.6	103.9	97	-0.1	16.7	3.6
2024 DC	MIL	MLB	28	593	69	23	76	4	.233/.316/.423	.288	.602	10.1%	26.6%							104	-0.1	9.4	3.4

2023 GP: SS (147), DH (2)   Comps: Derek Jeter (74), Alan Trammell (74), Tony Fernandez (74)

An escape from Tropicana Field boosted Adames' numbers in 2022. However, 2023 provided a mixed bag, filled mostly with licorice and those strawberry lozenge things your grandmother kept in a coffee table dish, crystalized into a single sugary fossil. The shortstop endured a frightening situation in May, as he was struck in the head with a line-drive foul. Whether due to the injury or just bad habits he picked up over the course of the season, his usual short slumps extended into longer versions. The main culprit was high whiff rates on fastballs and breaking pitches, at 24% and 37% respectively, that derailed his ability to reach base. Despite this being an off year offensively, his xWOBA continues to trend upwards (to a career-high .341), and the power is still very much there, as he led the team in home runs.

Brian Anderson 3B/RF Born: 05/19/93 Age: 31 Bats: R Throws: R Height: 6'2" Weight: 215 Origin: Round 3, 2014 Draft (#76 overall)

YEAR	TM	LVL	AGE	PA	R	HR	RBI	SB	AVG/OBP/SLG	BABIP	SLGCON	BB%	K%	ZSw%	ZCon%	OSw%	OCon%	LA	90th EV	DRC+	BRR	DRP	WARP
2021	MIA	MLB	28	264	24	7	28	5	.249/.337/.378	.317	.524	9.8%	24.6%	74.0%	81.8%	32.7%	55.4%	11.3	103.4	96	0.0	-0.2	0.7
2022	JAX	AAA	29	28	4	2	2	0	.231/.286/.538	.286	.875	7.1%	35.7%							89	-0.1	-0.6	0.0
2022	MIA	MLB	29	383	43	8	28	1	.222/.311/.346	.291	.494	9.7%	26.4%	75.9%	77.9%	32.8%	56.4%	7.8	105.8	88	-0.4	-1.0	0.3
2023	MIL	MLB	30	361	38	9	40	1	.226/.310/.368	.309	.557	10.0%	29.9%	70.7%	76.8%	32.5%	50.4%	10.3	104.7	80	-0.1	-2.4	-0.1
2024 non	MIL	MLB	31	251	25	6	26	1	.215/.301/.354	.292	.527	9.3%	29.7%							87	-0.1	-1.3	0.1

2023 GP: 3B (70), RF (39), DH (4)   Comps: Billy Nash (62), Don Wert (62), Bobby Byrne (62)

Milwaukee's hot corner served as a waystation for the damned all season; Anderson took residence for half the year before being dislodged by Andruw Monasterio. Like a pie on a windowsill, Anderson cooled off quickly after a hot start to the year. He found himself especially mystified by off-speed pitches, and was released by the Brewers in late September in favor of the brand name that is (or at least was) Josh Donaldson. A visible aroma wafting off a peach cobbler could cause an organization to levitate towards the windowsill and offer Anderson a one-year or two-year deal, given he's posted two north-of-.800 OPS seasons not too far in the past.

Jake Bauers RF Born: 10/06/95 Age: 28 Bats: L Throws: L Height: 5'11" Weight: 195 Origin: Round 7, 2013 Draft (#208 overall)

YEAR	TM	LVL	AGE	PA	R	HR	RBI	SB	AVG/OBP/SLG	BABIP	SLGCON	BB%	K%	ZSw%	ZCon%	OSw%	OCon%	LA	90th EV	DRC+	BRR	DRP	WARP
2021	SEA	MLB	25	202	20	2	13	6	.220/.297/.275	.295	.382	8.9%	25.2%	67.7%	83.4%	32.2%	61.2%	21.8	102.9	82	0.0	-0.1	0.1
2021	CLE	MLB	25	113	7	2	6	0	.190/.277/.280	.239	.384	10.6%	23.9%	71.0%	81.8%	26.9%	41.7%	16.7	103.2	91	0.1	0.1	0.1
2022	SWB	AAA	26	128	14	5	16	4	.226/.352/.406	.322	.683	15.6%	33.6%							96	0.1	-0.8	0.3
2022	LOU	AAA	26	116	7	3	12	4	.135/.276/.271	.164	.413	16.4%	28.4%							101	-0.2	-0.7	0.3
2023	SWB	AAA	27	97	19	11	23	6	.359/.485/.897	.333	1.129	19.6%	16.5%	64.9%	83.5%	24.7%	60.3%			163	0.6	1.0	1.1
2023	NYY	MLB	27	272	28	12	30	3	.202/.279/.413	.268	.680	9.9%	34.9%	67.2%	82.2%	32.0%	45.6%	14.9	106.7	87	-0.1	-0.6	0.2
2024 DC	MIL	MLB	28	442	50	17	55	11	.214/.308/.401	.273	.599	11.2%	29.3%							95	0.0	0.6	0.6

2023 GP: RF (33), LF (23), 1B (22), DH (2)   Comps: Daric Barton (49), Michael Saunders (48), Rusty Torres (40)

Picked up from the Reds in a forgotten June 2022 trade and re-signed to a minor-league deal, Bauers briefly reminded Yankees fans of the 2019 #NextManUp Era with an .891 OPS through his first 30 games. His lefty swing was a welcome relief in a lagging New York lineup at least for a little while. Of course, then he slumped over the next month, got hurt for a couple weeks, and spent the rest of 2023 reminding everyone why he's never been much of a threat at the plate despite his (long-expired) prospect pedigree. Bauers' quick flameout in the Bronx made the 2019 vibes of Luke Voit and Mike Ford seem protracted, and Kevin Maas' 1990 feel like a lifetime.

★ ★ ★ *2024 Top 101 Prospect* **#58** ★ ★ ★

Tyler Black **3B** Born: 07/26/00 Age: 23 Bats: L Throws: R Height: 5'10" Weight: 204 Origin: Round 1, 2021 Draft (#33 overall)

YEAR	TM	LVL	AGE	PA	R	HR	RBI	SB	AVG/OBP/SLG	BABIP	SLGCON	BB%	K%	ZSw%	ZCon%	OSw%	OCon%	LA	90th EV	DRC+	BRR	DRP	WARP
2021	CAR	A	20	103	11	0	6	3	.222/.388/.272	.346	.423	19.4%	28.2%							104	-1.3	-1.4	0.1
2022	WIS	A+	21	283	45	4	35	13	.281/.406/.424	.330	.524	15.9%	15.5%							120	0.5	-4.3	1.1
2023	BLX	AA	22	385	70	14	48	47	.273/.411/.513	.320	.684	15.8%	20.0%							132	-0.2	3.1	2.8
2023	NAS	AAA	22	173	35	4	25	8	.310/.428/.514	.345	.613	15.6%	13.3%	70.8%	86.9%	24.0%	66.3%			114	2.1	0.6	0.7
2024 DC	*MIL*	*MLB*	*23*	*360*	*36*	*6*	*35*	*23*	*.235/.330/.373*	*.289*	*.487*	*11.3%*	*20.8%*							*100*	*0.0*	*0*	*0.8*

2023 GP: 3B (97), 1B (16), DH (10)   *Comps: Abraham Toro (66), Miguel Andujar (61), Andy LaRoche (61)*

One of the Brewers' Minor League Co-Players of the Year in 2023, Black is already (and rightfully!) being recognized for his accomplishments, three years into his professional career. Versatility, variety's cousin, is also one of life's seasonings, and Black has played mostly third base at the Triple-A level but also has experience in other infield spots as well as the outfield—it's a matter of finding a position that sticks. He led the minors in triples with 12 and filled the Brewers' organizational leaderboards with his stolen bases and extra-base hits. These are all areas where a speedy, contact-over-power third-base prospect should excel, especially when there's a great chance he could be big league-ready in 2024.

★ ★ ★ *2024 Top 101 Prospect* **#6** ★ ★ ★

Jackson Chourio **OF** Born: 03/11/04 Age: 20 Bats: R Throws: R Height: 5'11" Weight: 165 Origin: IFA, 2021

YEAR	TM	LVL	AGE	PA	R	HR	RBI	SB	AVG/OBP/SLG	BABIP	SLGCON	BB%	K%	ZSw%	ZCon%	OSw%	OCon%	LA	90th EV	DRC+	BRR	DRP	WARP
2021	DSL BRW2	ROK	17	189	31	5	25	8	.296/.386/.447	.323	.542	12.2%	14.8%									8.8	
2022	ZUL	WIN	18	87	9	1	4	1	.256/.291/.354	.308	.439	4.6%	18.4%										
2022	CAR	A	18	271	51	12	47	10	.324/.373/.600	.423	.862	7.0%	28.0%							117	2.9	8.2	2.3
2022	WIS	A+	18	142	24	8	24	4	.252/.317/.488	.267	.646	7.7%	21.8%							120	0.4	2.0	1.0
2022	BLX	AA	18	26	0	0	4	2	.087/.154/.130	.154	.250	7.7%	42.3%							71	-0.1	-0.8	-0.1
2023	BLX	AA	19	559	84	22	89	43	.280/.336/.467	.311	.585	7.3%	18.4%							111	3.6	-9.1	2.0
2024 DC	*MIL*	*MLB*	*20*	*427*	*40*	*11*	*46*	*20*	*.238/.284/.380*	*.288*	*.500*	*5.3%*	*22.5%*							*84*	*0.0*	*0*	*0.5*

2023 GP: CF (113), DH (13), RF (8)   *Comps: Ronald Acuña Jr. (62), Mike Trout (60), Jason Heyward (56)*

When the top prospect in Milwaukee's system got a brief taste of Triple-A Nashville to conclude the 2023 season, it was a momentous occasion: The last teenage position player to achieve that was none other than Gary Sheffield, 35 years earlier. Chourio wields all five of the classic tools, using quick hands and feet to paper over any inexperience in his game while continuing to advance in skill as he progresses. The Brewers, craning their necks upward to look at the center fielder's floor, offered life-changing money in the form of an eight-year, $82-million contract that covers his years of team control. It also conveniently eliminated the need for another few months of unnecessary "development" in the high minors. Chourio does still have some plate discipline issues to iron out, not unexpected given that he was younger than the average age of the Brewers' rookie-league team last year. Could he use a month of Triple-A sliders to smooth out his development? Maybe. But now the decision can be based on baseball reasons instead of financial ones.

William Contreras **C** Born: 12/24/97 Age: 26 Bats: R Throws: R Height: 5'11" Weight: 216 Origin: IFA, 2015

YEAR	TM	LVL	AGE	PA	R	HR	RBI	SB	AVG/OBP/SLG	BABIP	SLGCON	BB%	K%	ZSw%	ZCon%	OSw%	OCon%	LA	90th EV	DRC+	BRR	DRP	WARP
2021	LAR	WIN	23	74	9	2	13	0	.215/.311/.338	.245	.431	10.8%	18.9%										
2021	GWN	AAA	23	171	26	9	29	0	.290/.357/.516	.327	.672	7.6%	21.1%							112	0.0	-1.6	0.7
2021	ATL	MLB	23	185	19	8	23	0	.215/.303/.399	.265	.596	10.3%	29.2%	72.8%	73.2%	36.6%	50.6%	9.2	108.2	91	-0.1	-5.5	0.0
2022	GWN	AAA	24	51	2	0	8	0	.292/.333/.354	.368	.447	5.9%	19.6%							98	-1.3	-1.0	-0.1
2022	ATL	MLB	24	376	51	20	45	2	.278/.354/.506	.344	.735	10.4%	27.7%	64.4%	75.5%	31.1%	52.4%	6.4	106.5	119	-0.3	-2.4	1.8
2023	MIL	MLB	25	611	86	17	78	6	.289/.367/.457	.348	.597	10.3%	20.6%	63.5%	81.5%	30.7%	59.9%	4.5	108.8	106	-0.4	8.0	3.3
2024 DC	*MIL*	*MLB*	*26*	*539*	*60*	*17*	*64*	*2*	*.253/.331/.417*	*.308*	*.558*	*9.6%*	*22.8%*							*110*	*-0.2*	*-1.3*	*2.4*

2023 GP: C (108), DH (33)   *Comps: Javy Lopez (66), Francisco Mejía (61), Earl Battey (60)*

Peering out from beneath his catcher's mask as if it were the lowered brim of a weathered Stetson hat, Wild Bill Contreras builds his legend. Truly a bandit with the mitt, Contreras assisted his pitching staff by reaching the top quartile in pitch framing—a vast improvement from his 2022 numbers, which were Statcast-blue as the Milwaukee sky on a summer day. He's yet another product of the Brewers catcher-improvement machine. Contreras brought both power and the ability to reach base to the second spot in the lineup, often moonlighting at DH when not behind the plate. His exit velocity and hard-hit numbers have been consistently galloping in the right direction throughout his career, and like the high noon sun over American Family Field on an oppressive July day, his bat continues to be scorching.

YEAR	TM	P. COUNT	FRM RUNS	BLK RUNS	THRW RUNS	TOT RUNS
2021	LAR	1492			0.0	0.0
2021	GWN	4102	-0.7	-0.1	-0.3	-1.1
2021	ATL	6935	-4.3	-0.3	0.1	-4.6
2022	GWN	1241	-0.3	0.0	-0.4	-0.8
2022	ATL	8525	-0.8	-0.1	-0.4	-1.2
2023	MIL	15428	9.5	0.1	-0.3	9.3
2024	*MIL*	*15632*	*-0.7*	*-0.1*	*-0.4*	*-1.3*

Josh Donaldson 3B
Born: 12/08/85 Age: 38 Bats: R Throws: R Height: 6'1" Weight: 210 Origin: Round 1, 2007 Draft (#48 overall)

YEAR	TM	LVL	AGE	PA	R	HR	RBI	SB	AVG/OBP/SLG	BABIP	SLGCON	BB%	K%	ZSw%	ZCon%	OSw%	OCon%	LA	90th EV	DRC+	BRR	DRP	WARP
2021	MIN	MLB	35	543	73	26	72	0	.247/.352/.475	.268	.633	13.6%	21.0%	70.6%	77.8%	26.9%	62.3%	14.6	108.5	134	-0.7	-0.4	4.0
2022	NYY	MLB	36	546	59	15	62	2	.222/.308/.374	.283	.542	9.9%	27.1%	69.0%	74.1%	31.4%	55.1%	12.2	105.5	86	-0.7	-0.4	0.2
2023	NYY	MLB	37	120	13	10	15	0	.142/.225/.434	.076	.622	10.0%	26.7%	68.9%	79.4%	30.4%	63.9%	11.5	107.6	110	0.0	-0.1	0.5
2023	MIL	MLB	37	69	5	3	11	0	.169/.290/.390	.184	.561	14.5%	26.1%	66.7%	77.6%	22.7%	62.5%	13.3	104.1	89	0.0	-0.1	0.1
2024 non	MIL	MLB	38	251	28	9	30	1	.221/.316/.396	.262	.540	11.1%	24.0%							101	-0.2	-0.4	0.7

2023 GP: 3B (38), DH (9), P (1)   Comps: Scott Rolen (74), Ron Cey (74), Brooks Robinson (73)

The late-season release of faltering Brian Anderson left a rookie (Andruw Monasterio) to man third base full-time, but while Monasterio's bat-to-ball skills were solid, his power upside was lacking. The Brewers signed Donaldson at the end of August, after the former MVP endured a disappointing season with the Yankees marred by injuries and streaky hitting and got released. It was a bet that his lopsided slugging percentage and 51.3% hard-hit rate could translate to that coveted power. Not only did it fail to do so, but the opportunity to regress in navy and gold robbed us of a truly hilarious seasonal BABIP. He's back on the market, and may be gone from MLB for good, but Milwaukee will always have those three homers to remember him by.

Sal Frelick OF
Born: 04/19/00 Age: 24 Bats: L Throws: R Height: 5'10" Weight: 182 Origin: Round 1, 2021 Draft (#15 overall)

YEAR	TM	LVL	AGE	PA	R	HR	RBI	SB	AVG/OBP/SLG	BABIP	SLGCON	BB%	K%	ZSw%	ZCon%	OSw%	OCon%	LA	90th EV	DRC+	BRR	DRP	WARP
2021	BRWG	ROK	21	17	4	0	4	3	.467/.529/.667	.538	.769	11.8%	11.8%									1.9	
2021	CAR	A	21	81	17	1	12	6	.437/.494/.592	.492	.689	11.1%	12.3%							128	0.3	2.3	0.8
2021	WIS	A+	21	71	7	1	5	3	.167/.296/.267	.196	.340	14.1%	18.3%							110	0.1	0.4	0.4
2022	WIS	A+	22	92	12	2	9	6	.291/.391/.456	.333	.554	14.1%	15.2%							128	0.3	2.7	0.9
2022	BLX	AA	22	253	40	5	25	9	.317/.380/.464	.351	.545	7.9%	13.0%							117	-1.0	3.3	1.5
2022	NAS	AAA	22	217	38	4	25	9	.365/.435/.508	.382	.555	8.8%	7.4%	69.8%	89.2%	25.0%	87.5%			133	1.6	-2.1	1.4
2023	NAS	AAA	23	183	25	2	18	8	.247/.333/.342	.266	.386	10.4%	9.8%	65.1%	93.2%	24.6%	80.8%			102	0.8	1.6	0.8
2023	MIL	MLB	23	223	29	3	24	7	.246/.341/.351	.286	.435	12.6%	16.6%	57.9%	91.0%	33.1%	79.0%	7.6	100.0	91	0.3	2.4	0.7
2024 DC	MIL	MLB	24	540	49	8	50	11	.240/.312/.352	.263	.407	8.8%	12.3%							89	0.2	6.3	1.3

2023 GP: RF (40), CF (30), LF (1), DH (1)   Comps: Jake Marisnick (59), Michael Hermosillo (55), Josh Reddick (54)

Before you can run, you should learn how to walk, and 2021's 15th-overall pick knows how to do plenty of both. The versatile outfielder managed to get to first base at least once in 19 consecutive games, Milwaukee's second-longest streak of 2023. His sprint speed of 28.6 feet per second and 100% success rate on steals has translated into value both on the basepaths and in the field. Since his heralded call-up in late July, he demonstrated those bat-to-ball skills he was lauded for in Triple-A, along with the plate discipline that contributed to that on-base streak ... but the power that was promised has yet to materialize. His production was sorely needed, especially with Garrett Mitchell's shoulder injury just slightly depleting Milwaukee's bounty of outfielders. The outfield can be crowded at times, but he'll make frequent appearances in the Brewers lineup.

Eric Haase C/LF
Born: 12/18/92 Age: 31 Bats: R Throws: R Height: 5'10" Weight: 210 Origin: Round 7, 2011 Draft (#218 overall)

YEAR	TM	LVL	AGE	PA	R	HR	RBI	SB	AVG/OBP/SLG	BABIP	SLGCON	BB%	K%	ZSw%	ZCon%	OSw%	OCon%	LA	90th EV	DRC+	BRR	DRP	WARP
2021	TOL	AAA	28	28	3	1	5	1	.348/.464/.609	.583	1.077	17.9%	35.7%							87	0.2	-0.3	0.0
2021	DET	MLB	28	381	48	22	61	2	.231/.286/.459	.278	.694	6.8%	31.2%	70.7%	75.9%	34.5%	52.3%	16.2	107.9	93	0.1	-8.6	0.3
2022	DET	MLB	29	351	41	14	44	0	.254/.305/.443	.316	.633	6.8%	27.6%	70.9%	77.8%	41.3%	57.6%	17.4	105.6	82	0.2	-7.8	-0.4
2023	COL	AAA	30	30	1	1	2	0	.154/.233/.269	.167	.389	10.0%	26.7%	61.0%	83.3%	33.3%	57.7%			90	-0.5	-0.1	0.0
2023	CLE	MLB	30	11	0	0	0	1	.200/.273/.200	.286	.286	9.1%	27.3%	73.7%	85.7%	40.7%	45.5%	0.2	101.7	79	0.0	0.0	0.0
2023	DET	MLB	30	282	22	4	26	3	.201/.246/.284	.268	.403	5.7%	27.7%	73.2%	79.5%	42.0%	54.8%	13.6	103.2	66	-0.1	-2.4	-0.4
2024 DC	MIL	MLB	31	123	12	4	14	1	.223/.282/.371	.290	.532	7.0%	28.6%							80	0.0	-3.1	-0.2

2023 GP: C (60), LF (23), DH (6), RF (1)   Comps: Tom Murphy (59), Jesús Sucre (57), Kelly Shoppach (57)

For two seasons, Haase's offensive production was held up by big-time home run power alongside a laundry list of below-average skills, particularly his ultra-clunky receiving. But in 2023, he simply stopped squaring up the ball, rendering him one of the least productive hitters in baseball. After it became clear he wasn't regaining his power stroke, the Tigers cut Haase loose and he joined Cleveland's revolving door of backup backstops. He's now a Brewer, and while it previously looked like he could hit well enough to stick around even if he became too much of a liability behind the plate, he'll now be challenged to get playing time.

YEAR	TM	P. COUNT	FRM RUNS	BLK RUNS	THRW RUNS	TOT RUNS
2021	DET	9170	-7.1	0.1	-0.1	-7.1
2022	DET	10053	-6.9	-0.7	0.5	-7.0
2023	COL	1181	0.2	0.0	0.1	0.2
2023	DET	7618	-1.6	0.0	0.2	-1.4
2023	CLE	463	-0.7	0.0		
2024	MIL	4810	-3.2	-0.1	0.2	-3.1

Garrett Mitchell CF   Born: 09/04/98   Age: 25   Bats: L   Throws: R   Height: 6'3"   Weight: 224   Origin: Round 1, 2020 Draft (#20 overall)

YEAR	TM	LVL	AGE	PA	R	HR	RBI	SB	AVG/OBP/SLG	BABIP	SLGCON	BB%	K%	ZSw%	ZCon%	OSw%	OCon%	LA	90th EV	DRC+	BRR	DRP	WARP
2021	WIS	A+	22	120	33	5	20	12	.359/.508/.620	.491	.919	23.3%	25.0%							126	0.8	-2.2	0.6
2021	BLX	AA	22	148	16	3	10	5	.186/.291/.264	.247	.386	12.2%	27.7%							84	-0.7	0.8	0.2
2022	BLX	AA	23	187	29	4	25	7	.277/.353/.428	.378	.623	8.6%	27.8%							93	1.0	0.7	0.6
2022	NAS	AAA	23	85	15	1	9	9	.342/.435/.466	.444	.618	11.8%	21.2%							106	1.7	-2.3	0.3
2022	MIL	MLB	23	68	9	2	9	8	.311/.373/.459	.548	.848	8.8%	41.2%	69.7%	80.2%	27.7%	39.5%	8.4	104.5	57	0.5	1.4	0.1
2023	NAS	AAA	24	35	3	0	0	3	.188/.257/.250	.231	.308	5.7%	17.1%	75.9%	90.9%	25.0%	37.5%			87	0.2		
2023	MIL	MLB	24	73	10	3	7	1	.246/.315/.446	.351	.744	9.6%	35.6%	69.7%	69.9%	27.6%	42.6%	6.7	104.4	69	0.0	1.4	0.1
2024 DC	MIL	MLB	25	407	37	8	38	15	.208/.286/.333	.293	.510	8.9%	31.1%							73	0.6	4	0.3

2023 GP: CF (19)   *Comps: Ramón Laureano (59), Jacoby Ellsbury (58), Eddie Rosario (57)*

Mitchell missed most of the 2023 season with a shoulder injury after an errant slide into third base back in April, but was cleared to return to the Brewers roster in late September. This was followed by a controversial decision to leave Mitchell off the postseason roster while doubts loomed about the potency of the Brewers offense. Mitchell posted Sal Frelick-like numbers in 2023, but with a dash of raw power included. A testament to his profile: He racked up a .431 wOBA off breaking pitches, which suggests a high upside if he can sustain it over a longer stretch of playing time. A healthy Mitchell should find his rightful place in center field, great arm and speed in tow.

Andruw Monasterio IF   Born: 05/30/97   Age: 27   Bats: R   Throws: R   Height: 5'11"   Weight: 186   Origin: IFA, 2014

YEAR	TM	LVL	AGE	PA	R	HR	RBI	SB	AVG/OBP/SLG	BABIP	SLGCON	BB%	K%	ZSw%	ZCon%	OSw%	OCon%	LA	90th EV	DRC+	BRR	DRP	WARP
2021	AKR	AA	24	304	49	7	51	6	.291/.365/.453	.374	.635	9.9%	25.0%							97	-0.2	3.1	1.1
2021	COL	AAA	24	130	23	1	10	1	.279/.385/.414	.411	.622	13.8%	28.5%							83	0.3	-2.0	0.0
2022	ORI	WIN	25	160	30	5	28	2	.317/.386/.482	.345	.578	10.6%	14.4%										
2022	BLX	AA	25	188	35	8	27	9	.316/.420/.513	.336	.614	13.3%	13.8%							140	2.3	-0.4	1.7
2022	NAS	AAA	25	249	34	1	17	6	.237/.321/.329	.327	.465	10.8%	25.7%	59.3%	75.0%	25.4%	66.7%			92	-0.4	4.1	0.8
2023	NAS	AAA	26	178	26	4	19	11	.271/.410/.400	.309	.505	18.0%	16.3%	60.7%	88.8%	22.7%	68.4%			118	1.4	3.2	1.3
2023	MIL	MLB	26	315	38	3	27	7	.259/.330/.348	.326	.454	8.9%	21.0%	62.6%	88.0%	27.7%	62.9%	17.8	100.9	87	0.1	1.2	0.6
2024 DC	MIL	MLB	27	347	33	5	32	8	.242/.324/.353	.294	.450	9.7%	19.5%							94	0.0	0.7	0.8

2023 GP: 3B (56), 2B (32), SS (5), DH (4)   *Comps: Adrián Sanchez (53), Alberto Gonzalez (49), Christian Colón (49)*

Signed as a minor-league free agent in 2021, Monasterio finally made his debut on May 28 to fill the void left when Willy Adames hit the injured list. His name graced the chyrons a few times during the season, as he mustered some torrid hot streaks at the plate in July and August, as well as fantastic numbers against lefty pitching. After Adames' return, he acquitted himself well at both second and third base. Late in the season, though, the team sidelined him in search of more power from the hot corner. As this book heads to print, the Brewers haven't done anything to solve either second or third base, leaving plenty of opportunities. Monasterio possesses plus speed and makes quality contact, albeit without power; his high sweet-spot numbers allowed him to find the outfield more, and opposing outfielders less.

Austin Nola C   Born: 12/28/89   Age: 34   Bats: R   Throws: R   Height: 6'0"   Weight: 197   Origin: Round 5, 2012 Draft (#167 overall)

YEAR	TM	LVL	AGE	PA	R	HR	RBI	SB	AVG/OBP/SLG	BABIP	SLGCON	BB%	K%	ZSw%	ZCon%	OSw%	OCon%	LA	90th EV	DRC+	BRR	DRP	WARP
2021	ELP	AAA	31	39	3	1	4	0	.303/.410/.424	.360	.538	12.8%	17.9%							102	-0.4	0.5	0.1
2021	SD	MLB	31	194	15	2	29	0	.272/.340/.376	.292	.422	7.2%	9.8%	71.4%	93.7%	23.5%	73.3%	14.5	102.7	101	-0.1	-2.9	0.5
2022	SD	MLB	32	397	40	4	40	2	.251/.321/.329	.284	.397	8.6%	15.1%	65.6%	92.2%	24.2%	70.3%	11.9	102.8	101	-0.6	-9.9	0.3
2023	ELP	AAA	33	30	5	0	2	0	.185/.267/.222	.263	.316	10.0%	26.7%	61.9%	80.8%	31.9%	68.2%			84	0.0	-0.7	0.0
2023	SD	MLB	33	154	9	1	8	0	.146/.260/.192	.184	.253	11.7%	20.1%	55.8%	92.4%	23.1%	67.9%	12.3	100.1	88	0.0	-3.5	0.0
2024 DC	MIL	MLB	34	27	3	0	2	0	.230/.311/.334	.260	.400	9.0%	14.9%							85	0.0	-0.5	0.0

2023 GP: C (52)   *Comps: A.J. Ellis (55), Manny Piña (54), Mike Rivera (54)*

When a player falls to pieces the way Nola did in 2023, the immediate instinct is to conduct a thorough forensic autopsy to identify the cause of career death. In his case, a Michael Fulmer fastball to the face near the end of spring training—one that broke his nose and required stitches—was likely the main culprit. Though the backstop never went on the injured list after his plunking, he hit a ghastly .156 in the month of April, then collected all of three hits total in the month of May. By mid-July, he'd been sent down to Triple-A, where he'd spend the rest of the season. In early September, Nola told Jeff Sanders of the *San Diego Union-Tribune* that he was struggling with oculomotor dysfunction, a vision problem that affects eye coordination, one that seems likely to have been caused by that errant spring pitch. Supplanted by Luis Campusano and non-tendered after the season, Nola faces an uncertain road back to the majors given his weak offense, indifferent glove, and possible injury after-effects.

YEAR	TM	P. COUNT	FRM RUNS	BLK RUNS	THRW RUNS	TOT RUNS
2021	SD	6719	-2.0	0.0	-0.1	-2.1
2022	SD	13572	-7.5	0.0	-1.2	-8.7
2023	ELP	1190		0.0	-0.1	
2023	SD	6477	-2.4	0.1	-0.3	-2.7
2024	MIL	1202	-0.5	0.0	0.0	-0.5

★ ★ ★ *2024 Top 101 Prospect* **#38** ★ ★ ★

Jeferson Quero C   Born: 10/08/02   Age: 21   Bats: R   Throws: R   Height: 5'11"   Weight: 215   Origin: IFA, 2019

YEAR	TM	LVL	AGE	PA	R	HR	RBI	SB	AVG/OBP/SLG	BABIP	SLGCON	BB%	K%	ZSw%	ZCon%	OSw%	OCon%	LA	90th EV	DRC+	BRR	DRP	WARP
2021	BRWB	ROK	18	83	15	2	8	4	.309/.434/.500	.339	.586	14.5%	12.0%									0.6	
2022	CAR	A	19	320	44	6	43	10	.278/.345/.412	.330	.525	8.8%	19.1%							103	0.5	12.8	2.3
2022	WIS	A+	19	85	10	4	14	0	.313/.329/.530	.344	.647	2.4%	17.6%							106	-0.1	1.0	0.4
2023	BLX	AA	20	381	47	16	49	5	.262/.339/.440	.281	.552	10.0%	17.8%							117	-2.1	9.5	2.5
2024 DC	MIL	MLB	21	28	3	1	3	0	.228/.282/.351	.280	.450	6.2%	22.4%							76	0.0	0	0.0

2023 GP: C (74), DH (16)

Comps: Gary Sánchez (68), Manuel Margot (68), Tommy Joseph (63)

The Brewers' no. 2 prospect gives a glimpse into the catching future of the organization: He offers plus arm strength and was named a Southern League All-Star after a 35% caught stealing rate for Double-A Biloxi in 2023, good for seventh-best at the level. In general, though, catchers aren't supposed to develop like this. They usually prove to be late bloomers because out of the eight textbooks' worth of responsibilities that get dumped on them in rookie ball, "Hitting, Vol. 1" tends to find the bottom of the stack. Quero, meanwhile, is not only advancing through the ranks quickly, he's improving incrementally in nearly every facet of his game. Prospect development *can* be linear once in a while.

YEAR	TM	P. COUNT	FRM RUNS	BLK RUNS	THRW RUNS	TOT RUNS
2021	BRWB	1021			0.4	0.4
2022	CAR	7853	7.7	1.2	4.8	13.8
2022	WIS	1659	-0.9	0.1	0.7	-0.2
2023	BLX	10331	7.3	-0.5	4.2	11.0
2024	MIL	1202	0.2	0.1	0.2	0.4

Darin Ruf DH/1B   Born: 07/28/86   Age: 37   Bats: R   Throws: R   Height: 6'2"   Weight: 232   Origin: Round 20, 2009 Draft (#617 overall)

YEAR	TM	LVL	AGE	PA	R	HR	RBI	SB	AVG/OBP/SLG	BABIP	SLGCON	BB%	K%	ZSw%	ZCon%	OSw%	OCon%	LA	90th EV	DRC+	BRR	DRP	WARP
2021	SF	MLB	34	312	41	16	43	2	.271/.385/.519	.344	.777	14.7%	27.9%	58.8%	84.5%	23.9%	59.2%	10.0	107.7	102	-0.3	-1.4	0.8
2022	NYM	MLB	35	74	6	0	7	0	.152/.216/.197	.208	.283	6.8%	27.0%	59.9%	81.7%	32.8%	55.9%	15.6	103.8	75	0.0	-0.5	-0.1
2022	SF	MLB	35	314	46	11	38	2	.216/.328/.373	.272	.546	12.7%	27.1%	58.2%	84.0%	25.6%	55.2%	14.8	105.5	93	-0.5	-1.1	0.3
2023	NAS	AAA	36	31	1	1	5	0	.120/.258/.280	.133	.467	16.1%	32.3%	51.4%	86.1%	20.8%	46.7%			86	-0.2		
2023	MIL	MLB	36	30	2	0	0	0	.192/.300/.231	.263	.316	13.3%	23.3%	60.7%	89.2%	15.8%	58.3%	4.8	103.4	82	0.0	0.0	0.0
2023	SF	MLB	36	27	1	0	3	0	.261/.370/.348	.429	.571	14.8%	33.3%	54.7%	86.2%	21.6%	25.0%	12.0	105.9	82	0.0	0.0	0.0
2024 non	MIL	MLB	37	251	27	8	28	1	.217/.316/.377	.263	.522	11.5%	24.1%							97	-0.2	-2	0.2

2023 GP: DH (14), 1B (4)

Comps: Steve Pearce (56), Tony Clark (52), Greg Vaughn (48)

Ruf had one job when the Brewers signed him: Serve as a platoon DH to clobber some left-handed pitching, a long-standing team weakness. This plan was soon thwarted when Ruf collided with some rolled-up tarp while going after a foul ball; he broke his kneecap and landed on the 60-day injured list. He can't defend, he's in his late 30s and his plan to never swing (even at strikes) looks like it'll easily be countered by pitchers simply putting it over the plate. Ruf's specific skill set could give him a very niche role on some rosters, especially if a stricter limit on pitchers rostered kicks in like, tomorrow. But we may have to view these past few years as a live-action demonstration of the "we are so back" to "it's so over" pipeline.

Brice Turang 2B   Born: 11/21/99   Age: 24   Bats: L   Throws: R   Height: 6'0"   Weight: 176   Origin: Round 1, 2018 Draft (#21 overall)

YEAR	TM	LVL	AGE	PA	R	HR	RBI	SB	AVG/OBP/SLG	BABIP	SLGCON	BB%	K%	ZSw%	ZCon%	OSw%	OCon%	LA	90th EV	DRC+	BRR	DRP	WARP
2021	BLX	AA	21	320	40	5	39	11	.264/.329/.385	.300	.463	8.8%	15.0%							107	0.4	2.4	1.5
2021	NAS	AAA	21	176	19	1	14	9	.245/.381/.315	.315	.417	18.2%	19.9%							100	0.1	2.1	0.8
2022	NAS	AAA	22	603	89	13	78	34	.286/.360/.412	.342	.529	10.8%	19.6%	71.4%	86.7%	31.7%	46.2%			109	1.6	0.3	2.6
2023	NAS	AAA	23	63	10	3	15	2	.298/.365/.561	.318	.681	9.5%	15.9%	61.7%	90.1%	24.4%	59.4%			116	0.0	1.4	0.4
2023	MIL	MLB	23	448	46	6	34	26	.218/.285/.300	.268	.390	8.5%	21.0%	67.9%	84.2%	30.1%	67.0%	12.1	100.6	86	0.9	-1.6	0.5
2024 DC	MIL	MLB	24	495	45	9	46	20	.231/.299/.345	.276	.439	8.4%	19.6%							81	0.8	-1.8	0.1

2023 GP: 2B (119), SS (22)

Comps: Erick Aybar (60), Tyler Wade (58), Luis Sardinas (57)

Like syndicated television on a day off from school, Turang was sufficient filler in a moment of profound need, even if he was longer on style than substance. After consistent production in Triple-A, his rookie season left much to be desired at the plate; he posted numbers worse than the Nielsen ratings of Matlock reruns opposite The Price is Right and not hitting the ball hard at all when he occasionally found it. Turang hit .200 and slugged .261 against fastballs, and (somehow more depressingly) slugged .140 on pitches in the direct center of the strike zone. He does offer speed and above-average defense—he once had a reputation of being able to get on base as well, but then, see the note above. His second season might be his last chance to break into prime time.

Joey Wiemer OF Born: 02/11/99 Age: 25 Bats: R Throws: R Height: 6'4" Weight: 220 Origin: Round 4, 2020 Draft (#121 overall)

YEAR	TM	LVL	AGE	PA	R	HR	RBI	SB	AVG/OBP/SLG	BABIP	SLGCON	BB%	K%	ZSw%	ZCon%	OSw%	OCon%	LA	90th EV	DRC+	BRR	DRP	WARP
2021	CAR	A	22	320	53	13	44	22	.276/.391/.478	.326	.643	14.1%	21.6%							126	-0.4	14.5	3.4
2021	WIS	A+	22	152	33	14	33	8	.336/.428/.719	.363	1.000	11.8%	23.7%							155	-0.1	-2.1	1.2
2022	BLX	AA	23	374	57	15	47	25	.243/.321/.440	.319	.665	9.1%	30.2%							90	4.1	12.6	2.5
2022	NAS	AAA	23	174	24	6	30	6	.287/.368/.520	.327	.672	12.1%	19.5%	82.5%	87.9%	25.9%	40.0%			106	-0.2	3.8	1.0
2023	MIL	MLB	24	410	48	13	42	11	.204/.283/.362	.258	.530	8.8%	28.3%	68.2%	77.7%	32.3%	49.7%	10.7	104.6	89	0.5	0.5	1.0
2024 DC	MIL	MLB	25	270	27	8	30	9	.215/.291/.369	.277	.529	8.3%	27.8%							84	0.1	1.1	0.2

2023 GP: CF (121), RF (13), LF (1) *Comps: Brian Anderson (62), Jake Marisnick (61), Michael Choice (58)*

Do we finally have an heir to the Hunter Pence aesthetic? With his mullet and wonky, wiggly batting stance, Wiemer moves something like a herky-jerky marionette come to life. In the field, it hardly matters—he was a wizard in the outfield, posting big Range and Arm numbers in the upper echelons of defensive leaderboards. His crazy legs carried him at 28.9 feet per second, but a series of slumps that no batting stance waggle could shake brought his offensive numbers down. He was victimized by an overly aggressive approach to sliders, turning in a .156 batting average and .067 ISO against the pitch, and a 39.7% whiff rate against breaking pitches generally. Despite the quality defense, Wiemer was sent to the minors in mid-September to yield at-bats to the likes of Sal Frelick and Mark Canha.

Jesse Winker DH Born: 08/17/93 Age: 30 Bats: L Throws: L Height: 6'2" Weight: 230 Origin: Round 1, 2012 Draft (#49 overall)

YEAR	TM	LVL	AGE	PA	R	HR	RBI	SB	AVG/OBP/SLG	BABIP	SLGCON	BB%	K%	ZSw%	ZCon%	OSw%	OCon%	LA	90th EV	DRC+	BRR	DRP	WARP
2021	CIN	MLB	27	485	77	24	71	1	.305/.394/.556	.324	.675	10.9%	15.5%	70.2%	85.1%	28.4%	71.3%	11.1	105.4	141	-0.3	-5.3	3.8
2022	SEA	MLB	28	547	51	14	53	0	.219/.344/.344	.251	.445	15.4%	18.8%	70.1%	86.4%	23.6%	66.4%	17.1	104.3	117	-0.8	-6.8	2.0
2023	NAS	AAA	29	93	13	4	7	0	.286/.462/.500	.302	.614	24.7%	14.0%	63.9%	81.7%	23.1%	63.5%			122	-2.0	-0.1	0.2
2023	MIL	MLB	29	197	16	1	23	0	.199/.320/.247	.278	.357	13.2%	25.9%	68.9%	81.1%	24.5%	62.8%	13.8	102.5	82	-0.1	-0.1	0.0
2024 DC	MIL	MLB	30	361	40	9	38	1	.235/.351/.378	.278	.492	13.7%	19.6%							110	-0.3	-6.7	0.7

2023 GP: DH (48), RF (4), LF (2) *Comps: Carl Yastrzemski (66), Rafael Palmeiro (64), Alvin Davis (64)*

Few things feel more certain than buying low on an ex-Mariners slugger emerging from the liquid air of Seattle's marine layer; Winker's decline defied the tradition of the post-Seattle offensive rebound. He struggled to stay on the field, and much of his year was spent bouncing between injured list stints and rehab assignments, including a setback in Triple-A Nashville where he injured his quad in September. When he played, it certainly *seemed* like he was hurt; his highest OPS in any month was .670 in June. Perhaps more memorably to fans, it was .000 in October, when Craig Counsell made the controversial decision to allow Winker two postseason at-bats after he hadn't faced major-league pitching since July.

Christian Yelich LF Born: 12/05/91 Age: 32 Bats: L Throws: R Height: 6'3" Weight: 207 Origin: Round 1, 2010 Draft (#23 overall)

YEAR	TM	LVL	AGE	PA	R	HR	RBI	SB	AVG/OBP/SLG	BABIP	SLGCON	BB%	K%	ZSw%	ZCon%	OSw%	OCon%	LA	90th EV	DRC+	BRR	DRP	WARP
2021	MIL	MLB	29	475	70	9	51	9	.248/.362/.373	.321	.521	14.7%	23.8%	67.8%	85.1%	23.3%	55.0%	2.9	106.9	95	0.4	1.1	1.6
2022	MIL	MLB	30	671	99	14	57	19	.252/.355/.383	.327	.533	13.1%	24.1%	67.2%	86.0%	25.3%	53.2%	3.2	107.8	101	0.5	3.0	2.5
2023	MIL	MLB	31	632	106	19	76	28	.278/.370/.447	.342	.600	12.3%	22.2%	69.8%	83.2%	27.0%	54.5%	3.5	107.6	107	0.9	2.4	2.6
2024 DC	MIL	MLB	32	615	67	15	67	16	.243/.343/.389	.306	.536	12.6%	23.8%							109	0.4	1.2	2.4

2023 GP: LF (122), DH (20) *Comps: Tim Raines (72), Carl Yastrzemski (68), Goose Goslin (67)*

One third of his nine-year contract is in the books; maybe it's worth asking what's Yelich's "deal?" You know, like *"What's the deal with corn nuts?"* It's a question so plain, but so loaded … we can merely attempt to answer it as best as we can. Yes, he's still "good," and has the xwOBA (.358) and xwOBACON (.419) numbers to prove that he can still clobber the ball. The four-seam fastball, in particular, remains his pitch of choice. He's battled a myriad of injuries the past few years, ranging from obliques to lower back, which have put a dent in those homer totals, but they haven't yet affected his range in left or his efficiency on the basepaths. (Nor can they be blamed for his arm, which rates alongside Johnny Damon encased in Jell-O.) Yelich may never again live up to his 2018 MVP year or his 44 home runs in 2019, but he's still lasering the ball and riding the attendant BABIP numbers. Heading into year four, that's all one can really ask for.

PITCHERS

Aaron Ashby LHP Born: 05/24/98 Age: 26 Height: 6'1" Weight: 188 Origin: Round 4, 2018 Draft (#125 overall)

YEAR	TM	LVL	AGE	G (GS)	IP	W-L	SV	K	WHIP	ERA	CSP	BB%	K%	HR%	GB%	ZSw%	ZCon%	OSw%	OCon%	BABIP	SLGCON	DRA-	WARP
2021	NAS	AAA	23	21 (12)	63¹	5-4	0	100	1.37	4.41		11.6%	36.2%	1.4%	66.9%					.370	.535	86	1.4
2021	MIL	MLB	23	13 (4)	31²	3-2	1	39	1.17	4.55	53.9%	9.0%	29.3%	3.0%	61.7%	57.7%	83.7%	37.0%	55.9%	.273	.487	80	0.6
2022	MIL	MLB	24	27 (19)	107¹	2-10	1	126	1.43	4.44	55.8%	9.9%	26.5%	3.2%	56.1%	58.6%	82.7%	33.1%	54.5%	.325	.596	92	1.5
2024 DC	MIL	MLB	26	52 (13)	93²	4-5	0	103	1.42	4.25	55.4%	12.5%	25.1%	2.2%	54.7%					.297	.498	93	1.0

2023 Arsenal: SI (92.1), FA (91.8), CH (85), SL (79), CU (75.9) *Comps: Brad Hand (46), Touki Toussaint (45), Felix Doubront (45)*

Fresh off a promising first full season, Ashby's only innings in 2023 were the rehab variety—he had shoulder surgery in April and underwent a slow journey to try and reclaim his pre-scalpel velocity. He's always had a well-balanced arsenal, but his plus slider seemed to mystify everything the light touched as it carried a 41.1% whiff rate in 2022. Ask not for whom the swingman tolls: Ashby lives in the shadowy land where he's not quite a starter but also not quite a reliever, but this versatility puts him at an advantage. With a potential rotation spot looming in the horizon and his velocity trending upward, spring training should provide Ashby with an opportunity to step out of the shadows to a place he fits in best.

J.B. Bukauskas RHP   Born: 10/11/96   Age: 27   Height: 6'0"   Weight: 208   Origin: Round 1, 2017 Draft (#15 overall)

YEAR	TM	LVL	AGE	G (GS)	IP	W-L	SV	K	WHIP	ERA	CSP	BB%	K%	HR%	GB%	ZSw%	ZCon%	OSw%	OCon%	BABIP	SLGCON	DRA-	WARP
2021	RNO	AAA	24	13(0)	12²	0-2	1	16	1.03	4.26		7.8%	31.4%	2.0%	46.7%					.276	.533	85	0.2
2021	AZ	MLB	24	21(0)	17¹	2-2	0	14	1.79	7.79	54.2%	8.6%	17.3%	4.9%	48.3%	68.1%	91.1%	34.7%	52.5%	.364	.724	107	0.1
2022	RNO	AAA	25	21(0)	20¹	0-1	1	19	1.23	2.66		5.0%	23.8%	1.3%	45.5%	65.1%	84.1%	31.9%	48.9%	.370	.545	95	0.2
2023	NAS	AAA	26	32(0)	37	5-2	6	42	1.22	2.92		6.4%	26.8%	1.3%	61.5%	61.7%	81.0%	34.7%	50.9%	.333	.480	74	1.1
2023	TAC	AAA	26	4(0)	5²	0-0	0	7	1.94	7.94		10.3%	24.1%	3.4%	68.4%	68.6%	75.0%	34.8%	69.6%	.389	.737	92	0.1
2023	MIL	MLB	26	5(0)	6	0-0	0	6	0.83	0.00	53.7%	4.3%	26.1%	0.0%	80.0%	70.6%	87.5%	30.8%	50.0%	.267	.267	88	0.1
2023	SEA	MLB	26	1(0)	1	0-0	0	1	4.00	9.00	42.0%	28.6%	14.3%	0.0%	75.0%	72.7%	75.0%	29.4%	40.0%	.500	.750	91	0.0
2024 DC	MIL	MLB	27	21(0)	23²	1-1	0	21	1.31	4.08	52.8%	8.0%	20.2%	2.5%	51.0%					.297	.500	92	0.2

2023 Arsenal: SI (95), SL (84.9), CH (88.8)   Comps: JC Ramírez (54), Brooks Pounders (52), José Ramírez (51)

A late-spring waiver claim from Seattle, Bakauskas went back to the old him, namely the broken one. Injuries kept him periodically shelved, then he was optioned to Triple-A a handful of times to make room for formerly injured pitchers returning to the roster. Like a celebrity making recurring appearances on a sitcom to move the plot forward (Bruce Willis on *Friends*? Clayton Kershaw on *New Girl*?), he made two cameo appearances in late September, both scoreless, just to have a finger tendon injury in his throwing hand to end his year. Though this may be a broken record at this point, he's certainly good when he's healthy.

Corbin Burnes RHP   Born: 10/22/94   Age: 29   Height: 6'3"   Weight: 246   Origin: Round 4, 2016 Draft (#111 overall)

YEAR	TM	LVL	AGE	G (GS)	IP	W-L	SV	K	WHIP	ERA	CSP	BB%	K%	HR%	GB%	ZSw%	ZCon%	OSw%	OCon%	BABIP	SLGCON	DRA-	WARP
2021	MIL	MLB	26	28(28)	167	11-5	0	234	0.94	2.43	51.9%	5.2%	35.6%	1.1%	49.3%	65.8%	80.7%	37.6%	43.3%	.309	.442	54	5.6
2022	MIL	MLB	27	33(33)	202	12-8	0	243	0.97	2.94	50.9%	6.4%	30.5%	2.9%	46.9%	64.3%	81.4%	36.4%	49.1%	.259	.510	70	5.1
2023	MIL	MLB	28	32(32)	193²	10-8	0	200	1.07	3.39	45.4%	8.4%	25.5%	2.8%	43.7%	67.8%	84.3%	33.0%	54.8%	.244	.452	94	2.9
2024 DC	MIL	MLB	29	29(29)	177²	12-9	0	195	1.16	3.42	48.3%	7.6%	26.6%	3.0%	45.2%					.286	.531	80	3.5

2023 Arsenal: HC (94.4), CU (79.9), CH (89.2), SI (95.3), SW (84.2), SL (88.1), FA (95.5)   Comps: Curt Schilling (77), Tyson Ross (72), David Cone (71)

The Brewers are at an awkward point in their relationship with Burnes, where whispers of trading him to focus on the future have bubbled to the surface of blogs and podcasts. The writing is certainly on the wall. Whether or not trading Burnes is a prudent idea, it's good to mention that since 2020, Burnes has ranked first amongst NL pitchers in strikeouts (765) and FIP (2.84), and fourth in innings pitched (622) and ERA (2.86). These numbers, along with another Burnes-ian 2023 (193 innings pitched and 200 strikeouts), garnered Milwaukee's ace a well-deserved most valuable pitcher accolade from the local chapter of the BBWAA. He remains under team control entering the 2024 season, and will be an obvious candidate for a third-straight Opening Day start, unless the team can't help themselves with their Tampa Bay cosplay.

Taylor Clarke RHP   Born: 05/13/93   Age: 31   Height: 6'4"   Weight: 217   Origin: Round 3, 2015 Draft (#76 overall)

YEAR	TM	LVL	AGE	G (GS)	IP	W-L	SV	K	WHIP	ERA	CSP	BB%	K%	HR%	GB%	ZSw%	ZCon%	OSw%	OCon%	BABIP	SLGCON	DRA-	WARP
2021	RNO	AAA	28	7(0)	7	1-0	0	8	1.14	0.00		7.4%	29.6%	0.0%	58.8%					.353	.438	84	0.1
2021	AZ	MLB	28	43(0)	43¹	1-3	0	39	1.52	4.98	54.1%	7.2%	20.1%	2.1%	37.6%	77.6%	81.9%	32.0%	69.5%	.350	.557	103	0.3
2022	KC	MLB	29	47(0)	49	3-1	3	48	1.18	4.04	54.7%	3.9%	23.6%	3.0%	36.3%	79.8%	84.1%	35.9%	60.9%	.314	.569	87	0.8
2023	KC	MLB	30	58(2)	59	3-6	3	65	1.61	5.95	46.2%	9.0%	24.4%	4.5%	30.6%	68.5%	82.2%	38.2%	61.3%	.369	.710	103	0.6
2024 DC	MIL	MLB	31	45(0)	47²	3-2	0	45	1.33	4.77	49.5%	8.3%	21.9%	4.2%	35.5%					.290	.603	106	0.1

2023 Arsenal: SL (88.7), FA (95.1), SW (84.1), CH (89.4)   Comps: Chris Stratton (67), Mike Wright Jr. (59), Matt Andriese (58)

You have to feel for Clarke, who must have looked around the Royals' bullpen in August with the dawning horror that he was now the lone adult in the room. Miscast as "stalwart veteran presence," Clarke is still trying to figure out himself as a pitcher, adding two distinct sliders last year: one a hard, cutterish jobbie that rides up, and the other the *en vogue* sweeper, this time with a dipping action reminiscent of his now-scrapped curveball. It's a good plan on paper, but batters weren't fooled by the tweaks to Clarke's arsenal, none of which addressed the core issue of his Very Hittable Fastball, which he threw less but should throw even less, if possible. Adulting is, as the t-shirts say, hard, but it's also hard to focus on a new arsenal when the bullpen phone won't stop ringing for you. Has he considered locking himself in the bathroom for a few moments' peace?

Robert Gasser LHP   Born: 05/31/99   Age: 25   Height: 6'0"   Weight: 192   Origin: Round 2, 2021 Draft (#71 overall)

YEAR	TM	LVL	AGE	G (GS)	IP	W-L	SV	K	WHIP	ERA	CSP	BB%	K%	HR%	GB%	ZSw%	ZCon%	OSw%	OCon%	BABIP	SLGCON	DRA-	WARP
2021	LE	A	22	5(5)	14	0-0	0	13	0.93	1.29		3.9%	25.5%	2.0%	52.8%					.286	.417	110	0.0
2022	FW	A+	23	18(18)	90¹	4-9	0	115	1.26	4.18		7.4%	30.5%	2.1%	41.2%					.356	.615	96	1.1
2022	BLX	AA	23	4(4)	20¹	1-1	0	26	1.08	2.21		9.6%	31.3%	2.4%	42.6%					.273	.478	89	0.3
2022	NAS	AAA	23	5(5)	26¹	2-2	0	31	1.59	4.44		13.4%	26.1%	0.8%	31.0%	67.6%	82.6%	36.1%	50.0%	.357	.521	109	0.2
2023	NAS	AAA	24	26(25)	135¹	9-1	0	166	1.28	3.79		8.4%	28.0%	2.0%	33.0%	68.3%	82.4%	33.3%	60.9%	.319	.546	93	2.4
2024 DC	MIL	MLB	25	16(16)	64²	2-5	0	62	1.36	4.75		8.9%	22.1%	3.5%	35.7%					.297	.568	105	0.4

2023 Arsenal: FA (93.5), SW (83.7), FC (89.4), SI (89.5)   Comps: Daniel Mengden (71), Daniel Gossett (70), Michael King (70)

Another dividend from the Josh Hader trade, Gasser pitched in both Double-A and Triple-A upon arriving in the Brewers organization and took steps forward immediately. His bread-and-butter consists of mixing his low-90s four-seam fastball in with off-speed stuff, and using his sinker early in counts. With his deep pitch mix, he's already tying up Triple-A hitters and offering Milwaukee a glimpse into their lefty-in-the-rotation future. The hold-up: while his sweeper is devastating against lefties, his cutter, subbed in for an ineffective change, has begun creating some platoon issues.

Bryan Hudson LHP Born: 05/08/97 Age: 27 Height: 6'8" Weight: 220 Origin: Round 3, 2015 Draft (#82 overall)

YEAR	TM	LVL	AGE	G (GS)	IP	W-L	SV	K	WHIP	ERA	CSP	BB%	K%	HR%	GB%	ZSw%	ZCon%	OSw%	OCon%	BABIP	SLGCON	DRA-	WARP
2021	TNS	AA	24	31(0)	54²	6-3	0	51	1.10	3.13		10.0%	23.3%	0.9%	64.8%					.259	.403	97	0.6
2022	TNS	AA	25	8(0)	13	3-1	3	18	1.15	2.08		9.6%	34.6%	1.9%	65.5%					.333	.519	78	0.3
2022	IOW	AAA	25	31(0)	46	1-2	1	58	1.35	4.11		10.8%	28.4%	2.0%	47.1%					.310	.565	88	0.9
2023	OKC	AAA	26	46(8)	55²	5-2	0	86	1.31	2.43		10.8%	35.7%	1.2%	45.3%	64.4%	76.1%	28.2%	60.0%	.355	.559	54	1.5
2023	LAD	MLB	26	6(0)	8²	0-0	0	7	1.85	7.27	58.0%	9.1%	15.9%	2.3%	56.2%	65.5%	72.7%	30.0%	79.2%	.355	.548	97	0.1
2024 DC	MIL	MLB	27	21(0)	23²	1-1	0	24	1.31	3.98	58.0%	10.6%	23.0%	2.6%	47.1%					.279	.500	89	0.2

2023 Arsenal: FA (91.9), FC (85.7), SW (79.5)   *Comps: Hoby Milner (46), Stephen Tarpley (46), Angel Perdomo (46)*

Say what you will about Hudson, but he's got one of the most fascinating 92-mph fastballs in MLB. He ranks in the 80th percentile in in-zone swing percentage, meaning he possesses the uncanny ability to get hitters to keep their bats on their shoulder, despite the low velo. For that, he can thank his funky delivery. Hudson uses his 6-foot-8 frame and long limbs to get extended 7.3 feet down the mound, which helps him create one of the lowest, widest release points in MLB. He has yet to pair his fastball with a strong secondary pitch, but if he were to do so, his called-strike savvy and ability to induce ground balls are a strong foundation.

Janson Junk RHP Born: 01/15/96 Age: 28 Height: 6'2" Weight: 202 Origin: Round 22, 2017 Draft (#662 overall)

YEAR	TM	LVL	AGE	G (GS)	IP	W-L	SV	K	WHIP	ERA	CSP	BB%	K%	HR%	GB%	ZSw%	ZCon%	OSw%	OCon%	BABIP	SLGCON	DRA-	WARP
2021	RCT	AA	25	5(5)	27¹	2-2	0	29	1.43	5.27		5.8%	24.0%	4.1%	43.5%					.338	.624	100	0.2
2021	SOM	AA	25	14(12)	65²	4-1	1	68	0.96	1.78		7.9%	26.8%	2.4%	43.6%					.233	.421	99	0.4
2021	LAA	MLB	25	4(4)	16¹	0-1	0	10	1.35	3.86	57.3%	2.8%	14.1%	7.0%	37.3%	71.7%	90.8%	33.3%	68.1%	.283	.621	127	-0.1
2022	SL	AAA	26	16(15)	73²	1-7	0	69	1.29	4.64		5.8%	22.1%	2.9%	32.3%	73.2%	82.3%	32.4%	66.5%	.318	.584	110	0.0
2022	LAA	MLB	26	3(2)	8¹	1-1	0	11	1.56	6.48	58.2%	8.1%	29.7%	2.7%	65.2%	65.8%	86.0%	27.7%	73.9%	.409	.652	81	0.2
2023	NAS	AAA	27	27(25)	140	7-10	0	94	1.35	4.18		7.4%	15.8%	2.4%	40.6%	72.5%	86.2%	32.9%	67.1%	.300	.493	105	1.6
2023	MIL	MLB	27	2(1)	7¹	0-1	0	5	1.36	4.91	53.2%	6.1%	15.2%	3.0%	53.8%	72.5%	94.6%	37.3%	86.4%	.292	.560	106	0.1
2024 DC	MIL	MLB	28	5(5)	19²	1-2	0	11	1.42	4.88	56.4%	7.1%	13.2%	2.8%	43.7%					.298	.507	108	0.1

2023 Arsenal: FA (92.5), SW (79.3), CU (82.5), FS (84.3), SI (91.8), SL (83.2)   *Comps: Brad Lincoln (49), Tyler Cloyd (49), Chase De Jong (48)*

There are few jokes in the name of nominative determinism that haven't already been made in Junk's lengthy nine-game tenure in the majors. In case you're wondering, Junk's fastball sits in the low-90s, and his lauded sweeper rings in at 80 mph. He spent most of 2023 in Triple-A Nashville, where he posted less-than-optimal numbers for a starter, with a few games going six-plus innings. The last day of the season found Junk recalled to Milwaukee, where he threw two-plus scoreless innings of relief and touched 96 miles per hour. Junk's future role with the big-league club could be in long relief, with his improved stuff playing up past his surname.

Eric Lauer LHP Born: 06/03/95 Age: 29 Height: 6'3" Weight: 209 Origin: Round 1, 2016 Draft (#25 overall)

YEAR	TM	LVL	AGE	G (GS)	IP	W-L	SV	K	WHIP	ERA	CSP	BB%	K%	HR%	GB%	ZSw%	ZCon%	OSw%	OCon%	BABIP	SLGCON	DRA-	WARP
2021	MIL	MLB	26	24(20)	118²	7-5	0	117	1.14	3.19	54.5%	8.4%	23.9%	3.3%	35.3%	70.3%	80.7%	31.5%	67.7%	.254	.486	97	1.3
2022	MIL	MLB	27	29(29)	158²	11-7	0	157	1.22	3.69	54.7%	8.9%	23.8%	4.1%	33.9%	68.2%	80.6%	30.0%	67.4%	.262	.559	115	0.3
2023	NAS	AAA	28	12(9)	43²	3-4	0	64	1.76	5.15		11.2%	31.1%	2.9%	36.8%	72.9%	77.1%	34.6%	59.4%	.436	.684	75	1.2
2023	MIL	MLB	28	10(9)	46²	4-6	0	43	1.67	6.56	49.2%	11.4%	20.4%	7.6%	25.0%	72.4%	83.5%	28.0%	67.6%	.297	.803	153	-0.8
2024 non	MIL	MLB	29	58(0)	50	2-2	0	47	1.41	4.80	53.1%	9.8%	21.7%	3.5%	32.6%					.296	.571	107	0.0

2023 Arsenal: FA (91.3), FC (87.1), CU (75.6), SL (83.2), CH (83.3)   *Comps: Jim Abbott (78), Danny Jackson (75), Jeff Francis (75)*

Lauer is a Brewer who's likely to have seen the last of the fermentation tanks, as he was waived in the offseason, outrighted to Triple-A Nashville, and then selected free agency. After two seasons of layered flavors from Lauer sours, 2023 was a bad batch. He was shelved in May due to an injury in his non-throwing shoulder, and struggled to shake it off in the minors after being activated in August. Lauer's fastball velocity dropped from 93.3 mph to 90, posting some rather hittable numbers for the four-seamer, with his peripherals not offering much solace beyond it. The numbers are inflated, but he's shown a deep arsenal and enough deception to rebound from this—if some of that velocity comes back, anyway.

Trevor Megill RHP Born: 12/05/93 Age: 30 Height: 6'8" Weight: 250 Origin: Round 7, 2015 Draft (#207 overall)

YEAR	TM	LVL	AGE	G (GS)	IP	W-L	SV	K	WHIP	ERA	CSP	BB%	K%	HR%	GB%	ZSw%	ZCon%	OSw%	OCon%	BABIP	SLGCON	DRA-	WARP
2021	IOW	AAA	27	12(0)	14	0-0	1	20	1.43	5.14		12.7%	31.7%	3.2%	44.1%					.313	.618	88	0.3
2021	CHC	MLB	27	28(0)	23²	1-2	0	30	1.86	8.37	55.4%	7.0%	26.1%	6.1%	38.2%	71.8%	89.0%	31.4%	53.9%	.426	.867	88	0.4
2022	STP	AAA	28	10(0)	12	0-2	2	16	1.25	3.00		8.5%	34.0%	4.3%	44.4%					.391	.826	79	0.3
2022	MIN	MLB	28	39(0)	45	4-3	0	49	1.49	4.80	58.0%	8.7%	25.0%	2.0%	44.2%	70.1%	84.9%	34.1%	58.9%	.368	.555	84	0.8
2023	NAS	AAA	29	11(0)	11	1-0	1	18	0.91	4.09		6.7%	40.0%	0.0%	36.4%	60.0%	74.5%	30.6%	53.3%	.318	.364	79	0.3
2023	STP	AAA	29	7(0)	9²	0-0	0	16	2.28	13.03		25.5%	31.4%	7.8%	50.0%	56.2%	75.6%	29.6%	42.5%	.278	1.095	104	0.1
2023	MIL	MLB	29	31(2)	34²	1-0	0	52	1.36	3.63	51.0%	8.1%	35.1%	1.4%	31.3%	62.6%	81.7%	34.4%	47.4%	.407	.637	77	0.8
2024 DC	MIL	MLB	30	39(0)	41²	2-2	0	49	1.27	4.18	54.7%	9.9%	27.7%	4.0%	37.9%					.285	.596	94	0.3

2023 Arsenal: FA (99.1), KC (85.6), SL (88.3)   *Comps: Tyler Kinley (69), JT Chargois (69), Hector Neris (68)*

After being optioned to Triple-A three times, Megill found himself locking down the middle innings. The Brewers had the luxury of a deep stock of high-leverage guys and once again were the beneficiaries of a reliever making minute adjustments to become near-unhittable. Megill's success goes a little bit deeper than "fastball go brrr," but rather pairing that incredible fastball and its improved command with a knuckle-curve he can control just as well. The curve notched an incredible 52.9% whiff rate and 33.8% put-away rate. As was the case with Josh Hader, on the off chance the fastball gets hit, it can get hit hard. But as with Hader, you happily take that tradeoff.

Wade Miley LHP Born: 11/13/86 Age: 37 Height: 6'1" Weight: 220 Origin: Round 1, 2008 Draft (#43 overall)

YEAR	TM	LVL	AGE	G(GS)	IP	W-L	SV	K	WHIP	ERA	CSP	BB%	K%	HR%	GB%	ZSw%	ZCon%	OSw%	OCon%	BABIP	SLGCON	DRA-	WARP
2021	CIN	MLB	34	28(28)	163	12-7	0	125	1.33	3.37	48.6%	7.2%	18.1%	2.5%	48.0%	70.3%	82.5%	35.3%	69.4%	.306	.510	105	1.1
2022	SB	A+	35	2(2)	6	0-0	0	3	2.00	9.00		3.3%	10.0%	0.0%	68.0%					.440	.520	111	0.0
2022	IOW	AAA	35	4(4)	16	0-0	0	12	1.06	2.81		6.3%	18.8%	1.6%	52.1%					.261	.362	98	0.2
2022	CHC	MLB	35	9(8)	37	2-2	0	28	1.22	3.16	49.6%	8.8%	17.6%	1.9%	51.3%	64.0%	85.4%	33.0%	62.1%	.250	.412	124	-0.1
2023	MIL	MLB	36	23(23)	120¹	9-4	0	79	1.14	3.14	47.8%	7.8%	16.1%	3.3%	46.6%	67.7%	88.2%	29.7%	70.2%	.236	.470	117	0.4
2024 DC	MIL	MLB	37	26(26)	134²	7-9	0	90	1.43	4.89	47.4%	8.1%	15.2%	2.8%	46.2%					.300	.510	107	0.7

2023 Arsenal: FC (87.1), CH (83.9), FA (90.4), SW (79.1), SI (90.7), CU (75.9)   Comps: Jason Vargas (77), Jimmy Key (77), Mark Buehrle (75)

Hands were wrung over the introduction of the pitch clock last spring, but not by Miley, who's never had to recharge for long between all those 87-mph cutters. Not counting Brandon Woodruff's 67 innings, Miley had the best ERA in the Brewers rotation (and the best in his 11-year tenure in MLB), making him a dependable back-end starter. While he's never been known for striking guys out, he did induce weak contact (his BABIP led all starters with 120+ IP), kept the ball on the ground, and tamped down the walks, despite his stubborn refusal to throw a single hittable strike. In perhaps the least surprising re-signing of the winter, Miley and the Brewers re-upped for one more year of junkball tomfoolery.

Hoby Milner LHP Born: 01/13/91 Age: 33 Height: 6'3" Weight: 184 Origin: Round 7, 2012 Draft (#248 overall)

YEAR	TM	LVL	AGE	G(GS)	IP	W-L	SV	K	WHIP	ERA	CSP	BB%	K%	HR%	GB%	ZSw%	ZCon%	OSw%	OCon%	BABIP	SLGCON	DRA-	WARP
2021	NAS	AAA	30	30(0)	32	1-1	5	48	0.66	1.69		1.7%	40.0%	1.7%	58.2%					.262	.400	71	0.9
2021	MIL	MLB	30	19(0)	21²	0-0	0	30	1.52	5.40	55.7%	3.0%	30.3%	8.1%	26.6%	61.0%	87.7%	33.5%	58.0%	.400	.905	90	0.3
2022	MIL	MLB	31	67(0)	64²	3-3	0	64	1.18	3.76	47.3%	5.5%	23.5%	1.8%	48.9%	57.1%	84.5%	32.3%	68.3%	.315	.511	93	0.9
2023	MIL	MLB	32	73(0)	64¹	2-1	0	59	0.96	1.82	47.5%	5.2%	23.4%	2.0%	50.0%	57.3%	85.0%	32.5%	72.7%	.254	.426	81	1.4
2024 DC	MIL	MLB	33	45(0)	47²	3-2	0	42	1.20	3.81	48.4%	6.0%	20.9%	2.9%	44.9%					.290	.510	88	0.5

2023 Arsenal: KC (79.7), SI (88.2), FA (89), CH (81.2)   Comps: Blaine Hardy (64), Jake Diekman (61), Aaron Loup (61)

Mourning the LOOGY doesn't necessarily follow the linear stages of grief. Bargaining is the stage to which pitchers like Milner naturally gravitate, adapting to use breaking and off-speed pitches to induce any outs they can get. The 2023 season was a very curveball-heavy year for Milner, with good reason: It's got an angry bite, holding hitters to a .192 wOBA. Weak contact was a huge part of Milner's game; he depressed expected production on batted balls as well as almost anyone in the game. Along with the back-end rotation fortification of Colin Rea, Milner was one of the quietly invaluable contributors to the Brewers' 2023 division title. He's gone from a fringe-average reliever to one of the better bullpen arms in the game. That's acceptance.

--- ★ ★ ★ *2024 Top 101 Prospect* **#63** ★ ★ ★ ---

Jacob Misiorowski RHP Born: 04/03/02 Age: 22 Height: 6'7" Weight: 190 Origin: Round 2, 2022 Draft (#63 overall)

YEAR	TM	LVL	AGE	G(GS)	IP	W-L	SV	K	WHIP	ERA	CSP	BB%	K%	HR%	GB%	ZSw%	ZCon%	OSw%	OCon%	BABIP	SLGCON	DRA-	WARP
2023	CAR	A	21	9(9)	26²	1-1	0	46	0.82	3.04		11.9%	45.5%	0.0%	39.0%					.244	.385	77	0.6
2023	WIS	A+	21	6(6)	23²	1-0	0	28	1.23	1.90		13.2%	26.4%	0.0%	37.3%					.254	.351	101	0.2
2023	BLX	AA	21	5(5)	21	2-1	0	36	1.57	5.57		15.0%	33.6%	1.9%	36.4%					.357	.581	106	
2024 non	MIL	MLB	22	58(0)	50	2-2	0	61	1.53	5.63		14.3%	26.7%	3.7%	34.4%					.294	.620	120	-0.3

Comps: Yadier Álvarez (76), Chris Archer (76), Mitch Keller (76)

The 2023 Biloxi Shuckers were something of a Double-A superteam, full of minor-league All-Star selections and ETAs in the very near future. Starting the year in Single-A, Misiorowski rose to become the organization's top pitching prospect, before a career-high workload led to a mid-August shutdown due to fatigue. He's had a few brushes with triple digits, including a sunny outing at the 2023 All-Stars Futures Game, but generally sits mid-90s with the fastball. He's also got a slider with depth that batters frequently chase out of the zone. He's started using his low-90s cutter, curveball and change more; with those pitches steadily developing Misiorowski is a candidate for yet another promotion in 2024.

Joel Payamps RHP Born: 04/07/94 Age: 30 Height: 6'2" Weight: 217 Origin: IFA, 2010

YEAR	TM	LVL	AGE	G(GS)	IP	W-L	SV	K	WHIP	ERA	CSP	BB%	K%	HR%	GB%	ZSw%	ZCon%	OSw%	OCon%	BABIP	SLGCON	DRA-	WARP
2021	OMA	AAA	27	8(0)	8	1-0	2	14	1.75	4.50		10.3%	35.9%	0.0%	19.0%					.476	.762	88	0.1
2021	TOR	MLB	27	22(0)	30	0-2	0	22	1.07	2.70	51.9%	9.2%	18.5%	2.5%	47.1%	70.4%	76.2%	33.3%	69.3%	.220	.388	99	0.3
2021	KC	MLB	27	15(1)	20¹	1-1	0	16	1.28	4.43	58.4%	3.5%	18.6%	3.5%	41.8%	64.7%	87.5%	41.8%	77.0%	.313	.582	101	0.2
2022	KC	MLB	28	29(0)	42²	2-3	0	33	1.45	3.16	55.0%	8.5%	17.6%	2.7%	52.6%	68.7%	81.5%	31.9%	68.5%	.313	.533	90	0.6
2022	OAK	MLB	28	12(0)	13	1-3	0	8	1.08	3.46	58.3%	0.0%	15.1%	3.8%	55.6%	74.4%	89.7%	32.5%	70.7%	.279	.500	85	0.2
2023	MIL	MLB	29	69(0)	70²	7-5	3	77	1.05	2.55	47.9%	5.9%	26.8%	2.8%	46.5%	64.9%	78.5%	28.4%	63.3%	.277	.486	79	1.6
2024 DC	MIL	MLB	30	56(0)	59²	4-3	2	54	1.25	3.98	51.7%	7.3%	21.5%	2.9%	46.1%					.291	.520	90	0.6

2023 Arsenal: SL (84.2), SI (95.3), FA (95.5), CH (89.2)   Comps: Tyler Duffey (54), Mike Mayers (53), Dylan Floro (52)

Payamps came to the Brewers as part of the three-team trade between the Brewers, A's and Braves that allowed the budding superstar William Contreras to land in Milwaukee. If Contreras cemented himself as the team's 2023 MVP, Payamps should get in on that recognition as well, considering he and Devin Williams have formed one of the better setup-closer combos in the game. His four-seamer is just another one of his secondaries, able to generate a high number of whiffs like his primary sinker. In a single year, Payamps pumped his strikeout rate from 17% to 26.8%, with a great deal of concomitant improvement in his overall run prevention. The Brewers bullpen has evolved to function like a poker hand: It's beneficial to start the betting with pocket kings.

Freddy Peralta RHP Born: 06/04/96 Age: 28 Height: 6'0" Weight: 196 Origin: IFA, 2013

YEAR	TM	LVL	AGE	G(GS)	IP	W-L	SV	K	WHIP	ERA	CSP	BB%	K%	HR%	GB%	ZSw%	ZCon%	OSw%	OCon%	BABIP	SLGCON	DRA-	WARP
2021	MIL	MLB	25	28(27)	144¹	10-5	0	195	0.97	2.81	52.7%	9.7%	33.6%	2.4%	32.1%	67.0%	74.8%	30.1%	51.4%	.232	.486	80	2.9
2022	MIL	MLB	26	18(17)	78	4-4	0	86	1.04	3.58	52.9%	8.5%	27.1%	1.9%	39.3%	64.6%	78.5%	31.2%	60.1%	.247	.434	87	1.3
2023	MIL	MLB	27	30(30)	165²	12-10	0	210	1.12	3.86	44.3%	7.9%	30.9%	3.8%	42.3%	70.8%	78.1%	33.1%	50.6%	.275	.587	83	3.4
2024 DC	MIL	MLB	28	29(29)	160¹	10-8	0	203	1.15	3.39	48.0%	8.7%	30.8%	3.4%	39.0%					.283	.577	79	3.2

2023 Arsenal: FA (94.5), CH (88.5), SW (82), CU (77.2), SL (83), SI (94.8)   Comps: Ubaldo Jiménez (82), Charlie Lea (82), Chris Archer (81)

Fastball Freddy may have to rebrand as Slider Freddy. The pitch stifled hitters to the tune of a .203 batting average, and they whiffed on it 45.8% of the time, a major improvement on prior years. As electric as Peralta was, however, it was a simpler stat that defined his success: 30 games started, the first time he'd reached that plateau. Without Brandon Woodruff, the Brewers needed (still need!) Peralta to be a constant presence in the rotation. Ignore the inflated ERA, as he's the same great pitcher he's always been. For years he played third banana to Woodruff and Corbin Burnes; now, unless Milwaukee can get its offense in order, he'll be a frontline starter on an invisible team.

Colin Rea RHP Born: 07/01/90 Age: 34 Height: 6'5" Weight: 218 Origin: Round 12, 2011 Draft (#383 overall)

YEAR	TM	LVL	AGE	G(GS)	IP	W-L	SV	K	WHIP	ERA	CSP	BB%	K%	HR%	GB%	ZSw%	ZCon%	OSw%	OCon%	BABIP	SLGCON	DRA-	WARP
2021	NAS	AAA	30	7(7)	35²	4-2	0	35	1.04	2.27		2.8%	24.6%	1.4%	49.0%					.310	.431	91	0.6
2021	MIL	MLB	30	1(0)	6	0-0	0	5	1.17	7.50	52.5%	0.0%	20.8%	8.3%	21.1%	77.8%	89.3%	29.1%	50.0%	.294	.833	109	0.0
2023	NAS	AAA	32	4(4)	18	0-0	0	21	0.94	2.50		1.4%	30.0%	1.4%	38.3%	65.3%	85.7%	32.1%	47.1%	.326	.543	87	0.4
2023	MIL	MLB	32	26(22)	124²	6-6	0	110	1.19	4.55	51.3%	7.4%	21.3%	4.4%	43.0%	68.5%	85.2%	31.7%	60.2%	.257	.567	99	1.6
2024 DC	MIL	MLB	33	23(23)	117²	6-8	0	104	1.31	4.63	51.4%	7.0%	20.8%	3.9%	35.4%					.295	.581	104	0.6

2023 Arsenal: SI (92.7), FC (86.7), FA (93.1), SW (83.4), KC (78.9), FS (86.1)   Comps: Brandon Duckworth (49), Tommy Milone (46), Wily Peralta (45)

Rea was one of the quieter contributors to the 2023 division title: He pitched at least five innings in 17 of his 22 games started, which is a compliment these days. Everything on the stat page whispers "average," because it doesn't inspire enough emotion to shout anything, but there's a certain virtue in knowing that a pitcher won't necessarily give the lineup a night off, but that the game will at least likely be in reach. Pretend there's a stat for anti-quality starts, giving up five runs or more. If so, Rea only did it twice. His numbers won't compel you to drop this book in astonishment, but he throws strikes, limits baserunners and covers starts, which is about as much as you can ask from a back-end starter. The Brewers agreed, giving him a quiet one-year contract early in the offseason.

Carlos F. Rodriguez RHP Born: 11/27/01 Age: 22 Height: 6'0" Weight: 206 Origin: Round 6, 2021 Draft (#177 overall)

YEAR	TM	LVL	AGE	G(GS)	IP	W-L	SV	K	WHIP	ERA	CSP	BB%	K%	HR%	GB%	ZSw%	ZCon%	OSw%	OCon%	BABIP	SLGCON	DRA-	WARP
2022	CAR	A	20	19(13)	71¹	3-4	1	84	1.12	3.53		9.4%	29.3%	2.4%	39.1%					.286	.515	80	1.5
2022	WIS	A+	20	7(7)	36¹	3-1	0	45	0.94	1.98		9.2%	31.9%	0.0%	38.3%					.259	.362	75	0.8
2023	BLX	AA	21	25(25)	123²	9-6	0	152	1.09	2.77		10.3%	29.5%	1.9%	37.9%					.249	.418	76	1.7
2024 DC	MIL	MLB	22	5(5)	21²	1-2	0	21	1.42	5.03		10.8%	21.9%	3.7%	34.2%					.288	.587	109	0.1

2023 Arsenal: FC (87.2), FA (93.4), SL (82.7), CH (85.9), SI (94.5), CU (74.4)

The Nashville Sounds starter is making waves with his mighty strikeout upside. He fanned 62 in 47 innings as a junior college pitcher, to later sign with the Brewers and be crowned the organization's 2022 Minor League Pitcher of the Year with a 30.1% strikeout rate. Rodriguez has quite the pitch mix: a mid-90's fastball accompanied by a mid-80's changeup, with an average slider that complements the other two pitches well. His curveball took a step forward in 2023, giving him a diverse arsenal. The development of those last two pitches will determine his fate as mid-rotation starter or swingman, since without a true out-pitch there's no real relief fallback here. He's already made strides in facing big-league hitters—he participated in the World Baseball Classic back in March 2023, toeing the rubber for Nicaragua.

Joe Ross RHP Born: 05/21/93 Age: 31 Height: 6'4" Weight: 232 Origin: Round 1, 2011 Draft (#25 overall)

YEAR	TM	LVL	AGE	G(GS)	IP	W-L	SV	K	WHIP	ERA	CSP	BB%	K%	HR%	GB%	ZSw%	ZCon%	OSw%	OCon%	BABIP	SLGCON	DRA-	WARP
2021	WAS	MLB	28	20(19)	108	5-9	0	109	1.22	4.17	55.7%	7.4%	23.7%	3.7%	42.7%	65.3%	81.7%	30.4%	62.8%	.280	.546	93	1.4
2023	SJ	A	30	4(4)	7	0-0	0	5	1.86	5.14		9.1%	15.2%	0.0%	58.3%					.455	.500	91	
2023	SAC	AAA	30	3(3)	6	0-0	0	5	1.83	6.00		17.9%	17.9%	0.0%	55.6%	61.2%	76.7%	29.1%	60.9%	.353	.562	90	
2024 DC	MIL	MLB	31	25(16)	99¹	5-6	0	85	1.43	5.09	53.7%	9.1%	19.3%	3.4%	42.5%					.299	.556	111	0.3

2023 Arsenal: SI (96.2), SL (87), FA (95.4), CH (91.1)   Comps: Jhoulys Chacín (51), Vance Worley (50), Zach McAllister (50)

Ross joined the Giants in the previous offseason to rehab his second Tommy John surgery and returned to game action in late August, reaching Triple-A by mid-September, where he had two reasonable appearances and a disastrous one. While partially attributable to the shorter stints of the rehab process, Ross reached his best velocity ever recorded by Brooks Baseball, rivaled only by a single-inning relief appearance in spring training of 2014. Perhaps more sustainably, he was getting more sink on his sinker, taking a flatter approach angle on his four-seamer (with some lost carry) and throwing a slightly more vertical, gyro-like slider. The strike-throwing was an issue and the strikeouts weren't there, but the former has been a strength in the past, so the first 14 innings off TJ might not be instructive, and he was getting enough whiffs and called strikes regardless. This all looks quite promising for a return to the majors in 2024, though it'll be in Milwaukee rather than San Francisco.

Julio Teheran RHP   Born: 01/27/91   Age: 33   Height: 6'2"   Weight: 205   Origin: IFA, 2007

YEAR	TM	LVL	AGE	G (GS)	IP	W-L	SV	K	WHIP	ERA	CSP	BB%	K%	HR%	GB%	ZSw%	ZCon%	OSw%	OCon%	BABIP	SLGCON	DRA-	WARP
2021	DET	MLB	30	1 (1)	5	1-0	0	3	1.40	1.80	55.8%	15.0%	15.0%	5.0%	35.7%	73.2%	83.3%	26.5%	84.6%	.231	.571	135	0.0
2022	TOR	WIN	31	8 (8)	38²	2-4	0	25	0.96	3.49		2.0%	16.3%	0.0%	52.9%					.281	.347		
2023	NAS	AAA	32	4 (4)	14¹	2-0	0	13	1.33	4.40		9.5%	20.6%	1.6%	51.2%	59.2%	87.9%	26.8%	58.8%	.300	.463	86	0.3
2023	ELP	AAA	32	8 (8)	40	4-2	0	45	1.68	5.63		8.6%	24.3%	3.8%	41.3%	68.4%	83.9%	28.7%	56.9%	.386	.689	106	0.2
2023	MIL	MLB	32	14 (11)	71²	3-5	0	50	1.13	4.40	51.6%	4.5%	17.4%	4.5%	40.3%	69.4%	84.1%	29.9%	70.9%	.266	.573	111	0.4
2024 non	MIL	MLB	33	58 (0)	50	2-2	0	36	1.34	4.78	49.5%	7.4%	16.7%	3.5%	38.7%					.285	.537	108	0.0

2023 Arsenal: SI (89.9), FC (86.5), CH (83.2), SW (77.6), FA (89.2)   Comps: Don Cardwell (64), Jake Peavy (64), Mike Torrez (63)

Van Gogh put on his first exhibit at 32. Chuck Berry was 32 when *Johnny B Goode* was released. *The Simpsons* were in season 32 when "The Last Barfighter" was aired, which a couple people probably think was as good as the old stuff. Teheran, at 32, looked like the oldest man ever to play baseball. The Brewers signed the veteran in May to plug a leaky rotation—which he sort of did, thanks to one of the league's lowest walk rates—and for half a dozen starts, he almost sort of looked like a copy of a reflection of an artist's rendition of his former self.

Abner Uribe RHP   Born: 06/20/00   Age: 24   Height: 6'3"   Weight: 225   Origin: IFA, 2018

YEAR	TM	LVL	AGE	G (GS)	IP	W-L	SV	K	WHIP	ERA	CSP	BB%	K%	HR%	GB%	ZSw%	ZCon%	OSw%	OCon%	BABIP	SLGCON	DRA-	WARP
2021	CAR	A	21	17 (4)	33²	1-0	3	52	1.46	4.01		16.7%	34.7%	1.3%	43.3%					.319	.521	70	0.8
2023	BLX	AA	23	15 (0)	15	1-0	7	28	1.07	1.80		14.8%	45.9%	1.6%	56.5%					.273	.478	71	0.5
2023	NAS	AAA	23	7 (0)	8	0-0	0	13	1.25	2.25		19.4%	36.1%	0.0%	73.3%	48.3%	85.7%	26.2%	37.0%	.200	.267	78	0.2
2023	MIL	MLB	23	32 (0)	30²	1-0	1	39	1.17	1.76	43.1%	15.7%	30.7%	0.0%	52.2%	62.6%	81.1%	27.2%	47.7%	.239	.308	92	0.5
2024 DC	MIL	MLB	24	45 (0)	47²	3-2	2	67	1.42	4.28	43.1%	15.1%	31.8%	2.8%	46.4%					.294	.564	92	0.4

2023 Arsenal: SI (99.3), SW (89.4), FA (100.8)   Comps: Ken Giles (74), Phillippe Aumont (73), Junior Fernández (72)

On August 23, Uribe sent a four-seamer screaming off the outer corner of the plate at 103.3 mph—just a few weeks after he repeatedly reached speeds of 102. Those were the fastest pitches in Brewers history, and quickly established him as a mainstay in an already talented Brewers bullpen. Uribe's sinker "only" sits 99 but features great vertical movement, contributing to his incredible strikeout rate and the complete lack of home runs. The 20 walks are a problem, sure, but they become a little more palatable when situated next to just the three extra-base hits. This is a major victory for player development; when his journey began he was an 18-year-old throwing in the low 90s. It's hard to imagine.

Devin Williams RHP   Born: 09/21/94   Age: 29   Height: 6'2"   Weight: 192   Origin: Round 2, 2013 Draft (#54 overall)

YEAR	TM	LVL	AGE	G (GS)	IP	W-L	SV	K	WHIP	ERA	CSP	BB%	K%	HR%	GB%	ZSw%	ZCon%	OSw%	OCon%	BABIP	SLGCON	DRA-	WARP
2021	MIL	MLB	26	58 (0)	54	8-2	3	87	1.19	2.50	48.2%	12.4%	38.5%	2.2%	45.0%	64.4%	69.6%	36.0%	44.5%	.301	.533	73	1.3
2022	MIL	MLB	27	65 (0)	60²	6-4	15	96	1.01	1.93	48.8%	12.5%	40.0%	0.8%	50.5%	64.5%	73.8%	38.0%	46.5%	.266	.385	67	1.6
2023	MIL	MLB	28	61 (0)	58²	8-3	36	87	0.92	1.53	41.7%	12.1%	37.7%	1.7%	47.8%	67.7%	71.2%	36.1%	46.7%	.198	.383	76	1.4
2024 DC	MIL	MLB	29	56 (0)	59²	4-7	37	94	1.11	2.72	45.6%	11.3%	38.2%	2.6%	47.4%					.284	.554	65	1.4

2023 Arsenal: CH (84), FA (94.3), FC (90.5)   Comps: Al Alburquerque (71), Greg Holland (70), Steve Cishek (70)

The Williams-Payamps one-two punch out of the powerhouse Brewers bullpen was a formidable barrier at the end of games. They're the toughest kids you know on the block, hands interlocked in an unwinnable game of Red Rover; elbows and wrists stiffened, no runs are crossing those bonded arms. Graduating from 2022's setup man to the Brewers' full-time closer, Williams managed to convert save opportunities by protecting tight leads well into the regular season. Games were saved and air was bent, even with a baserunner or two slipping his grasp due to occasional missteps with command. As this is his second year of arbitration availability, the hallowed closer, one of the best in the game, is set to get a much-deserved raise.

Bryse Wilson RHP   Born: 12/20/97   Age: 26   Height: 6'2"   Weight: 267   Origin: Round 4, 2016 Draft (#109 overall)

YEAR	TM	LVL	AGE	G (GS)	IP	W-L	SV	K	WHIP	ERA	CSP	BB%	K%	HR%	GB%	ZSw%	ZCon%	OSw%	OCon%	BABIP	SLGCON	DRA-	WARP
2021	GWN	AAA	23	10 (9)	55¹	5-2	0	42	1.39	4.23		6.8%	17.9%	3.4%	40.6%					.321	.590	109	0.5
2021	PIT	MLB	23	8 (8)	40¹	1-4	0	23	1.24	4.91	54.1%	5.9%	13.6%	4.7%	33.1%	74.2%	89.3%	38.2%	75.4%	.252	.564	134	-0.3
2021	ATL	MLB	23	8 (8)	33²	2-3	0	23	1.69	5.88	55.7%	7.8%	15.0%	4.6%	37.6%	67.7%	85.6%	31.9%	63.3%	.349	.640	127	-0.2
2022	IND	AAA	24	6 (6)	36¹	5-0	0	34	1.05	2.97		4.1%	23.1%	4.1%	47.2%					.263	.533	87	0.7
2022	PIT	MLB	24	25 (20)	115²	3-9	0	79	1.42	5.52	56.3%	6.3%	15.5%	3.9%	44.2%	69.7%	90.1%	30.5%	68.8%	.305	.585	122	-0.2
2023	MIL	MLB	25	53 (0)	76²	6-0	3	61	1.07	2.58	50.5%	7.0%	19.4%	2.9%	36.2%	72.9%	88.4%	30.1%	68.7%	.236	.480	102	0.8
2024 DC	MIL	MLB	26	45 (0)	47²	3-2	0	31	1.39	5.10	53.6%	7.1%	15.2%	3.8%	39.2%					.289	.550	112	0.0

2023 Arsenal: FC (89.3), SI (93.3), FA (93.8), CU (79.5), CH (87.8), FS (86.6)   Comps: Sean O'Sullivan (70), Tommy Hunter (69), Jacob Turner (65)

Chalk another one up to the Brewers' pitching development team. Purchased from Pittsburgh in January 2023 for what could only be assumed to be six pressed souvenir pennies and two matinee tickets to Gerard Butler's PLANE (2023), Milwaukee mapped out a new pitch mix for Wilson, bringing a newly fashioned cutter to the forefront. The result was like one of those little capsules children put in warm water and watch them expand into little foam tigers and crabs, except this time, he emerged as an excellent late-inning reliever. "Braves sophomore slump," "Pirates failed reclamation project," and "quality setup man" are all common archetypes, but rarely together, and even more rarely in that order.

LINEOUTS

Hitters

HITTER	POS	TM	LVL	AGE	PA	R	HR	RBI	SB	AVG/OBP/SLG	BABIP	SLGCON	BB%	K%	ZSw%	ZCon%	OSw%	OCon%	LA	90th EV	DRC+	BRR	DRP	WARP
Eric Bitonti	SS	BRW	ROK	17	48	8	2	9	0	.179/.333/.410	.227	.667	18.8%	31.3%										
Mike Boeve	2B	BRW	ROK	21	36	8	4	12	0	.500/.556/1.000	.524	1.250	11.1%	16.7%										
	2B	WIS	A+	21	84	11	1	18	1	.250/.333/.333	.315	.453	11.9%	22.6%							99	1.1	0.6	0.4
Eric Brown Jr.	SS	SUR	WIN	22	97	15	1	14	8	.289/.392/.410	.354	.515	11.3%	17.5%	75.0%	100.0%	25.0%	100.0%						
	SS	WIS	A+	22	287	48	4	25	37	.265/.362/.347	.311	.431	11.1%	16.7%							113	5.8	2.9	2.4
Vinny Capra	IF	IND	AAA	26	192	30	2	30	5	.329/.411/.439	.377	.526	12.5%	14.1%	49.4%	87.6%	25.8%	72.5%			112	-0.1	3.4	1.1
	IF	BUF	AAA	26	70	6	0	5	1	.167/.357/.222	.220	.293	20.0%	18.6%	36.2%	78.6%	19.7%	77.8%			109	-0.5	-0.7	0.2
	IF	PIT	MLB	26	21	3	0	1	0	.167/.250/.222	.231	.308	9.5%	23.8%	54.8%	82.4%	23.1%	66.7%	5.5	98.0	85	0.0	0.0	0.0
Filippo Di Turi	SS	DSL BRW2	ROK	17	222	35	0	27	12	.282/.414/.354	.342	.430	17.1%	14.4%										
Oliver Dunn	2B	SCO	WIN	25	83	17	2	10	12	.362/.470/.652	.548	1.023	16.9%	30.1%	42.1%	100.0%	28.2%	54.5%						
	2B	REA	AA	25	505	65	21	78	16	.271/.396/.506	.357	.759	16.2%	27.5%							121	1.0	-2.6	2.3
Daniel Guilarte	MI	CAR	A	19	265	35	0	31	26	.269/.377/.314	.377	.446	13.2%	24.9%							109	-1.6	-0.2	1.0
Keston Hiura	1B	NAS	AAA	26	367	55	23	77	0	.308/.395/.565	.359	.791	8.4%	24.5%	71.0%	79.8%	37.5%	53.2%			118	-0.9	0.8	1.8
Jahmai Jones	UT	NAS	AAA	25	182	31	3	14	10	.232/.392/.352	.306	.500	20.3%	23.1%	58.8%	81.7%	17.9%	43.2%			101	-0.5	-1.7	0.2
	UT	OKC	AAA	25	263	40	9	34	2	.292/.427/.542	.358	.732	17.5%	20.9%	64.6%	78.3%	20.9%	48.0%			116	0.5	0.1	1.3
	UT	MIL	MLB	25	11	2	0	3	1	.200/.273/.300	.400	.600	9.1%	45.5%	68.0%	76.5%	25.0%	50.0%	21.3	108.6	80	0.0	0.0	0.0
Luis Lara	CF	CAR	A	18	318	55	2	21	22	.285/.379/.354	.335	.425	12.3%	14.5%							115	1.4	1.4	1.7
	CF	WIS	A+	18	79	13	0	8	8	.290/.351/.377	.364	.481	6.3%	19.0%							101	1.8	-0.8	0.3
Owen Miller	2B	NAS	AAA	26	116	12	4	17	1	.283/.336/.472	.306	.568	5.2%	15.5%	66.1%	87.2%	36.0%	74.5%			100	0.6	-1.7	0.2
	2B	MIL	MLB	26	314	29	5	27	13	.261/.303/.371	.310	.470	5.4%	19.4%	64.3%	87.6%	37.2%	74.4%	13.4	102.3	92	0.5	0.2	0.6
Dylan O'Rae	CF/2B	BRW	ROK	19	178	44	0	15	28	.362/.522/.408	.431	.495	22.5%	12.9%										
	CF/2B	CAR	A	19	107	14	0	8	16	.330/.439/.375	.387	.446	15.9%	13.1%							133	1.7	1.2	1.0
Blake Perkins	OF	NAS	AAA	26	182	28	4	17	5	.308/.396/.500	.383	.667	13.2%	21.4%	60.8%	81.0%	25.7%	66.4%			110	0.3	4.0	1.2
	OF	MIL	MLB	26	168	28	4	20	5	.217/.325/.350	.290	.515	13.7%	27.4%	53.8%	85.3%	23.4%	63.7%	12.9	100.5	78	0.2	3.5	0.4
Cooper Pratt	SS	BRW	ROK	18	54	9	0	8	4	.356/.426/.444	.444	.588	9.3%	20.4%										
Yophery Rodriguez	CF	DSL BRW1	ROK	17	224	34	6	36	12	.253/.393/.449	.289	.580	18.3%	17.9%										
Brock Wilken	3B	BRW	ROK	21	28	3	1	6	1	.333/.464/.571	.400	.800	14.3%	21.4%										
	3B	WIS	A+	21	150	21	2	15	3	.289/.427/.438	.379	.596	18.0%	21.3%							120	-0.3	0.2	0.8
	3B	BLX	AA	21	25	3	2	8	0	.217/.280/.565	.250	.929	8.0%	36.0%							102	-0.1		

A six-foot-four lefty hitter with power: that's **Eric Bitonti** for you. He's shown to have good range at shortstop and is projected to be an above-average defender, if you happen to enjoy bigger dudes at the six. ⓪ **Mike Boeve** is one of those contact hitters who isn't afraid of hitting with two strikes, and who also isn't afraid of swinging to get to two strikes. He's adequate at second and third but not shortstop, and his bat-to-ball swing doesn't translate to bat-through-ball power. ⓪ He's speedy. He gets on base. He's **Eric Brown Jr.**, and he's here to play psychological war games with Double-A pitching staffs. His distinct swing could be replicated anywhere from backyards to batting cages; however, he's making small adjustments to alleviate the swing being the first thing mentioned about him in every scouting report. ⓪ **Vinny Capra** was traded from the Blue Jays to the Pirates for Tyler Heineman, a fourth-string catcher who was quickly cut loose. There are only a couple of player types that rate that sort of transaction, so you guessed it: He's a contact-first utility player destined to swing between the majors and minors. ⓪ A member of the 2023 international signing class, **Filippo Di Turi** is all about contact when it comes to his hitting. The 17-year-old has the strong arms and footwork to help him stick at the coveted shortstop position, and also wonders what a home run feels like. ⓪ **Oliver Dunn's** career was going nowhere in the Yankees system when the Phillies popped him in the minor-league phase of the Rule 5 Draft before last season. Given ample playing time, he made a four-grade jump in batted ball damage and vaulted his way into real prospectdom, and the Brewers picked him up in a prospects-for-prospect deal early in the offseason. ⓪ With an arcane knowledge of the strike zone, **Daniel Guilarte** gets on base via walks and makes contact with pitches in the zone, but similar to rolling a d20, he has a high tendency to keep the ball on the ground. The next quest is developing barbarian-like strength to add power to his hit tool. ⓪ As a prospect **Keston Hiura** promised a hit tool worth the defensive headaches, and failed to deliver on either. Not even the league's bottom feeders raised an eyebrow when the Brewers outrighted him, and he spent the rest of the season haunting Nashville, hitting just well enough to make them uninterested in opening old wounds. ⓪ Signed in July after yet another year frozen in Triple-A hell, **Jahmai Jones** hit a pinch-hit, three-run double in his first MLB game in two seasons. He got four more starts over the month and then the Brewers sent him back down to Triple-A, though he remains on the 40-man roster—where, thanks to just 12 innings in the field, he wound up listed by the Brewers as a DH. ⓪ Imagine this: You're a 19-year-old gifted with great hand-eye coordination and bat-to-ball skills. Your near-elite speed in the outfield and strong arm alongside your ability to seek great routes and out-read a library is pushing up the Brewers' ranks. Look at that. You're **Luis Lara**. ⓪ It's no longer the proverbial Miller Time at American Family Field, but the spirit lives on in **Owen Miller**, whose heavy workload as a utilityman proves the saying that it's always five o'clock somewhere. ⓪ Like a DJ spinning an arcane track, the Brewers dug into the crates for this 2022 third-round pick. Unranked on prospect lists at the time, **Dylan O'Rae** was considered a deep cut. His bat leaves much to be desired when it comes to power, but his great speed can turn singles into doubles, doubles into triples. ⓪ The Brewers have a great problem of having a surplus of outfielders that can roam the grass, **Blake Perkins** being the eye-catching centerpiece; he also came up in big spots at the plate in 2023. The position will need some clarity, but unless a trade is in the works, Perkins makes a viable option for the fourth spot. ⓪ Throw some time on your calendar for **Cooper Pratt**, whose name sounds like the world's most boring consulting firm. His collection of above-average tools shows some synergy with the shortstop position, and he has plenty of height and size to execute on his power-hitting KPIs. ⓪ At the advanced age of 17, **Yophery Rodriguez** has the balanced set of skills one might evenly distribute to an *MLB: The Show* player before deciding to go all-in on a facet. He possesses a flat swing path that's also loud and easy, and logs a wide range of velocities. ⓪ With great power comes great responsibility, and with the 2023 draft came **Brock Wilken**. The top prospect has raw power and consistently posts high exit velocities that many baseballs have filed personal grievances over. He finished 2023 at Double-A, but the bat alone could very well make him a Sound over a Shucker in 2024.

Pitchers

PITCHER	TM	LVL	AGE	G (GS)	IP	W-L	SV	K	WHIP	ERA	CSP	BB%	K%	HR%	GB%	ZSw%	ZCon%	OSw%	OCon%	BABIP	SLGCON	DRA-	WARP
Clayton Andrews	NAS	AAA	26	48 (1)	57	6-0	5	74	1.23	2.53		13.0%	31.1%	1.7%	46.2%	61.0%	76.1%	32.9%	47.9%	.276	.484	79	1.4
	MIL	MLB	26	4 (0)	3¹	0-1	0	4	3.60	27.00	45.2%	9.1%	18.2%	13.6%	43.8%	67.9%	94.7%	30.5%	66.7%	.538	1.375	104	0.0
Bradley Blalock	SAL	A	22	4 (4)	18	1-0	0	22	0.78	1.50		6.2%	33.8%	1.5%	34.2%					.243	.474	86	0.3
	WIS	A+	22	4 (4)	13²	0-0	0	17	1.46	5.27		11.5%	27.9%	4.9%	29.7%					.294	.917	103	0.2
	GVL	A+	22	7 (7)	35¹	5-1	0	36	1.13	2.55		6.2%	24.8%	2.1%	41.4%					.292	.495	97	0.3
Coleman Crow	RCT	AA	22	4 (4)	24	2-0	0	31	0.63	1.88		7.0%	36.0%	3.5%	44.9%					.133	.438	73	0.7
Logan Henderson	CAR	A	21	18 (18)	78²	4-3	0	106	0.97	2.75		8.6%	35.2%	2.7%	40.7%					.264	.530	80	1.6
Easton McGee	TAC	AAA	25	5 (5)	28²	3-0	0	24	1.22	3.14		7.6%	20.3%	0.8%	51.8%	66.7%	86.2%	31.7%	62.9%	.298	.440	96	0.3
	SEA	MLB	25	1 (1)	6²	0-0	0	2	0.30	0.00	56.9%	4.5%	9.1%	0.0%	47.4%	73.3%	90.9%	38.2%	61.5%	.053	.105	106	0.1
J.C. Mejía	NAS	AAA	26	23 (0)	30¹	2-1	0	32	1.25	3.86		10.2%	25.2%	1.6%	65.4%	67.2%	86.0%	31.2%	51.1%	.303	.532	85	0.7
	MIL	MLB	26	9 (0)	11¹	1-0	0	13	1.59	5.56	46.6%	6.0%	26.0%	4.0%	45.5%	62.5%	88.0%	34.3%	56.5%	.419	.667	91	0.2
Enoli Paredes	SUG	AAA	27	52 (0)	54¹	3-4	6	66	1.53	4.80		18.6%	27.3%	2.5%	46.0%	59.7%	78.5%	25.6%	53.9%	.260	.548	81	0.6
Chad Patrick	MID	AA	24	2 (2)	10²	0-1	0	14	2.16	8.44		3.8%	26.4%	11.3%	35.1%					.484	1.162	102	0.1
	AMA	AA	24	19 (19)	91²	4-7	0	90	1.39	4.71		9.2%	22.9%	2.8%	39.0%					.317	.562	93	1.3
	LV	AAA	24	6 (5)	21²	0-3	0	25	2.31	7.89		13.0%	21.7%	2.6%	33.3%	70.2%	74.6%	32.4%	67.1%	.471	.779	93	
Elvis Peguero	NAS	AAA	26	4 (0)	7¹	2-0	0	10	1.23	2.45		6.5%	32.3%	3.2%	42.1%	64.7%	69.7%	42.0%	41.4%	.333	.526	97	0.1
	MIL	MLB	26	59 (0)	61¹	4-5	1	54	1.22	3.38	42.9%	10.3%	21.4%	1.6%	56.0%	63.9%	85.5%	37.3%	54.4%	.274	.401	92	1.0
Ethan Small	NAS	AAA	26	38 (2)	51	2-4	3	61	1.25	3.18		11.2%	28.5%	2.3%	35.9%	66.9%	75.1%	31.7%	62.1%	.285	.523	92	0.9
	MIL	MLB	26	2 (0)	4	0-0	1	6	2.75	11.25	44.4%	8.7%	26.1%	4.3%	26.7%	63.6%	81.0%	35.0%	57.1%	.571	1.000	94	0.1
Thyago Vieira	NAS	AAA	30	33 (0)	37²	2-2	8	51	1.22	3.35		9.3%	31.7%	1.9%	39.1%	66.0%	72.9%	36.5%	56.9%	.315	.545	85	0.9
	MIL	MLB	30	2 (0)	3	0-1	0	2	0.33	0.00	55.7%	10.0%	20.0%	0.0%	14.3%	76.5%	84.6%	42.1%	62.5%	.000	.000	99	0.0
Justin Wilson	NAS	AAA	35	7 (0)	6¹	1-0	0	6	1.26	1.42		3.8%	23.1%	3.8%	26.3%	69.6%	75.0%	41.8%	67.9%	.333	.526	101	0.1

There's plenty of shoulder-shrugging to be done with the depth arms on the Brewers roster; in **Clayton Andrews'** case, he's a five-foot-six southpaw that can reach the upper-90s post-Tommy John surgery. If power-from-small-frame guys are interesting to you, well, here you go. ⊗ **Bradley Blalock** provides that storied player-development conundrum: the promising 22-year-old in the low minors, recovering from Tommy John. He'll be Rule 5 eligible, and he's also showing solid post-TJS command, making this a good problem for the Brewers to have, but still a problem. ⊗ **Coleman Crow** was off to a very strong start last year before an an elbow injury in early May and a trade to New York as part of the Eduardo Escobar deal shortly thereafter. After a three-month shutdown, it was finally announced that Crow needed Tommy John surgery, and we likely won't see him again until 2025. ⊗ When you say "changeup," you might think Devin Williams, but **Logan Henderson's** off-speed stuff may someday present a viable second option. He's a three-pitch mix guy at the Low-A level, and as he further develops, the tea leaves will reveal if he should work out of relief or blossom into a back-end starter. ⊗ 2023 draftee **Josh Knoth** was a fastball-curve guy at the high-school level, and with the Brewers' help, will one day be a fastball-curve-changeup guy. "Grip it and rip it" is one of his personal mottos, and it's hard to argue with the formula. ⊗ **Easton McGee** carried a no-hitter into the seventh inning of his first career MLB start on April 29 in Toronto. Unfortunately, it was also his final outing of 2023, as he hit the IL the very next day with a forearm strain that kept him on the shelf for the remainder of the season. ⊗ His shoulder was once injured, he's never played for the Reds: **J.C. Mejía** was suspended, once again for PEDs. He may return in late 2024. ⊗ **Enoli Paredes** walked or struck out half the batters he faced in 2023, so depending on how you look at it, his glass is either half full or mostly backwash. The Astros opted against taking another sip, letting the Brewers snag him off waivers. ⊗ The prospect prize in the Jace Peterson trade, **Chad Patrick**'s high walk rate did not follow him from the Diamondbacks to the Athletics organization because he threw it off his scent, a trick that he suspiciously learned from actual diamondback rattlesnakes. ⊗ In his first few appearances, **Elvis Peguero** was subject to the cruelty of hitters, but he eventually emerged as a reliable middle-reliever until a right elbow injury ended his first year with the Brewers. Our sources confirm that he's never caught a rabbit, but whether or not he's a friend of ours remains to be seen. ⊗ Architect Daniel Burnham was known for his influence on Neoclassical architecture and also the motto "make no little plans;" in **Ethan Small's** case, Burnham is talking about the wrong city, and certainly not referring to Small's ERA. ⊗ Spending an extended stay in Nashville was **Thyago Vieira**, signed in the 2022 offseason to a minor-league deal after spending three years pitching in Japan. The fastball is still fast, but a calf injury right after his callup prevented him from showing off more. ⊗ With his shiny new whiff-magnet of a slider in tow, the fresh-off-Tommy-John **Justin Wilson** stepped on the Brewers roster and faced 13 opponents, only for a new malady to befall him and abruptly delay his triumphant comeback to the big leagues. ⊗ The Brewers must covet something in **Jason Woodward**; he was drafted much earlier than expected, considering his recent Tommy John surgery. Many flattering things have been said about the ride on his fastball; rumor also has it his changeup is a well-liked secondary.

MINNESOTA TWINS

Essay by Zach Crizer

Player comments by Matt Trueblood and BP staff

When the particles settled and rendered the structure of Carlos Correa's ankle visible, a storm of interior images swirled unabated on the other side of the lens. The black-and-white snapshots of present anatomy morphed into florid premonitions of future anguish. Invested eyes in San Francisco and New York observed a fault line, but what they *saw*, crucially, was something more akin to the aftermath of a devastating quake.

You know the story by now. The Giants agreed to, then nixed, a $350 million deal. The Mets swooped in with a $315 million offer, then rescinded. Whatever they saw haunting the scans of his tibia, they couldn't bear. The Twins welcomed the shortstop back with a six-year, $200 million contract that could swell to 10 years and $270 million with options. They gave him a physical.

Maybe the Twins' doctors saw something different, something less concerning, in Correa's X-rays or MRIs. Or maybe they simply saw something familiar. This is a club and a fanbase that has known stars with faltering bodies, stars whose Jumbotron tributes inherently ring with minor-key overtones of what might have been. They didn't choose those fates, didn't wish them upon their heroes, didn't always endure their limitations gracefully. But they embraced them nonetheless.

Whatever the Twins saw in Correa's physical didn't shake them, didn't break the spell. They passed him. More than that, they accepted him. They accepted his ankle and his back and all the rest of the risk that can sink into a baseball player like snow into the spring soil. They accepted it as you might accept your reflection in the mirror first thing in the morning—hopefully, but with no illusions.

⚾   ⚾   ⚾

It would be easy to look upon the Twins' recent history with elite talent and despair.

An apparent savior, a Minnesota-born catcher with a magnificent bat taken no. 1 overall, was shunted over to first base by concussions, beaten down by maladies that left a likely Hall of Fame career feeling somehow lacking. Before he called it quits, a center field dynamo dropped into their laps, only to thrash against the hard boundaries of performance

MINNESOTA TWINS PROSPECTUS
2023 W-L: 87-75, 1ST IN AL CENTRAL

Pythag	.577	7th	DER	.701	11th
RS/G	4.80	10th	DRC+	92	25th
RA/G	4.07	3rd	DRA-	90	2nd
dWin%	.524	14th	FIP	3.90	3rd
Payroll	$154M	17th	B-Age	29.0	19th
M$/MW	$3.5M	12th	P-Age	29.4	16th

- Opened 2010
- Open air
- Natural surface
- Fence profile: 8' to 23"

Park Factors

Runs	Runs/RH	Runs/LH	HR/RH	HR/LH
100	100	99	98	87

Top Hitter WARP	2.2 Max Kepler
Top Pitcher WARP	4.8 Pablo López
2023 Top Prospect	Walker Jenkins

Payroll History (in millions)

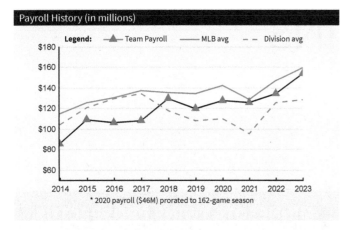

Legend: ▲ Team Payroll — MLB avg - - Division avg

* 2020 payroll ($46M) prorated to 162-game season

Future Commitments (in millions)

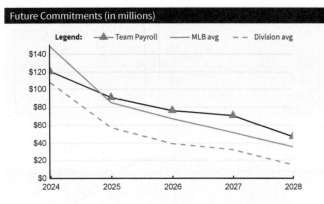

Legend: ▲ Team Payroll — MLB avg - - Division avg

Farm System Ranking

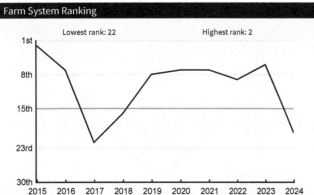

Lowest rank: 22   Highest rank: 2

Personnel

President, Baseball Operations
Derek Falvey

Senior Vice President, General Manager
Thad Levine

Vice President, Assistant General Manager
Daniel Adler

Vice President, Assistant General Manager
Jeremy Zoll

Vice President, Special Assistant to Baseball Operations
Rob Antony

Manager
Rocco Baldelli

BP Alumni
Bradley Ankrom
Kevin Goldstein
Ezra Wise

and human frailty with the violent speed that makes his game so transfixing. Then another first-overall pick, a new burst of promise, suffered two torn ACLs before outgrowing his rookie eligibility.

When Joe Mauer retired with a poignant flourish—donning his catcher's gear one last time, for one pitch, in the final game of the 2018 season—he rode out on the ripples of a rapturous ovation from the Minnesota faithful, from his lifelong neighbors.

Mauer lost all but 35 games of his rookie season—including one of those brief playoff bows to the Yankees—to a knee injury and the ensuing complications. He missed time in 2011 with weakness and pain in his legs. And of course he had to give up his valuable spot behind the plate because of concussions. But despite frequent dings and scares, he played at least 100 games in 13 of his remaining 14 seasons. He won an MVP award, three batting titles and earned six All-Star nods, but the Twins never won a postseason game in which he appeared.

When he retired, the Associated Press noted that, "staying healthy became a challenge" for Mauer, "and his popularity lessened some in a state usually fiercely proud of homegrown players due to the size of his contract and the amount of his absences."

In the moment, any latent disappointment was disguised, or perhaps redirected.

The day Mauer rode off into the sunset, Byron Buxton was watching from home in Georgia, simmering. In a tantalizing 2017 season, Buxton played 140 games, popped 16 homers, stole 29 bases while being caught just once, won a Gold Glove and registered MVP votes as Minnesota broke a six-year postseason drought. But his 2018 had been totally derailed by migraines, a wrist injury, a broken toe and a brutal .156 batting average in 28 games of intermittent playing time. The Twins front office sent him to Triple-A Rochester, then declined to add him to the roster at the end of the minor-league season, stopping his service clock short of a full year, pushing his free agency timeline back.

Over the next three seasons, Buxton mounted a case, via lightning-strike vignettes of excellence, for what could be. After the 2021 campaign in which Buxton blitzed the league for 19 homers and 23 doubles in only 61 games, Derek Falvey's front office remedied the earlier slight with an incentive-laden extension—seven years, $100 million guaranteed. It was a risk, but an honorable one.

By spring 2022, they had signed Correa to his first deal. By early May, Buxton had ripped eight homers in his first 17 games. Correa pronounced his new teammate "the best player in the world."

"Nobody hits the ball farther. Nobody plays better defense. Nobody throws harder. Nobody runs faster," Correa told the New York Times. "So when you talk about talent and you talk about tools, this is the most gifted out of all of them out there."

The next series, the Twins summoned Royce Lewis, their no. 1 overall pick in 2017, after his recovery from a torn ACL in his right knee. He played brilliantly, batting .300 with two homers in 12 games before tearing the same ACL again while playing center field, spelling Buxton on one of his DH days. Meanwhile, the less thoroughly defined knee issue that Buxton was dealing with at the time got progressively worse.

Over the past two seasons, Buxton has been limited to 177 total games, and even that understates his struggle to achieve peak form. In 2023, he batted 347 times, but the knee was so bothersome that he never set foot on the field as a defender.

⚾   ⚾   ⚾

"Every single thing I used to do on the baseball field, I used to do as hard as I could," the player said, reckoning with his diminished reality. "And now I don't."

A top pick and top prospect, he was only 26 years old when he said this. His name was Rocco Baldelli. After missing time early in his career due to a knee injury and an elbow injury, a disease called channelopathy (originally misdiagnosed as a mitochondrial disorder) left Baldelli's muscles depleted, often unable to summon the strength to play in two consecutive games.

At the height of his struggle with the mysterious ailment draining his stamina, Baldelli missed 240 consecutive games across 15 months. He returned fully aware of his limited capacity, but delivered the go-ahead hit in Game 7 of the 2008 ALCS, sending his Tampa Bay Rays to the World Series.

Baldelli retired two years later, 11 ½ months shy of his 30th birthday, went into coaching and took the Twins managerial job ahead of the 2019 season. Even before he hung up his spikes, though, he'd gained a new perspective on the hardship that changed the circumstances of how he wears a baseball uniform, of how he lives out his dream. Ahead of the 2010 season, his last go at playing, Baldelli wrote a letter that Jerry Crasnick published at ESPN relating a ritual for absorbing the scene during the national anthem ahead of the final game of the season, and what it had meant to him at the end of 2009. Recognizing, in an off-hand aside, that "neither the world nor the world of baseball are idealistic settings," he ticked off all of the rare occasions on which he had actually been present for his team's final game, a figure he could have counted on one hand.

"I will admit, as a professional athlete, your job is not to enjoy the moment. Your job is to perform and perform well. There is no time or place for rejoicing in your surroundings or in your fortuitous situation of being paid to play a game," Baldelli wrote. "I was always told as a child to appreciate what I had, whatever it may be. And this was an occasion I chose to actually do it."

As life thawed out after the worst of the COVID-19 pandemic, people began to reckon with the feeling that external forces were preventing them from even reaching for, much less attaining, whatever form of fulfillment they sought. From that sentiment sprang a boomlet of articles about "tragic optimism," a mindset Baldelli had demonstrated, if not specifically articulated. The concept traces to *Man's Search for Meaning*, Viktor Frankl's account of unbearable suffering during the Holocaust and stunning perseverance in its aftermath. In blending the two seemingly oxymoronic words, Frankl pushed readers to both accept their traumas and difficulties while simultaneously finding *reasons* to push toward something better.

Frankl wrote that it's "a characteristic of the American culture that, again and again, one is commanded and ordered to 'be happy.'" Yet he recognized and empathized with the impossibility of such an idea. He wrote that people should live not "in pursuit of happiness but rather in search of a reason to become happy." The pandemic stirred researchers and psychologists to build on that, to outline an action plan for the shellshocked masses whose lives were tugged asunder by grief or illness, or at the very least unpleasantly interrupted in a way that tracked to a chronically sidelined athlete. Most of the advice focused on locating those feelings of gratitude that Baldelli experienced during the national anthem.

"When individuals become aware that their advantages are not guaranteed," the cognitive scientist Scott Barry Kaufman wrote in The Atlantic, "many then come to appreciate them more."

Hiring Baldelli to helm their clubhouse now looks like a cosmically ordained move by the Twins—and not just because Baldelli and his wife welcomed twin boys in September. Few people are more qualified to understand the trials Lewis went through, that Buxton continues to go through, that at least a few doctors think Correa might eventually go through.

⚾   ⚾   ⚾

Professional athletes' contracts make people go a little bit crazy. Once a player's public finances hit a certain threshold, they're expected in some corners to achieve invincibility, to infuse the entire enterprise with the success such a big number signifies in America. Yet that initial golden spell is incredibly fragile, shattered by the first suboptimal day, or the first baseball that ricochets off a bone.

Mauer's eight-year, $184 million deal—the one that the AP said caused some fans to sour on him—coincided with Twitter's rise to ubiquity, when the opinions of fans began to escape the orbit of local sports radio and could sometimes reach the players and team themselves. Correa's six-year, $200 million deal is living in a slightly different world, where extreme scrutiny of value and luxury tax implications and roster structure pressurizes each major signing.

There's always a bust, an albatross whose salient quality has soured from the original intent—cornerstone—into something derogatory—an anchor. Someone's always grumbling about millionaires playing a kid's game, or dunking on a strawman who said Steph Curry couldn't shoot.

But there's no Jonny Flynn situation in recent Twins lore. When the Twins picked Mauer no. 1 overall, the alternative choice was the sterling pitcher the Cubs selected next: Mark Prior. When they took Buxton, the consensus top talent, at no. 2, they had the chance to do so only because the Astros had thrown their belief (and their bonus pool strategy) behind a savvy, striking young shortstop: Carlos Correa.

As Baldelli recognized when he was still playing, there's no ideal world. No matter how many alternative realities one tries to imagine, ligaments will still snap, muscles will still strain, bodies will still age, some more gracefully than others.

The 2023 season didn't proceed seamlessly. Correa dealt with plantar fasciitis and registered a career-worst .711 OPS. Buxton couldn't overcome his knee issue enough to man center field, and hit like someone who was only there to play defense. Minnesota went 19-27 in one-run games. But Baldelli spoke with constant candor about their little victories, their disappointments and their inner struggles. New characters rose up to lift the Twins, from trade addition Pablo López to on-base machine Edouard Julien.

And when the team found itself back in position to make good on its hopes, to confront its fears and conquer its infamous postseason struggles, there was a readiness, a fearlessness born not of reckless abandon but of self-aware understanding.

⚾   ⚾   ⚾

For the first time in a while, Twins fans have a positive "what if?" to ponder.

What if the Giants or Mets hadn't taken a doom and gloom approach to Correa's future? What if Lewis had been healthy enough to discourage the Twins from re-signing the two-time All-Star and clubhouse leader? What if Correa hadn't been there to make his mad dash to throw out Bo Bichette at home? What if he hadn't been in Minnesota to notice that Blue Jays runners couldn't hear their third-base coach during the American League Wild Card Series? What if Lewis hadn't pushed through an injury to make it onto the lineup card and hit massive homers as the Twins won their first postseason game since 2004, and then their first series since 2002?

After their Game 1 win over Toronto, Baldelli marveled at the rapturous roar of the Target Field crowd with a wink at one of his reasons to pursue happiness: "I thought the place was going to split open and melt," he said, referencing a song by one of his favorite musical acts, Phish. A jam band aficionado, Baldelli has said that learning to play the bass guitar was one of the ways he recharged his mind as his body failed his baseball career.

In that moment of triumph, he kept with him a relic of a struggle. Staring down the prospect of disappointment, the Twins chose to chase the sun.

Promise. Pain. Hope. Setback. Frustration. A telescoping cycle—of frailty, of playoff futility—got a new step: Release.

—Zach Crizer is a baseball writer based in New York.

HITTERS

Byron Buxton DH   Born: 12/18/93   Age: 30   Bats: R   Throws: R   Height: 6'2"   Weight: 190   Origin: Round 1, 2012 Draft (#2 overall)

YEAR	TM	LVL	AGE	PA	R	HR	RBI	SB	AVG/OBP/SLG	BABIP	SLGCON	BB%	K%	ZSw%	ZCon%	OSw%	OCon%	LA	90th EV	DRC+	BRR	DRP	WARP
2021	MIN	MLB	27	254	50	19	32	9	.306/.358/.647	.344	.879	5.1%	24.4%	78.4%	81.2%	36.3%	56.2%	14.1	109.2	132	0.5	7.3	2.9
2022	MIN	MLB	28	382	61	28	51	6	.224/.306/.526	.244	.799	8.9%	30.4%	68.9%	76.4%	30.3%	48.3%	22.0	108.9	111	0.3	2.2	2.0
2023	MIN	MLB	29	347	49	17	42	9	.207/.294/.438	.253	.682	10.1%	31.4%	76.7%	83.4%	31.6%	46.3%	20.5	108.5	96	0.3	0.0	0.6
2024 DC	MIN	MLB	30	499	61	25	71	6	.225/.305/.447	.268	.649	8.7%	28.0%						108	0.4	2.7	2.4

2023 GP: DH (80)   *Comps: Adam Jones (69), Andre Dawson (68), Carlos Gómez (64)*

Everyone wants this to work. The Twins invested in Buxton, and Buxton signed a deal that is wildly team-friendly—at least in theory. The two sides like and respect each other, and they've accommodated each other. In 2022, the Twins tried putting Buxton on a near-unprecedented schedule of proactive care, with off days as often as once or twice a week. It didn't work; Buxton went down with a hip injury in mid-August and never returned. In 2023, the team traded for a viable alternative center fielder, just so they could play him as their DH more often and keep him healthy. It didn't work. His hip fixed, Buxton saw his knee worsen instead. He didn't play an inning in center field and missed almost the entirety of the final two months—which was fine, because he had a .662 OPS after May 1. Everyone wants this to work. It isn't going to.

Noah Cardenas C   Born: 09/10/99   Age: 24   Bats: R   Throws: R   Height: 5'11"   Weight: 195   Origin: Round 8, 2021 Draft (#249 overall)

YEAR	TM	LVL	AGE	PA	R	HR	RBI	SB	AVG/OBP/SLG	BABIP	SLGCON	BB%	K%	ZSw%	ZCon%	OSw%	OCon%	LA	90th EV	DRC+	BRR	DRP	WARP
2022	FTM	A	22	401	42	9	43	11	.261/.421/.413	.308	.533	18.2%	17.5%	63.7%	85.2%	17.5%	75.3%			137	-1.0	5.0	3.2
2023	CR	A+	23	378	44	3	38	9	.272/.397/.382	.349	.509	14.6%	20.4%							114	0.2	19.0	3.9
2024 non	MIN	MLB	24	251	22	3	20	0	.219/.306/.311	.272	.399	9.8%	20.1%							79	0.0	0	0.2

2023 GP: C (69), DH (12), 1B (9)   *Comps: Bruce Maxwell (72), Clint Sammons (69), Donny Lucy (66)*

YEAR	TM	P. COUNT	FRM RUNS	BLK RUNS	THRW RUNS	TOT RUNS
2022	FTM	7181	3.0	1.0	1.6	5.6
2023	CR	9352	17.9	0.7	2.3	20.9
2024	MIN	6956	3.3	0.6	0.4	4.3

A 2021 eighth-rounder who didn't look like much of a hitter entering the draft, Cardenas has shown really encouraging plate discipline early in his professional career. He has a superabundance of defensive tools and skills: a good arm and great intangibles, but also general athleticism that soars far beyond that of most backstops. What he doesn't have (or even project to have) is power, and because of that, he might end up a backup. The bat has been more than good enough in the lower levels of the minors, but it's not just a lack of power that puts a ceiling on him. There's also the looming threat that advanced pitchers will crack open the sturdy casing of bat-to-ball skills that keeps his profile viable and shatter the whole thing.

Willi Castro LF
Born: 04/24/97   Age: 27   Bats: S   Throws: R   Height: 6'1"   Weight: 206   Origin: IFA, 2013

YEAR	TM	LVL	AGE	PA	R	HR	RBI	SB	AVG/OBP/SLG	BABIP	SLGCON	BB%	K%	ZSw%	ZCon%	OSw%	OCon%	LA	90th EV	DRC+	BRR	DRP	WARP
2021	DET	MLB	24	450	56	9	38	9	.220/.273/.351	.275	.477	5.1%	24.2%	75.9%	83.4%	43.2%	55.7%	11.1	104.3	81	0.4	-0.9	0.5
2022	TOL	AAA	25	36	2	0	1	3	.265/.306/.324	.375	.458	5.6%	27.8%							97	0.3	-0.8	0.1
2022	DET	MLB	25	392	47	8	31	9	.241/.284/.367	.288	.473	3.8%	20.9%	77.9%	83.2%	43.6%	56.6%	14.0	102.8	80	0.8	1.4	0.5
2023	MIN	MLB	26	409	60	9	34	33	.257/.339/.411	.328	.568	8.3%	24.2%	70.2%	83.2%	38.2%	57.7%	14.3	104.5	93	0.9	0.8	1.1
2024 DC	MIN	MLB	27	394	38	8	40	17	.237/.306/.369	.297	.493	7.0%	23.2%							91	0.6	-1.1	0.8

2023 GP: LF (54), CF (45), 3B (41), 2B (10), SS (8), RF (4), P (3), DH (1)   Comps: Reid Brignac (52), Yairo Muñoz (51), Travis Snider (51)

Signed to a minor-league deal after being cut by one of the worst offensive teams in baseball history, Castro entered 2023 with his career on life support. Then, a cascade of injuries and his own good performance saved it. Encouraged by the new rules and his new team, he trebled the frequency of his attempts to steal bases, and he was still successful at a very healthy rate. He modulated his approach just a little bit, to fit his new team's philosophy. He hunted fastballs, he was a bit more selective, and he tried the pull field more. The result was no star turn, but rather, the kind of solid big-league campaign that earns you three more as a role player—a pretty lucrative prize.

Carlos Correa SS
Born: 09/22/94   Age: 29   Bats: R   Throws: R   Height: 6'4"   Weight: 220   Origin: Round 1, 2012 Draft (#1 overall)

YEAR	TM	LVL	AGE	PA	R	HR	RBI	SB	AVG/OBP/SLG	BABIP	SLGCON	BB%	K%	ZSw%	ZCon%	OSw%	OCon%	LA	90th EV	DRC+	BRR	DRP	WARP
2021	HOU	MLB	26	640	104	26	92	0	.279/.366/.485	.308	.613	11.7%	18.1%	63.3%	88.7%	27.5%	64.0%	12.4	107.2	121	-0.8	0.0	4.0
2022	MIN	MLB	27	590	70	22	64	0	.291/.366/.467	.339	.608	10.3%	20.5%	63.7%	86.0%	31.0%	66.4%	12.0	106.1	122	-0.8	-0.4	3.4
2023	MIN	MLB	28	580	60	18	65	0	.230/.312/.399	.272	.535	10.2%	22.6%	63.1%	84.5%	29.9%	60.6%	10.8	107.1	94	-0.7	0.0	1.4
2024 DC	MIN	MLB	29	568	62	16	64	0	.246/.328/.398	.295	.526	10.1%	21.6%							106	0.0	2	2.7

2023 GP: SS (135)   Comps: Jim Fregosi (78), Travis Jackson (77), Cal Ripken Jr. (74)

When Correa joined the Twins for 2022, he changed his uniform number to 4. Scott Boras tried to make "C4" happen, in a press conference replete with puns about explosive weapons. That's all well and good, but in Minnesota, there's a more important C4: corn. Because corn is among the small group of plants on Earth that first fixes carbon into four-carbon compounds during photosynthesis, it's unusually resistant to drought and heat. It thrives better than other grains when the weather refuses to cooperate. It's become the dominant component of our diets because it's so adaptable, available, and energy-rich. Correa is, as far as we know, incapable of photosynthesis even in its simpler C3 form, and the first year of his long contract with the Twins was marred by plantar fasciitis. Still, he gave the team consistent leadership, even during the dry times, and earned unanimous praise for his energy production. The fireworks can still come, when he's healthy again.

Kyle Farmer IF
Born: 08/17/90   Age: 33   Bats: R   Throws: R   Height: 6'0"   Weight: 205   Origin: Round 8, 2013 Draft (#244 overall)

YEAR	TM	LVL	AGE	PA	R	HR	RBI	SB	AVG/OBP/SLG	BABIP	SLGCON	BB%	K%	ZSw%	ZCon%	OSw%	OCon%	LA	90th EV	DRC+	BRR	DRP	WARP
2021	CIN	MLB	30	529	60	16	63	2	.263/.316/.416	.296	.521	4.2%	18.3%	65.9%	89.8%	39.0%	68.8%	15.7	102.0	93	-0.1	0.5	1.5
2022	CIN	MLB	31	583	58	14	78	4	.255/.315/.386	.286	.475	5.7%	17.0%	66.7%	90.1%	38.7%	70.1%	12.4	101.0	99	-0.1	-0.6	1.6
2023	MIN	MLB	32	369	49	11	46	2	.256/.317/.408	.311	.548	6.2%	23.3%	62.9%	86.9%	35.9%	63.0%	13.4	101.8	89	-0.2	-1.2	0.6
2024 DC	MIN	MLB	33	195	19	5	20	2	.242/.308/.370	.284	.468	6.2%	19.2%							93	0.0	-0.5	0.3

2023 GP: 2B (45), 3B (43), SS (40), 1B (4), LF (3), DH (1)   Comps: Ivy Olson (51), Jordy Mercer (51), Ski Melillo (49)

If you carefully set about building a player to be beloved inside a big-league clubhouse, after months of work, you'd churn out Farmer. He's a Southern White guy, semi-famous for his Luke Bryan impression. He's the son of a pro who humped his way up to Triple-A as a lefty hurler, but who couldn't crack the bigs. He wanted to finish what his old man started so badly that he signed as a catcher, never believing it was really where he belonged, never wanting to do it at all but being willing to, if it would cash in his family's dreams. He didn't debut in MLB until he was almost 27, but here he is, half a decade later, still showing versatility but no longer compelled to squat any more than the rest of us. He's a ballplayer's ballplayer, but fans can find the charm there, too.

Ryan Jeffers C
Born: 06/03/97   Age: 27   Bats: R   Throws: R   Height: 6'4"   Weight: 235   Origin: Round 2, 2018 Draft (#59 overall)

YEAR	TM	LVL	AGE	PA	R	HR	RBI	SB	AVG/OBP/SLG	BABIP	SLGCON	BB%	K%	ZSw%	ZCon%	OSw%	OCon%	LA	90th EV	DRC+	BRR	DRP	WARP
2021	STP	AAA	24	103	13	5	16	0	.217/.340/.446	.236	.649	15.5%	25.2%							116	0.2	1.2	0.7
2021	MIN	MLB	24	293	28	14	35	0	.199/.270/.401	.269	.673	7.5%	36.9%	68.3%	77.4%	31.7%	48.7%	14.0	105.3	85	-0.2	4.3	1.1
2022	STP	AAA	25	39	5	3	7	1	.229/.308/.514	.179	.581	10.3%	10.3%							120	0.0	0.2	0.2
2022	MIN	MLB	25	236	25	7	27	0	.208/.285/.363	.259	.513	9.7%	26.3%	68.3%	83.6%	29.2%	66.2%	17.6	105.4	87	-0.2	3.0	0.8
2023	MIN	MLB	26	335	46	14	43	3	.276/.369/.490	.359	.725	9.9%	27.8%	63.5%	80.4%	33.0%	58.6%	16.2	106.1	95	-0.2	-2.8	0.7
2024 DC	MIN	MLB	27	244	26	8	28	1	.218/.302/.381	.272	.542	9.0%	26.5%							93	-0.1	2.8	1.0

2023 GP: C (82), DH (9)   Comps: Yasmani Grandal (65), Joe Oliver (61), Matt Wieters (59)

YEAR	TM	P. COUNT	FRM RUNS	BLK RUNS	THRW RUNS	TOT RUNS
2021	STP	2087	1.3	0.0	0.0	1.3
2021	MIN	11035	5.8	0.0	0.0	5.8
2022	MIN	8105	4.7	-0.1	-0.2	4.4
2023	MIN	10401	-2.0	-0.2	0.2	-2.0
2024	MIN	9620	2.7	-0.1	0.2	2.8

DRC+ is Jeffers' nemesis. In his breakout campaign, as he crushed 14 homers in a timeshare at catcher and put up an OPS north of .850, DRC+ pegged him as below-average. The huge and powerful catcher hit some true moonshots, but his profile was so dependent on home runs (and his approach seemingly so vulnerable to strikeouts, a long-standing problem for him) that this publication's flagship offensive metric dismissed it as an aberration. If you buy that lower estimate of his offense, it dents the overall value proposition more than it might have a year or two ago, because his framing value cratered and he'd always struggled with the rougher-grain aspects of catching. So, much rides on the question of whether you should buy that. Here's the most heartbreaking part, either way: Jeffers' nemesis barely knows he exists. Seventy-nine players had a wider differential between their actual run value and their Deserved Runs Above Average last year.

★ ★ ★ *2024 Top 101 Prospect* **#16** ★ ★ ★

Walker Jenkins CF/DH Born: 02/19/05 Age: 19 Bats: L Throws: R Height: 6'3" Weight: 210 Origin: Round 1, 2023 Draft (#5 overall)

YEAR	TM	LVL	AGE	PA	R	HR	RBI	SB	AVG/OBP/SLG	BABIP	SLGCON	BB%	K%	ZSw%	ZCon%	OSw%	OCon%	LA	90th EV	DRC+	BRR	DRP	WARP
2023	TWI	ROK	18	59	6	2	12	4	.333/.390/.537	.364	.630	8.5%	13.6%										
2023	FTM	A	18	56	10	1	10	2	.392/.446/.608	.432	.689	7.1%	10.7%	73.8%	91.5%	29.9%	68.6%			119	0.4	2.6	0.6
2024 non	MIN	MLB	19	251	19	2	20	0	.219/.269/.314	.282	.418	5.6%	23.0%							63	0.0	0	-0.3

2023 GP: DH (16), CF (10), RF (1)　　　　　　　　*Comps: Mike Trout (78), Courtney Hawkins (74), Juan Soto (71)*

The Twins will go down in history as the first-ever beneficiaries of the MLB Draft Lottery. They drew the lucky number and got to pick fifth, a year after finishing with the 13th-worst record in baseball. Their prize turned out to be Jenkins, the last on the board in a quintet of consensus elites atop the 2023 class. He's a rare combination of fluid and strong, hitterish but powerful, for a left-handed high-school hitter. He's a good all-around athlete. Most poignantly, though, he was a favorite of Mike Radcliff, the Twins' VP of Player Personnel—a scout so revered that he preceded the Terry Ryan regime in Minnesota and then survived the transition to their new leadership. Radcliff passed away in February 2023. Five months later, his team got one more of his Guys.

Edouard Julien 2B Born: 04/30/99 Age: 25 Bats: L Throws: R Height: 6'0" Weight: 195 Origin: Round 18, 2019 Draft (#539 overall)

YEAR	TM	LVL	AGE	PA	R	HR	RBI	SB	AVG/OBP/SLG	BABIP	SLGCON	BB%	K%	ZSw%	ZCon%	OSw%	OCon%	LA	90th EV	DRC+	BRR	DRP	WARP
2021	FTM	A	22	204	41	3	24	21	.299/.490/.456	.451	.720	24.5%	26.5%	59.1%	80.5%	14.5%	57.0%			128	0.1	-2.5	1.0
2021	CR	A+	22	310	52	15	48	13	.247/.397/.494	.322	.777	19.4%	29.0%							120	-1.0	-4.6	1.1
2022	WCH	AA	23	508	77	17	67	19	.300/.441/.490	.393	.713	19.3%	24.6%							128	-2.0	-8.2	2.2
2023	STP	AAA	24	170	29	5	22	3	.293/.435/.496	.386	.725	18.8%	24.7%	63.0%	87.0%	18.5%	58.3%			114	-0.2	2.3	0.8
2023	MIN	MLB	24	408	60	16	37	3	.263/.381/.459	.371	.738	15.7%	31.4%	62.9%	79.3%	17.1%	46.3%	8.0	104.7	86	-0.3	0.2	0.4
2024 DC	MIN	MLB	25	605	65	14	62	9	.222/.341/.367	.304	.550	14.4%	28.2%							105	-0.1	-0.1	1.7

2023 GP: 2B (75), DH (27), 1B (4)　　　　　　*Comps: Derek Dietrich (65), Brandon Lowe (63), Jason Kipnis (62)*

Imagine being a Québécois, arriving on the campus of Auburn University without the ability to speak English. It takes a certain intelligent and courageous patience to select a school so far from home, both geographically and culturally. In an exciting rookie showing, Julien demonstrated precisely that unflappable nous. Plenty of questions linger around his long-term profile. If he's a second baseman, he's going to be a bad fielder. If he's a first baseman, his power feels a little light—and he might also be a bad fielder. Sometimes, though, it's just a lot of fun to watch a player thrive in his element. Julien got 88% of his plate appearances against righties and 84% of them in the top two spots in the batting order. He ran a .381 OBP that feels sustainable, even if the rest of his production doesn't. Twins fans just want to know: What's French for "War Eagle?"

Luke Keaschall 2B Born: 08/15/02 Age: 21 Bats: R Throws: R Height: 6'1" Weight: 190 Origin: Round 2, 2023 Draft (#49 overall)

YEAR	TM	LVL	AGE	PA	R	HR	RBI	SB	AVG/OBP/SLG	BABIP	SLGCON	BB%	K%	ZSw%	ZCon%	OSw%	OCon%	LA	90th EV	DRC+	BRR	DRP	WARP
2023	FTM	A	20	94	20	1	9	8	.292/.426/.472	.370	.654	16.0%	21.3%	64.2%	86.8%	25.6%	65.0%			110	0.1	-1.9	0.2
2023	CR	A+	20	34	5	2	6	1	.313/.353/.563	.296	.621	5.9%	8.8%							127	-0.4	-1.0	0.0
2024 non	MIN	MLB	21	251	21	3	21	0	.217/.284/.314	.278	.419	7.5%	23.2%							70	0.0	0	-0.2

2023 GP: 2B (24), CF (4), 3B (2), DH (2)　　　　　　*Comps: Mookie Betts (85), Felix Valerio (85), Jesmuel Valentín (83)*

The Twins ponied up significantly to land Keaschall in the second round last summer, and immediately got a taste of what they hoped they were paying for. He's not going to cut it on the left side of the infield, and his potential utility in center field is uncertain, but he has the chops to be a plus second baseman, and he has above-average speed to leaven the profile. In the box, he's fun to watch, even though he's miles from a finished product. He shows good feel for contact, and as the pitcher stares in, he sets up and waggles in the box like an even more hitterish Juan Soto. His swing isn't that balanced or that violent, of course, but he pairs bat control with a pull-focused, fly-ball approach and good patience. In his first full pro season, the challenge will be to translate all that into real, live power.

Max Kepler RF Born: 02/10/93 Age: 31 Bats: L Throws: L Height: 6'4" Weight: 225 Origin: IFA, 2009

YEAR	TM	LVL	AGE	PA	R	HR	RBI	SB	AVG/OBP/SLG	BABIP	SLGCON	BB%	K%	ZSw%	ZCon%	OSw%	OCon%	LA	90th EV	DRC+	BRR	DRP	WARP
2021	MIN	MLB	28	490	61	19	54	10	.211/.306/.413	.225	.533	11.0%	19.6%	70.3%	86.6%	26.3%	58.4%	16.4	105.8	102	0.2	0.8	1.8
2022	MIN	MLB	29	446	54	9	43	3	.227/.318/.348	.249	.419	11.0%	14.8%	71.0%	90.0%	28.6%	63.1%	11.3	105.1	109	-0.3	3.9	2.2
2023	MIN	MLB	30	491	72	24	66	1	.260/.332/.484	.288	.639	9.2%	21.6%	72.7%	89.5%	28.5%	62.4%	15.1	106.5	111	0.1	2.9	2.2
2024 DC	MIN	MLB	31	569	61	17	65	2	.234/.318/.394	.259	.488	10.0%	17.3%							102	0.1	1.9	1.8

2023 GP: RF (124), DH (2)　　　　　　*Comps: Harry Hooper (69), Johnny Callison (66), Jose Cruz (65)*

They say the easiest way to hit the curveball is to hit the fastball. For a long time, Kepler tried to do things the hard way. Over the first several years of his career, he acquired and sustained the ability to keep his strikeout rate below the league average and his walk rate above the same line. It came at a cost, though: He was putting everything in play, but not punishing anything quite the way he needed to. In 2023, he finally found the Easy button. His whiff rate on off-speed stuff went through the roof, but his recompense was massive. He torched the fastball, and if he struck out a bit more often when pitchers fed him spin, the trade-off was a bargain. Now, all he has to do is keep doing all that damage, despite the league knowing full well about his change in hunting strategy.

Alex Kirilloff 1B
Born: 11/09/97 Age: 26 Bats: L Throws: L Height: 6'2" Weight: 195 Origin: Round 1, 2016 Draft (#15 overall)

YEAR	TM	LVL	AGE	PA	R	HR	RBI	SB	AVG/OBP/SLG	BABIP	SLGCON	BB%	K%	ZSw%	ZCon%	OSw%	OCon%	LA	90th EV	DRC+	BRR	DRP	WARP
2021	MIN	MLB	23	231	23	8	34	1	.251/.299/.423	.295	.558	6.1%	22.5%	73.8%	81.4%	41.5%	62.7%	7.3	104.4	104	0.0	0.4	0.8
2022	STP	AAA	24	157	33	10	32	1	.359/.465/.641	.389	.800	14.0%	16.6%							139	0.0	-1.3	1.0
2022	MIN	MLB	24	156	14	3	21	0	.250/.290/.361	.308	.481	3.2%	23.1%	70.8%	84.5%	34.9%	73.0%	6.3	103.3	78	0.0	-0.1	0.0
2023	STP	AAA	25	73	14	5	18	2	.369/.438/.662	.404	.827	8.2%	17.8%	74.6%	83.0%	27.8%	68.0%			118	0.2	0.1	0.4
2023	MIN	MLB	25	319	35	11	41	1	.270/.348/.445	.337	.622	8.8%	25.1%	65.5%	83.0%	34.3%	57.9%	12.6	102.2	83	-0.1	-0.1	0.0
2024 DC	MIN	MLB	26	467	49	13	52	2	.249/.321/.397	.305	.533	8.0%	22.9%							104	0.0	-0.6	1.1

2023 GP: 1B (75), RF (11), LF (10), DH (3)
Comps: Eric Hosmer (61), Eddie Rosario (60), Mike Carp (60)

Look, only one team can win the final game and hoist the trophy each baseball season. An individual player can finish their season lots of ways, though, and Kirilloff badly needs to stop ending his by cratering at the plate and, belatedly, having surgery. In 2023, it was a strained shoulder that cut his campaign one game short—and perhaps, since it contributed to his failure to collect an easy ground ball in a pivotal ALDS contest, curtailed the Twins' even more. Before disappearing in October, the former top prospect had begun finally to fulfill his promise. He's not one hitter, really, but two wholly distinct ones. The healthy Kirilloff has a graceful swing, generates all-fields power and could hit .300, to boot. The one who's playing hurt, and often, is almost useless, with too much chase and too much whiff in an underpowered profile. Dr. Jekyll is losing the battle, and with each new injury, Mr. Hyde gets stronger.

Trevor Larnach OF
Born: 02/26/97 Age: 27 Bats: L Throws: R Height: 6'4" Weight: 223 Origin: Round 1, 2018 Draft (#20 overall)

YEAR	TM	LVL	AGE	PA	R	HR	RBI	SB	AVG/OBP/SLG	BABIP	SLGCON	BB%	K%	ZSw%	ZCon%	OSw%	OCon%	LA	90th EV	DRC+	BRR	DRP	WARP
2021	STP	AAA	24	62	13	3	7	0	.176/.323/.373	.222	.633	9.7%	33.9%							90	0.8	0.8	0.3
2021	MIN	MLB	24	301	29	7	28	1	.223/.322/.350	.338	.583	10.3%	34.6%	65.8%	76.6%	29.4%	38.1%	13.1	108.4	74	-0.2	-3.3	-0.3
2022	STP	AAA	25	41	1	0	2	0	.222/.293/.222	.308	.320	9.8%	26.8%							88	-0.4	-0.5	0.0
2022	MIN	MLB	25	180	22	5	18	0	.231/.306/.406	.320	.631	10.0%	31.7%	62.9%	77.5%	27.2%	34.5%	13.5	106.5	83	0.1	-0.3	0.1
2023	STP	AAA	26	323	56	15	47	2	.271/.384/.504	.339	.767	15.5%	27.9%	63.0%	80.5%	23.8%	43.9%			101	1.5	-3.3	0.8
2023	MIN	MLB	26	212	26	8	40	1	.213/.311/.415	.295	.685	12.7%	34.0%	65.5%	78.4%	25.4%	38.7%	18.0	106.4	89	0.0	-1.1	0.2
2024 DC	MIN	MLB	27	156	16	4	16	1	.210/.310/.362	.294	.563	11.5%	31.4%							92	0.0	-1.5	0.1

2023 GP: LF (44), RF (20), DH (3)
Comps: Christin Stewart (60), Kirk Nieuwenhuis (59), Robbie Grossman (55)

You can almost get excited about Larnach, when he's healthy enough to get hot for a minute. He hits fastballs hard, and he hits them far. In 2023, he expanded the strike zone a little bit less, whiffed a little bit less and got the ball in the air more. He has almost the whole All-Star slugger kit. Alas, "almost" does the heaviest lifting in that sentence. There are two key ingredients of a great hitter's career missing from this stew. One is almost cliché, because everyone loves talking about it so much: Larnach can't hit the junk. Of 382 semi-regular hitters since 2021, only four have seen fastballs less often than Larnach, because the whole league knows he can't hit off-speed or breaking stuff. His deficiency is so obvious that pitchers found it really fast. The other missing ingredient, even more important and even more obvious but much less oft-discussed, is luck. Larnach has the buzzard's kind, and that's slowly killing his career, even more surely than his struggles with spin and dip.

─────────────── ★ ★ ★ *2024 Top 101 Prospect* **#52** ★ ★ ★ ───────────────

Brooks Lee SS
Born: 02/14/01 Age: 23 Bats: S Throws: R Height: 5'11" Weight: 205 Origin: Round 1, 2022 Draft (#8 overall)

YEAR	TM	LVL	AGE	PA	R	HR	RBI	SB	AVG/OBP/SLG	BABIP	SLGCON	BB%	K%	ZSw%	ZCon%	OSw%	OCon%	LA	90th EV	DRC+	BRR	DRP	WARP
2022	CR	A+	21	114	14	4	12	0	.289/.395/.454	.320	.557	14.0%	15.8%							114	-1.9	-1.0	0.3
2023	WCH	AA	22	399	63	11	61	6	.292/.365/.476	.325	.580	10.3%	15.8%							119	1.7	2.0	2.6
2023	STP	AAA	22	168	20	5	23	1	.237/.304/.428	.258	.524	8.9%	16.7%	67.6%	85.0%	39.2%	67.3%			97	0.8	0.2	0.4
2024 non	MIN	MLB	23	251	22	4	24	2	.229/.291/.351	.276	.450	7.5%	20.4%							81	0.0	0	0.3

2023 GP: SS (111), 3B (7), DH (6)
Comps: Eugenio Suárez (69), Nick Gordon (67), José Rondón (65)

When you think of a prized shortstop prospect everyone is worried will need to move off the position, you tend to picture the guys who look like they were just run through Willy Wonka's taffy stretcher: too long, too lean, too loose to be as quick as the position demands. That's not Lee. He's a mesomorph, with good strength and a paradoxically studied sort of quickness. He's the perfect shape for a shortstop. He's the perfect shape for a hitter, too, for that matter. He just moves strangely. His swing is unorthodox. So are some of his mechanics in the field—a surprising fact about a coach's kid and collegiate star. He's made the whole package work so far, but the ceiling will be slightly lowered by his peculiarities, unless and until he can correct them without losing the underlying athleticism and feel.

Royce Lewis 3B
Born: 06/05/99 Age: 25 Bats: R Throws: R Height: 6'2" Weight: 200 Origin: Round 1, 2017 Draft (#1 overall)

YEAR	TM	LVL	AGE	PA	R	HR	RBI	SB	AVG/OBP/SLG	BABIP	SLGCON	BB%	K%	ZSw%	ZCon%	OSw%	OCon%	LA	90th EV	DRC+	BRR	DRP	WARP
2022	STP	AAA	23	153	30	5	14	12	.313/.405/.534	.379	.707	11.8%	20.9%							116	-0.3	0.3	0.7
2022	MIN	MLB	23	41	5	2	5	0	.300/.317/.550	.303	.629	2.4%	12.2%	73.4%	89.4%	32.5%	72.0%	19.6	106.7	103	0.0	0.0	0.1
2023	STP	AAA	24	51	11	6	13	3	.356/.412/.778	.370	1.094	9.8%	25.5%	66.2%	83.0%	31.5%	47.5%			114	-0.8	0.1	0.2
2023	MIN	MLB	24	239	36	15	52	6	.309/.372/.548	.354	.735	8.4%	23.0%	69.4%	81.0%	31.5%	59.4%	16.3	107.4	114	0.2	-0.1	1.1
2024 DC	MIN	MLB	25	486	57	19	64	13	.263/.325/.445	.320	.609	7.3%	24.6%							116	0.3	-0.7	2.2

2023 GP: 3B (49), DH (9), SS (1)
Comps: Wilmer Flores (53), Ketel Marte (52), Nolan Arenado (50)

Even on a twice-repaired ACL, Lewis has demonstrated an ability to dominate the game with his pure talent. You can see the holes in his swing, sometimes. You can see the imperfect footwork at third base, where he slid in deference to Carlos Correa and where he might have found a long-term defensive home. Scouts who doubted that he'd be able to convert his raw tools into a polished, refined suite of skills haven't yet been proven wrong, exactly. It's just that they (and we all, perhaps) underestimated the potency of his athleticism. In particular, Lewis' power has been a revelation. He can lift and drive the ball with shocking authority, shockingly regularly. He hits like Juan Gonzalez. Of course, Gonzalez had played almost 600 MLB games by the same age.

Austin Martin   UT   Born: 03/23/99   Age: 25   Bats: R   Throws: R   Height: 6'0"   Weight: 185   Origin: Round 1, 2020 Draft (#5 overall)

YEAR	TM	LVL	AGE	PA	R	HR	RBI	SB	AVG/OBP/SLG	BABIP	SLGCON	BB%	K%	ZSw%	ZCon%	OSw%	OCon%	LA	90th EV	DRC+	BRR	DRP	WARP
2021	NH	AA	22	250	43	2	16	9	.281/.424/.383	.368	.524	14.8%	21.2%							116	0.8	5.6	1.9
2021	WCH	AA	22	168	24	3	19	5	.254/.399/.381	.304	.490	13.7%	17.9%							112	1.6	-1.3	0.8
2022	WCH	AA	23	406	59	2	32	34	.241/.367/.315	.280	.376	11.6%	13.3%							102	2.3	-1.7	1.4
2023	STP	AAA	24	252	33	6	28	16	.263/.386/.405	.302	.512	14.3%	17.1%	61.9%	92.3%	18.8%	57.3%			101	0.3	0.9	0.8
2024 DC	MIN	MLB	25	95	8	1	8	4	.227/.311/.315	.270	.391	9.2%	17.0%							82	0.0	0	0.1

2023 GP: 2B (39), LF (14), CF (12), DH (3)   Comps: Cliff Pennington (70), Hainley Statia (66), Sean Kazmar Jr. (66)

We'll see Martin in the big leagues this season, if he can just stay healthy enough. He lost the first half of his 2023 to an elbow injury, but once he returned, he looked like a big-leaguer at Triple-A: good contact skills, even better approach, adequate defense and enough speed to steal 20+ bases a year once he gets on. Right here, for a former top-five overall pick and premium trade chip who had to be added to the 40-man roster in November, you really want to see an "and." "And that's not all: He also has big power upside, if he can just tap into it." "And the cherry on top is that he might stick at shortstop after all." Alas, instead: a "but." Martin flashed all of the above, but without inspiring any increased confidence that he'll be more than a singles hitter with an average glove at a non-premium position. He'll be a big-leaguer this season. But that might be all he is.

Jose Miranda   3B   Born: 06/29/98   Age: 26   Bats: R   Throws: R   Height: 6'2"   Weight: 210   Origin: Round 2, 2016 Draft (#73 overall)

YEAR	TM	LVL	AGE	PA	R	HR	RBI	SB	AVG/OBP/SLG	BABIP	SLGCON	BB%	K%	ZSw%	ZCon%	OSw%	OCon%	LA	90th EV	DRC+	BRR	DRP	WARP
2021	WCH	AA	23	218	36	13	38	4	.345/.408/.588	.342	.675	7.8%	11.5%							148	0.9	2.3	2.2
2021	STP	AAA	23	373	61	17	56	0	.343/.397/.563	.362	.658	6.7%	13.1%							133	-2.7	-0.3	2.2
2022	STP	AAA	24	95	10	2	12	0	.256/.295/.442	.274	.528	5.3%	14.7%							103	0.3	2.3	0.5
2022	MIN	MLB	24	483	45	15	66	1	.268/.325/.426	.307	.535	5.8%	18.8%	73.9%	86.1%	36.0%	61.2%	13.9	103.7	105	-0.2	-1.3	1.2
2023	STP	AAA	25	181	24	3	23	2	.255/.326/.360	.290	.439	8.3%	16.0%	70.3%	90.2%	33.6%	61.8%			91	0.1	0.5	0.4
2023	MIN	MLB	25	152	12	3	13	0	.211/.263/.303	.235	.364	5.9%	15.8%	73.5%	84.9%	36.4%	61.2%	9.6	103.2	93	0.0	-0.5	0.3
2024 DC	MIN	MLB	26	31	3	1	3	0	.252/.311/.379	.294	.478	6.2%	18.3%							96	0.0	-0.1	0.1

2023 GP: 3B (38), DH (3), 1B (2)   Comps: Brandon Drury (59), Colin Moran (59), Kendrys Morales (54)

In an innovative tweak to the traditional hype model, Miranda let his teammates rave and remark upon his physical transformation over the winter of 2022-23, rather than give any quotes on the record about being in the best shape of his life. It's a good thing, too, since he immediately went to pieces, leaving us all to wonder if being just a tiny bit soft at the edges makes one a better hitter, after all. Miranda's arm is too weak (and his feet are too slow) for third base. He has to be a first baseman, which means he has to hit like one, which means he needs power. Since he showed a distinctly slider-speed bat and exactly zero punch in 2023, that (in turn) means he might very well have thrown away his shot at a long career by getting sexy.

Jorge Polanco   IF   Born: 07/05/93   Age: 31   Bats: S   Throws: R   Height: 5'11"   Weight: 208   Origin: IFA, 2009

YEAR	TM	LVL	AGE	PA	R	HR	RBI	SB	AVG/OBP/SLG	BABIP	SLGCON	BB%	K%	ZSw%	ZCon%	OSw%	OCon%	LA	90th EV	DRC+	BRR	DRP	WARP
2021	MIN	MLB	27	644	97	33	98	11	.269/.323/.503	.282	.630	7.0%	18.3%	70.6%	88.5%	35.9%	70.1%	19.0	104.6	121	0.4	-0.7	4.1
2022	MIN	MLB	28	445	54	16	56	3	.235/.346/.405	.269	.543	14.4%	21.3%	61.2%	84.8%	31.0%	62.2%	21.6	104.9	124	-0.3	-0.7	2.6
2023	STP	AAA	29	38	5	1	1	0	.281/.395/.406	.381	.591	13.2%	26.3%	43.1%	82.1%	36.6%	58.8%			105	-0.2	0.0	0.1
2023	MIN	MLB	29	343	38	14	48	4	.255/.335/.454	.310	.640	10.5%	25.7%	69.8%	85.6%	31.9%	60.6%	21.4	105.2	106	0.1	-0.1	1.2
2024 DC	MIN	MLB	30	554	61	17	64	7	.236/.326/.397	.287	.537	11.0%	23.2%							105	0.1	-0.3	1.9

2023 GP: 2B (58), 3B (15), DH (12)   Comps: Starlin Castro (77), Alan Trammell (75), Tony Fernandez (73)

Polanco has had to evolve in every aspect over the last few years. Nagging injuries progressed to more serious ones, and they compelled a change in approach from the formerly contact-centric, line drive-heavy switch-hitter. With some degradation in his bat-to-ball skills no longer avoidable, he's leaned into it. He's gotten more aggressive at the plate, trading some count leverage for more hard contact early in plate appearances. Just as an aging speedster can find an extra gear when they sniff an infield hit, though, Polanco showed the potential to sniff a walk and modulate his approach when the chance to get on base for free popped up. He's no longer as well-rounded as he was in his 20s, but Polanco has enough power and defensive aptitude to be an average or better contributor for another few years.

─────────────── ★ ★ ★ *2024 Top 101 Prospect* **#62** ★ ★ ★ ───────────────

Emmanuel Rodriguez   OF   Born: 02/28/03   Age: 21   Bats: L   Throws: L   Height: 5'10"   Weight: 210   Origin: IFA, 2019

YEAR	TM	LVL	AGE	PA	R	HR	RBI	SB	AVG/OBP/SLG	BABIP	SLGCON	BB%	K%	ZSw%	ZCon%	OSw%	OCon%	LA	90th EV	DRC+	BRR	DRP	WARP
2021	TWI	ROK	18	153	31	10	23	9	.214/.346/.524	.279	.943	15.0%	36.6%									3.7	
2022	FTM	A	19	199	35	9	25	11	.272/.492/.551	.364	.893	28.6%	26.1%	61.6%	79.2%	17.0%	43.8%			153	1.6	-2.0	1.7
2023	CR	A+	20	455	87	16	55	20	.240/.400/.463	.332	.745	20.2%	29.5%							122	0.3	5.7	3.0
2024 non	MIN	MLB	21	251	25	4	24	0	.222/.338/.352	.332	.564	14.2%	31.7%							100	0.0	0	0.9

2023 GP: CF (94), DH (5)   Comps: Akil Baddoo (78), Khalil Lee (73), Luis Alexander Basabe (68)

Everything here comes down to a simple question: Do you believe Rodriguez can make contact consistently against advanced pitching? If so, he's going to be a superstar. If not, then (as is almost always true) nothing else matters. At just 20 years old and coming off a major knee injury, Rodriguez hammered away at Midwest League pitching, and more than acquitted himself in center field. He's a power/speed combo not to be missed, but what really sets him apart is his plate discipline. He walks at rates that should barely be possible, and in the big leagues, they're almost sure not to be. He walks because opposing pitchers are afraid of him. He walks because they're bad. He walks because he whiffs enough to end up in deeper counts than similarly patient hitters—if such a creature exists, which is doubtful by now. Rodriguez could run .420 OBPs in MLB—or, if you think he'll never make enough contact, he could flame out before he even gets there.

Michael A. Taylor CF   Born: 03/26/91   Age: 33   Bats: R   Throws: R   Height: 6'4"   Weight: 215   Origin: Round 6, 2009 Draft (#172 overall)

YEAR	TM	LVL	AGE	PA	R	HR	RBI	SB	AVG/OBP/SLG	BABIP	SLGCON	BB%	K%	ZSw%	ZCon%	OSw%	OCon%	LA	90th EV	DRC+	BRR	DRP	WARP
2021	KC	MLB	30	528	58	12	54	14	.244/.297/.356	.319	.507	6.3%	27.3%	75.4%	79.7%	34.8%	52.6%	12.0	104.9	82	0.6	2.7	1.4
2022	KC	MLB	31	456	49	9	43	4	.254/.313/.357	.321	.485	7.7%	23.9%	73.5%	83.3%	34.4%	52.0%	12.5	103.7	104	0.2	5.5	2.5
2023	MIN	MLB	32	388	48	21	51	13	.220/.278/.442	.278	.698	6.7%	33.5%	69.9%	79.2%	34.0%	47.6%	11.7	106.3	75	0.4	1.3	0.4
2024 non	MIN	MLB	33	251	25	8	27	4	.217/.279/.362	.286	.535	7.0%	29.7%							79	0.1	0.7	0.3

2023 GP: CF (126), DH (1)   *Comps: Jim Busby (63), Dave Henderson (56), Tony Armas (55)*

It's almost impossible to predict what Taylor will do next. That's not because he's unusually volatile, per se, but rather because he underwent a major transformation in 2023 that wasn't really his own. We're all products of our environment; Taylor's environment last year was Minnesota, where they assiduously instill an approach that gives up contact in exchange for power. The whole plan for Twins hitters is to find the fastball in the zone and pummel. Taylor was, in a sense, perfect for it. Sitting on a pitch and attacking yielded a career high in homers. It also made him one of the most strikeout-prone hitters in baseball. The nastiest trick, though, is this: Once you put a player like Taylor through a change like that one, it's impossible to guess how lasting it will be—whether the circumstance changes or not.

Christian Vázquez C   Born: 08/21/90   Age: 33   Bats: R   Throws: R   Height: 5'9"   Weight: 205   Origin: Round 9, 2008 Draft (#292 overall)

YEAR	TM	LVL	AGE	PA	R	HR	RBI	SB	AVG/OBP/SLG	BABIP	SLGCON	BB%	K%	ZSw%	ZCon%	OSw%	OCon%	LA	90th EV	DRC+	BRR	DRP	WARP
2021	BOS	MLB	30	498	51	6	49	8	.258/.308/.352	.301	.430	6.6%	16.9%	67.7%	87.3%	34.3%	76.5%	13.6	101.3	99	-0.5	2.5	2.3
2022	HOU	MLB	31	108	8	1	10	0	.250/.278/.308	.294	.372	3.7%	16.7%	67.3%	93.8%	36.4%	67.8%	10.3	101.2	110	-0.2	0.1	0.5
2022	BOS	MLB	31	318	33	8	42	1	.282/.327/.432	.315	.523	5.7%	16.0%	69.5%	89.6%	36.1%	74.6%	10.9	101.6	102	-0.2	7.0	1.9
2023	MIN	MLB	32	355	34	6	32	1	.223/.280/.318	.279	.424	7.0%	23.1%	65.4%	80.9%	37.7%	65.3%	10.2	100.5	72	-0.3	7.4	0.8
2024 DC	MIN	MLB	33	377	34	6	35	2	.241/.297/.343	.295	.443	6.8%	20.9%							81	-0.4	3.3	0.8

2023 GP: C (94), 1B (7), 2B (2), DH (1)   *Comps: Dioner Navarro (68), Yadier Molina (66), Jim Sundberg (66)*

YEAR	TM	P. COUNT	FRM RUNS	BLK RUNS	THRW RUNS	TOT RUNS
2021	BOS	18097	3.3	0.1	1.3	4.7
2022	BOS	10710	8.3	0.2	0.6	9.0
2022	HOU	3647	0.6	-0.1	0.0	0.5
2023	MIN	13086	6.5	0.3	0.3	7.1
2024	MIN	13228	2.6	-0.1	0.8	3.4

Winning a mid-tier free-agent bidding war so often turns out to be a mixed blessing. The Twins had to pony up an eight-figure annual salary over three years to secure Vázquez's services, and by the time August came, he was in as programmed a timeshare at catcher as the game has seen in a long time. He and Ryan Jeffers alternated starts without deviation for four weeks near the end of the year. That Vázquez retained even that much playing time despite his putrid offensive numbers is telling. There's a gravity to Vázquez—his rich baritone carrying across the clubhouse effortlessly, his short, blockish frame cutting a sure swath through it and pulling guys into his wake like ducks in a row—that shows up in the way he conducts a defense and guides a pitcher through a game, too.

Matt Wallner OF   Born: 12/12/97   Age: 26   Bats: L   Throws: R   Height: 6'4"   Weight: 220   Origin: Round 1, 2019 Draft (#39 overall)

YEAR	TM	LVL	AGE	PA	R	HR	RBI	SB	AVG/OBP/SLG	BABIP	SLGCON	BB%	K%	ZSw%	ZCon%	OSw%	OCon%	LA	90th EV	DRC+	BRR	DRP	WARP
2021	CR	A+	23	294	39	15	47	0	.264/.350/.508	.363	.819	9.5%	33.3%							103	-1.2	-7.3	0.2
2022	WCH	AA	24	342	61	21	64	8	.299/.436/.597	.407	.994	18.1%	31.3%							111	1.3	8.5	2.7
2022	STP	AAA	24	229	29	6	31	1	.247/.376/.463	.339	.693	15.3%	27.5%							85	-2.2	1.0	0.2
2022	MIN	MLB	24	65	4	2	10	1	.228/.323/.386	.367	.688	9.2%	38.5%	71.0%	70.4%	26.8%	47.6%	12.0	105.4	72	0.0	0.1	0.0
2023	STP	AAA	25	305	50	11	47	0	.291/.403/.524	.399	.796	12.8%	28.5%	75.0%	75.5%	29.6%	41.3%			94	-0.3	3.9	1.1
2023	MIN	MLB	25	254	42	14	41	2	.249/.370/.507	.328	.812	11.0%	31.5%	75.3%	72.6%	27.9%	47.7%	21.4	111.0	116	0.1	0.7	1.2
2024 DC	MIN	MLB	26	497	53	13	54	3	.216/.324/.378	.321	.623	10.5%	34.0%							101	0.0	0.4	1.4

2023 GP: LF (43), RF (29), DH (9)   *Comps: Alex Presley (61), John Mayberry Jr. (57), Randy Arozarena (55)*

Bunyanesque power, and a surname that just begs to be mumbled, make Wallner the Platonic ideal of a hometown Minnesotan hero. His native Forest Lake is just a dozen miles up I-35W and a little jog over to Highway 61 from Target Field: half an hour tops, unless you're trying to fight Goin' Up North traffic on a Friday afternoon. In that case, you'd better budget an hour. It's been that kind of backed-up snarl of a trip to the big leagues for Wallner, with a bevy of left-hitting corner outfielders blocking his path, but he's made it. He whiffs too much on the fastball to ever be an elite slugger, but he doesn't whiff half the time on soft stuff or give away his power to put it in play, so he's set a nice, high floor for himself.

PITCHERS

Jordan Balazovic RHP   Born: 09/17/98   Age: 25   Height: 6'5"   Weight: 215   Origin: Round 5, 2016 Draft (#153 overall)

YEAR	TM	LVL	AGE	G(GS)	IP	W-L	SV	K	WHIP	ERA	CSP	BB%	K%	HR%	GB%	ZSw%	ZCon%	OSw%	OCon%	BABIP	SLGCON	DRA-	WARP
2021	WCH	AA	22	20(20)	97	5-4	0	102	1.40	3.62		8.9%	23.8%	2.1%	48.6%					.324	.504	86	1.4
2022	STP	AAA	23	22(21)	70²	0-7	0	76	1.94	7.39		10.2%	22.2%	5.8%	40.4%					.392	.829	126	0.0
2023	STP	AAA	24	22(3)	45²	1-1	0	54	1.73	5.32		15.2%	25.7%	2.4%	48.8%	60.1%	81.1%	33.3%	55.0%	.356	.636	89	1.0
2023	MIN	MLB	24	18(0)	24¹	1-0	0	17	1.56	4.44	51.2%	11.1%	15.7%	4.6%	44.3%	72.8%	90.3%	22.6%	57.4%	.284	.590	115	0.1
2024 DC	MIN	MLB	25	15(0)	48	3-2	0	41	1.53	5.34	51.2%	11.2%	19.1%	3.2%	42.4%					.300	.554	117	-0.2

2023 Arsenal: FA (95.2), KC (81.5), SL (86.4), FS (88.6)   *Comps: Jackson Stephens (73), Luke Jackson (70), Yency Almonte (69)*

It's not the arm that has betrayed this particular pitching prospect, but pretty much everything else. His back and knee have each cost Balazovic parts of seasons, and made him somewhat diminished even when he was on the mound. In 2023, he seasoned that stew of tsuris with some self-inflicted trouble, as he got punched in the mouth during a midnight fracas on the street during spring training. By now, the chances of Balazovic being a big-league starter have shrunk almost to zero. Instead, the race is on to find a breaking ball with which he can miss bats as a reliever, but he's getting out of the blocks slowly.

Jhoan Duran   RHP   Born: 01/08/98   Age: 26   Height: 6'5"   Weight: 230   Origin: IFA, 2014

YEAR	TM	LVL	AGE	G (GS)	IP	W-L	SV	K	WHIP	ERA	CSP	BB%	K%	HR%	GB%	ZSw%	ZCon%	OSw%	OCon%	BABIP	SLGCON	DRA-	WARP
2021	STP	AAA	23	5 (4)	16	0-3	0	22	1.81	5.06		17.3%	29.3%	1.3%	62.5%					.385	.550	85	0.3
2022	MIN	MLB	24	57 (0)	67²	2-4	8	89	0.98	1.86	55.4%	6.0%	33.5%	2.3%	59.2%	72.8%	79.6%	41.0%	46.2%	.295	.484	55	2.2
2023	MIN	MLB	25	59 (0)	62¹	3-6	27	84	1.14	2.45	45.9%	9.8%	32.9%	2.4%	64.1%	72.6%	78.3%	36.7%	45.9%	.301	.522	70	1.7
2024 DC	MIN	MLB	26	57 (0)	60	4-6	36	77	1.14	2.76	50.1%	9.7%	31.2%	1.8%	58.5%					.288	.469	67	1.3

2023 Arsenal: FA (101.8), KC (87.8), SI (98.3)   Comps: Jeurys Familia (78), Brandon Maurer (78), Zack Littell (74)

Duran is the size of an edge rusher. Every ballplayer is bigger than you think they are, especially in terms of thickness and musculature, but Duran dispenses even with the usual illusion of looseness or whip in the arms. He's all power, and he continues to absolutely overpower opposing batters. His fastball ranges from the top end of the 90s to the north side of 104 miles per hour, but that's only part of the story. His so-called splinker is evolving into more of a true splitter, in his usage of it, but it retains an unusual balance of whiff and ground-ball characteristics. Meanwhile, he's shaped his curveball into a third devastating weapon. His combination of strikeouts and weak grounders seems impossible to achieve, but once you see him pitch, it makes perfect sense. The only item on the task list is an occasional lack of control—but even that only makes hitters more uncomfortable.

David Festa   RHP   Born: 03/08/00   Age: 24   Height: 6'6"   Weight: 185   Origin: Round 13, 2021 Draft (#399 overall)

YEAR	TM	LVL	AGE	G (GS)	IP	W-L	SV	K	WHIP	ERA	CSP	BB%	K%	HR%	GB%	ZSw%	ZCon%	OSw%	OCon%	BABIP	SLGCON	DRA-	WARP
2022	FTM	A	22	5 (5)	24	2-1	0	33	0.75	1.50		6.8%	37.5%	1.1%	50.0%	74.8%	76.9%	37.7%	45.7%	.234	.312	75	0.7
2022	CR	A+	22	16 (13)	79²	7-3	0	75	1.19	2.71		8.6%	23.1%	1.5%	49.3%					.294	.432	92	1.1
2023	WCH	AA	23	21 (19)	80	3-3	0	104	1.36	4.39		9.6%	30.4%	2.3%	46.8%					.349	.537	70	2.0
2023	STP	AAA	23	3 (3)	12¹	1-1	0	15	1.54	2.92		16.7%	27.8%	1.9%	46.7%	74.5%	76.7%	26.9%	35.9%	.310	.533	85	0.3
2024 DC	MIN	MLB	24	5 (5)	21²	1-1	0	23	1.42	4.76		10.5%	23.5%	3.1%	39.8%					.306	.565	106	0.1

2023 Arsenal: SL (87.4), CH (87.4), FA (94.9), CU (78.7)   Comps: Nick Nelson (72), Rogelio Armenteros (71), Tyler Thornburg (68)

You can't get far in a book like this one without hearing about the rising usage of sliders, league-wide. Every year, the league throws more sliders. Even starters lean pretty heavily on them these days. Still, Festa seems to be pushing the envelope a bit. On the way up the ladder, he's made his slider his primary pitch, throwing it over 40% of the time and letting both his changeup and his four-seam heater play off of it, instead of the other way around. If you had to pick a slider with which to try this, this is the one you'd want. It's 84-88 with a lot of depth and relatively little horizontal movement, and from Festa's skyscraping release point, it can be around the zone enough to get chases and to set up the high fastball. Still, we're pushing new frontiers here.

Kody Funderburk   LHP   Born: 11/27/96   Age: 27   Height: 6'4"   Weight: 230   Origin: Round 15, 2018 Draft (#454 overall)

YEAR	TM	LVL	AGE	G (GS)	IP	W-L	SV	K	WHIP	ERA	CSP	BB%	K%	HR%	GB%	ZSw%	ZCon%	OSw%	OCon%	BABIP	SLGCON	DRA-	WARP
2021	CR	A+	24	11 (10)	45¹	1-3	1	59	1.19	3.18		10.9%	30.7%	0.5%	62.4%					.299	.402	74	1.1
2021	WCH	AA	24	7 (0)	21²	3-0	3	23	0.92	1.25		8.2%	27.1%	1.2%	50.0%					.226	.407	72	0.5
2022	WCH	AA	25	32 (17)	107	10-5	0	103	1.33	2.94		9.6%	22.4%	1.7%	48.8%					.307	.480	83	1.6
2023	WCH	AA	26	5 (0)	9	1-0	1	14	1.56	1.00		15.0%	35.0%	0.0%	65.0%					.400	.400	71	0.2
2023	MIN	MLB	26	11 (0)	12	2-0	0	19	0.92	0.75	47.8%	10.6%	40.4%	2.1%	54.5%	62.7%	76.9%	29.4%	46.9%	.238	.455	83	0.2
2024 DC	MIN	MLB	27	45 (0)	48	3-2	0	53	1.31	3.90	47.8%	10.2%	25.7%	2.3%	46.8%					.300	.512	89	0.5

2023 Arsenal: HC (91.5), SW (82), SI (93.2), CH (87.7)   Comps: Jeff Beliveau (38), Brad Wieck (36), Perci Garner (35)

His backstory is as intriguing as his surname is mellifluous. Funderburk was a 15th-round pick out of tiny collegiate pitching factory Dallas Baptist University and spent some time in limbo, on the brink of the kind of anonymous non-emergence that claims most 15th-rounders. An oblique strain interrupted his first pro season, and COVID-19 pulverized his second. As his name demands, he's a lefty with plenty of funk, especially in the disparate movement (out of very similar spin axes) on his two fastballs. He doesn't throw extraordinarily hard, but he knows how to set up his bat-missing slider. As a short reliever, even in the era of the three-batter minimum, he has a promising future.

Griffin Jax   RHP   Born: 11/22/94   Age: 29   Height: 6'2"   Weight: 195   Origin: Round 3, 2016 Draft (#93 overall)

YEAR	TM	LVL	AGE	G (GS)	IP	W-L	SV	K	WHIP	ERA	CSP	BB%	K%	HR%	GB%	ZSw%	ZCon%	OSw%	OCon%	BABIP	SLGCON	DRA-	WARP
2021	STP	AAA	26	8 (8)	40²	4-1	0	36	1.30	3.76		9.4%	21.2%	1.2%	39.8%					.302	.479	114	0.3
2021	MIN	MLB	26	18 (14)	82	4-5	0	65	1.35	6.37	55.3%	8.1%	18.1%	6.4%	31.8%	69.7%	88.0%	32.5%	64.3%	.248	.675	154	-1.6
2022	MIN	MLB	27	65 (0)	72¹	7-4	1	78	1.05	3.36	55.7%	6.9%	26.9%	2.4%	45.5%	64.1%	83.7%	36.8%	53.6%	.271	.473	74	1.7
2023	MIN	MLB	28	71 (0)	65¹	6-10	4	68	1.18	3.86	51.4%	6.9%	24.8%	1.8%	55.2%	64.4%	83.8%	33.5%	55.8%	.299	.473	78	1.5
2024 DC	MIN	MLB	29	51 (0)	54	3-2	2	52	1.28	4.02	54.0%	8.1%	22.7%	2.7%	45.4%					.296	.519	93	0.5

2023 Arsenal: SW (86.8), FA (96.5), SI (96.5), CH (91), FC (92.4)   Comps: Shane Greene (73), Craig Stammen (68), Tyler Lyons (67)

The numbers don't look all that different, and maybe they never will. Jax has a sweeper on which he relies heavily, but it's not one of those elite bat-missers. Adding a sinker that opened up the arm side of the plate for him against righties and tightening up the command of a couple of offerings didn't catapult him to relief ace status, but the Air Force captain became an exceptional ground-ball guy. He also became a whole lot more fun to watch—not only adding a tick to his fastball, but launching himself down the mound, lower to the ground and with greater ferocity. Greater stride length has yielded even more perceived velocity. His athleticism is on display, and the delivery itself is an act of aggression. Though stolid on the mound, Jax lets the latent competitor out each time he kicks and fires.

Cory Lewis RHP Born: 10/09/00 Age: 23 Height: 6'5" Weight: 220 Origin: Round 9, 2022 Draft (#264 overall)

YEAR	TM	LVL	AGE	G (GS)	IP	W-L	SV	K	WHIP	ERA	CSP	BB%	K%	HR%	GB%	ZSw%	ZCon%	OSw%	OCon%	BABIP	SLGCON	DRA-	WARP
2023	FTM	A	22	9(9)	39¹	4-3	0	55	1.04	2.75		9.2%	33.7%	1.8%	43.5%	71.1%	82.1%	33.6%	46.9%	.261	.489	63	1.1
2023	CR	A+	22	13(13)	62	5-1	0	63	1.06	2.32		7.2%	25.3%	1.2%	42.9%					.273	.412	79	1.3
2024 non	MIN	MLB	23	58(0)	50	2-2	0	42	1.46	5.27		9.9%	19.1%	3.8%	36.4%					.294	.574	116	-0.2

2023 Arsenal: FA (90.9), CU (79.9), CH (80.6), SL (81.5), KN (84)   Comps: Charles Brewer (87), Jack Leftwich (86), Chris Vallimont (86)

From the early 1930s through the end of the 1950s, there were a fistful of pitchers who made either primary or complementary use of a knuckleball in the majors. Beginning in the 1960s, though, it became the strict preserve of specialists. Some of that was, according to Rob Neyer, the (probably wrongheaded and self-interested) pronouncements by those very specialists that knuckleballs can't be thrown effectively except by those who make it their life's work. Some other, major part of it, though, was the fact that it ceased to be needed. In a world of relatively dead balls and big strike zones, as pitchers gained velocity and learned new, highly effective versions of the changeup, who needed the knuckler? Well, Lewis might. His fastball is just okay: good extension, good command at the top of the zone, but light on velocity. He has average secondaries. The knuckleball, as a fourth pitch, helped him break out in 2023. It's his upside play.

Pablo López RHP Born: 03/07/96 Age: 28 Height: 6'4" Weight: 225 Origin: IFA, 2012

YEAR	TM	LVL	AGE	G (GS)	IP	W-L	SV	K	WHIP	ERA	CSP	BB%	K%	HR%	GB%	ZSw%	ZCon%	OSw%	OCon%	BABIP	SLGCON	DRA-	WARP
2021	MIA	MLB	25	20(20)	102²	5-5	0	115	1.12	3.07	52.3%	6.2%	27.5%	2.6%	46.3%	67.0%	83.9%	39.2%	63.0%	.302	.551	75	2.3
2022	MIA	MLB	26	32(32)	180	10-10	0	174	1.17	3.75	52.3%	7.2%	23.6%	2.9%	46.7%	71.2%	80.9%	35.6%	60.3%	.283	.545	93	2.4
2023	MIN	MLB	27	32(32)	194	11-8	0	234	1.15	3.66	48.1%	6.0%	29.2%	3.0%	44.5%	69.4%	80.9%	39.0%	55.8%	.314	.563	75	4.8
2024 DC	MIN	MLB	28	29(29)	172	13-8	0	181	1.15	3.37	50.0%	6.9%	25.5%	2.8%	45.5%					.286	.518	81	3.2

2023 Arsenal: FA (94.9), SW (84.5), CH (88.4), CU (82.5), SI (94.5), SL (86.9)   Comps: Alex Fernandez (83), Bret Saberhagen (83), Ben Sheets (82)

Bob Gibson once said, "I think a ballplayer is just about the finest thing a man can be." It's a weighty and improbable statement, if you dismiss the idea that Gibson was being glib. He was a man not given to glibness, and his interlocutor was Roger Angell, a man not given to passing along glib remarks even when he heard them, so let's grant that dismissal. Thus, we have to consider the idea seriously. When we do, López becomes an interesting test of the theory. Articulate, intelligent and open-minded, he lends the game greater grace just by having chosen to play it. As a teenager in Venezuela, he chose baseball over a medical degree. Everything about him suggests that he'd have been a good doctor. More people would be alive today if López took a different path. Like Gibson, though, López might just be capable of enriching more lives by his artistry than he could have saved in the sciences.

Jovani Moran LHP Born: 04/24/97 Age: 27 Height: 6'1" Weight: 167 Origin: Round 7, 2015 Draft (#200 overall)

YEAR	TM	LVL	AGE	G (GS)	IP	W-L	SV	K	WHIP	ERA	CSP	BB%	K%	HR%	GB%	ZSw%	ZCon%	OSw%	OCon%	BABIP	SLGCON	DRA-	WARP
2021	WCH	AA	24	20(0)	37²	2-1	2	64	0.74	1.91		10.1%	46.0%	2.2%	42.6%					.190	.426	52	1.2
2021	STP	AAA	24	15(0)	29²	2-1	1	45	1.08	3.03		14.8%	36.9%	2.5%	46.4%					.212	.509	74	0.9
2021	MIN	MLB	24	5(0)	8	0-0	0	10	2.00	7.87	49.0%	18.4%	26.3%	0.0%	42.9%	86.7%	71.8%	35.0%	53.7%	.429	.476	105	0.1
2022	STP	AAA	25	20(0)	24	1-2	0	43	1.63	6.00		12.5%	38.4%	1.8%	50.9%					.451	.736	59	0.8
2022	MIN	MLB	25	31(0)	40²	0-1	1	54	1.06	2.21	52.6%	11.0%	32.9%	0.0%	50.0%	71.1%	73.4%	32.2%	44.9%	.272	.363	79	0.8
2023	STP	AAA	26	6(0)	8¹	0-0	1	8	1.92	1.08		23.1%	20.5%	0.0%	54.5%	59.4%	78.9%	22.9%	63.6%	.318	.364	101	0.1
2023	MIN	MLB	26	43(0)	42¹	2-2	0	48	1.46	5.31	44.5%	14.7%	26.1%	1.6%	40.4%	66.9%	76.1%	28.3%	44.1%	.308	.495	97	0.6
2024 non	MIN	MLB	27	58(0)	50	2-2	0	67	1.40	4.24	48.0%	13.1%	30.5%	2.7%	43.1%					.307	.570	94	0.4

2023 Arsenal: CH (83.2), FA (93.3), SW (81.8)   Comps: Paul Fry (70), Tanner Scott (67), J.B. Wendelken (67)

We should, perhaps, talk more about the inescapable quandary posed to opposing managers by a pitcher with reverse platoon splits. He has you where he wants you, and there's not much you can do about it. What are you going to do, swap in a lefty to face this funky lefty, just because his best pitch is a changeup that can be hell on right-handed batters? Your favorite lefty bench bat isn't going to feel more comfortable standing in there just because Moran leans on the change. Besides, you'd feel stupid. Double stupid, when your guy makes an out. Still, maybe you'd better... your bench coach is no help, feels like he's just waiting for your job. Ehhh. Okay, we'll try it. What? Moran walked *another* hitter while you were thinking? Well, cool. That was a freebie.

Bailey Ober RHP Born: 07/12/95 Age: 28 Height: 6'9" Weight: 260 Origin: Round 12, 2017 Draft (#346 overall)

YEAR	TM	LVL	AGE	G (GS)	IP	W-L	SV	K	WHIP	ERA	CSP	BB%	K%	HR%	GB%	ZSw%	ZCon%	OSw%	OCon%	BABIP	SLGCON	DRA-	WARP
2021	STP	AAA	25	4(4)	16	1-0	0	21	1.13	2.81		7.7%	32.3%	0.0%	48.7%					.333	.538	97	0.3
2021	MIN	MLB	25	20(20)	92¹	3-3	0	96	1.20	4.19	53.2%	5.0%	25.3%	5.3%	33.5%	68.4%	86.8%	37.0%	59.8%	.296	.669	104	0.7
2022	STP	AAA	26	2(2)	9²	0-1	0	13	0.72	4.66		5.4%	35.1%	5.4%	52.4%					.158	.524	79	0.2
2022	MIN	MLB	26	11(11)	56	2-3	0	51	1.05	3.21	53.3%	4.8%	22.5%	1.8%	28.8%	74.1%	82.3%	38.4%	59.7%	.278	.463	110	0.2
2023	STP	AAA	27	5(5)	22²	2-1	0	25	0.97	2.38		6.7%	27.8%	1.1%	32.2%	64.1%	82.7%	39.2%	51.2%	.259	.439	102	0.3
2023	MIN	MLB	27	26(26)	144¹	8-6	0	146	1.07	3.43	46.3%	5.0%	25.3%	3.8%	33.9%	73.6%	79.2%	39.8%	62.0%	.276	.552	99	1.8
2024 DC	MIN	MLB	28	28(28)	156²	11-8	0	151	1.19	3.89	49.1%	6.0%	23.2%	3.5%	33.0%					.291	.562	93	2.0

2023 Arsenal: FA (91.5), CH (83.8), SW (81.1), CU (77.5)   Comps: Dinelson Lamet (69), Scott Baker (68), Anthony DeSclafani (67)

The gigantic Ober gets an extra yard on the fastball, with excellent extension down the mound and a commitment to hammering the top of the zone with the pitch. His command of that offering in that region got better in 2023, which allowed him to establish himself as a mid-rotation starter. Around midseason, he tightened up his slider and found more consistent tilt on it, and late in the campaign, he discovered greater faith in his changeup, with sparkling results. The big man doesn't overpower hitters, so he has small margins for error, especially with that ground-ball rate. When he errs, he gives up long hits. Every indication, though, is that he's figured out how to avoid making enough mistakes to get truly hurt.

Chris Paddack RHP   Born: 01/08/96   Age: 28   Height: 6'5"   Weight: 217   Origin: Round 8, 2015 Draft (#236 overall)

YEAR	TM	LVL	AGE	G (GS)	IP	W-L	SV	K	WHIP	ERA	CSP	BB%	K%	HR%	GB%	ZSw%	ZCon%	OSw%	OCon%	BABIP	SLGCON	DRA-	WARP
2021	SD	MLB	25	23(22)	108¹	7-7	0	99	1.26	5.07	58.1%	4.8%	21.6%	3.3%	42.4%	70.7%	80.1%	32.1%	66.9%	.317	.579	93	1.4
2022	MIN	MLB	26	5(5)	22¹	1-2	0	20	1.21	4.03	62.4%	2.2%	21.5%	0.0%	44.3%	69.7%	77.0%	36.7%	69.6%	.357	.500	92	0.3
2023	MIN	MLB	27	2(0)	5	1-0	0	8	1.40	5.40	55.8%	4.5%	36.4%	4.5%	30.8%	70.3%	69.2%	31.0%	61.5%	.417	.769	85	0.0
2024 DC	MIN	MLB	28	32(23)	105	5-6	0	105	1.22	3.80	55.6%	6.3%	24.0%	2.9%	42.9%					.304	.538	90	1.4

2023 Arsenal: FA (95.5), CH (85), KC (79.9), SL (84.5)   Comps: Vance Worley (64), Danny Salazar (63), Scott Baker (61)

When Paddack underwent his second Tommy John surgery in May 2022, it could have spelled the end of his Twins tenure. Instead, the team doubled down on their bet on him, extending him through 2025. At the tail end of 2023, they got a sneak preview of the returns they still hope to realize on that investment. He was only working in short relief but, far from looking diminished, Paddack's stuff was better than ever. His fastball was three miles per hour livelier than in the past. His changeup regained the filthy factor that had waned even before his latest injury. Now, the question is: Why mess with it? Both Paddack and the Twins want him to start in 2024, but he's still a two-pitch guy with a reliever's cocksure intensity and no real scaffold on which to build a starter's workload. Maybe The Sheriff should stick to keeping the peace late in games, when the blood starts boilin' and the big guns come out.

Marco Raya RHP   Born: 08/07/02   Age: 21   Height: 6'1"   Weight: 170   Origin: Round 4, 2020 Draft (#128 overall)

YEAR	TM	LVL	AGE	G (GS)	IP	W-L	SV	K	WHIP	ERA	CSP	BB%	K%	HR%	GB%	ZSw%	ZCon%	OSw%	OCon%	BABIP	SLGCON	DRA-	WARP
2022	FTM	A	19	19(17)	65	3-2	0	76	1.08	3.05		8.7%	28.9%	3.0%	43.5%	70.9%	78.0%	33.7%	56.1%	.255	.506	96	1.2
2023	CR	A+	20	11(11)	33²	0-1	0	39	0.92	2.94		6.1%	29.5%	3.0%	39.8%					.241	.481	75	0.7
2023	WCH	AA	20	11(11)	29	0-3	0	26	1.24	5.28		11.2%	20.8%	1.6%	47.0%					.247	.390	98	0.3
2024 non	MIN	MLB	21	58(0)	50	2-2	0	43	1.50	5.57		10.1%	19.3%	3.9%	37.1%					.300	.587	122	-0.4

Comps: Arodys Vizcaíno (60), Aaron Sanchez (59), Ian Anderson (58)

There's being conservative with a young pitching prospect, and then there's whatever Minnesota is doing with Raya. He's an undersized right-hander who had shoulder trouble in 2021, and it seems to have scared his employers senseless. He appeared every seven days in the minors in 2023, ascending to Double-A, but he never got more than 12 outs or threw more than 55 pitches in a game. They say it's strictly about the cumulative lost work due to the pandemic and that previous shoulder trouble, but they haven't prepared him to be a big-league starter at all so far. That signals severe distrust that Raya will stick in the rotation, but his stuff is explosive enough to work gorgeously out of the bullpen—perhaps even in a multi-inning role, since he has a four-pitch mix and fair command. But they may be too overprotective to let him run in himself without the help of a cart.

Joe Ryan RHP   Born: 06/05/96   Age: 28   Height: 6'2"   Weight: 205   Origin: Round 7, 2018 Draft (#210 overall)

YEAR	TM	LVL	AGE	G (GS)	IP	W-L	SV	K	WHIP	ERA	CSP	BB%	K%	HR%	GB%	ZSw%	ZCon%	OSw%	OCon%	BABIP	SLGCON	DRA-	WARP
2021	MIN	MLB	25	5(5)	26²	2-1	0	30	0.79	4.05	56.4%	5.0%	30.0%	4.0%	26.2%	75.0%	80.1%	34.4%	70.1%	.197	.508	119	0.0
2022	MIN	MLB	26	27(27)	147	13-8	0	151	1.10	3.55	54.9%	7.8%	25.0%	3.3%	27.8%	72.7%	80.9%	33.3%	62.5%	.253	.524	110	0.7
2023	MIN	MLB	27	29(29)	161²	11-10	0	197	1.17	4.51	48.5%	5.1%	29.3%	4.8%	32.2%	73.7%	78.5%	40.0%	65.3%	.305	.660	87	3.1
2024 DC	MIN	MLB	28	29(29)	169	12-8	0	177	1.13	3.54	51.4%	6.6%	25.6%	3.6%	30.9%					.276	.563	86	2.8

2023 Arsenal: FA (92.3), FS (83.8), SW (79.7), CH (85.6), SL (83), CU (75.1)   Comps: Dinelson Lamet (71), Steven Matz (65), Kyle Hendricks (64)

This is not your 2023 BP *Annual* comment on Ryan. We're talking about an entirely new and different pitcher now. He has the same low-slung release point and high-riding fastball, but he throws it much less often. Gone are the curveball that was always a terrible fit for that delivery and the straight change that kinda was, but didn't do much. Here, instead, is a splitter that has become a staple of his arsenal, even against righties. He's throwing his old, sharp and vertical slider less, and a sweeper considerably more. He grew into one of the best strikeout mavens in baseball last year, with six regular-season starts in which he punched out at least 10. He doesn't walk people, either. Alas: the homers. This version of him is even more prone to them than the old ones. Oh, well. He joins the ranks of others who seem to do everything well except limiting power, along with Scott Baker, and Phil Hughes, and Kyle Lohse, and Jake Odorizzi and hey wait a minute—

Charlee Soto RHP   Born: 08/31/05   Age: 18   Height: 6'3"   Weight: 210   Origin: Round 1, 2023 Draft (#34 overall)

This is the archetype of the exciting young pitching prospect. Soto was born just five days before Francisco Liriano made his big-league debut. He's younger than *Wedding Crashers*, younger than all the *Star Wars* prequels. Until a very short time before the draft, he wasn't even focused on pitching, preferring to dabble in the art of shortstop. Now, he's soaring toward 6-foot-6, has a chance to throw 100 mph, has shown advanced feel for a slider and changeup as secondary options and possesses a bit more grace than a lot of the less fluidly athletic, more singularly trained fireballing high schoolers who pop up every year. He might just be the Chosen One—the one who can bring balance to the pitching universe. As far as he knows, that always ends well.

Brock Stewart RHP   Born: 10/03/91   Age: 32   Height: 6'3"   Weight: 220   Origin: Round 6, 2014 Draft (#189 overall)

YEAR	TM	LVL	AGE	G (GS)	IP	W-L	SV	K	WHIP	ERA	CSP	BB%	K%	HR%	GB%	ZSw%	ZCon%	OSw%	OCon%	BABIP	SLGCON	DRA-	WARP
2022	STP	AAA	30	7(0)	7¹	0-1	0	11	1.36	6.14		2.9%	32.4%	5.9%	38.1%					.368	.900	78	0.2
2023	MIN	MLB	31	28(0)	27²	2-0	1	39	1.08	0.65	49.9%	10.1%	35.8%	0.9%	36.2%	71.8%	64.7%	31.4%	45.1%	.316	.448	81	0.6
2024 DC	MIN	MLB	32	39(0)	42	2-2	0	55	1.25	4.17	49.3%	9.0%	30.9%	3.6%	37.6%					.307	.615	96	0.3

2023 Arsenal: FA (97.2), SW (84.7), FC (93.3), CH (89), SI (96.6), CU (81.2)   Comps: Anthony Bass (55), Casey Janssen (53), Shane Greene (51)

There were 615 pitchers who threw at least 50 fastballs at which hitters swung in 2023. That's 20 for every team in baseball, and a 21st for half of them. It's a lot of arms. The league churns through hurlers at an extraordinary rate. That's how broken-down former prospects like Stewart get enough chances to finally break out, and that's exactly what he did. How emphatically? Of those 615 pitchers, Stewart got the highest whiff rate on his heat. While he's roughly average-sized for a modern moundsman, Stewart cuts an intimidating figure on the mound. His fastball overpowers his opponents, and leaves only cleanup work for his cutter and sweeper. Alas, relievers are volatile. Not even late bloomers who figure out how to throw 100 and can command a breaking ball are guaranteed to sustain any value.

Caleb Thielbar LHP   Born: 01/31/87   Age: 37   Height: 6'0"   Weight: 205   Origin: Round 18, 2009 Draft (#556 overall)

YEAR	TM	LVL	AGE	G (GS)	IP	W-L	SV	K	WHIP	ERA	CSP	BB%	K%	HR%	GB%	ZSw%	ZCon%	OSw%	OCon%	BABIP	SLGCON	DRA-	WARP
2021	MIN	MLB	34	59(0)	64	7-0	0	77	1.17	3.23	59.1%	7.5%	28.9%	3.0%	30.7%	68.6%	80.9%	33.3%	61.1%	.303	.594	91	0.9
2022	MIN	MLB	35	67(0)	59¹	4-3	1	80	1.16	3.49	57.6%	7.3%	32.7%	2.0%	29.9%	73.8%	73.0%	38.3%	64.6%	.324	.514	75	1.3
2023	MIN	MLB	36	36(0)	30²	3-1	0	36	0.95	3.23	50.4%	5.0%	30.0%	5.8%	35.9%	70.8%	81.7%	32.5%	66.3%	.229	.662	85	0.6
2024 DC	MIN	MLB	37	45(0)	48	3-2	0	51	1.21	3.71	56.0%	7.7%	25.4%	3.2%	31.5%					.289	.557	88	0.5

2023 Arsenal: FA (93.1), SW (80.5), CU (73.5), SL (87.8)   Comps: Jake Diekman (53), Randy Choate (50), Pat Neshek (49)

At this rate, Thielbar will be as old as Jesse Orosco and Jamie Moyer were at the ends of their respective careers, but throwing as hard as Aroldis Chapman at the peak of his. Now 37 years old, the former soft-tosser is pumping in heat at 93 mph from the left side. He's become a sweeper maven against lefties, and he keeps spinning that achingly slow curveball, as lazy-looking and yet as lethal as the Cannon River as it carves through Northfield, MN. His body is starting to balk at all this. You can go to Driveline every winter and come back with a little bit more velocity and a new pitch for the mix, but you can't reverse the laws of nature in the process. Still, the news here is nothing but good. A kid from Northfield is now one of the anchors of his former hometown team, and he's hidden from Father Time for more than a decade.

Louie Varland   RHP   Born: 12/09/97   Age: 26   Height: 6'1"   Weight: 205   Origin: Round 15, 2019 Draft (#449 overall)

YEAR	TM	LVL	AGE	G (GS)	IP	W-L	SV	K	WHIP	ERA	CSP	BB%	K%	HR%	GB%	ZSw%	ZCon%	OSw%	OCon%	BABIP	SLGCON	DRA-	WARP
2021	FTM	A	23	10(8)	47¹	4-2	0	76	1.20	2.09		8.0%	38.0%	1.0%	45.7%	66.0%	74.4%	35.0%	46.5%	.379	.500	82	1.0
2021	CR	A+	23	10(10)	55²	6-2	0	66	0.99	2.10		6.3%	29.9%	1.8%	37.4%					.276	.489	87	0.9
2022	WCH	AA	24	20(19)	105	7-4	0	119	1.34	3.34		8.7%	26.4%	3.1%	40.3%					.320	.547	82	1.6
2022	STP	AAA	24	4(4)	21¹	1-1	0	27	0.84	1.69		3.6%	32.1%	1.2%	36.5%					.275	.431	81	0.5
2022	MIN	MLB	24	5(5)	26	1-2	0	21	1.23	3.81	58.1%	5.7%	19.8%	3.8%	38.5%	71.3%	88.5%	31.0%	62.7%	.297	.577	107	0.2
2023	STP	AAA	25	16(15)	81²	7-1	0	88	1.35	3.97		7.4%	25.1%	2.3%	43.8%	69.0%	81.2%	32.1%	59.6%	.338	.594	85	1.9
2023	MIN	MLB	25	17(10)	68	4-3	0	71	1.22	4.63	52.6%	6.0%	25.1%	5.7%	44.3%	73.8%	81.3%	36.5%	61.5%	.284	.675	87	1.3
2024 DC	MIN	MLB	26	40(19)	129	8-7	0	116	1.31	4.29	53.9%	7.4%	21.2%	3.0%	42.0%					.302	.536	99	1.2

2023 Arsenal: FA (95), SL (89.3), SW (83.9), CH (86), SI (95.6)   Comps: Tyler Cloyd (81), Jimmy Nelson (79), Tyler Duffey (77)

If Varland wants to cut it as a starter, he needs to either reengineer or reimagine his changeup. It was an utterly insufficient third weapon for him in 2023, and he needs one of those to work deep into games and get left-handed batters out. His fastball didn't do enough against big-leaguers when he was starting, either. Varland has a long, swooping arm action that gives him great extension, but which also seems to give opponents a great look at the ball. Late in the season, a crowded Twins rotation forced him to the bullpen—and everything changed. Varland's power cutter can bully lefties. His heater works much better in the uppermost reaches of the 90s, where he often put it in relief work. He's the rare young hurler who's stretched out to 150 innings per year in the minors, but it looks like his best future involves pitching half that much.

LINEOUTS

Hitters

HITTER	POS	TM	LVL	AGE	PA	R	HR	RBI	SB	AVG/OBP/SLG	BABIP	SLGCON	BB%	K%	ZSw%	ZCon%	OSw%	OCon%	LA	90th EV	DRC+	BRR	DRP	WARP
Danny De Andrade	SS	FTM	A	19	475	72	11	67	20	.244/.354/.396	.294	.536	12.2%	21.7%	68.0%	83.9%	31.5%	68.2%		106	3.0	2.6	2.6
Kyle Garlick	1B	STP	AAA	31	355	55	14	65	2	.242/.346/.450	.322	.713	12.1%	31.0%	63.1%	71.4%	29.4%	45.3%		89	0.2	3.1	0.9
	1B	MIN	MLB	31	30	2	2	4	0	.179/.233/.429	.200	.706	6.7%	36.7%	55.3%	80.8%	28.8%	38.1%	17.4	103.7	98	0.0	-0.4	0.0
Nick Gordon	UT	MIN	MLB	27	93	13	2	7	0	.176/.185/.319	.179	.362	1.1%	11.8%	80.1%	89.0%	42.2%	64.4%	9.6	102.4	97	0.0	-0.5	0.2
Jordan Luplow	RF	BUF	AAA	29	208	27	8	31	2	.239/.341/.438	.250	.546	12.0%	16.8%	69.7%	83.5%	25.3%	56.6%		111	0.8	2.0	1.1
	RF	MIN	MLB	29	73	10	2	4	2	.206/.315/.349	.262	.500	12.3%	26.0%	74.3%	77.4%	32.8%	59.0%	15.6	102.3	71	0.1	-0.3	-0.1
	RF	TOR	MLB	29	17	1	0	1	0	.214/.353/.214	.500	.500	17.6%	47.1%	81.8%	44.4%	29.2%	42.9%	18.3	102.6	80	0.0	-0.1	0.0
Yasser Mercedes	OF	TWI	ROK	18	105	14	4	17	6	.196/.248/.381	.211	.500	5.7%	21.9%	80.0%	75.0%	30.0%	33.3%						
Noah Miller	SS	CR	A+	20	526	71	8	60	12	.223/.309/.340	.271	.444	11.0%	20.5%						98	0.6	9.4	2.5
Jose Salas	IF	CR	A+	20	372	36	4	33	22	.190/.265/.272	.252	.385	7.3%	26.1%						77	-0.4	-0.2	-0.1
Tanner Schobel	3B/2B	CR	A+	22	347	53	14	61	9	.288/.366/.493	.319	.626	10.4%	18.4%						127	3.7	-3.5	2.4
	3B/2B	WCH	AA	22	207	19	2	18	3	.226/.329/.305	.277	.394	12.1%	19.3%						98	-0.1	-4.0	0.1
Yunior Severino	IF	WCH	AA	23	375	56	24	62	3	.287/.365/.560	.373	.862	9.6%	31.2%						106	-4.7	-1.9	0.6
	IF	STP	AAA	23	153	24	11	22	0	.233/.320/.511	.294	.883	9.8%	36.6%	67.9%	65.9%	31.3%	47.7%		85	-0.9	0.5	0.2
Brandon Winokur	OF	TWI	ROK	18	71	14	4	17	0	.288/.338/.545	.385	.837	5.6%	32.4%	100.0%	60.0%	50.0%	66.7%						

Athletic Venezuelan shortstop **Danny De Andrade** held his own impressively in full-season ball at age 19, but the tools are well ahead of the skills so far. ⓧ Like his namesake, lefty masher **Kyle Garlick** can be the perfect final ingredient in a well-balanced recipe, but comes with a severe risk of overuse. ⓧ Unable to keep any meat on his bones, **Nick Gordon** just keeps getting hurt, thwarting any hope that he'd continue his development into valuable utility man. ⓧ Platoon outfield bat **Jordan Luplow** has pitchers figured out. He can work them for walks, he hits them for power, and they can't strike him out much. It's just not the MLB pitchers we're describing here. ⓧ The Twins hope a lost year in the Complex League doesn't indicate a lasting bewilderment, because **Yasser Mercedes** has all the tools to be a star-caliber power/speed outfielder. ⓧ One of the dangers of metaphorical ceilings is that you can bump your head on them while standing still. Light-hitting infield **Noah Miller's** is no longer leaving room for tiptoes, let alone the leap he's been hoping for. ⓧ The Twins were excited to get **Jose Salas** as part of the Pablo López-Luis Arraez trade before the 2023 season, but he fell flatter than Arraez's bat path in the Midwest League. ⓧ Undersized **Tanner Schobel** earned the right to take the Double-A test midway through 2023, but the way those pitchers erased his power suggests that the ceiling here might be as a bench asset. ⓧ **Yunior Severino** is getting close to being a super senior in the minors, with strikeouts relentlessly thwarting his Jonathan Schoop-like blend of power and defensive utility. ⓧ Gangly power prospect **Brandon Winokur** cost the Twins a pretty penny in the third round of the draft, but if his skills keep up with his tools as he develops, he'll turn out to have been a terrific bargain.

Pitchers

PITCHER	TM	LVL	AGE	G (GS)	IP	W-L	SV	K	WHIP	ERA	CSP	BB%	K%	HR%	GB%	ZSw%	ZCon%	OSw%	OCon%	BABIP	SLGCON	DRA-	WARP
Jorge Alcala	STP	AAA	27	6 (0)	7²	2-1	0	10	1.17	1.17		13.3%	33.3%	3.3%	18.8%	68.5%	56.8%	35.2%	48.0%	.267	.562	97	0.1
	MIN	MLB	27	11 (0)	17¹	0-1	0	16	1.38	6.23	45.9%	13.3%	21.3%	6.7%	37.5%	62.7%	82.3%	26.4%	62.7%	.209	.681	107	0.1
C.J. Culpepper	FTM	A	21	11 (11)	46¹	4-3	0	53	1.01	2.33		8.3%	29.4%	1.1%	54.1%	66.4%	83.6%	36.7%	61.0%	.278	.355	63	1.2
	CR	A+	21	10 (10)	39²	2-2	0	36	1.41	4.99		9.0%	20.2%	1.1%	58.5%					.325	.449	93	0.4
José De León	STP	AAA	30	9 (4)	27¹	0-2	1	26	1.35	3.62		10.3%	22.2%	1.7%	41.0%	57.5%	83.5%	27.2%	50.8%	.303	.487	107	0.3
	MIN	MLB	30	12 (1)	17¹	0-1	0	17	1.21	4.67	49.6%	7.1%	24.3%	2.9%	40.4%	68.3%	83.3%	30.4%	57.1%	.311	.489	95	0.3
Randy Dobnak	STP	AAA	28	31 (26)	126¹	5-9	1	115	1.65	5.13		10.7%	20.2%	2.1%	45.6%	63.9%	85.8%	29.6%	55.4%	.362	.578	102	1.7
Brent Headrick	STP	AAA	25	19 (12)	75	4-2	0	83	1.31	4.68		8.1%	25.9%	3.4%	37.7%	70.9%	80.2%	34.2%	60.3%	.311	.583	88	1.5
	MIN	MLB	25	14 (0)	25²	3-0	1	30	1.44	6.31	50.4%	8.5%	25.9%	6.0%	17.8%	66.7%	83.1%	34.2%	63.5%	.303	.803	109	0.2
Ronny Henriquez	STP	AAA	23	37 (0)	57	5-3	1	49	1.58	5.68		13.7%	18.7%	2.3%	47.7%	74.2%	79.0%	31.4%	57.4%	.287	.477	97	0.9
Ryan Jensen	TNS	AA	25	14 (6)	32¹	2-5	0	40	1.79	5.57		14.5%	26.3%	2.6%	53.9%					.376	.602	90	0.4
	TAC	AAA	25	13 (0)	11¹	0-1	1	12	1.50	3.18		16.0%	24.0%	0.0%	40.0%	63.5%	79.6%	24.6%	68.6%	.300	.367	79	
	IOW	AAA	25	16 (0)	20²	0-2	0	26	2.03	6.10		22.0%	23.9%	1.8%	50.9%	61.8%	75.7%	23.8%	52.2%	.302	.545	104	0.3
Dallas Keuchel	STP	AAA	35	6 (6)	32	1-0	0	28	1.25	1.13		9.1%	21.2%	2.3%	62.0%	64.4%	79.3%	34.1%	53.5%	.281	.435	85	0.7
	MIN	MLB	35	10 (6)	37²	2-1	0	25	1.67	5.97	40.8%	10.5%	14.5%	1.7%	53.5%	64.3%	91.2%	31.9%	68.3%	.339	.548	123	0.0
Cole Sands	STP	AAA	25	19 (0)	30²	0-2	4	41	0.88	1.47		8.4%	34.5%	1.7%	44.1%	62.4%	76.4%	35.0%	51.0%	.227	.397	78	0.8
	MIN	MLB	25	15 (0)	21²	0-0	0	21	1.52	3.74	47.6%	13.3%	21.4%	4.1%	39.1%	63.3%	91.1%	28.5%	64.7%	.267	.578	111	0.1
Josh Staumont	KC	MLB	29	21 (1)	20	0-0	0	24	1.45	5.40	46.9%	14.6%	27.0%	1.1%	49.0%	70.6%	79.2%	30.4%	62.1%	.313	.429	95	0.3
Josh Winder	STP	AAA	26	18 (0)	30²	5-3	2	39	1.89	6.16		13.0%	26.7%	3.4%	46.0%	64.2%	76.5%	31.9%	44.5%	.415	.767	91	0.6
	MIN	MLB	26	19 (0)	34²	2-1	1	28	1.41	4.15	48.0%	9.5%	19.0%	2.0%	41.0%	74.2%	90.1%	32.2%	64.5%	.314	.553	107	0.3
Simeon Woods Richardson	STP	AAA	22	24 (22)	113²	7-6	0	96	1.50	4.91		12.3%	19.3%	2.6%	42.2%	68.9%	80.0%	29.7%	60.5%	.295	.543	101	1.5
	MIN	MLB	22	1 (0)	4²	0-0	0	5	2.14	9.64	47.2%	12.5%	20.8%	4.2%	37.5%	75.6%	93.5%	28.6%	68.8%	.429	.800	95	0.1

Elbow injuries have limited **Jorge Alcala** to very little work over the last two seasons, but his fastball-slider combo is still well clear of even increased modern standards. ⓧ He didn't make it back onto a mound in a competitive setting in 2023, so **Matt Canterino** enters 2024 just hoping to demonstrate that he can still overwhelm and overpower hitters when healthy. ⓧ The Twins have to be delighted with 2022 13th-rounder and breakout arm **C.J. Culpepper**, even if he's very unlikely to end up as the most notable slinger in Minnesota history with that surname. ⓧ Like an immortal trying to hide well enough in plain sight not to be captured and tortured by townsfolk, **José De León** tries to stay just below the detection radar of the Agents of Jobe. Alas, they got their scalpels into him again. ⓧ It's strange to think about a strained finger derailing a pitching career. How would you even go about avoiding one? And if you figure that out, could you please tell **Randy Dobnak**? ⓧ Crossfire southpaw **Brent Headrick** racks up strikeouts and limits walks, but has worse homer problems than early-seasons Marge Simpson. ⓧ Slider slinger **Ronny Henriquez** found more whiffs and the ability to land his breaking ball in the zone over the final two months in Triple-A, but it's far from guaranteed that his results are transferable to the majors. ⓧ Former Cubs first-rounder **Ryan Jensen**'s command struggles banished him first to the bullpen, then to waivers, where Seattle scooped him up as yet another reclamation project with draft pedigree. The 6-foot right-hander still throws the baseball quite hard without much clue where it's going, but it's no surprise the Mariners were the team eager to transform his crude arsenal into something more useful. ⓧ How many Cy Young winners have gone on to become lineouts in later Annuals? Technically, we're the ones making **Dallas Keuchel** an answer to that trivia question, but mostly, it was Keuchel who did so—with guile, a relentless competitive drive, and absolutely no actual stuff left to support either. ⓧ The Twins were only able to land **Connor Prielipp** in the second round in 2022 because of one Tommy John surgery, so they can't curse the baseball gods too sternly in the wake of his second one. He's allowed to, though. ⓧ His name sounds like a terrible idea for harvesting more fossil fuels, but in fact, **Cole Sands** is a decent little environmental initiative for a bullpen: He's the forgettable but durable guy who protects better pitchers from overuse. ⓧ 6-foot-3 reliever-only, fresh out of toxic relationship, seeks new team to learn and grow with. I have a triple-digit fastball, you have a coaching staff fluent in solving command issues. Must be okay with dogs, long hair, and TOS. No smokers or guys named John. - **Josh Staumont**'s personal ad, probably. ⓧ So far, neither a slide across the rubber nor a slide into the bullpen has allowed **Josh Winder** to turn a promising slider into a promising overall performance. Maybe the sinker he debuted in August will pair with it well enough. ⓧ Former top prospect **Simeon Woods Richardson** tried reinventing himself with a high-rise cutter thrown high over the top, but he needs about three more ticks on it to regain relevance.

NEW YORK METS

Essay by Ben Carsley

Player comments by Lucas Apostoleris and BP staff

"The expectations were really high this year, and my guess is next year will be a lot lower. But I can't speak to what's going to happen in the offseason...I'm opportunistic...But we also know that spending a fortune...doesn't guarantee you a trip to the playoffs...Hope's not a strategy."

Such was the message Steve Cohen delivered to a group of reporters on August 2, shortly after the dismantling of a 2023 Mets team that began the year with World Series aspirations and ended it with the fourth-worst record in the National League. It followed one hell of a Max Scherzer curveball, dropped via Ken Rosenthal: Scherzer had waived his no-trade clause upon being informed by Cohen and Billy Eppler that the Mets were backing away from their all-in approach and toward a "transitory year." If Scherzer wanted one last, best chance to win, he should want out of Queens.

Cohen's assessments—both to Scherzer and the public—were fair, if foreboding. The Mets spent big, shot for the moon and came up short. Rather than double down on an aging, top-heavy, injury-prone and *very* expensive roster—the priciest one in baseball history, at about $330 million for the Opening Day group alone—the organization needed to regroup to better position itself to achieve lasting, yearly relevance.

At face value, Cohen was doing little more than describing roster-building 101, an approach any armchair GM could appreciate. But his proclamation came amidst an era of baseball in which fans—and especially Mets fans—are justifiably prone to cynicism. For years, obscenely rich owners have cried poor as they've stripped their teams to the bones, saving money in the short-term while grifting on the promise of evergreen convention cycles that, most often, never materialize.

To some, Cohen's words begat a blend of *déjà vu*, ennui and malaise uniquely Metsian in its composition, but familiar to anyone who's had billionaires tell them: *I'm going to stop spending my money for you now, but you should keep spending yours for me.* Recent history suggested that this "transitory year" would see the LOLMets cycle begin anew as

NEW YORK METS PROSPECTUS
2023 W-L: 75-87, 4TH IN NL EAST

Pythag	.492	15th	DER	.695	17th
RS/G	4.43	20th	DRC+	103	8th
RA/G	4.50	18th	DRA-	103	20th
dWin%	.506	17th	FIP	4.49	23rd
Payroll	$331M	1st	B-Age	29.4	24th
M$/MW	$11.7M	27th	P-Age	32.2	30th

408'

379'　　　　370'

335'　　　　330'

- Opened 2009
- Open air
- Natural surface
- Fence profile: 8'

Park Factors

Runs	Runs/RH	Runs/LH	HR/RH	HR/LH
101	99	104	99	103

Top Hitter WARP	4.4 Brandon Nimmo
Top Pitcher WARP	2.6 Kodai Senga
2023 Top Prospect	Jett Williams

Payroll History (in millions)

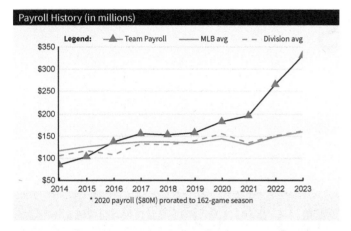

Legend: ▲ Team Payroll — MLB avg - - Division avg

* 2020 payroll ($80M) prorated to 162-game season

Future Commitments (in millions)

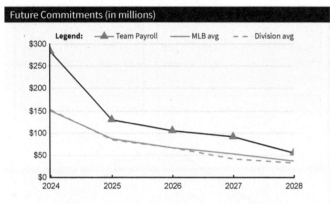

Legend: ▲ Team Payroll — MLB avg - - Division avg

Farm System Ranking

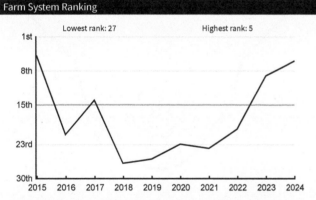

Lowest rank: 27   Highest rank: 5

Personnel

President, Baseball Operations
David Stearns

Senior Vice President, Baseball Operations
Jonathan Strangio

VP & Assistant General Manager, Baseball Operations
Ian Levin

VP & Assistant General Manager, Baseball Analytics
Ben Zauzmer

Vice President, International & Amateur Scouting
Tommy Tanous

Manager
Carlos Mendoza

BP Alumni
Tatiana DeRouen

the franchise once more inverted the myth of the phoenix, not rising from its ashes but collapsing in embers as soon as it threatened to take form.

And yet, despite all the events and entities involved that lend cause for concern—a billionaire owner lamenting sunk costs, an exodus of talent, a comically bad season and, chiefly, that all this is happening to the *New York Frickin' Mets*—an objective analysis of most of what's transpired from the trade deadline to present day should lead to a feeling far less familiar to most Mets faithful—guarded optimism. For the first time since becoming principal owner of the Mets, Cohen is taking steps toward his long-rumored dream of building the "East Coast Dodgers" through means other than writing blank checks to star players...though he's still trying to do that, too. (The Mets came up just short in the Yoshinobu Yamamoto sweepstakes, reportedly offering the potential ace over $300 million.) He's now building the infrastructure that should allow said check-writing to be far more impactful.

Though the Mets have lost three future Hall of Famers since July—two from their rotation and one from their clubhouse—their most impactful personnel change as they chart this new course came from the September hiring of former Brewers shot-caller David Stearns as president of baseball operations. It brought closure to a long-rumored dalliance between Cohen and Stearns, a Manhattan native who'd worked for the Mets earlier in his career. It also brought an end to Eppler's run within the organization; the former GM resigned in October as news broke that he was under investigation by MLB for reasons yet to be disclosed.

At the risk of encouraging the sport's continued fetishization of Theo Epstein types, Stearns' record as a baseball executive is inarguably impressive. Made the youngest GM in baseball at age 30 in 2015, Stearns orchestrated a dramatic overhaul of the Brewers organization. By 2018, he'd constructed a team that fell one win short of the World Series, and that would go on to make the playoffs five times in the next six years. It's one thing to grab another Ivy League grad, slap him on the hood and declare, "this baby can fit so many analytics in it." It's another to land the exemplar of the archetype. Stearns' hiring is especially refreshing given that, pending the results of Eppler's investigation, Brodie Van Wagenen may be the *least* embarrassing of the Mets' previous four front office leaders.

It's early days in Stearns' tenure, and, with all due respect to Joey Wendle, Luis Severino, Adrian Houser and Harrison Bader, we've yet to truly see his vision for the organization's major-league roster. He's wasted no time, however, in revamping its scouting and player development departments. Notable additions include Eduardo Brizuela, a top Stearns lieutenant in Milwaukee; Kris Gross, longtime scouting director for the Astros; and Andy Green, the former Cubs' bench coach. They'll join holdovers like Tommy Tanous and Drew Toussaint to form one of the more impressive collections of front office talent this side of Los Angeles.

Stearns also enacted change in the clubhouse, firing Buck Showalter at the season's end after a calamitous year in which the Mets underperformed PECOTA win projections by 12 games. To replace him as the fifth Mets manager of the last seven years, Stearns reportedly first tried for his former field general, Craig Conunsell, before shifting to Yankees bench coach Carlos Mendoza. Though not a household name, Mendoza filled a variety of roles in the Bronx over the course of seven years and, not coincidentally, boasts experience in player development. He'll be supported by new bench coach John Gibbons, ensuring that, in Showalter's absence, at least one sexagenerian will remain to glower at youths from the dugout, complain about spreadsheets and occasionally snip at the media.

Mendoza and Gibbons are now tasked with overseeing a team still laden with star power and high-priced veterans, yet built to facilitate the incorporation of younger, homegrown talent. Few teams figure to feature such dramatically top-heavy rosters in 2024 as the Mets, who must lick their wounds as they push through a year in which they'll pay nearly $50 million to three players—Scherzer, Justin Verlander and James McCann—who are no longer on the roster. (And another $1.4 million to Bobby Bonilla and Bret Saberhagen; perhaps some LOLMets DNA remains.)

The good news? While the '24 Mets won't win any $/WARP contests, a promising offensive nucleus remains. Francisco Lindor finished fifth among major-league shortstops in DRC+ and remains one of the game's better all-around players as he enters his age-30 season. Brandon Nimmo responded to his long-term deal by posting the second-best offensive season of his career. Despite a dramatic decline in batting average, Pete Alonso finished as a top-10 first baseman offensively, generating nearly as many extra-base hits as sullen headlines about his future. Is it a sign of measured roster-building that those three, plus Jeff McNeil, Omar Narváez and Starling Marte, will likely combine to earn north of $110 million this season? Perhaps not, but it's a group that should help the Mets score runs nonetheless.

Barring some offseason surprises, they'll be flanked by a collection of young position players that already cut its collective teeth in the bigs thanks to New York's veteran exodus last summer. Francisco Alvarez entered last year as BP's fourth-ranked overall prospect, then slugged the second-most homers of any primary catcher. While his batting average and strikeout rate may be "giving Gary Sánchez," as the kids would say, his season was quite promising. Fresh off an encouraging stint in Triple-A, fellow 22-year-old Ronny Mauricio flashed the tools that could make him an everyday regular with upside as an infielder, though a torn ACL suffered in winter ball will delay his ascension. Rookie third baseman Brett Baty also impressed in April before blissfully retiring for the remainder of the season, lending absolutely no cause for anyone to look up his statistics from May onward.

It's to Stearns' benefit he inherited a roster with offensive talent and promise intact, as there's substantial work to be done to the pitching staff. Among the 12 players who logged the most innings for the Mets last year, five—Verlander, Scherzer, Carlos Carrasco, David Robertson and Adam Ottavino—are no longer on the roster. Several who remain, such as Tylor Megill, Drew Smith and Joey Lucchesi, are coming off performances that put their long-term futures with the club in doubt.

Still, the cupboard in the arm barn is not entirely bare. Last winter's shopping spree netted Kodai Senga, who greatly impressed in his first tour of duty stateside, pacing Mets pitchers in WARP en route to finishing second in the NL Rookie of the Year vote. He'll front a rotation that features Houser, David Peterson, José Quintana and the newly inked Severino, poached from the cross-town Yankees on a one-year, $13 million boy-I-hope-you-rebound deal. The bullpen should benefit from the return of all-world closer Edwin Díaz, who missed all of last season with a torn patellar tendon suffered in the World Baseball Classic that, in hindsight, was an omen straight from the baseball gods. There's less short-term pitching help on the farm than the lineup boasts, but if Stearns proved he can do one thing during his time in Milwaukee, it's unearth and develop live arms.

The Mets are left with the core of a roster not too dissimilar in talent level from many of the Wild Card hopefuls around the league. Perhaps Stearns will tear it all down in time, but his early actions and Cohen's words suggest that the Mets will instead do the unthinkable: They will stay watchable and relevant even as they regroup for the future. Not only is that what the fanbase of any major-league team deserves, but it lends further credence to the notion that this organization is on a promising path.

When owners infer that they want to be the next Dodgers—or "the East Coast Dodgers," as Cohen purportedly desires—it's important to understand what they *really* mean. That they want to be perennially competitive, yes, but specifically via an inexhaustible pipeline of cheap, young talent that allows them to flex financial might if and when they choose.

Yet, a large part of what's made the Dodgers successful has been their willingness to pay for mistakes in cold, hard cash, rather than in talent or time. Since assuming control of the Dodgers' front office in late 2014, Andrew Friedman and company have swung and missed on player deals or acquisitions several times—Trevor Bauer, AJ Pollock, nearly a dozen failed pitching reclamation projects—yet have often eaten those sunk costs rather than allowing them to serve as anchors in future years. They've also leveraged their financial power to prey off the mistakes of others, like when they purposely acquired Homer Bailey to net prospects, or when they absorbed David Price's bloated contract in order to acquire Mookie Betts.

Even before Stearns' hiring, we saw the Mets begin to operate similarly last summer, when the way in which they shed their veterans suggested an emphasis on talent acquisition rather than financial relief. In eating about $35 million of the $58 million due to Scherzer through 2024, the Mets pried Luisangel Acuña, a top-100 prospect, from the Rangers. By absorbing more than $50 million of what's owed to Verlander through this season, they netted two of Houston's top-five prospects in Drew Gilbert and Ryan Clifford. Marco Vargas, acquired as part of the Robertson return from the Marlins, is also highly regarded in Extremely Online Scouting Circles.

Part of becoming Dodgers East also means using your resources to land true top-of-the-market talent. Though Cohen has spent lavishly in his time, he's swung and missed on some notable names the past two offseason. His mega-deal with Carlos Correa fell through due to medical concerns. He sat out the Aaron Judge and Shohei Ohtani sweepstakes. He also failed to sign former NPB ace Yoshinobu Yamamoto, losing out to Los Angeles on a 12-year, $325 million deal he reportedly matched, but for naught. Perhaps a leap of faith is required to believe Cohen can land the crown jewel of a free agent class, but it ought to be a small leap given the star-caliber players he's accumulated in his tenure. Plus, the Mets missing out on Yamamoto still leaves two very Dodgers-esque paths in front of them: They can reallocate some of that money on short-term, high-AAV deals to try and raise their roster's floor, or they can prepare to make a godfather offer to Juan Soto, prying a different generational talent from a cross-town rival.

Either way, the moves the Mets *did* make this winter, as much as the Stearns hiring or anything that's followed, clue us in as to where Cohen's "transitory year" falls within baseball's exhaustive lexicon of nebulous team-building jargon. A transitory year, it would seem, is far more palatable than the half-decades (or longer) "rebuilds" in fashion among owners praying to hit on the 400-leg parlay required to become The Next Astros. It's cleaner than the cross-town "retools" that've led to the average age of a New York Yankee landing at 57. It's more defined than the "bridge years" to nowhere in Boston, and more ambitious than Seattle's desire to "sustainably" win 54% of the time. It's more realistic than

the Sisyphean "retooling" in Anaheim, and more flexible than the slavish devotion to "achieving stability" that's paralyzed the shot-callers in San Francisco.

In truth, *this* is what building The Next Dodgers looks like. You hire the best people. You pay up, even when it's not sexy to do so. You take big swings, and when you get burned, you keep on swinging. You chase Correa one off-season and Yamamoto the next, but then you don't panic when you come up short. You invest in your farm system, to be sure, but to *enhance* your big-league roster—not solely to replace it. And you realize that you don't have to take 10 steps back to take a half-step forward.

Even now, in the face of substantial evidence that the organization is trending in the right direction, it can be hard to buy into the vision. Mets fans can't unlearn what the last decade of baseball—and baseball in Queens, in particular—have taught them. Believing that the Mets are on a good path requires taking the words of a billionaire ex-hedge fund manager and unwitting meme stock victim in good faith. It necessitates making peace with a roster that just lost two of the best pitchers of a generation. It means believing in Yet Another Ivy League Front Office Nerd. It means trusting that, maybe this time, the prospects won't break your heart. It means acknowledging that good things could be in store for the *New York Frickin' Mets*.

But really, if you're a Mets fan, what more do you have to lose? You can believe the same old LOLMets still lurk around the corner. Or you can look at this offseason, see the trajectory of the club, and recall what *else* Cohen told us last August:

> *"I don't want to roll a team out there that we're gonna be embarrassed by...We got our core. The baby Mets are going to be a year older...I'm not as negative. It won't be as star-studded a team as it was, but stars don't necessarily make for wins. I think we're going to be highly competitive."*

—Ben Carsley is an author of Baseball Prospectus.

HITTERS

★ ★ ★ *2024 Top 101 Prospect* **#77** ★ ★ ★

Luisangel Acuña SS   Born: 03/12/02   Age: 22   Bats: R   Throws: R   Height: 5'8"   Weight: 181   Origin: IFA, 2018

YEAR	TM	LVL	AGE	PA	R	HR	RBI	SB	AVG/OBP/SLG	BABIP	SLGCON	BB%	K%	ZSw%	ZCon%	OSw%	OCon%	LA	90th EV	DRC+	BRR	DRP	WARP
2021	DE	A	19	473	77	12	74	44	.266/.345/.404	.329	.551	10.4%	23.3%							106	1.9	2.5	2.1
2022	HIC	A+	20	240	45	8	29	28	.317/.417/.483	.416	.683	14.2%	25.0%							108	2.0	-2.3	1.0
2022	FRI	AA	20	169	21	3	18	12	.224/.302/.349	.274	.457	10.1%	21.3%							89	1.1	1.6	0.5
2023	BNG	AA	21	167	25	2	12	15	.243/.317/.304	.288	.381	9.0%	18.0%							91	1.4	0.4	0.6
2023	FRI	AA	21	402	68	7	51	42	.315/.377/.453	.381	.573	9.2%	18.9%							91	6.6	-0.6	1.4
2024 non	NYM	MLB	22	251	22	3	22	15	.233/.295/.333	.298	.445	7.4%	23.1%							79	0.0	0	0.2

2023 GP: SS (92), 2B (18), DH (10), CF (4)   Comps: Jorge Polanco (75), Alen Hanson (68), Alcides Escobar (66)

Last year, Acuña and his older brother, the eventual NL MVP, made a bet: whoever stole more bases in 2023 would owe the other $5,000. Though Ronald won this wager handily, 57 stolen bags from the younger Acuña is nothing to scoff at, and speed is a big part of both brothers' playbook. Hopes are high for Luisangel, who in addition to his proclivity for base thievery has shown a strong hit tool, good defense up the middle, and a high baseball IQ. He won't sock as many dingers as his more famous sibling, but he's an exciting player who could make an impact either as a middle infielder or in center field.

Pete Alonso 1B Born: 12/07/94 Age: 29 Bats: R Throws: R Height: 6'3" Weight: 245 Origin: Round 2, 2016 Draft (#64 overall)

YEAR	TM	LVL	AGE	PA	R	HR	RBI	SB	AVG/OBP/SLG	BABIP	SLGCON	BB%	K%	ZSw%	ZCon%	OSw%	OCon%	LA	90th EV	DRC+	BRR	DRP	WARP
2021	NYM	MLB	26	637	81	37	94	3	.262/.344/.519	.274	.671	9.4%	19.9%	71.2%	85.6%	36.1%	62.6%	14.9	110.0	137	-0.2	0.4	4.4
2022	NYM	MLB	27	685	95	40	131	5	.271/.352/.518	.279	.659	9.8%	18.7%	72.3%	85.4%	36.3%	64.5%	18.2	109.0	138	-0.3	-0.7	4.5
2023	NYM	MLB	28	658	92	46	118	4	.217/.318/.504	.205	.686	9.9%	22.9%	64.2%	82.9%	29.6%	60.4%	18.2	108.9	132	-0.1	-1.6	3.8
2024 DC	NYM	MLB	29	620	86	35	97	3	.249/.340/.494	.265	.653	9.9%	21.3%							133	-0.4	-0.6	3.7

2023 GP: 1B (144), DH (9)   *Comps: Boog Powell (80), Tony Clark (78), Richie Sexson (78)*

Since making his debut on Opening Day in 2019, the Polar Bear has been a steady presence in the Mets' lineup, appearing in almost 97% of his team's games over the past five seasons. What's more recently taken on a steady presence is the plethora of rumors surrounding Alonso's long-term future with the team. Will he be traded? Will he sign an extension? Despite the team's on-field disappointments in 2023, the Mets haven't seemed terribly interested in shipping Alonso off for a prospect package, though there also hasn't been much traction on an extension. As for his on-the-field production, the concerns over his career-worst batting average could be assuaged somewhat by more encouraging under-the-hood numbers, as his DRC and Statcast "expected" marks were right in line with his norms.

Francisco Alvarez C Born: 11/19/01 Age: 22 Bats: R Throws: R Height: 5'10" Weight: 233 Origin: IFA, 2018

YEAR	TM	LVL	AGE	PA	R	HR	RBI	SB	AVG/OBP/SLG	BABIP	SLGCON	BB%	K%	ZSw%	ZCon%	OSw%	OCon%	LA	90th EV	DRC+	BRR	DRP	WARP
2021	SLU	A	19	67	12	2	12	2	.417/.567/.646	.450	.756	22.4%	10.4%	72.2%	82.7%	28.4%	67.4%			143	0.1	-1.7	0.4
2021	BRK	A+	19	333	55	22	58	6	.247/.351/.538	.260	.761	12.0%	24.6%							154	0.8	-7.5	2.5
2022	BNG	AA	20	296	43	18	47	0	.277/.368/.553	.310	.769	12.2%	24.0%							115	-1.0	0.9	1.4
2022	SYR	AAA	20	199	31	9	31	0	.234/.382/.443	.283	.660	17.1%	26.1%	72.4%	71.4%	33.9%	28.6%			109	0.1	0.6	0.8
2022	NYM	MLB	20	14	3	1	1	0	.167/.286/.500	.143	.750	14.3%	28.6%	86.7%	92.3%	38.6%	35.3%	15.5	108.9	97	0.0	0.0	0.0
2023	NYM	MLB	21	423	51	25	63	2	.209/.284/.437	.222	.614	8.0%	26.0%	68.7%	81.4%	31.2%	51.6%	12.7	106.8	90	-0.6	10.1	2.0
2024 DC	NYM	MLB	22	463	55	20	61	1	.235/.314/.428	.292	.621	9.0%	27.9%							109	-0.6	10.5	3.2

2023 GP: C (108), DH (7)   *Comps: Freddie Freeman (44), Dilson Herrera (43), Willie Greene (41)*

In the history of the American and National Leagues, there has only been one catcher aged 21 or younger that hit more home runs than Alvarez did last year, and that was Johnny Bench in 1969—maybe you've heard of that guy? Sure, his team would love to see his average move further and further away from the Mendoza line, but there's a lot to like about what Alvarez brings to the table, including his improved receiving skills. In case you've forgotten over the last two sentences, he was only 21 last year, and plenty of room for development. The Mets and their fans have been waiting so long (since Gary Carter?) for a long-term answer at catcher, now they've finally caught a glimpse of that potential future.

YEAR	TM	P. COUNT	FRM RUNS	BLK RUNS	THRW RUNS	TOT RUNS
2021	SLU	1391	-1.3	-0.2	-0.3	-1.8
2021	BRK	6961	-6.7	-1.2	1.0	-6.8
2022	BNG	6924	0.1	0.1	1.0	1.2
2022	SYR	4873	-1.0	-0.2	1.8	0.6
2022	NYM	190	0.0	0.0	0.0	0.0
2023	NYM	15019	14.2	0.0	-0.6	13.6
2024	NYM	14430	11.5	-0.1	-1.0	10.4

Harrison Bader CF Born: 06/03/94 Age: 30 Bats: R Throws: R Height: 6'0" Weight: 210 Origin: Round 3, 2015 Draft (#100 overall)

YEAR	TM	LVL	AGE	PA	R	HR	RBI	SB	AVG/OBP/SLG	BABIP	SLGCON	BB%	K%	ZSw%	ZCon%	OSw%	OCon%	LA	90th EV	DRC+	BRR	DRP	WARP
2021	STL	MLB	27	401	45	16	50	9	.267/.324/.460	.306	.599	6.7%	21.2%	64.3%	87.1%	34.5%	59.1%	13.9	103.8	89	0.1	4.8	1.7
2022	STL	MLB	28	264	35	5	21	15	.256/.303/.370	.297	.457	4.9%	17.8%	63.1%	92.2%	36.1%	62.8%	17.5	101.7	87	1.0	2.6	0.9
2022	NYY	MLB	28	49	3	0	9	2	.217/.245/.283	.313	.419	4.1%	30.6%	69.7%	89.1%	38.2%	52.4%	13.9	100.8	91	0.0	0.2	0.1
2023	CIN	MLB	29	34	4	0	3	3	.161/.235/.194	.179	.214	8.8%	8.8%	71.2%	95.2%	26.7%	80.0%	17.3	100.0	109	0.1	0.2	0.2
2023	NYY	MLB	29	310	40	7	37	17	.240/.278/.365	.271	.453	4.5%	18.1%	67.9%	88.4%	35.8%	54.7%	17.4	103.5	103	1.0	1.2	1.5
2024 DC	NYM	MLB	30	352	33	8	36	17	.243/.298/.365	.292	.469	6.0%	20.8%							88	0.4	1.9	0.9

2023 GP: CF (95), DH (1)   *Comps: Carlos Gómez (72), Torii Hunter (70), B.J. Upton (66)*

After the Yankees waived the white flag on their 2023, Bader joined the Reds in late August as a waiver claim along with Hunter Renfroe. Oblique and hamstring strains kept him out of New York's lineup for the better part of two months combined, but Bader didn't hit much when available and didn't play his usually excellent defense according to some metrics. Like Renfroe, Bader played just 14 games with the Reds and posted an OPS under .450; he was shut down in mid-September with a groin strain. Lower-half injuries for players who make their living on speed and defense are unnerving, but the 29-year-old had a full offseason to heal up and look for a fresh start with a new club.

Brett Baty 3B/OF Born: 11/13/99 Age: 24 Bats: L Throws: R Height: 6'3" Weight: 210 Origin: Round 1, 2019 Draft (#12 overall)

YEAR	TM	LVL	AGE	PA	R	HR	RBI	SB	AVG/OBP/SLG	BABIP	SLGCON	BB%	K%	ZSw%	ZCon%	OSw%	OCon%	LA	90th EV	DRC+	BRR	DRP	WARP
2021	SRR	WIN	21	102	16	1	15	1	.292/.373/.404	.431	.621	10.8%	30.4%	65.8%	88.0%	25.6%	42.4%						
2021	BRK	A+	21	209	27	7	34	4	.309/.397/.514	.402	.727	11.5%	25.4%							118	-0.3	6.3	1.6
2021	BNG	AA	21	176	16	5	22	2	.272/.364/.424	.350	.604	12.5%	25.6%							91	0.0	0.6	0.4
2022	BNG	AA	22	394	73	19	59	2	.312/.406/.544	.390	.764	11.7%	24.9%							128	0.0	-1.0	2.2
2022	SYR	AAA	22	26	3	0	1	0	.364/.462/.364	.500	.500	11.5%	23.1%							99	-0.3	1.3	0.2
2022	NYM	MLB	22	42	4	2	5	0	.184/.244/.342	.179	.433	4.8%	19.0%	71.9%	91.3%	31.7%	50.0%	10.0	104.2	93	0.0	-0.2	0.0
2023	SYR	AAA	23	121	20	10	31	2	.298/.388/.625	.318	.867	13.2%	24.0%	69.3%	77.6%	27.5%	52.4%			115	-0.2	-0.2	0.5
2023	NYM	MLB	23	389	41	9	34	2	.212/.275/.323	.280	.467	7.5%	28.0%	66.2%	80.6%	30.8%	49.1%	7.0	107.6	79	0.0	-4.5	-0.2
2024 DC	NYM	MLB	24	442	46	12	48	4	.239/.314/.383	.324	.562	8.5%	28.7%							95	-0.3	-4.5	0.4

2023 GP: 3B (100), DH (4), LF (1)   *Comps: Abraham Toro (69), Andy LaRoche (62), Rio Ruiz (60)*

The Mets' decision to leave Baty off their Opening Day roster was met with a lot of … well, I guess the word "outrage" would apply here. Baty entered the season as one of the team's more exciting prospects in recent memory, and a strong spring—during which he hit for an .885 OPS across 50 plate appearances—seemed to give him a leg up on the third base job out of camp. He was ultimately recalled in mid-April to replace a struggling Eduardo Escobar, but his performance was anything but confidence-inspiring: He struggled so much that he was returned to Triple-A Syracuse in August as a "reset," according to manager Buck Showalter. He returned to the majors with the expanded rosters at the start of September, but his performance from then-on—a .514 OPS—was even worse than the paltry numbers he'd put up before. Between his inability to loft the ball and unspectacular defense, Baty will need to make big improvements across the board or the fans' anger will be directed at him, rather than the team's front office.

★ ★ ★ *2024 Top 101 Prospect* **#76** ★ ★ ★

Ryan Clifford 1B Born: 07/20/03 Age: 20 Bats: L Throws: L Height: 6'3" Weight: 200 Origin: Round 11, 2022 Draft (#343 overall)

YEAR	TM	LVL	AGE	PA	R	HR	RBI	SB	AVG/OBP/SLG	BABIP	SLGCON	BB%	K%	ZSw%	ZCon%	OSw%	OCon%	LA	90th EV	DRC+	BRR	DRP	WARP
2022	ASO	ROK	18	50	8	1	5	2	.222/.440/.389	.368	.700	24.0%	32.0%										
2022	FAY	A	18	51	5	1	5	0	.268/.412/.390	.400	.615	19.6%	29.4%							101	-0.2	0.8	0.2
2023	FAY	A	19	121	22	2	15	3	.337/.488/.457	.453	.646	20.7%	22.3%							136	-0.4	2.3	1.0
2023	ASH	A+	19	250	35	16	46	1	.271/.356/.547	.298	.770	8.4%	24.8%							116	-1.0	-1.8	0.9
2023	BRK	A+	19	140	13	6	20	1	.188/.307/.376	.258	.667	12.9%	36.4%							93	-0.7	1.6	0.3
2024 non	NYM	MLB	20	251	24	5	25	0	.226/.299/.348	.313	.516	8.3%	29.7%							83	0.0	0	0.0

2023 GP: 1B (52), RF (29), LF (26), DH (10) Comps: Chris Marrero (63), Jake Bauers (58), Randal Grichuk (58)

Coming over from Houston as the second prospect in the midseason Justin Verlander trade, Clifford has a lot of power in his bat (check out his minor-league damage rates) and has also shown an ability to take walks. He'll strike out his fair share and be somewhat limited defensively—he has experience in both outfield corners, but spent the plurality of his innings in both the Astros' and Mets' organizations last year at first base. Nevertheless, his significant offensive potential could make the Mets' ill-fated Verlander signing look wise in time.

Stanley Consuegra RF Born: 09/24/00 Age: 23 Bats: R Throws: R Height: 6'2" Weight: 167 Origin: IFA, 2017

YEAR	TM	LVL	AGE	PA	R	HR	RBI	SB	AVG/OBP/SLG	BABIP	SLGCON	BB%	K%	ZSw%	ZCon%	OSw%	OCon%	LA	90th EV	DRC+	BRR	DRP	WARP
2021	MET	ROK	20	83	10	2	10	3	.270/.325/.500	.340	.698	4.8%	25.3%									0.7	
2022	SLU	A	21	287	38	8	32	8	.251/.324/.431	.324	.618	9.1%	26.8%	75.5%	81.0%	34.8%	43.1%			100	-1.8	6.4	1.2
2022	BRK	A+	21	249	33	5	27	4	.239/.309/.381	.308	.524	7.2%	24.9%							90	-1.9	1.9	0.5
2023	BRK	A+	22	394	52	23	63	6	.232/.294/.489	.262	.703	7.4%	27.7%							119	-2.6	5.7	2.2
2024 non	NYM	MLB	23	251	22	6	25	0	.211/.263/.345	.290	.516	5.6%	31.1%							70	0.0	0	-0.3

2023 GP: RF (76), DH (10), LF (7), CF (4) Comps: Alexander Palma (59), Isiah Gilliam (56), Francisco Caraballo (56)

Solidly in the "post-hype" phase of his development, Consuegra has finally started to tap into the tools that made him a notable prospect out of the Dominican Republic in the 2017-2018 international free agent signing period. His lack of plate discipline is concerning—as is the fact that he's only made it to High-A since making his professional debut in 2018—but his power spike suggests that he's finally able to transfer some of his raw skills into tangible results. Better to be a late-bloomer than to never flower at all.

★ ★ ★ *2024 Top 101 Prospect* **#29** ★ ★ ★

Drew Gilbert CF Born: 09/27/00 Age: 23 Bats: L Throws: L Height: 5'9" Weight: 195 Origin: Round 1, 2022 Draft (#28 overall)

YEAR	TM	LVL	AGE	PA	R	HR	RBI	SB	AVG/OBP/SLG	BABIP	SLGCON	BB%	K%	ZSw%	ZCon%	OSw%	OCon%	LA	90th EV	DRC+	BRR	DRP	WARP
2022	FAY	A	21	22	4	1	2	3	.238/.273/.381	.200	.381	4.5%	0.0%							122	-0.1	0.3	0.1
2023	ASH	A+	22	95	21	6	18	4	.360/.421/.686	.424	.908	6.3%	22.1%							122	-0.2	-1.9	0.4
2023	BNG	AA	22	154	22	6	21	2	.325/.423/.561	.378	.742	12.3%	19.5%							115	0.1	1.6	0.9
2023	CC	AA	22	264	36	6	20	6	.241/.342/.371	.277	.466	12.5%	17.4%							114	2.4	2.2	1.7
2024 DC	NYM	MLB	23	62	6	1	6	1	.230/.301/.353	.287	.465	7.9%	22.2%							82	0.0	0	0.0

2023 GP: CF (51), DH (29), RF (25), LF (12) Comps: Jackie Bradley Jr. (72), Forrest Wall (70), Christian Marrero (69)

Former Mets' general manager Billy Eppler had this to say about Gilbert after acquiring him from the Astros last summer: "He plays the game with his hair on fire." Inflammatory scalp or no, the Mets are thrilled with what they've seen so far from Gilbert, who turned his season around after a slow start to put together an impressive showing with his new team. In addition to an appealing combination of bat-to-ball skills, plate discipline, and power, Gilbert also spent time in all three outfield positions last season. There's a good chance we'll see him debut in Queens in 2024; look for the exciting outfielder with smoke coming out from under his cap.

Francisco Lindor SS Born: 11/14/93 Age: 30 Bats: S Throws: R Height: 5'11" Weight: 190 Origin: Round 1, 2011 Draft (#8 overall)

YEAR	TM	LVL	AGE	PA	R	HR	RBI	SB	AVG/OBP/SLG	BABIP	SLGCON	BB%	K%	ZSw%	ZCon%	OSw%	OCon%	LA	90th EV	DRC+	BRR	DRP	WARP
2021	NYM	MLB	27	524	73	20	63	10	.230/.322/.412	.248	.522	11.1%	18.3%	71.4%	85.9%	32.8%	64.7%	13.3	104.3	108	0.4	1.5	2.7
2022	NYM	MLB	28	706	98	26	107	16	.270/.339/.449	.301	.569	8.4%	18.8%	68.7%	87.3%	35.5%	65.4%	13.9	103.7	123	0.4	-3.1	4.0
2023	NYM	MLB	29	687	108	31	98	31	.254/.336/.470	.277	.609	9.6%	19.9%	72.1%	86.4%	33.8%	65.6%	19.2	104.6	115	1.3	-5.0	3.2
2024 DC	NYM	MLB	30	635	73	22	78	19	.250/.333/.426	.284	.537	9.5%	18.7%							112	0.6	-1.6	3.2

2023 GP: SS (158), DH (1)   *Comps: Jim Fregosi (80), Arky Vaughan (78), Joe Sewell (78)*

In October, the Mets announced that Lindor had recently undergone surgery to remove a bone spur in his right elbow, which had reportedly been bothering him since the beginning of the season. Since Statcast began tracking arm strength numbers in 2015—which conveniently aligns with Lindor's debut—his maximum throwing velocity (83.3 mph) last year was the lowest of his career, and it's a fair assumption that the elbow injury contributed to that. Despite the busted wing, last season was a reminder that Lindor is one of the finest ballplayers of his generation; he added his first career 30/30 season to his mantle while playing in all but two of his team's games, in spite of his elbow injury. Perhaps not as flashy as he was in his early years, he's now the steady centerpiece of a historically chaotic franchise.

Starling Marte RF Born: 10/09/88 Age: 35 Bats: R Throws: R Height: 6'1" Weight: 195 Origin: IFA, 2007

YEAR	TM	LVL	AGE	PA	R	HR	RBI	SB	AVG/OBP/SLG	BABIP	SLGCON	BB%	K%	ZSw%	ZCon%	OSw%	OCon%	LA	90th EV	DRC+	BRR	DRP	WARP
2021	MIA	MLB	32	275	52	7	25	22	.305/.405/.451	.376	.597	11.6%	20.7%	69.8%	86.5%	31.5%	59.0%	3.6	105.9	113	1.2	1.0	1.9
2021	OAK	MLB	32	251	37	5	30	25	.316/.359/.466	.367	.568	4.4%	16.7%	71.0%	84.8%	37.5%	62.8%	4.8	105.4	118	0.8	0.9	1.8
2022	NYM	MLB	33	505	76	16	63	18	.292/.347/.468	.340	.591	5.1%	19.2%	68.8%	85.4%	36.4%	63.5%	7.3	105.7	116	1.1	3.4	2.9
2023	NYM	MLB	34	341	38	5	28	24	.248/.301/.324	.303	.415	4.7%	20.2%	71.4%	85.3%	40.4%	56.0%	5.4	105.6	90	0.7	1.3	0.6
2024 DC	NYM	MLB	35	489	49	11	51	25	.261/.322/.385	.320	.503	6.0%	21.4%							102	0.7	1.5	1.6

2023 GP: RF (84), CF (1)   *Comps: Carlos Lee (70), Willie McGee (69), Max Carey (67)*

Over the course of his career, one of the defining aspects of Marte's game has been his speed. Unfortunately, the wear and tear on his body after over a decade in the big leagues might finally be taking their toll on his greatest asset. After the 2022 season, Marte underwent surgery on *both* groins—if you're confused, well, so were we—and his resulting performance in 2023 was anything but clarifying. His offensive production cratered and his diminished speed was a big red flag: Per Statcast's sprint speed metric, his average competitive run in 2023 was 27.1 feet per second, putting him below the league average for the first time in his career. Sure, we should expect this sort of thing to happen as a player gets into his mid-30s, but it's still hard to watch it happen to a former All-Star like Marte.

Ronny Mauricio 2B Born: 04/04/01 Age: 23 Bats: S Throws: R Height: 6'3" Weight: 166 Origin: IFA, 2017

YEAR	TM	LVL	AGE	PA	R	HR	RBI	SB	AVG/OBP/SLG	BABIP	SLGCON	BB%	K%	ZSw%	ZCon%	OSw%	OCon%	LA	90th EV	DRC+	BRR	DRP	WARP
2021	LIC	WIN	20	94	8	2	8	1	.244/.277/.367	.299	.478	3.2%	22.3%										
2021	BRK	A+	20	420	55	19	63	9	.242/.290/.449	.278	.605	5.7%	24.0%							115	0.1	10.9	3.0
2021	BNG	AA	20	33	3	1	1	2	.323/.364/.452	.474	.700	6.1%	33.3%							89	-0.3	-0.4	0.0
2022	LIC	WIN	21	203	26	5	31	10	.287/.335/.468	.348	.607	4.9%	21.2%										
2022	BNG	AA	21	541	71	26	89	20	.259/.296/.472	.293	.625	4.4%	23.1%							107	0.7	-7.5	1.5
2023	SYR	AAA	22	532	76	23	71	24	.292/.346/.506	.323	.631	6.6%	18.2%	69.2%	86.1%	37.7%	65.0%			110	-0.9	-3.7	1.7
2023	NYM	MLB	22	108	11	2	9	7	.248/.296/.347	.338	.500	6.5%	28.7%	70.2%	78.8%	46.5%	61.2%	7.8	106.3	83	0.2	0.0	0.1
2024 DC	NYM	MLB	23	63	6	2	7	2	.222/.266/.363	.271	.489	4.9%	23.6%							72	0.0	0	0.0

2023 GP: 2B (21), 3B (5), SS (2)   *Comps: Brendan Rodgers (69), Alexi Casilla (66), Ketel Marte (65)*

With Francisco Lindor locked in as the Mets' shortstop, the team finally decided to try out Mauricio elsewhere on the diamond. A career shortstop, Mauricio now moves around the infield and even added 200 innings of work in left field for Syracuse last year. The prospect shine has worn off, but there's thump in Mauricio's bat—you may recall that 117-mph double he hit in his debut that stood as the Mets' hardest-hit ball of the season—and his increased defensive versatility gives him a better chance to stick on the Mets' roster. Patience is advised both for this player and his fans: His walk rate needs work, and he'll miss a good chunk of 2024 after tearing his ACL in the Dominican Winter League.

Jeff McNeil UT Born: 04/08/92 Age: 32 Bats: L Throws: R Height: 6'1" Weight: 195 Origin: Round 12, 2013 Draft (#356 overall)

YEAR	TM	LVL	AGE	PA	R	HR	RBI	SB	AVG/OBP/SLG	BABIP	SLGCON	BB%	K%	ZSw%	ZCon%	OSw%	OCon%	LA	90th EV	DRC+	BRR	DRP	WARP
2021	NYM	MLB	29	426	48	7	35	3	.251/.319/.360	.280	.424	6.8%	13.6%	86.1%	88.7%	33.4%	68.5%	11.9	101.7	110	0.2	1.4	2.3
2022	NYM	MLB	30	589	73	9	62	4	.326/.382/.454	.353	.513	6.8%	10.4%	79.9%	87.1%	32.2%	77.9%	12.6	99.9	125	-0.3	1.0	3.7
2023	NYM	MLB	31	648	75	10	55	10	.270/.333/.378	.288	.425	6.0%	10.0%	76.9%	92.6%	33.5%	76.0%	13.8	100.0	106	0.2	2.1	2.6
2024 DC	NYM	MLB	32	573	58	9	57	4	.278/.344/.392	.304	.442	6.9%	10.4%							107	0.0	-0.1	2.1

2023 GP: 2B (107), RF (41), LF (32), CF (3), 1B (1), SS (1)   *Comps: Johnny Ray (72), Billy Goodman (71), Glenn Beckert (69)*

At this point, we know who Jeff McNeil is. He shows up, he won't strike out and you can pretty much put him anywhere in the field (he added an inning apiece at first base and shortstop last season—two spots he hadn't played since his minor-league days). He's reliable, but his performance really isn't. We've come a long way since the days of BABIP stats as some kind of be-all, end-all … but sometimes the hits fall and sometimes they don't. McNeil's batting average oscillation from "great" to "not great" to "great" to "not great" over the past four seasons comes across as a perfect example of how a player who relies on lots of medium-strength contact is particularly susceptible to the whims of the BABIP gods, even if their underlying skills don't change from one moment to the next.

Omar Narváez C   Born: 02/10/92   Age: 32   Bats: L   Throws: R   Height: 5'11"   Weight: 220   Origin: IFA, 2008

YEAR	TM	LVL	AGE	PA	R	HR	RBI	SB	AVG/OBP/SLG	BABIP	SLGCON	BB%	K%	ZSw%	ZCon%	OSw%	OCon%	LA	90th EV	DRC+	BRR	DRP	WARP
2021	MIL	MLB	29	445	54	11	49	0	.266/.342/.402	.308	.511	9.2%	18.9%	77.0%	87.2%	37.7%	63.6%	18.1	100.1	96	-0.8	9.1	2.5
2022	MIL	MLB	30	296	21	4	23	0	.206/.292/.305	.248	.390	9.8%	19.3%	76.6%	84.9%	34.4%	66.3%	17.5	97.0	83	-0.5	3.0	0.7
2023	NYM	MLB	31	146	12	2	7	0	.211/.283/.297	.245	.376	9.6%	18.5%	71.7%	88.8%	28.0%	73.7%	20.7	100.4	90	-0.1	-0.7	0.3
2024 DC	NYM	MLB	32	156	15	3	15	0	.234/.321/.346	.272	.421	10.1%	16.4%							89	0.0	0.7	0.5

2023 GP: C (47)

Comps: Geno Petralli (70), Ron Hodges (69), Clay Dalrymple (68)

YEAR	TM	P. COUNT	FRM RUNS	BLK RUNS	THRW RUNS	TOT RUNS
2021	MIL	14925	11.8	-0.7	0.3	11.3
2022	MIL	11479	5.1	-0.1	0.0	5.0
2023	NYM	6089	0.2	0.1	0.0	0.3
2024	NYM	6012	1.1	-0.2	-0.2	0.7

A calf strain at the beginning of the season not only cost Narváez two months of his season, it effectively cost him his starting job with the Mets. Rookie Francisco Alvarez took the reins, pushing Narváez into the backup role he may be best suited for at this point in his career. It wasn't that long ago that Narváez had seemingly put it all together—he was an All-Star with Milwaukee in 2021, pairing his solid hitting profile with the defensive strides he'd made upon entering the Brewers' organization. But now, after a pair of lackluster offensive campaigns, it's much easier for him to be unseated by other up-and-coming backstops and start once or twice a week.

Tomás Nido C   Born: 04/12/94   Age: 30   Bats: R   Throws: R   Height: 6'0"   Weight: 211   Origin: Round 8, 2012 Draft (#260 overall)

YEAR	TM	LVL	AGE	PA	R	HR	RBI	SB	AVG/OBP/SLG	BABIP	SLGCON	BB%	K%	ZSw%	ZCon%	OSw%	OCon%	LA	90th EV	DRC+	BRR	DRP	WARP
2021	NYM	MLB	27	161	16	3	13	1	.222/.261/.327	.292	.459	3.1%	27.3%	84.8%	69.2%	53.8%	55.4%	10.6	102.5	79	-0.1	8.6	1.1
2022	NYM	MLB	28	313	31	3	28	0	.239/.276/.324	.314	.442	4.5%	24.3%	83.2%	74.6%	43.9%	53.5%	7.0	102.6	87	-0.7	14.1	2.0
2023	SYR	AAA	29	146	19	4	12	0	.281/.336/.393	.327	.491	7.5%	18.5%	80.6%	81.3%	44.8%	55.6%			89	0.1	-1.2	0.2
2023	NYM	MLB	29	61	5	0	1	0	.125/.153/.125	.179	.184	3.3%	29.5%	77.5%	80.0%	52.8%	52.2%	2.4	97.8	72	-0.1	1.4	0.1
2024 DC	NYM	MLB	30	29	2	0	3	0	.227/.275/.327	.300	.474	5.4%	26.7%							70	0.0	1.4	0.2

2023 GP: C (21)

Comps: Sandy León (60), Humberto Quintero (60), Jeff Mathis (57)

YEAR	TM	P. COUNT	FRM RUNS	BLK RUNS	THRW RUNS	TOT RUNS
2021	NYM	5964	8.9	0.0	0.6	9.4
2022	NYM	12294	15.3	0.6	0.9	16.7
2023	SYR	5539	-0.2	0.1	-0.5	-0.6
2023	NYM	2595	2.4	0.0	-0.2	2.2
2024	NYM	1202	1.4	0.0	0.0	1.4

Nido has been with the Mets' organization for over a decade and established himself as a ~~glove-first~~ glove-only catcher, both by the numbers and by the reaction from his pitchers. (You might recall a controversy from a few years back where Noah Syndergaard was reportedly quite vocal about preferring Nido behind the plate to recent free-agent-signing Wilson Ramos.) But no matter how great the leather is, or how much his pitching staff loves him, a catcher has to hit better than his battery-mates. With all three numbers in Nido's triple slash last year starting with "1," the Mets finally pulled the plug and removed Nido from the major-league roster in June.

Brandon Nimmo CF   Born: 03/27/93   Age: 31   Bats: L   Throws: R   Height: 6'3"   Weight: 206   Origin: Round 1, 2011 Draft (#13 overall)

YEAR	TM	LVL	AGE	PA	R	HR	RBI	SB	AVG/OBP/SLG	BABIP	SLGCON	BB%	K%	ZSw%	ZCon%	OSw%	OCon%	LA	90th EV	DRC+	BRR	DRP	WARP
2021	SYR	AAA	28	36	5	0	0	0	.172/.333/.207	.192	.231	13.9%	8.3%							116	-0.1	-1.2	0.1
2021	NYM	MLB	28	386	51	8	28	5	.292/.401/.437	.366	.577	14.0%	20.5%	67.4%	85.4%	20.9%	55.4%	8.7	103.5	108	0.6	2.9	2.4
2022	NYM	MLB	29	673	102	16	64	3	.274/.367/.433	.317	.541	10.5%	17.2%	66.6%	87.6%	25.0%	65.0%	6.1	104.8	124	0.7	5.2	5.1
2023	NYM	MLB	30	682	89	24	68	3	.274/.363/.466	.324	.619	10.9%	21.4%	63.8%	84.6%	23.5%	62.4%	12.3	105.2	121	-0.1	1.7	4.4
2024 DC	NYM	MLB	31	631	72	17	71	3	.256/.356/.412	.303	.527	11.4%	19.0%							117	0.2	3.9	3.8

2023 GP: CF (136), LF (10), DH (5)

Comps: Jim Edmonds (69), Ray Lankford (67), Lenny Dykstra (66)

Nimmo paired another excellent campaign with his outstanding platform year, and in between them was rewarded handsomely for his services to the borough of Queens. Those services are evolving, too—he's been long known for his excellent on-base ability, and now he's developing a power stroke as well. He just set a career high in homers, and it was buoyed in part by a nearly two-and-a-half mile per hour jump in average exit velocity, among the bigger leaps in the league last season. The Mets are committed to Nimmo as an important part of the team for the long term, and right now, he's looking like their faith in the boyish-faced center fielder is being rewarded.

Kevin Parada C   Born: 08/03/01   Age: 22   Bats: R   Throws: R   Height: 5'11"   Weight: 197   Origin: Round 1, 2022 Draft (#11 overall)

YEAR	TM	LVL	AGE	PA	R	HR	RBI	SB	AVG/OBP/SLG	BABIP	SLGCON	BB%	K%	ZSw%	ZCon%	OSw%	OCon%	LA	90th EV	DRC+	BRR	DRP	WARP
2022	SLU	A	20	41	5	1	5	0	.276/.463/.414	.412	.706	24.4%	29.3%	69.0%	85.0%	23.1%	51.9%			109	-0.3	-0.2	0.1
2023	GDD	WIN	21	71	7	3	9	0	.182/.239/.379	.250	.641	5.6%	38.0%	33.3%	100.0%	50.0%	20.0%						
2023	BRK	A+	21	382	44	11	42	1	.265/.340/.447	.336	.623	7.9%	25.1%							101	-1.0	-11.9	0.0
2023	BNG	AA	21	60	4	3	11	0	.185/.250/.389	.241	.677	6.7%	38.3%							71	0.3	0.5	0.1
2024 non	NYM	MLB	22	251	22	5	24	0	.215/.274/.334	.319	.534	6.2%	34.2%							71	0.0	0	0.0

2023 GP: C (86), DH (36)

Comps: Jorge Alfaro (52), Allan de San Miguel (51), Deivy Grullón (51)

YEAR	TM	P. COUNT	FRM RUNS	BLK RUNS	THRW RUNS	TOT RUNS
2023	GDD	1887				
2023	BRK	8958	-11.2	0.4	-1.9	-12.7
2023	BNG	1494	0.5	-0.1	0.3	0.8
2024	NYM	6956	-3.0	0.2	0.2	-2.7

Despite being a recent first-round pick, there are already legitimate concerns about Parada's development. He's generally regarded to be much stronger at the plate than behind it, and despite that his offensive performance in Brooklyn and Binghamton last year didn't exactly inspire confidence. Scouts are bearish on his likelihood at sticking at catcher, and the defensive metrics available to us would mesh with those assessments—especially when combined with fellow backstop Francisco Alvarez's productive debut in Queens. Time is still on Parada's side, but a shift off catcher seems like an increasingly likely outcome.

DJ Stewart RF Born: 11/30/93   Age: 30   Bats: L   Throws: R   Height: 6'0"   Weight: 210   Origin: Round 1, 2015 Draft (#25 overall)

YEAR	TM	LVL	AGE	PA	R	HR	RBI	SB	AVG/OBP/SLG	BABIP	SLGCON	BB%	K%	ZSw%	ZCon%	OSw%	OCon%	LA	90th EV	DRC+	BRR	DRP	WARP
2021	BAL	MLB	27	318	39	12	33	0	.204/.324/.374	.254	.558	13.8%	28.0%	72.8%	77.3%	27.1%	50.0%	19.5	104.8	98	0.0	-1.7	0.8
2022	NOR	AAA	28	105	18	6	17	2	.256/.390/.488	.308	.724	15.2%	26.7%							122	-0.2	2.0	0.7
2022	BAL	MLB	28	3	0	0	0	0	.000/.000/.000		.000	0.0%	66.7%	80.0%	75.0%	50.0%	0.0%	48.0	79.3	80		0.0	0.0
2023	SYR	AAA	29	229	35	16	41	0	.229/.362/.516	.213	.683	15.3%	20.1%	75.2%	78.6%	26.4%	64.4%			120	0.8	-2.4	1.1
2023	NYM	MLB	29	185	21	11	26	1	.244/.333/.506	.298	.779	8.1%	30.3%	76.8%	70.2%	32.0%	54.3%	16.0	105.2	99	0.0	-1.5	0.3
2024 DC	NYM	MLB	30	324	37	12	39	2	.209/.307/.388	.265	.569	10.3%	28.4%							93	-0.1	-2	0.3

2023 GP: RF (44), DH (7), LF (4)   Comps: Aaron Hicks (51), Lucas Duda (51), Xavier Paul (48)

Is there any bigger indicator of how the 2023 Mets' season had gone awry than a "DJ Stewart" chant breaking out in a late-August game at Citi Field? Stewart himself probably wouldn't have imagined that, let alone the rest of a disappointing Flushing crew. But after a handful of unimpressive part-time efforts on some bad Orioles teams, Stewart was an offensive bright spot for a bad Mets team, highlighted by that August 30th contest versus the Rangers in which he hit two homers, made an impressive running catch at the right field wall, and ultimately drove in the game-winning run on a walk-off hit-by-pitch. Good teams likely still shouldn't be relying heavily on Stewart's power-and-patience-only skillset, so if he's the Mets Opening Day left fielder or DH, that should give some early warning on what to expect for the 2024 Amazins.

Tyrone Taylor OF Born: 01/22/94   Age: 30   Bats: R   Throws: R   Height: 6'1"   Weight: 218   Origin: Round 2, 2012 Draft (#92 overall)

YEAR	TM	LVL	AGE	PA	R	HR	RBI	SB	AVG/OBP/SLG	BABIP	SLGCON	BB%	K%	ZSw%	ZCon%	OSw%	OCon%	LA	90th EV	DRC+	BRR	DRP	WARP
2021	NAS	AAA	27	35	10	3	10	0	.500/.543/.964	.478	1.125	14.3%	11.4%							136	0.9	0.4	0.4
2021	MIL	MLB	27	271	33	12	43	6	.247/.321/.457	.277	.603	7.4%	21.8%	70.9%	89.3%	35.4%	59.9%	15.9	104.7	95	0.0	-1.1	0.7
2022	MIL	MLB	28	405	49	17	51	3	.233/.286/.442	.272	.609	5.4%	25.2%	69.2%	86.1%	36.6%	55.1%	16.9	103.4	86	0.3	-4.3	0.3
2023	NAS	AAA	29	56	11	4	12	2	.245/.339/.571	.242	.757	7.1%	21.4%	74.7%	85.9%	41.9%	67.3%			113	0.4	2.9	0.5
2023	MIL	MLB	29	243	36	10	35	9	.234/.267/.446	.263	.585	3.3%	22.6%	69.2%	86.9%	37.7%	57.5%	17.8	104.6	94	0.2	-0.8	0.4
2024 DC	NYM	MLB	30	186	20	7	24	3	.244/.301/.426	.281	.557	5.9%	22.2%							103	0.0	-1.5	0.4

2023 GP: RF (60), LF (21), CF (8), DH (1)   Comps: Juan Rivera (54), Shane Victorino (52), Randal Grichuk (52)

From the producers of Craigtember comes …Tyronetember. (We're still workshopping the name.) As summer waned, Taylor's bat came alive, racking up a .912 OPS with five homers over the final month. Whenever his bat found the ball, it wrought havoc. He had a .360 BABIP in thag span, all high-leverage games with the likes of the Cubs and Reds breathing down Milwaukee's neck. The crown jewel, perhaps, was a physics-defying slide into home plate in a game versus the Marlins, circumventing the tag and somehow finding the plate. He's fast as heck, showcases the arm and leather and made a serviceable fill-in for Christian Yelich when he was limited by injuries. His next trick will be to stay healthy enough to extend the Tyronetember brand into Tyrune, Tyruly and Tyrogust.

Marco Vargas SS Born: 05/14/05   Age: 19   Bats: L   Throws: R   Height: 6'0"   Weight: 170   Origin: IFA, 2022

YEAR	TM	LVL	AGE	PA	R	HR	RBI	SB	AVG/OBP/SLG	BABIP	SLGCON	BB%	K%	ZSw%	ZCon%	OSw%	OCon%	LA	90th EV	DRC+	BRR	DRP	WARP
2022	DSL MIA	ROK	17	221	30	2	38	14	.319/.421/.456	.368	.553	15.8%	14.5%										
2023	MRL	ROK	18	162	32	2	19	8	.283/.457/.442	.327	.541	23.5%	13.6%										
2023	MET	ROK	18	57	9	0	5	2	.234/.368/.298	.289	.368	17.5%	15.8%										
2023	SLU	A	18	31	5	0	4	3	.308/.419/.308	.421	.421	16.1%	22.6%	65.3%	75.0%	27.4%	65.0%			94	0.4	-0.1	0.1
2024 non	NYM	MLB	19	251	18	2	19	0	.206/.261/.285	.304	.431	6.2%	31.8%							54	0.0	0	-0.6

2023 GP: SS (37), 2B (13), DH (4), 3B (3)

Vargas was the Mets' main prize in exchange for sending closer David Robertson to the Marlins at the trade deadline, and the deal immediately earned rave reviews as the young infielder's trajectory is on the way up. He started at the Florida Complex League upon entering the Mets' organization, but quickly earned a late-season promotion to Low-A St. Lucie. His plate discipline and bat-to-ball skills are advanced for a teeanger, and also he's been praised for exit velocities that are stronger than that of many of his peers. He's a name to keep an eye on over the next two years.

Mark Vientos 3B Born: 12/11/99   Age: 24   Bats: R   Throws: R   Height: 6'4"   Weight: 185   Origin: Round 2, 2017 Draft (#59 overall)

YEAR	TM	LVL	AGE	PA	R	HR	RBI	SB	AVG/OBP/SLG	BABIP	SLGCON	BB%	K%	ZSw%	ZCon%	OSw%	OCon%	LA	90th EV	DRC+	BRR	DRP	WARP
2021	BNG	AA	21	306	43	22	59	0	.281/.346/.580	.327	.850	8.5%	28.4%							123	-1.9	-4.7	1.1
2021	SYR	AAA	21	43	9	3	4	0	.278/.395/.583	.350	.913	16.3%	30.2%							110	-0.1	1.1	0.3
2022	SYR	AAA	22	427	66	24	72	0	.280/.358/.519	.350	.766	10.3%	28.6%	80.9%	76.3%	28.9%	38.5%			112	-0.7	-3.5	1.5
2022	NYM	MLB	22	41	3	1	3	0	.167/.268/.278	.217	.417	12.2%	29.3%	78.6%	72.7%	31.9%	66.7%	13.2	107.4	99	0.0	0.0	0.1
2023	SYR	AAA	23	269	38	16	50	0	.306/.387/.612	.340	.816	10.8%	21.6%	72.5%	76.7%	30.2%	56.6%			121	-1.1	-2.4	1.0
2023	NYM	MLB	23	233	19	9	22	1	.211/.253/.367	.264	.544	4.3%	30.5%	72.1%	74.1%	39.9%	49.2%	9.3	108.0	84	-0.2	-0.4	0.1
2024 DC	NYM	MLB	24	350	38	13	43	0	.233/.295/.404	.308	.605	7.0%	30.6%							96	0.0	-0.2	0.5

2023 GP: DH (37), 3B (19), 1B (10)   Comps: Jon Singleton (65), Aaron Cunningham (65), Brandon Wood (63)

It's easy to see why there's excitement surrounding Vientos' offensive profile: Look no further than an exit velocity leaderboard of Triple-A batters. In 2023, Vientos' average exit velo of 94.6 miles per hour was far and away the highest among his peers (setting a minimum of 100 balls in play tracked by the Hawkeye system). It's equally easy to see where the concerns lie: Vientos has generally struck out a fair amount at the expense of that great power, and his questionable fielding skills leaves him without a clear defensive home. (He roved between third base, first base, and designated hitter last season, without standing out at any spot.) In addition, the 53% ground-ball percentage he's shown in his major-league career far exceeds his recent minor-league rates, so he's not yet getting the equivalent results out of all that raw power.

Daniel Vogelbach DH   Born: 12/17/92   Age: 31   Bats: L   Throws: R   Height: 6'0"   Weight: 270   Origin: Round 2, 2011 Draft (#68 overall)

YEAR	TM	LVL	AGE	PA	R	HR	RBI	SB	AVG/OBP/SLG	BABIP	SLGCON	BB%	K%	ZSw%	ZCon%	OSw%	OCon%	LA	90th EV	DRC+	BRR	DRP	WARP
2021	MIL	MLB	28	258	30	9	24	0	.219/.349/.381	.255	.519	16.7%	22.1%	51.3%	88.3%	20.7%	68.2%	11.7	106.2	99	-0.6	0.0	0.5
2022	NYM	MLB	29	183	18	6	25	0	.255/.393/.436	.333	.637	18.0%	25.7%	46.3%	88.4%	23.9%	68.0%	15.0	103.0	107	-0.7	0.0	0.5
2022	PIT	MLB	29	278	29	12	34	0	.228/.338/.430	.264	.600	14.4%	24.1%	47.4%	89.1%	20.5%	64.1%	16.5	104.9	115	-0.6	0.0	1.1
2023	NYM	MLB	30	319	33	13	48	0	.233/.339/.404	.282	.572	13.2%	25.4%	52.4%	88.6%	23.6%	61.2%	14.3	104.6	88	-0.6	0.0	0.2
2024 DC	NYM	MLB	31	361	44	13	45	0	.238/.349/.415	.277	.554	14.0%	21.5%							117	0.0	-0.1	1.5

2023 GP: DH (85)   *Comps: Justin Smoak (62), Chris Davis (56), Ji Man Choi (55)*

Go back to 2016 and look at how lefty batters have performed against lefty pitchers (minimum 300 plate appearances). Vogelbach's .463 OPS in 323 PAs against lefties across his career is *far and away the worst in baseball* over the past seven seasons, with Jason Castro's .545 mark being the next in line. Vogelbach's one-dimensionality as a player apparently led to a rift between the Mets' former manager and general manager, with Buck Showalter wanting to free up the team's DH spot and not commit so much to Vogelbach, who, in addition to his issues with southpaws, has a limited profile beyond his patient batting eye. Billy Eppler, per reports, wanted to keep him in the lineup as the team's primary DH against righty pitchers. Even with his playing time against lefties limited to just 16 plate appearances last season, Vogelbach mustered an OPS just slightly above league-average; now all three participants in this drama are looking for new jobs.

Joey Wendle SS   Born: 04/26/90   Age: 34   Bats: L   Throws: R   Height: 6'1"   Weight: 195   Origin: Round 6, 2012 Draft (#203 overall)

YEAR	TM	LVL	AGE	PA	R	HR	RBI	SB	AVG/OBP/SLG	BABIP	SLGCON	BB%	K%	ZSw%	ZCon%	OSw%	OCon%	LA	90th EV	DRC+	BRR	DRP	WARP
2021	TB	MLB	31	501	73	11	54	8	.265/.319/.422	.327	.559	5.6%	22.6%	64.7%	86.2%	36.3%	61.1%	6.5	102.6	85	0.0	1.4	0.9
2022	MIA	MLB	32	371	27	3	32	12	.259/.297/.360	.293	.421	4.0%	13.5%	66.3%	90.8%	42.5%	74.3%	3.0	102.2	94	0.7	0.1	0.9
2023	MIA	MLB	33	318	33	2	20	7	.212/.248/.306	.264	.396	4.1%	21.1%	62.0%	85.9%	36.3%	60.6%	3.8	100.7	81	0.1	4.8	0.8
2024 DC	NYM	MLB	34	300	26	5	28	6	.247/.295/.364	.303	.466	4.8%	20.3%							82	0.0	0.8	0.3

2023 GP: SS (107)   *Comps: Billy Goodman (68), Orlando Hudson (64), Brian Roberts (62)*

Our batting-gloveless folk hero has provided far fewer Woey Jendle moments with Miami than he did before joining the team in 2022, and this past season represented another step down. And boy, he somehow still managed to play a lot. One look at his OPS and you'll see it's among the worst marks you'll ever see from anyone who gets on the field that much. Anyone who looks at an OPS like that should get a free bowl of soup. Of guys who registered at least 300 plate appearances, he ranked 292nd out of 293. He was ever-so-slightly above average in the field, which counts for something considering he was the club's primary shortstop, but there are questions to ask. Mainly, "Why?" or "How could you?" or "Won't somebody think of the children?"

★ ★ ★ *2024 Top 101 Prospect* **#23** ★ ★ ★

Jett Williams SS   Born: 11/03/03   Age: 20   Bats: R   Throws: R   Height: 5'6"   Weight: 175   Origin: Round 1, 2022 Draft (#14 overall)

YEAR	TM	LVL	AGE	PA	R	HR	RBI	SB	AVG/OBP/SLG	BABIP	SLGCON	BB%	K%	ZSw%	ZCon%	OSw%	OCon%	LA	90th EV	DRC+	BRR	DRP	WARP
2022	MET	ROK	18	41	7	1	6	6	.250/.366/.438	.259	.538	9.8%	14.6%										
2023	SLU	A	19	346	51	6	35	32	.249/.422/.410	.322	.578	19.9%	22.0%	56.8%	86.5%	18.8%	66.1%			128	0.3	-5.8	1.9
2023	BRK	A+	19	162	25	7	18	12	.299/.451/.567	.352	.758	20.4%	19.8%							136	0.3	-2.9	0.6
2023	BNG	AA	19	26	5	0	2	1	.227/.308/.273	.385	.500	7.7%	38.5%							76	0.4		
2024 non	NYM	MLB	20	251	24	4	23	6	.222/.316/.338	.285	.460	10.8%	23.2%							89	0.0	0	0.5

2023 GP: SS (92), CF (21), DH (8)   *Comps: Xander Bogaerts (60), Adam Jones (59), Vladimir Guerrero Jr. (54)*

A five-foot-six middle infielder with sneaky power? Fire up the unfair José Altuve comparisons! If Williams' career comes anything *close* to that of Houston's prospective Hall of Famer, it'd be a massive success. But what we *can* say to this point is that Williams impressed in his first full professional season, showing a discerning eye at the plate and a greater preponderance for hard-hit balls than you might expect given his frame. Though still primarily a shortstop, Williams spent some time in center field last year and expressed that if it helps him reach the big leagues faster, he's more than happy to flex his defensive versatility. So far, the high expectations are being met for this low-flying Jett.

PITCHERS

Austin Adams RHP   Born: 05/05/91   Age: 33   Height: 6'3"   Weight: 220   Origin: Round 8, 2012 Draft (#267 overall)

YEAR	TM	LVL	AGE	G (GS)	IP	W-L	SV	K	WHIP	ERA	CSP	BB%	K%	HR%	GB%	ZSw%	ZCon%	OSw%	OCon%	BABIP	SLGCON	DRA-	WARP
2021	SD	MLB	30	65 (0)	52²	3-2	0	76	1.20	4.10	49.1%	14.5%	31.5%	0.4%	33.0%	60.6%	80.7%	28.8%	47.7%	.265	.430	116	0.0
2022	SD	MLB	31	2 (0)	2¹	1-0	0	2	1.29	0.00	51.6%	33.3%	22.2%	0.0%	100.0%	53.3%	87.5%	28.1%	55.6%	.000	.000	104	0.0
2023	RNO	AAA	32	12 (0)	12²	1-0	3	20	1.18	2.84		11.1%	37.0%	0.0%	25.9%	60.2%	76.8%	29.4%	42.9%	.333	.407	85	0.2
2023	AZ	MLB	32	24 (0)	17¹	0-1	0	22	1.38	5.71	49.6%	9.9%	27.2%	1.2%	39.1%	63.8%	75.3%	31.9%	64.2%	.333	.435	93	0.3
2024 DC	NYM	MLB	33	28 (0)	31¹	2-1	0	40	1.30	4.48	48.7%	11.4%	29.1%	3.2%	38.6%					.288	.571	99	0.2

2023 Arsenal: SL (88.1), FA (93.9), SI (94.3)   *Comps: Ryan Buchter (57), Brad Brach (56), Blake Parker (56)*

Need a laugh? Check out Adams' splits by pitch type. Every season, without fail, his four-seam fastball records a .400-something wOBA, while his slider is in the .200s. And, mind you, that factors in the sheer number of batters Adams plunks with that slider. Still, 200 is less than 400, so the slider remains his weapon of choice; he threw it 90% of the time for the Diamondbacks before a fractured ankle abruptly ended his season. The true kicker, though, was the incredible gap between his slider wOBA (.276) and fastball wOBA (.687). Never mind that Adams only lasted 17 innings—that's absolutely horrifying, no matter the sample size. At this point, would it be surprising to see him go 100% sliders?

Phil Bickford RHP Born: 07/10/95 Age: 28 Height: 6'4" Weight: 200 Origin: Round 1, 2015 Draft (#18 overall)

YEAR	TM	LVL	AGE	G (GS)	IP	W-L	SV	K	WHIP	ERA	CSP	BB%	K%	HR%	GB%	ZSw%	ZCon%	OSw%	OCon%	BABIP	SLGCON	DRA-	WARP
2021	OKC	AAA	25	5 (0)	5	1-0	0	12	1.00	5.40		0.0%	57.1%	0.0%	44.4%					.556	.778	74	0.1
2021	LAD	MLB	25	56 (0)	50¹	4-2	1	59	1.03	2.50	57.6%	9.0%	29.5%	3.0%	47.1%	72.8%	79.7%	32.0%	50.8%	.243	.492	80	1.0
2021	MIL	MLB	25	1 (0)	1	0-0	0	0	3.00	18.00	51.3%	14.3%	0.0%	14.3%	20.0%	68.8%	81.8%	27.3%	66.7%	.250	1.250	96	0.0
2022	OKC	AAA	26	6 (0)	5	0-0	0	6	1.40	9.00		13.6%	27.3%	9.1%	53.8%	68.6%	83.3%	39.7%	73.9%	.182	1.000	90	0.1
2022	LAD	MLB	26	60 (0)	61	2-1	0	67	1.10	4.72	55.8%	5.7%	27.1%	4.9%	37.2%	71.6%	77.9%	32.0%	68.6%	.270	.637	81	1.2
2023	NYM	MLB	27	25 (0)	25¹	3-2	1	28	1.34	4.62	42.2%	11.4%	24.6%	2.6%	24.6%	70.1%	77.4%	36.3%	60.2%	.281	.522	115	0.1
2023	LAD	MLB	27	36 (0)	42	2-3	0	48	1.52	5.14	43.6%	13.7%	25.3%	2.6%	28.4%	74.5%	81.7%	30.3%	53.2%	.300	.579	114	0.2
2024 DC	NYM	MLB	28	53 (0)	56¹	4-2	0	62	1.30	4.34	49.9%	9.9%	25.8%	3.9%	34.2%					.283	.586	99	0.3

2023 Arsenal: FA (93.9), SL (84.1), FS (87.7)   Comps: J.J. Hoover (67), Arodys Vizcaíno (66), Nick Goody (66)

We're getting further and further away from the summer of 2021, when Bickford surprised everybody to become an integral part of the 106-win Dodgers' bullpen. While it's true that he did close out last season on a high note with nine consecutive scoreless relief outings, he has a 4.73 ERA across 137 innings dating back to September '21, with suspect control and a propensity to allow hard contact. Now with the Mets, the likelihood of him being an integral part of a 106-win bullpen have changed drastically for *two* reasons!

José Butto RHP Born: 03/19/98 Age: 26 Height: 6'1" Weight: 202 Origin: IFA, 2017

YEAR	TM	LVL	AGE	G (GS)	IP	W-L	SV	K	WHIP	ERA	CSP	BB%	K%	HR%	GB%	ZSw%	ZCon%	OSw%	OCon%	BABIP	SLGCON	DRA-	WARP
2021	BRK	A+	23	12 (12)	58¹	1-4	0	60	1.13	4.32		6.3%	25.1%	4.6%	44.1%					.267	.613	90	0.8
2021	BNG	AA	23	8 (8)	40¹	3-2	0	50	1.04	3.12		5.4%	29.9%	3.6%	42.7%					.284	.564	86	0.6
2022	BNG	AA	24	20 (18)	92¹	6-5	0	108	1.31	4.00		8.8%	27.2%	3.5%	38.9%					.313	.635	90	1.7
2022	SYR	AAA	24	8 (7)	36²	1-1	0	30	0.95	2.45		6.3%	21.0%	2.1%	47.1%	57.1%	100.0%	23.1%	100.0%	.232	.446	84	0.8
2022	NYM	MLB	24	1 (1)	4	0-0	0	5	2.75	15.75	53.7%	8.7%	21.7%	8.7%	25.0%	74.0%	83.8%	33.3%	56.2%	.500	1.000	119	0.0
2023	SYR	AAA	25	19 (19)	91	3-7	0	82	1.63	5.93		11.8%	19.8%	4.1%	38.5%	70.4%	82.9%	31.9%	53.4%	.314	.628	100	1.3
2023	NYM	MLB	25	9 (7)	42	1-4	0	38	1.33	3.64	43.5%	12.8%	21.2%	1.7%	41.5%	73.7%	80.7%	28.5%	56.5%	.261	.398	113	0.2
2024 DC	NYM	MLB	26	21 (5)	40	2-2	0	38	1.52	5.60	44.5%	10.1%	21.4%	3.9%	38.1%					.315	.607	123	-0.1

2023 Arsenal: FA (94.4), CH (85.8), FC (86.7), CU (80.6), SI (93)   Comps: Stephen Fife (71), Taylor Jungmann (69), Alex Colomé (66)

As was the case with many pitchers last year, Butto's walk rate spiked mightily during his time in Triple-A. Butto confirmed that the automatic ball/strike system was a hindrance to him and undoubtedly led to his unimpressive overall numbers. Nonetheless, he looked great when the Mets recalled him for a series of late-season starts, pitching to a 3.29 ERA across five starts and 27 ⅓ innings. With a lot of uncertainty surrounding the Mets' rotation, Butto will come into camp to compete for a starting job out of spring and might avoid the ABS system entirely in 2024.

Carlos Carrasco RHP Born: 03/21/87 Age: 37 Height: 6'4" Weight: 224 Origin: IFA, 2003

YEAR	TM	LVL	AGE	G (GS)	IP	W-L	SV	K	WHIP	ERA	CSP	BB%	K%	HR%	GB%	ZSw%	ZCon%	OSw%	OCon%	BABIP	SLGCON	DRA-	WARP
2021	NYM	MLB	34	12 (12)	53²	1-5	0	50	1.43	6.04	52.3%	7.6%	21.1%	5.1%	43.2%	71.8%	80.3%	37.2%	62.8%	.299	.653	107	0.3
2022	NYM	MLB	35	29 (29)	152	15-7	0	152	1.33	3.97	52.3%	6.4%	23.6%	2.6%	46.4%	71.7%	84.8%	39.2%	57.6%	.338	.571	95	1.9
2023	BNG	AA	36	2 (2)	7	0-0	0	5	1.00	1.29		7.7%	19.2%	0.0%	68.4%					.263	.263	95	0.1
2023	NYM	MLB	36	20 (20)	90	3-8	0	66	1.70	6.80	45.2%	9.1%	15.8%	4.3%	45.6%	69.1%	87.3%	33.6%	60.8%	.336	.646	128	-0.3
2024 non	NYM	MLB	37	58 (0)	50	2-2	0	43	1.43	4.99	49.0%	8.3%	19.6%	3.2%	44.8%					.311	.558	111	-0.1

2023 Arsenal: FA (92.9), CH (87.5), SL (84.4), SI (91.9), CU (80.3), FC (89.6), SW (82.6)   Comps: Johnny Cueto (71), Aníbal Sánchez (71), Pedro Astacio (71)

To say the least, 2023 was a disappointing season for Carrasco: he missed time with a bone spur at the beginning of the year, he broke his pinky in a weight room accident at the end of it, and in between, he pitched to one of the worst ERAs in the league. Carrasco isn't the same as he was during his peak in Cleveland; his slider and curveball no longer garner the swing-and-miss they used to, and his fastball is down a few ticks as well. While he's only a year removed from a solid season with the Mets, his lengthy injury history, age, and recent decline are all discouraging signs.

Edwin Díaz RHP Born: 03/22/94 Age: 30 Height: 6'3" Weight: 165 Origin: Round 3, 2012 Draft (#98 overall)

YEAR	TM	LVL	AGE	G (GS)	IP	W-L	SV	K	WHIP	ERA	CSP	BB%	K%	HR%	GB%	ZSw%	ZCon%	OSw%	OCon%	BABIP	SLGCON	DRA-	WARP
2021	NYM	MLB	27	63 (0)	62²	5-6	32	89	1.05	3.45	49.2%	8.9%	34.6%	1.2%	32.4%	70.6%	77.6%	35.4%	47.1%	.308	.477	80	1.3
2022	NYM	MLB	28	61 (0)	62	3-1	32	118	0.84	1.31	51.8%	7.7%	50.2%	1.3%	46.4%	64.8%	65.9%	42.5%	32.5%	.330	.484	44	2.4
2024 DC	NYM	MLB	30	59 (0)	62²	5-6	36	103	1.05	2.80	49.3%	9.1%	40.3%	3.3%	40.1%					.299	.621	69	1.3

2023 Arsenal: FA (97.2), SL (91)   Comps: Kenley Jansen (77), Ken Giles (76), David Robertson (75)

We often think of sports in a dichotomy of jubilation and anguish. Somebody has to win, somebody else has to lose. We less often think of those times where the jubilation and the anguish are one and the same. When Díaz sealed the win for Puerto Rico in last year's World Baseball Classic to earn a trip to the tournament's quarterfinals, the happiness of the victory was immediately overshadowed by the brutal knee injury Díaz suffered during the celebration. The loss of Díaz—coming off an absolutely brilliant 2022 campaign—set the tone for a season of disappointments in Flushing. Here's to a 2024 of joy without the pain for one of baseball's most dominant closers.

Dominic Hamel RHP   Born: 03/02/99   Age: 25   Height: 6'2"   Weight: 206   Origin: Round 3, 2021 Draft (#81 overall)

YEAR	TM	LVL	AGE	G(GS)	IP	W-L	SV	K	WHIP	ERA	CSP	BB%	K%	HR%	GB%	ZSw%	ZCon%	OSw%	OCon%	BABIP	SLGCON	DRA-	WARP
2022	SLU	A	23	14(13)	63¹	5-2	0	71	1.22	3.84		10.9%	26.6%	1.9%	44.1%	67.1%	82.2%	33.5%	56.0%	.276	.459	102	1.0
2022	BRK	A+	23	11(11)	55²	5-1	0	74	1.08	2.59		11.2%	33.2%	0.0%	36.9%					.287	.342	84	0.9
2023	BNG	AA	24	26(25)	124	8-6	0	160	1.27	3.85		9.3%	30.4%	2.3%	36.8%					.319	.561	91	2.4
2024 non	NYM	MLB	25	58(0)	50	2-2	0	49	1.43	4.93		10.8%	22.2%	3.5%	34.7%					.293	.569	109	0.0

Comps: Thaddeus Ward (80), Jimmy Nelson (80), Tyler Wagner (78)

Hamel refined his arsenal prior to the 2023 season, partitioning his slider into a hard cutter and slower sweeper, the latter of which Hamel admitted took some time getting acclimated to. But starting with a seven-inning, one-run effort against Reading on July 26th, he closed out his season with a 1.88 ERA over his final nine games. Binghamton should be decidedly in the rear-view mirror as he looks to consolidate his gains and get a chance at the back of a rotation.

Grant Hartwig RHP   Born: 12/18/97   Age: 26   Height: 6'5"   Weight: 235   Origin: Undrafted Free Agent, 2021

YEAR	TM	LVL	AGE	G(GS)	IP	W-L	SV	K	WHIP	ERA	CSP	BB%	K%	HR%	GB%	ZSw%	ZCon%	OSw%	OCon%	BABIP	SLGCON	DRA-	WARP
2021	MET	ROK	23	4(3)	7	0-1	0	9	1.43	3.86		9.7%	29.0%	3.2%	36.8%					.333	.556		
2022	SLU	A	24	10(0)	14²	3-0	3	21	1.36	4.30		7.8%	32.8%	0.0%	47.4%	56.4%	77.3%	42.6%	48.5%	.405	.432	85	0.3
2022	BRK	A+	24	11(0)	15¹	1-0	7	24	0.98	0.59		10.2%	40.7%	1.7%	72.4%					.296	.464	86	0.2
2022	BNG	AA	24	16(0)	23²	0-2	3	34	1.06	1.14		11.0%	34.0%	0.0%	52.9%					.275	.320	76	0.6
2023	SYR	AAA	25	24(0)	28²	4-3	3	37	1.85	5.02		13.1%	27.0%	2.2%	33.8%	65.0%	83.4%	26.0%	57.6%	.416	.667	107	0.4
2023	NYM	MLB	25	28(0)	35¹	5-2	0	30	1.39	4.84	45.1%	9.5%	19.0%	1.9%	47.7%	64.9%	90.7%	28.8%	63.2%	.298	.500	103	0.4
2024 DC	NYM	MLB	26	47(0)	50	3-2	0	43	1.40	4.58	45.1%	10.5%	19.5%	2.7%	44.3%					.286	.500	102	0.2

2023 Arsenal: SI (94.9), SL (82.7), HC (93.5), CH (86.7)   Comps: Ariel Hernández (75), Angel Nesbitt (71), Chad Sobotka (71)

After going undrafted in 2021, Hartwig was all set to go to medical school—he'd recently graduated from Miami University in Ohio with a major in microbiology and pre-med studies—until he got an unanticipated phone call from the Mets. He took them up on their offer and began pitching in the Florida Complex League shortly thereafter. Like he has with academia, Hartwig has taken a studious approach to pitching and has worked to improve the horizontal movement on his slider as well as developing a cut fastball, a pitch that was his primary offering to left-handed hitters last year. If he still wants to be a doctor after his playing career, he can do it for reasons other than the high salary: He's established himself as a viable major-league reliever.

Adrian Houser RHP   Born: 02/02/93   Age: 31   Height: 6'3"   Weight: 242   Origin: Round 2, 2011 Draft (#69 overall)

YEAR	TM	LVL	AGE	G(GS)	IP	W-L	SV	K	WHIP	ERA	CSP	BB%	K%	HR%	GB%	ZSw%	ZCon%	OSw%	OCon%	BABIP	SLGCON	DRA-	WARP
2021	MIL	MLB	28	28(26)	142¹	10-6	0	105	1.28	3.22	51.5%	10.7%	17.5%	2.0%	58.6%	65.4%	91.6%	30.8%	68.6%	.264	.426	94	1.8
2022	NAS	AAA	29	3(3)	8¹	0-1	0	10	1.56	3.24		18.9%	27.0%	2.7%	60.0%					.263	.550	95	0.1
2022	MIL	MLB	29	22(21)	102²	6-10	0	69	1.46	4.73	51.6%	10.3%	15.2%	1.8%	46.6%	66.0%	90.0%	30.1%	73.9%	.289	.468	123	-0.2
2023	NAS	AAA	30	4(4)	14²	0-1	0	12	1.50	3.07		8.6%	20.7%	3.4%	61.0%	66.0%	90.9%	28.3%	61.5%	.385	.585	89	0.3
2023	MIL	MLB	30	23(21)	111¹	8-5	0	96	1.39	4.12	49.5%	7.1%	20.0%	2.7%	46.3%	67.1%	87.5%	29.5%	72.0%	.320	.519	98	1.5
2024 DC	NYM	MLB	31	29(19)	109²	6-7	0	76	1.44	4.81	50.3%	8.9%	16.0%	2.7%	48.9%					.298	.503	107	0.6

2023 Arsenal: SI (92.1), FA (93.3), SL (82.1), KC (79.4), FS (84.5)   Comps: Al Fitzmorris (64), Jeff Samardzija (62), Mike Torrez (60)

Any great combo meal contains the unsung piece that complements the food. The zest of a startlingly carbonated lemon-lime soda makes a refreshing additive to a carbs-and-fat combo. Houser provides that kind of pleasant fizz. His stuff lacks some of the nutrients that make up a front-end starter, but you can't call his performance flat. You'd love more strikeouts and less vulnerability against lefties, but he ate at least five innings in 15 of his 21 games started, all while posting a league-average ERA. Given what the Mets had to sit through last year, "forgettable innings" sounds refreshing indeed.

Nate Lavender LHP   Born: 01/20/00   Age: 24   Height: 6'2"   Weight: 210   Origin: Round 14, 2021 Draft (#412 overall)

YEAR	TM	LVL	AGE	G(GS)	IP	W-L	SV	K	WHIP	ERA	CSP	BB%	K%	HR%	GB%	ZSw%	ZCon%	OSw%	OCon%	BABIP	SLGCON	DRA-	WARP
2021	MET	ROK	21	4(0)	6²	0-0	3	12	0.75	1.35		8.0%	48.0%	0.0%	36.4%					.273	.273		
2022	SLU	A	22	10(0)	18²	4-1	1	30	1.18	0.48		14.5%	39.5%	0.0%	48.5%	65.9%	64.2%	30.7%	47.3%	.344	.344	82	0.5
2022	BRK	A+	22	16(0)	29	2-2	2	37	1.24	2.48		12.2%	30.1%	0.8%	37.1%					.294	.433	94	0.3
2023	BNG	AA	23	7(0)	10¹	0-0	4	19	0.77	1.74		7.1%	45.2%	0.0%	50.0%					.278	.353	74	0.3
2023	SYR	AAA	23	35(1)	44	4-3	3	67	1.30	3.27		12.0%	35.1%	3.7%	29.2%	61.6%	73.1%	28.2%	47.9%	.303	.667	82	1.0
2024 non	NYM	MLB	24	58(0)	50	2-2	0	62	1.37	4.54		11.9%	28.6%	3.5%	34.2%					.294	.591	101	0.2

2023 Arsenal: FA (91.8), SL (81.5), CH (84.5)   Comps: Jared Miller (58), Dakota Mekkes (57), Daniel Webb (55)

Among Triple-A pitchers who threw at least 500 fastballs tracked by the Hawkeye system last season, Lavender's whiff rate of 36% ranked second, only behind noted Giants prospect Kyle Harrison. The University of Illinois product's heater averaged under 92 mph last year, but he's been able to rack up those impressive results given his deception and his advantageous release angle. He was an unheralded draft pick, but Light Purple has quickly risen up the Mets' minor-league system and should become a calming presence in the big league bullpen sometime during 2024.

Jorge López RHP   Born: 02/10/93   Age: 31   Height: 6'3"   Weight: 200   Origin: Round 2, 2011 Draft (#70 overall)

YEAR	TM	LVL	AGE	G (GS)	IP	W-L	SV	K	WHIP	ERA	CSP	BB%	K%	HR%	GB%	ZSw%	ZCon%	OSw%	OCon%	BABIP	SLGCON	DRA-	WARP
2021	BAL	MLB	28	33(25)	121²	3-14	0	112	1.63	6.07	55.7%	10.1%	20.2%	3.8%	50.4%	63.0%	85.8%	28.9%	69.0%	.341	.630	109	0.6
2022	BAL	MLB	29	44(0)	48¹	4-6	19	54	0.97	1.68	59.5%	8.7%	27.6%	1.5%	59.5%	66.7%	83.3%	29.2%	57.0%	.231	.390	78	1.0
2022	MIN	MLB	29	23(0)	22²	0-1	4	18	1.63	4.37	56.8%	13.7%	17.6%	1.0%	55.2%	60.7%	88.9%	34.6%	62.5%	.333	.463	92	0.3
2023	MIA	MLB	30	12(0)	11²	2-0	0	8	2.49	9.26	42.8%	14.8%	13.1%	1.6%	47.7%	69.0%	88.3%	31.1%	64.0%	.442	.643	103	0.1
2023	MIN	MLB	30	37(0)	35¹	4-2	3	27	1.27	5.09	49.0%	7.1%	17.4%	4.5%	47.7%	67.9%	91.3%	32.2%	58.2%	.267	.604	107	0.3
2023	BAL	MLB	30	12(0)	12	0-0	0	14	1.25	5.25	58.2%	4.0%	28.0%	8.0%	41.2%	60.4%	87.9%	37.0%	36.7%	.300	.794	91	0.2
2024 DC	NYM	MLB	31	53(0)	56¹	4-2	0	49	1.40	4.75	53.6%	9.1%	20.0%	2.9%	49.0%					.302	.523	105	0.1

2023 Arsenal: SI (96.8), KC (84.2), FA (96.9), SL (88.5), CH (89.2)   *Comps: Wily Peralta (57), Jason Grimsley (57), Phil Regan (56)*

López was a main character of the 2022 trade deadline, an All-Star closer dealt away from the upstart O's to a desperate Twins team for a quartet of pitching prospects. Alongside fan-favorite Trey Mancini, López's departure was yet another symbol of GM Mike Elias' deep, unyielding love for pragmatism over sentimentality. López hit a rough patch with the Twins, and one of the pitching prospects Baltimore received, Yennier Cano, became one of the best set-up men in baseball. López bounced to Miami at the deadline and continued to struggle before the Birds claimed him off waivers in September in a grand karmic gesture. The heartfelt Camden homecoming was short-lived, however, as López remained dinger-prone despite improved peripherals. It was a fairy-tale ending, but the Hans Christian Andersen kind.

Joey Lucchesi LHP   Born: 06/06/93   Age: 31   Height: 6'5"   Weight: 225   Origin: Round 4, 2016 Draft (#114 overall)

YEAR	TM	LVL	AGE	G (GS)	IP	W-L	SV	K	WHIP	ERA	CSP	BB%	K%	HR%	GB%	ZSw%	ZCon%	OSw%	OCon%	BABIP	SLGCON	DRA-	WARP
2021	NYM	MLB	28	11(8)	38¹	1-4	0	41	1.17	4.46	58.2%	7.0%	26.1%	2.5%	38.2%	71.5%	81.8%	24.9%	64.1%	.313	.592	95	0.5
2023	BRK	A+	30	2(2)	8	0-0	0	8	0.88	1.13		6.7%	26.7%	0.0%	50.0%					.250	.250	77	0.2
2023	SYR	AAA	30	15(14)	81²	6-5	0	75	1.42	4.74		11.1%	21.4%	3.4%	53.2%	64.2%	88.0%	31.8%	60.6%	.293	.571	88	1.8
2023	NYM	MLB	30	9(9)	46²	4-0	0	32	1.31	2.89	47.4%	8.7%	16.4%	2.1%	44.4%	64.1%	89.1%	29.9%	72.8%	.288	.483	126	-0.1
2024 DC	NYM	MLB	31	10(10)	44²	2-3	0	34	1.47	5.15	49.5%	8.7%	17.4%	3.2%	45.0%					.307	.545	114	0.0

2023 Arsenal: SI (90.2), CH (78.1), FA (90.6), FS (82.1)   *Comps: Brett Anderson (53), Alex Wood (52), Dave McNally (52)*

Lucchesi is trying to get his career back on track after a promising debut in San Diego was derailed by a combination of ineffectiveness and injury. Even as he returned from Tommy John, he still had to dodge the cartoon anvils life threw at him: a line drive to the neck in Triple-A, and a hit-and-run that struck his Uber ride while trying to flee the police. Despite the shenanigans he looked fine in a late-season return to the Mets' rotation, as long as you didn't look too closely, but his middling numbers for the majority of the season in Syracuse don't inspire a whole lot of confidence. He's essentially a depth option at this point.

Tylor Megill RHP   Born: 07/28/95   Age: 28   Height: 6'7"   Weight: 230   Origin: Round 8, 2018 Draft (#230 overall)

YEAR	TM	LVL	AGE	G (GS)	IP	W-L	SV	K	WHIP	ERA	CSP	BB%	K%	HR%	GB%	ZSw%	ZCon%	OSw%	OCon%	BABIP	SLGCON	DRA-	WARP
2021	BNG	AA	25	5(5)	26	2-1	0	42	1.08	3.12		6.7%	40.4%	1.0%	58.2%					.370	.547	73	0.6
2021	SYR	AAA	25	3(3)	14¹	0-0	0	17	1.12	3.77		8.3%	28.3%	3.3%	48.6%					.257	.486	101	0.2
2021	NYM	MLB	25	18(18)	89²	4-6	0	99	1.28	4.52	56.6%	7.1%	26.1%	5.0%	42.8%	73.0%	82.7%	31.9%	58.9%	.301	.654	82	1.7
2022	NYM	MLB	26	15(9)	47¹	4-2	0	51	1.25	5.13	56.3%	6.5%	25.5%	3.5%	40.0%	72.8%	80.2%	30.6%	58.1%	.310	.580	98	0.5
2023	SYR	AAA	27	6(6)	27	0-3	0	14	1.70	8.67		8.9%	11.4%	2.4%	41.7%	65.0%	92.5%	23.4%	56.1%	.344	.589	117	0.1
2023	NYM	MLB	27	25(25)	126¹	9-8	0	105	1.58	4.70	47.8%	10.2%	18.5%	3.2%	43.6%	70.2%	85.0%	27.1%	61.5%	.325	.557	116	0.5
2024 DC	NYM	MLB	28	16(16)	74¹	4-5	0	64	1.40	4.73	51.4%	8.8%	19.8%	3.1%	42.3%					.305	.541	106	0.4

2023 Arsenal: FA (95.1), SL (84.5), CH (88.2), CU (77.3), FS (85.3)   *Comps: Tyler Cloyd (66), Kendall Graveman (61), Jerad Eickhoff (60)*

You can say this about Megill: He certainly likes learning his teammates' pitches, even if he doesn't end up actually using them much. In March 2022, Megill told reporters that he was working on incorporating a new cutter into his pitch mix, inspired by the one thrown by former teammate (and childhood idol) Max Scherzer. He threw a few in some exhibition games and then put it on the shelf. Fast forward to last September, when he debuted a new splitter in his final start of the season. Megill grips it similar to how his rotation-mate Kodai Senga throws his famed "ghost fork"; Megill even punned on the name of the pitch, saying that he called it his "American spork." Whether or not the new pitch becomes an important part of his arsenal remains to be seen, but Megill is clearly in a "tinkering" phase. It's a good idea too; he needs something more to push him past "sixth-starter" to the next level.

Bryce Montes de Oca RHP   Born: 04/23/96   Age: 28   Height: 6'7"   Weight: 265   Origin: Round 9, 2018 Draft (#260 overall)

YEAR	TM	LVL	AGE	G (GS)	IP	W-L	SV	K	WHIP	ERA	CSP	BB%	K%	HR%	GB%	ZSw%	ZCon%	OSw%	OCon%	BABIP	SLGCON	DRA-	WARP
2021	BRK	A+	25	26(0)	32¹	1-3	6	42	1.52	4.73		18.0%	28.0%	0.7%	42.1%					.280	.400	107	0.1
2022	BNG	AA	26	14(1)	17¹	1-1	3	24	1.44	3.12		18.2%	31.2%	0.0%	65.8%					.289	.378	87	0.3
2022	SYR	AAA	26	30(0)	34	2-2	8	56	1.41	3.44		15.6%	36.4%	0.0%	38.2%	88.2%	80.0%	43.5%	30.0%	.353	.463	65	1.1
2022	NYM	MLB	26	3(0)	3¹	0-0	0	6	2.70	10.80	53.3%	10.5%	31.6%	0.0%	54.5%	75.0%	83.3%	32.7%	64.7%	.636	.636	87	0.1
2024 non	NYM	MLB	28	58(0)	50	2-2	0	59	1.51	5.06	53.3%	14.3%	26.1%	3.1%	40.9%					.295	.569	109	0.0

2023 Arsenal: SI (99), FC (95), SW (87.9), FA (99.2)   *Comps: Juan Jaime (48), Greg Weissert (47), Jon Edwards (46)*

There's never been any question about the stuff, and we got a quick look at it when Montes de Oca was promoted for a late-season cameo at the end of 2022: A cut fastball in the upper-90s and a sinking fastball *even harder than that* isn't easy to come by, even as pitchers find a way to throw faster and faster. Unfortunately for Montes de Oca, most of his professional career has been defined less by his stuff and more by his injury track record, and he'll be sidelined until at least the beginning of the 2024 season after undergoing his second career Tommy John surgery. When he comes back, he'll get every chance in the world ... until the next injury crops up.

David Peterson LHP   Born: 09/03/95   Age: 28   Height: 6'6"   Weight: 240   Origin: Round 1, 2017 Draft (#20 overall)

YEAR	TM	LVL	AGE	G (GS)	IP	W-L	SV	K	WHIP	ERA	CSP	BB%	K%	HR%	GB%	ZSw%	ZCon%	OSw%	OCon%	BABIP	SLGCON	DRA-	WARP
2021	NYM	MLB	25	15(15)	66²	2-6	0	69	1.40	5.54	51.7%	10.1%	24.0%	3.8%	47.3%	69.3%	83.2%	30.9%	61.7%	.310	.626	99	0.7
2022	SYR	AAA	26	6(6)	26	2-3	0	34	1.65	4.85		8.4%	28.6%	0.8%	50.7%					.432	.600	74	0.7
2022	NYM	MLB	26	28(19)	105²	7-5	0	126	1.33	3.83	48.9%	10.6%	27.8%	2.4%	49.1%	67.5%	83.9%	31.2%	52.0%	.315	.556	104	0.8
2023	SYR	AAA	27	7(7)	37	1-2	0	43	1.62	4.86		13.9%	25.9%	3.0%	45.5%	64.6%	82.2%	32.7%	45.1%	.340	.612	90	0.7
2023	NYM	MLB	27	27(21)	111	3-8	0	128	1.57	5.03	44.2%	10.2%	26.0%	3.3%	53.9%	68.3%	82.1%	32.3%	56.5%	.371	.648	94	1.6
2024 DC	NYM	MLB	28	20(10)	59	3-3	0	67	1.38	4.29	46.9%	10.6%	26.0%	2.5%	50.3%					.313	.531	96	0.6

2023 Arsenal: FA (93), SI (91.7), SL (85.5), CH (85.4), CU (79.1), SW (85.2)   Comps: Jordan Montgomery (67), Jeff Locke (67), Andrew Heaney (67)

Peterson seemed poised for a breakout after a strong showing in 2022, but his run prevention skills took a turn for the worse last year even as his peripherals improved. He showed increased movement on his sinker, which got a ground ball a whopping 70% of the time it was put into play. However, when balls were put into the air, he allowed an unsustainable rate of homers. He'll try to turn it around in 2024, but he'll have a late start to his campaign, as he underwent hip surgery in November that will sideline him into the start of the season.

José Quintana LHP   Born: 01/24/89   Age: 35   Height: 6'1"   Weight: 220   Origin: IFA, 2006

YEAR	TM	LVL	AGE	G (GS)	IP	W-L	SV	K	WHIP	ERA	CSP	BB%	K%	HR%	GB%	ZSw%	ZCon%	OSw%	OCon%	BABIP	SLGCON	DRA-	WARP
2021	LAA	MLB	32	24(10)	53¹	0-3	0	73	1.78	6.75	51.5%	11.4%	28.7%	3.5%	44.4%	69.5%	82.4%	33.0%	57.3%	.401	.718	90	0.8
2021	SF	MLB	32	5(0)	9²	0-0	0	12	1.45	4.66	53.3%	14.0%	27.9%	7.0%	48.0%	58.3%	92.9%	34.5%	44.7%	.227	.720	78	0.2
2022	STL	MLB	33	12(12)	62²	3-2	0	48	1.12	2.01	49.9%	6.5%	19.4%	0.4%	48.6%	69.8%	88.8%	37.0%	68.3%	.296	.374	108	0.3
2022	PIT	MLB	33	20(20)	103	3-5	0	89	1.27	3.50	50.5%	7.2%	20.6%	1.6%	45.5%	68.5%	87.3%	36.2%	62.0%	.307	.477	113	0.3
2023	SYR	AAA	34	2(2)	7	0-1	0	7	2.00	9.00		17.6%	20.6%	2.9%	28.6%	73.0%	92.6%	33.3%	48.6%	.350	.650	108	0.1
2023	NYM	MLB	34	13(13)	75²	3-6	0	60	1.31	3.57	42.5%	7.5%	18.8%	1.6%	41.5%	67.5%	88.9%	33.9%	67.4%	.307	.459	116	0.3
2024 DC	NYM	MLB	35	28(28)	140¹	8-9	0	123	1.43	4.81	48.0%	8.5%	20.2%	3.0%	43.3%					.315	.545	108	0.6

2023 Arsenal: SI (90.6), CU (77.4), FA (90.5), CH (86.1)   Comps: Jim Kaat (75), Claude Osteen (75), Andy Pettitte (74)

With the midseason departures of Justin Verlander and Max Scherzer during the team's deadline sell-off, Quintana will be serving as the veteran presence on a new-look Mets' staff ... unless he too gets dealt over the offseason. No matter where he suits up, he'll try to run back the solid run-prevention numbers of the past two years despite some concerns entering his age-35 season. Coming off of injury last year, his fastball velocity dipped to its lowest average of his career, and his strikeout percentage was his lowest since his rookie season in 2012. Quintana's managed to fight his way back to relevance multiple times over his career, so don't put yet another resurgence entirely out of play.

Brooks Raley LHP   Born: 06/29/88   Age: 36   Height: 6'3"   Weight: 200   Origin: Round 6, 2009 Draft (#200 overall)

YEAR	TM	LVL	AGE	G (GS)	IP	W-L	SV	K	WHIP	ERA	CSP	BB%	K%	HR%	GB%	ZSw%	ZCon%	OSw%	OCon%	BABIP	SLGCON	DRA-	WARP
2021	HOU	MLB	33	58(0)	49	2-3	2	65	1.20	4.78	49.2%	7.8%	31.7%	2.9%	44.6%	66.8%	77.7%	34.0%	54.2%	.325	.558	76	1.1
2022	TB	MLB	34	60(0)	53²	1-2	6	61	0.97	2.68	49.5%	6.8%	27.9%	1.4%	38.0%	63.5%	85.6%	36.2%	57.6%	.256	.400	89	0.8
2023	NYM	MLB	35	66(0)	54²	1-2	3	61	1.26	2.80	45.6%	10.6%	25.8%	1.7%	41.7%	62.4%	85.5%	30.5%	51.4%	.288	.472	94	0.8
2024 DC	NYM	MLB	36	53(0)	56¹	4-2	4	60	1.26	4.03	47.7%	8.9%	25.2%	3.0%	40.6%					.292	.539	92	0.5

2023 Arsenal: SW (81.8), SI (90.2), FC (87.1), CH (85), FA (90.6)   Comps: Andrew Miller (64), Joe Kelly (57), Anthony Bass (55)

Raley kept doing what he's been doing since returning from the Korea Baseball Organization prior to the 2020 season. The southpaw racks up strikeouts and elicits soft contact, befuddling hitters with a kitchen-sink mix of sinkers, cutters, changeups, and high-spin sweeping sliders. Despite his worst control numbers since returning to MLB, Raley was still a reliable option, frequently being used in short stints and facing three batters or fewer in his appearances. There aren't too many relievers exactly like him, either in terms of repertoire, history of travel, or consistency.

★ ★ ★ *2024 Top 101 Prospect* **#88** ★ ★ ★

Christian Scott RHP   Born: 06/15/99   Age: 25   Height: 6'4"   Weight: 215   Origin: Round 5, 2021 Draft (#142 overall)

YEAR	TM	LVL	AGE	G (GS)	IP	W-L	SV	K	WHIP	ERA	CSP	BB%	K%	HR%	GB%	ZSw%	ZCon%	OSw%	OCon%	BABIP	SLGCON	DRA-	WARP
2022	SLU	A	23	12(4)	37¹	3-3	0	52	1.39	4.82		7.3%	31.5%	1.2%	46.4%	70.7%	71.7%	36.0%	61.7%	.409	.579	82	0.9
2022	BRK	A+	23	6(5)	21¹	0-0	0	25	1.45	3.80		10.4%	26.0%	0.0%	43.3%					.350	.483	90	0.3
2023	BRK	A+	24	6(6)	23²	1-0	0	27	0.80	2.28		4.4%	30.0%	0.0%	51.7%					.259	.362	89	0.4
2023	BNG	AA	24	12(12)	62	4-3	0	77	0.84	2.47		3.4%	32.8%	2.1%	40.0%					.279	.490	78	1.5
2024 non	NYM	MLB	25	58(0)	50	2-2	0	45	1.29	4.36		7.6%	21.3%	3.4%	37.7%					.293	.550	100	0.2

2023 Arsenal: FA (95), CH (85.8), SL (84.5), CU (78.5)   Comps: Hiram Burgos (72), Jason Bahr (63), Garrett Hill (62)

After an unspectacular beginning to his professional career, Scott really took off in 2023. He views his brief stint in the Arizona Fall League in '22 as something of a turning point, and it was there that he refined a changeup that became his preferred secondary pitch last season. Improved control was also a big part of Scott's leap forward, as his 8.9 strikeout-to-walk ratio was second in all of minor-league baseball last year to only Tigers' prospect Jackson Jobe. Scott is on the older side for a prospect pitching at his level and, until this season, he hadn't been considered one of the Mets' more notable farmhands. However, his impressive numbers and development of an important out pitch are cause to stand up and take notice.

Kodai Senga RHP Born: 01/30/93 Age: 31 Height: 6'1" Weight: 202 Origin: IFA, 2022

YEAR	TM	LVL	AGE	G (GS)	IP	W-L	SV	K	WHIP	ERA	CSP	BB%	K%	HR%	GB%	ZSw%	ZCon%	OSw%	OCon%	BABIP	SLGCON	DRA-	WARP
2023	NYM	MLB	30	29(29)	166¹	12-7	0	202	1.22	2.98	44.0%	11.1%	29.1%	2.4%	43.5%	68.1%	84.7%	31.2%	51.4%	.279	.490	93	2.6
2024 DC	NYM	MLB	31	29(29)	163	10-9	0	184	1.27	3.90	44.0%	10.2%	26.7%	3.3%	35.0%					.283	.555	90	2.3

2023 Arsenal: FA (96), FC (91), FS (83.4), SW (81.4), SL (84.8), CU (73.1)   Comps: Dave Stewart (90), David Cone (90), Bob Veale (90)

As good as Senga's overall numbers look in his stateside debut, it was his in-season development that made it even more impressive. Even putting aside the challenges faced by anybody acclimating to a new culture and language, Senga needed to get used to the different baseball used in MLB. To do so, he severely limited usage of his legendary splitter—the "ghost fork"—during spring training to avoid excess stress on his fingers. By mid-season he'd introduced a new slider, as the sweeping breaking ball he'd thrown in Japan was neither missing bats nor getting good results when put into play. The harder slider has less horizontal movement, and it quickly became a reliable option for him in his repertoire. Then, after the early-season kid gloves, the ghost fork ultimately elicited a whiff on *59.6% of swings against it*, easily the highest rate of any pitch in the majors thrown at least 500 times. A strong new pitch to go with his unhittable old one, adapting to a new ball, and also greatly improved control numbers after his first few weeks of the season—Senga's transition to MLB may have taken a few months but was as successful as anyone could have expected.

Luis Severino RHP Born: 02/20/94 Age: 30 Height: 6'2" Weight: 218 Origin: IFA, 2011

YEAR	TM	LVL	AGE	G (GS)	IP	W-L	SV	K	WHIP	ERA	CSP	BB%	K%	HR%	GB%	ZSw%	ZCon%	OSw%	OCon%	BABIP	SLGCON	DRA-	WARP
2021	SOM	AA	27	2(2)	6¹	0-0	0	9	0.47	2.84		4.5%	40.9%	4.5%	50.0%					.091	.417	97	0.1
2021	NYY	MLB	27	4(0)	6	1-0	0	8	0.50	0.00	48.6%	4.5%	36.4%	0.0%	41.7%	71.4%	80.0%	34.3%	54.2%	.167	.250	86	0.1
2022	NYY	MLB	28	19(19)	102	7-3	0	112	1.00	3.18	55.7%	7.4%	27.7%	3.5%	43.6%	71.6%	80.8%	32.5%	58.2%	.239	.508	81	2.0
2023	NYY	MLB	29	19(18)	89¹	4-8	0	79	1.65	6.65	49.3%	8.2%	18.9%	5.5%	42.6%	74.1%	83.8%	33.3%	71.4%	.328	.703	114	0.4
2024 DC	NYM	MLB	30	19(19)	99	6-6	0	88	1.33	4.36	52.0%	8.1%	20.9%	3.1%	42.4%					.298	.534	99	0.8

2023 Arsenal: FA (96.6), SL (85.4), CH (86.7), FC (91.7), SI (95.7)   Comps: Yovani Gallardo (70), Don Drysdale (68), Matt Cain (68)

In the *Song of Ice and Fire* books, Dorne is far from the disaster it is in the television show. Prince Doran has another son, Quentyn, and he is so determined to bring Daenerys to Dorne that he endures a grueling journey to Meereen simply to get an audience with her. Quentyn continually fails in his attempt to convince her to return with him. Desperate to come home with something, he tries to take one of Dany's dragons—only to get absolutely cooked in the end. Poor Quentyn.

Anyway, that's what it was like for Yankees fans to watch Severino in 2023: Hope utterly incinerated. It was a brutal way for the erstwhile ace's career in pinstripes to end after peaking in 2018, so yeah, a Game of Thrones reference seemed appropriate.

Drew Smith RHP Born: 09/24/93 Age: 30 Height: 6'2" Weight: 190 Origin: Round 3, 2015 Draft (#99 overall)

YEAR	TM	LVL	AGE	G (GS)	IP	W-L	SV	K	WHIP	ERA	CSP	BB%	K%	HR%	GB%	ZSw%	ZCon%	OSw%	OCon%	BABIP	SLGCON	DRA-	WARP
2021	NYM	MLB	27	31(1)	41¹	3-1	0	41	1.06	2.40	55.0%	9.7%	24.8%	4.2%	34.0%	72.4%	81.0%	35.5%	55.6%	.212	.552	107	0.2
2022	NYM	MLB	28	44(0)	46	3-3	0	53	1.15	3.33	50.2%	8.0%	28.3%	4.8%	34.5%	73.5%	77.2%	32.8%	57.6%	.264	.585	86	0.8
2023	NYM	MLB	29	62(0)	56¹	4-6	3	60	1.40	4.15	43.2%	11.9%	24.6%	2.9%	30.7%	72.2%	82.2%	31.3%	62.8%	.301	.622	111	0.3
2024 DC	NYM	MLB	30	53(0)	56¹	4-2	2	59	1.35	4.63	47.3%	10.1%	24.3%	3.7%	33.5%					.291	.586	104	0.1

2023 Arsenal: FA (95.3), SL (84.7), CH (85.5), CU (76.9), SW (83.3)   Comps: Nick Wittgren (56), Ryan Dull (55), Evan Scribner (54)

It was a trying season for Smith, punctuated by a June suspension for breaking the league's foreign substance policy in a game against the Yankees (despite Smith's vehemence that the "stickiness" on his hands was just a buildup of rosin on a humid night). Beyond that, Smith's control and contact numbers both regressed from their 2022 levels. On the bright side, he was finally able to put up a fully healthy campaign, as his Mets tenure has been plagued by elbow, shoulder, and lat injuries. He also appears to have adhered himself to a regular mid-leverage relief role in Queens.

Blade Tidwell RHP Born: 06/08/01 Age: 23 Height: 6'4" Weight: 207 Origin: Round 2, 2022 Draft (#52 overall)

YEAR	TM	LVL	AGE	G (GS)	IP	W-L	SV	K	WHIP	ERA	CSP	BB%	K%	HR%	GB%	ZSw%	ZCon%	OSw%	OCon%	BABIP	SLGCON	DRA-	WARP
2022	SLU	A	21	4(4)	8¹	0-1	0	9	1.20	2.16		16.2%	24.3%	0.0%	40.0%	66.7%	80.4%	27.7%	53.8%	.200	.263	114	0.1
2023	BRK	A+	22	17(17)	81²	8-3	0	112	1.24	3.09		13.6%	33.0%	2.4%	33.3%					.275	.531	99	0.5
2023	BNG	AA	22	8(8)	34¹	3-3	0	41	1.43	4.72		11.5%	27.7%	4.1%	28.2%					.329	.706	101	0.5
2024 non	NYM	MLB	23	58(0)	50	2-2	0	52	1.55	5.61		13.2%	22.9%	3.9%	31.6%					.297	.606	121	-0.3

Comps: Ronald Bolaños (76), Parker Bridwell (72), Ben Lively (70)

There's no question about Tidwell's ability to rack up strikeouts: He has three bat-missing offerings with his riding mid-90s fastball, sweeping slider, and slow, screwball-like changeup—15 miles per hour slower than his heater—nicknamed "The Starfish." More cause for concern lies in his suspect control and in the fact that the nature of his repertoire leaves him susceptible to the long ball. That being said, there's a lot to like about Tidwell, and he seems fast-tracked to cut his way to Triple-A this season.

Michael Tonkin RHP   Born: 11/19/89   Age: 34   Height: 6'7"   Weight: 220   Origin: Round 30, 2008 Draft (#906 overall)

YEAR	TM	LVL	AGE	G (GS)	IP	W-L	SV	K	WHIP	ERA	CSP	BB%	K%	HR%	GB%	ZSw%	ZCon%	OSw%	OCon%	BABIP	SLGCON	DRA-	WARP
2022	GWN	AAA	32	47(0)	48¹	5-2	16	73	1.10	3.17		7.5%	36.5%	1.5%	48.6%	61.9%	92.3%	33.3%	66.7%	.343	.500	60	1.6
2023	ATL	MLB	33	45(0)	80	7-3	1	75	1.09	4.28	50.3%	7.1%	23.1%	4.0%	37.3%	69.6%	80.7%	33.6%	65.2%	.243	.509	94	1.2
2024 DC	NYM	MLB	34	41(0)	43²	3-2	0	39	1.30	4.52	50.3%	7.8%	21.0%	3.8%	34.6%					.287	.565	103	0.1

2023 Arsenal: SI (93.7), SL (83.2), SW (80)   *Comps: Rudy Seanez (48), Fernando Salas (47), Javy Guerra (47)*

After leaving Major League Baseball for the Hokkaido Nippon-Ham Fighters in Japan ahead of the 2018 season, it was completely reasonable to think that you'd never see Tonkin's name mentioned in these illustrious pages again. His stint in Japan didn't last longer than the one season, though, so he returned to America and bounced between affiliated organizations and the independent Long Island Ducks over the next three years. Eventually he left the States again and went to Tijuana to pitch for the Toros in 2022. He latched onto another MLB organization with the Braves last year, and this was when he finally got back to a big-league mound. He didn't just get a cup of coffee, either—he pitched 80 innings for Atlanta and even made a solitary postseason appearance, his first since his 2013 MLB debut. His sinker and slider were calling cards back when he was last in the bigs, a trait that hasn't changed in the intervening half-decade. They'll remain his calling cards if he wants to stick around.

Mike Vasil RHP   Born: 03/19/00   Age: 24   Height: 6'5"   Weight: 225   Origin: Round 8, 2021 Draft (#232 overall)

YEAR	TM	LVL	AGE	G (GS)	IP	W-L	SV	K	WHIP	ERA	CSP	BB%	K%	HR%	GB%	ZSw%	ZCon%	OSw%	OCon%	BABIP	SLGCON	DRA-	WARP
2021	MET	ROK	21	3(3)	7	0-0	0	10	0.43	1.29		0.0%	41.7%	0.0%	57.1%					.214	.357		
2022	SLU	A	22	9(8)	37	3-1	0	39	1.00	2.19		7.5%	26.5%	0.7%	45.4%	78.1%	79.9%	36.4%	50.0%	.260	.302	93	0.7
2022	BRK	A+	22	8(8)	33¹	1-1	0	44	1.17	5.13		10.7%	31.4%	2.1%	46.8%					.276	.500	93	0.4
2023	BNG	AA	23	10(10)	51	1-2	0	57	0.84	3.71		4.1%	28.9%	4.1%	36.6%					.220	.523	88	1.1
2023	SYR	AAA	23	16(16)	73	4-4	0	81	1.48	5.30		11.7%	24.9%	3.1%	33.5%	70.2%	79.9%	33.7%	57.8%	.314	.578	94	1.3
2024 DC	NYM	MLB	24	3(3)	12²	1-1	0	12	1.43	5.05		9.5%	20.7%	3.7%	36.1%					.299	.590	112	0.0

2023 Arsenal: FA (93.8), SL (85.8), CH (84.6), KC (79.3)   *Comps: Nick Nelson (82), Tyler Thornburg (82), Aaron Blair (80)*

Despite the infusion of young talent that the Mets added at the 2023 trade deadline, Vasil—entering his fourth year with the organization—is *still* the team's pitching prospect closest to contributing in the major-league rotation. He backs up his low-to-mid 90s fastball with a trio of secondaries: There's a hard, tight slider that's his preferred breaking pitch, a fading changeup that he prefers to throw to lefties and a biting spike curveball that comes in around 80 mph. Don't be surprised to see him making big league starts in the near future, and not *just* because holes need to be filled in the Mets' rotation.

LINEOUTS

Hitters

HITTER	POS	TM	LVL	AGE	PA	R	HR	RBI	SB	AVG/OBP/SLG	BABIP	SLGCON	BB%	K%	ZSw%	ZCon%	OSw%	OCon%	LA	90th EV	DRC+	BRR	DRP	WARP
Diego Castillo	UT	RNO	AAA	25	556	94	3	72	13	.313/.431/.410	.370	.496	17.4%	14.2%	49.1%	87.2%	25.4%	75.0%			106	2.2	-3.2	1.6
	UT	AZ	MLB	25	1	0	0	0	0	.000/.000/.000		.000	0.0%	0.0%	50.0%	100.0%			36.0	92.5	76		0.0	0.0
Carlos Cortes	LF	SYR	AAA	26	442	63	15	54	3	.241/.355/.428	.274	.564	14.7%	20.1%	62.9%	82.9%	29.3%	64.2%			106	-1.4	7.4	2.2
Luis Guillorme	IF	SYR	AAA	28	68	9	1	6	0	.241/.397/.352	.255	.396	19.1%	8.8%	62.0%	90.3%	25.6%	85.7%			118	0.2	-0.9	0.3
	IF	NYM	MLB	28	120	12	1	9	0	.224/.288/.327	.291	.443	8.3%	23.3%	59.4%	91.0%	28.6%	70.2%	11.1	99.2	84	0.1	-0.3	0.1
Tyler Heineman	C	BUF	AAA	32	142	21	1	13	5	.214/.331/.265	.282	.365	14.1%	22.5%	68.2%	82.7%	30.8%	72.2%			88	-1.1	1.1	0.3
	C	PIT	MLB	32	10	1	0	0	1	.111/.200/.111	.125	.125	10.0%	10.0%	92.3%	83.3%	31.8%	71.4%	17.6	98.2	111	0.0	0.0	0.1
	C	TOR	MLB	32	37	4	0	3	0	.276/.432/.379	.364	.500	18.9%	18.9%	57.1%	92.9%	35.9%	72.7%	20.0	97.7	108	0.0	0.1	0.2
Ronald Hernandez	C/DH	MRL	ROK	19	138	27	3	25	3	.298/.464/.452	.373	.610	23.2%	19.6%										
	C/DH	MET	ROK	19	53	6	1	11	1	.286/.509/.486	.360	.680	28.3%	18.9%										
	C/DH	SLU	A	19	39	3	0	7	0	.172/.333/.241	.278	.438	15.4%	33.3%	71.7%	63.2%	27.3%	63.6%			85	-0.1	0.1	0.0
Colin Houck	SS	MET	ROK	18	36	6	0	4	0	.241/.389/.310	.333	.429	19.4%	22.2%										
Cooper Hummel	1B	TAC	AAA	28	455	71	8	47	26	.262/.409/.435	.348	.615	18.0%	23.3%	65.7%	83.6%	24.8%	49.5%			102	-0.3	1.1	1.3
	1B	SEA	MLB	28	26	2	0	0	1	.087/.192/.130	.143	.214	7.7%	34.6%	73.3%	72.7%	28.2%	55.0%	6.9	101.2	80	0.0	0.0	0.0
José Iglesias	SS	ELP	AAA	33	135	22	4	27	0	.317/.356/.537	.350	.653	6.7%	16.3%	62.6%	86.6%	43.5%	71.9%			104	0.7	0.8	0.6
Taylor Kohlwey	OF	ELP	AAA	28	518	71	12	73	15	.276/.390/.437	.316	.547	14.5%	16.6%	59.7%	90.8%	25.0%	72.0%			104	-2.0	2.1	1.8
	OF	SD	MLB	28	13	0	0	0	0	.154/.154/.154	.250	.250	0.0%	38.5%	58.3%	85.7%	31.8%	42.9%	17.7	96.6	80		0.0	0.0
Tim Locastro	OF	SYR	AAA	30	66	8	2	10	0	.200/.313/.345	.225	.452	6.1%	19.7%	68.9%	80.8%	42.4%	67.2%			99	0.2	-0.2	0.2
	OF	NYM	MLB	30	67	13	2	3	6	.232/.338/.393	.344	.647	4.5%	32.8%	61.8%	73.5%	42.2%	59.3%	20.9	99.7	87	0.2	0.3	0.1
Danny Mendick	UT	SYR	AAA	29	425	62	11	57	14	.282/.369/.424	.311	.505	10.8%	14.1%	60.5%	88.2%	31.1%	71.8%			114	3.3	4.8	2.4
	UT	NYM	MLB	29	69	4	1	4	1	.185/.232/.277	.224	.360	5.8%	21.7%	62.9%	82.1%	28.9%	63.6%	10.9	100.4	87	-0.2	-0.1	0.1
Rafael Ortega	OF	RR	AAA	32	199	31	5	26	8	.226/.333/.381	.252	.478	13.6%	17.1%	69.0%	90.0%	30.3%	68.3%			108	-0.1	2.8	1.0
	OF	SYR	AAA	32	140	20	4	15	6	.230/.379/.398	.256	.500	19.3%	16.4%	63.8%	85.4%	30.1%	69.0%			109	0.0	3.4	0.9
	OF	NYM	MLB	32	136	16	1	8	6	.219/.341/.272	.300	.383	14.7%	24.3%	60.8%	81.2%	29.8%	71.7%	9.8	99.5	83	0.2	-2.2	-0.1
Alex Ramírez	CF	BRK	A+	20	521	66	7	53	21	.221/.310/.317	.277	.423	10.7%	21.9%							99		10.5	2.2
Zack Short	IF	TOL	AAA	28	100	20	5	12	1	.195/.340/.427	.244	.700	18.0%	32.0%	58.2%	79.1%	19.5%	42.3%			102	0.5	0.3	0.4
	IF	DET	MLB	28	253	17	7	33	5	.204/.292/.339	.255	.484	11.1%	26.1%	69.1%	84.4%	22.4%	54.8%	20.1	102.7	79	0.1	-0.8	0.1
Rhylan Thomas	OF	SLU	A	23	139	13	1	9	2	.303/.370/.434	.327	.486	10.1%	9.4%	77.0%	91.1%	36.1%	83.3%			120	-0.1	4.8	1.2
	OF	BRK	A+	23	148	19	2	16	3	.341/.432/.429	.357	.466	12.8%	6.8%							127	-1.0	-0.5	0.9
	OF	BNG	AA	23	59	8	0	2	2	.353/.431/.392	.391	.435	11.9%	8.5%							119	-0.3	0.5	0.2
Trayce Thompson	OF	CHW	MLB	32	92	5	1	3	2	.171/.261/.232	.317	.452	9.8%	43.5%	65.9%	63.6%	23.9%	41.1%	20.1	103.3	46	0.0	-1.1	-0.4
	OF	LAD	MLB	32	87	12	5	14	0	.155/.310/.366	.207	.765	17.2%	42.5%	63.2%	73.5%	22.6%	29.1%	24.1	108.2	75	0.0	-0.9	-0.1

Diego Castillo's claim to fame is his stellar contact rate, but with no other standout tool, he'll be hitting the bench more often than the baseball. ⊗ After joining the Mets organization in 2018, **Carlos Cortes** became known for his ambidexterity—combined with his defensive versatility, he would switch handedness based on where he played in the field. The novelty has worn off; he's mostly transitioned to a left-field role and he profiles as an organizational player on the 40-man roster bubble. ⊗ In 2021 and 2022, **Luis Guillorme** was a useful utility infielder with good on-base skills and a great defensive reputation. In 2023, Guillorme's walks went down, his strikeouts went up, and his defensive metrics faded, now he's more of a replacement-level fill-in. ⊗ The Clubhouse Magician (he is an actual magician, check out his TikTok) made some RBI appear out of thin air on the last day of the season: **Tyler Heineman** drove in all three of his runs last year during the season's final game, including notching his first career triple. ⊗ **Ronald Hernandez** has put up impressive plate discipline numbers so far in summer ball, both in the Dominican and stateside leagues; he's also known to have a solid throwing arm. With a late-season promotion to Low-A under his belt after his midseason trade to New York, it's safe to assume Hernandez will resume his development at St. Lucie. ⊗ Top draft pick **Colin Houck** was selected as a shortstop, but given his size, he's more likely to find a home at the hot corner—something the Mets already tasked him with for two of his nine games in his debut in the Florida Complex League. ⊗ Acquired for former Rookie of the Year Kyle Lewis, **Cooper Hummel** was banished to Tacoma three weeks into his Mariners tenure, where he continued to showcase his defensive versatility and OBP skills against Triple-A pitching. At 29, it's getting late to still consider him a late-bloomer. ⊗ Less a major leaguer and more a quarter found on the sidewalk, **José Iglesias** mashed for a month in Triple-A before opting out of his deal. No one came calling, making last season the first since 2014 where he didn't take a big-league PA. ⊗ **Taylor Kohlwey** made his major-league debut one day before his 29th birthday and, at 0 WARP, is now the second-most-valuable draft pick of the 21st round in 2016. John McMillon and his 0.1 WARP can't feel too comfortable right now. ⊗ Among active players who have attempted at least 50 stolen bases in their career, **Tim Locastro**'s success rate of 90% is ever-so-slightly behind the 90.3% rate of superstar Corbin Carroll. This is the *only* way that Locastro is like a superstar, but at least he's got one thing going for him. ⊗ In one of many low points for the 2023 Mets, infielder **Danny Mendick** was on the mound for the final inning of a 21-3 rout at the hands of the Braves. He gave up eight runs, pitching just about as well as he hit last season. ⊗ 2021 stands as the highlight of **Rafael Ortega**'s professional career, when he came out of nowhere to provide the Cubs with 330 quality plate appearances. Since then, he's bounced around between the Yankees', Rangers' and Mets' systems and has been unable to sustain what looked like a breakout, in part due to his .506 career OPS against southpaws. ⊗ One of the team's more prominent prospects for the past few seasons, **Alex Ramírez** had a very difficult 2023. He still spends most of his time in center field and you can dream on the tools, but after his unimpressive offensive showing at High-A, his future looks much murkier than it did a year ago. ⊗ The **Zack Short** nominative determinism lineouts will continue until his batting average improves. The Tigers designated the light-hitting utilityman for assignment this offseason, and his hometown Mets picked him up, which was nice of them. ⊗ There wasn't a whole lot of fanfare surrounding **Rhylan Thomas** as an 11th-round pick in 2022; he isn't young for the levels he's played at, and none of his batted balls tracked in Hawkeye-equipped parks last season exceeded 100 mph. Still, he's quickly made himself into the kind of organizational player that could get a cup of coffee thanks to his contact-oriented profile. ⊗ **Trayce Thompson's** bat-to-ball skill is so poor you almost want him to start swinging at the same place every time just in case it's thrown there, like answering B for every question on the multiple-choice test.

Pitchers

PITCHER	TM	LVL	AGE	G (GS)	IP	W-L	SV	K	WHIP	ERA	CSP	BB%	K%	HR%	GB%	ZSw%	ZCon%	OSw%	OCon%	BABIP	SLGCON	DRA-	WARP
Peyton Battenfield	AKR	AA	25	2 (2)	7²	0-0	0	5	1.04	1.17		13.8%	17.2%	0.0%	50.0%					.200	.250	103	0.1
	SYR	AAA	25	2 (2)	9	1-1	0	4	1.78	6.00		14.6%	9.8%	0.0%	38.7%	61.8%	97.1%	40.0%	69.0%	.323	.452	110	0.1
	COL	AAA	25	9 (9)	47²	0-5	0	24	1.38	5.66		10.3%	11.8%	6.4%	36.9%	75.0%	87.4%	29.4%	63.9%	.222	.592	119	0.2
	CLE	MLB	25	7 (6)	34²	0-5	0	27	1.33	5.19	46.3%	8.2%	18.5%	4.8%	42.1%	75.5%	84.9%	32.6%	60.2%	.270	.594	115	0.1
Jeff Brigham	SYR	AAA	31	10 (0)	9	0-1	0	6	2.56	10.00		19.1%	12.8%	6.4%	30.0%	73.1%	89.8%	31.8%	68.3%	.407	.897	135	0.0
	NYM	MLB	31	37 (0)	37²	1-3	0	42	1.17	5.26	45.7%	11.3%	26.3%	5.6%	35.8%	68.1%	77.9%	29.4%	62.7%	.198	.606	101	0.4
Nolan Clenney	BNG	AA	27	25 (0)	40¹	1-2	2	44	1.64	5.36		9.5%	23.3%	3.7%	46.0%					.345	.642	98	0.7
	SYR	AAA	27	12 (0)	23²	0-3	0	37	1.35	6.08		10.6%	35.6%	2.9%	38.9%	61.8%	80.0%	28.0%	46.7%	.353	.685	76	0.6
Sam Coonrod	SYR	AAA	30	9 (0)	7²	0-1	1	8	2.61	12.91		23.8%	19.0%	7.1%	39.1%	62.2%	82.6%	18.2%	66.7%	.350	1.000	113	0.0
	NYM	MLB	30	10 (0)	6²	0-0	0	6	1.95	9.45	41.8%	23.5%	17.6%	0.0%	61.1%	63.5%	78.8%	20.0%	73.7%	.278	.278	109	0.0
John Curtiss	SYR	AAA	30	18 (0)	21¹	1-2	0	21	1.69	7.17		9.9%	20.8%	5.9%	41.4%	71.2%	82.4%	27.7%	72.6%	.313	.700	102	0.3
	NYM	MLB	30	15 (0)	19²	0-0	0	16	1.27	4.58	47.0%	9.9%	19.8%	3.7%	40.4%	74.6%	90.1%	26.3%	48.9%	.259	.500	102	0.2
Reed Garrett	SYR	AAA	30	12 (0)	12²	0-0	0	12	1.89	5.68		14.5%	19.4%	3.2%	48.8%	70.1%	73.8%	33.5%	66.7%	.333	.625	90	0.2
	NOR	AAA	30	19 (0)	22²	5-1	3	27	1.28	1.59		10.5%	28.4%	2.1%	43.9%	67.3%	83.5%	37.9%	44.0%	.309	.491	86	0.5
	NYM	MLB	30	9 (0)	17	1-0	0	16	1.24	5.82	45.2%	8.5%	22.5%	4.2%	41.7%	72.6%	74.4%	36.6%	64.7%	.267	.574	94	0.3
	BAL	MLB	30	2 (0)	2²	0-0	0	0	3.00	10.12	55.0%	6.3%	0.0%	0.0%	53.3%	79.2%	84.2%	35.7%	80.0%	.467	.600	101	0.0
Justin Jarvis	BLX	AA	23	14 (14)	75²	6-4	0	91	1.26	3.33		8.2%	28.6%	3.1%	39.4%					.314	.599	82	1.7
	NAS	AAA	23	3 (3)	11²	0-2	0	11	2.49	10.80		19.4%	17.7%	3.2%	23.1%	68.2%	77.3%	23.9%	67.6%	.405	.784	119	0.0
	SYR	AAA	23	9 (9)	31¹	0-5	0	36	2.07	8.04		13.7%	22.4%	5.0%	36.9%	71.0%	84.1%	29.3%	65.5%	.368	.748	102	0.4
Luis Moreno	BNG	AA	24	25 (21)	119¹	9-6	0	117	1.48	4.98		11.2%	22.2%	2.3%	49.6%					.320	.549	117	0.9
Eric Orze	SYR	AAA	25	39 (1)	61	3-4	0	81	1.52	5.31		15.1%	29.8%	2.2%	39.2%	63.7%	78.7%	33.5%	46.7%	.324	.603	84	1.4
Yohan Ramirez	IND	AAA	28	18 (1)	22¹	1-1	0	32	1.21	4.43		12.4%	33.0%	0.0%	54.2%	59.2%	83.9%	28.2%	42.4%	.313	.457	80	0.6
	CHW	MLB	28	5 (0)	4	0-0	0	4	2.00	9.00	48.1%	14.3%	19.0%	0.0%	53.8%	41.5%	88.2%	12.3%	75.0%	.385	.667	86	0.1
	PIT	MLB	28	26 (0)	34¹	1-0	0	31	1.40	3.67	44.7%	9.0%	20.0%	1.9%	60.0%	69.7%	90.6%	26.7%	61.0%	.320	.450	99	0.4
Sean Reid-Foley	SYR	AAA	27	16 (0)	16¹	0-1	1	26	1.16	4.96		14.7%	38.2%	5.9%	40.6%	61.2%	78.4%	27.1%	46.7%	.179	.750	79	0.4
	NYM	MLB	27	8 (0)	7²	0-1	0	16	1.30	3.52	41.9%	17.6%	47.1%	0.0%	66.7%	68.3%	78.0%	31.7%	36.4%	.333	.455	78	0.2
Denyi Reyes	SYR	AAA	26	20 (18)	91²	2-3	0	72	1.42	5.79		8.2%	17.9%	6.0%	32.5%	70.0%	83.4%	34.2%	59.0%	.269	.678	114	0.6
	NYM	MLB	26	9 (3)	19²	0-2	0	17	1.68	7.78	48.3%	8.9%	18.9%	3.3%	39.1%	78.7%	79.3%	33.9%	70.8%	.361	.609	103	0.2
Cole Sulser	DUR	AAA	33	12 (0)	18²	2-0	0	19	1.39	3.86		5.9%	22.4%	3.5%	39.0%	73.1%	74.0%	33.7%	74.2%	.321	.559	90	0.4
	AZ	MLB	33	4 (0)	5¹	0-0	0	4	1.50	6.75	41.6%	13.0%	17.4%	8.7%	25.0%	78.6%	81.8%	28.6%	37.5%	.214	.750	111	0.0
Josh Walker	SYR	AAA	28	21 (0)	29¹	2-2	1	40	1.09	1.84		10.8%	33.3%	0.8%	40.0%	71.1%	77.3%	31.8%	55.3%	.281	.385	82	0.7
	NYM	MLB	28	14 (0)	10	0-1	0	12	1.80	8.10	43.5%	12.5%	25.0%	4.2%	23.3%	81.8%	84.7%	27.5%	47.2%	.357	.633	100	0.1

For someone who neither batted nor fielded after his midseason trade to the Mets, this wasn't really a strong showing for nominative determinism. Nor was it a strong showing for **Peyton Battenfield** himself, as the crafty righty will need to regain his domination of the strike zone that put him on the prospect map a few years ago. ⓦ A two-pitch pitcher for most of his career, **Jeff Brigham** began utilizing a cutter in 2023 that serves as a bridge between his fastball and his slider in terms of both movement and velocity. This middle-ground pitch hasn't graduated him from being a middle-ground reliever, as it hasn't yet made him any more effective. ⓦ **Nolan Clenney**'s professional debut was in the independent United Shore League in Michigan after he was passed by in the 2019 draft; two years later, he signed a free agent deal with the Mets. His preferred pitch to back up his mid-90s fastball is a hard gyro slider that sits in the upper-80s. ⓦ 2023 marked the second year in a row that **Sam Coonrod** was on the injured list from spring until August. His stuff is down a few ticks from 2021—by far his best major-league campaign to date—and he's continually been beset by significant injuries. ⓦ Despite a promising stint pitching in Florida in 2020 and 2021, **John Curtiss** is still looking to solidify a consistent role in a major-league bullpen as he enters his age-31 season. He missed 2022 recovering from TJS, and a follow-on elbow surgery cut 2023 short. ⓦ After returning from Japan to no particular fanfare, reliever **Reed Garrett** is trying to take the next step. In August, he swapped the power curve he'd used throughout his career for a horizontal sweeper, and drastically increased the usage of a sinking fastball he'd experimented with before. Maybe this next reinvention will be the one that propels him forward? ⓦ Since his debut in 2018, **Elieser Hernández**'s 2.13 home runs per nine is second-highest (minimum 250 innings pitched) only to Adam Plutko, who has since moved on to the Korea Baseball Organization. ⓦ Arriving from the Brewers as part of the Mark Canha trade, **Justin Jarvis** struggled mightily in his first exposure to Triple-A competition. The low-spin splitter that he added during the 2022 season looks like a decent bat-missing option, but the walk and home run issues that have plagued him throughout his career complicate his route to the big leagues. ⓦ Undersized **Luis Moreno** has leaned into a groundball-oriented approach recently, eschewing his four-seamer for more sinkers in addition to adding a cutter. Heading into his age-25 season, it might be time to try him as a reliever in an effort to coax some more velocity out of him and tame his control issues. ⓦ **Eric Orze** has already gotten through the hardest part—prior to being drafted, he overcame two cancer diagnoses in short succession. Finally mastering Triple-A in his third time through the league and finding a second offering to go with his calling-card splitter could be a cakewalk in comparison. ⓦ Since 2022, **Yohan Ramirez** has played for Seattle, Cleveland, Pittsburgh and Chicago, and will join the Mets in 2024. With that many homes, his career 3.99 ERA and league-average DRA- are a bit of a surprise, but his elite extension and spotty command make for an uncomfortable at-bat. ⓦ **Sean Reid-Foley** looked impressive in a late-season return from Tommy John surgery, maintaining the velocity bump he had displayed prior to his arm injury. A lat strain ended his season in the second week of September, and we're *still* waiting to see if he'll be a factor in the majors. ⓦ **Denyi Reyes** was a shuttle-arm for the Mets last season, spending most of his time in Syracuse but coming up to make some spot-starts and supply some low-leverage bullpen innings when needed. Given the quality of his pitches, that's likely his ceiling. ⓦ **Brandon Sproat** failed to reach a deal with the Mets when they drafted him in the third round in 2022, but when the Mets came calling again the following year, he couldn't resist putting pen to paper. He's a power pitcher with a traditional four-pitch arsenal and has reached triple digits during his time with the Florida Gators. ⓦ **Cole Sulser** spent time on the Rays' 40-man roster but never pitched for the big-league club. Now with the Mets as an NRI, the 34-year-old will need luck or a breakout to find another 40-man spot. ⓦ The most notable aspect of **Josh Walker**'s rookie season was when he allowed a walk-off balk to the Royals on August 1—without even throwing a pitch. ⓦ Injuries derailed **Calvin Ziegler**'s sophomore season in professional baseball, as he needed surgery to remove an elbow bone spur during spring training and then suffered a quadriceps strain while rehabbing. There's still a lot to like about Ziegler's arsenal, which includes a power curveball and a splitter that he developed after being drafted.

NEW YORK YANKEES

Essay by Russell A. Carleton

Player comments by Andrew Mearns and BP staff

One day while I was trawling around looking for the latest bluegrass music videos, the YouTube algorithm decided that I wanted to watch a short video featuring the famed astrophysicist Neil deGrasse Tyson. The good doctor was asked for an opinion about the most terrifying thing about the future. deGrasse Tyson pointed out that in the science fiction of the 1950s and 1960s, as people projected what the ideal future might look like in 2024, they imagined a world where energy and material production were plentiful and nearly unlimited. There were spaceships and the energy to push them faster than light and everyone seemed to have one. Poverty was largely eliminated and everyone's basic needs were met. deGrasse Tyson made the point that what sci-fi writers in the 1950s didn't anticipate was that it was information that has become wildly plentiful, rather than energy and material. That has produced a number of both problems and advantages that no one saw coming.

Before the internet—and I should probably say, before the "always on" internet, because I'm old enough to remember when getting "on-line" was a special occasion—the information that you had available was limited to whatever was in your memory and whatever books you might have at your house. Being "well read" was important because you didn't have a gadget in your pocket that could access the corpus of human knowledge. Not only has knowledge become democratized, but raw data have as well. With some basic training in stats, it's possible to conduct research that used to be only the realm of university professors. *Baseball Prospectus* wouldn't exist otherwise. Data have conquered baseball as well as the other, less important, parts of the world.

It's interesting to consider that dynamic as we look at the case of the New York Yankees fresh off an almost unthinkable 82-80 season. The Yankees haven't had a sub-.500 campaign since 1992, but in the 20 years that followed (1993-2012), the former Highlanders won at least 95 games in 15 of those years, and two of their failures to do so were seasons shortened by strikes. Then from 2013-2016, the Yankees had a relative dry spell, in which they made the playoffs only once (a loss in the 2015 Wild Card Game) in four years. It wasn't really until the emergence of Aaron Judge that they pulled

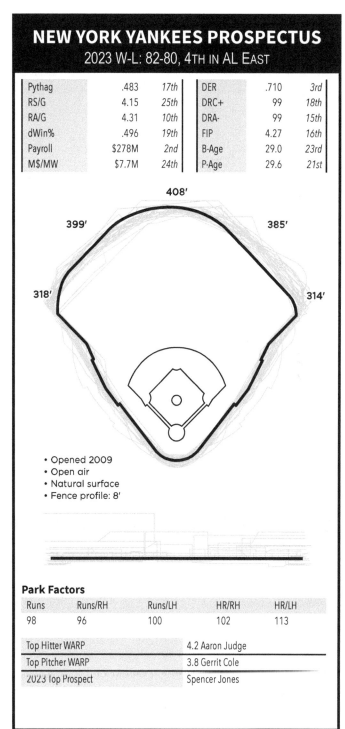

NEW YORK YANKEES PROSPECTUS
2023 W-L: 82-80, 4TH IN AL EAST

Pythag	.483	17th	DER	.710	3rd
RS/G	4.15	25th	DRC+	99	18th
RA/G	4.31	10th	DRA-	99	15th
dWin%	.496	19th	FIP	4.27	16th
Payroll	$278M	2nd	B-Age	29.0	23rd
M$/MW	$7.7M	24th	P-Age	29.6	21st

408'
399'   385'
318'   314'

- Opened 2009
- Open air
- Natural surface
- Fence profile: 8'

Park Factors

Runs	Runs/RH	Runs/LH	HR/RH	HR/LH
98	96	100	102	113

Top Hitter WARP	4.2 Aaron Judge
Top Pitcher WARP	3.8 Gerrit Cole
2023 Top Prospect	Spencer Jones

Payroll History (in millions)

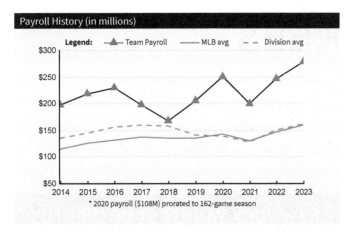

Legend: —▲— Team Payroll —— MLB avg - - - Division avg

* 2020 payroll ($108M) prorated to 162-game season

Future Commitments (in millions)

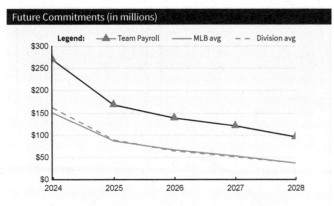

Legend: —▲— Team Payroll —— MLB avg - - - Division avg

Farm System Ranking

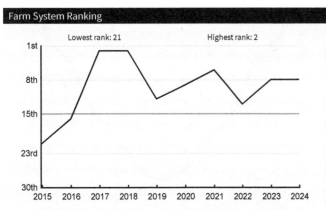

Lowest rank: 21   Highest rank: 2

Personnel

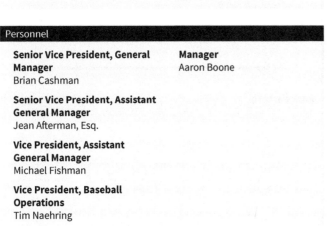

Senior Vice President, General Manager
Brian Cashman

Senior Vice President, Assistant General Manager
Jean Afterman, Esq.

Vice President, Assistant General Manager
Michael Fishman

Vice President, Baseball Operations
Tim Naehring

Manager
Aaron Boone

themselves back into the 90s both in wins and attitude. When Judge was sidelined for a good chunk of 2023, the Yankees suddenly looked like they were nothing special again.

Over the past half-century of the free agency era, the "Yankee problem" has been openly spoken of. They signed free agents, luring homegrown talent away from other teams while retaining their own with dizzying salary numbers. And they could do this because they had both the checkbook and the prestige that went with being the biggest media market in the United States. How could other teams possibly compete with that? Well, free agents are always a risky business. (Carlos Rodón on line one.) Players reach free agency around the time that we know their skills start to decline, and they tend to ask for contracts that last well into that decline phase. The Yankees were able to sustain some of their success because they could often sign another free agent who was likely to be good next season when the previous free agent was on the back end of their deal.

For a long time, the assumption was that the solution to the Yankee problem was to give everyone a spaceship to even things up. The words "salary cap" were thrown around, though never adopted. The competitive balance tax that did come into being was an attempt to level things out, though it hasn't had as much bite as some had hoped. With their big market advantage, the Yankees could land Gerrit Cole and re-sign Aaron Judge, and that turned out okay. But it was also the Yankees who took on Giancarlo Stanton's contract and signed both Carlos Rodón and Anthony Rizzo. It's not that the Yankees have been especially talented at signing the right free agents over the years. It's that when you have a bigger budget, you can take more chances—some of them are bound to work out.

But a moment ago, we said that it wasn't material and energy that had become abundant in the last few decades, but information. For the teams in the AL East that had to see the Bronx Bombers the most often, they sought out the advantage that information could bring. The Rays built up a powerhouse of an analytics department. The Red Sox hired Bill James. It's not like the Yankees stood still. Despite what general manager Brian Cashman has tried to claim, the Yankees don't have a small analytics department by any measure and are very invested in playing with numbers. Cashman specifically said that the Yankees have the smallest department in the AL East, which may or may not be true (it's impossible to really know who's doing what), but if it is factually true, it's because the other four teams in the division have built their own big departments to compete with the Bronx Bombers. The Blue Jays poached analytical pioneer Mark Shaprio and Ross Atkins, while the Orioles hired Mike Elias and Sig Mejdal from the Astros' infamous analytical juggernaut.

In fact, it's pretty much that way around the league, and that has some implications for a team like the Yankees. They will continue to have a large free agency budget and will likely be able to make more mistakes, but whom will they sign? As teams have gotten smarter, they've gotten better about identifying the good bets and the players that they should shy away from. Maybe the Yankee "problem" all along wasn't their ability to sign all the good free agents, but that the other teams weren't properly valuing their own players, and the Yankees had the resources to scoop up the tasty leftovers. What if there just aren't as many gems as there used to be in the free agency pool, because they never get there to begin with? Can a team really buy their way to a pennant in that environment? It would mean that the Yankees' fate would be much more dependent on their ability to draft and develop. They wouldn't be powerless, but the impact of information might have leveled things—at least somewhat—in a way that the competitive balance tax couldn't.

When information becomes the dominant currency of the game, it makes Cashman's statement that the Yankees would get away from being "too reliant" on analytics all the more concerning. Perhaps the Yankees should have hired Brian Infoman. But it's not entirely clear what Cashman meant by "too reliant on analytics." There's been plenty of backlash to the perceived—and sometimes real—excesses of analytical movement in baseball, both at the macro level (why is everyone on the roster a "swing for the fences" hitter?) and the micro level (why is "the spreadsheet" making pitching decisions rather than Aaron Boone's intestines?) Does Cashman mean that the Yankees will move toward more "small ball" and bunting? Perhaps pitch counts will be relaxed a bit?

In the press *post-mortem* of the season, in which the beat writers for 29 of the 30 teams angrily lament the fact that their team didn't win the World Series on behalf of their readers, there were all sorts of accusations against New York. Were the Yankees too reliant on pulling the ball? The data show that they weren't especially pull-happy compared to other MLB teams, nor were they especially reliant on lifting everything into the air. In fact, the Yankees had one of the highest home-run-to-fly-ball ratios in MLB in 2023, meaning that when they did lift the ball in the air, nice things tended to happen.

Were they too reliant on short-stint starters? Again, they were middle-of-the-pack on just about any measure of pitching staff usage. Maybe the thing that stuck out about the 2023 Yankees in the data was how ordinary they were. On most of the major indices of player behavior and strategy, they were...17th or so. There were teams who did more or less of what they allegedly did too much or too little of. There were teams who both succeeded and failed on both sides of that divide.

Maybe the problem with the Yankees relying on analytics isn't the analytics, but that in the modern day, it makes them ordinary. The Yankees aren't used to being ordinary. It's the age-old problem that in the same way that all of us believe we are above-average drivers, humans will quickly believe that they have some innate and inexpressible ability to make better decisions than we could by following the data. This is despite plenty of experimental evidence to the contrary, but of course, that evidence was gathered by studying the losers of the world. It's made even more tempting by the fact that baseball analytics can take you from being right 50% of the time to 52% of the time; even if you follow the wrong strategy, you're still right 48% of the time and you could still believe it's all working.

The Yankees face a world where they can be successful, but now, just coming to the ballpark and donning pinstripes doesn't protect you when Anthony Volpe shows up with a Gold Glove and a .283 OBP. The once-massive advantage that their deep pockets had afforded them has evaporated...somewhat. They will still snag a big-ticket, big-success free agent now and then but, more and more, they will need to lean into the same thing that all the other 29 teams are doing: Becoming the best information processors that they can. Running away from that because you had a tough year isn't going to solve anything.

—Russell A. Carleton is an author of Baseball Prospectus.

HITTERS

Roderick Arias SS
Born: 09/09/04   Age: 19   Bats: S   Throws: R   Height: 6'0"   Weight: 178   Origin: IFA, 2022

YEAR	TM	LVL	AGE	PA	R	HR	RBI	SB	AVG/OBP/SLG	BABIP	SLGCON	BB%	K%	ZSw%	ZCon%	OSw%	OCon%	LA	90th EV	DRC+	BRR	DRP	WARP
2022	DSL NYY	ROK	17	140	25	3	11	10	.194/.379/.370	.305	.645	20.0%	32.9%										
2023	YNK	ROK	18	130	32	6	26	17	.267/.423/.505	.313	.708	20.8%	22.3%	72.2%	69.2%	25.0%	55.6%						
2024									No projection														

2023 GP: SS (23), DH (4)

Arias looked much more like a top IFA signee in his second year than he did during his first foray in pro ball. Of course, the switch-hitter was also only 17 in 2022. In contrast, I spent much of that age wasting too much time watching Fuse and subsequently tweaking my MySpace page layout. (How else were people possibly going to learn about the next Snow Patrol hit?) Arias spent his age-18 season showing off a cannon at shortstop and posting the sixth-best OPS among all FCL players with at least 100 ABs—only one of the five players ahead of him was younger. Meanwhile, I simply moved on to wasting too much time on Facebook.

Oswaldo Cabrera LF Born: 03/01/99 Age: 25 Bats: S Throws: R Height: 5'11" Weight: 200 Origin: IFA, 2015

YEAR	TM	LVL	AGE	PA	R	HR	RBI	SB	AVG/OBP/SLG	BABIP	SLGCON	BB%	K%	ZSw%	ZCon%	OSw%	OCon%	LA	90th EV	DRC+	BRR	DRP	WARP
2021	SOM	AA	22	478	61	24	78	20	.256/.311/.492	.295	.674	7.5%	24.7%							111	2.0	7.9	3.1
2021	SWB	AAA	22	36	11	5	11	1	.500/.583/1.133	.625	1.619	13.9%	25.0%							134	-0.2	-0.4	0.2
2022	SWB	AAA	23	208	29	8	29	10	.262/.340/.492	.331	.703	9.1%	26.4%							97	0.2	5.8	1.1
2022	NYY	MLB	23	171	21	6	19	3	.247/.312/.429	.305	.600	8.8%	25.7%	73.4%	88.8%	39.6%	55.1%	21.3	102.7	89	-0.1	-0.1	0.2
2023	SWB	AAA	24	46	7	2	6	2	.225/.326/.400	.241	.516	10.9%	19.6%	65.8%	80.0%	27.5%	66.7%			102	0.6	0.4	0.2
2023	NYY	MLB	24	330	35	5	29	8	.211/.275/.299	.260	.394	7.6%	21.8%	74.6%	86.0%	33.8%	62.1%	12.3	101.9	82	0.1	-0.4	0.2
2024 DC	NYY	MLB	25	94	9	2	10	3	.231/.295/.371	.277	.492	7.9%	22.1%							87	0.0	-0.1	0.1

2023 GP: LF (51), RF (49), 3B (15), 2B (6), SS (5), DH (2), 1B (1), CF (1) Comps: Luis Valbuena (58), Junior Lake (54), Jorge Soler (54)

Cabrera rose from relative obscurity to become one of the Yankees' best stories late in 2022, inspiring hope for a potential new starting left fielder ... or at least a useful utility guy. Instead, the switch-hitter crashed with an atrocious .538 OPS through the first couple of months and was demoted on June 1. The Yankees' injury woes led to a quick recall, but Cabrera had fallen out of good graces and started only 13 MLB games between the start of June and mid-August. Once New York essentially waved the white flag and called up prospects, he got regular playing time but still couldn't hit much. A season without nearly as many expectations may do him some good, but there's a reason why every versatile switch-hitter can't immediately transform into Ben Zobrist.

★ ★ ★ *2024 Top 101 Prospect* **#39** ★ ★ ★

Jasson Domínguez OF Born: 02/07/03 Age: 21 Bats: S Throws: R Height: 5'9" Weight: 190 Origin: IFA, 2019

YEAR	TM	LVL	AGE	PA	R	HR	RBI	SB	AVG/OBP/SLG	BABIP	SLGCON	BB%	K%	ZSw%	ZCon%	OSw%	OCon%	LA	90th EV	DRC+	BRR	DRP	WARP
2021	YNK	ROK	18	27	5	0	1	2	.200/.407/.200	.286	.286	22.2%	22.2%									-0.4	
2021	TAM	A	18	214	26	5	18	7	.258/.346/.398	.371	.622	9.8%	31.3%	83.5%	74.4%	41.9%	57.4%			88	0.2	-4.4	0.1
2022	TAM	A	19	324	54	9	36	19	.265/.373/.440	.360	.651	14.2%	27.5%	77.1%	84.5%	33.8%	53.3%			104	0.1	-3.0	0.7
2022	HV	A+	19	184	33	6	22	17	.306/.397/.510	.353	.650	12.5%	18.5%							113	3.5	5.1	1.7
2023	SOM	AA	20	507	83	15	66	37	.254/.367/.414	.327	.597	15.2%	25.6%							97	0.9	-4.2	1.1
2023	SWB	AAA	20	37	6	0	10	3	.419/.514/.581	.464	.643	16.2%	8.1%	78.6%	95.5%	27.0%	75.0%			111	-0.4	-0.1	0.1
2023	NYY	MLB	20	33	6	4	7	1	.258/.303/.677	.211	.913	6.1%	24.2%	73.9%	76.5%	33.8%	52.0%	-0.1	102.8	101	0.0	-0.2	0.1
2024 DC	NYY	MLB	21	68	7	1	7	2	.245/.323/.373	.325	.535	9.9%	26.5%							99	0.0	-0.3	0.1

2023 GP: CF (8) Comps: Melky Cabrera (59), Rougned Odor (48), Jake Bauers (46)

In 1910, French astronomer Camille Flammarion warned that the coming Halley's Comet was powerful enough to "impregnate the atmosphere and possibly snuff out all life on the planet." A number of hucksters subsequently made a killing selling gas masks and "anti-comet pills." Some connections can probably be drawn between Halley's Comet and the Martian, not the least of which includes people profiting off the expected impacts. (Check out his baseball card market!) The 20-year-old rebounded from a pedestrian .702 OPS in the first three months at Double-A to catch fire at an .891 clip over the next 42 games, earning a promotion to Triple-A. The bump was brief because, with their season doomed, the Yankees got aggressive and moonshot Domínguez to The Show barely a week later. Jasson's Comet arrived in a blaze and awed with his power, but a torn UCL meant that his passing over the Bronx was short-lived. Although he should make a smooth recovery and return sometime in 2024—far sooner than the next appearance of Halley's Comet (2061)—fans should still be wary of modern anti-comet pill traders.

Oscar Gonzalez OF Born: 01/10/98 Age: 26 Bats: R Throws: R Height: 6'4" Weight: 240 Origin: IFA, 2014

YEAR	TM	LVL	AGE	PA	R	HR	RBI	SB	AVG/OBP/SLG	BABIP	SLGCON	BB%	K%	ZSw%	ZCon%	OSw%	OCon%	LA	90th EV	DRC+	BRR	DRP	WARP
2021	AKR	AA	23	199	31	13	41	1	.330/.367/.601	.353	.743	5.5%	18.1%							142	0.1	2.8	1.9
2021	COL	AAA	23	305	39	18	42	0	.269/.305/.503	.306	.682	3.6%	24.9%							106	-2.5	0.9	1.0
2022	COL	AAA	24	182	21	9	33	0	.282/.308/.506	.286	.595	3.3%	14.3%							120	-0.9	2.3	1.1
2022	CLE	MLB	24	382	39	11	43	1	.296/.327/.461	.345	.582	3.9%	19.6%	75.5%	82.0%	48.7%	64.4%	5.7	106.8	103	-0.2	-0.1	1.2
2023	COL	AAA	25	362	49	13	64	2	.287/.323/.496	.339	.659	5.2%	22.9%	72.0%	81.1%	45.0%	58.8%			89	0.1	-0.3	0.6
2023	CLE	MLB	25	180	15	2	12	0	.214/.239/.312	.278	.425	2.8%	25.6%	72.1%	81.7%	50.8%	59.6%	6.9	106.4	72	0.1	0.2	-0.2
2024 DC	NYY	MLB	26	31	3	1	3	0	.245/.280/.394	.297	.524	4.2%	24.2%							90	0.0	-0.1	0.0

2023 GP: RF (30), DH (19), LF (2) Comps: Nate Schierholtz (60), Aaron Cunningham (55), Anthony Santander (55)

After a productive rookie season in which his playoff heroics put him on the national stage, the freest swinger in baseball spent most of the season in Triple-A following an early-season demotion. While he was productive in 2022 despite swinging at everything and smashing balls straight into the ground, last summer Gonzalez was a shell of his rookie self. Most notable was his power outage compared to a year prior. In 2022, all 11 of his home runs were hit left of center; last year, the pull side of his spray chart looked like a ghost town, resulting in just two homers in 180 plate appearances. Gonzalez will likely continue to get big-league opportunities (though there is more outfield depth in the Bronx than Cleveland), but something will need to change in his offensive profile for him to stick around.

Trent Grisham CF Born: 11/01/96 Age: 27 Bats: L Throws: L Height: 5'11" Weight: 224 Origin: Round 1, 2015 Draft (#15 overall)

YEAR	TM	LVL	AGE	PA	R	HR	RBI	SB	AVG/OBP/SLG	BABIP	SLGCON	BB%	K%	ZSw%	ZCon%	OSw%	OCon%	LA	90th EV	DRC+	BRR	DRP	WARP
2021	SD	MLB	24	527	61	15	62	13	.242/.327/.413	.292	.557	10.2%	22.6%	65.5%	86.2%	23.9%	63.8%	11.9	103.2	90	0.5	1.0	1.7
2022	SD	MLB	25	524	58	17	53	7	.184/.284/.341	.231	.512	10.9%	28.6%	59.5%	83.4%	23.9%	57.1%	13.0	104.3	78	0.3	4.1	1.0
2023	SD	MLB	26	555	67	13	50	15	.198/.315/.352	.264	.524	13.5%	27.7%	64.5%	81.1%	24.1%	52.7%	17.2	104.8	86	0.4	-3.3	0.8
2024 DC	NYY	MLB	27	389	42	11	43	7	.211/.315/.372	.272	.545	12.0%	27.4%							94	0.1	-0.7	1.0

2023 GP: CF (153) Comps: Todd Dunwoody (65), Jay Johnstone (62), Milt Cuyler (59)

The ballast in December's trade that sent Juan Soto to the Yankees, Grisham arrives in the Bronx as the one-for-one replacement for his lost twin Harrison Bader. Both are slick fielders who showcase exceptional range in all directions. Both are looking to do maximum damage with every swing they take. Both are condemned to flirt with the Mendoza Line while occasionally running into flat fastballs and hanging breakers and sending them into low-Earth orbit. (To the surprise of no one, Bader is fourth on Baseball-Reference's list of Grisham's similar batters.) You could say Brian Cashman has a type but, to Grisham's credit, he's far more durable than Bader, having logged three straight seasons of at least 500 PA. While too many of those have ended in four pitches and three swings and misses, Grisham is also two years younger and a few million dollars cheaper than his counterpart. A lefty swing that should benefit from Yankee Stadium's short right field porch makes him ideal to hold down center and/or caddie for Aaron Judge in the late innings.

★ ★ ★ *2024 Top 101 Prospect* **#33** ★ ★ ★

Spencer Jones OF Born: 05/14/01   Age: 23   Bats: L   Throws: L   Height: 6'6"   Weight: 235   Origin: Round 1, 2022 Draft (#25 overall)

YEAR	TM	LVL	AGE	PA	R	HR	RBI	SB	AVG/OBP/SLG	BABIP	SLGCON	BB%	K%	ZSw%	ZCon%	OSw%	OCon%	LA	90th EV	DRC+	BRR	DRP	WARP
2022	TAM	A	21	95	18	3	8	10	.325/.411/.494	.387	.631	10.5%	18.9%	79.3%	88.6%	30.4%	55.8%			113	0.5	-0.5	0.4
2023	HV	A+	22	459	62	13	56	35	.268/.337/.450	.363	.665	9.2%	29.0%							99	2.3	5.3	2.2
2023	SOM	AA	22	78	9	3	10	8	.261/.333/.406	.333	.596	9.0%	28.2%							96	-0.3	-0.2	0.2
2024 non	NYY	MLB	23	251	21	4	23	16	.221/.279/.334	.311	.500	6.7%	30.2%							72	0.0	0	0.0

2023 GP: CF (101), DH (16)   *Comps: Tito Polo (71), Tyler Naquin (70), Brennon Lund (66)*

Now a second-year player in the Yankees' system, the Vandy product made enough progress to crack BP's midseason Top 50. Jones absolutely blisters the baseball, and Jasson Domínguez's ascent helped him get the late-season bump to Double-A for the final three weeks of 2023. Speed and defense are more of a factor in Jones' game than the average fan might think based on his size—he swiped 43 and played a smooth center field. Most of what Jones has done so far has been about as expected, so the true test of his approach against high-minors pitching awaits.

Aaron Judge RF Born: 04/26/92   Age: 32   Bats: R   Throws: R   Height: 6'7"   Weight: 282   Origin: Round 1, 2013 Draft (#32 overall)

YEAR	TM	LVL	AGE	PA	R	HR	RBI	SB	AVG/OBP/SLG	BABIP	SLGCON	BB%	K%	ZSw%	ZCon%	OSw%	OCon%	LA	90th EV	DRC+	BRR	DRP	WARP
2021	NYY	MLB	29	633	89	39	98	6	.287/.373/.544	.332	.763	11.8%	25.0%	66.6%	80.5%	27.8%	56.6%	11.7	111.6	142	-0.6	-7.0	4.5
2022	NYY	MLB	30	696	133	62	131	16	.311/.425/.686	.340	.990	15.9%	25.1%	66.1%	81.5%	26.9%	51.2%	15.0	111.6	184	0.3	-9.0	8.4
2023	NYY	MLB	31	458	79	37	75	3	.267/.406/.613	.300	.949	19.2%	28.4%	66.9%	73.9%	23.3%	41.9%	20.5	111.4	164	-0.4	-5.3	4.2
2024 DC	NYY	MLB	32	578	91	38	101	8	.261/.384/.553	.321	.868	16.0%	30.1%							160	-0.3	-10.3	4.9

2023 GP: RF (54), DH (38), CF (18)   *Comps: Sammy Sosa (80), Dwight Evans (77), Frank Howard (76)*

Like Roger Maris, Judge dropped from launching more than 60 bombs one year to hitting under 40 in the next. Then again, Maris didn't have to deal with an awkward toe injury on the concrete slab of the Dodger Stadium bullpen fence, which cost Judge nearly two months of his follow-up season. The Yankees floundered without their superstar, and by the time he returned in late July, there were enough other messes on the team that homering at a 50-dinger rate over the final 57 games was only enough to secure a winning record rather than anything meaningful. It's a testament to Judge's sheer talent that he finished third among all AL outfielders in homers despite the extended absence (just two behind league-leader Adolis García).

Without more lineup support, Judge will continue to face the challenge of maintaining his outstanding production while being pitched around like peak Mike Trout. He'll stay in pinstripes for the remainder of the 2020s; it will be up to the Yankees' front office to ensure that he doesn't become another Don Mattingly—a beloved captain whose prime was wasted on flawed teams that never even made the World Series, let alone won it.

DJ LeMahieu CI Born: 07/13/88   Age: 35   Bats: R   Throws: R   Height: 6'4"   Weight: 220   Origin: Round 2, 2009 Draft (#79 overall)

YEAR	TM	LVL	AGE	PA	R	HR	RBI	SB	AVG/OBP/SLG	BABIP	SLGCON	BB%	K%	ZSw%	ZCon%	OSw%	OCon%	LA	90th EV	DRC+	BRR	DRP	WARP
2021	NYY	MLB	32	679	84	10	57	4	.268/.349/.362	.301	.429	10.8%	13.8%	62.0%	90.2%	25.7%	77.3%	5.2	103.9	114	-0.7	0.1	3.4
2022	NYY	MLB	33	541	74	12	46	4	.261/.357/.377	.285	.444	12.4%	13.1%	54.2%	89.8%	27.3%	75.6%	3.4	103.2	126	-1.0	1.8	3.2
2023	NYY	MLB	34	562	55	15	44	2	.243/.327/.390	.295	.522	10.7%	22.2%	55.9%	87.6%	25.5%	67.4%	3.8	104.2	95	-1.2	-0.6	1.0
2024 DC	NYY	MLB	35	539	54	11	53	3	.242/.326/.361	.276	.445	10.5%	16.7%							100	-0.8	0.7	1.4

2023 GP: 3B (69), 1B (56), 2B (9), DH (4)   *Comps: Bill Mazeroski (68), Red Schoendienst (66), Omar Infante (66)*

Apologies in advance on the *Remember The '90s* anecdote, but I have distinct memories of hitting the power button on my parents' computer and walking away for a few minutes while it booted up, returning to connect to the internet, only to bounce again for a bit until I heard the dulcet tones of "You've got mail!" from the other room. That's what it was like for The Artist Formely Known as LeMachine in 2023, as he continued to look terrible in wake of his 2022 foot injury. He scuffled through the first half with a .643 OPS, but he did at least finally look like his old self once he finally booted up with a .273/.375/.432 triple slash in the second half. New York needs to upgrade to a better plan for LeMachine though because, given the state of their offense beyond Aaron Judge and Juan Soto, they can't afford for him to wait that long to log on in 2024.

Oswald Peraza IF Born: 06/15/00   Age: 24   Bats: R   Throws: R   Height: 6'0"   Weight: 200   Origin: IFA, 2016

YEAR	TM	LVL	AGE	PA	R	HR	RBI	SB	AVG/OBP/SLG	BABIP	SLGCON	BB%	K%	ZSw%	ZCon%	OSw%	OCon%	LA	90th EV	DRC+	BRR	DRP	WARP
2021	HV	A+	21	127	20	5	16	16	.306/.386/.532	.349	.678	9.4%	18.9%							127	1.0	4.9	1.4
2021	SOM	AA	21	353	51	12	40	20	.294/.348/.466	.362	.623	6.5%	23.2%							102	-2.2	-2.7	0.7
2021	SWB	AAA	21	31	5	1	2	2	.286/.323/.393	.304	.478	6.5%	16.1%							98	-0.3	1.5	0.2
2022	SWB	AAA	22	429	57	19	50	33	.259/.329/.448	.302	.605	7.9%	23.3%							100	3.1	-2.8	1.3
2022	NYY	MLB	22	57	8	1	2	2	.306/.404/.429	.359	.525	10.5%	15.8%	76.0%	89.5%	25.9%	63.6%	4.6	102.3	106	0.3	-0.2	0.2
2023	SWB	AAA	23	300	48	14	36	16	.268/.357/.479	.289	.607	9.7%	18.3%	75.9%	84.1%	32.9%	48.6%			107	0.7	-0.4	1.1
2023	NYY	MLB	23	191	15	2	14	4	.191/.267/.272	.256	.382	6.8%	26.2%	75.3%	79.6%	30.8%	45.4%	9.7	104.8	80	0.1	0.1	0.1
2024 DC	NYY	MLB	24	380	36	9	38	16	.224/.289/.350	.287	.496	6.7%	26.5%							84	0.2	-0.4	0.3

2023 GP: 3B (36), 2B (10), SS (6), DH (1)   *Comps: Eduardo Escobar (66), Gavin Cecchini (66), Erick Aybar (64)*

In a darkly amusing twist of fate, Anthony Volpe won the AL Gold Glove even though he's not the best defensive shortstop on his own team. (See, Volpe *is* the next Derek Jeter!) Regardless, it had to feel a little weird for Peraza, who is roughly the same age, skilled enough to play all around the infield and a whiz at the six. After starting playoff games in 2022, Peraza got leapfrogged by Volpe in the spring with the Yankees making it clear for all to see who they thought was the shortstop of the future. He didn't do nearly as much with his few chances in '23 as he did in '22, and even when given consistent time down the stretch, he mustered a mere .542 OPS in 32 starts. If he's not traded in the offseason, Peraza will enter 2024 with a big-league role since he's out of options and the onus will be on him to make strides at the plate. Otherwise, he's destined for a future as a utilityman who specializes at shortstop, the dollar-store Brendan Ryan to Volpe's dollar-store Jeter.

Everson Pereira OF Born: 04/10/01 Age: 23 Bats: R Throws: R Height: 5'11" Weight: 191 Origin: IFA, 2017

YEAR	TM	LVL	AGE	PA	R	HR	RBI	SB	AVG/OBP/SLG	BABIP	SLGCON	BB%	K%	ZSw%	ZCon%	OSw%	OCon%	LA	90th EV	DRC+	BRR	DRP	WARP
2021	TAM	A	20	83	17	5	22	4	.361/.446/.667	.457	.941	12.0%	25.3%	76.4%	69.1%	32.5%	42.2%			110	0.5	-1.3	0.3
2021	HV	A+	20	127	27	14	32	5	.259/.354/.676	.241	1.043	11.8%	29.9%							129	-1.0	-2.4	0.5
2022	HV	A+	21	325	55	9	43	19	.274/.354/.455	.363	.652	10.5%	26.8%							96	1.0	-6.9	0.3
2022	SOM	AA	21	123	21	5	13	2	.283/.341/.504	.380	.750	7.3%	30.1%							86	-0.8	-1.1	0.0
2023	SOM	AA	22	185	24	10	31	7	.291/.362/.545	.373	.811	10.3%	29.2%							99	-0.2	-0.2	0.5
2023	SWB	AAA	22	158	29	8	33	4	.312/.386/.551	.398	.809	8.2%	27.8%	78.3%	77.2%	31.3%	41.0%			94	2.0	-2.3	0.3
2023	NYY	MLB	22	103	6	0	10	4	.151/.233/.194	.264	.340	7.8%	38.8%	77.6%	74.6%	36.4%	32.6%	10.0	104.9	50	0.1	0.1	-0.3
2024 DC	NYY	MLB	23	30	3	1	3	0	.201/.267/.345	.288	.529	7.1%	34.8%							74	0.0	0	0.0

2023 GP: LF (27)

Comps: Aaron Cunningham (61), Lewis Brinson (56), David Dahl (51)

In 1995, both the Sega Saturn and the Sony PlayStation hit American shelves. Although the Saturn was first to release, the PlayStation (and later, the N64) soon blew it out of the water. But where the Saturn had a few months to itself in the States, Pereira only had 10 days before the Yankees hit the "Skip Scene" button and called up Jasson Domínguez. Fans who had been excited to see the toolsy prospect Pereira were quickly more captivated by the more dynamic Domínguez. Plus, the JayStation had the better release-day content: He homered in his first at-bat, whereas Pereira didn't go deep once during his six weeks in The Show. There's always new competition—even as Domínguez will go out of stock for almost a year, Juan Soto and Alex Verdugo are taking up shelf space in the Bronx. Pereira will need to cut the strikeouts and produce a *Panzer Dragoon Saga*-esque masterpiece to recapture some attention.

Anthony Rizzo 1B Born: 08/08/89 Age: 34 Bats: L Throws: L Height: 6'3" Weight: 240 Origin: Round 6, 2007 Draft (#204 overall)

YEAR	TM	LVL	AGE	PA	R	HR	RBI	SB	AVG/OBP/SLG	BABIP	SLGCON	BB%	K%	ZSw%	ZCon%	OSw%	OCon%	LA	90th EV	DRC+	BRR	DRP	WARP
2021	CHC	MLB	31	376	41	14	40	4	.248/.346/.446	.261	.545	9.6%	15.7%	65.1%	87.0%	32.8%	67.9%	14.1	106.4	123	-0.1	-0.4	1.9
2021	NYY	MLB	31	200	32	8	21	2	.249/.340/.428	.252	.510	8.0%	14.0%	67.4%	82.6%	32.3%	74.3%	16.3	104.6	116	-0.1	-0.1	0.8
2022	NYY	MLB	32	548	77	32	75	6	.224/.338/.480	.216	.613	10.6%	18.4%	66.4%	87.6%	31.8%	62.1%	19.7	104.4	123	-0.7	-0.9	2.4
2023	NYY	MLB	33	421	45	12	41	0	.244/.328/.378	.298	.511	8.3%	23.0%	64.9%	87.4%	36.9%	60.2%	17.6	104.0	89	-0.4	0.1	0.3
2024 DC	NYY	MLB	34	523	59	18	62	6	.227/.323/.395	.259	.519	9.1%	20.8%							102	-0.4	-1	1.0

2023 GP: 1B (92), DH (7)

Comps: Keith Hernandez (73), John Olerud (73), Joe Judge (72)

Rizzo must have felt great about his 2023 through May 28, as he was at .304/.376/.508 with 11 homers in 52 games and looking even better than he did during his 32-dinger 2022. That day, Fernando Tatis Jr.'s hip weirdly collided with Rizzo's head on a pickoff play. The veteran's season fell apart after that, as he descended into a horrible slump and was badly missing pitches while also waking up with the feeling of a hangover despite going to bed sober. It took far too long for the Yankees to connect the dots, and even after he complained of fogginess over the weekend of July 29, they still kept playing him. A few days later, they finally placed him on the IL with post-concussion syndrome, and on September 5, they conceded that he would not return in 2023. We'll hope for both a full recovery for Rizzo and an improvement in player health monitoring from the Yankees.

Ben Rortvedt C Born: 09/25/97 Age: 26 Bats: L Throws: R Height: 5'9" Weight: 191 Origin: Round 2, 2016 Draft (#56 overall)

YEAR	TM	LVL	AGE	PA	R	HR	RBI	SB	AVG/OBP/SLG	BABIP	SLGCON	BB%	K%	ZSw%	ZCon%	OSw%	OCon%	LA	90th EV	DRC+	BRR	DRP	WARP
2021	STP	AAA	23	136	18	5	22	0	.254/.324/.426	.313	.598	7.4%	25.7%							91	0.5	1.3	0.5
2021	MIN	MLB	23	98	8	3	7	0	.169/.229/.281	.211	.417	6.1%	29.6%	64.1%	81.3%	34.4%	54.7%	12.5	103.5	76	0.0	1.8	0.3
2022	SWB	AAA	24	177	21	6	20	0	.221/.307/.396	.301	.629	10.2%	32.2%							87	0.1	0.2	0.3
2023	SWB	AAA	25	124	19	6	22	2	.286/.395/.505	.353	.716	12.9%	25.0%	64.2%	82.6%	30.9%	58.1%			104	-0.8	-0.5	0.3
2023	NYY	MLB	25	79	6	2	4	0	.118/.241/.221	.128	.306	13.9%	24.1%	62.3%	84.0%	28.1%	53.7%	16.2	103.5	91	0.0	1.0	0.3
2024 DC	NYY	MLB	26	92	9	2	9	0	.216/.295/.346	.282	.500	9.2%	27.1%							80	0.0	1.6	0.3

2023 GP: C (31), DH (1)

Comps: Chance Sisco (52), Tucker Barnhart (49), Jeff Mathis (45)

The jokes on Yankees Twitter about Rortvedt not being a real person finally stopped when he made his Yankees debut in late May, but once Jose Trevino's season ended in July, most wished he was a hoax or Mandela Effect. Trevino battling through a shredded wrist ligament was still a better hitter than Rortvedt, but it's not all doom and gloom: He became Gerrit Cole's personal catcher for the final couple months while Cole polished off his Cy Young bid. Although they formed an amusingly aggressive rapport, Cole is really going to have to stump for Rortvedt to justify his noodle bat's presence on the healthiest version of the Yankees' roster. Otherwise he'll disappear just as quickly as he materialized.

YEAR	TM	P. COUNT	FRM RUNS	BLK RUNS	THRW RUNS	TOT RUNS
2021	STP	4304	2.0	0.0	0.0	2.0
2021	MIN	4482	2.2	0.1	0.1	2.4
2022	ESC	1569			0.0	0.0
2022	SWB	3722	0.8	0.0	-0.1	0.6
2023	SWB	2932	0.1	0.0	-0.4	-0.3
2023	NYY	3366	1.3	0.0	0.1	1.3
2024	NYY	3608	1.4	0.1	0.1	1.6

Juan Soto LF
Born: 10/25/98   Age: 25   Bats: L   Throws: L   Height: 6'2"   Weight: 224   Origin: IFA, 2015

YEAR	TM	LVL	AGE	PA	R	HR	RBI	SB	AVG/OBP/SLG	BABIP	SLGCON	BB%	K%	ZSw%	ZCon%	OSw%	OCon%	LA	90th EV	DRC+	BRR	DRP	WARP
2021	WAS	MLB	22	654	111	29	95	9	.313/.465/.534	.332	.655	22.2%	14.2%	62.3%	88.3%	16.2%	58.0%	6.0	109.4	166	0.4	4.5	8.0
2022	SD	MLB	23	228	31	6	16	0	.236/.388/.390	.261	.480	19.3%	14.9%	60.1%	87.7%	15.0%	65.8%	10.7	106.9	145	0.0	-0.4	1.9
2022	WAS	MLB	23	436	62	21	46	6	.246/.408/.485	.243	.593	20.9%	14.2%	62.7%	85.8%	18.9%	67.8%	8.6	107.4	159	-0.1	-0.5	4.3
2023	SD	MLB	24	708	97	35	109	12	.275/.410/.519	.296	.672	18.6%	18.2%	62.2%	87.7%	17.3%	59.1%	6.8	108.4	146	-0.2	-2.7	5.7
2024 DC	NYY	MLB	25	647	97	32	99	8	.274/.413/.517	.285	.639	18.6%	15.6%							161	-0.2	-2.2	6.5

2023 GP: LF (154), DH (6)   Comps: Bryce Harper (77), Mel Ott (69), Johnny Callison (64)

Why does no one want to keep Soto? The Nationals decided that the best way to build for the future was to trade away a 23-year-old coming off an 8-WARP season. The Padres, who made him the centerpiece of their World Series-or-bust plans, dealt him a scant 18 months later despite him putting up almost 7 WARP in San Diego. Just 25, Soto is already on the third team of his career and potentially headed for a fourth next winter. "It's not your fault!" Robin Williams bellows at him from *Good Will Hunting* purgatory, and it's really not. What more can he do, besides play defense at a level above "harmful?" After getting off to a slow start last season, he slashed .290/.418/.548 from May 1 onward. Only seven full-time hitters finished ahead of him in DRC+ in 2023; only two topped him in OBP, and they both won MVP awards. And yet here he is, getting handed off like a candle at a Yankee swap. The root of it all is his impending free agency and the $400 million-plus contract dreams he and Scott Boras are harboring. Everyone else's fiscal fears, though, are the Yankees' gain; he and Aaron Judge might make a pitcher cry in-game.

Giancarlo Stanton DH/RF
Born: 11/08/89   Age: 34   Bats: R   Throws: R   Height: 6'6"   Weight: 245   Origin: Round 2, 2007 Draft (#76 overall)

YEAR	TM	LVL	AGE	PA	R	HR	RBI	SB	AVG/OBP/SLG	BABIP	SLGCON	BB%	K%	ZSw%	ZCon%	OSw%	OCon%	LA	90th EV	DRC+	BRR	DRP	WARP
2021	NYY	MLB	31	579	64	35	97	0	.273/.354/.516	.324	.745	10.9%	27.1%	62.8%	78.6%	32.5%	53.4%	10.4	115.2	117	-0.8	-3.2	2.3
2022	NYY	MLB	32	452	53	31	78	0	.211/.297/.462	.227	.705	11.1%	30.3%	63.0%	72.9%	29.6%	49.7%	10.9	114.2	111	-0.8	-3.8	1.3
2023	NYY	MLB	33	415	43	24	60	0	.191/.275/.420	.210	.632	9.9%	29.9%	61.8%	78.4%	29.9%	48.9%	12.5	112.4	93	-0.5	-4.1	0.1
2024 DC	NYY	MLB	34	446	54	22	61	0	.220/.302/.426	.273	.653	10.0%	30.7%							103	0.0	-0.8	1.0

2023 GP: DH (65), RF (31), LF (2)   Comps: Jose Canseco (79), Jack Clark (72), Darryl Strawberry (65)

How do you solve a problem like Giancarlo?
How do you swing so hard and look so down?
How do you find a comment for Giancarlo?
A nonpareil talent! A hopeless approach! A frown!

Many a thing you know you'd like to tell him
Many a thing he ought to understand
But how do you make him stay
And lay off the curve away?
How do you stop a wave right through the zone?
Oh, how do you solve a problem like Giancarlo?
Does anyone have a handy philosopher's stone?

Enmanuel Tejeda SS
Born: 12/25/04   Age: 19   Bats: R   Throws: R   Height: 5'11"   Weight: 158   Origin: IFA, 2022

YEAR	TM	LVL	AGE	PA	R	HR	RBI	SB	AVG/OBP/SLG	BABIP	SLGCON	BB%	K%	ZSw%	ZCon%	OSw%	OCon%	LA	90th EV	DRC+	BRR	DRP	WARP
2022	DSL NYYB	ROK	17	188	35	3	22	11	.289/.463/.493	.333	.598	21.8%	13.3%										
2023	YNK	ROK	18	217	37	5	30	24	.307/.465/.458	.390	.623	20.3%	20.3%	68.8%	81.8%	30.8%	66.7%						
2024									No projection														

2023 GP: 3B (21), 2B (15), DH (14)

Tejeda followed up a loud summer of torching the DSL complex by doing the same stateside in Florida. Loud Trackman data in 2022 made his .956 OPS there all the more interesting, and those peripherals stayed exciting in 2023 as he was pegged with "lightning-quick bat speed" per BP's Smith Brickner. The jury's still out on whether or not the kid who turned 19 on Christmas will stay at shortstop; his arm strength isn't exactly where it needs to be just yet, though his instincts are good. Tejeda doubled as part of the FCL team's attack on Alek Manoah in his disastrous rehab start; the Yankees are hoping it won't be the first time he beats up on Toronto's pitchers.

Gleyber Torres 2B
Born: 12/13/96   Age: 27   Bats: R   Throws: R   Height: 6'1"   Weight: 205   Origin: IFA, 2013

YEAR	TM	LVL	AGE	PA	R	HR	RBI	SB	AVG/OBP/SLG	BABIP	SLGCON	BB%	K%	ZSw%	ZCon%	OSw%	OCon%	LA	90th EV	DRC+	BRR	DRP	WARP
2021	NYY	MLB	24	516	50	9	51	14	.259/.331/.366	.314	.473	9.7%	20.2%	71.8%	79.9%	28.1%	61.9%	14.5	103.3	106	0.1	-2.6	2.0
2022	NYY	MLB	25	572	73	24	76	10	.257/.310/.451	.295	.597	6.8%	22.6%	73.6%	78.9%	31.3%	62.4%	17.4	104.7	105	0.4	2.7	2.5
2023	NYY	MLB	26	672	90	25	68	13	.273/.347/.453	.288	.542	10.0%	14.6%	70.2%	83.0%	29.8%	70.0%	15.2	103.9	125	-0.4	-2.1	3.8
2024 DC	NYY	MLB	27	590	65	17	68	11	.263/.334/.413	.293	.507	9.4%	16.7%							114	-0.1	1.9	2.9

2023 GP: 2B (145), DH (12)   Comps: Carlos Correa (78), Jim Fregosi (75), Starlin Castro (73)

In seven seasons with the Yankees' organization, Torres has been a star prospect at age 20, a 38-homer phenom at age 22 and a disaster of a shortstop at age 24. The age-26 season offered no such extremes, as Torres was simply the most consistent hitter on a non-playoff team. While other players cycled in and out of the underachieving lineup, Torres and the divisive Anthony Volpe were the only ones to play over 140 games. Since he was always around, that made him an easy target whenever he did falter, and to be fair, he made his share of mental mistakes and worryingly regressed with his defense at the keystone. Whatever the expectations, don't take .800-OPS infielders for granted. Barring dramatic changes, which both Torres and the Yankees are accustomed to, a 2024 Yankees lineup that doesn't include him will be worse off for it.

Jose Trevino C Born: 11/28/92 Age: 31 Bats: R Throws: R Height: 5'10" Weight: 215 Origin: Round 6, 2014 Draft (#186 overall)

YEAR	TM	LVL	AGE	PA	R	HR	RBI	SB	AVG/OBP/SLG	BABIP	SLGCON	BB%	K%	ZSw%	ZCon%	OSw%	OCon%	LA	90th EV	DRC+	BRR	DRP	WARP
2021	TEX	MLB	28	302	23	5	30	1	.239/.267/.340	.279	.425	4.0%	18.9%	62.4%	88.2%	38.4%	65.1%	9.5	102.6	100	-0.2	12.8	2.5
2022	NYY	MLB	29	353	39	11	43	2	.248/.283/.388	.274	.476	4.2%	17.6%	61.5%	88.6%	42.4%	69.9%	13.4	103.0	92	-0.4	17.9	2.8
2023	NYY	MLB	30	168	15	4	15	0	.210/.257/.312	.221	.363	4.8%	13.1%	55.4%	91.5%	39.3%	76.5%	9.1	101.6	94	-0.1	6.0	1.1
2024 DC	NYY	MLB	31	250	23	5	25	1	.243/.286/.359	.270	.433	5.3%	15.7%							84	-0.2	7.8	1.2

2023 GP: C (54)

Comps: Toby Hall (65), Benny Bengough (63), Kevin Plawecki (63)

YEAR	TM	P. COUNT	FRM RUNS	BLK RUNS	THRW RUNS	TOT RUNS
2021	TEX	12070	14.2	0.1	-0.1	14.2
2022	NYY	13074	18.5	0.5	1.8	20.8
2023	NYY	7214	5.2	0.0	1.2	6.4
2024	NYY	9620	7.3	0.1	0.3	7.7

In 2022, Trevino was the opposite of Franchy Cordero: a last-second, end-of-spring addition who exceeded all expectations to become an essential contributor. Although his offense declined after an All-Star first half, Trevino's defense behind the dish was so phenomenal that he won a Platinum Glove. Fast forward to 2023, where his glovework was more solid than outstanding and the meager power in his bat went poof. The culprit was a torn ligament in his right wrist, which he admitted to battling for months after his season ended with surgery in July.

Alex Verdugo RF Born: 05/15/96 Age: 28 Bats: L Throws: L Height: 6'0" Weight: 209 Origin: Round 2, 2014 Draft (#62 overall)

YEAR	TM	LVL	AGE	PA	R	HR	RBI	SB	AVG/OBP/SLG	BABIP	SLGCON	BB%	K%	ZSw%	ZCon%	OSw%	OCon%	LA	90th EV	DRC+	BRR	DRP	WARP
2021	BOS	MLB	25	604	88	13	63	6	.289/.351/.426	.327	.518	8.4%	15.9%	65.2%	90.4%	30.5%	70.1%	7.9	104.1	117	-0.3	0.0	3.6
2022	BOS	MLB	26	644	75	11	74	1	.280/.328/.405	.309	.473	6.5%	13.4%	65.1%	92.5%	30.0%	71.4%	8.8	103.5	115	-0.6	1.0	3.3
2023	BOS	MLB	27	602	81	13	54	5	.264/.324/.421	.294	.508	7.5%	15.4%	58.8%	93.8%	26.3%	67.5%	9.2	103.7	104	0.4	2.8	2.1
2024 DC	NYY	MLB	28	458	47	10	49	2	.269/.329/.406	.294	.476	7.6%	13.4%							107	-0.1	1.2	1.7

2023 GP: RF (140)

Comps: Carl Crawford (78), Bill Buckner (78), Richie Ashburn (76)

Right field is Verdugo's Goldilocks zone. Center field was too big to cover. Left field was too small and cramped with weird, confusing caroms of the Green Monster. Right field was just right, and he had the best defensive season of his career. This kept his value afloat even as his offense lagged a bit. He's a fine player in aggregate, but defense is more volatile than offense, and in any case, how much excitement is there for a glove-first corner outfielder with an average bat? Enough for the rival Yankees to pluck him away in a rare divisional trade, where he'll come face-to-face with three bears of his own (Judge, Stanton and Soto) and try to find his place in New York's revamped outfield mix.

Anthony Volpe SS Born: 04/28/01 Age: 23 Bats: R Throws: R Height: 5'9" Weight: 180 Origin: Round 1, 2019 Draft (#30 overall)

YEAR	TM	LVL	AGE	PA	R	HR	RBI	SB	AVG/OBP/SLG	BABIP	SLGCON	BB%	K%	ZSw%	ZCon%	OSw%	OCon%	LA	90th EV	DRC+	BRR	DRP	WARP
2021	TAM	A	20	257	56	12	49	21	.302/.455/.623	.331	.795	19.8%	16.7%	66.3%	86.2%	23.5%	68.3%			153	0.4	-1.4	2.3
2021	HV	A+	20	256	57	15	37	12	.286/.391/.587	.319	.806	10.5%	22.7%							132	0.8	0.7	1.9
2022	SOM	AA	21	497	71	18	60	44	.251/.348/.472	.272	.596	11.5%	17.7%							123	-2.2	-1.8	2.5
2022	SWB	AAA	21	99	15	3	5	6	.236/.313/.404	.321	.610	8.1%	30.3%							87	0.2	-1.1	0.1
2023	NYY	MLB	22	601	62	21	60	24	.209/.283/.383	.259	.553	8.7%	27.8%	68.0%	82.8%	33.1%	56.2%	13.8	103.1	74	0.9	2.2	0.4
2024 DC	NYY	MLB	23	555	53	14	58	27	.208/.284/.358	.260	.504	8.6%	26.1%							84	0.8	0.1	0.9

2023 GP: SS (157)

Comps: Nick Franklin (59), Yamaico Navarro (52), J.P. Crawford (52)

The Yankees rolled out the red carpet for Volpe in a way not normally seen with their past rookies, as he made the Opening Day roster after just 22 games in Triple-A the previous season. The kid exceeded all possible expectations in two categories: Power and defense. Volpe's topped his preseason 99th-percentile PECOTA projection by six with 21 homers, and responded to skepticism about his shortstop ability by winning the Gold Glove. (This was a little surprising, but not egregious; he was third in the AL in DRP.) Regrettably, the rest of Volpe's game at the plate was so bad that even 2022 punching bag Isiah Kiner-Falefa had a far superior DRC+. The promising eye that he showed while drawing 16 walks in his first 100 PA clouded up, as he took just 36 free passes in his next 500 PA. A true baseball junkie who will put in the work, the talented Volpe will likely make more of an impact in his sophomore season.

Austin Wells C Born: 07/12/99 Age: 24 Bats: L Throws: R Height: 6'2" Weight: 220 Origin: Round 1, 2020 Draft (#28 overall)

YEAR	TM	LVL	AGE	PA	R	HR	RBI	SB	AVG/OBP/SLG	BABIP	SLGCON	BB%	K%	ZSw%	ZCon%	OSw%	OCon%	LA	90th EV	DRC+	BRR	DRP	WARP
2021	TAM	A	21	299	61	9	54	11	.258/.398/.479	.306	.649	17.1%	20.7%	70.2%	79.4%	24.0%	62.0%			122	-1.6	-2.0	1.3
2021	HV	A+	21	170	21	7	22	5	.274/.376/.473	.393	.758	11.8%	32.4%							97	0.4	4.4	0.9
2022	TAM	A	22	34	5	2	6	0	.231/.412/.538	.211	.667	23.5%	14.7%	76.0%	78.9%	19.8%	55.6%			127	-0.4	0.7	0.2
2022	HV	A+	22	121	21	6	16	9	.323/.429/.576	.388	.792	15.7%	22.3%							131	-0.5	6.1	1.4
2022	SOM	AA	22	247	34	12	43	7	.261/.360/.479	.301	.660	11.7%	23.5%							103	-0.8	4.7	1.2
2023	SOM	AA	23	263	28	11	50	5	.237/.327/.443	.269	.601	11.0%	22.8%							107	0.0	1.4	1.2
2023	SWB	AAA	23	146	16	5	20	2	.254/.349/.452	.307	.620	11.0%	23.3%	72.6%	83.7%	32.1%	59.8%			91	-0.5	-0.9	0.2
2023	NYY	MLB	23	75	8	4	13	0	.229/.257/.486	.226	.607	4.0%	18.7%	78.6%	80.4%	43.0%	58.4%	13.9	106.1	110	0.0	1.4	0.5
2024 DC	NYY	MLB	24	361	37	9	40	3	.248/.315/.396	.314	.544	8.0%	24.9%							99	0.2	5.5	1.8

2023 GP: C (19)

Comps: Yasmani Grandal (55), Danny Jansen (53), Mike Carp (47)

Between Nestor Cortes getting hurt and Carlos Rodón's disastrous debut in pinstripes, it was an awful year for the mustachioed Yankees contingent. Wells at least produced a mild salve (wax?) at the big league level when he was called up for his debut in September and sparked hirsute headlines not seen since Matt Carpenter found the Fountain of Youth for a couple months in 2022. Slugging a surprising .486 with four homers in 75 PA at catcher merits attention (especially after a 5-for-39 start to his career). Although Yankees pitchers and coaches praised the rookie's game-calling acumen and he remained an adequate framer, the questions about his ability to stick at catcher will linger until we get a longer look. New York is one of many teams without an obvious starting catcher in 2023, and Wells' lefty pop alone is enough to earn a serious shot in 2024, at least in an extended timeshare with Jose Trevino. With Kyle Higashioka finally relinquishing a roster slot, it's worth seeing what Wells (and his lip caterpillar) can do.

YEAR	TM	P. COUNT	FRM RUNS	BLK RUNS	THRW RUNS	TOT RUNS
2021	TAM	6825	-0.9	-0.5	-0.9	-2.2
2021	HV	3336	3.5	-0.3	0.5	3.8
2022	HV	3208	4.9	0.0	1.6	6.5
2022	SOM	5561	4.1	0.1	0.7	5.0
2023	SOM	5997	2.7	0.0	-1.7	1.0
2023	SWB	3433	-0.5	0.1	-0.7	-1.1
2023	NYY	2766	1.8	0.0	-0.1	1.7
2024	NYY	10822	5.9	0.0	-0.5	5.5

PITCHERS

Albert Abreu RHP   Born: 09/26/95   Age: 28   Height: 6'2"   Weight: 190   Origin: IFA, 2013

YEAR	TM	LVL	AGE	G(GS)	IP	W-L	SV	K	WHIP	ERA	CSP	BB%	K%	HR%	GB%	ZSw%	ZCon%	OSw%	OCon%	BABIP	SLGCON	DRA-	WARP
2021	NYY	MLB	25	28(0)	36²	2-0	1	35	1.25	5.15	52.2%	12.2%	22.4%	5.1%	45.5%	68.3%	83.2%	31.1%	61.2%	.209	.594	110	0.1
2022	NYY	MLB	26	22(0)	25²	2-2	0	26	1.21	3.16	53.8%	5.6%	24.1%	1.9%	49.3%	65.7%	84.4%	28.7%	58.8%	.319	.486	96	0.3
2022	KC	MLB	26	4(0)	4¹	0-0	0	3	2.31	4.15	54.8%	18.2%	13.6%	4.5%	64.3%	72.7%	75.0%	20.5%	77.8%	.385	.714	107	0.0
2022	TEX	MLB	26	7(0)	8²	0-0	0	9	1.85	3.12	44.4%	28.6%	21.4%	4.8%	55.0%	66.0%	85.7%	28.8%	55.3%	.111	.500	109	0.0
2023	NYY	MLB	27	45(0)	59	2-2	0	61	1.47	4.73	46.3%	13.1%	22.8%	3.4%	46.1%	65.9%	81.7%	26.0%	61.0%	.276	.555	105	0.5
2024 non	NYY	MLB	28	58(0)	50	2-2	0	51	1.43	4.72	48.8%	12.2%	23.1%	2.9%	45.9%					.287	.532	103	0.1

2023 Arsenal: SI (97.5), SL (87.7), CH (88.4), FA (97.3)   Comps: Austin Brice (62), José Ramirez (62), Ryne Stanek (62)

When I was in high school, I worked at a local pharmacy that liked to put out candy corn in a dish at the register around Halloween for customers to grab a piece or two if they so desired (yes, it was long before the days of COVID-19). I have never really liked candy corn but I would often find myself just noshing on it during slow times because, well, it was there and sugary. I wasn't exactly happy about eating it, but it helped move the shift along.

Abreu was the Yankees' candy corn in 2023—not a terrible reliever *per se*, because his stuff can still occasionally tantalize, but just someone to put out there because not every pitch can be thrown by a top relief arm. He was just there, grinding through low-leverage innings until something better came along.

Clayton Beeter RHP   Born: 10/09/98   Age: 25   Height: 6'2"   Weight: 220   Origin: Round 2, 2020 Draft (#66 overall)

YEAR	TM	LVL	AGE	G(GS)	IP	W-L	SV	K	WHIP	ERA	CSP	BB%	K%	HR%	GB%	ZSw%	ZCon%	OSw%	OCon%	BABIP	SLGCON	DRA-	WARP
2021	GL	A+	22	23(22)	37¹	0-4	0	55	1.15	3.13		9.9%	36.4%	2.0%	36.7%					.333	.571	71	1.0
2021	TUL	AA	22	5(5)	15	0-2	0	23	1.13	4.20		11.3%	37.1%	3.2%	53.3%					.286	.600	71	0.3
2022	TUL	AA	23	18(16)	51²	0-3	0	88	1.61	5.75		14.3%	36.1%	4.1%	39.8%					.352	.793	60	1.5
2022	SOM	AA	23	7(7)	25¹	0-0	0	41	1.07	2.13		10.6%	39.4%	1.0%	46.2%					.306	.440	72	0.7
2023	SOM	AA	24	12(12)	60²	6-2	0	76	1.24	2.08		12.1%	29.7%	1.2%	41.1%					.299	.436	91	1.1
2023	SWB	AAA	24	15(14)	71	3-5	0	89	1.48	4.94		13.9%	28.1%	4.7%	32.0%	69.1%	79.5%	30.6%	51.4%	.277	.689	84	1.3
2024 DC	NYY	MLB	25	18(3)	32¹	2-2	0	36	1.44	5.05		12.4%	25.2%	3.9%	34.5%					.284	.602	110	0.0

2023 Arsenal: FA (95.4), SL (85.1), CH (85.4)   Comps: Parker Dunshee (66), Conner Menez (65), Jimmy Nelson (63)

The strikeout stuff is clearly there for Beeter, who drew plenty of eyes by fanning 13 and generating 21 swings and misses in a five-inning effort against Buffalo on September 13. He did so with 97% of his pitches being a fastball or slider—the latter of which is especially good—just one of the reasons why he seems destined for a dynamic relief role. To complete the full picture of his performance, Beeter also gave up seven runs on eight hits and four walks in the previous outing, which was one of seven times out of his 26 starts that he issued at least four free passes.

Gerrit Cole RHP   Born: 09/08/90   Age: 33   Height: 6'4"   Weight: 220   Origin: Round 1, 2011 Draft (#1 overall)

YEAR	TM	LVL	AGE	G(GS)	IP	W-L	SV	K	WHIP	ERA	CSP	BB%	K%	HR%	GB%	ZSw%	ZCon%	OSw%	OCon%	BABIP	SLGCON	DRA-	WARP
2021	NYY	MLB	30	30(30)	181¹	16-8	0	243	1.06	3.23	53.5%	5.6%	33.5%	3.3%	42.5%	67.4%	77.8%	36.0%	55.5%	.305	.581	71	4.5
2022	NYY	MLB	31	33(33)	200²	13-8	0	257	1.02	3.50	52.6%	6.3%	32.4%	4.2%	42.0%	68.4%	78.8%	35.4%	50.7%	.269	.599	73	4.7
2023	NYY	MLB	32	33(33)	209	15-4	0	222	0.98	2.63	48.0%	5.8%	27.0%	2.4%	39.8%	72.3%	81.8%	33.9%	62.1%	.263	.455	88	3.8
2024 DC	NYY	MLB	33	31(31)	193²	15-8	0	213	1.11	3.30	50.5%	6.4%	27.0%	3.6%	39.7%					.278	.555	80	3.7

2023 Arsenal: FA (96.9), SL (89.2), KC (83.2), FC (92.7), CH (89.1), SI (94.7)   Comps: John Smoltz (84), Jim Palmer (83), Steve Rogers (83)

The disappointment of missing out on a major award is at least somewhat soothed by the knowledge that you'll be on voters' minds the next time you make your case. Mike Trout's 2014 will never be considered the best year of his career, but that was when he won his first MVP after the WAR Wars with Miguel Cabrera in 2012-13. Justin Verlander won his second Cy Young Award in 2019 even though he was arguably better in a handful of other campaigns.

Cole finished second to Verlander in that make-up 2019 and he was runner up to Robbie Ray in 2021. Was Cole as overwhelming in 2023 as he was then? Not really: His K% was its lowest since his two-seam days in Pittsburgh, and his DRA- was higher than all seasons following 2017 as well. Nevertheless, Cole was the bedrock for a shaky Yankees rotation, pacing the AL in IP and WHIP while throwing four different pitches that had positive run values. The not-so-secret sauce this time around involved slashing his home run total while posting his lowest-ball rate as a Yankee. Cole also lead the league in ERA, putting him in prime position to finally capture that elusive Cy. Better late than never!

Nestor Cortes LHP   Born: 12/10/94   Age: 29   Height: 5'11"   Weight: 210   Origin: Round 36, 2013 Draft (#1094 overall)

YEAR	TM	LVL	AGE	G (GS)	IP	W-L	SV	K	WHIP	ERA	CSP	BB%	K%	HR%	GB%	ZSw%	ZCon%	OSw%	OCon%	BABIP	SLGCON	DRA-	WARP
2021	SWB	AAA	26	5(1)	15	1-1	1	18	0.60	1.20		2.0%	35.3%	2.0%	37.5%					.226	.344	90	0.3
2021	NYY	MLB	26	22(14)	93	2-3	0	103	1.08	2.90	53.4%	6.7%	27.5%	3.7%	27.9%	72.1%	81.6%	31.3%	67.7%	.266	.550	108	0.5
2022	NYY	MLB	27	28(28)	158¹	12-4	0	163	0.92	2.44	55.3%	6.2%	26.5%	2.6%	34.2%	70.8%	81.4%	35.4%	67.1%	.232	.438	94	2.1
2023	NYY	MLB	28	12(12)	63¹	5-2	0	67	1.25	4.97	50.1%	7.5%	25.2%	4.1%	25.6%	74.2%	80.7%	30.6%	66.7%	.291	.611	125	-0.1
2024 DC	NYY	MLB	29	26(26)	137¹	9-6	0	136	1.19	3.81	53.1%	7.4%	23.8%	3.7%	30.9%					.275	.554	90	1.9

2023 Arsenal: FA (91.8), FC (86.8), SW (76.6), CH (83), SL (82.1)   Comps: *Derek Holland (44), Andrew Heaney (43), Blake Snell (42)*

Nasty Nestor had a dream 16-month run in the Bronx from his sudden ascension to the rotation in mid-2021 after beginning it in NRI purgatory, and a still-surprising All-Star 2022 to follow it up. When the Yankees hedged their bets a bit by signing another southpaw, Carlos Rodón, to be the no. 2 behind ace Gerrit Cole, they still envisioned great things from both lefties in their rotation. No one expected the dream to turn to a nightmare, as first-half injuries to Rodón and second-half injuries to Cortes meant that they shared a rotation for exactly one turn. (Oh, and they were both terrible when they were healthy.) Cortes has less of a track record than his new rotation-mate, so he'll get a little less leash to put things back together following his recovery from injury. At least he's already pulled himself up from mediocrity once before.

Scott Effross RHP   Born: 12/28/93   Age: 30   Height: 6'2"   Weight: 202   Origin: Round 15, 2015 Draft (#443 overall)

YEAR	TM	LVL	AGE	G (GS)	IP	W-L	SV	K	WHIP	ERA	CSP	BB%	K%	HR%	GB%	ZSw%	ZCon%	OSw%	OCon%	BABIP	SLGCON	DRA-	WARP
2021	TNS	AA	27	8(0)	18²	3-0	0	20	1.13	2.89		6.6%	26.3%	2.6%	50.0%					.292	.510	96	0.2
2021	IOW	AAA	27	23(2)	42	4-2	2	46	0.90	3.64		6.1%	28.2%	3.7%	57.8%					.232	.500	85	0.9
2021	CHC	MLB	27	14(0)	14²	2-1	0	18	0.95	3.68	56.5%	1.7%	31.0%	3.4%	47.2%	65.4%	73.5%	27.1%	62.5%	.324	.647	83	0.3
2022	NYY	MLB	28	13(0)	12²	0-0	3	12	1.03	2.13	54.7%	7.8%	23.5%	2.0%	41.2%	61.9%	78.8%	33.9%	70.3%	.242	.382	83	0.2
2022	CHC	MLB	28	47(1)	44	1-4	1	50	1.07	2.66	51.7%	6.2%	28.1%	1.1%	44.8%	61.2%	85.1%	37.4%	65.7%	.301	.430	73	1.1
2024 DC	NYY	MLB	30	50(0)	53²	4-2	0	49	1.30	4.45	53.1%	7.3%	21.1%	3.5%	42.4%					.292	.553	101	0.2

Comps: *Pedro Báez (65), Rob Wooten (63), Andrew Kittredge (62)*

As expected, Tommy John surgery in October 2022 kept Effross out for all of 2023, forcing him to a schedule of monotonous rehab and too much time at the Tampa complex for anyone's well-being. (Hopefully, he was into podcasts or hunting for favorite Bob Dylan deep tracks.) The Yankees' goal is to have him ready to rejoin the bullpen by early 2024; even after the procedure, his 2022 performance indicates that he can be a boon out there. Although he alone wouldn't be enough to salvage the much-maligned 2022 trade deadline, a resurgent upcoming season would at least make some people feel slightly better about it.

Yoendrys Gómez RHP   Born: 10/15/99   Age: 24   Height: 6'3"   Weight: 212   Origin: IFA, 2016

YEAR	TM	LVL	AGE	G (GS)	IP	W-L	SV	K	WHIP	ERA	CSP	BB%	K%	HR%	GB%	ZSw%	ZCon%	OSw%	OCon%	BABIP	SLGCON	DRA-	WARP
2021	TAM	A	21	9(9)	23²	0-0	0	29	0.97	3.42		9.4%	30.2%	3.1%	43.9%	69.9%	73.3%	32.4%	44.9%	.204	.491	90	0.4
2022	HV	A+	22	10(10)	28	0-0	0	27	1.14	1.93		10.6%	23.9%	0.0%	31.9%					.278	.324	104	0.1
2022	SOM	AA	22	4(4)	16¹	1-0	0	19	1.22	3.86		8.8%	27.9%	1.5%	26.2%					.317	.500	102	0.2
2023	SOM	AA	23	19(19)	65¹	0-3	0	78	1.29	3.58		13.5%	28.5%	2.2%	35.4%					.270	.490	96	1.0
2023	NYY	MLB	23	1(0)	2	0-0	0	4	0.50	0.00	42.3%	0.0%	50.0%	0.0%	33.3%	100.0%	87.5%	36.4%	62.5%	.333	.333	87	0.0
2024 DC	NYY	MLB	24	18(3)	32¹	2-2	0	31	1.55	5.66	42.3%	12.3%	21.1%	3.7%	33.4%					.296	.594	122	-0.2

2023 Arsenal: FA (94.4), FC (87.5), CU (79.8), SW (81.7), CH (89.5)   Comps: *Danny Salazar (40), Corbin Burnes (37), Walker Buehler (37)*

Gómez was born during the same month *Fight Club* was released in the United States, and both have had surprising staying power. He feels like he's been around forever, as he was added to the Yankees' 40-man roster for Rule 5 proection back in November 2020, but a COVID case, internal brace-assisted elbow surgery, and the organization's subsequent hesitance to push him too hard limited him to 70 ⅔ total innings between 2021-22. The Yankees remained quite cautious with him after a 2023 shoulder injury (even over the final couple months, he averaged just over four innings per start), before getting called upon for his MLB debut on September 28. He fanned Kevin Kiermaier and Matt Chapman in his late-season audition, causing rotation hope to spring eternal. Most likely, though, he'll call the bullpen home and hopefully build his own cult following there.

Ian Hamilton RHP   Born: 06/16/95   Age: 29   Height: 6'1"   Weight: 200   Origin: Round 11, 2016 Draft (#326 overall)

YEAR	TM	LVL	AGE	G (GS)	IP	W-L	SV	K	WHIP	ERA	CSP	BB%	K%	HR%	GB%	ZSw%	ZCon%	OSw%	OCon%	BABIP	SLGCON	DRA-	WARP
2021	STP	AAA	26	38(3)	59	4-3	4	86	1.44	4.12		15.2%	33.5%	1.9%	48.1%					.333	.571	75	1.6
2022	COL	AAA	27	15(0)	18²	0-4	1	24	1.50	6.27		13.1%	28.6%	3.6%	49.0%					.311	.646	82	0.4
2022	STP	AAA	27	23(0)	28²	2-3	1	36	0.84	1.88		7.1%	32.1%	2.7%	53.0%					.206	.431	70	0.8
2022	MIN	MLB	27	1(0)	2²	0-0	0	0	1.50	6.75	52.0%	9.1%	0.0%	9.1%	30.0%	70.6%	91.7%	28.0%	85.7%	.222	.700	107	0.0
2023	NYY	MLB	28	39(3)	58	3-2	2	69	1.22	2.64	44.1%	10.9%	28.9%	0.8%	56.0%	68.1%	77.0%	34.8%	51.9%	.309	.443	81	1.3
2024 DC	NYY	MLB	29	62(0)	65²	5-2	2	80	1.31	3.84	44.4%	11.2%	28.4%	2.5%	49.4%					.296	.527	87	0.8

2023 Arsenal: SL (88.3), SI (95.8), FA (96.4)   Comps: *Kevin Jepsen (41), Mike Morin (40), Dominic Leone (40)*

Hamilton spent quite a bit of time in the baseball wilderness after his rookie season in 2018, so it was a surprise when he made the Yankees' Opening Day roster despite just five big-league games to his name from 2019 to 2022. He had a secret weapon this time around: A slider/changeup mix dubbed the "slambio." Even with an IL stint from a groin strain mixed in, the pitch helped Hamilton dazzle through July, as he recorded a 1.60 ERA and a 29.9% K% in 33 ⅓ innings. His command faltered a bit down the stretch and he missed time due to yet another groin strain, so it will be fascinating to see if his slambio is good enough to ensure that Hamilton's more than a one-year wonder.

★ ★ ★ *2024 Top 101 Prospect* **#56** ★ ★ ★

Chase Hampton RHP Born: 08/07/01 Age: 22 Height: 6'2" Weight: 220 Origin: Round 6, 2022 Draft (#190 overall)

YEAR	TM	LVL	AGE	G (GS)	IP	W-L	SV	K	WHIP	ERA	CSP	BB%	K%	HR%	GB%	ZSw%	ZCon%	OSw%	OCon%	BABIP	SLGCON	DRA-	WARP
2023	HV	A+	21	9(9)	47	2-1	0	77	1.00	2.68		8.4%	40.5%	2.6%	32.0%					.283	.573	85	0.7
2023	SOM	AA	21	11(11)	59²	2-2	0	68	1.26	4.37		8.5%	27.4%	3.2%	32.7%					.305	.586	100	0.9
2024 DC	NYY	MLB	22	10(10)	45²	3-3	0	45	1.39	4.94		10.0%	22.9%	4.1%	32.8%					.288	.598	110	0.2

2023 Arsenal: FA (95), FC (87.5), SW (83.9) *Comps: Danny Duffy (80), Ryan Castellani (79), Edwin Díaz (78)*

The former Texas Tech Red Raider and sixth-round pick in 2022 made his pro debut in 2023 and steamrolled through Hudson Valley with overwhelming strikeout numbers. Then, Hampton arrived in Double-A before the first day of summer, and while the results there were a bit more moderate, his high-spin fastball still worked well with his slider and curve to make him one of the Yankees' top pitching prospects. The command will be what makes him either a difference-maker in the Bronx or just another trade chip for desperately needed big-league help.

Clay Holmes RHP Born: 03/27/93 Age: 31 Height: 6'5" Weight: 245 Origin: Round 9, 2011 Draft (#272 overall)

YEAR	TM	LVL	AGE	G (GS)	IP	W-L	SV	K	WHIP	ERA	CSP	BB%	K%	HR%	GB%	ZSw%	ZCon%	OSw%	OCon%	BABIP	SLGCON	DRA-	WARP
2021	NYY	MLB	28	25(0)	28	5-2	0	34	0.79	1.61	57.6%	3.9%	33.0%	1.9%	61.5%	55.9%	83.8%	29.3%	50.8%	.254	.375	69	0.7
2021	PIT	MLB	28	44(0)	42	3-2	0	44	1.43	4.93	56.0%	13.2%	23.3%	1.6%	70.7%	64.0%	84.9%	25.3%	51.4%	.286	.426	79	0.9
2022	NYY	MLB	29	62(0)	63²	7-4	20	65	1.02	2.54	54.2%	7.7%	25.0%	0.8%	77.0%	65.9%	83.0%	32.6%	52.1%	.264	.364	73	1.5
2023	NYY	MLB	30	66(0)	63	4-4	24	71	1.17	2.86	48.4%	8.8%	27.1%	0.8%	66.7%	64.9%	84.9%	27.7%	54.3%	.301	.417	76	1.6
2024 DC	NYY	MLB	31	62(0)	65²	5-6	41	66	1.23	3.32	51.9%	9.1%	23.5%	1.5%	65.2%					.286	.434	77	1.1

2023 Arsenal: SI (96.2), SL (87.7), SW (84.1), FA (97.4) *Comps: Matt Barnes (63), Ryan Pressly (62), Alex Colomé (62)*

For someone with a history of ups and downs like Holmes, he's been remarkably consistent once you zoom out. At the end of 2022, he suffered such an ugly walk-heavy second half that Wandy Peralta was recording the most important outs in October. Then, once the 2023 season kicked off, there was a bumpy start in early April led to a closer-by-committee dalliance, but with a 1.42 ERA, 30.3% K%, 62.4% GB% and .511 OPS against across his next 38 innings, Holmes regained the Yankees' confidence. That four-month run came to an end with a shockingly awful game in Miami that kicked off another shaky stretch more closely resembling a vintage What's Wrong With Mo Week situation than a true derailment. The final tally was rock-solid (despite again not having important innings to throw in October), and Holmes earned his third consecutive win-and-a-half season.

Tommy Kahnle RHP Born: 08/07/89 Age: 34 Height: 6'1" Weight: 230 Origin: Round 5, 2010 Draft (#175 overall)

YEAR	TM	LVL	AGE	G (GS)	IP	W-L	SV	K	WHIP	ERA	CSP	BB%	K%	HR%	GB%	ZSw%	ZCon%	OSw%	OCon%	BABIP	SLGCON	DRA-	WARP
2022	OKC	AAA	32	10(0)	9²	1-0	0	10	1.14	3.72		7.5%	25.0%	5.0%	48.1%	63.6%	77.1%	34.7%	50.0%	.240	.519	91	0.1
2022	LAD	MLB	32	13(0)	12²	0-0	1	14	0.63	2.84	58.3%	6.5%	30.4%	4.3%	65.4%	76.6%	72.9%	36.1%	60.0%	.125	.440	83	0.2
2023	NYY	MLB	33	42(0)	40²	1-3	2	48	1.11	2.66	43.7%	11.5%	29.1%	3.0%	48.5%	68.0%	74.7%	31.5%	51.9%	.231	.500	90	0.7
2024 DC	NYY	MLB	34	56(0)	59²	4-2	2	74	1.24	3.68	46.4%	9.5%	29.0%	2.8%	47.1%					.297	.550	85	0.7

2023 Arsenal: CH (89), FA (95.6), SI (94.5), SL (85) *Comps: Brad Boxberger (63), Greg Holland (61), Paul Shuey (60)*

Tommy Tightpants' season began with a couple months on the IL due to right biceps tendinitis, and it ended with him on the shelf as well in late September, when the Yankees shut him down with right shoulder inflammation. In between, there were changeups, changeups and oh yes, more changeups (75.8% of his total pitches). Most of them were good, but a few less so, particularly when batters got used to seeing too many in a row. Kahnle remains a perfectly cromulent relief arm, but he might never have the health to stomp around the mound again for an uninterrupted season.

Jonathan Loáisiga RHP Born: 11/02/94 Age: 29 Height: 5'11" Weight: 165 Origin: IFA, 2012

YEAR	TM	LVL	AGE	G (GS)	IP	W-L	SV	K	WHIP	ERA	CSP	BB%	K%	HR%	GB%	ZSw%	ZCon%	OSw%	OCon%	BABIP	SLGCON	DRA-	WARP
2021	NYY	MLB	26	57(0)	70²	9-4	5	69	1.02	2.17	53.7%	5.7%	24.4%	1.1%	60.5%	70.1%	81.4%	41.1%	61.3%	.279	.382	66	1.9
2022	NYY	MLB	27	50(0)	48	2-3	2	37	1.29	4.13	49.4%	9.4%	18.2%	1.5%	59.2%	69.9%	82.0%	38.3%	66.3%	.278	.367	90	0.7
2023	NYY	MLB	28	17(0)	17²	0-2	0	6	0.85	3.06	50.3%	1.4%	8.7%	2.9%	55.0%	76.5%	89.7%	38.1%	76.5%	.207	.362	98	0.2
2024 DC	NYY	MLB	29	56(0)	59²	4-2	2	48	1.34	4.25	50.8%	7.0%	18.6%	2.2%	54.1%					.306	.487	96	0.4

2023 Arsenal: SI (97.9), SW (86.3), CH (89.5), FA (97.8) *Comps: Justin Grimm (49), Michael Feliz (48), Addison Reed (47)*

Loáisiga's brilliant 2021 campaign is skittering further and further away. That gem of a season remains easily his career-high in MLB innings, and in 2023, he threw fewer than he did even in the COVID-shortened 2020. After a tough World Baseball Classic with Nicaragua, Loáisiga made it into just three games before enduring a four-month stay on the IL following surgery to remove bone spurs in his elbow. He looked like his old self at first upon returning, allowing nary a single earned run across the next month... only to then look awful in his early-September outings that preceded a return to the IL with elbow inflammation. With issues moving from shoulder (2022) to elbow (2023), here's hoping the injury bug stops crawling further down his arm—or worse, nibbles on his already-once-repaired UCL.

Ron Marinaccio RHP Born: 07/01/95 Age: 29 Height: 6'2" Weight: 205 Origin: Round 19, 2017 Draft (#572 overall)

YEAR	TM	LVL	AGE	G (GS)	IP	W-L	SV	K	WHIP	ERA	CSP	BB%	K%	HR%	GB%	ZSw%	ZCon%	OSw%	OCon%	BABIP	SLGCON	DRA-	WARP
2021	SOM	AA	25	22 (0)	39²	1-1	3	64	0.91	1.82		12.3%	41.3%	1.3%	30.4%					.224	.412	73	0.9
2021	SWB	AAA	25	18 (0)	26²	1-0	2	41	0.97	2.36		7.4%	38.0%	1.9%	31.6%					791	500	72	0.7
2022	SWB	AAA	26	8 (0)	9²	1-0	0	21	1.45	2.79		9.1%	47.7%	6.8%	31.6%					.438	1.158	63	0.3
2022	NYY	MLB	26	40 (0)	44	1-0	0	56	1.05	2.05	47.1%	13.3%	30.9%	1.1%	41.5%	65.6%	78.2%	33.5%	54.8%	.217	.380	97	0.5
2023	SWB	AAA	27	14 (0)	15¹	0-1	1	13	1.96	8.80		23.4%	16.9%	2.6%	31.8%	70.8%	74.1%	23.0%	52.2%	.244	.500	120	0.0
2023	NYY	MLB	27	45 (0)	47¹	4-5	2	56	1.31	3.99	42.4%	13.2%	27.3%	2.9%	36.8%	68.1%	75.0%	34.0%	68.1%	.271	.536	100	0.6
2024 DC	NYY	MLB	28	50 (0)	53²	4-2	0	63	1.35	4.45	44.3%	12.8%	26.9%	3.5%	37.2%					.266	.562	98	0.3

2023 Arsenal: FA (94), CH (83), SW (80.9), FC (85.2)   Comps: Vic Black (76), Giovanny Gallegos (74), Tanner Rainey (74)

The changeup that paired so well with Marinaccio's four-seamer in 2022 completely went to hell in 2023, as opposing hitters slugged nearly 200 percentage points higher against it on contact. The combination of a poor walk rate and his *cambio*'s rapid decline meant a midseason demotion—quite a fall for the rookie who was deeply missed after his injury kept him out of the 2022 postseason. The control problems only got worse in Triple-A, and even with rosters expanding in September, he made only one appearance that month while battling his woes. Both Yankee fans and eyebrow enthusiasts wept.

Keynan Middleton RHP Born: 09/12/93 Age: 30 Height: 6'3" Weight: 215 Origin: Round 3, 2013 Draft (#95 overall)

YEAR	TM	LVL	AGE	G (GS)	IP	W-L	SV	K	WHIP	ERA	CSP	BB%	K%	HR%	GB%	ZSw%	ZCon%	OSw%	OCon%	BABIP	SLGCON	DRA-	WARP
2021	TAC	AAA	27	7 (1)	7²	1-0	0	13	1.17	2.35		6.3%	40.6%	3.1%	23.5%					.375	.765	89	0.1
2021	SEA	MLB	27	32 (1)	31	1-2	4	24	1.58	4.94	54.5%	13.6%	17.1%	1.4%	31.6%	77.2%	76.0%	35.2%	59.0%	.301	.463	131	-0.2
2022	RNO	AAA	28	17 (0)	17	2-0	1	24	0.88	2.12		10.6%	36.4%	1.5%	45.7%	67.9%	75.0%	36.6%	46.7%	.206	.394	77	0.3
2022	AZ	MLB	28	18 (0)	17	1-2	0	15	1.12	5.29	60.2%	4.3%	21.7%	7.2%	26.0%	72.5%	73.4%	39.7%	48.1%	.250	.714	104	0.1
2023	CHW	MLB	29	39 (0)	36¹	2-2	2	47	1.35	3.96	47.0%	10.3%	30.1%	4.5%	50.0%	71.3%	80.4%	37.3%	43.3%	.310	.626	78	0.9
2023	NYY	MLB	29	12 (0)	14¹	0-0	0	17	0.98	1.88	44.2%	12.5%	30.4%	1.8%	68.8%	77.5%	75.8%	39.3%	49.1%	.194	.344	81	0.3
2024 non	NYY	MLB	30	58 (0)	50	2-2	0	60	1.27	3.84	49.9%	10.2%	28.3%	3.1%	40.9%					.290	.555	88	0.5

2023 Arsenal: CH (87.9), SL (86.1), FA (95.8)   Comps: Bryan Shaw (60), Ken Giles (59), Chris Resop (59)

At the trade deadline, the Yankees hemmed and hawed about whether to buy or sell with their mediocre team. Eventually, they threw their hands in the air, gave up and did neither, committing to their "mid" status by adding the Mid Man himself. Is that really fair to Middleton, who ticked up his slider usage with the Yankees and became a ground-ball machine? Kind of—he went on the IL in early September and didn't return to the team until the last series of the season. He's now a pending free agent, giving the Yankees nothing to show for their catastrophe of a trade deadline.

Cody Morris RHP Born: 11/04/96 Age: 27 Height: 6'4" Weight: 205 Origin: Round 7, 2018 Draft (#223 overall)

YEAR	TM	LVL	AGE	G (GS)	IP	W-L	SV	K	WHIP	ERA	CSP	BB%	K%	HR%	GB%	ZSw%	ZCon%	OSw%	OCon%	BABIP	SLGCON	DRA-	WARP
2021	AKR	AA	24	5 (5)	20	0-0	0	29	1.05	1.35		8.8%	36.3%	1.3%	38.1%					.317	.452	91	0.3
2021	COL	AAA	24	9 (8)	36²	2-2	0	52	1.01	1.72		8.3%	36.1%	0.7%	43.8%					.304	.456	76	0.9
2022	COL	AAA	25	6 (3)	15¹	0-0	1	30	0.72	2.35		10.3%	51.7%	3.4%	45.5%					.150	.545	59	0.5
2022	CLE	MLB	25	7 (5)	23²	1-2	0	23	1.39	2.28	53.7%	12.0%	23.0%	3.0%	36.9%	78.9%	77.8%	31.8%	59.5%	.290	.516	110	0.1
2023	COL	AAA	26	18 (1)	33²	2-1	0	40	1.34	3.74		17.4%	27.8%	3.5%	45.5%	60.3%	75.8%	29.4%	51.0%	.208	.468	91	0.6
2023	CLE	MLB	26	6 (0)	8	0-0	0	9	2.00	6.75	48.1%	15.8%	23.7%	7.9%	43.5%	72.5%	78.0%	25.0%	62.5%	.350	1.000	92	0.1
2024 DC	NYY	MLB	27	20 (5)	37¹	2-2	0	43	1.38	4.56	51.8%	11.7%	26.1%	3.4%	38.7%					.288	.576	101	0.2

2023 Arsenal: FA (95), FC (88.8), KC (79.4), CH (82.4)   Comps: Carlos Frías (47), Jefry Rodriguez (46), Domingo Germán (46)

The first half of Morris' season was knocked out by a teres major strain—the same barking shoulder muscle that cut his 2022 season short. For the first time in his injury-riddled professional career, he was moved to the bullpen, making regular two-inning appearances in Triple-A. While his fastball and cutter made a solid two-pitch whiff combination, Morris experienced the worst control issues of his career, walking over a sixth of batters and at times completely losing the zone. After spending a month in the big-league rotation in his debut season, Morris made just six short relief appearances at the highest level last year; he allowed walks in four and the devastating swing-and-miss stuff he showed off just a few seasons ago was nowhere to be found. Entering his final option year, his focus will likely shift to optimizing his stuff for short-burst relief.

Carlos Rodón LHP Born: 12/10/92 Age: 31 Height: 6'2" Weight: 255 Origin: Round 1, 2014 Draft (#3 overall)

YEAR	TM	LVL	AGE	G (GS)	IP	W-L	SV	K	WHIP	ERA	CSP	BB%	K%	HR%	GB%	ZSw%	ZCon%	OSw%	OCon%	BABIP	SLGCON	DRA-	WARP
2021	CHW	MLB	28	24 (24)	132²	13-5	0	185	0.96	2.37	53.7%	6.7%	34.6%	2.4%	37.5%	71.9%	76.7%	35.6%	52.9%	.271	.497	72	3.2
2022	SF	MLB	29	31 (31)	178	14-8	0	237	1.03	2.88	56.4%	7.3%	33.4%	1.7%	34.3%	69.9%	76.6%	35.3%	57.6%	.295	.485	79	3.7
2023	NYY	MLB	30	14 (14)	64¹	3-8	0	64	1.45	6.85	47.0%	9.8%	22.4%	5.2%	27.0%	78.2%	83.2%	35.6%	58.5%	.287	.670	147	-0.8
2024 DC	NYY	MLB	31	23 (23)	124²	8-6	0	135	1.21	3.90	53.2%	8.4%	25.8%	3.6%	32.8%					.277	.565	91	1.7

2023 Arsenal: FA (95.5), SL (85.8), CU (80.1), CH (85.4)   Comps: Madison Bumgarner (74), Shawn Estes (74), Kevin Appier (73)

Wastewater treatment plants were more aromatic than Rodón's first season in pinstripes after signing a six-year, $162 million deal in December 2022. It was a disaster by all measures, starting with a forearm strain and the reveal of a chronic back injury that delayed his debut until July 7. Once Rodón actually made it to the field, he looked little like the All-Star southpaw who excelled in Chicago and San Francisco. His DRA more than doubled, his home run rate more than tripled and his once-dynamic four-seamer went from a +22 Run Value pitch to -6 per Baseball Savant. Rodón capped his terrible year by allowing all eight Royals he faced in his 2023 finale to reach and score, failing to record a single out and taking his frustration out on pitching coach Matt Blake. It's no stretch to say there's nowhere to go but up in Yankee Year Two–even a catastrophic injury would be better than a 2023 repeat.

Clarke Schmidt RHP   Born: 02/20/96   Age: 28   Height: 6'1"   Weight: 200   Origin: Round 1, 2017 Draft (#16 overall)

YEAR	TM	LVL	AGE	G (GS)	IP	W-L	SV	K	WHIP	ERA	CSP	BB%	K%	HR%	GB%	ZSw%	ZCon%	OSw%	OCon%	BABIP	SLGCON	DRA-	WARP
2021	SOM	AA	25	2(2)	6¹	0-1	0	5	1.11	4.26		7.4%	18.5%	7.4%	47.4%					.176	.579	103	0.0
2021	SWB	AAA	25	6(5)	25²	0-1	0	32	1.29	2.10		7.2%	28.8%	3.6%	52.9%					.318	.557	89	0.5
2021	NYY	MLB	25	2(1)	6¹	0-0	0	6	2.53	5.68	49.1%	13.2%	15.8%	2.6%	57.7%	74.1%	95.0%	33.7%	63.3%	.417	.640	101	0.1
2022	SWB	AAA	26	8(8)	33	2-1	0	46	1.06	3.27		6.5%	33.1%	0.7%	50.0%					.313	.432	73	0.9
2022	NYY	MLB	26	29(3)	57²	5-5	2	56	1.20	3.12	55.5%	9.7%	23.7%	2.1%	41.9%	67.1%	83.8%	32.0%	57.2%	.279	.470	95	0.7
2023	NYY	MLB	27	33(32)	159	9-9	0	149	1.35	4.64	50.6%	6.6%	21.5%	3.5%	43.2%	66.1%	88.0%	31.7%	59.6%	.313	.590	99	1.9
2024 DC	*NYY*	*MLB*	*28*	*24(24)*	*121¹*	*8-7*	*0*	*101*	*1.35*	*4.65*	*51.6%*	*8.1%*	*19.1%*	*3.3%*	*43.1%*					*.290*	*.535*	*104*	*0.7*

2023 Arsenal: HC (91.5), SW (86.2), SI (93.6), KC (83.8), CH (89.9)   Comps: *Matt Andriese (57), Tyler Beede (54), Jerad Eickhoff (53)*

There is nothing *wrong* with enjoying a Trefoil. You're still eating a Girl Scout Cookie, and there are far worse things to consume than a nice little piece of shortbread. But there are so many superior Girl Scout Cookies available ... unless you're really craving Trefoils, you're missing out on something better. Schmidt is a Trefoil, but in the form of a full-season starting pitcher. He's fine! He's there! But don't you want something with a little more flavor in the rotation? Boy, I could go for a Tagalong or Samoa instead.

Will Warren RHP   Born: 06/16/99   Age: 25   Height: 6'2"   Weight: 175   Origin: Round 8, 2021 Draft (#243 overall)

YEAR	TM	LVL	AGE	G (GS)	IP	W-L	SV	K	WHIP	ERA	CSP	BB%	K%	HR%	GB%	ZSw%	ZCon%	OSw%	OCon%	BABIP	SLGCON	DRA-	WARP
2022	HV	A+	23	8(8)	35	2-3	0	42	1.11	3.60		6.4%	30.0%	1.4%	57.0%					.333	.500	95	0.3
2022	SOM	AA	23	18(18)	94	7-6	0	83	1.30	4.02		8.2%	20.6%	2.0%	52.5%					.302	.489	110	0.8
2023	SOM	AA	24	6(6)	29¹	3-0	0	39	1.30	2.45		9.9%	32.2%	0.0%	48.6%					.371	.443	86	0.6
2023	SWB	AAA	24	21(19)	99²	7-4	0	110	1.30	3.61		10.9%	25.6%	3.5%	53.2%	63.2%	83.4%	32.7%	53.5%	.271	.548	75	2.8
2024 DC	*NYY*	*MLB*	*25*	*22(13)*	*70*	*4-4*	*0*	*62*	*1.39*	*4.68*		*9.7%*	*20.2%*	*3.1%*	*43.9%*					*.288*	*.531*	*104*	*0.4*

2023 Arsenal: SI (95.3), SW (85.2), FA (95.1), CH (89.1), FC (85.3)   Comps: *Tyler Duffey (80), Taylor Jungmann (80), A.J. Griffin (78)*

After one clear breakout season in his first pro campaign of 2022, 2023 was a tale of three mini-seasons for Warren. The first was a clear maturation past Double-A, as he fanned 39 in six starts while allowing nary a dinger. The second was a two-month-long bumpy adjustment to Triple-A, where Warren struggled to find the plate (5.3 BB/9) and opponents took advantage by tagging him with a 5.52 ERA in 11 starts. His third act offered promise, as Warren toned down the free passes and allowed one run or less in six of his last seven starts, including a September 17 gem against Buffalo when his sweeper/sinker mix led to 10 K's. Will Warren debut in 2024? Probably!

LINEOUTS

Hitters

HITTER	POS	TM	LVL	AGE	PA	R	HR	RBI	SB	AVG/OBP/SLG	BABIP	SLGCON	BB%	K%	ZSw%	ZCon%	OSw%	OCon%	LA	90th EV	DRC+	BRR	DRP	WARP
Franchy Cordero	RF	SWB	AAA	28	350	53	13	61	8	.288/.403/.476	.350	.647	15.1%	22.0%	67.6%	81.6%	31.6%	42.1%		103	-2.0	0.4	0.9
	RF	NYY	MLB	28	71	9	6	13	0	.188/.211/.478	.184	.750	2.8%	35.2%	66.1%	74.4%	34.8%	41.3%	8.9	111.2	90	0.0	0.4	0.1
Jeter Downs	IF	ROC	AAA	24	193	29	3	18	11	.236/.358/.379	.313	.535	14.0%	24.4%	63.1%	83.6%	32.7%	63.6%		91	1.4	1.7	0.5
	IF	WAS	MLB	24	9	4	0	1	2	.400/.667/.400	.500	.500	44.4%	11.1%	58.3%	57.1%	19.4%	66.7%	3.9	99.5	105	0.0	0.0	0.2
George Lombard Jr.	SS	TAM	A	18	41	6	0	4	1	.273/.415/.303	.391	.435	19.5%	24.4%	65.8%	75.0%	19.4%	66.7%		94	0.9	0.1	0.2
Brando Mayea	OF	DSL NYY	ROK	17	170	27	3	18	22	.276/.382/.400	.322	.492	12.9%	15.9%										
Hans Montero	SS	YNK	ROK	19	234	41	5	23	17	.257/.419/.404	.323	.548	18.8%	20.5%	83.3%	90.0%	30.2%	46.2%						
Agustin Ramirez	C	TAM	A	21	232	35	7	35	7	.245/.384/.397	.271	.510	18.5%	17.7%	69.1%	89.6%	26.6%	50.7%		127	-3.1	4.4	1.5
	C	HV	A+	21	121	21	9	23	2	.384/.430/.714	.395	.842	6.6%	14.0%						148	-0.9	0.8	0.9
	C	SOM	AA	21	139	17	2	11	3	.211/.273/.313	.253	.396	7.2%	19.4%						92	0.0	-0.6	0.3
Ben Rice	C	TAM	A	24	42	7	2	10	1	.286/.405/.543	.348	.760	11.9%	23.8%	70.8%	94.1%	22.2%	40.0%		106	0.4	0.0	0.2
	C	HV	A+	24	68	15	2	10	3	.341/.559/.523	.394	.676	26.5%	14.7%						156	-0.6	-0.5	0.5
	C	SOM	AA	24	222	40	16	48	7	.327/.401/.648	.345	.825	9.5%	18.9%						140	-0.6	-0.7	1.3
Roc Riggio	2B	TAM	A	21	76	11	0	9	3	.193/.395/.228	.282	.333	23.7%	23.7%	66.1%	84.6%	27.9%	55.2%		101	0.5	-1.4	0.2
Bubba Thompson	OF	OMA	AAA	25	153	21	4	17	11	.259/.313/.410	.340	.582	5.2%	26.8%	74.0%	78.2%	31.8%	38.9%		76	0.5	0.3	0.2
	OF	RR	AAA	25	149	28	2	17	16	.260/.362/.378	.316	.485	12.8%	18.8%	70.0%	85.7%	26.7%	52.2%		94	1.4	-1.3	0.4
	OF	TEX	MLB	25	60	10	0	4	4	.170/.237/.283	.237	.405	6.7%	26.7%	75.0%	68.3%	33.8%	50.0%	1.0	97.8	79	0.1	0.3	0.1
Jorbit Vivas	2B	TUL	AA	22	491	82	12	54	21	.280/.391/.436	.292	.500	11.0%	10.6%						119	-0.7	5.2	2.8
	2B	OKC	AAA	22	121	16	1	9	4	.225/.339/.294	.265	.361	12.4%	15.7%	73.5%	92.0%	28.6%	59.7%		95	-0.6	2.2	0.3

It seems impossible that **Franchy Cordero** is not even 30 because it seems like he's been not living up to his potential for at least a decade. At this stage in his career his power still plays, but Mike Tyson would be envious of his punchouts. Call him Wily Less Peña. ⊗ **Jeter Downs** was unable to reclaim his prospect luster during a rough season, but a return to the majors was a feather in his cap. He might find it tough to manage doing it for a third straight season after landing with the Yankees, whose infield depth, uh...surpasses the Nationals'. ⊗ The son of a former second-round pick and six-year major leaguer, **George Lombard Jr.** did his father one round better when the Yankees nabbed the prep shortstop with the 26th-overall pick. Like Anthony Volpe, he passed up an offer to go to Vandy to join the Yankees; the team hopes he'll at least equal the big league performance of etiher Volpe or his father. ⊗ The Yankees landed the biggest name on the IFA market in January 2023 when they came to terms with **Brando Mayea** on a $4.4 million deal. He turned 18 years old in September and spent most of his Dominican Summer League season intriguing with remarkable tools. Keep an eye on his outstanding speed as he progresses through the system; he could be a contender. ⊗ Although not nearly as heralded during his IFA signing period as Roderick Arias or Jasson Domínguez were in theirs, the Yankees were glad to make **Hans Montero** their top signee in January 2021. He underwhelmed in the DSL for a couple years and while he did demonstrate good bat speed and put up numbers at the Florida complex in 2023, it's hard to envision him as their next great hope. ⊗ BP's Smith Brickner saw **Agustin Ramirez** in Hudson Valley and complimented his barrel control and ability to resist heaters and breakers, though the defense behind the dish needs work. He merited two promotions in 2023 after abandoning the complex leagues, so monitor him (and his rising strikeout rate) going forward. ⓧ **Ben Rice** is a 24-year-old catcher out of Dartmouth and a surprising choice as MLB Pipeline's Yankees Hitting Prospect of the Year. He's a modest defender, but his impressive numbers at three MiLB levels and solid pitch recognition give him the chance to be the first Big Green catcher to make the majors since Brad Ausmus. ⓧ Hard-nosed infielder **Roc Riggio** hit .335/.461/.679 with 18 homers in just 59 games at Oklahoma State, so the Yankees were leaning with it and Roccing it upon picking him in the fourth round of the 2023 MLB Draft. If he makes the majors, his bat will be what carries him—though his power doesn't project to be nearly that explosive. ⓧ **Bubba Thompson** went from competing with Leody Taveras to the top prospect in the Rangers system to getting squeezed out of the Royals outfield mix to Reds waiver claim. He retains excellent speed, but the power hasn't shown up in the higher levels of the game, or if it is has, it's been muffled by the sound of swings and misses, which is a doubba-bubba-bummer. ⓧ Most of us are incentivized to make our job look hard; baseball players, meanwhile, are praised for making it look easy. **Jorbit Vivas** certainly doesn't make it look easy, thanks to a coiled, heavy swing that looks like he's putting everything he's got into hitting it past infielders. He does hit it, though, which is the important part.

Pitchers

PITCHER	TM	LVL	AGE	G (GS)	IP	W-L	SV	K	WHIP	ERA	CSP	BB%	K%	HR%	GB%	ZSw%	ZCon%	OSw%	OCon%	BABIP	SLGCON	DRA-	WARP
Matt Bowman	SWB	AAA	32	49 (0)	58²	4-1	5	58	1.38	3.99		11.7%	22.6%	1.9%	52.7%	61.4%	87.6%	31.1%	60.0%	.288	.500	89	1.2
	NYY	MLB	32	3 (0)	4	0-0	0	3	2.00	9.00	46.9%	10.0%	15.0%	5.0%	46.7%	65.6%	95.2%	21.6%	72.7%	.357	.714	98	0.1
Jimmy Cordero	NYY	MLB	31	31 (1)	32²	3-2	0	34	1.07	3.86	47.0%	7.6%	25.8%	1.5%	55.8%	62.9%	84.7%	28.9%	62.6%	.274	.442	86	0.6
Yerry De Los Santos	IND	AAA	25	23 (0)	25	1-5	2	28	2.24	6.12		10.9%	21.7%	3.1%	50.0%	60.4%	84.1%	32.6%	59.6%	.463	.729	95	0.4
	PIT	MLB	25	22 (0)	24¹	1-1	0	18	1.23	3.33	47.8%	12.5%	17.3%	1.0%	54.2%	67.3%	92.2%	32.0%	71.8%	.225	.371	100	0.3
Victor González	OKC	AAA	27	20 (0)	20	2-1	1	22	1.60	5.40		17.4%	23.9%	0.0%	50.9%	64.2%	83.2%	23.6%	57.1%	.302	.346	89	0.3
	LAD	MLB	27	34 (1)	33²	3-3	0	30	1.10	4.01	47.7%	7.4%	22.2%	1.5%	54.3%	62.7%	81.0%	34.0%	59.0%	.278	.440	92	0.5
Matt Krook	SWB	AAA	28	27 (0)	34	1-1	0	55	1.06	1.32		18.4%	39.0%	0.0%	46.6%	55.3%	71.6%	32.5%	38.5%	.175	.214	72	1.0
	NYY	MLB	28	4 (0)	4	0-0	0	3	3.50	24.75	43.3%	22.2%	11.1%	3.7%	61.1%	56.8%	81.0%	31.4%	68.2%	.412	.706	112	0.0
Zach McAllister	RNO	AAA	35	37 (0)	38¹	1-2	3	54	1.59	4.93		11.2%	30.3%	2.2%	30.3%	66.3%	74.8%	20.5%	54.2%	.381	.636	87	0.8
	SWB	AAA	35	11 (3)	16²	1-1	0	20	0.60	1.62		6.7%	33.3%	3.3%	40.0%	57.4%	75.7%	31.7%	69.2%	.121	.343	87	0.4
	NYY	MLB	35	7 (0)	5¹	0-0	0	5	2.06	10.13	45.5%	6.9%	17.2%	6.9%	28.6%	79.6%	92.3%	40.5%	70.0%	.368	.857	103	0.1
Nick Ramirez	SWB	AAA	33	18 (1)	22¹	1-0	3	21	0.94	3.22		5.9%	24.7%	2.4%	59.3%	63.8%	72.3%	37.1%	56.9%	.246	.424	83	0.5
	NYY	MLB	33	32 (0)	40²	1-2	1	28	1.23	2.66	49.0%	5.2%	16.3%	0.6%	47.8%	64.8%	84.7%	33.2%	63.3%	.303	.432	98	0.5
Luis Serna	YNK	ROK	18	8 (8)	19¹	0-1	0	23	1.29	4.19		9.4%	27.1%	2.4%	44.0%	85.0%	70.6%	38.9%	42.9%	.313	.520		
Luke Weaver	LOU	AAA	29	2 (2)	9	0-0	0	9	0.78	3.00		12.1%	27.3%	3.0%	30.0%	60.6%	85.0%	32.4%	66.7%	.105	.368	117	0.1
	SEA	MLB	29	5 (1)	13¹	0-1	0	8	1.43	6.07	45.3%	5.2%	13.8%	3.4%	34.8%	75.3%	82.9%	33.3%	68.1%	.318	.609	109	0.1
	CIN	MLB	29	21 (21)	97	2-4	0	85	1.64	6.87	49.9%	7.6%	19.0%	5.4%	35.6%	69.6%	84.8%	28.8%	67.4%	.334	.724	115	0.4
	NYY	MLB	29	3 (3)	13¹	1-0	0	16	1.28	3.38	49.9%	5.3%	28.1%	5.3%	36.8%	74.0%	78.4%	26.4%	70.6%	.314	.703	108	0.1
Ryan Weber	SWB	AAA	32	7 (7)	34¹	3-3	0	26	1.40	5.77		4.1%	17.6%	4.1%	51.3%	65.8%	87.7%	35.7%	69.0%	.330	.623	98	0.5
	NYY	MLB	32	8 (0)	14¹	1-0	1	7	1.26	3.14	54.6%	1.7%	11.7%	3.3%	45.1%	70.5%	85.5%	28.7%	74.1%	.306	.540	102	0.2

The last time **Matt Bowman** pitched in the major leagues before his September cup of coffee in the Bronx, he was pitching out of the Cincinnati bullpen in the same game as Kevin Gausman. That's nearly a lifetime of a break, thanks to a 2020 Tommy John surgery that also wiped out his 2021 and 2022 seasons. ⓧ **Kyle Carr** is many things: A southpaw with a developing fastball, a former two-way player, a Tommy John surgery survivor, a Cali-born son of a Nova Scotian, a JuCo dominator and, if his social media likes are any indication, a Mickey Moniak 2023 renaissance appreciator. He contains multitudes. ⓧ **Jimmy Cordero**'s return to the majors in the Yankees bullpen abruptly ended on July 5 when he accepted a 76-game suspension for violating MLB's Joint Domestic Violence, Sexual Assault and Child Abuse Policy. ⓧ **Yerry de los Santos'** sinker jams hitters well inside, but all three of his pitches—he's a sinker/changeup/slider guy—misfire too often for him to consistently contribute in the short term. ⓧ 2021 standout **Luis Gil** spent 2023 rehabbing from early-2022 Tommy John surgery and only got into a smidge of minor-league action during September. ⓧ The Yankees essentially got a free **Victor González** when Shohei Ohtani stole his spot on the 40-man. He's a perfectly useful second lefty that belongs in some 'pen, somewhere; why not yours? ⓧ At least **Matt Krook** didn't debut during Chris Berman's prime, because he would've been tagged with the corny nickname Matt "I'm Not A" Krook. This statement presupposes he'd be relevant enough to appear on SportsCenter (unlikely). ⓧ 17 years after first being drafted by the Yankees and 13 years after getting dealt to Cleveland for Austin Kearns, **Zach McAllister** finally made his improbable pinstriped debut, throwing from a much lower arm slot than he once used. ⓧ Colten Brewer and **Nick Ramirez** were both taken in the fourth round of the 2011 draft; Brewer got the higher pick and slightly bigger bonus, but Ramirez got the belated prize (?) of pitching far more slightly-above-replacement-level innings for the 2023 Yankees. We'd have preferred a vacation in the Maldives, personally. ⓧ **Luis Serna**'s calling card is his changeup—which he used to rack up his share of punchies at the complex—but his other three pitches (fastball, curve and slider) are nothing to dismiss outright from a teenager. He should be ready for full-season ball in Tampa soon. ⓧ As if the 2022 Frankie Montas deal couldn't get uglier, solid reliever **Lou Trivino** missed all of 2023 due to Tommy John surgery. Worst of all, we were robbed of more action for the Trevino/Trivino battery. ⓧ Following disastrous stints in Cincinnati and Seattle, **Luke Weaver** popped up on the "Nothing Matters!" September Yankees. He pitched well enough not to rekindle memories of Jeff (no relation), which was kind of him. ⓧ **Ryan Weber** was a Scranton Shuttle veteran in 2022 and sat on the MLB roster for almost a full month in 2023. He earned his teammates' respect for his tenacity, but hit the IL with an ominous UCL strain in mid-June and was never heard from again.

OAKLAND ATHLETICS

Essay by Jeremy Koo

Player comments by Matt Sussman and BP staff

I thought, at the start of the 2023 season, that the Oakland Athletics might not lose 100 games—even if the projections marked that a distinct probability, the A's had beaten expectations time and again. I also thought I would be spending more time at the Oakland Coliseum in 2023 than I would in Carson City, Nevada legislative hearing rooms.

And at the start of 2017, I believed that Dave Kaval was the leader Oakland fans were looking for to push the team's stadium quest over the finish line. A fresh face for A's ownership represented a rebirth for fans' hopes for a new stadium after years under managing partner Lew Wolff. It was an end to a decade of proposals—Fremont, San Jose and every other locale in between—that were either dead on arrival or sent to die at the inaction of Bud Selig's blue-ribbon committee. I'm still waiting for that blue-ribbon committee report.

But seven years ago now, Kaval was introducing himself to A's fans at Fanfest by telling them that the A's were staying in Oakland, "We will make an announcement this year with not only the site but also the timeline that will include when we break ground and open a ballpark in Oakland." For once, the business side of the A's franchise was getting the fans excited, not the front office of *Moneyball* fame.

There was every reason to believe Kaval. He had helmed the San Jose Earthquakes, with John Fisher as owner, through the construction of its new stadium just a few years before. Kaval had even convinced Fisher to spend more money on the soccer stadium by getting him to build suites and other premium seating not part of the original plans. If anybody was going to get Fisher to write a check on the promise, "If you build it [in Oakland], they will come," it seemed to be Kaval.

And then, six years later, the betrayal. "We're turning our full attention to Las Vegas," Kaval said as news broke of the team's "binding agreement" to buy land in Las Vegas for a stadium. "We were on parallel paths before. But we're focused really on Las Vegas as our path to find a future home for the A's."

Kaval, it turned out, could not overcome Fisher's miserly instincts. And in retrospect, who could? Fisher is on record complaining about how their low payroll and consequent

OAKLAND ATHLETICS PROSPECTUS
2023 W-L: 50-112, 5TH IN AL WEST

Pythag	.296	30th	DER	.685	27th
RS/G	3.61	30th	DRC+	90	28th
RA/G	5.70	29th	DRA-	112	29th
dWin%	.394	29th	FIP	5.06	28th
Payroll	$57M	30th	B-Age	27.7	5th
M$/MW	$25.7M	30th	P-Age	28.0	5th

- Opened 1966
- Open air
- Natural surface
- Fence profile: 8' to 15'

Park Factors

Runs	Runs/RH	Runs/LH	HR/RH	HR/LH
98	98	98	92	97

Top Hitter WARP	1.9 Tony Kemp
Top Pitcher WARP	1.0 Paul Blackburn
2023 Top Prospect	Denzel Clarke

Payroll History (in millions)

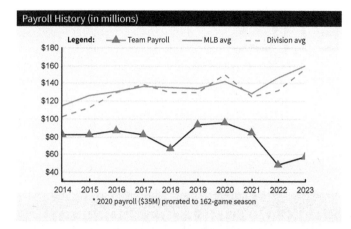

Legend: ▲ Team Payroll — MLB avg --- Division avg

* 2020 payroll ($35M) prorated to 162-game season

Future Commitments (in millions)

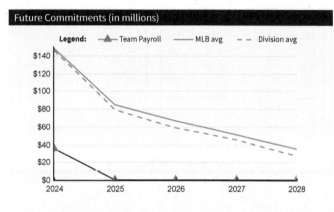

Legend: ▲ Team Payroll — MLB avg --- Division avg

Farm System Ranking

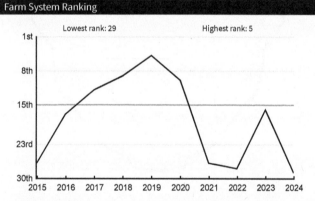

Lowest rank: 29   Highest rank: 5

Personnel

General Manager
David Forst

Manager
Mark Kotsay

AGM, Major League and International Operations
Dan Feinstein

AGM, Baseball Development & Technology
Rob Naberhaus

AGM, Director of Player Personnel
Billy Owens

losing record led to spending more money on the draft. "It's an expensive opportunity to sign high draft picks," Fisher told ESPN's Tim Keown on what was supposed to be a public relations rescue tour in September. Of his San Jose soccer stadium, he now complains—in the same interview where he's justifying building the smallest ballpark in what will be Major League Baseball's smallest television market—that PayPal Park "lacks the capacity and premium seating that drives the kind of revenue needed to compete for championships."

This billionaire, in his own words, "fell in love with the history and community around the A's from the beginning of my affiliation with the team." Put another way, Fisher professes having had no appreciation for the franchise's history and community *before* he bought the team. The native San Franciscan was 43 years old when he bought the team, but appeared to be focused more on the Giants, in which he and his family had owned a portion going back to 1992. Ironically, in that saga Fisher was part of the group that kept the club in San Francisco.

⚾   ⚾   ⚾

My personal history with the A's began before I can remember. My parents often recount one time they took me to the Coliseum when I was four or five years old. After I finished reading all of the advertising signage by the end of the second inning, I was ready to go home. Sensibly, my parents did not insist we stay. But afterward, I apparently told them, "I had a good time."

Later, my parents took me to the Oakland Coliseum on July 5, 1996, a month shy of my ninth birthday, for fireworks night. Both had finished full work weeks in San Francisco that Friday, so despite my eagerness to get in the car as soon as they walked in the door to make it in time for first pitch, they needed some time to settle down from their commute before we headed out. "Nothing happens in the first inning, anyway," my mom said. We arrived to discover the A's had tagged three California Angels pitchers in the first inning for 13 runs, provoking my complex about getting to the ballpark with plenty of time to spare.

I suppose that's why I was 30 minutes early to the hastily prepared joint meeting of the Nevada Senate and Assembly's appropriations committees on May 29, 2023, to discuss John Fisher's request for a taxpayer handout. I made the 136-mile journey from my home in Sacramento, feeling I was being called to a family member's deathbed. It was the least I could do.

I sat in that committee room and listened to extraordinary claim after extraordinary claim. "The state general fund will make money on this deal," said Ben Kieckhefer, Governor Joseph Lombardo's chief of staff. "If you build a stadium in most places in the United States, it is going to have a negative economic impact," said the A's retained analyst, Jeremy

Aguero of Applied Analysis. "While those statements are 100% right for markets that don't have 40 million visitors, they are 100% wrong for those that do."

I did not come to Carson City to testify on the bill, and was not going to. Then, asked about the appropriateness of arguing that Allegiant Stadium's purported success drawing Raiders fans visiting from California implied that A's fans would visit, given their recent low attendance, Aguero gave this answer: "Their attendance is abysmal now in Oakland...That is exactly why, I think, the A's are looking to find a new home."

Whose fault was that? The fans weren't the ones who did not even bother making a qualifying offer to Marcus Semien after the 2020 season, only to fall six games short of a postseason berth in 2021. The fans didn't double season-ticket prices ahead of a 2022 season in which the team would trade away Chris Bassitt, Matt Olson, Matt Chapman, Sean Manaea and Frankie Montas. The fans didn't take a 2023 revenue-sharing check and run out an Opening Day roster with a payroll $27 million below what it spent in 2021 without one.

And so for the A's brass to not even show up, to send their paid analysts and lobbyists to Carson City to tell these Nevada legislators that the A's had to move because of low attendance? Someone had to tell them that the fault in Oakland lies not with Oakland's fans but with the owner who did everything but tell A's fans to pound sand, John Fisher.

"I can't come here to convince you not to build an MLB stadium. I mean, I want a new MLB stadium in Oakland. But I do come with a warning, and it's to be wary of this ownership group," I said. "You can't trust these people. I would love to see a Major League Baseball team in Las Vegas and see the Oakland A's play...but if it's going to be this ownership group, you need to hold them down to everything. Absolutely everything. Because you can't trust these people."

⚾   ⚾   ⚾

June 5 was the nadir for the on-field A's. With 100 games to go, the A's finished the day 12-50, a .194 win percentage. The 36-117 Philadelphia Athletics of 1916 would have finished at least six games ahead of Oakland's pace. In eight days, A's fans were going to be visiting the Coliseum en masse, in a "Reverse Boycott," to tell the world that Fisher failed the Oakland Athletics, not its fans. I would not be among them.

Instead, I was back in Carson City on June 13, this time to ask the Nevada Assembly why it was settling for Fisher's idea of how to run a baseball team. It is a major news event if Mr. Fisher attends an A's game. He has not once indicated a scintilla of pride in the team he owns, nor shown an interest in building a franchise that its community can be proud of.

The day before, fewer than 5,000 people saw the 18-50 A's beat the Rays at the Coliseum. That night, with the help of social media and word of mouth, nearly 28,000 showed up to demonstrate that Oakland A's fans are ready to embrace and reward an owner willing to show *any sign at all* that an

MLB team isn't just another asset on his balance sheet. For better or for worse, Oakland A's fans are stuck with Fisher, but Oakland and Las Vegas deserve far better.

Despite the warnings to our neighbors to the east, despite the direct appeals sent to MLB owners by Oakland's fans and even its mayor ahead of the vote to approve A's relocation, the 2024 campaign could be the final season in Oakland. The Oakland 68's, the strident group of A's fans that organized the Reverse Boycott, are planning an Opening Day boycott after a second event drew nearly 38,000 spectators and rebuked Rob Manfred's snipe that the first drew "almost an average" attendance. The 68's will hand out 3-by-5 foot Kelly green flags emblazoned with the word "SELL" funded by the donations of fans who insist that Fisher cannot leave without hearing what a schmuck he is.

Perhaps John Fisher taking the A's from Oakland is the only way to get John Fisher out of Oakland baseball. And who knows, maybe MLB will come back to the East Bay sooner than we think. Kansas City was all too happy to embrace the newly established Royals just a year after Charlie Finley took the Athletics to Oakland in 1968. The league has some history of returning to abandoned cities: Since the American League's first season in 1901, big-league baseball has left and returned to Milwaukee (twice), Baltimore (once if you exclude the Federal League), Kansas City (once), Washington, D.C. (once or twice, depending on how you look at it) and Seattle.

But the Junior Circuit never returned to Philadelphia after Arnold Johnson took the A's to Kansas City for the 1955 season. St. Louis has been a Cardinals town since the Browns left for Baltimore ahead of 1954. On the NL ledger, New York only got one team back for the two that headed for the Pacific Coast for 1958; Boston never got a second club once the Braves decamped for Milwaukee in 1953. Montreal often gets mentioned as a potential expansion city, but even should a formal opportunity to expand come up for the first time since the Expos became the Washington Nationals in 2005, the return of a second team to Canada seems unlikely.

I fear that Rob Manfred and John Fisher have poisoned the well of enthusiasm for a new major-league club in Oakland. Having brought Oakland's fans and its civic leaders to the doorstep of hammering out a final deal to build Fisher's Howard Terminal fantasy, Fisher and Manfred instead opened the trap door.

What will remain are the memories. I remember the emotional on-field moments: the crushing defeat of ALDS Game 5 loss after ALDS Game 5 loss; literally rolling on the floor laughing, in 2005, once Jason Kendall scrambled home after Francisco Rodriguez dropped a return throw from his catcher; the high of actually making the 2006 ALCS only to be swept out of a World Series berth; the sheer elation I screamed witnessing Oakland's three-run comeback in Game 4 of the 2012 ALDS, days after making up a five-game deficit with nine to play to win the AL West.

I also remember—and treasure—the personal moments: downing a dozen dollar dogs on Dollar Dog Wednesdays; befriending an usher, known to us as Big Nick, who let my best friend and I sit in a lower-level row he knew belonged to A's scouting staff that never used them; developing my first celebrity crushes on players while I was still a closeted teen; handing Big Nick a letter telling him that as an openly gay man I wouldn't be able to converse with him on the National Day of Silence, to spread awareness about the effects of bullying on LGBTQ students, and his immediate acceptance and gratitude to me that I would share something like that with him.

What crushes me is that there are not going to be any chances for new memories, for me or anyone else in the community I grew up in. A generation of kids that were like me won't have their own moments growing up watching the Oakland A's, whatever they would have been.

—Jeremy Koo is an attorney based in Sacramento and formerly a contributor at http://athleticsnation.com.

HITTERS

Nick Allen SS Born: 10/08/98 Age: 25 Bats: R Throws: R Height: 5'8" Weight: 166 Origin: Round 3, 2017 Draft (#81 overall)

YEAR	TM	LVL	AGE	PA	R	HR	RBI	SB	AVG/OBP/SLG	BABIP	SLGCON	BB%	K%	ZSw%	ZCon%	OSw%	OCon%	LA	90th EV	DRC+	BRR	DRP	WARP
2021	MID	AA	22	229	31	6	31	8	.319/.374/.471	.381	.608	7.9%	20.1%							111	-0.8	1.4	1.1
2021	LV	AAA	22	151	17	0	10	4	.243/.302/.301	.308	.387	7.3%	19.9%							84	0.8	-1.4	0.1
2022	LV	AAA	23	206	31	2	16	10	.266/.371/.358	.321	.446	13.1%	16.5%	68.3%	85.6%	28.6%	60.4%			100	1.8	2.1	1.0
2022	OAK	MLB	23	326	31	4	19	3	.207/.256/.291	.250	.370	5.8%	19.6%	73.8%	88.2%	36.3%	60.2%	5.6	97.9	75	0.2	3.2	0.4
2023	LV	AAA	24	162	33	3	18	13	.333/.420/.519	.359	.588	12.3%	9.9%	65.0%	93.1%	25.5%	80.5%			119	2.6	0.6	1.1
2023	OAK	MLB	24	329	29	4	20	5	.221/.263/.287	.253	.347	5.2%	15.8%	68.9%	91.0%	33.5%	65.2%	5.0	99.7	88	0.0	2.0	0.8
2024 DC	OAK	MLB	25	241	21	3	22	6	.246/.303/.342	.281	.409	7.0%	15.0%							87	0.0	2	0.7

2023 GP: SS (104), 2B (1) 　　　　　　　*Comps: Dixon Machado (70), Luis Hernandez (65), Cristhian Adames (64)*

All teams are allowed one position player who can't hit, usually a catcher with intangibles or a slick-fielding shortstop. Allen, a practitioner of the latter of these two trades, is attempting to be the next Nick—like Ahmed before him and Punto before that—who hides low in the lineup and occasionally saves the game with his glove. It's the only way baseball will become his meal ticket. It's a loopy, lonely road that will lead him to several different franchises, usually with some audible groans and sayings like, "Oh, great, our primary shortstop has become stricken by calamity, so *Nick Allen* is here now." We recommend that he further improve his defense and start sliding into first base frequently enough that his shirsey sales skyrocket—cultivating a mystique is half the battle.

JJ Bleday OF Born: 11/10/97 Age: 26 Bats: L Throws: L Height: 6'2" Weight: 205 Origin: Round 1, 2019 Draft (#4 overall)

YEAR	TM	LVL	AGE	PA	R	HR	RBI	SB	AVG/OBP/SLG	BABIP	SLGCON	BB%	K%	ZSw%	ZCon%	OSw%	OCon%	LA	90th EV	DRC+	BRR	DRP	WARP
2021	MSS	WIN	23	115	20	5	24	2	.316/.435/.600	.373	.792	17.4%	20.0%	70.8%	82.4%	13.5%	57.1%						
2021	PNS	AA	23	468	52	12	54	5	.212/.323/.373	.250	.500	13.7%	21.6%							103	0.0	12.2	2.8
2022	JAX	AAA	24	367	54	20	52	1	.228/.365/.470	.268	.700	16.3%	27.0%	64.7%	86.4%	23.3%	63.3%			104	-1.5	-2.8	0.9
2022	MIA	MLB	24	238	21	5	16	4	.167/.277/.309	.216	.460	12.6%	28.2%	74.1%	80.1%	27.0%	56.2%	25.7	101.5	72	0.0	-0.9	-0.1
2023	LV	AAA	25	133	31	8	23	1	.333/.444/.667	.333	.800	17.3%	13.5%	67.3%	81.4%	18.3%	59.3%			134	1.6	-0.2	1.0
2023	OAK	MLB	25	303	35	10	27	5	.195/.310/.355	.226	.495	13.9%	23.8%	71.5%	80.4%	22.1%	51.0%	15.2	103.3	93	0.0	-3.2	0.4
2024 DC	OAK	MLB	26	430	46	13	47	3	.213/.318/.374	.263	.527	12.6%	25.0%							97	-0.3	-2.7	0.8

2023 GP: LF (39), CF (28), RF (12), DH (5) 　　　　　　*Comps: Jordan Schafer (61), Roger Bernadina (60), Alfredo Marte (59)*

Despite a batting average on the wrong side of .200, Bleday had the best on-base percentage of any outfielder on his team, and that includes the guy who stole 67 bases. These are low bars, but they're getting belted out like Thurl Ravenscroft singing that Grinch song. For someone to wield such a low batting average, power is almost a must. Bleday has it, but just barely enough to be one of the league's foursome who batted below .200 with a plus-.300 OBP and double-digit dingers. In other words, he could aspire to be Trent Grisham, but definitely not Kyle Schwarber or Joey Gallo. Right now he's a walk-hawk who can contribute to a team by stepping to the plate about 300 times—mostly against righties—and do damage that doesn't rise to the level of felony vandalism.

Henry Bolte OF Born: 08/04/03 Age: 20 Bats: R Throws: R Height: 6'3" Weight: 195 Origin: Round 2, 2022 Draft (#56 overall)

YEAR	TM	LVL	AGE	PA	R	HR	RBI	SB	AVG/OBP/SLG	BABIP	SLGCON	BB%	K%	ZSw%	ZCon%	OSw%	OCon%	LA	90th EV	DRC+	BRR	DRP	WARP
2022	ATH	ROK	18	39	5	0	2	0	.212/.333/.212	.500	.500	12.8%	48.7%										
2023	STK	A	19	491	77	14	68	32	.257/.356/.421	.382	.691	12.6%	33.4%							94	1.6	-9.5	0.3
2024 non	OAK	MLB	20	251	21	3	22	0	.221/.283/.325	.383	.586	7.1%	41.1%							73	0.0	0	-0.2

2023 GP: RF (72), CF (28), DH (9), LF (3) 　　　　　　*Comps: Yorman Rodriguez (87), Jack Herman (79), Josh Bell (78)*

The last name is two syllables (bolt-ee) but don't let that dissuade you from the electric adjectives; sportswriters and fans alike cannot help themselves when it comes to wordplay. He's more raw than ceviche but he flashed the potential of 1.21 gigawatts in a full Single-A season, not to mention lightning speed. Nobody in the California League matched his combination of homers and steals, but nobody matched the sheer volume of his strikeouts, either. The A's have all the reason in the world to take their time with his development and bolt Bolte until he's a bit more refined.

Seth Brown RF
Born: 07/13/92 Age: 31 Bats: L Throws: L Height: 6'1" Weight: 223 Origin: Round 19, 2015 Draft (#578 overall)

YEAR	TM	LVL	AGE	PA	R	HR	RBI	SB	AVG/OBP/SLG	BABIP	SLGCON	BB%	K%	ZSw%	ZCon%	OSw%	OCon%	LA	90th EV	DRC+	BRR	DRP	WARP
2021	OAK	MLB	28	307	43	20	48	4	.214/.274/.480	.230	.703	7.5%	29.0%	66.9%	82.6%	30.0%	45.2%	21.2	106.1	95	0.3	0.1	0.8
2022	OAK	MLB	29	555	55	25	73	11	.230/.305/.444	.273	.627	9.2%	26.3%	69.9%	84.8%	33.3%	49.5%	16.1	107.4	110	0.5	-2.8	1.9
2023	OAK	MLB	30	378	33	14	52	3	.222/.286/.405	.270	.574	7.9%	26.7%	71.7%	84.5%	35.3%	47.2%	17.5	105.6	99	-0.2	-2.0	0.7
2024 DC	OAK	MLB	31	471	53	19	61	7	.231/.300/.426	.283	.611	8.5%	27.1%							101	0.0	-3	0.9

2023 GP: RF (56), LF (25), DH (18), 1B (17)   Comps: Justin Bour (57), Luke Voit (56), Chris Heisey (51)

Brown is an ancient by A's standards, having traversed the organization's pathways for eight years. He's seen it all: the Khris Davis .247 Matrix Glitch. The Raiders leaving town. At least three players named Matt. Most recently he saw himself hit the ball harder without much to show for it, thanks to an increased propensity to chase. Finally he saw Ryan Noda show up, copy his exact same skill set (but with the walks) and take away his playing time. There's always going to be a demand for corner outfielders like Brown who can mash a respectable number of doubles and homers from the left side. If the A's haven't traded him by the time you read this sentence, he's hiding in the Coliseum's air ducts.

Lawrence Butler OF
Born: 07/10/00 Age: 23 Bats: L Throws: R Height: 6'3" Weight: 210 Origin: Round 6, 2018 Draft (#173 overall)

YEAR	TM	LVL	AGE	PA	R	HR	RBI	SB	AVG/OBP/SLG	BABIP	SLGCON	BB%	K%	ZSw%	ZCon%	OSw%	OCon%	LA	90th EV	DRC+	BRR	DRP	WARP
2021	STK	A	20	396	62	17	67	26	.263/.364/.499	.370	.819	13.9%	33.1%						104	0.6	-2.0	1.2
2021	LAN	A+	20	54	14	2	8	3	.340/.389/.540	.455	.771	7.4%	27.8%						95	-0.5	1.6	0.2
2022	LAN	A+	21	333	52	11	41	13	.270/.357/.468	.384	.729	12.0%	31.5%						104	-0.9	5.8	1.7
2023	MID	AA	22	318	53	10	47	13	.285/.352/.465	.327	.589	9.4%	18.9%						109	1.0	8.3	2.2
2023	LV	AAA	22	94	14	5	23	8	.280/.340/.512	.290	.656	8.5%	19.1%	66.5%	80.0%	28.5%	63.2%			96	-0.7	-1.2	0.1
2023	OAK	MLB	22	129	10	4	10	0	.211/.240/.341	.259	.477	3.1%	27.1%	65.5%	83.6%	32.5%	47.1%	15.9	106.1	92	0.0	-1.3	0.2
2024 DC	OAK	MLB	23	213	21	6	24	5	.244/.304/.396	.311	.550	7.5%	26.0%							96	0.0	-1.9	0.4

2023 GP: CF (41), RF (2)   Comps: Jake Marisnick (62), Josh Reddick (60), Aaron Cunningham (59)

The A's were extremely patient with Butler, a toolsy outfielder with power potential. The patience paid off as he trimmed his strikeout rate from horrific to just normal-power-hitter bad, first by making his mark in spring training then climbing three rungs on the organizational ladder, including an appearance in the Futures Game. His high swing rate is going to forever wound his on-base percentage, but a microdose of his energy showed Butler may have enough good days to validate the approach. He's already had one multi-homer game and has shown a lot of range in the outfield. He's going to be the starting center fielder, at least until someone more patient shows up.

───────────────── ★ ★ ★ *2024 Top 101 Prospect* **#99** ★ ★ ★ ─────────────────

Denzel Clarke OF
Born: 05/01/00 Age: 24 Bats: R Throws: R Height: 6'5" Weight: 220 Origin: Round 4, 2021 Draft (#127 overall)

YEAR	TM	LVL	AGE	PA	R	HR	RBI	SB	AVG/OBP/SLG	BABIP	SLGCON	BB%	K%	ZSw%	ZCon%	OSw%	OCon%	LA	90th EV	DRC+	BRR	DRP	WARP
2022	STK	A	22	193	37	7	26	14	.295/.420/.545	.411	.850	14.5%	29.0%							119	-1.5	-0.6	0.8
2022	LAN	A+	22	218	30	8	21	16	.209/.317/.406	.307	.704	12.8%	36.2%							105	1.0	2.5	1.2
2023	MID	AA	23	286	54	12	43	11	.261/.381/.496	.348	.779	12.9%	29.7%							116	2.4	2.3	2.0
2024 non	OAK	MLB	24	251	25	6	26	5	.223/.303/.366	.327	.589	8.8%	33.4%							90	0.0	0	0.5

2023 GP: CF (42), RF (15), DH (6)   Comps: Stuart Fairchild (69), Corey Brown (66), Greg Allen (66)

A lot of power and speed is packed into Clarke's 6-foot-5 torso. However, a recurring left shoulder injury caused the Canadian center fielder's season to start late and finish early. Between the injuries, he put on a show on both sides of the ball, conking four homers in his first four games, then playing an extremely adept outfield. He has largely roved cente, although it's very easy to picture him patrolling right field as his career and skill set evolve. He's cousins with the Naylors (Josh, Bo and recent draftee Miles) and there's nothing in the rulebook that says you can't have a family reunion barbecue in the outfield.

Aledmys Díaz IF
Born: 08/01/90 Age: 33 Bats: R Throws: R Height: 6'1" Weight: 195 Origin: IFA, 2014

YEAR	TM	LVL	AGE	PA	R	HR	RBI	SB	AVG/OBP/SLG	BABIP	SLGCON	BB%	K%	ZSw%	ZCon%	OSw%	OCon%	LA	90th EV	DRC+	BRR	DRP	WARP
2021	HOU	MLB	30	319	28	8	45	0	.259/.317/.405	.304	.513	5.0%	19.4%	73.2%	87.9%	38.0%	61.9%	13.4	105.9	99	-0.1	0.3	1.0
2022	HOU	MLB	31	327	35	12	38	1	.243/.287/.403	.256	.488	5.5%	16.2%	75.7%	85.9%	35.5%	63.7%	12.8	104.3	106	0.0	0.0	1.2
2023	OAK	MLB	32	344	25	4	24	1	.229/.280/.337	.273	.426	4.9%	19.2%	71.8%	86.4%	37.1%	63.7%	10.9	102.6	104	0.0	-1.4	1.1
2024 DC	OAK	MLB	33	259	24	6	26	1	.238/.293/.360	.275	.448	5.9%	18.3%							86	-0.1	-1.6	0.2

2023 GP: 3B (40), SS (40), LF (13), 2B (11), 1B (10), DH (5)   Comps: José Reyes (66), Tony Fernández (65), Jimmy Rollins (65)

Díaz was given 14 and a half million good reasons last winter to scooch over in the division from a 100-win team to a 100-loss team to play the exact same role, just a little worse. If a good team wanted to sign Díaz as a bench bat, sure, he's a fine choice. His shining strength at this point is avoiding strikeouts and playing a few innings at any defensive position. It's nice to be able to fill little holes! Unfortunately the Athletics' major-league roster had no little holes, or even big holes ... it was the motherloving Sea of Tranquility, and beyond leadership presence Díaz doesn't fit on this roster. His best chance at happiness is to have a couple of hot months at second base then be traded to a contender. His employers, who love sucking up prospects at the deadline, would love that too.

Jordan Diaz IF   Born: 08/13/00   Age: 23   Bats: R   Throws: R   Height: 5'10"   Weight: 175   Origin: IFA, 2016

YEAR	TM	LVL	AGE	PA	R	HR	RBI	SB	AVG/OBP/SLG	BABIP	SLGCON	BB%	K%	ZSw%	ZCon%	OSw%	OCon%	LA	90th EV	DRC+	BRR	DRP	WARP
2021	LAN	A+	20	365	46	13	56	2	.288/.337/.483	.311	.585	6.8%	15.9%							124	0.2	-3.3	1.8
2022	MID	AA	21	407	48	15	58	0	.319/.361/.507	.348	.604	5.4%	15.0%							111	0.8	-4.3	1.3
2022	LV	AAA	21	120	19	4	25	0	.348/.383/.545	.372	.629	5.0%	12.5%	77.1%	90.1%	36.3%	69.7%			109	-0.8	-1.1	0.3
2022	OAK	MLB	21	51	3	0	1	0	.265/.294/.327	.310	.381	3.9%	13.7%	87.1%	88.5%	45.7%	66.7%	-4.8	99.9	103	0.0	-0.1	0.1
2023	LV	AAA	22	169	18	6	31	0	.308/.351/.506	.347	.627	5.9%	17.8%	79.1%	88.1%	37.7%	58.7%			106	-0.3	-7.8	-0.2
2023	OAK	MLB	22	293	20	10	27	0	.221/.273/.364	.258	.488	5.8%	23.5%	75.8%	85.6%	43.3%	52.8%	5.3	106.4	86	-0.2	-1.4	0.2
2024 DC	OAK	MLB	23	358	34	9	39	0	.240/.285/.380	.286	.498	5.2%	22.2%							88	-0.3	-2.8	0.1

2023 GP: 3B (38), 2B (28), DH (16), 1B (7)   Comps: Luis Sardinas (58), Luis Urías (52), Andrés Blanco (50)

Exactly one visiting player hit three home runs in one game at Yankee Stadium last year, and it came from someone whose in-game power has been largely reclusive. (It's also worth mentioning his team still lost by five.) Diaz does not fit the mold of a utility infielder, but that's how he's been squeezed into the lineup instead of as a designated hitter, the profile he's carried for years. He's improved by hitting more liners than grounders, though he still pounds the ball into the dirt more than half the time. It's becoming harder to visualize the type of player Diaz will become, so let's just watch the three-homer game on a loop and manifest his best possible outcome.

Zack Gelof 2B   Born: 10/19/99   Age: 24   Bats: R   Throws: R   Height: 6'2"   Weight: 205   Origin: Round 2, 2021 Draft (#60 overall)

YEAR	TM	LVL	AGE	PA	R	HR	RBI	SB	AVG/OBP/SLG	BABIP	SLGCON	BB%	K%	ZSw%	ZCon%	OSw%	OCon%	LA	90th EV	DRC+	BRR	DRP	WARP
2021	STK	A	21	145	26	7	22	11	.298/.393/.548	.366	.773	13.1%	24.8%							120	1.5	-6.8	0.3
2021	LV	AAA	21	13	3	0	6	0	.583/.615/.667	.700	.800	7.7%	15.4%							90	0.8	0.2	0.1
2022	MID	AA	22	402	54	13	61	9	.271/.356/.438	.358	.635	11.7%	27.4%							102	-0.3	-3.8	0.8
2022	LV	AAA	22	38	7	5	5	1	.257/.316/.714	.211	1.042	7.9%	28.9%	68.3%	81.4%	27.7%	50.0%			103	0.5	-1.0	0.1
2023	LV	AAA	23	308	60	12	44	20	.304/.401/.529	.410	.785	13.3%	27.9%	69.9%	73.0%	23.7%	45.7%			95	0.7	-0.8	0.6
2023	OAK	MLB	23	300	40	14	32	14	.267/.337/.504	.331	.723	8.7%	27.3%	74.1%	73.1%	32.9%	55.0%	11.9	104.1	91	0.5	0.7	0.7
2024 DC	OAK	MLB	24	561	58	16	63	17	.234/.307/.389	.324	.596	8.8%	31.3%							98	-0.1	1.9	1.6

2023 GP: 2B (69)   Comps: Paul DeJong (64), Will Middlebrooks (63), Enrique Hernández (61)

You could make an argument that Gelof was the most valuable player on the A's last year, even though he didn't join the team until July. (You could probably make a similar argument that *you* were the most valuable player on the A's through July, since you weren't on the field and struggling.) Hailed as an infielder with a loud bat, he lived up to that promise by becoming the first A's rookie with 300 PA and a .500 slugging since Yoenis Cespedes. He was promoted the same time as top prospect Tyler Soderstrom and did far better, which stands out almost as much as that funny little hitch in his swing. As with any hot-hitting batter, there are going to be strikeouts, and averaged nearly two a game in the final eight days of the season. He won the 2024 second base job in August, and he'll be one of the most fun ones to watch in Oakland this year.

Darell Hernaiz SS   Born: 08/03/01   Age: 22   Bats: R   Throws: R   Height: 5'11"   Weight: 190   Origin: Round 5, 2019 Draft (#138 overall)

YEAR	TM	LVL	AGE	PA	R	HR	RBI	SB	AVG/OBP/SLG	BABIP	SLGCON	BB%	K%	ZSw%	ZCon%	OSw%	OCon%	LA	90th EV	DRC+	BRR	DRP	WARP
2021	DEL	A	19	410	62	6	52	22	.277/.333/.358	.323	.440	6.8%	17.1%							105	-1.6	10.5	2.3
2022	DEL	A	20	138	25	6	25	9	.283/.341/.512	.303	.619	5.8%	15.9%							126	2.6	-2.0	0.9
2022	ABD	A+	20	255	41	5	29	22	.305/.376/.456	.356	.563	8.6%	16.9%							107	-0.3	0.6	1.0
2022	BOW	AA	20	59	6	1	8	1	.113/.186/.189	.135	.270	8.5%	27.1%							90	0.4	-0.2	0.1
2023	MID	AA	21	308	43	5	43	7	.338/.393/.486	.394	.587	8.4%	15.6%							103	-1.9	-1.2	0.8
2023	LV	AAA	21	253	44	4	28	6	.300/.376/.418	.325	.477	9.5%	10.7%	68.7%	87.3%	33.0%	73.2%			100	-0.9	2.1	0.9
2024 DC	OAK	MLB	22	292	25	4	26	5	.233/.286/.333	.278	.417	6.0%	18.9%							77	0.0	0	0.2

2023 GP: SS (112), 2B (13), DH (4), 3B (1)   Comps: Luis Sardinas (64), Jorge Polanco (62), José Peraza (60)

As is standard fare in the Sisyphean woebegone baseball activity of the perpetual rebuild, Oakland traded away a perfectly serviceable pitcher (Cole Irvin) to Baltimore for Hernaiz, a mysterious toolsy low-minors prospect who may or may not be a true shortstop. A year later, he's playing shortstop more than ever, making terrific contact to all fields and was extremely close to a September call-up. There wasn't an Athletic minor leaguer who had a better season than him, so in 2024 it'll be hard to deny him a major-league presence. If all goes according to plan, he may even be dealt for another prospect!

Tony Kemp LF/2B   Born: 10/31/91   Age: 32   Bats: L   Throws: R   Height: 5'6"   Weight: 160   Origin: Round 5, 2013 Draft (#137 overall)

YEAR	TM	LVL	AGE	PA	R	HR	RBI	SB	AVG/OBP/SLG	BABIP	SLGCON	BB%	K%	ZSw%	ZCon%	OSw%	OCon%	LA	90th EV	DRC+	BRR	DRP	WARP
2021	OAK	MLB	29	397	54	8	37	8	.279/.382/.418	.304	.495	13.1%	12.8%	63.4%	89.4%	26.1%	75.8%	17.2	96.9	105	0.3	0.7	1.9
2022	OAK	MLB	30	558	61	7	46	11	.235/.307/.334	.259	.388	8.1%	12.4%	68.6%	92.8%	34.7%	78.7%	13.7	96.4	91	0.9	-0.2	1.2
2023	OAK	MLB	31	419	42	5	27	15	.209/.303/.304	.221	.342	10.5%	9.5%	66.3%	89.7%	28.5%	77.8%	9.6	97.3	115	0.6	-1.5	1.9
2024 DC	OAK	MLB	32	172	16	3	16	4	.243/.325/.350	.264	.402	9.8%	11.6%							95	0.1	-0.8	0.3

2023 GP: LF (65), 2B (57), DH (3)   Comps: Desi Relaford (59), Alex Cora (58), Ted Kubiak (56)

On May 22, Kemp struck out against Luis Castillo on three pitches, the third being a 98 mph heater up and away. Two innings later, Castillo blew him away a second time—same pitch, same location. This was the only time a starting pitcher got Kemp on strike three twice last season, as well as the only game all season in which Kemp recorded three Ks. The diminutive second baseman has lost a bit of his quickness, but he still had the best strikeout rate of anyone who batted as frequently and was not named Luis Arraez. It's one of the coolest skills, but didn't amount to much given his offensive output—his .209 average was MLB's lowest since 1984 with a strikeout rate below 10% (min. 400 PA). Kemp did get nominated for the Roberto Clemente Award for a fourth time, so there's ample reason to hope he can catch back up to his DRC+.

Shea Langeliers C   Born: 11/18/97   Age: 26   Bats: R   Throws: R   Height: 6'0"   Weight: 205   Origin: Round 1, 2019 Draft (#9 overall)

YEAR	TM	LVL	AGE	PA	R	HR	RBI	SB	AVG/OBP/SLG	BABIP	SLGCON	BB%	K%	ZSw%	ZCon%	OSw%	OCon%	LA	90th EV	DRC+	BRR	DRP	WARP
2021	MIS	AA	23	370	56	22	52	1	.258/.338/.498	.299	.707	9.7%	26.2%							136	0.3	-13.2	1.6
2021	GWN	AAA	23	14	3	0	1	0	.182/.357/.364	.400	.800	21.4%	42.9%							79	-0.3	0.3	0.0
2022	LV	AAA	24	402	62	19	56	5	.283/.366/.510	.327	.679	10.7%	21.9%	72.9%	80.8%	32.1%	54.0%			97	-2.2	-6.6	0.2
2022	OAK	MLB	24	153	14	6	22	0	.218/.261/.430	.294	.685	5.9%	34.6%	75.6%	70.0%	40.7%	42.1%	17.0	104.0	69	-0.1	-1.0	-0.3
2023	OAK	MLB	25	490	52	22	63	3	.205/.268/.413	.246	.607	6.9%	29.2%	71.7%	76.6%	34.7%	54.8%	19.6	107.7	88	-0.1	-10.6	0.0
2024 DC	OAK	MLB	26	373	39	14	45	4	.222/.285/.396	.276	.574	7.3%	28.0%							91	-0.1	-4	0.6

2023 GP: C (123), DH (8)   Comps: Tyler Flowers (70), Chris Iannetta (67), Kennys Vargas (64)

YEAR	TM	P. COUNT	FRM RUNS	BLK RUNS	THRW RUNS	TOT RUNS
2021	MIS	11234	-13.8	0.4	0.2	-13.3
2022	LV	11624	-7.0	0.1	1.3	-5.6
2022	OAK	2299	-0.5	-0.1	-0.1	-0.7
2023	OAK	18168	-8.6	-0.5	1.3	-7.8
2024	OAK	14430	-4.6	-0.3	0.9	-3.9

Every defensive catcher that has ever formed from the primordial goo of the amateur draft has been asked if they can hit. Langeliers can say "yes" when it comes to home runs but "no" to everything else—he became the first Oakland catcher in 20 years to bash 20 longballs. That went with some partial defensive success: his 38 runners thrown out was 11 more than anybody else, but he graded poorly on his framing and blocking skills. His video game comp is a Pong paddle directed by a slightly defective Atari controller.

Max Muncy SS   Born: 08/25/02   Age: 21   Bats: R   Throws: R   Height: 6'1"   Weight: 180   Origin: Round 1, 2021 Draft (#25 overall)

YEAR	TM	LVL	AGE	PA	R	HR	RBI	SB	AVG/OBP/SLG	BABIP	SLGCON	BB%	K%	ZSw%	ZCon%	OSw%	OCon%	LA	90th EV	DRC+	BRR	DRP	WARP
2021	ATH	ROK	18	34	3	0	4	1	.129/.206/.129	.211	.211	8.8%	35.3%	83.3%	60.0%	0.0%						-0.7	
2022	STK	A	19	365	50	16	51	6	.230/.352/.447	.298	.697	14.0%	29.9%							108	2.5	-1.0	1.6
2022	LAN	A+	19	190	19	3	19	13	.226/.305/.375	.327	.583	9.5%	31.6%							84	1.7	1.4	0.5
2023	MSS	WIN	20	87	13	4	14	7	.205/.287/.436	.226	.596	9.2%	24.1%										
2023	LAN	A+	20	312	36	6	31	9	.255/.327/.385	.356	.579	9.9%	29.5%							87	2.3	4.2	1.2
2023	MID	AA	20	233	40	4	31	4	.302/.387/.446	.396	.608	9.0%	23.2%							94	-0.4	0.4	0.5
2024 non	OAK	MLB	21	251	22	4	23	2	.224/.288/.337	.322	.517	7.3%	31.6%							77	0.0	0	0.2

2023 GP: SS (136), DH (7)   Comps: Javier Báez (59), Domingo Leyba (59), Alen Hanson (56)

At first it was funny that both Max Muncies started with the Athletics and share a birthday, but at some point one of them will have to blink and start going by Maxwell or Mad Dog or Scooter or Pudge. Throw in a middle initial or an umlaut, something...please. Muncy The Younger is forcing the decision after excelling during his Double-A promotion, showing extra-base power and more discipline to go with his already adept shortstop range. The strikeouts even went down a little bit. He just needs to work on a nickname, which, when it comes right down to the history of baseball, is the original fundamental.

Myles Naylor SS   Born: 04/15/05   Age: 19   Bats: R   Throws: R   Height: 6'2"   Weight: 195   Origin: Round 1, 2023 Draft (#39 overall)

YEAR	TM	LVL	AGE	PA	R	HR	RBI	SB	AVG/OBP/SLG	BABIP	SLGCON	BB%	K%	ZSw%	ZCon%	OSw%	OCon%	LA	90th EV	DRC+	BRR	DRP	WARP
2023	STK	A	18	132	16	6	17	2	.208/.280/.375	.306	.662	8.3%	39.4%							66	0.6	-0.6	-0.1
2024 non	OAK	MLB	19	251	19	3	21	0	.203/.252/.298	.370	.565	5.3%	44.6%							54	0.0	0	-0.6

2023 GP: SS (28), DH (5), 3B (1)   Comps: Jose Salas (71), Ketel Marte (66), Eduardo Garcia (65)

As soon as Myles' name was called on draft day, the Naylors joined the Drews on the complete list of families with three brothers drafted in the first round. Hopefully the "Family Feud" episode is in the works. Unlike eldest brother Josh, a pure slugger, and middle brother Bo, a catcher, Myles has separated himself from his former dinner table-mates by playing shortstop (at least for now), not playing for the Guardians (at least for now), batting right-handed (this one's likely permanent), and also being the tallest and most nimble of the trio. In his first couple months of pro ball, he went down on strike three far too often but made a boatload of noise when he connected. He's probably a future third baseman, which is awfully appropriate for the third brother.

Ryan Noda 1B   Born: 03/30/96   Age: 28   Bats: L   Throws: L   Height: 6'3"   Weight: 217   Origin: Round 15, 2017 Draft (#459 overall)

YEAR	TM	LVL	AGE	PA	R	HR	RBI	SB	AVG/OBP/SLG	BABIP	SLGCON	BB%	K%	ZSw%	ZCon%	OSw%	OCon%	LA	90th EV	DRC+	BRR	DRP	WARP
2021	TUL	AA	25	475	73	29	78	3	.250/.383/.521	.288	.778	15.6%	26.7%							120	0.4	-2.9	2.3
2022	OKC	AAA	26	574	86	25	90	20	.259/.395/.474	.339	.728	16.0%	28.2%	67.6%	77.8%	22.7%	49.4%			104	0.7	-4.7	1.5
2023	OAK	MLB	27	495	63	16	54	3	.229/.364/.406	.347	.699	15.6%	34.3%	67.7%	74.3%	21.8%	33.5%	15.7	106.8	82	0.1	0.2	0.0
2024 DC	OAK	MLB	28	595	65	18	65	10	.198/.322/.362	.284	.599	13.6%	33.5%							97	0.2	-0.1	0.9

2023 GP: 1B (119), RF (7), DH (5), LF (2)   Comps: Jeff Larish (70), Mauro Gomez (56), Christian Walker (56)

In fairness to the Dodgers, what were they going to do with two left-handed first basemen, make them ride a tandem bicycle to work? Noda went free-and-clear to the A's via the Rule 5 Draft and instantly imported his three-true-outcome game into a lineup that mostly had one true outcome: Debilitating ennui. With the potential for 20 homers and 80 walks a year, he's a set-it-and-forget-it lineup piece that already has an advanced approach. In other words, he's a poor (or at least crying-poor) team's Freddie Freeman though, to be fair, Freeman already had 133 home runs and 408 walks at the age of Noda's debut.

Carlos Pérez C   Born: 10/27/90   Age: 33   Bats: R   Throws: R   Height: 5'10"   Weight: 210   Origin: IFA, 2008

YEAR	TM	LVL	AGE	PA	R	HR	RBI	SB	AVG/OBP/SLG	BABIP	SLGCON	BB%	K%	ZSw%	ZCon%	OSw%	OCon%	LA	90th EV	DRC+	BRR	DRP	WARP
2021	MAG	WIN	30	81	11	2	10	1	.151/.235/.288	.161	.362	9.9%	18.5%										
2021	LV	AAA	30	418	61	31	89	0	.269/.337/.572	.246	.687	8.1%	15.1%							121	-2.5	0.6	2.2
2022	ABQ	AAA	31	522	75	31	87	0	.254/.341/.524	.258	.671	10.3%	19.2%	68.5%	92.5%	28.7%	64.1%			112	-3.5	1.4	2.1
2023	OAK	MLB	32	189	17	6	20	0	.226/.293/.357	.256	.469	6.9%	21.2%	65.5%	89.6%	33.7%	65.8%	16.1	104.5	93	-0.2	-6.7	-0.2
2024 non	OAK	MLB	33	251	25	8	28	0	.222/.285/.376	.243	.468	6.7%	17.9%							84	0.0	-9	-0.7

2023 GP: C (31), 1B (15), DH (12), P (2), LF (1)

Comps: Humberto Quintero (55), Jeff Mathis (51), Ryan Lavarnway (50)

YEAR	TM	P. COUNT	FRM RUNS	BLK RUNS	THRW RUNS	TOT RUNS
2021	MAG	2078			0.0	0.0
2021	LV	4485	-4.2	0.1	0.4	-3.8
2022	ABQ	4917	1.2	0.0	0.0	1.1
2023	OAK	4639	-6.6	0.0	0.4	-6.2
2024	OAK	6956	-9.7	0.0	0.8	-8.9

The Rangers game on September 30, 2018 signified the end of the careers of two All-Stars: Adrián Beltré and Yovani Gallardo. Until last year it was also going to be the final major-league game for Pérez, who caught Gallardo in that game. Despite hitting 31 Triple-A home runs in consecutive seasons, not even a scintilla of a promotion was on the horizon. He signed with a Mexican League team last March; three days later he changed tack and went to the A's, who then made him the backup catcher. He's got power potential, a decent throwing arm and, while Beltré and Gallardo are putting up their feet somewhere, another player more special (to him) is now in the league: his younger brother, also named Carlos. On July 1, he got to call pitches against his sibling, who entered the game as a pinch-hitter.

Brent Rooker DH   Born: 11/01/94   Age: 29   Bats: R   Throws: R   Height: 6'4"   Weight: 225   Origin: Round 1, 2017 Draft (#35 overall)

YEAR	TM	LVL	AGE	PA	R	HR	RBI	SB	AVG/OBP/SLG	BABIP	SLGCON	BB%	K%	ZSw%	ZCon%	OSw%	OCon%	LA	90th EV	DRC+	BRR	DRP	WARP
2021	STP	AAA	26	267	40	20	49	1	.245/.367/.564	.276	.886	14.2%	30.0%							119	-0.8	-6.1	0.8
2021	MIN	MLB	26	213	25	9	16	0	.201/.291/.397	.264	.630	7.0%	32.9%	68.5%	75.2%	33.7%	54.6%	13.7	107.8	85	-0.1	-1.6	0.1
2022	OMA	AAA	27	92	16	9	32	0	.338/.424/.775	.391	1.127	9.8%	27.2%							121	-1.1	-0.1	0.4
2022	ELP	AAA	27	273	55	19	55	5	.272/.385/.605	.323	.920	13.6%	28.6%	64.3%	80.1%	27.6%	43.2%			113	2.3	-0.4	1.4
2022	SD	MLB	27	7	0	0	0	0	.000/.000/.000		.000	0.0%	57.1%	54.5%	50.0%	54.5%	33.3%	24.4	102.4	108		0.0	0.0
2022	KC	MLB	27	29	1	0	2	0	.160/.276/.200	.222	.278	10.3%	24.1%	75.0%	82.1%	30.9%	52.4%	11.9	101.0	87	0.0	-0.1	0.0
2023	OAK	MLB	28	526	61	30	69	4	.246/.329/.488	.317	.777	9.3%	32.7%	66.8%	76.9%	31.5%	39.3%	18.0	106.7	94	-0.4	-3.3	0.5
2024 DC	OAK	MLB	29	527	63	23	70	4	.221/.309/.426	.302	.699	9.1%	34.6%							107	-1.1	-3.2	1.3

2023 GP: DH (75), RF (31), LF (29)

Comps: Lucas Duda (59), Nolan Reimold (58), Khris Davis (57)

Identity theft is no laughing matter. Just ask Chris Carter, the former right-handed slugger who basically saw Rooker lift a Chris Carter season, sand off the VIN and show it off as his own. The DH's power was previously kept secret in various sleepy minor-league ballparks around the country. His nine-homer, 1.245 OPS April, coupled with Oakland's ludicrous roster, made him the team's lone All-Star despite several months of regressing to the old Rooker, who was only permitted to hit home runs in places like Omaha and El Paso. The lack of consistency in his breakout season means he could still play himself back to the quaint hamlets of the PCL or proceed to hit 40 homers. Such is the seedy underbelly of the designated-hitter industrial complex.

Esteury Ruiz CF   Born: 02/15/99   Age: 25   Bats: R   Throws: R   Height: 6'0"   Weight: 169   Origin: IFA, 2015

YEAR	TM	LVL	AGE	PA	R	HR	RBI	SB	AVG/OBP/SLG	BABIP	SLGCON	BB%	K%	ZSw%	ZCon%	OSw%	OCon%	LA	90th EV	DRC+	BRR	DRP	WARP
2021	SA	AA	22	353	52	10	42	36	.249/.328/.411	.294	.538	7.9%	20.7%							106	1.7	7.3	2.2
2022	SA	AA	23	232	54	9	37	37	.344/.474/.611	.398	.786	13.8%	17.2%							141	1.1	-0.2	2.0
2022	NAS	AAA	23	167	30	3	19	25	.329/.402/.459	.395	.573	8.4%	17.4%	90.9%	90.0%	33.3%	50.0%			106	1.9	-1.3	0.7
2022	ELP	AAA	23	142	30	4	9	23	.315/.457/.477	.378	.616	14.1%	17.6%	67.6%	80.7%	29.6%	62.0%			111	0.3	-1.1	0.6
2022	MIL	MLB	23	9	2	0	0	0	.000/.111/.000		.000	11.1%	22.2%	64.7%	81.8%	41.2%	71.4%	14.1	99.7	102	-0.1	0.1	0.0
2022	SD	MLB	23	27	1	0	2	1	.222/.222/.333	.273	.409	0.0%	18.5%	66.0%	83.9%	40.4%	66.7%	22.6	94.5	93	-0.1	0.1	0.1
2023	OAK	MLB	24	497	47	5	47	67	.254/.309/.345	.315	.443	4.0%	19.9%	67.2%	84.9%	36.9%	58.8%	9.2	99.8	88	2.8	-1.2	1.2
2024 DC	OAK	MLB	25	422	41	8	41	52	.249/.316/.369	.304	.480	6.4%	21.0%							98	1.3	-0.6	1.3

2023 GP: CF (110), LF (15), RF (11), DH (3)

Comps: Johnny Giavotella (61), Eury Pérez (60), Adam Haseley (60)

It shouldn't be easy to establish stolen base records when you played for the same team as Rickey Henderson—let alone played the same sport as him—but Ruiz's 67 thefts as a rookie surpassed Henderson's 33 (in basically a half season) and just barely exceeded Kenny Lofton's major-league record by one. He also stole third 21 times; no single team had that many the previous year. The last player to steal the final square that often was Deion Sanders in 1997. But for all the times the new fellow pilfered a pillow, he scored just 47 runs. Yes, the team was bad, but nobody else has ever stolen 60 and scored fewer than 50. (A 50-SB-sub-50-run season has happened exactly twice, last in 1990 by Otis Nixon and the Expos.)

All of the speedy name-dropping aside, here's where the splash of cold water hits: Ruiz isn't a particularly gifted fielder, and he makes decent contact but hits neither for average nor for power. The pendulum swung hard toward the League of Extraordinary Leadoff Men thanks to the newly embiggened bases, and stolen bases will never not be cool, but the hot take on Ruiz is that he's only good for hot takes.

Tyler Soderstrom 1B/C   Born: 11/24/01   Age: 22   Bats: L   Throws: R   Height: 6'1"   Weight: 200   Origin: Round 1, 2020 Draft (#26 overall)

YEAR	TM	LVL	AGE	PA	R	HR	RBI	SB	AVG/OBP/SLG	BABIP	SLGCON	BB%	K%	ZSw%	ZCon%	OSw%	OCon%	LA	90th EV	DRC+	BRR	DRP	WARP
2021	STK	A	19	254	39	12	49	2	.306/.390/.568	.373	.783	10.6%	24.0%							125	-1.2	-5.1	0.9
2022	LAN	A+	20	371	47	20	71	0	.260/.323/.513	.306	.729	7.8%	26.7%							123	0.1	1.4	2.1
2022	MID	AA	20	147	17	8	28	0	.278/.327/.496	.305	.660	6.8%	22.4%							118	-0.3	-1.9	0.5
2022	LV	AAA	20	38	2	1	6	0	.297/.316/.405	.435	.625	2.6%	34.2%	64.2%	88.2%	44.2%	47.4%			82	0.3	0.1	0.1
2023	LV	AAA	21	335	49	21	62	2	.252/.307/.526	.280	.739	7.5%	26.3%	70.9%	85.9%	35.7%	57.0%			98	1.9	-3.4	0.8
2023	OAK	MLB	21	138	9	3	7	0	.160/.232/.240	.213	.366	8.0%	31.2%	71.3%	84.6%	35.2%	43.1%	6.1	106.9	75	0.0	-1.4	-0.2
2024 DC	OAK	MLB	22	344	34	12	40	1	.210/.266/.379	.258	.543	6.3%	27.5%							78	-0.2	-2.1	-0.2

2023 GP: DH (18), C (15), 1B (10)   Comps: Anthony Rizzo (73), Kyle Tucker (59), Adalberto Mondesi (52)

Much has been written over the past few years about Soderstrom's value as a hitter relative to his position. Yes, he's got power, but what if those 20-30 taters a year aren't from behind the plate? Rarely was the converse discussed: What if he can't hit at all? We are far from that conclusion, but Soderstrom's initial call-up was an atrocious one. Very little went right and even a quick errand back in Triple-A didn't improve his approach. He was particularly fooled by off-speed pitches, but he couldn't drive any type of pitch anywhere except into the ground. Mike Trout famously had a poor first year (.672 OPS) with similar playing time, but Soderstrom would need 200 points just to match him. Hopefully he will similarly shake off his staid start and perform more like a power-happy catching prospect, so we can dump a big bucket of liquid paper onto this paragraph.

Daniel Susac C/DH   Born: 05/14/01   Age: 23   Bats: R   Throws: R   Height: 6'4"   Weight: 218   Origin: Round 1, 2022 Draft (#19 overall)

YEAR	TM	LVL	AGE	PA	R	HR	RBI	SB	AVG/OBP/SLG	BABIP	SLGCON	BB%	K%	ZSw%	ZCon%	OSw%	OCon%	LA	90th EV	DRC+	BRR	DRP	WARP
2022	STK	A	21	107	14	1	13	0	.286/.346/.388	.375	.521	6.5%	23.4%							92	-1.2	-0.3	0.0
2023	LAN	A+	22	410	47	7	54	8	.303/.373/.437	.381	.576	9.5%	21.5%							108	2.8	-0.9	2.3
2023	MID	AA	22	56	2	1	8	1	.280/.304/.360	.342	.500	3.6%	25.0%							85	-0.3	-0.3	0.0
2024 non	OAK	MLB	23	251	20	3	21	4	.225/.277/.320	.287	.429	5.9%	23.4%							69	0.0	0	0.0

2023 GP: C (76), DH (36)   Comps: Argenis Raga (66), Jason Bour (64), Wilkin Castillo (62)

YEAR	TM	P. COUNT	FRM RUNS	BLK RUNS	THRW RUNS	TOT RUNS
2022	STK	1601	0.4	-0.3	-0.1	0.0
2023	LAN	9454	-0.7	0.1	0.9	0.2
2023	MID	1274	-0.5	0.0	0.2	-0.4
2024	OAK	6956	-1.8	-0.3	0.1	-2.0

Susac became the first catcher to win the Midwest League batting title since Robert Fick in 1997, Carlos Mendez in 1994, or possibly BJ Surhoff in 1985, depending on your definition of "catcher," "qualified," or "Midwest League." The point is, it's been an entire generation-and-a-half, and catchers who can hit are always en vogue, even if tall catchers are not. Susac is a large individual for the position, though his fielding and throwing arm are competent enough to possibly allow him some positional versatility. His brief foray into Double-A yielded modest results, but let's see if another year there could yield any more arcane catcher facts from the 1980s.

Abraham Toro IF   Born: 12/20/96   Age: 27   Bats: S   Throws: R   Height: 6'0"   Weight: 223   Origin: Round 5, 2016 Draft (#157 overall)

YEAR	TM	LVL	AGE	PA	R	HR	RBI	SB	AVG/OBP/SLG	BABIP	SLGCON	BB%	K%	ZSw%	ZCon%	OSw%	OCon%	LA	90th EV	DRC+	BRR	DRP	WARP
2021	SUG	AAA	24	68	10	2	11	2	.352/.485/.593	.386	.696	16.2%	11.8%							129	-1.1	0.8	0.4
2021	SEA	MLB	24	253	28	5	26	3	.252/.328/.367	.275	.430	8.7%	13.0%	66.3%	87.7%	34.3%	75.5%	14.5	103.2	109	0.1	-0.3	1.2
2021	HOU	MLB	24	122	17	6	20	3	.211/.287/.385	.205	.477	7.4%	17.2%	62.3%	85.8%	38.2%	77.0%	14.0	101.5	119	0.1	0.0	0.7
2022	TAC	AAA	25	69	6	2	12	3	.241/.353/.431	.273	.543	14.5%	17.4%	61.8%	79.4%	27.4%	67.4%			113	0.7	0.5	0.4
2022	SEA	MLB	25	352	36	10	35	2	.185/.239/.324	.198	.405	6.3%	18.5%	64.9%	85.7%	33.2%	67.1%	17.4	102.0	91	-0.1	0.4	0.6
2023	NAS	AAA	26	414	53	8	58	8	.291/.374/.471	.340	.592	11.8%	17.6%	60.9%	83.9%	25.9%	67.6%			113	-1.2	0.3	1.6
2023	MIL	MLB	26	21	4	2	9	0	.444/.524/.778	.545	1.077	9.5%	23.8%	53.1%	76.5%	32.4%	41.7%	11.1	104.9	108	0.0	-0.1	0.1
2024 DC	OAK	MLB	27	284	28	7	30	2	.237/.309/.376	.280	.485	8.2%	20.2%							95	-0.1	-0.4	0.5

2023 GP: 3B (4), 1B (2), DH (1)   Comps: Andy LaRoche (59), Gio Urshela (49), Brandon Wood (48)

A chance misspelling of Toro's name made it resemble that of a popular classic rock band, but the analysis applies regardless. Love isn't always on time, and neither is Toro's return to getting regular major-league minutes. He spent most of the year in Triple-A, where he demonstrated (for what seems like the eighth time) promising on-base skills, while fielding three different infield positions. Hold the line: the phone in Nashville rang occasionally for Toro's short visits to Milwaukee, where he appeared in lieu of an injured player on the active roster, just to be sent back down again. He's got skills, but's gonna to take a lot to drag him away from Triple-A purgatory; he does nothing that a hundred men or more (on MLB rosters) could ever do.

Jacob Wilson SS   Born: 03/30/02   Age: 22   Bats: R   Throws: R   Height: 6'3"   Weight: 190   Origin: Round 1, 2023 Draft (#6 overall)

YEAR	TM	LVL	AGE	PA	R	HR	RBI	SB	AVG/OBP/SLG	BABIP	SLGCON	BB%	K%	ZSw%	ZCon%	OSw%	OCon%	LA	90th EV	DRC+	BRR	DRP	WARP
2023	LAN	A+	21	99	13	1	8	4	.318/.378/.455	.346	.513	6.1%	10.1%							122	0.0	0.6	0.7
2024 non	OAK	MLB	22	251	19	3	20	0	.216/.270/.305	.251	.366	5.8%	15.7%							63	0.0	0	-0.3

2023 GP: SS (24), DH (2)   Comps: Imeldo Diaz (86), Lenyn Sosa (85), Didi Gregorius (85)

Wilson's father Jack was also a shortstop; the elder Wilson's long stretch with the Pirates included walking up to "Jumpin' Jack Flash." Jacob will likely not unfurl a Rolling Stones tune, not just because of the generational gap but because there isn't one that fits, least of all "Miss You."—Wilson struck out just 4.4% of the time during his college career. Power may or may not come, but in his first pro ballin' summer, he at least piled up the doubles. It's that precise bat-to-ball skill paired with his ability to fill the six-hole that made Wilson the first infielder off the 2023 draft board. He may not play shortstop as long as someone plays for the Stones, but no one does.

BASEBALL PROSPECTUS 2024

PITCHERS

Osvaldo Bido RHP   Born: 10/18/95   Age: 28   Height: 6'3"   Weight: 175   Origin: IFA, 2017

YEAR	TM	LVL	AGE	G(GS)	IP	W-L	SV	K	WHIP	ERA	CSP	BB%	K%	HR%	GB%	ZSw%	ZCon%	OSw%	OCon%	BABIP	SLGCON	DRA-	WARP
2021	ALT	AA	25	21(19)	93²	4-8	0	91	1.37	5.09		8.0%	22.1%	3.2%	34.6%					.307	.583	117	-0.1
2022	IND	AAA	26	32(25)	111¹	3-8	0	122	1.50	4.53		12.6%	24.1%	3.6%	37.8%	70.0%	85.7%	34.8%	81.2%	.296	.609	99	1.6
2023	IND	AAA	27	19(10)	62²	3-4	3	65	1.29	4.16		10.8%	24.3%	2.2%	40.2%	67.8%	79.6%	34.3%	58.1%	.282	.527	97	1.0
2023	PIT	MLB	27	16(9)	50²	2-5	0	48	1.50	5.86	48.2%	8.9%	20.3%	1.7%	35.8%	64.2%	84.1%	31.0%	67.6%	.329	.494	120	0.1
2024 DC	OAK	MLB	28	20(3)	34	1-2	0	30	1.44	5.18	48.2%	10.0%	19.5%	3.2%	35.7%					.293	.548	114	0.0

2023 Arsenal: SW (84.4), FA (94.8), SI (94.5), CH (89.2), SL (85.3)   Comps: Brent Suter (63), Shane Greene (62), Ben Lively (61)

Perhaps Bido could have been better than his 2023 results? His fastball and sinker were fairly effective, sitting just under 95 mph, and his changeup (just five miles slower than his four-seamer) was solid as well. The main problem was his slider, the most-used pitch in his repertoire. Due to its massive break compared to the rest of his arsenal, it needs support ... say from his occasional cutter which could help establish a tricky pitch tunnel. Until he either turns down his slider usage or turns up the use of his other pitches, he may not be a capable major-league starter.

Paul Blackburn RHP   Born: 12/04/93   Age: 30   Height: 6'1"   Weight: 196   Origin: Round 1, 2012 Draft (#56 overall)

YEAR	TM	LVL	AGE	G(GS)	IP	W-L	SV	K	WHIP	ERA	CSP	BB%	K%	HR%	GB%	ZSw%	ZCon%	OSw%	OCon%	BABIP	SLGCON	DRA-	WARP
2021	LV	AAA	27	17(16)	88²	4-7	0	80	1.59	4.97		6.8%	20.0%	2.0%	54.6%					.376	.568	91	0.8
2021	OAK	MLB	27	9(9)	38¹	1-4	0	26	1.62	5.87	50.2%	5.7%	14.9%	4.6%	51.1%	66.8%	94.3%	28.7%	71.7%	.341	.635	110	0.2
2022	OAK	MLB	28	21(21)	111¹	7-6	0	89	1.26	4.28	53.6%	6.4%	19.1%	3.2%	46.6%	66.4%	87.1%	30.6%	61.9%	.291	.556	111	0.5
2023	OAK	MLB	29	21(20)	103²	4-7	0	104	1.54	4.43	42.9%	9.3%	22.4%	2.4%	41.2%	68.5%	87.1%	32.6%	63.0%	.351	.584	104	1.0
2024 DC	OAK	MLB	30	24(24)	123²	6-9	0	98	1.38	4.70	47.7%	7.8%	18.1%	2.9%	43.8%					.299	.529	106	0.7

2023 Arsenal: SI (91.7), FC (89), SW (80.8), FA (92), KC (79), CH (86)   Comps: Iván Nova (65), Vance Worley (65), Nick Tropeano (64)

So often we see the story of a power pitcher turning to finesse in an attempt to stay in the rotation. Blackburn once was a sinker-oriented ground-ball pitcher, but over the last two years has transformed into a strikeout artist. (Somewhere, Frank Tanana is rolling in his Craftmatic adjustable bed.) He's added a tick of velocity but the real key has been trust in his auxiliary pitches: his curve, slider, and changeup all grade out at plus. For the first time, he averaged a K per inning and had more pitches hit in the air instead of the ground while maintaining a very good homer rate. He's not an ace but he can certainly improve a rotation's bell curve. It's hard to believe this is the same pitcher who cleared waivers three years ago.

Joe Boyle RHP   Born: 08/14/99   Age: 24   Height: 6'7"   Weight: 240   Origin: Round 5, 2020 Draft (#143 overall)

YEAR	TM	LVL	AGE	G(GS)	IP	W-L	SV	K	WHIP	ERA	CSP	BB%	K%	HR%	GB%	ZSw%	ZCon%	OSw%	OCon%	BABIP	SLGCON	DRA-	WARP
2022	DAY	A+	22	17(17)	74²	3-4	0	122	1.13	2.17		19.7%	40.7%	1.0%	42.6%					.198	.321	78	1.6
2022	CHA	AA	22	6(5)	26	0-2	0	31	1.77	4.85		21.0%	26.1%	2.5%	34.9%					.300	.525	120	0.0
2023	CHA	AA	23	19(19)	84	6-5	0	122	1.64	4.50		19.4%	31.5%	1.6%	42.9%					.326	.537	89	0.6
2023	MID	AA	23	3(3)	17¹	2-1	0	28	1.10	2.08		10.1%	40.6%	0.0%	51.5%					.364	.485	75	0.4
2023	LV	AAA	23	3(3)	16	0-2	0	18	1.19	2.25		16.7%	27.3%	1.5%	50.0%	58.9%	76.2%	27.4%	47.8%	.200	.400	86	
2023	OAK	MLB	23	3(3)	16	2-0	0	15	0.81	1.69	47.3%	8.3%	25.0%	1.7%	30.0%	60.2%	81.4%	36.6%	69.2%	.179	.359	107	0.1
2024 DC	OAK	MLB	24	36(13)	88	3-7	0	107	1.64	5.58	47.3%	17.1%	26.3%	3.4%	36.0%					.285	.591	119	-0.1

2023 Arsenal: FA (98), SL (88), CU (81.6)

Boyle has one of the most electric arms in the entire sport, regularly hitting 100 mph and spinning two different wicked breaking balls. He also has a long, long track record of walking the local populace everywhere he's been, including all levels of the minors (7.2 per nine for his career), out of the bullpen at Notre Dame (12 per 9), even in wood bat summer leagues (9.2 per 9 between two summers on the Cape and one in the Northwoods League). The Reds finally gave up on the "get Boyle to hit the zone" project and dealt him at the trade deadline for Sam Moll. Then a funny thing happened almost overnight: He started throwing strikes. Not a ton of strikes—one does not go from Steve Dalkowski to Greg Maddux on one trip from Chattanooga to Midland—but enough to get promoted to Triple-A and then the majors. He walked two or fewer in all three of his MLB outings, and if this is at all real and not a sample size fluke he's going to be a very good pitcher for a long time.

Lucas Erceg RHP   Born: 05/01/95   Age: 29   Height: 6'2"   Weight: 214   Origin: Round 2, 2016 Draft (#46 overall)

YEAR	TM	LVL	AGE	G(GS)	IP	W-L	SV	K	WHIP	ERA	CSP	BB%	K%	HR%	GB%	ZSw%	ZCon%	OSw%	OCon%	BABIP	SLGCON	DRA-	WARP
2021	BLX	AA	26	22(13)	47²	2-6	0	45	1.53	5.29		16.4%	21.1%	2.3%	58.1%					.266	.488	114	0.1
2022	BLX	AA	27	16(2)	22	1-3	1	27	2.00	6.55		12.4%	23.9%	2.7%	61.4%					.409	.710	83	0.4
2022	NAS	AAA	27	33(2)	39¹	2-1	1	42	1.45	3.43		13.5%	24.7%	1.8%	59.6%	81.8%	77.8%	47.1%	62.5%	.307	.476	88	0.8
2023	NAS	AAA	28	13(0)	15¹	3-1	0	16	1.57	6.46		14.9%	23.9%	4.5%	56.1%	64.7%	82.7%	26.6%	66.0%	.297	.600	100	0.2
2023	OAK	MLB	28	50(0)	55	4-4	0	68	1.58	4.75	45.1%	14.3%	27.1%	0.4%	44.0%	65.3%	80.2%	26.6%	58.4%	.357	.529	96	0.8
2024 DC	OAK	MLB	29	61(0)	64¹	4-5	15	67	1.50	5.03	45.1%	13.2%	22.9%	2.9%	44.6%					.289	.544	110	0.0

2023 Arsenal: SI (98), FA (98), CH (90.3), CU (85.6), SL (89.3)   Comps: Leonel Campos (78), Justin Miller (78), Gregory Infante (77)

It would have taken some real sorcery to predict Erceg would lead the Athletics in pitching appearances considering he began the season in Triple-A for another team and *three years ago was a third baseman*. Milwaukee and their league-leading ERA left him on the curb in mid-May. Yet, once acquired and promoted, not once was he optioned to Triple-A to work on anything. Erceg's upper-90s gas kept the ball in the park every time but one, and he can touch 100 in a pinch. By the end of the year he was receiving holds in the seventh inning and was the team's top strikeout shaman. The odometer has barely turned over on his arm and there are several high-leverage situations in his future. If the Brewers want him back, it's going to cost them.

332 - Oakland Athletics

Angel Felipe RHP Born: 08/30/97 Age: 26 Height: 6'5" Weight: 190 Origin: IFA, 2015

YEAR	TM	LVL	AGE	G (GS)	IP	W-L	SV	K	WHIP	ERA	CSP	BB%	K%	HR%	GB%	ZSw%	ZCon%	OSw%	OCon%	BABIP	SLGCON	DRA-	WARP
2021	CSC	A	23	21(0)	38	2-0	7	45	1.26	1.42		10.5%	27.8%	0.6%	68.8%					.323	.415	92	0.5
2021	BG	A+	23	15(0)	24²	1-0	1	33	1.46	4.38		14.3%	29.5%	2.7%	58.3%					.298	.542	88	0.4
2022	SA	AA	24	32(0)	39²	3-5	11	49	1.54	3.18		13.9%	27.2%	0.6%	50.0%					.350	.475	86	0.5
2022	ELP	AAA	24	19(0)	22¹	2-1	3	35	1.07	4.43		11.7%	37.2%	0.0%	59.1%	58.1%	75.6%	30.2%	55.2%	.295	.349	67	0.6
2023	ELP	AAA	25	25(0)	24²	0-2	1	39	1.78	6.20		14.9%	32.2%	1.7%	48.4%	56.9%	72.3%	26.3%	61.8%	.400	.613	72	0.7
2023	LV	AAA	25	5(0)	5	2-0	0	7	0.60	1.80		5.9%	41.2%	0.0%	44.4%	59.4%	84.2%	34.9%	53.3%	.222	.333	77	0.1
2023	OAK	MLB	25	14(0)	15	1-1	0	19	1.27	4.20	44.3%	20.3%	29.7%	0.0%	51.6%	54.0%	79.6%	22.8%	38.5%	.194	.226	99	0.2
2024 DC	OAK	MLB	26	36(0)	38²	2-2	3	49	1.37	4.11	44.3%	13.2%	28.5%	2.4%	47.0%					.290	.526	91	0.3

2023 Arsenal: SL (83.3), SI (94.6), FA (95.5), CH (85.4)   Comps: Reyes Moronta (85), Chad Sobotka (80), Kevin Quackenbush (79)

Felipe has a wild fastball and a slider that'll generate whiffs for weeks, but a disastrous first half in Triple-A led him astray from the Padres 40-man roster. He was not snuck through waivers, however, as the A's had no qualms about taking a chance on potential. Felipe, who began his career with the Rays in 2015, turned five magnificent Triple-A innings into a major-league debut. He showcased that wonderful out-pitch, as well as his command issues, and allowed more earned runs than hits before going on the injured list with a elbow strain. His health for the 2024 season resists prediction, which makes it a perfect pairing to go with his hellacious and randomized fastball.

Trevor Gott RHP Born: 08/26/92 Age: 31 Height: 5'11" Weight: 185 Origin: Round 6, 2013 Draft (#178 overall)

YEAR	TM	LVL	AGE	G (GS)	IP	W-L	SV	K	WHIP	ERA	CSP	BB%	K%	HR%	GB%	ZSw%	ZCon%	OSw%	OCon%	BABIP	SLGCON	DRA-	WARP
2021	SAC	AAA	28	43(1)	41²	1-3	3	53	1.27	4.10		9.4%	31.0%	2.3%	41.6%					.340	.566	79	0.7
2022	MIL	MLB	29	45(0)	45²	3-4	0	44	1.03	4.14	49.6%	6.5%	23.7%	4.3%	44.1%	65.3%	83.9%	34.7%	63.0%	.227	.528	91	0.7
2023	SEA	MLB	30	30(0)	29	0-3	0	32	1.41	4.03	52.3%	6.2%	24.8%	1.6%	42.5%	62.4%	79.0%	29.7%	65.8%	.365	.552	88	0.5
2023	NYM	MLB	30	34(0)	29	0-2	1	30	1.41	4.34	44.6%	8.3%	22.7%	1.5%	38.2%	66.1%	87.8%	30.1%	69.5%	.326	.483	90	0.5
2024 DC	OAK	MLB	31	55(0)	58	3-2	0	52	1.29	4.31	48.4%	8.2%	21.0%	3.2%	40.4%					.285	.535	99	0.3

2023 Arsenal: SL (89.5), SI (94), FA (93.7), KC (80.9), CH (87.4)   Comps: Jeremy Jeffress (61), Bryan Shaw (59), Brandon League (59)

Despite a modest dip in fastball velocity last year, Gott's heater had the best year of its career with whiffs on 34% of swings. He's finally locating his fastballs at the top of the strike zone, a particularly advantageous area for pitchers like Gott with a somewhat low release. Per data from Pitch Info, Gott threw 63% of his fastballs in the upper third of the strike zone or higher, by far the highest rate of his career and substantially above the 2023 league average of 52 percent. The Mets non-tendered him despite a projected $2 million arbitration price tag, so the Athletics will get to see if he can continue to hit his high marks and remain effective.

Hogan Harris LHP Born: 12/26/96 Age: 27 Height: 6'3" Weight: 230 Origin: Round 3, 2018 Draft (#85 overall)

YEAR	TM	LVL	AGE	G (GS)	IP	W-L	SV	K	WHIP	ERA	CSP	BB%	K%	HR%	GB%	ZSw%	ZCon%	OSw%	OCon%	BABIP	SLGCON	DRA-	WARP
2022	LAN	A+	25	7(7)	13	0-1	0	18	0.92	1.38		13.2%	34.0%	0.0%	42.3%					.192	.192	92	0.2
2022	MID	AA	25	8(7)	32¹	1-0	0	48	1.05	1.67		14.3%	36.1%	0.0%	43.5%					.242	.323	70	0.7
2022	LV	AAA	25	8(8)	28¹	1-3	0	39	1.69	6.35		12.9%	29.5%	4.5%	33.3%	68.7%	75.4%	28.9%	52.8%	.362	.781	93	0.3
2023	LV	AAA	26	15(14)	57	1-4	0	55	1.72	6.47		14.2%	20.6%	4.5%	37.6%	62.2%	81.4%	26.2%	63.6%	.304	.661	120	-0.2
2023	OAK	MLB	26	14(6)	63	3-6	0	56	1.51	7.14	53.8%	9.9%	19.7%	3.5%	38.3%	67.5%	81.6%	24.9%	65.0%	.308	.606	111	0.4
2024 DC	OAK	MLB	27	20(3)	33²	1-2	0	31	1.52	5.43	53.8%	11.5%	20.4%	3.4%	37.9%					.296	.569	119	-0.1

2023 Arsenal: FA (92.7), CH (80.1), FC (90.5), SL (77.5), CU (74)   Comps: Dillon Peters (71), Chris Rusin (68), Vidal Nuño (64)

The first ever major-league Hogan (proper name division) debuted last April with five walks in one-third of an inning, making it look like he was going to also become the last Hogan, potentially ruining it for all subsequent Hogans. However, he only walked four batters in his subsequent 30 innings saving his namesake from permanent tarnish. He eventually settled into a role where he would alternate between starting and relieving an opener for four or five innings. These former outings were decisively better (4.96 ERA) than the latter (7.80 ERA), and his changeup was so deceptive against righties that it gave him a reverse platoon split. There are ways a manager can make him useful, but they are extremely particular. Hopefully all Hogans aren't this finicky.

Gunnar Hoglund RHP Born: 12/17/99 Age: 24 Height: 6'4" Weight: 220 Origin: Round 1, 2021 Draft (#19 overall)

YEAR	TM	LVL	AGE	G (GS)	IP	W-L	SV	K	WHIP	ERA	CSP	BB%	K%	HR%	GB%	ZSw%	ZCon%	OSw%	OCon%	BABIP	SLGCON	DRA-	WARP
2023	STK	A	23	12(12)	43¹	1-5	0	27	1.52	7.48		5.2%	14.1%	4.7%	46.1%					.324	.645	107	0.2
2023	LAN	A+	23	3(3)	12²	1-0	0	14	0.55	1.42		4.3%	30.4%	0.0%	25.0%					.179	.214	100	0.1
2024 non	OAK	MLB	24	58(0)	50	2-2	0	33	1.58	6.27		8.0%	14.6%	4.0%	36.2%					.317	.595	136	-0.7

Comps: Josh Lucas (48), Jaison Vilera (48), Bowden Francis (48)

Hoglund still has a sizable journey ahead of him, and all these injuries really aren't helping shorten the trip. Still, he was given an extremely long leash to throw 60 pitches per start while getting thoroughly peppered in Low-A. The Athletics' front office showed faith in him, however, and he was given a promotion to High-A, where he threw five hitless and walkless innings in his debut. He even got a Double-A start before the season was up. Be patient with him, not only because it seems likely he will join a major-league rotation within a few years, but by that time 30% of the league will already be inhabited by fellow Gunnars. The future is a scary place.

Dany Jiménez RHP Born: 12/23/93 Age: 30 Height: 6'1" Weight: 182 Origin: IFA, 2015

YEAR	TM	LVL	AGE	G(GS)	IP	W-L	SV	K	WHIP	ERA	CSP	BB%	K%	HR%	GB%	ZSw%	ZCon%	OSw%	OCon%	BABIP	SLGCON	DRA-	WARP
2021	BUF	AAA	27	39(1)	44²	3-3	3	73	1.21	2.22		13.4%	39.0%	2.7%	39.3%					.289	.591	71	1.3
2022	OAK	MLB	28	34(0)	34¹	3-4	11	34	1.19	3.41	55.8%	12.4%	23.4%	1.4%	43.0%	61.9%	82.4%	29.7%	43.0%	.231	.348	104	0.3
2023	LV	AAA	29	9(1)	8²	1-0	1	14	1.62	10.38		17.5%	35.0%	5.0%	38.9%	52.5%	75.0%	30.3%	45.5%	.313	.722	85	0.0
2023	OAK	MLB	29	25(1)	23¹	0-2	1	21	1.07	3.47	44.6%	14.9%	22.3%	3.2%	27.1%	58.5%	79.1%	25.9%	64.2%	.145	.393	111	0.1
2024 DC	OAK	MLB	30	61(0)	64¹	4-5	15	74	1.43	4.87	50.3%	12.4%	25.8%	3.8%	36.3%					.286	.599	108	0.0

2023 Arsenal: SL (81.6), FA (93.6), CH (82.9)   *Comps: Tyler Kinley (57), Austin Adams (56), Spencer Patton (55)*

Laying off Jimenez's slider is probably your best chance of reaching first base. But it's basically all he throws, and you've got this giant chunk of smooth wood in your hands, and it feels like you oughta ... do *something* with it? Such is the tantalizing nature of this righty's breaking pitch; it finishes strong toward the earth in its final few feet of flight, and he channels its control just well enough to get the occasional save. He gives up more walks than base hits, and batters are hitting a career .086 against his slider, so you're left standing there in the batter's box, choosing your own adventure. Who knows, maybe the next pitch is that average fastball?

James Kaprielian RHP Born: 03/02/94 Age: 30 Height: 6'3" Weight: 225 Origin: Round 1, 2015 Draft (#16 overall)

YEAR	TM	LVL	AGE	G(GS)	IP	W-L	SV	K	WHIP	ERA	CSP	BB%	K%	HR%	GB%	ZSw%	ZCon%	OSw%	OCon%	BABIP	SLGCON	DRA-	WARP
2021	OAK	MLB	27	24(21)	119¹	8-5	0	123	1.22	4.07	52.4%	8.2%	24.5%	3.8%	33.6%	68.1%	79.6%	31.4%	63.2%	.276	.591	120	-0.1
2022	LV	AAA	28	2(2)	8²	0-1	0	7	1.96	9.35		11.9%	16.7%	2.4%	20.7%	70.8%	87.0%	26.8%	46.2%	.393	.741	131	-0.1
2022	OAK	MLB	28	26(26)	134	5-9	0	98	1.34	4.23	52.6%	10.2%	17.0%	2.8%	37.3%	71.9%	85.8%	30.1%	67.1%	.264	.513	135	-1.1
2023	LV	AAA	29	2(2)	8¹	1-0	0	7	1.08	1.08		6.1%	21.2%	0.0%	45.8%	70.6%	83.3%	25.0%	55.0%	.292	.333	107	0.1
2023	OAK	MLB	29	14(11)	61	2-6	0	57	1.59	6.34	51.0%	11.1%	20.4%	3.2%	31.2%	68.4%	81.3%	32.5%	64.5%	.324	.592	121	0.1
2024 non	OAK	MLB	30	58(0)	50	2-2	0	42	1.42	5.04	52.0%	9.7%	19.4%	3.7%	34.7%					.289	.562	112	-0.1

2023 Arsenal: FA (92.6), SW (80.8), SI (92.5), CH (83.5), CU (76.3), SL (83.1)   *Comps: Andrew Cashner (53), Matt Shoemaker (51), Jerad Eickhoff (51)*

We'll get to the surgical visits shortly. When he's healthy, Kaprielian is sometimes effective. Last year he battled through a slump that put his ERA nearly above a baker's dozen, only good for business when you're running a patisserie. Once he returned to the major-league staff he abandoned his sinking fastball and the rest of his repertoire earned him a 4.00 ERA down the stretch...at least until his name was scribbled onto the dreaded 60-day injured list with his second operation on his throwing shoulder in as many years. The former prize prospect in the 2017 Sonny Gray trade now needs one more shoulder surgery on his rewards card to receive a free tote bag which, it should be noted, must be held by his only functional arm.

Richard Lovelady LHP Born: 07/07/95 Age: 29 Height: 6'0" Weight: 185 Origin: Round 10, 2016 Draft (#313 overall)

YEAR	TM	LVL	AGE	G(GS)	IP	W-L	SV	K	WHIP	ERA	CSP	BB%	K%	HR%	GB%	ZSw%	ZCon%	OSw%	OCon%	BABIP	SLGCON	DRA-	WARP
2021	OMA	AAA	25	7(0)	8¹	0-0	0	9	1.08	1.08		12.1%	27.3%	0.0%	47.4%					.263	.368	94	0.1
2021	KC	MLB	25	20(0)	20²	2-0	1	23	1.06	3.48	55.5%	7.1%	27.4%	3.6%	55.6%	61.8%	87.6%	35.7%	45.9%	.255	.491	80	0.4
2023	GWN	AAA	27	4(0)	5	0-1	0	4	1.20	7.20		9.1%	18.2%	0.0%	40.0%	71.7%	84.8%	25.0%	50.0%	.267	.357	116	0.0
2023	OAK	MLB	27	27(0)	23¹	0-3	0	24	1.07	4.63	51.0%	10.4%	25.0%	3.1%	47.5%	62.6%	87.2%	29.4%	55.0%	.214	.536	90	0.4
2024 non	OAK	MLB	28	58(0)	50	2-2	0	47	1.29	3.96	52.4%	9.8%	22.0%	2.6%	46.4%					.279	.493	90	0.5

2023 Arsenal: SL (86), FA (91.1), SI (91.1), CH (86.3)   *Comps: Bruce Rondón (63), Eric O'Flaherty (61), Scott Elbert (60)*

After spending his entire career in the Kansas City organization, Richard made the first amicable departure from the Royals that involved a Lovelady since the abdication of Edward VIII in 1936. He took his Chris Sale-like sidearm delivery westward and weaved through traffic with a 2.16 ERA through May. It's admittedly the only number that matters in such limited innings, but unfortunately the axe of regression came swinging back to reality. Lovelady didn't toss a ball after July 8 due to a forearm strain, but he has the profile general managers covet when it comes to bullpen composition. The heart wants what it wants, so Lovelady will live to be loved again.

Adrián Martínez RHP Born: 12/10/96 Age: 27 Height: 6'2" Weight: 215 Origin: IFA, 2015

YEAR	TM	LVL	AGE	G(GS)	IP	W-L	SV	K	WHIP	ERA	CSP	BB%	K%	HR%	GB%	ZSw%	ZCon%	OSw%	OCon%	BABIP	SLGCON	DRA-	WARP
2021	SA	AA	24	17(13)	80²	7-3	0	83	1.09	2.34		7.3%	25.4%	1.2%	43.7%					.284	.435	74	1.7
2021	ELP	AAA	24	9(9)	44¹	1-2	0	39	1.51	5.28		8.7%	19.9%	3.1%	54.7%					.338	.609	86	0.5
2022	LV	AAA	25	18(18)	89²	5-7	0	100	1.42	5.72		8.5%	25.7%	6.2%	45.4%	67.7%	81.8%	31.0%	54.1%	.308	.758	81	1.5
2022	OAK	MLB	25	12(12)	57²	4-6	0	53	1.53	6.24	55.8%	7.3%	20.5%	5.0%	41.3%	68.9%	82.6%	32.5%	66.0%	.327	.652	106	0.4
2023	LV	AAA	26	13(12)	38¹	0-7	0	24	2.09	8.45		11.0%	12.6%	4.7%	43.0%	70.4%	89.6%	32.3%	69.0%	.379	.736	132	-0.1
2023	OAK	MLB	26	22(1)	55	0-2	0	47	1.42	4.75	47.0%	7.9%	19.5%	3.3%	38.2%	68.4%	86.2%	30.4%	63.2%	.315	.576	102	0.6
2024 DC	OAK	MLB	27	36(0)	38²	2-2	0	31	1.45	5.34	51.1%	8.5%	17.8%	3.5%	39.4%					.300	.569	119	-0.1

2023 Arsenal: SI (94.1), CH (82.8), SL (83.5)   *Comps: Joe Ross (69), Brad Lincoln (63), Tyler Duffey (62)*

At first glance, it looks like Martinez doesn't do anything particularly special. He's got an average fastball, average breaking stuff...average everything. He shows up, throws a couple innings when the team is behind, and gets brushed away—sometimes as far as Triple-A. All he's done in his two years as a major leaguer is bounce between the major-league bullpen and minor-league rotation (where he was notably worse). It's more than most players get, even if it's not what every little kid dreams of. Being mentally capable of enduring the constant changes of scenery is a skill that may allow him to stay on a 40-man roster and *possibly* luck into the occasional start.

Trevor May RHP
Born: 09/23/89 Age: 34 Height: 6'5" Weight: 240 Origin: Round 4, 2008 Draft (#136 overall)

YEAR	TM	LVL	AGE	G(GS)	IP	W-L	SV	K	WHIP	ERA	CSP	BB%	K%	HR%	GB%	ZSw%	ZCon%	OSw%	OCon%	BABIP	SLGCON	DRA-	WARP
2021	NYM	MLB	31	68(0)	62²	7-3	4	83	1.26	3.59	54.2%	9.0%	31.2%	3.8%	35.8%	73.7%	75.3%	34.5%	54.9%	.302	.610	82	1.2
2022	NYM	MLB	32	26(0)	25	2-0	1	30	1.44	5.04	57.0%	8.1%	27.0%	3.6%	29.2%	64.5%	78.0%	29.5%	55.7%	.338	.611	99	0.3
2023	OAK	MLB	33	49(0)	46²	4-4	21	40	1.37	3.28	46.7%	14.1%	19.5%	2.0%	30.8%	64.2%	83.4%	30.8%	66.7%	.246	.430	123	0.0
2024 non	OAK	MLB	34	58(0)	50	2-2	0	52	1.40	4.90	50.6%	10.2%	23.9%	3.8%	32.1%					.298	.599	109	0.0

2023 Arsenal: FA (94.8), SL (84.3), CH (87.8), SW (81.4)

Comps: Mike MacDougal (59), Jason Isringhausen (58), Tommy Hunter (58)

"Today I consider myself the luckiest man on the face of the earth." - Lou Gehrig, Yankee Stadium, July 4, 1939

"To the A's organization and every single person part of it, I love all of you. Every single one of you except for one guy. And we all know who that guy is. Sell the team, dude ... Take mommy and daddy's money somewhere else, dork. ... If you're gonna be a greedy f***, own it." - Trevor May, twitch.tv/iamtrevormay, October 16, 2023

Perfect retirement speeches can take several different forms. Happy streaming, Trev.

Luis Medina RHP
Born: 05/03/99 Age: 25 Height: 6'1" Weight: 175 Origin: IFA, 2015

YEAR	TM	LVL	AGE	G(GS)	IP	W-L	SV	K	WHIP	ERA	CSP	BB%	K%	HR%	GB%	ZSw%	ZCon%	OSw%	OCon%	BABIP	SLGCON	DRA-	WARP
2021	HV	A+	22	7(7)	32²	2-1	0	50	1.13	2.76		14.3%	37.6%	3.0%	50.0%					.241	.590	79	0.6
2021	SOM	AA	22	15(14)	73²	4-3	0	83	1.44	3.67		12.9%	26.1%	2.2%	50.5%					.314	.540	84	1.1
2022	TOR	WIN	23	10(10)	28	0-1	0	32	1.14	2.57		10.6%	28.3%	0.0%	53.7%					.299	.409		
2022	MID	AA	23	7(7)	20²	1-4	0	26	2.76	11.76		19.3%	22.8%	2.6%	46.2%					.516	.766	114	-0.1
2022	SOM	AA	23	17(17)	72	4-3	0	81	1.19	3.38		13.0%	26.4%	1.3%	51.4%					.240	.403	80	1.7
2023	LV	AAA	24	6(5)	16²	0-1	0	23	1.86	6.48		20.3%	29.1%	1.3%	31.6%	65.7%	81.5%	22.6%	62.2%	.389	.722	127	-0.3
2023	OAK	MLB	24	23(17)	109²	3-10	0	106	1.51	5.42	46.4%	11.5%	21.4%	2.8%	43.2%	69.9%	85.2%	29.4%	59.1%	.306	.586	109	0.8
2024 DC	OAK	MLB	25	21(21)	101	4-9	0	98	1.57	5.43	46.4%	13.6%	21.2%	3.0%	42.8%					.294	.549	117	-0.1

2023 Arsenal: FA (96.2), SL (85.3), SI (95.5), CU (79.8), CH (87.4)

Comps: Jharel Cotton (71), Mitch Keller (65), Touki Toussaint (65)

When the 2012 Astros lost 107 games, there was one play embodying their inferiority. IYKYK: it may be playing in your head right now. (Words fail to capture it, so just get online and search for "Roger Bernadina 2012 bunt.") Medina had such a play for the 110-loss A's, inducing a ground ball to himself, jogging toward first base, and then suddenly meandering a bit, only for the runner to beat him to first base. Brain toot aside, Medina flipped the script and made opposing hitters look like fools with his slider 48% of the time, and his changeup was also quite effective. Even if he can't consistently pull off the throw to first, it's okay; ask Jon Lester how that can sometimes work out.

Mason Miller RHP
Born: 08/24/98 Age: 25 Height: 6'5" Weight: 200 Origin: Round 3, 2021 Draft (#97 overall)

YEAR	TM	LVL	AGE	G(GS)	IP	W-L	SV	K	WHIP	ERA	CSP	BB%	K%	HR%	GB%	ZSw%	ZCon%	OSw%	OCon%	BABIP	SLGCON	DRA-	WARP
2021	ATH	ROK	22	3(2)	6	0-1	0	9	1.17	1.50		12.5%	37.5%	0.0%	66.7%					.333	.583		
2022	LAN	A+	23	3(3)	7	0-1	0	13	0.71	3.86		7.7%	50.0%	3.8%	45.5%					.200	.636	78	0.1
2023	LV	AAA	24	4(4)	12	1-0	0	23	0.50	0.00		7.1%	54.8%	0.0%	37.5%	74.6%	60.0%	29.6%	40.6%	.188	.250	71	0.1
2023	OAK	MLB	24	10(6)	33¹	0-3	0	38	1.20	3.78	46.8%	11.5%	27.3%	1.4%	24.4%	69.0%	84.7%	29.9%	55.7%	.275	.450	109	0.2
2024 DC	OAK	MLB	25	19(19)	93	4-6	0	108	1.23	3.93	46.8%	10.1%	27.4%	3.7%	29.4%					.266	.576	92	1.1

2023 Arsenal: FA (98.5), SL (86.1), FC (94.4), CH (90.2)

Comps: Adbert Alzolay (48), Tyler Glasnow (46), Lisalverto Bonilla (45)

If you've got a pitcher with gas, why not let him cook in a large open space, rather in the bush leagues where everything is flammable? Miller and his fastball with a peak speed of 102 mph were promoted after 17 career minor-league starts. He keeps hitters honest with a slider and changeup, so he's got the repertoire to be a starter. The bullpen is almost certainly his future, nevertheless, given that injuries have kept him under 60 innings every year. The A's will start him there in 2024, where he could be world-class once he recovers from his latest IL stint.

Luis Morales RHP
Born: 09/24/02 Age: 21 Height: 6'3" Weight: 190 Origin: IFA, 2023

YEAR	TM	LVL	AGE	G(GS)	IP	W-L	SV	K	WHIP	ERA	CSP	BB%	K%	HR%	GB%	ZSw%	ZCon%	OSw%	OCon%	BABIP	SLGCON	DRA-	WARP
2023	DSL ATH	ROK	20	4(3)	11	0-0	0	16	0.55	0.82		5.1%	41.0%	0.0%	57.1%					.190	.190		
2023	ATH	ROK	20	3(3)	9	0-2	0	11	1.33	6.00		5.0%	27.5%	0.0%	63.0%					.370	.654		
2023	STK	A	20	5(5)	16¹	0-3	0	18	1.29	2.20		11.6%	26.1%	0.0%	45.2%					.310	.381	87	0.0
2023	LAN	A+	20	2(2)	7²	0-0	0	8	1.17	3.52		9.4%	25.0%	6.3%	33.3%					.211	.571	104	0.1
2024 non	OAK	MLB	21	58(0)	50	2-2	0	44	1.66	6.43		11.8%	19.2%	4.1%	35.6%					.315	.624	137	-0.8

Comps: Trevor McDonald (50), Deryk Hooker (49), Dionys Rodriguez (49)

The stuff was there from the start. Four years ago Morales was the youngest pitcher in the Cuban National Series, striking out 12 batsmen per nine. The following year he defected from his national Under-23 team to Mexico, and trained there until he was declared a free agent. The Athletics were sufficiently enamored to break their international bonus record last January, paying him $3 million. Morales throws all the old standbys: fastball, slider, curve, change. He hits 97 routinely with the number one, and the curve and slider generate outs. Having received a nibble of stateside minors, he'll get a full entree this season and he might only be a year away from the majors.

www.baseballprospectus.com

Oakland Athletics - 335

Kyle Muller LHP Born: 10/07/97 Age: 26 Height: 6'7" Weight: 250 Origin: Round 2, 2016 Draft (#44 overall)

YEAR	TM	LVL	AGE	G (GS)	IP	W-L	SV	K	WHIP	ERA	CSP	BB%	K%	HR%	GB%	ZSw%	ZCon%	OSw%	OCon%	BABIP	SLGCON	DRA-	WARP
2021	GWN	AAA	23	17(17)	79²	5-4	0	93	1.36	3.39		12.2%	27.0%	2.6%	41.6%					.286	.527	78	2.0
2021	ATL	MLB	23	9(8)	36²	2-4	0	37	1.25	4.17	54.4%	12.9%	23.9%	1.3%	37.5%	65.0%	82.8%	32.1%	50.7%	.261	.413	107	0.2
2022	GWN	AAA	24	23(23)	134²	6-8	0	159	1.18	3.41		7.4%	29.3%	2.6%	46.6%	88.0%	81.8%	44.1%	46.7%	.325	.574	79	3.3
2022	ATL	MLB	24	3(3)	12¹	1-1	0	12	1.70	8.03	57.2%	13.6%	20.3%	3.4%	41.0%	67.6%	87.0%	29.8%	48.7%	.306	.553	135	-0.1
2023	LV	AAA	25	13(13)	62	2-3	0	51	1.89	7.26		12.6%	16.9%	4.0%	50.7%	69.4%	86.2%	28.7%	61.4%	.342	.675	115	0.5
2023	OAK	MLB	25	21(13)	77	1-5	0	56	1.96	7.60	49.7%	10.5%	15.1%	4.3%	42.3%	73.8%	87.8%	27.9%	60.2%	.375	.687	139	-0.7
2024 DC	OAK	MLB	26	52(10)	89²	4-6	0	70	1.56	5.53	51.3%	10.3%	17.2%	3.0%	41.6%					.307	.541	121	-0.3

2023 Arsenal: FA (93.8), SL (87.4), KC (81.4), CH (88.4), SI (93.9)   *Comps: Brett Oberholtzer (68), Jake Faria (65), Justin Nicolino (65)*

Like a candy orange slice that fell into the septic tank, there's no sugar-coating this one: Muller had a bad season. Generationally bad. The last time someone threw that many innings with such a high ERA was Chris Tillman in 2017. He was credited with the first starting pitching victory for his team on May 5, but despite his 5 ⅓ innings and five runs, there was no fiesta afterward. "I don't think the performance was worthy of the first win," Muller told reporters afterwards. The cosmos agreed, and withheld a second one. He did tinker, as pitchers are wont to do when their ERA can still buy a matinee movie ticket in most cities, and one bright spot at the end of the season was a retooled changeup that withstood right-handers. He'll need more than that to stay in a rotation, even Oakland's.

Zach Neal RHP Born: 11/09/88 Age: 35 Height: 6'3" Weight: 220 Origin: Round 17, 2010 Draft (#527 overall)

YEAR	TM	LVL	AGE	G (GS)	IP	W-L	SV	K	WHIP	ERA	CSP	BB%	K%	HR%	GB%	ZSw%	ZCon%	OSw%	OCon%	BABIP	SLGCON	DRA-	WARP
2022	ABQ	AAA	33	29(21)	116²	6-6	0	95	1.49	6.87		5.4%	18.3%	5.4%	41.6%	72.0%	84.9%	33.4%	64.6%	.327	.714	106	0.2
2023	LV	AAA	34	18(10)	74¹	4-2	1	54	1.43	5.21		4.8%	16.2%	5.4%	38.6%	72.6%	86.6%	35.5%	62.6%	.299	.633	112	0.5
2023	OAK	MLB	34	14(2)	27	1-1	0	25	1.63	6.67	49.0%	11.3%	20.2%	6.5%	33.7%	70.4%	88.6%	33.8%	58.4%	.297	.768	117	0.1
2024 non	OAK	MLB	35	58(0)	50	2-2	0	31	1.46	5.83	49.0%	6.7%	14.1%	4.3%	29.2%					.301	.593	129	-0.5

2023 Arsenal: SL (86.3), SI (89.3), CH (82.5), FA (89.2), CU (69.9)   *Comps: Casey Lawrence (47), Alfredo Simon (44), Josh Tomlin (42)*

Neal has played for five different organizations and has been around so long that the *Florida* Marlins drafted him. Yet, all but one of his major-league innings have been for one team. Some of that was predicated by a three-year sojourn in Japan, where his style of average-velocity with plus-movement generated a bunch of weak trajectories into the dirt, he's back in the states and topping out at 89. It's hard not to root for a guy with thousands of frequent flyer miles and bargain-bin stuff, unless he's on the mound wearing your team's colors with the bases loaded.

Austin Pruitt RHP Born: 08/31/89 Age: 34 Height: 5'10" Weight: 185 Origin: Round 9, 2013 Draft (#278 overall)

YEAR	TM	LVL	AGE	G (GS)	IP	W-L	SV	K	WHIP	ERA	CSP	BB%	K%	HR%	GB%	ZSw%	ZCon%	OSw%	OCon%	BABIP	SLGCON	DRA-	WARP
2021	HOU	MLB	31	2(0)	2²	0-1	0	1	1.13	6.75	39.1%	0.0%	8.3%	16.7%	30.0%	87.5%	85.7%	41.9%	84.6%	.125	.900	109	0.0
2021	MIA	MLB	31	4(0)	4²	0-0	0	4	0.86	1.93	62.5%	0.0%	23.5%	0.0%	38.5%	78.1%	80.0%	35.5%	54.5%	.308	.385	90	0.1
2022	LV	AAA	32	12(0)	22	1-0	1	20	1.00	3.27		2.2%	22.0%	0.0%	37.9%	65.1%	85.7%	35.0%	52.9%	.308	.422	89	0.3
2022	OAK	MLB	32	39(1)	55¹	0-1	1	38	1.03	4.23	52.4%	4.0%	17.0%	4.9%	46.0%	74.4%	82.3%	35.8%	65.7%	.224	.534	100	0.5
2023	LV	AAA	33	11(0)	16¹	1-1	0	18	1.10	2.76		7.6%	27.3%	3.0%	32.6%	72.2%	89.2%	34.2%	49.0%	.268	.512	99	0.1
2023	OAK	MLB	33	38(6)	48¹	2-6	0	30	1.16	2.98	46.1%	6.1%	15.3%	2.6%	36.6%	72.3%	87.1%	33.3%	69.2%	.264	.444	111	0.3
2024 non	OAK	MLB	34	58(0)	50	2-2	0	34	1.32	4.53	49.0%	6.1%	15.9%	3.2%	41.4%					.294	.524	103	0.1

2023 Arsenal: SL (87.7), FA (91.9), CU (81.1), SI (91.5), CH (87.4), SW (79.4)   *Comps: Brian Duensing (41), Javy Guerra (41), Craig Stammen (40)*

Pruitt, a modest and aging reliever who relies on generating soft contact and has never spent an entire year in the majors, had a career game last May 16 against the Diamondbacks. He strolled into the 10th inning and proceeded to pitch three innings—which meant a fresh-legged runner at second every time—and other than an intentional walk, he retired every batter he faced. His ninth and final out was a line-drive comebacker (accompanied by a large portion of bat helicoptering at his person) which he snagged while falling backwards. His team picked him up in the bottom half of the final inning with a walkoff single. That gave him a Win Probability Added of .916, the best by any pitcher in a single outing since 1996. His team then proceeded to lose their next 11 games.

JP Sears LHP Born: 02/19/96 Age: 28 Height: 5'11" Weight: 180 Origin: Round 11, 2017 Draft (#333 overall)

YEAR	TM	LVL	AGE	G (GS)	IP	W-L	SV	K	WHIP	ERA	CSP	BB%	K%	HR%	GB%	ZSw%	ZCon%	OSw%	OCon%	BABIP	SLGCON	DRA-	WARP
2021	SOM	AA	25	15(8)	50²	3-2	1	71	1.24	4.09		8.5%	33.6%	2.8%	47.5%					.351	.600	89	0.7
2021	SWB	AAA	25	10(10)	53¹	7-0	0	65	0.98	2.87		5.4%	31.9%	2.5%	39.8%					.298	.476	88	1.0
2022	SWB	AAA	26	11(9)	43	1-1	0	55	0.72	1.67		4.3%	33.7%	1.8%	41.0%					.216	.360	71	1.2
2022	NYY	MLB	26	7(2)	22	3-0	0	15	0.86	2.05	54.0%	6.0%	18.1%	1.2%	43.5%	64.3%	87.0%	28.0%	61.7%	.213	.328	116	0.0
2022	OAK	MLB	26	10(9)	48	3-3	0	36	1.48	4.69	54.3%	8.8%	17.6%	3.4%	39.3%	64.2%	88.0%	32.3%	69.1%	.322	.560	128	-0.2
2023	OAK	MLB	27	32(32)	172¹	5-14	0	161	1.26	4.54	49.0%	7.2%	21.9%	4.6%	29.5%	72.5%	80.5%	33.9%	66.4%	.279	.615	117	0.5
2024 DC	OAK	MLB	28	28(28)	148²	7-11	0	131	1.30	4.68	50.2%	7.3%	20.4%	3.8%	32.7%					.286	.570	107	0.7

2023 Arsenal: FA (93.2), SW (81.6), CH (84.3), SL (77.1), SI (91.6)   *Comps: Matthew Boyd (73), Steven Matz (67), Adam Plutko (65)*

As the game moves from a traditional rigid rotation to a cavalcade of multi-inning hurlers, pitching wins becomes a relic of the past. Also: Sears became the first starting pitcher to lead his team in wins with five since the 1899 Cleveland Spiders, a team that intentionally disposed of their best players. That sounds nothing like the A's, and is therefore a historical anomaly, right? Ownership is not to blame or take credit for Sears being a decent back-end starter who happened to be the *de facto* "ace." His entire pitch arsenal is solid, his walk-to-whiff rate is above-average and he uses every inch of the outfield dimensions with his changeup. He can round out a rotation, but probably shouldn't anchor one anytime soon.

Kirby Snead **LHP**   Born: 10/07/94   Age: 29   Height: 6'1"   Weight: 218   Origin: Round 10, 2016 Draft (#312 overall)

YEAR	TM	LVL	AGE	G(GS)	IP	W-L	SV	K	WHIP	ERA	CSP	BB%	K%	HR%	GB%	ZSw%	ZCon%	OSw%	OCon%	BABIP	SLGCON	DRA-	WARP
2021	BUF	AAA	26	36(1)	40	2-0	4	57	0.93	1.58		10.1%	36.1%	0.6%	59.0%					.244	.354	80	0.9
2021	TOR	MLB	26	7(0)	7²	0-1	0	7	1.17	2.35	52.6%	6.7%	23.3%	0.0%	35.0%	60.0%	87.5%	36.6%	69.2%	.350	.450	105	0.1
2022	LV	AAA	27	11(0)	13²	2-0	1	20	1.17	4.61		5.3%	35.1%	1.8%	51.5%	65.4%	83.8%	29.0%	34.5%	.375	.545	76	0.3
2022	OAK	MLB	27	46(0)	44²	1-1	1	35	1.75	5.84	53.6%	10.5%	16.7%	2.4%	43.0%	63.8%	86.3%	27.2%	68.1%	.352	.592	124	-0.1
2023	LV	AAA	28	23(0)	21¹	2-3	0	22	2.11	7.59		14.2%	19.5%	4.4%	48.6%	59.5%	87.6%	25.3%	61.5%	.369	.765	87	0.3
2023	OAK	MLB	28	15(0)	11²	1-2	0	9	1.71	4.63	49.1%	10.7%	16.1%	1.8%	46.3%	64.3%	87.0%	30.3%	57.6%	.325	.463	102	0.1
2024 non	OAK	MLB	29	58(0)	50	2-2	0	40	1.47	5.09	52.6%	10.2%	18.1%	3.0%	42.3%					.297	.526	112	-0.1

2023 Arsenal: SI (92.8), SL (81.3), CH (87.8)   *Comps: Tyler Webb (62), Yacksel Ríos (61), Scott Alexander (59)*

Snead is an aging lefty who gets a bunch of groundballs on a good day and faces one right-handed batter on a bad one. He has an effective slider to go with his signature sinker, but last year as a shoulder strain kept him out of action until June. Does any of that matter after he cut those extremely long blond locks? Baseball might be a game of numbers, but it is also an aesthetic endeavor. With his close-cropped coif, Snead looks like he has a job interview after the game instead of a righteous drum circle.

Ken Waldichuk **LHP**   Born: 01/08/98   Age: 26   Height: 6'4"   Weight: 220   Origin: Round 5, 2019 Draft (#165 overall)

YEAR	TM	LVL	AGE	G(GS)	IP	W-L	SV	K	WHIP	ERA	CSP	BB%	K%	HR%	GB%	ZSw%	ZCon%	OSw%	OCon%	BABIP	SLGCON	DRA-	WARP
2021	HV	A+	23	7(7)	30²	2-0	0	55	0.82	0.00		11.5%	48.7%	0.0%	31.1%					.267	.289	82	0.6
2021	SOM	AA	23	16(14)	79¹	4-3	0	108	1.29	4.20		11.2%	31.8%	3.8%	36.7%					.293	.618	87	1.2
2022	SOM	AA	24	6(6)	28²	4-0	0	46	0.91	1.26		8.9%	41.1%	1.8%	52.7%					.264	.436	78	0.7
2022	SWB	AAA	24	11(11)	47²	2-3	0	70	1.28	3.59		11.2%	34.0%	2.4%	40.7%					.333	.606	75	1.3
2022	LV	AAA	24	4(4)	18²	0-1	0	21	1.23	3.38		3.8%	26.6%	3.8%	38.9%	63.2%	82.6%	33.3%	48.4%	.333	.611	95	0.2
2022	OAK	MLB	24	7(7)	34²	2-2	0	33	1.21	4.93	53.7%	6.8%	22.6%	3.4%	36.4%	77.0%	82.7%	31.4%	60.4%	.287	.622	142	-0.3
2023	OAK	MLB	25	35(22)	141	4-9	1	132	1.56	5.36	46.1%	11.1%	20.7%	3.8%	40.1%	71.3%	84.5%	30.2%	58.6%	.313	.632	118	0.4
2024 DC	OAK	MLB	26	40(23)	125²	5-10	0	124	1.43	4.95	47.2%	10.5%	22.2%	3.3%	39.6%					.295	.562	110	0.4

2023 Arsenal: FA (93.6), SW (81.2), CH (84.4), CU (74.9)   *Comps: Matthew Boyd (81), Dillon Peters (73), Wade Miley (71)*

It's funny. So-called "doctors" all claim that walks are good for your health, but when your left-handed starter does it, suddenly it's bad for your heart? Science has refused to address this paradox. Waldichuk's horrendous May included more walks than innings, falling behind far too many batters for his sweeping slider to be of any use. He finished the season with positive steps, posting roughly league-average results for a team that barely aspires to average. His finest appearance was a hitless six-inning outing against the Astros. His manager slept good that night.

LINEOUTS

Hitters

HITTER	POS	TM	LVL	AGE	PA	R	HR	RBI	SB	AVG/OBP/SLG	BABIP	SLGCON	BB%	K%	ZSw%	ZCon%	OSw%	OCon%	LA	90th EV	DRC+	BRR	DRP	WARP
Miguel Andujar	RF	IND	AAA	28	465	63	16	86	5	.338/.404/.536	.358	.618	10.1%	11.8%	67.9%	88.2%	30.0%	67.0%			125	-2.9	-2.1	2.2
	RF	PIT	MLB	28	90	9	4	18	2	.250/.300/.476	.254	.563	6.7%	14.4%	66.9%	88.5%	40.6%	67.5%	5.7	103.5	105	0.0	-0.5	0.2
Jonah Bride	3B	LV	AAA	27	323	60	13	54	5	.305/.432/.544	.330	.671	17.3%	15.2%	40.5%	90.7%	23.3%	82.9%			124	-1.6	1.0	1.6
	3B	OAK	MLB	27	106	9	0	7	0	.170/.286/.205	.221	.273	10.4%	20.8%	48.5%	89.7%	24.2%	71.4%	5.2	100.0	85	-0.1	0.3	0.1
Brayan Buelvas	CF	STK	A	21	235	36	9	33	23	.290/.389/.515	.348	.691	13.2%	21.7%							124	0.4	-2.5	1.2
	CF	LAN	A+	21	123	6	2	10	8	.135/.211/.243	.181	.370	7.3%	30.9%							79	0.0	-0.4	0.1
	CF	MID	AA	21	83	13	1	19	0	.187/.241/.293	.236	.407	6.0%	25.3%							91	-0.6	-0.5	0.0
Brett Harris	3B	MID	AA	25	314	44	5	48	6	.283/.399/.426	.318	.509	12.7%	13.4%							124	-1.8	1.9	1.7
	3B	LV	AAA	25	147	19	4	14	4	.271/.347/.419	.316	.529	6.8%	18.4%	66.8%	93.6%	27.2%	52.4%			93	-0.5	3.8	0.5
Ryan Lasko	OF	ATH	ROK	21	30	3	0	3	1	.154/.233/.231	.182	.286	10.0%	16.7%											
Manny Piña	DH/C	LV	AAA	36	38	8	2	8	0	.324/.395/.559	.333	.655	7.9%	13.2%	57.1%	88.9%	28.9%	90.9%			111	-0.3	-0.1	0.1
	DH/C	OAK	MLB	36	12	1	1	1	0	.250/.250/.500	.250	.667	0.0%	25.0%	64.0%	100.0%	36.4%	62.5%	1.4	102.5	87	0.0	-0.1	0.0
Kevin Smith	SS/3B	LV	AAA	26	183	41	16	46	9	.324/.372/.653	.371	.917	7.1%	26.8%	69.9%	76.5%	35.8%	53.3%			107	0.8	-1.0	0.5
	SS/3B	OAK	MLB	26	146	15	5	11	1	.185/.220/.326	.253	.524	3.4%	34.9%	64.0%	79.2%	43.2%	55.1%	11.4	102.4	62	0.1	0.0	-0.2
Cody Thomas	RF	LV	AAA	28	477	67	23	109	5	.301/.361/.562	.338	.726	7.8%	20.3%	69.7%	84.5%	36.6%	65.3%			109	-0.5	4.2	2.4
	RF	OAK	MLB	28	46	1	1	2	0	.238/.304/.381	.375	.640	8.7%	37.0%	68.3%	73.2%	37.9%	54.5%	12.9	101.0	70	0.0	-0.2	-0.1

Remember when **Miguel Andújar** was considered for the Rookie of the Year Award over Shohei Ohtani? This former Bronx Bomber has almost bombed out of the league. ⊗ With an OPS nearly 500 points higher in the minor leagues than in the majors, infielder/emergency catcher **Jonah Bride** has definitely got that dog in him. (Specifically a Llasa apso, because it has triple A's.) ⊗ Swift-limbed Colombian center fielder **Brayan Buelvas** made it to Double-A after being aggressively promoted his entire career, and his batting line reflects that. His splits are slightly better against lefties, meaning he's a future platooner in the sense that Beetle Bailey is a future four-star general. ⊗ **Brett Harris** is too old to be a prospect and too young to be a senator, which means it's time to see what he can do in the majors. He will likely debut at third base this year, and could be the first position player from Gonzaga to play 50 career games since Jason Bay. ⊗ Thanks to two stints on the All-Big Ten team and Oakland's scouring of the mysterious turnpikes of New Jersey for prospects, **Ryan Lasko** became the highest draft pick from Rutgers University since Todd Frazier in 2007. ⊗ Ongoing issues with his non-throwing wrist have limited **Manny Piña** to nine games in the last two years. The career backup catcher can still swing the stick, but not with one arm, as entertaining as that would be to watch. ⊗ He hasn't translated his upward swing to any consistent power in the majors, but if **Kevin Smith** thrives in any two settings it's spring training and Las Vegas, just like your uncle. ⊗ Despite being a solid outfielder, **Cody Thomas** was not in Oakland's long- or short-term plans. After being outrighted off the roster, he proceeded to lead all of Triple-A with 109 RBI.

Pitchers

PITCHER	TM	LVL	AGE	G (GS)	IP	W-L	SV	K	WHIP	ERA	CSP	BB%	K%	HR%	GB%	ZSw%	ZCon%	OSw%	OCon%	BABIP	SLGCON	DRA-	WARP
Ryan Cusick	MID	AA	23	22 (22)	94¹	5-7	0	84	1.48	4.77		14.1%	20.7%	4.2%	39.2%					.268	.593	114	-0.8
Joey Estes	MID	AA	21	20 (17)	104²	6-6	0	100	1.10	3.28		7.2%	23.3%	3.3%	34.1%					.254	.514	106	0.9
	LV	AAA	21	7 (6)	32²	3-0	0	31	1.35	5.23		8.3%	21.5%	6.9%	34.3%	66.8%	85.0%	34.0%	70.2%	.247	.667	96	
	OAK	MLB	21	2 (2)	10	0-1	0	7	1.40	7.20	51.1%	4.3%	14.9%	8.5%	28.6%	72.1%	77.6%	39.2%	63.2%	.258	.771	129	0.0
Jeurys Familia	OAK	MLB	33	14 (0)	12²	0-1	2	9	2.05	6.39	45.4%	20.3%	14.1%	3.1%	53.7%	70.4%	81.2%	20.9%	48.5%	.289	.564	113	0.1
J.T. Ginn	MID	AA	24	6 (6)	22¹	1-2	0	11	1.79	8.06		12.0%	10.2%	1.9%	58.2%					.325	.545	129	-0.2
Zach Jackson	OAK	MLB	28	19 (0)	18	2-1	1	23	1.56	2.50	42.1%	12.5%	28.8%	1.3%	27.7%	66.9%	83.1%	28.9%	58.0%	.378	.500	98	0.2
Michael Kelly	COL	AAA	30	32 (0)	37²	1-3	2	58	1.59	3.58		12.8%	33.7%	1.7%	40.4%	55.8%	76.6%	32.4%	52.2%	.407	.667	84	0.9
	CLE	MLB	30	14 (0)	16²	1-0	0	16	1.32	3.78	48.3%	12.7%	22.5%	0.0%	39.1%	62.6%	84.7%	30.6%	64.6%	.283	.348	103	0.2
Easton Lucas	BOW	AA	26	11 (0)	17	1-0	0	24	0.76	1.59		6.5%	38.7%	3.2%	55.9%					.219	.500	72	0.5
	LV	AAA	26	15 (0)	16	0-0	0	13	2.00	5.62		5.3%	17.1%	3.9%	45.8%	70.8%	88.0%	31.6%	68.8%	.446	.793	80	0.1
	NOR	AAA	26	10 (0)	13²	0-0	1	14	1.39	4.61		15.0%	23.3%	6.7%	32.4%	76.0%	81.0%	31.5%	57.4%	.182	.730	104	0.1
	OAK	MLB	26	6 (0)	6²	0-0	0	7	2.10	8.10	46.5%	11.4%	20.0%	2.9%	37.5%	73.8%	81.2%	26.5%	63.6%	.391	.708	102	0.1
Sean Newcomb	SAC	AAA	30	18 (2)	31¹	0-1	0	40	1.40	3.16		15.3%	30.5%	1.5%	58.6%	60.2%	81.9%	26.1%	60.4%	.324	.500	72	0.7
	OAK	MLB	30	7 (2)	15	1-1	0	17	1.13	3.00	46.8%	14.8%	27.9%	1.6%	42.4%	62.0%	84.0%	31.4%	70.0%	.219	.394	97	0.2
Vinny Nittoli	SYR	AAA	32	19 (2)	22	0-1	1	25	1.59	5.73		13.4%	25.8%	9.3%	44.1%	66.2%	78.0%	27.8%	50.0%	.260	.862	93	0.4
	IOW	AAA	32	16 (0)	20²	1-1	0	22	1.21	3.48		7.8%	24.4%	2.2%	37.9%	60.5%	83.2%	24.8%	50.0%	.286	.509	100	0.3
	NYM	MLB	32	3 (0)	3²	0-0	0	3	1.09	2.45	48.4%	0.0%	20.0%	0.0%	27.3%	66.7%	92.9%	30.3%	60.0%	.364	.455	100	0.0
Spencer Patton	LV	AAA	35	44 (0)	46¹	4-2	5	50	1.47	4.66		11.0%	23.8%	1.9%	35.7%	64.1%	80.8%	33.7%	62.7%	.345	.587	88	0.7
	OAK	MLB	35	12 (0)	12¹	0-0	0	7	1.54	5.11	45.8%	10.9%	12.7%	5.5%	23.8%	69.4%	93.2%	28.3%	58.8%	.256	.675	120	0.0
Francisco Pérez	MID	AA	25	5 (0)	7¹	1-0	0	12	0.95	2.45		3.6%	42.9%	3.6%	33.3%					.357	.667	74	0.2
	LV	AAA	25	25 (0)	33¹	4-1	1	41	1.41	4.86		13.4%	28.9%	2.1%	45.7%	60.7%	82.4%	29.4%	42.5%	.321	.568	69	0.9
	OAK	MLB	25	17 (1)	16²	1-2	0	14	1.50	5.94	42.9%	10.8%	18.9%	0.0%	37.3%	74.3%	82.1%	31.8%	66.1%	.333	.500	109	0.1
Yacksel Ríos	GWN	AAA	30	22 (0)	25¹	1-2	7	30	0.87	2.49		8.1%	30.3%	2.0%	25.4%	72.9%	73.6%	29.0%	60.3%	.214	.393	99	0.4
	OAK	MLB	30	3 (0)	1²	0-0	0	2	5.40	37.80	41.0%	42.9%	14.3%	7.1%	33.3%	65.0%	76.9%	20.5%	50.0%	.400	1.000	113	0.0
Drew Rucinski	LV	AAA	34	3 (3)	9²	1-1	0	8	1.76	6.52		10.6%	17.0%	0.0%	37.5%	68.7%	84.8%	34.2%	68.4%	.364	.406	141	-0.2
	OAK	MLB	34	4 (4)	18	0-4	0	6	2.28	9.00	46.5%	14.7%	6.3%	5.3%	43.2%	61.3%	90.5%	26.8%	61.4%	.319	.653	136	-0.1
Royber Salinas	MID	AA	22	18 (16)	67¹	1-5	1	89	1.34	5.48		10.8%	30.9%	3.1%	39.5%					.316	.600	80	1.4
Chad Smith	LV	AAA	28	35 (0)	34²	1-3	4	42	2.00	7.53		17.3%	24.3%	3.5%	48.5%	66.5%	85.8%	28.3%	53.2%	.387	.649	92	0.5
	OAK	MLB	28	10 (0)	13²	1-2	0	9	1.61	6.59	49.3%	11.7%	15.0%	3.3%	54.8%	71.3%	81.8%	20.7%	72.4%	.325	.548	100	0.2
Mitch Spence	SWB	AAA	25	29 (29)	163	8-8	0	153	1.32	4.47		7.5%	21.8%	4.3%	49.7%	68.9%	86.3%	33.8%	49.6%	.288	.579	78	4.3
Freddy Tarnok	LV	AAA	24	5 (5)	19²	1-1	0	11	1.17	1.83		13.9%	13.9%	2.5%	31.6%	71.7%	81.3%	26.7%	70.4%	.182	.351	122	0.0
	OAK	MLB	24	5 (1)	14²	1-1	0	14	1.50	4.91	43.2%	16.9%	21.5%	6.2%	25.0%	76.0%	87.3%	27.5%	64.0%	.194	.675	115	0.1

Standing in at 6-foot-6, **Ryan Cusick** has a starter's build and a reliever's walk rate. It might be time to try out that fastball in the late innings. ⓧ **Steven Echavarria**, New Jersey's top high school player features mid-90s gas and excellent breaking pitches. He signed the 2023 draft's highest over-slot deal, setting the price for not making someone to go college; make your own student loan joke here. ⓧ **Joey Estes** has the upside of a back-of-the-rotation arm but more likely slots into an up-and-down role. Luckily for him, Oakland's planned move to Las Vegas should cut down on the travel. ⓧ In what may have been **Jeurys Familia**'s major-league denouement, the former 50-save closer had a relief victory revoked by the scorekeeper due to ineffectiveness. Two days later he walked four straight Mets, and three weeks later he was released from his second organization of the year. ⓧ After a tumultuous start, a mid-May forearm injury sidelined **J.T. Ginn** for multiple months before he returned to Double-A with promising results. Is this a description of his 2022 season or his 2023 season? The answer is "yes." ⓧ An elbow strain and an appendectomy kept **Zach Jackson** off the mound for most of the year—a shame, given batters were unable to square up his fastball for the month he wasn't constantly pointing to where it hurts. ⓧ After years of toiling in the minors, the 2011 first-round pick **Michael Kelly** performed admirably in a few short stints in the Guardians' bullpen, reinventing himself as a sweeper-heavy reliever. The 31-year old is a bit older than your typical up/down reliever—his most recent and only *Annual* appearance was in 2012—but he gets the job done just as well. ⓧ Left-handed late bloomer **Easton Lucas** stifled southpaws with an assortment of average pitches and even contributed to a minor-league no-hitter with two perfect innings. That led Oakland to acquire him for Shintaro Fujinami, after which he participated in several combined many-hitters. ⓧ Fourth-rounder **Cole Miller** is a extremely large right-handed teenager who offers a low 90s fastball with good movement, a nice slider, and a work-in-progress change. ⓧ For the first time since 1990, the A's and Giants completed a player-for-player trade. It was good news for diplomatic relations between the two Bay Area franchises, but bad news for **Sean Newcomb** as it means he's in the *Now You're On the Athletics* phase of his career. ⓧ As seems to be the case with many pitchers, **Vinny Nittoli** picked up a sweeper while in the Yankees' organization. Unfortunately, his new pitch didn't seem to help out his results that much and he once again stands to be on the fringes of a roster, looking for a fourth cup of coffee in as many years. ⓧ In limited action, journeyman reliever **Spencer Patton** finished with a 5.11 ERA to keep his career ERA at 5.11. PECOTA could phone this one in, but its technology has surpassed the use of landlines. ⓧ He's got the slider down, but young lefty **Francisco Pérez** hasn't found a complementary pitch for it. His latest attempt is a sinking fastball, but opponents hit .427 against it and therefore enjoyed it very much, tipping 25% and giving their compliments to the chef. ⓧ **Yacksel Ríos** is coming off surgery to repair a shoulder aneurysm, which caused blood clots to cascade into his pitching hand and induce numbness in his fingers. He was phenomenal a year ago during Puerto Rico winter ball, threw 3 ⅔ shutout innings in the World Baseball Classic, and was a formidable Triple-A reliever, but none of that has ever translated to major-league success for him. ⓧ A knee injury coupled with spinal lumbar surgery took **Drew Rucinski** from a KBO reclamation project to Cavity Sam in a few short months. Assuming he's all bandaged up, the 35-year-old righty will try to get through a full season without his nose flashing red. ⓧ There's an argument to be made for staying patient with professional thrower **Royber Salinas** to see if he progresses into a starter. There are also several bullpens in dire need of strikeout artists. Teach the controversy. ⓧ Normally a high-strikeout/high-walk tightrope act, **Chad Smith** was ineffective in a small sampling of innings, and equally ineffective in a large sample of minor-league games. Always sample before you try. ⓧ **Mitch Spence** is never going to be confused with Spencer Strider. He gets by with a low-90s fastball and a bevy of curves and cutters that led to a near-even ground-ball rate. He ultimately ended the year on the outside of the Yankees' patchwork rotation looking in, which might be for the best given how often Triple-A hitters put his non-grounders over the fence. ⓧ A shoulder sprain and a hip injury limited **Freddy Tarnok** to six starts last year. While his secondary selections were on point, his good hard fastball landed middle-middle far too often. Whether it's on a big league mound or in Congress, unabashed centrism is no way to make a living.

PHILADELPHIA PHILLIES

Essay by Kelsey McKinney

Player comments by Alex Chamberlain and BP staff

The 2023 Philadelphia Phillies came out of spring training sleepy, grumpy and playing terribly. They were kicking groundballs. They were striking out on pitch clock violations. They lost 6 of their first 10 games. This was the team that went to the World Series in 2022? Them?

Everyone was worried except for me, because I understood that the Phillies were first and foremost a vibes-based team, and I know that a vibe is a very precarious and special thing. Like a flame it must be sparked, and nourished, and never ever smothered. It must be given oxygen so that it can grow strong, and it should not burn too fast and too bright or it will die. Not all teams are vibes-based teams, but *this* one was.

By the All-Star break, things were a little better. The team was 48-41, which isn't an awful record, but they were 12 games back, and the games they lost, they lost terribly: never got that crucial hit, dropped a fly ball or forgot where the runners were. Sloppy, embarrassing: bad vibes.

Perhaps it will be helpful, before we continue, for me to explain how I think about baseball teams. To me, there are three axes on which to judge a team. First, is the team talented or untalented? This one is simple: either the team is talented in parts or it is not. For example, any team with Shohei Ohtani is a talented team, almost regardless of who else is there. The next axis is cohesion. Is the team harmonious? Do the members, in general, like each other? A team which is talented but incohesive will win fewer games than they are capable of, like 2023's New York Yankees or Cincinnati Reds. The Texas Rangers last year were both a talented team and a cohesive team. That can be a winning combination, but it fully depends on what is happening with the third axis.

The final axis is more complicated because it is more difficult to measure, and is the most powerful of them all. The third axis is what I call "volatility." At the bottom of the volatility axis is "ancient curse." Teams who are ancient cursed will always fight uphill no matter how talented or cohesive they are. Think: New York Mets, the Hanshin Tigers (until last year). The Atlanta Braves, a supremely talented and cohesive team, have proven themselves in the last two postseasons to be on the cursed end of this axis—a fate to which the Dodgers have become accustomed. You might

PHILADELPHIA PHILLIES PROSPECTUS
2023 W-L: 90-72, 2ND IN NL EAST

Pythag	.551	12th	DER	.697	15th
RS/G	4.91	8th	DRC+	100	13th
RA/G	4.41	12th	DRA-	90	3rd
dWin%	.562	7th	FIP	4.01	6th
Payroll	$243M	4th	B-Age	28.9	17th
M$/MW	$5.4M	19th	P-Age	30.1	27th

- Opened 2004
- Open air
- Natural surface
- Fence profile: 6' to 19'

Park Factors

Runs	Runs/RH	Runs/LH	HR/RH	HR/LH
102	101	102	109	111

Top Hitter WARP	3.6 Bryce Harper
Top Pitcher WARP	4.5 Zack Wheeler
2023 Top Prospect	Andrew Painter

Payroll History (in millions)

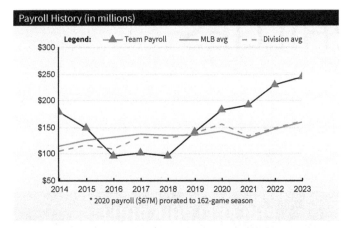

Legend: Team Payroll — MLB avg - - Division avg

* 2020 payroll ($67M) prorated to 162-game season

Future Commitments (in millions)

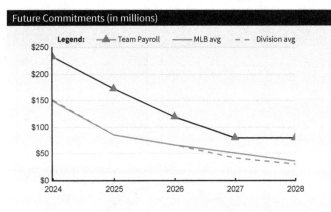

Legend: Team Payroll — MLB avg - - Division avg

Farm System Ranking

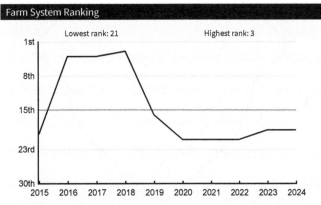

Lowest rank: 21   Highest rank: 3

Personnel

President, Baseball Operations
Dave Dombrowski

Vice President, General Manager
Sam Fuld

Assistant General Manager
Anirudh Kilambi

Assistant General Manager
Ned Rice

Assistant General Manager
Jorge Velandia

Manager
Rob Thomson

BP Alumni
Alex Rosen

expect "blessed" to be at the other end of the volatility axis, but you would be wrong. The baseball gods are cruel. They are relentless. They do not bless anyone. The best they can give you are vibes.

Take the Arizona Diamondbacks, the villain of this story. They too had high volatility, a vibe team, through and through. They're a young team, filled with quality players. They, too, beat a cursed team in the first round before arriving in the NLDS. But they showed up weak; vibes lost. They got destroyed in the first two games in Philadelphia, but when the vibes shifted, they hit four home runs in Game 3 at home. That kind of inconsistency is the hallmark of a vibes-based team. Of course, then the Diamondbacks lost to the Rangers in the World Series. The hot streak cannot last forever. When the vibe is misaligned, these teams are stupidly, embarrassingly bad. But when they are good...damn are they good.

Because I moved to Philadelphia at the very beginning of 2022, I have been a Phillies fan for two seasons. I have always chosen to root for the home team. But I do not intend to move again, so I plan to die a Phillies fan. I committed to this team the way a teen girl commits to a heartthrob, instantly, bodily, forever. I bought a season-ticket pack. I bought a Nick Castellanos jersey. I followed all of their wives on Instagram. And because I am famously blessed as a fan, the team has been good since my arrival. But they have also been unbelievably vibes-based.

I watched probably 120 of the 162 regular-season games last year. I attended 25. So I am more than qualified to tell you that no team has ever been closer to the top of the volatility axis. At no point in the 2023 season were the Philadelphia Phillies in first place in their division, which meant that it was never exactly a comfortable season to experience as a fan. Vibes-based teams are never comfortable, but that's part of what makes them so much fun.

A constant aura of fun and mischief permeated this team. Players began, at the beginning of the season, making a motion to indicate big balls (two hands moving up and down with various levels of aggression and size based on the hit). Everyone on the team, even the more reserved guys, did this when someone hit a double. The youngest players on the team (second baseman Bryson Stott, third baseman Alec Bohm and outfielder Brandon Marsh) were affectionately dubbed "the Phillies Daycare" in 2022. But the Daycare began committing "crimes" in 2023. The crimes were adding little bubblegums and snacks to cups of water, which they poured down the jerseys of whoever was being interviewed by the local broadcaster after the game. That's vibes behavior.

There are more examples. In a big-screen in-game video that premiered at the beginning of the season, Castellanos confidently declared that his favorite superhero was Scooby-Doo and, when pressed on it by a reporter, he doubled down, elaborating, "He's a dog who can talk." Castellanos also appeared to be the team's trend-setter in unbuttoning his jersey down to his sternum. Soon after, Bohm began to unbutton his jersey. Then so did Bryson Stott and new Phillie Trea Turner. When rookie Johan Rojas took the field sometime in August, video captured Castellanos helping to unbutton his jersey in the outfield, the better to help him "loosen up and chill out." When I reported a story on the team's consistently unbuttoned jerseys for Defector in October, Jess Castellanos (Nick's wife) read him the article aloud.

All of this silliness is the behavior of a vibes-based team with the vibes on their side. And boy were the vibes on their side. There is perhaps no better big example of the power of vibes on this team than the fairytale of Trea Turner.

Turner arrived in Philadelphia at the beginning of the season fresh from Los Angeles (cursed). He was signed to an 11-year, $300 million contract, a promise (most likely) to finish his career in Philadelphia. Turner is an incredible shortstop. He jumps high into the air like a spider monkey. He sprawls out for a racing groundball long and lean like a gazelle. He has a swing so beautiful and smooth it would move me to tears if I weren't so busy screaming. And when he arrived in Philadelphia, he forgot how to do all of those things instantly. He kicked groundballs. He whiffed easy pitches. In July, I listened to the girls behind me at the game yell "earn your paycheck; earn our love," at him over and over again. I wouldn't have known that he could hear them for sure if Bohm hadn't turned over his shoulder to glare. The vibes were not with Trea Turner. But vibes can change.

All of this culminated on August 2, in Miami, in a game where Turner went 0-for-5 and, in the 11th inning, missed a completely catchable groundball to cost the Phillies the game. He was at that point in the season batting .237 with 10 home runs and 34 RBIs.

Part of rooting for a vibes-based team, though, is understanding that while vibes are delicate, they can be fixed. Fans knew this, and on August 4 (the next home game), they gave Turner a standing ovation just for coming to the plate, a show of faith. He hit a home run. Over the rest of the season, he batted .337 with 16 homers and 42 RBIs. The magic was restored. On August 9, Michael Lorenzen, acquired at the trade deadline, threw a no-hitter at home. He wore Vans.

For all of August and September, the vibes were impeccable. By the time the Phillies arrived in the Wild Card Series to play the Marlins, it felt like they would never lose again despite having gone just 15-13 in September. I attended Game 2 of that series at Citizens Bank Park in Philadelphia. I have been to dozens of parks, attended playoff games for several different teams and even a few World Series games. I have never felt anything like the energy in the park that night. My cells felt like they might vibrate out of my body. People were kissing (with tongue!) after strikeouts in the first inning. The men behind me were high-fiving everyone they could reach for every single strike. I stood the whole time.

When Bryson Stott's bat shot the ball deep into right field for a grand slam in the bottom of the sixth inning, the stadium shook from people jumping. I should have gone hoarse from screaming so much, but the good vibes spared me. Nothing bad could happen. I couldn't sleep when I got home, my adrenaline was so high. I stayed up late watching clips of the team celebrating in the clubhouse. Plastic walls had been installed, as had a new floor. Team staff was opening dozens of cases of Budweiser. Turner was carrying around an entire handle of expensive tequila. Garrett Stubbs, backup catcher and vibesmith, was wearing overalls with the team logo on them, shirtless, with no fewer than 15 beer cans shoved into the pockets. He had an empty beer box on his head.

The team's post-game playlist, composed by Stubbs and designated hitter Kyle Schwarber, is on Spotify.[1] It is public. It is titled "Phils Win [dancing man emoji]" and includes the songs "Dicked Down in Dallas" by Trey Lewis, "My Dick" by Mickey Avalon and also "My Humps" by the Black Eyed Peas. The playlist is 6 hours and 21 minutes long. Say what you want about a vibes-based team, but they know how to party. When they beat Atlanta in the NLDS, for the second year in a row rendering a Braves NL East title hollow, I woke up with the worst hangover I've had in years and a smile plastered on my face that wouldn't leave for days.

But there is a reason that the volatility axis does not end in blessed. No team can ride the vibes forever. The vibes, as promised, are delicate. On my worst days, I choose to blame reliever Craig Kimbrel for the death of the vibes in the NLCS against the Arizona Diamondbacks. That's not entirely fair, though. The Phillies won Game 2, 10-0, and perhaps that exhausted what was left of the vibes. In that whole series, three of the team's best batters (Turner, Castellanos and Bryce Harper) went a combined 10-for-72. You cannot win a series, much less a World Series, with numbers like that.

The whole day before Game 7, I felt sick to my stomach. There's a deep kind of sports dread that can squish the diaphragm just right, so that you feel short of breath and nauseous all at the same time. The Philadelphia Phillies—my team, my guys—were not looking good. All day, I debated whether or not to use the tickets we had for the game. Sure, it was the first Game 7 in Philadelphia in the team's history, but something was off. We decided to go on the off chance that the ever-fickle vibes would return. The energy in the stadium was different, though. There was a permeating sense of dread. Everyone tried. We clapped and yelled so much. But you could feel that everyone knew it was over, even the team.

I wasn't surprised when they lost, and I wasn't mad. I was sad; not because I thought that winning the World Series would cure every mental illness I've ever had (though I hold out hope for that possibility), but because walking out of the stadium, I already missed them.

The baseball season is so long; 162 games is so many. Your team, whoever they are, plays almost every single day, and there is a liturgy to that. Unlike in other sports, you expect your team to lose. Losing is part of the deal. Even the best team in 2023 lost almost 60 games. Part of what I love about baseball as a sport is that it is communal. You commune with the team, these players you do not know and who do not know you, every single day. You watch them do their routines and rituals, make their plays and laugh and pout. The whole community sees it, as often as they can tune in. Fans care together. A team like this is an excuse to share emotions, more than anything else: to be happy in community, and sad in community.

In a late-season game, a new man sat behind my seats. He looked at his watch at 8:00 p.m. The Philies were down by one run. "Well," he said to everyone nearby, "it's the winning hour now." And when the Phillies came up to bat, Alec Bohm hit a home run on the first pitch. They were just that kind of team. The magic lived within them, and so often, it felt like their magic lived inside us as well.

While it's painful to root for a vibes-based team at times, it was also the most fun I've ever had with a team. This offseason has been longer than any I can remember since childhood. Perhaps a vibes-based team will always feel more communal because it is so easy to believe that we, the fans, matter too. Would Trea Turner have recovered without us? Maybe he would have, but it's so easy to believe that we, the fans, saved him. That's the narrative, but it also might be the truth. The magic has to be cultivated and maintained by all of us. And with almost all of this team returning for 2024, the vibes can reign once again. I cannot wait for them to return.

—Kelsey McKinney is a co-owner of Defector.

---

1. *https://open.spotify.com/playlist/78T1y2ulJlT3dhanfg5Y1v?si=3f42a4aef94344b8*

HITTERS

William Bergolla MI Born: 10/20/04   Age: 19   Bats: L   Throws: R   Height: 5'11"   Weight: 165   Origin: IFA, 2022

YEAR	TM	LVL	AGE	PA	R	HR	RBI	SB	AVG/OBP/SLG	BABIP	SLGCON	BB%	K%	ZSw%	ZCon%	OSw%	OCon%	LA	90th EV	DRC+	BRR	DRP	WARP
2022	DSL PHW	ROK	17	83	18	0	14	2	.380/.470/.423	.397	.441	13.3%	3.6%										
2023	CLR	A	18	228	26	0	20	2	.255/.351/.286	.275	.314	13.2%	7.5%	65.8%	98.3%	22.3%	88.5%			109	-2.9	1.2	0.9
2024 non	PHI	MLB	19	251	18	1	18	0	.209/.271/.280	.229	.316	7.2%	10.0%							57	0.0	0	-0.6

2023 GP: 2B (32), SS (22), DH (1)   *Comps: Luis Urías (70), Wilfredo Tovar (66), Reinaldo Ilarraza (65)*

It's impossible to know who the next Luis Arraez is, but Bergolla does a fine impression. The eponymous son of the former major leaguer, 18-year-old Bergolla has more than twice as many walks as strikeouts as a pro. His microscopic 2.2% swinging-strike rate paced the low minors among hitters with his number of plate appearances. His .031 isolated power, on the other hand, did, uh, whatever the opposite of pacing is. His precariously low .638 OPS speaks to the thumplessness of his bat—he barely hits doubles, let alone home runs, the latter of which he predictably has none—and at 5-foot-11, 165 pounds, it's hard to know how much more he'll fill out. It's clear, though, that the hit tool is advanced, regardless of his age and especially because of it. That, and his impressive defense at a premium position, can carry him up the organizational ladder. Check back in half a decade to see if he's being uttered in the same breath as Ted Williams some sweltering July.

Alec Bohm CI Born: 08/03/96   Age: 27   Bats: R   Throws: R   Height: 6'5"   Weight: 218   Origin: Round 1, 2018 Draft (#3 overall)

YEAR	TM	LVL	AGE	PA	R	HR	RBI	SB	AVG/OBP/SLG	BABIP	SLGCON	BB%	K%	ZSw%	ZCon%	OSw%	OCon%	LA	90th EV	DRC+	BRR	DRP	WARP
2021	LHV	AAA	24	68	8	1	6	3	.271/.353/.407	.341	.545	10.3%	22.1%							99	0.2	-0.4	0.2
2021	PHI	MLB	24	417	46	7	47	4	.247/.305/.342	.327	.483	7.4%	26.6%	74.7%	77.2%	30.8%	67.2%	5.8	105.6	76	-0.4	-0.1	0.1
2022	PHI	MLB	25	631	79	13	72	2	.280/.315/.398	.319	.489	4.9%	17.4%	74.2%	84.6%	35.6%	70.8%	10.4	104.8	104	-1.2	-1.1	1.6
2023	PHI	MLB	26	611	74	20	97	4	.274/.327/.437	.296	.526	6.9%	15.4%	69.9%	89.3%	34.9%	70.7%	11.4	104.8	124	-0.6	-2.8	3.1
2024 DC	PHI	MLB	27	568	58	13	61	4	.268/.325/.394	.301	.473	7.0%	15.4%							104	-0.7	-2	1.5

2023 GP: 3B (90), 1B (80), DH (3)   *Comps: Pablo Sandoval (64), Alex Bregman (63), Brooks Robinson (61)*

Bohm finally turned the corner offensively. He remains a free-swinger, but his contact skills have improved markedly each year, both in and out of the zone. It all culminated in career-best plate discipline coupled with career-best power, a long time coming for the former first-rounder who flashed an advanced hit tool in the Cape Cod League and demonstrated a feel for contact in the minors. "Career-best power" carries profound baggage, though, for someone whose raw once graded out plus, maybe even double-plus. Since his debut, Bohm's hard-hit rate ranks in the upper quartile, but his barrel rate ranks in the bottom third. A persistent and fundamental inability to elevate, especially to the pull side, underscores his failure—inability? refusal?—to capitalize. Development isn't linear, and it's important to celebrate the synthesis of this franchise cornerstone's two best tools. Let's also not overlook his modest glow-up at the hot corner, with his arm scrounging together defensive value to offset his poor range. Bohm's arrow points up, but it's easy to see how he's capped and hard not to feel like it's self-imposed.

Nick Castellanos   RF   Born: 03/04/92   Age: 32   Bats: R   Throws: R   Height: 6'4"   Weight: 203   Origin: Round 1, 2010 Draft (#44 overall)

YEAR	TM	LVL	AGE	PA	R	HR	RBI	SB	AVG/OBP/SLG	BABIP	SLGCON	BB%	K%	ZSw%	ZCon%	OSw%	OCon%	LA	90th EV	DRC+	BRR	DRP	WARP
2021	CIN	MLB	29	585	95	34	100	3	.309/.362/.576	.340	.746	7.0%	20.7%	79.2%	83.3%	40.7%	53.4%	14.3	105.6	116	-0.1	0.5	2.9
2022	PHI	MLB	30	558	56	13	62	7	.263/.305/.389	.326	.518	5.2%	23.3%	78.3%	80.6%	42.7%	52.4%	14.8	102.5	93	0.1	-3.0	0.8
2023	PHI	MLB	31	671	79	29	106	11	.272/.311/.476	.337	.676	5.4%	27.6%	76.1%	81.1%	43.0%	45.2%	14.6	105.0	83	-0.1	-2.2	0.0
2024 DC	PHI	MLB	32	584	63	21	73	5	.247/.299/.421	.313	.596	6.0%	27.6%							98	-0.2	-3.4	0.9

2023 GP: RF (148), DH (8)   *Comps: George Hendrick (71), Roberto Clemente (70), Adam Jones (69)*

In 2021 Castellanos synchronized his most-productive campaign with his foray into free agency, and the Walk Year™ narrative lived to see another day. Casty then succeeded what was possibly his career-best year with arguably his career-worst, at least since his early days in Detroit. It's not exactly the way one dreams of kicking off a five-year, nine-figure contract in a new city with newfound playoff aspirations.Castellanos' quality of contact mostly recovered last year. His hard-hit and barrel rates rebounded, and he tamped down a suddenly unsightly pop-up rate. The *frequency* of contact, though, eroded alarmingly, due largely to increasingly poor swing decisions. Castellanos historically has been hyper-aggressive, which is fine if the swing decision tree adds value. If it doesn't, the swings themselves better unleash hell consistently. The outfielder revealed that he hears an "evil" voice in his head when he's at the plate; maybe he needs to find the hidden angel that wants him to leave the bat on his shoulder.

Jake Cave   LF   Born: 12/04/92   Age: 31   Bats: L   Throws: L   Height: 6'0"   Weight: 200   Origin: Round 6, 2011 Draft (#209 overall)

YEAR	TM	LVL	AGE	PA	R	HR	RBI	SB	AVG/OBP/SLG	BABIP	SLGCON	BB%	K%	ZSw%	ZCon%	OSw%	OCon%	LA	90th EV	DRC+	BRR	DRP	WARP
2021	STP	AAA	28	36	6	1	5	0	.367/.472/.500	.526	.750	13.9%	27.8%							98	-0.4	0.3	0.1
2021	MIN	MLB	28	178	14	3	13	1	.189/.249/.293	.283	.471	5.6%	34.8%	68.5%	80.5%	27.4%	42.3%	8.2	101.5	60	-0.1	-0.7	-0.3
2022	STP	AAA	29	373	63	14	57	10	.273/.370/.509	.343	.716	11.5%	24.9%							107	0.7	-6.8	0.9
2022	MIN	MLB	29	177	17	5	20	2	.213/.260/.384	.268	.548	6.2%	27.7%	73.0%	77.3%	34.9%	46.9%	14.9	104.3	90	0.1	0.6	0.4
2023	LHV	AAA	30	275	61	16	49	2	.346/.429/.684	.395	.895	11.3%	20.4%	73.2%	83.5%	32.4%	60.1%			132	3.5	3.6	2.5
2023	PHI	MLB	30	203	18	5	21	3	.212/.272/.348	.270	.496	7.4%	27.1%	66.7%	82.2%	33.3%	58.0%	15.4	103.0	83	0.1	0.1	0.1
2024 DC	PHI	MLB	31	186	19	5	21	2	.230/.303/.397	.288	.540	8.2%	24.9%							92	0.0	-0.2	0.3

2023 GP: LF (35), 1B (17), RF (11), CF (1), DH (1)   *Comps: Alex Presley (50), Timo Perez (49), Roger Bernadina (47)*

It's all just an elaborate bit. Right? It has to be. Cave, who owns a .926 OPS at Triple-A since 2017, including a career-best 1.113 OPS at the level last year, mustered another lackluster installment at the major-league level. Plato's favorite ballplayer fulfilled his obligation as the guy who relieves Kyle Schwarber in left field to keep his glove off the field but his bat in the lineup. He did just enough damage against righties to make the endeavor worthwhile—which, presumably, is just enough to land him *another* part-time gig with a club needing to fill the strong ("strong," in air quotes) side of a platoon at a corner outfield or infield spot. Inevitably he'll latch on somewhere, where he'll attempt yet another time to break the shackles of the "Quad-A" moniker.

Kody Clemens   1B   Born: 05/15/96   Age: 28   Bats: L   Throws: R   Height: 6'1"   Weight: 200   Origin: Round 3, 2018 Draft (#79 overall)

YEAR	TM	LVL	AGE	PA	R	HR	RBI	SB	AVG/OBP/SLG	BABIP	SLGCON	BB%	K%	ZSw%	ZCon%	OSw%	OCon%	LA	90th EV	DRC+	BRR	DRP	WARP
2021	TOL	AAA	25	413	66	18	59	4	.247/.312/.466	.278	.625	8.7%	22.8%							105	0.1	6.1	2.1
2022	TOL	AAA	26	264	41	13	43	5	.274/.327/.535	.333	.759	7.6%	26.9%							105	1.5	0.4	1.1
2022	DET	MLB	26	127	13	5	17	1	.145/.197/.308	.148	.429	6.3%	26.0%	71.2%	81.0%	38.0%	60.4%	17.8	102.5	73	0.0	0.0	-0.1
2023	LHV	AAA	27	279	51	18	52	7	.256/.373/.564	.264	.750	15.4%	20.8%	65.1%	83.9%	25.4%	62.0%			124	1.5	-0.9	1.3
2023	PHI	MLB	27	148	15	4	13	0	.230/.277/.367	.295	.515	5.4%	27.0%	64.0%	80.3%	32.8%	57.5%	15.3	102.5	73	0.1	0.1	-0.1
2024 DC	PHI	MLB	28	28	3	1	4	0	.230/.299/.424	.271	.579	8.1%	24.0%							95	0.0	0	0.0

2023 GP: 1B (39), P (4), DH (2), SS (1), RF (1)   *Comps: Tyler Greene (53), Shawn O'Malley (51), Breyvic Valera (51)*

Clemens spent his first spring training as a Phillie working with hitting coach Kevin Long to close his stance and quiet his load. The ensuing change was spectacular: As an Iron Pig, Clemens put together a career-best line fueled by a rare combination of exceptional power and plate discipline: He dropped his swinging-strike rate into the single digits and more than doubled his walk rate. His fly-ball rate steepened and his BABIP plunged, underscoring the pitfalls of elevating *too* much. But the trade-off, per his 124 DRC+, was worth it. He was reborn. With rumblings of Bryce Harper possibly manning first base full-time post-Rhys Hoskins, it could be an enormous boon if Clemens capably filled this vacancy and enabled Harper to patrol a corner outfield spot where the Phillies endure mounting liabilities. It's a longer shot than it sounds: Clemens' limited Statcast data last year betrayed any evidence of his renaissance. The Phillies may ask for sustained excellence to lend further validation to his breakout. At the very least he's now much more than organizational filler.

Justin Crawford   CF   Born: 01/13/04   Age: 20   Bats: L   Throws: R   Height: 6'1"   Weight: 175   Origin: Round 1, 2022 Draft (#17 overall)

YEAR	TM	LVL	AGE	PA	R	HR	RBI	SB	AVG/OBP/SLG	BABIP	SLGCON	BB%	K%	ZSw%	ZCon%	OSw%	OCon%	LA	90th EV	DRC+	BRR	DRP	WARP
2022	PHI	ROK	18	43	6	0	5	8	.297/.395/.351	.355	.419	11.6%	14.0%										
2023	CLR	A	19	308	51	3	60	40	.344/.399/.478	.413	.592	8.1%	17.2%	76.0%	85.7%	37.2%	65.7%			115	2.4	-3.2	1.2
2023	JS	A+	19	82	20	0	4	7	.288/.366/.425	.368	.544	8.5%	19.5%							99	0.8	-1.4	0.1
2024 non	PHI	MLB	20	251	19	2	20	0	.223/.273/.317	.289	.418	5.7%	23.2%							65	0.0	0	-0.2

2023 GP: CF (77), DH (10)   *Comps: Estevan Florial (73), Jahmai Jones (66), Ronald Acuña Jr. (64)*

Prep outfielders are a fickle bunch, especially ones drafted by the Phillies. So it's reassuring that, after a summer of limited reps, Crawford got in a full season and performed admirably. His swing, aggressive but contact-oriented, produced a fairly robust OBP. His baserunning and fielding were as advertised (read: impressive). This is the part where we tell you he's Carl's son. The downside is Crawford hit only three home runs. That's arguably a *good* outcome, too, because he basically never hits the ball in the air (his 14% fly-ball rate is unfathomably low); his launch angle is so low it leaves one with an impression that he has a vendetta against the earth. The upshot, though, is that keeping the ball on the ground with plus-plus speed can play up a profile devoid of power. Crawford hit 33 extra-base hits in just 87 games and managed to record an ISO that starts with a 1, which, given the circumstances, is remarkable. However, the path to stardom for an outfielder carried by his legs and glove is not without its obstacles, even ones of their own making.

Darick Hall 1B
Born: 07/25/95   Age: 28   Bats: L   Throws: R   Height: 6'4"   Weight: 232   Origin: Round 14, 2016 Draft (#407 overall)

YEAR	TM	LVL	AGE	PA	R	HR	RBI	SB	AVG/OBP/SLG	BABIP	SLGCON	BB%	K%	ZSw%	ZCon%	OSw%	OCon%	LA	90th EV	DRC+	BRR	DRP	WARP
2021	LHV	AAA	25	471	46	14	60	0	.230/.338/.403	.270	.537	11.7%	21.2%							108	-3.3	4.6	1.5
2022	LHV	AAA	26	443	59	28	88	6	.254/.330/.528	.268	.707	9.5%	22.6%							129	-2.5	-1.8	2.3
2022	PHI	MLB	26	142	19	9	16	0	.250/.282/.522	.301	.772	3.5%	31.0%	73.8%	81.1%	35.6%	42.2%	18.8	106.7	85	0.0	0.0	0.1
2023	LHV	AAA	27	334	46	18	57	0	.311/.395/.545	.341	.706	12.6%	19.5%	71.3%	85.7%	30.7%	53.8%			117	-2.4	1.5	1.2
2023	PHI	MLB	27	56	2	1	3	0	.167/.196/.241	.229	.361	3.6%	32.1%	78.7%	81.4%	39.7%	67.4%	13.4	108.0	66	0.0	0.0	-0.1
2024 DC	PHI	MLB	28	64	7	2	8	0	.229/.300/.405	.272	.558	8.1%	23.6%							92	0.0	-0	0.1

2023 GP: 1B (16)

Comps: Chris Parmelee (64), Ben Paulsen (62), Jesús Aguilar (61)

If Hall's 2022 debut showed us a heater, his 2023 follow-up showed us a real cooler. Hall floundered miserably through two abbreviated MLB stints last year, demonstrating what happens when his trademark power dries up for a spell. As such, he spent much of his time in the minors, where he put together another commendable yet somewhat unremarkable offensive season. The plate discipline, while good enough as a farmhand, simply has not translated to the big stage. Time (and, perhaps, the Phillies' patience) is running out to see if it ever will. It also doesn't help that the Phillies have a couple guys they might want to consider trying at his position.

Bryce Harper DH
Born: 10/16/92   Age: 31   Bats: L   Throws: R   Height: 6'3"   Weight: 210   Origin: Round 1, 2010 Draft (#1 overall)

YEAR	TM	LVL	AGE	PA	R	HR	RBI	SB	AVG/OBP/SLG	BABIP	SLGCON	BB%	K%	ZSw%	ZCon%	OSw%	OCon%	LA	90th EV	DRC+	BRR	DRP	WARP
2021	PHI	MLB	28	599	101	35	84	13	.309/.429/.615	.359	.847	16.7%	22.4%	74.4%	77.5%	30.7%	53.8%	13.1	108.8	155	0.3	-2.0	5.8
2022	PHI	MLB	29	426	63	18	65	11	.286/.364/.514	.324	.671	10.8%	20.4%	80.7%	82.5%	40.0%	57.5%	11.7	108.3	139	0.1	-0.1	3.0
2023	PHI	MLB	30	546	84	21	72	11	.293/.401/.499	.352	.675	14.7%	21.8%	78.5%	79.2%	35.9%	51.6%	8.9	108.6	137	0.1	-0.1	3.6
2024 DC	PHI	MLB	31	595	74	22	76	12	.254/.363/.448	.318	.627	13.6%	24.6%							126	0.1	-0.1	3.2

2023 GP: DH (89), 1B (36)

Comps: Johnny Callison (72), Mel Ott (71), Jack Clark (64)

No one has ever recovered faster from Tommy John surgery—as if Harper needs more accolades. He returned to action May 2, recorded three hits in his second game back, and hit his first homer May 6. There could be no doubt: Harper was superhuman. What else could explain it? The next two months, however, would feel excruciatingly long. Harper hit only two more homers in May before a 37-game drought that ran through the All-Star Break, his original anticipated return window. It's not as if Harper was a liability; he far exceeded whatever else the Phillies would've deployed in Rhys Hoskins' absence. It's just that, well, perhaps this was all too soon. But then, like flicking a light switch, he went on a power barrage, launching 10 homers in August alone. It felt like an inauguration, like the exclamation mark that said, resolutely, his UCL tear was in the past. Which, of course, begs the question: Is it? He spent the better part of two seasons hampered by it, and these waters are largely uncharted. If anyone can overcome this kind of adversity, though, it's Harper. Whether or not he does will differentiate between his human and inhuman forms.

Rafael Marchán C
Born: 02/25/99   Age: 25   Bats: S   Throws: R   Height: 5'9"   Weight: 170   Origin: IFA, 2015

YEAR	TM	LVL	AGE	PA	R	HR	RBI	SB	AVG/OBP/SLG	BABIP	SLGCON	BB%	K%	ZSw%	ZCon%	OSw%	OCon%	LA	90th EV	DRC+	BRR	DRP	WARP
2021	LHV	AAA	22	265	28	0	19	1	.203/.283/.232	.249	.286	8.7%	17.0%							86	3.4	-4.2	0.5
2021	PHI	MLB	22	56	7	1	4	0	.231/.286/.346	.268	.429	7.1%	17.9%	60.8%	86.7%	37.7%	81.4%	18.0	98.9	94	0.0	-1.9	0.0
2022	LAG	WIN	23	88	14	0	16	1	.361/.477/.389	.441	.475	17.0%	14.8%										
2022	LHV	AAA	23	263	26	4	29	1	.233/.316/.358	.243	.399	7.6%	9.1%	40.0%	100.0%	33.3%	83.3%			116	0.1	10.4	2.2
2023	LHV	AAA	24	207	27	2	30	1	.297/.391/.440	.321	.497	11.6%	9.7%	62.9%	93.0%	31.8%	77.8%			113	0.7	2.2	1.1
2024 DC	PHI	MLB	25	63	5	1	5	0	.221/.290/.322	.247	.380	7.6%	13.2%							73	0.0	-0.8	-0.1

2023 GP: C (57), DH (4)

Comps: Rob Brantly (50), Alexi Casilla (49), Marwin Gonzalez (44)

YEAR	TM	P. COUNT	FRM RUNS	BLK RUNS	THRW RUNS	TOT RUNS
2021	LHV	8562	-3.6	0.0	0.2	-3.4
2021	PHI	2072	-1.9	0.0	0.4	-1.6
2022	LAG	1933			0.0	0.0
2022	LHV	8242	5.5	0.6	4.6	10.7
2023	LHV	7252	0.7	-0.1	3.7	4.4
2024	PHI	2405	-1.3	0.0	0.5	-0.8

Presently the only suitable heir to J.T. Realmuto's throne (one which Realmuto won't vacate for at least a couple more years), Marchán walked more than he struck out during his three healthy months in the minors, while an inordinate number of line drives paired with his slappy, gappy power underpinned his best pro season to date. It's hard to complain about a backup catcher whose bat profiles similarly to the Blue Jays' Alejandro Kirk, even the 2023 edition, rendering him a contact maven in his own right. Marchán's framing, unlike Kirk's, leaves much more to be desired. However, his arm has been nothing short of dazzling the last two years at Lehigh Valley, planting a seed of hope that he's more than just his bat, which isn't all that substantial to begin with. He really needs those line drives to stick.

Brandon Marsh CF
Born: 12/18/97   Age: 26   Bats: L   Throws: R   Height: 6'4"   Weight: 215   Origin: Round 2, 2016 Draft (#60 overall)

YEAR	TM	LVL	AGE	PA	R	HR	RBI	SB	AVG/OBP/SLG	BABIP	SLGCON	BB%	K%	ZSw%	ZCon%	OSw%	OCon%	LA	90th EV	DRC+	BRR	DRP	WARP
2021	SL	AAA	23	110	26	3	8	2	.255/.364/.468	.339	.677	14.5%	26.4%							99	2.0	0.0	0.5
2021	LAA	MLB	23	260	27	2	19	6	.254/.317/.356	.403	.579	7.7%	35.0%	64.9%	81.7%	31.2%	44.6%	7.9	105.1	58	0.6	1.3	-0.1
2022	PHI	MLB	24	138	15	3	15	2	.288/.319/.455	.398	.659	4.3%	29.7%	67.2%	82.1%	35.8%	65.5%	13.7	104.7	55	0.2	0.2	-0.2
2022	LAA	MLB	24	323	34	8	37	8	.226/.284/.353	.341	.589	6.8%	36.2%	65.2%	78.6%	33.5%	54.7%	9.3	104.9	71	0.6	3.6	0.3
2023	PHI	MLB	25	472	58	12	60	10	.277/.372/.458	.397	.712	12.5%	30.5%	61.5%	82.3%	27.9%	56.3%	12.1	104.2	89	0.8	-1.2	1.0
2024 DC	PHI	MLB	26	478	47	10	49	14	.227/.317/.375	.310	.548	10.5%	28.0%							92	0.7	2.2	1.3

2023 GP: CF (108), LF (29), RF (7), DH (1)

Comps: Michael Brantley (64), Felix Pie (58), Jim Edmonds (58)

Of the 18 combined triples and home runs Marsh hit in 2023, nearly half of them occurred in the season's first month. The rest of his campaign couldn't hold a candle to his torrid start, although it wasn't entirely a slog. The center fielder made meaningful discipline gains by being more selective: He doubled his walk rate and nearly got his strikeout rate below 30%. (Sometimes you have to celebrate the little things.) Unfortunately, DRC+ thinks there wasn't, and hasn't been, enough power to combat his weaknesses. The untenably high BABIP that keeps him afloat is understandably a subject of DRC's skepticism, and he suffers brutal platoon splits. Marsh's defense took a step back, too, putting a damper on his contributions wholesale. If his long-term fate is nothing more than the productive-but-flawed strong side of a center field platoon, he carries with him another honor more prestigious than any World Series ring or MVP award: He's the wettest, just the absolute wettest. So, so wet.

Cristian Pache OF Born: 11/19/98 Age: 25 Bats: R Throws: R Height: 6'2" Weight: 215 Origin: IFA, 2015

YEAR	TM	LVL	AGE	PA	R	HR	RBI	SB	AVG/OBP/SLG	BABIP	SLGCON	BB%	K%	ZSw%	ZCon%	OSw%	OCon%	LA	90th EV	DRC+	BRR	DRP	WARP
2021	GWN	AAA	22	353	50	11	44	9	.265/.330/.414	.347	.594	8.5%	27.5%							89	0.6	-3.8	0.5
2021	ATL	MLB	22	68	6	1	4	0	.111/.152/.206	.162	.342	2.9%	36.8%	76.5%	80.0%	43.3%	40.0%	4.6	100.9	59	0.0	-0.5	-0.1
2022	EST	WIN	23	66	8	0	5	1	.218/.308/.291	.255	.356	10.6%	15.2%										
2022	LV	AAA	23	171	15	4	20	1	.248/.298/.389	.302	.517	6.4%	22.8%	73.6%	83.6%	30.1%	50.5%			80	0.3	-4.7	-0.3
2022	OAK	MLB	23	260	18	3	18	2	.166/.218/.241	.220	.339	5.8%	26.9%	74.0%	80.9%	31.0%	48.2%	3.0	104.5	60	0.2	-1.3	-0.5
2023	LHV	AAA	24	60	10	1	6	3	.235/.350/.333	.297	.447	13.3%	21.7%	69.5%	78.8%	21.1%	46.2%			95	1.5	0.0	0.2
2023	PHI	MLB	24	95	12	2	11	2	.238/.319/.417	.327	.614	10.5%	28.4%	72.4%	70.7%	26.9%	52.6%	8.1	105.3	82	0.1	-0.4	0.1
2024 DC	PHI	MLB	25	218	19	4	20	4	.213/.279/.331	.288	.478	7.6%	28.6%							73	-0.1	-0.7	-0.2

2023 GP: LF (24), CF (19), RF (3), DH (1)   Comps: Jose Tabata (45), Byron Buxton (44), Carson Kelly (41)

Pache, like Kody Clemens who preceded him (and others who may follow), may be another Kevin Long success story. It's hard to wax poetic about an entirely unfulfilled former top prospect on his third team by his age-24 season. It's also hard to draw conclusions about 95 plate appearances. (It's somewhat easier to pass judgment on a 112-loss Athletics club that couldn't make room for him.) Yet, in that tiny sample, Pache exercised more patience than ever, cutting down on his brutally aimless swings. And, while not making *more* contact on a per-swing basis, he certainly made *much better* contact, roping line drives and pairing his wasted hard-hit rate with more-optimal launch angles. Again, maybe it's nothing. Maybe it's all noise. But it's noise that looks so substantially different from Pache's old miserable self that it's hard not to dream on him, even just a little bit.

J.T. Realmuto C Born: 03/18/91 Age: 33 Bats: R Throws: R Height: 6'1" Weight: 212 Origin: Round 3, 2010 Draft (#104 overall)

YEAR	TM	LVL	AGE	PA	R	HR	RBI	SB	AVG/OBP/SLG	BABIP	SLGCON	BB%	K%	ZSw%	ZCon%	OSw%	OCon%	LA	90th EV	DRC+	BRR	DRP	WARP
2021	PHI	MLB	30	537	64	17	73	13	.263/.343/.439	.325	.602	8.9%	24.0%	72.3%	78.7%	33.2%	64.3%	11.6	106.2	95	0.8	14.0	3.3
2022	PHI	MLB	31	562	75	22	84	21	.276/.342/.478	.318	.626	7.3%	21.2%	69.4%	81.5%	34.5%	64.2%	13.1	105.1	117	1.3	11.3	4.5
2023	PHI	MLB	32	540	70	20	63	16	.252/.310/.452	.307	.630	6.5%	25.6%	72.0%	82.7%	34.1%	60.0%	16.8	106.2	98	0.2	-7.0	1.2
2024 DC	PHI	MLB	33	500	53	16	58	15	.239/.309/.398	.286	.526	7.2%	22.5%							98	0.6	7	2.6

2023 GP: C (133)   Comps: Don Slaught (81), Ivan Rodríguez (79), Victor Martinez (78)

One of the league's best and most consistent catchers for years, Realmuto finally took a step back en route to his least-valuable campaign since his first full season. It's hard to overstate its magnitude, having ceded a whopping 19 framing runs. Defensive metrics are often conditional upon their opportunities and prone to variance, but this kind of whiplash is hard to ignore. Meanwhile, his bat continues to show signs of gradual erosion. The gulf between his strikeout and walk rates was at its widest, and a sudden shift in his launch

YEAR	TM	P. COUNT	FRM RUNS	BLK RUNS	THRW RUNS	TOT RUNS
2021	PHI	16465	15.0	0.2	0.9	16.1
2022	PHI	18477	10.2	0.8	3.5	14.4
2023	PHI	18919	-6.3	0.5	0.3	-5.5
2024	PHI	18038	6.6	0.4	0.1	7.1

angle-related batted ball metrics suggests a change in his swing path. That, or it's evidence of attrition in his swing decisions, or (*gulp*) both. Perhaps Realmuto was the victim of his own success—starting five-plus games a week, every week, for the better part of a decade—as he heads toward his mid-30s. No one staves off decline. The million dollar question is whether 2023 was simply a lower-percentile outcome or if the denouement has begun in earnest.

Gabriel Rincones Jr. RF Born: 03/03/01 Age: 23 Bats: L Throws: R Height: 6'3" Weight: 225 Origin: Round 3, 2022 Draft (#93 overall)

YEAR	TM	LVL	AGE	PA	R	HR	RBI	SB	AVG/OBP/SLG	BABIP	SLGCON	BB%	K%	ZSw%	ZCon%	OSw%	OCon%	LA	90th EV	DRC+	BRR	DRP	WARP
2023	SCO	WIN	22	96	20	2	13	14	.295/.427/.462	.429	.706	16.7%	28.1%	63.9%	78.3%	7.7%	25.0%						
2023	CLR	A	22	214	31	5	21	24	.264/.388/.444	.356	.642	13.1%	25.7%	67.4%	80.8%	25.6%	48.5%			108	0.4	1.6	1.1
2023	JS	A+	22	319	50	10	39	8	.238/.326/.416	.295	.579	10.3%	24.8%							109	1.6	4.6	2.0
2024 non	PHI	MLB	23	251	21	4	22	0	.216/.283/.331	.302	.487	7.4%	29.4%							73	0.0	0	-0.2

2023 GP: RF (65), DH (39), LF (38)   Comps: Ronnie Dawson (70), Nick Ciolli (68), Mitch Haniger (65)

Rincones Jr.'s first run through pro ball confirmed all expectations: He's a big, powerful kid with an unrefined feel for the zone. He's patient, bordering on passive, with the kind of walk rate that tries to disguise contact rate concerns, and the power wasn't quite where you'd like it to be given the former. But his unusual background—he grew up in Scotland and, despite a tremendous final college campaign, has significantly less lifetime baseball experience than his contemporaries—makes for an unusual projection. His lack of reps affords him the benefit of the doubt regarding pitch recognition, something that scouts hope he can improve as he marinates in the minors. It'll likely be his developmental linchpin, the trait that accelerates or stalls his ascent up the organizational ladder.

Johan Rojas CF   Born: 08/14/00   Age: 23   Bats: R   Throws: R   Height: 5'11"   Weight: 165   Origin: IFA, 2018

YEAR	TM	LVL	AGE	PA	R	HR	RBI	SB	AVG/OBP/SLG	BABIP	SLGCON	BB%	K%	ZSw%	ZCon%	OSw%	OCon%	LA	90th EV	DRC+	BRR	DRP	WARP
2021	CLR	A	20	351	51	7	38	25	.240/.305/.374	.283	.480	7.4%	19.7%	66.8%	86.7%	35.5%	62.5%			100	3.4	10.8	2.6
2021	JS	A+	20	74	16	3	11	8	.344/.419/.563	.352	.643	9.5%	10.8%							139	2.5	2.5	1.1
2022	JS	A+	21	292	40	3	22	33	.230/.287/.325	.278	.410	7.2%	18.8%							111	2.9	1.3	1.7
2022	REA	AA	21	264	42	4	16	29	.260/.333/.387	.305	.476	8.0%	16.7%							112	5.1	7.2	2.3
2023	REA	AA	22	354	56	9	45	30	.306/.361/.484	.349	.594	6.8%	16.7%							115	2.8	5.4	2.6
2023	PHI	MLB	22	164	24	2	23	14	.302/.342/.430	.410	.598	3.0%	25.6%	63.2%	88.7%	45.0%	57.2%	6.4	101.7	72	0.2	0.6	0.1
2024 DC	PHI	MLB	23	362	30	6	33	24	.223/.277/.335	.272	.433	5.5%	20.9%							72	0.6	1	0.2

2023 GP: CF (57), DH (1)   *Comps: Ryan Kalish (64), Raimel Tapia (57), Albert Almora Jr. (55)*

It might be easiest to simply quote BP lead prospect writer Jeffrey Paternostro. Per his prescient write-up of Rojas' call-up last July: "The glove and speed—each a 70 as well—give him some present major-league value even if I'd expect the bat to struggle mightily over the next few weeks." Indeed, in 59 games (nine of those as a pinch hitter or runner), Rojas stole bases and covered swaths of a neglected left and right center field. He hit an unconvincing .302, a product of chasing everything in arm's reach in hopes of poking it through the hole. In 113 batted ball events, he hit precisely one (1) barrel. We don't need to tell you where that ranks. Still, defense counts, and so in the season's waning weeks, he played most days, splitting time primarily with Brandon Marsh and Kyle Schwarber, facing (and flailing at) lefties and righties equally. The issue of if he can hit, let alone neutralize any platoon splits, will be resolved once his BABIP settles down from its lofty peak. Frankly, his swing decisions, which historically have been and evidently still are problematic, must improve. There's an abundance of talent here, but Rojas isn't a full-time regular yet.

Kyle Schwarber LF/DH   Born: 03/05/93   Age: 31   Bats: L   Throws: R   Height: 6'0"   Weight: 229   Origin: Round 1, 2014 Draft (#4 overall)

YEAR	TM	LVL	AGE	PA	R	HR	RBI	SB	AVG/OBP/SLG	BABIP	SLGCON	BB%	K%	ZSw%	ZCon%	OSw%	OCon%	LA	90th EV	DRC+	BRR	DRP	WARP
2021	WAS	MLB	28	303	42	25	53	1	.253/.340/.570	.273	.853	10.2%	29.0%	67.3%	76.1%	25.2%	61.4%	14.5	110.2	142	-0.2	-0.2	2.7
2021	BOS	MLB	28	168	34	7	18	0	.291/.435/.522	.364	.737	19.6%	23.2%	65.1%	81.5%	22.7%	54.1%	17.8	108.4	113	-0.1	-0.1	0.7
2022	PHI	MLB	29	669	100	46	94	10	.218/.323/.504	.240	.772	12.9%	29.9%	62.1%	80.8%	24.9%	52.9%	19.2	109.6	129	0.0	-4.0	4.0
2023	PHI	MLB	30	720	108	47	104	0	.197/.343/.474	.209	.749	17.5%	29.9%	56.7%	79.2%	24.1%	50.5%	18.9	108.1	118	-0.9	-5.7	2.8
2024 DC	PHI	MLB	31	614	87	36	95	3	.218/.348/.478	.261	.735	15.3%	29.7%							126	-0.5	-0.8	3.2

2023 GP: LF (103), DH (57)   *Comps: Adam Dunn (75), Willie Stargell (67), Pete Incaviglia (65)*

In 2023 Schwarber challenged us with perhaps *the* preeminent contemporary sabermetric thought experiment: Can a player hit nearly 50 home runs and actually be… bad? The question was prompted by Baseball-Reference's version of WAR, which in August described Schwarber as below replacement level despite encroaching upon 40 home runs. In our eyes it was never in dispute: Schwarber's 118 DRC+ carried him to a 2.5 WARP despite below-average defense (Rhys Hoskins' injury forcing him into a featured role at a position he wasn't intended to play) and a .197 batting average, built upon the glorious foundation of the most Three True Outcomes in a single season. Somewhere, Adam Dunn sheds a tear. Among active players with as many plate appearances as Schwarber, only Mike Trout and Giancarlo Stanton have a higher career ISO, and in the last half decade only Pete Alonso and Matt Olson have more home runs. Sure, his extremely passive approach and steep bat path leave him vulnerable to strikeouts and black hole batting averages. But Schwarber has evidently made it his life's work to ruffle the old school's feathers.

Edmundo Sosa 3B   Born: 03/06/96   Age: 28   Bats: R   Throws: R   Height: 6'0"   Weight: 210   Origin: IFA, 2012

YEAR	TM	LVL	AGE	PA	R	HR	RBI	SB	AVG/OBP/SLG	BABIP	SLGCON	BB%	K%	ZSw%	ZCon%	OSw%	OCon%	LA	90th EV	DRC+	BRR	DRP	WARP
2021	STL	MLB	25	326	39	6	27	4	.271/.346/.389	.326	.498	5.2%	19.3%	73.3%	81.7%	38.8%	58.6%	6.0	103.9	100	0.2	1.2	1.4
2022	STL	MLB	26	131	17	0	8	3	.189/.244/.270	.274	.393	3.1%	29.0%	69.5%	80.2%	48.3%	52.7%	11.1	102.2	73	0.4	0.5	0.1
2022	PHI	MLB	26	59	9	2	13	3	.315/.345/.593	.366	.762	1.7%	20.3%	72.4%	90.5%	46.2%	56.4%	11.3	104.0	91	0.2	0.1	0.1
2023	PHI	MLB	27	300	34	10	30	4	.251/.293/.427	.306	.580	2.7%	24.7%	76.6%	80.6%	44.8%	59.1%	13.8	104.8	88	0.2	-0.3	0.5
2024 DC	PHI	MLB	28	152	15	4	16	3	.238/.300/.372	.298	.500	4.8%	23.7%							90	0.1	0.4	0.3

2023 GP: 3B (82), SS (18), 2B (4), CF (1)   *Comps: Hernán Pérez (68), Eduardo Núñez (58), Erick Aybar (56)*

After Darick Hall's thumb surgery, the Phillies opted not to install surging Kody Clemens at first base. Instead, they moved Alec Bohm to first base to endear Sosa to the hot corner and, in manager Rob Thomson's words, "see what he's going to do against right-handed pitching." And what he did was fare quite poorly against them. He hit for more power—squint and you may see more of Kevin Long's fingerprints—but his approach remains a profound liability. Worse yet, the typically sure-handed and agile-footed Sosa showed below-average range and committed nine throwing errors. Endear himself, he did not. Sosa played sparingly during the second half, sometimes starting barely once a week, casting shadows over his future as anything more than a situational bench piece.

Bryson Stott 2B   Born: 10/06/97   Age: 26   Bats: L   Throws: R   Height: 6'3"   Weight: 200   Origin: Round 1, 2019 Draft (#14 overall)

YEAR	TM	LVL	AGE	PA	R	HR	RBI	SB	AVG/OBP/SLG	BABIP	SLGCON	BB%	K%	ZSw%	ZCon%	OSw%	OCon%	LA	90th EV	DRC+	BRR	DRP	WARP
2021	PEJ	WIN	23	119	20	2	31	5	.318/.445/.489	.333	.581	20.2%	11.8%	33.3%	100.0%	24.1%	85.7%						
2021	JS	A+	23	95	18	5	10	3	.288/.453/.548	.348	.784	23.2%	23.2%							134	1.5	0.1	0.8
2021	REA	AA	23	351	49	10	36	6	.301/.368/.481	.368	.641	10.0%	22.2%							109	1.9	-0.9	1.6
2021	LHV	AAA	23	41	4	1	3	1	.303/.439/.394	.375	.520	19.5%	19.5%							111	1.4	-2.4	0.1
2022	LHV	AAA	24	40	11	2	7	2	.333/.375/.611	.400	.846	7.5%	25.0%							101	0.3	0.8	0.2
2022	PHI	MLB	24	466	58	10	49	12	.234/.295/.358	.274	.453	7.7%	19.1%	61.0%	86.5%	31.6%	76.9%	12.7	101.7	84	0.9	-5.0	0.2
2023	PHI	MLB	25	640	78	15	62	31	.280/.329/.419	.312	.505	6.1%	15.6%	58.5%	88.6%	32.5%	78.8%	9.9	100.9	100	1.4	4.7	2.6
2024 DC	PHI	MLB	26	558	56	13	60	20	.260/.319/.394	.288	.466	7.2%	14.3%							99	0.8	3.5	2.0

2023 GP: 2B (149), DH (1)   *Comps: Anderson Hernandez (69), Kevin Newman (67), Erik González (67)*

During his 2022 debut, Stott's defensive metrics in his limited time at second base outshone those at his legacy position of shortstop, as if the keystone were his natural position all along. And in his first of perhaps many years as Trea Turner's double play partner, Stott flourished, showing the same superior range and arm that he did a year prior. At the plate, Stott roped line drives for days, spraying them to all fields. Always contact-forward, he notably cut back his pop-ups and legged out a few extra infield hits, pushing up his overall line into league-average territory. On the whole, he boasts middling power, but his pull-side homers aren't cheap, nor was the Stott Heard 'Round the World—his memorable grand slam that helped propel the Phillies past the Marlins in the Wild Card round. It could all be a delightful coincidence, what with his bat and glove rounding into form simultaneously. The Phillies bet on it, though, and it paid dividends.

Garrett Stubbs C   Born: 05/26/93   Age: 31   Bats: L   Throws: R   Height: 5'10"   Weight: 170   Origin: Round 8, 2015 Draft (#229 overall)

YEAR	TM	LVL	AGE	PA	R	HR	RBI	SB	AVG/OBP/SLG	BABIP	SLGCON	BB%	K%	ZSw%	ZCon%	OSw%	OCon%	LA	90th EV	DRC+	BRR	DRP	WARP
2021	SUG	AAA	28	146	25	2	15	4	.265/.418/.363	.333	.488	20.5%	19.9%							106	2.1	0.3	0.9
2021	HOU	MLB	28	38	2	0	3	0	.176/.222/.235	.222	.296	5.3%	18.4%	66.0%	90.9%	35.9%	56.5%	7.0	100.3	81	0.0	0.0	0.1
2022	PHI	MLB	29	121	19	5	16	2	.264/.350/.462	.324	.645	11.6%	24.8%	50.8%	90.0%	29.9%	65.2%	11.5	100.5	76	0.1	-4.6	-0.4
2023	PHI	MLB	30	125	15	1	12	2	.204/.274/.283	.265	.381	7.2%	23.2%	64.1%	89.4%	31.4%	58.2%	19.0	98.7	77	0.1	-7.4	-0.6
2024 DC	PHI	MLB	31	90	8	2	8	1	.223/.305/.337	.276	.435	9.6%	21.5%							81	0.0	-2.4	-0.1

2023 GP: C (40), LF (1)

Comps: Jesús Sucre (57), Sandy León (55), Brett Hayes (54)

The Phillies *love* their pop times. Stubbs' 1.87 seconds to second base tied for second-best in baseball, trailing only the immovable object himself, J.T. Realmuto. Unfortunately, Stubbs' elite hands didn't translate into elite baserunner prevention, and his pitch framing value could be characterized very generously as "bad." All of this is to say nothing of his bat, which might as well be a 34-inch stick of string cheese. Most teams don't have the luxury of wondering who, only once, maybe twice a week, will give their generational talent a breather. That said, even the Phillies can probably do better.

YEAR	TM	P. COUNT	FRM RUNS	BLK RUNS	THRW RUNS	TOT RUNS
2021	SUG	3981	0.3	-0.1	0.2	0.4
2021	HOU	1256	-0.4	0.0	0.0	-0.4
2022	PHI	4789	-4.0	-0.1	-0.1	-4.2
2023	PHI	4744	-6.1	-0.1	-0.1	-6.4
2024	PHI	3608	-2.2	-0.1	-0.1	-2.4

Trea Turner SS   Born: 06/30/93   Age: 31   Bats: R   Throws: R   Height: 6'2"   Weight: 185   Origin: Round 1, 2014 Draft (#13 overall)

YEAR	TM	LVL	AGE	PA	R	HR	RBI	SB	AVG/OBP/SLG	BABIP	SLGCON	BB%	K%	ZSw%	ZCon%	OSw%	OCon%	LA	90th EV	DRC+	BRR	DRP	WARP
2021	LAD	MLB	28	226	41	10	28	11	.338/.385/.565	.361	.672	6.6%	14.6%	76.0%	85.5%	33.6%	61.1%	12.6	107.5	123	0.7	0.2	1.6
2021	WAS	MLB	28	420	66	18	49	21	.322/.369/.521	.363	.650	6.2%	18.3%	71.1%	87.5%	30.7%	59.9%	10.8	104.8	127	1.6	1.9	3.4
2022	LAD	MLB	29	708	101	21	100	27	.298/.343/.466	.342	.583	6.4%	18.5%	73.3%	85.6%	36.5%	57.8%	10.7	104.4	119	1.7	5.8	4.7
2023	PHI	MLB	30	691	102	26	76	30	.266/.320/.459	.310	.599	6.5%	21.7%	75.0%	83.8%	38.0%	52.4%	13.4	104.8	96	1.1	-8.6	1.2
2024 DC	PHI	MLB	31	641	71	21	79	22	.270/.325/.437	.325	.578	6.7%	22.5%							112	1.3	0.5	3.5

2023 GP: SS (153), DH (2)

Comps: Nomar Garciaparra (79), José Reyes (76), Cal Ripken Jr. (74)

Turner's Philadelphia debut, first of a staggering 11 seasons, was not for the faint of heart. His first- and second-half splits were so starkly different—a .687 OPS prior to the All-Star Break, a .902 OPS after—they hardly reflected the same player. Turner's late burst was the nitrous that boosted the Phillies into a playoff berth and mostly redeemed what felt like a lost season for him. Meanwhile, he still flashed his same elite sprint speed, even if his stolen base count didn't keep pace with the league-wide bump under MLB's new rules. He simply had—or, more accurately, created for himself—fewer opportunities. In the last few seasons, however, we have witnessed the continued reddening of two flags: Turner's persistent increases in aggression, to the point where it now resembles blind impatience (with the Ks to show for it), and a steepening swing path, culminating this year in a glut of weak fly balls that undercut his usually high BABIP. Turner's skills are playing a game of chicken with his offensive tendencies, and the thing about aging is that time tends to travel in a pretty straight line.

PITCHERS

Mick Abel RHP   Born: 08/18/01   Age: 22   Height: 6'5"   Weight: 190   Origin: Round 1, 2020 Draft (#15 overall)

YEAR	TM	LVL	AGE	G (GS)	IP	W-L	SV	K	WHIP	ERA	CSP	BB%	K%	HR%	GB%	ZSw%	ZCon%	OSw%	OCon%	BABIP	SLGCON	DRA-	WARP
2021	CLR	A	19	14 (14)	44²	1-3	0	66	1.21	4.43		14.3%	34.9%	2.6%	40.0%	70.5%	78.4%	28.2%	42.5%	.259	.528	78	1.0
2022	JS	A+	20	18 (18)	85¹	7-8	0	103	1.32	4.01		10.2%	27.7%	1.6%	39.1%					.315	.502	101	0.5
2022	REA	AA	20	5 (5)	23	1-3	0	27	1.35	3.52		12.1%	27.3%	5.1%	27.6%					.264	.603	110	0.2
2023	REA	AA	21	22 (22)	108²	5-5	0	126	1.24	4.14		13.5%	27.5%	3.3%	36.2%					.233	.557	99	1.8
2024 DC	PHI	MLB	22	6 (6)	27	1-2	0	27	1.53	5.48		13.1%	22.1%	3.8%	35.6%					.288	.590	117	0.0

2023 Arsenal: FA (97.8), SW (86.9)

Comps: Archie Bradley (57), Jameson Taillon (57), Lucas Giolito (57)

Abel appeared on track to spend much of last year at Lehigh Valley, with a chance to crack the Phillies' roster in June or September. Instead, he made all but one start at Double-A Reading, putting up the sort of numbers that won't pay the rent. It's fine; you can scoff at minor-league ERA, especially when prospect's capital-S stuff grades out so handsomely. But at what point do you throw out year after year of mediocre results? In Abel's case, it's reflective of his transient control. He walked at least three hitters in 65% of his starts, capping his strikeout-to-walk ratio at 2-to-1. Scouts have long anticipated his command would lag his stuff given his large, lanky frame, and they'll continue to do so. Abel remains one of baseball's most-promising righty prospects, but any expectations of a 2024 debut should be put on ice in favor of hopes for further refinement.

José Alvarado LHP   Born: 05/21/95   Age: 29   Height: 6'2"   Weight: 245   Origin: IFA, 2012

YEAR	TM	LVL	AGE	G (GS)	IP	W-L	SV	K	WHIP	ERA	CSP	BB%	K%	HR%	GB%	ZSw%	ZCon%	OSw%	OCon%	BABIP	SLGCON	DRA-	WARP
2021	PHI	MLB	26	64 (0)	55²	7-1	5	68	1.60	4.20	52.7%	18.7%	27.1%	2.0%	55.8%	59.9%	80.7%	27.2%	47.1%	.298	.496	108	0.3
2022	PHI	MLB	27	59 (0)	51	4-2	2	81	1.22	3.18	47.2%	11.2%	37.9%	0.9%	56.5%	64.3%	77.7%	36.9%	45.9%	.343	.509	64	1.5
2023	PHI	MLB	28	42 (0)	41¹	0-2	10	64	1.16	1.74	46.7%	10.5%	37.2%	1.7%	54.4%	67.1%	76.4%	36.2%	52.6%	.314	.528	67	1.2
2024 DC	PHI	MLB	29	51 (0)	54¹	3-5	30	73	1.25	3.29	48.1%	12.3%	31.7%	2.3%	52.8%					.284	.504	75	1.0

2023 Arsenal: SI (98.9), FC (93.5), CU (86.2)   Comps: Ken Giles (60), Aroldis Chapman (60), Rex Brothers (59)

Delightful stories emerged this postseason of Alvarado's quirks. The man loves coffee and takes everyone's orders! He went through a "crafts era" and made necklaces for his teammates! They're stories that could redeem even the deadest weight on a roster; never mind that Alvarado is anything but. He's the Mod Podge that holds the Phillies' bullpen together. Rewind to January 2021, when the Rays shipped the lefty, plagued by control issues and inconsistent stuff, to Philadelphia. He promptly added three ticks to his cutter, helping to double the pitch's swinging-strike rate and giving him a legitimate, albeit sparsely used, swing-and-miss weapon. The seed was planted; all he had to do was nurture it (which, in this metaphor, means "throw it a heck of a lot more.") Nurture it he did—he took that hard cutter with its new bona fides and made it a feature of his arsenal, especially with two strikes. Now, he piles up strikeouts and ground balls in a way few others can. That's how Alvarado became baseball's most valuable left-handed reliever the last two years on a per-inning—and per-necklace—basis.

Andrew Bellatti RHP   Born: 08/05/91   Age: 32   Height: 6'1"   Weight: 190   Origin: Round 12, 2009 Draft (#379 overall)

YEAR	TM	LVL	AGE	G (GS)	IP	W-L	SV	K	WHIP	ERA	CSP	BB%	K%	HR%	GB%	ZSw%	ZCon%	OSw%	OCon%	BABIP	SLGCON	DRA-	WARP
2021	JAX	AAA	29	26 (0)	29²	1-2	11	38	0.84	1.52		8.7%	33.0%	1.7%	23.4%					.210	.444	85	0.6
2021	MIA	MLB	29	3 (0)	3¹	0-0	0	4	2.40	13.50	43.1%	10.5%	21.1%	0.0%	30.8%	70.4%	89.5%	51.8%	62.1%	.462	.538	104	0.0
2022	PHI	MLB	30	59 (1)	54¹	4-4	2	78	1.33	3.31	50.0%	10.9%	33.9%	2.2%	27.0%	70.6%	79.6%	35.1%	45.4%	.347	.626	86	0.9
2023	LHV	AAA	31	27 (0)	26	1-0	6	29	1.35	2.42		12.4%	25.7%	1.8%	37.3%	67.5%	80.4%	31.7%	45.5%	.292	.478	94	0.5
2023	PHI	MLB	31	27 (0)	24²	1-0	0	25	1.50	5.11	43.4%	10.6%	22.1%	3.5%	31.6%	68.2%	75.0%	36.4%	55.8%	.292	.587	102	0.3
2024 DC	PHI	MLB	32	35 (0)	38	2-2	0	47	1.33	4.47	47.3%	10.2%	28.3%	3.7%	30.4%					.303	.616	99	0.2

2023 Arsenal: FA (94.2), SL (86.3), CH (89.1)   Comps: Jeurys Familia (40), Jesus Colome (37), Jeremy Jeffress (37)

The Phillies optioned Bellatti twice last year amid a turbulent follow-up to his age-30 breakout. Important under-the-hood metrics remained largely unchanged, suggesting he probably deserved better. His slider-first approach amassed whiffs galore, just without the resultant K's to show for it. And although he did allow hard contact, it was generally the off-balance kind, heavily comprising pop-ups. His fly-ball slant will occasionally get him into trouble—home runs are exactly the kinds of mistakes you *don't* want to make in relief or, arguably, ever—but nonetheless it would behoove the Phillies to let Bellatti have another go at it, crowded as their roster is.

Connor Brogdon RHP   Born: 01/29/95   Age: 29   Height: 6'6"   Weight: 205   Origin: Round 10, 2017 Draft (#293 overall)

YEAR	TM	LVL	AGE	G (GS)	IP	W-L	SV	K	WHIP	ERA	CSP	BB%	K%	HR%	GB%	ZSw%	ZCon%	OSw%	OCon%	BABIP	SLGCON	DRA-	WARP
2021	PHI	MLB	26	56 (1)	57²	5-4	1	50	1.13	3.43	54.5%	7.7%	21.3%	2.6%	46.4%	77.3%	75.4%	35.4%	64.4%	.258	.472	91	0.8
2022	LHV	AAA	27	10 (1)	9¹	0-1	2	17	1.50	2.89		14.0%	39.5%	0.0%	52.6%	77.8%	85.7%	47.1%	75.0%	.421	.611	74	0.3
2022	PHI	MLB	27	47 (0)	44	2-2	2	50	1.25	3.27	53.7%	5.9%	26.6%	3.2%	31.7%	70.2%	74.9%	39.2%	57.0%	.319	.581	89	0.7
2023	LHV	AAA	28	26 (2)	28	1-1	1	34	1.36	5.46		12.9%	27.4%	3.2%	30.6%	70.9%	72.2%	35.8%	62.4%	.265	.603	98	0.4
2023	PHI	MLB	28	27 (1)	29	2-1	0	26	1.45	4.03	44.1%	10.2%	20.5%	3.9%	36.8%	67.8%	80.4%	33.9%	61.1%	.293	.619	106	0.2
2024 DC	PHI	MLB	29	24 (0)	27	1-1	0	28	1.34	4.53	50.5%	9.6%	24.1%	3.6%	37.3%					.294	.584	101	0.1

2023 Arsenal: CH (83.5), FA (95), FC (87.7)   Comps: Kevin Quackenbush (63), Ryan Dull (62), Juan Minaya (60)

Brogdon was *just* starting to look like a genuine bullpen weapon, breaking out in 2022 and burninating the countryside throughout the playoffs. Needless to say his 2023 encore left most of the thatched-roof cottages intact. His command betrayed him in a way his stuff couldn't redeem—if his stuff hadn't *also* betrayed him, too. His four-seamer, never particularly good, remained his weakest link. But his cutter took a huge step back, too, inducing less vertical break and altogether eroding its effectiveness. The Phillies optioned Brogdon in June for what would wind up being the rest of the season; there he walked another 16 batters in 28 innings. The Phillies' 'pen is the new pride and joy of Philly. Brogdon's going to have find to some majesty to earn his way back into that talented crew.

Seranthony Domínguez RHP   Born: 11/25/94   Age: 29   Height: 6'1"   Weight: 225   Origin: IFA, 2011

YEAR	TM	LVL	AGE	G (GS)	IP	W-L	SV	K	WHIP	ERA	CSP	BB%	K%	HR%	GB%	ZSw%	ZCon%	OSw%	OCon%	BABIP	SLGCON	DRA-	WARP
2021	REA	AA	26	4 (0)	5	1-0	0	3	2.20	14.40		10.7%	10.7%	14.3%	38.1%					.235	1.000	106	0.0
2021	LHV	AAA	26	12 (0)	12¹	0-1	0	16	1.70	7.30		12.7%	25.4%	1.6%	50.0%					.343	.500	81	0.3
2021	PHI	MLB	26	1 (0)	1	0-0	0	1	0.00	0.00	68.2%	0.0%	33.3%	0.0%	66.7%	75.0%	50.0%	75.0%	.000	.000	110	0.0
2022	PHI	MLB	27	54 (0)	51	6-5	9	61	1.14	3.00	51.3%	10.6%	29.5%	1.9%	47.2%	73.0%	76.7%	33.3%	54.9%	.269	.467	80	1.0
2023	PHI	MLB	28	57 (0)	50	5-5	2	48	1.40	3.78	45.3%	9.8%	21.4%	3.1%	41.2%	75.3%	76.2%	32.8%	64.5%	.291	.497	100	0.6
2024 DC	PHI	MLB	29	51 (0)	54¹	3-3	4	60	1.36	4.45	47.9%	10.5%	25.4%	3.1%	45.1%					.298	.557	98	0.3

2023 Arsenal: FA (97.7), SI (98.1), SL (90.1), CH (90.7)   Comps: Michael Feliz (61), Corey Knebel (61), Joe Smith (60)

Domínguez wasn't awful in 2023, but he certainly clouded the sunny outlook inspired by his impressive, long-awaited return from Tommy John surgery the year prior. His once-plump strikeout rate slimmed down considerably, fueled by living too much in the heart of the zone. Despite his downturn, Domínguez's high quality of stuff induced low quality of contact from hitters. There was evidence of misfortune, and Domínguez managed to remain serviceable despite it. The Phillies must have seen the signal through the noise and wisely trusted him enough to include him on their playoff roster—he recorded 16 scoreless outs, seven by strikeout—and odds are they'll trust him again this year to be another late-inning fixture.

Jeff Hoffman RHP Born: 01/08/93 Age: 31 Height: 6'5" Weight: 235 Origin: Round 1, 2014 Draft (#9 overall)

YEAR	TM	LVL	AGE	G (GS)	IP	W-L	SV	K	WHIP	ERA	CSP	BB%	K%	HR%	GB%	ZSw%	ZCon%	OSw%	OCon%	BABIP	SLGCON	DRA-	WARP
2021	LOU	AAA	28	4 (4)	15¹	0-0	0	20	0.98	1.76		6.6%	32.8%	3.3%	32.4%					.265	.556	86	0.3
2021	CIN	MLB	28	31 (11)	73	3-5	0	79	1.58	4.56	55.8%	13.4%	23.6%	3.6%	37.4%	69.2%	79.8%	28.4%	55.1%	.301	.606	114	0.1
2022	CIN	MLB	29	35 (1)	44²	2-0	0	45	1.41	3.83	53.2%	11.7%	22.8%	2.5%	28.6%	70.0%	83.6%	29.1%	60.8%	.289	.552	114	0.1
2023	LHV	AAA	30	9 (0)	9	0-2	0	16	1.33	7.00		17.9%	41.0%	2.6%	31.2%	58.5%	81.6%	34.0%	38.2%	.267	.733	95	0.2
2023	PHI	MLB	30	54 (0)	52¹	5-2	1	69	0.92	2.41	46.3%	9.1%	33.2%	1.4%	42.4%	71.2%	81.3%	37.5%	44.8%	.232	.412	75	1.3
2024 DC	PHI	MLB	31	46 (0)	49	3-3	4	60	1.31	4.44	51.0%	10.6%	28.5%	4.1%	36.5%					.288	.619	99	0.3

2023 Arsenal: SL (87.9), FA (97.2), FS (90.4), SW (86.7), SI (95.2)   Comps: Billy Buckner (58), Rafael Montero (56), Wily Peralta (55)

Imagine you're a committed baseball fan, someone well-versed enough in historical roster churn and prospect lore to have an opinion about Hoffman. Imagine further that you were prohibited from consuming any media about the Phillies—a "blackout," if you will. You are resigned to complete two tasks: (1) play out the Phillies' season in your head, and (2) make an educated guess specifically about the state of Hoffman's career. Obviously, the Phillies make a deep playoff run. *Duh*. As for Hoffman, you've seen 29 other teams play; he doesn't play for them, so odds are he doesn't play for Philadelphia either. He's probably in Triple-A somewhere, clinging desperately to the life raft that is The Dream™. Or maybe he found modest success overseas. You imagine, and you sleep soundly. Then, suddenly: The blackout is lifted. You feel you've awakened from a haze. The Phillies? An NLCS berth, check. Hoffman? He added six ticks to his slider and three to his four-seamer, and developed one of baseball's hardest splitters to become a top-15 reliever by DRA—*as a Phillie*. Hoffman was not just actively employed but a phoenix reborn. You? You were wrong. But you were happy to be.

Orion Kerkering RHP Born: 04/04/01 Age: 23 Height: 6'2" Weight: 204 Origin: Round 5, 2022 Draft (#152 overall)

YEAR	TM	LVL	AGE	G (GS)	IP	W-L	SV	K	WHIP	ERA	CSP	BB%	K%	HR%	GB%	ZSw%	ZCon%	OSw%	OCon%	BABIP	SLGCON	DRA-	WARP
2022	CLR	A	21	5 (0)	6	1-0	0	6	1.17	4.50		0.0%	24.0%	0.0%	31.6%	70.7%	75.9%	42.6%	69.2%	.368	.500	92	0.1
2023	CLR	A	22	9 (0)	10¹	1-0	4	18	0.29	0.00		2.9%	51.4%	0.0%	60.0%	56.9%	78.0%	38.6%	25.9%	.133	.133	67	0.2
2023	JS	A+	22	18 (0)	20¹	2-0	3	27	0.93	1.77		7.5%	33.8%	2.5%	39.1%					.250	.522	85	0.4
2023	REA	AA	22	21 (0)	22	0-1	7	33	1.09	2.05		5.7%	37.5%	2.3%	46.0%					.354	.540	76	0.5
2023	PHI	MLB	22	3 (0)	3	1-0	0	6	1.67	3.00	53.2%	14.3%	42.9%	0.0%	66.7%	43.5%	60.0%	32.4%	58.3%	.500	.667	88	0.1
2024 DC	PHI	MLB	23	40 (0)	43²	2-2	0	47	1.28	4.19	53.2%	8.6%	25.5%	·3.5%	38.6%					.295	.575	95	0.3

2023 Arsenal: SW (86.3), FA (97.9), SI (97.2)   Comps: Miles Mikolas (38), Michael Tonkin (37), Ian Hamilton (37)

Chalk up another W for nominative determinism: Orion already looks like a star. Kerkering's prospect stock went intergalactic after his transition into relief full-time. He added several ticks to a fastball that suddenly touched triple-digits routinely, and his 80-grade slider was commonly recognized as the minor leagues' best breaking pitch. Paired with exquisite command, Kerkering had the makings to impact the game immediately and to be an overnight relief ace, almost to the point that his dominance created urgency. Indeed, the Phillies called on him in September, barely a year after he was drafted, and trusted him enough for their playoff push. Philadelphia's bullpen was one of baseball's best last year, and that was without Kerkering, who is now the gratuitous (but no less delicious) extra tier at the top of a Great British Bake Off-caliber Phanatic-shaped cake.

Yunior Marte RHP Born: 02/02/95 Age: 29 Height: 6'2" Weight: 180 Origin: IFA, 2012

YEAR	TM	LVL	AGE	G (GS)	IP	W-L	SV	K	WHIP	ERA	CSP	BB%	K%	HR%	GB%	ZSw%	ZCon%	OSw%	OCon%	BABIP	SLGCON	DRA-	WARP
2021	SAC	AAA	26	43 (1)	56²	0-3	4	62	1.46	3.49		9.1%	24.6%	1.6%	51.5%					.348	.539	87	0.6
2022	SAC	AAA	27	25 (0)	25²	1-1	3	35	0.70	3.16		9.6%	37.2%	4.3%	40.0%	66.3%	81.5%	36.2%	39.8%	.109	.480	78	0.5
2022	SF	MLB	27	39 (0)	48	1-1	0	44	1.44	5.44	52.1%	10.3%	20.6%	2.3%	50.0%	68.1%	84.5%	35.7%	61.9%	.307	.514	102	0.4
2023	LHV	AAA	28	18 (0)	20	3-1	1	24	1.05	1.80		11.4%	30.4%	1.3%	66.7%	68.5%	77.5%	32.1%	36.1%	.250	.356	79	0.5
2023	PHI	MLB	28	40 (0)	39¹	1-1	2	38	1.63	5.03	45.9%	9.3%	20.9%	3.3%	49.2%	68.7%	87.4%	32.7%	57.2%	.342	.600	93	0.6
2024 DC	PHI	MLB	29	30 (0)	32²	2-1	0	31	1.35	4.29	49.0%	9.7%	21.8%	2.6%	48.7%					.295	.516	95	0.2

2023 Arsenal: SI (97.8), SL (87), FA (98.7)   Comps: Juan Minaya (70), Evan Scribner (70), Andrew Kittredge (70)

The Phillies love squeezing a fruit for all its juice. They saw something in Marte, a 27-year-old rookie with tepid production, enough to take a flyer on him and acquire him from the Giants. They created more differentiation among the movement profiles of his three pitches and had him focus primarily on his sinker and slider, his superior offerings. Pitch models already liked his specs, but they liked them more after these tweaks. Unfortunately, Marte lacked the results to show for it; in fact, his outcomes degraded. Reliever seasons can be erratic—anything can happen in 160 innings, let alone 40—but, like parts that exceed their sum, his ERA and its adjacent peripherals to date simply don't reflect his alleged ability. The gaudy numbers he compiled at Triple-A the last two years point to his upside.

Griff McGarry RHP Born: 06/08/99 Age: 25 Height: 6'2" Weight: 190 Origin: Round 5, 2021 Draft (#145 overall)

YEAR	TM	LVL	AGE	G (GS)	IP	W-L	SV	K	WHIP	ERA	CSP	BB%	K%	HR%	GB%	ZSw%	ZCon%	OSw%	OCon%	BABIP	SLGCON	DRA-	WARP
2021	CLR	A	22	5 (1)	11	0-0	1	22	1.18	3.27		15.2%	47.8%	0.0%	52.9%	58.3%	64.3%	33.3%	40.0%	.353	.471	84	0.2
2021	JS	A+	22	3 (3)	13¹	1-0	0	21	1.05	2.70		13.0%	38.9%	0.0%	34.6%					.269	.360	98	0.1
2022	JS	A+	23	12 (12)	46²	3-3	0	82	1.22	3.86		12.3%	42.1%	3.1%	35.3%					.342	.679	84	0.7
2022	REA	AA	23	8 (7)	32²	1-3	0	39	1.01	2.20		15.2%	29.5%	0.8%	44.9%					.176	.269	95	0.5
2022	LHV	AAA	23	7 (0)	8	0-2	0	9	2.00	9.00		24.3%	24.3%	5.4%	36.8%					.294	.789	101	0.1
2023	REA	AA	24	13 (13)	54²	1-1	0	74	1.23	3.13		15.6%	32.0%	1.7%	39.5%					.237	.457	83	1.2
2024 DC	PHI	MLB	25	6 (6)	27	1-2	0	34	1.63	5.67		16.3%	26.9%	3.6%	37.0%					.300	.623	119	0.0

2023 Arsenal: FA (95.9), SW (83.6), CH (89.4)   Comps: Dellin Betances (46), Pierce Johnson (44), Andrew Cashner (44)

Baseball has never been better-suited than it is now for pitchers with deficient command. To wit: Blake Snell just won a Cy Young Award with a 13% walk rate. "Deficient command" may characterize McGarry's issues rather charitably, however. In one start in particular, he faced only seven batters. He walked six of them and hit the seventh, and all of them scored without him recording an out. If McGarry's window to become a viable starter didn't slam shut right then and there, it's barely ajar. He possesses special stuff, though, a deep arsenal of high-velo fastballs and filthy secondaries. The command invariably betrays them, but a path forward in which he pares everything down in a high-leverage relief role faces the fewest obstructions.

McKinley Moore RHP   Born: 08/24/98   Age: 25   Height: 6'6"   Weight: 225   Origin: Round 14, 2019 Draft (#410 overall)

YEAR	TM	LVL	AGE	G (GS)	IP	W-L	SV	K	WHIP	ERA	CSP	BB%	K%	HR%	GB%	ZSw%	ZCon%	OSw%	OCon%	BABIP	SLGCON	DRA-	WARP
2021	KAN	A	22	19 (0)	22²	1-1	6	35	1.41	4.37		13.9%	34.7%	2.0%	50.0%					.327	.549	67	0.6
2021	WS	A+	22	18 (0)	18	1-1	3	24	1.44	4.00		8.8%	30.0%	2.5%	37.5%					.370	.583	96	0.2
2022	REA	AA	23	39 (1)	49²	4-5	0	71	1.53	4.35		11.5%	31.3%	1.3%	48.0%					.392	.570	77	1.2
2023	REA	AA	24	7 (0)	6¹	0-0	0	12	1.74	1.42		17.2%	41.4%	0.0%	50.0%					.500	.667	82	0.1
2023	LHV	AAA	24	12 (0)	13	2-1	0	22	1.69	1.38		29.3%	37.9%	0.0%	61.1%	67.0%	70.5%	28.7%	50.0%	.278	.333	92	0.3
2023	PHI	MLB	24	3 (0)	3¹	0-0	0	2	3.00	18.90	49.1%	23.8%	9.5%	4.8%	41.7%	61.1%	77.3%	18.0%	66.7%	.364	.917	109	0.0
2024 DC	PHI	MLB	25	19 (0)	21²	1-1	0	26	1.50	5.14	49.1%	14.2%	26.7%	3.5%	39.6%					.294	.579	110	0.0

2023 Arsenal: FA (97.5), SW (86.5), CH (91.2)   *Comps: Stephen Nogosek (42), César Vargas (42), Drew Smith (42)*

When healthy, Moore decimated the high minors, posting a 1.33 ERA and racking up both strikeouts and grounders. His fastball will threaten triple-digits, and his slider consistently shows up plus or better. He also walked 24% of hitters, an indictment of his control that may be prohibitively bad. The Phillies' relief corps made waves during the playoffs for its elite fastball velocities, top to bottom. There's a place in the bullpen for Moore, it's just a matter of establishing the time—and whether or not he can rein in his live arm in a way that makes him consistently reliable. The stuff alone (and his multiple remaining minor-league options) will buy him a couple more years of runway.

Nick Nelson RHP   Born: 12/05/95   Age: 28   Height: 6'1"   Weight: 205   Origin: Round 4, 2016 Draft (#128 overall)

YEAR	TM	LVL	AGE	G (GS)	IP	W-L	SV	K	WHIP	ERA	CSP	BB%	K%	HR%	GB%	ZSw%	ZCon%	OSw%	OCon%	BABIP	SLGCON	DRA-	WARP
2021	SWB	AAA	25	29 (5)	52	3-4	1	62	1.52	3.81		12.3%	26.3%	2.5%	54.5%					.324	.587	84	1.2
2021	NYY	MLB	25	11 (2)	14¹	0-2	0	22	2.16	8.79	53.8%	20.5%	28.2%	0.0%	35.1%	67.7%	81.0%	30.8%	54.5%	.405	.686	111	0.1
2022	PHI	MLB	26	47 (2)	68²	3-2	1	69	1.49	4.85	54.7%	11.8%	22.5%	0.3%	39.1%	70.8%	78.9%	30.4%	59.4%	.332	.479	114	0.2
2023	REA	AA	27	3 (3)	13	0-0	0	12	1.00	1.38		2.0%	24.0%	0.0%	52.8%					.333	.389	91	0.2
2023	LHV	AAA	27	20 (20)	97¹	7-3	0	75	1.48	4.35		9.9%	17.7%	3.1%	49.7%	72.2%	82.5%	31.1%	62.7%	.313	.532	92	1.8
2023	PHI	MLB	27	1 (0)	5¹	1-0	0	3	0.75	1.69	48.0%	10.0%	15.0%	5.0%	53.3%	78.6%	77.3%	39.0%	75.0%	.071	.333	102	0.1
2024 DC	PHI	MLB	28	27 (13)	72	3-5	0	61	1.53	5.47	53.1%	10.1%	18.9%	3.1%	42.8%					.315	.555	117	-0.3

2023 Arsenal: FA (94.3), CH (87.5), SI (93.3), SL (86.1)   *Comps: Drew VerHagen (55), José Ramírez (54), Lucas Sims (53)*

Nelson returned to the rotation, making 26 starts or bulk appearances following an opener—more than all his starts the previous four years combined. The outcomes were disappointing. But, as someone for whom the expectations of his stuff have long outstripped their results, it was at least interesting to see him tinker with his arsenal in a meaningful way. He lowered his release point several inches. Whether it caused or simply correlated with the three-tick dip in his velo is unclear, but considering his changeup remained quite hard by off-speed pitch standards, it seems like a conscious decision. Low-slot fastballs are all the rage right now, and the three-quarter release generated 90th-percentile carry on his changeup. All signs point to the Phillies trying to make *fetch* happen one last time, if just to have additional rotation depth.

Aaron Nola RHP   Born: 06/04/93   Age: 31   Height: 6'2"   Weight: 200   Origin: Round 1, 2014 Draft (#7 overall)

YEAR	TM	LVL	AGE	G (GS)	IP	W-L	SV	K	WHIP	ERA	CSP	BB%	K%	HR%	GB%	ZSw%	ZCon%	OSw%	OCon%	BABIP	SLGCON	DRA-	WARP
2021	PHI	MLB	28	32 (32)	180²	9-9	0	223	1.13	4.63	53.0%	5.2%	29.8%	3.5%	40.8%	66.2%	82.3%	36.0%	58.0%	.310	.596	73	4.3
2022	PHI	MLB	29	32 (32)	205	11-13	0	235	0.96	3.25	55.4%	3.6%	29.1%	2.4%	43.1%	64.3%	82.5%	37.4%	57.7%	.291	.501	68	5.4
2023	PHI	MLB	30	32 (32)	193²	12-9	0	202	1.15	4.46	48.1%	5.7%	25.5%	4.0%	42.6%	64.8%	85.5%	38.3%	60.4%	.286	.584	83	4.0
2024 DC	PHI	MLB	31	29 (29)	177²	12-8	0	178	1.15	3.56	50.8%	5.7%	24.6%	3.4%	43.0%					.290	.547	84	3.1

2023 Arsenal: KC (79.5), FA (93), SI (91.9), CH (86), FC (86.4)   *Comps: Justin Verlander (83), Juan Marichal (83), Kevin Appier (83)*

You have to admit, the commitment to the bit is spectacular. Alternating dazzlingly superb years with utterly aggravating ones? No one does it better. Nola tempted fate by entering his walk year with no contract extension and a brazen disregard for the very real curse cast upon him, and pitched to an abhorrent 4.46 ERA. Even the postseason couldn't withstand Nola's whiplash: He allowed two earned runs in his first three starts only to permit four in a crucial Game 6 NLCS loss—possibly his last as a Phillie. Despite his mediocrity, he delivered another 4.0-WARP season, his seventh straight (prorating his elite 2020 season). He also sports the second-widest gap between ERA and FIP the last three years. Both are claims few other active pitchers, if any, can make. Yet it begs the question: Why is Nola plagued so? Are we missing something? Whatever the diagnosis, the prescription could include scaling back his dual-fastball usage or cutting one of them all together. The Phillies had the fortitude to stomach Nola's tumult, signing him to a seven-year deal.

Luis F. Ortiz RHP   Born: 09/22/95   Age: 28   Height: 6'3"   Weight: 230   Origin: Round 1, 2014 Draft (#30 overall)

YEAR	TM	LVL	AGE	G (GS)	IP	W-L	SV	K	WHIP	ERA	CSP	BB%	K%	HR%	GB%	ZSw%	ZCon%	OSw%	OCon%	BABIP	SLGCON	DRA-	WARP
2021	RR	AAA	25	28 (4)	43	2-2	0	44	1.42	4.60		9.0%	23.4%	3.7%	33.6%					.314	.664	104	0.1
2022	SAC	AAA	26	35 (4)	67¹	4-3	2	72	1.20	4.54		4.6%	25.4%	2.8%	42.1%	71.2%	83.2%	34.2%	64.4%	.324	.553	80	1.2
2022	SF	MLB	26	6 (0)	8²	0-0	0	6	0.92	1.04	49.4%	9.1%	18.2%	0.0%	41.7%	73.3%	69.7%	35.6%	76.9%	.208	.208	107	0.1
2023	LHV	AAA	27	33 (1)	45	4-1	5	45	1.13	4.60		6.9%	23.9%	1.1%	54.5%	63.9%	87.0%	33.5%	59.3%	.300	.458	90	1.0
2023	PHI	MLB	27	14 (0)	19	0-0	1	16	1.47	3.32	54.4%	6.3%	20.0%	1.3%	50.8%	69.8%	83.7%	28.0%	69.0%	.386	.569	91	0.3
2024 DC	PHI	MLB	28	19 (0)	21²	1-1	0	17	1.29	4.28	52.9%	7.1%	18.7%	3.0%	45.2%					.291	.515	97	0.1

2023 Arsenal: SI (94.7), SW (82.3), FA (95.6), CU (79.9), CH (87.2), SL (86.3)   *Comps: A.J. Cole (53), Drew VerHagen (50), Carson Fulmer (49)*

A decade into a career that began with him being selected in the first round of the 2014 draft, Ortiz finally exhausted his rookie eligibility by throwing 19 decent innings in middle relief while bouncing back and forth between Philadelphia and Lehigh Valley. Ortiz's slider is slow and sweepy, possibly too slow for his mid-90s heat, but it's a solid pitch, certainly one suitable for headlining an arsenal. Everything else is substandard, but the steep approach angles and the high frequency of ground balls they produce will play. He's lost his shine, but he could still be a useful bullpen piece.

★ ★ ★ *2024 Top 101 Prospect* **#19** ★ ★ ★

Andrew Painter RHP   Born: 04/10/03   Age: 21   Height: 6'7"   Weight: 215   Origin: Round 1, 2021 Draft (#13 overall)

YEAR	TM	LVL	AGE	G (GS)	IP	W-L	SV	K	WHIP	ERA	CSP	BB%	K%	HR%	GB%	ZSw%	ZCon%	OSw%	OCon%	BABIP	SLGCON	DRA-	WARP
2021	PHI	ROK	18	4(4)	6	0-0	0	12	0.67	0.00		0.0%	57.1%	0.0%	88.9%	66.7%	50.0%	36.4%	50.0%	.444	.556		
2022	CLR	A	19	9(9)	38²	1-1	0	69	0.85	1.40		10.7%	46.3%	0.0%	38.1%	73.4%	69.7%	35.9%	48.9%	.270	.371	63	1.3
2022	JS	A+	19	8(8)	36²	3-0	0	49	0.87	0.98		4.9%	34.3%	1.4%	32.6%					.274	.442	83	0.6
2022	REA	AA	19	5(5)	28¹	2-1	0	37	0.95	2.54		1.8%	33.9%	2.8%	35.3%					.338	.588	82	0.6
2024 non	PHI	MLB	21	58(0)	50	2-2	0	48	1.31	4.50		8.9%	22.4%	3.9%	32.5%					.283	.576	101	0.2

2023 Arsenal: FA (96.6), FC (89.2), SW (85.4)   *Comps: Francis Martes (71), Julio Teheran (71), Dylan Bundy (68)*

Among Mick Abel, Griff McGarry, and Painter, the Phillies' three-headed pitching prospect monster, the latter's head is, uh, largest. Failed metaphors aside, Painter has a frontline starter's stuff: His fastball touches triple digits with significant carry, his two breaking pitches buckle knees, and his command already grades out as plus. He pulverized low-minors hitters and more than equipped himself to handle Double-A, all as a teenager. He inserts himself into the "best pitching prospect in baseball" discussion with little debate or resistance. Unfortunately, all of this describes Painter during his 2022 campaign, because 2023 was a lost one. After a UCL sprain in spring, he eventually succumbed to reconstructive surgery—which, unfortunately, didn't occur until July, thereby derailing much or all of his 2024 season as well. From a pure love-of-baseball perspective, the development stinks. But in the grand scheme of things, he'll return to baseball on what was previously an extremely accelerated trajectory, just slightly less so.

Cristopher Sánchez LHP   Born: 12/12/96   Age: 27   Height: 6'1"   Weight: 165   Origin: IFA, 2013

YEAR	TM	LVL	AGE	G (GS)	IP	W-L	SV	K	WHIP	ERA	CSP	BB%	K%	HR%	GB%	ZSw%	ZCon%	OSw%	OCon%	BABIP	SLGCON	DRA-	WARP
2021	LHV	AAA	24	19(17)	73	5-6	0	89	1.45	4.68		14.8%	27.4%	1.2%	59.4%					.297	.430	97	1.1
2021	PHI	MLB	24	7(1)	12²	1-0	0	13	1.82	4.97	54.7%	11.9%	22.0%	1.7%	59.0%	70.7%	87.9%	33.3%	60.5%	.417	.622	86	0.2
2022	LHV	AAA	25	15(14)	57¹	2-2	0	58	1.19	3.14		8.4%	24.4%	0.4%	62.8%	48.1%	84.6%	38.7%	83.3%	.305	.416	79	1.4
2022	PHI	MLB	25	15(3)	40	2-2	1	35	1.38	5.63	54.6%	9.6%	19.8%	2.8%	53.7%	62.7%	89.6%	33.3%	70.1%	.284	.512	112	0.1
2023	LHV	AAA	26	10(8)	49²	3-2	0	44	1.45	4.35		13.1%	19.8%	2.7%	53.8%	61.3%	86.6%	31.6%	57.1%	.268	.486	100	0.7
2023	PHI	MLB	26	19(18)	99¹	3-5	0	96	1.05	3.44	50.0%	4.0%	24.2%	4.0%	56.2%	62.4%	88.9%	37.4%	54.3%	.273	.566	81	2.2
2024 DC	PHI	MLB	27	24(24)	133¹	8-7	0	110	1.36	4.30	51.4%	8.8%	19.0%	2.3%	53.8%					.297	.487	96	1.2

2023 Arsenal: SI (92.4), CH (82.1), SL (82.9)   *Comps: Matt Andriese (57), Austin Gomber (56), Collin McHugh (55)*

It's difficult to overstate how critical Sánchez, inadvertent no. 3 starter, was for the playoff-bound Phillies as he picked up the considerable slack left by Aaron Nola, Ranger Suárez, and Taijuan Walker. By dropping his arm slot a hair and taking a little bit off everything, Sánchez created newfound plunging depth to his already steep, ground ball-oriented three-pitch repertoire. He shaved three ticks off his changeup, and, in becoming one of baseball's slowest, steepest off-speed pitches, it also became one of its filthiest, inducing whiffs and weak contact galore. His slider, more slurvy than sweepy, proved an effective third pitch with four more inches of drop. His new-look sinker lagged behind the rest, but he dialed back its usage about 15 percentage points, an exercise in picking the low-hanging fruit of optimization by simply throwing one's worst pitches less often. It cost Philadelphia a premium prospect in Curtis Mead to acquire Sánchez, but pitchers who perform at a prorated 4.0-WARP level don't grow on trees.

Gregory Soto LHP   Born: 02/11/95   Age: 29   Height: 6'1"   Weight: 234   Origin: IFA, 2012

YEAR	TM	LVL	AGE	G (GS)	IP	W-L	SV	K	WHIP	ERA	CSP	BB%	K%	HR%	GB%	ZSw%	ZCon%	OSw%	OCon%	BABIP	SLGCON	DRA-	WARP
2021	DET	MLB	26	62(0)	63²	6-3	18	76	1.35	3.39	55.6%	14.5%	27.5%	2.5%	44.0%	64.5%	81.1%	31.1%	50.5%	.258	.474	97	0.7
2022	DET	MLB	27	64(0)	60¹	2-11	30	60	1.38	3.28	54.0%	12.9%	22.8%	0.8%	47.5%	69.8%	80.4%	30.5%	64.6%	.296	.437	114	0.1
2023	PHI	MLB	28	69(0)	60¹	3-4	3	65	1.14	4.62	49.8%	8.8%	26.0%	2.4%	50.3%	63.4%	76.7%	35.3%	50.0%	.265	.472	78	1.4
2024 DC	PHI	MLB	29	51(0)	54¹	3-3	4	61	1.39	4.41	52.5%	11.2%	25.7%	2.8%	47.4%					.303	.541	97	0.3

2023 Arsenal: SI (98.4), SL (88.1), FA (99), CH (91.2)   *Comps: Andrew Chafin (71), Ryne Stanek (67), Matt Barnes (66)*

Soto managed to outrun some pretty dreadful peripherals as Detroit's de facto closer, so it only makes sense that Philadelphia offered him an exclusive, no-strings-attached invitation to its luxury spa for exiles and castaways. Like many before him, the Phillies tinkered with his arsenal—namely, by creating more depth to his slider (stop us if you've heard this one before). The pitch inarguably became one of baseball's best, full stop. And, in increasing its usage to nearly 40%, it added 4.5 percentage points to Soto's overall swinging-strike rate. Meanwhile he improved his first-pitch strike rate by 10(!) percentage points—an astonishing feat for someone allergic to single-digit walk rates. It's a shame that after leading his peripherals for a couple of years, his outcomes lagged, and he fell out of favor come playoff time.

Matt Strahm LHP   Born: 11/12/91   Age: 32   Height: 6'2"   Weight: 190   Origin: Round 21, 2012 Draft (#643 overall)

YEAR	TM	LVL	AGE	G (GS)	IP	W-L	SV	K	WHIP	ERA	CSP	BB%	K%	HR%	GB%	ZSw%	ZCon%	OSw%	OCon%	BABIP	SLGCON	DRA-	WARP
2021	SD	MLB	29	6(1)	6²	0-1	0	4	2.40	8.10	57.6%	2.8%	11.1%	0.0%	45.2%	69.6%	83.3%	43.3%	72.4%	.500	.667	98	0.1
2022	BOS	MLB	30	50(0)	44²	4-4	4	52	1.23	3.83	57.8%	8.8%	26.9%	2.6%	37.0%	65.9%	80.0%	30.8%	69.9%	.289	.508	97	0.5
2023	PHI	MLB	31	56(10)	87²	9-5	2	108	1.02	3.29	52.0%	6.0%	30.0%	3.1%	32.4%	68.4%	79.5%	33.9%	58.0%	.275	.566	84	1.8
2024 DC	PHI	MLB	32	51(0)	54¹	3-2	0	60	1.18	3.86	54.0%	7.4%	26.5%	3.8%	34.6%					.284	.578	89	0.6

2023 Arsenal: FA (93.7), SW (83.3), SI (93.4), FC (88), CH (86.6)   *Comps: Jake Diekman (61), Andrew Chafin (57), Sam Freeman (56)*

With Ranger Suárez missing the first month of the season, Strahm inhabited the role of mock fifth starter magnificently. When moved back into relief afterward, he was even better. He built on gains seen during his brief tenure with Boston, compiling his best season metrically in at least half a decade, and maybe ever. He abandoned his curve and paired his new-look four-seamer with a freshly sweepened slider from which he subtracted nearly five mph. It didn't become a huge swing-and-miss pitch, but its new horizontal movement profile kept hitters woefully off-balance, inducing harmless pop-ups at an elite clip. Highly capable swingmen are baseball's quiet symbol of opulence.

Ranger Suárez LHP   Born: 08/26/95   Age: 28   Height: 6'1"   Weight: 217   Origin: IFA, 2012

YEAR	TM	LVL	AGE	G (GS)	IP	W-L	SV	K	WHIP	ERA	CSP	BB%	K%	HR%	GB%	ZSw%	ZCon%	OSw%	OCon%	BABIP	SLGCON	DRA-	WARP
2021	PHI	MLB	25	39(12)	106	8-5	4	107	1.00	1.36	51.2%	7.9%	25.6%	1.0%	58.2%	68.2%	84.0%	32.6%	58.4%	.259	.357	74	2.5
2022	PHI	MLB	26	29(29)	155¹	10-7	0	129	1.33	3.65	49.8%	8.8%	19.5%	2.3%	55.2%	68.3%	88.7%	31.0%	64.8%	.294	.505	112	0.5
2023	LHV	AAA	27	2(2)	7	1-0	0	4	0.71	1.29		4.0%	16.0%	0.0%	55.0%	69.4%	76.0%	41.5%	70.6%	.200	.250	105	0.1
2023	PHI	MLB	27	22(22)	125	4-6	0	119	1.42	4.18	47.1%	8.9%	22.0%	2.4%	48.0%	62.6%	88.4%	33.4%	63.1%	.327	.549	98	1.6
2024 DC	PHI	MLB	28	26(26)	139	8-8	0	115	1.39	4.44	48.8%	8.9%	19.0%	2.6%	50.6%					.299	.505	99	1.3

2023 Arsenal: SI (92.9), FA (93.5), CU (75.9), CH (82.8), FC (87.7), SL (82.1)   *Comps: Felix Doubront (52), Jeff Locke (50), Patrick Corbin (49)*

Suárez's performance the last three years has been one of a magical carriage slowly reverting to its original pumpkin state. Not that pumpkins are bad; pumpkins are great. You can carve 'em. You can bake 'em. Drink them as spiced lattes. Delicious and versatile, those pumpkins. The former reliever had been outrunning his ERA estimators by several lengths, playing the part of mid-rotation starter admirably. He still did last year, but with heavier emphasis on *mid*. Suárez shuffled his pitch usage and, like everyone and their mothers in Philly, added more depth to his repertoire. Despite his ground-ball slant, the reboot seemed to work against Suárez. His changeup and cutter, both with steeper approach angles but sitting two ticks slower, got barreled up pretty badly. His locations weren't awful, though, and for someone who allows contact quality that's *mid*, a .327 BABIP was likely not representative of his talent. We're still testing this hypothesis, but Suárez's 2023 campaign could be a Type II error.

Taijuan Walker RHP   Born: 08/13/92   Age: 31   Height: 6'4"   Weight: 235   Origin: Round 1, 2010 Draft (#43 overall)

YEAR	TM	LVL	AGE	G (GS)	IP	W-L	SV	K	WHIP	ERA	CSP	BB%	K%	HR%	GB%	ZSw%	ZCon%	OSw%	OCon%	BABIP	SLGCON	DRA-	WARP
2021	NYM	MLB	28	30(29)	159	7-11	0	146	1.18	4.47	56.2%	8.4%	22.3%	4.0%	41.9%	65.0%	83.5%	30.4%	64.4%	.254	.532	100	1.5
2022	NYM	MLB	29	29(29)	157¹	12-5	0	132	1.19	3.49	53.4%	6.9%	20.3%	2.3%	45.9%	66.6%	85.9%	34.3%	64.3%	.284	.468	96	1.8
2023	PHI	MLB	30	31(31)	172²	15-6	0	138	1.31	4.38	45.6%	9.7%	18.8%	2.7%	44.4%	65.5%	88.7%	30.4%	67.0%	.273	.504	106	1.5
2024 DC	PHI	MLB	31	28(28)	154	9-9	0	123	1.41	4.93	50.5%	0.9%	10.4%	3.6%	43.6%					.292	.553	109	0.7

2023 Arsenal: FS (88.1), SI (92.6), FA (93.1), FC (87.6), KC (75.3), SL (86.3), SW (82.6)   *Comps: Pete Harnisch (74), Ramon Martinez (73), Andy Benes (72)*

At 30 years old, Walker set a personal record for innings and finally eclipsed the 20 start threshold. That's where the good news ends, because those 170+ innings were wildly mediocre, especially in the second half, an issue that seems to plague him perennially. None of his pitches by themselves were particularly terrible, but none stood out, either, which is not ideal since his splitter usually does. His velo continued to erode, and he finished the season with career-worst strikeout and walk rates underpinned by career-worst zone and contact rates. It made for a postseason where he was left unused, even when all other hands were on deck. Walker toyed with his pitch mix a bit, favoring his sinker over his four-seamer and subbing out his slider for his cutter, perhaps to tunnel the splitter more effectively. Neither of these tweaks can shoulder the blame, at least not by themselves. He's always managed to outperform his peripherals with middling stuff, but when the peripherals implode like a black hole, their gravitational pull may be too ruthless to escape.

Zack Wheeler RHP   Born: 05/30/90   Age: 34   Height: 6'4"   Weight: 195   Origin: Round 1, 2009 Draft (#6 overall)

YEAR	TM	LVL	AGE	G (GS)	IP	W-L	SV	K	WHIP	ERA	CSP	BB%	K%	HR%	GB%	ZSw%	ZCon%	OSw%	OCon%	BABIP	SLGCON	DRA-	WARP
2021	PHI	MLB	31	32(32)	213¹	14-10	0	247	1.01	2.78	53.9%	5.4%	29.1%	1.9%	49.1%	73.6%	82.3%	34.1%	58.0%	.291	.468	62	6.3
2022	PHI	MLB	32	26(26)	153	12-7	0	163	1.04	2.82	52.7%	5.6%	26.9%	2.1%	45.9%	69.5%	82.5%	35.8%	63.7%	.287	.495	74	3.5
2023	PHI	MLB	33	32(32)	192	13-6	0	212	1.08	3.61	47.2%	5.0%	26.9%	2.5%	40.8%	71.9%	81.7%	36.5%	56.6%	.292	.511	78	4.5
2024 DC	PHI	MLB	34	29(29)	174²	12-8	0	183	1.14	3.43	50.5%	5.9%	25.6%	3.2%	42.8%					.292	.540	81	3.3

2023 Arsenal: FA (96), SI (95.4), SL (91.1), SW (84.4), CU (81.5), CH (90.5)   *Comps: John Smoltz (77), Bob Welch (77), Bob Gibson (77)*

Wheeler is a true workhorse, combining quality and quantity in a way other pitchers can only dream of. Whereas some pitchers ride one or two elite pitches to success, the right-hander leverages one of baseball's deepest and most well-balanced arsenals, a repertoire of five solidly above-average pitches that all generate weak contact and double-digit swinging-strike rates. If we were to pick nits—as a precaution, but more out of boredom than anything else—it's that he leans heavily on his two fastballs that thrive on crisp velocity from a lower arm slot. That velocity won't last forever, and his breaking stuff isn't currently lethal enough to sustain him in a post-fastball world. Given that he's entering his age-34 season, it's anyone's best guess when his stuff starts to fade. Then again, he possesses the kind of command that would play up the inferior stuff he does not yet have. It's also difficult to succeed in this game without being adaptable, and Wheeler is definitely that: Last year he added a sweeper that bridged the gap (in both velocity and movement) between his slider and curve. Few pitchers are better-equipped to age gracefully through their 30s.

LINEOUTS

Hitters

HITTER	POS	TM	LVL	AGE	PA	R	HR	RBI	SB	AVG/OBP/SLG	BABIP	SLGCON	BB%	K%	ZSw%	ZCon%	OSw%	OCon%	LA	90th EV	DRC+	BRR	DRP	WARP
Starlyn Caba	SS	DSL PHW	ROK	17	164	29	0	17	16	.301/.423/.346	.339	.393	17.1%	9.8%										
Rodolfo Castro	IF	IND	AAA	24	57	7	2	10	0	.192/.246/.346	.267	.581	5.3%	36.8%	71.3%	73.1%	36.4%	50.9%			78	1.1	1.7	0.2
	IF	PIT	MLB	24	224	19	6	22	1	.228/.317/.355	.300	.519	9.4%	27.7%	72.3%	81.4%	28.6%	40.8%	9.1	104.4	83	-0.1	-1.4	0.1
	IF	PHI	MLB	24	32	2	0	2	0	.100/.156/.100	.167	.167	6.3%	37.5%	67.3%	87.9%	34.0%	43.8%	-5.5	105.6	66	0.0	-0.1	0.0
Carlos De La Cruz	1B	REA	AA	23	582	80	24	67	3	.259/.344/.454	.327	.662	9.3%	27.5%							91	-0.7	-5.8	0.6
Raylin Heredia	RF	PHL	ROK	19	164	30	4	25	7	.326/.415/.532	.438	.758	10.4%	25.6%										
	RF	CLR	A	19	73	9	1	9	4	.288/.342/.409	.419	.628	8.2%	31.5%	73.8%	80.6%	37.1%	36.7%			77	0.3	1.0	0.2
Scott Kingery	IF	LHV	AAA	29	466	68	13	47	24	.244/.325/.400	.328	.600	10.3%	29.0%	71.5%	77.2%	34.3%	55.5%			81	6.2	7.4	1.4
Matt Kroon	3B	SCO	WIN	26	68	12	1	13	5	.268/.368/.357	.368	.541	10.3%	27.9%	76.9%	50.0%	28.6%	50.0%						
	3B	REA	AA	26	344	53	8	44	22	.319/.387/.493	.375	.634	9.6%	19.2%							110	1.0	-8.0	0.6
	3B	LHV	AAA	26	76	12	3	13	4	.381/.447/.698	.457	.917	14.5%	19.7%	58.0%	87.0%	28.7%	51.0%			111	-0.3	-0.7	0.1
Aidan Miller	SS	PHL	ROK	19	36	6	0	2	0	.414/.528/.483	.500	.583	16.7%	13.9%										
	SS	CLR	A	19	44	4	0	0	4	.216/.341/.297	.296	.407	13.6%	22.7%	73.7%	92.9%	8.9%	100.0%			96	-0.9	1.5	0.2
Robert Moore	MI	WIS	A+	21	563	68	8	62	26	.233/.321/.361	.280	.463	9.8%	19.2%							104	-2.4	2.7	1.5
Símon Muzziotti	OF	LHV	AAA	24	524	67	7	61	26	.296/.358/.404	.343	.487	8.6%	15.5%	66.7%	87.5%	38.7%	74.8%			97	-0.9	3.4	1.8
Nick Podkul	IF	REA	AA	26	197	31	12	35	0	.285/.396/.588	.310	.782	13.7%	20.8%							128	-2.4	-0.9	0.8
	IF	LHV	AAA	26	34	9	2	5	0	.280/.471/.560	.278	.700	14.7%	14.7%	67.2%	82.9%	21.2%	44.4%			115	-1.1	-0.1	0.0
Caleb Ricketts	C	CLR	A	23	100	16	1	23	2	.368/.390/.547	.415	.634	3.0%	13.0%	69.7%	92.5%	30.5%	68.3%			114	0.8	3.1	0.8
	C	JS	A+	23	188	21	3	25	4	.218/.287/.300	.256	.378	8.0%	18.6%							105	-1.3	-2.9	0.1
Bryan Rincon	SS	CLR	A	19	348	49	8	45	23	.228/.369/.370	.261	.479	17.0%	18.1%	65.6%	88.7%	22.0%	65.6%			116	-0.7	1.4	2.1
	SS	JS	A+	19	77	13	0	7	4	.258/.364/.323	.308	.408	11.7%	16.9%							106	1.2	-1.7	0.2
Devin Saltiban	SS	PHL	ROK	18	46	10	1	7	5	.333/.391/.452	.382	.543	6.5%	15.2%	83.3%	60.0%	38.1%	37.5%						
Cal Stevenson	OF	SAC	AAA	26	58	8	1	1	2	.163/.293/.224	.241	.367	13.8%	32.8%	51.0%	84.0%	28.8%	61.9%			93	1.1	1.1	0.3
	OF	LHV	AAA	26	202	39	8	30	14	.271/.437/.472	.316	.687	22.8%	22.3%	54.2%	89.7%	19.6%	57.6%			123	1.9	-1.3	1.0
	OF	LV	AAA	26	29	7	0	2	3	.348/.483/.435	.400	.500	20.7%	10.3%	41.3%	100.0%	19.4%	75.0%			115	1.0	-0.2	0.2
	OF	SF	MLB	26	12	1	0	0	0	.000/.250/.000		.000	25.0%	16.7%	55.6%	100.0%	19.5%	62.5%	12.8	102.0	106	0.0	-0.2	0.0
Weston Wilson	SS	LHV	AAA	28	544	90	31	86	32	.259/.363/.515	.307	.755	13.8%	26.8%	64.3%	81.8%	24.8%	46.9%			116	3.8	-3.9	2.4
	SS	PHI	MLB	28	22	5	1	2	3	.313/.500/.500	.400	.727	27.3%	22.7%	70.3%	76.9%	18.6%	54.5%	7.3	101.6	99	0.1	0.1	0.1

Signed for $3 million out of the Dominican Republic, 17-year-old **Starlyn Caba** is a superlative defensive shortstop who, in his first taste of pro ball, hit .301 while walking nearly twice as often as he struck out. He's a long ways away, but he emphatically checks all the boxes. ⑩ Swapped for Bailey Falter at the deadline, **Rodolfo Castro** headed five hours east on I-76 so he could hop off the bench a couple of times a week when the Phillies needed a warm body at third or second. The good news is that Lehigh Valley is barely more than an hour, with good traffic. ⑩ **Carlos De La Cruz** is built like Oneil Cruz, but somehow taller and wirier. As you might imagine, the tools are loud (if not as loud as Oneil's) but volatile. He's crept up the organizational ladder, warranting cautious optimism that his power and athleticism in the field can overcome the lack of hit tool. ⑩ **Raylin Heredia** could prove the pull of the 2020-21 international signing class. Toolsy but unrefined, he has done nothing but hit the snot out of the ball… and strike out. A plus runner and above-average defender, he's a future corner outfielder if (big *if*) he can corral the Ks. ⑩ With the completion of his six-year contract, **Scott Kingery** is free. Or is it the Phillies who are free of Scott Kingery? In any sense, he is free to do whatever he wants—which *can* include baseball if he chooses. Given his inadequacy at Triple-A the last several years, perhaps it shouldn't. ⑩ After losing two of the last three developmental years to COVID-19 and injury, **Matt Kroon** mashed at Double-A and carried that momentum up to Triple-A. A third baseman and outfielder, his production and versatility could croon his way into a bench role. ⑩ The Phillies selected **Aidan Miller** as their 2023 first-rounder, and he immediately became their best hitting prospect. Does that say more about Miller, or about the Phillies' lack of impact talent? Are they mutually exclusive? ⑩ There's plenty to like about **Robert Moore**; having a low-ceiling-but-high-floor guy that can get on base, run and also bring some pop to the table never hurts. Fizziness aside, he's two or so years away, time for plenty of refills. ⑩ It was good to see **Símon Muzziotti** finally play a full professional season, uninterrupted by injury or administrative hurdles. Sadly, those unadulterated reps offered no new insight: He's a contact-oriented hitter with a capable glove and arm but virtually no power. ⑩ A longtime below-average hitter with Toronto, **Nick Podkul** became a Phillie farmhand at 26 and immediately hit for unforeseen average and power across the high minors. "*He can't keep getting away with it!!!*" —Jesse Pinkman, re: whoever is sprinkling magic pixie dust on all these retread hitters. ⑩ You can't spell **Caleb Ricketts** without "crickets," the sound heard after Ricketts' promotion to High-A Jersey Shore. With hopes that a solid hit tool could carry a glove that lags at a premium position, his bat went deafeningly silent. He has time, but he's old for his level and lacks pedigree. ⑩ **Bryan Rincon** demonstrates plate discipline, a good eye, and a complete dearth of power, reflecting both his current existence as a smaller-framed teenager and his future trajectory toward a low-ceiling but useful regular. ⑩ **Devin Saltiban** impressed the Phillies so much with his athleticism that they drafted him intent on making him a shortstop, a position he hasn't played since Little League. Should the experiment fail, they'll simply move him back to his natural position in center field. ⑩ The MLB ledger won't show it, but **Cal Stevenson**, in doing his best Edwin Jackson impression, is on his sixth team in as many years following three trades and DFAs last year. Let us hope, for him and for us, that 2024 makes it seven and counting. ⑩ Eight years into his professional career, **Weston Wilson** boasts intriguing power and speed but, most importantly, valuable defensive versatility that earned him a spot on the postseason roster. His plate discipline holds him back, but at 29, he fulfilled a lifelong dream. Let this be a memorial of that.

Pitchers

PITCHER	TM	LVL	AGE	G (GS)	IP	W-L	SV	K	WHIP	ERA	CSP	BB%	K%	HR%	GB%	ZSw%	ZCon%	OSw%	OCon%	BABIP	SLGCON	DRA-	WARP
Samuel Aldegheri	CLR	A	21	16 (15)	67²	3-1	0	79	1.32	3.86		10.3%	27.1%	2.7%	42.4%	70.1%	79.6%	34.5%	55.3%	.302	.555	76	1.2
	JS	A+	21	4 (4)	16	1-0	0	20	1.50	5.62		6.9%	27.8%	1.4%	32.6%					.400	.565	83	0.1
Shaun Anderson	LHV	AAA	28	11 (11)	52	4-2	0	35	1.42	4.85		6.5%	15.2%	4.8%	37.4%	67.8%	88.3%	28.5%	64.1%	.287	.588	106	0.5
Jean Cabrera	CLR	A	21	19 (13)	81¹	5-7	1	86	1.60	4.32		6.1%	24.0%	0.8%	47.2%	69.9%	82.2%	35.8%	58.5%	.432	.569	86	1.0
Dylan Covey	OKC	AAA	31	7 (6)	32	1-0	0	28	1.44	4.22		12.7%	19.7%	2.1%	63.2%	65.1%	90.4%	30.6%	61.4%	.272	.432	107	0.2
	LAD	MLB	31	1 (0)	4	0-0	0	3	1.50	4.50	50.5%	5.6%	16.7%	11.1%	57.1%	59.3%	87.5%	38.9%	85.7%	.250	.786	94	0.1
	PHI	MLB	31	28 (1)	39	1-3	0	27	1.51	3.69	45.0%	9.2%	15.6%	1.7%	53.1%	71.5%	90.7%	31.5%	74.0%	.320	.468	99	0.5
Drew Hutchison	BUF	AAA	32	9 (9)	35	2-2	0	31	1.80	5.66		17.9%	19.1%	1.9%	50.0%	63.5%	85.2%	24.7%	66.3%	.313	.510	116	0.2
	LHV	AAA	32	15 (15)	75¹	4-4	0	62	1.54	5.62		13.6%	18.3%	3.0%	42.2%	68.4%	85.9%	29.8%	63.1%	.280	.527	96	1.3
Alex McFarlane	CLR	A	22	16 (16)	50¹	0-4	0	69	1.67	5.72		16.3%	29.6%	1.7%	56.4%	66.3%	76.9%	29.5%	43.5%	.365	.576	85	0.6
Wen Hui Pan	CLR	A	20	27 (1)	57²	4-1	7	81	0.87	2.81		8.5%	36.2%	0.9%	45.0%	71.2%	73.9%	35.6%	59.0%	.246	.367	58	1.7
	JS	A+	20	6 (0)	6	0-0	0	7	3.00	15.00		13.9%	19.4%	2.8%	37.5%					.522	.792	110	0.0
Erich Uelmen	LHV	AAA	27	14 (0)	15²	1-2	1	14	1.66	4.02		11.3%	19.7%	1.4%	68.8%	65.9%	79.0%	31.9%	66.0%	.362	.542	92	0.3
	PHI	MLB	27	1 (0)	1	0-0	0	1	5.00	36.00	45.5%	25.0%	12.5%	0.0%	40.0%	54.5%	83.3%	13.6%	33.3%	.600	1.250	100	0.0
Jeremy Walker	LHV	AAA	28	47 (2)	68¹	6-2	0	52	1.24	2.90		11.1%	18.6%	2.9%	47.9%	66.7%	87.2%	28.3%	59.8%	.247	.438	97	1.0

A native of Italy, **Samuel Aldegheri** is a somewhat late convert to baseball. In his first full season his four-pitch mix piled up whiffs. He's unpolished due to circumstances both personal and global (he originally signed in 2019, pre-pandemic), but he's projectable. ⓧ **Shaun Anderson** returned stateside last summer after a short, unspectacular stint in the KBO. Despite his first go as a starter, the Phillies gave him another shot, inserting him into Lehigh Valley's rotation. The early returns were, at best, dubious. It's not "second time's the charm," after all. ⓧ After a forgettable 2022 campaign, **Jean Cabrera** got his control woes, uh, under control, cutting his walk rate in half and then some. He crucially added velocity, better delineating his breaking stuff, and showcased a hard, whiff-heavy changeup. He's old for his level but trending back toward being a back-end starter. ⓧ **Dylan Covey** made a two-year pit stop in Taiwan, starting 33 games for the Rakuten Monkeys. He was hardly an ace there, and when he returned stateside the Dodgers took a flier but quickly released him. Kudos to the Phillies for coaxing a 3.69 ERA out of his 7% swinging-strike rate. ⓧ **Drew Hutchison** spent most of 2023 bouncing between Triple-A and the Developmental List. What kind of developing Hutchison is doing at this point is unclear, but given the magic the Phillies worked on Jeff Hoffman and others at similar junctures you can't rule anything out, despite what your instincts demand. ⓧ The Phillies continued to try out former relief prospect **Alex McFarlane** as a starter. They succeeded in stretching him out: He completed 11 innings across two June starts. He also walked 14 of the last 50 hitters he faced. ⓧ Plucked from Taiwan during the 2023 international signing period, **Wen Hui Pan** flashed huge velo, scraping upper-90s with his fastball while showing a lethal splitter. His breaking and off speed pitches need refinement, but there may still be long-term starter aspirations here. ⓧ **Erich Uelmen** threw one (1) unmitigated disaster of an inning, strained a flexor and otherwise failed to fulfill the promise of his unique delivery that made him a vaguely interesting down-ballot Cubs prospect. ⓧ On his fourth team in five years, **Jeremy Walker** pitched to a sub-3.00 ERA in relief at Lehigh Valley but fundamentally lacked the requisite under-the-hood metrics to corroborate it. He can't miss bats, and at this rate, he'll never have a chance to miss Triple-A.

PITTSBURGH PIRATES

Essay by Michael Baumann

Player comments by Ben Hatch, Jarrett Seidler and BP staff

What's stopping the Pirates from being the Diamondbacks of 2026?

It's a serious question. We just saw an opportunistic Arizona club, composed mostly of castoffs and homegrown players, grab a Wild Card spot when preseason favorites faltered. And from there, the Diamondbacks dispatched three playoff regulars en route to the pennant. To borrow an exhortation from across the state: Why can't us?

The draft and amateur free agency are the most cost-effective ways to acquire talent. MLB has squeezed future players, unrepresented by a union, to a fraction of their potential value. Especially for an organization committed to toeing the line between frugality and penury as Pittsburgh does, making the most of the draft is one of the only avenues to sustainable success.

In any competition, an under-resourced competitor must be able to recognize an advantage when one arises. Unfortunately, Pittsburgh has too frequently done the opposite. Last June, the Pirates went to market with the equivalent of the 67th pick in the draft and simply chose not to use it.

Between Paul Skenes and second-round pick Mitch Jebb, the Pirates were close to $1 million under their bonus pool after two selections. They went $670,000 over with compensation round pick Zander Mueth, and exceeded slot by more than $100,000 just once for the rest of the draft.

All told, the Pirates left more than $300,000 of their bonus pool unspent. And when you consider that they could've gone 5% over without being penalized, that comes to roughly $1.1 million in bonus allotment left on the table. The Pirates can't afford to make unforced errors in the draft, because acquiring stars, surrounding them with supporting talent, is a difficult thing to accomplish under ideal circumstances. And circumstances are less ideal in Pittsburgh than anywhere else in the National League.

⚾   ⚾   ⚾

I don't really want to lead with the payroll and ownership. You've heard it all before. It's reductive. To use a different definition of the word, it's a little cheap.

PITTSBURGH PIRATES PROSPECTUS
2023 W-L: 76-86, 4TH IN NL CENTRAL

Pythag	.438	24th	DER	.691	21st
RS/G	4.27	22nd	DRC+	94	23rd
RA/G	4.88	22nd	DRA-	104	22nd
dWin%	.453	25th	FIP	4.41	21st
Payroll	$73M	27th	B-Age	27.9	8th
M$/MW	$1.9M	4th	P-Age	28.1	6th

- Opened 2001
- Open air
- Natural surface
- Fence profile: 6' to 21'

Park Factors

Runs	Runs/RH	Runs/LH	HR/RH	HR/LH
99	98	100	86	93

Top Hitter WARP	3.0 Bryan Reynolds
Top Pitcher WARP	3.4 Mitch Keller
2023 Top Prospect	Paul Skenes

Payroll History (in millions)

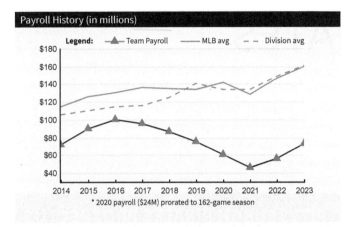

Legend: ▲ Team Payroll — MLB avg - - Division avg

$180
$160
$140
$120
$100
$80
$60
$40

2014 2015 2016 2017 2018 2019 2020 2021 2022 2023

* 2020 payroll ($24M) prorated to 162-game season

Future Commitments (in millions)

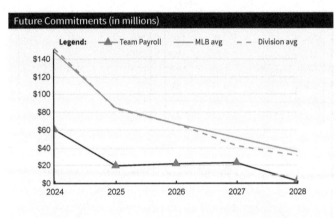

Legend: ▲ Team Payroll — MLB avg - - Division avg

$140
$120
$100
$80
$60
$40
$20
$0

2024 2025 2026 2027 2028

Farm System Ranking

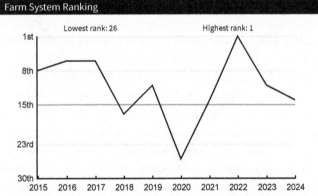

Lowest rank: 26   Highest rank: 1

1st
8th
15th
23rd
30th

2015 2016 2017 2018 2019 2020 2021 2022 2023 2024

Personnel

President
Travis Williams

General Manager
Ben Cherington

Assistant General Manager
Kevan Graves

Assistant General Manager
Steve Sanders

Senior Vice President, Baseball Operations
Bryan Stroh

Manager
Derek Shelton

BP Alumni
Dan Fox
Brendan Gawlowski
Grant Jones

Unfortunately, it determines everything about the Pittsburgh Pirates. It's bracing to look at a team's payroll in 2023 and see a full roster with nobody making more than $10 million. At the other end of the state, that's how much the Phillies spent as a gamble on an aging closer who couldn't throw strikes. The Pirates haven't been in the top 20 in payroll since at least 2000, which is as far back as the numbers at Cot's Contracts go. Those same numbers have year-end 40-man roster spending maxing out at $99.9 million in 2016.

A Major League Baseball team enters 2024, five years past the setting of *Blade Runner*, without running a $100 million payroll. Defenders of this practice might bring up that big players in free agency tend to be blessed with a shiny, fashionable market, like Los Angeles or New York. Pittsburgh, by contrast, has more in common with smaller postindustrial cities of the Midwest, and is fettered to this venerable franchise like a millstone.

At least that's what that cohort might say if anyone wanted to stand up and defend Bob Nutting, whose refusal to invest in his team has made him a pariah in western Pennsylvania and the target of an MLBPA grievance alleging the misappropriation of revenue-sharing funds. Never mind that the Reds and Guardians have gone into nine figures. So have the Twins, Rockies, Brewers and Royals. The Tigers and Orioles won championships in unfashionable markets in the 1980s and have been competitive recently, in spite of Fredo Corleone-like second-generation ownership. The Pirates are in a club with only two other teams: the Oakland Athletics and the Tampa Bay Rays. The A's are currently being moved from Oakland to Las Vegas as part of a process that has all the legitimacy of a money-laundering operation.

Then there's the Rays. Because you *can* win like this. If you're smart, ruthless and unsentimental, and make the most of every opportunity, you can win with a bottom-five payroll. Sure, the Rays' past two playoff appearances have involved going two-and-out in the Wild Card round, scoring a grand total of two runs over four games.

But the Pirates would kill for that. Maybe not Nutting himself; he seems indifferent to the whole making-the-playoffs thing. But Pirates players and fans? Yeah, getting smoked in the first round would be as good as it's been in almost a decade. By the end of this year, we'll be as far removed from the Pirates' last division title and trip to the NLCS as those events are from Bill Mazeroski's home run. And in the 31 years and counting since the Sid Bream slide and Barry Bonds' departure, the Pirates have had only four seasons of 80 or more wins.

So how do you win, on the...whatever comes beyond cheap?

Unless Nutting is visited by the ghost of his deceased business partner on Christmas Eve, the Pirates won't be able to do what the Rangers and Phillies have done of late: Buff up mediocre homegrown cores with hundreds of millions of dollars in superstar free agents. Lucky for them, the recent history of the NL Central suggests they won't have to.

It also would've been nice if the Pirates had strung together some ridiculous run in the draft. Think: The Astros grabbing George Springer, Carlos Correa, Lance McCullers Jr., Alex Bregman and Kyle Tucker with first-round picks in a five-draft span. Or the Orioles taking three no. 1 global prospect-type players (Adley Rutschman, Gunnar Henderson and Jackson Holliday) in four years, plus a number of other impactful big leaguers besides.

The Pirates have picked in the top five three years running, including no. 1 overall twice. Maybe in five years' time we'll look back on Skenes, Henry Davis and Termarr Johnson with similar awe, but we're getting ahead of ourselves.

What's a more replicable path to contenderdom for the Pirates? Well, how about we take a look at the Diamondbacks, who went to the World Series on a payroll of about $124 million, with a roster of roughly half homegrown players. That's about $50 million more than what the Pirates spent last year, but Arizona had about $40 million wrapped up in Madison Bumgarner, Mark Melancon and Nick Ahmed. If the Pirates don't make any mistakes, they might be able to get this done cheaper.

And you can build a team like that. When you drill down, what did the Diamondbacks actually have?

Type	Number	Players
Stars	2	Corbin Carroll, Zac Gallen
Supporting Players	5	Ketel Marte, Merrill Kelly, Christian Walker, Lourdes Gurriel Jr., Geraldo Perdomo
Cresting Prospects	3	Gabriel Moreno, Brandon Pfaadt Jordan Lawlar

That's two legitimate MVP- or Cy Young-type players and about five reliable position players or starters who range from useful on a good team to All-Star level. Add in three highly touted rookies—two of whom became major contributors in the playoffs—and the rest of the roster is made up of guys you can get.

In the postseason, the Diamondbacks platooned a lot. They made situational substitutions and leaned on their bullpen. You can get those guys on the cheap, even deadline pickups like Tommy Pham and Paul Sewald. Anyone can pick up these players, including the Pirates, who in 2023 had veterans with a little juice left in their bats, like Andrew McCutchen and Carlos Santana. Live-armed relievers like Dauri Moreta and Carmen Mlodzinski. The difference between the Pirates and Diamondbacks isn't roster spots no. 11 through 26, it's 1 through 10.

What do the Pirates have now?

Type	Number	Players
Stars	0	
Supporting Players	5	Bryan Reynolds, Ke'Bryan Hayes, David Bednar, Mitch Keller, Jack Suwinski
Cresting Prospects	4	Oneil Cruz, Quinn Priester, Henry Davis, Nick Gonzales

All of this is subjective, and obviously subject to change. It would've been nice to be able to count on Johan Oviedo for 2024, for instance. And all three of these listed prospects have wildly divergent possible outcomes, even for next year alone.

Out of the 10 Diamondbacks I highlighted, four have spent their entire professional careers with Arizona, including Carroll, who is a caliber of player the Pirates do not have at the moment. Walker bounced around a little, unable to break through into a starting job at various stops, before the Diamondbacks gave him enough playing time to blossom into a first-division starter.

Perhaps it's out of necessity, but the Pirates have given a lot of rope to potential diamonds in the rough. Walker was a waiver claim, but Pittsburgh has done good business finding these guys in trades: Bednar and Suwinski spring immediately to mind; even Connor Joe was pretty good in 2023, though I doubt he'll be the first baseman on the Pirates' next playoff team. It wasn't that long ago that the Astros used a similar process to find and develop Dallas Keuchel, Collin McHugh and Marwin Gonzalez.

The Diamondbacks have done two things the Pirates have not. The first is to capitalize on free agents from Asia, namely Kelly and Scott McGough. The Pirates have gone this route in the past, with Jung Ho Kang, before his rapidly expanding criminal record forced him to return to Korea. Ji Hwan Bae came over as a teenager, and is therefore more equivalent to an international signing from the Americas; either way, he hasn't hit a lick in the majors so it's all academic anyway.

Unless you're shopping at the top of the posting or free agent market in KBO or NPB, there's not much star power to be had. But Kelly is the perfect example of the kind of player who's available to teams that bother to look: An important supporting player, a mid-rotation starter, high-leverage relievers or useful position players. The Diamondbacks haven't spent that much money, but they've looked under every stone for talent; Pittsburgh would profit from following their example.

Most of the rest of Arizona's core came from an audacious but rare form of transaction: challenge trades. It's hard to find partners for this kind of trade, but Arizona GM Mike Hazen has won huge by doing this three times in six years, netting him Gallen, Marte, Gurriel and Moreno. The closest the Pirates have come to pulling off a move like that was the January 2018 deal that brought over Reynolds, Kyle Crick and international bonus money in exchange for McCutchen. Despite understandable uproar at the time, it's proved to be one of the best moves the Pirates have made in the past decade.

Making this kind of deal requires existing MLB talent, on which the Pirates have been short of late. But consider the disastrous trades Pittsburgh has made while the Diamondbacks were gobbling up young, talented big leaguers. Gerrit Cole turned into Joe Musgrove and a few other pieces, who turned into Bednar, Endy Rodríguez and a few other pieces. Tyler Glasnow, Shane Baz and Austin Meadows turned into Chris Archer, who came down with thoracic outlet syndrome.

Here's the real problem. In order to win on the cheap, you have to be lucky and smart. The Pirates haven't been lucky, but if we're using "smart" in the common front office shorthand for being good at scouting and player development, in general they haven't been smart either. Players they've acquired have stagnated, while players they've traded away have flourished.

And yet, there's an avalanche of young talent coming down the pipeline. Perhaps Suwinski's breakout is an omen that things are changing. But through all this, the Pirates still don't have a star on the level of a Carroll or a Gallen. There are candidates in the system: Cruz, most obviously, if he can stay healthy. Then there's 2022 no. 4 overall pick Termarr Johnson, and most recently Skenes.

In 2021, the Pirates drafted Davis first overall, in a seeming concession to the fact that you need stars as well as supporting players. Davis had a rough introduction to big-league baseball, but his under-slot bonus (only the fifth-highest in the class) funded the signings of talented high schoolers Anthony Solometo, Lonnie White Jr. and Bubba Chandler with the next three picks.

In 2023, in a much stronger draft with as many as five potential no. 1 selections, the Pirates went with chalk. Skenes was essentially co-favorite with his LSU teammate Dylan Crews, and the Pirates chose the more famous (and incidentally, more signable) of the two.

Year	Player	Bonus vs. Slot	Next 3 Picks vs. Slot
2021	Henry Davis	-$1.92M	+$3.38M
2023	Paul Skenes	-$520K	-$487K

Skenes went for the customary bonus for a no. 1 pick: Less than slot, but more than no. 2. If the Pirates had repeated their 2021 strategy, they probably would've taken high schooler Max Clark, who went third overall to the Tigers. Instead, they got a player who's as likely as anyone in his class to turn into a star.

Let's go back to that chart of stars and supporting players, and fast-forward three years into the future. Let's be optimistic, but not pie-in-the-sky, about how these players will develop over the next few years.

Type	Number	Players
Stars	2	Paul Skenes, Oneil Cruz
Supporting Players	6	Bryan Reynolds, Ke'Bryan Hayes, Jack Suwinski, Johan Oviedo, Nick Gonzales, Henry Davis
Cresting Prospects	2	Termarr Johnson, Bubba Chandler

However you want to project the next few years, the Pirates have two players—Skenes and Cruz—who could end up being as good as Gallen and Carroll, and soon. Reynolds and Hayes are locked down to long-term extensions, and there's plenty more talent where that came from.

Homegrown talent alone, however, is never enough. Even the Rays, Diamondbacks and Brewers supplement their prospects with established stars acquired through win-now trades and free agent signings. Among the 2023 playoff contenders, the closest thing to a true Dollar General contender was the Marlins, who still needed to build out their roster through challenge trades, the odd free agent signing and—crucially, in contrast to Pittsburgh—superior development of pitching.

Even then, Miami got bounced in two games, by an aggregate score of 11-2, by the team the Diamondbacks beat two rounds later. "Participate" might be too strong a word for what the Marlins did in the playoffs. And even that modest achievement would require investment and ingenuity beyond what the Pirates have exhibited in the past decade.

If offered the season Miami just had—84 wins and an uncompetitive "two-and-cue" in the playoffs—the median Pirates fan would probably bite your hand off to grab it. Is that achievable without breaking out of the bottom five in payroll? Maybe. Is a pennant achievable—or better yet, a consistent run of playoff appearances?

Every million dollars not spent, on major-league payroll or especially in the draft or on player development, is another bounce the Pirates need to get to make the playoffs. Another favorable call from the umpires, another late-night comeback, another well-timed rain delay. In short, another must-have that could've been accounted for but was otherwise left to chance.

You can win that way, sometimes, by being the smartest guys in the room. But it's the height of foolishness to tempt the caprices of the baseball gods, who help those who help themselves. It's not that it's impossible to imagine Pittsburgh contending in the near future, nor that their farm system couldn't grow into the sort of juggernaut Baltimore created. But it'd be a lot easier to dream if they stopped shooting themselves in the foot. ▪

—Michael Baumann is an author of FanGraphs.

HITTERS

Ji Hwan Bae 2B/CF   Born: 07/26/99   Age: 24   Bats: L   Throws: R   Height: 5'11"   Weight: 185   Origin: IFA, 2018

YEAR	TM	LVL	AGE	PA	R	HR	RBI	SB	AVG/OBP/SLG	BABIP	SLGCON	BB%	K%	ZSw%	ZCon%	OSw%	OCon%	LA	90th EV	DRC+	BRR	DRP	WARP
2021	ALT	AA	21	365	63	7	31	20	.278/.359/.413	.352	.557	10.4%	22.7%							103	3.2	-4.6	1.1
2022	IND	AAA	22	473	81	8	53	30	.289/.362/.430	.338	.531	10.1%	16.9%	70.2%	87.9%	26.6%	76.5%			106	5.3	-0.6	2.1
2022	PIT	MLB	22	37	5	0	6	3	.333/.405/.424	.407	.519	5.4%	16.2%	63.8%	75.7%	30.6%	89.5%	1.5	102.3	91	0.1	0.2	0.1
2023	PIT	MLB	23	371	54	2	32	24	.231/.296/.311	.310	.430	8.1%	24.8%	65.6%	83.1%	32.4%	63.3%	-0.6	102.8	75	1.0	1.8	0.4
2024 DC	PIT	MLB	24	282	25	4	25	14	.232/.304/.341	.295	.451	8.4%	22.1%							83	0.2	0.7	0.4

2023 GP: 2B (64), CF (62), SS (3) *Comps: Erick Aybar (70), Luis Sardinas (62), Yolmer Sánchez (59)*

Bae's speed is his selling point, and he proved it in a century's worth of games at the major-league level in 2023. He managed to post 24 steals despite pitiful offensive numbers, as a sky-high ground-ball rate led to a ground-floor OBP. He's flashed double-digit home run potential and passable discipline throughout his minor-league career; pair that with his 70-grade speed and you can see why the Pirates envision him as a solid MLB contributor. Bae could have made a better first impression in the majors, but his athleticism and consistency in the minors give him runway to learn on the job.

Jack Brannigan IF   Born: 03/11/01   Age: 23   Bats: R   Throws: R   Height: 6'0"   Weight: 190   Origin: Round 3, 2022 Draft (#83 overall)

YEAR	TM	LVL	AGE	PA	R	HR	RBI	SB	AVG/OBP/SLG	BABIP	SLGCON	BB%	K%	ZSw%	ZCon%	OSw%	OCon%	LA	90th EV	DRC+	BRR	DRP	WARP
2022	BRD	A	21	112	14	3	14	6	.211/.330/.337	.266	.478	13.4%	25.0%	60.7%	79.3%	30.2%	67.6%			117	0.1	1.9	0.8
2023	BRD	A	22	201	38	7	17	17	.253/.398/.451	.337	.676	15.9%	26.9%	59.9%	83.2%	27.4%	54.3%			113	2.2	6.9	1.8
2023	GBO	A+	22	173	26	12	37	7	.299/.382/.605	.395	1.000	12.1%	33.5%							102	-1.5	6.9	1.0
2024 non	PIT	MLB	23	251	23	5	24	0	.221/.294/.340	.317	.524	8.4%	31.8%							80	0.0	0	0.1

2023 GP: SS (48), 3B (47), 2B (11), DH (5) *Comps: Randy César (58), Ramon Morla (58), Nelson Ward (56)*

We were promised more two-way prospects in the wake of Ohtani but instead what we got is this: guys like Brannigan, who's focusing on hitting but can fall back on a fastball-slider combo if the hit tool never surfaces. Cynically, it makes sense. If the backup plan is a max-effort reliever bound to blow out his arm twice in six years, does it matter if those years start at 28 instead of 22? To his credit, Brannigan doesn't need to practice his grip yet. He's shown impressive game power and enough athleticism to stay on the dirt, though likely at third. He'll either have to cut down on the whiffs, though, or soon he'll have to start getting more of them.

Tsung-Che Cheng MI   Born: 07/26/01   Age: 22   Bats: L   Throws: R   Height: 5'7"   Weight: 173   Origin: IFA, 2019

YEAR	TM	LVL	AGE	PA	R	HR	RBI	SB	AVG/OBP/SLG	BABIP	SLGCON	BB%	K%	ZSw%	ZCon%	OSw%	OCon%	LA	90th EV	DRC+	BRR	DRP	WARP
2021	PIRG	ROK	19	157	32	4	31	16	.311/.449/.492	.321	.556	19.1%	8.9%									3.2	
2022	CAR	WIN	20	74	4	0	4	2	.182/.270/.242	.222	.296	9.5%	16.2%										
2022	BRD	A	20	458	79	6	52	33	.270/.376/.418	.340	.555	13.8%	20.7%	67.0%	82.7%	30.5%	67.7%			120	2.0	3.6	2.8
2023	GBO	A+	21	254	45	9	31	13	.308/.406/.575	.361	.737	13.8%	18.5%							130	-0.6	2.6	2.1
2023	ALT	AA	21	281	35	4	25	13	.251/.304/.352	.297	.448	6.0%	18.9%							95	2.0	0.4	1.0
2024 non	PIT	MLB	22	251	21	3	22	7	.225/.289/.335	.282	.440	7.6%	21.8%							76	0.0	0	0.1

2023 GP: SS (84), 2B (41), DH (2) *Comps: Didi Gregorius (67), Luis Rengifo (67), Yamaico Navarro (66)*

Cheng is a nifty prospect who, despite lacking a carrying tool, comes with a broad base of skills making the Pirates' 2019 signing for $380,000 look good already. After successful campaigns all the way through High-A Greensboro, Cheng graced the upper levels of the minors for the first time in 2023. Unfortunately, that's generally where pressure is applied to the "broad-based skill sets that lack carrying tools" and we see if, and how, they crack. Cheng's first foray against upper-level arms showed plenty of fissures: While his bat-to-ball remained solidly intact, his patience wore thin, as pitchers took advantage of his fringy bat speed and pounded the upper parts of the zone, where he couldn't keep up. Without the ability to truly impact the ball and the walks to buoy his offensive line, Cheng doesn't cut quite the profile. He'll only be 22 for the upcoming season, though, and can adequately man the six spot, though second base—or better yet, a utility role—may be his ultimate home.

Oneil Cruz SS   Born: 10/04/98   Age: 25   Bats: L   Throws: R   Height: 6'7"   Weight: 215   Origin: IFA, 2015

YEAR	TM	LVL	AGE	PA	R	HR	RBI	SB	AVG/OBP/SLG	BABIP	SLGCON	BB%	K%	ZSw%	ZCon%	OSw%	OCon%	LA	90th EV	DRC+	BRR	DRP	WARP
2021	ALT	AA	22	273	51	12	40	18	.292/.346/.536	.349	.720	7.3%	23.4%							120	2.6	-1.7	1.6
2021	IND	AAA	22	29	11	5	7	1	.524/.655/1.286	.545	1.688	27.6%	17.2%							147	0.0	1.1	0.3
2021	PIT	MLB	22	9	2	1	3	0	.333/.333/.667	.500	1.200	0.0%	44.4%	41.7%	80.0%	47.6%	30.0%	4.5	118.2	82		0.0	0.0
2022	IND	AAA	23	247	40	9	35	11	.232/.336/.422	.270	.574	12.1%	22.7%	61.4%	66.7%	34.2%	64.0%			114	1.5	1.6	1.4
2022	PIT	MLB	23	361	45	17	54	10	.233/.294/.450	.317	.727	7.8%	34.9%	52.8%	78.8%	32.6%	49.8%	8.3	111.5	91	0.8	-5.8	0.2
2023	PIT	MLB	24	40	7	1	4	3	.250/.375/.375	.292	.500	17.5%	20.0%	62.5%	72.5%	33.0%	65.6%	13.0	111.1	106	0.1	-0.1	0.2
2024 DC	PIT	MLB	25	524	55	17	61	20	.219/.294/.395	.276	.566	8.8%	27.2%							91	0.6	-6.4	0.6

2023 GP: SS (9) *Comps: Reid Brignac (60), Adalberto Mondesi (56), Corey Seager (53)*

Elly de la Cruz has taken the league by storm, but Pittsburgh has him at home with their own 6-foot-7 shortstop. Cruz, like his NL Central colleague, is all about bucking the trend. He holds the hardest-hit ball in major-league history and once had the hardest throw from an infielder in MLB history (you'll never guess who overtook him) at 97.8 mph. His power is astonishing in particular, due to the effortlessness in his swing, which is reminiscent of Giancarlo Stanton. His struggles come from plate discipline, evident by the fact that he struck out more than a third of the time in his debut season while also walking at a below-average rate. On the other side of the ball, his generational arm strength doesn't carry over to his range, leading to poor defensive numbers at shortstop. He's a clear work in progress, but with an entire offseason to rest up from the fibula injury he suffered in early April that kept him out for the whole year, he will have a chance to show his freakish talents in front of Pittsburgh's faithful.

Henry Davis   C   Born: 09/21/99   Age: 24   Bats: R   Throws: R   Height: 6'0"   Weight: 210   Origin: Round 1, 2021 Draft (#1 overall)

YEAR	TM	LVL	AGE	PA	R	HR	RBI	SB	AVG/OBP/SLG	BABIP	SLGCON	BB%	K%	ZSw%	ZCon%	OSw%	OCon%	LA	90th EV	DRC+	BRR	DRP	WARP
2021	GBO	A+	21	24	6	2	3	1	.263/.375/.684	.300	1.182	16.7%	33.3%							100	0.3	-0.5	0.1
2022	GBO	A+	22	100	18	5	22	5	.341/.450/.585	.383	.750	8.0%	18.0%							134	0.4	-0.9	0.7
2022	ALT	AA	22	136	19	4	18	3	.207/.324/.379	.244	.512	8.8%	22.1%							104	1.8	-1.8	0.5
2023	ALT	AA	23	187	25	10	27	7	.284/.433/.547	.311	.717	17.1%	18.7%							142	-0.4	0.9	1.5
2023	IND	AAA	23	63	7	2	5	3	.375/.516/.604	.485	.829	20.6%	20.6%	65.7%	83.6%	23.5%	51.4%			110	0.0	0.5	0.2
2023	PIT	MLB	23	255	27	7	24	3	.213/.302/.351	.273	.506	9.8%	27.1%	62.8%	86.9%	32.3%	54.8%	12.7	105.4	84	0.0	-2.2	-0.1
2024 DC	*PIT*	*MLB*	*24*	*486*	*49*	*12*	*51*	*10*	*.222/.312/.365*	*.274*	*.494*	*9.7%*	*23.3%*							*95*	*-0.3*	*-0.4*	*1.3*

2023 GP: RF (49), DH (11), C (2)   *Comps: Aaron Cunningham (62), Michael Hermosillo (61), Wendell Magee (58)*

People were puzzled when the Pirates drafted Davis first overall in the 2021 MLB Draft above higher-rated offensive prospects like Marcelo Mayer and Jordan Lawlar, a sentiment still held after being voted the MLB Pipeline's "Most Overrated Prospect" before last season by the league's scouts and executives. But Davis continues to improve at his role: an offensive force who can be serviceable behind the plate. His power and plate discipline both project to be excellent—his discipline is arguably already above league-average—and the revelation of Endy Rodriguez has allowed Davis to move to a more natural corner outfield spot with his elite arm, where he's been around league-average overall. His primary concern is now adjusting his swing path to translate that raw power to in-game results, and at the high level of games, after a quick summer promotion.

Nick Gonzales   MI   Born: 05/27/99   Age: 25   Bats: R   Throws: R   Height: 5'9"   Weight: 190   Origin: Round 1, 2020 Draft (#7 overall)

YEAR	TM	LVL	AGE	PA	R	HR	RBI	SB	AVG/OBP/SLG	BABIP	SLGCON	BB%	K%	ZSw%	ZCon%	OSw%	OCon%	LA	90th EV	DRC+	BRR	DRP	WARP
2021	PEJ	WIN	22	87	18	2	13	4	.380/.483/.549	.446	.684	14.9%	16.1%	75.0%	88.9%	10.0%	50.0%						
2021	GBO	A+	22	369	53	18	54	7	.302/.385/.565	.388	.821	10.8%	27.4%							112	-3.4	-0.8	1.2
2022	ALT	AA	23	316	47	7	33	5	.263/.383/.429	.367	.657	13.6%	28.5%							85	-0.5	-2.9	0.0
2023	IND	AAA	24	443	75	14	49	4	.281/.379/.507	.369	.737	12.0%	26.6%	77.9%	76.7%	32.8%	56.3%			93	-2.6	0.2	0.5
2023	PIT	MLB	24	128	12	2	13	0	.209/.268/.348	.278	.506	4.7%	28.1%	79.7%	79.5%	34.1%	48.5%	7.8	99.2	81	0.0	0.1	0.1
2024 DC	*PIT*	*MLB*	*25*	*185*	*18*	*4*	*19*	*2*	*.231/.309/.372*	*.322*	*.559*	*8.3%*	*29.6%*							*94*	*0.0*	*0.1*	*0.4*

2023 GP: 2B (29), SS (9)   *Comps: Cord Phelps (65), Ray Olmedo (63), J.D. Davis (62)*

Gonzales was part of a battalion of Pirates prospects that both debuted in 2023 and, for the most part, disappointed. The former first founder's calling card has always been power from an up-the-middle position, but he's going to be limited to the keystone defensively and his power comes at the expense of far too much in-zone swing-and-miss, when it opts to show up at all. It was there in spades in Triple-A and far too fleeting in the majors, adequately demonstrating the gulf between those two environs. Gonzales will surely earn another crack in the majors in the upcoming season, but the Pirates have a slew of players in a similar, ahem, boat, so he won't have the luxury of continuing to fail while receiving major-league playing time.

Ke'Bryan Hayes   3B   Born: 01/28/97   Age: 27   Bats: R   Throws: R   Height: 5'11"   Weight: 195   Origin: Round 1, 2015 Draft (#32 overall)

YEAR	TM	LVL	AGE	PA	R	HR	RBI	SB	AVG/OBP/SLG	BABIP	SLGCON	BB%	K%	ZSw%	ZCon%	OSw%	OCon%	LA	90th EV	DRC+	BRR	DRP	WARP
2021	PIT	MLB	24	396	49	6	38	9	.257/.316/.373	.321	.491	7.8%	22.0%	63.0%	91.2%	30.9%	64.4%	2.7	105.6	89	0.2	1.5	1.0
2022	PIT	MLB	25	560	55	7	41	20	.244/.314/.345	.307	.454	8.6%	21.8%	62.1%	90.3%	31.3%	64.9%	5.4	106.8	89	0.5	7.8	1.5
2023	PIT	MLB	26	525	65	15	61	10	.271/.309/.453	.315	.574	5.3%	19.8%	60.5%	91.2%	36.1%	65.6%	13.2	105.8	96	-0.2	4.0	1.8
2024 DC	*PIT*	*MLB*	*27*	*588*	*58*	*12*	*62*	*16*	*.257/.315/.394*	*.303*	*.497*	*7.2%*	*19.1%*							*101*	*0.0*	*8.6*	*2.6*

2023 GP: 3B (122), DH (2)   *Comps: Nolan Arenado (63), Jeimer Candelario (61), Evan Longoria (60)*

The Pirates' defensive wizard showed his potential to be a true franchise cornerstone in 2023, improving in nearly every offensive category. He's hitting the ball harder than ever while elevating it into the air more than ever, at only a slight cost in plate discipline—a recipe for almost certain success. That recipe bore great results this past season: He barreled up the ball at a league-average rate after languishing in the bottom quartile in 2022. He's known for his defensive capabilities and finally won his first Gold Glove this past year after six-time Platinum Glove winner Nolan Arenado generously relinquished his monopoly over them. With the great, proactive contract the Pirates gave him at the beginning of the 2022 season, Ke'Bryan will likely be able to continue enchanting audiences in the Burgh with his plays at the hot corner until 2030.

Mitch Jebb   MI   Born: 05/13/02   Age: 22   Bats: L   Throws: R   Height: 6'1"   Weight: 185   Origin: Round 2, 2023 Draft (#42 overall)

YEAR	TM	LVL	AGE	PA	R	HR	RBI	SB	AVG/OBP/SLG	BABIP	SLGCON	BB%	K%	ZSw%	ZCon%	OSw%	OCon%	LA	90th EV	DRC+	BRR	DRP	WARP
2023	BRD	A	21	153	26	1	13	11	.297/.382/.398	.308	.436	11.1%	7.2%	57.7%	95.6%	21.3%	81.1%			121	2.3	-1.4	1.0
2024 non	*PIT*	*MLB*	*22*	*251*	*19*	*2*	*19*	*0*	*.215/.276/.298*	*.243*	*.345*	*6.7%*	*12.9%*							*62*	*0.0*	*0*	*-0.4*

2023 GP: 2B (18), SS (18)   *Comps: Wenceel Pérez (91), Chris Getz (90), Hernan Iribarren (86)*

Jebb! was an underslot second-round pick out of Michigan State last year. He's an extreme contact-oriented middle infielder who made about as much impact after signing as his political namesake did in the 2016 Republican primary. He's not small of stature, but he makes himself small in the box and puts the ball in play with low energy. His glove and agility will play in the middle infield, although his arm is better suited for second base than shortstop. If this all sounds like "taller Nick Madrigal," well, at least he was the 42nd pick in the draft instead of the fourth. Please clap!

Connor Joe RF Born: 08/16/92 Age: 31 Bats: R Throws: R Height: 6'0" Weight: 205 Origin: Round 1, 2014 Draft (#39 overall)

YEAR	TM	LVL	AGE	PA	R	HR	RBI	SB	AVG/OBP/SLG	BABIP	SLGCON	BB%	K%	ZSw%	ZCon%	OSw%	OCon%	LA	90th EV	DRC+	BRR	DRP	WARP
2021	ABQ	AAA	28	110	20	9	25	1	.326/.418/.696	.333	.914	13.6%	20.0%							130	-0.3	-1.4	0.6
2021	COL	MLB	28	211	23	8	35	0	.285/.379/.469	.323	.609	12.3%	19.4%	70.0%	86.3%	23.2%	57.4%	14.9	104.0	112	-0.1	-0.8	0.9
2022	COL	MLB	29	467	56	7	28	6	.238/.338/.359	.296	.472	11.8%	20.8%	59.7%	87.4%	25.1%	62.5%	10.7	102.9	99	-0.1	-1.4	1.1
2023	PIT	MLB	30	472	63	11	42	3	.247/.339/.421	.311	.574	10.6%	23.3%	63.8%	84.7%	21.0%	58.4%	17.3	104.8	99	0.2	-2.6	0.8
2024 DC	PIT	MLB	31	419	43	9	43	6	.233/.325/.374	.280	.489	10.6%	20.6%							101	0.0	-1.7	0.7

2023 GP: RF (57), 1B (53), LF (32), DH (3)   *Comps: Brandon Guyer (59), Ryan Spilborghs (55), Ben Francisco (55)*

Connor-Eyed Joe has a great eye and a great arm. He takes his walks with the best of them and chips in a dozen home runs with passable corner outfield defense. That doesn't make him a star or anything: He's mediocre against righties, has one of the league's highest pop fly rates and lacks the muscle to hit the ball hard consistently. There's not much potential here, but much like with Rednex's famous diddy, you can do a whole lot worse at the ballpark.

★ ★ ★ *2024 Top 101 Prospect* **#90** ★ ★ ★

Termarr Johnson 2B Born: 06/11/04 Age: 20 Bats: L Throws: R Height: 5'8" Weight: 175 Origin: Round 1, 2022 Draft (#4 overall)

YEAR	TM	LVL	AGE	PA	R	HR	RBI	SB	AVG/OBP/SLG	BABIP	SLGCON	BB%	K%	ZSw%	ZCon%	OSw%	OCon%	LA	90th EV	DRC+	BRR	DRP	WARP
2022	PIR	ROK	18	29	0	0	0	2	.130/.310/.217	.200	.333	20.7%	27.6%										
2022	BRD	A	18	53	7	1	6	4	.275/.396/.450	.345	.667	18.9%	24.5%	61.8%	80.0%	20.3%	58.6%			114	0.0	-2.0	0.0
2023	BRD	A	19	330	57	13	44	7	.244/.419/.448	.318	.691	21.8%	26.7%	59.0%	76.2%	23.9%	52.8%			127	-1.0	-1.8	1.8
2023	GBO	A+	19	132	26	5	15	3	.242/.427/.414	.306	.612	22.0%	24.2%							117	1.3	-2.5	0.6
2024 non	PIT	MLB	20	251	24	4	23	0	.213/.317/.326	.325	.530	12.4%	33.4%							86	0.0	0	0.3

2023 GP: 2B (87), DH (11), SS (5)   *Comps: Delino DeShields (55), Nolan Gorman (52), Wendell Rijo (50)*

Johnson was hyped as an elite hitter coming out of the 2022 draft. Many scouts threw a plus-plus 70 grade on it; some even got to the vaunted 80 grade, which looked silly when he turned pro and started whiffing *a lot*. Johnson ran a 76.2% in-zone contact rate at Low-A last year, a number lower than all but one major-league qualifier and well below-average for the Florida State League. Simply put, Johnson is swinging and missing at far too many pitches in the zone to hit for even a decent batting average right now, let alone the top-of-the-league numbers expected of him so recently. He has time and other skills (like plate discipline and power) on his side, but as it stands entering 2024, he's more of an example about how little we know quantitatively about prep hitters compared to college and pro prospects than a projected future star.

Andrew McCutchen DH Born: 10/10/86 Age: 37 Bats: R Throws: R Height: 5'10" Weight: 190 Origin: Round 1, 2005 Draft (#11 overall)

YEAR	TM	LVL	AGE	PA	R	HR	RBI	SB	AVG/OBP/SLG	BABIP	SLGCON	BB%	K%	ZSw%	ZCon%	OSw%	OCon%	LA	90th EV	DRC+	BRR	DRP	WARP
2021	PHI	MLB	34	574	78	27	80	6	.222/.334/.444	.242	.611	14.1%	23.0%	66.0%	84.0%	25.1%	56.8%	14.8	103.8	102	0.1	0.7	2.4
2022	MIL	MLB	35	580	66	17	69	8	.237/.316/.384	.278	.506	9.8%	21.4%	70.4%	85.9%	27.8%	58.6%	13.4	104.1	97	-0.3	0.5	1.3
2023	PIT	MLB	36	473	55	12	43	11	.256/.378/.397	.312	.534	15.9%	21.1%	67.0%	82.3%	25.2%	55.8%	12.8	104.0	99	0.0	-0.1	0.9
2024 DC	PIT	MLB	37	411	45	11	44	6	.229/.334/.375	.281	.512	12.9%	22.9%							105	0.0	-0.1	1.1

2023 GP: DH (98), RF (8)   *Comps: Rickey Henderson (72), Gary Matthews (69), Amos Otis (68)*

Cutch returned to the Pirates for one last dance, and after a season that turned the clock back a year or two, he's ready for another year. While he was limited almost entirely to designated hitting, he demonstrated a vintage level of discipline while running into the occasional home run. The leading cause for concern for the captain of Pittsburgh's ship is his Achilles, which he ruptured in early September, costing him the last month of the year. He managed to maintain a healthy, above-average pace on the bases last year, but given another year of age and the injury, that may no longer be the case. All one can do is hope that Cutch has one last good run in him, Achilles tendon and all.

Edward Olivares LF/DH Born: 03/06/96 Age: 28 Bats: R Throws: R Height: 6'2" Weight: 190 Origin: IFA, 2014

YEAR	TM	LVL	AGE	PA	R	HR	RBI	SB	AVG/OBP/SLG	BABIP	SLGCON	BB%	K%	ZSw%	ZCon%	OSw%	OCon%	LA	90th EV	DRC+	BRR	DRP	WARP
2021	OMA	AAA	25	292	54	15	36	12	.313/.397/.559	.333	.681	9.9%	15.8%							133	-0.4	-4.4	1.6
2021	KC	MLB	25	111	14	5	12	2	.238/.291/.406	.244	.500	4.5%	17.1%	65.7%	86.2%	33.0%	63.9%	7.2	102.5	104	0.1	0.7	0.5
2022	EST	WIN	26	134	14	2	13	3	.267/.336/.408	.291	.471	9.7%	11.9%										
2022	OMA	AAA	26	86	13	1	11	2	.269/.337/.397	.317	.484	9.3%	16.3%							97	-1.8	0.0	0.1
2022	KC	MLB	26	174	24	4	15	2	.286/.333/.410	.344	.528	5.7%	20.7%	71.5%	83.7%	36.2%	63.2%	6.9	103.5	100	0.3	0.1	0.5
2023	OMA	AAA	27	59	10	3	12	4	.365/.424/.635	.410	.805	5.1%	18.6%	69.5%	83.3%	26.8%	46.2%			105	-0.4	0.2	0.2
2023	KC	MLB	27	385	47	12	36	11	.263/.317/.452	.289	.552	5.7%	16.6%	72.8%	88.4%	34.4%	59.4%	12.1	104.2	117	0.1	-1.0	1.7
2024 DC	PIT	MLB	28	226	23	6	25	6	.258/.314/.400	.299	.503	6.2%	18.9%							103	0.0	-0.4	0.6

2023 GP: LF (54), DH (42), RF (3), CF (2)   *Comps: Charlie Blackmon (66), Juan Rivera (56), Stephen Piscotty (55)*

It took 19 ⅔ innings for the 2023 Royals to score their first run of the season, and it was Olivares who delivered it, punishing a Joe Ryan fastball for a solo home run. That might have been his season highlight; the converse was, well, pick any time a ball was hit at him in the outfield. It's perplexing because Olivares is athletic, a good baserunner with a strong arm who can throw out runners once the ball is in hand, but the process of getting ball to hand looks less like an MLB outfielder and more like a cartoon character mid-electrocution; one half expects to see the outline of his skeleton light up as the ball is in flight. Still, Olivares was one of Kansas City's more consistent hitters, which is admittedly damning with faint praise but was enough to make up for his abject defense ahead of his trade to Pittsburgh.

Liover Peguero MI   Born: 12/31/00   Age: 23   Bats: R   Throws: R   Height: 6'0"   Weight: 220   Origin: IFA, 2017

YEAR	TM	LVL	AGE	PA	R	HR	RBI	SB	AVG/OBP/SLG	BABIP	SLGCON	BB%	K%	ZSw%	ZCon%	OSw%	OCon%	LA	90th EV	DRC+	BRR	DRP	WARP
2021	GBO	A+	20	417	67	14	45	28	.270/.332/.444	.337	.617	7.9%	25.2%							96	-0.6	8.1	1.7
2022	ALT	AA	21	521	65	10	58	28	.259/.305/.387	.316	.503	5.6%	21.3%							97	0.4	-4.7	1.0
2022	PIT	MLB	21	4	0	0	0	0	.333/.500/.333	1.000	1.000	25.0%	50.0%	75.0%	100.0%	41.7%	40.0%	3.0	106.7	86	0.0	0.0	0.0
2023	ALT	AA	22	318	50	11	34	19	.260/.333/.453	.290	.568	10.1%	18.2%							119	2.7	1.6	2.0
2023	IND	AAA	22	30	4	2	5	2	.259/.333/.556	.227	.625	10.0%	10.0%	66.7%	83.3%	21.0%	69.2%			112	0.6	0.0	0.2
2023	PIT	MLB	22	213	21	7	26	6	.237/.280/.374	.320	.565	5.2%	31.5%	72.7%	82.6%	34.6%	51.3%	3.7	105.2	65	0.0	-0.6	-0.3
2024 DC	PIT	MLB	23	362	30	7	34	14	.210/.264/.331	.258	.441	6.1%	23.0%							67	0.1	-1.6	-0.6

2023 GP: SS (39), 2B (33)   *Comps: Richard Urena (66), Alcides Escobar (62), Chris Owings (61)*

The critical piece in the Starling Marte deal nearly four years ago, Peguero hopes to be a toolsy middle infielder with average offensive production. Before 2022, he was listed as a top-100 prospect on every major prospect list and even as high as the top 40 in BP's. His ranking tumbled after he struggled in Double-A, before showing significant improvement in 2023 in his second spin at the level. He was surprisingly called into big-league action in July, a move that would proved premature. His lack of patience resurfaced and the power was inconsistent, but he did showcase elite sprint speed and flashed slick leather at second. At just 22, Peguero still has the chance to prove himself as a capable infielder up the middle, but in a system flush with middle-infield prospects, time is running out.

Bryan Reynolds LF   Born: 01/27/95   Age: 29   Bats: S   Throws: R   Height: 6'2"   Weight: 205   Origin: Round 2, 2016 Draft (#59 overall)

YEAR	TM	LVL	AGE	PA	R	HR	RBI	SB	AVG/OBP/SLG	BABIP	SLGCON	BB%	K%	ZSw%	ZCon%	OSw%	OCon%	LA	90th EV	DRC+	BRR	DRP	WARP
2021	PIT	MLB	26	646	93	24	90	5	.302/.390/.522	.345	.664	11.6%	18.4%	78.1%	87.8%	29.5%	56.2%	13.6	106.1	132	0.3	1.9	5.5
2022	PIT	MLB	27	614	74	27	62	7	.262/.345/.461	.306	.623	9.1%	23.0%	76.5%	86.2%	33.3%	52.2%	12.2	105.2	109	0.4	-3.7	2.5
2023	PIT	MLB	28	640	85	24	84	12	.263/.330/.460	.304	.606	8.3%	21.6%	74.6%	85.9%	30.1%	49.9%	11.2	105.1	116	0.3	-0.6	3.0
2024 DC	PIT	MLB	29	601	71	22	77	8	.260/.340/.450	.313	.605	9.4%	22.9%							122	0.1	0.9	3.5

2023 GP: LF (119), DH (19), CF (18)   *Comps: Jackie Brandt (81), Bob Skinner (80), Max Carey (80)*

Soon after demanding a trade that seemed to spell the end of his time in the Steel City, Reynolds signed a seven-year extension in late-April. Whether that about-face affected his play or not, it was a strange year for the former Commodore, as he hit the ball harder and chased outside the zone less than ever while still posting a career-low walk rate. He also continued his downward slide in admittedly noisy defensive metrics, like OAA, DRP and sprint speed, where he's now only slightly above average. He's already set for a corner outfield spot with Jack Suwinski in center field, where he may turn into more of a switch-hitting slugger than the all-around star that once seemed plausible. Given the current lack of non-platoon MLB-quality offensive talent on the Buccos though, that's enough to make last winter's unpleasantness water under the (Clemente) bridge.

Endy Rodríguez C/IF/OF   Born: 05/26/00   Age: 24   Bats: S   Throws: R   Height: 6'0"   Weight: 200   Origin: IFA, 2018

YEAR	TM	LVL	AGE	PA	R	HR	RBI	SB	AVG/OBP/SLG	BABIP	SLGCON	BB%	K%	ZSw%	ZCon%	OSw%	OCon%	LA	90th EV	DRC+	BRR	DRP	WARP
2021	BRD	A	21	434	73	15	73	2	.294/.380/.512	.333	.643	11.5%	17.7%	68.4%	85.8%	32.0%	72.2%			130	-2.3	-7.2	1.9
2022	GBO	A+	22	370	63	16	55	3	.302/.392/.544	.351	.718	11.4%	20.8%							117	-1.5	-0.4	1.8
2022	ALT	AA	22	138	27	8	32	1	.356/.442/.678	.378	.825	13.0%	15.2%							135	0.7	-1.3	0.9
2022	IND	AAA	22	23	2	1	8	0	.455/.435/.773	.474	.895	0.0%	13.0%							114	0.0	-0.1	0.1
2023	IND	AAA	23	315	54	6	38	4	.268/.356/.415	.300	.502	11.4%	14.9%	68.4%	86.1%	32.6%	69.3%			101	2.7	-2.7	1.1
2023	PIT	MLB	23	204	27	3	13	0	.220/.284/.328	.281	.445	8.3%	24.0%	67.2%	88.7%	32.7%	65.2%	16.5	100.9	85	0.0	4.4	0.8
2024 DC	PIT	MLB	24	29	3	1	3	0	.234/.303/.374	.283	.476	8.2%	20.5%							89	0.0	0	0.0

2023 GP: C (52), 1B (2), DH (1)   *Comps: Jason Castro (64), Christian Vázquez (64), Rob Brantly (61)*

When the Pirates traded Joe Musgrove before 2021, they could have only dreamed they'd find two critical pieces for their rebuild—which they did in star closer David Bednar and catcher Rodríguez. Despite being just 23, the latter has shown defensive aptitude with an elite pop time and average framing abilities. But just when it looked like the Pirates had found their backstop of the future, two stumbling blocks emerged. The first was tepid production in Pittsburgh last summer, a humbling showing that raised questions about how well his discerning eye and bat-to-ball skills would translate at the highest level. Even worse, December brought news that elbow surgery would cost Rodríguez all of the 2024 season. The injury couldn't have come at a worse time for club or player; sometimes baseball is a cruel game.

YEAR	TM	P. COUNT	FRM RUNS	BLK RUNS	THRW RUNS	TOT RUNS
2021	BRD	7963	-2.7	-0.3	-1.6	-4.6
2022	GBO	7648	-0.7	-2.5	2.3	-0.8
2022	ALT	2985	-1.2	-0.4	1.5	-0.1
2023	IND	8107	0.3	0.1	-1.5	-1.0
2023	PIT	6984	4.6	-0.2	0.6	4.9
2024	PIT	6956	4.5	-0.3	0.5	4.7

Jack Suwinski CF   Born: 07/29/98   Age: 25   Bats: L   Throws: L   Height: 6'2"   Weight: 215   Origin: Round 15, 2016 Draft (#444 overall)

YEAR	TM	LVL	AGE	PA	R	HR	RBI	SB	AVG/OBP/SLG	BABIP	SLGCON	BB%	K%	ZSw%	ZCon%	OSw%	OCon%	LA	90th EV	DRC+	BRR	DRP	WARP
2021	SA	AA	22	267	47	15	37	7	.269/.398/.551	.333	.838	16.9%	27.7%							135	-1.0	-2.2	1.7
2021	ALT	AA	22	182	21	4	21	4	.252/.359/.391	.343	.590	13.7%	28.0%							93	0.7	2.0	0.7
2022	ALT	AA	23	57	15	3	13	1	.353/.421/.686	.441	.946	8.8%	24.6%							116	0.9	-1.6	0.2
2022	IND	AAA	23	130	19	6	18	1	.214/.285/.410	.302	.706	8.5%	37.7%							81	0.9	-0.1	0.2
2022	PIT	MLB	23	372	45	19	38	4	.202/.298/.411	.242	.632	11.0%	30.6%	63.0%	81.8%	28.3%	49.8%	14.8	106.5	83	0.1	1.2	0.5
2023	PIT	MLB	24	534	63	26	74	13	.224/.339/.454	.290	.738	14.0%	32.2%	62.6%	81.8%	23.6%	48.9%	22.8	107.2	115	0.5	0.9	3.0
2024 DC	PIT	MLB	25	492	58	20	63	8	.219/.321/.421	.281	.636	11.9%	29.5%							107	0.1	0.2	2.2

2023 GP: CF (120), RF (28), LF (16), DH (2)   *Comps: Joc Pederson (59), Kyle Schwarber (56), Michael Conforto (54)*

The Pirates may have found their own Joey Gallo. Everybody knows the profile: strikeouts, stellar defense, and scorched balls off the bat. While it's a volatile way to play, it works so long as one can hit the fastball. Suwinski has obliged thus far, whiffing on heaters less than a quarter of the time when he swings, something Gallo never managed. Flawed and streaky as he is, the Midwesterner has played his way into an everyday role where he's 90% of Adam Dunn at the plate and competent in center field. With stalled prospects up and down the 40-man roster, Suwinski's development is a rare and rousing success story.

Rowdy Tellez 1B   Born: 03/16/95   Age: 29   Bats: L   Throws: L   Height: 6'4"   Weight: 270   Origin: Round 30, 2013 Draft (#895 overall)

YEAR	TM	LVL	AGE	PA	R	HR	RBI	SB	AVG/OBP/SLG	BABIP	SLGCON	BB%	K%	ZSw%	ZCon%	OSw%	OCon%	LA	90th EV	DRC+	BRR	DRP	WARP
2021	BUF	AAA	26	55	8	4	11	0	.298/.400/.638	.313	.833	10.9%	20.0%							121	0.0	1.2	0.4
2021	MIL	MLB	26	174	22	7	28	0	.272/.333/.481	.300	.603	8.0%	18.4%	71.4%	89.0%	36.6%	65.1%	14.3	108.4	104	-0.1	-0.2	0.5
2021	TOR	MLB	26	151	12	4	8	0	.209/.272/.338	.245	.443	6.0%	21.9%	65.8%	89.0%	35.8%	59.7%	12.3	109.4	108	0.0	-0.1	0.5
2022	MIL	MLB	27	599	67	35	89	2	.219/.306/.461	.215	.598	10.4%	20.2%	60.1%	85.4%	31.8%	63.9%	15.6	107.5	123	-0.5	-0.1	2.8
2023	NAS	AAA	28	34	4	1	5	0	.226/.294/.387	.261	.500	8.8%	20.6%	61.0%	80.6%	28.2%	77.3%			99	0.2	-0.1	0.1
2023	MIL	MLB	28	351	26	13	47	0	.215/.291/.376	.249	.520	10.0%	24.5%	51.9%	85.8%	28.3%	67.2%	15.6	107.1	79	-0.6	0.1	-0.2
2024 DC	PIT	MLB	29	363	42	14	46	1	.234/.314/.422	.258	.539	9.6%	19.8%							105	-0.4	-0.8	0.8

2023 GP: 1B (76), DH (20), P (1)   Comps: Mike Jorgensen (55), Carlos Pena (55), Mike Carp (55)

If you do one thing, do it well. For Tellez, that was taking the walk, which he did precisely 10% of the time, nearly matching his rate from a career year in 2022. Alas, that came by way of an overly passive approach at the plate, which led to more strikeouts as well as the free passes. Worse, beleaguered by injuries, he hit only one home run in the second half, with batted-ball numbers suggesting the power wasn't quite there anymore. It amounted to the worst DRC+ of his career. However, Tellez still managed to contribute to Brewers lore: He took the mound as a position player pitcher in a blowout versus the Marlins, pitching a clean inning minus a single, notching his first major-league strikeout and becoming the first position player in MLB history to close out a postseason-clinching game for the winning team. The outlook on the Milwaukee roster for such a two-way star proved murky, so Tellez headed to Pittsburgh on an inexpensive deal.

Jared Triolo IF   Born: 02/08/98   Age: 26   Bats: R   Throws: R   Height: 6'3"   Weight: 210   Origin: Round 2, 2019 Draft (#72 overall)

YEAR	TM	LVL	AGE	PA	R	HR	RBI	SB	AVG/OBP/SLG	BABIP	SLGCON	BB%	K%	ZSw%	ZCon%	OSw%	OCon%	LA	90th EV	DRC+	BRR	DRP	WARP
2021	GBO	A+	23	473	74	15	78	25	.304/.369/.480	.358	.618	8.9%	19.9%							117	2.5	-1.7	2.4
2022	ALT	AA	24	495	66	9	39	24	.282/.376/.419	.333	.527	12.7%	17.6%							114	2.1	3.2	2.7
2023	IND	AAA	25	226	39	2	25	10	.286/.412/.432	.411	.640	17.3%	26.5%	58.8%	80.7%	25.5%	50.0%			102	0.2	2.1	0.9
2023	PIT	MLB	25	209	30	3	21	6	.298/.388/.398	.440	.610	11.5%	30.1%	62.7%	79.3%	29.5%	49.7%	11.1	102.6	83	0.2	1.0	0.3
2024 DC	PIT	MLB	26	248	22	3	21	7	.215/.303/.325	.294	.471	10.1%	27.1%							80	0.1	0.6	0.1

2023 GP: 3B (35), 2B (13), 1B (7), DH (1)   Comps: Danny Valencia (58), David Bote (57), Antonio Perez (56)

Triolo has excellent discipline both at the plate and in the field, giving him elite walk rates and flowery evaluations by defensive metrics. But with an isolated-slugging measure of just over .100 and a propensity to swing and miss, those free passes will likely evaporate in due time. He's found most of his success against heaters, specifically, an always handy skill for the majors. Still, a lack of hard-hit balls outside of that pitch group leaves him few options when the adjustments by opposing hurlers inevitably come. With more breakers in the zone on the way, Triolo will need an adjustment in turn to stay afloat.

Lonnie White Jr. OF   Born: 12/31/02   Age: 21   Bats: R   Throws: R   Height: 6'3"   Weight: 212   Origin: Round 2, 2021 Draft (#64 overall)

YEAR	TM	LVL	AGE	PA	R	HR	RBI	SB	AVG/OBP/SLG	BABIP	SLGCON	BB%	K%	ZSw%	ZCon%	OSw%	OCon%	LA	90th EV	DRC+	BRR	DRP	WARP
2021	PIRB	ROK	18	33	6	2	5	0	.258/.303/.516	.400	.941	6.1%	42.4%									-2.3	
2023	PIR	ROK	20	76	13	1	10	6	.317/.434/.444	.442	.636	14.5%	25.0%										
2023	BRD	A	20	200	36	8	30	12	.259/.395/.488	.343	.745	16.0%	28.0%	64.5%	76.3%	24.6%	47.1%			109	1.9	-2.8	0.7
2024 non	PIT	MLB	21	251	21	4	22	0	.211/.284/.314	.346	.545	8.2%	38.2%							71	0.0	0	-0.1

2023 GP: CF (33), RF (16), DH (10), LF (5)   Comps: Pedro Gonzalez (84), Aaron Hicks (82), Jose Siri (80)

White can run and catch—that much is certain. He committed to Penn State out of Malvern Prep—a school on the wrong side of Pennsylvania—to run and catch on the football field. The Pirates gave him an over-slot bonus as their 2021 second-round pick to choose baseball instead, but a litany of ailments limited him to only 11 games in his first two years as a pro. When he finally got on the field in the second half of 2023, he showed that his best assets were still running and catching in the outfield. At the plate, he demonstrated a knack for drawing walks and hit for a little power in the low minors, but needs to show more offensive development—and stay healthy—as he climbs the ladder. Running and catching might be enough in football, but in baseball, you also need to hit. Okay, they hit in football too, just not with a bat. That would be dangerous.

Alika Williams SS   Born: 03/12/99   Age: 25   Bats: R   Throws: R   Height: 6'1"   Weight: 180   Origin: Round 1, 2020 Draft (#37 overall)

YEAR	TM	LVL	AGE	PA	R	HR	RBI	SB	AVG/OBP/SLG	BABIP	SLGCON	BB%	K%	ZSw%	ZCon%	OSw%	OCon%	LA	90th EV	DRC+	BRR	DRP	WARP
2021	CSC	A	22	263	37	1	34	5	.266/.317/.342	.313	.418	6.5%	16.3%							103	0.3	10.2	1.8
2021	BG	A+	22	63	12	3	9	1	.279/.302/.475	.304	.592	3.2%	19.0%							114	-0.2	0.6	0.3
2022	BG	A+	23	380	59	10	58	6	.254/.355/.390	.289	.494	12.4%	17.9%							124	-0.5	0.3	2.3
2023	MTG	AA	24	175	21	5	23	3	.237/.314/.417	.271	.533	8.6%	19.4%							113	-0.1	-2.2	0.5
2023	IND	AAA	24	148	25	7	20	3	.305/.384/.531	.320	.642	10.1%	14.9%	64.3%	89.9%	28.0%	65.5%			113	0.2	-4.4	0.3
2023	PIT	MLB	24	112	7	0	6	0	.198/.270/.248	.303	.379	8.0%	31.3%	69.1%	81.8%	31.5%	46.4%	9.2	101.6	62	0.0	-0.9	-0.2
2024 DC	*PIT*	*MLB*	*25*	*60*	*5*	*1*	*5*	*1*	*.200/.266/.302*	*.250*	*.415*	*7.2%*	*22.6%*							*61*	*0.0*	*-0.4*	*-0.2*

2023 GP: SS (45)
Comps: Brent Lillibridge (60), Chris Taylor (59), Luis Alfonso Cruz (55)

Generally speaking, it's not a bad gamble to swap a reliever with a 5.14 ERA, plucked off waivers the year prior, for a relatively recent first-round pick yet to debut in the majors. Generally speaking. The specifics in this case make the reliever one Robert Stephenson, who upon touching down in Tampa became a slider-breathing dragon. While Williams did rake in Triple-A and debut in the majors, his arrival probably won't linger in the memories of Pirates fans. Williams appeared at three different levels in 2023, and was a markedly different guy in each of them, hitting solidly in Double-A and catching fire in Triple-A before getting doused in the majors. Williams simply couldn't compete with MLB pitching, displaying a below-average ability to make contact and an utter inability to impact the ball when he did connect. Throw in a poor defensive showing that belied his quality athleticism and things start to look dour indeed. His MiLB slash lines and first-round pedigree lend a bit of hope, but as with any beans brewed after 5 pm, it wasn't an encouraging cup of coffee.

PITCHERS

Hunter Barco LHP   Born: 12/15/00   Age: 23   Height: 6'4"   Weight: 210   Origin: Round 2, 2022 Draft (#44 overall)

YEAR	TM	LVL	AGE	G (GS)	IP	W-L	SV	K	WHIP	ERA	CSP	BB%	K%	HR%	GB%	ZSw%	ZCon%	OSw%	OCon%	BABIP	SLGCON	DRA-	WARP
2023	PIR	ROK	22	3 (2)	7²	0-0	0	9	0.78	1.17		6.9%	31.0%	0.0%	61.1%					.222	.389		
2023	BRD	A	22	6 (6)	10²	0-2	0	19	1.59	5.06		8.2%	38.8%	0.0%	46.2%	72.2%	82.1%	37.3%	57.9%	.500	.615	63	0.3
2024 non	*PIT*	*MLB*	*23*	*58 (0)*	*50*	*2-2*	*0*	*46*	*1.49*	*5.33*		*10.8%*	*20.8%*	*3.7%*	*36.5%*					*.298*	*.580*	*117*	*-0.2*

2023 Arsenal: FA (91), SI (85), SL (81.9), CH (84)
Comps: Edwar Cabrera (26), Thomas Burrows (26), Gabriel Sequeira (26)

Drafted 44th overall in the 2022 draft, Barco has amassed fewer than 20 innings as a pro. That wasn't due to Barco lounging, but rather recovering from Tommy John surgery he underwent while at the University of Florida. When healthy he features an intriguing fastball-slider combination from the left side. We expected to know more about his ability to throw not only strikes, but quality ones at that, by this point. Unfortunately, 18 ⅓ innings just aren't enough to feel cozy with any definitive statements, though those minimal returns were pretty encouraging. We'll know more by this time next year, we hope.

David Bednar RHP   Born: 10/10/94   Age: 29   Height: 6'0"   Weight: 225   Origin: Round 35, 2016 Draft (#1044 overall)

YEAR	TM	LVL	AGE	G (GS)	IP	W-L	SV	K	WHIP	ERA	CSP	BB%	K%	HR%	GB%	ZSw%	ZCon%	OSw%	OCon%	BABIP	SLGCON	DRA-	WARP
2021	PIT	MLB	26	61 (0)	60²	3-1	3	77	0.97	2.23	56.6%	8.0%	32.5%	2.1%	42.1%	74.3%	78.8%	36.6%	48.4%	.259	.504	76	1.3
2022	PIT	MLB	27	45 (0)	51²	3-4	19	69	1.12	2.61	54.9%	7.6%	32.9%	1.9%	33.1%	73.5%	77.3%	33.4%	50.3%	.317	.524	80	1.0
2023	PIT	MLB	28	66 (0)	67¹	3-3	39	80	1.10	2.00	45.1%	7.6%	28.9%	1.1%	40.5%	75.6%	77.4%	40.2%	54.8%	.299	.467	84	1.4
2024 DC	*PIT*	*MLB*	*29*	*58 (0)*	*61*	*4-7*	*33*	*72*	*1.22*	*3.74*	*50.7%*	*8.3%*	*28.1%*	*3.2%*	*38.3%*					*.297*	*.572*	*88*	*0.7*

2023 Arsenal: FA (96.6), CU (77.8), FS (91.6)
Comps: Giovanny Gallegos (63), Nick Vincent (61), Luke Gregerson (60)

A major aspect of the modern closer aura is the entrance. This phenomenon is hardly new—Mariano Rivera is tied to Metallica's "Enter Sandman" as much as any baseball player is to any song—but it has recently evolved into a full stadium experience, with thumping bass, video packages and coordinated light displays. When local boy David Bednar was traded to the Pirates as an extra in the Joe Musgrove deal three years ago, he started warming up to the late-1970s anthem "Renegade" by Styx as an homage to his Steelers fandom. As Bednar has evolved into one of the league's best closers, so has his entrance, which is now one of those fancy-pants coordinated events telling fans and opposing hitters that "The Renegade" David Bednar is coming to steal hitters' souls. (For the most part, that's exactly what he does.) As the dominant closer on a perennially mediocre team, Bednar is naturally the subject of frequent trade rumors, but a move out of Pittsburgh would be unfortunate given his perfect yinzer presentation.

Ryan Borucki   LHP   Born: 03/31/94   Age: 30   Height: 6'4"   Weight: 210   Origin: Round 15, 2012 Draft (#475 overall)

YEAR	TM	LVL	AGE	G (GS)	IP	W-L	SV	K	WHIP	ERA	CSP	BB%	K%	HR%	GB%	ZSw%	ZCon%	OSw%	OCon%	BABIP	SLGCON	DRA-	WARP
2021	BUF	AAA	27	9 (0)	9¹	0-0	0	12	1.39	2.89		20.5%	30.8%	0.0%	52.6%					.263	.263	89	0.2
2021	TOR	MLB	27	24 (0)	23²	3-1	0	21	1.23	4.94	54.3%	11.2%	21.4%	5.1%	61.5%	58.4%	87.4%	31.8%	50.0%	.220	.571	88	0.4
2022	TOR	MLB	28	11 (0)	6¹	0-0	0	8	1.89	9.95	49.6%	15.2%	24.2%	6.1%	36.8%	61.2%	86.7%	28.9%	41.7%	.313	.778	98	0.1
2022	SEA	MLB	28	21 (0)	19	2-0	0	13	1.21	4.26	54.2%	7.7%	16.7%	5.1%	53.4%	73.9%	87.1%	34.7%	60.3%	.241	.534	101	0.2
2023	IND	AAA	29	8 (0)	8¹	1-0	0	4	1.08	0.00		16.7%	11.1%	0.0%	58.3%	72.9%	79.1%	27.2%	76.0%	.125	.167	104	0.1
2023	IOW	AAA	29	8 (0)	9	1-0	0	11	2.11	12.00		12.2%	22.4%	2.0%	53.3%	62.7%	82.7%	34.7%	48.8%	.414	.800	86	0.2
2023	PIT	MLB	29	38 (2)	40¹	4-0	0	33	0.74	2.45	53.3%	2.6%	21.7%	2.6%	45.9%	67.3%	81.4%	38.2%	57.9%	.210	.413	88	0.7
2024 DC	*PIT*	*MLB*	*30*	*52 (0)*	*54²*	*3-2*	*0*	*54*	*1.42*	*4.67*	*51.8%*	*9.4%*	*22.2%*	*2.5%*	*48.3%*					*.315*	*.531*	*104*	*0.1*

2023 Arsenal: SL (87.9), SI (94.1), SW (82.5), CH (84.5)   *Comps: Tyler Duffey (56), Zack Britton (55), Brett Cecil (54)*

The Pirates did another nifty piece of business, scooping Borucki off the street after he was released from the Cubs' Triple-A team in May. Their improvement was subtle but effective, turning his handedness-agnostic gyro slider usage into overdrive. Now thrown over two-thirds of the time, it elicits everything at an above-average level: chases, swings and misses, called strikes, ground balls, weak contact. With a host of formidable secondaries at his disposal, Borucki should see more high-leverage work in 2024.

JT Brubaker   RHP   Born: 11/17/93   Age: 30   Height: 6'3"   Weight: 180   Origin: Round 6, 2015 Draft (#187 overall)

YEAR	TM	LVL	AGE	G (GS)	IP	W-L	SV	K	WHIP	ERA	CSP	BB%	K%	HR%	GB%	ZSw%	ZCon%	OSw%	OCon%	BABIP	SLGCON	DRA-	WARP
2021	PIT	MLB	27	24 (24)	124¹	5-13	0	129	1.29	5.36	55.9%	7.1%	24.0%	5.2%	42.8%	69.0%	86.8%	31.8%	51.2%	.289	.654	94	1.6
2022	PIT	MLB	28	28 (28)	144	3-12	0	147	1.47	4.69	54.7%	8.4%	22.8%	2.6%	43.8%	66.0%	87.5%	33.4%	53.3%	.334	.580	110	0.6
2024 DC	*PIT*	*MLB*	*30*	*3 (3)*	*15¹*	*1-1*	*0*	*15*	*1.33*	*4.51*	*54.3%*	*8.4%*	*22.7%*	*3.1%*	*42.9%*					*.301*	*.556*	*102*	*0.1*

2023 Arsenal: SI (93.6), SL (86.7), CU (81), CH (88.3), FA (93.1)   *Comps: Anthony DeSclafani (69), Wade Miley (69), Corey Kluber (68)*

Brubaker missed the entirety of 2023 due to recovery from Tommy John surgery, but behind the curtain there's a host of quality pitches waiting in the wings. His sinker dances past barrels, his curve is a solid character actor, and the gyro slider handles physical comedy by making hitters look silly or getting banged around a bit. The fastball was relegated to a cameo role back in 2022, as it was his second-worst pitch by run value. We'll have to see when the show re-debuts, but the solid cast may lead to him eating innings at something close to a league-average rate.

Mike Burrows   RHP   Born: 11/08/99   Age: 24   Height: 6'1"   Weight: 190   Origin: Round 11, 2018 Draft (#324 overall)

YEAR	TM	LVL	AGE	G (GS)	IP	W-L	SV	K	WHIP	ERA	CSP	BB%	K%	HR%	GB%	ZSw%	ZCon%	OSw%	OCon%	BABIP	SLGCON	DRA-	WARP
2021	GBO	A+	21	13 (13)	49	2-2	0	66	0.90	2.20		10.4%	34.2%	1.6%	30.8%					.208	.412	93	0.6
2022	ALT	AA	22	12 (12)	52	4-2	0	69	1.10	2.94		8.9%	32.4%	1.4%	31.7%					.294	.492	93	0.9
2022	IND	AAA	22	12 (10)	42¹	1-4	0	42	1.35	5.31		6.7%	23.3%	2.8%	38.4%					.333	.565	99	0.6
2023	IND	AAA	23	2 (2)	6²	0-0	0	3	0.90	2.70		8.0%	12.0%	8.0%	35.0%	79.5%	80.0%	25.0%	86.7%	.111	.500	114	0.0
2024 non	*PIT*	*MLB*	*24*	*58 (0)*	*50*	*2-2*	*0*	*46*	*1.43*	*5.02*		*9.7%*	*20.8%*	*3.4%*	*32.8%*					*.300*	*.573*	*112*	*-0.1*

2023 Arsenal: FA (94), CH (86.2), CU (78.7), SL (86.3), FC (89)   *Comps: Marco Gonzales (72), Yency Almonte (71), Luis Gil (71)*

Burrows only pitched 6 ⅔ innings in 2023 before suffering a forearm injury that necessitated Tommy John surgery. It's a shame, given his repertoire's potential to go six innings with plenty of swings and misses. His primary arsenal contains a fastball that can hit the high 90s with great ride, a curve that can be reliably placed at the bottom of the zone and a changeup used to deal with pesky left-handed hitters. He also has played with a new slider last season, an addition considered vital by evaluators toward becoming a major-league starter. Given his significant injury history, one can only hope he can rebound late this year to finally get over the major-league hump in 2025.

Bubba Chandler   RHP   Born: 09/14/02   Age: 21   Height: 6'2"   Weight: 200   Origin: Round 3, 2021 Draft (#72 overall)

YEAR	TM	LVL	AGE	G (GS)	IP	W-L	SV	K	WHIP	ERA	CSP	BB%	K%	HR%	GB%	ZSw%	ZCon%	OSw%	OCon%	BABIP	SLGCON	DRA-	WARP
2022	PIR	ROK	19	6 (5)	15¹	0-0	0	27	0.85	0.00		16.9%	45.8%	0.0%	50.0%					.136	.136		
2022	BRD	A	19	8 (6)	26	1-1	0	33	1.46	4.15		15.8%	28.9%	2.6%	42.6%	69.3%	73.0%	28.3%	45.0%	.293	.533	104	0.4
2023	GBO	A+	20	24 (24)	106	9-4	0	120	1.50	4.75		10.9%	25.6%	3.2%	45.5%					.341	.594	98	0.9
2024 non	*PIT*	*MLB*	*21*	*58 (0)*	*50*	*2-2*	*0*	*47*	*1.64*	*6.28*		*12.2%*	*20.4%*	*4.0%*	*37.4%*					*.313*	*.621*	*134*	*-0.7*

Comps: Grant Holmes (51), Robert Stephenson (48), Germán Márquez (48)

A former four-star quarterback recruit to Clemson, Chandler was drafted for first-round money as a two-way player. The hitting part didn't work out—he hit .189 at the lowest levels of the minors in 2021 and 2022—so his bat was confiscated last year in spring training. He struggled with control early in his first full season as a pitcher, carrying a 6.79 ERA with 38 walks over his first 62 ⅓ innings, but he righted the ship in July and allowed only 10 runs over his last nine starts. Chandler has the classic projectable starting pitcher tool kit, with a mid-to-upper 90s fastball buttressed by a potentially above-average slider and changeup, but there's also the classic caveats. Like many pitching prospects, he needs to establish consistency and might be a candidate for pitch design improvements down the line.

Roansy Contreras RHP   Born: 11/07/99   Age: 24   Height: 6'1"   Weight: 205   Origin: IFA, 2016

YEAR	TM	LVL	AGE	G(GS)	IP	W-L	SV	K	WHIP	ERA	CSP	BB%	K%	HR%	GB%	ZSw%	ZCon%	OSw%	OCon%	BABIP	SLGCON	DRA-	WARP
2021	ALT	AA	21	12(12)	54¹	3-2	0	76	0.90	2.65		5.5%	34.9%	2.3%	48.4%					.267	.476	83	1.0
2021	PIT	MLB	21	1(1)	3	0-0	0	4	1.33	0.00	54.3%	8.3%	33.3%	0.0%	57.1%	76.5%	92.3%	31.0%	44.4%	.429	.571	91	0.0
2022	IND	AAA	22	9(9)	34¹	1-1	0	46	1.22	3.15		9.2%	32.6%	2.8%	45.1%	80.0%	87.5%	37.7%	60.0%	.321	.598	75	0.9
2022	PIT	MLB	22	21(18)	95	5-5	0	86	1.27	3.79	53.6%	9.6%	21.1%	3.2%	36.3%	65.3%	86.2%	36.6%	57.6%	.257	.541	121	-0.1
2023	IND	AAA	23	8(6)	32²	0-0	0	30	1.19	4.96		8.2%	22.4%	6.0%	34.1%	66.2%	85.3%	28.4%	52.5%	.241	.633	102	0.4
2023	PIT	MLB	23	19(11)	68¹	3-7	1	55	1.57	6.59	46.0%	10.6%	18.2%	3.6%	38.3%	69.4%	86.8%	32.9%	57.3%	.318	.588	124	-0.1
2024 DC	PIT	MLB	24	55(3)	70²	4-4	0	65	1.41	4.95	50.1%	9.3%	21.1%	3.6%	37.5%					.298	.580	111	0.1

2023 Arsenal: SL (83.6), FA (94.4), CU (76.9), CH (89.5), SW (82.6)   *Comps: Randall Delgado (51), Jacob Turner (50), Bryse Wilson (49)*

After a promising 2022 season, the Roansy hype train got derailed in 2023. While his curveball improved, his fastball lost over a mile per hour in velocity and got swings and misses at half the rate of a year ago. The slider also chipped in, but a continually erratic heater leaves him in no man's land against left-handed hitters. He retreated back to Indianapolis in August to find a left-handed hitter slayer, and a changeup that featured more in his brief MLB stint is the first candidate. He reminds one of fellow-touted pitching prospect Josiah Gray, with dominant secondaries, a horrific fastball, and no reliable changeup. The final remedy may, therefore, be the same: a cutter to pound lefties in.

Bailey Falter LHP   Born: 04/24/97   Age: 27   Height: 6'4"   Weight: 175   Origin: Round 5, 2015 Draft (#144 overall)

YEAR	TM	LVL	AGE	G(GS)	IP	W-L	SV	K	WHIP	ERA	CSP	BB%	K%	HR%	GB%	ZSw%	ZCon%	OSw%	OCon%	BABIP	SLGCON	DRA-	WARP
2021	PHI	MLB	24	22(1)	33²	2-1	0	34	1.19	5.61	56.1%	4.3%	24.5%	3.6%	37.1%	68.9%	82.1%	30.9%	66.7%	.315	.573	90	0.5
2022	LHV	AAA	25	9(9)	47	4-1	0	49	0.66	1.91		3.5%	28.8%	2.4%	33.6%	72.2%	96.2%	29.4%	40.0%	.196	.409	82	1.1
2022	PHI	MLB	25	20(16)	84	6-4	0	74	1.21	3.86	58.1%	4.9%	21.2%	4.6%	34.1%	67.1%	84.8%	32.8%	61.0%	.292	.618	126	-0.3
2023	LHV	AAA	26	11(11)	47	2-1	0	35	1.43	4.21		10.9%	17.4%	3.5%	30.8%	63.2%	88.2%	28.9%	65.9%	.279	.528	133	-0.2
2023	PIT	MLB	26	10(7)	40¹	2-2	0	32	1.39	5.58	51.4%	7.0%	18.6%	5.8%	39.1%	71.3%	85.8%	31.5%	70.0%	.288	.641	111	0.2
2023	PHI	MLB	26	8(7)	40¹	0-7	0	28	1.44	5.13	53.0%	4.6%	16.0%	4.0%	40.3%	73.4%	91.3%	31.9%	65.8%	.326	.594	122	0.0
2024 DC	PIT	MLB	27	59(13)	107	5-7	0	76	1.40	5.03	55.0%	7.1%	16.3%	3.4%	37.1%					.301	.551	114	0.0

2023 Arsenal: FA (90.9), CU (76.4), SL (84.2), CH (84.6), SI (91)   *Comps: Paul Blackburn (72), Gabriel Ynoa (71), Scott Diamond (71)*

Falter was at his worst in his third major-league season, losing a lot of the command that kept him afloat while working with stuff that struggles to deceive hitters. He uses all of his six-foot-four frame to get elite extension, but he's no Tyler Glasnow; Falter's 90-mph fastball is below-average in velocity, even with his biological advantage taken into account. His slider is a sore point, as it's entirely dropped off the map since 2022, and the culprit likely is the one-dimensional repertoire Falter now possesses. His primary pitches are a fastball, curveball and slider that all pack remarkably similar arm-side break, and none are overpowering. While his idea to drop his sinker isn't bad, he needs something in its place—the over-indexing of the heater last season didn't let him fare much better.

Marco Gonzales LHP   Born: 02/16/92   Age: 32   Height: 6'1"   Weight: 205   Origin: Round 1, 2013 Draft (#19 overall)

YEAR	TM	LVL	AGE	G(GS)	IP	W-L	SV	K	WHIP	ERA	CSP	BB%	K%	HR%	GB%	ZSw%	ZCon%	OSw%	OCon%	BABIP	SLGCON	DRA-	WARP
2021	SEA	MLB	29	25(25)	143¹	10-6	0	108	1.17	3.96	52.2%	7.2%	18.5%	5.0%	33.0%	68.7%	86.6%	34.0%	70.0%	.240	.583	139	-1.6
2022	SEA	MLB	30	32(32)	183	10-15	0	103	1.33	4.13	50.5%	6.4%	13.2%	3.8%	42.2%	71.4%	87.3%	37.4%	74.8%	.278	.534	137	-1.7
2023	SEA	MLB	31	10(10)	50	4-1	0	34	1.46	5.22	50.5%	8.4%	15.8%	2.3%	39.3%	66.4%	87.3%	35.6%	70.6%	.316	.522	127	-0.1
2024 DC	PIT	MLB	32	26(26)	129¹	6-10	0	85	1.40	4.99	51.2%	7.2%	15.1%	3.2%	39.6%					.297	.533	112	0.3

2023 Arsenal: FA (89.3), CH (80.2), KC (79.5), FC (86.1), SI (89.1)   *Comps: Jason Vargas (76), Jarrod Washburn (70), Scott McGregor (70)*

It was an unceremonious end to Gonzales' seven-year stint in Seattle on multiple fronts. A three-time Opening Day starter and the longest-tenured Mariner entering 2023, Gonzales had progressively descended the rotation hierarchy in recent years as the talent level had risen rapidly around him. But a forearm injury that limited Gonzales to just 10 starts and ultimately necessitated season-ending surgery pushed the veteran lefty even further into the background of the organization's pitching plans. Then, rather than retain him as valuable depth, Seattle included Gonzales and the $12M he was owed in a December deal with Atlanta as part of the organization's most dramatic cost-cutting move, AKA, The Salary Dump Heard 'Round The Winter Meetings. Atlanta flipped Gonzales to Pittsburgh, where he'll serve as a stabilizing force in a rotation full of young guns looking to find their footing.

Thomas Harrington RHP   Born: 07/12/01   Age: 22   Height: 6'2"   Weight: 185   Origin: Round 1, 2022 Draft (#36 overall)

YEAR	TM	LVL	AGE	G(GS)	IP	W-L	SV	K	WHIP	ERA	CSP	BB%	K%	HR%	GB%	ZSw%	ZCon%	OSw%	OCon%	BABIP	SLGCON	DRA-	WARP
2023	BRD	A	21	8(8)	39	4-1	0	40	1.10	2.77		8.0%	26.7%	2.0%	33.0%	69.4%	81.8%	38.9%	60.0%	.304	.516	84	0.5
2023	GBO	A+	21	18(18)	88¹	3-5	0	106	1.30	3.87		7.7%	28.2%	2.9%	27.7%					.335	.593	102	0.3
2024 non	PIT	MLB	22	58(0)	50	2-2	0	42	1.50	5.62		9.6%	19.0%	3.8%	30.5%					.306	.592	123	-0.4

2023 Arsenal: FA (93.2), SW (82.4), CH (87.5), CU (80.1)   *Comps: Tyler Viza (81), Joe Wieland (79), Pedro Avila (79)*

Harrington died in 1460 at the Battle of Wakefield, a minor knight in the service of the Duke of York during the War of the Roses. Given that medical setback, his limited ceiling as a starter doesn't seem so bad. A comp-round pick from 2022, Harrington is armed with a fastball that does just enough to slip by aggressive bats, and his low-80s slider has a nifty little downward bite to serve as a decent two-strike pitch. You could ask for the Pirates to aim a little higher, but a minor-knight fourth-starter role given to Harrington is one that *isn't* given, along with $8 million, to someone like Martín Pérez two years down the line. While there's value in that, it's okay to wish there were a little more.

Colin Holderman RHP Born: 10/08/95 Age: 28 Height: 6'4" Weight: 230 Origin: Round 9, 2016 Draft (#280 overall)

YEAR	TM	LVL	AGE	G (GS)	IP	W-L	SV	K	WHIP	ERA	CSP	BB%	K%	HR%	GB%	ZSw%	ZCon%	OSw%	OCon%	BABIP	SLGCON	DRA-	WARP
2021	BNG	AA	25	11 (2)	19¹	0-2	4	20	0.98	3.26		7.9%	26.3%	2.6%	38.0%					.229	.458	104	0.1
2022	SYR	AAA	26	11 (0)	14¹	1-0	3	17	0.84	2.51		5.4%	30.4%	3.6%	62.9%					.212	.471	78	0.4
2022	NYM	MLB	26	15 (0)	17²	4-0	0	18	1.02	2.04	53.4%	10.4%	26.9%	0.0%	47.6%	66.3%	83.1%	32.9%	58.0%	.262	.317	98	0.2
2022	PIT	MLB	26	9 (0)	10²	1-0	0	6	1.50	6.75	47.1%	13.7%	11.8%	0.0%	44.1%	72.7%	91.7%	26.4%	75.8%	.273	.344	122	0.0
2023	PIT	MLB	27	58 (0)	56	0-3	2	58	1.34	3.86	48.3%	8.3%	24.2%	1.7%	53.1%	71.5%	88.0%	29.6%	58.0%	.329	.497	82	1.2
2024 DC	PIT	MLB	28	58 (0)	61	3-3	0	54	1.36	4.37	48.9%	9.5%	20.4%	2.5%	48.8%					.294	.505	98	0.3

2023 Arsenal: SI (97.9), SW (84.6), FC (92.3) *Comps: Drew Steckenrider (68), Hunter Strickland (68), Rowan Wick (67)*

Holderman proved he could be a tremendous late-inning reliever in 2023, first by replacing his slider with a shiny new sweeper and then by tripling his cutter usage to improve tunneling between his tried-and-true sinker and the aforementioned boomerang. The results were spectacular all-around, with far more strikeouts and ground balls, while conceding far fewer free passes than ever before. His new sweeper is the star of the show, striking out more than half the batters it faces while giving up little hard contact—a feature the notoriously fickle sweeper archetype typically struggles to maintain—while also making his sinker far more elusive.

Andre Jackson RHP Born: 05/01/96 Age: 28 Height: 6'3" Weight: 210 Origin: Round 12, 2017 Draft (#370 overall)

YEAR	TM	LVL	AGE	G (GS)	IP	W-L	SV	K	WHIP	ERA	CSP	BB%	K%	HR%	GB%	ZSw%	ZCon%	OSw%	OCon%	BABIP	SLGCON	DRA-	WARP
2021	TUL	AA	25	15 (13)	63¹	3-2	0	75	1.04	3.27		7.9%	29.6%	4.7%	31.8%					.239	.565	82	1.0
2021	OKC	AAA	25	6 (5)	26¹	2-3	0	23	1.33	5.13		7.9%	20.2%	5.3%	35.4%					.263	.605	99	0.1
2021	LAD	MLB	25	3 (0)	11²	0-1	1	10	1.37	2.31	55.9%	12.0%	20.0%	2.0%	26.5%	76.0%	77.2%	32.3%	60.0%	.290	.500	103	0.1
2022	OKC	AAA	26	21 (19)	75²	2-7	1	76	1.70	5.00		17.2%	21.4%	2.8%	47.0%	71.7%	83.5%	29.3%	54.8%	.280	.516	86	1.0
2022	LAD	MLB	26	4 (0)	9²	0-0	1	9	1.34	1.86	61.7%	9.5%	21.4%	0.0%	48.3%	78.7%	86.4%	30.9%	44.0%	.321	.429	91	0.1
2023	PIT	MLB	27	12 (7)	43²	1-3	0	41	1.12	4.33	47.6%	10.7%	23.0%	3.4%	37.1%	68.6%	80.9%	30.8%	66.1%	.218	.491	107	0.3
2023	LAD	MLB	27	7 (0)	17²	0-0	2	16	1.42	6.62	54.4%	3.8%	20.3%	6.3%	36.7%	75.7%	79.5%	31.2%	69.4%	.309	.700	104	0.2
2024 non	PIT	MLB	28	58 (0)	50	2-2	0	47	1.46	5.13	51.5%	10.9%	21.1%	3.6%	36.9%					.292	.578	114	-0.1

2023 Arsenal: FA (94.8), CH (87), FC (87), CU (81.3) *Comps: Alec Mills (49), Shane Greene (48), Tyler Wilson (48)*

In Los Angeles, Jackson was one of many flat fastball-up/tumbling changeup down, could-be starters. Unable to distinguish himself from the pack, and running short on options amidst a broader roster crunch, Jackson was shipped off to Pittsburgh for cash. Jackson improved superficially in his new home, thanks mostly to nearly halving his rate of home runs allowed, but remained largely the same outcome-level pitcher despite a bunch of changes under the hood. The Pirates earned a reputation in 2023 for being pretty spin-heavy (alas, no ready-made nickname like Spincinnati was available), and Jackson followed suit upon his acquisition, seeing his changeup rate drop from 45% to 26%. He compensated by reintroducing a curveball, and increasing his slider and four-seam usage. Those types of adjustments will be crucial for Jackson, less because they'll unlock some heretofore unseen success, but rather because adapting to a new home is likely to be a common feature for his future. Expectations should be adjusted from "potential breakout" to "well-traveled" as he seeks to stay on the right side of replacement level when teams lack the ability to stash him in the minors.

Jared Jones RHP Born: 08/06/01 Age: 22 Height: 6'1" Weight: 190 Origin: Round 2, 2020 Draft (#44 overall)

YEAR	TM	LVL	AGE	G (GS)	IP	W-L	SV	K	WHIP	ERA	CSP	BB%	K%	HR%	GB%	ZSw%	ZCon%	OSw%	OCon%	BABIP	SLGCON	DRA-	WARP
2021	BRD	A	19	18 (15)	66	3-6	0	103	1.47	4.64		11.3%	34.1%	2.0%	45.5%	68.1%	75.9%	33.9%	45.9%	.385	.636	79	1.5
2022	GBO	A+	20	26 (26)	122²	5-7	0	142	1.35	4.62		9.6%	26.7%	3.6%	38.9%					.310	.594	94	1.3
2023	ALT	AA	21	10 (10)	44¹	1-4	0	47	1.08	2.23		8.9%	26.3%	1.7%	38.4%					.266	.429	98	0.7
2023	IND	AAA	21	16 (15)	82	4-5	0	99	1.32	4.72		9.7%	28.3%	2.6%	39.0%	70.7%	74.6%	32.3%	51.4%	.320	.574	79	2.1
2024 DC	PIT	MLB	22	13 (13)	62	3-5	0	63	1.45	5.25		10.1%	22.8%	3.6%	35.7%					.306	.600	116	0.0

2023 Arsenal: FA (97.9), CU (83), SL (87.6), CH (91.8)

Perhaps the next in a lengthy line of Pirates prospects to go from early-round 2020s pick to major-league debut, Jones spent 2023 conquering the upper minors. While the surface stats say he saw quite a bit of attrition in his production jumping from Double-A to Triple-A, league-wide context needs to be taken into account, namely an International League that played closer to the PCL. That's why, despite an ERA that more than doubled in the transition, Jones' Triple-A DRA- improved by nearly 20 points. Jones has a fastball and he likes to use it—with good reason, too. He flings it in the mid-to-upper 90s, regularly dotting 97 on the gun, and he's no stranger to triple digits. It's got carry and ride—he likes to pepper the upper third of the zone (and above), where it plays quite well. His secondaries (a slider and curve) both lag behind the fastball but at least flash solid-average, while his command acts as a drag on all his offerings thanks to some effort in his mechanics. He's prone to fly balls and will give up his share of homers, and his ability to limit them will be a significant factor as to how long he can stick as a starter. His 125+ innings last season are a great start to making it happen, though.

Mitch Keller RHP   Born: 04/04/96   Age: 28   Height: 6'3"   Weight: 220   Origin: Round 2, 2014 Draft (#64 overall)

YEAR	TM	LVL	AGE	G (GS)	IP	W-L	SV	K	WHIP	ERA	CSP	BB%	K%	HR%	GB%	ZSw%	ZCon%	OSw%	OCon%	BABIP	SLGCON	DRA-	WARP
2021	IND	AAA	25	8 (6)	28	1-1	0	39	1.43	3.21		10.2%	30.5%	1.6%	56.0%					.342	.562	83	0.6
2021	PIT	MLB	25	23 (23)	100²	5-11	0	92	1.79	6.17	57.0%	10.4%	19.6%	2.1%	39.4%	67.7%	87.8%	29.4%	65.3%	.392	.616	120	-0.1
2022	PIT	MLB	26	31 (29)	159	5-12	0	138	1.40	3.91	54.9%	8.7%	20.1%	2.0%	49.1%	66.5%	86.6%	30.1%	65.4%	.321	.501	95	1.9
2023	PIT	MLB	27	32 (32)	194¹	13-9	0	210	1.25	4.21	51.3%	6.7%	25.5%	3.0%	43.6%	67.4%	83.9%	30.8%	63.3%	.310	.561	89	3.4
2024 DC	PIT	MLB	28	29 (29)	177²	11-11	0	155	1.31	4.19	53.2%	8.5%	20.4%	2.6%	44.2%					.290	.507	95	2.0

2023 Arsenal: FA (95.4), FC (90.1), SI (94), SW (82.9), CU (78.1), CH (90.8)   *Comps: Rick Wise (79), Rick Porcello (78), Jim Slaton (76)*

While he saw success in 2022, Keller did so by the skin of his teeth. A 9% walk rate often got him into trouble, and he saw few chases despite so frequently missing the zone. Then 2023 happened. Adding a cutter in place of his slider, made obsolete by his sweeper, has been a welcome sight for sore eyes. The new pitch helped resolve his command problem more than he could ever imagine; it perfectly bridges his hard and soft stuff, pushing his fastball and sinker to new heights, while filling him with confidence to attack the zone. Everything a starter dreams of came in tow—more innings per outing, far more strikeouts, and significantly fewer walks. At 27, one can finally say that the Pirates' former top prospect is their new rotation anchor as they continue to turn the proverbial corner.

Michael Kennedy LHP   Born: 11/30/04   Age: 19   Height: 6'1"   Weight: 205   Origin: Round 4, 2022 Draft (#110 overall)

YEAR	TM	LVL	AGE	G (GS)	IP	W-L	SV	K	WHIP	ERA	CSP	BB%	K%	HR%	GB%	ZSw%	ZCon%	OSw%	OCon%	BABIP	SLGCON	DRA-	WARP
2023	PIR	ROK	18	11 (7)	42¹	2-1	0	55	1.04	2.13		11.1%	32.2%	0.6%	40.7%					.267	.396		
2024 non	PIT	MLB	19	58 (0)	50	2-2	0	50	1.84	7.03		16.3%	20.9%	3.9%	34.1%					.313	.628	146	-1.0

2023 Arsenal: FA (91), SL (81.4), CH (84.1)   *Comps: Orlando Castro (26), Julio Robaina (26), Dedgar Jimenez (26)*

If photography is the art that seeks beauty in the mundane, Kennedy embodies that spirit in the prospecting world. The scouting reports universally cast him as the idealized depiction of a humble object: a pitchability lefty lacking in top-end stuff; yet he earns raves for pitching beyond his years, showing advanced feel and command. His fastball maxes out in the low 90s with a healthy amount of movement, and his deception hides a low-80s change. It's not bat-missing stuff, but it's missing bats. It's like a black-and-white photograph of a broken chair that makes you miss your parents, somehow. Scouting and art are equally mysterious.

Carmen Mlodzinski RHP   Born: 02/19/99   Age: 25   Height: 6'2"   Weight: 220   Origin: Round 1, 2020 Draft (#31 overall)

YEAR	TM	LVL	AGE	G (GS)	IP	W-L	SV	K	WHIP	ERA	CSP	BB%	K%	HR%	GB%	ZSw%	ZCon%	OSw%	OCon%	BABIP	SLGCON	DRA-	WARP
2021	GBO	A+	22	14 (14)	50¹	2-3	0	64	1.29	3.93		9.4%	30.0%	3.3%	43.3%					.317	.595	81	0.9
2022	ALT	AA	23	27 (22)	105¹	6-8	0	111	1.41	4.78		8.7%	24.1%	2.2%	38.6%					.336	.584	100	1.4
2023	IND	AAA	24	20 (0)	26²	2-2	1	32	1.43	3.04		10.1%	26.9%	1.7%	40.0%	66.1%	83.1%	25.4%	54.5%	.329	.595	98	0.5
2023	PIT	MLB	24	35 (1)	36	3-3	1	34	1.28	2.25	45.5%	11.8%	22.4%	2.0%	47.5%	70.2%	85.9%	28.2%	66.0%	.260	.423	98	0.5
2024 DC	PIT	MLB	25	52 (0)	54²	3-2	0	46	1.43	4.72	45.5%	10.3%	19.0%	2.8%	43.5%					.293	.518	105	0.1

2023 Arsenal: FA (95.7), SW (83.9), CH (89.2), FC (92.1), SL (85.7), SI (93.8)   *Comps: Enoli Paredes (75), Maikel Cleto (74), Jonathan Hernández (73)*

The Polish Pirate showed real potential in 2023, first by pitching well in Triple-A Indianapolis, and second by maintaining good form at the big-league level. He keeps the ball on the turf well with four pitches that all can contribute, primarily his fastball and sweeper. With starting experience in High-A and Double-A, it's clear that with some consistency in his mix, he could be a back-end starter in the future for a Pirate rotation that could always use reinforcements. The move to relief was well supported, though—a double-digit walk rate hampered his ability to go deep into games, primarily from a lack of fooling hitters out of the zone. The crux of his success relies on his fastball, though. With its elite ride, his ability to unlock the rest of his repertoire with it will make or break his case to be a six-inning starter or 8th-inning setup man rather than be just another guy in the middle innings.

Dauri Moreta RHP   Born: 04/15/96   Age: 28   Height: 6'2"   Weight: 185   Origin: IFA, 2015

YEAR	TM	LVL	AGE	G (GS)	IP	W-L	SV	K	WHIP	ERA	CSP	BB%	K%	HR%	GB%	ZSw%	ZCon%	OSw%	OCon%	BABIP	SLGCON	DRA-	WARP
2021	CHA	AA	25	18 (0)	26²	4-0	0	37	0.82	1.35		5.0%	37.0%	3.0%	39.7%					.255	.466	86	0.5
2021	LOU	AAA	25	24 (0)	26¹	2-0	8	21	0.68	0.68		4.0%	21.2%	2.0%	36.5%					.169	.301	93	0.5
2021	CIN	MLB	25	4 (0)	3²	0-0	0	4	0.82	2.45	60.6%	7.1%	28.6%	7.1%	22.2%	80.8%	100.0%	38.7%	50.0%	.125	.556	109	0.0
2022	LOU	AAA	26	28 (0)	27¹	3-4	1	28	1.57	3.95		10.0%	23.3%	5.0%	30.4%					.352	.727	108	0.3
2022	CIN	MLB	26	35 (1)	38¹	0-2	1	39	1.17	5.40	54.1%	8.1%	24.4%	6.3%	32.7%	62.4%	83.5%	30.6%	55.1%	.234	.686	101	0.3
2023	IND	AAA	27	6 (1)	7²	0-1	1	13	1.96	9.39		23.7%	34.2%	2.6%	25.0%	59.3%	65.7%	33.7%	55.9%	.357	.733	87	0.2
2023	PIT	MLB	27	55 (0)	58	5-2	1	76	1.09	3.72	47.7%	10.0%	31.8%	1.7%	39.0%	65.6%	77.8%	29.6%	49.4%	.265	.519	85	1.1
2024 DC	PIT	MLB	28	58 (0)	61	4-3	4	74	1.25	4.02	50.1%	9.6%	28.8%	3.5%	35.8%					.291	.590	93	0.5

2023 Arsenal: SL (84.7), FA (95), CH (85.7)   *Comps: Juan Minaya (60), Hector Neris (57), Ryan Dull (57)*

Moreta was another astute piece of business from the Pirates, who acquired him from the Reds for bat-to-ball artist Kevin Newman. He's a one-pitch Pirate, but his one pitch is worth its weight in gold. His sweeping slider avoids barrels beautifully, mitigating contact while striking out more than a third of the batters it faces. Did I mention he's given up only one home run off it, despite being thrown a whopping two-thirds of the time? In tandem with Ryan Borucki, the Pirates seem to have their style of low-cost reliever pitching development figured out: grab pitchers with elite sliders and turn their usage up to 11.

Luis L. Ortiz RHP Born: 01/27/99 Age: 25 Height: 6'2" Weight: 235 Origin: IFA, 2018

YEAR	TM	LVL	AGE	G (GS)	IP	W-L	SV	K	WHIP	ERA	CSP	BB%	K%	HR%	GB%	ZSw%	ZCon%	OSw%	OCon%	BABIP	SLGCON	DRA-	WARP
2021	BRD	A	22	22(19)	87¹	5-3	0	113	1.26	3.09		7.4%	30.1%	1.3%	51.3%	69.0%	79.8%	33.2%	44.0%	.344	.502	89	1.5
2022	ALT	AA	23	24(23)	114¹	5-9	0	126	1.17	4.64		7.3%	26.9%	4.1%	46.5%					.288	.603	86	2.3
2022	IND	AAA	23	2(2)	10	0-0	0	12	0.80	3.60		9.5%	28.6%	2.4%	56.0%					.125	.280	81	0.2
2022	PIT	MLB	23	4(4)	16	0-2	0	17	1.13	4.50	52.2%	14.5%	24.6%	1.4%	42.9%	64.7%	83.3%	33.5%	55.2%	.171	.310	100	0.2
2023	IND	AAA	24	13(12)	56²	4-4	0	54	1.39	4.61		10.8%	21.7%	2.8%	48.5%	69.6%	79.0%	31.7%	60.2%	.281	.548	91	1.0
2023	PIT	MLB	24	18(15)	86²	5-5	0	59	1.70	4.78	44.9%	12.0%	14.8%	3.3%	48.1%	70.1%	86.9%	30.2%	64.1%	.309	.540	126	-0.2
2024 DC	PIT	MLB	25	23(23)	111	5-9	0	89	1.50	5.14	45.8%	10.1%	18.1%	2.8%	46.7%					.303	.530	113	0.2

2023 Arsenal: SL (85.8), SI (95.7), FA (96.3), CH (89.6) *Comps: Vance Worley (70), Nick Tropeano (67), Mitch Keller (66)*

Ortiz is a puzzling case. He combines mid to high-90s fastball velocity with elite extension, and possesses plus life on his secondaries, such as his fantastic gyro slider and sinker. However, he uses a random number generator to determine the location of his pitches, leading to incredibly high walk rates and crazy hard contact. To make matters worse, he has more than a 15-inch horizontal break difference between his great slider and his arm-side pitches. As a result, he struggles with deception and doesn't get anywhere near the whiffs his velocity and extension would suggest he should. His path to viable starter may be a long one, but the opportunity is clear for the former top-100 prospect. It all starts with interlocking his repertoire and keeping his pitches in the desired quadrant of the plate.

Johan Oviedo RHP Born: 03/02/98 Age: 26 Height: 6'5" Weight: 245 Origin: IFA, 2016

YEAR	TM	LVL	AGE	G (GS)	IP	W-L	SV	K	WHIP	ERA	CSP	BB%	K%	HR%	GB%	ZSw%	ZCon%	OSw%	OCon%	BABIP	SLGCON	DRA-	WARP
2021	MEM	AAA	23	12(11)	54¹	1-6	0	59	1.55	6.13		11.8%	24.1%	2.9%	52.0%					.331	.563	92	1.0
2021	STL	MLB	23	14(13)	62¹	0-5	0	51	1.57	4.91	53.7%	12.8%	17.7%	2.8%	49.0%	68.2%	84.8%	28.0%	55.6%	.286	.521	126	-0.3
2022	IND	AAA	24	5(4)	11¹	0-0	0	13	0.97	0.79		6.7%	28.9%	0.0%	39.3%					.286	.357	84	0.2
2022	MEM	AAA	24	10(10)	50	4-2	0	51	1.32	5.58		10.7%	23.8%	6.5%	45.6%	72.4%	85.7%	28.6%	42.9%	.238	.681	104	0.6
2022	STL	MLB	24	14(1)	25¹	2-1	0	26	1.30	3.20	57.4%	6.5%	24.1%	3.7%	43.2%	68.0%	83.3%	33.5%	53.8%	.314	.622	91	0.4
2022	PIT	MLB	24	7(7)	30²	2-2	0	28	1.27	3.23	54.9%	11.9%	20.9%	0.7%	56.8%	69.5%	90.4%	31.1%	56.7%	.253	.318	99	0.3
2023	PIT	MLB	25	32(32)	177²	9-14	0	158	1.37	4.31	47.6%	10.6%	20.2%	2.4%	44.5%	71.8%	84.2%	28.6%	56.2%	.281	.517	113	0.9
2024 non	PIT	MLB	26	58(0)	50	2-2	0	44	1.43	4.84	49.9%	10.7%	20.0%	2.8%	45.6%					.292	.530	107	0.0

2023 Arsenal: FA (96), SL (88.2), CU (81.1), CH (88.1), SI (95.2) *Comps: Jarred Cosart (74), Chris Archer (68), Joe Ross (68)*

It was more of the same for Oviedo: 96-mph fastballs all over the place, and curveballs and sliders in the zone *just* often enough to notch plenty of strikes while still going unpunished. He added a sinker, but it didn't really do anything—probably because it moves precisely like his changeup, which also contributed little. There were signs of progression for the 25-year-old after a stellar June saw him cut his walk rate in half and keep his ERA in the low threes, but a return to the "chuck it and pray" style ever since has kept that as an outlier, rather than a sign of good things to come. So long as he walks a tenth of those he faces, accept that Johan will be only OKiedo.

Martín Pérez LHP Born: 04/04/91 Age: 33 Height: 6'0" Weight: 200 Origin: IFA, 2007

YEAR	TM	LVL	AGE	G (GS)	IP	W-L	SV	K	WHIP	ERA	CSP	BB%	K%	HR%	GB%	ZSw%	ZCon%	OSw%	OCon%	BABIP	SLGCON	DRA-	WARP
2021	BOS	MLB	30	36(22)	114	7-8	0	97	1.51	4.74	53.0%	7.1%	19.1%	3.7%	43.3%	69.2%	86.9%	31.2%	71.6%	.337	.610	129	-0.7
2022	TEX	MLB	31	32(32)	196¹	12-8	0	169	1.26	2.89	48.3%	8.4%	20.6%	1.3%	50.2%	67.2%	85.3%	31.1%	70.9%	.298	.436	106	1.3
2023	TEX	MLB	32	35(20)	141²	10-4	0	93	1.40	4.45	45.7%	8.1%	15.3%	3.5%	44.9%	66.0%	89.6%	32.2%	74.1%	.295	.531	129	-0.5
2024 DC	PIT	MLB	33	26(26)	132	6-10	0	90	1.45	4.96	47.9%	8.4%	15.4%	2.6%	45.5%					.303	.510	110	0.4

2023 Arsenal: SI (91.8), CH (84.2), FC (89.4), FA (92.3), CU (79.2), SL (83.9) *Comps: Mark Buehrle (69), Claude Osteen (69), Jeff Suppan (69)*

All things considered, the Rangers probably wouldn't want a do-over on anything they did last season, for obvious reasons. But the decision to buy into Pérez's brief fling with stardom after his strong 2022 campaign and hand him no. 2 starter money for a year looks a little rough in hindsight. The upshot: Pérez managed to throw 141 innings for a rotation beleaguered by injuries. The downside: They were sub-replacement level innings, 28% worse than league average by DRA-. Pérez will take his World Series ring to Pittsburgh now, earning an $8 million contract to provide veteran presence and get a chance to once again bounce back to form. All's well that ends well, I suppose.

Quinn Priester RHP Born: 09/16/00 Age: 23 Height: 6'3" Weight: 210 Origin: Round 1, 2019 Draft (#18 overall)

YEAR	TM	LVL	AGE	G (GS)	IP	W-L	SV	K	WHIP	ERA	CSP	BB%	K%	HR%	GB%	ZSw%	ZCon%	OSw%	OCon%	BABIP	SLGCON	DRA-	WARP
2021	GBO	A+	20	20(20)	97²	7-4	0	98	1.24	3.04		9.6%	24.1%	2.0%	53.7%					.285	.446	85	1.6
2022	ALT	AA	21	15(15)	75¹	4-4	0	75	1.19	2.87		7.1%	24.0%	1.3%	50.2%					.314	.459	86	1.5
2022	IND	AAA	21	2(2)	9¹	1-1	0	10	1.29	3.86		17.5%	25.0%	2.5%	36.4%					.190	.409	99	0.1
2023	IND	AAA	22	22(20)	108	9-4	0	116	1.33	4.00		10.2%	25.3%	1.3%	54.6%	63.9%	85.6%	36.4%	52.4%	.319	.516	77	3.0
2023	PIT	MLB	22	10(8)	50	3-3	0	36	1.70	7.74	46.8%	11.5%	15.4%	5.1%	51.8%	67.1%	86.7%	29.1%	60.9%	.297	.677	117	0.1
2024 DC	PIT	MLB	23	16(16)	81	4-6	0	65	1.44	4.68	46.8%	10.1%	18.2%	2.3%	49.7%					.298	.498	104	0.5

2023 Arsenal: SI (93.4), SL (85.1), FA (93), CU (80.4), CH (89.1), FC (90.8) *Comps: Peter Lambert (72), Alex White (69), Bryse Wilson (66)*

Priester is the pitching prospect you've waited for since before the pandemic, but his pitch mix resembles your banana bread misadventure from quarantine. His curveball is the bananas—the star ingredient. His cutter is the vanilla extract that adds sweetness and flavor. But his fastball is the gloopy, misshapen dough you never mastered—and it was pounded just as hard. He couldn't rely on his four-seamer or sinker to get ahead in counts, leading to too many walks, not enough strikeouts and a whole lot of hard contact. He'll head back to the oven to bake a while longer, but just as there's no bread without dough, there's no rotation spot without a decent enough heater to set up his plus secondaries.

★ ★ ★ *2024 Top 101 Prospect* **#9** ★ ★ ★

Paul Skenes RHP Born: 05/29/02 Age: 22 Height: 6'6" Weight: 235 Origin: Round 1, 2023 Draft (#1 overall)

YEAR	TM	LVL	AGE	G(GS)	IP	W-L	SV	K	WHIP	ERA	CSP	BB%	K%	HR%	GB%	ZSw%	ZCon%	OSw%	OCon%	BABIP	SLGCON	DRA-	WARP
2024 DC	PIT	MLB	22	6(6)	25²	1-2	0	22	1.58	5.93		11.3%	18.7%	3.8%	36.6%					.302	.593	129	-0.2

2023 Arsenal: FA (98.2), FS (88.2), CU (84.2), SL (88), SI (96.6)   *Comps: David Hess (26), Bruce Rondón (26), Jordan Swagerty (26)*

Skenes is the fourth pitcher the Pirates have taken with the first overall pick, and the prior three ran the full gamut of prospect outcomes, from future Hall-of-Famer (Gerrit Cole) to oft-injured mid-rotation journeyman (Kris Benson) to complete bust (Bryan Bullington). The former LSU ace is coming off one of the greatest pitching seasons in collegiate baseball history, striking out a SEC-record 209 hitters on his road to a national championship and every relevant individual award, including the Men's College World Series Most Outstanding Player and the Dick Howser Award as college baseball's best player. Still, it was at least a mild surprise that the Pirates popped him ahead of similarly touted hitting prospects like teammate Dylan Crews or Florida outfielder Wyatt Langford.

Skenes is one of the hardest throwing starting pitching prospects ever, routinely hitting 100 mph and topping out at 102, and although his fastball has suboptimal movement it's still effective because of the absurd velocity. And that's not even his best pitch; his slider is one of the best breaking balls a prospect has thrown in the last decade. All in all, we think Skenes is trending more towards more of a Cole outcome right now—but the authors of this book's 1997 and 2003 editions thought Benson and Bullington were can't miss pitching prospects too.

Anthony Solometo LHP Born: 12/02/02 Age: 21 Height: 6'5" Weight: 220 Origin: Round 2, 2021 Draft (#37 overall)

YEAR	TM	LVL	AGE	G(GS)	IP	W-L	SV	K	WHIP	ERA	CSP	BB%	K%	HR%	GB%	ZSw%	ZCon%	OSw%	OCon%	BABIP	SLGCON	DRA-	WARP
2022	BRD	A	19	13(8)	47²	5-1	0	51	1.05	2.64		10.1%	27.1%	0.0%	51.8%	69.4%	77.7%	34.8%	58.9%	.272	.395	87	1.1
2023	GBO	A+	20	12(12)	58²	2-3	0	68	1.16	2.30		10.7%	29.1%	0.9%	49.6%					.295	.421	77	1.2
2023	ALT	AA	20	12(12)	51²	2-4	0	50	1.22	4.35		6.5%	23.0%	2.8%	40.0%					.299	.541	90	0.9
2024 non	PIT	MLB	21	58(0)	50	2-2	0	44	1.51	5.38		10.2%	19.7%	3.2%	37.8%					.310	.571	118	-0.2

Comps: Robbie Erlin (83), Danny Duffy (81), David Holmberg (78)

New Jersey is a northern state, but South Jersey doesn't always feel like it. The Mason-Dixon Line demarcates the Pennsylvania-Maryland border, and if it extended further east would cleave South Jersey from the rest of the state. It's a unique place, so it's fitting that Solometo—a lefty with a bizarre delivery—hails from Camden County. The Pirates pushed him aggressively in his age-20 season, more than doubling the previous year's innings total and promoting him to Double-A by midseason—and he met every challenge. His fastball sits in the low 90s but plays up due to his funky motion, and he has the frame to add more velo as he develops. His best secondary is a slider and he has an improving changeup that keeps right-handed hitters honest. He's ahead of schedule for a prep lefty with an unconventional release, but where he comes from folks do things their own way.

Vince Velasquez RHP Born: 06/07/92 Age: 32 Height: 6'3" Weight: 210 Origin: Round 2, 2010 Draft (#58 overall)

YEAR	TM	LVL	AGE	G(GS)	IP	W-L	SV	K	WHIP	ERA	CSP	BB%	K%	HR%	GB%	ZSw%	ZCon%	OSw%	OCon%	BABIP	SLGCON	DRA-	WARP
2021	CLR	A	29	4(2)	7	1-0	0	12	0.71	2.57		3.7%	44.4%	3.7%	30.8%	55.3%	76.2%	35.7%	48.0%	.250	.538	85	0.1
2021	LHV	AAA	29	2(2)	6²	0-0	0	12	0.75	2.70		12.5%	50.0%	4.2%	22.2%					.125	.667	87	0.1
2021	PHI	MLB	29	21(17)	81²	3-6	0	85	1.48	5.95	54.3%	12.5%	23.5%	4.7%	34.4%	70.8%	79.5%	28.8%	66.2%	.282	.681	122	-0.2
2021	SD	MLB	29	4(4)	12²	0-3	0	16	1.50	8.53	54.6%	7.1%	28.6%	10.7%	17.1%	74.7%	74.6%	35.3%	53.1%	.310	1.029	121	0.0
2022	CLT	AAA	30	4(0)	5²	0-0	0	7	1.59	4.76		15.4%	26.9%	0.0%	40.0%	84.6%	81.8%	17.6%	50.0%	.333	.400	93	0.1
2022	CHW	MLB	30	27(9)	75¹	3-3	0	69	1.23	4.78	55.7%	7.8%	21.6%	3.4%	35.9%	72.3%	82.0%	30.2%	61.8%	.270	.555	111	0.3
2023	PIT	MLB	31	8(8)	37¹	4-4	0	37	1.31	3.86	46.5%	8.6%	22.8%	2.5%	30.9%	69.2%	81.7%	32.1%	60.0%	.295	.514	122	0.0
2024 non	PIT	MLB	32	58(0)	50	2-2	0	47	1.40	5.03	51.8%	9.6%	21.7%	4.0%	34.8%					.293	.595	112	-0.1

2023 Arsenal: SL (83.8), FA (93.6), CH (88.8), SI (92.8), KC (80.5)   *Comps: Stan Bahnsen (65), Sterling Hitchcock (65), Scott Sanderson (63)*

Velasquez debuted in June 2015, the same day as the American premiere of *Jurassic World*. CBS was in the midst of the late-night transition between David Letterman and Stephen Colbert. The top television shows included *Scandal* and *The Big Bang Theory*. The series finale of *Mad Men* had just aired. The top song in the world was "Bad Blood" by Taylor Swift ... okay, some things actually don't change that much over time, do they? Since about five minutes after he was called up, Velasquez has been the epitome of tantalizing unrealized potential, constantly flashing the skills of a frontline pitcher without ever actually being one, through a long list of injuries, command-and-control problems and general underperformance. After the Phillies tried and tried and tried, in the rotation and the bullpen, he's become a pitching vagabond in his 30s, with a trio of new teams not good enough at pitch design to realize there just isn't anything left here. 2023 brought The Eras Tour (Vince's Version): he won a rotation job on a bad team out of camp, started off slow but then shoved a couple of times in late April, just enough to get the annual stories out about how *this* was finally the year, and then had successive IL stints that led to season-ending elbow surgery. It was his entire career in two months.

LINEOUTS

Hitters

HITTER	POS	TM	LVL	AGE	PA	R	HR	RBI	SB	AVG/OBP/SLG	BABIP	SLGCON	BB%	K%	ZSw%	ZCon%	OSw%	OCon%	LA	90th EV	DRC+	BRR	DRP	WARP
Seth Beer	1B	AMA	AA	26	359	58	13	54	0	.290/.387/.482	.353	.655	9.5%	22.6%							108	-1.7	-4.4	0.7
	1B	RNO	AAA	26	79	5	2	12	0	.200/.266/.314	.255	.468	7.6%	29.1%	76.2%	76.0%	34.6%	63.0%			91	-0.1	0.5	0.1
Gilberto Celestino	OF	STP	AAA	24	233	31	4	31	4	.243/.392/.389	.283	.486	18.0%	15.9%	69.7%	74.2%	21.9%	57.6%			101	-1.0	-1.7	0.3
Yordany De Los Santos	SS/3B	PIR	ROK	18	78	16	1	15	13	.328/.397/.463	.368	.554	9.0%	14.1%										
	SS/3B	BRD	A	18	153	20	1	10	9	.184/.322/.256	.338	.492	14.4%	39.2%	54.7%	69.4%	28.2%	44.4%			66	-0.1	0.6	-0.1
Jason Delay	C	IND	AAA	28	31	4	0	5	1	.357/.419/.500	.455	.636	9.7%	19.4%	66.7%	75.0%	36.0%	63.0%			93	0.3	0.7	0.2
	C	PIT	MLB	28	187	20	1	18	0	.251/.319/.347	.333	.472	7.5%	23.5%	72.4%	87.3%	37.3%	57.5%	11.6	99.0	79	-0.1	6.8	0.9
Tres Gonzalez	OF	BRD	A	22	82	15	1	12	6	.299/.427/.403	.345	.482	18.3%	13.4%	47.9%	92.9%	23.0%	81.6%			127	1.3	-0.9	0.5
	OF	GBO	A+	22	449	73	8	46	22	.287/.400/.402	.349	.521	14.5%	18.7%							128	0.3	-6.0	1.8
Billy McKinney	LF	SWB	AAA	28	160	20	9	25	3	.274/.388/.511	.298	.670	13.8%	20.0%	72.4%	88.1%	30.2%	56.9%			116	0.0	0.5	0.7
	LF	NYY	MLB	28	147	19	6	14	1	.227/.320/.406	.274	.584	11.6%	26.5%	66.4%	81.6%	28.4%	53.5%	12.2	104.2	106	0.0	-0.2	0.5
Chris Owings	UT	IND	AAA	31	371	50	15	41	4	.241/.349/.449	.311	.676	13.7%	28.6%	64.1%	81.6%	31.1%	56.2%			97	-1.0	-0.5	0.8
	UT	PIT	MLB	31	25	0	0	0	0	.160/.160/.160	.308	.308	0.0%	48.0%	73.8%	74.2%	43.4%	47.8%	22.7	104.0	58	0.0	0.0	0.0
Joshua Palacios	OF	ALT	AA	27	37	6	0	2	1	.265/.324/.324	.281	.344	5.4%	5.4%							118	0.2	-0.1	0.2
	OF	IND	AAA	27	90	19	8	27	4	.410/.489/.795	.407	.925	12.2%	12.2%	73.0%	85.6%	25.0%	67.9%			150	0.8	1.0	1.0
	OF	PIT	MLB	27	264	26	10	40	5	.239/.279/.413	.269	.534	4.5%	21.2%	73.0%	81.5%	34.8%	59.2%	7.4	104.8	105	-0.1	1.9	1.1
Ali Sánchez	C	RNO	AAA	26	267	37	11	43	0	.311/.375/.492	.335	.597	9.7%	15.7%	60.8%	88.5%	28.5%	70.8%			111	-1.8	2.0	1.2
Jhonny Severino	SS	BRW	ROK	18	52	12	4	10	5	.250/.288/.583	.229	.737	1.9%	19.2%										
Canaan Smith-Njigba	OF	IND	AAA	24	445	57	15	74	21	.280/.366/.473	.364	.679	11.9%	26.5%	61.7%	79.2%	28.1%	50.9%			101	-0.5	-10.3	0.3
	OF	PIT	MLB	24	37	3	0	5	1	.125/.216/.219	.235	.438	10.8%	43.2%	64.6%	81.0%	30.9%	37.9%	0.5	105.9	65	0.0	-0.3	-0.1
Estuar Suero	OF	PAD	ROK	17	160	22	4	23	7	.216/.306/.345	.295	.533	10.0%	30.6%										
	OF	PIR	ROK	17	58	7	1	6	2	.217/.379/.326	.273	.441	20.7%	20.7%										

Thanks to multiple clutch hits, the beginning of **Seth Beer**'s career was as strong and rich and sweet as a S'mores Barrel-Aged Framinghammer. His current body of work more resembles a lukewarm can of Coors Light. ⓧ Thumb surgery sidelined **Gilberto Celestino** for the first half of 2023, and better players sidelined him—even in Triple-A—for parts of the second half. ⓧ Through both levels of the complex, it really looked like the Pirates had something brewing in the bat of seven-figure IFA De Los Santos. Instead of letting him continue to thrive in the age-appropriate Florida Complex League, Pittsburgh inexplicably rushed him to face way more advanced pitchers at Low-A, where he posted the third-worst in-zone contact rate for any player who got 100 PAs at the level. You start to wonder if a David Zaslav-style tax write-off is involved in this kind of player development. ⓧ **Jason Delay** is the stereotypical backup catcher—he can receive the ball well but can't hit a lick. In fact, his current offensive numbers may even be a bit better than the regression to come. His future outlook with the Pirates lies squarely on how often they wish to utilize Henry Davis behind the plate. ⓧ Teams that aren't particularly good at drafting often use picks in the top five rounds on low-wattage position players with good on-base skills that obviously don't have enough pop to be impact major leaguers. **Tres Gonzalez** will likely play in bigs someday, and that's a kind of a win for a fifth-rounder, but his on-base percentage has exceeded his slugging in both his pro campaigns so far. ⓧ The problem wasn't necessarily what happened in **Billy McKinney**'s 48 games with the 2023 Yankees. No, the problem was that the former spring training NRI *had to play 48 games for the 2023 Yankees.* As Aaron Judge's emergency replacement, he hit like Aaron Judge for 52 plate appearances, then came back down to earth. ⓧ **Chris Owings** has reached the "one of our infielders got hurt and we don't want to call a prospect up" portion of his career, which means as long his agent does a good job he'll continue to hang out in a major-league clubhouse a couple weeks every year, at least until his new team remembers his bat-to-ball imploded around the same time as Hillary Clinton's presidential aspirations. ⓧ **Joshua Palacios** increased his pull rate considerably while clubbing the ball. However, a continued propensity to hit it on the ground with a poor swing path limits him to league-average offensive production from a corner outfield spot at best. At least he thought to develop a right-field arm. ⓧ Journeyman catcher **Ali Sánchez** signed a major-league deal with the Pirates as a minor-league free agent, something which happens a handful of times a year and usually means your previous team screwed up their self-scouting. Always a contact merchant, he started damaging the ball enough last year to become interesting again. ⓧ The Pirates traded Carlos Santana at the deadline and got back an eventual ex-shortstop in **Jhonny Severino**, who likely won't see the majors until two presidential elections from now. He's got plenty of power, and is overly willing to try and show it off on every pitch. ⓧ **Canaan Smith-Njigba** didn't do anything in 2023 to shake off any of the concerns about his game, and he added some new ones: The metrics have soured on his defense. He has one team option left, and after that, he may need to take stock of his personal ones. ⓧ **Estuar Suero** isn't simply a lottery ticket. He's a lottery ticket buried in a treasure chest marked by a map that's been torn apart and included in different chocolate bars, which are put in different crane machines whose locations are written in code in an ad in the back of a major newspaper. He might be good, though.

Pitchers

PITCHER	TM	LVL	AGE	G (GS)	IP	W-L	SV	K	WHIP	ERA	CSP	BB%	K%	HR%	GB%	ZSw%	ZCon%	OSw%	OCon%	BABIP	SLGCON	DRA-	WARP
Braxton Ashcraft	BRD	A	23	2 (2)	6^1	0-0	0	11	0.63	0.00		4.2%	45.8%	0.0%	50.0%	57.9%	68.2%	37.0%	65.0%	.250	.250	74	0.1
	GBO	A+	23	9 (9)	26^1	0-2	0	29	1.29	3.76		4.5%	26.4%	3.6%	42.1%					.347	.667	100	0.2
	ALT	AA	23	8 (8)	20	0-1	0	23	0.95	1.35		6.3%	29.1%	0.0%	42.0%					.280	.429	91	0.4
Po-Yu Chen	GBO	A+	21	25 (24)	119^2	5-8	0	124	1.38	4.44		8.5%	24.5%	4.2%	39.9%					.328	.682	100	1.1
Thomas Hatch	BUF	AAA	28	30 (3)	45	4-2	1	54	1.31	4.40		10.8%	27.8%	4.1%	41.9%	74.7%	80.9%	38.0%	45.5%	.278	.632	86	1.0
	PIT	MLB	28	12 (2)	22^1	1-1	0	16	1.34	4.03	44.1%	7.4%	17.0%	2.1%	55.1%	72.7%	88.2%	38.3%	54.9%	.313	.493	95	0.3
	TOR	MLB	28	6 (0)	6^1	0-0	0	10	2.37	4.26	43.1%	14.3%	28.6%	0.0%	45.0%	72.0%	86.1%	26.8%	27.3%	.526	.778	88	0.1
Ben Heller	DUR	AAA	31	18 (0)	27^1	3-2	1	34	1.39	3.95		6.1%	26.0%	1.5%	50.0%	68.9%	74.0%	34.9%	49.5%	.359	.610	85	0.6
	GWN	AAA	31	14 (0)	16^2	2-0	0	23	0.96	2.16		10.6%	34.8%	0.0%	55.9%	59.1%	73.8%	29.4%	52.0%	.265	.324	79	0.4
	ATL	MLB	31	19 (0)	18^2	0-0	0	16	1.45	3.86	47.3%	13.4%	19.5%	2.4%	50.9%	63.6%	89.0%	33.0%	50.8%	.275	.472	100	0.2
Jose Hernandez	PIT	MLB	25	50 (0)	50^2	1-3	0	62	1.36	4.97	46.8%	9.9%	27.8%	4.0%	38.4%	65.6%	81.3%	31.2%	54.8%	.299	.674	96	0.7
Owen Kellington	BRD	A	20	23 (18)	80	1-3	0	90	1.40	3.94		14.5%	26.2%	2.3%	36.0%	66.2%	75.3%	31.1%	57.5%	.277	.540	98	0.6
Max Kranick	IND	AAA	25	7 (7)	16^1	0-1	0	12	0.80	2.76		10.0%	20.0%	1.7%	35.7%	67.6%	84.5%	34.4%	55.4%	.146	.286	97	0.2
Kyle Nicolas	ALT	AA	24	12 (12)	53^2	3-5	0	63	1.47	4.36		9.6%	26.4%	3.3%	36.7%					.340	.639	97	0.9
	IND	AAA	24	23 (6)	45	1-2	2	64	1.58	6.20		13.9%	30.8%	3.8%	30.9%	70.8%	78.3%	30.8%	49.0%	.333	.706	92	0.9
	PIT	MLB	24	4 (0)	5^1	0-0	0	7	2.06	11.81	43.5%	15.4%	26.9%	3.8%	50.0%	71.1%	90.6%	30.3%	45.0%	.462	.857	97	0.1
Ryder Ryan	TAC	AAA	28	48 (1)	55	4-2	2	56	1.24	3.76		9.6%	24.3%	1.7%	46.0%	65.7%	86.7%	33.0%	51.6%	.290	.507	73	1.0
	SEA	MLB	28	1 (0)	1	0-0	0	2	1.00	0.00	37.9%	25.0%	50.0%	0.0%	0.0%	66.7%	0.0%	40.0%	75.0%	.000	.000	92	0.0
Colin Selby	IND	AAA	25	28 (0)	30^1	0-0	6	41	1.35	3.86		16.5%	30.8%	0.0%	59.7%	63.0%	76.0%	27.6%	38.1%	.284	.343	84	0.7
	PIT	MLB	25	21 (5)	24	2-2	0	30	1.83	9.00	45.3%	13.2%	26.3%	3.5%	47.8%	67.1%	87.5%	27.0%	45.2%	.391	.632	94	0.4
Hunter Stratton	IND	AAA	26	47 (2)	56^1	4-4	6	74	1.33	3.99		12.8%	30.6%	2.9%	37.3%	76.7%	74.5%	35.7%	49.5%	.294	.575	81	1.4
	PIT	MLB	26	8 (0)	12	0-0	0	10	1.00	2.25	54.4%	6.4%	21.3%	4.3%	48.5%	77.4%	83.1%	35.6%	50.0%	.226	.606	96	0.2
Jackson Wolf	SA	AA	24	18 (18)	88^1	8-9	0	105	1.09	4.08		6.3%	29.8%	3.4%	29.5%					.294	.603	90	1.9
	ALT	AA	24	8 (8)	36	0-4	0	30	1.17	4.25		6.6%	19.9%	3.3%	35.8%					.262	.565	101	0.5
	SD	MLB	24	1 (1)	5	1-0	0	1	1.40	5.40	52.1%	4.5%	4.5%	0.0%	60.0%	77.1%	96.3%	20.0%	87.5%	.300	.350	117	0.0

Braxton Ashcraft pitched just 26 times from 2018-2022 due to knee, shoulder, and elbow injuries. Finally healthy in 2023, he climbed through three levels with a four-pitch mix that he threw for strikes 70% of the time. The Pirates added him to the 40-man in November, clearing the runway for his major-league debut. ⓧ You could argue, even if a bit unfairly, that **Po-Yu Chen** is the entire Pirates organization in prospect form: low-ceiling, competent, demonstrating just enough of all the requisite skills to get by. He also probably won't ever put them all together, and in a few years we'll be saying all the same things about someone wearing a different jersey. ⓧ Described as "reliable" in last year's edition of this book before signing a sensible one-plus-an-option deal, **Jarlín García** came out of a March spring training soiree with the dreaded "arm tightness" diagnosis. It's unclear at publication time whether the lost year resolved the hex that has cursed Pirates pitching for decades, although signs point to no. ⓧ **Thomas Hatch**'s emphasis on sinkers and changeups over his horrible fastball has allowed him to look like an MLB-caliber middle reliever with his great cutter. Much of the chases he earns are on errant pitches, so when the book goes out, he'll likely be sent packing back to the waiver wire or minors. ⓧ **Ben Heller** returned to the bigs for the first time since 2020, and struck out eight batters in his first three innings back. Sadly, it took him 15 ⅔ more innings to double that strikeout tally, and he walked more than one in seven opponents in that span. ⓧ **Jose Hernandez** is a lefty reliever who throws a slider 49.3% of the time, but can't get lefties out. What? No. That's not how it's supposed to work. To escape the Pittsburgh-Indianapolis elevator on the top floor, he needs a better out pitch against same-side hitters. Usually that's a slider, but, well... ⓧ If **Owen Kellington** were in an organization remotely good at pitch design, we'd have real interest in a projectable young righty with big vertical movement on his fastball and interesting breaking stuff. Instead, he's a Pirates and walked over five-and-a-half per nine in Low-A. Please trade for him, executive from an enterprising team reading this. ⓧ **Max Kranick** skipped the entire 2023 major-league season recovering from June 2022 Tommy John surgery, although he did make nine minor-league starts late in the season. At his best, he throws a mid-90s fastball and a hard slider, although he's never really gotten the strikeouts one would expect. ⓧ Pittsburgh took high school right-hander **Zander Mueth** with the 67th pick of the 2023 draft. Instead of throwing him in the minors, however, the team conducted an experimental "Pirates Immersion Therapy," strapping him in a VR headset and making him answer questions from reporters after losses in a holographic clubhouse. ⓧ The Pirates gave a lot of their upper-minors guys cups of coffee last season, which felt distinctly old-fashioned in 2023. For **Kyle Nicolas**, it was battery acid, but the hard-thrower will have a rotation spot waiting for him this summer after he finishes writing his 20-page research assignment on the history and modern state of the strike zone. ⓧ Only two pitchers (Brian Moran and Silvino Bracho) have appeared in more Triple-A Games than **Ryder Ryan** over the last three seasons. He struck out Gunnar Henderson and Adley Rutschman in his MLB debut in August before immediately being sent back to Tacoma with his 0.00 career ERA intact. ⓧ **Colin Selby's** sinker/slider mix is reminiscent of Pirate expat Clay Holmes. While he does induce lots of soft contact, he also leaves very few pitches in the zone to be punished. Like Holmes, he's going to hit a critical crossroads in the near future. Can he refine his approach to get the sinker under control, or will he fall off the always-bumpy MLB wagon? ⓧ **Hunter Stratton** pitched all eight of his 2.25 ERA innings at night, which would make Robert Mitchum proud. Unfortunately, his minor-league command and 6-foot-4 stature are more aligned with a Joe Don Baker classic. ⓧ **Jackson Wolf** got shipped off from San Diego in the Rich Hill trade, but found Double-A much the same on the other side of the country. We could hype up his deceptive delivery and strikeout proclivity again, but we're afraid of doing that too many times.

SAN DIEGO PADRES

Essay by Lauren Theisen

Player comments by Jon Tayler and BP staff

Y ou can judge the magnitude of a team's disastrous season by how many games are left when the deeply-sourced, finger-pointing post-mortem in *The Athletic* gets published. Longform journalism takes time and effort—a writer can't start and end these things just on the day of mathematical elimination—so the date at the top of these articles, minus at least a few weeks, can clue a reader in on how early the team's grave got stuck in the ground and when those around the franchise got really, really eager to vent to a reporter about everything that went wrong. Some teams don't crave that catharsis until the very end of the year, but for others, the frustration boils over much, much earlier.

In a topsy-turvy MLB season where teams like the Diamondbacks and Orioles rose from the ashes while plenty of free-spending, ambitious franchises fell face first into the mud, *The Athletic* did not skimp on words while sifting through the wreckage of baseball's biggest disappointments. On September 29, Sam Blum published "How did Angels squander Mike Trout and Shohei Ohtani? It starts with the owner's frugality," about owner Arte Moreno's reluctance to invest in key areas beyond pure salary. Two days earlier, on September 27, Brendan Kuty and Chris Kirschner co-bylined "Behind the Yankees' most miserable season in 30 years," which investigated the many reasons that might explain New York's 17-win freefall in 2023. Even before those dropped, on September 21, Tim Britton and Will Sammon were able to finish "How the $445 million Mets crashed and burned."

Before any of those pieces went public, an even *more* depressing report got out ahead of all of them. On September 19, as 11 games still remained in the season, the San Diego Padres were toast enough for Ken Rosenthal and Dennis Lin to get the green light on "The Padres' disastrous season reveals shaky foundation and 'institutional failure.'" This was not some overnight hit job; it clocked in at over 4,000 words, and per the authors, the backbone of their work was "interviews over the past several weeks with more than two dozen current and former Padres employees as well as others."

The kind of parched heartbreak that a team like these Padres can bring is supposed to happen in the playoffs, with everybody watching from the edges of their seats. But in *August* it was clear that San Diego's 2023 would be so much

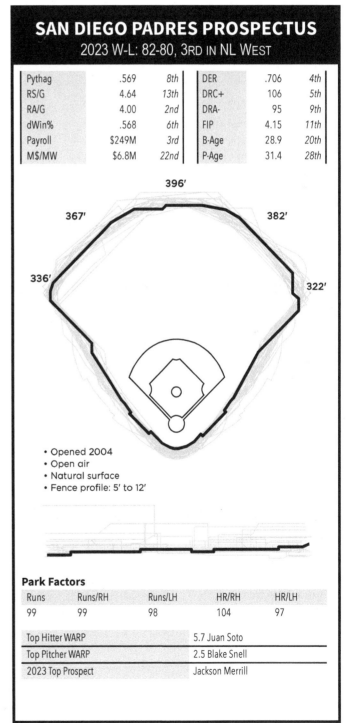

SAN DIEGO PADRES PROSPECTUS
2023 W-L: 82-80, 3RD IN NL WEST

Pythag	.569	8th	DER	.706	4th
RS/G	4.64	13th	DRC+	106	5th
RA/G	4.00	2nd	DRA-	95	9th
dWin%	.568	6th	FIP	4.15	11th
Payroll	$249M	3rd	B-Age	28.9	20th
M$/MW	$6.8M	22nd	P-Age	31.4	28th

- Opened 2004
- Open air
- Natural surface
- Fence profile: 5' to 12'

Park Factors

Runs	Runs/RH	Runs/LH	HR/RH	HR/LH
99	99	98	104	97

Top Hitter WARP	5.7 Juan Soto
Top Pitcher WARP	2.5 Blake Snell
2023 Top Prospect	Jackson Merrill

Payroll History (in millions)

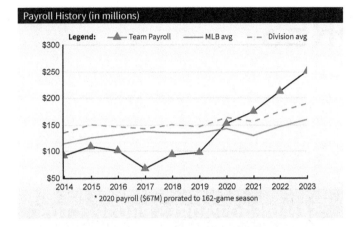

Legend: ▲ Team Payroll — MLB avg - - Division avg

* 2020 payroll ($67M) prorated to 162-game season

Future Commitments (in millions)

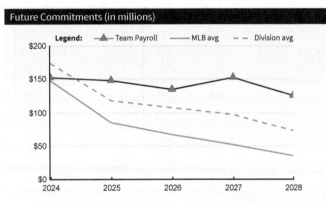

Legend: ▲ Team Payroll — MLB avg - - Division avg

Farm System Ranking

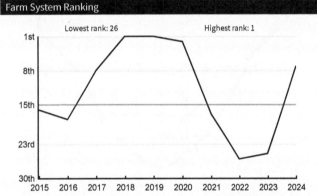

Lowest rank: 26   Highest rank: 1

Personnel

President of Baseball Operations & General Manager
A.J. Preller

Senior Vice President, Assistant General Manager
Josh Stein

Vice President, Assistant General Manager
Fred Uhlman, Jr.

Vice President, Baseball Operations
Nick Ennis

Senior Advisor/Director of Player Personnel
Logan White

Manager
Mike Schidt

of a flop that the public would demand an explanation. If anything, the recriminations on September 19 were overdue. But simply pointing out several organizational problems doesn't fully describe the damage done by this nightmare of a Padres season.

⚾   ⚾   ⚾

Expectations and the Padres were estranged for a long time, as much of the excitement about this team faded in the two decades after their 1998 World Series appearance. From 1999 to 2019, San Diego won one playoff game across two cameos, and heading into the plague season, they'd finished fourth or fifth in the NL West for five straight years. They were sleeping on a bed in the basement, and the door upstairs was sealed shut.

But after he was hired in 2014, Padres general manager A.J. Preller slowly assembled what would eventually become the best prospect core in baseball, led by Fernando Tatis Jr. In 2018, the team started spending—first on Eric Hosmer, and then a year later, much more impressively, on Manny Machado. The Padres beat the Cardinals in the Wild Card in 2020 before getting little-brothered by the Dodgers, and then in 2022, they struck gold at the trade deadline with a haul headlined by Juan Soto. This great leap in team construction started a bank run on their tickets and emphatically announced San Diego as yeah-duh contenders with dynastic ambitions. Their roster looked cool as hell.

Their management *and ownership* both seemed to actually, finally care about winning, which compared favorably with too many other clubs. And beating the Dodgers to get to the 2022 NLCS felt like a solid start that would precede even greater accomplishments in 2023. Xander Bogaerts entered the mix, Tatis returned from his combination motorcycle accident/steroid suspension and the Padres' $249 million payroll would stand in an unfamiliar spot as third-most in the majors.

Every fan, or at least every fan of a non-traditional power, should understand how rare this wave of enthusiasm is. If you're lucky, you get it maybe twice in a lifetime. It's not merely the feeling that comes when a perennial loser you love starts winning, or even shifts into higher gear—it's a rush of narcissistic joy upon realizing, suddenly, *the league revolves around us*. The Padres gave San Diego power in the form of attention and fear from the other 29 franchises. They united their fanbase behind the idea that, just down the street, perhaps the greatest baseball team they would ever cheer for had just been gathered. They were no longer a fourth-place team, nor a scrappy upstart underdog, nor even a "small-market" success. They were, as I vividly remember play-by-play announcer Don Orsillo shouting while I watched the Padres win their fifth straight to improve to 61-46, "*Slam Diego!*"

What the Padres did by building this lineup is the most good and noble act of love a franchise can demonstrate for its fans—better even than free hot dogs or a Shaggy concert at the end of the game. Snagging Soto and the others was unequivocally the right thing to do, from both a baseball perspective and an emotional perspective. But that's why what happened in 2023 is so tragic. The Padres' follow-up season broke the hearts of those who believed, squandered that all-too-rare thrill, and, worst of all, provided compelling evidence against ever surrendering to pure optimism again.

⚾   ⚾   ⚾

Thanks to a strong finish, last's Padres only finished with seven fewer wins than the previous version. It might as well have been 50. San Diego got out to a wobbly start, absorbed a bunch of hard-luck losses, struggled to find stability in the bullpen, and weathered underwhelming seasons from star hitters like Machado and Tatis. A middling start became a bad May which segued into a bleak June. It got so stressful that when I saw the Swinging Friar around the Fourth of July, he was missing most of his hair. But this Padres year didn't even warrant the awe of a horrific flameout, or a collapse at a critical juncture. This slow slide into irrelevancy, at least from the outside, felt more like watching a NASCAR driver try to run a whole race on three tires: It's weird for a while, and then it's mostly just sad.

If I had to pick the specific point when the sun went out and reverse-engineer when Rosenthal and Lin started pre-writing the autopsy, I think it would have to be the one-two punch of August 29 and 30. The Padres were gasping for air at this point, coming off a three-game sweep at the hands of the Brewers that featured, on that Sunday, Manny Machado repeatedly whalloping a dugout cooler as vengeance for a pop out with runners in the corners. On Monday, however, they slowed the momentum with a 4-1 win over the even-worse Cardinals, sticking them in a bad—but not unsalvageable—spot seven games back of the last Wild Card slot. That's when the universe told them to give up.

On both days, the Padres could have gained ground, but each time they let the Cardinals punk them. On Tuesday, they took a 5-3 lead into the bottom of the eighth, where Robert Suarez allowed a two-run shot to dead center by Willson Contreras. Then Bogaerts grounded into a double play to end their ninth, and two strikeouts plus a pop out with a man on third killed their tenth. After the sides switched, Josh Hader allowed the walk-off with a liner to left courtesy of Tommy Edman.

Wednesday, the walk-off happened an inning earlier, as a go-ahead Soto single in the seventh held only until Hader appeared to go for a save. The star closer got the first two outs, but Masyn Winn conjured up a double, and Edman topped himself with an opposite-field ball to the bullpen. Orsillo, who had wielded the triumphant, swaggering *Slam Diego* moniker, maintained his professional veneer as he summarized the outcome in a way that almost sounded like a question. But he could punctuate the facts of the conclusion with just one single editorialized word that stood alone amid the celebration: "Stunning."

The Padres were 62-72 at this point. What could they possibly do but sift through the wreckage and complain while reporters listened? And *The Athletic*'s post-mortem had no shortage of complaints from various interviewees. Among the gripes: Preller as a micromanager who struggles to communicate or maintain relationships; Machado as a "temperamental, inconsistent" facsimile of a leader; the overall star power of the locker room diffusing responsibility; and the unconventional hire of Kiwi softball coach Don Tricker—who had neither a medical background nor a baseball one—as director of player health and performance and later accused of being a "spy for the front office."

When it comes to these kinds of pieces, however, the juicy quotes are only part of the story. What's more compelling, as a baseball fan, is trying to divine the reasons behind those quotes—not just petty score-settling but deeper, less immediately legible feelings. On the surface, they attempt to portray a cause-and-effect in the way the Padres' year went down. If Preller was more chill, if the staff was in better tune with the players, if they had a focal point on the team who could really inspire them…maybe the Padres' would have won just a few more games and completely changed their season. It's almost a comforting narrative, even as it embeds itself in countless flaws, because it implies that all these issues can be fixed. But what this genre of sports journalism *really* captures is a large group of people who despise losing as they grapple with unthinkable failure. For as much blame that's been cast as a consequence of the team's fall, sometimes a team just breaks, in disastrous fashion, and all the actors involved can do is play their role in the tragedy.

⚾   ⚾   ⚾

Heading into 2024, everything about the Padres feels different from the can't-wait ecstasy of 12 months ago. The memories of the playoffs are long forgotten. Even before free-spending and well-liked team chairman Peter Seidler's passing, the team indicated they would cut payroll for 2024. Sure enough, Juan Soto was dealt to the Yankees for almost half a dozen unproven pitchers, and the team has replaced Josh Hader with high-risk imports in Yuki Matsui and Go Woo-Suk.

The Padres can still be a winning team, and they can improve on what they put to tape last year. But where a pennant run back then would have been a roller coaster zooming downhill from the very start, this season is a battle to win back the hearts and minds of many of their fans. The Padres sold out their 2023 season tickets based on the widespread belief among their supporters that their purchase would provide access to something special. This belief was backed by math and hard evidence—the sheer glee that resulted from summing the WARP their roster consistently provided and the Palomar Mountain high that came from vaporizing the Dodgers in October. A year later, 2024 now asks fans to believe without seeing—to forget the dreadful misery, cast off the burden of unfulfilled expectations, and risk disappointment while they embrace the possibility that this team could be real contenders once more.

To do that, you have to see some glimmer underneath the rubble. I don't believe that their futile September charge was anything worthwhile—the pointlessness of the wins made them even more painful—but I scoured the Padres' season for a silver lining and came away with footage of the team's May 5 win at home against the Dodgers, which put their record at 18-15. On this Friday night in front of a packed house, Yu Darvish outdueled Clayton Kershaw, Tatis rocketed two dingers over the fences, and Hader got the last two outs

on swings and misses while the whole crowd stood. After that final strike, an exuberant Tatis flipped his cap around, rotated to the right field seats, and gave the "rock on" gesture as he bounced on his cleats before turning to zip toward the infield in celebration. He never looked happier. *This*, I thought, *is the kind of reward everyone deserves when they give something their all*. For San Diego, and for their fans who've been knocked on their asses, 2024 is about trying to recapture the belief that a night this fun can be experienced again, dozens of times, all the way through October.

—Lauren Theisen is a co-owner of Defector.

HITTERS

José Azocar OF Born: 05/11/96 Age: 28 Bats: R Throws: R Height: 5'11" Weight: 181 Origin: IFA, 2012

YEAR	TM	LVL	AGE	PA	R	HR	RBI	SB	AVG/OBP/SLG	BABIP	SLGCON	BB%	K%	ZSw%	ZCon%	OSw%	OCon%	LA	90th EV	DRC+	BRR	DRP	WARP
2021	SA	AA	25	343	46	9	43	15	.276/.360/.432	.333	.565	10.2%	20.7%							121	0.3	-5.7	1.5
2021	ELP	AAA	25	201	26	0	27	17	.289/.308/.447	.369	.586	3.0%	22.4%							83	0.9	-1.6	0.2
2022	ORI	WIN	26	131	17	1	22	2	.294/.344/.387	.351	.479	4.6%	17.6%										
2022	ELP	AAA	26	105	11	5	16	3	.306/.352/.520	.362	.689	6.7%	22.9%	75.8%	86.7%	44.8%	62.5%			99	0.2	0.7	0.4
2022	SD	MLB	26	216	24	0	10	5	.257/.298/.332	.327	.424	5.6%	20.4%	75.5%	84.0%	42.4%	66.5%	10.1	102.3	86	0.2	0.6	0.4
2023	ELP	AAA	27	212	31	5	27	18	.269/.307/.388	.325	.500	4.2%	21.2%	68.4%	84.1%	43.9%	59.9%			86	1.4	0.9	0.6
2023	SD	MLB	27	102	16	2	9	8	.231/.278/.363	.292	.493	3.9%	23.5%	71.5%	81.7%	48.6%	71.0%	11.1	104.2	84	0.4	0.0	0.2
2024 DC	SD	MLB	28	499	43	9	47	37	.238/.284/.351	.297	.466	5.4%	23.1%							79	0.0	-2.5	0.1

2023 GP: RF (21), CF (17), LF (9), DH (2)   Comps: Noel Cuevas (53), Ryan Cordell (50), Abraham Almonte (49)

Have you noticed a decline in defensive substitutions for your compromised corner outfielder? Do you find yourself looking at your bench and wondering where your pinch-running specialist is? When it's time for a bunt, is it harder to get the sacrifice you need? If so, you may be suffering from FODS, or Fourth Outfielder Deficiency Syndrome. But the good news is, now there's a solution: Azocar. With a twice-weekly dose of Azocar, you can stabilize your outfield defense, experience a resurgence in stolen bases, and feel secure every time you square up. *Warning: Azocar is not intended for daily use. Do not use Azocar if you plan on hitting in high-leverage situations. If you experience dizziness, fatigue or the loss of a starting outfielder, stop using Azocar and contact your general manager.* Take control of your bench, with Azocar.

Xander Bogaerts SS Born: 10/01/92 Age: 31 Bats: R Throws: R Height: 6'2" Weight: 218 Origin: IFA, 2009

YEAR	TM	LVL	AGE	PA	R	HR	RBI	SB	AVG/OBP/SLG	BABIP	SLGCON	BB%	K%	ZSw%	ZCon%	OSw%	OCon%	LA	90th EV	DRC+	BRR	DRP	WARP
2021	BOS	MLB	28	603	90	23	79	5	.295/.370/.493	.333	.627	10.3%	18.7%	64.1%	85.8%	34.3%	68.9%	12.7	105.5	122	0.5	-2.5	3.7
2022	BOS	MLB	29	631	84	15	73	8	.307/.377/.456	.362	.579	9.0%	18.7%	66.4%	83.7%	32.8%	64.3%	10.2	104.8	119	1.1	-8.1	2.8
2023	SD	MLB	30	665	83	19	58	19	.285/.350/.440	.319	.539	8.4%	16.5%	60.8%	88.0%	28.7%	66.0%	8.2	103.3	119	0.6	2.5	4.1
2024 DC	SD	MLB	31	587	66	17	69	12	.272/.344/.424	.305	.520	8.9%	16.6%							118	0.6	-1.4	3.3

2023 GP: SS (146), DH (9)   Comps: Lou Boudreau (80), José Reyes (79), Alan Trammell (76)

Was Bogaerts' first year in Padres brown-and-mustard a disappointment or the latest in a long line of strong seasons? Depends on who you ask. By Baseball Prospectus' metrics, it was a career year, boosted by his best defensive numbers ever and a DRC+ bang on his last season in Boston. Head over to FanGraphs, and you'll see a dip in offense and defense both, albeit not so sharp, which added up to his sixth season of 4 or more WAR. If you check out Baseball Savant, you'll disappear amid a forest of red flags (or blue bars, as it were), with close-to-career-worst stats in barrel and hard-hit rate and expected numbers that will make you dry heave at the 10 years and $225 million or so left on his mondo-deal. The reality, as is usually the case, is somewhere in the middle, with his numbers damaged in part by a left wrist injury that bugged him all season, and clearly healed up before September (.417/.452/.670). On the bright side, his defense graded out mostly positive, and he's still top-tier at making great swing decisions. How well he and his wrist hold up as he delves deeper into his 30s will be the difference between future blurbs full of the usual praise and those that read increasingly like a desperate search for silver linings amidst darker and darker clouds.

Homer Bush Jr. OF Born: 10/13/01 Age: 22 Bats: R Throws: R Height: 6'3" Weight: 200 Origin: Round 4, 2023 Draft (#128 overall)

YEAR	TM	LVL	AGE	PA	R	HR	RBI	SB	AVG/OBP/SLG	BABIP	SLGCON	BB%	K%	ZSw%	ZCon%	OSw%	OCon%	LA	90th EV	DRC+	BRR	DRP	WARP
2023	PAD	ROK	21	53	16	2	4	10	.409/.509/.614	.457	.730	13.2%	13.2%										
2023	LE	A	21	105	16	1	10	11	.247/.369/.341	.286	.414	11.4%	14.3%							112	1.0	0.9	0.7
2023	SA	AA	21	29	2	0	3	1	.429/.448/.464	.462	.500	3.4%	6.9%							104		0.1	0.0
2024 non	SD	MLB	22	251	21	3	21	0	.223/.281/.317	.276	.413	6.2%	21.2%							70	0.0	0	-0.2

2023 GP: LF (20), CF (16), DH (6), RF (3)   Comps: Greg Golson (67), Juan Valdes (63), Alex Bregman (61)

The good news for Bush Jr. (or HoBuJu) is that outdoing his old man in the majors shouldn't be a challenge, what with Homer Sr.'s career DRC+ of 70. The bad news is that Junior's hit tool is a chip off the old block, with evaluators in agreement that his path to the big leagues will be built on speed and defense. He has the former in spades, grading out as a plus runner who'll rack up his fair share of infield hits and steals, and his fleet feet make him a natural fit in center field. It's a Billy Hamilton profile, where any offense will be a bonus. At least it'll only take Bush Jr. 364 MLB hits to pass his pops and give him family bragging rights.

Luis Campusano C   Born: 09/29/98   Age: 25   Bats: R   Throws: R   Height: 5'11"   Weight: 232   Origin: Round 2, 2017 Draft (#39 overall)

YEAR	TM	LVL	AGE	PA	R	HR	RBI	SB	AVG/OBP/SLG	BABIP	SLGCON	BB%	K%	ZSw%	ZCon%	OSw%	OCon%	LA	90th EV	DRC+	BRR	DRP	WARP
2021	ELP	AAA	22	326	47	15	45	1	.295/.365/.541	.335	.699	8.3%	20.2%							111	-0.8	-0.2	1.5
2021	SD	MLB	22	38	0	0	1	0	.088/.184/.088	.130	.130	10.5%	28.9%	63.5%	84.8%	37.1%	39.4%	15.0	106.5	73	0.0	-0.3	0.0
2022	ELP	AAA	23	358	62	14	60	0	.298/.363/.483	.328	.599	9.2%	17.3%	74.4%	85.4%	35.7%	63.4%			104	-0.5	-9.0	0.3
2022	SD	MLB	23	50	4	1	5	0	.250/.260/.333	.297	.432	2.0%	22.0%	78.6%	84.1%	54.3%	56.1%	15.7	104.9	99	-0.1	-0.5	0.1
2023	SD	MLB	24	174	27	7	30	0	.319/.356/.491	.331	.563	4.0%	12.1%	73.6%	88.8%	42.9%	74.0%	13.1	102.8	111	-0.3	-4.3	0.4
2024 DC	SD	MLB	25	348	36	9	39	0	.263/.316/.400	.295	.489	6.2%	16.7%							103	0.0	-3.6	0.9

2023 GP: C (42), DH (5)   Comps: Francisco Mejía (68), Javy Lopez (64), Buster Posey (63)

YEAR	TM	P. COUNT	FRM RUNS	BLK RUNS	THRW RUNS	TOT RUNS
2021	ELP	8976	2.6	-0.2	-1.1	1.2
2021	SD	1331	-0.2	0.0	0.0	-0.1
2022	ELP	9726	-7.7	-0.2	-0.3	-8.2
2022	SD	1357	-0.3	0.0	-0.1	-0.3
2023	SD	5405	-4.1	0.0	0.0	-4.1
2024	SD	9620	-3.3	0.0	-0.4	-3.7

A sprained left thumb cost Campusano three months of the season, and a sprained ankle brought it to an end a touch early, but when his joints were cooperating, he showed off the bat that made him a top prospect back in the day. Better still, all the peripherals pointed in the right direction: fewer swings, less chasing and whiffing, more and better contact (particularly in the strike zone), progress against breaking balls. The bad news is that none of the metrics thought Campusano's defense was anything other than poor; by CDA, he finished 83rd among qualified backstops. That said, no. 90 on that list is his best-case scenario: Willson Contreras. That kind of power-forward/glove-agnostic profile fits him to a T and meshes well with new battery-mate Kyle Higashioka. The big question for both him and San Diego, though, is how (and how often) it'll play alongside the position's heir apparent: Ethan Salas.

Matt Carpenter DH   Born: 11/26/85   Age: 38   Bats: L   Throws: R   Height: 6'4"   Weight: 210   Origin: Round 13, 2009 Draft (#399 overall)

YEAR	TM	LVL	AGE	PA	R	HR	RBI	SB	AVG/OBP/SLG	BABIP	SLGCON	BB%	K%	ZSw%	ZCon%	OSw%	OCon%	LA	90th EV	DRC+	BRR	DRP	WARP
2021	STL	MLB	35	249	18	3	21	2	.169/.305/.275	.250	.438	14.1%	30.9%	64.4%	75.8%	20.3%	57.9%	20.2	102.4	83	0.0	-0.1	0.3
2022	RR	AAA	36	95	15	6	19	1	.275/.379/.613	.291	.817	14.7%	21.1%	66.2%	84.9%	21.6%	60.0%			118	0.0	-2.1	0.3
2022	NYY	MLB	36	154	28	15	37	0	.305/.412/.727	.304	1.000	12.3%	22.7%	63.8%	85.0%	20.4%	51.3%	21.1	103.6	125	-0.1	-0.4	0.8
2023	SD	MLB	37	237	18	5	31	1	.176/.322/.319	.231	.496	17.3%	28.3%	59.7%	84.9%	25.6%	48.0%	24.6	103.0	104	-0.4	0.1	0.6
2024 non	SD	MLB	38	251	27	7	26	1	.198/.327/.355	.251	.514	14.1%	25.9%							96	-0.2	-0.5	0.4

2023 GP: DH (53), 1B (13)   Comps: Jason Giambi (61), Eddie Mathews (58), Joe Judge (58)

The pixie dust that covered Carpenter during his out-of-nowhere surge with the Yankees was apparently lost with the luggage en route to San Diego. Granted, expecting a 37-year-old to replicate a small sample of extreme performance without the benefit of Yankee Stadium's short porch was a fool's errand, but a Padres team short on left-handed power took the gamble anyway. To put it lightly, it didn't pay off: for $6.5 million, they received a DH who finished with a worse DRC+ than Sam Haggerty and Jon Berti, fewer home runs than Lenyn Sosa and René Pinto, and a lower wOBA than Ezequiel Tovar and Jurickson Profar. Was it all bad? Mostly, yes; you can only blame a wretched BABIP so much, and all the other peripherals suggest a hitter routinely getting beat in the strike zone and frequently expanding it. There might still be some magic in Carpenter's old silk bat; the Padres opted not to wait and find out, dealing him in mid-December to Atlanta, who also opted not to wait and find out, releasing him.

Ji Man Choi DH/1B   Born: 05/19/91   Age: 33   Bats: L   Throws: R   Height: 6'1"   Weight: 260   Origin: IFA, 2009

YEAR	TM	LVL	AGE	PA	R	HR	RBI	SB	AVG/OBP/SLG	BABIP	SLGCON	BB%	K%	ZSw%	ZCon%	OSw%	OCon%	LA	90th EV	DRC+	BRR	DRP	WARP
2021	DUR	AAA	30	27	4	0	2	0	.261/.333/.348	.353	.500	11.1%	25.9%							93	-1.1	0.3	0.0
2021	TB	MLB	30	305	36	11	45	0	.229/.348/.411	.300	.620	14.8%	28.5%	67.7%	76.9%	24.1%	50.6%	14.2	105.6	99	-0.1	0.1	0.6
2022	TB	MLB	31	419	36	11	52	0	.233/.341/.388	.320	.592	13.8%	29.4%	68.4%	72.7%	23.9%	57.9%	10.5	105.4	99	-0.5	0.2	0.1
2023	IND	AAA	32	29	7	3	9	0	.348/.448/.826	.357	1.188	17.2%	24.1%	71.4%	82.9%	24.2%	56.2%			111	0.0	-0.1	0.1
2023	ELP	AAA	32	29	1	0	1	0	.160/.276/.200	.222	.278	13.8%	24.1%	76.0%	78.9%	26.2%	58.8%			92	-0.4	-0.1	0.0
2023	PIT	MLB	32	76	9	6	11	0	.205/.224/.507	.220	.804	2.6%	35.5%	70.2%	75.8%	32.2%	54.5%	15.1	106.7	112	0.0	0.0	0.3
2023	SD	MLB	32	41	3	0	2	0	.065/.268/.097	.083	.130	19.5%	19.5%	74.3%	78.2%	23.7%	58.1%	5.5	106.2	80	0.0	0.0	0.0
2024 non	SD	MLB	33	251	25	7	26	0	.211/.303/.358	.268	.503	11.0%	25.9%							87	0.0	-0	0.1

2023 GP: 1B (17), DH (17)   Comps: Brandon Belt (52), Doug Mientkiewicz (50), J.T. Snow (49)

Between an Achilles tendon strain and a rib cage strain, Choi's season amounted to a month in Pittsburgh and two weeks in San Diego, the latter acquiring him at the trade deadline to try to paper over the Grand Canyon-sized chasm that was first base. That fortnight in southern California cratered his numbers, but the expected stats were overall positive, buying into him suddenly mashing the ball at a career-best level, including a whopping 59.2% hard-hit rate. That also came with a career-low walk rate, which dipped into the single digits for the first time—though that's an understandable result of a more aggressive approach, and one that didn't lead to more whiffs or strikeouts. That doesn't suggest a new ceiling or calling for Choi, though; he's still best-suited to be the strong side of a platoon at first base, and his injury-prone nature and so-so defense make him a bad bet as a full-time regular anyway.

Jake Cronenworth 1B   Born: 01/21/94   Age: 30   Bats: L   Throws: R   Height: 6'0"   Weight: 187   Origin: Round 7, 2015 Draft (#208 overall)

YEAR	TM	LVL	AGE	PA	R	HR	RBI	SB	AVG/OBP/SLG	BABIP	SLGCON	BB%	K%	ZSw%	ZCon%	OSw%	OCon%	LA	90th EV	DRC+	BRR	DRP	WARP
2021	SD	MLB	27	643	94	21	71	4	.266/.340/.460	.283	.547	8.6%	14.0%	63.0%	94.2%	27.9%	72.6%	12.3	103.5	118	0.0	-0.9	3.6
2022	SD	MLB	28	684	88	17	88	3	.239/.332/.390	.275	.502	10.2%	19.2%	61.3%	89.9%	25.5%	66.4%	18.7	102.0	104	0.6	0.1	2.5
2023	SD	MLB	29	522	54	10	48	6	.229/.312/.378	.267	.479	8.8%	18.6%	67.6%	91.3%	30.0%	69.9%	15.3	102.5	95	0.0	0.8	1.0
2024 DC	SD	MLB	30	548	57	13	59	3	.240/.325/.388	.265	.468	9.5%	15.2%							103	0.0	0.3	1.4

2023 GP: 1B (106), 2B (35)   *Comps: Aaron Hill (68), Johnny Evers (67), Billy Goodman (66)*

Turns out Jake is Cronenworthless when plying his trade at the cold corner instead of the keystone. The loser of all of San Diego's offseason machinations, the Michigan product was bumped over to first by the installation of Ha-seong Kim at second base and the Padres' total indifference to finding an actual first baseman. Asked to do a passable imitation of one, Cronenworth instead looked like, well, a middle infielder stuck in a corner. None of the major defensive metrics thought much of his work there, and while you can live with a so-so glove at first if the bat does the work, he simply doesn't have the stick to carry the position. His Statcast numbers were a sea of blue, and though he makes superb rates of in-zone contact, it's mostly harmless. It's a miscast performance up there with Jesse Eisenberg as Lex Luthor or Vin Diesel as anyone other than Dominic Torretto, and given the long-term presences of Kim, Bogaerts and Manny Machado in the rest of the infield, it severely muddies Cronenworth's future in San Diego. But who will take on that seven-year contract?

Nelson Cruz DH   Born: 07/01/80   Age: 44   Bats: R   Throws: R   Height: 6'2"   Weight: 230   Origin: IFA, 1998

YEAR	TM	LVL	AGE	PA	R	HR	RBI	SB	AVG/OBP/SLG	BABIP	SLGCON	BB%	K%	ZSw%	ZCon%	OSw%	OCon%	LA	90th EV	DRC+	BRR	DRP	WARP
2021	TB	MLB	40	238	35	13	36	0	.226/.283/.442	.252	.623	6.7%	26.5%	75.3%	77.5%	35.0%	53.1%	13.7	108.7	114	-0.1	0.0	0.9
2021	MIN	MLB	40	346	44	19	50	3	.294/.370/.537	.308	.682	10.1%	18.2%	75.4%	81.0%	34.8%	56.0%	10.9	110.8	133	-0.5	0.0	2.2
2022	WAS	MLB	41	507	50	10	64	4	.234/.313/.337	.295	.459	9.7%	23.5%	74.8%	78.5%	35.2%	53.5%	7.1	107.3	106	-0.5	0.0	1.4
2023	SD	MLB	42	152	9	5	23	1	.245/.283/.399	.323	.588	3.9%	30.3%	70.2%	79.1%	40.6%	45.7%	10.6	107.6	79	-0.1	0.0	-0.1
2024 non	SD	MLB	43	251	27	8	29	0	.240/.308/.391	.303	.546	7.6%	26.5%							97	-0.3	-0	0.3

2023 GP: DH (42), 1B (1)   *Comps: Hank Aaron (62), Tony Perez (61), Willie Stargell (59)*

Say goodbye to Cruz, whose 19th season in the majors turned out to be his last and, unfortunately, one of his worst. Hopes that an eye problem corrected with offseason surgery was the source of his woeful 2022 in Washington were dashed when he put up more or less the same season with San Diego, where he'd signed both to add some right-handed pop in the DH spot and be a clubhouse authority. In the latter role, he shined—"Everyone loves him, and the respect for him around the league is immense," said skipper Bob Melvin—but he was a zero at the plate, with the occasional surface-to-air missile off his bat surrounded by lots and lots of empty swings. And so on July 4, three days after his 43rd birthday, the Padres designated Cruz for assignment; after spending the back half of the season at home, he officially called it quits. His next stop: an advisor role with the Dodgers working primarily in Latin America, where his stature and popularity should go a long way with starstruck teens who were still in diapers when Cruz was obliterating MLB pitching. He'll be missed.

Dillon Head CF   Born: 10/11/04   Age: 19   Bats: L   Throws: L   Height: 6'0"   Weight: 185   Origin: Round 1, 2023 Draft (#25 overall)

YEAR	TM	LVL	AGE	PA	R	HR	RBI	SB	AVG/OBP/SLG	BABIP	SLGCON	BB%	K%	ZSw%	ZCon%	OSw%	OCon%	LA	90th EV	DRC+	BRR	DRP	WARP
2023	PAD	ROK	18	63	15	1	8	3	.294/.413/.471	.333	.571	17.5%	14.3%										
2023	LE	A	18	61	3	0	3	1	.241/.311/.333	.289	.409	6.6%	16.4%							96	-1.6	-0.3	-0.1
2024 non	SD	MLB	19	251	18	2	19	0	.204/.256/.285	.271	.390	5.7%	24.9%							52	0.0	0	-0.7

2023 GP: CF (26), DH (1)   *Comps: Jeisson Rosario (81), Wenceel Pérez (72), Anthony Gose (72)*

Head's speed is downright terrifying. Watch San Diego's 2023 first-round pick in action and you'll think that your video is either lagging or clipping; he covers acres of ground in the blink of an eye. The former no. 1 high school prospect in Illinois burned a 6.22 60-yard dash and made life a living hell for opposing catchers, going a perfect 31-for-31 in his senior season. Our staff rates him plus-plus in terms of wheels; toss in plus grades on the glove and you have an everyday center fielder profile. The trick will be his stick. Head has a clean lefty stroke that covers the strike zone, but his power lags behind and projects to be average at best. How much bop do you need, though, when you can just steal your way around the bases? If the offense holds, Head will rise as quickly through San Diego's system as he can fly on the field.

Kyle Higashioka C   Born: 04/20/90   Age: 34   Bats: R   Throws: R   Height: 6'1"   Weight: 202   Origin: Round 7, 2008 Draft (#230 overall)

YEAR	TM	LVL	AGE	PA	R	HR	RBI	SB	AVG/OBP/SLG	BABIP	SLGCON	BB%	K%	ZSw%	ZCon%	OSw%	OCon%	LA	90th EV	DRC+	BRR	DRP	WARP
2021	NYY	MLB	31	211	20	10	29	0	.181/.246/.389	.200	.560	8.1%	28.0%	71.1%	81.9%	30.2%	49.0%	21.8	105.2	106	-0.2	7.5	1.8
2022	NYY	MLB	32	248	27	10	31	0	.227/.264/.389	.246	.503	4.8%	21.0%	72.9%	85.5%	32.1%	50.3%	17.0	105.3	106	-0.2	8.1	1.9
2023	NYY	MLB	33	260	24	10	34	0	.236/.274/.413	.292	.595	5.4%	28.5%	67.6%	84.2%	35.0%	51.8%	15.2	105.0	90	-0.1	13.0	2.0
2024 DC	SD	MLB	34	185	18	6	21	1	.222/.275/.375	.269	.520	6.2%	25.4%							79	-0.2	5.6	0.8

2023 GP: C (90), DH (2)   *Comps: Doug Mirabelli (51), Yan Gomes (49), Nick Hundley (49)*

YEAR	TM	P. COUNT	FRM RUNS	BLK RUNS	THRW RUNS	TOT RUNS
2021	NYY	8429	8.5	0.0	-0.1	8.4
2022	NYY	10042	9.3	0.0	0.7	10.0
2023	NYY	10543	13.5	-0.3	-0.2	13.0
2024	SD	7215	6.0	-0.1	-0.3	5.6

Thrust into the primary receiver's role in 2023 almost essentially by default, Higashioka played about as well as expected considering the circumstances. He was far from the worst catcher in the league and his long-praised defense made him a productive player on the whole. Still, the Yankees needed more than that to compete in 2023, when their sagging lineup could really have used a catcher with at least a little punch (Austin Wells, anyone?). Higgy's 10 dingers were not enough to make him a helpful hitter, especially with a strikeout rate higher than anyone else on the team with at least 250 PA outside of Jake Bauers and Giancarlo Stanton. As part of the Juan Soto mega-trade, Higashioka finally finds himself in only his second organization entering his age-34 season; he'll likely slot into his familiar backup role on a brand new coast.

Ha-Seong Kim 2B/3B Born: 10/17/95 Age: 28 Bats: R Throws: R Height: 5'9" Weight: 168 Origin: IFA, 2020

YEAR	TM	LVL	AGE	PA	R	HR	RBI	SB	AVG/OBP/SLG	BABIP	SLGCON	BB%	K%	ZSw%	ZCon%	OSw%	OCon%	LA	90th EV	DRC+	BRR	DRP	WARP
2021	SD	MLB	25	298	27	8	34	6	.202/.270/.352	.241	.480	7.4%	23.8%	63.1%	83.5%	30.4%	70.0%	13.4	103.7	71	0.1	0.2	0.0
2022	SD	MLB	26	582	58	11	59	12	.251/.325/.383	.290	.475	8.8%	17.2%	62.2%	87.2%	30.4%	72.0%	15.8	102.4	107	0.8	7.8	3.3
2023	SD	MLB	27	626	84	17	60	38	.260/.351/.398	.306	.517	12.0%	19.8%	57.3%	88.7%	26.1%	72.5%	13.9	101.7	99	1.7	2.5	2.3
2024 DC	SD	MLB	28	580	61	15	62	25	.238/.327/.376	.264	.457	10.7%	15.8%							102	0.8	2.3	2.2

2023 GP: 2B (106), 3B (32), SS (20), DH (1)   *Comps: Freddie Patek (76), Carlos Guillen (75), Elvis Andrus (74)*

A.J. Preller's decision to give Xander Bogaerts enough money to finance and shoot his own Marvel movie forced a middle infield shuffle in San Diego, with Kim, who had more than held his own at shortstop, shifted over to second base. Not much worked out for the Padres last year, but Kim's move was a winner, as he earned a Gold Glove for what the metrics agreed was terrific work at the keystone. What's curious about his superficially stellar season, though, is that most of his peripherals were unimpressive. Kim's lack of barrels or hard contact doesn't translate well into expected or deserved stats, and his elite strikeout avoidance and plus eye at the plate only add up to so much offense. As such, he'll perpetually flirt with below-average outcomes at the plate. On the flip side, his combination of excellent defense, smart base running and superb strike zone judgment give him the kind of floor necessary to carry that kind of potentially fickle offense.

Manny Machado 3B Born: 07/06/92 Age: 32 Bats: R Throws: R Height: 6'3" Weight: 218 Origin: Round 1, 2010 Draft (#3 overall)

YEAR	TM	LVL	AGE	PA	R	HR	RBI	SB	AVG/OBP/SLG	BABIP	SLGCON	BB%	K%	ZSw%	ZCon%	OSw%	OCon%	LA	90th EV	DRC+	BRR	DRP	WARP
2021	SD	MLB	28	640	92	28	106	12	.278/.347/.489	.290	.597	9.8%	15.9%	72.2%	87.7%	32.7%	61.7%	14.1	109.3	128	0.0	1.6	4.7
2022	SD	MLB	29	644	100	32	102	9	.298/.366/.531	.337	.690	9.8%	20.7%	75.9%	83.9%	34.9%	63.0%	15.9	107.1	119	-0.1	-0.2	3.0
2023	SD	MLB	30	601	75	30	91	3	.258/.319/.462	.268	.578	8.3%	18.1%	71.5%	85.1%	33.4%	62.2%	15.2	107.6	115	-0.5	3.1	3.1
2024 DC	SD	MLB	31	598	78	30	88	4	.273/.341/.489	.295	.615	8.9%	18.6%							130	-0.3	1.7	4.0

2023 GP: 3B (105), DH (33)   *Comps: Brooks Robinson (71), Adrián Beltré (71), George Davis (70)*

The Padres' payroll situation can feel distressingly like a Ponzi scheme. Case in point: the 11-year, $350 million deal given to Machado before the 2023 season started, one that will pay him $39 million a year from 2027 through 2033, when he'll be 40 years old. It's a contract designed to circumvent luxury tax limits, with most of the money backloaded; it's less a statement of belief in Machado's longevity than a way to keep him on board without submarining the team's short-term finances. Nevertheless, year one of his mega-deal can't have Padres fans feeling good about that future, as Machado battled elbow trouble amidst his worst full-season offensive numbers since 2019. The big issues, beyond the balky joint and a broken left hand that cost him three weeks, were a drop in walk rate, suboptimal contact and struggles against pitches with big break like sweepers and splitters. None of that is enough to begin writing his epitaph, particularly as his defense remains elite. The hope for the Padres is that these scuffs will buff out.

Nathan Martorella 1B Born: 02/18/01 Age: 23 Bats: L Throws: L Height: 6'1" Weight: 224 Origin: Round 5, 2022 Draft (#150 overall)

YEAR	TM	LVL	AGE	PA	R	HR	RBI	SB	AVG/OBP/SLG	BABIP	SLGCON	BB%	K%	ZSw%	ZCon%	OSw%	OCon%	LA	90th EV	DRC+	BRR	DRP	WARP
2022	PAD	ROK	21	35	4	1	10	0	.387/.457/.613	.458	.760	11.4%	17.1%										
2022	LE	A	21	72	10	2	11	0	.288/.403/.458	.349	.614	16.7%	20.8%							101	-0.5	-1.8	0.0
2023	FW	A+	22	483	71	16	73	5	.259/.371/.450	.286	.576	15.1%	18.0%							129	-0.1	-2.8	2.3
2023	SA	AA	22	99	12	3	15	0	.236/.313/.382	.250	.453	9.1%	14.1%							115	-1.0	-1.2	0.1
2024 non	SD	MLB	23	251	23	5	24	0	.221/.300/.341	.273	.456	9.5%	22.2%							82	0.0	0	0.0

2023 GP: 1B (107), LF (29), DH (16)   *Comps: Ji Man Choi (65), Matt Thaiss (63), Hunter Morris (62)*

Martorella is your bog-standard first-base prospect: six feet tall, good power from the left side, runs like he's wearing the magnetic boots from the oil rig prison in *Face/Off*, might beble to fake it in an outfield corner if needed. That Martorella is straight out of central casting isn't necessarily a bad thing; for a Padres team lacking long-term first base options, the presence of a Spencer Torkelson/Andrew Vaughn-type player with room to grow would be a boon. And while Martorella's ceiling isn't as high as that of those former college superstars, he's shown above-average plate discipline so far in the minors, making it easier to envision him as a major-league regular. The main issue is that most of his contact is earth-bound, thanks to his deep, wide stance and low hand-load. The power is there; he'll need to tap into it more to continue being typecast.

────────────── ★ ★ ★ *2024 Top 101 Prospect* **#10** ★ ★ ★ ──────────────

Jackson Merrill SS Born: 04/19/03 Age: 21 Bats: L Throws: R Height: 6'3" Weight: 195 Origin: Round 1, 2021 Draft (#27 overall)

YEAR	TM	LVL	AGE	PA	R	HR	RBI	SB	AVG/OBP/SLG	BABIP	SLGCON	BB%	K%	ZSw%	ZCon%	OSw%	OCon%	LA	90th EV	DRC+	BRR	DRP	WARP
2021	PAD	ROK	18	120	19	0	10	5	.280/.339/.383	.370	.512	8.3%	22.5%									-1.9	
2022	PAD	ROK	19	31	5	1	6	3	.433/.452/.700	.444	.750	3.2%	6.5%										
2022	LE	A	19	219	33	5	34	8	.325/.387/.482	.393	.613	8.7%	19.2%							111	1.4	-1.3	0.9
2023	FW	A+	20	300	50	10	33	10	.280/.318/.444	.289	.512	5.7%	12.3%							118	0.5	-0.7	1.5
2023	SA	AA	20	211	26	5	31	5	.273/.338/.444	.288	.512	8.5%	11.8%							116	1.2	6.7	1.9
2024 DC	SD	MLB	21	30	3	1	3	0	.226/.272/.340	.256	.435	5.5%	16.5%							71	0.0	0	0.0

2023 GP: SS (99), DH (7), LF (5), 2B (2), 1B (1)   *Comps: Alen Hanson (84), Domingo Leyba (78), Oneil Cruz (77)*

For a small commuter suburb outside of Baltimore, Severna Park, MD has produced a surprising number of major leaguers; Mark Teixeira, Eric Milton, and Gavin Floyd have all called it home. Merrill (or Muhral, in proper Marylandese) msy soon join them on the "Notable People" section of the town's Wikipedia page. The 20-year-old kept chugging along with a 2023 season in which he showed off the elite bat and good defense that have made him one of the game's better middle-infield prospects. He continues to run excellent strikeout rates and gaudy contact numbers, and the baptism by fire that is Double-A couldn't slow him down. If there's a concern here, it's twofold: Merrill doesn't draw enough walks and hits too many grounders, giving him more of a Nico Hoerner feel than that of a franchise shortstop. Then again, you only have to look at the Padres' current shortstop to get a sense of what the 90th-percentile outcome for Merrill is, and why he remains an exciting player to dream on.

Rougned Odor 2B   Born: 02/03/94   Age: 30   Bats: L   Throws: R   Height: 5'11"   Weight: 200   Origin: IFA, 2011

YEAR	TM	LVL	AGE	PA	R	HR	RBI	SB	AVG/OBP/SLG	BABIP	SLGCON	BB%	K%	ZSw%	ZCon%	OSw%	OCon%	LA	90th EV	DRC+	BRR	DRP	WARP
2021	NYY	MLB	27	361	42	15	39	0	.202/.286/.379	.242	.550	7.5%	27.7%	74.9%	81.6%	35.1%	57.5%	18.3	104.6	80	0.1	-0.3	0.4
2022	BAL	MLB	28	472	49	13	53	6	.207/.275/.357	.244	.479	6.8%	23.1%	72.9%	84.1%	37.2%	60.0%	21.8	102.6	86	0.1	-3.9	0.3
2023	SD	MLB	29	157	21	4	18	2	.203/.299/.355	.247	.485	10.8%	23.6%	76.1%	88.5%	33.4%	53.5%	19.1	103.7	95	0.1	-0.2	0.3
2024 non	SD	MLB	30	251	26	8	28	3	.218/.300/.376	.266	.518	8.8%	24.4%							90	-0.1	-1.7	0.2

2023 GP: 2B (30), 3B (9), RF (9), DH (7), 1B (1)   Comps: Joe Morgan (66), Lou Bierbauer (58), Johnny Evers (57)

"I wish I knew how to quit you," A.J. Preller whispers to a headshot of Rougned Odor every night. Maybe 2023 will be the straw that breaks this particular back. Despite a putrid 2022 season in Baltimore, Odor landed a minor-league deal with the Padres to reunite with his former Texas boss, then beat out a punchless cast of Quad-A players and roster cast-offs to make the Opening Day roster as a backup infielder by slashing .316/.422/.474 in Cactus League play. Odor immediately went about proving the worthlessness of spring training stats by posting a .373 OPS in April before catching fire for the next six weeks, hitting .280/.372/.533. He even managed to draw nearly as many walks as strikeouts! Alas, that was a mirage: From June 20 through mid-July, he went 4-for-33 with 14 strikeouts before the spiraling Padres pulled the plug. Going back to 2017, Odor has hit .211/.280/.400; it's hard to imagine any team bothering with this particular song-and-dance anymore, and yet.

Jurickson Profar LF   Born: 02/20/93   Age: 31   Bats: S   Throws: R   Height: 6'0"   Weight: 184   Origin: IFA, 2009

YEAR	TM	LVL	AGE	PA	R	HR	RBI	SB	AVG/OBP/SLG	BABIP	SLGCON	BB%	K%	ZSw%	ZCon%	OSw%	OCon%	LA	90th EV	DRC+	BRR	DRP	WARP
2021	SD	MLB	28	412	47	4	33	10	.227/.329/.320	.266	.392	11.9%	15.8%	67.5%	87.8%	26.7%	71.7%	14.0	101.5	98	0.0	-2.8	1.0
2022	SD	MLB	29	658	82	15	58	5	.243/.331/.391	.272	.477	11.1%	15.7%	63.9%	86.9%	28.2%	71.5%	13.0	102.3	110	-0.2	-6.4	2.2
2023	SD	MLB	30	49	4	1	7	0	.295/.367/.409	.308	.450	10.2%	8.2%	70.9%	94.6%	29.1%	73.3%	21.5	101.5	120	0.0	-0.3	0.2
2023	COL	MLB	30	472	51	8	39	1	.236/.316/.364	.276	.459	9.5%	18.2%	69.7%	87.9%	29.0%	62.1%	14.0	101.8	98	-0.1	-3.4	0.8
2024 DC	SD	MLB	31	341	35	7	34	1	.241/.329/.370	.274	.449	10.5%	16.2%							100	-0.1	-4	0.5

2023 GP: LF (95), DH (18), 1B (5), RF (2), 2B (1)   Comps: Eddie Yost (49), Danny Heep (48), Tommy Thevenow (47)

It took until a week or so before Opening Day for Profar to find a free-agency fit, and in retrospect, it probably should have taken a little longer. The former top prospect (we are legally required to refer to him as such) was fine with the Padres in 2022, but last year he showed little power, bad defense, and none of the versatility that made him intermittently valuable in the past. Naturally, the one team willing to look past all of that was the Rockies, who handed him a one-year, $7.75 million deal, then watched him flail in the outfield and produce nothing at the plate despite getting to take his hacks at Coors Field. (Fun fact: Profar had a .793 OPS in Colorado and a .618 mark everywhere else. Coors is undefeated.) Released in late August, he returned to San Diego and, like the prodigal son, was welcomed with open arms to an injury-wracked roster in desperate need of bodies. His small-sample rally in September (.296/.367/.409) should earn him an NRI in the spring, but it will probably be another long winter of waiting by the phone for Profar.

★ ★ ★   *2024 Top 101 Prospect* **#12** ★ ★ ★

Ethan Salas C/DH   Born: 06/01/06   Age: 18   Bats: L   Throws: R   Height: 6'2"   Weight: 185   Origin: Undrafted Free Agent, 2022

YEAR	TM	LVL	AGE	PA	R	HR	RBI	SB	AVG/OBP/SLG	BABIP	SLGCON	BB%	K%	ZSw%	ZCon%	OSw%	OCon%	LA	90th EV	DRC+	BRR	DRP	WARP
2023	LE	A	17	220	35	9	35	5	.267/.350/.487	.328	.694	10.9%	25.9%							108	0.1	0.1	0.9
2023	FW	A+	17	37	3	0	3	0	.200/.243/.229	.280	.320	5.4%	27.0%							85	-0.1	-0.3	0.0
2023	SA	AA	17	33	2	0	3	0	.179/.303/.214	.250	.300	12.1%	24.2%							95	0.2	0.4	0.1
2024 non	SD	MLB	18	251	21	4	23	0	.213/.268/.325	.285	.463	6.2%	27.7%							65	0.0	0	-0.1

2023 GP: C (34), DH (32)   Comps: Angel Villalona (48), Fernando Martinez (45), Jose Tabata (33)

YEAR	TM	P. COUNT	FRM RUNS	BLK RUNS	THRW RUNS	TOT RUNS
2023	LE	3070	0.1	-0.3	0.2	0.0
2024	SD	6956	-3.7	-0.4	0.0	-4.0

Most 17-year-olds spend their summers mowing lawns or flipping burgers; Salas spent the last weeks of his season taking cuts against college grads and twentysomethings. That San Diego's catcher of the future made it all the way to Double-A as a teenager isn't a total surprise, given the aggressiveness with which the Padres promote their top prospects. But it's still unheard of for a kid not old enough to vote or buy a pack of cigarettes to be where Salas is. It's a testament to his drool-worthy tools, in particular a preternatural ability to cover the strike zone and go gap-to-gap with a gorgeous lefty swing. He's also earned plus grades across the board defensively. That's the kind of skill set that has A.J. Preller on the verge of breaking child labor laws. And if it doesn't break Salas in the process, the Padres may have found a permanent fixture behind the plate for the first time since the days of Terry Kennedy and Benito Santiago.

Fernando Tatis Jr. RF   Born: 01/02/99   Age: 25   Bats: R   Throws: R   Height: 6'3"   Weight: 217   Origin: IFA, 2015

YEAR	TM	LVL	AGE	PA	R	HR	RBI	SB	AVG/OBP/SLG	BABIP	SLGCON	BB%	K%	ZSw%	ZCon%	OSw%	OCon%	LA	90th EV	DRC+	BRR	DRP	WARP
2021	SD	MLB	22	546	99	42	97	25	.282/.364/.611	.324	.898	11.4%	28.0%	81.0%	77.9%	33.6%	46.8%	13.8	111.0	139	0.7	1.3	4.9
2023	ELP	AAA	24	39	11	7	15	2	.515/.590/1.212	.435	1.333	15.4%	7.7%	82.1%	89.1%	30.1%	72.0%			157	0.5	2.1	0.6
2023	SD	MLB	24	635	91	25	78	29	.257/.322/.449	.299	.594	8.3%	22.2%	81.9%	79.0%	35.6%	54.0%	10.7	107.2	120	1.2	4.8	3.8
2024 DC	SD	MLB	25	651	86	34	99	24	.265/.336/.495	.304	.672	8.9%	23.6%							130	0.6	6.2	4.9

2023 GP: RF (137), CF (5), DH (3), 2B (1)   Comps: Carlos Correa (67), Alex Rodriguez (63), Juan Gonzalez (62)

The would-be face of the Padres turned heel in 2022 with the double whammy of hurting his wrist in a motorcycle accident and then getting busted for a positive PED test; Tatis lost an entire season and a dump truck's worth of goodwill. Back in the fold and at a new position, thanks to the addition of Xander Bogaerts, Tatis' redemption tour was an uneven one. At the plate, he showed flashes of his dynamic self, but a big dip in his power output deadened his overall numbers. In particular, he struggled to square up four-seamers, going from a .750 slugging percentage against them to .490. But while he struggled to put the barrel on the ball, getting leather on it was another matter entirely. Moved to right field, Tatis was a revelation, showing off top-of-the-charts range to go with his nuclear-powered arm and elite speed. That helped keep his value from tanking, and should his offense rebound next season (and it should, given that he's still just 25 years old), that combo will go a long way toward restoring Tatis to his former heights.

Brandon Valenzuela C Born: 10/02/00 Age: 23 Bats: S Throws: R Height: 6'0" Weight: 225 Origin: IFA, 2017

YEAR	TM	LVL	AGE	PA	R	HR	RBI	SB	AVG/OBP/SLG	BABIP	SLGCON	BB%	K%	ZSw%	ZCon%	OSw%	OCon%	LA	90th EV	DRC+	BRR	DRP	WARP
2021	LE	A	20	378	50	6	62	3	.307/.389/.444	.386	.586	11.6%	21.2%							114	-0.8	12.3	2.8
2021	FW	A+	20	65	4	1	7	1	.245/.415/.327	.379	.552	23.1%	30.8%							98	-0.2	-1.7	0.0
2022	FW	A+	21	413	39	10	47	0	.209/.334/.348	.256	.480	15.3%	23.0%							109	-4.4	19.1	3.1
2023	FW	A+	22	156	22	4	15	0	.279/.372/.456	.358	.626	10.9%	23.7%							104	1.0	4.6	1.0
2023	SA	AA	22	108	10	1	6	2	.181/.287/.255	.250	.369	12.0%	26.9%							94	0.4	0.9	0.4
2024 DC	SD	MLB	23	30	3	0	3	0	.223/.297/.330	.310	.500	8.9%	28.6%							79	0.0	0	0.0

2023 GP: C (49), DH (16), 1B (1) *Comps: Argenis Raga (69), Chadwick Tromp (67), Julian Leon (66)*

YEAR	TM	P. COUNT	FRM RUNS	BLK RUNS	THRW RUNS	TOT RUNS
2021	LE	7058	9.7	-0.3	1.7	11.1
2021	FW	2117	-0.8	-0.6	-0.2	-1.5
2022	FW	9333	17.0	-1.2	5.4	21.2
2023	FW	4342	4.6	-0.3	1.1	5.4
2023	SA	2641	-0.3	-0.1	1.6	1.2
2024	SD	1202	0.3	-0.1	0.0	0.3

If Ethan Salas is San Diego's catcher of the future, then Valenzuela looks destined to be his backup. It's unlikely he can produce enough offense to give him a starter's profile; aside from his good batting eye, most of his contact is on the weaker side. As with most would-be second bananas behind the plate, Valenzuela grades out better with the glove. His arm is plus, which gives him a leg up in MLB's new go-go-go era of base running. No one seeks to be the second in line, but that looks like Valenzuela's lot with the Padres. Then again, he does just enough that he should have no trouble holding on to that understudy gig, and even the Kyle Higashiokas of the world will depart this game with a full bank account and a bunch of autographs in circulation. As the old Gershwin song goes, it's nice work if you can get it.

Samuel Zavala CF Born: 07/15/04 Age: 19 Bats: L Throws: L Height: 6'1" Weight: 175 Origin: IFA, 2021

YEAR	TM	LVL	AGE	PA	R	HR	RBI	SB	AVG/OBP/SLG	BABIP	SLGCON	BB%	K%	ZSw%	ZCon%	OSw%	OCon%	LA	90th EV	DRC+	BRR	DRP	WARP
2021	DSL PAD	ROK	16	235	44	3	40	11	.297/.400/.487	.344	.597	13.6%	15.3%									7.4	
2022	PAD	ROK	17	35	6	1	6	0	.345/.412/.621	.500	1.000	11.4%	31.4%										
2022	LE	A	17	141	24	7	26	5	.254/.355/.508	.308	.729	13.5%	26.2%							110	-1.8	-2.4	0.2
2023	LE	A	18	459	83	14	71	20	.267/.420/.451	.356	.692	19.4%	26.4%							126	1.5	-4.3	2.4
2023	FW	A+	18	56	4	0	6	1	.078/.161/.098	.125	.156	8.9%	33.9%							80	-1.5	2.4	0.1
2024 non	SD	MLB	19	251	23	4	23	0	.212/.295/.325	.320	.521	9.8%	33.9%							77	0.0	0	0.1

2023 GP: CF (101), RF (7), DH (6) *Comps: Estevan Florial (36), Mike Trout (34), Yorman Rodriguez (28)*

Of the Padres' top prospects, Zavala is the one with the most variance in his profile. Taking the glass half-full approach: He has an advanced eye at the plate and a ferocious hit tool, boasting a scythe of a swing and Formula 1-level bat speed. He ran a walk rate just shy of 20% as an 18-year-old in A-ball, and though that came with plenty of strikeouts, it speaks to a player with a good feel for the strike zone. Despite that, upon earning a promotion to High-A in early August, Zavala promptly went to pieces, striking out in a third of his plate appearances. Compounding that whiffery was average grades on defense and the bases, suggesting he doesn't have the speed to be a full-time center fielder. Zavala's overall package is less enticing if he's a corner outfielder with a so-so glove, but given that he won't turn 20 until July, there's plenty of time for him to tune up his tools and reduce the risk of an early flameout.

PITCHERS

Pedro Avila RHP Born: 01/14/97 Age: 27 Height: 5'11" Weight: 210 Origin: IFA, 2014

YEAR	TM	LVL	AGE	G (GS)	IP	W-L	SV	K	WHIP	ERA	CSP	BB%	K%	HR%	GB%	ZSw%	ZCon%	OSw%	OCon%	BABIP	SLGCON	DRA-	WARP
2021	ELP	AAA	24	13(1)	22¹	1-0	0	24	1.48	3.22		14.9%	23.8%	1.0%	44.8%					.298	.421	93	0.2
2021	SD	MLB	24	1(1)	4	0-1	0	5	1.75	2.25	55.0%	15.0%	25.0%	5.0%	33.3%	70.3%	88.5%	25.5%	66.7%	.273	.583	102	0.0
2022	ELP	AAA	25	30(24)	112	7-2	0	124	1.31	4.58		10.3%	26.1%	3.4%	44.1%	66.8%	80.0%	32.8%	53.1%	.290	.607	87	1.5
2022	SD	MLB	25	2(0)	4	0-0	0	5	1.00	4.50	64.0%	5.6%	27.8%	5.6%	54.5%	68.6%	70.8%	28.6%	60.0%	.200	.545	93	0.1
2023	ELP	AAA	26	19(15)	55²	1-6	0	48	1.85	8.57		11.5%	17.8%	4.8%	40.7%	71.4%	85.9%	31.8%	51.9%	.339	.720	127	-0.4
2023	SD	MLB	26	14(6)	50¹	2-2	0	54	1.35	3.22	45.7%	11.4%	24.5%	1.4%	56.6%	65.8%	83.6%	32.7%	55.2%	.305	.474	89	0.9
2024 DC	SD	MLB	27	27(16)	61²	1-5	0	58	1.45	4.82	47.3%	10.3%	21.0%	2.5%	49.5%					.306	.522	106	0.2

2023 Arsenal: FA (94.1), FS (83.7), CU (77.5), SI (93.4), SL (83.5), CH (84.7) *Comps: Rafael Montero (40), Bryan Mitchell (39), Gabriel Ynoa (38)*

Avila's 14th major-league game, in his third major-league season, marked a first: big-league win no. 1, earned by shutting out the Phillies over 6 ⅔ innings despite six walks. Touch-and-go command has been an issue throughout his career, and is the biggest obstacle between him and being a full-time starter. His solid '23 at least has him in the "viable option" bucket for San Diego. But even with better command, it's unlikely that he has a ceiling beyond the back of the rotation; with just one plus pitch to his name in his changeup, middle relief seems like a happier home. Still, given the departures among the Padres' pitching staff, it's a guarantee that he'll be busy in one role or another. After a decade of toiling in the minors, that qualifies as another happy ending.

Jhony Brito RHP Born: 02/17/98 Age: 26 Height: 6'2" Weight: 210 Origin: IFA, 2015

YEAR	TM	LVL	AGE	G (GS)	IP	W-L	SV	K	WHIP	ERA	CSP	BB%	K%	HR%	GB%	ZSw%	ZCon%	OSw%	OCon%	BABIP	SLGCON	DRA-	WARP
2021	HV	A+	23	14(14)	70	4-4	0	73	1.01	2.57		4.1%	25.1%	0.7%	53.3%					.292	.449	80	1.4
2021	SOM	AA	23	8(8)	46²	3-3	0	45	1.26	5.01		4.5%	22.6%	4.0%	41.5%					.316	.617	100	0.4
2022	SOM	AA	24	8(8)	42	5-2	0	38	1.12	2.36		6.6%	22.8%	2.4%	46.2%					.283	.462	100	0.6
2022	SWB	AAA	24	18(15)	70²	6-2	0	53	1.17	3.31		8.4%	18.5%	1.7%	52.9%					.266	.405	91	1.3
2023	SWB	AAA	25	7(7)	36¹	2-2	0	33	1.54	5.45		9.7%	20.0%	4.8%	48.7%	65.4%	82.9%	33.7%	62.8%	.299	.600	94	0.6
2023	NYY	MLB	25	25(13)	90¹	9-7	1	72	1.22	4.28	48.8%	7.5%	19.4%	3.8%	43.7%	68.0%	83.5%	33.8%	71.1%	.268	.553	105	0.8
2024 DC	SD	MLB	26	30(6)	57	3-3	0	41	1.37	4.74	48.8%	7.7%	16.7%	3.2%	43.5%					.290	.527	107	0.2

2023 Arsenal: SI (96.3), CH (88.9), FA (96.1), SW (82.5), SL (80.8), FC (86.6)   Comps: Cody Anderson (72), Tyler Wilson (71), Thomas Eshelman (68)

Unexpectedly thrust into the Yankees' rotation for the first couple months of 2023, Brito pitched about as well as most emergency starters would in that situation, but looked far better in shorter bursts out of the bullpen in August and September. In those months, he made 10 appearances of at least two innings, flashing improved command while notching a 1.43 ERA and 0.850 WHIP in relief. The best case scenario for 2024 is that the Padres snagged another relief version of Michael King, and at worst he'll serve the same role he did in 2023.

Tom Cosgrove LHP Born: 06/14/96 Age: 28 Height: 6'2" Weight: 190 Origin: Round 12, 2017 Draft (#348 overall)

YEAR	TM	LVL	AGE	G (GS)	IP	W-L	SV	K	WHIP	ERA	CSP	BB%	K%	HR%	GB%	ZSw%	ZCon%	OSw%	OCon%	BABIP	SLGCON	DRA-	WARP
2021	SA	AA	25	22(0)	26²	1-0	1	32	0.97	2.36		6.6%	30.2%	1.9%	44.8%					.262	.478	84	0.4
2022	SA	AA	26	20(0)	25²	6-1	0	39	0.97	2.45		12.7%	38.2%	2.9%	34.0%					.205	.511	66	0.6
2022	ELP	AAA	26	28(0)	30	2-1	0	43	1.23	4.80		11.7%	33.6%	4.7%	49.3%	64.7%	81.8%	34.3%	44.1%	.262	.627	73	0.6
2023	SD	MLB	27	54(0)	51¹	1-2	1	44	0.97	1.75	51.3%	9.3%	21.5%	1.5%	40.1%	66.4%	81.0%	27.0%	61.3%	.211	.326	101	0.6
2024 DC	SD	MLB	28	57(0)	60	4-3	2	58	1.37	4.66	51.3%	10.4%	22.1%	3.4%	39.3%					.282	.549	104	0.1

2023 Arsenal: SW (76.2), FA (92.1), SI (91.2), CH (85.3)   Comps: Brad Wieck (73), Ryan O'Rourke (71), Nefi Ogando (68)

Congrats to Cosgrove, who became MLB player no. 22,906 in late April. The Staten Island product brought the ruckus with a sub-2.00 ERA, but can his season be that simple? To a certain degree, yes: No one could put good wood on either his slider or his four-seamer, and while the latter is no fire-breather at just 92 mph, he throws it for strikes at the top of the zone. Small wonder that he's at the top of the charts in avoiding unwanted contact, ranking in the 100th percentile in average exit velocity and hard-hit rate and 98th In xwOBA. Every silver lining has a cloud—that strike pounding also means that hitters are neither chasing nor whiffing, and while Cosgrove does have a sinker, it hasn't turned him into a grounder-inducing machine. That's a tricky tightrope to walk; tweaking the slider, or perhaps developing a barely used changeup, might be necessary to keep the good times going in year two.

Yu Darvish RHP Born: 08/16/86 Age: 37 Height: 6'5" Weight: 220 Origin: IFA, 2012

YEAR	TM	LVL	AGE	G (GS)	IP	W-L	SV	K	WHIP	ERA	CSP	BB%	K%	HR%	GB%	ZSw%	ZCon%	OSw%	OCon%	BABIP	SLGCON	DRA-	WARP
2021	SD	MLB	34	30(30)	166²	8-11	0	199	1.09	4.22	57.6%	6.5%	29.2%	4.1%	36.5%	68.5%	82.6%	30.5%	54.7%	.274	.630	80	3.4
2022	SD	MLB	35	30(30)	194²	16-8	0	197	0.95	3.10	59.2%	4.8%	25.6%	2.9%	37.7%	66.6%	83.5%	34.4%	59.8%	.251	.458	82	3.6
2023	SD	MLB	36	24(24)	136¹	8-10	0	141	1.30	4.56	50.7%	7.5%	24.6%	3.1%	42.1%	65.9%	84.4%	30.8%	58.7%	.319	.577	90	2.3
2024 DC	SD	MLB	37	29(29)	166	10-10	0	165	1.21	4.00	55.0%	6.6%	23.7%	3.6%	39.4%					.288	.564	93	2.1

2023 Arsenal: SI (94.5), SW (82.6), SL (85.8), FA (94.9), FC (91), FS (89.3), KC (79.6), CU (72.6), CH (88.5)   Comps: Jim Bunning (84), Bert Blyleven (83), Justin Verlander (82)

The Padres re-upped Darvish on a six-year deal before the season started, a contract that probably caused eyeballs to bulge, but one that felt borderline necessary given the shambolic state of San Diego's rotation in 2024 and beyond. Some creative accounting made Darvish's deal more palatable as he goes from elder Millennial to plain old elder—it was substantially frontloaded and structured to lower the resulting tax hit—but it also felt like a worthwhile gamble given his durability and dependability. Or at least, it felt worthwhile before Darvish turned in his lowest full-season innings total and highest ERA since 2018. Oh, and he finished the year on the injured list with a stress reaction in his elbow. The main issue is that Darvish's swinging-strike rate has decreased for three straight seasons, forcing him to nibble, and that approach hurt him when the count went to three balls. A pitcher as clever as he is can hopefully turn back time, even if it's only a year or two, before it's all said and done in 2028.

Enyel De Los Santos RHP Born: 12/25/95 Age: 28 Height: 6'3" Weight: 235 Origin: IFA, 2014

YEAR	TM	LVL	AGE	G (GS)	IP	W-L	SV	K	WHIP	ERA	CSP	BB%	K%	HR%	GB%	ZSw%	ZCon%	OSw%	OCon%	BABIP	SLGCON	DRA-	WARP
2021	PHI	MLB	25	26(0)	28	1-1	0	42	1.71	6.75	54.3%	10.2%	30.7%	5.1%	41.0%	77.5%	71.5%	35.4%	58.7%	.391	.855	85	0.5
2021	PIT	MLB	25	7(0)	7¹	1-0	0	6	1.77	4.91	52.4%	11.1%	16.7%	2.8%	24.0%	70.0%	76.2%	37.5%	66.7%	.348	.583	100	0.1
2022	CLE	MLB	26	50(0)	53¹	5-0	1	61	1.07	3.04	58.3%	7.9%	28.4%	1.4%	40.0%	73.2%	80.4%	35.4%	52.4%	.280	.481	82	1.0
2023	CLE	MLB	27	70(0)	65²	5-2	0	62	1.14	3.29	49.9%	9.5%	23.7%	1.5%	40.4%	71.0%	86.1%	32.9%	50.3%	.275	.453	98	0.8
2024 DC	SD	MLB	28	57(0)	60	4-2	0	66	1.29	4.22	53.3%	9.7%	25.5%	3.3%	40.1%					.287	.562	96	0.4

2023 Arsenal: FA (95.8), SL (84.3), CH (88.1)   Comps: Lucas Sims (59), Jose Paniagua (57), Archie Bradley (56)

De Los Santos' transformation from struggling hurler on the minor-league shuttle to a consistently above-average middle reliever has been yet another win for Cleveland's pitching development system. For the second straight year, he posted an ERA below 3.5, and elevated himself into a setup role with 16 holds in 2023. The under-the-hood numbers declined as he got fewer swings and misses while inhabiting the zone less, and his platoon splits widened as his slider got better while his fastball regressed. Much of De Los Santos' success in the past two seasons has come thanks to a HR/FB rate about half the league average. In reliever sample sizes, even a few flyouts that become wall-scrapers can have an outsized impact on a season line. Until those concerns are realized, though, the quality breaking ball should make him a useful contributor to the Padres' bullpen.

Woo-Suk Go RHP   Born: 08/06/98   Age: 25   Height: 5'11"   Weight: 198   Origin: IFA, 2024

YEAR	TM	LVL	AGE	G (GS)	IP	W-L	SV	K	WHIP	ERA	CSP	BB%	K%	HR%	GB%	ZSw%	ZCon%	OSw%	OCon%	BABIP	SLGCON	DRA-	WARP
2024 DC	SD	MLB	25	50(0)	53¹	4-2	2	68	1.34	4.31		12.0%	29.2%	3.4%	41.5%					.287	.591	96	0.3

Go didn't make any of the free agent rankings that mark the beginning of the offseason, in part because no one would have predicted that his KBO team, the LG Twins, would post him. By releasing their closer out into the wild, the Twins reecived a whopping $900,000, 20% of the two-year, $4.5 million contract that he signed with the Padres. There he'll most likely fit in a set-up role; he struck out nearly a third of all batters in a league that likes to choke up with two strikes, relying primarily on a mid-90s heater and a low-90s cutter. But Go's never really mastered the command aspect of pitching, meaning that not only will he walk hitters, he'll also let some pitches bleed over the middle of the plate. A.J. Preller's willingness to look west has paid off so far, and while this might be his biggest stretch yet, the risk is minimal. One thing we do know: In a league where reliable relief pitching is hard to come by, Twins fans are going to miss him.

Rich Hill LHP   Born: 03/11/80   Age: 44   Height: 6'5"   Weight: 220   Origin: Round 4, 2002 Draft (#112 overall)

YEAR	TM	LVL	AGE	G (GS)	IP	W-L	SV	K	WHIP	ERA	CSP	BB%	K%	HR%	GB%	ZSw%	ZCon%	OSw%	OCon%	BABIP	SLGCON	DRA-	WARP
2021	TB	MLB	41	19(19)	95¹	6-4	0	91	1.16	3.87	57.1%	9.3%	23.4%	3.6%	39.8%	61.3%	82.7%	32.4%	65.6%	.255	.540	119	0.0
2021	NYM	MLB	41	13(12)	63¹	1-4	0	59	1.28	3.84	57.1%	7.0%	21.7%	2.6%	27.4%	65.5%	85.8%	29.7%	61.7%	.311	.544	111	0.2
2022	BOS	MLB	42	26(26)	124¹	8-7	0	109	1.30	4.27	56.8%	7.0%	20.7%	2.9%	39.6%	64.8%	86.1%	32.8%	64.8%	.305	.557	125	-0.4
2023	PIT	MLB	43	22(22)	119	7-10	0	104	1.48	4.76	50.5%	8.9%	19.6%	2.8%	37.8%	64.8%	87.5%	26.7%	69.6%	.320	.586	127	-0.3
2023	SD	MLB	43	10(5)	27¹	1-4	0	25	1.72	8.23	52.8%	8.5%	19.2%	6.2%	37.4%	65.9%	85.4%	32.4%	63.9%	.337	.784	119	0.1
2024 non	SD	MLB	44	58(0)	50	2-2	0	41	1.41	5.18	54.1%	8.2%	18.9%	3.7%	36.3%					.300	.573	115	-0.2

2023 Arsenal: FA (88.4), CU (71.9), FC (83.1), SL (69.8), SI (85.6), SW (78), CH (82.6), FS (83), CS (64.5) 　　　　*Comps: Steve Carlton (61), Jerry Koosman (59), Randy Johnson (58)*

Hill has been doing this for so long that his first BP Annual comment was written in Sanskrit (we complained that at 26 he was too *old*). Now 43 years old, he added two more teams and jerseys to his collection in 2023, making it a baker's dozen of clubs that have relied on his rubber arm and lollipop curveball to gobble up outs at the back of a rotation or in relief. With Pittsburgh, he was the definition of average, though he clearly began to run out of steam as the summer rolled on. Nonetheless, San Diego acquired him at the trade deadline to try to staunch some bleeding in the rotation. Hill was spent, completing five innings in just one of five starts before being unceremoniously demoted to the bullpen. His 88-mph fastball fools no one, his curve has lost a lot of its bite, and his late-career cutter got worked like a speed bag; among pitchers with 145 or more innings last year, only Jordan Lyles and Kyle Freeland recorded worse DRA- figures. It'll be something of a shock if Hill finds a team for his age-44 season, but then again, Hill's entire career has been something of a shock.

Jairo Iriarte RHP   Born: 12/15/01   Age: 22   Height: 6'2"   Weight: 160   Origin: IFA, 2018

YEAR	TM	LVL	AGE	G (GS)	IP	W-L	SV	K	WHIP	ERA	CSP	BB%	K%	HR%	GB%	ZSw%	ZCon%	OSw%	OCon%	BABIP	SLGCON	DRA-	WARP
2021	PAD	ROK	19	8(3)	21	0-1	0	25	1.19	4.71		8.2%	29.4%	1.2%	51.9%					.333	.529		
2021	LE	A	19	4(3)	9	0-4	0	9	3.44	27.00		10.0%	15.0%	8.3%	31.0%					.541	1.143	145	-0.2
2022	LE	A	20	21(18)	91¹	4-7	0	109	1.37	5.12		10.3%	26.7%	3.2%	39.2%					.304	.607	96	0.4
2023	FW	A+	21	14(14)	61	3-3	0	77	1.28	3.10		10.8%	29.7%	0.8%	41.2%					.331	.507	78	1.2
2023	SA	AA	21	13(7)	29¹	0-1	0	51	1.30	4.30		13.5%	40.5%	1.6%	45.5%					.358	.545	64	0.6
2024 DC	SD	MLB	22	22(5)	40²	2-3	0	42	1.51	5.61		11.9%	22.7%	4.1%	35.9%					.293	.615	122	-0.2

　　　　Comps: Roman Mendez (64), Luke Jackson (59), Touki Toussaint (55)

Iriarte flashes top-of-the-rotation stuff, keyed by a velocity jump that had him sitting in the mid-to-high 90s and touching 100 with his fastball. He also boasts a pair of plus secondaries in a sweeping slider and a changeup that he executes with good arm action and fade, so you can understand how he ran that ludicrous strikeout rate in Double-A. The problem so far has been the accompanying double-digit walk rate; control has been Iriarte's major weakness as a prospect, tailing him at every stop of the minors. Still, that's to be expected of a young pitcher with an arm like a railgun. Though Iriarte is likely to return to San Antonio to start 2024, there's a good chance he'll reach San Diego by season's end, assuming he masters the strike zone and keep his velo gains. That doesn't always happen, of course, but with the Padres holding open auditions for the back of their rotation they'll have every incentive to give him a try.

Michael King RHP   Born: 05/25/95   Age: 29   Height: 6'3"   Weight: 210   Origin: Round 12, 2016 Draft (#353 overall)

YEAR	TM	LVL	AGE	G (GS)	IP	W-L	SV	K	WHIP	ERA	CSP	BB%	K%	HR%	GB%	ZSw%	ZCon%	OSw%	OCon%	BABIP	SLGCON	DRA-	WARP
2021	NYY	MLB	26	22(6)	63¹	2-4	0	62	1.28	3.55	55.5%	8.7%	22.5%	2.2%	45.4%	68.3%	80.7%	30.4%	65.3%	.291	.478	98	0.7
2022	NYY	MLB	27	34(0)	51	6-3	1	66	1.00	2.29	53.6%	8.0%	33.2%	1.5%	48.7%	62.6%	76.4%	32.3%	46.3%	.281	.457	68	1.3
2023	NYY	MLB	28	49(9)	104²	4-8	6	127	1.15	2.75	46.5%	7.4%	29.5%	2.3%	42.3%	58.7%	85.9%	31.3%	50.8%	.307	.513	83	2.2
2024 DC	SD	MLB	29	23(23)	108²	6-6	0	123	1.20	3.61	49.8%	8.3%	27.0%	3.0%	43.1%					.288	.540	85	1.6

2023 Arsenal: SI (94.2), SW (81.8), FA (94.9), CH (87.3)　　　　*Comps: Adam Warren (55), Alex Colomé (55), Chad Green (55)*

For a few years, King has been an understudy of sorts on the Yankees' pitching staff. Even while mowing down hitters in relief, there was an acknowledgment that he probably still had the arsenal to be an MLB starter, and it was a common sight to see him picking the brains of savants like Gerrit Cole and Corey Kluber. In a perfect world, King would have loved to remain a starter. Fate forced the Yankees' hands when nearly the entire ~~cast~~ rotation went down with various maladies. With so few alternatives, New York conceded that the show must go on, and the understudy got eight starts. He built up stamina, fanned 30 batters across one three-start stretch and used a well-commanded sinker as his primary offering. Now ensconced as a starter in San Diego, we'll see if King's rotation performance with have the staying power of a *The Lion King* or will end up more like the short run of Stephen Sondheim's *Passion*.

★ ★ ★ *2024 Top 101 Prospect* **#46** ★ ★ ★

Dylan Lesko RHP Born: 09/07/03 Age: 20 Height: 6'2" Weight: 195 Origin: Round 1, 2022 Draft (#15 overall)

YEAR	TM	LVL	AGE	G(GS)	IP	W-L	SV	K	WHIP	ERA	CSP	BB%	K%	HR%	GB%	ZSw%	ZCon%	OSw%	OCon%	BABIP	SLGCON	DRA-	WARP
2023	LE	A	19	5(5)	16	0-3	0	23	1.31	4.50		11.8%	33.8%	1.5%	34.3%					.353	.588	86	0.0
2023	FW	A+	19	3(3)	12	1-1	0	20	1.58	4.50		20.8%	37.7%	1.9%	36.4%					.333	.591	103	0.1
2024 non	SD	MLB	20	58(0)	50	2-2	0	54	1.62	6.01		14.6%	23.2%	4.1%	33.0%					.292	.626	128	-0.5

Comps: Luis Patiño (78), Sean Reid-Foley (78), Simeon Woods Richardson (77)

Despite Tommy John surgery wiping out his 2022 and most of '23, Lesko doesn't seem to have missed a beat. His fastball still clocks in with mid-90s velocity; his changeup still disappears under bats; his curveball still spins like a seasoned Washington press flack. The one notable laggard is his command, but that's a tool that graded out above-average pre-Tommy John, and one he should be able to regain over time. Even better, Lesko didn't turn 20 until September; he was blowing away hitters four or five years older than him on average in High-A. It's as good a return as the Padres could have imagined, raising the question of whether that Tommy John surgery came with a free vial of the Super Soldier Serum.

Yuki Matsui LHP Born: 10/30/95 Age: 28 Height: 5'8" Weight: 165 Origin: IFA, 2024

YEAR	TM	LVL	AGE	G(GS)	IP	W-L	SV	K	WHIP	ERA	CSP	BB%	K%	HR%	GB%	ZSw%	ZCon%	OSw%	OCon%	BABIP	SLGCON	DRA-	WARP
2024 DC	SD	MLB	28	57(0)	60	4-5	26	81	1.11	2.98		9.5%	32.9%	3.2%	24.0%					.271	.565	73	1.1

How do the Padres replace Josh Hader? With the Japanese version of Hader. Well, not really. They're both undersized lefty closers with gaudy strikeout rates, minuscule ERAs and more walks allowed than you'd like, but that's where the similarities end. Matsui throws in the low-to-mid 90s with good life on his fastball. His best knockout punch is a splitter, which isn't a pitch most MLB batters are used to seeing from a lefty—especially a 5-foot-8 lefty. Only eight southpaws in MLB threw a splitter in 2023 and 6-foot-4 Chasen Shreve was the only one who utilized the pitch more than 8% of the time. Whether he'll automatically ascend to the closer role in San Diego remains to be seen, but the five-time NPB All-Star should fill some of the high-leverage void left by Hader. As for the other 600 innings that walked away in free agency, there's not much he can do about that.

Adam Mazur RHP Born: 04/20/01 Age: 23 Height: 6'2" Weight: 180 Origin: Round 2, 2022 Draft (#53 overall)

YEAR	TM	LVL	AGE	G(GS)	IP	W-L	SV	K	WHIP	ERA	CSP	BB%	K%	HR%	GB%	ZSw%	ZCon%	OSw%	OCon%	BABIP	SLGCON	DRA-	WARP
2023	FW	A+	22	12(11)	58	4-1	0	47	1.03	2.02		4.3%	20.4%	0.9%	39.3%					.281	.387	86	0.8
2023	SA	AA	22	12(7)	38	2-3	0	43	1.42	4.03		4.3%	26.2%	1.8%	36.8%					.396	.602	95	0.6
2024 non	SD	MLB	23	58(0)	50	2-2	0	37	1.46	5.48		7.2%	16.7%	3.7%	35.5%					.312	.582	121	-0.3

Comps: Jonathan Loáisiga (84), Brant Hurter (82), Tim Sexton (80)

Mazur's rise from "JAG on a Summit League team" to "best pitcher in the Big Ten" to "big-bonus draft pick" to "in the conversation for best Padres pitching prospect" has been wild to watch, and 2023 was yet another progression of the plot. The lanky righty won't blow batters away with his arsenal, but he pounds the strike zone—his walk rate ranked sixth best among all pitchers with 90 or more innings in the minors—with a mid-90s fastball that can touch 99. To that, he adds a hard slider and an improving changeup. The lack of true swing-and-miss stuff keeps him a step behind Dylan Lesko and Jairo Iriarte in San Diego's system, but the floor is rock solid, and as he keeps showing, there still might be more ceiling than expected.

Joe Musgrove RHP Born: 12/04/92 Age: 31 Height: 6'5" Weight: 230 Origin: Round 1, 2011 Draft (#46 overall)

YEAR	TM	LVL	AGE	G(GS)	IP	W-L	SV	K	WHIP	ERA	CSP	BB%	K%	HR%	GB%	ZSw%	ZCon%	OSw%	OCon%	BABIP	SLGCON	DRA-	WARP
2021	SD	MLB	28	32(31)	181¹	11-9	0	203	1.08	3.18	54.9%	7.2%	27.1%	2.9%	44.2%	62.7%	83.9%	34.7%	52.9%	.268	.524	84	3.2
2022	SD	MLB	29	30(30)	181	10-7	0	184	1.08	2.93	54.0%	5.7%	24.9%	3.0%	44.9%	60.6%	85.4%	35.9%	60.6%	.277	.525	81	3.5
2023	SD	MLB	30	17(17)	97¹	10-3	0	97	1.14	3.05	46.1%	5.3%	24.3%	2.5%	45.6%	63.0%	87.6%	40.3%	59.8%	.305	.511	84	2.0
2024 DC	SD	MLB	31	26(26)	147²	9-8	0	141	1.18	3.76	51.6%	6.5%	22.8%	2.9%	44.4%					.287	.519	88	2.2

2023 Arsenal: CU (81.3), FA (93.2), FC (90.2), SW (82.2), CH (87.1), SI (92.8), SL (83.8)   *Comps: Johnny Cueto (78), Marcus Stroman (75), Chris Carpenter (75)*

Musgrove's 2023 was a Three Stooges greatest hits package. He missed the start of the season after dropping a kettlebell on his left big toe, breaking it, landed on his right shoulder during a rehab assignment while fielding a bunt, burned his feet on the super-heated turf of Mexico's Estadio Alfredo by walking on it sans shoes or socks and spent the last two months of the season on the injured list with capsule inflammation in that shoulder. That last one is no laughing matter, and while the righty said after the season that everything feels fine, the Padres have to be a little nervous about his health. In between all those maladies, Musgrove was brilliant; after his Mexico City disaster, he posted a 2.33 ERA over his final 15 starts. His four-seamer and cutter are a dynamic duo, and his curveball drew lots of awkward swings and empty cuts, making up for a slider that went AWOL. So long as the Padres make sure there are no black cats or broken mirrors in Petco Park, he should be good to go as the team's ace in residence. It probably wouldn't hurt to have a priest bless him, too.

★ ★ ★ *2024 Top 101 Prospect* **#55** ★ ★ ★

Robby Snelling   LHP   Born: 12/19/03   Age: 20   Height: 6'3"   Weight: 210   Origin: Round 1, 2022 Draft (#39 overall)

YEAR	TM	LVL	AGE	G (GS)	IP	W-L	SV	K	WHIP	ERA	CSP	BB%	K%	HR%	GB%	ZSw%	ZCon%	OSw%	OCon%	BABIP	SLGCON	DRA-	WARP
2023	LF	A	19	11(11)	51²	5-1	0	59	1.01	1.57		6.5%	29.6%	1.0%	47.2%					.296	.460	73	1.0
2023	FW	A+	19	7(7)	34²	4-2	0	40	1.21	2.34		7.6%	27.8%	0.7%	35.9%					.333	.462	80	0.7
2023	SA	AA	19	4(4)	17¹	2-0	0	19	1.27	1.56		13.7%	26.0%	1.4%	45.5%					.256	.477	91	0.2
2024 non	SD	MLB	20	58(0)	50	2-2	0	43	1.49	5.33		9.9%	19.3%	3.5%	36.3%					.302	.574	117	-0.2

Comps: Julio Teheran (78), Tyler Skaggs (75), Dylan Bundy (70)

So far, there's not much deception or intrigue to Snelling's game. Here's a fastball, anywhere from 93 to 97 mph; here's a curveball, big with lots of spin. Mix and match, rinse and repeat over five innings. That strategy has paid dividends so far, with the lefty climbing three levels in his first pro season and posting the lowest overall ERA of any pitcher in the minors in the process (min. 100 IP). There's still work to be done; a consistent third pitch—Snelling is developing a changeup that's touch-and-go so far—would be a start. But it's hard to argue with the results to date, especially given his youth and relative inexperience as a former two-sport athlete. Even if Snelling slows down, there's enough here to make him a viable back-of-the-rotation possibility, with the chance to be far more.

Robert Suarez   RHP   Born: 03/01/91   Age: 33   Height: 6'2"   Weight: 210   Origin: IFA, 2021

YEAR	TM	LVL	AGE	G (GS)	IP	W-L	SV	K	WHIP	ERA	CSP	BB%	K%	HR%	GB%	ZSw%	ZCon%	OSw%	OCon%	BABIP	SLGCON	DRA-	WARP
2022	SD	MLB	31	45(0)	47²	5-1	1	61	1.05	2.27	52.6%	11.0%	31.9%	2.1%	42.9%	70.5%	78.7%	32.3%	69.1%	.250	.452	78	1.0
2023	SD	MLB	32	26(0)	27²	4-3	0	24	0.90	4.23	51.5%	9.3%	22.2%	3.7%	50.0%	69.8%	78.4%	32.8%	65.9%	.157	.397	91	0.5
2024 DC	SD	MLB	33	57(0)	60	4-3	10	54	1.28	4.12	52.1%	8.8%	21.1%	3.2%	39.0%					.277	.523	94	0.4

2023 Arsenal: FA (97.7), CH (89.8), SI (97.5), SL (87), FC (91.9)   *Comps: Steve Cishek (68), Pedro Strop (68), Ryan Pressly (67)*

It was a good winter and a bad year for Suarez, who turned his out-of-nowhere rookie season into a five-year deal worth $46 million, then missed the first half of 2023 with elbow pain and earned a 10-game sticky-stuff suspension to boot. That ban came in late August, when umpires tossed him from a relief outing against the Marlins after inspecting him for illegal substances on his arm—a charge that Suarez denied, saying that it was simply a regular amount of sunscreen. A Coppertone sponsorship failed to materialize; neither did the version of Suarez who flummoxed hitters in 2022. He lost 10 points of strikeout rate en route to league-average numbers. Oddly, a decision to throw his changeup more didn't result in more whiffs despite that being his best swing-and-miss pitch. Like a lot of the Padres' roster, a hard reset seems in order for a theoretically integral part of San Diego's post-Josh Hader bullpen.

★ ★ ★ *2024 Top 101 Prospect* **#45** ★ ★ ★

Drew Thorpe   RHP   Born: 10/01/00   Age: 23   Height: 6'4"   Weight: 212   Origin: Round 2, 2022 Draft (#61 overall)

YEAR	TM	LVL	AGE	G (GS)	IP	W-L	SV	K	WHIP	ERA	CSP	BB%	K%	HR%	GB%	ZSw%	ZCon%	OSw%	OCon%	BABIP	SLGCON	DRA-	WARP
2023	HV	A+	22	18(18)	109	10-2	0	138	1.07	2.81		7.7%	32.4%	2.3%	48.2%					.303	.536	71	2.8
2023	SOM	AA	22	5(5)	30¹	4-0	0	44	0.66	1.48		4.5%	40.0%	2.7%	53.3%					.211	.500	70	0.9
2024 non	SD	MLB	23	58(0)	50	2-2	0	51	1.33	4.53		8.8%	23.8%	3.7%	39.3%					.295	.585	103	0.2

2023 Arsenal: CH (83.9), FA (92.9), SW (82.3)   *Comps: Parker Dunshee (81), Bailey Ober (81), Erik Johnson (80)*

Thorpe didn't pitch in 2022 after being taken in the second round of that year's draft, as the Yankees elected to have him rest after the Cal Poly season and get ready for fall ball work in their instructional program. Fast-forward to the end of the 2023 campaign, and Thorpe was named Minor League Baseball's Pitching Prospect of the Year. That's a neat trick! Thorpe is up front about the fact that he's not a flamethrower and the secret to his success lies in command; still, his five-pitch mix (especially his changeup) flummoxed the High-A and Double-A competition as he paced the minors with 182 strikeouts. Of course, the biggest vote of confidence he received following the breakout wasn't his MiLB award—it was that he was chosen to be the centerpiece (sorry, Michael King) of the latest Juan Soto blockbuster.

Randy Vásquez   RHP   Born: 11/03/98   Age: 25   Height: 6'0"   Weight: 165   Origin: IFA, 2018

YEAR	TM	LVL	AGE	G (GS)	IP	W-L	SV	K	WHIP	ERA	CSP	BB%	K%	HR%	GB%	ZSw%	ZCon%	OSw%	OCon%	BABIP	SLGCON	DRA-	WARP
2021	TAM	A	22	13(11)	50	3-3	0	58	1.16	2.34		10.8%	27.4%	0.9%	54.7%	68.5%	79.0%	31.6%	50.9%	.262	.433	80	1.1
2021	HV	A+	22	6(6)	36	3-0	0	53	1.14	1.75		5.5%	36.6%	0.0%	65.9%					.393	.512	75	0.8
2021	SOM	AA	22	4(4)	21¹	2-1	0	19	1.41	4.22		7.2%	19.6%	2.1%	52.9%					.309	.500	104	0.1
2022	SOM	AA	23	25(25)	115¹	2-7	0	120	1.27	3.90		8.3%	24.2%	2.2%	47.1%					.304	.508	95	1.8
2023	SWB	AAA	24	17(17)	80¹	3-8	0	96	1.47	4.59		11.2%	26.9%	2.8%	45.5%	63.7%	83.9%	30.9%	61.4%	.340	.614	83	1.9
2023	NYY	MLB	24	11(5)	37²	2-2	0	33	1.27	2.87	46.0%	10.8%	19.9%	3.0%	37.3%	66.0%	89.0%	32.9%	73.1%	.238	.477	121	0.0
2024 DC	SD	MLB	25	16(16)	74¹	3-6	0	62	1.42	5.02	46.0%	10.0%	18.9%	3.3%	39.8%					.287	.544	111	0.1

2023 Arsenal: FA (94.6), SW (80.6), SI (94.4), FC (87.6), CH (88.1)   *Comps: John Gant (81), Alex Colomé (73), Brandon Cumpton (71)*

Much like Jhony Brito, the average Yankees fan grew more familiar with Vásquez than they ever could have dreamed at the start of spring training 2023. He acquitted himself nicely in three spot starts before taking on more of an adequate swingman role in mid-August and beyond. Although the six-pitch mix gives Vásquez a number of options and he gets his share of strikeouts, he'll need more than just a nice breaking ball to carve out a long-term role. On the bright side, he's the first Randy V. in the majors since Randy Velarde, so maybe Action Bronson will keep "the young Randy Vásquez" in mind for his next random baseball namedrop. Also, much like Jhony Brito, he filled out the Juan Soto trade, and will now vie for a spot in San Diego's re-tooled pitching staff. (Maybe he's more likely to show up in Rob $tone's bars than Action Bronson's?)

Matt Waldron RHP Born: 09/26/96 Age: 27 Height: 6'2" Weight: 185 Origin: Round 18, 2019 Draft (#550 overall)

YEAR	TM	LVL	AGE	G (GS)	IP	W-L	SV	K	WHIP	ERA	CSP	BB%	K%	HR%	GB%	ZSw%	ZCon%	OSw%	OCon%	BABIP	SLGCON	DRA-	WARP
2021	FW	A+	24	13(13)	72¹	3-4	0	72	1.22	3.24		6.3%	23.9%	2.0%	45.5%					.318	.515	102	0.7
2021	SA	AA	24	7(7)	31¹	0-4	0	31	1.63	6.61		11.1%	21.5%	1.4%	40.4%					.359	.495	132	-0.4
2022	SA	AA	25	9(9)	44¹	2-1	0	38	1.17	2.84		5.6%	21.5%	1.1%	47.2%					.320	.416	93	0.4
2022	ELP	AAA	25	16(16)	69¹	3-9	0	58	1.75	8.44		8.7%	17.3%	3.6%	37.2%	67.4%	82.2%	29.6%	73.0%	.354	.668	125	-0.6
2023	ELP	AAA	26	20(18)	92¹	2-10	0	99	1.60	7.31		7.2%	23.8%	4.3%	37.1%	62.4%	82.6%	32.4%	57.6%	.379	.770	97	0.9
2023	SD	MLB	26	8(6)	41¹	1-3	0	31	1.23	4.35	51.3%	6.9%	17.9%	5.2%	40.0%	67.9%	85.0%	30.2%	73.1%	.248	.597	107	0.3
2024 DC	SD	MLB	27	27(16)	78	3-6	0	54	1.42	5.20	51.3%	7.7%	15.7%	3.6%	39.2%					.295	.550	116	0.0

2023 Arsenal: KN (76.6), SI (91.5), FA (91.6), SW (80.2), FC (86.8) *Comps: Greg Reynolds (76), Adam Plutko (74), Chase De Jong (71)*

Every now and again, as if to underscore how huge and remote parts of this world can be, scientists will "rediscover" species previously thought lost to time. From the coelacanth (a prehistoric fish believed to have disappeared with the dinosaurs but that was found off the coast of South Africa in 1938) to Wallace's Giant Bee (a, uh, giant bee last seen in the late 1970s before turning up in Indonesia in 2019), there are plenty of creatures who didn't vanish so much as go into the hiding. So it was for the knuckleball, which, on June 24, 2023, returned to the majors after a two-year absence out of the right hand of Waldron, who in his first MLB start tossed 13 of them against the Nationals. The results were nothing special, which is also true of Waldron's season as a whole, but regardless, he is now keeper of the knuckleball flame, the torch passed to him for as long as he can keep it burning. Given his otherwise pedestrian arsenal (a 91-mph fastball and some dubious breakers), that may not be for long.

Steven Wilson RHP Born: 08/24/94 Age: 29 Height: 6'3" Weight: 221 Origin: Round 8, 2018 Draft (#231 overall)

YEAR	TM	LVL	AGE	G (GS)	IP	W-L	SV	K	WHIP	ERA	CSP	BB%	K%	HR%	GB%	ZSw%	ZCon%	OSw%	OCon%	BABIP	SLGCON	DRA-	WARP
2021	ELP	AAA	26	28(0)	39¹	4-0	0	63	0.92	3.43		8.9%	40.1%	4.5%	26.9%					.211	.610	72	0.8
2022	SD	MLB	27	50(1)	53	4-2	1	53	1.06	3.06	53.6%	9.3%	24.8%	3.3%	22.5%	70.2%	81.6%	31.4%	56.4%	.223	.481	115	0.1
2023	SD	MLB	28	52(0)	53	1-2	0	57	1.17	3.91	48.8%	12.3%	26.0%	3.2%	25.8%	67.0%	80.5%	27.4%	60.1%	.224	.508	104	0.5
2024 DC	SD	MLB	29	50(0)	53¹	4-2	0	57	1.28	4.28	50.8%	10.2%	25.1%	3.8%	26.8%					.271	.576	98	0.3

2023 Arsenal: SW (81.1), FA (94.7), CH (84.8), FC (89.7) *Comps: Brad Brach (79), Tanner Rainey (77), Ryne Stanek (77)*

As far as names go, "Steven Wilson" isn't the most common in existence, but neither is it particularly distinctive. Get on an airport public address system and send out a page for Steven Wilson, and within minutes you'll have a dozen men standing around, confused and probably chatting with each other about tax law or the Battle of the Bulge. And who knows, maybe one of them will be America's most famous Steven Wilson, the one who's done yeoman's work out of San Diego's bullpen for the last two seasons. Both years are near-carbon copies of each other, save for a spike in walks in 2023, that fit firmly in the category of "anonymous yet useful middle relief." Appropriately, Wilson's arsenal is as standard as his name: a fastball thrown at 94 mph at the top of the zone and a sweeper that's now his primary pitch, one that ran a good strikeout rate and is a nightmare for right-handers. None of this will make Wilson a household name, but it will keep him employed in the Padres' bullpen as a valuable late-innings piece.

LINEOUTS

Hitters

HITTER	POS	TM	LVL	AGE	PA	R	HR	RBI	SB	AVG/OBP/SLG	BABIP	SLGCON	BB%	K%	ZSw%	ZCon%	OSw%	OCon%	LA	90th EV	DRC+	BRR	DRP	WARP
Matthew Batten	IF	ELP	AAA	28	413	71	12	50	27	.235/.341/.399	.291	.555	13.3%	24.0%	53.1%	90.1%	28.2%	63.0%			93	4.3	0.7	1.3
	IF	SD	MLB	28	139	19	2	11	2	.258/.355/.358	.330	.478	12.2%	21.6%	48.7%	81.2%	34.3%	65.8%	13.3	100.1	82	0.1	-0.1	0.1
Ben Gamel	LF	ELP	AAA	31	82	14	5	13	2	.314/.402/.600	.340	.778	13.4%	19.5%	65.5%	93.1%	27.3%	66.7%			111	-0.4	-0.3	0.3
	LF	DUR	AAA	31	250	37	8	31	4	.276/.402/.463	.343	.644	16.8%	22.8%	62.6%	83.0%	23.9%	54.0%			107	0.2	0.9	1.1
	LF	SD	MLB	31	15	2	0	2	0	.200/.200/.267	.231	.308	0.0%	13.3%	84.6%	81.8%	21.7%	80.0%	0.2	102.5	102	0.0	0.0	0.0
Bryce Johnson	CF	SAC	AAA	27	298	48	8	29	18	.280/.373/.455	.358	.626	11.4%	23.5%	62.0%	88.3%	26.2%	55.3%			93	1.3	-2.1	0.7
	CF	SF	MLB	27	48	7	1	3	3	.163/.229/.256	.214	.393	8.3%	31.3%	59.5%	84.1%	32.4%	48.5%	5.9	101.3	83	0.1	-0.5	0.0
Tucupita Marcano	SS	IND	AAA	23	48	8	1	10	3	.422/.458/.689	.500	.838	6.3%	16.7%	61.6%	91.1%	25.0%	45.5%			112	-0.6	-0.1	0.1
	SS	PIT	MLB	23	220	16	3	18	5	.233/.276/.356	.265	.431	4.5%	15.9%	73.5%	91.8%	31.4%	70.6%	12.1	101.7	90	0.0	-3.9	0.1
Jakob Marsee	CF	PEJ	WIN	22	104	22	4	17	14	.378/.490/.671	.482	.948	17.3%	23.1%	65.6%	81.0%	24.6%	46.7%						
	CF	FW	A+	22	499	91	13	41	41	.273/.413/.425	.313	.535	17.4%	16.4%							135	5.4	5.6	4.4
	CF	SA	AA	22	69	12	3	5	5	.286/.412/.446	.342	.610	15.9%	21.7%							110	-0.6	-1.7	0.1
Cal Mitchell	OF	IND	AAA	24	316	46	9	55	6	.261/.333/.414	.354	.620	9.2%	29.4%	64.1%	82.3%	29.9%	52.4%			89	1.6	-2.1	0.5
	OF	PIT	MLB	24	5	0	0	0	0	.200/.200/.000		.000	20.0%	20.0%	80.0%	100.0%	37.5%	33.3%	3.6	103.3	94		0.0	0.0
Tirso Ornelas	OF	NAV	WIN	23	83	8	1	9	1	.284/.349/.378	.345	.483	4.8%	19.3%										
	OF	SA	AA	23	312	38	11	51	4	.284/.381/.473	.323	.610	14.1%	18.9%							128	0.5	-3.7	1.9
	OF	ELP	AAA	23	240	34	4	24	4	.285/.358/.425	.348	.545	9.6%	19.6%	66.9%	86.4%	33.6%	65.6%			90	2.0	-1.4	0.4
Graham Pauley	3B	PEJ	WIN	22	81	13	4	17	4	.253/.284/.467	.268	.603	4.9%	21.0%										
	3B	LE	A	22	276	50	4	36	12	.309/.422/.465	.360	.563	14.5%	14.5%							130	2.0	2.6	2.2
	3B	FW	A+	22	187	33	16	46	8	.300/.358/.629	.307	.829	7.0%	21.9%							142	0.1	0.9	1.7
	3B	SA	AA	22	88	15	3	12	2	.321/.375/.556	.348	.652	8.0%	13.6%							120	0.1	1.4	0.4
Eguy Rosario	3B/2B	ELP	AAA	23	187	24	5	28	4	.265/.348/.422	.320	.551	10.7%	20.9%	72.5%	80.8%	39.6%	63.0%			88	-0.4	0.5	0.2
	3B/2B	SD	MLB	23	37	6	2	6	0	.250/.270/.500	.318	.750	2.7%	32.4%	64.7%	75.0%	34.8%	61.3%	15.2	102.3	81	0.0	-0.1	0.0
Brett Sullivan	C	ELP	AAA	29	279	45	7	41	9	.328/.401/.517	.336	.583	11.5%	9.7%	71.9%	94.6%	30.0%	75.1%			111	-0.2	1.1	1.4
	C	SD	MLB	29	86	7	1	6	0	.210/.244/.284	.258	.371	4.7%	22.1%	67.2%	89.3%	33.1%	69.0%	15.3	99.7	75	0.0	-5.0	-0.4
Preston Tucker	LF/DH	ELP	AAA	32	240	47	11	40	1	.293/.433/.565	.326	.730	17.9%	17.9%	68.3%	85.3%	20.1%	54.5%			125	-1.8	-1.0	1.2

Good plate discipline will only get you so far if you hit with less power than a blindfolded boxer; of **Matthew Batten's** 91 batted balls last year, just one qualified as a barrel. He whiffed on one of every four fastballs, and got the bat knocked out of his hands by two of the other three. ⓧ **Ben Gamel** is baseball's equivalent of filling up a bunch of old two-liter bottles with water, throwing them in the garage and calling it an emergency kit. Which sounds like a knock, and maybe is, but remember: There's also a baseball equivalent of having to drink your own urine. ⓧ **J.D. Gonzalez** is the Padres' latest high-ceiling catcher, added to the system as an underslot third-round pick last summer. Blessed with big bat speed but raw just about everywhere else, he'll need time to grow into his gear. ⓧ Last year's *Annual* noted that "If **Bryce Johnson** can hit even a little bit, there's a spot for him in San Francisco's slow-footed outfield." It turns out, by the end of his brief tenure with the big-league club, that spot was as a designated bunter; he was outrighted in September and elected free agency a month later. ⓧ **Tucupita Marcano** filled in for Oneil Cruz at shortstop during his extended convalescence, and his offensive performance earned him the rating of true utility man. He can get the ball off the ground well, but he needs more power to utilize that skill effectively from the left side of the plate. His defensive performance at shortstop could have inspired more confidence, but he can play all over the infield and outfield at a major-league level, particularly in left. Here's a random fun fact: he was born in Tucupita, Venezuela. That might be the most remarkable thing about him. ⓧ **Jakob Marsee** should trade in the K in his name for a BB after drawing more walks on the year than all but 10 hitters in the entirety of the minors. An average athlete with average power, he'll need to continue to operate as Jabbob to stay memorable. ⓧ Once a Top 101 prospect, **Cal Mitchell** just hasn't hit enough in the majors—and hasn't always done so in the upper-minors either. Outrighted by the Pirates in September, he signed an early minor-league deal in San Diego, where A.J. Preller has never met a former blue chip with a great-looking swing he didn't take a crack at resurrecting. ⓧ **Tirso Ornelas** has twice been exposed to the Rule 5 draft, and twice been passed over. But his stock is up, making him a name to watch for 2024, or at least a name to potentially recognize in December if you're a Rule 5 sicko. ⓧ **Graham Pauley** is a bat-first utilityman who can capably handle plenty of spots around the diamond. Call him Victorinox, because he profiles as a first-rate Swiss Army knife. ⓧ A broken ankle suffered in winter ball scrambled **Eguy Rosario's** season; he only made it to the majors in September. Once there, he hit for some power, but never walked and struck out too much. Given his past results, it's probably best to give him a mulligan. ⓧ **Brett Sullivan's** bat appears to be made of balsa wood, marrying a plus hit tool with some of the weakest exit velocities in the majors. Approaching 30 and offering little defensively, he seems destined to remain a depth piece long-term. ⓧ Brought stateside by the Braves from Korea after mashing KBO pitching but never getting out of Triple-A in 2022, **Preston Tucker** took it up a notch and nuked PCL hurlers last year, only for the Padres to release him in August when his plantar fasciitis wouldn't heal.

Pitchers

PITCHER	TM	LVL	AGE	G (GS)	IP	W-L	SV	K	WHIP	ERA	CSP	BB%	K%	HR%	GB%	ZSw%	ZCon%	OSw%	OCon%	BABIP	SLGCON	DRA-	WARP
Ryan Bergert	FW	A+	23	14 (12)	61²	5-2	0	75	1.18	2.63		11.0%	29.5%	1.2%	36.2%					.288	.473	82	1.2
	SA	AA	23	9 (8)	44	1-2	0	51	1.14	2.86		10.2%	28.8%	0.6%	48.1%					.298	.413	81	0.9
Drew Carlton	ELP	AAA	27	15 (0)	18	2-1	0	21	1.11	3.00		6.9%	29.2%	1.4%	51.1%	68.9%	76.5%	32.1%	70.0%	.318	.523	79	0.3
	SD	MLB	27	11 (0)	20²	2-1	0	18	1.16	4.35	51.7%	7.1%	21.2%	2.4%	42.4%	66.0%	77.2%	36.2%	78.1%	.291	.500	96	0.3
Jeremiah Estrada	IOW	AAA	24	26 (0)	28²	1-1	1	43	1.74	5.97		18.8%	31.2%	5.8%	28.4%	73.4%	75.2%	31.5%	43.8%	.271	.818	93	0.3
	CHC	MLB	24	12 (0)	10²	0-0	0	13	2.25	6.75	49.2%	21.4%	23.2%	7.1%	22.6%	75.2%	81.0%	26.5%	62.9%	.296	.867	116	0.0
Jay Groome	ELP	AAA	24	30 (30)	134²	4-10	0	137	2.10	8.55		16.7%	20.5%	3.7%	39.2%	65.8%	83.4%	28.4%	65.7%	.374	.703	133	-0.9
Jagger Haynes	LE	A	20	11 (11)	25¹	0-3	0	29	1.34	3.91		11.0%	26.6%	1.8%	41.8%					.317	.431	90	0.3
Nick Hernandez	SA	AA	28	24 (0)	28¹	3-1	6	43	1.06	3.18		7.0%	37.7%	0.9%	39.7%					.344	.435	68	0.8
	ELP	AAA	28	23 (0)	32²	2-0	1	39	1.19	4.41		9.5%	28.5%	2.2%	25.3%	64.6%	75.6%	41.7%	53.0%	.291	.568	77	0.4
	SD	MLB	28	2 (0)	3	0-0	0	5	2.33	12.00	42.8%	22.2%	27.8%	5.6%	42.9%	79.3%	82.6%	30.8%	62.5%	.333	.857	103	0.0
Alek Jacob	SA	AA	25	18 (0)	27¹	1-0	5	32	0.99	1.32		7.3%	29.4%	0.9%	56.7%					.273	.388	84	0.6
	SD	MLB	25	3 (0)	3	0-0	0	5	0.33	0.00	41.3%	10.0%	50.0%	0.0%	75.0%	52.9%	66.7%	50.0%	60.0%	.000	.000	89	0.1
Reiss Knehr	ELP	AAA	26	18 (1)	36²	4-1	0	41	1.17	3.93		7.3%	27.3%	3.3%	42.3%	65.7%	85.9%	32.5%	57.6%	.293	.567	79	0.8
	SD	MLB	26	4 (1)	5²	0-1	0	4	2.65	15.88	48.2%	15.6%	12.5%	9.4%	26.1%	68.8%	93.9%	24.0%	66.7%	.350	1.000	125	0.0
Victor Lizarraga	FW	A+	19	21 (21)	94²	4-7	0	78	1.26	4.09		8.4%	19.2%	1.2%	44.6%					.289	.436	97	0.9
Adrian Morejon	ELP	AAA	24	19 (2)	23²	2-1	0	26	1.73	6.08		10.6%	23.0%	2.7%	37.0%	68.4%	87.3%	30.0%	49.4%	.371	.562	86	0.1
	SD	MLB	24	8 (1)	9	0-0	0	8	2.11	7.00	49.6%	11.4%	18.2%	2.3%	41.9%	68.1%	91.8%	22.5%	60.0%	.448	.700	98	0.1
Glenn Otto	RR	AAA	27	10 (6)	29¹	1-1	0	39	1.06	3.38		10.8%	32.5%	3.3%	28.8%	63.0%	78.4%	31.0%	50.0%	.230	.508	74	0.4
	TEX	MLB	27	6 (0)	10²	0-0	0	11	1.88	10.12	41.8%	11.8%	21.6%	11.8%	44.1%	75.0%	80.4%	36.3%	51.1%	.286	.941	95	0.2
Luis Patiño	DUR	AAA	23	27 (6)	45¹	3-4	0	38	1.72	6.75		13.4%	17.5%	4.6%	41.5%	73.3%	82.6%	32.5%	62.2%	.285	.650	123	0.1
	CLT	AAA	23	5 (5)	14¹	0-1	0	12	1.67	5.65		20.3%	18.8%	4.7%	30.8%	65.4%	83.0%	27.7%	69.6%	.222	.632	102	0.2
	CHW	MLB	23	7 (1)	17²	0-1	0	13	1.58	3.57	46.4%	15.0%	16.3%	1.3%	43.6%	70.6%	80.9%	22.8%	68.3%	.278	.382	113	0.1
	TB	MLB	23	2 (0)	4	0-0	0	5	1.75	9.00	44.2%	10.5%	26.3%	10.5%	25.0%	64.0%	100.0%	30.8%	68.8%	.300	.917	107	0.0
Sean Reynolds	PNS	AA	25	24 (0)	30²	1-1	9	37	1.21	2.35		12.3%	28.5%	0.8%	36.0%					.274	.438	96	0.5
	ELP	AAA	25	17 (0)	16	0-1	0	19	3.31	13.50		26.7%	18.8%	3.0%	50.0%	68.0%	91.2%	27.3%	54.8%	.451	.870	138	0.0
	JAX	AAA	25	14 (0)	18	2-0	3	17	1.17	3.50		9.3%	22.7%	1.3%	38.0%	70.1%	70.8%	27.4%	66.7%	.265	.99	133	0.3

The further **Ryan Bergert** gets from his 2021 Tommy John surgery, the better he looks. A strong Double-A debut gives him a boost in his quest to remain a starter, but even if that dream doesn't come to be, a regular relief role seems likely.   Ⓣ   Elbow inflammation cut **Drew Carlton's** 2023 short. A replacement-level reliever—if healthy—he'll keep trying to make his way / make his way through the crowd in San Diego's bullpen.   Ⓣ   Handed a big bonus out of a Virginia high school, **Blake Dickerson** offers lots to dream on as a tall lefty with an above-average fastball and slider, sound mechanics and a lanky frame tailor-made for Padres pinstripes.   Ⓣ   The Cubs hoped **Jeremiah Estrada** might be the answer to their biggest question—who takes the ball in the ninth inning—but instead answered a different one: What's the baseball equivalent of an seven-year-old playing Stratego against an adult?   Ⓣ   **Jay Groome's** collapse continued apace in 2023; his Triple-A walk rate was the worst of any pitcher with 100 or more innings. To take a line from a book about a descent into hell: Let us not speak of him, but look and pass on.   Ⓣ   Tommy John surgery and rehab kept 2020 draft pick **Jagger Haynes** off the mound until last season, but the lefty looked good in limited time, throwing 93–96 mph with his fastball and racking up whiffs. High-A, Jagger, is just a shot away.   Ⓣ   An eighth-round draft pick in 2016, 28-year-old rookie **Nick Hernandez** threw his slider nearly 75% of the time in his brief major-league stay in September—a sensible strategy, given that his fastball putters in at 90 mph.   Ⓣ   **Alek Jacob** has two first names and one bum elbow that impeded the sidearmer's quest to become this generation's Brad Ziegler, or at least a lesser Craig Breslow. If healthy, he's a good bet to contribute useful relief innings in 2024.   Ⓣ   Tabbed for a spot start in June, reliever **Reiss Knehr** was hammered for five runs in two innings, hurt his elbow, and ended up needing Tommy John surgery. Outrighted in November, he's Reiss Fahr from a major-league roster spot.   Ⓣ   San Diego has aggressively pushed young **Victor Lizarraga**, and he's responded by throwing tons of strikes wherever he goes, making him the first teenage boy in history who isn't obsessed with balls.   Ⓣ   Elbow and knee problems were **Adrian Morejon's** undoing in 2023, and he was battered while rehabbing in Triple-A at season's end. "I'm not a bust!" he continues to insist as he slowly shrinks and transforms into Adrian Lessjon.   Ⓣ   Claimed off waivers from the Rangers in September, **Glenn Otto** walked over a third of the batters he faced in his short time with Triple-A El Paso, which is like starting a job interview by spilling coffee all over the hiring manager.   Ⓣ   **Luis Patiño** is now in the long, dark post-prospect hype phase of the soul. He's spent the last two years shuffling through pitch mixes and shapes like a teenager in a slasher flick fumbling through a set of keys, as his own mortality comes bearing down on him.   Ⓣ   The final season of **Drew Pomeranz's** four-year, $34 million deal with San Diego was spent mostly on the injured list, as his balky elbow continued to trouble him. He hasn't set foot on a major-league mound since August 2021 and may not again.   Ⓣ   A converted infielder, **Sean Reynolds** now throws 97 off the mound with a good slider to boot, going from a guy who couldn't stop whiffing to one who, if everything breaks right, could soon be racking them up in middle relief.

SAN FRANCISCO GIANTS

SAN FRANCISCO GIANTS PROSPECTUS
2023 W-L: 79-83, 4TH IN NL WEST

Essay by Jon Hegglund

Player comments by Alexandra Whitley and BP staff

For better or worse, the Giants are the major-league organization most spiritually and geographically proximate to the tech milieu of Silicon Valley. When Farhan Zaidi was hired as president of baseball operations in 2018, it was an alignment of the Valley's self-justifying narratives of bleeding-edge innovation with a refreshed Giants organization that would leave behind its previous, old-school regime. (On looks alone, former GM Brian Sabean and manager Bruce Bochy could very well be cast as high-level Teamster operators in a *Hoffa* remake). The Giants shed the anachronistic, if thrice successful, methods of the elder statesmen and supplanted them with Data Guys who brought their Harvard MBAs to the land of full-stack developers and tricked-out Teslas.

One of the most ubiquitous Valley buzzwords of this late-teens cultural moment was "disruption." Uber would disrupt the taxicab industry. Theranos would disrupt health care. Cryptocurrency would disrupt the fiat currency system. If you didn't delve too deeply into who was behind this disruption, who was being disrupted, why disruption was necessary and whether or not disruption could lead to stable, sustainable enterprises—well, then, it all sounded pretty cool.

Much of the shine has worn off of the idea of disruption. Despite the best efforts of Mark Zuckerberg, Sam Altman and a host of other white dudes clad in T-shirts, sneakers and dead eyes, most of us are not yet using AI to trade cryptocurrency in the metaverse. At their best, disruptors have simply immiserated people like taxi drivers and renters while scooping up short-term profit. At their worst, yesterday's disruptors, like Elizabeth Holmes and Sam Bankman-Fried, are today's convicts. Disruption and innovation, writes Ed Zitron of the Silicon Valley context, "may seem synonymous, but they're fundamentally different. One refers to actual technological advancement, whereas the other refers to the appearance of innovation, whether it exists or doesn't."

Offering a slicker update of the Moneyball philosophy that he studied in Oakland under Billy Beane, and then in its wealthier 2.0 version in Los Angeles with Andrew Friedman, Zaidi rode the wave of the disruption zeitgeist to the peninsular side of the Bay. After a few years of grace while the franchise built its farm system and began to cycle out its

Pythag	.470	20th	DER	.687	26th
RS/G	4.16	24th	DRC+	92	27th
RA/G	4.44	15th	DRA-	91	4th
dWin%	.504	18th	FIP	3.92	4th
Payroll	$188M	10th	B-Age	28.9	12th
M$/MW	$5.5M	21st	P-Age	30.5	26th

- Opened 2000
- Open air
- Natural surface
- Fence profile: 8' to 25'

Park Factors

Runs	Runs/RH	Runs/LH	HR/RH	HR/LH
100	100	99	92	82

Top Hitter WARP	2.9 Wilmer Flores
Top Pitcher WARP	5.5 Logan Webb
2023 Top Prospect	Marco Luciano

Payroll History (in millions)

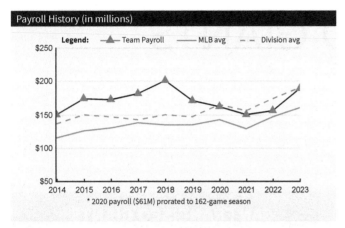

Legend: ▲ Team Payroll ── MLB avg – – Division avg

* 2020 payroll ($61M) prorated to 162-game season

Future Commitments (in millions)

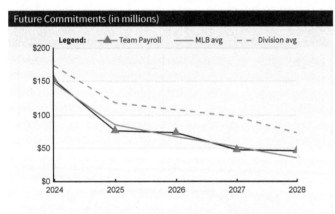

Legend: ▲ Team Payroll ── MLB avg – – Division avg

Farm System Ranking

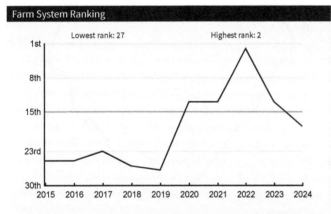

Lowest rank: 27   Highest rank: 2

Personnel

President of Baseball Operations
Farhan Zaidi

General Manager
Pete Putila

Vice President & Assistant General Manager
Jeremy Shelley

Vice President of Baseball Resources & Development
Yeshayah Goldfarb

Vice President, Baseball Analytics
Paul Bien

Manager
Bob Melvin

veterans, the fruits of disruption seemed to sprout. In 2021, the Giants platooned, mixed, matched, optimized and veteran scrapheaped their way to a 107-win season as improbable as it was intoxicating. By the end of the 2023 season, however, Zaidi's micromanaging of the margins had soured into something that looked less like disruption than dysfunction.

When manager Gabe Kapler, the chiseled facade of the Giants' corporate edifice, was dismissed with only three games left in the season, it was clear that the bubble had burst, or at least deflated to an alarming degree. There had been rumblings of a disinterested clubhouse and a dissatisfied ownership group. But to dismiss the most public-facing member of the organization in September—a walking algorithm of Zaidi's strategic imperatives—read as a scapegoating pure and simple, a toss of the square-jawed manager under an electric Muni bus. Moreover, only weeks before the firing, club chairman Greg Johnson had promised that both Zaidi and Kapler would return in 2024. Even as Kapler took the fall, Zaidi apparently convinced Johnson to give him one more bite at the sourdough loaf, as the embattled POBO agreed to a three-year extension in October.

Did Zaidi and company move too fast and break a team? It's easy to be in autopsy mode when the 2023 season ended on such a downer: a patched-together roster, an indifferent clubhouse, a dismissed manager. How did the Giants get from the *anni mirabili* era of 2010-14, to the improbable ride of 2021, to the bummed-out, exhausted vibes of 2023? And where does it go from here?

⚾   ⚾   ⚾

PECOTA gives us an alternate timeline for the last three years. The Giants' projected win totals from 2021-23 come in at steadily improving intervals of three: 75, 78 and 81. Absent any other context, you'd think of a team slowly and methodically scaling the upside of a rebuild. If we wipe 2021 from our minds and hard drives, then, does the narrative look any different? Yes and no. In retrospect, 2021 may have just been a blind alley of history, a *trompe-l'œil* open door that was just a painting on a brick wall. Somehow, the Giants still spent most of 2023 trying to find a key.

To be fair to Zaidi and the Giants brass, after a disappointing 81-81 follow-up to the magic of 2021, they recognized the Buster Posey-sized hole in the team's lineup and personality. After the future Hall-of-Famer retired at the end of 2021, the team was bereft of anything resembling a franchise-anchoring superstar. Logan Webb, with his boyish, Jesse-Plemonsesque face and ace-level consistency, is the de facto centerpiece of the club but, if we're being honest, is not someone that fires the imagination outside of the Northern California media market.

With the need for a towering figure that could carry both marketing campaigns and lineups, they assembled an appropriately gargantuan offer for Aaron Judge in the 2022 offseason. For the time it took Jon Heyman to send, and then retract, his infamous "Arson Judge" tweet, it appeared the slugger from Linden, California might be coming back to his home region. Then, after Judge re-upped with the Yankees, the next-best free-agent superstar option, Carlos Correa, appeared to be headed to the Bay. But upon seeing Correa's dodgy medicals, the Giants backed out of the 13-year deal with the alarmed haste of a nauseous diner excusing themselves from the table after gorging on some questionable shellfish.

The Giants swung hard for two of the biggest free agents on the market, but in the end they were just loud outs. Like a desperate spouse shopping as the stores close on Christmas Eve, Zaidi rushed to backfill the team's lineup with two injury-discounted corner outfielders in Michael Conforto and Mitch Haniger. In the least surprising turn of events ever, Haniger subsequently spent 107 games on the IL, while Conforto was uneven in his first full year back from shoulder surgery. The stopgaps that so recently seemed like brilliant opportunism suddenly just felt like stopgaps.

In the absence of a star or two, the 2023 Giants felt optimized for mediocrity, the output of an algorithm perfectly constructed to get a team as close to .500 as possible without going over. This grimly engineered efficiency, combined with the lack of highlight-reel talent, made for baseball that was competent but often excruciating to watch. While "disruption" sounds edgy and exciting—and in 2021 it was—the 2023, late-stage iteration of the Giants was little more than an ersatz version of the Rays, a team painstakingly designed to win precisely 78 games. Mission accomplished.

Much of the ennui induced by Giants baseball in 2023 came from a roster that felt like a hastily assembled crew of gig workers rather than a team with an identity and a core. Position players were fungible, with a compulsive platooning, pinch-hitting and part-timing that yielded few of what anyone would call "everyday players." Quick—who led the Giants in plate appearances in 2023? While you're furrowing your brow and scratching your head, I'll reveal the utterly underwhelming answer: J.D. Davis, with 546 (and only two other players, Thairo Estrada and Lamonte Wade, topped 500). What began as careful skill maximization and load management plunged into mere juggling. Injuries and lineup machinations gave far too much time to players who may as well have been AI-generated: Bryce Johnson. Wade Meckler. Blake Sabol. For God's sake, *Brett Wisely*.

If the offense felt like output from a ChatGPT query—minimally competent but utterly devoid of personality—there was hope that the pitching would hang together with the addition of Sean Manaea and Ross Stripling, along with the return of Alexes Cobb and Wood, as well as Anthony DeSclafani. Unfortunately, the "get seven starters to have five" strategy yielded precisely two rotation fixtures in Webb and Cobb. After a luckless April, Manaea was repurposed for spot starts and bulk relief, while Stripling, Wood and DeSclafani were by turns injured and ineffective.

Zaidi and Kapler countered with a tactic that would have seemed innovative five years ago but in 2023 simply read as desperate: rather than one bullpen game per week, how about three? Forget about "Spahn, Sain and pray for rain," the Giants updated the old saying with "Webb, Cobb and RyanWalkerJakeJunisSeanManaeaSeanHjelleTristanBeck and probably some guy named Bob." The staff was dominated by piece work, with a group that was more Fiverr than starting five. Forget about the jock tax; hopefully these players managed to file their 1099-MISC forms.

⚾   ⚾   ⚾

The most interesting, if not always successful, element of the 2023 Giants was the major-league promotion of several prospects. The combined 883 plate appearances given to Patrick Bailey, Luis Matos and Casey Schmitt should have been the culmination of some grand plan, but instead it was largely just another round of slapped-together bug fixes. Out of this mish-mash of underripe prospects, the one who will stick was the precociously well-rounded catcher Bailey, who quickly had Giants fans thinking the bridesmaid of the organization's catching prospects should have been the one at the altar all along.

The two prized prospects of the organization, lefty pitcher Kyle Harrison and shortstop Marco Luciano, dipped their toes in the major-league pond and demonstrated both franchise-anchoring potential and the considerable distance to be covered to meet this promise. If these two are to be a bridge to the future, they'll need support more substantial than the floating pontoons of Mitch Haniger and Mike Yastrzemski to reach the other side.

Don't get me wrong—it's nice to see a cohort of prospects graduate together, even if some might be headed back for a few remedial credits. The problem is that behind Luciano, Matos, Harrison and Bailey, the water pressure in the minor-league pipeline is disappointingly weak. The prospects that were supposed to be the mainstays of a new Giants era are arriving, more or less on schedule, but onto a major-league squad that is bereft of a strong, coherent core.

Even if it wasn't exciting baseball—what with the regular parade of bulk relievers and the lineup cards filled out with dim stars no brighter than Wilmer Flores or Joc Pederson—the flurry of platoons and fresh-faced callups and bullpen games was good enough to keep them churning above .500 until the middle of July. On July 18, after an 11-10 victory at Great American Ballpark, they sat at 54-41, with a roughly 60% chance of landing a Wild Card spot. If you squinted just right, you could see an even scrappier, greener, more jerry-rigged version of the 2021 squad. But even then something seemed faintly off, and regression hung in the air like the fog. Even post-2021 Bitcoin had its minor rallies, too.

After the All-Star break, the Giants collapsed in two ways: gradually, and then suddenly. From July 19th until the end of August, they went 16-23 but still retained the inside track for a Wild Card spot, thanks to the expanded playoff format.

From the beginning of September, they went 9-19, essentially falling out of contention before the season's final homestand, a funereal 2-4 slog against the Padres (who ended up nipping them at the wire for third place in the West) and Dodgers. Suddenly forced to try to stop the bleeding, Kapler's crew discovered that they'd forgotten to reinvent bandages.

In the wake of Kapler's dismissal, the Giants pivoted from his techbro influencer energy to the best available substitute for Bruce Bochy in former A's and Padres manager Bob Melvin—and indeed if Boch hadn't been busy leading the Rangers to a world championship it's possible that Zaidi would have sent him a "miss u, wyd rn" text or two. Whether the move to Melvin was Zaidi's or ownership's idea, it's difficult not to read this as at least a partial repudiation of the organization's Silicon Valley ethos of the past six years.

⚾   ⚾   ⚾

"The concept of disruption," writes cultural critic Adrian Daub, is a way for companies, the press or simply individuals to think about questions of continuity and discontinuity—what lasts and what doesn't, what is genuinely new and what is just the next version of something older." Disruption is just another iteration of Marx's dictum that "all that is solid melts into air." The innovation that got the Giants to 107 wins has evaporated into a confused roster overloaded with too many situational options. Perhaps the hiring of Melvin heralds a more traditional model of team building. Nurture your youth. Trade from strength to need. Build a rotation of pitchers who can go deep—or at least five innings—into a game. It's not sexy, and it's definitely not tech-y, but it might be the best way to reverse the trend of an overthought and underperforming team.

The farther we get from 2021, the longer, more measured view we have of it: when an alarming number of people thought cryptocurrency was a good investment, the Metaverse represented a step forward, and the San Francisco Giants won 107 regular-season games. The Giants have exited the blinding starburst of 2021 and expectations have receded like a low tide at Candlestick Point. Zaidi's vision has lurched into a dead end like a Roomba circling endlessly in a closet. The slick, statuesque Kapler has given way to grizzled baseball lifer Melvin. The team has a smattering of credible veterans and some young players with promise. The marine layer's thick blanket is still there, as are the gulls that raid the scraps left behind at the end of a night game. Tony Bennett will warble through the fog, win or lose. It could be 1976. Or 1985. Or 2006. For the Giants, everything new is old again, and maybe that's where the next wave of innovation lies.

—Jon Hegglund is a professor at Washington State University.

HITTERS

Patrick Bailey C Born: 05/29/99 Age: 25 Bats: S Throws: R Height: 6'0" Weight: 210 Origin: Round 1, 2020 Draft (#13 overall)

YEAR	TM	LVL	AGE	PA	R	HR	RBI	SB	AVG/OBP/SLG	BABIP	SLGCON	BB%	K%	ZSw%	ZCon%	OSw%	OCon%	LA	90th EV	DRC+	BRR	DRP	WARP
2021	SJ	A	22	207	45	7	24	1	.322/.415/.531	.403	.723	13.5%	22.7%							122	0.8	19.5	3.1
2021	EUG	A+	22	155	13	2	15	6	.185/.290/.296	.256	.435	11.6%	27.7%							84	0.8	5.8	0.8
2022	EUG	A+	23	325	49	12	51	1	.225/.342/.419	.253	.574	15.1%	22.2%							118	-0.2	18.3	3.5
2023	RIC	AA	24	60	9	2	10	2	.333/.400/.481	.410	.634	10.0%	21.7%							116	0.3	0.7	0.4
2023	SAC	AAA	24	60	5	2	6	1	.216/.317/.353	.257	.500	11.7%	25.0%	76.6%	76.4%	33.6%	67.4%			102	0.1	1.4	0.4
2023	SF	MLB	24	353	29	7	48	1	.233/.285/.359	.314	.518	5.9%	28.3%	66.0%	83.7%	31.1%	57.3%	10.0	103.7	75	-0.3	25.3	2.8
2024 DC	SF	MLB	25	323	28	6	30	2	.219/.287/.335	.282	.456	7.9%	24.6%							76	-0.2	20.9	2.4

2023 GP: C (94), DH (1)

Comps: Omar Narváez (61), Chris Herrmann (60), Cameron Rupp (59)

YEAR	TM	P. COUNT	FRM RUNS	BLK RUNS	THRW RUNS	TOT RUNS
2021	SJ	5450	17.4	0.6	1.3	19.4
2021	EUG	3744	3.5	0.1	1.2	4.9
2022	EUG	9831	16.8	0.6	2.9	20.4
2023	RIC	1286	0.6	-0.1	0.6	1.0
2023	SAC	1736	0.4	0.0	0.4	0.8
2023	SF	12144	23.6	-0.2	2.2	25.7
2024	SF	12025	20.0	0.0	1.0	21.0

Bailey is responsible for what has widely been hailed as the most memorable moment of the Giants' 2023 campaign, his game-ending backpick of Geraldo Perdomo on August 1. He didn't get the Gold Glove because no one respects framing, and didn't hit very well, but his 2022 Minor League Gold Glove is probably more prestigious given the additional 90 teams to compete with. Bailey walked quite a bit more in the minors, and in the majors significantly underachieved his quality of contact—and even underperformed his deserved strikeout and walk rates—so there's a lot more offensive promise here than the surface numbers suggest. If you don't buy any of that, the NC State University product admitted to being tired down the stretch after catching more than he ever had before. And even if that's all nonsense, he's a switch-hitting Austin Hedges, which might be enough to get down-ballot MVP votes.

Michael Conforto   RF   Born: 03/01/93   Age: 31   Bats: L   Throws: R   Height: 6'1"   Weight: 215   Origin: Round 1, 2014 Draft (#10 overall)

YEAR	TM	LVL	AGE	PA	R	HR	RBI	SB	AVG/OBP/SLG	BABIP	SLGCON	BB%	K%	ZSw%	ZCon%	OSw%	OCon%	LA	90th EV	DRC+	BRR	DRP	WARP
2021	NYM	MLB	28	479	52	14	55	1	.232/.344/.384	.276	.517	12.3%	21.7%	68.2%	83.0%	28.2%	66.3%	13.3	104.0	106	-0.2	-4.3	1.3
2023	SF	MLB	30	470	58	15	58	4	.239/.334/.384	.284	.520	11.3%	22.6%	69.1%	86.4%	28.0%	55.5%	12.5	104.9	94	-0.3	-6.1	0.2
2024 DC	SF	MLB	31	543	59	13	57	4	.238/.340/.377	.293	.504	11.5%	21.8%							107	-0.3	-5.5	1.2

2023 GP: RF (96), LF (18), DH (13)   *Comps: Steve Kemp (62), Ken Singleton (61), Mike Lum (61)*

One of the more entertaining factoids of the year: Among bounceback lefty outfielders, Conforto actually led Cody Bellinger in xwOBA. That didn't make its way into the line because the former couldn't pull his fly balls enough and struggled down the stretch after a strong start. There can be few players less exciting than a corner outfielder with below-average speed and three home runs after June 8. This is best illustrated by Game 162, in which Conforto saw 10 pitches in the zone and swung at seven, essentially a league-average rate. He somehow managed to be called out on strikes three times in four trips to the plate; even forgiving that two were borderline calls, it was a truly remarkable way to end the season. In a game with no impact on the standings, watching strike three on three separate occasions is fully distinct from how any fan would approach the sport, and the last ? came on a fastball right over the middle of the plate. It's not hard to imagine that Conforto simply wore down in his return to the league, but he's hit a lot more ground balls his last two campaigns and seems like a low-end regular at this point.

J.D. Davis   3B   Born: 04/27/93   Age: 31   Bats: R   Throws: R   Height: 6'3"   Weight: 218   Origin: Round 3, 2014 Draft (#75 overall)

YEAR	TM	LVL	AGE	PA	R	HR	RBI	SB	AVG/OBP/SLG	BABIP	SLGCON	BB%	K%	ZSw%	ZCon%	OSw%	OCon%	LA	90th EV	DRC+	BRR	DRP	WARP
2021	SYR	AAA	28	49	8	4	7	0	.316/.469/.737	.400	1.167	20.4%	28.6%							112	0.3	-0.1	0.2
2021	NYM	MLB	28	211	18	5	23	1	.285/.384/.436	.426	.703	11.4%	32.2%	77.6%	69.0%	30.6%	40.9%	13.0	105.4	87	-0.1	-0.9	0.3
2022	NYM	MLB	29	207	26	4	21	1	.238/.324/.359	.345	.565	9.7%	31.9%	77.9%	68.8%	29.5%	50.4%	10.0	107.9	68	-0.5	-0.1	-0.4
2022	SF	MLB	29	158	20	8	14	0	.263/.361/.496	.384	.840	12.0%	35.4%	79.4%	70.6%	31.1%	46.2%	15.6	107.5	99	-0.1	-0.3	0.3
2023	SF	MLB	30	546	61	18	69	1	.248/.325/.413	.320	.604	9.5%	27.8%	81.8%	75.4%	31.4%	47.2%	7.8	105.8	73	-0.5	-1.1	-0.3
2024 DC	SF	MLB	31	537	57	14	58	1	.229/.321/.374	.314	.558	10.0%	29.4%							99	-0.5	-4.7	0.8

2023 GP: 3B (116), 1B (15), DH (14)   *Comps: Chris Taylor (60), Ray Knight (56), Mike Lowell (56)*

On June 13, Davis was hitting .286/.369/.476 with enough defensive improvement to no longer be a DH, a hard-hit rate still over 50%, more contact and patience and not as much good luck as one might suspect. In that game against the Cardinals, he rolled his ankle on a slide into third base; though he returned a few days later for a pinch-hit grand slam in a legendary 15-0 win against the Dodgers, the injury might as well have ended his season. Even including the grand slam, Davis slumped to an ugly .219/.290/.363 line for the remaining three-plus months, hitting the ball on the ground regularly and whiffing even more than usual as he tried to swing his way out of it. He still has a 118 OPS+ over the last five seasons, so it's not all bad, but two out of four defensive metrics (DRP and DRS, but not OAA & the eye test) still think he's an awful defender. Davis needs to start elevating again pretty quickly to get a guaranteed contract when he escapes arbitration next winter.

─────────── ★ ★ ★ *2024 Top 101 Prospect* **#97** ★ ★ ★ ───────────

Bryce Eldridge   RF   Born: 10/20/04   Age: 19   Bats: L   Throws: R   Height: 6'7"   Weight: 223   Origin: Round 1, 2023 Draft (#16 overall)

YEAR	TM	LVL	AGE	PA	R	HR	RBI	SB	AVG/OBP/SLG	BABIP	SLGCON	BB%	K%	ZSw%	ZCon%	OSw%	OCon%	LA	90th EV	DRC+	BRR	DRP	WARP
2023	GNTO	ROK	18	61	8	5	13	0	.294/.393/.647	.323	.943	14.8%	26.2%										
2023	SJ	A	18	69	7	1	5	1	.293/.406/.379	.410	.550	15.9%	26.1%							99	-0.7	-0.9	0.0
2024 non	SF	MLB	19	251	19	2	19	0	.207/.271/.289	.321	.462	7.4%	34.3%							59	0.0	0	-0.7

2023 GP: RF (26), DH (5)   *Comps: Ramón Flores (73), Isael Soto (70), Yorman Rodriguez (68)*

Eldridge is one of the more real two-way prospects around, even if the Giants didn't ramp back up his pitching after taking him with their first-round pick in 2023. Most people are understandably enamored with the power and patience a 6-foot-7 high schooler might offer at the plate, but before a spring ankle injury, he had a mid-90s fastball with tail on the mound to go with a solid slider, flashes of a changeup and reasonable strike-throwing capabilities. It probably helps his chance of being a true two-way player that he's coming out of high school instead of college, as his youth should allow him to be slow played—unlike Brendan McKay or Reggie Crawford.

Thairo Estrada   2B   Born: 02/22/96   Age: 28   Bats: R   Throws: R   Height: 5'10"   Weight: 185   Origin: IFA, 2012

YEAR	TM	LVL	AGE	PA	R	HR	RBI	SB	AVG/OBP/SLG	BABIP	SLGCON	BB%	K%	ZSw%	ZCon%	OSw%	OCon%	LA	90th EV	DRC+	BRR	DRP	WARP
2021	SAC	AAA	25	233	37	9	40	6	.333/.399/.538	.367	.646	8.6%	15.0%							123	-1.0	-3.8	1.0
2021	SF	MLB	25	132	19	7	22	1	.273/.333/.479	.286	.592	6.8%	17.4%	67.4%	90.8%	33.3%	69.2%	6.7	104.1	112	0.0	0.0	0.7
2022	SF	MLB	26	541	71	14	62	21	.260/.322/.400	.290	.489	6.1%	16.5%	67.0%	90.0%	37.2%	68.9%	7.7	101.3	104	0.8	0.0	2.1
2023	SF	MLB	27	530	63	14	49	23	.271/.315/.416	.331	.549	4.2%	22.6%	65.6%	91.0%	42.5%	67.2%	11.2	102.9	90	0.9	-1.2	0.9
2024 DC	SF	MLB	28	577	58	14	62	21	.251/.311/.385	.292	.482	5.7%	18.5%							97	0.3	-1.1	1.4

2023 GP: 2B (102), SS (24), LF (3), DH (2)   *Comps: Howie Kendrick (66), Felix Millan (60), Rennie Stennett (59)*

Estrada is a capable bat with a capable glove, or a weak bat with a strong glove or a strong bat with a weak glove, depending on what one's narrative desires. He again overperformed his expected Statcast output notably, and DRC+ is displeased with his more free-swinging approach, which sent his walk rate down to half of league average and his strikeout rate up to that level. DRP and DRS see his defense as roughly average, too. On the other hand, if not for missing a month with a hit-by-pitch injury, Estrada likely would have led all infielders in Statcast's Fielding Run Value, and he did improve his quality of contact notably. At this point, Estrada either has a lackluster 3.1 WARP in two full seasons, a reasonable 4.0 rWAR, or an exceptional 6.7 fWAR.

Tyler Fitzgerald SS   Born: 09/15/97   Age: 26   Bats: R   Throws: R   Height: 6'3"   Weight: 205   Origin: Round 4, 2019 Draft (#116 overall)

YEAR	TM	LVL	AGE	PA	R	HR	RBI	SB	AVG/OBP/SLG	BABIP	SLGCON	BB%	K%	ZSw%	ZCon%	OSw%	OCon%	LA	90th EV	DRC+	BRR	DRP	WARP
2021	EUG	A+	23	432	71	19	65	12	.262/.342/.495	.360	.778	8.8%	32.2%							102	0.1	1.5	1.6
2022	RIC	AA	24	519	74	21	58	20	.229/.310/.424	.310	.680	7.1%	32.9%							89	3.8	-3.2	1.0
2023	RIC	AA	25	78	15	2	9	3	.324/.410/.588	.455	.870	11.5%	28.2%							93	0.0	-0.2	0.1
2023	SAC	AAA	25	466	72	20	69	29	.287/.358/.499	.346	.681	9.7%	23.8%	72.9%	80.4%	33.8%	53.7%			100	2.1	-2.8	1.1
2023	SF	MLB	25	34	3	2	5	2	.219/.265/.469	.250	.682	5.9%	29.4%	72.7%	85.4%	22.2%	44.4%	18.7	100.8	84	0.3	-0.3	0.1
2024 DC	SF	MLB	26	59	6	1	6	2	.230/.291/.371	.318	.541	6.7%	30.6%							85	0.0	0	0.1

2023 GP: CF (9), 3B (3)   *Comps: Tim Locastro (55), Andy Parrino (54), Justin Ruggiano (53)*

Fitzgerald is a speedy utility player who lacks an obvious offensive strength: His 90th-percentile exit velocity in Triple-A was below-average, but not by miles, his in-zone contact rate wasn't all that bad but still sat nearly 4% below the MLB average and his chase rate, while not ruinous, was 5% above the big-league average. This is somewhat true on defense, too, where his arm can be a bit light for a lockdown defender on the left side and he's only recently gotten time in the outfield. If we push the qualifiers threshold all the way down to 30 plate appearances to include his 10-game MLB debut, Fitzgerald shockingly would have had the sixth-lowest chase rate (15.9%) in the league. He still had contact issues with non-fastballs, and overachieved his quality of contact dramatically, but if any of that patience is real he's probably a useful depth piece.

Wilmer Flores 1B   Born: 08/06/91   Age: 32   Bats: R   Throws: R   Height: 6'2"   Weight: 213   Origin: IFA, 2007

YEAR	TM	LVL	AGE	PA	R	HR	RBI	SB	AVG/OBP/SLG	BABIP	SLGCON	BB%	K%	ZSw%	ZCon%	OSw%	OCon%	LA	90th EV	DRC+	BRR	DRP	WARP
2021	SF	MLB	29	436	57	18	53	1	.262/.335/.447	.264	.523	9.4%	12.8%	69.1%	89.3%	30.0%	74.1%	18.0	102.3	111	-0.7	-0.7	1.9
2022	SF	MLB	30	602	72	19	71	0	.229/.316/.394	.246	.491	9.8%	17.1%	67.9%	89.0%	29.3%	68.0%	20.6	101.6	99	-1.5	-0.6	1.3
2023	SF	MLB	31	454	51	23	60	0	.284/.355/.509	.286	.602	9.0%	13.9%	64.5%	90.2%	30.2%	74.5%	22.3	101.9	134	-0.7	-0.3	2.9
2024 DC	SF	MLB	32	488	56	17	60	0	.256/.332/.425	.269	.501	9.0%	13.6%							113	0.0	-0.6	1.8

2023 GP: 1B (61), DH (41), 3B (22), 2B (6)   *Comps: Pie Traynor (68), Brooks Robinson (67), Buddy Bell (66)*

With the Giants offense completely dead in the second half, it was easy for outside observers to assume widespread failure. Let's clear up that misconception right now: From June 1 through September 8, Flores hit .323/.398/.610, making him one of six players with an OPS surpassing 1.000 in that span (over at least 250 plate appearances). The other five were Shohei Ohtani, Mookie Betts, Corey Seager, Matt Olson and Ronald Acuña Jr. Will this carry over into Flores' age-32 season? He only needed the benefit of a .306 BABIP in that stretch, so it's not exactly unthinkable.

Jung Hoo Lee OF   Born: 08/20/98   Age: 25   Bats: L   Throws: R   Height: 6'1"   Weight: 192   Origin: IFA, 2023

YEAR	TM	LVL	AGE	PA	R	HR	RBI	SB	AVG/OBP/SLG	BABIP	SLGCON	BB%	K%	ZSw%	ZCon%	OSw%	OCon%	LA	90th EV	DRC+	BRR	DRP	WARP
2024 DC	SF	MLB	25	531	55	9	55	0	.275/.351/.413	.302	.471	9.6%	11.3%							117	0.0	0	3.0

Nicknamed "The Grandson of the Wind" by virtue of his bloodlines (his father, the titular son of said wind, was considered the best all-round player of his own era), Lee collected KBO Rookie of the Year and MVP awards of his own before coming stateside. His 2023 season was actually a bit of a down year comparatively, thanks to a fractured ankle. But the Giants—and plenty of other teams—recognized an incontrovertible truth: free-agent stars are uncommon, but 25-year-old free-agent stars are rare. Lee can play a solid center field, something the Giants have lacked for a while now, and while there's some question to how (and how quickly) his power will translate against MLB-quality velocity, his bat-to-ball skills are impeccable. Scouting for overseas pitching is ahead of hitting right now, since each pitch can basically be evaluated and quantified in a vacuum, while hitting remains reactive, and thus more of a mystery. The common wisdom is that Lee will likely go through an adjustment phase, as former teammate Ha-seong Kim did. But hitting isn't Lee's only tool, and the rest should translate easily in the meantime.

★ ★ ★ *2024 Top 101 Prospect* **#43** ★ ★ ★

Marco Luciano SS   Born: 09/10/01   Age: 22   Bats: R   Throws: R   Height: 6'1"   Weight: 178   Origin: IFA, 2018

YEAR	TM	LVL	AGE	PA	R	HR	RBI	SB	AVG/OBP/SLG	BABIP	SLGCON	BB%	K%	ZSw%	ZCon%	OSw%	OCon%	LA	90th EV	DRC+	BRR	DRP	WARP
2021	SCO	WIN	19	87	7	3	13	0	.253/.356/.373	.364	.596	12.6%	32.2%	77.8%	71.4%	11.8%	100.0%						
2021	SJ	A	19	308	52	18	57	5	.278/.373/.556	.309	.747	12.3%	22.1%							129	-0.9	-0.1	1.9
2021	EUG	A+	19	145	16	1	14	1	.217/.283/.295	.351	.507	6.9%	37.2%							69	-0.1	-1.2	-0.3
2022	GNTB	ROK	20	27	6	1	6	0	.318/.444/.545	.429	.800	14.8%	25.9%										
2022	EUG	A+	20	230	27	10	30	0	.263/.339/.459	.303	.610	9.6%	22.2%							112	-0.1	2.1	1.3
2023	RIC	AA	21	242	32	11	32	6	.228/.339/.450	.285	.700	14.9%	29.8%							105	1.7	2.3	1.2
2023	SAC	AAA	21	78	10	4	8	0	.209/.321/.418	.286	.718	12.8%	35.9%	69.4%	66.7%	23.2%	46.3%			79	-0.6	0.7	0.1
2023	SF	MLB	21	45	4	0	0	1	.231/.333/.308	.409	.545	13.3%	37.8%	65.7%	72.7%	24.8%	27.6%	-4.7	107.5	66	0.0	0.1	0.0
2024 DC	SF	MLB	22	440	40	11	43	4	.195/.273/.329	.279	.524	8.6%	33.6%							70	0.0	-5	-0.7

2023 GP: SS (13), DH (1)   *Comps: Javier Báez (53), Corey Seager (52), Jorge Polanco (51)*

Luciano is a three-true-outcomes shortstop, if you're willing to count hard-hit balls rather than home runs; he's also not a lock to stick at short. For the 576 MLB hitters who put at least 20 balls in play, his 93-mph average exit velocity ranked inside the top 20. He also made less contact than Joey Gallo in his brief debut, even with a langorous approach. He's already been named the Giants starting shortstop for 2024, but don't be surprised if they sneak a more experienced option onto the roster: Luciano's career-high in games played at shortstop is 107 in 2021, and that required a stint in the Arizona Fall League. Still, he's been their top prospect for over four years now, Joey Bart infatuation aside, so as Izzy Mandelbaum would say, it's go time.

Walker Martin SS Born: 02/20/04 Age: 20 Bats: L Throws: R Height: 6'2" Weight: 188 Origin: Round 2, 2023 Draft (#52 overall)

A 2023 second-rounder, Martin received a bonus commensurate with the first-round grades most public analysts had on him. There's some mystery here because he didn't make his pro debut after signing, but assuming health, there's a lot of intrigue in a possible shortstop with some power and feel for line-drive contact. Martin had critics because he was a high schooler halfway to 20 on draft day and played in the low-competition, high-elevation state of Colorado, but his appeal isn't based on the sort of polish that is often a red flag for older high school bats. For the believers, that puts him in a similar class as White Sox super-prospect Colson Montgomery.

Luis Matos OF Born: 01/28/02 Age: 22 Bats: R Throws: R Height: 5'11" Weight: 160 Origin: IFA, 2018

YEAR	TM	LVL	AGE	PA	R	HR	RBI	SB	AVG/OBP/SLG	BABIP	SLGCON	BB%	K%	ZSw%	ZCon%	OSw%	OCon%	LA	90th EV	DRC+	BRR	DRP	WARP
2021	SJ	A	19	491	84	15	86	21	.313/.358/.494	.332	.572	5.7%	12.4%							129	1.2	-7.6	3.0
2022	EUG	A+	20	407	55	11	43	11	.211/.275/.344	.226	.418	6.6%	16.0%							98	0.5	0.1	1.3
2023	RIC	AA	21	133	18	3	16	9	.304/.398/.443	.320	.495	12.8%	9.0%							129	1.0	1.7	1.1
2023	SAC	AAA	21	152	23	9	22	6	.353/.404/.626	.336	.680	7.2%	7.2%	69.6%	95.5%	38.5%	76.7%			131	-0.2	-3.2	0.8
2023	SF	MLB	21	253	24	2	14	3	.250/.319/.342	.285	.400	7.9%	13.0%	69.1%	91.7%	31.7%	70.3%	6.5	103.3	105	0.0	-3.5	0.7
2024 DC	SF	MLB	22	126	12	2	12	4	.248/.305/.366	.274	.430	6.5%	13.5%							90	0.0	-1.2	0.1

2023 GP: CF (57), RF (15), LF (14), DH (2)   Comps: Byron Buxton (69), Matt Kemp (59), Vernon Wells (53)

Matos had a well-earned reputation as a contact-driven free-swinger, but showed up in the spring of 2023 bat-flipping after walks, and as a result he reached the majors by early June despite a .619 OPS in 91 High-A games the year prior. What makes this transformation most incredible is that it wasn't just Matos being passive; his in-zone swing rate remained above average while his chase rate was a few points better than the mean, so he's just making good decisions now. He had strong contact rates across all pitch types, hit a bunch of line drives, wasn't into the slap-hitter range of exit velocities, is 22 in January and was close to competent offensively, so one can imagine improvement. The trouble is that by DRP, DRS, and OAA, Matos was the worst or second-worst defensive center fielder on a rate basis. This appears almost entirely due to an inability to catch bloops; Matos was essentially average in the other three cardinal directions, and his sprint speed is acceptable, but on every batted ball his first step was backwards so he rarely got to anything in front of him. If you're going to be awful on defense, it probably helps to have one clear area for improvement, but it's a lot harder to fit someone with an .092 ISO onto the big-league roster if they can't play an average center field.

Wade Meckler OF Born: 04/21/00 Age: 24 Bats: L Throws: R Height: 5'10" Weight: 178 Origin: Round 8, 2022 Draft (#256 overall)

YEAR	TM	LVL	AGE	PA	R	HR	RBI	SB	AVG/OBP/SLG	BABIP	SLGCON	BB%	K%	ZSw%	ZCon%	OSw%	OCon%	LA	90th EV	DRC+	BRR	DRP	WARP
2022	GNTB	ROK	22	50	12	0	6	1	.289/.460/.395	.367	.500	22.0%	16.0%										
2022	SJ	A	22	50	9	1	8	1	.439/.540/.683	.531	.848	18.0%	16.0%							116	0.6	-1.0	0.2
2023	EUG	A+	23	87	14	2	17	2	.456/.494/.633	.493	.714	6.9%	10.3%							131	1.0	0.2	0.7
2023	RIC	AA	23	174	36	2	23	4	.336/.431/.450	.407	.558	14.4%	16.7%							124	0.6	-2.7	0.8
2023	SAC	AAA	23	102	12	2	10	7	.354/.465/.500	.443	.661	17.6%	19.6%	61.2%	87.1%	23.6%	59.0%			102	0.6	0.7	0.3
2023	SF	MLB	23	64	6	0	4	0	.232/.328/.250	.419	.452	9.4%	39.1%	53.1%	75.0%	25.4%	47.7%	6.3	97.8	61	-0.1	-1.0	-0.2
2024 DC	SF	MLB	24	30	3	0	2	0	.214/.301/.314	.268	.381	9.8%	20.6%							75	0.0	-0.4	-0.1

2023 GP: CF (18), LF (4)   Comps: Magneuris Sierra (60), Omar Quintanilla (55), Mallex Smith (54)

Meckler is a decidedly Arraez-ian player, which is to say that he is addicted to hitting line-drive singles. For a minimum of 50 plate appearances at a given level, Luis Arraez's career-high line-drive rate is 29.4%, a mark comfortably beaten by Meckler at three of the four levels he visited in 2023. Despite a major-league OPS of .578, Meckler's 36.7% line-drive rate was the second-best among the 542 MLB hitters with at least 50 plate appearances. Even just collecting 82-mph singles, Meckler should be able to add value as a solid defensive center fielder and one of the faster players in baseball. The question is where the non-fastball contact rates and plate discipline end up. Meckler's in-zone and out-of-zone swing rates are approximately three-fourths of the average, which is to say that he does not so much have good discipline as extreme patience. He would benefit from a more aggressive approach: 15 of his 29 whiffs against breaking balls and off-speed, and one-third of his total pitches seen, came with two strikes. Despite a disastrous week to open his career (a 51% contact rate), he recovered to something close to average offensively thereafter.

Tom Murphy C Born: 04/03/91 Age: 33 Bats: R Throws: R Height: 6'1" Weight: 206 Origin: Round 3, 2012 Draft (#105 overall)

YEAR	TM	LVL	AGE	PA	R	HR	RBI	SB	AVG/OBP/SLG	BABIP	SLGCON	BB%	K%	ZSw%	ZCon%	OSw%	OCon%	LA	90th EV	DRC+	BRR	DRP	WARP
2021	SEA	MLB	30	325	35	11	34	0	.202/.304/.350	.265	.545	12.3%	30.5%	68.7%	78.9%	28.2%	47.1%	16.0	103.9	89	-0.2	0.9	1.0
2022	SEA	MLB	31	42	9	1	1	0	.303/.439/.455	.474	.750	19.0%	31.0%	71.4%	76.0%	27.9%	51.6%	13.7	108.9	83	0.0	0.2	0.1
2023	SEA	MLB	32	159	19	8	17	0	.290/.335/.538	.358	.772	6.3%	27.7%	74.2%	81.1%	34.4%	50.0%	13.9	106.3	93	-0.3	-2.6	0.2
2024 DC	SF	MLB	33	155	15	4	16	0	.215/.294/.358	.281	.515	9.1%	27.9%							84	0.0	-0.5	0.2

2023 GP: C (41), DH (5)   Comps: David Ross (60), Travis d'Arnaud (59), George Gibson (56)

YEAR	TM	P. COUNT	FRM RUNS	BLK RUNS	THRW RUNS	TOT RUNS
2021	SEA	12065	1.8	0.1	0.6	2.5
2022	SEA	1582	0.5	0.0	0.0	0.5
2023	SEA	5360	-2.2	0.0	-0.4	-2.5
2024	SF	4810	0.0	0.0	-0.4	-0.4

In many respects, Murphy is the ideal backup catcher. His bat packs more than a respectable punch for the position, especially against lefties. His presence in the clubhouse is felt as both a beloved teammate and in a strong reputation as a game-planner for his pitching staff. While his advanced defensive metrics may not shine especially bright, pitchers have routinely expressed a high level of comfort throwing to Murphy. But if the inherent nature of being a backup is to, you know, *be around to back up the starter*, that's where Murphy has fallen short recently. A thumb sprain in August ended his season early, making it the third time in four seasons an injury has kept Murphy on the shelf for significant time. Perhaps even more troublesome for his future was the initial response to MLB's new rules introducing a new era of Baserunners Gone Wild: Murphy cut down *just one* of the 28 baserunners who attempted a steal during his time behind the plate, which was comfortably the worst rate of any catcher who logged as many innings as he did.

Heliot Ramos OF Born: 09/07/99 Age: 24 Bats: R Throws: R Height: 6'1" Weight: 188 Origin: Round 1, 2017 Draft (#19 overall)

YEAR	TM	LVL	AGE	PA	R	HR	RBI	SB	AVG/OBP/SLG	BABIP	SLGCON	BB%	K%	ZSw%	ZCon%	OSw%	OCon%	LA	90th EV	DRC+	BRR	DRP	WARP
2021	RIC	AA	21	266	36	10	26	7	.237/.323/.432	.301	.626	10.2%	27.4%							104	0.0	-3.2	0.7
2021	SAC	AAA	21	229	30	4	30	8	.272/.323/.399	.375	.574	6.6%	28.4%							78	2.9	-1.2	0.3
2022	SAC	AAA	22	475	61	11	45	6	.227/.305/.349	.283	.473	8.6%	23.6%	72.4%	80.0%	35.0%	54.2%			76	0.2	-6.6	-0.5
2022	SF	MLB	22	22	4	0	0	0	.100/.182/.100	.143	.143	9.1%	27.3%	86.2%	68.0%	33.3%	43.8%	2.3	106.0	104	0.0	-0.2	0.1
2023	SAC	AAA	23	263	44	12	45	9	.300/.382/.546	.368	.770	10.3%	25.1%	70.5%	79.9%	33.8%	49.2%			100	1.3	-0.7	0.9
2023	SF	MLB	23	60	5	1	2	0	.179/.233/.304	.257	.472	6.7%	33.3%	71.8%	83.5%	32.4%	43.2%	13.1	106.9	70	0.0	-0.6	-0.1
2024 DC	SF	MLB	24	123	11	3	12	2	.217/.281/.346	.292	.500	7.2%	28.4%							76	-0.1	-1.8	-0.3

2023 GP: LF (13), RF (10), CF (3), DH (1) *Comps: Chad Hermansen (45), Tony Scott (44), Carlos Tocci (43)*

Giants fans may best remember Ramos for a mid-August stretch when he scalded three extra-base hits with triple-digit exit velocities for a completely dead offense, two over 110 mph and each coming in the bottom of the ninth. The quieter part of these highlights was that all three came on middle-middle fastballs from lefty relievers, which did little to dispel the perception of Ramos as a platoon prospect. He missed much of the first half with an oblique injury but had a strong second half in the minors, earning periodic chances with the big club. From the time of his return to Triple-A on July 3, Ramos hit .315/.401/.611, though with a slightly below-average walk rate and much worse-than-average strikeout rate. It's unsurprising, then, that the Giants have tried to protect him from same-handed sliders at the major-league level, but that's left things in a tricky spot: Ramos has one option year left, and even with strong quality of contact—especially against lefties—there just hasn't been enough plate discipline to stick. At the same time, he's a 24-year-old with 82 major-league plate appearances, hardly the sort of sample that offers a definitive conclusion. He's a corner outfielder only and doesn't even offer much defensive value there; the moment to show out is now or never.

Blake Sabol C/LF Born: 01/07/98 Age: 26 Bats: L Throws: R Height: 6'4" Weight: 225 Origin: Round 7, 2019 Draft (#214 overall)

YEAR	TM	LVL	AGE	PA	R	HR	RBI	SB	AVG/OBP/SLG	BABIP	SLGCON	BB%	K%	ZSw%	ZCon%	OSw%	OCon%	LA	90th EV	DRC+	BRR	DRP	WARP
2021	BRD	A	23	59	11	2	12	0	.370/.508/.543	.469	.735	20.3%	20.3%	76.7%	73.9%	21.9%	53.1%			124	0.6	-0.5	0.4
2021	GBO	A+	23	229	39	11	33	6	.296/.380/.553	.407	.866	11.8%	31.4%							104	0.1	3.1	1.1
2022	ALT	AA	24	412	61	14	60	9	.281/.347/.486	.355	.687	9.2%	26.0%							102	-0.3	2.5	1.5
2022	IND	AAA	24	101	13	5	15	1	.296/.426/.543	.345	.746	16.8%	21.8%							118	-0.7	-1.7	0.3
2023	SF	MLB	25	344	36	13	44	4	.235/.301/.394	.330	.632	7.0%	34.0%	75.5%	75.7%	31.6%	40.8%	14.4	104.2	68	0.2	1.4	-0.1
2024 DC	SF	MLB	26	189	18	5	20	2	.222/.294/.369	.310	.558	8.0%	31.4%							86	0.0	1.3	0.4

2023 GP: C (55), LF (43), DH (10) *Comps: Austin Allen (53), José Briceño (51), Nick Hundley (50)*

YEAR	TM	P. COUNT	FRM RUNS	BLK RUNS	THRW RUNS	TOT RUNS
2021	GBO	3710	1.8	0.1	-0.1	1.8
2022	ALT	8366	4.5	-1.1	-0.4	3.0
2022	IND	1104	-0.9	0.0	-0.2	-1.0
2023	SF	6472	2.1	-0.4	0.0	1.7
2024	SF	4810	1.3	-0.3	0.2	1.3

Sabol was baseball's worst blocker by a wide margin, but he was a decent framer and thrower, and can play a little left field, so it wasn't enough to kick him out of a backup catcher role. What probably got close was picking up four catcher's interference calls in his first eight starts at the position (though he avoided logging another in the subsequent five months), but Sabol's offense was solid enough to complete the improbable feat of sticking on the roster for the whole year as a Rule 5 selection and converted catcher. The underlying numbers were scary (67 DRC+), but that's not what's important. It's fundamentally cool to have a backup catcher stealing bases in the ninth or 10th inning of a tied game, which happened in two of three September contests against the Guardians, one of which came as a pinch-runner and the other of which allowed him to score as the walk-off run.

Casey Schmitt 3B Born: 03/01/99 Age: 25 Bats: R Throws: R Height: 6'2" Weight: 215 Origin: Round 2, 2020 Draft (#49 overall)

YEAR	TM	LVL	AGE	PA	R	HR	RBI	SB	AVG/OBP/SLG	BABIP	SLGCON	BB%	K%	ZSw%	ZCon%	OSw%	OCon%	LA	90th EV	DRC+	BRR	DRP	WARP
2021	SJ	A	22	280	36	8	29	2	.247/.318/.406	.269	.493	7.9%	15.7%							110	0.4	6.0	1.7
2022	EUG	A+	23	383	58	17	59	1	.273/.363/.474	.319	.640	11.0%	22.5%							127	1.1	-3.6	2.1
2022	RIC	AA	23	127	13	3	16	2	.342/.378/.517	.432	.681	4.7%	22.8%							92	1.3	-1.1	0.3
2023	SAC	AAA	24	217	28	4	33	3	.300/.346/.435	.364	.558	6.5%	20.3%	72.8%	82.9%	42.9%	63.9%			94	0.6	-1.2	0.4
2023	SF	MLB	24	277	28	5	30	2	.206/.255/.324	.253	.436	4.7%	23.5%	73.0%	86.2%	41.2%	56.6%	14.6	103.8	91	0.0	-1.6	0.5
2024 DC	SF	MLB	25	184	16	4	18	2	.230/.284/.346	.288	.457	5.7%	23.2%							77	-0.1	-1.1	-0.1

2023 GP: SS (42), 3B (35), 2B (19) *Comps: Chris Taylor (62), Luis Alfonso Cruz (60), Chase d'Arnaud (59)*

Known as the sort of goofball everyone wants around, the rookie Schmitt shared Brandon Crawford's defensive reputation (though as a third baseman) and the two bonded in the spring. On October 1, perhaps his final day on the field, Crawford selected "Just the Two of Us" as Schmitt's walk-up song; when Crawford was replaced in the ninth, Schmitt told him, "I love you, Papa." The loving tribute continued with Schmitt's two-homer day raising his season-long OPS to .580, within range of Crawford's .587. What's worse, Schmitt's defensive reputation didn't quite show up as the Giants experimented with him as a middle infielder, and he needed 69 plate appearances to draw his first walk. In his first three-month crack at the big leagues, he swung at 43% of pitches outside the zone, which thankfully swooned to 22.9% over 59 scattered PA as the season waned. His contact rate ballooned, too, but this sample is a bit of a cheat because pitchers went back to challenging him with fastballs and he was platooned more. His in-zone swing rate remained a steadily above-average 71%, so there still may have been some pitch recognition improvement. If you think Schmitt can provide Gold Glove-level defense at third base, the question is really whether he can improve the offense enough to mimic 2021-2022 Ke'Bryan Hayes as a contact-driven defensive specialist.

Austin Slater OF   Born: 12/13/92   Age: 31   Bats: R   Throws: R   Height: 6'1"   Weight: 204   Origin: Round 8, 2014 Draft (#238 overall)

YEAR	TM	LVL	AGE	PA	R	HR	RBI	SB	AVG/OBP/SLG	BABIP	SLGCON	BB%	K%	ZSw%	ZCon%	OSw%	OCon%	LA	90th EV	DRC+	BRR	DRP	WARP
2021	SF	MLB	28	306	39	12	32	15	.241/.320/.423	.303	.611	9.2%	27.5%	67.2%	77.4%	27.1%	54.2%	7.7	104.0	90	0.6	-1.7	0.7
2022	SF	MLB	29	325	49	7	34	12	.264/.366/.408	.361	.601	12.3%	27.4%	68.2%	77.2%	28.5%	54.5%	6.1	104.7	91	0.6	-0.7	0.8
2023	SF	MLB	30	207	24	5	20	2	.270/.348/.400	.369	.583	9.7%	28.0%	65.7%	80.8%	24.6%	49.6%	7.5	105.6	90	0.0	-1.0	0.3
2024 DC	SF	MLB	31	212	22	5	22	4	.232/.320/.372	.305	.530	10.0%	26.6%							98	0.1	-1	0.5

2023 GP: CF (39), LF (34), RF (9), DH (5)   *Comps: Chris Taylor (52), George Springer (52), Dexter Fowler (51)*

Slater is currently the second-best pinch-hitter of all time by OPS, for a minimum of 200 opportunities and excluding subsequent plate appearances with a defensive position, sitting at .911. The rest of that list is full of Chase Utleys and others who simply were very good and played long enough to pinch hit a lot, whereas the lefty-masher Slater makes regular appearances in that role. There are some worrying signs: He's lost power the last two years and finally had a long-needed elbow surgery over the winter, but he's an above-average hitter when used carefully and can spend time at all three outfield spots.

LaMonte Wade Jr. 1B   Born: 01/01/94   Age: 30   Bats: L   Throws: L   Height: 6'1"   Weight: 205   Origin: Round 9, 2015 Draft (#260 overall)

YEAR	TM	LVL	AGE	PA	R	HR	RBI	SB	AVG/OBP/SLG	BABIP	SLGCON	BB%	K%	ZSw%	ZCon%	OSw%	OCon%	LA	90th EV	DRC+	BRR	DRP	WARP
2021	SF	MLB	27	381	52	18	56	6	.253/.326/.482	.289	.656	8.7%	23.4%	69.8%	89.1%	28.1%	63.5%	18.6	104.6	107	-0.1	-3.2	1.1
2022	SAC	AAA	28	58	11	2	11	0	.250/.397/.477	.237	.553	17.2%	10.3%	79.8%	82.3%	24.4%	72.7%			112	0.5	-0.8	0.2
2022	SF	MLB	28	251	29	8	26	1	.207/.305/.359	.233	.470	10.4%	20.3%	66.1%	88.9%	27.9%	69.4%	20.7	102.8	99	-0.2	-1.8	0.4
2023	SF	MLB	29	519	64	17	45	2	.256/.373/.417	.290	.536	14.6%	18.3%	62.5%	88.1%	21.4%	59.5%	16.3	103.4	121	-0.4	-0.9	2.3
2024 DC	SF	MLB	30	571	64	15	62	2	.239/.348/.388	.279	.499	12.9%	19.1%							112	-0.5	-0.1	1.9

2023 GP: 1B (116), LF (14), RF (7), DH (3), CF (2)   *Comps: Abraham Almonte (53), Jackie Bradley Jr. (50), Jerry White (46)*

Through June, Wade carried an .867 OPS, putting him among the more valuable first baseman in baseball, thanks in part to an uncharacteristically high .331 BABIP. Still, he owns an above-average bat for the position with tremendous plate discipline, solid contact skills and average power. The main question is how locked he is at the cold corner, where the Giants kept him at the cost of putting Joc Pederson in left or Wilmer Flores at third base in the late-season search for offense; this seemed related to persistent knee issues in 2022, which did not show up last season. Wade is an ordinary defender at first base and has been a tick below-average in an outfield corner, but if getting a full season of health into the legs give him a chance to play more outfield, it opens up first base as a spot for the Giants to fit another bat into the lineup.

Mike Yastrzemski OF   Born: 08/23/90   Age: 33   Bats: L   Throws: L   Height: 5'10"   Weight: 178   Origin: Round 14, 2013 Draft (#429 overall)

YEAR	TM	LVL	AGE	PA	R	HR	RBI	SB	AVG/OBP/SLG	BABIP	SLGCON	BB%	K%	ZSw%	ZCon%	OSw%	OCon%	LA	90th EV	DRC+	BRR	DRP	WARP
2021	SF	MLB	30	532	75	25	71	4	.224/.311/.457	.254	.635	9.6%	24.6%	68.8%	85.9%	30.8%	61.0%	19.6	103.1	96	0.2	-0.4	1.4
2022	SF	MLB	31	558	73	17	57	5	.214/.305/.392	.261	.552	10.9%	25.3%	64.2%	87.0%	27.6%	61.8%	19.5	103.8	98	0.2	0.6	1.8
2023	SF	MLB	32	381	54	15	43	2	.233/.330/.445	.286	.636	11.8%	26.0%	63.5%	86.0%	26.9%	61.9%	19.2	104.7	83	0.1	-1.5	0.3
2024 DC	SF	MLB	33	574	61	16	64	5	.224/.320/.391	.274	.535	11.3%	23.5%							102	0.1	-0.7	1.5

2023 GP: RF (56), CF (51), LF (17), DH (1)   *Comps: Jeromy Burnitz (78), Bill Nicholson (75), Kole Calhoun (73)*

In the midst of a season dotted with three left hamstring injuries, Giants strength and conditioning coach Brad Lawson explained the plan for Yaz to sidestep the issue, to San Francisco Chronicle writer Susan Slusser: "it's just his ability to maintain what I call a projection angle throughout the course of his mechanics, where the upright posture happens gradually." This is the most interesting thing there is to say about Yastrzemski. That sounds meaner than it is; he's a consistent, well-rounded contributor, and seemingly a clubhouse leader, but there's not a lot to guess about other than whether the hamstring will continue to be an issue.

PITCHERS

Tristan Beck RHP   Born: 06/24/96   Age: 28   Height: 6'4"   Weight: 165   Origin: Round 4, 2018 Draft (#112 overall)

YEAR	TM	LVL	AGE	G (GS)	IP	W-L	SV	K	WHIP	ERA	CSP	BB%	K%	HR%	GB%	ZSw%	ZCon%	OSw%	OCon%	BABIP	SLGCON	DRA-	WARP
2021	RIC	AA	25	4 (4)	18¹	2-2	0	17	1.47	5.89		8.5%	20.7%	4.9%	29.8%					.308	.696	113	0.0
2022	RIC	AA	26	3 (3)	14	0-1	0	19	1.21	2.57		11.9%	32.2%	1.7%	46.9%					.290	.531	100	0.2
2022	SAC	AAA	26	20 (19)	97¹	5-8	0	97	1.38	5.64		6.8%	22.7%	2.3%	42.0%	69.3%	84.1%	33.2%	56.6%	.335	.572	95	0.8
2023	SAC	AAA	27	9 (6)	26	3-3	0	26	1.42	5.88		12.4%	23.0%	8.0%	35.2%	62.6%	81.5%	31.9%	40.8%	.226	.826	114	0.0
2023	SF	MLB	27	33 (3)	85	3-3	2	68	1.22	3.92	48.8%	5.9%	19.2%	2.8%	41.4%	70.3%	85.9%	34.0%	62.1%	.290	.489	96	1.1
2024 DC	SF	MLB	28	49 (8)	78¹	4-4	0	63	1.39	4.79	48.8%	7.8%	18.6%	3.1%	40.8%					.305	.544	108	0.1

2023 Arsenal: FA (94.7), SL (87.7), SW (82.4), CU (79.4), CH (86.3)   *Comps: Kyle McGowin (62), A.J. Schugel (55), Zach Neal (53)*

Beck's rookie season peaked as the calendar flipped into August: He retired every batter asked of him in the 10th and 11th innings against the Red Sox on July 30, striking out three, and in his next appearance, he went one over the minimum in four innings against the fellow Wild Card hopeful Diamondbacks as the day's bulk pitcher. He was subsequently roughed up by the Angels, Rays and Padres, pushing his ERA back toward the 4.00 mark his peripherals already suggested. Beck's prospect reputation was as someone with several pitches but no particularly impressive ones, and to some degree this remains true. The big breakthrough for Beck was a small velo boost and adding a sweeper, which allowed him to throw three distinct breakers 63% of the time (a more common slider and the occasional curve); his fastball didn't grade out well for pure stuff, but the results were fairly strong and there's a wide enough band of shapes to imagine an uncoded grip or two. There's also a changeup, if you want a full six pitches. The tricky portion for Beck will be how much confidence you put in a mix-and-match approach, as his 19.2% strikeout rate and ordinary ground-ball rate don't leave much room for regression.

Mason Black RHP Born: 12/10/99 Age: 24 Height: 6'3" Weight: 230 Origin: Round 3, 2021 Draft (#85 overall)

YEAR	TM	LVL	AGE	G(GS)	IP	W-L	SV	K	WHIP	ERA	CSP	BB%	K%	HR%	GB%	ZSw%	ZCon%	OSw%	OCon%	BABIP	SLGCON	DRA-	WARP
2022	SJ	A	22	8(8)	34¹	1-1	0	44	0.96	1.57		5.9%	32.6%	0.7%	60.2%					.293	.415	81	0.5
2022	EUG	A+	22	16(16)	77²	5-3	0	92	1.26	3.94		8.5%	28.0%	3.4%	43.5%					.312	.570	97	0.8
2023	RIC	AA	23	16(16)	63	1-5	0	83	1.05	3.57		8.3%	32.7%	2.8%	40.8%					.273	.514	80	1.5
2023	SAC	AAA	23	13(13)	60²	3-4	0	72	1.38	3.86		12.0%	27.9%	3.5%	39.6%	61.2%	86.0%	29.8%	55.1%	.314	.626	82	0.4
2024 DC	SF	MLB	24	13(3)	26²	1-2	0	26	1.37	4.65		9.8%	22.7%	3.4%	38.2%					.294	.558	105	0.1

2023 Arsenal: FA (93.9), SW (82.1), SL (85.4), SI (93.3), CH (87.6) Comps: Nick Nelson (80), Rogelio Armenteros (80), Daniel Mengden (78)

The Giants' third-round pick in 2021, Black has been steady but not dominant across High-A, Double-A and Triple-A as he mixes two fastball shapes and two slider shapes, as well as the occasional changeup. His drop-and-drive delivery gives him a flat approach angle to get whiffs with his 94-mph four-seamer, despite it having notable arm-side run, and he will shave off some carry for a somewhat distinct sinker. At the start of 2023, he was messing with a sweeper and more crossfire in his delivery, but he straightened out the approach and reintegrated the gyro slider ahead of a strong mid-season run that got him out of the muggy Richmond summer. The purer heat of Sacramento sent his walk rate up from 8.3% to 12.0%, but the average Pacific Coast League walk rate was at 12.3%, so it's not as if he was ridiculously wild. With 13 Triple-A starts under his belt, Black is pretty close to auditioning for the Giants rotation. Breaking ball consistency has long been the question here, and that remains the case; most of his wild misses come with wide variance in the shape of both slides, and it's also why he doesn't get many in-zone whiffs. There's a decent argument for him to just drop the sinker, too, since it doesn't have enough run or sink to collect ground balls.

Alex Cobb RHP Born: 10/07/87 Age: 36 Height: 6'3" Weight: 205 Origin: Round 4, 2006 Draft (#109 overall)

YEAR	TM	LVL	AGE	G(GS)	IP	W-L	SV	K	WHIP	ERA	CSP	BB%	K%	HR%	GB%	ZSw%	ZCon%	OSw%	OCon%	BABIP	SLGCON	DRA-	WARP
2021	LAA	MLB	33	18(18)	93¹	8-3	0	98	1.26	3.76	50.4%	8.4%	24.9%	1.3%	53.3%	60.0%	85.3%	35.9%	62.4%	.316	.465	85	1.6
2022	SF	MLB	34	28(28)	149²	7-8	0	151	1.30	3.73	53.2%	6.8%	23.9%	1.4%	60.3%	61.2%	87.7%	34.1%	60.5%	.338	.473	65	4.0
2023	SF	MLB	35	28(28)	151¹	7-7	0	131	1.32	3.87	46.3%	5.7%	20.3%	2.9%	57.2%	62.0%	88.5%	33.7%	66.1%	.319	.557	89	2.7
2024 DC	SF	MLB	36	21(21)	113²	7-7	0	95	1.32	4.02	49.4%	7.2%	19.6%	2.2%	55.5%					.307	.487	93	1.5

2023 Arsenal: SI (94.4), FS (89.4), KC (83.5), SW (86), FA (95) Comps: Freddy Garcia (77), Tim Hudson (75), Justin Verlander (73)

Cobb's 2023 contains one of the great games in major-league history: five innings, three runs, seven strikeouts, and no walks in Mexico City—situated at 7,349 feet above sea level. Most remarkably, he allowed only one home run to 22 batters, whereas no other pitcher in the pair of games faced more than 15 without allowing multiple. No one took on more than eight opponents without allowing one long fly. It's concerning that all of Cobb's pitches got hit harder in 2023 than 2022, and also that his strikeout and ground-ball rates fell notably, and also that he's a 36-year-old who underwent major hip surgery at the end of October. But none of that will get recorded in the Hall of Fame, or the career retrospective, and the Mexico City game will (or at least *should*).

Reggie Crawford LHP Born: 12/04/00 Age: 23 Height: 6'4" Weight: 235 Origin: Round 1, 2022 Draft (#30 overall)

YEAR	TM	LVL	AGE	G(GS)	IP	W-L	SV	K	WHIP	ERA	CSP	BB%	K%	HR%	GB%	ZSw%	ZCon%	OSw%	OCon%	BABIP	SLGCON	DRA-	WARP
2023	SJ	A	22	7(7)	11	0-0	0	18	1.18	4.09		8.7%	39.1%	6.5%	60.9%					.300	.870	75	0.2
2023	EUG	A+	22	6(6)	8	0-0	0	14	1.50	1.13		16.7%	38.9%	0.0%	20.0%					.400	.467	86	0.1
2024 non	SF	MLB	23	58(0)	50	2-2	0	52	1.50	5.42		12.2%	23.3%	3.9%	36.1%					.294	.603	118	-0.3

Comps: Andy Otero (26), Jorge Benitez (26), Nick Dombkowski (26)

Crawford was never going to rack up the innings after pitching fewer than 15 total in each of the previous three years, but because of spring mononucleosis and an August oblique issue, he ended up with a mere 19 frames in his first pro season. That the oblique issue seems to have followed his first appearance as a hitter in nearly two months likely foreshadows the end of the two-way experiment, though he did get perhaps a last chance with the bat after being sent to the Arizona Fall League in a hitter-only capacity. The lack of innings will likely always make it difficult to bet on him being a starter, but the stuff—a mid-90s fastball and power slurve, primarily—is still there for major-league success.

Camilo Doval RHP Born: 07/04/97 Age: 27 Height: 6'2" Weight: 185 Origin: IFA, 2015

YEAR	TM	LVL	AGE	G(GS)	IP	W-L	SV	K	WHIP	ERA	CSP	BB%	K%	HR%	GB%	ZSw%	ZCon%	OSw%	OCon%	BABIP	SLGCON	DRA-	WARP
2021	SAC	AAA	23	28(0)	30²	3-0	1	44	1.70	4.99		16.7%	30.6%	2.1%	50.7%					.362	.611	86	0.4
2021	SF	MLB	23	29(0)	27	5-1	3	37	1.04	3.00	53.1%	8.3%	33.9%	3.7%	50.0%	62.2%	84.3%	33.0%	43.2%	.259	.532	74	0.6
2022	SF	MLB	24	68(0)	67²	6-6	27	80	1.24	2.53	51.5%	10.5%	28.0%	1.4%	57.2%	66.7%	81.4%	34.5%	54.2%	.298	.470	77	1.5
2023	SF	MLB	25	69(0)	67²	6-6	39	87	1.14	2.93	44.5%	9.3%	31.0%	1.1%	51.9%	68.3%	77.6%	32.7%	50.0%	.308	.446	78	1.5
2024 DC	SF	MLB	26	66(0)	70	5-7	33	86	1.22	3.29	48.2%	10.6%	29.1%	2.1%	51.6%					.290	.491	77	1.2

2023 Arsenal: SL (89), FA (99.8), SI (98) Comps: Ken Giles (85), Kelvin Herrera (82), Henry Alberto Rodriguez (82)

Doval opened the season with more carry on his four-seamer (often called a cutter), getting strikeouts commensurate with his velocity. Over the course of 2023, that carry evaporated until September saw the lowest four-seamer induced vertical break of Doval's career, with his delivery getting progressively more slingy. That caused issues throughout the second half as the four-seamer stole usage from his excellent slider; Doval's K-rate dropped from 33.5% to 27.0%, which is too significant a decrease to offset a 2% dip in walk rate. The loss of carry also brought a decline in pop ups, and accordingly a 75-point increase in opponents' BABIP. Still, for as negative as this might sound, Doval retained an ERA under 3.50 after the All-Star break. As such, he's still the closer, and still a very good one.

★ ★ ★ *2024 Top 101 Prospect* **#44** ★ ★ ★

Kyle Harrison LHP Born: 08/12/01 Age: 22 Height: 6'2" Weight: 200 Origin: Round 3, 2020 Draft (#85 overall)

YEAR	TM	LVL	AGE	G (GS)	IP	W-L	SV	K	WHIP	ERA	CSP	BB%	K%	HR%	GB%	ZSw%	ZCon%	OSw%	OCon%	BABIP	SLGCON	DRA-	WARP
2021	SJ	A	19	23(23)	98²	4-3	0	157	1.40	3.19		11.8%	35.7%	0.7%	49.1%					.393	.547	82	1.6
2022	EUG	A+	20	7(7)	29	0-1	0	59	1.00	1.55		8.5%	50.0%	1.7%	43.8%					.378	.574	63	0.8
2022	RIC	AA	20	18(18)	84	4-2	0	127	1.18	3.11		11.2%	36.4%	3.2%	34.1%					.301	.614	84	1.8
2023	SAC	AAA	21	20(20)	65²	1-3	0	105	1.52	4.66		16.3%	35.6%	3.4%	36.5%	58.3%	72.5%	25.7%	53.2%	.331	.759	76	1.2
2023	SF	MLB	21	7(7)	34²	1-1	0	35	1.15	4.15	49.4%	7.5%	23.8%	5.4%	27.8%	67.4%	82.4%	28.7%	64.9%	.236	.625	121	0.0
2024 DC	*SF*	*MLB*	*22*	*24(24)*	*109¹*	*5-7*	*0*	*124*	*1.31*	*4.16*	*49.4%*	*11.9%*	*26.4%*	*3.3%*	*30.8%*					*.271*	*.550*	*95*	*1.3*

2023 Arsenal: FA (93.5), CU (82.2), CH (86.7), SL (86.5), FC (89.2) Comps: Luis Severino (70), Deivi García (66), Jacob Turner (64)

Harrison debuted with a reputation for strikeouts and wildness but was largely the opposite in his seven starts. In the first three, Harrison used his exceptionally flat vertical approach angle and solid fastball carry to rack up 27 whiffs on 70 swings—nearly double the average fastball whiff rate, and truly otherworldly for a starter throwing fastballs 68.8% of the time. Only 14 whiffs in 95 swings followed, as Harrison's velo and carry gradually declined, with his release point moving further out and lower with each start. Late-season fatigue and mechanical issues are reasonable explanations, but Harrison may have lost his best stuff in the search for better command. His in-zone rate was a steady and expectedly below-average 44.5% in the first three outings, and shot up to 56.3% thereafter. Assuming Harrison's fastball whiffs return, he still has to figure out a second pitch. His slurvy primary breaker hasn't worked well in Triple-A or MLB because it's too slow (82 mph), with too much break to fool batters into swinging. The cutter-ish gyro slider he's toyed with looks pretty good, but it's not clear he can throw it for strikes. There's also a changeup that he doesn't trust but which has some promising moments. It's a lot of moving parts for a 22-year-old with big expectations, though it's likely he'll get plenty of big-league starts this year to figure things out.

Sean Hjelle RHP Born: 05/07/97 Age: 27 Height: 6'11" Weight: 228 Origin: Round 2, 2018 Draft (#45 overall)

YEAR	TM	LVL	AGE	G (GS)	IP	W-L	SV	K	WHIP	ERA	CSP	BB%	K%	HR%	GB%	ZSw%	ZCon%	OSw%	OCon%	BABIP	SLGCON	DRA-	WARP
2021	RIC	AA	24	14(14)	65²	3-2	0	69	1.20	3.15		6.9%	25.2%	2.9%	55.2%					.299	.517	93	0.8
2021	SAC	AAA	24	10(10)	53¹	2-6	0	35	1.80	5.74		11.7%	14.1%	2.4%	54.6%					.345	.563	111	-0.1
2022	SAC	AAA	25	22(22)	97	6-8	0	80	1.55	4.92		8.6%	18.1%	2.5%	56.1%	66.4%	90.2%	28.0%	58.5%	.334	.561	103	0.4
2022	SF	MLB	25	8(0)	25	1-2	0	28	1.64	5.76	59.1%	7.0%	24.3%	2.6%	59.0%	63.3%	89.3%	25.7%	58.5%	.400	.577	82	0.5
2023	SAC	AAA	26	22(19)	93	3-7	0	70	1.53	6.00		9.5%	16.7%	3.3%	55.5%	63.6%	88.7%	25.9%	59.6%	.313	.579	99	1.1
2023	SF	MLB	26	15(0)	29	2-1	0	31	1.76	6.52	48.1%	9.4%	22.3%	2.2%	52.7%	64.1%	90.6%	30.1%	57.8%	.402	.618	90	0.5
2024 DC	*SF*	*MLB*	*27*	*54(6)*	*78*	*4-4*	*0*	*60*	*1.51*	*5.25*	*52.7%*	*8.8%*	*17.1%*	*2.4%*	*53.0%*					*.321*	*.514*	*115*	*-0.1*

2023 Arsenal: SI (94.9), SL (85.6), CH (89.9) Comps: Casey Kelly (62), Andrew Suárez (61), Shaun Anderson (60)

Hjelle was the talk of the spring as a new, sharper version of his knuckle-curve and some new velocity sent the sinkerballer's K-rate through the roof. Unfortunately, as soon as the season began it was clear he could not control this shape, repeatedly missing to the same down-and-away location. Four wild pitches and five hit-by-pitches in 15 relief appearances is no easy feat. When combined with poor strand and batted-ball luck, Hjelle looked unusable at times for Gabe Kapler, but he still ended the season with reasonable peripherals. He will always run higher walk rates than most sinkerballers because unusual release points make batters cautious, but the best version of Hjelle is a fairly straightforward vision of pounding the zone with sinkers, clipping the corner with knuckling curves and standing four or five feet taller than anyone in the vicinity.

Luke Jackson RHP Born: 08/24/91 Age: 32 Height: 6'2" Weight: 210 Origin: Round 1, 2010 Draft (#45 overall)

YEAR	TM	LVL	AGE	G (GS)	IP	W-L	SV	K	WHIP	ERA	CSP	BB%	K%	HR%	GB%	ZSw%	ZCon%	OSw%	OCon%	BABIP	SLGCON	DRA-	WARP
2021	ATL	MLB	29	71(0)	63²	2-2	0	70	1.16	1.98	55.2%	11.1%	26.8%	2.3%	52.5%	67.6%	84.2%	36.7%	53.7%	.255	.459	84	1.1
2023	SF	MLB	31	33(0)	33¹	2-2	0	43	1.23	2.97	45.3%	10.5%	30.1%	2.1%	51.2%	69.4%	80.7%	35.2%	55.0%	.284	.518	84	0.7
2024 DC	*SF*	*MLB*	*32*	*60(0)*	*63²*	*4-2*	*0*	*69*	*1.27*	*3.59*	*48.5%*	*10.2%*	*25.8%*	*2.3%*	*52.2%*					*.289*	*.488*	*83*	*0.8*

2023 Arsenal: SL (87.3), FA (94.5), CU (83) Comps: Jeremy Jeffress (60), Liam Hendriks (50), Fernando Rodney (50)

Jackson's fastball velocity was slightly down in his return from Tommy John surgery, sitting 94.5 mph on average rather than 95.8, and it both did and did not affect his results. To argue for the latter, he pushed his slider usage to nearly 70% and picked up a huge whiff rate with the fastball. And to argue for the former, for any four-seamer thrown at least 125 times, he yielded the 13th-worst quality of contact, as measured by xwOBAcon. Because he picked up so, so many whiffs (and also got more called strikes than before), this ends up resembling a tiny sample of 12 batted balls. As such, Jackson's 2.97 ERA overperformed only barely against a 3.20 xERA. But this is still concerning, even forgiving the also large xwOBAcon in 2021, as Jackson finds the zone at a below-average rate and relies almost entirely on getting chases with his excellent slider to prevent walks. One wonders what would happen if batters sat on the fastball and dared Jackson to throw three sliders for strikes: He does have a curveball, but batters love that pitch even more because his slider is already a sharp vertical breaker, so the curve presents as a slower version of what's already been seen. Still, he's a good middle-innings option for a strong bullpen, and a nervy back-end option for a weak one.

Robbie Ray   LHP   Born: 10/01/91   Age: 32   Height: 6'2"   Weight: 225   Origin: Round 12, 2010 Draft (#356 overall)

YEAR	TM	LVL	AGE	G (GS)	IP	W-L	SV	K	WHIP	ERA	CSP	BB%	K%	HR%	GB%	ZSw%	ZCon%	OSw%	OCon%	BABIP	SLGCON	DRA-	WARP
2021	TOR	MLB	29	32 (32)	193¹	13-7	0	248	1.04	2.84	55.3%	6.7%	32.1%	4.3%	37.1%	73.7%	79.2%	35.7%	50.0%	.269	.614	87	3.2
2022	SEA	MLB	30	32 (32)	189	12-12	0	212	1.19	3.71	52.6%	8.0%	27.4%	4.1%	38.5%	75.7%	80.7%	35.2%	54.6%	.284	.604	96	2.2
2023	SEA	MLB	31	1 (1)	3¹	0-1	0	3	2.70	8.10	39.2%	26.3%	15.8%	0.0%	54.5%	76.9%	90.0%	35.4%	69.6%	.364	.500	100	0.0
2024 DC	SF	MLB	32	11 (11)	60	4-4	0	66	1.35	4.57	51.5%	9.4%	25.5%	3.7%	38.6%					.304	.596	104	0.4

2023 Arsenal: FA (93.4), SL (85.5)   *Comps: Jon Lester (78), Mark Langston (76), Gio González (75)*

Motivated by the bitter taste of his unexpected bullpen appearance in the 2022 ALDS, and a prompt dispatch courtesy of one thunderous Yordan Alvarez swing, Ray arrived in Peoria eager to turn to the page. By his third spring training start, Ray's heater was averaging 95 mph—a marked jump from the 91-93 he had exhibited for much of his first year with the M's. He was flashing a promising splitter, introduced as an intriguing complement to the fastball-slider combo for which he was known. The revenge tour appeared to be on track.

Then, after just one start in which he looked out of sorts for 3 ⅓ uninspiring innings, Ray reported soreness and was diagnosed with a flexor tendon strain. Further testing revealed damage to the UCL, prompting season-ending surgery. As highly variable as Ray's performance has been over the years, durability had rarely been a concern. But such is the nature of his profession, and the baseball gods responsible for dictating pitching injuries have never set much store by proper timing. It was the first truly lost season of Ray's career, and will delay the start to this one as well.

Randy Rodríguez   RHP   Born: 09/05/99   Age: 24   Height: 6'0"   Weight: 166   Origin: IFA, 2017

YEAR	TM	LVL	AGE	G (GS)	IP	W-L	SV	K	WHIP	ERA	CSP	BB%	K%	HR%	GB%	ZSw%	ZCon%	OSw%	OCon%	BABIP	SLGCON	DRA-	WARP
2021	SJ	A	21	32 (0)	62	6-3	2	101	1.08	1.74		8.9%	39.1%	0.0%	36.2%					.346	.488	88	0.8
2022	EUG	A+	22	16 (13)	50²	2-3	0	71	1.16	3.38		11.1%	32.9%	2.3%	22.3%					.280	.555	96	0.6
2022	RIC	AA	22	6 (0)	10	0-1	0	19	1.50	6.30		16.7%	39.6%	4.2%	36.8%					.294	.737	77	0.2
2022	SAC	AAA	22	5 (0)	6	0-1	0	7	2.33	10.50		33.3%	21.2%	0.0%	57.1%	57.8%	73.1%	19.8%	57.1%	.214	.214	101	0.0
2023	RIC	AA	23	16 (0)	30¹	2-1	1	40	1.22	2.97		14.0%	31.0%	0.8%	32.4%					.273	.424	96	0.5
2023	SAC	AAA	23	27 (0)	37²	0-1	0	41	1.83	5.73		20.7%	22.9%	1.7%	50.5%	62.4%	80.4%	24.9%	56.4%	.296	.520	88	0.2
2024 DC	SF	MLB	24	35 (0)	38	2-2	0	42	1.58	5.47		14.7%	24.2%	3.2%	34.3%					.297	.577	118	-0.2

2023 Arsenal: FA (96.8), SL (84.4), SI (96.6), CH (89.2)   *Comps: Johan Yan (71), Wilmer Font (71), Ken Giles (68)*

Rodríguez is often compared to Camilo Doval, who also bears down into a slingy release with high velocity, runs huge walk rates and added a sinker to complement his four-seamer. Maybe it will click in the same way someday, but he diverges in two important respects: Doval has a bit more velocity (as well as a truer sinker), and his slider has the more neutral gyro shape that encourages chases, but Rodríguez's slower, almost sweepy breaker encourages batters to lay off. It's almost impossible to run reasonable walk rates while running a swing rate near 40%, even accepting that the automated strike zone made batters more cautious in Triple-A. Rodríguez needs a slider that encourages swings, better slider feel, a truer sinker shape to enable pitching to contact or two out of three, but he's already lost two option years without getting an MLB debut.

Taylor Rogers   LHP   Born: 12/17/90   Age: 33   Height: 6'3"   Weight: 190   Origin: Round 11, 2012 Draft (#340 overall)

YEAR	TM	LVL	AGE	G (GS)	IP	W-L	SV	K	WHIP	ERA	CSP	BB%	K%	HR%	GB%	ZSw%	ZCon%	OSw%	OCon%	BABIP	SLGCON	DRA-	WARP
2021	MIN	MLB	30	40 (0)	40¹	2-4	9	59	1.14	3.35	56.5%	4.8%	35.5%	2.4%	48.5%	63.6%	78.1%	38.1%	60.3%	.366	.600	59	1.3
2022	SD	MLB	31	42 (0)	41¹	1-5	28	48	1.11	4.35	55.1%	5.2%	27.6%	0.6%	44.0%	59.3%	84.3%	33.8%	49.2%	.333	.505	90	0.6
2022	MIL	MLB	31	24 (0)	23	3-3	3	36	1.30	5.48	58.0%	10.0%	36.0%	6.0%	37.3%	54.5%	80.4%	29.5%	48.4%	.318	.896	80	0.5
2023	SF	MLB	32	60 (0)	51²	6-4	2	64	1.24	3.83	48.3%	11.6%	29.6%	2.8%	40.3%	55.6%	82.3%	30.4%	60.1%	.282	.545	86	1.0
2024 DC	SF	MLB	33	60 (0)	63²	4-3	4	77	1.18	3.53	53.2%	8.5%	28.8%	2.9%	42.4%					.292	.543	83	0.8

2023 Arsenal: SL (79.3), SI (93.6), FC (87.3)   *Comps: Justin Wilson (70), Jake Diekman (69), Ryan Pressly (68)*

In the first two weeks of the season, Rogers walked six (31.6% of batters faced), struck out one (5.3%) and allowed two home runs, giving him a variety of unenviable numbers—an 18.90 ERA, 15.86 FIP, 12.02 xFIP and 11.15 SIERA. That was capped off by an April 12 game versus the Dodgers in which he entered with a 3-3 tie in the sixth and walked all four batters faced, inspiring the frustrated twin to calmly deposit his glove in the dugout trash can. Excluding a back-tightness-induced struggle in the final game of the season, Rogers was brilliant from then on, with an ERA of 2.25 and strong peripherals, mostly due to an extra half-tick of velocity and tighter break on his sweeper. There's still some room for concern because Rogers' velo was down two ticks from 2021 and one from 2022, but he's comfortably making it worthwhile to roster identical twins.

Tyler Rogers   RHP   Born: 12/17/90   Age: 33   Height: 6'3"   Weight: 181   Origin: Round 10, 2013 Draft (#312 overall)

YEAR	TM	LVL	AGE	G (GS)	IP	W-L	SV	K	WHIP	ERA	CSP	BB%	K%	HR%	GB%	ZSw%	ZCon%	OSw%	OCon%	BABIP	SLGCON	DRA-	WARP
2021	SF	MLB	30	80 (0)	81	7-1	13	55	1.07	2.22	56.9%	4.0%	16.9%	1.5%	57.3%	70.0%	86.5%	33.4%	77.6%	.279	.400	79	1.7
2022	SF	MLB	31	68 (0)	75²	3-4	0	49	1.27	3.57	55.2%	7.2%	15.4%	0.9%	55.6%	63.0%	86.8%	28.3%	68.9%	.294	.439	96	0.9
2023	SF	MLB	32	68 (0)	74	4-5	2	60	1.15	3.04	50.7%	6.1%	19.4%	2.3%	52.0%	72.1%	80.4%	31.4%	71.4%	.274	.468	87	1.4
2024 DC	SF	MLB	33	60 (0)	63²	4-3	4	45	1.29	4.04	53.7%	6.6%	16.6%	2.1%	53.0%					.297	.468	93	0.5

2023 Arsenal: SI (82.8), SL (72.9)   *Comps: Blake Parker (74), Hector Neris (69), Brad Brach (69)*

One of the enduring lessons of the 2023 season is that submarine pitchers don't perform as well in the Mexico City elevation: Rogers allowed four earned runs, including a homer, to eight batters against the south-of-the-border Friars. At other elevations, the opposition required 139 plate appearances to tally their first four earned runs, and 171 for the first pair of home runs. Some second-half scuffles still meant that his career total in home runs allowed nearly doubled (from 10 to 17), but Rogers remains a good late-inning option.

Landen Roupp   RHP   Born: 09/10/98   Age: 25   Height: 6'2"   Weight: 205   Origin: Round 12, 2021 Draft (#356 overall)

YEAR	TM	LVL	AGE	G (GS)	IP	W-L	SV	K	WHIP	ERA	CSP	BB%	K%	HR%	GB%	ZSw%	ZCon%	OSw%	OCon%	BABIP	SLGCON	DRA-	WARP
2021	GNTB	ROK	22	4 (0)	6	0-0	0	12	1.00	3.00		4.3%	52.2%	0.0%	57.1%					.500	.600		
2022	SJ	A	23	14 (2)	48²	5-2	0	69	1.03	2.59		8.6%	35.0%	1.0%	49.5%					.295	.477	80	0.7
2022	EUG	A+	23	7 (7)	32¹	3-0	0	52	0.87	1.67		7.2%	41.6%	0.8%	54.7%					.286	.460	79	0.7
2022	RIC	AA	23	5 (5)	26¹	2-1	0	31	1.14	3.76		10.0%	28.2%	2.7%	51.5%					.246	.463	82	0.6
2023	RIC	AA	24	10 (10)	31	0-0	0	42	1.00	1.74		7.5%	35.0%	0.8%	45.5%					.323	.477	78	0.7
2024 non	SF	MLB	25	58 (0)	50	2-2	0	55	1.33	4.38		9.8%	25.7%	3.3%	40.6%					.298	.574	99	0.3

Comps: Domingo Acevedo (76), Erik Davis (72), Mike Baumann (72)

A 12th-round pick in 2021 after four years at UNC Wilmington, Roupp had perhaps the best results of any minor-league pitcher in 2022, posting big strikeout rates, ground-ball rates over 50% and reasonable walk rates across three levels—all despite beginning the year as the back-half of a tandem starting combo. He returned to Double-A for the 2023 season and dealt with repeated leg issues that prevented him from ever getting enough momentum for a promotion, but was just as dominant when on the field. In 10 starts, Roupp had excellent numbers and backed them up with matching estimators (2.15 FIP, 2.61 xFIP, 80 DRA-). He does it mostly with a beautiful sweeping curveball, which isn't thrown particularly hard but mirrors exceptionally with a low-to-mid 90s sinker, as Tieran Alexander described for Prospects Live in November of 2022. He can manipulate the curve into a sweeper and does have a changeup, and how he rounds out the repertoire will likely dictate whether his MLB future is at the end of a rotation or in the bullpen. Roupp is already 25 years old and clearly ready for the daunting Pacific Coast League, so he should be part of the Giants' pitching depth moving forward.

Carson Seymour   RHP   Born: 12/16/98   Age: 25   Height: 6'6"   Weight: 260   Origin: Round 6, 2021 Draft (#172 overall)

YEAR	TM	LVL	AGE	G (GS)	IP	W-L	SV	K	WHIP	ERA	CSP	BB%	K%	HR%	GB%	ZSw%	ZCon%	OSw%	OCon%	BABIP	SLGCON	DRA-	WARP
2022	SLU	A	23	7 (4)	30¹	4-0	0	27	1.05	1.19		7.3%	22.0%	0.0%	60.7%	70.0%	84.9%	33.1%	56.7%	.277	.301	101	0.5
2022	BRK	A+	23	11 (9)	51¹	1-5	0	65	1.11	3.68		5.7%	30.7%	3.8%	55.3%					.298	.583	82	0.9
2022	EUG	A+	23	6 (6)	29¹	2-3	0	43	1.19	3.99		8.0%	34.4%	0.8%	50.7%					.358	.455	82	0.5
2023	RIC	AA	24	28 (23)	112²	5-3	0	114	1.23	3.99		9.2%	24.5%	1.7%	49.0%					.297	.490	91	2.2
2024 DC	SF	MLB	25	10 (0)	12²	1-1	0	11	1.43	4.88		9.2%	19.8%	3.0%	42.5%					.305	.538	109	0.0

Comps: Alec Mills (78), Sean Hjelle (76), John Simms (76)

Seymour joined the Giants as part of the Darin Ruf trade and exploded for a 34.4% strikeout rate in his time with High-A Eugene, alongside a big ground-ball rate. For his first six starts of 2023 at Double-A Richmond, the velocity was down a bit and he was getting less than 10% of opposing batters to K. In an interview with Giants prospect expert Roger Munter, Seymour said he was having trouble keeping on muscle—sure enough, he exhibited a clear improvement over the course of the season. His next eight starts saw a 20% strikeout rate, and his final 13 got all the way up to 34.1%. That puts him on a course to the majors sooner rather than later, where his mid-90s fastball and hard slider should play. He's generally evaluated as a future reliever, but Seymour has controlled the walks well enough in the minors (9.2% in 2023) to stay in the rotation for now; he also toys with a second fastball shape, another breaking ball shape and a changeup.

Ross Stripling   RHP   Born: 11/23/89   Age: 34   Height: 6'1"   Weight: 215   Origin: Round 5, 2012 Draft (#176 overall)

YEAR	TM	LVL	AGE	G (GS)	IP	W-L	SV	K	WHIP	ERA	CSP	BB%	K%	HR%	GB%	ZSw%	ZCon%	OSw%	OCon%	BABIP	SLGCON	DRA-	WARP
2021	TOR	MLB	31	24 (19)	101¹	5-7	0	94	1.27	4.80	57.5%	7.0%	21.8%	5.3%	35.4%	71.4%	83.1%	28.5%	61.9%	.270	.641	115	0.1
2022	TOR	MLB	32	32 (24)	134¹	10-4	1	111	1.02	3.01	55.8%	3.7%	20.7%	2.2%	44.2%	69.5%	84.3%	38.1%	66.1%	.269	.453	86	2.3
2023	GNTO	ROK	33	2 (2)	6	0-1	0	6	1.33	4.50		3.7%	22.2%	0.0%	65.0%					.350	.421		
2023	SF	MLB	33	22 (11)	89	0-5	0	70	1.35	5.36	49.2%	4.2%	18.4%	5.2%	44.4%	69.7%	81.1%	32.9%	69.4%	.308	.616	102	1.0
2024 DC	SF	MLB	34	28 (28)	126²	6-9	0	102	1.30	4.37	53.4%	5.7%	19.1%	3.2%	42.3%					.307	.542	101	0.9

2023 Arsenal: SL (87.2), CH (83.7), FA (92.6), KC (75.9), SI (90.3)   Comps: Kevin Jarvis (69), Jordan Zimmermann (69), Ed Whitson (69)

Stripling followed up arguably the best season of his career by allowing 20 home runs in 89 innings. The primary issue was that his fastball shape regressed considerably amid season-long back issues, falling from 18.8 inches of induced vertical break to 17.3 while also shedding a few inches of horizontal movement (though it oddly picked up a lot of whiffs despite getting crushed on contact). His changeup and sinker also regressed, while the slider and knuckle-curve looked about the same. There were just two positives to take away: In his first stint off the IL (for a back strain), Stripling went 46 innings with just one walk allowed, a level of command that allows for success despite bad stuff; similarly, his season-long strikeout and walk rates were quite close to an impressive 2022. In his second return off the IL after suffering the same malady, his velocity was as high as it had ever been in his big-league career, even if it was only three games and the shapes were awful. Looking only at the middle 10 appearances, there's room for optimism.

Thomas Szapucki   LHP   Born: 06/12/96   Age: 28   Height: 6'2"   Weight: 210   Origin: Round 5, 2015 Draft (#149 overall)

YEAR	TM	LVL	AGE	G (GS)	IP	W-L	SV	K	WHIP	ERA	CSP	BB%	K%	HR%	GB%	ZSw%	ZCon%	OSw%	OCon%	BABIP	SLGCON	DRA-	WARP
2021	SYR	AAA	25	10 (9)	41²	0-4	0	41	1.68	4.10		14.5%	21.2%	2.6%	36.1%					.322	.546	114	0.3
2021	NYM	MLB	25	1 (0)	3²	0-0	0	4	2.73	14.73	49.1%	15.0%	20.0%	10.0%	38.5%	73.1%	78.9%	21.4%	58.3%	.455	1.154	116	0.0
2022	SYR	AAA	26	18 (16)	64	2-6	0	87	1.30	3.38		10.8%	32.3%	1.9%	44.6%					.343	.554	73	1.8
2022	SAC	AAA	26	7 (0)	8¹	0-0	0	15	1.20	1.08		8.8%	44.1%	0.0%	37.5%	63.6%	65.3%	26.1%	39.1%	.438	.500	79	0.1
2022	SF	MLB	26	10 (0)	13²	0-0	0	16	1.17	1.98	56.4%	7.4%	29.6%	3.7%	32.4%	67.6%	80.3%	30.7%	69.0%	.313	.676	99	0.1
2022	NYM	MLB	26	1 (1)	1¹	0-1	0	2	7.50	60.75	47.7%	23.1%	15.4%	30.8%	12.5%	64.3%	100.0%	22.9%	50.0%	.750	2.750	143	0.0
2024 non	SF	MLB	28	58 (0)	50	2-2	0	50	1.38	4.60	54.0%	11.0%	23.2%	3.4%	34.0%					.283	.553	103	0.2

Comps: T.J. McFarland (49), Nik Turley (47), Sean Gilmartin (46)

Szapucki broke out after the Giants acquired him from the Mets at the 2022 trade deadline and moved him to full-time relief duty, with a sub-two ERA in both Triple-A and MLB plus strong peripherals. He missed all of last season following surgery for Thoracic Outlet Syndrome, and it's a pretty concerning development given his lengthy injury history with the Mets. Still, he's a lefty with an option year remaining and the stuff to fit in the middle of a bullpen—a mid-90s four-seamer and a curveball that bolsters it. He should find his way into the big leagues in 2024, even though the Giants moved him off their 40-man roster for the winter.

Kai-Wei Teng RHP   Born: 12/01/98   Age: 25   Height: 6'4"   Weight: 260   Origin: IFA, 2017

YEAR	TM	LVL	AGE	G(GS)	IP	W-L	SV	K	WHIP	ERA	CSP	BB%	K%	HR%	GB%	ZSw%	ZCon%	OSw%	OCon%	BABIP	SLGCON	DRA-	WARP
2021	EUG	A+	22	21(21)	95²	5-6	0	142	1.35	4.33		12.7%	34.1%	2.6%	47.8%					.328	.597	97	0.9
2022	RIC	AA	23	28(28)	136¹	6-12	0	169	1.52	5.22		13.7%	27.2%	2.3%	46.4%					.323	.591	97	2.0
2023	RIC	AA	24	12(12)	47¹	1-3	0	68	1.23	4.75		9.9%	33.7%	2.0%	40.4%					.340	.624	88	1.0
2023	SAC	AAA	24	17(16)	79	6-5	0	96	1.44	4.22		13.8%	27.6%	1.1%	43.8%	62.9%	80.3%	30.6%	44.8%	.328	.542	77	0.9
2024 DC	SF	MLB	25	28(5)	46¹	2-3	0	52	1.44	4.82		12.8%	25.2%	3.0%	38.5%					.293	.556	106	0.1

2023 Arsenal: SW (86.1), FA (93.2), SI (92), CU (82.3), CH (87)   *Comps: Ariel Peña (78), Pedro Payano (70), Mike Baumann (70)*

I'm convinced that Teng could hit every combination of vertical break and horizontal break if he was asked. Those who are picky about classifying pitches could probably pick up nine distinct offerings, the most common of which would be some form of breaker and sinker. At times, the breaker shows up with cutter movement, other times gyro, other times half or full sweeper and, quite often, as a slurve or traditional 12-6 curveball. Sometimes it ventures into the unnamed territory of 5+ inches of induced vertical break and 5+ inches of gloveside break, which usually gets classified as a slider. There's also a changeup and four-seamer, though sometimes the four-seam can straighten up a bit more and look like two separate pitches. He's throwing more breakers than hard stuff, so he's naturally out of the zone a lot and walking plenty of batters, but Teng keeps hitters off balance well enough to stick around as a depth piece and eventually get a shot in the majors.

Cole Waites RHP   Born: 06/10/98   Age: 26   Height: 6'3"   Weight: 180   Origin: Round 18, 2019 Draft (#536 overall)

YEAR	TM	LVL	AGE	G(GS)	IP	W-L	SV	K	WHIP	ERA	CSP	BB%	K%	HR%	GB%	ZSw%	ZCon%	OSw%	OCon%	BABIP	SLGCON	DRA-	WARP
2022	EUG	A+	24	13(0)	12²	1-1	1	27	1.11	3.55		7.7%	51.9%	1.9%	42.9%					.450	.667	70	0.3
2022	RIC	AA	24	18(0)	21	2-2	4	38	1.29	1.71		16.3%	41.3%	0.0%	34.2%					.324	.389	75	0.6
2022	SAC	AAA	24	7(0)	8	1-0	1	11	0.75	0.00		10.7%	39.3%	0.0%	50.0%	64.0%	71.9%	29.7%	63.6%	.214	.286	84	0.1
2022	SF	MLB	24	7(0)	5²	0-0	0	4	1.76	3.18	55.4%	16.0%	16.0%	4.0%	41.2%	75.0%	90.9%	31.7%	68.4%	.313	.765	112	0.0
2023	SAC	AAA	25	32(3)	30²	3-4	1	32	1.73	6.16		18.8%	22.2%	2.1%	35.3%	64.4%	81.6%	30.0%	51.4%	.280	.524	120	0.1
2023	SF	MLB	25	3(0)	2¹	0-0	0	2	3.43	15.43	49.9%	13.3%	13.3%	0.0%	54.5%	75.0%	81.0%	27.0%	80.0%	.545	.636	100	0.0
2024 non	SF	MLB	26	58(0)	50	2-2	0	54	1.49	4.93	53.0%	13.9%	24.3%	3.4%	38.3%					.283	.563	108	0.0

2023 Arsenal: FA (95.9), SL (83.5)   *Comps: James Bourque (49), Ricardo Rodríguez (49), Ariel Hernández (48)*

Waites' fastball looks like an 80-grade pitch, sitting above 95 mph with 18 inches of induced vertical break (carry), an extremely flat vertical approach angle (-4.1), and over seven feet of extension when things are right. He had a chance to break camp in the big-league bullpen but missed most of the spring with a lat strain and never looked right, with wide swings in velocity, pitch shape and even release point. Most puzzlingly, his fastball just never got any whiffs, and while his slider certainly lets batters sit on the four-seam, that rarely mattered in past years. Waites probably needs better command or a new secondary to be a meaningful MLB reliever, but that will have to wait after a right elbow strain turned into Tommy John surgery in September.

Ryan Walker RHP   Born: 11/26/95   Age: 28   Height: 6'2"   Weight: 200   Origin: Round 31, 2018 Draft (#916 overall)

YEAR	TM	LVL	AGE	G(GS)	IP	W-L	SV	K	WHIP	ERA	CSP	BB%	K%	HR%	GB%	ZSw%	ZCon%	OSw%	OCon%	BABIP	SLGCON	DRA-	WARP
2021	EUG	A+	25	31(0)	40	1-0	0	56	1.23	4.28		5.8%	32.7%	2.3%	50.0%					.357	.680	81	0.7
2022	RIC	AA	26	43(0)	45²	7-2	2	56	1.34	3.35		11.8%	27.5%	0.5%	53.3%					.305	.397	85	0.9
2022	SAC	AAA	26	7(0)	7¹	0-1	0	9	1.77	6.14		7.9%	23.7%	0.0%	48.0%	62.7%	92.9%	32.0%	54.2%	.400	.500	95	0.1
2023	SAC	AAA	27	15(3)	20¹	1-0	1	23	0.84	0.89		10.8%	31.1%	0.0%	50.0%	58.3%	80.2%	24.9%	55.8%	.214	.310	81	0.4
2023	SF	MLB	27	49(13)	61¹	5-3	1	78	1.39	3.23	47.4%	9.1%	29.7%	3.0%	42.8%	60.5%	80.8%	35.2%	52.7%	.356	.632	76	1.4
2024 DC	SF	MLB	28	48(0)	50²	3-2	0	59	1.28	3.89	47.4%	9.4%	27.1%	2.7%	42.4%					.304	.541	90	0.6

2023 Arsenal: SW (83.2), SI (94.8)   *Comps: Tim Peterson (65), Juan Jaime (61), Adam Cimber (61)*

Starting from the extreme first base side of the rubber, Walker steps toward the third base dugout, makes eye contact with the manager and then squares his hips toward home plate, sometimes hitting 98 mph. His mid-90s sinker has slightly positive induced vertical break and veers 14.4 inches to the arm side, while the low-80s slider has slightly positive induced vertical break and veers 14.6 inches glove side. Among righty non-sidearmers, Walker's slider had the second-most extreme horizontal approach angle of any pitch, at -6.0 (min. 50 pitches). The result was one of the best relievers in baseball, with a 76 DRA- that ranked between Andrés Muñoz and Devin Williams. Additionally, Walker's usage was quite versatile: He served as an opener in 13 of 49 appearances, got at least seven outs on five occasions and didn't require the careful platoon usage expected of those with unusual deliveries.

Logan Webb RHP   Born: 11/18/96   Age: 27   Height: 6'1"   Weight: 220   Origin: Round 4, 2014 Draft (#118 overall)

YEAR	TM	LVL	AGE	G(GS)	IP	W-L	SV	K	WHIP	ERA	CSP	BB%	K%	HR%	GB%	ZSw%	ZCon%	OSw%	OCon%	BABIP	SLGCON	DRA-	WARP
2021	SF	MLB	24	27(26)	148¹	11-3	0	158	1.11	3.03	53.7%	6.0%	26.5%	1.5%	60.9%	61.0%	85.9%	37.1%	55.8%	.312	.466	63	4.3
2022	SF	MLB	25	32(32)	192¹	15-9	0	163	1.16	2.90	52.9%	6.2%	20.7%	1.4%	56.6%	63.7%	87.2%	35.5%	61.9%	.294	.446	82	3.6
2023	SF	MLB	26	33(33)	216	11-13	0	194	1.07	3.25	48.2%	3.6%	22.8%	2.4%	62.0%	62.7%	89.9%	36.8%	67.0%	.303	.491	74	5.5
2024 DC	SF	MLB	27	29(29)	189¹	14-10	0	146	1.22	3.43	50.6%	5.8%	18.5%	1.7%	59.3%					.298	.449	81	3.6

2023 Arsenal: CH (87.5), SI (92.3), SL (84.3), FA (92.7)   *Comps: Dan Haren (79), Roy Halladay (78), Matt Garza (77)*

It's appropriate Webb comes near the end of this chapter because, well, what is there to say? People thought he was good, and he proved them right again. Maybe there were some who worried about the jump from a 63 DRA- breakout in 2021 to an 82 in 2022, but that latter figure isn't exactly dire. The Cy Young field was slightly weaker last year, enough for the midpoint 74 DRA- to stand out as exceptional. Of course, what truly stands out is the volume of innings. If Game 162 had been more important, he would have needed to last just four frames to exceed 220 on the season, a mark only met three times in the last six full seasons. The only downside here is that there is just one repeat appearance (Justin Verlander, who then needed TJ the following summer) among the 15 player seasons of 210+ innings in that span. It's not just injury risk, but also sequencing fortune; Webb had the second-fewest pitches per inning among qualified starters, and there isn't much stability to that statistic.

★ ★ ★ *2024 Top 101 Prospect* **#68** ★ ★ ★

Carson Whisenhunt LHP   Born: 10/20/00   Age: 23   Height: 6'3"   Weight: 209   Origin: Round 2, 2022 Draft (#66 overall)

YEAR	TM	LVL	AGE	G (GS)	IP	W-L	SV	K	WHIP	ERA	CSP	BB%	K%	HR%	GB%	ZSw%	ZCon%	OSw%	OCon%	BABIP	SLGCON	DRA-	WARP
2023	SJ	A	22	4 (4)	13²	0-0	0	20	1.17	3.29		7.0%	35.1%	1.8%	50.0%					.355	.562	72	0.3
2023	EUG	A+	22	6 (6)	25¹	1-0	0	36	0.67	1.42		8.5%	38.3%	1.1%	35.4%					.170	.292	82	0.4
2023	RIC	AA	22	6 (6)	19²	0-1	0	27	1.37	3.20		13.1%	32.1%	1.2%	41.3%					.333	.543	81	0.5
2024 non	SF	MLB	23	58 (0)	50	2-2	0	54	1.36	4.45		10.8%	25.1%	3.4%	35.5%					.289	.566	100	0.2

Comps: Alec Hansen (64), Sean Newcomb (64), Tyler Ivey (62)

Whisenhunt was completely dominant in the lower minors, including a stretch where he allowed one hit or fewer in six of seven starts. A June promotion to Double-A yielded slightly diminished velocity and admissions of fatigue—he didn't pitch much in his draft year due to a collegiate PED suspension, and the season ended with the scare of an elbow sprain. Still, it was a successful campaign that set him up for a possible big-league debut in 2024. That may seem ambitious for a pitcher who walked five per nine innings in a half-dozen starts above A-ball, but lefties with great changeups don't really abide by normal development timelines. The remaining obstacles for Whisenhunt are fastball shape, fastball command and a breaking ball. He'll need improvement in one or both of the latter in order to make the jump to the majors in 2024.

Keaton Winn RHP   Born: 02/20/98   Age: 26   Height: 6'4"   Weight: 238   Origin: Round 5, 2018 Draft (#136 overall)

YEAR	TM	LVL	AGE	G (GS)	IP	W-L	SV	K	WHIP	ERA	CSP	BB%	K%	HR%	GB%	ZSw%	ZCon%	OSw%	OCon%	BABIP	SLGCON	DRA-	WARP
2022	SJ	A	24	13 (11)	40²	1-1	0	55	1.33	4.87		9.2%	31.6%	1.7%	50.5%					.357	.616	83	0.5
2022	EUG	A+	24	8 (8)	37	3-2	0	46	1.30	3.16		6.3%	28.9%	1.3%	62.6%					.371	.571	88	0.6
2022	RIC	AA	24	6 (6)	30¹	2-3	0	24	1.35	4.15		4.7%	18.8%	3.1%	40.6%					.341	.558	101	0.4
2023	SAC	AAA	25	17 (14)	58	0-6	0	66	1.59	4.81		9.9%	25.1%	2.7%	47.3%	68.5%	79.4%	32.2%	54.0%	.369	.639	81	1.2
2023	SF	MLB	25	9 (5)	42¹	1-3	1	35	1.04	4.68	50.3%	4.7%	20.3%	3.5%	56.1%	71.5%	78.7%	39.0%	57.5%	.259	.537	89	0.8
2024 DC	SF	MLB	26	33 (23)	103¹	4-7	0	101	1.37	4.45	50.3%	8.0%	22.5%	2.3%	50.8%					.323	.526	100	0.8

2023 Arsenal: FS (88.8), FA (96.1), SI (95.4), SL (85.7) *Comps: Shane Greene (67), Colin Rea (64), Josh Collmenter (63)*

Winn probably throws more splitters than anyone else ever has. In his first 42 ⅓ MLB innings, they made up 55.4% of his pitches, easily beating Alex Cobb's 2022 mark of 42.5% for the most on record by someone who turns the lineup over. He gets whiffs, he gets chases, he gets ground balls (58% in MLB) and he's consistently in and around the zone. The problem here is how many of those whiffs are real and can turn into strikeouts. Both of Winn's 95+ mph fastball types allowed a good deal more contact in Triple-A than MLB, and his four-seamer gets crushed on contact because he's throwing from an elevated release with limited carry. His sinker has a pretty generic shape, too. What has most prospect writers pushing Winn to the bullpen is that he has never really had a breaking ball that he trusts: He had already thrown 185 MLB pitches before his first breaker, and he only added one more in his next 145. As such, the 6.3% slider usage in September was close to revolutionary. The shape looks good; it's mid-80s with extra depth and limited horizontal movement. If he can throw it more often or improve one of the fastball shapes, Winn will be a starter, and possibly a very good one. But right now he's in an in-between zone, getting grounders with ease off the sinker and splitter but still giving up extra-base damage due to the four-seamer. In any case, he's a big-league pitcher because he's been able to show batters the same splitter 10 times a night and end up with average results.

LINEOUTS

Hitters

HITTER	POS	TM	LVL	AGE	PA	R	HR	RBI	SB	AVG/OBP/SLG	BABIP	SLGCON	BB%	K%	ZSw%	ZCon%	OSw%	OCon%	LA	90th EV	DRC+	BRR	DRP	WARP
Rayner Arias	OF	DSL GIB	ROK	17	76	19	4	21	4	.414/.539/.793	.455	.979	19.7%	14.5%										
Aeverson Arteaga	SS	EUG	A+	20	546	66	17	73	8	.235/.299/.410	.283	.560	7.3%	24.2%							94	0.5	2.3	1.6
Joey Bart	C	SAC	AAA	26	244	33	6	28	1	.248/.357/.393	.338	.591	12.3%	28.3%	58.7%	83.4%	26.8%	56.8%			84	0.2	-0.3	0.3
	C	SF	MLB	26	95	9	0	5	0	.207/.263/.264	.277	.359	3.2%	24.2%	64.0%	85.4%	37.0%	57.7%	15.3	103.2	76	0.0	2.6	0.3
Vaun Brown	OF	RIC	AA	25	208	27	8	34	15	.221/.284/.421	.324	.714	6.3%	37.5%							67	3.2	1.6	0.2
TJ Hopkins	OF	LOU	AAA	26	393	63	16	55	2	.308/.411/.514	.386	.717	14.0%	23.9%	74.8%	78.0%	28.7%	47.5%			107	2.5	0.5	2.0
	OF	CIN	MLB	26	44	7	0	1	1	.171/.227/.171	.292	.292	4.5%	38.6%	64.3%	77.8%	31.7%	48.5%	-1.6	103.2	58	0.0	0.1	-0.1
Grant McCray	CF	EUG	A+	22	584	101	14	66	52	.255/.360/.417	.357	.638	12.3%	29.3%							92	1.3	3.9	1.7
AJ Pollock	LF/DH	SF	MLB	35	6	0	0	0	0	.000/.000/.000		.000	0.0%	33.3%	58.3%	85.7%	23.5%	75.0%	32.6	99.1	98		0.1	0.0
	LF/DH	SEA	MLB	35	138	15	5	15	0	.173/.225/.323	.181	.423	6.5%	21.7%	72.2%	84.0%	38.5%	60.8%	12.0	103.4	99	0.0	0.0	0.3
Diego Velasquez	MI	SJ	A	19	517	76	8	69	23	.298/.387/.434	.344	.538	10.8%	15.9%							119	-0.5	0.9	3.0
David Villar	IF	SAC	AAA	26	334	54	17	51	5	.272/.371/.498	.335	.722	13.2%	26.6%	68.8%	78.1%	26.8%	53.7%			100	-1.8	-2.3	0.2
	IF	SF	MLB	26	140	15	5	12	1	.145/.236/.315	.173	.494	7.9%	32.1%	61.9%	74.2%	27.7%	38.6%	19.6	103.1	86	-0.1	-0.1	0.1
Brett Wisely	UT	SAC	AAA	24	280	40	6	31	7	.285/.417/.466	.370	.656	16.8%	22.9%	64.9%	84.1%	27.3%	61.0%			100	1.8	0.9	0.7
	UT	SF	MLB	24	131	10	2	8	2	.175/.231/.267	.241	.400	6.9%	30.5%	68.9%	77.4%	40.4%	58.8%	15.1	100.7	71	0.1	0.0	0.0

Rayner Arias received one of the larger bonuses in the 2023 international amateur class and hit a comical .414/.539/.793 in 16 DSL games before he picked up a reported wrist injury in the outfield. Though he's played only center so far, Arias is frequently comped to a young Eloy Jiménez and projects as a corner bat. He's got a chance to skip the ACL entirely and become one of the better prospects in baseball this year. ⓧ **Aeverson Arteaga** raised his ISO and lowered his strikeout rate in the move from Low-A to High-A, but his offense declined anyway because he walked a little less and lost 79 points of BABIP. Still, he's a solid shortstop who will be 21 and (probably) in Double-A. ⓧ The 2022 story of **Joey Bart** was about excellent quality of contact being undone by poor swing decisions and contact abilities, leaving average catcher offense that appeared sustainable (a 92 wRC+ but a 64 DRC+). In 2023, the defense was much better and he was making more contact, but the quality of batted balls was so dreadful that Patrick Bailey quickly took his job during an IL stint. A trade seems probable now that he's out of options and Tom Murphy is in town. ⓧ He struck out a ton and didn't walk much in Double-A, but **Vaun Brown** only got into 50 games due to recovery from offseason knee surgery, subsequent soreness in the spring and an August fracture in his left leg (per Giants prospect expert Roger Munter). He's 26 years old in June, so things are starting to stack up against the owner of 2022's best minor-league batting line (.346/.437/.623, with 23 homers and 44 steals in 103 games). ⓧ A Triple-A slash line that surpassed each component of the vaunted .300/.400/.500 thresholds earned **TJ Hopkins** his big-league debut, but he left the Bats in Louisville, punching out 17 times and tallying just seven hits in 41 at-bats. ⓧ **Grant McCray**'s 2023 at High-A Eugene looked quite similar to his 2022 at Single-A San Jose, with his walk rate rising from 11.9% to 12.3%, strikeout rate rising from 29.2% to 29.3% and BABIP falling from .391 to .357. His power output declined more notably, but was still solid for a good defensive center fielder. Double-A Richmond will be the real test. ⓧ Farhan Zaidi was already testing the limits of the Giants faithful by making **AJ Pollock** and Mark Mathias the trade deadline acquisitions for a team nine games over .500 and in the first Wild Card spot. When Gabe Kapler penciled the 35-year-old into the starting center field slot a week later, the dam broke almost instantly, with Pollock picking up an oblique injury before he could step to the plate. By the time he was healthy again, Mitch Haniger was back, and Pollock was released. ⓧ **Diego Velasquez** finally posted a ground-ball rate below 57% in his third pro season, and it resulted in a solid all-around season for San Jose. It takes quite a bit of imagination to dream on low strikeout rates in Single-A, but he'll be 20 all of this season and the offensive bar at second base isn't very high, not to mention that he's a switch-hitter. ⓧ **David Villar** entered the year as the Giants' slugging third baseman and struggled so much that he only appeared in 16 of the team's final 110 games. He just doesn't have the exit velocities to guarantee the big power needed to justify a passive and whiff-heavy approach, but that might be writing him off too quick: Villar has managed 78 home runs across his last 363 Double-A, Triple-A, and major-league games. ⓧ Presenting something of a conundrum, the only way the Giants can use **Brett Wisely** would be to not use him at all.

Pitchers

PITCHER	TM	LVL	AGE	G (GS)	IP	W-L	SV	K	WHIP	ERA	CSP	BB%	K%	HR%	GB%	ZSw%	ZCon%	OSw%	OCon%	BABIP	SLGCON	DRA-	WARP
Scott Alexander	SF	MLB	33	55 (8)	48¹	7-3	1	31	1.37	4.66	50.6%	5.3%	14.9%	1.0%	60.6%	72.4%	91.0%	36.0%	62.6%	.327	.439	93	0.7
Will Bednar	GNTO	ROK	23	4 (3)	10²	1-2	0	15	1.50	4.22		14.3%	30.6%	0.0%	32.0%					.360	.560		
Hayden Birdsong	SJ	A	21	12 (10)	41²	0-0	0	70	1.34	2.16		12.0%	38.0%	0.0%	41.4%					.391	.547	59	1.2
	EUG	A+	21	8 (7)	36	2-2	0	46	0.92	3.25		6.5%	33.1%	2.9%	35.8%					.260	.562	88	0.4
	RIC	AA	21	8 (8)	23	0-3	0	33	1.48	5.48		12.5%	31.7%	1.9%	29.8%					.345	.625	90	0.4
John Brebbia	SF	MLB	33	40 (10)	38¹	3-5	0	47	1.17	3.99	47.5%	8.7%	29.2%	3.7%	30.0%	68.5%	81.7%	32.8%	59.2%	.266	.598	95	0.5
William Kempner	SJ	A	22	14 (5)	27	1-3	1	29	1.33	4.67		12.1%	23.4%	0.0%	44.6%					.284	.403	105	0.1
	EUG	A+	22	23 (0)	34	3-2	0	47	1.21	2.91		9.0%	32.6%	3.5%	44.3%					.311	.615	78	0.6
Gerelmi Maldonado	SJ	A	19	19 (16)	65	1-1	0	81	1.42	4.71		13.9%	28.2%	1.7%	46.8%					.307	.519	86	0.6
Trevor McDonald	GNTB	ROK	22	4 (4)	8²	0-1	0	11	1.15	1.04		5.7%	31.4%	0.0%	72.7%					.364	.429		
	EUG	A+	22	9 (8)	37²	3-1	0	39	0.85	0.96		5.7%	27.7%	0.7%	73.6%					.256	.319	68	0.7
Erik Miller	RIC	AA	25	6 (0)	10¹	1-0	1	15	0.68	0.87		11.1%	41.7%	0.0%	41.2%					.176	.294	84	0.2
	SAC	AAA	25	48 (0)	52	2-1	14	73	1.31	2.77		18.5%	32.9%	0.9%	41.1%	61.8%	68.6%	29.7%	45.2%	.238	.352	70	0.9
Devin Sweet	ARK	AA	26	27 (0)	35	4-1	5	47	0.91	1.54		5.9%	34.6%	0.7%	32.5%					.291	.392	78	0.9
	TAC	AAA	26	7 (0)	7	0-0	0	7	1.29	2.57		10.0%	23.3%	6.7%	40.0%	56.8%	80.0%	36.8%	52.0%	.222	.600	83	
	OAK	MLB	26	5 (0)	6²	1-0	0	5	1.95	10.80	42.6%	14.7%	14.7%	8.8%	36.4%	70.5%	83.9%	31.0%	65.5%	.263	.773	111	0.0
	SEA	MLB	26	2 (0)	2	0-0	0	1	1.50	9.00	35.4%	11.1%	11.1%	11.1%	42.9%	80.0%	100.0%	39.3%	72.7%	.167	.714	109	0.0

Scott Alexander throws his sinker a ridiculous three-quarters of the time and gets predictable results, which is to say tons of ground balls and very few of the three true outcomes. His 4.66 ERA is mostly attributable to a 57.6% strand rate, as his peripherals all suggested a figure somewhere in the 3.00s. ⓧ Despite back issues spanning the entirety of his first two full pro seasons, it's not as if **Will Bednar** has failed as a prospect. Even acccepting the slightly diminished fastball velocity and awful control as influenced by the bad back, his slider has gotten all the whiffs one might expect from a collegiate star in the lower minors. His brother, David, is the closer for the Pirates, which seems a more likely outcome for Will than taking on a starter's workload unless his back problems are massaged away. ⓧ **Hayden Birdsong** struggles with walks and doesn't get many ground balls, but throws a mid-90s fastball with carry, a hard slider and a solid curveball. He was a reliever for Eastern Illinois in 2022, so more growth could be coming if the shift to the rotation holds, which is quite encouraging after his first full pro season that saw him climb from Single-A to Double-A. ⓧ Through mid-June, **John Brebbia** was enjoying something of a breakout season, with an ERA around 3.00 and peripherals to back it up. When he returned from a lat strain, some home run-rate regression hit and batters were more aggressive on his slider, but he should be able to latch on in middle relief somewhere. ⓧ **R.J. Dabovich** has an untouchable knuckle-curve but struggled for fastball whiffs and velocity over the last two years, with season-ending hip surgery early in 2023 offering a possible explanation. ⓧ **William Kempner** is a sidearmer who throws hard but with little precision. A third-round pick in 2022, he was tried as a starter but quickly moved to the 'pen, where he's excelled enough to earn a promotion to Double-A for a single outing at the end of last season. ⓧ **Gerelmi Maldonado** is a fireballing starter who walked a lot of batters at the lowest level of full-season ball. He could break out further in his age-20 season, or scuffle so much with command that he turns to the bullpen. ⓧ **Trevor McDonald** is a well-rounded starter prospect with a Southern drawl as deep as his repertoire. He's missed a lot of time since being drafted in 2019, though none of it seems to be related to arm issues and he'll still be just 23 this spring. ⓧ **Erik Miller**'s command and fastball shape are hit or miss (literally), but he's a lefty with two good secondaries (slider, changeup) and can scrape 99. His walk rate in Triple-A was bloated, though the average PCL walk rate was over 12%—and higher than that in Sacramento, which was rumored to have a tight automatic strike zone. ⓧ I was told that writing at least one sentence here would get **Sergio Romo** into one last edition of the *Annual*, marking 17 straight, so that's what I did. Congratulations on a wonderful career. ⓧ It took changeup specialist **Devin Sweet** nearly six years to advance from an undrafted prospect to The Show, and his game has always lived in the air for better or worse. In limited major-league usage, no other Athletics pitcher gave up more homers or pop-ups on a rate basis. ⓧ **Joe Whitman** broke out at Kent State, ending up as a possible first-round pick thanks to his slurvy slider. He nearly made it to the third round instead, but put in the sort of strong innings as a pro to suggest that may have been the Giants feasting on the mistakes of others.

SEATTLE MARINERS

Essay by Grant Brisbee

Player comments by Jordan Shusterman and BP staff

It's hard to win 54% of your games over an extended stretch of time.

Since 1977, the Boston Red Sox have won exactly 54% of their regular-season games. During those 46 seasons, they've won five pennants and four World Series, and their winning percentage was the third-best in baseball, behind only the Yankees and Dodgers. It's been a very successful half-century for the Red Sox, with some of the greatest experiences found in professional sports.

Since the Seattle Mariners came into the league in 1977, they've won 47.7% of their games. To get to that same .540 winning percentage the Red Sox have enjoyed, they would have needed to earn almost exactly 10 extra wins per season since the franchise's inception. Those victories sure would have been helpful in a lot of those seasons. Last year's 88-win season would have turned into a 98-win triumph, the dull third-place finish from 2014 would have become a raucous AL West battle. Sure, the Mariners' extra wins in 1995 would have meant an ALDS matchup against the Red Sox, not Yankees, and some serious magic would have been lost. They'd also lose the highlight of Edgar Martinez's double and the magic of watching those highlights over and over for 30 years. But the 2001 Mariners would have gone from charming fluke to legitimate dynasty, and we'd have the thrill of Alvin Davis and Mark Langston, as rookies, clinching a Game 163 on the last day of 1984 by outdueling Tom Seaver in one of those cheap White Sox pullovers.

Jerry Dipoto, Mariners president of baseball operations, knows this. His goal is for the Mariners to win 54% games over any given 10-year stretch, saying "54% is—one year, you're going to win 60%, another year you're going to win 50%. It's whatever it is. But over time, that type of mindset gets you there."

What he was trying to say: *"I have a plan to secure flour, eggs and sugar, and I will continue the deliveries on a regular schedule. Trust in me! I will deliver on this promise and ease your hunger pangs!"*

How it came out: *"Let them eat 54% of their cake."*

Also, there have been several seasons with weevils in the flour and beaks poking out of the eggshells.

SEATTLE MARINERS PROSPECTUS
2023 W-L: 88-74, 3RD IN AL WEST

Pythag	.565	9th	DER	.705	7th
RS/G	4.68	12th	DRC+	95	21st
RA/G	4.07	4th	DRA-	92	5th
dWin%	.526	13th	FIP	3.89	2nd
Payroll	$137M	18th	B-Age	28.4	21st
M$/MW	$3.0M	9th	P-Age	27.6	3rd

401'
378'
381'
331'
326'

- Opened 1999
- Retractable roof
- Natural surface
- Fence profile: 8'

Park Factors

Runs	Runs/RH	Runs/LH	HR/RH	HR/LH
97	98	97	106	112

Top Hitter WARP	4.2 Cal Raleigh
Top Pitcher WARP	3.7 Logan Gilbert
2023 Top Prospect	Harry Ford

Payroll History (in millions)

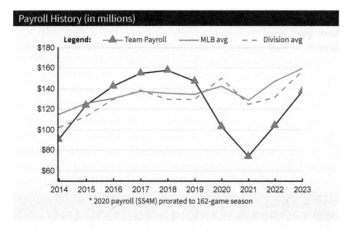

Legend: ▲ Team Payroll — MLB avg - - Division avg

* 2020 payroll ($54M) prorated to 162-game season

Future Commitments (in millions)

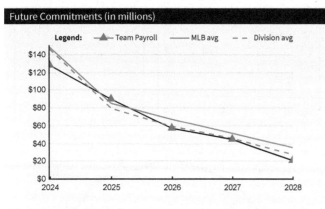

Legend: ▲ Team Payroll — MLB avg - - Division avg

Farm System Ranking

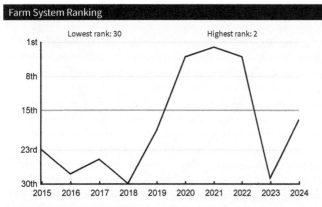

Lowest rank: 30   Highest rank: 2

Personnel

President, Baseball Operations
Jerry Dipoto

Executive Vice President & General Manager, Baseball Operations
Justin Hollander

Assistant General Manager
Andy McKay

Senior Director, Analytics
Jesse Smith

Manager
Scott Servais

BP Alumni
Trevor Andresen
Dave Cameron
John Choiniere

The 54% gaffe was a bumbling, inelegant way of speaking about some uncontroversial baseball truths, like your kid explaining that there are *lots* of times they turn the homework in. But the biggest problem was that the philosophy hasn't always applied to the Mariners under Dipoto's tenure. Sometimes they win 44% of their games and sometimes they win 54%. That's a wee bit different than what Dipoto's stated goal was, even if the 54% seasons have happened more often in recent seasons. (The last time the franchise got to 60, in 2001, Dipoto was a year removed from his final appearance in the majors, in which he didn't throw a pitch. Picked Reggie Sanders off first.)

A better way to frame the philosophy would have been, "We want long-term success. We want to be in it every season. Some years we'll be up and winning 100 games, and some years we'll fall short and finish .500, but we need continuity. We need to go all-in when the roster justifies it, and we need to build up through the farm system at all times. The championships will find us if we do this. Don't panic. Value sustainability. All we are is transactions in the wind."

Dipoto's comments didn't just cause a brouhaha because they were articulated poorly, but because they also ignored the fact that the Mariners' fan experience has been 54% of what they've been hoping for over the years. It's only 54% of what other teams have experienced right in front of them. Diving into the top end of the free-agent market is risky? Here come the Texas Rangers, showing off their fancy new ring and saying things like, "Oh, the World Series? You've never *been*?"[1] The Rangers are a team that took some wild risks and got a parade.

⚾   ⚾   ⚾

Mariners fans have received 54% of what they've been promised, but it's worth appreciating that 54% because it's some of the greatest stuff that baseball can give. Consider the overall baseball experience that the Mariners have offered their fans.

Ken Griffey Jr., the darling of baseball, a worldwide superstar and a cultural pivot point, one of the greatest talents you could ever imagine, playing for your team and grinning the entire time. He was perfect, and everyone knew it.

Alex Rodriguez, who got weird and complicated when he left, but was the purest embodiment of youth, talent and hope since Griffey. They were on the same team together. There was no way it wasn't going to work.

Randy Johnson, a pitcher whose delivery reminded you of a box of toothpicks dropped into a Cuisinart, but who turned into one of the most fearsome pitchers in baseball history.

Ichiro, who excelled in one of the most exciting skills the sport has to offer: Contact. Balls in play. Hittin' 'em where they ain't. There's something about expecting a guy to get a hit and then getting validated for that expectation, with his almost dismissive effortlessness. Those kinds of endorphins are unmatched. Also, he could zip around the bases and throw a sunflower seed through a brick wall, all of which helped with the excitement factor.

Félix Hernández, one of the last practitioners of the old way, a 200-inning maestro who made people excited every time he stepped on the mound. Starting pitchers can still be stars in the modern game, but not like that, not alone. Hernández was one of the last starting pitchers who threw enough to be an absolute phenomenon, like Fernando Valenzuela, Dontrelle Willis or Tim Lincecum. The modern game has moved on from this kind of pitcher, but not without regret.

Julio Rodríguez, a college-age player who's started his career as well as anyone could have possibly expected. He's a maelstrom of baseball talent, signed for the next decade, and he gives the Mariners the best possible chance of shaking President Grohl's hand at the White House in 2034.

This is overlooking some great players, including literal Hall of Famers like Edgar Martinez, but you get the idea. Some teams go decades between players who electrify the fanbase like that. The Mariners have had a mostly uninterrupted string since the '80s. They're leaders in the field of individual baseball spectacles, and don't you forget it.

If half the baseball experience is appreciating the moment, any given moment, and revering the pure, singular baseball talents in front of you, absolute legends who warm your heart while they're playing and for decades after, the Mariners get 100% of that 50%. Heck, they get extra credit. When it comes to the overall experience of a baseball fan, the Mariners have an AP-inflated grade-point average with the players they've enjoyed. They go above the 4.0 GPA. They're at 5.4, easy. Look at those Hall of Fame names cycling through and giving people a reason to watch and fall in love with the sport.

The other 46% of the baseball experience, though, is team success, the kind that hangs on a banner somewhere in the ballpark. Here are the banners the Mariners have hung, physically and metaphorically, over the last half-century:

- A glorious 116-win season (2001)
- Three-time AL West champions (1995, 1997, 2001)
- A super exciting postseason series win, followed by pain (1995)
- A postseason series win that's...pretty hazy, followed by...actually, maybe it's just déjà vu (2000)
- A kinda exciting postseason series win, followed by pain (2001)

Those were fun, but we're talking about a team that's been around for 47 seasons. They're trailing the Diamondbacks in division titles, postseason wins, pennants and

championships, even though the Mariners got a two-decade head start. The Rockies have been to the World Series, and the Mariners haven't. The *Rockies*.

Every team has been to the World Series, except for the Mariners, which means that even the hint of 87 wins, forever and ever, doesn't sound exciting. It sounds like the punishment the Greek gods gave the Mariners for stealing Ken Griffey Jr. from Mount Olympus.

The 46% of pain and malaise has been constant because even though the Mariners have had a cavalcade of baseball icons pass through their orbit, they've often dedicated the rest of the roster to awful ideas and disappointing players. Griffey played for the Mariners (the first time) from 1989 through 1999. During that period, Rich Amaral, Dave Valle, Pete O'Brien and Greg Briley each ranked in the top-20 for plate appearances as a Mariner.

King Félix played for the Mariners from 2005 through 2019, and the most valuable pitchers beside him in the rotation in that time were Hisashi Iwakuma (12.6 WARP over six seasons) and James Paxton (10.6 WARP over six seasons), with a whole lot of eh, meh and yuck after that. Even the pitchers who had good seasons for the Mariners didn't always have good *careers* for them. Consider that Marco Gonzales and Jarrod Washburn combined for 179 starts during the Félix era, and their combined WARP (1.8) was lower than Cliff Lee's career WARP with the Mariners (2.2) in 13 starts. Jason Vargas' WARP in 110 starts was slightly higher than Lee's, but only by decimal points.

The Mariners have forever needed more than Griffey, Ichiro, Félix and now Julio Rodríguez. They needed more Cliff Lees. One time they had the actual Cliff Lee, and they traded him after 13 starts for Blake Beavan, Josh Lueke and Justin Smoak. Some of their Lees broke, like Ryan Anderson and Kyle Lewis. Others were handed away. Never forget that Asdrubal Cabrera and Shin-soo Choo were given away at the deadline for two halves of a first base platoon in two different deals a month apart with *the same team*. When it comes to failure, the Mariners demonstrate an endless supply of ingenuity.

This is the 46-% bogeyman lurking under the bed of every Mariners fan. Winning 54% of your games in baseball over a decade gets you in a good position to win a World Series. A 54-% return on your overall baseball experience is just 87 wins for the soul on a good day.

⚾   ⚾   ⚾

The Mariners are close. That's another reason why the 54% quote was so scandalous to so many people, beyond the fact that it came amidst a naked, early-offseason salary dump that as of this writing has been spent on...Mitch Haniger and Anthony DeSclafani? While saving money along the way, of course. Still, they're closer to being a World Series champion than the Rangers looked like a couple of seasons ago. They're closer than a lot of teams today. Seattle has put together a winning percentage over .540 for three seasons in a row, which is just the second time they've done that in franchise history. A tweak there, a surprise development there, a cagey acquisition there, and they're in. Mitch Garver, signed to a two-year deal, should help.

The foundation is there. Julio Rodríguez's season was a little disappointing, which shows how great he already is, considering he was just 22 (!) and finished fourth in the American League MVP voting. He's the favorite to win the MVP this season as well as the next five.

J.P. Crawford is a fantastically underrated cornerstone at a crucial position, leading the league in walks and finally translating his patience into extra-base hits. His defense leaves a little to be desired (-2.6 DRP), but if the Mariners are hanging a banner—any banner—he'll be a huge reason why. He and lunch-pail framing craftsman Cal Raleigh have established themselves as the veteran leadership in the clubhouse.

The rotation is the best reason to have hopes beyond a .540 winning percentage, though. The Mariners had three starting pitchers with a top-20 WARP last season, in Luis Castillo, George Kirby and Logan Gilbert. If you look at just the AL, they had three out of the top 11 starters, which is bananas. And it's not as if the pitchers after that troika are back end types, either. Bryce Miller and Bryan Woo still have plenty of ceiling left, which means the Mariners are one of those freakiest of teams: the kind that can feel confident about their starting pitcher every single day. A fun way to describe the 2023 Mariners rotation is their starting pitchers walked just 62 batters more than Randy Johnson did himself in 1991. They throw strikes. So many strikes.

It's a rotation worth making silly moves to support, and you know that Dipoto has silly moves on his brain. He has a pull-down flowchart detailing his plan to make a 30-team trade that works for everyone, and when other people come into his office, he quickly pulls the string to roll it back up. The world isn't ready for it yet. Yet. But he has plans.

The silly moves will come, but until then, there's still the unending parade of exhausting ones. The decision to trade Jarred Kelenic and Evan White in the same deal to clear payroll space made a modicum of baseball sense, but it was also the equivalent of Dipoto crumpling up a piece of paper reading "Your hopes and dreams from just a couple years ago" and tossing it over his shoulder into the wastebasket. Despite years of promises, despite hanging on the cusp, Seattle's payroll still sits below where it did in 2019. And 2018...and 2017...and 2016.

This is a team that can win 57% of their games with just a little run support. Or even just some support in general. Maybe even 60%. Heck, maybe even...

"Just a little run support" is doing a lot of work, though, which is why the 54% quote was received so poorly. This should be one of those seasons for the Mariners that buoys the winning percentage over the 10-year stretch and covers for the disappointing seasons. Instead, as of this writing, and you'll never believe it, the Mariners look like an 87-win team. Hang that banner.

Another season like that would be an absolute shame. Mariners fans have had 54% of the best possible baseball experience imaginable. It's time for them to experience some of the other 46%, like almost every other franchise has. Dipoto is so, so close to getting there, while also being as far away as any executive has been in the history of the sport.

—Grant Brisbee is a writer for The Athletic.

---

1. Note that "been" here rhymes with the last syllable of Wladimir Balentien's name.

HITTERS

Ryan Bliss MI
Born: 12/13/99   Age: 24   Bats: R   Throws: R   Height: 5'6"   Weight: 165   Origin: Round 2, 2021 Draft (#42 overall)

YEAR	TM	LVL	AGE	PA	R	HR	RBI	SB	AVG/OBP/SLG	BABIP	SLGCON	BB%	K%	ZSw%	ZCon%	OSw%	OCon%	LA	90th EV	DRC+	BRR	DRP	WARP
2021	VIS	A	21	175	22	6	23	11	.259/.322/.443	.310	.593	7.4%	22.9%							108	-1.5	-0.8	0.5
2022	HIL	A+	22	484	68	10	37	31	.214/.298/.343	.268	.474	8.9%	24.4%							87	0.7	4.4	1.3
2023	PEJ	WIN	23	73	15	0	5	9	.241/.397/.259	.341	.366	19.2%	23.3%										
2023	AMA	AA	23	324	67	12	47	30	.358/.414/.594	.408	.731	7.4%	17.0%							109	2.1	3.4	1.7
2023	RNO	AAA	23	62	6	1	4	5	.196/.274/.357	.233	.455	8.1%	19.4%	76.7%	78.3%	35.0%	70.8%			97	-1.2	-0.2	0.0
2023	TAC	AAA	23	226	37	10	35	20	.251/.356/.466	.290	.640	12.8%	23.0%	68.8%	83.2%	31.0%	58.9%			100	1.9	-1.6	0.4
2024 DC	SEA	MLB	24	29	3	1	3	1	.222/.282/.345	.274	.450	6.7%	23.5%							79	0.0	0	0.0

2023 GP: 2B (90), SS (51), DH (4)   Comps: Yadiel Rivera (57), Matt Reynolds (55), David Fletcher (54)

Though his potential future impact in Seattle cannot undo the disdain much of the fan base demonstrated in response to Seattle's trade of closer Paul Sewald to Arizona, Bliss may eventually prove to be the key piece of the return for the popular closer. After hitting a serious roadbump offensively in 2022, Bliss exploded with one of the loudest statlines of any hitter in the entire minor leagues. He scuffled initially post-trade but finished with a strong September and an invite to the Arizona Fall League, putting him squarely in position to battle for the second base job out of spring training. The bar for 5-foot-6 second basemen in the AL West is famously high, but Bliss' dynamic skill set could make him a fan favorite in short order if he hits, in every sense of the word.

Dominic Canzone LF   Born: 08/16/97   Age: 26   Bats: L   Throws: R   Height: 5'11"   Weight: 190   Origin: Round 8, 2019 Draft (#242 overall)

YEAR	TM	LVL	AGE	PA	R	HR	RBI	SB	AVG/OBP/SLG	BABIP	SLGCON	BB%	K%	ZSw%	ZCon%	OSw%	OCon%	LA	90th EV	DRC+	BRR	DRP	WARP
2021	SRR	WIN	23	78	13	3	15	1	.319/.397/.507	.388	.673	10.3%	21.8%	67.7%	83.3%	33.3%	47.4%						
2021	HIL	A+	23	193	22	7	25	18	.263/.337/.468	.309	.625	8.8%	22.3%							115	0.6	-3.6	0.7
2021	AMA	AA	23	146	25	7	27	1	.354/.425/.592	.411	.755	10.3%	19.2%							121	0.6	2.6	1.1
2022	AMA	AA	24	63	18	6	20	1	.400/.476/.855	.372	.959	12.7%	9.5%							131	2.0	1.1	0.7
2022	RNO	AAA	24	364	61	16	68	14	.284/.349/.489	.324	.630	7.7%	20.3%	67.6%	82.6%	37.7%	59.9%			112	1.8	-0.9	1.7
2023	RNO	AAA	25	304	61	16	71	2	.354/.431/.634	.361	.751	12.8%	13.2%	63.7%	86.4%	37.4%	73.4%			136	0.5	-0.8	2.3
2023	SEA	MLB	25	141	19	5	13	1	.215/.248/.407	.226	.495	4.3%	17.0%	65.9%	79.2%	47.1%	67.9%	17.3	105.4	111	0.0	0.0	0.6
2023	AZ	MLB	25	41	4	1	8	0	.237/.293/.368	.276	.467	4.9%	19.5%	68.9%	90.5%	43.4%	63.9%	12.7	102.2	108	0.0	0.0	0.1
2024 DC	SEA	MLB	26	194	21	7	24	3	.261/.316/.435	.289	.542	7.1%	18.2%							110	0.0	-0.2	0.7

2023 GP: LF (26), DH (17), RF (13)   Comps: Andy Dirks (56), Adam Frazier (55), John Bowker (54)

The latest in a long line of average prospects to produce a cartoonish slash line in the hitter-haven known as Triple-A Reno, Canzone earned his first cup of coffee with the Snakes in July before being shipped to Seattle as part of the Paul Sewald trade. A former eighth-rounder from Ohio State, Canzone was often lost in the shuffle of Arizona's deep array of young outfielders, but eventually his production was too loud to ignore. While his lack of speed and defensive impact squeezed him out of Arizona's big-league picture, Seattle, ever in search of any semblance of offensive impact that costs as little as possible, was eager to take a gamble on Canzone's pull-happy power profile. The early returns, albeit in a small sample, were stark: Canzone torched four-seam fastballs and was roughly hopeless against everything else. Without a serious adjustment to the spinny stuff, Canzone's viability as a regular will remain wobbly at best.

Felnin Celesten SS   Born: 09/15/05   Age: 18   Bats: S   Throws: R   Height: 6'1"   Weight: 175   Origin: IFA, 2023

Only Padres phenom Ethan Salas received a higher signing bonus in the 2022-2023 signing period than Celesten, who garnered $4.7 million from Seattle as the organization's latest and most lucrative commitment to an international amateur prospect. A hamstring strain during extended spring training robbed Celesten the opportunity to make his professional debut, though he did appear in some unofficial games in Arizona by the end of the summer. A switch-hitting shortstop with projectable power, Celesten checks every box in the What They Look Like column of the scouting report; as with any tooled-up teenager, the looks mean little if the player can't put the bat on the ball with regularity. And without any initial stats from which to glean promise or concern on that front, Celesten's offensive aptitude relative to his peers remains something of a mystery box. Whether Seattle sends him back to the DSL as an 18-year-old or pushes him to a stateside assignment out of the gate will shed crucial light on his trajectory.

Jonatan Clase CF   Born: 05/23/02   Age: 22   Bats: S   Throws: R   Height: 5'9"   Weight: 150   Origin: IFA, 2018

YEAR	TM	LVL	AGE	PA	R	HR	RBI	SB	AVG/OBP/SLG	BABIP	SLGCON	BB%	K%	ZSw%	ZCon%	OSw%	OCon%	LA	90th EV	DRC+	BRR	DRP	WARP
2021	MRN	ROK	19	57	12	2	10	16	.245/.333/.388	.303	.559	10.5%	26.3%									-1.3	
2022	MOD	A	20	499	91	13	49	55	.267/.373/.463	.358	.676	13.0%	26.7%							101	3.6	0.3	1.8
2023	EVE	A+	21	106	23	7	17	17	.333/.453/.701	.423	1.034	17.0%	26.4%							141	-1.8	0.3	0.7
2023	ARK	AA	21	489	79	13	51	62	.222/.331/.396	.294	.592	13.1%	28.0%							101	2.2	-2.7	1.4
2024 DC	SEA	MLB	22	65	6	1	6	4	.225/.301/.358	.311	.538	9.3%	29.8%							88	0.0	0	0.1

2023 GP: CF (137), LF (2), DH (1)   Comps: Brandon Nimmo (68), Ryan McKenna (64), Brett Jackson (64)

Clase offers a growing number of positive traits to help distract from the glaring red flag commonly associated with young hitters who strike out at such an alarming rate. His freaky speed has been well-known since he signed as an amateur, and has only been accentuated as stolen bases have skyrocketed across the game: Clase's 79 successful swipes in 2023 ranked third in all of MiLB. He remains in center field, where his quickness enables plus range that compensates for inconsistent instincts. Fast Guy Does Fast Things is hardly news, though—it's the degree to which the Clase continues to demonstrate real power when he does make contact that is both encouraging and vital to his profile sustaining value. Add in the stellar walk-rate and increasingly balanced splits as a switch-hitter and suddenly the whiffs become a lot more digestible. Contact issues sink prospects with regularity, but Clase appears to have enough else going to ensure a big-league role in the not-so-distant future.

J.P. Crawford SS   Born: 01/11/95   Age: 29   Bats: L   Throws: R   Height: 6'2"   Weight: 202   Origin: Round 1, 2013 Draft (#16 overall)

YEAR	TM	LVL	AGE	PA	R	HR	RBI	SB	AVG/OBP/SLG	BABIP	SLGCON	BB%	K%	ZSw%	ZCon%	OSw%	OCon%	LA	90th EV	DRC+	BRR	DRP	WARP
2021	SEA	MLB	26	687	89	9	54	3	.273/.338/.376	.320	.461	8.4%	16.6%	65.2%	90.4%	26.6%	72.5%	9.7	102.8	94	-0.3	2.2	2.2
2022	SEA	MLB	27	603	57	6	42	3	.243/.339/.336	.275	.397	11.3%	13.3%	64.2%	91.2%	23.7%	74.5%	8.7	102.0	108	-0.5	2.1	2.7
2023	SEA	MLB	28	638	94	19	65	2	.266/.380/.438	.314	.572	14.7%	19.6%	59.3%	88.3%	22.2%	67.0%	15.1	104.1	105	-0.2	-1.0	2.5
2024 DC	SEA	MLB	29	625	66	12	62	1	.246/.348/.373	.278	.460	12.7%	16.0%							109	-0.5	3.8	3.3

2023 GP: SS (144)   Comps: Ed Brinkman (69), Everth Cabrera (67), Jose Offerman (66)

Having already signed an extension that secured his spot in the Seattle infield through 2026, Crawford seemed to have found his offensive niche as someone whose stellar on-base skills compensated for a severe lack of power potential. But rather than settle as merely a shortstop who can get on base and occasionally rope a double down the line, Crawford went to work in the winter at Driveline in search of more impact—and boy did he find it. Though his jump in average exit velocity from the third percentile in 2022 (85.1 mph) to the 29th (88.3) in 2023 may not seem like much, the results speak for themselves: Crawford more than doubled his previous career-high in homers and added more than 100 points to his slugging percentage from the year before. Most importantly, his keen eye sustained, as Crawford drew an AL-best 94 free passes. With the right drills and an admirable commitment to improving upon an already stable profile, Crawford has blasted through his previously understood ceiling to become one of the better all-around shortstops in the league.

─── ★ ★ ★ *2024 Top 101 Prospect* **#50** ★ ★ ★ ───

Colt Emerson **MI** Born: 07/20/05 Age: 18 Bats: L Throws: R Height: 6'1" Weight: 195 Origin: Round 1, 2023 Draft (#22 overall)

YEAR	TM	LVL	AGE	PA	R	HR	RBI	SB	AVG/OBP/SLG	BABIP	SLGCON	BB%	K%	ZSw%	ZCon%	OSw%	OCon%	LA	90th EV	DRC+	BRR	DRP	WARP
2023	MRN	ROK	17	35	10	1	5	4	.536/.629/.786	.667	1.000	17.1%	17.1%										
2023	MOD	A	17	79	17	1	8	4	.302/.436/.444	.375	.571	13.9%	17.7%							117	-0.2	-0.2	0.3
2024 non	SEA	MLB	18	251	19	2	19	0	.210/.272/.293	.285	.412	7.0%	26.2%							60	0.0	0	-0.4

2023 GP: SS (14), 2B (8), DH (2) *Comps: Carlos Triunfel (62), Jose Tabata (59), Wilmer Flores (57)*

A year after spending the 21st-overall pick on a high school shortstop with a sweet lefty swing in Cole Young, Seattle went back to the well with the selection of a similar profile in Emerson at pick no. 22. Like Young, Emerson—hailing from an Ohio high school about two hours west of Young's Pittsburgh-area alma mater—exhibited exceptionally advanced offensive ability from both a contact and approach standpoint throughout his time on the amateur showcase circuit. What Emerson had in his favor that Young did not, was, ironically, youth: Emerson didn't even turn 18 until after the Draft whereas Young turned 19 shortly after signing pro. Not only does being young for the class tend to display a precocious ability to compete against older competition, it also affords a player additional time to find their footing in pro ball before needing to worry about performing up the age-appropriate standards of each level. However, a strong showing in Emerson's debut—just as Young delivered with the opposite age-related pressure to perform immediately—suggests patience may not be necessary for a hitter of his caliber. Like Young, he could hit his way onto Top-100 lists by mid-summer.

Jonny Farmelo **OF** Born: 09/09/04 Age: 19 Bats: L Throws: R Height: 6'2" Weight: 205 Origin: Round PPI, 2023 Draft (#29 overall)

One of the more fascinating wrinkles of the new CBA was the introduction of "Prospect Promotion Incentive" picks, an effort to curb service-time gaming by awarding draft picks to teams who put top prospects on Opening Day rosters. Should those players go on to win Rookie of the Year, the team receives a pick at the end of the first round of the following year's Draft—a tremendously valuable asset. Julio Rodríguez's award-winning campaign garnered the first ever "PPI" pick for the Mariners, which they fittingly used on Farmelo, another center fielder on whom everyone can dream big. It took a $3.2 million signing bonus to lure him away from his University of Virginia commitment, but a potent power/speed profile rendered Farmelo a crucial part of Seattle's prep-heavy Draft haul. While his offensive skill set is more crude than what Harry Ford, Cole Young or Colt Emerson brought to the table as amateurs, Farmelo's physical tools stand out loud and clear. It's a scouting report that simultaneously elicits memories of future All-Stars and spectacular busts, but it's a gamble teams will continue to happily take. Worst-case scenario, he'll be excellent Draft trivia one day.

─── ★ ★ ★ *2024 Top 101 Prospect* **#34** ★ ★ ★ ───

Harry Ford **C** Born: 02/21/03 Age: 21 Bats: R Throws: R Height: 5'10" Weight: 200 Origin: Round 1, 2021 Draft (#12 overall)

YEAR	TM	LVL	AGE	PA	R	HR	RBI	SB	AVG/OBP/SLG	BABIP	SLGCON	BB%	K%	ZSw%	ZCon%	OSw%	OCon%	LA	90th EV	DRC+	BRR	DRP	WARP
2021	MRN	ROK	18	65	12	3	10	3	.291/.400/.582	.342	.780	13.8%	21.5%									0.8	
2022	MOD	A	19	499	89	11	65	23	.274/.425/.438	.358	.622	17.6%	23.0%							116	-0.6	8.2	3.3
2023	EVE	A+	20	563	89	15	67	24	.257/.410/.430	.307	.570	18.3%	19.4%							124	-1.0	28.7	5.7
2024 non	SEA	MLB	21	251	23	3	22	0	.224/.322/.327	.298	.459	11.6%	24.8%							90	0.0		0.6

2023 GP: C (83), DH (42) *Comps: Miguel Amaya (80), Austin Hedges (74), Neil Walker (71)*

YEAR	TM	P. COUNT	FRM RUNS	BLK RUNS	THRW RUNS	TOT RUNS
2022	MOD	8140	5.7	0.8	1.0	7.5
2023	EVE	11296	27.4	0.3	2.3	30.0
2024	SEA	6956	6.4	0.5	0.2	7.2

You could argue anyone choosing the life of a catcher is a glutton for punishment, but Ford managed to take the grueling responsibilities of a backstop to the extreme in 2023. He sandwiched a successful season in High-A with two different stints starring for Team Great Britain, whom he proudly represents as the son of two British nationals. Ford was a driving force behind Team GB's first-ever World Baseball Classic victory in March and their runner-up finish at the European Baseball Championship in Czechia in late September. You'd think that amount of globetrotting after six months of squatting for his day job would warrant a well-deserved rest, but no: Ford returned from Europe to log another five games behind the dish in the Arizona Fall League, where he also somehow had enough energy to hit three more homers. We can only hope he took it relatively easy over the winter. And without any international competition on the calendar in 2024, Ford can focus fully on his steady climb to Seattle as one of baseball's premier catching prospects.

Mike Ford **DH** Born: 07/04/92 Age: 32 Bats: L Throws: R Height: 6'0" Weight: 225 Origin: Undrafted Free Agent, 2013

YEAR	TM	LVL	AGE	PA	R	HR	RBI	SB	AVG/OBP/SLG	BABIP	SLGCON	BB%	K%	ZSw%	ZCon%	OSw%	OCon%	LA	90th EV	DRC+	BRR	DRP	WARP
2021	SWB	AAA	28	29	3	0	1	0	.083/.207/.083	.118	.125	10.3%	27.6%							92	-0.2	-0.1	0.0
2021	ROC	AAA	28	116	10	3	12	0	.202/.284/.337	.261	.486	9.5%	27.6%							91	0.3	-0.8	0.1
2021	DUR	AAA	28	162	22	11	31	1	.243/.346/.529	.261	.747	13.0%	25.3%							120	-0.2	-0.2	0.7
2021	NYY	MLB	28	72	6	3	5	0	.133/.278/.283	.147	.459	15.3%	31.9%	56.4%	79.0%	20.9%	55.3%	16.5	105.7	90	0.0	0.0	0.1
2022	TAC	AAA	29	47	10	2	5	0	.317/.404/.488	.314	.541	10.6%	8.5%	61.4%	88.4%	20.6%	72.7%			119	0.5	-0.6	0.3
2022	GWN	AAA	29	53	2	0	3	0	.238/.396/.381	.286	.457	20.8%	13.2%							119	-2.0	-0.6	0.0
2022	SF	MLB	29	4	0	0	2	0	.250/.250/.250	.250	.250	0.0%	0.0%	75.0%	66.7%	22.2%	100.0%	50.2	110.4	99		0.0	0.0
2022	SEA	MLB	29	38	1	0	3	0	.172/.368/.207	.294	.353	21.1%	31.6%	47.7%	83.9%	13.3%	42.9%	10.6	107.0	85	-0.1	0.0	0.0
2022	ATL	MLB	29	8	0	0	0	0	.000/.125/.000		.000	12.5%	25.0%	52.9%	77.8%	18.8%	100.0%	4.0	105.1	86		0.0	0.0
2022	LAA	MLB	29	99	8	3	5	0	.231/.293/.374	.290	.523	8.1%	26.3%	60.4%	89.9%	23.9%	62.1%	19.9	103.3	84	-0.2	0.1	0.0
2023	TAC	AAA	30	211	35	13	56	2	.302/.427/.605	.300	.732	16.1%	14.2%	66.3%	89.1%	23.8%	65.3%			138	1.0	-0.9	1.6
2023	SEA	MLB	30	251	32	16	34	0	.228/.323/.475	.276	.754	9.6%	32.3%	66.7%	83.6%	26.9%	46.1%	21.6	105.1	90	-0.3	0.0	0.2
2024 non	SEA	MLB	31	251	27	9	29	0	.205/.301/.376	.241	.522	10.5%	24.6%							90	0.0	0.1	0.2

2023 GP: DH (64), 1B (10), P (2) *Comps: Carlos Pena (52), Justin Smoak (52), Lucas Duda (49)*

After an absurd 2022 in which he was involved in 32 different transactions across four different organizations, Ford's 2023 was staggeringly straightforward. He destroyed Triple-A for two months (again), then was called up by Seattle in June where he stuck on the big-league roster for the remainder of the season. No injuries, no DFAs, no minor trades that were mentioned in fleeting fashion at the bottom of an MLB Trade Rumors news and notes post. He was down, then he was up, then the season ended, with some memorable moonshots mixed in along the way. While it was the most convincing sample of big-league success Ford has delivered thus far, his severely limited skillset still cost him his roster spot in November, sending him back out into the baseball wilderness.

Ty France   1B   Born: 07/13/94   Age: 29   Bats: R   Throws: R   Height: 5'11"   Weight: 215   Origin: Round 34, 2015 Draft (#1017 overall)

YEAR	TM	LVL	AGE	PA	R	HR	RBI	SB	AVG/OBP/SLG	BABIP	SLGCON	BB%	K%	ZSw%	ZCon%	OSw%	OCon%	LA	90th EV	DRC+	BRR	DRP	WARP
2021	SEA	MLB	26	650	85	18	73	0	.291/.368/.445	.327	.546	7.1%	16.3%	74.4%	91.9%	36.3%	67.8%	11.2	104.1	124	-1.1	0.4	3.4
2022	SEA	MLB	27	613	65	20	83	0	.274/.338/.436	.296	.525	5.7%	15.3%	77.8%	92.5%	38.2%	67.1%	10.2	104.4	116	-0.9	-0.1	2.3
2023	SEA	MLB	28	665	79	12	58	1	.250/.337/.366	.294	.457	6.5%	17.6%	75.0%	91.5%	40.2%	63.4%	13.7	104.6	111	-1.3	1.0	2.2
2024 DC	SEA	MLB	29	596	63	14	64	0	.257/.336/.391	.293	.487	7.0%	17.2%							110	-0.8	1.2	2.0

2023 GP: 1B (158)   *Comps: Dave Magadan (76), Walter Holke (75), Gregg Jefferies (69)*

For those who can endure the bruises and avoid the broken bones, being hit by a ton of pitches can indeed be a valuable skill for a hitter—it just can't be the *only* skill. France's statline as Seattle's everyday first baseman in 2023 was reduced to an underwhelming array of mediocrity headlined by yet another historic year of pain: His 34 plunkings tied 1997 Craig Biggio for the third-most in a single season in the past century. As long as France can continue to weather the pain, the consistent free trips to first will be a welcome part of his profile. That can't be it, though—especially at his position, and even more crucially, as a notoriously slow runner who brings zero additional value once he's actually on the bases. To sustain as a viable daily option, France must rediscover the average power he consistently married with his excellent contact ability during his initial breakout. France's similar batted-ball data to previous years were something of an encouraging sign his fall-off wasn't as severe as the surface stats suggest. But anything resembling a repeat of a .116 ISO at first base is a no-go on a contending team, and a dangerous step towards non-tender territory.

Mitch Garver   DH/C   Born: 01/15/91   Age: 33   Bats: R   Throws: R   Height: 6'1"   Weight: 220   Origin: Round 9, 2013 Draft (#260 overall)

YEAR	TM	LVL	AGE	PA	R	HR	RBI	SB	AVG/OBP/SLG	BABIP	SLGCON	BB%	K%	ZSw%	ZCon%	OSw%	OCon%	LA	90th EV	DRC+	BRR	DRP	WARP
2021	MIN	MLB	30	243	29	13	34	1	.256/.358/.517	.320	.787	12.8%	29.2%	61.1%	80.3%	23.7%	52.1%	19.1	107.5	96	-0.2	0.0	0.8
2022	TEX	MLB	31	215	23	10	24	1	.207/.298/.404	.228	.563	10.7%	24.7%	61.5%	79.6%	26.7%	65.5%	18.8	103.9	93	-0.2	0.1	0.4
2023	RR	AAA	32	25	7	2	4	0	.316/.480/.737	.400	1.167	24.0%	28.0%	69.6%	71.9%	13.8%	55.6%			103	0.1	-0.2	0.1
2023	TEX	MLB	32	344	45	19	50	0	.270/.370/.500	.313	.692	12.8%	23.8%	63.3%	85.3%	21.2%	56.5%	20.9	106.6	114	-0.4	1.7	1.6
2024 DC	SEA	MLB	33	399	48	17	52	1	.228/.320/.422	.262	.578	11.0%	23.7%							109	-0.4	0	1.4

2023 GP: DH (57), C (28), 1B (1)   *Comps: Travis d'Arnaud (57), Kevin Millar (56), Mike Macfarlane (55)*

YEAR	TM	P. COUNT	FRM RUNS	BLK RUNS	THRW RUNS	TOT RUNS
2021	MIN	7509	1.0	0.0	0.0	1.0
2022	TEX	2081	0.5	0.0	-0.1	0.4
2023	TEX	3708	1.7	0.0	0.0	1.7
2024	SEA	3608	0.1	-0.1	0.0	0.1

For years the analysis on Garver has begun with the same two words: "When healthy...". In 2023, the 32-year-old appeared in just 87 games, only one of which came as a catcher after the calendar turned to September. He all but officially completed a transition to a full-time designated hitter by the end of the year, which is where he figures to be best deployed by the Mariners; over the last three regular seasons, he's accumulated 802 plate appearances, whereas his former teammate Marcus Semien put up 835 in the 2023 season and postseason alone.

It takes significant ability to retain a place in a major-league lineup with that spotty of a medical history, and that underscores the second half of the typical Garver assessment: He's awfully productive. He sports one of the game's very best eyes—his chase rate was in the 98th percentile and his walk rate in the 90th—and the power has never been in question. Seattle will be happy to insert that kind of right-handed bat into the middle of their order, even if it may only be for a half-season at a time.

Gabriel Gonzalez   RF   Born: 01/04/04   Age: 20   Bats: R   Throws: R   Height: 5'10"   Weight: 165   Origin: IFA, 2021

YEAR	TM	LVL	AGE	PA	R	HR	RBI	SB	AVG/OBP/SLG	BABIP	SLGCON	BB%	K%	ZSw%	ZCon%	OSw%	OCon%	LA	90th EV	DRC+	BRR	DRP	WARP
2021	DSL SEA	ROK	17	221	39	7	36	9	.287/.371/.521	.313	.645	9.5%	16.3%									1.3	
2022	MRN	ROK	18	140	20	5	17	5	.357/.421/.548	.400	.657	5.7%	15.0%										
2022	MOD	A	18	150	31	2	17	4	.286/.400/.389	.330	.467	8.7%	14.0%							113	0.4	0.1	0.7
2023	MOD	A	19	335	51	9	54	8	.348/.403/.530	.379	.628	6.9%	13.7%							135	-0.3	0.5	2.5
2023	EVE	A+	19	200	27	9	30	2	.215/.290/.387	.233	.507	6.5%	21.5%							101	-2.3	-1.9	0.3
2024 non	SEA	MLB	20	251	20	4	22	0	.217/.267/.316	.273	.416	4.9%	22.9%							64	0.0	0	-0.5

2023 GP: RF (88), DH (21), LF (7)   *Comps: Dylan Carlson (60), Victor Robles (57), Juremi Profar (55)*

Only Jackson Holliday, Jackson Chourio and Junior Caminero collected more hits in 2023 among teenage position players than Gonzalez, who, unsurprisingly, loves swinging the bat with high frequency. Still just 20 on Opening Day, Gonzalez remains plenty ahead of schedule, though his ultra-aggressive approach is sure to be exploited further as he climbs the minor-league ladder. How he responds will be the difference between an eventual spot on a Top 101 list and a debilitating stint in Double-A.

Sam Haggerty UT   Born: 05/26/94   Age: 30   Bats: S   Throws: R   Height: 5'11"   Weight: 175   Origin: Round 24, 2015 Draft (#724 overall)

YEAR	TM	LVL	AGE	PA	R	HR	RBI	SB	AVG/OBP/SLG	BABIP	SLGCON	BB%	K%	ZSw%	ZCon%	OSw%	OCon%	LA	90th EV	DRC+	BRR	DRP	WARP
2021	SEA	MLB	27	94	15	2	5	5	.186/.247/.291	.250	.431	6.4%	29.8%	71.4%	85.3%	33.2%	45.7%	6.8	104.4	82	0.2	0.9	0.2
2022	TAC	AAA	28	179	28	6	25	15	.283/.369/.500	.325	.644	10.1%	19.0%	71.3%	85.8%	32.0%	55.1%			109	1.5	0.6	0.9
2022	SEA	MLB	28	201	29	5	23	13	.256/.335/.403	.333	.577	9.0%	26.4%	70.1%	82.4%	33.2%	55.8%	12.1	102.6	88	0.6	2.1	0.6
2023	TAC	AAA	29	222	41	8	29	19	.324/.419/.578	.361	.723	13.1%	16.7%	69.3%	87.7%	28.7%	57.8%			119	-0.7	0.6	1.1
2023	SEA	MLB	29	108	13	1	5	10	.253/.364/.341	.301	.419	13.9%	15.7%	76.6%	86.4%	30.9%	66.2%	11.8	101.3	107	0.5	0.2	0.5
2024 DC	SEA	MLB	30	212	22	6	23	15	.233/.317/.385	.272	.500	10.0%	20.3%							100	0.6	0.1	0.7

2023 GP: LF (16), DH (14), 2B (10), 1B (4), CF (4), RF (2)   Comps: Ryan Langerhans (47), Rob Ducey (47), Jace Peterson (46)

Haggerty has amalgamated enough secondary skills to make it increasingly hard to argue against his worthiness on the bottom of an active big-league roster. He's both exceptionally quick and a savvy baserunner. His switch-hitting offers more flexibility when it comes to pinch-hitting assignments. He's played every defensive position besides catcher as a pro. And in 2023, Haggerty's plate discipline improved markedly, as he cut down on strikeouts while continuing to take a healthy number of free passes, enabling more opportunities for his speed to advance bases in ways his bat rarely allows. With 30-grade power at best, he should never be Plan A at any position, but plenty of managers would happily take Haggerty on their bench.

Mitch Haniger OF   Born: 12/23/90   Age: 33   Bats: R   Throws: R   Height: 6'2"   Weight: 214   Origin: Round 1, 2012 Draft (#38 overall)

YEAR	TM	LVL	AGE	PA	R	HR	RBI	SB	AVG/OBP/SLG	BABIP	SLGCON	BB%	K%	ZSw%	ZCon%	OSw%	OCon%	LA	90th EV	DRC+	BRR	DRP	WARP
2021	SEA	MLB	30	691	110	39	100	1	.253/.318/.485	.281	.667	7.8%	24.5%	65.3%	82.5%	33.1%	52.8%	14.9	105.5	105	-0.2	-3.1	2.0
2022	TAC	AAA	31	33	5	2	6	0	.238/.515/.524	.188	.611	30.3%	9.1%	58.8%	96.7%	22.3%	61.9%			125	0.5	0.6	0.3
2022	SEA	MLB	31	247	31	11	34	0	.246/.308/.429	.293	.604	8.1%	26.3%	67.3%	81.4%	29.8%	52.6%	18.3	106.5	99	-0.2	-1.2	0.5
2023	SAC	AAA	32	35	3	2	3	0	.167/.286/.367	.125	.423	5.7%	11.4%	62.9%	82.1%	40.9%	77.8%			112	-0.3	-0.1	0.1
2023	SF	MLB	32	229	27	6	28	1	.209/.266/.365	.270	.527	6.6%	28.4%	64.5%	84.0%	30.5%	51.6%	16.1	104.5	83	-0.1	-2.8	-0.1
2024 DC	SEA	MLB	33	478	51	17	57	1	.224/.291/.390	.262	.525	7.5%	23.7%							91	-0.4	-6.2	0.0

2023 GP: LF (46), RF (14), DH (3)   Comps: Jose Cruz (68), Jermaine Dye (64), Brad Hawpe (62)

Haniger was always set up for failure. The way that this came together was sometimes predictable: he missed 10 weeks with a right forearm fracture that required surgery, yet another significant injury over which he had no control. It also came in unusual ways, in that much of the surrounding information suggests he was the same player, except he had a .631 OPS. He swung slightly less at both out-of-zone and in-zone pitches, and he made more contact in both areas. But his walk and strikeout rates slipped to a career-worst 6.6% and second-worst 28.4% marks, respectively. The only clear difference is that pitchers pounded the zone on the first pitch to Haniger, up above 60% in a realm only exceeded by a few light-hitting infielders and catchers, and he also swung at a below-average number of in-zone first pitches. In addition to setting himself back with the early called strike, Haniger pulled his fly balls much less, which partially explains why he underperformed his strong quality of contact so severely.

Tommy La Stella DH   Born: 01/31/89   Age: 35   Bats: L   Throws: R   Height: 5'11"   Weight: 180   Origin: Round 8, 2011 Draft (#266 overall)

YEAR	TM	LVL	AGE	PA	R	HR	RBI	SB	AVG/OBP/SLG	BABIP	SLGCON	BB%	K%	ZSw%	ZCon%	OSw%	OCon%	LA	90th EV	DRC+	BRR	DRP	WARP
2021	SF	MLB	32	242	26	7	27	0	.250/.308/.405	.255	.459	7.4%	10.7%	56.6%	91.5%	26.8%	81.9%	13.5	101.6	104	-0.1	-0.6	0.9
2022	SF	MLB	33	195	17	2	14	0	.239/.282/.350	.272	.420	5.6%	15.4%	55.4%	92.5%	30.8%	72.3%	14.8	101.2	92	-0.1	0.0	0.3
2023	SEA	MLB	34	24	2	0	2	0	.190/.292/.238	.250	.312	12.5%	20.8%	58.3%	76.2%	27.9%	73.7%	19.4	97.8	98	0.0	0.0	0.1
2024 non	SEA	MLB	35	251	24	4	25	0	.251/.324/.371	.282	.440	9.1%	14.4%							97	0.0	-1.5	0.5

2023 GP: DH (6)   Comps: Brian Roberts (56), Orlando Hudson (53), Jim Gantner (50)

Inexplicably the starting DH on Opening Day, La Stella started just six times before Seattle waived him, hoping no one would remember his Mariners tenure ever happened. Despite receiving far less run than far more promising veteran additions Kolten Wong and AJ Pollock, La Stella was routinely lumped in with them as a representative triumvirate of the front office's abject failure to meaningfully improve the offense during the previous winter. Unlike his fellow flops, La Stella failed to latch on with any other organization following his release—hence his unwelcome presence in this chapter.

Cade Marlowe OF   Born: 06/24/97   Age: 27   Bats: L   Throws: R   Height: 6'1"   Weight: 210   Origin: Round 20, 2019 Draft (#606 overall)

YEAR	TM	LVL	AGE	PA	R	HR	RBI	SB	AVG/OBP/SLG	BABIP	SLGCON	BB%	K%	ZSw%	ZCon%	OSw%	OCon%	LA	90th EV	DRC+	BRR	DRP	WARP
2021	MOD	A	24	160	35	6	29	11	.301/.406/.556	.382	.796	15.0%	25.0%							127	0.9	-4.2	0.8
2021	EVE	A+	24	325	52	20	77	12	.259/.345/.566	.307	.831	11.1%	28.0%							113	-3.5	-0.9	1.2
2022	ARK	AA	25	518	75	20	86	36	.291/.380/.483	.369	.688	10.6%	25.7%							101	2.0	1.2	2.0
2022	TAC	AAA	25	60	8	3	16	6	.250/.350/.519	.385	.931	11.7%	38.3%	72.4%	76.2%	33.1%	40.9%			79	0.7	1.4	0.2
2023	TAC	AAA	26	379	59	11	52	29	.257/.338/.443	.330	.630	10.3%	26.1%	74.2%	82.7%	28.0%	43.8%			88	2.3	-0.3	1.0
2023	SEA	MLB	26	100	14	3	11	4	.239/.330/.420	.346	.673	12.0%	33.0%	72.8%	78.6%	33.9%	57.6%	21.0	101.3	74	0.1	0.4	0.0
2024 DC	SEA	MLB	27	185	17	5	19	11	.208/.280/.357	.270	.513	8.4%	28.3%							78	0.4	0.1	0.0

2023 GP: LF (24), CF (4), RF (2), DH (1)   Comps: Chris Dickerson (55), Seth Brown (53), Kirk Nieuwenhuis (53)

"You've got Shohei, we've got Cade Marlowe!" bellowed teammate Bryan Woo as Marlowe entered the visiting clubhouse in Anaheim after the highlight of his season. Ohtani had provided some insurance in the eighth inning with his 40th blast of the year but, in another twist of Tungsten Arm fate, Marlowe—with one homer in 11 career games to that point—had other plans for the Angels that night. He launched a go-ahead grand slam in the ninth inning off a 100-mph, elevated fastball from Angels closer Carlos Estévez, sending the Seattle bench into chaos and prompting Woo's emphatic, if unintentionally hilarious, postgame proclamation. The novelty of a former 20th-round pick from a Division-II school delivering such heroics eventually wore off, as Marlowe failed to make enough contact to carve out a regular role down the stretch. Still, his lauded work ethic and knack for adjustments make him particularly beloved within the organization, increasing the likelihood he'll have more opportunities to prove his worth.

Lazaro Montes RF Born: 10/22/04 Age: 19 Bats: L Throws: R Height: 6'3" Weight: 210 Origin: IFA, 2022

YEAR	TM	LVL	AGE	PA	R	HR	RBI	SB	AVG/OBP/SLG	BABIP	SLGCON	BB%	K%	ZSw%	ZCon%	OSw%	OCon%	LA	90th EV	DRC+	BRR	DRP	WARP
2022	DSL SEA	ROK	17	223	34	10	41	3	.284/.422/.585	.421	1.010	15.7%	33.2%										
2023	MRN	ROK	18	146	31	6	31	1	.282/.452/.555	.368	.836	22.6%	25.3%										
2023	MOD	A	18	156	27	7	30	1	.321/.429/.565	.412	.804	13.5%	25.0%							126	-0.6	1.4	1.1
2024 non	SEA	MLB	19	251	20	3	21	0	.211/.276/.308	.327	.500	7.4%	35.0%							65	0.0	0	-0.5

2023 GP: RF (58), DH (12)   *Comps: Bryce Harper (90), Jason Heyward (80), Julio Rodríguez (78)*

Montes is comically enormous. The fact that he's the same age as the high school seniors who just heard their names called in the 2023 draft only adds to the absurdity of his size (we'll take the over on the listed 210 pounds) and strength (he's already registered exit velocities as high as 118 mph). The massive Cuban slugger with a thunderous left-handed cut doesn't shy away from the inevitable Yordan Alvarez comps, instead embracing the similarities and confirming in interviews that the Astros star does indeed represent his ideal player type. Montes is even ahead of where Alvarez was at the same age: Alvarez's pro debut in the DSL did not come until after his 19th birthday; Montes just played all of 2023 at 18, finishing the year with 33 productive games in Low-A. He still whiffed a good amount, though less than in his pro debut, and punished southpaws just as consistently as he teed off on right-handers. The degree to which his bat continues to shine will dictate how much longer the organization allows him to lumber around the outfield. For now, Montes' lopsided yet ludicrously fun prospect profile is one of the lower minors' most intriguing.

Dylan Moore UT Born: 08/02/92 Age: 31 Bats: R Throws: R Height: 6'0" Weight: 205 Origin: Round 7, 2015 Draft (#198 overall)

YEAR	TM	LVL	AGE	PA	R	HR	RBI	SB	AVG/OBP/SLG	BABIP	SLGCON	BB%	K%	ZSw%	ZCon%	OSw%	OCon%	LA	90th EV	DRC+	BRR	DRP	WARP
2021	SEA	MLB	28	377	42	12	43	21	.181/.276/.334	.229	.502	10.6%	29.4%	61.7%	80.2%	25.1%	62.4%	20.6	103.8	77	0.8	0.5	0.4
2022	SEA	MLB	29	255	41	6	24	21	.224/.368/.385	.320	.608	13.3%	29.4%	61.6%	78.5%	21.1%	58.4%	20.6	103.5	90	1.4	-0.7	0.6
2023	TAC	AAA	30	30	5	0	4	1	.200/.333/.240	.313	.375	13.3%	30.0%	67.3%	75.8%	22.7%	40.0%			87	0.7	0.4	0.1
2023	SEA	MLB	30	165	18	7	19	7	.207/.303/.428	.280	.697	9.7%	33.9%	66.6%	77.2%	30.9%	49.6%	22.1	105.2	82	0.2	-0.1	0.1
2024 DC	SEA	MLB	31	313	32	9	33	24	.199/.300/.350	.263	.531	10.0%	29.7%							86	0.6	-0.9	0.4

2023 GP: 2B (23), LF (22), SS (9), DH (6), RF (5), 1B (4), CF (3), 3B (1)   *Comps: Jayson Nix (51), Hernán Pérez (46), Ryan Flaherty (45)*

The novelty of Moore's superutility schtick has somewhat worn off as Sam Haggerty emerged to occupy a similar role, often leaving both waiting in the dugout for the first five innings, pointing at each other like Spiderman. There's markedly more impact on contact for Moore than when Haggerty connects, but the former was aggressive as ever at the plate in 2023, and his overall output suffered for it. While he remains a far more attractive pinch-hitting option or occasional down-order starter against lefties than Haggerty, Moore's path to more consistent at-bats in any context must include a more refined approach.

Tai Peete 3B/DH Born: 08/11/05 Age: 18 Bats: L Throws: R Height: 6'2" Weight: 193 Origin: Round 1, 2023 Draft (#30 overall)

YEAR	TM	LVL	AGE	PA	R	HR	RBI	SB	AVG/OBP/SLG	BABIP	SLGCON	BB%	K%	ZSw%	ZCon%	OSw%	OCon%	LA	90th EV	DRC+	BRR	DRP	WARP
2023	MRN	ROK	17	42	4	0	6	3	.351/.429/.432	.500	.615	11.9%	26.2%										
2023	MOD	A	17	67	7	2	14	3	.242/.299/.387	.317	.558	7.5%	28.4%							95	-0.6	-0.3	0.0
2024 non	SEA	MLB	18	251	18	2	19	0	.202/.253/.287	.293	.427	5.6%	31.0%							51	0.0	0	-0.9

2023 GP: 3B (7), SS (6), DH (6), 2B (5)   *Comps: Angel Villalona (52), Carlos Triunfel (47), Adalberto Mondesi (46)*

Peete may one day join the likes of Todd Frazier, Michael Conforto and Cody Bellinger as former Little League World Series participants to reach the sport's highest level. He starred for the Peachtree City, Ga. team that reached Williamsport in 2018 (the same year Big Al told America he hits dingers, in case you want to feel old), and shortly after established himself as one of the most exciting amateur prospects in the Atlanta area. Peete's exceptional athleticism buoyed significant promise as a two-way player for much of his prep career until an elbow injury as a senior ensured a full focus on shortstop entering the draft. Seattle was thrilled to include him in their prep bat parade and it didn't take long for Peete to make a name for himself after signing: His first two pro homers came in back-to-back innings amidst a furious Modesto comeback from a 6-0 deficit—*and they were both grand slams.*

Cal Raleigh C Born: 11/26/96 Age: 27 Bats: S Throws: R Height: 6'3" Weight: 235 Origin: Round 3, 2018 Draft (#90 overall)

YEAR	TM	LVL	AGE	PA	R	HR	RBI	SB	AVG/OBP/SLG	BABIP	SLGCON	BB%	K%	ZSw%	ZCon%	OSw%	OCon%	LA	90th EV	DRC+	BRR	DRP	WARP
2021	TAC	AAA	24	199	34	9	36	3	.324/.377/.608	.327	.709	7.0%	12.6%							124	0.4	7.3	2.1
2021	SEA	MLB	24	148	6	2	13	0	.180/.223/.309	.267	.494	4.7%	35.1%	80.0%	72.9%	48.2%	59.5%	17.1	105.0	49	-0.1	3.2	0.0
2022	TAC	AAA	25	30	4	1	4	0	.286/.333/.464	.350	.619	6.7%	23.3%	73.1%	100.0%	40.7%	54.2%			98	0.0	-0.2	0.1
2022	SEA	MLB	25	415	46	27	63	1	.211/.284/.489	.226	.730	9.2%	29.4%	78.3%	77.3%	36.3%	55.0%	22.8	105.4	105	-0.1	8.8	2.7
2023	SEA	MLB	26	569	78	30	75	0	.232/.306/.456	.273	.659	9.5%	27.8%	71.7%	81.4%	35.3%	54.7%	20.8	106.4	109	-0.5	14.9	4.2
2024 DC	SEA	MLB	27	460	54	22	63	1	.225/.298/.440	.263	.623	8.9%	26.6%							102	-0.3	13.3	3.2

2023 GP: C (128), DH (14)   *Comps: J.P. Arencibia (71), Yan Gomes (69), Sean Murphy (69)*

YEAR	TM	P. COUNT	FRM RUNS	BLK RUNS	THRW RUNS	TOT RUNS
2021	TAC	5098	7.4	0.0	0.1	7.5
2021	SEA	5497	4.1	-0.1	0.1	4.0
2022	SEA	14649	11.4	0.1	-0.1	11.4
2023	SEA	16945	15.2	0.3	1.8	17.2
2024	SEA	14430	12.0	0.1	1.3	13.4

At a position where high-level offensive production is not only rare but nearly impossible to rely upon on a year-to-year basis, Raleigh leading all big-league backstops in homers for a second consecutive season is no small feat. A switch-hitter by definition, Raleigh remains far more productive from the left side, though that continues to serve him better than if the reverse were true. That preferred platoon advantage, combined with a severe lack of suitable alternatives on the roster, enabled Raleigh to amass a huge workload behind the plate: His 1,038 innings in the tools of ignorance were second only to J.T. Realmuto during the regular season. And unlike Realmuto, whose framing and control of the running game has started to suffer, Raleigh's defensive chops seem to only be improving.

Yet for all Raleigh offers between the lines, it was his status off the field that soared even higher in 2023. Almost exactly a year after electrifying T-Mobile Park by ending the franchise's infamous playoff drought with one swing, Raleigh provided the fan base with a different kind of jolt: **"We've got to commit to winning,"** said Raleigh in the moments after Seattle was officially eliminated during the season's final weekend. "We have to commit to going and getting those players you see other teams going out and getting. We've done a great job of growing some players here and within the farm system, but sometimes you've got to go out and you have to buy."

"You look at the other locker room," Raleigh said in reference to the Rangers team that just ended their regular season. "They've added more than anybody else and you saw where it got them this year." Painfully prescient would perhaps be the best way to describe Raleigh's season-ending address, as Seattle watched Texas storm through the postseason en route to its first-ever World Series title. The M's, meanwhile, were in store for another winter of frugality and uninspiring payroll maneuvering. Raleigh's words of urgency loomed over Seattle's winter in every sense, a reflection of the disconnect between fans'—and players'—dreams and ambitions, and ownership's financial priorities. Nevertheless, Raleigh forges ahead as Seattle's franchise catcher. He's certainly doing his part.

Luke Raley RF   Born: 09/19/94   Age: 29   Bats: L   Throws: R   Height: 6'4"   Weight: 235   Origin: Round 7, 2016 Draft (#221 overall)

YEAR	TM	LVL	AGE	PA	R	HR	RBI	SB	AVG/OBP/SLG	BABIP	SLGCON	BB%	K%	ZSw%	ZCon%	OSw%	OCon%	LA	90th EV	DRC+	BRR	DRP	WARP
2021	OKC	AAA	26	318	60	19	69	8	.294/.393/.570	.339	.783	8.5%	23.3%							122	0.9	4.0	2.4
2021	LAD	MLB	26	72	5	2	4	0	.182/.250/.288	.256	.463	2.8%	34.7%	79.8%	75.8%	32.0%	31.9%	3.2	103.9	84	-0.1	-0.7	0.0
2022	DUR	AAA	27	268	39	14	50	7	.300/.401/.529	.383	.779	10.1%	27.2%	86.2%	76.8%	34.1%	51.6%			104	-2.7	-1.6	0.5
2022	TB	MLB	27	72	7	1	4	0	.197/.306/.279	.297	.459	9.7%	33.3%	75.2%	73.6%	31.7%	35.3%	17.0	105.4	76	-0.1	-0.2	0.0
2023	TB	MLB	28	406	56	19	49	14	.249/.333/.490	.330	.764	6.9%	31.5%	75.8%	78.7%	37.0%	39.0%	16.0	107.8	95	0.3	0.9	0.9
2024 DC	SEA	MLB	29	462	51	17	55	8	.216/.303/.396	.299	.636	7.3%	33.5%							96	-0.1	-2	0.6

2023 GP: RF (36), 1B (35), LF (18), DH (18), CF (11), P (2)   Comps: Nelson Cruz (52), Lucas Duda (51), Andre Ethier (51)

Raley has always had the look that made you wonder … *what if we gave this guy 400 plate appearances?* It turns out that the answer is 40+ extra-base hits and a strikeout once in every three times up. Granted, the Rays made sure the majority of those 400 chances came against right-handed pitchers, to the tune of a .357 wOBA against them. He did fare better than you would think against lefties, but it's probably best to continue a similar usage at the plate going forward, as the total package was a slightly below-average overall hitter per DRC+. No longer just a corner outfielder, he picked up 233 innings at first base; although the versatility is a nice wrinkle, Raley's job is hit first, field later. If his late-season neck injury is fully behind him, he may get another 400 attempts to cement himself as a full-time starter.

Julio Rodríguez CF   Born: 12/29/00   Age: 23   Bats: R   Throws: R   Height: 6'3"   Weight: 228   Origin: IFA, 2017

YEAR	TM	LVL	AGE	PA	R	HR	RBI	SB	AVG/OBP/SLG	BABIP	SLGCON	BB%	K%	ZSw%	ZCon%	OSw%	OCon%	LA	90th EV	DRC+	BRR	DRP	WARP
2021	EVE	A+	20	134	29	6	21	5	.325/.410/.581	.390	.773	10.4%	21.6%							114	0.6	1.5	0.8
2021	ARK	AA	20	206	35	7	26	16	.362/.461/.546	.431	.693	14.1%	18.0%							125	0.9	2.5	1.6
2022	SEA	MLB	21	560	84	28	75	25	.284/.345/.509	.345	.710	7.1%	25.9%	70.9%	83.6%	37.7%	53.7%	10.1	109.0	112	1.1	-2.0	2.8
2023	SEA	MLB	22	714	102	32	103	37	.275/.333/.485	.330	.662	6.6%	24.5%	73.1%	84.7%	41.0%	56.3%	8.6	108.7	109	1.7	1.6	3.7
2024 DC	SEA	MLB	23	600	72	25	81	23	.263/.328/.458	.313	.624	7.4%	23.9%							122	0.6	-0.5	3.7

2023 GP: CF (152), DH (3)   Comps: Mookie Betts (69), Mike Trout (66), Juan Gonzalez (64)

Even in a sport overflowing with postgame cliches, few refrains get recycled more often than a hitter describing their recipe for success as simply "not trying to do too much." While this is unquestionably a sentiment Rodríguez has already echoed on numerous occasions over the course of his young career, he appeared to spend the first half of his sophomore season trying to do the absolute most. And yet, because Rodríguez is one of the most naturally gifted players our game has seen in quite some time, the final results were still largely sensational.

For a few months, though, it wasn't pretty. With the weight of the franchise on his shoulders and little surrounding star power to support him, Rodríguez's admirable determination to come through in every big spot was often undone by wildly aggressive hacks at non-competitive pitches. While he was hardly the team's only severely underperforming member, his own late-game failures seemed to wear on him more than most. He carried a .721 OPS into the break, though a much-needed rest wasn't even an option: Rodríguez remained the center of attention at the All-Star festivities in Seattle, where he put on another memorable show in the Home Run Derby.

Exhausted, surely, Rodríguez returned to his regular-season responsibilities, and finally found his stride. No longer was he trying to do too much and failing. Suddenly, he was trying to do it all—and succeeding spectacularly. An otherworldly August (1.198 OPS) featured an MLB-record 17 hits in a four-game span, the hottest peak of a month-long heater that helped launch Seattle back into the playoff picture. His fearlessness on the basepaths helped him secure the first of what should be many 30/30 seasons. His spectacular defense in center field continued to stun, considering his humble beginnings as a corner outfield prospect, ultimately tabbing him as a Gold Glove finalist. A fourth-place AL MVP finish aptly summarized his immense value to his team, even in a year that ended short of October. While his final line may not have represented the comprehensive leap from his rookie year that some may have hoped, Year Two of The J-Rod Show was still a bold reminder of how bright Rodríguez's star can burn when things fall into place. His ceiling remains undefined, for all the right reasons.

Josh Rojas 3B/2B   Born: 06/30/94   Age: 30   Bats: L   Throws: R   Height: 6'1"   Weight: 207   Origin: Round 26, 2017 Draft (#781 overall)

YEAR	TM	LVL	AGE	PA	R	HR	RBI	SB	AVG/OBP/SLG	BABIP	SLGCON	BB%	K%	ZSw%	ZCon%	OSw%	OCon%	LA	90th EV	DRC+	BRR	DRP	WARP
2021	AZ	MLB	27	550	69	11	44	9	.264/.341/.411	.345	.573	10.5%	24.9%	64.4%	84.4%	25.7%	61.6%	8.3	101.2	85	0.6	-0.5	0.9
2022	AZ	MLB	28	510	66	9	56	23	.269/.349/.391	.323	.501	10.8%	19.2%	64.5%	83.9%	23.2%	64.9%	10.9	101.5	109	1.2	-1.5	1.9
2023	SEA	MLB	29	134	24	4	14	6	.272/.321/.400	.330	.526	6.7%	22.4%	63.7%	80.6%	27.4%	65.9%	15.1	101.2	86	0.1	0.3	0.2
2023	AZ	MLB	29	216	23	0	26	6	.228/.292/.296	.303	.406	8.3%	23.6%	62.1%	84.8%	30.7%	62.3%	10.1	100.4	77	0.0	0.1	0.1
2024 DC	SEA	MLB	30	514	49	10	50	18	.240/.308/.360	.289	.470	8.9%	20.9%							91	0.4	-1.8	0.7

2023 GP: 2B (49), 3B (48), DH (5), P (2), LF (2)   Comps: Tony Kemp (49), Fernando Vina (48), Dee Strange-Gordon (47)

A paragon of mediocrity and versatility over the previous two seasons, Rojas' bat cratered to start 2023. Having already endured the darkest depths of second base production via Kolten Wong's catastrophic first half, the Mariners identified Rojas as a viable bounce-back candidate from his ugly start and included him in the deadline haul from Arizona for closer Paul Sewald. As Rojas settled in as the strong side of Seattle's keystone platoon, a more familiar version of his modest offensive profile began to re-emerge while his glove exhibited enhanced steadiness after a rash of errors the year prior. In turn, Rojas managed to re-establish his sufficiency as a useful role player before his career veered too far off track.

Taylor Trammell CF   Born: 09/13/97   Age: 26   Bats: L   Throws: L   Height: 6'2"   Weight: 220   Origin: Round 1, 2016 Draft (#35 overall)

YEAR	TM	LVL	AGE	PA	R	HR	RBI	SB	AVG/OBP/SLG	BABIP	SLGCON	BB%	K%	ZSw%	ZCon%	OSw%	OCon%	LA	90th EV	DRC+	BRR	DRP	WARP
2021	TAC	AAA	23	323	43	12	49	8	.263/.362/.456	.313	.625	12.4%	22.9%							95	1.1	-3.0	0.7
2021	SEA	MLB	23	178	23	8	18	2	.160/.256/.359	.233	.691	9.6%	42.1%	70.3%	67.6%	30.6%	37.9%	14.1	104.3	47	0.1	0.3	-0.4
2022	TAC	AAA	24	98	18	5	12	8	.333/.408/.575	.369	.714	11.2%	17.3%	74.0%	83.3%	27.9%	53.2%			114	1.2	-0.9	0.5
2022	SEA	MLB	24	117	15	4	10	2	.196/.284/.402	.242	.594	11.1%	28.2%	72.2%	80.8%	28.8%	40.3%	18.6	104.6	81	0.1	0.5	0.1
2023	TAC	AAA	25	391	59	21	63	17	.268/.390/.530	.323	.789	16.1%	26.6%	70.6%	79.1%	26.0%	43.1%			106	-0.3	-2.2	1.3
2023	SEA	MLB	25	56	7	3	11	0	.130/.286/.326	.143	.625	16.1%	39.3%	66.0%	68.2%	23.7%	33.3%	26.5	104.7	87	0.0	0.1	0.1
2024 DC	SEA	MLB	26	185	20	6	21	5	.185/.290/.359	.242	.569	11.6%	31.5%							82	0.2	0.6	0.1

2023 GP: LF (11), DH (8), CF (1)   Comps: Derek Fisher (57), Jackie Bradley Jr. (55), Aaron Hicks (49)

The strides Trammell made at the plate in 2023—unlocking more game power, drawing more walks and proving more competent against left-handers—would be received far more favorably were he four years younger and tackling Triple-A pitching for the first time. But as a 25-year-old on his third stint in the PCL, Trammell's progress was viewed through a far less enthusiastic lens. A dramatic grand slam in Toronto in his first big-league plate appearance of the season provided a spark of false hope, but Trammell quickly reverted to an untenable amount of flailing at pitches with which he could do nothing. For as much as we bemoan the overreliance on traditional offensive statistics, at some point, batting average does matter.

Luis Urías 2B/3B   Born: 06/03/97   Age: 27   Bats: R   Throws: R   Height: 5'10"   Weight: 202   Origin: IFA, 2013

YEAR	TM	LVL	AGE	PA	R	HR	RBI	SB	AVG/OBP/SLG	BABIP	SLGCON	BB%	K%	ZSw%	ZCon%	OSw%	OCon%	LA	90th EV	DRC+	BRR	DRP	WARP
2021	MIL	MLB	24	570	77	23	75	5	.249/.345/.445	.280	.583	11.1%	20.4%	68.7%	84.1%	30.5%	66.4%	14.3	103.3	106	0.1	-0.7	2.4
2022	MIL	MLB	25	472	54	16	47	1	.239/.335/.404	.274	.534	10.6%	21.0%	66.8%	82.4%	27.5%	70.6%	18.3	101.4	102	-0.2	-0.7	1.4
2023	NAS	AAA	26	139	20	4	16	1	.233/.345/.379	.288	.537	13.7%	24.5%	71.9%	80.1%	30.9%	65.2%			93	-1.7	-3.4	-0.2
2023	MIL	MLB	26	68	5	1	5	0	.145/.299/.236	.179	.325	10.3%	22.1%	55.5%	81.8%	26.6%	62.2%	17.6	99.4	92	0.0	0.0	0.1
2023	BOS	MLB	26	109	13	2	13	0	.225/.361/.337	.295	.476	12.8%	23.9%	58.9%	84.9%	28.2%	57.1%	13.7	100.5	99	-0.1	-0.3	0.3
2024 DC	SEA	MLB	27	450	47	12	47	2	.224/.320/.361	.271	.488	10.2%	22.7%							97	-0.3	-0.5	1.0

2023 GP: 2B (39), 3B (19)   Comps: Rubén Tejada (46), Mark Lewis (45), Jurickson Profar (45)

Urías' 2023 season was like wandering around a parking lot trying to catch a glint of phone reception. The previous two years, he had full bars as he bashed 39 home runs, but all of a sudden he couldn't even send a text out of the ballpark. There was a momentary blip when he tapped into his latent power: He slugged grand slams on consecutive pitches across two games on July 17 and 19. After that, he went dark again, becoming frustratingly punchless at the plate for the rest of the season. He remains a capable infielder who can draw a walk, so he'll get a chance in Seattle to reconnect with his home-run stroke. If not, remember that a phone without service is just an overpriced flashlight.

———————————   ★ ★ ★ *2024 Top 101 Prospect* **#61** ★ ★ ★   ———————————

Cole Young SS   Born: 07/29/03   Age: 20   Bats: L   Throws: R   Height: 6'0"   Weight: 180   Origin: Round 1, 2022 Draft (#21 overall)

YEAR	TM	LVL	AGE	PA	R	HR	RBI	SB	AVG/OBP/SLG	BABIP	SLGCON	BB%	K%	ZSw%	ZCon%	OSw%	OCon%	LA	90th EV	DRC+	BRR	DRP	WARP
2022	MRN	ROK	18	26	6	0	5	3	.333/.423/.476	.389	.588	15.4%	15.4%										
2022	MOD	A	18	45	11	2	9	1	.385/.422/.538	.371	.600	8.9%	8.9%							118	-0.3	0.0	0.2
2023	MOD	A	19	376	60	5	39	17	.267/.396/.429	.303	.518	14.4%	13.8%							130	-0.9	2.7	3.1
2023	EVE	A+	19	230	32	6	23	5	.292/.404/.479	.336	.597	14.8%	16.5%							130	-4.1	1.1	1.2
2024 non	SEA	MLB	20	251	21	3	21	0	.224/.298/.329	.269	.414	8.6%	18.3%							79	0.0	0	0.2

2023 GP: SS (114), 2B (12), DH (1)   Comps: J.P. Crawford (71), Royce Lewis (65), Geraldo Perdomo (63)

Introducing: Gen Z Daniel Murphy. Young's reputation as one of the more advanced hitters in the 2022 prep class only strengthened as he confidently handled both levels of A-ball without much fuss, running a nearly even strikeout-to-walk ratio while turning in a top-five DRC+ at both levels (min. 200 PA). The only red flag at the plate thus far has been a noticeable lack of power production against lefties, but his .394 OBP against southpaws in 2023 suggests he was hardly overmatched, just somewhat nerfed. Added muscle has begun to unlock more power potential for Young on the whole, though it's come more in the form of doubles than homers. While he's comfortable and largely dependable at shortstop, increased bulk as he ages may necessitate a move to the other side of second base. These are nitpicks, though. For now, Young appears well on track to someday elicit compliments from broadcasts about how he's just a **professional hitter**—just as Murphy did for many years.

PITCHERS

Prelander Berroa RHP Born: 04/18/00 Age: 24 Height: 5'11" Weight: 170 Origin: IFA, 2016

YEAR	TM	LVL	AGE	G(GS)	IP	W-L	SV	K	WHIP	ERA	CSP	BB%	K%	HR%	GB%	ZSw%	ZCon%	OSw%	OCon%	BABIP	SLGCON	DRA-	WARP
2021	SJ	A	21	24(24)	98²	5-6	0	135	1.34	3.56		12.6%	32.2%	3.1%	39.2%					.310	.598	94	0.9
2022	EVE	A+	22	13(13)	52¹	2-2	0	81	1.17	2.41		14.9%	37.7%	0.9%	49.0%					.276	.440	78	1.1
2022	EUG	A+	22	4(4)	13¹	0-0	0	16	0.83	0.67		12.8%	34.0%	0.0%	32.0%					.200	.280	88	0.2
2022	ARK	AA	22	9(9)	35	2-1	0	53	1.29	4.37		16.8%	35.6%	2.0%	46.4%					.262	.478	69	0.8
2023	ARK	AA	23	43(5)	65¹	5-1	6	101	1.29	2.89		14.1%	36.6%	0.7%	40.3%					.326	.485	78	1.6
2023	SEA	MLB	23	2(0)	1²	0-0	0	3	1.80	0.00	37.1%	37.5%	37.5%	0.0%	50.0%	43.8%	85.7%	20.0%	0.0%	.000	.000	95	0.0
2024 DC	SEA	MLB	24	18(0)	21	1-1	0	28	1.45	4.67	37.1%	14.5%	29.6%	3.5%	37.0%					.283	.608	102	0.1

2023 Arsenal: SL (85.7), FA (96.2) *Comps: Wilmer Font (38), Michel Baez (38), Dylan Cease (38)*

Even an optimistic outcome for this wiry but electric right-hander projects to have his outings referred to by fans as "The Prelander Berroa Experience." In an era littered with bullpen arms unleashing plus-plus stuff with minus-minus command, Berroa takes things to an extreme. Among 446 pitchers with at least 150 MiLB innings over the past two seasons, only prized Giants lefty Kyle Harrison (38.4%) struck out a higher percentage of opposing batters than Berroa (36.5%), but only a handful issued free passes with greater frequency (14.8%). The sizable workload is attributable to the fact that, somewhat miraculously, Berroa was still being developed as a starter a month into the 2023 season. After a few too many flammable starts in Double-A forced the long-anticipated move to the bullpen, Berroa's vicious vertical fastball-slider combo continued to shine in high-leverage situations, and the control improved steadily as the summer went on. That an arm with Berroa's volatile yet substantial upside was acquired for the most vanilla utility infielder imaginable in Donovan Walton was amusing enough at the time, but what happens next will determine whether it was merely a deal of hilarious contrast or one of the finest swaps among Jerry Dipoto's vast collection.

Matt Brash RHP Born: 05/12/98 Age: 26 Height: 6'1" Weight: 173 Origin: Round 4, 2019 Draft (#113 overall)

YEAR	TM	LVL	AGE	G(GS)	IP	W-L	SV	K	WHIP	ERA	CSP	BB%	K%	HR%	GB%	ZSw%	ZCon%	OSw%	OCon%	BABIP	SLGCON	DRA-	WARP
2021	EVE	A+	23	10(9)	42¹	3-2	1	62	1.32	2.55		13.7%	33.9%	1.6%	51.1%					.315	.478	92	0.5
2021	ARK	AA	23	10(10)	55	3-2	0	80	1.00	2.13		10.4%	36.0%	1.4%	45.8%					.252	.398	78	1.0
2022	TAC	AAA	24	22(0)	26	0-1	3	41	1.27	3.46		13.1%	38.3%	3.7%	50.0%	67.0%	77.9%	28.1%	47.4%	.319	.686	65	0.7
2022	SEA	MLB	24	39(5)	50²	4-4	0	62	1.56	4.44	52.6%	14.9%	27.9%	1.4%	51.2%	58.7%	82.2%	31.3%	51.1%	.355	.492	89	0.8
2023	SEA	MLB	25	78(0)	70²	9-4	4	107	1.33	3.06	43.6%	9.4%	34.7%	1.0%	45.2%	60.3%	77.9%	33.2%	41.8%	.380	.537	70	1.9
2024 DC	SEA	MLB	26	49(0)	52²	3-3	4	74	1.25	3.59	46.9%	11.6%	32.9%	2.9%	46.2%					.291	.562	82	0.8

2023 Arsenal: SW (89.1), FA (98.2), KC (86), SI (98.6), FC (94.6), CH (87.8) *Comps: Ryan Cook (76), Ty Buttrey (72), Brayan Villarreal (72)*

That the wiry frame and lightning-quick arm of Brash has transitioned splendidly to a vital relief role is hardly a surprise. But for the slender Canadian to sustain his ferocious arsenal with such consistency as to enable his participation in nearly half of Seattle's games? That's a much more difficult reality to comprehend. With dreams of starting officially in the rearview, Brash found a different way to rack up innings via more frequent intervals of concentrated electricity; his 78 appearances led all big-league bullpen arms in 2023. Along the way, Brash cranked up the usage of his outrageous slider to great effect, further establishing the pitch as one of baseball's most dynamic breakers. The command remains fair at best, but it matters little when the stuff is this good. Brash is the ideal modern relief weapon, one who blends high-leverage with high-usage, affording his manager an exceptionally valuable late-inning button to press multiple times a week.

Luis Castillo RHP Born: 12/12/92 Age: 31 Height: 6'2" Weight: 200 Origin: IFA, 2012

YEAR	TM	LVL	AGE	G(GS)	IP	W-L	SV	K	WHIP	ERA	CSP	BB%	K%	HR%	GB%	ZSw%	ZCon%	OSw%	OCon%	BABIP	SLGCON	DRA-	WARP
2021	CIN	MLB	28	33(33)	187²	8-16	0	192	1.36	3.98	50.2%	9.3%	23.9%	2.4%	55.6%	70.5%	80.4%	35.6%	59.7%	.323	.551	81	3.7
2022	LOU	AAA	29	2(2)	8	0-0	0	12	1.25	0.00		14.7%	35.3%	0.0%	58.8%					.294	.412	85	0.2
2022	CIN	MLB	29	14(14)	85	4-4	0	90	1.07	2.86	53.7%	8.0%	25.8%	2.0%	46.9%	68.2%	81.7%	33.2%	60.4%	.257	.446	80	1.7
2022	SEA	MLB	29	11(11)	65¹	4-2	0	77	1.10	3.17	54.2%	6.4%	28.9%	2.3%	45.8%	70.5%	78.4%	35.7%	59.2%	.302	.512	72	1.6
2023	SEA	MLB	30	33(33)	197	14-9	0	219	1.10	3.34	46.4%	7.0%	27.3%	3.5%	38.9%	74.2%	78.6%	36.2%	55.9%	.268	.562	92	3.2
2024 DC	SEA	MLB	31	31(31)	184²	12-9	0	190	1.22	3.91	48.9%	8.1%	24.5%	3.6%	43.3%					.278	.553	91	2.5

2023 Arsenal: FA (96.4), SL (85.8), SI (96), CH (88.5) *Comps: Jake Peavy (85), Camilo Pascual (84), Bob Welch (84)*

Castillo's 2023 was the equivalent of a plane skidding off the tarmac after a transatlantic flight that featured minimal turbulence. After logging at least five innings in each of his first 31 starts, Castillo's command uncharacteristically abandoned him at the worst possible time in Game 161 against Texas, forcing an early exit in the third inning to set the stage for the loss that officially eliminated Seattle from postseason contention. It was an unfortunate end to a campaign in which Castillo largely looked like the ace the Mariners paid a hefty price for at the 2022 deadline. Amidst the steady success, a few changes to Castillo's profile emerged. He threw more four-seamers than ever before, and for good reason: By Run Value, it was one of baseball's best, ranking behind only Gerrit Cole and Zac Gallen among traditional heaters. On the flip side, a de-emphasis of both his sinker and changeup in favor of the slider as his go-to secondary appeared to contribute to a less favorable trend: the lowest ground-ball rate of Castillo's career. Granted, there are worse home venues in which to exhibit such a shift in batted-ball distribution than the spacious T-Mobile Park.

Assuming health, Castillo doesn't need to change a thing in order to offer tremendous value. Nevertheless, how he and the organization choose to optimize his attack as he enters his 30s will be fascinating to monitor. It seems absurd to yearn for more from a pitcher as accomplished as Castillo, but his high-powered arsenal makes it hard not to dream even bigger.

Anthony DeSclafani RHP   Born: 04/18/90   Age: 34   Height: 6'2"   Weight: 195   Origin: Round 6, 2011 Draft (#199 overall)

YEAR	TM	LVL	AGE	G (GS)	IP	W-L	SV	K	WHIP	ERA	CSP	BB%	K%	HR%	GB%	ZSw%	ZCon%	OSw%	OCon%	BABIP	SLGCON	DRA-	WARP
2021	SF	MLB	31	31 (31)	167²	13-7	0	152	1.09	3.17	56.5%	6.2%	22.5%	2.8%	43.3%	69.3%	85.3%	32.5%	60.2%	.268	.473	84	3.0
2022	SF	MLB	32	5 (5)	19	0-2	0	17	2.00	6.63	57.0%	4.3%	18.1%	4.3%	43.1%	63.7%	89.5%	34.5%	61.2%	.448	.824	98	0.2
2023	SF	MLB	33	19 (18)	99²	4-8	0	79	1.25	4.88	47.9%	4.8%	18.9%	3.6%	41.0%	69.1%	89.1%	30.7%	65.5%	.303	.573	104	0.9
2024 DC	SEA	MLB	34	34 (16)	105¹	6-6	0	78	1.32	4.60	51.3%	6.5%	17.3%	3.5%	41.0%					.289	.538	104	0.7

2023 Arsenal: SL (87.4), SI (93.2), FA (93.3), CH (86.4), KC (82.4)   Comps: *Rick Wise (80), Frank Lary (80), Charles Nagy (80)*

DeSclafani had a nice rebound to start the year, with a miniscule 3.2% walk rate offsetting a low K-rate in his first nine starts for a 3.09 ERA. When the BABIP ticked up and the home runs started flowing in his remaining 10 appearances, he had a 7.11 ERA. One could argue that DeSclafani was a bit unlucky with all the homers and a low strand rate, but he got so few whiffs that it's hard to believe better is coming. Like teammate Ross Stripling, his best hope moving forward seems to be walking so few batters that things work out okay; unlike the now-healthy Stripling, DeSclafani ended the season on the IL with a flexor strain. If you're in the mood for optimism, there was a clear loss of carry on the fastball and decline in cut on the slider over the course of the season, so it's pretty clear how to get the early-season Disco back.

Logan Gilbert RHP   Born: 05/05/97   Age: 27   Height: 6'6"   Weight: 215   Origin: Round 1, 2018 Draft (#14 overall)

YEAR	TM	LVL	AGE	G (GS)	IP	W-L	SV	K	WHIP	ERA	CSP	BB%	K%	HR%	GB%	ZSw%	ZCon%	OSw%	OCon%	BABIP	SLGCON	DRA-	WARP
2021	SEA	MLB	24	24 (24)	119¹	6-5	0	128	1.17	4.68	57.5%	5.6%	25.4%	3.4%	32.6%	75.5%	79.0%	32.0%	61.7%	.295	.586	104	0.9
2022	SEA	MLB	25	32 (32)	185²	13-6	0	174	1.18	3.20	57.6%	6.4%	22.7%	2.5%	36.3%	73.5%	80.9%	31.9%	66.4%	.294	.519	97	2.0
2023	SEA	MLB	26	32 (32)	190²	13-7	0	189	1.08	3.73	51.3%	4.7%	24.5%	3.8%	41.4%	73.1%	83.8%	34.0%	55.1%	.274	.553	86	3.7
2024 DC	SEA	MLB	27	29 (29)	174²	12-9	0	162	1.20	3.96	54.8%	6.1%	22.2%	3.6%	39.0%					.284	.554	93	2.2

2023 Arsenal: FA (95.9), SL (88.8), FS (85.6), KC (80.3), SI (94.7)   Comps: *Homer Bailey (83), Jered Weaver (82), Dylan Bundy (82)*

Still yet to miss a start since making his debut in 2021, Gilbert has methodically munched innings in a manner that is something of a marvel relative to his generation of five-and-dive artists. However, Gilbert's proclivity for allowing loud, often airborne contact has thus far limited an elevation in his status from workhorse to something greater. While a shift from a pedestrian changeup to a gnarly splitter in Year Three was a legitimate breakthrough in Gilbert's search for more whiffs, his four-seamer continued to get punished with alarming regularity. Whether he adjusts the specs on his heater or simply continues to de-emphasize its overall usage, his best bet at avoiding more barrels almost certainly lies in his secondaries. It's not just the fresh new splitter, either: Gilbert ratcheted up the velo on his slider a couple ticks and threw it more than ever, with great results. With plus command already in store, Gilbert has all the ingredients necessary to take another leap.

Emerson Hancock RHP   Born: 05/31/99   Age: 25   Height: 6'4"   Weight: 213   Origin: Round 1, 2020 Draft (#6 overall)

YEAR	TM	LVL	AGE	G (GS)	IP	W-L	SV	K	WHIP	ERA	CSP	BB%	K%	HR%	GB%	ZSw%	ZCon%	OSw%	OCon%	BABIP	SLGCON	DRA-	WARP
2021	EVE	A+	22	9 (9)	31	2-0	0	30	1.03	2.32		10.5%	24.2%	0.8%	57.0%					.231	.364	100	0.2
2021	ARK	AA	22	3 (3)	13²	1-1	0	13	1.02	3.29		7.3%	23.6%	0.0%	36.8%					.263	.289	95	0.1
2022	ARK	AA	23	21 (21)	98¹	7-4	0	92	1.20	3.75		9.2%	22.3%	3.9%	34.5%					.245	.526	91	1.0
2023	ARK	AA	24	20 (20)	98	11-5	0	107	1.23	4.32		9.2%	26.0%	2.2%	41.7%					.298	.531	88	1.6
2023	SEA	MLB	24	3 (3)	12	0-0	0	6	1.33	4.50	48.1%	6.1%	12.2%	2.0%	50.0%	70.9%	85.7%	40.9%	76.6%	.308	.400	109	0.1
2024 DC	SEA	MLB	25	10 (10)	43²	2-3	0	34	1.44	4.93	48.1%	9.7%	17.5%	3.0%	43.1%					.288	.518	109	0.2

2023 Arsenal: SI (92.8), FC (86.8), FA (92.9), CH (84.8)   Comps: *Taylor Jungmann (48), Luis Castillo (45), Tyler Duffey (44)*

Whether the biggest barrier to Hancock achieving a higher ceiling is his contact-prone arsenal or his ongoing struggles to stay healthy remains somewhat unclear. His first go at big-league bats following an early August call-up was a reminder that his sinker-forward repertoire profiles more as that of a useful arm than an impact one despite his top-six pick pedigree. A shoulder strain after just three starts with the big-league club to end the season on the 60-day was another check in favor of an ever-expanding injury-prone reputation, the kind more commonly ascribed to pitchers without the sturdy build or clean mechanics Hancock exhibits. Pitching can hurt anyone, though, so here we are. There's still plenty of value in a healthy Hancock, though his path to regular run in a rotation would be much clearer in another organization.

George Kirby RHP   Born: 02/04/98   Age: 26   Height: 6'4"   Weight: 215   Origin: Round 1, 2019 Draft (#20 overall)

YEAR	TM	LVL	AGE	G (GS)	IP	W-L	SV	K	WHIP	ERA	CSP	BB%	K%	HR%	GB%	ZSw%	ZCon%	OSw%	OCon%	BABIP	SLGCON	DRA-	WARP
2021	EVE	A+	23	9 (9)	41²	4-2	0	52	0.98	2.38		4.9%	31.7%	0.6%	58.3%					.317	.471	83	0.7
2021	ARK	AA	23	6 (6)	26	1-1	0	28	1.23	2.77		6.4%	25.5%	0.0%	48.6%					.338	.452	83	0.4
2022	ARK	AA	24	5 (5)	24²	2-0	0	32	0.89	1.82		5.4%	34.4%	3.2%	43.6%					.269	.564	65	0.6
2022	SEA	MLB	24	25 (25)	130	8-5	0	133	1.21	3.39	56.6%	4.1%	24.5%	2.4%	45.3%	73.0%	82.6%	35.2%	72.3%	.332	.532	75	3.0
2023	SEA	MLB	25	31 (31)	190²	13-10	0	172	1.04	3.35	52.6%	2.5%	22.7%	2.9%	44.1%	71.0%	84.8%	39.8%	64.8%	.293	.517	87	3.6
2024 DC	SEA	MLB	26	29 (29)	180²	12-9	0	143	1.21	4.01	54.1%	4.8%	18.9%	3.3%	44.4%					.288	.527	94	2.2

2023 Arsenal: FA (96.2), SI (95.9), SW (86.2), KC (82), FS (84.8), CH (86.7), KN (73)   Comps: *Luis Castillo (69), A.J. Griffin (69), Zach Plesac (66)*

While Blake Snell plows ahead with his abstract interpretation of the strike zone, Kirby continues to chart a drastically different course as his generation's most advanced strike-thrower. It didn't take long for his long-standing hatred of free passes to be on full display against the game's best: his 9.05 K/BB in just his second season slots in fifth on the all-time single-season leaderboard among qualified starting pitchers, a touch behind 2002 Curt Schilling and a hair above 2000 Pedro Martinez, if you're curious of the statistical company he already keeps. As long as Kirby lives in the zone to such an extreme degree, his run prevention—and in turn, his chance at awards—may always be beholden to the strength of his defense and the whims of the BABIP gods. But considering Kirby's aptitude for his craft and unrelenting desire to optimize every ounce of his arsenal—on top of a renowned knack for learning new tricks on a whim—it would seem foolish to bet against him finding a way to work in more whiffs without falling too far off the no-walk wagon.

Jackson Kowar   RHP   Born: 10/04/96   Age: 27   Height: 6'5"   Weight: 200   Origin: Round 1, 2018 Draft (#33 overall)

YEAR	TM	LVL	AGE	G (GS)	IP	W-L	SV	K	WHIP	ERA	CSP	BB%	K%	HR%	GB%	ZSw%	ZCon%	OSw%	OCon%	BABIP	SLGCON	DRA-	WARP
2021	OMA	AAA	24	17(16)	80²	9-4	0	115	1.24	3.46		10.1%	34.0%	2.1%	43.8%					.331	.568	76	2.1
2021	KC	MLB	24	9(8)	30¹	0-6	0	29	2.08	11.27	52.2%	13.0%	18.8%	4.5%	35.0%	69.3%	85.2%	25.6%	59.6%	.375	.758	150	-0.5
2022	OMA	AAA	25	20(20)	83¹	4-10	0	88	1.66	6.16		11.1%	22.7%	3.6%	42.7%					.348	.617	108	0.8
2022	KC	MLB	25	7(0)	15²	0-0	0	17	2.43	9.77	54.1%	13.4%	20.7%	4.9%	50.0%	63.2%	89.9%	33.9%	54.0%	.460	.889	95	0.2
2023	OMA	AAA	26	30(1)	45¹	2-5	2	49	1.83	5.96		14.5%	22.3%	1.8%	43.6%	67.9%	77.0%	27.6%	52.3%	.370	.594	108	0.5
2023	KC	MLB	26	23(0)	28	2-0	0	29	1.93	6.43	45.0%	14.6%	21.2%	2.9%	43.7%	68.3%	86.1%	28.2%	53.1%	.361	.609	109	0.2
2024 DC	*SEA*	*MLB*	*27*	*18(0)*	*21*	*1-1*	*0*	*20*	*1.51*	*5.31*	*49.2%*	*11.9%*	*21.4%*	*3.4%*	*41.5%*					*.292*	*.565*	*115*	*0.0*

2023 Arsenal: FA (97), CH (86.7), SL (86.5)   *Comps: Shaun Anderson (70), Anthony Bass (67), Jake Faria (67)*

He shares a first name and intense spirit with action painter Jackson Pollock, but unfortunately also Pollock's spotty sense of a strike zone. Kowar's formerly hard-but-hittable fastball played up out of the bullpen, jumping up to 97 mph on average and inducing more whiffs. Command issues are keeping that much-ballyhooed changeup from being effective and hampering the development of the slider, which looks to be a swing-and-miss weapon when it's not hanging over the middle of the plate. Kowar and the Royals worked intensely on improving his command but, well, *that* didn't work; they finally flipped him to Atlanta over the offseason for Kyle Wright to let the Braves try to help Jackson find his Rhythm, Autumn or otherwise.

Bryce Miller   RHP   Born: 08/23/98   Age: 25   Height: 6'2"   Weight: 200   Origin: Round 4, 2021 Draft (#113 overall)

YEAR	TM	LVL	AGE	G (GS)	IP	W-L	SV	K	WHIP	ERA	CSP	BB%	K%	HR%	GB%	ZSw%	ZCon%	OSw%	OCon%	BABIP	SLGCON	DRA-	WARP
2021	MOD	A	22	5(3)	9¹	0-0	0	15	1.82	4.82		4.4%	33.3%	0.0%	53.6%					.556	.741	81	0.1
2022	EVE	A+	23	16(15)	77²	3-3	0	99	1.02	3.24		7.9%	31.3%	2.2%	45.7%					.264	.506	80	1.5
2022	ARK	AA	23	10(10)	50²	4-1	0	61	1.05	3.20		9.3%	29.9%	1.5%	43.0%					.263	.393	64	1.3
2023	ARK	AA	24	4(4)	19²	0-2	0	18	1.32	6.41		3.5%	21.2%	5.9%	40.6%					.305	.734	106	0.2
2023	SEA	MLB	24	25(25)	131¹	8-7	0	119	1.14	4.32	51.3%	4.8%	22.2%	3.4%	33.8%	74.0%	81.6%	34.0%	64.8%	.290	.560	108	1.0
2024 DC	*SEA*	*MLB*	*25*	*24(24)*	*128²*	*8-8*	*0*	*113*	*1.32*	*4.77*	*51.3%*	*7.2%*	*20.3%*	*3.9%*	*34.8%*					*.290*	*.581*	*108*	*0.6*

2023 Arsenal: FA (95.2), FC (86.6), SW (81.3), SI (95.2), CH (85.1), CU (78.3)   *Comps: David Buchanan (76), Anthony DeSclafani (73), Wade Miley (72)*

Is Miller a One-Pitch Pony? Few starters relied on their four-seamer more heavily (58.5%) than he did as a rookie, and to no surprise: Few hurlers' heaters possess a similar combination of velocity and explosive carry capable of making a Rapsodo unit sing. But while the metrics for the right-hander's fastball continued to jump off the iPad, big-league bats weren't quite as impressed, forcing Miller to wean off his go-to offering as the season went on, prompting struggles that suggest strengthening his secondaries will be paramount moving forward. But while the depth of Miller's arsenal may have underwhelmed, his control of it far exceeded expectations: He filled up in the strike zone a ton in his debut campaign, especially for someone who was walking nearly five batters per nine innings in college not too long ago. The strides with control and durability in pro ball give Miller a great chance to beat the longstanding "he's a reliever" allegations, but he'll need further tweaks to re-establish the reputation he earned as a prospect as a swing-and-miss merchant.

Andrés Muñoz   RHP   Born: 01/16/99   Age: 25   Height: 6'2"   Weight: 222   Origin: IFA, 2015

YEAR	TM	LVL	AGE	G (GS)	IP	W-L	SV	K	WHIP	ERA	CSP	BB%	K%	HR%	GB%	ZSw%	ZCon%	OSw%	OCon%	BABIP	SLGCON	DRA-	WARP
2021	SEA	MLB	22	1(0)	0²	0-0	0	1	3.00	0.00	44.3%	50.0%	25.0%	0.0%	100.0%	16.7%	100.0%	27.3%	66.7%	.000	.000	99	0.0
2022	SEA	MLB	23	64(0)	65	2-5	4	96	0.89	2.49	49.9%	6.0%	38.7%	2.0%	52.6%	71.8%	70.7%	42.9%	44.8%	.297	.473	52	2.2
2023	SEA	MLB	24	52(0)	49	4-7	13	67	1.27	2.94	45.1%	10.4%	31.8%	0.9%	59.0%	65.3%	69.7%	36.3%	49.5%	.330	.479	75	1.2
2024 DC	*SEA*	*MLB*	*25*	*49(0)*	*52²*	*3-6*	*35*	*77*	*1.11*	*2.86*	*47.4%*	*9.5%*	*35.2%*	*2.4%*	*51.5%*					*.291*	*.526*	*69*	*1.1*

2023 Arsenal: SL (88.3), FA (99.1), SI (98.5)   *Comps: Francisco Rodríguez (63), Tim Collins (62), Huston Street (62)*

Long known for his routine visits into triple-digits with his fastball, it was Muñoz's slider that stole the show in his first full year as one of Scott Servais' preferred high-leverage options: In 2022, the right-hander opted for the spinny stuff nearly two-thirds of the time, and with a 51% whiff-rate, it was tough to argue against it as Muñoz's best pitch. Still, it was natural to wonder how Muñoz could better maximize his ability to throw the baseball faster than 99.9999999% of people on the planet. Though his slider remained his most-used offering in 2023, Muñoz identified a new way to leverage his elite heat with the mid-summer introduction of a two-seamer, which quickly stood out visually due to its absurd combination of vertical and horizontal movement that differed greatly from his traditional four-seamer. As if gearing up for a coin flip between 99 mph and a vicious slider wasn't difficult enough, suddenly hitters have to worry about which direction the 99 mph was going. With the help of his nasty new pitch, Muñoz has put himself in the ultra-rare category of pitchers who can rack up grounders as well as they can rack up whiffs. In a bullpen chock full of reclamation projects and unlikely development stories, Muñoz is its most naturally gifted.

Tayler Saucedo LHP   Born: 06/18/93   Age: 31   Height: 6'4"   Weight: 205   Origin: Round 21, 2015 Draft (#632 overall)

YEAR	TM	LVL	AGE	G (GS)	IP	W-L	SV	K	WHIP	ERA	CSP	BB%	K%	HR%	GB%	ZSw%	ZCon%	OSw%	OCon%	BABIP	SLGCON	DRA-	WARP
2021	BUF	AAA	28	12 (0)	18¹	2-1	0	25	0.93	1.96		2.9%	36.2%	0.0%	47.5%					.375	.450	80	0.4
2021	TOR	MLB	28	29 (0)	25²	0-0	0	19	1.25	4.56	45.2%	9.2%	17.4%	0.9%	59.0%	70.2%	90.2%	36.9%	49.5%	.273	.442	95	0.3
2022	BUF	AAA	29	20 (0)	19	1-0	1	28	1.26	2.37		12.2%	34.1%	1.2%	38.1%					.317	.476	74	0.5
2022	TOR	MLB	29	4 (0)	2²	0-0	0	0	2.63	13.50	54.2%	6.7%	0.0%	20.0%	50.0%	78.9%	100.0%	27.6%	50.0%	.273	1.143	100	0.0
2023	TAC	AAA	30	5 (0)	7²	2-0	0	8	0.52	0.00		7.7%	30.8%	0.0%	50.0%	61.4%	77.8%	40.0%	50.0%	.125	.125	94	0.1
2023	SEA	MLB	30	52 (0)	47²	3-2	1	43	1.34	3.59	44.5%	11.1%	20.8%	1.0%	56.0%	60.4%	87.2%	36.5%	53.1%	.300	.409	96	0.7
2024 DC	SEA	MLB	31	49 (0)	52²	3-2	0	55	1.32	4.09	45.0%	9.7%	23.8%	2.3%	52.6%					.294	.497	92	0.5

2023 Arsenal: SI (92.4), CH (86.1), SL (82.8), SW (82.5), CU (77.3), FA (93)   Comps: Tommy Layne (66), Richard Bleier (63), Adam Kolarek (62)

Waiver claims in January aren't often vehicles for lifelong dreams coming true, but that was exactly the case when Saucedo found out his childhood team had acquired him to compete for a relief role. Though he didn't make the Opening Day roster, five nearly flawless outings in Tacoma prompted a quick April promotion to Seattle, where he stuck all year as Scott Servais' go-to option when a ground ball was needed. While it's much more likely Saucedo grew up in Maple Valley fantasizing of one day becoming Ken Griffey Jr. or Randy Johnson than the second lefty out of the Mariners bullpen, it's hard to imagine he's too disappointed with the latter actually coming to fruition.

Gabe Speier LHP   Born: 04/12/95   Age: 29   Height: 5'11"   Weight: 200   Origin: Round 19, 2013 Draft (#563 overall)

YEAR	TM	LVL	AGE	G (GS)	IP	W-L	SV	K	WHIP	ERA	CSP	BB%	K%	HR%	GB%	ZSw%	ZCon%	OSw%	OCon%	BABIP	SLGCON	DRA-	WARP
2021	OMA	AAA	26	45 (0)	45¹	3-0	5	57	1.19	2.98		4.7%	29.8%	2.6%	53.7%					.345	.529	81	1.1
2021	KC	MLB	26	7 (0)	7²	0-0	0	5	1.30	1.17	63.4%	0.0%	15.2%	0.0%	44.4%	61.5%	90.6%	34.0%	55.6%	.370	.370	94	0.1
2022	OMA	AAA	27	30 (0)	26²	1-3	0	34	2.36	14.51		8.3%	23.4%	7.6%	42.7%					.482	1.022	104	0.3
2022	KC	MLB	27	17 (1)	19¹	0-1	0	14	1.09	2.33	55.0%	6.5%	18.2%	2.6%	44.8%	69.9%	87.2%	26.9%	66.0%	.250	.439	96	0.2
2023	SEA	MLB	28	69 (0)	54²	2-2	1	64	1.06	3.79	46.2%	5.1%	29.6%	3.2%	54.3%	65.5%	84.2%	42.7%	53.6%	.305	.551	73	1.4
2024 DC	SEA	MLB	29	49 (0)	52²	3-2	0	52	1.25	3.89	48.7%	7.0%	23.1%	2.7%	47.6%					.299	.520	90	0.5

2023 Arsenal: SI (94.5), SL (84.4), FA (95.1), CH (88.5)   Comps: Scott Alexander (52), Sam Freeman (50), Xavier Cedeño (50)

Bad news for Jesse Pinkman: The Mariners keep getting away with this. *This*, of course, being the development of effective bullpen arms from the most unlikely of places. Speier was claimed off waivers from Kansas City not long after a hellish few months in Triple-A to finish 2022 in which his ERA ballooned to laughable levels, even by Pacific Coast League standards. Undeterred by the ugly statline, Seattle identified Speier's pitch mix as ripe for their vaunted bullpen lab to tweak to their liking. Speier upped the usage of his sinker and the velo on his slider, and voila: He flat-out bullied left-handed hitters, coaxed a ton of grounders and posted the second-highest chase-rate among relievers behind only Robert Stephenson. A few ill-timed homers inflated his ERA to a more pedestrian mark, but the rest of his peripherals suggest Speier's performance was far from a mirage.

Trent Thornton RHP   Born: 09/30/93   Age: 30   Height: 6'0"   Weight: 190   Origin: Round 5, 2015 Draft (#139 overall)

YEAR	TM	LVL	AGE	G (GS)	IP	W-L	SV	K	WHIP	ERA	CSP	BB%	K%	HR%	GB%	ZSw%	ZCon%	OSw%	OCon%	BABIP	SLGCON	DRA-	WARP
2021	BUF	AAA	27	10 (0)	10¹	1-0	3	8	0.97	0.00		5.0%	20.0%	0.0%	50.0%					.267	.367	90	0.2
2021	TOR	MLB	27	37 (3)	49	1-3	0	52	1.43	4.78	53.8%	7.4%	24.1%	5.6%	41.0%	69.4%	82.5%	32.5%	67.4%	.321	.732	102	0.4
2022	BUF	AAA	28	21 (0)	28	2-2	3	30	1.36	2.89		9.8%	24.6%	0.8%	41.8%					.325	.455	97	0.4
2022	TOR	MLB	28	32 (0)	46	0-2	0	37	1.24	4.11	61.2%	9.0%	19.6%	3.7%	36.6%	65.6%	89.8%	28.8%	60.0%	.260	.508	105	0.3
2023	BUF	AAA	29	22 (0)	28	5-1	0	26	1.64	4.18		13.7%	19.8%	3.1%	43.7%	59.3%	81.5%	31.0%	57.7%	.293	.548	112	0.2
2023	SEA	MLB	29	23 (1)	26	1-2	0	21	1.08	2.08	51.2%	4.9%	20.4%	4.9%	37.7%	64.7%	84.5%	33.3%	66.7%	.250	.584	98	0.3
2023	TOR	MLB	29	4 (0)	5¹	0-0	0	5	1.50	1.69	44.8%	4.5%	22.7%	0.0%	50.0%	64.7%	90.9%	36.2%	64.7%	.438	.438	94	0.1
2024 DC	SEA	MLB	30	49 (0)	52²	3-3	0	43	1.39	4.87	52.2%	8.7%	18.6%	3.6%	37.4%					.286	.549	109	0.0

2023 Arsenal: SW (79.5), FA (93.9), CU (79.7), SI (93.3), FC (87.5), FS (85.5)   Comps: Tyler Duffey (67), Luis Cessa (58), Tommy Hunter (58)

Thornton puts the "mid" in "middle relief." Cast aside by Toronto, Seattle was the perfect landing spot for Thornton to make the necessary tweaks and be reminded of what all the cool kids are doing in the bullpen nowadays: just throw a bunch of sweepers, dude. Thornton also threw a higher percentage of sinkers than ever before, a long overdue transition after years of his four-seamer getting punished. He's still a bit too homer-prone to trust in high-leverage, but a continued shift away from hittable heaters in favor of breaking balls and ground-pounding two-seamers could do wonders for the bespectacled right-hander.

Justin Topa   RHP   Born: 03/07/91   Age: 33   Height: 6'4"   Weight: 200   Origin: Round 17, 2013 Draft (#509 overall)

YEAR	TM	LVL	AGE	G (GS)	IP	W-L	SV	K	WHIP	ERA	CSP	BB%	K%	HR%	GB%	ZSw%	ZCon%	OSw%	OCon%	BABIP	SLGCON	DRA-	WARP
2021	NAS	AAA	30	10(0)	9	1-0	0	9	1.00	3.00		5.6%	25.0%	0.0%	68.0%					.280	.280	93	0.2
2021	MIL	MLB	30	4(0)	3¹	0-0	0	1	3.90	29.70	58.7%	4.3%	4.3%	8.7%	42.9%	64.4%	93.1%	35.9%	78.6%	.526	1.000	106	0.0
2022	NAS	AAA	31	17(0)	18²	2-0	0	17	1.66	4.34		9.2%	19.5%	0.0%	59.3%					.390	.431	100	0.2
2022	MIL	MLB	31	7(0)	7¹	0-0	0	4	1.77	4.91	47.3%	11.4%	11.4%	0.0%	74.1%	56.8%	96.0%	32.1%	76.9%	.333	.370	92	0.1
2023	SEA	MLB	32	75(0)	69	5-4	3	61	1.14	2.61	53.0%	6.5%	21.9%	1.4%	55.8%	63.3%	86.4%	30.3%	70.3%	.297	.430	80	1.5
2024 DC	SEA	MLB	33	49(0)	52²	3-3	4	37	1.30	4.01	52.9%	7.5%	16.2%	2.2%	53.5%					.282	.458	92	0.5

2023 Arsenal: SI (95.1), SW (83), FC (92.7), CH (86.7)   Comps: Pat Venditte (34), Blake Parker (32), James Hoyt (32)

Topa's success in 2023 may be as much of a triumph for the Seattle training staff as their vaunted pitching development apparatus. His stuff has impressed dating back to 2019, when Milwaukee scooped him out of indy ball, but staying on the mound had been a challenge to say the least. After appearing in 84 total games between the minors and majors across four seasons between 2019 and 2022, Topa pitched in an astonishing 75 MLB games in his first year as a Mariner, tied with Emmanuel Clase and Miguel Castro for the second-most in baseball behind only his teammate Matt Brash. While the rest of his bullpen-mates racked up the whiffs, Topa neutralized opposing batters with different tactics. His sinker-slider-cutter attack induced weak contact with tremendous consistency, earning him regular high-leverage responsibilities. Whether his newfound durability sustains remains uncertain, but Topa's ability to get late-inning outs proved fairly convincing.

Bryan Woo   RHP   Born: 01/30/00   Age: 24   Height: 6'2"   Weight: 205   Origin: Round 6, 2021 Draft (#174 overall)

YEAR	TM	LVL	AGE	G (GS)	IP	W-L	SV	K	WHIP	ERA	CSP	BB%	K%	HR%	GB%	ZSw%	ZCon%	OSw%	OCon%	BABIP	SLGCON	DRA-	WARP
2022	MOD	A	22	6(6)	20¹	0-1	0	29	1.18	3.98		7.1%	34.1%	2.4%	37.5%					.356	.717	86	0.2
2022	EVE	A+	22	7(7)	32	1-3	0	46	1.50	4.78		10.8%	31.1%	1.4%	35.4%					.375	.600	92	0.4
2023	ARK	AA	23	9(9)	44	3-2	0	59	0.89	2.05		7.0%	34.3%	1.2%	32.3%					.266	.375	85	1.0
2023	SEA	MLB	23	18(18)	87²	4-5	0	93	1.21	4.21	49.7%	8.4%	25.1%	3.5%	40.0%	73.4%	77.6%	32.0%	61.3%	.274	.546	100	1.0
2024 DC	SEA	MLB	24	23(23)	111	6-6	0	118	1.29	4.27	49.7%	9.2%	24.7%	3.2%	38.7%					.287	.554	96	1.2

2023 Arsenal: FA (95.3), SI (95.2), FC (87.7), SW (83.3), CH (89.9)   Comps: Griffin Canning (77), Danny Salazar (74), Cristian Javier (72)

If you're wondering how Woo snuck up on much of the industry, consider this: across 27 starts in 2023 (18 in MLB), the right-hander accrued more innings (131 ⅔) than he had in the previous four years combined between his collegiate career at Cal Poly and his MILB debut in 2022 (126 ⅓). It was this staggering jump in workload that Seattle was tasked with managing, balancing the urge to run the ultra-talented Woo out every fifth day with the need to responsibly preserve the young pitcher's bright future. Considering the interruptions he endured early in his career—the pandemic wrecked his sophomore season before Tommy John surgery cut his junior year short going into the Draft—no one would have held a more gradual development against Woo. Instead, his picturesque delivery and a deep repertoire headlined by two different highly effective heaters rocketed Woo to the big-league rotation in a relative blink. While his fastball-forward attack worked wonders as a rookie, a more consistent dose of something slower may make Woo even more of a headache for opponents. Having already come so far so quickly, Woo's ability to make that adjustment in short order should probably not be doubted.

LINEOUTS

Hitters

HITTER	POS	TM	LVL	AGE	PA	R	HR	RBI	SB	AVG/OBP/SLG	BABIP	SLGCON	BB%	K%	ZSw%	ZCon%	OSw%	OCon%	LA	90th EV	DRC+	BRR	DRP	WARP
Michael Arroyo	SS	MOD	A	18	265	45	2	23	5	.234/.389/.373	.301	.500	13.6%	20.0%							115	2.0	-2.6	1.3
Zach DeLoach	RF	TAC	AAA	24	623	90	23	88	8	.286/.387/.481	.380	.715	13.3%	27.8%	69.9%	77.1%	26.1%	44.2%			98	-1.1	4.4	1.9
Isiah Gilliam	DH	ARK	AA	26	422	70	22	66	22	.281/.393/.523	.391	.852	14.7%	32.2%							104	-0.5	-0.4	1.4
	DH	TAC	AAA	26	101	8	3	14	3	.253/.386/.410	.327	.586	14.9%	24.8%	74.7%	80.3%	25.3%	60.3%			96	-0.6	-0.8	-0.1
Blake Hunt	C	MTG	AA	24	155	22	6	18	2	.250/.342/.455	.297	.638	9.0%	24.5%							110	0.4	-1.7	0.5
	C	DUR	AAA	24	126	18	6	23	0	.263/.317/.518	.276	.648	6.3%	18.3%	69.4%	88.8%	40.1%	60.6%			103	0.4	-0.2	0.5
Tyler Locklear	1B	PEJ	WIN	22	85	13	3	16	1	.290/.400/.493	.370	.723	12.9%	25.9%	80.0%	83.3%	31.8%	57.1%						
	1B	EVE	A+	22	275	40	12	44	10	.305/.422/.549	.365	.747	13.1%	21.8%							122	1.3	0.3	1.6
	1B	ARK	AA	22	94	11	1	8	2	.260/.383/.403	.302	.492	11.7%	14.9%							104	0.2	0.0	0.2
Brian O'Keefe	C	TAC	AAA	29	403	63	23	67	2	.238/.328/.504	.262	.701	11.4%	24.6%	71.5%	75.8%	27.8%	51.7%			106	-0.6	4.3	1.7
	C	SEA	MLB	29	21	0	0	2	0	.105/.190/.211	.167	.333	9.5%	33.3%	78.8%	65.4%	30.2%	23.1%	31.5	102.9	74	0.0	-0.5	0.0
Alberto Rodriguez	RF	EVE	A+	22	322	61	11	58	3	.306/.393/.580	.373	.769	9.6%	21.4%							125	-1.7	-0.5	1.9
	RF	ARK	AA	22	202	17	3	27	5	.291/.361/.385	.386	.539	9.9%	25.2%							93	0.5	2.3	0.6
Jake Scheiner	IF	TAC	AAA	27	553	91	30	105	5	.252/.369/.509	.286	.718	14.6%	24.2%	62.3%	80.5%	23.6%	43.2%			112	-3.9	-8.4	1.2
Aidan Smith	CF	MRN	ROK	18	30	7	0	3	6	.261/.433/.435	.400	.667	20.0%	26.7%										
	CF	MOD	A	18	54	11	1	5	0	.184/.259/.327	.250	.485	7.4%	29.6%							88	0.8	1.9	0.3
Luis Suisbel	IF	MRN	ROK	20	140	28	6	25	4	.291/.471/.573	.407	.922	18.6%	27.9%										
	IF	MOD	A	20	144	26	6	32	0	.290/.375/.492	.390	.753	8.3%	29.9%							106	0.2	1.3	0.6
Seby Zavala	C	CHW	MLB	29	176	15	7	16	1	.155/.207/.304	.205	.527	5.7%	38.6%	71.8%	76.0%	43.2%	44.8%	14.1	101.8	49	-0.2	4.8	0.1
	C	AZ	MLB	29	17	2	0	2	0	.357/.471/.429	.417	.500	11.8%	11.8%	50.0%	76.9%	35.3%	58.3%	15.4	96.8	51	0.0	0.3	0.0

The recipient of a $1.3 million signing bonus out of Colombia in 2021, **Michael Arroyo** more than held his own as one of the youngest hitters in the California League. Perhaps more importantly, he continued to spend the bulk of his time in the field at shortstop, a trend that will need to sustain if his long-lauded bat ends up being more good than great. ⊗ That **Zach DeLoach** was added to the 40-man after the season to shield him from a potential Rule 5 selection would seem to indicate a level of confidence that he could contribute at the MLB level sooner rather than later. The fact that DeLoach was never considered a viable option in Seattle at any point across his PCL-leading 623 plate appearances in Triple-A suggests otherwise. ⊗ A longtime Yankees farmhand who never quite actualized a toolset lauded by scouts since his amateur days, **Isiah Gilliam** enjoyed a productive campaign after signing with Seattle as a minor-league free agent. The switch-hitting outfielder was one of just five MiLB players to collect at least 25 homers and 25 steals. ⊗ The Mariners traded for **Blake Hunt** and immediately added him to the 40-man roster, which means he will compete for the role of backup dumper. ⊗ Right-right 1B/DH-types are a notoriously tenuous prospect profile, but 2022 second-round pick **Tyler Locklear** is off to a promising start in pro ball since his days pummeling Atlantic-10 pitching at VCU. He takes his walks, hits the ball hard and doesn't whiff an ugly amount. A big year in Double-A (or beyond) could help further clarify whether he's on a Rhys Hoskins track or if he's destined to be launching dingers for the Doosan Bears in 2027. ⊗ While Cal Raleigh was busy leading all major-league catchers in homers in 2023, **Brian O'Keefe** was the gold standard among power production for Pacific Coast League backstops. His 23 home runs for the Rainiers brought his career MiLB total to 116. His first big-league big fly still awaits. ⊗ **Alberto Rodriguez** did what you'd hope a bat-first prospect would do in a return trip to High-A as a 22-year-old: dominate. His production in Double-A after a promotion, however, reverted to a more underwhelming level more in line with his track record of hitting without really *raking*. ⊗ Acquired from Philadelphia for Jay Bruce back in 2019, **Jake Scheiner** was one of just four hitters across all of MiLB to clear 30 home runs and 100 RBI in 2023. He was named Co-Hitter of the Year among Mariners farmhands alongside Lazaro Montes, an amusing pair to share an award considering the nine-year age gap. ⊗ **Aidan Smith** was the last of four high school hitters to receive a seven-figure bonus from Seattle in the 2023 Draft. In a relatively down year for amateur talent in the Lone Star State, Smith's well-rounded game stood out as especially good value for the Mariners to land in the fourth round. ⊗ The switch-hitting **Luis Suisbel** showed little evidence of a pending breakout across two summers of middling production in the Dominican Summer League. That changed upon his arrival stateside: The stocky infielder torched the complex competition before a late-season call-up to Low-A, where the raking continued. The bat demands some level of attention, though the whiffs are a concern and he'll need to avoid falling too far down the defensive spectrum to stay relevant. ⊗ **Seby Zavala** approaches hitting like it's a technical challenge on the Great British Bake Off: there's a general sense of knowing what to do but a much more specific sense of not knowing how to do it, and further, not being able to.

Pitchers

PITCHER	TM	LVL	AGE	G (GS)	IP	W-L	SV	K	WHIP	ERA	CSP	BB%	K%	HR%	GB%	ZSw%	ZCon%	OSw%	OCon%	BABIP	SLGCON	DRA-	WARP
Ty Adcock	EVE	A+	26	6 (0)	7	1-0	1	9	0.43	0.00		8.3%	37.5%	0.0%	66.7%					.083	.083	85	0.1
	ARK	AA	26	13 (0)	13²	0-0	2	13	0.80	2.63		5.9%	25.5%	2.0%	32.4%					.212	.382	104	0.1
	SEA	MLB	26	12 (0)	15²	0-0	0	11	0.70	3.45	53.0%	0.0%	19.0%	6.9%	36.2%	81.2%	87.2%	37.8%	61.9%	.163	.553	98	0.2
Eduard Bazardo	TAC	AAA	27	10 (0)	9¹	1-0	0	15	1.61	3.86		11.6%	34.9%	2.3%	59.1%	49.4%	82.5%	31.2%	57.1%	.429	.636	67	
	NOR	AAA	27	27 (1)	38¹	4-1	2	43	1.10	3.05		7.0%	27.2%	0.6%	38.0%	59.9%	83.5%	33.5%	54.0%	.303	.424	97	0.6
	SEA	MLB	27	9 (0)	13²	0-0	0	14	0.95	2.63	47.3%	7.4%	25.9%	3.7%	41.7%	71.8%	85.2%	39.0%	56.2%	.206	.500	99	0.2
	BAL	MLB	27	3 (0)	2¹	0-0	0	1	2.57	15.43	44.1%	0.0%	7.7%	0.0%	33.3%	72.7%	81.2%	45.0%	66.7%	.500	.750	103	0.0
Cody Bolton	IND	AAA	25	34 (2)	46²	3-4	1	47	1.22	3.86		9.2%	24.1%	1.0%	35.7%	68.5%	78.2%	28.9%	55.0%	.301	.475	100	0.7
	PIT	MLB	25	16 (0)	21¹	1-0	0	22	2.11	6.33	42.3%	14.0%	20.6%	2.8%	36.2%	76.3%	87.4%	23.1%	58.0%	.415	.691	109	0.2
Darren Bowen	MOD	A	22	19 (15)	55²	4-2	0	59	1.10	3.88		10.9%	25.7%	0.9%	37.6%					.246	.388	85	0.5
Taylor Dollard	TAC	AAA	24	3 (3)	8¹	0-2	0	8	1.44	7.56		8.3%	22.2%	11.1%	44.0%	64.8%	89.1%	31.5%	64.3%	.238	1.000	116	0.0
Walter Ford	MRN	ROK	18	9 (8)	22²	0-0	0	23	1.54	3.57		9.7%	22.3%	1.0%	31.3%					.364	.569		
Dominic Leone	RR	AAA	31	8 (0)	11¹	2-0	2	15	1.15	1.59		4.3%	31.9%	2.1%	46.7%	75.3%	82.8%	41.3%	55.8%	.345	.600	81	0.2
	SEA	MLB	31	9 (0)	10¹	0-0	0	10	1.45	4.35	42.4%	17.0%	21.3%	10.6%	42.9%	69.6%	77.1%	30.2%	42.9%	.087	.857	111	0.1
	NYM	MLB	31	31 (0)	30²	1-3	0	33	1.24	4.40	42.8%	8.7%	26.0%	5.5%	35.4%	77.5%	75.8%	39.3%	54.6%	.267	.667	102	0.3
	LAA	MLB	31	11 (0)	13	0-0	1	11	1.85	5.54	38.9%	14.8%	18.0%	3.3%	36.6%	75.3%	83.6%	39.1%	55.7%	.333	.634	114	0.1
Jeter Martinez	DSL SEA	ROK	17	10 (8)	47	2-2	0	55	0.79	1.72		11.2%	30.7%	0.6%	58.4%					.160	.248		
Darren McCaughan	TAC	AAA	27	25 (25)	139	7-8	0	130	1.42	5.83		7.2%	21.2%	4.9%	33.3%	62.9%	87.0%	34.5%	64.9%	.312	.697	111	0.4
	SEA	MLB	27	3 (0)	5	0-0	0	10	2.00	5.40	50.2%	11.1%	37.0%	3.7%	64.3%	57.1%	71.4%	23.8%	46.7%	.462	.786	71	0.1
Michael Morales	MOD	A	20	22 (22)	101¹	5-4	0	106	1.30	4.53		9.2%	24.4%	1.6%	44.7%					.308	.507	82	1.2
Casey Sadler	TAC	AAA	32	18 (0)	15¹	1-0	0	15	1.76	7.63		7.0%	21.1%	4.2%	36.0%	62.4%	90.4%	26.6%	51.4%	.404	.720	80	0.0
Carlos Vargas	RNO	AAA	23	38 (0)	42¹	1-1	2	36	2.10	7.02		15.1%	17.0%	1.4%	60.1%	62.3%	87.9%	27.9%	59.0%	.386	.546	96	0.3
	AZ	MLB	23	5 (0)	4²	0-0	0	7	1.93	5.79	51.6%	18.2%	31.8%	9.1%	50.0%	57.1%	80.0%	28.3%	46.2%	.375	1.100	85	0.1

A former two-way player at Elon where he was teammates with George Kirby, **Ty Adcock** ditched the bat upon entering pro ball at the behest of his employer, who viewed him as a potential impact reliever. The canceled 2020 season and Tommy John surgery delayed his journey substantially. Finally healthy to start 2023, Adcock flew through the minors in a flash. He found immediate success in the big leagues with his high-90's heater and sharp slider, but three straight outings allowing a homer in late July sent him packing back to Double-A, where his season was cut short for good after with an undisclosed injury. ⓧ **Eduard Bazardo** showed promise as a low-leverage slider specialist after arriving via midseason trade from Baltimore. Sorry, nothing bizzar-do say here (no, that's now how you pronounce it). ⓧ **Cody Bolton's** sweeper is suitable for righties, but his fastball's volatility allows lefties to eat him alive. You don't need a math degree to figure that seven strikeouts plus three home runs and 10 walks in 44 batters faced equals disaster. ⓧ In his pro debut, **Darren Bowen** exhibited a lot of what you'd want in a starting pitching prospect (athletic delivery, mid-90's heater, wicked slider) without any of the pedigree (he's a 13th-round pick from a Division II school in North Carolina.) These humble beginnings are important context for what could be a slow developmental burn for a prospect who will already be 23 on Opening Day. ⓧ Labrum surgery forced right-hander **Taylor Dollard** to the IL for the remainder of the season after just three April starts in Triple-A, immediately derailing the momentum carried over from a breakout 2022. His prospects as a prospect are firmly pending a return from a particularly challenging injury. ⓧ **Walter Ford** spent the summer ironing out his complicated delivery on the complex with mixed results in games along the way. Still a teenager for all of 2024, there is ample time for the self-proclaimed Vanilla Missile to make the tweaks necessary to finally launch out of Arizona and bring his unmistakable, undeniably hilarious brand to full-season ball. ⓧ The late-August Angels waiver purge enabled a return to Seattle for **Dominic Leone,** the righty reliever who made his MLB debut with the Mariners back in 2014. The home crowd quickly became disenchanted with the homecoming story when Leone allowed four homers across his first three appearances. ⓧ The $600,000 signing bonus Seattle gave **Jeter Martinez** was one of the largest bonuses given to any pitcher in the 2022 international class. That might say more about teams' increased hesitation to dole out seven-figure bonuses to 16-year-old arms than Martinez's ceiling as a prospect, but the projectable right-hander from Mexico certainly performed like a top prospect in his pro debut in the Dominican Summer League. ⓧ Only one pitcher on the planet has logged more than 300 innings in the Pacific Coast League over the past three seasons, and that's **Darren McCaughan,** whose 408 ⅔ frames completed in MiLB's anti-paradise for pitchers exemplify a profound level of courage and resilience. His prospects as viable big-league depth appear to be waning, but he certainly checks every box of what a future ace in the Dominican Winter League looks like should he have interest in such an opportunity. ⓧ Of the 1,269 major leaguers born in the state of New York, not one has their birthplace listed as Cooperstown. That could change if third-rounder **Teddy McGraw,** who grew up in nearby Oneonta, ever pitches his way to the big leagues. Some scouts thought McGraw's explosive sinker/slider combo could vault him ahead future eighth-overall pick Rhett Lowder on draft boards. Unfortunately, the second Tommy John surgery of his young career wiped out McGraw's junior-year spring. ⓧ A repeat stint in the California League for **Michael Morales** yielded modest improvements across the board statistically, though his pure stuff remains surprisingly stuck in neutral despite a prototypical frame that has long had evaluators yearning for more. ⓧ As expected, **Cole Phillips** didn't throw a single pitch in a 2023 pro game. He did spend some time throwing with the Atlanta coaching staff ahead of his inclusion in the Jackson Kowar-Marco Gonzales-Evan White-Jarred Kelenic deal; if his velocity is still upper-90s, as it was pre-injury, he'll be getting plenty of attention in Seattle. ⓧ Just as he had multiple times earlier in his career, **Casey Sadler** once again persevered through a lengthy rehab, returning to the mound following shoulder surgery that wiped out the entirety of his 2022. Unfortunately, his Tacoma showings never warranted the return to Seattle he truly sought. ⓧ If baseball were an RPG, **Carlos Vargas** is a character you'd create out of boredom and morbid curiosity. "What if I put all my points into velocity and none into command?"

ST. LOUIS CARDINALS

Essay by Ben Clemens

Player comments by Justin Klugh and BP staff

This isn't how it's supposed to work. Whether you were a team employee, player or simply a fan, that sentiment pervaded the 2023 Cardinal season. For almost the entirety of the 21st century, St. Louis has fallen out of bed and into the upper tier of the NL Central. Hiccups were so rare as to feel nonexistent. From 2000 through 2022, the team missed the playoffs seven times; only the Yankees made it to the postseason more consistently. Their worst year was 2007, and even then they won 78 games. The 2023 disaster—a 71-91 record that ended in their first last-place division finish since the days of Joe Magrane—feels like a nightmare or a misprint. These are the *Cardinals*. That kind of stuff doesn't happen here.

The exact mechanics behind the team's long and fruitful run have changed through the years. The equally notorious and nebulous "Cardinal Way" is about baserunning and defense—except when it's about developing positionless hitters like Allen Craig or Matt Carpenter and training them just enough defensively to handle tough positions. It's about homegrown talent—except when it's about trading for Marcell Ozuna, Paul Goldschmidt and Nolan Arenado. It's about pitching well and winning 3-2 games—except when it's about leading the league in runs scored. Mostly, it's about the fact that St. Louis doesn't operate like the rest of the NL Central, or really the rest of the major leagues.

Most successful modern franchises have a clear method at work. The Yankees use their financial might to supplement their homegrown talent with stars, and their minor-league coaching staff is adept at getting the most out of pitching prospects. The Dodgers use money to chase every last edge, whether it's player acquisition or training, and then sign Shohei Ohtani. The Rays trade for profit and unlock new potential in players they acquire. The Orioles draft a million guys, teach them all to pull home runs and then hold onto every single one of them. The Braves scout well and lock up hometown players to extensions that work out for everyone involved. The very best teams combine financial acumen with cutting-edge analysis.

None of those descriptions quite fit the Cardinals. They spend, but not at the top of the league. They draft well, but not exceptionally well. Their minor-league pitching development feels antiquated; they consistently grade out

ST. LOUIS CARDINALS PROSPECTUS
2023 W-L: 71-91, 5TH IN NL CENTRAL

Pythag	.432	25th	DER	.672	30th
RS/G	4.44	19th	DRC+	106	6th
RA/G	5.12	25th	DRA-	105	25th
dWin%	.516	15th	FIP	4.45	22nd
Payroll	$177M	15th	B-Age	27.9	7th
M$/MW	$7.0M	23rd	P-Age	30.6	24th

- Opened 2006
- Open air
- Natural surface
- Fence profile: 8'

Park Factors

Runs	Runs/RH	Runs/LH	HR/RH	HR/LH
97	97	97	89	86

Top Hitter WARP	3.1 Paul Goldschmidt
Top Pitcher WARP	1.4 Steven Matz
2023 Top Prospect	Masyn Winn

Payroll History (in millions)

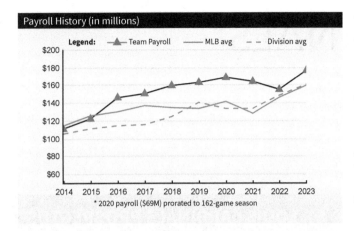

Legend: ▲ Team Payroll —— MLB avg - - Division avg

* 2020 payroll ($69M) prorated to 162-game season

Future Commitments (in millions)

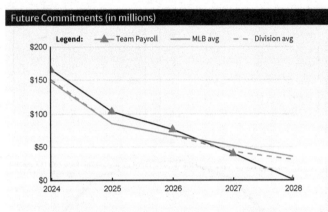

Legend: ▲ Team Payroll —— MLB avg - - Division avg

Farm System Ranking

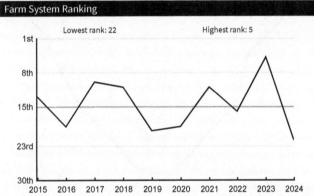

Lowest rank: 22   Highest rank: 5

Personnel

President of Baseball Operations
John Mozeliak

Vice President & General Manager
Mike Girsch

Assistant General Manager
Moisés Rodriguez

Assistant General Manager & Director of Scouting
Randy Flores

Assistant General Manager & Director of Player Development
Gary LaRocque

Manager
Oliver Marmol

BP Alumni
Keanan Lamb
Zach Mortimer
Christopher Rodriguez
Mauricio Rubio
Chaim Bloom

toward the bottom of the barrel whether you're looking at swing-and-miss results or pitch-level modeling. They haven't had much luck in free agency, either; the last Cardinals free agent signee to exceed 2.0 WARP in a single season was Mike Leake in 2016, and his tenure with the team ended so badly that they gave him away for salary relief the very next year.

In fact, the constants in the Cardinals' recent run were players more so than systems. At least one of Yadier Molina, Albert Pujols or Adam Wainwright has appeared on every Cardinals team of the 21st century. Molina in particular felt like a linchpin; he debuted in 2004 and retired after 2022, and seemed to start every game in between. The 2024 season will be the first with none of these veterans left; Wainwright, the last active member of the bunch, rode into the sunset after the 2023 season to the twang of his own soundtrack.

What remains feels like a band without their frontman. It's easy to pinpoint what went wrong in 2023: pitching and defense. Cardinals pitchers allowed the third-most runs in the NL last year, ahead of only the hapless Nationals and mile-high Rockies. They did so despite playing in Busch Stadium, one of the pitcher-friendliest stadiums in the majors. Meanwhile, the defense, long one of St. Louis' strengths, added fuel to the fire. The Cardinals finished 22nd in team DRP, 26 runs worse than the 2022 edition. Things were so bad that 21-year-old phenom Jordan Walker was sent down in late April to work on his defense, and the reasoning wasn't even ironic.

You can't fix the kind of pitching deficit the team faces with half measures, but the Cardinals are certainly trying. Sonny Gray, the gem of their offseason acquisition spree, fits the bill as their number one starter, but things fall off quickly from there. Lance Lynn led the league in home runs allowed last year. Kyle Gibson is the kind of pitcher that teams who can't get top-flight pitching turn to as a contingency plan, except the Cardinals signed him before Thanksgiving. Both of them will throw a lot of innings, but it's hard to tell if that's a relief or a threat. They join holdovers Miles Mikolas and Steven Matz, the latter of whom has performed exactly how Brodie Van Wagenen characterized Zack Wheeler.

It almost seems as though the Cardinals looked at their roster and decided it needed pure bulk volume of outs rather than quality—or perhaps realized they didn't have the budget to get both. In the 18 years from 2006 through 2023, they've had an Opening Day payroll that ranked between 10th and 15th in the majors 16 times. They're headed for another year of the same, but while that might be good for Bill DeWitt's pocketbook, it feels like an insufficient response to the questions posed by the 2023 season.

Mercifully, the hitting side is already in place. The St. Louis farm system has been all hitters in recent years, and the team's blockbuster trades have focused on cornerstone bats as well. Heck, their biggest recent free agent signing is Willson Contreras. The result is a lineup that doesn't need improving, and one that's built to succeed for years to come. Between a predictable, if graying, core and a collection of solid younger talent led by Walker and Nolan Gorman, that's eight of nine positions accounted for, and it doesn't count top prospects Masyn Winn and Iván Herrera. Some of those hitters will likely end up as trade bait, but the vast majority of the group will crowd the lineup in 2024.

That impressive list of returning contributors is part of the solution, but it also helps explain the problem. The Cardinals had all those guys last year, and they stunk. Having achieved consistent results through varied means for two decades, they're now trying to flip last year's results while relying mostly on the same team, a complete reversal of script. This year will be a test of the entire organization; how will a team that hangs its hat on repeating the same solid performance year after year handle its first big failure?

It's not a given that they'll bounce back. "This isn't how it's supposed to work" isn't just what Cardinals fans thought about 2023; it's what fans of every other team in baseball have been thinking about the Cardinals for most of their recent run. Sure, the Pujols/Scott Rolen/Jim Edmonds teams were awesome, and Pujols continued to power the team until he departed after 2011. But then they were supposed to falter, not build a whole new team out of mid-round draft picks. How did they survive Mike Matheny? How did they survive Randal Grichuk playing the outfield without being able to throw, or Matt Adams playing the outfield at all? How did they survive trading away Sandy Alcantara, Zac Gallen and Randy Arozarena? How did they survive stripping Contreras of his catching duties less than a year into his tenure, only to reinstate him a week later?

It *isn't* supposed to work this way. Teams *aren't* supposed to be this consistent. Bumps in the road are completely normal. The sky isn't falling in St. Louis, at least not yet, even if it might feel that way to everyone who spent the last two decades getting used to things working out the redbirds' way. Baseball alternately lifts teams up and brings them low. But not the Cardinals; they've been able to justify every strange roster decision by simply pointing at the scoreboard.

In 2024, these two competing "this isn't how it's supposed to work"s will do battle. The stakes couldn't be higher, at least if you limit the world to St. Louis and its environs. A 90-win season and a return to the playoffs would be vindication for the Cardinal Way. "Oh, 2023? Just a fluke, look at how quickly we bounced back." It's easy to rationalize failure when it a) isn't happening anymore and b) only happened briefly.

Another bad season, however, could lead to a seismic shift in the organization. John Mozeliak has been at the helm, either as GM or POBO, since 2007. Under his direction, the never-all-in, never-rebuilding model has flourished. The organization didn't end up this way by random chance; Mozeliak is constantly nudging it toward the center, avoiding trades that mortgage too much of the future and eschewing rebuilds even when the natural ebb and flow of talent might encourage one. The results have been spectacular, so much so that the bar has been raised; the Cards can't go back to a boom/bust style of team-building because they've conditioned everyone in St. Louis to expect something better, or at least less worse.

The importance of this upcoming year will undoubtedly put stress on the Cardinals' way of doing things. Their front office largely speaks and acts in corporate jargon, emphasizing long-term plans, sustainable growth and process over everything else, even while they leave the specifics of the process conspicuously undefined. It's an organization blessed by its results with never having to explain itself too openly. That process might not matter if they lose 90 games again, though. It might not matter if they lose 80. The promise of never having a bad season loses a lot of its shine after one bad season; it's nearly worthless after two. The amorphous, undefinable Cardinal Way is on the ropes, and somehow, this watershed season is going to depend in no small part on Lance Lynn and Kyle Gibson delivering the goods. Perhaps it never existed at all.

Everything looks like the result of an orderly plan when you win more than your opponents, but it's hard to tell the difference between a plan so inscrutable that it looks like randomness and actual randomness. But the Cardinals have never really needed a plan, because they had a Way. The illusion that there truly was some devil magic, some divine intervention guiding the franchise through peril, was shattered in a single April. Not only did players like Walker and Contreras suddenly look mortal, so did the folks charged with managing them. It's like being a kid and realizing one day that your parents are actually fallible: a sort of magic that's hard to put back in the bottle.

—Ben Clemens is an author of FanGraphs.

HITTERS

Nolan Arenado 3B   Born: 04/16/91   Age: 33   Bats: R   Throws: R   Height: 6'2"   Weight: 215   Origin: Round 2, 2009 Draft (#59 overall)

YEAR	TM	LVL	AGE	PA	R	HR	RBI	SB	AVG/OBP/SLG	BABIP	SLGCON	BB%	K%	ZSw%	ZCon%	OSw%	OCon%	LA	90th EV	DRC+	BRR	DRP	WARP
2021	STL	MLB	30	653	81	34	105	2	.255/.312/.494	.249	.590	7.7%	14.7%	68.0%	91.1%	33.2%	68.7%	20.4	103.3	110	-0.3	0.9	3.1
2022	STL	MLB	31	620	73	30	103	5	.293/.358/.533	.290	.612	8.4%	11.6%	67.7%	89.2%	35.6%	70.4%	22.0	103.8	140	-0.5	4.5	4.9
2023	STL	MLB	32	612	71	26	93	3	.266/.315/.459	.279	.560	6.7%	16.5%	65.7%	89.9%	36.9%	67.7%	16.8	104.2	116	-0.5	-0.5	3.0
2024 DC	STL	MLB	33	621	71	24	81	3	.260/.317/.444	.272	.532	7.2%	14.9%							115	-0.4	2.8	3.1

2023 GP: 3B (128), DH (15)   Comps: Brooks Robinson (86), Ron Santo (83), Aramis Ramirez (83)

Arenado had won a Gold Glove every season of his career until 2023. In fact, coming into Game 1 of the 2022 NL Wild Card Series, Arenado simply wasn't the kind of third baseman who would let a ball just slip under his glove—and then, in the ninth inning, he was. By the end of the following season, he wasn't the kind of third baseman who had 30+ homers or 100+ RBI, either. He did, at age 32, have some aches in his back and a desire to not sit through a full rebuild. Arenado's second-half swoon ended with him on the IL after not homering in his final 26 games of the season. An enduring professional who would play through almost anything, Arenado took himself out of commission in September after the Cardinals had taken themselves out of commission in July. When a guy who refuses to quit knocks on the manager's door, there's more than a little wrong. And whatever the Cardinals are planning to do next, they better do it fast—Arenado played in Colorado too long to not be traumatized by any utterance of the word "rebuild."

Luken Baker 1B   Born: 03/10/97   Age: 27   Bats: R   Throws: R   Height: 6'4"   Weight: 280   Origin: Round 2, 2018 Draft (#75 overall)

YEAR	TM	LVL	AGE	PA	R	HR	RBI	SB	AVG/OBP/SLG	BABIP	SLGCON	BB%	K%	ZSw%	ZCon%	OSw%	OCon%	LA	90th EV	DRC+	BRR	DRP	WARP
2021	SPR	AA	24	391	51	26	68	0	.248/.322/.530	.270	.754	9.7%	26.3%							114	-1.0	-7.8	0.9
2022	MEM	AAA	25	513	52	21	66	0	.228/.288/.394	.265	.546	7.2%	25.1%	77.5%	83.6%	26.0%	40.0%			88	-2.2	-2.4	0.3
2023	MEM	AAA	26	380	71	33	98	0	.334/.439/.720	.344	.950	15.5%	20.0%	65.8%	80.6%	27.6%	61.1%			158	-4.2	-2.2	3.1
2023	STL	MLB	26	99	9	2	10	0	.209/.313/.314	.302	.491	13.1%	31.3%	64.6%	79.6%	27.1%	51.4%	16.8	108.9	86	0.0	0.0	0.0
2024 DC	STL	MLB	27	230	25	9	28	0	.213/.289/.391	.251	.547	8.7%	25.5%							92	0.0	-0	0.2

2023 GP: DH (16), 1B (12)   Comps: Mark Hamilton (66), Marc Krauss (62), Chris Gimenez (58)

More plate discipline, fewer strikeouts and 33 home runs in 54 games with Memphis were enough to make Baker the International League MVP. This was the kind of development that the Cardinals and their fans latched onto in 2023, as Baker appeared in the majors, predominantly in the second half, and got his first big-league homer out of the way (because it was the 2023 Cardinals, it was the only St. Louis run in a 12-1 loss). For a team looking to pivot while maintaining its balance, Baker has positioned himself as a marketable name for 2024: Fans want to see more of the 27-year-old slugger.

Alec Burleson LF   Born: 11/25/98   Age: 25   Bats: L   Throws: L   Height: 6'2"   Weight: 212   Origin: Round 2, 2020 Draft (#70 overall)

YEAR	TM	LVL	AGE	PA	R	HR	RBI	SB	AVG/OBP/SLG	BABIP	SLGCON	BB%	K%	ZSw%	ZCon%	OSw%	OCon%	LA	90th EV	DRC+	BRR	DRP	WARP
2021	SPR	AA	22	282	34	14	44	2	.288/.333/.488	.321	.632	6.7%	20.9%							113	-0.7	-1.9	1.0
2021	MEM	AAA	22	172	19	4	22	0	.234/.310/.357	.260	.433	9.9%	15.7%							106	-0.4	-1.2	0.5
2022	MEM	AAA	23	470	68	20	87	4	.331/.372/.532	.350	.630	6.2%	14.3%	89.4%	83.1%	49.5%	66.0%			121	1.6	2.6	2.8
2022	STL	MLB	23	53	4	1	3	1	.188/.264/.271	.211	.333	9.4%	17.0%	81.9%	83.1%	31.4%	62.2%	3.9	102.8	108	0.0	-0.1	0.2
2023	STL	MLB	24	347	34	8	36	3	.244/.300/.390	.261	.456	6.6%	13.0%	72.0%	89.4%	38.2%	73.1%	11.9	104.2	134	-0.3	-2.6	2.0
2024 DC	STL	MLB	25	165	17	4	18	1	.257/.309/.396	.280	.473	6.4%	14.5%							99	-0.1	-0.5	0.3

2023 GP: LF (44), DH (24), 1B (17), RF (13), P (2)   Comps: Andrew Stevenson (57), Anthony Santander (55), Aaron Cunningham (53)

Luck is a cycle. When Burleson joined the Cardinals near the end of 2022, it was because Dylan Carlson had sprained his thumb. He spent a lot more time in the majors last year, where it was hoped that his ability to hit the ball as hard, as often and as not-on-the-ground as Carlson could make him a monster. But the bigger monster in 2023 was bad luck, which kept Burleson's numbers below where they deserved to be, as did his annoying habit of not quite making solid contact with the barrel. After knocking a high fastball for a double in September, he tried his luck at stealing third, something he'd never yet done in the majors. He paid for the attempt with a broken thumb and an instantaneous end to his season. Here's hoping the new cycle starts on a good note.

Dylan Carlson OF   Born: 10/23/98   Age: 25   Bats: S   Throws: L   Height: 6'2"   Weight: 205   Origin: Round 1, 2016 Draft (#33 overall)

YEAR	TM	LVL	AGE	PA	R	HR	RBI	SB	AVG/OBP/SLG	BABIP	SLGCON	BB%	K%	ZSw%	ZCon%	OSw%	OCon%	LA	90th EV	DRC+	BRR	DRP	WARP
2021	STL	MLB	22	619	79	18	65	2	.266/.343/.437	.332	.608	9.2%	24.6%	67.1%	81.3%	29.0%	56.9%	14.6	101.8	95	0.1	-0.5	1.7
2022	STL	MLB	23	488	56	8	42	5	.236/.316/.380	.281	.485	9.2%	19.3%	70.2%	80.5%	29.1%	64.0%	12.7	101.1	99	0.1	0.0	1.6
2023	STL	MLB	24	255	27	5	27	3	.219/.318/.333	.256	.429	10.2%	19.2%	70.3%	83.8%	28.9%	66.3%	14.3	102.2	104	0.0	-0.5	0.9
2024 DC	STL	MLB	25	265	27	5	27	2	.239/.326/.376	.281	.478	10.0%	18.8%							101	0.0	-1.1	0.8

2023 GP: CF (50), RF (20), LF (5), DH (2)   Comps: Byron Buxton (56), Lastings Milledge (52), Adam Jones (50)

There was a Dylan Carlson who could hit the ball so hard, you'd forgive him if he forgot his glove. Then there was another Dylan Carlson who'd hurt his wrist, couldn't hit as hard and played spectacular defense in center field. Here's the twist: I'm talking about *the same Dylan Carlson*. Pick your jaw up off the floor. Even with a healed wrist in 2023 he had his playing time limited in the outfield by Tommy Edman, Lars Nootbaar and Jordan Walker—which, when the Cardinals started selling, made Carlson an interesting case. Interesting to us, anyway. To him, it might have been annoying and stressful, producing struggles at the plate as he tried to figure things out with inconsistent playing time and a potential impending move. In early August, he opted for season-ending ankle surgery. But at 24, Carlson's young enough that some team—the Cardinals or to whomever they might yet trade him—will believe he can bounce back.

Willson Contreras C Born: 05/13/92 Age: 32 Bats: R Throws: R Height: 6'1" Weight: 225 Origin: IFA, 2009

YEAR	TM	LVL	AGE	PA	R	HR	RBI	SB	AVG/OBP/SLG	BABIP	SLGCON	BB%	K%	ZSw%	ZCon%	OSw%	OCon%	LA	90th EV	DRC+	BRR	DRP	WARP
2021	CHC	MLB	29	483	61	21	57	5	.237/.340/.438	.298	.658	10.8%	28.6%	65.9%	78.9%	31.1%	46.5%	9.6	108.5	106	0.3	-4.9	1.9
2022	CHC	MLB	30	487	65	22	55	4	.243/.349/.466	.270	.620	9.2%	21.1%	72.6%	80.0%	36.4%	54.5%	8.5	108.0	132	0.2	-2.8	3.1
2023	STL	MLB	31	495	55	20	67	6	.264/.358/.467	.311	.631	10.3%	22.4%	69.5%	82.1%	35.6%	57.5%	10.1	109.7	116	-0.3	-7.4	1.9
2024 DC	STL	MLB	32	563	66	20	69	5	.239/.337/.415	.284	.563	9.7%	22.9%							117	-0.1	-3.5	2.9

2023 GP: C (97), DH (30)

Comps: Geovany Soto (76), Ozzie Virgil (75), Victor Martinez (75)

YEAR	TM	P. COUNT	FRM RUNS	BLK RUNS	THRW RUNS	TOT RUNS
2021	CHC	15657	-4.2	0.1	1.6	-2.6
2022	CHC	10500	-2.5	-0.2	1.1	-1.6
2023	STL	13034	-7.1	0.1	0.5	-6.4
2024	STL	15632	-4.6	0.1	1.0	-3.5

You know that feeling you get sometimes, that all the people you work with are talking trash about you? And then you convince yourself you're being sensitive and paranoid, and that you just need to take a nap or eat a salad? And then a bunch of major news outlets report that all the people you work with definitely are talking trash about you, and then, months later, you get tendonitis? Willson Contreras lived that extremely relatable situation in 2023. The first season of his five-year contract with the Cardinals started on the wrong note, with that missive written by a bunch of Cardinals pitchers who didn't like pitching to him and handed to Oli Marmol in early May. So the Cardinals said fine, not-Yadier Molina, you can play in the outfield instead. But Contreras didn't wind up out there, either, and was back catching a week later, where he did manage to provide some above-average offensive and caught stealing numbers, but struggled with pitch framing, blocking and game-calling in a way that might've made him feel less paranoid than afflicted.

★ ★ ★ *2024 Top 101 Prospect* #101 ★ ★ ★

Chase Davis CF Born: 12/05/01 Age: 22 Bats: L Throws: L Height: 6'1" Weight: 216 Origin: Round 1, 2023 Draft (#21 overall)

YEAR	TM	LVL	AGE	PA	R	HR	RBI	SB	AVG/OBP/SLG	BABIP	SLGCON	BB%	K%	ZSw%	ZCon%	OSw%	OCon%	LA	90th EV	DRC+	BRR	DRP	WARP
2023	PMB	A	21	131	15	0	23	3	.212/.366/.269	.310	.400	19.1%	26.0%	75.9%	89.0%	25.1%	60.9%			95	0.3	0.1	0.3
2024 non	STL	MLB	22	251	20	2	19	0	.208/.292/.291	.290	.411	9.7%	26.9%							68	0.0	0	-0.1

2023 GP: CF (28), DH (6)

Comps: Chris Curran (88), Reece Hampton (83), Jay Austin (82)

Nothing gets the people going like a smooth left-handed swing. Foregoing contact for power, Davis has the muscles and the bat speed to crush one. The Cardinals certainly liked what they saw, taking the 21-year-old outfielder at no. 21 overall in the 2023 draft, having been impressed by his ability to mash at the University of Arizona and the adjustments he made between his sophomore and junior seasons to cut down on his strikeouts. The thunder didn't translate from metal to wood-bat production, but he continued to sting the ball when he did make contact, while showing plenty of patience. His well-rounded skill set should serve him well, but there's more variance here than it looked like on draft day.

Brendan Donovan UT Born: 01/16/97 Age: 27 Bats: L Throws: R Height: 6'1" Weight: 195 Origin: Round 7, 2018 Draft (#213 overall)

YEAR	TM	LVL	AGE	PA	R	HR	RBI	SB	AVG/OBP/SLG	BABIP	SLGCON	BB%	K%	ZSw%	ZCon%	OSw%	OCon%	LA	90th EV	DRC+	BRR	DRP	WARP
2021	PEO	A+	24	109	15	2	13	7	.295/.385/.421	.333	.500	9.2%	13.8%							118	0.0	-1.1	0.5
2021	SPR	AA	24	219	35	4	28	8	.319/.411/.449	.379	.568	11.4%	17.8%							117	-1.3	0.3	1.0
2021	MEM	AAA	24	131	23	6	25	4	.288/.389/.495	.313	.625	11.5%	17.6%							123	0.7	-5.2	0.3
2022	MEM	AAA	25	65	12	1	6	0	.298/.385/.404	.333	.469	12.3%	12.3%	70.6%	95.8%	23.9%	72.7%			120	1.3	2.0	0.6
2022	STL	MLB	25	468	64	5	45	2	.281/.394/.379	.330	.461	12.8%	15.0%	57.2%	92.1%	23.2%	70.1%	5.9	101.5	121	0.3	0.5	2.6
2023	STL	MLB	26	371	48	11	34	5	.284/.365/.422	.311	.504	8.9%	14.3%	62.7%	90.7%	26.8%	74.8%	9.8	103.2	114	-0.1	-0.2	1.6
2024 DC	STL	MLB	27	279	30	5	28	2	.267/.356/.390	.297	.457	9.8%	13.3%							116	-0.1	-0.1	1.3

2023 GP: 2B (34), LF (21), DH (17), 1B (14), RF (9), 3B (6), SS (1)

Comps: Adam Frazier (58), Alberto Callaspo (57), Ray Durham (57)

It's not tough to see what went right for the Cardinals last year, if only because of how isolated the examples are. But cases like Donovan illustrate why St. Louis will be retooling rather than rebuilding in the seasons ahead. The 26-year-old made it into 95 games before being shut down to undergo surgery on his sore throwing arm, and in 238 PA out of the leadoff spot he hit .300, seventh among NL hitters who hit in that slot at least 90 times. But that many qualifiers are unnecessary to perceive Donovan's effectiveness in the outfield, where he could be comfortably placed in either corner and perform passably at worst (He also made at least one appearance at each infield position). His versatility makes him valuable to St. Louis *and* renders him even more tradeable as they sort out what's next.

Tommy Edman UT Born: 05/09/95 Age: 29 Bats: S Throws: R Height: 5'10" Weight: 180 Origin: Round 6, 2016 Draft (#196 overall)

YEAR	TM	LVL	AGE	PA	R	HR	RBI	SB	AVG/OBP/SLG	BABIP	SLGCON	BB%	K%	ZSw%	ZCon%	OSw%	OCon%	LA	90th EV	DRC+	BRR	DRP	WARP
2021	STL	MLB	26	691	91	11	56	30	.262/.308/.387	.291	.454	5.5%	13.7%	65.7%	92.1%	35.4%	76.4%	9.3	101.9	97	1.4	4.5	2.8
2022	STL	MLB	27	630	95	13	57	32	.265/.324/.400	.308	.496	7.3%	17.6%	64.0%	90.0%	36.0%	67.3%	8.8	103.3	109	2.3	1.0	3.0
2023	STL	MLB	28	528	69	13	47	27	.248/.307/.399	.275	.484	6.6%	15.9%	62.6%	93.1%	33.9%	72.2%	7.5	104.1	109	1.0	1.1	2.5
2024 DC	STL	MLB	29	585	60	15	65	24	.261/.316/.409	.285	.481	6.7%	14.1%							106	1.1	1.6	2.7

2023 GP: 2B (51), SS (48), CF (42), RF (8)

Comps: Cookie Rojas (80), Jerry Adair (78), Tito Fuentes (77)

The Cardinals' base-stealing, ball-nabbing, super-utility wonderboy who just showed up out of nowhere now seems critical to their future plans. Or, he could be part of a trade package out of town. That's kind of where the Cardinals left it in 2023. Edman is 28 years old, plays spectacular defense, and until 2023, had played in the postseason every year of his career. But last year he, like the Cardinals, lost some altitude, seeing a drop in his batting average and stolen base numbers—though he did go on a bit of a tear after returning from a wrist injury in August. Oli Marmol has been open about what he and the organization saw in Edman. Any talk about him turns into a discussion about whether "clutch" is a talent or a gene, but as long as we're having intangi-talk, his versatility and experience are also part of why the Cardinals value him as they do. Maybe someday he'll even get a position all to himself.

St. Louis Cardinals - 427

José Fermín   IF   Born: 03/29/99   Age: 25   Bats: R   Throws: R   Height: 5'9"   Weight: 200   Origin: IFA, 2015

YEAR	TM	LVL	AGE	PA	R	HR	RBI	SB	AVG/OBP/SLG	BABIP	SLGCON	BB%	K%	ZSw%	ZCon%	OSw%	OCon%	LA	90th EV	DRC+	BRR	DRP	WARP
2021	AKR	AA	22	336	40	6	39	4	.258/.329/.383	.276	.440	6.8%	11.3%							114	0.4	-3.1	1.3
2022	COL	AAA	23	330	60	6	31	9	.215/.336/.322	.235	.388	12.7%	13.9%							112	2.3	3.0	1.9
2023	MEM	AAA	24	81	16	4	7	1	.227/.358/.485	.190	.525	14.8%	6.2%	60.5%	93.6%	27.3%	87.2%			123	-0.7	2.2	0.6
2023	STL	MLB	24	61	2	0	4	0	.235/.339/.255	.279	.302	9.8%	13.1%	63.3%	91.2%	25.6%	81.8%	7.6	99.8	100	0.1	0.0	0.2
2024 DC	STL	MLB	25	61	6	1	6	1	.228/.307/.337	.243	.375	8.5%	11.0%							87	0.0	0	0.1

2023 GP: 2B (10), 3B (8)   *Comps: Alexi Casilla (58), Luis Hernandez (55), Max Moroff (55)*

Like almost everyone else among these Cardinal player comments, Fermín got his chance in 2023 due to an injury to the guy in front of him—in this case, Tommy Edman in July. An unranked journeyman prospect, the 25-year-old was one of those guys whom the Cardinals were said to be hoping would "make the most of the opportunity"—which really just means, "whatever, give him a bat." Early in his career, Fermín had been known as a natural, mature hitter with a good ability to make contact. Last year, he introduced himself to the fans by going 4-for-25 in his first 12 games, though he did pick up the pace offensively a little in September.

Paul Goldschmidt   1B   Born: 09/10/87   Age: 36   Bats: R   Throws: R   Height: 6'3"   Weight: 220   Origin: Round 8, 2009 Draft (#246 overall)

YEAR	TM	LVL	AGE	PA	R	HR	RBI	SB	AVG/OBP/SLG	BABIP	SLGCON	BB%	K%	ZSw%	ZCon%	OSw%	OCon%	LA	90th EV	DRC+	BRR	DRP	WARP
2021	STL	MLB	33	679	102	31	99	12	.294/.365/.514	.331	.664	9.9%	20.0%	65.1%	79.4%	29.1%	68.2%	17.2	107.3	139	0.2	0.9	4.9
2022	STL	MLB	34	651	106	35	115	7	.317/.404/.578	.368	.771	12.1%	21.7%	62.0%	78.9%	27.9%	64.4%	15.9	107.0	148	0.2	0.1	5.2
2023	STL	MLB	35	687	89	25	80	11	.268/.363/.447	.327	.613	12.7%	23.4%	63.5%	76.4%	29.4%	66.5%	13.1	106.3	118	-0.3	1.2	3.1
2024 DC	STL	MLB	36	645	79	24	83	5	.258/.351/.442	.308	.599	12.0%	22.8%							126	0.0	1.9	3.6

2023 GP: 1B (133), DH (21)   *Comps: Eddie Murray (82), Jeff Bagwell (82), Mark Teixeira (79)*

Every day of your thirties, you wake up with a worm wriggling in your brain. *Is this it?* it asks. *Is this all that you will be?* When you look around and see a stale-smelling den with a bunch of weathered old BP Annuals in it, you might feel something other than good. But Paul Goldschmidt looked around at 34 years old and saw three Gold Gloves, five Silver Sluggers, seven all-star appearances (six of them consecutive) and, oh yeah, a 2022 NL MVP trophy. Goldschmidt's high-level, well-rounded career is why the Cardinals snagged him from the Diamondbacks, but he was not immune to the plummet from relevance the franchise took in 2023. His power and on-base numbers dropped to levels not seen since 2019, his pedestrian first season in St. Louis—and you know what kind of questions a struggling mid-thirties slugger gets. Which means as the sun rises on his age-36 season, Goldschmidt will wake up with a whispering worm in his ear, asking… *Is this it?*

Moisés Gómez   RF   Born: 08/27/98   Age: 25   Bats: R   Throws: R   Height: 5'11"   Weight: 200   Origin: IFA, 2015

YEAR	TM	LVL	AGE	PA	R	HR	RBI	SB	AVG/OBP/SLG	BABIP	SLGCON	BB%	K%	ZSw%	ZCon%	OSw%	OCon%	LA	90th EV	DRC+	BRR	DRP	WARP
2021	MTG	AA	22	301	34	8	23	5	.171/.256/.309	.259	.539	9.0%	38.2%							68	0.8	0.4	-0.1
2022	SPR	AA	23	257	53	23	54	7	.321/.401/.705	.434	1.179	10.5%	35.0%							109	-0.1	3.3	1.5
2022	MEM	AAA	23	244	36	16	40	3	.266/.340/.541	.353	.881	10.2%	34.4%							90	2.8	3.0	1.1
2023	MEM	AAA	24	567	77	30	79	5	.232/.293/.457	.287	.704	6.9%	31.7%	76.8%	75.3%	41.7%	51.0%			82	-0.9	-10.6	-0.5
2024 non	STL	MLB	25	251	26	9	30	3	.232/.286/.395	.335	.639	6.0%	35.5%							89	0.0	0	0.3

2023 GP: RF (81), DH (30), LF (27), CF (4)   *Comps: Moisés Sierra (61), Jorge Bonifacio (57), Teoscar Hernández (55)*

The 25-year-old Gómez got off to a softer start in 2023, making contact with more air than ball in spring training and into April, homering once in his first 99 plate appearances. Something about the late spring air got the pistons firing, and suddenly Gómez hit more home runs (12) in May than any other minor leaguer. His numbers looked even better than they'd been the year before, when they'd been good; combined with other hard-hitting Cardinals prospects Luken Baker and Chandler Redmond, a slugging cerberus was born within the St. Louis farm system. Gómez gets dinged for his defense and still has to learn how to strike out less, but what big bopper doesn't?

Nolan Gorman   2B   Born: 05/10/00   Age: 24   Bats: L   Throws: R   Height: 6'1"   Weight: 210   Origin: Round 1, 2018 Draft (#19 overall)

YEAR	TM	LVL	AGE	PA	R	HR	RBI	SB	AVG/OBP/SLG	BABIP	SLGCON	BB%	K%	ZSw%	ZCon%	OSw%	OCon%	LA	90th EV	DRC+	BRR	DRP	WARP
2021	SPR	AA	21	195	26	11	27	4	.288/.354/.508	.351	.720	9.2%	26.7%							114	0.5	1.5	1.1
2021	MEM	AAA	21	328	45	14	48	3	.274/.320/.465	.301	.588	6.1%	19.2%							109	0.2	8.6	2.2
2022	MEM	AAA	22	188	35	16	26	3	.275/.330/.585	.352	.980	7.4%	36.7%	60.0%	66.7%	39.4%	65.4%			107	0.0	2.9	0.9
2022	STL	MLB	22	313	44	14	35	1	.226/.300/.420	.301	.661	8.9%	32.9%	75.1%	74.7%	34.6%	52.2%	20.5	105.4	91	0.0	-1.1	0.5
2023	STL	MLB	23	464	59	27	76	7	.236/.328/.478	.296	.752	11.4%	31.9%	75.2%	74.3%	31.2%	48.4%	22.6	106.5	103	0.3	0.7	1.6
2024 DC	STL	MLB	24	477	55	21	62	5	.221/.298/.417	.298	.669	9.2%	33.8%							100	0.0	-0.9	1.2

2023 GP: 2B (75), DH (27), 3B (18)   *Comps: Rougned Odor (54), Robinson Canó (54), Yoán Moncada (53)*

The Cardinals' Opening Day DH was named NL Player of the Week in late May, following a week in which he'd hit .458. When he homered twice in a game and Jordan Walker homered once, the Cardinals became the only team in baseball with two players aged 23 or younger possessing at least 15 home runs—one of which he'd hit off Shohei Ohtani. Gorman finished the year with the team lead in home runs and SLG, though at that point he was watching from the 10-day IL, his power already having established him as a slugger of the future in St. Louis. He was no stranger to the injured reserve, though, with back, foot, back again, and finally hamstring issues taking him out of commission at various points.

Iván Herrera   C   Born: 06/01/00   Age: 24   Bats: R   Throws: R   Height: 5'11"   Weight: 220   Origin: IFA, 2016

YEAR	TM	LVL	AGE	PA	R	HR	RBI	SB	AVG/OBP/SLG	BABIP	SLGCON	BB%	K%	ZSw%	ZCon%	OSw%	OCon%	LA	90th EV	DRC+	BRR	DRP	WARP
2021	SPR	AA	21	437	50	17	63	2	.231/.346/.408	.261	.554	13.7%	22.0%							106	-1.7	3.5	2.0
2022	MEM	AAA	22	278	41	6	34	5	.268/.374/.396	.318	.508	13.7%	18.7%	64.3%	85.2%	20.3%	76.9%			119	-1.3	4.0	1.7
2022	STL	MLB	22	22	0	0	1	0	.111/.190/.111	.182	.200	9.1%	36.4%	56.8%	88.0%	25.9%	42.9%	3.6	100.9	72	-0.1	-0.2	0.0
2023	MEM	AAA	23	375	66	10	60	11	.297/.451/.500	.371	.681	20.0%	20.5%	61.1%	82.5%	23.3%	61.0%			126	2.1	1.4	2.4
2023	STL	MLB	23	44	6	0	4	0	.297/.409/.351	.423	.500	11.4%	25.0%	63.5%	85.1%	30.2%	63.2%	11.1	108.8	83	0.0	-0.2	0.1
2024 DC	STL	MLB	24	187	18	4	17	3	.210/.316/.331	.268	.457	11.6%	24.2%							89	-0.1	0.1	0.5

2023 GP: C (13)

Comps: Christian Bethancourt (59), Jeff Mathis (59), Carson Kelly (54)

YEAR	TM	P. COUNT	FRM RUNS	BLK RUNS	THRW RUNS	TOT RUNS
2021	SPR	11099	1.7	-0.4	-0.2	1.0
2022	MEM	8682	3.4	0.6	0.0	4.0
2022	STL	994	0.0	0.0	0.0	0.0
2023	MEM	10024	-0.2	0.2	0.6	0.6
2023	STL	1590	-0.4	0.0	0.1	-0.3
2024	STL	7215	-0.2	0.0	0.3	0.2

Herrera's numbers at Triple-A were good enough for the Cardinals to bump him up to the majors for an eight-game look in July. He hit .348 with an .814 OPS. That was enough to bring him back up in September for 11 more games, when he looked capable of producing more of the same. Willson Contreras is still St. Louis' starting catcher, but Andrew Knizner is no longer around, setting up Herrera for his third—and potentially much longer—look by the organization as it works out who will and won't be part of the future.

Andrew Knizner   C   Born: 02/03/95   Age: 29   Bats: R   Throws: R   Height: 6'1"   Weight: 225   Origin: Round 7, 2016 Draft (#226 overall)

YEAR	TM	LVL	AGE	PA	R	HR	RBI	SB	AVG/OBP/SLG	BABIP	SLGCON	BB%	K%	ZSw%	ZCon%	OSw%	OCon%	LA	90th EV	DRC+	BRR	DRP	WARP
2021	STL	MLB	26	185	18	1	9	0	.174/.281/.236	.223	.311	10.8%	21.1%	69.8%	84.2%	32.3%	64.9%	7.6	103.2	88	-0.2	-6.2	-0.2
2022	STL	MLB	27	293	28	4	25	0	.215/.301/.300	.268	.394	8.9%	21.2%	65.4%	85.6%	36.7%	66.8%	15.2	102.9	90	-0.1	-7.7	-0.1
2023	STL	MLB	28	241	30	10	31	2	.241/.288/.424	.288	.586	5.0%	25.7%	71.2%	80.0%	40.9%	62.4%	14.8	105.1	96	-0.2	-7.5	0.0
2024 non	STL	MLB	29	251	24	5	25	1	.225/.298/.346	.278	.462	7.8%	22.7%							83	-0.2	-7.6	-0.4

2023 GP: C (68), 1B (1)

Comps: Josh Bard (60), Chris Iannetta (59), Jarrod Saltalamacchia (59)

YEAR	TM	P. COUNT	FRM RUNS	BLK RUNS	THRW RUNS	TOT RUNS
2021	STL	6775	-4.8	0.0	-0.3	-5.1
2022	STL	11293	-7.0	0.2	0.2	-6.6
2023	STL	9551	-7.3	-0.1	-0.2	-7.6
2024	STL	6956	-7.6	0.1	-0.2	-7.6

Knizner did his job as a backup catcher: He became beloved by the fans. People are tough. They form wrong, dumb opinions. The more those opinions are believed, the more the cycle perpetuates. It can be tough talking over the ever-banging gavel in the court of public opinion, but not for Knizner. People loved it when he saved a run by surging forward to field a trickler and dove back toward home to tag a runner trying to score; they gushed when he became the third player in modern MLB history to pinch-run and hit a grand slam in the same inning; they were concerned when he took a ball to his midsection and ended up in the ER. Once they decide to, fans love latching onto second-string backstops, and Knizner kept giving them reasons to; following his non-tender, Knizner now has to win over a new fanbase.

Lars Nootbaar   OF   Born: 09/08/97   Age: 26   Bats: L   Throws: R   Height: 6'3"   Weight: 210   Origin: Round 8, 2018 Draft (#243 overall)

YEAR	TM	LVL	AGE	PA	R	HR	RBI	SB	AVG/OBP/SLG	BABIP	SLGCON	BB%	K%	ZSw%	ZCon%	OSw%	OCon%	LA	90th EV	DRC+	BRR	DRP	WARP
2021	MEM	AAA	23	136	21	6	19	1	.308/.404/.496	.349	.630	12.5%	18.4%							129	-0.2	1.3	1.0
2021	STL	MLB	23	124	15	5	15	2	.239/.317/.422	.273	.568	10.5%	22.6%	60.7%	82.8%	22.9%	56.5%	9.3	104.3	95	0.1	1.4	0.5
2022	MEM	AAA	24	77	13	4	14	2	.222/.325/.476	.233	.682	13.0%	24.7%							111	0.2	0.1	0.4
2022	STL	MLB	24	347	53	14	40	4	.228/.340/.448	.248	.594	14.7%	20.5%	60.6%	84.7%	23.7%	60.8%	10.2	106.4	121	0.6	3.6	2.4
2023	STL	MLB	25	503	74	14	46	11	.261/.367/.418	.307	.544	14.3%	19.7%	55.2%	85.9%	20.1%	72.8%	7.0	106.3	113	0.6	1.8	2.7
2024 DC	STL	MLB	26	590	66	17	67	11	.240/.341/.402	.269	.504	12.9%	17.4%							113	0.6	2.5	3.0

2023 GP: CF (73), RF (34), LF (24), DH (2)

Comps: Max Kepler (59), Von Hayes (53), Nate Schierholtz (52)

"LARS NOOTBAAR IS FOR REAL" could have been painted on the abandoned buildings and bridge overpasses of St. Louis last spring, as though they were foretellings of a great arrival. And with more playing time than ever in 2023, the 25-year-old outfielder did more Lars Nootbaar-ing than ever, proving that he was indeed not the fading illusion of desperation-fevered Cardinals fans. Like Edman in the infield, Nootbaar gives the Cardinals versatility and skill they can deploy anywhere: Left, right, center, an ad for Japanese energy bars, etc. In 2023, Nootbaar had to battle his rostering on a struggling Cardinals team *and* newfound celebrity after playing for Team Japan in the WBC *and* having reporters from Japan assigned to follow him during the MLB season. Despite it all, look for "LARS NOOTBAAR STILL LIVES" on closed shutters across St. Louis this spring.

★ ★ ★ *2024 Top 101 Prospect* **#83** ★ ★ ★

Thomas Saggese   IF   Born: 04/10/02   Age: 22   Bats: R   Throws: R   Height: 5'11"   Weight: 175   Origin: Round 5, 2020 Draft (#145 overall)

YEAR	TM	LVL	AGE	PA	R	HR	RBI	SB	AVG/OBP/SLG	BABIP	SLGCON	BB%	K%	ZSw%	ZCon%	OSw%	OCon%	LA	90th EV	DRC+	BRR	DRP	WARP
2021	DE	A	19	288	44	10	37	11	.256/.372/.463	.351	.713	14.6%	29.5%							104	0.8	-0.5	1.0
2022	HIC	A+	20	419	56	14	61	11	.308/.359/.487	.372	.647	6.9%	22.4%							102	-1.5	3.3	1.5
2023	FRI	AA	21	418	67	15	78	8	.313/.379/.512	.380	.694	8.1%	23.0%							109	-1.7	0.1	1.2
2023	SPR	AA	21	149	25	10	29	3	.331/.403/.662	.375	.896	10.1%	22.8%							124	-0.1	0.3	0.8
2023	MEM	AAA	21	63	9	1	4	1	.207/.270/.345	.256	.455	4.8%	22.2%	72.0%	91.7%	39.9%	67.8%			87	0.5	-0.6	0.0
2024 non	STL	MLB	22	251	24	6	27	3	.243/.299/.386	.309	.529	6.4%	25.0%							92	0.0	0	0.5

2023 GP: 2B (77), 3B (40), SS (13), DH (10)

Comps: Adrian Cardenas (60), Yolmer Sánchez (59), Brendan Rodgers (56)

Saggese went from Texas to St. Louis at the trade deadline as the Rangers prepped for their World Series run. While he's been a longtime beneficiary of BABIP, the 21-year-old has been a skilled hitter at every level where he's played. He's a slick enough fielder at enough positions to be considered "versatile," which is one of those labels that can get a front office salivating. Beloved by his teammates and a great guy to have around by reputation, St. Louis will presumably want to find him a position someday, should his solid approach and love of routine find him in the majors.

★ ★ ★ *2024 Top 101 Prospect* **#64** ★ ★ ★

Victor Scott II   CF   Born: 02/12/01   Age: 23   Bats: L   Throws: L   Height: 5'10"   Weight: 190   Origin: Round 5, 2022 Draft (#157 overall)

YEAR	TM	LVL	AGE	PA	R	HR	RBI	SB	AVG/OBP/SLG	BABIP	SLGCON	BB%	K%	ZSw%	ZCon%	OSw%	OCon%	LA	90th EV	DRC+	BRR	DRP	WARP
2022	PMB	A	21	142	20	2	12	13	.222/.358/.389	.262	.512	16.9%	18.3%	70.6%	90.8%	23.9%	58.5%			116	0.3	-1.7	0.5
2023	PEO	A+	22	308	44	2	29	50	.282/.365/.398	.338	.495	9.1%	16.9%							108	3.9	-1.6	1.2
2023	SPR	AA	22	310	51	7	34	45	.323/.373/.450	.362	.536	5.8%	14.5%							105	3.3	4.3	1.9
2024 non	STL	MLB	23	251	20	3	21	19	.227/.286/.330	.277	.415	6.5%	19.7%							74	0.0	0	0.0

2023 GP: CF (149), DH (2)   *Comps: Julio Borbon (71), Luis Barrera (71), Jacoby Ellsbury (64)*

If you thought Won-Bin Cho was a base-stealing threat, wait until you meet Scott, the co-leader in stolen bases across all of minor-league baseball in 2023 (94). And when that's who you are, you're going to want to show off. At the Arizona Fall League Fall-Stars game, Scott led off and played center field, stealing a base each and every time he got on. He finished the day with a double, two walks and three steals—exactly what the Cardinals wanted to see from their left-handed center field prospect. His AFL numbers were on par with his 2023 numbers, which remained consistently productive as the 22-year-old made the jump from High-A to Double-A.

Jordan Walker   OF/3B   Born: 05/22/02   Age: 22   Bats: R   Throws: R   Height: 6'6"   Weight: 245   Origin: Round 1, 2020 Draft (#21 overall)

YEAR	TM	LVL	AGE	PA	R	HR	RBI	SB	AVG/OBP/SLG	BABIP	SLGCON	BB%	K%	ZSw%	ZCon%	OSw%	OCon%	LA	90th EV	DRC+	BRR	DRP	WARP
2021	PMB	A	19	122	24	6	21	1	.374/.475/.687	.419	.872	14.8%	17.2%	75.8%	85.1%	35.1%	59.5%			145	-0.3	-3.6	0.6
2021	PEO	A+	19	244	39	8	27	13	.292/.344/.487	.382	.688	6.1%	27.0%							101	-0.5	-3.6	0.4
2022	SPR	AA	20	536	100	19	68	22	.306/.388/.510	.365	.681	10.8%	21.6%							98	-1.3	1.2	1.4
2023	MEM	AAA	21	135	14	4	16	4	.239/.348/.398	.291	.556	11.9%	23.7%	63.0%	84.7%	31.7%	60.2%			99	0.1	0.7	0.5
2023	STL	MLB	21	465	51	16	51	7	.276/.342/.445	.331	.592	8.0%	22.4%	72.7%	83.3%	37.0%	51.8%	10.3	107.1	96	0.1	-3.9	0.6
2024 DC	STL	MLB	22	585	60	15	64	9	.253/.322/.397	.320	.545	8.0%	24.6%							106	-0.2	-4.3	1.4

2023 GP: RF (93), LF (19), DH (7)   *Comps: Victor Robles (57), Nomar Mazara (55), Rafael Devers (53)*

A lot could have gone better in 2023. Walker worked to make sure it did. You could find him in the outfield before Cardinals games, checking the length of the grass and ensuring he had his routes right, regardless of the species of fly ball coming at him. It was all part of an effort to rise beyond the label he'd already received: Lots of raw talent, not a lot of execution—he can throw the ball far, but couldn't hit the cut-off man. It's the kind of thing that gets worked out rep by rep, and Walker got plenty of those. Some personal attention from the Cardinals coaching staff helped, too. He isn't clearing space for a Gold Glove on his mantle, but one of the good qualities of a season like St. Louis had is that at some point, it goes from being a campaign to a laboratory; the 21-year-old rookie was able to experiment, learn and become a better outfielder. Not the best, but… better.

★ ★ ★ *2024 Top 101 Prospect* **#53** ★ ★ ★

Masyn Winn   SS   Born: 03/21/02   Age: 22   Bats: R   Throws: R   Height: 5'11"   Weight: 180   Origin: Round 2, 2020 Draft (#54 overall)

YEAR	TM	LVL	AGE	PA	R	HR	RBI	SB	AVG/OBP/SLG	BABIP	SLGCON	BB%	K%	ZSw%	ZCon%	OSw%	OCon%	LA	90th EV	DRC+	BRR	DRP	WARP
2021	PMB	A	19	284	50	3	34	16	.262/.370/.388	.331	.520	14.1%	21.1%	61.8%	83.0%	30.0%	67.9%			108	3.8	6.5	2.0
2021	PEO	A+	19	154	26	2	10	16	.209/.240/.304	.274	.417	3.9%	26.0%							87	0.7	1.3	0.4
2022	PEO	A+	20	147	22	1	15	15	.349/.404/.566	.431	.730	8.8%	19.7%							132	0.8	-0.4	1.1
2022	SPR	AA	20	403	69	11	48	28	.258/.349/.432	.308	.575	12.4%	21.3%							102	5.9	4.5	2.4
2023	MEM	AAA	21	498	99	18	61	17	.288/.359/.474	.318	.583	8.8%	16.7%	59.8%	88.8%	33.5%	72.6%			116	3.9	3.4	2.9
2023	STL	MLB	21	137	8	2	12	2	.172/.230/.238	.196	.302	7.3%	19.0%	60.0%	81.5%	29.8%	73.9%	13.1	100.4	77	0.1	-0.4	0.0
2024 DC	STL	MLB	22	494	44	8	47	15	.239/.298/.356	.284	.448	7.3%	19.2%							88	0.3	-1.9	0.8

2023 GP: SS (37)   *Comps: Javier Báez (60), Richard Urena (58), Adalberto Mondesi (58)*

From Grant Balfour to Burke Badenhop, baseball has a history of players with bad baseball outcomes as their surname. That already puts Winn on a better path than all of them. The 21-year-old rookie spent half of August and all of September with the Cardinals at shortstop. He certainly didn't figure out major-league hitting, but his defense was a literal game-changer—enough to get Cardinals fans to lift their heads out of their hands, at least. When the Cardinals lost their 90th game, guaranteeing the kind of season their poor, poor fans haven't suffered through more than seven times in the last 110 years, their hopes immediately leapt to Winn, whose natural talent, instincts and unshatterable confidence made it easy to believe in the near future, in which *hopefully* they won't have to undergo such a horrific experience an eighth time.

PITCHERS

Giovanny Gallegos   RHP   Born: 08/14/91   Age: 32   Height: 6'2"   Weight: 215   Origin: IFA, 2011

YEAR	TM	LVL	AGE	G (GS)	IP	W-L	SV	K	WHIP	ERA	CSP	BB%	K%	HR%	GB%	ZSw%	ZCon%	OSw%	OCon%	BABIP	SLGCON	DRA-	WARP
2021	STL	MLB	29	73(0)	80¹	6-5	14	95	0.88	3.02	54.9%	6.5%	30.6%	1.9%	32.3%	71.2%	82.7%	39.3%	46.4%	.247	.459	86	1.3
2022	STL	MLB	30	57(0)	59	3-6	14	73	1.02	3.05	57.0%	7.7%	31.1%	2.6%	27.1%	72.7%	79.4%	39.0%	48.1%	.263	.514	87	0.9
2023	STL	MLB	31	56(0)	55	2-4	10	59	1.20	4.42	44.1%	5.2%	25.8%	4.8%	34.8%	73.4%	82.5%	38.3%	41.1%	.297	.645	88	1.0
2024 DC	STL	MLB	32	46(0)	49¹	3-2	0	59	1.20	3.83	51.2%	7.1%	28.5%	3.5%	33.1%					.301	.597	91	0.4

2023 Arsenal: FA (93.9), SL (85.2), CH (87.5)   Comps: Louis Coleman (66), Nick Vincent (66), Pedro Strop (65)

For everything to fall apart, first one must have everything together. That's what the Cardinals thought they had in Gallegos after four seasons of reliable high-leverage bullpen work, strengthened by his ability to keep the ball in the yard. Instead, batters hit Gallegos in 2023, and they hit him *hard*. It isn't viewed as damaging to his overall reputation, however—the 32-year-old still kept his walk rates and swings-and-misses down. Maybe he was missing the rosin on his glove arm that an umpire kept making him wipe off in July. Some right rotator cuff tendonitis ended Gallegos' season a few weeks early as he joined a growing mob of Cardinals on the IL—which, honestly, playing for the Cardinals in 2023, may have been just what the doctor ordered.

Kyle Gibson   RHP   Born: 10/23/87   Age: 36   Height: 6'6"   Weight: 200   Origin: Round 1, 2009 Draft (#22 overall)

YEAR	TM	LVL	AGE	G (GS)	IP	W-L	SV	K	WHIP	ERA	CSP	BB%	K%	HR%	GB%	ZSw%	ZCon%	OSw%	OCon%	BABIP	SLGCON	DRA-	WARP
2021	PHI	MLB	33	12(11)	69	4-6	0	61	1.29	5.09	47.5%	7.8%	20.7%	2.7%	53.1%	70.4%	88.1%	33.3%	64.2%	.294	.547	100	0.6
2021	TEX	MLB	33	19(19)	113	6-3	0	94	1.18	2.87	47.4%	8.9%	20.4%	2.0%	50.9%	66.7%	86.4%	32.7%	61.4%	.267	.423	95	1.4
2022	PHI	MLB	34	31(31)	167²	10-8	0	144	1.34	5.05	52.4%	6.7%	20.1%	3.3%	45.8%	69.4%	87.4%	34.5%	58.5%	.309	.557	98	1.8
2023	BAL	MLB	35	33(33)	192	15-9	0	157	1.32	4.73	45.7%	6.8%	19.5%	2.9%	48.6%	67.3%	86.4%	31.2%	58.3%	.311	.557	99	2.4
2024 DC	STL	MLB	36	29(29)	169	11-9	0	135	1.37	4.55	47.3%	7.6%	18.4%	2.7%	47.4%					.302	.519	104	1.2

2023 Arsenal: SI (92.1), CH (85.6), FC (90), FA (92.3), SW (81.5), CU (79.5), SL (82.2)   Comps: Jake Westbrook (75), Johnny Cueto (75), Esteban Loaiza (74)

One of Gen-Z's largest contributions (thus far) to the mainstream English lexicon is the term "mid," shorthand for "middling" or "mediocre." But when it comes to big-league starting pitchers, "mid" is actually "good." Delivering 150+ below-average innings is a well-above-average trait, one that can get the mid amongst us handsomely paid. Last season Gibson hoovered up 192 underwhelming frames for the Orioles and parlayed that into a one-year, $10 million deal with St. Louis early in free agency. From an entertainment perspective, Gibson has the electricity of an 18th-century woodshop, but is equally useful. Just make sure he isn't starting a postseason game for you come October. Even the Orioles, who allowed 21 runs to Texas in their brief postseason "run," escorted Gibby into mop up duty.

Sonny Gray   RHP   Born: 11/07/89   Age: 34   Height: 5'10"   Weight: 195   Origin: Round 1, 2011 Draft (#18 overall)

YEAR	TM	LVL	AGE	G (GS)	IP	W-L	SV	K	WHIP	ERA	CSP	BB%	K%	HR%	GB%	ZSw%	ZCon%	OSw%	OCon%	BABIP	SLGCON	DRA-	WARP
2021	CIN	MLB	31	26(26)	135¹	7-9	0	155	1.22	4.19	54.8%	8.7%	27.0%	3.3%	48.2%	62.8%	86.5%	30.6%	57.7%	.282	.552	79	2.8
2022	MIN	MLB	32	24(24)	119²	8-5	0	117	1.13	3.08	55.1%	7.4%	24.0%	2.3%	44.1%	63.3%	87.1%	29.8%	64.6%	.278	.475	90	1.8
2023	MIN	MLB	33	32(32)	184	8-8	0	183	1.15	2.79	47.9%	7.3%	24.3%	1.1%	47.3%	69.0%	87.5%	32.3%	53.5%	.295	.435	86	3.6
2024 DC	STL	MLB	34	29(29)	163	10-8	0	155	1.28	3.98	50.5%	8.2%	22.3%	2.7%	46.2%					.293	.514	92	2.1

2023 Arsenal: FA (92.8), SW (84.3), CU (79.6), SI (92.8), FC (88.3), CH (87.9), SL (86.7), HC (90.8)   Comps: Bob Welch (80), Jim Palmer (80), Roger Clemens (79)

Gray enjoyed his best season in over half a decade in 2023, and entered free agency in perfect position to capitalize. Still a thoughtful tinkerer as he entered his mid-30s, he traded in his middle-of-the-road slider for a newfangled sweeper and much heavier usage of his cutter. He also tweaked his fastball to have more cut and a bit less ride. Almost everything works to the glove side, but even with only spotty command of his sinker and changeup, the damage on mistakes was minimal. Gray missed to the arm side much less often with his new arsenal, and it paid off to the tune of much less power and newfound dominance of right-handed batters. He also pitched a ton, and showed no signs of tiring in September or October. He's found a confluence of pitch mix, mechanics and mentality that works gorgeously. Gray will get the chance to deploy these new skills in St. Louis on a new three-year contract.

Ryan Helsley   RHP   Born: 07/18/94   Age: 29   Height: 6'2"   Weight: 230   Origin: Round 5, 2015 Draft (#161 overall)

YEAR	TM	LVL	AGE	G (GS)	IP	W-L	SV	K	WHIP	ERA	CSP	BB%	K%	HR%	GB%	ZSw%	ZCon%	OSw%	OCon%	BABIP	SLGCON	DRA-	WARP
2021	STL	MLB	26	51(0)	47¹	6-4	1	47	1.42	4.56	56.3%	13.1%	22.8%	1.9%	41.7%	70.4%	83.2%	28.9%	55.7%	.283	.465	109	0.2
2022	STL	MLB	27	54(0)	64²	9-1	19	94	0.74	1.25	57.9%	8.4%	39.3%	2.5%	34.4%	72.7%	76.9%	38.5%	41.6%	.185	.416	66	1.7
2023	STL	MLB	28	33(0)	36²	3-4	14	52	1.06	2.45	47.9%	11.6%	35.6%	0.7%	40.8%	69.3%	75.9%	36.2%	50.4%	.280	.452	78	0.9
2024 DC	STL	MLB	29	46(0)	49¹	3-5	34	60	1.22	3.61	53.9%	10.5%	29.1%	3.5%	37.5%					.269	.566	86	0.6

2023 Arsenal: FA (99.7), SL (89.3), CU (82.4), CH (89.5)   Comps: Brad Boxberger (64), Trevor Rosenthal (62), Matt Barnes (62)

On June 7, the Cardinals' All-Star closer struck out two Rangers en route to a one-run victory in which he got the save. Two days prior, he'd pitched a clean eighth and struck out two in another one-run win over Texas. They were Helsley's 21st and 22nd games out of the Cardinals bullpen in 2023, well under half the number of games he'd nailed down for St. Louis the previous year. He didn't pitch again until September. Pain shooting up and down the arm is exactly when a pitcher should take some time off, and Helsley was on the shelf for months as his team fell deeper and deeper into last place. The absence of the closer who'd finished 33 games with 19 saves the year prior was only one of many reasons for the decline, but it certainly didn't help. He would eventually return on September 1 and allow only two hits and one run across his last 10 ⅔ innings of the season, but during his absence, the Cardinals allowed the fourth-most earned runs in the majors—a metric by which they barely squeaked into the league's lower third prior to his absence.

★ ★ ★ *2024 Top 101 Prospect* **#54** ★ ★ ★

Tink Hence RHP Born: 08/06/02 Age: 21 Height: 6'1" Weight: 185 Origin: Round 2, 2020 Draft (#63 overall)

YEAR	TM	LVL	AGE	G (GS)	IP	W-L	SV	K	WHIP	ERA	CSP	BB%	K%	HR%	GB%	ZSw%	ZCon%	OSw%	OCon%	BABIP	SLGCON	DRA-	WARP
2021	CAR	ROK	18	8(1)	8	0-1	1	14	1.75	9.00		7.3%	34.1%	2.4%	31.8%					.476	.773		
2022	PMB	A	19	16(16)	52¹	0-1	0	81	0.88	1.38		7.7%	41.5%	0.5%	54.1%	62.7%	77.8%	35.4%	45.7%	.309	.433	73	1.5
2023	PEO	A+	20	11(11)	41²	2-1	0	46	1.10	2.81		7.3%	27.9%	2.4%	41.5%					.294	.453	78	0.8
2023	SPR	AA	20	12(12)	54¹	2-5	0	53	1.51	5.47		9.2%	22.2%	3.3%	39.5%					.342	.629	100	0.3
2024 non	STL	MLB	21	58(0)	50	2-2	0	44	1.44	5.19		9.5%	20.3%	4.0%	36.8%					.295	.586	115	-0.2

2023 Arsenal: FA (97), SL (83.5), CH (83.4), CU (80.7)   *Comps: Ariel Jurado (80), Sean Reid-Foley (77), Jen-Ho Tseng (75)*

Chest and oblique tightness kept Hence off the field for a month, but he still managed to pitch well enough for a promotion to Double-A in July. From there, the 21-year-old's seasoned tanked. After a sizzling July when Hence appeared to be everything the Cardinals had dreamed, with a 2.25 ERA and 20 Ks in four starts, he imploded in August as opponents hit .400 against him and blasted the command right out of his arm. But everybody just chalked that up to his development as he fine-tuned his fastball against a deeper pool of hitting talent.

John King LHP Born: 09/14/94 Age: 29 Height: 6'2" Weight: 215 Origin: Round 10, 2017 Draft (#314 overall)

YEAR	TM	LVL	AGE	G (GS)	IP	W-L	SV	K	WHIP	ERA	CSP	BB%	K%	HR%	GB%	ZSw%	ZCon%	OSw%	OCon%	BABIP	SLGCON	DRA-	WARP
2021	TEX	MLB	26	27(0)	46	7-5	0	40	1.15	3.52	51.4%	6.2%	20.7%	1.6%	57.7%	69.9%	85.1%	37.2%	61.0%	.286	.426	86	0.8
2022	RR	AAA	27	14(0)	17¹	2-1	0	18	1.56	7.27		8.8%	22.5%	6.3%	57.4%	62.9%	85.5%	30.9%	69.6%	.306	.698	83	0.3
2022	TEX	MLB	27	39(0)	51¹	1-4	0	30	1.46	4.03	53.4%	6.3%	13.5%	2.3%	63.3%	67.8%	87.2%	35.8%	70.7%	.327	.480	92	0.7
2023	RR	AAA	28	12(3)	21²	2-2	1	13	1.57	3.32		6.2%	13.4%	1.0%	65.4%	62.9%	91.0%	30.7%	59.3%	.355	.421	95	0.3
2023	TEX	MLB	28	15(0)	18²	1-1	0	10	1.61	5.79	50.4%	4.9%	12.3%	1.2%	65.7%	64.8%	94.3%	39.9%	69.8%	.379	.500	93	0.3
2023	STL	MLB	28	20(0)	18²	1-0	0	10	1.34	1.45	46.2%	7.9%	13.2%	1.3%	63.3%	61.7%	81.0%	40.1%	67.2%	.310	.407	93	0.3
2024 DC	STL	MLB	29	46(0)	49¹	3-2	0	31	1.47	4.78	51.1%	7.3%	14.1%	1.6%	60.2%					.320	.465	106	0.1

2023 Arsenal: SI (93.8), CH (84.2), SL (85.3), FA (92.7)   *Comps: T.J. McFarland (65), Sam Dyson (62), Michael Feliz (62)*

The news was that Jordan Montgomery had been traded by the Cardinals. Of seemingly less importance was that three prospects, including King, were coming back from the Rangers. A zone-pounder who prefers to keep things grounded, King went on an obligatory pilgrimage to the giant parenthesis for which his new city was known and offered a proper amount of veneration. With that out of the way, he was free to start pitching, the curve of St. Louis' haunting monolith looming in the background. In 20 appearances after his shift to the senior circuit, King only entered four times prior to the seventh inning, meaning he had the honor of eating a terrible team's late innings. Thing is, he appeared in 10 games in September, of which the Cardinals won nine. Throwing principally a sinker and a change, King slowly deflated the bulbous numbers he accrued in Texas and allowed only three earned runs in 18 ⅔ innings down the season's homestretch. This is why even aristocracy pays fealty to the Arch.

Andrew Kittredge RHP Born: 03/17/90 Age: 34 Height: 6'1" Weight: 230 Origin: Round 45, 2008 Draft (#1360 overall)

YEAR	TM	LVL	AGE	G (GS)	IP	W-L	SV	K	WHIP	ERA	CSP	BB%	K%	HR%	GB%	ZSw%	ZCon%	OSw%	OCon%	BABIP	SLGCON	DRA-	WARP
2021	TB	MLB	31	57(4)	71²	9-3	8	77	0.98	1.88	54.5%	5.3%	27.3%	2.5%	53.5%	69.3%	82.9%	45.5%	55.8%	.268	.470	72	1.8
2022	TB	MLB	32	17(0)	20	3-1	5	14	0.85	3.15	53.0%	2.7%	18.7%	5.3%	45.8%	74.7%	90.1%	43.5%	56.7%	.200	.508	93	0.3
2023	TB	MLB	33	14(0)	11²	2-0	1	10	1.20	3.09	54.6%	4.0%	20.0%	2.0%	37.8%	73.9%	89.2%	42.9%	69.0%	.306	.486	95	0.2
2024 DC	STL	MLB	34	41(0)	43²	3-2	0	34	1.28	4.03	53.0%	6.3%	18.3%	2.5%	46.5%					.297	.493	94	0.3

2023 Arsenal: SI (94.9), SL (88.8), HC (94)   *Comps: Nick Vincent (59), Javy Guerra (56), Mark Melancon (56)*

Voted the pitcher with a face most resembling a 19th century American President (and a name to match), Kittredge returned to the mound in August after a 14-month recovery from Tommy John surgery. He was very much the same pitcher as he was before the zipper, featuring a mid-90s fastball and hard slider. The Rays eased the righty back into use with mostly low-leverage outings to favorable results. Kittredge should see an uptick in responsibility as he puts more distance between himself and a surgeon. He may no longer ride the top of the team's closer ticket, but should grab some down-ballot holds as he heads towards unrestricted free agency after the 2024 season.

Adam Kloffenstein RHP Born: 08/25/00 Age: 23 Height: 6'5" Weight: 243 Origin: Round 3, 2018 Draft (#88 overall)

YEAR	TM	LVL	AGE	G (GS)	IP	W-L	SV	K	WHIP	ERA	CSP	BB%	K%	HR%	GB%	ZSw%	ZCon%	OSw%	OCon%	BABIP	SLGCON	DRA-	WARP
2021	VAN	A+	20	23(23)	101¹	7-7	0	107	1.55	6.22		13.1%	23.0%	2.1%	52.9%					.306	.580	87	1.5
2022	VAN	A+	21	6(6)	26	0-2	0	30	1.46	3.81		8.6%	25.9%	3.4%	41.9%					.343	.649	95	0.3
2022	NH	AA	21	19(18)	86	2-5	0	88	1.66	6.07		11.3%	22.2%	3.0%	48.2%					.354	.617	99	1.2
2023	NH	AA	22	17(17)	89	5-5	0	105	1.27	3.24		8.9%	27.6%	2.1%	51.5%					.316	.539	79	2.2
2023	MEM	AAA	22	9(8)	39	2-1	0	35	1.28	3.00		12.7%	21.2%	3.6%	45.2%	63.5%	90.9%	29.9%	49.6%	.235	.519	95	0.5
2024 DC	STL	MLB	23	11(3)	23²	1-1	0	21	1.53	5.53		11.4%	19.7%	3.3%	40.6%					.299	.562	121	-0.1

2023 Arsenal: SI (91.1), SL (88.4), SW (81.6), CH (86.5), FA (92.6)   *Comps: Joe Ross (78), Wily Peralta (74), Robert Stephenson (74)*

The Cardinals got young, sinkerballing Kloffenstein back from the Blue Jays in the Jordan Hicks trade and sent him right to Triple-A, the highest level at which the 23-year-old righty had ever pitched. It was a show of faith, or at least curiosity, after he had struggled with the command and velocity that had gotten scouts to call. Kloffenstein trained himself to pitch with a less-pressurized mindset and wound up throwing more strikes in 2023, setting a career high in punch-outs from Double- to Triple-A. In his first 29 innings with Memphis, he was getting an encouraging rate of ground balls and held opponents to a .190 batting average with a 2.17 ERA, thanks in part to a cutter he developed to handle lefties.

Casey Lawrence   RHP   Born: 10/28/87   Age: 36   Height: 6'0"   Weight: 180   Origin: Undrafted Free Agent, 2010

YEAR	TM	LVL	AGE	G (GS)	IP	W-L	SV	K	WHIP	ERA	CSP	BB%	K%	HR%	GB%	ZSw%	ZCon%	OSw%	OCon%	BABIP	SLGCON	DRA-	WARP
2021	NH	AA	33	4 (4)	21	1-1	0	18	0.86	3.00		5.2%	23.4%	2.6%	44.4%					.231	.481	103	0.1
2021	BUF	AAA	33	21 (10)	65	7-2	0	62	1.20	4.85		4.9%	23.1%	3.7%	42.1%					.306	.585	102	0.8
2022	BUF	AAA	34	23 (23)	126	9-5	0	106	0.89	2.79		3.5%	21.9%	3.7%	42.3%					.227	.479	84	2.7
2022	TOR	MLB	34	6 (0)	18	0-1	0	11	1.50	7.50	51.2%	5.1%	13.9%	6.3%	39.7%	67.3%	90.3%	42.1%	78.8%	.310	.677	107	0.1
2023	BUF	AAA	35	18 (18)	90²	3-7	0	81	1.39	4.67		7.3%	20.5%	3.8%	45.4%	66.9%	84.8%	34.4%	63.2%	.305	.603	99	1.3
2023	MEM	AAA	35	3 (3)	13¹	1-1	0	9	1.43	5.40		3.4%	15.5%	5.2%	28.9%	61.2%	88.9%	32.4%	68.9%	.333	.644	99	0.2
2023	STL	MLB	35	15 (0)	27¹	1-0	0	20	1.54	6.59	47.1%	8.2%	16.4%	5.7%	32.2%	67.5%	86.4%	33.8%	69.8%	.305	.724	113	0.1
2024 non	STL	MLB	36	58 (0)	50	2-2	0	32	1.36	5.07	48.5%	6.0%	14.7%	3.9%	38.8%					.290	.560	115	-0.2

2023 Arsenal: SW (80.4), SI (89.6), FA (90.1), CH (83), FC (83), CU (78.5)   *Comps: Paolo Espino (39), Richard Bleier (38), Josh Tomlin (37)*

Welcome to the St. Louis Cardinals 2023 bullpen! You have arrived here after [BEING SIGNED AS A 35-YEAR-OLD FREE AGENT], following a career of [BEING ACQUIRED BY THE BLUE JAYS THREE SEPARATE TIMES]. It is [AUGUST] and we are in [VERY LAST PLACE], so you have been brought here to [ALLOW A TON OF FLY BALLS] and you will finish with the [FOURTH-HIGHEST ERA] out of guys on this team who will make double-digit appearances. Don't worry, though; it may be a tough slog that you just have to bear down and pitch through, but we can offer you [A NARRATIVE ABOUT HOW YOU'RE 'NOT AFRAID' TO PITCH TO RONALD ACUÑA JR., EVEN THOUGH THE ALTERNATIVE WOULD JUST BE GIVING UP AND LEAVING]. Thank you for your interest and we look forward to you [EATING ALL THESE INNINGS BECAUSE, AGAIN, SOMEONE HAS TO].

Matthew Liberatore   LHP   Born: 11/06/99   Age: 24   Height: 6'4"   Weight: 200   Origin: Round 1, 2018 Draft (#16 overall)

YEAR	TM	LVL	AGE	G (GS)	IP	W-L	SV	K	WHIP	ERA	CSP	BB%	K%	HR%	GB%	ZSw%	ZCon%	OSw%	OCon%	BABIP	SLGCON	DRA-	WARP
2021	MEM	AAA	21	22 (18)	124²	9-9	0	123	1.25	4.04		6.3%	23.7%	3.7%	38.3%					.308	.580	104	1.4
2022	MEM	AAA	22	22 (22)	115	7-9	0	116	1.38	5.17		8.3%	23.4%	3.2%	41.8%	75.0%	72.2%	39.4%	58.5%	.328	.582	111	0.9
2022	STL	MLB	22	9 (7)	34²	2-2	0	28	1.73	5.97	53.4%	11.2%	17.4%	3.1%	37.7%	69.0%	84.2%	28.2%	69.0%	.346	.664	148	-0.5
2023	MEM	AAA	23	13 (13)	64²	4-3	0	84	1.48	4.18		13.4%	29.7%	2.8%	45.6%	62.4%	78.0%	30.2%	57.3%	.333	.613	84	1.4
2023	STL	MLB	23	22 (11)	61²	3-6	0	46	1.48	5.25	48.5%	9.1%	16.7%	1.8%	43.7%	68.0%	91.8%	27.8%	62.1%	.314	.549	121	0.0
2024 DC	STL	MLB	24	13 (5)	32²	2-2	0	26	1.43	4.88	50.1%	9.8%	18.2%	3.1%	41.9%					.288	.529	109	0.1

2023 Arsenal: FA (94.5), CU (76.5), SI (94.5), SL (86.8), CH (87.4)   *Comps: Logan Allen (76), Kyle Ryan (69), Yohander Méndez (68)*

The plan was to give the rookie starts. He stopped getting them after August. The fastball had dropped in velocity and the curveball was curving over the fence instead of the plate. So the Cardinals gently escorted the 24-year-old lefty out to the bullpen, and he was dropped into situations of varying stress levels (though by September in St. Louis, nobody was really feeling the heat). But Liberatore responded well to the change; his ERA in September (1.54) looked a lot different than over the rest of the season (6.12). Not having to manage his stamina through five or six frames, the velocity returned to Liberatore's fastball. The curve returned, as well... returned to being shaken off in favor of the fastball.

Lance Lynn   RHP   Born: 05/12/87   Age: 37   Height: 6'5"   Weight: 270   Origin: Round 1, 2008 Draft (#39 overall)

YEAR	TM	LVL	AGE	G (GS)	IP	W-L	SV	K	WHIP	ERA	CSP	BB%	K%	HR%	GB%	ZSw%	ZCon%	OSw%	OCon%	BABIP	SLGCON	DRA-	WARP
2021	CHW	MLB	34	28 (28)	157	11-6	0	176	1.07	2.69	52.4%	7.0%	27.5%	2.8%	38.8%	73.5%	80.9%	32.4%	60.3%	.265	.483	84	2.8
2022	CHW	MLB	35	21 (21)	121²	8-7	0	124	1.13	3.99	51.5%	3.7%	24.2%	3.7%	42.3%	76.0%	79.0%	35.1%	59.6%	.294	.549	87	2.0
2023	CHW	MLB	36	21 (21)	119²	6-9	0	144	1.46	6.47	46.6%	8.4%	26.9%	5.2%	37.5%	75.0%	77.5%	33.4%	55.6%	.328	.709	106	1.1
2023	LAD	MLB	36	11 (11)	64	7-2	0	47	1.27	4.36	44.3%	8.1%	17.2%	5.9%	31.3%	76.8%	85.1%	31.1%	62.6%	.232	.567	127	-0.2
2024 DC	STL	MLB	37	28 (28)	156²	10-8	0	157	1.26	4.28	48.8%	7.1%	23.5%	3.6%	37.1%					.294	.576	100	1.4

2023 Arsenal: FA (92.7), FC (88.9), SI (91.5), SW (81.3), CH (85.1), CU (83.2)   *Comps: Yu Darvish (79), Zack Greinke (76), Jim Bunning (76)*

The only thing that stood between Lynn and the title of Worst Starting Pitcher in MLB was Jordan Lyles. Eight times last season, Lynn gave up three or more home runs. Six times, he surrendered seven or more earned runs. He threw the straightest four-seam of his career, the pitch that had been his bread-and-butter forever. And yet—and yet!—during one fateful game, Lynn proceeded to strike out 16 Mariners hitters, which has got to be the first time such a thing has happened during such a miserable season. Someone in the Cardinals' organization must have been watching that game, because they jumped on him early in the offseason, providing him with a $10 million homecoming.

Steven Matz   LHP   Born: 05/29/91   Age: 33   Height: 6'2"   Weight: 201   Origin: Round 2, 2009 Draft (#72 overall)

YEAR	TM	LVL	AGE	G (GS)	IP	W-L	SV	K	WHIP	ERA	CSP	BB%	K%	HR%	GB%	ZSw%	ZCon%	OSw%	OCon%	BABIP	SLGCON	DRA-	WARP
2021	TOR	MLB	30	29 (29)	150²	14-7	0	144	1.33	3.82	57.1%	6.6%	22.3%	2.8%	45.6%	67.0%	84.0%	30.3%	66.4%	.321	.534	91	2.1
2022	MEM	AAA	31	6 (4)	14²	0-0	0	19	0.82	1.84		5.4%	33.9%	1.8%	45.5%					.250	.375	87	0.3
2022	STL	MLB	31	15 (10)	48	5-3	0	54	1.25	5.25	57.8%	4.8%	26.1%	3.9%	38.3%	65.9%	80.4%	35.6%	59.5%	.316	.596	96	0.6
2023	STL	MLB	32	25 (17)	105	4-7	0	98	1.33	3.86	50.9%	7.1%	21.8%	2.4%	45.3%	68.3%	82.1%	31.4%	62.1%	.320	.532	97	1.4
2024 DC	STL	MLB	33	31 (23)	128²	7-7	0	117	1.29	4.27	53.5%	7.0%	21.2%	3.1%	43.5%					.299	.537	99	1.2

2023 Arsenal: SI (94.4), CH (84.3), CU (78.6), SL (89.2)   *Comps: Scott McGregor (75), Jim Kaat (75), Kirk Rueter (74)*

By late May 2023, the Cardinals pitching staff had an ERA over 5.00. They were far from alone in this statistic, but that didn't mean they weren't trying to solve the problem. Or at least, they were aware that it needed to be solved. Matz was a big part of that problem, with opposing hitters barely letting him get to the mound before knocking his pitches all over the field—through 17 games, his first inning ERA was 6.35. But after a brutal April and May, plus a relegation to the pen to get his head on straight, the 32-year-old lefty started his best stretch of pitching since joining the Cardinals, allowing only two runs in six games and 11 innings in June. There were a few more crooked numbers allowed in the weeks that followed, but his resurgence and plummeting ERA from June to August were noted prior to him suffering the fate of just about every 2023 Cardinal being shut down with a left lat strain.

Miles Mikolas RHP Born: 08/23/88   Age: 35   Height: 6'4"   Weight: 230   Origin: Round 7, 2009 Draft (#204 overall)

YEAR	TM	LVL	AGE	G(GS)	IP	W-L	SV	K	WHIP	ERA	CSP	BB%	K%	HR%	GB%	ZSw%	ZCon%	OSw%	OCon%	BABIP	SLGCON	DRA-	WARP
2021	PEO	A+	32	1(1)	7	1-0	0	8	0.86	3.86		0.0%	30.8%	0.0%	44.4%					.333	.333	91	0.1
2021	SPR	AA	32	2(2)	10¹	1-0	0	7	1.74	6.97		7.0%	16.3%	7.0%	51.5%					.400	.788	113	0.0
2021	MEM	AAA	32	5(5)	19¹	1-1	0	13	1.03	2.33		4.1%	17.8%	2.7%	36.8%					.273	.456	111	0.1
2021	STL	MLB	32	9(9)	44²	2-3	0	31	1.21	4.23	59.3%	5.9%	16.7%	3.2%	52.1%	65.7%	87.0%	33.9%	75.2%	.276	.496	97	0.5
2022	STL	MLB	33	33(32)	202¹	12-13	0	153	1.03	3.29	57.6%	4.8%	19.0%	3.1%	45.5%	68.8%	88.1%	31.6%	69.1%	.250	.468	91	2.9
2023	STL	MLB	34	35(35)	201¹	9-13	0	137	1.32	4.78	53.5%	4.5%	15.9%	3.0%	38.7%	68.6%	87.8%	32.5%	74.6%	.309	.547	114	0.9
2024 DC	STL	MLB	35	29(29)	169	11-10	0	99	1.31	4.59	55.1%	5.4%	13.7%	3.2%	41.0%					.289	.516	106	1.0

2023 Arsenal: FA (93.6), SI (93), SL (86.7), CU (76.1), CH (85.7), CS (66.1)   *Comps: Pat Hentgen (73), Kyle Lohse (72), Scott Erickson (71)*

There have been plenty of farewells for the Cardinals since 2022. Their sneeze of a postseason appearance that year saw the final hacks of both Albert Pujols and Yadier Molina, and 2023 was the last ride for Adam Wainwright. But the future was still there, waiting to be reached, and part of the Cardinals' future was going to involve Mikolas, whom they signed to a three-year extension through 2025 for $55.75 million. By the time he'd thrown his last pitch of a lost year, for him and his club, it felt less like an extension and more like a regret as he led all of baseball in hits allowed and paced the National League in earned runs. No one was ready to totally give up on the 35-year-old—it's not like he's never had a down year before—but some were starting to think about where else the $16 million Mikolas will make in 2024 could have gone. For some guys, a year like this in their age-35 season would be signaling some kind of end. For others, it's nothing some work over the winter and a target with Ian Happ's face on the bullseye won't fix.

Packy Naughton LHP Born: 04/16/96   Age: 28   Height: 6'2"   Weight: 195   Origin: Round 9, 2017 Draft (#257 overall)

YEAR	TM	LVL	AGE	G(GS)	IP	W-L	SV	K	WHIP	ERA	CSP	BB%	K%	HR%	GB%	ZSw%	ZCon%	OSw%	OCon%	BABIP	SLGCON	DRA-	WARP
2021	SL	AAA	25	13(9)	56²	2-2	0	53	1.45	4.76		5.3%	21.7%	2.9%	47.8%					.363	.607	94	0.4
2021	LAA	MLB	25	7(5)	22²	0-4	0	12	1.81	6.35	47.8%	13.0%	11.1%	2.8%	50.6%	68.0%	92.0%	36.5%	66.7%	.308	.481	134	-0.2
2022	MEM	AAA	26	11(0)	21²	2-1	0	25	1.20	2.08		5.6%	28.1%	2.2%	43.1%	76.9%	75.0%	50.0%	50.0%	.345	.596	90	0.4
2022	STL	MLB	26	26(3)	32	0-2	1	31	1.44	4.78	50.5%	5.0%	22.0%	2.1%	50.0%	64.1%	82.0%	36.5%	61.1%	.367	.574	94	0.4
2023	STL	MLB	27	4(0)	5	0-0	0	5	0.60	0.00	38.8%	5.9%	29.4%	0.0%	63.6%	56.5%	84.6%	35.6%	62.5%	.182	.273	91	0.1
2024 non	STL	MLB	28	58(0)	50	2-2	0	43	1.38	4.48	48.6%	7.8%	19.9%	2.4%	47.9%					.312	.516	101	0.2

2023 Arsenal: CH (85.6), SI (93.9), FC (87.0), ГА (93.7)   *Comps: Tyler Duffey (59), Andrew Suárez (58), Jalen Beeks (56)*

We can trace the name "Packy" in baseball back to Packy Dillon, who played three games for the St. Louis Red Stockings in 1875. Packy Rogers took up the mantle for 23 games with the 1938 Brooklyn Dodgers. Guys named "Packy" have a hard time sticking around. And that brings us to today: Naughton finally broke the trend in 2022 when he got tuned up a few times but still managed to pile up strikeouts, limit walks and keep the ball on the ground. In 2023 he was ready to build off of what had worked the previous year and log his third consecutive season in the major leagues, running a victory lap around the other Packies. But he paid for his hubris with a left forearm strain in June, after which he was sidelined and scheduled for a surgical procedure.

Andre Pallante RHP Born: 09/18/98   Age: 25   Height: 6'0"   Weight: 203   Origin: Round 4, 2019 Draft (#125 overall)

YEAR	TM	LVL	AGE	G(GS)	IP	W-L	SV	K	WHIP	ERA	CSP	BB%	K%	HR%	GB%	ZSw%	ZCon%	OSw%	OCon%	BABIP	SLGCON	DRA-	WARP
2021	SPR	AA	22	21(21)	94¹	4-7	0	82	1.53	3.82		10.0%	19.4%	1.9%	60.3%					.331	.497	109	0.1
2022	STL	MLB	23	47(10)	108	6-5	0	73	1.42	3.17	58.1%	8.8%	16.0%	2.0%	64.4%	68.5%	90.3%	26.3%	65.8%	.313	.471	85	1.9
2023	MEM	AAA	24	5(0)	9²	0-0	0	14	0.72	2.79		5.3%	36.8%	0.0%	72.7%	72.4%	71.4%	29.6%	50.0%	.227	.286	80	0.2
2023	STL	MLB	24	62(0)	68	4-1	0	43	1.56	4.76	49.1%	9.9%	14.2%	2.0%	76.5%	70.2%	90.3%	25.9%	63.6%	.320	.493	87	1.3
2024 DC	STL	MLB	25	46(0)	49¹	3-2	0	32	1.49	4.52	54.1%	9.7%	14.6%	1.3%	67.9%					.305	.433	99	0.3

2023 Arsenal: FA (96.3), SL (87.6), KC (77.1), SI (96.8), CH (87.4)   *Comps: Trevor Bell (57), Zack Littell (54), Fernando Romero (54)*

In 2022, Pallante was the first Cardinals rookie in 10 years to pitch more than 100 innings in his debut season. The theory for his struggles in 2023 came down to new rules about defensive shifts: He was keeping the ball on the ground more than ever, but also giving up more hits. Like your least-dateable friend, Pallante's problem is being single. Or at least, giving them up—especially to righties, who hit .357 against him and tuned him up for a 7.24 ERA. The 25-year-old finally slowed down the stream of earned runs coming across in September but continued to give up hits, including four in one inning during his final appearance of the season.

Sem Robberse RHP Born: 10/12/01   Age: 22   Height: 6'1"   Weight: 185   Origin: IFA, 2019

YEAR	TM	LVL	AGE	G(GS)	IP	W-L	SV	K	WHIP	ERA	CSP	BB%	K%	HR%	GB%	ZSw%	ZCon%	OSw%	OCon%	BABIP	SLGCON	DRA-	WARP
2021	DUN	A	19	14(12)	57²	5-4	0	61	1.14	3.90		8.4%	25.5%	1.7%	49.4%	67.3%	89.1%	35.4%	53.3%	.273	.468	101	0.5
2021	VAN	A+	19	7(7)	31	0-3	0	29	1.84	5.23		12.0%	19.3%	2.0%	52.0%					.367	.616	114	0.0
2022	VAN	A+	20	17(17)	86²	4-4	0	78	1.15	3.12		6.7%	21.8%	2.0%	48.6%					.280	.490	95	1.0
2022	NH	AA	20	5(5)	24²	0-3	0	19	1.18	3.65		9.6%	18.3%	3.8%	47.9%					.217	.493	104	0.3
2023	NH	AA	21	18(18)	88²	3-5	0	86	1.17	4.06		8.9%	23.1%	3.8%	42.0%					.242	.520	95	1.5
2023	MEM	AAA	21	8(7)	35¹	2-1	0	44	1.78	4.84		14.3%	26.2%	3.6%	36.5%	64.9%	78.9%	36.2%	50.0%	.367	.708	91	0.6
2024 DC	STL	MLB	22	11(3)	25²	1-2	0	23	1.52	5.59		10.1%	19.7%	3.7%	37.6%					.306	.588	124	-0.1

2023 Arsenal: FA (93.6), CH (89.8), FC (88.4), SW (86.5)   *Comps: Jacob Turner (67), Germán Márquez (67), Carlos Martinez (67)*

The Netherlands-born Robberse leans on his four-seamer and slider the vast majority of the time, with a changeup he typically brings out as a special treat for lefties. The 22-year-old came to St. Louis last July by way of the Jordan Hicks trade with the Blue Jays, at which point the Cardinals promoted him from Double- to Triple-A. His history of delayed development—he didn't even throw a curveball until reaching the highest level of play in the Netherlands—made him even more appealing to the Cardinals, who were patient as he struggled through his first month at Memphis.

★ ★ ★ *2024 Top 101 Prospect* **#93** ★ ★ ★

Tekoah Roby RHP   Born: 09/18/01   Age: 22   Height: 6'1"   Weight: 185   Origin: Round 3, 2020 Draft (#86 overall)

YEAR	TM	LVL	AGE	G (GS)	IP	W-L	SV	K	WHIP	ERA	CSP	BB%	K%	HR%	GB%	ZSw%	ZCon%	OSw%	OCon%	BABIP	SLGCON	DRA-	WARP
2021	DE	A	19	6(6)	22	2-2	0	35	0.95	2.45		7.8%	38.9%	1.1%	46.7%					.295	.455	68	0.6
2022	HIC	A+	20	22(21)	104²	3-11	0	126	1.24	4.64		7.9%	28.4%	4.3%	38.5%					.298	.653	96	1.0
2023	FRI	AA	21	10(10)	46¹	2-3	0	50	1.32	5.05		6.2%	25.6%	2.6%	40.5%					.349	.636	91	0.8
2023	SPR	AA	21	4(4)	12	0-0	0	19	0.75	3.00		6.8%	43.2%	2.3%	31.8%					.238	.545	79	0.3
2024 non	STL	MLB	22	58(0)	50	2-2	0	47	1.40	5.19		8.8%	21.5%	4.2%	35.3%					.297	.611	116	-0.2

Comps: Joe Ross (83), Nick Neidert (82), Zach Lee (82)

A new arrival in the Jordan Montgomery trade, Roby showed up with three pitches—a four-seamer, curve and change—he could throw for strikes. In four starts after switching organizations, Roby made an impression by ratcheting up the strikeouts—to which the org only recently become partial—but hurt his image in the Arizona Fall League by appearing to throw all of his stuff too hard, losing control in the process. Health and consistency have been sticking points (he was actually injured at the time of the trade), but Roby's stuff has remained intact and a full season in 2024 could see him debut in the majors.

Drew Rom LHP   Born: 12/15/99   Age: 24   Height: 6'2"   Weight: 215   Origin: Round 4, 2018 Draft (#115 overall)

YEAR	TM	LVL	AGE	G (GS)	IP	W-L	SV	K	WHIP	ERA	CSP	BB%	K%	HR%	GB%	ZSw%	ZCon%	OSw%	OCon%	BABIP	SLGCON	DRA-	WARP
2021	ABD	A+	21	14(13)	67²	8-0	0	73	1.14	2.79		6.2%	26.5%	2.2%	56.0%					.307	.481	103	0.4
2021	BOW	AA	21	9(7)	40	3-1	0	47	1.10	3.83		5.5%	28.8%	3.7%	53.3%					.293	.552	88	0.6
2022	BOW	AA	22	19(18)	82¹	7-2	0	101	1.47	4.37		7.9%	27.6%	2.5%	42.9%					.374	.596	110	0.7
2022	NOR	AAA	22	7(7)	37²	1-1	0	43	1.49	4.54		10.9%	26.1%	0.6%	47.1%					.370	.535	94	0.6
2023	MEM	AAA	23	2(2)	11	2-0	0	18	0.55	0.82		9.8%	43.9%	2.4%	44.4%	59.7%	69.6%	33.0%	46.7%	.059	.278	74	0.3
2023	NOR	AAA	23	19(18)	86	7-6	0	100	1.70	5.34		11.5%	25.1%	1.8%	48.2%	63.6%	83.9%	26.2%	64.8%	.391	.578	95	1.4
2023	STL	MLB	23	8(8)	33²	1-4	0	32	2.08	8.02	53.0%	11.2%	18.8%	4.1%	39.5%	62.9%	89.5%	25.8%	64.8%	.393	.780	128	-0.1
2024 DC	STL	MLB	24	29(5)	50	3-3	0	41	1.47	5.10	53.0%	9.8%	18.5%	3.0%	40.0%					.301	.535	113	0.1

2023 Arsenal: FA (90.7), SI (87.5), SL (79.5), FS (83.7), CH (82.3)   Comps: Justus Sheffield (70), Ariel Jurado (69), Robert Stephenson (69)

The Orioles seemed dead set on keeping every young piece of talent in their farm system so that in the future, John Angelos doesn't have to pay to keep anyone because there will always be new talent to replace the old. But at the trade deadline, Angelos signed off on a deal that sent Rom to St. Louis for Jack Flaherty—not the deal for which O's fans were necessarily looking, but one that might get them to do Angelos' favorite thing for fans to do: Shut up. That gave Rom an opportunity in a new organization, and as fate would have it, he got to pitch against his old club in the fifth appearance of his big-league career. He made the O's regret the swap with 5 ⅓ innings of shutout ball featuring two hits and seven strikeouts. Unfortunately, it was the only start of its kind in the majors for Rom: Without revenge in his veins, his low-velocity fastball and poor bat-missing capabilities got hit hard.

JoJo Romero LHP   Born: 09/09/96   Age: 27   Height: 5'11"   Weight: 200   Origin: Round 4, 2016 Draft (#107 overall)

YEAR	TM	LVL	AGE	G (GS)	IP	W-L	SV	K	WHIP	ERA	CSP	BB%	K%	HR%	GB%	ZSw%	ZCon%	OSw%	OCon%	BABIP	SLGCON	DRA-	WARP
2021	PHI	MLB	24	11(0)	9	0-0	0	8	1.78	7.00	58.5%	9.1%	18.2%	9.1%	54.8%	71.1%	87.0%	31.2%	66.7%	.296	.839	91	0.1
2022	STL	MLB	25	15(0)	14¹	0-0	0	16	1.26	3.77	47.2%	15.8%	28.1%	3.5%	56.2%	55.7%	77.3%	31.6%	48.0%	.241	.548	97	0.2
2023	MEM	AAA	26	17(0)	21	2-1	2	33	1.33	3.00		10.2%	37.5%	3.4%	41.3%	61.8%	77.7%	36.2%	43.4%	.372	.652	77	0.6
2023	STL	MLB	26	27(0)	36²	4-2	3	42	1.06	3.68	50.5%	6.8%	28.6%	0.7%	57.4%	65.2%	74.8%	32.9%	45.5%	.304	.435	76	0.9
2024 DC	STL	MLB	27	41(0)	43²	3-2	9	51	1.27	3.71	50.5%	8.6%	27.5%	2.2%	51.6%					.314	.521	86	0.5

2023 Arsenal: SI (94.9), CH (86.1), SW (84.6), FA (95.1), FC (87.8)   Comps: Kyle Ryan (49), Renyel Pinto (48), Chasen Shreve (47)

Before Romero became a part of the Cardinals' injured masses, he got an opportunity because of them. With Packy Naughton hurt and Zack Thompson struggling, Romero started getting the ball in high-leverage situations more often. After Jordan Hicks was dealt at the deadline, an increasingly confident Romero started showing up even more, often pitching more than one inning while leading with an effective sinker and change. And, because he was spotted drinking a Red Bull and crushing the can one time in 2020, that's now his entire personality! Hey, every late-inning reliever needs a quirk, and now Romero will be answering questions about energy drinks for the rest of his career. Eventually, Romero suffered an injury Red Bull couldn't solve and joined the IL corps with patellar tendonitis in his left knee.

Zack Thompson LHP   Born: 10/28/97   Age: 26   Height: 6'2"   Weight: 215   Origin: Round 1, 2019 Draft (#19 overall)

YEAR	TM	LVL	AGE	G (GS)	IP	W-L	SV	K	WHIP	ERA	CSP	BB%	K%	HR%	GB%	ZSw%	ZCon%	OSw%	OCon%	BABIP	SLGCON	DRA-	WARP
2021	MEM	AAA	23	22(19)	93	2-10	2	82	1.84	7.06		12.8%	18.5%	4.1%	38.5%					.343	.659	131	-0.2
2022	MEM	AAA	24	19(10)	53¹	2-3	0	67	1.22	4.73		9.2%	29.4%	2.6%	44.9%	74.6%	75.0%	18.5%	60.0%	.292	.567	85	1.1
2022	STL	MLB	24	22(1)	34²	1-1	1	27	0.98	2.08	57.3%	10.3%	19.9%	2.2%	54.7%	66.8%	87.4%	29.4%	72.8%	.185	.337	99	0.3
2023	MEM	AAA	25	11(9)	34¹	1-4	0	41	2.36	8.65		21.8%	22.9%	2.8%	42.7%	65.0%	82.6%	22.6%	58.2%	.411	.734	118	0.1
2023	STL	MLB	25	25(9)	66¹	5-7	0	72	1.42	4.48	48.6%	8.7%	25.1%	2.8%	43.6%	63.1%	85.2%	29.0%	62.2%	.341	.587	95	1.0
2024 DC	STL	MLB	26	22(3)	38	2-2	0	36	1.45	4.68	51.1%	11.7%	21.3%	2.7%	45.2%					.290	.514	104	0.2

2023 Arsenal: FA (94), CU (75.8), SL (86.2), CH (87), CS (62.9)   *Comps: Cody Reed (65), Sean Gilmartin (59), Steve Johnson (58)*

Thompson was going to be an important lefty reliever for St. Louis, but the club quickly realized they had more use for him as a starter. So, it was down to Memphis to learn how to sit him in the dugout instead of the bullpen. This went terribly; he racked up an 8.65 ERA in 11 games (and nine starts) against Triple-A hitters. But speaking of terrible, Steven Matz strained his left lat in mid-August and became one of those guys who was around but generally considered done for the season. Thompson made eight starts in Matz's stead and, barring one gem against the Pirates on September 3, generally lasted four or five innings, gave up five or six hits and surrendered at least a couple runs. The 25-year-old's primary issue seemed to be losing a few ticks on his fastball the later into a start he lasted, with the radar gun chirping excitedly as he hit 96-97 in the first and sighing exasperatedly as he dropped to 91-92 by the fifth.

Drew VerHagen RHP   Born: 10/22/90   Age: 33   Height: 6'6"   Weight: 230   Origin: Round 4, 2012 Draft (#154 overall)

YEAR	TM	LVL	AGE	G (GS)	IP	W-L	SV	K	WHIP	ERA	CSP	BB%	K%	HR%	GB%	ZSw%	ZCon%	OSw%	OCon%	BABIP	SLGCON	DRA-	WARP
2022	STL	MLB	31	19(0)	21²	3-1	0	18	1.89	6.65	50.8%	13.2%	17.0%	4.7%	34.2%	70.9%	84.1%	31.0%	55.4%	.324	.639	124	-0.1
2023	STL	MLB	32	60(0)	61	5-1	0	60	1.28	3.98	47.7%	9.7%	22.4%	3.4%	41.0%	65.3%	81.4%	31.9%	51.3%	.262	.535	97	0.8
2024 non	STL	MLB	33	58(0)	50	2-2	0	52	1.39	5.01	48.7%	9.4%	23.6%	3.6%	35.9%					.304	.592	111	-0.1

2023 Arsenal: SW (81.6), FA (93.8), SI (92.9), FS (88.9), FC (89.8), SL (86.9)   *Comps: Anthony Bass (43), Jim Johnson (42), Bryan Shaw (42)*

VerHagen was not the guy Cardinals fans wanted to see coming through that bullpen gate in 2022. So the staff messed with him a little bit, breaking his slider in half and converting it into a sweeper and a cutter while having him begin using his four-seam fastball more than his sinker. The results were positive: The 32-year-old ate the middle innings for the Cardinals when a starter would leave them empty, and even got dropped into a few high-leverage late spots. There is a bullpen out there in which VerHagen will find a home in free agency; probably one for whom an assistant excitedly pitches the idea of acquiring a durable righty to a GM looking to add relief help (which is the GM of every team).

Adam Wainwright RHP   Born: 08/30/81   Age: 42   Height: 6'7"   Weight: 230   Origin: Round 1, 2000 Draft (#29 overall)

YEAR	TM	LVL	AGE	G (GS)	IP	W-L	SV	K	WHIP	ERA	CSP	BB%	K%	HR%	GB%	ZSw%	ZCon%	OSw%	OCon%	BABIP	SLGCON	DRA-	WARP
2021	STL	MLB	39	32(32)	206¹	17-7	0	174	1.06	3.05	56.1%	6.0%	21.0%	2.5%	47.9%	60.6%	89.4%	30.6%	66.5%	.257	.455	90	3.1
2022	STL	MLB	40	32(32)	191²	11-12	0	143	1.28	3.71	56.5%	6.7%	17.8%	2.0%	43.7%	62.9%	90.5%	29.2%	71.8%	.302	.474	108	1.1
2023	STL	MLB	41	21(21)	101	5-11	0	55	1.90	7.40	49.9%	8.5%	11.4%	4.1%	40.3%	62.8%	92.0%	25.8%	78.1%	.359	.655	141	-1.0
2024 non	STL	MLB	42	58(0)	50	2-2	0	29	1.48	5.44	53.7%	7.3%	13.1%	3.4%	41.2%					.303	.540	120	-0.3

2023 Arsenal: SI (87.1), CU (71.9), FC (83), FA (85.8), FS (82.4), CH (79.7), SW (75.9), CS (63.1)   *Comps: Justin Verlander (71), Tom Glavine (69), Bert Blyleven (69)*

The worst season of the 42-year-old Wainwright's career was also his last. It happens. At least he managed to pitch most of the season and didn't Aaron Rodgers himself 75 seconds into the schedule. By the time he was recording his 200th career win—a 1-0 victory over the Brewers in which his offense provided all support of which they were capable—his back was spasming so hard Wainwright had considered missing the start. But it wound up being the best effort of his season: In the only appearance where he completed seven innings of work, he shut down a division rival on its way to the postseason and got people thinking more about his own glorious past than the Cardinals' ambiguous future. Things—even the best things—don't always have the ending one imagines, desires, or earns. Sometimes they're just over, and all that's left is to simply wrap up the past and enjoy that at one point it was the present.

Guillermo Zuñiga RHP   Born: 10/10/98   Age: 25   Height: 6'5"   Weight: 230   Origin: IFA, 2016

YEAR	TM	LVL	AGE	G (GS)	IP	W-L	SV	K	WHIP	ERA	CSP	BB%	K%	HR%	GB%	ZSw%	ZCon%	OSw%	OCon%	BABIP	SLGCON	DRA-	WARP
2021	TUL	AA	22	25(0)	35¹	7-2	2	49	1.08	3.06		9.0%	33.8%	3.4%	32.1%					.263	.588	65	0.9
2022	TUL	AA	23	48(0)	54²	4-4	11	66	1.41	4.77		12.4%	27.4%	5.0%	38.5%					.269	.631	83	0.8
2023	MEM	AAA	24	29(0)	30²	0-2	5	37	1.70	7.63		13.7%	25.3%	4.1%	31.4%	69.1%	76.9%	27.4%	54.8%	.325	.788	113	0.2
2023	STL	MLB	24	2(0)	2	0-0	0	4	1.00	4.50	50.2%	0.0%	50.0%	0.0%	0.0%	65.0%	84.6%	30.4%	71.4%	.500	.750	91	0.0
2024 DC	STL	MLB	25	30(0)	32²	2-2	0	33	1.49	5.36	50.2%	11.7%	22.3%	3.8%	32.0%					.292	.600	119	-0.2

2023 Arsenal: FA (99.4), SL (88.9), CH (91)   *Comps: Joey Krehbiel (46), Evan Phillips (45), Jake Barrett (45)*

The world got to know Zuñiga last year at the World Baseball Classic, when, pitching for Colombia, he sent his screaming high-90s fastball past Mike Trout and Paul Goldschmidt. Clearly, the Cardinals thought highly of the 24-year-old Dodger cast-off, having given him a big-league deal over the winter leading up to the WBC. Spending most of the season at Triple-A, he allowed walks and strikeouts at higher and lower rates, respectively; with that below-average control that guys always have when they can throw a baseball through a wall, he wound up with an ERA that ballooned dramatically enough to lift him off the ground. Nevertheless, Zuñiga's three-pitch mix (which contains his slider and changeup) remains encouragingly effective as the massive lad prepares to throw further major-league fastballs down the line.

LINEOUTS

Hitters

HITTER	POS	TM	LVL	AGE	PA	R	HR	RBI	SB	AVG/OBP/SLG	BABIP	SLGCON	BB%	K%	ZSw%	ZCon%	OSw%	OCon%	LA	90th EV	DRC+	BRR	DRP	WARP
Leonardo Bernal	C	PMB	A	19	323	45	3	44	4	.265/.381/.362	.319	.455	15.2%	17.0%	69.5%	82.3%	27.5%	70.0%			113	-1.4	-3.6	0.9
Won-Bin Cho	OF	PMB	A	19	452	64	7	52	32	.270/.376/.389	.341	.525	14.2%	21.7%	68.5%	83.2%	24.4%	54.0%			111	2.1	4.0	2.5
Jimmy Crooks	C	PEO	A+	21	477	71	12	73	2	.271/.358/.433	.329	.574	10.9%	21.2%							114	2.5	23.3	4.8
Zach Levenson	OF	PMB	A	21	139	24	6	22	2	.268/.331/.480	.307	.648	8.6%	23.0%	72.0%	78.9%	29.4%	69.2%			104	-0.9	-4.0	0.1
Jonathan Mejia	SS	CAR	ROK	18	131	16	2	8	7	.173/.331/.288	.242	.448	18.3%	28.2%										
	SS	PMB	A	18	33	3	0	2	1	.107/.242/.143	.167	.222	12.1%	30.3%	65.9%	85.2%	31.2%	50.0%			91	0.4	2.0	0.3
Taylor Motter	IF	MEM	AAA	33	236	31	8	26	8	.255/.343/.438	.319	.611	11.4%	25.0%	63.5%	80.4%	25.6%	63.4%			96	1.0	2.5	0.8
	IF	STL	MLB	33	82	3	0	2	0	.171/.232/.211	.289	.356	6.1%	37.8%	70.4%	78.5%	32.0%	56.4%	19.2	107.4	57	-0.1	0.2	-0.2
Pedro Pagés	C	SPR	AA	24	497	63	16	72	3	.267/.362/.443	.305	.573	11.9%	19.3%							117	-2.5	23.2	4.3
César Prieto	IF	BOW	AA	24	249	33	4	29	5	.364/.406/.476	.379	.514	6.0%	6.8%							126	-1.3	6.1	1.8
	IF	MEM	AAA	24	176	24	4	20	2	.270/.314/.387	.296	.457	4.0%	14.2%	72.0%	90.1%	46.9%	70.1%			90	0.2	1.3	0.4
	IF	NOR	AAA	24	115	16	2	20	2	.317/.365/.471	.330	.521	7.0%	8.7%	70.5%	90.8%	43.1%	73.4%			107	-2.0	-1.8	0.1
Juniel Querecuto	2B	MEM	AAA	30	440	53	13	57	12	.269/.343/.418	.331	.564	9.1%	23.0%	75.3%	86.2%	37.2%	61.9%			91	-0.6	0.5	0.7
	2B	STL	MLB	30	21	2	0	0	0	.100/.143/.150	.143	.214	4.8%	28.6%	58.1%	77.8%	37.5%	55.6%	7.7	95.7	87	0.0	0.0	0.0
Michael Siani	CF	LOU	AAA	23	454	63	9	47	22	.228/.344/.354	.292	.498	15.2%	24.0%	60.6%	83.1%	24.3%	51.9%			92	2.6	2.5	1.4
	CF	MEM	AAA	23	39	6	0	1	1	.226/.385/.290	.304	.391	17.9%	20.5%	47.7%	90.3%	31.0%	61.3%			93	1.5	0.1	0.0
	CF	CIN	MLB	23	1	1	0	0	0	.000/1.000/.000			100.0%	0.0%	0.0%		0.0%				86	0.0	0.0	0.0
	CF	STL	MLB	23	5	0	0	0	1	.000/.000/.000		.000	0.0%	20.0%	54.5%	83.3%	15.4%	0.0%	12.7	98.7	98	0.0	0.0	0.0
William Sullivan	1B	PMB	A	22	119	14	1	16	2	.308/.395/.433	.392	.562	12.6%	20.2%	68.6%	86.7%	30.4%	60.4%			105	-2.2	-1.1	0.0
Jared Young	1B	IOW	AAA	27	376	71	21	72	7	.310/.417/.577	.359	.792	13.3%	22.3%	71.9%	83.6%	25.1%	53.3%			121	1.9	-1.2	1.9
	1B	CHC	MLB	27	47	8	2	8	2	.186/.255/.465	.214	.667	6.4%	27.7%	75.9%	76.2%	31.9%	51.7%	11.1	107.2	88	0.1	0.0	0.0

Projected to reach High-A last year, **Leonardo Bernal** instead stayed in Palm Beach. A plus defender with a solid plate approach, the teenage power-hitting catcher struggles with contact. As far as stopping the ball, he's solid; as far as throwing it, there remains room to grow. He's currently buried near the bottom of the Cardinals' deep catching pool. ⓪ The Cardinals are going to want to send **Won-Bin Cho**. The 20-year-old made headlines last summer when he had three hits and stole four bases in one game—three of the steals came with two outs, including one of home. The outfielder's 32 swipes only tied for eighth in the Florida State League, but he showcased the consistent contact and searing exit velocity that made him the first amateur player the Cardinals have signed out of Asia. ⓪ **Jimmy Crooks** has typically put on a show every time he swings: It starts with an aggressive leg kick, evolves into a violent follow-through and, should he make contact, the resulting *crack* is satisfying to every ear. The 22-year-old catcher, an average defender with adequate arm strength, showed this off when he homered in three straight games for Peoria. ⓪ "CARDINALS TAKE 'PEQUA'S HONEYMAN," read the headlines. It sounded as if the beekeeping vendor at a local farmers' market had been carried off by birds. Instead, it meant a junior at Boston College had been drafted by St. Louis in the third round. **Travis Honeyman** had been projected to go as early as the first round when the 2023 season was getting underway, but a shoulder injury ruined all that. A skilled barreler, Honeyman was shifted from third base to the outfield by his former college coach, but the move never broke his concentration at the plate. Hopefully it can outlast his labrum and rotator cuff rehabilitation as well. ⓪ **Zach Levenson**'s bat is what will get him to the majors, as an agreeable hitter for both contact and power. His 2023 Miami Hurricanes had the third-highest home run total in the program's history coming into the regular-season finale against Duke. It was Levenson's grand slam—his 14th home run of the season—that helped them get into second. ⓪ **Jonathan Mejia** had established a reputation as a slugging, switch-hitting teenage shortstop ahead of the 2023 season. Especially after such a resounding showcase in the 2022 Dominican Summer League, the Cardinals just wanted to see *more* of that beautiful swing, and the defense that comes with it, so they put Mejia in the Florida State League; his numbers, like a lot of things in Florida, dropped off the face of the earth. ⓪ In his third go-around with the Cardinals, **Taylor Motter** was used for his defensive flexibility over the course of 29 games—the most exposure to big-league pitching the 34-year-old has had since 2017. He had a good handle on the bat—by which we mean, he knew which end of it to hold. ⓪ Both George R.R. Martin and this catching prospect have an elite ability to frame things in a compelling way. While the latter has shown a more recent ability to impact the ball, improving his prospect status in the process, perhaps the biggest difference between two is that **Pedro** has **Pagés**. ⓪ The Cardinals got to tap into more than one fertile farm system as they embraced their role as "sellers" at the trade deadline. **César Prieto** came from the Orioles as part of the Jack Flaherty deal; while he possesses a bat which has produced elite contact rates, he's eager to chase out of the zone and has struggled to correct this approach flaw. The 24-year-old infielder is viewed as just about major-league ready, though his Triple-A slash line dropped significantly post-trade. ⓪ Pretty close to six years went by between big-league appearances for **Juniel Querecuto**; when he grounded out in the seventh inning for the Rays in 2017, he may not have known he wouldn't jog back onto the field again until he was pinch running for Willson Contreras in 2023. We never know how the years will change us. They did not change Querecuto's output at the plate. ⓪ Defense! Speed! These were things the Cardinals did not have much of in 2023. They claimed **Michael Siani**, who'd appeared in 12 major-league games, off waivers from the Reds in September and jammed him into five games in hopes he'd provide a little bit of both. Then again, they were also running out the clock on 2023 and needed some fresh meat bags to shove onto the diamond as the IL continued to fill up. The 24-year-old went 0-for-5 with a stolen base. ⓪ The Good: **William Sullivan** knows what pitches he can damage, whacking fastballs in his nitro zone to produce high exit velocities. The Bad: He's probably limited to first base, and mechanical deficiencies cause him to mistime the ball and put it straight into the ground. The Ugly: His barrel control is a mess and he struggles badly making contact on breakers, which he'll see more of as he moves up the chain. ⓪ **Jared Young** finished two games for Triple-A Iowa last season. Is this his Sean Doolittle turn? Of course not. Unless it is, in which case, you heard it in these pages first.

Pitchers

PITCHER	TM	LVL	AGE	G (GS)	IP	W-L	SV	K	WHIP	ERA	CSP	BB%	K%	HR%	GB%	ZSw%	ZCon%	OSw%	OCon%	BABIP	SLGCON	DRA-	WARP
Ian Bedell	PEO	A+	23	27 (19)	96	4-2	0	106	1.15	2.44		8.7%	27.2%	1.8%	39.1%					.292	.459	78	1.7
Gordon Graceffo	MEM	AAA	23	21 (18)	86	4-3	0	81	1.53	4.92		11.6%	20.9%	2.3%	41.9%	66.0%	88.4%	31.7%	56.8%	.313	.556	103	1.2
Cooper Hjerpe	PEO	A+	22	10 (8)	41	2-3	0	51	1.24	3.51		14.6%	29.8%	4.7%	45.1%					.217	.604	100	0.1
Brycen Mautz	PMB	A	21	23 (23)	104	4-9	0	115	1.34	3.98		9.9%	25.2%	0.9%	49.5%	72.5%	84.8%	32.6%	57.3%	.320	.473	75	1.9
Michael McGreevy	SPR	AA	22	3 (3)	18²	2-0	0	16	0.96	1.45		1.4%	22.5%	0.0%	67.9%					.321	.396	85	0.4
	MEM	AAA	22	24 (24)	134¹	11-6	0	107	1.47	4.49		6.2%	18.0%	2.9%	52.2%	63.6%	87.9%	34.2%	67.1%	.335	.553	91	2.5
Edwin Nunez	PMB	A	21	19 (0)	27¹	3-3	5	35	1.35	3.62		11.7%	29.2%	0.8%	47.1%	76.7%	75.7%	36.7%	54.9%	.319	.500	82	0.4
	PEO	A+	21	22 (0)	36¹	3-1	5	30	1.35	3.22		10.1%	19.0%	2.5%	39.6%					.271	.509	114	0.1
Max Rajcic	PMB	A	21	12 (12)	62	6-3	0	68	0.81	1.89		3.8%	28.6%	1.7%	36.3%	68.9%	82.9%	32.8%	69.4%	.243	.410	66	1.6
	PEO	A+	21	11 (11)	61¹	3-3	0	55	1.22	3.08		7.2%	21.9%	0.8%	35.6%					.320	.419	95	0.6
Nick Robertson	WOR	AAA	24	15 (0)	14¹	2-1	2	16	1.26	4.40		6.3%	25.4%	4.8%	42.9%	77.9%	78.4%	33.6%	57.1%	.282	.619	83	0.3
	OKC	AAA	24	27 (0)	28¹	2-0	7	42	0.99	2.54		8.0%	37.5%	1.8%	50.8%	65.5%	74.6%	36.5%	43.7%	.288	.459	60	0.9
	LAD	MLB	24	9 (0)	10¹	0-1	0	13	2.03	6.10	49.9%	8.0%	26.0%	2.0%	48.5%	67.9%	81.8%	29.2%	57.6%	.500	.788	88	0.2
	BOS	MLB	24	9 (1)	12	0-0	0	13	1.50	6.00	49.2%	8.9%	23.2%	3.6%	45.9%	71.1%	84.4%	40.4%	43.2%	.314	.667	89	0.2
Wilking Rodríguez	MEM	AAA	33	7 (0)	5²	0-0	0	6	1.24	0.00		8.7%	26.1%	0.0%	53.3%	64.3%	92.6%	26.9%	50.0%	.333	.333	88	0.1
Zack Showalter	ORI	ROK	19	3 (3)	10	0-0	0	16	1.10	0.90		10.0%	40.0%	0.0%	50.0%					.350	.400		
	DEL	A	19	6 (5)	20¹	0-2	0	25	1.43	3.10		11.2%	28.1%	1.1%	43.1%					.360	.580	92	0.3
Connor Thomas	MEM	AAA	25	21 (17)	94¹	5-4	1	69	1.75	5.53		7.0%	15.7%	2.3%	49.9%	68.5%	87.8%	34.0%	63.2%	.382	.598	101	1.3
Jake Woodford	SPR	AA	26	3 (3)	8	1-0	0	11	0.75	3.38		3.3%	36.7%	6.7%	38.9%					.188	.667	89	0.1
	MEM	AAA	26	7 (6)	20²	0-2	0	23	1.21	2.61		11.1%	25.6%	3.3%	38.9%	60.8%	87.1%	30.1%	66.2%	.235	.500	95	0.4
	STL	MLB	26	15 (8)	47²	2-3	0	29	1.74	6.23	50.9%	9.9%	13.1%	5.0%	51.2%	66.7%	86.7%	22.4%	78.3%	.318	.673	116	0.2

Ian Bedell pitches from a low arm slot that provides the trickery needed to cover for his lack of velocity. The 24-year-old has been much more fortunate with his health of late (he's a TJ survivor) and a new slider seems primed to move Bedell up the organizational ladder. ☉ When his shoulder inflamed last year, 23-year-old **Gordon Graceffo** said it was the first injury he'd experienced since high school. That meant he'd be "digging up" mentally and physically as he recovered over a seven-week window. He returned out of the bullpen for Triple-A Memphis—which required another mental adjustment—and while his curveball looked pretty delectable to opposing hitters, he was able to get his fastball back into the high nineties. ☉ **Cooper Hjerpe**'s 2023 season was hijacked by a loose body in his elbow, to which he lost all of June, July and August as he went under the knife. The Cardinals sent the 23-year-old to the Arizona Fall League to get back some of the innings he'd lost, where he not only stayed healthy but racked up a lot of strikeouts for a guy who was just trying to re-establish his muscle memory. ☉ The Cardinals grabbed **Quinn Mathews** in the fourth round of the 2023 draft after he'd made a name for himself by throwing 156 pitches in a complete-game, 16-strikeout performance in the NCAA Super Regionals. With a deep arsenal, a commanding fastball and a plus changeup, Mathews' marathon showcase was reflective of his overall reputation as a grinder. ☉ Coming out of the University of San Diego, **Brycen Mautz** profiled as a mystifying lefty with a slider that worked, a changeup that didn't and a fastball that topped out around 93 mph. After shutting him down subsequent to his 2022 second-round selection, last spring the Cardinals assigned him to the famously gentle (for pitchers) Florida State League. Batters nevertheless found his four-seamer hittable, though he was named the Cardinals' Minor League Pitcher of the Month for July. ☉ **Michael McGreevy** lets his fastball and his slider feed off of each other; while the heater is mediocre in velocity and movement, the slider gets a lot of hitters to chase. The 23-year-old roasted Double-A hitters through three starts, so the Cardinals bumped him up to Triple-A Memphis, where he struggled against a higher class of hitters. ☉ **Edwin Nunez** was dispatched to the desert last fall with the intention of cutting down on walks. It had been a focus of his development since 2022, when he walked nearly 30% of batters across five Low-A contests. The 2023 season saw him keep that rate at a career-lows at both halves of A-ball, and with only four free passes over 10 ⅔ AFL frames, the Cardinals have to be encouraged by the flamethrowing 22-year-old's progress. ☉ **Max Rajcic** comes at batters with a sinister curveball and an arsenal deep enough to keep them guessing. He saved his best performance for the Midwest League Division Series, striking out nine batters—a career high—and allowing only one hit. It wasn't really a stunning performance for a guy who'd been named the Cardinals Minor League Pitcher of the Month in 2023—twice. ☉ **Nick Robertson**, nicknamed Big Country, was part of the return package for Kiké Hernández before 2023. "Big Country Goes to Beantown'' could be the title of a children's book in which the main character struggles to adjust to a new city. The sequel, "Big Country and the Gateway to the West," will see him try to leverage his upper-90s heater into more chances for a happy ending in St. Louis. ☉ The Cardinals used a Rule 5 pick to get **Wilking Rodríguez** from the Yankees, and he spent the whole season on the injured list with a sore shoulder. The 34-year-old underwent arthroscopic surgery in May as he tried to get into his first big-league game in eight years, and put a shot in his arm in September in the hopes he'd be able to make one major-league appearance in 2023. It didn't happen. ☉ **Zack Showalter** was attractive to the Orioles during the 2022 draft because of velocity that topped out at 95 mph and an ability to get batters to swing and miss. While a hardened strike-thrower, his secondary offerings have a ways to go. Baltimore sent him to St. Louis as part of the Jack Flaherty trade, and the Cardinals stationed him in Palm Beach before he hit the injured list. ☉ **Connor Thomas** was back for his third year with Triple-A Memphis in 2023, though "back" was not a permanent status as he missed two months on the injured list. He finished the year with some unsatisfying numbers through 21 appearances, diminishing his prospect status. ☉ **Jake Woodford** shares his name with the mayor of Appleton, Wisconsin. Perhaps *that* Woodford has the shoulder that the Cardinals' Jake could have used multiple times last season, when he hit the IL thanks to a right shoulder strain. His numbers weren't encouraging, but he did keep the ball on the ground. The pitcher, not the mayor. We don't have stats on him.

TAMPA BAY RAYS

Essay by Ginny Searle and Patrick Dubuque

Player comments by Tommy Rancel and BP staff

The Tampa Bay Rays are the World Champions of being the Tampa Bay Rays.

A beaver has to make a dam. Even separated from running water, the availability of typical materials and any necessity to create lodging, countless videos exist of pet beavers turning to their natural instincts and fashioning makeshift dams of Charlie Brown Christmas trees, SpongeBob SquarePants stuffed animals, and whatever other materials they might get their forepaws on. Sundered from the realities of nature, in the pristine hallways of those who foster beavers, rescued rodents will build, watch their work erased and build again. It's what they do. Perhaps Tampa Bay shouldn't have dealt in half-measures when they de-apostatized their name.

The last five years of Rays baseball have been the best in the franchise's Gen-Z history. In a sport as fickle as baseball, where teams with historic run differentials routinely get bounced 72 hours after all their dreams seemed within reach, there might be shame in coming up short year after year, but there's no shock value. Just ask the Dodgers, who responded to their poor dice rolls by buying every die they could get their hands on. The Rays, meanwhile, are content to wait it out; they even sold one of their dice to Los Angeles, in Tyler Glasnow. This is a group that's mastered graduate-level statistical analysis; they can handle the gambler's fallacy.

Banners would be nice; they'd certainly add some color to the Tropicana Field skyline, such as it is. But they've always been a secondary concern. The Rays have, in many ways, completed what they set out to do. What began as a sustainability drive has become an ethos, so slowly that it took the entire sabermetric community time to notice. Tampa Bay is no longer the plucky underdog, just happy to punch above its weight against the likes of New York and Los Angeles. They've lost players, lost masterminds, lost everything and regrown it all, less like a delicate flower and more like thistle. Someday, introductory poetry classes will eschew Elizabeth Bishop in favor of the Rays' transaction logs.

Attendance is no longer the measurement of team success, either on the field or in the bank; this is another advanced statistic that the Rays understand better than most. Their

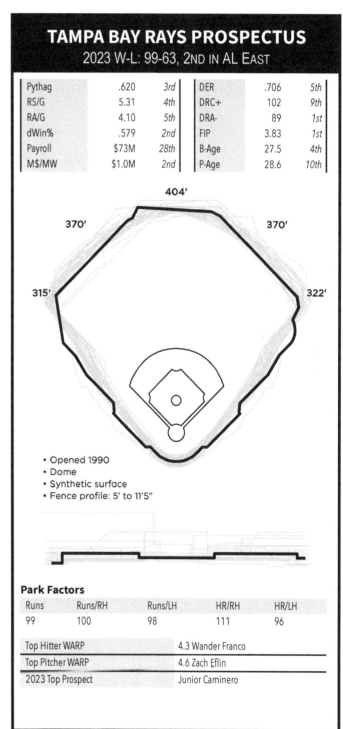

TAMPA BAY RAYS PROSPECTUS
2023 W-L: 99-63, 2ND IN AL EAST

Pythag	.620	3rd	DER	.706	5th
RS/G	5.31	4th	DRC+	102	9th
RA/G	4.10	5th	DRA-	89	1st
dWin%	.579	2nd	FIP	3.83	1st
Payroll	$73M	28th	B-Age	27.5	4th
M$/MW	$1.0M	2nd	P-Age	28.6	10th

404'
370'   370'
315'   322'

- Opened 1990
- Dome
- Synthetic surface
- Fence profile: 5' to 11'5"

Park Factors

Runs	Runs/RH	Runs/LH	HR/RH	HR/LH
99	100	98	111	96

Top Hitter WARP	4.3 Wander Franco
Top Pitcher WARP	4.6 Zach Eflin
2023 Top Prospect	Junior Caminero

Payroll History (in millions)

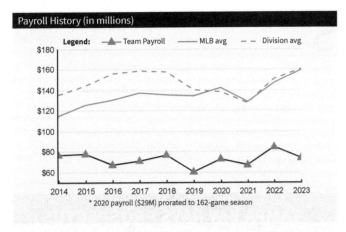

Legend: ▲ Team Payroll — MLB avg -- Division avg

* 2020 payroll ($29M) prorated to 162-game season

Future Commitments (in millions)

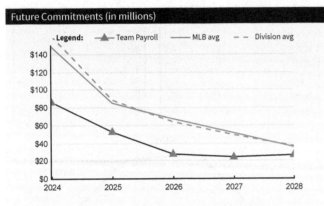

Legend: ▲ Team Payroll — MLB avg -- Division avg

Farm System Ranking

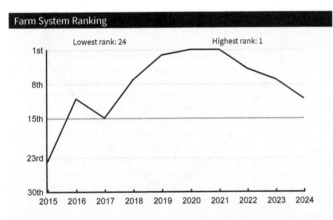

Lowest rank: 24   Highest rank: 1

Personnel

President, Baseball Operations
Erik Neander

Vice President, Assistant General Manager
Will Cousins

Vice President, Assistant General Manager
Chana Lawdermilk

Vice President, Assistant General Manager
Carlos Rodriguez

Manager
Kevin Cash

BP Alumni
Jason Cole

television deal is quite lucrative and their ratings are strong. Even in the stadium, not all seats are equal, and gate revenues pale against the growing alternative revenue streams available to MLB and its franchises. But at the same time, Tampa's turnstiles swung 1,440,301 times in 2023, their highest total in a decade. That ranked 27th in baseball; the last time they exceeded that figure was in 2010, when the franchise was still basking in the afterglow of its first World Series appearance.

Those numbers have always defined baseball in Tampa Bay: restricted its options, dictated its behavior. It drove owner Stuart Sternberg to threaten relocation and, failing that, to propose his wild time-share idea with Montreal. (If a single parent with full custody suddenly wants to hand off the kids to Dad half the time, the kids are likely to wonder whether they've done anything wrong.) But this, just as with everything the Rays do, was never about winning. It was a means to an end, and that end is in sight: a new stadium, and the promise of not success, but eternal sustainability. The secret to happiness isn't happiness. It's about staying alive.

⚾   ⚾   ⚾

In rattling off 13 consecutive wins to start their season, the Rays secured the hottest start of the Wild Card era and matched the best starts of any campaigns postdating the establishment of the American League. The impenetrable pitching that would become the club's signature—the staff ranked first in MLB, undergirded by an 87 DRA- for starters—was in evidence from the get-go, with the six shutouts compiled through 19 games as many (or more) than seven teams logged all year. By the time April was out, Tampa Bay had a +103 run differential at a point when just one other team had even broken +50. Over the next 133 games, the Rays' run differential would be +92.

Through 23 games, the Rays had taken just three losses. The energy surrounding Randy Arozarena was capable of charging handheld devices in a 200-foot radius. They stretched their AL East lead to 6.5 games a half-dozen times between May 8 and July 1. Just a few weeks later, in a stretch that included the All-Star break, losing streaks of seven and five games had erased that lead and handed it over to Baltimore, who would never relinquish (at least partial) control of the division. The pixie dust that had floated the Rays through a historic start went missing in the dog days of summer, and there simply weren't enough fans in the stands to clap them back to life. The playoffs came around and dealt another quick exit, with Tampa Bay now 1-7 in their last three postseason series.

One wonders if this is as good as things get for the Rays. It's not that this paper dynasty could never produce a championship, but that the front office has marked the complete realization of their guiding principles. It was widely assumed that a blazing start to the season would finally cement the team's place among the league's true elite, and that an era of Tampa Bay as perennial favorites, rather than afterthoughts who continued to pleasantly surprise, was upon us. Then April ended, and the Rays faded entirely from the collective consciousness.

The asymptotic approach to success could certainly still produce a World Series title eventually, but should that day come the victory will taste as much as happenstance as all the disappointment leading to it. No one could have expected the Rays to exit the 2020 World Series with a commitment to build and spend like the Dodgers, but the contrast to the Diamondbacks—another low-payroll, surprise pennant winner—is telling. Whereas Arizona has committed to spending more and delivering on the expectations a World Series appearance implies, nothing—not coming within two games of a title, not the best start to a season in a third of a century—could persuade ownership to bring payroll out of the league's bottom third. Glasnow's salary was set to jump some 467% from last year's $5.35 million, meaning that his being traded was as foregone of a conclusion as a battleground-state television becoming unwatchable in an election year. If there was ever a time to retain a Cy Young-caliber (when healthy) starter, it'd be the offseason after Shane McClanahan, Jeffrey Springs and Drew Rasmussen all went down with elbow injuries that required surgery. Instead, Ryan Pepiot came on in the Dodgers trade to provide timber for the next estuarine dam.

⚾   ⚾   ⚾

The dam is complete. The Rays have a new home. It's a copy of their old home.

After years of casting about for alternatives, mourning the demographic challenges of the Tampa Bay region and its bridge-connected, spread-out populace, the team announced that its new stadium would be built in St. Petersburg after all, near Tropicana. It will feature a non-retractable dome. It will seat around 30,000, a figure they topped once at home all year in 2023, a Sunday afternoon matchup against the Yankees. Faced with a similar problem of an unworkable location, Indonesia has undertaken the process of moving its capital from Jakarta to Nusantara—a city which does not yet exist. The question of whether the Rays' decision to hunker down is a better one will also unravel over a span of decades.

The difference, of course, is not what's inside the stadium—shiny as the surfaces will certainly be—but what sits outside it. The Rays have been given the opportunity to build their own shopping complex—sorry, village—in a revitalized region of downtown. This has basically become a mandatory step in the stadium-shopping process; the infeasibility of the Oakland Waterfall Ballpark District played a central role in the A's decision to relocate, while the Orioles harbored similar hopes in the Camden Yards renovation and played out nearly every inch of string they possessed in an attempt to get their way.

If this all sounds a little familiar, it's understandable; after excitement over the rule changes wore off, the dominant national storyline outside the action on the field was the protracted and inevitable relocation of the Athletics to Las Vegas. Oakland and Tampa Bay were considered commissioner Rob Manfred's two "problem spots," situations that needed to be resolved before the league could entertain expansion. And while John Fisher has bungled every step of his crusade, Tampa quietly and efficiently extracted every single thing they needed. Months after the A's promised renderings, still struggling to find a site and the backing to afford a stadium to put on it, the Rays are just...done. They have their niche market. They have their guaranteed revenue sharing. They're set.

The Rays are the best version of the Rays they've ever been. On January 5 the team announced a couple of minor trades, the kind that summon sarcastic "PRINT THE CHAMPIONSHIP SHIRTS" responses on social media. They traded their fourth outfielder Luke Raley for a utility infielder in José Caballero, and then traded a middle reliever, Andrew Kittredge, for a fourth outfielder in Richie Palacios. The key: Raley was out of options, and Kittredge was due a large raise in arbitration. Caballero and Palacios offered team control and options. It was the sort of move the Rays make all the time, and get praised or derided for, depending on the audience.

It's not entirely clear whether it matters how successful the Rays are. Attendance in 2023 was up more than 27% year-over-year, but that likely has more to do with rule changes than it did the team's fifth straight postseason run; 90- and 96-win showings in the final two pre-COVID seasons were met with even more dismal gate receipts than the four seasons preceding them, in which Tampa Bay averaged 76 wins. Getting to the playoffs, perhaps, might not matter especially much to fans when there's nothing being built in the long-term, when long-term itself is nothing more than another dream to be traded away for future value.

The Rays front office, which has been and remains one of the league's most talented and enviable, will continue to build. They're slated to be the next focus of GEICO's "It's What You Do" ad campaign. One may as well mock or root for the Krebs cycle. The sort of moves for which they've become renowned aren't art, or blasphemy: They're just part of the life cycle, a franchise trained by hardship and evolution to be themselves, as much as possible, to flourish. Everything else is a product of that survival instinct, not an input. The championship will come, some day, and the profits will come, tomorrow. What the Rays have built will provide it all.

—Patrick Dubuque and Ginny Searle are editors of Baseball Prospectus.

HITTERS

Jonathan Aranda   2B   Born: 05/23/98   Age: 26   Bats: L   Throws: R   Height: 6'0"   Weight: 210   Origin: IFA, 2015

YEAR	TM	LVL	AGE	PA	R	HR	RBI	SB	AVG/OBP/SLG	BABIP	SLGCON	BB%	K%	ZSw%	ZCon%	OSw%	OCon%	LA	90th EV	DRC+	BRR	DRP	WARP
2021	OBR	WIN	23	137	12	2	9	2	.284/.382/.362	.341	.457	12.4%	17.5%										
2021	BG	A+	23	89	20	4	7	1	.351/.449/.554	.379	.672	10.1%	14.6%							129	0.6	1.6	0.8
2021	MTG	AA	23	322	53	10	58	4	.325/.410/.540	.383	.701	10.2%	19.6%							129	0.8	-0.5	2.0
2022	DUR	AAA	24	465	71	18	85	4	.318/.394/.521	.377	.693	9.7%	21.5%	58.3%	75.0%	23.4%	73.3%			124	2.6	1.4	2.9
2022	TB	MLB	24	87	10	2	6	0	.192/.276/.321	.245	.455	9.2%	26.4%	64.1%	80.6%	28.6%	72.2%	5.8	104.0	79	-0.1	-0.1	0.0
2023	DUR	AAA	25	434	82	25	81	2	.339/.449/.613	.387	.811	14.7%	20.0%	57.0%	81.6%	24.9%	73.1%			141	0.5	-3.3	3.1
2023	TB	MLB	25	103	13	2	13	0	.230/.340/.368	.327	.571	12.6%	30.1%	58.9%	75.9%	33.6%	63.2%	8.6	103.0	83	0.0	0.0	0.0
2024 DC	TB	MLB	26	164	18	5	18	0	.238/.326/.397	.286	.523	9.7%	21.9%							105	-0.1	-0.1	0.5

2023 GP: DH (12), 1B (11), 2B (4), 3B (2)   Comps: Jason Botts (68), Taylor Green (64), Ji Man Choi (63)

The Rays have about 10 players that fit Aranda's profile: A good minor-league hitter with a track record at the lower levels, but not much success in the bigs and no real place on the diamond. Some of those guys will work out and some won't. Aranda, 26 in May, is looking like he may fall in the "won't" category. He was closer to average in 2023 than he was in 2022 despite an unacceptable amount of strikeouts for his skill set. He does not have over-the-wall power and is pretty stationary on the bases. Defensively, he can play anything with the word "base" after it with no particular aptitude for any of them. Therefore, he's the platonic ideal of a *Rays* placement-level infielder.

Randy Arozarena   LF   Born: 02/28/95   Age: 29   Bats: R   Throws: R   Height: 5'11"   Weight: 185   Origin: IFA, 2016

YEAR	TM	LVL	AGE	PA	R	HR	RBI	SB	AVG/OBP/SLG	BABIP	SLGCON	BB%	K%	ZSw%	ZCon%	OSw%	OCon%	LA	90th EV	DRC+	BRR	DRP	WARP
2021	TB	MLB	26	604	94	20	69	20	.274/.356/.459	.363	.677	9.3%	28.1%	68.8%	76.4%	29.7%	55.4%	8.1	106.0	98	1.5	4.2	2.4
2022	TB	MLB	27	645	72	20	89	32	.263/.327/.445	.325	.607	7.1%	24.2%	66.0%	79.8%	34.2%	61.7%	8.7	106.4	102	1.3	2.2	2.5
2023	TB	MLB	28	654	95	23	83	22	.254/.364/.425	.310	.592	12.2%	23.9%	63.5%	79.2%	31.4%	61.4%	11.5	106.7	112	0.8	4.5	3.3
2024 DC	TB	MLB	29	588	67	18	69	28	.243/.339/.409	.301	.566	10.3%	24.3%							113	-0.1	2.6	2.9

2023 GP: LF (139), DH (12)   Comps: Roy White (74), Steve Henderson (74), Jason Bay (73)

For the third straight season, Arozarena joined Trea Turner and José Ramírez in the Roaring 20s Club. These three are the only players to achieve at least 20 home runs and 20 steals in each of the last three seasons. Impressive as that is, it's worth noting that Arozarena also led the league in getting caught red-handed each of those seasons—until last year. While that may look like an improvement, he still got caught 10 times while pilfering only 22 bags, a drop of 10 stolen bases despite the new running-friendly rules. While his counting stats remain consistent, the percentages bounce around a bit—his batting average dipped slightly last season but his OBP popped thanks to a career high in walks. And he's settled in as a left fielder, not making an error in over 1,200 innings on patrol. There's consistency with a few gentle ups and downs, and he remains a three-win player, even if his rising salary might mean a uniform change is in the offing.

Osleivis Basabe   IF   Born: 09/13/00   Age: 23   Bats: R   Throws: R   Height: 5'11"   Weight: 188   Origin: IFA, 2017

YEAR	TM	LVL	AGE	PA	R	HR	RBI	SB	AVG/OBP/SLG	BABIP	SLGCON	BB%	K%	ZSw%	ZCon%	OSw%	OCon%	LA	90th EV	DRC+	BRR	DRP	WARP
2021	ZUL	WIN	20	142	21	0	20	3	.262/.336/.397	.284	.431	9.2%	7.0%										
2021	CSC	A	20	309	51	2	35	18	.284/.347/.385	.322	.448	8.4%	12.6%							120	-1.6	2.0	1.7
2022	BG	A+	21	236	41	4	22	7	.315/.370/.463	.360	.549	6.8%	14.4%							121	1.3	2.8	1.7
2022	MTG	AA	21	259	39	0	25	14	.333/.399/.461	.369	.517	9.3%	9.7%							122	2.2	1.2	1.7
2023	DUR	AAA	22	426	45	4	58	16	.296/.351/.426	.344	.514	7.3%	15.5%	66.5%	82.7%	40.1%	71.6%			96	-2.2	-0.1	0.8
2023	TB	MLB	22	94	15	1	12	0	.218/.277/.310	.295	.435	6.4%	26.6%	73.2%	81.2%	44.2%	68.1%	-2.1	101.8	75	0.2	0.1	0.0
2024 DC	TB	MLB	23	192	15	2	16	4	.222/.275/.318	.267	.401	5.9%	18.7%							70	0.0	-0.5	-0.1

2023 GP: SS (20), 3B (5), 2B (4), RF (2), LF (1)   Comps: Gavin Cecchini (68), Erick Aybar (66), Cole Tucker (64)

Circumstances led to Basabe getting regular playing time in the infield down the stretch: Wander Franco's administrative leave and Brandon Lowe's injury opened the door, but Basabe's bat helped him walk through it. He is a legit hit tool guy and maintained a batting average above .300 in over 1,600 minor-league plate appearances, though that did not exactly translate in his small sample at the highest level. Perhaps he was a bit overzealous, as his strikeout rate jumped upon promotion with more chases and whiffs than advertised. (That explanation should be the hope, since the alternative means he was overwhelmed by the quality of MLB pitching.) Defensively, he seems better suited as a rover than a pillar at one position. He is a decent runner which is important since he hits a lot of ground balls. As the Oni Mystake once explained, true power is never lost, only given away when you think you have none ... Basabe has none. Provided he can maintain an average glove and find his bat-to-ball skills, he should be a semi-regular until better options become available.

José Caballero IF Born: 08/30/96 Age: 27 Bats: R Throws: R Height: 5'9" Weight: 185 Origin: Round 7, 2017 Draft (#202 overall)

YEAR	TM	LVL	AGE	PA	R	HR	RBI	SB	AVG/OBP/SLG	BABIP	SLGCON	BB%	K%	ZSw%	ZCon%	OSw%	OCon%	LA	90th EV	DRC+	BRR	DRP	WARP
2021	PEJ	WIN	24	65	4	1	11	4	.224/.308/.293	.316	.436	7.7%	29.2%	66.7%	75.0%	25.0%	25.0%						
2021	MRN	ROK	24	29	6	2	9	1	.280/.345/.600	.313	.882	10.3%	27.6%									-0.1	
2021	ARK	AA	24	28	3	1	3	2	.200/.393/.400	.188	.500	25.0%	14.3%							103	0.2	-1.4	0.0
2022	ARK	AA	25	134	20	2	12	15	.227/.440/.330	.274	.427	26.1%	16.4%							127	2.2	1.0	1.2
2023	TAC	AAA	26	40	8	2	9	5	.333/.550/.593	.333	.696	30.0%	10.0%	58.1%	91.7%	19.1%	72.2%			135	-0.2	1.0	0.3
2023	SEA	MLB	26	280	37	4	26	26	.221/.343/.320	.285	.448	10.0%	23.6%	59.9%	86.2%	31.3%	64.8%	22.2	99.8	91	1.1	0.9	0.8
2024 DC	TB	MLB	27	181	19	4	17	16	.217/.339/.339	.260	.448	11.9%	19.9%							99	0.6	-0	0.6

2023 GP: 2B (64), SS (21), 3B (9), DH (7), LF (1)   Comps: Breyvic Valera (61), Andy Parrino (56), David Adams (55)

A former national champion at the junior college level at powerhouse Chipola in Marianna, Florida, Caballero grinded his way to the big leagues in every sense of the word. The Panama native battled numerous injuries which repeatedly delayed his development, though they did help earn him the tremendously rare distinction of having appeared in the Arizona Fall League three different times. He bounced around every position on the dirt to prop up an otherwise uninspiring offensive profile and, once finally healthy, surfaced in Seattle as a viable role player. Though never mistaken as a real threat in the batter's box, Caballero capably hit lefties and played stellar defense wherever Scott Servais needed him. Most entertaining was how much Caballero asserted himself as a genuine pain in the ass for opponents, a Patrick Beverley-style irritant. He regularly found ways to use the pitch timer rules to mess with opposing pitchers by stepping in at the last possible second or calling unexpected timeouts. He crowded the plate and got plunked at a rate that surely made his teammate Ty France proud. He ran the bases aggressively in every sense. His chirps led to benches being cleared. He was a problem for the other dugout, and beloved in his own. You know, one of *those* guys. Such an act's sustainability will always depend first and foremost on more tangible baseball skills, but it appears Caballero has enough of those to keep it up for a while.

★ ★ ★ *2024 Top 101 Prospect* **#3** ★ ★ ★

Junior Caminero 3B Born: 07/05/03 Age: 21 Bats: R Throws: R Height: 6'1" Weight: 157 Origin: IFA, 2019

YEAR	TM	LVL	AGE	PA	R	HR	RBI	SB	AVG/OBP/SLG	BABIP	SLGCON	BB%	K%	ZSw%	ZCon%	OSw%	OCon%	LA	90th EV	DRC+	BRR	DRP	WARP
2021	DSL INDR	ROK	17	171	26	9	33	2	.295/.380/.534	.304	.661	11.7%	16.4%									0.8	
2022	RAY	ROK	18	154	18	5	31	7	.326/.403/.492	.349	.586	9.7%	13.6%										
2022	CSC	A	18	117	19	6	20	5	.299/.359/.505	.329	.635	6.8%	18.8%							117	1.3	-0.8	0.6
2023	BG	A+	19	159	30	11	32	2	.356/.409/.685	.432	.943	6.3%	25.2%							130	-0.1	-2.2	0.8
2023	MTG	AA	19	351	55	20	62	3	.309/.373/.548	.325	.677	9.1%	17.1%							133	-1.1	-1.6	1.9
2023	TB	MLB	19	36	4	1	7	0	.235/.278/.353	.280	.462	5.6%	22.2%	63.8%	76.7%	41.4%	63.9%	-1.2	108.6	89	0.0	0.0	0.1
2024 DC	TB	MLB	20	175	18	6	21	2	.251/.300/.412	.305	.554	5.8%	24.2%							99	-0.1	-0.1	0.5

2023 GP: 3B (3), SS (2), DH (2), 2B (1)   Comps: Adrián Beltré (58), Jesus Montero (57), Justin Upton (56)

Caminero had a tremendous breakout campaign in 2023. He torched the South Atlantic League before mashing his way through Montgomery. The Rays, in need of some star power, promoted Caminero to the big leagues in September about two months after his 20th birthday. He fared well enough in the brief cameo, but more important than what he did in his first 34 at-bats is what he is going to do in his next 500. Shortstop is now a glaring need for the team, and the lineup, while improved from 2022, could always use another bat. Caminero does work at the plate with a bat that plays like it was cleansed in the waters of Lake Minnetonka. He hits blistering line drives and his pull-side power went from developing to demolishing opposing pitchers in a year's time. He's an adequate runner with average speed and has work to do when his feet touch the clay. This includes on defense, where although he may get some opportunities at shortstop out of necessity in the interim, he is more likely to hold down the hot corner like Avon Barksdale long-term. His stay near the apex of top 100 lists may be short, as the need for offense in Tampa Bay could lead to an early graduation.

Jonny DeLuca OF Born: 07/10/98 Age: 25 Bats: R Throws: R Height: 6'0" Weight: 200 Origin: Round 25, 2019 Draft (#761 overall)

YEAR	TM	LVL	AGE	PA	R	HR	RBI	SB	AVG/OBP/SLG	BABIP	SLGCON	BB%	K%	ZSw%	ZCon%	OSw%	OCon%	LA	90th EV	DRC+	BRR	DRP	WARP
2021	RC	A	22	255	48	15	43	13	.287/.376/.592	.306	.754	12.2%	18.8%							135	-0.4	1.1	2.0
2021	GL	A+	22	182	27	7	21	7	.232/.308/.421	.254	.535	8.2%	19.2%							111	0.2	-1.3	0.8
2022	GL	A+	23	321	51	18	51	12	.245/.343/.516	.244	.647	11.5%	17.4%							137	-1.7	-2.0	2.1
2022	TUL	AA	23	119	22	7	20	5	.298/.359/.606	.293	.724	6.7%	14.3%							121	0.8	-1.3	0.7
2023	TUL	AA	24	142	29	10	18	9	.279/.380/.590	.279	.750	9.9%	18.3%							130	1.6	-1.4	0.9
2023	OKC	AAA	24	184	27	7	35	3	.306/.397/.548	.333	.672	11.4%	15.8%	74.5%	89.2%	29.7%	65.2%			114	-0.5	-0.4	0.6
2023	LAD	MLB	24	45	5	2	6	1	.262/.311/.429	.281	.529	6.7%	17.8%	70.0%	89.8%	45.4%	56.8%	9.3	98.7	106	0.0	0.4	0.2
2024 DC	TB	MLB	25	287	30	10	34	5	.228/.296/.399	.250	.500	7.5%	18.4%							95	0.1	1.5	0.8

2023 GP: LF (9), CF (8), RF (7), DH (2)   Comps: Aaron Altherr (63), Tim Locastro (62), Randy Arozarena (61)

If there's one player who epitomized the Dodgers' development and procurement system, it's DeLuca. He struggled to consistently square up the ball in his shot of espresso, but it wasn't for lack of trying—DeLuca sent 58.8% of his batted balls to his pull side, just too often at extreme launch angles. His plus bat control ought to alleviate the preliminary mishits he's struggled with, and his elite speed should buy him a few extra bases as well. And if you're wondering how he's been able to squeeze as much game power as he's been able to out of his frame—his isolated slugging percentage over the past two years is in the top 10 of all minor-league hitters—it's by being one of the most pull-heavy hitters in the minor leagues. The aggregate of his skillset led to his inclusion as a secondary piece to Ryan Pepiot in the Dodgers' trade for Tyler Glasnow and Manuel Margot. Those "Dodgers skills" will fit in just fine in Tampa.

Yandy Díaz 1B   Born: 08/08/91   Age: 32   Bats: R   Throws: R   Height: 6'2"   Weight: 215   Origin: IFA, 2013

YEAR	TM	LVL	AGE	PA	R	HR	RBI	SB	AVG/OBP/SLG	BABIP	SLGCON	BB%	K%	ZSw%	ZCon%	OSw%	OCon%	LA	90th EV	DRC+	BRR	DRP	WARP
2021	TB	MLB	29	541	62	13	64	1	.256/.353/.387	.286	.474	12.8%	15.7%	69.7%	87.6%	22.3%	64.7%	6.7	108.0	112	-0.3	0.4	2.3
2022	TB	MLB	30	558	71	9	57	3	.296/.401/.423	.323	.484	14.0%	10.8%	66.1%	91.1%	22.9%	73.9%	7.8	108.1	141	0.2	0.9	4.2
2023	TB	MLB	31	600	95	22	78	0	.330/.410/.522	.367	.636	10.8%	15.7%	67.5%	89.0%	23.3%	65.2%	6.0	108.9	134	0.1	0.1	3.9
2024 DC	TB	MLB	32	621	70	14	68	2	.274/.364/.408	.303	.486	11.6%	14.0%							124	-0.1	0.4	3.1

2023 GP: 1B (118), DH (13), 3B (6)   Comps: Terry Pendleton (69), Jeff Cirillo (63), Ken McMullen (62)

Díaz finally put it all together in 2023. His slugging percentage matched his biceps: *huge*. He was on base more than most members of the military. He was a constant contributor for a lineup that was in a state of constant flux, and he did it all with a smile and infectious attitude. Díaz traded in fewer walks and slightly more strikeouts in favor of more barrels and even more exit velocity. Now established as one of the game's hardest hitters and a Silver Slugger winner, will his (sort of) great power come with greater responsibility? Will Díaz be able to sustain this surge? Some things suggest ... maybe not. First, he hit even more ground balls than he did in 2021 and 2022, and his much-discussed launch angle was his lowest since 2020. But even if the home runs come down a bit, he is still a tremendously talented hitter with an understanding for the zone. He played much more cold corner than hot, which is probably the best thing for him, and as long as there is value in his bat, he's an ideal Rays player: locked into a contract paying much less than his production.

Wander Franco SS   Born: 03/01/01   Age: 23   Bats: S   Throws: R   Height: 5'10"   Weight: 189   Origin: IFA, 2017

YEAR	TM	LVL	AGE	PA	R	HR	RBI	SB	AVG/OBP/SLG	BABIP	SLGCON	BB%	K%	ZSw%	ZCon%	OSw%	OCon%	LA	90th EV	DRC+	BRR	DRP	WARP
2021	DUR	AAA	20	180	31	7	35	5	.313/.372/.583	.324	.669	7.8%	11.7%							134	0.6	0.5	1.4
2021	TB	MLB	20	308	53	7	39	2	.288/.347/.463	.311	.533	7.8%	12.0%	72.8%	91.0%	35.4%	74.6%	10.1	104.7	106	0.2	0.2	1.4
2022	DUR	AAA	21	25	3	0	2	0	.429/.520/.524	.500	.611	16.0%	12.0%	81.8%	100.0%	23.1%	100.0%			117	-0.1	0.0	0.1
2022	TB	MLB	21	344	46	6	33	8	.277/.328/.417	.290	.466	7.6%	9.6%	74.2%	93.7%	38.1%	78.4%	8.4	102.8	120	0.5	0.7	2.0
2023	TB	MLB	22	491	65	17	58	30	.281/.344/.475	.297	.563	8.6%	14.1%	66.1%	90.8%	31.8%	78.3%	8.9	104.2	128	1.0	8.1	4.3
2024 non	TB	MLB	23	251	27	6	29	10	.276/.341/.438	.297	.503	8.4%	12.2%							120	0.0	4.5	2.0

2023 GP: SS (111), DH (1)   Comps: Carlos Correa (73), Francisco Lindor (69), Jim Fregosi (67)

Franco is currently on Major League Baseball's indefinite administrative leave list. Both MLB and a specialized Minor and Gender Violence division of law enforcement in the Dominican Republic are investigating alleged relationships with minors. As of the time of publication, both his baseball status for the 2024 season and his personal legal status are pending the results of these investigations.

─────────────── ★ ★ ★ *2024 Top 101 Prospect* **#60** ★ ★ ★ ───────────────

Xavier Isaac 1B   Born: 12/17/03   Age: 20   Bats: L   Throws: L   Height: 6'3"   Weight: 240   Origin: Round 1, 2022 Draft (#29 overall)

YEAR	TM	LVL	AGE	PA	R	HR	RBI	SB	AVG/OBP/SLG	BABIP	SLGCON	BB%	K%	ZSw%	ZCon%	OSw%	OCon%	LA	90th EV	DRC+	BRR	DRP	WARP
2023	CSC	A	19	376	58	13	56	10	.266/.380/.462	.314	.621	14.9%	21.3%							126	3.8	1.8	2.5
2023	BG	A+	19	57	13	6	16	2	.408/.491/.898	.452	1.189	14.0%	21.1%							124	-0.2	1.2	0.3
2024 non	TB	MLB	20	251	23	5	24	0	.224/.295/.349	.321	.541	8.4%	31.8%							82	0.0	0	-0.1

2023 GP: 1B (82), DH (18)   Comps: Anthony Rizzo (64), Josh Naylor (62), Juan Soto (60)

In last year's edition, we said Isaac is *really* going to have to hit to justify his draft position as a first-base-only prospect. So far, so good—he mashed in his first full-season of professional baseball. He was one of the Carolina League's best sluggers and finished fifth in home runs despite not spending the entire year in Charleston. Upon promotion to Bowling Green he was even better, pummeling everything in sight for a dozen games. (Also, he did this as a teenager when most players in the South Atlantic League can buy their own beer after the game.) He showed a mature approach, taking first base around 14% of the time with a manageable strikeout rate. His power went from projection to production rapidly and, despite having catcher speed, he even collected four triples. This enormous frame also glues him to first base, and he is barely passable defensively despite attempts to improve his footwork. To reiterate, he will really have to slangoo the ball to prove worthy of the 29th pick but, based off his early production, you can see why the Rays might think he will do just that.

Colton Ledbetter CF   Born: 11/15/01   Age: 22   Bats: L   Throws: R   Height: 6'2"   Weight: 205   Origin: Round 2, 2023 Draft (#55 overall)

YEAR	TM	LVL	AGE	PA	R	HR	RBI	SB	AVG/OBP/SLG	BABIP	SLGCON	BB%	K%	ZSw%	ZCon%	OSw%	OCon%	LA	90th EV	DRC+	BRR	DRP	WARP
2023	CSC	A	21	74	11	1	8	2	.254/.356/.397	.326	.532	13.5%	21.6%							107	-0.4	1.0	0.3
2024 non	TB	MLB	22	251	19	2	19	0	.210/.277/.297	.292	.425	7.7%	27.9%							63	0.0	0	-0.4

2023 GP: CF (9), RF (5), DH (5), LF (2)   Comps: Troy Montgomery (83), Ray-Patrick Didder (82), Kameron Misner (80)

Ledbetter transferred to Mississippi State after two collegiate seasons at Samford, and the move did him good: He established himself as one of the Southeastern Conference's top hitters and played himself into a $1.3 million bonus as the 55th pick in the draft. Ledbetter has a solid build and maintains good athleticism, springing fluidly like a kangaroo in sauce. His power has an average floor with a chance to pop like a Pringles can with some additional strength. Sticking in center field would maximize his value, however, some have him pegged for further sinistral movement, and hey ... it worked well when he went west in college, right? There is an outside chance he spends part of his summer back in Alabama (Montgomery, this time) with a fast start.

Brandon Lowe 2B   Born: 07/06/94   Age: 30   Bats: L   Throws: R   Height: 5'10"   Weight: 185   Origin: Round 3, 2015 Draft (#87 overall)

YEAR	TM	LVL	AGE	PA	R	HR	RBI	SB	AVG/OBP/SLG	BABIP	SLGCON	BB%	K%	ZSw%	ZCon%	OSw%	OCon%	LA	90th EV	DRC+	BRR	DRP	WARP
2021	TB	MLB	26	615	97	39	99	7	.247/.340/.523	.280	.761	11.1%	27.2%	80.8%	78.2%	36.2%	53.4%	17.1	105.9	119	0.2	-1.2	3.6
2022	TB	MLB	27	266	31	8	25	1	.221/.308/.383	.263	.517	10.2%	22.9%	79.0%	80.9%	37.0%	47.2%	16.8	105.1	96	0.1	-0.4	0.6
2023	TB	MLB	28	436	58	21	68	7	.231/.328/.443	.275	.647	11.5%	27.3%	75.9%	85.0%	37.5%	47.9%	16.1	105.6	106	0.1	0.0	1.6
2024 DC	TB	MLB	29	531	63	21	68	5	.230/.324/.427	.280	.611	11.1%	26.4%							111	0.0	-1.5	2.1

2023 GP: 2B (105), DH (4)   *Comps: Roberto Alomar (68), Joe Gordon (68), Lou Whitaker (68)*

Lowe is starting to near the territory of "will he ever be what he was" and is currently on a detour of "if he's ever healthy enough." After hitting nearly 40 home runs in 2021, he has just 28 over the last two seasons due playing in just 51% of the games his team played. An aching back has been responsible for most of the missed time, but it was a fractured patella that ended his season for good in late September. Although he still cleared the wall his fair share, there has to be concern about a dip in power coinciding with a bad vertebra. His ISO and slugging have been below his career mark and that aging back will see its 30th year in June. On the positive side, Lowe still hits the ball very hard. His exit velocity was the second highest of his career and he hit more balls harder than ever. His ability to hit and show up to hit, will remain key as he is average at best at the keystone and doesn't run much. He enters 2024 on the last guaranteed year of his contract with the Rays, who hold a few options should be regain his previous form.

Josh Lowe RF   Born: 02/02/98   Age: 26   Bats: L   Throws: R   Height: 6'4"   Weight: 205   Origin: Round 1, 2016 Draft (#13 overall)

YEAR	TM	LVL	AGE	PA	R	HR	RBI	SB	AVG/OBP/SLG	BABIP	SLGCON	BB%	K%	ZSw%	ZCon%	OSw%	OCon%	LA	90th EV	DRC+	BRR	DRP	WARP
2021	DUR	AAA	23	470	76	22	78	26	.291/.381/.535	.361	.771	13.0%	26.2%							119	4.5	-1.7	2.9
2021	TB	MLB	23	2	0	0	0	1	1.000/1.000/1.000	1.000	1.000	50.0%	0.0%	100.0%	50.0%	14.3%	100.0%	-63.0	43.3	104	0.0	0.0	0.0
2022	DUR	AAA	24	351	51	14	67	25	.315/.402/.556	.460	.898	12.5%	32.8%	67.8%	72.5%	24.1%	31.6%			101	-0.9	1.4	1.2
2022	TB	MLB	24	198	24	2	13	3	.221/.284/.343	.336	.539	7.6%	33.3%	65.7%	72.5%	30.5%	59.3%	11.5	103.1	76	0.1	1.8	0.2
2023	TB	MLB	25	501	71	20	83	32	.292/.335/.500	.357	.681	6.2%	24.8%	74.8%	82.5%	39.0%	53.8%	14.5	105.1	102	1.4	3.9	2.0
2024 DC	TB	MLB	26	493	52	14	57	24	.257/.319/.422	.336	.597	7.8%	27.0%							107	1.1	3.3	2.1

2023 GP: RF (101), DH (21), CF (14), LF (3)   *Comps: Clint Frazier (68), Corey Hart (61), Eddie Rosario (60)*

Lowe beat the Kevin Kiermaier allegations, producing offensive output for which the blue-eyed devil would have sold his soul. Taking over as the club's primary right fielder, he produced a 20-30 season while approaching a .300 batting average, which was almost unimaginable based off his 2022 output. Even though he swung at more pitches out of the zone in 2023, he cut his strikeout rate to a more tolerable 25% as he increased his contact—especially within the zone—and barreled the ball much more frequently. Perhaps the greatest thief since The Tinder Swindler, he was successful on 91% of his base thefts, which is quite the rate for the volume. Now we have one abbreviated season that was not good and one mostly full season that was very good. If we end up with Matt Joyce rather than Kiermaier, that's not bad; Ol' Sweet Swingin' throttled right-handed pitching. Lowe did so too—he hit .300/.343/.511 in 434 plate appearances against righties, accounting for 87% of his trips to the plate. For reference, Hall-of-Famer Al Kaline finished his *career* with an .855 OPS. A pre-arbitration player, the Rays say "Do it right for less. Start with Lowe."

★ ★ ★ *2024 Top 101 Prospect* **#42** ★ ★ ★

Curtis Mead 3B   Born: 10/26/00   Age: 23   Bats: R   Throws: R   Height: 6'0"   Weight: 171   Origin: IFA, 2018

YEAR	TM	LVL	AGE	PA	R	HR	RBI	SB	AVG/OBP/SLG	BABIP	SLGCON	BB%	K%	ZSw%	ZCon%	OSw%	OCon%	LA	90th EV	DRC+	BRR	DRP	WARP
2021	SCO	WIN	20	90	16	3	11	1	.313/.360/.530	.343	.629	4.4%	14.4%	57.1%	100.0%	50.0%	100.0%						
2021	CSC	A	20	211	36	7	35	9	.356/.408/.586	.391	.696	7.1%	14.2%							134	-1.0	1.7	1.5
2021	BG	A+	20	233	38	7	32	2	.282/.348/.466	.309	.571	8.2%	16.3%							119	0.4	1.2	1.4
2021	DUR	AAA	20	14	3	1	2	0	.429/.429/.786	.500	1.000	0.0%	21.4%							97	0.2	0.3	0.1
2022	MTG	AA	21	246	35	10	36	6	.305/.394/.548	.342	.697	10.2%	18.3%							133	-0.3	0.0	1.6
2022	DUR	AAA	21	85	8	3	14	1	.278/.376/.486	.321	.636	12.9%	20.0%	64.3%	85.2%	31.0%	72.2%			111	0.1	-1.2	0.3
2023	DUR	AAA	22	278	41	9	45	4	.294/.385/.515	.328	.647	12.6%	17.3%	66.3%	87.1%	28.7%	70.0%			114	0.7	-1.5	1.1
2023	TB	MLB	22	92	12	1	5	0	.253/.326/.349	.328	.468	7.6%	22.8%	66.9%	83.9%	37.9%	66.2%	13.2	100.3	82	0.0	0.1	0.1
2024 DC	TB	MLB	23	132	12	3	13	1	.232/.301/.366	.271	.463	7.7%	19.1%							89	0.0	0.1	0.1

2023 GP: 3B (19), 2B (4), SS (1)   *Comps: Mike Moustakas (54), Ketel Marte (54), Evan Longoria (54)*

The Meadelaide Machine made his major-league debut on the strength of his bat and weakness in the Rays' late-season lineup. He carries a plus hit-stick with the potential to add more in-game power as he progresses. Mead fared much better against lefties than righties in limited time with the Rays, and this has been a trend since reaching the upper levels of the system. Is he more than a short-side platoon player? Possibly, but he's not really a fit at any infield position aside from first base, even though he saw plenty of reps at third in 2023. There's still enough potential in his bat for him to play every day, but he'll need to be exceptional if his best position is going to be "in the batter's box."

Richie Palacios OF   Born: 05/16/97   Age: 27   Bats: L   Throws: R   Height: 5'10"   Weight: 180   Origin: Round 3, 2018 Draft (#103 overall)

YEAR	TM	LVL	AGE	PA	R	HR	RBI	SB	AVG/OBP/SLG	BABIP	SLGCON	BB%	K%	ZSw%	ZCon%	OSw%	OCon%	LA	90th EV	DRC+	BRR	DRP	WARP
2021	SCO	WIN	24	93	17	3	11	4	.269/.387/.513	.300	.635	14.0%	16.1%	70.0%	100.0%	10.0%	100.0%						
2021	AKR	AA	24	283	53	6	36	10	.299/.389/.496	.338	.599	11.7%	14.8%							128	2.3	5.5	2.6
2021	COL	AAA	24	145	19	1	12	10	.292/.434/.416	.376	.553	17.2%	19.3%							107	0.8	0.4	0.7
2022	MAY	WIN	25	91	16	1	8	4	.217/.393/.290	.264	.370	17.6%	16.5%										
2022	COL	AAA	25	206	34	4	36	12	.279/.371/.458	.348	.603	11.7%	20.9%							103	1.3	1.4	0.9
2022	CLE	MLB	25	123	7	0	10	2	.232/.293/.286	.280	.348	7.3%	16.3%	70.0%	89.0%	32.7%	75.0%	13.3	100.4	91	-0.1	0.0	0.2
2023	MEM	AAA	26	195	34	5	29	3	.299/.418/.459	.311	.526	16.4%	10.3%	68.8%	89.9%	26.4%	69.4%			113	-2.8	-2.3	0.5
2023	COL	AAA	26	269	42	3	30	6	.217/.351/.318	.249	.392	15.2%	15.2%	71.3%	85.1%	30.0%	71.9%			99	-0.2	0.5	0.9
2023	STL	MLB	26	102	9	6	16	2	.258/.307/.516	.234	.585	5.9%	10.8%	69.1%	91.2%	25.6%	72.4%	5.9	101.1	103	0.1	0.9	0.5
2024 DC	TB	MLB	27	126	13	2	12	3	.264/.343/.390	.306	.478	10.0%	16.0%							110	0.0	0.2	0.6

2023 GP: LF (17), CF (8), RF (2), DH (2), 2B (1)   *Comps: Alex Presley (55), Ryan Church (55), Trevor Crowe (53)*

St. Louis gave Palacios a shot after an ignoble 2022 season in Cleveland, and now they've got on their hands a left-handed hitter who can play all three outfield positions plus second base. After the Cardinals began resolving (but did not entirely solve) their glut of position players by trading Tyler O'Neill for pitchers over the winter, the 26-year-old could step into a spot recently or soon to be vacated. Over another brief big-league sample, he was 8-for-19 against left-handed pitching with two home runs, hit .412 with RISP and rarely got himself in trouble at the plate with only 11 strikeouts in 102 PA. The Cardinals will find a use for that.

Isaac Paredes 3B   Born: 02/18/99   Age: 25   Bats: R   Throws: R   Height: 5'11"   Weight: 213   Origin: IFA, 2015

YEAR	TM	LVL	AGE	PA	R	HR	RBI	SB	AVG/OBP/SLG	BABIP	SLGCON	BB%	K%	ZSw%	ZCon%	OSw%	OCon%	LA	90th EV	DRC+	BRR	DRP	WARP
2021	MAZ	WIN	22	181	26	4	23	0	.282/.436/.408	.305	.475	20.4%	11.0%										
2021	TOL	AAA	22	315	39	11	42	0	.265/.397/.451	.281	.553	17.8%	14.9%							128	-2.9	5.4	2.2
2021	DET	MLB	22	85	7	1	5	0	.208/.306/.319	.226	.377	11.8%	12.9%	63.8%	90.5%	24.9%	78.9%	18.7	100.6	105	-0.1	0.1	0.3
2022	HER	WIN	23	101	9	2	7	0	.125/.297/.238	.127	.297	17.8%	15.8%										
2022	DUR	AAA	23	113	15	4	18	0	.263/.354/.484	.280	.605	11.5%	16.8%							118	0.0	3.5	0.9
2022	TB	MLB	23	381	48	20	45	0	.205/.304/.435	.195	.545	11.5%	17.6%	61.7%	88.9%	26.9%	76.1%	16.1	102.6	103	-0.6	0.6	1.1
2023	TB	MLB	24	571	71	31	98	1	.250/.352/.488	.257	.619	10.2%	18.2%	67.5%	90.2%	32.9%	72.1%	22.0	101.0	104	-0.5	0.1	2.0
2024 DC	TB	MLB	25	530	65	22	70	1	.239/.334/.434	.251	.536	10.3%	16.5%							116	-0.5	1.4	2.5

2023 GP: 3B (116), 1B (25), 2B (14), DH (3), SS (1)   *Comps: Wilmer Flores (57), Maikel Franco (55), Luis Urías (51)*

The Rays' pickup of Paredes has been one of the slicker moves of the past few years, as the 25-year-old is one of the most unique right-handed sluggers in the game. Everything he puts over the wall—and there's *a lot* of balls clearing the fence here—is straight down the line, as he's one of the most pull-happy hitters in baseball. Since the tradeoff appears to cause a woeful batting average on balls in play, Paredes has to come to the plate with patience to remain an above-average hitter and reach base. The total offensive package resulted in reverse splits last year; against same-siders he hit .247/.347/.513 with 27 home runs. Last season he was the team's primary third baseman, though he retained flexibility by making cameos at first, second, and even shortstop for good measure. Though you can't be too sure where he'll play on the diamond next year, everyone knows where the ball is going after he hits it.

René Pinto C   Born: 11/02/96   Age: 27   Bats: R   Throws: R   Height: 5'10"   Weight: 195   Origin: IFA, 2013

YEAR	TM	LVL	AGE	PA	R	HR	RBI	SB	AVG/OBP/SLG	BABIP	SLGCON	BB%	K%	ZSw%	ZCon%	OSw%	OCon%	LA	90th EV	DRC+	BRR	DRP	WARP
2021	MTG	AA	24	171	25	8	25	2	.242/.322/.458	.326	.722	8.8%	32.7%							101	-1.0	2.1	0.7
2021	DUR	AAA	24	211	25	12	35	2	.299/.327/.532	.364	.748	3.3%	27.5%							101	-2.3	4.4	0.9
2022	DUR	AAA	25	306	39	14	54	1	.266/.320/.521	.326	.735	7.2%	26.8%	84.6%	69.7%	50.0%	50.0%			93	-0.7	9.5	1.4
2022	TB	MLB	25	83	5	2	10	0	.213/.241/.325	.349	.578	2.4%	42.2%	75.8%	77.3%	43.1%	47.1%	12.5	105.1	37	-0.1	0.8	-0.2
2023	DUR	AAA	26	160	25	9	24	1	.253/.306/.521	.301	.760	6.3%	28.8%	76.7%	75.0%	38.8%	56.8%			94	0.1	0.0	0.4
2023	TB	MLB	26	105	10	6	16	0	.252/.267/.456	.317	.681	1.9%	32.4%	78.0%	72.5%	37.6%	44.6%	17.2	105.6	88	-0.1	0.7	0.3
2024 DC	TB	MLB	27	363	34	12	41	1	.212/.258/.372	.288	.575	4.7%	33.1%							72	-0.2	6.1	0.7

2023 GP: C (38), P (1)   *Comps: Josh Phegley (64), Carlos Pérez (60), Héctor Sánchez (58)*

Pinto worked himself into a timeshare at the catcher's position toward the end of the season largely because his bat was closer to average than most backstops. Whether that average-ness is sustainable is to be determined: Below the surface, it does not look great. The Venezuelan native walked twice (as in the number two) in 105 plate appearances. In those same plate appearances, he struck out 34 times. Not to spill the beans (pun intended) here, but that's not going to work. Defensively he is a bit better than average, especially when it comes to catching the ball and presenting it for a strike; he should steal a few runs over the course of a season. That's a fair trade-off, as base-stealers ran all over him in a limited sample. The Rays don't have many options at the position, which may af*Ford Pinto* more opportunities to grow.

YEAR	TM	P. COUNT	FRM RUNS	BLK RUNS	THRW RUNS	TOT RUNS
2021	MTG	3712	2.9	0.0	0.4	3.2
2021	DUR	4551	4.5	0.1	0.3	4.9
2022	ESC	1102			0.0	0.0
2022	DUR	7553	8.4	-0.5	1.1	8.9
2022	TB	3312	1.7	0.0	-0.3	1.4
2023	DUR	4639	0.6	-0.2	0.2	0.7
2023	TB	4242	1.9	-0.1	-0.3	1.5
2024	TB	14430	7.5	-0.2	-1.1	6.2

Harold Ramírez DH   Born: 09/06/94   Age: 29   Bats: R   Throws: R   Height: 5'10"   Weight: 232   Origin: IFA, 2011

YEAR	TM	LVL	AGE	PA	R	HR	RBI	SB	AVG/OBP/SLG	BABIP	SLGCON	BB%	K%	ZSw%	ZCon%	OSw%	OCon%	LA	90th EV	DRC+	BRR	DRP	WARP
2021	CLE	MLB	26	361	33	7	41	3	.268/.305/.398	.301	.477	3.9%	15.5%	67.7%	89.4%	48.1%	65.4%	6.0	108.2	102	0.0	0.9	1.4
2022	TB	MLB	27	435	46	6	58	3	.300/.343/.404	.350	.492	4.4%	16.6%	72.9%	86.4%	46.7%	63.8%	5.0	106.2	103	-0.3	0.3	1.2
2023	TB	MLB	28	434	58	12	68	5	.313/.353/.460	.359	.573	5.1%	18.2%	71.9%	84.5%	48.2%	61.6%	6.2	105.2	112	0.1	0.2	1.6
2024 DC	TB	MLB	29	416	41	9	43	4	.264/.315/.388	.316	.495	5.6%	20.1%							101	-0.2	0.2	0.9

2023 GP: DH (91), LF (7), RF (7), 1B (6)   Comps: Alex Ochoa (58), Dmitri Young (56), Eddie Rosario (55)

Ramírez has sneakily become one of the more underrated pure hitters in baseball, earning a slash line of .289/.329/.419 in over 1,500 career plate appearances. He did his best work this past season off the strength of a .359 BABIP, but that's not far off the .350 he posted in 2022. The right-handed hitter mashed southpaws to the turn of .387/.411/.555 and, while not quite a superstar against same-siders, he did produce a reasonable .281/.329/.420 against righties. As you might guess from the BABIP, he does most of his work on balls in play; his strikeout rate is manageable and he lives and dies as a contact machine. He's no longer a speedy outfielder, but a station-to-station designated hitter with occasional cameos in a corner or at first base. He's eminently Rays: Talented but flawed, affordable and quietly solid.

Austin Shenton CI   Born: 01/22/98   Age: 26   Bats: L   Throws: R   Height: 6'0"   Weight: 205   Origin: Round 5, 2019 Draft (#156 overall)

YEAR	TM	LVL	AGE	PA	R	HR	RBI	SB	AVG/OBP/SLG	BABIP	SLGCON	BB%	K%	ZSw%	ZCon%	OSw%	OCon%	LA	90th EV	DRC+	BRR	DRP	WARP
2021	EVE	A+	23	273	55	11	53	1	.295/.418/.576	.362	.796	15.0%	22.7%							124	-0.1	1.4	1.7
2021	ARK	AA	23	48	6	1	8	0	.326/.396/.512	.406	.667	8.3%	20.8%							104	-0.8	0.7	0.1
2021	MTG	AA	23	51	5	2	9	0	.271/.294/.458	.344	.667	3.9%	29.4%							79	-0.1	-0.1	0.0
2022	MTG	AA	24	228	28	8	29	0	.236/.338/.415	.319	.648	12.3%	30.7%							96	0.2	-1.6	0.4
2023	MTG	AA	25	306	45	15	49	0	.307/.415/.567	.387	.823	15.0%	25.8%							125	0.3	-2.6	1.6
2023	DUR	AAA	25	271	57	14	50	0	.301/.432/.603	.397	.917	17.7%	27.7%	59.4%	77.4%	24.5%	46.7%			120	-1.5	-0.7	0.9
2024 DC	TB	MLB	26	65	7	2	7	0	.239/.329/.392	.336	.595	10.9%	30.2%							105	0.0	0	0.2

2023 GP: 3B (86), 1B (37), DH (8), LF (1)   Comps: J.D. Davis (56), Rhyne Hughes (56), Chris Shaw (55)

A former fifth-round pick out of Florida International University, Shenton stands a good chance to return to the Sunshine State relatively soon. He is a solid left-handed swinger with above-average power, and while the hit tool might not hold out enough to replicate his minor-league results at the highest level, it could allow him to produce 60 or more extra-base hits. If he displays 29-homer power again like he did across two levels in 2023, then that will play. He's probably destined for a four-corner role with a focus on first base, and that's promising given that Kyle Manzardo plays for the Guardians and Yandy Díaz's age and salary are climbing. The way his bat is currently producing, it may not matter what glove he carries.

Jose Siri CF   Born: 07/22/95   Age: 28   Bats: R   Throws: R   Height: 6'2"   Weight: 175   Origin: IFA, 2012

YEAR	TM	LVL	AGE	PA	R	HR	RBI	SB	AVG/OBP/SLG	BABIP	SLGCON	BB%	K%	ZSw%	ZCon%	OSw%	OCon%	LA	90th EV	DRC+	BRR	DRP	WARP
2021	GIG	WIN	25	77	11	2	3	6	.217/.289/.333	.271	.460	9.1%	24.7%										
2021	SUG	AAA	25	397	70	16	72	24	.318/.369/.552	.436	.833	6.5%	30.7%							96	2.6	-2.7	1.1
2021	HOU	MLB	25	49	10	4	9	3	.304/.347/.609	.400	.966	2.0%	34.7%	76.7%	69.6%	47.6%	58.3%	16.3	106.4	93	0.1	0.4	0.2
2022	GIG	WIN	26	85	15	2	6	9	.315/.398/.507	.404	.685	10.6%	22.4%										
2022	SUG	AAA	26	78	17	9	22	2	.296/.346/.775	.279	1.078	7.7%	25.6%	71.1%	73.3%	37.5%	52.2%			121	0.7	2.9	0.8
2022	HOU	MLB	26	147	18	3	10	6	.178/.238/.304	.247	.471	6.1%	32.7%	69.8%	74.7%	40.6%	48.1%	16.8	106.3	56	0.4	2.4	0.0
2022	TB	MLB	26	178	35	4	14	8	.241/.292/.367	.353	.575	6.2%	33.7%	68.4%	74.7%	39.4%	54.7%	14.3	106.3	64	0.8	4.1	0.4
2023	TB	MLB	27	364	58	25	56	12	.222/.267/.494	.269	.803	5.5%	35.7%	72.2%	71.0%	39.4%	45.0%	14.7	105.5	81	0.5	3.2	0.8
2024 DC	TB	MLB	28	406	44	17	53	19	.221/.276/.416	.310	.686	5.9%	36.3%							89	0.7	3.9	1.3

2023 GP: CF (100), DH (1)   Comps: Keon Broxton (62), Jake Marisnick (61), Michael A. Taylor (56)

Lots of MLB players fit into neat player-type buckets. You have your plodding first-base sluggers, your 95-and-a-slider relief arms, your contact-first second basemen. Siri defies categorization and denies taxonomy, showing up like a duck-billed platypus. Known for his prowess as a defender in center field, metrics vary in their assessment of his glove skills, with DRP judging him as good, but not elite. His other carrying skills are power and speed, and despite hitting 25 homers he was a god-awful offensive player in 2023, while only stealing 12 bases in a run-heavy environment. His contact and on-base skills—rather, his total lack thereof—would make him nigh-unplayable if it weren't for his defense, which would be a shame because he's aesthetically great fun to watch. (Well, most of the time. Some of his swing decisions are … not good.) The fleet, defensive-replacement center fielder is a prototype, sure … but Siri's surprising pop and inability to find first base make him an outlier even on a team full of mold-breakers.

Brayden Taylor 3B   Born: 05/22/02   Age: 22   Bats: L   Throws: R   Height: 6'1"   Weight: 180   Origin: Round 1, 2023 Draft (#19 overall)

YEAR	TM	LVL	AGE	PA	R	HR	RBI	SB	AVG/OBP/SLG	BABIP	SLGCON	BB%	K%	ZSw%	ZCon%	OSw%	OCon%	LA	90th EV	DRC+	BRR	DRP	WARP
2023	CSC	A	21	96	15	5	15	9	.244/.354/.512	.326	.824	14.6%	32.3%							104	0.8	0.5	0.3
2024 non	TB	MLB	22	251	21	4	22	0	.212/.283/.319	.308	.487	8.2%	31.5%							70	0.0	0	-0.3

2023 GP: 3B (21), DH (4)   Comps: Luis Yanel Diaz (75), Justin Baum (72), Brett Wallace (72)

The 19th selection in the 2023 draft, Taylor was the first player to be selected in the first round out of TCU and the first selection for Tampa Bay under new scouting director Chuck Ricci. The former Horned Frog is one of those jack-of-all-trades, master-of-none prospects: His scouting report features more fives than the afternoon shift at your local "entertainment" establishment. He hits for both average and power, flashing the latter tool with a school single-season record of 23 homers as well as his school's career mark of 48. (He popped five more in just 22 games with the Charleston Riverdogs, where he seemed to trade some discipline for power.) He has enough arm and glove to play the hot corner at the highest level—the Rays are hoping for an Alex Bregman type, but shouldn't be too upset if they end up with another Joe Crede.

Taylor Walls IF Born: 07/10/96 Age: 27 Bats: S Throws: R Height: 5'10" Weight: 185 Origin: Round 3, 2017 Draft (#79 overall)

YEAR	TM	LVL	AGE	PA	R	HR	RBI	SB	AVG/OBP/SLG	BABIP	SLGCON	BB%	K%	ZSw%	ZCon%	OSw%	OCon%	LA	90th EV	DRC+	BRR	DRP	WARP
2021	DUR	AAA	24	222	41	8	29	10	.247/.387/.444	.316	.658	18.0%	26.1%							114	1.5	0.6	1.2
2021	TB	MLB	24	176	15	1	15	4	.211/.314/.296	.304	.437	13.1%	27.8%	62.3%	80.5%	25.2%	61.5%	11.7	101.4	84	0.0	1.3	0.4
2022	TB	MLB	25	466	53	8	33	10	.172/.268/.285	.221	.404	11.2%	25.8%	66.2%	83.3%	26.3%	58.8%	16.1	100.4	70	1.2	4.9	0.4
2023	TB	MLB	26	349	50	8	36	22	.201/.305/.333	.261	.479	12.6%	26.4%	66.4%	82.5%	27.7%	58.1%	19.1	100.2	77	0.9	1.6	0.4
2024 DC	TB	MLB	27	353	34	7	33	16	.206/.305/.333	.266	.466	12.0%	25.2%							83	0.4	2.4	0.8

2023 GP: 3B (39), 2B (37), SS (32) Comps: Omar Quintanilla (64), Deven Marrero (64), Pedro Florimón (62)

Walls raised his batting average by 30% in 2023. For most, that would be an awesome jump—in this case it moved him *just* above Mendoza Line (Taylor's Version). A surprisingly hot start to the year matched the whole team's surge, but he started flailing long before the Rays as a whole flagged, and instead of getting surpassed by the Orioles, Walls got lapped all but a dozen hitters in baseball in terms of batting average. At BP we know that stat's not the end-all-be-all, but the Rays' defensive ace has no considerable power to go with his dynamic glove. Defense plays, but over the last 45 years there have been two non-pitchers to accumulate over 990 plate appearances with an average below .190: Walls and Austin Hedges. Hedges is one of the top defensive catchers of his generation, while Walls is just a great shortstop. Unless he takes up the tools of ignorance, his chances in the field are likely coming to an end.

───────── ★ ★ ★ *2024 Top 101 Prospect* **#18** ★ ★ ★ ─────────

Carson Williams SS Born: 06/25/03 Age: 21 Bats: R Throws: R Height: 6'1" Weight: 180 Origin: Round 1, 2021 Draft (#28 overall)

YEAR	TM	LVL	AGE	PA	R	HR	RBI	SB	AVG/OBP/SLG	BABIP	SLGCON	BB%	K%	ZSw%	ZCon%	OSw%	OCon%	LA	90th EV	DRC+	BRR	DRP	WARP
2021	RAY	ROK	18	47	8	0	8	2	.282/.404/.436	.423	.654	12.8%	27.7%									1.2	
2022	CSC	A	19	523	81	19	70	28	.252/.347/.471	.354	.750	10.9%	32.1%							112	-0.5	0.8	2.3
2023	PEJ	WIN	20	78	9	0	6	5	.262/.385/.292	.472	.528	14.1%	37.2%	61.0%	64.0%	30.0%	55.6%						
2023	BG	A+	20	462	69	23	77	17	.254/.351/.506	.341	.799	11.5%	31.8%							108	-0.1	0.4	1.5
2023	MTG	AA	20	26	4	0	4	3	.429/.538/.524	.563	.688	15.4%	19.2%							104	0.0		
2024 non	TB	MLB	21	251	23	5	25	10	.223/.289/.359	.342	.586	7.6%	35.7%							83	0.0	0	0.3

2023 GP: SS (127), DH (5) Comps: Carter Kieboom (61), Javier Báez (60), Richard Urena (58)

Williams finds himself entering the 2024 season as the potential heir apparent to the Rays' shortstop situation. That's a wild statement for a guy who only rated a lineout last year, but we said he had the chance to earn a full comment and here we are. As a former pitcher who threw mid-90s he has more than enough arm for the left side and possesses both foot speed and range. Although he has a wiry frame, he is power-over-hit at the plate with plus pop from the right side. And like many young hitters, he still has issues with strikeouts, which could limit his offensive ceiling. He may skip over Montgomery to begin 2024—or at least make it a quick stop—and spend most of his season in North Carolina waiting for the call to the majors.

PITCHERS

Jason Adam RHP Born: 08/04/91 Age: 32 Height: 6'3" Weight: 229 Origin: Round 5, 2010 Draft (#149 overall)

YEAR	TM	LVL	AGE	G (GS)	IP	W-L	SV	K	WHIP	ERA	CSP	BB%	K%	HR%	GB%	ZSw%	ZCon%	OSw%	OCon%	BABIP	SLGCON	DRA-	WARP
2021	IOW	AAA	29	5 (0)	6¹	1-0	1	6	0.79	0.00		4.2%	25.0%	0.0%	23.5%					.235	.353	100	0.1
2021	CHC	MLB	29	12 (0)	10²	1-0	0	19	1.50	5.91	50.4%	12.0%	38.0%	2.0%	36.4%	69.3%	80.8%	29.4%	47.6%	.429	.773	85	0.2
2022	TB	MLB	30	67 (0)	63¹	2-3	8	75	0.76	1.56	54.2%	7.2%	31.6%	2.1%	44.2%	64.8%	71.3%	39.1%	49.3%	.195	.375	75	1.4
2023	TB	MLB	31	56 (0)	54¹	4-2	12	69	1.01	2.98	46.8%	9.0%	31.1%	3.2%	41.1%	65.4%	72.5%	32.4%	55.8%	.239	.532	85	1.1
2024 DC	TB	MLB	32	51 (0)	54	3-2	2	70	1.16	3.69	49.4%	8.9%	30.9%	3.5%	38.7%					.280	.580	86	0.6

2023 Arsenal: CH (89.8), FA (94.9), SW (79.2), SL (83.9) Comps: Chaz Roe (59), Jose Veras (56), Jeremy Jeffress (55)

Despite remaining near the top of the Rays' bullpen food chain, Adam wasn't the apex predator he was in 2022. Everything was just a tick down: More hits, more free passes and more homers allowed than a year ago. Still, the bar he'd set in his breakout year was so high that he was still very effective in high-leverage situations. His three-pitch mix is led by his upper-80s change, which was the out pitch as he whiffed 31% of batters faced. He backed the *cambio* up with a mid-90s heater and a slider that dipped slightly below the temperature on Christmas in St. Petersburg (low 80s). The 32-year-old found himself used as Kevin Cash's high-leverage safety valve, and in save situations when Petey Fireball wasn't available. Of course, Adam had his own availability issues, as an oblique strain landed him on the injured list twice late in the season. Still effective and cost-efficient, he'll likely hunt big game from the Rays' bullpen again this year.

Tyler Alexander LHP Born: 07/14/94 Age: 29 Height: 6'2" Weight: 203 Origin: Round 2, 2015 Draft (#65 overall)

YEAR	TM	LVL	AGE	G (GS)	IP	W-L	SV	K	WHIP	ERA	CSP	BB%	K%	HR%	GB%	ZSw%	ZCon%	OSw%	OCon%	BABIP	SLGCON	DRA-	WARP
2021	DET	MLB	26	41 (15)	106¹	2-4	0	87	1.26	3.81	53.6%	6.2%	19.3%	3.5%	38.0%	69.0%	84.4%	35.0%	73.1%	.285	.543	114	0.2
2022	TOL	AAA	27	5 (1)	9	1-1	0	8	1.44	8.00		2.4%	19.5%	2.4%	45.2%					.367	.581	98	0.1
2022	DET	MLB	27	27 (17)	101	4-11	0	61	1.32	4.81	55.7%	5.9%	14.3%	4.2%	35.9%	71.1%	87.1%	34.7%	76.4%	.281	.560	144	-1.3
2023	DET	MLB	28	25 (1)	44	2-1	0	44	1.11	4.50	55.3%	2.8%	24.3%	4.4%	32.6%	66.8%	86.3%	32.5%	72.8%	.298	.609	94	0.7
2024 DC	TB	MLB	29	51 (0)	54	3-2	0	37	1.33	4.92	54.1%	6.0%	15.8%	3.9%	36.4%					.289	.559	111	0.0

2023 Arsenal: FC (86.3), FA (89.9), CH (83), SI (89.7), SL (81.3) Comps: Daniel Norris (61), Robbie Erlin (60), Aaron Laffey (60)

Able to work out of the bullpen or rotation? Check. Full arsenal of acceptable-ish pitches? Check. Doesn't walk anyone? Check. Left-handed? Check. Generic, witness-protection-style name? Check and check again. Alexander spent his career toiling in Detroit until a lat strain prematurely ended his season; the Tigers tried to sneak him through waivers, but the Rays, as they do, said "this is our kind of guy" and snatched him up. Look forward to a healthy and retooled Alexander becoming the latest in a long line of nameless, faceless, brutally effective relievers in Tampa Bay.

Shawn Armstrong RHP Born: 09/11/90 Age: 33 Height: 6'2" Weight: 225 Origin: Round 18, 2011 Draft (#548 overall)

YEAR	TM	LVL	AGE	G (GS)	IP	W-L	SV	K	WHIP	ERA	CSP	BB%	K%	HR%	GB%	ZSw%	ZCon%	OSw%	OCon%	BABIP	SLGCON	DRA-	WARP
2021	DUR	AAA	30	14(0)	14	2-1	2	20	0.86	2.57		3.8%	37.7%	1.9%	45.2%					.310	.500	75	0.3
2021	NOR	AAA	30	15(0)	17	1-3	0	21	1.47	3.18		7.6%	26.6%	3.8%	49.0%					.333	.620	90	0.4
2021	BAL	MLB	30	20(0)	20	0-0	0	22	1.90	8.55	51.3%	10.0%	22.0%	5.0%	31.3%	71.5%	76.3%	33.2%	57.7%	.371	.773	106	0.1
2021	TB	MLB	30	11(0)	16	1-0	0	22	1.00	4.50	53.8%	7.7%	33.8%	7.7%	32.4%	76.8%	78.1%	30.6%	44.9%	.188	.730	100	0.1
2022	DUR	AAA	31	7(0)	7	0-0	2	10	1.00	2.57		7.4%	37.0%	0.0%	66.7%					.333	.467	79	0.2
2022	TB	MLB	31	43(3)	55	2-3	2	61	1.27	3.60	58.7%	6.0%	26.0%	2.6%	50.0%	71.2%	77.1%	37.8%	67.8%	.336	.570	76	1.2
2022	MIA	MLB	31	7(0)	6²	0-0	0	5	1.95	10.80	50.2%	8.8%	14.7%	2.9%	38.5%	83.3%	91.4%	35.8%	55.2%	.360	.720	80	0.1
2023	DUR	AAA	32	7(0)	9	1-0	0	8	0.44	2.00		6.5%	25.8%	3.2%	33.3%	65.3%	84.4%	35.1%	50.0%	.050	.238	108	0.1
2023	TB	MLB	32	39(6)	52	1-0	0	54	0.90	1.38	50.9%	5.3%	26.1%	1.0%	39.1%	72.1%	79.5%	37.8%	63.8%	.250	.380	89	0.9
2024 DC	TB	MLB	33	57(0)	60	4-2	0	58	1.23	4.03	53.5%	7.1%	22.8%	3.3%	39.7%					.286	.549	93	0.5

2023 Arsenal: FC (91.5), SI (94.9), FA (94.6), SL (85.2)   Comps: Heath Hembree (51), Brad Boxberger (51), Javy Guerra (50)

The New Bern, NC rattlesnake picked up where he left off in 2022, despite missing the first two months of the season with a neck injury. Once healthy, Armstrong was one of the better relievers in all of baseball. For what it's worth, he had the second lowest ERA amongst American League pitchers with a minimum of 50 innings tossed. Even when you factor in fielding independent metrics, his season still holds up as one of better ones for a non-closer. On average, nine of every 10 pitches out of his hand topped 90 mph, led by a mid-90s fastball and a cutter just a few ticks slower. Armstrong did most of his work on the edge of the zone, living on the outskirts about six percent more than the average pitcher. Working on the margins allowed him to stay away from the thick part of the wood and just four percent of the balls in play against him were barrelled up. Considering the counting stats and his advancing age, he should be an affordable piece of a bullpen tasked with getting its share of outs in the first six frames of the game.

Taj Bradley RHP Born: 03/20/01 Age: 23 Height: 6'2" Weight: 190 Origin: Round 5, 2018 Draft (#150 overall)

YEAR	TM	LVL	AGE	G (GS)	IP	W-L	SV	K	WHIP	ERA	CSP	BB%	K%	HR%	GB%	ZSw%	ZCon%	OSw%	OCon%	BABIP	SLGCON	DRA-	WARP
2021	CSC	A	20	15(14)	66²	9-3	0	81	0.85	1.76		8.0%	32.5%	1.6%	50.3%					.237	.399	79	1.5
2021	BG	A+	20	8(8)	36²	3-0	0	42	1.06	1.96		7.4%	28.4%	2.7%	47.4%					.267	.473	85	0.6
2022	MTG	AA	21	16(16)	74¹	3-1	0	88	0.91	1.70		6.3%	30.9%	1.4%	39.5%					.266	.435	84	1.4
2022	DUR	AAA	21	12(12)	59	4-3	0	53	1.19	3.66		6.1%	21.5%	4.0%	34.1%	73.8%	85.4%	42.2%	65.8%	.271	.545	93	1.0
2023	DUR	AAA	22	10(10)	37²	2-5	0	37	1.57	6.45		11.6%	21.5%	5.2%	45.1%	70.3%	78.9%	29.5%	57.0%	.288	.643	90	0.7
2023	TB	MLB	22	23(21)	104²	5-8	0	129	1.39	5.59	50.2%	8.5%	28.0%	5.0%	36.1%	72.5%	82.8%	32.5%	60.4%	.310	.718	93	1.6
2024 DC	TB	MLB	23	21(21)	103	6-6	0	99	1.32	4.64	50.2%	8.6%	22.4%	4.1%	36.7%					.284	.590	105	0.6

2023 Arsenal: FA (96.3), FC (89), CU (78.9), FS (89.4)   Comps: Randall Delgado (73), Bryse Wilson (73), Matt Wisler (72)

Bradley was on target to make a 2023 debut no matter what happened; however, after a nasty, itchy rash of injuries in the rotation, the Rays had to lean on him more than anyone expected. He allowed a lot of runs, especially on balls that left the yard, and he was a bit generous with free passes, but nothing unexpected from your typical hard-throwing 22-year-old. Bradley's average heater landed in the 85th percentile and his strikeout rate was comfortably above league-average. Unfortunately, the hard-thrown balls were hit almost as hard. The average ball hit off him came off the bat at 91 mph; the league-average was around 87. Around the fastball, he threw a hard cutter and a hard changeup. A slow breaking ball exists, but around 85% of his tosses were of the firmer variety. Bradley was not included in the Rays' postseason roster, but is a likely candidate for the Opening Day one.

Aaron Civale RHP Born: 06/12/95 Age: 29 Height: 6'2" Weight: 215 Origin: Round 3, 2016 Draft (#92 overall)

YEAR	TM	LVL	AGE	G (GS)	IP	W-L	SV	K	WHIP	ERA	CSP	BB%	K%	HR%	GB%	ZSw%	ZCon%	OSw%	OCon%	BABIP	SLGCON	DRA-	WARP
2021	AKR	AA	26	2(2)	7	1-0	0	8	1.00	1.29		10.7%	28.6%	0.0%	41.2%					.250	.312	94	0.1
2021	CLE	MLB	26	21(21)	124¹	12-5	0	99	1.12	3.84	53.4%	6.2%	19.9%	4.6%	44.2%	68.5%	86.2%	33.9%	68.5%	.250	.565	111	0.4
2022	COL	AAA	27	4(4)	13¹	0-0	0	18	1.35	4.72		6.7%	30.0%	3.3%	60.0%					.364	.714	81	0.3
2022	CLE	MLB	27	20(20)	97	5-6	0	98	1.19	4.92	52.3%	5.4%	24.1%	3.4%	41.4%	66.5%	89.5%	34.0%	58.5%	.297	.575	95	1.2
2023	COL	AAA	28	3(3)	11	0-0	0	16	1.55	4.91		8.5%	34.0%	4.3%	44.4%	65.9%	81.5%	31.2%	44.1%	.440	.852	83	0.3
2023	CLE	MLB	28	13(13)	77	5-2	0	58	1.04	2.34	46.4%	7.2%	19.0%	1.6%	40.4%	64.0%	89.1%	34.3%	65.0%	.243	.392	110	0.5
2023	TB	MLB	28	10(10)	45¹	2-3	0	58	1.37	5.36	47.8%	5.6%	29.3%	3.5%	36.5%	64.9%	83.2%	35.5%	66.5%	.373	.648	93	0.7
2024 DC	TB	MLB	29	28(28)	145²	9-8	0	127	1.22	4.01	49.7%	6.7%	20.7%	3.4%	41.0%					.281	.533	93	1.8

2023 Arsenal: FC (87.9), CU (78.3), SI (92.5), FA (92), SW (82.6), CH (85.4)   Comps: Anthony DeSclafani (63), Jerad Eickhoff (59), Steven Matz (56)

The Rays are notorious for being in the "we tried" camp at the trade deadline so the mid-season acquisition of Civale, an above-average starting pitcher with two more years of arbitration, qualifies as the closest thing to a Tampa Bay Blockbuster since the days of "be kind, rewind." The right-hander allowed a fair amount of home runs in this time with the Rays—about 15 percent of the fly balls he allowed left the yard. On the flip side, the peripherals were fine. It is unlikely he carries a BABIP of .370 in a full season, and his strikeout rate went from just under 20% with Cleveland to just under 30% with the Rays. How? Under the eye of Kyle Snyder, Civale threw more sinkers and sliders in lieu of fastballs and cutters. The Rays relinquished Kyle Manzardo to complete the deal, but if Civale pitches the way he did after the trade over the next two seasons, it is a long-term rental that they will likely be happy with.

Chris Devenski RHP   Born: 11/13/90   Age: 33   Height: 6'3"   Weight: 211   Origin: Round 25, 2011 Draft (#771 overall)

YEAR	TM	LVL	AGE	G (GS)	IP	W-L	SV	K	WHIP	ERA	CSP	BB%	K%	HR%	GB%	ZSw%	ZCon%	OSw%	OCon%	BABIP	SLGCON	DRA-	WARP
2021	AZ	MLB	30	8 (0)	7¹	1-0	1	5	1.77	8.59	50.7%	5.7%	14.3%	5.7%	37.0%	65.5%	84.2%	31.0%	59.3%	.360	.704	121	0.0
2022	PHI	MLB	31	3 (0)	4	0-0	0	3	1.75	11.25	55.5%	0.0%	15.8%	5.3%	43.8%	79.3%	69.6%	44.7%	64.7%	.400	.733	99	0.0
2022	AZ	MLB	31	10 (0)	10²	2-1	0	9	1.41	7.59	62.0%	2.1%	18.8%	4.2%	40.5%	69.6%	87.3%	30.5%	55.2%	.343	.829	98	0.1
2023	TB	MLB	32	9 (0)	8²	3-2	0	9	0.81	2.08	43.7%	6.1%	27.3%	3.0%	9.1%	77.4%	80.5%	35.3%	40.0%	.190	.476	94	0.1
2023	LAA	MLB	32	29 (0)	33²	3-2	0	33	1.19	5.08	44.8%	6.4%	23.6%	3.6%	46.4%	65.4%	86.0%	35.2%	58.1%	.286	.532	90	0.6
2024 DC	TB	MLB	33	57 (0)	60	4-3	0	59	1.31	4.67	47.9%	7.2%	22.9%	3.9%	37.3%					.301	.593	106	0.1

2023 Arsenal: CH (83.2), FA (94), SW (79.5), SL (82.1)   *Comps: Bob Howry (55), Grant Balfour (54), Jim Johnson (54)*

Devenski was a late-season addition, signing with the Rays just before September after being let loose by the Angels. Despite the short stay, the veteran was tasked with several high-leverage assignments, including during the post-season. In Game 1 of the Wild Card series against the Rangers, the Rays were faced with a two-on, nobody out situation, already trailing 2-0. Kevin Cash called on the newcomer, but unfortunately after a single and an error, Texas was able to double their lead. Devo has an unconventional approach to pitching, leading his attack with a low-80s changeup. This was only emphasized more when he got to Tampa Bay, as nearly 60% of his pitches for the Rays were changeups. After five seasons with Houston, he has settled into the life of a journeyman making four stops in the last two seasons. The Rays liked what they saw enough to give him a break from riding the rails, signing him to a one-year deal.

Jake Diekman LHP   Born: 01/21/87   Age: 37   Height: 6'4"   Weight: 195   Origin: Round 30, 2007 Draft (#923 overall)

YEAR	TM	LVL	AGE	G (GS)	IP	W-L	SV	K	WHIP	ERA	CSP	BB%	K%	HR%	GB%	ZSw%	ZCon%	OSw%	OCon%	BABIP	SLGCON	DRA-	WARP
2021	OAK	MLB	34	67 (0)	60²	3-3	7	83	1.34	3.86	52.1%	13.0%	31.7%	3.8%	34.8%	64.9%	75.2%	29.5%	49.5%	.282	.621	99	0.6
2022	BOS	MLB	35	44 (0)	38¹	5-1	1	51	1.49	4.23	48.4%	17.5%	29.8%	2.9%	35.7%	62.1%	84.2%	27.7%	44.9%	.278	.610	115	0.1
2022	CHW	MLB	35	26 (0)	19¹	0-3	0	28	1.91	6.52	52.9%	12.2%	28.6%	4.1%	44.6%	73.4%	78.8%	29.6%	48.5%	.404	.727	96	0.2
2023	CHW	MLB	36	13 (0)	11¹	0-1	0	11	2.12	7.94	43.1%	22.4%	19.0%	1.7%	47.1%	63.0%	89.7%	21.5%	64.5%	.303	.500	106	0.1
2023	TB	MLB	36	50 (0)	45¹	0-1	0	53	1.13	2.18	48.2%	13.5%	28.6%	1.1%	45.3%	60.0%	75.3%	28.3%	66.4%	.233	.356	96	0.6
2024 non	TB	MLB	37	58 (0)	50	2-2	0	59	1.47	4.94	49.0%	13.7%	26.2%	3.3%	41.2%					.290	.577	107	0.0

2023 Arsenal: FA (95.6), SW (83.9), CH (88.1), FC (89.4)   *Comps: Gary Lavelle (83), Jesse Orosco (82), Randy Choate (80)*

The White Sox quickly moved on from Diekman last year, which made sense after allowing 10 earned runs and issuing 13 walks in his first 11 ⅓ innings. But the Rays were desperate for pitching, so he latched on and still allowed a lot of free baserunners, but at a much more palatable clip. More importantly, he struck out two hitters for every one he walked. Diekman also specialized in weak contact after the move from the South Side to the Southeast, giving up an average exit velocity of less than 84 mph. His next pitch will come from a 37-year-old arm, but as long as that arm can pump out mid-summer temperatures from the left side, he will continue to find regular work.

Zach Eflin RHP   Born: 04/08/94   Age: 30   Height: 6'6"   Weight: 220   Origin: Round 1, 2012 Draft (#33 overall)

YEAR	TM	LVL	AGE	G (GS)	IP	W-L	SV	K	WHIP	ERA	CSP	BB%	K%	HR%	GB%	ZSw%	ZCon%	OSw%	OCon%	BABIP	SLGCON	DRA-	WARP
2021	PHI	MLB	27	18 (18)	105²	4-7	0	99	1.25	4.17	55.1%	3.6%	22.4%	3.4%	43.2%	68.4%	85.1%	36.2%	66.2%	.328	.602	87	1.7
2022	PHI	MLB	28	20 (13)	75²	3-5	1	65	1.12	4.04	52.3%	4.8%	20.8%	2.6%	45.2%	66.2%	87.5%	34.8%	65.2%	.282	.507	95	0.9
2023	TB	MLB	29	31 (31)	177²	16-8	0	186	1.02	3.50	51.0%	3.4%	26.5%	2.7%	49.2%	65.6%	84.6%	37.5%	64.4%	.296	.524	73	4.6
2024 DC	TB	MLB	30	29 (29)	166	12-8	0	146	1.13	3.34	51.6%	4.9%	21.5%	2.6%	46.9%					.287	.497	81	3.2

2023 Arsenal: SI (92.4), FC (88.7), CU (79.3), FA (93.1), CH (86.4), SW (80), SL (85.2)   *Comps: Rick Porcello (80), Rick Wise (79), Charles Nagy (78)*

Somewhat of a hometown kid, Eflin grew up about two and a half hours away from Tropicana Field. If you want to feel really old, he waxed poetically about how much of a fan he was as a youth during the Rays' 2008 run to the World Series. After signing the richest free agent contract in team history, a number that itself carried strong 2008 vibes, Eflin, the man, was making memories on the mound in Tropicana Field in 2023. He was the team's starting pitcher in Game 2 of the Wild Card series and, although he didn't win that game, he won plenty of others, pacing the American League in wins while turning in a career-best ERA. Those standard metrics are backed by advanced ones that say he might have been even better than his baseball card stats. The Rays let Eflin embrace more of his secondary offerings, resulting in the highest ground-ball rate of his career, as he threw more cutters and changeups than ever before. In a year with a ton of uncertainty, Eflin was a stabilizing force in the Rays' rotation, and will occupy a similar role moving forward.

Pete Fairbanks RHP   Born: 12/16/93   Age: 30   Height: 6'6"   Weight: 225   Origin: Round 9, 2015 Draft (#258 overall)

YEAR	TM	LVL	AGE	G (GS)	IP	W-L	SV	K	WHIP	ERA	CSP	BB%	K%	HR%	GB%	ZSw%	ZCon%	OSw%	OCon%	BABIP	SLGCON	DRA-	WARP
2021	TB	MLB	27	47 (0)	42²	3-6	5	56	1.43	3.59	56.5%	11.1%	29.6%	1.1%	42.3%	67.9%	76.2%	31.8%	59.6%	.349	.500	81	0.8
2022	TB	MLB	28	24 (0)	24	0-0	8	38	0.67	1.13	56.2%	3.4%	43.7%	1.1%	53.3%	67.1%	73.6%	39.7%	51.9%	.273	.386	54	0.8
2023	TB	MLB	29	49 (0)	45¹	2-4	25	68	1.01	2.58	51.0%	10.9%	37.0%	1.6%	48.9%	61.9%	75.7%	33.9%	59.6%	.261	.407	72	1.2
2024 DC	TB	MLB	30	57 (0)	60	4-6	38	77	1.13	3.07	52.2%	9.7%	31.0%	3.0%	45.4%					.270	.531	74	1.1

2023 Arsenal: FA (98.9), SL (86.7), CH (94.4), FS (92.7)   *Comps: Ryne Stanek (64), Giovanny Gallegos (62), Steve Cishek (60)*

Ol' Petey Fireball was one of the better relievers in baseball once again, despite a little bit of regression. Fairbanks worked around forearm and hip issues to post gaudy strikeout numbers with a fastball that tickles triple-digits. Meanwhile, for the first time since his maiden voyage in the majors, the heater ever-so slightly took a backseat to his mid-80s slider. The change in usage led to more walks, but it was still a manageable amount given those strikeout and groundball metrics. Despite being one of the club's better arm barners over the past few seasons, Fairbanks racked up just 13 saves in his first 111 appearances with the Rays. Saves cost money in arbitration, after all. By signing Fairbanks to a three-year deal covering his arbitration years, the Rays were freed from their own tyranny and he magically converted 25 saves on the year. He should occupy a similar role for the next few seasons as his contract takes him through 2025 with a club option for 2026.

Kevin Kelly RHP   Born: 11/28/97   Age: 26   Height: 6'2"   Weight: 200   Origin: Round 19, 2019 Draft (#580 overall)

YEAR	TM	LVL	AGE	G (GS)	IP	W-L	SV	K	WHIP	ERA	CSP	BB%	K%	HR%	GB%	ZSw%	ZCon%	OSw%	OCon%	BABIP	SLGCON	DRA-	WARP
2021	LC	A+	23	40 (0)	56	5-5	7	81	1.14	4.66		3.4%	34.5%	3.0%	48.3%					.366	.686	85	1.0
2022	AKR	AA	24	16 (0)	24¹	3-2	3	32	0.95	1.11		8.8%	31.4%	0.0%	57.9%					.246	.333	86	0.5
2022	COL	AAA	24	32 (1)	33	2-0	1	43	1.24	2.73		8.7%	28.9%	0.7%	61.9%					.325	.417	80	0.8
2023	TB	MLB	25	57 (0)	67	5-2	1	56	1.01	3.09	51.7%	5.4%	20.3%	0.7%	48.2%	62.5%	82.8%	29.5%	68.6%	.264	.395	91	1.1
2024 DC	TB	MLB	26	51 (0)	54	3-2	0	47	1.27	4.28	51.7%	7.3%	20.2%	2.8%	46.5%					.289	.509	97	0.3

2023 Arsenal: SI (90.8), SW (76.4), FC (87.3), FA (91.8), CH (84.4), CU (72.4)   Comps: Kevin Quackenbush (84), Brian Ellington (84), Jacob Webb (82)

This baby-faced reliever bounced around prior to the season, but may have found a permanent home in the Rays bullpen. After landing in Tampa from Cleveland by way of a waiver claim from Colorado, Kelly proved to be a reliable arm capable of going longer than one inning. He recorded four or more outs in 21 of his appearances and topped six or more in 10 of those. Working off a very low-90s fastball with a mid-70s slider (and a slightly harder cutter), he posted modest strikeout rates. However, he rarely issued a walk and allowed just two balls to leave the yard in 67 innings; he kept hitters closer to the ground and had a knack for missing barrels. After a strong performance in lower-leverage situations, the 26-year-old could be in line for more important work.

Zack Littell RHP   Born: 10/05/95   Age: 28   Height: 6'4"   Weight: 220   Origin: Round 11, 2013 Draft (#327 overall)

YEAR	TM	LVL	AGE	G (GS)	IP	W-L	SV	K	WHIP	ERA	CSP	BB%	K%	HR%	GB%	ZSw%	ZCon%	OSw%	OCon%	BABIP	SLGCON	DRA-	WARP
2021	SF	MLB	25	63 (2)	61²	4-0	2	63	1.14	2.92	55.4%	9.5%	25.0%	2.8%	46.6%	77.3%	77.6%	33.6%	61.3%	.253	.522	85	1.1
2022	SAC	AAA	26	13 (1)	13¹	0-1	0	13	1.35	6.75		7.1%	23.2%	5.4%	46.2%	78.9%	76.1%	34.2%	53.8%	.306	.667	94	0.1
2022	SF	MLB	26	39 (0)	44¹	3-3	1	39	1.38	5.08	54.6%	6.8%	20.5%	4.2%	43.1%	75.0%	76.9%	36.1%	66.5%	.310	.622	94	0.6
2023	RR	AAA	27	8 (0)	12	2-0	0	16	0.92	2.25		4.2%	33.3%	2.1%	43.3%	70.0%	91.1%	44.8%	44.2%	.276	.433	79	0.2
2023	TB	MLB	27	26 (14)	87	3-6	0	72	1.15	3.93	51.9%	2.5%	19.8%	3.6%	42.3%	75.3%	88.1%	34.8%	61.4%	.294	.543	98	1.1
2023	BOS	MLB	27	2 (0)	3	0-0	0	2	2.00	9.00	52.7%	20.0%	13.3%	0.0%	30.0%	76.7%	82.6%	28.1%	77.8%	.300	.500	96	0.0
2024 DC	TB	MLB	28	38 (23)	133²	7-8	0	106	1.35	4.72	53.3%	7.0%	18.3%	3.4%	41.8%					.297	.550	106	0.4

2023 Arsenal: SL (88.7), FA (94.1), FS (84.3), SI (92.9), SW (80.6)   Comps: Michael Bowden (53), J.B. Wendelken (51), Bruce Rondón (49)

A former starter in the minors, Littell spent most of the last five seasons in relief, first for the Twins and more recently for the Giants. But in 2023, he started the year with the Rangers, got traded to the Red Sox and soon after that claimed by the Rays. Oh ye of Littell faith! Coming out of this chaotic background, Littell was what he pretended to be: When the Rays lost a pair of former relievers-turned-starters early in the season, they tapped Littell for a similar transition out of necessity. He threw a career-high 90 innings and was mostly effective—especially as a strike thrower—using modest means to achieve those results. His fastball velocity was shockingly similar to his pure relief days and Littell added a sweeper to go along with a harder cutter/slider while also mixing in more off-speed. The Rays also shifted his horizontal release with a move toward the first base side of the rubber. Littell has certainly earned a spot on the major-league roster, but his role remains anything but determined. He'll roll with it.

Jacob Lopez LHP   Born: 03/11/98   Age: 26   Height: 6'4"   Weight: 220   Origin: Round 26, 2018 Draft (#766 overall)

YEAR	TM	LVL	AGE	G (GS)	IP	W-L	SV	K	WHIP	ERA	CSP	BB%	K%	HR%	GB%	ZSw%	ZCon%	OSw%	OCon%	BABIP	SLGCON	DRA-	WARP
2021	BG	A+	23	14 (10)	54²	3-1	2	88	1.04	2.30		7.6%	39.5%	2.7%	50.0%					.321	.586	67	1.4
2023	MTG	AA	25	8 (6)	28	0-0	0	45	0.82	2.57		8.3%	41.7%	1.9%	50.0%					.240	.442	57	1.1
2023	DUR	AAA	25	18 (18)	79¹	4-5	0	87	1.32	2.72		14.0%	26.0%	2.1%	41.1%	63.2%	80.3%	31.3%	58.0%	.270	.513	89	1.6
2023	TB	MLB	25	4 (1)	12¹	1-0	1	8	1.30	4.38	45.6%	3.7%	14.8%	0.0%	35.7%	64.8%	84.8%	41.8%	66.7%	.333	.476	118	0.0
2024 DC	TB	MLB	26	14 (5)	33²	2-2	0	35	1.36	4.60	45.6%	10.3%	23.9%	3.5%	37.3%					.287	.568	102	0.2

2023 Arsenal: FA (90.9), SL (78.8), CH (83.6)   Comps: Michael King (60), Matthew Boyd (59), Framber Valdez (59)

Lopez is an unassuming lefty born in the Golden State who stayed home for college, ending up at College of the Canyons (Santa Clarita, CA). He was then drafted by the San Francisco Giants before they shipped him to the east coast's version of the Bay Area in exchange for Joe McCarthy. And if McCarthy's name has you thinking politics, here you go: He throws a three-pitch mix leading with a fastball that hovers around the first Bush administration (88-92) and can sometimes pop into the Clinton years. His Jimmy Carter slider (77-81) is his out-pitch against leftists and his Reaganomics changeup covers the right wing of the plate. With several defections from the Tampa bullpen, he should be in the mix for a role—maybe bulk reliever, maybe starter—heading into election season.

Shane McClanahan LHP Born: 04/28/97 Age: 27 Height: 6'1" Weight: 200 Origin: Round 1, 2018 Draft (#31 overall)

YEAR	TM	LVL	AGE	G (GS)	IP	W-L	SV	K	WHIP	ERA	CSP	BB%	K%	HR%	GB%	ZSw%	ZCon%	OSw%	OCon%	BABIP	SLGCON	DRA-	WARP
2021	TB	MLB	24	25 (25)	123¹	10-6	0	141	1.27	3.43	57.0%	7.2%	27.3%	2.7%	45.7%	67.7%	84.3%	36.7%	45.1%	.330	.552	89	1.9
2022	TB	MLB	25	28 (28)	166¹	12-8	0	194	0.93	2.54	55.4%	5.9%	30.3%	3.0%	49.9%	67.5%	76.7%	36.4%	50.7%	.252	.469	68	4.3
2023	TB	MLB	26	21 (21)	115	11-2	0	121	1.18	3.29	49.5%	8.7%	25.8%	3.2%	44.0%	70.2%	78.2%	36.2%	49.3%	.274	.541	91	1.9
2024 non	TB	MLB	27	58 (0)	50	2-2	0	58	1.22	3.67	53.6%	8.0%	27.9%	3.0%	45.8%					.302	.556	86	0.6

2023 Arsenal: FA (97), CH (87), CU (83.7), SL (89.5)   *Comps: Blake Snell (75), David Price (75), Walker Buehler (75)*

Similar to his former teammate Tyler Glasnow in 2021, McClanahan was one of the best pitchers in the league at the time of his torn UCL. The lefty was not as dominant as he was in his 2022 campaign, but was still pretty freaking good and sitting around 97 mph when he went down. He maintained elite stuff, including a hard slider, a hook and a stout off-speed pitch in the upper 80s. McClanahan's control and command took a slight step back, but elite stuff means that he can miss and still be dangerous. The late-season surgery means he will miss most of the upcoming year, but if the Rays have meaningful games in September and October, he could figure into those contests.

Mason Montgomery LHP Born: 06/17/00 Age: 24 Height: 6'2" Weight: 195 Origin: Round 6, 2021 Draft (#191 overall)

YEAR	TM	LVL	AGE	G (GS)	IP	W-L	SV	K	WHIP	ERA	CSP	BB%	K%	HR%	GB%	ZSw%	ZCon%	OSw%	OCon%	BABIP	SLGCON	DRA-	WARP
2021	RAY	ROK	21	5 (4)	10²	1-0	0	20	0.47	0.84		2.7%	54.1%	0.0%	12.5%					.250	.267		
2022	BG	A+	22	16 (16)	69²	3-2	0	118	1.09	1.81		9.6%	41.8%	2.1%	43.7%					.333	.570	73	1.6
2022	MTG	AA	22	11 (11)	54¹	3-1	0	53	1.03	2.48		7.3%	24.3%	2.3%	45.6%					.245	.412	90	0.8
2023	MTG	AA	23	25 (25)	107²	5-4	0	131	1.37	4.18		10.5%	28.0%	3.8%	36.4%					.305	.607	93	1.4
2023	DUR	AAA	23	4 (4)	16²	2-0	0	13	1.08	2.70		15.9%	18.8%	2.9%	31.0%	75.6%	87.8%	29.7%	56.8%	.125	.333	110	0.1
2024 DC	TB	MLB	24	14 (5)	33²	1-2	0	33	1.48	5.37		10.9%	21.9%	3.9%	34.3%					.298	.590	117	-0.1

2023 Arsenal: FA (94.1), SL (85.9), CH (84.7)   *Comps: Sean Nolin (83), Jordan Montgomery (78), Andrew Heaney (76)*

Montgomery signed for under-slot money as sixth-round pick out of Texas Tech in 2021, but he's pitched well over his slot. His best offering is a mid-90s fastball that plays up because of a deceptive delivery; he gets good velocity separation on his changeup and his slider continues to be in development but also flashes above-average potential. Montgomery had been a strike-thrower prior to 2023, but appears to be having GPS issues at the upper levels. If he can recalibrate, he is a three-pitch starter with solid size and pitchability. If his control remains iffy, he could find himself in a slightly more limited bulk role where his flaws can be hidden a bit more.

Ryan Pepiot RHP Born: 08/21/97 Age: 26 Height: 6'3" Weight: 215 Origin: Round 3, 2019 Draft (#102 overall)

YEAR	TM	LVL	AGE	G (GS)	IP	W-L	SV	K	WHIP	ERA	CSP	BB%	K%	HR%	GB%	ZSw%	ZCon%	OSw%	OCon%	BABIP	SLGCON	DRA-	WARP
2021	TUL	AA	23	15 (13)	59²	3-4	0	81	0.94	2.87		11.2%	34.8%	3.0%	32.5%					.198	.438	70	1.4
2021	OKC	AAA	23	11 (9)	41²	2-5	0	46	1.80	7.13		10.4%	22.8%	5.9%	40.6%					.350	.802	99	0.2
2022	OKC	AAA	24	19 (17)	91¹	9-1	0	114	1.07	2.56		9.8%	30.9%	2.7%	39.4%	66.6%	76.9%	35.0%	57.0%	.263	.507	80	1.6
2022	LAD	MLB	24	9 (7)	36¹	3-0	0	42	1.46	3.47	47.4%	16.9%	26.3%	3.8%	26.1%	62.1%	77.8%	30.6%	64.3%	.244	.545	121	0.0
2023	OKC	AAA	25	6 (6)	22²	0-2	0	26	1.15	3.97		5.4%	28.0%	4.3%	33.9%	68.3%	80.0%	36.9%	54.4%	.293	.590	86	0.3
2023	LAD	MLB	25	8 (3)	42	2-1	0	38	0.76	2.14	48.0%	3.1%	23.9%	4.4%	34.5%	69.8%	82.5%	37.2%	58.9%	.189	.487	99	0.4
2024 DC	TB	MLB	26	23 (23)	113¹	6-7	0	112	1.32	4.56	47.7%	9.3%	22.9%	3.7%	32.2%					.282	.575	103	0.7

2023 Arsenal: FA (94), CH (86.4), FC (88.5)   *Comps: Adbert Alzolay (74), Dinelson Lamet (73), John Gant (72)*

It's tough to know what to make of Pepiot, which is perhaps an assessment in and of itself. He added velocity to his cutter while adding more depth to his changeup, which now creates about 14 inches of separation from his fastball in induced vertical break. The slight raising of his arm slot has made his changeup more devastating, but his fastball even more generic—a good tradeoff, since his changeup was borderline unusable last year, and his fastball still plays well towards the top of the zone. While DRA- thinks he had a middling season, we can say that he did himself a solid by suppressing walks and hitter-friendly contact, while striking out just enough batters. Given that just 12 months ago he would have had trouble throwing strikes from 20 feet, it's a happy improvement. Just in time to be the headliner of a weird Tyler Glasnow trade.

Colin Poche LHP Born: 01/17/94 Age: 30 Height: 6'3" Weight: 225 Origin: Round 14, 2016 Draft (#419 overall)

YEAR	TM	LVL	AGE	G (GS)	IP	W-L	SV	K	WHIP	ERA	CSP	BB%	K%	HR%	GB%	ZSw%	ZCon%	OSw%	OCon%	BABIP	SLGCON	DRA-	WARP
2022	DUR	AAA	28	6 (0)	6	0-0	1	11	0.50	0.00		9.5%	52.4%	0.0%	25.0%					.125	.125	81	0.1
2022	TB	MLB	28	65 (0)	58²	4-2	7	64	1.16	3.99	55.7%	9.0%	26.1%	4.5%	31.6%	73.5%	77.6%	36.6%	64.5%	.238	.578	107	0.4
2023	TB	MLB	29	66 (0)	60²	12-3	1	61	1.09	2.23	46.2%	9.8%	24.8%	1.6%	33.8%	69.3%	80.0%	34.9%	59.0%	.247	.426	100	0.7
2024 DC	TB	MLB	30	57 (0)	60	4-3	4	71	1.31	4.31	50.4%	9.7%	27.5%	3.5%	31.2%					.300	.597	97	0.4

2023 Arsenal: FA (92.7), SL (84.5)   *Comps: Jake Diekman (77), Sam Freeman (73), Craig Breslow (69)*

Do you want to know how awesome pitcher wins are? Poche had more wins (12) than $700-million man Shohei Ohtani (10) despite the latter making 23 starts and the former making zero. Obviously, the lefty wasn't 12-win good, but he showed improvement from his disappointing 2022 campaign and seems to be fully beyond the injuries that robbed him of 2020 and 2021 seasons. Poche still throws a mid-90 fastball about two-thirds of the time, but did go to slider a bit more, which was more of a biter instead of a cutter with tight movement and more velocity. His strikeout-to-walk rate was relatively static; however, he missed more barrels and had an exit velocity against that was lower than the league average. His next meaningful pitch will come on the other side of 30 and arrives with an increased paycheck, which puts him on some sort of watchlist within the organization.

Erasmo Ramírez   RHP   Born: 05/02/90   Age: 34   Height: 6'0"   Weight: 220   Origin: IFA, 2007

YEAR	TM	LVL	AGE	G (GS)	IP	W-L	SV	K	WHIP	ERA	CSP	BB%	K%	HR%	GB%	ZSw%	ZCon%	OSw%	OCon%	BABIP	SLGCON	DRA-	WARP
2021	TOL	AAA	31	5 (0)	8	1-0	0	10	0.88	3.38		9.4%	31.3%	0.0%	47.4%					.211	.263	91	0.1
2021	DET	MLB	31	17 (0)	26²	1-1	0	20	1.09	5.74	61.3%	4.6%	18.3%	3.7%	37.3%	71.6%	85.8%	31.3%	77.0%	.253	.506	109	0.1
2022	WAS	MLB	32	60 (2)	86¹	4-2	0	61	1.08	2.92	57.2%	4.0%	17.6%	3.2%	45.1%	71.7%	85.0%	34.8%	67.5%	.268	.481	89	1.4
2023	DUR	AAA	33	9 (1)	23	2-1	0	29	1.52	5.87		7.9%	28.7%	4.0%	45.3%	67.8%	79.3%	35.5%	60.5%	.383	.778	79	0.6
2023	WAS	MLB	33	23 (0)	27	2-3	0	13	1.56	6.33	55.9%	4.8%	10.3%	3.2%	43.3%	71.5%	89.9%	22.5%	76.6%	.320	.545	105	0.2
2023	TB	MLB	33	15 (2)	33¹	1-0	0	30	1.59	6.48	49.1%	4.7%	20.3%	4.7%	43.6%	78.8%	84.4%	35.3%	60.0%	.379	.704	95	0.5
2024 non	TB	MLB	34	58 (0)	50	2-2	0	34	1.32	4.60	55.1%	6.1%	15.9%	3.2%	42.0%					.293	.524	105	0.1

2023 Arsenal: FC (88.8), SI (91.7), CU (80), CH (84), SL (81.7), FA (92.2), SW (79.2)   Comps: Anthony Swarzak (61), Mudcat Grant (59), Jason Grimsley (58)

They say if you love something let it go, and if it comes back to you then it was truly meant to be. After nearly five years and a similar number of employers, Ramírez was back with the Rays at the end of 2023. But just because something is fated does not guarantee it will be a *good* thing, and The Eraser's return was more grim (Grimm?) than fairy tale: He gave up a lot of runs on a lot of hits with several of them leaving the yard. However, there were also enough positives that the Rays decided not to let him go again, bringing him back on a minor-league deal for 2024. He ended his season showing more control and an upgraded pitch mix (more sliders and changeups, fewer sinkers), and he's famous for a rubber arm that can soak up innings in a variety of roles. Here's to their happily ever after.

Drew Rasmussen   RHP   Born: 07/27/95   Age: 28   Height: 6'1"   Weight: 211   Origin: Round 6, 2018 Draft (#185 overall)

YEAR	TM	LVL	AGE	G (GS)	IP	W-L	SV	K	WHIP	ERA	CSP	BB%	K%	HR%	GB%	ZSw%	ZCon%	OSw%	OCon%	BABIP	SLGCON	DRA-	WARP
2021	DUR	AAA	25	8 (1)	11¹	2-0	1	23	0.62	0.00		4.8%	54.8%	0.0%	60.0%					.333	.533	66	0.3
2021	TB	MLB	25	20 (10)	59	4-0	0	48	0.97	2.44	56.8%	5.7%	20.9%	1.3%	50.9%	70.8%	84.5%	33.7%	63.6%	.248	.377	92	0.8
2021	MIL	MLB	25	15 (0)	17	0-1	1	25	1.47	4.24	55.3%	15.6%	32.5%	2.6%	32.5%	60.2%	73.0%	29.0%	65.6%	.289	.575	85	0.3
2022	TB	MLB	26	28 (28)	146	11-7	0	125	1.04	2.84	55.6%	5.3%	21.4%	2.2%	47.0%	73.2%	85.9%	38.3%	59.6%	.264	.450	80	2.8
2023	TB	MLB	27	8 (8)	44²	4-2	0	47	1.05	2.62	53.4%	6.2%	26.6%	1.1%	51.7%	66.7%	90.2%	34.9%	52.8%	.296	.414	79	1.0
2024 DC	TB	MLB	28	8 (8)	39²	2-2	0	35	1.21	3.59	54.9%	7.2%	21.1%	2.7%	47.7%					.281	.496	84	0.7

2023 Arsenal: SL (88.7), FA (96.4), SW (85.2), SI (95.6), CU (80.7)   Comps: Andrew Cashner (60), Brandon Woodruff (56), Pete Vuckovich (55)

The plan in 2022 was to limit Rasmussen's innings to keep him healthy in 2023. Like most plans, it went great until it didn't, which took about 45 innings. Rasmussen was pumping mid-90s heaters with a slider/cutter combo and a changeup, peaking with an outing of seven shutout innings before feeling something "off." He should've known. His UCL has been through the wringer before, and he chose an internal brace procedure rather than submitting to a third (and likely final) Tommy John surgery. The brace repair will still cost him a good chunk of 2024, but he could return in the middle of the season and provide a cheap trade deadline boost for the perennially contending Rays.

Jeffrey Springs   LHP   Born: 09/20/92   Age: 31   Height: 6'3"   Weight: 218   Origin: Round 30, 2015 Draft (#888 overall)

YEAR	TM	LVL	AGE	G (GS)	IP	W-L	SV	K	WHIP	ERA	CSP	BB%	K%	HR%	GB%	ZSw%	ZCon%	OSw%	OCon%	BABIP	SLGCON	DRA-	WARP
2021	TB	MLB	28	43 (0)	44²	5-1	2	63	1.10	3.43	52.6%	7.8%	35.2%	5.0%	33.3%	64.1%	76.9%	35.3%	48.5%	.283	.727	72	1.1
2022	TB	MLB	29	33 (25)	135¹	9-5	0	144	1.07	2.46	53.3%	5.6%	26.2%	2.6%	41.0%	66.3%	80.2%	39.8%	59.8%	.280	.491	83	2.5
2023	TB	MLB	30	3 (3)	16	2-0	0	24	0.50	0.56	54.3%	7.3%	43.6%	1.8%	50.0%	51.0%	76.5%	35.5%	44.7%	.120	.269	80	0.4
2024 DC	TB	MLB	31	10 (10)	50¹	3-3	0	58	1.17	3.52	52.7%	7.3%	27.7%	3.4%	38.4%					.289	.564	84	0.8

2023 Arsenal: FA (92.2), CH (81.4), SL (85.1), SW (79.6)   Comps: C.J. Wilson (51), Fernando Abad (48), Brian Bohanon (48)

Springs and Drew Rasmussen were similarly transformed by the Rays from average-ish bullpen arms to quality members of what might have been baseball's best rotation when healthy. But at what cost? They both went down like dominoes, one after the other, but Springs could not avoid Tommy John surgery like Rasmussen did. Since he was first to the IL, he has a chance to pitch for Tampa Bay around Memorial Day; when that time comes, he'll serve up a modest fastball to go with a slider and changeup that have both been proven to succeed at the highest level. The 32-year-old signed a contract extension in January that will guarantee him over $25 million in the next three years regardless of health or effectiveness, and neither of those are certain.

Cole Wilcox   RHP   Born: 07/14/99   Age: 24   Height: 6'5"   Weight: 232   Origin: Round 3, 2020 Draft (#80 overall)

YEAR	TM	LVL	AGE	G (GS)	IP	W-L	SV	K	WHIP	ERA	CSP	BB%	K%	HR%	GB%	ZSw%	ZCon%	OSw%	OCon%	BABIP	SLGCON	DRA-	WARP
2021	CSC	A	21	10 (10)	44¹	1-0	0	52	0.86	2.03		2.9%	29.9%	0.6%	61.7%					.281	.389	80	0.9
2022	CSC	A	22	4 (4)	11	0-1	0	15	0.91	2.45		4.4%	33.3%	2.2%	66.7%					.269	.407	66	0.3
2023	MTG	AA	23	25 (25)	106²	6-8	0	99	1.30	5.23		9.7%	21.8%	3.1%	54.0%					.281	.548	92	1.6
2024 non	TB	MLB	24	58 (0)	50	2-2	0	40	1.49	5.39		9.0%	17.8%	3.2%	43.6%					.308	.556	118	-0.3

Comps: Harold Arauz (69), Yonny Chirinos (67), Mikey O'Brien (67)

Considered one of the top arms in his draft class, Wilcox is the Rays' last hope of turning the Blake Snell trade into something other than a rare L for the club. Injuries limited him to just around 60 innings over his first two years as a professional, but he was healthy in 2023 and that is more impressive than his middling results were. His mid-90s fastball and slider are potentially 60-grade offerings, while his changeup and control rate closer to average grades. If he can eventually maintain health, he's got the frame to be a three-pitch starter with two plus pitches, an average third offering and some navigation skills. Otherwise perhaps the slider would be a weapon out of the bullpen. Would either of these outcomes make the Snell trade a winner? Probably not, but they're much better outcomes than continued rehab and recovery from injury

LINEOUTS

Hitters

HITTER	POS	TM	LVL	AGE	PA	R	HR	RBI	SB	AVG/OBP/SLG	BABIP	SLGCON	BB%	K%	ZSw%	ZCon%	OSw%	OCon%	LA	90th EV	DRC+	BRR	DRP	WARP
Mason Auer	OF	MTG	AA	22	511	59	11	51	47	.205/.292/.348	.315	.585	9.6%	36.0%							75	2.7	1.7	0.3
Carlos Colmenarez	SS	CSC	A	19	346	42	6	28	10	.201/.344/.304	.349	.570	15.0%	38.2%							82	0.4	5.0	1.1
Brailer Guerrero	OF	DSL RAY	ROK	17	29	3	0	5	0	.261/.379/.391	.333	.529	13.8%	20.7%										
Billy Hamilton	CF	CLT	AAA	32	89	14	1	4	3	.147/.261/.253	.217	.413	12.4%	32.6%	63.2%	80.6%	32.2%	52.7%			82	1.3	-0.8	0.1
	CF	CHW	MLB	32	2	2	0	0	2	.000/.000/.000		.000	0.0%	50.0%	80.0%	25.0%	0.0%		83.0	36.2	96	0.0	-0.1	0.0
Brock Jones	OF	BG	A+	22	372	49	15	49	10	.201/.309/.412	.268	.672	12.9%	33.1%							87	0.5	-0.9	0.7
Greg Jones	CF/SS	MTG	AA	25	92	11	3	9	12	.173/.264/.358	.262	.644	9.8%	39.1%							79	1.6	1.9	0.4
	CF/SS	DUR	AAA	25	189	32	7	26	12	.278/.344/.467	.440	.823	7.9%	38.6%	70.6%	74.1%	36.6%	29.4%			68	0.9	-0.9	-0.1
Dominic Keegan	C	PEJ	WIN	22	62	8	3	12	0	.360/.459/.620	.429	.838	14.5%	21.0%	57.1%	87.5%	26.3%	40.0%						
	C	CSC	A	22	241	34	5	35	2	.315/.402/.475	.377	.625	12.9%	19.9%							144	-0.1	8.8	2.7
	C	BG	A+	22	207	26	8	30	0	.254/.367/.457	.288	.603	13.5%	20.3%							117	-0.2	5.3	1.3
Tre' Morgan	1B	CSC	A	20	44	7	0	2	4	.389/.500/.472	.412	.500	18.2%	4.5%							127	-0.2	-0.6	0.2
Adrian Santana	SS	RAY	ROK	17	47	6	0	3	3	.205/.340/.256	.267	.333	14.9%	19.1%										
Chandler Simpson	OF	CSC	A	22	397	66	0	24	81	.285/.358/.333	.317	.370	9.6%	8.8%							122	9.1	-0.2	3.0
	OF	BG	A+	22	106	22	0	7	13	.326/.429/.393	.363	.438	15.1%	8.5%							120	0.5	1.5	0.8
Raimel Tapia	OF	DUR	AAA	29	124	19	4	11	7	.269/.371/.413	.324	.566	14.5%	22.6%	57.9%	79.2%	34.5%	69.2%			97	-1.0	-1.9	0.2
	OF	MIL	MLB	29	61	10	2	3	2	.173/.267/.288	.226	.469	9.8%	32.8%	67.7%	73.1%	41.2%	63.5%	3.5	101.4	92	0.1	0.4	0.1
	OF	TB	MLB	29	11	4	0	0	2	.333/.455/.333	.375	.375	18.2%	9.1%	75.0%	41.7%	29.0%	77.8%	-16.9	106.2	89	0.0	0.1	0.0
	OF	BOS	MLB	29	97	14	1	10	6	.264/.333/.368	.328	.471	9.3%	19.6%	56.0%	85.3%	42.9%	66.7%	1.3	105.0	92	0.2	0.3	0.2
Willy Vasquez	3B/2B	BG	A+	21	472	53	16	62	17	.233/.310/.393	.275	.531	9.7%	23.1%							96	-3.8	-2.5	0.8

Mason Auer could not capitalize on his strong showing in the lower levels in the minors and looked real soggy in his Biscuits debut. ⓦ **Carlos Colmenarez** is looking real Rey Ordonez-ish. The glove looks good, but the bat looks like dead wood. (And not in the "critically acclaimed" way, but rather in the "let's use extensive profanity" way.) ⓦ **Brailer Guerrero** is a super-swaggy member of the 2006 birth class. He's already a big kid with projectable size that should grow into plus power, a potentially plus stick and solid defense in right field. At the hefty (for Tampa) price tag of $3.7 million, both parties hope all that projection comes true. ⓦ **Billy Hamilton** appeared in a major-league game for the 11th straight season. Check back next year to see if he gets to 12. (The odds are not in his favor.) ⓦ **Brock Jones** is a pretty good-looking dude. He'd also look good in St. Petersburg as a poor man's Kevin Kiermaier: A defensive-minded center fielder with speed, power and a tough time making contact. ⓦ **Greg Jones** hit better in 2023; finally reaching Triple-A in advance of his 26th birthday. He remains fast. ⓦ **Dominic Keegan** might be the best catcher in the Rays' organization. Not the best *prospect*, but the best *overall*. Right now. Today. April 17, 2024. (Someone just got really creeped out reading this.) ⓦ Fresh off a National Championship, **Tre' Morgan** is a solid hitter and tremendous athlete. He's limited to first base on the dirt because he throws left-handed and limited left field on the grass because that left hand is attached to a below-average left arm. ⓦ **Adrian Santana** is as true of a traditional shortstop prospect as they come. The 34th pick in the recent draft is a double-plus runner with a plus arm and a plus glove. Will he hit? Maybe. Will he hit for power? Probably not. ⓦ The 70th overall pick in 2022, **Chandler Simpson** has top-of-the-order skills with a plus hit tool and elite speed. A former middle infielder in college, the Rays moved him to the outfield where he is expected to be a blanket in center field. ⓦ **Raimel Tapia** suited up for three different teams in 2023, ending the year with the Rays. He'll catch on somewhere as a fill-in fifth or sixth outfielder that can also run a bit. ⓦ **Willy Vasquez** carries himself like a gallivanting boulevardier. It is impressive confidence for a dude who has struggled to hit consistently in A-ball. He does have some pop and a big arm that shines like the diamond studs in his headshots.

Pitchers

PITCHER	TM	LVL	AGE	G (GS)	IP	W-L	SV	K	WHIP	ERA	CSP	BB%	K%	HR%	GB%	ZSw%	ZCon%	OSw%	OCon%	BABIP	SLGCON	DRA-	WARP
Garrett Cleavinger	TB	MLB	29	15 (0)	12	1-0	0	14	1.00	3.00	42.7%	12.5%	29.2%	4.2%	40.7%	58.3%	88.1%	34.3%	61.2%	.160	.481	93	0.2
Josh Fleming	DUR	AAA	27	14 (4)	31	1-1	0	15	1.77	4.35		5.6%	10.4%	2.1%	62.5%	72.3%	84.6%	37.0%	68.1%	.379	.555	101	0.4
	TB	MLB	27	12 (3)	51²	2-0	0	25	1.45	4.70	44.2%	8.6%	11.3%	4.1%	61.0%	66.5%	92.1%	35.0%	72.3%	.280	.534	109	0.4
Marcus Johnson	CSC	A	22	26 (24)	130	5-6	0	114	1.16	3.74		3.9%	21.3%	2.2%	39.1%					.308	.533	98	1.4
Trevor Kelley	DUR	AAA	30	27 (3)	32²	1-0	2	28	1.50	5.23		7.3%	18.7%	4.7%	48.1%	61.0%	83.1%	33.1%	69.9%	.307	.593	100	0.4
	TB	MLB	30	10 (3)	15¹	0-1	0	11	1.43	5.87	47.2%	8.7%	15.9%	5.8%	34.0%	51.9%	73.2%	36.6%	80.0%	.261	.660	113	0.1
Ian Seymour	RAY	ROK	24	4 (4)	6²	0-0	0	11	1.20	1.35		14.3%	39.3%	0.0%	69.2%					.308	.385		
	CSC	A	24	6 (6)	22	1-0	0	22	0.77	1.64		6.5%	28.6%	1.3%	32.7%					.234	.354	91	0.3
	BG	A+	24	2 (2)	8²	0-0	0	9	1.04	2.08		14.7%	26.5%	2.9%	40.0%					.158	.421	93	
Colby White	RAY	ROK	24	11 (5)	10¹	0-0	0	12	1.35	1.74		28.9%	31.6%	0.0%	46.7%					.200	.200		
	BG	A+	24	5 (0)	5	1-0	0	4	1.20	3.60		10.0%	20.0%	0.0%	42.9%					.286	.429	103	0.0
	MTG	AA	24	8 (0)	6²	0-0	0	8	1.20	0.00		13.8%	27.6%	0.0%	47.1%					.235	.235	91	

Shane Baz missed the entire season recovering from Tommy John surgery. One of the better pitching prospects prior to his injury, he should be good to go in early 2024 and could take a turn in the rotation not long after Opening Day, assuming everything returns intact. ⓦ Hard-throwing southpaw **Garrett Cleavinger** missed most of the season with a torn ACL, but should be ready to go to start 2024. ⓦ **Josh Fleming** kinda stunk for 50+ innings. He'll look to smell better for the Phillies in 2024. ⓦ A former college reliever, the Rays are giving **Marcus Johnson**'s 6-foot-6 frame all the opportunities to prove he belongs in the rotation and not the arm barn. ⓦ **Trevor Kelley** is proof that not every fringe reliever touched by the Rays turns to gold. ⓦ **Andrew Lindsey**'s circuitous path to pro ball included taking a year off in college and later transferring to Tennessee, where he pitched his way into weekend starts. He brings a mid-90s fastball and biting, high-80s slider that provides a major-league ceiling—if he can throw enough strikes, which has been a problem. ⓦ **Ian Seymour** looked very good in his return to the mound following Tommy John surgery. If he repeats this performance, he'll have a full comment in the next year's edition of this book! ⓦ **Colby White** returned to the mound after missing the 2022 season. His advanced age and previous advancement to Durham means he could be a regular on the shuttle to Tropicana Field this year.

TEXAS RANGERS

Essay by Shaker Samman

Player comments by Robert Orr and BP staff

Josh Sborz made two throws. First, the hanging curveball that won the Texas Rangers their first World Series. Then his glove, which he launched into the dirt with enough force it could've permanently embedded in Chase Field.

Do you remember what it felt like? When you close your eyes, can you feel yourself shifting to the edge of your seat, watching the ball arc downward like it was descending from the heavens, freezing Ketel Marte in his place before nestling in Jonah Heim's outstretched glove? That perfect, holy snapshot in time, when Sborz understands what he's done—understands the weight of the moment—and the wait required to get here. And then, the pandemonium.

For 52 years in Texas and 11 before that as the Washington Senators, the franchise was synonymous with failure. It wasn't for lack of trying. Stars like Alex Rodriguez, Rafael Palmeiro and Pudge swept into town, racking up prestige and individual accolades only to spend each October on their couches watching better teams play. It took 36 years for the Rangers to reach the postseason, and 14 more to win a series. Even this time, it nearly all fell apart: Sborz himself earned the win in Game 161, as the team that led the AL West most of the year finally, barely clinched a playoff berth. They reached the postseason gasping like a man who's just received the Heimlich.

Losing festers. It creeps into the walls and the water, poisons the air. It suffocates hope, and swallows excitement, over, and over and over again. Once it gets in, it's almost impossible to get out. At their best, the Rangers were a shave from history, bested by only one team in the 2010 and 2011 seasons—but close isn't good enough, and being runner-up is just a nicer way of saying they were the most exemplary losers. And yet these wheezing, panting Rangers never stopped breathing. Winning a World Series goes beyond the record books. It's a collective sigh of relief; decades of effort validated in an instant. Fans were given proof that the near-constant cycle of heartbreak and unfulfilled hope was worth it, that good things can actually happen to those who wait. It's catharsis on a diamond—the sort of breakthrough that admittedly takes about this long but usually requires an uncomfortable amount of therapy.

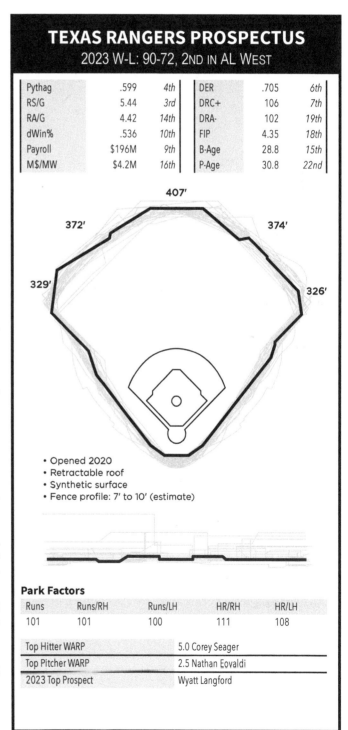

TEXAS RANGERS PROSPECTUS
2023 W-L: 90-72, 2ND IN AL WEST

Pythag	.599	4th	DER	.705	6th
RS/G	5.44	3rd	DRC+	106	7th
RA/G	4.42	14th	DRA-	102	19th
dWin%	.536	10th	FIP	4.35	18th
Payroll	$196M	9th	B-Age	28.8	15th
M$/MW	$4.2M	16th	P-Age	30.8	22nd

407'
372'   374'
329'   326'

- Opened 2020
- Retractable roof
- Synthetic surface
- Fence profile: 7' to 10' (estimate)

Park Factors

Runs	Runs/RH	Runs/LH	HR/RH	HR/LH
101	101	100	111	108

Top Hitter WARP	5.0 Corey Seager
Top Pitcher WARP	2.5 Nathan Eovaldi
2023 Top Prospect	Wyatt Langford

Payroll History (in millions)

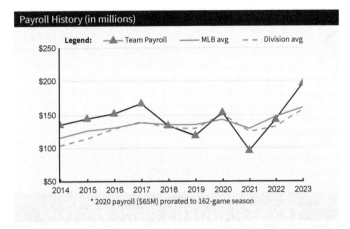

Legend: —▲— Team Payroll ——— MLB avg – – – Division avg

* 2020 payroll ($65M) prorated to 162-game season

Future Commitments (in millions)

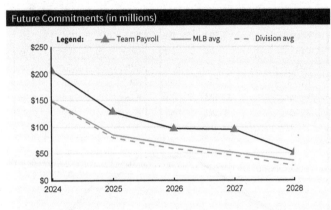

Legend: —▲— Team Payroll ——— MLB avg – – – Division avg

Farm System Ranking

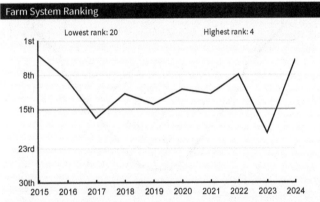

Lowest rank: 20   Highest rank: 4

Personnel

**Executive Vice President &
General Manager**
Chris Young

**Vice President/Assistant
General Manager**
Josh Boyd

**Vice President/Assistant
General Manager**
Ross Fenstermaker

**Senior Director, Research &
Development/Applications**
Daren Willman

Manager
Chris Woodward

In pictures, and videos, and retellings of that night, you can see the pain leave fans and players' bodies. Ghosts swirled and evaporated, visages of David Clyde and Oddibe McDowell and Hank Blalock. Decades of disappointment ejected in an instant; the culmination of a lifetime of work. Work that often seemed pointless and futile; work that left them with half as many seasons with at least 90 wins as it did campaigns with 90 losses.

It was the kind of failure that ate at any remnants of joy, and left those cursed with Rangers fandom with an insatiable hunger for something that would never come. Even respectability was preferable to continued disaster. The first half of the 2010s had delivered just that; the Rangers were always on the cusp of something noteworthy. But those teams gave way to miserable and middling squads trapped in the shadow of their Lone Star State rivals. As the Astros ascended, winning their first World Series in 2017 and then reaching the ALCS the next six seasons, the Rangers floundered. Only the Pirates won fewer games in the pandemic-shortened 2020 season, and only the Diamondbacks and Orioles were worse the year after.

Escaping the treadmill of mediocrity is no small thing, even for teams that experienced recent success. The Detroit Tigers won four AL Central crowns and 336 games from 2011 to 2014, and have only broken .500 once since. The Kansas City Royals won the World Series in 2015—seriously, it happened, I swear—and have had seasons of 97, 103, 104 and 106 in the loss column. The Washington Nationals promptly imploded after reaching the mountaintop in 2019, and the Red Sox, who won it all the year before, have finished four of the past five seasons dead last in the AL East.

Even in a sport where one player can change a team's fortune's overnight, champions aren't built over a single winter. They take planning, patience and also an astounding amount of money. To be fair, that last part wasn't ever Texas' problem. The Rangers haven't ever been strangers to spending—as far as I'm concerned, 252 is a bigger number than 700—but for much of their history, they struggled to spend on the right guys at the right time. A-Rod's Rangers never broke 73 wins. Michael Young didn't make the postseason until he was 33. Palmeiro only saw playoff action once in red and blue, in his second stint with the team. And Mark Teixeira's only taste of October baseball came long after he left the heart of Texas.

It's always darkest before the dawn. The Rangers won 60 games the year before they spent half of a billion dollars on their two infield superstars, Corey Seager and Marcus Semien. They won eight more the next year—moving from fifth in the AL West to fourth, only by the grace of Oakland's unparalleled implosion. It wasn't the sort of improvement that shouts "eventual World Series champions," so much as it seemed to offer a referendum on money in baseball; proof for the peanut gallery that you couldn't buy a winner, despite the fact that others had managed the feat for decades. But the Rangers didn't waver.

They spent more. Like so much more. The Rangers took potential lessons gleaned from the failed A-Rod or Palmeiro seasons, and shoved them in a locker. Then they made it rain cash. They leaned into the skid, handing Jacob deGrom a contract nearly three-times larger than the Civil War cost, and bolstered the pitching staff even further with Nathan Eovaldi, Andrew Heaney and Will Smith. Where others might've balked at what seemed like *more* proof that big contracts just didn't lead to big wins in Dallas, the Rangers took a page from their peers, and said to hell with logic and reason—and signed another check.

There's a version of this story that's centered around the idea of hubris. Where the Rangers once again go all-in and then watch their dreams crumble before them. It's a common scenario, especially in 2023. Both the Mets and the Padres doled out massive deals, and then pressed the eject button en route to disappointing seasons. Given their history, it'd be understandable if, in the wake of an underwhelming 2022 campaign, Texas cut bait with their big signings and trudged down another path, as they did. Instead, they committed to the bit. They spent more money. They chased more talent.

But there's a difference between Texas and those other cautionary tales in New York and San Diego: timing. Both those teams had their depth challenged—because that's exactly what a six-month baseball season is designed to do—and folded under it. The Rangers lost Seager for a time, but Ezequiel Duran filled in. A battered Sam Huff was replaced, and upgraded, by Jonah Heim. Evan Carter became an overnight sensation. It was never just the money. It was also the money.

The Rangers sprinted to an early division lead, and then carried it into the late summer despite failing to encase deGrom in a hyperbaric chamber and then losing him to a season-ending elbow tear. They doubled down again, trading for two aces—Jordan Montgomery and Max Scherzer—essential to surviving a four-way fight for the American League's final three postseason spots. Semien and Seager didn't just make good on their contracts—they came one Shohei Ohtani away from finishing 1-2 in MVP voting.

It didn't matter that they'd lost the division to the Astros, or had seen their 2-0 ALCS lead transform into a 3-2 deficit on the ninth-inning heroics of Jose Altuve, the same way it didn't matter when the Diamondbacks bludgeoned them to knot the World Series after two games. Or that José Leclerc was somehow pitching his 22nd game in 17 postseason contests. When it mattered most, the Rangers just kept winning. It wasn't destiny, so much as that same stubbornness.

"The whole thing just doesn't make a lot of sense," Bochy said after Texas won the Commissioner's Trophy.

He wasn't wrong. One more loss against the Mariners in the regular season's closing days, and the Rangers would've watched the postseason from home. One stray pitch, and the Astros might've knocked them out before the World Series. They thrived in moments with the crowd against them and their backs to the wall, playing 11 games on the road in the playoffs and winning each and every one of them.

That level of resolve is intimidating. Even scarier still: the Rangers could do it all over again. Semien and Seager show no signs of slowing down, Carter and Josh Jung are ascendant, and key contributors like Eovaldi, Adolis García and Dane Dunning are gearing up for a title defense. Wyatt Langford, one of the top prospects in the game, will likely start 2024 in Triple-A, but won't stay there long. At some point in the year, they'll get reinforcements in the form of new signing Tyler Mahle, and both Scherzer and deGrom—two of the defining hurlers of the 21st century. And Bochy, the man who tied it all together, is back, too.

Victory isn't just the end of something; it's also a beginning. There will be more losing seasons—there always are. Heartbreak is closest immediately after a triumph. But unlike in the Before Times, when those failed seasons felt like just another chapter in an endless history of despair, the ones to come will feel different. The long wait is over; the Rangers have nothing left to prove. They won.

—Shaker Samman is a writer and editor in Los Angeles.

HITTERS

─── ★　★　★ *2024 Top 101 Prospect* **#4** ★　★　★ ───

Evan Carter　OF　Born: 08/29/02　Age: 21　Bats: L　Throws: R　Height: 6'2"　Weight: 190　Origin: Round 2, 2020 Draft (#50 overall)

YEAR	TM	LVL	AGE	PA	R	HR	RBI	SB	AVG/OBP/SLG	BABIP	SLGCON	BB%	K%	ZSw%	ZCon%	OSw%	OCon%	LA	90th EV	DRC+	BRR	DRP	WARP
2021	DE	A	18	146	22	2	12	12	.236/.438/.387	.299	.526	23.3%	19.2%							121	-2.0	-4.0	0.4
2022	HIC	A+	19	447	78	11	66	26	.287/.388/.476	.329	.595	13.2%	16.8%							137	-2.1	-0.9	3.1
2022	FRI	AA	19	28	8	1	7	2	.429/.536/.714	.533	1.000	17.9%	21.4%							104	0.2	0.3	0.2
2023	FRI	AA	20	462	68	12	62	22	.284/.411/.451	.360	.620	16.0%	22.3%							118	-1.0	3.2	2.7
2023	RR	AAA	20	39	8	0	3	3	.353/.436/.382	.429	.464	10.3%	15.4%	59.3%	88.6%	22.9%	62.5%			90	1.6	-1.1	0.1
2023	TEX	MLB	20	75	15	5	12	3	.306/.413/.645	.412	1.053	16.0%	32.0%	59.7%	77.9%	14.6%	46.4%	8.7	105.2	93	0.3	1.5	0.3
2024 DC	*TEX*	*MLB*	*21*	*488*	*47*	*9*	*47*	*15*	*.219/.315/.356*	*.279*	*.492*	*11.4%*	*24.0%*							*93*	*0.4*	*7.6*	*1.7*

2023 GP: LF (18), CF (4), RF (2)　　　　　　　　　　　*Comps: Juan Soto (55), Ronald Acuña Jr. (55), Giancarlo Stanton (51)*

Star player goes down, rookie steps in and plays a larger-than-life role in a fairy tale run to a championship. Along the way he displays a superlative, almost supernatural feel for the game and an uncanny ability to rise to the moment. Script of your favorite 90s baseball movie filling air time on MLB Network in November, or the story of Carter's rookie season? It was that kind of a magical ride for the lefty from Elizabethton, Tennessee. He started the season taking ABs for the Frisco RoughRiders in Double-A and ended it hitting third in the clinching game of the World Series as a 21-year-old. That's not to say that everything is roses and sunshine from here; Carter had dramatically worse splits against southpaws at all levels, still hasn't demonstrated a sustainable ability to hit for pop, and will need to do something about the strikeouts he suddenly started racking up after reaching the majors. Those are minor quibbles, though. Carter's Soto-ian sense of the zone and contact skills should be enough to make him an above-average regular for the Rangers going forward.

Ezequiel Duran　UT　Born: 05/22/99　Age: 25　Bats: R　Throws: R　Height: 5'11"　Weight: 185　Origin: IFA, 2017

YEAR	TM	LVL	AGE	PA	R	HR	RBI	SB	AVG/OBP/SLG	BABIP	SLGCON	BB%	K%	ZSw%	ZCon%	OSw%	OCon%	LA	90th EV	DRC+	BRR	DRP	WARP
2021	HIC	A+	22	174	25	7	31	7	.229/.287/.408	.309	.653	6.9%	33.9%							81	-0.9	2.4	0.3
2021	HV	A+	22	297	42	12	48	12	.290/.374/.533	.354	.734	9.4%	23.9%							124	-2.2	5.5	2.0
2022	FRI	AA	23	200	34	7	31	7	.317/.365/.574	.359	.714	7.0%	18.0%							113	0.2	-2.7	0.7
2022	RR	AAA	23	155	18	9	26	7	.283/.316/.531	.337	.755	4.5%	27.7%	68.5%	84.9%	42.2%	63.5%			95	-0.7	-0.6	0.2
2022	TEX	MLB	23	220	25	5	25	4	.236/.277/.365	.295	.494	5.5%	24.5%	72.4%	82.4%	45.0%	60.1%	9.4	105.2	81	0.3	-0.8	0.0
2023	TEX	MLB	24	439	55	14	46	8	.276/.324/.443	.358	.629	5.2%	27.3%	72.2%	83.4%	42.6%	59.0%	13.8	106.6	85	0.3	0.4	0.6
2024 DC	*TEX*	*MLB*	*25*	*376*	*36*	*10*	*41*	*11*	*.235/.288/.383*	*.297*	*.530*	*5.7%*	*25.8%*							*86*	*0.0*	*-0.2*	*0.3*

2023 GP: SS (37), LF (34), 3B (22), DH (21), 2B (9), 1B (2), RF (1)　　*Comps: Eduardo Núñez (60), Yuniesky Betancourt (55), Marcus Semien (52)*

Part of the return for erstwhile face of the franchise Joey Gallo, Duran began to reveal why he was a highly regarded prospect. Stepping in for an injured Corey Seager, he became a pivotal cog in a deep lineup in the first half of the season, then transitioned into a utility role once the Rangers' talisman returned from injury. He didn't play much in the postseason, only making it onto the roster after Adolis García was forced off the World Series squad with an oblique injury, but Duran's midseason contribution is exactly the sort of reinforcement that every aspiring champion needs at some point.

Justin Foscue　2B/3B　Born: 03/02/99　Age: 25　Bats: R　Throws: R　Height: 5'11"　Weight: 205　Origin: Round 1, 2020 Draft (#14 overall)

YEAR	TM	LVL	AGE	PA	R	HR	RBI	SB	AVG/OBP/SLG	BABIP	SLGCON	BB%	K%	ZSw%	ZCon%	OSw%	OCon%	LA	90th EV	DRC+	BRR	DRP	WARP
2021	HIC	A+	22	150	34	14	35	1	.296/.407/.736	.315	1.070	10.7%	26.0%							127	0.7	-0.2	1.0
2021	FRI	AA	22	104	14	2	13	0	.247/.317/.387	.333	.562	7.7%	27.9%							84	-1.6	-0.7	-0.1
2022	FRI	AA	23	460	60	15	81	3	.288/.367/.483	.308	.578	9.8%	14.3%							118	0.3	2.0	2.5
2023	RR	AAA	24	563	94	18	84	14	.266/.394/.468	.279	.551	15.1%	12.4%	59.1%	91.0%	29.1%	71.4%			119	0.6	1.7	2.7
2024 non	*TEX*	*MLB*	*25*	*251*	*25*	*6*	*25*	*3*	*.225/.310/.363*	*.254*	*.448*	*9.3%*	*16.7%*							*92*	*0.0*	*0*	*0.4*

2023 GP: 2B (70), 3B (35), 1B (9), DH (9)　　　　　　　　*Comps: Tony Kemp (72), Nick Solak (70), José Pirela (65)*

Foscue has always been able to rake and just completed a full season at Triple-A where he drew more walks than strikeouts. So what's keeping him down? His problem is twofold: First, the Rangers lineup is absolutely loaded and only getting more difficult to break into. Second—and perhaps more significantly—it's become a challenge to figure out where he can play in the field. With the team's "if-it's-not-broke-don't-fix-it" approach to the offseason and Wyatt Langford also looming in the minors, Foscue may be the one to fix things if one of the team's steady infield contributors breaks down.

Adolis García　RF　Born: 03/02/93　Age: 31　Bats: R　Throws: R　Height: 6'1"　Weight: 205　Origin: IFA, 2017

YEAR	TM	LVL	AGE	PA	R	HR	RBI	SB	AVG/OBP/SLG	BABIP	SLGCON	BB%	K%	ZSw%	ZCon%	OSw%	OCon%	LA	90th EV	DRC+	BRR	DRP	WARP
2021	TEX	MLB	28	622	77	31	90	16	.243/.286/.454	.306	.682	5.1%	31.2%	75.5%	75.5%	39.2%	52.8%	14.8	104.8	90	0.1	1.8	1.6
2022	TEX	MLB	29	657	88	27	101	25	.250/.300/.456	.309	.654	6.1%	27.9%	74.3%	73.9%	40.0%	57.7%	13.5	106.8	103	2.1	0.7	2.5
2023	TEX	MLB	30	632	108	39	107	9	.245/.328/.508	.280	.742	10.3%	27.7%	72.5%	76.8%	32.9%	56.1%	16.2	107.3	124	0.6	0.1	3.6
2024 DC	*TEX*	*MLB*	*31*	*581*	*72*	*29*	*84*	*15*	*.239/.310/.458*	*.286*	*.654*	*8.2%*	*27.4%*							*110*	*0.4*	*0.3*	*2.3*

2023 GP: RF (135), CF (8), DH (7)　　　　　　　　　　*Comps: Nelson Cruz (70), Jayson Werth (64), Dwight Evans (61)*

He faced his close friend Randy Arozarena in the Home Run Derby, then did an homage to Randy by turning October into his personal dinger showcase. García set a new record for RBI in the postseason, but the biggest hit of his season may not have come with the bat: He was plunked by Bryan Abreu in the ALCS' most heated moment, one that seemingly swung the series in the Astros' favor after Jose Altuve's go-ahead ninth-inning homer. García would have the last laugh, however, hitting three homers in Houston to clinch the series and punctuating his postseason with a walkoff opposite-field laser in Game 1 of the World Series. His series was cut short by an oblique injury, but García was unquestionably the face of the 2023 postseason.

Robbie Grossman LF Born: 09/16/89 Age: 34 Bats: S Throws: L Height: 6'0" Weight: 209 Origin: Round 6, 2008 Draft (#174 overall)

YEAR	TM	LVL	AGE	PA	R	HR	RBI	SB	AVG/OBP/SLG	BABIP	SLGCON	BB%	K%	ZSw%	ZCon%	OSw%	OCon%	LA	90th EV	DRC+	BRR	DRP	WARP
2021	DET	MLB	31	671	88	23	67	20	.239/.357/.415	.286	.575	14.6%	23.1%	61.1%	84.9%	21.8%	65.2%	20.8	101.9	106	0.8	1.9	3.0
2022	ATL	MLB	32	157	16	5	22	3	.217/.306/.370	.263	.515	11.5%	24.8%	60.5%	85.4%	26.8%	59.6%	23.7	99.8	83	-0.1	0.6	0.2
2022	DET	MLB	32	320	24	2	23	3	.205/.313/.282	.293	.421	11.9%	28.1%	59.2%	84.2%	25.1%	60.0%	19.9	100.1	85	0.1	1.4	0.6
2023	TEX	MLB	33	420	56	10	49	1	.238/.340/.394	.292	.545	13.6%	23.3%	60.1%	86.6%	20.1%	63.7%	20.5	101.8	83	-0.2	0.0	0.1
2024 non	TEX	MLB	34	251	26	6	25	2	.219/.324/.353	.264	.467	12.4%	20.8%							94	0.0	-0.1	0.5

2023 GP: LF (48), DH (39), RF (28)   Comps: Dave Collins (59), Greg Gross (56), Luis Gonzalez (53)

Among active players with 1000+ plate apps since his debut in 2013, Grossman's 18.6% O-Swing rate is 10th-best, putting him in the midst of plate discipline icons Juan Soto and Joey Votto. Rumor has it his parents couldn't take him to any restaurants as a kid because of how picky he is. However, in an unfortunate victory for nominative determinism, Grossman's DRC+ the last two seasons has been an unsavory 84 and 83, as his quality of contact has not kept up with his discerning eye. That didn't keep manager Bruce Bochy from beginning the postseason with Grossman hitting third in the Rangers order, but his .308 OPS (yes, you read that right) eventually prompted a change and might sour his suitors.

Dustin Harris LF/1B Born: 07/08/99 Age: 24 Bats: L Throws: R Height: 6'3" Weight: 185 Origin: Round 11, 2019 Draft (#344 overall)

YEAR	TM	LVL	AGE	PA	R	HR	RBI	SB	AVG/OBP/SLG	BABIP	SLGCON	BB%	K%	ZSw%	ZCon%	OSw%	OCon%	LA	90th EV	DRC+	BRR	DRP	WARP
2021	DE	A	21	306	54	10	53	20	.301/.389/.483	.329	.592	11.1%	15.7%							130	0.1	1.0	1.9
2021	HIC	A+	21	160	32	10	32	5	.372/.425/.648	.396	.783	8.1%	15.6%							144	-0.6	-2.0	1.0
2022	FRI	AA	22	382	58	17	66	19	.257/.346/.471	.279	.607	11.0%	19.4%							112	-1.1	-3.0	1.3
2023	FRI	AA	23	278	42	5	29	24	.245/.374/.406	.319	.567	15.8%	23.4%							103	3.7	-0.8	1.2
2023	RR	AAA	23	288	47	9	31	17	.273/.382/.455	.331	.615	13.9%	21.9%	70.2%	87.6%	28.8%	57.0%			99	1.4	0.7	0.8
2024 DC	TEX	MLB	24	168	16	3	16	8	.224/.306/.352	.281	.482	9.5%	23.6%							88	0.0	0	0.1

2023 GP: LF (79), 1B (32), DH (17), CF (1)   Comps: Domonic Brown (50), Jake Cave (50), Brandon Jones (50)

On the surface, Harris appears to still be about as productive as expected, looking something like a three-true-outcomes type who can offer some utility on the basepaths and in the corners. Beneath the surface, his star has dimmed a bit. His exit velocities are unexceptional for a prospect expected to hit for legit pop and who pretty much has to in order to shoulder his way into his major-league team's lineup. He was only average in the hitter-friendly PCL, and he's no longer young for the level he's playing at. It's not beyond the realm of reason for Harris to recoup some of the shine that made him one of the Rangers' top prospects as recently as a year ago, but the projections are much less exciting than they used to be.

Jonah Heim C Born: 06/27/95 Age: 29 Bats: S Throws: R Height: 6'4" Weight: 220 Origin: Round 4, 2013 Draft (#129 overall)

YEAR	TM	LVL	AGE	PA	R	HR	RBI	SB	AVG/OBP/SLG	BABIP	SLGCON	BB%	K%	ZSw%	ZCon%	OSw%	OCon%	LA	90th EV	DRC+	BRR	DRP	WARP
2021	TEX	MLB	26	285	22	10	32	3	.196/.239/.358	.210	.459	5.3%	20.4%	73.9%	83.6%	33.6%	70.5%	15.5	104.4	89	-0.1	9.9	1.8
2022	TEX	MLB	27	450	51	16	48	2	.227/.298/.399	.249	.508	9.1%	19.3%	75.2%	86.1%	33.6%	66.6%	17.0	103.4	99	-0.4	8.4	2.4
2023	TEX	MLB	28	501	61	18	95	2	.258/.317/.438	.289	.554	8.0%	19.2%	75.0%	84.3%	34.8%	67.1%	17.4	104.0	110	-0.4	15.9	4.0
2024 DC	TEX	MLB	29	495	53	16	58	1	.239/.308/.401	.270	.508	8.5%	19.1%							97	-0.5	11.6	2.9

2023 GP: C (124), DH (7)

Comps: Steve Clevenger (62), Travis d'Arnaud (61), Michael McKenry (61)

Long considered one of the game's premier defensive backstops, Heim improved his skills with the stick for the third consecutive season, earning himself an All-Star selection in the process. His 4.3 WARP tied him with Cal Raleigh for second among catchers, and his 95 RBI were 15 more than any other backstop managed to rack up. If he continues improving at this rate, he'll be an MVP candidate in 2024 and a no-doubt Hall of Famer by 2030, enshrined under the moniker of "Jonah Him." Failing all of that, Rangers fans would just be happy with a repeat of his terrific 2023.

YEAR	TM	P. COUNT	FRM RUNS	BLK RUNS	THRW RUNS	TOT RUNS
2021	TEX	10395	11.3	-0.4	0.4	11.2
2022	TEX	14678	12.2	-0.2	-0.8	11.2
2023	TEX	16067	15.2	-0.1	2.1	17.2
2024	TEX	16835	10.0	-0.4	2.0	11.7

Sam Huff C Born: 01/14/98 Age: 26 Bats: R Throws: R Height: 6'4" Weight: 240 Origin: Round 7, 2016 Draft (#219 overall)

YEAR	TM	LVL	AGE	PA	R	HR	RBI	SB	AVG/OBP/SLG	BABIP	SLGCON	BB%	K%	ZSw%	ZCon%	OSw%	OCon%	LA	90th EV	DRC+	BRR	DRP	WARP
2021	FRI	AA	23	191	24	10	23	0	.237/.309/.439	.360	.792	8.4%	40.3%							70	-0.1	-0.8	-0.3
2022	RR	AAA	24	274	46	21	50	0	.260/.336/.533	.307	.814	9.1%	31.0%	70.0%	80.3%	36.7%	46.9%			110	-1.7	3.5	1.3
2022	TEX	MLB	24	132	9	4	10	1	.240/.303/.372	.333	.570	8.3%	31.8%	75.8%	76.9%	39.1%	41.7%	10.0	107.6	74	-0.1	-0.3	0.0
2023	RR	AAA	25	321	48	17	67	0	.298/.399/.548	.358	.768	13.7%	24.3%	69.6%	83.4%	32.9%	48.1%			111	-1.0	3.1	1.6
2023	TEX	MLB	25	45	5	3	6	0	.256/.289/.512	.348	.846	4.4%	37.8%	74.2%	75.5%	44.9%	31.8%	5.8	108.0	84	0.0	-0.2	0.0
2024 DC	TEX	MLB	26	218	24	8	27	0	.228/.299/.402	.306	.615	8.2%	31.8%							94	0.0	-1.5	0.4

2023 GP: C (10), DH (9), 1B (4)   Comps: Michael Barrett (52), Nick Hundley (50), Nick Evans (49)

In 2021, the pecking order at catcher for the Rangers was supposed to be Huff #1, Jose Trevino #2 and Jonah Heim #3. Huff hurt his knee and couldn't catch at all that year—even in the minors—and got permanently bypassed on the depth chart. Fast forwarding to 2024, Trevino is long gone and so is Mitch Garver, which finally gives the out-of-options Huff a clear path to sticking around in Texas all year. Ignore those 45 plate appearances he had for the Rangers last season—his plate discipline improved in Triple-A. Sure, he was repeating the level, but striking out less and walking more is always a positive sign. Since he frames and blocks pitches with all the finesse of a bulldozer, he needs to squeeze every drop of

YEAR	TM	P. COUNT	FRM RUNS	BLK RUNS	THRW RUNS	TOT RUNS
2022	RR	6770	3.3	-0.5	0.4	3.1
2022	TEX	3846	0.5	-0.2	-0.1	0.2
2023	RR	9060	0.4	0.1	1.4	1.9
2023	TEX	663	-0.2	0.0	0.0	-0.2
2024	TEX	4810	-1.5	0.0	-0.1	-1.6

value he can get out of his bat. He's unlikely to overtake Heim, who's now an All-Star and Gold Glover, for playing time, but the backup gig is his for the taking.

Josh Jung   3B   Born: 02/12/98   Age: 26   Bats: R   Throws: R   Height: 6'2"   Weight: 214   Origin: Round 1, 2019 Draft (#8 overall)

YEAR	TM	LVL	AGE	PA	R	HR	RBI	SB	AVG/OBP/SLG	BABIP	SLGCON	BB%	K%	ZSw%	ZCon%	OSw%	OCon%	LA	90th EV	DRC+	BRR	DRP	WARP
2021	FRI	AA	23	186	25	10	40	2	.308/.366/.544	.356	.724	7.0%	22.6%							114	-1.9	0.2	0.7
2021	RR	AAA	23	156	29	9	21	0	.348/.436/.652	.413	.871	11.5%	21.8%							125	-0.4	1.3	1.1
2022	RAN	ROK	24	29	4	3	5	0	.240/.345/.600	.176	.750	10.3%	17.2%										
2022	RR	AAA	24	106	15	6	24	1	.273/.321/.525	.333	.754	3.8%	28.3%	69.6%	80.7%	38.1%	56.2%			97	-0.2	-0.2	0.2
2022	TEX	MLB	24	102	9	5	14	2	.204/.235/.418	.278	.695	3.9%	38.2%	65.4%	83.0%	35.0%	54.2%	14.5	103.6	62	-0.1	-0.1	-0.3
2023	TEX	MLB	25	515	75	23	70	1	.266/.315/.467	.340	.682	5.8%	29.3%	72.5%	82.0%	37.2%	54.3%	15.3	105.3	99	-0.5	4.6	2.0
2024 DC	TEX	MLB	26	567	61	21	70	4	.235/.291/.410	.297	.585	6.0%	27.9%							93	-0.4	4.7	1.5

2023 GP: 3B (121)   Comps: Chris Johnson (75), Matt Chapman (74), Juan Francisco (73)

Jung got off to a scalding start to his rookie season, filling an archetype popular in the modern game: lots of power and lots of Ks. He had 19 HR and a .504 SLG at the All-Star Break, earning him a seat in the festivities, but his season went off the rails shortly after that. His OPS was just .638 down the stretch, and his already elevated strikeout rate of 28% in the first half sneaked its way to 32%. You don't need to be a psychoanalyst to figure out why: he suffered a fractured thumb in his top hand that required surgery to fix and limited him to just 140 trips to the plate after the break, effectively knocking him out of the AL Rookie of the Year race. It wasn't all lost for Jung, however; when he sits down and reviews 2023, he'll have Memories, Dreams, and Reflections of a mostly encouraging debut and a promising future as a middle-of-the-order bopper for an annual contender.

★ ★ ★ *2024 Top 101 Prospect* **#2** ★ ★ ★

Wyatt Langford   LF/DH   Born: 11/15/01   Age: 22   Bats: R   Throws: R   Height: 6'1"   Weight: 225   Origin: Round 1, 2023 Draft (#4 overall)

YEAR	TM	LVL	AGE	PA	R	HR	RBI	SB	AVG/OBP/SLG	BABIP	SLGCON	BB%	K%	ZSw%	ZCon%	OSw%	OCon%	LA	90th EV	DRC+	BRR	DRP	WARP
2023	HIC	A+	21	106	22	5	15	7	.333/.453/.644	.375	.812	17.0%	17.0%							127	0.5	0.0	0.6
2023	FRI	AA	21	54	7	4	10	1	.405/.519/.762	.406	.914	20.4%	13.0%							130	-1.1	0.9	0.2
2023	RR	AAA	21	26	4	0	1	3	.368/.538/.526	.538	.769	23.1%	23.1%	56.2%	88.9%	19.2%	80.0%			87	0.3		
2024 DC	TEX	MLB	22	337	34	7	34	11	.234/.317/.365	.274	.464	9.9%	18.8%							95	0.0	0	0.5

2023 GP: LF (30), DH (12), CF (2)   Comps: Eloy Jiménez (70), Lewis Brinson (61), Luis Robert Jr. (60)

Today's baseball vocabulary test: Define "meteoric" and use it in a sentence.

Meteoric: Resembling a meteor in speed or in sudden and temporary brilliance. Langford enjoyed a meteoric ascent to the top of prospect lists during the 2023 season.

No longer viewed as the consolation prize for the teams that missed out on LSU's Dylan Crews or Paul Skenes, the outfielder from Gainesville, FL went from playing in the College World Series in June to being in serious contention for MLB's Fall Classic as an injury replacement for Adolis García four short months later. After the Rangers snapped him up with the fourth pick in the draft, Langford went on to lay waste to four different levels in the minors in the months that followed, flashing every tool you could ever want from a young hitter. He has elite power, speed and swing decisions at just 21 years old. Barring something completely unexpected, one of the most dangerous offenses in the league will add perhaps the best hitting prospect in baseball to their lineup sometime early in 2024. Then we'll discover which half of the definition of meteoric applies here: Has he rapidly accelerated into a blossoming superstar, or is his brilliance sudden and temporary?

Nathaniel Lowe   1B   Born: 07/07/95   Age: 29   Bats: L   Throws: R   Height: 6'4"   Weight: 220   Origin: Round 13, 2016 Draft (#390 overall)

YEAR	TM	LVL	AGE	PA	R	HR	RBI	SB	AVG/OBP/SLG	BABIP	SLGCON	BB%	K%	ZSw%	ZCon%	OSw%	OCon%	LA	90th EV	DRC+	BRR	DRP	WARP
2021	TEX	MLB	25	642	75	18	72	8	.264/.357/.415	.339	.585	12.5%	25.2%	68.9%	83.2%	26.9%	63.8%	5.2	106.3	101	0.0	0.4	1.5
2022	TEX	MLB	26	645	74	27	76	2	.302/.358/.492	.363	.655	7.4%	22.8%	75.4%	83.1%	34.1%	61.4%	8.5	106.7	120	-0.9	-1.9	2.6
2023	TEX	MLB	27	724	89	17	82	1	.262/.360/.414	.329	.563	12.8%	22.8%	69.3%	87.8%	25.6%	63.2%	7.5	106.1	103	-0.9	0.9	1.8
2024 DC	TEX	MLB	28	616	70	17	70	0	.255/.346/.408	.302	.529	11.7%	20.2%							115	0.0	-0.3	2.3

2023 GP: 1B (161)   Comps: Eric Hosmer (80), Chris Chambliss (78), Brandon Belt (76)

Long a player thought to hit the ball on the ground too much ... too Lowe, if you will (I'm sorry), Lowe seemingly learned how to elevate in his breakout 2022, smashing 27 long balls in a career-best season. Unfortunately, he regressed to his pre-2022 production last year—still above-average, but nowhere near as potent a slugger—but it wasn't because he had returned to his worm-killing ways. Instead, Lowe's roller-coaster power seems to be tied to how aggressive he is. Over the last three seasons, when he's been more patient than the league average, he's been a credible on-base machine without much pop, drawing walks at a 12% or better clip. When he has swung the bat more aggressively—both in and out of the zone—his walk rate dipped but he hit the aforementioned career-high in home runs on his way to a near .500 slugging percentage. Entering year four as an everyday starter, we still aren't sure which version is the *real* Lowe; is he the cog that keeps a lineup ticking over and posts every day at first but doesn't supply much pop, or is he the corner bat capable of carrying a lineup for stretches at a time with extra-base hits?

Abimelec Ortiz 1B   Born: 02/22/02   Age: 22   Bats: L   Throws: L   Height: 6'0"   Weight: 230   Origin: Undrafted Free Agent, 2021

YEAR	TM	LVL	AGE	PA	R	HR	RBI	SB	AVG/OBP/SLG	BABIP	SLGCON	BB%	K%	ZSw%	ZCon%	OSw%	OCon%	LA	90th EV	DRC+	BRR	DRP	WARP
2021	DSL RGR1	ROK	19	172	33	11	33	5	.233/.419/.581	.216	.765	19.2%	18.0%										3.6
2022	DE	A	20	331	37	11	39	6	.226/.308/.380	.288	.558	9.7%	28.1%							97	-1.7	3.0	1.2
2023	DE	A	21	121	19	7	20	0	.307/.392/.604	.393	.938	13.2%	29.8%							132	-1.4	-1.6	0.4
2023	HIC	A+	21	333	59	26	81	1	.290/.363/.624	.322	.905	9.9%	27.0%							124	0.4	2.6	2.2
2024 non	TEX	MLB	22	251	24	7	27	0	.223/.283/.373	.309	.573	7.0%	32.2%							82	0.0	0	-0.1

2023 GP: 1B (89), DH (18), RF (15)   *Comps: Mike Ford (69), Dustin Harris (64), Mike McDade (62)*

Ortiz's transaction log is...odd, to say the least. A Puerto Rican native, he went to the Carlos Beltrán Baseball Academy—New Yorkers may remember that as the project Beltrán skipped a visit to Walter Reed Army Medical Center to work on, spawning a huge local controversy (Beltrán would later win the Roberto Clemente Award for his work to revive Puerto Rican youth baseball and other charitable efforts)—and then matriculated stateside at Florida Southwestern State, a junior college with a pipeline from Beltrán's high school. Ortiz wasn't drafted in 2021 after a solid freshman season and signed as an undrafted free agent with Texas, which is normal enough, but the playing time the organization had for him was in the Dominican Summer League, somewhere players coming out of domestic high schools and colleges basically never go. He jumped straight from the DSL to Low-A in 2022 and was overmatched, and basically nothing as of last offseason indicated Ortiz was on the track to ever getting a comment in this book series. Except then he shortened up his swing and walloped 33 homers between the A-ball levels as one of the top breakout prospects across the minors, an emergence that continued in the Arizona Fall League. Ortiz is a real prospect now, albeit one still limited defensively and with some contact concerns.

Corey Seager SS   Born: 04/27/94   Age: 30   Bats: L   Throws: R   Height: 6'4"   Weight: 215   Origin: Round 1, 2012 Draft (#18 overall)

YEAR	TM	LVL	AGE	PA	R	HR	RBI	SB	AVG/OBP/SLG	BABIP	SLGCON	BB%	K%	ZSw%	ZCon%	OSw%	OCon%	LA	90th EV	DRC+	BRR	DRP	WARP
2021	LAD	MLB	27	409	54	16	57	1	.306/.394/.521	.336	.641	11.7%	16.1%	84.2%	84.7%	33.2%	50.9%	10.9	106.4	136	-0.3	0.4	3.4
2022	TEX	MLB	28	663	91	33	83	3	.245/.317/.455	.242	.551	8.7%	15.5%	82.7%	88.1%	35.8%	50.8%	13.9	105.8	131	-0.4	-0.8	4.5
2023	TEX	MLB	29	536	88	33	96	2	.327/.390/.623	.340	.763	9.1%	16.4%	85.9%	89.6%	35.7%	53.0%	13.1	107.4	150	-0.6	-1.1	5.0
2024 DC	TEX	MLB	30	577	77	28	86	0	.281/.357/.502	.303	.623	9.6%	17.5%							138	-0.5	-1.1	4.7

2023 GP: SS (112), DH (7)   *Comps: Arky Vaughan (79), Joe Sewell (76), José Reyes (74)*

There are certain colloquialisms unique to baseball that transcend the simple diction of the English language and tap into the romanticism deeper within the sport. When we say "smooth fielder" or "powerful slugger" certain actions emerge from the description before you even watch them play, and a certain nuance emerges beyond the words themselves. Otherwise innocuous terms can damn with faint praise or sell the reader or listener on rare skill. The term "pure hitter" is one of those phrases, and it is truly just about the highest compliment a batter can receive. Describing what it really means to call somebody that is a tall order, since it involves each part of hitting, but transcends those parts individually. To paraphrase Supreme Court Justice Potter Stewart: you know one when you see one. The names associated with "pure hitter" are spoken with reverence: Ichiro. Gwynn. Williams.

Now on the exclusive list of two-time World Series MVPs and last year's runner-up to Shohei Ohtani in the American League MVP voting, can we begin to reserve Seager's place in that rarefied air? Just two seasons into his decade-long contract, he's already delivered more than could've been hoped for; everything the Rangers get from here is just myth-making. What will he do for an encore? Are we watching a Hall-of-Fame career? One thing is certain though: the next time somebody asks you what a pure hitter is, you can point to Seager.

Marcus Semien 2B   Born: 09/17/90   Age: 33   Bats: R   Throws: R   Height: 6'0"   Weight: 195   Origin: Round 6, 2011 Draft (#201 overall)

YEAR	TM	LVL	AGE	PA	R	HR	RBI	SB	AVG/OBP/SLG	BABIP	SLGCON	BB%	K%	ZSw%	ZCon%	OSw%	OCon%	LA	90th EV	DRC+	BRR	DRP	WARP
2021	TOR	MLB	30	724	115	45	102	15	.265/.334/.538	.276	.694	9.1%	20.2%	71.3%	87.9%	26.3%	60.1%	20.7	103.0	106	0.5	0.0	3.3
2022	TEX	MLB	31	724	101	26	83	25	.248/.304/.429	.263	.525	7.3%	16.6%	74.2%	88.5%	28.0%	62.4%	20.2	101.6	104	1.2	4.1	3.2
2023	TEX	MLB	32	753	122	29	100	14	.276/.348/.478	.291	.571	9.6%	14.6%	75.7%	89.6%	25.6%	65.3%	19.3	102.2	113	1.1	4.2	4.0
2024 DC	TEX	MLB	33	663	78	26	87	15	.257/.327/.443	.271	.532	8.9%	15.1%							114	0.4	4.2	3.6

2023 GP: 2B (162)   *Comps: Asdrúbal Cabrera (70), Barry Larkin (68), Alan Trammell (67)*

Sixty seconds in a minute. Sixty minutes in an hour. Twenty-four hours in a day. Three hundred sixty-five days in a year. 2+2=4. The persistence of sales calls. Leadoff walks. Taxes. Inflation. Leadoff doubles. The rising of the sun in the east. The setting of the sun in the west. Wallscrapers pulled just inside the foul pole. Rain in May. That little tickle in your nose after that rain when the pollen is thick in the air. The fall of leaves in September. Traffic at 9 AM. Seven hundred trips to the plate. Traffic at 5 PM. The smell at the gas pump. School buses. Every routine grounder gobbled up at second. Sand everywhere after a day at the beach. The interminable passage of time. Marcus Semien.

Josh H. Smith SS   Born: 08/07/97   Age: 26   Bats: L   Throws: R   Height: 5'10"   Weight: 172   Origin: Round 2, 2019 Draft (#67 overall)

YEAR	TM	LVL	AGE	PA	R	HR	RBI	SB	AVG/OBP/SLG	BABIP	SLGCON	BB%	K%	ZSw%	ZCon%	OSw%	OCon%	LA	90th EV	DRC+	BRR	DRP	WARP
2021	TAM	A	23	50	15	6	15	5	.333/.480/.795	.259	.939	14.0%	12.0%	56.2%	85.4%	23.0%	89.7%			138	1.1	-0.4	0.4
2021	HIC	A+	23	49	10	1	7	2	.295/.367/.432	.353	.543	4.1%	18.4%							105	-0.1	1.0	0.3
2021	HV	A+	23	125	29	3	9	12	.320/.435/.583	.411	.789	12.8%	21.6%							109	-0.3	3.6	0.8
2021	FRI	AA	23	127	12	3	10	7	.294/.425/.431	.338	.537	14.2%	15.7%							124	-0.1	-1.8	0.6
2022	RR	AAA	24	261	45	6	45	9	.290/.395/.466	.358	.617	12.6%	20.7%	60.5%	85.5%	26.1%	69.8%			112	0.1	-2.0	1.0
2022	TEX	MLB	24	253	23	2	16	4	.197/.307/.249	.244	.325	11.1%	19.8%	63.6%	85.7%	25.2%	60.4%	18.2	99.7	90	0.1	0.7	0.5
2023	TEX	MLB	25	232	29	6	15	1	.185/.304/.328	.222	.457	10.8%	23.7%	61.6%	88.1%	28.4%	64.2%	12.4	105.3	91	0.1	0.2	0.5
2024 DC	TEX	MLB	26	157	15	3	15	4	.219/.316/.339	.261	.443	9.7%	19.6%							89	0.1	0.1	0.3

2023 GP: SS (33), 3B (25), LF (20), DH (8), 2B (3)   *Comps: Tony Kemp (62), Cord Phelps (59), Luis Valbuena (59)*

Handy. Hustle. Hearty. Heady. Any of these could be what the "H." in Smith's name stands for; the man with the most anonymous name in baseball occupies an equally anonymous role, filling in as the versatile glove at the end of the bench capable of playing nearly anywhere. Unfortunately for him, it's never likely to stand for "hard-hitting" as the utility man's career ISO is below .100, and he has yet to hit above the Mendoza line at the highest level. Still, a strong sense of the zone and the ability to stand basically anywhere—he started games at shortstop, third base, second base, and the outfield in 2023—make him a useful bit of depth for just about any club. Helpful, indeed.

Leody Taveras CF Born: 09/08/98 Age: 25 Bats: S Throws: R Height: 6'2" Weight: 195 Origin: IFA, 2015

YEAR	TM	LVL	AGE	PA	R	HR	RBI	SB	AVG/OBP/SLG	BABIP	SLGCON	BB%	K%	ZSw%	ZCon%	OSw%	OCon%	LA	90th EV	DRC+	BRR	DRP	WARP
2021	AGU	WIN	22	175	27	2	19	11	.274/.379/.363	.309	.431	13.7%	13.1%										
2021	RR	AAA	22	381	57	17	55	13	.245/.343/.475	.287	.674	12.9%	24.9%							98	1.2	7.9	2.1
2021	TEX	MLB	22	185	14	3	9	10	.161/.207/.270	.225	.412	4.9%	32.4%	68.5%	77.5%	31.4%	65.6%	5.4	103.1	60	0.3	2.4	0.1
2022	RR	AAA	23	221	34	7	29	7	.294/.335/.485	.349	.635	6.3%	21.7%	68.9%	87.2%	36.9%	66.1%			99	-0.2	-1.9	0.5
2022	TEX	MLB	23	341	39	5	34	11	.261/.309/.366	.344	.509	6.2%	25.8%	67.4%	82.4%	33.3%	53.9%	10.5	103.9	87	0.5	3.3	1.1
2023	TEX	MLB	24	554	67	14	67	14	.266/.312/.421	.318	.546	6.3%	21.1%	70.7%	86.4%	33.0%	58.5%	10.0	105.4	92	0.7	2.2	1.8
2024 DC	TEX	MLB	25	499	48	12	52	14	.241/.298/.378	.293	.497	7.0%	22.2%							89	0.6	3.7	1.5

2023 GP: CF (140), DH (2) *Comps: Byron Buxton (63), Carlos Gómez (52), Melky Cabrera (52)*

"Player development isn't linear" is a maxim that Taveras has done his very best to disprove over the long arc of his early career. A touted prospect dating back to 2018, his has been a journey of stops and starts with a steady march towards competence, culminating in a 2023 season that saw him make incremental gains in enough areas to finally realize his potential as a solid major leaguer. He walked more, struck out less, hit for more power, stole more bases and amassed a career-high tally in games played and plate appearances, all while playing his typically stellar center field. On a team with no shortage of starpower, his brand of yeoman's work in the field and on the bases is especially important, and he emerged as the ultimate role player in 2023—even homering off Justin Verlander in the ALCS.

★ ★ ★ *2024 Top 101 Prospect* **#75** ★ ★ ★

Sebastian Walcott DH Born: 03/14/06 Age: 18 Bats: R Throws: R Height: 6'4" Weight: 190 Origin: IFA, 2023

YEAR	TM	LVL	AGE	PA	R	HR	RBI	SB	AVG/OBP/SLG	BABIP	SLGCON	BB%	K%	ZSw%	ZCon%	OSw%	OCon%	LA	90th EV	DRC+	BRR	DRP	WARP
2023	DSL RNGB	ROK	17	42	4	0	3	3	.161/.381/.323	.217	.435	23.8%	19.0%										
2023	RAN	ROK	17	157	26	7	19	9	.273/.325/.524	.368	.815	6.4%	32.5%										
2024 non	TEX	MLB	18	251	18	2	19	0	.205/.258/.290	.305	.447	5.8%	32.8%							55	0.0	0	-0.7

2023 GP: DH (25), SS (23)

If Walcott were American, he wouldn't even be eligible for the draft until this upcoming season, but the Bahamian blew through the DSL in a couple weeks last summer on his way to flashing huge power as the youngest player at the domestic complex level. He hits the ball harder than any player in his age cohort, and with another half-decade or so of growth he projects out to be a true impact thumper way down the road. Everything else in his profile is a bit up for grabs; he's very aggressive at the plate and prone to chase and contact issues. Defensively, he's a shortstop for now, but everyone's a shortstop at his age, and he could certainly grow off the position. Walcott is one of the highest upside prospects in the game given his rare pop at such a young age, yet so much remains unknown.

PITCHERS

Grant Anderson RHP Born: 06/21/97 Age: 27 Height: 6'0" Weight: 180 Origin: Round 21, 2018 Draft (#628 overall)

YEAR	TM	LVL	AGE	G(GS)	IP	W-L	SV	K	WHIP	ERA	CSP	BB%	K%	HR%	GB%	ZSw%	ZCon%	OSw%	OCon%	BABIP	SLGCON	DRA-	WARP
2021	HIC	A+	24	15(0)	27¹	0-3	3	35	1.32	4.61		11.9%	29.7%	2.5%	58.8%					.297	.567	86	0.4
2021	FRI	AA	24	20(0)	27¹	2-1	0	26	1.72	6.91		11.4%	19.7%	3.8%	40.2%					.329	.659	103	0.1
2022	FRI	AA	25	39(0)	54²	5-0	6	75	1.19	2.80		6.8%	32.1%	2.6%	38.4%					.328	.569	77	1.0
2022	RR	AAA	25	8(0)	12²	0-0	0	16	1.66	6.39		8.8%	28.1%	3.5%	50.0%	56.5%	88.5%	29.3%	59.0%	.412	.694	87	0.2
2023	FRI	AA	26	4(0)	6²	1-0	0	9	1.05	2.70		3.6%	32.1%	7.1%	23.5%					.267	.824	95	0.1
2023	RR	AAA	26	21(2)	34	3-1	1	54	1.18	3.71		9.9%	38.3%	3.5%	50.7%	63.5%	73.8%	37.8%	55.5%	.328	.731	57	0.8
2023	TEX	MLB	26	26(0)	35²	2-1	0	30	1.46	5.05	49.6%	9.1%	19.5%	3.2%	45.9%	61.0%	87.7%	30.0%	63.0%	.317	.551	96	0.5
2024 DC	TEX	MLB	27	44(0)	47	3-2	0	43	1.29	4.14	49.6%	9.3%	21.5%	3.1%	44.3%					.277	.511	94	0.4

2023 Arsenal: SL (85.2), SI (92.9), FA (93), CH (86.8) *Comps: Tyler Kinley (62), Evan Reed (62), Colton Murray (62)*

As a somewhat anonymous, older rookie reliever out of McNeese State, Anderson made quite the first impression in his debut. The righty with the high leg kick and low arm slot punched out seven of the nine Tigers he faced, tossing 2 ⅔ scoreless innings and picking up the W in his first game as a big leaguer. Unfortunately, that proved to be the highlight of his season; he hung around for three months, but eventually the walks started outnumbering the strikeouts two-to-one, and the Rangers cut bait and let him drift back to Round Rock.

Cody Bradford LHP Born: 02/22/98 Age: 26 Height: 6'4" Weight: 197 Origin: Round 6, 2019 Draft (#175 overall)

YEAR	TM	LVL	AGE	G (GS)	IP	W-L	SV	K	WHIP	ERA	CSP	BB%	K%	HR%	GB%	ZSw%	ZCon%	OSw%	OCon%	BABIP	SLGCON	DRA-	WARP
2021	HIC	A+	23	13(13)	61²	4-4	0	87	1.17	4.23		6.5%	33.2%	3.4%	31.0%					.315	.645	104	0.4
2021	FRI	AA	23	7(7)	34²	2-0	0	41	1.30	3.89		2.7%	28.1%	0.7%	41.0%					.404	.525	103	0.2
2022	FRI	AA	24	26(26)	118²	10-7	0	124	1.24	5.01		6.6%	24.7%	3.6%	35.0%					.298	.585	89	1.3
2023	RR	AAA	25	14(14)	74¹	9-2	0	65	1.17	3.63		5.2%	21.3%	2.0%	31.1%	72.0%	81.8%	34.2%	61.4%	.301	.471	101	0.5
2023	TEX	MLB	25	20(8)	56	4-3	0	51	1.21	5.30	49.9%	5.1%	21.8%	4.7%	32.9%	68.9%	83.9%	32.8%	67.8%	.285	.655	113	0.3
2024 DC	TEX	MLB	26	26(11)	66¹	3-4	0	52	1.31	4.58	49.9%	6.5%	18.4%	3.7%	32.6%					.294	.557	104	0.3

2023 Arsenal: FA (90.4), CH (82.1), FC (86.3), SL (82.4)   Comps: Logan Darnell (69), Brooks Raley (66), Michael King (65)

Bradford was the pitching embodiment of the It's so over/We're so back trope that pervades whatever Twitter's called today. Being optioned three times: it's so over. But being called up four times? We're so back. The final time he was called up, he stayed up and made it onto Texas' postseason roster. After yeoman's work as an emergency depth starter in the regular season, the lanky lefty put together a strong postseason that included zero walks and only four baserunners in 7 ⅔ innings as the long man out of the pen. Bradford is a typical command lefty with a funky delivery, and because he doesn't have the pure stuff to overwhelm hitters, the ERA estimators and peripherals have never bought what he's selling. He'll never be an ace, but his ability to work quickly and chew up innings for the Rangers makes him a valuable member of their staff, and likely guarantees him a place on the major-league roster in 2024. We're so back.

Brock Burke LHP Born: 08/04/96 Age: 27 Height: 6'4" Weight: 210 Origin: Round 3, 2014 Draft (#96 overall)

YEAR	TM	LVL	AGE	G (GS)	IP	W-L	SV	K	WHIP	ERA	CSP	BB%	K%	HR%	GB%	ZSw%	ZCon%	OSw%	OCon%	BABIP	SLGCON	DRA-	WARP
2021	RR	AAA	24	21(20)	77²	1-5	0	97	1.38	5.68		9.2%	28.9%	3.9%	42.2%					.330	.650	86	1.1
2022	TEX	MLB	25	52(0)	82¹	7-5	0	90	1.06	1.97	53.5%	7.3%	27.4%	2.7%	37.7%	69.4%	81.5%	30.4%	64.9%	.271	.510	86	1.4
2023	TEX	MLB	26	53(0)	59²	5-3	0	52	1.22	4.37	52.2%	3.6%	20.8%	5.2%	38.0%	78.2%	81.6%	36.7%	70.1%	.295	.603	101	0.7
2024 DC	TEX	MLB	27	61(0)	64²	4-3	0	55	1.32	4.51	52.7%	7.2%	19.7%	3.4%	39.0%					.297	.545	102	0.2

2023 Arsenal: FA (94.8), SL (87.1), CH (88.2), SI (93)   Comps: Lucas Sims (63), Cody Reed (61), Robert Gsellman (58)

Last year in this space, we pointed out how improbable Burke's dominance was in the 2022 season. The 2023 campaign was much more in line with what we expected from him, coming in at exactly league-average by DRA-. There's nothing wrong with that! Burke fills a valuable role in the structure of a modern bullpen as the lower-leverage lefty who can also deal with right-handed hitters competently and pitch multiple innings at a time. What makes the variation in Burke's last two years particularly interesting is just how little actually changed: He threw his fastball over 60% of the time, turning to the slider for around 20% of offerings with changeups to righties comprised the rest of his arsenal. It's just that hitters slugged in the .300s against all three of those pitches in 2022 and in the .400s in 2023. The truth probably lies somewhere in between those extremes, but in the meantime Burke can continue to come in, walk absolutely nobody—he improved his walk rate to 3.6%, putting him in the 99th percentile of pitchers—and plug along as the quietly competent long man in the Rangers' bullpen.

Jacob deGrom RHP Born: 06/19/88 Age: 36 Height: 6'4" Weight: 180 Origin: Round 9, 2010 Draft (#272 overall)

YEAR	TM	LVL	AGE	G (GS)	IP	W-L	SV	K	WHIP	ERA	CSP	BB%	K%	HR%	GB%	ZSw%	ZCon%	OSw%	OCon%	BABIP	SLGCON	DRA-	WARP
2021	NYM	MLB	33	15(15)	92	7-2	0	146	0.55	1.08	45.6%	3.4%	45.1%	1.9%	44.6%	74.3%	75.2%	43.7%	40.7%	.213	.457	52	3.2
2022	SYR	AAA	34	2(2)	8	0-1	0	10	1.00	4.50		12.9%	32.3%	6.5%	23.5%					.133	.647	93	0.1
2022	NYM	MLB	34	11(11)	64¹	5-4	0	102	0.75	3.08	49.7%	3.3%	42.7%	3.8%	38.8%	73.9%	71.7%	41.9%	42.7%	.261	.583	61	1.9
2023	TEX	MLB	35	6(6)	30¹	2-0	0	45	0.76	2.67	41.1%	3.5%	39.1%	1.7%	37.9%	69.8%	72.1%	41.4%	44.6%	.266	.545	79	0.7
2024 DC	TEX	MLB	36	8(8)	42²	3-2	0	62	0.95	2.36	45.8%	5.6%	36.8%	3.5%	40.2%					.286	.589	62	1.2

2023 Arsenal: FA (99.2), SL (92.4), CH (92), CU (84.9)   Comps: Bob Gibson (87), Tom Seaver (86), Max Scherzer (84)

When the Rangers inked deGrom to his $185 million deal in the winter of 2022, the contract was notable for just how many provisions were included concerning the state of his right elbow. Those clauses quickly proved prescient, as the two-time Cy Young award winner only managed six starts for Texas before suffering from the all-too-familiar forearm tightness that inevitably leads to Tommy John surgery. He's seemingly been headed for this fate for years now, with his last "full" season coming during the pandemic-shortened 2020 season. The fact he's been able to pitch to a 2.03 ERA and amass 293 strikeouts in 186 innings across three partial seasons since, while constantly battling the mortal limitations of his own right arm, underscores just how obscenely dominant deGrom is still capable of being when he is able to take the mound. The next time he does will likely have to wait until late 2024—if it's next season, at all—but with any luck we'll get to watch a more sustained run of starts from deGrom when he does return.

Dane Dunning RHP Born: 12/20/94 Age: 29 Height: 6'4" Weight: 225 Origin: Round 1, 2016 Draft (#29 overall)

YEAR	TM	LVL	AGE	G (GS)	IP	W-L	SV	K	WHIP	ERA	CSP	BB%	K%	HR%	GB%	ZSw%	ZCon%	OSw%	OCon%	BABIP	SLGCON	DRA-	WARP
2021	TEX	MLB	26	27(25)	117²	5-10	0	114	1.44	4.51	55.2%	8.4%	22.3%	2.5%	53.6%	65.8%	86.2%	32.4%	63.4%	.339	.568	93	1.5
2022	TEX	MLB	27	29(29)	153¹	4-8	0	137	1.43	4.46	50.1%	9.2%	20.4%	3.0%	51.5%	62.6%	87.9%	33.9%	62.7%	.314	.577	109	0.8
2023	TEX	MLB	28	35(26)	172²	12-7	0	140	1.26	3.70	48.5%	7.6%	19.4%	2.8%	47.0%	68.5%	88.5%	31.7%	61.1%	.288	.500	104	1.7
2024 DC	TEX	MLB	29	36(21)	137²	9-8	0	116	1.38	4.62	50.1%	8.4%	19.3%	2.8%	48.6%					.302	.520	103	1.0

2023 Arsenal: SI (91), SL (82), HC (89), CH (85.6), KC (77.8), FA (90.9), SW (77.9)   Comps: Doc Medich (83), Kris Benson (82), Aaron Sele (80)

Dunning pretty much nailed the retro pitcher aesthetic in 2023: Donning goggles and pitching to contact with a 90-mph sinker, he successfully chewed up innings in a way you just don't see much any more. After a year of pretending he was something more, Dunning went back to throwing strikes, doing a fair job of scraping the edges of the zone with his cutter and changeup, while letting his excellent sinker do the work in the middle of the zone. He was especially effective in the first half of the season, posting a 2.84 ERA that all your favorite ERA estimators called an optical illusion. Maybe they were onto something: his second half ERA jumped nearly two full runs as he sputtered down the stretch and found himself in long relief by the time the postseason rolled around. Nevertheless, the innings he did provide were crucial to a rotation otherwise plagued by chronic trips to the IL.

Nathan Eovaldi RHP   Born: 02/13/90   Age: 34   Height: 6'2"   Weight: 217   Origin: Round 11, 2008 Draft (#337 overall)

YEAR	TM	LVL	AGE	G (GS)	IP	W-L	SV	K	WHIP	ERA	CSP	BB%	K%	HR%	GB%	ZSw%	ZCon%	OSw%	OCon%	BABIP	SLGCON	DRA-	WARP
2021	BOS	MLB	31	32(32)	182¹	11-9	0	195	1.19	3.75	57.8%	4.6%	25.5%	2.0%	42.3%	69.1%	83.5%	36.5%	58.7%	.327	.552	81	3.6
2022	WOR	AAA	32	2(2)	6	0-0	0	8	1.67	7.50		6.7%	26.7%	6.7%	31.6%					.400	.941	93	0.1
2022	BOS	MLB	32	20(20)	109¹	6-3	0	103	1.23	3.87	54.9%	4.3%	22.4%	4.6%	47.3%	73.5%	85.1%	36.5%	58.8%	.300	.599	79	2.3
2023	TEX	MLB	33	25(25)	144	12-5	0	132	1.14	3.63	45.3%	8.1%	22.9%	2.6%	51.0%	69.1%	84.1%	34.0%	60.2%	.271	.512	89	2.5
2024 DC	TEX	MLB	34	29(29)	169	12-8	0	156	1.20	3.68	51.6%	6.6%	22.3%	3.0%	47.5%					.287	.515	86	2.7

2023 Arsenal: FA (95.4), FS (88.2), FC (91), CU (76.4), SL (84.2)   Comps: Rick Wise (72), Homer Bailey (69), Doyle Alexander (68)

At this point in his career, the book is pretty much already written on the big righty from Alvin, TX: oft-injured, with top-of-the-rotation upside and bottom-of-the-rotation risk when his velo wanes, but also a knack for coming up aces in the biggest moments. All of it was on display in 2023, as Eovaldi's return to the Lone Star State featured a Cy Young-caliber first half, an injury that saw him miss most of the second half, and struggles with dipping velo in his return. The only pages left are more entries to his already-impressive postseason ledger. Scuffling as he was in September after coming off the IL, that all disappeared the minute the calendar flipped to October. Once in his element, "Nasty Nate" was back delivering when it counted, becoming the first starter to win five games in a single postseason, three of those series clinchers. He completed six or more innings in five of his six playoff starts, manna from heaven for a Rangers team that desperately needed to hide as much of its relief staff as possible. At 34 years young and entrenched as starter on the World Series champs, here's hoping there's still another chapter or two on the way.

Jon Gray RHP   Born: 11/05/91   Age: 32   Height: 6'4"   Weight: 225   Origin: Round 1, 2013 Draft (#3 overall)

YEAR	TM	LVL	AGE	G (GS)	IP	W-L	SV	K	WHIP	ERA	CSP	BB%	K%	HR%	GB%	ZSw%	ZCon%	OSw%	OCon%	BABIP	SLGCON	DRA-	WARP
2021	COL	MLB	29	29(29)	149	8-12	0	157	1.33	4.59	56.8%	9.0%	24.4%	3.3%	47.7%	67.9%	84.0%	27.6%	52.9%	.299	.578	89	2.3
2022	TEX	MLB	30	24(24)	127¹	7-7	0	134	1.13	3.96	55.1%	7.5%	25.7%	3.3%	43.9%	67.0%	83.8%	34.6%	59.7%	.271	.524	84	2.3
2023	TEX	MLB	31	29(29)	157¹	9-8	0	142	1.29	4.12	48.5%	8.2%	21.6%	3.4%	39.9%	69.3%	84.2%	36.6%	58.8%	.299	.530	103	1.6
2024 DC	TEX	MLB	32	28(28)	148²	9-9	0	133	1.34	4.57	52.3%	8.3%	20.9%	3.5%	41.6%					.294	.552	103	1.1

2023 Arsenal: FA (95.8), SL (87.9), CH (88.9), SW (83.9), CU (78.5)   Comps: Steve Trachsel (77), Ricky Nolasco (77), Jeff Suppan (76)

Gray's time as a Ranger has been a fine example of nominative determinism: His career can't be easily divided into black-and-white sections for Colorado and post-Coors. There are those who thought he was an ace-in-waiting once freed from the pitching torture chamber known as Coors Field, and those who declared him just another average starter—both have been validated. At times, Gray has been a revelation, mixing in multiple distinct breakers with his upper-90s heat to put together stretches like May 2023, when he tossed 32 ⅓ innings of a 1.95 ERA and looked every bit the starter Texas thought could front its staff if when Jacob deGrom is injured. At other times he was indistinguishable from your typical product of the Rockies staff, like when he had a 5.32 ERA for the entire second half of the season. He lived in a bit of a gray area in the postseason too, not trusted enough to start but shuffling out of the pen to soak up critical innings like his three scoreless frames relieving Max Scherzer in Game 3 of the World Series.

Andrew Heaney LHP   Born: 06/05/91   Age: 33   Height: 6'2"   Weight: 200   Origin: Round 1, 2012 Draft (#9 overall)

YEAR	TM	LVL	AGE	G (GS)	IP	W-L	SV	K	WHIP	ERA	CSP	BB%	K%	HR%	GB%	ZSw%	ZCon%	OSw%	OCon%	BABIP	SLGCON	DRA-	WARP
2021	NYY	MLB	30	12(5)	35²	2-2	0	37	1.35	7.32	50.2%	6.4%	23.6%	8.3%	32.7%	69.7%	82.9%	32.8%	67.6%	.266	.857	115	0.1
2021	LAA	MLB	30	18(18)	94	6-7	0	113	1.31	5.27	49.2%	7.7%	28.2%	4.0%	34.0%	68.6%	79.4%	37.0%	60.0%	.319	.623	103	0.7
2022	OKC	AAA	31	2(2)	7¹	0-1	0	10	0.55	1.23		0.0%	40.0%	0.0%	60.0%	72.3%	79.4%	40.7%	54.5%	.267	.333	77	0.1
2022	LAD	MLB	31	16(14)	72²	4-4	0	110	1.09	3.10	50.8%	6.1%	35.5%	4.5%	34.9%	67.7%	78.0%	39.2%	47.6%	.293	.706	81	1.4
2023	TEX	MLB	32	34(28)	147¹	10-6	0	151	1.38	4.15	44.7%	9.4%	23.6%	3.6%	41.2%	69.9%	82.7%	33.8%	61.4%	.302	.598	113	0.7
2024 DC	TEX	MLB	33	30(21)	114²	6-6	0	124	1.26	4.37	47.5%	7.9%	25.5%	4.1%	38.2%					.291	.597	99	1.0

2023 Arsenal: FA (92.6), SL (81.9), CH (84)   Comps: Jason Vargas (73), Jarrod Washburn (72), José Quintana (71)

If you prompted an AI image generator to print you an effective, modern pitcher, odds are the output would look a lot like Heaney. Rising four-seam fastball? Check. Fancy, sweeping breaker? Check. High spin rates and unusual release traits? Check and check. At first glance, he looks great, like in 2022 with the Dodgers. Upon closer inspection, nothing works together the way it should; the fastball gets hit on the screws constantly, the sweeping slider loses its shape, and the weird release point leads to losing the zone for stretches at a time. Like some seven-fingered, three-armed monstrosity from Bing AI, your modern "ace" ends up 12% worse than league average by DRA and barely above replacement level despite throwing nearly 150 innings.

Jonathan Hernández RHP   Born: 07/06/96   Age: 28   Height: 6'3"   Weight: 190   Origin: IFA, 2013

YEAR	TM	LVL	AGE	G (GS)	IP	W-L	SV	K	WHIP	ERA	CSP	BB%	K%	HR%	GB%	ZSw%	ZCon%	OSw%	OCon%	BABIP	SLGCON	DRA-	WARP
2022	RR	AAA	25	15(0)	13¹	0-2	0	16	1.95	4.05		20.0%	24.6%	1.5%	55.6%	62.7%	76.6%	28.3%	37.8%	.343	.528	87	0.2
2022	TEX	MLB	25	29(0)	30¹	2-3	4	27	1.42	2.97	52.3%	13.0%	20.6%	1.5%	60.5%	73.8%	82.6%	26.5%	47.7%	.289	.435	102	0.3
2023	RR	AAA	26	24(0)	32	1-1	2	32	1.13	1.13		16.3%	24.8%	0.8%	56.6%	64.8%	76.8%	30.7%	44.1%	.187	.267	84	0.3
2023	TEX	MLB	26	33(0)	31²	1-2	0	34	1.58	5.40	44.3%	10.2%	23.1%	2.7%	51.1%	64.3%	88.3%	30.0%	44.1%	.348	.593	92	0.5
2024 DC	TEX	MLB	27	50(0)	53	3-2	0	57	1.44	4.57	46.6%	11.8%	24.1%	2.6%	51.4%					.303	.524	100	0.2

2023 Arsenal: SI (97.8), SL (87.6), CH (90.3)   Comps: Jeremy Jeffress (65), Dominic Leone (63), Bruce Rondón (60)

If a pitcher had a changeup with similar characteristics to Devin Williams' airbender, but threw it with seven more ticks of velocity, how often do you think he would use that pitch? Somewhere closing in on 100% of the time, right? Hernández's killer cambio averaged 11.2 inches of arm-side run, which trailed only Williams' 11.5 inches among MLB changeups (minimum 50 thrown). Throwing a change at 90 mph isn't always a good thing, but he still had an eight-mph difference between the off-speed pitch and his fastball. It's a potentially elite pitch, but he only used it 9.8% of the time in the regular season and he didn't throw it whatsoever in the playoffs. If you're looking for an explanation for why he didn't spam the pitch like your most annoying friend in the group chat, you won't find one here. His slider is a real bat-misser too. His sinker definitely isn't, and it was the culprit for most of the hard contact against him. But Jonathan, dude, don't overthink this. Just throw the changeup!

José Leclerc   RHP   Born: 12/19/93   Age: 30   Height: 6'0"   Weight: 195   Origin: IFA, 2010

YEAR	TM	LVL	AGE	G (GS)	IP	W-L	SV	K	WHIP	ERA	CSP	BB%	K%	HR%	GB%	ZSw%	ZCon%	OSw%	OCon%	BABIP	SLGCON	DRA-	WARP
2022	RR	AAA	28	7 (0)	6²	0-1	0	8	1.50	5.40		16.1%	25.8%	0.0%	37.5%	74.5%	68.4%	36.1%	56.7%	.313	.438	97	0.1
2022	TEX	MLB	28	39 (0)	47²	0-3	7	54	1.13	2.83	48.8%	10.6%	27.3%	2.5%	29.2%	70.8%	77.2%	36.2%	47.9%	.243	.492	108	0.3
2023	TEX	MLB	29	57 (0)	57	0-2	4	67	1.14	2.68	40.3%	12.0%	28.8%	2.1%	28.7%	73.9%	76.1%	34.6%	52.4%	.244	.437	100	0.7
2024 DC	TEX	MLB	30	55 (0)	58²	4-6	37	77	1.28	4.14	43.5%	10.7%	30.5%	3.6%	30.5%					.294	.611	94	0.5

2023 Arsenal: FA (95.5), SL (83), FC (90.3), CH (88.6), SI (95.6)   Comps: Ken Giles (55), Dominic Leone (52), Joakim Soria (52)

In October 2010, the Rangers were in the process of losing a World Series to Bruce Bochy's Giants—their first of two consecutive losses in the Fall Classic. They didn't know it at the time, but in December of that year they first began assembling the roster of the team that would finally get over the hump. That's when they signed an undersized pitcher from Esperanza in the Dominican Republic, one who would go on to pitch in 13 of 17 postseason games as the most trusted bullpen arm of Bochy, who was now guiding Texas to a title. As the longest-tenured player in the organization—and one who battled through more than his fair share of adversity—Leclerc playing such a vital role in bringing a title to Arlington was one of the best parts of their run, and a nice example of things coming full circle.

Jack Leiter   RHP   Born: 04/21/00   Age: 24   Height: 6'1"   Weight: 205   Origin: Round 1, 2021 Draft (#2 overall)

YEAR	TM	LVL	AGE	G (GS)	IP	W-L	SV	K	WHIP	ERA	CSP	BB%	K%	HR%	GB%	ZSw%	ZCon%	OSw%	OCon%	BABIP	SLGCON	DRA-	WARP
2022	FRI	AA	22	23 (22)	92²	3-10	0	109	1.55	5.54		13.2%	25.6%	2.6%	36.0%					.322	.548	88	1.1
2023	FRI	AA	23	19 (19)	81²	2-6	0	110	1.40	5.07		13.4%	31.3%	4.0%	33.9%					.303	.663	87	0.7
2024 DC	TEX	MLB	24	5 (5)	20²	1-2	0	21	1.54	5.60		13.2%	22.1%	4.1%	33.9%					.285	.600	120	0.0

2023 Arsenal: FA (95.4), SL (85.3), CU (78.8), CH (87.4)   Comps: Joey Murray (89), Austin Brice (89), Carson Fulmer (86)

Plans are a fickle thing. When the Rangers took Leiter second overall in the 2021 draft, they had visions of him fronting their rotation within a few short seasons, starting him off with an aggressive assignment in Double-A in 2022. It made sense; he was considered one of the most MLB-ready starters to come out of college in recent memory. The early returns were ominous, including a bloated ERA and several bouts of wildness leading to a ghastly walk rate. At different points in his second year in the minors, he appeared to be turning it around—from May 5 to June 17 he threw 40 ⅓ innings of 2.68 ERA ball with a 17.4% strikeout-minus-walk percentage—but by the end of Year 2 he was once again battling wildness while making intermittent trips to the developmental list in an effort to fix his mechanics.

Now the plan is ... well, there is none. Leiter's future is unclear, and his prospect luster has worn off. There are still flashes of the premium stuff that made him such a promising arm to begin with, but now they're accompanied by questions about whether he can throw enough strikes to remain a starter. Maybe the third year will be the charm, and we'll finally see the Rangers' plan of a future ace come to fruition. Maybe not. Plans are a fickle thing.

Brock Porter   RHP   Born: 06/03/03   Age: 21   Height: 6'4"   Weight: 208   Origin: Round 4, 2022 Draft (#109 overall)

YEAR	TM	LVL	AGE	G (GS)	IP	W-L	SV	K	WHIP	ERA	CSP	BB%	K%	HR%	GB%	ZSw%	ZCon%	OSw%	OCon%	BABIP	SLGCON	DRA-	WARP
2023	DE	A	20	21 (21)	69¹	0-3	0	95	1.17	2.47		14.3%	32.4%	0.3%	43.2%					.259	.331	77	1.5
2024 non	TEX	MLB	21	58 (0)	50	2-2	0	51	1.63	6.13		13.9%	21.9%	4.0%	35.0%					.298	.618	130	-0.6

Comps: Chris Anderson (91), Bryan Abreu (90), Joe Boyle (88)

We imagine the Rangers scouting process has just a few boxes: Taller than 6'4"? Check. Long, wiry frame? Check. Right-handed arm? Check. Sits mid-90s, touching high-90 or even triple digits? Check. It's no surprise then, that they were so gung-ho to acquire Porter in the draft, and they'll only be reinforced by the way his first professional season went. A microscopic ERA and 95 Ks in 69 1/3 innings speak to his potential dominance on the mound, and to do so at the age of 20 makes it even more impressive. Porter now faces the very real possibility of reaching Double-A by the end of 2024, which could put him on the doorstep of the majors when he's a 22-year-old. That's all in the future, but in the meantime Porter will have to clean up his command a bit to cement his place in the Rangers' future rotation; unless you're Blake Snell, walking 5.5 per nine isn't a great recipe for success.

Kumar Rocker   RHP   Born: 11/22/99   Age: 24   Height: 6'5"   Weight: 245   Origin: Round 1, 2022 Draft (#3 overall)

YEAR	TM	LVL	AGE	G (GS)	IP	W-L	SV	K	WHIP	ERA	CSP	BB%	K%	HR%	GB%	ZSw%	ZCon%	OSw%	OCon%	BABIP	SLGCON	DRA-	WARP
2023	HIC	A+	23	6 (6)	28	2-2	0	42	1.00	3.86		6.3%	37.8%	1.8%	51.6%					.317	.548	77	0.6
2024 non	TEX	MLB	24	58 (0)	50	2-2	0	46	1.38	4.78		9.7%	21.0%	3.7%	38.3%					.286	.565	107	0.0

Comps: Beau Brieske (92), Alan Rangel (91), Chris Vallimont (90)

Ahead of the 2021 season, Vanderbilt's pitching staff featured a pair of arms who each had a claim to be top pick in the draft, in Rocker and his teammate Jack Leiter. Both appeared destined to star in big-league rotations soon; some would have guessed both would be in the majors by now. Instead, both find themselves languishing in the Rangers farm, their star turns delayed by injuries, inconsistency, and draft day shenanigans. Rocker got his first taste of pro ball in 2023, showing off the slider that made him such a promising arm to begin with, especially in terms of strikeouts. That brief flash of potential was cut short by an elbow injury that required Tommy John surgery, meaning we'll have to wait until 2025 to see if he can live up to the expectations he's trudged under for nearly a half-decade.

Josh Sborz RHP   Born: 12/17/93   Age: 30   Height: 6'3"   Weight: 215   Origin: Round 2, 2015 Draft (#74 overall)

YEAR	TM	LVL	AGE	G (GS)	IP	W-L	SV	K	WHIP	ERA	CSP	BB%	K%	HR%	GB%	ZSw%	ZCon%	OSw%	OCon%	BABIP	SLGCON	DRA-	WARP
2021	TEX	MLB	27	63(0)	59	4-3	1	69	1.42	3.97	52.9%	12.5%	26.8%	2.7%	41.7%	73.2%	82.1%	35.0%	48.8%	.302	.556	96	0.7
2022	RR	AAA	28	19(1)	22¹	3-0	1	30	0.99	1.61		12.4%	33.7%	2.2%	36.2%	68.2%	76.7%	29.1%	35.9%	.205	.400	82	0.4
2022	TEX	MLB	28	19(1)	22¹	1-0	0	32	1.61	6.45	51.6%	11.0%	32.0%	4.0%	29.8%	68.5%	75.5%	31.2%	52.3%	.396	.768	90	0.3
2023	TEX	MLB	29	44(0)	52¹	6-7	0	66	1.15	5.50	46.1%	7.9%	30.7%	3.7%	46.9%	64.7%	75.2%	35.2%	48.6%	.287	.577	79	1.2
2024 DC	TEX	MLB	30	61(0)	64²	5-3	7	80	1.24	3.65	49.7%	9.8%	29.5%	3.1%	40.7%					.294	.558	84	0.8

2023 Arsenal: FA (96.8), SL (88.6), KC (85.2)   *Comps: Ryan Cook (58), Hector Neris (56), Danny Farquhar (56)*

We all know the kid who skated on raw talent in school. They didn't study, didn't do homework and their grades never reflected their raw book smarts, which frustrated their teachers and parents to no end. If that kid grew up to be a middle reliever, he might look like Sborz. A career ERA most estimators agree should be about a run lower than it is and a sterling 22% strikeout minus walk rate over the last two seasons are somehow paired with an ERA a shade under six. All the signs of potential are there, but rarely do the results match. Then, for one glorious stretch of three weeks in October, Sborz completed every assignment: He gave up just one run and four hits in 12 innings of postseason work, including the last seven outs of the clinching game of the World Series. Maybe Sborz now turns the corner and becomes a straight-A student. The more likely outcome is that he continues to frustrate, but onlookers will at least have fresh glimpses of his potential when he does.

Max Scherzer RHP   Born: 07/27/84   Age: 39   Height: 6'3"   Weight: 208   Origin: Round 1, 2006 Draft (#11 overall)

YEAR	TM	LVL	AGE	G (GS)	IP	W-L	SV	K	WHIP	ERA	CSP	BB%	K%	HR%	GB%	ZSw%	ZCon%	OSw%	OCon%	BABIP	SLGCON	DRA-	WARP
2021	WAS	MLB	36	19(19)	111	8-4	0	147	0.89	2.76	52.9%	6.5%	34.3%	4.2%	33.1%	70.0%	75.5%	33.9%	47.6%	.235	.568	75	2.5
2021	LAD	MLB	36	11(11)	68¹	7-0	0	89	0.82	1.98	54.2%	3.0%	33.6%	1.9%	34.9%	74.8%	78.8%	36.1%	51.2%	.269	.455	70	1.7
2022	NYM	MLB	37	23(23)	145¹	11-5	0	173	0.91	2.29	52.9%	4.2%	30.6%	2.3%	31.1%	70.5%	81.0%	37.8%	52.6%	.279	.477	80	2.9
2023	TEX	MLB	38	8(8)	45	4-2	0	53	0.96	3.20	45.5%	8.5%	29.9%	2.8%	38.0%	69.6%	80.2%	37.7%	58.2%	.223	.463	101	0.5
2023	NYM	MLB	38	19(19)	107²	9-4	0	121	1.19	4.01	48.4%	6.8%	27.3%	5.2%	31.0%	73.2%	81.3%	35.0%	57.6%	.281	.632	97	1.4
2024 DC	TEX	MLB	39	13(13)	72¹	5-4	0	83	1.16	3.77	50.4%	6.7%	27.8%	3.9%	32.1%					.292	.596	89	1.1

2023 Arsenal: FA (93.9), SL (84.1), CH (83.8), CU (75.3), FC (88.5)   *Comps: Don Sutton (77), Roger Clemens (77), Bob Gibson (77)*

In many ways, Scherzer is the same inner-circle Hall of Famer he's always been. You can watch him for one start and see all the same traits that made him one of his generation's greatest pitchers: overwhelming stuff with the same mid-90s velo, an array of punchout secondaries that make him nigh-unhittable and pinpoint command that makes it nearly impossible to get on base against him. In other ways, the cracks in his armor are more apparent. The dominant starts are slightly less frequent now, and while he's always been slightly vulnerable to the long ball, he's now graduated to being homer-prone. And a pitcher who threw 200 or more innings in six consecutive seasons at his peak hasn't cleared 180 since 2018. These last three seasons have ended with a familiar sight: A physically compromised Scherzer laboring through a playoff start, looking nothing like the once-dominant ace. This time his manager got him out in time for it to end pleasantly...at least for a little while; Scherzer had surgery in the offseason to repair a herniated disc in his back, and won't pitch until the middle of the 2024 season at the earliest.

Josh Stephan RHP   Born: 11/01/01   Age: 22   Height: 6'3"   Weight: 185   Origin: Undrafted Free Agent, 2020

YEAR	TM	LVL	AGE	G (GS)	IP	W-L	SV	K	WHIP	ERA	CSP	BB%	K%	HR%	GB%	ZSw%	ZCon%	OSw%	OCon%	BABIP	SLGCON	DRA-	WARP
2021	RAN	ROK	19	7(6)	28	2-1	0	31	1.14	3.86		10.4%	27.0%	2.6%	44.1%					.262	.493		
2021	DE	A	19	3(3)	12	0-1	0	19	1.58	8.25		7.0%	33.3%	7.0%	25.0%					.393	.906	110	0.0
2022	DE	A	20	18(16)	91²	4-4	1	102	1.10	3.34		6.4%	27.2%	2.7%	51.8%					.286	.539	97	1.1
2022	HIC	A+	20	3(3)	11²	2-1	0	13	1.20	1.54		14.9%	27.7%	2.1%	55.6%					.231	.423	101	0.1
2023	HIC	A+	21	12(11)	62¹	6-3	0	73	0.80	2.17		5.1%	31.2%	3.4%	50.0%					.221	.493	87	1.1
2024 non	TEX	MLB	22	58(0)	50	2-2	0	43	1.39	5.09		8.3%	19.5%	3.9%	39.8%					.293	.578	114	-0.1

Comps: Zack Littell (54), Robert Gsellman (52), Tyler Viza (51)

Signed as a free agent out of high school after going undrafted in the pandemic-shortened 2020 draft, Stephan has established himself as one of the more advanced arms in the Rangers system in his two seasons as a pro. With a uniquely low-slung release for a starter, Stephan creates awkward visuals for opposing hitters; he features a pair of fastballs with divergent shapes and a biting low-80s slidepiece that he uses for whiffs. The word *pitchability* comes to mind when describing him, a somewhat surprising moniker for such a young pitcher. Despite not possessing overwhelming velo, Stephan has proven to be far too much for low minors hitters to handle: His 26% K-BB difference was the sixth-best in the minors for pitchers who tallied as many innings as he did.

Owen White RHP   Born: 08/09/99   Age: 24   Height: 6'3"   Weight: 199   Origin: Round 2, 2018 Draft (#55 overall)

YEAR	TM	LVL	AGE	G (GS)	IP	W-L	SV	K	WHIP	ERA	CSP	BB%	K%	HR%	GB%	ZSw%	ZCon%	OSw%	OCon%	BABIP	SLGCON	DRA-	WARP
2021	DE	A	21	8(8)	33¹	3-1	0	54	1.11	3.24		8.9%	40.0%	1.5%	41.2%					.348	.515	68	0.7
2022	HIC	A+	22	11(10)	58²	6-2	0	81	1.19	3.99		7.8%	33.3%	2.9%	43.7%					.326	.631	87	0.9
2022	FRI	AA	22	4(4)	21²	3-0	0	23	1.06	2.49		4.7%	27.1%	1.2%	50.9%					.327	.446	80	0.4
2023	FRI	AA	23	12(12)	56¹	2-3	0	48	1.12	3.51		10.1%	21.1%	2.2%	44.4%					.243	.415	94	0.7
2023	RR	AAA	23	13(12)	52¹	2-2	0	32	1.61	4.99		13.5%	13.5%	4.2%	44.9%	67.6%	86.5%	27.3%	66.7%	.269	.558	127	-0.1
2023	TEX	MLB	23	2(0)	4	0-1	0	4	1.75	11.25	45.8%	10.5%	21.1%	10.5%	46.2%	66.7%	88.9%	36.6%	66.7%	.300	.917	91	0.1
2024 DC	TEX	MLB	24	23(8)	52¹	2-3	0	43	1.54	5.72	45.8%	10.5%	18.3%	3.8%	39.2%					.301	.578	123	-0.3

2023 Arsenal: FC (88.4), FA (93.4), SW (81.9), SI (93.3), CH (88.1), SL (84.8), KC (77.8)   *Comps: Chris Flexen (45), John Gant (45), Dan Straily (45)*

First, the good: White eclipsed 100 innings in 2023, no small feat for a pitcher beset by injuries and circumstances as much as he has been in his young career. Now, the bad: pretty much everything else. White declined in just about every facet, losing nearly half his strikeouts while nearly doubling his walks. Each of those would be bad enough on their own; in tandem, they turned White from promising hurler to something of an organizational afterthought in the blink of an eye. Thanks to Texas' addiction to oft-broken starters, White could get some run in the major-league rotation, though he's unlikely to find MLB hitters any easier to get out than the ones he saw at Round Rock. The consolation: It can only get better from here (probably).

Kirby Yates RHP Born: 03/25/87 Age: 37 Height: 5'10" Weight: 205 Origin: Round 26, 2005 Draft (#798 overall)

YEAR	TM	LVL	AGE	G (GS)	IP	W-L	SV	K	WHIP	ERA	CSP	BB%	K%	HR%	GB%	ZSw%	ZCon%	OSw%	OCon%	BABIP	SLGCON	DRA-	WARP
2022	GWN	AAA	35	5(0)	5¹	0-0	0	4	0.75	1.69		9.5%	19.0%	0.0%	64.3%	80.0%	83.3%	50.0%	75.0%	.143	.143	93	0.1
2022	ATL	MLB	35	9(0)	7	0-0	0	6	1.57	5.14	50.4%	15.2%	18.2%	6.1%	36.4%	62.7%	87.5%	29.1%	48.0%	.200	.714	114	0.0
2023	ATL	MLB	36	61(0)	60¹	7-2	5	80	1.19	3.28	42.8%	14.6%	31.5%	3.5%	35.6%	66.3%	80.7%	32.6%	55.3%	.213	.508	91	1.0
2024 DC	TEX	MLB	37	50(0)	53	3-2	0	70	1.38	4.72	43.8%	12.1%	30.1%	4.0%	38.6%					.297	.631	104	0.1

2023 Arsenal: FA (93.7), FS (86.2), SW (76.6), SL (85.6)   Comps: Darren O'Day (57), Santiago Casilla (57), Steve Cishek (56)

It was a long, winding and painful road for Yates, but he was finally able to pitch a full season for the first time since 2019. We did see flashes of what he was like back in the first act of his career, as one of the top relievers in the game—his fastball is still sitting around 94 mph and he's still getting plenty of whiffs with both the four-seamer and his splitter. What's different is the free passes. With the high walk rate from Yates' 2022 cameo seemingly here to stay, it became easy to see which way the wind was blowing in any given appearance. It seemed he was equally likely to either strike out the side or walk himself into a dire situation in any given inning. Still, his strikeout rate was high enough to merit plenty of high-leverage, high-stress opportunities.

LINEOUTS

Hitters

HITTER	POS	TM	LVL	AGE	PA	R	HR	RBI	SB	AVG/OBP/SLG	BABIP	SLGCON	BB%	K%	ZSw%	ZCon%	OSw%	OCon%	LA	90th EV	DRC+	BRR	DRP	WARP
Cameron Cauley	SS	DE	A	20	275	43	7	35	22	.244/.331/.405	.354	.641	10.9%	32.4%							94	3.9	1.2	1.4
	SS	HIC	A+	20	146	25	5	24	14	.248/.336/.424	.329	.654	11.6%	30.1%							91	1.2	-0.5	0.2
Anthony Gutierrez	CF	DE	A	18	325	39	2	34	30	.259/.326/.338	.335	.448	7.7%	22.2%							98	1.4	1.2	1.1
Trevor Hauver	RF	FRI	AA	24	471	58	12	59	1	.260/.374/.429	.361	.654	15.1%	28.7%							109	-1.4	-5.3	1.2
Jesus Lopez	C	RAN	ROK	18	53	8	3	8	0	.289/.396/.644	.345	.906	9.4%	24.5%										
Maxton Martin	OF	RAN	ROK	18	45	8	1	7	0	.243/.378/.378	.320	.538	17.8%	24.4%										
J.P. Martínez	OF	RR	AAA	27	353	54	14	59	38	.298/.418/.543	.367	.755	15.6%	22.9%	67.9%	80.6%	25.7%	57.3%			111	4.4	5.0	2.1
	OF	TEX	MLB	27	44	7	1	4	0	.225/.250/.325	.320	.542	4.5%	36.4%	62.7%	72.3%	33.7%	54.5%	20.3	102.2	71	0.0	-0.2	-0.1
Brad Miller	DH/1B	TEX	MLB	33	67	8	1	6	0	.214/.328/.339	.244	.422	14.9%	16.4%	59.3%	83.6%	27.5%	69.4%	7.9	102.3	103	0.1	0.0	0.2
Braylin Morel	CF	DSL RNGR	ROK	17	204	40	7	43	2	.344/.417/.644	.444	.892	10.3%	24.5%										
Yeison Morrobel	OF	DE	A	19	151	16	1	13	12	.273/.384/.313	.366	.426	14.6%	22.5%							109	2.5	5.8	1.4
Jonathan Ornelas	SS	RR	AAA	23	517	78	8	52	15	.253/.368/.359	.332	.498	14.3%	23.4%	52.7%	85.0%	25.7%	58.6%			91	-0.5	1.6	1.0
	SS	TEX	MLB	23	8	2	0	0	0	.143/.250/.143	.333	.333	0.0%	50.0%	41.7%	60.0%	36.8%	57.1%	24.1	97.7	76	0.0	0.0	0.0
Hector Osorio	CF	DSL RNGB	ROK	18	223	42	1	29	17	.293/.466/.376	.326	.450	22.0%	11.7%										
Echedry Vargas	SS	RAN	ROK	18	222	46	11	39	17	.315/.387/.569	.383	.783	9.5%	24.3%										
Aaron Zavala	OF	FRI	AA	23	426	47	5	40	7	.194/.343/.284	.335	.533	16.9%	37.3%							88	0.4	-7.6	0.1

A typically excellent fielder up the middle, **Cameron Cauley** had struggled to get his bat going his first few years as a pro. The worm started to turn in 2023, when the 20-year-old popped a .400+ slugging percentage for the first time. He definitely needs to cut down on the strikeouts, but Cauley doesn't need to make huge strides to become a viable major-leaguer. ⓧ **Anthony Gutierrez** signed for just under $2 million two years ago as a toolsy boom-or-bust lottery ticket. His .079 ISO in the Carolina League indicates that he hasn't boomed, but he's still a teenager so let's not call him the other thing just yet. ⓧ The *other* other piece in the the Joey Gallo deal, **Trevor Hauver** has taken to doing his best impersonation of Gallo in Double-A: Nearly half (46 percent) of his plate appearances in Frisco ended with a walk, strikeout or home run. This is rare patience for a minor-leaguer, but he's 25 and still in Double-A. ⓧ **Jesus Lopez** is a defense-first, lefty-hitting catcher who played stateside as an 18-year-old. He's got some power in his bat, and if he proves he can make enough contact as he faces more advanced pitching, he'll generate some recognition on prospect lists. ⓧ The Rangers gave 11th-round pick **Maxton Martin** an over-slot bonus to skip out on his commitment to the University of Oregon. The young outfielder didn't distinguish himself in the complex leagues, but he'll still be 18 at the beginning of the 2024 season. You won't see him for a while. ⓧ A decorated slugger from the Tigers who won a World Series with the Red Sox, Martinez put up a monster year as the Dodgers DH in 2023. [holds hand to earpiece] Oh, excuse me ... this is a lineout for **J.P. Martínez**. At least he has a ring too, after appearing in 17 games for the Rangers last year. Close enough. ⓧ **Brad Miller** clobbered 30 home runs while playing shortstop and first base for the 2016 Rays and finished in last place. He hit just one homer for the 2023 Rangers, tallying only 11 innings on defense—including two as a pitcher—and received a World Series ring. Baseball. ⓧ **Braylin Morel** was named Top MLB Prospect in the Dominican Summer League after posting video game numbers that increased as the season went along. He's got corner outfielder written all over him, but he could be the fun kind. ⓧ **Yeison Morrobel** is a year away from making that transition all awkward prospects have to go through: Double-A pitching. He put it off a little by suffering a season-ending injury in June, but reports wafted up that his athleticism was already in conflict with awkward mechanics and stiffness. And that's before the pitchers start throwing strikes. ⓧ **Jonathan Ornelas'** best tool is his ability to play shortstop, which he does quite well. Ironically, he won't hit enough to play shortstop all the time in MLB, so he'll have to find playing time at other positions further down the defensive spectrum to justify a roster spot. ⓧ Teenagers' stats in the Dominican Summer League don't translate to future MLB success. Don't expect **Hector Osorio** to maintain his 22% walk rate as he progresses through the system, but the fact that he only swatted one home run in that many tries might be a problem. ⓧ **Echedry Vargas** won the Top MLB Prospect Award in the Arizona Complex League. Presumably, there's some kind of trophy to go with that, or at least a Fry's Food Stores gift card, which he won't be able to use since he was already promoted to the Carolina League at the end of the season. ⓧ Remember that one freakishly horrible Adam Dunn season? That's what **Aaron Zavala** did while repeating Double-A. Dunn played three more years after his 2011 collapse, but Zavala won't last that long unless he cuts his strikeout rate by two thirds.

Pitchers

PITCHER	TM	LVL	AGE	G (GS)	IP	W-L	SV	K	WHIP	ERA	CSP	BB%	K%	HR%	GB%	ZSw%	ZCon%	OSw%	OCon%	BABIP	SLGCON	DRA-	WARP
Diego Castillo	TAC	AAA	29	43 (1)	47¹	5-5	0	50	1.80	5.13		15.5%	22.1%	2.2%	40.9%	61.0%	83.6%	25.3%	53.2%	.349	.609	96	0.1
	SEA	MLB	29	8 (0)	8²	0-0	0	7	1.62	6.23	51.1%	17.1%	17.1%	4.9%	53.8%	77.5%	78.2%	29.7%	63.0%	.208	.538	103	0.1
Marc Church	FRI	AA	22	13 (0)	18	2-3	0	31	1.33	4.00		13.2%	40.8%	2.6%	32.4%					.375	.676	74	0.4
	RR	AAA	22	30 (2)	44	7-1	2	48	1.55	3.48		14.6%	25.0%	2.6%	34.2%	66.4%	80.9%	30.7%	41.6%	.321	.555	91	0.5
Aidan Curry	DE	A	20	19 (15)	82	6-3	0	99	0.93	2.30		9.0%	30.8%	1.2%	35.1%					.230	.353	83	1.5
	HIC	A+	20	2 (2)	6¹	0-0	0	5	3.00	8.53		27.8%	13.9%	8.3%	28.6%					.333	.905	134	
Skylar Hales	DE	A	21	5 (0)	8¹	0-1	0	7	0.48	2.16		7.1%	25.0%	3.6%	42.1%					.056	.263	97	0.1
Antoine Kelly	FRI	AA	23	43 (0)	50²	3-1	11	69	1.16	1.95		10.1%	31.8%	1.8%	47.9%					.277	.443	64	1.4
	RR	AAA	23	6 (0)	6²	0-0	0	10	1.35	2.70		3.4%	34.5%	0.0%	58.8%	68.3%	78.0%	32.7%	62.5%	.471	.529	57	
Ian Kennedy	RR	AAA	38	22 (0)	25²	1-0	3	30	1.13	3.51		8.8%	29.4%	4.9%	38.7%	68.6%	83.9%	32.9%	48.8%	.263	.645	74	0.4
	TEX	MLB	38	16 (0)	16¹	0-1	0	21	1.41	7.16	44.7%	9.3%	28.0%	5.3%	35.6%	74.8%	77.9%	29.4%	45.5%	.293	.705	92	0.3
Zak Kent	RAN	ROK	25	3 (3)	6²	0-0	0	9	1.65	9.45		9.7%	29.0%	9.7%	52.6%					.313	.944		
	RR	AAA	25	10 (10)	34	0-1	0	34	1.06	3.97		7.1%	24.3%	2.9%	42.6%	66.2%	86.1%	31.3%	56.9%	.244	.484	81	0.0
Tyler Mahle	MIN	MLB	28	5 (5)	25²	1-2	0	28	1.05	3.16	43.4%	4.9%	27.5%	4.9%	37.7%	63.8%	82.7%	32.9%	65.9%	.266	.594	89	0.5
Yerry Rodríguez	RR	AAA	25	38 (2)	48¹	3-0	8	63	1.39	5.03		12.0%	29.0%	4.1%	48.8%	71.4%	74.4%	27.7%	62.5%	.276	.581	69	0.8
	TEX	MLB	25	13 (1)	13²	0-1	0	15	1.90	7.90	53.2%	9.1%	22.7%	1.5%	28.9%	72.1%	80.2%	26.7%	51.4%	.432	.682	104	0.1
Cole Winn	RR	AAA	23	29 (13)	101	9-8	0	97	1.91	7.22		16.0%	19.7%	3.4%	35.4%	68.9%	82.6%	29.3%	58.2%	.328	.606	133	-1.0

A cautionary tale for front offices flaunting acquiring relievers with multiple years of team control, **Diego Castillo**'s stuff and command regressed to the point of full-fledged relegation to Triple-A. Though he didn't throw a big-league pitch after April, he did look much better over the final two months, hinting that a return to a major-league bullpen somewhere could still be in the cards. ⓧ **Marc Church** is a 95-and-a-slider reliever with control issues. He'll try to distinguish himself from all 4,136 of the other 95-and-a-slider relievers with control issues the Rangers will bring to spring training. ⓧ Former undrafted free agent **Carson Coleman** missed the entire 2023 season after undergoing Tommy John surgery. Prior to the injury, he was striking out the world with a hellacious fastball; Texas will get a(n almost) free look at his rehab after picking him up in the Rule 5 Draft. ⓧ Unpicked in the shortened five-round draft in 2020, whippy righty **Aidan Curry** now finds himself turning heads in their low minors. Having just turned 21 and already displaying good command of a low-to-mid 90s fastball and a slider that Low-A hitters haven't been able to figure out, he could move up prospect lists quickly in 2024. ⓧ The Rangers fourth-round selection in the June MLB draft, **Skylar Hales** features both a fastball that touches triple digits and surprising command of the strike zone. He'll look to join alums Penn Murfee, Steven Wilson and Mitch White as the next Santa Clara Bronco to make the bigs. ⓧ **Antoine Kelly** is a lefty who's the opposite of crafty. He bludgeons opponents with a sinking high-90s heater and mixes in a few sliders. It's a borderline unhittable combination when he locates his pitches in the vicinity of the strike zone, which he often doesn't. ⓧ **Ian Kennedy** called it a career after the 2023 season, but thanks to his 16 games out of the Rangers 'pen in the regular season, he received a World Series championship ring as a parting gift. Not a bad ending to a long, winding, and probably better-than-you-remember career. ⓧ Some players burst through the minors, while others graduate to MLB because they have no place left to go. **Zak Kent** is the latter, and he's going to be a mainstay in the Round Rock rotation once again. He's on the 40-man now, so he'll probably make a spot start or two in Texas. ⓧ Less than a year from what could have been a very lucrative free agency, **Tyler Mahle** fell out of the frying pan of shoulder inflammation into the fire of Tommy John surgery. He'll be back at some point in 2024. ⓧ Seemingly beset nonstop by injuries and inconsistency since his All-Star season in 2019, **Jake Odorizzi** had a 2023 to forget. You might be straining to remember anything he did, and there's good reason: He didn't throw a single pitch after undergoing surgery in his throwing shoulder in the first week of April. Be like Jake—take a Tylenol and try to move on from this whole experience. ⓧ Don't look at **Yerry Rodríguez's** ERA above. Don't look! No pitcher deserves a .432 BABIP against. He's out of options now, so the Rangers should give him an extended chance to show what his blazing fastball can do. Ugh, you looked anyway, didn't you? ⓧ A quick glance at **Alejandro Rosario**'s college statistics at Miami—a 7.11 ERA in 74 ⅔ innings as a junior and a 7.05 ERA in 65 innings as a sophomore—would have one wondering what the Rangers saw in him that made them take him in the fifth round of the 2023 MLB Draft. A closer inspection reveals that Rosario struck out 143 hitters in his last two years and sits between 97 and 98 mph as a starter. ⓧ A sixth-round overslot signee in the 2023 draft, **Caden Scarborough** follows a familiar formula for a Rangers draftee. He's a tall righty with room to fill out who comes out of high school already featuring a good slider to go along with a mid-90s fastball. ⓧ There is an alternate universe buried in the forgotten files of an old version of Out of the Park edition in which **Cole Winn** became a Cy Young winner and a Hall of Famer. That future was plausible a few years ago in this universe, but no longer.

TORONTO BLUE JAYS

Essay by Steve Sladkowski

Player comments by Michael Clair and BP staff

*with so many people
in the cities, and so few geese, nobody is
silly as a goose anymore[1]*

It doesn't seem like A.R. Ammons cared much about baseball. Nowhere in his oeuvre is there a poem as ubiquitous to the American pastime as Ernest Thayer's "Casey at the Bat" or Walt Whitman's observations of the nascent game that served as the opening monologue for Ken Burns' masterpiece.[2] Instead, Archie Randolph Ammons seemed content to pass his time finding the sublime in the everyday; his was a metaphysics of the mundane. Or, as *The New Yorker* once put it, Ammons is "the Great American Poet of Daily Chores."[3] Whatever the subject and however long the composition—short poems written on adding-machine tape, book-length poems about garbage, many poems of various length about the natural world—Ammons' works are unified by his sharp wit and sage appreciation of time's elastic nature, leading to memorable observations like the poem "Their Sex Life": "*One failure on/Top of another*"[4] and "Pebble's Story": "*Wearing away/wears/wearing/away away*"[5]

Whenever I return to Ammons' work (which is frequently), I remain deeply moved by the palpable sense of joy he derived from the act of writing in and of itself. Deriving a sense of joy from the very act of doing your job is difficult in any field; it is especially difficult to do in professional creative and performative fields such as writing, music or baseball. As a long-suffering Toronto Blue Jays fan and musician who has been fortunate enough to perform in 25 countries over the past decade,I have found the most difficult-to-manage element of performing for a living is the knowledge that your life's passion is also your meal ticket. With that knowledge, an ugly question emerges from the murky depths of existence like a three-eyed-fish on Bart Simpson's line: How can you find and sustain joy, while doing the thing you love, when the thing you love is also your f***in' job? I've been interrogating this concept for a decade-plus; Ammons wrote poetry for 46 years. That's probably why I identified the phenomenon using a *Simpsons* reference, and he wrote

TORONTO BLUE JAYS PROSPECTUS
2023 W-L: 89-73, 3RD IN AL EAST

Pythag	.549	13th	DER	.696	16th
RS/G	4.60	14th	DRC+	106	4th
RA/G	4.14	6th	DRA-	94	8th
dWin%	.575	4th	FIP	4.08	7th
Payroll	$210M	7th	B-Age	29.3	26th
M$/MW	$4.7M	17th	P-Age	31.1	29th

- Opened 1989
- Retractable roof
- Synthetic surface
- Fence profile: 8'-14'4"

Park Factors

Runs	Runs/RH	Runs/LH	HR/RH	HR/LH
99	99	100	107	102

Top Hitter WARP	4.5 Vladimir Guerrero Jr.
Top Pitcher WARP	4.1 Kevin Gausman
2023 Top Prospect	Ricky Tiedemann

Payroll History (in millions)

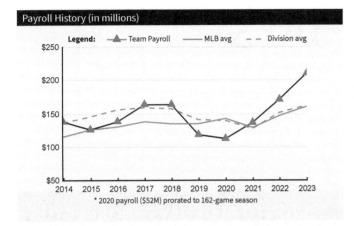

Legend: ▲ Team Payroll — MLB avg -- Division avg

* 2020 payroll ($52M) prorated to 162-game season

Future Commitments (in millions)

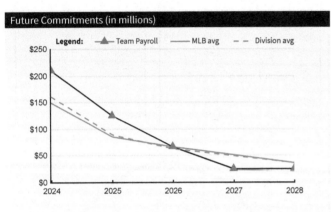

Legend: ▲ Team Payroll — MLB avg -- Division avg

Farm System Ranking

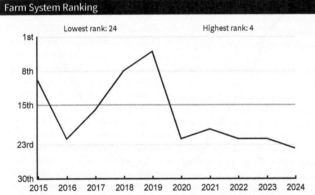

Lowest rank: 24   Highest rank: 4

Personnel

President & CEO
Mark A. Shapiro

Executive Vice President, Baseball Operations & General Manager
Ross Atkins

Senior Vice President, Player Personnel
Tony Lacava

Vice President, International Scouting & Baseball Operations
Andrew Tinnish

Vice President, Baseball Strategy
James Click

Assistant General Manager
Joe Sheehan

Assistant General Manager
Michael Murov

Manager
John Schneider

BP Alumni
James Click

things like: "*on/one side/of their goofiness is carnal misery/ and on the other the prettiest high slides/glee ever broke out of.*"[6]

The logic of capitalism dictates that an individual's time and skills can be bought, sold and exploited in myriad ways to the financial benefit of...well, usually someone else. Ask anyone working in the arts or any member of the MLBPA about that. Of course, there are real material rewards that exist for individuals working hard on a baseball diamond or in a concert club. However, in making the kinds of sacrifices necessary to perform for a paying audience in a stadium or theater, you run the real risk of experiencing what Ammons identified in his poem "Success Story": "*I never got on good/ relations with the world/first I had nothing/the world wanted/ then the world had/nothing I wanted.*"[7] The world having nothing one wants, that emptying of joy in the context of the 2023 Toronto Blue Jays, seems to have become clear in a late-season series against the eventual World Series champion Texas Rangers. In hindsight, the true end to the Jays' season occurred from September 11-14 when the team and their fans—in the thick of a Wild Card chase!—conducted themselves in shocking ways: The team by surrendering 35 runs in a demoralizing four-game sweep and their fans by setting a season-low in attendance for Game 1 of the pivotal series and booing nearly everything they saw on the field in the three games following the first. For 2024, the question becomes: If the pursuit of one's passion as livelihood empties a world of joy, where are the worlds-within-worlds where joy can be (re-)discovered?

⚾   ⚾   ⚾

You may be sitting here, reading this, thinking to yourself: "Well, that's all well and good, Steve. I don't really know you or your band PUP, and I think poetry is goofy, *and* I think professional athletes and rockstars are coddled little babies. I have a tough job, too, and this sort of navel-gazing isn't what I've come to expect when I crack the Baseball Prospectus *Annual*. Sure, I'm a nerd just like you. But the *Annual* is something that affords me some momentary reprieve from the unceasing horrors of the world, or the world-within-a-world, or whatever. The team essays should not be used as a portal to look directly at those same horrors, especially with a close reading of the opaque linguistic insights of a poet! At best, your first three paragraphs are beside-the-point; at worst, they are needlessly self-indulgent even by the generous standards of baseball writing. Plus, what do poetics and loss of joy really have to do with the aforementioned 2024 Toronto Blue Jays?"

⚾   ⚾   ⚾

Established in 1977 on the freezing cold northern shore of Lake Ontario, my belovèd hometown ballclub has remained a complementary franchise[8] over their 46 years on the Junior Circuit. Nevertheless, this dumb team has contributed a few moments of psychotically joyful baseball poetry that left an indelible mark on the game's long historical record.[9] One of my earliest memories, full-stop, is Joe Carter's 1993 World Series-clinching homer: I was five years old, watching with my Belarusian immigrant grandparents at their apartment in Toronto's Junction neighborhood, wearing pajamas modeled after the Jays' home uniforms. Knowing WAMCO could win it all again that evening—and embodying a DIY aesthetic that would help launch my career in punk rock two decades later—I had excitedly made my own confetti in anticipation of the big moment. Little did I know how big that moment would be for my little squares of paper. "Touch 'em all, Joe!" the great Tom Cheek was yelling, as I launched myself from my grandparents' deep-set gray couches, criss-crossing the wall-to-wall carpeting and ~~making a giant mess~~ throwing confetti everywhere. The DVD recaps of those World Series victories came with me to college where, having lost the joy of playing competitive baseball as a teenager, I took the first step on the stereotypically Millennial path of monetizing my passion: I majored in music.

You must be
nearly lost to
be (if
found) nearly
found[10]

After the first guitar lesson I took in college, I walked out into the autumnal Southern Ontario air and thought I was going to burst into tears. What little confidence I had as an 18-year-old musician was completely gone: I had no rhythm, I couldn't get my hands to work together to play anything coherent at all, so naturally I should just quit...or so went the logic in my not-fully-developed teenage mind. Instead, I threw myself into my new major, and had something of a brainwave while watching the Baseball Gryphons (my school's abysmal baseball team) a few weeks after that disastrous first guitar lesson. "But no! I'm studying to be a jazz musician now. An artiste! The type of person who simply doesn't have time for sports. This type of person cannot think about the 83-79 2007 Toronto Blue Jays, managed by John Gibbons, that featured team-leading OPS from Matt Stairs and Frank Thomas both in their age-39 seasons."[11]

So I didn't think about Matt Stairs or Frank Thomas or Roy Halladay or A.J. Burnett. I didn't even think about the legendary 2006 clubhouse fight between John Gibbons and Shea Hillenbrand![12] Instead, like a serious artist, I smoked weed and drank beer and went to almost every class sober and played a lot of guitar...like, *a lot* of guitar. I played so much guitar (and smoked so much weed) that in 2010, graduating on the heels of the Great Recession, I got it into my head that joining a rock band—turning whatever was left of my teenage passion and joy into a career—was an economically feasible (and therefore incredibly smart) idea. A professor told me that I was probably making a mistake—that the academy was a cushy gig and I had the right makeup for it—but if I really wanted to play rock'n'roll, I should give it three years and see what happens. I did exactly that and now routinely joke that I'm on Year 13 of a three-

year plan. This plan, like some of the best moments of Toronto Blue Jays baseball, included a helluva lot of loss and almost as much (re-)discovery of the worlds-within-worlds where joy resides.

The first appearance of that world-within-a-world came while making *The Dream Is Over*. I was still doing odd jobs in catering and sales to make rent between tours but the band had become my full-time concern, if not yet my full-time job. My ideas about the role of a musician-artiste were dissipating faster than a cloud of weed smoke; I was working odd jobs and routinely found myself at Rogers Centre (SkyDome) with my dad, drinking overpriced Budweisers and gradually reconnecting with my joyful love of the game and José Bautista's Toronto Blue Jays. My fandom was returning with a vengeance in that world-within-a-world. I was wearing a Jays hat throughout the United States, excitedly talking to PUP-and-baseball fans over post-show beers in shitty punk venues. I autographed a guy's ass in Cleveland as the Jays were busy dispensing with the city's then-horribly-named team in extra innings, screaming and pointing at my hat to people who had just paid to scream and point at me.

The Jays traded for David Price and Troy Tulowitzki as we were driving home from a tour to finish writing the songs for *TDIO*. We were in the studio recording that album when, on October 14, 2015, we stopped for a full hour to watch the seventh-inning chaos that ended in José Bautista's bat flip. There, at the most rock'n'roll age possible (27 years old), it finally became clear to me: You can love art, music and sports all at the same time because there is joyful poetry in every world as long as you are willing to find it. Bautista's bat flip was a sonnet:

don't you know you
have an unaccomplished mission unaccomplished?[13]

The intervening years have led to some strange times for the Blue Jays—and for everyone who loves the team. Free agent pitchers and position player signings have come and gone while some of the biggest what-ifs have gone on to compete for, and win, the World Series. Even more significant than that, the shiny debut of the Jays' talented young core of sons-of-former-big-leaguers has seemingly lost its luster in the long shadow of the COVID-19 pandemic. A writer looking for a parable might say that the Blue Jays and their fans are no longer looking to put on a fun jacket after hitting a home run.

While you'd be well within your rights to wonder—as many have—whether or not the Blue Jays are the worst best team in baseball, this greater question remains: For a team with so much talent, why is it so...joyless? Indeed, you could go as far as to say that when it comes to the Toronto Blue Jays, *no one is silly as a goose anymore*. As it is my unimpeachable right as a fan to psychoanalyze on-field talent, and given that I have made my living as someone who monetizes their passion and been lucky enough to lose and rediscover the things about it that bring me joy, please believe me when I say that these sons-of-former-big-leaguers, these Blue Jays, need to (re-)discover their own passion and joy. For the 2024 team, more than anything analytic or statistical or personnel-y in nature, the real breakthrough will come if the team can find an irrepressibly carefree and joyful way to play the game of baseball. (Or go back in time and put Shohei Ohtani on that plane to Toronto. That would've helped too.)

If they do? No-one will remember Vlad's solid-but-still-disappointing season, or José Berríos' untimely exit from Game 2 of the AL Wild Card, or Lourdes Gurriel Jr., Gabriel Moreno and Marcus Semien all playing in the 2023 World Series. It's a truism to say that a major-league season is a grinding rollercoaster ride; there are obviously many ups and downs for every team and thus not every gameday can be joyful. But the joy I'm talking about here is a joy of the game that exists within the larger world of the season. That joy is one that is irrepressible in the best teams, even when they're struggling. It is a simple eye test that will never be usurped by analytics. It's the kind of joy that makes loser baseball conservatives mad, y'know? Frankly, I'm not sure that I want to think too deeply about what happens to the Blue Jays if they aren't able to find that joyful world-within-a-world this year. In the AL East, as in baseball generally, it can get joyless

in every world really fast. However, since that sentiment is far too depressing to leave you with, let's allow one of America's greatest poets to have the final words on the 2024 Toronto Blue Jays:

> May happiness
> pursue you,
>
> catch you
> often, and,
>
> should it
> lose you,
>
> be waiting
> ahead, making
>
> a clearing
> for you.[14]

—Steve Sladkowski is a member of the punk rock band PUP.

---

1. Ammons, A.R. 2017. "Clabblebabble." In *The Complete Poems of A.R. Ammons, Vol. 2: 1978-2005*, edited by Robert M. West, 874. New York: W.W. Norton & Company.

2. Thorn, John. 2012. "Whitman, Melville, and Baseball." Published June 15, 2012.
https://ourgame.mlblogs.com/whitman-melville-and-baseball-662f5ef3583d/

3. Chiasson, Dan. 2017. "The Great American Poet of Daily Chores." *The New Yorker*, November 27, 2017.
https://www.newyorker.com/magazine/2017/12/04/the-great-american-poet-of-daily-chores

4. Ammons, A.R. 2006. "Their Sex Life." In *A.R. Ammons selected poems*, edited by David Lehman, 84. New York: The Library of America.

5. Ammons, A.R. 2017. "Pebble's Story." In *The Complete Poems of A.R. Ammons, Vol. 2: 1978-2005*, edited by Robert M. West, 205. New York: W.W. Norton & Company.

6. Ammons, A.R. 2017. "Glare." In *The Complete Poems of A.R. Ammons, Vol. 2: 1978-2005*, edited by Robert M. West, 654. New York: W.W. Norton & Company

7. Ammons, A.R. 2017. "Success Story." In *The Complete Poems of A.R. Ammons, Vol. 2: 1978-2005*, edited by Robert M. West, 192. New York: W.W. Norton & Company

8. 3687-3700, .499 W-L% all-time. If that's not the epitome of mediocre, what is?

9. The franchise also launched the career of Dan Shulman alongside Buck Martinez in 1995. You're welcome, baby!

10. Ammons, A.R. 2017. "Poetry to the Rescue." In *The Complete Poems of A.R. Ammons, Vol. 2: 1978-2005*, edited by Robert M. West, 204. New York: W.W. Norton & Company

11. Alex Rios and Troy Glaus finished third and fourth on the team in OPS that year. A few years later in 2009, mired in a horrible slump and with a contract looking increasingly like an albatross, Rios cold-shouldered a fan asking for an autograph outside a Toronto charity event. In an early showing of social media's power, Rios was called a bum on camera and shipped out of town to the White Sox shortly thereafter. Glaus was traded for Scott Rolen in 2008, a sentence that still feels crazy to type 15 years later.

12. As it turns out, John Gibbons' memoir *Gibby: Tales of a Baseball Lifer* was published by Toronto's ECW Press in 2023. The infamous fight between Gibby and Hillenbrand was brought on by an anonymously written message on a clubhouse whiteboard. The memoir reveals that the message was written by the worst former player television analyst the Jays ever had: Gregg Zaun.

13. Ammons, A.R. 2017. "Garbage." In *The Complete Poems of A.R. Ammons, Vol. 2: 1978-2005*, edited by Robert M. West, 220. New York: W.W. Norton & Company.

14. Ammons, A.R. 2017. "Salute." In *The Complete Poems of A.R. Ammons, Vol. 2: 1978-2005*, edited by Robert M. West, 210. New York: W.W. Norton & Company.

HITTERS

Bo Bichette SS Born: 03/05/98 Age: 26 Bats: R Throws: R Height: 6'0" Weight: 190 Origin: Round 2, 2016 Draft (#66 overall)

YEAR	TM	LVL	AGE	PA	R	HR	RBI	SB	AVG/OBP/SLG	BABIP	SLGCON	BB%	K%	ZSw%	ZCon%	OSw%	OCon%	LA	90th EV	DRC+	BRR	DRP	WARP
2021	TOR	MLB	23	690	121	29	102	25	.298/.343/.484	.339	.616	5.8%	19.9%	82.2%	86.3%	41.3%	66.0%	7.6	107.4	125	0.9	0.7	4.8
2022	TOR	MLB	24	697	91	24	93	13	.290/.333/.469	.347	.616	5.9%	22.2%	79.2%	86.1%	39.6%	64.2%	8.6	106.6	106	-0.8	-6.5	2.0
2023	TOR	MLB	25	601	69	20	73	5	.306/.339/.475	.355	.594	4.5%	19.1%	79.1%	87.6%	40.6%	66.5%	6.6	106.6	113	-0.1	1.5	3.1
2024 DC	TOR	MLB	26	607	68	21	76	12	.283/.326/.446	.320	.556	5.5%	18.3%							117	0.2	1.1	3.6

2023 GP: SS (130), DH (5)   *Comps: Francisco Lindor (82), Alex Rodriguez (81), Garry Templeton (80)*

Bo Bichette swings—a fluid motion of absolute aggression—and lines the ball down the line. Bo Bichette swings and his hair—cleaned with shampoo made for horses—flutters in the breeze as he drives a ball to the gap. Bo Bichette swings—the fans intuit the ball's imminent ascent and feel the torque from his hips up in the cheap seats—and the moon rises over the roof of the Rogers Centre. Bo Bichette swings and a butterfly takes off in Kansas—the oceans rise and the world spins—both the ballgame and the universe come closer and closer to chaos. Bo Bichette swings—he has no time to simply *look* at pitches—because man was not put on earth to merely look at things. Bo Bichette swings.

Cavan Biggio 2B Born: 04/11/95 Age: 29 Bats: L Throws: R Height: 6'2" Weight: 200 Origin: Round 5, 2016 Draft (#162 overall)

YEAR	TM	LVL	AGE	PA	R	HR	RBI	SB	AVG/OBP/SLG	BABIP	SLGCON	BB%	K%	ZSw%	ZCon%	OSw%	OCon%	LA	90th EV	DRC+	BRR	DRP	WARP
2021	BUF	AAA	26	90	15	3	11	0	.182/.289/.325	.224	.490	12.2%	28.9%							85	0.3	-1.9	0.0
2021	TOR	MLB	26	294	27	7	27	3	.224/.322/.356	.290	.517	12.6%	26.5%	64.5%	86.2%	22.7%	46.8%	15.3	101.2	82	0.0	0.1	0.3
2022	BUF	AAA	27	39	9	0	3	2	.276/.462/.379	.348	.478	25.6%	15.4%							114	0.6	-0.4	0.2
2022	TOR	MLB	27	303	43	6	24	2	.202/.318/.350	.275	.523	12.5%	28.1%	64.6%	84.7%	21.0%	48.7%	20.1	101.6	80	-0.1	0.5	0.1
2023	TOR	MLB	28	338	54	9	40	5	.235/.340/.370	.304	.532	11.8%	26.0%	65.5%	88.6%	19.4%	43.4%	15.8	101.1	87	0.0	-0.2	0.4
2024 DC	TOR	MLB	29	349	36	8	35	4	.215/.323/.354	.269	.486	12.4%	23.5%							94	0.0	-0.5	0.5

2023 GP: 2B (49), RF (27), 1B (20), 3B (13), DH (7), SS (1)   *Comps: Danny Espinosa (60), Greg Garcia (57), Pat Kelly (53)*

Biggio started the season about as cold as possible: He was 4-for-25 in the first few weeks and carried a sub-.450 OPS into the middle of May. The Blue Jays long had found uses for Biggio thanks to his defensive versatility, easily shifting all across the infield and outfield. But there comes a time when the stick needs to show up, too. Fortunately, Biggio always had the support of his former minor-league manager and current big-league skipper, John Schneider.

"I just said, 'Dude, I'm not going to ever give up on you,'" Schneider told Yahoo Sports Canada.

After working with hitting coach Hunter Mense, Biggio flattened out his swing and focused on his key skills: Contact and controlling the strike zone. By the end of the year, Biggio was an everyday player even if he didn't have an everyday position, hitting .272/.404/.361 in the second half of the season.

Enmanuel Bonilla OF Born: 01/22/06 Age: 18 Bats: R Throws: R Height: 6'1" Weight: 180 Origin: IFA, 2023

YEAR	TM	LVL	AGE	PA	R	HR	RBI	SB	AVG/OBP/SLG	BABIP	SLGCON	BB%	K%	ZSw%	ZCon%	OSw%	OCon%	LA	90th EV	DRC+	BRR	DRP	WARP
2023	DSL BLJ	ROK	17	226	41	3	22	5	.307/.407/.429	.410	.604	11.9%	24.3%										
2024									No projection														

2023 GP: CF (49), 3B (1), DH (1)

Signed to a $4.1 million bonus last January, Bonilla's bat speed has scouts salivating and the Blue Jays front office thinking they've got *next decade*'s middle-of-the-order hitter figured out. Just 17 years old, he impressed in the Dominican Summer League, but while Bonilla has the raw stuff, he also comes with the usual caveats when regarding ballplayers who could otherwise be thinking about prom dates: Will he fill out and need to move to a corner outfield spot? Will he close the holes in his swing and control the strike zone? Will he have a change of heart and decide that animal husbandry is really his life's purpose? Those are all questions best answered years from now.

Ernie Clement IF Born: 03/22/96 Age: 28 Bats: R Throws: R Height: 6'0" Weight: 170 Origin: Round 4, 2017 Draft (#132 overall)

YEAR	TM	LVL	AGE	PA	R	HR	RBI	SB	AVG/OBP/SLG	BABIP	SLGCON	BB%	K%	ZSw%	ZCon%	OSw%	OCon%	LA	90th EV	DRC+	BRR	DRP	WARP
2021	COL	AAA	25	138	11	1	10	2	.250/.294/.387	.288	.471	6.5%	15.9%							95	0.2	1.7	0.5
2021	CLE	MLB	25	133	16	3	9	0	.231/.285/.339	.253	.402	5.3%	14.3%	62.6%	89.1%	36.9%	76.3%	14.3	100.8	99	0.2	0.0	0.5
2022	COL	AAA	26	87	13	4	17	0	.238/.291/.438	.221	.486	6.9%	9.2%							124	0.3	0.5	0.6
2022	OAK	MLB	26	18	1	0	0	0	.056/.056/.111	.063	.125	0.0%	11.1%	76.9%	100.0%	42.9%	75.0%	20.7	97.1	119	0.0	0.0	0.1
2022	CLE	MLB	26	161	18	0	6	0	.200/.264/.221	.238	.264	6.8%	14.9%	64.3%	85.4%	37.5%	81.6%	10.1	100.3	97	-0.1	0.7	0.5
2023	BUF	AAA	27	320	57	11	58	12	.348/.401/.544	.338	.576	8.1%	5.0%	66.2%	93.6%	37.7%	82.9%			129	2.0	-1.3	1.9
2023	TOR	MLB	27	52	7	1	10	1	.380/.385/.500	.391	.543	1.9%	7.7%	70.8%	92.2%	44.6%	86.5%	16.1	99.9	108	0.0	0.0	0.2
2024 DC	TOR	MLB	28	92	9	2	9	1	.262/.312/.381	.274	.434	6.2%	9.9%							98	0.0	0.2	0.3

2023 GP: SS (15), 2B (6), 3B (3), DH (2), P (1)   *Comps: Donovan Solano (54), Jeff Bianchi (53), Jonathan Herrera (53)*

Clement hails from Rochester, New York—home of the Garbage Plate. The Garbage Plate looks as its name implies: It's hot dogs or cheeseburgers over a plate—or, usually, a styrofoam box—featuring home fries, macaroni salad and meat sauce. It shouldn't all come together and yet, it does. (Especially if you've had a few Genny Cream Ales.) Clement's 2023 was very Garbage Plate-esque. The former fourth-round pick found himself bouncing between Toronto or Buffalo, which is a quick drive from his hometown and those Nick Tahou's Garbage Plates. Clement swung at almost everything and hit almost everything, too. His contact rate would have been second in the league with enough plate appearances—just behind Luis Arraez—despite a ridiculously high 45% rate of swinging at pitches outside the strike zone. Just like the garbage plate, when looked at from afar, it doesn't make sense...until it does.

Alex De Jesus 3B/SS Born: 03/22/02   Age: 22   Bats: R   Throws: R   Height: 6'1"   Weight: 170   Origin: IFA, 2018

YEAR	TM	LVL	AGE	PA	R	HR	RBI	SB	AVG/OBP/SLG	BABIP	SLGCON	BB%	K%	ZSw%	ZCon%	OSw%	OCon%	LA	90th EV	DRC+	BRR	DRP	WARP
2021	RC	A	19	422	67	12	73	1	.268/.386/.447	.385	.704	16.4%	30.3%							106	0.0	-8.3	0.8
2022	RC	A	20	176	34	7	22	2	.259/.398/.483	.349	.742	18.2%	28.4%							115	-0.7	0.7	0.9
2022	GL	A+	20	226	27	4	26	0	.282/.376/.421	.402	.631	12.4%	28.8%							90	-0.3	-0.5	0.2
2022	VAN	A+	20	104	10	2	13	0	.211/.298/.333	.315	.556	11.5%	34.6%							79	-0.4	-0.2	0.0
2023	VAN	A+	21	344	56	11	59	5	.248/.340/.466	.313	.675	11.6%	26.5%							107	-1.4	-0.7	1.0
2024 non	TOR	MLB	22	251	22	4	23	0	.229/.300/.342	.330	.520	8.6%	31.0%							83	0.0	0	0.3

2023 GP: 3B (42), SS (29), DH (9)   *Comps: Juan Silverio (64), Aderlin Rodríguez (63), Jeimer Candelario (61)*

There was plenty of teeth gnashing among Blue Jays fans over the acquisition of De Jesus—and it had nothing to do with the infield prospect at all! Rather, it's that the Blue Jays gave up top pitching prospect Nick Frasso for Mitch White and De Jesus at the 2022 deadline and have watched as Frasso and his big fastball are now on the cusp of the majors. While White was sent to Triple-A for much of the year, De Jesus repeated Single-A, where he kept getting on base and showed off some increased power. He'll need that if a move to third base is in his future.

Santiago Espinal IF Born: 11/13/94   Age: 29   Bats: R   Throws: R   Height: 5'10"   Weight: 185   Origin: Round 10, 2016 Draft (#298 overall)

YEAR	TM	LVL	AGE	PA	R	HR	RBI	SB	AVG/OBP/SLG	BABIP	SLGCON	BB%	K%	ZSw%	ZCon%	OSw%	OCon%	LA	90th EV	DRC+	BRR	DRP	WARP
2021	TOR	MLB	26	246	32	2	17	6	.311/.376/.405	.353	.469	8.9%	12.2%	67.4%	93.1%	33.1%	72.9%	12.5	99.9	113	0.2	0.6	1.4
2022	TOR	MLB	27	491	51	7	51	6	.267/.322/.370	.300	.436	7.3%	13.8%	66.4%	90.3%	32.9%	76.8%	13.5	101.0	101	-0.1	1.9	1.8
2023	TOR	MLB	28	254	30	2	25	2	.248/.310/.335	.285	.397	7.1%	14.2%	62.7%	89.0%	31.9%	73.8%	10.8	100.7	103	0.1	-0.5	0.9
2024 DC	TOR	MLB	29	220	21	3	21	4	.260/.322/.362	.292	.427	7.8%	13.8%							97	0.0	0.2	0.5

2023 GP: 2B (47), 3B (26), SS (16), DH (1)   *Comps: Alberto Gonzalez (56), Brock Holt (54), César Hernández (54)*

The season started rough for Espinal and never got much better. After making his first All-Star Game appearance last year, the super-utility player found himself with a sub-.100 batting average 17 games into the season. A month later, and just as soon as he had got his average over the Mendoza line, he *was* on the IL with a hamstring strain. While he was never known for his skills at the plate—the second-half of last year's All-Star campaign saw Espinal hit just .258/.328/.315— the more alarming part is what happened to Espinal's glove. He'd previously passed both the eye test and the advanced stats exam no matter where he lined up on the field, but both standard stats (nine errors) and advanced numbers saw him backslide on the field. Entering his first year of arbitration and with plenty of infield options coming up from the minors, Espinal may find himself on a new team looking for a bounceback.

Vladimir Guerrero Jr. 1B Born: 03/16/99   Age: 25   Bats: R   Throws: R   Height: 6'2"   Weight: 245   Origin: IFA, 2015

YEAR	TM	LVL	AGE	PA	R	HR	RBI	SB	AVG/OBP/SLG	BABIP	SLGCON	BB%	K%	ZSw%	ZCon%	OSw%	OCon%	LA	90th EV	DRC+	BRR	DRP	WARP
2021	TOR	MLB	22	698	123	48	111	4	.311/.401/.601	.313	.735	12.3%	15.8%	75.3%	84.9%	29.2%	51.0%	9.5	112.7	157	-0.5	0.3	6.6
2022	TOR	MLB	23	706	90	32	97	8	.274/.339/.480	.289	.586	8.2%	16.4%	73.0%	85.5%	34.5%	61.9%	4.2	111.0	129	-0.5	-0.7	3.8
2023	TOR	MLB	24	682	78	26	94	5	.264/.345/.444	.277	.532	9.8%	14.7%	77.3%	86.8%	32.7%	61.6%	10.5	109.1	138	-0.3	-0.9	4.5
2024 DC	TOR	MLB	25	601	78	27	86	5	.278/.354/.483	.292	.585	9.5%	15.6%							136	-0.3	-0.1	3.9

2023 GP: 1B (121), DH (34)   *Comps: Fred Merkle (75), Stuffy McInnis (70), Freddie Freeman (69)*

Just like all those aging millennials who have created countless "gifted child" memes, so too has the Blue Jays' gifted slugger been weighed down with the burdens of hope and heightened expectations. Ever since the big-boned bruiser emerged on this planet and was given his Hall-of-Fame father's moniker, people have been waiting for Vlad to—if not ascend to heaven—then get awfully close. He pulled it off two years ago, showing the kind of game-changing power that he was fated for. Though his power dropped off in 2022, he made up for it by willing himself to a Gold Glove. Now, though? 26 HRs and a 4.5 WARP were simply not good enough for the chosen one. Like he was burdened with a horrid curse, Guerrero didn't even hit a home run at the Rogers Centre until June 23, depriving his legions of fans from such exquisite ecstasy. Guerrero showed that his world-breaking power was still there when he collected the HR Derby trophy, but when Guerrero was picked off in the Blue Jays' final game of the postseason, it made people begin to wonder: Is it possible that he's simply mortal?

Spencer Horwitz 1B Born: 11/14/97   Age: 26   Bats: L   Throws: R   Height: 5'10"   Weight: 190   Origin: Round 24, 2019 Draft (#717 overall)

YEAR	TM	LVL	AGE	PA	R	HR	RBI	SB	AVG/OBP/SLG	BABIP	SLGCON	BB%	K%	ZSw%	ZCon%	OSw%	OCon%	LA	90th EV	DRC+	BRR	DRP	WARP
2021	MSS	WIN	23	74	14	1	12	4	.375/.459/.484	.442	.585	12.2%	14.9%	75.0%	100.0%	0.0%							
2021	VAN	A+	23	469	65	10	62	4	.290/.401/.445	.324	.536	14.9%	14.1%							131	1.2	5.9	3.8
2022	NH	AA	24	281	46	10	39	3	.297/.413/.517	.347	.674	15.3%	19.2%							128	0.8	-0.9	1.6
2022	BUF	AAA	24	202	31	2	12	4	.246/.361/.363	.313	.477	14.9%	20.3%							101	-1.2	-1.7	0.3
2023	BUF	AAA	25	484	61	10	72	9	.337/.450/.495	.386	.606	16.1%	14.9%	68.6%	88.6%	29.1%	70.0%			123	-1.5	2.9	2.7
2023	TOR	MLB	25	44	5	1	7	0	.256/.341/.385	.346	.556	9.1%	27.3%	70.0%	81.0%	35.8%	61.5%	1.8	103.3	88	0.0	0.0	0.0
2024 DC	TOR	MLB	26	199	20	3	19	2	.241/.338/.369	.287	.464	11.6%	18.1%							103	-0.1	0	0.5

2023 GP: DH (6), 1B (5)   *Comps: Andy Wilkins (71), Mark Hamilton (67), Jared Walsh (63)*

Horwitz may not be the prototypical first baseman, having never topped 12 home runs in a minor-league season, but that's okay when you can get on base the way he does. His .450 OBP was fifth-best in the minors for all hitters with at least 350 plate appearances, and he's drawn more walks than strikeouts in two of his last three seasons. Naturally, during his first call-up this summer, Horwitz didn't just pick up his first big league hit, but he drew his first two walks as well. Don't be surprised if you see a lot more of Horwitz's name in the press this winter, too. While his performance on the field certainly deserves it, he's also the grandson of legendary Mets PR stud, Jay Horwitz. The elder Horwitz is retired now, but do you really think he won't make a few phone calls on behalf of his grandson?

Danny Jansen C   Born: 04/15/95   Age: 29   Bats: R   Throws: R   Height: 6'2"   Weight: 215   Origin: Round 16, 2013 Draft (#475 overall)

YEAR	TM	LVL	AGE	PA	R	HR	RBI	SB	AVG/OBP/SLG	BABIP	SLGCON	BB%	K%	ZSw%	ZCon%	OSw%	OCon%	LA	90th EV	DRC+	BRR	DRP	WARP
2021	BUF	AAA	26	26	5	1	4	0	.238/.346/.381	.222	.444	15.4%	11.5%							117	-0.1	0.0	0.1
2021	TOR	MLB	26	205	32	11	28	0	.223/.299/.473	.233	.621	8.3%	21.5%	74.6%	79.2%	28.1%	65.1%	20.7	105.4	101	0.0	0.7	1.0
2022	TOR	MLB	27	248	34	15	44	1	.260/.339/.516	.255	.649	10.1%	17.7%	69.1%	82.5%	25.5%	67.9%	22.1	105.0	134	-0.3	-0.9	1.8
2023	TOR	MLB	28	301	38	17	53	0	.228/.312/.474	.233	.617	7.6%	20.6%	71.0%	83.9%	28.8%	64.0%	20.5	103.6	111	0.0	3.1	1.8
2024 DC	TOR	MLB	29	375	46	17	52	0	.243/.322/.449	.263	.575	8.7%	19.8%							115	0.0	1.3	2.1

2023 GP: C (73), DH (9)

Comps: Yasmani Grandal (58), Francisco Cervelli (58), Devin Mesoraco (58)

YEAR	TM	P. COUNT	FRM RUNS	BLK RUNS	THRW RUNS	TOT RUNS
2021	TOR	8117	1.7	0.2	0.0	1.9
2022	TOR	8444	-1.1	0.3	0.8	0.0
2023	TOR	9548	3.5	0.1	0.3	3.8
2024	TOR	10822	1.0	0.3	-0.1	1.3

Despite missing the last month of the season with a fractured finger, Jansen still put up career highs in home runs, total bases and RBI all while getting the short end of a timeshare with Alejandro Kirk for the catching job. His 43 home runs over the last three years is 10th-most among all catchers, just behind Jonah Heim and William Contreras. His OPS in that time is sixth-best among all catchers with at least 500 PA in the period, just three points behind Adley Rutschman for fourth-best. That's all to say that the bespectacled Jansen is one of the most underrated players in the game, and that the Blue Jays just may have the greatest catching duo in the sport. Equally adept at hitting righties and lefties and entering his final year of arbitration, don't be surprised if Jansen ends up having quite the payday in 2025.

Leo Jimenez MI   Born: 05/17/01   Age: 23   Bats: R   Throws: R   Height: 5'10"   Weight: 215   Origin: IFA, 2017

YEAR	TM	LVL	AGE	PA	R	HR	RBI	SB	AVG/OBP/SLG	BABIP	SLGCON	BB%	K%	ZSw%	ZCon%	OSw%	OCon%	LA	90th EV	DRC+	BRR	DRP	WARP
2021	DUN	A	20	242	35	1	19	4	.315/.517/.381	.388	.481	21.1%	14.5%	65.4%	84.2%	23.2%	65.2%			145	-0.7	-3.8	1.6
2022	VAN	A+	21	294	45	6	40	7	.230/.340/.385	.269	.505	9.2%	19.7%							122	-0.3	-0.7	1.6
2023	NH	AA	22	333	54	8	44	8	.287/.372/.436	.325	.534	9.6%	15.9%							125	0.2	-2.3	1.7
2023	BUF	AAA	22	77	8	0	3	0	.190/.338/.238	.250	.312	11.7%	19.5%	60.3%	92.4%	29.8%	63.2%			96	0.5	-2.3	0.0
2024 DC	TOR	MLB	23	30	3	0	3	0	.222/.301/.317	.263	.364	8.0%	17.9%							81	0.0	0	0.0

2023 GP: SS (62), 2B (25), DH (8)

Comps: Yamaico Navarro (56), Edmundo Sosa (55), Eugenio Suárez (53)

Anytime a shortstop is a wizard with glove and can hit even the tiniest amount, GMs perk up the way one does in a restaurant upon seeing a waiter holding a tray with what could be your meal. Add in just a touch of power and those same GMs might tackle their servers trying to get a bite. Already carrying an MLB-ready glove, the big concern was if Jimenez could add enough strength to hold pitchers accountable. He did that last year, hitting a career-high eight home runs while continuing to display the same advanced approach at the plate. It made him a highly prized commodity, so Jays fans weren't too surprised when he was pulled for what was assumed to be a trade on July 30th. Instead of being shipped out, the Jays held onto Jimenez, and will roll the dice on what they have: If the bat plays, it will be a full meal, piping hot and filled with All-Star games in the future.

Kevin Kiermaier CF   Born: 04/22/90   Age: 34   Bats: L   Throws: R   Height: 6'1"   Weight: 210   Origin: Round 31, 2010 Draft (#941 overall)

YEAR	TM	LVL	AGE	PA	R	HR	RBI	SB	AVG/OBP/SLG	BABIP	SLGCON	BB%	K%	ZSw%	ZCon%	OSw%	OCon%	LA	90th EV	DRC+	BRR	DRP	WARP
2021	TB	MLB	31	390	54	4	37	9	.259/.328/.388	.345	.542	8.5%	25.4%	77.6%	79.8%	33.1%	50.2%	1.5	102.6	76	0.4	6.2	1.1
2022	TB	MLB	32	221	28	7	22	6	.228/.281/.369	.290	.524	6.3%	27.6%	76.3%	80.9%	32.1%	44.0%	5.7	102.9	87	0.3	2.5	0.7
2023	TOR	MLB	33	408	58	8	36	14	.265/.322/.419	.321	.546	7.1%	21.1%	72.7%	81.0%	31.7%	50.0%	5.8	102.6	88	0.4	3.9	1.4
2024 DC	TOR	MLB	34	449	42	8	44	9	.235/.302/.361	.307	.500	7.8%	25.5%							87	0.6	4.8	1.4

2023 GP: CF (127)

Comps: Mark Kotsay (68), Bill Virdon (62), Carlos Beltrán (62)

What is the ideal baseball highlight? Is it a 450-foot home run to the moon? Is it a crisply turned 6-4-3 double play? Is it a player delightfully sneaking a fart in the dugout—only to realize with horror that it has been captured by the TV cameras? I would like to submit that it is the center fielder's gazelle-like sprint across the outfield, punctuating in a headfirst leap for the baseball, that is brightest in the mind's eye. And if that *is* the highlight of highlights, then Kiermaier deserves a special honor for his place in the canon. Staying healthy enough to play in 129 games—he lost time after getting his arm chewed up in Fenway Park's outfield wall—Kiermaier earned his fourth Gold Glove after another year of backbreaking, physics-defying highlights. Now a free agent, Kiermaier will hope he can turn his successful bet-on-me season into a trip to a ballpark with natural grass. The longer he plays, the longer we can watch him launch himself into our memories.

Isiah Kiner-Falefa CF   Born: 03/23/95   Age: 29   Bats: R   Throws: R   Height: 5'11"   Weight: 190   Origin: Round 4, 2013 Draft (#130 overall)

YEAR	TM	LVL	AGE	PA	R	HR	RBI	SB	AVG/OBP/SLG	BABIP	SLGCON	BB%	K%	ZSw%	ZCon%	OSw%	OCon%	LA	90th EV	DRC+	BRR	DRP	WARP
2021	TEX	MLB	26	677	74	8	53	20	.271/.312/.357	.304	.417	4.1%	13.3%	63.0%	93.7%	36.1%	76.4%	5.3	100.9	98	0.9	3.6	2.8
2022	NYY	MLB	27	531	66	4	48	22	.261/.314/.327	.296	.384	6.6%	13.6%	59.2%	95.7%	34.7%	80.8%	4.0	100.5	102	0.9	8.1	2.8
2023	NYY	MLB	28	361	39	6	37	14	.242/.306/.340	.289	.434	7.8%	19.4%	62.2%	89.5%	32.5%	68.0%	6.5	103.4	93	0.7	0.9	1.0
2024 DC	TOR	MLB	29	384	35	5	35	15	.252/.311/.344	.288	.412	6.9%	15.0%							90	0.4	1.4	0.8

2023 GP: CF (41), LF (37), 3B (31), RF (7), P (4), 2B (1), SS (1)

Comps: Jose Vizcaino (70), Hal Lanier (69), Adeiny Hechavarría (68)

One of the most finicky ingredients on "The Great British Bake Off" is rose water. Every season, various contestants try to mix it into their recipes in hopes of winning Star Baker, only to use either too much, overpowering their recipe's other flavors, or too little, leading to Paul Hollywood grumbling "I'm not getting any of the rose water!" It's just so rare to see anyone hit the Goldilocks-esque "just right" level that it hardly seems worth it. That's the IKF problem too, but the Yankees seemed to get the proportions a little better in 2023, avoiding an ugly reaction from the fanbase. In the smaller dose of a super-utility role, which it looks like he'll occupy in Toronto as well, Kiner-Falefa is a lot more palatable.

Alejandro Kirk C Born: 11/06/98 Age: 25 Bats: R Throws: R Height: 5'8" Weight: 245 Origin: IFA, 2016

YEAR	TM	LVL	AGE	PA	R	HR	RBI	SB	AVG/OBP/SLG	BABIP	SLGCON	BB%	K%	ZSw%	ZCon%	OSw%	OCon%	LA	90th EV	DRC+	BRR	DRP	WARP
2021	BUF	AAA	22	56	7	2	13	0	.347/.393/.531	.375	.650	8.9%	16.1%							110	0.0	-1.0	0.2
2021	TOR	MLB	22	189	19	8	24	0	.242/.328/.436	.234	.503	10.1%	11.6%	65.1%	86.7%	31.4%	72.1%	14.6	105.2	138	-0.1	0.0	1.7
2022	TOR	MLB	23	541	59	14	63	0	.285/.372/.415	.299	.473	11.6%	10.7%	61.5%	91.0%	27.5%	75.1%	8.4	105.1	137	-1.4	10.5	5.1
2023	TOR	MLB	24	422	34	8	43	0	.250/.334/.358	.265	.407	10.0%	10.7%	58.8%	93.3%	30.1%	79.1%	6.6	102.9	141	-0.7	7.1	4.3
2024 DC	TOR	MLB	25	466	52	12	51	0	.269/.349/.402	.280	.455	10.0%	10.3%							117	0.0	3.2	3.0

2023 GP: C (99), DH (17)

Comps: Milt May (67), Salvador Perez (63), Jerry May (61)

YEAR	TM	P. COUNT	FRM RUNS	BLK RUNS	THRW RUNS	TOT RUNS
2021	BUF	1421	-0.7	-0.1	0.0	-0.8
2021	TOR	5494	0.6	0.0	0.2	0.8
2022	TOR	10231	11.0	0.4	1.1	12.5
2023	TOR	12618	5.4	0.3	0.6	6.3
2024	TOR	13228	2.9	0.2	0.1	3.1

For the fans who are particularly enthralled by the huskier members of the Blue Jays team—those who take the term Beefy Boy as a compliment—2023 was not your year. Vladimir Guerrero Jr.'s numbers dipped and, for the first few months of the season, it appeared that Kirk had dropped off the edge as well. (While Guerrero struggled for months to hit a home run *at home*, Kirk had the opposite problem: Only one of his eight dingers came on the road.) The biggest culprit is clear: Kirk's exit velocity sunk, going from 92.3 mph in 2021 to 90.5 in 2022 and dropping all the way to 87.6 last year. Fortunately, his defense was once again splendid; the squat-bodied catcher has become one of the game's very best at blocking balls in the dirt.

Rafael Lantigua UT Born: 04/28/98 Age: 26 Bats: R Throws: R Height: 5'7" Weight: 153 Origin: IFA, 2016

YEAR	TM	LVL	AGE	PA	R	HR	RBI	SB	AVG/OBP/SLG	BABIP	SLGCON	BB%	K%	ZSw%	ZCon%	OSw%	OCon%	LA	90th EV	DRC+	BRR	DRP	WARP
2021	VAN	A+	23	347	65	11	43	26	.280/.375/.470	.341	.629	12.1%	21.9%							123	1.6	-1.9	2.0
2022	NH	AA	24	368	53	5	35	6	.268/.345/.402	.327	.512	10.1%	19.0%							95	0.8	4.4	1.3
2022	BUF	AAA	24	179	20	2	29	9	.286/.346/.373	.349	.476	8.9%	19.6%							95	1.3	-1.9	0.4
2023	BUF	AAA	25	578	101	12	85	28	.305/.425/.469	.366	.609	17.0%	18.5%	70.1%	82.2%	24.0%	58.6%			113	0.3	-7.4	1.6
2024 non	TOR	MLB	26	251	24	4	23	6	.235/.319/.348	.299	.467	10.2%	22.5%							92	0.0	0	0.5

2023 GP: LF (39), 3B (34), SS (24), RF (14), 2B (10), DH (9), CF (5)

Comps: Brian Horwitz (61), Breyvic Valera (57), Ty Kelly (55)

In an earlier, more Jack Cust-y version of Baseball Twitter, there would be a #FreeRafaelLantigua movement with t-shirts and fan meetups. Long known for his patient approach at the plate, Lantigua set career highs in homers, batting average, on-base percentage and slugging, while his 98 walks were ninth-most in all of the minors. Where he's not like Cust is that Lantigua played six different positions last year, including shortstop and center field. Entering his age-26 season, expect to see him in the majors next year as a super-utility guy, or maybe even something more.

★ ★ ★ *2024 Top 101 Prospect* **#95** ★ ★ ★

Orelvis Martinez IF Born: 11/19/01 Age: 22 Bats: R Throws: R Height: 5'11" Weight: 200 Origin: IFA, 2018

YEAR	TM	LVL	AGE	PA	R	HR	RBI	SB	AVG/OBP/SLG	BABIP	SLGCON	BB%	K%	ZSw%	ZCon%	OSw%	OCon%	LA	90th EV	DRC+	BRR	DRP	WARP
2021	DUN	A	19	326	49	19	68	4	.279/.369/.572	.333	.818	10.1%	26.1%	83.1%	83.6%	37.5%	49.5%			130	-1.8	-5.1	1.5
2021	VAN	A+	19	125	17	9	19	0	.214/.282/.491	.197	.655	8.0%	22.4%							125	-0.4	-1.6	0.6
2022	NH	AA	20	492	57	30	76	6	.203/.286/.446	.217	.659	8.1%	28.5%							96	-3.3	-1.8	0.8
2023	NH	AA	21	292	33	17	46	0	.226/.339/.485	.223	.648	14.0%	20.5%							120	-1.8	-2.6	1.1
2023	BUF	AAA	21	246	37	11	48	2	.263/.340/.507	.317	.741	10.6%	26.8%	76.2%	84.1%	34.2%	39.8%			92	-0.1	-3.5	0.0
2024 DC	TOR	MLB	22	131	14	5	15	0	.217/.288/.385	.288	.590	8.1%	31.3%							89	0.0	0	0.2

2023 GP: SS (43), 3B (37), 2B (30), DH (25)

Comps: Nick Franklin (53), Corey Seager (52), Ketel Marte (51)

Here's the list of big league shortstops with at least 28+ HRs in each of the last two seasons: Corey Seager. That's the list. Meanwhile, Martinez has now done that in back-to-back seasons in the minors, perhaps explaining why the youngster is so highly valued. Just 21 years old, the Blue Jays continued to be aggressive in their promotion of the infielder, and they watched as his OPS leaped by 100 points while playing across two levels. His average will always be ghastly and the production will come with plenty of whiffs, but the combination of power, on-base skills and the ability to play both short and third means Martinez's big-league time is coming.

Arjun Nimmala SS Born: 10/16/05 Age: 18 Bats: R Throws: R Height: 6'1" Weight: 170 Origin: Round 1, 2023 Draft (#20 overall)

YEAR	TM	LVL	AGE	PA	R	HR	RBI	SB	AVG/OBP/SLG	BABIP	SLGCON	BB%	K%	ZSw%	ZCon%	OSw%	OCon%	LA	90th EV	DRC+	BRR	DRP	WARP
2023	BLU	ROK	17	40	7	0	3	1	.200/.500/.320	.294	.471	35.0%	20.0%			75.0%	33.3%						
2024									No projection														

2023 GP: SS (9)

Every first round athlete has an aura of expectations hung around their neck. It's certainly not fair: These are teenagers who happen to have an impressive collection of skills, who quickly have to become franchise faces. The hopes for Nimmala are even higher than normal: The 20th-overall selection in the past draft isn't just expected to carry the Blue Jays into the future, but he could also become the first player of Indian descent to reach the majors. Not only is this something that is on his mind—he already told MLB Network that he can hopefully "inspire young Indian-Americans to play [baseball],"—but he has also already starred in a four-episode TV series that aired in India showcasing the youngster traveling through the country and getting in touch with his roots. Could Nimmala be the type of player that changes the future of baseball forever in one of the world's most populous countries? And is it even fair to ask that of him?

Damiano Palmegiani 3B Born: 01/24/00 Age: 24 Bats: R Throws: R Height: 6'0" Weight: 195 Origin: Round 14, 2021 Draft (#422 overall)

YEAR	TM	LVL	AGE	PA	R	HR	RBI	SB	AVG/OBP/SLG	BABIP	SLGCON	BB%	K%	ZSw%	ZCon%	OSw%	OCon%	LA	90th EV	DRC+	BRR	DRP	WARP
2021	BLU	ROK	21	48	11	2	9	1	.333/.458/.538	.393	.700	14.6%	18.8%										1.7
2022	DUN	A	22	228	30	11	37	2	.256/.351/.508	.279	.669	10.1%	20.6%	70.9%	88.4%	28.0%	53.5%			132	1.3	-2.6	1.4
2022	VAN	A+	22	272	44	13	46	3	.224/.335/.443	.239	.601	11.4%	22.1%							118	0.9	0.1	1.4
2023	SUR	WIN	23	93	19	4	17	1	.260/.366/.521	.313	.809	11.8%	28.0%	76.2%	87.5%	28.6%	33.3%						
2023	NH	AA	23	461	57	19	71	6	.249/.351/.463	.312	.679	12.6%	27.1%							117	-7.0	-0.6	1.4
2023	BUF	AAA	23	96	13	4	22	1	.284/.427/.554	.386	.891	15.6%	29.2%	69.0%	82.7%	20.8%	34.8%			97	-0.4	0.4	0.1
2024 DC	TOR	MLB	24	29	3	1	3	0	.218/.297/.363	.289	.500	8.6%	28.9%							88	0.0	0	0.0

2023 GP: 3B (87), 1B (33), DH (29)   Comps: Edwin Ríos (62), Christian Walker (55), Nicholas Torres (54)

The Blue Jays have had that Canadian pipeline on lock in recent years. Born in Caracas, Venezuela, Palmegiani moved to British Columbia when he was five years old and has seemingly been on Toronto's radar since then. He made his Canadian youth debut in 2016, played in Canadian Futures Showcases in '16 and '17, and the Jays even drafted him twice—taking Palmegiani in the 35th round in 2018 and then the 14th round in 2021. The corner infielder has tremendous power, finishing second in the system in home runs with 23 and increased his on-base percentage by 25 points from the season prior. That Jays' love is returned by Palmegiani, who grew up a Blue Jays obsessive. As for his favorite players, prepare to feel ancient: "José Bautista when I was a little younger," Palmegiani told MiLB.com. "Then when I started to get a little older, like high school, it was Josh Donaldson. He was the man."

Alan Roden OF Born: 12/22/99 Age: 24 Bats: L Throws: R Height: 5'11" Weight: 215 Origin: Round 3, 2022 Draft (#98 overall)

YEAR	TM	LVL	AGE	PA	R	HR	RBI	SB	AVG/OBP/SLG	BABIP	SLGCON	BB%	K%	ZSw%	ZCon%	OSw%	OCon%	LA	90th EV	DRC+	BRR	DRP	WARP
2022	DUN	A	22	115	17	1	9	5	.233/.374/.311	.253	.364	14.8%	11.3%	68.5%	95.7%	22.6%	69.0%			130	0.6	1.1	0.9
2023	VAN	A+	23	323	57	4	41	15	.321/.437/.459	.353	.521	13.0%	9.9%							150	-0.4	1.2	3.1
2023	NH	AA	23	209	35	6	27	9	.310/.421/.460	.350	.563	12.4%	15.3%							132	1.1	-2.9	1.2
2024 DC	TOR	MLB	24	29	3	0	3	1	.233/.313/.332	.260	.409	8.9%	12.9%							85	0.0	0	0.0

2023 GP: LF (52), RF (45), DH (19), 1B (1)   Comps: Drew Avans (71), Tim Smith (68), Terone Harris III (67)

Alan Rodent is a fast-talking wiseguy, the main character in my children's show I'm trying to pitch. *Alan Roden* was the Blue Jays' hitting prospect of the year. Alan Rodent is *really really* cool and he's got a ton of catchphrases like "This mouse is in the house!" Alan Roden is also cool, because he makes impressive contact, striking out only 9.9% of the time in High-A and earning an aggressive promotion to Double-A. Alan Rodent is the kind of in-your-face character that screams virality and marketing opportunities, while Alan Roden is pretty viral himself, sure to quickly rise up Blue Jays' prospect rankings for his high baseball IQ and ability to swipe bags despite otherwise pedestrian speed. Alan Rodent could be the new Spongebob if someone at Nickelodeon would just give me a call. Alan Roden is much more likely to be on your television in the near future.

Davis Schneider UT Born: 01/26/99 Age: 25 Bats: R Throws: R Height: 5'9" Weight: 190 Origin: Round 28, 2017 Draft (#849 overall)

YEAR	TM	LVL	AGE	PA	R	HR	RBI	SB	AVG/OBP/SLG	BABIP	SLGCON	BB%	K%	ZSw%	ZCon%	OSw%	OCon%	LA	90th EV	DRC+	BRR	DRP	WARP
2021	VAN	A+	22	179	26	9	22	0	.231/.348/.476	.305	.795	14.5%	33.0%							110	-2.2	-0.5	0.5
2022	VAN	A+	23	189	26	8	25	6	.229/.354/.459	.280	.673	15.3%	26.5%							122	0.2	2.6	1.4
2022	NH	AA	23	190	22	6	22	10	.283/.368/.476	.357	.658	11.6%	24.2%							106	0.8	0.5	0.8
2022	BUF	AAA	23	75	18	2	9	1	.233/.387/.400	.316	.600	18.7%	26.7%							100	0.3	1.0	0.3
2023	BUF	AAA	24	392	61	21	64	9	.275/.416/.553	.309	.767	18.4%	21.9%	66.0%	84.2%	23.5%	55.5%			133	-1.7	0.3	2.5
2023	TOR	MLB	24	141	23	8	20	1	.276/.404/.603	.369	.959	14.9%	30.5%	65.2%	72.6%	22.9%	45.1%	25.9	104.3	91	-0.1	0.1	0.2
2024 DC	TOR	MLB	25	445	49	15	52	8	.209/.314/.386	.266	.571	11.7%	28.3%							99	0.0	-0.3	1.1

2023 GP: 2B (23), DH (7), 3B (3), LF (3)   Comps: Randy Arozarena (60), Aaron Judge (57), Will Smith (50)

Schneider might be your favorite baseball nerd's favorite player, seemingly gifted to hardball sickos by the baseball gods. His fit is extraordinary, with the bushiest mustache this side of Tom Selleck and the thickest goggles since Chris Sabo. To make things even better, he became the first player to record at least nine hits and two home runs in his first three games *and* he set the record for best OPS after 15 games (1.379). Not only are these records, but they're insane records, the kinds of things someone who might dress up like Schneider for Halloween might yell to you over the punch bowl. If you know any of these people, please send them a copy of this book and a Schneider shirsey.

George Springer RF Born: 09/19/89 Age: 34 Bats: R Throws: R Height: 6'3" Weight: 220 Origin: Round 1, 2011 Draft (#11 overall)

YEAR	TM	LVL	AGE	PA	R	HR	RBI	SB	AVG/OBP/SLG	BABIP	SLGCON	BB%	K%	ZSw%	ZCon%	OSw%	OCon%	LA	90th EV	DRC+	BRR	DRP	WARP
2021	TOR	MLB	31	342	59	22	50	4	.264/.352/.555	.286	.755	10.8%	23.1%	74.3%	82.9%	26.4%	54.5%	19.2	107.7	109	0.2	-0.3	1.5
2022	TOR	MLB	32	583	89	25	76	14	.267/.342/.472	.285	.586	9.3%	17.2%	80.3%	81.4%	30.1%	53.7%	13.9	106.9	116	0.8	-0.2	3.0
2023	TOR	MLB	33	683	87	21	72	20	.258/.327/.405	.291	.508	8.8%	18.3%	76.3%	85.5%	27.5%	60.3%	12.1	105.5	109	0.6	1.3	2.6
2024 DC	TOR	MLB	34	627	72	22	77	15	.251/.326/.419	.277	.522	8.9%	17.7%							110	0.3	-0.1	2.4

2023 GP: RF (131), DH (21), CF (1)   Comps: Carlos Beltrán (77), Amos Otis (76), Chet Lemon (75)

After the Blue Jays added two of the best defensive outfielders in baseball—Daulton Varsho and Kevin Kiermaier—to their team, it allowed them to move the injury-prone Springer over to right field. It was the right choice: By taking off a little of the defensive responsibility, Springer managed to play more than 140 games for the first time since 2016. Unfortunately, that extra time on the field came with a downturn in production at the plate, which is concerning for a player with three more years under contract. He still has that undeniable flair for the dramatic, though, whether it's a diving catch in the outfield or a dinger just as everyone takes their seats. Springer smashed his 57th leadoff blast last year, the second-most all-time behind Rickey Henderson. He should still thrill even as he enters his mid-30s, if perhaps a little less often as he did in his youth.

Daulton Varsho OF   Born: 07/02/96   Age: 28   Bats: L   Throws: R   Height: 5'10"   Weight: 207   Origin: Round 2, 2017 Draft (#68 overall)

YEAR	TM	LVL	AGE	PA	R	HR	RBI	SB	AVG/OBP/SLG	BABIP	SLGCON	BB%	K%	ZSw%	ZCon%	OSw%	OCon%	LA	90th EV	DRC+	BRR	DRP	WARP
2021	RNO	AAA	24	87	18	9	25	2	.313/.368/.750	.291	.938	8.0%	18.4%							126	0.7	0.0	0.7
2021	AZ	MLB	24	315	41	11	38	6	.246/.318/.437	.286	.571	9.5%	21.3%	72.6%	82.4%	36.2%	66.2%	17.4	104.6	100	0.4	-3.2	1.0
2022	AZ	MLB	25	592	79	27	74	16	.235/.302/.443	.269	.609	7.8%	24.5%	70.6%	81.0%	36.1%	65.9%	14.2	104.2	96	0.7	1.8	1.9
2023	TOR	MLB	26	581	65	20	61	16	.220/.285/.389	.256	.523	7.7%	23.2%	71.4%	84.2%	35.9%	64.2%	19.4	106.2	95	0.7	2.1	1.7
2024 DC	TOR	MLB	27	541	60	21	68	14	.232/.303/.419	.266	.552	8.3%	22.1%							99	0.3	2.8	1.9

2023 GP: LF (117), CF (64), DH (1) *Comps: Josh Reddick (57), Aaron Cunningham (52), Felix Pie (51)*

While the Blue Jays spent October at home, Lourdes Gurriel and Gabriel Moreno—the other side of the trade that brought Varsho to Toronto—put on a show during the D'Backs pennant run. None of that is Varsho's fault. A true world-class athlete with the kind of neck that scouts would call "thicc," Varsho was the same player he always was, providing power, speed and an unbelievable glove. Unfortunately for the Blue Jays, no player seemed able to hit in the Rogers Centre last year—Varsho hit just .182 at home—and though an outfield with Varsho and Kevin Kiermaier stole plenty of hits, they couldn't save enough. Assume that Varsho's numbers should improve a little simply because there was nothing that speaks to his power decline other than simple bad luck and team-wide chaos. Whether that will ever be enough for Blue Jays fans to re-evaluate the trade will be a harder question to answer. Just don't blame Varsho for it.

PITCHERS

Brandon Barriera LHP   Born: 03/04/04   Age: 20   Height: 6'2"   Weight: 180   Origin: Round 1, 2022 Draft (#23 overall)

YEAR	TM	LVL	AGE	G (GS)	IP	W-L	SV	K	WHIP	ERA	CSP	BB%	K%	HR%	GB%	ZSw%	ZCon%	OSw%	OCon%	BABIP	SLGCON	DRA-	WARP
2023	DUN	A	19	6(6)	18¹	0-2	0	23	0.98	4.42		11.0%	31.5%	0.0%	73.7%	67.6%	73.3%	26.3%	54.3%	.263	.289	68	0.4
2024 non	TOR	MLB	20	58(0)	50	2-2	0	44	1.60	5.82		12.5%	19.3%	3.3%	40.6%					.301	.562	124	-0.4

2023 Arsenal: FA (92.7), SL (82.8), CH (86.8) *Comps: Kodi Medeiros (85), Aaron Sanchez (82), Jaime Melendez (80)*

Taken 23rd overall in the 2022 MLB Draft, Barriera has the left-handed fastball that scouts salivate over. Sitting in the mid-90s, but reaching 98 mph in his professional debut last year, Barriera looked as dominant as expected in limited innings. Unfortunately for someone who already had durability concerns, Barreiera was shut down in May for elbow soreness and then—after his velocity dropped—went on the IL for a bicep issue. And those, dear reader, are the kinds of words that keep those same scouts up all night.

Chris Bassitt RHP   Born: 02/22/89   Age: 35   Height: 6'5"   Weight: 217   Origin: Round 16, 2011 Draft (#501 overall)

YEAR	TM	LVL	AGE	G (GS)	IP	W-L	SV	K	WHIP	ERA	CSP	BB%	K%	HR%	GB%	ZSw%	ZCon%	OSw%	OCon%	BABIP	SLGCON	DRA-	WARP
2021	OAK	MLB	32	27(27)	157¹	12-4	0	159	1.06	3.15	57.1%	6.1%	25.0%	2.4%	41.6%	67.9%	83.9%	31.0%	62.4%	.271	.479	88	2.5
2022	NYM	MLB	33	30(30)	181²	15-9	0	167	1.14	3.42	57.0%	6.6%	22.4%	2.6%	49.1%	65.3%	81.3%	30.1%	67.4%	.282	.476	89	2.8
2023	TOR	MLB	34	33(33)	200	16-8	0	186	1.18	3.60	51.5%	7.1%	22.5%	3.4%	41.8%	67.1%	86.0%	31.3%	64.4%	.274	.536	93	3.1
2024 DC	TOR	MLB	35	29(29)	177²	13-9	0	154	1.23	3.96	54.3%	7.1%	20.6%	3.0%	42.5%					.282	.512	92	2.4

2023 Arsenal: SI (91.9), FC (88.1), CU (70.7), FA (92.5), SW (73.3), CH (84.2), SL (80.4), FS (82.8) *Comps: Lance Lynn (77), Todd Stottlemyre (74), Yu Darvish (74)*

The bassist is the least flashy member of most rock bands. They never get asked to pose in the center of the band photograph, they're given no solos, and there is hardly ever a person in the crowd who turns to a friend and says, "I want to shtup that guy keeping the low end steady."

That's who Chris Bassistt—ahem, sorry, *Bassitt*—is: always overlooked and yet a crucially important member of any pitching staff. Since 2019, when Bassitt turned 30 and—like athletes and band members, this is supposed to be when you're no longer relevant—he has been remarkably productive despite limited attention. His 58 wins are the third-most in baseball, his 746 innings are 14th, and his 3.39 ERA is 16th among all pitchers with at least 500 innings in that span. Yet, when the Blue Jays' season came down to the end, he was left out once again. The team opted to use José Berríos for only three-plus innings before giving the ball to Yusei Kikuchi in Game 2 of the team's Wild Card series which ended in a two-game sweep. Hey, maybe he can become a rockabilly dude; everyone loves the bassist there.

José Berríos RHP   Born: 05/27/94   Age: 30   Height: 6'0"   Weight: 205   Origin: Round 1, 2012 Draft (#32 overall)

YEAR	TM	LVL	AGE	G (GS)	IP	W-L	SV	K	WHIP	ERA	CSP	BB%	K%	HR%	GB%	ZSw%	ZCon%	OSw%	OCon%	BABIP	SLGCON	DRA-	WARP
2021	TOR	MLB	27	12(12)	70¹	5-4	0	78	1.09	3.58	53.4%	4.5%	26.8%	2.7%	42.5%	66.6%	85.0%	33.8%	66.5%	.303	.571	90	1.0
2021	MIN	MLB	27	20(20)	121²	7-5	0	126	1.04	3.48	54.0%	6.5%	25.7%	2.9%	43.2%	64.3%	84.0%	34.5%	66.2%	.263	.508	96	1.4
2022	TOR	MLB	28	32(32)	172	12-7	0	149	1.42	5.23	54.2%	6.0%	19.8%	3.9%	39.7%	66.0%	88.2%	35.9%	66.1%	.329	.593	109	0.9
2023	TOR	MLB	29	32(32)	189²	11-12	0	184	1.19	3.65	48.6%	6.6%	23.5%	3.2%	41.5%	63.7%	85.4%	34.4%	60.5%	.290	.535	93	3.0
2024 DC	TOR	MLB	30	29(29)	172	12-9	0	158	1.26	4.21	51.3%	6.9%	21.8%	3.4%	41.1%					.293	.546	97	1.8

2023 Arsenal: SI (93.9), SW (83), FA (94.3), CH (84.5), SL (83.6) *Comps: Freddy Garcia (80), Alex Cobb (80), Mark Gubicza (79)*

Berríos threw 2,937 pitches in the regular season, but the only ones people are going to focus on are the 47 he tossed in the Blue Jays' final postseason game against his former ballclub. The right-hander had been cruising for three innings, striking out five batters and keeping Minnesota off the board. But when he walked Royce Lewis to lead off the fourth inning, Toronto manager John Schneider pulled his right-hander for Yusei Kikuchi.

You could argue—as Schneider did after the game—that in this must-win game, the Blue Jays wanted to optimize every possible advantage. Maybe there was reason to be skeptical of how long Berríos could keep it up when he had given up four-plus runs in four of his final seven starts to end the season and that his expected ERA was a run higher than what he actually posted. Rarely do you get unanimous disagreement from a team's ballplayers, especially publicly, but Blue Jays players like Whit Merrifield and Vlad Guerrero Jr. admitted they were surprised by the move. As for Berríos: "I just control what I can control," he said. "I pitched my ass off." It's a good descriptor for the workhorse's bounceback season, even if it didn't end as the team wished.

Génesis Cabrera LHP Born: 10/10/96 Age: 27 Height: 6'2" Weight: 180 Origin: IFA, 2013

YEAR	TM	LVL	AGE	G(GS)	IP	W-L	SV	K	WHIP	ERA	CSP	BB%	K%	HR%	GB%	ZSw%	ZCon%	OSw%	OCon%	BABIP	SLGCON	DRA-	WARP
2021	STL	MLB	24	71(0)	70	4-5	0	77	1.26	3.73	54.3%	12.2%	26.0%	1.0%	41.0%	71.0%	82.6%	29.2%	57.5%	.287	.448	96	0.8
2022	STL	MLB	25	39(0)	44²	4-2	1	32	1.32	4.63	53.0%	10.3%	16.5%	4.1%	44.9%	71.2%	84.0%	31.6%	65.2%	.238	.518	122	-0.1
2023	STL	MLB	26	32(0)	32	1-1	0	38	1.56	5.06	45.6%	12.6%	26.6%	4.2%	37.9%	66.5%	81.3%	33.6%	53.0%	.325	.663	91	0.5
2023	TOR	MLB	26	29(0)	23²	1-0	0	20	0.97	2.66	46.8%	6.3%	20.8%	2.1%	38.2%	75.0%	78.9%	39.4%	61.9%	.227	.433	102	0.3
2024 DC	TOR	MLB	27	46(0)	49²	3-2	0	50	1.43	4.90	50.2%	10.8%	22.5%	3.3%	40.6%					.296	.559	108	0.0

2023 Arsenal: FA (95.9), SL (89.7), SI (95.4), CU (79.6), CH (88.8) Comps: Renyel Pinto (59), Michael Bowden (58), Franklin Morales (57)

Genesis—the 1980s prog-rock band—had two drummers, giving the group its epic pop sound. This Génesis had two *seasons*: In the first part of the year with the Cardinals, Cabrera was his usually confounding self. He mixed dominant mid-90s stuff with lots of strikeouts and walks. After he was DFA'd and then traded to Toronto in exchange for catcher Sammy Hernandez, he went "No Jacket Required"; his second half was as smooth as Phil Collins' pop masterpiece. The Jays asked him to throw more of his electric four-seamer and brought his release angle up a little, then watched as he cut his walk rate in half, dropping below 10% for the first time in his career.

The question now: Will Cabrera go the way of Genesis' Chester Thompson, known only by obsessive enthusiasts, or will he keep up his Phil Collins act, grab hold of the closer's job, and make a break for a solo career? He's probably been waiting for this moment all his life, oh lord.

Connor Cooke RHP Born: 11/02/99 Age: 24 Height: 6'1" Weight: 203 Origin: Round 10, 2021 Draft (#302 overall)

YEAR	TM	LVL	AGE	G(GS)	IP	W-L	SV	K	WHIP	ERA	CSP	BB%	K%	HR%	GB%	ZSw%	ZCon%	OSw%	OCon%	BABIP	SLGCON	DRA-	WARP
2022	DUN	A	22	14(8)	46¹	2-5	1	63	1.25	4.86		7.1%	32.0%	1.5%	33.6%	68.0%	73.2%	32.2%	55.5%	.376	.568	89	1.0
2022	VAN	A+	22	11(0)	10²	0-2	8	12	1.13	6.75		6.5%	26.1%	4.3%	26.7%					.250	.586	110	0.0
2023	VAN	A+	23	9(0)	9¹	0-0	1	19	1.07	2.89		7.7%	48.7%	2.6%	47.1%					.375	.647	75	0.2
2023	NH	AA	23	20(0)	24²	1-2	3	46	1.46	4.38		6.3%	41.1%	2.7%	24.6%					.481	.842	72	0.7
2023	BUF	AAA	23	9(0)	10¹	2-0	0	15	1.45	4.35		19.6%	32.6%	2.2%	33.3%	54.9%	71.8%	28.3%	55.6%	.250	.667	95	0.2
2024 DC	TOR	MLB	24	8(0)	11	0-0	0	12	1.27	4.26		9.6%	25.9%	3.8%	31.8%					.279	.567	97	0.1

2023 Arsenal: FA (96.9), SW (84.4), CH (84.7) Comps: Bryan Dobzanski (44), Adam Hofacket (40), Isaac Mattson (40)

The sexiest thing on baseball Twitter—apart from the brotherly love the Phillies have for each other—are strikeout reels filled with unbelievable, jaw-dropping, physics-defying sliders shared by the likes of @PitchingNinja. Cooke just may have the most alluring slider of the bunch. The former 10th-round pick catapulted his way through three levels last year thanks to a mid-90s fastball that has picked up five or six ticks since college, and a wiffleball slider that touches 3,000 RPMs. Once Maxim Magazine starts highlight the Hottest 100 Relief Pitching Prospects, expect Cooke to get a centerfold.

Chad Dallas RHP Born: 06/26/00 Age: 24 Height: 5'11" Weight: 206 Origin: Round 4, 2021 Draft (#121 overall)

YEAR	TM	LVL	AGE	G(GS)	IP	W-L	SV	K	WHIP	ERA	CSP	BB%	K%	HR%	GB%	ZSw%	ZCon%	OSw%	OCon%	BABIP	SLGCON	DRA-	WARP
2022	VAN	A+	22	21(21)	88	1-7	0	86	1.55	4.60		12.6%	21.2%	3.2%	45.8%					.287	.552	115	0.1
2023	VAN	A+	23	5(5)	26²	2-0	0	37	0.94	2.03		11.8%	36.3%	1.0%	46.2%					.235	.385	95	0.3
2023	NH	AA	23	18(18)	96²	7-3	0	107	1.26	4.10		8.9%	25.8%	3.6%	44.9%					.283	.580	100	1.5
2024 non	TOR	MLB	24	58(0)	50	2-2	0	43	1.55	5.64		11.6%	19.3%	3.8%	37.7%					.296	.578	122	-0.4

Comps: Robert Dugger (75), Jackson Kowar (75), Jerad Eickhoff (75)

With a name straight out of an early internet meme and a mustache that would make Tom Selleck proud, don't be surprised if Dallas soon becomes a trendy cult player. The 5-foot-11 starter has a slider worth salivating over, throwing it in the mid-80s with plenty of spin, and he added a cutter last season. He'll sit in the low 90s with his fastball, admitting to *The Orange Leader* that he's hoping to add a few more ticks onto it. Perhaps most impressively, Dallas continued to cut his walk rate upon reaching Double-A. His brother Jack is in the Phillies system, so we may be seeing the best Dallas brothers since *Dynasty*.

Hagen Danner RHP Born: 09/30/98 Age: 25 Height: 6'1" Weight: 215 Origin: Round 2, 2017 Draft (#61 overall)

YEAR	TM	LVL	AGE	G(GS)	IP	W-L	SV	K	WHIP	ERA	CSP	BB%	K%	HR%	GB%	ZSw%	ZCon%	OSw%	OCon%	BABIP	SLGCON	DRA-	WARP
2021	VAN	A+	22	25(0)	35²	2-1	3	42	0.93	2.02		8.4%	29.4%	1.4%	35.4%					.232	.370	92	0.4
2023	NH	AA	24	8(0)	9	1-1	0	16	1.22	3.00		5.4%	43.2%	0.0%	36.8%					.474	.474	78	0.2
2023	BUF	AAA	24	23(1)	28¹	0-1	1	35	0.95	3.81		6.3%	31.5%	7.2%	37.7%	69.7%	84.7%	33.3%	45.2%	.197	.667	85	0.7
2023	TOR	MLB	24	1(0)	0¹	0-0	0	0	0.00	0.00	98.0%	0.0%	0.0%	0.0%	0.0%	50.0%	100.0%			.000	.000	93	0.0
2024 DC	TOR	MLB	25	8(0)	11	0-0	0	10	1.39	4.98	98.0%	9.2%	21.6%	3.9%	34.5%					.294	.576	111	0.0

2023 Arsenal: FA (96.6), SL (85.9), CU (80.2)

A former catcher converted to pitching, the right-hander affectionately called "The Ice Cream Man" had a hellish major-league debut. Danner threw seven pitches to retire Seiya Suzuki before grabbing his back and exiting the game. The resulting oblique injury would eventually get him put on the 60-day IL to end his season. Hopefully he'll return to the majors soon and not become the latest Ben and Jerry's flavor: Moonlight Graham Cracker Crunch.

Bowden Francis   RHP   Born: 04/22/96   Age: 28   Height: 6'5"   Weight: 220   Origin: Round 7, 2017 Draft (#204 overall)

YEAR	TM	LVL	AGE	G(GS)	IP	W-L	SV	K	WHIP	ERA	CSP	BB%	K%	HR%	GB%	ZSw%	ZCon%	OSw%	OCon%	BABIP	SLGCON	DRA-	WARP
2021	BLX	AA	25	4(4)	21	3-1	0	26	1.10	3.86		5.7%	29.9%	5.7%	29.1%					.260	.655	107	0.1
2021	NAS	AAA	25	7(7)	38²	4-2	0	39	0.98	3.49		7.9%	25.8%	2.6%	27.6%					.237	.505	107	0.4
2021	BUF	AAA	25	14(13)	73	6-4	0	71	1.19	4.19		10.0%	23.0%	4.9%	28.0%					.223	.569	107	0.7
2022	CAG	WIN	26	9(9)	35¹	1-2	0	47	0.79	1.51		6.6%	34.6%	0.7%	35.9%					.234	.312		
2022	BUF	AAA	26	37(23)	98¹	5-10	0	110	1.54	6.59		9.5%	24.3%	5.1%	27.3%					.326	.759	123	0.1
2022	TOR	MLB	26	1(0)	0²	0-0	0	1	1.50	0.00	70.9%	0.0%	33.3%	0.0%	100.0%	100.0%	100.0%	50.0%	0.0%	.500	1.000	87	0.0
2023	BUF	AAA	27	9(7)	27	0-2	0	42	1.30	2.67		6.2%	37.2%	5.3%	23.8%	66.7%	74.2%	34.2%	45.8%	.386	.794	83	0.6
2023	TOR	MLB	27	20(0)	36¹	1-0	1	35	0.83	1.73	49.0%	5.9%	25.7%	3.7%	34.8%	68.5%	84.8%	33.9%	62.4%	.195	.440	94	0.5
2024 DC	TOR	MLB	28	36(6)	59	3-3	0	53	1.31	4.79	49.3%	8.0%	21.0%	4.4%	34.6%					.280	.591	108	0.1

2023 Arsenal: FA (94.2), CU (74.1), SL (84.7), SW (78.8) • *Comps: A.J. Schugel (65), Chad Green (62), Joel Payamps (60)*

Plenty of MLBers rock sick custom cleats these days, but Francis' were a little different: Rather than rocking some special Jordans or bejeweling his kicks with diamonds and precious gems, his kicks had splashes of Blue Jays blue paint on them. Those didn't come from a customizer, though, but rather his two-year-old son. Like the magical shoes in "Like Mike," the shoes did the job. Though he was used primarily in long relief and low leverage situations, Francis dominated by filling up the strike zone. His 5.3% walk rate would have been top-15 among relief pitchers—tying Emmanuelle Clase—had he thrown enough innings in his signature shoes.

Yimi García   RHP   Born: 08/18/90   Age: 33   Height: 6'1"   Weight: 230   Origin: IFA, 2009

YEAR	TM	LVL	AGE	G(GS)	IP	W-L	SV	K	WHIP	ERA	CSP	BB%	K%	HR%	GB%	ZSw%	ZCon%	OSw%	OCon%	BABIP	SLGCON	DRA-	WARP
2021	HOU	MLB	30	23(0)	21¹	1-2	0	25	1.08	5.48	54.3%	5.8%	29.1%	3.5%	44.6%	70.6%	75.2%	34.5%	68.6%	.288	.545	87	0.4
2021	MIA	MLB	30	39(0)	36¹	3-7	15	35	1.21	3.47	56.4%	8.6%	23.2%	3.3%	39.2%	72.2%	78.8%	31.9%	62.4%	.271	.582	91	0.5
2022	TOR	MLB	31	61(0)	61	4-5	1	58	1.05	3.10	54.5%	6.5%	23.5%	2.4%	40.2%	67.5%	80.4%	31.5%	68.1%	.258	.467	89	0.9
2023	TOR	MLB	32	73(0)	66	3-4	3	79	1.24	4.09	46.1%	5.3%	28.0%	2.8%	45.6%	68.4%	77.1%	33.7%	56.4%	.345	.584	75	1.6
2024 DC	TOR	MLB	33	52(0)	55¹	3-3	5	56	1.21	3.91	50.7%	7.0%	24.0%	3.3%	41.2%					.288	.545	91	0.5

2023 Arsenal: FA (95.9), SL (83.6), SI (95.5), FC (90), CH (88.6), SW (84.1) • *Comps: Joe Smith (56), Brad Boxberger (55), Bryan Shaw (54)*

It was a season of contradictions for García. The right-handed reliever was actually better against lefties than righties—.686 vs. 739 OPS—was unhittable at home but crushable on the road (.218 BAA at the Rogers Centre vs. .301 on the road) and his splits couldn't be more different, either. After posting a 6.20 ERA through the season's first two months, he posted a 2.83 mark the rest of the year. What does that all mean? Is there some method to this madness? Or is it merely an example of that xkcd comic about sports fans creating narratives out of a random number generator? No matter the answer, while García may not have been the automatic, set-it-and-forget-it reliever that fans and managers dream of, he still put up above-average numbers and was 90th percentile in walks among relievers. After appearing in his 110th career game with the Blue Jays in July, his 2024 option vested.

Kevin Gausman   RHP   Born: 01/06/91   Age: 33   Height: 6'2"   Weight: 205   Origin: Round 1, 2012 Draft (#4 overall)

YEAR	TM	LVL	AGE	G(GS)	IP	W-L	SV	K	WHIP	ERA	CSP	BB%	K%	HR%	GB%	ZSw%	ZCon%	OSw%	OCon%	BABIP	SLGCON	DRA-	WARP
2021	SF	MLB	30	33(33)	192	14-6	0	227	1.04	2.81	58.2%	6.5%	29.3%	2.6%	41.1%	72.3%	79.7%	36.8%	51.9%	.275	.506	77	4.2
2022	TOR	MLB	31	31(31)	174²	12-10	0	205	1.24	3.35	55.3%	3.9%	28.3%	2.1%	39.5%	73.8%	82.6%	43.4%	56.5%	.364	.569	70	4.4
2023	TOR	MLB	32	31(31)	185	12-9	0	237	1.18	3.16	46.5%	7.2%	31.1%	2.5%	42.3%	70.6%	84.0%	35.7%	54.8%	.324	.572	80	4.1
2024 DC	TOR	MLB	33	29(29)	174²	13-8	0	196	1.12	3.34	51.8%	6.5%	27.6%	3.5%	40.7%					.286	.557	81	3.3

2023 Arsenal: FA (94.9), FS (86.5), SL (84), SW (78) • *Comps: Rick Rhoden (75), Chris Carpenter (73), Esteban Loaiza (72)*

People talk a lot about how baseball is a game of constant adjustment and there may be no better example than this formerly long-locked hurler. 10 years ago, Gausman made his debut as a fireballing top prospect with the Orioles and now, four teams and multiple post-hype sleeper columns later, he continues to reinvent himself. Gausman has thrown at least 174 innings for each of the last three years, has a miniscule 3.10 ERA in that time and continues to tinker with his unhittable split-finger. Gausman started throwing it more than ever this past year and even changed his armslot, giving the pitch more arm-side run. Suddenly, the 32-year-old starter did something he had never done in the previous 10 years: He led the league in strikeouts.

"I miss those guys already. This one hurts," Gausman wrote on Twitter after the Blue Jays were bounced from the postseason. "The last two years have been heartbreaking but I am still so proud and honored to be a Blue Jay. We will be better."

If anyone has proven that they can will themselves to do it, it's Gausman.

Chad Green   RHP   Born: 05/24/91   Age: 33   Height: 6'3"   Weight: 215   Origin: Round 11, 2013 Draft (#336 overall)

YEAR	TM	LVL	AGE	G(GS)	IP	W-L	SV	K	WHIP	ERA	CSP	BB%	K%	HR%	GB%	ZSw%	ZCon%	OSw%	OCon%	BABIP	SLGCON	DRA-	WARP
2021	NYY	MLB	30	67(0)	83²	10-7	6	99	0.88	3.12	56.4%	5.4%	31.4%	4.4%	27.1%	74.5%	73.5%	35.5%	58.8%	.234	.582	88	1.3
2022	NYY	MLB	31	14(0)	15	1-1	1	16	1.20	3.00	58.3%	8.1%	25.8%	1.6%	25.0%	80.4%	73.3%	39.7%	73.1%	.308	.500	97	0.2
2023	BUF	AAA	32	9(0)	9	0-0	0	11	1.00	2.00		2.8%	30.6%	2.8%	33.3%	75.7%	81.1%	38.0%	56.7%	.304	.583	89	0.2
2023	TOR	MLB	32	12(0)	12	3-0	0	16	1.33	5.25	48.2%	7.7%	30.8%	1.9%	34.4%	77.4%	67.7%	39.6%	56.8%	.355	.625	90	0.2
2024 DC	TOR	MLB	33	46(0)	49²	3-2	0	56	1.19	3.83	54.2%	7.0%	27.0%	3.7%	31.1%					.293	.590	90	0.5

2023 Arsenal: FA (95.6), SL (85.7), FS (87.6) • *Comps: Liam Hendriks (60), Tommy Hunter (59), Shane Greene (58)*

By the time you read this comment, Chad Green's contract situation has been all figured out. However, it's important to realize the kind of strategical masterwork *someone* fashioned here. (It's unclear whether it's the Blue Jays who came out ahead here or if it's Green.) Basically, here is the structure: Toronto held a club option for $27 million over three years. When the Jays declined that one in November, Green could have selected a $6.25 million player option for this season. After he opted not to take that, the Blue Jays had another choice, a $21 million, two-year club option. Frankly, it's upsetting that this didn't continue until eventually reaching the point where the Blue Jays could ink Green to a mutual option that included a free froyo card, but Toronto did exercise their final option and bring Green back.

Jay Jackson   RHP   Born: 10/27/87   Age: 36   Height: 6'1"   Weight: 195   Origin: Round 9, 2008 Draft (#281 overall)

YEAR	TM	LVL	AGE	G (GS)	IP	W-L	SV	K	WHIP	ERA	CSP	BB%	K%	HR%	GB%	ZSw%	ZCon%	OSw%	OCon%	BABIP	SLGCON	DRA-	WARP
2021	SAC	AAA	33	10 (0)	14	1-0	0	24	0.43	1.29		2.1%	50.0%	2.1%	65.2%					.182	.348	67	0.3
2021	SF	MLB	33	23 (1)	21²	2-1	0	28	1.25	3.74	51.2%	13.3%	31.1%	3.3%	28.0%	65.4%	82.4%	30.6%	52.8%	.261	.604	98	0.2
2022	GWN	AAA	34	19 (0)	19²	2-0	1	25	1.12	2.29		5.0%	31.3%	2.5%	39.2%	50.0%	75.0%	45.0%	66.7%	.327	.540	78	0.5
2022	ATL	MLB	34	2 (0)	1¹	0-0	0	1	0.75	0.00	64.0%	0.0%	20.0%	0.0%	0.0%	83.3%	80.0%	16.7%	0.0%	.250	.250	99	0.0
2023	BUF	AAA	35	25 (0)	29	1-3	2	43	1.28	6.21		5.6%	34.4%	6.4%	20.8%	71.2%	72.0%	37.2%	47.9%	.349	.817	101	0.4
2023	TOR	MLB	35	25 (0)	29²	3-1	0	27	0.91	2.12	46.8%	7.8%	23.3%	3.4%	44.3%	74.1%	81.4%	32.5%	51.7%	.189	.423	92	0.4
2024 DC	TOR	MLB	36	54 (0)	57¹	3-2	0	62	1.24	4.13	47.5%	7.7%	25.9%	3.9%	32.3%					.292	.595	96	0.4

2023 Arsenal: SL (84.8), FA (93.5), SI (92.7), CH (87.9)   *Comps: Blake Parker (53), Tyler Clippard (52), Tommy Hunter (51)*

When Jackson was called back up to pitch for the Blue Jays on July 6th—his third stint in the majors—baseball was probably the furthest thing from his mind. That's because on that same day, his third child was born nearly four months premature. Jackson would stay in the Blue Jays bullpen for most of the season from then on, FaceTiming with his family every night and using every off day possible to travel back to Utah to visit before rejoining the big-league squad the next day. Jackson finished the year as one of the standout performers in the Blue Jays' bullpen, but far more importantly, one update the right-hander's fiancee, Sam Bautista, shared after the season ended was of the pitcher sharing some "tummy time" with little JR for the first time.

Hayden Juenger   RHP   Born: 08/09/00   Age: 23   Height: 6'0"   Weight: 180   Origin: Round 6, 2021 Draft (#182 overall)

YEAR	TM	LVL	AGE	G (GS)	IP	W-L	SV	K	WHIP	ERA	CSP	BB%	K%	HR%	GB%	ZSw%	ZCon%	OSw%	OCon%	BABIP	SLGCON	DRA-	WARP
2021	VAN	A+	20	11 (0)	20	2-0	0	34	0.75	2.70		5.4%	45.9%	0.0%	37.1%					.314	.412	80	0.4
2022	NH	AA	21	20 (17)	56	0-5	0	67	1.09	4.02		9.3%	29.5%	5.3%	32.1%					.224	.635	99	0.8
2022	BUF	AAA	21	18 (2)	32²	3-2	2	33	1.19	3.31		11.9%	24.6%	4.5%	42.4%					.215	.553	91	0.6
2023	BUF	AAA	22	54 (5)	75¹	5-2	2	92	1.66	6.33		11.2%	26.4%	3.2%	29.9%	67.4%	79.0%	28.9%	60.2%	.375	.652	106	0.8
2024 non	TOR	MLB	23	58 (0)	50	2-2	0	50	1.41	5.00		10.2%	22.7%	3.9%	32.5%					.292	.597	111	-0.1

2023 Arsenal: FA (95.8), CH (87.1), SW (84)   *Comps: Kelvin Herrera (59), Eduardo Sanchez (53), Joe Jiménez (51)*

A trendy sleeper prospect after a fast rise across two levels in 2022, Juenger (pronounced Ying-er) struggled all year in Buffalo. One of the Blue Jays' most versatile relievers, he often shifts across bullpen roles in the minors to stay stretched out and prepared for a variety of uses in the majors. If Juenger can prove that the .375 BABIP was a mirage rather than a sign of his stuff topping out, a future in the bigs as a swingman or multi-inning reliever likely awaits.

Yusei Kikuchi   LHP   Born: 06/17/91   Age: 33   Height: 6'0"   Weight: 210   Origin: IFA, 2019

YEAR	TM	LVL	AGE	G (GS)	IP	W-L	SV	K	WHIP	ERA	CSP	BB%	K%	HR%	GB%	ZSw%	ZCon%	OSw%	OCon%	BABIP	SLGCON	DRA-	WARP
2021	SEA	MLB	30	29 (29)	157	7-9	0	163	1.32	4.41	57.1%	9.3%	24.5%	4.1%	48.9%	67.5%	82.0%	33.7%	57.2%	.289	.594	98	1.7
2022	TOR	MLB	31	32 (20)	100²	6-7	1	124	1.50	5.19	54.5%	12.8%	27.3%	5.1%	44.1%	69.8%	77.4%	31.5%	55.6%	.293	.730	117	0.1
2023	TOR	MLB	32	32 (32)	167²	11-6	0	181	1.27	3.86	48.0%	6.9%	25.9%	3.9%	39.4%	68.8%	82.9%	33.4%	55.2%	.315	.591	96	2.4
2024 DC	TOR	MLB	33	29 (29)	151¹	9-9	0	163	1.36	4.65	51.9%	9.0%	24.9%	3.7%	41.1%					.306	.594	104	1.0

2023 Arsenal: FA (95.1), SL (88.4), CH (88.9), SW (83.3), CU (82.6), SI (92.6)   *Comps: Ricky Nolasco (77), Gary Peters (76), Floyd Bannister (75)*

On Sept. 19, Kikuchi removed himself from his start against the Yankees due to a cramp. Afterward, he blamed the injury on not getting enough sleep. Hey, who hasn't been there, trying to squeeze in a day of work after you took part in 2-for-1 shots, waking up the next morning with a half-eaten doner kebab on the pillow next to you? The difference here is that Kikuchi "only" slept 11 hours instead of his customary 13-to-14. So while we *could* talk about Kikuchi's best MLB season—he posted career bests in ERA, walks per nine and innings—and sure, we could say it's because he finally figured his sleep schedule out, I think this is a moment we need to ask: Is this really worth it? Would it not be better to sacrifice a little of the quality in our professional leagues to return to the days when guys would stumble to the park, bleary-eyed from the night before? I know which one I find more inspiring.

Alek Manoah   RHP   Born: 01/09/98   Age: 26   Height: 6'6"   Weight: 285   Origin: Round 1, 2019 Draft (#11 overall)

YEAR	TM	LVL	AGE	G (GS)	IP	W-L	SV	K	WHIP	ERA	CSP	BB%	K%	HR%	GB%	ZSw%	ZCon%	OSw%	OCon%	BABIP	SLGCON	DRA-	WARP
2021	BUF	AAA	23	3(3)	18	3-0	0	27	0.56	0.50		4.5%	40.9%	1.5%	40.6%					.194	.375	90	0.3
2021	TOR	MLB	23	20(20)	111²	9-2	0	127	1.05	3.22	53.2%	8.7%	27.7%	2.6%	39.5%	69.6%	78.5%	32.7%	57.7%	.246	.460	99	1.1
2022	TOR	MLB	24	31(31)	196²	16-7	0	180	0.99	2.24	53.9%	6.5%	22.9%	2.0%	37.5%	69.4%	84.1%	35.0%	62.3%	.245	.420	100	1.9
2023	TOR	MLB	25	19(19)	87¹	3-9	0	79	1.74	5.87	44.9%	14.2%	19.0%	3.6%	37.7%	70.0%	86.4%	30.8%	66.9%	.308	.596	146	-1.1
2024 DC	TOR	MLB	26	19(19)	93	5-6	0	87	1.40	4.95	50.8%	10.6%	21.1%	3.5%	38.0%					.282	.555	109	0.4

2023 Arsenal: SW (80.9), FA (92.9), SI (92.8), CH (86.4)   Comps: Jack Flaherty (75), Zac Gallen (74), Jarred Cosart (72)

Once seen as the future of the Jays rotation, Manoah enters next year in a battle for a rotation spot…if he's even a Blue Jay at that point. The year started off with all the fun of the end of "Ethan Frome," with Manoah rushing headlong into a metaphorical tree holding a 6.36 ERA on June 5 after surrendering six runs in one-third of an inning against the Astros. That earned the starter's first demotion. Called back up a month later when the Toronto rotation was in a bind, Manoah made one solid start against the Tigers before earning his second demotion. This time, Manoah didn't immediately report to his club. Once he did, he chose to get a shoulder injection that the team didn't recommend, which ended his season. "We supported him. Our medical staff wasn't suggesting that. He made the decision on his own to move in that direction. There were no structural issues," Ross Atkins said. This is exactly the kind of thing you *don't* want to hear from your boss before going on sabbatical for the winter, especially if you intend on coming back.

Tim Mayza   LHP   Born: 01/15/92   Age: 32   Height: 6'3"   Weight: 215   Origin: Round 12, 2013 Draft (#355 overall)

YEAR	TM	LVL	AGE	G (GS)	IP	W-L	SV	K	WHIP	ERA	CSP	BB%	K%	HR%	GB%	ZSw%	ZCon%	OSw%	OCon%	BABIP	SLGCON	DRA-	WARP
2021	TOR	MLB	29	61(0)	53	5-2	1	57	0.98	3.40	52.9%	5.7%	27.1%	2.4%	57.2%	65.7%	87.0%	32.4%	58.4%	.265	.438	72	1.3
2022	TOR	MLB	30	63(0)	48²	8-1	2	44	1.11	3.14	50.1%	6.2%	22.8%	3.6%	56.6%	67.0%	87.3%	32.8%	64.2%	.273	.534	80	1.0
2023	TOR	MLB	31	69(0)	53¹	3-1	1	53	1.22	1.52	45.6%	7.0%	24.7%	0.9%	58.5%	63.2%	85.2%	30.7%	67.3%	.331	.466	77	1.3
2024 DC	TOR	MLB	32	46(0)	49²	3-2	0	43	1.24	3.54	47.9%	7.2%	20.6%	2.1%	54.7%					.292	.463	83	0.7

2023 Arsenal: SI (93.5), SL (86.3)   Comps: Jake Diekman (71), Sam Freeman (66), Danny Coulombe (65)

Since returning from Tommy John surgery in 2019, Mayza has been like the broom in your closet: Dependable, reliable, but less flashy than the Roomba that keeps smashing itself directly into the wall. All that flipped last year as Mayza changed how he *thought* about throwing his slider. Proving that the brain is the best organ of all, Mayza began thinking of it as a curveball. He watched as its RPM ticked up, its break got deeper and its velo went *lower*—add it all up and batters went from slugging .704 against it in '22 to just .327 in '23. Use your brain; remember the broom.

Nate Pearson   RHP   Born: 08/20/96   Age: 27   Height: 6'6"   Weight: 255   Origin: Round 1, 2017 Draft (#28 overall)

YEAR	TM	LVL	AGE	G (GS)	IP	W-L	SV	K	WHIP	ERA	CSP	BB%	K%	HR%	GB%	ZSw%	ZCon%	OSw%	OCon%	BABIP	SLGCON	DRA-	WARP
2021	BUF	AAA	24	12(6)	30²	1-3	0	44	1.11	4.40		10.1%	34.1%	3.1%	36.8%					.266	.597	91	0.6
2021	TOR	MLB	24	12(1)	15	1-1	0	20	1.73	4.20	49.7%	16.9%	28.2%	2.8%	41.0%	64.5%	76.1%	23.0%	50.0%	.324	.590	98	0.2
2022	BUF	AAA	25	11(0)	12²	2-1	0	18	1.11	3.55		14.0%	36.0%	4.0%	36.0%					.217	.640	84	0.3
2023	BUF	AAA	26	20(0)	20²	0-1	2	34	1.40	1.74		16.5%	37.4%	1.1%	45.2%	60.8%	74.3%	29.1%	40.9%	.317	.429	80	0.6
2023	TOR	MLB	26	35(0)	42²	5-2	1	43	1.27	4.85	47.2%	9.9%	23.6%	3.8%	30.5%	67.9%	83.5%	24.0%	52.0%	.261	.560	109	0.3
2024 DC	TOR	MLB	27	41(0)	44	2-2	0	50	1.40	4.83	47.3%	11.7%	25.8%	4.0%	35.0%					.286	.610	107	0.0

2023 Arsenal: FA (98), SL (87.5), CU (80.7)   Comps: Lucas Sims (66), Casey Coleman (59), Michael Lorenzen (58)

Here's the good news: Through his first 13 games with the Blue Jays in 2023, Pearson had a 1.59 ERA and 20 K's in 17 innings. He was looking every bit the dominant arm the Jays took in the first round in the 2017 draft.

Here's the bad news: Over his next 22 appearances—sandwiched around four separate trips to Triple-A—he had a 7.01 ERA in 25 ⅔ innings, striking out 23 but also walking 13.

Here's the best news of all: For the first time since 2019, Pearson pitched a full season, not having it be interrupted by a pandemic or a series of unfortunate injuries. After throwing just 61 innings total in 2021-22, you could understand if the former Top-10 prospect had simply run out of gas over the summer. He can still throw 97. Batters still struggle to get good wood on his fastball. If he can build up some stamina and work on his secondary offerings, the Blue Jays may still have a valuable reliever in their system.

Zach Pop   RHP   Born: 09/20/96   Age: 27   Height: 6'4"   Weight: 220   Origin: Round 7, 2017 Draft (#220 overall)

YEAR	TM	LVL	AGE	G (GS)	IP	W-L	SV	K	WHIP	ERA	CSP	BB%	K%	HR%	GB%	ZSw%	ZCon%	OSw%	OCon%	BABIP	SLGCON	DRA-	WARP
2021	MIA	MLB	24	50(0)	54²	1-0	0	51	1.43	4.12	47.5%	9.8%	20.7%	1.2%	55.8%	63.8%	84.6%	36.1%	64.1%	.321	.475	92	0.8
2022	JAX	AAA	25	19(0)	24¹	0-1	0	20	1.48	2.22		7.8%	19.4%	0.0%	59.5%	78.3%	94.4%	33.3%	57.1%	.378	.500	101	0.3
2022	TOR	MLB	25	17(0)	19	2-0	0	11	1.05	1.89	52.0%	2.7%	14.9%	1.4%	50.0%	66.3%	88.4%	39.9%	74.6%	.288	.383	85	0.3
2022	MIA	MLB	25	18(0)	20	2-0	0	14	1.25	3.60	48.9%	2.4%	16.9%	1.2%	62.1%	64.0%	95.3%	44.5%	68.8%	.338	.455	83	0.4
2023	BUF	AAA	26	31(0)	32²	1-2	1	32	1.50	5.51		9.0%	22.1%	2.8%	57.6%	67.0%	89.2%	36.4%	54.3%	.337	.592	86	0.7
2023	TOR	MLB	26	15(0)	13²	1-1	0	14	1.24	6.59	43.3%	10.7%	25.0%	7.1%	38.9%	63.6%	91.8%	35.8%	52.3%	.219	.667	100	0.2
2024 DC	TOR	MLB	27	14(0)	16¹	1-1	0	14	1.39	4.59	47.8%	8.3%	18.7%	2.3%	51.8%					.306	.510	102	0.1

2023 Arsenal: SI (96.3), SL (85.9), CH (85.3)   Comps: Evan Phillips (64), Dominic Leone (63), Bruce Rondón (63)

In some ways, Pop had a very bad 2023. The right-handed reliever hurt his hamstring in May and then spent the rest of the year in Triple-A—first rehabbing and then being optioned back down once healthy as Toronto had better options already on the big league roster. However, in another way, the hard-throwing righty had a great year: As reported by much of the Canadian Press, Pop made his pitch of the year when he asked his girlfriend Taye Anita to marry him in October. (She said yes.) Sometimes it's important to recognize the *human* side of baseball, especially when there isn't much on-field performance to dwell on.

Trevor Richards RHP Born: 05/15/93 Age: 31 Height: 6'2" Weight: 205 Origin: Undrafted Free Agent, 2016

YEAR	TM	LVL	AGE	G (GS)	IP	W-L	SV	K	WHIP	ERA	CSP	BB%	K%	HR%	GB%	ZSw%	ZCon%	OSw%	OCon%	BABIP	SLGCON	DRA-	WARP
2021	TOR	MLB	28	32(0)	32²	4-2	0	37	0.80	3.31	45.2%	8.2%	30.3%	5.7%	32.0%	71.1%	81.4%	37.4%	50.4%	.132	.507	107	0.2
2021	TB	MLB	28	6(0)	12	0-0	1	16	1.00	4.50	53.9%	6.4%	34.0%	4.3%	28.6%	66.2%	79.6%	35.0%	55.8%	.269	.607	103	0.1
2021	MIL	MLB	28	15(0)	19²	3-0	0	25	1.22	3.20	51.2%	11.0%	30.5%	3.7%	18.8%	66.4%	74.7%	32.1%	61.8%	.273	.596	96	0.2
2022	TOR	MLB	29	62(4)	64	3-2	0	82	1.44	5.34	46.1%	12.5%	29.2%	3.2%	34.4%	65.9%	79.4%	35.5%	53.1%	.314	.601	95	0.8
2023	TOR	MLB	30	56(3)	72²	2-1	0	105	1.35	4.95	39.1%	11.1%	33.3%	4.1%	31.2%	62.1%	79.5%	40.7%	51.7%	.313	.684	87	1.4
2024 DC	TOR	MLB	31	52(0)	55¹	3-2	0	72	1.22	3.72	44.0%	10.3%	31.2%	3.8%	32.7%					.280	.602	87	0.6

2023 Arsenal: CH (82.6), FA (92.8) *Comps: Joe Kelly (71), Jose Mesa (70), Kendall Graveman (70)*

2023 was the year that Richards finally gave in and emerged from his pitching cocoon as the pitcher he was always meant to be: Known ever since his rookie year for his stupendously fantastical changeup, Richards threw the pitch a remarkable 56.6% of the time— only Devin Williams and Tommy Kahnle threw their changeups more often. While the increased usage saw hangers get crushed for nine homers, batters actually saw their batting averages *decrease*, all the way down to .165 against the change of pace. For a pitcher who spurns a designated job and who has fought his way to the majors all the way from a DII school and the independent leagues, it just makes too much sense that he would eventually pitch backwards, too.

Jordan Romano RHP Born: 04/21/93 Age: 31 Height: 6'5" Weight: 210 Origin: Round 10, 2014 Draft (#294 overall)

YEAR	TM	LVL	AGE	G (GS)	IP	W-L	SV	K	WHIP	ERA	CSP	BB%	K%	HR%	GB%	ZSw%	ZCon%	OSw%	OCon%	BABIP	SLGCON	DRA-	WARP
2021	TOR	MLB	28	62(0)	63	7-1	23	85	1.05	2.14	53.4%	9.9%	33.6%	2.8%	46.5%	69.6%	79.0%	34.9%	52.2%	.254	.496	76	1.4
2022	TOR	MLB	29	63(0)	64	5-4	36	73	1.02	2.11	55.2%	8.1%	28.3%	1.6%	44.0%	70.7%	79.7%	37.6%	55.9%	.258	.384	82	1.2
2023	TOR	MLB	30	59(0)	59	5-7	36	72	1.22	2.90	46.7%	9.7%	29.0%	2.4%	36.7%	68.8%	77.7%	37.4%	46.8%	.296	.520	85	1.2
2024 DC	TOR	MLB	31	52(0)	55¹	3-6	36	70	1.27	4.10	51.0%	9.4%	29.7%	3.5%	41.5%					.302	.600	93	0.4

2023 Arsenal: SL (87), FA (96.9) *Comps: Pierce Johnson (70), Brad Brach (69), Hector Neris (66)*

When it's Romano's time to enter the game, the Rogers Centre lights turn a threatening, glowing red and the epic sounds of DVBBS & Borgeous' "Tsunami" pump out of the speakers. Even as other closer entrances continue to get better and better, Romano's is one of the very best. If fans get chills in the stands, what chance does a batter have? Armed with an unhittable two-pitch mix that generates elite whiff rates, Romano has the second-most saves in the league over the last two years behind only Cleveland's Emmanuel Clase—a remarkable total for the former Rule 5 draft pick. One more year like this and Romano should slide into second all-time on the Blue Jays in saves, behind only the legendary Tom Henke. Cue up the red lights!

Erik Swanson RHP Born: 09/04/93 Age: 30 Height: 6'3" Weight: 225 Origin: Round 8, 2014 Draft (#246 overall)

YEAR	TM	LVL	AGE	G (GS)	IP	W-L	SV	K	WHIP	ERA	CSP	BB%	K%	HR%	GB%	ZSw%	ZCon%	OSw%	OCon%	BABIP	SLGCON	DRA-	WARP
2021	SEA	MLB	27	33(2)	35¹	0-3	1	35	1.08	3.31	56.4%	6.9%	24.3%	3.5%	32.7%	77.9%	75.4%	36.1%	67.5%	.247	.546	103	0.3
2022	SEA	MLB	28	57(1)	53²	3-2	3	70	0.91	1.68	56.6%	4.9%	34.0%	1.5%	32.8%	72.9%	72.7%	39.0%	67.2%	.300	.455	71	1.3
2023	TOR	MLB	29	69(0)	66²	4-2	4	75	1.10	2.97	46.1%	8.0%	28.6%	3.1%	39.8%	70.1%	75.6%	36.9%	56.5%	.280	.521	83	1.4
2024 DC	TOR	MLB	30	52(0)	55¹	3-3	5	63	1.20	3.89	51.2%	7.5%	27.4%	3.9%	36.8%					.290	.592	91	0.5

2023 Arsenal: FS (85), FA (93.7), SW (86.6) *Comps: Tyler Duffey (52), Nick Wittgren (50), Dylan Floro (50)*

Swanson was made for his new franchise. The hurler grew up in Fargo, North Dakota—a state with only 20 big-leaguers to its credit that's located only 160 miles from the Canadian border. When the big right-hander learned he had been traded to Toronto, he was only about a five-minute drive from the border in the middle of a deeply off-the-grid hunting trip. It also fits that he joined the Jays' staff, given that credit for his success can be split (foreshadowing pun) between his pitching coach with the Mariners (Paul Davis) who suggested he add a new split-finger pitch, and the hurler from whom Swanson borrowed the grip. His model was, unknowingly, Jays ace Kevin Gausman; Swanson took it upon himself to find videos online and, with smaller hands than Gausman, practiced stretching his fingers on long drives from his rural home. He took his splitter to a new level once he found himself in Toronto where he was meant to be, as batters hit just .162 off his signature pitch.

──────────────── ★ ★ ★ *2024 Top 101 Prospect* **#26** ★ ★ ★ ────────────────

Ricky Tiedemann LHP Born: 08/18/02 Age: 21 Height: 6'4" Weight: 220 Origin: Round 3, 2021 Draft (#91 overall)

YEAR	TM	LVL	AGE	G (GS)	IP	W-L	SV	K	WHIP	ERA	CSP	BB%	K%	HR%	GB%	ZSw%	ZCon%	OSw%	OCon%	BABIP	SLGCON	DRA-	WARP
2022	DUN	A	19	6(6)	30	3-1	0	49	0.80	1.80		11.8%	44.5%	0.9%	46.8%	71.4%	68.3%	39.7%	38.0%	.217	.362	68	1.0
2022	VAN	A+	19	8(8)	37²	2-2	0	54	0.93	2.39		8.0%	36.0%	1.3%	46.2%					.276	.442	87	0.6
2022	NH	AA	19	4(4)	11	0-1	0	14	0.82	2.45		9.8%	34.1%	0.0%	63.6%					.227	.400	90	0.2
2023	NH	AA	20	11(11)	32	0-5	0	58	1.50	5.06		13.7%	39.7%	0.7%	48.5%					.422	.557	65	1.0
2024 DC	TOR	MLB	21	10(10)	46¹	3-2	0	60	1.25	3.77		11.9%	30.5%	3.3%	38.4%					.271	.559	86	0.8

2023 Arsenal: FA (97.5), SW (83.5), CH (86.1) *Comps: Deivi García (40), Tyler Skaggs (37), Forrest Whitley (37)*

Consider Tiedemann the ortolan in the Blue Jays system. He is that most cherished of things: The dominant pitching prospect, a man with a golden arm that could single-handedly deliver great things to a team, striking out a remarkable 44% of the batters he faced. Unfortunately, he is also as delicate and scarce as that special songbird. Tiedemann was limited to just 44 innings, never reaching five innings in a start during the year, as he battled biceps issues that kept him out from May 5 until July 21. He re-appeared in the Arizona Fall League and flashed dominance, but you may need to put a napkin over your head as you watch his performances to hide your sinful excitement.

LINEOUTS

Hitters

HITTER	POS	TM	LVL	AGE	PA	R	HR	RBI	SB	AVG/OBP/SLG	BABIP	SLGCON	BB%	K%	ZSw%	ZCon%	OSw%	OCon%	LA	90th EV	DRC+	BRR	DRP	WARP
Addison Barger	UT	BUF	AAA	23	397	53	9	46	5	.250/.353/.403	.308	.539	13.1%	21.7%	65.8%	88.6%	29.7%	54.2%			94	0.6	0.0	0.9
Manuel Beltre	SS	DUN	A	19	431	67	6	50	12	.231/.335/.340	.280	.439	11.1%	19.3%	69.5%	82.5%	32.6%	62.9%			100	1.2	2.9	2.1
Jace Bohrofen	RF	DUN	A	21	77	17	6	16	0	.306/.442/.677	.342	.955	19.5%	23.4%	65.6%	81.0%	17.2%	52.4%			123	0.8	2.2	0.8
Dasan Brown	CF	SUR	WIN	21	79	11	1	9	4	.282/.342/.408	.404	.617	7.6%	30.4%	61.1%	54.5%	31.8%	14.3%						
	CF	VAN	A+	21	463	59	7	39	26	.218/.309/.315	.286	.443	8.9%	25.1%							96	-0.4	1.2	1.3
Cade Doughty	IF	VAN	A+	22	424	61	18	68	4	.264/.342/.459	.346	.691	8.3%	29.7%							98	-0.1	-1.1	0.7
Josh Kasevich	SS	VAN	A+	22	383	46	4	50	11	.284/.363/.365	.310	.416	9.9%	10.7%							122	-1.0	1.6	2.2
Otto Lopez	UT	BUF	AAA	24	346	48	2	35	13	.258/.313/.343	.305	.414	6.6%	15.9%	63.9%	90.6%	36.1%	67.9%			89	2.9	0.7	0.8
Nathan Lukes	RF	BUF	AAA	28	222	39	5	32	3	.366/.423/.530	.401	.605	7.7%	11.3%	71.5%	90.7%	36.1%	74.7%			116	0.3	0.2	1.1
	RF	TOR	MLB	28	31	4	0	2	0	.192/.290/.308	.278	.471	12.9%	29.0%	72.3%	91.2%	43.1%	67.9%	14.5	102.5	82	0.0	-0.1	0.0
Brennan Orf	1B	DUN	A	21	148	18	0	11	1	.224/.439/.308	.353	.485	24.3%	26.4%	65.4%	82.1%	14.5%	53.8%			103	-0.1	-1.6	0.3
Sam Shaw	2B	BLU	ROK	18	40	4	0	0	0	.207/.425/.276	.261	.348	25.0%	15.0%	100.0%	100.0%								
Tucker Toman	3B/SS	DUN	A	19	503	59	5	51	7	.208/.320/.313	.289	.457	12.5%	26.8%	68.0%	78.6%	32.0%	54.2%			86	-1.3	-1.1	0.3

Nominally a bat-first shortstop prospect, **Addison Barger** has experience all over the infield and added corner outfield play to his back of tricks last year, revealing his true lot in life: potentially very nifty utility player. ⓧ Given a $2.35 million bonus in 2021, 19-year-old **Manuel Beltre** already gets tagged with terms usually reserved for mid-30s utility guys. He's renowned for his work ethic and baseball IQ, but the hope is that he adds some strength while staying at shortstop as he moves up the developmental ladder. ⓧ A breakout junior season saw **Jace Bohrofen** fly up draft charts. The Jays plucked the outfielder with good raw power for a just-below-slot deal in the sixth round, then watched as he put up one of the best performances from anyone in the 2023 draft class. ⓧ A third-round selection in the 2019 Draft, **Dasan Brown** is still a work-in-progress for the Jays. His 80-grade speed could mean the team could easily add outfield range and oodles of stolen bases if the center fielder manages to figure it all out, but until then he's only representing Canada at the World Baseball Classic, not the AL East. ⓧ With a strong arm, powerful bat, and the ability to play both second and third base, **Cade Doughty** is the kind of jack-of-all-trades that organizations like having in their systems. He still strikes out too much, but the Blue Jays are likely content with his full-season debut. ⓧ **Josh Kasevich** may have a slugging percentage that matches his OBP, but at least it is a very good OBP. He's going to need his quality approach, contact skills and glove to continue to push him up the chain. ⓧ **Otto Lopez** balled out for Team Canada in the World Baseball Classic, building off his successful 2022 campaign by hitting .294/.333/.588 with the maple leaf on his cap. Unfortunately, that would be the high point of his season: After starting the year cold, Lopez's year ended in July with an oblique injury. ⓧ After amassing over 2,500 professional plate appearances, **Nathan Lukes** finally made his big-league debut on Opening Day last year. He wouldn't spend much time in Toronto but did get to play hero at least once: On July 9, Lukes hit the game-winning 10th-inning double to push the Jays past the Tigers. ⓧ A power-hitting first baseman, **Brennan Orf** displayed great exit velos in the MLB Draft League. Unfortunately, the third-best HR hitter in SIU history only showed off his plate discipline in his pro debut, failing to homer in his 35-game audition.

ⓧ Arguably the best Canadian bat in the draft, lifelong Blue Jays fan **Sam Shaw** was snagged for an over-slot bonus in the ninth round. ⓧ **Tucker Toman** is the definition of a baseball rat, working so hard and frequently at team facilities that the team sent him home to give him a break. He'll also need to catch a break at the plate next year, as the switch-hitter known for his contact-savvy ways struggled in that department, and to impact the ball in any way whatsoever.

Pitchers

PITCHER	TM	LVL	AGE	G (GS)	IP	W-L	SV	K	WHIP	ERA	CSP	BB%	K%	HR%	GB%	ZSw%	ZCon%	OSw%	OCon%	BABIP	SLGCON	DRA-	WARP
Mason Fluharty	VAN	A+	21	12 (0)	15¹	1-0	1	21	0.78	0.59		8.6%	36.2%	1.7%	43.8%					.194	.375	95	0.1
	NH	AA	21	36 (0)	42¹	2-5	4	54	1.58	4.25		9.3%	28.0%	3.1%	36.4%					.387	.678	89	0.8
Ryan Jennings	DUN	A	24	9 (7)	33	2-3	0	44	1.24	4.36		10.1%	31.7%	1.4%	35.9%	67.5%	85.5%	34.6%	46.6%	.329	.551	81	0.5
	VAN	A+	24	3 (3)	10	0-1	0	11	1.20	2.70		7.7%	28.2%	2.6%	40.0%					.333	.560	99	0.0
Connor O'Halloran	DUN	A	20	6 (1)	10	3-1	0	9	1.60	6.30		16.7%	18.8%	2.1%	53.3%	66.7%	82.4%	37.3%	41.9%	.241	.467	119	0.0
Kendry Rojas	DUN	A	20	20 (15)	84	4-6	0	82	1.24	3.75		9.4%	23.4%	2.3%	35.5%	79.4%	79.8%	35.1%	53.1%	.279	.478	88	0.8
Dahian Santos	VAN	A+	20	12 (12)	48¹	3-3	0	56	1.18	3.54		13.1%	27.2%	2.4%	34.2%					.223	.444	106	0.1
Mitch White	BUF	AAA	28	17 (12)	55²	1-2	0	67	1.56	5.50		12.0%	26.7%	3.6%	39.6%	63.5%	84.2%	32.2%	55.4%	.343	.639	91	1.1
	TOR	MLB	28	10 (0)	12²	0-1	0	13	1.74	7.11	44.3%	11.7%	21.7%	3.3%	20.0%	70.5%	85.1%	34.2%	61.1%	.342	.711	114	0.1
Yosver Zulueta	BUF	AAA	25	45 (7)	64	4-4	0	73	1.53	4.08		15.7%	25.4%	0.3%	52.8%	57.8%	85.8%	24.6%	52.5%	.329	.465	95	1.2

As long as there is baseball, then there will be guys whose purpose on earth is to make life hell for left-handed batters. **Mason Fluharty's** four-seamer scrapes the low 90s, but his cutter and slider are practically unhittable for left-handed hitters, giving Fluharty the kind of direct line to the majors otherwise reserved for top prospects. ⓧ A fourth-round pick in 2022, **Ryan Jennings** ended his college career in the bullpen but was moved back to the rotation with a breakout performance last year. He was dominant when he returned to High-A for the season's final weeks, including a hitless, five-strikeout, three-inning outing in the championship series. ⓧ $1.5 million was enough to sign this two-way high school star away from NC State. While **Landen Maroudis** lined up at shortstop in high school, that money is more for his 96 mph fastball and emerging changeup. ⓧ The only pitcher in Michigan history to post back-to-back 100 strikeout seasons, **Connor O'Halloran**—another member of Toronto's Canadian pipeline—is the rare pitching prospect who doesn't flirt with triple digit heat. Instead, he pairs a low-90s fastball to go with a sweeping slider and developing changeup. ⓧ **Kendry Rojas'** fastball ticked up and his walk rate dipped, all while doubling his innings total from the season before. Rojas did display mid-summer fatigue, but the former outfielder is still getting a feel for pitching and will need to add a third offering to his fastball/slider combo. ⓧ **Dahian Santos** and his high-spin slider returned to Vancouver and, though he still needs to work on getting his walks under control, he acquitted himself well at the level. Unfortunately, Santos went on the IL just 12 starts into his season. ⓧ Signed to an above-slot bonus in the third round, **Juaron Watts-Brown's** Oklahoma State numbers may not look great, but they hide that the pitcher led the Big 12 in K's. With a low-90s fastball and standout mid-80s slider, the player who entered college games to 50 Cent's "Outta Control" will want to find some, as he also led his conference in wild pitches. ⓧ **Mitch White** suffered a shoulder impingement during the offseason, hurt his elbow trying to build up the shoulder in time for Opening Day, then hurt his shoulder again rehabbing the elbow. It was like a nesting doll of misery, with a tiny little pink slip tucked in the middle. ⓧ Finally healthy after years of dealing with injuries, **Yosver Zulueta** pitched in the Futures Game in Seattle in July. While he is still striking out more than a batter per inning, the control still hasn't shown up. He spent a few weeks in August back in Dunedin, suggesting he was in need of a mechanical tune-up at Toronto's pitching lab.

WASHINGTON NATIONALS

Essay by Davy Andrews

Player comments by Mike Gianella and BP staff

It may be helpful to think of the 2024 season as an experiment. When the Washington Nationals finished at the bottom of the National League East in 2023, they became the first team since Connie Mack's 1940-1943 Philadelphia Athletics to record four straight last-place seasons without firing either their manager or general manager. The A's couldn't fire the 80-year-old Mack because he owned the team. The 15 other teams with stretches of four-plus seasons in the cellar averaged two GMs and three managers during their prolonged slumps. In Washington, not only have general manager Mike Rizzo and manager Davey Martinez kept their jobs, they've signed contract extensions.

You could quibble with including the 2020 season in this run, as it lasted just 60 games and the Nationals tied with the Mets for last place, but the fact remains that the Nationals are trying something that's virtually unprecedented in the history of baseball. After four years as the worst team in the game, and with no notable additions to the roster, they are simply running it back in 2024. Even before Rizzo and Martinez signed their extensions, the only team that had ever been so bad for so long without a change in leadership was the team whose leader was cutting the checks. It was 80 years ago, and the leader in question wore a bowler hat in the dugout.

A unique set of circumstances conspired to allow Rizzo and Martinez to survive for this long. For the most part, GMs and managers hold onto their jobs when their teams are either winning or rebuilding. Firings tend to come when the winning peters out or when the rebuild looks like it's not working out. The Nationals plunged into the cellar immediately after winning the 2019 World Series, skipping the traditional years of aimless decline that set the scene for most front office turnover.

Rizzo is the architect who built the Nationals into a powerhouse from scratch and Martinez is the manager who finally got them over the hump. The quick descent means that the memory of their triumph is still fresh, and the resultant goodwill has insulated them from much of the usual clamor for regime change. Now they can point to shoots of hope emerging from the wreckage. The Nationals have a highly ranked farm system and a core of young big-

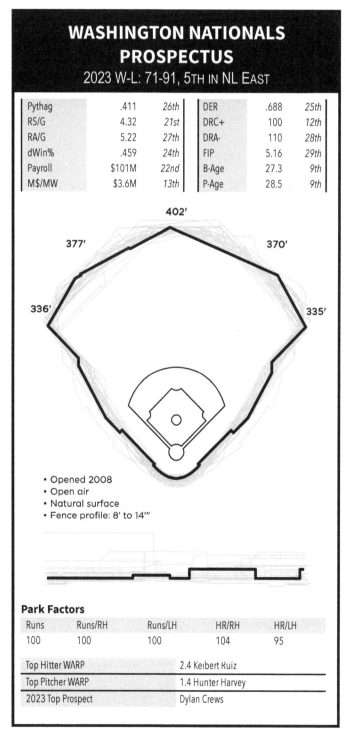

WASHINGTON NATIONALS PROSPECTUS
2023 W-L: 71-91, 5TH IN NL EAST

Pythag	.411	26th	DER	.688	25th
RS/G	4.32	21st	DRC+	100	12th
RA/G	5.22	27th	DRA-	110	28th
dWin%	.459	24th	FIP	5.16	29th
Payroll	$101M	22nd	B-Age	27.3	9th
M$/MW	$3.6M	13th	P-Age	28.5	9th

402'

377'   370'

336'   335'

- Opened 2008
- Open air
- Natural surface
- Fence profile: 8' to 14'"

Park Factors

Runs	Runs/RH	Runs/LH	HR/RH	HR/LH
100	100	100	104	95

Top Hitter WARP	2.4 Keibert Ruiz
Top Pitcher WARP	1.4 Hunter Harvey
2023 Top Prospect	Dylan Crews

485

Payroll History (in millions)

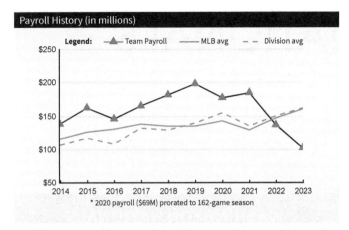

Legend: ▲ Team Payroll — MLB avg - - - Division avg

* 2020 payroll ($69M) prorated to 162-game season

Future Commitments (in millions)

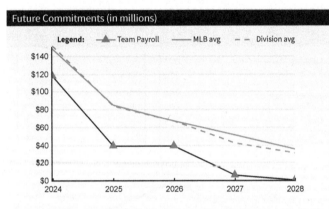

Legend: ▲ Team Payroll — MLB avg - - - Division avg

Farm System Ranking

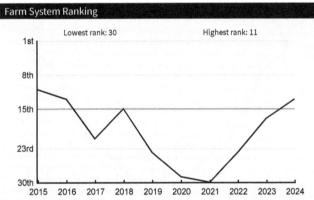

Lowest rank: 30   Highest rank: 11

Personnel

General Manager & President of Baseball Operations
Mike Rizzo

Manager
Dave Martinez

Vice President & Assistant General Manager, Baseball Operations
Michael DeBartolo

Assistant General Manager, Player Personel
Mark Scialabba

Senior Director, Baseball Research & Development
Lee Mendelowitz

leaguers who took a step forward in 2023. Their 71-91 record was a 16-win improvement over 2022, and it included a second-half stretch of 23 victories in 34 games.

There is another factor that has contributed to the longevity of Rizzo and Martinez. While this may seem like an essay about organizational stability, it is anything but: The truth is that the extent to which anyone is actually in charge of the Washington Nationals is unclear. Owner Mark Lerner announced his intention to sell the team in April of 2022. Since then, he hasn't spoken to reporters, and his few public statements have scrupulously avoided any mention of the sale process.

That uncertainty continues on down the ladder. It's hard to tell how much control Rizzo actually has. He received his contract extension in September, but only after initiating sweeping firings throughout the scouting and player development departments. Among those let go or reassigned were Rizzo's minor-league roommate and at least one member of his wedding party. It's hard to imagine he would have made those moves of his own volition. Martinez got his extension in August, but much of his coaching staff won't be returning, either. Even if ownership didn't mandate these firings, why bring Rizzo and Martinez back without their most trusted lieutenants? Ken Rosenthal proposed a cynical answer. "With the team for sale," he wrote, "ownership seemingly does not want to create a perception of chaos."

Here's what avoiding the perception of chaos looks like. In September and October, the team let go of 26 people who were prominent enough to be mentioned by name in *The Washington Post*. Together they read like a litany of fallen soldiers from the *Iliad*: Special assistants Willie Fraser, Jeff Harris, John Mirabelli, Mike Pagliarulo, Matt Ruebel and Jon Weil. International scouting director Jonny DiPuglia along with scouts Mike Cadahia, Greg Hunter, David Leer, Alan Marr, Jose Pepe Ortega and Alex Rodriguez (not that Alex Rodriguez). Director of player development De Jon Watson, along with minor-league coordinators Coco Crisp (yes, that Coco Crisp), Joe Dillon, Tim Doherty, Micah Franklin, Troy Gingrich, Mark Grater, Cody Ransom and Michael Tejera. Major-league coaches Tim Bogar, Gary DiSarcina, Pat Roessler and Eric Young Jr. The Internet Archive's Wayback Machine reveals four more scouts and two senior advisers who were listed in the staff directory in May but gone by November. In all, that makes 32 members of the scouting, player development and coaching departments gone.

In last year's *Annual*, Jarret Seidler's entire essay was devoted to Washington's deficiencies in those very departments. Once you wrap your head around the carnage, it should be reassuring that the Nationals have recognized their shortcomings and decided to act. However, Rizzo was at the wheel while the rest of baseball whizzed by and this isn't his first attempt to catch up. During 2022's similar (though less extreme) bloodletting, Rizzo listed his goals: "New ideas, outside-the-box thinking and new technology and people to handle the new technologies." This offseason, he offered the same platitudes, saying that "new technologies and analytics" would be "a big impetus in our development moving forward." At the very least, this shakeup is a tacit admission the previous one failed.

At the big-league level, question marks surround every member of the team's young core. CJ Abrams has yet to hit left-handed pitching, develop any plate discipline or turn his abundant athleticism into decent defense. By DRP, Keibert Ruiz was the third-worst defender in all of baseball in 2023. Josiah Gray seemingly remade himself into a contact manager, but DRA- is understandably skeptical of his 3.91 ERA. Lane Thomas is 28 years old and entering arbitration. In order to field a competitive team, the Nationals would need all of those players, along with MacKenzie Gore and Luis García, to take another step forward, and that's just not how things tend to work. Ruiz is the only National with a PECOTA projection above 2.0 WARP. Gray's forecasted 0.7 WARP ranks 176th among pitchers, making him the only National in the top 250. No other team has fewer than three pitchers in the top 250.

While that's not an ideal position to be in, testing young players and giving them a chance to prove their mettle is what the Nationals should be doing at this point in the rebuild. The team's cynical, pump-and-dump approach to free agency is also geared toward making sure that what little money is spent goes toward accruing more prospects. Over the offseason, the Nationals signed bounceback candidates Dylan Floro and Nick Senzel to one-year deals with the hope of exchanging them for a lottery ticket or two at the trade deadline. This is what a rebuilding team does while it waits for its prospects to mature and open the contention window. The problem is that it will all be for naught if the prospects don't actually perform, and the Nationals have a terrible track record in that department. With 2.0 WARP in 2023, García became the first National to graduate from the minors and post a replacement-level season since Juan Soto, who debuted in 2018.

While the farm system is highly-ranked it lacks depth. James Wood and Dylan Crews are truly excellent prospects, but too many of the players behind them bear the hallmarks of the club's systemic blind spots: hard-throwing right-handers who miss spots but not bats, or hitters with sweet swings, sour batted-ball metrics and unsavory plate discipline. In 2023, five of the team's six minor-league affiliates had losing records, and three finished dead last in their divisions. Four posted either the worst or second-worst OPS in their respective leagues. None ranked higher than seventh in ERA or 11th in K/9. The underlying metrics are even scarier. When *Baseball America* released organizational rankings based on minor-league Statcast data, Washington finished 28th in both hitting and pitching. Even if Rizzo were to wake up tomorrow and assemble the best scouting and player development systems in baseball, it would take a while to catch up.

Rizzo built the Nationals from nothing into a perennial contender and a champion, but he also presided as they became one of the worst organizations in baseball from top to bottom. That's the experiment the Nationals are conducting: Is someone who allowed a team to become this bad in the first place capable of turning it around again?

There are already some troubling inconsistencies: While the team has brought in outside hires to lead the scouting department, they have filled some of their most prominent player development openings with internal candidates. Somehow the department was so deficient that it needed to be completely gutted, but also contained the very people who were best suited to step in and turn things around. Rizzo is a baseball lifer with a vast network, and he has a tendency to trust his people. That policy has worked in the past. The signing of Max Scherzer, with whose promise Rizzo fell in love as Arizona's scouting director in 2006, serves as a shining example. But relying on people you know is also the path to homogeneity and stagnation. The Nationals desperately need to learn from the rest of the league, and promoting from within while restocking the lower rungs of the org chart from the usual sources won't help them do so.

Modernizing operations isn't the only impetus for the firings, however. The Lerners are cutting personnel in order to save money. Rizzo has said publicly that all player development jobs will be filled. Notably, he has not said the same about the scouting jobs. "I don't think the Lerner family necessarily wants to sell the team," wrote Brittany Ghiroli of *The Athletic*. "Rather, it's become a financial burden that necessitates new ownership, which can hopefully figure out a path out of the MASN TV right mess and has deep enough pockets to handle the team's multitude of deferred salary payments along with affording a competitive team."

The fight over television revenues won't be ending any time soon, and the Nationals will be paying Patrick Corbin until 2026, Scherzer until 2028 and Stephen Strasburg until 2029. The same issues that are motivating the Lerners to sell will make potential buyers hesitant to meet their asking price, which is reportedly well above the $2 billion valuation that *Forbes* gave the club. The organization has maintained that the Lerners are fully committed to winning for as long as they're in charge. Even if that's true, between the financial restraints and Rizzo's hiring tendencies, it's hard to imagine that the team is exploring every avenue to find the right person for the job, and that's just for the jobs that will actually be filled.

The Nationals won't get their results in 2024. Much as it was in 2023, the focus will be on monitoring the development of the young players, hoping for reasons to hope. Regardless of whether the experiment succeeds, it's important to remember what was lost when the Nationals tore it all down. It may be tempting to view the last four years of futility as similar to the team's initial struggles upon moving to Washington in 2005, but to those who care about the team the two situations couldn't be more different.

In the beginning, people were just glad to have baseball in DC. They understood that the team would need to be built from the ground up, and they didn't mind the ugly uniforms or the decrepit ballpark. It felt like a miracle when the Nationals went 81-81 in their inaugural season. In the lean years that followed, fans celebrated milestones including opening a new ballpark, drafting can't-miss prospects and signing coveted free agents. Watching Rizzo build the team from nothing gave more meaning to the successes that came later.

It feels different to watch a championship team suddenly implode and get sold off for parts. If retained, any one of Bryce Harper, Max Scherzer, Trea Turner or Juan Soto could have become the greatest player in franchise history. Instead, the first four players on the Washington Nationals Baseball-Reference page are wearing Montreal Expos hats, and their positions will remain secure for the rest of this decade at the very least. Not every championship team turns into a dynasty, but few have hacked at the bonds that linked them to the good times with such gusto.

—Davy Andrews is an author of FanGraphs.

HITTERS

CJ Abrams SS   Born: 10/03/00   Age: 23   Bats: L   Throws: R   Height: 6'2"   Weight: 191   Origin: Round 1, 2019 Draft (#6 overall)

YEAR	TM	LVL	AGE	PA	R	HR	RBI	SB	AVG/OBP/SLG	BABIP	SLGCON	BB%	K%	ZSw%	ZCon%	OSw%	OCon%	LA	90th EV	DRC+	BRR	DRP	WARP
2021	SA	AA	20	183	26	2	23	13	.296/.363/.420	.365	.540	8.2%	19.7%							104	2.7	-1.1	0.8
2022	ROC	AAA	21	35	7	0	2	4	.290/.343/.355	.375	.478	5.7%	22.9%							92	0.1	-0.4	0.0
2022	ELP	AAA	21	151	35	7	28	10	.314/.364/.507	.343	.617	5.3%	16.6%	76.4%	84.2%	44.6%	66.0%			107	1.3	-1.7	0.5
2022	SD	MLB	21	139	16	2	11	1	.232/.285/.320	.276	.408	2.9%	19.4%	70.6%	85.6%	46.3%	63.7%	5.6	101.6	99	0.1	0.2	0.5
2022	WAS	MLB	21	163	17	0	10	6	.258/.276/.327	.301	.382	0.6%	14.1%	73.9%	88.8%	42.9%	66.9%	6.5	103.0	83	0.0	0.4	0.2
2023	WAS	MLB	22	614	83	18	64	47	.245/.300/.412	.279	.521	5.2%	19.2%	72.5%	84.8%	39.7%	68.6%	13.1	103.7	93	2.6	0.4	1.9
2024 DC	WAS	MLB	23	553	54	12	58	32	.252/.308/.382	.297	.479	5.3%	18.8%							94	1.0	0.9	1.8

2023 GP: SS (151)
Comps: José Ramírez (71), Ketel Marte (64), Amed Rosario (63)

In the 1994 movie *Clerks*, Randal Graves argued that title doesn't dictate behavior. Maybe so, but having someone else put you into a position to succeed can positively reinforce an existing skill set. More promise than polish entering 2023, Abrams came out of the blocks with more of the same, swinging at everything and looking lost at the plate for two-and-a-half months. He turned his season around by laying off fastballs outside of the zone and focusing on offerings he could drive. The results weren't extreme, but Abrams went from a bottom-of-the-barrel offensive player to an above-average one, along with a massive boost in stolen bases. From June 19 onward, Abrams stole a nearly incomprehensible 35 bags in 36 attempts; only Ronald Acuña Jr. had more steals in that time frame. Abrams attributed his improvement to the confidence and comfort he felt after the Nats moved him to the top of the batting order. It's easy to forget he is just 22, barely played in the minors and was younger than nearly every other starting shortstop. The arrow is pointing up for a young, dynamic player who is must-see entertainment every time he reaches first.

Jake Alu UT   Born: 04/06/97   Age: 27   Bats: L   Throws: R   Height: 5'10"   Weight: 186   Origin: Round 24, 2019 Draft (#723 overall)

YEAR	TM	LVL	AGE	PA	R	HR	RBI	SB	AVG/OBP/SLG	BABIP	SLGCON	BB%	K%	ZSw%	ZCon%	OSw%	OCon%	LA	90th EV	DRC+	BRR	DRP	WARP
2021	WIL	A+	24	157	22	5	19	8	.303/.357/.490	.361	.628	5.1%	20.4%							111	0.4	0.4	0.8
2021	HBG	AA	24	213	26	5	23	5	.264/.315/.411	.313	.526	6.1%	20.2%							99	-0.5	-2.7	0.3
2022	HBG	AA	25	325	44	9	36	9	.281/.360/.470	.323	.593	9.8%	18.2%							122	0.6	6.2	2.3
2022	ROC	AAA	25	242	37	11	45	6	.323/.372/.553	.353	.694	7.9%	18.2%							123	0.8	-0.2	1.4
2023	ROC	AAA	26	330	46	5	43	16	.298/.360/.428	.333	.508	8.8%	13.9%	58.7%	90.4%	34.7%	74.6%			106	0.9	0.5	1.4
2023	WAS	MLB	26	175	14	2	16	5	.226/.282/.289	.291	.393	5.7%	24.0%	64.2%	83.0%	40.1%	63.0%	4.7	101.6	79	0.0	-0.1	0.1
2024 DC	WAS	MLB	27	158	14	3	15	3	.231/.289/.350	.272	.432	6.4%	18.5%							79	0.0	-0.2	0.0

2023 GP: LF (27), 2B (24), 3B (5)
Comps: Roger Kieschnick (50), Cameron Perkins (48), Todd Cunningham (47)

Like many Nationals in the team's post-championship era, Alu is a useful role player who was overexposed in 2023 because the team had few palatable options. Advertised as a good contact hitter with limited power potential, he couldn't even live up to the "good" part of the bargain, struggling with the big club after they sent off Jeimer Candelario at the trade deadline to give Alu an extended look. He's versatile and can play lots of positions, but nothing about the bat or the glove stands out. There's an excellent chance Alu winds up back at Triple-A as a depth piece.

Darren Baker 2B/LF   Born: 02/11/99   Age: 25   Bats: L   Throws: R   Height: 5'10"   Weight: 180   Origin: Round 10, 2021 Draft (#293 overall)

YEAR	TM	LVL	AGE	PA	R	HR	RBI	SB	AVG/OBP/SLG	BABIP	SLGCON	BB%	K%	ZSw%	ZCon%	OSw%	OCon%	LA	90th EV	DRC+	BRR	DRP	WARP
2021	FBG	A	22	74	3	0	5	2	.318/.352/.394	.362	.456	5.4%	12.2%							120	-0.7	-0.1	0.3
2022	WIL	A+	23	273	43	2	25	10	.273/.333/.367	.335	.464	8.1%	18.7%							112	-0.7	5.1	1.6
2022	HBG	AA	23	191	23	1	14	5	.290/.356/.361	.345	.439	9.4%	15.7%							106	1.3	1.8	0.9
2023	ROC	AAA	24	448	49	3	41	19	.273/.338/.340	.329	.419	8.7%	17.0%	57.6%	90.8%	32.4%	71.8%			92	0.6	0.7	0.9
2024 non	WAS	MLB	25	251	20	2	20	4	.230/.285/.308	.274	.379	6.5%	17.1%							68	0.0	0	-0.3

2023 GP: 2B (68), LF (33), DH (3), CF (1)   *Comps: Juan Francia (62), Billy Fleming (58), Colin Walsh (56)*

The son of Astros manager Dusty Baker, Darren has been around the game his entire life, serving as the Giants batboy in 2002 and famously getting rescued at home plate by J.T. Snow during Game Five of the World Series. Baker is a solid if unspectacular prospect in his own right, a contact hitter with a fluid swing whose limited power potential will probably limit him to a bench role when he does make the majors. While batted-ball elevation isn't everything, a 17% fly-ball rate at Triple-A Rochester doesn't bode well, particularly for a player who doesn't have game-breaking speed. Baker's baseball instincts and knowledge of the game might not be enough to overcome his modest physical ceiling.

Alex Call   OF   Born: 09/27/94   Age: 29   Bats: R   Throws: R   Height: 5'11"   Weight: 189   Origin: Round 3, 2016 Draft (#86 overall)

YEAR	TM	LVL	AGE	PA	R	HR	RBI	SB	AVG/OBP/SLG	BABIP	SLGCON	BB%	K%	ZSw%	ZCon%	OSw%	OCon%	LA	90th EV	DRC+	BRR	DRP	WARP
2021	AKR	AA	26	180	34	5	23	12	.310/.389/.503	.339	.605	11.7%	14.4%							131	2.4	0.9	1.6
2021	COL	AAA	26	269	34	10	27	3	.229/.335/.394	.234	.472	12.3%	14.1%							117	0.3	6.7	2.1
2022	COL	AAA	27	305	56	11	46	6	.280/.418/.494	.306	.624	16.1%	16.4%							131	-2.5	2.8	2.0
2022	CLE	MLB	27	16	2	0	0	0	.167/.375/.167	.250	.250	25.0%	25.0%	56.5%	84.6%	32.8%	47.4%	6.8	102.1	97	0.0	0.0	0.1
2022	WAS	MLB	27	115	16	5	13	3	.245/.330/.441	.282	.592	9.6%	22.6%	64.4%	86.9%	31.0%	61.8%	19.0	100.4	87	0.0	0.1	0.2
2023	ROC	AAA	28	50	5	1	3	3	.275/.388/.425	.278	.472	14.0%	8.0%	61.1%	90.9%	35.2%	73.0%			110	0.5	-1.1	0.2
2023	WAS	MLB	28	439	43	8	38	9	.200/.307/.307	.230	.387	12.1%	17.8%	62.4%	89.6%	24.7%	67.6%	17.8	101.6	95	0.7	0.2	1.3
2024 DC	WAS	MLB	29	225	23	5	23	6	.231/.326/.363	.260	.450	11.0%	16.5%							98	0.2	-0	0.6

2023 GP: CF (81), LF (34), RF (9)   *Comps: Keon Broxton (54), Casper Wells (51), Greg Allen (51)*

A briefly successful stint roaming the Nationals outfield at the tail end of 2022 led to the hope that Call could be a decent center fielder for the 2023 squad, serving as a capable stopgap until the jewels of their system started arriving to the majors in 2024. Instead, like most things associated with the 2023 Nationals it was a miserable experience for everyone involved. Call has a good batting eye and decent bat-to-ball skills, but that's about all he has going for him. He doesn't hit the ball particularly hard, isn't fast enough to grind out infield hits or steal a bunch of bases and grades out as defensively average at best. Despite their desperate need for a placeholder until top prospect Dylan Crews arrives, by the end of the season Washington had pulled the plug and relegated Call to a reserve role.

★ ★ ★ *2024 Top 101 Prospect* **#5** ★ ★ ★

Dylan Crews   CF   Born: 02/26/02   Age: 22   Bats: R   Throws: R   Height: 6'0"   Weight: 205   Origin: Round 1, 2023 Draft (#2 overall)

YEAR	TM	LVL	AGE	PA	R	HR	RBI	SB	AVG/OBP/SLG	BABIP	SLGCON	BB%	K%	ZSw%	ZCon%	OSw%	OCon%	LA	90th EV	DRC+	BRR	DRP	WARP
2023	FBG	A	21	71	16	5	24	1	.355/.423/.645	.436	.930	8.5%	26.8%							123	-2.0	1.7	0.3
2023	HBG	AA	21	85	7	0	5	3	.208/.318/.278	.278	.377	9.4%	22.4%							88	1.0	-1.1	0.1
2024 DC	WAS	MLB	22	96	8	2	9	2	.219/.274/.327	.304	.483	5.9%	30.1%							70	0.0	0	-0.1

2023 GP: CF (27), RF (4), LF (2), DH (2)   *Comps: Sean Henry (68), Josh Flores (62), Jake Marisnick (60)*

The second-overall pick in last year's Amateur Draft, Crews is viewed by many as the best collegiate position prospect since Adley Rutschman. He already looks like a polished, five-tool player, flashing strong exit velocities with regularity, showing great bat-to-ball skills and excellent strike zone judgment. The glove should play in center field and Crews' speed should make him a threat on the basepaths. You need to squint to find a weakness in his game, but it's possible that a propensity to hit the ball on the ground might make his over-the-fence power simply good as opposed to elite. Crews demolished low-minors pitching before finishing the season with a brief stop at Double-A. He has an outside chance of making his major-league debut late this year and should be thrilling fans in the District of Columbia for years to come.

Luis García 2B Born: 05/16/00 Age: 24 Bats: L Throws: R Height: 6'2" Weight: 220 Origin: IFA, 2016

YEAR	TM	LVL	AGE	PA	R	HR	RBI	SB	AVG/OBP/SLG	BABIP	SLGCON	BB%	K%	ZSw%	ZCon%	OSw%	OCon%	LA	90th EV	DRC+	BRR	DRP	WARP
2021	ROC	AAA	21	159	26	13	25	1	.303/.371/.599	.288	.733	9.4%	16.4%								147	0.8	-0.8	1.3
2021	WAS	MLB	21	247	29	6	22	0	.242/.275/.411	.273	.503	4.5%	17.4%	70.7%	87.6%	39.2%	60.5%	4.1	102.7	91	-0.1	0.1	0.6
2022	ROC	AAA	22	205	39	8	32	3	.308/.366/.519	.343	.644	8.8%	17.6%							121	-0.9	-1.1	0.9
2022	WAS	MLB	22	377	29	7	45	3	.275/.295/.408	.337	.533	2.9%	22.3%	67.8%	80.7%	43.0%	64.6%	5.7	103.7	95	-0.4	-8.4	0.0
2023	ROC	AAA	23	108	15	1	13	2	.268/.315/.381	.291	.440	7.4%	12.0%	72.3%	93.9%	44.0%	70.7%			97	1.2	0.2	0.4
2023	WAS	MLB	23	482	61	9	50	9	.266/.304/.385	.286	.444	5.6%	12.4%	74.8%	89.3%	34.2%	71.5%	4.6	103.8	111	0.3	-1.5	2.0
2024 DC	WAS	MLB	24	430	42	10	46	5	.266/.313/.397	.300	.474	5.8%	15.3%							99	-0.2	-0.5	1.1

2023 GP: 2B (121) *Comps: José Reyes (56), Rougned Odor (53), Ozzie Albies (53)*

García is one of two players who missed out on the fun of the Nationals World Series title in 2019 but has been with the team for all four years of their ensuing rebuild (the other is Kyle Finnegan), and for better or worse he is emblematic of the team's fortunes over that span. There are moments where you can see glimpses of why García was a BP Top 101 prospect, but on a surface level it has mostly been a disappointing run for both the team and their once-promising middle infielder. García improved his plate discipline but still only managed a meager 27 walks. His proponents point to how hard he hits the ball when he puts it in the air, but he doesn't elevate nearly enough for it to matter and those batted-ball metrics fell off last year. He's still young but the clock is ticking, and it doesn't help that García's glove is a liability up the middle.

Stone Garrett LF Born: 11/22/95 Age: 28 Bats: R Throws: R Height: 6'2" Weight: 224 Origin: Round 8, 2014 Draft (#227 overall)

YEAR	TM	LVL	AGE	PA	R	HR	RBI	SB	AVG/OBP/SLG	BABIP	SLGCON	BB%	K%	ZSw%	ZCon%	OSw%	OCon%	LA	90th EV	DRC+	BRR	DRP	WARP
2021	AMA	AA	25	443	65	25	81	17	.280/.317/.516	.332	.727	4.5%	26.6%							99	0.2	-3.2	0.9
2022	RNO	AAA	26	440	73	28	95	15	.275/.332/.568	.302	.778	7.5%	23.9%	71.6%	83.1%	38.3%	52.4%			110	0.0	5.4	2.4
2022	AZ	MLB	26	84	13	4	10	3	.276/.309/.539	.370	.837	3.6%	32.1%	75.8%	70.0%	42.8%	58.4%	22.4	104.8	96	0.1	-0.5	0.2
2023	WAS	MLB	27	271	40	9	40	3	.269/.343/.457	.365	.704	9.6%	30.3%	76.5%	79.7%	37.1%	50.9%	17.7	106.4	83	0.1	-0.7	0.1
2024 DC	WAS	MLB	28	536	54	19	63	11	.213/.274/.381	.270	.555	6.7%	28.8%							81	0.2	-1.5	-0.2

2023 GP: LF (77), RF (12), DH (4) *Comps: Tommy Pham (66), Scott Van Slyke (57), Lane Adams (55)*

If names were everything, Homer Simpson would forever be known as Max Power and Stone Garrett would be a perennial All-Star on his way to a Hall of Fame career. Instead, Garrett is a late-blooming prospect with some power potential, a propensity to swing and miss plus loads of bad luck. The "knife prank" that derailed him as a prospect is well-documented, while last year's misfortune was a fractured fibula in late August that ended his season prematurely. Garrett's defense limits him to a corner infield slot, so the bat will have to play up at the level it did in the second half last year if he hopes for his career to skyrocket. If he sustains that performance, we can all strap ourselves in and feel the G's.

Elijah Green CF Born: 12/04/03 Age: 20 Bats: R Throws: R Height: 6'3" Weight: 225 Origin: Round 1, 2022 Draft (#5 overall)

YEAR	TM	LVL	AGE	PA	R	HR	RBI	SB	AVG/OBP/SLG	BABIP	SLGCON	BB%	K%	ZSw%	ZCon%	OSw%	OCon%	LA	90th EV	DRC+	BRR	DRP	WARP
2022	NAT	ROK	18	52	9	2	9	1	.302/.404/.535	.524	1.045	11.5%	40.4%										
2023	NAT	ROK	19	29	9	1	3	1	.318/.483/.591	.600	1.182	24.1%	37.9%										
2023	FBG	A	19	332	36	4	36	30	.210/.323/.306	.393	.606	13.6%	41.9%							68	-0.3	-2.8	-0.6
2024 non	WAS	MLB	20	251	19	2	20	0	.209/.273/.293	.439	.636	7.3%	49.5%							62	0.0	0	-0.4

2023 GP: CF (75), DH (6), RF (2) *Comps: Kenny Wilson (84), D.J. Davis (83), Wilderd Patiño (82)*

An impressive, mammoth athletic specimen, the knock on Green when the Nationals used their first-round pick on him in 2022 was that he had severe contact issues that didn't bode well for his long-term future. Sure enough, his first minor-league experience away from the complex went poorly. Everything else about Green speaks to an elite athlete, but if you can't hit the baseball none of that matters. He's lightning fast both on the bases and in the field and has a surprisingly good batting eye for someone with strikeout issues. There isn't much precedent, however, for players like this making it to the majors, let alone having long and successful careers, without significant bat-to-ball improvement. Even the prodigious power that wowed scouts when Green was a prep player was absent, although that might have been due to a wrist injury that sidelined him for six weeks.

Robert Hassell III OF Born: 08/15/01 Age: 22 Bats: L Throws: L Height: 6'1" Weight: 195 Origin: Round 1, 2020 Draft (#8 overall)

YEAR	TM	LVL	AGE	PA	R	HR	RBI	SB	AVG/OBP/SLG	BABIP	SLGCON	BB%	K%	ZSw%	ZCon%	OSw%	OCon%	LA	90th EV	DRC+	BRR	DRP	WARP
2021	LE	A	19	429	77	7	65	31	.323/.415/.482	.385	.605	13.3%	17.2%							125	3.1	-3.9	2.9
2021	FW	A+	19	87	10	4	11	3	.205/.287/.410	.245	.604	10.3%	28.7%							102	-0.3	-0.9	0.2
2022	WIL	A+	20	45	9	0	3	3	.211/.311/.237	.296	.346	13.3%	26.7%							86	0.5	0.0	0.1
2022	FW	A+	20	346	49	10	55	20	.299/.379/.467	.352	.597	11.0%	19.1%							118	1.7	0.2	2.1
2022	HBG	AA	20	122	9	1	12	1	.222/.311/.296	.319	.438	10.7%	28.7%							82	0.6	-0.2	0.2
2023	FBG	A	21	69	12	1	4	2	.189/.377/.302	.209	.364	23.2%	13.0%							132	1.1	-0.4	0.5
2023	HBG	AA	21	476	54	8	37	13	.225/.316/.324	.331	.511	10.9%	31.9%							84	-0.6	-0.3	0.3
2024 non	WAS	MLB	22	251	22	4	22	4	.228/.300/.332	.313	.481	8.6%	27.9%							80	0.0	0	0.2

2023 GP: CF (57), LF (38), RF (35), DH (8) *Comps: Engel Beltre (62), Xavier Avery (48), Austin Meadows (45)*

It's generally wise to avoid hyperbole or extreme statements, particularly when it comes to prospects, but it's fair to say that 2023 was an utter disaster for Hassell. A broken hamate bone in the 2022 Arizona Fall League followed by a wrist injury during spring training led to an extended rehab, eventually succeeded by a promotion to Double-A Harrisburg. While there were flashes of promise, the problems that have plagued Hassell throughout his professional career were exacerbated by a combination of lingering injury aftereffects and the challenge of facing more advanced arms. He has a sweet swing but a rigid stance that lends itself to far too much weak, opposite-field contact. To his credit, Hassell is an intelligent, driven and self-aware player who has the right makeup to work through these challenges and plenty of time to do so.

★ ★ ★ *2024 Top 101 Prospect* **#69** ★ ★ ★

Brady House 3B   Born: 06/04/03   Age: 21   Bats: R   Throws: R   Height: 6'4"   Weight: 215   Origin: Round 1, 2021 Draft (#11 overall)

YEAR	TM	LVL	AGE	PA	R	HR	RBI	SB	AVG/OBP/SLG	BABIP	SLGCON	BB%	K%	ZSw%	ZCon%	OSw%	OCon%	LA	90th EV	DRC+	BRR	DRP	WARP
2021	NAT	ROK	18	66	14	4	12	0	.322/.394/.576	.357	.739	10.6%	19.7%									0.8	
2022	FBG	A	19	203	24	3	31	1	.278/.356/.375	.393	.564	5.9%	29.1%							99	2.9	-1.1	0.7
2023	FBG	A	20	158	22	6	22	5	.297/.369/.500	.350	.663	10.1%	21.5%							118	0.9	3.2	1.1
2023	WIL	A+	20	68	11	3	13	3	.317/.368/.540	.362	.680	4.4%	19.1%							112	0.6	-1.7	0.2
2023	HBG	AA	20	148	19	3	12	1	.324/.358/.475	.442	.680	4.7%	28.4%							76	-0.8	0.1	-0.2
2024 non	*WAS*	*MLB*	*21*	*251*	*21*	*4*	*23*	*2*	*.232/.278/.344*	*.327*	*.509*	*4.9%*	*30.7%*							*74*	*0.0*	*0*	*-0.1*

2023 GP: 3B (87), DH (1)   Comps: *Maikel Franco (59), Ryan Mountcastle (59), Wilmer Flores (55)*

After slumping through most of 2022 due to a lingering back injury, House mostly put those concerns to bed with a rebound season in 2023, dominating low-minors pitching at two levels before earning a promotion to Double-A Harrisburg midseason. His transition from shortstop to third base not only went well but showed that, despite his size, House has the agility and speed to be an elite defender at the hot corner. Offensively, while the raw numbers were good there were some concerns both with his swing mechanics as well as his breaking ball recognition. While these concerns are valid, he was a 20-year old who was a well-above-average player at Double-A who put himself back on the road to being a potential long-term fixture for the Nationals.

Daylen Lile OF   Born: 11/30/02   Age: 21   Bats: L   Throws: R   Height: 5'11"   Weight: 195   Origin: Round 2, 2021 Draft (#47 overall)

YEAR	TM	LVL	AGE	PA	R	HR	RBI	SB	AVG/OBP/SLG	BABIP	SLGCON	BB%	K%	ZSw%	ZCon%	OSw%	OCon%	LA	90th EV	DRC+	BRR	DRP	WARP
2021	NAT	ROK	18	80	16	0	10	2	.219/.363/.250	.311	.364	18.8%	25.0%										
2023	FBG	A	20	294	49	7	48	21	.291/.381/.510	.347	.663	12.2%	19.7%							123	6.2	-1.6	2.1
2023	WIL	A+	20	171	16	2	18	2	.234/.310/.357	.306	.487	9.4%	24.0%							93	-1.0	0.6	0.4
2024 non	*WAS*	*MLB*	*21*	*251*	*20*	*3*	*22*	*0*	*.220/.281/.334*	*.295*	*.467*	*7.0%*	*26.2%*							*73*	*0.0*	*0*	*-0.1*

2023 GP: LF (59), CF (31), RF (8), DH (8)   Comps: *Mason Williams (70), Angel Morales (60), Pablo Olivares (60)*

After missing all of 2022 post-Tommy John surgery, Lile hit the ground running in his first full season as a professional, dominating Low-A pitching before receiving a well-earned promotion to High-A Wilmington. He struggled there, but Delaware's largest city offers a famously rough offensive environment and Lile had all of 80 plate appearances as a professional entering 2023. He possesses a gorgeous swing with lots of torque, but doesn't generate as much power as one might expect. Lile's defense will likely limit him to left field, so there's even more pressure on him to either generate more power or be a generationally great batting average hitter. He's only 21, so it's unfair to say this is all he is or that there isn't room for plenty of growth, but Lile has toiled for an organization that hasn't exactly excelled on the developmental front.

Joey Meneses DH   Born: 05/06/92   Age: 32   Bats: R   Throws: R   Height: 6'3"   Weight: 240   Origin: IFA, 2011

YEAR	TM	LVL	AGE	PA	R	HR	RBI	SB	AVG/OBP/SLG	BABIP	SLGCON	BB%	K%	ZSw%	ZCon%	OSw%	OCon%	LA	90th EV	DRC+	BRR	DRP	WARP
2021	CUL	WIN	29	240	23	7	47	4	.290/.358/.467	.301	.532	9.2%	10.8%										
2021	POR	AA	29	207	31	10	43	0	.303/.348/.590	.320	.725	5.8%	16.9%							130	-0.2	-4.4	0.9
2021	WOR	AAA	29	162	14	5	27	0	.260/.315/.452	.314	.617	8.0%	24.1%							88	-1.2	1.0	0.2
2022	ROC	AAA	30	414	51	20	64	1	.286/.341/.489	.321	.642	7.7%	21.5%							123	-1.4	2.5	2.3
2022	WAS	MLB	30	240	33	13	34	1	.324/.367/.563	.371	.735	6.3%	21.7%	68.1%	83.6%	34.1%	66.5%	9.6	105.4	121	-0.1	-1.4	1.0
2023	WAS	MLB	31	657	71	13	89	0	.275/.321/.401	.329	.509	5.8%	19.8%	66.0%	87.8%	34.7%	60.8%	9.5	104.0	92	-0.7	0.0	0.6
2024 DC	*WAS*	*MLB*	*32*	*588*	*60*	*16*	*66*	*0*	*.253/.303/.396*	*.299*	*.509*	*5.9%*	*20.8%*							*96*	*-0.5*	*0.3*	*0.8*

2023 GP: DH (131), 1B (19), RF (1)   Comps: *Chris Colabello (45), Oscar Salazar (44), Angel Echevarria (41)*

While PECOTA is frequently right, it isn't infallible. Its rare whiffs commonly occur when a player has an outlier season and then repeats or even improves upon it. Meneses' 2022—a year that saw him stomp major-league pitching for two months after spending a decade of his life wandering around the minors, Mexico and Japan—was about as much of an outlier as you'll ever see. Analysts noted that while PECOTA's dour 2023 prediction could come to pass, he made legitimate improvements that meant he could beat the odds and be this generation's Raul Ibanez: a journeyman who emerged in his 30s and made a big-league career of it.

Meneses didn't completely fall off the face of the earth, but looked far more like the minor-league yeoman he had been than the burgeoning superstar many hoped he had become. Pitchers threw him more breaking stuff and Meneses became a singles hitter with very little pop. He traded batting average for power in the second half, but didn't sock enough balls over the fence to justify the exchange. Everyone roots for the underdog, but sometimes hard math splashes cold water to the face. Meneses didn't play himself out of baseball, but the long odds of him becoming anything more than a placeholder never really went away.

Drew Millas   C   Born: 01/15/98   Age: 26   Bats: S   Throws: R   Height: 6'0"   Weight: 198   Origin: Round 7, 2019 Draft (#224 overall)

YEAR	TM	LVL	AGE	PA	R	HR	RBI	SB	AVG/OBP/SLG	BABIP	SLGCON	BB%	K%	ZSw%	ZCon%	OSw%	OCon%	LA	90th EV	DRC+	BRR	DRP	WARP
2021	SUR	WIN	23	64	8	1	5	3	.196/.359/.275	.196	.298	20.3%	6.3%	72.7%	87.5%	14.8%	25.0%						
2021	WIL	A+	23	118	15	0	20	5	.284/.373/.324	.326	.375	11.0%	11.9%							119	0.4	-0.3	0.6
2021	LAN	A+	23	266	34	3	28	10	.255/.372/.359	.293	.436	15.4%	14.7%							125	0.0	5.5	2.1
2022	FBG	A	24	75	15	2	10	6	.246/.387/.377	.283	.479	18.7%	17.3%							126	0.3	0.5	0.5
2022	WIL	A+	24	98	13	1	10	1	.237/.408/.434	.309	.589	22.4%	20.4%							119	-0.3	-0.6	0.4
2022	HBG	AA	24	169	12	3	16	1	.211/.280/.296	.299	.455	8.9%	31.4%							85	-0.7	-2.7	-0.1
2023	HBG	AA	25	99	14	4	19	2	.341/.455/.537	.387	.667	16.2%	16.2%							140	-0.4	0.1	0.7
2023	ROC	AAA	25	229	26	3	24	4	.270/.362/.403	.307	.485	11.4%	14.4%	67.3%	91.8%	28.0%	62.9%			103	1.2	0.9	1.0
2023	WAS	MLB	25	33	1	1	6	0	.286/.375/.464	.318	.565	12.1%	15.2%	70.0%	88.1%	31.1%	60.9%	1.5	102.4	108	0.0	-0.5	0.1
2024 DC	*WAS*	*MLB*	*26*	*62*	*6*	*1*	*6*	*1*	*.240/.320/.348*	*.296*	*.432*	*9.7%*	*20.0%*							*91*	*-0.1*	*-0.3*	*0.1*

2023 GP: C (10)

Comps: Curt Casali (56), Carson Blair (52), Austin Barnes (47)

YEAR	TM	P. COUNT	FRM RUNS	BLK RUNS	THRW RUNS	TOT RUNS
2021	LAN	7132	3.3	-0.4	2.4	5.3
2021	WIL	2929	-0.9	0.0	1.0	0.0
2022	WIL	2513	-1.4	-0.2	0.8	-0.7
2022	HBG	4797	-3.5	0.3	0.6	-2.6
2023	HBG	3423	-0.9	-0.1	1.3	0.3
2023	ROC	7848	0.6	-0.3	1.6	2.0
2023	WAS	1321	-0.1	0.0	0.0	-0.1
2024	*WAS*	*2405*	*-0.2*	*-0.1*	*0.0*	*-0.3*

Millas is arguably the most intriguing prospect in the Nationals' minor-league system. "Intriguing" isn't synonymous with "best," and he poses the challenge of figuring out if his combination of elite athletic skills behind the plate and decent minor-league results thus far will be enough to overcome an underwhelming hit tool and a body type that typically doesn't hold up well to the rigors of catching at the major-league level. A few short years ago, the seemingly imminent arrival of an automated strike zone led to assumptions that the position would be deemed mostly irrelevant, but the new baserunning rules could make catchers with excellent range and rocket arms vital. Health permitting, Millas has a future as a backup; how much further he goes depends on the continued evolution of the sport itself.

Yohandy Morales   3B   Born: 10/09/01   Age: 22   Bats: R   Throws: R   Height: 6'4"   Weight: 225   Origin: Round 2, 2023 Draft (#40 overall)

YEAR	TM	LVL	AGE	PA	R	HR	RBI	SB	AVG/OBP/SLG	BABIP	SLGCON	BB%	K%	ZSw%	ZCon%	OSw%	OCon%	LA	90th EV	DRC+	BRR	DRP	WARP
2023	FBG	A	21	87	18	0	17	1	.390/.448/.571	.500	.746	9.2%	20.7%							98	0.1	0.0	0.2
2023	WIL	A+	21	80	12	0	14	0	.314/.400/.443	.407	.574	10.0%	20.0%							99	0.2	-0.1	0.2
2024 non	*WAS*	*MLB*	*22*	*251*	*20*	*3*	*21*	*0*	*.230/.287/.332*	*.305*	*.458*	*6.4%*	*25.4%*							*75*	*0.0*	*0*	*-0.1*

2023 GP: 3B (34), DH (6), 1B (3)

Comps: Sam Travis (69), Dawel Lugo (63), Brandon Drury (62)

Expected by some analysts to go in the first round of the 2022 Amateur Draft, Morales slipped to the Nationals at the beginning of the second round in part due to his relatively advanced age for a college junior but mostly due to significant chase and swing-and-miss issues. Morales' prodigious collegiate power (20 home runs and a .713 slugging percentage in 278 PA) didn't translate to his first taste of professional ball, as he didn't hit a single home run across four minor-league levels. On the positive side, it was his first taste of affiliated ball, and the whiff rate was manageable. Morales ended the year at Double-A, so while the Nationals aren't going to rush him the glide path has been an aggressive one.

Victor Robles   CF   Born: 05/19/97   Age: 27   Bats: R   Throws: R   Height: 6'0"   Weight: 194   Origin: IFA, 2013

YEAR	TM	LVL	AGE	PA	R	HR	RBI	SB	AVG/OBP/SLG	BABIP	SLGCON	BB%	K%	ZSw%	ZCon%	OSw%	OCon%	LA	90th EV	DRC+	BRR	DRP	WARP
2021	ROC	AAA	24	93	14	4	8	6	.301/.370/.566	.396	.825	7.5%	28.0%							100	0.5	2.5	0.6
2021	WAS	MLB	24	369	37	2	19	8	.203/.310/.295	.271	.404	8.9%	23.0%	69.4%	84.6%	30.5%	57.0%	17.1	101.8	82	0.0	-3.5	0.4
2022	AGU	WIN	25	61	9	1	3	7	.204/.295/.259	.256	.350	4.9%	23.0%										
2022	WAS	MLB	25	407	42	6	33	15	.224/.273/.311	.292	.435	4.2%	25.6%	74.9%	83.0%	35.2%	55.1%	12.6	101.0	71	0.9	-2.5	-0.1
2023	WAS	MLB	26	126	15	0	8	8	.299/.385/.364	.360	.438	8.7%	14.3%	80.3%	84.1%	32.0%	67.1%	7.2	103.4	104	0.2	-1.6	0.4
2024 DC	*WAS*	*MLB*	*27*	*362*	*34*	*6*	*34*	*15*	*.228/.307/.338*	*.283*	*.447*	*7.2%*	*21.9%*							*86*	*0.1*	*-4.7*	*0.1*

2023 GP: CF (36)

Comps: Rick Manning (49), Milt Cuyler (48), Cesar Cedeno (46)

"He had a breakout year and finally lived up to the promise he had long ago as a prospect" is what we might be saying about Robles had he not suffered a back injury in May, tried returning in June and then been shut down a mere five games later. Robles' rookie campaign back in 2019 offered a tantalizing glimpse of what might have been—since then, he has been hurt, ineffective, or both. He started hitting the ball harder and striking out less, but it's difficult to know whether this was the product of a legitimate change or a small sample size blip. Likewise, his defense slipped, which could have been a product of the injury or an insufficient data set. Fair assessment or not, Robles hasn't been a viable major-leaguer this decade and enters a now-or-never season at the age of 27, with "never" the odds-on favorite.

Keibert Ruiz   C   Born: 07/20/98   Age: 25   Bats: S   Throws: R   Height: 6'0"   Weight: 227   Origin: IFA, 2015

YEAR	TM	LVL	AGE	PA	R	HR	RBI	SB	AVG/OBP/SLG	BABIP	SLGCON	BB%	K%	ZSw%	ZCon%	OSw%	OCon%	LA	90th EV	DRC+	BRR	DRP	WARP
2021	ROC	AAA	22	85	11	5	14	0	.308/.365/.577	.284	.625	8.2%	7.1%							135	-1.3	0.6	0.6
2021	OKC	AAA	22	231	39	16	45	0	.311/.381/.631	.293	.726	10.0%	11.7%							140	-1.0	2.2	2.2
2021	LAD	MLB	22	7	1	1	1	0	.143/.143/.571		2.000	0.0%	71.4%	50.0%	50.0%	50.0%	40.0%	16.0	106.5	139		0.0	0.1
2021	WAS	MLB	22	89	9	2	14	0	.284/.348/.395	.280	.416	6.7%	4.5%	66.7%	93.6%	41.7%	87.1%	18.7	99.3	108	-0.1	-0.2	0.4
2022	WAS	MLB	23	433	33	7	36	6	.251/.313/.360	.271	.413	6.9%	11.5%	72.0%	92.6%	36.7%	74.9%	14.9	101.6	109	-0.2	1.4	2.2
2023	WAS	MLB	24	562	55	18	67	1	.260/.308/.409	.263	.460	5.5%	10.3%	68.0%	93.2%	39.2%	76.8%	15.4	101.8	123	-0.6	-12.2	2.4
2024 DC	*WAS*	*MLB*	*25*	*532*	*59*	*17*	*64*	*3*	*.273/.330/.428*	*.283*	*.484*	*6.6%*	*10.8%*							*113*	*-0.5*	*-3.5*	*2.3*

2023 GP: C (117), DH (16)

Comps: Al Lopez (55), Salvador Perez (55), Jose Tabata (53)

Perhaps more than any other non-pitcher, Ruiz had a legitimate gripe that the abrupt changes in major-league baseball's rules had an outsized impact on his 2023 performance. An adequate albeit unspectacular defender in his 2022 breakout campaign, every aspect of Ruiz's defensive game collapsed last year. He allowed a whopping 119 stolen bases, 20 more than any other backstop and more than any catcher since Josh Bard in 2007. Every other part of his defensive skill set eroded as well, which is bad news for a catcher who isn't an offensive powerhouse. Ruiz's contact skills are well-documented, but so is his lack of in-game power: He had some home run success in the first half, which led to him selling out, trying to pull the ball more and seeing his batted-ball metrics plummet as a result. Ruiz inked a $50 million, eight-year extension in March 2023. What seemed like a team-friendly deal at the time now looks like an insurance policy that paid off handsomely for the player.

YEAR	TM	P. COUNT	FRM RUNS	BLK RUNS	THRW RUNS	TOT RUNS
2021	OKC	6748	3.7	-0.2	-0.2	3.3
2021	ROC	2573	1.1	0.1	0.1	1.2
2021	WAS	3216	0.3	0.1	-0.2	0.2
2021	LAD	67	0.0	0.0	0.0	0.0
2022	WAS	15128	1.4	0.2	2.0	3.7
2023	WAS	17748	-9.0	-0.3	-1.1	-10.4
2024	WAS	14430	-1.9	-0.3	-1.4	-3.6

Nick Senzel 3B
Born: 06/29/95   Age: 29   Bats: R   Throws: R   Height: 6'1"   Weight: 218   Origin: Round 1, 2016 Draft (#2 overall)

YEAR	TM	LVL	AGE	PA	R	HR	RBI	SB	AVG/OBP/SLG	BABIP	SLGCON	BB%	K%	ZSw%	ZCon%	OSw%	OCon%	LA	90th EV	DRC+	BRR	DRP	WARP
2021	LOU	AAA	26	39	5	0	2	0	.286/.316/.429	.294	.455	5.1%	5.1%							105	-0.4	0.0	0.1
2021	CIN	MLB	26	124	18	1	8	2	.252/.323/.315	.284	.368	9.7%	12.9%	78.4%	90.6%	36.1%	70.7%	10.6	102.2	101	0.0	-0.4	0.5
2022	CIN	MLB	27	420	45	5	25	8	.231/.296/.306	.276	.384	7.1%	18.1%	69.7%	85.9%	30.7%	65.1%	11.2	102.0	92	0.2	-4.5	0.7
2023	LOU	AAA	28	70	11	1	3	4	.224/.348/.362	.286	.488	12.9%	21.4%	60.8%	79.5%	24.0%	54.3%			100	0.9	3.9	0.6
2023	CIN	MLB	28	330	49	13	42	6	.236/.297/.399	.269	.529	7.9%	22.4%	72.4%	85.5%	30.0%	64.5%	15.3	102.9	84	0.5	-1.4	0.3
2024 DC	WAS	MLB	29	355	34	8	35	6	.231/.299/.348	.270	.440	8.1%	18.9%							85	0.1	-2.9	0.1

2023 GP: 3B (57), LF (23), CF (18), RF (18), 2B (6), DH (4)   *Comps: Cameron Maybin (61), Brian McRae (49), Coco Crisp (48)*

Senzel has been a breakout candidate for about half a decade now, but at this point he might just be who he appears: a speedy, light-hitting utility player with a lengthy and unlucky injury history, who can stand at a handful of positions even if he's not particularly effective at any of them. That's a bit of a dour assessment, but it's hard to argue Senzel is a more appealing option on either side of the ball than any of the players who've leapfrogged him on the depth chart. Perhaps there's still a chance Senzel can unlock the talent that led the Reds to draft him second overall in 2016, and find a niche as a Chris Taylor-esque role player. A classic change-of-scenery candidate, Washington signed him for the 2024 season.

Dominic Smith 1B
Born: 06/15/95   Age: 29   Bats: L   Throws: L   Height: 6'0"   Weight: 224   Origin: Round 1, 2013 Draft (#11 overall)

YEAR	TM	LVL	AGE	PA	R	HR	RBI	SB	AVG/OBP/SLG	BABIP	SLGCON	BB%	K%	ZSw%	ZCon%	OSw%	OCon%	LA	90th EV	DRC+	BRR	DRP	WARP
2021	NYM	MLB	26	493	43	11	58	2	.244/.304/.363	.298	.485	6.5%	22.7%	73.4%	84.5%	38.0%	57.3%	15.1	103.9	86	0.0	-1.1	0.8
2022	SYR	AAA	27	248	42	10	38	4	.284/.367/.472	.306	.575	10.1%	15.7%	75.6%	91.2%	34.0%	77.8%			119	-0.5	1.0	1.2
2022	NYM	MLB	27	152	11	0	17	0	.194/.276/.284	.263	.392	7.9%	24.3%	70.6%	86.7%	26.8%	49.4%	11.4	103.0	79	0.0	0.0	-0.1
2023	WAS	MLB	28	586	57	12	46	1	.254/.326/.366	.286	.443	8.0%	15.5%	68.9%	87.4%	34.0%	70.0%	13.3	102.0	111	-0.7	0.2	2.0
2024 non	WAS	MLB	29	251	25	5	26	1	.249/.323/.376	.285	.462	8.2%	16.8%							99	-0.2	0.1	0.5

2023 GP: 1B (151), DH (1)   *Comps: Casey Kotchman (55), Adrián González (53), Anthony Rizzo (51)*

Everybody had those friends in 2020 who were living their best lives and incessantly posting updates on social media. You know the types: They organized every room of their houses, did genealogy projects where they traced their lineage to Charlamagne and completed macaroni art installations of the United States Constitution with their two perfect children, Borthany and Tharthanial. Smith had that kind of 2020 in real life when he hit .316, displayed power to all fields and even managed to pummel his fellow portsiders. Since then, he has been less like the person living his best life and more like the guy who hasn't been able to readjust after everything started reopening. Even for a low-rent gamble, he was a major disappointment in his first year for the Nationals. He displayed far more patience, but all this translated to pitchers throwing more strikes early in the count knowing he wouldn't take the bat off his shoulder. Maybe Smith survives another year as an everyday player, but it's unlikely we're ever going to see another macaroni art project from him.

Lane Thomas RF
Born: 08/23/95   Age: 28   Bats: R   Throws: R   Height: 6'0"   Weight: 198   Origin: Round 5, 2014 Draft (#144 overall)

YEAR	TM	LVL	AGE	PA	R	HR	RBI	SB	AVG/OBP/SLG	BABIP	SLGCON	BB%	K%	ZSw%	ZCon%	OSw%	OCon%	LA	90th EV	DRC+	BRR	DRP	WARP
2021	MEM	AAA	25	127	18	4	20	3	.265/.339/.451	.347	.654	9.4%	27.6%							98	-0.3	1.7	0.5
2021	STL	MLB	25	58	2	0	1	2	.104/.259/.125	.161	.194	17.2%	29.3%	54.7%	75.9%	23.3%	66.7%	8.5	105.8	82	0.0	0.1	0.1
2021	WAS	MLB	25	206	33	7	27	4	.270/.364/.489	.325	.659	13.1%	22.3%	62.2%	88.8%	24.7%	64.8%	13.0	103.4	106	0.1	-1.0	0.9
2022	WAS	MLB	26	548	62	17	52	8	.241/.301/.404	.291	.549	7.5%	24.1%	63.5%	86.1%	29.0%	67.1%	12.6	103.9	88	0.0	-0.1	1.0
2023	WAS	MLB	27	682	101	28	86	20	.268/.315/.468	.325	.650	5.3%	25.8%	64.1%	87.0%	28.0%	60.2%	11.2	105.5	97	1.2	0.0	1.6
2024 DC	WAS	MLB	28	587	62	20	70	13	.236/.297/.402	.281	.540	6.9%	23.6%							95	0.1	0.3	1.2

2023 GP: RF (151), CF (11), P (1), DH (1)   *Comps: Harrison Bader (61), Dexter Fowler (58), Franklin Gutierrez (54)*

Knowing your strengths minimizes your weaknesses. While this might sound like the sort of jargon-y claptrap to be found on an inspirational poster in an office cubicle, it was the key to Thomas' success in 2023. He took his strengths—solid center field defense, a pull-oriented approach, and a fastball-focused attack—and parlayed them into a modest breakout campaign. Thomas obliterated southpaws and did enough against his fellow right-handers to keep him in the lineup, thanks to a swing-happy approach that led to more strikeouts but also more over-the-fence power: Seven of his 28 home runs came on the first pitch he saw. The new baserunning rules were also a big help for a player who is fast, but was previously not overtly confident on the basepaths. Thomas isn't a superstar but has cemented himself as a useful cog who can hold his own in any big-league lineup.

Cristhian Vaquero OF   Born: 09/13/04   Age: 19   Bats: S   Throws: R   Height: 6'3"   Weight: 180   Origin: IFA, 2022

YEAR	TM	LVL	AGE	PA	R	HR	RBI	SB	AVG/OBP/SLG	BABIP	SLGCON	BB%	K%	ZSw%	ZCon%	OSw%	OCon%	LA	90th EV	DRC+	BRR	DRP	WARP
2022	DSL NAT	ROK	17	216	33	1	22	17	.256/.379/.341	.317	.435	15.3%	17.6%										
2023	NAT	ROK	18	182	34	1	16	15	.279/.410/.393	.352	.524	15.9%	19.2%										
2023	FBG	A	18	78	10	1	9	7	.197/.321/.288	.255	.396	15.4%	23.1%							99	1.1	-0.1	0.4
2024 non	WAS	MLB	19	251	20	2	20	0	.214/.277/.305	.311	.458	7.5%	30.9%							65	0.0	0	-0.4

2023 GP: CF (43), RF (14), DH (3), LF (1)   Comps: Starling Heredia (75), Michael Harris II (74), Zach Collier (73)

It's completely unjust that the amount of virtual ink that is (or isn't) devoted to adolescent athletes is contingent upon how much money they're paid up front by their soon-to-be major-league organizations. The signees who receive the most money aren't set up to fail, but they also have practically nowhere to go but down from that wonderful moment when they're paid entirely for the promise of a future that hasn't happened yet. Two years after signing a contract with nearly a $5 million bonus, Vaquero has done little in the minors besides steal bases. His contact and swing decisions are very good, but he still can't drive the ball. He also doesn't turn 20 until September. Being nicknamed "The Phenomenon" before even logging a moment in the minors depicts a future filled of nothing but accolades, but it's easy to forget that having any kind of big-league career is an achievement.

Ildemaro Vargas IF   Born: 07/16/91   Age: 32   Bats: S   Throws: R   Height: 6'0"   Weight: 195   Origin: IFA, 2008

YEAR	TM	LVL	AGE	PA	R	HR	RBI	SB	AVG/OBP/SLG	BABIP	SLGCON	BB%	K%	ZSw%	ZCon%	OSw%	OCon%	LA	90th EV	DRC+	BRR	DRP	WARP
2021	LAR	WIN	29	204	37	11	40	3	.319/.377/.566	.294	.613	9.3%	6.9%										
2021	RNO	AAA	29	268	50	10	39	3	.313/.351/.518	.316	.581	6.0%	10.1%							116	1.3	2.8	1.8
2021	PIT	MLB	29	13	0	0	1	0	.077/.077/.077	.100	.100	0.0%	23.1%	67.9%	94.7%	35.3%	16.7%	0.7	100.3	99		-0.1	0.0
2021	CHC	MLB	29	24	3	0	2	1	.143/.250/.238	.214	.357	12.5%	29.2%	64.7%	77.3%	26.8%	60.0%	13.2	98.4	101	0.0	0.0	0.1
2021	AZ	MLB	29	46	4	0	4	0	.186/.239/.256	.222	.306	6.5%	15.2%	57.3%	90.7%	44.1%	73.2%	-1.1	99.7	94	0.0	-0.1	0.1
2022	LAR	WIN	30	189	33	1	22	6	.342/.429/.478	.360	.517	13.2%	6.3%										
2022	IOW	AAA	30	112	16	1	7	1	.279/.321/.413	.304	.467	6.3%	10.7%							116	0.4	0.9	0.6
2022	ROC	AAA	30	197	21	2	18	2	.224/.301/.322	.248	.376	10.2%	12.7%							111	1.0	1.6	1.1
2022	CHC	MLB	30	26	4	1	4	0	.130/.231/.348	.100	.381	11.5%	7.7%	66.7%	100.0%	24.6%	75.0%	4.8	100.5	126	0.1	0.1	0.2
2022	WAS	MLB	30	196	15	3	19	3	.280/.308/.398	.301	.448	2.6%	10.7%	66.7%	92.7%	32.6%	79.2%	7.0	100.3	109	0.0	0.0	0.7
2023	WAS	MLB	31	286	32	4	31	1	.252/.304/.363	.259	.393	6.6%	7.0%	65.0%	95.1%	30.8%	76.1%	3.8	102.0	145	0.2	-0.7	2.5
2024 DC	WAS	MLB	32	310	28	5	29	3	.254/.307/.362	.273	.407	6.5%	10.5%							90	0.0	-1.2	0.3

2023 GP: 3B (45), 2B (18), SS (15), LF (11), P (2), RF (1)   Comps: Brock Holt (47), Don Blasingame (45), Adam Rosales (45)

Earlier iterations of this tome frequently derided players like Vargas, role players whose impact on team chemistry were perhaps overstated generations ago. But while this was true once upon a time, savvy front offices and their minions of analytic geniuses have arguably course-corrected too far in the other direction. Perhaps on paper Vargas was nothing more than a forgettable utility player on a last-place team, but for the Nationals and their fans he was an inspiration: the guy whose joyous shouts of "Campeon!" echoed through the clubhouse, the veteran presence who was a role model both on and off the field for the up-and-coming young guard. Vargas quietly signed a one-year extension right before the close of the 2023 season; even if he isn't part of the next winning Nationals squad, he'll certainly help to mold it.

★ ★ ★ *2024 Top 101 Prospect* **#7** ★ ★ ★

James Wood OF   Born: 09/17/02   Age: 21   Bats: L   Throws: R   Height: 6'6"   Weight: 240   Origin: Round 2, 2021 Draft (#62 overall)

YEAR	TM	LVL	AGE	PA	R	HR	RBI	SB	AVG/OBP/SLG	BABIP	SLGCON	BB%	K%	ZSw%	ZCon%	OSw%	OCon%	LA	90th EV	DRC+	BRR	DRP	WARP
2021	PAD	ROK	18	101	18	3	22	10	.372/.465/.535	.569	.852	12.9%	31.7%									-2.5	
2022	FBG	A	19	93	14	2	17	4	.293/.366/.463	.400	.679	10.8%	28.0%							99	0.8	-0.2	0.3
2022	LE	A	19	236	55	10	45	15	.337/.453/.601	.387	.768	15.7%	17.8%							138	1.9	-0.6	2.0
2023	WIL	A+	20	181	32	8	36	8	.293/.392/.580	.371	.861	14.4%	27.1%							149	0.2	-1.7	1.4
2023	HBG	AA	20	368	48	18	55	10	.248/.334/.492	.339	.799	10.6%	33.7%							105	1.5	-4.2	1.1
2024 DC	WAS	MLB	21	161	16	4	18	3	.231/.306/.392	.328	.606	8.8%	32.1%							95	0.0	0	0.3

2023 GP: CF (67), RF (46), DH (18)   Comps: Carlos González (72), Kyle Tucker (68), Cameron Maybin (66)

Hype and hyperbole are frequent bedfellows, but in Wood's case the former is justified while the latter is virtually nonexistent. He continued to wreck minor-league pitching, and even though he slipped somewhat at Double-A it was still an impressive run for a 20-year-old against much older competition. His power isn't merely a product of facing minor-league arms, as he's a behemoth who generates high exit velocities to go along with excellent barrel control—particularly surprising given his mammoth frame. There are long-term questions about whether he'll ever be able to cut down on his strikeouts and if his size will eventually lead to reduced mobility that moves him out of center field, but when you can square it up like Wood these aren't dealbreakers. He has a solid chance of making his Nationals debut this year and, even if he doesn't reach the perennial 40-homer upside some are dreaming on, it's going to be incredibly fun to watch him try.

Juan Yepez LF Born: 02/19/98 Age: 26 Bats: R Throws: R Height: 6'1" Weight: 200 Origin: IFA, 2014

YEAR	TM	LVL	AGE	PA	R	HR	RBI	SB	AVG/OBP/SLG	BABIP	SLGCON	BB%	K%	ZSw%	ZCon%	OSw%	OCon%	LA	90th EV	DRC+	BRR	DRP	WARP
2021	GDD	WIN	23	103	15	7	26	1	.302/.388/.640	.297	.809	11.7%	17.5%	82.6%	89.5%	24.3%	66.7%						
2021	SPR	AA	23	77	11	5	14	0	.270/.387/.571	.267	.720	11.7%	16.9%							128	-0.7	-1.2	0.3
2021	MEM	AAA	23	357	56	22	63	1	.289/.382/.589	.304	.762	11.8%	19.3%							146	-0.2	-4.1	2.3
2022	MEM	AAA	24	208	34	16	53	0	.277/.341/.580	.283	.768	8.2%	22.1%	69.4%	84.0%	46.2%	62.5%			126	-0.8	-1.2	1.0
2022	STL	MLB	24	274	27	12	30	0	.253/.296/.447	.283	.589	5.8%	22.3%	74.2%	85.5%	40.0%	58.2%	17.6	103.7	112	-0.2	-1.3	1.0
2023	MEM	AAA	25	384	44	9	69	2	.255/.323/.413	.294	.526	8.6%	19.0%	68.4%	83.7%	32.6%	66.4%			91	-1.1	-1.3	0.3
2023	STL	MLB	25	65	5	2	2	0	.183/.246/.300	.237	.450	6.2%	30.8%	68.6%	84.0%	37.3%	59.6%	26.3	105.2	75	-0.1	-1.0	-0.1
2024 non	WAS	MLB	26	251	25	8	29	1	.236/.295/.392	.278	.517	6.9%	21.9%							92	-0.2	-1.9	0.1

2023 GP: LF (9), DH (9), RF (3)   *Comps: José Osuna (56), Nick Evans (55), Josh Bell (54)*

The hardest part was figuring out where Yepez fit in St. Louis. He was blocked in every direction: by Goldschmidt at first base, by his defensive shortcomings plus the Cardinals' greater interest in RIchie Palacios in the outfield and by everyone else at DH. The 25-year-old appeared in about 50 fewer big-league games in 2023 than the preceding campaign. Therefore, he didn't get to do what he does best: Hit the ball hard. After the Cardinals chose not to offer him a contract in November, Yepez landed a minor-league deal with Washington, where opportunity abounds for a corner bat.

Jacob Young OF Born: 07/27/99 Age: 24 Bats: R Throws: R Height: 5'11" Weight: 180 Origin: Round 7, 2021 Draft (#203 overall)

YEAR	TM	LVL	AGE	PA	R	HR	RBI	SB	AVG/OBP/SLG	BABIP	SLGCON	BB%	K%	ZSw%	ZCon%	OSw%	OCon%	LA	90th EV	DRC+	BRR	DRP	WARP
2021	FBG	A	21	114	16	0	5	13	.208/.283/.267	.247	.321	8.8%	14.9%							108	2.5	2.4	1.0
2022	FBG	A	22	542	118	2	46	52	.262/.360/.331	.313	.402	10.9%	15.1%							125	10.9	3.0	4.5
2023	WIL	A+	23	248	28	2	28	22	.307/.383/.401	.346	.470	10.1%	12.5%							127	-1.7	4.9	1.7
2023	HBG	AA	23	231	30	3	28	17	.304/.374/.431	.355	.527	7.4%	16.0%							117	0.5	11.3	2.3
2023	WAS	MLB	23	121	9	0	12	13	.252/.322/.336	.318	.424	8.3%	18.2%	61.3%	88.9%	33.5%	66.3%	1.4	100.8	87	0.6	1.0	0.4
2024 DC	WAS	MLB	24	179	15	2	15	9	.233/.292/.319	.283	.402	6.6%	18.6%							76	0.5	0.2	0.0

2023 GP: CF (32), DH (1)   *Comps: César Hernández (52), Coco Crisp (52), Ramon Nivar (51)*

Even accounting for the Nationals' many deficiencies, it didn't seem likely that Young would make it to the majors last year after finishing 2022 in A-ball, but he literally and figuratively sped through three minor-league stops and found himself making his big-league debut in late August. He's one of the fastest players in the game and parlayed that speed into 13 steals in a mere 33 major-league games, with excellent center field defense thrown in for good measure. He'll need to squeeze every morsel out of this skill, as Young has very little power and creates more worm burners than a sadistic eight-year-old with a magnifying glass. Young might get a chance to start the season manning center, but even so is more of a placeholder for the next wave of Nationals outfielders than a future starter.

PITCHERS

Joan Adon RHP Born: 08/12/98 Age: 25 Height: 6'2" Weight: 245 Origin: IFA, 2016

YEAR	TM	LVL	AGE	G (GS)	IP	W-L	SV	K	WHIP	ERA	CSP	BB%	K%	HR%	GB%	ZSw%	ZCon%	OSw%	OCon%	BABIP	SLGCON	DRA-	WARP
2021	WIL	A+	22	17 (17)	87	6-4	0	91	1.25	4.97		8.6%	24.4%	1.9%	46.1%					.299	.511	87	1.3
2021	HBG	AA	22	3 (3)	14	1-2	0	24	1.43	6.43		7.8%	37.5%	1.6%	37.1%					.412	.727	79	0.3
2021	WAS	MLB	22	1 (1)	5¹	0-0	0	9	1.69	3.38	60.2%	12.5%	37.5%	4.2%	72.7%	51.5%	88.2%	31.1%	47.4%	.500	.818	75	0.1
2022	ROC	AAA	23	10 (10)	42¹	2-2	0	43	1.54	4.68		12.7%	22.8%	2.6%	50.4%					.316	.578	102	0.5
2022	WAS	MLB	23	14 (14)	64²	1-12	0	55	1.78	7.10	54.4%	12.6%	17.7%	2.6%	47.1%	66.8%	87.4%	27.0%	75.4%	.338	.609	132	-0.4
2023	ROC	AAA	24	17 (17)	87²	3-5	0	80	1.51	4.62		10.4%	20.7%	2.6%	48.5%	66.1%	85.5%	33.6%	61.1%	.324	.582	95	1.5
2023	WAS	MLB	24	12 (10)	51²	2-4	0	48	1.63	6.45	46.3%	10.0%	20.0%	3.3%	37.6%	69.1%	87.0%	33.2%	66.5%	.333	.626	116	0.2
2024 DC	WAS	MLB	25	13 (13)	62	2-6	0	45	1.52	5.38	50.7%	10.7%	16.1%	3.1%	42.5%					.293	.530	118	0.0

2023 Arsenal: FA (94.5), CU (80.6), CH (88), SI (94.2), SL (87.2)   *Comps: Jeff Hoffman (74), Erik Johnson (73), Liam Hendriks (72)*

I have been in your minor-league system for many years, but this is the first time you've come to me for innings or quality pitches. I can't remember the last time you invited me to your offices for a cup of coffee, even though I struck out nine in my major-league debut. But let's be frank here. You never wanted my friendship. And you feared to be with a gaping hole in your rotation. I understand. You found paradise in the 2019 World Series. You had a good rotation, you made a good living. The luxury tax protected you and there were arbitrators keeping salaries down. So you didn't need a pitcher like me. Now you come and say "Adon, give me quality starts." But you don't ask it with respect. You don't offer friendship. You don't even think to call me Godfather. You come onto my mound on the day I am supposed to be a starter and you ask me to throw pitches—for money.

Oops, wrong (A)don. This one throws a mid-90s fastball, is better suited to relief and wasn't featured in an Academy Award-winning film.

Jake Bennett LHP Born: 12/02/00 Age: 23 Height: 6'6" Weight: 234 Origin: Round 2, 2022 Draft (#45 overall)

YEAR	TM	LVL	AGE	G (GS)	IP	W-L	SV	K	WHIP	ERA	CSP	BB%	K%	HR%	GB%	ZSw%	ZCon%	OSw%	OCon%	BABIP	SLGCON	DRA-	WARP
2023	FBG	A	22	9 (9)	42	1-3	0	54	1.00	1.93		4.9%	32.9%	1.2%	52.5%					.330	.465	75	1.0
2023	WIL	A+	22	6 (6)	21	0-3	0	19	1.62	5.57		8.5%	20.2%	2.1%	53.0%					.375	.578	86	0.3
2024 non	WAS	MLB	23	58 (0)	50	2-2	0	44	1.47	5.29		9.0%	20.0%	3.4%	39.1%					.313	.568	116	-0.2

Comps: Luis Perdomo (79), D.J. Snelten (79), Bryan Sammons (79)

You wouldn't expect a team in Washington, D.C. to have a thing for Oklahoma prospects, but over the last decade only the nearby Astros have drafted more prospects from the Sooner State than the Nationals. A 2022 second-round pick, Bennett fits the profile of a polished college arm: He doesn't throw particularly hard but locates, has two plus off-speed offerings and sequences everything well. He predictably breezed through Low-A ball in his first taste of professional action before struggling with the tougher assignment to High-A. Given his relatively advanced age and limited ceiling the hope was that Bennett would move quickly through the system, but he's probably going to be less like the wind sweepin' down the plain and more like a gentle breeze that only requires a lightweight jacket.

★ ★ ★ *2024 Top 101 Prospect* **#85** ★ ★ ★

Cade Cavalli RHP Born: 08/14/98 Age: 25 Height: 6'4" Weight: 232 Origin: Round 1, 2020 Draft (#22 overall)

YEAR	TM	LVL	AGE	G (GS)	IP	W-L	SV	K	WHIP	ERA	CSP	BB%	K%	HR%	GB%	ZSw%	ZCon%	OSw%	OCon%	BABIP	SLGCON	DRA-	WARP
2021	WIL	A+	22	7 (7)	40²	3-1	0	71	0.89	1.77		7.6%	44.9%	0.6%	49.3%					.329	.449	63	1.2
2021	HBG	AA	22	11 (11)	58	3-3	0	80	1.28	2.79		14.4%	32.9%	0.8%	38.3%					.296	.433	80	1.1
2021	ROC	AAA	22	6 (6)	24²	1-5	0	24	1.86	7.30		10.7%	19.8%	1.7%	52.5%					.397	.525	109	0.2
2022	ROC	AAA	23	20 (20)	97	6-4	0	104	1.18	3.71		9.7%	25.9%	0.7%	42.6%					.293	.420	85	2.0
2022	WAS	MLB	23	1 (1)	4¹	0-1	0	6	1.85	14.54	56.7%	8.7%	26.1%	0.0%	50.0%	73.8%	74.2%	24.6%	64.3%	.500	.750	103	0.0
2024 DC	WAS	MLB	25	10 (10)	46¹	2-4	0	47	1.42	4.81	56.7%	10.5%	22.8%	3.0%	40.2%					.303	.552	106	0.3

2023 Arsenal: FA (96.5), KC (87.1), SL (89), CH (88.5) *Comps: Erik Johnson (49), Daniel Mengden (48), Dylan Cease (48)*

The injury concerns that had dogged Cavalli since high school because of his size and delivery rapidly collided with reality in spring training last year. On track to join the Nationals rotation, Cavalli threw a fastball nearly 10 miles-per-hour below his usual velocity in his third spring and was quickly pulled. An examination revealed a blown-out UCL and led to Tommy John surgery, knocking him out for all of 2023. When he returns in mid-2024, Cavalli will be a 25-year-old with a mere 224 ⅔ professional innings under his belt and an unclear future trajectory. Some scouts believe his build and athleticism will eventually provide strong results, while others see an inconsistent arm that will never develop the consistency necessary to be more than a back-end starter or late-inning relief weapon.

Patrick Corbin LHP Born: 07/19/89 Age: 34 Height: 6'4" Weight: 226 Origin: Round 2, 2009 Draft (#80 overall)

YEAR	TM	LVL	AGE	G (GS)	IP	W-L	SV	K	WHIP	ERA	CSP	BB%	K%	HR%	GB%	ZSw%	ZCon%	OSw%	OCon%	BABIP	SLGCON	DRA-	WARP
2021	WAS	MLB	31	31 (31)	171²	9-16	0	143	1.47	5.82	53.5%	8.0%	19.0%	4.9%	46.0%	67.8%	88.4%	35.4%	59.5%	.312	.648	112	0.5
2022	WAS	MLB	32	31 (31)	152²	6-19	0	128	1.70	6.31	54.8%	6.9%	18.0%	3.8%	44.6%	67.6%	88.1%	33.0%	66.5%	.365	.638	139	-1.6
2023	WAS	MLB	33	32 (32)	180	10-15	0	124	1.48	5.20	47.3%	7.2%	15.7%	4.2%	43.6%	66.1%	91.4%	31.7%	61.6%	.311	.582	124	-0.1
2024 DC	WAS	MLB	34	28 (28)	154	6-13	0	108	1.52	5.58	50.1%	7.5%	15.8%	3.5%	43.7%					.319	.562	123	-0.5

2023 Arsenal: SI (92.2), SL (80.8), FA (91.8), CH (81.2) *Comps: Livan Hernandez (75), Jordan Zimmermann (74), Mark Buehrle (72)*

Since nearly the dawn of free agency, there has been vigorous debate about if it's worth throwing gobs of money and committing to years and years of a player currently in his prime whose performance will inexorably fall off a cliff. To the sort of fan inexplicably rooting for the local squad's bottom line above anything else, Corbin is a massive disappointment, a one-year wonder whose best case scenario the last four seasons has been a replacement-level innings eater. For fans who care about winning above all else, that 2019 World Series banner flying over Nationals Park is everything, and it is impossible to imagine it's there without Corbin's strong season and especially without those three gutty relief innings he provided in Game 7, which not only kept Washington in the game but allowed them to rally. Corbin has one more year on what turned out to be a gobsmackingly awful contract, but if you're a Washington fan, who cares? It's not your money and those memories will stick with you for the rest of your time on this big blue marble.

Matt Cronin LHP Born: 09/20/97 Age: 26 Height: 6'2" Weight: 210 Origin: Round 4, 2019 Draft (#123 overall)

YEAR	TM	LVL	AGE	G (GS)	IP	W-L	SV	K	WHIP	ERA	CSP	BB%	K%	HR%	GB%	ZSw%	ZCon%	OSw%	OCon%	BABIP	SLGCON	DRA-	WARP
2021	WIL	A+	23	10 (0)	14²	2-0	4	28	0.89	1.23		9.1%	50.9%	0.0%	28.6%					.381	.476	79	0.3
2021	HBG	AA	23	10 (0)	11¹	0-1	0	18	1.68	5.56		19.6%	35.3%	3.9%	21.7%					.333	.739	84	0.2
2022	HBG	AA	24	14 (0)	16¹	1-0	0	22	0.73	0.00		11.9%	37.3%	0.0%	26.7%					.167	.167	92	0.3
2022	ROC	AAA	24	34 (0)	35²	3-1	0	34	1.26	3.53		10.1%	22.8%	2.0%	35.4%					.281	.474	100	0.5
2023	ROC	AAA	25	14 (0)	14¹	1-1	0	13	1.88	5.02		20.9%	19.4%	3.0%	27.5%	67.8%	76.9%	26.7%	66.0%	.289	.615	128	0.0
2024 DC	WAS	MLB	26	10 (0)	12	0-1	0	13	1.52	5.19		12.9%	23.6%	3.4%	31.2%					.299	.588	113	0.0

2023 Arsenal: FA (89.5), CU (74.2) *Comps: Mitch Lambson (75), Kyle McGrath (75), Paul Fry (74)*

Relievers drafted out of college are typically about as interesting as people who drone on about the wonder of cold press coffee, but Cronin's mid-90s heater and high-spin curveball made him an exception to the rule. Despite this promise, he was stuck in the minors for years and in 2023 was shut down with a shoulder/arm injury. Or so the Nationals initially thought: A more thorough examination revealed a herniated disk in his back that he had been pitching through for almost two years. He's already 26 years old, but pitchers don't follow nearly the same linear path to the majors as their offensive counterparts, so Cronin could eventually make an impact on the Nats bullpen assuming a full recovery.

Sean Doolittle LHP
Born: 09/26/86 Age: 37 Height: 6'2" Weight: 218 Origin: Round 1, 2007 Draft (#41 overall)

YEAR	TM	LVL	AGE	G (GS)	IP	W-L	SV	K	WHIP	ERA	CSP	BB%	K%	HR%	GB%	ZSw%	ZCon%	OSw%	OCon%	BABIP	SLGCON	DRA-	WARP
2021	CIN	MLB	34	45(0)	38¹	3-1	1	41	1.51	4.46	57.2%	10.4%	23.7%	3.5%	18.6%	75.9%	78.7%	35.2%	72.6%	.324	.670	118	0.0
2021	SEA	MLB	34	11(0)	11¹	0-0	0	12	1.32	4.76	57.0%	10.0%	24.0%	2.0%	21.9%	75.3%	75.9%	40.2%	63.4%	.290	.469	120	0.0
2022	WAS	MLB	35	6(0)	5¹	0-0	0	6	0.19	0.00	56.4%	0.0%	35.3%	0.0%	27.3%	73.1%	78.9%	41.4%	41.7%	.091	.182	94	0.1
2024 non	WAS	MLB	37	58(0)	50	2-2	0	51	1.49	5.59	54.3%	10.3%	22.9%	4.2%	23.3%					.309	.644	123	-0.4

2023 Arsenal: FA (92), SL (77.9), FS (82.2) *Comps: Jake McGee (55), Jake Diekman (54), Tony Sipp (54)*

"When I was a kid, I remember my parents would say, 'Baseball is what you do, but that's not who you are'—like that might be my job, but that's not the end-all, be-all. I feel like I might even be able to use it to help other people or open some doors or explore more opportunities."

On September 22, 2023, Doolittle announced his retirement from Major League Baseball. His on-the-field accomplishments—a 3.20 ERA, 112 saves and a stellar 2019 postseason run over which he posted a 1.74 ERA including three shutout innings in the World Series—are certainly memorable, but the most important thing to know about Doolittle is that he lived up to that quote every day. Whether it was supporting Operation Finally Home—a nonprofit dedicated to finding housing for U.S. military veterans and their families—his work with LGBT+ organizations or hosting a Thanksgiving dinner for Syrian refugees and their families, Doolittle used his fame and platform to give so much back to the community and the world at large. Baseball needs awesome humans like him, but what the sport is losing the world is gaining, as he'll surely continue his tireless efforts to make it the best place it can possibly be.

Kyle Finnegan RHP
Born: 09/04/91 Age: 32 Height: 6'2" Weight: 200 Origin: Round 6, 2013 Draft (#191 overall)

YEAR	TM	LVL	AGE	G (GS)	IP	W-L	SV	K	WHIP	ERA	CSP	BB%	K%	HR%	GB%	ZSw%	ZCon%	OSw%	OCon%	BABIP	SLGCON	DRA-	WARP
2021	WAS	MLB	29	68(0)	66	5-9	11	68	1.48	3.55	55.8%	11.6%	23.1%	3.1%	47.6%	66.2%	83.0%	33.4%	62.8%	.309	.551	97	0.7
2022	WAS	MLB	30	66(0)	66²	6-4	11	70	1.14	3.51	56.8%	8.2%	26.1%	3.4%	47.7%	71.4%	77.9%	30.8%	61.8%	.269	.534	78	1.4
2023	WAS	MLB	31	67(0)	69¹	7-5	28	63	1.30	3.76	51.3%	8.3%	21.9%	3.8%	45.5%	72.6%	84.1%	29.6%	56.2%	.294	.558	89	1.2
2024 DC	WAS	MLB	32	58(0)	61¹	3-7	26	59	1.38	4.43	54.1%	9.3%	22.4%	2.9%	45.7%					.306	.536	100	0.3

2023 Arsenal: FA (97.4), FS (89.6), SL (90) *Comps: Blake Parker (63), Andrew Kittredge (63), Brad Brach (62)*

Lingering beneath the pejorative expression "the wheels are coming off" is the optimistic notion that the wheels are still working for the moment, and things could somehow be worse. Last year, Finnegan's wheels wobbled but managed to stay firmly attached. His whiff rate declined while batters' hard-hit rate against him skyrocketed. After a terrible April, he mostly abandoned his slider as a secondary offering in favor of his splitter, which worked for a while until it didn't, as hitters started teeing off once again down the stretch in September. He managed to hang on as Washington's primary closer, but mostly because there weren't many other palatable options, particularly after Hunter Harvey got hurt in mid-July. Some analysts were surprised the Nats didn't move Finnegan at last year's deadline, but potential suitors surely saw those wobbly wheels and decided on a sturdier model.

Dylan Floro RHP
Born: 12/27/90 Age: 33 Height: 6'2" Weight: 203 Origin: Round 13, 2012 Draft (#422 overall)

YEAR	TM	LVL	AGE	G (GS)	IP	W-L	SV	K	WHIP	ERA	CSP	BB%	K%	HR%	GB%	ZSw%	ZCon%	OSw%	OCon%	BABIP	SLGCON	DRA-	WARP
2021	MIA	MLB	30	68(0)	64	6-6	15	62	1.22	2.81	51.9%	9.3%	23.0%	0.7%	49.2%	69.6%	83.7%	33.4%	67.0%	.282	.385	94	0.8
2022	MIA	MLB	31	56(0)	53²	1-3	10	48	1.17	3.02	52.9%	6.8%	21.8%	1.8%	43.9%	65.8%	85.0%	36.0%	68.2%	.288	.442	89	0.8
2023	MIA	MLB	32	43(0)	39²	3-5	7	41	1.49	4.54	47.1%	6.4%	24.0%	1.2%	55.1%	62.3%	82.0%	32.6%	68.8%	.397	.559	81	0.9
2023	MIN	MLB	32	19(0)	17	2-1	0	17	1.65	5.29	44.2%	7.8%	22.1%	1.3%	51.9%	67.5%	82.7%	34.3%	64.5%	.412	.529	86	0.3
2024 DC	WAS	MLB	33	40(0)	43	2-2	0	36	1.31	4.02	49.7%	7.8%	19.8%	2.6%	49.3%					.297	.492	92	0.4

2023 Arsenal: SI (92.8), FA (92.4), SL (84.1), CH (85.5) *Comps: Tommy Hunter (60), Ryan Pressly (59), Nick Vincent (59)*

The unassuming middle reliever is a player type in crisis. Maybe it's a marketing problem. "Middle reliever" doesn't really tell me what makes you pop, does it? Let's try some rebranding. Floro is the exemplar of the modern utility reliever. You can use him in a dirty inning, because he doesn't walk people and he keeps the ball on the ground. You can use him as an opener, because he has three pitches for righties and four for lefties, and can change eye levels as well as lanes. He can pitch on zero days' rest without going to pieces. He's a really solid, versatile bullpen tool. You just need to have three or four guys who are better in your pen.

MacKenzie Gore LHP
Born: 02/24/99 Age: 25 Height: 6'2" Weight: 192 Origin: Round 1, 2017 Draft (#3 overall)

YEAR	TM	LVL	AGE	G (GS)	IP	W-L	SV	K	WHIP	ERA	CSP	BB%	K%	HR%	GB%	ZSw%	ZCon%	OSw%	OCon%	BABIP	SLGCON	DRA-	WARP
2021	PAD	ROK	22	3(3)	16¹	1-0	0	22	1.04	1.65		6.3%	34.4%	0.0%	45.9%					.351	.378		
2021	SA	AA	22	2(2)	9	0-0	0	16	1.56	3.00		19.5%	39.0%	0.0%	47.1%					.353	.471	92	0.1
2021	ELP	AAA	22	6(6)	20	0-2	0	18	1.80	5.85		12.5%	18.8%	3.1%	46.2%					.339	.646	105	0.0
2022	ROC	AAA	23	4(4)	12	0-1	0	9	1.67	5.25		7.3%	16.4%	5.5%	48.8%					.342	.756	113	0.1
2022	SD	MLB	23	16(13)	70	4-4	0	72	1.47	4.50	55.4%	12.0%	23.3%	2.3%	37.8%	70.4%	83.1%	29.4%	63.8%	.312	.515	127	-0.3
2023	WAS	MLB	24	27(27)	136¹	7-10	0	151	1.40	4.42	45.4%	9.8%	25.9%	4.6%	38.1%	71.7%	82.9%	33.0%	56.7%	.310	.647	105	1.3
2024 DC	WAS	MLB	25	23(23)	113¹	4-10	0	120	1.46	5.16	48.3%	10.8%	24.0%	3.9%	38.6%					.306	.607	114	0.2

2023 Arsenal: FA (95.1), SL (88.7), CU (83.3), CH (86.6), SW (84.9) *Comps: Brett Oberholtzer (63), Justus Sheffield (62), Robbie Erlin (62)*

The words "control" and "Gore" have been bandied about so much on the sports pages of *The Washington Post* the last two seasons that one would think they were writing about a gritty reboot of *Get Smart* and not a promising young Nationals pitcher who has too little of the former and is named the latter. The last two seasons have been more like *Mission: Impossible* for the promising young southpaw, who managed to mostly put the injury whispers from his prospect days behind him but still hasn't managed to parlay a mid-90s heater with movement and high-80s slider with bite into results. Gore toyed around throwing more changeups in the second half of the season, which mitigated the command issue but made him far more hittable before a blister shut him down in early September. He will be 25 years old on Opening Day, but the Nationals are hoping that this pitcher with a very particular set of skills isn't going to need a similarly long career to capitalize on that potential and promise.

Josiah Gray   RHP   Born: 12/21/97   Age: 26   Height: 6'1"   Weight: 210   Origin: Round 2, 2018 Draft (#72 overall)

YEAR	TM	LVL	AGE	G (GS)	IP	W-L	SV	K	WHIP	ERA	CSP	BB%	K%	HR%	GB%	ZSw%	ZCon%	OSw%	OCon%	BABIP	SLGCON	DRA-	WARP
2021	OKC	AAA	23	4 (3)	15²	1-1	0	22	0.64	2.87		3.5%	38.6%	5.3%	36.4%					.167	.545	85	0.2
2021	WAS	MLB	23	12 (12)	62²	2-2	0	63	1.34	5.31	51.7%	10.3%	23.2%	5.5%	29.6%	71.4%	85.4%	35.5%	55.5%	.258	.669	123	-0.2
2021	LAD	MLB	23	2 (1)	8	0-0	0	13	1.50	6.75	45.6%	14.3%	37.1%	11.4%	29.4%	68.9%	74.2%	40.5%	42.2%	.231	1.118	96	0.1
2022	WAS	MLB	24	28 (28)	148²	7-10	0	154	1.36	5.02	52.5%	10.2%	23.7%	5.9%	32.9%	65.1%	83.4%	31.4%	59.3%	.257	.670	123	-0.3
2023	WAS	MLB	25	30 (30)	159	8-13	0	143	1.46	3.91	45.1%	11.5%	20.5%	3.2%	37.8%	69.8%	83.8%	31.6%	60.3%	.293	.539	119	0.3
2024 DC	WAS	MLB	26	29 (29)	160¹	7-13	0	159	1.42	4.90	48.6%	10.9%	22.6%	3.6%	35.3%					.293	.572	109	0.7

2023 Arsenal: SL (86.4), FA (93.8), KC (82.4), SI (93.1), FC (89.5), SW (82), CH (88.8)   Comps: Jarred Cosart (74), Drew Hutchison (72), Mitch Keller (72)

There were some improvements on the margins for the Nationals' perennially promising right-hander but for the most part it was more of the same for a pitcher whose tantalizing parts have not quite added up to an acceptable sum. Gray managed to procure an All-Star appearance based on an appealing first-half ERA and the reality that someone from the Nationals was required to be there by rule, but his DRA tells the tale of a hurler spinning his wheels in the mud. To his credit, Gray continues attempting to reinvent himself as something better. He moved away from his four-seamer in favor of a cutter/sinker combination, but the larger problem is that his curve and slider both don't have enough movement to keep hitters from teeing off when the pitches miss in the zone. On a better, deeper team Gray might be at risk of getting shifted to the bullpen, but in a shallow Nationals organization the pitcher and team are stuck with each other every fifth day.

Hunter Harvey   RHP   Born: 12/09/94   Age: 29   Height: 6'3"   Weight: 239   Origin: Round 1, 2013 Draft (#22 overall)

YEAR	TM	LVL	AGE	G (GS)	IP	W-L	SV	K	WHIP	ERA	CSP	BB%	K%	HR%	GB%	ZSw%	ZCon%	OSw%	OCon%	BABIP	SLGCON	DRA-	WARP
2021	NOR	AAA	26	8 (1)	10	2-1	0	7	2.10	8.10		3.9%	13.7%	3.9%	54.8%					.436	.659	104	0.1
2021	BAL	MLB	26	9 (0)	8²	0-0	0	6	1.27	4.15	58.4%	8.3%	16.7%	2.8%	48.1%	72.9%	95.3%	31.2%	76.0%	.269	.556	100	0.1
2022	WAS	MLB	27	38 (0)	39¹	2-1	0	45	1.14	2.52	55.4%	7.6%	28.7%	0.6%	39.0%	70.2%	80.7%	32.0%	57.4%	.323	.490	81	0.8
2023	WAS	MLB	28	57 (0)	60²	4-4	10	67	0.94	2.82	49.3%	5.5%	28.5%	3.0%	43.1%	70.1%	79.3%	34.1%	64.0%	.253	.480	78	1.4
2024 DC	WAS	MLB	29	46 (0)	49	2-2	2	47	1.23	3.91	51.7%	7.4%	22.7%	3.3%	41.5%					.287	.535	91	0.4

2023 Arsenal: FA (98.4), FS (89.6), SL (86.7), CU (83.3)   Comps: Ryne Stanek (60), Giovanny Gallegos (59), Jared Hughes (58)

For most pitchers, missing a month with an elbow strain would be anything between a red flag and cause for moderate concern, but for Harvey it represented progress. He finally eclipsed 60 innings as a major leaguer, and for the first time across all professional levels since 2019. If you're wondering why this matters for an oft-injured bullpen piece heading into his age-29 season, that just means you haven't seen this dude pitch. Harvey dials his fastball into the upper 90s and locates it so well that hitters have extreme difficulty squaring it up. He complements it with a splitter that generates lots of swings and misses. Harvey was on his way to taking over as Washington's closer before the injury put him on the shelf, and it seems inevitable he eventually claims the role—assuming health, no minor caveat.

Cole Henry   RHP   Born: 07/15/99   Age: 24   Height: 6'4"   Weight: 215   Origin: Round 2, 2020 Draft (#55 overall)

YEAR	TM	LVL	AGE	G (GS)	IP	W-L	SV	K	WHIP	ERA	CSP	BB%	K%	HR%	GB%	ZSw%	ZCon%	OSw%	OCon%	BABIP	SLGCON	DRA-	WARP
2021	WIL	A+	21	9 (8)	43	3-3	0	63	0.79	1.88		6.7%	38.7%	1.8%	46.4%					.247	.458	74	1.0
2022	HBG	AA	22	7 (7)	23²	0-0	0	28	0.59	0.76		10.6%	32.9%	1.2%	42.6%					.087	.170	92	0.4
2022	ROC	AAA	22	2 (2)	8	1-0	0	6	1.38	4.50		5.9%	17.6%	2.9%	38.5%					.320	.462	108	0.1
2023	FBG	A	23	2 (2)	7	0-0	0	11	0.57	0.00		0.0%	42.3%	0.0%	30.8%					.308	.385	87	0.1
2023	WIL	A+	23	2 (2)	8	0-1	0	5	1.13	2.25		9.7%	16.1%	3.2%	43.5%					.227	.565	119	-0.1
2023	HBG	AA	23	10 (6)	18¹	0-2	0	21	1.96	10.31		14.3%	23.1%	5.5%	42.6%					.367	.792	107	0.2
2024 non	WAS	MLB	24	58 (0)	50	2-2	0	47	1.39	4.80		9.9%	21.3%	3.4%	36.9%					.290	.562	107	0.0

Comps: Jeremy Jeffress (38), Yency Almonte (38), Edward Cabrera (36)

Last season was essentially a season-long rehab assignment for Henry, who spent the year following brief bursts of activity with rest and recuperation on the long road back from thoracic outlet surgery. Early reports said his mid-90s fastball velocity had returned, but by the end of the season Henry was struggling both with velocity and in-game endurance. The Nationals shut him down in late July. When he returned in early September, Henry was a permanent fixture in the Harrisburg Senators relief corps. The results were terrible but can mostly be ignored. When he was drafted, there were questions about whether Henry would make it as a starter or reliever; now the goal is simply to get him back in any capacity whatsoever.

DJ Herz   LHP   Born: 01/04/01   Age: 23   Height: 6'2"   Weight: 175   Origin: Round 8, 2019 Draft (#252 overall)

YEAR	TM	LVL	AGE	G (GS)	IP	W-L	SV	K	WHIP	ERA	CSP	BB%	K%	HR%	GB%	ZSw%	ZCon%	OSw%	OCon%	BABIP	SLGCON	DRA-	WARP
2021	MB	A	20	17 (17)	65²	3-4	0	105	1.07	3.43		14.6%	40.4%	2.3%	30.9%					.252	.557	81	1.4
2021	SB	A+	20	3 (3)	16	1-0	0	26	1.00	2.81		9.4%	40.6%	1.6%	51.6%					.300	.581	76	0.4
2022	SB	A+	21	17 (17)	63²	2-2	0	99	1.10	2.26		14.2%	38.1%	1.2%	41.8%					.252	.380	77	1.4
2022	TNS	AA	21	9 (9)	31²	1-4	0	42	1.80	8.24		20.9%	26.6%	3.2%	35.1%					.275	.630	127	-0.1
2023	HBG	AA	22	8 (8)	35¹	2-2	0	53	1.13	2.55		13.6%	36.1%	0.7%	38.0%					.271	.408	75	0.8
2023	TNS	AA	22	14 (14)	59	1-1	0	80	1.42	3.97		14.0%	30.3%	1.5%	35.0%					.314	.493	85	0.6
2024 DC	WAS	MLB	23	13 (3)	18²	0-2	0	23	1.55	5.15		15.2%	26.7%	3.2%	33.6%					.294	.583	111	0.0

Comps: Stephen Gonsalves (72), Luke Jackson (71), Yordano Ventura (71)

Herz was part of the only deadline deal the Nationals completed last season, a swap of third base rental Jeimer Candelario to the Cubs for the southpaw and infielder Kevin Made. He is your prototypical lefty who relies on deception, in the form of a funky delivery that keeps hitters off balance. He features a changeup that is inconsistent but utterly nasty when working, getting hitters to flail as the pitch drops out of the zone right before it reaches the plate. The fastball is far too hittable and command is a significant issue, but Herz continues to succeed as a starter even though every scouting report out there says his future is probably in ~~mega~~ middle relief.

Jake Irvin RHP Born: 02/18/97 Age: 27 Height: 6'6" Weight: 227 Origin: Round 4, 2018 Draft (#131 overall)

YEAR	TM	LVL	AGE	G (GS)	IP	W-L	SV	K	WHIP	ERA	CSP	BB%	K%	HR%	GB%	ZSw%	ZCon%	OSw%	OCon%	BABIP	SLGCON	DRA-	WARP
2022	WIL	A+	25	9(9)	30	0-0	0	29	1.07	1.50		6.8%	24.6%	0.0%	53.2%					.304	.392	110	0.1
2022	HBG	AA	25	15(15)	73¹	0-4	0	78	1.17	4.79		6.5%	25.5%	2.9%	37.3%					.297	.604	105	0.8
2023	ROC	AAA	26	5(5)	22¹	2-2	0	20	1.52	5.64		11.2%	20.4%	3.1%	41.5%	67.8%	81.2%	33.6%	76.4%	.323	.538	104	0.3
2023	WAS	MLB	26	24(24)	121	3-7	0	99	1.42	4.61	50.1%	10.2%	18.7%	3.8%	42.0%	66.2%	88.1%	25.9%	70.1%	.281	.548	118	0.3
2024 DC	*WAS*	*MLB*	*27*	*19(19)*	*93*	*3-8*	*0*	*67*	*1.46*	*5.14*	*50.1%*	*9.6%*	*16.3%*	*3.3%*	*41.6%*					*.290*	*.533*	*114*	*0.2*

2023 Arsenal: FA (94.7), CU (81.2), SI (94.1), CH (87.9)   *Comps: Aaron Civale (71), Chris Stratton (70), Seth Lugo (68)*

A fourth-round draft pick way back in 2018 out of the University of Oklahoma, a combination of the pandemic year and Tommy John surgery stole two seasons and made Irvin mostly a forgotten arm in the Nationals system. The long layoff didn't take anything away from his polished delivery and repeatability, but the stuff speaks more to a back-end starter who will need to find a little extra oomph to avoid the dreaded mid-career move to middle relief. Irvin's size and delivery make it difficult for hitters to pick up his low-90s heater until it's right up on them, but deception can only do so much for you in Washington unless you're up on Capitol Hill. He will need to refine his changeup or come up with another, quality third pitch to keep his spot in a big-league rotation.

Jackson Rutledge RHP Born: 04/01/99 Age: 25 Height: 6'8" Weight: 251 Origin: Round 1, 2019 Draft (#17 overall)

YEAR	TM	LVL	AGE	G (GS)	IP	W-L	SV	K	WHIP	ERA	CSP	BB%	K%	HR%	GB%	ZSw%	ZCon%	OSw%	OCon%	BABIP	SLGCON	DRA-	WARP
2021	FBG	A	22	7(7)	22	1-2	0	26	1.32	5.32		9.2%	26.5%	1.0%	49.2%					.317	.475	84	0.4
2021	WIL	A+	22	4(4)	10²	0-3	0	10	2.44	12.66		15.5%	17.2%	0.0%	39.5%					.447	.528	107	0.0
2022	FBG	A	23	20(20)	97¹	8-6	0	99	1.39	4.90		6.9%	23.4%	1.7%	51.2%					.354	.519	89	1.6
2023	HBG	AA	24	12(12)	68¹	6-1	0	62	1.10	3.16		9.2%	22.8%	1.8%	39.4%					.257	.452	100	1.1
2023	ROC	AAA	24	11(11)	50²	2-3	0	44	1.50	4.44		13.3%	19.6%	3.1%	36.8%	67.9%	83.3%	25.8%	63.3%	.285	.557	106	0.5
2023	WAS	MLB	24	4(4)	20	1-1	0	12	1.50	6.75	50.0%	6.8%	13.6%	4.5%	26.5%	75.0%	80.7%	27.8%	75.9%	.313	.612	130	-0.1
2024 DC	*WAS*	*MLB*	*25*	*11(11)*	*56²*	*2-5*	*0*	*44*	*1.55*	*5.82*	*50.0%*	*10.0%*	*17.1%*	*3.6%*	*32.2%*					*.306*	*.574*	*127*	*-0.3*

2023 Arsenal: FA (95.9), SL (85.1), SI (94.8), CH (88.8), CU (80.4), SW (82.7)   *Comps: Hiram Burgos (76), James Marvel (74), Adrián Martínez (74)*

"The Shape of His Heater" might sound like the title of an edgy arthouse romance, but is actually a rough way of measuring the viability of a pitcher's fastball. Rutledge is a mammoth human being with an intimidating mound presence, but that won't be enough to cement a major-league role if he can't improve his heater. The pitch is a mid-to-upper 90s offering that sinks but doesn't have enough horizontal or vertical break, meaning hitters find it relatively easy to track. Rutledge breezed through his first taste of the high minors at Double-A, but then struggled with command at Triple-A and got bombarded in a September call-up based far more on need than merit. He did improve his off-speed offerings, doing just enough to perhaps survive as a fourth or fifth starter on a second-division squad.

Stephen Strasburg RHP Born: 07/20/88 Age: 35 Height: 6'5" Weight: 239 Origin: Round 1, 2009 Draft (#1 overall)

YEAR	TM	LVL	AGE	G (GS)	IP	W-L	SV	K	WHIP	ERA	CSP	BB%	K%	HR%	GB%	ZSw%	ZCon%	OSw%	OCon%	BABIP	SLGCON	DRA-	WARP
2021	WAS	MLB	32	5(5)	21²	1-2	0	21	1.38	4.57	52.6%	14.7%	22.1%	4.2%	37.3%	56.7%	89.1%	22.8%	56.1%	.218	.525	111	0.1
2022	FBG	A	33	2(2)	7²	1-1	0	9	1.04	3.52		16.1%	29.0%	0.0%	35.3%					.176	.235	102	0.1
2022	ROC	AAA	33	1(1)	6	0-0	0	4	0.33	0.00		5.0%	20.0%	0.0%	46.7%					.067	.067	92	0.1
2022	WAS	MLB	33	1(1)	4²	0-1	0	5	2.14	13.50	60.2%	8.7%	21.7%	4.3%	40.0%	51.4%	94.4%	25.0%	58.3%	.500	.933	109	0.0
2024 non	*WAS*	*MLB*	*35*	*58(0)*	*50*	*2-2*	*0*	*51*	*1.43*	*4.98*	*47.2%*	*10.2%*	*23.0%*	*3.4%*	*42.2%*					*.305*	*.576*	*110*	*0.0*

Comps: Bob Welch (84), Don Sutton (83), Roger Clemens (82)

Despite the three years and $105 million remaining on his contract (not including deferred money, please don't ask us to calculate deferrals), it's effectively over for Strasburg, who was all set to announce his retirement last September before the Nationals abruptly canceled his press conference and said he'll remain on the team's roster. When a player's career ends like this it's common for fans to get wistful about what might have been or mad about the money he's "stealing" from the team, but this glosses over how good Stras was when he was able to take the mound. From 2010—his rookie season—until 2023, he ranked sixth in pitching WARP despite being only 41st in innings pitched. This doesn't even account for his greatness in the postseason, where he posted a miniscule 1.46 ERA in 55 ⅓ innings with 71 strikeouts and earned a well-deserved World Series MVP award in 2019. Despite the lack of Cy Young awards or anything close to Hall of Fame credentials, Strasburg gave Nationals fans plenty to be happy about and for a brief while delivered on the promise we all saw in his rookie campaign.

Jarlin Susana RHP Born: 03/23/04 Age: 20 Height: 6'6" Weight: 235 Origin: IFA, 2022

YEAR	TM	LVL	AGE	G (GS)	IP	W-L	SV	K	WHIP	ERA	CSP	BB%	K%	HR%	GB%	ZSw%	ZCon%	OSw%	OCon%	BABIP	SLGCON	DRA-	WARP
2022	PAD	ROK	18	8(7)	29¹	0-0	0	44	0.89	2.45		9.9%	39.6%	0.9%	56.6%					.269	.434		
2022	FBG	A	18	3(3)	10¹	0-0	0	13	1.35	2.61		11.4%	29.5%	2.3%	38.5%					.320	.538	93	0.1
2023	FBG	A	19	17(17)	63	1-6	0	62	1.52	5.14		14.1%	21.8%	1.1%	51.7%					.308	.441	102	0.4
2024 non	WAS	MLB	20	58(0)	50	2-2	0	41	1.82	7.27		13.7%	17.0%	4.1%	37.2%					.317	.626	152	-1.1

Comps: Kohl Stewart (87), Valente Bellozo (86), Daniel Corcino (84)

An afterthought in the Padres/Nationals Juan Soto blockbuster, Susanna almost immediately generated buzz once video of his 100+ mile-per-hour fastball and hard slider that sits in the low 90s (and has touched 95) started making its way acros the web. The fastball velocity led to immediate Jacob deGrom comparisons, although the complete lack of movement on the pitch is more reminiscent of another onetime Mets stud, Noah Syndergaard, who threw extremely hard but was hittable once major-league batters figured out how to time the heater. Susanna comes with all the usual "he's a teenager, it's way too soon to make any concrete judgments yet" caveats, both good and bad, but the history of pitchers who throw this hard in the minors at this early of an age frequently ends with some sort of injury. Even that glosses over Susanna's struggles in 2023, both with command and overall results.

Travis Sykora RHP Born: 04/28/04 Age: 20 Height: 6'6" Weight: 232 Origin: Round 3, 2023 Draft (#71 overall)

Don't be fooled by the fact that he was "only" a third-round pick in the 2023 Amateur Draft; Sykora was a first-round talent whose draft stock fell primarily due to a commitment to the University of Texas and signability questions. The Nationals lured him away with a $2.6 million bonus that was more than double the pick's slot value. Sykora's fastball sits in the mid-90s and can hit 101, but his secondary pitches are as unrefined as might be expected from a prep arm with no professional experience. Right now, what he has going for him is tremendous arm speed, which isn't nothing, but plenty of developmental work lies ahead.

Thaddeus Ward RHP Born: 01/16/97 Age: 27 Height: 6'3" Weight: 204 Origin: Round 5, 2018 Draft (#160 overall)

YEAR	TM	LVL	AGE	G (GS)	IP	W-L	SV	K	WHIP	ERA	CSP	BB%	K%	HR%	GB%	ZSw%	ZCon%	OSw%	OCon%	BABIP	SLGCON	DRA-	WARP
2021	POR	AA	24	2(2)	8	0-0	0	11	2.00	5.62		12.8%	28.2%	0.0%	60.9%					.478	.696	96	0.1
2022	SAL	A	25	2(2)	6	0-0	0	10	0.50	0.00		4.8%	47.6%	0.0%	60.0%					.200	.200	84	0.1
2022	GVL	A+	25	2(2)	7	0-1	0	6	1.86	5.14		11.4%	17.1%	0.0%	56.0%					.375	.458	98	0.1
2022	POR	AA	25	7(7)	33¹	0-1	0	4¹	1.26	2.43		10.1%	29.5%	2.2%	40.0%					.321	.531	84	0.7
2023	WIL	A+	26	2(2)	8	0-0	0	7	1.25	3.38		8.8%	20.6%	2.9%	65.2%					.273	.478	87	0.1
2023	HBG	AA	26	2(2)	10	0-2	0	6	1.20	3.60		2.3%	13.6%	4.5%	48.6%					.290	.576	103	0.1
2023	WAS	MLB	26	26(0)	35¹	0-0	0	30	1.61	6.37	47.3%	17.5%	18.8%	4.4%	45.0%	59.6%	83.8%	23.7%	64.2%	.237	.545	111	0.2
2024 DC	WAS	MLB	27	40(0)	43	2-2	0	38	1.54	5.30	47.3%	11.9%	19.6%	3.0%	44.2%					.300	.534	115	-0.1

2023 Arsenal: SW (81.2), SI (93.3), FC (87.6), FA (93.5), CH (87.8)

Comps: Pierce Johnson (54), Jaime Schultz (54), Kyle Funkhouser (52)

Ward's surface numbers, awful (albeit brief) major-league career to date and extremely advanced age might make it seem like he's a fringy reliever. Instead, he remains a promising prospect who struggled to acclimate himself to part-time work in the Nationals bullpen after being taken in the Rule 5 draft in 2022 from the Boston Red Sox. When he is at his best, he features a mid-90s fastball and complements the heater with two plus breaking pitches. Given his ceiling and the Nationals' desperate need for pitching, it's likely he'll get a shot at breaking into their rotation at some point in 2024.

Trevor Williams RHP Born: 04/25/92 Age: 32 Height: 6'3" Weight: 231 Origin: Round 2, 2013 Draft (#44 overall)

YEAR	TM	LVL	AGE	G (GS)	IP	W-L	SV	K	WHIP	ERA	CSP	BB%	K%	HR%	GB%	ZSw%	ZCon%	OSw%	OCon%	BABIP	SLGCON	DRA-	WARP
2021	SYR	AAA	29	2(2)	12	1-0	0	10	0.92	2.25		4.3%	21.3%	2.1%	38.2%					.242	.382	101	0.2
2021	IOW	AAA	29	2(2)	7	1-0	0	5	0.43	0.00		3.7%	18.5%	0.0%	60.0%					.111	.167	99	0.1
2021	CHC	MLB	29	13(12)	58²	4-2	0	61	1.53	5.06	54.2%	8.3%	23.1%	3.8%	46.6%	69.4%	85.2%	31.8%	62.9%	.345	.650	91	0.8
2021	NYM	MLB	29	10(3)	32¹	0-0	0	29	1.42	3.06	49.3%	6.4%	20.6%	0.7%	42.2%	73.1%	84.4%	38.6%	64.8%	.367	.545	88	0.5
2022	NYM	MLB	30	30(9)	89²	3-5	1	84	1.23	3.21	50.8%	6.2%	22.6%	3.2%	35.8%	74.6%	86.4%	32.9%	62.2%	.302	.546	103	0.8
2023	WAS	MLB	31	30(30)	144¹	6-10	0	111	1.60	5.55	45.3%	8.0%	16.8%	5.2%	39.2%	72.2%	89.0%	31.4%	70.3%	.316	.656	123	0.0
2024 DC	WAS	MLB	32	26(26)	127	4-11	0	93	1.42	5.11	47.6%	7.6%	16.9%	3.5%	38.9%					.303	.553	114	0.1

2023 Arsenal: FA (89.8), CH (83.5), SI (88.4), SL (81.8), CU (76.9), SW (76.8)

Comps: Josh Fogg (83), Jeff Weaver (81), Dave Bush (81)

Beyond the money and the two-year guarantee, a big reason Williams signed with the Nationals was because he was promised a spot in a major-league rotation. Perhaps he should have read the fine print, because he might have been better off on a team that could have shifted him to a long relief role when the going got rough. Williams started off the year OK but from June through the closing bell he endured a nightmare stretch, posting a 6.55 ERA in his final 19 starts. His fastball dropped nearly two miles per hour from where it was in 2022. While it made sense for him to start using it less, his other pitches weren't particularly effective either. He has another year on his deal and while he might not survive it as a starter, the Nationals may not have much of a choice.

LINEOUTS

Hitters

HITTER	POS	TM	LVL	AGE	PA	R	HR	RBI	SB	AVG/OBP/SLG	BABIP	SLGCON	BB%	K%	ZSw%	ZCon%	OSw%	OCon%	LA	90th EV	DRC+	BRR	DRP	WARP
Riley Adams	C	WAS	MLB	27	158	8	4	21	0	.273/.331/.476	.368	.694	7.0%	28.5%	72.8%	83.8%	37.0%	53.8%	18.1	106.1	76	-0.1	-7.3	-0.6
Travis Blankenhorn	LF	ROC	AAA	26	455	67	23	75	0	.262/.360/.517	.307	.717	11.2%	24.2%	68.5%	83.4%	32.7%	54.7%			116	-0.4	-1.7	1.9
	LF	WAS	MLB	26	37	2	1	1	0	.161/.297/.258	.167	.320	16.2%	16.2%	63.0%	82.8%	34.4%	54.8%	6.4	105.5	105	0.0	-0.1	0.1
Michael Chavis	IF	WAS	MLB	27	96	16	2	5	1	.242/.281/.341	.357	.534	5.2%	34.4%	71.9%	80.0%	42.7%	51.5%	9.2	103.0	52	-0.1	0.3	-0.3
Jeremy De La Rosa	OF	WIL	A+	21	383	44	7	42	13	.240/.324/.361	.363	.584	10.7%	33.7%							90	-0.3	-6.4	-0.1
Corey Dickerson	LF	WAS	MLB	34	152	12	2	17	0	.250/.283/.354	.296	.440	4.6%	18.4%	71.9%	86.0%	52.2%	69.3%	9.9	101.6	92	0.0	0.3	0.3
Carter Kieboom	3B	HER	WIN	25	61	9	1	12	0	.306/.443/.449	.359	.550	16.4%	14.8%										
	3B	ROC	AAA	25	161	24	5	23	1	.264/.360/.429	.317	.566	11.8%	21.1%	56.6%	88.6%	22.1%	54.3%			103	1.4	3.6	1.0
	3B	WAS	MLB	25	94	12	4	11	0	.207/.266/.368	.250	.533	6.4%	28.7%	74.3%	80.2%	29.4%	41.9%	14.1	102.2	78	0.0	-0.4	0.0
Trey Lipscomb	IF	SCO	WIN	23	76	9	0	4	1	.200/.211/.227	.254	.288	1.3%	21.1%	87.5%	42.9%	61.1%	63.6%						
	IF	WIL	A+	23	212	19	4	27	6	.251/.311/.387	.297	.497	7.1%	19.8%							105	-0.4	2.6	1.0
	IF	HBG	AA	23	335	40	10	45	4	.284/.310/.438	.323	.541	3.6%	18.2%							100	-0.3	3.3	1.2
Nasim Nuñez	SS	PEJ	WIN	22	84	11	0	13	14	.246/.369/.290	.333	.400	15.5%	22.6%	66.7%	100.0%	21.7%	100.0%						
	SS	PNS	AA	22	585	84	5	43	52	.224/.341/.286	.275	.366	14.9%	18.3%							97	-0.5	-5.7	0.7
Israel Pineda	C	SCO	WIN	23	61	5	2	11	0	.250/.295/.393	.300	.537	6.6%	24.6%	62.5%	93.3%	52.4%	54.5%						
	C	WIL	A+	23	40	3	1	4	0	.205/.225/.308	.250	.414	2.5%	25.0%							93	-0.3	-0.4	0.0
	C	HBG	AA	23	107	6	1	9	0	.153/.215/.214	.219	.328	6.5%	31.8%							70	-0.8	0.2	-0.2
Franmil Reyes	DH	ESC	WIN	27	64	12	4	14	1	.321/.391/.625	.368	.854	10.9%	23.4%	76.1%	80.4%	34.2%	50.0%						
	DH	ROC	AAA	27	149	18	5	19	0	.219/.322/.383	.261	.533	13.4%	24.2%	67.1%	77.9%	30.3%	57.6%			97	-0.9	-0.5	0.2
	DH	KC	MLB	27	65	5	2	7	0	.186/.231/.288	.257	.486	6.2%	36.9%	69.3%	74.7%	35.2%	52.4%	-1.7	110.9	86	-0.1	-0.3	0.0
Blake Rutherford	OF	HBG	AA	26	141	23	7	28	2	.341/.390/.612	.378	.760	6.4%	17.7%							122	3.3	-2.9	0.8
	OF	ROC	AAA	26	172	16	5	21	5	.331/.395/.536	.381	.675	8.7%	18.0%	80.7%	78.7%	45.9%	51.5%			103	-0.1	-2.0	0.3
	OF	WAS	MLB	26	36	4	0	2	0	.171/.194/.171	.240	.240	2.8%	27.8%	78.8%	82.9%	49.4%	53.7%	-1.0	99.8	83	0.0	-0.2	0.0

A gifted all-around athlete, **Riley Adams** earned a second-degree black belt in karate as a 13-year-old and excelled in both baseball and basketball in high school. Alas, his chopping skills are limited to large wooden boards and don't parlay into chopping runs onto pitchers' ERAs. ⊗ It's difficult to illustrate a fringe major leaguer with power potential and defensive deficiencies, so in the extremely unlikely event **Travis Blankenhorn** is a Pictionary prompt you'll have to draw a tiny horn, a plus sign and nothing else. ⊗ Years ago, **Michael Chavis** was given the sobriquet "Ice Horse" on a Boston sports podcast because of his purported ability to hit in the clutch. The Nationals took the "ice" part of that moniker far too literally, putting Chavis into cold storage on the deepest recesses of their bench and saying "neigh" to the idea of more playing time. ⊗ You can almost see the electricity in **Jeremy De La Rosa**'s bat when he connects, but all too often it looks like someone didn't pay their utility bill. He's still very young, but runs the risk of being overtaken by the teeming multitudes of talented young outfielders in the Nationals system. ⊗ **Corey Dickerson** has made a career out of punishing right-handed pitching, but had been cruising on reputation more than results for a couple years and may have finally reached the end of the line when the Nationals released him last August. ⊗ **Carter Kieboom's** hot August and cold September gave boomers fond memories of what the weather used to be like before climate change ruined everything, but also sad reminders of olden times when weak-hitting players manned the hot corner. Ok, Grandpa, let's get you to bed. ⊗ **Trey Lipscomb** showed some surprising and uncharacteristic pop after he was promoted to Double-A Harrisburg last year, but it's his versatility and improved defensive skills that will probably get him to the majors—most likely as a reserve. ⊗ With how **Nasim Nuñez** plays defense at an elite level, fans will go buckwild when he works a walk and swipes a bag at the dish. Beyond that, they won't expect much, but his overall profile will float him as a fan favorite who inevitably bugs opposing teams. ⊗ It was a lost season for **Israel Pineda,** who broke a finger in spring training, strained an oblique during a May rehab assignment and never got it going offensively after he was activated in the minors in July. ⊗ A mere two seasons removed from a 30-home run campaign, **Franmil Reyes** couldn't manage to crack the starting lineup for two rebuilding teams and was cast aside by the Nationals in August. Even at 28 years old, it might be difficult for the beefy, defensively challenged DH to find another opportunity. ⊗ **Blake Rutherford** finally reached the majors after nearly a decade toiling in the minors, but the soundtrack to his long-awaited arrival was more sad trombone than triumphant fanfare.

Pitchers

PITCHER	TM	LVL	AGE	G (GS)	IP	W-L	SV	K	WHIP	ERA	CSP	BB%	K%	HR%	GB%	ZSw%	ZCon%	OSw%	OCon%	BABIP	SLGCON	DRA-	WARP
Cory Abbott	ROC	AAA	27	13 (13)	56	3-4	0	69	1.38	4.98		14.6%	28.8%	3.3%	34.1%	64.0%	83.2%	32.6%	50.3%	.270	.591	91	1.0
	WAS	MLB	27	22 (0)	39^1	1-2	0	40	1.70	6.64	48.7%	10.4%	21.9%	4.9%	39.2%	64.3%	85.5%	33.6%	55.4%	.351	.692	102	0.4
Carl Edwards Jr.	WAS	MLB	31	32 (0)	31^2	1-3	2	24	1.52	3.69	43.8%	12.0%	16.9%	0.7%	45.0%	68.1%	84.8%	34.4%	70.2%	.303	.440	108	0.2
Jose A. Ferrer	ROC	AAA	23	34 (0)	40	4-3	0	33	1.55	3.83		11.2%	18.4%	2.2%	52.0%	64.8%	80.4%	29.1%	64.7%	.319	.563	103	0.5
	WAS	MLB	23	39 (0)	34	3-0	0	25	1.47	5.03	50.0%	9.2%	17.6%	2.8%	55.3%	68.1%	86.0%	28.9%	74.2%	.333	.524	94	0.5
Robert Garcia	JAX	AAA	27	31 (1)	41	2-0	2	62	1.34	2.85		12.6%	35.4%	2.3%	37.9%	65.6%	80.4%	34.7%	44.2%	.358	.619	74	1.2
	MIA	MLB	27	1 (0)	0^1	0-0	0	0	6.00	0.00	45.2%	33.3%	0.0%	0.0%	50.0%	66.7%	100.0%	11.1%	100.0%	.500	.500	101	0.0
	WAS	MLB	27	24 (0)	31^2	2-2	0	33	1.14	3.69	47.1%	8.9%	26.6%	2.4%	45.6%	71.3%	83.1%	35.1%	63.7%	.297	.474	88	0.6
Hobie Harris	ROC	AAA	30	27 (0)	32^1	2-3	1	24	1.89	5.57		15.2%	15.2%	1.9%	43.5%	66.5%	82.0%	29.6%	55.4%	.355	.559	110	0.3
	WAS	MLB	30	16 (0)	19^1	0-0	0	9	1.76	5.12	46.5%	14.3%	9.9%	2.2%	35.3%	66.9%	93.3%	30.4%	63.6%	.288	.471	131	-0.1
Joe La Sorsa	ROC	AAA	25	12 (0)	12^2	0-0	0	14	1.66	4.26		8.6%	24.1%	1.7%	25.6%	61.2%	87.3%	31.1%	63.2%	.395	.615	93	0.3
	DUR	AAA	25	9 (3)	21	2-1	0	13	1.57	3.86		8.4%	13.7%	4.2%	48.6%	67.7%	76.6%	30.5%	63.8%	.300	.554	130	0.0
	WAS	MLB	25	23 (0)	28^1	1-0	0	25	1.24	4.76	52.4%	4.8%	20.0%	2.4%	40.4%	65.7%	82.1%	31.9%	66.7%	.302	.472	99	0.3
	TB	MLB	25	2 (0)	4^1	0-0	0	3	1.38	2.08	59.5%	15.0%	15.0%	0.0%	46.2%	60.4%	82.8%	18.6%	75.0%	.231	.308	97	0.1
Andrés Machado	ROC	AAA	30	24 (0)	28^2	1-0	3	35	1.19	4.08		5.0%	28.9%	0.8%	42.3%	63.2%	76.6%	33.7%	65.5%	.355	.571	83	0.7
	WAS	MLB	30	44 (0)	50	4-1	0	43	1.32	5.22	49.0%	6.3%	20.8%	5.8%	41.3%	70.8%	84.2%	34.9%	63.2%	.304	.676	91	0.8
Tanner Rainey	ROC	AAA	30	8 (0)	7^2	0-0	0	8	1.43	3.52		12.5%	25.0%	3.1%	30.0%	86.0%	77.6%	32.1%	42.3%	.316	.632	97	0.1
	WAS	MLB	30	1 (0)	1	0-0	1	2	2.00	0.00	36.4%	20.0%	20.0%	0.0%	33.3%	57.1%	100.0%	36.4%	50.0%	.333	.333	115	0.0
Mason Thompson	WAS	MLB	25	51 (0)	54	4-4	1	44	1.56	5.50	49.9%	9.2%	18.3%	1.7%	49.4%	63.0%	87.2%	28.5%	62.7%	.352	.527	94	0.8
Spenser Watkins	LV	AAA	30	7 (5)	24^2	0-3	0	29	1.66	6.93		9.5%	25.0%	5.2%	44.0%	69.5%	82.6%	31.1%	51.3%	.348	.720	76	
	NOR	AAA	30	8 (6)	26	2-1	0	20	1.92	7.27		13.4%	15.7%	0.8%	55.2%	68.4%	86.6%	31.6%	68.4%	.372	.488	109	0.2
	SUG	AAA	30	6 (5)	20^1	1-3	0	16	2.21	9.74		13.5%	15.4%	1.9%	37.8%	66.3%	88.8%	24.2%	58.9%	.403	.753	120	0.1
	OAK	MLB	30	1 (1)	4^1	0-1	0	4	2.08	10.38	50.7%	9.5%	19.0%	9.5%	33.3%	76.3%	89.7%	28.8%	66.7%	.385	1.067	112	0.0
Jordan Weems	ROC	AAA	30	22 (0)	24	1-1	6	24	1.08	3.75		13.4%	24.7%	2.1%	37.3%	65.7%	83.0%	36.1%	45.2%	.193	.393	105	0.3
	WAS	MLB	30	51 (0)	54^2	5-1	0	60	1.21	3.62	46.8%	12.1%	25.9%	3.9%	37.6%	68.2%	82.2%	28.2%	58.1%	.223	.566	97	0.7
Amos Willingham	HBG	AA	24	10 (0)	10^2	2-5	0	14	0.66	0.00		2.5%	35.0%	0.0%	44.0%					.240	.240	86	0.2
	ROC	AAA	24	18 (0)	25	3-1	0	22	1.40	2.88		11.3%	20.8%	0.0%	40.8%	69.3%	86.9%	33.8%	68.2%	.314	.443	99	0.3
	WAS	MLB	24	18 (0)	24^1	0-2	0	15	1.81	6.66	44.8%	7.8%	12.9%	6.9%	35.2%	68.6%	90.0%	34.8%	64.3%	.325	.730	119	0.0

Cory Abbott has reached the point of his career where starting no longer looks like an option and the bullpen is his most realistic hope of hanging onto a major-league role. A lack of top-line velocity and questionable command put his future in doubt, even if he does know Who's on First. ⓑ It's hard to believe that **Victor Arano** has been kicking around organized baseball for over a decade, but a series of injuries have kept him under the radar. This time around it was shoulder surgery that knocked him completely out of commission. ⓑ The opportunity for major-league announcers to mispronounce **Zach Brzykcy** in the late innings was put on hold, as the flamethrowing reliever suffered an elbow injury in spring training and had Tommy John surgery in April. He's a future middle innings dude if his stuff returns post-rehab. ⓑ A drop in velocity isn't always a harbinger of a future injury, but for **Carl Edwards Jr.** the dip and a corresponding falloff in strikeouts were giant red flags. He was shut down in June due to shoulder inflammation, then suffered a stress fracture in that same shoulder during an August rehab assignment that ended his season. ⓑ Not to the confused with the late Tony- and Academy Award-winning actor with the same name, **Jose Ferrer** throws hard and possesses a plus changeup, but his stiff delivery and struggle to consistently locate make him a LOOGY in a LOOGY-less world. ⓑ **Robert Garcia** looks like just another forgettable midseason middle relief waiver claim, but the Nationals see a pitcher with a potentially elite changeup that didn't get enough utilization in his previous locales. If nothing else, Garcia was the only pitcher in baseball to strike out contact marvel Luis Arraez twice in 2023. ⓑ **Hobie Harris** picked up his nickname when he grew up sailing with his father and grandfather on Hobie Cat boats. It was the furthest thing from smooth sailing for the situational reliever, who was anything but a Master and Commander of his pitch arsenal last year. ⓑ Scooped up from the Rays last June on waivers, **Joe La Sorsa** is a soft-tossing lefty who made his mark in the 2023 World Baseball Classic representing Italy and was a useful cog for the Nats in the second half, thanks to a plus slider he leaned on more heavily as the season progressed. ⓑ Nominative determinism might have you believe that **Andrés Machado** is a light-hitting, slick-fielding middle infielder; in reality, he's a hard-throwing reliever who has never had enough of a second pitch to stick in the majors for more than a few short bursts. ⓑ Despite all the advances in forecast modeling, weather remains as unpredictable as ever, which makes it all the more appropriate that **Tanner Rainey** is a complete wild card entering 2024 after missing 14 months post-Tommy John surgery and pitching just one big-league inning last year. ⓑ The good news for **Mason Thompson** is that he managed to stay healthy for a full season. The bad news was almost everything else, as the fastball velocity dropped and led to him being predictably hittable in a late-inning role where strikeouts are generally a must. ⓑ A helpful mnemonic to help cement **Spenser Watkins**' name in the mind: Spenser as in "dispenser," like the Pez plastic candy holder that *also* delivers treats from a predictable release point to hungry onlookers. ⓑ As a human-interest story (former minor-league catcher makes a go of it as a major-league pitcher) **Jordan Weems** is a rousing success; as a major-league pitcher Weems' lack of command has thus far kept him from being anything more. ⓑ Adding five miles per hour to his fastball got **Amos Willingham** all the way to the majors, but he's going to need to improve his slider command if he wants to be more than a fringe reliever who bounces between the majors and minors.

FREE AGENTS

HITTERS

Tim Anderson   SS
Born: 06/23/93   Age: 31   Bats: R   Throws: R   Height: 6'1"   Weight: 185   Origin: Round 1, 2013 Draft (#17 overall)

YEAR	TM	LVL	AGE	PA	R	HR	RBI	SB	AVG/OBP/SLG	BABIP	SLGCON	BB%	K%	ZSw%	ZCon%	OSw%	OCon%	LA	90th EV	DRC+	BRR	DRP	WARP
2021	CHW	MLB	28	551	94	17	61	18	.309/.338/.469	.372	.605	4.0%	21.6%	80.4%	83.1%	41.5%	61.3%	4.5	104.5	104	0.8	1.2	2.5
2022	CHW	MLB	29	351	50	6	25	13	.301/.339/.395	.347	.473	4.0%	15.7%	76.3%	87.4%	44.9%	64.2%	3.7	102.3	107	0.8	-3.0	1.2
2023	CHW	MLB	30	524	52	1	25	13	.245/.286/.296	.323	.394	5.0%	23.3%	71.8%	84.4%	40.0%	62.1%	2.1	103.2	71	0.6	-2.3	-0.3
2024 DC	FA	MLB	31	477	44	8	46	9	.257/.302/.362	.312	.460	5.2%	20.4%							89	0.4	-2.4	0.8

2023 GP: SS (119), 2B (2)   *Comps: Shawon Dunston (78), Bert Campaneris (74), José Reyes (73)*

Anderson's 2023 season was perplexing for a variety of reasons, most notably in that his offense took a huge step back from his usual standards. From 2019-2022, he put up a 123 wRC+ with .318 batting average, .376 BABIP and .404 xwOBACON. His contact-oriented approach seemed quite sustainable; his steep bat path, combined with an elite feel for the barrel, was reminiscent of the old-school model for contact hitting. His 2023 line is just not what you'd ever expect to see from a hitter this talented. Yes, there were obviously things going on in Anderson's life outside the game of baseball, but this performance was perhaps one of the most surprising of 2023. Anderson is by no means a home run hitter, but only running into a single dinger in over 500 plate appearances is historically shocking for a player with this level of barrel awareness. The league is better with Anderson spraying the ball around the park; fingers crossed for a big turnaround in 2024.

Elvis Andrus   MI
Born: 08/26/88   Age: 35   Bats: R   Throws: R   Height: 6'0"   Weight: 210   Origin: IFA, 2005

YEAR	TM	LVL	AGE	PA	R	HR	RBI	SB	AVG/OBP/SLG	BABIP	SLGCON	BB%	K%	ZSw%	ZCon%	OSw%	OCon%	LA	90th EV	DRC+	BRR	DRP	WARP
2021	OAK	MLB	32	541	60	3	37	12	.243/.294/.320	.283	.382	5.7%	15.0%	67.9%	90.8%	34.8%	65.8%	7.8	102.6	98	0.7	-1.5	1.7
2022	CHW	MLB	33	191	25	9	28	11	.271/.309/.464	.282	.556	4.7%	15.7%	64.1%	92.7%	32.9%	58.7%	8.3	102.8	120	0.5	0.1	1.1
2022	OAK	MLB	33	386	41	8	30	7	.237/.301/.373	.268	.452	7.8%	16.1%	63.3%	86.2%	31.8%	67.5%	13.3	102.5	102	0.0	0.3	1.4
2023	CHW	MLB	34	406	39	6	44	12	.251/.304/.358	.294	.442	6.2%	17.5%	63.2%	89.7%	30.9%	64.9%	5.3	102.7	96	0.3	-0.9	1.0
2024 DC	FA	MLB	35	477	44	9	46	17	.243/.299/.359	.277	.436	6.6%	16.2%							87	0.5	-0.4	0.9

2023 GP: 2B (63), SS (52), 3B (3), DH (1)   *Comps: Edgar Renteria (66), Don Kessinger (65), Bill Russell (64)*

Andrus probably spent significantly more time at shortstop in 2023 than Chicago anticipated. While for most 35-year-olds that statement would usually be followed by something negative, that isn't the case for the longtime defensive savant. DRP, OAA and DRAA all agreed on the quality of Andrus' defense. Add that to the high-level eye test, and you have yourself a player who will continue to stick around the big leagues despite the evaporation of his 2022 power mirage. Above-average middle infield defense is valuable, especially in a part-time role. If Andrus wants to continue playing, no shortage of teams could make use of his defensive skills. And if not, then 2023 wound up a very entertaining and successful 15-year career.

Cody Bellinger   CF/1B
Born: 07/13/95   Age: 28   Bats: L   Throws: L   Height: 6'4"   Weight: 203   Origin: Round 4, 2013 Draft (#124 overall)

YEAR	TM	LVL	AGE	PA	R	HR	RBI	SB	AVG/OBP/SLG	BABIP	SLGCON	BB%	K%	ZSw%	ZCon%	OSw%	OCon%	LA	90th EV	DRC+	BRR	DRP	WARP
2021	LAD	MLB	25	350	39	10	36	3	.165/.240/.302	.196	.430	8.9%	26.9%	74.9%	76.6%	35.7%	61.4%	22.1	103.3	67	0.2	1.7	0.1
2022	LAD	MLB	26	550	70	19	68	14	.210/.265/.389	.255	.554	6.9%	27.3%	70.6%	79.3%	34.7%	63.1%	20.4	102.3	75	1.0	4.5	0.9
2023	CHC	MLB	27	556	95	26	97	20	.307/.356/.525	.319	.636	7.2%	15.6%	68.3%	86.2%	35.6%	70.6%	17.5	103.0	112	0.5	3.0	2.9
2024 DC	FA	MLB	28	511	56	17	62	16	.246/.309/.411	.273	.512	7.8%	18.1%							101	0.4	2.2	2.0

2023 GP: CF (84), 1B (59), DH (3)   *Comps: Ken Griffey Jr. (64), Mickey Mantle (64), Joe Pepitone (62)*

If his life were a movie, you'd be checking your watch: Bellinger is too young to already be in the third act. It's impossible to look at the past seven seasons and not draw a distinct line between 2019 and 2020 and another one between 2022 and 2023, like one of those lesser constellations that are supposed to make a swordfish. And yet, even though last year was a smashing success by any measure, the way he got there—with an abundance of contact, even if the majority of that contact was subpar—also forces us to wonder whether it's a particularly repeatable feat. It certainly doesn't seem so, although some team is going to pay a lot of money this winter to find out. That is, after all, what makes the great sports underdog movies so enjoyable—we know the Monstars are victorious on most days, but every once in a while, Michael Jordan and his elastic arm win one for the good guys.

Brandon Belt DH Born: 04/20/88 Age: 36 Bats: L Throws: L Height: 6'3" Weight: 230 Origin: Round 5, 2009 Draft (#147 overall)

YEAR	TM	LVL	AGE	PA	R	HR	RBI	SB	AVG/OBP/SLG	BABIP	SLGCON	BB%	K%	ZSw%	ZCon%	OSw%	OCon%	LA	90th EV	DRC+	BRR	DRP	WARP
2021	SF	MLB	33	381	65	29	59	3	.274/.378/.597	.309	.874	12.6%	27.0%	77.1%	75.7%	25.1%	63.7%	23.0	105.5	121	-0.2	-0.3	1.8
2022	SF	MLB	34	298	25	8	23	1	.213/.326/.350	.277	.514	12.4%	27.2%	75.7%	75.6%	24.9%	48.8%	23.3	102.9	86	-0.2	-0.5	0.0
2023	TOR	MLB	35	404	53	19	43	0	.254/.369/.490	.370	.838	15.1%	34.9%	67.7%	74.5%	20.4%	49.3%	20.4	105.7	87	-0.8	0.1	0.1
2024 DC	FA	MLB	36	361	44	15	47	0	.223/.336/.428	.298	.673	13.3%	31.2%							114	0.0	-0.4	1.3

2023 GP: DH (69), 1B (29)   *Comps: Tony Clark (72), Justin Morneau (72), Mark Teixeira (69)*

"This could be the end for me." That was the statement from an otherwise reliably goofy and charming Belt after the Blue Jays lost in the Wild Card round.

If it is the end, not after a boat parade around Oracle Park with the Giants but after a disappointing 0-for-8 performance in the playoffs with the Blue Jays, then baseball will be worse off. His power numbers—or perhaps the stadium he played in—and his inability to stay healthy meant that he was always going to be more beloved by his real-life ballclubs than the world of baseball fandom at large. And so, the Baby Giraffe himself never earned the accolades of a Tim Lincecum, nor did he become an internet oddity like Hunter Pence. Though you could never count on Belt to be healthy, you could *always* count on him to get on base—it's simply up to Belty Bob on if he wants to put his body through the ringer again.

Matt Chapman 3B Born: 04/28/93 Age: 31 Bats: R Throws: R Height: 6'0" Weight: 215 Origin: Round 1, 2014 Draft (#25 overall)

YEAR	TM	LVL	AGE	PA	R	HR	RBI	SB	AVG/OBP/SLG	BABIP	SLGCON	BB%	K%	ZSw%	ZCon%	OSw%	OCon%	LA	90th EV	DRC+	BRR	DRP	WARP
2021	OAK	MLB	28	622	75	27	72	3	.210/.314/.403	.272	.651	12.9%	32.5%	68.4%	72.1%	26.5%	57.6%	19.2	106.2	98	0.2	6.2	2.6
2022	TOR	MLB	29	621	83	27	76	2	.229/.324/.433	.277	.633	11.0%	27.4%	66.2%	76.8%	23.1%	59.4%	19.2	107.2	109	0.3	1.5	2.4
2023	TOR	MLB	30	581	66	17	54	4	.240/.330/.424	.319	.628	10.7%	28.4%	68.8%	74.4%	22.7%	55.2%	18.9	107.8	109	0.1	1.7	2.7
2024 DC	FA	MLB	31	580	64	20	68	3	.218/.311/.393	.280	.583	10.7%	28.5%							98	0.1	4	1.9

2023 GP: 3B (137), DH (2)   *Comps: Doug Rader (75), Sal Bando (74), Scott Rolen (74)*

Chapman has long terrorized batters with his ability to snare line drives meant for outfield corners, stab at grounders with seeing eyes, and use his strong arm to nail runners at first base. Despite having an unbelievably hot April—he was hitting .385/.465/.687 with five homers at the end of the month—Chapman had to pay for all those stolen hits as the season wore on. Despite being in the 98th and 100th percentile for barrel percentage and hard-hit percentage, respectively, Chapman had perhaps his worst season by outcomes. His 17 HRs are his fewest in a full season and his .424 slugging percentage was second-worst of his career. If you accept process over results, then Chapman should be fine as he steps out on the free agent market this winter.

Garrett Cooper 1B/DH Born: 12/25/90 Age: 33 Bats: R Throws: R Height: 6'5" Weight: 235 Origin: Round 6, 2013 Draft (#182 overall)

YEAR	TM	LVL	AGE	PA	R	HR	RBI	SB	AVG/OBP/SLG	BABIP	SLGCON	BB%	K%	ZSw%	ZCon%	OSw%	OCon%	LA	90th EV	DRC+	BRR	DRP	WARP
2021	MIA	MLB	30	250	30	9	33	1	.284/.380/.465	.374	.680	12.0%	27.2%	67.2%	80.8%	31.4%	61.2%	8.2	107.7	110	-0.2	-2.0	0.8
2022	MIA	MLB	31	469	37	9	50	0	.261/.337/.415	.340	.583	8.5%	25.4%	62.7%	83.7%	32.0%	62.1%	9.2	106.9	102	-0.1	0.1	1.1
2023	MIA	MLB	32	324	28	13	46	0	.256/.296/.426	.332	.625	5.2%	29.9%	67.1%	80.6%	43.2%	55.8%	12.8	105.1	72	-0.6	0.1	-0.5
2023	SD	MLB	32	133	14	4	15	0	.239/.323/.402	.304	.573	10.5%	26.3%	66.8%	84.9%	39.8%	55.0%	14.4	107.5	71	-0.1	0.0	-0.2
2024 non	FA	MLB	33	251	26	7	28	0	.236/.307/.389	.308	.563	8.0%	27.8%							96	0.0	0	0.4

2023 GP: 1B (82), DH (36)   *Comps: Jeff Conine (55), David Freese (54), Michael Morse (54)*

Pity poor Cooper, who timed his most pedestrian season with his first trip into free agency. For the last few years, he's been as dependable and underrated as a glass of cold water in the middle of the night: decent pop from the right side, enough plate patience to stay afloat, capable of standing at first base and not muffing 98% of the plays that involve him. And for the second straight year, he even managed to avoid a long injured list stay. Sadly, all it took was a slight rise in strikeouts keyed by a more aggressive approach for his offense to sink perilously below league average. For a right-handed first baseman old enough to know the words to "Pumped Up Kicks," that's a potentially terminal problem that he needs to fix in order to keep drawing MLB paychecks.

Brandon Crawford SS Born: 01/21/87 Age: 37 Bats: L Throws: R Height: 6'1" Weight: 223 Origin: Round 4, 2008 Draft (#117 overall)

YEAR	TM	LVL	AGE	PA	R	HR	RBI	SB	AVG/OBP/SLG	BABIP	SLGCON	BB%	K%	ZSw%	ZCon%	OSw%	OCon%	LA	90th EV	DRC+	BRR	DRP	WARP
2021	SF	MLB	34	549	79	24	90	11	.298/.373/.522	.334	.667	10.2%	19.1%	79.1%	81.2%	34.0%	54.9%	14.8	103.7	123	-0.2	3.8	4.0
2022	SF	MLB	35	458	50	9	52	1	.231/.308/.344	.280	.453	8.5%	21.4%	76.9%	78.1%	31.3%	50.3%	12.1	101.5	91	-0.4	-1.5	0.8
2023	SF	MLB	36	320	31	7	38	3	.194/.273/.314	.241	.441	8.8%	25.3%	77.4%	83.6%	34.6%	49.6%	14.0	103.4	81	-0.1	-3.0	0.0
2024 DC	FA	MLB	37	375	37	9	38	1	.229/.310/.360	.285	.490	9.3%	23.4%							90	-0.2	-1.7	0.7

2023 GP: SS (92), P (1)   *Comps: Don Kessinger (69), Dave Bancroft (66), Dick Groat (61)*

Crawford was still a capable defender for portions of 2023, but pretty much everything else about his send-off, including the Correa-related events preceding it, seemed pretty unceremonious. Even his pitching appearance came early enough in the season to get buried under IL stints and an (unsuccessful) struggle to keep his OPS above .600. And the nice goodbye at the end of the season was tarnished a bit by Crawford's 15-second speech to the fans, which makes perfect sense because he hadn't made a decision on retirement but nevertheless offers a rather empty conclusion to his Giants career. He hopes to play again in 2024, but it will likely be elsewhere.

Adam Duvall OF   Born: 09/04/88   Age: 35   Bats: R   Throws: R   Height: 6'1"   Weight: 233   Origin: Round 11, 2010 Draft (#348 overall)

YEAR	TM	LVL	AGE	PA	R	HR	RBI	SB	AVG/OBP/SLG	BABIP	SLGCON	BB%	K%	ZSw%	ZCon%	OSw%	OCon%	LA	90th EV	DRC+	BRR	DRP	WARP
2021	MIA	MLB	32	339	41	22	68	5	.229/.277/.478	.263	.718	6.2%	31.0%	66.1%	82.8%	37.7%	56.8%	24.2	105.2	90	-0.1	0.5	0.7
2021	ATL	MLB	32	216	26	16	45	0	.226/.287/.513	.254	.785	6.5%	31.9%	69.5%	83.0%	38.0%	53.5%	23.6	105.9	103	0.1	-0.9	0.8
2022	ATL	MLB	33	315	39	12	36	0	.213/.276/.401	.278	.618	6.7%	32.1%	66.7%	79.5%	39.6%	60.9%	23.5	105.4	73	0.0	-1.8	-0.1
2023	WOR	AAA	34	29	5	2	3	0	.208/.345/.500	.214	.750	17.2%	27.6%	61.9%	79.5%	21.1%	68.8%			96	-0.2	-0.9	0.0
2023	BOS	MLB	34	353	45	21	58	4	.247/.303/.531	.299	.810	6.2%	31.2%	64.3%	80.7%	37.2%	55.1%	29.5	106.0	92	0.0	-3.8	0.4
2024 DC	FA	MLB	35	375	44	18	52	2	.223/.288/.435	.270	.638	7.1%	29.2%							98	-0.1	-3.4	0.7

2023 GP: CF (61), RF (26), LF (7), DH (5)   Comps: Gary Redus (61), Gus Zernial (60), Dave Kingman (60)

Duvall lives at the extremes—extreme fly-ball rates, extreme whiff rates, extreme dingers and extremely low walk totals for a power hitter—and 2023 was his most Duvallian season yet. His average launch angle obliterated the single-season record of 26.8 set by Joey Gallo in 2020. Correspondingly, his 20.9% groundball rate was 6.7 points lower than anyone else's in MLB (minimum 300 plate appearances). He also finished fourth in pull rate (54.9%) and had the third-lowest oppo rate (19.5%). His home-road OPS splits were .933-.745, because there's no better place to play than Fenway Park for a guy who hits everything in the air to left field.

Joey Gallo 1B   Born: 11/19/93   Age: 30   Bats: L   Throws: R   Height: 6'5"   Weight: 250   Origin: Round 1, 2012 Draft (#39 overall)

YEAR	TM	LVL	AGE	PA	R	HR	RBI	SB	AVG/OBP/SLG	BABIP	SLGCON	BB%	K%	ZSw%	ZCon%	OSw%	OCon%	LA	90th EV	DRC+	BRR	DRP	WARP
2021	TEX	MLB	27	388	57	25	55	6	.223/.379/.490	.275	.822	19.1%	32.2%	66.7%	72.4%	23.7%	39.3%	20.0	109.3	124	-0.1	-1.6	2.1
2021	NYY	MLB	27	228	33	13	22	0	.160/.303/.404	.193	.760	16.2%	38.6%	66.8%	70.8%	21.1%	40.5%	24.5	108.7	94	-0.1	-0.7	0.6
2022	LAD	MLB	28	137	16	7	23	1	.162/.277/.393	.222	.767	11.7%	41.6%	64.1%	73.0%	33.0%	42.2%	22.7	106.2	82	-0.1	-1.6	-0.1
2022	NYY	MLB	28	273	32	12	24	2	.159/.282/.339	.217	.622	14.7%	38.8%	73.0%	74.2%	33.1%	38.9%	24.6	109.2	79	-0.1	-2.1	-0.1
2023	STP	AAA	29	34	2	2	6	0	.172/.265/.414	.176	.667	11.8%	32.4%	80.0%	65.9%	25.0%	52.4%			91	0.1	0.4	0.1
2023	MIN	MLB	29	332	39	21	40	1	.177/.301/.440	.244	.886	14.5%	42.8%	73.1%	68.3%	29.0%	33.5%	27.0	108.2	84	-0.1	-2.2	0.0
2024 DC	FA	MLB	30	341	41	16	45	2	.181/.304/.395	.271	.765	14.0%	41.3%							95	-0.1	-3.4	0.3

2023 GP: 1B (51), LF (51), CF (11), RF (10), DH (1)   Comps: Adam Dunn (58), Barry Bonds (55), Christian Yelich (55)

Why does it ache so deeply to ponder the protracted demise of Gallo? Perhaps it's because we see the anxiety it's inflicted upon him, and the frustration of such a talented player begets a visceral reaction. Then again, maybe it's the fact that his mental approach really had nothing to do with this: that, whatever imperfections might exist in his head, the trouble ultimately lied in his inability to sustain the athleticism that once gave him the fluid bat speed to beat big-league pitchers. The best answer, though, combines the two. We feel deeply for Gallo's ruined career, because he didn't deserve it and he saw it coming, but he was helpless to stop it. In these times, what player's experience could be more hideously relatable?

Aaron Hicks OF   Born: 10/02/89   Age: 34   Bats: S   Throws: R   Height: 6'1"   Weight: 205   Origin: Round 1, 2008 Draft (#14 overall)

YEAR	TM	LVL	AGE	PA	R	HR	RBI	SB	AVG/OBP/SLG	BABIP	SLGCON	BB%	K%	ZSw%	ZCon%	OSw%	OCon%	LA	90th EV	DRC+	BRR	DRP	WARP
2021	NYY	MLB	31	126	13	4	14	0	.194/.294/.333	.224	.462	11.1%	23.8%	64.2%	81.2%	23.0%	48.5%	19.2	103.2	108	0.0	-1.4	0.5
2022	NYY	MLB	32	453	54	8	40	10	.216/.330/.313	.279	.436	13.7%	24.1%	63.3%	82.2%	24.5%	59.1%	14.1	102.9	100	0.3	1.6	1.8
2023	NYY	MLB	33	76	9	1	5	0	.188/.263/.261	.250	.367	9.2%	26.3%	72.7%	81.2%	21.1%	50.0%	14.0	100.3	100	0.1	0.4	0.3
2023	BAL	MLB	33	236	35	7	31	6	.275/.381/.425	.331	.563	14.8%	20.8%	58.7%	83.4%	25.0%	60.1%	11.5	102.9	105	0.1	0.4	0.9
2024 DC	FA	MLB	34	327	33	6	31	6	.220/.323/.341	.273	.458	12.6%	22.1%							92	0.1	-0.8	0.6

2023 GP: CF (44), LF (30), RF (21), DH (8)   Comps: Jim Busby (55), Paul Blair (55), Richie Ashburn (54)

Baseball players are, for the most part, not like the rest of us. They are physical freaks who make millions of dollars and travel in private planes and eat at steakhouses multiple times a week. But Hicks' 2023 was very relatable. Initially, he was on the Yankees, an employer he appeared to hate going to work for each day. After a few months of subpar performance, the Yanks cut him loose, eating the $40 million-plus remaining on his deal. He was then scooped up by the Orioles, an employer who gave him the regular playing time he coveted, and his performance improved. With the Yankees he was a target for scorn; with the Orioles he was just another above-average contributor to a larger machine. Baltimore bounceback aside, Hicks is still a flawed player as he hits free agency for the first time. At 34, he's no longer a good center fielder and his damage on contact didn't improve that much after leaving the Yankees. But his "never swing" approach should land him a job somewhere, anywhere, but The Bronx.

Rhys Hoskins 1B   Born: 03/17/93   Age: 31   Bats: R   Throws: R   Height: 6'4"   Weight: 245   Origin: Round 5, 2014 Draft (#142 overall)

YEAR	TM	LVL	AGE	PA	R	HR	RBI	SB	AVG/OBP/SLG	BABIP	SLGCON	BB%	K%	ZSw%	ZCon%	OSw%	OCon%	LA	90th EV	DRC+	BRR	DRP	WARP
2021	PHI	MLB	28	443	64	27	71	3	.247/.334/.530	.270	.733	10.6%	24.4%	64.5%	83.3%	30.1%	59.2%	22.0	106.6	118	-0.1	-0.1	1.9
2022	PHI	MLB	29	672	81	30	79	2	.246/.332/.462	.292	.648	10.7%	25.1%	64.3%	83.5%	25.9%	57.8%	18.3	105.1	116	-1.1	0.2	2.6
2024 DC	FA	MLB	31	498	59	20	64	2	.232/.320/.424	.270	.577	10.3%	23.4%							109	-0.4	-0.1	1.5

Comps: Mark McGwire (77), Andre Thornton (69), Paul Konerko (67)

Hoskins tore his ACL during spring training and, in one fell swoop, ended his 2023 season and possibly his tenure with the Phillies. The team held its own without him but, with a power-sapped Bryce Harper holding it down at first base and Kyle Schwarber, bless his heart, bastardizing the left field position four days a week, Hoskins' absence was felt. It stands to reason that, other than now officially being on the wrong side of 30, his outlook hasn't substantially changed. Before the injury he'd traded liners for loft, and the result was essentially an even swap. He just is what he is at this point. Regardless of which version of Hoskins appears this year, he'll probably continue to do what he does best: clobber the ball, hit roughly .246, and play a passable first base.

Travis Jankowski OF   Born: 06/15/91   Age: 33   Bats: L   Throws: R   Height: 6'2"   Weight: 190   Origin: Round 1, 2012 Draft (#44 overall)

YEAR	TM	LVL	AGE	PA	R	HR	RBI	SB	AVG/OBP/SLG	BABIP	SLGCON	BB%	K%	ZSw%	ZCon%	OSw%	OCon%	LA	90th EV	DRC+	BRR	DRP	WARP
2021	LHV	AAA	30	72	16	0	6	4	.304/.451/.375	.362	.447	20.8%	12.5%							125	0.5	-0.6	0.4
2021	PHI	MLB	30	157	24	1	10	5	.252/.364/.351	.317	.451	14.0%	18.5%	61.3%	88.3%	21.8%	65.2%	2.5	98.3	97	-0.1	0.7	0.7
2022	SYR	AAA	31	165	27	1	6	15	.237/.387/.298	.319	.411	18.8%	21.8%	71.9%	87.0%	24.4%	45.5%			116	2.6	-1.5	0.9
2022	NYM	MLB	31	63	11	0	2	3	.167/.286/.167	.200	.200	12.7%	14.3%	61.8%	96.8%	20.1%	73.3%	-4.5	98.4	94	0.2	0.7	0.2
2022	SEA	MLB	31	1	0	0	0	0	.000/.000/.000			0.0%	100.0%	33.3%	100.0%	0.0%				105		0.0	0.0
2023	TEX	MLB	32	287	34	1	30	19	.263/.357/.332	.311	.400	12.2%	14.6%	60.7%	90.1%	18.7%	73.3%	7.6	100.5	104	0.9	2.5	1.3
2024 non	FA	MLB	33	251	23	2	21	15	.240/.338/.324	.279	.388	12.1%	14.5%							94	0.5	1.7	0.8

2023 GP: LF (78), RF (16), CF (14), DH (2)   Comps: Otis Nixon (47), Craig Gentry (46), Jarrod Dyson (46)

The lefty from Lancaster, PA ended up playing a larger role for the champs than even he could have imagined when he latched on with Texas on an invite to spring training. A typical glove-first slap-hitter, Jankowski has always been a little better at getting on base than you remember. That skill, plus his typically steady defense in center, earned him a career-high in plate appearances, and that led to a career year across the board offensively. His season culminated with a two-hit, two-RBI day in Game 4 of the World Series as the replacement for Adolis García in the Rangers' lineup. We won't pretend to know how that compares to getting a picture taken with Shakira, as he did when she visited Citi Field in 2022, but surely that performance on baseball's biggest stage is at least a top-two moment in Jankowski's career so far.

J.D. Martinez DH   Born: 08/21/87   Age: 36   Bats: R   Throws: R   Height: 6'3"   Weight: 230   Origin: Round 20, 2009 Draft (#611 overall)

YEAR	TM	LVL	AGE	PA	R	HR	RBI	SB	AVG/OBP/SLG	BABIP	SLGCON	BB%	K%	ZSw%	ZCon%	OSw%	OCon%	LA	90th EV	DRC+	BRR	DRP	WARP
2021	BOS	MLB	33	634	92	28	99	0	.286/.349/.518	.340	.702	8.7%	23.7%	78.4%	81.9%	37.8%	54.9%	17.0	106.4	115	-0.4	-3.4	2.5
2022	BOS	MLB	34	596	76	16	62	0	.274/.341/.448	.345	.616	8.7%	24.3%	77.0%	80.9%	34.9%	53.4%	14.4	105.6	111	-1.2	0.0	2.0
2023	LAD	MLB	35	479	61	33	103	1	.271/.321/.572	.324	.873	7.1%	31.1%	77.3%	80.8%	36.0%	42.8%	17.0	107.3	104	-0.2	0.0	1.2
2024 DC	FA	MLB	36	532	62	23	71	0	.241/.307/.441	.306	.648	8.0%	29.1%							106	-0.5	-2.7	1.6

2023 GP: DH (110), LF (3)   Comps: Willie Horton (70), Bob Watson (70), Joe Adcock (69)

For all that was made of his demise, Martinez posted a wOBA and xwOBA that were both in the top nine percent of the league—his best offensive campaign since 2019—despite the relative ambivalence of DRC+. There's truth to both sides. Martinez ranked among the tops in exit velocity, exit velocity on fly balls and line drives, dynamic hard-hit percentage, and had the lowest mishit percentage in MLB outside of Aaron Judge. That's all to say that Martinez's results were more than deserved, perhaps because he made some adjustments to stave off age-related decline, like catching the ball out front more often to lift it to his pull side. This didn't come without consequence—although we're not necessarily claiming causality—as Martinez also became more susceptible to the swing-and-miss than he's ever been. The new whiffs seem like more of a feature than a bug, especially since slow bat speed comes for us all, but a higher strikeout percentage is more than palatable when it comes with the type of damage Martinez is doing on contact.

Whit Merrifield 2B/LF   Born: 01/24/89   Age: 35   Bats: R   Throws: R   Height: 6'1"   Weight: 195   Origin: Round 9, 2010 Draft (#269 overall)

YEAR	TM	LVL	AGE	PA	R	HR	RBI	SB	AVG/OBP/SLG	BABIP	SLGCON	BB%	K%	ZSw%	ZCon%	OSw%	OCon%	LA	90th EV	DRC+	BRR	DRP	WARP
2021	KC	MLB	32	720	97	10	74	40	.277/.317/.395	.309	.467	5.6%	14.3%	73.8%	86.7%	32.3%	73.5%	14.0	100.2	95	1.8	-1.3	2.2
2022	KC	MLB	33	420	51	6	42	15	.240/.290/.352	.266	.419	7.1%	14.5%	73.1%	87.2%	33.6%	70.9%	15.3	99.2	95	0.6	-0.1	1.1
2022	TOR	MLB	33	130	19	5	16	1	.281/.323/.446	.312	.557	6.2%	18.5%	71.2%	84.8%	31.7%	66.2%	15.2	99.9	106	0.0	-0.3	0.5
2023	TOR	MLB	34	592	66	11	67	26	.272/.318/.382	.313	.469	6.1%	17.1%	70.3%	86.4%	36.1%	71.6%	14.7	99.0	96	1.0	0.7	1.6
2024 DC	FA	MLB	35	511	49	10	51	19	.257/.310/.371	.293	.449	6.6%	16.0%							93	0.7	-1.7	0.9

2023 GP: 2B (84), LF (81), RF (6)   Comps: Red Schoendienst (73), Placido Polanco (73), Brandon Phillips (71)

"Wit, my dear Merrifield, is like a baseball game: At its best when it's quick, but quickly overstays its welcome on a hot summer day."

Just as our friendly narrator in Oscar Wilde's (somehow unproduced) play, "Lady Windermere's (a Blue Jays) Fan," noted above, our charming rogue Whit Merrifield certainly did see the heat of late summer sap away his strength. While the first-half of the season saw Merrifield return to his All-Star form, the second half was miserable. Merrifield hit just .212/.250/.288 from August onward. Entering free agency entering his age-35 season, Merrifield's best days may be behind him, but he still offers plenty of speed to infield-deficient ball clubs. As Wilde surely would have written, "It is absurd to divide ballplayers into good and bad. Players are either charming or tedious." When they're in their mid-to-late 30s, sometimes they are both.

Joc Pederson DH/LF   Born: 04/21/92   Age: 32   Bats: L   Throws: L   Height: 6'1"   Weight: 220   Origin: Round 11, 2010 Draft (#352 overall)

YEAR	TM	LVL	AGE	PA	R	HR	RBI	SB	AVG/OBP/SLG	BABIP	SLGCON	BB%	K%	ZSw%	ZCon%	OSw%	OCon%	LA	90th EV	DRC+	BRR	DRP	WARP
2021	ATL	MLB	29	194	20	7	22	0	.249/.325/.428	.290	.569	8.8%	22.2%	68.3%	80.6%	33.0%	65.3%	10.0	105.7	101	0.1	-0.2	0.7
2021	CHC	MLB	29	287	35	11	39	2	.230/.300/.418	.274	.588	7.7%	25.8%	67.0%	80.9%	37.5%	64.3%	17.4	107.4	104	0.1	0.2	1.2
2022	SF	MLB	30	433	57	23	70	3	.274/.353/.521	.310	.707	9.7%	23.1%	65.7%	85.8%	32.2%	61.1%	15.1	107.8	133	-0.1	-1.3	3.0
2023	SF	MLB	31	425	59	15	51	0	.235/.348/.416	.268	.554	13.4%	20.9%	67.0%	82.8%	31.1%	65.2%	15.4	106.8	114	0.1	-0.6	1.6
2024 DC	FA	MLB	32	436	50	15	53	1	.234/.332/.412	.273	.547	11.1%	21.6%							110	-0.1	-2.5	1.5

2023 GP: DH (79), LF (32), RF (6), 1B (2)   Comps: Dexter Fowler (63), Lou Brock (62), Luis Gonzalez (62)

By our measure of baserunning runs, Pederson was the 40th-most valuable baserunner in 2023. That aside, his season was essentially a repeat of his excellent 2022 but with the sort of rotten luck that a left-handed batter in San Francisco might. He hit a few more ground balls but also narrowed the gap between his strikeout and walk rates, while also spending much less time in the field. This latter point was vital to the Giants' much-improved defense. In 2022, with Pederson spending nearly four times as many innings in the outfield, the Giants ranked 28th in DRP, 28th in OAA and 30th in DRS. In 2023, with Wilmer Flores seeing second and third base a fraction as frequently, the Giants ranked 15th in DRP, 9th in OAA and 22nd in DRS, with the latter two marks not factoring in Patrick Bailey's league-best framing. They still ended up leading baseball in errors, which drives most things written about the Giants defense, but it just goes to show the importance of remembering that there's a designated hitter spot when filling out the lineup card.

Tommy Pham LF/DH   Born: 03/08/88   Age: 36   Bats: R   Throws: R   Height: 6'1"   Weight: 223   Origin: Round 16, 2006 Draft (#496 overall)

YEAR	TM	LVL	AGE	PA	R	HR	RBI	SB	AVG/OBP/SLG	BABIP	SLGCON	BB%	K%	ZSw%	ZCon%	OSw%	OCon%	LA	90th EV	DRC+	BRR	DRP	WARP
2021	SD	MLB	33	561	74	15	49	14	.229/.340/.383	.280	.524	13.9%	22.8%	63.3%	84.9%	19.1%	55.8%	7.7	106.0	103	-0.3	-4.0	1.9
2022	CIN	MLB	34	387	57	11	39	7	.238/.320/.374	.300	.529	10.9%	25.8%	64.4%	84.2%	24.6%	47.7%	8.9	106.1	86	0.2	-3.5	0.2
2022	BOS	MLB	34	235	32	6	24	1	.234/.298/.374	.310	.544	6.0%	28.5%	61.2%	87.8%	24.5%	53.6%	7.0	106.5	89	0.2	-2.1	0.2
2023	NYM	MLB	35	264	29	10	36	11	.268/.348/.472	.310	.623	11.0%	21.2%	64.1%	88.1%	22.6%	52.2%	8.1	108.1	118	0.2	-2.3	1.1
2023	AZ	MLB	35	217	26	6	32	11	.241/.304/.415	.289	.559	8.3%	23.0%	60.4%	86.6%	25.2%	56.6%	3.3	107.4	92	0.3	-0.9	0.2
2024 DC	FA	MLB	36	477	50	13	52	10	.233/.315/.378	.282	.503	9.9%	22.4%							97	0.1	-6.3	0.5

2023 GP: LF (71), DH (44), RF (10), CF (7)   Comps: Tim Raines (68), Hoot Evers (67), Gary Matthews (67)

There's a lot of slap involved in the career of Pham, whether it refers adjectivally to the prospect for whom he was traded, or to that gratuitous altercation with outfielder Joc Pederson. But with the Mets and Diamondbacks last season, he returned to the type of physical exertion he was originally known for: slapping baseballs. In truth, it never made much sense why Pham struggled after departing the Rays. His batted ball metrics stayed consistent, and it just seemed like his hard-hit balls found gloves at a rate higher than the league average. But at last, the veteran outfielder's thunderous slaps have been landing for hits. A respectable 2023 slashline suggests that he'll stick around for at least an additional season, helping stretch out the lineup of some postseason hopeful.

Amed Rosario SS   Born: 11/20/95   Age: 28   Bats: R   Throws: R   Height: 6'2"   Weight: 190   Origin: IFA, 2012

YEAR	TM	LVL	AGE	PA	R	HR	RBI	SB	AVG/OBP/SLG	BABIP	SLGCON	BB%	K%	ZSw%	ZCon%	OSw%	OCon%	LA	90th EV	DRC+	BRR	DRP	WARP
2021	CLE	MLB	25	588	77	11	57	13	.282/.321/.409	.340	.523	5.3%	20.4%	64.1%	84.9%	38.1%	63.4%	5.7	104.4	88	0.8	1.7	1.6
2022	CLE	MLB	26	670	86	11	71	18	.283/.312/.403	.326	.489	3.7%	16.6%	67.5%	85.0%	42.8%	72.1%	5.2	104.7	114	1.4	-0.4	3.4
2023	CLE	MLB	27	412	51	3	40	9	.265/.306/.369	.321	.461	5.3%	18.7%	69.3%	86.5%	41.9%	66.0%	8.5	104.2	97	0.3	-2.7	1.0
2023	LAD	MLB	27	133	19	3	18	6	.256/.301/.408	.290	.495	5.3%	16.5%	72.2%	87.2%	43.3%	67.2%	5.7	103.2	120	0.1	0.0	0.8
2024 DC	FA	MLB	28	545	51	9	54	13	.266/.311/.386	.314	.478	5.6%	18.3%							97	0.5	-1.5	1.6

2023 GP: SS (104), 2B (36), DH (7)   Comps: Granny Hamner (73), Xander Bogaerts (72), José Reyes (72)

Cleveland's decision to collect every single middle-infield prospect born between 1997-2000 was probably going to spell doom for Rosario eventually, but he accelerated matters through a grisly first half of 2023. The Dodgers included him in their deadline junkyard field trip, and among the one-eyed dolls and rusty oil cans, he was probably the best acquisition of the bunch. LA helped him by judiciously shifting him over to second, where his defense was workable, and handing him the platoon advantage for the bulk of his plate appearances. It wasn't quite enough, for player or for team, so now he wades into free agency as a rebound candidate whose single best statistic is probably 28, his playing age next season.

Eddie Rosario LF   Born: 09/28/91   Age: 32   Bats: L   Throws: R   Height: 6'1"   Weight: 180   Origin: Round 4, 2010 Draft (#135 overall)

YEAR	TM	LVL	AGE	PA	R	HR	RBI	SB	AVG/OBP/SLG	BABIP	SLGCON	BB%	K%	ZSw%	ZCon%	OSw%	OCon%	LA	90th EV	DRC+	BRR	DRP	WARP
2021	GWN	AAA	29	53	7	4	16	0	.196/.226/.471	.146	.533	3.8%	11.3%							124	0.3	2.6	0.6
2021	ATL	MLB	29	106	13	7	16	2	.271/.330/.573	.250	.671	8.5%	13.2%	78.9%	85.7%	39.3%	76.6%	19.9	102.1	112	0.1	0.6	0.7
2021	CLE	MLB	29	306	29	7	46	9	.254/.296/.389	.280	.466	5.6%	15.4%	75.4%	84.0%	39.2%	76.2%	13.8	101.7	92	0.2	2.3	1.1
2022	GWN	AAA	30	37	4	0	5	0	.273/.351/.333	.409	.500	10.8%	29.7%							91	-1.1	0.2	0.0
2022	ATL	MLB	30	270	27	5	24	3	.212/.259/.328	.267	.451	6.3%	25.2%	71.5%	78.4%	41.6%	56.7%	15.0	100.6	70	0.2	1.1	0.0
2023	ATL	MLB	31	516	64	21	74	3	.255/.305/.450	.300	.604	6.6%	23.6%	74.7%	77.2%	45.5%	61.9%	14.3	103.7	94	0.2	3.5	1.4
2024 DC	FA	MLB	32	409	41	13	47	3	.235/.290/.391	.286	.527	6.9%	24.3%							89	0.2	1.8	0.7

2023 GP: LF (130), DH (10)   Comps: Carl Crawford (83), Tim Raines (78), Lou Brock (76)

At least in the memories of Atlanta fans, 2021 is still fresh, as made evident by the vast number of "Eddie! Eddie! Eddie!" chants that rang out around the ballpark in Cobb County each time Rosario came to the plate last year. While it's extremely unlikely that he'll ever sustain across a full season the form that made him an NLCS MVP, he's still a productive hitter—particularly against right-handed pitching. Rosario filled his platoon role about as well as could be expected, threatening righties all season. His defense also flew under the radar as he returned to the positive side of DRP for the first time since that magical championship stretch. That stint may be getting further and further away, but the Rosario we have in the here and now is plenty capable.

Gary Sánchez C   Born: 12/02/92   Age: 31   Bats: R   Throws: R   Height: 6'2"   Weight: 230   Origin: IFA, 2009

YEAR	TM	LVL	AGE	PA	R	HR	RBI	SB	AVG/OBP/SLG	BABIP	SLGCON	BB%	K%	ZSw%	ZCon%	OSw%	OCon%	LA	90th EV	DRC+	BRR	DRP	WARP
2021	NYY	MLB	28	440	54	23	54	0	.204/.307/.423	.230	.618	11.8%	27.5%	64.2%	78.3%	30.5%	59.7%	20.4	106.9	104	-0.3	-2.9	1.8
2022	MIN	MLB	29	471	42	16	61	2	.205/.282/.377	.257	.558	8.5%	28.9%	60.7%	81.6%	31.8%	51.7%	14.2	108.5	98	-0.3	3.9	1.8
2023	SYR	AAA	30	37	3	1	5	0	.308/.514/.500	.467	.812	24.3%	27.0%	57.1%	77.5%	16.2%	47.1%			108	-0.8	0.1	0.1
2023	SAC	AAA	30	69	6	0	8	1	.164/.319/.182	.243	.278	15.9%	27.5%	53.3%	93.8%	26.1%	48.9%			98	0.1	1.0	0.3
2023	NYM	MLB	30	7	0	0	1	0	.167/.143/.167	.250	.333	0.0%	42.9%	27.3%	100.0%	37.5%	50.0%	22.8	90.8	92		0.0	0.0
2023	SD	MLB	30	260	33	19	46	0	.218/.292/.500	.211	.688	8.1%	24.6%	60.4%	84.2%	28.4%	54.6%	16.5	105.9	115	-0.3	4.3	1.9
2024 DC	FA	MLB	31	273	30	10	33	1	.214/.303/.392	.258	.556	9.8%	26.1%							95	-0.2	-0.8	0.8

2023 GP: C (66), DH (7)   Comps: Steve Yeager (71), Yasmani Grandal (69), Frankie Hayes (69)

If it spins or dips, Sánchez can't hit it and might not catch it either. Then again, after a short yet resurgent stint with the Padres, maybe those flaws aren't such a big deal. The backstop went through three different teams in 2023, going from San Francisco to Queens to San Diego (apparently he booked with the same travel agency that scheduled the Steve Miller Band's concerts in "Rock'n Me"). At his final stop the weary traveler stepped up as the starter in place of the demoted Austin Nola and the injured Luis Campusano, AKA his displaced time-traveling self. Somehow he straightened out his swing; his power reappeared and he clobbered fastballs until a broken wrist knocked him out in early September. The book on Sánchez remains the same: he's a howitzer at and behind the plate who will go days between base hits, and blocking is still something to which he takes a Bartleby the Scrivener approach. But his willingness to don the tools of ignorance, frame pitches with increasing deftness and blast the occasional moonshot should give him enough value to carve out a career as a catcher-for-hire.

YEAR	TM	P. COUNT	FRM RUNS	BLK RUNS	THRW RUNS	TOT RUNS
2021	NYY	14761	-0.9	-0.4	0.1	-1.2
2022	MIN	11847	4.8	0.0	0.9	5.7
2023	SAC	1590	0.5	-0.1	0.0	0.4
2023	NYM	303	0.0	0.0		
2023	SD	8780	3.4	0.1	0.9	4.4
2024	FA	6956	-1.1	0.0	0.4	-0.8

Carlos Santana 1B Born: 04/08/86 Age: 38 Bats: S Throws: R Height: 5'11" Weight: 210 Origin: IFA, 2004

YEAR	TM	LVL	AGE	PA	R	HR	RBI	SB	AVG/OBP/SLG	BABIP	SLGCON	BB%	K%	ZSw%	ZCon%	OSw%	OCon%	LA	90th EV	DRC+	BRR	DRP	WARP
2021	KC	MLB	35	659	66	19	69	2	.214/.319/.342	.227	.417	13.1%	15.5%	69.0%	86.2%	29.4%	67.2%	12.9	105.4	111	-0.2	0.3	2.3
2022	SEA	MLB	36	294	35	15	39	0	.192/.293/.400	.187	.523	11.9%	20.4%	66.7%	81.9%	30.1%	71.0%	17.0	105.9	120	0.0	0.1	1.4
2022	KC	MLB	36	212	17	4	21	0	.216/.349/.341	.236	.405	17.0%	13.2%	64.3%	85.3%	25.4%	73.1%	13.0	105.7	118	-0.1	0.1	0.9
2023	MIL	MLB	37	226	33	11	33	0	.249/.314/.459	.250	.553	8.8%	15.5%	70.1%	85.5%	28.5%	71.7%	13.2	102.4	113	0.1	-0.1	0.8
2023	PIT	MLB	37	393	45	12	53	6	.235/.321/.412	.258	.514	11.5%	17.6%	70.8%	85.2%	30.1%	64.2%	12.3	105.5	106	0.0	-0.3	1.1
2024 DC	FA	MLB	38	477	53	15	55	2	.231/.320/.389	.252	.482	11.2%	17.1%							101	0.0	0.4	1.0

2023 GP: 1B (135), DH (11)   Comps: Earl Torgeson (67), Wally Joyner (65), Tino Martinez (64)

We're not sure if there's a snappy acronym for the Veteran Slugger Acquired at the Deadline Brought On to Mash Before Entering Free Agency in the Offseason. (VSYADBOMBEFAO?) Santana fulfilled the role bestowed on him by Matt Arnold, offering a power bat and solid defense at first base. As with any slugger in the twilight years of his career, we'll continue to see a litany of one-year deals with non-contending teams just to see a flip at the deadline to a contender in need of an extra slugger; the exciting thing is that he's been in this role so long that some of the good teams when he started are tanking now. There's still much to like about Santana's game; given the remaining pop in his bat, if his contact rate holds steady, he'll outlive us all.

Donovan Solano IF Born: 12/17/87 Age: 36 Bats: R Throws: R Height: 5'8" Weight: 210 Origin: IFA, 2005

YEAR	TM	LVL	AGE	PA	R	HR	RBI	SB	AVG/OBP/SLG	BABIP	SLGCON	BB%	K%	ZSw%	ZCon%	OSw%	OCon%	LA	90th EV	DRC+	BRR	DRP	WARP
2021	SF	MLB	33	344	35	7	31	2	.280/.344/.404	.321	.498	7.3%	16.9%	72.4%	90.2%	35.3%	66.0%	11.2	102.0	109	-0.1	0.3	1.7
2022	LOU	AAA	34	34	2	1	3	0	.345/.412/.586	.360	.680	5.9%	11.8%							108	-0.2	-0.6	0.1
2022	CIN	MLB	34	304	22	4	24	0	.284/.339/.385	.349	.493	6.3%	20.1%	67.0%	89.1%	38.3%	67.2%	10.9	103.7	93	-0.2	0.2	0.5
2023	MIN	MLB	35	450	43	5	38	0	.282/.369/.391	.366	.524	8.9%	22.2%	66.1%	86.6%	35.3%	60.1%	13.2	104.1	94	-0.5	0.1	0.7
2024 DC	FA	MLB	36	273	25	4	25	0	.245/.319/.348	.306	.455	7.7%	21.0%							92	0.0	0.4	0.4

2023 GP: 1B (85), 2B (28), 3B (19), DH (13)   Comps: Julian Javier (68), Brandon Phillips (64), Frank White (61)

At the twilight of his career, Solano is the Late Fernando Rodney of hitters. Each year he hits the market anew, and each year, he inspires zero enthusiasm, because the modern front office is always looking for the next player they can mill into a star. There is no star here. There's no upside. He's going to hit the ball solidly but unspectacularly, over and over again. He's going to use the big part of the field and he's not going to clear the deep fences. He's going to hit it toward the gaps but rarely reach second base on the play. He's extraordinary, but his extraordinary achievement is in the field of ordinariness. For those who see past that, though, there's tremendous value, as there always was with Rodney. Solano is a productive player and beloved teammate. He just needs to be used well, and not ceaselessly dreamed upon.

Jorge Soler DH Born: 02/25/92 Age: 32 Bats: R Throws: R Height: 6'4" Weight: 235 Origin: IFA, 2012

YEAR	TM	LVL	AGE	PA	R	HR	RBI	SB	AVG/OBP/SLG	BABIP	SLGCON	BB%	K%	ZSw%	ZCon%	OSw%	OCon%	LA	90th EV	DRC+	BRR	DRP	WARP
2021	ATL	MLB	29	242	36	14	33	0	.269/.358/.524	.278	.669	12.0%	18.6%	70.2%	86.4%	24.8%	52.1%	13.6	107.5	118	-0.3	-3.0	0.9
2021	KC	MLB	29	360	38	13	37	0	.192/.288/.370	.229	.540	10.6%	26.9%	72.2%	83.0%	29.4%	45.3%	17.4	109.6	111	-0.4	-2.9	1.1
2022	MIA	MLB	30	306	32	13	34	0	.207/.295/.400	.256	.600	10.1%	29.4%	71.2%	79.7%	29.5%	50.9%	14.0	109.9	97	0.0	-1.8	0.6
2023	MIA	MLB	31	580	77	36	75	1	.250/.341/.512	.272	.711	11.4%	24.3%	68.4%	82.1%	28.1%	56.7%	17.8	108.0	117	-0.5	-1.9	2.2
2024 DC	FA	MLB	32	498	63	25	71	1	.237/.325/.457	.271	.632	10.5%	24.5%							118	-0.3	-10.1	1.3

2023 GP: DH (102), RF (32)   Comps: Jeff Burroughs (69), Danny Tartabull (62), Giancarlo Stanton (60)

A year after unusual injuries limited him to less than 400 plate appearances, Soler was healthy in 2023. He posted his best offensive performance since 2019 the way he always does: by mashing as many homers as possible. That wasn't the only way he was locked in, though. He had a career-low rate of infield fly balls and squared it up in the zone as well as he ever has in the bigs. His defense remains something more to tolerate than celebrate, but should be palatable so long as he continues socking dingers. And the dingers, boy, were they there. He led the team with 16 pops at home this past season, a year after tying for the team lead with just eight in his first campaign in spacious loanDepot Park. For a team that struggles with the long ball—Miami ranked 23rd in home runs last year, and 27th at home—he was a critical piece. In any case, Soler utilized the opt-out available to him over the winter, being well-positioned to test a dim free agent market.

Justin Turner DH/1B   Born: 11/23/84   Age: 39   Bats: R   Throws: R   Height: 5'11"   Weight: 208   Origin: Round 7, 2006 Draft (#204 overall)

YEAR	TM	LVL	AGE	PA	R	HR	RBI	SB	AVG/OBP/SLG	BABIP	SLGCON	BB%	K%	ZSw%	ZCon%	OSw%	OCon%	LA	90th EV	DRC+	BRR	DRP	WARP
2021	LAD	MLB	36	612	87	27	87	3	.278/.361/.471	.292	.577	10.0%	16.0%	67.6%	87.7%	29.5%	74.5%	19.1	103.0	118	-1.1	0.7	3.5
2022	LAD	MLB	37	532	61	13	81	3	.278/.350/.438	.313	.541	9.4%	16.7%	70.9%	87.2%	34.7%	70.5%	18.6	103.0	122	-1.0	-1.4	2.4
2023	BOS	MLB	38	626	86	23	96	4	.276/.345/.455	.304	.567	8.1%	17.6%	63.3%	90.3%	33.1%	72.8%	16.8	102.2	106	-0.5	0.1	1.7
2024 DC	FA	MLB	39	545	61	16	63	2	.263/.338/.414	.287	.495	8.4%	14.7%							113	-0.7	-1.5	2.1

2023 GP: DH (98), 1B (41), 2B (10), 3B (7)   *Comps: Adrián Beltré (76), Chipper Jones (72), Pete Rose (70)*

Turner inadvertently won the 2023 Pedro-Zimmer Aggression Against a Yankees Senior Citizen Award, one of the most prestigious honors a Red Sox player can achieve. On June 10, he fouled a ball into the New York radio booth that struck 84-year-old play-by-play man John Sterling. (Important note: He was okay.) On August 20, he bombarded Sterling with another foul ball, though the spry announcer dodged that one and it caromed off his chair.

Turner's pull-side batted balls in *fair* territory were nearly as dangerous. His 44.3% pull rate was the highest of his career—moving to Fenway Park will do that—and 71.4% of his hits were to the left of second base including all but one of his home runs. He autographed a baseball for Sterling after the first foul-ball barrage. The inscription says, "To John, no matter where you sit at a ballgame, you're never safe!" When he's at bat, the same still holds true for both opposing fielders and the fans beyond the fences.

Gio Urshela CI   Born: 10/11/91   Age: 32   Bats: R   Throws: R   Height: 6'0"   Weight: 215   Origin: IFA, 2008

YEAR	TM	LVL	AGE	PA	R	HR	RBI	SB	AVG/OBP/SLG	BABIP	SLGCON	BB%	K%	ZSw%	ZCon%	OSw%	OCon%	LA	90th EV	DRC+	BRR	DRP	WARP
2021	NYY	MLB	29	442	42	14	49	1	.267/.301/.419	.329	.566	4.5%	24.7%	72.5%	82.5%	40.7%	65.3%	8.1	104.1	93	-0.4	-0.6	1.1
2022	MIN	MLB	30	551	61	13	64	1	.285/.338/.429	.326	.531	7.4%	17.4%	71.8%	84.6%	40.0%	71.1%	12.0	103.4	114	-0.3	0.3	2.3
2023	LAA	MLB	31	228	22	2	24	3	.299/.329/.374	.346	.449	4.4%	15.8%	74.0%	88.4%	41.4%	72.1%	8.8	100.4	102	-0.2	0.5	0.7
2024 DC	FA	MLB	32	368	36	8	38	2	.263/.314/.383	.302	.468	6.5%	17.1%							97	-0.2	-0.2	0.8

2023 GP: 3B (37), 1B (22), SS (9), 2B (1)   *Comps: Carney Lansford (68), George Kell (67), Sal Bando (66)*

Another young life cut short too soon. Urshela isn't dead, but may have wished he was after his season was shortened halfway through by a pelvis fracture sustained while trying to leg out a GIDP. Sent to be with the Angels indeed. Urshela should be ready for play at the onset of the season, and his defensive prowess and versatility will find him a home, but a four-mph dip in exit velocity and a career-high ground-ball rate might make teams look askance even putting aside the old-man injury sustained at the ripe old age of 31.

Joey Votto 1B   Born: 09/10/83   Age: 40   Bats: L   Throws: R   Height: 6'2"   Weight: 220   Origin: Round 2, 2002 Draft (#44 overall)

YEAR	TM	LVL	AGE	PA	R	HR	RBI	SB	AVG/OBP/SLG	BABIP	SLGCON	BB%	K%	ZSw%	ZCon%	OSw%	OCon%	LA	90th EV	DRC+	BRR	DRP	WARP
2021	CIN	MLB	37	533	73	36	99	1	.266/.375/.563	.287	.785	14.4%	23.8%	70.1%	78.9%	26.2%	55.9%	18.3	106.1	133	-0.8	-0.1	3.3
2022	CIN	MLB	38	376	31	11	41	0	.205/.319/.370	.257	.529	11.7%	25.8%	70.9%	78.4%	29.4%	56.5%	14.3	104.5	84	-0.5	0.0	0.0
2023	LOU	AAA	39	103	10	3	13	0	.185/.340/.346	.261	.596	18.4%	33.0%	57.2%	72.1%	22.9%	46.6%			90	0.1	1.3	0.2
2023	CIN	MLB	39	242	26	14	38	0	.202/.314/.433	.212	.616	11.2%	25.6%	70.7%	77.2%	29.9%	55.1%	13.9	104.6	97	-0.1	0.1	0.4
2024 DC	FA	MLB	40	273	31	10	33	0	.215/.317/.389	.270	.568	11.5%	27.7%							99	0.0	-0.1	0.5

2023 GP: 1B (47), DH (16)   *Comps: Todd Helton (77), Eddie Murray (75), Rafael Palmeiro (74)*

It's possible that this is the last time Votto appears in the *Annual* as a player, as 2023 was the last guaranteed year of his 10-year contract extension. If this is it, let us admire that Votto went out in an extremely fitting way: getting tossed in the first inning by umpire Shane Livensparger for correctly arguing that a fastball off the plate had been wrongly called a strike. Votto later apologized to those who wanted to see him play for more than five minutes in his final Reds game, and that's admirable of him. But if anyone had to close out their career by knowing the strike zone better than anyone else, it makes sense that it was Votto.

PITCHERS

Ryan Brasier RHP   Born: 08/26/87   Age: 36   Height: 6'0"   Weight: 223   Origin: Round 6, 2007 Draft (#208 overall)

YEAR	TM	LVL	AGE	G (GS)	IP	W-L	SV	K	WHIP	ERA	CSP	BB%	K%	HR%	GB%	ZSw%	ZCon%	OSw%	OCon%	BABIP	SLGCON	DRA-	WARP
2021	BOS	MLB	33	13 (0)	12	1-1	0	9	1.33	1.50	59.6%	8.0%	18.0%	4.0%	56.8%	77.9%	80.6%	29.7%	60.6%	.286	.528	96	0.1
2022	BOS	MLB	34	68 (0)	62¹	0-3	1	64	1.30	5.78	57.9%	4.9%	24.3%	3.4%	41.1%	72.4%	84.8%	40.9%	61.4%	.335	.654	88	1.0
2023	LAD	MLB	35	39 (0)	38²	2-0	1	38	0.72	0.70	48.9%	7.0%	26.6%	0.7%	51.1%	70.6%	85.3%	36.3%	53.6%	.183	.275	89	0.7
2023	BOS	MLB	35	20 (0)	21	1-0	1	18	1.57	7.29	46.6%	9.5%	18.9%	2.1%	34.8%	77.3%	82.4%	31.7%	71.0%	.344	.530	96	0.3
2024 DC	FA	MLB	36	47 (0)	50	3-2	0	46	1.28	4.20	52.0%	7.8%	21.6%	3.4%	41.1%					.287	.544	97	0.3

2023 Arsenal: SL (85.2), FA (96), SI (96.1), FC (92.2), CH (80.4)   *Comps: Anthony Bass (53), Brad Boxberger (51), Tommy Hunter (51)*

Historically speaking, Brasier has been very good against righties. He's also been equally bad against lefties, because he hadn't had an adequate secondary pitch to use against them. In order to even out his career-long platoon woes, Brasier folded in a hard 92-mph cutter in 2023 to get up and in on lefties and serve as a bridge between his flat four-seamer and steep slider. And although it hardly missed any bats, it was his best pitch by run value, whether straight up in the air or on the ground. Braiser picking up a new trick at the ripe old age of 36 is like a septuagenarian penning a bestselling debut novel. Consider his platoon split closed.

Aroldis Chapman LHP Born: 02/28/88 Age: 36 Height: 6'4" Weight: 235 Origin: IFA, 2010

YEAR	TM	LVL	AGE	G(GS)	IP	W-L	SV	K	WHIP	ERA	CSP	BB%	K%	HR%	GB%	ZSw%	ZCon%	OSw%	OCon%	BABIP	SLGCON	DRA-	WARP
2021	NYY	MLB	33	61(0)	56¹	6-4	30	97	1.31	3.36	55.0%	15.6%	39.9%	3.7%	41.9%	65.9%	69.4%	29.4%	46.3%	.287	.703	80	1.1
2022	NYY	MLB	34	43(0)	36¹	4-4	9	43	1.43	4.46	53.7%	17.5%	26.9%	2.5%	35.6%	64.9%	70.9%	26.3%	58.7%	.241	.482	129	-0.2
2023	TEX	MLB	35	30(0)	29	2-3	4	50	1.28	3.72	48.0%	12.6%	39.4%	3.1%	50.0%	62.5%	73.3%	31.0%	36.1%	.304	.600	75	0.7
2023	KC	MLB	35	31(0)	29¹	4-2	2	53	1.23	2.45	49.9%	16.4%	43.4%	0.0%	44.9%	66.7%	61.3%	26.4%	46.7%	.327	.396	70	0.8
2024 DC	FA	MLB	36	50(0)	53²	3-2	0	86	1.27	3.66	51.5%	13.6%	37.6%	3.4%	40.7%					.292	.633	84	0.7

2023 Arsenal: FA (99.2), SW (88.1), SI (101.1), FS (90.8), CH (94.2)　　　*Comps: Craig Kimbrel (85), Kenley Jansen (81), Randy Myers (79)*

"Flags fly forever," Texas fans will say, as they watch Cole Ragans twirl another double-digit strikeout gem in Kansas City.

"First time?" Cubs fans will ask, watching Gleyber Torres send another ball into the left field seats at Yankee Stadium.

It was a familiar refrain for Chapman in 2023, the second time he was traded to the eventual champs in the middle of the season, and the second time the player that went the other way made that decision look questionable shortly thereafter. Chapman wasn't bad for Texas, but he was hardly the kind of lockdown reliever you feel great about trading away a young stud for, either, especially once October rolled around. He once again enters free agency surrounded by a ton of questions, so there's every chance of him being traded at midseason for the fourth time in his career in 2024.

Mike Clevinger RHP Born: 12/21/90 Age: 33 Height: 6'4" Weight: 215 Origin: Round 4, 2011 Draft (#135 overall)

YEAR	TM	LVL	AGE	G(GS)	IP	W-L	SV	K	WHIP	ERA	CSP	BB%	K%	HR%	GB%	ZSw%	ZCon%	OSw%	OCon%	BABIP	SLGCON	DRA-	WARP
2022	SD	MLB	31	23(22)	114¹	7-7	0	91	1.20	4.33	55.9%	7.2%	18.8%	4.1%	35.5%	68.9%	83.0%	32.3%	63.7%	.250	.520	119	0.0
2023	CHW	MLB	32	24(24)	131¹	9-9	0	110	1.23	3.77	49.4%	7.3%	20.0%	2.9%	30.8%	70.6%	86.5%	32.6%	60.8%	.282	.523	124	-0.1
2024 DC	FA	MLB	33	19(19)	102	6-7	0	89	1.32	4.64	51.3%	7.7%	20.3%	3.6%	33.5%					.293	.566	105	0.6

2023 Arsenal: FA (94.7), SW (79.8), CH (86.4), FC (85.3), SI (93.3), CU (75.8), SL (78.2)　　　*Comps: Bronson Arroyo (74), Kevin Appier (73), Chris Young (72)*

On August 29, just ahead of the postseason roster deadline, the White Sox put Clevinger and his 3.32 ERA (let's set aside the other statistics for a moment) on waivers. And yet despite postseason contenders like the Reds and Diamondbacks set to give a prospective Game 3 start to TBA, Clevinger found himself showing back up to work at Guaranteed Rate in September. Was it the fading peripherals throwing out more red flags than an overconfident bullfighter? The $4 million guaranteed buyout on his option year, one the White Sox wound up paying themselves when Clevinger elected free agency? Or perhaps it stemmed from the accusations of domestic abuse made by the mother of his children, which MLB investigated and decided not to punish? Whatever the reason, he'll seek a multi-year contract this offseason, despite not looking like the same pitcher he used to be, except in the ways that, he, regretfully, very much does.

Domingo Germán RHP Born: 08/04/92 Age: 31 Height: 6'2" Weight: 181 Origin: IFA, 2009

YEAR	TM	LVL	AGE	G(GS)	IP	W-L	SV	K	WHIP	ERA	CSP	BB%	K%	HR%	GB%	ZSw%	ZCon%	OSw%	OCon%	BABIP	SLGCON	DRA-	WARP
2021	NYY	MLB	28	22(18)	98¹	4-5	0	98	1.18	4.58	52.2%	6.6%	23.9%	4.1%	42.8%	67.3%	82.2%	38.8%	55.5%	.271	.574	94	1.2
2022	SOM	AA	29	2(2)	7¹	0-0	0	6	0.55	1.23		0.0%	24.0%	0.0%	52.6%					.211	.368	98	0.1
2022	SWB	AAA	29	2(2)	10	1-0	0	5	0.50	0.00		2.9%	14.7%	0.0%	55.6%					.148	.185	104	0.1
2022	NYY	MLB	29	15(14)	72¹	2-5	0	58	1.16	3.61	56.8%	6.4%	19.5%	3.7%	40.1%	69.3%	88.5%	34.8%	56.3%	.262	.530	110	0.3
2023	NYY	MLB	30	20(19)	108²	5-7	0	114	1.08	4.56	47.7%	7.7%	25.7%	4.5%	39.7%	70.6%	80.7%	37.3%	55.5%	.233	.578	100	1.3
2024 DC	FA	MLB	31	19(17)	95¹	6-5	0	95	1.23	4.03	50.9%	7.4%	23.6%	3.5%	40.1%					.287	.557	94	1.1

2023 Arsenal: CU (83.1), FA (92.6), CH (85.9), SI (92.7)　　　*Comps: Shaun Marcum (73), Steve Stone (72), Rick Helling (72)*

There are strange years, and then there is the lunacy of Germán's 2023. No other player over the decade prior had twirled a perfecto until Germán went 27 up, 27 down in his *first career complete game* on June 28. Of course during the start before, he got pummeled by Seattle for 10 runs in 3 ⅓ innings; during the start after his career-defining achievement, he didn't make it out of the fifth. Other than his gem, his performance was pretty underwhelming across his other 19 games, and included both a substance-check ejection on May 16 and another incident a month prior that probably should've been a heave-ho as well—especially if you ask Twins skipper Rocco Baldelli, who got tossed in protest.

On August 2, Germán's bizarre season ended abruptly when he accepted an assignment to the restricted list after entering an alcohol abuse treatment program. It was yet another serious brush with problems beyond baseball in his career; we can only hope that Germán—and more importantly, his family—emerges on the other side better off for it.

Zack Greinke RHP Born: 10/21/83 Age: 40 Height: 6'2" Weight: 200 Origin: Round 1, 2002 Draft (#6 overall)

YEAR	TM	LVL	AGE	G(GS)	IP	W-L	SV	K	WHIP	ERA	CSP	BB%	K%	HR%	GB%	ZSw%	ZCon%	OSw%	OCon%	BABIP	SLGCON	DRA-	WARP
2021	HOU	MLB	37	30(29)	171	11-6	0	120	1.17	4.16	53.4%	5.2%	17.2%	4.3%	44.9%	67.7%	89.9%	33.1%	64.4%	.264	.532	104	1.3
2022	OMA	AAA	38	2(2)	12	2-0	0	8	0.67	2.25		2.4%	19.0%	2.4%	45.5%					.188	.333	98	0.2
2022	KC	MLB	38	26(26)	137	4-9	0	73	1.34	3.68	53.5%	4.6%	12.5%	2.4%	41.1%	65.3%	88.3%	33.4%	75.3%	.306	.481	121	-0.1
2023	KC	MLB	39	30(27)	142¹	2-15	0	97	1.27	5.06	49.0%	3.9%	16.4%	4.2%	43.1%	65.7%	90.7%	33.5%	71.7%	.300	.565	108	1.1
2024 non	FA	MLB	40	58(0)	50	2-2	0	30	1.35	4.80	50.8%	5.0%	13.8%	3.4%	41.7%					.300	.535	109	0.0

2023 Arsenal: FA (89.7), SW (79.4), CH (86.7), SI (89.9), CU (73.1), FC (85.6), SL (82.1), CS (58)　　　*Comps: Greg Maddux (73), Bert Blyleven (72), Don Sutton (71)*

When *The Oprah Winfrey Show* went off the air in 2011 after 25 seasons, it created something media psychologists termed "Empty Oprah": a void in people's daily routines with real mental health consequences. While Greinke, in typically reserved fashion, waited until mid-December to announce (via his representation) he plans to pitch in 2024, the specter of Empty Greinke nevertheless looms. After nearly 20 seasons of Greinke curveballs, Greinke dingers (hit by him, not off him, we come here to praise), Greinke grunts, Greinke defense and, of course, Greinke one-liners, which deserve their own book, one of baseball's most interesting chapters seems slated to come to an end someday soon. He'll never again get guacamole, and we'll never again get a pitcher like Zack Greinke.

Josh Hader LHP
Born: 04/07/94 Age: 30 Height: 5'11" Weight: 180 Origin: Round 19, 2012 Draft (#582 overall)

YEAR	TM	LVL	AGE	G(GS)	IP	W-L	SV	K	WHIP	ERA	CSP	BB%	K%	HR%	GB%	ZSw%	ZCon%	OSw%	OCon%	BABIP	SLGCON	DRA-	WARP
2021	MIL	MLB	27	60(0)	58²	4-2	34	102	0.84	1.23	47.5%	10.7%	45.5%	1.3%	31.2%	72.5%	66.8%	37.0%	39.6%	.237	.400	71	1.5
2022	SD	MLB	28	19(0)	16	1-1	7	22	1.63	7.31	52.5%	11.5%	28.2%	1.3%	31.8%	73.0%	71.0%	29.1%	57.9%	.372	.561	91	0.2
2022	MIL	MLB	28	37(0)	34	1-4	29	59	1.12	4.24	48.0%	8.5%	41.8%	5.0%	30.4%	65.6%	67.6%	35.7%	55.4%	.306	.783	85	0.6
2023	SD	MLB	29	61(0)	56¹	2-3	33	85	1.10	1.28	40.4%	13.0%	36.8%	1.3%	34.5%	69.6%	77.2%	38.4%	55.7%	.269	.396	81	1.2
2024 DC	FA	MLB	30	55(0)	58²	4-2	0	89	1.14	3.24	45.1%	11.1%	36.6%	3.6%	32.5%					.272	.618	77	1.0

2023 Arsenal: SI (96.3), SL (85.8), CH (88.2)   Comps: Aroldis Chapman (71), Jeurys Familia (69), Scott Williamson (67)

Here's how Hader ranks among all qualified relievers from 2017, his debut season, through '23: first in strikeout rate (an astronomical 42.2%); first in strikeout-minus-walk rate (32%); first in batting average against (.155); third in WHIP (0.94, two points behind Félix Bautista, who won't pitch next year, and five behind Roberto Osuna, who hasn't pitched in the majors since 2020); third in swinging-strike rate (18.7%); and first in Win Probability Added (15.40). In 2023, he finished fifth in strikeout rate; batters came up empty on over half the Hader sliders they swung at. Right-handers slugged .217 against him. From the beginning of June until the end of July, he allowed a single run and eight hits, one for extra bases. With two strikes, batters posted an OPS against him of .287. He gave up all of six extra-base hits on the season. He is going to make his new team very, very happy in the ninth inning for the next three or four years.

Liam Hendriks RHP
Born: 02/10/89 Age: 35 Height: 6'0" Weight: 235 Origin: IFA, 2007

YEAR	TM	LVL	AGE	G(GS)	IP	W-L	SV	K	WHIP	ERA	CSP	BB%	K%	HR%	GB%	ZSw%	ZCon%	OSw%	OCon%	BABIP	SLGCON	DRA-	WARP
2021	CHW	MLB	32	69(0)	71	8-3	38	113	0.73	2.54	55.3%	2.6%	42.3%	4.1%	32.4%	78.7%	78.2%	42.1%	40.2%	.254	.566	56	2.3
2022	CHW	MLB	33	58(0)	57²	4-4	37	85	1.04	2.81	51.4%	6.8%	36.2%	3.0%	34.6%	69.1%	73.6%	34.7%	41.5%	.303	.592	67	1.5
2023	CHW	MLB	34	5(0)	5	2-0	1	3	1.00	5.40	37.0%	5.0%	15.0%	5.0%	50.0%	74.1%	80.0%	35.0%	57.1%	.200	.533	100	0.1
2024 non	FA	MLB	35	58(0)	50	2-2	0	66	1.12	3.54	51.7%	6.3%	32.4%	4.0%	33.7%					.306	.634	85	0.6

2023 Arsenal: FA (95.6), SL (88), KC (84)   Comps: Tommy Hunter (69), Jason Isringhausen (68), Don Aase (65)

On January 8, 2023, Liam Hendricks announced on his Instagram account that he was fighting non-Hodgkin Lymphoma. On May 29, having beaten cancer, he was pitching the eighth of a major-league ballgame. On August 2 he was back in a hospital bed, going under the knife for Tommy John surgery, ending his White Sox tenure and putting his 2024 season in jeopardy. By declining his option, the White Sox will pay his full salary in 2024 anyway. The move frees up an offseason roster spot for the team, since the IL only kicks in on Opening Day, and freed up some cash flow in the short term, while allowing the closer to sign a two-year deal with another team while he rehabs. Injured or not, hopeless as the White Sox might be, the AL Comeback Player of the Year did provide the team and its fans a lot of value without stepping on the mound. You can't put a price on that, until suddenly you have to.

Jordan Hicks RHP
Born: 09/06/96 Age: 27 Height: 6'2" Weight: 220 Origin: Round 3, 2015 Draft (#105 overall)

YEAR	TM	LVL	AGE	G(GS)	IP	W-L	SV	K	WHIP	ERA	CSP	BB%	K%	HR%	GB%	ZSw%	ZCon%	OSw%	OCon%	BABIP	SLGCON	DRA-	WARP
2021	STL	MLB	24	10(0)	10	0-0	0	10	1.50	5.40	48.1%	22.7%	22.7%	0.0%	70.8%	56.2%	86.1%	29.7%	68.3%	.208	.333	92	0.1
2022	STL	MLB	25	35(8)	61¹	3-6	0	63	1.32	4.84	55.1%	13.3%	24.0%	1.9%	58.2%	61.5%	86.1%	28.0%	60.7%	.268	.455	90	0.9
2023	STL	MLB	26	40(0)	41²	1-6	8	59	1.51	3.67	45.9%	12.7%	31.2%	1.1%	59.2%	55.6%	81.1%	30.0%	54.4%	.366	.535	70	1.1
2023	TOR	MLB	26	25(0)	24	2-3	4	22	1.08	2.63	46.9%	8.3%	22.9%	2.1%	58.5%	57.7%	86.0%	33.3%	65.2%	.254	.431	83	0.5
2024 DC	FA	MLB	27	47(0)	50²	3-2	0	55	1.35	3.86	49.8%	12.4%	24.9%	1.9%	58.2%					.284	.470	86	0.6

2023 Arsenal: SI (100.4), SW (87.1), FA (100.4), SL (87.5), FS (91.9)   Comps: Francisco Rodríguez (71), Michael Jackson (70), Matt Mantei (70)

If you had a life away from the internet, you may have missed one of those hallucinatory periods when fans, players, and former players all got together to argue over some fine points of baseball. In this case, it was Brent Rooker and Jeff Frye arguing over which was more effective: A blazing fastball over the heart of the plate or a more pedestrian offering that clips the corners. Because this was an argument on the internet, there was no consensus reached but plenty of hurt feelings all around. Jordan Hicks and his famed triple-digit heat are a perfect case study. Acquired for two pitching prospects by the Blue Jays at the trade deadline, you may see his dip in strikeouts as a reason not to believe the corresponding dip in ERA he had with Toronto. But, the Blue Jays also seemingly asked Hicks to pitch differently: As noted by SportsNet's Nick Ashbourne, Hicks upped his first strike percentage by 20 points after moving to Toronto and started throwing his sinker in the zone more than ever. That seemed to work pretty well from an outcomes standpoint. Now, would this be enough to settle an argument on social media? Absolutely not...have you ever *been* on the internet?

Jakob Junis RHP
Born: 09/16/92 Age: 31 Height: 6'3" Weight: 220 Origin: Round 29, 2011 Draft (#876 overall)

YEAR	TM	LVL	AGE	G(GS)	IP	W-L	SV	K	WHIP	ERA	CSP	BB%	K%	HR%	GB%	ZSw%	ZCon%	OSw%	OCon%	BABIP	SLGCON	DRA-	WARP
2021	KC	MLB	28	16(6)	39¹	2-4	0	41	1.40	5.26	54.3%	7.1%	24.4%	4.2%	43.5%	65.2%	83.3%	29.7%	59.8%	.333	.628	95	0.4
2022	SF	MLB	29	23(17)	112	5-7	0	98	1.29	4.42	56.5%	5.2%	20.5%	2.7%	42.7%	61.1%	88.1%	32.8%	63.7%	.318	.569	98	1.2
2023	SF	MLB	30	40(4)	86	4-3	1	96	1.29	3.87	48.7%	5.7%	26.2%	3.3%	42.8%	61.6%	87.9%	35.1%	53.0%	.338	.632	85	1.7
2024 DC	FA	MLB	31	43(9)	76	4-4	0	69	1.24	4.15	52.1%	6.5%	21.7%	3.5%	42.1%					.290	.549	96	0.7

2023 Arsenal: SW (84.3), SI (93.7), CH (87.1), FA (93.9)   Comps: Luke Hochevar (78), Dick Drago (75), Sidney Ponson (74)

Junis made waves in 2022 by breaking the 50% breaking ball usage barrier as a starting pitcher, and that slider usage went all the way up to 62.5% last season as a full-time long relief option. On the surface, it would seem that a two-tick velo jump for his sinker helped it play better, giving him an ERA, xERA, FIP and xFIP between 3.66 and 3.87, with a DRA nearby at 4.00. But even adjusting for some misfortune, batters preferred his 2023 sinker to the 2022 one, making more contact and turning that into more damage even as he avoided the heart of the zone better. Instead, the answer seems to be that his sweeping slider was thrown at 84 mph instead of 83 and got more whiffs even as it was thrown more often. The contact against it was a bit more damaging, too, but batters also chased it more and swung at in the zone less, so this is really just a slider story. He was destined to be overlooked in free agency and probably couldn't throw so many sliders as a starter, but Junis can go three innings with the best of them.

Clayton Kershaw LHP   Born: 03/19/88   Age: 36   Height: 6'4"   Weight: 225   Origin: Round 1, 2006 Draft (#7 overall)

YEAR	TM	LVL	AGE	G (GS)	IP	W-L	SV	K	WHIP	ERA	CSP	BB%	K%	HR%	GB%	ZSw%	ZCon%	OSw%	OCon%	BABIP	SLGCON	DRA-	WARP
2021	LAD	MLB	33	22(22)	121²	10-8	0	144	1.02	3.55	57.0%	4.3%	29.5%	3.1%	48.0%	70.0%	82.3%	37.5%	44.0%	.292	.544	67	3.3
2022	LAD	MLB	34	22(22)	126¹	12-3	0	137	0.94	2.28	55.2%	4.7%	27.8%	2.0%	47.1%	68.0%	85.1%	37.8%	53.1%	.269	.439	79	2.5
2023	LAD	MLB	35	24(24)	131²	13-5	0	137	1.06	2.46	48.0%	7.6%	26.2%	3.6%	47.5%	68.8%	84.4%	36.3%	56.1%	.250	.515	92	2.0
2024 non	FA	MLB	36	58(0)	50	2-2	0	53	1.11	3.23	51.8%	6.1%	26.4%	3.3%	46.4%					.284	.537	77	0.8

2023 Arsenal: SL (86.8), FA (91.1), CU (73.6), FS (84.1), CH (86.5), SI (90.4)   Comps: Don Sutton (79), Roger Clemens (79), Steve Carlton (77)

Through his first 15 starts, Kershaw continued to defy the aging curve as a pitcher who literally debuted the same season as the pitch-tracking era. Through that point, Kershaw ranked in the top seven of all qualified starters in K-BB% and strike percentage. That all changed in a hurry after leaving a June 27th start against the Rockies with "cranky" shoulder inflammation. Upon returning, Kershaw surrendered six home runs in his first five games back, and sat a full two ticks below his fastball's season average. The Dodgers legend was clearly operating with compromised command of his fastball-protective curveball and slider—so much so that he started mixing in an old changeup with a new grip toward the season's completion. He didn't throw any in his postseason start, perhaps because he never got the chance. Instead he suffered through the worst start of his career, a six-run, one-out disaster. He swore afterward that he was healthy. Not long after, Kershaw elected to undergo a procedure to repair gleno-humeral ligaments and capsule in his shoulder—both ostensibly real things—with the hopes to return to the mound in the summertime. Only then will we find out if he can continue to bolster his Hall of Fame case.

Michael Lorenzen RHP   Born: 01/04/92   Age: 32   Height: 6'3"   Weight: 217   Origin: Round 1, 2013 Draft (#38 overall)

YEAR	TM	LVL	AGE	G (GS)	IP	W-L	SV	K	WHIP	ERA	CSP	BB%	K%	HR%	GB%	ZSw%	ZCon%	OSw%	OCon%	BABIP	SLGCON	DRA-	WARP
2021	CIN	MLB	29	27(0)	29	1-2	4	21	1.38	5.59	51.9%	11.2%	16.8%	1.6%	42.7%	72.3%	85.2%	33.6%	58.8%	.279	.425	115	0.0
2022	LAA	MLB	30	18(18)	97²	8-6	0	85	1.28	4.24	52.2%	10.7%	20.7%	2.7%	50.7%	70.4%	84.7%	33.4%	62.0%	.262	.477	99	1.0
2023	DET	MLB	31	18(18)	105²	5-7	0	83	1.10	3.58	50.5%	6.5%	19.9%	2.6%	41.6%	70.5%	84.6%	33.9%	65.2%	.268	.468	108	0.8
2023	PHI	MLB	31	11(7)	47¹	4-2	1	28	1.46	5.51	49.0%	9.7%	13.6%	4.4%	39.2%	68.4%	89.3%	33.3%	67.6%	.268	.548	119	0.1
2024 DC	FA	MLB	32	23(18)	114¹	7-7	0	89	1.43	4.87	49.9%	9.2%	17.7%	3.2%	43.3%					.293	.535	109	0.5

2023 Arsenal: FA (94.5), CH (84.7), SL (85.2), SI (93.9), SW (83.4), FC (89.9), CU (82.6)   Comps: Tyler Clippard (68), Kyle Farnsworth (65), Randy Moffitt (64)

Lorenzen, in his first two games as a Phillie, stifled the Marlins for eight innings before completing the franchise's 14th no-hitter five days later—nearly seven years to the day after his father's passing. It's the kind of performance that prompts the eternal question: How can you not be romantic about baseball? Typically a rhetorical question, this time it regrettably had an answer. Over his next six appearances, Lorenzen allowed more earned runs than he completed innings, prompting his employer to not only pull him from the rotation in mid-September but also omit him from the playoff roster. It was a bittersweet affair, but at least he and the Phillies will always have that balmy August evening to share.

Sean Manaea LHP   Born: 02/01/92   Age: 32   Height: 6'5"   Weight: 245   Origin: Round 1, 2013 Draft (#34 overall)

YEAR	TM	LVL	AGE	G (GS)	IP	W-L	SV	K	WHIP	ERA	CSP	BB%	K%	HR%	GB%	ZSw%	ZCon%	OSw%	OCon%	BABIP	SLGCON	DRA-	WARP
2021	OAK	MLB	29	32(32)	179¹	11-10	0	194	1.23	3.91	57.5%	5.4%	25.7%	3.3%	41.8%	72.5%	79.6%	32.4%	59.8%	.318	.573	91	2.6
2022	SD	MLB	30	30(28)	158	8-9	0	156	1.30	4.96	56.7%	7.5%	23.2%	4.3%	37.4%	72.8%	81.9%	32.4%	59.8%	.292	.611	110	0.7
2023	SF	MLB	31	37(10)	117²	7-6	1	128	1.24	4.44	49.4%	8.4%	25.7%	2.8%	41.4%	72.5%	83.6%	31.6%	61.9%	.293	.554	98	1.5
2024 DC	NYM	MLB	32	51(23)	140	8-8	0	135	1.26	4.20	54.1%	7.6%	22.8%	3.6%	40.5%					.289	.558	97	1.3

2023 Arsenal: FA (93.6), CH (86.7), SL (84.4), SW (79.5), SI (93.3)   Comps: Jimmy Key (77), Claude Osteen (77), Joe Blanton (77)

On May 17, Manaea stood with his heel in the middle of the rubber and swept out over three feet to the left; five days later, Manaea stood with his heel on the third base side of the rubber and swept out a much more typical two feet. Even throwing fastballs 65% of the time, Manaea led baseball with a 1.84 FIP from May 18 through August 20. Because he had been relegated to a multi-inning bullpen role, that span only totaled 53 ⅓ innings, but that FIP was nearly a full run better than runner-up Pablo López (2.81). This was a pretty remarkable development, as to that point Manaea had yielded the worst contact quality in the league, a .518 xwOBAcon that was nearly 40 points worse than the runner up (minimum 100 batters faced). The dramatic change in delivery allowed his sinker-shaped fastball to sink more, without losing any of a two-tick velo bump from the offseason, and significantly improved his command. He then switched his gyro slider to a sweeper and tinkered with his changeup, eventually pitching his way back into the rotation in September. That end-of-season run saw some regression, mostly due to the velo declining a tick, the sinker losing its shape ever so slightly and the return of the not-so-good gyro slider. But it's still quite the transformation. It's unclear how long the 65% fastball, 25% sweeper, and 10% experimentation combo would last as a traditional starter, but Manaea can get through 15 to 18 batters at a strong level.

Collin McHugh RHP   Born: 06/19/87   Age: 37   Height: 6'2"   Weight: 191   Origin: Round 18, 2008 Draft (#554 overall)

YEAR	TM	LVL	AGE	G (GS)	IP	W-L	SV	K	WHIP	ERA	CSP	BB%	K%	HR%	GB%	ZSw%	ZCon%	OSw%	OCon%	BABIP	SLGCON	DRA-	WARP
2021	TB	MLB	34	37(7)	64	6-1	1	74	0.94	1.55	57.0%	4.9%	30.0%	1.2%	42.8%	63.2%	78.3%	37.4%	55.9%	.290	.424	73	1.5
2022	ATL	MLB	35	58(0)	69¹	3-2	0	75	0.94	2.60	52.3%	5.1%	27.6%	1.8%	40.4%	69.6%	82.8%	37.1%	60.9%	.266	.426	79	1.4
2023	ATL	MLB	36	41(1)	58²	4-1	0	47	1.57	4.30	46.1%	8.2%	17.5%	1.9%	43.3%	67.2%	81.0%	32.7%	65.0%	.348	.495	104	0.6
2024 DC	FA	MLB	37	49(2)	52²	3-2	0	48	1.27	4.15	50.5%	7.1%	21.4%	3.0%	40.2%					.295	.535	95	0.4

2023 Arsenal: SW (79.9), HC (89.1), FA (91.2), CU (73.8), CH (84.1), CS (63.2)   Comps: Stan Bahnsen (63), Dave Giusti (61), Joe Blanton (60)

McHugh continued to abandon his four-seamer in favor of his sweeper and cutter; while that may have been a recipe for success in 2021 and 2022, the ingredients just weren't there in 2023. McHugh's sweeper was nowhere near as effective, and his cut fastball wasn't getting the job done, either. McHugh's pitches were no longer enticing hitters outside of the zone, which resulted in his walk rate leaping to levels unseen since he was in Houston and his strikeout rate plummeting to its lowest since he was a rookie. It's definitely a concerning turn of events: McHugh isn't getting any younger and all his peripherals are trending in the wrong direction.

Jordan Montgomery LHP   Born: 12/27/92   Age: 31   Height: 6'6"   Weight: 228   Origin: Round 4, 2014 Draft (#122 overall)

YEAR	TM	LVL	AGE	G(GS)	IP	W-L	SV	K	WHIP	ERA	CSP	BB%	K%	HR%	GB%	ZSw%	ZCon%	OSw%	OCon%	BABIP	SLGCON	DRA-	WARP
2021	NYY	MLB	28	30(30)	157¹	6-7	0	162	1.28	3.83	55.8%	7.7%	24.5%	2.9%	42.6%	72.1%	81.6%	35.8%	56.7%	.308	.521	93	2.1
2022	NYY	MLB	29	21(21)	114²	3-3	0	97	1.10	3.69	53.9%	4.9%	20.7%	3.2%	45.3%	70.4%	80.4%	36.5%	57.1%	.271	.496	104	0.9
2022	STL	MLB	29	11(11)	63²	6-3	0	61	1.08	3.11	55.3%	5.1%	23.9%	2.4%	48.9%	72.6%	79.9%	37.0%	70.4%	.287	.511	98	0.7
2023	TEX	MLB	30	11(11)	67²	4-2	0	58	1.09	2.79	44.6%	4.9%	21.6%	2.2%	42.1%	70.4%	84.7%	36.4%	54.9%	.288	.459	108	0.5
2023	STL	MLB	30	21(21)	121	6-9	0	108	1.25	3.42	47.8%	6.9%	21.2%	2.4%	43.9%	67.4%	83.4%	32.2%	64.8%	.299	.539	109	0.8
2024 DC	FA	MLB	31	29(29)	166	10-9	0	141	1.26	4.01	51.2%	6.6%	20.2%	3.0%	43.1%					.294	.520	93	2.1

2023 Arsenal: SI (93.3), CU (80.4), CH (83.5), FA (93.4), FC (88.3)   Comps: Aaron Sele (79), José Quintana (78), Cliff Lee (77)

There's something about a lefty painting the corners with low-90s heat and mixing four pitches flawlessly that just feels right. It's timeless; it's a baseball tradition. Quickly approaching similarly traditional status is this *particular* crafty southpaw moving at the deadline and going on an absolute tear for the team that acquires him. In 2022 it was the Cardinals enjoying his 3.11 ERA in 11 starts after the trade; in 2023, Texas said "thank you very much!" as Montgomery carried their battered rotation down the stretch with a 2.79 ERA in 11 starts post-deadline. Something will have gone very wrong if he moves at the 2024 deadline, as Montgomery is one of the biggest arms available in free agency and should sign on to a long-term deal elsewhere. He certainly put a flourish on his resume with the 2.90 ERA he put up in 31 postseason innings for Texas. Montgomery offers his teammates in the 'pen a much needed reprieve every fifth day: He completed six innings 21 times in the regular season, then three more times in the postseason. He isn't a prototypical modern starter, but in an era of flamethrowers taxing their bullpens after only going five innings, what manager wouldn't love this throwback?

Matt Moore LHP   Born: 06/18/89   Age: 35   Height: 6'3"   Weight: 210   Origin: Round 8, 2007 Draft (#245 overall)

YEAR	TM	LVL	AGE	G(GS)	IP	W-L	SV	K	WHIP	ERA	CSP	BB%	K%	HR%	GB%	ZSw%	ZCon%	OSw%	OCon%	BABIP	SLGCON	DRA-	WARP
2021	LHV	AAA	32	5(5)	19¹	0-2	0	22	1.60	4.66		12.6%	25.3%	5.7%	20.8%					.313	.755	124	0.0
2021	PHI	MLB	32	24(13)	73	2-4	0	63	1.59	6.29	52.0%	11.4%	18.9%	4.5%	37.7%	71.8%	85.1%	29.8%	65.9%	.303	.653	122	-0.2
2022	RR	AAA	33	2(0)	5	1-0	0	7	0.60	0.00		5.9%	41.2%	0.0%	33.3%	59.3%	68.8%	42.5%	52.9%	.250	.375	90	0.1
2022	TEX	MLB	33	63(0)	74	5-2	5	83	1.18	1.95	53.6%	12.5%	27.3%	1.0%	44.0%	71.9%	77.6%	36.6%	57.4%	.257	.402	97	0.8
2023	MIA	MLB	34	4(0)	4	1-0	0	3	1.25	0.00	48.9%	5.6%	16.7%	0.0%	38.5%	66.7%	77.8%	38.9%	71.4%	.308	.462	96	0.1
2023	CLE	MLB	34	5(0)	4²	0-0	0	8	2.36	3.86	47.9%	8.0%	32.0%	4.0%	33.3%	78.6%	87.9%	36.5%	42.1%	.571	.867	87	0.1
2023	LAA	MLB	34	41(0)	44	4-1	0	49	1.02	2.66	49.1%	6.9%	28.0%	3.4%	33.0%	70.2%	80.0%	38.2%	58.9%	.257	.545	91	0.7
2024 non	FA	MLB	35	58(0)	50	2-2	0	52	1.34	4.46	51.6%	10.0%	24.0%	3.5%	36.4%					.289	.568	101	0.2

2023 Arsenal: FA (94.1), CH (84.3), KC (84.3)   Comps: Greg Swindell (63), Oliver Pérez (63), Derek Holland (61)

Moore has had a whirlwind of a career, which prior to 2022 included a ranking as the no. 1 overall prospect, an All-Star selection, several years as a terrible starter, and relief work that briefly pushed him out of the league. His first decade as a major leaguer spanned five MLB teams and a stint in NPB. But he figured something out in the Texas bullpen, and last season added three more stamps to his MLB passport. Moore started the season with the Angels and was their best pitcher by ERA, but joined a few teammates on a flight to Cleveland when it became clear Anaheim's venture over the luxury tax wouldn't net a playoff appearance. He was subsequently waived by the Guardians after they fell impossibly behind in their own playoff race, and joined the Marlins. Although ineligible for the playoff roster, he still put together four scoreless appearances down the stretch, helping his new friends achieve their dreams.

Hector Neris RHP   Born: 06/14/89   Age: 35   Height: 6'2"   Weight: 227   Origin: IFA, 2010

YEAR	TM	LVL	AGE	G(GS)	IP	W-L	SV	K	WHIP	ERA	CSP	BB%	K%	HR%	GB%	ZSw%	ZCon%	OSw%	OCon%	BABIP	SLGCON	DRA-	WARP
2021	PHI	MLB	32	74(0)	74¹	4-7	12	98	1.17	3.63	52.1%	10.3%	31.6%	3.9%	48.9%	70.2%	73.3%	36.6%	56.9%	.264	.598	77	1.6
2022	HOU	MLB	33	70(0)	65¹	6-4	3	79	1.01	3.72	57.1%	6.5%	30.0%	1.1%	34.2%	67.1%	82.6%	36.1%	51.4%	.293	.456	85	1.1
2023	HOU	MLB	34	71(0)	68¹	6-3	2	77	1.05	1.71	46.8%	11.4%	28.2%	2.6%	31.7%	71.3%	77.3%	36.0%	59.2%	.222	.434	95	1.0
2024 DC	FA	MLB	35	47(0)	50	3-2	0	59	1.26	4.12	50.0%	9.7%	27.9%	3.7%	36.0%					.284	.585	94	0.4

2023 Arsenal: FA (93.1), FS (82.9), SI (93.1), SL (86.4)   Comps: Grant Balfour (76), Darren O'Day (74), Justin Speier (74)

Hector was the greatest of the Trojans, but even he couldn't being killed by Achilles and dragged around the walls of his city as his horrified father and mother looked on. Neris' time in Houston was less gruesome, but he exits stage left after a season spent battling the foe he's never been able to best: walks. His 30-grade control reared its ugly head in 2023, undoing his superlative stuff and making him as hard to trust as a giant wooden horse left temptingly outside the gates. That's been the case with Neris throughout a career about as long as the Trojan War. A new wrinkle, though, was his fastball losing almost a mile per hour in velocity, though that didn't stop him from throwing it over half the time (a 10-point jump from 2022). None of this bodes well for Neris' future, though his ability to avoid hard contact remains excellent, and he can pile up whiffs with the best of them thanks to his still strong splitter.

Adam Ottavino RHP Born: 11/22/85 Age: 38 Height: 6'5" Weight: 246 Origin: Round 1, 2006 Draft (#30 overall)

YEAR	TM	LVL	AGE	G (GS)	IP	W-L	SV	K	WHIP	ERA	CSP	BB%	K%	HR%	GB%	ZSw%	ZCon%	OSw%	OCon%	BABIP	SLGCON	DRA-	WARP
2021	BOS	MLB	35	69(0)	62	7-3	11	71	1.45	4.21	53.5%	12.7%	25.7%	1.8%	39.9%	60.7%	83.6%	26.5%	54.4%	.321	.541	102	0.5
2022	NYM	MLB	36	66(0)	65²	6-3	3	79	0.97	2.06	55.1%	6.2%	30.6%	2.3%	51.3%	60.8%	82.7%	31.3%	51.6%	.276	.487	68	1.7
2023	NYM	MLB	37	66(0)	61²	1-7	12	62	1.22	3.21	47.6%	11.1%	23.8%	2.7%	54.9%	60.3%	85.2%	28.2%	56.0%	.255	.472	91	1.0
2024 DC	FA	MLB	38	53(0)	56¹	4-2	0	60	1.29	4.01	51.5%	9.9%	24.9%	2.7%	47.2%					.289	.523	91	0.5

2023 Arsenal: SI (92.8), SW (79.8), FC (88.1), CH (87.9), FA (93.4)   Comps: David Weathers (77), Fernando Rodney (76), Octavio Dotel (75)

On the whole, it was a fine season for Ottavino, as his run prevention numbers were solid and he became a reliable option closing out games for New York after their midseason trade of David Robertson. There is some cause for concern, as there almost always is when a veteran pitcher enters his age-38 season: Ottavino's usually strong strikeout rate dipped in 2023 to its lowest point in a decade, which won't pair well with his chronic command-and-control issues. His signature sweeping slider only elicited whiffs on 23.3% of swings against it last year; that's far below the 34.6% mark it's generated over the course of Ottavino's career. Even with the dip, he still for now is a reliable setup option who can plug-and-play in any contender's bullpen.

James Paxton LHP Born: 11/06/88 Age: 35 Height: 6'4" Weight: 212 Origin: Round 4, 2010 Draft (#132 overall)

YEAR	TM	LVL	AGE	G (GS)	IP	W-L	SV	K	WHIP	ERA	CSP	BB%	K%	HR%	GB%	ZSw%	ZCon%	OSw%	OCon%	BABIP	SLGCON	DRA-	WARP
2021	SEA	MLB	32	1(1)	1¹	0-0	0	2	0.75	6.75	44.6%	20.0%	40.0%	0.0%	50.0%	80.0%	75.0%	43.8%	71.4%	.000	.000	103	0.0
2023	WOR	AAA	34	6(5)	21²	2-3	0	26	1.57	6.23		16.0%	26.0%	2.0%	34.5%	78.1%	83.3%	24.3%	55.0%	.286	.544	97	0.4
2023	BOS	MLB	34	19(19)	96	7-5	0	101	1.31	4.50	47.7%	8.0%	24.6%	4.4%	42.5%	71.9%	83.0%	34.4%	57.0%	.294	.620	93	1.5
2024 non	FA	MLB	35	58(0)	50	2-2	0	51	1.35	4.55	47.2%	9.1%	24.0%	3.6%	39.7%					.299	.580	103	0.1

2023 Arsenal: FA (95.3), KC (81.3), SL (85.8), CH (84.5), SI (94.4)   Comps: Mickey Lolich (68), CC Sabathia (67), Erik Bedard (66)

Since Paxton's greatest foe has always been his own body, does that make him the victim or the assailant? Last year, he avenged himself against … himself … simply by staying off the IL from May through August and throwing so many innings. Most of those innings were pretty good! His 95.3 mph fastball velo was back up to his 2017-2019 standard. His 24.6% strikeout rate, 8.0% walk rate, 39.9% hard-hit rate and 12.7% whiff rate were all around the league averages. If you ignore the reality that he barely pitched at all from 2020-2022, his age-34 season would represent a graceful, gradual aging curve based on how well he pitched in his 20s. His injury ledger sounds like the leadup to a punchline, but living well is the best revenge—even when it's against one's own scar tissue.

Wandy Peralta LHP Born: 07/27/91 Age: 32 Height: 6'0" Weight: 227 Origin: IFA, 2009

YEAR	TM	LVL	AGE	G (GS)	IP	W-L	SV	K	WHIP	ERA	CSP	BB%	K%	HR%	GB%	ZSw%	ZCon%	OSw%	OCon%	BABIP	SLGCON	DRA-	WARP
2021	NYY	MLB	29	46(1)	42²	3-3	3	35	1.31	2.95	47.9%	9.9%	19.2%	2.7%	57.0%	70.5%	80.8%	40.0%	60.9%	.268	.465	94	0.6
2021	SF	MLB	29	10(0)	8¹	2-1	2	8	1.68	5.40	55.0%	8.1%	21.6%	2.7%	53.8%	61.1%	72.7%	40.0%	55.9%	.400	.640	94	0.1
2022	NYY	MLB	30	56(0)	56¹	3-4	4	47	1.05	2.72	48.7%	7.6%	21.1%	0.9%	53.2%	78.9%	79.0%	38.0%	52.9%	.260	.342	90	0.8
2023	NYY	MLB	31	63(0)	54	4-2	4	51	1.22	2.83	37.3%	13.2%	22.5%	3.1%	55.0%	71.2%	85.1%	36.0%	57.5%	.220	.442	100	0.6
2024 DC	FA	MLB	32	47(0)	50	3-2	0	50	1.36	4.12	43.9%	10.2%	23.1%	2.1%	51.4%					.301	.486	92	0.4

2023 Arsenal: CH (89.1), SI (96.1), SL (88.9), FA (95.8)   Comps: Sam Freeman (66), Xavier Cedeño (66), Jake Diekman (64)

Unwanted jumps in walk and home run rates led to a very small dip in results for Peralta—still, he remained a gutsy competitor, stranding 23 of 28 inheriting runners while handling high-leverage innings as Aaron Boone's go-to southpaw. When Clay Holmes and Michael King were going through rough stretches, it felt like Peralta had a chance to bail them out until he went down in late September with a triceps injury. Now the Yankees will have to consult their inner Shania Twain and decide if he's still the Wandy they run to, the Wandy they belong to, the Wandy they want for life.

Hyun Jin Ryu LHP Born: 03/25/87 Age: 37 Height: 6'3" Weight: 250 Origin: IFA, 2013

YEAR	TM	LVL	AGE	G (GS)	IP	W-L	SV	K	WHIP	ERA	CSP	BB%	K%	HR%	GB%	ZSw%	ZCon%	OSw%	OCon%	BABIP	SLGCON	DRA-	WARP
2021	TOR	MLB	34	31(31)	169	14-10	0	143	1.22	4.37	53.1%	5.3%	20.4%	3.4%	46.2%	65.5%	85.2%	35.1%	67.6%	.296	.555	98	1.8
2022	TOR	MLB	35	6(6)	27	2-0	0	16	1.33	5.67	57.3%	3.5%	14.2%	4.4%	45.2%	68.6%	90.0%	28.2%	69.4%	.307	.634	126	-0.1
2023	BUF	AAA	36	2(2)	11	2-0	0	10	0.64	2.45		2.6%	26.3%	7.9%	59.3%	63.3%	92.0%	29.0%	50.0%	.125	.556	88	0.2
2023	TOR	MLB	36	11(11)	52	3-3	0	38	1.29	3.46	50.4%	6.3%	17.0%	4.0%	45.0%	67.7%	84.5%	34.7%	72.1%	.275	.548	114	0.2
2024 DC	FA	MLB	37	13(13)	63	3-4	0	44	1.31	4.38	51.3%	5.9%	16.3%	2.9%	45.3%					.298	.512	100	0.6

2023 Arsenal: FA (88.8), CH (78.3), FC (85.3), CU (69.5), SI (87.6)   Comps: Jim Kaat (70), Jon Lester (69), Andy Pettitte (66)

We never really appreciate greatness in its time and I worry we may have taken Ryu for granted. The KBO superstar—the only one to win Rookie of the Year and MVP in the same season—came to the states and absolutely dominated. Between 2017-20, Ryu went 31-19 with a 2.71 ERA and nearly a strikeout per inning. All that work earned him one All-Star Game nod and the pride of coming in second and third in the Cy Young Award voting.

Time and its withering effects on the body stop for no man, Ryu and his amazing ramen commercials included. Always susceptible to injuries, Ryu worked his way back from Tommy John surgery to make 11 solid starts for Toronto, though wise readers of the stones will see that his strikeout rate continues to dip while his average fastball dropped below 89 mph last year. There could be free agent offers in MLB available to Ryu next year, but the pitcher has always vowed to finish his career back where it started with the Hanwha Eagles. "I haven't changed my mind on that," Ryu told Yonhap News' Jeeho Yoo. "I will absolutely make that happen."

Blake Snell LHP Born: 12/04/92 Age: 31 Height: 6'4" Weight: 225 Origin: Round 1, 2011 Draft (#52 overall)

YEAR	TM	LVL	AGE	G (GS)	IP	W-L	SV	K	WHIP	ERA	CSP	BB%	K%	HR%	GB%	ZSw%	ZCon%	OSw%	OCon%	BABIP	SLGCON	DRA-	WARP
2021	SD	MLB	28	27(27)	128²	7-6	0	170	1.32	4.20	54.6%	12.5%	30.9%	2.9%	39.0%	67.2%	82.7%	30.7%	49.7%	.296	.586	96	1.5
2022	SD	MLB	29	24(24)	128	8-10	0	171	1.20	3.38	53.5%	9.5%	32.0%	2.1%	36.7%	70.6%	79.0%	33.7%	51.6%	.308	.534	81	2.5
2023	SD	MLB	30	32(32)	180	14-9	0	234	1.19	2.25	39.3%	13.3%	31.5%	2.0%	43.6%	66.7%	79.3%	31.4%	45.6%	.256	.453	97	2.5
2024 DC	FA	MLB	31	29(29)	153²	10-8	0	211	1.24	3.45	46.3%	11.3%	32.6%	2.9%	41.6%					.293	.561	80	3.0

2023 Arsenal: FA (95.8), CU (81.2), CH (87.2), SL (88.6)   Comps: Gio González (79), Mark Langston (79), Steve Carlton (78)

Inside of you are two Snells. One is a two-time Cy Young winner blessed with off-the-charts stuff and the ability to go on Bob Gibson-level heaters; from June 5 through the end of the season, this Snell's ERA was a ridiculous 1.23 to go with a strikeout rate of 35% over 124 innings. The other Snell churns out three-ball counts and four-inning starts with frustrating regularity; prior to that Peak Koufaxian stretch, he put up a 4.50 ERA with 34 walks in 56 innings. Which Snell you get is a coin flip; all you know for sure is that you're going to get lots of whiffs (98th percentile in 2023) and lots of walks (fourth percentile). Is Snell worth a nine-figure plunge? There are few if any starters with his kind of talent, even on an intermittent basis. All four of his pitches finished in the red in run value last season, with his curveball as the fifth-most valuable offering overall (and second-best curve behind Charlie Morton's). But Snell has only twice cracked 180 innings or 30 starts. Is he an ace or an enigma? He's an ace and an enigma, which is going to give one general manager plenty of sleepless nights.

Robert Stephenson RHP Born: 02/24/93 Age: 31 Height: 6'3" Weight: 205 Origin: Round 1, 2011 Draft (#27 overall)

YEAR	TM	LVL	AGE	G (GS)	IP	W-L	SV	K	WHIP	ERA	CSP	BB%	K%	HR%	GB%	ZSw%	ZCon%	OSw%	OCon%	BABIP	SLGCON	DRA-	WARP
2021	COL	MLB	28	49(0)	46	2-1	1	52	1.30	3.13	54.3%	9.1%	26.4%	2.5%	37.6%	63.9%	81.3%	32.9%	60.6%	.311	.582	95	0.6
2022	COL	MLB	29	45(0)	44²	2-1	0	37	1.48	6.04	55.3%	6.6%	18.8%	4.1%	27.2%	76.0%	82.6%	37.1%	61.9%	.324	.662	117	0.0
2022	PIT	MLB	29	13(0)	13¹	0-1	0	18	0.83	3.38	58.4%	2.0%	36.0%	4.0%	23.3%	55.7%	86.4%	50.0%	50.8%	.296	.655	100	0.1
2023	PIT	MLB	30	18(0)	14	0-3	0	17	1.43	5.14	43.6%	13.1%	27.9%	4.9%	36.1%	61.6%	88.7%	35.8%	42.6%	.273	.657	84	0.3
2023	TB	MLB	30	42(0)	38¹	3-1	1	60	0.68	2.35	45.6%	5.7%	42.9%	3.6%	31.9%	72.7%	71.1%	46.7%	26.4%	.197	.557	74	1.0
2024 non	FA	MLB	31	58(0)	50	2-2	0	63	1.16	3.53	50.5%	8.5%	30.4%	3.7%	32.2%					.283	.593	84	0.6

2023 Arsenal: FC (88.5), SL (84.6), FA (97), CH (88.8), CU (78.4)   Comps: Liam Hendriks (62), Anthony Swarzak (58), Tommy Hunter (58)

Stephenson came to Tampa Bay from Pittsburgh in a June '23 deal and immediately baptized himself in the Rays' magical pitching waters located in the touch tank in right-center field—he emerged reborn as an effective hurler. He struck out an astounding 43% of the batters he faced while handing a free pass to fewer than six percent of those same stickmen. A simple change in approach and grip transformed his previously east-to-west slider into one with more drop, more velocity and different letters in the name, as it was re-classified as a cutter by most pitching data trackers. There is also a splitter to keep the opposite hand honest and a fastball that still lives uptown somewhere in the high 90s. The short time in Florida was mutually beneficial as the Rays got the best work of his career to date and the former first-round pick is now free to spread the good word and cash in on the free agent market.

Marcus Stroman RHP Born: 05/01/91 Age: 33 Height: 5'7" Weight: 180 Origin: Round 1, 2012 Draft (#22 overall)

YEAR	TM	LVL	AGE	G (GS)	IP	W-L	SV	K	WHIP	ERA	CSP	BB%	K%	HR%	GB%	ZSw%	ZCon%	OSw%	OCon%	BABIP	SLGCON	DRA-	WARP
2021	NYM	MLB	30	33(33)	179	10-13	0	158	1.15	3.02	54.9%	6.0%	21.6%	2.3%	49.5%	67.7%	84.8%	35.2%	57.9%	.289	.475	82	3.4
2022	CHC	MLB	31	25(25)	138²	6-7	0	119	1.15	3.50	56.0%	6.3%	20.9%	2.8%	51.5%	65.0%	88.4%	32.2%	62.2%	.272	.488	86	2.3
2023	CHC	MLB	32	27(25)	136²	10-9	0	119	1.26	3.95	47.3%	9.0%	20.7%	1.6%	57.4%	67.3%	88.2%	31.3%	63.9%	.283	.435	94	2.0
2024 DC	FA	MLB	33	26(26)	142¹	9-8	0	114	1.31	3.94	51.6%	7.9%	18.8%	2.3%	53.9%					.293	.478	90	2.0

2023 Arsenal: SI (91.6), SW (84.9), FC (90.1), FA (92.3), CH (86.7), SL (86.1)   Comps: Roy Oswalt (78), Tim Hudson (77), Johnny Cueto (77)

You can draw the line on Stroman's season through June 21, coincidentally the exact midpoint of his season. The night before, in start no. 16, he'd shut out the Pirates for seven innings, dropping his ERA to 2.28 with a 60% ground-ball rate. He only got through six frames once in his 11 starts after that, trudging through an ugly July before acquiescing to an IL stint to deal with hip inflammation and some right rib cartilage fracture. He even pitched a couple times out of the bullpen, clearly broken but with his team in dire need of help; he posted an 8.29 ERA and got 51.5% of balls on the ground the rest of the way. Neither side of the coin is typical of Stroman, who's probably the most consistent starter, by DRA, in baseball. While he's gotten nicked up some more in his 30s, he might be the safest bet among the pitchers on the market this winter.

Alex Wood LHP Born: 01/12/91 Age: 33 Height: 6'4" Weight: 215 Origin: Round 2, 2012 Draft (#85 overall)

YEAR	TM	LVL	AGE	G (GS)	IP	W-L	SV	K	WHIP	ERA	CSP	BB%	K%	HR%	GB%	ZSw%	ZCon%	OSw%	OCon%	BABIP	SLGCON	DRA-	WARP
2021	SF	MLB	30	26(26)	138²	10-4	0	152	1.18	3.83	54.2%	6.7%	26.0%	2.4%	50.0%	63.5%	82.7%	34.3%	57.9%	.305	.523	83	2.6
2022	SF	MLB	31	26(26)	130²	8-12	0	131	1.24	5.10	53.2%	5.4%	23.6%	3.1%	48.7%	66.3%	82.8%	34.1%	63.4%	.317	.550	100	1.3
2023	SAC	AAA	32	2(2)	6²	0-1	0	2	1.50	2.70		3.6%	7.1%	0.0%	36.0%	76.1%	91.4%	24.5%	76.9%	.360	.440	115	0.0
2023	SF	MLB	32	29(12)	97²	5-5	0	74	1.43	4.33	46.9%	9.8%	17.2%	2.1%	44.6%	69.7%	84.3%	29.6%	68.9%	.303	.525	122	0.0
2024 DC	FA	MLB	33	39(19)	113¹	6-7	0	96	1.37	4.70	51.0%	7.7%	19.4%	2.8%	45.7%					.306	.526	105	0.6

2023 Arsenal: SI (91.6), CH (85.2), SL (82.6)   Comps: Mike Hampton (72), Johnny Podres (71), Bob Knepper (69)

In 2021, Wood had a solid sinker and a good slider. In 2022, Wood had a solid sinker and a good changeup, as well as some rough looks that produced a 5.10 ERA. In 2023, Wood had a solid sinker that he controlled worse. It's pretty difficult to watch 97 ⅔ innings of a pitcher with a 17.2% strikeout rate and 9.8% walk rate, both career-worsts if not for his 2015 K-rate. The velo was down a tick, too, and Wood's slider transformed into a slurvy beast that regularly ended in an uncompetitive location. He was still within shouting distance of league-average run prevention, but it's not clear that he'll get a guaranteed MLB rotation spot for 2024, wherever he lands.

Brandon Woodruff RHP

Born: 02/10/93   Age: 31   Height: 6'4"   Weight: 244   Origin: Round 11, 2014 Draft (#326 overall)

YEAR	TM	LVL	AGE	G (GS)	IP	W-L	SV	K	WHIP	ERA	CSP	BB%	K%	HR%	GB%	ZSw%	ZCon%	OSw%	OCon%	BABIP	SLGCON	DRA-	WARP
2021	MIL	MLB	28	30(30)	179¹	9-10	0	211	0.96	2.56	55.3%	6.1%	29.8%	2.5%	41.6%	70.1%	78.6%	35.5%	60.8%	.264	.469	71	4.4
2022	MIL	MLB	29	27(27)	153¹	13-4	0	190	1.07	3.05	54.5%	6.8%	30.6%	2.9%	37.4%	69.1%	79.2%	35.0%	54.1%	.287	.550	76	3.4
2023	WIS	A+	30	2(2)	7	0-0	0	7	0.86	1.29		0.0%	28.0%	0.0%	55.6%					.333	.389	90	0.1
2023	MIL	MLB	30	11(11)	67	5-1	0	74	0.82	2.28	51.5%	5.9%	29.2%	3.6%	36.0%	68.9%	78.0%	33.9%	60.9%	.204	.472	87	1.3
2024 non	FA	MLB	31	58(0)	50	2-2	0	57	1.16	3.61	53.5%	6.9%	27.9%	3.5%	39.3%					.292	.571	86	0.6

2023 Arsenal: FA (96), SI (95), CH (85.9), SL (86.7), KC (83.1)   Comps: Adam Wainwright (87), Stephen Strasburg (86), Bob Gibson (85)

Do you remember Woodruff's complete-game shutout? The Brewers' first in over two years? No? Put this book down. Find some video. Grab a refreshing beverage and come back to this later. Woodruff threw nine strong innings versus the Marlins on September 11, and followed that performance with a quality start. (Okay. Admittedly, we started in the middle of this story.) Woodruff missed the first four months of the season with a subscapular shoulder injury, arriving just in time to save Milwaukee's season. To the chagrin fans and the severe detriment of the Brewers' playoff hopes, he was shut down on the eve of the Wild Card, and his team was shut down shortly thereafter. The two-time All-Star underwent surgery in October to repair the anterior capsule in his right shoulder. We won't see much of Woodruff in 2024, if any.

The Road to Sin City is Paved with Bad Intentions

by Marc Normandin

Let's set aside, for the sake of admitting the gap between when this essay was written and edited and when you'll actually be reading it, that it's unclear whether or not the Oakland A's will actually become the Las Vegas A's, or if the last year has just been a very infuriating waste of everyone's time. That the move was approved by Major League Baseball's 30 owners at their annual offseason meetings is enough for our purposes: The Athletics, and their owner John Fisher, received the blessing they needed to pack up the furniture and head a little ways east, where they'll be the second-most popular baseball team in town behind the Los Angeles Dodgers, in the smallest media-market in the league, squeezed into a 30,000-seat park that will be too small the moment the A's create a product anyone would actually want to see.

Given the way the A's have been run for decades now—and especially the somehow even more miserly way they've been run since the revenue-sharing tap was shut off[1] by the 2016 collective bargaining agreement—"a product anyone would actually want to see" isn't something you'll want to bet money on, even if you'd be in the city built for that purpose. So maybe that's not a concern anyone will actually need to have. The real problem here isn't the specifics, but the generalities; regardless of why, or for how much, a social contract has been broken with the approval of the A's relocation. And with the way MLB's current class of owners zeroes in on any exploitable bit of, well, *anything*, it's not difficult not to imagine that threats to relocate are going to become increasingly common, now that everyone has watched Fisher orchestrate his own departure from Oakland simply by being a guy who lies as often as he pockets other people's tax payments.

The last team to relocate in Major League Baseball was the Montreal Expos, which became the Washington Nationals. That was never going to be the start of a trend, though, as it was just a broken situation which MLB made worse in different ways than with the A's. The Expos peaked in popularity in the early '80s, made the postseason exactly one time—during the strike-shortened and odd 1981 campaign—and their lone first-place finish came during another strike year, 1994, that famously ended without a postseason. That came in the midst of an attendance resurgence, and it lasted a few years more despite the ensuing decline, but once Greatest Living Pitcher™ and 1997 Cy Young recipient Pedro Martinez was dealt to the Red Sox

for prospects, attendance cratered. Montreal would only exceed one million paying customers once more before packing up after the 2004 season and heading south.

Montreal was *maybe* too far gone before MLB figured out the magic formulas for revenue-sharing that allowed bad teams no one wanted to watch to still make absurd amounts of money. Not to excuse the MLB-led takeover of the club that allowed for a game of musical chairs among owners and the migration to Washington D.C., but the context was at least a little different in 2004 than it is now, two decades later. (Outside of the desire for a new ballpark to be built on someone else's dime, anyway.) The A's had no such issues, however. They refused to spend when times were a little tough decades ago, and then kept that up even as times stopped being so tough, thanks to the kind of bottom line backstopping provided by things like MLBAM (and its sale), RSN and national television boosts, and other collectively bargained benefits that were never available to the same magnitude for the Expos. The franchise then got pissy when the rest of the owners agreed that they didn't deserve revenue-sharing checks just because they shared a densely populated part of California featuring 7,000 square miles and 7.5 million people with another team, and this even though their owner really, really wanted to get those checks.

With apologies to the surviving fans of the Expos, the last *true* relocation for our purposes—performed by an owner of a team and not just MLB attempting to solve a problem partially of its own making—was in 1971, when the Washington Senators became the Texas Rangers. Two years prior, the Seattle Pilots became the Milwaukee Brewers, and two years before that, the Kansas City Athletics shipped off to Oakland—amusingly, a major reason for the move was to play in a larger market[2], which the Bay Area provided even then despite the presence of the Giants, who had moved from New York a decade prior. Two years before that, the Milwaukee Braves became the Atlanta Braves, which had been what necessitated the push for another Milwaukee club to arrive, and five years before that, the original Senators left for Minnesota to become the Twins. The Brooklyn Dodgers headed west for Los Angeles in '57, the same year the Giants went to San Francisco. The Philadelphia Athletics had become the Kansas City A's just 13 years before they skipped town a second time, the St. Louis Browns headed east to become the Baltimore Orioles a year before that, and the move that kick-started this whole two-decade rush of relocation came in 1952, when the Boston Braves moved to Milwaukee. You couldn't tell the teams without a scorecard. Before all this, the last relocation in MLB had come in 1901, when the Milwaukee Brewers—no, not that one—moved to St. Louis to become the Browns.

In fact, that was the lone relocation in league history until that enormous wave of them in the '50s and '60s: Every other major change was due to a team simply shuttering due to disinterest, a league folding or someone in charge deciding New York needed a team more than Baltimore did, but that New York did not need the team Baltimore had. This is all to explain that this sort of thing wasn't normal until it was, with many decades passing before it became the norm, and also to note that MLB actually *did* put a stop to this constant shuffling.

Until now. Oakland may prove to be another Montreal, an isolated incident. But at the very least, owners like the White Sox' Jerry Reinsdorf[3] are going to make threats that, to local public officials, will feel far more credible than they did prior to Fisher's exodus. And local public officials, as a rule, do not need any help being convinced to do what sports teams want: This change in approach will exhaust what little fight does exist within their halls.

Given how regularly MLB's teams now demand nine-figure bounties of public subsidies[4] in order to pay for their new ballparks, these threats to relocate can't be ignored as they were before. It was clear the Rays weren't actually going to move, that their weirdo scheme to split the season between Montreal and St. Petersburg was a desperation move thrown out to prompt their hometown to blink, or maybe get Tampa proper's attention.

Now, though? Reinsdorf probably won't actually move the White Sox to Nashville, no matter how many lunches he has with the mayor of that city, but other owners might be happy to make good on the threat if they think the situation merits it. John Angelos, who moves with all the political acumen of a toddler demanding chocolate milk, bargained his way into a parcel of the warehouse district outside Camden. Rays co-president Brian Auld threatened to quash a ballpark deal should St. Petersburg, where the stadium is located, desire their name be on the jersey. Meanwhile, Wisconsin governor Tony Evers approved $500 million in public aid for renovations, little of which will actually go toward renovations. As Rob Baade, a retired economics professor, told the *Wisconsin State Journal*[5], "The new stadium model is one that spills over the stadium walls."

Everything about the A's moving to Vegas is going to be worse for the team itself, given the smaller population, smaller park and smaller media market. But it allows Fisher to play god-king in a state whose largest newspaper publishes specifically to make men like him feel special, and he also gets his precious revenue-sharing checks back, seemingly forever, by heading to a market as small as he likes to pretend Oakland is. Fisher isn't the only owner who, if given the opportunity, would be happy to prove themselves to be as terrible and self-centered, if it guaranteed they were also paid easy money for the privilege.

And what is MLB going to tell those teams if that occurs, and their home city calls their bluff enough for a deal to be made under cover of night, or the equipment trucks rerouted on their way back from spring training? No, you're not allowed to? John Fisher is a special boy just like *The Las Vegas-Review Journal* wrote in their latest issue dedicated to him, and therefore gets special treatment? Remember, MLB is its owners: Just like with Fisher, they'll allow it, because they want to leave the door open for their own machinations when the opportunity presents. The A's moving to Oakland is bad for business, both in terms of public relations for the league, and in the strangulation of a large and devoted fanbase, and yet, here we are. What's to stop all of this from happening again, maybe with more subtlety than Fisher is capable of, but with the end result otherwise the same?

The answer is "nothing," unless Congress intervenes, anyway. And they very well could, given that MLB commissioner Rob Manfred used the need for keeping teams from relocating as the most significant reason that the league needed to retain the antitrust exemption established for them over a century ago. MLB waived the A's relocation fee to make their move from Oakland to Las Vegas that much simpler for Fisher, a fact that did not go unnoticed by California Representative Barbara Lee[6] this past summer. With MLB still in the hot seat located in the Senate chambers[7], expect more questions about what the antitrust exemption is and is not for, now that the central premise of the league's defense of it was ignored by Manfred and co. at the first opportunity. While sabres have been rattled, and bought off, before, one hopes the league can only say one thing and do another for so long in this arena before an adult, any adult, puts a stop to it.

That's not as dispiriting a paragraph ender as it would have been a few years ago, with the league's owners on the defensive. The MLB Players Association managed to repel multiple significant attacks on labor during the shortened 2020 season and in the lockout that followed the 2021 campaign, before bringing organized minor leaguers under its umbrella for the long overdue minor-league players union a year after that. The league *can't* just do what it wants all the time; it *can* be defeated when challenged.

Maybe, similarly, someone or some group with the power to do something about the John Fishers of the world will actually utilize said power, avoiding another chain reaction of relocation—or relocation threats designed to extract wealth from the lower classes to the upper one. We can hope, at least, in the same way we can hope that, between the writing of this and the reading of it, Fisher has already been foiled somehow. Perhaps it's by a failure to secure the hundreds of millions of dollars in private financing he needs for the park to be built, or because the political action committee, Schools Over Stadiums, is right about Nevada's citizenry not being thrilled about the allocation of what's really $600 million in public funds, or simply because the Senate actually manages to put their foot down on the antitrust exemption instead of merely teasing its removal. Something could give, is the point, and something *has* to. Otherwise, the relocation seal truly will have been broken, and we aren't going to like what comes crawling out from behind it any more than all those newly baseball-less cities of the mid-20th century did.

—Marc Normandin is an author of Baseball Prospectus.

1. "The A's Could Have Made Money in Oakland"
https://www.baseballprospectus.com/news/article/83419/prospectus-feature-the-as-could-have-made-money-in-oakland/

2. "Losing a sports team: The relocation of the Kansas City Athletics"
https://www.royalsreview.com/2016/1/20/10761476/losing-a-sports-team-the-relocation-of-the-kansas-city-athletics/

3. "You don't have to buy what Jerry Reinsdorf is selling"
https://www.marcnormandin.com/2023/12/08/jerry-reinsdorf-white-sox-nashville/

4. "The Stadium Schemes Keep Getting Bigger"
https://www.baseballprospectus.com/news/article/84890/prospectus-feature-the-stadium-schemes-keep-getting-bigger-royals-brewers-diamondbacks-orioles/

5. "Milwaukee Brewers deal is part of costly trend of publicly funded stadium construction projects"
https://madison.com/news/local/government-politics/professional-stadiums-public-funding-trend/article_2ba24bcc-a20a-11ee-827e-9b988c923455.html

6. "The A's relocation and MLB's antitrust exemption don't fit together"
https://www.marcnormandin.com/2023/06/12/the-as-relocation-and-mlbs-antitrust-exemption-dont-fit-together/

7. "The Senate Has Some Labor Questions for Rob Manfred"
https://www.baseballprospectus.com/news/article/86750/the-senate-has-some-labor-questions-for-rob-manfred/

Men, How Often Do You Think About Roman Anthony?

by Jarrett Seidler

Roman Anthony endured a dismal April last year. Aggressively assigned to Low-A Salem in the Carolina League as a prep second-rounder, the then-18-year-old Red Sox outfield prospect hit just .200 with a .250 slugging percentage to start the season, and went on an 0-for-17 skid from April 23 to May 2 before sitting for four games. His robust walk rate indicated he wasn't totally confounded by the pitching, but his baseball card wouldn't tell you he was about to become one of the top prospects in baseball.

We start canvassing for our Midseason Top 50 Prospects list around the first week of May. It's too early to pay attention to topline results; sabermetric forefather Voros McCracken noted several decades ago that "anybody can hit just about anything in 60 at-bats," an axiom that has withstood the test of time. Anthony, in fact, had exactly 60 ABs in April and pretty much sucked. But around May Day is when we can start considering who *looks* good and, in this new age of data-driven scouting analysis, whose underlying data traits have really popped. It was around this time a year earlier that an industry veteran suggested to me that Gunnar Henderson was the top prospect left in the minors, a take that initially seemed bizarre since we'd ranked him no. 88 before the season without much consternation in any direction—but also a take that turned out to be completely correct.

Even still, it was surprising when a scout told me in May 2023 that he now considered Anthony one of the top prospects in the game. He was hitting an empty .200 in Low-A; how could that be right? In 2022, Henderson was an established Top 101 prospect off to a scorching start. A year later, Anthony was a second-round pick in his first full season carrying the slash line of a struggling kid about to get demoted back to the complex.

One of my rules of thumb, though, is that it's wise to trust the instincts of people who are paid to evaluate players, so I went to work trying to figure out *why* a good scout would believe Anthony made such a leap in the face of obvious evidence. A second source confirmed that Anthony's batted-ball and swing-decision metrics had spiked huge year-over-year and were now exemplary: the traits you'd expect from a prospect putting up a .300/.400/.500 line, not someone struggling to stay above the Mendoza Line. His in-zone contact rate was in the high 80s, very strong for a prospect who was perceived to have potential swing-and-miss issues. His average exit velocity was pushing 90 mph, his 90th-percentile exit velocity was around 108 and he was maxing out at 112 mph, all very impressive figures for his age. He was hitting too many balls on the ground overall, yet elevating enough of his hardest contact. His chase rate was minuscule, in the teens. Few teenage prospects in baseball at any given time display that combination of hitting traits—sometimes none at all—and it's a skill set which portends not just success, but future MLB stardom. I threw on as much video as I could find, and everything looked right to my scouting eye too. Anthony took flawless swings at exactly the right pitches...except that he was smashing the ball directly at fielders almost every time.

The more data I studied, the more video I watched, the more industry contacts I spoke to, the more I became convinced that Roman Anthony was the best-kept secret in the game. He was a global top prospect with pedestrian statistics.

⚾ ⚾ ⚾

We have often said—dating back to the Up and In era of Kevin Goldstein and Jason Parks—that the backbone of the Baseball Prospectus Prospect Team is our live looks. For well over a decade, we've canvassed the country's minor-league ballparks, getting eyes on hundreds and hundreds of games each year, and scouting nearly every relevant prospect in person to evaluate their tools, skills and overall projection. We've always considered other information, especially sourcing within the industry for undiscovered talent. But over the years, we've hewn closely towards an old player evaluation maxim: Don't scout the stat line.

This approach was the best way to evaluate prospects from the media side in the 2000s and for most of the 2010s. It was also the closest a public outlet could replicate how teams were doing it at that time. Indeed, more than a dozen of my Prospect Team predecessors and colleagues at BP have been hired as talent evaluators for major-league clubs, including Goldstein and Parks themselves.

Yet the data revolution was coming for all of us. MLBAM began releasing public pitch-by-pitch data in the 2007 major-league season with the introduction of the PITCHf/x camera system. For the first time, there was a comprehensive database of pitch speed, location and movement at the player and single-event levels. The PITCHf/x data led to a number of great sabermetric discoveries across the scope of player valuation; for one, we were now able to quantify pitch framing as a skill. Over time, the original camera system was deprecated for TrackMan radar and more recently the Hawk-Eye optical system, each advancement adding new inputs, including point-of-contact hitting data like exit velocity and launch angle. By 2015, MLB's Statcast Era was here; what had begun as simple pitch tracking fully evolved to include granular batted-ball data that meaningfully quantified important hitting traits.

Early on in baseball's big data revolution, this tracking was limited to major-league games in major-league parks. But by the mid-2010s, TrackMan installations expanded at all levels of scouted baseball—not just the affiliated minors but spring training facilities, college stadiums, the prep showcase circuit, even high-school fields. Unlike in the majors, this data was not public, and indeed, aggressive organizations were hoarding it for a time. Major-league teams started bringing amateur players of interest to work out in parks where they had access to TrackMan units, and there were even whispers of major-league clubs offering free analytic setups to colleges in exchange for exclusive access to the results.

Over time, smart teams drifted away from putting scout butts in stadium seats in favor of a new flavor of hybrid scouting analysis that combines video, qualitative looks at data and quantitative modeling. The COVID-19 pandemic sped up this shift across the industry; there was nothing else for scouts to do other than watch video and look at spreadsheets. About 20 teams shared data and video with each other from their 2020 alternate sites.[1] By the end of that dreadful non-season, most scouts were adept at discussing modern data trends and much of the secrecy surrounding it vanished.

When recognizable baseball returned in 2021, minor-league and amateur TrackMan and Hawk-Eye data became more freely available to us on background. Additionally, MLBAM started publicly releasing Statcast data from some minor-league parks. Every year, more and more minor-league games get added to streaming platforms like MiLB.tv and ESPN+, with increasingly high broadcast quality. In short, with each successive season, the quantity and quality of our video and data access improves. We can now watch an entire season of at-bats from a player in the time it takes to drive to a ballpark to watch a single game. And more importantly, we have the data to form a superior evaluation of that player.

⚾   ⚾   ⚾

While it isn't necessarily outcome-determinative, the single most important factor in modern hitting evaluation is damage on contact, frequently expressed as average, 90th-percentile and maximum exit velocity. For years, the best way to determine a player's raw power potential was to watch a batting practice session. But you can get a better sense of long-term power potential just by looking at the same player's in-game 90th-percentile exit velocity, let alone

a holistic approach that also includes average and maximum exit velocities. What constitutes a good set of exit velocities very much depends on age and the rest of their skill set, but typically for full-season prospects you want to see 90th-percentile exit velocities over 101-102 mph and max exit velocities over 107 to project considerable major-league power outcomes. Anthony exceeded those figures by about 5-6 mph despite his youth.

Research last year by *Baseball America* showed that the average minor leaguer added about 3.5 mph on their average and 90th-percentile exit velocities between the ages of 18 and 22. That doesn't mean *every* prospect can be expected to gain that much; some players are maxed out at 18 and some make even greater gains later in their careers. But that's why players like Anthony (and even moreso Junior Caminero) who hit the ball very hard as teenagers against pro pitching are clear-cut top global prospects: You can reasonably expect them to hit the ball even harder with a few more years of physical and skill development.

But exit velocity doesn't tell the whole story of damage; both vertical and horizontal launch components matter here too. Hitters who pull the ball in the air evoke much better game-power outcomes as a group than players who push the ball or tend to hit it on the ground. For example, Isaac Paredes clubbed 31 home runs in the majors last year despite very mediocre average (86.9 mph) and 90th-percentile (101 mph) exit velocity numbers. He hit an extraordinary amount of balls in the air at optimal launch angles (22.1-degree average, among the highest marks in the league), and his pulled-contact rate led the league. They make the walls closer at the corners.

The amount of contact matters to power outputs, too. That seems obvious; if you make more contact and don't sacrifice any power doing it, you'll hit more balls hard. Duh. But for years, we've evaluated power, hit and swing decisions in individual silos. These skills actually interact quite a lot; if you identify better pitches to swing at, you're going to make more and better contact.

The best measure of bat-to-ball ability is in-zone contact rates, often shortened to "Z-Contact." In-zone contact is a better measure than overall contact rate because out-of-zone contact is pretty noisy and duplicative; players with incredible out-of-zone bat-to-ball skills, like Luis Arraez, also have incredible in-zone contact ability anyway. (It's also far more difficult to convert non-strike pitches into positive balls in play; not everyone can be a bad-ball hitter.) Z-Contact rates in the mid-80s and higher (like Anthony's) are indicative of future strong hit tool outcomes, while Z-Contact below 80% is a problem.

Swing decisions require a finer tooth comb. The best surface-level analysis tools are chase rate and in-zone swing rate. Chasing pitches outside the strike zone at a rate much above 30% is a red flag, while higher in-zone swing rates separate out the selectively aggressive from the passive.

Players who have a significantly elevated chase rate without a correspondingly high in-zone swing rate have major issues identifying pitches.[2]

Everything mentioned in the preceding half-dozen paragraphs is still qualitative analysis. We aren't quants, and we don't have full data sets covering the entire minor leagues to manipulate anyway. And by design, we're still doing it in concert with what our eyes tell us. As a data-adept scout pointed out, anyone with any level of baseball knowledge can look at the red and blue bubbles on Baseball Savant player pages and figure out the red is good and the blue is bad, but it takes a pretty good baseball mind to tell you what it means and how, in context, it projects into the future.

The reds and the blues can tell you that Angels first baseman Nolan Schanuel doesn't hit the ball that hard but makes a ton of contact, yet it can't tell you why or what that means for his overall future projection. Watching Schanuel swing the bat tells me that his extremely upright stance and strange hand path lead to a really slow bat that stays in the zone forever, juicing his contact at the cost of damage. That's going to be hard for him to change, which is why he's not a top global prospect despite having performed quite well in the majors just a few months after the draft.

⚾   ⚾   ⚾

Roman Anthony warmed up as last spring turned into summer. Yet he was still only hitting .228 and slugging .317 when the Red Sox promoted him to High-A in mid-June, a decision which on the surface looked completely absurd for a struggling player a month after his 19th birthday. But the batted-ball data remained incredibly strong, and by that point we'd already identified him as one of the ten best prospects in the minors for our Midseason 50 list released a few weeks later.

He'd go on to hit .294/.412/.569 at High-A, and then .343/.477/.543 over a two-week cameo at Double-A as one of the youngest players all season at the level. He's now clearly one of the very best prospects in the game, and this time the back of his baseball card tells you that, too.

—*Jarrett Seidler is an author of Baseball Prospectus.*

1. For a broader discussion of the effects of the pandemic on scouting, I co-wrote the "Ordinality in an Unordinary World" essay with Jeffrey Paternostro and Keanan Lamb in the 2021 *Annual*.

2. Robert Orr's SEAGER metric, introduced last fall at the Baseball Prospectus website and named after selective aggression kingpin Corey Seager, is a cutting edge swing decision model using public Statcast data. Orr's research found increased value on top of chase and in-zone swing rates for players who excel at attacking certain high-value hittable pitches and have stronger approaches in two-strike and three-ball counts. We've incorporated Orr's modeling into our evaluations where it's available.

Top 101 Prospects

by Jeffrey Paternostro, Jarrett Seidler, Nathan Graham and Ben Spanier

1.) Jackson Holliday, SS, Baltimore Orioles

Holliday spent time at all four full-season levels of the minors last year, crushing the first three and performing well enough at Triple-A that a contender less awash in quality infielders probably would've started him in the major-league playoffs. And he didn't turn 20 until months after the season ended. Holliday is unusually skilled, not just for his own age but any age, possessing a strong combination of bat-to-ball ability, plate discipline and quality of contact that hints at a potentially huge hit tool outcome. While he doesn't have tons of loft in his swing or possess elite strength (and correspondingly his max and 90th-percentile exit velocities are only decent for his age), he's stinging the ball reasonably hard on the regular already. The Orioles organization excels at hitting development and Holliday has shown a propensity for rapid improvements, so he's as likely to reach his offensive upside as any prospect in the game. Defensively, he projects as a solid shortstop in a vacuum, but the aforementioned embarrassment of infield riches in Baltimore might slide him to second or third. He's tracking for likely stardom, and at the current rate seven-time All-Star Matt Holliday is going to be known as "Jackson's father" in short order—at least until potential 2025 top draft pick Ethan Holliday enters the scene.

2.) Wyatt Langford, OF, Texas Rangers

Most years, Langford would have been the consensus first-overall pick. He was a potential up-the-middle defender and middle-of-the-order hitter who destroyed the SEC his sophomore and junior seasons at Florida. In 2023, though, he had to play third fiddle to Dylan Crews—who had an even better campaign for LSU—and Paul Skenes, who might have had the best college pitching season in a decade-plus. Then a funny thing happened. Only a few months after the draft, it became clear to us that Langford should have been the first-overall pick *that* year too. He functionally stopped swinging and missing in the zone in the pros, turning what was already a skill into a bona fide strength, and he hits the ball hard—harder than Crews at the high end—and in the air when he makes contact. His minor-league performance was so dominant, Chris Young got asked if he'd be a World Series replacement for an injured Adolis García. That would have been a tough assignment for Langford, but a much more reasonable one will be Opening Day outfielder for the defending champs. A bushel of All-Star appearances should

follow soon after, and the gap between Holliday and Langford on this list is smaller than you would have thought on draft day.

3.) Junior Caminero, 3B/SS, Tampa Bay Rays

Caminero showed up in full-season ball at the end of 2022, flashing impressive power in the Carolina League. He continued to mash down under during winter ball in Australia, but that was just an *amuse bouche* for his 2023 breakout. The 20-year-old made it all the way to Tampa—and the Rays playoff roster—swatting 31 dingers in 117 minor-league games along the way. That gaudy home run rate doesn't oversell his power either, Caminero can hit the ball as hard as anyone in the minors *or* majors, and while he doesn't have elite bat-to-ball or swing decisions, his approach and contact rates are both plenty fine given the explosive damage he can do once barrel meets rawhide. He played mostly third base in 2023, but he's spotted some at shortstop and second, and probably could take a turn in a corner outfield spot if needed. Defensive flexibility is all well and good—and something the Rays value—but Caminero's true home will be the cleanup spot in Tampa's lineup for years to come.

4.) Evan Carter, OF, Texas Rangers

The only aspect of baseball that Carter isn't great at—aside from his defense, and he should be fine in center—is impacting the baseball. We mean this in the modern sense of the word, of course. His swing decisions are in the elite of the elite, he makes more than enough contact and he even manages to lift the ball enough to pop some opportunistic homers. Additionally, he performed very well in both the regular and postseason after a late-year call-up to the big leagues. Questions about the ultimate power projection remain, questions that will only become louder the longer his outputs there remain status quo, and this does legitimately limit his upside. On the other hand, Carter has already basically "made it" as a productive everyday big leaguer, which is something that cannot be said of anyone else near the top of this list.

5.) Dylan Crews, OF, Washington Nationals

Although Crews was generally considered the top player in the 2023 draft, the Pirates were never perceived as strong on him as the public, and it wasn't a huge surprise when he fell to the Nationals with the second pick. Crews is a prototypical Mike Rizzo selection: famous, with incredibly strong college production and big, flashy tools. He hit a mind-boggling

.426/.567/.713 in his junior year at LSU, the type of slash line you'd expect from a mid-major player at significant altitude, not against a SEC schedule at sea level. As you'd expect, he hits the ball quite hard, with his average exit velocity as a pro only falling off a few ticks from the 95 mph he dialed up with metal bats. He makes excellent swing decisions and is likely to stick in center field. His offensive profile can be nitpicked a bit, which is also a Rizzo archetype; Crews only has average contact ability and too many of his harder batted balls are at suboptimal launch angles. He's still overwhelmingly likely to be a good regular, as likely as anyone save Holliday, and has a chance to be a star.

6.) Jackson Chourio, OF, Milwaukee Brewers

Chourio has blasted through the minors over the last two years like he was shot out of a cannon—he reached Triple-A as a 19-year-old—and signed an extension with $82 million in guarantees in December, which could allow him to slip into Milwaukee's Opening Day lineup a few weeks after his 20th birthday. Few prospects have moved as fast up the ladder, and that itself is generally a trait that bodes well for future major-league success. Chourio played most of the season in the Double-A Southern League and hit significantly better in the second half after the league stopped using the pre-tacked baseball, so his .280/.336/.467 line at the level is even more impressive when further contextualized. He demonstrates significant bat speed and hits the ball very, very hard for a teenager—he's popped 20 or more homers in each of the last two seasons. He still chases bad pitches way, way too much and sometimes beats the ball into the ground. His contact rate significantly improved in 2023, which could be a precursor to skill consolidation given his youth. He's a capable center fielder at present, although Milwaukee's outfield depth could push him to a corner. Chourio's skill set is imperfect, but his massive upside is more than worthy of his pre-debut extension.

7.) James Wood, OF, Washington Nationals

Many players struggle in their jump from High-A to Double-A and Wood was no exception. After having a breakout 2022 in which his performance catapulted him into consideration for the top prospect in baseball, he gave back some of the gains, as he was somewhat exposed by Eastern League pitching. The swing-and-miss, which was a concern going into the 2021 Draft, spiked again at Double-A, where he ran a 33.7% strikeout rate over 87 games. Given his extreme size and long levers, whiffs are always going to be part of his game; he'll just need to keep them in check enough to continue getting to his massive power. It's that aforementioned pop that keeps Wood high on the list, with his ability to demolish baseballs and post elite-level exit velocities. The concerns with the hit tool are real, but there was a glimmer of hope at the end of 2023, with Wood slashing .353/.421/.569 over the last month of the season. If he can carry that hot bat into

2024 and show the ability to make the proper adjustments, Wood will again be in the team picture for best prospect in baseball.

8.) Roman Anthony, OF, Boston Red Sox

If you want a beautiful lefty swing with almost every positive hitting trait you can name, Anthony is your guy. The 2022 second-rounder burst through pedestrian top-line numbers at Low-A to scorch High-A as a teenager, ending the season with a .343 cup-of-coffee in Double-A. He does most things well at the plate, and some very well: He has clear plus power potential with a shot for more, excellent swing decisions and very solid bat-to-ball since he's turned professional, fixing his biggest issue as an amateur. He could stand to elevate and pull the ball a little more, although that's true for most hitters on this list, especially the younger ones. He played mostly in center last year, although he probably projects as more of a right fielder long term. If there's one finite concern, Anthony struggled in a small sample against lefties, although his batted-ball and swing-decision data showed only typical platoon splits there. All-in-all, he's one of the most well-rounded hitting prospects in the minors and unusually advanced for a teenager.

9.) Paul Skenes, RHP, Pittsburgh Pirates

After a historic and dominant run at LSU, the Pirates made Skenes the top overall selection in last year's draft, inking him to a slightly under-slot deal. He's a physical freak, built like Paul Bunyon with his 6-foot-6, 235-pound frame. His NFL body type and electric arm speed help him generate triple-digit heat on the fastball, which he pairs with a plus-plus, swing-and-miss slider. Skenes rounds out the arsenal with a slower-breaking curve and a developing change—each is seldom used but will be nurtured along to help attack big-league hitters. The top-end fastball velocity helps him bully hitters but there's still some gains to be had in terms of movement which could help the heater play up even more. A sneaky-good athlete, Skenes repeats his delivery well, making for solid command. It's electric stuff, which gives Skenes the possibility of becoming a future top-of-the-rotation arm.

10.) Jackson Merrill, SS, San Diego Padres

Ever since being a pop-up prep draftee in 2021, Merrill has hit, showing an innate ability to put bat to ball, even against older, more advanced pitching. Each year he has improved the quality of contact, honing his approach and trying to maximize his swing to take full advantage of his plus raw pop. Merrill showed up stronger this spring and also found a way to lift the ball more often over the course of the season. There's still some power left to unlock as he continues to be more selective in choosing when to attack. Defensively, even with the added bulk, there wasn't a loss of athleticism and it still looks like a safe bet that he remains at the six. There was talk at the end of last season about Merrill being promoted to the big-league club to help save a sinking Padres' season, even to the point of him getting playing time at multiple positions in preparation for the promotion. However, a late-September hamstring strain ended that discussion along with Merrill's season. He'll be back this spring, on the cusp of a San Diego debut once more as the Padres choose to shed.

11.) Colson Montgomery, SS, Chicago White Sox

Montgomery has been elevated to a significantly higher position on this list than last year's, due largely to attrition and graduations, but we really don't know much more about him as a player. Felled early in the season by not-unconcerning injury issues, he returned in July to dominate High-A (which he had essentially already conquered in 2022) and...actually not play all that well in Double-A following a promotion. The 21-year-old has a whole lot going for him, of course. The swing decisions are excellent, he makes plenty of contact, and he hits the ball in the air from the left side with enough consistency and strength that we really do think the power is coming. He also plays a credible shortstop, even if third base and second base continue to be bandied about as eventual landing spots. Nevertheless, there remains plenty to prove this upcoming season in terms of both durability and concrete production.

12.) Ethan Salas, C, San Diego Padres

The most advanced 16-year-old international free agent signing in the last decade, Salas showed up in both major-league spring training games and then Low-A before his 17th birthday. For some context on just how far along Salas is, if he was an American high schooler, he'd be one of the youngest top prospects in the *2024* draft class. He performed extraordinarily well for a catcher in his age-17 season, showing advanced skills both at and behind the dish, and earning a late-season promotion to High-A. His second promotion a few weeks later to Double-A was frankly pretty bizarre; the always aggressive Padres can drift towards a "burn the ships" approach to player development. Salas is so young and already so good that you can dream on basically any outcome, including truly elite ones, though the rigors of the position are a huge wild card to any teenage catcher's projection.

13.) Samuel Basallo, C, Baltimore Orioles

A team might not tell you what they truly think about one of their prospects, but they will always show you. First, the Orioles gave Basallo the largest IFA signing bonus in team history. Next, they brought him stateside for his age-17 season. Then...well, you don't really need Baltimore or us to tell you an aggregate line over .300/.400/.500 for a teenage catcher who ended the season in Double-A is good, do you? Basallo won't overwhelm with bat speed, but few 19-year-olds hit the ball this hard or have this good an approach. Many Orioles prospects do, although not many of them are or were catchers—one notable exception there. But on that note, Basallo played almost as many games last year at first base or DH, so perhaps Baltimore is telling us something.

Basallo's arm is strong, but he already has a large frame for catcher and is a below-average receiver. So the bat may force his way to the majors before the defensive skills are ready behind the plate. That downside possibility is baked into this ranking, though: The bat really is that.

14.) Jordan Lawlar, SS, Arizona Diamondbacks

Like Evan Carter, Lawlar got to experience a World Series run before exhausting his rookie eligibility. Unlike Carter, who became a national star overnight as a regular no. 3 hitter for a championship club, Lawlar was used as a "last man on the bench" type utility player. He did acquit himself well by working a pinch-hit walk against Will Smith in the ninth inning of Game 4 after a series of back-and-forth managerial volleys by Bruce Bochy and Torey Lovullo. For the bulk of the season, Lawlar continued to consolidate his jack-of-all-trades skill set; he's above-average or better at nearly everything. He's improved his contact traits, and while he doesn't post huge exit velocities, he projects to maximize his physical hit and power tools with an optimized vertical spray. On defense, he's gained enough reliability with his throws to where he may play shortstop long-term in the majors, though Geraldo Perdomo beat him there and is probably a better defender right now. He's a speedy runner and base-stealing threat, to top it all off.

15.) Coby Mayo, 3B/1B, Baltimore Orioles

Mayo would be the no. 1 prospect for more than half the teams in baseball. He clocks in at third for the Orioles, but offensively at least, he bears a very close resemblance to a former overall no. 1 prospect. Now, one could argue that Baltimore player dev is a lab designed to build once and future Gunnar Hendersons, but not many prospects have that kind of potential. Mayo, however, fits the mold well. He continued to add power in 2023, improved his swing decisions and contact ability, and his line in the upper minors looked eerily similar to Henderson's in 2022. Mayo is not a shortstop—nor a particularly good third baseman—and that's a large part of why he's 15th overall while Henderson was first, but even for Baltimore, future 30-home-run hitters don't just roll off the factory line every year.

16.) Walker Jenkins, OF, Minnesota Twins

The pro debut was short for Jenkins, just a little over 100 at-bats, but in it he showed enough to raise his stock more than any other 2023 draftee. The production matched his aesthetically pleasing left-handed swing, with very little swing-and-miss and a refusal to expand the zone. It's a short track record for contact ability but prior to the draft, the only real concern was how he would hit, and the early results are extremely positive. His swing is not currently optimized for power but it's not hard to envision the pop showing up down the road with Jenkins' quick bat and projectable 6-foot-3 frame. Defensively, despite his large frame, Jenkins is an excellent athlete, capable of covering enough ground and showing the instincts necessary to handle center field.

There's as much upside here as anyone in last year's draft class and even if the power numbers don't fully show up in-game, Jenkins has enough game to still be a good, everyday player.

17.) Jackson Jobe, RHP, Detroit Tigers

"If he were healthy all year, he might be the top pitching prospect in baseball." You'll be hearing that line again, but despite being limited to a smidge under 80 innings due to lumbar spine inflammation, Jobe still checks in as the second-best pitching prospect in the sport. He's added an above-average cutter to go with his plus, high-spin slider. That would be more than enough off-speed options to back his upper-90s heat, yet there's more—his change emerged as arguably his best secondary, with plus-plus potential due to its velocity differential and power sink and fade. Jobe has a clear and obvious top-of-the-rotation arsenal, and has ironed out most of the command concerns from this time last year. So that brings us back to the opening line. Back injuries don't tend to recur, right?

18.) Carson Williams, SS, Tampa Bay Rays

Sometimes the most important skill improvements aren't getting a tool to plus or plus-plus, they're turning a hindrance into playability. Williams has had trouble making contact dating back to his prep days, but he's steadily improved his bat-to-ball ability as a pro, and it's honing in on fringe-average with a shot to get to average. He's never going to be Luis Arraez, but he doesn't have to be. Williams hits the ball quite hard in the air, the foundational skill of hitting prospects, and he does it while playing a nifty shortstop with a cannon arm. The Rays could push him quickly depending on need; they gave him a week's trial at Triple-A last August straight out of High-A. He's likely never going to be a strong hitter for average, but plus power from a plus shortstop is still a hell of a player as long as his hit tool stays afloat.

19.) Andrew Painter, RHP, Philadelphia Phillies

Painter was ramping up to make a run at breaking camp with the Phillies last March when he was sidelined with an elbow sprain. Four months later, he had Tommy John surgery; the bad timing means he'll miss most or all of two straight seasons. Before the injury, he'd emerged as the clear top pitching prospect in the minors—and he's still not that far off even though it's likely he'll throw few if any pitches in anger this year. The healthy version of Painter sat in the upper-90s and touched triple digits with tough movement, threw two plus breaking balls that worked off each other and was working on changeup development. His advanced command and pitchability have belied his youth; he'll still only be 21 on Opening Day 2025 if it takes him that long to return.

20.) Pete Crow-Armstrong, OF, Chicago Cubs

A poor showing in his major-league debut where inconsistent playing time limited him to just 19 plate appearances isn't something for the Cubs to panic about—but there was a slide in Crow-Armstrong's upper-level metrics that warrant keeping an eye on. The swing is geared for hard contact in the air but the power on contact dipped slightly as he faced more advanced upper-minors arms, making us question his future power output. You can live with slightly below-average pop if PCA is hitting rocket line drives to all fields, but there was also a concerning rise in the chase rate as he climbed the ladder. Despite the trends, he doesn't have to hit all that much, as his Gold Glove-caliber center field defense and speed make for a pretty high floor. Crow-Armstrong has also shown the ability to make adjustments in the past and with some nominal improvements to his swing decisions and a return of some high-end contact. He'll be back on track to becoming a standout top-of-the-order table setter in Chicago.

21.) Matt Shaw, SS, Chicago Cubs

In any other draft year Shaw might have been a top-five selection but, fortunately for the Cubs, a historically deep class allowed them to nab him 13th overall last summer. Shaw has hit at every stop: high school, Maryland, on the Cape and post-draft over three levels. He boasts near-elite contact ability, but there's room for some refinement in his approach and more selectivity in when to attack. When Shaw does pounce, he makes loud contact, with his strong, compact frame and quick bat producing consistent above-average exit velocities. The swing won't produce gaudy over-the-fence power numbers but the hard line drives will help him rack up tons of gap-to-gap doubles. Defensively, he's passable at short but his limited range and arm makes him a better fit for second or third. It doesn't really matter, since Dansby Swanson isn't going anywhere anytime soon on the North Side, and Chicago will be anxious to get Shaw's bat in the lineup soon—no matter where they have to put him on the diamond.

22.) Colt Keith, 3B/2B, Detroit Tigers

Keith was in the midst of a breakout in 2022 when a shoulder injury put him on the shelf. He proved it wasn't a fluke with an excellent full season across two levels last year. There's potential for big-time offensive production in the profile, with Keith showing the ability to produce over-the-fence power numbers while maintaining a knack for contact. He's not an exit-velocity monster but more of a complete hitter who is close to major-league ready. The knock on Keith has long been the glove and his deficiencies in the field. He split time between second and third last season, showing enough improvements with his hands and instincts to no longer be considered a defensive liability. There are no longer any major red flags to Keith's profile and he's likely to get his shot in the Tigers lineup early in 2024.

23.) Jett Williams, SS/OF, New York Mets

Overlooked no more for his stature, the 5-foot-6 (listed) Williams combines a bunch of intriguing skills into a package that outpunches his height. He just doesn't swing outside the zone, and that discipline, combined with his short levers—that one's not a joke, he really is very direct to the ball—allow him to take a dead uppercut swing path without sacrificing any contact, creating a truly maximized contact/damage interaction. While he's not tall, he's pretty well built and has surprising pop which improved over the course of the season. His approach can verge on passive at times, limiting the offensive upside, but if he can make moderate adjustments on which pitches to ambush and which ones to foul off, he could be an offensive force. He played most of the 2023 season at shortstop but his arm projects to be a little light for the position. He looked playable in his initial pro exposure to center field, and second base is an obvious fallback position as well.

24.) Max Clark, OF, Detroit Tigers

Clark's advanced swing decisions, paired with an ability to make good contact, made him the highest ever prep drafted out of Indiana, and the Tigers were able to lure him away from a Vanderbilt commitment with a slightly under-slot deal. There are high-ceiling tools across the board with the bat a potential double-plus. On the showcase circuit against the top competition, Clark showed an aptitude for laying off pitches out of the zone and the ability to smoke hard line drives on stuff in the zone. It's a swing currently geared for those line drives, but Clark has more than enough bat speed and projection remaining in his frame to see the power numbers eventually playing above-average or higher. He's an excellent athlete with some quick-twitch that helps him steal a base and cover plenty of ground in center field. We can give him a pass for his post-draft performance at the complex after a long prep season, but the true test will come next year as he faces advanced pitching for the first time. If he can handle the soft stuff down and away and refrain from chasing, Clark will continue to be one of the brightest stars in the organization.

25.) Noelvi Marte, IF, Cincinnati Reds

Marte signed for a seven-figure bonus in 2018, making him a notable prospect for six list cycles now. He's developed in steady and predictable—frankly downright boring—ways, turning more of his raw power into game power, sliding down the defensive spectrum from shortstop to third base, and logging a series of eerily consistent seasons all the way from the complex leagues to the upper minors. Unlike the power bats a bit ahead of him on this list, Marte doesn't elevate the ball consistently enough to translate all of his raw power into game power, hence the consistent sub-.500 slugging percentages in the minors. Otherwise, Marte has functionally no weakness in his offensive game. It doesn't make for the most exciting prospect to talk about—especially for the sixth time—but it makes for a very good major leaguer.

26.) Ricky Tiedemann, LHP, Toronto Blue Jays

"If he were healthy all year, he might be the top pitching prospect in baseball." Well, perhaps not in this case, because if Tiedemann were healthy all year, he might have been in the Jays rotation by the second half, and not even eligible for this list. Instead a biceps issue limited him to just 62 innings on the mound in 2023. Even in small doses, the stuff shines. Tiedemann slings mid-to-upper-90s heat, a wipeout sweeper, and a developing—but potential plus—change, striking out 105 batters over those 62 innings. In the taxonomy of pitching injuries, biceps is scarier than back, but Tiedemann should be a full go for 2024, and in contention for a spot on Toronto's staff in short order.

27.) Cade Horton, RHP, Chicago Cubs

It didn't take long for Horton to show that he was more than just an under-slot, cost-saving draft selection. He bullied younger, less-experienced Carolina League hitters during his brief time at Myrtle Beach, with his fastball-slider combination punching out 21 in just 14 innings of work. After his promotion to High-A, he continued to hold the upper-90s velocity and command of the mid-80s slider. But it was mid-season when Horton really took off, emphasizing his changeup and adding a curve to the mix. Both offerings are still inconsistent and he'll need to continue to refine them, but the foundation is there for an advanced four-pitch mix. It's the best pure stuff in the organization and rivals any other pitcher in minor-league baseball. No longer is Horton considered a two-pitch, likely bullpen arm; he has the look of a safe, durable, frontline starter.

28.) Adael Amador, SS/2B, Colorado Rockies

The Rockies' major-league team often seems to approach the sport like postmodern art, while their farm system bounces around the bottom half of our organizational rankings. In the midst of mostly mediocre chaos, Colorado has managed to stumble upon two operational strengths: catcher defense and international scouting. Amador—signed for $1.5 million out of the Dominican Republic in 2019—has hit at every stop since putting pen to paper and may have the best overall hit tool in this year's class of prospects. He's quick and direct to the ball with a bit more thump than his frame or mostly level swing would suggest. He's aggressive in the zone, patient enough out of it and able to spoil enough pitches to work a walk when he doesn't find an offering to square. Amador is fast but not a great basestealer. He's rangy, but a better fit for second than shortstop. Oh, and he also had hamate surgery in the middle of 2023 and struggled in Double-A after it. So let's just close with this: "if he were healthy all year, he'd be a top-20 prospect in baseball."

29.) Drew Gilbert, OF, New York Mets

On first impression Gilbert strikes one almost as a kind of supercharged Brett Gardner. He's similarly small and pesky in a way that may annoy opposing teams and fans, though it would be difficult to project a similar level of plate discipline against big-league pitching. He should make a lot of contact, though, and his swing is optimized in a way that the Yankee stalwart's wasn't until later in his career when many of his physical tools had waned. Gilbert plays with a large amount of swagger, intensity and visual *jouissance*, often taking huge swings and showing a tendency to stand on it when he connects. Perhaps most importantly, he's performed extraordinarily well throughout his professional career, both before and after he was exchanged for Justin Verlander. The former Tennessee man will be volunteering his services to the Mets outfield in relatively short order.

30.) Hurston Waldrep, RHP, Atlanta Braves

Waldrep's high-80s splitter is just a sick, sick pitch; it's basically a get out of jail free card whenever swing and misses are required. He completely kills its spin and it dives and dances with unusual motion, running some of the highest whiff rates you'll ever see; it's one of the clearest 80-grade offerings from a prospect imaginable. His other offerings aren't *that* good—there's no pitch in the entire minors that is—but even if he didn't have the split, he'd be a cromulent standard 95-and-a-high-spin-slider type. His usage and location was a bit odd in college, with a lot of fastballs in places where we know fastballs shouldn't be thrown, but the Braves immediately cleaned his locations up and he blasted through all four minor-league levels while most of his draft cohort made token appearances or were on deload programs. While his command isn't all the way there yet, and may never be, Waldrep's stuff is up there with anyone's and he's likely to make an impact this year. And no, we have no idea how the rest of the league let Atlanta scoop him up with the 24th pick either.

31.) Chase DeLauter, OF, Cleveland Guardians

A James Madison alum with a funky swing and recurring foot problems, it's not hard to see why DeLauter was a divisive draft prospect in 2022. He may still be a divisive pro prospect this year, but it's hard to argue with the production when he was on the field. You won't find a motion-captured version of his "scissor swing" front and center in future ads for MLB The Show, but it's not "how," it's "how many hits," and DeLauter's bat contains multitudes. If you include his Arizona Fall League time, he hit well over .300 and walked almost as often as he struck out. One would like to see him stay on the field for a full year in 2024 and hit for a little more power—given he's likely destined for a corner outfield spot—but if you hit .300, everything else becomes a relatively minor quibble on a good major-league resume.

32.) Marcelo Mayer, SS, Boston Red Sox

Mayer entered 2023 as the clear top prospect in the Red Sox system and exited it as clearly not the top prospect in the Red Sox system. That change in status was affected primarily by the actions of Roman Anthony, to be fair, but it is worth more than a passing note—it wasn't only Anthony's explosion that reversed their roles, but also an incomplete and inconsistent

campaign on Mayer's part. He conquered High-A early in the season, as a 20-year-old former fourth-overall pick should, but was faced with considerably more turbulence following a promotion to Double-A Portland. Some of Mayer's struggles were likely due to attempting to play through the shoulder issues that eventually shut him down for the year, but he also developed a troubling tendency to whiff against breaking stuff down in the zone. He handles shortstop well enough, and it's a really nice-looking swing that should allow him to tap into more power than he's shown thus far. If a healthy Mayer can assuage those hit tool concerns, he could be back near the top of this list by midseason. If he can't, the outcome is indeterminate.

33.) Spencer Jones, OF, New York Yankees

Jones' average exit velocity last year was just a touch under 94 mph. There were only three major-league hitters who hit the ball harder: Shohei Ohtani, Ronald Acuña and Aaron Judge. Probably not coincidentally, those are arguably the three best hitters in the sport. That's the crux of why Jones is among the game's better prospects; he can liquify the ball on contact, as a 22-year-old who can handle center. Both his ground-ball and swing-and-miss rates are mediocre, which is how you end up slugging .444 in the minors while hitting the ball almost as hard as Ohtani. They're not horrid markers though, and Jones could have more developmental runway left than his age indicates given that he didn't hit full-time until his last year at Vanderbilt as a two-way player recovering from Tommy John surgery. With some late development, his power upside would be completely absurd.

34.) Harry Ford, C, Seattle Mariners

Ford's 2023 WBC performance for Great Britain may have him well on his way to an OBE, but the rest of his season made it clear he has a big future in MLB as well. The 20-year-old spent the whole year at High-A Everett—where he was, per our metrics, by far the best defensive catcher at the level—and walked almost as often as he struck out. Ford has started stinging the ball a bit harder, popping 15 homers last season despite a reputation as a hit-over-power player. If anything, he has a fly-ball problem rather than a ground-ball one, as he can pop up pitches he's trying to deposit into the bleachers. That's more of a barrel control issue than a selection or contact issue at present, and even if Ford continues to run .250 batting averages, his on-base ability, burgeoning pop and viable catcher glove would make him a good regular regardless.

35.) Tommy Troy, SS, Arizona Diamondbacks

For many years, Stanford was well known in the scouting community for producing players with the "Stanford swing," a slow poke—trading damage for opposite-field contact—designed to hit for high averages with metal bats against college velocity, and not at all with wood against pro pitching. After a change at head coach and several on the staff overall, the Stanford swing is gone, and in its place evolved Troy, a quick-bat demon who can square up any fastball. What really unlocked Troy's potential in the year leading up to the draft was a major improvement in his swing decisions: He went from an all-or-nothing free swinger to a reasonably patient slugger, a trend which carried over to his professional debut. He played mostly third as a junior at Stanford and then moved to shortstop full-time as a pro, which may not be his ultimate home. Wherever he lands, expect him to take some majestic swings.

36.) Dalton Rushing, C, Los Angeles Dodgers

Rushing's stock continued to gain helium last year, especially with his scorching-hot hitting early on. However, the physical rigors of catching took their toll, with Rushing suffering a rash of injuries after the Futures Game which affected his overall performance. When healthy, he puts together consistently professional at-bats where he shows a patient approach and the ability to find his way on base. Rushing also knows when to attack and can do damage with his above-average bat speed, physical strength and a swing geared to generate loft. Defensively, he's still relatively raw, despite coming from a major college program, but has the tools to stick long term at the position. Catching will wear a man down, as evidenced by his 2023 season, but Rushing is already one of the top offensive-minded backstops in the minors.

37.) Kyle Manzardo, 1B, Cleveland Guardians

We wish we had a better answer for why Manzardo hit .237 last year. Unlike with Harry Ford, that kind of batting average would be a real issue given that Manzardo resides at the opposite end of the defensive spectrum. He's not an exit-velocity king, but he still hit the ball more than hard enough given his optimized swing path. He has a downright good in-zone and overall contact rates for a slugger, too. He doesn't—and didn't—chase too much. Manzardo passed the eye test in 2023, as well. In just a few at-bats you'll confirm that he's a big bopper with a good eye who swings with wicked intent. And sure, sometimes you just have a down season. It would be easy to write off 2023 for Manzardo, except when you are a first-base-only prospect without elite or even plus-plus raw power, almost everything has to go right for you. And even when you don't really do anything wrong, the margins can be this thin.

38.) Jeferson Quero, C, Milwaukee Brewers

Jeferson has pulled ahead of Edgar in the race between the two catching Queros, reversing the ordinal relationship they had on the midseason list. Why is that? Consistency, basically, and continued improvement. Jeferson now grades out exceptionally well in our catching defense metrics, and he has begun to really tap into what was previously latent home run pop. A .262/.339/.441 line with 16 homers in 381 plate appearances as a (good!) 20-year-old catcher in Double-A is nothing to scoff at, and as a result he's gone from the guy you incidentally see and kind of like while watching Jackson Chourio's Carolina League team to the second-best prospect in the Brewers system behind only Chourio. There is some downside in his hit tool, but given the defense and pop it's hard to see him not being a big-league contributor. The question now is: How significant an impact will he make?

39.) Jasson Domínguez, OF, New York Yankees

The Martian has landed! Well, sort of. Domínguez's much-ballyhooed major-league debut was cut short after just eight games with Tommy John surgery. The bulk of his 2023 was spent at Double-A, where he had a nice season making reasonably loud contact that didn't actually go for a ton of extra-base hits—he slugged .414 there—because of moderate ground-ball and swing-and-miss tendencies. Essentially, his analytic profile is pretty similar to Spencer Jones'—right down to the batted-ball data looking more appealing than his actual slugging percentage—but with higher valleys and lower peaks. The Yankees do have their type. Of course, since his entire career has been a rollercoaster, Domínguez went on the best three-week run of his life starting in mid-August: Two four-hit games in three days at Double-A earned him a promotion to Triple-A, where he continued to be red hot (.419 average over nine games) and earned a promotion to the majors, where he clonked four home runs in his first eight games. Without the injury, he almost assuredly would've been playing center in the Bronx this year—and would've been a bunch of spots higher here too—but instead the Yankees decided not to wait for him and traded for Juan Soto and Alex Verdugo, bumping Aaron Judge to center. Domínguez should be able to hit somewhere by this summer, though what outfield spot he'll return to, when he'll be able to play the field and whether the Yankees will send him to the minors is cloudier. But he does seem to be tracking towards a quality major-leaguer again, if not quite up to the card collector hype.

40.) Zach Dezenzo, 3B, Houston Astros

Dezenzo represents a nifty bit of modern scouting and player development synergy by the Astros. As a junior and senior at Ohio State, he posted some of the nation's best exit velocity metrics, and he did much the same with wood bats in the MLB Draft League for two summers. But his contact metrics stunk, and it was easy to see why: A heavily exaggerated leg kick and a long swing path just stopped him from getting the bat on the ball, even on hittable pitches in the zone. The Astros scooped him up in the 2022 draft in the 12th round for a Day Three slot bonus—just $125,000 that year. They quickly went to work on a swing change, quieting down the leg kick and shortening up his barrel path. The changes didn't substantially impact his exit velocities—he was over 92 mph average with similarly impressive 90th-percentile and max figures in 2023—but they did get his bat-to-ball issues to a manageable state, and that launched him into huge offensive production (he was hitting over .400 as late as the last week of May). Defensively, he moved off shortstop and might have a home at third, although first and/or the outfield corners are possibilities too. Dezenzo is never going to have a plus hit tool despite the adjustments, but he has one of the higher power upsides around and has already taken huge steps towards fully actualizing it.

41.) Heston Kjerstad, 1B/OF, Baltimore Orioles

Shortly after being selected second overall in the 2020 draft, Kjerstad was diagnosed with myocarditis and missed the next season and a half. Just getting back on the field was an accomplishment, but he made it all the way to the majors in his first full season. He posted a .900 OPS in the upper minors and didn't look particularly overmatched in his 33 major-league plate appearances. Like every good Orioles hitting prospect, Kjerstad has plenty of pull-side thump in his bat and doesn't sacrifice too much contact ability to get to it, despite a bit of a stiff, forearm-heavy swat. Kjerstad does expand the zone more than you'd like given he's going to be a three-true-outcomes, power-hitting first baseman. Sometimes when you are trying to design another Gunnar Henderson, you just end up with better Ryan Mountcastle.

42.) Curtis Mead, IF, Tampa Bay Rays

Last offseason, in this space, we wrote the following about Mead: "[he] is an extremely good hitting prospect…[h]e hits the ball early, hits it often and hits it very hard. He has a longish swing but a quick bat, and a plus power outcome is well within reason. What position will he be playing? TBD." All of that remains true, essentially, but Mead ranks significantly lower on this list than last year's edition, in part because there were guys who broke out and jumped him, because he spent a lot of time on the injured list in 2023 and because his is an extremely bat-driven profile whose underlying metrics went in some concerning directions in a nearly 100 PA big-league sample. The latter is hardly out of the ordinary for players making their debut, of course, and Mead's Triple-A outputs remained status quo with 2022. As the Rays continue to shift around their chess pieces, we're interested to see how they deploy Mead going forward, after mostly using him primarily as a weak-side platoon option in his debut.

43.) Marco Luciano, SS, San Francisco Giants

Luciano's 2022 back issues carried into 2023, and he missed the first month of the season. He got off to a dreadfully cold start at Double-A, which certainly could be attributed to rust, but then forced promotions to Triple-A and then the majors. While a hamstring injury cost him a bunch of time in the late summer, he still impressed enough to set himself up as the likely starting shortstop for San Francisco moving forward. Luciano has impressive, impressive power from a lightning-quick bat, but he swings through everything in the universe. We've continually projected over the past half-decade that he could improve his bat-to-ball ability, but the improvements never arrived, and we're reaching the point now where this is probably just the kind of player he is. His shortstop defense has turned out to be surprisingly solid, and a nice outcome now would be enough dingers from the six spot to make the sea of strikeouts worthwhile.

44.) Kyle Harrison, LHP, San Francisco Giants

Harrison's stuff is somewhat unremarkable these days for a top pitching prospect. It's a mid-90s fastball, a low-80s slurve that is plus when he locates it and a changeup that he doesn't use all that frequently. His command is often scattershot. After dominating High-A and Double-A in 2022, he wasn't great statistically at Triple-A in 2023. But he was more than fine against big-league hitters throughout an extended late-season look. The whole is greater than the sum of the parts here. Why? First of all, it's a really good fastball. Really good fastball meaning, in this case, that its characteristics are such that it gets bad swings from big leaguers despite only sitting mid-90s. He throws it quite a bit, and the secondaries play well off of it. The whole ensemble plays up thanks to deception created by a tough release point and good extension, and here we are: instant mid-rotation starter.

45.) Drew Thorpe, RHP, San Diego Padres

Thorpe's changeup was one of the most valuable pitches in minor-league baseball in 2023, running an enormous whiff rate both in the zone and out of it. The change was a clear plus projection for him already coming out of the 2022 draft, but the Yankees coaxed a few extra ticks on his fastball and sharpened his slider, leaving hitters to just get devastated by that killer changeup and command. Changeups are notoriously hard to project based on their properties alone, since so much of the deception is in how the pitcher sells and tunnels it, so separating out the elite of the elite—like Thorpe's appears to be now—from the merely very good requires proof of concept. Traded in December to San Diego in the Juan Soto deal, the weight of high expectations will now be squarely on Thorpe's off-speed continuing to whiff the world.

46.) Dylan Lesko, RHP, San Diego Padres

One of the most talented prep righties in recent memory, the Padres popped Lesko with the 15th pick in 2022 less than three months after he underwent Tommy John surgery. They brought him back very slowly in 2023, and his initial pro outings at the Arizona complex in June and July got rave reviews even though his ERA was over 10 and he was pitching two innings or less. By September, Lesko got ramped up to twice through the order in High-A. His raw stuff is absolutely huge: A mid-90s fastball that can beat hitters up in the zone with a changeup flashing plus-plus and a high-spin curveball. But his command looked quite rusty—he walked six batters per nine between his various stops—and he's going to need to tighten everything up to continue his ascension to the game's true top-tier pitching prospects.

47.) Kyle Teel, C, Boston Red Sox

Teel has dominated nearly from the moment he was selected 14th overall out of the University of Virginia, small samples notwithstanding. It's a very pretty overall stat line, .363/.483/.495, and most of that damage was done between

High-A and Double-A. We'd like to see him actualize a bit more pop, but his ability to make quality contact bodes well moving forward even if he swings a bit more than is strictly necessary. Teel is a lefty-hitting catcher who is actually very good defensively, so this should be a somewhat airtight thing. He is still a catcher, of course, so be on the alert for possible attrition in the skill set. He'll probably just end up being an everyday player for years, though.

48.) Josue De Paula, OF, Los Angeles Dodgers

If De Paula had been eligible for last summer's amateur draft—he was born in Brooklyn—his athletic, projectable frame and ability to do damage at the plate would have made him a slam dunk top-10 pick. Instead, the 18-year-old signed out of the Dominican in January 2022 as an international free agent, and is coming off a season where he flashed big potential against older Cal League competition. It's easy to dream on the sweet, lefty swing, but he backs it up with a solid approach and the ability to make hard contact. Never overmatched at the plate and possessing an excellent command of the zone and recognizing spin well, De Paula showed the swing decisions of a much more seasoned player. Tall and athletic, there's loads of projectable good growth coming to a player that already hits the ball extremely hard and has a swing geared for getting the ball in the air. It makes for an exciting profile; one of an athletic corner outfield bat who hits for a combination of average and power.

49.) Rhett Lowder, RHP, Cincinnati Reds

One of the most polished college arms of last year's draft, Lowder was nabbed by the Reds at number seven with the hopes that they could squeeze some additional development out of the big righty. At Wake Forest, Lowder's sinking low to mid-90s fastball, plus-plus change and quality slider were more than enough to get hitters out and helped make him ACC pitcher of the year in consecutive seasons. Cincinnati has done a nice job of late in helping pitchers maximize their heaters, adding a few extra ticks of velocity to fastballs. A broken fingernail caused him to rely on the two-seamer this past spring but, now healed, he can return to adding the four-seam fastball to the mix. There's little else to improve upon and even if they can't work their magic with Lowder's number one, his quality arsenal is strong enough to carry him to Great American Ballpark with haste.

50.) Colt Emerson, SS, Seattle Mariners

The Mariners took Emerson in last year's first round, coaxing him out of an Auburn commitment and, after an absurdly dominant stint on the complex, he found himself making his full-season debut as a just-turned 18-year-old. He acquitted himself quite well there too, slashing .302/.436/.444 in 79 plate appearances with Low-A Modesto in the Cal League. We are still early in observing Emerson's development (the kid was born in 2005), but as the stats imply, the hit tool projection is quite promising. He's hardly wispy for his age,

either, so there should be some pop lurking as he acclimates himself to more advanced competition. There is still a pretty broad delta of outcomes in the offing here, but he's certainly off to a good start as a lefty hitter who should stick in the middle infield.

51.) Colton Cowser, OF, Baltimore Orioles

Cowser was a darling of all statistical persuasions during his time at Sam Houston State, pushing his way up to the fifth-overall pick with stellar traditional stats and great batted-ball data. He's continued some aspects of that in the pros—he still has excellent plate discipline and hits the ball reasonably hard. Beyond that, he's actually been a bit better than advertised defensively, capable of taking major-league reps in center. But one significant problem has emerged: Cowser's bat-to-ball has been surprisingly mediocre in the pros, not just against slow stuff but also against some harder pitches, which has led to both a ton of whiffs and more topped balls into the ground than you'd like. That followed him all the way up the ladder, and led to a tough major-league debut last summer. The Orioles are one of the best hitting development organizations around, so there's some hope for improvement on that front, and even as-is he's got some nifty traits likely to lead to utility. Nonetheless his stock is down a bit despite a facially impressive Triple-A campaign.

52.) Brooks Lee, SS, Minnesota Twins

The first full professional season for Lee was not without its ups and downs. After a solid showing at Wichita, Lee struggled to take advantage of the hitter friendly International League environment and ended the year on a somewhat down note. We can overlook some of the performance at St. Paul—the jump to Triple-A can be tough, even for an advanced college bat like Lee. He still makes tons of contact with his unorthodox swing, but the quality can be lacking, especially when he expands the zone too much. The power is also looking to play more in the average range rather than plus, putting more pressure on the contact ability. Defensively, the glove is good enough to stick in the dirt but it appears more suited for second or third rather than at the six. Lee is still clearly a future everyday big-league player, but we are seeing the limits to his upside more clearly.

53.) Masyn Winn, SS, St. Louis Cardinals

It should never require a ton of thought before you give a tool a top-of-the-scale, 80 grade. After all, if you have to ruminate too long, is it really elite? But even using that guidepost, Winn's throwing arm is an easy eight. That should come as no shock as he was drafted in 2022 as a two-way player who was mid-90s on the mound as a prep. What's more of a (pleasant) surprise is how rapidly his bat has developed in the pros since he ditched pitching to become a full-time shortstop. While he'll always be a defense-first player—he's a plus glove in addition to the howitzer of a throwing arm—he made enough contact and did enough damage in the upper minors to project for average offense. That projection might not be met with the same rapidity though, as his first 122 major-league at-bats were downright awful. It leaves him eligible for this list and his stock a bit down from this time last year, but if he can bounce back in 2024 and keep the bat from getting knocked out of his hands as much in the majors, the Cards may have found another core piece of their next division-winning roster.

54.) Tink Hence, RHP, St. Louis Cardinals

Last year we wrote that Hence was one full, healthy season away from being one of the top pitching prospects in baseball. He went out and made his first start in April, his last well after Labor Day, and 21 in between. The stuff looked as sharp as ever, so what gives? Well, those 23 starts totaled 96 innings, which is right in line with what you'd expect from a 20-year-old pitching prospect who has dealt with intermittent injuries during his teenage years. This is just how baseball teams develop young pitching prospects now, but it injects a lot of uncertainty into Hence's future projection. His mid-90s—touching higher—fastball has plenty of giddy up and comes from a tough angle when he's landing it at the top of the zone. Hence's low-80s curve flashes plus-plus, and he's teased out a solid slider from it as well. His change is coming along fine. The issue is this all happens in four- or five-inning bursts and his delivery has a bit of late arm effort and can lead to corresponding command wobbles. And Hence still cuts a willowy frame on the mound, so you do wonder how many more innings than those 96 he might be able to throw over a full season. Then again, we can nitpick this for another 200 words, worry about what it looks like when he has to stretch out more, but it's not like last year's NL Cy Young winner even averaged six innings a start. This is just how teams use major-league starters now. Hence, Hence remains a well-regarded pitching prospect, if not quite a tip-top one.

55.) Robby Snelling, LHP, San Diego Padres

The Padres went over slot in 2022 to lure Snelling away from a LSU commitment and he rewarded them with one of the minor league's best seasonal pitching performances. Despite still being a teenager, he mowed down hitters across three levels culminating with a dominant four-game stretch in the hitter-friendly Texas League. There he allowed just three earned runs in 17 innings of work. He's a physical and athletic strike-thrower who pounds the zone and has shown the ability to make adjustments in-game. Hitters have a tough time squaring up the fastball and the breaking ball has a chance to be a true swing-and-miss offering. Despite his youth, Snelling already looks like a mid-rotation starter, but could be a rotation climber as he gains experience and continues to refine the secondaries.

56.) Chase Hampton, RHP, New York Yankees

Is Hampton the last Yankees pitching prospect standing after the ritual sacrifice required to consummate the Juan Soto trade? No, actually, because Will Warren also almost made this list. He is the best remaining one, though, and perhaps the exemplar of the Sam Briend makeover challenge. A sixth-rounder in 2022 out of Texas Tech (a southern non-directional school this time), Hampton found a consistent arm slot and corresponding command jump upon joining the Yankees system, rocketing out of the gate last season and beginning his professional career with a 2.68 ERA and K rate north of 40% in High-A. Hampton was more terrestrial following a promotion to Double-A, with the ERA bloating to over 4.00 and the strikeout rate dropping below 30%. Nevertheless, he pitched the entirety of last season at age 21 and could debut late next year if his ascension continues apace. The fastball is a strong pitch, sitting mid-90s and touching higher, and generating whiffs. The gyro slider is excellent with tight, hard movement, and his beautiful curveball gives him an additional vital weapon against both lefties and righties. This is an organization that is traditionally loath to give homegrown pitchers long-form rotation opportunities, but Hampton just might be the best they've had in the last half-decade.

57.) Noah Schultz, LHP, Chicago White Sox

Schultz was a high-risk, high-ceiling proposition when the Sox nabbed him late in 2022's first round, and thus far they've been rewarded for their audacity. He's only thrown 27 professional innings, sure, but his 1.33 ERA and a mid-30s strikeout rate have created a strong impression. The former Illinois prep sits mid- and touches upper-90s with a pair of fastballs that he throws from an extremely difficult angle—he's very tall and slings from a low three-quarters, almost sidearm slot. He also has a slider that he shows exceptionally advanced feel for, shifting its shape and varying it vertically and horizontally. With the changeup also offering promise, this is potentially a very exciting profile. That buzz is harshed just a bit by Schultz's lack of innings, though. It isn't only caution on the organization's part that's limited them, but rather the cropping up of a mildly worrisome set of injuries. In addition to taking on a full workload next season we'd also like to see Schultz hold his velo deep into outings and continue to improve his command.

58.) Tyler Black, 3B, Milwaukee Brewers

Prior to last season, we were pretty sure Black would hit, but his prospect status was somewhat muted due to his questionable ability to impact the ball and his lack of defensive home. He answered both this past year, posting career-high slugging numbers and playing a passable third base. Both the pop and glove should land around at least fringe-average, giving a high floor to the profile. However, the carrying tool continues to be the bat. Black's near-elite contact ability and above-average swing decisions allow him to spray hard line drives to all fields and get on base at a high clip. Once on base, Black is a threat to steal and, while not the most efficient of base stealers, he has the aggressiveness and raw foot speed to swipe multiple bags. Black is about as close to major-league ready as anyone on the 101 and even if the power never fully develops, he's a fairly safe bet to have a lengthy big-league career.

59.) Ceddanne Rafaela, OF/SS, Boston Red Sox

Rafaela suffered from the perfunctory MLB debut slump following his late-season promotion. But broadly speaking he only continued to make the case he's been making since the beginning of 2022: that he's likely a solid big leaguer despite an extremely low signing bonus and infinitesimal hype early on in his minor-league career. He chases too much, sure. He's been chasing too much forever, actually. It hasn't hurt him all that much yet, because he makes a lot of contact and makes up for this shortcoming in other ways. He is an absolutely excellent center fielder, cuts the bases well and somewhat inexplicably also plays a good shortstop. He would likely be able to extend this versatility to other spots around the field, if necessary, but his outfield defense is strong enough that he may just be an everyday center fielder. It's a nifty set of skills, and we're looking forward to seeing how it plays across a full big-league campaign.

60.) Xavier Isaac, 1B, Tampa Bay Rays

Isaac's minimal experience on the showcase circuit and position made his selection at 29th overall in 2022 a bit of a head scratcher. He rewarded the scouting department by putting together one of the best (non-Junior Caminero) offensive seasons in the system, slugging .521 between the A-ball levels. There's enough length in his swing to cover the zone and he's shown the ability to punish mistakes. Isaac is still honing his approach to take full advantage of his plus raw pop and, if he can get to it, has the potential to post big-time power numbers. Originally seen as just a first baseman, Isaac has taken advantage of Tampa's strength programs, and his increased athleticism could help him get some future playing time at a corner outfield spot. There was a lot to like about Isaac's first full professional season but there might be even more in the tank, making him a potential breakout performer in 2024.

61.) Cole Young, SS, Seattle Mariners

It's Young's highly promising hit tool that has earned him his placement on this list, and his performance between Low-A and High-A as a 19-year-old made him impossible to ignore. The profile is not dissimilar to that of his org mate Colt Emerson, actually, only Young is further along in his development and thus a bit less of a mystery box. Slashing .277/.399/.449 in full-season ball as a teenager who also happens to be a lefty hitter while playing almost exclusively shortstop? That's very good! His barrel ability is excellent, and he has really strong control of the strike zone. While Young makes a lot of contact, it often lacks impact, and that does limit his upside. His frame doesn't scream physical projection, but the potential exists for Emerson's game power to eventually exceed the raw given his perspicacity in

the box. How much more pop he can wring out of his bat may determine whether he is a fringy everyday guy or a player on the cuspy edge of stardom.

62.) Emmanuel Rodriguez, OF, Minnesota Twins

Rodriguez's 2022 was cut short by a knee injury, and it took him a bit of time to really get off the mat last year. Once spring turned to summer in Cedar Rapids, though, he was back to looking like a breakout prospect once again. His final line in the Midwest League looks merely good, but there was plenty of power and patience on display—especially in the second half—while Rodriguez only took two plate appearances against a pitcher younger than him. He was also back to manning center field and still runs well despite the still-recent knee injury. Rodriguez has only logged a little over 180 games across his three pro seasons, so 2024 will hopefully see him make good on his deferred 2022 breakout campaign. If so, his power/speed/patience combo could make him one of the top outfield prospects in baseball this time next year.

63.) Jacob Misiorowski, RHP, Milwaukee Brewers

Even before he was drafted, baseball analysts and scouts raved about how impressive Misiorowski's TrackMan data was. The amount of breathless praise for his amateur pitch data might lead you to think the spreadsheets were hand drawn by Mondrian. It would have even been prettier if Steve Wynn put his elbow through the cell with Misiorowski's Zone% though. While he had unhittable stuff it was often put in unswingable locations. He still walked five per nine in his full pro debut in 2023, but that's enough control and command to make Misiorowski very effectively wild. He can top 100 mph from a tough angle and with bat-missing shape, and boasts a potential plus cutter and slider backing the elite fastball. But while you can hang the TrackMan in the Louvre, it comes with a delivery that is more violent than Carvaggio's *Judith Beheading Holoferenes*, and after *The Treachery of Late Season Arm Fatigue*, we remain inclined to write "Ceci n'est pas une starting pitcher."

64.) Victor Scott II, OF, St. Louis Cardinals

Speed doesn't slump and Scott has as much as anyone in all of baseball. His speed is game-changing, the type of wheels not seen in St. Louis since the Whiteyball days in the '80s. Not only does it help Scott rack up gaudy stolen base numbers, but also allows him to patrol wide swaths of real estate in center field. He shows good instincts on the grass and has enough of an arm to keep runners honest, giving him the potential to become a plus defender. The speed and defense give Scott a high floor, but his increased prospect profile relies on his much improved hit tool. A former fifth round selection out of West Virginia in 2022, Scott struggled post-draft to make quality contact, but broke out in his first full-season assignment. His improved swing decisions, along with his feel for contact, helped Scott post career highs in most offensive categories and put him on the prospect map as a potential top of the order spark plug for St. Louis.

65.) Owen Caissie, OF, Chicago Cubs

The Cubs handed Caissie arguably the toughest challenge in the system by starting the teenager off in the tacky ball-using Southern League. His strikeouts spiked early but Caissie made adjustments and showed some improvements to his approach, helping bring the K-rate back down to a more manageable clip. He's still learning how to maximize his swing and take advantage of the high-end exit velocities it produces, but the plus raw pop is beginning to find its way into games with more frequency. Despite Caissie's size, he's no slouch in the field, with some sneaky athleticism and a strong arm, making him an above-average defender in a corner. Caissie will provide Chicago with outfield depth in 2024 but could be called upon soon to offer some thunder to the Cubs' lineup.

66.) Jace Jung, 2B, Detroit Tigers

The younger Jung continues to follow in big brother Josh's footsteps, first in the Big 12, then as a first-round draft selection, now hitting his way up the minor-league ladder and on the cusp of a Detroit call-up. After a lackluster post-draft performance, the bat came alive in his first full-season assignment, maintaining the average and producing a surprising amount of power. There's some swing-and-miss to his game but Jung has a firm grasp of the strike zone and has the plate discipline to draw his fair share of walks. Defensively, Jung got some reps at third during his time in the Arizona Fall League and was fine, but his limited range and arm strength make him better suited for second. It's a tough profile, but there's enough in the bat for Jung to make it work. A strong start this spring at Toledo will likely earn Jung a mid-summer look in the Tigers' infield.

67.) Nick Frasso, RHP, Los Angeles Dodgers

One of the top bits of evidence on just how far ahead the Dodgers really are at putting everything together is the 2022 trade deadline heist where Toronto coughed up a mid-breakout Frasso for Mitch White and Alex De Jesus. In his return from elbow surgery, the gangly right-hander was running monstrous whiff and chase numbers with his slider and changeup but was leaning more on his fastball, which itself was touching triple-digits from a tough arm slot. The Blue Jays just didn't know what they had, and Los Angeles scooped him in a minor challenge trade. Frasso has continued to consolidate his gains in the Dodgers system, with increasing emphasis on his secondary stuff. His velocity did take a slight step back in 2023, thanks to a more traditional starting workload, and he suffered a bit of a summer swoon. But he made it through the season and hurled 93 innings. Frasso is on the older side for a prospect—he's just three months younger than new

teammate Yoshinobu Yamamoto—and there's still some bullpen risk present, although he has quite a strong relief fallback.

68.) Carson Whisenhunt, LHP, San Francisco Giants

Whisenhunt's primary weapon is his changeup, beautiful at its best, with sharp dive and a dead-fish disappearing act. A great change really is fun to watch, even if there's a (well-deserved) stigma attached to minor-league changeup artists who lean on the pitch to dominate future history teachers. Fortunately for Whisenhunt, the former second-rounder also tosses a mid-90s heater from the left side and breaking stuff that appears well on its way to big-league cromulence. After 25 ⅓ innings of dominance against High-A competition—a 1.42 ERA and high-30s strikeout percentage—the 22-year-old was promoted to Double-A Richmond, where he took the ball four times before bowing out for the season with an elbow injury. This injury was not as bad as initially feared, and he ought to be more than ready for spring training. Whisenhunt should be joining his former ECU Pirates staffmate Gavin Williams in the bigs relatively shortly.

69.) Brady House, 3B, Washington Nationals

House achieved a strong bounceback campaign in 2023 after a back injury wrecked his 2022 season. Moved over to third base and protected with ample rest—he only played 88 games over a full uninterrupted season—House thrived offensively. He hit .312 and pushed his way up two levels from Low-A to Double-A, getting things mostly back on track as if 2022 never happened. He also started hitting the ball a lot harder without the injuries, over 10 mph on average, playing back to the high school reports that had him as one of the top power prospects in the 2021 draft. He's still quite rough around the edges, with a red-flag chase rate, too much swing-and-miss and too much contact on the ground, and he needs to keep this quality of contact up while actually playing a full-time schedule. But flashing his hit and power abilities again to this extent was quite a course correction for a prospect who looked in dire straits just a year ago.

70.) Thayron Liranzo, C, Los Angeles Dodgers

There were some whispers last year at this time from Dodgers' staff about Liranzo and his performance during the 2022 complex league season and the way the ball jumped off the bat despite his mediocre slash line. That talk grew louder last year as Liranzo broke out offensively in his first full-season assignment. Granted, Rancho Cucamonga is a hitter's paradise but the gaudy power numbers were backed up by elite exit velocities from both sides of the plate. There's going to be some swing-and-miss to the profile and it's not a given that Liranzo will make enough contact from the right side to continue to switch hit, but he'll get to enough of the raw pop to produce big-time power numbers. Like most young catchers, Liranzo is still raw as a framer and receiver, but showed improvements in both facets during his time in

Low-A. His solid athleticism and strong throwing arm will get him plenty of opportunity to develop behind the dish, but a move to the cold corner is also in play. He'll be tested next season in the cold-weather, less-hitter-friendly environment of the Midwest League. The contact issues might get exposed but if Liranzo can make the necessary adjustments, his huge power potential will strap a rocket to his prospect status.

71.) Michael Busch, IF/OF, Los Angeles Dodgers

A crowded major-league roster might make playing time hard to come by for Busch (you may have heard that they signed a new DH), especially after last season's struggles during his brief time with the Dodgers. That doesn't change the fact that Busch is a near-major-league ready bat who would be already penciled into a starting lineup on a team with less depth. His patient approach and ability to do damage from the left side make him a solid bet to produce offensive numbers when given the opportunity. Defensively, he can be plugged into multiple positions, even getting some run in the outfield last season. He's not going to win any Gold Gloves, but is also not a liability anywhere he gets placed on the diamond. It's a fairly safe bet that Busch winds up having a solid big-league career, one where he profiles as a versatile lefty run producer; it just might not be in Los Angeles.

72.) Connor Phillips, RHP, Cincinnati Reds

Phillips throws an incredible fastball, and this is borne out by virtually every metric available on the subject: It sits middle-upper and reaches upper-upper 90s, is high-spin and creates the illusion of rising action using the magic of superior induced vertical break. If you are guessing along, you may be expecting us to tell you next that his secondaries are well behind his fastball, need further refinement, so on and so forth. [Bzzzzzzt] Phillips throws an awesome sweeper that garnered huge whiffs both in the minors and in the big leagues, and his curveball is pretty good too. His brief late-season stretch in the bigs was kind of rocky, though, and you may be wondering why, given the preceding description of his stuff. Well, let's just say that in-zone command is still at least somewhat important, even when the pure stuff is excellent. Although he turned the ship around a bit during his last few starts, Phillips was knocked around more than one might have expected and presently runs the risk of being a bit too homer-prone for a high-end starter's role. A great breaker still needs to be landed consistently, and a great fastball still needs to be kept out of the dead zone.

73.) Noble Meyer, RHP, Miami Marlins

The Marlins went back to their strengths in last year's draft, selecting two prep pitchers within the first 35 selections, popping Meyer at 10 and lefty Thomas White with their second pick. Meyer brings a nice mix of stuff, polish and physical projection, even if the likely mid-rotation-ish outcome isn't the most thrilling thing to hear about a top-10 pick. Long and lean, he throws a mid-90s fastball with room for more, along with an already-advanced secondary mix that includes a slider, a curve and a change. The command and fastball shape will both require refinement, and there should be plenty of time to do it. It was encouraging to see Meyer make his full-season debut in his draft year, and he showed well in the short outings he was afforded.

74.) Yu-Min Lin, LHP, Arizona Diamondbacks

Lin sits around 90 mph with his sinking fastball. His best secondary is a potential plus change with above-average fade and feel, and he has two average-to-above breaking balls as well. This draws a picture of a certain type of pitching prospect. Pitching to contact, spotting all four quadrants of the strike zone, working backwards as needed, flashing that change when he absolutely needs a strikeout, but mixing his whole arsenal to keep hitters off balance. Well, the truth will muddy that image. Lin's fastball has an outlier shape and misses plenty of bats on its own, despite the below-average velocity. His twisty, torque-heavy delivery with a corresponding long arm action can mean occasional bouts of wildness, and his K and walk rates were closer to that of Jacob Misiorowski than Bob Tewksksbury. It still shakes out as two plus pitches and enough command to start, just perhaps not the polaroid you imagined.

75.) Sebastian Walcott, SS, Texas Rangers

For fake or real GMs, making decisions on prospects, the question can often come down to something like this: Would you prefer the high-performing, low-upside, sure big-leaguer college bat? Or would you like to trade it all in for what's in the mystery box? Walcott is the box. It's true that there are certain empirical trends working in the Bahamian's favor—he made it to full-season ball as a 17-year-old, for one, and he certainly hits the ball hard enough. He's also the type of athlete who makes difficult baseball actions look natural. On the other hand, he's tall and fairly broad-framed, which means that the contents of this metaphorical box could change—he might in the future become a third baseman, or a corner outfielder. Will his offensive game develop enough to make him an everyday player there? A star? There are hit tool doubts that need to be extinguished, typical for players of this age and experience level. If we see strong swing decisions and steady shortstop play in full-season ball, he could be near the top of this list a year from now. Please don't disregard the "if."

76.) Luisangel Acuña, SS/2B, New York Mets

Acuña was a great deadline return for the now aged and frequently unavailable Max Scherzer. The questions now become: Who is Luisangel Acuña, really, as a prospect, and what type of player will he be as a big leaguer? The 21-year-old is the kind of talent who can cause a minor civil war among a team of prospect writers. Some put a lot of weight on his contact ability, speed, defensive skills, and confident bearing, while others caution that his batted-ball profile is hardly ideal and may lead not only to a paucity of home runs, but also to a dip in batting average once he is faced with superior big-league defense. Fortunately, his floor is pretty high, even if his ceiling can be seen as limited. Acuña could soon slide right into an everyday role near the bottom of the lineup and at second base, or near the top of the lineup—if things break right.

77.) Ryan Clifford, 1B/OF, New York Mets

The second man involved in the Verlander exchange, Clifford already created a good return on the investment the Astros made in him when they lured him out of a Vanderbilt commitment in 2022 with an extremely over-slot bonus. Clifford attended a Research Triangle high school that specializes in educating future pro athletes, and he was ready for his moment—his trips south to Low-A Fayetteville and west to High-A Asheville produced both strong numbers and strong under-the-hood plate discipline and contact metrics. Hence the high-profile flip. He didn't do nearly as well following the trade, struggling with Brooklyn's large dimensions and difficult hitting background, though we are not talking about a huge sample of games and the underlying skill set remains intact. There truly is big power potential here, and his pitch selection is also generally strong. He will need to prove beyond all doubt his offensive abilities, however, because he isn't really an outfielder and is merely passable at first base at present.

78.) Edgar Quero, C, Chicago White Sox

All the big rule changes you saw debuted in the majors last season were first tested in the minors. Every level of organized ball has become a lab environment, which can make for tricky evaluation contexts. And no league was trickier to evaluate—for both pitchers and hitters—than the 2023 Southern League. The first half of the season featured a pre-tacked baseball, the second half, the standard specs. And no prospect was trickier to evaluate even in this context than Edgar Quero, who not only had to figure out the movement patterns for two different baseballs—both at the plate and behind it—but who was also jumping straight from Low-A in the process. You can even toss in an org switch in the middle of the year—he was dealt from the Angels to the White Sox for Lucas Giolito—to even further complicate things. Quero was a little bit better in the second half, but overall he struggled to damage the ball as much as he did in the more age-appropriate and friendlier confines of the Cal League in 2022. He did make important strides defensively, but everything else is a bit more muddled going forward. Expect the 21-year-old backstop to be back in Birmingham this year, for what hopefully will be a clarifying season with just one baseball on offer.

79.) Kevin McGonigle, SS/2B, Detroit Tigers

The superlative "best prep hit tool in the draft class" has been a bit of a prospect curse. You'll have to read further for last year's edition, Termarr Johnson, who hit .244 across two A-ball levels. McGonigle went much later in his draft than Johnson, lasting to the 37th pick. He's likely to end up at

second base and as a cold-weather prep hitter, perhaps didn't get the looks in the spring that might have helped raise his stock. Regardless, we had him ranked as a top-20 prospect in the draft class, and his strong pro debut did nothing to dissuade us from doubling down on this prospect list. It's a small sample, but if you are going to be a future .300 hitter in the majors, hitting .355 in the Florida State League while making a ton of contact is a decent start. Everything else checks out here, as McGonigle has a simple, in-sync swing with plenty of bat speed, but we may have also written those things about Forrest Wall and Trent Grisham after they were drafted.

80.) Kevin Alcántara, OF, Chicago Cubs

Few in minor-league baseball possess the upside of Alcántara. It's been a theme since signing with the Yankees in 2018 and a large reason the Cubs made him the key return when trading franchise cornerstone Anthony Rizzo in 2021. There are potential plus tools across the board, but so far Alcántara has shown them only in spurts during his professional career. As a 20-year-old in High-A he looked overmatched early but made enough adjustments to become one of the Midwest League's hottest hitters by the end of the season. Alcántara will need to continue that consistent contact if he's to take advantage of his plus raw pop, which is currently curtailed by his propensity to hit the ball on the ground. Defensively, if not for Pete Crow-Armstrong, Alcántara would be considered the top glove in the organization. He moves well in center, shows good instincts and has enough arm strength to handle the position. There's enough speed and defense to give Alcántara a floor of a reserve outfielder but if the impact ability begins to show up more consistently, there's a chance he can reach All-Star levels.

81.) Druw Jones, OF, Arizona Diamondbacks

The biggest problem for Jones since he was picked second overall in the 2022 draft has been just staying on the field. As has become a troubling tradition for Diamondbacks first-round picks, Jones was quickly felled by a major shoulder injury, tearing his labrum before he could debut in the complex. In 2023 two leg injuries limited him to just 41 games. Normally we would just lament the lost development time and mostly default to the pre-draft report, but there have been some worrying signs in his limited on-field action. Jones has struggled to greet pitches out in front of the plate despite plus bat speed (continuing a concerning trend dating back to high school where he rarely pulls the ball in the air), leading to questions about his pitch recognition—also a concern in those pre-draft reports. And he struggled against A-ball spin, which okay, maybe you give him a pass on for now because of the lack of reps. The one thing you won't have to worry about is the defensive profile. Jones should challenge for Gold Gloves in center as he already glides from gap-to-gap with the greatest of ease. If you know you have at least a plus center field glove, you'll be more forgiving on the offensive evaluation, but we will need to see more from (and more of) Jones in 2024.

82.) Enrique Bradfield, OF, Baltimore Orioles

Bradfield is one of the fastest runners and best defenders in the entire minors, and that's not all of his game whatsoever—he also possesses truly elite contact ability and makes tremendous swing decisions. What he doesn't do is drive the ball in the air *at all*; his ground-ball rate was astronomical (subterranean?) in his pro debut and his swing is geared for low, opposite-field contact. That said, given his speed, a moderately hit grounder to short is a potential infield hit for Bradfield nearly every time, so that overall offensive profile isn't *necessarily* a bad thing. It's extremely, extremely unusual in the modern game to see a true slap-and-dash hitter, and it remains to be seen whether the Orioles will try to coax some pulled fly-ball contact out of it. That sort of swing plane change certainly could make Bradfield more valuable if he starts dumping balls in the gap and flying around the bases, but also could turn grounders to short that he can beat out into grounders to second that he can't.

83.) Thomas Saggese, IF, St. Louis Cardinals

Saggese had one of the bigger prospect glow-ups in 2023, completing the journey from borderline personal cheeseball type to centerpiece of a major deadline deal. The Cardinals clearly liked what we liked in Saggese: great feel for contact and a shockingly authoritative swing considering his size. The former fifth-rounder didn't miss a beat after changing Texas League locales, hitting over .300 and whacking 25 homers at Double-A before scuffling a bit after a promotion to Triple-A. Saggese isn't an everyday shortstop but he can play there in a pinch, and still broadly profiles as a utility type who should be fine at both second and third. The increased power output has bolstered the ceiling of a player who already had a pretty high floor, but there are one or two issues to interrogate as the 21-year-old finishes his development. He swings quite a lot, and although he very frequently squares the ball up, his high-end exits aren't extraordinary. We tend to think he'll be fine, though, and that he'll fit in quite well for someone who was only recently given access to Cardinals devil magic.

84.) Moises Ballesteros, C, Chicago Cubs

Signed out of Venezuela in 2021, Ballesteros showed flickers in his previous two professional seasons but the light turned on in a breakout offensive performance in 2023. As a 19-year-old he started the year in the extremely pitcher-friendly environment of Myrtle Beach, slugging his way through South Bend before landing on Double-A Tennessee's playoff roster. Ballesteros combines an excellent ability to make contact with his advanced approach at the plate, recognizing spin well and keeping the chase to a minimum. It's not weak contact either; he utilizes a quick bat and his strong physical frame to produce high exit velocities which should lead to above-average power numbers at the big-league level. The body will require maintenance if he's to stick behind the plate, but Ballesteros is a sneaky-good athlete who showed improvement as a receiver in 2023. If the defensive skills continue to develop, Ballesteros will be one of the few catchers that don't need to be hidden at the back of a lineup.

85.) Cade Cavalli, RHP, Washington Nationals

Cavalli had Tommy John surgery towards the end of the 2022 season, and in the intervening 18 months or so, he hasn't pitched and we've taken a closer look at how we evaluate pitching prospects. Cavalli would have been the best pitching prospect of 2014—which also explains why Mike Rizzo took him in the first round in 2020—showing a mid-90s fastball that could touch triple digits, two potential above-average breaking balls and a developing change. He looks the part too, a broad 6-foot-4 frame that appears built to log innings. Cavalli hasn't really done that though—before his Tommy John surgery he had recurring arm injuries dating back to his college years at Oklahoma. When he gets back on the mound sometime this summer we'll be keeping an eye on that fastball, as despite his ability to redline a radar gun, his heater has a rather anonymous shape and spin profile. Plus-plus velocity does not a plus-plus fastball make. Yeah, in this case it's not Cavalli, it's us. We've just changed (while Nationals pitching development has not). But at worst the triple-digit heat and plus power curve should play in the late innings.

86.) Max Meyer, RHP, Miami Marlins

Cavalli and Meyer are once again paired together; Meyer also missed all of 2023 after summer 2022 Tommy John surgery. Both pitchers were 2020 first-round draft picks with exceptional arm strength, and both had upper-minors whiff concerns relating to command and pitch design issues. Meyer is shorter and leans a lot on his exceptional plus-plus slider, so he's carried the "potential relief conversion" since before he was drafted, though his less-utilized changeup did jump a bit under Miami's pitching development. Meyer is a bit ahead of Cavalli on his recovery as his surgery was earlier, and should be back early in 2024.

87.) Yanquiel Fernandez, OF, Colorado Rockies

Fernandez hit a ball 119 mph in 2023, before he could legally drink. You can count the number of *major* leaguers who are capable of posting an exit velocity that high on one hand, and they're all no-doubt 80-grade power guys. Returning to our discussion about how easy it should be to discern an elite tool, one batting practice session from Fernandez should suffice. What you won't see at 5 o'clock, though, is how often he chases and whiffs. Despite the high swing-and-miss, low walk rate and indifferent corner outfield defense, Fernandez just hits the ball so hard at such a young age that he tantalizes regardless. Fernandez hit just .206/.262/.362 after his promotion to Double-A, where the pitching gets a lot better; he'll get another shot at the Eastern League in 2024 as a still young-for-his-level 21-year-old. So beware of flying objects if you are stuck on I-91 in downtown Hartford during rush hour.

88.) Christian Scott, RHP, New York Mets

Scott started the 2023 season completely off the national radar. A 2021 fifth-round college reliever out of Florida, he had a solid, if unspectacular, first full pro campaign in 2022 as an A-ball swingman; he was a mildly compelling relief prospect with interesting arm strength and a cool slider, no more and no less. But in obscurity he worked on maxing out intriguing four-seam fastball characteristics—he now attacks hitters with an extremely difficult movement and vertical approach angle profile—while downplaying his sinkers, and his command and changeup feel jumped several grades. Moving into a full-time starting role for the first time since high school, Scott suddenly emerged over the summer as one of the better pitchers in the minors, running a 107:12 K:BB ratio while spending most of the season at Double-A. He still only threw 87 ⅔ innings, which is quite light for a starter even in today's climate, but he's going to be a good major-league starting pitcher soon if he can take the ball consistently enough.

89.) Nolan Schanuel, 1B, Los Angeles Angels

When you've struggled to develop prospects as mightily as the Angels have for the past decade, we suppose there are worse draft strategies than just taking the most advanced college player on the board and then getting them to the majors as quickly as possible. Reid Detmers, Sam Bachman and Zach Neto all fit that bill and all are likely to be significant parts of the Angels' 2024 major-league roster. So will Schanuel, who played just 22 games in the minors before taking over the everyday first base gig in Anaheim. Owner of a ludicrous 14:71 K:BB ratio his junior season at Florida Atlantic, Schanuel has Evan Carter-quality swing decisions and strong contact ability, but does even less damage on contact. It's an amusing juxtaposition, given that he's a 6-foot-4 first baseman that swings like he's Luis Arraez, but that can work if he hits like Luis Arraez. He did in the minors, but less so in the majors, where his in-zone contact rate was merely "above-average" rather than "Luis Arraez." Schanuel also hits the ball...not as hard as Luis Arraez. Jumping from Conference USA to the AL West in the space of a few months was always going to be a challenge, and you'd expect him to make those first-order adjustments in time, but Schanuel will need to have his OBP *and* slugging start with a 4 in order to be more than a second-division starter on a second-division Angels team.

90.) Termarr Johnson, 2B, Pittsburgh Pirates

Whatever the opposite of a prospect glow-up might be called, that's what happened last year. That isn't to say that there aren't things to like here, and they will be enumerated, but Johnson's star has nevertheless dimmed to such an extent that the former fourth-overall pick was in danger of dropping off of this list entirely. The primary takeaway here ought to be that what was once a hit tool-driven offensive profile—a generational hit tool, according to some reports—has done a near-complete 180 into a power-driven profile with significant hit tool concerns. Let's first acknowledge the positives: The former Atlanta prep is still quite young, having played all of last season at age 19. The power is legit, as evidenced by a quick, explosive swing and the 18 homers he whacked over 462 plate appearances between Low-A Bradenton and High-A Greensboro. Most impressively, his eye at the plate is incredibly advanced for his age and he commands the zone extraordinarily well. There are really only a couple of issues, though unfortunately they are of the kind that can sink a profile if they are not corrected. A bad in-zone contact rate has led to quite a few whiffs, and the second base-only defensive profile doesn't help matters. Still, Johnson is quite talented and may be able to turn things around if he can begin to adapt his aggressive, stomp-and-lift swing to different situations.

91.) James Triantos, 2B, Chicago Cubs

The hallmark for Triantos is his elite bat-to-ball ability and advanced approach. The former second-round selection sprays hard line drives to all fields, and while there's not much in terms of over-the-fence power, Triantos racks up plenty of gap-to-gap doubles. Listed as a third baseman when the Cubs went over slot to draft him in 2021, he's been shuffled around to multiple positions trying to find a permanent defensive home. Nothing really stuck until Triantos showed up to camp in better physical shape last year and seemed to settle in at the keystone. He'll be an average to slightly above defender at second, with lateral quickness, soft hands and enough arm strength to finish off double plays. A right-handed hit tool-driven profile is tough and there's not much of a floor for Triantos if his bat doesn't continue to progress but so far, as a professional, he's shown the ability to make consistent, quality contact.

92.) Chase Dollander, RHP, Colorado Rockies

Going into the 2023 NCAA season, Dollander was every bit the draft prospect as Paul Skenes. Their subsequent college campaigns took them in opposite directions, as Skenes capped a historic pitching season by being voted Most Outstanding Player in the College World Series, while Dollander struggled to consistently land his stuff and posted a near 5.00 ERA for Tennessee. He still flashed an analytically-friendly arsenal, led by a mid-90s fastball that can miss bats in the zone and a potential plus-plus slider every bit as good as Skenes when it's at its best. Dollander wasn't at his best much in 2023, but in a pitching savvy org that can find the right tweaks to get his command back, Dollander could quickly move up this list. We will leave it as an exercise for the reader to determine if the Colorado Rockies are that organization going into 2024.

93.) Tekoah Roby, RHP, St. Louis Cardinals

Taken in the third round in the 2020 draft by the Rangers (turns out that was a pretty good draft for them), Roby has battled injuries and inconsistency throughout his professional career—he rebuilt his arm action over the past couple of years only to be beset by a shoulder issue last season. He was actually out of action when the Jordan Montgomery trade flipped him into the Cardinals organization. Despite the setbacks, he's retained a collection of good stuff that includes a strong and riding mid-90s fastball, a sharp curve that projects plus and a potentially above-average changeup. Roby was innings-limited but effective when he returned to Double-A action in late August, and a full campaign in 2024 would put him on the fast track to a big-league starter outcome.

94.) Jordan Wicks, LHP, Chicago Cubs

Wicks provided just what the Cubs needed down the stretch, stringing together six solid starts before his unfortunate clunker in Game 161. Despite the sour end to the season, Wicks still looks to be a future rotation stalwart on the North Side. It's a classic crafty-lefty profile with his low-90s fastball likely his fifth-best pitch, relying instead on a change and a trio of breakers to keep hitters off-balance. The changeup was the calling card coming out of Kansas State but has yet to turn it into a true swing-and-miss offering at the professional level. The Cubs helped him fine-tune the other secondaries and the three distinct and improving benders give Wicks an arsenal deep enough to profile him as a back-of-the-rotation innings-eater. If the command of the change improves enough to take advantage of its movement, he'll have enough strikeout ability to become a mid-rotation starter.

95.) Orelvis Martinez, IF, Toronto Blue Jays

"If I can change, and you can change, everybody can change." That line from *Rocky IV* is perhaps the quintessential 80s quote, but 40 years later Martinez took it to heart. Mostly off prospect radars after hitting .203 in Double-A in 2022, he improved his swing decisions by two full grades, cutting his chase rate to more than acceptable levels given how much damage Martinez can do when he finds a pitch in his nitro zone. Never likely to stick at shortstop, he bounced around the infield in 2023, and the Jays have short-term needs at both second and third—his likely best position. A year ago, Martinez breaking camp as a 2024 starter seemed less likely than Rocky Balboa downing Ivan Drago in Moscow, but Martinez's changes have him in line to be a power-hitting third baseman for the Jays for the balance of the decade

96.) Blake Mitchell, C, Kansas City Royals

"Mama, don't let your children grow up to draft prep catchers." We get why Mitchell is tempting. He's a plus athlete that could grow into above-average hit and power tools. He has defensive fallbacks other than first base if the bat develops ahead of the glove, or the glove just doesn't develop enough. The list of good two-way catchers is short and generally populated by players that make a few All-Star games. That list is also very rarely populated by former prep picks, and Mitchell is more likely to be Neil Walker than Joe Mauer. And, well, Neil Walker was once no. 94 on this list, so there ya go.

97.) Bryce Eldridge, TWP, San Francisco Giants

Eldridge is the second consecutive two-way player the Giants have taken in the first round, although top 2022 pick Reggie Crawford seems destined for life as a left-handed pitcher only. San Francisco had Eldridge focus on hitting after the draft, converting him from his amateur position of first base to right field. He terrorized the complex league with sweet blasts from the left side of the plate, slugging .647 before a late promotion to Low-A. He's a huge kid and he might end up back at first long-term, but for now he has the speed and agility to amble around the grass, and he's showing plus-plus power potential and strong swing decisions already. His bat might be too valuable for the Giants to follow through on his development as a pitcher—there just aren't many teenagers who hit the ball this hard—but he's also a projectable pitching prospect, up to the mid-90s with a plus slider.

98.) Ignacio Alvarez, SS, Atlanta Braves

Alvarez is the vaunted "professional hitter" type. He's got excellent feel for contact and great plate discipline, and he actually does decent damage for his age. The issue stopping him from having significant game power at this point is his level swing plane; he comes through the zone pretty flat and just doesn't get a ton of lift on the ball, limiting him to moderate gap power at present. This is often something young hitters improve at, and Alvarez is only 20 with many of the other tools for all-around offensive success. He's very likely to move off the shortstop position due to lack of agility and speed, although he should remain somewhere on the dirt.

99.) Denzel Clarke, OF, Oakland Athletics

A fourth-rounder out of a small school (Cal State Northridge) in 2021, the now 23-year-old Clarke has the characteristics of a late bloomer who nevertheless works himself into the big leagues on an everyday basis. The Canadian is a big man with many talents—he runs well, has both power and patience and handles center field ably. He debuted well in Low-A in 2022, struggled a bit upon a promotion to High-A, and was doing more than well enough (.261/.381/.496 with 12 homers in 286 plate appearances) at Double-A this past season before a shoulder ailment cut his season short in July. The primary concern here is the strikeout rate, which hovers around 30% even after some recent improvement in that regard. Lost development time is never welcome, especially so when a player possesses this particular set of traits. The A's will hope that Clarke's good work continues apace upon his return, and that he will soon be able to add some excitement to their lineup.

100.) Juan Brito, 2B, Cleveland Guardians

The Guardians' swap of Nolan Jones for Brito last winter did not go well in the short term. Jones' 122 DRC+ would have been third-best on Cleveland's roster, but trades are long-term value plays, especially when dealing for a prospect that hadn't seen High-A yet. Well, Brito dispatched that level by Memorial Day, kept hitting in Double-A, and made it all the way to the International League for a last-week-of-the-season cameo. He's a pretty good second baseman, but mostly limited to the keystone. The switch-hitting Brito has been better from the left side throughout his pro career, and covers the zone much better against righties. If you are going to have a platoon split though, that's the one to have—and not an uncommon one for a young switch-hitter. Brito is an absolutely annoying at-bat, fouling stuff off until he gets something he can line into the gap, and there's potentially average over-the-fence power in his stick as well. Living up to being traded for Jones has gotten a lot tougher in the last year, but Brito has a broad set of skills that could add up to the same three or four wins per season.

101.) Chase Davis, OF, St. Louis Cardinals

Davis had a true breakout in his junior year at Arizona in 2023, with a huge jump in contact ability sparking even more power and hit prowess than he'd already shown. He displayed top-end exit velocities and swing decisions on par with the top college bats like Langford and Crews, and was nearly as good, ultimately posting a .362/.489/.742 line for the Wildcats. Sent to Low-A after signing, he really struggled in 34 games, slugging just .269 with his average exit velocity tanking down to 85 mph. We don't have a great explanation as to why Davis' game power just evaporated, and his 90th-percentile exit velocity remained near 103 mph (which points to a weird small sample fluke), but he did struggle in a small sample with wood bats on the Cape in 2022 as well. For now we're giving him a partial mulligan, because the well-rounded offensive potential he showed in college was so enticing.

MLB Managers

Rocco Baldelli   wRM+: 103

TEAM	YEAR	W	L	Pythag +/-	Avg PC	100+ P	120+ P	QS	REL	REL w Zero R	IBB	PH	PH Avg	PH HR	SB2	CS2	SB3	CS3	SAC Att	SAC %	POS SAC	Squeeze
MIN	2023	87	75	-7	88.2	20	0	76	490	340	16	185	.228	7	68	18	15	0	27	44	12	4

David Bell   wRM+: 102

TEAM	YEAR	W	L	Pythag +/-	Avg PC	100+ P	120+ P	QS	REL	REL w Zero R	IBB	PH	PH Avg	PH HR	SB2	CS2	SB3	CS3	SAC Att	SAC %	POS SAC	Squeeze
CIN	2023	82	80	5	84.6	30	0	44	605	422	13	146	.278	9	153	37	35	12	32	59	19	1

Brandon Hyde   wRM+: 102

TEAM	YEAR	W	L	Pythag +/-	Avg PC	100+ P	120+ P	QS	REL	REL w Zero R	IBB	PH	PH Avg	PH HR	SB2	CS2	SB3	CS3	SAC Att	SAC %	POS SAC	Squeeze
BAL	2023	101	61	6	88.9	13	0	68	560	403	16	135	.237	1	97	20	17	2	26	81	21	0

Craig Counsell   wRM+: 102

TEAM	YEAR	W	L	Pythag +/-	Avg PC	100+ P	120+ P	QS	REL	REL w Zero R	IBB	PH	PH Avg	PH HR	SB2	CS2	SB3	CS3	SAC Att	SAC %	POS SAC	Squeeze
MIL	2023	92	70	1	87.9	18	0	68	518	387	7	122	.221	4	114	26	15	2	13	54	7	0

Oliver Marmol   wRM+: 101

TEAM	YEAR	W	L	Pythag +/-	Avg PC	100+ P	120+ P	QS	REL	REL w Zero R	IBB	PH	PH Avg	PH HR	SB2	CS2	SB3	CS3	SAC Att	SAC %	POS SAC	Squeeze
STL	2023	71	91	1	89.2	26	0	48	484	312	6	104	.207	2	77	27	22	6	19	68	13	0

Derek Shelton   wRM+: 101

TEAM	YEAR	W	L	Pythag +/-	Avg PC	100+ P	120+ P	QS	REL	REL w Zero R	IBB	PH	PH Avg	PH HR	SB2	CS2	SB3	CS3	SAC Att	SAC %	POS SAC	Squeeze
PIT	2023	76	86	6	83.3	21	0	53	529	356	25	152	.241	4	90	29	27	12	44	57	25	1

Skip Schumaker   wRM+: 101

TEAM	YEAR	W	L	Pythag +/-	Avg PC	100+ P	120+ P	QS	REL	REL w Zero R	IBB	PH	PH Avg	PH HR	SB2	CS2	SB3	CS3	SAC Att	SAC %	POS SAC	Squeeze
MIA	2023	84	78	10	82.3	13	0	52	544	379	20	112	.282	4	71	20	14	0	34	65	22	0

Mark Kotsay   wRM+: 101

TEAM	YEAR	W	L	Pythag +/-	Avg PC	100+ P	120+ P	QS	REL	REL w Zero R	IBB	PH	PH Avg	PH HR	SB2	CS2	SB3	CS3	SAC Att	SAC %	POS SAC	Squeeze
OAK	2023	50	112	4	80.9	17	0	32	532	323	33	204	.246	5	116	26	33	5	50	56	28	2

A. J. Hinch   wRM+: 101

TEAM	YEAR	W	L	Pythag +/-	Avg PC	100+ P	120+ P	QS	REL	REL w Zero R	IBB	PH	PH Avg	PH HR	SB2	CS2	SB3	CS3	SAC Att	SAC %	POS SAC	Squeeze
DET	2023	78	84	6	79.5	8	0	44	535	356	8	173	.204	7	80	24	5	0	18	72	13	0

Scott Servais   wRM+: 101

TEAM	YEAR	W	L	Pythag +/-	Avg PC	100+ P	120+ P	QS	REL	REL w Zero R	IBB	PH	PH Avg	PH HR	SB2	CS2	SB3	CS3	SAC Att	SAC %	POS SAC	Squeeze
SEA	2023	88	74	-4	88.0	18	0	74	550	398	22	149	.206	5	100	27	17	3	7	57	4	0

Buck Showalter   wRM+: 100

TEAM	YEAR	W	L	Pythag +/-	Avg PC	100+ P	120+ P	QS	REL	REL w Zero R	IBB	PH	PH Avg	PH HR	SB2	CS2	SB3	CS3	SAC Att	SAC %	POS SAC	Squeeze
NYM	2023	75	86	-5	89.8	34	0	59	522	361	13	124	.170	5	102	14	16	1	27	70	19	1

Matt Quatraro   wRM+: 100

TEAM	YEAR	W	L	Pythag +/-	Avg PC	100+ P	120+ P	QS	REL	REL w Zero R	IBB	PH	PH Avg	PH HR	SB2	CS2	SB3	CS3	SAC Att	SAC %	POS SAC	Squeeze
KC	2023	56	106	-6	78.9	17	0	32	526	327	8	100	.155	1	139	38	26	11	24	58	14	2

David Ross   wRM+: 100

TEAM	YEAR	W	L	Pythag +/-	Avg PC	100+ P	120+ P	QS	REL	REL w Zero R	IBB	PH	PH Avg	PH HR	SB2	CS2	SB3	CS3	SAC Att	SAC %	POS SAC	Squeeze
CHC	2023	83	79	-8	84.8	12	0	71	510	355	5	124	.218	3	125	29	16	2	23	65	15	1

Pedro Grifol   wRM+: 100

TEAM	YEAR	W	L	Pythag +/-	Avg PC	100+ P	120+ P	QS	REL	REL w Zero R	IBB	PH	PH Avg	PH HR	SB2	CS2	SB3	CS3	SAC Att	SAC %	POS SAC	Squeeze
CHW	2023	61	101	1	91.5	43	0	51	521	330	14	107	.187	1	69	20	15	2	24	62	16	0

Alex Cora wRM+: 100

TEAM	YEAR	W	L	Pythag +/-	Avg PC	100+ P	120+ P	QS	REL	REL w Zero R	IBB	PH	PH Avg	PH HR	SB2	CS2	SB3	CS3	SAC Att	SAC %	POS SAC	Squeeze
BOS	2023	78	84	-3	80.3	18	0	47	514	335	21	149	.215	2	107	24	7	0	14	79	11	1

Gabe Kapler wRM+: 100

TEAM	YEAR	W	L	Pythag +/-	Avg PC	100+ P	120+ P	QS	REL	REL w Zero R	IBB	PH	PH Avg	PH HR	SB2	CS2	SB3	CS3	SAC Att	SAC %	POS SAC	Squeeze
SF	2023	78	81	3	71.7	21	1	51	489	307	22	216	.207	6	54	13	3	1	31	55	17	3

Aaron Boone wRM+: 100

TEAM	YEAR	W	L	Pythag +/-	Avg PC	100+ P	120+ P	QS	REL	REL w Zero R	IBB	PH	PH Avg	PH HR	SB2	CS2	SB3	CS3	SAC Att	SAC %	POS SAC	Squeeze
NYY	2023	82	80	4	84.1	21	0	48	503	357	6	81	.227	1	84	27	14	3	22	41	9	1

Torey Lovullo wRM+: 99

TEAM	YEAR	W	L	Pythag +/-	Avg PC	100+ P	120+ P	QS	REL	REL w Zero R	IBB	PH	PH Avg	PH HR	SB2	CS2	SB3	CS3	SAC Att	SAC %	POS SAC	Squeeze
AZ	2023	84	78	5	84.7	12	0	57	547	382	13	150	.189	2	137	19	29	5	50	72	36	1

Terry Francona wRM+: 99

TEAM	YEAR	W	L	Pythag +/-	Avg PC	100+ P	120+ P	QS	REL	REL w Zero R	IBB	PH	PH Avg	PH HR	SB2	CS2	SB3	CS3	SAC Att	SAC %	POS SAC	Squeeze
CLE	2023	76	86	-1	87.0	17	0	57	545	375	9	91	.163	0	136	34	13	4	26	50	13	0

Rob Thomson wRM+: 99

TEAM	YEAR	W	L	Pythag +/-	Avg PC	100+ P	120+ P	QS	REL	REL w Zero R	IBB	PH	PH Avg	PH HR	SB2	CS2	SB3	CS3	SAC Att	SAC %	POS SAC	Squeeze
PHI	2023	90	72	0	89.4	42	1	70	523	377	6	93	.228	4	121	23	21	3	24	54	13	1

Dave Martinez wRM+: 99

TEAM	YEAR	W	L	Pythag +/-	Avg PC	100+ P	120+ P	QS	REL	REL w Zero R	IBB	PH	PH Avg	PH HR	SB2	CS2	SB3	CS3	SAC Att	SAC %	POS SAC	Squeeze
WAS	2023	71	91	5	90.2	28	0	50	526	339	25	79	.273	2	112	26	13	1	36	56	20	1

Bud Black wRM+: 99

TEAM	YEAR	W	L	Pythag +/-	Avg PC	100+ P	120+ P	QS	REL	REL w Zero R	IBB	PH	PH Avg	PH HR	SB2	CS2	SB3	CS3	SAC Att	SAC %	POS SAC	Squeeze
COL	2023	59	103	0	78.6	2	0	39	544	336	13	107	.245	1	66	25	10	1	22	50	11	0

Bruce Bochy wRM+: 99

TEAM	YEAR	W	L	Pythag +/-	Avg PC	100+ P	120+ P	QS	REL	REL w Zero R	IBB	PH	PH Avg	PH HR	SB2	CS2	SB3	CS3	SAC Att	SAC %	POS SAC	Squeeze
TEX	2023	90	72	-8	85.8	14	0	66	467	312	19	71	.233	0	73	18	6	1	14	71	10	0

Dusty Baker wRM+: 99

TEAM	YEAR	W	L	Pythag +/-	Avg PC	100+ P	120+ P	QS	REL	REL w Zero R	IBB	PH	PH Avg	PH HR	SB2	CS2	SB3	CS3	SAC Att	SAC %	POS SAC	Squeeze
HOU	2023	90	72	-5	91.9	18	0	70	513	373	6	82	.194	1	95	31	12	3	24	58	14	2

John Schneider wRM+: 99

TEAM	YEAR	W	L	Pythag +/-	Avg PC	100+ P	120+ P	QS	REL	REL w Zero R	IBB	PH	PH Avg	PH HR	SB2	CS2	SB3	CS3	SAC Att	SAC %	POS SAC	Squeeze
TOR	2023	89	73	-1	90.9	36	0	70	550	401	29	114	.232	3	80	27	19	6	12	33	4	0

Kevin Cash wRM+: 99

TEAM	YEAR	W	L	Pythag +/-	Avg PC	100+ P	120+ P	QS	REL	REL w Zero R	IBB	PH	PH Avg	PH HR	SB2	CS2	SB3	CS3	SAC Att	SAC %	POS SAC	Squeeze
TB	2023	99	63	-2	75.8	8	0	49	536	372	10	105	.305	2	131	37	29	5	12	50	6	1

Brian Snitker wRM+: 98

TEAM	YEAR	W	L	Pythag +/-	Avg PC	100+ P	120+ P	QS	REL	REL w Zero R	IBB	PH	PH Avg	PH HR	SB2	CS2	SB3	CS3	SAC Att	SAC %	POS SAC	Squeeze
ATL	2023	104	58	1	88.3	33	0	60	532	367	14	71	.179	1	115	21	17	5	3	67	2	0

Phil Nevin wRM+: 98

TEAM	YEAR	W	L	Pythag +/-	Avg PC	100+ P	120+ P	QS	REL	REL w Zero R	IBB	PH	PH Avg	PH HR	SB2	CS2	SB3	CS3	SAC Att	SAC %	POS SAC	Squeeze
LAA	2023	73	89	1	88.1	35	0	48	491	306	41	113	.172	3	64	25	9	7	20	40	8	1

Bob Melvin wRM+: 98

TEAM	YEAR	W	L	Pythag +/-	Avg PC	100+ P	120+ P	QS	REL	REL w Zero R	IBB	PH	PH Avg	PH HR	SB2	CS2	SB3	CS3	SAC Att	SAC %	POS SAC	Squeeze
SD	2023	82	80	-11	89.2	33	1	75	508	360	14	114	.113	2	108	27	27	4	37	60	22	2

Dave Roberts wRM+: 97

TEAM	YEAR	W	L	Pythag +/-	Avg PC	100+ P	120+ P	QS	REL	REL w Zero R	IBB	PH	PH Avg	PH HR	SB2	CS2	SB3	CS3	SAC Att	SAC %	POS SAC	Squeeze
LAD	2023	100	62	-2	79.5	9	0	53	551	399	20	176	.230	5	99	22	7	2	9	56	5	0

2024 PECOTA Projected Standings

AL East	Sim W	Sim L	Sim W%	RS	RA	Div %	WC %	Playoff %	WS %
New York Yankees	92.6	69.4	.572	823	697	51.4	35.6	87.0	10.1
Toronto Blue Jays	87.6	74.4	.541	772	696	18.6	43.4	62.0	5.8
Tampa Bay Rays	86.6	75.4	.535	742	676	17.7	39.8	57.5	3.7
Baltimore Orioles	85.0	77.0	.525	740	692	10.1	36.7	46.8	4.0
Boston Red Sox	80.3	81.7	.496	769	759	2.2	18.0	20.2	0.2
AL Central	**Sim W**	**Sim L**	**Sim W%**	**RS**	**RA**	**Div %**	**WC %**	**Playoff %**	**WS %**
Minnesota Twins	88.8	73.2	.548	745	684	68.7	9.4	78.1	6.5
Cleveland Guardians	83.9	78.1	.518	734	712	27.6	16.8	44.4	2.5
Detroit Tigers	74.0	88.0	.457	653	721	2.4	2.3	4.7	0.1
Kansas City Royals	70.9	91.1	.438	692	794	1.3	0.8	2.1	0.0
Chicago White Sox	66.1	95.9	.408	690	841	0.0	0.1	0.1	0.0
AL West	**Sim W**	**Sim L**	**Sim W%**	**RS**	**RA**	**Div %**	**WC %**	**Playoff %**	**WS %**
Houston Astros	95.0	67.0	.586	843	713	74.7	18.5	93.2	11.0
Texas Rangers	86.4	75.6	.533	767	715	14.9	41.0	55.9	3.6
Seattle Mariners	85.1	76.9	.525	733	694	10.3	35.4	45.7	2.1
Los Angeles Angels	73.4	88.6	.453	733	804	0.1	2.2	2.3	0.0
Oakland Athletics	64.1	97.9	.396	678	835	0.0	0.0	0.0	0.0

NL East	Sim W	Sim L	Sim W%	RS	RA	Div %	WC %	Playoff %	WS %
Atlanta Braves	101.2	60.8	.625	857	668	93.3	6.6	99.9	16.1
Philadelphia Phillies	84.5	77.5	.522	768	732	2.8	51.0	53.8	1.5
New York Mets	83.9	78.1	.518	779	752	2.7	47.5	50.2	2.5
Miami Marlins	81.1	80.9	.501	734	732	1.2	31.8	33.0	1.2
Washington Nationals	58.6	103.4	.362	664	881	0.0	0.0	0.0	0.0
NL Central	**Sim W**	**Sim L**	**Sim W%**	**RS**	**RA**	**Div %**	**WC %**	**Playoff %**	**WS %**
St. Louis Cardinals	85.0	77.0	.525	778	748	45.4	14.9	60.3	2.9
Chicago Cubs	81.1	80.9	.501	766	773	20.9	14.8	35.7	1.7
Milwaukee Brewers	80.8	81.2	.499	694	702	22.2	12.5	34.7	0.9
Cincinnati Reds	77.8	84.2	.480	795	831	9.9	8.4	18.3	0.3
Pittsburgh Pirates	71.3	90.7	.440	708	803	1.6	1.8	3.4	0.0
NL West	**Sim W**	**Sim L**	**Sim W%**	**RS**	**RA**	**Div %**	**WC %**	**Playoff %**	**WS %**
Los Angeles Dodgers	102.7	59.3	.634	887	675	95.9	3.9	99.8	19.7
Arizona Diamondbacks	84.5	77.5	.522	782	747	2.4	51.9	54.3	1.9
San Francisco Giants	80.8	81.2	.499	719	723	1.2	30.6	31.8	0.8
San Diego Padres	79.2	82.8	.489	732	746	0.5	24.3	24.8	0.9
Colorado Rockies	57.6	104.4	.356	678	907	0.0	0.0	0.0	0.0

2024 PECOTA Leaderboards

Catcher DRC+

Rank	Name	Team	DRC+
1	Adley Rutschman	BAL	123
2	Will Smith	LAD	122
3	Alejandro Kirk	TOR	117
3	W. Contreras	STL	117
5	Danny Jansen	TOR	115
6	Keibert Ruiz	WAS	113
7	Sean Murphy	ATL	112
7	Yainer Diaz	HOU	112
9	W. Contreras	MIL	110
10	Salvador Perez	KC	109
10	F. Alvarez	NYM	109
12	Luis Campusano	SD	103
13	Cal Raleigh	SEA	102
13	Bo Naylor	CLE	102
13	Gabriel Moreno	AZ	102

First Base DRC+

Rank	Name	Team	DRC+
1	Matt Olson	ATL	145
2	V. Guerrero	TOR	136
3	Freddie Freeman	LAD	134
4	Pete Alonso	NYM	133
5	Paul Goldschmidt	STL	126
6	Yandy Díaz	TB	124
7	V. Pasquantino	KC	118
8	Christian Walker	AZ	117
9	Josh Naylor	CLE	116
10	Nathaniel Lowe	TEX	115
11	Wilmer Flores	SF	113
12	LaMonte Wade Jr.	SF	112
13	Triston Casas	BOS	111
14	Ty France	SEA	110
14	C.J. Cron	LAA	110

Second Base DRC+

Rank	Name	Team	DRC+
1	Luis Arraez	MIA	130
2	Jose Altuve	HOU	123
3	Ketel Marte	AZ	120
4	Gleyber Torres	NYY	114
4	Marcus Semien	TEX	114
4	Ozzie Albies	ATL	114
7	Brandon Lowe	TB	111
7	Andrés Giménez	CLE	111
9	Jonathan India	CIN	109
10	Jeff McNeil	NYM	107
11	Tommy Edman	STL	106
12	Jorge Polanco	MIN	105
12	Edouard Julien	MIN	105
12	Nico Hoerner	CHC	105
15	Luis Rengifo	LAA	102

Shortstop DRC+

Rank	Name	Team	DRC+
1	Corey Seager	TEX	138
2	Xander Bogaerts	SD	118
3	Bobby Witt Jr.	KC	117
3	Bo Bichette	TOR	117
5	Trea Turner	PHI	112
5	Francisco Lindor	NYM	112
7	J.P. Crawford	SEA	109
8	Carlos Correa	MIN	106
9	Dansby Swanson	CHC	105
10	Matt McLain	CIN	104
10	Willy Adames	MIL	104
12	Vaughn Grissom	BOS	101
13	Amed Rosario	FA	97
14	Geraldo Perdomo	AZ	95
14	Orlando Arcia	ATL	95

Third Base DRC+

Rank	Name	Team	DRC+
1	José Ramírez	CLE	136
2	Manny Machado	SD	130
2	Rafael Devers	BOS	130
4	Austin Riley	ATL	126
5	Alex Bregman	HOU	125
6	Isaac Paredes	TB	116
6	Max Muncy	LAD	116
6	Royce Lewis	MIN	116
9	Nolan Arenado	STL	115
10	Gunnar Henderson	BAL	114
11	Nick Madrigal	CHC	109
12	J. Candelario	CIN	105
13	Patrick Wisdom	CHC	104
13	Alec Bohm	PHI	104
15	Jake Burger	MIA	103

Designated Hitter DRC+

Rank	Name	Team	DRC+
1	Shohei Ohtani	LAD	153
1	Yordan Alvarez	HOU	153
3	Bryce Harper	PHI	126
4	Jorge Soler	FA	118
4	Eloy Jiménez	CHW	118
6	Daniel Vogelbach	NYM	117
6	Marcell Ozuna	ATL	117
8	Brandon Belt	FA	114
9	Justin Turner	FA	113
10	Jesse Winker	MIL	110
10	Joc Pederson	FA	110
10	Josh Bell	MIA	110
13	Mitch Garver	SEA	109
14	Byron Buxton	MIN	108
15	Brent Rooker	OAK	107

Left Field DRC+

Rank	Name	Team	DRC+
1	Juan Soto	NYY	161
2	Corbin Carroll	AZ	127
3	Kyle Schwarber	PHI	126
4	Bryan Reynolds	PIT	122
5	Masataka Yoshida	BOS	119
6	Steven Kwan	CLE	116
7	Ian Happ	CHC	113
7	Randy Arozarena	TB	113
9	Taylor Ward	LAA	112
10	Mark Canha	DET	111
11	Christian Yelich	MIL	109
12	L. Gurriel	AZ	108
13	Nolan Jones	COL	105
14	Tyler O'Neill	BOS	104
14	Chas McCormick	HOU	104

Center Field DRC+

Rank	Name	Team	DRC+
1	Mike Trout	LAA	135
2	Julio Rodríguez	SEA	122
3	Luis Robert Jr.	CHW	115
4	Lars Nootbaar	STL	113
5	J. Chisholm	MIA	110
6	M. Harris	ATL	108
7	Jack Suwinski	PIT	107
8	Cedric Mullins	BAL	105
9	TJ Friedl	CIN	103
10	James Outman	LAD	101
10	Cody Bellinger	FA	101
12	Esteury Ruiz	OAK	98
12	Adam Duvall	FA	98
14	Alek Thomas	AZ	96
14	Riley Greene	DET	96

Right Field DRC+

Rank	Name	Team	DRC+
1	Aaron Judge	NYY	160
2	Ronald Acuña Jr.	ATL	151
3	Mookie Betts	LAD	138
4	Kyle Tucker	HOU	132
5	F. Tatis	SD	130
6	Seiya Suzuki	CHC	120
7	Brandon Nimmo	NYM	117
8	Jake Fraley	CIN	114
9	A. Santander	BAL	111
10	George Springer	TOR	110
10	Adolis García	TEX	110
12	Will Benson	CIN	109
13	Alex Verdugo	NYY	107
13	Jesús Sánchez	MIA	107
13	Josh Lowe	TB	107

Catcher DRP

Rank	Name	Team	DRP
1	Patrick Bailey	SF	20.9
2	Cal Raleigh	SEA	13.3
3	Adley Rutschman	BAL	12.9
4	Jonah Heim	TEX	11.6
5	F. Alvarez	NYM	10.5
6	Austin Hedges	CLE	8.4
7	Jose Trevino	NYY	7.8
8	J.T. Realmuto	PHI	7.0
9	René Pinto	TB	6.1
10	Sean Murphy	ATL	6.0
11	Kyle Higashioka	SD	5.6
12	Austin Wells	NYY	5.5
13	Reese McGuire	BOS	4.2
14	Bo Naylor	CLE	3.7
15	Miguel Amaya	CHC	3.6

First Base DRP

Rank	Name	Team	DRP
1	Paul Goldschmidt	STL	1.9
2	Ty France	SEA	1.2
3	Freddie Freeman	LAD	1.0
4	Christian Walker	AZ	0.7
4	Ryan Mountcastle	BAL	0.7
6	Donovan Solano	FA	0.4
6	Carlos Santana	FA	0.4
6	Matt Olson	ATL	0.4
6	Yandy Díaz	TB	0.4
10	Jake Cronenworth	SD	0.3
11	José Abreu	HOU	0.2
12	Andrew Vaughn	CHW	0.1
12	Michael Toglia	COL	0.1
12	Alfonso Rivas	LAA	0.1
12	Josh Naylor	CLE	0.1

Second Base DRP

Rank	Name	Team	DRP
1	Marcus Semien	TEX	4.2
2	Bryson Stott	PHI	3.5
3	Brendan Rodgers	COL	3.1
4	Luis Arraez	MIA	2.5
5	Ha-Seong Kim	SD	2.3
5	Andrés Giménez	CLE	2.3
7	Gleyber Torres	NYY	1.9
7	Zack Gelof	OAK	1.9
9	Tommy Edman	STL	1.6
9	Jose Altuve	HOU	1.6
11	Ji Hwan Bae	PIT	0.7
12	Ozzie Albies	ATL	0.5
13	Mauricio Dubón	HOU	0.4
14	Andy Ibáñez	DET	0.3
14	Adam Frazier	BAL	0.3

Shortstop DRP

Rank	Name	Team	DRP
1	Willy Adames	MIL	9.4
2	Dansby Swanson	CHC	8.9
3	J.P. Crawford	SEA	3.8
4	Zach Neto	LAA	3.7
5	Javier Báez	DET	3.4
6	Ezequiel Tovar	COL	2.7
7	Orlando Arcia	ATL	2.5
8	Geraldo Perdomo	AZ	2.2
9	Carlos Correa	MIN	2.0
9	Nick Allen	OAK	2.0
11	Matt McLain	CIN	1.8
12	Bo Bichette	TOR	1.1
13	CJ Abrams	WAS	0.9
14	Joey Wendle	NYM	0.8
14	Miguel Rojas	LAD	0.8

Third Base DRP

Rank	Name	Team	DRP
1	Ke'Bryan Hayes	PIT	8.6
2	Austin Riley	ATL	6.7
3	Yoán Moncada	CHW	5.6
4	Josh Jung	TEX	4.7
5	Matt Chapman	FA	4.0
6	Nick Madrigal	CHC	3.1
7	Alex Bregman	HOU	3.0
8	Gunnar Henderson	BAL	2.8
8	Nolan Arenado	STL	2.8
10	Taylor Walls	TB	2.4
11	Manny Machado	SD	1.7
12	Isaac Paredes	TB	1.4
13	A. Monasterio	MIL	0.7
13	DJ LeMahieu	NYY	0.7
15	Jared Triolo	PIT	0.6

Rich Hill Annual Comments

Rank	Name	Team	Year
1	Rich Hill	CHC	2006
2	Rich Hill	SD	2024
3	Rich Hill	MIN	2021
4	Rich Hill	LAD	2017
5	Rich Hill	BOS	2023
6	Rich Hill	NYY	2015
7	Rich Hill	LAD	2019
8	Rich Hill	BOS	2016
9	Rich Hill	LAD	2018
10	Rich Hill	NYM	2022
11	Rich Hill	LAD	2020
12	Rich Hill	CHC	2009
13	Rich Hill	CHC	2008
14	Rich Hill	CLE	2014
15	Rich Hill	BOS	2012

Left Field DRP

Rank	Name	Team	DRP
1	Corbin Carroll	AZ	11.6
2	Evan Carter	TEX	7.6
3	Steven Kwan	CLE	7.2
4	Akil Baddoo	DET	3.9
5	Daulton Varsho	TOR	2.8
6	Randy Arozarena	TB	2.6
7	Tyler O'Neill	BOS	2.1
8	Eddie Rosario	FA	1.8
9	Jonny DeLuca	TB	1.5
10	Ian Happ	CHC	1.4
11	Christian Yelich	MIL	1.2
12	Forrest Wall	ATL	0.9
12	Bryan Reynolds	PIT	0.9
14	Chas McCormick	HOU	0.7
15	Taylor Trammell	SEA	0.6

Center Field DRP

Rank	Name	Team	DRP
1	Myles Straw	CLE	5.7
2	Parker Meadows	DET	5.0
3	Kevin Kiermaier	TOR	4.8
4	Jarren Duran	BOS	4.7
5	Alek Thomas	AZ	4.2
6	Garrett Mitchell	MIL	4.0
7	Jose Siri	TB	3.9
7	Cedric Mullins	BAL	3.9
7	J. Chisholm	MIA	3.9
10	Leody Taveras	TEX	3.7
11	Riley Greene	DET	3.3
12	Brenton Doyle	COL	2.7
13	Lars Nootbaar	STL	2.5
14	Mickey Moniak	LAA	2.2
14	Brandon Marsh	PHI	2.2

Right Field DRP

Rank	Name	Team	DRP
1	Sal Frelick	MIL	6.3
2	F. Tatis	SD	6.2
3	Ronald Acuña Jr.	ATL	4.7
4	Brandon Nimmo	NYM	3.9
5	Josh Lowe	TB	3.3
6	MJ Melendez	KC	2.6
7	Joshua Palacios	PIT	2.2
8	Seiya Suzuki	CHC	1.9
8	Max Kepler	MIN	1.9
10	Jake McCarthy	AZ	1.5
10	Starling Marte	NYM	1.5
12	Jake Fraley	CIN	1.3
13	Alex Verdugo	NYY	1.2
14	Blake Perkins	MIL	0.9
14	Ryan McKenna	BAL	0.9

Catcher WARP

Rank	Name	Team	WARP
1	Adley Rutschman	BAL	5.2
2	Will Smith	LAD	3.2
2	Cal Raleigh	SEA	3.2
2	F. Alvarez	NYM	3.2
5	Sean Murphy	ATL	3.0
5	Alejandro Kirk	TOR	3.0
7	Jonah Heim	TEX	2.9
7	W. Contreras	STL	2.9
9	J.T. Realmuto	PHI	2.6
10	W. Contreras	MIL	2.4
10	Patrick Bailey	SF	2.4
12	Keibert Ruiz	WAS	2.3
13	Danny Jansen	TOR	2.1
14	Bo Naylor	CLE	2.0
14	Gabriel Moreno	AZ	2.0

First Base WARP

Rank	Name	Team	WARP
1	Matt Olson	ATL	4.9
2	Freddie Freeman	LAD	4.3
3	V. Guerrero	TOR	3.9
4	Pete Alonso	NYM	3.7
5	Paul Goldschmidt	STL	3.6
6	Yandy Díaz	TB	3.1
7	Christian Walker	AZ	2.7
8	Josh Naylor	CLE	2.4
9	Nathaniel Lowe	TEX	2.3
10	V. Pasquantino	KC	2.1
11	Ty France	SEA	2.0
12	LaMonte Wade Jr.	SF	1.9
13	Andrew Vaughn	CHW	1.8
13	Wilmer Flores	SF	1.8
13	José Abreu	HOU	1.8

Second Base WARP

Rank	Name	Team	WARP
1	Luis Arraez	MIA	4.2
2	Jose Altuve	HOU	3.7
3	Marcus Semien	TEX	3.6
4	Ketel Marte	AZ	3.1
5	Gleyber Torres	NYY	2.9
6	Ozzie Albies	ATL	2.8
7	Andrés Giménez	CLE	2.7
7	Tommy Edman	STL	2.7
9	Ha-Seong Kim	SD	2.2
10	Jeff McNeil	NYM	2.1
10	Brandon Lowe	TB	2.1
12	Bryson Stott	PHI	2.0
12	Nico Hoerner	CHC	2.0
14	Jorge Polanco	MIN	1.9
15	Edouard Julien	MIN	1.7

Shortstop WARP

Rank	Name	Team	WARP
1	Corey Seager	TEX	4.7
2	Dansby Swanson	CHC	3.6
2	Bo Bichette	TOR	3.6
4	Trea Turner	PHI	3.5
5	Willy Adames	MIL	3.4
6	J.P. Crawford	SEA	3.3
6	Xander Bogaerts	SD	3.3
8	Francisco Lindor	NYM	3.2
9	Bobby Witt Jr.	KC	3.0
10	Carlos Correa	MIN	2.7
11	Matt McLain	CIN	2.1
12	CJ Abrams	WAS	1.8
13	Zach Neto	LAA	1.7
13	Orlando Arcia	ATL	1.7
15	Amed Rosario	FA	1.6

Third Base WARP

Rank	Name	Team	WARP
1	José Ramírez	CLE	4.7
2	Austin Riley	ATL	4.5
3	Alex Bregman	HOU	4.1
4	Manny Machado	SD	4.0
5	Rafael Devers	BOS	3.6
6	Nolan Arenado	STL	3.1
7	Gunnar Henderson	BAL	3.0
8	Ke'Bryan Hayes	PIT	2.6
9	Isaac Paredes	TB	2.5
10	Max Muncy	LAD	2.3
11	Royce Lewis	MIN	2.2
12	Nick Madrigal	CHC	1.9
12	Matt Chapman	FA	1.9
14	Ryan McMahon	COL	1.6
15	Yoán Moncada	CHW	1.5

Designated Hitter WARP

Rank	Name	Team	WARP
1	Shohei Ohtani	LAD	5.6
2	Yordan Alvarez	HOU	5.0
3	Bryce Harper	PHI	3.2
4	Eloy Jiménez	CHW	2.5
5	Byron Buxton	MIN	2.4
6	Marcell Ozuna	ATL	2.3
7	Justin Turner	FA	2.1
8	Josh Bell	MIA	1.9
9	J.D. Martinez	FA	1.6
10	Daniel Vogelbach	NYM	1.5
10	Joc Pederson	FA	1.5
12	C. Morel	CHC	1.4
12	Mitch Garver	SEA	1.4
14	Jorge Soler	FA	1.3
14	Brent Rooker	OAK	1.3

Left Field WARP

Rank	Name	Team	WARP
1	Juan Soto	NYY	6.5
2	Corbin Carroll	AZ	5.0
3	Steven Kwan	CLE	4.0
4	Bryan Reynolds	PIT	3.5
5	Kyle Schwarber	PHI	3.2
6	Masataka Yoshida	BOS	2.9
6	Ian Happ	CHC	2.9
6	Randy Arozarena	TB	2.9
9	Christian Yelich	MIL	2.4
10	Taylor Ward	LAA	2.2
11	Daulton Varsho	TOR	1.9
11	Tyler O'Neill	BOS	1.9
11	Chas McCormick	HOU	1.9
11	A. Benintendi	CHW	1.9
15	Nolan Jones	COL	1.7

Center Field WARP

Rank	Name	Team	WARP
1	Mike Trout	LAA	3.9
2	Julio Rodríguez	SEA	3.7
3	J. Chisholm	MIA	3.4
4	Lars Nootbaar	STL	3.0
5	Cedric Mullins	BAL	2.8
6	Luis Robert Jr.	CHW	2.6
7	M. Harris	ATL	2.5
8	Jack Suwinski	PIT	2.2
9	TJ Friedl	CIN	2.1
10	Cody Bellinger	FA	2.0
11	Alek Thomas	AZ	1.9
11	James Outman	LAD	1.9
13	Jarren Duran	BOS	1.7
14	Leody Taveras	TEX	1.5
14	Riley Greene	DET	1.5

Right Field WARP

Rank	Name	Team	WARP
1	Ronald Acuña Jr.	ATL	6.8
2	Mookie Betts	LAD	5.1
3	F. Tatis	SD	4.9
3	Aaron Judge	NYY	4.9
5	Kyle Tucker	HOU	4.0
6	Brandon Nimmo	NYM	3.8
7	Seiya Suzuki	CHC	3.1
8	George Springer	TOR	2.4
9	Adolis García	TEX	2.3
10	Josh Lowe	TB	2.1
11	Max Kepler	MIN	1.8
12	Alex Verdugo	NYY	1.7
12	Jesús Sánchez	MIA	1.7
12	Will Benson	CIN	1.7
15	MJ Melendez	KC	1.6

Batting Average

Rank	Name	Team	BA
1	Luis Arraez	MIA	.321
2	Ronald Acuña Jr.	ATL	.294
3	Freddie Freeman	LAD	.287
4	Nick Madrigal	CHC	.284
5	Masataka Yoshida	BOS	.283
5	Bo Bichette	TOR	.283
7	Corey Seager	TEX	.281
8	Steven Kwan	CLE	.279
9	José Ramírez	CLE	.278
9	Jeff McNeil	NYM	.278
9	V. Guerrero	TOR	.278
12	Yordan Alvarez	HOU	.276
13	Jung Hoo Lee	SF	.275
14	Juan Soto	NYY	.274
14	Josh Naylor	CLE	.274
14	Yandy Díaz	TB	.274
17	Keibert Ruiz	WAS	.273
17	Manny Machado	SD	.273
19	Xander Bogaerts	SD	.272
20	Kyle Tucker	HOU	.271
20	Eloy Jiménez	CHW	.271
20	Rafael Devers	BOS	.271
23	Trea Turner	PHI	.270
23	Mookie Betts	LAD	.270
25	Alex Verdugo	NYY	.269

On-Base Percentage

Rank	Name	Team	OBP
1	Juan Soto	NYY	.413
2	Aaron Judge	NYY	.384
3	Ronald Acuña Jr.	ATL	.382
4	Yordan Alvarez	HOU	.380
5	Luis Arraez	MIA	.377
6	Shohei Ohtani	LAD	.374
7	Freddie Freeman	LAD	.371
8	Mookie Betts	LAD	.368
9	Matt Olson	ATL	.366
10	Yandy Díaz	TB	.364
10	Alex Bregman	HOU	.364
12	Bryce Harper	PHI	.363
13	Adley Rutschman	BAL	.359
14	Corey Seager	TEX	.357
14	José Ramírez	CLE	.357
16	Brandon Nimmo	NYM	.356
17	Masataka Yoshida	BOS	.355
17	Kyle Tucker	HOU	.355
17	Will Smith	LAD	.355
20	V. Guerrero	TOR	.354
20	Corbin Carroll	AZ	.354
22	Steven Kwan	CLE	.352
23	Jesse Winker	MIL	.351
23	Jung Hoo Lee	SF	.351
23	Paul Goldschmidt	STL	.351

Slugging Percentage

Rank	Name	Team	SLG
1	Aaron Judge	NYY	.553
2	Shohei Ohtani	LAD	.549
3	Matt Olson	ATL	.530
4	Yordan Alvarez	HOU	.526
5	Juan Soto	NYY	.517
6	Mike Trout	LAA	.502
6	Corey Seager	TEX	.502
8	Ronald Acuña Jr.	ATL	.500
9	F. Tatis	SD	.495
10	Pete Alonso	NYM	.494
11	Mookie Betts	LAD	.493
12	Manny Machado	SD	.489
13	José Ramírez	CLE	.483
13	V. Guerrero	TOR	.483
15	Rafael Devers	BOS	.481
16	Kyle Schwarber	PHI	.478
16	Corbin Carroll	AZ	.478
18	Kyle Tucker	HOU	.473
19	Luis Robert Jr.	CHW	.472
20	Austin Riley	ATL	.466
21	Freddie Freeman	LAD	.460
22	Julio Rodríguez	SEA	.458
22	Adolis García	TEX	.458
24	Jorge Soler	FA	.457
25	Yainer Diaz	HOU	.456

Isolated Slugging Percentage

Rank	Name	Team	ISO
1	Aaron Judge	NYY	.292
2	Shohei Ohtani	LAD	.282
3	Matt Olson	ATL	.271
4	Kyle Schwarber	PHI	.260
5	Mike Trout	LAA	.254
6	Yordan Alvarez	HOU	.250
7	Pete Alonso	NYM	.245
8	Juan Soto	NYY	.243
9	Patrick Wisdom	CHC	.238
10	F. Tatis	SD	.230
11	Mookie Betts	LAD	.223
12	Byron Buxton	MIN	.222
13	Corey Seager	TEX	.221
14	Jorge Soler	FA	.220
15	Adolis García	TEX	.219
16	Manny Machado	SD	.216
17	Cal Raleigh	SEA	.215
18	Luis Robert Jr.	CHW	.214
18	Joey Gallo	FA	.214
20	Adam Duvall	FA	.212
21	Corbin Carroll	AZ	.211
22	Rafael Devers	BOS	.210
22	J. Chisholm	MIA	.210
24	C. Morel	CHC	.209
25	Max Muncy	LAD	.208

OPS

Rank	Name	Team	OPS
1	Aaron Judge	NYY	.936
2	Juan Soto	NYY	.930
3	Shohei Ohtani	LAD	.923
4	Yordan Alvarez	HOU	.906
5	Matt Olson	ATL	.896
6	Ronald Acuña Jr.	ATL	.883
7	Mookie Betts	LAD	.862
8	Corey Seager	TEX	.859
9	Mike Trout	LAA	.850
10	José Ramírez	CLE	.840
11	V. Guerrero	TOR	.837
12	Pete Alonso	NYM	.833
13	Freddie Freeman	LAD	.832
13	Rafael Devers	BOS	.832
13	Corbin Carroll	AZ	.832
16	F. Tatis	SD	.831
17	Kyle Tucker	HOU	.829
17	Manny Machado	SD	.829
19	Kyle Schwarber	PHI	.826
20	Bryce Harper	PHI	.811
21	Luis Arraez	MIA	.809
22	Austin Riley	ATL	.801
23	Jose Altuve	HOU	.796
24	Paul Goldschmidt	STL	.793
25	Will Smith	LAD	.792

BABIP

Rank	Name	Team	BABIP
1	Josh Lowe	TB	.336
1	Luis Arraez	MIA	.336
3	P. Crow-Armstrong	CHC	.326
4	Trea Turner	PHI	.325
5	Zack Gelof	OAK	.324
5	Brett Baty	NYM	.324
7	M. Harris	ATL	.323
8	J. Chisholm	MIA	.322
9	Matt Wallner	MIN	.321
9	Aaron Judge	NYY	.321
9	Eloy Jiménez	CHW	.321
12	Jordan Walker	STL	.320
12	Starling Marte	NYM	.320
12	Royce Lewis	MIN	.320
12	Freddie Freeman	LAD	.320
12	Bo Bichette	TOR	.320
17	Shohei Ohtani	LAD	.319
17	T. Hernandez	LAD	.319
19	Bryce Harper	PHI	.318
19	Riley Greene	DET	.318
19	Corbin Carroll	AZ	.318
22	Will Benson	CIN	.317
23	Harold Ramírez	TB	.316
23	Ronald Acuña Jr.	ATL	.316
25	Austin Wells	NYY	.314

Runs Scored

Rank	Name	Team	R
1	Juan Soto	NYY	97
2	Matt Olson	ATL	95
3	Shohei Ohtani	LAD	93
4	Aaron Judge	NYY	91
4	Ronald Acuña Jr.	ATL	91
6	Mookie Betts	LAD	88
7	Kyle Schwarber	PHI	87
8	F. Tatis	SD	86
8	Pete Alonso	NYM	86
10	Yordan Alvarez	HOU	82
11	Freddie Freeman	LAD	80
11	Rafael Devers	BOS	80
13	Austin Riley	ATL	79
13	José Ramírez	CLE	79
13	Paul Goldschmidt	STL	79
16	Marcus Semien	TEX	78
16	Manny Machado	SD	78
16	V. Guerrero	TOR	78
19	Kyle Tucker	HOU	77
19	Corey Seager	TEX	77
19	Alex Bregman	HOU	77
22	Christian Walker	AZ	75
23	Bryce Harper	PHI	74
24	Mike Trout	LAA	73
24	Francisco Lindor	NYM	73

Runs Batted In

Rank	Name	Team	RBI
1	Matt Olson	ATL	106
2	Shohei Ohtani	LAD	105
3	Aaron Judge	NYY	101
4	F. Tatis	SD	99
4	Juan Soto	NYY	99
6	Pete Alonso	NYM	97
7	Ronald Acuña Jr.	ATL	96
8	Kyle Schwarber	PHI	95
9	Mookie Betts	LAD	94
10	Yordan Alvarez	HOU	90
11	Austin Riley	ATL	89
11	Rafael Devers	BOS	89
13	Manny Machado	SD	88
14	Marcus Semien	TEX	87
14	José Ramírez	CLE	87
16	Corey Seager	TEX	86
16	V. Guerrero	TOR	86
18	Luis Robert Jr.	CHW	85
19	Kyle Tucker	HOU	84
19	Adolis García	TEX	84
21	Christian Walker	AZ	83
21	Paul Goldschmidt	STL	83
23	Bobby Witt Jr.	KC	82
23	Mike Trout	LAA	82
23	Freddie Freeman	LAD	82

Home Runs

Rank	Name	Team	HR
1	Matt Olson	ATL	39
2	Shohei Ohtani	LAD	38
2	Aaron Judge	NYY	38
4	Kyle Schwarber	PHI	36
5	Pete Alonso	NYM	35
6	F. Tatis	SD	34
7	Juan Soto	NYY	32
8	Mookie Betts	LAD	31
9	Mike Trout	LAA	30
9	Manny Machado	SD	30
9	Yordan Alvarez	HOU	30
12	Patrick Wisdom	CHC	29
12	Luis Robert Jr.	CHW	29
12	Adolis García	TEX	29
12	Ronald Acuña Jr.	ATL	29
16	Corey Seager	TEX	28
16	Austin Riley	ATL	28
18	V. Guerrero	TOR	27
18	Rafael Devers	BOS	27
20	Christian Walker	AZ	26
20	Marcus Semien	TEX	26
20	Marcell Ozuna	ATL	26
20	J. Chisholm	MIA	26
24	Jorge Soler	FA	25
24	Julio Rodríguez	SEA	25

Stolen Bases

Rank	Name	Team	SB
1	Esteury Ruiz	OAK	52
2	Ronald Acuña Jr.	ATL	49
3	Elly De La Cruz	CIN	42
4	Bobby Witt Jr.	KC	41
5	José Azocar	SD	37
6	J. Chisholm	MIA	33
7	Jon Berti	MIA	32
7	CJ Abrams	WAS	32
9	Corbin Carroll	AZ	31
10	Kyle Tucker	HOU	30
11	Randy Arozarena	TB	28
12	Anthony Volpe	NYY	27
12	José Ramírez	CLE	27
12	Nico Hoerner	CHC	27
15	Cedric Mullins	BAL	26
16	Starling Marte	NYM	25
16	Ha-Seong Kim	SD	25
18	F. Tatis	SD	24
18	Johan Rojas	PHI	24
18	Dylan Moore	SEA	24
18	Josh Lowe	TB	24
18	Andrés Giménez	CLE	24
18	Tommy Edman	STL	24
24	Julio Rodríguez	SEA	23
24	Jake McCarthy	AZ	23

Walk Rate

Rank	Name	Team	BB%
1	Juan Soto	NYY	18.6
2	Aaron Judge	NYY	16.0
3	Kyle Schwarber	PHI	15.3
4	Edouard Julien	MIN	14.4
4	Max Muncy	LAD	14.4
6	Daniel Vogelbach	NYM	14.0
6	Joey Gallo	FA	14.0
8	Shohei Ohtani	LAD	13.8
9	Jesse Winker	MIL	13.7
10	Bryce Harper	PHI	13.6
10	Will Benson	CIN	13.6
10	Ryan Noda	OAK	13.6
13	Matt Olson	ATL	13.4
14	Brandon Belt	FA	13.3
15	LaMonte Wade Jr.	SF	12.9
15	Andrew McCutchen	PIT	12.9
15	Lars Nootbaar	STL	12.9
18	Yordan Alvarez	HOU	12.8
19	Adley Rutschman	BAL	12.7
19	J.P. Crawford	SEA	12.7
19	Ian Happ	CHC	12.7
22	Christian Yelich	MIL	12.6
22	JJ Bleday	OAK	12.6
22	Aaron Hicks	FA	12.6
25	Triston Casas	BOS	12.5

Strikeout Rate

Rank	Name	Team	K%
1	Luis Arraez	MIA	5.9
2	Nick Madrigal	CHC	7.7
3	Steven Kwan	CLE	9.0
4	Alejandro Kirk	TOR	10.3
5	Nico Hoerner	CHC	10.4
5	Jeff McNeil	NYM	10.4
7	Ildemaro Vargas	WAS	10.5
8	Keibert Ruiz	WAS	10.8
9	Jung Hoo Lee	SF	11.3
10	Alex Bregman	HOU	11.4
11	Masataka Yoshida	BOS	11.8
12	José Ramírez	CLE	12.2
13	Sal Frelick	MIL	12.3
14	V. Pasquantino	KC	13.1
15	Alex Verdugo	NYY	13.4
16	Adley Rutschman	BAL	13.5
17	Wilmer Flores	SF	13.6
18	Yandy Díaz	TB	14.0
19	Tommy Edman	STL	14.1
20	Bryson Stott	PHI	14.3
21	Mookie Betts	LAD	14.4
21	Myles Straw	CLE	14.4
23	Kyle Tucker	HOU	14.5
24	Adam Frazier	BAL	14.6
25	Justin Turner	FA	14.7

BASEBALL PROSPECTUS 2024

Catcher Defense Added

Rank	Name	Team	Total Runs
1	Patrick Bailey	SF	21.0
2	Cal Raleigh	SEA	13.4
3	Adley Rutschman	BAL	12.8
4	Jonah Heim	TEX	11.7
5	F. Alvarez	NYM	10.4
6	Austin Hedges	CLE	8.4
7	Jose Trevino	NYY	7.7
8	J.T. Realmuto	PHI	7.1
9	René Pinto	TB	6.2
10	Sean Murphy	ATL	5.9
11	Kyle Higashioka	SD	5.6
12	Austin Wells	NYY	5.5
13	Reese McGuire	BOS	4.2
14	Bo Naylor	CLE	3.8
15	Miguel Amaya	CHC	3.6
16	C. Vazquez	MIN	3.4
17	Alejandro Kirk	TOR	3.1
18	Gabriel Moreno	AZ	3.0
19	Ryan Jeffers	MIN	2.8
19	Austin Barnes	LAD	2.8
21	Victor Caratini	HOU	2.3
21	Seby Zavala	SEA	2.3
23	Carson Kelly	DET	2.1
23	Travis d'Arnaud	ATL	2.1
25	Ben Rortvedt	NYY	1.6

Framing Runs

Rank	Name	Team	Framing Runs
1	Patrick Bailey	SF	20.0
2	Adley Rutschman	BAL	12.7
3	Cal Raleigh	SEA	12.0
4	F. Alvarez	NYM	11.5
5	Jonah Heim	TEX	10.0
6	Austin Hedges	CLE	8.3
7	René Pinto	TB	7.5
8	Jose Trevino	NYY	7.3
9	J.T. Realmuto	PHI	6.6
10	Kyle Higashioka	SD	6.0
11	Austin Wells	NYY	5.9
12	Sean Murphy	ATL	4.8
13	Bo Naylor	CLE	4.7
14	Reese McGuire	BOS	3.9
14	Miguel Amaya	CHC	3.9
16	Austin Barnes	LAD	3.4
17	Alejandro Kirk	TOR	2.9
18	Ryan Jeffers	MIN	2.7
19	C. Vazquez	MIN	2.6
19	Victor Caratini	HOU	2.6
19	Seby Zavala	SEA	2.6
22	Travis d'Arnaud	ATL	2.5
23	Carson Kelly	DET	1.9
24	Jason Delay	PIT	1.5
25	Tomás Nido	NYM	1.4

Called Strikes Above Average

Rank	Name	Team	CSAA
1	Patrick Bailey	SF	.024
2	Tomás Nido	NYM	.017
3	Austin Hedges	CLE	.016
4	Brian Serven	CHC	.015
5	Kyle Higashioka	SD	.012
5	Cal Raleigh	SEA	.012
5	Adley Rutschman	BAL	.012
8	F. Alvarez	NYM	.011
8	Jose Trevino	NYY	.011
10	Jonah Heim	TEX	.009
11	Austin Barnes	LAD	.008
11	Austin Wells	NYY	.008
13	René Pinto	TB	.007
13	Miguel Amaya	CHC	.007
15	Seby Zavala	SEA	.006
15	Reese McGuire	BOS	.006
15	Jason Delay	PIT	.006
15	Ben Rortvedt	NYY	.006
19	J.T. Realmuto	PHI	.005
19	Bo Naylor	CLE	.005
19	Sean Murphy	ATL	.005
22	Travis d'Arnaud	ATL	.004
22	Joey Bart	SF	.004
22	Ryan Jeffers	MIN	.004
22	Blake Sabol	SF	.004

Throwing Runs

Rank	Name	Team	Throwing Runs
1	Gabriel Moreno	AZ	3.1
2	Jonah Heim	TEX	2.0
3	Cal Raleigh	SEA	1.3
3	Yan Gomes	CHC	1.3
5	Elias Díaz	COL	1.0
5	W. Contreras	STL	1.0
5	Patrick Bailey	SF	1.0
8	Shea Langeliers	OAK	0.9
8	Sean Murphy	ATL	0.9
10	C. Vazquez	MIN	0.8
11	Yainer Diaz	HOU	0.7
12	James McCann	BAL	0.6
13	Freddy Fermin	KC	0.4
13	Connor Wong	BOS	0.4
15	Iván Herrera	STL	0.3
15	Jose Trevino	NYY	0.3
15	C. Bethancourt	MIA	0.3
18	Blake Sabol	SF	0.2
18	Eric Haase	MIL	0.2
18	Ryan Jeffers	MIN	0.2
18	Luke Maile	CIN	0.2
22	Reese McGuire	BOS	0.1
22	Jose Herrera	AZ	0.1
22	Alejandro Kirk	TOR	0.1
22	J.T. Realmuto	PHI	0.1

Blocking Runs

Rank	Name	Team	Blocking Runs
1	J.T. Realmuto	PHI	0.4
1	Gabriel Moreno	AZ	0.4
3	Danny Jansen	TOR	0.3
3	Sean Murphy	ATL	0.3
3	Will Smith	LAD	0.3
6	Jacob Stallings	COL	0.2
6	Carson Kelly	DET	0.2
6	Alejandro Kirk	TOR	0.2
9	Adley Rutschman	BAL	0.1
9	Austin Hedges	CLE	0.1
9	Victor Caratini	HOU	0.1
9	Ben Rortvedt	NYY	0.1
9	W. Contreras	STL	0.1
9	Jose Trevino	NYY	0.1
9	Reese McGuire	BOS	0.1
9	Yainer Diaz	HOU	0.1
9	Cal Raleigh	SEA	0.1
9	Nick Fortes	MIA	0.1
19	Yan Gomes	CHC	0.0
19	Freddy Fermin	KC	0.0
19	Brett Sullivan	SD	0.0
19	Tomás Nido	NYM	0.0
19	César Salazar	HOU	0.0
19	Tyler Heineman	NYM	0.0
19	Austin Wells	NYY	0.0

Swipe Rate Above Average

Rank	Name	Team	SRAA
1	Gabriel Moreno	AZ	-.076
2	Jonah Heim	TEX	-.045
3	Cal Raleigh	SEA	-.034
4	Yan Gomes	CHC	-.033
5	Patrick Bailey	SF	-.030
6	Elias Díaz	COL	-.028
7	James McCann	BAL	-.025
8	Shea Langeliers	OAK	-.024
8	C. Vazquez	MIN	-.024
10	Sean Murphy	ATL	-.022
10	W. Contreras	STL	-.022
12	Freddy Fermin	KC	-.021
13	Yainer Diaz	HOU	-.019
14	Iván Herrera	STL	-.017
14	Blake Sabol	SF	-.017
16	Eric Haase	MIL	-.016
17	C. Bethancourt	MIA	-.015
18	Jose Trevino	NYY	-.013
19	Connor Wong	BOS	-.010
19	Ben Rortvedt	NYY	-.010
21	Luke Maile	CIN	-.008
21	Jose Herrera	AZ	-.008
23	Tyler Heineman	NYM	-.007
24	Ryan Jeffers	MIN	-.006
25	Reese McGuire	BOS	-.005

AL Hitter WARP

Rank	Name	Team	WARP
1	Juan Soto	NYY	6.5
2	Adley Rutschman	BAL	5.2
3	Yordan Alvarez	HOU	5.0
4	Aaron Judge	NYY	4.9
5	Corey Seager	TEX	4.7
5	José Ramírez	CLE	4.7
7	Alex Bregman	HOU	4.1
8	Kyle Tucker	HOU	4.0
8	Steven Kwan	CLE	4.0
10	Mike Trout	LAA	3.9
10	V. Guerrero	TOR	3.9
12	Julio Rodríguez	SEA	3.7
12	Jose Altuve	HOU	3.7
14	Marcus Semien	TEX	3.6
14	Rafael Devers	BOS	3.6
14	Bo Bichette	TOR	3.6
17	J.P. Crawford	SEA	3.3
18	Cal Raleigh	SEA	3.2
19	Yandy Díaz	TB	3.1
20	Bobby Witt Jr.	KC	3.0
20	Alejandro Kirk	TOR	3.0
20	Gunnar Henderson	BAL	3.0
23	Masataka Yoshida	BOS	2.9
23	Gleyber Torres	NYY	2.9
23	Jonah Heim	TEX	2.9

NL Hitter WARP

Rank	Name	Team	WARP
1	Ronald Acuña Jr.	ATL	6.8
2	Shohei Ohtani	LAD	5.6
3	Mookie Betts	LAD	5.1
4	Corbin Carroll	AZ	5.0
5	F. Tatis	SD	4.9
5	Matt Olson	ATL	4.9
7	Austin Riley	ATL	4.5
8	Freddie Freeman	LAD	4.3
9	Luis Arraez	MIA	4.2
10	Manny Machado	SD	4.0
11	Brandon Nimmo	NYM	3.8
12	Pete Alonso	NYM	3.7
13	Dansby Swanson	CHC	3.6
13	Paul Goldschmidt	STL	3.6
15	Trea Turner	PHI	3.5
15	Bryan Reynolds	PIT	3.5
17	J. Chisholm	MIA	3.4
17	Willy Adames	MIL	3.4
19	Xander Bogaerts	SD	3.3
20	Will Smith	LAD	3.2
20	Kyle Schwarber	PHI	3.2
20	Francisco Lindor	NYM	3.2
20	Bryce Harper	PHI	3.2
20	F. Alvarez	NYM	3.2
25	Seiya Suzuki	CHC	3.1

WARP

Rank	Name	Team	WARP
1	Ronald Acuña Jr.	ATL	6.8
2	Juan Soto	NYY	6.5
3	Shohei Ohtani	LAD	5.6
4	Adley Rutschman	BAL	5.2
5	Mookie Betts	LAD	5.1
6	Corbin Carroll	AZ	5.0
6	Yordan Alvarez	HOU	5.0
8	F. Tatis	SD	4.9
8	Matt Olson	ATL	4.9
8	Aaron Judge	NYY	4.9
11	Corey Seager	TEX	4.7
11	José Ramírez	CLE	4.7
13	Austin Riley	ATL	4.5
14	Freddie Freeman	LAD	4.3
15	Luis Arraez	MIA	4.2
16	Alex Bregman	HOU	4.1
17	Kyle Tucker	HOU	4.0
17	Manny Machado	SD	4.0
17	Steven Kwan	CLE	4.0
20	Mike Trout	LAA	3.9
20	V. Guerrero	TOR	3.9
22	Brandon Nimmo	NYM	3.8
23	Julio Rodríguez	SEA	3.7
23	Jose Altuve	HOU	3.7
23	Pete Alonso	NYM	3.7
26	Dansby Swanson	CHC	3.6
26	Marcus Semien	TEX	3.6
26	Paul Goldschmidt	STL	3.6
26	Rafael Devers	BOS	3.6
26	Bo Bichette	TOR	3.6
31	Trea Turner	PHI	3.5
31	Bryan Reynolds	PIT	3.5
33	J. Chisholm	MIA	3.4
33	Willy Adames	MIL	3.4
35	J.P. Crawford	SEA	3.3
35	Xander Bogaerts	SD	3.3
37	Will Smith	LAD	3.2
37	Kyle Schwarber	PHI	3.2
37	Cal Raleigh	SEA	3.2
37	Francisco Lindor	NYM	3.2
37	Bryce Harper	PHI	3.2
37	F. Alvarez	NYM	3.2
43	Seiya Suzuki	CHC	3.1
43	Ketel Marte	AZ	3.1
43	Yandy Díaz	TB	3.1
43	Nolan Arenado	STL	3.1
47	Bobby Witt Jr.	KC	3.0
47	Lars Nootbaar	STL	3.0
47	Sean Murphy	ATL	3.0
47	Jung Hoo Lee	SF	3.0

DRC+

Rank	Name	Team	DRC+
1	Juan Soto	NYY	161
2	Aaron Judge	NYY	160
3	Shohei Ohtani	LAD	153
3	Yordan Alvarez	HOU	153
5	Ronald Acuña Jr.	ATL	151
6	Matt Olson	ATL	145
7	Corey Seager	TEX	138
7	Mookie Betts	LAD	138
9	José Ramírez	CLE	136
9	V. Guerrero	TOR	136
11	Mike Trout	LAA	135
12	Freddie Freeman	LAD	134
13	Pete Alonso	NYM	133
14	Kyle Tucker	HOU	132
15	F. Tatis	SD	130
15	Manny Machado	SD	130
15	Rafael Devers	BOS	130
15	Luis Arraez	MIA	130
19	Corbin Carroll	AZ	127
20	Kyle Schwarber	PHI	126
20	Austin Riley	ATL	126
20	Bryce Harper	PHI	126
20	Paul Goldschmidt	STL	126
24	Alex Bregman	HOU	125
25	Yandy Díaz	TB	124
26	Adley Rutschman	BAL	123
26	Jose Altuve	HOU	123
28	Will Smith	LAD	122
28	Julio Rodríguez	SEA	122
28	Bryan Reynolds	PIT	122
31	Seiya Suzuki	CHC	120
31	Ketel Marte	AZ	120
33	Masataka Yoshida	BOS	119
34	Jorge Soler	FA	118
34	V. Pasquantino	KC	118
34	Eloy Jiménez	CHW	118
34	Xander Bogaerts	SD	118
38	Bobby Witt Jr.	KC	117
38	Christian Walker	AZ	117
38	Daniel Vogelbach	NYM	117
38	Marcell Ozuna	ATL	117
38	Brandon Nimmo	NYM	117
38	Jung Hoo Lee	SF	117
38	Alejandro Kirk	TOR	117
38	W. Contreras	STL	117
38	Bo Bichette	TOR	117
47	Isaac Paredes	TB	116
47	Josh Naylor	CLE	116
47	Max Muncy	LAD	116
47	Royce Lewis	MIN	116

Earned Run Average - Starters

Rank	Name	Team	ERA
1	Tyler Glasnow	LAD	2.81
2	Tarik Skubal	DET	3.03
3	Spencer Strider	ATL	3.10
4	Y. Yamamoto	LAD	3.12
5	Gerrit Cole	NYY	3.30
6	Zach Eflin	TB	3.34
6	Kevin Gausman	TOR	3.34
6	G. Rodriguez	BAL	3.34
9	Pablo López	MIN	3.37
10	Freddy Peralta	MIL	3.39
11	Max Fried	ATL	3.41
12	Corbin Burnes	MIL	3.42
13	Logan Webb	SF	3.43
13	Zack Wheeler	PHI	3.43
15	Blake Snell	FA	3.45
16	Joe Ryan	MIN	3.54
17	Aaron Nola	PHI	3.56
18	Framber Valdez	HOU	3.58
19	Michael King	SD	3.61
20	Hunter Brown	HOU	3.68
20	Nathan Eovaldi	TEX	3.68
22	Zac Gallen	AZ	3.69
23	Kyle Bradish	BAL	3.74
24	Joe Musgrove	SD	3.76
25	Chris Paddack	MIN	3.80

Strikeout Percentage - Starters

Rank	Name	Team	K%
1	Spencer Strider	ATL	35.5%
2	Tyler Glasnow	LAD	33.8%
3	Blake Snell	FA	32.6%
4	Freddy Peralta	MIL	30.8%
5	Emmet Sheehan	LAD	29.6%
6	Hunter Greene	CIN	29.0%
7	Eury Pérez	MIA	28.8%
8	Charlie Morton	ATL	28.4%
9	Dylan Cease	CHW	27.8%
10	Kevin Gausman	TOR	27.6%
11	Tarik Skubal	DET	27.5%
12	Mason Miller	OAK	27.4%
12	Chris Sale	ATL	27.4%
14	Jesús Luzardo	MIA	27.0%
14	Michael King	SD	27.0%
14	Gerrit Cole	NYY	27.0%
14	Edward Cabrera	MIA	27.0%
18	Kodai Senga	NYM	26.7%
19	Corbin Burnes	MIL	26.6%
20	Kyle Harrison	SF	26.4%
21	Cole Ragans	KC	26.1%
22	Nick Pivetta	BOS	25.9%
23	Carlos Rodón	NYY	25.8%
24	Zack Wheeler	PHI	25.6%
24	Joe Ryan	MIN	25.6%

Walk Percentage - Starters

Rank	Name	Team	BB%
1	George Kirby	SEA	4.8%
2	Zach Eflin	TB	4.9%
3	Miles Mikolas	STL	5.4%
4	Ross Stripling	SF	5.7%
4	Cole Irvin	BAL	5.7%
4	Aaron Nola	PHI	5.7%
7	Logan Webb	SF	5.8%
8	Kyle Hendricks	CHC	5.9%
8	Zack Wheeler	PHI	5.9%
10	Bailey Ober	MIN	6.0%
11	Logan Gilbert	SEA	6.1%
12	Max Fried	ATL	6.2%
12	John Means	BAL	6.2%
12	Shota Imanaga	CHC	6.2%
12	Brandon Pfaadt	AZ	6.2%
16	Justin Verlander	HOU	6.3%
16	Chris Paddack	MIN	6.3%
18	Y. Yamamoto	LAD	6.4%
18	Gerrit Cole	NYY	6.4%
20	Joe Musgrove	SD	6.5%
20	Kevin Gausman	TOR	6.5%
20	Jameson Taillon	CHC	6.5%
20	A. DeSclafani	SEA	6.5%
24	Nathan Eovaldi	TEX	6.6%
24	Joe Ryan	MIN	6.6%

Earned Run Average - Relievers

Rank	Name	Team	ERA
1	Devin Williams	MIL	2.72
2	Jhoan Duran	MIN	2.76
3	Edwin Díaz	NYM	2.80
4	Andrés Muñoz	SEA	2.86
5	Yuki Matsui	SD	2.98
6	Pete Fairbanks	TB	3.07
7	Ryan Pressly	HOU	3.10
8	Josh Hader	FA	3.24
9	Aaron Bummer	ATL	3.27
10	José Alvarado	PHI	3.29
10	Camilo Doval	SF	3.29
12	Joe Kelly	LAD	3.30
13	Raisel Iglesias	ATL	3.31
14	Clay Holmes	NYY	3.32
15	Emmanuel Clase	CLE	3.37
16	Tanner Scott	MIA	3.43
17	A.J. Minter	ATL	3.51
18	Taylor Rogers	SF	3.53
19	G. Cleavinger	TB	3.54
19	Tim Mayza	TOR	3.54
21	Bryan Abreu	HOU	3.57
22	Matt Brash	SEA	3.59
22	Kevin Ginkel	AZ	3.59
22	Luke Jackson	SF	3.59
25	Ryan Helsley	STL	3.61

Strikeout Percentage - Relievers

Rank	Name	Team	K%
1	Edwin Díaz	NYM	40.3%
2	Devin Williams	MIL	38.2%
3	Aroldis Chapman	FA	37.6%
4	Josh Hader	FA	36.6%
5	John McMillon	KC	35.4%
6	Andrés Muñoz	SEA	35.2%
7	Bryan Abreu	HOU	35.0%
8	Yuki Matsui	SD	32.9%
8	Matt Brash	SEA	32.9%
10	James Karinchak	CLE	32.8%
11	Alex Lange	DET	31.8%
11	Abner Uribe	MIL	31.8%
13	José Alvarado	PHI	31.7%
14	Luke Little	CHC	31.4%
14	Lucas Sims	CIN	31.4%
16	Tanner Scott	MIA	31.3%
17	Trevor Richards	TOR	31.2%
17	Jhoan Duran	MIN	31.2%
19	Pete Fairbanks	TB	31.0%
20	Jason Adam	TB	30.9%
20	Brock Stewart	MIN	30.9%
22	Fernando Cruz	CIN	30.8%
23	José Leclerc	TEX	30.5%
24	Alexis Díaz	CIN	30.4%
25	Kirby Yates	TEX	30.1%

Walk Percentage - Relievers

Rank	Name	Team	BB%
1	Chris Martin	BOS	5.0%
2	Ryan Yarbrough	LAD	5.5%
3	Garrett Whitlock	BOS	5.8%
4	Tyler Alexander	TB	6.0%
4	Hoby Milner	MIL	6.0%
6	Michael McGreevy	STL	6.2%
7	Adam Cimber	LAA	6.3%
7	Andrew Kittredge	STL	6.3%
9	Raisel Iglesias	ATL	6.4%
10	Emmanuel Clase	CLE	6.6%
10	Tyler Rogers	SF	6.6%
10	Tanner Banks	CHW	6.6%
13	Joe Mantiply	AZ	6.8%
13	Dylan Lee	ATL	6.8%
15	Ryan Pressly	HOU	6.9%
15	Brusdar Graterol	LAD	6.9%
17	Bryan Hoeing	MIA	7.0%
17	Gabe Speier	SEA	7.0%
17	J. Loaisiga	NYY	7.0%
17	Yimi García	TOR	7.0%
17	Chad Green	TOR	7.0%
22	Nick Ramirez	NYY	7.1%
22	Shawn Armstrong	TB	7.1%
22	Collin McHugh	FA	7.1%
22	G. Gallegos	STL	7.1%

Wins

Rank	Name	Team	W
1	Framber Valdez	HOU	15
1	Gerrit Cole	NYY	15
3	Logan Webb	SF	14
3	Spencer Strider	ATL	14
5	Pablo López	MIN	13
5	Kevin Gausman	TOR	13
5	Zac Gallen	AZ	13
5	Chris Bassitt	TOR	13
9	Y. Yamamoto	LAD	12
9	Zack Wheeler	PHI	12
9	Joe Ryan	MIN	12
9	Aaron Nola	PHI	12
9	George Kirby	SEA	12
9	Merrill Kelly	AZ	12
9	Logan Gilbert	SEA	12
9	Max Fried	ATL	12
9	Nathan Eovaldi	TEX	12
9	Zach Eflin	TB	12
9	Luis Castillo	SEA	12
9	Corbin Burnes	MIL	12
9	José Berríos	TOR	12
22	Justin Verlander	HOU	11
22	Bailey Ober	MIN	11
22	Charlie Morton	ATL	11
22	Miles Mikolas	STL	11

Strikeouts

Rank	Name	Team	K
1	Spencer Strider	ATL	245
2	Gerrit Cole	NYY	213
3	Blake Snell	FA	211
4	Freddy Peralta	MIL	203
5	Kevin Gausman	TOR	196
6	Corbin Burnes	MIL	195
7	Cole Ragans	KC	194
8	Dylan Cease	CHW	190
8	Luis Castillo	SEA	190
10	Tyler Glasnow	LAD	189
11	Framber Valdez	HOU	186
11	Lucas Giolito	BOS	186
13	Kodai Senga	NYM	184
14	Zack Wheeler	PHI	183
15	Charlie Morton	ATL	182
15	Zac Gallen	AZ	182
17	Pablo López	MIN	181
18	Aaron Nola	PHI	178
19	Tarik Skubal	DET	177
19	Joe Ryan	MIN	177
21	Jesús Luzardo	MIA	176
22	Shane Bieber	CLE	171
23	G. Rodriguez	BAL	167
23	Reid Detmers	LAA	167
25	Yu Darvish	SD	165

WHIP - Starters

Rank	Name	Team	WHIP
1	Tyler Glasnow	LAD	1.10
1	Spencer Strider	ATL	1.10
3	Gerrit Cole	NYY	1.11
3	Tarik Skubal	DET	1.11
3	Y. Yamamoto	LAD	1.11
6	Kevin Gausman	TOR	1.12
7	Zach Eflin	TB	1.13
7	Joe Ryan	MIN	1.13
9	Zack Wheeler	PHI	1.14
10	Pablo López	MIN	1.15
10	Aaron Nola	PHI	1.15
10	Freddy Peralta	MIL	1.15
13	Corbin Burnes	MIL	1.16
14	Joe Musgrove	SD	1.18
14	Chris Sale	ATL	1.18
16	Nestor Cortes	NYY	1.19
16	Zac Gallen	AZ	1.19
16	Bailey Ober	MIN	1.19
19	Nathan Eovaldi	TEX	1.20
19	Max Fried	ATL	1.20
19	Logan Gilbert	SEA	1.20
19	Michael King	SD	1.20
19	Kenta Maeda	DET	1.20
24	Yu Darvish	SD	1.21
24	George Kirby	SEA	1.21

Saves

Rank	Name	Team	SV
1	Raisel Iglesias	ATL	41
1	Clay Holmes	NYY	41
3	Ryan Pressly	HOU	38
3	Pete Fairbanks	TB	38
5	Devin Williams	MIL	37
5	José Leclerc	TEX	37
7	Jordan Romano	TOR	36
7	Kenley Jansen	BOS	36
7	Jhoan Duran	MIN	36
7	Edwin Díaz	NYM	36
7	Emmanuel Clase	CLE	36
12	Paul Sewald	AZ	35
12	Andrés Muñoz	SEA	35
12	Craig Kimbrel	BAL	35
15	Ryan Helsley	STL	34
15	Carlos Estévez	LAA	34
17	Camilo Doval	SF	33
17	David Bednar	PIT	33
19	Alexis Díaz	CIN	32
20	Tanner Scott	MIA	31
20	Evan Phillips	LAD	31
22	Alex Lange	DET	30
22	José Alvarado	PHI	30
24	Adbert Alzolay	CHC	28
25	Yuki Matsui	SD	26

Holds

Rank	Name	Team	HLD
1	Chris Martin	BOS	24
1	Ian Hamilton	NYY	24
3	Josh Sborz	TEX	23
3	Tyler Rogers	SF	23
3	Taylor Rogers	SF	23
3	A.J. Puk	MIA	23
3	Andrew Nardi	MIA	23
3	Tyler Kinley	COL	23
9	Dauri Moreta	PIT	22
10	Colin Poche	TB	21
10	Joel Payamps	MIL	21
10	A.J. Minter	ATL	21
10	J. Merryweather	CHC	21
10	J. Loaisiga	NYY	21
10	Mark Leiter Jr.	CHC	21
10	Tommy Kahnle	NYY	21
10	Joe Jiménez	ATL	21
10	Danny Coulombe	BAL	21
10	Tom Cosgrove	SD	21
10	Yennier Cano	BAL	21
21	Will Vest	DET	20
21	Erik Swanson	TOR	20
21	Drew Smith	NYM	20
21	Brooks Raley	NYM	20
21	Jimmy Herget	LAA	20

WHIP - Relievers

Rank	Name	Team	WHIP
1	Edwin Díaz	NYM	1.05
2	Yuki Matsui	SD	1.11
2	Andrés Muñoz	SEA	1.11
2	Devin Williams	MIL	1.11
5	Raisel Iglesias	ATL	1.12
6	Pete Fairbanks	TB	1.13
7	Jhoan Duran	MIN	1.14
7	Josh Hader	FA	1.14
7	Ryan Pressly	HOU	1.14
10	Jason Adam	TB	1.16
11	Mark Leiter Jr.	CHC	1.18
11	A.J. Minter	ATL	1.18
11	Taylor Rogers	SF	1.18
11	Matt Strahm	PHI	1.18
15	Chad Green	TOR	1.19
15	Paul Sewald	AZ	1.19
17	G. Gallegos	STL	1.20
17	Hoby Milner	MIL	1.20
17	Erik Swanson	TOR	1.20
17	Garrett Whitlock	BOS	1.20
21	G. Cleavinger	TB	1.21
21	Yimi García	TOR	1.21
21	Chris Martin	BOS	1.21
21	Evan Phillips	LAD	1.21
21	Caleb Thielbar	MIN	1.21

Fastball Velocity - Starters

Rank	Name	Team	FB Velo
1	Bobby Miller	LAD	99
1	Hunter Greene	CIN	99
1	Jacob deGrom	TEX	99
4	Sixto Sánchez	MIA	98
4	Mason Miller	OAK	98
4	Joe Boyle	OAK	98
4	Spencer Strider	ATL	98
8	Eury Pérez	MIA	97
8	Dustin May	LAD	97
8	Gerrit Cole	NYY	97
8	G. Rodriguez	BAL	97
8	Luis Castillo	SEA	97
8	Tyler Glasnow	LAD	97
8	Huascar Ynoa	ATL	97
8	Graham Ashcraft	CIN	97
8	Dylan Cease	CHW	97
17	Luis Severino	NYM	96
17	Luis Gil	NYY	96
17	Jesús Luzardo	MIA	96
17	Shane Baz	TB	96
17	Zack Wheeler	PHI	96
17	Luis L. Ortiz	PIT	96
17	Edward Cabrera	MIA	96
17	Nick Nelson	PHI	96
17	Frankie Montas	CIN	96

Groundball Rate - Starters

Rank	Name	Team	GB%
1	Logan Webb	SF	59.3%
2	Framber Valdez	HOU	57.8%
3	Alex Cobb	SF	55.5%
4	Brayan Bello	BOS	55.1%
5	Aaron Ashby	MIL	54.7%
6	Marcus Stroman	FA	53.9%
7	C. Sanchez	PHI	53.8%
8	Max Fried	ATL	52.8%
9	Dakota Hudson	COL	52.6%
10	Hunter Brown	HOU	52.0%
11	Tanner Houck	BOS	51.3%
12	Keaton Winn	SF	50.8%
13	Ranger Suárez	PHI	50.6%
14	Edward Cabrera	MIA	49.9%
15	Bryce Elder	ATL	49.7%
16	Graham Ashcraft	CIN	49.6%
17	Adrian Houser	NYM	48.9%
18	Justin Steele	CHC	48.8%
19	Dane Dunning	TEX	48.6%
20	Brady Singer	KC	48.5%
20	Tyler Glasnow	LAD	48.5%
22	Kyle Bradish	BAL	47.6%
23	Nathan Eovaldi	TEX	47.5%
24	Kyle Gibson	STL	47.4%
24	Braxton Garrett	MIA	47.4%

Whiff Rate - Starters

Rank	Name	Team	Whiff%
1	Spencer Strider	ATL	36.4%
2	Blake Snell	FA	34.8%
3	Tyler Glasnow	LAD	34.0%
4	Eury Pérez	MIA	32.3%
4	Freddy Peralta	MIL	32.3%
6	Jesús Luzardo	MIA	31.2%
7	Corbin Burnes	MIL	31.0%
8	Dylan Cease	CHW	30.9%
9	Hunter Greene	CIN	30.8%
10	Emmet Sheehan	LAD	30.2%
11	Charlie Morton	ATL	30.1%
12	Edward Cabrera	MIA	29.7%
13	Griffin Canning	LAA	29.4%
14	Chris Sale	ATL	29.3%
14	Luis Castillo	SEA	29.3%
16	Keaton Winn	SF	28.9%
17	Kodai Senga	NYM	28.8%
17	Tanner Houck	BOS	28.8%
17	Lucas Giolito	BOS	28.8%
20	Pablo López	MIN	28.7%
20	Michael King	SD	28.7%
22	Patrick Sandoval	LAA	28.6%
22	Cole Ragans	KC	28.6%
24	Tarik Skubal	DET	28.5%
24	Kevin Gausman	TOR	28.5%

Fastball Velocity - Relievers

Rank	Name	Team	FB Velo
1	Jhoan Duran	MIN	101
1	Justin Martinez	AZ	101
3	Ben Joyce	LAA	100
3	Jordan Hicks	FA	100
3	Emmanuel Clase	CLE	100
3	Andrés Muñoz	SEA	100
7	Guillermo Zuñiga	STL	99
7	Abner Uribe	MIL	99
7	Brusdar Graterol	LAD	99
7	Carlos Vargas	SEA	99
7	Ryan Helsley	STL	99
7	Gregory Santos	CHW	99
7	John McMillon	KC	99
7	Camilo Doval	SF	99
7	Edwin Díaz	NYM	99
7	Aroldis Chapman	FA	99
7	Daniel Palencia	CHC	99
7	Orion Kerkering	PHI	99
19	Pete Fairbanks	TB	98
19	José Alvarado	PHI	98
19	Hunter Harvey	WAS	98
19	Joe Kelly	LAD	98
19	Gregory Soto	PHI	98
19	Trevor Megill	MIL	98
19	Carlos Hernández	KC	98

Groundball Rate - Relievers

Rank	Name	Team	GB%
1	Andre Pallante	STL	67.9%
2	Clay Holmes	NYY	65.2%
3	Aaron Bummer	ATL	62.0%
4	Brusdar Graterol	LAD	60.9%
5	John King	STL	60.2%
6	Jhoan Duran	MIN	58.5%
6	Emmanuel Clase	CLE	58.5%
8	Jordan Hicks	FA	58.2%
9	Andrew Saalfrank	AZ	56.8%
10	Tim Hill	CHW	56.7%
11	Joe Kelly	LAD	56.0%
12	Dillon Tate	BAL	54.9%
13	Tim Mayza	TOR	54.7%
14	Jason Foley	DET	54.5%
15	Cionel Pérez	BAL	54.4%
16	J. Loaisiga	NYY	54.1%
17	Yennier Cano	BAL	54.0%
18	Justin Topa	SEA	53.5%
19	Tyler Rogers	SF	53.0%
20	L. McCullers	HOU	52.8%
20	Sam Hentges	CLE	52.8%
20	José Alvarado	PHI	52.8%
23	Tayler Saucedo	SEA	52.6%
24	Victor González	NYY	52.4%
25	Luke Jackson	SF	52.2%

Whiff Rate - Relievers

Rank	Name	Team	Whiff%
1	Edwin Díaz	NYM	40.8%
2	Devin Williams	MIL	39.3%
3	Andrés Muñoz	SEA	37.7%
4	John McMillon	KC	37.5%
5	Alex Lange	DET	37.4%
6	Bryan Abreu	HOU	37.1%
7	Aroldis Chapman	FA	36.3%
8	Josh Hader	FA	35.3%
9	Tanner Scott	MIA	35.0%
10	José Leclerc	TEX	34.8%
11	Matt Brash	SEA	34.7%
12	Yuki Matsui	SD	34.2%
12	Alexis Díaz	CIN	34.2%
14	G. Gallegos	STL	33.8%
14	Jhoan Duran	MIN	33.8%
16	José Alvarado	PHI	33.5%
17	Trevor Richards	TOR	33.3%
17	Raisel Iglesias	ATL	33.3%
19	Josh Sborz	TEX	33.2%
20	Abner Uribe	MIL	33.0%
20	Tanner Rainey	WAS	33.0%
20	Jason Adam	TB	33.0%
23	Tommy Kahnle	NYY	32.8%
24	Brock Stewart	MIN	32.7%
24	Fernando Cruz	CIN	32.7%

Batting Average Against

Rank	Name	Team	AVG
1	Devin Williams	MIL	.181
2	Edwin Díaz	NYM	.188
2	Josh Hader	FA	.188
4	James Karinchak	CLE	.190
5	Aroldis Chapman	FA	.191
6	Andrés Muñoz	SEA	.196
7	Yuki Matsui	SD	.198
7	John McMillon	KC	.198
9	José Alvarado	PHI	.199
10	Jacob deGrom	TEX	.200
11	Jhoan Duran	MIN	.201
11	Pete Fairbanks	TB	.201
13	Spencer Strider	ATL	.202
14	Bryan Abreu	HOU	.203
14	Ricky Tiedemann	TOR	.203
16	Matt Brash	SEA	.205
17	Tyler Glasnow	LAD	.206
17	Abner Uribe	MIL	.206
19	G. Cleavinger	TB	.207
19	Joe Kelly	LAD	.207
21	Blake Snell	FA	.208
22	Luke Little	CHC	.209
23	Camilo Doval	SF	.210
23	Ryan Helsley	STL	.210
23	Tanner Scott	MIA	.210

AL WARP

Rank	Name	Team	WARP
1	Gerrit Cole	NYY	3.7
2	Framber Valdez	HOU	3.5
3	Tarik Skubal	DET	3.4
4	Kevin Gausman	TOR	3.3
5	Pablo López	MIN	3.2
5	Zach Eflin	TB	3.2
7	G. Rodriguez	BAL	3.1
8	Joe Ryan	MIN	2.8
9	Nathan Eovaldi	TEX	2.7
10	Luis Castillo	SEA	2.5
10	Kyle Bradish	BAL	2.5
12	Chris Bassitt	TOR	2.4
13	Hunter Brown	HOU	2.3
13	Shane Bieber	CLE	2.3
15	Cole Ragans	KC	2.2
15	George Kirby	SEA	2.2
15	Logan Gilbert	SEA	2.2
18	Bailey Ober	MIN	2.0
18	Lucas Giolito	BOS	2.0
18	Erick Fedde	CHW	2.0
21	Nestor Cortes	NYY	1.9
21	Brayan Bello	BOS	1.9
23	Justin Verlander	HOU	1.8
23	Aaron Civale	TB	1.8
23	Dylan Cease	CHW	1.8

Slugging Percent Against

Rank	Name	Team	SLG
1	Aaron Bummer	ATL	.303
2	Jhoan Duran	MIN	.304
3	Devin Williams	MIL	.313
4	Clay Holmes	NYY	.318
5	Andrés Muñoz	SEA	.319
6	José Alvarado	PHI	.320
7	Camilo Doval	SF	.327
7	Joe Kelly	LAD	.327
9	Jordan Hicks	FA	.330
10	Tanner Scott	MIA	.331
11	Andrew Saalfrank	AZ	.337
12	Edwin Díaz	NYM	.340
13	Pete Fairbanks	TB	.345
14	Alex Lange	DET	.346
15	Edward Cabrera	MIA	.347
15	Tyler Glasnow	LAD	.347
17	Matt Brash	SEA	.348
18	Luke Jackson	SF	.349
19	Luke Little	CHC	.350
20	Aroldis Chapman	FA	.351
21	G. Rodriguez	BAL	.352
21	Abner Uribe	MIL	.352
23	Emmanuel Clase	CLE	.353
23	Blake Snell	FA	.353
25	Bryan Abreu	HOU	.354

NL WARP

Rank	Name	Team	WARP
1	Logan Webb	SF	3.6
2	Tyler Glasnow	LAD	3.5
2	Corbin Burnes	MIL	3.5
4	Y. Yamamoto	LAD	3.4
4	Spencer Strider	ATL	3.4
6	Zack Wheeler	PHI	3.3
7	Freddy Peralta	MIL	3.2
8	Aaron Nola	PHI	3.1
9	Zac Gallen	AZ	2.9
10	Max Fried	ATL	2.8
11	Kodai Senga	NYM	2.3
11	Merrill Kelly	AZ	2.3
13	Justin Steele	CHC	2.2
13	Joe Musgrove	SD	2.2
15	Sonny Gray	STL	2.1
15	Yu Darvish	SD	2.1
17	Mitch Keller	PIT	2.0
18	Eury Pérez	MIA	1.9
18	Jesús Luzardo	MIA	1.9
20	Edward Cabrera	MIA	1.7
21	Chris Sale	ATL	1.6
21	Michael King	SD	1.6
21	Braxton Garrett	MIA	1.6
21	Walker Buehler	LAD	1.6
25	Charlie Morton	ATL	1.5

BASEBALL PROSPECTUS 2024

WARP

Rank	Name	Team	WARP
1	Gerrit Cole	NYY	3.7
2	Logan Webb	SF	3.6
3	Framber Valdez	HOU	3.5
3	Tyler Glasnow	LAD	3.5
3	Corbin Burnes	MIL	3.5
6	Y. Yamamoto	LAD	3.4
6	Spencer Strider	ATL	3.4
6	Tarik Skubal	DET	3.4
9	Zack Wheeler	PHI	3.3
9	Kevin Gausman	TOR	3.3
11	Freddy Peralta	MIL	3.2
11	Pablo López	MIN	3.2
11	Zach Eflin	TB	3.2
14	G. Rodriguez	BAL	3.1
14	Aaron Nola	PHI	3.1
16	Blake Snell	FA	3.0
17	Zac Gallen	AZ	2.9
18	Joe Ryan	MIN	2.8
18	Max Fried	ATL	2.8
20	Nathan Eovaldi	TEX	2.7
21	Luis Castillo	SEA	2.5
21	Kyle Bradish	BAL	2.5
23	Chris Bassitt	TOR	2.4
24	Kodai Senga	NYM	2.3
24	Merrill Kelly	AZ	2.3
24	Hunter Brown	HOU	2.3
24	Shane Bieber	CLE	2.3
28	Justin Steele	CHC	2.2
28	Cole Ragans	KC	2.2
28	Joe Musgrove	SD	2.2
28	George Kirby	SEA	2.2
28	Logan Gilbert	SEA	2.2
33	J. Montgomery	FA	2.1
33	Sonny Gray	STL	2.1
33	Yu Darvish	SD	2.1
36	Marcus Stroman	FA	2.0
36	Bailey Ober	MIN	2.0
36	Mitch Keller	PIT	2.0
36	Lucas Giolito	BOS	2.0
36	Erick Fedde	CHW	2.0
41	Eury Pérez	MIA	1.9
41	Jesús Luzardo	MIA	1.9
41	Nestor Cortes	NYY	1.9
41	Brayan Bello	BOS	1.9
45	Justin Verlander	HOU	1.8
45	Aaron Civale	TB	1.8
45	Dylan Cease	CHW	1.8
45	José Berríos	TOR	1.8
49	Carlos Rodón	NYY	1.7
49	Nick Pivetta	BOS	1.7

DRA- Starters

Rank	Name	Team	DRA-
1	Tyler Glasnow	LAD	69
2	Tarik Skubal	DET	75
2	Y. Yamamoto	LAD	75
4	Spencer Strider	ATL	76
5	Freddy Peralta	MIL	79
6	Corbin Burnes	MIL	80
6	Gerrit Cole	NYY	80
6	G. Rodriguez	BAL	80
6	Blake Snell	FA	80
10	Zach Eflin	TB	81
10	Max Fried	ATL	81
10	Kevin Gausman	TOR	81
10	Pablo López	MIN	81
10	Logan Webb	SF	81
10	Zack Wheeler	PHI	81
16	Framber Valdez	HOU	83
17	Aaron Nola	PHI	84
18	Hunter Brown	HOU	85
18	Michael King	SD	85
20	Nathan Eovaldi	TEX	86
20	Joe Ryan	MIN	86
22	Zac Gallen	AZ	87
23	Kyle Bradish	BAL	88
23	Edward Cabrera	MIA	88
23	Joe Musgrove	SD	88
26	Chris Sale	ATL	89
27	Nestor Cortes	NYY	90
27	Chris Paddack	MIN	90
27	Eury Pérez	MIA	90
27	Kodai Senga	NYM	90
27	Marcus Stroman	FA	90
32	Shane Bieber	CLE	91
32	Luis Castillo	SEA	91
32	Carlos Rodón	NYY	91
35	Chris Bassitt	TOR	92
35	Erick Fedde	CHW	92
35	Sonny Gray	STL	92
35	Merrill Kelly	AZ	92
35	Mason Miller	OAK	92
35	Cole Ragans	KC	92
35	Justin Steele	CHC	92
42	Aaron Ashby	MIL	93
42	Aaron Civale	TB	93
42	Alex Cobb	SF	93
42	Yu Darvish	SD	93
42	Logan Gilbert	SEA	93
42	Tanner Houck	BOS	93
42	Kenta Maeda	DET	93
42	J. Montgomery	FA	93
42	Bailey Ober	MIN	93

DRA- Relievers

Rank	Name	Team	DRA-
1	Devin Williams	MIL	65
2	Jhoan Duran	MIN	67
3	Edwin Díaz	NYM	69
3	Andrés Muñoz	SEA	69
5	Yuki Matsui	SD	73
6	Pete Fairbanks	TB	74
7	José Alvarado	PHI	75
7	Aaron Bummer	ATL	75
7	Ryan Pressly	HOU	75
10	Joe Kelly	LAD	76
11	Camilo Doval	SF	77
11	Josh Hader	FA	77
11	Clay Holmes	NYY	77
14	Tanner Scott	MIA	79
15	Emmanuel Clase	CLE	80
15	Raisel Iglesias	ATL	80
17	Bryan Abreu	HOU	82
17	Matt Brash	SEA	82
17	G. Cleavinger	TB	82
20	Kevin Ginkel	AZ	83
20	Luke Jackson	SF	83
20	Tim Mayza	TOR	83
20	Taylor Rogers	SF	83
24	Aroldis Chapman	FA	84
24	Mark Leiter Jr.	CHC	84
24	A.J. Minter	ATL	84
24	Josh Sborz	TEX	84
28	Tommy Kahnle	NYY	85
28	James Karinchak	CLE	85
28	John Schreiber	BOS	85
28	Paul Sewald	AZ	85
32	Jason Adam	TB	86
32	Ryan Helsley	STL	86
32	Sam Hentges	CLE	86
32	Jordan Hicks	FA	86
32	Evan Phillips	LAD	86
32	JoJo Romero	STL	86
32	Ryan Thompson	AZ	86
39	Brusdar Graterol	LAD	87
39	Ian Hamilton	NYY	87
39	Pierce Johnson	ATL	87
39	Chris Martin	BOS	87
39	Trevor Richards	TOR	87
39	Andrew Saalfrank	AZ	87
39	Greg Weissert	BOS	87
39	Garrett Whitlock	BOS	87
47	David Bednar	PIT	88
47	Hoby Milner	MIL	88
47	Caleb Thielbar	MIN	88
50	Caleb Ferguson	LAD	89

Team Codes

CODE	TEAM	LG	AFF	NAME
ABD	Aberdeen	SAL	Orioles	IronBirds
ABQ	Albuquerque	PCL	Rockies	Isotopes
ADE	Adelaide	ABL	-	Giants
AGU	Aguilas	LIDOM	-	Aguilas
AKL	Auckland	ABL	-	Tuatara
AKR	Akron	EAS	Guardians	RubberDucks
ALT	Altoona	EAS	Pirates	Curve
AMA	Amarillo	TEX	D-backs	Sod Poodles
ANG	ACL Angels	ACL	Angels	ACL Angels
ARA	Aragua	LVBP	-	Tigres
ARK	Arkansas	TEX	Mariners	Travelers
ASB	FCL Astros Blue	FCL	Astros	FCL Astros Blue
ASH	Asheville	SAL	Astros	Tourists
ASO	FCL Astros Orange	FCL	Astros	FCL Astros Orange
AST	FCL Astros	FCL	Astros	FCL Astros
ATH	ACL Athletics	ACL	Athletics	ACL Athletics
ATL	Atlanta	NL	-	Braves
AUG	Augusta	CAR	Braves	GreenJackets
AZ	Arizona	NL	-	D-backs
BAL	Baltimore	AL	-	Orioles
BEL	Beloit	MID	Marlins	Sky Carp
BEL	Beloit	A+ C	Marlins	Snappers
BG	Bowling Green	SAL	Rays	Hot Rods
BIR	Birmingham	SOU	White Sox	Barons
BLU	FCL Blue Jays	FCL	Blue Jays	FCL Blue Jays
BLX	Biloxi	SOU	Brewers	Shuckers
BNG	Binghamton	EAS	Mets	Rumble Ponies
BOS	Boston	AL	-	Red Sox
BOW	Bowie	EAS	Orioles	Baysox
BRA	FCL Braves	FCL	Braves	FCL Braves
BRD	Bradenton	FSL	Pirates	Marauders
BRI	Brisbane	ABL	-	Bandits
BRK	Brooklyn	SAL	Mets	Cyclones
BRW	ACL Brewers	ACL	Brewers	ACL Brewers
BRWB	ACL Brewers Blue	ACL	Brewers	ACL Brewers Blue
BRWG	ACL Brewers Gold	ACL	Brewers	ACL Brewers Gold
BUF	Buffalo	INT	Blue Jays	Bisons
CAG	Caguas	PWL	-	Caguas
CAN	Canberra	ABL	-	Cavalry
CAR	Carolina	CAR	Brewers	Mudcats
CAR	FCL Cardinals	FCL	Cardinals	FCL Cardinals
CAR	Carolina	PWL	-	Carolina
CAR	Caracas	LVBP	-	Leones
CC	Corpus Christi	TEX	Astros	Hooks
CHA	Chattanooga	SOU	Reds	Lookouts
CHC	Chi Cubs	NL	-	Cubs
CHW	Chi White Sox	AL	-	White Sox
CIN	Cincinnati	NL	-	Reds
CLE	Cleveland	AL	-	Guardians
CLE	Cleveland	AL	-	Guardians
CLR	Clearwater	FSL	Phillies	Threshers

CODE	TEAM	LG	AFF	NAME
CLT	Charlotte	INT	White Sox	Knights
COL	Colombia	CS	-	Colombia
COL	Colorado	NL	-	Rockies
COL	Columbia	CAR	Royals	Fireflies
COL	Columbus	INT	Guardians	Clippers
CR	Cedar Rapids	MID	Twins	Kernels
CSC	Charleston	CAR	Rays	RiverDogs
CUB	ACL Cubs	ACL	Cubs	ACL Cubs
CUB	Cuba	CS	-	Cuba
CUL	Culiacan	LMP	-	Culiacan
CW	Curacao	CS	-	Curacao
CHW	Chi White Sox	AL	-	White Sox
DAY	Dayton	MID	Reds	Dragons
DBT	Daytona	FSL	Reds	Tortugas
DE	Down East	CAR	Rangers	Wood Ducks
DEL	Delmarva	CAR	Orioles	Shorebirds
DET	Detroit	AL	-	Tigers
DIA	ACL D-backs	ACL	D-backs	ACL D-backs
DIA2	ACL D-backs 2	ACL	D-backs	ACL D-backs 2
DIAB	ACL D-backs Black	ACL	D-backs	ACL D-backs Black
DIAR	ACL D-backs Red	ACL	D-backs	ACL D-backs Red
DOD	ACL Dodgers	ACL	Dodgers	ACL Dodgers
DR	Dom. Rep.	CS	-	Dom. Rep.
DSL ANG	DSL Angels	DSL	Angels	DSL Angels
DSL AST	DSL Astros	DSL	Astros	DSL Astros
DSL ASTB	DSL Astros Blue	DSL	Astros	DSL Astros Blue
DSL ASTO	DSL Astros Orange	DSL	Astros	DSL Astros Orange
DSL ATH	DSL Athletics	DSL	Athletics	DSL Athletics
DSL AZB	DSL Arizona Black	DSL	D-backs	DSL Arizona Black
DSL AZR	DSL Arizona Red	DSL	D-backs	DSL Arizona Red
DSL BALB	DSL BAL Black	DSL	Orioles	DSL BAL Black
DSL BALO	DSL BAL Orange	DSL	Orioles	DSL BAL Orange
DSL BAU	DSL Dodgers Bautista	DSL	Dodgers	DSL Dodgers Bautista
DSL BLJ	DSL Blue Jays	DSL	Blue Jays	DSL Blue Jays
DSL BOSB	DSL BOS Blue	DSL	Red Sox	DSL BOS Blue
DSL BOSR	DSL BOS Red	DSL	Red Sox	DSL BOS Red
DSL BRA	DSL Braves	DSL	Braves	DSL Braves
DSL BRW1	DSL Brewers 1	DSL	Brewers	DSL Brewers 1
DSL BRW1	DSL Brewers1	DSL	Brewers	DSL Brewers1
DSL BRW2	DSL Brewers 2	DSL	Brewers	DSL Brewers 2
DSL BRW2	DSL Brewers2	DSL	Brewers	DSL Brewers2
DSL CAR	DSL Cardinals	DSL	Cardinals	DSL Cardinals
DSL CARB	DSL Cardinals Blue	DSL	Cardinals	DSL Cardinals Blue
DSL CARR	DSL Cardinals Red	DSL	Cardinals	DSL Cardinals Red
DSL CLEB	DSL CLE Blue	DSL	Guardians	DSL CLE Blue
DSL CLER	DSL CLE Red	DSL	Guardians	DSL CLE Red
DSL COL	DSL Colorado	DSL	Rockies	DSL Colorado
DSL CUBB	DSL Cubs Blue	DSL	Cubs	DSL Cubs Blue
DSL CUBR	DSL Cubs Red	DSL	Cubs	DSL Cubs Red
DSL DB1	DSL D-backs1	DSL	D-backs	DSL D-backs1

CODE	TEAM	LG	AFF	NAME	CODE	TEAM	LG	AFF	NAME
DSL DB2	DSL D-backs2	DSL	D-backs	DSL D-backs2	DSL TIG1	DSL Tigers 1	DSL	Tigers	DSL Tigers 1
DSL DBB	DSL D-backs Black	DSL	D-backs	DSL D-backs Black	DSL TIG2	DSL Tigers 2	DSL	Tigers	DSL Tigers 2
DSL DBR	DSL D-backs Red	DSL	D-backs	DSL D-backs Red	DSL TWI	DSL Twins	DSL	Twins	DSL Twins
DSL GIB	DSL Giants Black	DSL	Giants	DSL Giants Black	DSL WSX	DSL White Sox	DSL	White Sox	DSL White Sox
DSL GIO	DSL Giants Orange	DSL	Giants	DSL Giants Orange	DUN	Dunedin	FSL	Blue Jays	Blue Jays
DSL GUAB	DSL Guardians Blue	DSL	Guardians	DSL Guardians Blue	DUR	Durham	INT	Rays	Bulls
DSL GUAR	DSL Guardians Red	DSL	Guardians	DSL Guardians Red	ELP	El Paso	PCL	Padres	Chihuahuas
DSL HOUB	DSL HOU Blue	DSL	Astros	DSL HOU Blue	ERI	Erie	EAS	Tigers	SeaWolves
DSL HOUO	DSL HOU Orange	DSL	Astros	DSL HOU Orange	ESC	Escogido	LIDOM	-	Leones
DSL INDB	DSL Guardians Blue	DSL	Guardians	DSL Guardians Blue	EST	Estrellas	LIDOM	-	Estrellas
DSL INDR	DSL Guardians Red	DSL	Guardians	DSL Guardians Red	EUG	Eugene	NWL	Giants	Emeralds
DSL KCG	DSL KC Glass	DSL	Royals	DSL KC Glass	EVE	Everett	NWL	Mariners	AquaSox
DSL KCS	DSL KC Stewart	DSL	Royals	DSL KC Stewart	FAY	Fayetteville	CAR	Astros	Woodpeckers
DSL LADB	DSL LAD Bautista	DSL	Dodgers	DSL LAD Bautista	FBG	Fredericksburg	CAR	Nationals	Nationals
DSL LADM	DSL LAD Mega	DSL	Dodgers	DSL LAD Mega	FRE	Fresno	CAL	Rockies	Grizzlies
DSL MET1	DSL Mets 1	DSL	Mets	DSL Mets 1	FRI	Frisco	TEX	Rangers	RoughRiders
DSL MET1	DSL Mets1	DSL	Mets	DSL Mets1	FTM	Fort Myers	FSL	Twins	Mighty Mussels
DSL MET2	DSL Mets 2	DSL	Mets	DSL Mets 2	FW	Fort Wayne	MID	Padres	TinCaps
DSL MET2	DSL Mets2	DSL	Mets	DSL Mets2	GBO	Greensboro	SAL	Pirates	Grasshoppers
DSL METB	DSL Mets Blue	DSL	Mets	DSL Mets Blue	GDD	Glendale	AFL	-	Desert Dogs
DSL METO	DSL Mets Orange	DSL	Mets	DSL Mets Orange	GEE	Geelong-Korea	ABL	-	Geelong-Korea
DSL MIA	DSL Miami	DSL	Marlins	DSL Miami	GIG	Gigantes	LIDOM	-	Gigantes
DSL MRL	DSL Marlins	DSL	Marlins	DSL Marlins	GL	Great Lakes	MID	Dodgers	Loons
DSL NAT	DSL Nationals	DSL	Nationals	DSL Nationals	GNTB	ACL Giants Black	ACL	Giants	ACL Giants Black
DSL NYY	DSL NYY Yankees	DSL	Yankees	DSL NYY Yankees	GNTO	ACL Giants Orange	ACL	Giants	ACL Giants Orange
DSL NYY1	DSL Yankees1	DSL	Yankees	DSL Yankees1	GSV	Guasave	LMP	-	Guasave
DSL NYY2	DSL Yankees2	DSL	Yankees	DSL Yankees2	GUA	ACL Guardians	ACL	Guardians	ACL Guardians
DSL NYYB	DSL NYY Bombers	DSL	Yankees	DSL NYY Bombers	GVL	Greenville	SAL	Red Sox	Drive
DSL OR1	DSL Orioles1	DSL	Orioles	DSL Orioles1	GWN	Gwinnett	INT	Braves	Stripers
DSL OR2	DSL Orioles2	DSL	Orioles	DSL Orioles2	HBG	Harrisburg	EAS	Nationals	Senators
DSL ORIB	DSL Orioles Black	DSL	Orioles	DSL Orioles Black	HER	Hermosillo	LMP	-	Hermosillo
DSL ORIO	DSL Orioles Orange	DSL	Orioles	DSL Orioles Orange	HFD	Hartford	EAS	Rockies	Yard Goats
DSL PAD	DSL Padres	DSL	Padres	DSL Padres	HIC	Hickory	SAL	Rangers	Crawdads
DSL PADB	DSL Padres Brown	DSL	Padres	DSL Padres Brown	HIL	Hillsboro	NWL	D-backs	Hops
DSL PADG	DSL Padres Gold	DSL	Padres	DSL Padres Gold	HOU	Houston	AL	-	Astros
DSL PHR	DSL Phillies Red	DSL	Phillies	DSL Phillies Red	HV	Hudson Valley	SAL	Yankees	Renegades
DSL PHW	DSL Phillies White	DSL	Phillies	DSL Phillies White	IE	Inland Empire	CAL	Angels	66ers
DSL PIRB	DSL Pirates Black	DSL	Pirates	DSL Pirates Black	IND	ACL Guardians	ACL	Guardians	ACL Guardians
DSL PIRG	DSL Pirates Gold	DSL	Pirates	DSL Pirates Gold	IND	Indianapolis	INT	Pirates	Indianapolis
DSL PITB	DSL PIT Black	DSL	Pirates	DSL PIT Black	IOW	Iowa	INT	Cubs	Cubs
DSL PITG	DSL PIT Gold	DSL	Pirates	DSL PIT Gold	JAL	Jalisco	LMP	-	Jalisco
DSL RAY	DSL Rays	DSL	Rays	DSL Rays	JAX	Jacksonville	INT	Marlins	Jumbo Shrimp
DSL RAY1	DSL Rays1	DSL	Rays	DSL Rays1	JS	Jersey Shore	SAL	Phillies	BlueClaws
DSL RAY2	DSL Rays2	DSL	Rays	DSL Rays2	JUP	Jupiter	FSL	Marlins	Hammerheads
DSL REDS	DSL Reds	DSL	Reds	DSL Reds	KAN	Kannapolis	CAR	White Sox	Cannon Ballers
DSL RGR1	DSL Rangers1	DSL	Rangers	DSL Rangers1	KC	Kansas City	AL	-	Royals
DSL RGR2	DSL Rangers2	DSL	Rangers	DSL Rangers2	LAA	LA Angels	AL	-	Angels
DSL RNGB	DSL Rangers Blue	DSL	Rangers	DSL Rangers Blue	LAD	LA Dodgers	NL	-	Dodgers
DSL RNGR	DSL Rangers Red	DSL	Rangers	DSL Rangers Red	LAG	La Guaira	LVBP	-	Tiburones
DSL ROC	DSL Rockies	DSL	Rockies	DSL Rockies	LAK	Lakeland	FSL	Tigers	Flying Tigers
DSL ROYB	DSL Royals Blue	DSL	Royals	DSL Royals Blue	LAN	Lansing	MID	Athletics	Lugnuts
DSL ROYG	DSL Royals Gold	DSL	Royals	DSL Royals Gold	LAR	Lara	LVBP	-	Cardenales
DSL ROYW	DSL Royals White	DSL	Royals	DSL Royals White	LBPRC	LBPRC All-Stars	PWL	-	LBPRC All-Stars
DSL RSB	DSL Red Sox Blue	DSL	Red Sox	DSL Red Sox Blue	LC	Lake County	MID	Guardians	Captains
DSL RSR	DSL Red Sox Red	DSL	Red Sox	DSL Red Sox Red	LE	Lake Elsinore	CAL	Padres	Storm
DSL RSXB	DSL Red Sox Blue	DSL	Red Sox	DSL Red Sox Blue	LHV	Lehigh Valley	INT	Phillies	IronPigs
DSL RSXR	DSL Red Sox Red	DSL	Red Sox	DSL Red Sox Red	LIC	Licey	LIDOM	-	Tigres
DSL SEA	DSL Mariners	DSL	Mariners	DSL Mariners	LIDOM	LIDOM All-Stars	LIDOM	-	LIDOM All-Stars
DSL SHO	DSL Dodgers Shoemaker	DSL	Dodgers	Dodgers Shoemaker	LOU	Louisville	INT	Reds	Bats
DSL TB	DSL Tampa Bay	DSL	Rays	DSL Tampa Bay	LV	Las Vegas	PCL	Athletics	Aviators
DSL TEXB	DSL TEX Blue	DSL	Rangers	DSL TEX Blue	LYN	Lynchburg	CAR	Guardians	Hillcats
DSL TEXR	DSL TEX Red	DSL	Rangers	DSL TEX Red	MAG	Magallanes	LVBP	-	Navegantes
DSL TIG	DSL Tigers	DSL	Tigers	DSL Tigers	MAR	Margarita	LVBP	-	Bravos
					MAY	Mayaguez	PWL	-	Mayaguez

CODE	TEAM	LG	AFF	NAME
MAZ	Mazatlan	LMP	-	Mazatlan
MB	Myrtle Beach	CAR	Cubs	Pelicans
MEL	Melbourne	ABL	-	Aces
MEM	Memphis	INT	Cardinals	Redbirds
MET	FCL Mets	FCL	Mets	FCL Mets
MEX	Mexico	CS	-	Mexico
MIA	Miami	NL	-	Marlins
MID	Midland	TEX	Athletics	RockHounds
MIL	Milwaukee	NL	-	Brewers
MIN	Minnesota	AL	-	Twins
MIS	Mississippi	SOU	Braves	Braves
MOC	Los Mochis	LMP	-	Los Mochis
MOD	Modesto	CAL	Mariners	Nuts
MRL	FCL Marlins	FCL	Marlins	FCL Marlins
MRN	ACL Mariners	ACL	Mariners	ACL Mariners
MSS	Mesa	AFL	-	Solar Sox
MTG	Montgomery	SOU	Rays	Biscuits
MTY	Monterrey	LMP	-	Sultanes
MXC	Mexicali	LMP	-	Mexicali
NAS	Nashville	INT	Brewers	Sounds
NAT	FCL Nationals	FCL	Nationals	FCL Nationals
NAV	Navojoa	LMP	-	Navojoa
NCA	Nicaragua	CS	-	Nicaragua
NH	New Hampshire	EAS	Blue Jays	Fisher Cats
NOR	Norfolk	INT	Orioles	Tides
NWA	NW Arkansas	TEX	Royals	Naturals
NYM	NY Mets	NL	-	Mets
NYY	NY Yankees	AL	-	Yankees
OAK	Oakland	AL	-	Athletics
OBR	Obregon	LMP	-	Obregon
OKC	Okla. City	PCL	Dodgers	Dodgers
OMA	Omaha	INT	Royals	Storm Chasers
ORI	Caribes	LVBP	-	Caribes
ORI	FCL Orioles	FCL	Orioles	FCL Orioles
ORIB	FCL Orioles Black	FCL	Orioles	FCL Orioles Black
ORIO	FCL Orioles Orange	FCL	Orioles	FCL Orioles Orange
PAD	ACL Padres	ACL	Padres	ACL Padres
PAN	Panama	CS	-	Panama
PEJ	Peoria	AFL	-	Javelinas
PEO	Peoria	MID	Cardinals	Chiefs
PER	Perth	ABL	-	Heat
PHI	FCL Phillies	FCL	Phillies	FCL Phillies
PHI	Philadelphia	NL	-	Phillies
PHL	FCL Phillies	FCL	Phillies	FCL Phillies
PIR	FCL Pirates	FCL	Pirates	FCL Pirates
PIRB	FCL Pirates Black	FCL	Pirates	FCL Pirates Black
PIRG	FCL Pirates Gold	FCL	Pirates	FCL Pirates Gold
PIT	Pittsburgh	NL	-	Pirates
PMB	Palm Beach	FSL	Cardinals	Cardinals
PNS	Pensacola	SOU	Marlins	Blue Wahoos
PON	Ponce	PWL	-	Ponce
POR	Portland	EAS	Red Sox	Sea Dogs
PUR	Puerto Rico	CS	-	Puerto Rico
QC	Quad Cities	MID	Royals	River Bandits
RA12	RA12	PWL	-	RA12
RAN	ACL Rangers	ACL	Rangers	ACL Rangers
RAY	FCL Rays	FCL	Rays	FCL Rays
RC	Rancho Cuca.	CAL	Dodgers	Quakes
RCK	ACL Rockies	ACL	Rockies	ACL Rockies
RCT	Rocket City	SOU	Angels	Trash Pandas
REA	Reading	EAS	Phillies	Fightin Phils
RED	ACL Reds	ACL	Reds	ACL Reds
RIC	Richmond	EAS	Giants	Flying Squirrels
RNO	Reno	PCL	D-backs	Aces

CODE	TEAM	LG	AFF	NAME
ROC	Rochester	INT	Nationals	Red Wings
ROM	Rome	SAL	Braves	Braves
ROM	Rome	SAL	Braves	Emperors
ROY	ACL Royals	ACL	Royals	ACL Royals
ROYB	ACL Royals Blue	ACL	Royals	ACL Royals Blue
ROYG	ACL Royals Gold	ACL	Royals	ACL Royals Gold
RR	Round Rock	PCL	Rangers	Express
RSX	FCL Red Sox	FCL	Red Sox	FCL Red Sox
SA	San Antonio	TEX	Padres	Missions
SAC	Sacramento	PCL	Giants	River Cats
SAL	Salem	CAR	Red Sox	Red Sox
SAN	Santurce	PWL	-	Santurce
SB	South Bend	MID	Cubs	Cubs
SCO	Scottsdale	AFL	-	Scorpions
SD	San Diego	NL	-	Padres
SEA	Seattle	AL	-	Mariners
SF	San Francisco	NL	-	Giants
SJ	San Jose	CAL	Giants	Giants
SL	Salt Lake	PCL	Angels	Bees
SLU	St. Lucie	FSL	Mets	Mets
SOM	Somerset	EAS	Yankees	Patriots
SPO	Spokane	NWL	Rockies	Spokane
SPR	Springfield	TEX	Cardinals	Cardinals
SRR	Salt River	AFL	-	Rafters
STK	Stockton	CAL	Athletics	Ports
STL	St. Louis	NL	-	Cardinals
STP	St. Paul	INT	Twins	Saints
SUG	Sugar Land	AAA W	Astros	Skeeters
SUG	Sugar Land	PCL	Astros	Space Cowboys
SUR	Surprise	AFL	-	Saguaros
SWB	Scranton/WB	INT	Yankees	RailRiders
SYD	Sydney	ABL	-	Blue Sox
SYR	Syracuse	INT	Mets	Mets
TAC	Tacoma	PCL	Mariners	Rainiers
TAM	Tampa	FSL	Yankees	Tarpons
TB	Tampa Bay	AL	-	Rays
TDN	Tren del Norte		-	Tren del Norte
TEX	Texas	AL	-	Rangers
TIG	FCL Tigers	FCL	Tigers	FCL Tigers
TIGE	FCL Tigers East	FCL	Tigers	FCL Tigers East
TIGW	FCL Tigers West	FCL	Tigers	FCL Tigers West
TNS	Tennessee	SOU	Cubs	Smokies
TOL	Toledo	INT	Tigers	Mud Hens
TOR	Toronto	AL	-	Blue Jays
TOR	Toros	LIDOM	-	Toros
TRI	Tri-City	NWL	Angels	Dust Devils
TUL	Tulsa	TEX	Dodgers	Drillers
TWI	FCL Twins	FCL	Twins	FCL Twins
VAN	Vancouver	NWL	Blue Jays	Canadians
VEN	Venezuela	CS	-	Venezuela
VIS	Visalia	CAL	D-backs	Rawhide
WAS	Washington	NL	-	Nationals
WCH	Wichita	TEX	Twins	Wind Surge
WIL	Wilmington	SAL	Nationals	Blue Rocks
WIS	Wisconsin	MID	Brewers	Timber Rattlers
WM	West Michigan	MID	Tigers	Whitecaps
WOR	Worcester	INT	Red Sox	Red Sox
WS	Winston-Salem	SAL	White Sox	Dash
WAS	Washington	NL	-	Nationals
WSX	ACL White Sox	ACL	White Sox	ACL White Sox
YNK	FCL Yankees	FCL	Yankees	FCL Yankees
ZUL	Zulia	LVBP	-	Aguilas

Contributors

Biographies

Mikey Ajeto is a community organizer struggling for national sovereignty and genuine democracy in the Philippines. He moonlights as a contributor at Baseball Prospectus and still watches the Mariners on purpose.

Martín Alonso is a data analyst living in St. Paul, MN, with his wife, soon to be two kids, and dog. When he isn't thinking about sports, bad jokes and puns, he's playing music in a Smashing Pumpkins cover band and a separate blues-rock band.

Maitreyi Anantharaman is a staff writer at Defector. She lives in Detroit.

Davy Andrews is a contributing writer at FanGraphs, editorial assistant at SABR and guitarist in The Subway Ghosts. In 2020 and 2021 he recorded 64 songs about moribund minor-league teams for Baseball Prospectus' Too Far From Town project. He lives in Brooklyn with all the other baseball writers.

Lucas Apostoleris is a musician living in Miami, FL. Baseball is his other lifelong passion, and he has worked as a writer and researcher for Baseball Prospectus since 2019. Previously, he has been published in other outlets such as ESPN and FanGraphs.

Robert Au is the Director of Operations at Baseball Prospectus. His San Francisco Bay Area household includes three other humans and a heat-seeking cat.

Lindsay Ballant is an art director, designer and very occasional writer. She has won numerous industry awards in magazine and editorial design, though none as prestigious as that one time she won free beer from a random Yankee fan in the concession line at Yankee Stadium, who, upon seeing her vintage graphic Cal Ripken tee, challenged her on the spot to name three other Oriole players from the 1980s.

Michael Baumann is a writer at FanGraphs, the winner of the 2023 SABR Analytics Conference Research Award for Contemporary Baseball Commentary and author of the Wheelysports cycling newsletter on Substack. His work has also appeared at The Ringer, Grantland, Sports Illustrated and The Atlantic.

Demetrius Bell is a freelance writer whose work has appeared in publications such as SB Nation MLB, Vice Sports, Forbes, FanGraphs and Baseball Prospectus. He can be found in Lithia Springs, Georgia, watching nearly every single second of Braves baseball during the summer and any given game of Premier League football during the winter. If you care, you can follow him on Twitter (@fergoe) and Bluesky (fergoe.bsky.social).

Grant Brisbee is a writer for The Athletic, where he covers the San Francisco Giants and Major League Baseball.

Shawn Brody is a former writer for Beyond the Box Score and BP Mets. He now works for the BP Stats team on PECOTA and other assorted projects, happy he gets to do research without the need to write about it. He lives with his wife and daughter in Austin, Texas.

Zach Buchanan is a freelancer who has covered Major League Baseball for more than a decade, both on the beat writing about the Reds and Diamondbacks and nationally as a prospects writer. He lives in Phoenix, Arizona, where his summer electric bill would give you heart palpitations.

Russell A. Carleton is an author of Baseball Prospectus, and *The New Ballgame: The Not-So-Hidden Forces Shaping Modern Baseball*. He lives in Atlanta with his wife, who is awesome, and their kids.

Ben Carsley is a Senior Author at Baseball Prospectus. When he's not writing about baseball, Ben can be found cooking, drinking wine, making nihilistic puns and losing NFL parlays. By day, he manages a team of SEO analysts and content writers who are fairly convinced he's Ron Swanson.

Alex Chamberlain maintains the Pitch Leaderboard and writes infrequently for FanGraphs. He spends most of his precious little free time wondering how anyone with toddlers could possibly have so much of it.

Justin Choi is an undergraduate student at Washington University in St. Louis, majoring in data science. He is a former contributor to FanGraphs. This is his second time participating in the Baseball Prospects *Annual*, so he hopes to have avoided the dreaded sophomore slump.

Michael Clair writes for MLB.com with a special focus on the wild and weird in global baseball. Follow him @michaelsclair on whatever social media platform is still alive by the time you read this. He plays in the Brooklyn band The Subway Ghosts with three other baseball writers (two of whom are in this book!).

Ben Clemens is a writer for FanGraphs. He lives in San Francisco with his wife and dog. His hobbies include running, traveling and trying to convince friends to move to California.

Alex Convery is a screenwriter, who wrote *AIR* (2023), but got his start as a baseball blogger. He's been featured on the Hollywood Blacklist three times and was named one of Variety's 10 screenwriters to watch in 2022. He lives in Venice Beach with his wife, Quinn.

Zach Crizer is a baseball writer in New York. A former national reporter for Yahoo Sports and columnist for Baseball Prospectus, he unmasks the monster known as "analytics."

Mario Delgado Genzor is a baseball writer and professional pitching nerd who's mainly written for Baseball Prospectus and SB Nation's Purple Row. He was born and raised in Spain, and learned to speak English at a young age through music and sports. He's also, somewhat unfortunately, a big fan of the Colorado Rockies.

Patrick Dubuque is the managing editor of Baseball Prospectus. This is his fourth time co-editing the *Annual*. He lives in the Pacific Northwest with his wife, two children and the everpresent gray that has permeated the townsfolk, buildings and plants.

Alex Eisert is a baseball writer and researcher. He's been on staff at FanGraphs, Pinstripe Alley, Pitcher List and Sports Info Solutions, with the Blue Jays joining that list in 2024. He is especially interested in how and why players make decisions, something he struggles with in his own life.

Daniel R. Epstein is an elementary special education teacher and union president in Central Jersey. He is a contributor at Baseball Prospectus, Forbes SportsMoney and Off the Bench Baseball. He also serves as co-director of the Internet Baseball Writers Association of America.

James Fegan hails from the South Side of Chicago. His written work has appeared at Baseball Prospectus, the Chicago Sun-Times, The Athletic, ESPN, FanSided and all the places that run AP wire copy. He was named the 2021 NSMA Illinois Sportswriter of the Year; probably due to quarreling on Zoom with Tony La Russa.

Catherine Galanti is a journalism major who thought that, by becoming a writer, she could avoid doing math as part of her job. Her most contentious opinions include: bunts are good, it's always morally correct to yell "good pitch" at a pitcher who can't find the zone and that every team should have powder blue uniforms again. This is her first BP *Annual*.

Mike Gianella is a business project manager for a healthcare company who writes about fantasy baseball at Baseball Prospectus. He lives in Southeast Pennsylvania and has spent more time worrying about the fortunes of the New York Mets than any adult should.

Steven Goldman, former BP editor-in-chief and current consulting editor, has been part of BP for much of the past 20-plus years. He edited, co-edited, and contributed to multiple volumes of this book and was responsible for BP's books *Mind Game*, *It Ain't Over 'Til It's Over* and *Extra Innings: More Baseball Between the Numbers*. He's also the author of the Casey Stengel biography *Forging Genius* and *Baseball's Brief Lives: Player Stories Inspired by the Infinite Inning*, presented by BP. His work has appeared in numerous other places ranging from *Deadspin* to *The Daily Beast*. He's the host of the long-running *Infinite Inning* podcast, which sits at the crossroads of baseball, history, politics and culture. All of the above originates from New Jersey, where he resides with his wife, son, occasionally his daughter, two cats and an unmanageable number of books, but shame him not for this most scholarly and benign of addictions (assuming a stack doesn't fall on him).

Craig Goldstein is the editor-in-chief of Baseball Prospectus. His work has appeared in Sports Illustrated, Vice Sports, Fox Sports MLB and SB Nation MLB. He lives in Maryland, where he spends just the right amount of time becoming the joker.

Nathan Graham is a native Hoosier who covers the Midwest League for the Baseball Prospectus prospect team. He also co-hosts the "Heat Check" podcast, the bi-weekly, in-season wrap-up of minor-league baseball.

Nathan Grimm is a fantasy writer at Baseball Prospectus. Before joining BP, his work was featured at Rotoworld for the better part of a decade. He lives in southwestern Illinois and asks that you please don't hold that against him.

Bryan Grosnick is Baseball Prospectus' Fantasy Editor and has consulted for an MLB franchise. He lives in New England with his stunning wife (who is perpetually entering her age-29 season) and their three wonderful children.

Ben Hatch is a graduate student at Hunter College, studying statistics. He lives in New York City and writes about baseball when he isn't stressing about how to use Python and R properly.

Jon Hegglund is the only current Idaho resident who remembers Atlee Hammaker's disastrous 1983 All-Star Game appearance. In many ways, it has shaped the course of his (Jon's, not Atlee's) life. Jon teaches at one of the top universities in the Pac-2 and is more passionate about than successful at fantasy baseball.

Scott Hines is the publisher of the widely beloved Action Cookbook Newsletter. He is an architect, blogger and proficient internet user based in Louisville, Kentucky.

Tim Jackson is a writer and educator from New Jersey. He was at Veterans Stadium for Robert Person's two-homer game in 2002 and thinks about it at least once a month. (One was an upper decker!)

Jonathan Judge is a lawyer who also designs statistics and models for Baseball Prospectus. He believes in hierarchical (modeling) structures, full paragraph justification and two spaces between sentences. *[We did not leave this in for him. -ed.]*

Kyle Kishimoto is a writer for FanGraphs. He's a California native now residing in the Bay Area, where he teaches at a science museum by day.

Justin Klugh is a copy and feature writer who can only drink beer out of plastic bats now, so good job, MLB marketing. His "work" has appeared in Baseball Prospectus, FanGraphs, SB Nation, the Philadelphia Inquirer and

Baltimore Magazine. He has never caught a foul ball or home run presumably because of some sort of hex of which he is too oblivious to be afflicted.

Jeremy Koo is an attorney for the State of California's investment and financial services regulator who once upon a time wrote blogs at athleticsnation.com but now just blueskys or whatever about the A's. Having grown up in Alameda and attended law school in San Francisco, he now resides in Sacramento, where he misses being able to hop on BART on a whim for yet another ballgame at the Oakland Coliseum.

Rob Mains is a writer at Baseball Prospectus, where his career in finance is distressingly handy in discussing the game today. He lives in a redoubt in update New York, surrounded by Finger Lakes wine, waging a lonely battle to preserve the Chicago Manual of Style usage of the word *only*. He has never played Wordle.

Kelsey McKinney is a writer and co-owner at Defector Media where she also hosts the podcast Normal Gossip. Her first book, *God Spare The Girls* was published in 2021, and she is always, always keeping boxscore in pen like an idiot.

Andrew Mearns is the managing editor of Pinstripe Alley, the Yankees' SB Nation blog, where he first started writing in 2012. He has also written for Baseball Prospectus, Cut4 at MLB.com, Sports on Earth and the 2008 Madison High School bowling yearbook page. If you knew that last one, then, uh, go Dodgers? (They sadly did not feature Mookie Betts.)

Sam Miller is a former editor of the Baseball Prospectus *Annual*. He publishes a newsletter on Substack called Pebble Hunting.

Jake Mintz is the more irritating half of the Céspedes Family BBQ. He also writes baseball for Fox Sports and co-hosts Baseball Bar-B-Cast on the SiriusXM Podcast Network. Most importantly though, he runs the sharpest little league practice in Uptown Manhattan.

Dan Moore is a contributor to The Ringer and Baseball Prospectus. His work has appeared most recently in Oaklandside Magazine. He is, unfortunately, an A's fan. He lives in the Bay Area.

Marc Normandin writes on baseball's labor issues and more at marcnormandin.com, which you can read for free but support through his Patreon. He writes regularly for Baseball Prospectus, and his other baseball work has appeared at SB Nation, Defector, Deadspin, Sports Illustrated, ESPN, Sports on Earth, The Guardian, The Nation, FAIR, TalkPoverty and other places, too, but please don't make him remember how long he's been doing this. You can also read his takes on video games at Retro XP and Paste Magazine.

Robert Orr notionally works as a data analyst in Philadelphia. At night, he (mostly) enjoys the local nine and moonlights as a baseball analyst.

Jeffrey Paternostro is the Lead Prospect Writer and Multimedia Production Manager for Baseball Prospectus. He has written for the site since 2015. He really misses his 32 oz.

iced coffee with a randomized amount of sugar from Dunkin Donuts Park in Hartford, CT, but the post-shift cocktail at Water Witch in Salt Lake City does the trick well enough.

Harry Pavlidis is the Director of R&D for Baseball Prospectus and an unrelenting reviewer of pitch tracking data.

Mike Piellucci is the sports editor at D Magazine. He is a former staffer at The Athletic, Front Office Sports and Vice Sports, and his freelance work has been featured in Sports Illustrated, The New York Times, Los Angeles Magazine and The Year's Best Sports Writing. He lives in Dallas with his wife and rescue dog.

Amy Pircher is a software designer for NASA JPL by day and Baseball Prospectus by night. Her cats think she should do neither.

Kate Preusser is the editor-in-chief at Lookout Landing, where she spends too much time pondering the black hole of second base for the Seattle Mariners. When not at the ballpark, she is the world's Okayest Dog-Sitter.

Tommy Rancel a.k.a. Pen Griffey Jr has previously written for ESPN, The Athletic, FanGraphs and the Baseball Prospectus *Annual*. He lives in the Tampa Bay area with his wife Jamie and their five children.

Esteban Rivera is a New York City-based data scientist. He is a contributor at FanGraphs and Pinstripe Alley. In his downtime, he collects bat sensor data in the hopes of constructing the best softball swing in NY.

David Roth is an editor at and co-owner of Defector. His writing has appeared in The New Yorker, New York, The New Republic and other publications without the word "new" in their name, but mostly appears at Defector. He is from New Jersey and lives in New York with his wife and turtle.

Shaker Samman is a writer based in Los Angeles. His work has previously appeared in Sports Illustrated, The Ringer, The Guardian and Slate, and was selected as part of The Year's Best Sports Writing 2022. His time at Baseball Prospectus was mostly spent googling the first 13 games of Chris Shelton's 2006 season, just to make sure they actually happened. Don't follow him on Twitter.

Janice Scurio is an IT professional with degrees in English literature and library science. Her work has appeared in SB Nation (South Side Sox), Baseball Prospectus, Sports Illustrated, CHGO Sports and NBC Sports. She lives in Chicago, where she continues her quest to create the platonic ideal of a hot dog.

Ginny Searle is a writer and editor for Baseball Prospectus. Her work has appeared in various outlets. She lives in Los Angeles.

Jarrett Seidler is the Senior Prospect Writer for Baseball Prospectus. He also co-hosts For All You Kids Out There, a weekly BP podcast which is occasionally about the Mets. As a lifelong New Jersey resident, he has begrudgingly accepted that Taylor Swift is in the same tier of artist as Bruce Springsteen.

Jordan Shusterman is one half of Céspedes Family BBQ and the co-host of Baseball Bar-B-Cast. His work has appeared on Baseball Prospectus, Cut4, MLB Pipeline, The Ringer, D1Baseball.com and FOXSports.com. When he's not covering every conceivable level of professional baseball, he's podcasting about Division-III baseball. No, seriously.

Steve Sladkowski is a guitarist and member of the Canadian punk rock band PUP. When not touring the world strumming his little guitar, he can usually be found wallowing in the misery of Toronto sports fandom.

Ben Spanier is a writer and evaluator for the Prospect Team at Baseball Prospectus. He lives in a mid-size North Carolina city, where he enjoys visiting local libraries and looking at pine trees.

Matt Sussman writes about MLB players' 50th birthdays for Baseball Prospectus and otherwise does IT work in Toledo, Ohio. He can be found on the internet, and if you find him, please return him to his rightful owner.

Jon Tayler is formerly of FanGraphs and Sports Illustrated and now makes his living smashing together trains for the MTA. If you're ever in New York City, come get a slice with him.

Lauren Theisen is a co-owner and a blog girl at defector.com.

Matthew Trueblood is the Managing Editor of Twins Daily, Brewer Fanatic and North Side Baseball. He lives in the Twin Cities, trying to survive enough winters to get to the good part of climate change.

Eli Walsh is a reporter and contributes to Baseball Prospectus' prospect team with coverage of the California League's North Division. He lives in San Diego and serves as BP's resident emo music scholar.

Alexandra Whitley is a student and researcher of education histories and curriculum. Most of her time is spent reading 20th century journal articles, watching *Star Trek: The Next Generation* and considering the implications of various Giants minor-league signings.

Roy Wood Jr. is an Emmy-nominated producer, comedian and writer. He resides in New York City, where he often reminisces about his glory days riding the bench for his high school baseball team in Birmingham, AL.

Acknowledgments

This book is dedicated to our friend Rob McQuown.
Thanks for the research, and for everything else.

Mikey Ajeto: My dad, Cesar, who forged my love for Mariners baseball; Patrick Dubuque, who kindly dealt with my procrastination, and to whom I now owe several beers; the Seattle Mariners, who traded Paul Sewald and make me want to watch baseball less every single day; the National Democratic movement of the Philippines, which changed the way I view the world.

Martin Alonso: My wife Dani, who has always supported my not-so-well-thought-out ideas. Our daughters Liv, Victoria for inspiring me to always keep improving, and Louie who is such a good bud. Thanks to my mum and dad for nurturing my interests and hobbies. Thank you to Rob Mains and the BP Español crew; Harry Pavlidis, Jen Ramos Eisen, Rob Arthur, Jonathan Judge, Kendall Guillemette, and the rest of the Baseball Prospectus stats team for always welcoming and suffering my idiotic comments. And special thanks to Rob McQuown, without whom I would not be at Baseball Prospectus.

Maitreyi Anantharaman: Conversations in Defector baseball Slack; coverage of the team from the Kansas City Star; and Mark Dent and Rustin Dodd's *Kingdom Quarterback* all informed this essay.

Davy Andrews: Thank you to my wife for shooting down an extended metaphor of Mike Rizzo as Penelope of Ithaca. Thank you to Mike Clair, Dan Epstein, and Mike Petriello for being incredible friends despite completely ruining Immaculate Grid for me. Thank you to Roger Cormier, Patrick Dubuque, Craig Goldstein, Jacob Pomrenke, Meg Rowley, Ginny Searle, Cecilia Tan, and Jon Taylor for making my writing better and for letting me write in the first place.

Lucas Apostoleris: I'm grateful to the editorial staff (Craig, Bryan, Ginny and Patrick) for inviting me to write for this publication, and also for making my words sound less bad. I owe a lot in particular to Harry Pavlidis, whom I've worked with in some capacity or another for over a decade and has been helpful to me ever since I was just a high schooler trying to learn more about PITCHf/x.

Robert Au: Thank you to the human and feline members of my family for bringing me joy and love. To those of you who have departed, I miss you. Thanks again to everyone on the BP stats team for your camaraderie and hard work, to Kathy Woolner and Rob Mains for their patience and diligence, and to Craig Goldstein for inviting me to this crazy world in the first place.

Lindsay Ballant: To Justin, for his unconditional support and encouragement of my emotional swings based on win-loss ratios from 2014 to present, and for picking up extra walking duties of Luna while I wrestled with this. To my late father, who patiently answered every annoying question about the rules of baseball I threw at him as a child. To the late Wild Bill Hagy, who introduced my parents to each other. To the OrSoc group chat for their camaraderie, endless sourcing of stats, and terminally online antics. To David Roth, and to the BP editors, for taking a chance. And to Melanie Newman, for being an inspiration to all of Birdland's fellow daughters of proud fathers.

Michael Baumann: My wife, Kate White, who has an endless capacity to tolerate my ridiculousness. And my work spouse, Craig Goldstein, who has an endless capacity to fill my life with ridiculousness that must be tolerated.

Demetrius Bell: Patricia Bell, Garry Bell, Sheretha Bell, Deronne Floyd, Joanne Thimot, Gaurav Vedak, Kris Willis, the entire team at Battery Power and everybody who's given my work a read, a click, or even just a passing glance. Thanks to everybody mentioned for believing in me and continuing to give me the motivation to move forward.

Grant Brisbee: It was a dark and stormy night. Suddenly, a shot rang out! A door slammed. The maid screamed. Suddenly, a pirate ship appeared on the horizon! While millions of people were starving, the king lived in luxury. Meanwhile, in a suburb of Oakland, a baseball writer thanked his friends, family and coworkers.

Shawn Brody: Thank you to my wife, Grace, for your patience in tolerating my perpetually inconsistent schedule and incoherent rants. Thank you to my daughter, Cece, for giving me a reason to get work done early this year. Thank you to my mom, dad, brother, friends and family for all the support. Thank you to R.J. Anderson, Harry Pavlidis, Robert Au, Cory Frontin and the rest of the BP Stats team for all the help and assistance in solving any problem.

Zach Buchanan: Derrick Hall, Nick Piecoro, my wife Taryn and my three-year-old daughter Fallon who would *really* test my patience if she weren't so cute.

Russell A. Carleton: I'd like to thank the fine folks at Retrosheet, who should be in the Hall of Fame. This is not hyperbole.

Ben Carsley: The ever-patient Allyson Carsley, Bob, Bernadette, Elizabeth and PTBNL Carsley, Bret Sayre, Craig Goldstein, Sam Miller, Patrick Dubuque, Xander Bogaerts, Mary Donovan, Daniel Ohman and the C-4 Content Team.

Alex Chamberlain: Remi, you are the most hard-headed, most delightful child. May you never inherit my baseball-induced brain rot. I love you so much. Jill, thanks for supporting this absurd hobby (and nodding and smiling politely when I'm really on one). Patrick, thanks for trusting me to ruin another chapter. Meg, thanks for making my work at FanGraphs readable. To those on Twitter doing superb research on the public side, thanks for inadvertently pushing me forward.

Justin Choi: Patrick Dubuque, who is not only a fantastic editor but also an invaluable mentor. Dr. Arch, whose course on the Reed-Kellogg diagramming system improved my writing in ways I previously would not have thought of. Previous contributors to Baseball Prospectus Annuals, whose comments I consulted numerous times. RosterResource, Baseball Savant, Microsoft Excel, and R Studio. And finally, Mom and Dad, who are always there for me.

Michael Clair: Thanks to my wife, Marissa, for putting up with the endless sound of gloves popping at all hours of the day, my MLB.com colleagues for advice, support, and amazing stories, the wonderful people who do so much for baseball and the growth of the game all across the world, and my baseball-writing bandmates for getting wild together.

Ben Clemens: Jenna Hovel, Libby Clemens, Bruce Clemens, Roy Clemens, Jenny Xiao, Ruby Hovmens, Chris Lin, Cheng Zhao, Matt Jakobovits.

Alex Convery: My family and my wife Quinn, all of whom put up with too much baseball. My Dad, who always let me stay up late on school nights in October. And my friends, all of whom I've dragged to a random Dodgers game at some point, especially when the starting pitching matchup is good.

Zach Crizer: Craig Goldstein, R.J. Anderson, Hannah Keyser, Stein, Catania, Jefe, Steph, Scott and Amy.

Mario Delgado Genzor: My first thanks go to my family, because as outlandish as this kind of thing is for someone living in a country that barely knows what baseball is, they've always been supportive and excited for me. I'd also like to thank my friend Patrick Ellington Jr., a talented writer himself, for encouraging me to begin doing this years ago, as well as every editor and member of both Baseball Prospectus and the Purple Row staff I've ever crossed paths with. I've learned a lot from many different places, but I'd like to particularly shout out the folks at Tread Athletics, as their content and in-depth breakdowns on pitching really helped me connect the dots and come up with my own ideas. And of course, what would a pitching nerd like me be without tools like PITCHf/x and Baseball Savant? Lastly, I wish to sneak one last thanks to a close friend of mine who I won't name, but who'll know this refers to him if he reads it. Huge thanks to all of you.

Patrick Dubuque: Kjersten, Sylvie, and Felix Dubuque; Craig Goldstein, Ginny Searle, and Bryan Grosnick; Steve Goldman, Kate Pruesser, Dan Epstein, RJ Anderson, Brendan Gawlowski, Andrew Rice, Robert Au, Amy Pircher, Tom Gieryn, and all the folks who have channeled their time and love into this project, year after year; Eric Nusbaum, Carson Cistulli, Bret Sayre, Sam Miller; Von Hayes.

Alex Eisert: Thank you to FanGraphs, not only for providing me with most of the data I used for this book (Baseball Savant and BP being the other major sources), but also for their willingness to publish my kooky ideas. Thank you to the BP editorial staff for inviting me to contribute and for guiding me through the process. Thank you to Mario Delgado Genzor for publishing a great series on pitching at altitude, which I drew heavily from. Lastly, thank you to my family, friends and Grace for encouraging me to continue pursuing a career in baseball, no matter how unprofitable.

Daniel R. Epstein: Thanks to Heather, Andrew, Sofia, Ronni and Ray, Theresa and Joe, The Subway Ghosts (Davy Andrews, Michael Clair, and Mike Petriello), the GhostWives, Jonathan Becker and the IBWAA, the NASA and Rany's Rejects Strat-O-Matic leagues, the Somerset County Education Association and public school educators in general.

James Fegan: I would like to thank my wife Jacqueline, who successfully argues against me quitting writing once per year on average.

Catherine Galanti: Thank you to my parents for teaching me to love baseball, and for your unwavering support through every pursuit. Thanks for giving me the grit needed to endure being an Angels fan. To Miles, for filling in the gaps in my copyediting knowledge and for reminding me that someone always knows more about sports than I do. To Elliot, Meena, Tam and Bri for being my biggest cheerleaders and for originating countless inside jokes. I'm so glad to have found a community with y'all—everything I write is for you. To all the BP staff, but especially Craig, Patrick and Ginny; thanks for taking a chance on me. Thank you to countless others for believing in me, pointing me in the right direction and putting up with late night texts about obscure facts you don't care about. I appreciate you more than you know.

Mike Gianella: To the great editorial and writing team at Baseball Prospectus, who make my words sound much better than they do after I put them on the page. My friends at UUCWC, who lift my heart and my spirits. Jon Hegglund and Samuel Hale, my podcast partners who are also my friends. Tristan Cockcroft, Peter Kreutzer, Eric Karabell, Alex Patton, Jeff Erickson and the many, many people who make the fantasy community what it is. Colleen, Lucy and Elliot, whose love and patience make me a better person.

Steven Goldman: As always, immeasurable gratitude to Stefanie, Sarah, Clemens, Reuven, Eliane, Ilana, Andy, Rick, Cliff, Raven and Charity for their unvarying support and timely distractions.

Craig Goldstein: Katherine, Charlie and Theo Pappas, Laurie Gross, Harvey Goldstein, Alexis Goldstein, Tony and Dale Pappas, Patrick Dubuque, Ben Carsley, Ginny Searle, R.J. Anderson, Bret Sayre, Sam Miller, Jason Wojciechowski, Marc Normandin, Steven Goldman, Tim Jackson, Rob McQuown, Jacob Raim, Harry Pavlidis, Jeffrey Paternostro, Tom Gieryn, Robert Orr, Mikey Ajeto, Jonathan Judge, Rob Mains, Jason Parks, Ben Lindbergh, the BP Prospect Team, Jarrett Seidler, Zach Mortimer, Tucker Blair, Mike Ferrin, Tommy Rancel, Michael Baumann, Meg Rowley, James Fegan, Emma Baccellieri, Shakeia Taylor, Mauricio Rubio, Zach Crizer, Robert Au.

Nathan Graham: Thanks to Emily Graham, Jeffrey Paternostro, Jarrett Seidler, the entire prospect team, Smith Brickner, Jay Matthews, Eric Foerg, Leo Foerg, Jack and Judy Graham, and all of the wonderful public school teachers that I had over the years.

Nathan Grimm: Even if I had received help, showing weakness and acknowledging it goes against my personal set of beliefs.

Bryan Grosnick: Thanks to Sarah Grosnick first, always, for everything. Thanks to Phil, Debbie, Lucas, Miles, and Jack Grosnick, for their love, support, and tolerance. Thanks to Craig Goldstein, Patrick Dubuque, Ginny Searle, Robert Au, Bret Sayre, Andrew Mearns, Jarrett Seidler, Jeffrey Paternostro, the BP Stats team and the dozens of other people whose brilliance and effort made this book a reality.

Ben Hatch: My friends and family for always supporting my passion for baseball. Bryan Grosnick and the BP Staff for giving me the opportunity to contribute to this great yearly project. Jarrett Seidler for guiding me through the writing process. PitcherList, Alex Chamberlain, BaseballSavant and FanGraphs for resources that were invaluable to my research.

Jon Hegglund: Thanks to Craig G. for letting me try my hand at an essay, to Patrick D. for giving the essay two of its best lines, and to Mike G. and Samuel H. for continued camaraderie regarding baseball and so much more. Thanks to my family, who remain tolerant of my bad habits even as they help me nurture better ones.

Tim Jackson: Thanks to my wife, Teresa, and my dog, Nox, for accepting my compulsive baseball neuroses, which include watching up to five games at a time during the season.

Kyle Kishimoto: Thank you to Meg Rowley and Jon Tayler of FanGraphs for making me more capable as a writer, to my family for supporting my wide array of professional interests, and to the Effectively Wild Discord group for being a source of community in the baseball world.

Justin Klugh: My wife for her constant support despite a complete disinterest in baseball and my writing about it, my wonderful father, mother, and two sisters for being a baseball family, my grandparents for bringing me to so many games, and the Phillie Phanatic for being a symbol of the last goodness in the world.

Jeremy Koo: Without journalists, whether they be baseball reporters in the clubhouse or political reporters in state capitols, little about the entire process that is the A's stadium saga sees the light of day. This includes Tim Keown of ESPN, the political reporting team at the *Nevada Independent*, and the reporters at the *East Bay Times* and the *San Francisco Chronicle*. Thank you also to the A's fans that cheered me on from afar in my adventures to Carson City. And to my parents, for taking me or letting me go to all of those A's games. Thanks, I had a good time.

Rob Mains: My mother, Rhoda Mains, for instilling a love of the game, and my wife, Amy Durland, for encouraging me to pursue it and often not regretting having done so. Martín Alonso, José Hernández, Marco Gámez, Pepe Latorre, Fernando Battaglini, and Rohanna Pacheco for making BP en español, our daily Spanish-language content, a reality. Craig Goldstein, Ginny Searle, Marc Normandin, and Patrick Dubuque for putting up with my overuse of charts and tables. AM and PM for who they are.

Andrew Mearns: Ali, the cats who keep us sane (Piccolo and Hugo), my family writ large, the Pinstripe Alley writing staff, the 2013 Yankees for numbing me to how weird a season can truly get, and my late grandfather, Al Mearns. He wasn't much of a baseball fan, but he still humored my dad's fascination by obliging in long family road trips to distant ballparks.

Sam Miller: Andy O'Hara, Craig Goldstein, R.J. Anderson and the editors of this book.

Jake Mintz: To Jordan Shusterman, who was my muse when I wrote uncut comments. Tamar Eisen, for being my actual life partner. Kevin Brown for watching most of the 2023 Orioles.

Dan Moore: Thank you to my wife, Alex, for her patience, support, and inspiration. To my parents for the same. And thank you to Oliver, our son, who at seven months is neither patient nor supportive but everyday inspires. May he, somehow, grow up an Oakland A's fan.

Marc Normandin: Thanks to my friends and family for their support both this year and in others. I'd also like to curse my enemies and assume everyone knows which of these groups they belong to.

Robert Orr: I'm obligated to thank my editors for their unwavering patience and my fiancée, Jayne, for putting up with and enabling my BS.

Jeffrey Paternostro: Jess for supporting me no matter how cranky I get during list season. Evelyn, for mercifully preferring soccer to baseball (I'll explain about Sheffield Wednesday in due time). Jarrett for supporting me no matter how cranky I get during list season. Craig, take care of Nabil Crismatt for me, won't you? The prospect team for supporting me no matter how crank...eh, you get the idea. And the Terminal Passage YouTube Channel for providing the soundtrack for said prospect list season.

Harry Pavlidis: To Jill Santos for many things, including being so understanding of my schedule. Shirley Barkovich, who does not care about my schedule as long as it complies with her canine needs. The PitchInfo team and the entire BP Stats community for all their work, humor and creativity.

Mike Piellucci: Thank you to my parents, Joe and Doreen, and my wife, Sarah—the three people without whom none of this would be possible. Thank you to my friends and family both in and out of the business, all of whom have created community in what can be an isolating profession. Lastly, thank you, for reading.

Amy Pircher: Thanks to my parents who started my baseball fandom at a young age, and all of the support they've given me throughout the years. Also to Mike Petriello and Harry Pavlidis, without whom my career would be dramatically different.

Kate Preusser: I would like to acknowledge my SB Nation colleagues at Royals Review and Bless You Boys for helping me understand what, exactly, is afoot in the AL Central.

Tommy Rancel: Jamie, Alexis, Vincent, Jarek, Brooklyn, Dakota, Rebecca Basse, Carlos Alvarez, R.J. Anderson, Erik Hahmann, Craig Goldstein, Keith Law, Chris Crawford, Randy Lemery, Charles Saul, Rayne Dakota Prescott, Thomas Klevanosky, Son Heung-min, Harry Fraud, Max Winn and Benito Antonio Martínez Ocasio.

Esteban Rivera: Many thanks to Patrick Dubuque for his help throughout this process. Also, thanks to Meg Rowley and Andrew Mearns for their help in developing my writing over the last few years. Lastly, none of this could have done without the many baseball publications or my other half, Emily.

Shaker Samman: Shoutout to Craig Goldstein, Patrick Dubuque and Ginny Searle for once again saving me from myself; to the Rangers for not blowing it for once; to the two dogs wailing like banshees throughout my attempts to finish writing this essay; and to Lani Kim, who did her best to corral them.

Janice Scurio: The great folks at Brewer Fanatic and their meticulous prospect evaluations. Michael Ajeto, Jordan White and Zach Hayes for their collective "no, that's not crazy at all, you should definitely say that" reassurances.

Ginny Searle: Tori. Mom, Dad, Keenan, Joanie, Katie, and Erin. Nicole, Emery, Rae, Vanessa, Payton. Craig, Patrick and Marc. To everyone in the dark, who came to need, who would do it again.

Jarrett Seidler: To Kate, in paper rings, in picture frames, in dreams.

Jordan Shusterman: Bailey Bowers, David Shusterman, Rebecca Shusterman, Gila Shusterman, Alan Shusterman, Jake Mintz, Ryan Divish, Adam Jude, Larry Stone, Daniel Kramer, Aaron Goldsmith, Kinza Baad, Bailey Freeman, Sarah Langs.

Steve Sladkowski: I'd like to thank my wife Bailey Jensen for the constant inspiration and for adopting the Blue Jays (much to the chagrin of her Red Sox Dad). I'll also send three cheers to Dr. David B. Hobbs for the input and advice on all things Ammons.

Ben Spanier: Thanks to those who tolerate and interact with my musings on baseball, including but not limited to: Jon, David, Matt, Ian, and Wilson and also those who prefer other avenues of discussion, including but not limited to: Jen, Abby, Charlie, Joe and James.

Matt Sussman: Max, Mom, Lauren, Chief.

Jon Tayler: Thanks to Kristin and the girls, Rachel and the nephew to be named later, the fine folks at FanGraphs and the very patient people who edit this wonderful book.

Lauren Theisen: Nook Logan.

Matthew Trueblood: Thanks to my wife, Maria, for encouraging me in all facets of life and specifically supporting this occasionally insupportable passion. Thanks to Sorkin and Lincoln Trueblood, who played my favorite baseball of 2023 and talk the game smarter than I can. Thanks to Anna Trueblood, for her relentless enthusiasm and for building me up when I most need it. I love you all. Thanks to the BP editors for enfolding me back into the family this year and to the crew at Diamond Centric who made it possible for me to wade back into these waters.

Eli Walsh: Special thanks to my wife, Sam; and parents, Prov and Rory, for their boundless support; and to my BP colleagues, whose talent and creativity consistently drives me to improve my own work.

Index of Names

You may have reached the end of the book, but this is only the **beginning** of our 2024 baseball coverage.

Head over to **www.baseballprospectus.com** today and see what you get with an annual membership. Here are some highlights:

- Updated in-season PECOTA projections, both at the individual player and team levels;
- Daily features on what you need to know about baseball, including BP's Transaction Analysis series;
- Fantasy content and rankings from our expert staff, including both redraft and dynasty formats;
- The AX, BP's customizable fantasy auction valuation tool;
- Prospect content from BP's dedicated team, including our 101 and Top Prospect lists, along with all flavors of in-season live looks;
- PECOTA percentiles ranging from 1st to 99th;
- Leaderboards and Player Cards with up-to-date stats;
- The Bat Signal, our fantasy answering service (for Super-Premium members only);
- All that, and so much more!

Thank you again for your support and we look forward to providing you with even more baseball content in the future!

www.baseballprospectus.com/subscriptions

Since 2016, THIRTY81 Project has partnered with Baseball Prospectus to provide readers with detailed field illustrations based on our series of full size posters and custom prints. Visit our web shop to explore the full collection including our popular "Century of Ballparks" print.

THIRTY81PROJECT.COM